The
HOLY
BIBLE

1611
EDITION

❖

King James Version

Presented To

_____

_____

By

_____

Date

_____

The HOLY BIBLE

1611 EDITION

King James Version

THE HOLY BIBLE,
KING JAMES VERSION

A reprint of the edition of 1611

Hendrickson Publishers, Inc.
P.O. Box 3473
Peabody, MA 01961-3473

First Printing Hendrickson Publisher's Edition—October 2003

ISBN 1-56563-160-9 (Bonded Leather Hardcover)
ISBN 1-56563-162-5 (Genuine Leather, Black)
ISBN 1-56563-175-7 (Genuine Leather, Burgundy)
ISBN 1-56563-194-3 (Genuine Leather, Brown)

Printed in the United States of America

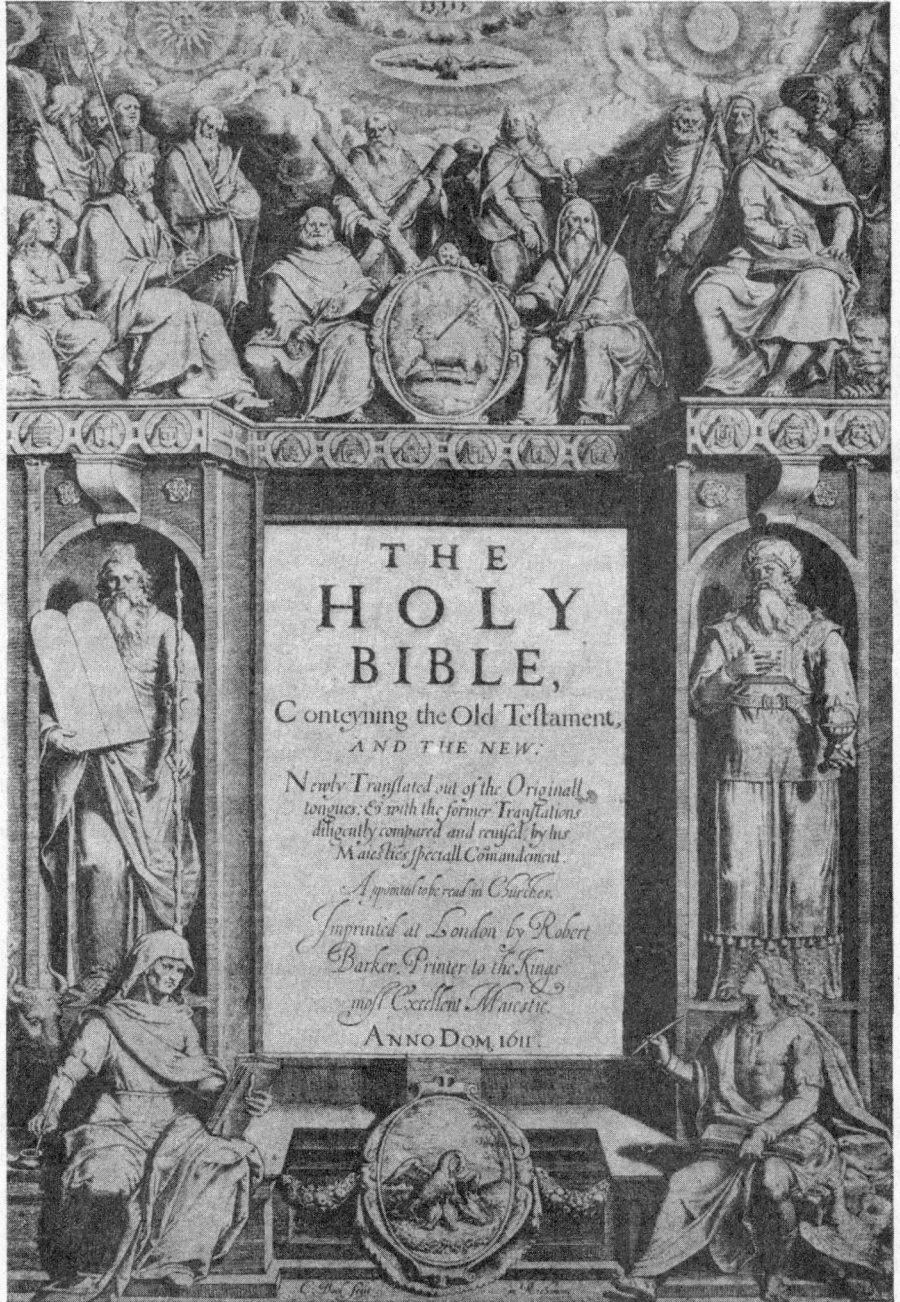

THE
HOLY
BIBLE,

Conteyning the Old Testament,
AND THE NEW:

Newly Translated out of the Originall
tongues: & with the former Translations
diligently compared and reuised, by his
Maiesties speciall Comandement.

Appointed to be read in Churches.

Imprinted at London by Robert
Barker, Printer to the Kings
most Excellent Maiestie.

ANNO DOM. 1611

CONTENTS

CONTENTS

BIBLIOGRAPHICAL INTRODUCTION

I. THE EARLIER ENGLISH TRANSLATIONS
(1380–1582)

MAINLY, no doubt, because of the predominance of French as the language of educated people in England from the time of the Norman Conquest until the middle of the fourteenth century, the Bible, as a whole, remained untranslated into English until the last years of the life of Wyclif. A version was then made, about 1380–3, and some years later this was revised and substantially rewritten in a simpler style by another hand. That the reformer himself took any personal share in either of these versions which pass popularly under his name is unlikely, and in the case of the second is not seriously contended. We know from a manuscript at the Bodleian Library, Oxford, that Nicholas of Hereford, who up to the time of the final defeat of Wyclif's cause at Oxford (June 1382) figured as one of his strongest supporters at the University, was the author of the first version as far as Baruch iii. 20, where it breaks off in the manuscript abruptly, presumably because of Hereford's flight. The authorship of the rest of this version is unknown, and being unknown has been ascribed to Wyclif himself, with more piety than probability, since the master does not often take up the work of the disciple, and Wyclif, after June 1382, was both old and ill. The authorship of the second version was tentatively ascribed to one of Wyclif's followers, John Purvey, by Daniel Waterton in 1729 (*Waterton's Works*, vol. x, p. 361), and although Waterton says himself that he merely guessed and 'pitched upon' Purvey as the author, and his reason for doing so has not been confirmed, the suggestion was accepted by Forshall and Madden in their splendid edition of the two versions in 1850, and is now frequently stated as a fact.

A name which long before Waterton's time was connected with an English version of the Bible was that of John of Trevisa, of whom Caxton wrote in the preface to his edition of Higden's *Polychronicon* that at the request of 'one Sir Thomas lord barkley', to whom he acted as priest, he had translated the *Polychronicon*, the Bible, and the *De Proprietatibus Rerum* of Bartholomaeus Anglicus, one of the best known of mediaeval encyclopaedias. The first and third of these translations survive. Of that of the Bible (mentioned also, probably on Caxton's authority, in the preface to the Bible of 1611) nothing is known, unless it can be identified either with the completion of the first version begun by Nicholas of

Hereford or with the second version which has somewhat lightly
been assigned to Purvey. For our present purpose it is unneces-
sary to enter further into these questions of authorship. It is
sufficient to note that the translator of the second of the two
extant versions worked, according to his own account, 'with
diverse felawis and helpars' and had 'manie gode felawis and
kunnynge at the correccioun of his translacioun'. It thus seems
certain that there was something of the nature of an informal
board or company of translators, and if piety did not constrain
us to speak of these two versions, not indeed as the Wyclif, but
as the Wyclifite Bible, we might well have been content, as the
present writer suggested ten years ago, to have called this the
Oxford Bible, since it was with the reform party at Oxford that it
took its inception and, despite its origin among Wyclif's followers,
there was no attempt in either version to translate in any party
spirit, or to do anything else than give a faithful rendering of the
Vulgate Latin.

As early as 1397 at least one copy of this English Bible was in the
possession of a royal duke, and the names of other noble owners
during the fifteenth century, as well as fine manuscripts decorated
so as to be worthy of such ownership, remain on record. In 1408
the Convocation held at Oxford had forbidden the possession of
any English version of the Bible without licence from a bishop, but
it is plain that such a licence could be procured, and we even hear
of a copy belonging to such an eminently orthodox community as
the Bridgetine house of Sion, at Isleworth. But the existence of
Lollardy had reawakened such fears as Aelfric had expressed lest his
epitome of the Pentateuch should entrap the unwary to believe in
the lawfulness of polygamy, and a reader of the merchant class who
had asked his priest to get him a licence to own an English Bible
towards the end of the fifteenth century would probably have met
but small encouragement. Add to this the fact that by this time
the language of the Wyclifite versions was fast becoming obsolete,
and also the vast expense of such an enterprise, and we have no
reason to wonder that Caxton neither printed either of the existing
translations, nor set himself to procure, or (hardened translator as
he was) to make, a new one. But a generation later, other ideas had
sprung up, and at least one man in England, William Tyndale, was
determined that there should be an English Bible which not merely
merchants but ploughboys could buy and read.

Tyndale's New Testament. William Tyndale had come to London, with a translation of
a speech of Isocrates as a proof of his ability, in the hope of finding
encouragement from the Bishop of London (Cuthbert Tunstall) to
make a new translation of the New Testament not, as the 'Wyclifite'
translators had done, from the Latin Vulgate, but from the original
Greek. Erasmus had published his famous edition of the Greek

Testament in 1516, and this had been revised and reprinted in 1519 and 1522. Along with it he had printed a new translation into Latin. Tyndale had probably heard Erasmus lecture at Cambridge, and he must have been prepared, if Tunstall had given him any encouragement, to make his English version in the spirit of Erasmus. But there was no room for a translator of the Bible in the Bishop's house, nor indeed, as Tyndale said bitterly, in all England, so in 1524 he betook himself to Hamburg, with the help of a subsidy of £10 given him by a generous and devout London merchant, Henry Monmouth, and completed his translation undisturbed. There are references to what may have been trial issues of Matthew and Mark, but if, which is doubtful, these ever had a separate existence, no traces of them remain. But before December, 1525, copy had been handed to a Cologne printer, probably connected in some way with the important printing house of Peter Quentell, founded some fifty years earlier, and ten quires (eighty pages) of an edition of 3,000 copies in small quarto had been printed off, when an anti-Lutheran controversialist, Johann Dobneck,[1] better known as Cochlaeus, anxious to ingratiate himself with the king of England, persuaded the magistrates of Cologne to interfere. To escape arrest, Tyndale and his amanuensis, William Roy, fled along the Rhine to Worms, taking the printed quires with them, and it was thus at Worms, not at Cologne, that the first printed edition of the New Testament in English was brought out.

By a lucky chance a single copy of eight of the ten quires of Tyndale's New Testament printed at Cologne has been preserved, wanting only the first leaf, and is now in the British Museum, to which it was bequeathed by Thomas Grenville. According to Dobneck, a quarto edition was published at Worms, but whether this incorporated and completed the sheets printed at Cologne, or was entirely reset, is unknown, as no copy has survived. Our knowledge of Tyndale's Testament in its unrevised form thus rests on an octavo edition which has been identified from its types and illustrations as printed at Worms by Peter Schoeffer, the second son of the Schoeffer of the same name who had helped to make the art of printing a practical success at Mainz some seventy years before. This has survived in a copy at the Baptist College, Bristol, lacking only the first leaf, and another, much more imperfect, at St. Paul's Cathedral. According to Dobneck, Tyndale printed 6,000 New Testaments at Worms; it is thus probable that both the Worms quarto edition and the octavo, like the projected Cologne quarto, consisted of 3,000 copies.

The thirty-one leaves still extant of the Cologne fragment contain

---

[1] Dobneck has left three accounts of his exploit, of which he seems to have been more than a little proud, written respectively in 1533 and 1538 and (the fullest) in his *De actis et scriptis Martini Lutheri* of 1549.

Tyndale's Prologue and the text of St. Matthew down to the middle of chapter xxii. To the text are attached marginal notes, some of them vehemently anti-Roman. In the Worms octavo the marginal notes have been removed, but the prefaces are largely based on those of Luther, and the translation of the text shows abundant traces of Luther's German version. It is clear that Tyndale worked with this, the Vulgate, the Latin version of Erasmus, and the Greek text all before him, but it is also clear that it was primarily from the Greek that he translated, and that the other three books were only aids in the use of which he exercised his own very competent judgement. We have his personal assurance ('I had no man to counterfet, nether was holpe with englysshe of eny that had interpreted the same, or soche lyke thinge in the scripture beforetyme') that among his aids there was no copy of either of the 'Wyclifite' versions, and though some resemblances have been quoted between his translation and these, they are not sufficient to cast any doubt on his statement. On the other hand, Tyndale's own work fixed, once for all, the style and tone of the English Bible, and supplied not merely the basis of all subsequent Protestant renderings of the books (with unimportant exceptions) on which he laboured, but their very substance and body, so that those subsequent versions must be looked upon as revisions of his, not as independent translations.

After the octavo printed at Worms, no fragment of the text of any subsequent edition earlier than August 1534 is known to exist. Tyndale was at work on the Old Testament and refused all requests to supervise reprints of his version of the New. Copies of this are heard of as selling in England as early as the spring of 1526, and they were episcopally denounced in the following autumn. We hear of English Testaments sold the next year at five and seven groats apiece (1s. 8d. and 2s. 4d., answering to a modern value of ten or twelve times as much), and the profit on these prices may have been sufficient of itself to evoke unauthorized reprints, though it is equally probable that the unauthorized reprinters were enthusiasts who did not make pecuniary profit their chief object. According to George Joye, the editor of the unauthorized edition of August 1534, 'anon after' Tyndale's own issue (i. e. of 1525), the 'Dutchmen' got a copy and printed it again in a small volume, adding the Kalendar at the beginning, concordances (i. e. references to parallels) in the margins, and a Table at the end.[1] A second reprint was in

---

[1] This edition was apparently printed at Antwerp in 1526 by Christoffel van Endhoven, who was in trouble about it with the city authorities by the end of the year, and in 1531 died in prison at Westminster as a result of trying to sell Testaments in England. Endhoven also called himself Van Ruremond (in various spellings) and until Mr. Gordon Duff cleared up the matter in his *Century of the English Book Trade,* much confusion was caused by the natural assumption that the two names belonged to different men.

a larger form, and with larger type[1] and with figures, i. e. wood-cuts, in the Apocalypse. Of these two editions there were about 5,000 copies printed and these were all sold out some time in 1533. A third reprint, consisting of 2,000 copies, Joye was asked to revise, but refused. When, however, yet another was in preparation, rather, according to his own account, than allow 2,000 additional copies to be placed on the market with the errors which by this time a succession of Dutch compositors had introduced, he undertook to correct the edition which appeared in August 1534. For doing this he was paid at the rate of $4\frac{1}{2}d.$ for sixteen leaves, a small enough sum even when multiplied by ten to give it its modern value, but probably the full market-price of press-correction at that day. Unhappily, Joye did not confine himself to press-correction, but not only botched Tyndale's English in places where he thought it obscure, but in certain passages gave practical effect to views which he had expressed in private controversy with Tyndale by substituting the words 'the life after this' and similar phrases for Tyndale's 'the resurrection'. This edition was very neatly printed in sextodecimo at Antwerp by the widow of Christoffel van Endhoven, whose husband's share in Bible printing has been already mentioned in a note to page 8.

Meanwhile, Tyndale himself had at last revised his translation, and his new edition was printed as an octavo at Antwerp in November 1534 by Martin Emperour, otherwise known as Martin Caesar or Keysere. Tyndale had time to insert into this a vigorous and deserved denunciation of Joye, whom, however, he probably wronged in depicting him as actuated by merely mercenary motives. In 1904 the British Museum, which possesses both these editions, was fortunate enough to acquire yet another, previously unknown, 'prynted now agayne at Antwerpe by me Catharyn wydowe [the words 'of Christoffel of Endhouen' appear to have dropped out] in the yere of our lorde M. ccccc. and xxxv, the ix. daye of Januarye.' This contains a letter from Joye 'Unto the Reader' written at a moment when friends had brought the two men together, and Tyndale had agreed to withdraw his 'uncharitable pistle', as Joye calls it, and substitute a 'reformed' one in which they were both to 'salute the readers with one salutacion'. But the reconciliation was shortlived, the appearance of Joye's new edition being probably itself a fresh cause of offence ; Tyndale drew back, and on February 27, 1535, Joye sent to press an *Apology*, in which he made out the best case he could for himself and

---

[1] This may be the edition of 1532 of which Dr. Angus possessed a mutilated title-page. Joye certainly seems to be enumerating all the editions of which he knew, and, although he may have missed one or more which actually appeared, statements like that of Anderson (*Annals of the English Bible*), that there were six editions before the end of 1530, seem based on very slender evidence.

incidentally tells us that Tyndale was paid £10 for his edition of November 1534.

In December 1534 the Upper House of Convocation of the province of Canterbury had departed so far from its attitude of mere resistance as to petition the King that the Bible might be translated by authorized translators, and the progress which this denotes accounts for the rapidity with which one edition of Tyndale's New Testament follows another at this period. Tyndale himself revised one more, printed for him by G. H., i. e. Godfrid van der Haghen, ere he was enticed from the house of the English merchants at Antwerp in May 1535, with the result that once beyond the walls of the free city he was arrested by the imperial authorities and carried to imprisonment and death at Vilvorde. Yet another 1535 edition may be noticed (probably printed by Hans van Ruremond), because its strange spellings (faether, moether, &c.) at one time were imagined to have been adopted to assimilate its language to the dialect of the ploughboys for whom Tyndale had declared that he would write. More prosaic commentators attributed it to the vagaries of Flemish compositors. But several similar spellings are found in a letter written this year by Tyndale's friend, Thomas Poyntz, with whom he lodged at the 'English house' at Antwerp, and it is possible that they should be looked upon as among the phonetic devices by which many bookish people in the sixteenth century tried to express their views on pronunciation. All these phonetic devices without exception were bad, and it would be well if we could get rid of them, but while many remained to trouble us in the twentieth century, some were rejected very quickly, and those of the Antwerp press-corrector (possibly Thomas Poyntz himself) were among those which never obtained currency. It may be noted that the Van der Haghen edition of 1535 has sometimes been confused with that which has the strange spellings, and also that the spellings are repeated in a reprint known only from a fragment in the British Museum. Seven different issues or editions of Tyndale's New Testament appeared in 1536, the year of his martyrdom (October 6), and between 1525 and 1566, when the last dated edition was issued, more than forty editions were printed, of which definite evidence has been preserved. From the fact that many of these are known only from a single copy, or fragment of a copy, we may be sure that other editions have perished entirely.

Coverdale's
Bible. Had Tyndale escaped his enemies for but a few more years he would assuredly have translated the whole Bible. He had published an English Pentateuch in January 1530 [1531?], purporting to be printed by Luther's favourite printer, Hans Luft, not at Wittenberg but at 'Malborow [Marburg] in the land of Hesse' (an imprint of which the genuineness has been alternately accepted and denied by

bibliographers for a fatiguing number of years[1]),and a second edition
of this without date, or imprint (? Antwerp, Martin Keysere, 1531);
also, 'The prophete Ionas, with an introduccion before, teachinge
to understande him and the right use also of all the scripture.' To
his New Testament of November 1534, moreover, he had appended
English versions of all the lessons from the Old Testament appointed
to be read in the liturgy instead of Epistles. As we shall see, he
had also left behind him, in all probability, a manuscript translation
of the Old Testament as far as the end of Chronicles. But the
completion of an English Bible was reserved for a man of far less
scholarship, but an equally happy style, Miles Coverdale, a York-
shireman born in 1488, and educated at Cambridge, where he had
taken the degree of Bachelor of Canon Law as recently as 1531.

The most explicit information which Coverdale's Bible offers as to
its provenance is that of its colophon, which reads : 'Prynted in
the yeare of oure LORDE M.D.XXXV. and fynished the fourth
daye of October.' Its earliest title-page begins with the word
'Biblia' in roman majuscules, followed in German script type of
various sizes by the explanation : 'The Bible, that ‖ is, the holy
Scripture of the ‖ Olde and New Testament, faith ‖ fully and truly
translated out ‖ of Douche and Latyn in to Englishe ‖ M.D.XXXV.'
Subsequently this was replaced by another title in English black-
letter with the shortened formula, 'faythfully translated in ‖ to
Englyshe.' The whole of the text of the book is in a small German
script, and it had originally preliminary leaves in the same type (of
which only one has survived) ; these, however, were reprinted in
English black-letter at the same time as the title-page.

In his dedication to the king Coverdale protests 'I haue nether
wrested nor altered so moch as one worde for the mayntenaunce of
any maner of secte : but haue with a cleare conscience purely and
faythfully translated this out of fyue sundry interpreters, hauyng
onely the manyfest trueth of the scripture before myne eyes.'
Investigation has shown that of the five 'interpreters' here mentioned two must have been 'Douche' i.e. (i) the Swiss-German
version of Zwingli and Leo Juda, first printed at Zurich by

---

[1] The recent investigations of Mr. Steele have tended to connect the types
and ornaments with some firm at Antwerp, but Fox states circumstantially that
Tyndale took his translation to be printed at Hamburg, lost the manuscript by
shipwreck on the coast of Holland, and when he reached Hamburg in another
ship was obliged to begin his work anew, completing it with the aid of Miles
Coverdale. There are some difficulties in this account, but the hue and cry for
Lutheran books raised by Wolsey's agents in Antwerp at the end of 1526 and
beginning of 1527 make it not at all improbable that a press and materials may
have been shipped from Antwerp to Hamburg (also a Free City and under
ordinary circumstances comparatively safe) in 1527, and that books may have
been produced there until printing at Antwerp could be resumed. The attribution
of them to Luther's printer would have gained ready credence at the time, as
Tyndale's adversaries had greatly exaggerated Luther's influence on his work.

Christopher Froschouer in the years 1527–9, and (ii) Luther's German, of which the New Testament was printed in 1522, the Old Testament as far as the Song of Songs in 1523–4, and a complete edition in 1534 ; two Latin, i. e. (iii) the new rendering of Sanctes Pagninus, an Italian Catholic theologian, published with papal sanction at Lyons in 1527–8, and (iv) the Vulgate; and one English, i. e. (v) the New Testament and Pentateuch translated by Tyndale.

Coverdale graduated as Bachelor of Canon Law at Cambridge in 1531, but thereafter until 1536 his movements are unknown.[1] There has consequently been much dispute as to where and by what firm his Bible was printed in 1535. Early in the 18th century, however, Humphrey Wanley, the librarian of Robert Harley, Earl of Oxford, suggested that the printer was probably Christopher Froschouer of Zürich, who fifteen years later produced another edition of it. Investigation showed that two of the larger types of the English Bible of 1535 were in the possession of Froschouer, but these were used also by other German printers, and the matter remained undecided until, in his article on Coverdale in the *Dictionary of National Biography*, Mr. H. R. Tedder by the kindness of Dr. Christian Ginsburg was enabled to state that he had seen two leaves of a Swiss-German Bible printed in the same German type as the text of Coverdale's English version. The complete book, an unrecorded edition of 1529–30 from the press of Froschouer, had once been in Dr. Ginsburg's possession, but I learn from Dr. Ginsburg himself that this disappeared from his library in a very painful manner, and only these leaves remain. While it is regrettable that the complete evidence can no longer be produced, they may be taken as sufficiently establishing that it was at Zurich and by Froschouer that the first printed English Bible was issued.

The problem presented by the reprinted preliminary leaves is not very difficult. These, as printed at Zurich, probably did not exceed four, of which the first was occupied by the title with a list of the books of the Bible printed on the back, the second and third by Coverdale's Prologue, the fourth by the statement as to ' The first boke of Moses, called Genesis, what this boke conteyneth.' When it was ascertained that the book would be allowed to circulate in England it was very desirable to distinguish it from the Antwerp New Testaments which had brought such trouble on their purchasers. The word ' Douche ' was therefore eliminated from the title-page (' Latyn ' going with it),[1] a dedication to the king was

---

[1] If the story that he was subsidized while translating by Jacob van Meteren of Antwerp be believed he was probably part of the time at Antwerp.

[2] The space thus saved was devoted to extending the third of three texts quoted in the title by an additional two lines. It has been contended that the mention of ' Douche and Latyn ' was removed expressly to make room for this. Such a view surely reverses the relative importance of the two changes.

inserted and the whole quire was printed in English black-letter, almost certainly by James Nycholson at Southwark, first with the date M D X X X V on the title, afterwards with that of the following year. There would be the less difficulty in doing this, as under an Act passed in 1534 books printed abroad could not be imported into England ready bound, but only in sheets (so that English binders might make their profit off them), and there was thus no need to pull the book to pieces in order to make the change. In the revised form the preliminary quire was made up as follows :

> 1ᵃ, title ; 1ᵇ, blank ; 2ᵃ–4ᵃ, an Epistle || Unto the Kynges High-nesse ; 4ᵇ–7ᵃ, A prologe || To the reader ; 7ᵇ–8ᵃ, The bokes of the hole Byble || how they are named in Englyssh, etc. ; 8ᵇ, The first boke of || Moses, called || Genesis || what this book conteyneth.

Coverdale's version was reprinted in folio and quarto by James Nycholson in 1537, each edition bearing on its title, not over truth-fully, the words ' newly ouersene and corrected ', or, as the last word stands in the quarto, ' correcte.' The quarto title, which must thus be the later of the two, bears also the still more reassuring announcement, ' Set foorth with the Kynges moost gracious licence.' When as much favour was shown to it as this, it is surprising that this text of 1537 was not taken as the official version, since Coverdale was a much suppler and more conciliatory translator than Tyndale, and whereas the latter had consistently substituted (even going out of his way, at times, to do so), the less ecclesiastical terms *congregation, elder, favour, knowledge, love, repentance,* for *church, priest, grace, confession, charity, penance,* Coverdale was ready to use either or both. While, however, his folio and quarto were being printed at South-wark, a new Bible was being set up, almost certainly at Antwerp, which used Coverdale's version of the Old Testament from the end of Chronicles, including the Apocrypha, but Tyndale's New Testa-ment, as revised by him for the edition of May 1535, and also his Pentateuch and a hitherto unprinted version of Joshua—2 Chronicles, which has been conjectured with every appearance of reason to be Tyndale's continuation of his translation to the point, or very near the point,[1] which he had reached at the time of his arrest. This

Matthew's Bible.

---

[1] According to Halle's Chronicle, printed by Richard Grafton in 1548, Tyndale also translated Nehemiah, ' the Prophet Jonas and no more of the holy scripture.' Why Coverdale's version was preferred to his for Nehemiah is hard to see, but the statement strongly confirms the attribution of Joshua —2 Chronicles to Tyndale. The manuscript of this may have been handed by Thomas Poyntz, Tyndale's host at Antwerp, either to Rogers, the editor, or to the two English printers, Grafton and Whitchurch, who are known to have superin-tended the production of the edition. Poyntz and Grafton were both members of the Grocers' Company, at this time apparently very favourable to Protestantism. The attribution of the edition to a press at Antwerp is confirmed by Grafton sending Bibles to Cromwell by the hands of a servant who, as he tells Cromwell, had just arrived from Flanders.

version was corrected for the press by Tyndale's disciple, John Rogers, and was put forward as 'truly and purely translated into Englysh by Thomas Matthew', a probably fictitious and certainly deceptive attribution, the name serving at the time to cover the share of Tyndale, but being afterwards unequivocally treated as the alias of the real editor, Rogers.

Almost childish as the device of attributing a translation of the Bible made up of the work of Tyndale and Coverdale to a fictitious or man-of-straw Thomas Matthew[1] now appears, it served to save the face of the king and the bishops by the pretence that this was a new version, and so one which might be considered to have been made in compliance with the petition sent to the king by the Upper House of Convocation in December 1534. Cranmer had originally planned that such a version should be made by the English bishops, sharing the task between them, and there is evidence to show that some steps in this direction had actually been taken. But while some of the bishops had little fitness for such a task, others had still less inclination, and the work made no progress. Thus when the Matthew Bible was submitted to Cranmer, he wrote urgently to Cromwell (August 1537), entreating him to use his influence to get from the king 'a license that the same may be sold and redde of every person withoute danger of any acte, proclamacion or ordinaunce heretofore graunted to the contrary, untill such tyme that we the Bishops shall set forth a better translation, which I thinke will not be till a day after Domesday.' The petition thus made was granted, Cromwell's goodwill having apparently been already secured, and, with a lightheartedness which is really amazing, official sanction was given to a Bible largely made up of the work of Tyndale, and which included his markedly Protestant Prologue to Romans (based on Luther), and equally Protestant side-notes, some of them supplied by Rogers from the version of the French reformer Olivetan. In his letter to Cromwell Cranmer characterizes the book as 'a Bible in Englishe both of a new translation [which, save for the portion Joshua—2 Chronicles, from Tyndale's unpublished manuscript, it was not] and of a new prynte [Antwerp!], dedicated unto the Kinges Majestie, as farther apperith by a pistle unto His Grace in the begynnyng of the boke,' and further remarks, 'as for the translation, so farre as I have redde thereof I like it better than any other translation hertofore made.' No doubt in 1537 the king had moved a long way in the direction of Protestantism— for the moment—but considering his character, the whole transaction bore a remarkable resemblance to playing with gunpowder. From a letter of Grafton's it appears that 1,500 copies of this Bible were printed, and that it had cost him £500.

---

[1] A few years earlier there was a real Thomas Matthew at Colchester.

As was inevitable, the Matthew Bible was quickly superseded, but its importance was very great, since it formed the starting-point of the successive revisions which resulted in the version of 1611, a matter for sincere congratulation, as it contained (save for the rejection of his version of Nehemiah, Jonah, and the 'Epistles' from the Old Testament) the greatest possible amount of the work of Tyndale, who was a far better scholar than Coverdale. It was, however, to the latter, who is known to have been in England early in 1538, that the task of revising it, and expunging all controversial annotation, was entrusted. It was intended, at first, to substitute new notes, but although signs drawing attention to these were printed, the notes themselves were suppressed. For the revision of the text, great use was made in the Old Testament of a new Latin translation from the Hebrew by Sebastian Münster, published in 1534-5, while the New Testament was compared afresh with the translation of Erasmus and the Complutensian Polyglott. No English office being considered sufficiently well equipped to produce so large a book in a handsome manner, or with the speed desired, it was resolved to have recourse to the great Paris firm of François Regnault, who up to 1534 had been accustomed to print service-books for the English market. Coverdale and Grafton went to Paris to see the work through the press, and an edition of 2,000 copies was put in hand, the funds being provided wholly or mainly by Cromwell. Letters written by Coverdale and Grafton to Cromwell in June, August, and September, 1538, speak of the rapid progress of the book, and its arrival in England seemed to be only a matter of a few months. In November the king issued a proclamation which reflects the scandal caused to the less progressive Churchmen by the notes and prologues in Matthew's Bible. The contents of the earlier sections are thus summarized by Mr. Robert Steele (*Bibliography of Royal Proclamations of the Tudor and Stuart Sovereigns*, No. 176):

> In consequence of the import of certain printed books from abroad and the publication of others here 'with privilege' containing annotations in the margins, &c., imagined by the makers and printers of these books, dissension has been set up concerning the sacraments, &c. It is therefore ordered (1) that no English books printed abroad be brought into the country on pain of forfeiture of all goods and imprisonment. (2) No person to print any English book except after examination by some of the Privy Council or other persons appointed. The words 'cum privilegio regali' not to be used without 'ad imprimendum solum', and the whole copy or the effect of the licence to be printed underneath. No copies of Scripture with annotations to be printed except they are first examined, but only the plain sentence with a table. No translations to be printed without the name of the translator, unless the printer answer for it as his own. (3) No printer to publish any books of Scripture in English till they are examined by the King, or one of the Privy Council, or a bishop.

The Great Bibles.

While these provisions were clearly directed to prevent a recurrence of the scandal of 1537, some of them naturally caused great alarm to Grafton and Coverdale, who wrote at once to Cromwell to know how they were to be met. But a heavier blow was awaiting them. The relations between England and France were becoming critical, and the French ambassador, learning of Cromwell's personal interest in the English Bible which was being printed at Paris, wrote home suggesting that it should be seized. On December 9 the crisis was intensified by the execution of Cardinal Pole's relations on a charge of treason. On December 13 Coverdale became alarmed and wrote to Cromwell that he had deposited some of the printed sheets (quantity unspecified) with the English ambassador, Bishop Bonner, that something at least might be saved from the threatened wreck. Four days later the Inquisitors were let loose on the printing office, Regnault was arrested, the English correctors had to flee for their lives, and all the stock on the premises was seized for conveyance to the custody of the University of Paris. As early as December 31 we find Cromwell asking the French ambassador in London to secure its return. He had spent, he said, £400 on the work, and any good offices rendered in this matter should meet with due acknowledgement. Mention of the Bibles recurs in the ambassador's correspondence, and as late at least as July 1539 it is evident that the stock still lay at the University, and that the negotiations for its return were at a standstill. Yet the printed copies of the book bear a colophon which reads: 'The ende of the New Testament and of the whole Byble. Fynisshed in Apryll Anno M. CCCCC. XXXIX. A domino factum est istud.'

It seems probable that in the colophon just quoted there was at least a touch of bravado. Doubtless the completion in any form of the edition in April 1539 was indeed 'the Lord's doing', and doubtless its editors desired that it should appear marvellous in the eyes of their enemies. But it is far from certain that the existence of the colophon denotes the existence of sufficient copies for an edition to have been issued anywhere near the date named. In the later editions of his *Actes and Monumentes*, John Foxe added to his 'Story of the L[ord] Cromwell' a section 'Of the Bible in English printed in the large volume', and although almost every statement in this which can be tested can be shown to be inexact, his account of what happened in Paris is worth quoting:

> And so the printer went forward and printed forth the booke euen to the last part, and then was the quarell picked to the printer, and he was sent for to the inquisitors of the fayth, and there charged with certaine articles of heresie. Then were sent for the Englishmen that were at the cost and charge thereof, and also such as had the correction of the same, which was Myles Coverdale, but having some warning what would folow the said Englishmen posted away as fast as they could to saue themselves, leauing behynd them all their Bibles, which

were to the number of 2500, called the Bibles of the great volume, and neuer recouered any of them, sauing that the Lieftenaunt criminal hauing them delivered vnto him to burne in a place of Paris (like Smithfield) called Maulbert place, was somewhat mooued with couetousnes, and sold 4 great dry fattes of them to a Haberdassher to lap in caps, and those were bought againe, but the rest were burned, to the great and importunate losse of those that bare the charge of them. But notwithstandyng the sayd losse after they had recouered some part of the foresayd bookes, and were comforted and encouraged by the Lord Cromwell, the said Englishmen went agayne to Paris, and there got the presses, letters, and seruaunts of the aforesayd Printer and brought them to London, and there they became printers themselues (which before they neuer entended) and printed out the said Bible in London, and after that printed sundry impressions of them ; but yet not without great trouble and losse, for the hatred of the Bishops, namely, Stephen Gardiner, and his fellowes, who mightily did stomacke and maligne the printing thereof. (*Acts and Monuments*, newly recognised and inlarged by the Authour, John Foxe, 1583, page 1191).

It is clear from this narrative that the French authorities, while holding the bulk of the stock as an asset in their negotiations with Cromwell, made a pretence of burning it, and that of the copies set aside to be burnt, Grafton rescued a certain number, possibly sixty or eighty, as it would need a large vat to hold more than a score of them. Add the copies deposited with Bonner before the raid, and there may have been a hundred or so available for issue, enough for distribution, but not a quantity which could be put on the market. When, therefore, on the arrival of type and printers from France, the missing sheets were printed and the first edition finished, a new one, answering to the first page for page, so that sheets would be interchangeable, was put in hand, at the expense this time, not of Cromwell, but of a member of the haberdashers' company, Anthony Marler. In November 1539 there is good evidence that Grafton was once more in Paris and nothing is likely to have taken him there save the business of the Bible. It seems probable that this time he succeeded in rescuing the remains of the confiscated stock, and that this first Great Bible was thus ready for issue some time before the end of the year 1539, which, it must be remembered, answered to March 24, 1540, the more prevalent English reckoning at this time being from the Incarnation, not the Nativity, nor the Jan. 1 of the Roman Civil Year. Thus the issue of 'April 1539' was probably followed within a few weeks by that of April 1540, and this by a third in July, and a fourth in November, while yet others followed in May, November, and December, 1541, making seven Great Bibles in all. Only by an output on this scale could it be possible for every parish church to supply itself with a copy, as Cromwell had bade in the Injunctions which, as Vicar-General, he issued (before the trouble in Paris) in September 1538, and as the king commanded afresh by a proclamation of May 6, 1541, the limit of date being then fixed at the feast of All Saints (November 1), under penalty of a fine of forty shillings for each month's delay.   In order to lighten the obligation, the price of the book was fixed as low as 10s. unbound, or 12s. well and sufficiently bound, trimmed and clasped.   This price of ten shillings was only formally imposed by the Privy Council on April 25, 1541, but as early as November 1539 we find Cranmer writing to Cromwell that Berthelet (the king's printer) and Whitchurch had been with him, and that he had sanctioned a charge of 13s. 4d., but that as the printers understood that Cromwell desired it to be 10s., they were contented to sell them for that, if they could be protected against competition.   This Cromwell effected the same day, by getting a patent from the king made out to himself, which enabled him to make the authorized printers and publishers his deputies.   All the same, the substitution of 10s. for 13s. 4d. as the price must have hit the producers rather heavily, as from a curious lawsuit decided—such were the law's delays in Tudor times —in 1560, it appears that Anthony Marler had actually agreed to repurchase Bibles from a stationer named Philip Scapulis at the rate of 10s. 4d. apiece, or 4d. more than the price which he was himself allowed to charge (see 'Anthony Marler and the Great Bible ', by H. R. Plomer.   The Library, 3rd Series, i. 200–6).   If he had made many such contracts the vellum copy of the issue of April 1540, which Marler presented to the king, can hardly have been paid for out of profits.

In the fine wood-cut title-page, designed, it is said, by Holbein, for these Great Bibles, the king is shown seated while Cranmer and Cromwell stand distributing copies to the people, who receive them with shouts of 'Vivat Rex'.   For the 1539 Bible Cranmer had done nothing, and it is accordingly called Cromwell's.   That of April 1540 and the subsequent issues are enriched 'with a prologe thereinto, made by the reuerende father in God, Thomas archbysshop of Cantorbury,' and these are usually called Cranmer's.[1] The April 1540 text shows fairly numerous signs of further revision by Coverdale, and that of July of a few further changes ; the remaining editions were reprints.   The first, third, and fourth of the seven editions bear the name of Grafton, the second and fifth that of Whitchurch, the sixth mostly Whitchurch with a few Grafton titles, the seventh mostly Grafton with a few for Whitchurch.   The second, third, fifth, and seventh bear only the notice, 'This is the Bible appoynted to the vse of the churches ' ; the fourth and sixth bear title-pages specially worded to comply with the proclamations, viz. :

The Byble in Englyshe of the largest and greatest volume, auctorised and apoynted by the commaundement of oure moost redoubted prynce

---

[1] After Cromwell's execution in July 1540 his arms were cut out from this title-page.

and soueraygne Lorde, Kynge Henry the VIII, supreme head of this his churche and realme of Englande : to be frequented and vsed in euery church w 'in this his sayd realme, accordynge to the tenoure of hys former Iniunctions geuen in that behalfe. Ouersene and perused at the comaundement of the kinges hyghnes by the ryght reuerende fathers in God, Cuthbert, bysshop of Duresme, and Nicholas bisshop of Rochester. Printed by Rycharde Grafton [*in other copies* by Edwarde Whitchurch]. Cum priuilegio ad imprimendum solum, 1541.

Diligent investigation has not yet discovered in what the episcopal revision consisted.

A smaller folio edition was printed in 1540 by Petit and Redman for Berthelet, who, from his presence at the interview between Cranmer and Whitchurch as to the price of the Great Bible, seems to have helped Whitchurch with funds. It should be mentioned also that in 1539 an independent version by Richard Taverner, a barrister with a considerable knowledge of Greek, was printed by Petit for Berthelet, but this as attaining little success at the time and having no influence on the version of 1611 need not detain us here.

After December 1541 no more English Bibles were printed during the reign of Henry VIII. Proposals were made for a more conservative rendering, with due retention of ecclesiastical phrases, but these came to nothing. During the short reign of Edward VI the idea was entertained of a new revision by Fagius and Bucer, but this also fell through. Reprints, however, were very numerous, Matthew's Bible, the Great Bible, and Tyndale's Testament (revised and unrevised) being the most favoured, but Coverdale's Bible was also reprinted, and even Taverner's version of the Old Testament was touched up and reissued with Tyndale's of the New.

Under the reign of Mary there was no Bible-printing in England, but the number of Protestant exiles, holding extreme views and interested in scholarship, who found themselves congregated at Geneva, led to a new revision of great importance in the history of the English Bible. The Geneva Bible itself did not appear until 1560 but it was preluded in 1557 by a New Testament, obviously the work of a single translator, identifiable with practical certainty as William Whittingham, a senior student of Christ Church, Oxford, who subsequently (1563) became Dean of Durham, although he had received no episcopal ordination. While working on his translation Whittingham was acting as a 'senior' or elder of the Church at Geneva, of which in 1559 he became deacon and the following year minister. He is said to have been connected by marriage with Calvin, who contributed to the New Testament of 1557 'The Epistle declaring that Christ is the end of the Lawe', and he was undoubtedly the moving spirit of the Bible of 1560, which he stayed at Geneva to complete when other exiles were hurrying home on the accession of Elizabeth. Moreover, while the 1557 translation of the New Testament was very thoroughly

The Geneva Bible.

revised when reprinted in the Bible of 1560, the general lines of the earlier book were carefully followed in the later, and even some phrases were taken over from its preface. There is thus a very strong presumption that the new translation, destined to so great a popularity, originated with Whittingham, and that the trial New Testament was his individual work. The printing of this was completed at Geneva 'this x. of Iune' 1557, by Conrad Badius, the book being a pretty little 32°, in the style at that time specially popular at Lyons, with ornamental capitals and headpieces, printed in a small clear roman type, with a still smaller type of the same class for the marginal notes, and italics as a subsidiary fount. The title of the book reads :

> The || New Testa- || ment of our Lord Ie || sus Christ. ||| Conferred diligently with the Greke, and best ap- || proued translations. ||| With the arguments, aswel before the Chapters, as for euery Boke || & Epistle, also diuersities of readings, and moste proffitable || annotations of all harde places : wherunto is added a copi- || ous Table. [Woodcut illustrating the theme [1] : God by time restoreth Truth || and maketh her victorious.] At Geneva || Printed by Conrad Badius, || M.D. LVII.

In the preface, which deserves quotation in full, Whittingham says that in his translation he has chiefly had respect to the 'simple lambes, which partely are already in the folde of Christ, and so willingly heare their Shepeheards voyce, and partly wandering astray by ignorance, tary the tyme tyll the Shepeherde fynde them and bring them vnto his flocke', being himself 'moued with zeale, counselled by the godly, and drawen by occasion, both of the place where God hath appointed vs to dwel, and also of the store of heauenly learning & iudgement, which so abundeth in this Citie of Geneua, that iustely it may be called the patron and mirrour of true religion and godlynes'.

> To these therfore which are of the flocke of Christ which knowe their Fathers wil, and are affectioned to the trueth, I rendre a reason of my doing in fewe lines. First as touching the perusing of the text, it was diligently reuised by the moste approued Greke examples, and conference of translations in other tonges as the learned may easily iudge, both by the faithful rendering of the sentence, and also by the proprietie of the wordes and perspicuitie of the phrase. Furthermore that the Reader might be by all meanes proffited, I haue deuided the text into verses and sections, according to the best editions in other langages, and also, as to this day the ancient Greke copies mencion, it was wont to be vsed. And because the Hebrew and Greke phrases which are strange to rendre in other tongues, and also shorte, shulde not be so harde, I haue sometyme interpreted them without any whit diminishing the grace of the sense, as our langage doth vse them,

---

[1] It is evident that we have here the inspiration for the pageant of Time, Truth, and the Bible at 'the Little Conduit in Cheape' which attracted so much attention at the progress of Queen Elizabeth from Westminster to the Tower the next year.

and sometyme haue put to that worde, which lacking made the sentence obscure, but haue set it in such letters as may easely be discerned from the commun texte.

He goes on to explain his system of annotation, and the critical marks by which he drew attention to differences in the Greek manuscripts, either in single words or 'in the sentence', and finally expatiates at some length on the value of the Arguments 'aswel they which conteyne the summe of euery chapter, as the other which are placed before the bookes and epistles, wherof the commoditie is so great that they may serue in stede of a Commentarie to the Reader.'

Space forbids more quotation, but it will be evident from these extracts that it is to Whittingham's New Testament that the Version of 1611 owes two of its prominent features, its division into verses (taken by Whittingham from Étienne's Greek-Latin Testament of 1551) and the use of italics for explanatory and connective words and phrases (taken from Beza's New Testament of 1556). Whittingham's chapter-summaries, moreover, were much fuller than those of the Great Bible.

All the features in the New Testament of 1557 are repeated in the Bible of 1560, in preparing which Whittingham had the help of Anthony Gilby and Thomas Sampson, afterwards (from 1561 till his deprivation in 1565) Dean of Christ Church. The funds for this were apparently subscribed by the Protestant exiles or sent out by friends in England, since the translator speaks of 'being earnestly desired and by diuers, whose learning and godlynes we reuerence, exhorted and also incouraged by the ready willes of suche, whose heartes God likewise touched, not to spare any charges for the fortherance of suche a benefite and fauour of God toward his Churche.' One of these helpers was John Bodley (father of Sir Thomas), who in January 1561 received an exclusive patent from Elizabeth for printing this Bible for seven years, a grant which in March 1565 (? 1566) Parker and Grindal recommended should be extended for another twelve, but subject to a condition of episcopal supervision which apparently Bodley could not accept. By the help of these funds the translators were able to borrow or buy woodcuts to illustrate the descriptions of the tabernacles, &c., in Exodus, 1 Kings, and Ezekiel from Antoine Rebul, the publisher of the French Bible printed at Geneva in the same year. They allude to these cuts in their preface and also to the addition of verse-numbers in the chapter-summaries, by which these were brought into the form used in 1611.

As regards the literary influences which afiected the Geneva version, it is clear that increased use was made of the Latin translation of Pagninus, the revised Bible of Leo Juda, and that of Sebastian Münster, also of the French revisions of Olivetan. For the New Testament Whittingham had constant recourse to the French version of Beza (Théodore de Bèze), published in 1556; further use was made of this in 1560, while in 1576 Laurence Tomson (a Fellow of Magdalen College, Oxford, who sat for fourteen years, 1575–89, in the House of Commons) used the Geneva version as the basis of a direct translation from the French of Beza, and editions of this were often bound up with the Geneva Old Testament.

After Elizabeth's accession the Great Bible was once again, by the Injunctions of 1559, ordered to be set up in churches, and new editions were printed by R. Harrison at London in 1562, and at Rouen in 1566 by Cardin Hamillon, at the expense of Richard Carmarden (an Englishman connected with the customs), this foreign edition disarming suspicion by stating on its title-page that it was 'According to the translation apoynted by the Queenes Majesties Iniunctions to be read in all Churches with in her Majesties Realme'. Archbishop Parker had shown no ill-will to the Geneva version, was even, indeed, subject to conditions, ready to support John Bodley's application for an extension of his privilege for it, but the use of a translation with bitterly controversial notes in the public services of the Church was contrary both to Tudor ideals of uniformity and to Parker's own preference for the *via media*. In or before 1566, therefore, perhaps at the instigation of Richard Cox, Bishop of Ely, he revived the project, which had come to naught in Cranmer's day, of a new revision to be mainly the work of the Anglican bishops. Beyond two or three quotations in Strype's Life of Parker from letters of prelates engaged in the task we know curiously little about its progress until October 5, 1568, when Parker was able to send to Sir William Cecil a bound copy for presentation to the Queen, and enclosed with it a dedicatory letter, and (for Cecil's information) a list of the revisers and a copy of the 'Observations respected' by them. The observations tell us that the revisers were to follow the Great Bible 'and not to recede from it but where it varyeth manifestly from the Greek or Hebrew original', to make use of the versions of Pagninus and Münster, to abstain from bitter or controversial notes, to mark sections not edifying for public reading, and to substitute more convenient terms and phrases for 'all such words as sound [tend] in the old translation to any offence of lightnes or obscenity'.

As regards the personality of the revisers, Parker tells Cecil 'because I would you knew all, I here send you a note to signify who first travailed in the divers books, though after them some other perusing was had; the letters of their names be partly affixed in the end of their books; which I thought a policy to show them, to make them more diligent, as answerable for their doings.' When we turn to the Bible itself we find initials such as Parker thus leads

The
Bishops'
Bible.

us to expect not only at the end of certain books, but also in certain cases printed in or under the ornamental capital with which a book or chapter begins. We may thus construct the following table :

	Parker's Note.	Indications in the Bible.	Author.
The sum of the Scripture . The Tables of Christ's Line The Arguments of the Scripture The first Preface unto the Whole Bible The Preface unto the Psalter The Preface unto the New Testament	M. Cant. .	The Archbishop's arms quartered with those of Christ Church, Canterbury, in the capital before the Table of Christ's Line ; his personal arms in the capital before the general preface or prologue	Matthew Parker, Archbishop of Canterbury.
Genesis . . . Exodus . . .	M. Cant. .	Initials M. C. under capitals	Matthew Parker.
Leviticus . . . Numbers . . .	Cantuariae .		Andrew Pierson, Prebend. of Canterbury.
Deuteronomy . .	W. Exon. .	W. E. at end . .	William Alley, Bishop of Exeter.
Joshua . . . Judges . . . Ruth . . . Kings (Samuel) I, II .	R. Meneven .	R. M. at end . .	Richard Davies, Bishop of St. Davids.
Kings III, IV (I, II) . Chronicles I, II .	Ed. Wigorn .	E. W. under capital and at end	Edwin Sandys, Bishop of Worcester.
Job . . . Proverbs . . .	Cantuariae .	A. P C at end of each book	Andrew Pierson, Prebend. of Canterbury.
Ecclesiastes . . Cantica . . .	Cantabrigiae .	A P E at end . .	Andrew Perne, Dean of Ely.
Ecclesiasticus . Susanna . . . Baruch . . . Maccabees . .	J. Norwic .	J. N. . . .	John Parkhurst, Bishop of Norwich.
Esdras . . . Judith . . . Tobias . . . Wisdom . . .	W. Cicestren. .	W. C. (in some copies) at end of Wisdom	William Barlow, Bishop of Chichester.
Isaiah . . . Jeremiah . . . Lamentations . .	R. Winton .	R. W. at end . .	Robert Horne, Bishop of Winchester.
Ezekiel . . . Daniel . . .	J. Lich. and Covent.	T. C. L. at end .	Thomas Bentham, Bishop of Coventry and Lichfield.
Minor Prophets .	Ed. London .	E. L. at end . .	EdmundGrindal, Bishop of London.
Matthew . . . Mark . . .	M. Cant. .	M. C. under first capital	Matthew Parker.
Luke . . . John . . .	Ed. Peterb. .		Edmund Scambler, Bishop of Peterborough.
Acts . . . Romans . . .	R. Eliensis .	R. E. at end of both .	Richard Cox, Bishop of Ely.

	Parker's Note.	Indications in the Bible.	Author.
1 Corinthians . . .	D. Westmon.	G. G. at end . .	Gabriel Goodman, Dean of Westminster.
2 Corinthians . . .			
Galatians . . .		M. C. under capitals beginning 2 Corinth. Galatians (in some copies), Ephesians, Philipp., 1, 2 Coloss., 1, 2 Thessal., Titus, Philemon, Hebrews	Matthew Parker.
Ephesians . . .			
Philippians . .	} M. Cant.		
Colossians . .			
Thessalonians . .			
Timothy . . .			
Titus . . .			
Philemon . . .			
Hebrews . . .			
Canonical Epistles .	} N. Lincoln .	H. L. under capitals beginning 1 Peter v, 2 Peter iii, 1 John v, 3 John, Jude and Apocalypse xxii	Nicholas Bullingham, Bishop of Lincoln (? completed by Hugh Jones, Bishop of Llandaff).
Apocalypse . .			

The Bishops' Bible (continued).

It will be noticed that in the above list (the books in which are given in Parker's order, but with English instead of Latin names) there is no mention of the Psalms. These had originally been assigned to Guest, Bishop of Rochester, but the intention he expressed in a letter quoted by Strype of bringing his translation into violent conformity with the New Testament quotations had apparently alarmed Parker, and the initials at the end of the book are T. B. These Strype interpreted as standing for Thomas Becon, a prebendary of Canterbury, but a very unlikely man. Dr. Aldis Wright, in his revision of Westcott's *General View of the History of the English Bible* assigns them, no doubt rightly, to Thomas Bickley, one of Parker's chaplains, afterwards Bishop of Chichester. The only other difficulty is as to the responsibility for the Canonical Epistles and the Apocalypse. Until Dr. Wright drew attention to them, the initials beneath the capitals in such seemingly haphazard positions had escaped notice. His conjecture that the revision was begun by the Bishop of Lincoln and completed by his brother of Llandaff meets the case, though it is strange that the first worker should have left so many of his books unfinished.

Portioned out, as it was, among a number of individual revisers who, as far as we know, never checked each other's work, the Bishops' Bible, as it came to be called from the number of prelates who collaborated in it, while an improvement on the Great Bible, more especially in the New Testament, can hardly be regarded as much more than a makeshift. In form, on the other hand, it is a handsome book,[1] and Parker highly commended Richard Jugge, the

[1] Messrs. Darlow and Moule note that 27s. 8d. was paid for a copy by St. John's College, Cambridge, in 1571.

printer, to Cecil for the pains he had taken with it, even to the point of printing the New Testament on thicker paper to withstand the extra amount of wear it was likely to receive. The Bible is embellished with numerous woodcuts, and also with a fine engraved title-page, attributed to Franciscus Hogenberg, bearing in the centre a rather pleasing portrait of the Queen. Before the Book of Judges, there is another engraved portrait, representing the Earl of Leicester, in whom the bishops apparently found some resemblance to Joshua, and at the beginning of the Psalms a third portrait, of Lord Burghley holding a B, which thus at once does duty for a capital and helps to identify its holder. Punning capitals, of which this may claim to be one of the least pleasing, had been for some time in vogue, but in the second folio edition, published in 1572, the B was taken out of the plate and Burleigh divorced from his immediate connexion with the Psalter. A little further revision was bestowed on the New Testament in this reprint, and the Psalter is printed twice over, once as revised, and once in the text of the Great Bible, still familiar to all churchgoers as the ' Prayer-book version '.

The struggle for supremacy between the Geneva and the Bishops' version leads so directly to the undertaking of that of 1611 that we must leave the discussion of it to our next chapter. Meanwhile there is still another translation to be noticed here.

The years which followed the publication of the Bishops' Bible witnessed a devoted attempt by the Jesuits to win back England to the faith. It appears to have been in connexion with this attempt that the New Testament was rendered into English by members of the English College at Douay early in their temporary exile to Rheims which began in 1578. In a Latin letter written by Cardinal Allen to Dr. Vendeville, September 16 in that year,[1] we find this interesting passage, in a description of the life of the college :

On every Sunday and festival English sermons are preached by the more advanced students on the gospel, epistle or subject proper to the day. . . . We preach in English, in order to acquire greater power and grace in the use of the vulgar tongue. . . . In this respect the heretics, however ignorant they may be in other points, have the advantage over many of the more learned Catholics, who having been educated in the universities and the schools do not commonly have at command the text of Scripture or quote it except in Latin. Hence when they are preaching to the unlearned and are obliged on the spur of the moment to translate some passage which they have quoted into the vulgar tongue, they often do it inaccurately and with unpleasant hesitation, because either there is no English version of the words or it does not then and there occur to them. Our adversaries on the other hand have at their

The Rheims New Testament.

[1] The text is given on pp. 52–67 of *Letters and Memorials of William Cardinal Allen* by T. F. Knox (1882) the translation on p. xl. sq. of the *First and Second Diaries of the English College at Douay* by the same editor (1878).

fingers' ends all those passages of Scripture which seem to make for them, and by a certain deceptive adaptation and alteration of the sacred words produce the effect of appearing to say nothing but what comes from the bible. This evil might be remedied if we too had some catholic version of the bible, for all the English versions are most corrupt. I do not know what kind you have in Belgium. But certainly we on our part, if his Holiness shall think proper, will undertake to produce a faithful, pure and genuine version of the bible in accordance with the edition approved by the Church, for we already have men most fitted for the work.

The man of all others most fitted for the work in Allen's eyes was Gregory Martin, one of the original scholars (1557) of St. John's College, Oxford, when Edmund Campion was a Fellow, now in 1578 lecturer in Hebrew and Holy Scripture at the Douay-Rheims College. According to the entry in the College Diaries he began to translate the Bible on or about October 16 (i.e. just a month after Allen's letter), and in order to get on with it rapidly, made a practice of translating two chapters daily, his version being corrected by Allen himself and by Richard Bristow, Moderator of the College. His work occupied him altogether three years and a half, the entry, ' Hoc ipso mense extrema manus Nouo Testamento Anglice edito imposita est' occurring in the Diary under March, 1582, and in the same year the New Testament was published with the title :

> The New Testament of Iesus Christ, translated faithfully into English, out of the authentical Latin, according to the best corrected copies of the same, diligently conferred with the Greeke and other editions in diuers languages : With Arguments of bookes and chapters, Annotations, and other necessarie helpes, for the better vnderstanding of the text, and specially for the discouerie of the corruptions of diuers late translations, and for cleering the controuersies in religion of these daies : in the English College of Rhemes. [Quotations [1] in Latin and English]. Printed at Rhemes by Iohn Fogny. 1582. Cum priuilegio.

On the back of the title is ' The Censure and Approbation ' signed by four licensers, and this is followed by twenty-two pages of small print containing ' The Preface to the Reader treating of these three points : of the translation of Holy Scriptures into the vulgar tongues, and namely into English ; of the causes why this new Testament is translated according to the auncient vulgar Latin text :

---

[1] The first from Psalm 118 ' Give me vnderstanding, and I wil searche thy law, and wil keepe it with my whole hart ', the second from St. Augustine, tract 2, on the Epistles of St. John ' al things that are readde in holy Scriptures we must heare with great attention, to our instruction and saluation : but those things specially must be commended to memorie, which make most against Heretikes : whose deceites cease not to circumuent and beguile al the weaker sort and the more negligent persons.'

& of the maner of translating the same.' Interesting as this preface
is, there is no need to quote from it here, though it may be well to
remind any reader struck with the superficial absurdity of translating
from a translation instead of an original, that if St. Jerome worked
from better Greek manuscripts than any which were known in the
sixteenth century, his Latin translation might, at least theoretically,
represent the original Greek better than any manuscript used by
Erasmus. Practically, of course, the question would be one of the
balance between loss and gain, and in striking this balance Gregory
Martin, or whoever wrote the preface, was probably very insufficiently
conscious that if the available Greek texts were corrupt the available
Latin texts were very corrupt also, and far from representing what
St. Jerome really wrote. Thus from the point of view of scholarship the decision to translate from the Vulgate was doubtless wrong,
but it was not absurd, and there is ample evidence that Martin and
his supervisors were good Graecists, and on any point, such as the
use of the article, on which they felt free to interpret the Latin
by the Greek, did so with conspicuous success.

Another point which must be made is that the translation is
much simpler than popular accounts of it make out. It is quite
true that the translators acted up to their declaration, ' we presume
not in hard places to mollifie the speaches or phrases, but religiously
keepe them word for word, and point for point, for feare of missing
or restraining the sense of the holy Ghost to our phantasie,' and it is
possible to quote verses, especially from the Epistles, which remain
utterly unintelligible until we know the original. In this the
translators seem to have forgotten the needs of popular preaching
which Cardinal Allen made the main ground for setting Gregory
Martin to work. But ' hard places ' do not occur on every page
of the New Testament, and it is easy to find long passages in the
Gospels without a difficult word in them, and which a good reader
could make all the more dramatic because of the abruptness of some
of the constructions and transitions.

The Jesuit New Testament was reprinted at Antwerp in 1600.
In 1593 the College returned from Rheims to Douai, and in 1609-
10, a press having been set up in the town, the Old Testament
was printed there. This had been mentioned in the Introduction
of 1582 as ' lying by us for lacke of good meanes to publish the
whole in such sort as a worke of so great charge and importance
requireth,' and it was doubtless the news of the forthcoming
new Anglican version which at last brought it to the light.
No use was made of the Old Testament by the Anglican revisers,
but in his excellent study, *The Part of Rheims in the making of the
English Bible* (1902), Dr. James G. Carleton has shown that the
influence of the Rheims New Testament on the version of 1611
was very considerable. That it attained this influence was mainly

due to the exertions of the Rev. William Fulke, D.D., who in 1589 published 'The Text of the New Testament of Iesus Christ, translated out of the vulgar Latine by the Papists of the traiterous Seminarie at Rhemes', and very honestly reprinted the whole translation with its notes, parallel with the Bishops' version and alternated with his own confutations. Fulke's folio (reprinted in 1601, 1617, and 1633) was regarded for over forty years as a standard work on the Protestant side, and probably every reviser of the New Testament for the edition of 1611 possessed it. Along with Tyndale, Coverdale, Whittingham, and Parker, the exiled Jesuit, Gregory Martin, must be thus recognized as one of the builders of the version of the Bible which after three centuries is still in scarcely disturbed possession of the affections of the English people.

II. THE BIBLE OF 1611

IN his letter of October 5, 1568, to Cecil, forwarding a copy of the Bishop's Bible for presentation to the Queen, Archbishop Parker writes with obvious timidity : 'The printer hath honestly done his diligence ; if your honour would obtain of the Queen's Highness that this edition might be licensed and only [1] commended in public reading in churches, to draw to one uniformity, it were no great cost to the most parishes, and a relief to him for his great charges sustained.' That the adoption of the new version for use in churches should thus be urged mainly on the ground of an obligation to recoup the printer is certainly strange, but the very half-hearted canons on the subject passed by the Province of Canterbury in 1571 show that there was not much enthusiasm to be reckoned on. The passage usually quoted (Cardwell, *Synodalia*, 115) is indeed almost malicious, since it merely lays down that every archbishop and bishop is to have the book ('sacra Biblia in amplissimo volumine, uti nuperrime Londini excusa sunt') in his own house along with Fox's *Book of Martyrs* and other similar works, and that deans were to see that it was bought and placed in their cathedrals in order that vicars, minor canons, the servants of the church, strangers, and wayfarers might read and hear it, and were also to buy it for their own households, i. e. the chief obligation imposed was on the bishops and other 'superior clergy' to buy their own revision. In a later canon (Cardwell, *Synodalia*, 123) churchwardens are enjoined to see that a copy of the new edition is placed in every church [2], but the proviso, 'if it can be done con-

---

[1] i.e. to the exclusion of any other.

[2] ' Curabunt etiam ut sacra Biblia sint in singulis ecclesiis in amplissimo volumine (si commode fieri possit) qualia nunc nuper Londini excusa sunt.'

veniently,' is in striking contrast with the royal order to provide
a copy by a certain day under penalty of a fine of four times its cost
for every month of delay, which had been issued by Proclamation
in the case of the Great Bible.

With little backing, either from the State or from his own Convocation, Parker was left to deal with the question of the circulation
of the Bible by means of his own resources, and these, it must be
remembered, owing to the duties cast on him in connexion with
the licensing of books for the press, were, for any negative purpose,
very great. In March 1565 (? 1566) he and Grindal, who as Bishop
of London shared these duties, had recommended Cecil to extend
John Bodley's exclusive privilege for printing the Geneva Bible for
another twelve years on the ground that ' thoughe one other speciall
Bible for the churches be meant by us to be set forthe, as convenient time and leysor hereafter will permytte: yet shall it nothing
hindre, but rather do moch good to have diversitie of translacions
and readings.' They had added, however, ' and if his licence, hereafter to be made, goe simplye foorthe withowt proviso of owr over-
sight, as we thinke it maye so passe well ynoughe, yet shall we take
suche ordre in writing withe the partie, that no impression shall passe
but by our direccion, consent and advise.' In the face of this last
sentence it is highly significant that during Parker's life no edition
of the Geneva Bible was printed in England, although at Geneva
itself one was published by John Crispin in 1570. At variance
with the Privy Council over the question of ' prophesyings ' during
1574, Parker was unable during the last months of his life to
attend its meeting owing to his rapidly failing health. He died
on May 17, 1575, and as the first Geneva New Testament printed
in London is dated in this year without specifying the month, we
cannot say with complete certainty that he was dead before its
publication, although there are good reasons for placing this in the
latter half of the year. It is impossible, however, to avoid the
conviction that to the very end of his life Parker used his control
over the Stationers' Company to prevent the Geneva version being
printed in England, and also to secure for Jugge the monopoly of
printing the Bishops' Bible.

According to the ideas of the day the exclusion of the Geneva
Bible was perhaps justified by the character of a few of the notes.
The monopoly secured for Jugge might also have been defended
from the Tudor standpoint, if it had been accompanied by an insistence that the Bishops' version should be effectively circulated; but,
as far as the evidence before us shows, there was no such insistence.
Editions in large folio were printed in 1568, 1572, and 1574; others
in large quarto in 1569 and 1573. Evidence as to editions in octavo,
either of the whole Bible or of the New Testament, is much less
exact, owing on the one hand to the curious absence of dates from

the two or three editions probably of this period of which copies remain, and on the other to the possibility of one or more entire editions having perished. But taking the most favourable view possible, it seems certain that the Archbishop cared little for providing Bibles for private reading. He saw and met the need of suitable editions for the service of the church, but to use a phrase which, though it has a ring of these present times, is taken from the preface to the version of 1611 (where it is applied to the Roman Catholic position) he did not 'trust the people' with cheap editions of the Bible, and his lack of confidence sealed the fate of the Bishops' Bible.

Immediately after the death of Archbishop Parker, the other printers of London, who had previously acquiesced in Jugge's monopoly of Bible-printing, took courage to urge their right to share it. A compromise was patched up by which Jugge was left with the exclusive right of printing editions of the Bible in quarto, and of the New Testament in sextodecimo, while the other sizes were left free, subject (presumably to secure responsibility for accuracy) to a licence from the Stationers' Company. Licences were obtained, and on November 24, 1575, there appeared a folio edition of the Bishops' Bible, printed by Jugge, but on behalf of William Norton, Luke Harrison, and other stationers, each of whom put his name on a portion of the edition. This was apparently the beginning of the 'Bible Stock' of the Stationers' Company, a company within a company, the subsequent history of which is very obscure, but which is said to have earnt profits and possessed funds which enabled it, on occasion, to lend money at interest to the Stationers' Company itself. If, as is usually said, the revisers of 1611 received any payment from the Company, it must have been from this separate Bible Stock that it was derived. The existence of this Stock also offers a strong ground for believing that the compromise of 1575 continued to affect the business of Bible-printing in ways of which we have no knowledge. But for this we should be bound to believe that it had no other result than the folio edition of the Bishops' Bible already mentioned. In this same year, 1575, under the powerful patronage of Sir Francis Walsingham, Christopher Barker, who had been in Walsingham's service, and was himself a man of some means, employed Thomas Vautrollier to print for him an edition in duodecimo of the Geneva Bible, hitherto unprinted in England, and printed another edition himself in octavo. Barker advertised his connexion with Walsingham by taking the latter's crest, a tiger's head, as the sign of his house, and used a cut of it as an ornament in his books. He also printed in 1576 the already mentioned translation of Beza's French New Testament, on the basis of the Geneva version, made by Laurence Tomson, who was in Walsingham's service. He further printed two folio editions of the Geneva Bible in 1576 and another in 1577. In that year Richard Jugge made his will, on August 17 and 18, and died. From subsequent allusions we know that his patent as Queen's printer must immediately have been obtained (if the reversion had not already been secured) by Thomas Wilkes, a diplomatist of some ability. The new patent extended to all editions of the Bible, and Wilkes must have tried at first to work it through John Jugge, the son of Richard, since John, who had begun business for himself the previous May by copyrighting two insignificant books, is actually called Queen's Printer about this time in a largely signed petition against monopolies. He disappears, however, possibly by death, possibly because Wilkes learnt that he was receiving under his father's will the inconsiderable sum of 10s., and was thus not a person to be dealt with. On September 28, at Wilkes's instance, a new patent conferring complete monopoly of Bible-printing was granted to Christopher Barker. Five years later, in 1582, when monopolies were again challenged, Barker wrote as follows :

> The whole bible together requireth so great a somme of money to be employed in the imprinting thereof : as Master Iugge kept the Realme twelue yere withoute, before he Durst aduenture to print one [1] impression[1]; but I considering the great somme I paide to Master Wilkes, Did (as some haue termed it since) gyue a Desperate aduenture to imprint fower sundry impressions for all ages, wherein I employed to the value of three thowsande pounde in the terme of one yere and an halfe, or thereaboute : in which tyme if I had died, my wife and children had ben vtterlie vndone, and many of my frendes greatlie hindered by disbursing round sommes of money for me, by suertiship and other meanes : as my late good master Master Secretary for one, so that nowe this gappe being stopped, I haue little or nothing to doe, but aduenture a needlesse charge; to keepe many Journemen in worke, most of them seruauntes to my predicessours.

The 'fower sundry impressions' to which Barker here alludes, comprised a small folio and octavo in 1577, and two large folios in 1578. One of the large folios was of the Bishops' version but of this we find him writing to the City Companies as 'another Bible, which was begon before I had authoritie, as it is affirmed, which could not be finished but by my consent and therefore hath the name to be printed by the assignment of Christopher Barker'. All the other three impressions were of the Geneva version, and the large folio is a very notable volume since it was clearly intended for use in churches and was ccompanied by a prayer-book in which the word 'minister' was throughout substituted for 'priest , and references to the books from which they come printed instead of the text of the Gospels and Epistles. All this surely shows that, despite the suspension of Grindal, the extremer Protestant party were very strong, and that behind these

---

[1] This must refer to the period before 1568

printing ventures, for which Walsingham helped to find money, there was something more than ordinary trading. Numerous other editions of the Geneva version were printed during the next five years, but I can find no single Bishops' Bible to balance them. When, however, Whitgift succeeded Grindal as Archbishop, Barker was awakened from his dream that the 'gappe' was stopped, and ordered to put in hand a smaller and larger edition of the Bishops' Bible, as to which when they were both ready (the quarto in 1584, the folio in 1585), and apparently had not sold very quickly, Whitgift wrote (July 16, 1587) to the Bishop of Lincoln :

> Whereas I am credibly informed, that divers, as well parish churches, as chapels of ease, are not sufficiently furnished with Bibles, but some have either none at all, or such as be torn and defaced, and yet not of the translation authorized by the synods of bishops : these are therefore to require you strictly in your visitations, or otherwise, to see that all and every the said churches and chapels in your diocese be provided of one Bible, or more, at your discretion, of the translation allowed as aforesaid, and one book of Common Prayer, as by the laws of this realm is appointed. And for the performance thereof, I have caused her highness's printer to imprint two volumes of the said translation of the Bible aforesaid, a bigger and a less, the largest for such parishes as are of ability, and the lesser for chapels and very small parishes ; both which are now extant and ready.

One other folio of the Bishops' Bible was printed by Christopher Barker himself in 1588. In August, 1589, he secured a fresh patent from the queen for his own life and that of his son Robert, and thenceforth entrusted his Bible-printing to deputies, until his death in 1599. During the fourteen years 1589–1603 three more folio editions of the Bishops' Bible appeared, no quarto, and three or four octavos. Against this, during the entire period from 1575 onwards, on an average three editions of the Geneva version were produced each year, the majority of them in small sizes for private reading. How far this superiority was the result of demand, how far it was produced by a control of the supply, is a question which, difficult as it is to answer, deserves more attention than it has received. It is clear, on the one hand, that during Parker's life the circulation of the Geneva version was artificially barred, and nothing was done to popularize its rival. It is clear, I think, also, that from the death of Parker to the appointment of Whitgift, the positions were reversed, and that in these eight years the Geneva version, which was not only favoured, but pushed, by the aid of Walsingham and his friends, with a zeal in which politics, religion, and desire for gain (closely allied in those days) were all combined, was put on the market in such quantities as to give it a real hold on the English people. After Whitgift's accession it is possible that, as the scales were more evenly held, the editions of each version came gradually to be issued mainly in accordance with the demand, although until nearly the end of the century the rarity of octavo editions of the Bishops' version is very noticeable. But taking the period as a whole it is obvious that other influences than those of publishers merely anxious to make money were contending over the fortunes of the two versions, and that the short-sighted policy of Parker gave Walsingham and his friends a chance of which they availed themselves to the full. Interpret the evidence as we may, the fact must steadily be borne in mind that throughout the reign of Elizabeth, the production of editions of the Bible was always a controlled production, and when we come to consider the fortunes of the version of 1611 it will be well to remember that the control still went on.

The lack of agreement between the Bible which men read in their houses and that which they heard in church must have caused annoyance to both parties. It is creditable to the scholarship, and perhaps also to the foresight, of the Puritan party, that at the Conference at Hampton Court, which James I called together (quite informally) in January 1604 to ascertain how far the Puritan complaints could be met, the demand for a new translation, which would command the assent of the whole church, came from their spokesman, Dr. John Reynolds, President of Corpus Christi College, Oxford. According to the fullest account of the Conference which has come down to us, Reynolds began by raising questions about the Catechism, &c.

After that, he moued his Maiestie, that there might bee a newe *translation* of the *Bible*, because, those which were allowed in the raignes of *Henrie* the eight, and *Edward* the sixt, were corrupt and not aunswerable to the truth of the Originall. For example, first, *Galathians*, 4, 25, the Greeke word συστοιχεῖ is not well translated, as nowe it is, *Bordreth*, neither expressing the force of the worde, nor the Apostles sense, nor the situation of the place.

Secondly, *Psalme*, 105, 28, *they were not obedient*; the Originall beeing, *They were not disobedient*.

Thirdly, *Psalme*, 106, verse 30. Then stood up *Phinees* and *prayed*, the Hebrew hath *Executed iudgement*. To which motion, there was, at the present, no gainsaying, the obiections beeing triuiall and old, and alreadie, in print, often aunswered; onely, my Lord of *London* well added, that if euery mans humour should be followed, there would be no ende of translating. Whereupon his Highnesse wished that some especiall paines should be taken in that behalfe for one vniforme translation (professing that hee could neuer, yet see a Bible well translated in English; but the worst of all, his Maiestie thought the *Geneua* to bee) and this to bee done by the best learned in both the Vniuersities, after them to be reuiewed by the Bishops, and the chiefe learned of the Church; from them to bee presented to the *Priuie-Councell*; and lastly to bee ratified by his *Royall authoritie*;

and so this whole Church to be bound vnto it, and none other ; Marry, withall, hee gaue this caueat (vpon a word cast out by my Lord of London) that no marginall notes should be added, hauing found in them which are annexed to the *Geneua* translation (which he sawe in a Bible giuen him by an English Lady) some notes very partiall, vntrue, seditious, and sauouring too much of daungerous, and trayterous conceites. As for example, *Exod.* 1, 19, where the marginal note alloweth *disobedience to Kings.* And 2. *Chron.* 15, 16, the note taxeth *Asa* for deposing his mother, *onely,* and *not killing* her : And so concludeth this point, as all the rest with a graue and iudicious aduise. First, that errours in matters of faith might bee rectified and amended. Secondly, that matters indifferent might rather be interrupted and a glosse added ; alleaging from *Bartolus de regno,* that as better a King with some weaknesse, then still a chaunge ; so rather, a Church with some faultes, then an *Innouation.* And surely, sayth his Maiestie, if these bee the greatest matters you be grieued with, I neede not haue beene troubled with such importunities and complaintes, as haue beene made vnto me ; some other more priuate course might haue bene taken for your satisfaction, and withall looking vppon the Lords, he shooke his head, smiling.[1]

It is evident from every page in the narrative that the writer of it, William Barlow, had no love for the Puritans, and that his report is highly prejudiced. We cannot, therefore, feel sure that Reynolds ignored the Bishops' Bible by referring only to the versions allowed in the reigns of Henry VIII and Edward VI, in the rather insulting way that the text represents. The renderings to which he objected are found also in the Bishops' Bible, and if Reynolds passed over this, either as a mere reprint, or as not formally 'allowed' (i. e. approved), he was needlessly provocative. But the genuine interest which the king at once took in the proposal swept away any difficulty which might have been raised by its form. Nor was that interest transient. The Dean of Westminster and the Regius Professors of Hebrew at the Universities of Oxford and Cambridge must have been instructed with little delay to suggest the names of revisers, and by June 30 Bancroft, Bishop of London, with whom (in the vacancy of the see of Canterbury) the King communicated, was able to write :

His Majesty being made acquainted with the choice of all them to be employed in the translating of the Bible, in such sort as

<hr>

[1] 'The Summe and Substance of the Conference, which it pleased his Excellent Maiestie to haue with the Lords, Bishops and other of his Clergie, (at which the most of the Lordes of the Councell were present) in his Maiesties Priuy-Chamber, at Hampton Court, Ianuary 14, 1603. Contracted by William Barlow, Doctor of Diuinity, and Deane of Chester. Whereunto are added, some Copies, (scattered abroad), vnsauory, and vntrue. London, Printed by Iohn Windet, for Matthew Law and are to be sold at his shop in Paules Churchyeard, neare S. Austens Gate. 1604.' It should be noted that a different turn is given to the Puritan complaint in the preface to the 1611 Bible.

Mr. Lively can inform you, doth greatly approve of the said choice. And for as much as his Highness is very anxious that the same so religious a work should admit of no delay, he has commanded me to signify unto you in his name that his pleasure is, you should with all possible speed meet together in your University and begin the same.

The Mr. Lively here named was the Professor of Hebrew at Cambridge, and must have specially attracted the notice of the king, by whom he was presented to the rectory of Purleigh, Essex, in September 1604. His death the following May was a great blow to the work. The interest taken by James is further shown by a circular sent out by Bancroft to the other Bishops on July 31 enclosing a letter of the 22nd from the king, stating that he had appointed ' certain learned men to the number of four and fifty [1] for the translating of the Bible, and that in this number divers of them have either no ecclesiastical preferment at all, or else so very small, as the same is far unmeet for men of their deserts '. The king himself being unable to remedy this ' in any convenient time ', enjoins all patrons of parsonages or prebends, of the value of twenty pounds at least, to certify him of the next vacancy in order that he may commend to them ' some such of the learned men as we shall think fit to be preferred unto it '. In another circular of the same date Bancroft asks each bishop ' not only to think yourself what is meet for you to give for this purpose, but likewise to acquaint your dean and chapter ' that they might subscribe also. The response to the first of these circulars seems to have been very slight ; that to the second *nil*.

Of the lists of the translators which have come down to us, the most trustworthy is that printed by Bishop Burnet in his *History of the Reformation*,[2] which is here given together with the Rules by which the revisers were to be guided, and brief biographical notes, based on those by Cardwell, supplemented from the *Dictionary of National Biography* and other sources :

[1] Only about fifty names in all have come down to us, and only forty-seven in any one list. It may have been intended at first that there should be nine revisers on each board.

[2] *The History of the Reformation of the Church of England.* By Gilbert Burnett. The Fourth Edition, with Additions &c. London, 1715. Part II. A Collection of Records, p. 333 sqq. The document has the side-note ' Ex MS. D. Borlase ', i. e. Edmund Borlase, the physician and historian. There are several similar lists in MS. in the British Museum, with unimportant variants. One of these (Add. 34218) is dated ' Anno secundi regis Iacobi 1604 ', and there is no doubt that the lists refer to that year, although Cardwell, from a mistake as to the date of Barlow being made Dean of Chester, thought otherwise.

An Order set down for the Translating of the Bible, by
King James.

*The Places and Persons agreed upon for the Hebrew, with the
particular Books by them undertaken.*

Westminster.

Mr. Dean of *Westminster*
Mr. Dean of *Paul's*
Mr. Doctor *Saravia*
Mr. Doctor *Clark*
Mr. Doctor *Leifield*
Mr. Doctor *Teigh*
Mr. *Burleigh*
Mr. *King*
Mr. *Thompson*
Mr. *Beadwell*

Penteteuchon.
The Story from *Joshua*
to the first Book of
Chronicles, exclusive.

Cambridge.

Mr. Lively
Mr. Richardson
Mr. Chatterton
Mr. Dillingham
Mr. Harrison
Mr. Andrews
Mr. Spalding
Mr. Binge

From the First of the
Chronicles, with the
rest of the Story, and
the *Hagiographi*, viz.
Job, *Psalms*, *Pro-
verbs*, *Canticles*, Ec-
clesiastes.

Mr. Dean of Westminster: Lancelot Andrewes, made Bishop of Chichester in 1605.

Mr. Dean of Pauls: John Overall, made Bishop of Coventry, 1614.

Mr. Dr. Saravia: born at Hesdin in Artois in 1531, Professor of Divinity at Leyden, 1582; Rector of Tattenhill, Staffs, 1588; Prebendary of Canterbury and Vicar of Lewisham, 1595; Prebendary of Worcester and Westminster, 1601; died, 1612.

Mr. Dr. Clark: Dr. Richard Clark, Fellow of Christ's College, Cambridge.

Mr. Dr. Leifield: Dr. John Layfield, Fellow of Trinity College, Cambridge (resigned 1603), Rector of St. Clement Danes, London, 1601.

Mr. Dr. Teigh: Robert Tighe, Vicar of All Hallows, Barking, and Archdeacon of Middlesex.

Mr. Burleigh, probably the Dr. Francis Burley, who was one of the first Fellows of Chelsea College.

Mr. King: Geoffrey King, Fellow of King's College, Cambridge, and Regius Professor of Hebrew (1607–8) in succession to Spalding.

Mr. Thompson: Richard Tomson, of Clare Hall, Cambridge, B.D. 1593.

Mr. Beadwell: William Bedwell, Arabic Scholar, Rector of St. Ethelburga's, Bishopsgate Street, 1601.

Mr. Lively: Edward Lively, appointed Regius Professor of Hebrew at Cambridge, 1580; presented by the king to the rectory of Purleigh, Essex, September 20, 1604; died, May 1605.

Mr. Richardson: Dr. John Richardson, Fellow of Emmanuel College, Regius Professor of Divinity, 1607; Master of Peterhouse, 1609–15; then of Trinity.

Mr. Chatterton: Laurence Chaderton, Master of Emmanuel College, 1584–1622. Took part as a Puritan in the Hampton Court Conference.

Oxford.	⎧ Doctor *Harding* ⎪ Dr. *Reynolds* ⎪ Dr. *Holland* ⎨ Dr. *Kilbye* ⎪ Mr. *Smith* ⎪ Mr. *Brett* ⎩ Mr. *Fairclough*	The four, or greater Prophets, with the *Lamentations*, and the twelve lesser Prophets.

Cambridge.	⎧ Doctor *Dewport* ⎪ Dr. *Branthwait* ⎪ Dr. *Radclife* ⎨ Mr. *Warde*, Eman. ⎪ Mr. *Downs* ⎪ Mr. *Boyes* ⎩ Mr. *Warde*, Reg.	The Prayer of *Manasses* and the rest of the *Apocrypha*.

Mr. Dillingham: Francis Dillingham, Fellow of Christ's, author of numerous books, 1599–1609 (or later); Incumbent of Wilden, Beds.

Mr. Harrison: Thomas Harrison, a noted Hebraist, Vice-Master of Trinity College, Cambridge.

Mr. Andrews: Roger Andrewes, brother of Lancelot, Fellow of Pembroke, Master of Jesus College, Cambridge.

Mr. Spalding: Robert Spalding, Fellow of St. John's College, Cambridge, Regius Professor of Hebrew in succession to Lively (1605–7).

Mr. Binge: Andrew Byng, Regius Professor of Hebrew at Cambridge in succession to King, 1608. 'About 1605 we find a decree of the Chapter of York to keep a residentiary's place for him.' [*D.N.B.*]

Dr. Harding: John Harding, Regius Professor of Hebrew (1591–8, 1604–10) and President of Magdalen College, Oxford.

Dr. Reynolds: John Reynolds or Rainolds, President of Corpus Christi College, Oxford, from 1598. Died, 1607.

Dr. Holland: Thomas Holland, Regius Professor of Divinity, 1589; Rector of Exeter College, 1592. Died, 1612.

Dr. Kilbye: Richard Kilbye, Rector of Lincoln College, 1590; Regius Professor of Hebrew, 1610–21.

Mr. Smith: Miles Smith, of Brasenose, Prebendary of Hereford and Exeter Cathedrals, a noted Orientalist, one of the two final revisers of the version of 1611, and the writer of the preface; made Bishop of Gloucester, 1612.

Mr. Brett: Richard Brett, Fellow of Lincoln College, Rector of Quainton, Bucks, 1595.

Mr. Fairclough: Richard Fairclough, Fellow of New College, Rector of Bucknell, Oxford, 1593.

Dr. Dewport: John Duport, Master of Jesus College, Cambridge, 1590; Prebendary of Ely, 1609.

Dr. Branthwait: William Branthwait, Fellow of Emmanuel College, 1584; Master of Gonville and Caius, 1607.

Dr. Radcliffe: Jeremiah Radcliffe, Fellow of Trinity College, Cambridge.

Mr. Warde: Samuel Ward, Fellow of Sidney Sussex, 1599; master, 1610; King's Chaplain, 1611.

Mr. Downs: Andrew Downes, Fellow of St. John's College, Cambridge, 1581; Regius Professor of Greek, 1585–1624.

Mr. Boyes: John Boys, Fellow of Clare Hall, 1593; Dean of Canterbury, 1619.

The Places and Persons agreed upon for the Greek, with the particular Books by them undertaken.

Ⓞⓧⓕⓞⓡⓓ.
{
Mr. Dean of *Christchurch*
Mr. Dean of *Winchester*
Mr. Dean of *Worcester*
Mr. Dean of *Windsor*
Mr. *Savile*
Dr. *Perne*
Dr. *Ravens*
Mr. *Harmer*
}
The four Gospels. *Acts of the Apostles. Apocalyps.*

Ⓦⓔⓢⓣⓜⓘⓝⓢⓣⓔⓡ.
{
Dean of *Chester*
Dr. *Hutchinson*
Dr. *Spencer*
Mr. *Fenton*
Mr. *Rabbett*
Mr. *Sanderson*
Mr. *Dakins*
}
The Epistles of St. *Paul*. The Canonical Epistles.

Mr. *Dean of Christchurch*: Thomas Ravis, Dean of Christ Church, 1596; Bishop of Gloucester, 1605; Bishop of London, 1607; died, 1609.

Mr. *Dean of Winchester*: George Abbot, Master of University College, 1597; Dean of Winchester, 1600; Bishop of Coventry and Lichfield, 1609; of London, 1610; Archbishop of Canterbury, 1611.

Mr. *Dean of Worcester*: Richard Edes, Dean of Worcester, 1597; Chaplain to James I.; died, November 19, 1604. Edes was succeeded by James Montague, afterwards (1608) Bishop of Bath and Wells, &c. Fuller is the authority for identifying Edes as the (intended) reviser.

Mr. *Dean of Windsor*: Giles Thompson, or Tomson, Fellow of All Souls, Bishop of Gloucester, 1611; died, 1612.

Mr. *Savile*: Sir Henry Savile, Warden of Merton, 1585–1622; Provost of Eton, 1596; knighted, 1604; edited works of Chrysostom, 1610–13.

Dr. *Perne*: John Perin, Fellow of St. John's, Oxford; Regius Professor of Greek, 1597–1615; Canon of Christ Church, November 24, 1604.

Dr. *Ravens*: apparently an error. See below.

Mr. *Harmer*: John Harmer, Fellow of New College, 1582; Regius Professor of Greek, 1585; Head Master of Winchester, 1588; Warden of St. Mary's College, 1596; died, 1613.

Dean of *Chester*: William Barlow, Fellow of Trinity Hall, Dean, 1602; Bishop of Rochester, 1605; died, 1613.

Dr. *Hutchinson*: Ralph Hutchinson, President of St. John's College, Oxford.

Dr. *Spencer*: John Spenser, Editor of Hooker, 1604; President of Corpus Christi College, Oxford, 1607.

Mr. *Fenton*: Roger Fenton, Fellow of Pembroke Hall, Cambridge, Vicar of Chigwell, 1606; Prebendary of St. Paul's, 1609.

Mr. *Rabbett*: Michael Rabbett, Rector of St. Vedast Foster, 1603.

Mr. *Sanderson*: Thomas Sanderson, Rector of All Hallows the Great, Thames Street, 1603; Archdeacon of Rochester, 1606.

Mr. *Dakins*: William Dakins, Fellow of Trinity College, Cambridge, Professor of Divinity, Gresham College, London, 1604, died in 1607.

In other lists the name of J. Aglionby, Principal of St. Edmund Hall, is substituted for that of the Dean of Worcester, and that of L. Hutten, Canon of Christ-Church, for the mysterious Dr. Ravens. The choice of the revisers seems to have been determined solely by their fitness, and both parties in the Church were represented by some of their best men.

The Rules to be observed in the Translation of the Bible.

1. THE ordinary Bible read in the Church, commonly called the *Bishops Bible*, to be followed, and as little altered as the Truth of the original will permit.

2. The Names of the Prophets, and the Holy Writers, with the other Names of the Text, to be retained, as nigh as may be, accordingly as they were vulgarly used.

3. The old Ecclesiastical Words to be kept, *viz.* the Word *Church* not to be translated *Congregation* &c.

4. When a Word hath divers Significations, that to be kept which hath been most commonly used by the most of the Ancient Fathers, being agreeable to the Propriety of the Place, and the Analogy of the Faith.

5. The Division of the Chapters to be altered, either not at all, or as little as may be, if Necessity so require.

6. No Marginal Notes at all to be affixed, but only for the Explanation of the *Hebrew* or *Greek* Words, which cannot, without some circumlocution, so briefly and fitly be express'd in the Text.

7. Such Quotations of Places to be marginally set down as shall serve for the fit Reference of one Scripture to another.

8. Every particular Man of each Company, to take the same Chapter, or Chapters, and having translated or amended them severally by himself, where he thinketh good, all to meet together, confer what they have done, and agree for their Parts what shall stand.

9. As any one Company hath dispatched any one Book in this Manner they shall send it to the rest, to be consider'd of seriously and judiciously, for His Majesty is very careful in this Point.

10. If any Company, upon the Review of the Book so sent, doubt or differ upon any Place, to send them Word thereof; note the Place, and withal send the Reasons, to which if they consent not, the Difference to be compounded at the General Meeting, which is to be of the chief Persons of each Company, at the end of the Work.

11. When any Place of special Obscurity is doubted of, Letters to be directed, by Authority, to send to any Learned Man in the Land, for his Judgement of such a Place.

12. Letters to be sent from every Bishop to the rest of his Clergy, admonishing them of this Translation in hand; and to move and charge as many as being skilful in the Tongues; and having taken Pains in that kind, to send his particular Observations to the Company, either at *Westminster*, *Cambridge* or *Oxford*.

13. The Directors in each Company, to be the Deans of *Westminster* and *Chester* for that Place; and the King's Professors in the *Hebrew* or *Greek* in either University.

14. These translations to be used when they agree better with the Text than the Bishops Bible.

> *Tindoll's.*
> *Matthews.*
> *Coverdale's.*
> *Whitchurch's.*
> *Geneva.*

15. Besides the said Directors before mentioned, three or four of the most Ancient and Grave Divines, in either of the Universities, not employed in Translating, to be assigned by the Vice-Chancellor, upon Conference with the rest of the Heads, to be Overseers of the Translations as well *Hebrew* as *Greek*, for the better Observation of the 4th Rule above specified.

In contrast with all these preparatory arrangements and rules, we may now quote the only nearly contemporary account of the experiences of one of the revisers which has come down to us. This relates to one of the second Cambridge group, to whom was committed the translation of the Apocrypha, Dr. John Boys, afterwards (1619) Dean of Canterbury, but at this time the holder of a living at Boxworth, which, it is to be feared, he rather neglected during his work as a translator. His biographer, Dr. Anthony Walker, writes :

> When it pleased God to move King James to that excellent work, the translation of the Bible ; when the translators were to be chosen for Cambridge, he was sent for thither by those therein employed, & was chosen one ; some university men thereat repining (it may be not more able, yet more ambitious to have born [a] share in that service) disdaining that it should be thought they needed any help from the country.—Forgetting that Tully was the same man at Tusculan[um] as he was at Rome. Sure I am, that part of the Apocrypha was allotted to him (for he hath shewed me the very copy he translated by), but to my grief I know not which part.
>
> All the time he was about his own part, his commons were given him at St. John's ; where he abode all the week, till Saturday night ; & then went home to discharge his cure : returning thence on Monday morning. When he had finished his own part, at the earnest request of him to whom it was assigned, he undertook a second ; and then he was in commons in another college : but I forbear to name both the person and the house.
>
> Four years were spent in this first service ; at the end whereof the whole work being finished, & three copies of the whole Bible sent from Cambridge, Oxford & Westminster, to London ; a new choice was to be made of six in all, two out of every company, to review the whole work ; & extract one [copy] out of all three, to be committed to the presse.
>
> For the dispatch of which business Mr. Downes & Mr. Bois were sent for up to London. Where meeting (though Mr. Downes would not go till he was either fetcht or threatned with a pursivant) their four fellow labourers, they went dayly to Stationers Hall, & in three quarters of a year, finished their task. All which time they had from the Company of Stationers xxx[s] [each] per week, duly paid them : tho' they had nothing before but the self-rewarding, ingenious industry. Whilst they were imployed in this last businesse, he & he only, took notes of their proceedings : which notes he kept till his dying day.[1]

Dr. Boys's biographer seems ignorant of the fact that alike at Oxford, Cambridge, and Westminster, there were two companies, making six in all, so that if two revisers went to Stationers' Hall

---

[1] From *Desiderata Curiosa*: or a collection of divers scarce and curious pieces. By Francis Peck. New ed., 1779. Part viii, p. 325 sqq. 'The life of that famous Grecian, Mr. John Bois, S.T.B. one of the translators of the Bible, temp. Jac. I. . . . By Anthony Walker, M.A., of St. John's College, Cambridge. From a 4° MS. in the hands of the publisher. The gift of the Rev. Mr. Thomas Baker.'

from each company, this final board of revision must have had
twelve members instead of the six of which he speaks. We know
this indeed as a fact from the report of the English delegates to
the Synod of Dort, among whom was Samuel Ward, one of the
revisers.[1] On the basis of a board of twelve, paid 30s. each a week
for 39 weeks, the sum disbursed would be £702. That this sum
was paid by the Company is incredible; it is just possible, however,
that it was the contribution of the proprietors of the 'Bible Stock'
already mentioned, which can only have continued in existence all
these years if its owners were admitted by the holder of the royal
patent to share a portion of the expenses and profits either of all
editions or of those in particular sizes. Even, however, if this were
so it is evident that such a payment would only be made in pursuance
of a private agreement with Robert Barker, and forty years after
the Bible was published we meet with a definite statement [2] that
Barker had, in fact, 'paid for the amended or corrected Translation
of the Bible £3,500 : by reason whereof the translated copy did of
right belong to him and his assignes.' If, as the statement should
mean, this sum was actually paid to the translators, it would have
represented between £50 and £60 apiece for the work done during
the sittings of the six companies. Now the preface to the Bible
says of the translation that it 'hath cost the workemen, as light as
it seemeth, the paines of twise seven times seventy-two dayes and
more', or about two years and nine months. On the basis of the
prebend of the value of £20 at least which the King desired to secure
for the translators, this would mean a payment of just £55, either to
the translators direct or to the colleges which boarded them. But
neatly as these figures work out, the hypothesis thus suggested is
quite uncorroborated, and we have really no sound basis even for
guessing how the £3,500 was paid. The sessions of the six companies, it may be noted, are usually supposed to have begun (although doubtless there were preliminary meetings) in 1607, the
years 1605, 1606 being thus allotted to private research, 1607-9
to the work of the six boards, part of 1610 to that of the twelve
revisers at Stationers' Hall, and the rest of 1610 and part of 1611
to printing. From the Report to the Synod of Dort (November 16,
1618) already mentioned, we learn that the final touches to the
translation were given by Bilson, Bishop of Winchester, and Miles

---

[1] 'Post peractum a singulis pensum, ex hisce omnibus duodecim selecti viri in
unum locum convocati integrum opus recognoverunt ac recensuerunt.'

[2] In William Ball's *Briefe treatise concerning the regulating of printing*,
1651. On May 10, 1612, Robert Barker obtained an extended patent, and on
February 11, 1617, this was re-granted to him for his own life and for thirty
years after his death to his son, Robert II. In 1635 the reversion was re-granted
to Charles and Matthew Barker. Robert died in 1646, and in 1664 a moiety of
these rights was valued at £1,300. See the article by H. R. Plomer 'The King's
Printing House under the Stuarts' in *The Library*, 2nd Series, vol. 8. (1901).

Smith, afterwards Bishop of Gloucester.[1] The former was not
a member of any of the boards of revisers, but that the work of the
revisers should subsequently be 'reviewed by the Bishops and the
chiefe learned of the Church' was part of the scheme which the
King had sketched out at the Hampton Court Conference, and
another Bishop, Bancroft of London, is said to have insisted on
fourteen alterations. Whether in further pursuance of the King's
programme the version was presented by the bishops to the Privy
Council, and lastly ratified by his Royal authority, we cannot say.
As is well known no authority has ever been discovered for the
words 'Appointed to be read in Churches' which appear on the
title-page of all editions, nor for the phrase, the 'Authorized
Version', by which the Bible is usually known. When, however,
this point was raised at the time of the Revision of 1881, Lord
Chancellor Selborne wrote to the *Times* (June 3, 1881), giving it
as his opinion that if the version

> was 'appointed to be read in churches' (as is expressly stated on the
> title-page of 1611), at the time of its first publication, nothing is more
> probable than that this may have been done by Order in Council.
> If so, the authentic record of that order would now be lost, because all
> the Council books and registers from the year 1600 to 1613 inclusive
> were destroyed by a fire at Whitehall, on the 12th of January, 1618
> (O.S.). Nothing, in my opinion, is less likely than that the King's
> printer should have taken upon himself (whether with a view to his
> own profit or otherwise) to issue the book (being what it was, a transla-
> tion unquestionably made by the King's commandment to correct
> defects in earlier versions of which the use had been authorized by
> Royal injunctions, &c. in preceding reigns) with a title-page asserting
> that it was 'Appointed to be read in Churches' if the fact were not
> really so.

Lord Selborne proceeds to speak of the terrors of the Court of High
Commission and the Star Chamber as making it 'incredible' that
Barker should have taken any risks. But he does not seem sufficiently to have distinguished between what may be done when
authorities are amiable and when they are the reverse. The
Version of 1611 was produced to take the place of the Bishops'
Bible, on the title-pages of which, in the editions from 1585 to
1602 (the last) inclusive, had been printed the words 'Authorised
and Appointed to be read in Churches'. In the small folio edition
of 1584 the phrase runs, 'Of that Translation authorised to be
read in Churches.' Previously to this (1574–8) we find only
'Set foorth by aucthoritie'. In 1568, 1569, and 1572, there are
no words to this effect of any sort or kind, although we know that

---

[1] Postremo Reverendissimus Episcopus Wintoniensis Bilsonus una cum Doctore
Smitho nunc Episcopo Glocestriensi, viro eximio, et ab initio in toto hoc opere
versatissimo, omnibus mature pensitatis et examinatis, extremam manum huic
versioni imposuerunt.'

Parker would have liked to use them. Parker had even had to
endure the sight of an edition following the text of the Great Bible,
which was published in 1569 by Cawood, and advertized itself as
'According to the translation that is appointed to be read in the
Churches', a phrase which he might not use of his own. None
the less, the Bishops' Bible superseded the Great Bible, and as the
need for distinguishing it from the Geneva version made itself felt
we find Jugge (and the assigns of Christopher Barker in the folio
of 1578) using the words, 'Set foorth by aucthoritie'. When
Whitgift became Archbishop we get first the phrase of 1584 and
then the fuller 'Authorised and Appointed to be read in Churches'
of 1585–1602. As far as I know it has never been contended that
there was any Order in Council passed in 1584 or 1585 to justify
this, and it seems therefore far from safe to postulate the existence
of such an Order in 1611. There is indeed negative evidence that
there was no such order, for the word 'Appointed', is considerably
weaker than the 'Authorised and Appointed' which it replaced.
By itself 'Appointed' means little more than 'assigned' or
'provided', and the words 'Appointed to be read in Churches'
literally expressed the facts that this Bible was printed by the
King's printer with the approval of the King and the Bishops for
use in churches, and that no competing edition 'of the largest
volume' was allowed to be published. Theoretically this justifica-
tion by facts may have been insufficient; but when all the parties
are agreed, legal formalities are often omitted.

If the notes which Dr. Boys treasured so carefully to the end of
his life had been preserved, it might be possible to trace, if only for
a single section, the work done at the different stages of the revision.
As it is we have nothing but the finished result and a few remarks
on it in the preface. As far as ecclesiastical politics were concerned
the task of the revisers was with the smallest possible amount of
disturbance to harmonize the Bishops' version with the Geneva
wherever the latter was more correct, and the desire to do this
accounts for the vast majority of the changes which in any way
affect the sense. The revisers were concerned also, although pride
prevented any reference to the fact, to meet the objections which
had been urged in the preface and notes to the Rheims New
Testament, and it is to their credit that they not only did this, but
took from that version much that was good, though with no other
acknowledgement than a gibe. Other changes were due to the
study of two new Latin versions, that by Arias Montanus of the Old
Testament printed in the Antwerp Polyglott, and that by Tremellius
of the Old and New Testament, with the Apocrypha by his son-in-
law, Franciscus Junius; yet others from the Geneva French
version (1587–8), Diodati's Italian (1607), and the Spanish (1602)
of Cipriano de Valera. These three foreign translations seem to

have attracted considerable attention, as they are mentioned not only in the Preface, but by Selden, in whose *Table-Talk* we read (clearly of the meetings of the final board of twelve) that :

> The translators in king James's time took an excellent way. That part of the Bible was given to him who was most excellent in such a tongue (as the Apocrypha to Andrew Downs) and then they met together, and one read the translation, the rest holding in their hands some Bible, either of the learned tongues, or French, Spanish, Italian, etc. If they found any fault they spoke; if not, he read on.

Whether the wonderful felicity of phrasing should be attributed to the dexterity with which, after meanings had been settled and the important words in each passage chosen, either the board of twelve or the two final revisers put their touches to the work, or whether, as seems more likely, the rhythm, first called into being by Tyndale and Coverdale, reasserted itself after every change, only gathering strength and melody from the increasing richness of the language, none can tell. All that is certain is that the rhythm and the strength and the melody are there.

The Bible of 1611, being only a revised edition, was not entered on the Stationers' Registers, nor have we any information as to the month in which it was issued. In its original form it is a handsome, well-printed book, set up apparently with newly cast type yielding a clean and sharp impression, and on excellent paper. It begins with an engraved title-page signed ' C. Boel fecit in Richmont ', i.e. by Cornelis Boel, an Antwerp artist, who about this time produced portraits of the Queen, the Princess Elizabeth, and Prince Henry. In the upper panel SS. Peter and James sit, holding between them an oval frame within which is a representation of the Lamb; at the sides are SS. Matthew and Mark. On the two sides of the title stand Moses and Aaron in niches. At the foot are seated SS. Luke and John, while between them is another oval frame containing a picture of a pelican feeding her young. The title reads :

> ' The Holy Bible, conteyning the Old Testament and the New. Newly Translated out of the Originall tongues : & with the former Translations diligently compared and reuised by his Maiesties speciall Comandement. Appointed to be read in Churches. Imprinted at London by Robert Barker, Printer to the Kings most Excellent Maiestie. Anno Dom. 1611.'

Leaves 2 and 3ª are occupied with the Dedication : ' To the most High and Mightie Prince, Iames by the grace of God King of Great Britaine, France and Ireland, Defender of the Faith, &c.' ; 3ᵇ–8, by the preface headed ' The Translators to the Reader ', 9–14 by a Calendar ; 15ª, by ' An Almanacke for xxxix. yeeres ', 1603–1641; 15ᵇ, by Directions 'To finde Easter for euer'; 16–18ª, by ' The Table and Kalendes, expressing the order of Psalmes and Lessons to be said at Morning and Euening prayer ', and a table headed, ' These to be obserued for Holy dayes, and none other ; ' 18[b], by ' The names and order of all the Bookes of the Olde and New Testament, with the Number of their Chapters '. Inserted at the binder's pleasure after the preface, after leaf 18 or elsewhere, are usually eighteen leaves of the Genealogies of Holy Scripture and a sheet containing a Map of Canaan with a table of the places named printed on the reverse. In October 1610 John Speed had obtained a privilege from the king enabling him for ten years to saddle every edition of the Scriptures with his decoratively printed but useless Genealogies, and so the cost of the book was needlessly increased by from sixpence to two shillings a copy, according to the size. In some copies, it may be mentioned, the Genealogies begin with a blank page ; in others this is occupied by a fine cut of the royal arms, subscribed Cum Priuilegio Regiæ Maiestatis.

The text of the Bible is printed in black-letter with the inserted words (now printed in italics) in small roman, and roman type is also used for the summaries at the head of each chapter, for the subject headlines at the top of each page, and for the references to parallel passages in the margin ; the alternative renderings in the margins are in italics.[1] The text is printed in double columns enclosed within rules, with ornamental headpieces and a few tailpieces and capitals at the beginning of each chapter and psalm. At the outset it was clearly intended that the capital at the beginning of a book should occupy the depth of nine lines of text, that at the beginning of each chapter after the first the depth of five ; but the run on capitals in the Psalter caused four- and six-line blocks to be used, and after this the arrangement is more frequently disturbed,[2] though it still remains the normal one. In order to begin the Psalter (one of the old five sections into which Bibles used to be divided), on a right-hand page, the page before it is left blank, but there is no typographical break throughout the Old Testament. The New Testament has a separate title-page, with a woodcut previously used in editions of the Bishops' Bible. It was also taken as a new typographical starting-point. The book consists in all of 366 sheets of two leaves, or four pages each, grouped in 123 quires or gatherings signed as follows :

Preliminaries : A-D.

---

[1] The alternative renderings and references to parallels are probably the work of the six companies ; the chapter summaries and subject headlines are usually attributed to the two final revisers. In later editions the subject headlines, which are based on the chapter summaries, have usually been left to the printer's reader.

[2] In the New Testament two of the mythological ten-line set, the use of which in the Bishops' Bible had justly been censured, reappear at the beginning of Matthew and Romans ; and small pictorial capitals of an evangelist writing, at the beginning of the gospels according to S. Luke and S. John.

Old Testament : A-Z, Aa-Zz, Aaa-Zzz, Aaaa-Zzzz, Aaaaa-Ccccc.

New Testament : A-Z, Aa.

With the exception of B and D in the preliminaries, of which the former has only one sheet, the latter only two, every quire is regularly made up of three sheets or six leaves. The whole book is homogeneous, and was almost certainly set up and printed in its own sequence, not in different sections worked simultaneously. Of the Bible thus set up only a single issue was printed. The so-called second issue is an entirely distinct and separate edition, save that a few leaves of the original edition, of which an excessive number had been printed by some mistake, are sometimes found used in it. It is the exact text of this first edition that the present reprint reproduces.

III. THE LATER HISTORY OF THE BIBLE OF 1611

AS we have seen, every parish in England had been obliged to provide itself with a Bible of the 'largest volume' in 1541 under penalty of a fine of 40s. for every month of delay, the book costing 10s. in sheets and 12s. bound. Beyond the words on the title-page, 'Appointed to be read in Churches,' which, as they stand, are purely affirmative, not exclusive (unlike, for instance, the 'These to be obserued for Holy dayes, and none other' of this very volume), there is no tittle of evidence for any Order in Council having enjoined parishes to buy copies with inconvenient haste. In the year of issue the Dean and Chapter of Worcester bought 'a Great Bible of the new translation' for £2 18s., which probably represents the cost of the book in a binding good enough for cathedral use. From a book printed in 1641 (Michael Sparke's *Scintilla*) we learn that the price of Church Bibles had then recently been raised from 30s. to 40s., and that 'in former times' these were sold in quires at 25s., to which must be added the cost of binding. It would have been highly unpopular to force an expenditure of this kind on every parish, however small. To do so, moreover, would have been alike impolitic and needless ; impolitic, because any haste in the matter would have suggested that very slur on the Bishops' version which the Preface so earnestly disclaims [1] ; needless, because the supply of Bibles being, as we have pointed out, a regulated and controlled supply, whenever an old Church Bible was worn out, it was neces-

---

[1] 'Truly (good Christian Reader) wee neuer thought from the beginning, that we should neede to make a new Translation, nor yet to make of a bad one a good one, (for then the imputation of *Sixtus* had bene true in some sort, that our people had bene fed with gall of Dragons instead of wine, with whey instead of milke:) but to make a good one better.'

sarily replaced by a new one of the version of 1611, because no other Bible in large folio was purchasable. In an interesting article on *The Authorisation of the English Bible*, contributed by the present Archbishop of Canterbury to *Macmillan's Magazine* for June 1881, we find it stated :

> Of twenty-four [25 ?] 'inquiries' between 1612 and 1641 thirteen Bishops and Archdeacons, ask for 'a Bible of the latest edition', or 'of the last translation', while twelve ask only for 'a Bible of the largest volume', in accordance with what had been the usual form of the question prior to 1611. Among the latter are Bishop Neile of Lincoln (1614) ; Bishop Williams of Lincoln (1631) ; Bishop Duppa of Chichester (1638) ; and the Archdeacons of London, York and Colchester (1640). Archbishop Abbot in his metropoliticall visitation in 1616 asks only for 'the whole Bible of the largest volume', though three years later, in a visitation of the Diocese of Canterbury, he carefully refers to 'the Bible of the New Translation, lately set forth by His Majesty's authority'. Archbishop Laud, however, in a Diocesan visitation in 1634, departing from the form adopted by his predecessor, asks only for 'the whole Bible of the largest volume'.

With the policy of patience and quiet penetration which the bishops as a body (some, no doubt, being more urgent than others) thus seem to have pursued, the bibliographical evidence is in entire agreement. Misapprehension of the ecclesiastical position has indeed caused some bibliographers to go astray, and to imagine the simultaneous printing of two issues in 1611 to meet a demand for 20,000 copies, such as Grafton and Whitchurch had to provide for in 1540 and 1541. But the demand for 20,000 copies and the double issue are equally imaginary. After the first edition, completed in 1611, an entirely new one was put in hand, the issue of the bulk of which belongs to 1613, and in this year there appeared also a folio reprint for church use in smaller type ;[1] a third edition in the largest type was published in 1617, a fourth in 1634, a fifth in 1640. It is clear that if every parish had acquired a copy in 1611, there could have been no demand for new editions in 1613 and 1617. It is also clear, from the seventeen years interval before a reprint, that the 1617 edition did substantially complete the necessary supply. If so, the editions may have been of as many as 5,000 copies apiece.

To understand the trouble which has arisen it must be remembered that in the case of Bibles all editions of the same size were so printed that, the contents of corresponding sheets being the same, the sheets should be interchangeable. This probably made for correctness in reprinting, and the reprints follow each other so closely, mostly line for line, and always leaf for leaf, that they can only be distinguished from the copy they follow by careful collation.

---

[1] By printing 72 instead of 59 lines to a column, and a corresponding lateral saving, the number of leaves was reduced from 732 to 508.

But the printer's object in this arrangement was probably the lower one of being able to use up sheets which had been printed in excess of the requirements of one edition by printing fewer copies for the next, and also, when any sheets of a nearly exhausted edition had accidentally been spoilt, by printing these particular sheets in advance of the next edition, to make one setting serve for both purposes. In a well-managed printing-office, neither class of accident would recur with sufficient frequency to be worth providing against; but Barker's office was not well managed, and from his plea in one of the interminable lawsuits which made him end his days in a debtor's prison, we learn that about 1616–18 he owed over £200 to various booksellers as compensation for having supplied imperfect books.[1]

Before the end of 1611 the stock of the first edition of the new Bible was sufficiently low to cause a second to be put in hand. The engraved plate from which the title had been printed must by this time have been much worn and (possibly after some hesitation) henceforth Barker preferred the woodcut border which appears in the New Testament for the general title as well. The easiest hypothesis to account for the peculiarities which we find in the edition which he now proceeded to print is that he first reprinted the sheet which bears the title, and a few other sheets at various points, to complete imperfect copies of the first edition, and then settled down to reprint the rest, completing this, if we are bound to press the date 1611 found on the New Testament, within the year, somewhat ahead of the demand. Before this became urgent a serious accident must have happened in his warehouse, which rendered unusable a large part of the stock (about 119 out of 138 sheets) in one part of the book, viz. the quires signed Aa–Zz and Aaa–Zzz. A few sheets,[2] which I conjecture to have been among those printed in advance of the rest and kept in a different place, escaped, but the stock of the rest had to be completed by a second reprinting, and the completed stock was then stored according to the exigencies of the warehouse. By 1613 the supply of the title-sheet, of which only a small number seems to have been printed in 1611 (possibly because Barker at first thought of re-engraving the original copper-plate[3]) was exhausted, and this sheet was then reprinted and dated 1613. During the next three or four years the copies sold exhibit so many combinations of the two printings

[1] See Mr. H. R. Plomer's article in *The Library* (Second Series, vol. ii, pp. 353–375), on ' The King's Printing House under the Stuarts '.

[2] Viz. (probably) Aa$_1$, Ff$_2$, Gg$_{1, 2}$, Kk$_1$, Tt$_{1-3}$, Aaa$_2$, Bbb$_3$, Iii$_2$, Lll$_1$, Ooo$_{2, 3}$, Qqq$_3$, Sss$_{1-3}$, Zzz$_3$.

[3] I may note that the engraved title is said to be found in a ' very few ' copies of the cheaper Church folio (72 line) of 1613. In one at least of these it is clearly inserted. But as long as the plate existed it might be used on an emergency to complete copies.

of the sheets bearing the double and treble signatures (Aa and Aaa, &c.), that with the exception of a group of about twenty hardly any two copies agree. The inference is that this score of copies represent the part of the edition sold to the booksellers when first it was ready, since these copies would all be made up at the same time, and the sheets required for them would be extracted from the same part of each bundle. On the other hand, copies made up at later dates in response to the casual daily demand would naturally differ according to the whim of the man who picked out the sheets for them.

The above explanation is based [1] on the very able paper by the Rev. Walter E. Smith, published in three numbers of *The Library* for 1890 under the title *The Great She-Bible*, and is intended to account for the following facts :

(i) While the great majority of the extant title-pages of the second edition are dated 1613, those in at least three copies are dated 1611, and this title with the woodcut border and the date 1611 has also been found on some copies of the editio princeps. The title-page of the New Testament in all copies is dated 1611.

(ii) Out of a total of 357 sheets of text, four of those singly signed (E_3, $P_{2, 3}$, X_2), and 119 of those doubly and trebly signed (Aa, &c., Aaa, &c.) are found in two different forms, constituting different editions of these individual sheets, one of which can almost always be positively proved to have been set up from the other.

(iii) The sheets of these signatures first printed are not, as a rule, all found together in some copies, and the reprints of them in others, but the two printings are very much mixed together, and in very various ways.

The explanation is probably only a very rough approximation to the truth, and further investigation is rendered almost hopeless by the fact that collectors like Lea Wilson and Francis Fry (the latter of whom bought and sold an extraordinary number of copies), and many much more easily forgivable booksellers, have transferred sheets from one copy to another to bring them into accord with their own mistaken ideas of perfection, and the evidence has thus been hopelessly confused. Nor if, as I believe, the way in which copies of this second edition were made up depended mainly on the whim of Barker's storekeeper, is it possible as regards the bulk of the copies [2] to say with any probability that one is earlier than another.

---

[1] I use this word because Mr. Smith did not fully express his views on the significance of the 1611 printed title-page, as to which he obtained additional information after his text was printed, and in some points I think I interpret the evidence he collected a little differently. His paper settled the main question quite finally.

[2] Those with one or more 1611 sheets used in them may perhaps be set down as earlier, and those with 1617 sheets as later. But even this is not always certain.

The important point is that we must repudiate altogether the misuse of bibliographical terms by which Mr. Fry constantly wrote of a certain type of copy of the second edition as the second 'issue' of the first. A sheet of the first edition may here and there be found (for the reasons given) in a copy of the second, but the second edition as a whole, whether it bears a 1611 title or a 1613 title, was printed from a new setting up of the type, whereas the essence of a new 'issue' is that it is printed from the same setting up, but with additions, cancels, or other subordinate changes. The only first edition is that which is here reprinted.

A still more serious error was committed by the distinguished scholar, Dr. F. H. A. Scrivener, who in 1884, in his book entitled *The Authorised Edition of the English Bible* (1611) : *its subsequent reprints and modern representatives* (an enlargement of his Introduction to the *Cambridge Paragraph Bible* of 1873) argued strenuously, but in entire ignorance of the customs of the book trade in the seventeenth century, that copies of the (second) edition with the woodcut title dated 1611 preceded the (first) edition with the engraved title, here reprinted. Dr. Scrivener was led to this conclusion by the idea, natural to a modern scholar, that the opportunity of a new edition would be used for making the text more correct. So far from this being the case it is a practically invariable experience that for every error corrected in a seventeenth-century reprint, at least two are introduced. Dr. Scrivener allowed that the accepted editio princeps was the finer and better, but did not see how incredible it is that an eagerly expected book like the version of 1611, of which copies would at once be given to the king and other great persons, should have been put on the market in the first instance in an inferior form, have been then improved in almost every respect in a second edition, and then have gone back to its original state, or a little worse, in a third. The relations of the copies with the 1611 and 1613 woodcut titles constitute another insuperable difficulty to his theory, but the priority of the true editio princeps can be proved bibliographically in a dozen different ways. A few of these may be indicated :

(i) Dr. Scrivener himself noted a blunder in the editio princeps by which three lines are repeated in Exodus xiv. 10. In the second edition we can see the printer, who could not ignore this particular error, bringing a couple of words on to another line, and leaving extra space at the head of chapter xv, in order to fill the gap created by omitting the three repeated lines.

(ii) The editio princeps, as we have seen, begins with a regular system of nine-line capitals at the beginning of the first chapter of each book, and five-line capitals at the beginning of other chapters, and only gradually departs from it. In the second edition the printer is careless all the way through, using additional capitals from other sets, and making changes in the line-arrangements obviously dictated by the different sizes of the new capitals.

(iii) In the editio princeps the word 'Lord' is printed throughout the book of Genesis as LORD, afterwards as LORD. In the second edition it is always printed LORD.

All of these changes are intelligible if the second edition was printed from the first. None of them can be explained if the first edition was printed from the second. Add the fact that the type of the second edition is distinctly more worn, and the true sequence is obvious. This is now generally recognized, and it is only just to say that on this point Mr. Francis Fry was quite sound.

It remains to be added that the first edition of the new translation is frequently called the He-Bible and the second the She-Bible, from the fact that in Ruth iii. 15 the former reads 'He went into the city', and the latter 'She'. All such nicknames for editions of the Bible are objectionable, and this, which suggests that the two editions form a pair, is mischievous. Their relation is not that of equality as between man and woman, but the second is derived from the first, as a child from its parents, an entirely new and distinct edition, reprinted from the original, and not a contemporaneous issue.

Turning now from the Church Bibles to those for private use we find that two quartos and two octavos were issued in 1612, one quarto and one octavo following the editio princeps, and the other quarto and octavo following the second edition. A quarto and octavo were printed at the turn of the years 1612–13, two other quartos and an octavo in 1613, two quartos in 1613–14, and two more quartos and an octavo in 1614, almost all of these following the text of the second edition. These fourteen editions (there may have been more) seem to have satisfied the immediate demand, and after this we find one, two, and three editions printed in different years. Very few editions of the New Testament seem at first to have been printed separately, and it is interesting to find Messrs. Darlow and Moule, in their catalogue of the treasures of the Bible Society, recording editions of the Bishops' version as being printed in 1613, 1614, 1615, and 1617. After this New Testaments of the new translation became more common.

As regards the Geneva Bible, of which a folio and quarto had been printed in 1611, we find another folio published in 1612, three quartos in 1614, two more quartos in 1615, and a folio in 1616. After this, although for another fifteen or twenty years eminent ecclesiastics, ordained before 1611, continued to take into the pulpit their old Geneva pocket editions, no doubt marked and familiar to their hands, and had no hesitation in using this version for their texts, the king's printers were encouraged to print no more Geneva Bibles, and the production of them was thus driven underground. It has long been a puzzle to bibliographers why there should be so many different editions (at least six), of the Geneva Bible asserting themselves on their title-pages to have been ' Imprinted at London by the Deputies of Christopher Barker, Printer to the Queenes most excellent Maiestie. 1599.' One of these editions is found also bearing the much more truthful statement, ' By Iohn Fredericksz. Stam, dwelling by the South Churche at the signe of the Hope. 1633 ' (see Bible Society Catalogue, Nos. 191 and 364). Mr. N. Pocock, who wrote on the subject in the *Bibliographer*, vol. iii, stated as his conclusion that ' the whole investigation seems to show that these editions of the Geneva-Tomson [Bible] were published at different times at Amsterdam and Dort, and adopted afterwards by Barker, who affixed the date 1599, probably because this was a well-known and popular edition '. A still more probable reason for the selection of the date 1599 is surely that in 1600 Robert Barker took over his father's business, and the deputies vanished. Thus this particular imprint was the latest with which editions could circulate freely in England, without Robert Barker being personally implicated. Whether Robert himself was always in the position of having ' a few remaining copies ' of one or other of these editions in stock we can only surmise. But the complete, or nearly complete, cessation of English-printed editions of the Geneva Bible after 1616, combined with the appearance of Dutch-printed editions, one at least of which belongs to the year 1633, disguised by spurious imprints, is fair proof that the Geneva Bible was now again subjected to the silent boycott by which Parker had repressed it until the year of his death. Fortunately, lethargy no longer accompanied repression, and the supply of Bibles of every size was abundant, although we hear murmurs that the king's printers were allowed to charge too much for them.

Although there can be no doubt that the price of Bibles gradually rose, in 1629 buyers of small folios and large quartos were for a short time able to obtain them cheap enough, as, on the Cambridge University Press for the first time exercising its right to print a Bible, and putting a small folio on the market at 10*s*. instead of 12*s*., the king's printers sold a specially printed folio edition and a thousand copies in quarto at 5*s*. apiece, ' to overthrow the Cambridge printing, and so to keep all in their own hands' (Sparke's *Scintilla*, 1641). This Cambridge edition of 1629 is noteworthy also, not only as exceptionally well printed, but as bearing marks of careful revision, carried still further in an edition of 1638, which went so far as to improve the text (I quote from Dr. Scrivener) ' by inserting words or clauses, especially in the Old Testament, overlooked by the editors of 1611 ; by amending manifest errors ; by rendering the italic notation at once more self-consistent, and more agreeable to the design of the original translators.' According to a contemporary note the revisers were Dr. Goad, of Hadley, Dr. Joseph Mede, Dean Boys, and Dr. Samuel Ward, of Sidney Sussex, of whom the last two were survivors of the original Cambridge board of 1611. Between these two Cambridge editions came one from the king's printers in 1631, for which the firm was fined £300 for omitting the word *not* in the seventh commandment. After 1638 carelessness still continued, and the London market was also flooded with incorrect editions printed in Holland. In the eighteenth century even Baskett, as a rule a careful printer, in aiming at sumptuousness could produce the Bible of 1716–17 [1] with its 'basketfull' of errors. In 1762 a Bible revised by Dr. Thomas Paris of Trinity College was printed at Cambridge, and seven years later a similar revision was carried through at Oxford by Dr. Benjamin Blayney, of Hertford College. It must be remembered that no copy of the version of 1611 had been 'sealed' as a standard, as was done in the case of the Prayer-book, and these attempts to increase consistency and to remove errors were wholly laudable. On the other hand it is obvious that under cover of such minor revisions more serious changes might be introduced, and in 1831, in a pamphlet entitled *The Existing Monopoly an inadequate protection of the Authorised Version of the Scripture,* Thomas Curtis, of Islington, called public attention to a number of departures from the original text. The uneasiness thus created was effectually dispelled by the Oxford University Press producing, in 1833, a line for line reprint of the editio princeps, the extraordinary accuracy of which has been everywhere acknowledged. It is this edition which is now reproduced by a mechanical process.

ALFRED W. POLLARD.

---

[1] The so-called Vinegar Bible, from the misprint Vinegar for Vineyard in the headline to Luke xx.

TO THE MOST
HIGH AND MIGHTIE
Prince, IAMES by the grace of God
King of Great Britaine, France and Ireland,
Defender of the Faith, &c.

THE TRANSLATORS OF *THE BIBLE,*
wish Grace, Mercie, and Peace, through IESVS
CHRIST *our* LORD.

Reat and manifold were the blessings (most dread Soueraigne) which Almighty GOD, the Father of all Mercies, bestowed vpon vs the people of ENGLAND, when first he sent your Maiesties Royall person to rule and raigne ouer us. For whereas it was the expectation of many, who wished not well vnto our SION, that vpon the setting of that bright *Occidentall Starre* Queene ELIZABETH of most happy memory, some thicke and palpable cloudes of darkenesse would so haue ouershadowed this land, that men should haue bene in doubt which way they were to walke, and that it should hardly be knowen, who was to direct the vnsetled State : the appearance of your MAIESTIE, as of the *Sunne* in his strength, instantly dispelled those supposed and surmised mists, and gaue vnto all that were well affected, exceeding cause of comfort; especially when we beheld the gouernment established in your HIGHNESSE, and your hopefull Seed, by an vndoubted Title, and this also accompanied with Peace and tranquillitie, at home and abroad.

But amongst all our Ioyes, there was no one that more filled our hearts, then the blessed continuance of the Preaching of GODS sacred word amongst vs, which is that inestimable treasure, which excelleth all the riches of the earth, because the fruit thereof extendeth it selfe, not onely to the time spent in this transitory world, but directeth and disposeth men vnto that Eternall happinesse which is aboue in Heauen.

Then, not to suffer this to fall to the ground, but rather to take it vp, and to continue it in that state, wherein the famous predecessour of your HIGH-NESSE did leaue it ; Nay, to goe forward with the confidence and reso-
lution

lution of a man in maintaining the trueth of CHRIST, and propagating it farre and neere, is that which hath so bound and firmely knit the hearts of all your MAIESTIES loyall and Religious people vnto you, that your very Name is precious among them, their eye doeth behold you with comfort, and they blesse you in their hearts, as that sanctified person, who vnder GOD, is the immediate authour of their true happinesse. And this their contentment doeth not diminish or decay, but euery day increaseth and taketh strength, when they obserue that the zeale of your Maiestie towards the house of GOD, doth not slacke or goe backward, but is more and more kindled, manifesting it selfe abroad in the furthest parts of *Christendome*, by writing in defence of the Trueth, (which hath giuen such a blow vnto that man of Sinne, as will not be healed) and euery day at home, by Religious and learned discourse, by frequenting the house of GOD, by hearing the word preached, by cherishing the teachers therof, by caring for the Church as a most tender and louing nourcing Father.

There are infinite arguments of this right Christian and Religious affection in your MAIESTIE: but none is more forcible to declare it to others, then the vehement and perpetuated desire of the accomplishing and publishing of this Worke, which now with all humilitie we present vnto your MAIESTIE. For when your Highnesse had once out of deepe iudgment apprehended, how conuenient it was, That out of the Originall sacred tongues, together with comparing of the labours, both in our owne and other forreigne Languages, of many worthy men who went before vs, there should be one more exact Translation of the holy Scriptures into the *English tongue*; your MAIESTIE did neuer desist, to vrge and to excite those to whom it was commended, that the worke might be hastened, and that the businesse might be expedited in so decent a maner, as a matter of such importance might iustly require.

And now at last, by the Mercy of GOD, and the continuance of our Labours, it being brought vnto such a conclusion, as that we haue great hope that the Church of *England* shall reape good fruit thereby; we hold it our duety to offer it to your MAIESTIE, not onely as to our King and Soueraigne, but as to the principall moouer and Author of the Worke. Humbly crauing of your most Sacred Maiestie, that since things of this quality haue euer bene subiect to the censures of ill meaning and discontented persons, it may receiue approbation and Patronage from so learned and iudicious a Prince as your Highnesse is, whose allowance and acceptance of our Labours, shall more honour and incourage vs, then all the calumniations and hard interpretations of other men shall dismay vs. So that, if on the one side we shall be traduced by Popish persons at home or abroad, who therefore will maligne vs, because we are poore Instruments to make GODS holy Trueth to be yet more and more knowen vnto the people, whom they desire still to keepe in ignorance and darknesse: or if on the other

other side, we shall be maligned by selfe-conceited brethren, who runne
their owne wayes, and giue liking vnto nothing but what is framed by
themselues, and hammered on their Anuile; we may rest secure, supported
within by the trueth and innocencie of a good conscience, hauing walked
the wayes of simplicitie and integritie, as before the Lord; And sustained
without, by the powerfull Protection of your Maiesties grace and fauour,
which will euer giue countenance to honest and Christian endeuours, a-
gainst bitter censures, and vncharitable imputations.

The LORD of Heauen and earth blesse your Maiestie with many and
happy dayes, that as his Heauenly hand hath enriched your Highnesse
with many singular, and extraordinary Graces; so you may be the
wonder of the world in this later age, for happinesse and true
felicitie, to the honour of that Great GOD, and the
good of his Church, through IESVS CHRIST
our Lord and onely Sauiour.

(∵)

¶ THE

THE TRANSLATORS
TO THE READER.

Eale to promote the common good, whether it be by deuising any thing our selues, or reuising that which hath bene laboured by others, deserueth certainly much respect and esteeme, but yet findeth but cold intertainment in the world. It is welcommed with suspicion in stead of loue, and with emulation in stead of thankes: and if there be any hole left for cauill to enter, (and cauill, if it doe not finde a hole, will make one) it is sure to bee misconstrued, and in danger to be condemned. This will easily be granted by as many as know story, or haue any experience. For, was there euer any thing proiected, that sauoured any way of newnesse or renewing, but the same endured many a storme of gaine-saying, or opposition? A man would thinke that Ciuilitie, holesome Lawes, learning and eloquence, Synods, and Church-maintenance, (that we speake of no more things of this kinde) should be as safe as a Sanctuary, and ‖ out of shot, as they say, that no man would lift vp the heele, no, nor dogge mooue his tongue against the motioners of them. For by the first, we are distinguished from bruit-beasts led with sensualitie: By the second, we are bridled and restrained from outragious behauiour, and from doing of iniuries, whether by fraud or by violence: By the third, we are enabled to informe and reforme others, by the light and feeling that we haue attained vnto our selues: Briefly, by the fourth being brought together to a parle face to face, we sooner compose our differences then by writings, which are endlesse: And lastly, that the Church be sufficiently prouided for, is so agreeable to good reason and conscience, that those mothers are holden to be lesse cruell, that kill their children assoone as they are borne, then those noursing fathers and mothers (wheresoeuer they be) that withdraw from them who hang vpon their breasts (and vpon whose breasts againe themselues doe hang to receiue the Spirituall and sincere milke of the word) liuelyhood and support fit for their estates. Thus it is apparent, that these things which we speake of, are of most necessary vse, and therefore, that none, either without absurditie can speake against them, or without note of wickednesse can spurne against them.

Yet for all that, the learned know that certaine worthy men haue bene brought to vntimely death for none other fault, but for seeking to reduce their Countrey-men to good order and discipline: and that in some Common-weales it was made a capitall crime, once to motion the making of a new Law for the abrogating of an old, though the same were most pernicious: And that certaine, which would be counted pillars of the State, and paternes of Vertue and Prudence, could not be brought for a long time to giue way to good Letters and refined speech, but bare themselues as auerse from them, as from rocks or boxes of poison: And fourthly, that hee was no babe, but a great clearke, that gaue foorth (and in writing to remaine to posteritie) in passion peraduenture, but yet he gaue foorth, that hee had not seene any profit to come by any Synode, or meeting of the Clergie, but rather the contrary: And lastly, against Church-maintenance and allowance, in such sort, as the Embassadors and messengers of the great King of Kings should be furnished, it is not vnknowen what a fiction or fable (so it is esteemed, and for no better by the reporter himselfe, though superstitious) was deuised; Namely, that at such time as the professours and teachers of Christianitie in the Church of Rome, then a true Church, were liberally endowed, a voyce forsooth was heard from heauen, saying: Now is poison powred down into the Church, &c. Thus not only as oft as we speake, as one saith, but also as oft as we do any thing of note or consequence, we subiect our selues to euery ones censure, and happy is he that is least tossed vpon tongues; for vtterly to escape the snatch of them it is impossible. If any man conceit, that this is the lot and portion of the meaner sort onely, and that Princes are priuiledged by their high estate, he is deceiued. As *the sword deuoureth aswell one as the other*, as it is in *Samuel*; nay as the great Commander charged his souldiers in a certaine battell, to strike at no part of the enemie, but at the face; And as the King of *Syria* commanded his chiefe Captaines *to fight neither with small nor great, saue onely against the King of Israel*: so it is too true, that Enuie striketh most spitefully at the fairest, and at the chiefest. *Dauid* was a worthy Prince, and no man to be compared to him for his first deedes; and yet for as worthy an acte as euer he did (euen for bringing backe the Arke of God in solemnitie) he was scorned and scoffed at by his owne wife. *Solomon* was greater then *Dauid*, though

Margin notes (left):

ἔξω βέλους.

Anacharsis with others.

Locri.

Cato the elder.

Gregory the Diuine.

Nauclerus.

2. Sam. 11. 25.

1. King. 22. 31.

2. Sam. 6. 16.

Margin note (right): The best things haue been calumniated.

To the Reader.

though not in vertue, yet in power: and by his power and wisdome he built a Temple to the LORD, such a one as was the glory of the land of Israel, and the wonder of the whole world. But was that his magnificence liked of by all? We doubt of it. Otherwise, why doe they lay it in his sonnes dish, and call vnto him for || easing of the burden, *Make*, say they, *the grieuous seruitude of thy father, and his sore yoke, lighter.* Belike he had charged them with some leuies, and troubled them with some cariages; Hereupon they raise vp a tragedie, and wish in their heart the Temple had neuer bene built. So hard a thing it is to please all, euen when we please God best, and doe seeke to approue our selues to euery ones conscience. *oeioaxθειαν.* 1.King.12.4.

The highest personages haue been calumniated. If wee will descend to later times, wee shall finde many the like examples of such kind, or rather vnkind acceptance. The first Romane Emperour did neuer doe a more pleasing deed to the learned, nor more profitable to posteritie, for conseruing the record of times in true supputation; then when he corrected the Calender, and ordered the yeere according to the course of the Sunne: and yet this was imputed to him for noueltie, and arrogancie, and procured to him great obloquie. So the first Christened Emperour (at the leastwise that openly professed the faith himselfe, and allowed others to doe the like) for strengthening the Empire at his great charges, and prouiding for the Church, as he did, got for his labour the name *Pupillus*, as who would say, a wastefull Prince, that had neede of a Guardian, or ouerseer. So the best Christened Emperour, for the loue that he bare vnto peace, thereby to enrich both himselfe and his subiects, and because he did not seeke warre but find it, was iudged to be no man at armes, (though in deed he excelled in feates of chiualrie, and shewed so much when he was prouoked) and condemned for giuing himselfe to his ease, and to his pleasure. To be short, the most learned Emperour of former times, (at the least, the greatest politician) what thanks had he for cutting off the superfluities of the lawes, and digesting them into some order and method? This, that he hath been blotted by some to bee an Epitomist, that is, one that extinguished worthy whole volumes, to bring his abridgements into request. This is the measure that hath been rendred to excellent Princes in former times, euen, *Cum benè facerent, malè audire*, For their good deedes to be euill spoken of. Neither is there any likelihood, that enuie and malignitie died, and were buried with the ancient. No, no, the reproofe of *Moses* taketh hold of most ages; *You are risen vp in your fathers stead, an increase of sinfull men. What is that that hath been done? that which shall be done: and there is no new thing vnder the Sunne*, saith the wiseman: and S. *Steuen, As your fathers did, so doe you.* This, and more to this purpose, His Maiestie that now reigneth (and long, and long may he reigne, and his offspring for euer, *Himselfe and children, and childrens children alwayes*) knew full well, according to the singular wisedome giuen vnto him by God, and the rare learning and experience that he hath attained vnto; namely that whosoeuer attempteth any thing for the publike (specially if it pertaine to Religion, and to the opening and clearing of the word of God) the same setteth himselfe vpon a stage to be glouted vpon by euery euil eye, yea, he casteth himselfe headlong vpon pikes, to be gored by euery sharpe tongue. For he that medleth with mens Religion in any part, medleth with their custome, nay, with their freehold; and though they finde no content in that which they haue, yet they cannot abide to heare of altering. Notwithstanding his Royall heart was not daunted or discouraged for this or that colour, but stood resolute, *as a statue immoueable, and an anuile not easie to be beaten into plates*, as one sayth; he knew who had chosen him to be a Souldier, or rather a Captaine, and being assured that the course which he intended made much for the glory of God, & the building vp of his Church, he would not suffer it to be broken off for whatsoeuer speaches or practises. It doth certainely belong vnto Kings, yea, it doth specially belong vnto them, to haue care of Religion, yea, to know it aright, yea, to professe it zealously, yea to promote it to the vttermost of their power. This is their glory before all nations which meane well, and this will bring vnto them a farre most excellent weight of glory in the day of the Lord Iesus. For the Scripture saith not in vaine, *Them that honor me, I will honor*, neither was it a vaine word that *Eusebius* deliuered long agoe, that pietie towards God was the weapon, and the onely weapon that both preserued *Constantines* person, and auenged him of his enemies. C.Cæsar. Plutarch. Constantine. Aurel.Victor. Theodosius. Zosimus. Iustinian. Numb 32.14. Eccles.1.9. Acts 7.51. Αυτοὶ, καὶ παιδες, καὶ παιδων πάντοτε παιδες. Suidas. ὥσπερ τις ἀνδριὰς ἀπερίτρεπτος καὶ ἄκμων ἀνὴ Αατος. 1 Sam 2.30. θεοσέβεια. Eusebius lib.10 cap.8.

His Maiesties constancie, notwithstanding calumniation, for the suruey of the English translations.

The praise of the holy Scriptures. But now what pietie without trueth? what trueth (what sauing trueth) without the word of God? what word of God (whereof we may be sure) without the Scripture? The Scriptures we are commanded to search. Ioh.5.39. Esa.8.20. They are commended that searched & studied them. Act.17.11. and 8.28,29. They are reproued that were vnskilful in them, or slow to beleeue them. Mat.22.29. Luk.24.25. They can make vs wise vnto saluation.2.Tim.3.15. If we be ignorant, they will instruct vs; if out of the way, they will bring vs home; if out of order, they will reforme vs, if in heauines, comfort vs; if dull, quicken vs; if colde, inflame vs. *Tolle, lege; Tolle, lege*, Take vp and read, take vp and read the Scriptures, (for vnto them was the direction) it was said vnto S. *Augustine* by a supernaturall voyce. *Whatsoeuer is in the Scriptures, beleeue me*, saith the same S. *Augustine, is high and diuine; there is verily trueth, and a doctrine most fit for the refreshing and renewing of mens mindes, and truely so tempered, that euery* S. August confess.lib.8.cap.12 S. August.de vtilit. credendi cap.6.

The Translators

S.Hieronym. ad
Demetriad.

S.Cyril.7°. con-
tra Iulianum.

Tertul.aduers.
Hermo.
Testul de car-
ne Christi.
Iustin προτρεπτ-
πρὸς ἕλληνα,
οἷόν τε—
S. Basil. περὶ
πίστεως.
ὑπερηφανίας κατη-
γορία.

Εἰρεσιῶνη σῦκα
φέρει, καὶ πίονας
ἄρτους, καὶ μέλιτν
κοτύλῃ, καὶ ἔλαι-
ον,&c.
An oliue bow
wrapped a-
bout with
wooll, where-
vpon did hang
figs,& bread,
and honie in
a pot,& oyle.

κοινὸν ἰατρεῖον.
S. Basil. in
Psal.primum.

1.Cor.14.

Clem.Alex.1°.
Strom.

S. Hieronym.
Damaso.
Michael, Theo-
phili fil.
2.Tom. Concil.
ex edit. Petri
Crab.
Cicero 5°.de fi-
nibus.

euery one may draw from thence that which is sufficient for him, if hee come to draw with a deuout and pious minde, as true Religion requireth. Thus S. Augustine. And S. Hierome: Ama scripturas, & amabit te sapientia &c. Loue the Scriptures, and wisedome will loue thee. And S. Cyrill against Iulian; Euen boyes that are bred vp in the Scriptures, become most religious, &c. But what mention wee three or foure vses of the Scripture, whereas whatsoeuer is to be beleeued or practised, or hoped for, is contained in them? or three or foure sentences of the Fathers, since whosoeuer is worthy the name of a Father, from Christs time downeward, hath likewise written not onely of the riches, but also of the perfection of the Scripture? I adore the fulnesse of the Scripture, saith Tertullian against Hermogenes. And againe, to Apelles an Heretike of the like stampe, he saith; I doe not admit that which thou bringest in (or con-cludest) of thine owne (head or store, de tuo) without Scripture. So Saint Iustin Martyr before him; Wee must know by all meanes, saith hee, that it is not lawfull (or possible) to learne (any thing) of God or of right pietie, saue onely out of the Prophets, who teach vs by diuine inspiration. So Saint Basill after Tertullian, It is a manifest-falling away from the Faith, and a fault of presumption, either to reiect any of those things that are written, or to bring in (vpon the head of them, ἐπεισάγειν) any of those things that are not written. Wee omit to cite to the same effect, S. Cyrill B. of Hierusalem in his 4. Cataches. Saint Hierome against Heluidius, Saint Augustine in his 3. booke against the letters of Petilian, and in very many other places of his workes. Also we forbeare to descend to latter Fathers, because wee will not wearie the reader. The Scriptures then being acknowledged to bee so full and so perfect, how can wee excuse our selues of negligence, if we doe not studie them, of curiositie, if we be not content with them? Men talke much of εἰρεσιῶνη, how many sweete and goodly things it had hanging on it; of the Philosophers stone, that it turneth copper into gold; of Cornu-copia, that it had all things necessary for foode in it; of Panaces the herbe, that it was good for all diseases; of Catholicon the drugge, that it is in stead of all purges; of Vulcans armour, that is was an armour of proofe against all thrusts, and all blowes,&c. Well, that which they falsly or vainely attributed to these things for bodily good, wee may iustly and with full measure ascribe vnto the Scripture, for spirituall. It is not onely an armour, but also a whole armorie of weapons, both offensiue, and defensiue; whereby we may saue our selues and put the enemie to flight. It is not an herbe, but a tree, or rather a whole paradise of trees of life, which bring foorth fruit euery moneth, and the fruit thereof is for meate, and the leaues for medi-cine. It is not a pot of Manna, or a cruse of oyle, which were for memorie only, or for a meales meate or two, but as it were a showre of heauenly bread sufficient for a whole host, be it neuer so great; and as it were a whole cellar full of oyle vessels; whereby all our necessities may be prouided for, and our debts discharged. In a word, it is a Panary of holesome foode, against fenowed traditions; a Physi-ons-shop (Saint Basill calleth it) of preseruatiues against poisoned heresies; a Pandect of profitable lawes, against rebellious spirits; a treasurie of most costly iewels, against beggarly rudiments; Finally a fountaine of most pure water springing vp vnto euerlasting life. And what maruaile? The originall thereof being from heauen, not from earth; the authour being God, not man; the enditer, the holy spirit, not the wit of the Apostles or Prophets; the Pen-men such as were sanctified from the wombe, and endewed with a principall portion of Gods spirit; the matter, veritie, pietie, puritie, vprightnesse; the forme, Gods word, Gods testimonie, Gods oracles, the word of trueth, the word of saluation, &c. the effects, light of vnderstanding, stablenesse of perswasion, repentance from dead workes, newnesse of life, holinesse, peace, ioy in the holy Ghost; lastly, the end and reward of the studie thereof, fellow-ship with the Saints, participation of the heauenly nature, fruition of an inheritance immortall, vnde-filed, and that neuer shall fade away: Happie is the man that delighteth in the Scripture, and thrise happie that meditateth in it day and night.

But how shall men meditate in that, which they cannot vnderstand? How shall they vnderstand Translation
necessarie. that which is kept close in an vnknowen tongue? as it is written, Except I know the power of the voyce, I shall be to him that speaketh, a Barbarian, and he that speaketh, shalbe a Barbarian to me. The Apostle ex-cepteth no tongue; not Hebrewe the ancientest, not Greeke the most copious, not Latine the finest. Nature taught a naturall man to confesse, that all of vs in those tongues which wee doe not vnder-stand, are plainely deafe; wee may turne the deafe eare vnto them. The Scythian counted the Athe-nian, whom he did not vnderstand, barbarous: so the Romane did the Syrian, and the Iew, (euen S. Hierome himselfe calleth the Hebrew tongue barbarous, belike because it was strange to so many) so the Emperour of Constantinople calleth the Latine tongue, barbarous, though Pope Nicolas do storme at it: so the Iewes long before Christ, called all other nations, Lognazim, which is little better then bar-barous. Therefore as one complaineth, that alwayes in the Senate of Rome, there was one or other that called for an interpreter: so lest the Church be driuen to the like exigent, it is necessary to haue translations in a readinesse. Translation it is that openeth the window, to let in the light; that brea-keth the shell, that we may eat the kernel; that putteth aside the curtaine, that we may looke into the most Holy place; that remooueth the couer of the well, that wee may come by the water, euen as

Iacob

To the Reader.

Gen.29.10.

Iacob rolled away the stone from the mouth of the well, by which meanes the flockes of *Laban* were watered. Indeede without translation into the vulgar tongue, the vnlearned are but like children at *Iacobs* well (which was deepe) without a bucket or some-thing to draw with: or as that person men-tioned by *Esay*, to whom when a sealed booke was deliuered, with this motion, *Reade this, I pray thee*, hee was faine to make this answere, *I cannot, for it is sealed.*

Ioh.4.11.
Esay 29. 11.

The translati-
on of the olde
Testament
out of the He-
brew into
Greeke.

While God would be knowen onely in *Iacob*, and haue his Name great in *Israel*, and in none o-ther place, while the dew lay on *Gideons* fleece onely, and all the earth besides was drie ; then for one and the same people, which spake all of them the language of *Canaan*, that is, *Hebrewe*, one and the same originall in *Hebrew* was sufficient. But when the fulnesse of time drew neere, that the Sunne of righteousnesse, the Sonne of God should come into the world, whom God ordeined to be a recon-ciliation through faith in his blood, not of the *Iew* onely, but also of the *Greeke*, yea, of all them that were scattered abroad ; then loe, it pleased the Lord to stirre vp the spirit of a *Greeke* Prince (*Greeke* for descent and language) euen of *Ptolome Philadelph* King of *Egypt*, to procure the translating of the Booke of God out of *Hebrew* into *Greeke*. This is the translation of the *Seuentie* Interpreters, com-monly so called, which prepared the way for our Sauiour among the Gentiles by written preaching, as Saint *Iohn* Baptist did among the *Iewes* by vocall. For the *Grecians* being desirous of learning, were not wont to suffer bookes of worth to lye moulding in Kings Libraries, but had many of their ser-uants, ready scribes, to copie them out, and so they were dispersed and made common. Againe, the *Greeke* tongue was wellknowen and made familiar to most inhabitants in *Asia*, by reason of the con-quest that there the *Grecians* had made, as also by the Colonies, which thither they had sent. For the same causes also it was well vnderstood in many places of *Europe*, yea, and of *Affrike* too. Therefore the word of God being set foorth in *Greeke*, becommeth hereby like a candle set vpon a candlesticke, which giueth light to all that are in the house, or like a proclamation sounded foorth in the market place, which most men presently take knowledge of ; and therefore that language was fittest to con-taine the Scriptures, both for the first Preachers of the Gospel to appeale vnto for witnesse, and for the learners also of those times to make search and triall by. It is certaine, that that Translation was not so sound and so perfect, but that it needed in many places correction ; and who had bene so sufficient for this worke as the Apostles or Apostolike men? Yet it seemed good to the holy Ghost and to them, to take that which they found, (the same being for the greatest part true and sufficient) rather then by making a new, in that new world and greene age of the Church, to expose themselues to ma-ny exceptions and cauillations, as though they made a Translation to serue their owne turne, and therefore bearing witnesse to themselues, their witnesse not to be regarded. This may be supposed to bee some cause, why the Translation of the *Seuentie* was allowed to passe for currant. Notwith-standing, though it was commended generally, yet it did not fully content the learned, no not of the *Iewes*. For not long after *Christ*, *Aquila* fell in hand with a new Translation, and after him *Theodo-tion*, and after him *Symmachus* : yea, there was a fift and a sixt edition, the Authours wherof were not knowen. These with the *Seuentie* made vp the *Hexapla*, and were worthily and to great purpose compiled together by *Origen*. Howbeit the Edition of the *Seuentie* went away with the credit, and therefore not onely was placed in the midst by *Origen* (for the worth and excellencie thereof aboue the rest, as *Epiphanius* gathereth) but also was vsed by the *Greeke* fathers for the ground and founda-tion of their Commentaries. Yea, *Epiphanius* aboue named doeth attribute so much vnto it, that he holdeth the Authours thereof not onely for Interpreters, but also for Prophets in some respect: and *Iustinian* the Emperour enioyning the *Iewes* his subiects to vse specially the Translation of the *Seuen-tie*, rendreth this reason thereof, because they were as it were enlightened with propheticall grace. Yet for all that, as the *Egyptians* are said of the Prophet to bee men and not God, and their horses flesh and not spirit: so it is euident, (and Saint *Hierome* affirmeth as much) that the *Seuentie* were Interpreters, they were not Prophets ; they did many things well, as learned men ; but yet as men they stumbled and fell, one while through ouersight, another while through ignorance, yea, some-times they may be noted to adde to the Originall, and sometimes to take from it ; which made the Apostles to leaue them many times, when they left the *Hebrew*, and to deliuer the sence thereof ac-cording to the trueth of the word, as the spirit gaue them vtterance. This may suffice touching the Greeke Translations of the old Testament.

See S. August.
lib. 12. contra
Faust.c.32.

Epiphan. de
mensur.& pon-
deribus.

See S. August
2°. de doctrin.
Christian.c.15°.
Nouell. diatax.
146.
προφητικῆς ὥσπερ
χάριτος περι-
λαμψάσης αὐτούς
Essa. 38.3.
S. Hieron.de
optimo genero
interpret.

Translation
out of Hebrew
and Greeke
into Latine.

There were also within a few hundreth yeeres after CHRIST, translations many into the Latine tongue: for this tongue also was very fit to conuey the Law and the Gospel by, because in those times very many Countreys of the West, yea of the South, East and North, spake or vnderstood Latine, being made Prouinces to the *Romanes*. But now the Latine Translations were too many to be all good, for they were infinite (*Latini Interpretes nullo modo numerari possunt*, saith *S.Augustine*.) Againe they were not out of the *Hebrew* fountaine (wee speake of the *Latine* Translations of the Old Testa-ment) but out of the *Greeke* streame, therefore the *Greeke* being not altogether cleare, the *Latine* deri-ued

S.Augustin. de
doctr. Christ.lib.
2.cap.11.

*C

The Translators

ued from it must needs be muddie. This moued *S. Hierome* a most learned father, and the best linguist without controuersie, of his age, or of any that went before him, to vndertake the translating of the Old Testament, out of the very fountaines themselues; which hee performed with that euidence of great learning, iudgement, industrie and faithfulnes, that he hath for euer bound the Church vnto him, in a debt of speciall remembrance and thankefulnesse.

S. Hieronym.
Marcell.
Zosim.
2.King.7.9.

S. Hieron. præf.
in 4.Euangel.

S. Hieron.So-
phronio.

Six.Sen.lib.4.
Alphon.à Ca-
stro lib.1.ca.23.
S. Chrysost. in
Iohan. cap.1.
bom.1.

Theodor. 5.
Therapeut.

P.Diacon.li.12.
Isidor.in Chron.
Goth. Sozom.li.
6. cap. 37.
Vaseus in
Chron Hispan.
Polydor.Virg.
5.histor. Anglo-
rum testatur i-
dem de Aluredo
nostro.
Auentin. lib.4.
* Circa annum
900. B.Rbenan.
rerum German.
lib.2.
Beroald.

Tbuan.

Psal.48.8.

ἄδρον ἄδωρον
κοὐκ ὀνήσιμον
Sophocles.

Now though the Church were thus furnished with *Greeke* and *Latine* Translations, euen before the faith of CHRIST was generally embraced in the Empire: (for the learned know that euen in *S. Hieroms* time, the Consul of *Rome* and his wife were both Ethnicks, and about the same time the greatest part of the Senate also) yet for all that the godly-learned were not content to haue the Scriptures in the Language which themselues vnderstood, *Greeke* and *Latine*, (as the good Lepers were not content to fare well themselues, but acquainted their neighbours with the store that God had sent, that they also might prouide for themselues) but also for the behoofe and edifying of the vnlearned which hungred and thirsted after Righteousnesse, and had soules to be saued aswell as they, they prouided Translations into the vulgar for their Countreymen, insomuch that most nations vnder heauen did shortly after their conuersion, heare CHRIST speaking vnto them in their mother tongue, not by the voyce of their Minister onely, but also by the written word translated. If any doubt hereof, he may be satisfied by examples enough, if enough wil serue the turne. First *S.Hierome* saith, *Multarum gentiū linguis Scriptura antè translata, docet falsa esse quæ addita sunt,&c.i. The Scripture being translated before in the languages of many Nations, doth shew that those things that were added* (by Lucian or Hesychius) *are false.* So *S.Hierome* in that place. The same *Hierome* elsewhere affirmeth that he, the time was, had set forth the translation of the *Seuenty, suæ linguæ hominibus.i.* for his countreymen of *Dalmatia.* Which words not only *Erasmus* doth vnderstand to purport, that *S. Hieronie* translated the Scripture into the *Dalmatian* tongue, but also *Sixtus Senensis*, and *Alphonsus à Castro* (that we speake of no more) men not to be excepted against by them of *Rome*, doe ingenuously confesse as much. So, *S. Chrysostome* that liued in *S. Hieromes* time, giueth euidence with him: *The doctrine of* S. Iohn (saith he) *did not in such sort* (as the Philosophers did) *vanish away: but the Syrians, Egyptians, Indians, Persians, Ethiopians, and infinite other nations being barbarous people, translated it into their(mother) tongue,and haue learned to be* (true) *Philosophers,* he meaneth Christians. To this may be added *Theodorit*, as next vnto him, both for antiquitie, and for learning. His words be these, *Euery Countrey that is vnder the Sunne, is full of these wordes* (of the Apostles and Prophets) *and the Hebrew tongue* (he meaneth the Scriptures in the *Hebrew* tongue) *is turned not onely into the Language of the Grecians, but also of the Romanes, and Egyptians,and Persians,and Indians, and Armenians,and Scythians, and Sauromatians, and briefly into all the Languages that any Nation vseth.* So he. In like maner, *Vlpilas* is reported by *Paulus Diaconus* and *Isidor* (and before them by *Sozomen*) to haue translated the Scriptures into the *Gothicke* tongue: *Iohn* Bishop of *Siuil* by *Vasseus*, to haue turned them into *Arabicke*, about the yeere of our Lord 717: *Beda* by *Cistertiensis*, to haue turned a great part of them into *Saxon: Efnard* by *Trithemius*, to haue abridged the French Psalter, as *Beda* had done the *Hebrew*, about the yeere 800: King *Alured* by the said *Cistertiensis*, to haue turned the Psalter into *Saxon: Methodius* by *Auentinus* (printed at Ingolstad) to haue turned the Scriptures into ‖ *Sclauonian: Valdo*, Bishop of *Frising* by *Beatus Rhenanus*, to haue caused about that time, the Gospels to be translated into *Dutch*-rithme, yet extant in the Library of *Corbinian: Valdus*, by diuers to haue turned them himselfe, or to haue gotten them turned into *French*, about the yeere 1160: *Charles* the 5. of that name, surnamed *The wise*, to haue caused them to be turned into *French*, about 200. yeeres after *Valdus* his time, of which translation there be many copies yet extant, as witnesseth *Beroaldus.* Much about that time, euen in our King *Richard* the seconds dayes, *Iohn Treuisa* translated them into *English*, and many *English* Bibles in written hand are yet to be seene with diuers, translated as it is very probable, in that age. So the *Syrian* translation of the New Testament is in most learned mens Libraries, of *Widminstadius* his setting forth, and the Psalter in *Arabicke* is with many, of *Augustinus Nebiensis* setting foorth. So *Postel* affirmeth, that in his trauaile he saw the Gospels in the *Ethiopian* tongue; And *Ambrose Thesius* alleageth the Psalter of the *Indians*, which he testifieth to haue bene set forth by *Potken* in *Syrian* characters. So that, to haue the Scriptures in the mother-tongue is not a quaint conceit lately taken vp, either by the Lord *Cromwell* in *England*, or by the Lord *Radeuil* in *Polonie*, or by the Lord *Vngnadius* in the Emperours dominion, but hath bene thought vpon, and put in practise of old, euen from the first times of the conuersion of any Nation; no doubt, because it is esteemed most profitable, to cause faith to grow in mens hearts the sooner, and to make them to be able to say with the words of the Psalme, *As we haue heard, so we haue seene.*

Now the Church of Rome would seeme at the length to beare a motherly affection towards her children, and to allow them the Scriptures in their mother tongue: but indeed it is a gift, not deseruing to be called a gift, an vnprofitable gift: they must first get a Licence in writing before they may vse

The translating of the Scripture into the vulgar tongues.

The vnwillingnes of our chiefe Aduersaries, that the Scriptures should be di-

To the Reader.

uulged in the mother tongue, &c.

vse them, and to get that, they must approue themselues to their Confessor, that is, to be such as are, if not frozen in the dregs, yet sowred with the leauen of their superstition. Howbeit, it seemed too much to *Clement. the* 8. that there should be any Licence granted to haue them in the vulgar tongue, and therefore he ouerruleth and frustrateth the grant of *Pius* the fourth. So much are they afraid of the light of the Scripture, (*Lucifugæ Scripturarum*, as *Tertullian* speaketh) that they will not trust the people with it, no not as it is set foorth by their owne sworne men, no not with the Licence of their owne Bishops and Inquisitors. Yea, so vnwilling they are to communicate the Scriptures to the peoples vnderstanding in any sort, that they are not ashamed to confesse, that wee forced them to translate it into English against their wills. This seemeth to argue a bad cause, or a bad conscience, or both. Sure we are, that it is not he that hath good gold, that is afraid to bring it to the touch-stone, but he that hath the counterfeit; neither is it the true man that shunneth the light, but the malefactour, lest his deedes should be reproued: neither is it the plaine dealing Merchant that is vnwilling to haue the waights, or the meteyard brought in place, but he that vseth deceit. But we will let them alone for this fault, and returne to translation.

See the obseruation. (set forth by Clemen. his authority) vpon the 4. rule of Pius the 4. his making in the Index, *lib.prohib.pag.*15. *ver.*5.
Tertul. de reuur. carnit.
Ioan 3.20.

The speaches and reasons, both of our brethren, and of our Aduersaries against this worke.

Many mens mouths haue bene open a good while (and yet are not stopped) with speeches about the Translation so long in hand, or rather perusals of Translations made before: and aske what may be the reason, what the necessitie of the employment: Hath the Church bene deceiued, say they, all this while? Hath her sweet bread bene mingled with leauen, her siluer with drosse, her wine with water, her milke with lime? (*Lacte gypsum malè miscetur*, saith *S. Ireney*,) We hoped that we had bene in the right way, that we had had the Oracles of God deliuered vnto vs, and that though all the world had cause to be offended and to complaine, yet that we had none. Hath the nurse holden out the breast, and nothing but winde in it? Hath the bread bene deliuered by the fathers of the Church, and the same proued to be *lapidosus*, as *Seneca* speaketh? What is it to handle the word of God deceitfully, if this be not? Thus certaine brethren. Also the aduersaries of *Iudah* and *Hierusalem*, like Sanballat in *Nehemiah*, mocke, as we heare, both at the worke and workemen, saying; *What doe these weake Iewes, &c. will they make the stones whole againe out of the heapes of dust which are burnt? although they build, yet if a foxe goe vp, he shall euen breake downe their stony wall.* Was their Translation good before? Why doe they now mend it? Was it not good? Why then was it obtruded to the people? Yea, why did the Catholicks (meaning Popish *Romanists*) alwayes goe in ieopardie, for refusing to goe to heare it? Nay, if it must be translated into English, Catholicks are fittest to doe it. They haue learning, and they know when a thing is well, they can *manum de tabulâ*. Wee will answere them both briefly: and the former, being brethren, thus, with *S. Hierome*, *Damnamus veteres? Minimè, sed post priorum studia in domo Domini quod possumus laboramus.* That is, *Doe we condemne the ancient? In no case: but after the endeuours of them that were before vs, wee take the best paines we can in the house of God.* As if hee said, Being prouoked by the example of the learned that liued before my time, I haue thought it my duetie, to assay whether my talent in the knowledge of the tongues, may be profitable in any measure to Gods Church, lest I should seeme to haue laboured in them in vaine, and lest I should be thought to glory in men, (although ancient,) aboue that which was in them. Thus *S. Hierome* may be thought to speake.

*S.Iren.*3.*lib. cap.*19.

*Neh.*4.3.

S.Hieron. Apolog. aduers. Ruffin.

A satisfaction to our brethren.

And to the same effect say wee, that we are so farre off from condemning any of their labours that traueiled before vs in this kinde, either in this land or beyond sea, either in King *Henries* time, or King *Edwards* (if there were any translation, or correction of a translation in his time) or Queene *Elizabeths* of euer-renowned memorie, that we acknowledge them to haue beene raised vp of God, for the building and furnishing of his Church, and that they deserue to be had of vs and of posteritie in euerlasting remembrance. The Iudgement of *Aristotle* is worthy and well knowen: *If Timotheus had not bene, we had not had much sweet musicke; but if Phrynis* (*Timotheus* his master) *had not beene, wee had not had Timotheus.* Therefore blessed be they, and most honoured be their name, that breake the yce, and glue th onset vpon that which helpeth forward to the sauing of soules. Now what can bee more auaileable thereto, then to deliuer Gods booke vnto Gods people in a tongue which they vnderstand? Since of an hidden treasure, and of a fountaine that is sealed, there is no profit, as *Ptolomee Philadelph* wrote to the Rabbins or masters of the Iewes, as witnesseth *Epiphanius*: and as *S. Augustine* saith; *A man had rather be with his dog then with a stranger* (whose tongue is strange vnto him.) Yet for all that, as nothing is begun and perfited at the same time, and the later thoughts are thought to be the wiser: so, if we building vpon their foundation that went before vs, and being holpen by their labours, doe endeuour to make that better which they left so good; no man, we are sure, hath cause to mislike vs; they, we perswade our selues, if they were aliue, would thanke vs. The vintage of *Abiezer*, that strake the stroake: yet the gleaning of grapes of *Ephraim* was not to be despised. See *Iudges* 8. *verse* 2. *Ioash* the king of *Israel* did not satisfie himselfe, till he had smitten the ground three times; and yet hee offended the Prophet, for giuing ouer then. *Aquila*, of whom wee spake before, translated

*Arist.*2.*metaphys.cap.*1.

S. Epiphan. loco antè citato.
S. Augustin.lib. 19. *de ciuit. Dei c.*7.

Iudges 8. 2.
2 *Kings* 13. 18, 19.

The Translators

S.Hieron.in
Eseeb.cap.3.

ted the Bible as carefully, and as skilfully as he could; and yet he thought good to goe ouer it againe, and then it got the credit with the Iewes, to be called κατα ἀκρίβειαν, that is, accuratly done, as Saint *Hierome* witnesseth. How many bookes of profane learning haue bene gone ouer againe and againe, by the same translators, by others? Of one and the same booke of *Aristotles* Ethikes, there are extant not so few as sixe or seuen seuerall translations. Now if this cost may bee bestowed vpon the goord, which affordeth vs a little shade, and which to day flourisheth, but to morrow is cut downe; what may we bestow, nay what ought we not to bestow vpon the Vine, the fruite whereof maketh glad the conscience of man, and the stemme whereof abideth for euer? And this is the word of God, which we

Ierem. 23. 28.
Tetul. ad Mar-
tyr.
Si tanti vilissi-
mum vitrum,
quanti pretiosis-
simum Marga-
ritum: Hieron.
ad Sulnin.

translate. *What is the chaffe to the wheat, saith the Lord? Tanti vitreum, quanti verum margaritum* (saith *Tertullian*,) if a toy of glasse be of that rekoning with vs, how ought wee to value the true pearle? Therefore let no mans eye be euill, because his Maiesties is good; neither let any be grieued, that wee haue a Prince that seeketh the increase of the spirituall wealth of Israel (let *Sanballats* and *Tobiahs* doe so, which therefore doe beare their iust reproofe) but let vs rather blesse God from the ground of our heart, for working this religious care in him, to haue the translations of the Bible maturely conside- red of and examined. For by this meanes it commeth to passe, that whatsoeuer is sound alreadie (and all is sound for substance, in one or other of our editions, and the worst of ours farre better then their autentike vulgar) the same will shine as gold more brightly, being rubbed and polished; also, if any thing be halting, or superfluous, or not so agreeable to the originall, the same may bee corrected, and the trueth set in place. And what can the King command to bee done, that will bring him more true honour then this? and wherein could they that haue beene set a worke, approue their duetie to the King, yea their obedience to God, and loue to his Saints more, then by yeelding their seruice, and all that is within them, for the furnishing of the worke? But besides all this, they were the principall motiues of it, and therefore ought least to quarrell it: for the very Historicall trueth is, that vpon the importunate petitions of the Puritanes, at his Maiesties comming to this Crowne, the Conference at Hampton Court hauing bene appointed for hearing their complaints: when by force of reason they were put from all other grounds, they had recourse at the last, to this shift, that they could not with good conscience subscribe to the Communion booke, since it maintained the Bible as it was there translated, which was as they said, a most corrupted translation. And although this was iudged to be but a very poore and emptie shift; yet euen hereupon did his Maiestie beginne to bethinke him- selfe of the good that might ensue by a new translation, and presently after gaue order for this Trans- lation which is now presented vnto thee. Thus much to satisfie our scrupulous Brethren.

Now to the later we answere; that wee doe not deny, nay wee affirme and auow, that the very meanest translation of the Bible in English, set foorth by men of our profession (for wee haue seene none of theirs of the whole Bible as yet) containeth the word of God, nay, is the word of God. As the Kings Speech which hee vttered in Parliament, being translated into *French*, *Dutch*, *Italian* and *Latine*, is still the Kings Speech, though it be not interpreted by euery Translator with the like grace, nor peraduenture so fitly for phrase, nor so expresly for sence, euery where. For it is confessed, that things are to take their denomination of the greater part; and a naturall man could say, *Verùm vbi*

An answere to
the imputati-
ons of our ad-
uersaries.

Hora.t.

Iames 3. 2.

multa nitent in carmine, non ego paucis offendor maculis, &c. A man may be counted a vertuous man, though hee haue made many slips in his life, (els, there were none vertuous, for *in many things we of- fend all*) also a comely man and louely, though hee haue some warts vpon his hand, yea, not onely freakles vpon his face, but also skarres. No cause therefore why the word translated should bee de- nied to be the word, or forbidden to be currant, notwithstanding that some imperfections and blemi- shes may be noted in the setting foorth of it. For what euer was perfect vnder the Sunne, where A- postles or Apostolike men, that is, men indued with an extraordinary measure of Gods spirit, and priuiledged with the priuiledge of infallibilitie, had not their hand? The Romanistes therefore in refusing to heare, and daring to burne the Word translated, did no lesse then despite the spirit of grace, from whom originally it proceeded, and whose sense and meaning, as well as mans weakenesse

Plutarch.14
Camilis.

would enable, it did expresse. Iudge by an example or two. *Plutarch* writeth, that after that *Rome* had beene burnt by the *Galles*, they fell soone to builde it againe: but doing it in haste, they did not cast the streets, nor proportion the houses in such comely fashion, as had bene most sightly and con- uenient; was *Catiline* therefore an honest man, or a good Patriot, that sought to bring it to a combu- stion? or *Nero* a good Prince, that did indeed set it on fire? So, by the story of *Ezrah*, and the pro- phesie of *Haggai* it may be gathered, that the Temple built by *Zerubbabel* after the returne from *Ba- bylon*, was by no meanes to bee compared to the former built by *Solomon* (for they that remembred the former, wept when they considered the later) notwithstanding, might this later either haue bene

Eztah 3. 12.

abhorred and forsaken by the *Iewes*, or prophaned by the *Greekes*? The like were we to thinke of Translations. The translation of the *Seuentie* dissenteth from the Originall in many places, neither doeth it come neere it, for perspicuitie, grauitie, maiestie; yet which of the Apostles did condemne

it?

it? Condemne it? Nay, they vsed it, (as it is apparent, and as Saint *Hierome* and most learned men doe confesse) which they would not haue done, nor by their example of vsing it, so grace and commend it to the Church, if it had bene vnworthy the appellation and name of the word of God. And whereas they vrge for their second defence of their vilifying and abusing of the *English* Bibles, or some pieces thereof, which they meete with, for that heretikes (forsooth) were the Authours of the translations, (heretikes they call vs by the same right that they call themselues Catholikes, both being wrong) wee marueile what diuinitie taught them so. Wee are sure *Tertullian* was of another minde : *Ex personis probamus fidem, an ex fide personas?* Doe we trie mens faith by their persons? we should trie their persons by their faith. Also S. *Augustine* was of an other minde : for he lighting vpon certaine rules made by *Tychonius* a *Donatist*, for the better vnderstanding of the word, was not a-shamed to make vse of them, yea, to insert them into his owne booke, with giuing commendation to them so farre foorth as they were worthy to be commended, as is to be seene in S. *Augustines* third booke *De doctrina Christiana*. To be short, *Origen*, and the whole Church of God for certain hundred yeeres, were of an other minde : for they were so farre from treading vnder foote, (much more from burning) the Translation of *Aquila* a Proselite, that is, one that had turned *Iew;* of *Symmachus*, and *Theodotion*, both *Ebionites*, that is, most vile heretikes, that they ioyned them together with the *Hebrew* Originall, and the Translation of the *Seuentie* (as hath bene before signified out of *Epiphanius*) and set them forth openly to be considered of and perused by all. But we weary the vnlearned, who need not know so much, and trouble the learned, who know it already.

Yet before we end, we must answere a third cauill and obiection of theirs against vs, for altering and amending our Taanslations so oft; wherein truely they deale hardly, and strangely with vs. For to whom euer was it imputed for a fault (by such as were wise) to goe ouer that which hee had done, and to amend it where he saw cause? Saint *Augustine* was not afraide to exhort S. *Hierome* to a *Palinodia* or recantation; the same S. *Augustine* was not ashamed to retractate, we might say reuoke, many things that had passed him, and doth euen glory that he seeth his infirmities. If we will be sonnes of the Trueth, we must consider what it speaketh, and trample vpon our owne credit, yea, and vpon other mens too, if either be any way an hinderance to it. This to the cause : then to the persons we say, that of all men they ought to bee most silent in this case. For what varieties haue they, and what alterations haue they made, not onely of their Seruice bookes, Portesses and Breuiaries, but also of their *Latine* Translation? The Seruice booke supposed to be made by S. *Ambrose* (*Officium Ambrosianum*) was a great while in speciall vse and request : but Pope *Hadrian* calling a Councill with the ayde of *Charles* the Emperour, abolished it, yea, burnt it, and commanded the Seruice-booke of Saint *Gregorie* vniuersally to be vsed. Well, *Officium Gregorianum* gets by this meanes to be in credit, but doeth it continue without change or altering? No, the very *Romane* Seruice was of two fashions, the New fashion, and the Old, (the one vsed in one Church, the other in another) as is to bee seene in *Pamelius* a Romanist, his Preface, before *Micrologus*. The same *Pamelius* reporteth out of *Radulphus de Riuo*, that about the yeere of our Lord, 1277. Pope *Nicolas* the third remoued out of the Churches of *Rome*, the more ancient bookes (of Seruice) and brought into vse the Missals of the Friers Minorites, and commaunded them to bee obserued there; insomuch that about an hundred yeeres after, when the aboue named *Radulphus* happened to be at *Rome*, he found all the bookes to be new, (of the new stampe.) Neither was there this chopping and changing in the more ancient times onely, but also of late : *Pius Quintus* himselfe confesseth, that euery Bishopricke almost had a peculiar kind of seruice, most vnlike to that which others had : which moued him to abolish all other Breuiaries, though neuer so ancient, and priuiledged and published by Bishops in their Dioceses, and to establish and ratifie that onely which was of his owne setting foorth, in the yeere 1568. Now, when the father of their Church, who gladly would heale the soare of the daughter of his people softly and sleightly, and make the best of it, findeth so great fault with them for their odds and iarring; we hope the children haue no great cause to vaunt of their vniformitie. But the difference that appeareth betweene our Translations, and our often correcting of them, is the thing that wee are specially charged with; let vs see therefore whether they themselues bee without fault this way, (if it be to be counted a fault, to correct) and whether they bee fit men to throw stones at vs : *O tandem maior parcas insane minori* : they that are lesse sound themselues, ought not to obiect infirmities to others. If we should tell them that *Valla, Stapulensis, Erasmus*, and *Viues* found fault with their vulgar Translation, and consequently wished the same to be mended, or a new one to be made, they would answere peraduenture, that we produced their enemies for witnesses against them; albeit, they were in no other sort enemies, then as S. *Paul* was to the *Galatians*, for telling them the trueth : and it were to be wished, that they had dared to tell it them plainlier and oftner. But what will they say to this, that Pope *Leo* the tenth allowed *Erasmus* Translation of the New Testament, so much different from the vulgar, by his Apostolike Letter & Bull; that the same *Leo* exhorted *Pagnin* to translate the whole Bible,

Tertul.de præscript. contra hæreses.

S.August.3.de doct.Christ.cap. 30.

S.Aug.Epist.9. S.Aug.lib.Retractat. Video interdum vitia mea, S. Aug.Epist.8.

Durand.lib.5. cap.2.

Horat.

Galat.4.16.

Sixtus Senens.

The Translators

Heb.7.11.
& 8.7.

Bible, and bare whatsoeuer charges was necessary for the worke? Surely, as the Apostle reasoneth to the *Hebrewes*, that *if the former Law and Testament had bene sufficient, there had beene no need of the latter*: so we may say, that if the olde vulgar had bene at all points allowable, to small purpose had labour and charges bene vndergone, about framing of a new. If they say, it was one Popes priuate opinion, and that he consulted onely himselfe; then wee are able to goe further with them, and to a-uerre, that more of their chiefe men of all sorts, euen their owne *Trent*-champions *Paiua* & *Vega*, and their owne Inquisitors, *Hieronymus ab Oleastro*, and their own Bishop *Isidorus Clarius*, and their owne Cardinall *Thomas à Vio Caietan*, doe either make new Translations themselues, or follow new ones of other mens making, or note the vulgar Interpretor for halting; none of them feare to dissent from him, nor yet to except against him. And call they this an vniforme tenour of text and iudgement a-bout the text, so many of their Worthies disclaiming the now receiued conceit? Nay, we wil yet come neerer the quicke: doth not their *Paris*-edition differ from the *Louaine*, and *Hentenius* his from them both, and yet all of them allowed by authoritie? Nay, doth not *Sixtus Quintus* confesse, that cer-taine Catholikes (he meaneth certaine of his owne side) were in such an humor of translating the Scriptures into *Latine*, that Satan taking occasion by them, though they thought of no such matter, did striue what he could, out of so vncertaine and manifold a varietie of Translations, so to mingle all things, that nothing might seeme to be left certaine and firme in them, &c? Nay further, did not the same *Sixtus* ordaine by an inuiolable decree, and that with the counsell and consent of his Cardinals, that the *Latine* edition of the olde and new Testament, which the Councill of *Trent* would haue to be authenticke, is the same without controuersie which he then set forth, being diligently corrected and printed in the Printing-house of *Vatican*? Thus *Sixtus* in his Preface before his Bible. And yet *Cle-ment* the eight his immediate successour, publisheth another edition of the Bible, containing in it in-finite differences from that of *Sixtus*, (and many of them waightie and materiall) and yet this must be authentike by all meanes. What is to haue the faith of our glorious Lord IESVS CHRIST with Yea and Nay, if this be not? Againe, what is sweet harmonie and consent, if this be? Therfore, as *Demara-tus of Corinth* aduised a great King, before he talked of the dissentions among the *Grecians*, to com-pose his domesticke broiles (for at that time his Queene and his sonne and heire were at deadly fuide with him) so all the while that our aduersaries doe make so many and so various editions themselues, and doe iarre so much about the worth and authoritie of them, they can with no show of equitie challenge vs for changing and correcting.

Sixtns 5.præfat.
fixæ Biblijs.

The purpose
of the Tran-
slators, with
their number,
furniture, care
&c.

But it is high time to leaue them, and to shew in briefe what wee proposed to our selues, and what course we held in this our perusall and suruay of the Bible. Truly (good Christian Reader) wee ne-uer thought from the beginning, that we should neede to make a new Translation, nor yet to make of a bad one a good one, (for then the imputation of *Sixtus* had bene true in some sort, that our peo-ple had bene fed with gall of Dragons in stead of wine, with whey in stead of milke:) but to make a good one better, or out of many good ones, one principall good one, not iustly to be excepted against; that hath bene our indeauour, that our marke. To that purpose there were many chosen, that were greater in other mens eyes then in their owne, and that sought the truth rather then their own praise. Againe, they came or were thought to come to the worke, not *exercendi causâ* (as one saith) but *exer-citati*, that is, learned, not to learne: For the chiefe oueruseer and ἐργοδιώκτης vnder his Maiestie, to whom not onely we, but also our whole Church was much bound, knew by his wisedome, which thing also *Nazianzen* taught so long agoe, that it is a preposterous order to teach first and to learne after, yea that τὸ ἐν πίθῳ κεραμίαν μανθάνειν to learne and practise together, is neither commendable for the workeman, nor safe for the worke. Therefore such were thought vpon, as could say modestly with Saint *Hierome*, *Et Hebræum Sermonem ex parte didicimus, & in Latino penè ab ipsis incunabulis &c. detriti sumus*. Both we haue learned the Hebrew tongue in part, and in the Latine wee haue beene exercised almost from our verie cradle. S. *Hierome* maketh no mention of the *Greeke* tongue, wherein yet hee did excell, because hee translated not the old Testament out of *Greeke*, but out of *Hebrewe*. And in what sort did these as-semble? In the trust of their owne knowledge, or of their sharpenesse of wit, or deepenesse of iudge-ment, as it were in an arme of flesh? At no hand. They trusted in him that hath the key of *Dauid*, opening and no man shutting; they prayed to the Lord the Father of our Lord, to the effect that S. *Augustine* did; *O let thy Scriptures be my pure delight, let me not be deceiued in them, neither let me deceiue by them*. In this confidence, and with this deuotion did they assemble together; not too many, lest one should trouble another; and yet many, lest many things haply might escape them. If you aske what they had before them, truely it was the *Hebrew* text of the Olde Testament, the *Greeke* of the New. These are the two golden pipes, or rather conduits, where-through the oliue branches emp-tie themselues into the golde. Saint *Augustine* calleth them precedent, or originall tongues; Saint *Hierome*, fountaines. The same Saint *Hierome* affirmeth, and *Gratian* hath not spared to put it into his Decree, That *as the credit of the olde Bookes* (he meaneth of the Old Testament) *is to bee tryed by the*

Nazianzen, εἰς
ρν. ἀσπασ. γαρος.ς.

Idem in Apo-
loget.

S. Aug. lib. 11.
Confess. cap. 2.

S. August. 3. de
doctr. c.3. &c.
S. Hieron. ad
Suniam &
Fretel.
S. Hieron. ad
Lucinium, Dist.
9. vt veterum.

the Hebrewe Volumes, so of the New by the Greeke tongue, he meaneth by the originall *Greeke.* If trueth be to be tried by these tongues, then whence should a Translation be made, but out of them? These tongues therefore, the Scriptures wee say in those tongues, wee set before vs to translate, being the tongues wherein God was pleased to speake to his Church by his Prophets and Apostles. Neither did we run ouer the worke with that posting haste that the *Septuagint* did, if that be true which is reported of them, that they finished it in 72. dayes; neither were we barred or hindered from going ouer it againe, hauing once done it, like S.*Hierome*, if that be true which himselfe reporteth, that he could no sooner write any thing, but presently it was caught from him, and published, and he could not haue leaue to mend it: neither, to be short, were we the first that fell in hand with trāslating the Scripture into English, and consequently destitute of former helpes, as it is written of *Origen*, that hee was the first in a maner, that put his hand to write Commentaries vpon the Scriptures, and therefore no maruelle, if he ouershot himselfe many times. None of these things: the worke hath not bene hudled vp in 72. dayes, but hath cost the workemen, as light as it seemeth, the paines of twise seuen times seuentie two dayes and more: matters of such weight and consequence are to bee speeded with maturitie: for in a businesse of moment a man feareth not the blame of conuenient slacknesse. Neither did wee thinke much to consult the Translators or Commentators, *Chaldee, Hebrewe, Syrian, Greeke,* or *Latine,* no nor the *Spanish, French, Italian,* or *Dutch;* neither did we disdaine to reuise that which we had done, and to bring backe to the anuill that which we had hammered: but hauing and vsing as great helpes as were needfull, and fearing no reproch for slownesse, nor coueting praise for expedition, wee haue at the length, through the good hand of the Lord vpon vs, brought the worke to that passe that you see.

Some peraduenture would haue no varietie of sences to be set in the margine, lest the authoritie of the Scriptures for deciding of controuersies by that shew of vncertaintie, should somewhat be shaken. But we hold their iudgmēt not to be so sound in this point. For though, *whatsoeuer things are necessary are manifest,* as S. *Chrysostome* saith, and as S. *Augustine, In those things that are plainely set downe in the Scriptures, all such matters are found that concerne Faith, hope, and Charitie.* Yet for all that it cannot be dissembled, that partly to exercise and whet our wits, partly to weane the curious from loathing of them for their euery-where-plainenesse, partly also to stirre vp our deuotion to craue the assistance of Gods spirit by prayer, and lastly, that we might be forward to seeke ayd of our brethren by conference, and neuer scorne those that be not in all respects so complete as they should bee, being to seeke in many things our selues, it hath pleased God in his diuine prouidence, heere and there to scatter wordes and sentences of that difficultie and doubtfulnesse, not in doctrinall points that concerne saluation, (for in such it hath beene vouched that the Scriptures are plaine) but in matters of lesse moment, that fearefulnesse would better beseeme vs then confidence, and if we will resolue, to resolue vpon modestie with S. *Augustine,* (though not in this same case altogether, yet vpon the same ground) *Melius est dubitare de occultis, quàm litigare de incertis,* it is better to make doubt of those things which are secret, then to striue about those things that are vncertaine. There are many words in the Scriptures, which are neuer found there but once, (hauing neither brother nor neighbour, as the *Hebrewes* speake) so that we cannot be holpen by conference of places. Againe, there be many rare names of certaine birds, beastes and precious stones, &c. concerning which the *Hebrewes* themselues are so diuided among themselues for iudgement, that they may seeme to haue defined this or that, rather because they would say somthing, thē because they were sure of that which they said, as S. *Hierome* somewhere saith of the *Septuagint.* Now in such a case, doth not a margine do well to admonish the Reader to seeke further, and not to conclude or dogmatize vpon this or that peremptorily? For as it is a fault of incredulitie, to doubt of those things that are euident: so to determine of such things as the Spirit of God hath left (euen in the iudgment of the iudicious) questionable, can he no lesse then presumption. Therfore as S. *Augustine* saith, that varietie of Translations is profitable for the finding out of the sense of the Scriptures: so diuersitie of signification and sense in the margine, where the text is not so cleare, must needes doe good, yea, is necessary, as we are perswaded. We know that *Sixtus Quintus* expresly forbiddeth, that any varietie of readings of their vulgar edition, should be put in the margine, (which though it be not altogether the same thing to that we haue in hand, yet it looketh that way) but we thinke he hath not all of his owne side his fauourers, for this conceit. They that are wise, had rather haue their iudgements at libertie in differences of readings, then to be captiuated to one, when it may be the other. If they were sure that their hie Priest had all lawes shut vp in his brest, as *Paul* the second bragged, and that he were as free from errour by speciall priuiledge, as the Dictators of *Rome* were made by law inuiolable, it were an other matter; then his word were an Oracle, his opinion a decision. But the eyes of the world are now open, God be thanked, and haue bene a great while, they find that he is subiect to the same affections and infirmities that others be, that his skin is penetrable, and therefore so much as he prooueth, not as much as he claimeth, they grant and embrace.

An

Ioseph. Antiq.
lib.12.
S. Hieron. ad
Pammac. pro
libr. aduers. Io-
uinian
πρωτόπειρος.

φιλεῖ γὰρ ὀκνεῖν
πρᾶγμα ἀνὴρ
πράσσων μεγα.
Sophoc. in E-
lect.

πάντα τὰ ἀναγ-
καῖα δῆλα.
S. Chrysost. in 2.
Thess. cap.2.
S. Aug.2. de
doctr. Christ.
cap.9.

S. August. li.8.
de Genes. ad Li-
ter. cap.5.
ἅπαξ λεγόμενα.

S. Aug.2ª.de
doctr. Christian.
cap.14.

Sixtus 5.præf.
Bibliæ.

Plat. in Pau-
lo secundo.

ὁμοιοπαθὴς,
τρωτός γ᾽ οἱ
χρὼς ἐστι.

reasons mo-
 [u]ng vs to set
uersitie of
[se]nces in the
[m]argin, where
[th]ere is great
[pr]obability for
[e]ach.

The Translators

Reasons inducing vs not to stand curiously vpon an identitie of phrasing.

An other thing we thinke good to admonish thee of (gentle Reader) that wee haue not tyed our selues to an vniformitie of phrasing, or to an identitie of words, as some peraduenture would wish that we had done, because they obserue, that some learned men some where, haue beene as exact as they could that way. Truly, that we might not varie from the sense of that which we had translated before, if the word signified the same thing in both places (for there bee some wordes that bee not of the same sense euery where) we were especially carefull, and made a conscience, according to our duetie. But, that we should expresse the same notion in the same particular word; as for example, if we translate the *Hebrew* or *Greeke* word once by *Purpose*, neuer to call it *Intent*; if one where *Iourneying*, neuer *Traueiling*; if one where *Thinke*, neuer *Suppose*; if one where *Paine*, neuer *Ache*; if one where *Ioy*, neuer *Gladnesse*, &c. Thus to minse the matter, wee thought to sauour more of curiositie then wisedome, and that rather it would breed scorne in the Atheist, then bring profite to the godly Reader. For is the kingdome of God become words or syllables? why should wee be in bondage to them if we may be free, vse one precisely when wee may vse another no lesse fit, as commodiously? A godly Father in the Primitiue time shewed himselfe greatly moued, that (or dangerous) one of newfanglenes called κράββατον σκίμπους, though the difference be little or none; and another reporteth, that he was much abused for turning *Cucurbita* (to which reading the people had beene vsed) into *Hedera*. Now if this happen in better times, and vpon so small occasions, wee might iustly feare hard censure, if generally wee should make verball and vnnecessary changings. We might also be charged (by scoffers) with some vnequall dealing towards a great number of good English wordes. For as it is written of a certaine great Philosopher, that he should say, that those logs were happie that were made images to be worshipped; for their fellowes, as good as they, lay for blockes behinde the fire: so if wee should say, as it were, vnto certaine words, Stand vp higher, haue a place in the Bible alwayes, and to others of like qualitie, Get ye hence, be banished for euer, wee might be taxed peraduenture with S. *Iames* his words, namely, *To be partiall in our selues and iudges of euill thoughts*. Adde hereunto, that nicenesse in wordes was alwayes counted the next step to trifling, and so was to bee curious about names too: also that we cannot follow a better patterne for elocution then God himselfe; therefore hee vsing diuers words, in his holy writ, and indifferently for one thing in nature: we, if wee will not be superstitious, may vse the same libertie in our English versions out of *Hebrew* & *Greeke*, for that copie or store that he hath giuen vs. Lastly, wee haue on the one side auoided the scrupulositie of the Puritanes, who leaue the olde Ecclesiasticall words, and betake them to other, as when they put *washing* for *Baptisme*, and *Congregation* in stead of *Church*: as also on the other side we haue shunned the obscuritie of the Papists, in their *Azimes, Tunike, Rational, Holocausts, Præpuce, Pasche*, and a number of such like, whereof their late Translation is full, and that of purpose to darken the sence, that since they must needs translate the Bible, yet by the language thereof, it may bee kept from being vnderstood. But we desire that the Scripture may speake like it selfe, as in the language of *Canaan*, that it may bee vnderstood euen of the very vulgar.

Many other things we might giue thee warning of (gentle Reader) if wee had not exceeded the measure of a Preface alreadie. It remaineth, that we commend thee to God, and to the Spirit of his grace, which is able to build further then we can aske or thinke. Hee remoueth the scales from our eyes, the vaile from our hearts, opening our wits that wee may vnderstand his word, enlarging our hearts, yea correcting our affections, that we may loue it aboue gold and siluer, yea that we may loue it to the end. Ye are brought vnto fountaines of liuing water which yee digged not; doe not cast earth into them with the Philistines, neither preferre broken pits before them with the wicked Iewes. Others haue laboured, and you may enter into their labours; O receiue not so great things in vaine, O despise not so great saluation! Be not like swine to treade vnder foote so precious things, neither yet like dogs to teare and abuse holy things. Say not to our Sauiour with the *Gergesites*, Depart out of our coasts; neither yet with *Esau* sell your birthright for a messe of potage. If light be come into the world, loue not darkenesse more then light; if foode, if clothing be offered, goe not naked, starue not your selues. Remember the aduise of *Naẑianzene, It is a grieuous thing* (or dangerous) *to neglect a great faire, and to seeke to make markets afterwards*: also the encouragement of S. *Chrysostome, It is altogether impossible, that he that is sober (and watchfull) should at any time be neglected*: Lastly, the admonition and menacing of S. *Augustine, They that despise Gods will inuiting them, shal feele Gods will taking vengeance of them*. It is a fearefull thing to fall into the hands of the liuing God; but a blessed thing it is, and will bring vs to euerlasting blessednes in the end, when God speaketh vnto vs, to hearken; when he setteth his word before vs, to reade it; when hee stretcheth out his hand and calleth, to answere, Here am I; when he sweareth by the wil, O God. The Lord worke a care and conscience in vs to know him and serue him, that we may be acknowledged of him at the appearing of our Lord Iesus Christ, to whom with the holy Ghost, be all prayse and thankesgiuing. Amen.

πολύσημα.

Abed.
*Niceph. Calist.
lib. 8. cap. 42.
S. Hieron. in 4.
Iona. See S.
Aug: epist: 10.*

λεπτολογία.
ἀδολεσχία.
τὸ σπουδάζειν ἐπὶ ὀνόμασι.
See Euseb. προπαρασκευ lit. 12.
εν Platon.

Gen. 26. 15.
Ierem. 2. 13.

Matth. 8. 34.
Hebr. 12. 16.

Nazianz. περὶ ἁγ. βαπτ.
δεινὸν πανήγυριν παρελθεῖν καὶ τηνικαῦτα πραγματείαν ἐπιζητεῖν.

S. August. ad artic. sibi falsò obiect.
Artic. 16.
Heb. 10. 31.

S. Chrysost. in epist ad Rom.
Cap. 14. orat.
26. ἴν ἠδὲ ἀμήχανον σφόδρα ἀμήχανον.

❧ Ianuary hath xxxj. dayes,

¶ The Moone xxx.

					Plalmes.	¶ Morning Prayer.		¶ Euening Prayer.	
Sunne { riseth } houre { 8. mi. 4. / falleth } { 3. mi. 56. }						1. Lesson.	2. Lesson.	1. Lesson.	2. Lesson.
xix	1	A	Kalend.	Circumcision.	j	Gen.17.	Rom.2.	Deu.10.	Col.ii.
viii	2	b	iiii No.		ij	Gen.1.	Matth.1.	Gene.2.	Rom.1.
	3	c	iii No.		iij	iii	ii	iiii	ii
xvi	4	d	prid. No.		iiij	v	iii	vi	iii
	5	e	Nonas.		v	vii	iiii	viii	iiii
xiii	6	f	viii Id.	Epiphanie.	vj	Esa.60	Luke3.	Esa.49.	John ii.
xiii	7	g	vii Id.		vij	Gene.9.	Matth.5.	Gen.12.	Rom.v.
ii	8	A	vi Id.	Lucian.	viii	xiii	vi	xiiii	vi
	9	b	v Id.		ix	xv	vii	xvi	vii
x	10	c	iiii Id.		x	xvii	viii	xviii	viii
	11	d	iii Id.		xj	xix	ix	xx	ix
xviii	12	e	prid. Id.	Sol in Aquario.	xij	xxi	x	xxii	x
vii	13	f	Idus.	Hillarii.	xiij	xxiii	xi	xxiiii	xi
	14	g	xix Kl.	Februarii.	xiiij	xxv	xii	xxvi	xii
xv	15	A	xviii Kl.		xv	xxvii	xiii	xxviii	xiii
iiii	16	b	xvii Kl.		xvj	xxix	xiiii	xxx	xiiii
	17	c	xvi Kl.		xvij	xxxi	xv	xxxii	xv
xii	18	d	xv Kl.	Prisca.	xviij	xxxiii	xvi	xxxiiii	xvi
i	19	e	xiiii Kl.		xix	xxxv	xvii	xxxvii	1.Cor.i.
	20	f	xiii Kl.	Fabian.	xx	xxxvii	xviii	xxxix	ii
ix	21	g	xii Kl.	Agnes.	xxj	xl	xix	xli	iii
	22	A	xi Kl.	Vincent.	xxij	xlii	xx	xliii	iiii
xvii	23	b	x Kl.		xxiij	xliiii	xxi	xlv	v
vi	24	c	ix Kl.		xxiiij	xlvi	xxii	xlvii	vi
	25	d	viii Kl.	Conuers. Paul.	xxv	Wisd.v.	Acts.22.	Wisd.6.	Acts.26.
xiiii	26	e	vii Kl.		xxvj	Gene.48.	Matt.23.	Gen.49.	1.Cor.7.
iii	27	f	vi Kl.		xxvij	l	xxiiii	Exod.i.	viii
	28	g	v Kl.		xxviij	Exod.2.	xxv	iii	ix
xi	29	A	iiii Kl.		xxix	iiii	xxvi	v	x
xix	30	b	iii Kl.		xxx	vii	xxvii	viii	xi
viii	31	c	prid. Kl.		xxx	ix	xxviii	x	xii

❧ February hath xxviij. dayes.

¶ The Moone xxix.

Sunne { riseth / falleth } houre { 7.mi. 15 / 4.mi. 45 }					Psalmes.	¶ Morning Prayer.		¶ Euening Prayer.	
						1. Lesson.	2. Lesson.	1.Lesson.	2.Lesson.
	1	d	Kalend.	Fast.	ij	Exod.xi.	Marke i.	Exo.xii.	1.Cor.xiij.
xvi	2	e	iiii No.	Purification of Mary.	iij	wild.9.	ii	wild.xii.	xiiii
v	3	f	iii No.	Blasij.	iiij	Exod.xiii.	iii	Exo.xiiii.	xv
	4	g	prid.No.		h	xv	iiii	xvi	xvi
xiii	5	A	Nonas	Agathe.	vj	xvij	v	xviii	2.Cor.i.
ij	6	b	viii Id.		vij	xix	vi	xx	ii
	7	c	vii Id.		vuj	xxi	vii	xxii	iii
x	8	d	vi Id.		ix	xxiii	viii	xxiiii	iiii
	9	e	v Id.		x	xxxii	ix	xxxiii	v
xviii	10	f	iiii Id.		xj	xxxiiii	x	Leu.18.	vi
vij	11	g	iii Id.	Sol in Piscibus.	xij	Leui.xix.	xi	xx	vij
	12	A	prid.Id.		xiij	xxvi	xii	Num.11.	viij
xv	13	b	Idus.		xiiij	Num.xii.	xiii	xiii	ix
xiiii	14	c	xvi Kl.	Valentine.	xv	iiii	iiii	xvi	x
	15	d	xv Kl.	March.	xvi	xvii	xv	xx	xi
xij	16	e	xiiii Kl.		xvij	xxi	xvi	xxii	xii
	17	f	xiii Kl.		xviij	xxiij	Luk.i.j.	xxiiii	xiii
	18	g	xii Kl.		xix	xxv	i.i.	xxvij	Galat.i.
x	19	A	xi Kl.		xx	xxx	ii	xxxi	ii
	20	b	x Kl.		xxj	xxxij	iii	xxxii	iii
xvij	21	c	ix Kl.		xxij	xxxvi	iiii	Deut.i.	iiii
vi	22	d	viii Kl.		xxiij	Deut.ij.	v	iii	v
	23	e	vii Kl.	Fast.	xxiiij	iiij	vi	v	vi
xiiij	24	f	vi Kl.	S.Matthias.	xxv	wild.xix.	vii	Eccles.i.	Ephes.i.
iij	25	g	v Kl.		xxvj	Deut.vi.	viii	Deut.vij.	ii
	26	A	iiii Kl.		xxvij	viij	ix	ix	iii
vi	27	b	iii Kl.		xxviij	x	x	xi	iiii
	28	c	prid. Kl.		xxix	xiij	xi	xv	v

❧ March hath xxxj. dayes.

¶ The Moone xxx.

Sunne	riseth } houre	6.mi.18.
	falleth } houre	5.mi.42.

					Psalmes.	¶ Morning Prayer		¶ Euening Prayer	
						1.Lesson.	2.Lesson.	1.Lesson.	Ephes.vi.
xx	1	D	Kalend.	Dauid.	xxx	Deut.xvj.	Luke xii.	Deut.17.	Phil.i.
vij	2	e	vi No.	Cedde.	i	xviij	xiii	xix	ii
	3	f	v No.		ij	xx	xiiii	xxi	iii
xvj	4	g	iiii No.		iij	xxij	xv	xxiij	iiii
v	5	A	iii No.		iiij	xxv	xvi	xxvi	Colos. i.
	6	b	prid.No.		v	xxvij	xvii	xxviii	ii
xiij	7	c	Nonas.	Perpetue.	vi	xxix	xviii	xxx	iii
ij	8	d	viii Id.		vij	xxxj	xix	xxxij	iiii
	9	e	vii Id.		vuj	xxxiij	xx	xxxiiii	i. Thes.i.
x	10	f	vi Id.		ix	Iosua.i.	xxi	Iosua. ii	ii
	11	g	v Id.		x	iij	xxii	iiii	iii
xviij	12	A	iiii Id.	Gregorie.	xi	v	xxiii	vi	iiii
vij	13	b	iii Id.	Sol in Aries.	xij	vij	xxiiii	viii	v
	14	c	prid.Id.		xiij	ix	John i.	x	ii. Thes.i.
xv	15	D	Idus.		xiiij	xxiij	ii	xxiiii	ii
iiij	16	e	xvii Kl.	Aprilis.	xv	Iudg.i.	iii	Iudg.ii.	iii
	17	f	xvi Kl.		xvi	iii	iiii	iiii	i. Tim. i.
xij	18	g	xv Kl.	Edward.	xvij	v	v	vi	ii.iii.
j	19	A	xiiii Kl.		xviij	vij	vi	viii	iiii
	20	b	xiii Kl.		xix	ix	vii	x	v
ix	21	c	xii Kl.	Benedict.	xx	xj	viii	xii	vi
	22	d	xi Kl.		xxi	xiij	ix	xiiii	ii. Tim. i.
xvij	23	e	x Kl.		xxij	xv	x	xvi	ii
vi	24	f	ix Kl	Init.Reg.Iacob. Fast.	xxiij	xvij	xi	xviii	iii
	25	g	viii Kl.	Annun. of Marie.	xxiiij	Eccle.2.	xii	Eccle.iii.	iiii
xiiij	26	A	vii Kl.		xxv	Iudg.xix.	xiii	Iudg.xx	Titus i.
iij	27	b	vi Kl.		xxvj	xxi	xiiii	Ruth i	ii
	28	c	v Kl.		xxvij	Ruth ij.	xv	iii	iii
xi	29	d	iiii Kl.		xxviij	iiii	xvi	i.King.i.	Philem.
	30	e	iii Kl.		xxix	i.king.i.	xvii	iii	Hebr.i.
xix	31	f	prid. Kl.		xxx	iiii	xviii	v	ii.

Sunne { riseth / falleth } houre { 5.mi.15 / 6.mi.45 }					Pſalmes	¶ Morning Prayer.		¶ Euening Prayer.	
						1. Leſſon.	2. Leſſon.	1. Leſſon.	2. Leſſon.
vii	1	g	Kalend.		ii	1.King.vi	John xii.	1.King.vii	Hebꝛe.iii.
xvi	2	A	iiii No.		ii	viii	xx	xi	iiii
v	3	b	iii No.	Richard.	iii	x	xxi	xiii	v
	4	c	pꝛid.No.	Ambꝛoſe.	iiii	xii	Actes.i.	xiii	vi
xiii	5	D	Nonas.		v	xiiii	ii	xv	vii
ii	6	e	viii Jd.		vi	xvi	iii	xvii	viii
	7	f	vii Jd.		vii	xviii	iiii	xix	ix
	8	g	vi Jd.		viii	xx	v	xxi	x
x	9	A	v Jd.		ix	xxii	vi	xxiii	xi
xviii	10	b	iiii Jd.		x	xxiiii	vii	xxv	xii
vii	11	c	iii Jd.	Sol in Tauru.	xi	xxvi	viii	xxvii	xiii
	12	D	pꝛid. Jd.		xii	xxviii	ix	xxix	James.i.
xv	13	e	Idus.		xiii	xxx	x	xxxi	ii
iiii	14	f	xviii Kl.	Matt.	xiiii	ii. King.i.	xi	2.King.2.	iii
	15	g	xvii Kl.		xv	iii	xii	iiii	iiii
xii	16	A	xvi Kl.		xvi	v	xiii	vi	v
	17	b	xv Kl.		xvii	vii	xiiii	viii	1.Pet.1.
	18	c	xiiii Kl.		xviii	ix	xv	x	ii
ix	19	D	xiii Kl.	Alphege.	xix	xi	xvi	xii	iii
	20	e	xii Kl.		xx	xiii	xvii	xiiii	iiii
xvii	21	f	xi Kl.		xxi	xv	xviii	xvi	v
vi	22	g	x Kl.		xxii	xvii	xix	xviii	ii.Pet.i.
	23	A	ix Kl.	S.George.	xxiii	xix	xx	xx	ii
xiiii	24	b	viii Kl.		xxiiii	xxi	xxi	xxii	iii
iii	25	c	vii Kl.	Marke Euang.	xxv	Eccle.iiii.	xxii	Eccle.v.	1.Joh.i.
	26	D	vi Kl.		xxvi	2.Kin.23.	xxiii	2.Kin.24.	ii
xi	27	e	v Kl.		xxvii	3.King.i.	xxiiii	3.King.ii.	iii
	28	f	iiii Kl.		xxviii	iii	xxv	iiii	iiii
xix	29	g	pꝛid. Kl.		xxix	v	xxvi	vi	v
viii	30	A	pꝛid. Kl.		xxx	vii	xxvii	viii	2.3.Joh.

☙ May hath xxxj. dayes.

¶ The Moone xxx.

Sunne riseth/falleth houre 4.mi.36./7.mi.24.					Psalmes.	¶ Morning Prayer.		¶ Euening Prayer.	
						1. Lesson.	2. Lesson.	1. Lesson.	2. Lesson.
	1	b	Kalend	Philip and Iacob.	i	Eccle.7.	Acts.3.	Eccle.9.	Iude 1.
xbi	2	c	bi No.		ij	3.king.9.	xxbij	3.Kin.10.	Rom.1.
b	3	d	b No.	Inu. of the Crosse	iij	xi	Matth.1.	xii	ii
	4	e	iiii No.		iiii	riij	ii	xiiii	iii
xiii	5	f	iii No.		b	xb	iii	xbi	iiii
ii	6	g	piid. No.	John Euang.	bi	xbij	iiii	xbiij	b
	7	A	Nonas		bij	xix	b	xx	bi
x	8	b	biii Id.		biij	xxi	bi	xxii	bij
xbiii	9	c	bii Id.		ix	4.King.1.	bii	4.King.2	biij
bii	10	d	bi Id.		x	iij	biii	iiii	ix
	11	e	b Id.		xi	b	ix	bi	x
xb	12	f	iiii Id.	Sol in Gemini.	xij	bij	x	biii	xi
iiii	13	g	iii Id.		xiij	ix	xi	x	xii
	14	A	piid. Id.		xiiij	xi	xii	xii	xiii
	15	b	Idus		xb	xiij	xiii	xiiii	xiiii
xii	16	c	xbii Kl.	Iunii.	xbi	xb	xiiii	xbi	xb
i	17	d	xbi Kl.		xbij	xbij	xb	xbiij	xbi
	18	e	xb Kl.		xbiij	xix	xbi	xx	I.Cor.1.
x	19	f	xiiii Kl.	Dunstane.	xix	xxi	xbii	xxii	ii
	20	g	xiii Kl.		xx	xxiij	xbiii	xxiiii	iii
xbij	21	A	xii Kl.		xxi	xxb	xix	I.Esd.2.	iiii
bi	22	b	xi Kl.		xxij	I.Esd.3.	xx	iiii	b
	23	c	x Kl.		xxiij	b	xxi	bi	bi
xiiii	24	d	ix Kl.		xxiiij	bij	xxii	ix	bii
iii	25	e	biii Kl.		xxb	2.Esd.1.	xxiii	2.Esd.2.	biii
	26	f	bii Kl.	Augustine.	xxbi	xxiii	xxiiii	b	ix
xi	27	g	bi Kl.		xxbij	bi	xxb	biii	x
	28	A	b Kl.		xxbiij	ix	xxbi	x	xi
xix	29	b	iiii Kl.		xxix	xiij	xxbii	Ester 1.	xii
biii	30	c	iii Kl.		xxx	Ester 2.	xxbiii	iii	xiii
xbi	31	d	piid. Kl.		xxx	iiii	Marke 1.	b	xiiii

☜ Iune hath xxx. dayes.

¶ The Moone xxix.

Sunne { riseth / falleth } houre { 3.mi.34. / 8.mi.26. }

					Psalmes.	Morning Prayer.		Euening Prayer.	
						1.Lesson.	2.Lesson.	1.Lesson.	2.Lesson.
b	1	e	Kalend.		i	Ester.6.	Marke ii.	Ester 7.	1.Cor.15.
	2	f	iiii No.		ii	viii	iii	ix	xvi
xiii	3	g	iii No.	Nichomede.	iii	Job i.	iiii	Job ii.	2.Cor.i.
ii	4	A	prid.No.		iiii	iii	v	iiii	ii
	5	h	Nonas.	Boniface.	v	v	vi	vi	iii
x	6	c	viii Id.		vi	vii	vii	viii	iiii
xviii	7	d	vii Id.		vii	ix	viii	x	v
vii	8	e	vi Id.		viii	xi	ix	xii	vi
	9	f	v Id.		ix	xiii	x	xiiii	vii
	10	g	iiii Id.		x	xv	xi	xvi	viii
xv	11	A	iii Id.	Barnabe.	xi	Eccle.x.	Acts.xvii.	Eccle.xii.	Acts.15.
xiiii	12	b	prid.Id.	Sol in Cancro.	xii	Job 17.18	Mar.xii.	Job xix.	2.Cor.ix.
	13	c	Idus.	Solstiti. æstiuum.	xiii	xx	xiii	xxi	x
xi	14	d	xviii Kl.	Iulii.	xiiii	xxii	xiiii	xxiii	xi
i	15	e	xvii Kl.		xv	xxiiii.xxv.	xv	xxvi.xxvii.	xii
	16	f	xvi Kl.		xvi	xxviii	xvi	xxix	xiii
ix	17	g	xv Kl.		xvii	xxx	Luke i.	xxxi	Gala.i.
	18	A	xiiii Kl.		xviii	xxxi	ii	xxxiii	ii
xviii	19	b	xiii Kl.	Nati.of King Iames.	xix	xxxiiii	iii	xxxv	iii
vi	20	c	xii Kl.	Edward.	xx	xxxvi	iiii	xxxvii	iiii
	21	d	xi Kl.		xxi	xxxviii	v	xxxix	v
xiiii	22	e	x Kl.		xxii	xl	vi	xli	vi
ii	23	f	ix Kl.	Fast.	xxiii	xlii	vii	Prou.i.	Ephes.i.
	24	g	viii Kl.	Iohn Baptist.	xxiiii	Gala.iii.	Matth.3.	Prou.ii.	Matt.14.
ii	25	A	vii Kl.		xxv	Prou.ii.	Luke 8.	Prou.iii.	Ephes.2.
	26	b	vi Kl.		xxvi	iiii	ix	v	iii
xix	27	c	v Kl.		xxvii	vi	x	vii	iiii
	28	d	iiii Kl.	Fast.	xxviii.viii	xi	ix	v	
viii	29	e	iii Kl.	S.Peter Apostle.	xxix	Ecclus.xv	Acts.iii.	Ecclus.19.	Acts.4.
xvi	30	f	prid. Kl.		xxx	Prou.x.	Luke xii.	Prou.xi.	Ephes.6.

¶ The Moone xxx.

| Sunne ⎰ riseth ⎱ houre ⎰ 7. mi. 34 | | | | | Psalmes. | ¶ Morning Prayer. | | ¶ Euening Prayer. | |
⎱ falleth ⎰ ⎱ 4. mi. 26						1. Lesson.	2. Lesson.	1. Lesson.	2. Lesson.
b	1	g	Kalend.	Visitat. of Mary.	i	Prou. rij.	Luke rij.	Prou. riij.	Phil. i.
	2	A	vi No.		ii	riiij	riiij	rb	ii
riij	3	b	v No.	Martin.	iii	rbj	rb	rbii	iii
ij	4	c	iiij No.		iiii	rbiij	rbi	rir	iiii
	5	D	iii No.		b	rr	rbii	rref	Colof. i.
r	6	e	prid No.	Dog dayes.	bi	rri	rbiii	rriii	ii
rbiij	7	f	Nonas.		bii	rriiij	rir	rrb	iii
vij	8	g	viij Jd.		biii	rrbj	rr	rrbi	iiii
	9	A	vii Jd.		ir	rrbiij	rri	rrir	i. Thef. i.
	10	b	bi Jd.		r	rrri	rrii	Ecclef. i.	ii
rb	11	c	v Jd.		ri	Ecclef. ij.	rriii	iii	iii
uiij	12	D	iiij Jd.	Sol in Leone.	rii	iiij	rriiii	b	iiii
	13	e	iii Jd.		riii	ib	Iohn j.	bii	b
rj	14	f	prid. Jd.		riiii	biij	ii	ir	ii. Thef. i.
i	15	g	Idus.	Swithune.	rb	r	iii	ri	ii
ir	16	A	rbii Kl.	Augufti.	rbi	rij	iiii	Iere. i.	iii
	17	b	rbi Kl.		rbii	Ierem. ij.	b	iii	i. Tim. i.
	18	c	rb Kl		rbiii	iiij	bi	b	ii. iii.
rbij	19	D	riiii K..		rir	bj	bii	bii	iiii
bi	20	e	riii Kl.	Margaret.	rr	biij	biii	ir	b
	21	f	rii Kl.		rri	r	ir	ri	bi
riiij	22	g	ri Kl.	Magdalen.	rrii	rij	r	riii	ii. Tim. i.
iii	23	A	r Kl.		rriii	riiij	ri	rb	ii
	24	b	ir Kl.	Faft.	rriiii	rbj	rii	rbii	iii
ri	25	c	biij Kl.	Iames Apoftle.	rrb	Ecclus. rri	riiii	Ecclus. 29	iiii
rir	26	D	bii Kl.	Anne.	rrbi	Iere. rbiij	rb	Iere. rir.	Titus. i.
biij	27	e	bi Kl.		rrbii	rr	rb	rri	ii. iij.
	28	f	b Kl.		rrbiij rrir	rbi	rriii	Phlem.
rbi	29	g	iiij Kl.		rrir	rriiij	rbii	rrb	Hebz. i.
	30	A	iii Kl.		rrr	rrbj	rbiii	rrbii	ii
b	31	b	prid. Kl.		rrri	rrbiii	rir	rrir	iii

❧ Auguſt hath xxxj. dayes.

¶ The Moone xxx.

Sunne { riſeth / falleth } houre { 4.mi.34 / 7.mi.26 }	Pſalmes.		¶ Morning Prayer.		¶ Euening Prayer.	
				1. Leſſon.	2. Leſſon.	1. Leſſon.	2. Leſſon.

					Pſal.	1. Leſſon.	2. Leſſon.	1. Leſſon.	2. Leſſon.
xiii	1	c	Kalend.	Lammas.	i	Jere.xxx.	John.xx.	Jere.xxxi.	Heb2.iiii.
ii	2	d	iiii No.		ii	xxxii	xxi	xxxiii	v
	3	e	iii No.		iii	xxxiiii	Actes.i.	xxxv	vi
x	4	f	prid.No.		iiii	xxxvi	ii	xxxvii	vii
xviii	5	g	Nonas.		v	xxxviii	iii	xxxix	viii
vii	6	A	viii Id.	Transfiguration.	vi	xl	iiii	xli	ix
	7	b	vii Id.	Name of Jesus.	vii	xlii	v	xliii	x
	8	c	vi Id.		viii	xliiii	vi	xlv,xlvi.	xi
xv	9	d	v Id.		ix	xlvii	vii	xlviii	xii
iiii	10	e	iiii Id.	Laurence.	x	xlix	viii	l	xiii
	11	f	iii Id.	Sol in virgine.	xi	li	ix	lii	James i.
xi	12	g	prid. Id.		xii	Lamen.i.	x	Lamen.ii.	ii
	13	A	Idus.		xiii	iii	xi	iiii	iii
xix	14	b	xix Kl.	Septembris.	xiiii	v	xii	Ezek.ii.	iiii
viii	15	c	xviii Kl.		xv	Ezek.iii.	xiii	vi	v
	16	d	xvii Kl.		xvi	vii	xiiii	xiii	1.Pet.i.
xvi	17	e	xvi Kl.		xvii	xiii	xv	xviii	ii
v	18	f	xv Kl.		xviii	xxxiii	xvi	xxxiiii	iii
	19	g	xiiii Kl.		xix	Dan.i.	xvii	Daniel ii.	iiii
xiii	20	A	xiii Kl.		xx	iii	xviii	iiii	v
ii	21	b	xii Kl.		xxi	v	xix	vi	ii.Pet.i.
	22	c	xi Kl.		xxii	vii	xx	viii	ii
x	23	d	x Kl.	Faſt.	xxiii	ix	xxi	x	iii
xviii	24	e	ix Kl.	Barthol. Apoſtle.	xxiiii	Ecclus.25	xxii	Ecclus.29	1.Joh.i.
viii	25	f	viii Kl.		xxv	Dan.xi.	xxiii	Dan.xii.	ii
	26	g	vii Kl.		xxvi	xiii	xxiiii	xiiii	iii
xvi	27	A	vi Kl.		xxvii	Oſe.i.	xxv	Oſe.ii.iii.	iiii
v	28	b	v Kl.	Auguſtine	xxviii	iiii	xxvi	v.vi.	v
	29	c	iiii Kl.	Behead. of John.	xxix	vii	xxvii	viii	2.3. John.
	30	d	iii Kl.		xxx	ix	xxviii	x	Jude.
xiii	31	e	prid. Kl.		xxxi	xi	Matth.i.	xii	Rom.i.

☞ Note, that the 13. of Daniel, touching the hiſtory of Suſanna, is to be read vntill theſe words: (And King Aſtyages, &c.)

❧ September hath xxx. dayes.

¶ The Moone xxix.

		Sunne { riseth / falleth } houre { 5.mi.36 / 6.mi.24 }	Pſalmes	¶ Morning Prayer.		¶ Euening Prayer.	
				1. Leſſon.	2. Leſſon.	1. Leſſon.	2. Leſſon.
ij	1	f	Kalend.	Gyles.	i	Oſe. riii.	Mat. ii.	Oſe. riiii.	Rom. ii.
	2	g	iiii No.		ii	Joel.	iii	Joel ii.	iii
r	3	A	iii No.		iii	iiii	iiii	Amos i.	iiii
rbiij	4	b	prid. No.		iiii	Amos ii.	b	iii	b
bij	5	c	Nonas.	Dog dayes end.	b	iiii	bi	b	bi
	6	d	biii Id.		bi	bi	bii	bii	bii
	7	e	bii Id.	Enurchus biſhop.	bij	biii	biii	ir	biii
rb	8	f	bi Id.	Natiuit. of Mary.	biij	Abdi.	ir	Jona i.	ir
iiij	9	g	b Id.		ir	Ion. ii. iii. r	r	iiii	r
	10	A	iiii Id.		r	Miche. i.	ri	Mich. ii.	ri
rij	11	b	iii Id.		ri	iii	rii	iiii	rii
j	12	c	prid. Id.	Sol in Libra.	rij	b	riii	bi	riii
ir	13	d	Idus.		riij	bii	riiii	Naum i.	riiii
	14	e	rbiii Kl.	Holy croſſe.	riiij	Naum. ii.	rb	iii	rb
	15	f	rbii Kl.	Æquinoctium.	rb	Abac. i.	rbi	Abac ii.	rbi
rbij	16	g	rbi Kl.	Autumnale.	rbi	rbii	rbii	Soph. i.	i. Cor. i.
bj	17	A	rb Kl.	Lambert.	rbij	Soph. ii.	rbiii	iii	ii
	18	b	riiii Kl.		rbiij	Agge. i.	rir	Agge. ii.	iii
riiij	19	c	riii Kl.		rir	Zach. i.	rr	Zac. ii. iii.	iiii
iij	20	d	rii Kl.	Faſt.	rr	iiii. b	rri	bi	b
	21	e	ri Kl.	S. Matthew.	rri	Eccle. 35.	rrii	Eccl. 38.	bi
rj	22	f	r Kl.		rrij	Zach. bii.	rriii	Zac. bii.	biii
rir	23	g	ir Kl.		rriij	riiii	rriiii	r	biii
biij	24	A	biii Kl.		rriiij	ri	rrb	rii	ir
	25	b	bii Kl.		rrb	riii	rrbi	riiii.	r
	26	c	bi Kl.	Cyprian.	rrbi	Mala. i.	rrbii	Mala. ii.	ri
rbj	27	d	b Kl.		rrbij	iii.	rrbiii	iiii	rii
b	28	e	iiii Kl.		rrbiij	Tob. i.	Mark. i.	Tob. ii.	riii
riiij	29	f	iii Kl.	S. Michael.	rrir	Eccl. rrrir	ii	Eccle. 44.	riiii
ij	30	g	prid. Kl.	Hieronꝰ.	rrr	Tob. iii.	iii	Tob. iiii.	rb

¶ The Moone xxx.

| Sunne { riseth } houre { 6.mi.35 |
| falleth } 5.mi.25 |

						Psalmes.	¶ Morning Prayer.		¶ Euening Prayer.	
							1. Lesson.	2. Lesson.	1. Lesson.	2. Lesson.
	1	A		Kalend.	Remige.	i	Tob.v.	Marke 4.	Tob.vi	1.Cor.xvi.
x	2	b	vi	No.		ii	vii	v	viii	2.Cor 1.
	3	c	v	No.		iii	ix	vi	x	ii
xviii	4	d	iiii	No.		iiii	xi	vii	xii	iii
vii	5	e	iii	No.		v	xiii	viii	xiii	iiii
	6	f	prid.No.		Faith.	vi	Judit.i.	ix	Judit.ii.	v
xv	7	g		Nonas.		vii	iii	x	iiii	vi
iiii	8	A	viii	Id.		viii	v	xi	vi	vii
	9	b	vii	Id.	Dennis.	ix	vii	xii	viii	viii
xii	10	c	vi	Id.		x	ix	xiii	x	ix
i	11	d	v	Id.		xi	xi	xiiii	xii	x
	12	e	iiii	Id.	Sol in Scorpio.	xii	xiii	xv	xiii	xi
ix	13	f	iii	Id.	Edward.	xiii	xv	xvi	xvi	xii
	14	g	prid. Id.			xiiii	Wisd.1.	Luk.vi.i.	Wisd.ii.	xiii
xvii	15	A		Idus.		xv	iii	vi.i.	iiii	Galat.i.
vi	16	b	xvii	Kl.	Nouembris.	xvi	v	ii	vi	ii
vi	17	c	xvi	Kl.	Etheldrede.	xvii	vii	iii	viii	iii
xiiii	18	d	xv	Kl.	Luke Euang.	xviii	Ecclu.li.	iiii	Iob.i.	iiii
iii	19	e	xiiii	Kl.		xix	Wisd.ix.	v	Wisd.x	v
	20	f	xiii	Kl.		xx	xi	vi	xii	vi
xi	21	g	xii	Kl.		xxi	xiii	vii	xliii	Ephes.i.
xix	22	A	xi	Kl.		xxii	xv	viii	xvi	ii
	23	b	x	Kl.		xxiii	xvii	ix	xviii	iii
viii	24	c	ix	Kl.		xxiiii	xix	x	Eccle.i.	iiii
	25	d	viii	Kl.	Crispine.	xxv	Eccle.ii.	xi	iii	v
xvi	26	e	vii	Kl.		xxvi	iiii	xii	v	vi
v	27	f	vi	Kl.	Fast.	xxvii	vi	xiii	vii	Phil.i.
	28	g	v	Kl.	Simon and Iude.	xxviii	Iob.24.25.	xiiii	Iob.xlii.	ii
xiii	29	A	iiii	Kl.		xxix	Eccle.8.	xv	Eccle.ix.	iii
ii	30	b	iii	Kl.		xxx	x	xvi	xi	iiii
	31	c	prid. Kl.		Fast.	xxx	xii	xvii	xiii	Colos.i.

❧ Nouember hath xxx.dayes.

¶ The Moone xxix.

Sunne { riseth falleth } houre {	7.mi.34. 4.mi.26.	Pſalmes.	¶ Morning Prayer.		¶ Euening Prayer.	

						1.Leſſon.	2. Leſſon.	1.Leſſon.	2. Leſſon.
c	1	d	Kalend.	All Saints	i	Wiſd.3.	Heb.11.12.	Wiſd.5.	Reuel.19.
	2	e	iiii No.		ii	Eccluſ.14.	Luke 18.	Eccluſ.15.	Col.ii.
xb	3	f	iii No.		iii	xbi	xix	xbii	iii
bii	4	g	prid.No.		iiii	xbiii	xx	xix	iiii
	5	A	Nonas.	Papiſts conſpiracie.	b	xx	xxi	xxi	1.Theſ.1.
xb	6	b	biii Id.	Leonard.	bi	xxii	xxii	xxiii	ii
iiii	7	c	bii Id.		bii	xxiiii	xxiii	xxb	iii
	8	d	bi Id.		biii	xxbi	xxiiii	xxbiii	iiii
xii	9	e	b Id.		ix	xxix	John 1.	xxx	b
i	10	f	iiii Id.		x	xxxi	ii	xxxii	2.Theſ.1.
ix	11	g	iii Id.	S.Martine.	xi	xxxiii	iii	xxxiiii	ii
	12	A	prid. Id.	Sol in Sagit.	xii	xxxb	iiii	xxxbi	iii
	13	b	Idus.	Brice.	xiii	xxxbii	b	xxxbiii	1.Tim.1.
xbii	14	c	xbiii Kl.	Decembris.	xiiii	xxxix	bi	xl	ii.iii.
bi	15	d	xbii Kl.	Machute.	xb	xli	bii	xlii	iiii
	16	e	xbi Kl.		xbi	xliii	biii	xliiii	b
xiiii	17	f	xb Kl.	Hugh biſhop.	xbii	xlb	ix		bi
iii	18	g	xiiii Kl.		xbiii	xlbii	x	xlbiii	2.Tim.1.
	19	A	xiii Kl.		xix	xlix	xi	l	ii
xi	20	b	xii Kl.	Edmund King.	xx	li	xii	Baruc.1.	iii
xix	21	c	xi Kl.		xxi	Baruc.2.	xiii	iii	iiii
biii	22	d	x Kl.	Cicilie.	xxii	iiii	xiiii	b	Titus j.
	23	e	ix Kl.	Clement.	xxiii	bi	xb	Eſa.i.	ii.iii.
	24	f	biii Kl.		xxiiii	Eſa. ii.	xbi	iii	Philem.
xbi	25	g	bii Kl.	Katherine.	xxb	iiii	xbii	b	Hebr.1.
b	26	A	bi Kl.		xxbi	bi	xbiii	bii	ii
	27	b	b Kl.		xxbii	biii	xix	ix	iii
xiii	28	c	iiii Kl.		xxbiii	x	xx	xi	iiii
ii	29	d	iii Kl.	Faſt.	xxix	xii	xxi	xiii	b
c	30	e	prid. Kl.	Andrew Apoſtle.	xxx	Prou.20.	Actes.1.	Prou.21.	bi

☞ Note that the beginning of the xxij. Chapter of Eccleſiaſticus (vnto verſ.6.) But a griefe of heart, &c. muſt be read with the xxv. Chapter.

☞ Note that the xlvj Chapter of Eccleſiaſticus is to be read vnto theſe words : And after his death, &c.

❧ December hath xxxj. dayes.

¶ The Moone xxx.

Sunne { riseth / falleth } houre { 8.mi.12 / 3.mi.48 }					Psalmes.	¶ Morning Prayer.		¶ Euening Prayer.	
						1.Lesson.	2.Lesson.	1.Lesson.	2.Lesson.
	1	f	Kalend.		i	Esa.xiiij.	Actes ij.	Esa.xv.	Heb2.7.
rbiii	2	g	iiij No.		ij	rbj	iij	rbij	biij
bij	3	A	iij No.		iij	rbiij	iiij	rir	ir
	4	b	pziD. No.		iiij	rr.rri	b	rrij	r
rb	5	c	Nonas.		b	rriij	bi	rriiij	rj
iiij	6	d	biij Jd.	Nicolas bish.	bi	rrb	Di.bij.	rrbi	rij
	7	e	bij Jd.		bij	rrbij	Di.bij.	rrbiij	riij
rij	8	f	bi Jd.	Conc. of Mary.	biij	rir	biij	rrr	Psalm 2.1.
	9	g	b Jd.		ir	rrrj	ir	rrrij	ij
	10	A	iiij Jd.		r	rrriij	r	rrriiij	iij
ir	11	b	iij Jd.		rj	rrrb	rj	rrrbi	iiij
	12	c	pziD. Jd.	Sol in Capricor.	rij	rrrbij	rij	rrrbiij	b
rbii	13	D	Idu.	Luci virgin.	riij	rrrir	riij	rl	1.Pet.1.
	14	e	rir Kl.	Januarii.	riiij	rlj	riiij	rlij	ij
bi	15	f	rbiij Kl.		rb	rliij	rb	rliiij	iij
riij	16	g	rbij Kl.	O sapientia.	rbi	rlb	rbi	rlbi	iiij
iij	17	A	rbi Kl.		rbij	rlbij	rbij	rlbiij	b
	18	b	rb Kl.		rbiij	rlir	rbiij	l	2.Pet.1.
rj	19	c	riiij Kl.		rir	lj	rir	lij	ij
rir	20	D	riij Kl.	Fast.	rr	liiij	rr	liiij	iij
	21	e	rij Kl.	Thomas Apost.	rrj	P20.rriij.	rrj	Prou.24.	1. John 1.
biij	22	f	rj Kl.		rrij	Esa.lb.	rrij	Esa.56.	ij
	23	g	r Kl.		rriij	lbij	rriiij	lbiij	iij.
rbi	24	A	ir Kl.	Fast.	rriiij	lir	rriiij	lr	iiij
b	25	b	biij Kl.	Christmas.	rrb	Esa.ir.	Luke ij.	Esa.7.	Titus.iij.
	26	c	bij Kl.	S Steuen.	rrbi	Prou.28.	Acts 6.7.	Eccles.4.	Acts.7.
riij	27	D	bi Kl.	S.Iohn.	rrbij	Eccles.b.	Reuel.i.	Eccle.6.	Reuel.22.
ij	28	e	b Kl.	Innocents.	rrbiij	Ierem.31.	Acts 25	Wisd.1.	1.Joh.us.
	29	f	iiij Kl.		rrir	Esa.lri.	rrbi	Esa.62.	2.John.
r	30	g	iij Kl.		rrr	lriij	rrbij	lriiij	3.John.
	31	A	pziD. Kl.	Siluester bish.	rrr	lrb	rrbiij	lrbi	Iude.

¶ An Almanacke for xxxix. yeeres.

The yeere of our Lord.	The Golden number.	The Epact.	Dominicall Letter.	Septuagesima.	The first day of Lent.	Easter day.	Rogation weeke.	Ascension day.	Whitsunday.	Advent Sunday.
1603	viii	xxviii	B	20.Febru.	9.March	24.April	30.Maii	2.Iunii	12.Iune	27.Nou.
1604	ix	ix	AG	5.	22.Febru.	8.		17.Maii	27.Maii	2.Decem.
1605	x	xx	F	27.Ianu.	13.	31.March	vi	ix	xix	i
1606	xi	i	E	16.Febru.	5.March	20.April	xix	xxix	8.Iune	30.Nou.
1607	xii	xii	D	1.Febru.	18.Febru.	5.	xi	xxi	24.Maii	xxix
1608	xiii	xxiii	CB	24.Ianu.	10.	27.March	ii	v	xv	iii
1609	xiiii	iiii	A	12.Febru.	1.March	16.April	xxii	xxv	4.Iune	3.Decem.
1610	xv	xv	G	4.	21.Febru.	8.	xiii	xvi	xxvii	ii
1611	xvi	xxvi	F	20.Ianu.	6.	24.March	29.April	ii	xii	i
1612	xvii	vii	ED	9.Febru.	25.	12.April	18.Maii	xxi	xxii	29.Nou.
1613	xviii	xviii	C	31.Ianu.	17.	4.	x	xiii	xxiii	xxviii
1614	xix	xix	B	20.Febru.	9.March	24.	xxii	2.Iunii	12.Iune	xxvii
1615	i	xi	A	5.	22.Febru.	9.	xv	18.Maii	28.Maii	3.Decem.
1616	ii	xii	GF	28.Ianu.	14.	31.March	vi	ix	xix	ii
1617	iii	iii	E	16.Febru.	7.March	20.April	xxiii	xxix	3.Iune	30.Nou.
1618	iiii	xiiii	DC		18.Febru.	5.	xi	xxi	24.Maii	xxix
1619	v	xxv	B	24.Ianu.	10.	28.March	iii	iii	xv	xxviii
1620	vi	vi	A	13.Febru.	1.March	16.April	xxii	vi	4.Iune	3.Decem.
1621	vii	xvii	G	28.Ianu.	14.Febru.	1.	ii	vii	20.Maii	ii
1622	viii	xxviii	F	17.Febru.	6.March	21.	xxvi	xxx	9.Iune	i
1623	ix	ix	ED		16.Febru.	13.	xvi	xxii	i	30.Nou.
1624	x	xx	C	25.Ianu.	11.	28.March	iii.Maii	vi	16.Maii	xxviii
1625	xi	i	B	13.Febru.	2.March	17.April	xxxi	vii	7.Iune	xxvii
1626	xii	xii	A	5.	22.Febru.	9.	xv	xvi	28.Maii	3.Decem.
1627	xiii	xxiii	G	21.Ianu.	7.	25.March	30.April	iii	xiii	ii
1628	xiiii	iiii	FE	10.Febru.	27.	13.April	19.Maii	xxii	1.Iune	30.Nou.
1629	xv	xv	D	1.	18.	5.	x	xi	24.Maii	xxix
1630	xvi	xxvi	C	24.Ianu.	10.	28.March	iii	vi	xv	xxviii
1631	xvii	vii	B	6.Febru.	23.	10.April	xvi	xix	xxix	xxvii
1632	xviii	xviii	AG	29.Ianu.	20.	1.	vii	x	xx	2.Decem.
1633	xix	xix	F	17.Febru.	6.March	21.April	xxvi	xxx	9.Iune	i
1634	i	xi	E	2.Febru.	19.Febru.	6.	xii	xv	25.Maii	30.Nou.
1635	ii	xxii	DC	25.Febru.	11.Febru.	March 29	vii	vii	17.Maii	xxix
1636	iii	iii	B	14.Febru.	2.March	April, 17.	xxiii	xxvi	5.Iune	xxviii
1637	iiii	xiiii	A	5.	22.Febru.	9.	xv	xxviii	28.Maii	3.Decem.
1638	v	xxv	G	21.Ianu.	7.	25.March	30.April	iii	xiii	ii
1639	vi	vi	FE	10.Febru.	27.	13.April	20.Maii	xxii	1.Iune	t
1640	vii	xvii	D	2.	19.	5.	xxi	xxiii	24.Maii	29.No.n
1641	iii	xxviii	C	21.Ianu.	10.March	25.	xxxi	3.June	13.June	xxviii

¶ Of the Golden number.

The Golden number is so called, because it was written in the Kalender with letters of gold, right at the day whereon the Moone changed: and it is the space of 19. yeeres, in the which the Moone returneth to the selfe same day of the yeere of the Sunne: and therefore is also called the Cycle of the Moone, in the which the Solstices and Equinoctials vp returne to all one point in the Zodiaque.

To finde it euery yeere, you must adde one yeere to the yeere of Christ, (for Christ was borne one yeere of the 19. already past) then diuide the whole vp 19. and that which resteth, is the Golden number for that yeere: if there be no surplusage, it is then 19.

¶ The Epact

Epacte hemera in Greeke, doth signifie in English, dayes set betweene, and therefore the 11. dayes and 3. houres that are added to the yeere of the Moone, are called Epacts, and are added to make the yeere of the Moone, which is but 354. dayes, iust with the yeere of the Sunne, which hath 365. dayes and a quarter.

To finde out the Epact of each yeere, doe thus: To the Epact of the yeere that last went before that yeere for which you would finde the Epact, adde 11. and the summe of these two make the Epact. If it surmount 30. then take 30. out, and that which resteth aboue 30. is the Epact you desire.

¶ The vse of the Epact.

To know how old the Moone is at any time by the Epact, do thus: Adde vnto the dayes of your moneth wherein you would know this, the Epact, and as many dayes moe as are moneths from March to that moneth, including both moneths, out of the which substract 30. as often as you may, the age remaineth: if nothing remaine, the Moone changeth that day.

For the more ease of the Reader, we haue placed here ouer an Almanacke, inclusiuely comprehending, not onely how to finde the Epact for the space of 30. yeeres to come, but also the Golden number afore specified, together with the Dominicall letter, Leape yeere, and seuen other moueable feasts, or dayes in the yeere, during the same time, as may appeare.

¶ Note that the Golden number and Dominicall letter doeth change euery yeere the first day of Ianuary, and the Epact the first day of March for euer. Note also, that the yeere of our Lord beginneth the xxv. day of March, the same day supposed to be the first day vpon which the world was created, and the day when Christ was conceiued in the wombe of the Virgine Mary.

To

❧ To finde Easter for euer.

Golden number.	A.	B.	C.	D.	E.	F.	G.
i	April xix.	x	xi	xij	vi	vii	viij
ii	March xxvi.	xxvii	xxviii	xix	xxx	xxxi	April i.
iii	April xvi.	xvii	xviii	xix	xx	vi	xv
iiii	April ix.	iii	iiii	v	vi	vii	viij
v	March xxvi.	xxvii	xxviii	xxix	xxxiii	xxiiii	xxv
vi	April xvi.	xvii	xi	xii	xiii	xiiii	xv
vii	April ii.	iii	iiii	v	vi	Mar. 31.	April i.
viii	April xxiii.	xxiiii	xxv	xix	xx	xxi	xxij
ix	April ix.	x	xi	xii	iiii	iiii	viij
x	April ii.	iii	Mar. 28.	xviii	xxix	xxxi	April i.
xi	April xvi.	xvii	xi	v	xix	vij	xxii
xii	April ix.	x	xi	xxviii	xix	xxxi	xxv
xiii	March xxvi.	xvii	xviii	xix	xiii	xiiii	xv
xiiii	April xvi.	iii	iiii	v	vi	vij	viij
xv	April ii.	xxvii	xxviii	xxii	xii	xxiiii	xv
xvi	March xxvi.	x	iiii	v	Mar. 30.	xxxi	April i.
xvij	April xvi.	iii	iiii	v	xx	xx	xxij
xviij	April ii.	xxiiii	xviii	xix			
xix	April xxiii.	xxiiii	xviii	xix	xx		xxij

W Hen ye haue found the Sunday letter in the vppermost line, guide your
eye downeward from the same, till yee come right ouer against the
Prime, and there is shewed both what Moneth, and what day of the
Moneth Easter falleth that yeere.

¶ The

The Table and Kalender, expreſsing the order of
Pſalmes and Leſſons to be ſaid at Morning and Euening prayer
throughout the yeere, except certaine proper feaſts , as the rules
following more plainely declare.

The order how the Pſalter is appointed to be read.

He Pſalter ſhall bee read through once euery Moneth. And be-
cauſe that ſome Moneths be longer then ſome other be, it is thought
good to make them euen by this meanes.

To euery moneth ſhal be appointed (as concerning this purpoſe)
iuſt thirtie dayes.

And becauſe Ianuary and March haue one day aboue the ſayd
number, and February, which is placed betweene them both, hath
onely xxviij. dayes: February ſhall borrowe of either of the Moneths
(of Ianuary and March) one day : and ſo the Pſalter which ſhall bee
read in February, muſt begin at the laſt day of Ianuary, and end the firſt day of March.

And whereas May, Iuly, Auguſt, Octobor, and December haue xxxj. dayes apieee : It is ordered
that the Pſalmes ſhal be read the laſt day of the ſaid Moneths, which were read the day before, ſo that
the Pſalter may begin againe the firſt day of the next moneth enſuing.

Now to know what Pſalmes ſhall be read euery day : Looke in the Kalender the number that is
appointed for the Pſalmes, and then finde the ſame number in this Table , and vpon that number you
ſhall ſee what Pſalmes ſhall be ſayd at Morning and Euening prayer.

And where the Cxix. Pſalme is diuided into xxij. portions, and is ouerlong to be read at one time :
it is ſo ordered, that at one time ſhall not be read aboue foure or fiue of the ſaid portions, as you ſhall
perceiue to be noted in this Table following.

And here is alſo to bee noted , that in this Table , and in all other parts of the Seruice where any
Pſalms are appointed, the number is expreſſed after the great Engliſh Bible, which from the ix. Pſalme
vnto the Cxviij. Pſalme, (following the diuiſion of the Hebrewes) doeth varie in numbers from the
common Latine Tranſlation.

The order how the reſt of holy Scripture (beſide the Pſalter)
is appointed to bee read.

He old Teſtament is appointed for the firſt Leſſons at Morning and Euening prayer,
and ſhalbe read through euery yeere once , except certaine Bookes and Chapters,
which be leaſt edifying, and might beſt be ſpared, and therfore are left vnread.

The New Teſtament is appointed for the ſecond Leſſons at Morning and Euening prayer, and ſhall be read ouer orderly euery yeere thriſe, beſides the Epiſtles and
Goſpels : except the Apocalypſe, out of the which there be onely certaine Leſſons appointed vpon
diuers proper Feaſtes.

And to know what Leſſons ſhall be read euery day, finde the day of the Moneth in the Kalender,
going before and there ye ſhall perceiue the Bookes and Chapters that ſhall be read for the Leſſons
both at Morning and Euening prayer.

And here is to be noted, that whenſoeuer there be any proper Pſalmes or Leſſons appointed for
the Sundayes, or for any Feaſt , moueable or vnmoueable : then the Pſalmes and Leſſons appointed
in the Kalender, ſhall be omitted for that time.

Ye muſt note alſo, that the Collect, Epiſtle, and Goſpel , appointed for the Sunday , ſhall ſerue all
the weeke after, except there fall ſome Feaſt that hath his proper.

When

When the yeeres of our Lord may be diuided into foure euen parts, which is euery fourth yeere: then the Sunday letter leapeth, and that yeere the Psalmes and Lessons which serue for the xxiij. day of February, shall be read againe the day following, except it be Sunday, which hath proper Lessons of the old Testament, appointed in the Table seruing to that purpose.

Also, wheresoeuer the beginning of any Lesson, Epistle, or Gospel is not expressed, there yee must begin at the beginning of the Chapter.

And wheresoeuer is not expressed how farre shall be read, there shall you reade to the ende of the Chapter.

Item, so oft as the first Chapter of Saint Matthew is read either for Lesson or Gospel, ye shall begin the same at (**Now the birth of Iesus Christ was on this wise, &c.**) And the third Chapter of S. Lukes Gospel, shalbe read vnto, **Being as was supposed, the sonne of Ioseph, &c.**

☙ Proper Lessons to bee read for the first
Lessons, both at Morning and Euening prayer, on
the Sundayes throughout the yeere, and for some
also the second Lessons.

Sundayes of Aduent.	¶ Mattens.	¶ Euensong.		¶ Mattens.	¶ Euensong.
The first.	Esa.j.	Esa.ij.	Whitsunday.		
ij.	v	xxiiij	j.Lesson.	Deut.xvi.	Wisedom.t.
iij.	xxv	xxvj	ij.Lesson.	Acts x.	Acts xix. It
iiij.	xxx	xxxij		Then Peter	fortuned ye
Sundayes after Christmas.				opened his	while Apol-
The first.	xxxvij	xxxviij		mouth, &c.	lo was at
ij.	xlj	xliij			Corinth, &c.
Sundayes after the Epiphany			Trinitie Sunday.		(vnto) After these things.
The first.	xliiij	xlvj	j.Lesson.	Gen.xviij.	Ioshua.j.
ij.	lj	liij	ij.Lesson.	Matt.iij.	
iij.	lv	lvj	Sundayes after Trinitie.		
iiij.	lvij	lviij	First.	Iosh.x.	Iosh.xxiij
v.	lix	lxiiij	ij.	Iudg.iiij.	Iudg.v.
Septuagesima.	Gen.j.	Gen.ij.	iij.	i.King.ii.	i.King.iij.
Sexagesima.	iij.	vj.	iiij.	xij	xiij
Quinquagesima.	ix	xij	v.	xv	xvj
			vj.	ii.King.xij.	ii.King.xxi.
Lent.			vij.	xij	xxiiij
First Sunday.	Gen.xix.	Gen.xxij.	viij.	iii.King.xiij.	iii.King.xvij
ij.	xxvij	xxxiiij	ix.	xviij	xix
iij.	xxxix	xlij	x.	xxj	xxij
iiij.	xliij	xlv	xj.	iiij.King.v.	iiij.King.ix.
v.	Exod.iij.	Exod.v.	xij.	x	xviij
vj.	ix	x	xiij.	xix	xxiij
Easter day.			xiiij.	Ierem.v.	Ierem.xxij.
j.Lesson.	Exod.xij.	Exod.xiiij.	xv.	xxxv.	xxxvj
ij.Lesson.	Rom.vj.	Act.ij.	xvj.	Ezech.ii.	Ezech.xiiij.
Sundayes after Easter.			xvij.	xviij	xxiij
The first.	Num.xvi.	Num.xxij.	xviij.	xx	xxiiij
ij.	xxiij	xxv	xix.	Dan.iij.	Daniel.vj.
iij.	Deut.iiij.	Deut.v.	xx.	Ioel ij.	Mich.vj.
iiij.	vj	vij	xxj.	Abacuc ii.	Prouerb.j
v.	viij	ix	xxij.	Prouerb.ii.	Prouerb.iij.
Sunday after Ascension day.	Deut.xij.	Deut.xiij.	xxiij.	xj	xij
			xxiiij.	xiij	xiiij
			xxv.	xv	xvj
			xxvj.	xvij	xix

¶ Lessons

	¶Mattens.	¶Euenfong.
S. Andrew. / S. Thomas the Apostle.	Prouerb.rr. rriii	Prou.rri. rriiii
Christmas day. j.Lesson.	Esa.ir	Esa. vii. Moreouer p̄ Lord fpake once &c.
ij.Lesson.	Luke ii. vnto Good will toward me.	Titus iii. The kindnes & loue &c.
S.Steuen. j.Lesson.	Prou. rrviii.	Ecclef.iiii.
ij.Lesson.	Act.6.and 7. And Steuen ful of faith & power,&c. (vnto) And when forty yeeres,&c.	Acts 7. And whe rl.yeres Were expired there appearedvntoMoses, &c. vnto, But he being full of the holy Ghoft,&c.
S.Iohn. j.Lesson.	Ecclef.v.	Ecclef.vi.
ij.Lesson.	Apoc.i.	Apoc.rrii.
Innocents day.	Jerem. rrri. vnto, I haue furely heard	wild.i.
Circumcifion. j.Lesson.	Ephraim.	
ii.Lesson.	Gen.rvii.	Deu.r.(vnto) And now Ifrael,&c.
Epiphanie. i.Lesson.	Rom.ii.	Esa.rl.
ii.Lesson.	Luk.3.(vnto) Beeing as was suppofed,the sonne of Iofeph.	Esa.rlix. John ii. (vnto)After this he went to Capernaum
Conuerfion of S.Paul. i.Lesson.	wifd.v.	wifd.vi.
ii.Lesson.	Acts rrii.(vnto) They heard him.	Act.rrvi.
Purification of the virgin Mary.	wifd.ir.	wifd.rii.
S.Matthias.	wild.rir.	Ecclef.i.
Annunciation of our Lady.	Ecclef.ii.	Ecclef.iii.
Wednefday a-fore Easter.	Ofee riiii	Ofee riiii
Thurfday afore Easter.	Dan.ir.	Jerem.rrri.
Good Friday.	Gen.rrii.	Esa.liii.
Easter Euen.	Zach.ir.	Erod.riii.
Munday in Eafter weeke. i.Lesson.	Erod.rvi.	Erod.rvii.

	¶Mattens.	¶Euenfong.
ij.Lesson. Tuesday in Eafter weeke.	Matt. rrviii.	Acts. iij.
i.Lesson.	Erod.rr.	Erod.rrrvi.
ij.Lesson.	Luke rriiii. (vnto) And behold two of them.	i.Corinth.rv.
S.Marke.	Eccle.iiii.	Eccle.v.
Philip & Iacob	Eccle.vij.	Eccle.ir.
Ascenfion day.	Deut.r.	iiii.Ring.ij.
Munday in Whitfun-weeke. i.Lesson.	Gen.ri. (vnto These are the generations of She m.	Num.ri Gather vnto me 70. men,&c. (vnto) Mofes gate him into p̄ camp,&c.
ij.Lesson.	i.Cor.rij.	Deut.rrr.
Tuesday in Whitfun-weeke.	i.King.rir. Dauid came to Samuel to Rama.&c.	
S.Barnabe. i.Lesson.	Eccle.r.	Eccle.rii.
ij.	Acts.riii.	Act.rv.(vnto) After certain dayes.
S. Iohn Baptift. i.Lesson.	Mala.iii.	Mala.4.
ij.Lesson.	Matth.iii.	Mat. riiii. (vnto) when Iefus heard
S.Peter. i.Lesson.	Ecclu.rv.	Ecclu.rir.
ij.Lesson.	Acts.iij.	Acts.iiii.
S.Iames.	Ecclus.rri.	Ecclus.rriij.
S. Bartholomew.	rrv.	rrir.
S.Matthew.	Ecclus.rrrv.	rrrviij.
S.Michael.	rrrir.	rliiij.
S.Luke.	Ecclus.li.	Iob i.
Simon and Iude. i.Lesson.	Iob rriii.25.	rlij.
All Saints. i.Lesson.	wifdome iii. (vnto) wher-fore bleffedis the barren.	wifedome v. (vnto)He fhal take to &c.
ij.Lesson.	Hebr.ri.rij. Saints by faith (vnto) If ye indure chaftening	Apocalyp. rir.(vnto)And I faw an Angel ftand.

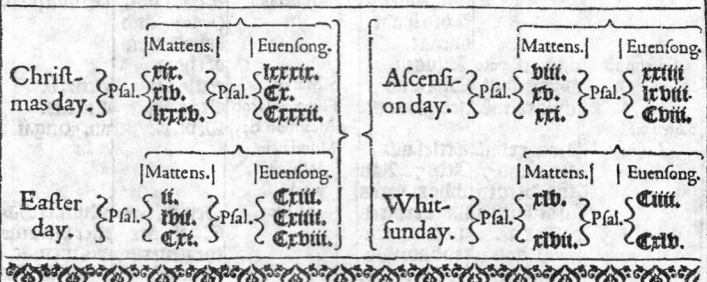

		Mattens.	Euensong.				Mattens.	Euensong.
Christmas day.	Psal.	xix. xlv. lxxxv.	Psal.	lxxxix. cx. cxxxii.	Ascension day.	Psal.	viii. xv. xxi.	Psal.	xxiiii. xlviii. cviii.
Easter day.	Psal.	ii. lvii. cxi.	Psal.	cxiii. cxiiii. cxviii.	Whitsunday.	Psal.	xlv. xlvii.	Psal.	ciiii. cxlv.

¶ The table for the order of the Psalmes,
to be said at Morning and Euening prayer.

Dayes of the Moneth.	¶ Psalmes for Morning prayer.	¶ Psalmes for Euening Prayer.
1.	i.ii.iii.iiii.v.	vi.vii.viii.
2.	ix.x.xi.	xii.xiii.xiiii.
3.	xv.xvi.xvii.	xviii.
4.	xix.xx.xxi.	xxii.xxiii.
5.	xxiiii.xxv.xxvi.	xxvii.xxviii.xxix.
6.	xxx.xxxi.	xxxii.xxxiii.xxxiiii.
7.	xxxv.xxxvi.	xxxvii.
8.	xxxviii.xxxix.xl.	xli.xlii.xliii.
9.	xliiii.xlv.xlvi.	xlvii.xlviii.xlix.
10.	l.li.lii.	liii.liiii.lv.
11.	lvi.lvii.lviii.	lix.lx.lxi.
12.	lxii.lxiii.lxiiii.	lxv.lxvi.lxvii.
13.	lxviii.	lxix.lxx.
14.	lxxi.lxxii.	lxxiii.lxxiiii.
15.	lxxv.lxxvi.lxxvii.	lxxviii.
16.	lxxix.lxxx.lxxxi.	lxxxii.lxxxiii.lxxxiiii.lxxxv.
17.	lxxxvi.lxxxvii.lxxxviii.	lxxxix.
18.	xc.xci.xcii.	xciii.xciiii.
19.	xcv.xcvi.xcvii.	xcviii.xcix.c.ci.
20.	cii.ciii.	ciiii.
21.	cv.	cvi.
22.	cvii.	cviii.cix.
23.	cx.cxi.cxii.cxiii.	cxiiii.cxv.
24.	cxvi.cxvii.cxviii.	cxix. Inde iiii.
25.	Inde v.	Inde iiii.
26.	Inde v.	Inde iiii.
27.	cxx.cxxi.cxxii.cxxiii.cxxiiii.cxxv.	cxxvi.cxxvii.cxxviii.cxxix.cxxx.cxxxi.
28.	cxxvi.cxxvii.cxxviii.cxxix.cxxx.	cxxxii.cxxxiii.cxxxiiii.cxxxviii.
29.	cxxxix.cxl.cxli.	cxlii.cxliii.
30.	cxliiii.cxlv.cxlvi.	cxlvii.cxlviii.cxlix.cl.

Septuagesima

 Eptuagesima
Sexagesima
Quinquagesima } before Easter { ix
viij
viij
vj } weekes.
Quadragesima

 Ogations
Whitsunday } after Easter { v
vij
viij } weekes.
Trinitie Sunday

❧ These to be obſerued for Holy
dayes, and none other.

 Hat is to ſay : All Sun-
dayes in the yeere.

The dayes of the feaſts
of the Circumciſion of our
Lord Jeſus Chriſt.

Of the Epiphanie.

Of the Purification of the bleſſed
Virgin.

Of Saint Matthias the Apoſtle.

Of the Annunciation of the bleſſed
Virgin.

Of Saint Marke the Euangeliſt.

Of S. Philip and Jacob the Apoſtles.

Of the Aſcenſion of our Lord Jeſus
Chriſt.

Of the Natiuity of Saint John
Baptiſt.

Of S. Peter the Apoſtle.

Of S. James the Apoſtle.

Of S. Bartholomew the Apoſtle.

Of S. Matthew the Apoſtle.

Of S. Michael the Archangel.

Of S. Luke the Euangeliſt.

Of S. Simon & Jude the Apoſtles.

Of All Saints.

Of S. Andrew the Apoſtle.

Of S. Thomas the Apoſtle.

Of the Natiuitie of our Lord.

Of S. Steuen the Martyr.

Of S. John the Euangeliſt.

Of the Holy Innocents.

Munday and Tueſday in Eaſter
weeke.

Munday and Tueſday in Whitſun
weeke.

¶ The

¶ The names and order of all the Bookes of the Olde and New Testament, with the Number of their Chapters.

Genesis hath Chapters	50	Ecclesiastes hath Chapters	12
Exodus	40	The song of Solomon	8
Leuiticus	27	Isaiah	66
Numbers	36	Ieremiah	52
Deuteronomie	34	Lamentations	5
Ioshua	24	Ezekiel	48
Iudges	21	Daniel	12
Ruth	4	Hosea	14
1.Samuel	31	Ioel	3
2.Samuel	24	Amos	9
1.Kings	22	Obadiah	1
2.Kings	25	Ionah	4
1.Chronicles	29	Micah	7
2.Chronicles	36	Nahum	5
Ezrah	10	Habakkuk	3
Nehemiah	13	Zephaniah	3
Ester	10	Haggai	2
Iob	42	Zechariah	14
Psalmes	150	Malachi	4
Prouerbs	31		

✠ The Bookes called Apocrypha.

1. Esdras hath Chapters	9	Baruch with the Epistle of Ieremiah	6
2.Esdras	16	The song of the three children.	
Tobit	14	The story of Susanna.	
Iudeth	16	The idole Bel and the Dragon.	
The rest of Esther	6	The prayer of Manasseh.	
Wisedome	19	1.Maccabees	16
Ecclesiasticus	51	2.Maccabees	15

✠ The Bookes of the New Teſtament.

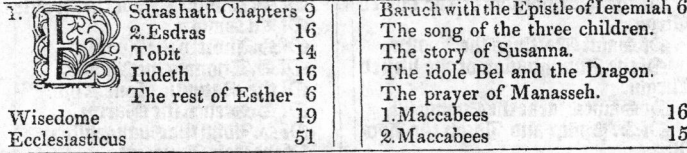

Matthew hath Chap.	28	2.Thessalonians hath Chapters	3
Marke	16	1.Timotheus	6
Luke	24	2.Timotheus	4
Iohn	21	Titus	3
The Actes	26	Philemon	1
The Epistle to the Romanes	16	To the Hebrewes	13
1.Corinthians	16	The Epistle of Iames	5
2.Corinthians	13	1.Peter	5
Galatians	6	2.Peter	3
Ephesians	6	1.Iohn	5
Philippians	4	2.Iohn	1
Colossians	4	3.Iohn	1
1.Thessalonians	5	Iude	1
		Reuelation	22

THE

THE

FIRST BOOKE

OF MOSES,

called GENESIS.

CHAP. I.

1 The creation of Heauen and Earth, 3 of the light, 6 of the firmament, 9 of the earth separated from the waters, 11 and made fruitfull, 14 of the Sunne, Moone, and Starres, 20 of fish and fowle, 24 of beasts and cattell, 26 of Man in the Image of God. 29 Also the appointment of food.

* Psal. 33. 6. and 136. 5. acts. 14. 15. and 17. 24. hebr. 11. 3.

IN *the beginning God created the Heauen, and the Earth.

2 And the earth was without forme, and voyd, and darkenesse *was* vpon the face of the deepe : and the Spirit of God mooued vpon the face of the waters.

* 2. Cor. 4. 6.

3 And God said, *Let there be light: and there was light.

4 And God saw the light, that *it was* good: and God diuided †the light from the darkenesse.

† Hebr. betweene the light and betweene the darkenesse.
† Hebr. and the euening was, and the morning was &c.
* Psal. 136.
5. Ier. 10. 12 and 51. 15.
† Hebr. Expansion.

5 And God called the light, Day, and the darkenesse he called Night: †and the euening and the morning were the first day.

6 ¶ And God said, * Let there be a †firmament in the midst of the waters: and let it diuide the waters from the waters.

7 And God made the firmament; and diuided the waters, which *were* vnder the firmament, from the waters, which *were* aboue the firmament: and it was so.

8 And God called the * firmament, Heauen: and the euening and the morning were the second day.

* Ier. 51. 15.

9 ¶ And God said, *Let the waters vnder the heauen be gathered together vnto one place, and let the dry land appeare : and it was so.

* Psal. 33. 7. iob. 38. 8.

10 And God called the drie land, Earth, and the gathering together of the waters called hee, Seas : and God saw that *it was* good.

11 And God said, Let the Earth bring foorth †grasse, the herbe yeelding seed, *and* the fruit tree, yeelding fruit after his kinde, whose seed *is* in it selfe, vpon the earth : and it was so.

† Heb. tender grasse.

12 And the earth brought foorth grasse, *and* herbe yeelding seed after his kinde, and the tree yeelding fruit, whose seed *was* in it selfe, after his kinde: and God saw that *it was* good.

13 And the euening and the morning were the third day.

14 ¶ And God said, Let there bee *lights in the firmament of the heauen, to diuide †the day from the night: and let them be for signes and for seasons, and for dayes and yeeres.

* Deu. 4. 19 psal. 136. 7.
† Hebr. betweene the day and betweene the night.

15 And let them be for lights in the firmament of the heauen, to giue light vpon the earth: and it was so.

16 And God made two great lights: the greater light † to rule the day, and the lesser light to rule the night: *he made* the starres also.

† Hebr. for the rule of the day, &c.

17 And God set them in the firmament of the heauen, to giue light vpon the earth:

18 And to * rule ouer the day, and ouer

* Ier. 31. 35

ouer the night, and to diuide the light from the darkenesse: and God saw that *it was* good

19 And the euening and the morning were the fourth day.

20 And God said, * Let the waters bring foorth aboundantly the ‖ mouing creature that hath †life, and foule *that* may flie aboue the earth in the † open firmament of heauen.

21 And God created great whales, and euery liuing creature that moueth, which the waters brought forth aboundantly after their kinde, and euery winged foule after his kinde: and God saw that *it was* good.

22 And God blessed them, saying, *Be fruitfull, and multiply, and fill the waters in the Seas, and let foule multiply in the earth.

23 And the euening and the morning were the fift day.

24 ¶ And God said, Let the earth bring forth the liuing creature after his kinde, cattell, and creeping thing, and beast of the earth after his kinde: and it was so.

25 And God made the beast of the earth after his kinde, and cattell after their kinde, and euery thing that creepeth vpon the earth, after his kinde: and God saw that *it was* good.

26 ¶ And God said, * Let vs make man in our Image, after our likenesse: and let them haue dominion ouer the fish of the sea, and ouer the foule of the aire, and ouer the cattell, and ouer all the earth, and ouer euery creeping thing that creepeth vpon the earth.

27 So God created man in his owne Image, in the Image of God created hee him; *male and female created hee them.

28 And God blessed them, and God said vnto them, *Be fruitfull, and multiply, and replenish the earth, and subdue it, and haue dominion ouer the fish of the sea, and ouer the foule of the aire, and ouer euery liuing thing that †mooueth vpon the earth.

29 ¶ And God said, Behold, I haue giuen you euery herbe †bearing seede, which *is* vpon the face of all the earth, and euery tree, in the which *is* the fruit of a tree yeelding seed, *to you it shall be for meat:

30 And to euery beast of the earth, and to euery foule of the aire, and to euery thing that creepeth vpon the earth,

wherein there *is* †life, *I haue giuen* euery greene herbe for meat: and it was so.

31 And * God saw euery thing that hee had made: and behold, *it was* very good. And the euening and the morning were the sixth day.

CHAP. II.

1 The first Sabbath. 4 The maner of the creation. 8 The planting of the garden of Eden, 10 and the riuer thereof. 17 The tree of knowledge onely forbidden. 19. 20 The naming of the creatures. 21 The making of woman, and institution of Mariage.

Hus the heauens and the earth were finished, and all the hoste of them.

2 *And on the seuenth day God ended his worke, which hee had made: And he rested on the seuenth day from all his worke, which he had made.

3 And God blessed the seuenth day, and sanctified it: because that in it he had rested from all his worke, which God † created and made.

4 ¶ These *are* the generations of the heauens, & of the earth, when they were created; in the day that the LORD God made the earth, and the heauens,

5 And euery plant of the field, before it was in the earth, and euery herbe of the field, before it grew: for the LORD God had not caused it to raine vpon the earth, and there *was* not a man to till the ground.

6 ‖ But there went up a mist from the earth, and watered the whole face of the ground.

7 And the LORD God formed man † * of the dust of the ground, & breathed into his nostrils the breath of life; and *man became a liuing soule.

8 ¶ And the LORD God planted a garden Eastward in Eden; and there he put the man whom he had formed.

9 And out of the ground made the LORD God to grow euery tree that is pleasant to the sight, and good for food: the tree of life also in the midst of the garden, and the tree of knowledge of good and euill.

10 And a riuer went out of Eden to water the garden, and from thence it was parted, and became into foure heads.

11 The name of the first *is* * Pison: that *is* it which compasseth the whole land of Hauilah, where *there is* gold.

12 And

Margin notes (left column)

* 4. Esdr. 6. 47.
‖ Or, creeping.
† Heb. soule.
† Heb. face of the firmament of heauen.

* Chap. 8. 17. and 9. 1.

* Chap. 5. 1. and 9. 6.
1. corin. 11. 7. ephes. 4. 14. col. 3. 10.

* Matth. 19 4. wisd. 2. 23.

* Chap. 9. 1.

† Heb. creepeth.

† Hebr. seeding seed.

* Chap. 9. 3.

Margin notes (right column)

† Hebr. a liuing soule.

* Ecclus. 39 16.

* Exod. 20. 11. and 31. 17. deut. 5. 14. hebr. 4. 4.

† Heb. created to make.

‖ Or, a mist which went vp from &c.

† Heb. dust of the ground.
* 1. Cor. 15 47.
* 1. Corin. 15. 45.

* Ecclus. 24. 29.

12 And the gold of that land *is* good : There *is* Bdellium and the Onix stone.

13 And the name of the second riuer *is* Gihon: the same *is* it that compasseth the whole land of † Ethiopia.

† *Heb. Cush.*

14 And the name of the third riuer *is* Hiddekel: that *is it* which goeth ||toward the East of Assyria: and the fourth riuer is Euphrates.

|| *Or, Eastward to Assyria.*

15 And the LORD God tooke || the man, and put him into the garden of Eden, to dresse it, and to keepe it.

|| *Or, Adam.*

16 And the LORD God commanded the man, saying, Of euery tree of the garden thou mayest †freely eate.

† *Hebr. eating thou shalt eate.*

17 But of the tree of the knowledge of good and euill, thou shalt not eate of it: for in the day that thou eatest thereof, thou shalt † surely die.

† *Hebr. dying thou shalt die.*

18 ¶ And the LORD God said, It *is* not good that the man should be alone: I will make him * an helpe †meet for him.

* *Ecclus. 17. 5.*
† *Hebr. as before him.*

19 And out of ỹ ground the LORD God formed euery beast of the field, and euery foule of the aire, and brought *them* vnto ||Adam, to see what he would call them : and whatsoeuer Adam called euery liuing creature, that *was* the name thereof.

|| *Or, the man.*

20 And Adam †gaue names to all cattell, and to the foule of the aire, and to euery beast of the fielde: but for Adam there was not found an helpe meete for him.

† *Hebr. called.*

21 And the LORD God caused a deepe sleepe to fall vpon Adam, and hee slept; and he tooke one of his ribs, and closed vp the flesh in stead thereof.

22 And the rib which the LORD God had taken from man, †made hee a woman, & brought her vnto the man.

† *Hebr. builded.*

23 And Adam said, This is now bone of my bones, and flesh of my flesh: she shalbe called woman, because shee was * taken out of man.

24 * Therefore shall a man leaue his father and his mother, and shall cleaue vnto his wife: and they shalbe one flesh.

* *1. Corin. 11. 8.*
* *Matt. 19. 5. mar. 10. 7. 1. corin. 6. 16. ephe. 5. 31.*

25 And they were both naked, the man & his wife, and were not ashamed.

CHAP. III.

1 The serpent deceiueth Eue. 6 Mans shamefull fall. 9 God arraigneth them. 14 The serpent is cursed. 15 The promised Seed. 16 The punishment of Mankind. 21 Their first clothing. 22 Their casting out of Paradise.

NOw the serpent was more subtill then any beast of the field, which the LORD God had made, and he said vnto the woman, † Yea, hath God said, Ye shall not eat of euery tree of the garden ?

† *Heb. Yea, because, &c.*

2 And the woman said vnto the serpent, Wee may eate of the fruite of the trees of the garden:

3 But of the fruit of the tree, which *is* in the midst of the garden, God hath said, Ye shal not eate of it, neither shall ye touch it, lest ye die.

4 And the Serpent said vnto the woman, Ye shall not * surely die.

* *2. Cor. 11. 3. 1. tim. 2. 14.*

5 For God doeth know, that in the day ye eate thereof, then your eyes shalbee opened: and yee shall bee as Gods, knowing good and euill.

6 And when the woman saw, that the tree *was* good for food, and that it *was* †pleasant to the eyes, and a tree to be desired to make one wise, she tooke of the fruit thereof, *and did eate, and gaue also vnto her husband with her, and hee did eate.

† *Heb. a desire.*
* *Ecclus. 25. 26. 1. tim. 2. 14.*

7 And the eyes of them both were opened, & they knew that they *were* naked, and they sewed figge leaues together, and made themselues ||aprons.

|| *Or, things to gird about.*

8 And they heard the voyce of the LORD God, walking in the garden in the †coole of the day: and Adam and his wife hid themselues from the presence of the LORD God, amongst the trees of the garden.

† *Heb. wind.*

9 And the LORD God called vnto Adam, and said vnto him, Where *art* thou ?

10 And he said, I heard thy voice in the garden: and I was afraid, because I *was* naked, and I hid my selfe.

11 And he said, Who told thee, that thou *wast* naked? Hast thou eaten of the tree, whereof I commanded thee, that thou shouldest not eate ?

12 And the man said, The woman whom thou gauest *to be* with mee, shee gaue me of the tree, and I did eate.

13 And the LORD God said vnto the woman, What *is* this *that* thou hast done? And the woman said, The Serpent beguiled me, and I did eate.

14 And the LORD God said vnto the Serpent, Because thou hast done this, thou *art* cursed aboue all cattel, and aboue euery beast of the field: vpon thy belly shalt thou goe, and dust shalt thou eate,

eate, all the dayes of thy life.

15 And I will put enmitie betweene thee and the woman, and betweene thy seed and her seed: it ſhal bruiſe thy head, and thou ſhalt bruiſe his heele.

16 Unto the woman he said, I will greatly multiply thy ſorowe and thy conception. In ſorow thou ſhalt bring forth children: and thy deſire *shall be* ||to thy husband, and hee ſhall * rule ouer thee.

|| Or, ſubiect to thy huſband.
* 1. Corin. 14. 34.

17 And vnto Adam he said, Because thou haſt hearkened vnto the voyce of thy wife, and haſt eaten of the tree, of which I commaunded thee, ſaying, Thou ſhalt not eate of it: curſed *is* the ground for thy ſake: in ſorow ſhalt thou eate of it all the dayes of thy life.

18 Thornes also and thiſtles ſhall it † bring forth to thee: and thou ſhalt eate the herbe of the field.

† Heb. cauſe to bud.

19 In the ſweate of thy face ſhalt thou eate bread, till thou returne vnto the ground: for out of it waſt thou taken, for duſt thou *art*, and vnto duſt ſhalt thou returne.

20 And Adam called his wiues name † Eue, because she was the mother of all liuing.

† Heb. Cha-uah.

21 Unto Adam also, and to his wife, did the LORD God make coates of ſkinnes, and cloathed them.

22 ¶ And the LORD God said, Behold, the man is become as one of us, to know good & euill. And now leſt hee put foorth his hand, and take also of the tree of life, and eate and liue for euer:

23 Therefore the LORD God ſent him foorth from the garden of Eden, to till the ground, from whence he was taken.

24 So he droue out the man: and he placed at the Eaſt of the garden of Eden, Cherubims, and a flaming ſword, which turned euery way, to keepe the way of the tree of life.

CHAP. IIII.

1 The birth, trade, and religion of Cain and Abel. 8 The murder of Abel. 9 The curse of Cain. 17 Enoch the firſt citie. 19 Lamech and his two wiues. 25 The birth of Seth, 26 and Enos.

Nd Adam knew Eue his wife, and ſhee conceiued, and bare Cain, and said, I haue gotten a man from the LORD.

2 And ſhe againe bare his brother † Abel, and Abel was a † keeper of ſheep, but Cain was a tiller of the ground.

† Heb. Hebel.
† Heb. a feeder.
† Heb. at the end of dayes.

3 And † in proceſſe of time it came to paſſe, that Cain brought of the fruite of the ground, an offering vnto the LORD.

4 And Abel, he also brought of the firſtlings of his † flocke, and of the fat thereof: and the LORD had *respect vnto Abel, and to his offering.

† Heb. ſheep, or goates.
* Heb. 11. 4

5 But vnto Cain, and to his offring he had not reſpect: and Cain was very wroth, and his countenance fell.

6 And the LORD said vnto Cain, Why art thou wroth? And why is thy countenance fallen?

7 If thou doe well, ſhalt thou not ||be accepted? and if thou doeſt not well, ſinne lieth at the doore: And || vnto thee *shall be* his deſire, and thou ſhalt rule ouer him.

|| Or, haue the excellencie?
|| Or, ſubiect vnto thee.

8 And Cain talked with Abel his brother: and it came to paſſe * when they were in the field, that Cain roſe vp against Abel his brother, and ſlew him.

* Wis. 10. 3 matth. 23. 35. 1. iohn 3. 12. iude 11.

9 ¶ And the LORD said vnto Cain, Where *is* Abel thy brother? And hee said, I know not: Am I my brothers keeper?

10 And he said, What haſt thou done? the voyce of thy brothers † blood cryeth vnto me, from the ground.

† Heb. bloods

11 And now *art* thou curſed from the earth, which hath opened her mouth to receiue thy brothers blood from thy hand.

12 When thou tilleſt the ground, it ſhall not henceforth yeeld vnto thee her ſtrength: A fugitiue and a vagabond ſhalt thou be in the earth.

13 And Cain said vnto the LORD, ||My puniſhment *is* greater, then I can beare.

|| Or, my iniquitie is greater, then that it may be forgiuen.

14 Behold, thou haſt driuen me out this day from the face of the earth, and from thy face ſhall I be hid, and I ſhall be a fugitiue, and a vagabond in the earth: and it ſhall come to paſſe, *that* euery one that findeth me, ſhall ſlay me.

15 And the LORD said vnto him, Therefore whoſoeuer ſlayeth Cain, vengeance ſhalbe taken on him ſeuen fold. And the LORD ſet a marke vpon Cain, leſt any finding him, ſhould kill him.

16 ¶ And Cain went out from the preſence of the LORD, and dwelt in the land of Nod, on the Eaſt of Eden.

17 And Cain knew his wife, and she concei-

† *Heb. Cha-noch.*

conceiued and bare †Enoch, and hee builded a City, and called the name of the City, after the name of his sonne, Enoch.

18 And vnto Enoch was borne Irad: and Irad begate Mehuiael, and Mehuiael begate Methusael, and Methusael begate †Lamech.

† *Hebr. Le-mech.*

19 ¶ And Lamech tooke vnto him two wiues: the name of the one *was* Adah, and the name of the other Zillah.

20 And Adah bare Jabal: he was the father of such as dwell in tents, and *of such as haue* cattell.

21 And his brothers name was Jubal: hee was the father of all such as handle the harpe and organ.

† *Heb. whet-ter.*

22 And Zillah, she also bare Tubal-Cain, an †instructer of euery artificer in brasse and iron: and the sister of Tubal-Cain *was* Naamah.

23 And Lamech sayd vnto his wiues, Adah and Zillah, Heare my voyce, yee wiues of Lamech, hearken vnto my speech: for ‖ I haue slaine a man to my wounding, and a yong man to my ‖hurt.

‖ *Or, I would slay a man in my wound, &c.*
‖ *Or, in my hurt.*

24 If Cain shall bee auenged seuen fold, truely Lamech seuenty and seuen folde.

25 ¶ And Adam knew his wife againe, and she bare a sonne, & called his name †Seth: For God, *said she*, hath appointed mee another seed in stead of Abel, whom Cain slew.

† *Hebr. Sheth.*

26 And to Seth, to him also there was borne a sonne, and he called his name †Enos: then began men to ‖call vpon the Name of the LORD.

† *Hebr. E-nosh.*
‖ *Or, to call themselues by the Name of the* LORD.

CHAP. V.

1 The genealogie, age, and death of the Patriarchs from Adam vnto Noah. 24 The godlinesse and translation of Enoch.

* 1. Chron. 1. 1.

His *is* the *booke of the generations of Adam : In the day that God created man, in the likenes of God made he him.

* Wisd. 2. 23.

2 * Male and female created hee them, and blessed them, and called their name Adam, in the day when they were created.

3 ¶ And Adam liued an hundred and thirtie yeeres, and begate *a sonne* in his owne likenesse, after his image; and called his name Seth.

* 1. Chron. 1. 1. &c.

4 * And the dayes of Adam, after he had begotten Seth, were eight hundred yeeres: and he begate sonnes and daughters.

5 And all the dayes that Adam liued, were nine hundred and thirtie yeeres: and he died.

6 And Seth liued an hundred and fiue yeeres: and begate †Enos.

† *Hebr. E-nosh.*

7 And Seth liued, after he begate Enos, eight hundred and seuen yeeres, and begate sonnes and daughters.

8 And all the dayes of Seth, were nine hundred and twelue yeeres, and he died.

9 ¶ And Enos liued ninetie yeeres, and begate †Cainan.

† *Heb. Ke-nan.*

10 And Enos liued after hee begate Cainan, eight hundred and fifteene yeeres, and begate sonnes & daughters.

11 And all the dayes of Enos were nine hundred & fiue yeres; and he died.

12 ¶ And Cainan liued seuentie yeeres, and begate †Mahalaleel.

† *Greeke, Maleleel.*

13 And Cainan liued after he begate Mahalaleel, eight hundred and fourtie yeeres, & begate sonnes and daughters.

14 And al the dayes of Cainan were nine hundred & ten yeres; and he died.

15 ¶ And Mahalaleel liued sixtie and fiue yeeres, and begat †Jared.

† *Heb, Iered.*

16 And Mahalaleel liued after he begate Jared, eight hundred and thirtie yeeres, and begate sonnes & daughters.

17 And all the dayes of Mahalaleel, were eight hundred ninetie and fiue yeeres, and he died.

18 ¶ And Jared liued an hundred sixtie and two yeeres, & he begat Enoch.

19 And Jared liued after he begate Enoch, eight hundred yeres, and begate sonnes and daughters.

20 And all the dayes of Jared were nine hundred sixtie and two yeeres, and he died.

21 ¶ And Enoch liued sixtie and fiue yeeres, and begate ‖Methuselah.

‖ *Gr. Ma-thusala.*

22 And Enoch walked with God, after he begate Methuselah, three hundred yeeres, and begate sonnes and daughters.

23 And all the dayes of Enoch, were three hundred sixtie and fiue yeeres.

24 And * Enoch walked with God: and he was not; for God tooke him.

* Ecclus. 44. 16. heb. 11. 5.

25 And Methuselah liued an hundred eightie and seuen yeeres, and begat Lamech.

26 And Methuselah liued, after hee begate †Lamech, seuen hundred, eightie and

† *Hebr. Le-mech.*

and two yeeres, and begate sonnes and daughters.

27 And all the dayes of Methuselah were nine hundred, sixtie and nine yeeres, and he died.

28 ¶ And Lamech liued an hundred eightie and two yeeres: and begate a sonne.

‖ Gr. Noe.

29 And he called his name ‖ Noah, saying; This *same* shall comfort vs, concerning our woorke and toyle of our hands, because of the ground, which the LORD hath cursed.

30 And Lamech liued, after hee begate Noah, fiue hundred ninetie and fiue yeeres, and begate sonnes and daughters.

31 And all the dayes of Lamech were seuen hundred seuentie and seuen yeeres, and he died.

32 And Noah was fiue hundred yeeres olde: and Noah begate Sem, Ham, and Japheth.

CHAP. VI.

1 The wickednesse of the world, which prouoked Gods wrath, and caused the Flood. 8 Noah findeth grace. 13 The order, forme, and end of the Arke.

Nd it came to passe, when men began to multiply on the face of the earth, and daughters were borne vnto them:

2 That the sonnes of God saw the daughters of men, that they were faire, and they took them wiues, of all which they chose.

3 And the LORD said, My Spirit shall not alwayes striue with man; for that hee also *is* flesh: yet his dayes shalbe an hundred and twenty yeeres.

4 There were Giants in the earth in those daies: and also after that, when the sonnes of God came in vnto the daughters of men, & they bare *children* to them; the same became mightie men, which *were* of old, men of renowme.

5 ¶ And God saw, that the wickednes of man was great in the earth, and ‖ *that* euery imagination of the thoughts of his * heart was onely euill † continually.

‖ Or, the whole imagination. The Hebr.word signifieth not onely the imagination, but also the purposes and desires.
** Chap. 8. 21. mat 15. 19.*
† Hebr. euery day.

6 And it repented the LORD that he had made man on the earth, and it grieued him at his heart.

7 And the LORD said, I will destroy man, whom I haue created,

from the face of the earth: † both man and beast, and the creeping thing, and the foules of the aire: for it repenteth me that I haue made them.

† Hebr. from man vnto beast.

8 But Noah found grace in the eyes of the LORD.

9 ¶ These *are* the generations of Noah: * Noah was a iust man, *and* ‖ perfect in his generations, *and* Noah walked with God.

** Ecclus. 44 17. 2. pet. 2. 5.*
‖ Or, vpright.

10 And Noah begate three sonnes: Sem, Ham, and Japheth.

11 The earth also was corrupt before God; and the earth was filled with violence.

12 And God looked vpon the earth, and behold, it was corrupt: for all flesh had corrupted his way vpon the earth.

13 And God said vnto Noah, The end of all flesh is come before mee; for the earth is filled with violence through them; and behold, I will destroy them ‖ with the earth.

‖ Or, from the earth.

14 ¶ Make thee an Arke of Gopher-wood: † roomes shalt thou make in the arke, and shalt pitch it within and without with pitch.

† Heb. nests

15 And this is the *fashion*, which thou shalt make it of: the length of the arke *shalbe* three hundred cubits, the breadth of it fifty cubits, and the height of it thirtie cubits.

16 A window shalt thou make to the arke, and in a cubite shalt thou finish it aboue; and the doore of the arke shalt thou set in the side thereof: With lower, second, and third stories shalt thou make it.

17 And behold, I, euen I, doe bring a flood of waters vpon the earth, to destroy all flesh, wherein is the breath of life from vnder heauen, *and* euery thing that is in the earth shall die.

18 But with thee wil I establish my Couenant: and thou shalt come into the Arke, thou, and thy sonnes, and thy wife, and thy sonnes wiues with thee.

19 And of euery liuing thing of all flesh, two of euery *sort* shalt thou bring into the Arke, to keepe *them* aliue with thee: they shall be male and female.

20 Of fowles after their kinde, and of cattel after their kinde: of euery creeping thing of the earth after his kinde, two of euery *sort* shall come vnto thee, to keepe *them* aliue.

21 And take thou vnto thee of all food that is eaten, and thou shalt gather *it* to thee; and it shall be for food, for

for thee, and for them.

22 * Thus did Noah ; according to all that God commanded him, so did he.

* Heb. 11. 7.

CHAP. VII.

1 Noah, with his familie, and the liuing creatures, enter into the Arke. 17 The beginning, increase, and continuance of the Flood.

2. Pet. 2. 5.

Nd the * LORD saide vnto Noah, Come thou and all thy house into the Arke: for thee haue I seene righteous before me, in this generation.

2 Of euery cleane beast thou shalt take to thee † by seuens, the male and his female: and of beastes that are not cleane, by two, the male and his female.

Hebr. seuen seuen.

3 Of fowles also of the aire, by seuens, the male & the female; to keepe seed aliue vpon the face of all the earth.

4 For yet seuen dayes, and I will cause it to raine vpon the earth, fortie dayes, and forty nights: and euery liuing substance that I haue made, will I † destroy, fro off the face of the earth.

Hebr. blot out.

5 And Noah did according vnto all that the LORD commanded him.

6 And Noah was sixe hundred yeeres old, when the flood of waters was vpon the earth.

7 ¶ And Noah went in, and his sonnes, and his wife, and his sonnes wiues with him, into the Arke, because of the waters of the Flood.

8 Of cleane beasts, & of beasts that are not cleane, & of fowles, and of euery thing that creepeth vpon the earth,

9 There went in two and two vnto Noah into the Arke, the male & the female, as God had commanded Noah.

10 And it came to passe ||after seuen dayes, that the waters of the Flood were vpon the earth.

Or, on the ||uenth day.

11 ¶ In the sixe hundredth yeere of Noahs life, in the second moneth, the seuenteenth day of the moneth, the same day, were al the fountaines of the great deepe broken vp, and the || windowes of heauen were opened.

Or, floodgates.

12 And the raine was vpon the earth, fortie dayes, and fortie nights.

13 In the selfe same day entred Noah, and Sem, and Ham, and Japheth, the sonnes of Noah, and Noahs wife, and the three wiues of his sonnes with them, into the Arke,

14 They, and euery beast after his kinde, & all the cattell after their kinde: and euery creeping thing that creepeth vpon the earth after his kinde, and euery foule after his kinde, euery birde of euery † sort.

† Heb. wing.

15 And they went in vnto Noah into the Arke, two and two of all flesh, wherein is the breath of life.

16 And they that went in, went in male and female of all flesh, as God had commaunded him : and the LORD shut him in.

17 And the Flood was fortie dayes vpon the earth, and the waters increased, and bare vp the Arke, and it was lift vp aboue the earth.

18 And the waters preuailed, and were encreased greatly vpon the earth : and the Arke went vpon the face of the waters.

19 And the waters preuailed exceedingly vpon the earth, and all the high hils, that *were* vnder the whole heauen, were couered.

20 Fifteene cubits vpward, did the waters preuaile ; and the mountaines were couered.

21 * And all flesh died, that mooued vpon the earth, both of fowle, & of cattell, and of beast, and of euery creeping thing that creepeth vpon the earth, and euery man.

* Wisd. 10. 4.

22 All in whose nosethrils *was* the † breath of life, of all that was in the dry land, died.

† Hebr. the breath of the spirit of life.

23 And euery liuing substance was destroyed, which was vpon the face of the ground, both man and cattell, and the creeping things, and the foule of the heauen ; and they were destroyed from the earth : and * Noah onely remained aliue, and they that *were* with him in the Arke.

* Wisd. 10. 4. 2. pet. 2. 5

24 And the waters preuailed vpon the earth, an hundred and fifty dayes.

CHAP. VIII.

1 The waters asswage. 4 The Arke resteth on Ararat. 7 The rauen and the doue. 15 Noah, being commanded, 18 goeth forth of the Arke. 20 He buildeth an Altar, and offereth sacrifice, 21 which God accepteth, and promiseth to curse the earth no more.

Nd God remembred Noah, and euery liuing thing, and all the cattell that *was* with him in the Arke : and God made a winde to

to passe ouer the earth, and the waters asswaged.

2 The fountaines also of the deepe, and the windowes of heauen were stopped, and the raine from heauen was restrained.

3 And the waters returned from off the earth, †continually: and after the end of the hundred and fiftie dayes, the waters were abated.

† Hebr. in going and returning.

4 And the Arke rested in the seuenth moneth, on the seuenteenth day of the moneth, vpon the mountaines of Ararat.

5 And the waters † decreased continually vntill the tenth moneth: in the tenth moneth, on the first *day* of the moneth, were the tops of the mountaines seene.

† Hebr. were in going and decreasing.

6 ¶ And it came to passe at the end of forty dayes, that Noah opened the window of the Arke which he had made.

7 And he sent forth a Rauen, which went foorth †to and fro, vntill the waters were dryed vp from off the earth.

† Hebr. in going foorth, and returning.

8 Also hee sent foorth a doue from him, to see if the waters were abated from off the face of the ground.

9 But the doue found no rest for the sole of her foote, and she returned vnto him into the Arke: for the waters *were* on the face of the whole earth. Then he put foorth his hand, and tooke her, and †pulled her in vnto him, into the Arke.

† Hebr. caused her to come.

10 And hee stayed yet other seuen dayes; and againe hee sent foorth the doue out of the Arke.

11 And the doue came in to him in the euening, and loe, in her mouth *was* an Oliue leafe pluckt off: So Noah knew that the waters were abated from off the earth.

12 And hee stayed yet other seuen dayes, and sent forth the doue, which returned not againe vnto him any more.

13 ¶ And it came to passe in the sixe hundredth and one yeere, in the first *moneth*, the first *day* of the moneth, the waters were dryed vp from *off* the earth: and Noah remooued the couering of the Arke, and looked, and behold, the face of the ground was drie.

14 And in the second moneth, on the seuen and twentieth day of the moneth, was the earth dried.

15 ¶ And God spake vnto Noah, saying,

16 Goe foorth of the Arke, thou, and thy wife, and thy sonnes, and thy sonnes wiues with thee:

17 Bring foorth with thee euery liuing thing that *is* with thee, of all flesh, *both* of fowle, and of cattell, and of euery creeping thing that creepeth vpon the earth, that they may breed abundantly in the earth, and be fruitfull, and multiply vpon the earth.

18 And Noah went foorth, and his sonnes, and his wife, and his sonnes wiues with him:

19 Euery beast, euery creeping thing, and euery fowle, *and* whatsoeuer creepeth vpon the earth, after their †kinds, went foorth out of the Arke.

† Hebr. families.

20 ¶ And Noah builded an Altar vnto the LORD, and tooke of euery cleane beast, and of euery cleane fowle, and offred burnt offrings on the Altar.

21 And the LORD smelled a †sweete sauour, and the LORD said in his heart, I will not againe curse the ground any more for mans sake; for the *imagination of mans heart *is* euil from his youth: neither will I againe smite any more euery thing liuing, as I haue done.

† Hebr. a sauour of rest.

* Chap. 6. 5. matt. 15. 19.

22 †While the earth remaineth, seedtime and haruest, and cold, and heat, and Summer, and Winter, and day and night, shall not cease.

† Heb. as yet all the dayes of the earth.

CHAP. IX.

1 God blesseth Noah. 4 Blood and murder are forbidden. 9 Gods Couenant 13 signified by the Rainebow. 18 Noah replenisheth the world, 20 planteth a Vineyard, 21 is drunken, and mocked of his sonne: 25 Curseth Canaan, 26 Blesseth Shem, 27 prayeth for Iaphet, 28 and dieth.

Nd God blessed Noah, and his sonnes, and said vnto them, * Bee fruitfull and multiply, and replenish the earth.

* Chap. 1. 28. and 8. 17.

2 And the feare of you, & the dread of you shall be vpon euery beast of the earth, and vpon euery fowle of the aire, vpon all that mooueth *vpon* the earth, and vpon all the fishes of the sea; into your hand are they deliuered.

3 Euery mouing thing that liueth, shalbe meat for you; euen as the *greene herbe haue I giuen you all things.

* Chap. 1. 29.

4 * But flesh with the life thereof, *which is* the blood thereof, shall you not eate.

* Leuit. 17. 14.

5 And surely your blood of your liues

* Matt. 26.
52. reuel.
13. 10.
* Chap. 1.
27.

liues will I require: at the hand of euery beast will I require it, & at the hand of man, at the hand of euery mans brother will I require the life of man.

6 *Who so sheddeth mans blood, by man shall his blood be shed: *for in the image of God made he man.

7 And you, be ye fruitfull, and multiply, bring foorth aboundantly in the earth, and multiply therein.

8 ¶ And God spake vnto Noah, and to his sonnes with him, saying;

9 And I, behold, I establish my couenant with you, and with your seede after you:

10 And with euery liuing creature that is with you, of the fowle, of the cattell, and of euery beast of the earth with you, from all that goe out of the Arke, to euery beast of the earth.

* Esa. 54. 9.

11 And *I will establish my couenant with you, neither shal all flesh be cut off any more, by the waters of a flood, neither shall there any more be a flood to destroy the earth.

12 And God said, This is the token of the Couenant which I make betweene mee and you, and euery liuing creature that is with you, for perpetuall generations.

13 I doe set my bow in the cloud, and it shall be for a token of a couenant, betweene me and the earth.

* Ecclus. 43.
11, 12.

14 *And it shall come to passe, when I bring a cloud ouer the earth, that the bow shall be seene in the cloud.

15 And I will remember my couenant, which is betweene mee and you, and euery liuing creature of all flesh: and the waters shall no more become a flood to destroy all flesh.

16 And the bow shalbe in the cloud; and I will looke vpon it, that I may remember the euerlasting couenant betweene God and euery liuing creature, of all flesh that is vpon the earth.

17 And God said vnto Noah, This is the token of the couenant, which I haue established betweene mee and all flesh, that is vpon the earth.

18 ¶ And the sonnes of Noah that went forth of the Arke, were Shem, and Ham, and Iaphet: and Ham is the father of ‖ Canaan.

‖ Heb. Che-
naan.

19 These are the three sonnes of Noah: and of them was the whole earth ouerspread.

20 And Noah began to bee an husbandman, and he planted a vineyard.

21 And he dranke of the wine, and was drunken, and hee was vncouered within his tent.

22 And Ham, the father of Canaan, saw the nakednesse of his father, and told his two brethren without.

23 And Shem and Iaphet tooke a garment, and layed it vpon both their shoulders, and went backward, and couered the nakednesse of their father, and their faces were backward, and they saw not their fathers nakednesse.

24 And Noah awoke from his wine, and knew what his yonger sonne had done vnto him.

25 And he said, Cursed bee Canaan: a seruant of seruants shall hee be vnto his brethren.

26 And hee saide, Blessed bee the LORD God of Shem, and Canaan shalbe ‖ seruant.

27 God shall ‖ enlarge Iaphet, and he shal dwel in the tents of Shem, and Canaan shalbe his seruant.

‖ Or, seruant
to them.
¶ Or, per-
swade.

28 ¶ And Noah liued after the flood, three hundred and fifty yeeres.

29 And all the dayes of Noah were nine hundred & fifty yeeres, and he died.

CHAP. X.

1 The generations of Noah. 2 The sonnes of Iaphet. 6 The sonnes of Ham. 8 Nimrod the first Monarch. 21 The sonnes of Shem.

Ow these are the generations of the sonnes of Noah; Shem, Ham, and Iaphet: and vnto them were sonnes borne after the Flood.

2 * The sonnes of Iaphet: Gomer, and Magog, and Madai, and Iauan, & Tubal, and Meshech, & Tiras.

* 1. Chron.
1. 5.

3 And the sonnes of Gomer: Ashkenaz, and Riphath, and Togarmah.

4 And the sons of Iauan: Elishah, and Tarshish, Kittim, and Dodanim.

5 By these were the Iles of the Gentiles diuided in their lands, euery one after his tongue: after their families, in their nations.

6 ¶ *And the sonnes of Ham: Cush, and Mizraim, and Phut, and Canaan.

* 1. Chron.
1. 8.

7 And the sonnes of Cush, Seba, and Hauilah, and Sabtah, and Raamah, and Sabtecha: and the sonnes of Raamah: Sheba, and Dedan.

8 And Cush begat Nimrod: he began to be a mighty one in the earth.

9 He was a mighty hunter before the

the LORD: wherefore it is saide, Euen as Nimrod the mightie hunter before the LORD.

10 And the beginning of his king-dome was † Babel, and Erech, and Ac-cad, and Calneh, in the land of Shinar.

11 Out of that land ‖ went forth As-shur, and builded Nineueh, and the ‖ci-tie Rehoboth, and Calah,

12 And Resen betweene Nineueh and Calah: the same is a great citie.

13 And Mizraim begat Ludim, and Anamim, and Lehabim, and Naph-tuhim,

14 And Pathrusim, and Casluhim (out of whome came Philistiim) and Caphtorim.

15 ¶ And Canaan begate † Sidon his first borne, and Heth,

16 And the Jebusite, and the Emo-rite, and the Girgasite,

17 And the Hiuite, and the Arkite, and the Sinite,

18 And the Aruadite, and the Ze-marite, and the Hamathite: and after-ward were the families of the Canaa-nites spread abroad.

19 And the border of the Canaa-nites, was from Sidon, as thou com-mest to Gerar, vnto †Gaza, as thou go-est vnto Sodoma and Gomorah, and Admah, & Zeboim, euen vnto Lasha.

20 These are the sonnes of Ham, af-ter their families, after their tongues, in their countries, and in their nations.

21 ¶ Vnto Shem also the father of all the children of Eber, the brother of Iaphet the elder, euen to him were children borne.

22 The *children of Shem: Elam, and Asshur, and † Arphaxad, and Lud, and Aram.

23 And the children of Aram: Vz, and Hul, and Gether, and Mash.

24 And Arphaxad begate † Salah, and Salah begate Eber.

25 * And vnto Eber were borne two sonnes: the name of one was Peleg, for in his dayes was the earth diuided, and his brothers name was Joktan.

26 And Joktan begate Almodad, and Sheleph, and Hazarmaueth, and Ierah,

27 And Hadoram, and Vzal, and Diklah,

28 And Obal, and Abimael, and Sheba,

29 And Ophir, and Hauilah, & Io-bab: all these were the sonnes of Ioktan.

Marginal notes (left column):
† Gr. Baby-lon.
‖ Or, he went out into As-syria.
‖ Or, the streetesofthe Citie.

† Heb. Tzi-don.

† Hebr. Az-zah.

*1.Chron. 1.17.
† Hebr. Ar-pachshad.

† Hebr. She-lah.
* 1.Chron. 1. 19.

30 And their dwelling was from Mesha, as thou goest vnto Sephar, a mount of the East.

31 These are the sonnes of Shem, af-ter their families, after their tongues, in their lands after their nations.

32 These are the families of the sonnes of Noah after their generati-ons, in their nations: and by these were the nations diuided in the earth after the Flood.

CHAP. XI.

1 One language in the world. 3 The building of Babel. 5 The confusion of tongues. 10 The generations of Shem. 27 The genera-tions of Terah the father of Abram. 31 Te-rah goeth from Vr to Haran.

ANd *the whole earth was of one †language, and of one †speach.

2 And it came to passe as they iourneyed from the East, that they found a plaine in the land of Shinar, and they dwelt there.

3 And † they sayd one to another; Goe to, let vs make bricke, and † burne them thorowly. And they had bricke for stone, and slime had they for morter.

4 And they said; Goe to, let vs build vs a city and a tower, whose top may reach vnto heauen, and let vs make vs a name, lest we be scattered abroad vpon the face of the whole earth.

5 And the LORD came downe to see the city and the tower, which the children of men builded.

6 And the LORD said; Behold, the people is one, and they haue all one language: and this they begin to doe: and now nothing will be restrained from them, which they haue imagined to doe.

7 Goe to, let vs go downe, and there cōfound their language, that they may not vnderstand one anothers speech.

8 So the LORD scattered them abroad from thence, vpon the face of all the earth: and they left off to build the Citie.

9 Therefore is the name of it called † Babel, because the LORD did there confound the language of all the earth: and from thence did the LORD scat-ter them abroad vpon the face of all the earth.

10 ¶ * These are the generations of Shem. Shem was an hundred yeres old, and

Marginal notes (right column):
* Wis. 10.
† Hebr.lipp
†Heb.worɒ

† Heb.a me said to his neighbour
† Heb. bur them to a burning.

† That is, Confusio

* 1.Chron 1.17.

and begate Arphaxad two yeeres after the Flood.

11 And Shem liued, after he begate Arphaxad, fiue hundred yeeres, and begate sonnes and daughters.

12 And Arphaxad liued fiue and thirtie yeeres, and begate Salah.

13 And Arphaxad liued, after he begate Salah, foure hundred and three yeeres, and begate sonnes and daughters.

14 And Salah liued thirtie yeeres, and begate Eber.

15 And Salah liued, after hee begate Eber, foure hundred and three yeeres, and begate sonnes and daughters.

16 *And Eber liued foure and thirty yeeres, and begate * Peleg.

17 And Eber liued, after hee begate Peleg, foure hundred and thirtie yeres, and begate sonnes and daughters.

18 And Peleg liued thirtie yeeres, and begate Reu.

19 And Peleg liued, after hee begate Reu, two hundred and nine yeeres, and begate sonnes and daughters.

20 And Reu liued two and thirtie yeeres, and begate * Serug.

21 And Reu liued, after hee begate Serug, two hundreth and seuen yeres, and begate sonnes and daughters.

22 And Serug liued thirtie yeeres, and begate Nahor.

23 And Serug liued, after he begate Nahor, two hundred yeeres, and begat sonnes and daughters.

24 And Nahor liued nine and twentie yeeres, and begate * Terah.

25 And Nahor liued, after he begate Terah, an hundred & nineteene yeeres, and begate sonnes and daughters.

26 And Terah liued seuenty yeeres, and *begate Abram, Nahor, & Haran.

27 ¶ Now these *are* the generations of Terah: Terah begate Abram, Nahor, and Haran: And Haran begate Lot.

28 And Haran died, before his father Terah in the land of his natiuity, in Vr of the Chaldees.

29 And Abram and Nahor tooke them wiues: the name of Abrams wife *was* Sarai, and the name of Nahors wife, Milcah, the daughter of Haran, the father of Milcah, and the father of Iscah.

30 But Sarai was barren; she *had* no childe.

31 And Terah tooke Abram his

sonne, and Lot the sonne of Haran his sonnes sonne, and Sarai his daughter in lawe, his sonne Abrams wife, and they went foorth with them from * Vr of the Chaldees, to goe into the land of Canaan: and they came vnto Haran, and dwelt there.

32 And the dayes of Terah, were two hundred and fiue yeres: and Terah died in Haran.

CHAP. XII.

1 God calleth Abram, and blesseth him with a promise of Christ. 4 He departeth with Lot from Haran. 6 He iourneyeth through Canaan, 7 which is promised him in a vision. 10 Hee is driuen by a famine into Egypt. 11 Feare maketh him faine his wife to be his sister. 14 Pharaoh hauing taken her from him, by plagues is compelled to restore her.

Ow the * LORD had said vnto Abram, Get thee out of thy countrey, and from thy kinred, and from thy fathers house, vnto a land that I will shew thee.

2 And I will make of thee a great nation, and I wil blesse thee, and make thy name great; and thou shalt bee a blessing.

3 And I will blesse them that blesse thee, and curse him, that curseth thee: *and in thee shal all families of the earth be blessed.

4 So Abram departed, as the LORD had spoken vnto him, and Lot went with him: And Abram was seuentie and fiue yeeres old when he departed out of Haran.

5 And Abram tooke Sarai his wife, and Lot his brothers sonne, and all their substance that they had gathered, and the soules that they had gotten in Haran, and they went foorth to goe into the land of Canaan: and into the land of Canaan they came.

6 ¶ And Abram passed through the land, vnto the place of Sichem, vnto the plaine of Moreh. And the Canaanite *was* then in the land.

7 And the LORD appeared vnto Abram, and said, * Vnto thy seed wil I giue this land: and there builded hee an * altar vnto the LORD, who appeared vnto him.

8 And he remoued from thence vnto a mountaine, on the East of Beth-el, and pitched his tent *hauing* Beth-el on the

Marginal notes (left column)

Chron. 9.
'alled ke 3. 35. alec.

Luc. 5. 35 uch.

Luc. 3. 34. ara.

osh. 24. 2 'hron. 1.

Marginal notes (right column)

* Nehem. 9. 7. Iudith. 5. 7. acts. 7. 4.

* Acts. 7. 3.

* Chap. 18. 18. and 22. 18. acts. 3. 25. galat. 3. 8.

* Chap. 13. 15.

* Chap. 13 4.

the West, and Hai on the East: and there hee builded an altar vnto the LORD, and called vpon the Name of the LORD.

9 And Abram iourneyed, ‖going on still toward the South.

† Heb. in going and iourneying.

10 ¶ And there was a famine in the land, and Abram went downe into Egypt, to soiourne there: for the famine was grieuous in the land.

11 And it came to passe when he was come neere to enter into Egypt, that he said vnto Sarai his wife, Behold now, I know that thou art a faire woman to looke vpon.

12 Therefore it shall come to passe, when the Egyptians shall see thee, that they shall say, This is his wife: and they will kill me, but they will saue thee aliue.

13 Say, I pray thee, thou art my sister, that it may be wel with me, for thy sake; and my soule shall liue, because of thee.

14 ¶ And it came to passe, that when Abram was come into Egypt, the Egyptians beheld the woman, that shee was very faire.

15 The Princes also of Pharaoh saw her, and commended her before Pharaoh: and the woman was taken into Pharaohs house.

16 And he entreated Abram well for her sake: and he had sheepe, and oxen, and hee asses, and men seruants, and maid seruants, and shee asses, and camels.

17 And the LORD plagued Pharaoh & his house with great plagues, because of Sarai Abrams wife.

18 And Pharaoh called Abram, and said, What is this that thou hast done vnto me? Why diddest thou not tell me, that she was thy wife?

19 Why saidest thou, Shee is my sister? so I might haue taken her to mee to wife: now therfore behold, thy wife, take *her* and goe thy way.

20 And Pharaoh comanded *his* men concerning him: and they sent him away, and his wife, and all that he had,

CHAP. XIII.

1 Abram and Lot returne out of Egypt. 7 By disagreement they part asunder. 10 Lot goeth to wicked Sodom. 14 God renueth the promise to Abram. 18 He remoueth to Hebron, and there buildeth an Altar.

Nd Abram went vp out of Egypt, he and his wife, and all that he had, and Lot with him, into the South.

2 And Abram was very rich in cattell, in siluer, and in gold.

3 And hee went on his iourneyes from the South, euen to Beth-el, vnto the place where his tent had bene at the beginning, betweene Beth-el and Hai:

4 Vnto the *place of the altar, which he had made there at the first: and there Abram called on the Name of the LORD.

* Chap. 12. 7.

5 ¶ And Lot also which went with Abram, had flocks and heards, & tents.

6 And the land was not able to beare them, that they might dwell together: for their substance was great, so that they could not dwell together.

7 And there was a strife betweene the heardmen of Abrams cattell, and the heardmen of Lots cattell: And the Canaanite, and the Perizzite dwelled then in the land.

8 And Abram said vnto Lot, Let there be no strife, I pray thee, betweene mee and thee, and betweene my heardmen and thy heardmen: for wee bee † brethren.

† Hebr. men brethren.

9 Is not the whole land before thee? Separate thy selfe, I pray thee, from mee: if thou *wilt take* the left hand, then I will goe to the right: or if thou *depart* to the right hand, then I will goe to the left.

10 And Lot lifted vp his eyes, and beheld all the plaine of Iordane, that it was well watered euery where before the Lord destroyed Sodome and Gomorah, *euen* as the garden of the LORD, like the land of Egypt, as thou commest vnto Zoar.

11 Then Lot chose him all the plaine of Iordane: and Lot iourneyed East; and they separated themselues the one from the other.

12 Abram dwelled in the land of Canaan, and Lot dwelled in the cities of the plaine, and pitched his tent toward Sodome.

13 But the men of Sodome were wicked, and sinners before the LORD exceedingly.

14 ¶ And the LORD said vnto Abram, after that Lot was separated from him, Lift vp now thine eyes, and looke from the place where thou art, North-

Northward, and Southward, and Eastward, and Westward.

Chap. 12.
and 26.
deut. 34.

15 For all the land which thou seest, * to thee will I giue it, and to thy seede for euer.

16 And I will make thy seede as the dust of the earth: so that if a man can number the dust of the earth, then shall thy seed also be numbred.

17 Arise, walke through the land, in the length of it, and in the breadth of it: for I will giue it vnto thee.

Hebr.
ines.

18 Then Abram remoued his tent, and came and dwelt in the † plaine of Mamre, which is in Hebron, and built there an altar vnto the LORD.

CHAP. XIIII.

1 The battell of foure Kings against fiue. 11 Lot is taken prisoner. 14 Abram rescueth him. 18 Melchi-zedek blesseth Abram. 20 Abram giueth him tithe. 22 The rest of the spoile, his partners hauing had their portions, he restoreth to the King of Sodom.

Nd it came to passe in the dayes of Amraphel King of Shinar, Arioch King of Ellasar, Chedorlaomer King of Elam, and Tidal King of nations:

2 That these made warre with Bera King of Sodome, and with Birsha King of Gomorrah, Shinab King of Admah, and Shemeber King of Zeboiim, and the King of Bela, which is Zoar.

3 All these were ioyned together in the vale of Siddim; which is the salt Sea.

4 Twelue yeeres they serued Chedorlaomer, and in the thirteenth yeere they rebelled.

5 And in the fourteenth yeere came Chedorlaomer, and the Kings that were with him, and smote the Rephaims, in Ashteroth Karnaim, & the Zuzims in Ham, and the Emims in ‖Shaueh Kiriathaim;

r, the
ine of Ki-
athaim.

6 And the Horites in their mount Seir, vnto ‖El-Paran, which is by the wildernesse.

r, the
ine of
aran.

7 And they returned, and came to En-mishpat, which is Kadesh, & smote all the countrey of the Amalekites, and also the Amorites, that dwelt in Hazezon-tamar.

8 And there went out the King of Sodome, and the King of Gomorrah, and the King of Admah, and the King of Zeboiim, and the King of Bela, (the same is Zoar) and they ioyned battell with them, in the vale of Siddim,

9 With Chedorlaomer the King of Elam, and with Tidal King of nations, and Amraphel King of Shinar, and Arioch King of Ellasar; foure Kings with fiue.

10 And the vale of Siddim was full of slime-pits: and the Kings of Sodome & Gomorrah fled, and fell there: and they that remained, fled to the mountaine.

11 And they tooke all the goods of Sodome and Gomorrah, and all their victuals, and went their way.

12 And they tooke Lot, Abrams brothers sonne, (who dwelt in Sodome) and his goods, and departed.

13 ¶ And there came one that had escaped, and told Abram the Hebrew, for hee dwelt in the plaine of Mamre the Amorite, brother of Eshcol, and brother of Aner: and these were confederate with Abram.

14 And when Abram heard that his brother was taken captiue, he ‖ armed his ‖trained seruants borne in his owne house, three hundred and eighteene, and pursued them vnto Dan.

‖ Or, led foorth.
‖ Or, instructed.

15 And hee diuided himselfe against them, he and his seruants by night, and smote them, and pursued them vnto Hoba, which is on the left hand of Damascus:

16 And hee brought backe all the goods, and also brought againe his brother Lot, and his goods, and the women also, and the people.

17 ¶ And the king of Sodome went out to meete him, (after his returne from the slaughter of Chedorlaomer, and of the Kings that were with him) at the valley of Saueh, which is the * Kings dale.

* 2. Sam. 18.
18.
* Heb. 7. 1.

18 And * Melchizedek King of Salem brought foorth bread and wine: and he was the Priest of the most high God.

19 And hee blessed him, and saide; Blessed bee Abram of the most high God, possessour of heauen and earth,

20 And blessed bee the most high God, which hath deliuered thine enemies into thy hand: and hee gaue him * tithes of all.

* Heb. 7. 4.

21 And the King of Sodome said vnto Abram, giue me the † persons, and take

† Hebr.
soules.

take the goods to thy selfe.

22 And Abram said to the King of Sodome, I haue lift vp my hand vnto the LORD, the most high God, the possessour of heauen and earth,

23 That I wil not take from a threed euen to a shoe latchet, and that I will not take any thing that is thine, lest thou shouldest say, I haue made A-brain rich:

24 Saue onely that which the yong men haue eaten, and the portion of the men which went with mee, Aner, Es-chol, and Mamre; let them take their portion.

CHAP. XV.

1 God encourageth Abram. 2 Abram com-plaineth for want of an heire. 4 God pro-miseth him a sonne, and a multiplying of his seed. 6 Abram is iustified by faith. 7 Ca-naan is promised againe, and confirmed by a signe, 12 and a vision.

Fter these things, the word of the LORD came vnto Abram in a vi-sion, saying; Feare not, Abram: I am thy shield,

* Psal. 16. 16 *and* thy exceeding * great reward.

2 And Abram said, Lord GOD, what wilt thou giue me, seeing I goe childlesse? and the steward of my house *is* this Eliezer of Damascus.

3 And Abram said; Behold, to mee thou hast giuen no seed: and loe, one borne in my house is mine heire.

4 And behold, the word of the LORD *came* vnto him, saying; This shall not be thine heire: but he that shall come foorth out of thy owne bowels, shalbe thine heire.

5 And he brought him forth abroad, and said, Looke now towards hea-uen, and tell the starres, if thou be able to number them. And hee said vnto

* Rom. 4. 18. him, *So shall thy seed be.

* Rom. 4. 3. galat. 3. 6. iam. 2. 23. 6 And he *beleeued in the LORD; and hee counted it to him for righte-ousnesse.

7 And he said vnto him; I am the LORD that brought thee out of Vr of the Caldees, to giue thee this land, to inherit it.

8 And he said, Lord GOD, where-by shal I know that I shall inherit it?

9 And he said vnto him, Take me an heifer of three yeeres old, and a shee goat of three yeeres old, and a ramme of three yeeres old, and a turtle doue, and a yong pigeon.

10 And he tooke vnto him all these, and diuided them in the midst, and layd each peece one against another: but the birds diuided he not.

11 And when the fowles came downe vpon the carcases, Abram droue them away.

12 And when the Sunne was go-ing downe, a deepe sleepe fell vpon A-bram: and loe, an horrour of great darkenesse fell vpon him.

13 And he said vnto Abram, Know of a surety, *that thy seed shalbe a stran-ger, in a land that is not theirs, and shal serue them, and they shall afflict them foure hundred yeeres.

* Acts 7.

14 And also that nation whom they shall serue, wil I iudge: and afterward shall they come out with great sub-stance.

15 And thou shalt goe to thy fathers in peace; thou shalt be buried in a good old age.

16 But in the fourth generation they shall come hither againe: for the iniqui-tie of the Amorites is not yet full.

17 And it came to passe that when the Sunne went downe, and it was *darke*, behold, a smoking furnace, and a † burning lampe that passed betweene those pieces.

‖ Hebr. a lampe fire.

18 In that same day the LORD made a couenant with Abram, saying; *Vnto thy seed haue I giuen this land from the riuer of Egypt vnto the great riuer, the riuer Euphrates:

* Chap 7. and 15. & 20 deut. 34

19 The Kenites, and the Kenizites, and the Kadmonites:

20 And the Hittites, and the Pe-rizzites, and the Rephaims,

21 And the Amorites, and the Ca-naanites, and the Girgashites, and the Iebusites.

CHAP. XVI.

1 Sarai, being barren, giueth Hagar to Abram. 4 Hagar being afflicted for despising her mi-stresse, runneth away. 7 An Angel sendeth her backe to submit her selfe, 11 and telleth her of her child. 15 Ishmael is borne.

Ow Sarai Abrams wife bare him no children: and she had an handmaide, an Egyptian, whose name was Hagar.

2 And Sarai said vnto Abram, Be-hold now, the LORD hath restrai-ned me from bearing: I pray thee go in vnto my maid: it may bee that I may
† obtaine

† *Heb. bee builded by her.*

† obtaine children by her: and Abram hearkened to the voice of Sarai.

3 And Sarai Abrams wife, tooke Hagar her maid, the Egyptian, after Abram had dwelt ten yeeres in the land of Canaan, and gaue her to her husband Abram, to be his wife.

4 ¶ And he went in vnto Hagar, and she conceiued: And when shee saw that shee had conceiued, her mistresse was despised in her eyes.

5 And Sarai said vnto Abram, My wrong be vpon thee: I haue giuen my maid into thy bosome, and when shee saw that she had conceiued, I was despised in her eyes: the LORD iudge betweene me and thee.

6 But Abram said vnto Sarai, Behold, thy maid *is* in thy hand; doe to her † as it pleaseth thee. And when Sarai † dealt hardly with her, shee fled from her face.

† *Heb. that which is good in thy eyes.*
† *Heb. afflicted her.*

7 ¶ And the Angel of the LORD found her by a fountaine of water, in the wildernesse, by the fountaine, in the way to Shur:

8 And he said, Hagar Sarais maid, whence camest thou? and whither wilt thou goe? And she said, I flee from the face of my mistresse Sarai.

9 And the Angel of the LORD said vnto her, Returne to thy mistresse, and submit thy selfe vnder her hands.

10 And the Angel of the LORD said vnto her, I will multiply thy seede exceedingly, that it shall not be numbred for multitude.

11 And the Angel of the LORD said vnto her, Behold, thou art with child, and shalt beare a sonne, and shalt call his name ‖ Ishmael; because the LORD hath heard thy affliction.

‖ *That is, God shall heare.*

12 And he will be a wilde man; his hand will be against euery man, and euery mans hand against him: *and he shal dwell in the presence of all his brethren.

* *Chap. 25. 18.*

13 And shee called the name of the LORD that spake vnto her, Thou God seest me: for she said, Haue I also here looked after him that seeth me?

14 Wherefore the well was called, * ‖ Beer-lahai-roi: Behold, It is betweene Cadesh and Bered.

* *Chap. 24. 62.*
‖ *That is, the well of him that liueth and seeeth me.*

15 ¶ And Hagar bare Abram a sonne: and Abram called his sonnes name, which Hagar bare, Ishmael.

16 And Abram was fourescore and sixe yeeres old, when Hagar bare Ishmael to Abram.

CHAP XVII.

1 God reneweth the Couenant. 5 Abram his name is changed, in token of a greater blessing. 10 Circumcision is instituted. 15 Sarai her name is changed, and she blessed. 17 Izsaac is promised. 23 Abram and Ishmael are circumcised.

Nd when Abram was ninetie yeres old and nine, the LORD appeared to Abram, and said vnto him, I am the almightie God, *walke before me, and be thou ‖ perfect.

* *Chap. 5. 22.*
‖ *Or, vpright or sincere.*

2 And I wil make my couenant betweene me and thee, and will multiply thee exceedingly.

3 And Abram fell on his face, and God talked with him, saying,

4 As for me, behold, my couenant is with thee, and thou shalt be a *father of ‖ many nations.

† *Heb. multitude of nations.*

5 Neither shall thy name any more be called Abram, but thy name shall bee Abraham: *for a father of many nations haue I made thee.

* *Rom. 4. 17*

6 And I will make thee exceeding fruitfull, and I will make nations of thee, and Kings shall come out of thee.

7 And I will establish my couenant betweene me and thee, and thy seede after thee, in their generations for an euerlasting couenant, to bee a God vnto thee, and to thy seed after thee.

8 And I will giue vnto thee, and to thy seed after thee, the land † wherein thou art a stranger, all the land of Canaan, for an euerlasting possession, and I will be their God.

† *Heb. of thy soiournings.*

9 ¶ And God said vnto Abraham, Thou shalt keepe my couenant therefore, thou, and thy seede after thee, in their generations.

10 This is my couenant, which yee shall keepe betweene me and you, and thy seed after thee: *euery man-child among you shall be circumcised.

* *Acts 7. 8.*

11 And ye shall circumcise the flesh of your foreskinne: and it shal be a *token of the couenant betwixt me and you.

* *Acts 7. 8. rom. 4. 11.*

12 And he that is † eight dayes olde, *shalbe circumcised among you, euery man child in your generations, he that is borne in the house, or bought with money of any stranger, which is not of thy seed.

† *Hebr. a sonne of eight dayes.*
* *Leuit. 12. 3. luke 2. 21 iohn 7. 22.*

13 He that is borne in thy house, and he that is bought with thy money, must needs

needs be circumcised: and my couenant shall be in your flesh, for an euerlasting couenant.

14 And the vncircumcised man-child, whose flesh of his foreskinne is not circumcised, that soule shall be cut off from his people: hee hath broken my couenant.

15 ¶ And God said vnto Abraham, As for Sarai thy wife, thou shalt not call her name Sarai, but Sarah *shall her name be.*

16 And I will blesse her, and giue thee a sonne also of her: yea I wil blesse † *Hebr. she* her, and ‖she shalbe a *mother* of nations; *shall become nations.* Kings of people shall be of her.

17 Then Abraham fell vpon his face, and laughed, and said in his heart, Shall *a child* be borne vnto him that is an hundred yeeres old? and shal Sarah that is ninetie yeeres old, beare?

18 And Abraham said vnto God, O that Ishmael might liue before thee.

* *Chap. 18.* 19 And God said, * Sarah thy wife *10. and 21.* shall beare thee a sonne in deede, and *2.* thou shalt call his name Isaac: and I will establish my couenant with him, for an euerlasting couenant, *and* with his seed after him.

20 And as for Ishmael, I haue heard thee: behold, I haue blessed him, and will make him fruitfull, and will * *Gene. 25.* multiplie him exceedingly: * Twelue *12.* princes shall he beget, and I will make him a great nation.

21 But my couenant wil I establish with Isaac, which Sarah shall beare vnto thee, at this set time, in the next yeere.

22 And he left off talking with him, and God went vp from Abraham.

23 ¶ And Abraham tooke Ishmael his sonne, and all that were borne in his house, and all that were bought with his money, euery male, among the men of Abrahams house, and circumcised the flesh of their foreskinne, in the selfesame day, as God had said vnto him.

24 And Abraham *was* ninety yeeres old and nine, when he was circumcised in the flesh of his foreskinne.

25 And Ishmael his sonne *was* thirteene yeeres old, when he was circumcised in the flesh of his foreskinne.

26 In the selfe same day was Abraham circumcised, and Ishmael his sonne.

27 And all the men of his house, borne in the house, and bought with money of the stranger, were circumcised with him.

CHAP. XVIII.

1 Abraham entertaineth three Angels. 9 Sarah is reproued for laughing at the strange promise. 17 The destruction of Sodome is reuealed to Abraham. 23 Abraham maketh intercession for the men thereof.

ANd the * LORD appeared vnto him, in the * *Hebr. 13.* *2.* plaines of Mamre: and he sate in the tent doore, in the heat of the day.

2 And he lift vp his eyes and looked, and loe, three men stood by him: and when he saw *them*, hee ranne to meete them from the tent doore, and bowed himselfe toward the ground,

3 And said, My Lord, If now I haue found fauour in thy sight, passe not away, I pray thee, fro thy seruant:

4 Let a little water, I pray you, be fetched, and wash your feete, and rest your selues vnder the tree:

5 And I will fetch a morsell of bread; and † comfort ye your hearts, af- † *Hebr. stay* ter that you shall passe on: for therefore *†* are you come to your seruant. And † *Hebr. you haue passed* they said; So doe, as thou hast said.

6 And Abraham hastened into the tent, vnto Sarah, & said; † Make ready † *Hebr. Hasten.* quickly three measures of fine meale, knead *it*, and make cakes vpon the hearth.

7 And Abraham ranne vnto the heard, and fetcht a calfe, tender and good, and gaue it vnto a yong man: and he hasted to dresse it.

8 And he tooke butter, and milke, and the calfe which he had dressed, and set it before them; and he stood by them vnder the tree: and they did eate.

9 ¶ And they said vnto him, Where is Sarah thy wife? And he said, Behold, in the tent.

10 And he said, I will certainly returne vnto thee according to the time of life; and loe, * Sarah thy wife shall * *Chap. 17.* haue a sonne. And Sarah heard *it* in *19. and 21.* *2.* the tent doore, which was behind him.

11 Now Abraham and Sarah were old, and well stricken in age: *and* it ceased to be with Sarah after the maner of women.

12 Therefore Sarah laughed within her selfe, saying, After I am waxed old, shall I haue pleasure, my * lord be- * *1. Pet. 3.* ing old also? *6.*

13 And

13 And the LORD said vnto Abraham, Wherefore did Sarah laugh, saying; Shall I of a surety beare a childe, which am old?

14 Is any thing too hard for the LORD? At the time appointed will I returne vnto thee, according to the time of life, and Sarah shall haue a sonne.

15 Then Sarah denied, saying, I laughed not: for she was afraid. And he said, Nay, but thou diddest laugh.

16 ¶ And the men rose vp from thence, and looked toward Sodome: and Abraham went with them, to bring them on the way.

17 And the LORD said, Shall I hide from Abraham that thing which I doe;

18 Seeing that Abraham shall surely become a great and mighty nation, and all the nations of the earth shall be * blessed in him?

* Chap. 12. 3. and 22. 10. acts. 3. 25. galat. 3. 8.

19 For I know him, that hee will command his children, and his houshold after him, and they shall keepe the way of the LORD, to doe iustice and iudgement, that the LORD may bring vpon Abraham, that which hee hath spoken of him.

20 And the LORD said, Because the cry of Sodome and Gomorrah is great, and because their sinne is very grieuous:

21 I will goe downe now, and see whether they haue done altogether according to the cry of it, which is come vnto me: and if not, I will know.

22 And the men turned their faces from thence, and went toward Sodome: but Abraham stood yet before the LORD.

23 ¶ And Abraham drew neere, and said, Wilt thou also destroy the righteous with the wicked?

24 Peraduenture there be fifty righteous within the citie; wilt thou also destroy, and not spare the place for the fiftie righteous, that are therein?

25 That be farre from thee, to do after this maner, to slay the righteous with the wicked, and that the righteous should be as the wicked, that be farre from thee: Shall not the Iudge of all the earth doe right?

26 And the LORD said, If I find in Sodom fiftie righteous, within the citie, then I will spare all the place for their sakes.

27 And Abraham answered, and said, Behold now, I haue taken vpon me to speake vnto the LORD, which am but dust and ashes.

28 Peraduenture there shall lacke fiue of the fiftie righteous: wilt thou destroy all the citie for *lacke* of fiue? And he said, If I find there fourtie and fiue, I will not destroy *it.*

29 And hee spake vnto him yet againe, and said, Peraduenture there shall be fourtie found there: and he said, I will not doe *it* for fourties sake.

30 And he said vnto him, Oh let not the Lord be angry, and I will speake: Peraduenture there shall thirtie bee found there. And he said, I will not doe *it*, if I find thirtie there.

31 And he said, Behold now, I haue taken vpon mee to speake vnto the Lord: Peraduenture there shall bee twenty found there. And he said, I will not destroy *it* for twenties sake.

32 And hee saide, Oh let not the Lord be angry, and I will speake yet but *this* once: Peraduenture ten shall be found there. And he said, I will not destroy *it* for tennes sake.

33 And the LORD went his way, assoone as hee had left communing with Abraham: and Abraham returned vnto his place.

CHAP. XIX.

1 Lot entertaineth two Angels. 4 The vicious Sodomites are striken with blindnesse. 12 Lot is sent for safety into the mountaines. 18 Hee obtaineth leaue to goe into Zoar. 24 Sodome and Gomorrah are destroyed. 26 Lots wife is a pillar of salt. 30 Lot dwelleth in a caue. 31 The incestuous originall of Moab and Ammon.

Nd there came two Angels to Sodome at euen, and Lot sate in the gate of Sodome: and Lot seeing *them*, rose vp to meet them, and he bowed himselfe with his face toward the ground.

2 And he said, Beholde now my Lords, turne in, I pray you, into your seruants house, and tarie all night, and *wash your feete, and ye shall rise vp early and goe on your wayes. And they said, Nay: but we wil abide in the street all night.

* Chap. 18. 4.

3 And he pressed vpon them greatly, and they turned in vnto him, and entred into his house: and he made them
a feast,

a feast, and did bake vnleauened bread, and they did eate.

4 ¶ But before they lay downe, the men of the citie, *euen* the men of Sodom, compassed the house round, both old and yong, all the people from euery quarter.

5 And they called vnto Lot, and said vnto him, Where are the men which came in to thee this night? bring them out vnto vs, that we may know them.

6 And Lot went out at the doore vnto them, & shut the doore after him,

7 And said, I pray you, brethren, doe not so wickedly.

8 Behold now, I haue two daughters, which haue not knowen man; let mee, I pray you, bring them out vnto you, and doe ye to them, as is good in your eyes: onely vnto these men do nothing: for therefore came they vnder the shadow of my roofe.

9 And they said, Stand backe. And they said againe, This one *fellow* came in to soiourne, and he will needs bee a Iudge: Now wil we deale worse with thee, then with them. And they pressed sore vpon the man, *euen* Lot, and came neere to breake the doore.

10 But the men put forth their hand, and pulled Lot into the house to them, and shut to the doore.

* Wisd. 19. 16.

11 And they smote the men * that *were* at the doore of the house, with blindnes, both small and great: so that they wearied themselues to finde the doore.

12 ¶ And the men said vnto Lot, Hast thou here any besides? sonne in law, and thy sonnes, and thy daughters, and whatsoeuer thou hast in the citie, bring *them* out of this place.

* Chap. 18. 20.

13 For we will destroy this place, because the * crie of them is waxen great before the face of the LORD: and the LORD hath sent vs to destroy it.

14 And Lot went out, and spake vnto his sonnes in law, which married his daughters, and said, Vp, get yee out of this place: for the LORD wil destroy this citie: but hee seemed as one that mocked, vnto his sonnes in law.

15 ¶ And when the morning arose, then the Angels hastened Lot, saying, Arise, take thy wife, & thy two daughters, which † are here, lest thou be consumed in the ‖iniquitie of the citie.

† Heb. are found.
‖ Or, punishment.
* Wisd. 10. 6.

16 And * while he lingred, the men laid hold vpon his hand, and vpon the hand of his wife, and vpon the hand of his two daughters, the LORD being mercifull vnto him: and they brought him forth, and set him without the citie.

17 ¶ And it came to passe, when they had brought them forth abroad, that he said, Escape for thy life, looke not behind thee, neither stay thou in all the plaine: escape to the mountaine, lest thou bee consumed.

18 And Lot said vnto them, Oh not so, my Lord.

19 Beholde now, thy seruant hath found grace in thy sight, and thou hast magnified thy mercy, which thou hast shewed vnto me, in sauing my life, and I cannot escape to the mountaine, lest some euill take me, and I die.

20 Behold now, this citie is neere to flee vnto, and it is a litle one: Oh let me escape thither, (is it not a litle one?) and my soule shall liue.

21 And he said vnto him, See, I haue accepted † thee concerning this thing, that I will not ouerthrow this citie, for the which thou hast spoken.

† Heb. thy face.

22 Haste thee, escape thither: for I cannot doe any thing till thou bee come thither: therefore the name of the citie was called Zoar.

23 ¶ The sunne was † risen vpon the earth, when Lot entred into Zoar.

† Hebr. gone forth.

24 Then * the LORD rained vpon Sodome & vpon Gomorrah, brimstone and fire, from the LORD out of heauen.

* Deut. 29. 23. luk. 17. 29. isa. 13. 19. ier. 50. 40. amos 4. 11. Iude 7.

25 And he ouerthrew those cities, and all the plaine, and all the inhabitants of the cities, and that which grew vpon the ground.

26 ¶ But his wife looked backe from behind him, and she became a pillar of salt.

27 ¶ And Abraham gate vp earely in the morning, to the place, where hee stood before the LORD.

28 And he looked toward Sodome and Gomorrah, & toward all the land of the plaine, and beheld, and loe, the smoke of the countrey went vp as the smoke of a furnace.

29 ¶ And it came to passe, when God destroyed the cities of the plaine, that God remembred Abraham, and sent Lot out of the midst of the ouerthrow, when he ouerthrew the cities, in the which Lot dwelt.

30 ¶ And Lot went vp out of Zoar, and dwelt in the mountaine, and his two

two daughters with him: for hee feared to dwell in Zoar, and he dwelt in a caue, he and his two daughters.

31 And the first borne saide vnto the yonger, Our father is old, and there is not a man in the earth, to come in vnto vs, after the maner of all the earth.

32 Come, let vs make our father drinke wine, and we will lye with him, that we may preserue seed of our father.

33 And they made their father drinke wine that night, & the first borne went in, and lay with her father: and he perceiued not, when shee lay downe, nor when she arose.

34 And it came to passe on the morrow, that the first borne said vnto the yonger, Behold, I lay yesternight with my father: let vs make him drinke wine this night also, and goe thou in, and lye with him, that we may preserue seed of our father.

35 And they made their father drinke wine that night also, and the yonger arose, and lay with him: and he perceiued not, when she lay downe, nor when she arose.

36 Thus were both the daughters of Lot with childe by their father.

37 And the first borne bare a sonne, and called his name Moab: the same is the father of the Moabites vnto this day.

38 And the yonger, she also bare a sonne, and called his name, Ben-ammi: the same is the father of the children of Ammon, vnto this day.

CHAP. XX.

1 Abraham soiourneth at Gerar, 2 denieth his wife, and loseth her. 3 Abimelech is reproued for her in a dreame. 9 He rebuketh Abraham, 14 restoreth Sarah, 16 and reprooueth her. 17 Hee is healed by Abrahams prayer.

ANd Abraham iourneyed from thence, toward the South - Countrey, and dwelled betweene Cadesh and Shur, and soiourned in Gerar.

2 And Abraham said of Sarah his wife, She is my sister: And Abimelech King of Gerar sent, and tooke Sarah.

3 But God came to Abimelech in a dreame by night, and said to him, Behold, thou *art but* a dead man, for the woman which thou hast taken: for shee is † a mans wife.

† Heb. married to an husband.

4 But Abimelech had not come neere her: and he said, LORD, wilt thou slay also a righteous nation?

5 Said he not vnto me, She is my sister? and she, euen she herselfe said, Hee is my brother: in the ||integritie of my heart, and innocencie of my hands haue I done this.

|| Or, simplicitie or sinceritie.

6 And God saide vnto him in a dreame, Yea, I know that thou didst this in the integritie of thy heart: for I also withheld thee from sinning against mee, therefore suffered I thee not to touch her.

7 Now therefore restore the man his wife: for he is a Prophet, and he shal pray for thee, and thou shalt liue: and if thou restore her not, know thou that thou shalt surely die, thou, and all that are thine.

8 Therefore Abimelech rose earely in the morning, and called all his seruants, and told all these things in their eares: and the men were sore afraid.

9 Then Abimelech called Abraham, and said vnto him, What hast thou done vnto vs? and what haue I offended thee, that thou hast brought on me, and on my kingdome a great sinne? thou hast done deeds vnto mee that ought not to be done.

10 And Abimelech said vnto Abraham, What sawest thou, that thou hast done this thing?

11 And Abraham said, Because I thought, Surely the feare of God is not in this place: and they will slay mee for my wiues sake.

12 And yet indeed shee is my sister: she *is* the daughter of my father, but not the daughter of my mother; and shee became my wife.

13 And it came to passe when God caused me to wander from my fathers house, that I said vnto her, This *is* thy kindnesse which thou shalt shew vnto me; at euery place whither wee shall come, *say of me, He is my brother.

* Chap. 12. 13.

14 And Abimelech tooke sheepe and oxen, and men-seruants, and women-seruants, and gaue them vnto Abraham, and restored him Sarah his wife.

15 And Abimelech said, Behold, my land *is* before thee; dwel † where it pleaseth thee.

† Heb. as is good in thine eyes.

16 And vnto Sarah hee said, Behold, I haue giuen thy brother a thousand *pieces* of siluer: behold, he *is* to thee a couering of the eyes, vnto all that are with

with thee, and with all *other*: thus shee was reproued.

17 ¶ So Abraham prayed vnto God: and God healed Abimelech, and his wife, and his maid-seruants, and they bare children.

18 For the LORD had fast closed vp all the wombes of the house of Abimelech, because of Sarah Abrahams wife.

CHAP. XXI.

1 Isaac is borne. 4 He is circumcised. 6 Sarahs ioy. 9 Hagar & Ishmael are cast forth. 15 Hagar in distresse. 17 The Angel comforteth her. 22 Abimelechs couenant with Abraham at Beer-sheba.

*Chap. 17. 19. and 18. 10.
*Acts 7. 8. Gal. 4. 22. Heb. 11. 11

ANd the LORD visited Sarah as he had said, and the LORD did vnto Sarah *as he had spoken.

2 For Sarah *conceiued, and bare Abraham a sonne in his old age, at the set time, of which God had spoken to him.

3 And Abraham called the name of his sonne, that was borne vnto him, whom Sarah bare to him, Isaac.

*Chap. 17. 12.

4 And Abraham circumcised his sonne Isaac, being eight dayes old, *as God had commanded him.

5 And Abraham was an hundred yeeres old, when his sonne Isaac was borne vnto him.

6 ¶ And Sarah said, God hath made me to laugh, *so that* all that heare, will laugh with me.

7 And she said, Who would haue said vnto Abraham, that Sarah should haue giuen children sucke? for I haue borne *him* a sonne in his old age.

8 And the child grew, and was weaned: and Abraham made a great feast, the *same* day that Isaac was weaned.

9 ¶ And Sarah saw the sonne of Hagar the Egyptian, which shee had borne vnto Abraham, mocking.

*Gal. 4. 30

10 Wherfore she said vnto Abraham, *Cast out this bond woman, and her sonne: for the sonne of this bond woman shall not be heire with my sonne, *euen* with Isaac.

11 And the thing was very grieuous in Abrahams sight, because of his sonne.

12 ¶ And God said vnto Abraham, Let it not be grieuous in thy sight, because of the lad, and because of thy bond woman. In all that Sarah hath said

vnto thee, hearken vnto her voice: for in Isaac shall thy seed be called.

13 And also, of the sonne of the bond woman will I make a nation, because he is thy seed.

14 And Abraham rose vp earely in the morning, and tooke bread, and a bottle of water, and gaue it vnto Hagar, (putting it on her shoulder,) and the child, and sent her away: and shee departed, and wandered in the wildernesse of Beer-sheba.

15 And the water was spent in the bottle, and shee cast the child vnder one of the shrubs.

16 And she went, and sate her downe ouer against *him*, a good way off, as it were a bow shoot: for she said, Let me not see the death of the child. And shee sate ouer against *him*, and lift vp her voice, and wept.

17 And God heard the voice of the lad, and the Angel of God called to Hagar out of heauen, and said vnto her, What aileth thee, Hagar? feare not: for God hath heard the voice of the ladde, where he is.

18 Arise, lift vp the lad, and hold him in thine hand: for I will make him a great nation.

19 And God opened her eyes, and she saw a well of water, and shee went, and filled the bottle with water, and gaue the lad drinke.

20 And God was with the lad, and he grew, and dwelt in the wildernesse, and became an archer.

21 And hee dwelt in the wildernesse of Paran: and his mother tooke him a wife out of the land of Egypt.

22 ¶ And it came to passe at that time, that Abimelech and Phichol the chiefe captaine of his hoste spake vnto Abraham, saying, God *is* with thee in all that thou doest.

23 Now therefore sweare vnto mee here by God, that thou wilt not †deale falsly with me, nor with my sonne, nor with my sonnes sonne: *but* according to the kindnesse that I haue done vnto thee, thou shalt doe vnto me, and to the land wherein thou hast soiourned.

† Hebrew, if thou shalt lie vnto me.

24 And Abraham saide, I will sweare.

25 And Abraham reproued Abimelech, because of a well of water, which Abimelechs seruants had violently taken away.

26 And Abimelech saide, I wote not

not who hath done this thing: neither didſt thou tell me, neither yet heard I of it, but to day.

27 And Abraham tooke sheepe and oxen, and gaue them vnto Abimelech: and both of them made a couenant.

28 And Abraham set seuen ewe lambes of the flocke by themselues

29 And Abimelech said vnto Abraham , What meane these seuen ewe lambes, which thou hast set by themselues?

30 And he said, For these seuen ewe lambs shalt thou take of my hand, that they may be a witnesse vnto me, that I haue digged this well

That is, the well of the othe.

31 Wherefore he called that place, ||Beer-sheba: because there they sware both of them.

32 Thus they made a couenant at Beeer-sheba: then Abimelech rose vp, and Phichol the chiefe captaine of his hoste, and they returned into the land of the Philistines.

Or, Tree

33 ¶ And *Abraham* planted a ||groue in Beer-sheba, and called there on the Name of the LORD, the euerlaſting God.

34 And Abraham soiourned in the Philistines land, many dayes.

CHAP. XXII

1 Abraham is tempted to offer Isaac. 3 Hee giueth proofe of his faith and obedience. 11 The Angel stayeth him. 13 Isaac is exchanged with a ramme. 14 The place is called Iehouah-ijreh. 15 Abraham is blessed againe. 20 The generation of Nahor vnto Rebekah.

Hebr. 11.

Hebr. Behold me.

ANd it came to passe after these things, that *God did tempt Abraham, and said vnto him, Abraham. And hee said, †Beholde, heere I am.

2 And he said, Take now thy ſonne, thine onely *ſonne* Isaac, whom thou loueſt, and get thee into the land of Moriah: and offer him there for a burnt offering vpon one of the Mountaines which I will tell thee of.

3 ¶ And Abraham rose vp earely in the morning, and sadled his asse, and tooke two of his yong men with him, and Isaac his ſonne, and claue the wood for the burnt offering, and rose vp, and went vnto the place of which God had told him.

4 Then on the third day Abraham lift vp his eyes, and saw the place afarre off

5 And Abraham said vnto his yong men, Abide you here with the asse, and I and the lad will goe yonder and worship, and come againe to you.

6 And Abraham tooke the wood of the burnt offering, and layd it vpon Isaac his sonne: and he tooke the fire in his hand, and a knife: and they went both of them together.

7 And Isaac spake vnto Abraham his father, and said, My father: and he said, †Here am I, my sonne. And hee said, Behold the fire and wood: but where is the ||lambe for a burnt offring?

† Hebr. behold me.

‖ Or, kidde.

8 And Abraham said , My sonne, God will prouide himselfe a lambe for a burnt offering: so they went both of them together.

9 And they came to the place which God had tolde him of, and Abraham built an Altar there, and layd the wood in order, and bound Isaac his sonne, and *layde him on the Altar vpon the wood.

* Iam. 2. 21.

10 And Abraham stretched foorth his hand, and tooke the knife to slay his sonne.

11 And the Angel of the LORD called vnto him out of heauen, and said, Abraham, Abraham. And he said, Here am I.

12 And he said, Lay not thine hand vpon the lad, neither do thou any thing vnto him : for now I know that thou fearest God, seeing thou hast not withhelde thy sonne , thine onely sonne from mee.

13 And Abraham lifted vp his eyes, and looked, and beholde, behinde *him* a Ramme caught in a thicket by his hornes: And Abraham went and tooke the Ramme, and offered him vp for a burnt offering, in the stead of his sonne.

14 And Abraham called the name of that place ||Iehouah-ijreh, as it is said to this day, In the Mount of the LORD it shalbe seene.

‖ That is, The LORD will see, or, prouide.

15 ¶ And the Angel of the LORD called vnto Abraham out of heauen the second time,

16 And said, * By my selfe haue I sworne, saith the LORD, for because thou hast done this thing, and hast not withheld thy sonne, thine onely sonne,

* Psal. 105. 9. ecclus. 44. 21. luke 1. 73. hebr. 6. 13.

17 That in blessing I will blesse thee, and in multiplying, I will multiply

tiply thy seed as the starres of the heauen, and as the sand which is vpon the sea †shore, and thy seed shall possesse the gate of his enemies.

† Heb. lippe.

18 * And in thy seed shall all the nations of the earth be blessed, because thou hast obeyed my voice.

* Chap. 12.
3. and 18.
18. ecclus.
44. 22. acts.
3. 25, galat.
3. 8.

19 So Abraham returned vnto his yong men, and they rose vp, and went together to Beer-sheba, and Abraham dwelt at Beer-sheba.

20 ¶ And it came to passe after these things, that it was told Abraham, saying, Behold Milcah, shee hath also borne children vnto thy brother Nahor,

21 Huz his first borne, and Buz his brother, and Kemuel the father of Aram,

22 And Chesed, and Hazo, and Pildash, and Iidlaph, and Bethuel.

23 And Bethuel begate * Rebekah: these eight Milcah did beare to Nahor, Abrahams brother.

* Called
Rom. 9.10.
Rebecca.

24 And his concubine whose name was Reumah, she bare also to Tebah, and Gaham, and Thahash, and Maachah.

CHAP. XXIII.

1 The age and death of Sarah. 3 The purchase of Machpelah, 19 where Sarah was buried.

 Nd Sarah was an hundred and seuen and twenty yeeres olde: *these were* the yeeres of the life of Sarah.

2 And Sarah died in Kiriath-arba, the same is Hebron in the land of Canaan: And Abraham came to mourne for Sarah, and to weepe for her.

3 ¶ And Abraham stood vp from before his dead, & spake vnto the sonnes of Heth, saying,

4 I am a stranger and a soiourner with you: giue me a possession of a burying place with you, that I may bury my dead out of my sight.

5 And the children of Heth answered Abraham, saying vnto him,

6 Heare vs, my Lord, thou art a † mightie Prince amongst vs: in the choise of our sepulchres bury thy dead: none of vs shall withhold from thee his sepulchre, but that thou mayest bury thy dead.

† Hebr. a
Prince of
God.

7 And Abraham stood vp and bowed himselfe to the people of the land, *euen* to the children of Heth.

8 And hee communed with them,

saying, if it be your mind that I should bury my dead out of my sight, heare me, and entreat for me to Ephron the sonne of Zohar:

9 That he may giue me the caue of Machpelah, which he hath, which *is* in the end of his field: for †as much money as it is worth he shall giue it mee, for a possession of a burying place amongst you.

† Hebr. full
money.

10 And Ephron dwelt amongst the children of Heth. And Ephron the Hittite answered Abraham in the †audience of the children of Heth, *euen* of all that went in at the gates of his citie, saying,

† Hebr. eare

11 Nay, my lord, heare mee: the field giue I thee, and the caue that *is* therein, I giue it thee, in the presence of the sonnes of my people giue I it thee: bury thy dead.

12 And Abraham bowed downe himselfe before the people of the land.

13 And he spake vnto Ephron in the audience of the people of the land, saying, But if thou wilt *giue it*, I pray thee, heare mee: I will giue thee money for the field: take it of me, and I will bury my dead there.

14 And Ephron answered Abraham, saying vnto him,

15 My lord, hearken vnto mee: the land is worth foure hundred shekels of siluer: what is that betwixt mee and thee? bury therefore thy dead.

16 And Abraham hearkened vnto Ephron, and Abraham weighed to Ephron the siluer, which he had named, in the audience of the sonnes of Heth, foure hundred shekels of siluer, currant *money* with the merchant.

17 ¶ And the field of Ephron which *was* in Machpelah, which *was* before Mamre, the fielde and the caue which *was* therein, and all the trees that were in the field, that were in all the borders round about, were made sure

18 Vnto Abraham for a possession in the presence of the children of Heth, before all that went in at the gates of his Citie.

19 And after this Abraham buried Sarah his wife in the caue of the field of Machpelah, before Mamre: the same is Hebron in the land of Canaan.

20 And the field, and the caue that *is* therein, were made sure vnto Abraham, for a possession of a burying place, by the sonnes of Heth.

CHAP.

CHAP. XXIIII.

1 Abraham sweareth his seruant. 10 The seruants iourney: 12 His prayer: 14 His
signe. 15 Rebekah meeteth him, 18 ful-
filleth his signe, 22 receiueth iewels, 23
sheweth her kinred, 25 and inuiteth him
home. 26 The seruant blesseth God. 28 Laban enterteineth him. 34 The seruant sheweth his message. 50 Laban and Bethuel approue it. 58 Rebekah consenteth to goe.
62 Isaac meeteth her.

*Hebr. gone
into dayes.

ANd Abraham was olde
and † well stricken in age:
And the LORD had
blessed Abraham in all
things.

*Chap. 47.
29.

2 And Abraham said vnto his eldest
seruant of his house, that ruled ouer all
that he had, * Put, I pray thee, thy
hand vnder my thigh:

3 And I will make thee sweare by
the LORD the God of heauen, and
the God of the earth, that thou shalt
not take a wife vnto my sonne of the
daughters of the Canaanites amongst
whom I dwell.

4 But thou shalt go vnto my countrey, and to my kinred, and take a wife
vnto my sonne Isaac.

5 And the seruant said vnto him,
Peraduenture the woman will not bee
willing to follow mee vnto this land:
must I needes bring thy sonne againe,
vnto the land from whence thou camest?

6 And Abraham said vnto him, Beware thou, that thou bring not my
sonne thither againe.

7 ¶ The LORD God of heauen
which tooke mee from my fathers
house, and from the land of my kindred,
and which spake vnto me, and that

*Chap. 12.
7. and 13.
15. and 15.
18. and 26.
4.

sware vnto me, saying, * Vnto thy seed
will I giue this land, he shall send his
Angel before thee, and thou shalt take a
wife vnto my sonne from thence.

8 And if the woman wil not be willing to follow thee, then thou shalt bee
cleare from this my othe: onely bring
not my sonne thither againe.

9 And the seruant put his hand vnder the thigh of Abraham his master,
and sware to him concerning that
matter.

|Or, And

10 ¶ And the seruant tooke ten camels, of the camels of his master, and
departed, (||for all the goods of his ma-
ster were in his hand) and he arose, and

went to Mesopotamia, vnto the citie
of Nahor.

11 And he made his camels to kneele
downe without the citie, by a well of
water, at the time of the euening, *euen*
the time † that women goe out to draw
water.

† Hebr. that
wome which
draw water,
goe foorth.

12 And he said, O LORD, God of
my master Abraham, I pray thee send
me good speed this day, and shew kindnesse vnto my master Abraham.

13 Behold, * I stand here by the well
of water; and the daughters of the
men of the Citie come out to draw
water:

* Vers. 43.

14 And let it come to passe, that the
damsell to whom I shall say, Let
downe thy pitcher, I pray thee, that I
may drinke, and she shall say, Drinke,
and I will giue thy camels drinke also;
let the same be shee that thou hast appointed for thy seruant Isaac: and
thereby shall I know that thou hast
shewed kindnesse vnto my master.

15 ¶ And it came to passe before hee
had done speaking, that behold, Rebekah came out, who was borne to Bethuel, sonne of Milcah, the wife of Nahor Abrahams brother, with her pitcher vpon her shoulder.

16 And the damsell was † very faire
to looke vpon, a virgine, neither had a-
ny man knowen her; and shee went
downe to the wel, and filled her pitcher,
and came vp.

† Hebr. good
of counte-
nance.

17 And the seruant ranne to meete
her, and said, Let mee (I pray thee)
drinke a little water of thy pitcher.

18 And she said, Drinke, my lord: and
she hasted, and let downe her pitcher
vpon her hand, and gaue him drinke.

19 And when shee had done giuing
him drinke, she said, I will draw water
for thy camels also, vntill they haue
done drinking.

20 And she hasted and emptied her
pitcher into the trough, and ranne a-
gaine vnto the well to draw *water*, and
drew for all his camels.

21 And the man wondering at her,
helde his peace, to wit, whether the
LORD had made his iourney prosperous, or not.

22 And it came to passe as the camels
had done drinking, that the man tooke
a golden || eare-ring, of halfe a shekel
weight, & two bracelets for her handes,
of ten *shekels* weight of gold,

|| Or, iewell
for the fore-
head.

23 And said, Whose daughter art
thou?

thou? tell mee, I pray thee: is there roome in thy fathers house for vs to lodge in?

24 And she said vnto him, I am the daughter of Bethuel the sonne of Milcah, which she bare vnto Nahor:

25 She said moreouer vnto him, We haue both straw & prouender ynough, and roome to lodge in.

26 And the man bowed downe his head, and worshipped the LORD.

27 And hee saide, Blessed *bee* the LORD God of my master Abraham, who hath not left destitute my master of his mercy, and his trueth: I being in the way, the LORD led me to the house of my masters brethren.

28 And the damsell ranne, and told *them of* her mothers house, these things.

29 ¶ And Rebekah had a brother, and his name *was* Laban: and Laban ranne out vnto the man, vnto the well.

30 And it came to passe when he saw the eare-ring, and bracelets vpon his sisters hands, and when hee heard the wordes of Rebekah his sister, saying, Thus spake the man vnto me, that he came vnto the man; and behold, hee stood by the camels, at the well.

31 And he said, Come in, thou blessed of the LORD, wherefore standest thou without? for I haue prepared the house, and roome for the camels.

32 ¶ And the man came into the house: and he vngirded his camels, and gaue straw and prouender for the camels, and water to wash his feet, and the mens feet that *were* with him.

33 And there was set *meat* before him to eate: but he said, I will not eate, vntill I haue tolde mine errand. And hee said, Speake on.

34 And he said, I *am* Abrahams seruant.

35 And the LORD hath blessed my master greatly, and hee is become great: and hee hath giuen him flocks, and heards, and siluer, and gold, and men seruants, and mayd seruants, and camels, and asses.

36 And Sarah my masters wife bare a sonne to my master when shee was old: and vnto him hath hee giuen all that he hath.

37 And my master made me sweare, saying, Thou shalt not take a wife to my sonne, of the daughters of the Canaanites, in whose land I dwell:

38 But thou shalt goe vnto my fa-

thers house, and to my kinred, and take a wife vnto my sonne.

39 And I said vnto my master, Peraduenture the woman will not followe me.

40 And hee saide vnto me, The LORD, before whom I walke, will send his Angel with thee, and prosper thy way: and thou shalt take a wife for my sonne, of my kinred, and of my fathers house.

41 Then shalt thou bee cleare from this my oath, when thou commest to my kinred, and if they giue not thee *one,* thou shalt be cleare from my oath.

42 And I came this day vnto the well, and said, O LORD God of my master Abraham, if now thou doe prosper my way, which I goe:

43 *Behold, I stand by the well of water; and it shall come to passe, that when the virgine commeth foorth to draw *water*, and I say to her, Giue me, I pray thee, a litle water of thy pitcher to drinke;

44 And she say to me, Both drinke thou, and I will also draw for thy camels: let the same be the woman, who the LORD hath appointed out for my masters sonne.

45 And before I had done speaking in mine heart, behold, Rebekah came forth, with her pitcher on her shoulder; and she went downe vnto the well, and drew *water:* and I said vnto her, Let me drinke, I pray thee.

46 And she made haste, & let downe her pitcher from her *shoulder*, and saide, Drinke, and I will giue thy camels drinke also: so I dranke, and she made the camels drinke also.

47 And I asked her, and said, Whose daughter art thou? and she said, The daughter of Bethuel, Nahors sonne, whom Milcah bare vnto him: and I put the earering vpon her face, and the bracelets vpon her hands.

48 And I bowed downe my head, and worshipped the LORD, and blessed the LORD God of my master Abraham, which had led mee in the right way to take my masters brothers daughter vnto his sonne.

49 And now if you wil deale kindly and truely with my master, tell me: and if not, tell me, that I may turne to the right hand, or to the left.

50 Then Laban and Bethuel answered and said, The thing proceedeth from

* Verse 13.

from the LORD: we cannot speake
vnto thee bad or good.

51 Behold, Rebekah is before thee,
take *her*, and goe, and let her be thy masters sonnes wife, as the LORD hath
spoken.

52 And it came to passe, that when
Abrahams seruant heard their words,
he worshipped the LORD, *bowing*
himselfe to the earth.

53 And the seruant brought foorth
† iewels of siluer, and iewels of gold,
and raiment, and gaue *them* to Rebekah: He gaue also to her brother, and
to her mother precious things.

54 And they did eate and drinke, he
and the men that were with him, and
taried all night, and they rose vp in the
morning, and he said, * Send me away
vnto my master.

55 And her brother and her mother
said, Let the damsell abide with vs
|| *a few* dayes, at the least ten; after that,
she shall goe.

56 And he said vnto them, Hinder
me not, seeing the LORD hath prospered my way: send me away, that I
may goe to my master.

57 And they said, Wee will call the
Damsell, and enquire at her mouth.

58 And they called Rebekah, and said
vnto her, Wilt thou go with this man?
and she said, I will goe.

59 And they sent away Rebekah
their sister, and her nurse, and Abrahams seruant, and his men.

60 And they blessed Rebekah, and
said vnto her, Thou art our sister, bee
thou *the mother* of thousands of milli-
ons, and let thy seed possesse the gate of
those which hate them.

61 ¶ And Rebekah arose, and her
damsels, & they rode vpon the camels,
and followed the man: and the seruant
tooke Rebekah, and went his way.

62 And Isaac came from the way
of the *well Lahai-roi, for he dwelt in
the South countrey.

63 And Isaac went out, to || meditate
in the field, at the euentide: and hee lift
vp his eyes, and saw, and behold, the
camels were comming.

64 And Rebekah lift vp her eyes,
and when she saw Isaac, she lighted off
the camel.

65 For she had said vnto the seruant,
What man is this that walketh in the
field to meet vs? and the seruant had
said, It is my master: therefore shee

tooke a vaile and couered her selfe.

66 And the seruant tolde Isaac all
things that he had done.

67 And Isaac brought her into his
mother Sarahs tent, and tooke Rebekah, and she became his wife, and he loued her: and Isaac was comforted after his mothers *death*.

CHAP. XXV.

1 The sonnes of Abraham by Keturah. 5 The
diuision of his goods. 7 His age and death.
9 His buriall. 12 The generations of Ishmael. 17 His age, and death. 19 Isaac
prayeth for Rebekah being barren. 22 The
children striue in her wombe. 24 The birth
of Esau and Iacob. 27 Their difference. 29
Esau selleth his birthright.

Hen againe Abraham
tooke a wife, & her name
was Keturah.

2 And shee bare him
Zimran, and Iokshan,
and Medan, and Midian, and Ishbak,
and Shuah.

3 And * Iokshan begat Sheba, and
Dedan. And the sonnes of Dedan *were*
Asshurim, and Letushim, and Leum-
mim.

4 And the sonnes of Midian, E-
phah, and Epher, and Hanoch, and A-
bida, and Eldaah: all these were the
children of Keturah.

5 ¶ And Abraham gaue all that he
had, vnto Isaac.

6 But vnto the sonnes of the concubines which Abraham had, Abraham gaue gifts, and sent them away
from Isaac his sonne (while he yet liued) Eastward, vnto the East country.

7 And these *are* the dayes of the
yeres of Abrahams life which he liued;
an hundred, threescore & fifteene yeeres.

8 Then Abraham gaue vp the ghost,
and died in a good old age, an old man,
and full *of yeeres*, and was gathered to
his people.

9 And his sonnes Isaac and Ishmael buried him in the caue of Machpelah, in the field of Ephron the sonne
of Zohar the Hittite, which *is* before
Mamre;

10 *The field which Abraham purchased of the sonnes of Heth: there was
Abraham buried, and Sarah his wife.

11 ¶ And it came to passe after the
death of Abraham, that God blessed
his sonne Isaac, and Isaac dwelt
by the *well Lahai-roi.

12 ¶ Now

Margin notes

† *Hebr. ves-
sels.*

* Vers. 56.
and 59.

|| Or, *a full
yeere, or, ten
noneths.*

Chap. 16.
4. and 25.
1.
Or, *to pray.*

* 1. Chro. 1.
32.

* Chap. 23.
16.

* Chap. 16.
14. and 24.
62.

12 ¶ Now these *are* the generations of Ishmael Abrahams sonne, whom Hagar the Egyptian Sarahs handmayd, bare vnto Abraham:

13 And *these are the names of the sonnes of Ishmael, by their names, according to their generations; The first borne of Ishmael, Nebaioth, and Kedar, and Adbeel, and Mibsam,

*1. Chron. 1. 29.

14 And Mishma, and Dumah, and Massa,

15 Hadar, and Tema, Jetur, Naphish, and Kedemah.

16 These are the sonnes of Ishmael, and these are their names, by their townes and by their castels; twelue princes according to their nations.

17 And these *are* the yeeres of the life of Ishmael; an hundred and thirty and seuen yeeres: and he gaue vp the ghost and died, and was gathered vnto his people.

18 And they dwelt from Hauilah vnto Shur, that *is* before Egypt, as thou goest towards Assyria: *and* hee †died in the presence of all his brethren.

†*Hebr.* fell.

19 ¶ And these *are* the generations of Isaac, Abrahams sonne: Abraham begate Isaac.

20 And Isaac was fortie yeeres old when hee tooke Rebekah to wife, the daughter of Bethuel the Syrian of Padan Aram, the sister to Laban the Syrian.

21 And Isaac intreated the LORD for his wife, because she *was* barren: and the LORD was intreated of him, and Rebekah his wife conceiued.

22 And the children struggled together within her; and she said, If it be so, why am I thus? and shee went to enquire of the LORD.

23 And the LORD said vnto her, Two nations are in thy wombe, and two maner of people shall be separated from thy bowels: and the one people shalbe stronger then the other people: and *the elder shall serue the yonger.

*Rom. 9. 12

24 ¶ And when her dayes to be deliuered were fulfilled, behold, there *were* twinnes in her wombe.

25 And the first came out red, all ouer like an hairy garment: and they called his name, Esau.

26 And after that came his brother out, and *his hand tooke holde on Esaus heele; and his name was called Iacob: and Isaac was threescore yeres old, when shee bare them.

*Ose. 12. 3.

27 And the boyes grew; and Esau was a cunning hunter, a man of the fielde: and Iacob was a plaine man, dwelling in tents.

28 And Isaac loued Esau, because †he did eate of his venison: but Rebekah loued Iacob.

†*Hebr.* venison was in his mouth.

29 ¶ And Iacob sod pottage: and Esau came from the field, and hee was faint.

30 And Esau said to Iacob, Feed me, I pray thee, † with that same red *pottage:* for I am faint; therefore was his name called Edom.

†*Hebr.* with that red, with that re pottage.

31 And Iacob said, Sell me this day thy birthright.

32 And Esau said, Behold, I am † at the point to die: and what profit shall this birthright doe to me?

†*Hebr.* going to die.

33 And Iacob said, Sweare to mee this day: and he sware to him: and *he sold his birthright vnto Iacob.

*Hebr. 12. 16.

34 Then Iacob gaue Esau bread and pottage of lentiles; and he did eate and drinke, and rose vp, and went his way: thus Esau despised *his* birthright.

CHAP. XXVI.

1 Isaac because of famine went to Gerar. 2 God instructeth, and blesseth him. 7 Hee is reproued by Abimelech for denying his wife. 12 He groweth rich. 18 He diggeth Esek, Sitnah, and Rehoboth. 23 Abimelech maketh a couenant with him at Beersheba. 34 Esaus wiues.

Nd there was a famine in the land, besides the first famine that was in the dayes of Abraham. And Isaac went vnto Abimelech King of the Philistims, vnto Gerar.

2 And the LORD appeared vnto him and said, Goe not downe into Egypt; dwell in the land which I shall tell thee of.

3 Soiourne in this land, and I wil be with thee, and will blesse thee: for vnto thee, and vnto thy seed *I will giue all these countreys, and I wil performe the othe, which I sware vnto Abraham thy father.

*Chap. 1: 15. and 15 18.

4 And I wil make thy seed to multiply as the starres of heauen, and will giue vnto thy seed all these countreys: and in thy Seed shall all the nations of the earth be *blessed:

*Chap. 1 3. and 15. 18. and 22 18.

5 Because that Abraham obeyed my voyce, and kept my charge, my Com-

Commandements, my Statutes and my Lawes.

6 ¶ And Isaac dwelt in Gerar.

7 And the men of the place asked *him* of his wife: and he said, She is my sister: for he feared to say, *She is* my wife; lest, *said he*, the men of the place should kill me for Rebekah, because shee was faire to looke vpon.

8 And it came to passe when he had bene there a long time, that Abimelech king of the Philistims looked out at a window, and saw, and behold, Isaac was sporting with Rebekah his wife.

9 And Abimelech called Isaac and said, Behold, of a suretie she is thy wife: and how saidst thou, She is my sister? And Isaac said vnto him, Because I said, Lest I die for her.

10 And Abimelech said, What is this thou hast done vnto vs? one of the people might lightly haue lien with thy wife, and thou shouldest haue brought guiltinesse vpon vs.

11 And Abimelech charged all his people, saying, Hee that toucheth this man or his wife, shall surely bee put to death.

12 Then Isaac sowed in that land, and †receiued in the same yeere an hundred fold: & the LORD blessed him.

13 And the man waxed great, and †went forward, and grew vntill he became very great.

14 For he had possession of flocks, and possession of heards, and great store of ||seruants, and the Philistims enuied him.

15 For all the wels which his fathers seruants had digged in the dayes of Abraham his father, the Philistims had stopped them, & filled them with earth.

16 And Abimelech said vnto Isaac, Goe from vs: for thou art much mightier then we.

17 ¶ And Isaac departed thence, and pitched his tent in the valley of Gerar, and dwelt there.

18 And Isaac digged againe the wels of water, which they had digged in the dayes of Abraham his father: for the Philistims had stopped them after the death of Abraham, and he called their names after the names by which his father had called them.

19 And Isaacs seruants digged in the valley, and found there a well of † springing water.

20 And the heardmen of Gerar did striue with Isaacs heardmen, saying, The water is ours; and hee called the name of the well, ||Esek, because they stroue with him.

21 And they digged another well, and stroue for that also: and hee called the name of it, ||Sitnah.

22 And he remoued from thence, and digged another well, and for that they stroue not: and he called the name of it ||Rehoboth: and he said, For now the LORD hath made roome for vs, and we shall be fruitfull in the land.

23 And he went vp from thence to Beer-sheba.

24 And the LORD appeared vnto him the same night, and saide, I *am* the God of Abraham thy father: feare not, for I am with thee, and will blesse thee, and multiply thy seede, for my seruant Abrahams sake.

25 And he builded an altar there, and called vpon the name of the LORD, and pitched his tent there: and there Isaacs seruants digged a well.

26 ¶ Then Abimelech went to him from Gerar, and Ahuzzath one of his friends, and Phichol the chiefe captaine of his armie.

27 And Isaac saide vnto them, Wherefore come ye to me, seeing ye hate me, and haue sent me away from you?

28 And they said, †We saw certainly that the LORD was with thee: and wee said, Let there be now an othe betwixt vs, euen betwixt vs and thee, and let vs make a couenant with thee,

29 †That thou wilt doe vs no hurt, as we haue not touched thee, and as we haue done vnto thee nothing but good, and haue sent thee away in peace: thou art now the blessed of the LORD.

30 And he made them a feast, and they did eate and drinke.

31 And they rose vp betimes in the morning, and sware one to another: and Isaac sent them away, and they departed from him in peace.

32 And it came to passe the same day, that Isaacs seruants came, and tolde him concerning the well which they had digged, and said vnto him, We haue found water.

33 And he called it ||Shebah: therefore the name of the citie is ||Beer-sheba vnto this day.

34 ¶ And Esau was forty yeeres old, when he tooke to wife Iudith, the daughter of Beeri the Hittite, and Bashe-

Marginal notes:

Heb. found.

Heb. went oing.

Or, husandry.

Heb. liuing

‖ *That is, Contention.*

‖ *That is, Hatred.*

‖ *That is, roome.*

†*Heb. seeing we saw.*

†*Heb. if thou shalt &c.*

‖ *That is, an oath.*
‖ *That is, the well of the oath.*

*Chap. 27.
46.
† Hebr. bit-
ternesse of
spirit.

Bashemath the daughter of Elon the Hittite:

35 Which *were † a griefe of minde vnto Isaac and to Rebekah.

CHAP. XXVII.

1 Isaac sendeth Esau for venison. 5 Rebekah instructeth Iacob to obtaine the blessing. 15 Iacob vnder the person of Esau obteineth it. 30 Esau bringeth venison. 33 Isaac trembleth. 34 Esau complaineth, and by importunitie obtaineth a blessing. 41 He threatneth Iacob. 42 Rebekah disappointeth it.

Nd it came to passe that when Isaac was old, and his eyes were dimme, so that he could not see, hee called Esau his eldest son, and said vnto him, My sonne. And hee said vnto him, Behold, here am I.

2 And he said, Behold now, I am old, I know not the day of my death.

3 Now therefore take, I pray thee, thy weapons, thy quiuer, and thy bow, and goe out to the field, and † take mee *some* venison.

† Heb. hunt.

4 And make me sauoury meat, such as I loue, and bring it to mee, that I may eate, that my soule may blesse thee before I die.

5 And Rebekah heard when Isaac spake to Esau his sonne: and Esau went to the fielde to hunt *for* venison, *and to* bring *it.*

6 ¶ And Rebekah spake vnto Jacob her sonne, saying, Behold, I heard thy father speake vnto Esau thy brother, saying,

7 Bring me venison, and make mee sauoury meat, that I may eate, and blesse thee before the LORD, before my death.

8 Now therefore, my sonne, obey my voyce, according to that which I command thee.

9 Goe now to the flocke, and fetch me from thence two good kids of the goates, and I will make them sauoury meat for thy father, such as he loueth.

10 And thou shalt bring *it* to thy father, that he may eate, and that he may blesse thee, before his death.

11 And Iacob said to Rebekah his mother, Behold, Esau my brother is a hairy man, and I am a smooth man.

12 My father peraduenture will feele me, and I shall seeme to him as a deceiuer, and I shall bring a curse vpon me, and not a blessing.

13 And his mother said vnto him, Vpon me be thy curse, my sonne: onely obey my voice, and goe fetch me *them.*

14 And hee went, and fetched, and brought *them* to his mother, and his mother made sauoury meat, such as his father loued.

15 And Rebekah tooke †goodly raiment of her eldest sonne Esau, which were with her in the house, and put them vpon Iacob her yonger sonne:

† Hebr. de-
sireable.

16 And shee put the skinnes of the kids of the goats vpon his hands, and vpon the smooth of his necke.

17 And she gaue the sauoury meate, and the bread, which she had prepared, into the hand of her sonne Iacob

18 ¶ And he came vnto his father, and said, My father: And he said, Here am I: who art thou, my sonne?

19 And Iacob said vnto his father, I am Esau, thy first borne; I haue done according as thou badest mee: arise, I pray thee, sit, and eate of my venison, that thy soule may blesse me.

20 And Isaac said vnto his sonne, How is it that thou hast found it so quickly, my sonne? And he said, Because the LORD thy God brought it †to me.

† Hebr. be-
fore me.

21 And Isaac saide vnto Iacob, Come neere, I pray thee, that I may feele thee, my sonne, whether thou bee my very sonne Esau, or not.

22 And Iacob went neere vnto Isaac his father: and hee felt him, and said, The voyce *is* Iacobs voyce, but the hands *are* the hands of Esau.

23 And he discerned him not, because his hands were hairie, as his brother Esaus hands: So he blessed him.

24 And he said, Art thou my very sonne Esau? and he said, I am.

25 And he said, Bring *it* neere to me, and I will eate of my sonnes venison, that my soule may blesse thee: and hee brought *it* neere to him, and he did eate: and he brought him wine, & he dranke.

26 And his father Isaac saide vnto him, Come neere now, and kisse me, my sonne.

27 And hee came neere, and kissed him: and he smelled the smell of his raiment, and blessed him, and said, See, the smell of my sonne is as the smell of a field, which the LORD hath blessed.

28 Therefore *God giue thee of the dew of heauen, and the fatnesse of the earth, and plenty of corne and wine.

*Heb. 11.
20.

29 Let

29 Let people serue thee, and nations bow downe to thee: bee lord ouer thy brethren, & let thy mothers sonnes bow downe to thee: Cursed bee euery one that curseth thee, and blessed be hee that blesseth thee.

30 ¶ And it came to passe, as soone as Isaac had made an ende of blessing Iacob, and Iacob was yet scarce gone out from the presence of Isaac his father, that Esau his brother came in from his hunting.

31 And hee also had made sauoury meate, and brought it vnto his father, and said vnto his father, Let my father arise, and eat of his sonnes venison, that thy soule may blesse me.

32 And Isaac his father said vnto him, Who *art* thou? and he said, I am thy sonne, thy first borne Esau.

33 And Isaac †trembled very exceedingly, and said, Who? where *is* he that hath †taken venison, and brought it me, and I haue eaten of all before thou camest, and haue blessed him? yea and he shalbe blessed.

† Hebr. trembled with a great trembling greatly.
† Hebr. hunted.

34 And when Esau heard the words of his father, he cried with a great and exceeding bitter cry, and said vnto his father, Blesse mee, *euen* me also, O my father.

35 And hee said, Thy brother came with subtilty, and hath taken away thy blessing.

36 And he said, Is not he rightly naned ||Iacob? for he hath supplanted me these two times: hee tooke away my birthright, and behold, now he hath taken away my blessing: and hee said, Hast thou not reserued a blessing for mee?

|| That is, *A supplanter.*

37 And Isaac answered and saide vnto Esau, Behold, I haue made him thy lord, and all his brethren haue I giuen to him for seruants: and with corne and wine haue I ||susteined him: and what shall I doe now vnto thee, my sonne?

|| *Or, supported.*

38 And Esau said vnto his father, Hast thou but one blessing, my father? blesse mee, *euen* mee also, O my father. And Esau lift vp his voyce, * and wept.

* Heb. 12. 17.

39 And Isaac his father answered, and said vnto him, Behold, * thy dwelling shall be ||the fatnesse of the earth, and of the dew of heauen from aboue.

* Verse 28.
|| *Or, of the fatnesse.*

40 And by thy sword shalt thou liue, and shalt serue thy brother: and it shall come to passe when thou shalt haue the dominion, that thou shalt breake his yoke from off thy necke.

41 ¶ And Esau hated Iacob, because of the blessing, wherewith his father blessed him: and Esau said in his heart, The dayes of mourning for my father are at hand; * then will I slay my brother Iacob.

* Obad. 10.

42 And these words of Esau her elder sonne were told to Rebekah: And shee sent and called Iacob her yonger sonne, and said vnto him, Behold, thy brother Esau, as touching thee, doeth comfort himselfe, *purposing* to kill thee.

43 Now therefore my sonne, obey my voice: and arise, flee thou to Laban my brother, to Haran.

44 And tary with him a few dayes, vntill thy brothers furie turne away;

45 Vntill thy brothers anger turne away from thee, and hee forget that, which thou hast done to him: then I will send, and fetch thee from thence: why should I be depriued also of you both in one day?

46 And Rebekah said to Isaac, * I am weary of my life, because of the daughters of Heth: If Iacob take a wife of the daughters of Heth, such as these which are of the daughters of the land, what good shall my life doe me?

* Chap. 26. 35.

CHAP. XXVIII.

1 Isaac blesseth Iacob, and sendeth him to Padan Aram. 6 Esau marrieth Mahalal the daughter of Ishmael. 10 The Vision of Iacobs ladder. 18 The stone of Bethel. 20 Iacobs vow.

ANd Isaac called Iacob, and blessed him, and charged him, and saide vnto him, Thou shalt not take a wife, of the daughters of Canaan.

2 * Arise, goe to Padan Aram, to the house of Bethuel thy mothers father, and take thee a wife from thence, of the daughters of Laban thy mothers brother.

* Ose. 12. 12.

3 And God Almighty blesse thee, and make thee fruitfull, and multiply thee, that thou mayest be †a multitude of people:

† *Hebr. an assembly of people.*

4 And giue thee the blessing of Abraham, to thee and to thy seede with thee, that thou mayest inherit the lande †wherein thou art a stranger, which God gaue vnto Abraham.

† *Hebr of thy soiournings*

5 And

5 And Isaac sent away Iacob, and hee went to Padan-Aram vnto Laban, sonne of Bethuel the Syrian, the brother of Rebekah, Iacobs and Esaus mother.

6 ¶ When Esau sawe that Isaac had blessed Iacob, and sent him away to Padan-Aram, to take him a wife from thence; and that as he blessed him, he gaue him a charge, saying, Thou shalt not take a wife of the daughters of Canaan;

7 And that Iacob obeyed his father, and his mother, and was gone to Padan-Aram;

8 And Esau seeing that the daughters of Canaan † pleased not Isaac his father.

† Heb. were euill in the eyes, &c.

9 Then went Esau vnto Ishmael, and tooke vnto the wiues which hee had, Mahalath the daughter of Ishmael Abrahams sonne, the sister of Nebaioth, to be his wife.

＊ Called Acts 7. 2. Charran.

10 ¶ And Iacob went out from Beer-sheba, and went toward *Haran.

11 And hee lighted vpon a certaine place, and taried there all night, because the sunne was set: and hee tooke of the stones of that place, and put them for his pillowes, and lay downe in that place to sleepe.

12 And he dreamed, and beholde, a ladder set vp on the earth, and the top of it reached to heauen: and beholde the Angels of God ascending and descending on it.

＊ Chap. 35 1. & 48. 3

13 *And behold, the LORD stood aboue it, and said, I am the LORD God of Abraham thy father, and the God of Isaac: the land whereon thou liest, to thee will I giue it, and to thy seede.

14 And thy seed shall be as the dust of the earth, and thou shalt † spread abroad *to the West, and to the East, and to the North, and to the South: and in thee, and *in thy seed, shall all the families of the earth be blessed.

† Heb. break forth.
＊ Deut. 12. 3.
＊ Cha. 12. 3 and 18. 18. and 22. 18. and 26 4.

15 And behold, I am with thee, and will keepe thee in all *places* whither thou goest, and will bring thee againe into this land: for I will not leaue thee, vntill I haue done that which I haue spoken to thee of.

16 ¶ And Iacob awaked out of his sleepe, and he said, Surely the LORD is in this place, and I knew it not.

17 And he was afraid, and said, How dreadfull *is* this place? this is none other,

but the house of God, and this *is* the gate of heauen.

18 And Iacob rose vp earely in the morning, and tooke the stone that hee had put for his pillowes, and set it vp for a pillar, and powred oile vpon the top of it.

19 And hee called the name of that place † Beth-el: but the name of that citie was called Luz, at the first.

† That is, the house of God.

20 And Iacob vowed a vow, saying, If God will be with me, and will keepe me in this way that I goe, and will giue me bread to eate, and raiment to put on,

21 So that I come againe to my fathers house in peace: then shall the LORD be my God.

22 Aud this stone which I haue set for a pillar, shall be Gods house: and of all that thou shalt giue me, I will surely giue the tenth vnto thee.

CHAP. XXIX.

1 Iacob commeth to the well of Haran. 9 He taketh acquaintance of Rachel. 13 Laban enterteineth him. 18 Iacob couenanteth for Rachel. 23 He is deceiued with Leah. 28 He marrieth also Rachel, and serueth for her seuen yeeres more. 32 Leah beareth Reuben, 33 Simeon, 34 Leui, 35 and Iudah.

Hen Iacob † went on his iourney, and came into the land of the † people of the East.

† Heb. lift vp his feet.
† Heb. children.

2 And he looked, and behold, a well in the field, and loe, there *were* three flocks of sheepe lying by it: for out of that wel they watered the flocks: and a great stone was vpon the welles mouth.

3 And thither were all the flockes gathered, and they rolled the stone from the wels mouth, & watered the sheepe, and put the stone againe vpon the wels mouth in his place.

4 And Iacob said vnto them, My brethren, whence be ye? and they saide, Of Haran are we.

5 And he said vnto them, Know ye Laban the sonne of Nahor? And they sayde, We knowe *him.*

6 And he said vnto them, † Is hee well? and they said, He is well: and behold, Rachel his daughter commeth with the sheepe.

† Hebr. Is there peace to him?

7 And hee said, Loe, † *it is* yet high day, neither is it time that the cattell should

† Heb. yet the day is great.

should be gathered together: water yee the sheepe, and goe and feed *them*.

8 And they said, We cannot, vntill all the flockes bee gathered together, and till they rolle the stone from the welles mouth: then wee water the sheepe.

9 ¶ And while hee yet spake with them, Rachel came with her fathers sheepe: for she kept them.

10 And it came to passe, when Iacob saw Rachel the daughter of Laban his mothers brother, and the sheepe of Laban his mothers brother; that Iacob went neere, and rolled the stone from the wels mouth, and watered the flocke of Laban his mothers brother.

11 And Iacob kissed Rachel, and lifted vp his voyce, and wept.

12 And Iacob told Rachel, that hee was her fathers brother, and that hee was Rebekahs sonne: and she ranne, and told her father.

13 And it came to passe, when Laban heard the † tidings of Iacob his sisters sonne, that he ranne to meete him, and imbraced him, and kissed him, & brought him to his house: and hee tolde Laban all these things.

14 And Laban said to him, Surely thou art my bone and my flesh: and he abode with him the † space of a moneth.

15 ¶ And Laban said vnto Iacob, Because thou art my brother, shouldest thou therefore serue me for nought? tell me, what shall thy wages be?

16 And Laban had two daughters: the name of the elder was Leah, and the name of the yonger *was* Rachel.

17 Leah was tender eyed: but Rachel was beautiful and well fauoured.

18 And Iacob loued Rachel, and said, I will serue thee seuen yeeres for Rachel thy yonger daughter.

19 And Laban said, It is better that I giue her to thee, then that I should giue her to another man: abide with mee.

20 And Iacob serued seuen yeeres for Rachel: and they seemed vnto him but a few dayes, for the loue hee had to her.

21 ¶ And Iacob said vnto Laban, Giue me my wife (for my dayes are fulfilled) that I may goe in vnto her.

22 And Laban gathered together all the men of the place, and made a feast.

23 And it came to passe in the eue-

ning, that he tooke Leah his daughter, and brought her to him, and he went in vnto her.

24 And Laban gaue vnto his daughter Leah, Zilpah his mayde, for a handmayd.

25 And it came to passe, that in the morning, behold it was Leah: and he said to Laban, What is this thou hast done vnto mee? did not I serue with thee for Rachel? wherefore then hast thou beguiled me?

26 And Laban said, It must not be so done in our †countrey, to giue the yonger, before the first borne.

27 Fulfill her weeke, and wee will giue thee this also, for the seruice which thou shalt serue with mee, yet seuen other yeeres.

28 And Iacob did so, and fulfilled her weeke: and he gaue him Rachel his daughter to wife also.

29 And Laban gaue to Rachel his daughter, Bilhah his handmayd, to be her mayd.

30 And hee went in also vnto Rachel, and he loued also Rachel more then Leah, and serued with him yet seuen other yeeres.

31 ¶ And when the LORD saw that Leah was hated, hee opened her wombe: but Rachel was barren.

32 And Leah conceiued and bare a sonne, and shee called his name ‖ Reuben: for she said, Surely, the LORD hath looked vpon my affliction; now therefore my husband will loue me.

33 And shee conceiued againe, and bare a sonne, and saide, Because the LORD hath heard that I was hated, hee hath therefore giuen mee this *sonne* also, and she called his name ‖ Simeon.

34 And shee conceiued againe, and bare a sonne, and said, Now this time will my husband be ioyned vnto me, because I haue borne him three sonnes: therefore was his name called ‖ Leui.

35 And shee conceiued againe, and bare a sonne: and she said, Now wil I praise the LORD: therefore she called his name *‖ Iudah, and †left bearing.

CHAP. XXX.

1 Rachel in griefe for her barrennesse, giueth Bilhah her mayd vnto Iacob. 5 She beareth Dan and Naphtali. 9 Leah giueth Zilpah her mayd, who beareth Gad and Asher. 14 Reuben

Marginal notes:

† *Heb. hearing.*

† *Hebr. a moneth of daies.*

† *Heb. place.*

‖ *That is, See a sonne.*

‖ *That is, Hearing.*

‖ *That is, ioyned.*

* *Matth. 1. 2.*

‖ *That is, Praise.*

† *Hebr. stood from bearing.*

Reuben findeth Mandrakes, with which Leah buyeth her husband of Rachel. 17 Leah beareth Issachar, Zebulun, and Dinah. 22 Rachel beareth Ioseph. 25 Iacob desireth to depart. 27 Laban stayeth him on a new couenant. 37 Iacobs policie, whereby hee became rich.

Nd when Rachel saw that shee bare Iacob no children, Rachel enuied her sister, and said vnto Iacob, Giue mee children, or els I die.

2 And Iacobs anger was kindled against Rachel, and he said, Am I in Gods stead, who hath withheld from thee the fruit of the wombe?

3 And she said, Behold my mayde Bilhah: goe in vnto her, and she shall beare vpon my knees, that I may also †haue children by her.

† Hebr. be built by her.

4 And shee gaue him Bilhah her handmayd to wife: and Iacob went in vnto her.

5 And Bilhah conceiued and bare Iacob a sonne.

6 And Rachel said, God hath iudged me, and hath also heard my voyce, and hath giuen me a sonne; therefore called she his name ‖Dan.

‖ That is, Iudging.

7 And Bilhah Rachels mayd conceiued againe, and bare Iacob a second sonne.

8 And Rachel saide, With †great wrastlings haue I wrastled with my sister, and I haue preuailed: and she called his name ‖*Naphtali.

† Heb. wrastlings of God.

‖ That is, My wrastling.
* Called Matt. 4. 13. Nephthalim.

9 When Leah saw that she had left bearing, shee tooke Zilpah her mayde, and gaue her Iacob to wife.

10 And Zilpah Leahs mayde bare Iacob a sonne.

11 And Leah said, A troupe commeth: and she called his name ‖Gad.

‖ That is, A troupe, or company.

12 And Zilpah Leahs mayde bare Iacob a second sonne.

13 And Leah said, †Happy am I, for the daughters will call me blessed: and she called his name ‖Asher.

† Hebr. in my happines.

‖ That is, Happy.

14 ¶ And Reuben went in the dayes of wheat haruest, & found Mandrakes in the field, and brought them vnto his mother Leah. Then Rachel saide to Leah, Giue me, I pray thee, of thy sonnes Mandrakes.

15 And shee said vnto her, Is it a small matter, that thou hast taken my husband? and wouldst thou take away my sonnes Mandrakes also? and Rachel said, Therefore hee shall lye with thee to night, for thy sonnes Mandrakes.

16 And Iacob came out of the field in the euening, and Leah went out to meet him, and said, Thou must come in vnto mee: for surely I haue hired thee with my sonnes Mandrakes. And hee lay with her that night.

17 And God hearkened vnto Leah, and she conceiued, and bare Iacob the fift sonne.

18 And Leah said, God hath giuen mee my hire, because I haue giuen my mayden to my husband: and she called his name ‖Issachar.

‖ That is, An hire.

19 And Leah conceiued againe, and bare Iacob the sixth sonne.

20 And Leah said, God hath endued me *with* a good dowry: Now will my husband dwel with me, because I haue borne him sixe sonnes: and shee called his name ‖ *Zebulun.

‖ That is, Dwelling.
* Called Matth. 4. 13. Zobulon.

21 And afterwardes shee bare a daughter, and called her name ‖Dinah.

22 ¶ And God remembred Rachel, and God hearkened to her, and opened her wombe.

‖ That is, Iudgement.

23 And shee conceiued and bare a sonne, and said; God hath taken away my reproch:

24 And shee called his name ‖Ioseph, and saide, The LORD shall adde to me another sonne.

‖ That is, Adding.

25 ¶ And it came to passe when Rachel had borne Ioseph, that Iacob said vnto Laban, Send me away, that I may goe vnto mine owne place, and to my countrey.

26 Giue *mee* my wiues and my children, for whom I haue serued thee, and let me goe: for thou knowest my seruice which I haue done thee.

27 And Laban said vnto him, I pray thee, if I haue found fauour in thine eyes, *tary:* for I haue learned by experience, that the LORD hath blessed me for thy sake.

28 And he said, Appoint me thy wages, and I will giue it.

29 And hee said vnto him, Thou knowest how I haue serued thee, and how thy cattell *was* with me.

30 For it was little which thou hadst before I *came;* and it is *now* †increased vnto a multitude; and the LORD hath blessed thee †since my comming: and now when shall I prouide for mine owne house also?

† Hebr. broken foorth.

† Hebr. at my foote.

31 And

31 And hee said, What shall I giue thee? and Iacob said, Thou shalt not giue me any thing; if thou wilt doe this thing for mee, I will againe feed *and* keepe thy flocke.

32 I wil passe through all thy flocke to day, remoouing from thence all the speckled and spotted cattell: and all the browne cattell among the sheepe, and the spotted and speckled among the goates, and *of such* shalbe my hire.

33 So shall my righteousnesse answere for mee †in time to come, when it shall come for my hire, before thy face: euery one that is not speckled and spotted amongst the goates, and browne amongst the sheepe, that shalbe counted stollen with me.

† Hebr. to morrow.

34 And Laban saide, Beholde, I would it might bee according to thy word.

35 And he remoued that day the hee goates that were ring-straked, and spotted, and all the shee goats that were speckled and spotted, *and* euery one that had *some* white in it, and all the browne amongst the sheepe, and gaue *them* into the hand of his sonnes.

36 And hee set three dayes iourney betwixt himselfe and Iacob: and Iacob fed the rest of Labans flocks.

37 ¶ And Iacob tooke him rods of greene poplar, and of the hasel and chesnut tree, and pilled white strakes in them, and made the white appeare which was in the rods.

38 And he set the rods which he had pilled, before the flockes in the gutters in the watering troughes when the flocks came to drinke, that they should conceiue when they came to drinke.

39 And the flockes conceiued before the rods, and brought forth cattell ring-straked, speckled and spotted.

40 And Iacob did separate the lambes, and set the faces of the flockes toward the ring-straked, and all the browne in the flocke of Laban: and he put his owne flocks by themselues, and put them not vnto Labans cattell.

41 And it came to passe whensoeuer the stronger cattell did conceiue, that Iacob layd the rods before the eyes of the cattell in the gutters, that they might conceiue among the rods.

42 But when the cattel were feeble, hee put *them* not in: so the feebler were Labans, and the stronger Iacobs.

43 And the man increased exceedingly, and had much cattell, and maydseruants, and men seruants, and camels, and asses.

CHAP. XXXI.

1 Iacob vpon displeasure departeth secretly. 19 Rachel stealeth her fathers images. 22 Laban pursueth after him, 26 and complaineth of the wrong. 34 Rachels policie to hide the images. 36 Iacobs complaint of Laban. 43 The couenant of Laban and Iacob at Galeed.

 Nd he heard the words of Labans sonnes, saying, Iacob hath taken away all that was our fathers; and of that which was of our fathers, hath hee gotten all this glory.

2 And Iacob behelde the countenance of Laban, and behold, it *was* not toward him †as before.

† Hebr. as yesterday and the day before.

3 And the LORD said vnto Iacob, Returne vnto the land of thy fathers, and to thy kindred; and I wil be with thee.

4 And Iacob sent and called Rachel and Leah, to the field vnto his flocke,

5 And said vnto them, I see your fathers countenance, that it is not toward mee as before: but the God of my father hath bene with me.

6 And yee know, that with all my power I haue serued your father.

7 And your father hath deceiued mee, and changed my wages ten times: but God suffered him not to hurt me.

8 If hee said thus, The speckled shall be thy wages, then all the cattell bare speckled: and if he said thus, The ring-straked shalbe thy hire, then bare all the cattell ring-straked.

9 Thus God hath taken away the cattell of your father, and giuen *them* to mee.

10 And it came to passe at the time that the cattell conceiued, that I lifted vp mine eyes and saw in a dreame, and behold, the ‖rammes which leaped vp-on the cattell *were* ring-straked, speckled and grisled.

‖ Or, hee goates.

11 And the Angel of God spake vnto me in a dreame, *saying*, Iacob; And I said, Here am I.

12 And hee said, Lift vp now thine eyes, and see, all the rammes which leape vpon the cattell *are* ring-straked, speckled and grisled: for I haue seene all

all that Laban doeth vnto thee.

* Chap. 28.
18.

13 I am the God of Bethel, *where thou annoyntedst the pillar, *and* where thou vowedst a vow vnto mee: now a-rise, get thee out from this land, and re-turne vnto the land of thy kindred.

14 And Rachel and Leah answe-red, and said vnto him; Is there yet any portion or inheritance for vs in our fathers house?

15 Are we not counted of him stran-gers? for he hath sold vs, and hath quite deuoured also our money.

16 For all the riches which God hath taken from our father, that is ours, and our childrens: now then whatsoe-uer God hath said vnto thee, doe.

17 ¶ Then Iacob rose vp, and set his sonnes and his wiues vpon camels.

18 And he caried away all his cattell, and all his goods which he had gotten, the cattell of his getting, which hee had gotten in Padan Aram, for to goe to I-saac his father in the land of Canaan.

† Hebr. Te-raphim.

19 And Laban went to sheare his sheepe: and Rachel had stollen the † I-mages that *were* her fathers.

† Hebr. the heart of La-ban.

20 And Iacob stale away † vna-wares to Laban the Syrian, in that he told him not that he fled.

21 So hee fled with all that hee had, and he rose vp and passed ouer the Ri-uer, and set his face *toward* the mount Gilead.

22 And it was tolde Laban on the third day, that Iacob was fled.

23 And hee tooke his brethren with him, and pursued after him seuen dayes iourney, and they ouertooke him in the mount Gilead.

24 And God came to Laban the Syrian in a dreame by night, and saide vnto him, Take heed that thou speake not to Iacob †either good or bad.

† Hebr. from good to bad.

25 ¶ Then Laban ouertooke Ia-cob. Now Iacob had pitched his tent in the mount: and Laban with his bre-thren pitched in the mount of Gilead.

26 And Laban said to Iacob, What hast thou done, that thou hast stollen a-way vnawares to me, and caried away my daughters, as captiues *taken* with the sword?

† Hebr. hast stollen me.

27 Wherefore didst thou flie away secretly, and †steale away from me, and didst not tell mee? that I might haue sent thee away with mirth, and with songs, with tabret, and with harpe,

28 And hast not suffered me to kisse

my sonnes and my daughters? thou hast now done foolishly in *so* doing.

29 It is in the power of my hand to doe you hurt: but the God of your father spake vnto mee yesternight, say-ing, Take thou heed, that thou speake not to Iacob either good or bad.

30 And now *though* thou wouldest needes bee gone, because thou sore lon-gedst after thy fathers house; *yet* where-fore hast thou stollen my gods?

31 And Iacob answered and said to Laban, Because I was afraid: for I said, Peraduenture thou wouldest take by force thy daughters from me.

32 With whomsoeuer thou findest thy gods, let him not liue: before our brethren discerne thou what is thine with me, and take it to thee: for Iacob knew not that Rachel had stollen them.

33 And Laban went into Iacobs tent, and into Leahs tent, and into the two maid seruants tents: but he found *them* not. Then went he out of Leahs tent, and entred into Rachels tent.

34 Now Rachel had taken the i-mages, and put them in the camels fur-niture, and sate vpon them: and La-ban †searched all the tent, but found *them* not.

† Hebr. felt.

35 And shee said to her father, Let it not displease my lord, that I cannot rise vp before thee; for the custome of women is vpon mee: and he searched, but found not the images.

36 ¶ And Iacob was wroth, and chode with Laban: and Iacob answe-red and said to Laban, What *is* my tres-passe? what *is* my sinne, that thou hast so hotly pursued after me?

37 Whereas thou hast †searched all my stuffe, what hast thou found of all thy houshold stuffe? set it here before my brethren, and thy brethren, that they may iudge betwixt vs both.

† Hebr. felt.

38 This twentie yeeres *haue* I *bene* with thee: thy ewes and thy shee goates haue not cast their yong, and the rammes of thy flocke haue I not eaten.

39 That which was torne *of beasts*, I brought not vnto thee: I bare the losse of it; of *my hand didst thou require it, whether stollen by day, or stollen by night.

* Exod. 22.
12.

40 *Thus* I was in ỹ day, the drought consumed mee, and the frost by night, aud my sleep departed from mine eyes.

41 Thus

41 Thus haue I bene twentie yeres in thy house: I serued thee fourteene yeeres for thy two daughters, and sixe yeres for thy cattel; and thou hast changed my wages ten times.

42 Except the God of my father, the God of Abraham, and the feare of Isaac had bin with me, surely thou hadst sent me away now emptie: God hath seene mine affliction, and the labour of my hands, & rebuked *thee* yesternight.

43 ¶ And Laban answered and said vnto Iacob, These daughters are my daughters, and these children are my children, and these cattell are my cattell, and all that thou seest, is mine: and what can I doe this day vnto these my daughters, or vnto their children which they haue borne?

44 Now therefore come thou, let vs make a couenant, I and thou: and let it be for a witnesse betweene me and thee.

45 And Iacob tooke a stone, and set it vp for a pillar.

46 And Iacob saide vnto his brethren, Gather stones: and they tooke stones, and made an heape, and they did eate there vpon the heape.

47 And Laban called it || Iegar-Sahadutha: but Iacob called it Galeed.

|| That is, The heape of witnesse.

48 And Laban said, This heape is a witnesse betweene mee and thee this day. Therefore was the name of it called Galeed,

49 And || Mizpah: for he said, The LORD watch betweene me and thee when we are absent one from another.

|| That is, A beacon: or, watch tower.

50 If thou shalt afflict my daughters, or if thou shalt take *other* wiues beside my daughters, no *man* is with vs; See, God is witnesse betwixt mee and thee.

51 And Laban said to Iacob, Behold this heape, and behold this pillar, which I haue cast betwixt me and thee.

52 This heape be witnesse, and this pillar be witnesse, that I will not passe ouer this heape to thee, and that thou shalt not passe ouer this heape, and this pillar vnto me, for harme.

53 The God of Abraham, and the God of Nahor, the God of their father, iudge betwixt vs. And Iacob sware by the feare of his father Isaac.

54 Then Iacob || offred sacrifice vpon the mount, and called his brethren to eate bread, and they did eate bread, and

|| Or, killed beasts.

taried all night in the mount.

55 And earely in the morning, Laban rose vp and kissed his sonnes, and his daughters, and blessed them: and Laban departed, and returned vnto his place.

CHAP. XXXII.

1 Iacobs vision at Mahanaim. 3 His message to Esau. 6 He is afraid of Esaus comming. 9 He prayeth for deliuerance. 13 Hee sendeth a present to Esau. 24 He wrestleth with an Angel at Peniel, where hee is called Israel. 31 He halteth.

Nd Iacob went on his way, and the Angels of God met him.

2 And when Iacob saw them, he said, This *is* Gods hoste: and hee called the name of that place || Mahanaim.

|| That is, two hostes or campes.

3 And Iacob sent messengers before him, to Esau his brother, vnto the land of Seir, the †countrey of Edom.

† Heb. Field.

4 And he commaunded them, saying, Thus shall ye speake vnto my lord Esau, Thy seruant Iacob saith thus, I haue soiourned with Laban, and stayed there vntill now.

5 And I haue oxen, and asses, flockes, and men seruants and women seruants: and I haue sent to tell my lord, that I may find grace in thy sight.

6 ¶ And the messengers returned to Iacob, saying, Wee came to thy brother Esau, and also he commeth to meet thee, and foure hundred men with him.

7 Then Iacob was greatly afraid, and distressed, and he diuided the people that *was* with him, and the flockes, and herdes, and the camels into two bands,

8 And said, If Esau come to the one company, and smite it, then the other company which is left, shall escape.

9 ¶ And Iacob said, O God of my father Abraham, and God of my father Isaac, the LORD which saidst vnto me, * Returne vnto thy countrey, and to thy kinred, and I will deale well with thee:

* Chap. 31. 13.

10 † I am not worthy of the least of all the mercies, and of all the trueth, which thou hast shewed vnto thy seruant: for with my staffe I passed ouer this Iordan, and now I am become two bands.

† Heb. I am lesse then all &c.

11 Deliuer me, I pray thee, from the hand of my brother, from the hand of Esau:

† *Heb. vpon.*

Esau: for I feare him, lest he will come, and smite me, and the mother †with the children.

12 And thou saidst, I will surely doe thee good, and make thy seed as the sand of the sea, which cannot be numbred for multitude.

13 ¶ And he lodged there that same night, and tooke of that which came to his hand, a present for Esau his brother:

14 Two hundred shee goats, and twentie hee goats, two hundred ewes, and twentie rammes,

15 Thirtie milch camels with their colts, fortie kine, and ten bulles, twenty shee asses, and ten foales.

16 And hee deliuered *them* into the hand of his seruants, euery droue by themselues, and said vnto his seruants, Passe ouer before me, and put a space betwixt droue and droue.

17 And he commanded the formost, saying, When Esau my brother meeteth thee, and asketh thee, saying, Whose *art* thou? and whither goest thou? and whose *are* these before thee?

18 Then thou shalt say, They *be* thy seruant Iacobs: it is a present sent vnto my lord Esau: and behold also, he is behind vs.

19 And so commanded he the second, and the third, and all that followed the droues, saying, On this maner shal you speake vnto Esau, when you find him.

20 And say ye moreouer, Beholde, thy seruant Iacob is behind vs: for he said, I will appease him with the present that goeth before me, and afterward I will see his face; peraduenture he will accept †of me.

† *Heb. my face.*

21 So went the present ouer before him: and himselfe lodged that night in the company.

22 And hee rose vp that night, and tooke his two wiues, and his two women seruants, and his eleuen sonnes, and passed ouer the foord Iabbok.

† *Heb. caused to passe.*

23 And he tooke them, and †sent them ouer the brooke, and sent ouer that hee had.

24 ¶ And Iacob was left alone: and there wrestled a man with him, vntill the †breaking of the day.

† *Hebr. Ascending of the morning.*

25 And when he saw, that he preuailed not against him, he touched the hollow of his thigh: and the hollow of Iacobs thigh was out of ioynt, as hee wrestled with him.

26 And he said, Let me goe, for the day breaketh: and he said, *I will not let thee goe, except thou blesse me.

* *Ose. 12. 4.*

27 And he said vnto him, What is thy name? and he said, Iacob.

28 And he said, * Thy name shall be called no more Iacob, but Israel: for as a prince hast thou power with God, and with men, and hast preuailed.

* *Chap. 35. 10.*

29 And Iacob asked *him*, and saide, Tell me, I pray thee, thy name: and he said, Wherefore is it, that thou doest aske after my name? and he blessed him there.

30 And Iacob called the name of the place ||Peniel: for I haue seene God face to face, and my life is preserued.

‖ *That is, The face of God.*

31 And as he passed ouer Penuel, the sunne rose vpon him, and he halted vpon his thigh.

32 Therefore the children of Israel eate not of the sinewe which shranke, which is vpon the hollow of the thigh, vnto this day: because hee touched the hollow of Iacobs thigh, in the sinewe that shranke.

CHAP. XXXIII.

1 The kindnesse of Iacob and Esau at their meeting. 17 Iacob commeth to Succoth. 18 At Salem he buyeth a field, and buildeth an Altar called Elohe Israel.

And Iacob lifted vp his eyes, and looked, and behold, Esau came, and with him foure hundreth men: and hee diuided the children vnto Leah, and vnto Rachel, and vnto the two handmaids.

2 And he put the handmaides, and their chidren foremost, and Leah and her children after, and Rachel and Ioseph hindermost.

3 And hee passed ouer before them, and bowed himselfe to the ground seuen times, vntill hee came neere to his brother.

4 And Esau ran to meete him, and imbraced him, and fell on his necke, and kissed him, and they wept.

5 And he lift vp his eyes, and sawe the women, and the children, and said, Who are those †with thee? And he said, The children which God hath graciously giuen thy seruant.

† *Heb. To thee.*

6 Then the handmaidens came neere; they and their children, and they bowed themselues.

7 And

7 And Leah also with her children came neere, and bowed themselues: and after came Ioseph neere and Rachel, and they bowed themselues.

8 And he said, †What meanest thou by all this droue, which I met? And he said, *These are* to find grace in the sight of my lord.

Heb. what all this and to thee?

9 And Esau said, I haue enough: my brother, †keepe that thou hast vnto thy selfe.

Heb. bee vnto thee that is thine.

10 And Iacob saide, Nay, I pray thee: if now I haue found grace in thy sight, then receiue my present at my hand: for therefore I haue seene thy face, as though I had seene the face of God; and thou wast pleased with me.

11 Take, I pray thee, my blessing that is brought to thee; because God hath dealt graciously with mee, and because I haue enough: and hee vrged him, and he tooke *it*.

12 And he said, Let vs take our iourney, and let vs goe, and I will goe before thee.

13 And hee said vnto him, My lord knoweth, that the children are tender, and the flockes and heards with yong are with mee: and if men should ouer-driue them one day, all the flocke will die.

14 Let my lord, I pray thee, passe ouer before his seruant, and I will leade on softly, according †as the cattell that goeth before me, and the children be able to endure, vntill I come vnto my lord vnto Seir.

Heb. accor-ding to the foote of the worke, &c. according to the foot of the children.

Heb. Set, or place.

Heb. where-fore is this?

15 And Esau said, Let me now †leaue with thee *some* of the folke that are with me: And hee said, †What needeth it? let me finde grace in the sight of my lord.

16 ¶ So Esau returned that day, on his way vnto Seir.

17 And Iacob iourneyed to Succoth, and built him an house, and made boothes for his cattell: therefore the name of the place is called ‖Succoth.

That is, boothes.

18 ¶ And Iacob came to Shalem, a citie of * Shechem, which is in the land of Canaan, when he came from Padan Aram, and pitched his tent before the Citie.

* Called Acts. 7. 16. Sychem.

19 And he bought a parcell of a field where hee had spread his tent, at the hand of the children of * Hamor Shechems father, for an hundred ‖pieces of money.

* Called Acts. 7. 16. Emor. Or, lambes. That is, God, the God of Is-rael.

20 And hee erected there an Altar, and called it ‖El-Elohe-Israel.

CHAP. XXXIIII.

1 Dinah is rauished by Shechem. 4 He sueth to marry her. 13 The sonnes of Iacob offer the condition of Circumcision to the Shechemites. 20 Hamor and Shechem perswade them to accept it. 25 The sonnes of Iacob vpon that aduantage slay them, 27 and spoile their citie. 30 Iacob reproueth Simeon and Leui.

Nd Dinah the daughter of Leah, which shee bare vnto Iacob, went out to see the daughters of the land.

2 And when Shechem the sonne of Hamor the Hiuite, prince of the countrey saw her, he tooke her, and lay with her, and †defiled her.

† Hebr. hum-bled her.

3 And his soule claue vnto Dinah the daughter of Iacob, and hee loued the damsell, and spake †kindly vnto the damsell.

† Hebr. to her heart.

4 And Shechem spake vnto his father Hamor, saying, Get mee this damsell to wife.

5 And Iacob heard that he had defiled Dinah his daughter (now his sonnes were with his cattel in the field) and Iacob helde his peace vntill they were come.

6 ¶ And Hamor the father of Shechem went out vnto Iacob to commune with him.

7 And the sonnes of Iacob came out of the field when they heard *it*, and the men were grieued: and they were very wroth, because hee had wrought folly in Israel, in lying with Iacobs daughter; which thing ought not to be done.

8 And Hamor communed with them, saying, The soule of my sonne Shechem longeth for your daughter: I pray you giue her him to wife.

9 And make ye mariages with vs, and giue your daughters vnto vs, and take our daughters vnto you.

10 And ye shall dwell with vs, and the land shall be before you: dwell and trade you therein, and get you possessions therein.

11 And Shechem said vnto her father, and vnto her brethren, Let mee finde grace in your eyes, and what yee shall say vnto me, I will giue.

12 Aske mee neuer so much dowrie and gift, and I will giue according as yee

yee shall say vnto mee: but giue me the damsell to wife.

13 And the sonnes of Iacob answered Shechem, and Hamor his father deceitfully, and said, because he had defiled Dinah their sister.

14 And they saide vnto them, Wee cannot doe this thing, to giue our sister to one that is vncircumcised : for that were a reproch vnto vs.

15 But in this will we consent vnto you : If ye will be as we *be*, that euery male of you be circumcised :

16 Then wil we giue our daughters vnto you, and we wil take your daughters to vs, and we will dwell with you, and we will become one people.

17 But if ye will not hearken vnto vs, to be circumcised, then will we take our daughter, and we will be gone.

18 And their words pleased Hamor, and Shechem Hamors sonne.

19 And the yong man deferred not to doe the thing, because he had delight in Iacobs daughter : and he was more honourable then all the house of his father.

20 ¶ And Hamor and Shechem his sonne came vnto the gate of their citie, and communed with the men of their citie, saying :

21 These men are peaceable with vs, therefore let them dwel in the land, and trade therein: for the land, behold, it is large enough for them : let vs take their daughters to vs for wiues, and let vs giue them our daughters.

22 Onely herein will the men consent vnto vs, for to dwell with vs to be one people, if euery male among vs bee circumcised, as they are circumcised.

23 Shall not their cattell, and their substance, and euery beast of theirs bee ours ? onely let vs consent vnto them, and they will dwell with vs.

24 And vnto Hamor and vnto Shechem his sonne, hearkened all that went out of the gate of his citie ; and euery male was circumcised, all that went out of the gate of his citie.

25 ¶ And it came to passe on the thirde day when they were sore, that two of the sonnes of Iacob, Simeon and Leui, Dinahs brethren, tooke each man his sword and came vpon the citie boldly, and *slew all the males. *Chap. 49. 6.

26 And they slew Hamor and Shechem his sonne, with the †edge of the sword, and tooke Dinah out of She- †Hebr. mouth.

chems house, and went out.

27 The sonnes of Iacob came vpon the slaine, and spoiled the citie, because they had defiled their sister.

28 They tooke their sheepe, and their oxen, and their asses, and that which *was* in the citie, and that which *was* in the field.

29 And all their wealth, and all their little ones, and their wiues tooke they captiue, and spoiled euen all that *was* in the house.

30 And Iacob said to Simeon and Leui, Ye haue troubled me to make me to stinke among the inhabitants of the land, amongst the Canaanites, and the Perizzites : and I being few in number, they shall gather themselues together against me, and slay me, and I shal be destroyed, I and my house.

31 And they said, Should hee deale with our sister, as with an harlot ?

CHAP. XXXV.

1 God sendeth Iacob to Bethel. 2 He purgeth his house of idols. 6 He buildeth an Altar at Bethel. 8 Deborah dieth at Allon Bachuth. 9 God blesseth Iacob at Bethel. 16 Rachel traueileth of Beniamin, and dieth in the way to Edar. 22 Reuben lieth with Bilhah. 23 The sonnes of Iacob. 27 Iacob commeth to Isaac at Hebron. 28 The age, death, and buriall of Isaac.

Nd God said vnto Iacob, Arise, goe vp to Bethel, and dwel there: and make there an Altar vnto God, that appeared vnto thee, *when thou fleddest from the face of Esau thy brother. *Chap. 27. 43.

2 Then Iacob said vnto his household, and to all that were with him, Put away the strange gods that are among you, and bee cleane, and change your garments,

3 And let vs arise, and goe vp to Bethel, and I will make there an Altar vnto God, who answered me in the day of my distresse, and was with me in the way which I went.

4 And they gaue vnto Iacob all the strange gods which *were* in their hand, and all their eare-rings which *were* in their eares, and Iacob hid them vnder the oke which was by Shechem.

5 And they iourneyed : and the terrour of God was vpon the cities that were

were round about them, and they did not pursue after the sonnes of Iacob.

6 ¶ So Iacob came to Luz, which *is* in the land of Canaan (that *is* Bethel) hee and all the people that *were* with him.

7 And hee built there an Altar, and *called the place ||El-Bethel,because there God appeared vnto him, when he fled from the face of his brother.

* Chap. 28. 19.
That is,
The God of Bethel.

8 But Deborah Rebekahs nurse died, and she was buried beneath Bethel vnder an oke: and the name of *it* was called ||Allon Bachuth.

That is,
The oke of weeping.

9 ¶ And God appeared vnto Iacob againe, when he came out of Padan Aram, and blessed him.

10 And God said vnto him, Thy name is Iacob: thy name shall not bee called any more Iacob, * but Israel shall bee thy name; and hee called his name Israel.

Chap. 32. 28.

11 And God saide vnto him, I am God Almightie: be fruitfull and multiply: a nation and a company of nations shall be of thee, and Kings shall come out of thy loynes.

12 And the land which I gaue Abraham, and Isaac, to thee I will giue it, and to thy seed after thee will I giue the land.

13 And God went vp from him, in the place where he talked with him.

14 And Iacob set vp a pillar in the place where he talked with him, *euen* a pillar of stone: and hee powred a drinke offering thereon, and he powred oile thereon.

15 And Iacob called the name of the place where God spake with him, Bethel.

16 ¶ And they iourneyed from Bethel: and there was but a †litle way to come to Ephrath; and Rachel traueiled, and she had hard labour.

Hebr. a litle piece of ground.

17 And it came to passe when shee was in hard labour, that the midwife said vnto her, Feare not: thou shalt haue this sonne also.

18 And it came to passe as her soule was in departing, (for she died) that she called his name ||Ben-oni: but his father called him ||Beniamin.

That is,
he sonne of my sorrow.
That is,
he sonne of e right and.

19 And Rachel died, and was buried in the way to Ephrath, which *is* Bethlehem.

20 And Iacob set a pillar vpon her graue: that is the pillar of Rachels graue vnto this day.

21 ¶ And Israel iourneyed and spread his tent beyond the towre of Edar.

22 And it came to passe when Israel dwelt in that land, that Reuben went & * lay with Bilhah his fathers concubine: and Israel heard *it*. Now the sonnes of Iacob were twelue.

* Chap. 49. 4.

23 The sonnes of Leah: Reuben Iacobs first borne, and Simeon, and Leui, and Iudah, and Issachar, and Zebulun.

24 The sonnes of Rachel: Ioseph, and Beniamin.

25 And the sonnes of Bilhah, Rachels handmaid: Dan and Naphtali.

26 And the sonnes of Zilpah, Leahs handmaid: Gad, and Asher. These *are* the sonnes of Iacob, which were borne to him in Padan Aram.

27 ¶ And Iacob came vnto Isaac his father vnto Mamre, vnto the citie of Arbah (which is Hebron) where Abraham and Isaac soiourned.

28 And the dayes of Isaac were an hundred and fourescore yeeres.

29 And Isaac gaue vp the ghost and died, and was * gathered vnto his people, being old and full of dayes: and his sonnes Esau and Iacob buried him.

* Chap. 25. 8.

CHAP. XXXVI.

1 Esaus three wiues. 6 His remouing to mount Seir. 9 His sonnes. 15 The Dukes which descended of his sonnes. 20 The sonnes and dukes of Seir. 24 Anah findeth mules. 31 The kings of Edom. 40 The dukes that descended of Esau.

Ow these are the generations of Esau, who *is* Edom.

2 Esau tooke his wiues of the daughters of Canaan: Adah the daughter of Elon the Hittite, and Aholibamah the daughter of Anah the daughter of Zibeon the Hiuite:

3 And Bashemath Ishmaels daughter, sister of Nebaioth.

4 And * Adah bare to Esau, Eliphaz: and Bashemath bare Reuel.

* 1. Chron. 1. 35.

5 And Aholibamah bare Ieush, and Iaalam, and Korah: these are the sonnes of Esau, which were borne vnto him in the land of Canaan.

6 And Esau tooke his wiues, and his sonnes, and his daughters, and all the †persons of his house, and his cattell,

† Heb. soules.

tell, and all his beasts, and all his substance, which he had got in the lande of Canaan: and went into the countrey from the face of his brother Iacob.

7 For their riches were more then that they might dwell together: and the land wherein they were strangers, could not beare them, because of their cattell.

8 Thus dwelt Esau in *mount Seir: Esau is Edom.

*Iosh. 24. 4.

9 ¶ And these are the generations of Esau, the father of †the Edomites in mount Seir.

† Hebr. Edom.

10 These are the names of Esaus sonnes: *Eliphaz the sonne of Adah the wife of Esau, Reuel the sonne of Bashemath, the wife of Esau.

* 1. Chro. 1. 35. &c.

11 And the sonnes of Eliphaz were, Teman, Omar, Zepho, and Gatam, and Kenaz.

12 And Timna was concubine to Eliphaz Esaus sonne, and shee bare to Eliphaz Amalek: these were the sonnes of Adah Esaus wife.

13 And these are the sonnes of Reuel: Nahath and Zerah, Shammah, and Mizzah: these were the sonnes of Bashemath, Esaus wife.

14 ¶ And these were the sonnes of Aholibamah, the daughter of Anah, daughter of Zibeon Esaus wife: and she bare to Esau, Ieush and Iaalam, and Korah.

15 ¶ These were dukes of the sonnes of Esau: the sonnes of Eliphaz the first borne sonne of Esau, duke Teman, duke Omar, duke Zepho, duke Kenaz,

16 Duke Korah, duke Gatam, and duke Amalek: These are the dukes that came of Eliphaz, in the land of Edom: These were the sonnes of Adah.

17 ¶ And these are the sonnes of Reuel Esaus sonne: duke Nahath, duke Zerah, duke Shammah, duke Mizzah. These are the dukes that came of Reuel, in the land of Edom: these are the sonnes of Bashemath, Esaus wife.

18 ¶ And these are the sonnes of Aholibamah Esaus wife: duke Ieush, duke Iaalam, duke Korah: these were the dukes that came of Aholibamah the daughter of Anah Esaus wife.

19 These are the sonnes of Esau, (who is Edom) and these are their dukes.

* 1. Chro. 1. 38.

20 ¶ *These are the sonnes of Seir the Horite, who inhabited the land, Lo-tan, and Shobal, and Zibeon, and A-nah.

21 And Dishon, and Ezer, and Dishan: these are the dukes of the Horites the children of Seir in the lande of Edom.

22 And the children of Lotan, were Hori, and Hemam: and Lotans sister was Timna.

23 And the children of Shobal were these: Aluan, and Manahath, and Ebal, Shepho, and Onam.

24 And these are the children of Zibeon, both Aiah, and Anah: this was that Anah that found the mules in the wildernesse, as he fed the asses of Zibeon his father.

25 And the children of Anah were these: Dishon, and Aholibamah the daughter of Anah.

26 And these are the children of Dishon: Hemdan and Eshban, & Ithran, and Cheran.

27 The children of Ezer are these: Bilhan and Zaauan, and Akan.

28 The children of Dishan are these: Vz, and Aran.

29 These are the dukes that came of the Horites: duke Lotan, duke Shobal, duke Zibeon, duke Anah,

30 Duke Dishon, duke Ezer, duke Dishan: these are the dukes that came of Hori, among their dukes in the land of Seir.

31 ¶ And these are the kings that reigned in the land of Edom, before there reigned any king ouer the children of Israel.

32 And Bela the sonne of Beor reigned in Edom: and the name of his citie was Dinhabah.

33 And Bela died, and Iobab the sonne of Zerah of Bozra reigned in his stead.

34 And Iobab died, and Husham of the land of Temani reigned in his stead.

35 And Husham died, and Hadad the sonne of Bedad, (who smote Midian in the field of Moab,) reigned in his stead: & the name of his citie was Auith.

36 And Hadad died, and Samlah of Masrekah, reigned in his stead.

37 And Samlah died, and Saul of Rehoboth, by the riuer, reigned in his stead.

38 And Saul died, and Baal-hanan the sonne of Achbor reigned in his stead.

39 And Baal-hanan the sonne of Achbor

Achbor died, and Hadar reigned in his stead: and the name of his citie *was* Pau, and his wiues name *was* Mehetabel, the daughter of Matred, the daughter of Mezahab.

40 And these *are* the names of the dukes that came of Esau, according to their families, after their places, by their names: duke Timnah, duke Aluah, duke Ietheth,

41 Duke Aholibamah, duke Elah, duke Pinon,

42 Duke Kenaz, duke Teman, duke Mibzar,

43 Duke Magdiel, duke Iram. These *be* the dukes of Edom, according to their habitations, in the land of their possession: he is Esau the father of † the Edomites.

Heb. Edom

CHAP. XXXVII.

2 Ioseph is hated of his brethren. 5 His two dreames. 13 Iacob sendeth him to visite his brethren. 18 His brethren conspire his death. 21 Reuben saueth him. 26 They sell him to the Ishmeelites. 31 His father, deceiued by the bloodie coat, mourneth for him. 36 Hee is sold to Potiphar in Egypt.

ANd Iacob dwelt in the land †wherein his father was a stranger, in the land of Canaan.

† Heb. of his fathers so-iournings.

2 These *are* the generations of Iacob: Ioseph being seuenteene yeeres old, was feeding the flocke with his brethren, and the lad was with the sonnes of Bilhah, and with the sonnes of Zilpah, his fathers wiues: and Ioseph brought vnto his father their euill report.

3 Now Israel loued Ioseph more then all his children, because he was the sonne of his old age: and he made him a coat of many ||colours.

‖ Or, peeces.

4 And when his brethren saw that their father loued him more then all his brethren, they hated him, and could not speake peaceably vnto him.

5 ¶ And Ioseph dreamed a dreame, and he told it his brethren, and they hated him yet the more.

6 And he said vnto them, Heare, I pray you, this dreame which I haue dreamed.

7 For beholde, wee were binding sheaues in the field, and loe, my sheafe arose, and also stood vpright; and behold, your sheaues stood round about,

and made obeisance to my sheafe.

8 And his brethren saide to him, Shalt thou indeed reigne ouer vs? or shalt thou indeed haue dominion ouer vs? and they hated him yet the more, for his dreames, and for his words.

9 ¶ And hee dreamed yet another dreame, and told it his brethren, and said, Behold, I haue dreamed a dreame more: and behold, the sunne and the moone, and the eleuen starres made obeisance to me.

10 And he told *it* to his father, and to his brethren: and his father rebuked him, and said vnto him, What *is* this dreame that thou hast dreamed? shal I, and thy mother, and thy brethren indeed come to bow downe our selues to thee, to the earth?

11 And his brethren enuied him: but his father obserued the saying.

12 ¶ And his brethren went to feed their fathers flocke in Shechem.

13 And Israel saide vnto Ioseph, Doe not thy brethren feed the flocke in Shechem? Come, and I will send thee vnto them: & he said to him, Here am I.

14 And he said to him, Goe, I pray thee, † see whether it bee well with thy brethren, and well with the flockes, and bring me word againe: so hee sent him out of the vale of Hebron, and he came to Shechem.

† Hebr. see the peace of thy brethren &c.

15 ¶ And a certaine man found him, and behold, hee was wandring in the field, and the man asked him, saying, What seekest thou?

16 And he said, I seeke my brethren: tell me, I pray thee, where they feede their *flockes*.

17 And the man said, They are departed hence: for I heard them say, Let vs goe to Dothan. And Ioseph went after his brethren, and found them in Dothan.

18 And when they saw him a farre off, euen before he came neere vnto them, they conspired against him, to slay him.

19 And they said one to another, Behold, this †dreamer commeth.

† Hebr. master of dreames.

20 Come now therefore, and let vs slay him, and cast him into some pit, and we will say, Some euill beast hath deuoured him: and we shall see what will become of his dreames.

21 And *Reuben heard *it*, and he deliuered him out of their hands, and said; Let vs not kill him.

* Chap. 42. 22.

22 And

22 And Reuben saide vnto them, Shed no blood, *but* cast him into this pit that is in the wildernesse, and lay no hand vpon him; that he might rid him out of their hands, to deliuer him to his father againe.

23 ¶ And it came to passe when Ioseph was come vnto his brethren, that they stript Ioseph out of his coate, his coat of many ||colours that *was* on him.

|| Or, pieces.

24 And they tooke him and cast him into a pit: and the pit *was* emptie, *there was* no water in it.

25 And they sate downe to eat bread: and they lift vp their eyes and looked, and behold, a company of Ishmeelites came from Gilead, with their camels, bearing spicery, & baulme, and myrrhe, going to cary *it* downe to Egypt.

26 And Iudah saide vnto his brethren, What profit *is it* if we slay our brother, and conceale his blood?

27 Come, and let vs sell him to the Ishmeelites, and let not our hand bee vpon him: for he is our brother, and *our* flesh; and his brethren †were content.

† Hebr. hearkened.

28 Then there passed by Midianites merchant men, and they drew and lift vp Ioseph out of the pit, and *sold Ioseph to the Ishmeelites for twentie pieces of siluer: and they brought Ioseph into Egypt.

* Psal 105. 17. wis. 10. 13. acts. 7. 9.

29 ¶ And Reuben returned vnto the pit, and behold, Ioseph was not in the pit: and he rent his clothes.

30 And hee returned vnto his brethren and said, The childe is not, and I, whither shall I goe?

31 And they tooke Iosephs coat, and killed a kid of the goats, and dipped the coat in the blood.

32 And they sent the coat of many colours, and they brought it to their father, and said, This haue we found: know now whether it bee thy sonnes coat or no.

33 And he knew *it*, and said, *It is* my sonnes coat: an *euil beast hath deuoured him; Ioseph is without doubt rent in pieces.

* Chap. 44. 28.

34 And Iacob rent his clothes, and put sackcloth vpon his loines, & mourned for his sonne many dayes.

35 And all his sonnes, and all his daughters rose vp to comfort him: but he refused to be comforted: and he said, For I will goe downe into the graue vnto my sonne, mourning; thus his father wept for him.

36 And the Medanites sold him into Egypt vnto Potiphar, an † officer of Pharaohs, *and* †||captaine of the guard.

† Hebr. Eunuch. But the word doeth signifie notonly Eunuches, but also Chamberlaines, Courtiers, and Officers.

† Hebr. chiefe of theslaughtermen, or executioners.

|| Or, chiefe Marshall.

CHAP. XXXVIII.

1 Iudah begetteth Er, Onan, and Shelah. 6 Er marrieth Tamar. 8 The trespasse of Onan. 11 Tamar stayeth for Shelah. 13 She deceiueth Iudah. 27 She beareth twinnes, Pharez and Zarah.

And it came to passe at that time, that Iudah went downe from his brethren, and turned in to a certaine Adullamite, whose name *was* Hirah:

2 And Iudah saw there a daughter of a certaine Canaanite, whose name was *Shuah: and he tooke her, and went in vnto her.

* 1. Chron. 2. 3.

3 And she conceiued & bare a sonne, and he called his name Er.

4 *And shee conceiued againe, and bare a sonne, and shee called his name, Onan.

* Num. 26. 19.

5 And she yet againe conceiued and bare a sonne, and called his name Shelah: and hee was at Chezib, when shee bare him.

6 And Iudah tooke a wife for Er his first borne, whose name *was* Tamar.

7 And *Er, Iudahs first borne was wicked in the sight of the LORD, and the LORD slew him.

* Num. 26. 19.

8 And Iudah said vnto Onan, Goe in vnto thy brothers wife, and marrie her, and raise vp seed to thy brother.

9 And Onan knew that the seed should not be his; and it came to passe when hee went in vnto his brothers wife, that hee spilled it on the ground, least that hee should giue seed to his brother.

10 And the thing which he did, †displeased the LORD: wherefore hee slew him also.

† Hebr. wa euill in the eyes of the Lord.

11 Then said Iudah to Tamar his daughter in law, Remaine a widow at thy fathers house, til Shelah my sonne be growen: (for he said, Lest peraduenture he die also as his brethren *did*) and Tamar went and dwelt in her fathers house.

12 ¶ And †in processe of time, the daughter of Shuah Iudahs wife died: and Iudah was comforted, and went vp vnto his sheepe-shearers to Timnath,

† Hebr. Th dayes were multiplied.

nath, he and his friend Hirah the Adullamite.

13 And it was told Tamar, saying,
Behold, thy father in law goeth vp to
Timnath to sheare his sheepe.

14 And shee put her widowes garments off from her, and couered her
with a vaile, and wrapped her selfe, and
sate in †an open place, which is by the
way to Timnath: for shee sawe that
Shelah was growen, and she was not
giuen vnto him to wife.

Heb. the
ooreofeyes,
r, of E-
aïm.

15 When Iudah saw her, he thought
her to be an harlot: because she had couered her face.

16 And hee turned vnto her by the
way, and said, Goe to, I pray thee, let
me come in vnto thee: (for he knew not
that she *was* his daughter in law) and
she said, What wilt thou giue mee, that
thou mayest come in vnto me?

Heb. a kid
f the goats.

17 And hee said, I will send thee
†a kid from the flocke: and shee saide,
Wilt thou giue *mee* a pledge, till thou
send it?

18 And he said, What pledge shall I
giue thee? And she said, Thy signet, and
thy bracelets, and thy staffe, that is in
thine hand: and he gaue it her, & came
in vnto her, and she conceiued by him.

19 And shee arose and went away,
and laid by her vaile from her, and put
on the garments of her widowhood.

20 And Iudah sent the kidde by the
hand of his friend the Adullamite, to
receiue *his* pledge from the womans
hand: but he found her not.

Or, in E-
aïm.

21 Then hee asked the men of that
place, saying, Where is the harlot, that
was ||openly by the way side? And they
said, There was no harlot in this *place.*

22 And he returned to Iudah, and
said, I cannot finde her: and also the
men of the place said, That there was
no harlot in this *place.*

Heb. be-
ome a con-
empt.

23 And Iudah said, Let her take it
to her, lest we †bee shamed: behold, I
sent this kidde, and thou hast not found
her.

24 ¶ And it came to passe about
three moneths after, that it was tolde
Iudah, saying, Tamar thy daughter
in law hath played the harlot, and also
behold, she is with child by whoredom:
and Iudah said, Bring her foorth, and
let her be burnt.

25 When she was brought forth, she
sent to her father in law, saying, By the
man whose these are, am I with child:

and shee said, Discerne, I pray thee,
whose are these, the signet, and bracelets, and staffe.

26 And Iudah acknowledged *them,*
and said, She hath bin more righteous
then I: because that I gaue her not to
Shelah my sonne: and he knew her a-
gaine no more.

27 ¶ And it came to passe in the time
of her trauaile, that beholde, twinnes
were in her wombe.

28 And it came to passe when shee
trauailed, that *the one* put out his hand,
and the midwife tooke and bound vpon
his hand a skarlet threed, saying, This
came out first.

29 And it came to passe as he drewe
backe his hand, that behold, his brother
came out: and she said, ||How hast thou
broken foorth? *this* breach *bee* vpon
thee: Therefore his name was called
||*Pharez.

30 And afterward came out his
brother that *had* the skarlet threed vpon his hand, and his name was called
Zarah.

||*Or, where-*
fore hast
thou made
this breach
againstthee?
|| *That is,*
a breach.
* 1. Chron.
2. 4. matt.
1. 3.

CHAP. XXXIX.

1 Ioseph aduanced in Potiphars house. 7 Hee
resisteth his mistresses temptation. 13 He is
falsly accused. 19 Hee is cast in prison. 21
God is with him there.

ANd Ioseph was brought
downe to Egypt, and Po-
tiphar an Officer of Pha-
raoh, captaine of ŷ guard,
an Egyptian, bought him
of the hand of the Ishmeelites, which
had brought him downe thither.

2 And the LORD was with Ioseph, and hee was a prosperous man,
and hee was in the house of his master
the Egyptian.

3 And his master sawe that the
LORD *was* with him, and that the
LORD made all that he did, to pro-
sper in his hand.

4 And Ioseph found grace in his
sight, and he serued him; and hee made
him ouerseer ouer his house, and all
that he had he put into his hand.

5 And it came to passe from the time
that hee had made him ouerseer in his
house, and ouer all that he had, that the
LORD blessed the Egyptians house
for Iosephs sake: and the blessing of
the LORD was vpon all that he had
in the house, and in the field.

6 And he left all that he had, in Iosephs

sephs hand: and he knew not ought he had, saue the bread which he did eate: and Ioseph was a goodly person, and well fauoured.

7 ¶ And it came to passe after these things, that his masters wife cast her eyes vpon Ioseph, and shee said, Lie with me.

8 But he refused, and said vnto his masters wife, Behold, my master wotteth not what *is* with mee in the house, and he hath committed all that he hath, to my hand.

9 There is none greater in this house then I : neither hath hee kept backe any thing from me, but thee, because thou *art* his wife: how then can I doe this great wickednesse, and sinne against God ?

10 And it came to passe as she spake to Ioseph day by day, that hee hearkened not vnto her, to lie by her, *or* to bee with her.

11 And it came to passe about this time, that Ioseph went in to the house, to doe his busines, and there was none of the men of the house there within.

12 And shee caught him by his garment, saying, Lie with me: and he left his garment in her hand, and fled, and got him out.

13 And it came to passe, when she saw that hee had left his garment in her hand, and was fled forth ;

14 That she called vnto the men of her house, and spake vnto them, saying, See, he hath brought in an Hebrew vnto vs, to mocke vs: he came in vnto me to lie with me, and I cried with a † loud voice.

† *Heb. great.*

15 And it came to passe, when hee heard that I lifted vp my voice, and cried, that he left his garment with mee, and fled, and got him out.

16 And she laid vp his garment by her, vntill her lord came home.

17 And she spake vnto him, according to these words, saying, The Hebrew seruant which thou hast brought vnto vs, came in vnto me to mocke me.

18 And it came to passe as I lift vp my voice, and cried, that he left his garment with me, and fled out.

19 And it came to passe when his master heard the words of his wife, which she spake vnto him, saying, After this maner did thy seruant to me, that his wrath was kindled.

20 And Iosephs master tooke him, and put him into the prison, a place, where ỹ kings prisoners were bound: and he was there in the prison.

21 ¶ But the LORD was with Ioseph, and †shewed him mercie, and gaue him fauour in the sight of the keeper of the prison.

† *Heb. extended kindnes vnto him.*

22 And the keeper of the prison committed to Iosephs hand all the prisoners that *were* in the prison, and whatsoeuer they did there, he was the doer *of it :*

23 The keeper of the prison looked not to any thing, *that was* vnder his hand, because the LORD was with him: & that which he did, the LORD made *it* to prosper.

CHAP. XL.

1 The Butler and Baker of Pharaoh in prison. 4 Ioseph hath charge of them. 5 He interpreteth their dreames. 20 They come to passe according to his interpretation. 23 The ingratitude of the Butler.

Nd it came to passe after these things , that the Butler of the King of Egypt, and *his* Baker, had offended their lord the King of Egypt.

2 And Pharaoh was wroth against two of his officers, against the chiefe of the Butlers, and against the chiefe of the Bakers.

3 And he put them in ward in the house of the captaine of the guard, into the prison, the place where Ioseph was bound.

4 And the captaine of the guard charged Ioseph with them, and he serued them, and they continued a season in warde.

5 ¶ And they dreamed a dreame both of them, each man his dreame in one night, each man according to the interpretation of his dreame, the Butler and the Baker of the king of Egypt, which were bound in the prison.

6 And Ioseph came in vnto them in the morning, and looked vpon them, and behold, they *were* sad.

7 And he asked Pharaohs officers that were with him in the warde of his lords house, saying, Wherefore †looke ye so sadly to day?

† *Heb. are your faces euill ?*

8 And they said vnto him, We haue dreamed a dreame, and there is no interpreter of it. And Ioseph said vnto them,

them, Doe not interpretations belong to God? tell me them, I pray you.

9 And the chiefe Butler tolde his dreame to Ioseph, and said to him; In my dreame, beholde, a vine was before mee:

10 And in the vine *were* three branches, and it *was* as though it budded, and her blossoms shot foorth; *and* the clusters thereof brought forth ripe grapes.

11 And Pharaohs cup was in my hand, and I tooke the grapes and pressed them into Pharaohs cup: and I gaue the cup into Pharaohs hand.

12 And Ioseph said vnto him, This is the interpretation of it: the three branches are three dayes,

13 Yet within three dayes shall Pharaoh ||lift vp thine head, and restore thee vnto thy place, and thou shalt deliuer Pharaohs cup into his hand, after the former manner when thou wast his Butler.

14 But ||thinke on me, when it shall be well with thee, and shew kindenesse, I pray thee, vnto mee, and make mention of me vnto Pharaoh, and bring me out of this house.

15 For indeed I was stollen away out of the land of the Hebrewes: and here also haue I done nothing, that they should put me into the dungeon.

16 When the chiefe Baker saw, that the interpretation was good, he said vnto Ioseph, I also was in my dreame, and behold, I had three ||white baskets on my head.

17 And in the vppermost basket there was of all maner of †bake-meats for Pharaoh, and the birds did eate them out of the basket vpon my head.

18 And Ioseph answered, and said, This is the interpretation thereof: the three baskets are three dayes:

19 Yet within three dayes shall Pharaoh ||lift vp thy head from off thee, and shall hang thee on a tree, and the birds shall eate thy flesh from off thee.

20 ¶ And it came to passe the third day, *which was* Pharaohs birth day, that hee made a feast vnto all his seruants: and he ||lifted vp the head of the chiefe Butler, and of the chiefe Baker among his seruants.

21 And he restored the chiefe Butler vnto his Butlership againe, and hee gaue the cup into Pharaohs hand.

22 But he hanged the chiefe Baker, as Ioseph had interpreted to them.

23 Yet did not the chiefe Butler remember Ioseph, but forgate him.

CHAP. XLI.

1 Pharaohs two dreames. 9 Ioseph interpreteth them. 33 Hee giueth Pharaoh counsell. 38 Ioseph is aduanced. 50 Hee begetteth Manasseh and Ephraim. 54 The famine beginneth.

Nd it came to passe at the end of two ful yeeres, that Pharaoh dreamed: and beholde, hee stood by the riuer.

2 And behold, there came vp out of the riuer seuen well fauoured kine, and fat fleshed, and they fed in a medow.

3 And behold, seuen other kine came vp after them out of the riuer, ill fauoured and leane fleshed, and stood by the other kine, vpon the brinke of the riuer.

4 And the ill fauoured and leane fleshed kine, did eate vp the seuen well fauoured and fat kine: So Pharaoh awoke.

5 And hee slept and dreamed the second time: and beholde, seuen eares of corne came vp vpon one stalke, †ranke and good.

6 And beholde, seuen thinne eares and blasted with the Eastwind, sprang vp after them.

7 And the seuen thinne eares deuoured the seuen ranke and full eares: and Pharaoh awoke, and behold, it was a dreame.

8 And it came to passe in the morning, that his spirit was troubled, and he sent and called for all the Magicians of Egypt, and all the wise men thereof: and Pharaoh tolde them his dreame; but there was none that could interprete them vnto Pharaoh.

9 ¶ Then spake the chiefe Butler vnto Pharaoh, saying, I doe remember my faults this day.

10 Pharaoh was wroth with his seruants, and put mee in warde, in the captaine of the guards house, *both* mee, and the chiefe Baker.

11 And we dreamed a dreame in one night, I and he: we dreamed each man according to the interpretation of his dreame.

12 And *there was* there with vs a yong man an Hebrew, seruant to the captaine of the guard: and wee told him, and he *interpreted to vs our dreames,

to

Or, reckon.

† *Hebr. Remember mee with thee.*

|| *Or, full of holes.*

† *Hebr. meat of Pharaoh, the worke of a baker, or cooke.*

|| *Or, reckon thee, and take thy office from thee.*

|| *Or, reckoned.*

† *Hebr. fat.*

* *Chap. 40. 12. &c.*

to each man according to his dreame, he did interpret.

13 And it came to passe, as he interpreted to vs, so it was; mee he restored vnto mine office, and him he hanged.

* Psal. 105. 20.
† Hebr.made him runne.

14 ¶ * Then Pharaoh sent and called Ioseph, and they † brought him hastily out of the dungeon: And he shaued himselfe, and changed his raiment, and came in vnto Pharaoh.

15 And Pharaoh said vnto Ioseph, I haue dreamed a dreame, and there is none that can interpret it: and I haue heard say of thee, that ||thou canst vnderstand a dreame, to interpret it.

|| Or, When thou hearest a dreame, thou canst interpret it.

16 And Ioseph answered Pharaoh, saying; It is not in me: God shall giue Pharaoh an answere of peace.

17 And Pharaoh said vnto Ioseph; In my dreame, behold, I stood vpon the banke of the riuer.

18 And behold, there came vp out of the riuer seuen kine, fat fleshed and well fauoured, and they fed in a medow.

19 And behold, seuen other kine came vp after them, poore and very ill fauoured, and leane fleshed, such as I neuer saw in all the land of Egypt for badnes.

† Hebr. come to the inward parts of them.

20 And the leane, & the ill fauoured kine, did eate vp the first seuen fat kine.

21 And when they had † eaten them vp, it could not bee knowen that they had eaten them, but they were still ill fauoured, as at the beginning: So I awoke.

22 And I saw in my dreame, and behold, seuen eares came vp in one stalke, full and good.

|| Or, small.

23 And behold, seuen eares ||withered, thin & blasted with the East wind, sprung vp after them.

24 And the thin eares deuoured the seuen good eares: and I told this vnto the magicians, but there was none that could declare it to me.

25 ¶ And Ioseph said vnto Pharaoh, The dreame of Pharaoh is one; God hath shewed Pharaoh what he is about to doe.

26 The seuen good kine are seuen yeeres: and the seuen good eares are seuen yeeres: the dreame is one.

27 And the seuen thin and ill fauoured kine that came vp after them, are seuen yeeres: and the seuen emptie eares blasted with the East wind, shall bee seuen yeeres of famine.

28 This is the thing which I haue spoken vnto Pharaoh: what God is a-

bout to doe, he sheweth vnto Pharaoh.

29 Behold, there come seuen yeeres of great plentie, throughout all the land of Egypt.

30 And there shall arise after them, seuen yeeres of famine, and all the plentie shall be forgotten in the land of Egypt: and the famine shall consume the land.

31 And the plentie shal not be knowen in the land, by reason of that famine following · for it shalbe very † grieuous.

† Heb. heauy

32 And for that the dreame was doubled vnto Pharaoh twice, it is because the thing is ||established by God: and God will shortly bring it to passe.

|| Or, prepared of God.

33 Now therfore let Pharaoh looke out a man discreet and wise, and set him ouer the land of Egypt.

34 Let Pharaoh doe this, and let him appoint ||officers ouer the land, & take vp the fift part of the land of Egypt, in the seuen plenteous yeeres.

|| Or, ouerseers,

35 And let them gather all the food of those good yeeres that come, and lay vp corne vnder the hand of Pharaoh, and let them keepe food in the cities.

36 And that food shall be for store to the land, against the seuen yeeres of famine, which shall bee in the land of Egypt, that the land † perish not through the famine.

† Heb. be no cut off.

37 ¶ And the thing was good in the eyes of Pharaoh, and in the eyes of all his seruants.

38 And Pharaoh said vnto his seruants, Can we find such a one, as this is, a man in whom the spirit of God is?

39 And Pharaoh said vnto Ioseph, Forasmuch as God hath shewed thee all this, there is none so discreete and wise, as thou art:

40 * Thou shalt be ouer my house, and according vnto thy word shall all my people be † ruled: only in the throne will I be greater then thou.

* Psal. 105. 21. 1. mac. 2. 53. act. 7. 10.
† Heb. armed: or, kisse.

41 And Pharaoh said vnto Ioseph, See, I haue set thee ouer all the land of Egypt.

42 And Pharaoh tooke off his ring from his hand, & put it vpon Iosephs hand, and arayed him in vestures of ||fine linnen, and put a gold chaine about his necke.

|| Or, silke.

43 And he made him to ride in the second charet which he had: and they cried before him, || Bow the knee: and he made him ruler ouer all the land of Egypt.

|| Or, Tender father Heb. Abrech.

44 And

44 And Pharaoh said vnto Ioseph, I am Pharaoh, and without thee shall no man lift vp his hand or foote, in all the land of Egypt.

45 And Pharaoh called Iosephs name, Zaphnath-Paaneah, and he gaue him to wife Asenath the daughter *Or, Prince* of Poti-pherah, ||priest of On: and Ioseph went out ouer all the lande of Egypt.

46 (¶ And Ioseph was thirtie yeeres old when he stood before Pharaoh king of Egypt) and Ioseph went out from the presence of Pharaoh, and went thorowout all the land of Egypt.

47 And in the seuen plenteous yeres the earth brought forth by handfuls.

48 And he gathered vp all the foode of the seuen yeeres, which were in the land of Egypt, and laid vp the foode in the cities: the foode of the field which was round about euery citie, laid he vp in the same.

49 And Ioseph gathered corne as the sand of the sea, very much, vntill he left numbring: for it was without number.

50 *And vnto Ioseph were borne two sonnes, before the yeeres of famine came: which Asenath the daughter of Poti-pherah, ||Priest of On bare vnto him.

51 And Ioseph called the name of the first borne||Manasseh: for God, *said hee,* hath made me forget all my toile, and all my fathers house.

52 And the name of the second called he ||Ephraim: for God hath caused mee to be fruitfull in the land of my affliction.

53 ¶ And the seuen yeeres of plenteousnesse, that was in the land of Egypt, were ended.

54 *And the seuen yeeres of dearth beganne to come according as Ioseph had saide, and the dearth was in all lands: but in all the land of Egypt there was bread.

55 And when all the land of Egypt was famished, the people cried to Pharaoh for bread: and Pharaoh said vnto all the Egyptians, Goe vnto Ioseph: what he saith to you, doe.

56 And the famine was ouer all the face of the earth; and Ioseph opened all †the storehouses, and solde vnto the Egyptians: and the famine waxed sore in the land of Egypt.

57 And all countreys came into E-

Or, Prince
Chap. 46.
20. & 48. 5.
Or, Prince.
That is, Forgetting.
That is, Fruitfull.
Psal. 105. 6.
Hebr. All wherein was.

gypt to Ioseph, for to buy corne, because that the famine was so sore in all lands.

Now when * Iacob saw that there was corne in Egypt, Iacob said vnto his sonnes, Why doe ye looke one vpon an other?

2 And hee said, Beholde, I haue heard that there is corne in Egypt: get you downe thither and buy for vs from thence, that we may liue, and not die.

3 ¶ And Iosephs ten brethren went downe to buy corne in Egypt.

4 But Beniamin Iosephs brother, Iacob sent not with his brethren: for he said, Lest peraduenture mischiefe befall him.

5 And the sonnes of Israel came to buy corne among those that came: for the famine was in the land of Canaan.

6 And Ioseph was the gouernour ouer the land, *and* hee *it was* that sold to all the people of the land: and Iosephs brethren came, & bowed downe themselues before him, *with* their faces to the earth.

7 And Ioseph saw his brethren, and he knew them, but made himselfe strange vnto them, and spake †roughly vnto them; and hee saide vnto them, Whence come ye? And they said, From the land of Canaan, to buy food.

8 And Ioseph knew his brethren, but they knew not him.

9 And Ioseph *remembred the dreames which hee dreamed of them, and said vnto them, Ye are spies: to see the nakednes of the land you are come.

10 And they said vnto him, Nay, my lord, but to buy food *are* thy seruants come.

11 We are all one mans sonnes; we are true men: thy seruants are no spies.

12 And he said vnto them, Nay: but to see the nakednesse of the land, you are come.

13 And they said, Thy seruants are twelue

*Acts. 7. 12.
†Hebr. hard things with them.
*Chap. 37. 5.

twelue brethren, the ſonnes of one man in the land of Canaan: and behold, the yongeſt *is* this day with our father, and one is not.

14 And Ioſeph ſaid vnto them, That is it that I ſpake vnto you, ſaying, Ye *are* ſpies.

15 Hereby ye ſhall be proued: by the life of Pharaoh ye ſhall not goe foorth hence, except your yongeſt brother come hither.

16 Send one of you, and let him fetch your brother, and ye ſhalbe †kept in priſon, that your wordes may be proued, whether there be any trueth in you: or els by the life of Pharaoh ſurely ye are ſpies.

† Heb. bound

17 And he †put them all together into warde, three dayes.

† Hebr. gathered.

18 And Ioſeph ſaid vnto them the third day, This doe, and liue: *for* I feare God.

19 If ye be true men, let one of your brethren be bound in the houſe of your priſon: goe ye, carry corne for the famine of your houſes.

20 But * bring your yongeſt brother vnto mee, ſo ſhall your wordes be verified, and yee ſhall not die: and they did ſo.

* Chap. 43. 5.

21 ¶ And they ſaid one to another, We are verily guiltie concerning our brother, in that we ſaw the anguiſh of his ſoule, when he beſought vs, and we would not heare: therefore is this diſtreſſe come vpon vs.

22 And Reuben anſwered them, ſaying, * Spake I not vnto you, ſaying, Doe not ſinne againſt the childe, and ye would not heare? therefore behold alſo, his blood is required.

* Chap. 37. 21.

23 And they knew not that Ioſeph vnderſtood them: for †hee ſpake vnto them by an interpreter.

† Hebr. an interpreter was betweene them.

24 And hee turned himſelfe about from them and wept, and returned to them againe, and communed with them, and tooke from them Simeon, and bound him before their eyes.

25 ¶ Then Ioſeph commanded to fill their ſackes with corne, and to reſtore euery mans money into his ſacke, and to giue them prouiſion for the way: and thus did he vnto them.

26 And they laded their aſſes with the corne, and departed thence.

27 And as one of them opened his ſacke, to giue his aſſe prouender in the Inne, he eſpied his money: for behold, it *was* in his ſackes mouth.

28 And he ſaid vnto his brethren, My money is reſtored, and loe, *it is* euen in my ſacke: and their heart †failed them, and they were afraid, ſaying one to an other, What is this that God hath done vnto vs?

† Hebr. went foorth.

29 ¶ And they came vnto Iacob their father, vnto the land of Canaan, and told him all that befell vnto them, ſaying;

30 The man *who is* the lord of the land, ſpake †roughly to vs, and tooke vs for ſpies of the countrey.

† Hebr. with vs hard things.

31 And we ſaid vnto him, We are true men; we are no ſpies.

32 We be twelue brethren, ſonnes of our father: one *is* not, and the yongeſt *is* this day with our father, in the land of Canaan.

33 And the man the lord of the countrey ſaid vnto vs, Hereby ſhall I know that ye are true men: leaue one of your brethren here with me, and take *foode* for the famine of your houſholds, and be gone.

34 And bring your yongeſt brother vnto me: then ſhall I know that you *are* no ſpies, but *that* you *are* true men: *ſo* will I deliuer you your brother, and ye ſhall traffique in the land.

35 ¶ And it came to paſſe as they emptied their ſacks, that behold, euery mans bundle of money *was* in his ſacke: and when both they and their father ſaw the bundels of money, they were afraid.

36 And Iacob their father ſaid vnto them, Me haue ye bereaued of my children: Ioſeph is not, and Simeon is not, and ye wil take Beniamin *away*: all theſe things are againſt me.

37 And Reuben ſpake vnto his father, ſaying; Slay my two ſonnes, if I bring him not to thee: deliuer him into my hand, and I will bring him to thee againe.

38 And he ſaid, My ſonne ſhall not goe downe with you, for his brother is dead, and he is left alone: if miſchiefe befall him by the way in the which yee goe, then ſhall ye bring downe my gray haires with ſorrow to the graue.

CHAP. XLIII.

1 Iacob is hardly perſwaded to ſend Beniamin. 15 Ioſeph entertaineth his brethren. 31 Hee maketh them a feaſt.

And

ANd the famine was sore in the land.

2 And it came to passe when they had eaten vp the corne, which they had brought out of Egypt, their father said vnto them, Goe againe, buy vs a little foode.

3 And Iudah spake vnto him, saying, The man did †solemnly protest vnto vs, saying, Ye shall not see my face, except your * brother *be* with you.

4 If thou wilt send our brother with vs, we will goe downe and buy thee food.

5 But if thou wilt not send *him*, we will not goe downe : for the man saide vnto vs, Ye shall not see my face, except your brother *be* with you.

6 And Israel said, Wherefore dealt ye so ill with me, as to tell the man whether ye had yet a brother ?

7 And they said, The man † asked vs straitly of our state, and of our kindred, saying, Is your father yet aliue ? haue yee *another* brother ? and we tolde him according to the †tenour of these words : † Could we certainely knowe that he would say, Bring your brother downe ?

8 And Iudah said vnto Israel his father, Send the lad with me, and wee will arise and go, that we may liue, and not die, both we, and thou, and also our little ones.

9 I will be surety for him ; of my hand shalt thou require him : * if I bring him not vnto thee, and set him before thee, then let me beare the blame for euer.

10 For except we had lingred, surely now wee had returned ‖ this second time.

11 And their father Israel said vnto them, If it must *bee* so now, doe this : take of the best fruits in the land in your vessels, and carie downe the man a Present, a litle balme, and a litle honie, spices, and myrrhe, nuts, and almonds.

12 And take double money in your hand, and the money that was brought againe in the mouth of your sackes : carie *it* againe in your hand, peraduenture it was an ouersight.

13 Take also your brother, and arise, goe againe vnto the man.

14 And God Almightie giue you mercie before the man, that he may send away your other brother, and Benia-

min : ‖ If I be bereaued of my children, I am bereaued.

15 ¶ And the men tooke that Present, and they tooke double money in their hand, and Beniamin, and rose vp, and went downe to Egypt, and stood before Ioseph.

16 And when Ioseph sawe Beniamin with them, hee said to the ruler of his house, Bring these men home, and †slay, and make ready : for these men shall †dine with me at noone.

17 And the man did as Ioseph bade : and the man brought the men into Iosephs house.

18 And the men were afraid, because they were brought into Iosephs house, and they said, Because of the money that was returned in our sackes at the first time are we brought in, that hee may †seeke occasion against vs, and fall vpon vs, and take vs for bondmen, and our asses.

19 And they came neere to the steward of Iosephs house, and they communed with him at the doore of the house,

20 And said, O Sir, * we came indeed downe at the first time to buy food.

21 And it came to passe when wee came to the Inne, that wee opened our sackes, and behold, euery mans money *was* in the mouth of his sacke, our money in ful weight : and we haue brought it againe in our hand.

22 And other money haue wee brought downe in our handes to buy food : we cannot tell who put our money in our sackes.

23 And he said, Peace *be* to you, feare not : your God, and the God of your father, hath giuen you treasure in your sackes : †I had your money. And hee brought Simeon out vnto them.

24 And the man brought the men into Iosephs house, and *gaue *them* water, and they washed their feete, and he gaue their asses prouender.

25 And they made ready the Present against Ioseph came at noone : for they heard that they should eate bread there.

26 ¶ And when Ioseph came home, they brought him the Present which was in their hand, into the house, and bowed themselues to him to the earth.

27 And he asked them of their †welfare, and said, *Is your father well, the old man of whom ye spake ? Is he yet aliue ?

28 And

Marginal notes (left column):

† Heb. protesting he protested.
* Chap. 42. 20.

† Heb. asking he asked vs.

† Heb. mouth
† Heb. knowing could we know ?

* Chap. 44. 32.

‖ Or, twice by this.

Marginal notes (right column):

‖ Or, and I, as I haue bene &c.

† Heb. kill a killing.
† Hebr. eate.

† Heb. roll himselfe vpon vs.

* Cha. 42. 3
† Heb. comming downe we came downe.

† Heb. your money came to mee.

* Chap. 18. 4. & 24. 32.

† Heb. peace
† Hebr. Is there peace to your father ?

28 And they answered, Thy seruant our father *is* in good health, hee *is* yet a-liue: & they bowed downe their heads, and made obeisance.

29 And he lift vp his eyes, and sawe his brother Beniamin, his mothers sonne, and said, Is this your yonger brother, of whom yee spake vnto mee? and he said, God be gracious vnto thee, my sonne.

30 And Ioseph made haste: for his bowels did yerne vpon his brother: and he sought where to weepe, and hee entred into his chamber, & wept there.

31 And he washed his face, and went out, and refrained himselfe, and saide, Set on bread.

32 And they set on for him by himselfe, and for them by themselues, and for the Egyptians which did eate with him, by themselues: because the Egyptians might not eate bread with the Hebrewes: for that *is* an abomination vnto the Egyptians.

33 And they sate before him, the first borne according to his birthright, and the yongest according to his youth: and the men marueiled one at another.

34 And hee tooke and *sent* measses vnto them from before him: but Beniamins measse *was* fiue times so much as any of theirs: and they drunke, and †were merry with him.

† *Heb. they dranke largely*

CHAP. XLIIII.

1 Iosephs policie to stay his brethren. 14 Iudahs humble supplication to Ioseph.

 Nd hee commaunded the †steward of his house, saying, Fill the mens sackes *with* food, as much as they can carie, and put euery mans money in his sacks mouth

† *Heb. him that was o-uer his house*

2 And put my cup, the siluer cup, in the sackes mouth of the yongest, and his corne money: and he did according to the word that Ioseph had spoken.

3 Assoone as the morning was light, the men were sent away, they, and their asses.

4 And when they were gone out of the citie, and not *yet* farre off, Ioseph said vnto his steward, Vp, follow after the men; and when thou doest ouertake them, say vnto them, Wherefore haue ye rewarded euill for good?

5 Is not this it, in which my lord drinketh? and whereby indeed he ‖diuineth? ye haue done euill in so doing.

‖ *Or, maketh triall.*

6 ¶ And he ouertooke them, and he spake vnto them these same words.

7 And they said vnto him, Wherefore saith my lord these words? God forbid that thy seruants should doe according to this thing.

8 Behold, the money which wee found in our sackes mouthes, wee brought againe vnto thee, out of the land of Canaan: how then should wee steale out of thy lords house, siluer or golde?

9 With whom *soeuer* of thy seruants it be found, both let him die, and we also will be my lords bondmen.

10 And he said, Now also let it be according vnto your wordes · hee with whom it is found, shall be my seruant: and ye shall be blamelesse.

11 Then they speedily tooke downe euery man his sacke to the ground, and opened euery man his sacke.

12 And he searched, and began at the eldest, and left at the yongest: and the cup was found in Beniamins sacke.

13 Then they rent their clothes, and laded euery man his asse, and returned to the citie

14 ¶ And Iudah and his brethren came to Iosephs house: (for he was yet there) and they fell before him on the ground.

15 And Ioseph said vnto them, What deed is this that ye haue done? wote ye not, that such a man as I can certainely ‖diuine?

‖ *Or, make triall?*

16 And Iudah said, What shall wee say vnto my lord? what shal we speake? or how shall we cleare our selues? God hath found out the iniquitie of thy seruants: beholde, wee are my lords seruants, both we, and he also with whom the cup is found.

17 And he said, God forbid that I should doe so: *but* the man in whose hand the cup is found, he shal be my seruant; and as for you, get you vp in peace vnto your father.

18 ¶ Then Iudah came neere vnto him, and said, Oh my lord, let thy seruant, I pray thee, speake a word in my lords eares, & let not thine anger burne against thy seruant: for thou art euen as Pharaoh.

19 My lord asked his seruants, saying, Haue ye a father, or a brother?

20 And we said vnto my lord, Wee haue a father, an olde man, and a childe of

of his old age, a little one: and his brother is dead, and he alone is left of his mother, and his father loueth him.

21 And thou saidst vnto thy seruants, Bring him downe vnto mee, that I may set mine eyes vpon him.

22 And we said vnto my lord, The lad cannot leaue his father: for *if* hee should leaue his father, *his father* would die.

23 And thou saidst vnto thy seruants, * Except your yongest brother come downe with you, you shall see my face no more.

* Chap. 43. 3.

24 And it came to passe when wee came vp vnto thy seruant my father, we told him the words of my lord.

25 And our father said, Goe againe, and buy vs a little food.

26 And we saide, Wee cannot goe downe: if our yongest brother be with vs, then will we goe downe: for wee may not see the mans face, except our yongest brother be with vs.

27 And thy seruant my father said vnto vs, Ye know that my wife bare me two *sonnes.*

28 And the one went out from me, and I said, * Surely he is torne in pieces: and I saw him not since.

* Chap. 37. 33.

29 And if ye take this also from me, and mischiefe befall him, ye shall bring downe my gray haires with sorrow to the graue.

30 Now therefore when I come to thy seruant my father, and the lad *bee* not with vs: (seeing that his life is bound vp in the lads life.)

31 It shall come to passe, when he seeth that the lad *is* not with vs, that he will die, and thy seruants shall bring downe the gray haires of thy seruant our father with sorrow to the graue.

32 For thy seruant became surety for the lad vnto my father, saying, * If I bring him not vnto thee, then I shall beare the blame to my father, for euer.

* Chap. 43. 9.

33 Now therefore, I pray thee, let thy seruant abide in stead of the lad, a bondman to my lord, and let the lad goe vp with his brethren.

34 For how shall I goe vp to my father, and the lad be not with mee, lest peraduenture I see the euill that shall †come on my father?

† Hebr. finde my father.

CHAP. XLV.

1 Ioseph maketh himselfe knowen to his brethren. 5 Hee comforteth them in Gods prouidence. 9 Hee sendeth for his father. 16 Pharaoh confirmeth it. 21 Ioseph furnisheth them for their iourney, and exhorteth them to concord. 25 Iacob is reuiued with the newes.

Hen Ioseph could not refraine himselfe before all them that stood by him: and he cried, Cause euery man to goe out from me; and there stood no man with him, while Ioseph made himselfe knowen vnto his brethren.

2 And he †wept aloud: and the Egyptians, and the house of Pharaoh heard.

† Hebr. Gaue foorth his voice in weeping.

3 And Ioseph said vnto his brethren, *I am Ioseph; Doeth my father yet liue? and his brethren could not answere him: for they were ||troubled at his presence.

* A&s. 7. 13.
|| Or, terrified.

4 And Ioseph said vnto his brethren, Come neere to me, I pray you: and they came neere; and he said, I *am* Ioseph your brother, whom ye sold into Egypt.

5 Now therefore bee not grieued, †nor angry with your selues, that yee sold me hither: *for God did send me before you, to preserue life.

† Hebr. neither let there be anger in your eyes.
* Chap. 50. 20.

6 For these two yeeres hath the famine bene in the land: and yet there are fiue yeeres, in the which there shall neither be earing nor haruest.

7 And God sent me before you, to †preserue you a posteritie in the earth, and to saue your liues by a great deliuerance.

† Hebr. to put for you a remnant.

8 So now it was not you *that* sent me hither, but God: and he hath made me a father to Pharaoh, and lord of all his house, and a ruler throughout all the land of Egypt.

9 Haste you, and goe vp to my father, and say vnto him, Thus saith thy sonne Ioseph; God hath made me lord of all Egypt; come downe vnto me, tary not.

10 And thou shalt dwell in the land of Goshen, and thou shalt be neere vnto me, thou, and thy children, and thy childrens children, and thy flockes, and thy heards, and all that thou hast.

11 And there wil I nourish thee, (for yet there are fiue yeeres of famine) lest thou and thy houshold, and all that thou hast, come to pouertie.

12 And behold, your eyes see, and the eyes of my brother Beniamin, that *it is* my

my mouth that ſpeaketh vnto you.

13 And you ſhall tell my father of all my glory in Egypt, and of all that you haue ſeene, and ye ſhall haſte, and bring downe my father hither.

14 And he fel vpon his brother Beniamins necke, and wept: and Beniamin wept vpon his necke.

15 Moreouer hee kiſſed all his brethren, and wept vpon them: and after that, his brethren talked with him.

16 ¶ And the fame thereof was heard in Pharaohs houſe, ſaying, Ioſephs brethren are come: and it †pleaſed Pharaoh well, and his ſeruants.

† Hebr. was good in the eyes of Pharaoh.

17 And Pharaoh ſaid vnto Ioſeph, Say vnto thy brethren, This doe yee, lade your beaſts and goe, get you vnto the land of Canaan.

18 And take your father, and your houſholds, and come vnto mee: and I wil giue you the good of the land of Egypt, and ye ſhall eat the fat of the land.

19 Now thou art commanded, this doe yee; Take you wagons out of the land of Egypt for your little ones, and for your wiues, and bring your father, and come.

† Hebr. Let not your eye ſpare, &c.

20 Also †regard not your ſtuffe: for the good of all the land of Egypt is yours.

21 And the children of Iſrael did ſo: and Ioſeph gaue them wagons, according to the † commandement of Pharaoh, and gaue them prouiſion for the way.

† Hebr. mouth.

22 To all of them he gaue each man changes of raiment: but to Beniamin hee gaue three hundred *pieces* of ſiluer, and fiue changes of raiment.

23 And to his father hee ſent after this maner: ten aſſes †laden with the good things of Egypt, and ten ſhee aſſes laden with corne, and bread and meat for his father by the way.

† Hebr. carrying.

24 So he ſent his brethren away, and they departed: and hee ſaid vnto them, See that yee fall not out by the way.

25 ¶ And they went vp out of Egypt, and came into the land of Canaan vnto Iacob their father,

26 And told him, ſaying, Ioſeph is yet aliue, and he is gouernour ouer all the land of Egypt. And †Iacobs heart fainted, for he beleeued them not.

† Hebr. his.

27 And they told him all the words of Ioſeph, which hee had ſaide vnto them: and when hee ſaw the wagons which Ioſeph had ſent to carie him, the ſpirit of Iacob their father reuiued.

28 And Iſrael ſaid, It is enough; Ioſeph my ſonne is yet aliue: I will goe and ſee him before I die.

CHAP. XLVI.

1 Iacob is comforted by God at Beerſheba. 5 Thence hee with his company goeth into Egypt. 8 The number of his family that went into Egypt. 28 Ioſeph meeteth Iacob. 31 Hee inſtructeth his brethren how to anſwere to Pharaoh.

ANd Iſrael tooke his iourney with all that hee had, and came to Beerſheba, and offered ſacrifices vnto the God of his father Iſaac.

2 And God ſpake vnto Iſrael in the viſions of the night, and ſaid, Iacob, Iacob. And he ſaid, Here am I.

3 And he ſaid, I am God, the God of thy father, feare not to goe downe into Egypt: for I will there make of thee a great nation.

4 I will goe downe with thee into Egypt; and I will alſo ſurely bring thee vp *againe:* and Ioſeph ſhall put his hand vpon thine eyes.

5 And Iacob roſe vp from Beerſheba: and the ſonnes of Iſrael caried Iacob their father, and their litle ones, and their wiues, in the wagons which Pharaoh had ſent to cary him.

6 And they tooke their cattell, and their goods which they had gotten in the land of Canaan, and came into Egypt, *Iacob, and all his ſeed with him:

Iosh. 24. 4. psal. 105. 23. esal. 52. 4.

7 His ſonnes, and his ſonnes ſonnes with him, his daughters, and his ſonnes daughters, and all his ſeed brought he with him into Egypt.

8 ¶ And *theſe *are* the names of the children of Iſrael, which came into Egypt, Iacob and his ſonnes: *Reuben Iacobs firſt borne.

*Exod. 1. 1. and 6. 14. num. 26. 8. and 1. chro. 5. 1.
* Num. 26. 5.*

9 And the ſonnes of Reuben, Hanoch, and Phallu, and Hezron, and Carmi.

10 ¶ * And the ſonnes of Simeon: Iemuel, and Iamin, and Ohad, and Iachin, and Zohar, and Shaul the ſonne of a Canaanitiſh woman.

Exod. 6. 15. 1. chro. 4. 24.

11 ¶ And the ſonnes of *Leui: Gerſhon, Kohath, and Merari.

1. Chro. 6. 1.

12 ¶ And the ſonnes of * Iudah: Er,

1. Chro. 2. 3. and 4. 21. chap. 38. 3.

Er, and Onan, and Shelah, and Pharez, and Zerah : But Er & Onan died in the land of Canaan. And the sonnes of Pharez, were Hezron, and Hamul.

1. Chron. 7. 1.

13 ¶ And the sonnes of Issachar : Tola, and Phuuah, and Job, and Shimron.

14 ¶ *And the sonnes of Zebulun : Sered, and Elon, and Iahleel.

15 These *bee* the sonnes of Leah, which she bare vnto Iacob in Padan-Aram, with his daughter Dinah : all the soules of his sonnes and his daughters, were thirtie and three.

16 ¶ And the sonnes of Gad : Ziphion, and Haggi, Shuni, and Ezbon, Eri, and Arodi, and Areli.

1. Chro. 7. 40.

17 ¶ * And the sonnes of Asher : Iimnah, and Ishuah, and Isui, and Beriah, and Serah their sister : And the sonnes of Beriah : Heber, and Malchiel.

18 These *are* the sonnes of Zilpah, whome Laban gaue to Leah his daughter : and these she bare vnto Iacob, euen sixteene soules.

19 The sonnes of Rachel Iacobs wife : Ioseph, and Beniamin.

Chap. 41. 50.
Or, Prince.

20 ¶ And vnto Ioseph in the lande of Egypt, were borne Manasseh and Ephraim, * which Asenath the daughter of Poti-pherah ‖ Priest of On bare vnto him.

1. Chron. 7. 6. & 8. 1.

21 ¶ * And the sonnes of Beniamin *were* Belah, and Becher, and Ashbel, Gera, and Naaman, Ehi and Rosh, Muppim, and Huppim, and Ard.

22 These are the sonnes of Rachel which were borne to Iacob : all the soules were fourteene.

23 ¶ And the sonnes of Dan : Hushim.

24 ¶ And the sonnes of Naphtali : Iahzeel, and Guni, and Iezer, and Shillem.

25 These are the sonnes of Bilhah, which Laban gaue vnto Rachel his daughter, and she bare these vnto Iacob : all the soules were seuen.

Deut. 10. 22.
Heb. thigh.

26 All the * soules that came with Iacob into Egypt, which came out of his †loines, besides Iacobs sonnes wiues, all the soules *were* threescore and sixe.

27 And the sonnes of Ioseph, which were borne him in Egypt, *were* two soules : all the soules of the house of Iacob, which came into Egypt, were threescore and ten.

28 ¶ And he sent Iudah before him vnto Ioseph, to direct his face vnto Goshen, and they came into the lande of Goshen.

29 And Ioseph made ready his charet, and went vp to meet Israel his father, to Goshen, and presented himselfe vnto him : and he fell on his necke, and wept on his necke a good while.

30 And Israel saide vnto Ioseph, Now let me die, since I haue seene thy face, because thou art yet aliue.

31 And Ioseph said vnto his brethren, and vnto his fathers house, I will goe vp, and shew Pharaoh, and say vnto him, My brethren, & my fathers house, which *were* in the land of Canaan, are come vnto me.

32 And the men *are* sheapheards, for †their trade hath bene to feed cattell : and they haue brought their flocks, and their heards, and all that they haue.

† Hebr. they are men of cattell.

33 And it shall come to passe when Pharaoh shall call you, and shall say, What is your occupation ?

34 That ye shall say, Thy seruants trade hath bene about cattell, from our youth euen vntill now, both we, and also our fathers : that ye may dwell in the land of Goshen ; for euery shepheard is an abomination vnto the Egyptians.

CHAP. XLVII.

1 Ioseph presenteth fiue of his brethren, 7 and his father, before Pharaoh. 11 Hee giueth them habitation and maintenance. 13 He getteth all the Egyptians money, 16 their cattell, 18 their lands to Pharaoh. 22 The Priestes land was not bought. 23 Hee letteth the land to them for a fift part. 28 Iacobs age. 29 Hee sweareth Ioseph to burie him with his fathers.

Hen Ioseph came and tolde Pharaoh, and saide, My father and my brethren, and their flockes, and their heards, and all that they haue, are come out of the land of Canaan : and behold, they are in the land of Goshen.

2 And hee tooke some of his brethren, euen fiue men, & presented them vnto Pharaoh.

3 And Pharaoh said vnto his brethren, What is your occupation ? And they said vnto Pharaoh, Thy seruants are shepheards, both wee and also our fathers.

4 The

4 They said moreouer vnto Pharaoh, For to soiourne in the land are we come: for thy seruants haue no pasture for their flockes, for the famine is sore in the land of Canaan: now therefore we pray thee, let thy seruants dwel in the land of Goshen.

5 And Pharaoh spake vnto Ioseph, saying, Thy father and thy brethren are come vnto thee.

6 The land of Egypt is before thee: in the best of the land make thy father and brethren to dwell, in the lande of Goshen let them dwell: and if thou knowest any man of actiuitie amongst them, then make them rulers ouer my cattell.

7 And Ioseph brought in Iacob his father, and set him before Pharaoh: and Iacob blessed Pharaoh.

8 And Pharaoh said vnto Iacob, † How old art thou?

† Heb. how many are the dayes of the yeeres of thy life?
* Heb. 11. 9, 13.

9 And Iacob said vnto Pharaoh, * The dayes of the yeeres of my pilgrimage are an hundred & thirtie yeres: few and euill haue the dayes of the yeeres of my life bene, and haue not attained vnto the dayes of the yeeres of the life of my fathers, in the dayes of their pilgrimage.

10 And Iacob blessed Pharaoh, and went out from before Pharaoh.

11 ¶ And Ioseph placed his father, and his brethren, and gaue them a possession in the land of Egypt, in the best of the land, in the land of Rameses, as Pharaoh had commanded.

12 And Ioseph nourished his father and his brethren, and all his fathers houshold with bread, ||according to *their* families.

‖ Or, as a litle childe is nourished.
Heb. according to the little ones.

13 ¶ And there was no bread in all the land: for the famine was very sore, so that the land of Egypt and all the land of Canaan fainted by reason of the famine.

14 And Ioseph gathered vp all the money that was found in the land of Egypt, and in the land of Canaan, for the corne which they bought: and Ioseph brought the money into Pharaohs house.

15 And when money failed in the land of Egypt, and in the land of Canaan, all the Egyptians came vnto Ioseph, and said, Giue vs bread: for why should we die in thy presence? for the money faileth.

16 And Ioseph said, Giue your cat-

tell: and I will giue you for your cattell, if money faile.

17 And they brought their cattel vnto Ioseph: and Ioseph gaue them bread *in exchange* for horses, and for the flockes, and for the cattell of the heards, and for the asses, and † he fed them with bread, for all their cattel, for that yeere.

† Heb. led them.

18 When that yeere was ended, they came vnto him the second yeere, and said vnto him, We will not hide it from my lord, how that our money is spent, my lord also had our heards of cattell: there is not ought left in the sight of my lord, but our bodies, and our lands.

19 Wherfore shall we die before thine eyes, both we, and our land? buy vs and our land for bread, and we and our land will be seruants vnto Pharaoh: and giue *vs* seede that we may liue and not die, that the land be not desolate.

20 And Ioseph bought all the land of Egypt for Pharaoh: for the Egyptians sold euery man his field, because the famine preuailed ouer them: so the land became Pharaohs.

21 And as for the people, he remoued them to cities from one end of the borders of Egypt, euen to the *other* ende thereof.

22 Onely the land of the ‖ Priests bought he not: for the priests had a portion assigned them of Pharaoh, and did eate their portion which Pharaoh gaue them: wherefore they solde not their lands.

‖ Or, Princes

23 Then Ioseph said vnto the people, Behold, I haue bought you this day, and your land for Pharaoh: Loe, here is seed for you, and ye shall sow the land.

24 And it shall come to passe in the increase, that you shall giue the fift part vnto Pharaoh, and foure parts shall be your owne, for seed of the field, and for your food, and for them of your households, and for food for your litle ones.

25 And they said, Thou hast saued our liues: let vs find grace in the sight of my lord, and we will be Pharaohs seruants.

26 And Ioseph made it a law ouer the land of Egypt vnto this day, that Pharaoh should haue the fift part: except the land of the ‖ priests onely, *which* became not Pharaohs.

‖ Or, Princes

27 ¶ And Israel dwelt in the land of Egypt in the countrey of Goshen, and they had possessions therein, and grew,

grew, and multiplied exceedingly.

28 And Iacob liued in the land of Egypt seuenteene yeres: so †the whole age of Iacob was an hundred fourtie and seuen yeeres.

Hebr. the ayes of the eeres of his fe.

29 And the time drew nigh that Israel must die, and he called his sonne Ioseph, and said vnto him, If now I haue found grace in thy sight, * put, I pray thee, thy hand vnder my thigh, and deale kindly and truely with mee, bury me not, I pray thee, in Egypt.

Chap. 4. 2.

30 But I will lie with my fathers, and thou shalt carie mee out of Egypt, and bury me in their burying place: and he said, I will doe as thou hast said.

31 And he said, Sweare vnto mee: and he sware vnto him. And * Israel bowed himselfe vpon the beds head.

Heb. 11. 4.

CHAP. XLVIII.

1 Ioseph with his sonnes visiteth his sicke father. 2 Iacob strengtheneth himselfe to blesse them. 3 He repeateth the promise. 5 He taketh Ephraim and Manasseh as his owne. 7 Hee telleth him of his mothers graue. 9 Hee blesseth Ephraim and Manasseh. 17 Hee preferreth the yonger before the elder. 21 He prophesieth their returne to Canaan.

ANd it came to passe after these things, that one told Ioseph, Behold, thy father is sicke: and he tooke with him his two sonnes, Manasseh and Ephraim.

2 And one told Iacob, and said, Behold, thy sonne Ioseph commeth vnto thee: and Israel strengthened himselfe, and sate vpon the bed.

3 And Iacob saide vnto Ioseph, God Almightie appeared vntò mee at *Luz in the land of Canaan, and blessed mee,

Chap. 28. 4. & 35. 6.

4 And said vnto me, Behold, I wil make thee fruitfull, and multiplie thee, and I will make of thee a multitude of people, and will giue this land to thy seede after thee, for an euerlasting possession.

5 ¶ And now thy * two sonnes, Ephraim and Manasseh, which were borne vnto thee in the land of Egypt, before I came vnto thee into Egypt, *are* mine: as Reuben and Simeon, they shalbe mine.

Chap. 41.). iosh. 3. 7.

6 And thy issue which thou begettest after them, shall be thine, and shall be called after the name of their brethren in their inheritance.

7 And as for me, when I came from *Padan, Rachel died by me in the land of Canaan, in the way, when yet *there was* but a little way to come vnto Ephrath: and I buried her there in the way of Ephrath, the same is Bethlehem.

Gen. 35. 19.

8 And Israel behelde Iosephs sonnes, and said, Who *are* these?

9 And Ioseph said vnto his father, They are my sonnes, whom God hath giuen me in this *place:* and he said, Bring them, I pray thee, vnto me, and I will blesse them.

10 (Now the eyes of Israel were †dimme for age, *so that* he could not see,) and hee brought them neere vnto him, and he kissed them, and imbraced them.

† Heb. heauy

11 And Israel said vnto Ioseph, I had not thought to see thy face: and loe, God hath shewed me also thy seed.

12 And Ioseph brought them out from betweene his knees, and hee bowed himselfe with his face to the earth.

13 And Ioseph tooke them both, Ephraim in his right hand, toward Israels left hand, and Manasseh in his left hand towards Israels right hand, and brought *them* neere vnto him.

14 And Israel stretched out his right hand, and layd *it* vpon Ephraims head who *was* the yonger; and his left hand vpon Manassehs head, guiding his hands wittingly: for Manasseh *was* the first borne.

15 ¶ And * he blessed Ioseph and said, God before whom my fathers Abraham and Isaac did walke, the God which fedde mee all my life long vnto this day,

Hebr. 11. 21.

16 The Angel which redeemed mee from all euill, blesse the laddes, and let my name be named on them, and the name of my fathers Abraham and Isaac, and let them grow †into a multitude in the midst of the earth.

† Hebr. as fishes doe increase.

17 And when Ioseph saw that his father laide his right hand vpon the head of Ephraim, it displeased him: and he held vp his fathers hand, to remoue it from Ephraims head, vnto Manassehs head.

18 And Ioseph saide vnto his father, Not so my father: for this *is* the first borne; put thy right hand vpon his head.

19 And his father refused, and said, I know *it,* my sonne, I know *it:* he also shall become a people, and he also shall be

be great: but truely his yonger brother shall be greater then he; and his seede shall become a †multitude of nations.

† Hebr. ful-nesse.

20 And he blessed them that day, saying, In thee shall Israel blesse, saying, God make thee as Ephraim, and as Manasseh: and he set Ephraim before Manasseh.

21 And Israel saide vnto Ioseph, Behold, I die: but God shall be with you, and bring you againe vnto the land of your fathers.

22 Moreouer I haue giuen to thee one portion aboue thy brethren, which I tooke out of the hand of the Amorite with my sword, and with my bow.

CHAP. XLIX.

1 Iacob calleth his sonnes to blesse them. 3 Their blessing in particular. 29 He chargeth them about his buriall. 33 He dieth.

Nd Iacob called vnto his sonnes, and said, Gather your selues together, that I may tell you that which shall befall you in the last dayes.

2 Gather your selues together, and heare ye sonnes of Iacob, and hearken vnto Israel your father.

3 ¶ Reuben, thou art my first borne, my might, and the beginning of my strength, the excellencie of dignitie, and the excellencie of power:

† Hebr. doe not thou excell.
* Chap. 35. 22. 1. chro. 5. 1.
‖ Or, my cowche is gone.
‖ Or, their swords are weapons of violence.

4 Vnstable as water, †thou shalt not excell, because thou *wentest vp to thy fathers bed: then defiledst thou it. ‖He went vp to my couche.

5 ¶ Simeon and Leui are brethren, ‖instruments of crueltie are in their habitations.

6 O my soule, come not thou into their secret: vnto their assembly mine honour be not thou vnited: for in their anger they slew a man, and in their selfe will they ‖digged downe a wall.

‖ Or houghed oxen.

7 Cursed be their anger, for it was fierce; and their wrath, for it was cruell: I will diuide them in Iacob, and scatter them in Israel.

8 ¶ Iudah, thou art he whom thy brethren shall praise: thy hand shall be in the necke of thine enemies, thy fathers children shall bow downe before thee.

9 Iudah is a Lyons whelpe: from the pray my sonne thou art gone vp: he stouped downe, hee couched as a Lyon, and as an old Lyon: who shall rouse him vp?

10 The scepter shall not depart from Iudah, nor a Law-giuer from betweene his feete, vntill Shiloh come: and vnto him shall the gathering of the people be:

11 Binding his foale vnto the vine, and his asses colt vnto the choice vine; he washed his garments in wine, and his clothes in the blood of grapes.

12 His eyes shall be red with wine, and his teeth white with milke.

13 ¶ Zebulun shall dwell at the hauen of the sea, and hee shall be for an Hauen of ships: and his border shall be vnto Zidon.

14 ¶ Issachar is a strong asse, couching downe betweene two burdens.

15 And he saw that rest was good, and the land that it was pleasant: and bowed his shoulder to beare, and became a seruant vnto tribute.

16 ¶ Dan shall iudge his people, as one of the tribes of Israel.

17 Dan shalbe a serpent by the way, an †adder in the path, that biteth the horse heeles, so that his rider shall fall backward.

† Heb. an arrow-snake.

18 I haue waited for thy saluation, O LORD.

19 ¶ Gad, a troupe shall ouercome him: but he shall ouercome at the last.

20 ¶ Out of Asher his bread shall be fat, and he shall yeeld royall dainties.

21 ¶ Naphtali is a hinde let loose: He giueth goodly words.

22 ¶ Ioseph is a fruitfull bough, euen a fruitfull bough by a well, whose †branches runne ouer the wall.

† Hebr. daughters.

23 The archers haue sorely grieued him, and shot at him, and hated him.

24 But his bow abode in strength, and the armes of his hands were made strong, by the hands of the mighty God of Iacob: from thence is the Sheapheard, the stone of Israel,

25 Euen by the God of thy father who shall helpe thee, and by the Almightie, who shall blesse thee with blessings of heauen aboue, blessings of the deepe that lyeth vnder, blessings of the breasts and of the wombe.

26 The blessings of thy father haue preuailed aboue the blessings of my progenitors: vnto the vtmost bound of the euerlasting hils, they shall bee on the head of Ioseph, and on the crowne of the head of him that was separate from his brethren.

27 ¶ Beniamin shall rauine as a wolfe:

wolfe: In the morning hee shall deuoure the pray, and at night he shall diuide the spoile.

28 ¶ All these are the twelue tribes
of Israel, and this is it that their father
spake vnto them, and blessed them: euery one according to his blessing he blessed them.

29 And hee charged them and said
vnto them, I am to bee gathered vnto
my people: *burie me with my fathers,
in the caue that is in the field of Ephron
the Hittite,

Chap. 47.
).

30 In the caue that is in the field of
Machpelah, which is before Mamre, in
the land of Canaan, * which Abraham
bought with the field of Ephron the
Hittite, for a possession of a burying
place.

Chap. 23.
5.

31 (There they buried Abraham and
Sarah his wife, there they buried I-
saac and Rebekah his wife, and there
I buried Leah.)

32 The purchase of the field and of
the caue that is therein, *was* from the
children of Heth.

33 And when Iacob had made an
end of commanding his sonnes, he gathered vp his feete into the bed, and
yeelded vp the ghost, and was gathered
vnto his people.

CHAP. L.

1 The mourning for Iacob. 4 Ioseph getteth
leaue of Pharaoh to goe to bury him. 7 The
funerall. 15 Ioseph comforteth his brethren,
who craued his pardon. 22 His age. 23 He
seeth the third generation of his sonnes. 24
He prophesieth vnto his brethren of their returne. 25 He taketh an oath of them for his
bones. 26 He dieth, and is chested.

ANd Ioseph fell vpon his
fathers face, and wept vpon him, and kissed him.

2 And Ioseph com-
manded his seruants the
physicians to imbalme his father: and
the physicians imbalmed Israel.

3 And fortie dayes were fulfilled for
him, (for so are fulfilled the dayes of
those which are imbalmed) and the E-
gyptians †mourned for him threescore
and ten dayes.

† Heb. wept.

4 And when the dayes of his mourning were past, Ioseph spake vnto the
house of Pharaoh, saying, If now I
haue found grace in your eyes, speake,

I pray you, in the eares of Pharaoh,
saying,

5 * My father made me sweare, saying, Loe, I die: in my graue which I
haue digged for me, in the land of Canaan, there shalt thou bury me. Now
therfore let me goe vp, I pray thee, and
bury my father, and I will come a-
gaine.

* Chap. 47.
29.

6 And Pharaoh said, Goe vp, and
bury thy father, according as he made
thee sweare.

7 ¶ And Ioseph went vp to bury
his father: and with him went vp all
the seruants of Pharaoh, the elders of
his house, and all the elders of the land
of Egypt,

8 And all the house of Ioseph, and
his brethren, and his fathers house:
onely their litle ones, and their flockes,
and their heards, they left in the land of
Goshen.

9 And there went vp with him both
charets and horsemen: and it was a
very great company.

10 And they came to the threshing
floore of Atad, which is beyond Iordan, and there they mourned with a
great and very sore lamentation: and
he made a mourning for his father seuen dayes.

11 And when the inhabitants of the
land, the Canaanites sawe the mourning in the floore of Atad, they saide,
This is a grieuous mourning to the E-
gyptians: wherfore the name of it was
called, ‖Abel Mizraim, which is beyond
Iordan.

‖ That is,
the mour-
ning of the
Egyptians.

12 And his sonnes did vnto him according as he commanded them.

13 For * his sonnes caried him into
the land of Canaan, and buried him in
the caue of the field of Machpelah,
which Abraham * bought with the field
for a possession of a burying place, of E-
phron the Hittite, before Mamre.

* Act. 7. 16

* Chap. 23.
16.

14 ¶ And Ioseph returned into E-
gypt, he and his brethren, and all that
went vp with him, to bury his father,
after he had buried his father.

15 ¶ And when Iosephs brethren
saw that their father was dead, they
said, Ioseph will peraduenture hate
vs, and will certainely requite vs all the
euill which we did vnto him.

16 And they †sent a messenger vnto
Ioseph, saying, Thy father did command before he died, saying,

† Heb. char-
ged.

17 So shall ye say vnto Ioseph, Forgiue,

giue, I pray thee now, the trespasse of thy brethren, and their sinne: for they did vnto thee euill: And now wee pray thee, forgiue the trespasse of the seruants of the God of thy father. And Ioseph wept, when they spake vnto him.

18 And his brethren also went and fell downe before his face, and they said, Behold, we *be* thy seruants.

*Chap. 45. 5.

19 And Ioseph saide vnto them, * Feare not: for *am* I in the place of God?

20 But as for you, yee thought euill against me, *but* God meant it vnto good, to bring to passe, as it is this day, to saue much people aliue.

21 Now therefore feare yee not: I will nourish you, and your litle ones. And hee comforted them, and spake †kindly vnto them.

† Hebr. to their hearts.

22 ¶ And Ioseph dwelt in Egypt, he, and his fathers house: and Ioseph liued an hundred and ten yeeres.

23 * And Ioseph sawe Ephraims children, of the third generation: the children also of Machir, the sonne of Manasseh were †brought vp vpon Iosephs knees.

*Num. 32. 39.

†Heb. borne

24 And Ioseph saide vnto his brethren, *I die: and God will surely visit you, and bring you out of this land, vnto the land which hee sware to Abraham, to Isaac, and to Iacob.

*Heb. 11. 22.

25 And Ioseph tooke an othe of the children of Israel, saying, * God will surely visite you, and ye shal carie vp my bones from hence.

*Exod. 1 19.

26 So Ioseph died, being an hundred and ten yeeres old: and they imbalmed him, and he was put in a coffin, in Egypt.

THE
SECOND BOOKE OF
Moses, called Exodus.

CHAP. I.

1 The children of Israel after Iosephs death do multiply. 8 The more they are oppressed by a new King, the more they multiply. 15 The godlines of the Midwiues, in sauing the men children aliue. 22 Pharaoh commandeth the male children to be cast into the riuer.

*Gen. 46. 8. exod. 6. 14.

Owe these are the names of the * children of Israel, which came into Egypt, euery man & his household, came with Iacob.

2 Reuben, Simeon, Leui, and Iudah,

3 Issachar, Zebulun and Beniamin,

4 Dan, and Naphtali, Gad, and Asher.

5 And all the soules that came out

of the †loynes of Iacob, were *seuentie soules: for Ioseph was in Egypt *already.*

† Heb. thigh
*Gen. 46. 27. deut. 10. 22.

6 And Ioseph died, and all his brethren, and all that generation.

7 ¶ * And the children of Israel were fruitfull, and increased aboundantly, and multiplied, and waxed exceeding mighty, and the land was filled with them.

*Acts. 7. 17.

8 Now there arose vp a new King ouer Egypt, which knew not Ioseph.

9 And he said vnto his people, Behold, the people of the children of Israel are moe and mightier then we.

10 Come on, let vs deale wisely with them, lest they multiply, and it come to passe that when there falleth out any warre, they ioyne also vnto our enemies, and fight against vs, and *so* get them vp out of the land.

11 Therefore they did set ouer them task-masters, to afflict them with their burdens:

burdens: And they built for Pharaoh treasure-cities, Pithom and Raamses.

*Hebr. and as they afflicted them, ſo they multiplied, &c.

12 † But the more they afflicted them, the more they multiplied and grew: and they were grieued because. of the children of Israel.

13 And the Egyptians made the children of Israel to serue with rigour.

14 And they made their liues bitter, with hard bondage, in morter and in bricke, and in all maner of seruice in the fielde: all their seruice wherein they made them serue, *was* with rigour.

15 ¶ And the King of Egypt spake to the Hebrew midwiues, (of which the name of one was Shiphrah, and the name of the other Puah.)

16 And he said, When ye do the office of a midwife to the Hebrew - women, and see them vpon the stooles, if it be a sonne, then ye shall kill him: but if it be a daughter, then shee shall liue.

17 But the midwiues feared God, and did not as the King of Egypt commanded them, but saued the men children aliue.

18 And the King of Egypt called for the midwiues, & said vnto them, Why haue ye done this thing, and haue saued the men children aliue?

19 And the midwiues said vnto Pharaoh, Because the Hebrew women are not as the Egyptian women: for they are liuely, and are deliuered ere the midwiues come in vnto them.

20 Therefore God dealt well with the midwiues: and the people multiplied and waxed very mighty.

21 And it came to passe, because the midwiues feared God, that hee made them houses.

22 And Pharaoh charged all his people, saying, Euery sonne that is borne, yee shall cast into the riuer, and euery daughter ye shall saue aliue.

CHAP. II.

1 Moses is borne, 3 and in an arke cast into the flags. 5 He is found, and brought vp by Pharaohs daughter. 11 He slayeth an Egyptian. 13 He reproueth an Hebrew. 15 He fleeth into Midian. 21 Hee marrieth Zipporah. 22 Gershom is borne. 23 God respecteth the Israelites cry.

*Chap. 6.
20. num.
26. 59.

ANd there went *a man of the house of Leui, & tooke *to wife* a daughter of Leui.

2 And the woman conceiued, and bare a sonne:

and when shee saw him that hee was a goodly childe, shee *hid him three moneths.

*Acts 7.
20. heb. 11.
23.

3 And when shee could not longer hide him, she tooke for him an arke of bul-rushes, and daubed it with slime, and with pitch, and put the childe therein, and shee layd it in the flags by the riuers brinke.

4 And his sister stood afarre off, to wit what would be done to him.

5 ¶ And the daughter of Pharaoh came downe to wash *her selfe* at the riuer, and her maydens walked along by the riuer side: and when shee saw the arke among the flags, she sent her maid to fetch it.

6 And when she had opened *it*, she saw the childe: and beholde, the babe wept. And she had compassion on him, and said, This is *one* of the Hebrewes children.

7 Then said his sister to Pharaohs daughter, Shall I goe, and call to thee a nurse of the Hebrew-women, that she may nurse the childe for thee?

8 And Pharaohs daughter said to her, Goe: And the mayd went and called the childs mother.

9 And Pharaohs daughter said vnto her, Take this child away, and nurse it for me, and I will giue thee thy wages. And the woman tooke the childe, and nursed it.

10 And the childe grew, and shee brought him vnto Pharaohs daughter, and he became her sonne. And she called his name || Moses: And she said, Because I drew him out of the water.

|| That is, *Drawen out.*

11 ¶ And it came to passe in those dayes, when Moses was growen, that he went out vnto his brethren, and looked on their burdens, and he spied an Egyptian smiting an Hebrew, one of his brethren.

12 And he looked this way and that way, and when he saw that there was no man, he slew the Egyptian, and hid him in the sand.

13 And when he went out the second day, behold, two men of the Hebrewes stroue together: And hee said to him that did the wrong, Wherefore smitest thou thy fellow?

14 And he said, Who made thee †a Prince and a iudge ouer vs? intendest thou to kill me, as thou killedst the Egyptian? And Moses feared, and said, Surely this thing is knowen.

†Hebr. a Man a Prince.

15 Now

15 Now when Pharaoh heard this thing, he sought to slay Moses. But Moses fled from the face of Pharaoh, and dwelt in the land of Midian: and he sate downe by a well.

‖ Or, Prince.

16 Now the ‖ Priest of Midian had seuen daughters, and they came and drew water, and filled the troughes to water their fathers flocke.

17 And the shepheards came and droue them away: but Moses stood vp and helped them, & watred their flocke.

18 And when they came to Reuel their father, he said, How is it that you are come so soone to day?

19 And they said, An Egyptian deliuered vs out of the hand of the shepheards, and also drew water enough for vs, and watered the flocke.

20 And he said vnto his daughters, And where is he? why is it that yee haue left the man? Call him, that hee may eate bread.

21 And Moses was content to dwel with the man, and he gaue Moses Zipporah his daughter.

* Chap. 18. 3.

22 And she bare him a sonne, and he called his name * Gershom: for he said, I haue bene a stranger in a strange land.

23 ¶ And it came to passe in processe of time, that the king of Egypt died, and the children of Israel sighed by reason of the bondage, and they cried, and their cry came vp vnto God, by reason of the bondage.

* Gene. 15. 14. and 46. 4.

24 And God heard their groning, and God remembred his * Couenant with Abraham, with Isaac, and with Iacob.

† Heb. knew.

25 And God looked vpon the children of Israel, and God †had respect vnto *them.*

CHAP. III.

1 Moses keepeth Iethros flocke. 2 God appeareth to him in a burning bush. 9 He sendeth him to deliuer Israel. 14 The name of God. 15 His message to Israel.

Owe Moses kept the flocke of Iethro his father in law, the Priest of Midian: and hee led the flocke to the backeside of the desert, and came to the mountaine of God, *euen* to Horeb.

* A&s. 7 30.

2 And the Angel of the LORD appeared vnto him, in a *flame of fire out of the midst of a bush, and he loo-

ked, and behold, the bush burned with fire, and the bush was not consumed.

3 And Moses saide, I will nowe turne aside, and see this great sight, why the bush is not burnt.

4 And when the LORD sawe that he turned aside to see, God called vnto him out of the midst of the bush, and said, Moses, Moses. And he saide, Here am I.

* Iosh. 5. 15 acts. 7. 53.

5 And he said, Drawe not nigh hither: * put off thy shooes from off thy feete, for the place whereon thou standest, is holy ground.

* Matth. 22 32. acts 7. 32.

6 Moreouer hee said, * I am the God of thy father, the God of Abraham, the God of Isaac, and the God of Iacob. And Moses hid his face: for he was afraid to looke vpon God.

7 ¶ And the LORD said, I haue surely seene the affliction of my people which are in Egypt, and haue heard their crie, by reason of their taske-masters: for I know their sorrowes,

8 And I am come downe to deliuer them out of the hand of the Egyptians, and to bring them vp out of that land, vnto a good land and a large, vnto a lande flowing with milke and hony, vnto the place of the Canaanites, and the Hittites, and the Amorites, and the Perizzites, and the Hiuites, and the Iebusites.

9 Now therefore behold, the crie of the children of Israel is come vnto me: and I haue also seene the oppression wherewith the Egyptians oppresse them.

10 Come now therefore, and I will send thee vnto Pharaoh, that thou mayest bring forth my people the children of Israel out of Egypt.

11 ¶ And Moses saide vnto God, Who am I, that I should goe vnto Pharaoh, and that I should bring forth the children of Israel out of Egypt?

12 And he said, Certainely I will be with thee, and this shall be a token vnto thee, that I haue sent thee: When thou hast brought foorth the people out of Egypt, ye shall serue God vpon this mountaine.

13 And Moses saide vnto God, Behold, *when* I come vnto the children of Israel, and shall say vnto them, The God of your fathers hath sent me vnto you; and they shall say to me, What is his name? what shall I say vnto them?

14 And

14 And God saide vnto Moses, I AM THAT I AM: And he said, Thus shalt thou say vnto the children of Israel, I AM hath sent me vnto you.

15 And God said moreouer vnto Moses, Thus shalt thou say vnto the children of Israel; The Lord God of your fathers, the God of Abraham, the God of Isaac, and the God of Iacob hath sent me vnto you: this is my name for euer, and this is my memoriall vnto all generations.

16 Goe and gather the Elders of Israel together, and say vnto them, The Lord God of your fathers, the God of Abraham, of Isaac, and of Iacob appeared vnto me, saying, I haue surely visited you, and *seene* that which is done to you in Egypt.

17 And I haue said, I will bring you vp out of the affliction of Egypt, vnto the land of the Canaanites, and the Hittites, and the Amorites, and the Perizzites, and the Hiuites, and the Iebusites, vnto a land flowing with milke and hony.

18 And they shall hearken to thy voyce: and thou shalt come, thou and the Elders of Israel vnto the King of Egypt, and you shall say vnto him, The Lord God of the Hebrewes hath met with vs: and now let vs goe, (wee beseech thee) three dayes iourney into the wildernes, that we may sacrifice to the Lord our God.

19 ¶ And I am sure that the King of Egypt will not let you goe, ‖ no not by a mightie hand.

*, but by ng hand.

20 And I will stretch out my hand, and smite Egypt with all my wonders which I will doe in the midst thereof: and after that he will let you goe.

21 And I will giue this people fauour in the sight of the Egyptians, and it shall come to passe that when ye goe, ye shall not goe empty:

hap. 11. c 12. 35.

22 *But euery woman shal borrow of her neighbour, and of her that soiourneth in her house, iewels of siluer, and iewels of gold, and rayment: and ye shall put *them* vpon your sonnes and vpon your daughters, and yee shall spoile ‖ the Egyptians.

, Egypt.

CHAP. III.

1 Moses rod is turned into a Serpent. 6 His hand is leprous. 10 He is loath to bee sent. 14 Aaron is appointed to assist him. 18 Moses departeth from Iethro. 21 Gods message to Pharaoh. 24 Zipporah circumciseth her sonne. 27 Aaron is sent to meet Moses. 31 The people beleeueth them.

Nd Moses answered, and said, But behold, they will not beleeue mee, nor hearken vnto my voice: for they will say, The Lord hath not appeared vnto thee.

2 And the Lord said vnto him, What is that in thine hand? and hee said, A rod.

3 And he said, Cast it on the ground: And he cast it on the ground, and it became a serpent: and Moses fled from before it.

4 And the Lord said vnto Moses, Put forth thine hand, and take it by the taile: And he put foorth his hand, and caught it, and it became a rod in his hand:

5 That they may beleeue that the Lord God of their fathers, the God of Abraham, the God of Isaac, and the God of Iacob hath appeared vnto thee.

6 ¶ And the Lord said furthermore vnto him, Put now thine hand into thy bosome. And he put his hand into his bosome: and when hee tooke it out, behold, his hand was leprous as snowe.

7 And he said, Put thine hand into thy bosome againe. And hee put his hand into his bosome againe, and plucked it out of his bosome, and behold, it was turned againe as his *other* flesh.

8 And it shall come to passe, if they wil not beleeue thee, neither hearken to the voice of the first signe, that they will beleeue the voice of the latter signe.

9 And it shall come to passe, if they will not beleeue also these two signes, neither hearken vnto thy voice, that thou shalt take of the water of the riuer, and powre it *vpon* the drie land: and the water which thou takest out of the riuer, †shall become blood vpon the drie land.

† Heb. shalbe and shall be.

10 ¶ And Moses saide vnto the Lord, O my lord, I am not †eloquent, neither heretofore, nor †since thou hast spoken vnto thy seruant: but I am slow of speach, and of a slow tongue.

† Heb. a man of words. † Heb. since yesterday nor since the third day.

11 And the Lord said vnto him, Who hath made mans mouth? or who maketh the dumbe or deafe, or the seeing, or ẙ blind? haue not I the Lord?

12 Now

* Matth. 10
19. mar. 13.
11. luk. 12.
11.

‖ Or, shouldest.

12 Now therefore goe, and I will be * with thy mouth, and teach thee what thou shalt say.

13 And he said, O my Lord, send, I pray thee, by the hand *of him whom* thou ‖ wilt send.

14 And the anger of the LORD was kindled against Moses, and hee said, Is not Aaron the Leuite thy brother? I know that he can speake well. And also behold, he commeth foorth to meet thee: and when he seeth thee, hee will be glad in his heart.

15 And thou shalt speake vnto him, and put words in his mouth, and I wil be with thy mouth, & with his mouth, and will teach you what ye shall doe.

16 And he shal be thy spokesman vnto the people: and he shall be, *euen* hee shall be to thee in stead of a mouth, and

* Chap. 7. 1.

*thou shalt be to him in stead of God.

17 And thou shalt take this rod in thine hand, wherewith thou shalt doe signes.

18 ¶ And Moses went and returned to Iethro his father in law, and said vnto him, Let me goe, I pray thee, and returne vnto my brethren, which are in Egypt, and see whether they bee yet aliue. And Iethro said to Moses, Goe in peace.

19 And the LORD said vnto Moses in Midian, Goe, returne into Egypt: for all the men are dead which sought thy life.

20 And Moses tooke his wife, and his sonnes, and set them vpon an asse, and he returned to the land of Egypt. And Moses tooke the rod of God in his hand.

21 And the LORD said vnto Moses, When thou goest to returne into Egypt, see that thou doe all those wonders before Pharaoh, which I haue put in thine hand: but I wil harden his heart, that hee shall not let the people goe.

22 And thou shalt say vnto Pharaoh, Thus saith the LORD, Israel is my sonne, *euen* my first borne.

23 And I say vnto thee, let my sonne goe, that he may serue mee: and if thou refuse to let him goe, behold, I will slay thy sonne, *euen* thy first borne.

24 ¶ And it came to passe by the way in the Inne, that the LORD met him, and sought to kill him.

‖ Or, knife.

25 Then Zipporah tooke a sharpe ‖ stone, and cut off the foreskinne of her

sonne, and †cast it at his feete, and said, Surely a bloody husband art thou to mee.

† Heb. made it touch.

26 So he let him goe. then she said, A bloody husband thou art, because of the Circumcision.

27 ¶ And the LORD said to Aaron, Goe into the wildernesse to meete Moses. And hee went and met him in the mount of God, and kissed him.

28 And Moses tolde Aaron all the wordes of the LORD, who had sent him, and all the signes which hee had commanded him.

29 ¶ And Moses and Aaron went, and gathered together all the elders of the children of Israel.

30 And Aaron spake all the wordes which the LORD had spoken vnto Moses, and did the signes in the sight of the people.

31 And the people beleeued. And when they heard that the LORD had visited the children of Israel, and that he had looked vpon their affliction, then they bowed their heads and worshipped.

CHAP. V.

1 Pharaoh chideth Moses and Aaron for their message. 5 Hee encreaseth the Israelites taske. 15 Hee checketh their complaints. 19 They cry out vpon Moses and Aaron. 22 Moses complaineth to God.

Nd afterward Moses and Aaron went in, and tolde Pharaoh, Thus saith the LORD God of Israel, Let my people goe, that they may holde a feast vnto mee in the wildernesse.

2 And Pharaoh said, Who is the LORD, that I should obey his voyce to let Israel goe? I know not the LORD, neither will I let Israel goe.

3 And they said, * The God of the Hebrewes hath met with vs: let vs goe, we pray thee, three dayes iourney into the desert, and sacrifice vnto the LORD our God, lest hee fall vpon vs with pestilence, or with the sword.

* Chap. 3. 18.

4 And the King of Egypt said vnto them, Wherfore doe ye, Moses and Aaron, let the people from their workes? get you vnto your burdens.

5 And Pharaoh said, Behold, the people of the land now *are* many, & you make them rest from their burdens.

6 And Pharaoh commanded the same

same day the taske-masters of the people, and their officers, saying;

7 Yee shall no more giue the people straw to make bricke, as heretofore: let them goe and gather straw for themselues.

8 And the tale of the brickes which they did make heretofore, you shall lay vpon them: you shall not diminish *ought* thereof: for they be idle; therefore they cry, saying, Let vs goe *and* sacrifice to our God.

Heb. let
e worke be
eauy vpon
e men.

9 † Let there more worke be layde vpon the men, that they may labour therein, and let them not regard vaine wordes.

10 ¶ And the taske-masters of the people went out, and their officers, and they spake to the people, saying, Thus saith Pharaoh, I will not giue you straw.

11 Goe ye, get you straw where you can find it: yet not ought of your worke shall be diminished.

12 So the people were scattered abroad throughout all the land of Egypt, to gather stubble in stead of straw.

Hebr. a
atter of a
ay in his
ay.

13 And the taske-masters hasted *them*, saying; Fulfill your workes, your † dayly taskes, as when there was straw.

14 And the officers of the children of Israel, which Pharaohs task-masters had set ouer them, were beaten, *and* demanded, Wherefore haue ye not fulfilled your taske, in making bricke, both yesterday and to day, as heretofore?

15 ¶ Then the officers of the children of Israel came and cryed vnto Pharaoh, saying, Wherefore dealest thou thus with thy seruants?

16 There is no straw giuen vnto thy seruants, and they say to vs, Make bricke: and beholde, thy seruants are beaten; but the fault is in thine owne people.

17 But he said, Ye are idle, *ye are* idle: therefore ye say, Let vs goe *and* doe sacrifice to the LORD.

18 Goe therefore now *and* worke: for there shall no straw bee giuen you, yet shall ye deliuer the tale of brickes.

19 And the officers of the children of Israel did see that they were in euill case, after it was said, Yee shall not minish *ought* from your brickes of your dayly taske.

20 ¶ And they met Moses and Aaron, who stood in the way, as they came foorth from Pharaoh.

21 And they said vnto them; The LORD looke vpon you, and iudge, because you haue made our sauour † to be abhorred in the eyes of Pharaoh, and in the eyes of his seruants, to put a sword in their hand to slay vs.

† Hebr. to
stinke.

22 And Moses returned vnto the LORD, and said, Lord, Wherefore hast thou *so* euill intreated this people? why is it that thou hast sent me?

23 For since I came to Pharaoh to speake in thy Name, he hath done euill to this people, neither hast thou † deliuered thy people at all.

† Heb. deli-
uering thou
hast not de-
liuered.

CHAP. VI.

1 God renueth his promise by his Name IEHOVAH. 14 The genealogie of Reuben, 15 of Simeon, 16 of Leui, of whom came Moses and Aaron.

Hen the LORD said vnto Moses, Now shalt thou see what I will doe to Pharaoh: for with a strong hand shall hee let them goe, and with a strong hand shall he driue them out of his land.

2 And God spake vnto Moses, and said vnto him, I *am* the LORD.

3 And I appeared vnto Abraham, vnto Isaac, and vnto Iacob, by *the Name of* God Almighty, but by my name *IEHOVAH* was I not knowen to them.

4 And I haue also established my Couenant with them, to giue them the land of Canaan, the land of their pilgrimage, wherein they were strangers.

5 And I haue also heard the groning of the children of Israel, whom the Egyptians keepe in bondage: and I haue remembred my Couenant.

6 Wherefore say vnto the children of Israel, I am the LORD, and I will bring you out from vnder the burdens of the Egyptians, and I will rid you out of their bondage: and I will redeeme you with a stretched out arme, and with great iudgements.

7 And I will take you to mee for a people, and I will be to you a God: and ye shall know that I am the LORD your God, which bringeth you out from vnder the burdens of the Egyptians.

8 And I will bring you in vnto the lande concerning the which I did

† sweare

† Heb. lift vp my hand.

†sweare to giue it, to Abraham, to Isaac, and to Iacob, and I will giue it you for an heritage, I *am* the LORD

9 ¶ And Moses spake so vnto the children of Israel: but they hearkened not vnto Moses, for †anguish of spirit, and for cruell bondage.

† Heb. shortnesse: or, straitnes.

10 And the LORD spake vnto Moses, saying,

11 Goe in, speake vnto Pharaoh King of Egypt, that he let the children of Israel goe out of his land.

12 And Moses spake before the LORD, saying, Behold, the children of Israel haue not hearkened vnto me: how then shal Pharaoh heare me, who am of vncircumcised lips?

13 And the LORD spake vnto Moses and vnto Aaron, & gaue them a charge vnto the children of Israel, and vnto Pharaoh King of Egypt, to bring the children of Israel out of the land of Egypt.

* Gen. 46. 9 1. chro. 5. 3.

14 ¶ These *be* the heads of their fathers houses: * The sonnes of Reuben the first borne of Israel, Hanoch, and Pallu, Hezron, and Carmi: these *be* the families of Reuben.

* 1. Chron. 4. 24.

15 * And the sonnes of Simeon: Iemuel, and Iamin, and Ohad and Iachin, and Zohar, and Shaul the sonne of a Canaanitish woman: these are the families of Simeon.

* Num. 3. 17 1 chron. 6. 1

16 ¶ And these are the names of the * sonnes of Leui, according to their generations: Gershon and Kohath and Merari: and the yeeres of the life of Leui, were an hundred, thirtie and seuen yeeres.

17 The sonnes of Gershon: Libni and Shimi, according to their families.

* Num. 26. 57. 1. chro. 6..1.

18 And * the sonnes of Kohath: Amram, and Izhar, and Hebron, and Uzziel. And the yeeres of the life of Kohath, were an hundred thirtie and three yeeres.

19 And the sonnes of Merari: Mahali and Mushi: these are the families of Leui, according to their generations.

* Chap. 2. 2. num. 26. 59

20 And * Amram tooke him Iochebed his fathers sister to wife, and shee bare him Aaron and Moses: and the yeeres of the life of Amram were an hundred, and thirtie and seuen yeeres.

21 ¶ And the sonnes of Izhar: Korah and Nepheg, and Zichri.

22 And the sonnes of Uzziel: Mishael, and Elzaphan, and Zithri.

23 And Aaron tooke him Elisheba daughter of Amminadab sister of Naashon to wife, and she bare him Nadab and Abihu, Eleazar and Ithamar.

24 And the sonnes of Korah, Assir, and Elkanah, and Abiasaph: these *are* the families of the Korhites.

25 And Eleazar Aarons sonne tooke him *one* of the daughters of Putiel to wife, and * she bare him Phinehas: these *are* the heads of the fathers of the Leuites, according to their families.

* Num. 25. 11.

26 These *are* that Aaron and Moses, to whom the LORD said, Bring out the children of Israel from the land of Egypt, according to their armies.

27 These *are* they which spake to Pharaoh king of Egypt, to bring out the children of Israel from Egypt: These *are* that Moses and Aaron.

28 ¶ And it came to passe on the day when the LORD spake vnto Moses in the land of Egypt,

29 That the LORD spake vnto Moses, saying, I am the LORD: speake thou vnto Pharaoh king of Egypt, all that I say vnto thee.

30 And Moses said before the LORD, Behold, I am of vncircumcised lips, and how shall Pharaoh hearken vnto mee?

CHAP. VII.

1 Moses is encouraged to go to Pharaoh. 7 His age. 8 His rod is turned into a Serpent. 11 The sorcerers do the like. 13 Pharaohs heart is hardened. 14 Gods message to Pharaoh. 19 The riuer is turned into blood.

Nd the LORD said vnto Moses, See, I haue made thee a god to Pharaoh, and Aaron thy brother shalbe thy prophet.

2 Thou shalt speake all that I command thee, and Aaron thy brother shall speake vnto Pharaoh, that he send the children of Israel out of his land.

3 And I will harden Pharaohs heart, and multiplie my signes and my wonders in the land of Egypt.

4 But Pharaoh shall not hearken vnto you, that I may lay my hand vpon Egypt, and bring forth mine armies, *and* my people the children of Israel, out of the land of Egypt, by great iudgments.

5 And the Egyptians shall knowe that I *am* the LORD, when I stretch forth mine hand vpon Egypt, and bring out

out the children of Israel from among them.

6 And Moses and Aaron did as the LORD commanded them, so did they.

7 And Moses was fourescore yeres olde, and Aaron fourescore and three yeeres old, when they spake vnto Pharaoh.

8 ¶ And the LORD spake vnto Moses, and vnto Aaron, saying:

9 When Pharaoh shall speake vnto you, saying, Shew a miracle for you: then thou shalt say vnto Aaron, Take thy rod and cast it before Pharaoh, *and* it shall become a serpent.

10 ¶ And Moses and Aaron went in vnto Pharaoh, and they did so as the Lord had commanded: and Aaron cast downe his rod before Pharaoh, and before his seruants, and it became a serpent.

11 Then Pharaoh also called the wise men and the sorcerers; now the Magicians of Egypt, they also did in like maner with their enchantments.

12 For they cast downe euery man his rod, and they became serpents: but Aarons rod swallowed vp their rods.

13 And hee hardened Pharaohs heart, that hee hearkened not vnto them, as the LORD had said.

14 ¶ And the LORD saide vnto Moses, Pharaohs heart is hardened: he refuseth to let the people goe.

15 Get thee vnto Pharaoh in the morning, loe, he goeth out vnto the water, and thou shalt stand by the riuers brinke, against hee come: and the rod which was turned to a serpent, shalt thou take in thine hand.

16 And thou shalt say vnto him, The LORD God of the Hebrewes hath sent me vnto thee, saying; Let my people goe, that they may serue mee in the wildernesse: and beholde, hitherto thou wouldest not heare.

17 Thus saith the LORD, In this thou shalt know that I am the LORD: behold, I will smite with the rod that is in my hand, vpon the waters which are in the riuer, and they shalbe turned to blood.

18 And the fish that is in the riuer shall die, and the riuer shall stincke, and the Egyptians shall loathe to drinke of the water of the riuer.

19 ¶ And the LORD spake vnto Moses, Say vnto Aaron, Take thy rod, & stretch out thine hand vpon the waters of Egypt, vpon their streames, vpon their riuers, and vpon their ponds, and vpon all their † pooles of water, that they may become blood, and that there may be blood throughout all the land of Egypt, both in *vessels of* wood, and in *vessels of* stone.

† Heb. Gathering of their waters.

20 And Moses and Aaron did so, as the LORD commanded: and he * lift vp the rod and smote the waters that were in the riuer, in the sight of Pharaoh, and in the sight of his seruants: and all the * waters that were in the riuer, were turned to blood.

* Chap. 17. 5.

* Psal. 78. 44.

21 And the fish that *was* in the riuer died: and the riuer stunke, and the Egyptians could not drinke of the water of the riuer: and there was blood throughout all the land of Egypt.

22 * And the Magicians of Egypt did so, with their enchantments: and Pharaohs heart was hardened, neither did he hearken vnto them, as the LORD had said.

* Wis. 17. 7.

23 And Pharaoh turned and went into his house, neither did hee set his heart to this also.

24 And all the Egyptians digged round about the riuer for water to drinke: for they could not drinke of the water of the riuer.

25 And seuen dayes were fulfilled after that the LORD had smitten the riuer.

CHAP. VIII.

1 Frogges are sent. 8 Pharaoh sueth to Moses, 12 and Moses by prayer remoueth them away. 16 The dust is turned into lice, which the Magicians could not doe. 20 The swarmes of flies. 25 Pharaoh inclineth to let the people goe, 32 but yet is hardened.

A Nd the LORD spake vnto Moses, Goe vnto Pharaoh, and say vnto him; Thus sayeth the LORD, Let my people goe, that they may serue me.

2 And if thou refuse to let them goe, beholde, I will smite all thy borders with frogges.

3 And the riuer shall bring foorth frogges abundantly, which shall goe vp and come into thine house, and into thy bed-chamber, and vpon thy bed, and into the house of thy seruants, and vpon thy people, and into thine ouens, and into thy ‖kneading troughes.

‖ Or, dough.

4 And

4 And the frogges shall come vp both on thee, and vpon thy people, and vpon all thy seruants.

5 ¶ And the Lord spake vnto Moses; Say vnto Aaron, Stretch foorth thine hand with thy rodde ouer the streames, ouer the riuers, and ouer the ponds, and cause frogges to come vp vpon the land of Egypt.

6 And Aaron stretched out his hand ouer the waters of Egypt, and the frogges came vp, and couered the land of Egypt.

*Wisd. 17. 7.

7 * And the Magicians did so with their inchantments, and brought vp frogges vpon the land of Egypt.

8 ¶ Then Pharaoh called for Moses, and Aaron, and said, Intreat the Lord, that hee may take away the frogges from me, and from my people: and I will let the people goe, that they may doe sacrifice vnto the Lord.

‖ Or haue this honour ouer me, &c.
‖ Or, against when.
† Hebr. to cut off.
‖ Or, against to morrow.

9 And Moses saide vnto Pharaoh, ‖Glory ouer mee: ‖when shall I entreat for thee, and for thy seruants, and for thy people, to †destroy the frogges from thee, and thy houses, that they may remaine in the riuer onely?

10 And he said, ‖To morrow. And hee said, *Bee it* according to thy word: That thou mayest know that there is none like vnto the Lord our God.

11 And the frogs shall depart from thee, and from thy houses, and from thy seruants, and from thy people; they shall remaine in the riuer onely.

12 And Moses and Aaron went out from Pharaoh, and Moses cried vnto the Lord because of the frogs which he had brought against Pharaoh.

13 And the Lord did according to the word of Moses: and the frogges died out of the houses, out of the villages, and out of the fields.

14 And they gathered them together vpon heapes, and the land stanke.

15 But when Pharaoh saw that there was respit, he hardned his heart, and hearkened not vnto them, as the Lord had said.

16 ¶ And the Lord saide vnto Moses, Say vnto Aaron, Stretch out thy rod, and smite the dust of the land, that it may become lice, thorowout all the land of Egypt.

17 And they did so: for Aaron stretched out his hand with his rod, and smote the dust of the earth, and it became lice, in man and in beast: all the dust of the land became lice throughout all the land of Egypt.

18 And the Magicians did so with their enchantments to bring foorth lice, but they could not: so there were lice vpon man and vpon beast.

19 Then the Magicians said vnto Pharaoh; This *is* the finger of God. And Pharaohs heart was hardned, and he hearkened not vnto them, as the Lord had said.

20 ¶ And the Lord saide vnto Moses, Rise vp early in the morning, and stand before Pharaoh: loe, he commeth foorth to the water, and say vnto him; Thus saith the Lord, Let my people goe, that they may serue me.

† Or, a mixture of noysome beasts &c.

21 Els, if thou wilt not let my people goe, beholde, I will send ‖swarmes of flies vpon thee, and vpon thy seruants, and vpon thy people, and into thy houses: and the houses of the Egyptians shall bee full of swarmes of flies, and also the ground whereon they are.

22 And I will seuer in that day the lande of Goshen in which my people dwell, that no swarmes of flies shall be there, to the end thou maiest know that I *am* the Lord in the midst of the earth.

† Hebr. a redemption.
‖ Or, by to morrow.

23 And I will put †a diuision betweene my people and thy people: ‖to morrow shall this signe be.

*Wisd. 16. 9.

24 And the Lord did so: and *there came a grieuous swarme of flies into the house of Pharaoh, and into his seruants houses, and into all the lande of Egypt: the land was ‖corrupted by reason of the swarme of flies.

‖ Or, destroyed.

25 ¶ And Pharaoh called for Moses and for Aaron, and said, Goe yee, sacrifice to your God in the land.

26 And Moses said, It is not meete so to doe; for we shal sacrifice the abomination of the Egyptians, to the Lord our God: Loe, shall we sacrifice the abomination of the Egyptians before their eyes, and will they not stone vs?

27 We will goe three dayes iourney into the wildernesse, and sacrifice to the Lord our God, as * he shall command vs.

*Chap. 3. 18.

28 And Pharaoh said, I wil let you goe that ye may sacrifice to the Lord your God, in the wildernes: onely you shall not goe very farre away: intreate for me.

29 And Moses said, Behold, I goe out

out from thee, and I will intreate the LORD that the swarmes of flies may depart from Pharaoh, from his seruants, and from his people to morrow: but let not Pharaoh deale deceitfully any more, in not letting the people goe to sacrifice to the LORD.

30 And Moses went out from Pharaoh, and intreated the LORD:

31 And the LORD did according to the word of Moses: and he remooued the swarmes of flies from Pharaoh, from his seruants, and from his people: there remained not one.

32 And Pharaoh hardened his heart at this time also, neither would hee let the people goe.

CHAP. IX.

1 The murraine of beasts.   8 The plague of boyles, and blaines.   13 His message about the haile.   22 The plague of haile.   27 Pharaoh sueth to Moses, 35 but yet is hardened.

Hen the LORD said vnto Moses, Goe in vnto Pharaoh, and tell him, Thus saith the LORD God of the Hebrewes, Let my people goe, that they may serue me.

2 For if thou refuse to let *them* goe, and wilt hold them still,

3 Behold, the hand of the LORD is vpon thy cattell which is in the field, vpon the horses, vpon the asses, vpon the camels, vpon the oxen, and vpon the sheepe: there *shall be* a very grieuous murraine.

4 And the LORD shall seuer betweene the cattel of Israel, and the cattell of Egypt, and there shall nothing die of all that is the childrens of Israel.

5 And the LORD appointed a set time, saying, To morrow the LORD shall doe this thing in the land.

6 And the LORD did that thing on the morrow; and all the cattell of Egypt died, but of the cattell of the children of Israel died not one.

7 And Pharaoh sent, and beholde, there was not one of the cattell of the Israelites dead. And the heart of Pharaoh was hardened, and he did not let the people goe.

8 ¶ And the LORD saide vnto Moses, and vnto Aaron, Take to you handfuls of ashes of the fornace, and let Moses sprinkle it towards the heauen, in the sight of Pharaoh:

9 And it shall become small dust in all the land of Egypt, and shall bee a boyle breaking forth *with* blaines, vpon man and vpon beast, throughout all the land of Egypt.

10 And they tooke ashes of the fornace, and stood before Pharaoh, and Moses sprinkled it vp toward heauen: and it became a boile breaking forth *with* blaines, vpon man and vpon beast.

11 And the Magicians could not stand before Moses, because of the boiles: for the boile was vpon the magicians, and vpon all the Egyptians.

12 And the LORD hardened the heart of Pharaoh, and hee hearkened not vnto them, * as the LORD had spoken vnto Moses.   * Chap. 4. 21.

13 ¶ And the LORD saide vnto Moses, Rise vp earely in the morning, and stand before Pharaoh, and say vnto him, Thus saith the LORD God of the Hebrewes, Let my people goe, that they may serue me.

14 For I will at this time send all my plagues vpon thine heart, and vpon thy seruaunts, and vpon thy people: that thou mayest knowe that *there is* none like me in all the earth.

15 For now I will stretch out my hand, that I may smite thee and thy people, with pestilence, and thou shalt be cut off from the earth.

16 And in very deede, for * this *cause* haue I †raised thee vp, for to shewe in thee my power, and that my name may be declared throughout all the earth.   * Rom. 9. 17. ‖ *Heb. made thee stand.*

17 As yet exaltest thou thy selfe against my people, that thou wilt not let them goe?

18 Behold, to morrow about this time, I wil cause it to raine a very grieuous haile, such as hath not bene in Egypt, since the foundation thereof euen vntill now.

19 Send therefore now, and gather thy cattell, and all that thou hast in the field: for *vpon* euery man and beast which shal be found in the field, and shal not bee brought home, the haile shall come downe vpon them, and they shall die.

20 Hee that feared the word of the LORD amongst the seruants of Pharaoh, made his seruants and his cattell flee into the houses.

21 And he that † regarded not the word of the LORD, left his seruants and his cattell in the field.   † *Heb. set not his heart vnto.*

22 ¶ And

22 ¶ And the LORD saide vnto Moses, Stretch forth thine hand toward heauen, that there may be haile in all the land of Egyyt, vpon man and vpon beast, and vpon euery herbe of the field, thorowout the land of Egypt.

23 And Moses stretched foorth his rod toward heauen, and the LORD sent thunder and haile, and the fire ranne along vpon the ground, and the LORD rained haile vpon the land of Egypt.

24 So there was haile, and fire mingled with the haile, very grieuous, such as there was none like it in all the land of Egypt, since it became a nation.

25 And the haile smote throughout all the land of Egypt, all that *was* in the field, both man and beast: and the haile smote euery herbe of the fielde, and brake euery tree of the field.

26 Onely in the land of Goshen where the children of Israel *were*, was there no haile.

27 ¶ And Pharaoh sent, and called for Moses and Aaron, and said vnto them, I haue sinned *this* time: the LORD is righteous, and I and my people are wicked.

28 Entreat the LORD, (for it is enough) that there be no more † mighty thunderings and haile, and I will let you goe, and ye shall stay no longer.

† *Hebr. voyces of God.*

29 And Moses saide vnto him, Assoone as I am gone out of the citie, I will spread abroad my hands vnto the LORD, *and* the thunder shall cease, neither shall there be any more haile: that thou mayest know how that the * earth *is* the LORDS.

* *Psal. 24. 1.*

30 But as for thee and thy seruants, I know that ye will not yet feare the LORD God.

31 And the flaxe, and the barley was smitten: for the barley *was* in the eare, and the flaxe *was* bolled:

32 But the wheat and the rye were not smitten: for they were † not growen vp.

† *Hebr. hidden: or, darke.*

33 And Moses went out of the city from Pharaoh, and spread abroad his hands vnto the LORD: and the thunders and haile ceased, and the raine was not powred vpon the earth.

34 And when Pharaoh saw that the raine, and the haile and the thunders were ceased, hee sinned yet more, and hardened his heart, he and his seruants.

35 And the heart of Pharaoh was hardened, neither would he let the children of Israel goe, as the LORD had spoken † by Moses.

† *Hebr. by the hand of Moses.*

CHAP. X.

A Nd the LORD said vnto Moses, Goe in vnto Pharaoh: for *I haue hardned his heart, and the heart of his seruants, that I might shew these my signes before him:

* *Chap. 4. 21.*

2 And that thou mayest tell in the eares of thy sonne, and of thy sonnes sonne, what things I haue wrought in Egypt, and my signes which I haue done amongst them, that ye may know how that I am the LORD.

3 And Moses and Aaron came in vnto Pharaoh, and saide vnto him, Thus saith the LORD God of the Hebrewes, How long wilt thou refuse to humble thy selfe before mee? Let my people goe, that they may serue me.

4 Els, if thou refuse to let my people goe, behold, to morrow will I bring the * locusts into thy coast.

* *Wisd. 16. 9.*

5 And they shall couer the † face of the earth, that one cannot be able to see the earth, and they shall eate the residue of that which is escaped, which remaineth vnto you from the haile, and shall eate euery tree, which groweth for you out of the field.

† *Hebr. eye*

6 And they shall fill thy houses, and the houses of all thy seruants, and the houses of all the Egyptians, which neither thy fathers, nor thy fathers fathers haue seene, since the day that they were vpon the earth, vnto this day. And he turned himselfe, and went out from Pharaoh.

7 And Pharaohs seruants said vnto him, How long shall this man be a snare vnto vs? Let the men goe, that they may serue the LORD their God: Knowest thou not yet, that Egypt is destroyed?

8 And Moses and Aaron were brought againe vnto Pharaoh: and he said vnto them, Goe, serue the LORD your

† Heb. who
& who, &c.

your God: *but* †who *are* they that shall goe?

9 And Moses said, We wil goe with our yong, and with our old, with our sonnes and with our daughters, with our flockes and with our heards will we goe: for we *must hold* a feast vnto the Lord.

10 And he said vnto them; Let the Lord bee so with you, as I will let you goe, and your litle ones. Looke to it, for euill is before you.

11 Not so: goe now yee *that are* men, and serue the Lord, for that you did desire: and they were driuen out from Pharaohs presence.

12 ¶ And the Lord said vnto Moses, Stretch out thine hand ouer the land of Egypt for the locusts, that they may come vp vpon the land of Egypt, and eate euery herbe of the land, euen all that the haile hath left.

13 And Moses stretched forth his rod ouer the land of Egypt, and the Lord brought an East wind vpon the land all that day, and all that night: and when it was morning, the East wind brought the locusts.

14 And the locusts went vp ouer all the land of Egypt, and rested in all the coasts of Egypt: very grieuous were they: before them there were no such locusts as they, neither after them shall be such.

15 For they couered the face of the whole earth, so that the land was darkned, and they did eate euery herbe of the land, and all the fruit of the trees, which the haile had left, and there remained not any greene thing in the trees, or in the herbes of the field, through all the land of Egypt.

† Heb. haste-
ned to call.

16 ¶ Then Pharaoh †called for Moses and Aaron in haste: and he said, I haue sinned against the Lord your God, and against you.

17 Now therefore forgiue, I pray thee, my sinne onely this once, and intreat the Lord your God, that hee may take away from mee this death onely.

18 And he went out from Pharaoh, and intreated the Lord.

19 And the Lord turned a mighty strong West wind, which tooke away the locusts, and †cast them into the red sea: there remained not one locust in all the coasts of Egypt.

† Heb. faste-
ned.

20 But the Lord hardened Pha-

raohs heart, so that hee would not let the children of Israel goe.

21 ¶ And the Lord said vnto Moses, Stretch out thine hand toward heauen, that there may be darkenesse ouer the land of Egypt, †euen darkenes which may be felt.

† Heb. that
one may feele
darkenesse.

22 And Moses stretched foorth his hand toward heauen: and there was a thicke darkenesse in all the land of Egypt three dayes.

23 They saw not one another, neither rose any from his place for three dayes: *but all the children of Israel had light in their dwellings.

*Wisd. 18.1

24 ¶ And Pharaoh called vnto Moses, and said, Goe ye, serue the Lord: onely let your flockes and your herds be stayed: let your litle ones also goe with you.

25 And Moses saide, Thou must giue †vs also sacrifices, and burnt offerings, that we may sacrifice vnto the Lord our God.

† Heb. into
our hands.

26 Our cattell also shall goe with vs: there shall not an hoofe bee left behind: for thereof must we take to serue the Lord our God: and we knowe not with what wee must serue the Lord, vntill we come thither.

27 ¶ But the Lord hardened Pharaohs heart, and he would not let them goe.

28 And Pharaoh said vnto him, Get thee from me, take heed to thy selfe: see my face no more: for in that day thou seest my face, thou shalt die.

29 And Moses said, Thou hast spoken well, I will see thy face againe no more.

CHAP. XI.

1 Gods message to the Israelites to borrow iewels of their neighbours. 4 Moses threatneth Pharaoh with the death of the first borne.

Nd the Lord said vnto Moses, Yet will I bring one plague more vpon Pharaoh, and vpon Egypt, afterwards hee will let you goe hence: when hee shall let *you* goe, he shall surely thrust you out hence altogether.

2 Speake now in the eares of the people, and let euery man borrowe of his neighbour, and euery woman of her neighbour, * iewels of siluer, and iewels of gold.

* Chap. 3.
22. & 12.
35.

3 And the Lord gaue the people fauour

* Ecclus.
45. 1.

fauour in the sight of the Egyptians. Moreouer the man * Moses was very great in the land of Egypt, in the sight of Pharaohs seruants, and in the sight of the people.

4 And Moses said, Thus saith the LORD, * about midnight will I goe out into the midst of Egypt.

* Chap. 12.
29.

5 And all the first borne in the lande of Egypt shall die, from the first borne of Pharaoh, that sitteth vpon his throne, euen vnto the first borne of the maid seruant that is behind the mill, and all the first borne of beasts.

6 And there shall bee a great crie throughout all the land of Egypt, such as there was none like it, nor shall bee like it any more.

7 But against any of the children of Israel, shal not a dog moue his tongue, against man or beast: that ye may know how that the LORD doth put a difference betweene the Egyptians and Israel.

8 And all these thy seruants shall come downe vnto me, and bow downe themselues vnto me, saying, Get thee out, and all the people that † follow thee; and after that I wil goe out: and he went out from Pharaoh in † a great anger.

† Hebr. that
is at thy feet.
† Heb. heat
of anger.

9 And the LORD said vnto Moses, Pharaoh shall not hearken vnto you, that my wonders may be multiplied in the land of Egypt.

10 And Moses and Aaron did all these wonders before Pharaoh: and the LORD hardened Pharaohs heart, so that he would not let the children of Israel goe out of his land.

CHAP. XII.

1 The beginning of the yeere is changed. 3 The Passeouer is instituted. 11 The Rite of the Passeouer. 15 Vnleauened bread. 29 The first borne are slaine. 31 The Israelites are driuen out of the lande. 37 They come to Succoth. 43 The ordinance of the Passeouer.

 Nd the LORD spake vnto Moses and Aaron in the land of Egypt, saying, 2 This moneth shalbe vnto you the beginning of moneths: it shall be the first moneth of the yeere to you.

3 ¶ Speake ye vnto all the Congregation of Israel, saying, In the tenth day of this moneth they shall take to them euery man a lambe, according to the house of their fathers, a ‖ lambe for an house.

‖ Or, kidde

4 And if the houshold be too little for the lambe, let him and his neighbour next vnto his house, take it according to the number of the soules: euery man according to his eating shall make your count for the lambe.

5 Your lambe shall be without blemish, a male †of the first yeere: yee shall take it out from the sheepe or from the goates.

† Heb, son
of a yeere

6 And ye shall keepe it vp vntill the fourteenth day of the same moneth: and the whole assembly of the congregation of Israel shall kill it †in the euening.

7 And they shall take of the blood and strike it on the two side postes, and on the vpper doore poste, of the houses wherin they shall eate it.

† Hebr. be
tweene th
two eue-
nings.

8 And they shall eat the flesh in that night roste with fire, and vnleauened bread, and with bitter herbes they shall eate it.

9 Eate not of it raw, nor sodden at all with water, but roste with fire: his head, with his legs, and with the purtenance thereof.

10 And ye shall let nothing of it remaine vntill the morning: and that which remaineth of it vntill the morning, ye shall burne with fire.

11 ¶ And thus shall ye eate it: with your loines girded, your shooes on your feet, and your staffe in your hand: and ye shall eate it in haste: it is the LORDS Passeouer.

12 For I will passe through the land of Egypt this night, and will smite all the first borne in the land of Egypt, both man & beast, and against all the ‖gods of Egypt I will execute iudgement: I am the LORD.

‖ Or, prin
ces.

13 And the blood shall be to you for a token vpon the houses where you are: and when I see the blood, I will passe ouer you, and the plague shall not bee vpon you †to destroy you, when I smite the land of Egypt.

† Heb. fo
a destruc
on.

14 And this day shall be vnto you for a memoriall: and you shall keepe it a feast to the LORD, throughout your generations: you shall keepe it a feast by an ordinance for euer.

15 Seuen dayes shall ye eate vnleauened bread, euen the first day yee shall put away leauen out of your houses: For

For whosoeuer eateth leauened bread, from the first day vntil the seuenth day, that soule shall be cut off from Israel.

16 And in the first day there *shalbe* an holy conuocation, and in the seuenth day there shall be an holy conuocation to you: no maner of worke shalbe done in them, saue that which euery †man must eate, that onely may bee done of you.

Heb. soule.

17 And yee shall obserue the *feast of* vnleauened bread: for in this selfe same day haue I brought your armies out of the land of Egypt; therefore shall ye obserue this day in your generations, by an ordinance for euer.

18 ¶ * In the first *moneth*, on the fourteenth day of the moneth at euen, ye shall eate vnleauened bread vntill the one and twentieth day of the moneth at euen.

Leuit. 23. num. 28. 5.

19 Seuen dayes shall there bee no leauen found in your houses: for whosoeuer eateth that which is leauened, euen that soule shall be cut off from the congregation of Israel, whether he be a stranger, or borne in the land.

20 Yee shall eate nothing leauened: in all your habitations shall ye eate vnleauened bread.

21 ¶ Then Moses called for all the Elders of Israel, and said vnto them ; Draw out and take you a ‖ lambe, according to your families, and kill the Passeouer.

Or, kidde.

22 * And ye shall take a bunch of hysope, and dip it in the blood that *is* in the bason, and strike the lintel and the two side postes with the blood that is in the bason : and none of you shall goe out at the doore of his house, vntill the morning.

Heb. 11. 8.

23 For the LORD wil passe through to smite the Egyptians : and when hee seeth the blood vpon the lintel, and on the two side-postes, the LORD will passe ouer the doore, and will not suffer the destroyer to come in vnto your houses to smite *you.*

24 And ye shall obserue this thing for an ordinance to thee, and to thy sonnes for euer.

25 And it shall come to passe when yee bee come to the land, which the LORD will giue you, according as he hath promised, that ye shall keepe this seruice.

26 * And it shall come to passe, when your children shall say vnto you, What

Iosh. 4. 6.

meane you by this seruice ?

27 That ye shall say, It is the sacrifice of the LORDS Passeouer, who passed ouer the houses of the children of Israel in Egypt, when he smote the Egyptians, and deliuered our houses. And the people bowed the head, and worshipped.

28 And the children of Israel went away, and did as the LORD had commanded Moses and Aaron, so did they.

29 ¶ * And it came to passe that at midnight the LORD smote all the first borne in the land of Egypt, * from the first borne of Pharaoh that sate on his throne, vnto the first borne of the captiue that was in the †dungeon, and all the first borne of cattell.

Chap. 11. 4.
Wisd. 18. 11.
†*Heb. house of the pit.*

30 And Pharaoh rose vp in the night, hee and all his seruants, and all the Egyptians ; and there was a great cry in Egypt: for there was not a house, where there was not one dead.

31 ¶ And hee called for Moses and Aaron by night, and said, Rise vp, *and* get you forth from amongst my people, both you and the children of Israel : and goe, serue the LORD, as ye haue said.

32 Also take your flockes and your heards, as ye haue said : and bee gone, and blesse me also.

33 And the Egyptians were vrgent vpon the people that they might send them out of the land in haste: for they said, We be all dead *men.*

34 And the people tooke their dough before it was leauened, their ‖ kneading troughes beeing bound vp in their clothes vpon their shoulders.

‖ *Or, dough.*

35 And the children of Israel did according to the word of Moses: and they borrowed of the Egyptians * iewels of siluer, and iewels of gold, and raiment.

Chap. 3. 22. and 11. 2.

36 And the LORD gaue the people fauour in the sight of the Egyptians, so that they lent vnto them such things as they required : and they spoiled the Egyptians.

37 ¶ And * the children of Israel iourneyed from Rameses to Succoth, about sixe hundred thousand on foote *that were* men, beside children.

Num. 33. 3.

38 And a †mixed multitude went vp also with them, and flocks and heards, euen very much cattell.

†*Hebr. a great mixture.*

39 And they baked vnleauened cakes of the dough, which they brought forth out of Egypt ; for it was not leauened : because

because they were thrust out of Egypt, and could not tarry, neither had they prepared for themselues any victuall.

40 ¶ Now the soiourning of the children of Israel, who dwelt in Egypt, *was* * foure hundred and thirtie yeeres

41 And it came to passe at the end of the foure hundred and thirtie yeeres, *euen* the selfe same day it came to passe, that all the hosts of the LORD went out from the land of Egypt.

42 It is a †night to be much obserued vnto the LORD, for bringing them out from the land of Egypt: This is that night of the LORD to be obserued of all the children of Israel, in their generations.

43 ¶ And the LORD saide vnto Moses and Aaron, This is the ordinance of the Passeouer: there shall no stranger eate thereof.

44 But euery mans seruant that is bought for money, when thou hast circumcised him, then shall he eate thereof.

45 A forreiner, and an hired seruant shall not eate thereof.

46 * In one house shall it be eaten, thou shalt not carie foorth ought of the flesh abroad out of the house, * neither shall ye breake a bone thereof.

47 All the Congregation of Israel shall †keepe it.

48 And when a stranger shall soiourne with thee, and will keepe the Passeouer to the LORD, let all his males be circumcised, and then let him come neere, and keepe it: and he shall be as one that is borne in the land: for no vncircumcised person shall eate thereof.

49 One law shall be to him that is home-borne, and vnto the stranger that soiourneth among you.

50 Thus did all the children of Israel: as the LORD commanded Moses and Aaron, so did they.

51 And it came to passe the selfe same day, that the LORD did bring the children of Israel out of the land of Egypt, by their armies.

CHAP. XIII.

Nd the LORD spake vnto Moses, saying,

2 * Sanctifie vnto me all the first borne, whatsoeuer openeth the wombe, among the children of Israel, both of man and of beast: it is mine.

3 ¶ And Moses said vnto the people, Remember this day, in which yee came out from Egypt, out of the house of †bondage: for by strength of hand the LORD brought you out from this *place:* there shall no leauened bread be eaten.

4 This day came yee out, in the moneth Abib.

5 ¶ And it shalbe when the LORD shall bring thee into the land of the Canaanites, and the Hittites, and the Amorites, and the Hiuites, and the Iebusites, which he sware vnto thy fathers to giue thee, a land flowing with milke and hony, that thou shalt keepe this seruice in this moneth.

6 Seuen dayes thou shalt eate vnleauened bread, and in the seuenth day *shall be* a feast to the LORD.

7 Vnleauened bread shall be eaten seuen dayes: and there shall no leauened bread bee seene with thee: neither shall there be leauen seene with thee in all thy quarters.

8 ¶ And thou shalt shew thy sonne in that day, saying, *This is done* because of that *which* the LORD did vnto mee, when I came forth out of Egypt.

9 And it shall bee for a signe vnto thee, vpon thine hand, and for a memoriall betweene thine eyes, that the LORDs law may be in thy mouth: for with a strong hande hath the LORD brought thee out of Egypt.

10 Thou shalt therfore keepe this ordinance in his season from yeere to yere.

11 ¶ And it shalbe when the LORD shall bring thee into the land of the Canaanites as he sware vnto thee, and to thy fathers, and shall giue it thee:

12 * That thou shalt †set apart vnto the LORD all that openeth the matrix, and euery firstling that commeth of a beast, which thou hast, the males shall be the LORDs.

13 And euery firstling of an asse thou shalt redeeme with a ‖lambe: and if thou wilt not redeeme it, then thou shalt breake his necke, and all the first borne of man amongst thy children shalt thou redeeme.

14 ¶ And

* Gen. 15. 13. acts 7. 6 gal. 3. 17.

† Hebr. a night of obseruations.

* Numb. 9. 12.

* Ioh. 19. 36.

† Heb. doe it.

* Chap. 22. 29. and 34. 19. leuit. 27. 26. num. 3. 13. & 8. 16 luke 2. 23.

† Hebr. seruants.

* Chap. 22 29. and 34. 19. ezek. 44. 30.
† Heb. cau to passe ou

‖ Or, kidd

Hebr. to morrow.

14 ¶ And it shalbe when thy sonne asketh thee †in time to come, saying, What is this? that thou shalt say vnto him; By strength of hand the LORD brought vs out from Egypt, from the house of bondage.

15 And it came to passe when Pharaoh would hardly let vs goe, that the LORD slew all the first borne in the land of Egypt, both the first borne of man, and the first borne of beast: Therefore I sacrifice to the LORD all that openeth the matrix, being males: but all the first borne of my children I redeeme.

16 And it shall be for a token vpon thine hand, and for frontlets betweene thine eyes. For by strength of hand the LORD brought vs foorth out of Egypt.

17 ¶ And it came to passe when Pharaoh had let the people goe, that God led them not through the way of the land of the Philistines, although that was neere: For God saide, Lest peraduenture the people repent when they see warre, and they returne to Egypt:

Or, by fiue in a ranke.

18 But God ledde the people about through the way of the wildernesse of the Red-sea: and the children of Israel went vp ||harnessed out of the land of Egypt.

Gene. 50. 25. iosh. 24. 2.

19 And Moses tooke the bones of Ioseph with him: for hee had straitly sworne the children of Israel, saying; * God will surely visite you, and ye shall cary vp my bones away hence with you.

Num. 33.

20 ¶ And *they tooke their iourney from Succoth, and encamped in Etham, in the edge of the wildernesse.

Num. 14. 14. deut. 1. 33. psal. 78. 14. 1. cor. 10. 1.

21 And * the LORD went before them by day in a pillar of a cloud, to lead them the way, and by night in a pillar of fire, to giue them light to goe by day and night.

Nehem. 9. 19.

22 He tooke not away the pillar of the cloud by day, * nor the pillar of fire by night, *from* before the people.

CHAP. XIIII.

1 God instructeth the Israelites in their iourney. 5 Pharaoh pursueth after them. 10 The Israelites murmure. 13 Moses comforteth them. 15 God instructeth Moses. 19 The cloud remoueth behinde the campe. 21 The Israelites passe through the Red-sea, 23 which drowneth the Egyptians.

And the LORD spake vnto Moses, saying,

2 Speake vnto the children of Israel, that they turne and encampe before * Pi-hahiroth, betweene Migdol and the sea, ouer against Baal-zephon: before it shall ye encampe by the sea.

Num. 33. 7.

3 For Pharaoh will say of the children of Israel, They *are* intangled in the land, the wildernesse hath shut them in.

4 And I will harden Pharaohs heart, that he shall follow after them, and I will be honoured vpon Pharaoh, and vpon all his hoste, That the Egyptians may know that I am the LORD. And they did so.

5 ¶ And it was told the King of Egypt, that the people fled: And the heart of Pharaoh and of his seruants was turned against the people, and they said, Why haue wee done this, that we haue let Israel goe from seruing vs?

6 And hee made ready his charet, and tooke his people with him:

7 And hee tooke sixe hundred chosen charets, and all the charets of Egypt, and captaines ouer euery one of them.

8 And the LORD hardened the heart of Pharaoh King of Egypt, and he pursued after the children of Israel: and the children of Israel went out with an high hand.

9 But the * Egyptians pursued after them (all the horses and charets of Pharaoh, and his horsemen, and his army) and ouertooke them encamping by the sea, beside Pi-hahiroth before Baal-zephon.

Iosh. 24. 6. 1. macc. 4. 9.

10 ¶ And when Pharaoh drew nigh, the children of Israel lift vp their eyes, and behold, the Egyptians marched after them, and they were sore afraid: and the children of Israel lift vp their eyes, and beholde, the Egyptians marched after them, and they were sore afraid`: and the children of Israel cried out vnto the LORD.

11 And they said vnto Moses, Because there were no graues in Egypt, hast thou taken vs away to die in the wildernesse? Wherefore hast thou dealt thus with vs, to cary vs foorth out of Egypt?

12 * Is not this the word that wee did tell thee in Egypt, saying, Let vs alone, that we may serue the Egyptians?
For

Chap. 6. 9,

For it had bene better for vs to ſerue the Egyptians, then that wee ſhould die in the wildernesse.

13 ¶ And Moſes ſaide vnto the people, Feare ye not, ſtand ſtill, and ſee the ſaluation of the LORD, which he will ſhew to you to day: ||for the Egyptians whom ye haue ſeene to day, ye ſhall ſee them againe no more for euer.

|| Or, For whereas you haue ſeene the Egyptians to day, &c.

14 The LORD ſhall fight for you, and ye ſhall hold your peace.

15 ¶ And the LORD ſaide vnto Moſes, Wherefore crieſt thou vnto me? Speake vnto the children of Iſrael, that they goe forward.

16 But lift thou vp thy rodde, and ſtretch out thine hand ouer the Sea, and diuide it : and the children of Iſrael ſhall goe on dry ground thorow the mids of the Sea.

17 And I, beholde, I will harden the hearts of the Egyptians, and they ſhall follow them : and I will get mee honour vpon Pharaoh, and vpon all his hoſte, vpon his charets, and vpon his horſemen.

18 And the Egyptians ſhall know that I am the LORD, when I haue gotten me honour vpon Pharaoh, vpon his charets, and vpon his horſemen.

19 ¶ And the Angel of God which went before the campe of Iſrael, remoued and went behind them, and the pillar of the cloud went from before their face, and ſtood behinde them.

20 And it came betweene the campe of the Egyptians, and the campe of Iſrael, and it was a cloud and darkeneſſe to them, but it gaue light by night to these : ſo that the one came not neere the other all the night.

21 And Moſes ſtretched out his hand ouer the Sea, and the LORD cauſed the Sea to goe backe by a ſtrong Eaſt winde all that night, and made the Sea dry land, and the waters were * diuided.

* Ioſh. 4. 23. pſalme 114. 3. * Pſal. 78. 13. 1. cor. 10. 1. hebr. 11. 29.

22 And * the children of Iſrael went into the midſt of the Sea vpon the dry ground, and the waters were a wall vnto them on their right hand, and on their left.

23 ¶ And the Egyptians purſued, and went in after them, to the midſt of the Sea, euen all Pharaohs horſes, his charets and his horſemen.

24 And it came to paſſe, that in the morning watch the LORD looked vnto the hoſte of the Egyptians, through the pillar of fire, and of the cloude, and troubled the hoſte of the Egyptians,

25 And tooke off their charet wheeles, ||that they draue them heauily: So that the Egyptians ſaid, Let vs flee from the face of Iſrael : for the LORD fighteth for them, againſt the Egyptians.

|| Or, made them to goe heauily.

26 ¶ And the LORD ſaide vnto Moſes, Stretch out thine hand ouer the Sea, that the waters may come againe vpon the Egyptians, vpon their charets, and vpon their horſemen.

27 And Moſes ſtretched foorth his hand ouer the ſea, and the ſea returned to his ſtrength when the morning appeared : and the Egyptians fled againſt it : and the Lord †ouerthrew the Egyptians in the midſt of the ſea.

† Hebr. ſhooke off.

28 And the waters returned, and couered the charets, and the horſemen, and all the hoſte of Pharaoh that came into the ſea after them : there remained not ſo much as * one of them.

* Pſal. 106. 11.

29 But the children of Iſrael walked vpon drie land, in the midſt of the ſea, and the waters were a wall vnto them on their right hand, and on their left.

30 Thus the LORD ſaued Iſrael that day out of the hand of the Egyptians : and Iſrael ſawe the Egyptians dead vpon the ſea ſhore.

31 And Iſrael ſaw that great †worke which the LORD did vpon the Egyptians : & the people feared the LORD, and beleeued the LORD, and his ſeruant Moſes.

† Hebr. hand.

CHAP. XV.

1 Moſes ſong. 22 The people want water. 23 The waters at Marah are bitter. 25 A tree ſweetneth them. 27 At Elim are twelue wels, and ſeuentie palme trees.

 Hen ſang * Moſes and the children of Iſrael this ſong vnto the LORD, and ſpake, ſaying, I will ſing vnto the LORD : for he hath triumphed gloriouſly, the horſe and his rider hath he throwen into the Sea.

* Wiſd. 1. 20.

2 The LORD is my ſtrength and ſong, and he is become my ſaluation : he is my God, and I will prepare him an habitation, my fathers God, and I will exalt him.

3 The LORD is a man of warre : the LORD is his Name.

4 Pha-

4 Pharaohs charets and his hoſte hath he caſt into the sea : his choſen captaines also are drowned in the red Sea.

5 The depths haue couered them: they sanke into the bottome as a stone.

6 Thy right hand, O Lord, is become glorious in power, thy right hand, O Lord, hath dashed in pieces the enemie.

7 And in the greatnesse of thine excellencie thou hast ouerthrowen them, that rose vp against thee : thou sentest forth thy wrath, *which* consumed them as stubble.

8 And with the blast of thy nostrils the waters were gathered together : the floods stood vpright as an heape, *and* the depths were congealed in the heart of the Sea.

9 The enemie said, I will pursue, I wil ouertake, I wil diuide the spoile: my lust shall be satisfied vpon them: I will draw my sword, mine hand shall ||destroy them.

r, repos-se.

10 Thou didst blow with thy wind, the sea couered them, they sanke as lead in the mighty waters.

11 Who *is* like vnto thee, O Lord, amongst the ||gods? who *is* like thee, glorious in holinesse, fearefull in praises, doing wonders!

r, mighty es ?

12 Thou stretchedst out thy right hand, the earth swallowed them.

13 Thou in thy mercie hast led forth the people which thou hast redeemed : thou hast guided *them* in thy strength vnto thy holy habitation.

14 *The people shall heare, *and* be afraid : sorrow shall take hold on the inhabitants of Palestina.

Deut. 2. Iosh. 2.

15 Then the dukes of Edom shal be amased : the mighty men of Moab trembling shall take hold vpon them : all the inhabitants of Canaan shal melt away.

16 *Feare and dread shall fall vpon them, by the greatnesse of thine arme they shall be as still as a stone, till thy people passe ouer, O Lord, till the people passe ouer which thou hast purchased.

Deut 2. Iosh. 2.

17 Thou shalt bring them in, and plant them in the mountaine of thine inheritance, in the place, O Lord, *which* thou hast made for thee to dwell in, in the Sanctuary, O Lord, *which* thy hands haue established.

18 The Lord shal reigne for euer and euer.

19 For the horse of Pharaoh went in with his charets and with his horsemen into the sea, and the Lord brought againe the waters of the Sea vpon them : But the children of Israel went on drie land in the mids of the sea.

20 ¶ And Miriam the prophetesse the sister of Aaron, tooke a timbrell in her hand, and all the women went out after her, with timbrels & with dances.

21 And Miriam answered them, Sing ye to the Lord, for he hath triumphed gloriously : the horse and his rider hath he throwen into the sea.

22 So Moses brought Israel from the red sea, and they went out into the wildernesse of Shur : and they went three dayes in the wildernesse, and found no water.

23 ¶ And when they came to Marah, they could not drinke of the waters of Marah, for they were bitter : therefore the name of it was called ||Marah.

|| That is, Bitternesse.

24 And the people murmured against Moses, saying, What shall wee drinke ?

25 And he cried vnto the Lord : and the Lord shewed him a * tree, which when hee had cast into the waters, the waters were made sweete : there he made a statute & an ordinance, and there he proued them,

** Ecclus. 38. 5.*

26 And said, If thou wilt diligently hearken to the voice of the Lord thy God, and wilt doe that which is right in his sight, and wilt giue eare to his Commandements, and keepe all his Statutes, I will put none of these diseases vpon thee, which I haue brought vpon the Egyptians : for I am the Lord that healeth thee.

27 ¶ * And they came to Elim : where *were* twelue wels of water, and threescore and ten palme-trees, and they encamped there by the waters.

** Num. 33. 9.*

CHAP. XVI.

And they tooke their iourney from Elim, and all the Congregation of the children of Israel came vnto the wildernesse of Sin, which

which is betweene Elim and Sinai, on the fifteenth day of the second moneth after their departing out of the land of Egypt.

2 And the whole Congregation of the children of Israel murmured against Moses and Aaron in the wildernesse.

3 And the children of Israel saide vnto them, Would to God wee had died by the hand of the LORD in the land of Egypt, when wee sate by the flesh pots, *and* when we did eate bread to the full: for ye haue brought vs forth into this wildernesse, to kill this whole assembly with hunger.

4 ¶ Then said the LORD vnto Moses, Behold, I will raine bread from heauen for you : and the people shall goe out, and gather †a certaine rate euery day, that I may proue them, whether they will walke in my Law, or no.

5 And it shall come to passe, that on the sixt day, they shall prepare that which they bring in, and it shall be twice as much as they gather dayly.

6 And Moses and Aaron said vnto all the children of Israel, At euen, then ye shall know that the LORD hath brought you out from the land of Egypt.

7 And in the morning, then ye shall see the glory of the LORD, for that he heareth your murmurings against the LORD : And what are wee, that yee murmure against vs?

8 And Moses said, *This shalbe* when the LORD shal giue you in the euening flesh to eate, and in the morning bread to the full : for that the LORD heareth your murmurings which ye murmure against him; and what *are* wee? your murmurings are not against vs, but against the LORD.

9 ¶ And Moses spake vnto Aaron, Say vnto all the Congregation of the children of Israel, Come neere before the LORD : for hee hath heard your murmurings.

10 And it came to passe as Aaron spake vnto the whole Congregation of the children of Israel, that they looked toward the wildernesse, and behold, the glory of the LORD * appeared in the cloude.

11 ¶ And the LORD spake vnto Moses, saying,

12 I haue heard the murmurings

of the children of Israel : Speake vnto them, saying, At euen ye shall eat flesh, and in the morning ye shalbe filled with bread : and ye shal know that I am the LORD your God.

13 And it came to passe, that at euen * the Quailes came vp, and couered the campe: and in the morning the dew lay round about the hoste.

14 And when * the dewe that lay was gone vp, behold, vpon the face of the wildernesse there lay a small round thing, *as* small as the hoare frost on the ground.

15 And when the children of Israel saw it, they said one to another, ‖ It is Manna : for they wist not what it *was*. And Moses said vnto them, * This is the bread which the LORD hath giuen you to eate.

16 ¶ This *is* the thing which the LORD hath commanded : gather of it euery man according to his eating : an Omer †for euery man, according to the number of your †persons, take yee euery man for them which *are* in his tents.

17 And the children of Israel did so, and gathered some more, some lesse.

18 And when they did mete *it* with an Omer, * he that gathered much, had nothing ouer, and he that gathered litle, had no lacke : they gathered euery man according to his eating.

19 And Moses saide, Let no man leaue of it till the morning.

20 Notwithstanding they hearkened not vnto Moses, but some of them left of it vntill the morning, and it bred wormes, and stanke : and Moses was wroth with them.

21 And they gathered it euery morning, euery man according to his eating : and when the Sunne waxed hot, it melted.

22 ¶ And it came to passe that on the sixt day they gathered twice as much bread, two Omers for one *man:* and all the rulers of the Congregation came and told Moses.

23 And he said vnto them, This is that which the LORD hath said, To morrow *is* the rest of the holy Sabbath vnto the LORD : bake that which you will bake, to day, and seethe that ye will seethe, and that which remaineth ouer, lay vp for you to be kept vntill the morning.

24 And they laid it vp till the morning,

Marginal notes:

† Hebr. the portion of a day in his day.

* Chap. 13. 21.

* Numb. 31.

* Numb 7. psal. 24. wisd. 20.

‖ Or, *what* this? or a portio * Ioh. 6 1. Cor. ‖

† Heb. t polle or † Heb. so

* 2. Co 15.

ning, as Moses bade : and it did not stinke, neither was there any worme therein.

25 And Moses saide, Eate that to day, for to day is a Sabbath vnto the LORD : to day yee shall not finde it in the field.

26 Sixe dayes ye shall gather it, but on the seuenth day *which is* the Sabbath, in it there shall be none.

27 ¶ And it came to passe, that there went out *some* of the people on the seuenth day for to gather, and they found none.

28 And the LORD said vnto Moses, How long refuse yee to keepe my Commandements, and my Lawes ?·

29 See, for that the LORD hath giuen you the Sabbath, therefore hee giueth you on the sixt day the bread of two dayes : abide yee euery man in his place : let no man goe out of his place on the seuenth day.

30 So the people rested on the seuenth day.

31 And the house of Israel called the name thereof Manna : and it *was* like Coriander seed, white : and the taste of it *was* like wafers made with hony.

32 ¶ And Moses said, This *is* the thing which the LORD commandeth : Fill an Omer of it to bee kept for your generations, that they may see the bread wherewith I haue fed you in the wildernesse, when I brought you forth from the land of Egypt.

33 And Moses sayd vnto Aaron, Take a pot, and put an Omer full of Manna therein, and lay it vp before the LORD, to be kept for your generations.

34 As the LORD commaunded Moses, so Aaron layd it vp before the Testimonie, to be kept.

35 And the children of Israel did eat Manna fortie yeeres, *vntill they came to a land inhabited : they did eate Manna, vntill they came vnto the borders of the land of Canaan.

*Iosh. 5.
2. nehem.
. 15.*

36 Now an Omer is the tenth part of an Ephah.

CHAP. XVII.

1 The people murmure for water at Rephidim.
5 God sendeth him for water to the rocke in
Horeb. 8 Amalek is ouercome by the holding vp of Moses hands. 15 Moses buildeth the Altar IEHOVAH Nissi.

Nd all the Congregation of the children of Israel iourneyed from the wildernesse of Sin after their iourneys, according to the commandement of the LORD, and pitched in Rephidim : and *there was* no water for the people to drinke.

2 Wherefore *the people did chide with Moses and said, Giue vs water that wee may drinke. And Moses said vnto them, Why chide you with mee ? Wherefore doe ye tempt the LORD ?

*Num. 20.
4.*

3 And the people thirsted there for water, and the people murmured against Moses, and said, Wherefore is this that thou hast brought vs vp out of Egypt, to kill vs and our children, and our cattell with thirst ?

4 And Moses cried vnto the LORD, saying, What shall I doe vnto this people? they be almost ready to stone me.

5 And the LORD said vnto Moses, Goe on before the people, and take with thee of the Elders of Israel : and thy rod wherewith *thou smotest the riuer, take in thine hand, and goe.

*Chap. 7.
20.*

6 *Behold, I will stand before thee there, vpon the rocke in Horeb, and thou shalt smite the rocke, and there shall come water out of it, that the people may drinke. And Moses did so, in the sight of the Elders of Israel.

*Num. 20.
9. psal. 78.
15. and 105
41. wis. 11.
4. 1. cor. 10.
4.*

7 And hee called the name of the place ‖ Massah, and ‖ Meribah, because of the chiding of the children of Israel, and because they tempted the LORD, saying, Is the LORD amongst vs, or not ?

‖ *That is,
Tentation.*
‖ *That is,
Chiding: or,
strife.*

8 ¶ *Then came Amalek, & fought with Israel in Rephidim.

*Deut. 25.
17. wis. 11.
3.*

9 And Moses said vnto *Ioshua, Choose vs out men, and goe out, fight with Amalek : to morrow I will stand on the top of the hill, with the rodde of God in mine hand.

*Called Ie-
sus, Acts. 7.
45.*

10 So Ioshua did as Moses had said to him, and fought with Amalek : and Moses, Aaron, and Hur went vp to the top of the hill.

11 And it came to passe when Moses held vp his hand, that Israel preuailed : and when he let downe his hand, Amalek preuailed.

12 But Moses hands were heauie, and they tooke a stone, and put it vnder him, and he sate thereon : and Aaron and Hur stayed vp his hands, the one on the one side, and the other on the other

ther side, and his handes were steady vntill the going downe of the Sunne.

13 And Ioshua discomfited Amalek, and his people, with the edge of the sword.

14 And the LORD said vnto Moses, Write this for a memoriall in a booke, and rehearse it in the eares of Ioshua: for *I will vtterly put out the remembrance of Amalek from vnder heauen.

15 And Moses built an Altar, and called the name of it ‖IEHOVAH Nissi.

16 For he said, ‖Because the LORD hath sworne *that* the LORD will haue warre with Amalek from generation to generation.

CHAP. XVIII.

1 Iethro bringeth to Moses his wife and two sonnes. 7 Moses entertaineth him. 13 Iethros counsell is accepted. 27 Iethro departeth.

Hen *Iethro the Priest of Midian, Moses father in law, heard of all that God had done for Moses, and for Israel his people, *and* that the LORD had brought Israel out of Egypt:

2 Then Iethro Moses father in law tooke Zipporah Moses wife, after he had sent her backe,

3 And her two sonnes, of which the *name of the one *was* ‖Gershom: for he said, I haue bene an alien in a strange land.

4 And the name of the other *was* ‖Eliezer: for the God of my father, *said he,* *was* mine helpe, and deliuered me from the sword of Pharaoh.

5 And Iethro Moses father in law came with his sonnes and his wife vnto Moses into the wildernes, where he encamped at the mount of God.

6 And he said vnto Moses, I thy father in law Iethro am come vnto thee, and thy wife, and her two sonnes with her.

7 ¶ And Moses went out to meete his father in law, and did obeysance, and kissed him: and they asked each other of *their* † welfare, and they came into the tent.

8 And Moses told his father in law, all that the LORD had done vnto Pharaoh, and to the Egyptians for Israels sake, *and* all the trauaile that had

†come vpon them by the way, and *how* the LORD deliuered them.

9 And Iethro reioyced for all the goodnesse which the LORD had done to Israel: whom he had deliuered out of the hand of the Egyptians.

10 And Iethro said, Blessed *be* the LORD, who hath deliuered you out of the hand of the Egyptians, and out of the hand of Pharaoh, who hath deliuered the people from vnder the hand of the Egyptians.

11 Now I know that the LORD is greater then all gods: *for in the thing wherein they dealt proudly, *hee* *was* aboue them.

12 And Iethro, Moses father in law, tooke a burnt offering and sacrifices for God: and Aaron came, and all the Elders of Israel, to eat bread with Moses father in law before God.

13 ¶ And it came to passe on the morrow, that Moses sate to iudge the people: and the people stood by Moses, from the morning vnto the euening.

14 And when Moses father in law saw all that he did to the people, he said, What is this thing that thou doest to the people? Why sittest thou thy selfe alone, and all the people stand by thee from morning vnto euen?

15 And Moses said vnto his father in law, Because the people come vnto me to enquire of God.

16 When they haue a matter, they come vnto mee, and I iudge betweene †one and another, and I doe make them know the statutes of God and his Lawes.

17 And Moses father in law saide vnto him, The thing that thou doest, is not good.

18 †Thou wilt surely weare away, both thou, and this people that is with thee: for this thing is too heauy for thee; *thou art not able to performe it thy selfe alone.

19 Hearken now vnto my voyce, I will giue thee counsell, and God shall be with thee: Be thou for the people to Godward, that thou mayest bring the causes vnto God:

20 And thou shalt teach them ordinances and lawes, and shalt shew them the way wherein they must walke, and the worke that they must doe.

21 Moreouer thou shalt prouide out of all the people able men, such as feare God, men of trueth, hating couetousnesse,

* Num. 24.
20. 1. sam,
15, 3.
‖ That is,
The LORD
my banner.
‖ Or, because
the hand of
Amalek is
against the
throne of the
LORD, therefore &c.
Hebr. The
hand vpon
the throne of
the Lord.

* Chap. 2.
16.

* Chap. 2.
22.
‖ That is,
A stranger
there.
‖ That is,
my God is an
helpe.

† Heb. peace.

† Heb. fou
them.

* Chap.
10, 16, 22
and 5. 7.
and 14. 1

† Hebr.
man and
fellow.

† Hebr.
ding thou
will fade
* Deut.

neſſe, and place *such* ouer them, *to bee* rulers of thousands, and rulers of hundreds, rulers of fifties, and rulers of tennes.

22 And let them iudge the people at all seasons: and it shall bee that euery great matter they shall bring vnto thee, but euery small matter they shal iudge: so shall it be easier for thy selfe, and they shall beare *the burden* with thee.

23 If thou shalt doe this thing, and God command thee so, then thou shalt bee able to endure, and all this people shall also goe to their place in peace.

24 So Moses hearkened to the voice of his father in law, and did all that he had said.

25 And Moses chose able men out of all Israel, and made them heads ouer the people, rulers of thousands, rulers of hundreds, rulers of fifties, and rulers of tennes.

26 And they iudged the people at all seasons: the hard causes they brought vnto Moses, but euery small matter they iudged themselues.

27 ¶ And Moses let his father in law depart, and he went his way into his owne land.

CHAP. XIX.

1 The people come to Sinai. 3 Gods message by Moses vnto the people out of the mount. 8 The peoples answere returned againe. 10 The people are prepared against the third day. 12 The mountaine must not be touched. 16 The fearefull presence of God vpon the Mount.

N the third moneth when the children of Israel were gone forth out of the land of Egypt, the same day came they into the wildernesse of Sinai.

2 For they were departed from Rephidim, and were come to the desert of Sinai, and had pitched in the wildernesse, and there Israel camped before the mount.

Acts 7. 38　3 And *Moses went vp vnto God: and the Lord called vnto him out of the mountaine, saying, Thus shalt thou say to the house of Iacob, and tell the children of Israel:

Deut. 29.　4 *Ye haue seene what I did vnto the Egyptians, and how I bare you on Eagles wings, and brought you vnto my selfe.

5 Now *therfore if ye will obey my voice indeed, and keepe my couenant, then ye shall be a peculiar treasure vnto me aboue all people: for *all the earth *is* mine.

6 And ye shall be vnto me a *kingdome of Priests, and an holy nation. These *are* the wordes which thou shalt speake vnto the children of Israel.

7 ¶ And Moses came and called for the Elders of the people, and layd before their faces all these wordes which the Lord commanded him.

8 And *all the people answered together, and said, All that the Lord hath spoken, we will doe. And Moses returned the wordes of the people vnto the Lord.

9 And the Lord said vnto Moses, Loe, I come vnto thee in a thicke cloud, that the people may heare when I speake with thee, and beleeue thee for euer: And Moses told the wordes of the people vnto the Lord.

10 ¶ And the Lord saide vnto Moses, Goe vnto the people, and sanctifie them to day and to morrow, and let them wash their clothes.

11 And be ready against the thirde day: for the third day the Lord will come downe in the sight of all the people, vpon mount Sinai.

12 And thou shalt set bounds vnto the people round about, saying, Take heed to your selues, that ye goe not vp into the mount, or touch the border of it: *whosoeuer toucheth the mount, shall be surely put to death.

13 There shall not a hand touch it, but he shall surely be stoned or shot thorow, whether it be beast, or man, it shall not liue: when the ‖trumpet soundeth long, they shall come vp to the mount.

14 ¶ And Moses went downe from the mount vnto the people, and sanctified the people; and they washed their clothes.

15 And hee said vnto the people, Be ready against the third day: come not at your wiues.

16 ¶ And it came to passe on the third day in the morning, that there were thunders and lightnings, and a thicke cloud vpon the mount, and the voyce of the trumpet exceeding lowd, so that all the people that was in the campe, trembled.

17 And Moses brought foorth the people out of the campe to meete with God,

* Deut. 5. 2.

* Deut. 10. 14. psal. 24.

* I. Pet. 2. 9. reuel. 1. 6.

* Chap. 24. 3; 7. deut. 5. 27. & 26. 17.

* Heb. 12. 20.

‖ Or, *Cornet*

God, and they stood at the nether part of the mount.

* Deut. 4. 11.

18 And *mount Sinai was altogether on a smoke, because the LORD descended vpon it in fire: and the smoke thereof ascended as the smoke of a furnace, and the whole mount quaked greatly.

19 And when the voyce of the trumpet sounded long, and waxed lowder and lowder, Moses spake, and God answered him by a voyce.

20 And the LORD came downe vpon mount Sinai, on the top of the mount: and the LORD called Moses vp to the top of the mount, and Moses went vp.

† Heb. contest.

21 And the LORD said vnto Moses, Goe downe, † charge the people, lest they breake thorow vnto the LORD to gaze, and many of them perish.

22 And let the Priests also which come neere to the LORD, sanctifie themselues, lest the LORD breake foorth vpon them.

23 And Moses said vnto the LORD, The people cannot come vp to mount Sinai: for thou chargedst vs, saying, Set bounds about the mount, and sanctifie it.

24 And the LORD said vnto him, Away, get thee downe, and thou shalt come vp, thou, and Aaron with thee: but let not the Priests and the people breake through, to come vp vnto the LORD, lest hee breake foorth vpon them.

25 So Moses went downe vnto the people, and spake vnto them.

CHAP. XX.

1 The ten Commandements. 18 The people are afraid. 20 Moses comforteth them. 22 Idolatrie is forbidden. 24 Of what sort the Altar should be.

* Deut. 5. 6. psal. 81. 10.

A Nd God spake all these words, saying,

2 *I am the LORD thy God, which haue brought thee out of the land of Egypt, out of the house of † bondage:

† Hebr. seruants.

3 Thou shalt haue no other Gods before me.

* Leuit. 26. 1. psal. 97. 7.

4 *Thou shalt not make vnto thee any grauen Image, or any likenesse of any thing that is in heauen aboue, or that is in the earth beneath, or that is in the

water vnder the earth.

5 Thou shalt not bow downe thy selfe to them, nor serue them: For I the LORD thy God am a iealous God, visiting the iniquitie of the fathers vpon the children, vnto the thirde and fourth generation of them that hate me:

6 And shewing mercy vnto thousands of them that loue mee, and keepe my Commandements.

* Leuit. 19. 12. deut. 5. 11. matt. 5. 33.

7 *Thou shalt not take the Name of the LORD thy God in vaine: for the LORD will not holde him guiltlesse, that taketh his Name in vaine.

8 Remember the Sabbath day, to keepe it holy.

* Chap. 23. 12. ezech. 20. 12. luke 13. 14.

9 *Sixe dayes shalt thou labour, and doe all thy worke:

10 But the seuenth day is the Sabbath of the LORD thy God: in it thou shalt not doe any worke, thou, nor thy sonne, nor thy daughter, thy man seruant, nor thy mayd seruant, nor thy cattell, nor thy stranger that is within thy gates:

* Gene. 2.

11 For *in sixe dayes the LORD made heauen and earth, the sea, and all that in them is, and rested the seuenth day: wherefore the LORD blessed the Sabbath day, and halowed it.

* Deut. 5. 16. mat. 15. 4. ephes. 6. 2.

12 ¶ *Honour thy father and thy mother: that thy dayes may bee long vpon the land, which the LORD thy God giueth thee.

* Matth. 5. 21.

13 *Thou shalt not kill.

14 Thou shalt not commit adultery.

15 Thou shalt not steale.

16 Thou shalt not beare false witnes against thy neighbour.

* Rom. 7.

17 *Thou shalt not couet thy neighbours house, thou shalt not couet thy neighbours wife, nor his man seruant, nor his maid seruant, nor his oxe, nor his asse, nor any thing that is thy neighbours.

* Hebr. 12. 18.

18 ¶ And *all the people saw the thundrings, and the lightnings, and the noise of the trumpet, and the mountaine smoking: and when the people saw it, they remooued, and stood a farre off.

* Deut. 5. 24. and 18. 16.

19 And they saide vnto Moses, *Speake thou with vs, and wee will heare: But let not God speake with vs, lest we die.

20 And Moses said vnto the people, Feare not: for God is come to prooue you, and that his feare may bee before your faces, that ye sinne not.

21 And

21 And the people stood afarre off, and Moses drew neere vnto the thicke darkenes, where God was.

22 ¶ And the LORD said vnto Moses, Thus thou shalt say vnto the children of Israel, Yee haue seene that I haue talked with you from heauen.

23 Ye shall not make with me gods of siluer, neither shall ye make vnto you gods of gold.

24 ¶ An Altar of earth thou shalt make vnto me, and shalt sacrifice thereon thy burnt offerings, and thy peace offerings, thy sheepe, and thine oxen: In all places where I record my Name, I will come vnto thee, and I will blesse thee.

*eut. 27.
sh. 8.

*br. build
* *with
* *ng.*

25 And * if thou wilt make mee an Altar of stone, thou shalt not † build it of hewen stone : for if thou lift vp thy toole vpon it, thou hast polluted it.

26 Neither shalt thou goe vp by steps vnto mine Altar, that thy nakednesse be not discouered thereon.

CHAP. XXI.

*euit. 25.
*eut. 15
ere. 34.

Ow these are the Iudgements which thou shalt set before them.

2 * If thou buy an Hebrew seruant, sixe yeeres he shall serue, and in the seuenth he shall goe out free for nothing.

*br. with
* *ody.*

3 If he came in † by himselfe, he shal goe out by himselfe : if he were married, then his wife shall goe out with him.

4 If his master haue giuen him a wife, and she haue borne him sonnes or daughters ; the wife and her children shall be her masters, and he shall go out by himselfe.

*br. say-
shallsay.

5 And if the seruant † shall plainely say, I loue my master, my wife, and my children, I will not goe out free :

6 Then his master shall bring him vnto the Iudges, hee shall also bring him to the doore, or vnto the doore post, and his master shall boare his eare through with an aule, and he shall serue him for euer.

7 ¶ And if a man sell his daughter to be a mayd seruant, shee shall not goe out as the men seruants doe.

8 If she † please not her master, who hath betrothed her to himselfe, then shall he let her be redeemed: To sell her vnto a strange nation hee shall haue no power, seeing he hath dealt deceitfully with her.

† *Hebr. be
euill in the
eyes of, &c.*

9 And if he haue betrothed her vnto his sonne, he shall deale with her after the maner of daughters.

10 If he take him another *wife*, her food, her rayment, and her duety of mariage shall he not diminish.

11 And if he doe not these three vnto her, then shall she goe out free without money.

12 ¶ * He that smiteth a man, so that he die, shalbe surely put to death.

* *Leuit. 24.
17.*

13 And if a man lye not in wait, but God deliuer *him* into his hand, then * I will appoint thee a place whither hee shall flee :

* *Deut. 19.
3.*

14 But if a man come presumptuously vpon his neighbour to slay him with guile, thou shalt take him from mine Altar, that he may die.

15 ¶ And he that smiteth his father, or his mother, shall bee surely put to death.

16 ¶ And he that stealeth a man, and selleth him, or if he be found in his hand, he shall surely be put to death.

17 ¶ And * hee that ‖ curseth his father or his mother, shall surely bee put to death.

* *Leuit. 20.
9. prou. 20.
20. matth.
15. 4. marke
7. 10.*
‖ *Or, reuileth.*
‖ *Or, his
neighbour.*

18 ¶ And if men striue together, and one smite ‖ another with a stone, or with his fist, and he die not, but keepeth his bed :

19 If hee rise againe, and walke abroad vpon his staffe, then shall hee that smote him, be quit : onely he shall pay for † the losse of his time, and shall cause *him* to be throughly healed.

† *Hebr. ceasing.*

20 ¶ And if a man smite his seruant, or his mayd, with a rod, and hee die vnder his hand, hee shall bee surely † punished :

† *Hebr. auenged.*

21 Notwithstanding, if he continue a day or two, hee shall not be punished, for he is his money.

22 ¶ If men striue, and hurt a woman with child, so that her fruit depart from her, and yet no mischiefe follow, he shalbe surely punished, according as the womans husband will lay vpon him, and hee shall pay as the Iudges *determine*.

23 And

23 And if any mischiefe follow, then thou shalt giue life for life,

* Leuit. 24. 20. deut. 19 21. matth. 5. 38.

24 *Eye for eye, tooth for tooth, hand for hand, foote for foote,

25 Burning for burning, wound for wound, stripe for stripe.

26 ¶ And if a man smite the eye of his seruant, or the eye of his mayd, that it perish, hee shall let him goe free for his eyes sake.

27 And if he smite out his man seruants tooth, or his mayde seruants tooth, hee shal let him goe free for his tooths sake.

* Gene. 9. 5.

28 ¶ If an oxe gore a man, or a woman, that they die, then *the oxe shal be surely stoned, and his flesh shall not be eaten : but the owner of the oxe shall be quitte.

29 But if the oxe were wont to push with his horne in time past, and it hath bene testified to his owner, and he hath not kept him in, but that he hath killed a man or a woman; the oxe shall be stoned, and his owner also shall bee put to death.

30 If there be layed on him a summe of money, then he shall giue for the ransome of his life, whatsoeuer is layd vpon him.

31 Whether hee haue gored a sonne, or haue gored a daughter, according to this iudgement shall it bee done vnto him.

32 If the oxe shall push a man seruant, or a mayd seruant, hee shall giue vnto their master thirty shekels, and the oxe shalbe stoned.

33 ¶ And if a man shall open a pit, or if a man shall digge a pit, and not couer it, and an oxe or an asse fall therein :

34 The owner of the pit shall make it good, and giue money vnto the owner of them, and the dead beast shalbe his.

35 ¶ And if one mans oxe hurt anothers, that he die, then they shall sell the liue oxe, and diuide the money of it, and the dead oxe also they shall diuide.

36 Or if it bee knowen that the oxe hath vsed to push in time past, and his owner hath not kept him in, hee shall surely pay oxe for oxe, and the dead shall be his owne.

CHAP. XXII.

‖ Or, goa.

* 2. Sam. 6.

I F a man shal steale an oxe, or a ‖sheepe, and kill it, or sell it; he shall restore fiue oxen for an oxe, and *foure sheepe for a sheepe.

2 ¶ If a thiefe bee found breaking vp, and be smitten that he die, there shal no blood be shed for him.

3 If the Sunne be risen vpon him, there shall be bloodshed for him : for hee should make full restitution : if he haue nothing, then he shall bee sold for his theft.

4 If the theft be certainely found in his hand aliue, whether it bee oxe or asse, or sheepe, he shall restore double.

5 ¶ If a man shall cause a field or vineyard to be eaten, and shall put in his beast, and shall feede in another mans field : of the best of his owne field, and of the best of his owne vineyard shall he make restitution.

6 ¶ If fire breake out, and catch in thornes, so that the stackes of corne, or the standing corne, or the field be consumed therewith; hee that kindled the fire, shall surely make restitution.

7 ¶ If a man shal deliuer vnto his neighbour money or stuffe to keepe, and it be stollen out of the mans house; if the thiefe be found, let him pay double.

8 If the thiefe be not found, then the master of the house shall be brought vnto the Iudges, to see whether he haue put his hande vnto his neighbours goods.

9 For all maner of trespasse, whether it be for oxe, for asse, for sheepe, for raiment, or for any maner of lost thing, which another challengeth to be his : the cause of both parties shall come before the Iudges, and whome the Iudges shall condemne, he shall pay double vnto his neighbour.

10 If a man deliuer vnto his neighbour an asse, or an oxe, or a sheepe, or any beast to keepe, and it die, or be hurt, or driuen away, no man seeing it,

11 Then shall an othe of the LORD be betweene them both, that hee hath not put his hand vnto his neighbours goods : and the owner of it shall accept thereof, and he shall not make it good.

* Gene. 39.

12 And *if it be stollen from him, he shall make restitution vnto the owner thereof.

13 If

13 If it be torne in pieces, then let him bring it *for* witnesse, and hee shall not make good that which was torne.

14 ¶ And if a man borrowe ought of his neighbour, and it be hurt, or die, the owner thereof being not with it, he shall surely make it good.

15 But if the owner thereof be with it, he shall not make it good: If it bee an hired *thing*, it came for his hire.

eut. 22.

16 ¶ And * if a man entice a maide that is not betrothed, and lie with her, he shall surely endow her to be his wife.

17 If her father vtterly refuse to giue her vnto him, he shall † pay money according to the dowrie of virgins.

eb. weigh

18 ¶ Thou shalt not suffer a witch to liue.

19 ¶ Whosoeuer lieth with a beast, shall surely be put to death.

20 ¶ * Hee that sacrificeth vnto *any* god saue vnto the LORD onely, hee shall be vtterly destroyed.

eut. 13. 14, 15. lac. 2. 24

21 ¶ * Thou shalt neither vexe a stranger, nor oppresse him: for ye were strangers in the land of Egypt.

euit. 19.

22 ¶ * Yee shall not afflict any widow, or fatherlesse child.

ac. 7. 10.

23 If thou afflict them in any wise, and they crie at all vnto mee, I will surely heare their crie.

24 And my wrath shall waxe hote, and I will kill you with the sword: and your wiues shall be widowes, and your children fatherlesse.

25 ¶ * If thou lend money to any of my people that is poore by thee, thou shalt not be to him as an vsurer, neither shalt thou lay vpon him vsurie.

euit. 25. deut. 23 psal. 15.

26 If thou at all take thy neighbors raiment to pledge, thou shalt deliuer it vnto him by that the sun goeth downe.

27 For that is his couering onely, it is his raiment for his skinne: wherein shal he sleepe? and it shal come to passe, when he crieth vnto mee, that I will heare: for I am gracious.

28 ¶ * Thou shalt not reuile the || Gods, nor curse the ruler of thy people.

cts 23. 5

r, *Judges*

29 ¶ Thou shalt not delay *to offer* the † first of thy ripe fruits, and of thy † liquors: * the first borne of thy sonnes shalt thou giue vnto me.

Ieb. thy nesse.
eb. Teare
hap. 13. 2. & 34.

30 Likewise shalt thou do with thine oxen, *and* with thy sheepe: seuen dayes it shall be with his damme, on the eight day thou shalt giue it me.

31 ¶ And ye shall be holy men vnto me: * neither shall ye eate any flesh that is torne of beasts in the field: yee shall cast it to the dogs.

Leuit. 22. zek. 44.

CHAP. XXIII.

1 Of slander and false witnesse. 3.6 Of iustice. 4 Of charitablenesse. 10 Of the yeere of rest. 12 Of the Sabbath. 13 Of idolatrie. 14 Of the three feasts. 18 Of the blood and the fat of the sacrifice. 20 An Angel is promised, with a blessing, if they obey him.

THou shalt not || raise a false report: put not thine hand with the wicked to bee an vnrighteous witnesse.

|| *Or, receiue*

2 ¶ Thou shalt not follow a multitude to doe euill: neither shalt thou † speake in a cause, to decline after many, to wrest *iudgement:*

† *Heb. answere.*

3 ¶ Neither shalt thou countenance a poore man in his cause.

4 ¶ If thou meete thine enemies oxe or his asse going astray, thou shalt surely bring it backe to him againe.

5 * If thou see the asse of him that hateth thee, lying vnder his burden, || and wouldest forbeare to helpe him, thou shalt surely helpe with him.

* Deu. 22. 4

|| *Or, wilt thou cease to helpe him? or, & wouldest cease to leaue thy* businesse *for him: thou shalt surely leaue* it to ioyne *with him.*

6 Thou shalt not wrest the iudgement of thy poore in his cause.

7 Keepe thee farre from a false matter: and the innocent and righteous slay thou not: for I will not iustifie the wicked.

8 ¶ And * thou shalt take no gift: for the gift blindeth † the wise, and peruerteth the words of the righteous.

* Deut. 16. 19. ecclus. 20. 28.

† *Hebr. the seeing.*

9 ¶ Also thou shalt not oppresse a stranger: for yee know the † heart of a stranger, seeing yee were strangers in the land of Egypt.

† *Heb. soule.*

10 And * sixe yeres thou shalt sow thy land, and shalt gather in the fruites thereof:

* Leuit. 25. 3.

11 But the seuenth *yeere* thou shalt let it rest, and lie still, that the poore of thy people may eate, and what they leaue, the beasts of the field shall eate. In like maner thou shalt deale with thy vineyard, *and* with thy || oliue yard.

|| *Or, oliue trees.*

12 * Sixe dayes thou shalt doe thy worke, and on the seuenth day thou shalt rest: that thine oxe and thine asse may rest, and the sonne of thy handmayd, & the stranger may be refreshed.

* Chap. 20. 8. deut. 5. 13. luke 13. 14.

13 And in all things that I haue said vnto you, be circumspect: and make no mention of the names of other gods, neither let it be heard out of thy mouth.

14 ¶ * Three

* Deut. 16.
16.

* Chap. 13.
3. & 34. 18.

* Deut. 16.
16. ecclus.
35. 4.

‖ Or, feast.

* Chap. 34.
26. deut. 14
22.

† Chap. 33.
2.

‖ Or, I will
afflict them
that afflict
thee.
† Chap. 33.
2.
* Iosh. 24.
11.

* Deut. 7.
25.

* Deut. 7.
14.

14 ¶ *Three times thou shalt keepe a feast vnto me in the yeere.

15 *Thou shalt keepe the feast of vnleauened bread: thou shalt eate vnleauened bread seuen daies, as I commanded thee in the time appointed of the moneth Abib: for in it thou camest out from Egypt: *and none shall appeare before me emptie:

16 And the feast of haruest, the first fruits of thy labours, which thou hast sowen in the field: and the feast of ingathering *which is* in the end of the yeere, when thou hast gathered in thy labours out of the field.

17 Three times in the yeere all thy males shall appeare before the LORD God.

18 Thou shalt not offer the blood of my sacrifice with leauened bread, neither shall the fat of my ‖ sacrifice remaine vntill the morning.

19 *The first of the first fruits of thy land thou shalt bring into the house of the LORD thy God: thou shalt not seethe a kid in his mothers milke.

20 ¶ *Behold, I send an Angel before thee to keepe thee in the way, and to bring thee into the place which I haue prepared.

21 Beware of him, and obey his voice, prouoke him not: for he will not pardon your transgressions: for my name is in him.

22 But if thou shalt indeed obey his voice, and doe all that I speake, then I wil be an enemie vnto thine enemies, and ‖ an aduersarie vnto thine aduersaries.

23 *For mine Angel shall goe before thee, and *bring thee in vnto the Amorites, and the Hittites, and the Perizzites, and the Canaanites, the Hiuites, and the Iebusites: and I will cut them off.

24 Thou shalt not bow downe to their gods, nor serue them, nor doe after their workes: *but thou shalt vtterly ouerthrowe them, and quite breake downe their images.

25 And yee shall serue the LORD your God, and he shall blesse thy bread, and thy water: and I will take sicknes away from the midst of thee.

26 ¶ *There shall nothing cast their yong, nor bee barren in thy land: the number of thy dayes I will fulfill.

27 I will send my feare before thee, and will destroy all the people to whom

thou shalt come, and I will make all thine enemies turne their † backes vnto thee.

28 And *I will send hornets before thee, which shall driue out the Hiuite, the Canaanite, and the Hittite from before thee.

29 I will not driue them out from before thee in one yeere, lest the land become desolate, and the beast of the field multiply against thee.

30 By little and little I will driue them out from before thee, vntill thou be increased and inherit the land.

31 And I will set thy bounds from the Red sea, euen vnto the sea of the Philistines, and from the desert vnto the riuer: for I will deliuer the inhabitants of the land into your hand: and thou shalt driue them out before thee.

32 *Thou shalt make no couenant with them, nor with their gods.

33 They shall not dwell in thy land, lest they make thee sinne against me: for if thou serue their gods, *it will surely be a snare vnto thee.

† Heb. neck.

* Iosh. 24.
12.

* Chap. 34
15. deut. 7.
2.

* Deut. 7.
16. iosh. 23.
13. iudg. 2.
3.

CHAP. XXIIII.

1 Moses is called vp into the Mountaine. 3 The people promise obedience. 4 Moses buildeth an Altar, and twelue pillars. 6 Hee sprinkleth the blood of the Couenant. 9 The glory of God appeareth. 14 Aaron and Hur haue the charge of the people. 15 Moses goeth into the Mountaine, where he continueth 40.dayes,and 40.nights.

Nd hee said vnto Moses, Come vp vnto ỹ LORD, thou, and Aaron, Nadab and Abihu, and seuentie of the Elders of Israel: and worship ye a farre off.

2 And Moses alone shall come neere the LORD: but they shall not come nigh, neither shall the people goe vp with him.

3 ¶ And Moses came and told the people all the words of the LORD, and all the iudgements: and all the people answered with one voyce, and said, *All the words which the LORD hath said, will we doe.

4 And Moses wrote all the words of the LORD, and rose vp early in the morning, and builded an Altar vnder the hill, and twelue pillars, according to the twelue tribes of Israel.

5 And he sent yong men of the children

* Chap. 19.
8, and 24.
3, 7. deut.
27.

dren of Israel, which offered burnt offerings, and sacrificed peace offerings of oxen, vnto the LORD.

6 And Moses tooke halfe of the blood, and put it in basons, and halfe of the blood he sprinkled on the Altar.

7 And he tooke the booke of the couenant, and read in the audience of the _{rſe 3.} people: and they saide, * All that the LORD hath said, will we doe, and be obedient.

8 And Moses tooke the blood and sprinkled it on the people, and said, Be- _{Pet. 1.} hold * the blood of the Couenant which _{br. 9.} the LORD hath made with you, concerning all these words.

9 ¶ Then went vp Moses and Aaron, Nadab and Abihu, and seuenty of the Elders of Israel:

10 And they saw the God of Israel: and there was vnder his feet, as it were a paued worke of a Saphire stone, and as it were the body of heauen in his clearenesse.

11 And vpon the Nobles of the children of Israel he layd not his hand: also they saw God, and did eate and drinke.

12 ¶ And the LORD sayd vnto Moses, Come vp to me into the mount, and be there, and I will giue thee Tables of stone, and a Law, and Commandements which I haue written, that thou mayest teach them.

13 And Moses rose vp, and his minister Ioshua: and Moses went vp into the mount of God.

14 And hee saide vnto the Elders, Tary ye here for vs, vntill wee come againe vnto you: and behold, Aaron and Hur *are* with you · If any man haue any matters to doe, let him come vnto them.

15 And Moses went vp into the Mount, and a cloud couered the Mount.

16 And the glory of the LORD abode vpon mount Sinai, and the cloud couered it six dayes: and the seuenth day hee called vnto Moses out of the midst of the cloud.

17 And the sight of the glory of the LORD *was* like deuouring fire, on the top of the mount, in the eyes of the children of Israel.

18 And Moses went into the midst of the cloud, and gate him vp into the _{ıap. 34.} mount: and * Moses was in the mount _{leut. 9.} forty dayes, and forty nights.

CHAP. XXV.

1 What the Israelites must offer for the making of the Tabernacle. 10 The forme of the Arke. 17 The Mercy-seat, with the Cherubims. 23 The table, with the furniture thereof. 31 The candlesticke, with the instruments thereof.

Nd the LORD spake vnto Moses, saying,

2 Speake vnto the children of Israel, that they †bring me an ||offering: *of euery man that giueth it willingly with his heart, ye shall take my offering.

3 And this is the offering which ye shall take of them; Gold, and siluer, and brasse,

4 And blew, and purple, and scarlet, and fine ||linnen, and goats *haire:*

5 And rammes skinnes died red, and badgers skinnes, and Shittim wood:

6 Oile for the light, spices for anointing oile, and for sweet incense:

7 Onix stones, and stones to be set in the *Ephod, and in the * brest plate.

8 And let them make mee a Sanctuary, that I may dwell amongst them:

9 According to all that I shew thee, after the patterne of the Tabernacle, and the patterne of all the instruments thereof, euen so shall ye make *it.*

10 ¶ * And they shall make an Arke of Shittim wood: two cubites and a halfe *shalbe* the length thereof, and a cubite and an halfe the breadth thereof, and a cubite & a halfe the height thereof.

11 And thou shalt ouerlay it with pure gold, within and without shalt thou ouerlay it: and shalt make vpon it a crowne of gold round about.

12 And thou shalt cast foure rings of gold for it, and put them in the foure corners thereof, and two rings *shal be* in the one side of it, and two rings in the other side of it.

13 And thou shalt make staues of Shittim wood, and ouerlay them with gold.

14 And thou shalt put the staues into the rings, by the sides of the Arke, that the Arke may be borne with them.

15 The staues shall be in the rings of the Arke: they shal not be taken from it.

16 And thou shalt put into the Arke the Testimonie which I shall giue thee.

17 And

_{† Hebr. take for me.}
_{|| Or, heaue offering.}
_{* Chap. 35. 5.}

_{|| Or, silke.}

_{* Chap. 28. 4.}
_{* Chap. 28. 15.}

_{* Chap. 37. 1.}

17 And thou shalt make a Mercie-seat of pure gold : two cubites and a halfe *shalbe* the length thereof, and a cubite and a halfe the breadth thereof.

18 And thou shalt make two Cherubims of gold : of beaten worke shalt thou make them, in the two endes of the Mercie-seat.

19 And make one Cherub on the one end, and the other Cherub on the other end: *euen* ||of the Mercie-seat shall yee make the Cherubims, on the two ends thereof.

|| *Or, of the matter of the Mercie seate.*

20 And the Cherubims shall stretch forth their wings on high, couering the Mercie-seat with their wings, and their faces *shall looke* one to another: totoward the Mercie-seat shall the faces of the Cherubims be.

21 And thou shalt put the Mercie-seat aboue vpon the Arke, and in the Arke thou shalt put the Testimonie that I shall giue thee.

22 And there I wil meet with thee, and I will commune with thee, from aboue the Mercie-seat, from *betweene the two Cherubims which are vpon the Arke of the Testimonie, of all things which I will giue thee in commaundement vnto the children of Israel.

* *Numb. 7. 89.*

23 ¶ * Thou shalt also make a table of Shittim wood: two cubites *shall bee* the length thereof, and a cubite the bredth thereof, and a cubite and a halfe the height thereof.

* *Chap. 37. 10.*

24 And thou shalt ouerlay it with pure gold, and make thereto a crowne of gold round about.

25 And thou shalt make vnto it a border of an hand bredth round about, and thou shalt make a golden crowne to the border thereof round about.

26 And thou shalt make for it foure rings of gold, and put the rings in the foure corners that *are* on the foure feete thereof.

27 Ouer against the border shall the rings be for places of the staues to beare the table.

28 And thou shalt make the staues of Shittim wood, and ouerlay them with gold, that the table may be borne with them.

29 And thou shalt make the dishes thereof, and spoones therof, and couers thereof, and bowles thereof, ||to couer withall : of pure gold shalt thou make them.

|| *Or, to powre out withall.*

30 And thou shalt set vpon the Table Shew-bread before me alway.

31 ¶ * And thou shalt make a Candlesticke of pure gold : of beaten worke shall the candlesticke bee made ; his shaft and his branches, his bowles, his knops, and his flowers shall be of the same.

* *Chap. 17.*

32 And six branches shall come out of the sides of it : three branches of the candlesticke out of the one side, and three branches of the candlesticke out of the other side :

33 Three bowles made like vnto almonds, with a knop and a flower in one branch: and three bowles made like almonds in the other branch, with a knop and a flower: so in the sixe branches that come out of the candlesticke.

34 And in the candlesticke *shall bee* foure bowles made like vnto almonds, with their knops and their flowers.

35 And *there shal be* a knop vnder two branches of the same, and a knop vnder two branches of the same, and a knop vnder two branches of the same, according to the sixe branches that proceede out of the candlesticke.

36 Their knops and their branches shall be of the same: all it shall bee one beaten worke of pure gold.

37 And thou shalt make the seuen lamps thereof: and they shall ||light the lampes thereof, that they may giue light ouer against †it.

|| *Or, cause to ascend.*
† *Heb. the face of it.*

38 And the tongs thereof, and the snuffe dishes therof *shalbe* of pure gold.

39 Of a talent of pure gold shall hee make it, with all these vessels.

40 And * looke that thou make them after their patterne, †which was shewed thee in the mount.

* *Acts 7. heb. 8. 5*
† *Heb. which thou wast caused to see.*

CHAP. XXVI.

1 The ten curtaines of the Tabernacle. 7 The eleuen curtaines of goats haire. 14 The couering of Rammes skinnes. 15 The boards of the Tabernacle, with their sockets and barres. 31 The Vaile for the Arke. 36 The hanging for the doore.

Oreouer thou shalt make the Tabernacle with ten curtaines of fine twined linnen, and blew, and purple, and scarlet: with Cherubims of †cunning worke shalt thou make them.

† *Heb. the worke of cunning workeman or Embroderer.*

2 The length of one curtaine *shalbe* eight

eight and twenty cubits, and the bredth of one curtaine, foure cubits: and euery one of the curtaines shall haue one measure.

3 The fiue curtaines shalbe coupled together one to another: and *other* fiue curtaines *shalbe* coupled one to another.

4 And thou shalt make loopes of blew vpon the edge of the one curtaine, from the seluedge in the coupling, and likewise shalt thou make in the vttermost edge of *another* curtaine, in the coupling of the second.

5 Fiftie loopes shalt thou make in the one curtaine, and fiftie loopes shalt thou make in the edge of the curtaine, that is in the coupling of the second, that the loopes may take hold one of another.

6 And thou shalt make fiftie taches of gold, and couple the curtaines together with the taches: and it shall be one tabernacle.

7 ¶ And thou shalt make curtaines of goats *haire*, to be a couering vpon the tabernacle : eleuen curtaines shalt thou make.

8 The length of one curtaine *shalbe* thirtie cubites, and the bredth of one curtaine foure cubites: and the eleuen *shalbe* all of one measure.

9 And thou shalt couple fiue curtaines by themselues, and six curtaines by themselues, and shalt double the sixt curtaine in the forefront of the tabernacle.

10 And thou shalt make fiftie loopes on the edge of the one curtaine, that is outmost in the coupling , and fiftie loopes in the edge of the curtaine which coupleth the second.

11 And thou shalt make fiftie taches of brasse , and put the taches into the loopes , and couple the ||tent together, that it may be one.

12 And the remnant that remaineth of the curtaines of the tent, the halfe curtaine that remaineth shall hang ouer the backe side of the tabernacle.

13 And a cubite on the one side, and a cubite on the other side †of that which remaineth in the length of the curtaines of the tent, it shall hang ouer the sides of the tabernacle, on this side, and on that side to couer it.

14 And thou shalt make a couering for the tent of rammes skinnes died red, and a couering aboue of badgers skinnes.

15 ¶ And thou shalt make boards for the Tabernacle of Shittim wood standing vp.

16 Ten cubits shall be the length of a board, and a cubite and an halfe shall be the breadth of one board.

17 Two †tenons *shall there be* in one board set in order one against another: thus shalt thou make for all the boards of the Tabernacle.

18 And thou shalt make the boards for the Tabernacle, twentie boards on the Southside Southward.

19 And thou shalt make fourtie sockets of siluer, vnder the twenty boards: two sockets vnder one board for his two tenons , and two sockets vnder another board for his two tenons.

20 And for the second side of the Tabernacle on the Northside *there shall bee* twentie boards,

21 And their fourtie sockets of siluer: two sockets vnder one board, and two sockets vnder another board.

22 And for the sides of the Tabernacle Westward thou shalt make sixe boards.

23 And two boards shalt thou make for the corners of the tabernacle in the two sides.

24 And they shall be †coupled together beneath, and they shall be coupled together aboue the head of it vnto one ring: thus shall it bee for them both ; they shall be for the two corners.

25 And they shall be eight boards, and their sockets of siluer sixteene sockets: two sockets vnder one board, and two sockets vnder another board.

26 ¶ And thou shalt make barres of Shittim wood : fiue for the boards of the one side of the Tabernacle,

27 And fiue barres for the boards of the other side of the Tabernacle, and fiue barres for the boards of the side of the Tabernacle for the two sides Westward.

28 And the middle barre in the mids of the boards, shall reach from ende to ende.

29 And thou shalt ouerlay the boards with gold, and make their rings of gold for places for the barres: and thou shalt ouerlay the barres with gold.

30 And thou shalt reare vp the Tabernacle *according to the fashion therof, which was shewed thee in the mount.

31 ¶ And thou shalt make a Vaile of blew,

† *Heb. hands*

† *Heb. twinned.*

* Chap. 25 9, 40. acts 7. 44. heb. 8. 5.

blew, and purple, and scarlet, and fine twined linnen of cunning worke: with Cherubims shall it be made.

32 And thou shalt hang it vpon foure pillars of Shittim wood, ouerlayd with gold: their hookes shalbe of gold, vpon the foure sockets of siluer.

33 ¶ And thou shalt hang vp the Vaile vnder the taches, that thou maist bring in thither within the Vaile, the Arke of the Testimony: and the Vaile shall diuide vnto you, betweene the holy *place* and the most holy.

34 And thou shalt put the Mercieseat vpon the Arke of the Testimony, in the most holy *place*.

35 And thou shalt set the table without the Vaile, and the candlesticke ouer against the table, on the side of the Tabernacle toward the South: and thou shalt put the table on the North side.

36 And thou shalt make an Hanging for the doore of the Tent, of blew, and purple and scarlet, and fine twined linnen, wrought with needle worke.

37 And thou shalt make for the Hanging fiue pillars of Shittim wood, and ouerlay them with gold, and their hookes shalbe of gold: and thou shalt cast fiue sockets of brasse for them.

CHAP. XXVII.

1 The Altar of burnt offering, with the vessels thereof. 9 The Court of the Tabernacle inclosed with hangings and pillars. 18 The measure of the Court. 20 The oile for the lampe.

And thou shalt make an Altar of Shittim wood, fiue cubits long, and fiue cubites broad: the Altar shall be foure square, and the height thereof *shalbe* three cubits.

2 And thou shalt make the hornes of it vpon the foure corners thereof: his hornes shall be of the same: and thou shalt ouerlay it with brasse.

3 And thou shalt make his pannes to receiue his ashes, and his shouels, and his basons, and his fleshhooks, and his firepannes: all the vessels thereof thou shalt make of brasse.

4 And thou shalt make for it a grate of networke of brasse; and vpon the net shalt thou make foure brasen rings in the foure corners thereof.

5 And thou shalt put it vnder the compasse of the Altar beneath, that the net may bee euen to the midst of the Altar.

6 And thou shalt make staues for the Altar, staues of Shittim wood, and ouerlay them with brasse.

7 And the staues shalbe put into the rings, and the staues shall be vpon the two sides of the Altar, to beare it.

8 Hollow with boards shalt thou make it: as †it was shewed thee in the mount, so shall they make it. † *Hebr. he shewed.*

9 ¶ And thou shalt make the Court of the Tabernacle for the Southside, Southward: there shall be hangings for the Court, of fine twined linnen of an hundred cubits long, for one side.

10 And the twenty pillars thereof, and their twenty sockets, *shall be* of brasse: the hookes of the pillars, and their fillets *shalbe* of siluer.

11 And likewise for the Northside in length, there shall be hangings of an hundred cubits long, and his twenty pillars, and their twenty sockets of brasse: the hookes of the pillars, and their fillets of siluer.

12 ¶ And for the breadth of the Court, on the Westside shalbe hangings of fifty cubits: their pillars tenne, and their sockets ten.

13 And the breadth of the Court on the Eastside Eastward, shall bee fiftie cubits.

14 The hangings of one side *of the gate* shalbe fifteene cubits: their pillars three, and their sockets three.

15 And on the other side *shalbe* hangings, fifteene *cubits*: their pillars three, and their sockets three.

16 ¶ And for the gate of the Court *shall be* an hanging of twenty cubits of blew, and purple, and scarlet, and fine twined linnen, wrought with needle worke: and their pillars *shall be* foure, and their sockets foure.

17 All the pillars round about the Court *shalbe* filletted with siluer: their hookes *shalbe* of siluer, and their sockets of brasse.

18 ¶ The length of the Court *shalbe* an hundred cubits, and the breadth †fiftie euery where, and the height fiue cubits of fine twined linnen, and their sockets of brasse. † *Hebr. fif by fiftie.*

19 All the vessels of the Tabernacle in all the seruice thereof, and all the pinnes thereof, and all the pinnes of the Court, *shalbe* of brasse.

20 ¶ And thou shalt command the children

children of Israel, that they bring thee pure oyle Oliue beaten, for the light, to cause the lampe †to burne alwayes.

Hebr. to scend vp.

21 In the Tabernacle of the Congregation without the Vaile, which is before the Testimony, Aaron and his sonnes shall order it from euening to morning before the LORD: It shall be a statute for euer, vnto their generations, on the behalfe of the children of Israel.

CHAP. XXVIII.

1 Aaron and his sonnes are set apart for the Priests office. 2 Holy garments are appointed. 6 The Ephod. 15 The breastplate, with twelue precious stones. 30 The Vrim and Thummim. 31 The robe of the Ephod, with pomegranates and belles. 36 The plate of the Miter. 39 The imbroidered coate. 40 The garments for Aarons sonnes.

Nd take thou vnto thee Aaron thy brother, and his sonnes with him, from among the children of Israel, that he may minister vnto me in the Priests office, *euen* Aaron, Nadab, and Abihu, Eleazar, and Ithamar, Aarons sonnes.

2 And thou shalt make holy garments for Aaron thy brother, for glory and for beauty.

3 And thou shalt speake vnto all that are wise hearted, whom I haue filled with the spirit of wisedome, that they may make Aarons garments to consecrate him, that hee may minister vnto me in the Priests office.

4 And these are the garments which they shall make; a breastplate, and an Ephod, and a robe, and a broidered coat, a Miter, and a girdle: and they shall make holy garments for Aaron thy brother, and his sonnes, that hee may minister vnto mee in the Priestes office.

5 And they shall take gold, and blew, and purple, and scarlet, and fine linnen.

6 ¶ And they shall make the Ephod of gold, of blew and of purple, of scarlet, and fine twined linnen, with cunning worke.

7 It shall haue the two shoulder pieces thereof, ioyned at the two edges thereof; and so it shall bee ioyned together.

‖ *Or, Imbroidered.*

8 And the ‖curious girdle of the E-

phod which is vpon it, shall bee of the same, according to the worke thereof, euen of gold, of blew, and purple, and scarlet, and fine twined linnen.

9 And thou shalt take two Onix stones, and graue on them the names of the children of Israel:

10 Sixe of their names on one stone, and the other sixe names of the rest on the other stone, according to their birth:

11 * With the worke of an engrauer in stone; *like* the engrauings of a signet shalt thou engraue the two stones, with the names of the children of Israel; thou shalt make them to be set in ouches of gold.

* Wisd. 18. 24.

12 And thou shalt put the two stones vpon the shoulders of the Ephod, for stones of memoriall vnto the children of Israel. And Aaron shall beare their names before the LORD, vpon his two shoulders for a memoriall.

13 ¶ And thou shalt make ouches of gold;

14 And two chaines of pure gold at the ends; of wreathen worke shalt thou make them, and fasten the wreathen chaines to the ouches.

15 ¶ And thou shalt make the brestplate of Iudgement, with cunning worke, after the worke of the Ephod thou shalt make it: of gold, of blew, and of purple, and of scarlet, and of fine twined linnen shalt thou make it.

16 Foure square it shall be *being* doubled; a spanne *shalbe* the length thereof, and a span shalbe the breadth thereof.

17 And thou shalt †set in it settings of stones; *euen* foure rowes of stones: *the first* row *shalbe* a ‖Sardius, a Topaz, and a Carbuncle: this shall be the first row.

† *Hebr. fill in it fillings of stone.* ‖ *Or, Ruby.*

18 And the second row *shall be* an Emeraude, a Saphir, and a Diamond.

19 And the third row a Lygure, an Agate, and an Amethist.

20 And the fourth row, a Berill, and an Onix, and a Iasper: they shalbe set in gold in their †inclosings.

† *Hebr. filings.*

21 And the stones shall bee with the names of the children of Israel, twelue, according to their names, *like* the engrauings of a signet: euery one with his name shall they bee according to the twelue tribes.

22 ¶ And thou shalt make vpon the brestplate chaines at the ends, of wreathen worke, of pure gold.

23 And thou shalt make vpon the brest-

brestplate two rings of gold, and shalt put the two rings on the two endes of the brestplate.

24 And thou shalt put the two wreathen *chaines* of gold in the two rings, *which are* on the ends of the brestplate.

25 And the other two endes of the two wreathen *chaines*, thou shalt fasten in the two ouches, and shalt put them on the shoulder pieces of the Ephod before it.

26 ¶ And thou shalt make two rings of gold, and thou shalt put them vpon the two ends of the breastplate, in the border thereof, which is in the side of the Ephod inward.

27 And two *other* rings of gold thou shalt make, and shalt put them on the two sides of the Ephod vnderneath towards the forepart thereof, ouer against *the other* coupling thereof, aboue the curious girdle of the Ephod.

28 And they shall bind the brestplate by the rings thereof, vnto the rings of the Ephod with a lace of blewe, that it may be aboue the curious girdle of the Ephod, and that the breastplate be not loosed from the Ephod.

29 And Aaron shal beare the names of the children of Israel in the breastplate of iudgement, vpon his heart, when hee goeth in vnto the holy *place*, for a memoriall before the LORD continually.

30 ¶ And thou shalt put in the breastplate of iudgement, the Vrim and the Thummim, and they shall bee vpon Aarons heart, when he goeth in before the LORD: and Aaron shall beare the iudgement of the children of Israel vpon his heart, before the LORD continually.

31 ¶ And thou shalt make the robe of the Ephod all of blew.

32 And there shall bee an hole in the top of it, in the mids thereof: it shall haue a binding of wouen worke, round about the hole of it, as it were the hole of an habergeon, that it be not rent.

_{‖ Or, skirts.}

33 ¶ And beneath vpon the ‖hemme of it thou shalt make pomegranates of blew, and of purple, and of scarlet, round about the hemme thereof, and belles of gold betweene them round about.

34 A golden bell and a pomegranate, a golden bell and a pomegranate, vpon the hemme of the robe round about.

_{* Ecclus. 45. 10.}

35 * And it shall be vpon Aaron, to

minister: and his sound shall be heard when he goeth in vnto the holy *place* before the LORD, and when he commeth out, that he die not.

36 ¶ And thou shalt make a plate of pure gold, and graue vpon it, *like* the engrauings of a signet, HOLINES TO THE LORD.

37 And thou shalt put it on a blewe lace, that it may be vpon the miter; vpon the forefront of the miter it shall be.

38 And it shall be vpon Aarons forehead, that Aaron may beare the iniquitie of the holy things, which the children of Israel shall hallow, in all their holy gifts: and it shall be alwayes vpon his forehead, that they may be accepted before the LORD.

39 ¶ And thou shalt embroider the coat of fine linnen, and thou shalt make the miter of fine linnen, and thou shalt make the girdle of needle worke.

40 ¶ And for Aarons sonnes thou shalt make coats, and thou shalt make for them girdles, and bonnets shalt thou make for them, for glory and for beautie.

41 And thou shalt put them vpon Aaron thy brother, and his sonnes with him: and shalt annoint them, and †consecrate them, and sanctifie them, that they may minister vnto mee in the Priests office.

_{† Heb. fill their hand}

42 And thou shalt make them linnen breeches, to couer †their nakednes, from the loines euen vnto the thighes they shall †reach.

_{† Heb. fle... of their n... kednesse.
† Heb. bee...}

43 And they shall be vpon Aaron, & vpon his sonnes, when they come in vnto the Tabernacle of the Congregation, or when they come neere vnto the Altar to minister in the holy place, that they beare not iniquitie, and die. *It shall be* a statute for euer vnto him and his seede after him.

CHAP. XXIX.

1 The sacrifice and ceremonies of consecrating the Priests. 38 The continuall burnt offering. 45 Gods promise to dwell among the children of Israel.

Nd this is the thing that thou shalt doe vnto them, to hallow them, to minister vnto me in the Priests office: * Take one yong bullocke, and two rammes without blemish,

_{* Leuit. 9.}

2 And vnleauened bread, and cakes vnlea-

vnleauened, tempered with oyle, and wafers vnleauened, annointed with oile: of wheaten flowre shalt thou make them.

3 And thou shalt put them into one basket, and bring them in the basket, with the bullocke and the two rammes.

4 And Aaron and his sonnes thou shalt bring vnto the doore of the Tabernacle of the Congregation, and shalt wash them with water.

5 And thou shalt take the garments, and put vpon Aaron the coat, and the robe of the Ephod, and the Ephod, and the brestplate, and gird him with the curious girdle of the Ephod.

6 And thou shalt put the Miter vpon his head, and put the holy Crowne vpon the Miter.

Chap. 30.

7 Then shalt thou take the annointing *oyle, and powre it vpon his head, and annoint him.

8 And thou shalt bring his sonnes, and put coats vpon them.

Heb. bind.

Heb. fill the hand of. Chap. 28.

9 And thou shalt gird them with girdles, (Aaron and his sonnes) and †put the bonnets on them: and the priests office shall be theirs for a perpetuall statute: and thou shalt †*consecrate Aaron and his sonnes.

Leuit. 1. 4

10 And thou shalt cause a bullocke to bee brought before the Tabernacle of the Congregation : and *Aaron and his sonnes shall put their hands vpon the head of the bullocke.

11 And thou shalt kill the bullocke before the Lord, by the doore of the Tabernacle of the Congregation.

12 And thou shalt take of the blood of the bullocke, and put it vpon the hornes of the altar with thy finger, and powre all the blood beside the bottome of the Altar.

Leuit. 3. 3
It seemeth by Anatomy, and the Hebrewe Doctours, to be the midriffe.

13 And *thou shalt take all the fat that couereth the inwards, and ||the caule that is aboue the liuer, and the two kidneis, and the fat that is vpon them, and burne them vpon the altar.

14 But the flesh of the bullocke, and his skinne, and his doung shalt thou burne with fire without the campe, it is a sinne offering.

15 ¶ Thou shalt also take one ram, and Aaron and his sonnes shall put their hands vpon the head of the ram.

16 And thou shalt slay the ramme, and thou shalt take his blood, and sprinkle it round about vpon the altar.

17 And thou shalt cut the ramme in pieces, and wash the inwards of him, and his legs, and put them vnto his pieces, and ||vnto his head.

|| Or, vpon.

18 And thou shalt burne the whole ramme vpon the Altar: it is a burnt offering vnto the Lord: It is a sweet sauour, an offering made by fire vnto the Lord.

19 ¶ And thou shalt take the other ramme : and Aaron and his sonnes shall put their hands vpon the head of the ramme.

20 Then shalt thou kill the ramme, and take of his blood, and put it vpon the tip of the right eare of Aaron, and vpon the tip of the right eare of his sonnes, and vpon the thumbe of their right hand, and vpon the great toe of their right foot, and sprinckle the blood vpon the Altar round about.

21 And thou shalt take of the blood that is vpon the Altar, and of the anointing oyle, and sprinkle it vpon Aaron, and vpon his garments, and vpon his sonnes, and vpon the garments of his sonnes with him : and hee shall be hallowed, and his garments, and his sonnes, and his sonnes garments with him.

22 Also thou shalt take of the ram the fat and the rumpe, and the fat that couereth the inwards, & the caule aboue the liuer, and the two kidneis, and the fat that is vpon them, and the right shoulder, for it is a ram of consecration:

23 And one loafe of bread, and one cake of oyled bread, and one wafer out of the basket of the vnleauened bread, that is before the Lord.

24 And thou shalt put all in the hands of Aaron, and in the hands of his sonnes, and shalt ||waue them for a waue-offering before the Lord.

|| Or, shake to and fro.

25 And thou shalt receiue them of their hands, and burne them vpon the Altar for a burnt offering, for a sweet sauour before the Lord : it is an offering made by fire vnto the Lord.

26 And thou shalt take the brest of the ramme of Aarons consecrations, and waue it for a waue-offering before the Lord, and it shalbe thy part.

27 And thou shalt sanctifie the brest of the waue-offering, and the shoulder of the heaue offering, which is waued, and which is heaued vp of the ramme of the consecration, euen of that which is for Aaron, and of that which is for his sonnes.

28 And

28 And it shalbe Aarons, and his sonnes by a statute for euer, from the children of Israel : for it *is* an heaue offering: and it shall be an heaue offering from the children of Israel, of the sacrifice of their peace offrings, euen their heaue offering vnto the LORD.

29 ¶ And the holy garments of Aaron shall be his sonnes after him, to bee anoynted therein, and to be consecrated in them.

† *Hebr. He of his sonnes.* 30 And † that sonne that is Priest in his stead, shal put them on seuen dayes, when he commeth into the Tabernacle of the Congregation to minister in the holy place.

31 ¶ And thou shalt take the ramme of the consecration, and seethe his flesh in the holy place.

* *Leuit. 8. 31. matth. 12. 4.* 32 And Aaron and his sonnes shall eate the flesh of the ramme, and the *bread that is in the basket, by the doore of the Tabernacle of the Cōgregation.

33 And they shall eate those things, wherewith the atonement was made, to consecrate and to sanctifie them : but a stranger shall not eate *thereof,* because they are holy.

34 And if ought of the flesh of the consecrations, or of the bread remaine vnto the morning, then thou shalt burne the remainder with fire : it shall not be eaten, because it is holy.

35 And thus shalt thou doe vnto Aaron, and to his sonnes, according to all things which I haue commaunded thee: seuen dayes shalt thou consecrate them.

36 And thou shalt offer euery day a bullocke for a sinne offering, for atonement : and thou shalt clense the Altar, when thou hast made an atonement for it, and thou shalt anoynt it, to sanctifie it.

37 Seuen dayes shalt thou make an atonement for the Altar, and sanctifie it: and it shalbe an Altar most holy: whatsoeuer toucheth the Altar, shalbe holy.

* *Num. 28. 3.* 38 ¶ Now this is that which thou shalt offer vpon the Altar; *two lambs of the first yere, day by day continually.

39 The one lambe thou shalt offer in the morning : and the other lambe thou shalt offer at euen :

40 And with the one lambe a tenth deale of flowre mingled with the fourth part of an Hin of beaten oyle : and the fourth part of an Hin of wine for a drinke offering.

41 And the other lambe thou shalt offer at Euen, and shalt doe thereto, according to the meat offering of the morning, and according to the drinke offering thereof, for a sweet sauour, an offering made by fire vnto the LORD.

42 *This shalbe* a continuall burnt offering throughout your generations, at the doore of the Tabernacle of the Congregation, before the LORD, where I wil meete you, to speake there vnto thee.

43 And there I will meet with the children of Israel : and ‖ *the Tabernacle* shalbe sanctified by my glory.

‖ *Or,* Israel

44 And I will sanctifie the Tabernacle of the Congregation, and the Altar : I will sanctifie also both Aaron and his sonnes, to minister to me in the Priests office.

* *Leuit.26. 12. 2. cor. 6. 16.* 45 ¶ And * I will dwell amongst the children of Israel, and will be their God.

46 And they shall know that I am the LORD their God, that brought them foorth out of the land of Egypt, that I may dwell amongst them : I am the LORD their God.

CHAP. XXX.

1 The Altar of incense. 11 The ransome of soules. 17 The brasen lauer. 22 The holy anoynting oyle. 34 The composition of the perfume.

A Nd thou shalt make an Altar to burne incense vpon : of Shittim wood shalt thou make it.

2 A cubite *shall bee* the length thereof, and a cubite the breadth thereof, (foure square shall it bee) and two cubits *shalbe* the height thereof: the hornes thereof *shalbe* of the same.

3 And thou shalt ouerlay it with pure gold, the † top therof, and the † sides thereof round about, and the hornes thereof: and thou shalt make vnto it a crowne of gold round about.

† *Hebr. the roofe and th walls.* † *Heb. walls.*

4 And two golden rings shalt thou make to it vnder the crowne of it, by the two † corners thereof, vpon the two sides of it shalt thou make it : and they shalbe for places for the staues to beare it withall.

† *Heb. Ribs*

5 And thou shalt make the staues of Shittim wood, and ouerlay them with gold.

6 And thou shalt put it before the Vaile,

Hebr. in-
cēse of spi-
 s.

Vaile, that is by the Arke of the Testimonie before the Mercie-seat, that is, o-
uer the Testimonie where I will meet
with thee.

7 And Aaron shall burne thereon
†sweet incense euery morning : when he
dresseth the lamps he shal burne incense
vpon it.

r, setteth
heb. cau-
h to as-
d.
leb. be-
ene the
euens.

8 And when Aaron ‖ lighteth the
lampes †at euen, he shall burne incense
vpon it, a perpetuall incense before the
LORD , throughout your generations.

9 Ye shall offer no strange incense
thereon, nor burnt sacrifice, nor meate
offering, neither shall ye powre drinke
offering thereon.

10 And Aaron shall make an atonement vpon the hornes of it once in a
yeere, with the blood of the sinne offering of atonements : once in the yeere
shall hee make atonement vpon it,
throughout your generations : it is most
holy vnto the LORD.

Num. 1.

eb. them
t are to be
mbred.

11 ¶ And the LORD spake vnto
Moses, saying,

12 *When thou takest the summe of
the children of Israel, after †their number, then shall they giue euery man a
ransome for his soule vnto the LORD,
when thou numbrest them, that there
be no plague amongst them, when thou
numbrest them.

euit. 27.
num. 3.
ezek.
2.

13 This they shall giue, euery one
that passeth among them that are
numbred : halfe a shekel after the shekel
of the Sanctuary : *A shekel is twenty
gerahs : an halfe shekel shall be the offering of the LORD.

14 Euery one that passeth among
them that are numbred from twentie
yeeres old and aboue, shall giue an offering vnto the LORD.

eb. mul-
e.
eb. dimi-
.

15 The rich shal not †giue more, and
the poore shall not †giue lesse then halfe
a shekel, when they giue an offering vnto the LORD, to make an atonement
for your soules.

16 And thou shalt take the atonement money of the children of Israel,
and shalt appoint it for the seruice of the
Tabernacle of the Congregation, that
it may be a memoriall vnto the children
of Israel before the LORD, to make
an atonement for your soules.

17 ¶ And the LORD spake vnto
Moses, saying,

18 Thou shalt also make a Lauer of
brasse , and his foote also of brasse, to
wash withall, and thou shalt put it betweene the Tabernacle of the Congregation, and the altar, and thou shalt put
water therein.

19 For Aaron and his sonnes shall
wash their hands and their feet thereat.

20 When they goe into the Tabernacle of the Congregation, they shall
wash with water, that they die not : or
when they come neere to the altar to
minister, to burne offering made by fire
vnto the LORD.

21 So they shall wash their handes
and their feet, that they die not : and it
shall be a statute for euer to them, euen to
him and to his seed throughout their generations.

22 ¶ Moreouer the LORD spake
vnto Moses, saying,

23 Take thou also vnto thee principall spices, of pure myrrhe fiue hundred
shekels, and of sweet cinamon halfe so
much, euen two hundred and fifty shekels, and of sweet calamus two hundred
and fiftie shekels,

24 And of Cassia fiue hundred shekels,
after the shekel of the Sanctuary, and
of oyle oliue an *Hin.

25 And thou shalt make it an oyle of
holy oyntment, an oyntment com-
pound after the arte of the ‖ Apothecarie : it shalbe an holy anointing oyle.

26 And thou shalt anoint the Tabernacle of the Congregation therewith , and the Arke of the Testimonie .

27 And the Table and all his vessels,
and the Candlesticke , and his vessels,
and the Altar of incense :

28 And the Altar of burnt offering
with all his vessels, and the Lauer and
his foot.

29 And thou shalt sanctifie them, that
they may bee most holy : whatsoeuer
toucheth them, shall be holy,

30 And thou shalt annoint Aaron
and his sonnes, and consecrate them,
that they may minister vnto mee in the
priests office.

31 And thou shalt speake vnto the
children of Israel, saying, This shall
bee an holy anointing oile vnto mee,
throughout your generations.

32 Vpon mans flesh shall it not bee
powred, neither shall ye make any other
like it, after the composition of it : it is
holy, and it shall be holy vnto you.

33 Whosoeuer compoundeth any
like it, or whosoeuer putteth any of it
vpon

* Chap. 29.
40.

‖ Or, perfu-
mer.

vpon a stranger, shall euen be cut off from his people.

34 ¶ And the Lord said vnto Moses, Take vnto thee sweete spices, Stacte, and Onicha, and Galbanum: *these* sweete spices with pure frankincense, of each shall there be a like *weight*.

35 And thou shalt make it a perfume, a confection after the arte of the Apothecarie, †tempered together, pure *and* holy.

† *Heb. salted*

36 And thou shalt beat *some* of it very small, and put of it before the testimony in the tabernacle of the Congregation, where I will meet with thee: it shalbe vnto you most holy.

37 And as for the perfume which thou shalt make, you shall not make to your selues, according to the composition thereof: it shall be vnto thee holy for the Lord.

38 Whosoeuer shall make like vnto that, to smell thereto, shall euen bee cut off from his people.

CHAP. XXXI.

1 Bezaleel and Aholiab are called and made meet for the worke of the Tabernacle. 12 The obseruation of the Sabbath is againe commanded. 18 Moses receiueth the two Tables.

Nd the Lord spake vnto Moses, saying,

2 See, I haue called by name, Bezaleel the *sonne of Vri, the sonne of Hur, of the tribe of Iudah:

* 1. Chron. 2. 20.

3 And I haue filled him with the Spirit of God, in wisedome, and in vnderstanding, and in knowledge, and in all maner of workemanship,

4 To deuise cunning workes, to worke in golde, and in siluer, and in brasse,

5 And in cutting of stones, to set them, and in caruing of timber, to worke in all maner of workemanship.

6 And I, behold, I haue giuen with him, Aholiab the sonne of Ahisamach, of the tribe of Dan, and in the hearts of all that are wise hearted I haue put wisedome, that they may make all that I haue commanded thee:

7 The Tabernacle of the Congregation, and the Arke of the Testimony, and the Mercie-seat that is thereupon, & all the †furniture of the Tabernacle:

† *Heb. vessels*

8 And the Table, and his furniture, and the pure Candlesticke, with all his furniture, and the Altar of incense:

9 And the Altar of burnt offering, with all his furniture, and the Lauer and his foote:

10 And the clothes of seruice, and the holy garments for Aaron the Priest, and the garments of his sonnes, to minister in the Priests office:

11 And the anointing oyle, and sweet incense for the Holy *place:* according to all that I haue commanded thee, shall they doe.

12 ¶ And the Lord spake vnto Moses, saying,

13 Speake thou also vnto the children of Israel, saying, Verely my Sabbaths ye shall keepe: for it *is* a signe betweene me and you, throughout your generations, that *ye* may know that I am the Lord, that doth sanctifie you.

14 * Yee shall keepe the Sabbath therefore: for it is holy vnto you: Euery one that defileth it, shall surely be put to death: for whosoeuer doth *any* worke therein, that soule shall be cut off from amongst his people.

* Chap. 20. 8. deut. 5. 12. ezek. 20. 12.

15 Six dayes may worke bee done, but in the seuenth *is* the Sabbath of rest, † holy to the Lord: whosoeuer doth *any* worke in the Sabbath day, he shall surely be put to death.

† *Heb. holinesse.*

16 Wherefore the children of Israel shall keepe the Sabbath, to obserue the Sabbath throughout their generations, for a perpetuall couenant.

17 It *is* a signe betweene me and the children of Israel for euer: for *in sixe dayes the Lord made heauen and earth, and on the seuenth day he rested, and was refreshed.

* Gen. 1. 3 and 2. 2.

18 ¶ And he gaue vnto Moses, when hee had made an end of communing with him vpon mount Sinai, * two tables of Testimonie, tables of stone, written with the finger of God.

* Deut. 9. 10.

CHAP. XXXII.

1 The people in the absence of Moses, cause Aaron to make a calfe. 7 God is angred thereby. 11 At the intreatie of Moses he is appeased. 15 Moses commeth downe with the Tables. 19 He breaketh them. 20 He destroyeth the calfe. 22 Aarons excuse for himselfe. 25 Moses causeth the Idolaters to bee slaine. 30 He prayeth for the people.

Nd when the people saw that Moses delayed to come downe out of the mount, the people gathered themselues together vnto

vnto Aaron, and said vnto him, * Vp, make vs gods which shall goe before vs : for as for this Moses, the man that brought vs vp out of the land of Egypt, we wot not what is become of him.

2 And Aaron saide vnto them, Breake off the golden earerings which are in the eares of your wiues, of your sonnes, and of your daughters, and bring *them* vnto me.

3 And all the people brake off the golden earerings, which were in their eares, and brought *them* vnto Aaron.

4 * And hee receiued *them* at their hand, and fashioned it with a grauing toole, after hee had made it a molten calfe : and they said, These be thy gods, O Israel, which brought thee vp out of the land of Egypt.

5 And when Aaron saw it, he built an altar before it, and Aaron made proclamation, and said, To morrow *is* a feast to the LORD.

6 And they rose vp early on the morrow, and offered burnt offerings, and brought peace offerings : and the *people sate downe to eate and to drinke, and rose vp to play.

7 ¶ And the LORD said vnto Moses, *Goe, get thee downe : for thy people which thou broughtest out of the land of Egypt, haue corrupted *themselues.*

8 *They haue turned aside quickly out of the way which I commaunded them : they haue made them a molten Calfe, and haue worshipped it, and haue sacrificed thereunto, and saide, These bee thy gods, O Israel, which haue brought thee vp out of the land of Egypt.

9 And the LORD said vnto Moses, * I haue seene this people, and behold, it is a stiffenecked people.

10 Now therefore let me alone, that my wrath may waxe hot against them, and that I may consume them : and I will make of thee a great nation.

11 * And Moses besought †the LORD his God, and said, LORD, why doeth thy wrath waxe hot against thy people, which thou hast brought foorth out of the land of Egypt, with great power, and with a mighty hand ?

12 * Wherefore should the Egyptians speake and say, For mischiefe did he bring them out, to slay them in the mountaines, & to consume them from the face of the earth ? Turne from thy fierce wrath, and repent of this euill against thy people.

13 Remember Abraham, Isaac, and Israel thy seruants, to whom thou swarest by thine owne selfe, and saidest vnto them, * I will multiply your seed as the starres of heauen : and all this land that I haue spoken of, will I giue vnto your seed, and they shall inherit it for euer.

14 And the LORD repented of the euill which he thought to doe vnto his people.

15 ¶ And Moses turned, and went downe from the Mount, and the two Tables of the Testimony were in his hand : the Tables were written on both their sides; on the one side, and on the other were they written.

16 And the * Tables were the worke of God ; and the writing was the writing of God, grauen vpon the Tables.

17 And when Ioshua heard the noise of the people as they shouted, hee said vnto Moses, *There is* a noise of warre in the campe.

18 And he said, *It is* not the voyce of them that shout for mastery, neither *is it* the voyce of them that cry for †being ouercome : *but* the noyse of them that sing doe I heare.

19 ¶ And it came to passe, assoone as he came nigh vnto the campe, that he saw the Calfe, and the dancing : and Moses anger waxed hot, and he cast the Tables out of his hands, and brake them beneath the mount.

20 * And he tooke the Calfe which they had made, and burnt *it* in the fire, and ground *it* to powder, and strawed *it* vpon the water, and made the children of Israel drinke *of it.*

21 And Moses said vnto Aaron, What did this people vnto thee, that thou hast brought so great a sinne vpon them ?

22 And Aaron said, Let not the anger of my lord waxe hot : thou knowest the people, that they are set on mischiefe.

23 For they said vnto me, Make vs gods which shall goe before vs : for as for this Moses, the man that brought vs vp out of the land of Egypt, we wot not what is become of him.

24 And I said vnto them, Whosoeuer hath any gold, let them breake it off : So they gaue it mee : then I cast it into the fire, & there came out this Calfe.

25 ¶ And

Acts. 7.
0.

* Psal. 106.
9. 1. king.
2. 28.

* 1. Cor. 10.

* Deut. 9.
2.

* Deut. 9. 8.

* Chap. 33.
3. deut. 9.
13.

* Psal. 106,
25.
† Hebr. the
face of the
Lord.

* Num. 14.
13.

* Gene. 12.
7. and 15. 7.
and 48. 16.

* Chap. 31.
18.

† Heb. weaknesse.

* Deut. 9.
21.

† Hebr. those
that rose vp
against
them.

25 ¶ And when Moses saw that the people were naked, (for Aaron had made them naked vnto their shame, amongst †their enemies)

26 Then Moses stood in the gate of the campe, and saide, Who is on the LORDS side? *let him come* vnto mee. And all the sonnes of Leui gathered themselues together vnto him.

27 And hee said vnto them, Thus saith the LORD God of Israel, Put euery man his sword by his side, and go in and out from gate to gate throughout the campe, and slay euery man his brother, and euery man his companion, and euery man his neighbour.

28 And the children of Leui did according to the word of Moses; and there fell of the people that day about three thousand men.

‖ Or, And
Moses said,
Consecrate
your selues to
day to the
LORD, be-
cause euery
man hath
bene against
his sonne,
and against
his brother,
&c.
† Hebr. fill
your hands.

29 ‖For Moses had said, †Consecrate your selues to day to the LORD, *euen* euery man vpon his sonne, and vpon his brother, that he may bestow vpon you a blessing this day.

30 ¶ And it came to passe on the morrow, that Moses said vnto the people, Ye haue sinned a great sinne: And now I will goe vp vnto the LORD; peraduenture I shall make an atonement for your sinne.

31 And Moses returned vnto the LORD, and said, Oh, this people haue sinned a great sinne, and haue made them gods of gold.

32 Yet now, if thou wilt forgiue their sinne; and if not, blot me, I pray thee, out of thy Booke, which thou hast written.

33 And the LORD said vnto Moses, Whosoeuer hath sinned against me, him will I blot out of my Booke.

34 Therefore now goe, leade the people vnto *the place* of which I haue spoken vnto thee: Behold, mine Angel shall goe before thee; Neuerthelesse in the day when I visit, I will visit their sinne vpon them.

35 And the LORD plagued the people, because they made the Calfe, which Aaron made.

CHAP. XXXIII.

1 The Lord refuseth to goe as he had promised with the people. 4 The people murmure thereat. 7 The Tabernacle is remoued out of the Campe. 9 The Lord talketh familiarly with Moses. 12 Moses desireth to see the Glory of God.

Nd the LORD said vnto Moses, Depart, *and goe vp* hence, thou and the people which thou hast brought vp out of the land of Egypt, vnto the land which I sware vnto Abraham, to Isaac, & to Iacob, saying, *Vnto thy seed will I giue it.

2 *And I will send an Angel before thee, and I will driue out the Canaanite, the Amorite, and the Hittite, and the Perizzite, the Hiuite, and the Iebusite:

3 Vnto a land flowing with milke and hony: For I will not goe vp in the midst of thee: for thou art a*stiffenecked people, lest I consume thee in the way.

4 ¶ And when the people heard these euill tidings, they mourned: and no man did put on him his ornaments.

5 For the LORD had saide vnto Moses, Say vnto the children of Israel, Ye are a stiffenecked people: I wil come vp into the midst of thee in a moment, & consume thee: Therefore now put off thy ornaments from thee, that I may know what to doe vnto thee.

6 And the children of Israel stript themselues of their ornaments, by the mount Horeb.

7 And Moses tooke the Tabernacle, & pitched it without the campe, a farre off from the campe, and called it the Tabernacle of the Congregation: And it came to passe, that euery one which sought the LORD, went out vnto the Tabernacle of the Congregation, which *was* without the campe.

8 And it came to passe when Moses went out vnto the Tabernacle, *that* all the people rose vp, and stood euery man at his tent doore, and looked after Moses, vntill he was gone into the Tabernacle.

9 And it came to passe as Moses entred into the Tabernacle, the cloudy pillar descended, and stood at the doore of the Tabernacle, and *the Lord* talked with Moses.

10 And all the people saw the cloudy pillar stand at the Tabernacle doore: and all the people rose vp, and worshipped euery man in his tent doore.

11 And the LORD spake vnto Moses face to face, as a man speaketh vnto his friend. And he turned againe into the campe, but his seruant Ioshua the sonne of Nun, a yong man, departed not out of the Tabernacle.

* Gene. 12
7.
* Deut. 7.
22. iosh. 24
11.

* Chap. 32
9. deut. 9.
13.

12 ¶ And

12 ¶ And Moses saide vnto the Lord, See, thou sayest vnto mee, Bring vp this people, and thou hast not let mee know whome thou wilt send with me. Yet thou hast said, I knowe thee by name, and thou hast also found grace in my sight.

13 Now therefore, I pray thee, If I haue found grace in thy sight, shewe mee now thy way that I may know thee, that I may find grace in thy sight: and consider that this nation is thy people.

14 And he said, My presence shall go *with thee*, and I will giue thee rest.

15 And he said vnto him, If thy presence goe not *with mee*, carie vs not vp hence.

16 For wherein shall it bee knowen here, that I and thy people haue found grace in thy sight? is it not in that thou goest with vs? So shall we be separated, I and thy people, from all the people that *are* vpon the face of the earth.

17 And the Lord said vnto Moses, I will doe this thing also that thou hast spoken : for thou hast found grace in my sight, and I know thee by name.

18 And he said, I beseech thee, shew me thy glory.

19 And he said, I will make all my goodnesse passe before thee, and I will proclaime the name of the Lord before thee : *and I wil bee gracious to whom I wil be gracious, and wil shew mercie on whom I will shew mercie. [Rom. 9.]

20 And he said, Thou canst not see my face : for there shall no man see mee, and liue.

21 And the Lord said, Beholde, there is a place by mee, and thou shalt stand vpon a rocke.

22 And it shall come to passe, while my glory passeth by, that I will put thee in a clift of the rocke, and will couer thee with my hand, while I passe by.

23 And I wil take away mine hand, and thou shalt see my backe parts: but my face shall not be seene.

CHAP. XXXIIII.

1 The Tables are renued. 5 The Name of the Lord proclaimed. 8 Moses intreateth God to go with them. 10 God maketh a couenant with them, repeating certaine dueties of the first Table. 28 Moses after fourtie dayes in the Mount commeth downe with the Tables. 29 His face shineth, and he couereth it with a vaile.

And the Lord said vnto Moses, *Hew thee two Tables of stone, like vnto the first : and I will write vpon *these* Tables, the words that were in the first Tables which thou brakest. [* Deut. 10. 1.]

2 And be ready in the morning, and come vp in the morning vnto mount Sinai, and present thy selfe there to me, in the top of the mount.

3 And no man shall *come vp with thee, neither let any man bee seene throughout all the mount, neither let the flockes nor herds feede before that mount. [* Chap. 19. 12.]

4 ¶ And he hewed two Tables of stone, like vnto the first, and Moses rose vp earely in the morning, and went vp vnto mount Sinai, as the Lord had commanded him, and tooke in his hand the two tables of stone.

5 And the Lord descended in the cloud, and stood with him there, and proclaimed the Name of the Lord.

6 And the Lord passed by before him, and proclaimed, The Lord, The Lord God, mercifull and gracious, long suffering, and abundant in goodnesse and trueth,

7 Keeping mercie for thousands, forgiuing iniquitie and transgression and sinne, and that will by no meanes cleere *the guiltie,* *visiting the iniquitie of the fathers vpon the children, and vpon the childrens children, vnto the third and to the fourth generation. [* Exod. 20. 5. deut. 5. 9. ierem. 32. 18.]

8 And Moses made haste, and bowed his head toward the earth, and worshipped.

9 And he said, If now I haue found grace in thy sight, O Lord, let my Lord, I pray thee, goe amongst vs, (for it is a stiffenecked people,) and pardon our iniquitie, and our sinne, and take vs for thine inheritance.

10 ¶ And he said, Behold, *I make a couenant: before all thy people, I wil doe marueiles, such as haue not beene done in all the earth, nor in any nation: and all the people amongst which thou art, shall see the worke of the Lord: for it is a terrible thing that I will doe with thee. [* Deut. 5. 2.]

11 Obserue thou that which I command thee this day: Behold, I driue out before thee the Amorite, and the Canaanite, and the Hittite, and the Perizzite, and the Hiuite, and the Iebusite:
12 *Take

* Chap. 23.
32. deut. 7.
2.

12 *Take heed to thy selfe, lest thou make a couenant with the inhabitants of the land whither thou goest, lest it be for a snare in the midst of thee.

† Hebr. sta-
tues.

13 But ye shall destroy their altars, breake their †images, and cut downe their groues.

* Chap. 20.
5.

14 For thou shalt worship no other god : for the LORD, whose name is Ielous, is a *Ielous God:

15 Lest thou make a couenant with the inhabitants of the land, and they goe a whoring after their gods, and doe sacrifice vnto their gods, and *one* call thee, and thou eate of his sacrifice,

* 1. King.
11. 2.

16 And thou take of * their daughters vnto thy sonnes, and their daughters goe a whoring after their gods, and make thy sonnes goe a whoring after their gods.

17 Thou shalt make thee no molten gods.

* Chap. 23.
15.

18 ¶ The feast of * vnleauened bread shalt thou keepe : Seuen dayes thou shalt eate vnleauened bread, as I commanded thee in the time of the moneth Abib : for in the * moneth Abib thou camest out from Egypt.

* Chap. 13.
4.

* Chap. 22.
29. ezech.
44. 30.

19 * All that openeth the matrixe *is* mine : and euery firstling amongst thy cattell, whether oxe or sheepe, *that is male.*

‖ Or, kid.

20 But the firstling of an Asse thou shalt redeeme with a ‖ lambe : and if thou redeeme him not, then shalt thou breake his necke. All the first borne of thy sonnes thou shalt redeeme : and none shall appeare before me * empty.

* Chap. 23.
15.
* Chap. 23.
12. deut. 5.
12. luke 13.
14.

21 ¶ * Sixe dayes thou shalt worke, but on the seuenth day thou shalt rest: in earing time and in haruest thou shalt rest.

* Chap. 23.
16.

22 ¶ * And thou shalt obserue the feast of weekes, of the first fruits of wheat haruest, and the feast of ingathering at the †yeeres end.

† Hebr. re-
uolution of
the yeere.
* Chap. 23.
14, 17. deu.
16. 16.

23 ¶ * Thrice in the yeere shall all your men children appeare before the Lord GOD, the God of Israel.

24 For I will cast out the nations before thee, and enlarge thy borders : neither shall any man desire thy land, when thou shalt goe vp to appeare before the LORD thy God, thrice in the yeere.

* Chap. 23.
18.

25 * Thou shalt not offer the blood of my sacrifice with leauen, neither shall the sacrifice of the feast of Passeouer be left vnto the morning.

26 The first of the first fruits of thy land thou shalt bring vnto the house of the LORD thy God. Thou shalt not seethe a *kid in his mothers milke.

* Exod. 23
19. deut.
14 21.
* Deut. 4.
13.

27 And the LORD said vnto Moses, Write thou * these words : for after the tenour of these wordes, I haue made a couenant with thee, and with Israel.

28 * And hee was there with the LORD forty dayes and forty nights : he did neither eat bread, nor drinke water ; and he wrote vpon the Tables the words of the couenant, the ten †Commandements.

* Chap. 24
18. deut. 9
9.

† Hebr.
words.

29 ¶ And it came to passe when Moses came downe from mount Sinai (with the two Tables of Testimony in Moses hand, when hee came downe from the mount) that Moses wist not that the skin of his face shone, while he talked with him.

30 And when Aaron and all the children of Israel saw Moses, behold, the skinne of his face shone, and they were afraid to come nigh him.

31 And Moses called vnto them, and Aaron and all the rulers of the Congregation returned vnto him, and Moses talked with them.

32 And afterward all the children of Israel came nigh : and he gaue them in commandement all that the LORD had spoken with him in mount Sinai.

33 And *till* Moses had done speaking with them, he put * a vaile on his face.

* 2. Cor. 3
13.

34 But when Moses went in before the LORD to speake with him, hee tooke the vaile off, vntill he came out: And hee came out and spake vnto the children of Israel, that which he was commanded.

35 And the children of Israel saw the face of Moses, that the skinne of Moses face shone : and Moses put the vaile vpon his face againe, vntill hee went in to speake with him.

CHAP. XXXV.

1 The Sabbath. 4 The free gifts for the Tabernacle. 20 The readinesse of the people to offer. 30 Bezaleel and Aholiab are called to the worke.

Nd Moses gathered all the Congregation of the children of Israel together, and said vnto them; These are the wordes which the LORD hath commanded, that

that yee should doe them.

2 * Sixe dayes shall worke be done, but on the seuenth day there shall be to you an †holy day, a Sabbath of rest to the Lord: whosoeuer doeth worke therein, shall be put to death.

3 Ye shall kindle no fire throughout your habitations vpon the Sabbath day.

4 ¶ And Moses spake vnto all the Congregation of the children of Israel, saying, This *is* the thing which the Lord commanded, saying,

5 Take ye from amongst you an offring vnto the Lord: * Whosoeuer is of a willing heart, let him bring it, an offering of the Lord, gold, and siluer, and brasse,

6 And blew, and purple, and scarlet, and fine linnen, and goats *haire*,

7 And rammes skinnes died red, & badgers skinnes, and Shittim wood,

8 And oyle for the light, and spices for anoynting oyle, and for the sweet incense:

9 And Onix stones, and stones to be set for the Ephod, and for the brestplate.

10 And euery wise hearted among you, shall come and make all that the Lord hath commanded:

11 *The Tabernacle, his tent, and his couering, his taches, & his barres, his pillars, and his sockets:

12 The Arke and the staues thereof, with the Mercy seat, and the Vaile of the couering:

13 The Table and his staues, and all his vessels, and the Shewbread,

14 The Candlesticke also for the light, and his furniture, and his lamps, with the oyle for the light,

15 *And the incense Altar, and his staues, and the anoynting oyle, and the sweet incense, and the hanging for the doore, at the entring in of the Tabernacle:

16 * The Altar of burnt offering with his brasen grate, his staues, and all his vessels, the Lauer and his foot:

17 The hangings of the Court, his pillars, and their sockets, and the hanging for the doore of the Court:

18 The pinnes of the Tabernacle, and the pinnes of the Court, and their coards:

19 The cloathes of seruice, to doe seruice in the holy *place*, the holy garments for Aaron the Priest, and the garments

of his sonnes to minister in the Priests office.

20 ¶ And all the Congregation of the children of Israel departed from the presence of Moses.

21 And they came euery one whose heart stirred him vp, and euery one whom his spirit made willing, and they brought the Lords offering to the worke of the Tabernacle of the Congregation, and for all his seruice, and for the holy garments.

22 And they came both men and women, as many as were willing hearted, *and* brought bracelets, and earerings, and rings, & tablets, all iewels of gold: and euery man that offered, *offered* an offering of gold vnto the Lord.

23 And euery man with whom was found blew, and purple, and scarlet, and fine linnen, and goates *haire*, and red skinnes of rammes, and badgers skinnes, brought *them*.

24 Euery one that did offer an offering of siluer and brasse, brought the Lords offering: and euery man with whom was found Shittim wood for any worke of the seruice, brought *it*.

25 And all the women that were wise hearted, did spin with their hands, and brought that which they had spun, both of blew, and of purple, and of scarlet, and of fine linnen.

26 And all the women whose heart stirred them vp in wisedome, spunne goats *haire*.

27 And the rulers brought Onix stones, and stones to be set for the Ephod, and for the brestplate:

28 And * spice and oyle for the light, and for the anoynting oyle, and for the sweet incense.

29 The children of Israel brought a willing offering vnto the Lord, euery man and woman, whose heart made them willing to bring for all maner of worke, which the Lord had commanded to be made by the hands of Moses.

30 ¶ And Moses said vnto the children of Israel, See, * the Lord hath called by name Bezaleel the sonne of Vri, the sonne of Hur, of the tribe of Iudah.

31 And he hath filled him with the Spirit of God, in wisedome, in vnderstanding, and in knowledge, and in all maner of workemanship:

32 And to deuise curious workes, to worke

Chap. 20.
. leuit. 23.
, deut. 5.
2. luke 13.
4
Hebr. Hollnesse.

Chap. 25.

Chap. 26.
.

Chap. 30.

Chap. 27.

* Chap. 30.
23.

* Chap. 31.
2.

worke in gold, & in siluer, and in brasse,

33 And in the cutting of stones, to set *them*, and in caruing of wood, to make any maner of cunning worke.

34 And he hath put in his heart that he may teach, *both* he and Aholiab the sonne of Ahisamach of the tribe of Dan.

35 Them hath hee filled with wisedome of heart, to worke all manner of worke, of the ingrauer, and of the cunning workeman, and of the embroiderer, in blew, and in purple, in scarlet, and in fine linnen, and of the weauer, euen of them that doe any worke, and of those that deuise cunning worke.

CHAP. XXXVI.

1 The offerings are deliuered to the workemen. 5 The liberalitie of the people is restrained. 8 The curtaines of Cherubims. 14 The curtaines of goats haire. 19 The couering of skinnes. 20 The boards with their sockets. 31 The barres. 35 The vaile. 37 The hanging for the doore.

HEn wrought Bezaleel and Aholiab, and euery wise hearted man, in whome the Lord put wisedome and vnderstanding, to know how to worke all maner of worke for the seruice of the Sanctuary, according to all that the Lord had commanded.

2 And Moses called Bezaleel and Aholiab, and euery wise hearted man, in whose heart the Lord had put wisedome, *euen* euery one whose heart stirred him vp to come vnto the worke to doe it.

3 And they receiued of Moses all the offering which the children of Israel had brought, for the worke of the seruice of the Sanctuarie, to make it *withall*. And they brought yet vnto him free offerings euery morning.

4 And al the wise men that wrought all the worke of the Sanctuary, came euery man from his worke which they made.

5 ¶ And they spake vnto Moses, saying, The people bring much more then enough for the seruice of the worke which the Lord commaunded to make.

6 And Moses gaue commandement, and they caused it to bee proclaimed throughout the campe, saying, Let neither man nor woman make any more

worke for the offering of the Sanctuarie : so the people were restrained from bringing.

7 For the stuffe they had was sufficient for all the worke to make it, and too much.

8 ¶ * And euery wise hearted man, among them that wrought the worke of the Tabernacle, made ten curtaines, of fine twined linnen, and blew, and purple, and scarlet : with Cherubims of cunning worke made he them. ** Chap. 26. 3,4.*

9 The length of one curtaine was twentie & eight cubites, and the breadth of one curtaine foure cubites : the curtaines *were* all of one cise.

10 And he coupled the fiue curtaines one vnto another : and *the other* fiue curtaines he coupled one vnto another.

11 And he made loopes of blew, on the edge of one curtaine, from the seluedge in the coupling : likewise hee made in the vttermost side of *another* curtaine, in the coupling of the second.

12 * Fiftie loopes made he in one curtaine, and fiftie loopes made hee in the edge of the curtaine which *was* in the coupling of the second : the loopes held one curtaine to another. ** Chap. 26 10.*

13 And he made fiftie taches of gold, and coupled the curtaines one vnto another with the taches. So it became one tabernacle.

14 ¶ And he made curtaines of goats *haire*, for the tent ouer the Tabernacle : eleuen curtaines he made them.

15 The length of one curtaine was thirtie cubites, and foure cubites was the breadth of one curtaine : the eleuen curtaines were of one cise.

16 And he coupled fiue curtaines by themselues, and sixe curtaines by themselues.

17 And he made fiftie loopes vpon the vttermost edge of the curtaine in the coupling, and fiftie loopes made he vpon the edge of the curtaine, which coupleth the second.

18 And he made fiftie taches of brasse to couple the tent together that it might be one.

19 And he made a couering for the tent of rammes skinnes died red, and a couering of badgers skinnes aboue *that.*

20 ¶ And hee made boards for the Tabernacle of Shittim wood, standing vp.

21 The length of a board *was* ten cubites,

cubites, and the breadth of a board one cubite and a halfe.

22 One board had two tenons, equally distant one from another : thus did he make for all the boards of the tabernacle.

23 And he made boards for the Tabernacle : twentie boards for the South side, Southward.

24 And fourtie sockets of siluer hee made vnder the twentie boards : two sockets vnder one board for his two tenons, and two sockets vnder another board, for his two tenons.

25 And for the other side of the Tabernacle *which is* toward the North corner, he made twentie boards.

26 And their fourtie sockets of siluer : two sockets vnder one board, and two sockets vnder another board.

27 And for the sides of the Tabernacle Westward, he made sixe boards.

28 And two boards made he for the corners of the Tabernacle , in the two sides.

29 And they were †coupled beneath and coupled together at the head thereof, to one ring: thus hee did to both of them in both the corners.

30 And there were eight boards, and their sockets were sixteene sockets of siluer : vnder †euery board two sockets.

31 ¶ And he made *barres of Shittim wood : fiue for the boards of the one side of the Tabernacle,

32 And fiue barres for the boards of the other side of the Tabernacle, and fiue barres for the boards of the Tabernacle for the sides Westward.

33 And he made the middle barre to shoot thorow the boards from the one end to the other.

34 And he ouerlaid the boards with gold, and made their rings of golde to be places for the barres, and ouerlaide the barres with gold.

35 ¶ And he made a Vaile of blew, and purple, and scarlet, and fine twined linnen : with Cherubims made he it of cunning worke.

36 And he made thereunto foure pillars of Shittim *wood*, and ouerlaide them with golde: their hookes *were* of gold : and he cast for them foure sockets of siluer.

37 ¶ And hee made an hanging for the Tabernacle doore of blew and purple, and scarlet, and fine twined linnen, †of needle worke,

38 And the fiue pillars of it with their hooks : and he ouerlaid their chapiters and their fillets with gold : but their fiue sockets were of brasse.

CHAP. XXXVII.

1 The Arke. 6 The Mercie seat with Cherubims. 10 The Table with his vessels. 17 The Candlesticke with his lamps and instruments. 25 The Altar of incense. 29 The anointing oyle and sweet incense.

A Nd Bezaleel made * the Arke of Shittim wood : two cubites and a halfe was the length of it, and a cubite and a halfe the breadth of it, and a cubite and a halfe the height of it.

2 And he ouerlaid it with pure gold within & without, and made a crowne of gold to it round about.

3 And hee cast for it foure rings of gold, *to be set* by the foure corners of it: euen two rings vpon the one side of it. and two rings vpon the other side of it.

4 And he made staues of Shittim wood, and ouerlaid them with gold.

5 And hee put the staues into the rings, by the sides of the Arke, to beare the Arke.

6 ¶ And he made the * Mercie seat of pure gold : two cubites and an halfe *was* the length thereof, and one cubite and an halfe the breadth thereof.

7 And he made two Cherubims of gold, beaten out of one piece made hee them, on the two endes of the Mercie seate :

8 One Cherub ‖on the end on this side, and another Cherub ‖on the *other* end, on that side: out of the Mercie seat made hee the Cherubims on the two ends thereof.

9 And the Cherubims spread out their wings on high, *and* couered with their wings ouer the Mercie seat with their faces one to another : *euen* to the Mercie seat ward were the faces of the Cherubims.

10 ¶ And hee made the Table of Shittim wood : two cubites *was* the length thereof, and a cubite the breadth thereof, and a cubite and a halfe the height thereof.

11 And he ouerlaid it with pure gold, and made thereunto a crowne of gold round about.

12 Also he made thereunto a border of
an

eb. twin-

eb. two kets, two kets vn- one rd. hap. 25. & 30. 5.

Iebr. the rke of a edle wor- , or em- iderer.

* Chap. 25. 10.

* Chap. 25. 17.

‖ Or, out of &c.
‖ Or, out of &c.

an handbreadth, round about: and made a crowne of gold for the border thereof round about.

13 And hee cast for it foure rings of gold, and put the rings vpon the foure corners that *were* in the foure feete thereof.

14 Ouer against the border were the rings, the places for the staues, to beare the Table.

15 And he made the staues of Shittim wood, and ouerlayed them with gold, to beare the Table.

16 And hee made the vessels which *were* vpon the Table, his * dishes, and his spoones, and his bowles, and his couers ||to couer withall, of pure gold.

* Chap. 25. 29.

|| Or, to powre out withall.

* Chap. 25. 31.

17 ¶ And he made the *Candlesticke of pure gold, of beaten worke made he the Candlesticke, his shaft & his branch, his bowles, his knops, and his flowers were of the same.

18 And six branches going out of the sides thereof: three branches of the candlesticke out of the one side thereof, and three branches of the candlesticke out of the other side thereof.

19 Three bowles made he after the fashion of almonds, in one branch, a knop and a flower: and three bowles made like almonds, in another branch, a knop and a flower: so throughout the six branches, going out of the Candlesticke.

20 And in the candlesticke *were* foure bowles made like almonds, his knops, and his flowers:

21 And a knop vnder two branches of the same, & a knop vnder two branches of the same, and a knop vnder two branches of the same, according to the six branches going out of it.

22 Their knops and their branches were of the same: all of it *was* one beaten worke of pure gold.

23 And he made his seuen lampes, and his snuffers, and his snuffe-dishes of pure gold.

24 Of a talent of pure gold made he it, and all the vessels thereof.

* Chap. 30 34.

25 ¶ *And he made the incense Altar of Shittim wood: the length of it *was* a cubit, and the breadth of it a cubit: it *was* foure square, and two cubites *was* the height of it; the hornes thereof were of the same.

26 And he ouerlayed it with pure gold, *both* the top of it and the sides thereof round about, and the hornes of

it: also he made vnto it a crowne of gold round about.

27 And he made two rings of gold for it vnder the crowne thereof, by the two corners of it, vpon the two sides thereof, to bee places for the staues to beare it withall.

28 And he made the staues of Shittim wood, and ouerlayed them with gold.

29 ¶ And he made *the holy anoynting oyle, and the pure incense of sweet spices, according to the worke of the Apothecary.

* Chap. 3 35.

CHAP. XXXVIII.

1 The Altar of burnt offerings. 8 The Lauer of brasse. 9 The Court. 21 The summe of that the people offered.

 Nd *he made the Altar of burnt offring of Shittim wood: fiue cubits *was* the length thereof, and fiue cubites the breadth thereof: it *was* foure square, and three cubits the height thereof.

* Chap. 2 1.

2 And hee made the hornes thereof on the foure corners of it: the hornes thereof were of the same, and he ouerlayed it with brasse.

3 And he made all the vessels of the Altar, the pots and the shouels, and the basons, *and* the fleshhookes, and the firepannes: all the vessels thereof made he of brasse.

4 And he made for the Altar a brasen grate of networke, vnder the compasse thereof, beneath vnto the midst of it.

5 And hee cast foure rings for the foure ends of the grate of brasse, to bee places for the staues.

6 And he made the staues of Shittim wood, and ouerlayed them with brasse.

7 And hee put the staues into the rings on the sides of the Altar, to beare it withall; hee made the Altar hollow with boards.

8 ¶ And hee made the Lauer of brasse, and the foot of it of brasse, of the ||looking glasses of *the women* †assembling, which assembled at the doore of the Tabernacle of the Congregation.

|| Or, brasse glasses. † Hebr. sembling troupes.

9 ¶ And he made the Court: on the Southside Southward, the hangings of the Court *were* of fine twined linnen, a hundred cubits.

10 Their

10 Their pillars *were* twenty, and their braſen ſockets twentie : the hooks of the pillars, and their fillets *were* of ſiluer.

11 And for the North ſide, *the hangings were* an hundred cubites, their pillars *were* twentie, and their ſockets of braſſe twentie : the hoopes of the pillars, and their fillets of ſiluer.

12 And for the Weſt ſide *were* hangings of fiftie cubites, their pillars ten, and their ſockets ten : the hookes of the pillars, and their fillets of ſiluer.

13 And for the Eaſt ſide Eaſtward fiftie cubites.

14 The hangings of the one ſide *of the gate were* fifteene cubites, their pillars three, and their ſockets three.

15 And for the other ſide of the court gate on this hand and that hand *were* hangings of fifteene cubites, their pillars three, and their ſockets three.

16 All the hangings of the court round about, *were* of fine twined linnen.

17 And the ſockets for the pillars *were* of braſſe, the hookes of the pillars, and their fillets of ſiluer, and the ouerlaying of their chapiters of ſiluer, and all the pillars of the court were filleted with ſiluer.

18 And the hanging for the gate of the Court was needle worke, of blew, and purple, and ſcarlet, and fine twined linnen : and twentie cubites was the length, and the height in the breadth was fiue cubites, anſwerable to the hangings of the Court.

19 And their pillars were foure, and their ſockets of braſſe foure, their hookes of ſiluer, and the ouerlaying of their chapiters, & their fillets of ſiluer.

* Chap. 27.
19. 20 And all the * pinnes of the Tabernacle, and of the court round about, *were* of braſſe.

21 ¶ This is the ſumme of the Tabernacle, *euen* of the Tabernacle of Teſtimonie, as it was counted, according to the commaundement of Moſes, *for* the ſeruice of the Leuites, by the hand of Ithamar, ſon to Aaron the Prieſt.

22 And Bezaleel the ſonne of Vri, the ſonne of Hur, of the tribe of Iudah, made all that the LORD commanded Moſes.

23 And with him *was* Aholiab, ſonne of Ahiſamach, of the tribe of Dan, an engrauer, and a cunning workeman, and an embroiderer in blew, and in purple, and in ſcarlet, and fine linnen.

24 All the gold that was occupied for the worke in all the worke of the holy place, euen the gold of the offring, *was* twentie and nine talents, and ſeuen hundred and thirtie ſhekels, after the ſhekel of the Sanctuary.

25 And the ſiluer of them that were numbred of the Congregation, *was* an hundred talents, and a thouſand, ſeuen hundred and threeſcore and fifteene ſhekels, after the ſhekel of the Sanctuary.

26 A Bekah for †euery man, *that is,* halfe a ſhekel, after the ſhekel of the Sanctuary, for euery one that went to be numbred, from twentie yeeres olde and vpward, for ſixe hundred thouſand, and three thouſand, and fiue hundred, and fiftie *men.*   † *Heb. a poll.*

27 And of the hundred talents of ſiluer, were caſt the ſockets of the Sanctuary, and the ſockets of the vaile: an hundred ſockets of the hundred talents, a talent for a ſocket.

28 And of the thouſand, ſeuen hundred, ſeuentie and fiue ſhekels, he made hookes for the pillars, and ouerlaide their chapiters, and filleted them.

29 And the braſſe of the offring was ſeuentie talents, and two thouſand and foure hundred ſhekels.

30 And therewith he made the ſockets to the doore of the Tabernacle of the Congregation, and the braſen Altar, and the braſen grate for it, and all the veſſels of the Altar,

31 And the ſockets of the court round about, and the ſockets of the court gate, and all the pinnes of the Tabernacle, and all the pinnes of the court round about.

CHAP. XXXIX.

1 The clothes of ſeruice and holy garments. 2 The Ephod. 8 The Breſtplate. 22 The robe of the Ephod. 27 The Coates, Miter and girdle of fine linnen. 30 The plate of the holy Crowne. 32 All is viewed and approued by Moſes.

And of the blew, and purple, and ſcarlet, they made clothes of ſeruice, to doe ſeruice in the holy place, and * made the holy garments for Aaron, as the LORD commanded Moſes.   * Chap. 31. 10. and 35. 19.

2 And he made the Ephod of gold, blew, and purple, and ſcarlet, and fine twined linnen.

3 And they did beate the golde into thinne

thinne plates, and cut it into wiers, to worke it in the blew, and in the purple, and in the scarlet, and in the fine linnen, with cunning worke.

4 They made shoulder pieces for it, to couple *it* together: by the two edges was it coupled together.

5 And the curious girdle of his Ephod that *was* vpon it, was of the same, according to the worke thereof: of gold, blew, and purple, and scarlet, and fine twined linnen, as the Lord commanded Moses.

* Chap. 28. 9.

6 ¶ * And they wrought Onix stones enclosed in ouches of gold, grauen as signets are grauen, with the names of the children of Israel.

* Chap. 28. 12.

7 And hee put them on the shoulders of the Ephod, that they should be stones for a * memoriall to the children of Israel, as the Lord commanded Moses.

8 ¶ And he made the brestplate of cunning worke, like the worke of the Ephod, of gold, blew, and purple, and scarlet, and fine twined linnen.

9 It was foure square, they made the brestplate double : a spanne was the length therof, and a spanne the breadth thereof *being* doubled.

|| Or, Ruby.

10 And they set in it foure rowes of stones. the *first* row *was* a ||Sardius, a Topaz, and a Carbuncle: this *was* the first row.

11 And the second row an Emeraude, a Saphire and a Diamond.

12 And the third row a Lygure, an Agate, and an Amethist.

13 And the fourth row, a Berill, an Onix and a Iasper : they were enclosed in ouches of gold in their inclosings.

14 And the stones *were* according to the names of the children of Israel, twelue according to their names, like the ingrauings of a signet, euery one with his name, according to the twelue tribes.

15 And they made vpon the brestplate chaines, at the ends, of wrethen worke of pure gold.

16 And they made two ouches of gold, and two gold rings : and put the two rings in the two ends of the brestplate.

17 And they put the two wreathen chaines of golde in the two rings on the ends of the brestplate.

18 And the two endes of the two wreathen chaines they fastened in the two ouches, and put them on the shoulder pieces of the Ephod, before it.

19 And they made two rings of gold, and put *them* on the two endes of the brest plate vpon the border of it, which *was* on the side of the Ephod inward.

20 And they made two *other* golden rings, and put them on the two sides of the Ephod vnderneath, toward the forepart of it, ouer against the *other* coupling thereof, aboue the curious girdle of the Ephod.

21 And they did bind the brest plate by his rings vnto the rings of the Ephod, with a lace of blew, that it might be aboue the curious girdle of the Ephod, and that the brest plate might not bee loosed from the Ephod, as the Lord commanded Moses.

22 ¶ And he made the robe of the Ephod of wouen worke, all of blew.

23 And there was a hole in the midst of the robe as the hole of an habergeon, with a band round about the hole, that it should not rent.

24 And they made vpon the hemmes of the robe pomegranates, of blew, and purple, and scarlet, *and* twined linnen.

* Chap. 28. 33.

25 And they made * belles of pure gold, and put the belles betweene the pomegranates, vpon the hemme of the robe, round about betweene the pomegranates.

26 A bell and a pomegranate, a bell and a pomegranate round about the hemme of the robe to minister *in*, as the Lord commanded Moses.

27 ¶ And they made coats of fine linnen, of wouen worke, for Aaron and for his sonnes.

* Chap.. 28. 42.

28 And a miter of fine linnen, and goodly bonnets of fine linnen, and *linnen breeches of fine twined linnen,

29 And a girdle of fine twined linnen and blew, and purple, and scarlet of needle worke, as the Lord commanded Moses.

30 ¶ And they made the plate of the holy Crowne of pure gold, and wrote vpon it a writing, *like to* the engrauings of a signet, * HOLINES TO THE LORD.

* Chap. 28. 36.

31 And they tied vnto it a lace of blew to fasten it on high vpon the mitre, as the Lord commanded Moses.

32 ¶ Thus was all the worke of the Tabernacle of the tent of the Congregation finished : and the children of Israel did according to al that the Lord commanded Moses, so did they.

33 ¶ And

33 ¶ And they brought the Tabernacle vnto Moses, the tent, and all his furniture, his taches, his boards, his barres, and his pillars, and his sockets,

34 And the couering of rammes skinnes died red, and the couering of badgers skinnes, and the vaile of the couering:

35 The Arke of the Testimony, and the staues thereof, and the Mercie seat,

36 The Table, *and* all the vessels thereof, and the Shew bread:

37 The pure Candlesticke, with the lampes thereof, euen with the lampes to be set in order, and all the vessels thereof, and the oyle for light:

38 And the golden altar, and the anointing oyle, and the †sweet incense, and the hanging for the Tabernacle doore:

† Heb. the incense of sweet spices.

39 The brasen altar, and his grate of brasse, his staues, and all his vessels, the lauer and his foote:

40 The hangings of the Court, his pillars, and his sockets, and the hanging for the court gate, his coards, and his pinnes, and all the vessels of the seruice of the Tabernacle, for the tent of the Congregation:

41 The clothes of seruice to doe seruice in the holy place, and the holy garments for Aaron the Priest, and his sonnes garments to minister in the Priests office.

42 According to all that the LORD commanded Moses, so the children of Israel made all the worke.

43 And Moses did looke vpon all the worke, and behold, they had done it as the LORD had commanded, euen so had they done it: and Moses blessed them.

CHAP. XL.

1 The Tabernacle is commanded to be reared, 9 and anointed. 13 Aaron and his sonnes to be sanctified. 16 Moses performeth all things accordingly. 34 A cloude couereth the Tabernacle.

Nd the LORD spake vnto Moses, saying,

2 On the first day of the first moneth shalt thou set vp the Tabernacle of the Tent of the Congregation.

3 And thou shalt put therein the Arke of the Testimonie, and couer the Arke with the Vaile:

* Chap. 26. 35.
† Heb. the order thereof.

4 And *thou shalt bring in the Table, and set in order † the things that are

to be set in order vpon it, and thou shalt bring in the Candlesticke, and light the lampes thereof.

5 And thou shalt set the Altar of gold for the incense before the Arke of the Testimonie, and put the hanging of the doore to the Tabernacle.

6 And thou shalt set the Altar of the burnt offering, before the doore of the Tabernacle of the Tent of the Congregation.

7 And thou shalt set the Lauer betweene the Tent of the Congregation and the Altar, and shalt put water therein.

8 And thou shalt set vp the Court round about, and hang vp the hanging at the Court gate.

9 And thou shalt take the annoynting oyle, and annoynt the Tabernacle and all that *is* therein, and shalt hallow it, and all the vessels thereof: and it shalbe holy.

10 Aud thou shalt annoynt the Altar of the burnt offering, and all his vessels, and sanctifie the Altar: and it shalbe an Altar †most Holy.

† Heb. Holines of Holinesses.

11 And thou shalt annoynt the Lauer and his foot, and sanctifie it.

12 And thou shalt bring Aaron and his sonnes vnto the doore of the Tabernacle of the Congregation, and wash them with water.

13 And thou shalt put vpon Aaron the holy garments, and anoynt him, and sanctifie him, that he may minister vnto me in the Priests office.

14 And thou shalt bring his sonnes, and clothe them with coats.

15 And thou shalt anoynt them, as thou didst anoynt their father, that they may minister vnto mee in the Priests office: For their anoynting shall surely be an euerlasting Priesthood, throughout their generations.

16 Thus did Moses: according to all that the LORD commanded him, so did he.

17 ¶ And it came to passe in the first moneth, in the second yeere, on the first *day* of the moneth, that the * Tabernacle was reared vp.

* Num. 7. 1.

18 And Moses reared vp the Tabernacle, and fastened his sockets, and set vp the boards thereof, and put in the barres thereof, and reared vp his pillars.

19 And he spread abroad the tent ouer the Tabernacle, and put the couering

ring of the Tent aboue vpon it, as the LORD commanded Moses.

20 ¶ And he tooke and put the testimony into the Arke, and set the staues on the Arke, and put the Mercie-seat aboue vpon the Arke.

21 And he brought the Arke into the Tabernacle, and * set vp the Vaile of the couering, and couered the Arke of the Testimony, as the LORD commanded Moses.

*Chap. 35. 12.

22 ¶ And hee put the Table in the Tent of the Congregation, vpon the side of the Tabernacle Northwaed, without the Vaile.

23 And he set the bread in order vpon it, before the LORD, as the LORD had commanded Moses.

24 ¶ And he put the candlesticke in the Tent of the Congregation, ouer against the Table, on the side of the Tabernacle Southward.

25 And he lighted the lampes before the LORD, as the LORD commanded Moses.

26 ¶ And he put the golden Altar in the Tent of the Congregation, before the Vaile.

27 And he burnt sweet incense thereon, as the LORD commanded Moses.

28 ¶ And hee set vp the hanging, at the doore of the Tabernacle.

29 And he put the Altar of burnt offering by the doore of the Tabernacle of the Tent of the Congregation, and offered vpon it the burnt offering, and

the meat offring, as * the LORD commanded Moses.

* Exod. 30. 9.

30 ¶ Antl he set the Lauer betweene the Tent of the Congregation and the Altar, & put water there, to wash *withall.*

31 And Moses, and Aaron and his sonnes, washed their hands, and their feet thereat.

32 When they went into the Tent of the Congregation, and when they came neere vnto the Altar, they washed, as the LORD commanded Moses.

33 And hee reared vp the Court round about the Tabernacle, and the Altar, & set vp the hanging of the Court gate : so Moses finished the worke.

34 ¶ * Then a cloud couered the Tent of the Congregation, and the glory of the LORD filled the Tabernacle.

* Numb. 9. 15. 1. king. 8. 10.

35 And Moses was not able to enter into the Tent of the Congregation, because the cloud abode thereon, and the glory of the LORD filled the Tabernacle.

36 And when the cloud was taken vp from ouer the Tabernacle, the children of Israel †went onward in all their iourneys :

† Hebr. iourneyed.

37 But if the cloud were not taken vp, then they iourneyed not, till the day that it was taken vp.

38 For the cloud of the LORD *was* vpon the Tabernacle by day, and fire was on it by night, in the sight of all the house of Israel, throughout all their iourneys.

¶ THE THIRD BOOKE

of Moses, called Leuiticus.

CHAP. I.

1 The burnt offerings 3 Of the herd, 10 Of the flockes, 13 Of the foules.

Nd the LORD called vnto Moses, and spake vnto him out of the Tabernacle of the Congregation, saying,

2 Speake vnto the children of Israel, and say vnto them, If any man of you bring an offering vnto the LORD, ye shall bring your offering of the cattell, euen of the herd, and of the flocke.

3 * If his offering be a burnt sacrifice of the herd, let him offer a male without blemish : he shall offer it of his owne voluntary will, at the doore of the Tabernacle of the Congregation before the LORD.

* Exod. 29 10.

4 And he shall put his hand vpon the

the head of the burnt offering: and it shall be accepted for him to make atonement for him.

5 And he shall kill the bullocke before the LORD: and the Priests Aarons sonnes shall bring the blood, and sprinkle the blood round about vpon the altar, that *is* by the doore of the Tabernacle of the Congregation.

6 And hee shall flay the burnt offering, and cut it into his pieces.

7 And the sonnes of Aaron the Priest shall put fire vpon the Altar, and lay the wood in order vpon the fire.

8 And the Priests Aarons sonnes shall lay the parts, the head and the fat in order vpon the wood that *is* in the fire which *is* vpon the altar.

9 But the inwards and his legges shall he wash in water, and the Priest shall burne all on the altar, to *be* a burnt sacrifice, an offering made by fire, of a sweet sauour vnto the LORD.

10 ¶ And if his offring be of the flocks, *namely* of the sheepe, or of the goates for a burnt sacrifice, he shall bring it a male without blemish.

11 And hee shall kill it on the side of the Altar Northward, before the LORD: and the Priestes Aarons sonnes shall sprinkle his blood round about vpon the altar.

12 And he shall cut it into his pieces, with his head and his fat: and the Priest shall lay them in order on the wood that *is* on the fire, which *is* vpon the altar:

13 But hee shall wash the inwards and the legs with water, and the Priest shall bring *it* all, and burne *it* vpon the altar: it *is* a burnt sacrifice, an offering made by fire, of a sweet sauour vnto the LORD.

14 ¶ And if the burnt sacrifice for his offring to the LORD *be* of foules, then he shall bring his offering of turtle doues, or of yong pigeons.

15 And the Priest shall bring it vnto the altar, and ‖wring off his head, and burne it on the altar: and the blood thereof shall be wrung out at the side of the altar.

‖ Or, *pinch off the head with the naile.*

16 And he shall plucke away his crop with ‖his feathers, and cast it beside the altar on the East part, by the place of the ashes.

‖ Or the *filth thereof.*

17 And hee shall cleaue it with the wings thereof, *but* shall not diuide it asunder: And the Priest shall burne it

vpon the altar, vpon the wood that is vpon the fire: it is a burnt sacrifice, an offering made by fire of a sweet sauour vnto the LORD.

CHAP. II.

1 The meate offering of flower with oile and incense, 4 either baken in the ouen, 5 or on a plate, 7 or in a frying pan, 12 Or of the first fruits in the eare. 13 The salt of the meate offering.

Nd when any will offer a meate offering vnto the LORD, his offring shall be of fine flowre: and hee shall powre oyle vpon it, and put frankincense thereon.

2 And he shall bring it to Aarons sonnes the Priests: and hee shall take thereout his handfull of the flowre thereof, and of the oile thereof, with all the frankincense thereof, and the Priest shall burne the memoriall of it vpon the altar, to *be* an offering made by fire *of* a sweet sauour vnto the LORD.

3 And *the remnant of the meat offering *shall be* Aarons and his sonnes: *it is* a thing most holy of the offerings of the LORD made by fire.

* Ecclus. 7. 31.

4 ¶ And if thou bring an oblation of a meate offering baken in the ouen, *it shall bee* an vnleauened cake of fine flowre mingled with oyle, or vnleauened wafers anointed with oyle.

5 ¶ And if thy oblation be a meate offering *baken* ‖in a panne, it shall bee of fine flowre vnleauened, mingled with oyle.

‖ Or, on *a flat plate* or, *slice.*

6 Thou shalt part it in pieces, and powre oyle thereon: it *is* a meate offering.

7 ¶ And if thy oblation be a meate offering *baken* in the frying pan, it shalbe made of fine flowre with oyle.

8 And thou shalt bring the meat offering that is made of these things vnto the LORD, and when it is presented vnto the Priest, he shall bring it vnto the Altar.

9 And the Priest shall take from the meat offering *a memoriall thereof, and shall burne it vpon the Altar, *it is* an *offering made by fire of a sweet sauour vnto the LORD.

* Verse 2.
* Exod. 29. 18.

10 And that which is left of the meat offering, *shalbe* Aarons and his sonnes: *It is* a thing most holy, of the offerings of the LORD made by fire.

11 No

11 No meat offering, which ye shall bring vnto the LORD, shall be made with leauen: For ye shall burne no leauen, nor any hony, in any offering of the LORD made by fire.

12 ¶ As for the oblation of the first fruits, yee shall offer them vnto the LORD, but they shall not † be burnt on the Altar for a sweet sauour.

13 And euery oblation of thy meat offering * shalt thou season with salt; neither shalt thou suffer the salt of the Couenant of thy God to bee lacking from thy meat offering: with all thine offerings thou shalt offer salt.

14 And if thou offer a meat offering of thy first fruits vnto the LORD, thou shalt offer for the meat offering of thy first fruits, greene eares of corne dried by the fire, *euen* corne beaten out of full eares.

15 And thou shalt put oyle vpon it, and lay frankincense theron; it *is* a meat offering.

16 And the Priest shall burne the memoriall of it, part of the beaten corne thereof, and part of the oyle thereof, with all the frankincense thereof : *it is* an offering made by fire vnto the LORD.

CHAP. III.

1 The meat offering of the herde, 6 of the flocke, 7 either a lambe, 12 or a goat.

Nd if his oblation *be* a sacrifice of peace offering, if hee offer *it* of the herd, whether it be a male or female, he shal offer it without blemish before the LORD.

2 And he shall lay his hand vpon the head of his offering, and kil it at the doore of the Tabernacle of the Congregation : and Aarons sonnes the Priests shall sprinckle the blood vpon the Altar round about.

3 And he shall offer of the sacrifice of the peace offering, an offering made by fire vnto the LORD ; *the ‖fat that coucreth the inwards, and all the fat that *is* vpon the inwards.

4 And the two kidneys, and the fat that *is* on them, which *is* by the flanks: and the ‖caule aboue the liuer with the kidneys, it shall he take away.

5 And Aarons sonnes shall burne it on the Altar vpon the burnt sacrifice, which *is* vpon the wood that *is* on the fire : *it is* an offering made by fire of a sweet sauour vnto the LORD.

6 ¶ And if his offering for a sacrifice of peace offering vnto the LORD, be of the flocke, male or female, he shall offer it without blemish.

7 If hee offer a lambe for his offering, then shall he offer it before the LORD.

8 And he shall lay his hand vpon the head of his offering, and kill it before the Tabernacle of the Congregation: Aud Aarons sonnes shall sprinkle the blood thereof, round about vpon the Altar.

9 And he shall offer of the sacrifice of the peace offering, an offering made by fire vnto the LORD : the fat thereof *and* the whole rumpe, it shall he take off hard by the backe bone : and the fat that coucreth the inwards, and all the fat that *is* vpon the inwards.

10 And the two kidneys, and the fat that is vpon them, which *is* by the flankes, and the caule aboue the liuer, with the kidneys, it shall he take away.

11 And the Priest shall burne it vpon the Altar : *it is* the food of the offering made by fire vnto the LORD.

12 ¶ And if his offering be a goat, then he shall offer it before the LORD.

13 And he shall lay his hand vpon the head of it, and kill it before the Tabernacle of the Congregation : and the sonnes of Aaron shall sprinckle the blood thereof vpon the Altar, round about.

14 And he shall offer thereof his offering, *euen* an offering made by fire vnto the LORD ; the fat that coucreth the inwards, and al the fat that is vpon the inwards.

15 And the two kidneys, and the fat that is vpon them, which *is* by the flancks, and the caule aboue the liuer with the kidneys, it shall he take away.

16 And the Priest shall burne them vpon the Altar : *it is* the food of the offering made by fire, for a sweet sauour : * All the fat *is* the LORDS.

17 *It shall be* a perpetuall statute for your generations, throughout all your dwellings, that ye eat neither fat, nor *blood.

CHAP. IIII.

1 The sinne offering of ignorance, 3 for the Priest, 13 for the Congregation, 22 for the Ruler, 27 for any of the people.

And

---

† *Hebr. ascend.*

* Marke 9. 49.

* Exod. 29. 22.
‖ *Or, suet.*

‖ *Or, Midriffe ouer the liuer, and ouer the kidneys.*

* Chap. 7. 25.

* Gene. 9. 4. chap. 7 26. and 17 14.

And the Lord spake vnto Moses, saying,

2 Speake vnto the children of Israel, saying, If a soule shall sinne through ignorance against any of the commandements of the Lord (concerning things which ought not to bee done) and shall do against any of them:

3 If the Priest that is anointed, doe sinne according to the sinne of the people, then let him bring for his sinne which he hath sinned, a yong bullock without blemish, vnto the Lord for a sinne offering.

4 And hee shall bring the bullocke vnto the doore of the Tabernacle of the Congregation before the Lord, and shall lay his hand vpon the bullockes head, and kill the bullocke before the Lord.

5 And the Priest that is anointed, shall take of the bullocks blood, and bring it to the Tabernacle of the Congregation.

6 And the Priest shall dip his finger in the blood, and sprinkle of the blood seuen times before the Lord, before the Vaile of the Sanctuary.

7 And the Priest shall put some of the blood vpon the hornes of the Altar of sweet incense before the Lord, which *is* in the Tabernacle of the Congregation, and shal powre *all the blood of the bullocke at the bottome of the altar of the burnt offering, which *is* at the doore of the Tabernacle of the Congregation.

* Chap. 5. 9.

8 And he shall take off from it all the fat of the bullocke for the sinne offering: the fat that couereth the inwards, and all the fat that is vpon the inwards,

9 And the two kidneis, and the fat that *is* vpon them, which *is* by the flankes, and the caule aboue the liuer with the kidneis, it shall he take away,

10 As it was taken off from the bullocke of the sacrifice of peace offerings: and the Priest shall burne them vpon the altar of the burnt offering.

* Exod. 29.
4. numb.
9. 5.

11 * And the skinne of the bullocke, and all his flesh, with his head, and with his legs, and his inwards, and his doung,

Hebr. To without the campe.
Heb. 13.
1.

12 Euen the whole bullocke shall he carie foorth †without the campe, vnto a cleane place, where the ashes are powred out, and * burne him on the wood with fire: †where the ashes are powred out, shall he be burnt.

† *Heb. at the powring out of the ashes.*

13 ¶ And if the whole Congregation of Israel sinne through ignorance, *and the thing be hid from the eyes of the assembly, and they haue done somewhat against any of the Commandements of the Lord, concerning things which should not be done, and are guiltie:

* Chap :.5.
2, 3, 4.

14 When the sinne which they haue sinned against it, is knowen, then the Congregation shall offer a yong bullocke for the sinne, and bring him before the Tabernacle of the Congregation.

15 And the Elders of the Congregation shall lay their hands vpon the head of the bullocke, before the Lord: and the bullocke shall be killed before the Lord.

16 And the Priest that is anointed, shall bring of the bullockes blood to the Tabernacle of the Congregation.

17 And the Priest shall dip his finger in some of the blood, and sprinkle *it* seuen times before the Lord, *euen* before the vaile.

18 And he shal put some of the blood vpon the hornes of the altar, which *is* before the Lord, that *is* in the Tabernacle of the Congregation, and shall powre out all the blood at the bottome of the altar of the burnt offring, which *is at* the doore of the Tabernacle of the Congregation.

19 And he shall take all his fat from him, and burne it vpon the altar.

20 And he shall do with the bullocke as he did with the bullocke for a sinne offring, so shall he do with this: And the Priest shall make an atonement for them, and it shall be forgiuen them.

21 And he shall carie foorth the bullocke without the campe, and burne him as he burned the first bullocke: it *is* a sinne offering for the Congregation.

22 ¶ When a ruler hath sinned and done somewhat through ignorance against any of the Commandements of the Lord his God, concerning things which should not be done, and is guilty:

23 Or if his sinne wherein hee hath sinned, come to his knowledge: he shall bring his offering, a kid of the goates, a male without blemish.

24 And hee shall lay his hand vpon the head of the goate, and kill it in the place where they kill the burnt offering before the Lord: it *is* a sinne offring.

25 And

25 And the Priest shall take of the blood of the sinne offering with his finger, and put *it* vpon the hornes of the Altar of burnt offring, and shall powre out his blood at the bottome of the Altar of burnt offering

26 And he shall burne all his fat vpon the Altar, as the fat of the sacrifice of peace offerings : and the Priest shall make an atonement for him, as concerning his sinne, and it shall be forgiuen him.

† *Hebr. any soule.*
† *Hebr. people of the land.*

27 ¶ And if †any one of the †common people sinne through ignorance, while he doeth somewhat against any of the commandements of the LORD, concerning things which ought not to be done, and be guiltie :

28 Or if his sinne which he hath sinned come to his knowledge, then hee shall bring his offering, a kidde of the goats, a female without blemish, for his sinne which he hath sinned.

29 And he shall lay his hand vpon the head of the sinne offering, and slay the sin offering in the place of the burnt offering.

30 And the Priest shall take of the blood thereof with his finger, and put it vpon the hornes of the Altar of burnt offering, and shall powre out all the blood thereof at the bottome of the Altar.

* *Leuit. 3, 14.*

31 And *he shall take away all the fat thereof, as the fat is taken away from off the sacrifice of peace offerings: and the Priest shall burne *it* vpon the

* *Exod. 29. 18.*

Altar, for a * sweet sauour vnto the LORD, and the Priest shall make an atonement for him, and it shall be forgiuen him.

32 And if he bring a lambe for a sinne offering, he shall bring it a female without blemish.

33 And he shall lay his hand vpon the head of the sinne offering, and slay it for a sinne offering, in the place where they kill the burnt offering.

34 And the Priest shall take of the blood of the sinne offering with his finger, and put *it* vpon the hornes of the Altar of burnt offring, and shall powre out all the blood thereof at the bottome of the Altar.

35 And he shall take away all the fat thereof, as the fat of the lambe is taken away from the sacrifice of the peace offerings: and the Priest shall burnt them vpon the Altar, according to the offerings made by fire vnto the LORD, and the Priest shall make an atonement for his sinne that he hath committed, and it shalbe forgiuen him.

CHAP. V

1 He that sinneth in concealing his knowledge, 2 in touching an vncleane thing, 4 or in making an oath. 6 His trespasse offering, of the flocke, 7 of foules, 11 or of flowre. 14 The trespasse offering in sacriledge, 17 and in sinnes of ignorance.

ANd if a soule sinne, and heare the voyce of swearing, and is a witnesse, whether he hath seene or knowen *of it*, if he doe not vtter it, then he shall beare his iniquity.

2 Or if a soule touch any vncleane thing, whether it be a carcase of an vncleane beast, or a carcase of vncleane cattell, or the carcase of vncleane creeping things, and if it be hidden from him, he also shall be vncleane, and guilty:

3 Or if he touch the vncleannesse of man, whatsoeuer vncleannesse it be that a man shalbe defiled withall, and *it* be hid from him, when he knoweth *of it*, then he shalbe guilty.

4 Or if a soule sweare, pronouncing with his lips to do euill, or to do good, whatsoeuer it be that a man shall pronounce with an oath, and *it* be hid from him, when he knoweth *of it*, then he shalbe guilty in one of these.

5 And it shalbe when he shalbe guiltie in one of these things, that he shall confesse that hee hath sinned in that thing.

6 And he shall bring his trespasse offering vnto the LORD for his sinne which he hath sinned, a female from the flocke, a lambe, or a kidde of the goates, for a sinne offering : And the Priest shal make an atonement for him concerning his sinne.

† *Hebr. his hand cannot reach to the sufficiencie of a lambe.*

7 And if †hee be not able to bring a lambe, then he shall bring for his trespasse which hee hath committed, two turtle doues, or two yong pigeons vnto the LORD: one for a sinne offring, and the other for a burnt offering.

8 And he shall bring them vnto the Priest, who shall offer that which is for the sinne offering first, and *wring off his head from his necke, but shall not diuide *it* asunder.

* *Chap. 1. 15.*

9 And he shall sprinckle of the blood of the sinne offering vpon the side of the Altar,

Altar, and the rest of the blood shall be wrung out at the bottome of the altar: it *is* a sinne offering.

10 And hee shall offer the second for a burnt offering, according to the ‖manner: and the Priest shal make an atonement for him for his sinne, which he had sinned, and it shall be forgiuen him.

11 ¶ But if hee be not able to bring two turtle doues, or two yong pigeons; then he that sinned, shall bring for his offring the tenth part of an Ephah of fine flowre for a sinne offering: hee shall put no oyle vpon it, neither shall he put any frankincense thereon: for it is a sinne offering.

12 Then shall hee bring it to the Priest, and the Priest shall take his handfull of it, * *euen* a memoriall thereof, and burne *it* on the altar, *according to the offerings made by fire vnto the LORD: it is a sinne offering.

13 And the Priest shall make an atonement for him as touching his sinne that he hath sinned in one of these, and it shall be forgiuen him: and *the remnant* shall be the Priests, as a meat offering.

14 ¶ And the LORD spake vnto Moses, saying,

15 If a soule commit a trespasse, and sinne through ignorance, in the holy things of the LORD; then hee shall bring for his trespasse vnto the LORD, a ramme without blemish, out of the flockes, with thy estimation by shekels of siluer, after the shekel of the Sanctuarie, for a trespasse offering.

16 And hee shall make amends for the harme that he hath done in the holy thing, and shall adde the fift part thereto, and giue it vnto the Priest: and the Priest shall make an atonement for him with the ramme of the trespasse offering, and it shall be forgiuen him.

17 ¶ And if a *soule sinne, and commit any of these things which are forbidden to be done by the commaundements of the LORD, though he wist it not, yet is hee guiltie, and shall beare his iniquitie.

18 And he shall bring a ramme without blemish out of the flocke, with thy estimation, for a trespasse offering vnto the Priest: and the Priest shall make an atonement for him concerning his ignorance wherein he erred, and wist it not: and it shall be forgiuen him.

19 It is a trespasse offring: he hath certainly trespassed against the LORD.

CHAP. VI.

1 The trespasse offering for sinnes done wittingly. 8 The Law of the burnt offering, 14 and of the meate offering. 19 The offering at the consecration of a Priest. 24 The Law of the sinne offering.

And the LORD spake vnto Moses, saying,

2 If a soule sinne, and commit a trespasse against the LORD, and lie vnto his neighbour in that which was deliuered him to keepe, or in ‖fellowship, or in a thing taken away by †violence, or hath deceiued his neighbour:

3 Or haue found that which was lost, and lieth concerning it, and *sweareth falsly: in any of all these that a man doth, sinning therein:

4 Then it shall be, because he hath sinned, and is guiltie, that hee shall restore that which he tooke violently away, or the thing which he hath deceitfully gotten, or that which was deliuered him to keepe, or the lost thing which he found:

5 Or all that about which hee hath sworne falsly: hee shall euen * restore it in the principall, and shall adde the fift part more thereto, and giue it vnto him to whom it apperteineth, ‖in the day of his trespasse offering.

6 And hee shall bring his trespasse offering vnto the LORD, a ramme without blemish out of the *flocke, with thy estimation, for a trespasse offering vnto the Priest.

7 And the Priest shall make an atonement for him, before the LORD: and it shall bee forgiuen him, for any thing of all that he hath done, in trespassing therein.

8 ¶ And the LORD spake vnto Moses, saying,

9 Command Aaron and his sonnes, saying, This *is* the law of the burnt offring: (It is the burnt offring, ‖because of the burning vpon the Altar all night vnto the morning, and the fire of the altar shall be burning in it.)

10 And the Priest shal put on his linnen garment, & his linnen breeches shal he put vpon his flesh, and take vp the ashes which the fire hath consumed with the burnt offering on the Altar, and he shall put them besides the Altar.

11 And he shal put off his garments, and put on other garments, and carry forth

Margin notes

Or, ordinance.

* Chap. 2. 2.

Chap. 4. 5.

* Chap. 4. 2.

‖ Or, in dealing.

† Heb. putting of the hand.

* Num. 5. 6.

* Chap. 5. 15.

‖ Or, in the day of his being found guilty. Heb. the day of his trespasse.

* Chap. 5. 15.

‖ Or, for the burning.

foorth the ashes without the Campe, vnto a cleane place.

12 And the fire vpon the Altar shall be burning in it : it shall not be put out; And the Priest shall burne wood on it euery morning, and lay the burnt offering in order vpon it, and he shall burne thereon the fatte of the peace offerings.

13 The fire shall euer be burning vpon the Altar : it shall neuer goe out.

^{* Chap. 21. 1. num. 15, 4.} 14 ¶ *And this is the law of the meat offering : the sonnes of Aaron shall offer it before the LORD, before the Altar.

15 And he shall take of it his handfull, of the flowre of the meat offering, and of the oyle therof, and all the frankincense which *is* vpon the meat offring, and shall burne *it* vpon the Altar, for a ^{* Chap. 2. 9.} sweet sauour, *euen* the *memoriall of it vnto the LORD.

16 And the remainder thereof shall Aaron and his sonnes eat : with vnleauened bread shall it be eaten in the holy place : in the court of the Tabernacle of the Congregation they shall eat it.

17 It shall not be baken with leauen : I haue giuen it vnto them for their portion of my offerings made by fire : it *is* most holy, as *is* the sin offering, and as the trespasse offering.

18 All the males among the children of Aaron shall eat of it : It shalbe a statute for euer in your generations concerning the offerings of the LORD ^{* Exod. 29. 37.} made by fire : *euery one that toucheth them shalbe holy.

19 ¶ And the LORD spake vnto Moses, saying,

20 This *is* the offering of Aaron, and of his sonnes which they shall offer vnto the LORD, in the day when he ^{* Exod. 16. 36.} is anoynted : The tenth part of an *Ephah of fine flowre for a meat offering perpetuall, halfe of it in the morning, and halfe thereof at night.

21 In a panne it shalbe made with oyle, and when it is baken, thou shalt bring it in : and the baken pieces of the meat offering shalt thou offer for a sweet sauour vnto the LORD.

22 And the Priest of his sonnes that is anoynted in his stead, shal offer it : It is a statute for euer vnto the LORD, it shalbe wholly burnt.

23 For euery meat offering for the Priest shal be wholly burnt : it shall not be eaten.

24 ¶ And the LORD spake vnto Moses, saying,

25 Speake vnto Aaron and to his sonnes, saying, This *is* the law of the sinne offering : In the place where the burnt offering is killed, shall the sinne offering be killed before the LORD : it *is* most holy.

26 The Priest that offereth it for sinne, shall eat it : In the holy place shal it be eaten, in the court of the Tabernacle of the Congregation.

27 Whatsoeuer shall touch the flesh thereof, shalbe holy : and when there is sprinckled of the blood thereof vpon any garment, thou shalt wash that whereon it was sprinckled, in the holy place.

28 But the earthen vessell wherein it is sodden, *shall be broken : And if it ^{* Chap. 11. 33.} be sodden in a brasen pot, it shall be both scowred, and rinsed in water.

29 All the males among the Priests shall eate thereof : it *is* most holy.

30 *And no sinne offering whereof ^{* Hebr. 13. 11.} any of the blood is brought into the Tabernacle of the Congregation to reconcile *withall* in the holy place, shall be eaten : it shall be burnt in the fire.

CHAP. VII.

1 The law of the trespasse offering, 11 and of the Peace offerings, 12 whether it be for a Thankesgiuing, 16 or a Vow, or a Freewill-offering. 22 The fat, 26 and the blood are forbidden. 28 The Priests portion in the Peace offerings.

Ikewise this *is* the lawe of the trespasse offering : it is most Holy.

2 In the place where they kil the burnt offring, shall they kil the trespasse offering; and the blood thereof shall hee sprinckle round about vpon the Altar.

3 And he shall offer of it, all the fat thereof; the rumpe, and the fat that couereth the inwards,

4 And the two kidneys, and the fat that *is* on them, which *is* by the flankes, and the caule *that is* aboue the liuer, with the kidneys, it shall he take away.

5 And the Priest shall burne them vpon the Altar, for an offering made by fire vnto the LORD : it *is* a trespasse offering.

6 Euery male among the Priestes shall eate thereof : it shall be eaten in the holy place : it *is* most holy.

7 As

7 As the sinne offering *is*, so *is* the trespasse offering: there is one law for them: the Priest that maketh atonement therewith, shall haue *it*.

8 And the Priest that offereth any mans burnt offering, euen the Priest shall haue to himselfe the skinne of the burnt offering which he hath offered.

9 And all the meate offering that is baken in the ouen, and all that is dressed in the frying panne, and ||in the panne, shall be the Priests that offereth it.

Or, on the flat plate, or, slice.

10 And euery meate offering mingled with oyle, and drie, shall all the sonnes of Aaron haue, one as much as another.

11 And this *is* the law of the sacrifice of peace offerings, which he shall offer vnto the LORD.

12 If hee offer it for a thankesgiuing, then he shall offer with the sacrifice of thankesgiuing vnleauened cakes mingled with oyle, and vnleauened wafers anointed with oile, and cakes mingled with oyle of fine flowre fried.

13 Besides the cakes, hee shall offer for his offring leauened bread, with the sacrifice of thankesgiuing of his peace offerings.

14 And of it he shall offer one out of the whole oblation, for an heaue offering vnto the LORD, and it shall bee the Priests that sprinkleth the blood of the peace offerings.

15 And the flesh of the sacrifice of his peace offerings for thankesgiuing, shall be eaten the same day that it is offered: he shall not leaue any of it vntill the morning.

16 But if the sacrifice of his offering be a vow, or a voluntary offering, it shall be eaten the same day that he offereth his sacrifice: and on the morrowe also the remainder of it shall be eaten.

17 But the remainder of the flesh of the sacrifice on the third day shall bee burnt with fire.

18 And if any of the flesh of the sacrifice of his peace offerings be eaten at all on the third day, it shall not be accepted, neither shal it be imputed vnto him that offereth it: it shall be an abomination, and the soule that eateth of it, shall beare his iniquitie.

19 And the flesh that toucheth any vncleane thing, shal not be eaten: it shall be burnt with fire, and as for the flesh, all that be cleane shall eate thereof.

20 But the soule that eateth of the flesh of the sacrifice of peace offerings, that pertaine vnto the LORD, * hauing his vncleannesse vpon him, euen that soule shall be cut off from his people.

* Chap. 15. 3.

21 Moreouer, the soule that shall touch any vncleane thing, *as* the vncleannesse of man, or *any* vncleane beast, or any abominable vncleane thing, and eate of the flesh of the sacrifice of peace offerings which pertaine vnto the LORD, euen that soule shall be cut off from his people.

22 ¶ And the LORD spake vnto Moses, saying,

23 Speake vnto the children of Israel, saying, * Ye shall eat no maner fat of oxe, or of sheepe, or of goat.

* Chap. 3. 17.

24 And the fat of the † beast that dieth of it selfe, and the fat of that which is torne with beasts, may be vsed in any other vse: but yee shall in no wise eate of it.

† Heb. carcaise.

25 For whosoeuer eateth the fat of the beast, of which men offer an offring made by fire vnto the LORD, euen the soule that eateth *it*, shall be cut off from his people.

26 * Moreouer ye shall eat no maner of blood, whether it bee of foule or of beast in any of your dwellings.

* Gene. 9. 4 chap. 3. 17. and 17. 14.

27 Whatsoeuer soule it be that eateth any maner of blood, euen that soule shalbe cut off from his people.

28 ¶ And the LORD spake vnto Moses, saying,

29 Speake vnto the children of Israel, saying, Hee that offereth the sacrifice of his peace offerings vnto the LORD, shall bring his oblation vnto the LORD, of the sacrifice of his peaceofferings.

30 His owne hands shall bring the offerings of the LORD made by fire, the fat with the brest, it shall hee bring, that *the brest may be waued for a waue offering before the LORD.

* Exod. 29. 24.

31 And the Priest shall burne the fat vpon the Altar: but the brest shalbe Aarons and his sonnes.

32 And the right shoulder shall ye giue vnto the Priest for an heaue offering of the sacrifices of your peace offerings.

33 Hee among the sonnes of Aaron that offereth the blood of the peace offerings, and the fat, shall haue the right shoulder for his part.

34 For

34 For the waue brest and the heaue shoulder haue I taken of the children of Israel, from off the sacrifices of their peace offerings, and haue giuen them vnto Aaron the Priest, and vnto his sonnes, by a statute for euer, from among the children of Israel.

35 ¶ This *is the portion* of the anointing of Aaron, and of the anointing of his sonnes, out of the offerings of the LORD made by fire, in the day when he presented them, to minister vnto the LORD in the Priests office:

36 Which the LORD commanded to be giuen them of the children of Israel, in the day that hee anointed them, *by* a statute for euer, throughout their generations.

37 This *is* the law of the burnt offering, of the meate offering, and of the sinne offering, and of the trespasse offering, and of the consecrations, and of the sacrifice of the peace offerings ·

38 Which the LORD commanded Moses in mount Sinai, in the day that he commanded the children of Israel to offer their oblations vnto the LORD, in the wildernesse of Sinai.

CHAP. VIII.

1 Moses consecrateth Aaron and his sonnes. 14 Their sinne offering. 18 Their burnt offring. 22 The ram of consecrations. 31 The place and time of their consecration.

* Exod. 28. 2, 4.
* Exod. 30. 24.

ANd the LORD spake vnto Moses, saying,

2 * Take Aaron and his sonnes with him, and the garments, and * the anointing oyle, and a bullocke for the sinne offering, and two rammes, and a basket of vnleauened bread.

3 And gather thou all the Congregation together vnto the doore of the Tabernacle of the Congregation.

4 And Moses did as the LORD commanded him, & the assembly was gathered together vnto the doore of the Tabernacle of the Congregation.

* Exod. 29. 4.

5 And Moses saide vnto the Congregation, * This is the thing which the LORD commanded to be done.

6 And Moses brought Aaron and his sonnes, and washed them with water.

7 And he put vpon him the coate, and girded him with the girdle, and clothed him with the robe, and put the E-

phod vpon him, and he girded him with the curious girdle of the Ephod, and bound *it* vnto him therewith.

8 And hee put the brest plate vpon him: also he * put in the brest plate the Vrim and the Thummim.

* Exod. 28. 30.

9 And he put the miter vpon his head; also vpon the miter, euen vpon his forefront did hee put the golden plate, the holy crowne, as the LORD * commanded Moses.

* Exod. 28. 39. &c.

10 And Moses tooke the anointing oile, and anointed the tabernacle and all that was therein, and sanctified them.

11 And he sprinkled thereof vpon the altar seuen times, and anointed the altar and all his vessels, both the lauer and his foot, to sanctifie them.

12 And he * powred of the anointing oile vpon Aarons head, and anointed him, to sanctifie him.

* Ecclus. 45. 15. psal. 133. 2.

13 And Moses brought Aarons sonnes, and put coats vpon them, and girded them with girdles, and † put bonnets vpon them, as the LORD commanded Moses.

† *Heb. bound*

14 * And he brought the bullocke for the sinne offering, and Aaron and his sonnes laid their hands vpon the head of the bullocke for the sinne offering.

* Exod. 29. 1.

15 And he slew it, and Moses tooke the blood, and put it vpon the hornes of the altar round about with his finger, and purified the altar, and powred the blood at the bottome of the altar, and sanctified it, to make reconciliation vpon it.

16 And he tooke all the fat that was vpon the inwards, and the kall *aboue* the liuer, and the two kidneis, and their fat, and Moses burned it vpon the Altar.

17 But the bullocke, and his hide, his flesh and his doung, he burnt with fire without the campe, as the LORD * commanded Moses.

* Exod. 29. 14.

18 ¶ And he brought the ramme for the burnt offring: and Aaron and his sonnes laid their hands vpon the head of the ramme.

19 And he killed it, and Moses sprinkled the blood vpon the Altar round about.

20 And he cut the ramme into pieces, and Moses burnt the head, and the pieces, and the fat.

21 And he washed the inwards and the legges in water, and Moses burnt the

the whole ramme vpon the Altar: It *was* a burnt sacrifice for a sweet sauour, *and* an offering made by fire vnto the Lord, as the Lord commanded Moses.

22 ¶ And * hee brought the other ramme, the ramme of consecration: and Aaron and his sonnes layd their hands vpon the head of the ramme.

23 And he slew it, and Moses tooke of the blood of it, and put it vpon the tip of Aarons right eare, and vpon the thumbe of his right hand, and vpon the great toe of his right foot.

24 And he brought Aarons sonnes, and Moses put of the blood vpon the tippe of their right eare, and vpon the thumbs of their right hands, and vpon the great toes of their right feete: and Moses sprinkled the blood vpon the Altar round about.

25 And hee tooke the fat, and the rumpe, and all the fat that was vpon the inwards, and the caule *aboue* the liuer, and the two kidneys and their fat, and the right shoulder.

26 And out of the basket of vnleauened bread, that *was* before the Lord, he tooke one vnleauened cake, and a cake of oyled bread, and one wafer, and put them on the fat, and vpon the right shoulder.

27 And hee put all * vpon Aarons hands, and vpon his sonnes hands, and waued them for a waue offering before the Lord.

28 And Moses tooke them from off their hands, and burnt *them* on the Altar, vpon the burnt offering: They *were* consecrations for a sweet sauour: It is an offering made by fire vnto the Lord.

29 And Moses tooke the brest, and waued it for a waue offering before the Lord: *For* of the ramme of consecration it was Moses *part, as the Lord commanded Moses.

30 And Moses tooke of the anoynting oyle, and of the blood which was vpon the Altar, and sprinckled it vpon Aaron, *and* vpon his garments, and vpon his sonnes, and vpon his sunnes garments with him: and sanctified Aaron, *and* his garments, and his sonnes, and his sonnes garments with him.

31 ¶ And Moses said vnto Aaron and to his sonnes, Boile the flesh at the doore of the Tabernacle of the Congregation: and there *eat it with the bread

that is in the basket of consecrations, as I commanded, saying, Aaron and his sonnes shall eat it.

32 And that which remaineth of the flesh, and of the bread, shall yee burne with fire.

33 And ye shall not goe out of the doore of the Tabernacle of the Congregation *in* seuen dayes, vntill the dayes of your consecration be at an end: for * seuen dayes shall he consecrate you.

34 As he hath done this day, *so* the Lord hath commanded to doe, to make an atonement for you.

35 Therefore shall ye abide at the doore of the Tabernacle of the Congregation day and night, seuen dayes, and keepe the charge of the Lord, that ye die not: for so I am commanded.

36 So Aaron and his sonnes did all things which the Lord commanded by the hand of Moses.

CHAP IX.

1 The first offerings of Aaron, for himselfe and the people. 8 The sinne-offering, 12 and the burnt offering for himselfe. 15 The offerings for the people. 23 Moses and Aaron blesse the people. 24 Fire commeth from the Lord, vpon the Altar.

And it came to passe on the eight day, that Moses called Aaron and his sonnes, and the elders of Israel.

2 And hee saide vnto Aaron, * Take thee a yong calfe for a sinne offering, and a ramme for a burnt offering, without blemish, and offer *them* before the Lord.

3 And vnto the children of Israel thou shalt speake, saying, Take ye a kid of the goats, for a sinne offering, and a calfe, and a lambe, both of the first yeere without blemish, for a burnt offering.

4 Also a bullocke and a ramme, for peace offerings, to sacrifice before the Lord, and a meat offring mingled with oyle: for to day the Lord will appeare vnto you.

5 ¶ And they brought that which Moses commanded, before the Tabernacle of the Congregation: and all the Congregation drew neere and stood before the Lord.

6 And Moses said, This is the thing which the Lord commanded that ye should doe: and the glory of the Lord shall appeare vnto you.

7 And

*Exod. 29.
1.

*Exod. 29.
34. &c.

*Exod. 29.
26.

*Exod. 29.
32.

*Exod. 29.
35.

*Exod. 29.
1.

7 And Moses said vnto Aaron, Goe vnto the Altar, and offer thy sinne offering, and thy burnt offering, and make an atonement for thy selfe, and for the people : and offer the offering of the people, and make an atonement for them, as the LORD commanded.

8 ¶ Aaron therefore went vnto the Altar, and slew the calfe of the sinne offering, which *was* for himselfe.

9 And the sonnes of Aaron brought the blood vnto him, and he dipt his finger in the blood, and put it vpon the hornes of the Altar, and powred out the blood at the bottome of the Altar.

10 But the fat and the kidneys; and the caule *aboue* the liuer of the sinne offering he burnt vpon the Altar, as the LORD commanded Moses.

11 And the flesh and the hide he burnt with fire, without the campe.

12 And hee slew the burnt offering, and Aarons sonnes presented vnto him the blood, which he sprinckled about vpon the Altar.

13 And they presented the burnt offering vnto him, with the pieces thereof, and the head : and he burnt *them* vpon the Altar.

14 And he did wash the inwards, and the legs, and burnt *them* vpon the burnt offering on the Altar.

15 ¶ And he brought the peoples offering, and tooke the goat, which was the sinne offering for the people, and slew it, and offered it for sinne, as the first.

16 And he brought the burnt offring, and offered it according to the ‖ maner.

17 And he brought the meat offring, and †tooke an handfull thereof, and burnt it vpon the Altar, * beside the burnt sacrifice of the morning.

18 He slew also the bullocke and the ramme, for a sacrifice of peace offerings, which *was* for the people : And Aarons sonnes presented vnto him the blood, (which hee sprinckled vpon the Altar round about)

19 And the fat of the bullocke and of the ramme, the rumpe, and that which couereth *the inwards*, and the kidneys, and the caule *aboue* the liuer.

20 And they put the fat vpon the brests, & he burnt the fat vpon the altar:

21 And the breasts and the right shoulder, Aaron waued for a waue offering before the LORD, as Moses commanded.

margin notes:
‖ *Or, ordinance.*
† *Hebr. filled his hand out of it.*
* *Exod. 29. 38.*

22 And Aaron lift vp his hand towards the people, and blessed them, and came downe from offering of the sinne offering, and the burnt offering, and peace offerings.

23 And Moses and Aaron went into the Tabernacle of the Congregation, and came out, and blessed the people : and the glory of the LORD appeared vnto all the people.

24 And * there came a fire out from before the LORD, and consumed vpon the Altar the burnt offering, and the fat : which when all the people saw, they shouted, and fell on their faces.

*margin: * Gen. 4. 4. 1. king. 18. 38. 2. chro. 7. 1. 2. macc. 10. 11.*

CHAP. X.

1 Nadab and Abihu, for offering of strange fire, are burnt by fire. 6 Aaron and his sonnes are forbidden to mourne for them. 8 The Priests are forbidden wine when they are to goe into the Tabernacle. 12 The law of eating the holy things. 16 Aarons excuse for transgressing thereof.

ANd * Nadab and Abihu, the sonnes of Aaron, tooke either of them his censer, and put fire therein, and put incense thereon, and offered strange fire before the LORD, which hee commaunded them not.

2 And there went out fire from the LORD and deuoured them, and they died before the LORD.

3 Then Moses said vnto Aaron, This *is it* that the LORD spake, saying, I will bee sanctified in them that come nigh me, and before all the people I will be glorified : And Aaron held his peace.

4 And Moses called Mishael and Elzaphan the sonnes of Vzziel, the vncle of Aaron, and said vnto them, Come neere, cary your brethren from before the Sanctuary, out of the campe.

5 So they went neere, and caried them in their coats out of the campe, as Moses had said.

6 And Moses said vnto Aaron, and vnto Eleazar and vnto Ithamar his sonnes, Vncouer not your ·heads, neither rend your clothes, lest you die, and lest wrath come vpon all the people : But let your brethren, the whole house of Israel, bewaile the burning which the LORD hath kindled.

7 And ye shal not goe out from the doore

*margin: * Num. 3. 4. and 26. 61. 1. chron. 24. 2.*

doore of the Tabernacle of the Congregation, lest you die : for the anointing oyle of the Lord is vpon you : and they did according to the word of Moses.

8 ¶ And the Lord spake vnto Aaron, saying,

9 Doe not drinke wine nor strong drinke, thou, nor thy sonnes with thee, when ye goe into the Tabernacle of the Congregation, lest yee die : It shall bee a statute for euer, throughout your generations :

10 And that ye may put difference betweene holy and vnholy, and betweene vncleane and cleane :

11 And that ye may teach the children of Israel all the statutes which the Lord hath spoken vnto them by the hand of Moses.

12 ¶ And Moses spake vnto Aaron, and vnto Eleazar and vnto Ithamar his sonnes that were left, Take the meate offering that remaineth of the offerings of the Lord made by fire, and eate it without leauen, beside the altar : for it is most holy.

13 And ye shal eat it in the holy place, because it is thy due, and thy sonnes due of the sacrifices of the Lord, made by fire : for so I am commanded.

14 And * the waue breast and heaue shoulder shall ye eate in a cleane place, thou, and thy sonnes, and thy daughters with thee : For they be thy due and thy sonnes due, which are giuen out of the sacrifice of peace offerings, of the children of Israel:

15 The heaue shoulder, and the waue breast shal they bring, with the offrings made by fire of the fat, to waue it for a waue offering before the Lord : and it shall bee thine, and thy sonnes with thee, by a statute for euer, as the Lord hath commanded.

16 ¶ And Moses diligently sought the goate of the sinne offering, and behold, it was burnt : and he was angry with Eleazar and Ithamar, the sonnes of Aaron, which were left aliue, saying,

17 Wherefore haue ye not eaten the sinne offering in the holy place, seeing it is most holy, and God hath giuen it you to beare the iniquitie of the Congregation, to make atonement for them, before the Lord ?

18 Behold, the blood of it was not brought in, within the holy place : yee

Exod. 29. 4.

should indeed haue eaten it in the holy place, *as I commanded.

19 And Aaron said vnto Moses, Behold, this day haue they offered their sinne offering, and their burnt offering before the Lord : and such things haue befallen me : and if I had eaten the sinne offering to day, should it haue bin accepted in the sight of the Lord ?

20 And when Moses heard that, he was content.

CHAP. XI.

1 What beasts may, 4 and what may not bee eaten. 9 What fishes. 13 What foules. 29 The creeping things which are vncleane.

And the Lord spake vnto Moses, and to Aaron, saying vnto them,

2 Speake vnto the children of Israel, saying, * These are the beasts which ye shal eat among all the beasts that are on the earth :

3 Whatsoeuer parteth the hoofe, and is clouen footed, & cheweth cud among the beasts, that shall ye eate.

4 Neuerthelesse, these shall ye not eate, of them that chewe the cud, or of them that diuide the hoofe: as the camel, because hee cheweth the cud, but diuideth not the hoofe, he is vncleane vnto you.

5 And the conie, because he cheweth the cud, but diuideth not the hoofe, he is vncleane vnto you.

6 And the hare, because he cheweth the cud, but diuideth not the hoofe, he is vncleane vnto you.

7 And * the swine, though he diuide the hoofe, and be clouen footed, yet hee cheweth not the cud: he is vncleane to you.

8 Of their flesh shall ye not eat, and their carcase shall ye not touch : they are vncleane to you.

9 ¶ These shal ye eat, of all that are in the waters : whatsoeuer hath finnes and scales in the waters, in the seas, and in the riuers, them shall ye eate.

10 And all that haue not finnes nor scales in the seas, and in the riuers, of all that moue in the waters, and of any liuing thing which is in the waters, they shalbe an abomination vnto you :

11 They shalbe euen an abomination vnto you: ye shall not eat of their flesh, but you shall haue their carcases in abomination.

12 What-

Chap. 6. 26.

Deut. 14. 4. act. 10. 14.

2. Macc. 6. 18.

12 Whatsoeuer hath no finnes nor scales in the waters, that shalbe an abomination vnto you.

13 ¶ And these are they which ye shall haue in abomination among the foules, they shall not be eaten, they *are* an abomination : The Eagle, and the Ossifrage, and the Ospray,

14 And the Vulture, and the Kite, after his kinde :

15 Euery Rauen after his kinde :

16 And the Owle, and the night-hauke, & the Cuckow, and the Hawke after his kinde,

17 And the little Owle, and the Cormorant, and the great Owle,

18 And the Swanne, and the Pellicane, and the Gier-eagle,

19 And the Storke, the Heron after her kinde, and the Lapwing, and the Batte.

20 All foules that creepe, going vpon all foure, shalbe an abomination vnto you.

21 Yet these may ye eat, of euery flying creeping thing that goeth vpon *all* foure, which haue legges aboue their feet, to leape withall vpon the earth.

22 *Euen* these of them ye may eate : the Locust, after his kinde, and the Bald-locust after his kinde, and the Beetle after his kinde, and the Grassehopper after his kinde.

23 But al *other* flying creeping things which haue foure feet, shall be an abomination vnto you.

24 And for these ye shalbe vncleane : whosoeuer toucheth the carkasse of them, shall be vncleane vntill the euen.

25 And whosoeuer beareth ought of the carkasse of them, shall wash his clothes, & be vncleane vntill the euen.

26 *The carkasses* of euery beast which diuideth the hoofe, and is not clouen footed, nor cheweth the cud, are vncleane vnto you : euery one that toucheth them, shalbe vncleane.

27 And whatsoeuer goeth vpon his pawes, among all maner of beasts, that goe on *all* foure, those *are* vncleane vnto you : who so toucheth their carkasse, shall be vncleane vntill the Euen.

28 And he that beareth the carkasse of them, shall wash his clothes, and be vncleane vntill the Euen : they are vncleane vnto you.

29 ¶ These also shalbe vncleane vnto you, among the creeping things that creepe vpon the earth : the Weasell, and the Mouse, and the Tortois, after his kinde,

30 And the Ferret, and the Cameleon, and the Lyzard, and the Snaile, and the Molle.

31 These are vncleane to you among all that creepe : whosoeuer doth touch them when they bee dead, shall be vncleane vntill the Euen.

32 And vpon whatsoeuer any of them, when they are dead, doeth fall, it shalbe vncleane, whether *it be* any vessel of wood, or raiment, or skinne, or sacke, whatsoeuer vessell *it be*, wherein any worke is done, it must be put into water, and it shall be vncleane vntill the Euen ; so it shalbe cleansed.

33 And euery earthen vessel, whereinto any of them falleth, whatsoeuer *is* in it shall bee vncleane ; and *yee shall break it.   * Chap. 6. 28.

34 Of all meat which may be eaten, that on which *such* water commeth, shall be vncleane : And all drinke that may be drunkein euery *such* vessell, shalbe vncleane.

35 And euery thing, whereupon any part of their carkasse falleth, shall be vncleane, *whether it be* ouen, or ranges for pots, they shalbe broken downe : for they are vncleane, and shall be vncleane vnto you.

36 Neuerthelesse, a fountaine or pit, †*wherein* there is plenty of water, shalbe cleane : but that which toucheth their carkasse shalbe vncleane.   † Hebr. a gathering toge ther of waters.

37 And if any part of their carkasse fall vpon any sowing seed which is to be sowen, it shalbe cleane :

38 But if any water be put vpon the seed, and any part of their carkasse fall thereon, it shalbe vncleane vnto you.

39 And if any beast of which ye may eat, die, he that toucheth the carkasse thereof, shall be vncleane vntill the Euen.

40 And hee that eateth of the carkasse of it, shall wash his clothes, and be vncleane vntil the Euen : he also that beareth the carkasse of it, shal wash his clothes, and bee vncleane vntill the Euen.

41 And euery creeping thing that creepeth vpon the earth, shalbe an abomination : it shall not be eaten.

42 Whatsoeuer goeth vpon the bellie, and whatsoeuer goeth vpon *all* foure, or whatsoeuer †hath more feet among all creeping things that creepe vpon   † Hebr. doth multiply feet.

vpon the earth, them ye shall not eate, for they are an abomination.

43 Yee shall not make your †selues abominable with any creeping thing that creepeth, neither shall ye make your selues vncleane with them, that ye should be defiled thereby.

† Heb. soules

44 For I am the LORD your God: yee shall therefore sanctifie your selues, and *ye shall be holy, for I am holy: neither shall ye defile your selues with any maner of creeping thing that creepeth vpon the earth.

* Chap. 19.
2. and 20. 7.
1. pet. 1. 15

45 For I am the LORD that bringeth you vp out of the land of Egypt to be your God: ye shal therefore be holy, for I am holy.

46 This is the law of the beasts, and of the foule, and of euery liuing creature that moueth in the waters, and of euerie creature that creepeth vpon the earth:

47 To make a difference betweene the vncleane and the cleane, & betweene the beast that may be eaten, and the beast that may not be eaten.

CHAP. XII.

1 The purification of women after childbirth.
6 Her offerings for her purifying.

Nd the LORD spake vnto Moses, saying,

2 Speake vnto the children of Israel, saying, If a *woman haue conceiued seed, and borne a man child, then she shal be vncleane seuen dayes: according to the dayes of the separation for her infirmitie shall she be vncleane.

* Chap. 15.
19.

3 And in the *eight day, the flesh of his foreskinne shall be circumcised.

Luk. 2. 21
Iohn 7. 22.

4 And she shal then continue in the blood of her purifying three and thirtie dayes: Shee shall touch no hallowed thing, nor come into the Sanctuary, vntill the dayes of her purifying be fulfilled.

5 But if she beare a maid child, then she shalbe vncleane two weekes, as in her separation: and she shall continue in the blood of her purifying threescore and sixe dayes.

6 And when the dayes of her purifying are fulfilled, for a sonne, or for a daughter, she shall bring a lambe of the †first yeere for a burnt offring, & a yong pigeon, or a turtle doue for a sinne offering, vnto the doore of the Tabernacle

Heb. sonne
of his yeere.

of the Congregation, vnto the Priest:

7 Who shall offer it before the LORD, and make an atonement for her, and she shall be cleansed from the issue of her blood. This is the law for her that hath borne a male or a female.

8 *And if †she be not able to bring a lambe, then she shall bring two turtles, or two yong pigeons, the one for the burnt offering, and the other for a sinne offering: and the Priest shall make an atonement for her, and shee shall bee cleane.

* Luke 2.
24.
† Hebr. her
hand find not
sufficiencie
of.

CHAP. XIII.

1 The Lawes and tokens whereby the Priest is to be guided in discerning the Leprosie.

Nd the LORD spake vnto Moses and Aaron, saying,

2 When a man shall haue in the skinne of his flesh, a ‖rising, a scabbe, or bright spot, and it bee in the skinne of his flesh like the plague of leprosie, then he shall bee brought vnto Aaron the Priest, or vnto one of his sonnes the Priests.

‖ Or, swel-
ling.

3 And the Priest shall looke on the plague in the skinne of the flesh: and when the haire in the plague is turned white, and the plague in sight be deeper then the skin of his flesh, it is a plague of leprosie: and the Priest shall looke on him, and pronounce him vncleane.

4 If the bright spot be white in the skinne of his flesh, and in sight bee not deeper then the skinne, and the haire thereof be not turned white, then the Priest shall shut vp him that hath the plague, seuen dayes.

5 And the Priest shall looke on him the seuenth day: and beholde, if the plague in his sight be at a stay, and the plague spread not in the skinne, then the Priest shall shut him vp seuen dayes more.

6 And the Priest shall looke on him againe the seuenth day · and beholde, if the plague be somewhat darke, and the plague spread not in the skin, the Priest shall pronounce him cleane: it is but a scab: and he shall wash his clothes, and be cleane.

7 But if the scab spread much abroad in the skinne after that hee hath beene seene of the Priest, for his cleansing hee shall be seene of the Priest againe.

8 And if the Priest see, that behold, the scab spreadeth in the skin, then the Priest

Priest shall pronounce him vncleane: it *is* a leprosie.

9 ¶ When the plague of leprosie is in a man, then he shall be brought vnto the Priest;

10 And the Priest shall see him : and behold, if the rising *be* white in the skin, and it haue turned the haire white, and there be †quicke raw flesh in the rising:

† *Hebr. the quickening of liuing flesh.*

11 It is an old leprosie in the skinne of his flesh, and the Priest shall pronounce him vncleane, and shal not shut him vp : for he is vncleane.

12 And if a leprosie breake out abroad in the skin, and the leprosie couer all the skin of *him that hath* the plague, from his head euen to his foot, wheresoeuer the Priest looketh :

13 Then the Priest shall consider: and behold, if the leprosie haue couered al his flesh, he shal pronounce *him* cleane *that hath* the plague, it is all turned white; he *is* cleane.

14 But when raw flesh appeareth in him, he shall be vncleane.

15 And the Priest shall see the raw flesh, and pronounce him to bee vncleane: for the raw flesh is vncleane: it is a leprosie.

16 Or if the raw flesh turne againe, and bee changed vnto white, hee shall come vnto the Priest:

17 And the Priest shall see him: and beholde, if the plague bee turned into white, then the Priest shall pronounce *him* cleane *that hath* the plague; hee *is* cleane.

18 ¶ The flesh also, in which, *euen* in the skinne thereof was a bile, and is healed,

19 And in the place of the bile there be a white rising, or a bright spot white, and somewhat reddish, and it be shewed to the Priest :

20 And if when the Priest seeth it, behold, it be in sight lower then the skinne, and the haire thereof be turned white, the Priest shall pronounce him vncleane : it is a plague of leprosie broken out of the bile.

21 But if the Priest looke on it, and behold, there be no white haires therein, and if it be not lower then the skin, but be somewhat darke; then the Priest shall shut him vp seuen dayes.

22 And if it spread much abroad in the skinne, then the Priest shall pronounce him vncleane; it is a plague.

23 But if the bright spot stay in his place, and spread not, it *is* a burning bile; and the Priest shall pronounce him cleane.

24 ¶ Or if there be any flesh in the skin whereof there is a †hot burning, and the quicke flesh that burneth haue a white bright spot, somewhat reddish, or white;

† *Hebr. a burning of fire.*

25 Then the Priest shall looke vpon it : and behold, if the haire in the bright spot be turned white, and it bee in sight deeper then the skinne, it *is* a leprosie broken out of the burning : wherefore the Priest shal pronounce him vncleane: it *is* the plague of leprosie.

26 But if the Priest looke on it, and behold, there be no white haire in the bright spot, and it be no lower then the *other* skin, but be somewhat darke, then the Priest shal shut him vp seuen dayes.

27 And the Priest shall looke vpon him the seuenth day : and if it be spread much abroad in the skin, then the Priest shall pronounce him vncleane; it *is* the plague of leprosie.

28 And if the bright spot stay in his place, *and* spread not in the skin, but it be somewhat darke; it *is* a rising of the burning, and the Priest shall pronounce him cleane: for it is an inflammation of the burning.

29 ¶ If a man or woman hath a plague vpon the head or the beard,

30 Then the Priest shall see the plague: and behold, if it be in sight deeper then the skin, *and* there be in it a yellow thin haire, then the Priest shall pronounce him vncleane, it *is* a dry skall, *euen* a leprosie vpon the head or beard.

31 And if the Priest looke on the plague of the skall, and behold, it be not in sight deeper then the skin, and that there is no blacke haire in it; then the Priest shall shut vp *him that hath* the plague of the skall, seuen dayes.

32 And in the seuenth day the Priest shall looke on the plague : and behold, if the skall spread not, and there be in it no yellow haire, and the skall be not in sight deeper then the skin;

33 He shall be shauen, but the skall shall he not shaue : and the Priest shall shut vp *him that hath* the skall, seuen dayes more.

34 And in the seuenth day the Priest shall looke on the skall: and behold, if the skall be not spread in the skin, nor be in sight deeper then the skin, then the Priest shall pronounce him cleane: and he

he ſhall waſh his clothes, and be cleane.

35 But if the ſkall ſpread much in the ſkinne after his cleanſing,

36 Then the Prieſt ſhall looke on him, and behold, if the ſkall be ſpread in the ſkinne, the Prieſt ſhall not ſeeke for yellow haire : he is vncleane.

37 But if the ſkall be in his ſight at a ſtay, and *that there* is blacke haire growen vp therein : the ſkall is healed, he *is* cleane, and the Prieſt ſhall pronounce him cleane.

38 ¶ If a man alſo or a woman haue in the ſkinne of their fleſh bright ſpots, *euen* white bright ſpots,

39 Then the Prieſt ſhall looke : and behold, if the bright ſpots in the ſkinne of their fleſh bee darkiſh white, it *is* a freckled ſpot that groweth in the ſkin: he *is* cleane.

Hebr. head pilled.   40 And the man whoſe †haire is fallen off his head, he is bald : *yet is* hee cleane.

41 And he that hath his haire fallen off from the part of his head toward his face, he is forehead-bald : *yet is* hee cleane.

42 And if there be in the bald head, or bald forehead a white reddiſh ſore, it *is* a leproſie ſprung vp in his bald-head, or his bald forehead.

43 Then the Prieſt ſhall looke vpon it : and beholde, if the riſing of the ſore bee white reddiſh in his balde head, or in his bald forehead, as the leproſie appeareth in the ſkinne of the fleſh,

44 Hee *is* a leprous man, he *is* vncleane: the Prieſt ſhall pronounce him vtterly vncleane, his plague *is* in his head.

45 And the leper in whom the plague *is*, his clothes ſhall be rent, and his head bare, and he ſhall put a couering vpon his vpper lip, and ſhall cry, Vncleane, vncleane.

Num. 5. 2. king. 15.   46 All the dayes wherein the plague ſhall bee in him, he ſhall bee defiled, hee *is* vncleane: he ſhall dwell alone, *without the campe ſhall his habitation be.

47 ¶ The garment alſo, that the plague of leproſie *is* in, whether it bee a woollen garment, or a linnen garment,

Iebr. rke of.   48 Whether it bee in the warpe, or woofe of linnen or of woollen, whether in a ſkin, or in any †thing made of ſkinne:

49 And if the plague be greeniſh or reddiſh in the garment, or in the ſkin, either in the warpe, or in the woofe, or in any †thing of ſkinne, it is a plague of leproſie, and ſhall be ſhewed vnto the Prieſt.   †*Heb. veſſell or inſtrument.*

50 And the Prieſt ſhall looke vpon the plague, and ſhut vp *it that hath* the plague, ſeuen dayes.

51 And he ſhall looke on the plague on the ſeuenth day : if the plague be ſpread in the garment, either in the warpe, or in the woofe, or in a ſkin, *or* in any worke that is made of ſkinne, the plague *is* a fretting leproſie; it *is* vncleane.

52 Hee ſhall therefore burne that garment, whether warpe or woofe, in wollen or in linnen, or any thing of ſkinne, wherein the plague *is :* for it *is* a fretting leproſie; it ſhall bee burnt in the fire.

53 And if the Prieſt ſhall looke, and behold the plague be not ſpread in the garment, either in the warpe, or in the woofe, or in any thing of ſkinne ;

54 Then the Prieſt ſhall command that they waſh the thing wherein the plague is, and he ſhall ſhut it vp ſeuen dayes more.

55 And the Prieſt ſhall looke on the plague after that it is waſhed : and behold, if the plague haue not changed his colour, and the plague be not ſpread, it is vncleane, thou ſhalt burne it in the fire, it *is* fret inward, whether it be †bare within or without.   † *Heb. whether it be bauld in the head thereof, or in the forehead thereof.*

56 And if the Prieſt looke, and behold, the plaine be ſomewhat darke after the waſhing of it, then he ſhall rend it out of the garment, or out of the ſkin, or out of the warpe, or out of the woofe.

57 And if it appeare ſtill in the garment, either in the warpe, or in the woofe, or in any thing of ſkinne, it *is* a ſpreading *plague*, thou ſhalt burne that wherein the plague *is*, with fire.

58 And the garment, either warpe, or woofe, or whatſoeuer thing of ſkin it *bee*, which thou ſhalt waſh, if the plague be departed from them, then it ſhall be waſhed the ſecond time, and *ſhalbe* cleane.

59 This *is* the law of the plague of leproſie in a garment of woollen or linnen, either *in* the warpe, or woofe, or any thing of ſkinnes, to pronounce it cleane, or to pronounce it vncleane.

CHAP

CHAP. XIIII.

1 The rites and sacrifices in clensing of the Leper. 33 The signes of leprosie in a house. 43 The clensing of that house.

Nd the Lord spake vnto Moses, saying,

2 This shalbe the law of the leper, in the day of his cleansing: he *shall be brought vnto the Priest.

*Matt. 8. 2. mark. 1. 40. luke 5. 12.

3 And the Priest shall goe forth out of the campe, and the Priest shall looke: and beholde, if the plague of leprosie be healed in the leper,

4 Then shall the Priest command to take for him that is to bee cleansed, two ‖birds aliue, *and* cleane, and Cedar w⌐od, and scarlet, and hysope.

‖ Or, *sparrowes.*

5 And the Priest shall command that one of the birds bee killed in an earthen vessell, ouer running water.

6 As for the liuing bird, he shal take it, and the Cedar wood, and the scarlet, and the hysope, and shall dip them and the liuing bird in the blood of the bird that was killed ouer the running water.

7 And he shall sprinckle vpon him that is to be cleansed from the leprosie, seuen times, and shall pronounce him cleane, and shall let the liuing bird loose †into the open field.

† Hebr. vpon the face of the field.

8 And he that is to be cleansed shall wash his clothes, and shaue off all his haire, and wash himselfe in water, that he may be cleane: And after that hee shall come into the Campe, and shall tarry abroad out of his tent seuen dayes.

9 But it shall be on the seuenth day, that he shall shaue all his haire off his head and his beard, and his eyebrowes, euen all his haire he shal shaue off: And he shall wash his clothes, also he shall wash his flesh in water, and he shall be cleane.

10 And on the eight day he shall take two hee lambes without blemish, and one ewe-lambe of †the first yeere, without blemish, and three tenth deales of fine flowre for a meat offering, mingled with oyle, and one log of oyle.

† Hebr. the daughter of her yeere.

11 And the Priest that maketh *him* cleane, shall present the man that is to be made cleane, and those things before the Lord, *at* the doore of the Tabernacle of the Congregation:

12 And the Priest shall take one hee lambe, and offer him for a trespasse offering, and the log of oile, and *waue them for a waue offering before the Lord.

*Exod. 29. 24.

13 And he shall slay the lambe in the place where he shall kil the sin-offering, and the burnt offring in the holy place: for *as the sinne offering is the Priests, so is the trespasse offering: it *is* most Holy.

*Chap. 7.

14 And the Priest shall take some of the blood of the trespasse offering, and the Priest shall put it vpon the tip of the right eare of him that is to be cleansed, and vpon the thumbe of his right hand, and vpon the great toe of his right foot.

15 And the Priest shall take some of the log of oile, and powre it into the palme of his owne left hand:

16 And the Priest shall dip his right finger in the oile that is in his left hand, and shall sprinckle of the oile with his finger, seuen times before the Lord.

17 And of the rest of the oile that *is* in his hand, shall the Priest put vpon the tip of the right eare of him that is to be cleansed, and vpon the thumbe of his right hande, and vpon the great toe of his right foot, vpon the blood of the trespasse offering.

18 And the remnant of the oile that is in the Priests hand, he shall powre vpon the head of him that is to be cleansed: and the Priest shall make an atonement for him before the Lord.

19 And the Priest shal offer the sinne offering, and make an atonement for him that is to be cleansed from his vncleannesse, and afterward he shall kill the burnt offering.

20 And the Priest shall offer the burnt offering, and the meat offering vpon the Altar: and the Priest shall make an atonement for him, and he shalbe cleane.

21 And if he be poore, and †cannot get so much, then hee shall take one lambe for a trespasse offring †to be waued, to make an atonement for him, and one tenth deale of fine flowre mingled with oile, for a meat offering, and a log of oile,

† Hebr. h hand reac not.
† Hebr. F a wauing

22 And two turtle doues, or two yong pigeons, such as he is able to get: and the one shalbe a sinne offering, and the other a burnt offering.

23 And hee shall bring them on the eight day, for his cleansing vnto the Priest,

Priest, vnto the doore of the Tabernacle of the Congregation, before the LORD.

24 And the Priest shall take the lambe of the trespasse offering, and the log of oile, and the Priest shall waue them for a waue offering before the LORD.

25 And he shall kill the lambe of the trespasse offering, and the Priest shall take some of the blood of the trespasse offering, and put it vpon the tip of the right eare of him that is to be cleansed, and vpon the thumbe of his right hand, and vpon the great toe of his right foote.

26 And the Priest shall powre of the oyle into the palme of his owne left hand.

27 And the Priest shal sprinkle with his right finger, some of the oile that is in his left hand, seuen times before the LORD.

28 And the Priest shall put of the oile that is in his hand, vpon the tip of the right eare of him that is to be cleansed, and vpon the thumbe of his right hand, and vpon the great toe of his right foot; vpon the place of the blood of the trespasse offering.

29 And the rest of the oile that is in the Priests hand, he shall put vpon the head of him that is to bee cleansed, to make an atonement for him before the LORD.

30 And he shall offer the one of the turtle doues, or of the yong pigeons, such as he can get:

31 *Euen* such as he is able to get, the one for a sinne offering, and the other for a burnt offering, with the meat offering. And the Priest shall make an atonement for him that is to be cleansed, before the LORD.

32 This *is* the law of him in whom *is* the plague of leprosie, whose hand is not able to get that which pertaineth to his cleansing.

33 ¶ And the LORD spake vnto Moses, and vnto Aaron, saying,

34 When ye be come into the land of Canaan, which I giue to you for a possession, and I put the plague of leprosie in a house of the land of your possession;

35 And hee that oweth the house shall come, and tell the Priest, saying, It seemeth to me there is as it were a plague in the house:

36 Then the Priest shall command that they ‖ emptie the house, before the Priest goe into it to see the plague, that all that is in the house be not made vncleane: and afterward the Priest shall goe in, to see the house.

‖ Or, prepare.

37 And he shal looke on the plague: and behold, if the plague be in the walls of the house, with hollow strakes, greenish or reddish, which in sight are lower then the wall;

38 Then the Priest shall goe out of the house, to the doore of the house, and shut vp the house seuen dayes.

39 And the Priest shall come againe the seuenth day, and shall looke: and behold, if the plague bee spread in the walls of the house;

40 Then the Priest shall command that they take away the stones in which the plague *is*, and they shall cast them into an vncleane place without the Citie.

41 And hee shall cause the house to be scraped within round about, and they shall powre out the dust that they scrape off, without the citie into an vncleane place.

42 And they shall take other stones, and put *them* in the place of those stones; and hee shall take other morter, and shall plaister the house.

43 And if the plague come againe, and breake out in the house, after that he hath taken away the stones, and after he hath scraped the house, and after it is plastered;

44 Then the Priest shall come and looke, and behold, *if* the plague bee spread in the house, it *is* a fretting leprosie in the house: it *is* vncleane.

45 And he shall breake downe the house, the stones of it, and the timber thereof, and all the morter of the house: and he shall cary them foorth out of the city into an vncleane place.

46 Moreouer, he that goeth into the house all the while that it is shut vp, shalbe vncleane vntill the Euen.

47 And hee that lieth in the house, shall wash his clothes: and hee that eateth in the house, shall wash his clothes.

48 And if the Priest †shall come in, and looke *vpon it*, and behold, the plague hath not spread in the house, after the house was plastered: then the Priest shall pronounce the house cleane, because the plague is healed.

† Hebr. in comming in, shall come in, &c.

49 And

49 And he shall take to cleanse the house, two birds, and Cedar wood, and scarlet, and hyssope.

50 And he shall kill the one of the birds in an earthen vessell, ouer running water.

51 And he shall take the Cedar-wood and the hyssope, and the scarlet, and the liuing bird, and dip them in the blood of the slaine bird, and in the running water, and sprinkle the house seuen times.

52 And he shall clense the house with the blood of the bird, and with the running water, and with the liuing bird, and with the Cedar wood, and with the hyssope, and with the scarlet.

53 But hee shall let goe the liuing bird out of the citie into the open fields, and make an atonement for the house: and it shall be cleane.

54 This *is* the law for all manner * plague of leprosie and *skall,

55 And for the leprosie of a garment, and of an house,

56 And for a rising, and for a scabbe, and for a bright spot:

57 To teach †when *it is* vncleane, and when *it is* cleane: this *is* the lawe of leprosie.

*Chap. 13. 30.

†Heb. in the day of the vncleane, and in the day of the cleane

CHAP. XV.

1 The vncleannes of men in their issues. 13 The clensing of them. 19 The vncleannesse of women in their issues. 28 Their clensing.

And the LORD spake vnto Moses, and to Aaron, saying,

2 Speake vnto the children of Israel, and say vnto them, When any man hath a ‖running issue out of his flesh, because of his issue he *is* vncleane.

‖Or, running of the reines.

3 And this shall be his vncleannesse in his issue: whether his flesh run with his issue, or his flesh be stopped from his issue, it *is* his vncleannesse.

4 Euery bed whereon he lieth, that hath the issue, is vncleane: and euery †thing whereon he sitteth, shall bee vncleane.

†Heb. vessel.

5 And whosoeuer toucheth his bed, shall wash his clothes, and bath *himselfe* in water, and bee vncleane vntill the Euen.

6 And hee that sitteth on *any* thing whereon hee sate that hath the issue, shall wash his clothes, and bath *himselfe* in water, and bee vncleane vntill the Euen.

7 And he that toucheth the flesh of him that hath the issue, shall wash his clothes, and bathe *himselfe* in water, and be vncleane vntill the Euen.

8 And if he that hath the issue, spit vpon him that is cleane, then hee shall wash his clothes, and bathe *himselfe* in water, and bee vncleane vntill the Euen.

9 And what saddle soeuer he rideth vpon, that hath the issue, shall bee vncleane.

10 And whosoeuer toucheth any thing that was vnder him, shall be vncleane vntill the Euen: And he that beareth any of those things, shall wash his clothes, and bathe *himselfe* in water, and be vncleane vntill the Euen.

11 And whomsoeuer hee toucheth that hath the issue (and hath not rinsed his hands in water) he shall wash his clothes, and bathe *himselfe* in water, and be vncleane vntill the Euen.

12 And the *vessell of earth that hee toucheth which hath the issue, shall bee broken: and euery vessell of wood shall be rinsed in water.

*Chap. 6. 28.

13 And when hee that hath an issue, is cleansed of his issue, then hee shall number to himselfe seuen dayes for his cleansing, and wash his clothes, and bathe his flesh in running water, and shall be cleane.

14 And on the eight day hee shall take to him two turtle doues, or two yong pigeons, and come before the LORD, vnto the doore of the Tabernacle of the Congregation, and giue them vnto the Priest.

15 And the Priest shall offer them, the one for a sinne offering, and the other for a burnt offering, and the Priest shall make an atonement for him before the LORD for his issue.

16 And if any mans seede of copulation goe out from him, then hee shall wash all his flesh in water, and bee vncleane vntill the Euen.

17 And euery garment and euery skinne whereon is the seede of copulation, shall be washed with water, and be vncleane vntill the Euen.

18 The woman also with whom man shall lie with seed of copulation, they shall both bath *themselues* in water, and be vncleane vntill the Euen.

19 ¶ And if a woman haue an issue, *and*

Hebr. in er separa-ion.

and her issue in her flesh be blood, shee shall bee † put apart seuen dayes: and whosoeuer toucheth her, shall bee vncleane vntill the Euen.

20 And euery thing that she lieth vpon in her separation, shall be vncleane: euery thing also that she sitteth vpon, shalbe vncleane.

21 And whosoeuer toucheth her bed, shall wash his clothes, and bathe *himselfe* in water, and be vncleane vntill the Euen.

22 And whosoeuer toucheth any thing that she sate vpon, shall wash his clothes, and bathe *himselfe* in water, and be vncleane vntill the Euen.

23 And if it be on *her* bed, or on any thing whereon she sitteth, when hee toucheth it, he shall be vncleane vntill the Euen.

24 And if any man lye with her at all, and her flowers be vpon him, hee shall be vncleane seuen dayes: and all the bed whereon he lyeth, shall be vncleane.

25 And if a woman haue an issue of her blood many dayes out of the time of her separation, or if it runne beyond the time of her separation, all the dayes of the issue of her vncleannesse, shall be as the dayes of her separation: she shal-be vncleane.

26 Euery bed whereon she lyeth all the dayes of her issue, shall be vnto her as the bed of her separation: and whatsoeuer shee sitteth vpon, shall bee vncleane, as the vncleannesse of her separation.

27 And whosoeuer toucheth those things, shalbe vncleane, and shall wash his clothes, and bathe *himselfe* in water, and be vncleane vntill the Euen.

28 But if she be cleansed of her issue, then she shall number to her selfe seuen dayes: and after that, she shalbe cleane.

29 And on the eight day she shall take vnto her two turtles or two yong pigeons, & bring them vnto the Priest, to the doore of the Tabernacle of the Congregation.

30 And the Priest shall offer the one for a sinne offering, and the other for a burnt offering, and the Priest shall make an atonement for her before the Lord, for the issue of her vncleannesse.

31 Thus shall yee separate the children of Israel from their vncleannesse, that they die not in their vncleannesse,

when they defile my Tabernacle that is among them.

32 This is the law of him that hath an issue, and *of him* whose seed goeth from him, and is defiled therewith;

33 And of her that is sicke of her flowers, and of him that hath an issue, of the man, and of the woman, & of him that lyeth with her which is vncleane.

CHAP. XVI.

1 How the hie Priest must enter into the Holy place. 11 The sinne-offering for himselfe. 15 The sinne-offering for the people. 20 The Scape Goat. 29 The yeerely Feast of the Expiations.

Nd the Lord *spake vnto Moses, after the death of the two sonnes of Aaron, when they offered before the Lord, and died.   *Leuit. 10. 2.

2 And the Lord sayd vnto Moses, Speake vnto Aaron thy brother, that hee *come not at all times into the Holy place within the Vaile, before the Mercy seat, which is vpon the Arke, that hee die not: for I will appeare in the cloud vpon the Mercy seat.   * Exod. 30. 10. heb. 9. 7.

3 Thus shall Aaron come in to the Holy place: with a yong bullocke for a sinne offering, and a ramme for a burnt offering.

4 Hee shall put on the holy linnen coate, and he shall haue the linnen breeches vpon his flesh, and shall be girded with a linnen girdle, and with the linnen Miter shall hee be attired. These *are* holy garments: therefore shall he wash his flesh in water, and so put them on.

5 And he shall take of the Congregation of the children of Israel, two kiddes of the Goates for a sinne offering, and one ramme for a burnt offering.

6 And Aaron shall offer his bullocke of the sinne offering, which is for himselfe, and *make an atonement for himselfe, and for his house.   * Hebr. 9. 7.

7 And he shall take the two goats, and present them before the Lord at the doore of the Tabernacle of the Congregation.

8 And Aaron shall cast lottes vpon the two Goates: one lot for the Lord, and the other lot for the †Scape goat.   † *Hebr.* A-zazel.

9 And

† *Hebr. went vp.*

9 And Aaron shall bring the goate vpon which the Lords lot †fell, and offer him for a sinne offering.

10 But the goat on which the lot fell to be the Scape goate, shalbe presented aliue before the Lord, to make an atonement with him, and to let him goe for a Scape goate into the wildernesse.

11 And Aaron shal bring the bullocke of the sinne offering, which is for himselfe, and shall make an atonement for himselfe, and for his house, and shal kill the bullocke of the sinne offering which *is* for himselfe.

12 And he shall take a censer full of burning coales of fire from off the Altar before the Lord, and his handes full of sweet incense beaten small, and bring *it* within the vaile.

13 And he shall put the incense vpon the fire before the Lord, that the cloud of the incense may couer the mercie seate that *is* vpon the testimonie, that he die not.

* Heb. 9. 13 and 10. 4.
* Chap. 4. 6

14 And *he shall take of the blood of the bullocke, and *sprinkle *it* with his finger vpon the Mercie seat Eastward: and before the Mercie seate shall hee sprinkle of the blood with his finger seuen times.

15 ¶ Then shall he kill the goate of the sinne offering that *is* for the people, and bring his blood within the Vaile, and doe with that blood as he did with the blood of the bullocke, and sprinkle it vpon the Mercie seat, and before the Mercie seat.

16 And he shall make an atonement for the holy place, because of the vncleannesse of the children of Israel, and because of their transgressions in all their sinnes: and so shall hee doe for the Tabernacle of the Congregation that †remaineth among them, in the middest of their vncleannesse.

† *Heb. dwelleth.*

* Luk. 1. 10.

17 *And there shall bee no man in the Tabernacle of the Congregation, when hee goeth in to make an atonement in the holy place, vntill hee come out, and haue made an atonement for himselfe, and for his houshold, and for all the Congregation of Israel.

18 And he shall goe out vnto the Altar that *is* before the Lord, and make an atonement for it, & shall take of the blood of the bullocke, and of the blood of the goate, and put *it* vpon the hornes of the Altar round about.

19 And he shall sprinkle of the blood vpon it with his finger seuen times, and clense it, and hallow it from the vncleannesse of the children of Israel.

20 ¶ And when hee hath made an end of reconciling the holy place, and the Tabernacle of the Congregation, and the Altar, hee shall bring the liue goate.

21 And Aaron shall lay both his hands vpon the head of the liue goate, and confesse ouer him all the iniquities of the children of Israel, and all their transgressions in all their sinnes, putting them vpon the head of the goate, and shall send him away by the hand of †a fit man into the wildernesse

† *Hebr. a man of opportunitie.*
‡ *Heb. of separation.*

22 And the goate shall beare vpon him all their iniquities, vnto a land †not inhabited; and he shall let goe the goat in the wildernesse.

23 And Aaron shall come into the Tabernacle of the Congregation, and shal put off the linnen garments which he put on, when he went in to the holy place, and shall leaue them there.

24 And he shall wash his flesh with water in the holy place, and put on his garments, and come foorth, and offer his burnt offering, and the burnt offering of the people, and make an atonement for himselfe, and for the people.

25 And the fat of the sinne offering shall he burne vpon the Altar

26 And he that let goe the goat for the Scape-goat, shal wash his clothes, and bathe his flesh in water, and afterward come into the Campe

27 And the bullocke for the sinne offering, and the goat for the sin offering, whose blood was brought in, to make atonement in the holy place, shall one cary foorth *without the Campe, and they shal burne in the fire their skinnes and their flesh, and their doung.

* Leuit. 6 30. heb. 13 11.

28 And he that burneth them, shall wash his clothes, and bathe his flesh in water, and afterward he shall come into the Campe.

29 ¶ And this shall be a statute for euer vnto you: that in the seuenth moneth, on the tenth day of the moneth, ye shall afflict your soules, & doe no worke at all, whether it bee one of your owne countrey, or a stranger that soiourneth among you.

30 For on that day shal *the Priest* make an atonement for you, to cleanse you,
that

Hebr. fill is hand.

that yee may bee cleane from all your sinnes before the LORD.

31 It *shall be* a Sabbath of rest vnto you, and ye shall afflict your soules by a statute for euer.

32 And the Priest whom he shall anoynt, and whom he shall †consecrate to minister in the Priests office in his fathers stead, shall make the atonement, and shal put on the linnen clothes, euen the holy garments.

33 And he shall make an atonement for the holy Sanctuary, and hee shall make an atonement for the Tabernacle of the Congregation, and for the Altar: and he shall make an atonement for the Priests, and for all the people of the Congregation.

34 And this shall be an euerlasting statute vnto you, to make an atonement for the children of Israel, for all their sinnes *once a yeere. And he did as the LORD commanded Moses.

*Exod. 30.
). heb 9.*

CHAP. XVII.

1 The blood of all slaine beasts must be offered to the Lord at the doore of the Tabernacle. 7 They must not offer to deuils. 10 All eating of blood is forbidden, 15 and all that dieth alone, or is torne.

ANd the LORD spake vnto Moses, saying,

2 Speake vnto Aaron and vnto his sonnes, and vnto all the children of Israel, and say vnto them; This is the thing which the LORD hath commanded, saying;

3 What man soeuer *there bee* of the house of Israel, that killeth an oxe, or lambe, or goat in the Campe, or that killeth *it* out of the Campe,

4 And bringeth it not vnto the doore of the Tabernacle of the Congregation, to offer an offering vnto the LORD before the Tabernacle of the LORD, blood shall be imputed vnto that man; he hath shed blood, and that man shall be cut off from among his people:

5 To the end that the children of Israel may bring their sacrifices, which they offer in the open field, euen that they may bring them vnto the LORD, vnto the doore of the Tabernacle of the Congregation vnto the Priest, and offer them for peace offerings vnto the LORD.

6 And the Priest shall sprinckle the blood vpon the Altar of the LORD, *at* the doore of the Tabernacle of the Congregation, and burne the fat for a *sweet sauour vnto the LORD.

*Exod. 29.
18. chap. 4.
31.*

7 And they shall no more offer their sacrifices vnto deuils, after whom they haue gone a whoring: This shall be a statute for euer vnto them throughout their generations.

8 ¶ And thou shalt say vnto them, Whatsoeuer man *there be* of the house of Israel, or of the strangers which soiourne among you, that offreth a burnt offering or sacrifice,

9 And bringeth it not vnto the doore of the Tabernacle of the Congregation, to offer it vnto the LORD, euen that man shall be cut off from among his people.

10 ¶ And whatsoeuer man *there be* of the house of Israel, or of the strangers that soiourne among you, that eateth any maner of blood, I will euen set my face against that soule that eateth blood, and will cut him off from among his people.

11 For the life of the flesh is in the blood, and I haue giuen it to you vpon the Altar, to make an atonement for your soules: for it *is* the blood, *that* maketh an atonement for the soule.

12 Therefore I said vnto the children of Israel, No soule of you shall eat blood, neither shall any stranger that soiourneth among you, eat blood.

13 And whatsoeuer man there be of the children of Israel, or of the strangers that soiourne among you, which †hunteth and catcheth any beast or foule that may be eaten, he shall euen powre out the blood thereof, and couer it with dust.

† Heb. that hunteth any hunting.

14 For *it is* the life of all flesh, the blood of it is for the life thereof: therefore I said vnto the children of Israel, *Ye shall not eat the blood of no maner of flesh: for the life of all flesh is the blood thereof: whosoeuer eateth it, shalbe cut off.

Gen. 9. 4.

15 And euery soule that eateth that which †died *of it selfe*, or that which was torne *with beasts*, whether it bee one of your owne countrey, or a stranger, he shall both wash his clothes, and bathe *himselfe* in water, and be vncleane vntill the Euen: then shall he be cleane.

† Heb. a carcqise.

16 But if he wash *them* not, nor bathe his flesh, then he shal beare his iniquity.

CHAP.

CHAP. XVIII.

1 Vnlawfull Marriages. 19 Vnlawfull lusts.

Nd the LORD spake vnto Moses, saying,

2 Speake vnto the children of Israel, and say vnto them, I *am* the LORD your God.

3 After the doings of the land of Egypt wherein ye dwelt, shal ye not doe: and after the doings of land of Canaan whither I bring you, shall ye not doe: neither shall yee walke in their ordinances.

4 Ye shall doe my iudgements, and keepe mine ordinances, to walke therein : I *am* the LORD your God.

5 *Yee shall therefore keepe my statutes, and my iudgements : which if a man doe, hee shall liue in them : I *am* the LORD.

6 ¶ None of you shall approche to any that is †neere of kinne to him, to vncouer *their* nakednesse : I *am* the LORD.

7 The nakednesse of thy father, or the nakednesse of thy mother, shalt thou not vncouer : she is thy mother, thou shalt not vncouer her nakednesse.

8 *The nakednesse of thy fathers wife shalt thou not vncouer : it *is* thy fathers nakednesse.

9 The nakednesse of thy sister, the daughter of thy father, or daughter of thy mother, whether shee be borne at home, or borne abroad, *euen* their nakednesse thou shalt not vncouer.

10 The nakednesse of thy sonnes daughter, or of thy daughters daughter, *euen* their nakednesse thou shalt not vncouer : for theirs *is* thine owne nakednesse.

11 The nakednesse of thy fathers wiues daughter, begotten of thy father, (she *is* thy sister,) thou shalt not vncouer her nakednesse.

12 *Thou shalt not vncouer the nakednesse of thy fathers sister : she *is* thy fathers neere kinswoman.

13 Thou shalt not vncouer the nakednesse of thy mothers sister : for she *is* thy mothers neere kinswoman.

14 *Thou shalt not vncouer the nakednesse of thy fathers brother, thou shalt not approche to his wife : shee is thine aunt.

15 *Thou shalt not vncouer the nakednesse of thy daughter in law : shee *is* thy sonnes wife, thou shalt not vncouer her nakednesse.

16 *Thou shalt not vncouer the nakednesse of thy brothers wife : it *is* thy brothers nakednesse.

17 Thou shalt not vncouer the nakednesse of a woman and her daughter, neither shalt thou take her sonnes daughter, or her daughters daughter, to vncouer her nakednesse : For they are her neere kinsewomen : it *is* wickednesse.

18 Neither shalt thou take a wife ||to her sister, to vexe *her*, to vncouer her nakednes besides the other, in her life *time*.

19 *Also thou shalt not approche vnto a woman to vncouer her nakednes, as long as shee is put apart for her vncleannesse.

20 Moreouer, thou shalt not lie carnally with thy neighbours wife, to defile thy selfe with her.

21 And thou shalt not let any of thy seed *passe through *the fire* to *Molech, neither shalt thou prophane the Name of thy God : I am the LORD.

22 Thou shalt not lie with mankinde, as with womankinde : it *is* abomination.

23 *Neither shalt thou lie with any beast, to defile thy selfe therewith : neither shall any woman stand before a beast to lie downe thereto : It *is* confusion.

24 Defile not you your selues in any of these things : for in all these, the nations are defiled which I cast out before you.

25 And the land is defiled : Therefore I doe visit the iniquitie thereof vpon it, and the land it selfe vomiteth out her inhabitants.

26 Ye shall therefore keepe my Statutes and my Iudgements, and shall not commit any of these abominations; *neither* any of your owne nation, nor any stranger that soiourneth among you :

27 (For all these abominations haue the men of the land done, which were before you, and the land is defiled.)

28 That the land spew not you out also, when ye defile it, as it spewed out the nations that were before you.

29 For whosoeuer shall commit any of these abominations, euen the soules that commit *them*, shall be cut off from among their people.

30 There-

Marginal notes

* Ezek. 20. 11. rom. 10. 5. galat. 3. 12.

† Hebr. remainder of his flesh.

* Chap. 20. 11.

* Chap. 20. 19.

* Chap. 20. 20.

* Chap. 20. 12.

* Chap. 20. 21.

‖ Or, one wife to another.

* Chap. 20. 18.

* Chap. 20 2. 2. king. 23. 10.
* Called Acts. 7. 43. Moloc.

* Chap. 20 15.

30 Therefore shal ye keepe mine Ordinance, that ye commit not any one of these abominable customes, which were committed before you, and that ye defile not your selues therein: I *am* the LORD your God.

CHAP. XIX.

1 A repetition of sundry Lawes.

Nd the LORD spake vnto Moses, saying,

2 Speake vnto all the Congregation of the children of Israel, and say vnto them, * Ye shalbe holy: for I the LORD your God *am* holy.

3 ¶ Yee shall feare euery man his mother, and his father, and keepe my Sabbaths: I *am* the LORD your God.

4 ¶ Turne ye not vnto idoles, nor make to your selues molten gods: I *am* the LORD your God.

5 ¶ And if ye offer a sacrifice of peace offerings vnto the LORD, ye shall offer it, at your owne will.

6 It shall be eaten the same day ye offer it, and on the morrow: and if ought remaine vntill the third day, it shalbe burnt in the fire.

7 And if it be eaten at all on the third day, it is abominable; it shall not be accepted.

8 Therefore *euery one* that eateth it, shal beare his iniquitie, because he hath prophaned the halowed thing of the LORD; and that soule shalbe cut off from among his people.

9 ¶ And * when ye reape the haruest of your land, thou shalt not wholly reape the corners of thy field, neither shalt thou gather the gleanings of thy haruest.

10 And thou shalt not gleane thy vineyard, neither shalt thou gather euery grape of thy vineyard; thou shalt leaue them for the poore and stranger: I *am* the LORD your God.

11 ¶ Ye shall not steale, neither deale falsly, neither lie one to another.

12 ¶ And ye shall not * sweare by my Name falsly, neither shalt thou prophane the Name of thy God: I *am* the LORD.

13 ¶ * Thou shalt not defraud thy neighbour, neither rob him: the wages of him that is hired, shal not abide with thee all night, vntill the morning.

14 ¶ Thou shalt not curse the deafe, * nor put a stumbling blocke before the blind, but shalt feare thy God: I *am* the LORD.

15 ¶ Ye shall doe no vnrighteousnes in iudgement; thou shalt not * respect the person of the poore, nor honour the person of the mightie: *but* in righteousnesse shalt thou iudge thy neighbour.

16 ¶ Thou shalt not goe vp and downe as a tale-bearer among thy people: neither shalt thou stand against the blood of thy neighbour: I *am* the LORD.

17 ¶ * Thou shalt not hate thy brother in thine heart: thou shalt in any wise rebuke thy neighbour, ‖ and not suffer sinne vpon him.

18 ¶ Thou shalt not auenge nor beare any grudge against the children of thy people, * but thou shalt loue thy neighbor as thy selfe: I *am* the LORD.

19 ¶ Yee shall keepe my Statutes: Thou shalt not let thy cattell gender with a diuerse kinde: Thou shalt not sowe thy field with mingled seed: Neither shall a garment mingled of linnen and woollen come vpon thee.

20 ¶ And whosoeuer lieth carnally with a woman that is a bondmaid, ‖ betrothed to an husband, and not at all redeemed, nor freedome giuen her, ‖ she shall be scourged: they shall not be put to death, because she was not free:

21 And he shall bring his trespasse offering vnto the LORD, vnto the doore of the Tabernacle of the Congregation, *euen* a ramme for a trespasse offering.

22 And the Priest shall make an atonement for him with the ramme of the trespasse- offering before the LORD for his sinne which hee hath done: and the sinne which he hath done shall bee forgiuen him.

23 ¶ And when yee shall come in to the land, and shall haue planted all maner of trees for food, then ye shall count the fruit therof as vncircumcised: three yeeres shall it be as vncircumcised vnto you: it shall not be eaten of.

24 But in the fourth yeere all the fruit thereof shall be † holy to praise the LORD *withall.*

25 And in the fift yeere shall ye eate of the fruit thereof, that it may yeelde vnto you the increase thereof: I *am* the LORD your God.

26 ¶ Ye shall not eate *any thing* with the

Marginal notes

* Chap. 11.
4. & 20. 7.
. pet. 1. 16.

Chap. 23.
2.

Exod. 20.
deut. 5.
. matt. 5.
. iam. 5.
.

Eccles. 10.
deut. 24.
. tobi. 4
.

* Deut. 27.
18.

* Exod. 23.
3. deut. 1.
17. and 16.
16. prou. 24
23. iam. 2. 9

* 1. Ioh. 2.
11. mat. 8. 5
ecclu. 19. 13
‖ Or, *that*
thou beare
not sinne for
him.

* Matt. 5. 43
and 22. 39.
rom. 13. 9.
galat. 5. 14.
iam. 2. 8.

‖ Or, *abused*
by any. Heb.
reproched
by [*or for*]
man.
‖ Or, *they.*
Heb. there
shall bee a
scourging.

† *Holines of*
praises to the
LORD.

the blood, neither shall ye vse inchantment, nor obserue times.

27 * Ye shall not round the corners of your heads, neither shalt thou marre the corners of thy beard.

28 Ye shall not * make any cuttings in your flesh for the dead, nor print any markes vpon you: I *am* the LORD.

29 ¶ Doe not † prostitute thy daughter, to cause her to be a whore, lest the land fall to whoredome, and the land become full of wickednesse.

30 ¶ Ye shall keepe my Sabbaths, and reuerence my Sanctuary: I *am* the LORD.

31 ¶ Regard not them that haue familiar spirits, neither seeke after Wizards, to be defiled by them: I *am* the LORD your God.

32 ¶ Thou shalt rise vp before the hoary head, and honour the face of the old man, and feare thy God: I *am* the LORD.

33 ¶ And * if a stranger soiourne with thee in your land, yee shall not || vexe him.

34 * But the stranger that dwelleth with you, shalbe as one borne amongst you, and thou shalt loue him as thy selfe, for ye were strangers in the land of Egypt: I *am* the LORD your God.

35 ¶ Ye shall doe no vnrighteousnes in iudgment, in meteyard, in weight, or in measure.

36 * Iust ballances, iust † weights, a iust Ephah, and a iust Hin shall ye haue: I *am* the LORD your God, which brought you out of the land of Egypt.

37 Therefore shall ye obserue all my Statutes, and all my Iudgements, and doe them: I *am* the LORD.

CHAP. XX.

1 Of him that giueth of his seed to Molech. 4 of him that fauoureth such an one. 6 Of going to Wizards. 7 Of sanctification. 9 Of him that curseth his parents. 10 Of adulterie. 11. 14. 17. 19 Of Incest. 13 Of Sodomie. 15 Of Beastialitie. 18 Of vncleannesse. 22 Obedience is required with holinesse. 27 Wizards must be put to death.

ANd the LORD spake vnto Moses, saying,

2 * Againe, thou shalt say to the children of Israel; Whosoeuer he be of the children of Israel, or of the strangers that soiourne in Israel, that giueth any of his seed vnto Molech, he shall surely be put to death: the people of the land shall stone him with stones.

3 And I wil set my face against that man, and will cut him off from among his people: because he hath giuen of his seed vnto Molech, to defile my Sanctuary, and to prophane my holy Name.

4 And if the people of the land doe any wayes hide their eyes from the man, when he giueth of his seed vnto Molech, and kill him not:

5 Then I will set my face against that man, and against his family, and will cut him off, and all that goe a whoring after him, to commit whoredome with Molech, from among their people.

6 ¶ And the soule that turneth after such as haue familiar spirits, and after wizards, to goe a whoring after them, I will euen set my face against that soule, and will cut him off from among his people.

7 ¶ * Sanctifie your selues therefore, and bee yee holy: for I *am* the LORD your God.

8 And ye shall keepe my Statutes, and do them: I *am* the LORD which sanctifie you.

9 ¶ * For euery one that curseth his father or his mother, shalbe surely put to death: hee hath cursed his father or his mother; his blood *shalbe* vpon him.

10 ¶ And * the man that committeth adulterie with another mans wife, *euen* he that committeth adulterie with his neighbours wife, the adulterer, and the adulteresse shall surely bee put to death.

11 * And the man that lieth with his fathers wife, hath vncouered his fathers nakednesse: both of them shalbe put to death; their blood *shalbe* vpon them.

12 And if a man lie with his daughter in law, both of them shall surely be put to death: they haue wrought confusion; their blood *shall be* vpon them.

13 * If a man also lie with mankind, as hee lyeth with a woman, both of them haue committed an abomination: they shall surely be put to death; their blood *shalbe* vpon them.

14 And if a man take a wife, and her mother, it *is* wickednesse: They shalbe burnt with fire, both he and they, that there be no wickednesse among you.

15 * And if a man lie with a beast, he shall

Marginal notes (left column)
* Chap. 21. 5.

* Deut. 14. 1.

† *Hebr. prophane.*

* Exod. 22. 21.

||*Or, oppresse.*

* Exod. 22. 21.

* Prou. 11. 1. and 16. 11. and 20. 10.

†*Heb. stones.*

* Chap. 18. 21.

Marginal notes (right column)
* Chap. 11. 44. and 19. 2. 1. pet. 1. 16.

* Exod. 21. 17. pro. 20. 20. matth. 15. 4.

* Deut. 22. 22. iohn 8. 4.

* Chap. 18. 8.

* Chap. 18. 23.

* Chap. 18. 9.

shall surely be put to death: and ye shall slay the beast.

16 And if a woman approch vnto any beast, and lie downe thereto, thou shalt kill the woman and the beast: they shall surely be put to death, their blood *shalbe* vpon them.

17 And if a man shall take his sister, his fathers daughter, or his mothers daughter, and see her nakednesse, and she see his nakednesse, it is a wicked thing, and they shall bee cut off in the sight of their people: he hath vncouered his sisters nakednesse, he shall beare his iniquitie.

18 * And if a man shall lie with a woman hauing her sickenesse, and shal vncouer her nakednesse: he hath †discouered her fountaine, and she hath vncouered the fountaine of her blood: and both of them shall bee cut off from among their people.

19 And thou shalt not vncouer the nakednesse of thy mothers sister, nor of thy fathers sister: for hee vncouereth his neere kinne: they shall beare their iniquitie.

20 And if a man shall lie with his vncles wife, he hath vncouered his vncles nakednesse: they shall beare their sinne, they shall die childlesse.

21 And if a man shall take his brothers wife, it *is* †an vncleane thing: hee hath vncouered his brothers nakednesse, they shall be childlesse.

22 ¶ Ye shall therefore keepe all my *Statutes, and all my Iudgements, and doe them: that the lande whither I bring you to dwell therein, *spue you not out.

23 And ye shall not walke in the maners of the nation, which I cast out before you: for they committed all these things, & *therefore I abhorred them.

24 But I haue said vnto you, Yee shall inherit their land, and I will giue it vnto you, to possesse it, a land that floweth with milke and hony: I *am* the Lord your God, which haue separated you from *other* people.

25 * Ye shall therefore put difference betweene cleane beasts, and vncleane, and betweene vncleane foules, and cleane: & ye shall not make your soules abominable by beast or by foule, or by any maner of liuing thing, that ‖creepeth on the ground, which I haue separated from you as vncleane.

26 And ye shal be holy vnto me: *for

I the Lord *am* holy, & haue seuered you from *other* people, that ye should be mine.

27 ¶ * A man also or woman that hath a familiar spirit, or that is a wizzard, shall surely be put to death: they shall stone them with stones: their blood *shalbe* vpon them.

CHAP XXI.

1 Of the Priests mourning. 6 Of their holinesse. 8 Of their estimation. 7. 13 Of their Mariages. 16 The Priests that haue blemishes must not minister in the Sanctuarie.

And the Lord said vnto Moses; Speake vnto the Priests the sonnes of Aaron, and say vnto them, There shall none be defiled for the dead among his people:

2 But for his kinne, that is neere vnto him, *that is,* for his mother, and for his father, and for his sonne, and for his daughter, and for his brother,

3 And for his sister a virgin, that is nigh vnto him, which hath had no husband: for her may he be defiled.

4 But hee shall not defile himselfe ‖being a chiefe man among his people, to prophane himselfe.

5 * They shall not make baldnesse vpon their head, neither shall they shaue off the corner of their beard, nor make any cuttings in their flesh:

6 They shalbe holy vnto their God, and not prophane the name of their God: for the offrings of the Lord made by fire, *and* the bread of their God they doe offer: therefore they shall be holy.

7 They shall not take a wife that is a whore, or profane, neither shall they take a woman put away from her husband: for he *is* holy vnto his God.

8 Thou shalt sanctifie him therfore, for he offereth the bread of thy God: he shalbe holy vnto thee: for I the Lord which sanctifie you, *am* holy.

9 ¶ And the daughter of any Priest, if she profane her selfe, by playing the whore, she profaneth her father: shee shall be burnt with fire.

10 And he that is the high Priest among his brethren, vpon whose head the anointing oyle was powred, and that is consecrated to put on the garments, shall not vncouer his head, nor rent his clothes:

11 Neither shall he goe in to any dead body,

Margin notes (left column)
* Chap. 18. 9.

Heb. made naked.

Heb. a separation.

Chap. 18. 3.

Chap. 18. 5.

Deut. 9.5.

Chap. 11. deut. 14.

‖Or, moueth

Chap. 19. and 20.7. pet. 1. 16.

Margin notes (right column)
* Deut. 18. 11. 1. Sam. 28. 7.

‖Or, being an husband among his people hee shall not defile himselfe for his wife &c.
* Chap. 19. 27.

body, nor defile himselfe for his father, or for his mother :

12 Neither shall hee goe out of the Sanctuary, nor prophane the Sanctuary of his God ; for the crowne of the anointing oile of his God *is* vpon him : I *am* the LORD.

13 And he shall take a wife in her virginitie.

14 A widow, or a diuorced woman, or prophane, *or* an harlot, these shall he not take : but he shall take a virgine of his owne people to wife.

15 Neither shal he prophane his seed among his people : for I the LORD doe sanctifie him.

16 ¶ And the LORD spake vnto Moses, saying,

17 Speake vnto Aaron, saying, Whosoeuer *he be* of thy seed in their generations, that hath any blemish, let him not approche to offer the ‖bread of his God :

‖ *Or, food.*

18 For whatsoeuer man *hee be* that hath a blemish, he shall not approche: a blind man, or a lame, or he that hath a flat nose, or any thing *superfluous,

* *Chap. 22. 23.*

19 Or a man that is broken footed, or broken handed,

20 Or crooke-backt, or a ‖dwarfe, or that hath a blemish in his eye, or be scuruy, or scabbed, or hath his stones broken :

‖ *Or, too slender.*

21 No man that hath a blemish, of the seed of Aaron the Priest, shall come nigh to offer the offrings of the LORD made by fire: he hath a blemish; he shall not come nigh to offer the bread of his God.

22 He shall eat the bread of his God, *both* of the most Holy, and of the holy:

23 Onely he shall not goe in vnto the Vaile, nor come nigh vnto the Altar, because he hath a blemish, that he prophane not my Sanctuaries : for I the LORD doe sanctifie them.

24 And Moses told it vnto Aaron, and to his sonnes, and vnto all the children of Israel.

CHAP. XXII.

1 The Priests in their vncleannesse must abstaine from the holy things. 6 How they shall bee cleansed. 6 Who of the Priests house may eate of the holy things. 17 The sacrifices must be without blemish. 26 The age of the sacrifice. 29 The law of eating the sacrifice of thankesgiuing.

 Nd the LORD spake vnto Moses, saying,

2 Speake vnto Aaron, and to his sonnes, that they separate themselues from the holy things of the children of Israel, and that they prophane not my holy Name, *in those things* which they halow vnto me : I *am* the LORD.

3 Say vnto them, Whosoeuer he be of all your seed, among your generations, that goeth vnto the holy things, which the children of Israel hallow vnto the LORD, hauing his vncleannesse vpon him, that soule shalbe cut off from my presence : I *am* the LORD.

4 What man soeuer of the seed of Aaron is a leper, or hath a †running issue, he shall not eat of the holy things, vntill he be cleane. And *who so touch-eth any thing *that is* vncleane *by* the dead, or a man whose seed goeth from him :

† *Hebr. running of the reines.*
* *Chap. 15. 2.*

5 Or whosoeuer toucheth any creeping thing, whereby he may be made vncleane, or a man of whom hee may take vncleannesse, whatsoeuer vncleannesse he hath :

6 The soule which hath touched any such, shalbe vncleane vntill Euen, and shall not eate of the holy things, vnlesse he wash his flesh with water.

7 And when the Sunne is downe, he shall be cleane, and shall afterward eate of the holy things, because it *is* his food.

8 *That which dieth of it selfe, or is torne *with beasts*, hee shall not eate to defile himselfe therewith : I *am* the LORD.

* *Exod. 22. 31. ezech. 44. 31.*

9 They shall therefore keepe mine Ordinance, lest they beare sinne for it, and die therefore, if they prophane it : I the LORD doe sanctifie them.

10 There shall no stranger eat of the holy thing ; a soiourner of the Priests, or an hired seruant shall not eate of the holy thing.

11 But if the Priest buy any soule †with his money, he shall eat of it, and he that is borne in his house : they shall eat of his meat.

† *Hebr. with the purchase of his money*

12 If the Priests daughter also bee married vnto †a stranger, she may not eate of an offering of the holy things.

† *Heb. a man a stranger.*

13 But if the Priests daughter be a widow, or diuorced, and haue no childe, and is returned vnto her fathers house, *as in her youth, she shall eat of her fathers

* *Chap. 10. 14.*

thers meat, but there shall no stranger eate thereof.

14 ¶ And if a man eate of the holy thing vnwittingly, then he shall put the fift part thereof vnto it, and shall giue *it* vnto the Priest, with the holy thing.

15 And they shall not profane the holy things of the children of Israel, which they offer vnto the LORD:

16 Or ‖suffer them to beare the iniquitie of trespasse, when they eate their holy things: for I the LORD do sanctifie them.

Or, lade themselues with the iniuity of trespasse in their eating.

17 ¶ And the LORD spake vnto Moses, saying,

18 Speake vnto Aaron and to his sonnes, and vnto all the children of Israel, and say vnto them, Whatsoeuer he be of the house of Israel, or of the strangers in Israel, that will offer his oblation for all his vowes, and for all his free will offerings, which they will offer vnto the LORD for a burnt offering:

19 *Ye shal offer* at your owne wil a male without blemish, of the beeues, of the sheepe, or of the goats.

20 *But* whatsoeuer hath a blemish, that shall ye not offer: for it shall not be acceptable for you.

Deut. 15. 1. & 17. 1.

21 *And whosoeuer offereth a sacrifice of peace offerings vnto the LORD, to accomplish his vow, or a free will offring in beeues or ‖sheepe, it shalbe perfect, to be accepted: there shall be no blemish therein.

Or, goats.

22 Blind, or broken, or maimed, or hauing a wenne, or scuruie, or scabbed, ye shal not offer these vnto the LORD, nor make an offring by fire of them vpon the Altar vnto the LORD.

23 Either a bullocke, or a ‖lambe that hath any thing *superfluous or lacking in his parts, that mayest thou offer for a free will offring: but for a vow it shal not be accepted.

Or, kidde.
Chap. 21. 18.

24 Ye shal not offer vnto the LORD that which is bruised, or crushed, or broken, or cut, neither shall you make any offering thereof in your land.

25 Neither from a strangers hand shall ye offer the bread of your God of any of these; because their corruption is in them, *and* blemishes bee in them: they shall not be accepted for you.

26 ¶ And the LORD spake vnto Moses, saying,

27 When a bullocke, or a sheepe, or a goat is brought forth, then it shall bee

seuen dayes vnder the damme, and from the eight day and thencefoorth, it shal be accepted for an offering made by fire vnto the LORD.

28 And whether it be cowe or ‖ewe, ye shall not kill it, *and her yong, both in one day.

Or, shee goat.
Deu. 22. 6

29 And when yee will offer a sacrifice of thankesgiuing vnto the LORD, offer it at your owne will.

30 On the same day it shall be eaten vp, ye shall leaue *none of it vntill the morrow: I *am* the LORD.

Chap. 7. 15.

31 Therefore shall ye keepe my Commandements, and doe them: I *am* the LORD.

32 Neither shal ye *profane my holy Name, but I will be hallowed among the children of Israel: I *am* the LORD which hallow you,

Leuit. 10. 3.

33 That brought you out of the land of Egypt, to be your God: I *am* the LORD.

CHAP. XXIII.

1 The feasts of the Lord. 3 The Sabbath. 4 The Passeouer. 9 The Sheafe of first fruits. 15 The Feast of Pentecost. 22 Gleanings to be left for the poore. 23 The Feast of Trumpets. 26 The day of atonement. 33 The Feast of Tabernacles.

Nd the LORD spake vnto Moses, saying,

2 Speake vnto the children of Israel, and say vnto them, Concerning the feasts of the LORD, which yee shall proclaime *to be* holy conuocations, *euen* these are my feasts.

3 *Sixe dayes shall worke be done, but the seuenth day is the Sabbath of rest, an holy conuocation; ye shall doe no worke therein: it is the Sabbath of the LORD in all your dwellings.

Exo. 20. 9 deut. 5. 13. luke 13. 14.

4 ¶ These *are* the feastes of the LORD, *euen* holy conuocations, which ye shall proclaime in their seasons.

5 *In the fourteenth day of the first moneth at euen, *is* the LORDS Passeouer.

Exod. 12. 18. num. 28 17.

6 And on the fifteenth day of the same moneth, *is* the feast of vnleauened bread vnto the LORD: seuen dayes ye must eate vnleauened bread.

7 In the first day ye shall haue an holy conuocation: ye shall do no seruile worke therein.

8 But ye shal offer an offring made by fire vnto the LORD seuen dayes:
in

in the seuenth day *is* an holy conuocation, Ye shall doe no seruile worke *therein.*

9 ¶ And the LORD spake vnto
Moses, saying,

10 Speake vnto the children of Israel, and say vnto them, When yee be
come into the land which I giue vnto
you, and shal reape the haruest thereof,
then ye shall bring a ||sheafe of the first
fruits of your haruest vnto the Priest:

|| *Or, hand-*
full: Hebr.
an Omer.

11 And hee shall waue the sheafe before the LORD to be accepted for you:
on the morrow after the Sabbath the
Priest shall waue it.

12 And ye shall offer that day, when
ye waue the sheafe, an hee lambe without blemish of the first yeere, for a burnt
offering vnto the LORD.

13 And the meat offring thereof *shall*
be two tenth deales of fine flowre, mingled with oile, an offering made by fire
vnto the LORD, for a sweet sauour:
and the drinke offering thereof *shalbe* of
wine, the fourth part of an Hin.

14 And ye shall eate neither bread,
nor parched corne, nor greene eares,
vntill the selfe same day that yee haue
brought an offering vnto your God:
It shalbe a statute for euer, throughout
your generations, in all your dwellings.

* Deut. 16.
9.

15 ¶ And *ye shall count vnto you
from the morrow after the Sabbath,
from the day that ye brought the sheafe
of the waue offering; seuen Sabbaths
shalbe complete.

16 Euen vnto the morrow after the
seuenth Sabbath, shall ye number fifty
dayes, and ye shall offer a new meat offering vnto the LORD.

17 Ye shall bring out of your habitations two waue-loaues, of two tenth
deales: they shalbe of fine flowre, they
shall be baken with leauen, *they are* the
first fruits vnto the LORD.

18 And ye shall offer with the bread
seuen lambes without blemish, of the
first yeere, and one yong bullocke and
two rammes: they shall be for a burnt
offering vnto the LORD, with their
meat offring and their drinke offrings,
euen an offering made by fire of sweet
sauour vnto the LORD.

19 Then ye shall sacrifice one kid of
the goates, for a sinne offering, and two
lambes of the first yeere, for a sacrifice of
peace offerings.

20 And the Priest shall waue them
with the bread of the first fruits, for a

waue-offring before the LORD, with
the two lambs: they shalbe holy to the
LORD for the Priests.

21 And ye shal proclaime on the selfe
same day, *that* it may be an holy conuocation vnto you: ye shall doe no seruile
worke *therein: it shall be* a statute for euer
in all your dwellings throughout your
generations.

22 ¶ And *when ye reape the haruest of your land, thou shalt not make
cleane riddance of the corners of the
field, when thou reapest, *neither shalt
thou gather any gleaning of thy haruest: thou shalt leaue them vnto the
poore, and to the stranger: I *am* the
LORD your God.

* Chap. 19.
9.

* Deut. 24.
19.

23 ¶ And the LORD spake vnto
Moses, saying,

24 Speake vnto the children of Israel, saying, In the *seuenth moneth,
in the first day of the moneth shall yee
haue a Sabbath, a memoriall of blowing of trumpets, an holy conuocation.

* Num. 29.
1.

25 Ye shall do no seruile worke *therein;* but ye shall offer an offering made
by fire vnto the LORD.

26 ¶ And the LORD spake vnto
Moses, saying,

27 *Also on the tenth day of this seuenth moneth, there shalbe a day of atonement, it shalbe an holy conuocation
vnto you, & ye shall afflict your soules,
and offer an offering made by fire vnto
the LORD.

* Chap. 16.
30. num.
29. 7.

28 And ye shall doe no worke in that
same day: for it is a day of atonement,
to make an atonement for you, before
the LORD your God.

29 For whatsoeuer soule *it bee* that
shall not bee afflicted in that same day,
hee shall bee cut off from among his
people.

30 And whatsoeuer soule *it bee* that
doeth any worke in that same day, the
same soule will I destroy from among
his people.

31 Ye shall doe no maner of worke:
it shall be a statute for euer throughout
your generations, in all your dwellings.

32 It *shalbe* vnto you a Sabbath of
rest, and yee shall afflict your soules in
the ninth *day* of the moneth at Euen,
from Euen vnto Euen shall ye †cele-
brate your Sabbath.

† *Hebr. reſt.*

33 ¶ And the LORD spake vnto
Moses, saying,

34 Speake vnto the children of
Israel,

Num. 29.
2. Iohn 7.

Israel, saying, * The fifteenth day of this seuenth moneth, *shall be* the feast of Tabernacles *for* seuen dayes vnto the LORD.

35 On the first day *shalbe* an holy conuocation: ye shall doe no seruile worke therein.

36 Seuen dayes ye shall offer an offring made by fire vnto the LORD, on the eight day shall be an holy conuocation vnto you, and ye shall offer an offering made by fire vnto the LORD: It is a † solemne assembly, and ye shall doe no seruile worke therein.

Heb. day
† restraint.

37 These are the feasts of the LORD which ye shall proclaime *to be* holy conuocations, to offer an offering made by fire vnto the LORD, a burnt offering, and a meat offering, a sacrifice, & drinke offerings, euery thing vpon his day;

38 Beside the Sabbaths of the LORD, and beside your gifts, and beside all your vowes, and beside all your free will offerings, which ye giue vnto the LORD.

39 Also in the fifteenth day of the seuenth moneth when yee haue gathered in the fruit of the land, ye shall keepe a feast vnto the LORD seuen dayes. On the first day *shall bee* a Sabbath, and on the eight day *shall bee* a Sabbath.

Heb. fruit.

40 And ye shall take you on the first day the † boughes of goodly trees, branches of Palme trees, and the boughes of thicke trees, and willowes of the brooke, and yee shall reioyce before the LORD your God seuen dayes.

41 And yee shall keepe it a feast vnto the LORD seuen dayes in the yeere: It *shalbe* a Statute for euer in your generations, ye shall celebrate it in the seuenth moneth.

42 Ye shall dwell in boothes seuen dayes: all that are Israelites borne, shall dwell in boothes;

43 That your generations may know that I made the children of Israel to dwell in boothes, when I brought them out of the land of Egypt: I *am* the LORD your God.

44 And Moses declared vnto the children of Israel the feastes of the LORD.

CHAP. XXIIII.

ANd the LORD spake vnto Moses, saying,

2 Command the children of Israel, that they bring vnto thee pure oyle Oliue, beaten, for the light, † to cause the lampes to burne continually.

† Hebr. to
cause to as-
cend.

3 Without the Vaile of the Testimonie, in the Tabernacle of the Congregation, shal Aaron order it from the euening vnto the morning, before the LORD continually: It *shall be* a Statute for euer in your generations.

4 He shall order the lampes vpon * the pure Candlesticke before the LORD continually.

* Exo. 31. 8

5 ¶ And thou shalt take fine flowre, and bake twelue * cakes thereof: two tenth deales shall be in one cake.

* Exod. 25.
30.

6 And thou shalt set them in two rowes, sixe on a row vpon the pure Table, before the LORD.

7 And thou shalt put pure frankincense vpon ech row, that it may bee on the bread for a memoriall, *euen* an offering made by fire vnto the LORD.

8 Euery Sabbath he shall set it in order before the LORD continually, *being taken* from the children of Israel by an euerlasting couenant.

9 And * it shall be Aarons and his sonnes, and they shall eate it in the holy place: for it *is* most holy vnto him, of the offerings of the LORD made by fire, by a perpetuall statute.

* Exod. 29.
33. chap. 8.
31. mat. 12.
1, 5.

10 ¶ And the sonne of an Israelitish woman, whose father was an Egyptian, went out among the children of Israel: and this sonne of the Israelitish woman, and a man of Israel stroue together in the campe.

11 And the Israelitish womans sonne blasphemed the name of the LORD, and cursed, and they brought him vnto Moses: and his mothers name was Shelomith, the daughter of Dibri, of the tribe of Dan.

12 And they * put him in ward, † that the minde of the LORD might bee shewed them.

* Numb. 15
34.
† Heb. to ex-
pound vnto
them accor-
ding to the
mouth of the
LORD.

13 ¶ And the LORD spake vnto Moses, saying,

14 Bring forth him that hath cursed, without the Campe, and let all that heard him, * lay their hands vpon his head, and let all the Congregation stone him.

* Deut. 13.
9. and 17. 7

15 And thou shalt speake vnto the children of Israel, saying, Whosoeuer curseth

curseth his God, shall beare his sinne.

16 And hee that blasphemeth the Name of the LORD, he shall surely be put to death, and all the Congregation shall certainly stone him: Aswell the stranger, as he that is borne in the land, when he blasphemeth the Name of the LORD, shall be put to death.

17 ¶ *And he that †killeth any man, shall surely be put to death.

18 And he that killeth a beast, shall make it good; †beast for beast.

19 And if a man cause a blemish in his neighbour; as *he hath done, so shal it be done to him:

20 Breach, for breach, eye for eye, tooth for tooth: as he hath caused a blemish in a man, so shall it be done to him againe.

21 And hee that killeth a beast, hee shall restore it: and hee that killeth a man, he shall be put to death.

22 Ye shall haue *one maner of law, aswell for the stranger, as for one of your owne countrey : for I *am* the LORD your God.

23 ¶ And Moses spake to the children of Israel, that they should bring foorth him that had cursed, out of the Campe, and stone him with stones: and the children of Israel did as the LORD commanded Moses.

CHAP. XXV.

1 The Sabbath of the seuenth yeere. 8 The Iubile in the fiftieth yeere. 14 Of oppression. 18 A blessing of obedience. 23 The redemption of land, 29 Of houses. 35 Compassion of the poore. 39 The vsage of bondmen. 47 The redemption of seruants.

ANd the LORD spake vnto Moses in Mount Sinai, saying,

2 Speake vnto the children of Israel, and say vnto them : When yee come into the land which I giue you, then shall the land †keepe *a Sabbath vnto the LORD.

3 Sixe yeeres thou shalt sow thy field, and sixe yeeres thou shalt prune thy Vineyard, and gather in the fruit thereof.

4 But in the seuenth yeere shalbe a Sabbath of rest vnto the land, a Sabbath for the LORD : thou shalt neither sow thy field, nor prune thy Vineyard.

5 That which groweth of it owne

accord of thy haruest, thou shalt not reape, neither gather the grapes †of thy Vine vndressed: for it is a yeere of rest vnto the land.

6 And the Sabbath of the land shall be meat for you; for thee, and for thy seruant, and for thy mayd, and for thy hired seruant, and for the stranger that soiourneth with thee,

7 And for thy cattel, and for the beast that are in thy land, shal all the encrease thereof be meat.

8 ¶ And thou shalt number seuen Sabbaths of yeeres vnto thee, seuen times seuen yeeres, and the space of the seuen Sabbaths of yeeres, shall be vnto thee fourtie and nine yeeres.

9 Then shalt thou cause the trumpet †of the Iubile to sound, on the tenth day of the seuenth moneth; in the day of atonement shall ye make the trumpet sound throughout all your land.

10 And ye shall hallow the fiftieth yeere, and proclaime libertie throughout all the land, vnto al the inhabitants thereof: It shalbe a Iubile vnto you, and ye shall returne euery man vnto his possession, and ye shall returne euery man vnto his family.

11 A Iubile shall that fiftieth yeere be vnto you : Ye shall not sow, neither reape that which groweth of it selfe in it, nor gather *the grapes* in it of thy Vine vndressed.

12 For it is the Iubile, it shall be holy vnto you : ye shall eate the encrease thereof out of the field.

13 In the yeere of this Iubile yee shall returne euery man vnto his possession.

14 And if thou sell ought vnto thy neighbour, or buyest ought of thy neighbours hand, ye shall not oppresse one another.

15 According to the number of yeres after the Iubile, thou shalt buy of thy neighbour, and according vnto the number of yeeres of the fruits, he shall sell vnto thee.

16 According to the multitude of yeeres, thou shalt encrease the price thereof, and according to the fewnesse of yeeres, thou shalt diminish the price of it: for *accoridmg* to the number *of the yeeres* of the fruites doeth hee sell vnto thee.

17 Yee shall not therefore oppresse one another; but thou shalt feare thy God: For I *am* the LORD your God.

18 ¶ Where-

---

*Exod. 21. 12. deu. 19. 21.
† *Hebr smiteth the life of a man.*
† *Hebr. life for life.*
* Exod. 21. 24. deu. 19. 21. matth. 5. 38.

* Exod. 12. 49.

* Exod. 23. 10.
† *Hebr. rest.*

† *Hebr. of thy separations.*

† *Hebr. lowde of sound.*

18 ¶ Wherefore ye shall do my Statutes, and keepe my Iudgements, and doe them, and ye shall dwell in the land in safetie.

19 And the land shall yeeld her fruit, and ye shal eat your fill, and dwell therin in safetie.

20 And if ye shall say, What shall we eate the seuenth yeere ? Behold, we shall not sow, nor gather in our increase :

21 Then I will command my blessing vpon you in the sixt yeere, and it shall bring forth fruit for three yeeres.

22 And ye shall sow the eight yeere, and eat yet of old fruit, vntill the ninth yeere : vntill her fruits come in, ye shall eate of the old store.

23 ¶ The land shall not be sold ||for euer : for the land is mine, for ye were strangers and soiourners with me.

24 And in all the land of your possession, ye shall grant a redemption for the land.

25 ¶ If thy brother be waxen poore, and hath sold away some of his possession, and if any of his kinne come to redeeme it, then shall hee redeeme that which his brother sold.

26 And if the man haue none to redeeme it, and †himselfe bee able to redeeme it :

27 Then let him count the yeeres of the sale therof, and restore the ouerplus vnto the man, to whom he sold it, that he may returne vnto his possession.

28 But if he be not able to restore it to him, then that which is sold, shall remaine in the hand of him that hath bought it, vntill the yeere of Iubile : and in the Iubile it shall goe out, and he shall returne vnto his possession.

29 And if a man sell a dwelling house in a walled citie, then he may redeeme it within a whole yeere after it is solde : within a full yeere may he redeeme it.

30 And if it be not redeemed within the space of a full yeere, then the house that is in the walled citie, shall be stablished for euer to him that bought it, throughout his generations : it shall not goe out in the Iubile.

31 But the houses of the villages which haue no walles round about them, shall bee counted as the fields of the countrey : †they may ee redeemed, and they shall goe out in the Iubile.

32 Notwithstanding, the cities of the Leuites, and the houses of the cities

of their possession, may the Leuites redeeme at any time.

33 And if ‖ a man purchase of the Leuites, then the house that was sold, and the citie of his possession shall goe out in the yeere of Iubile : for the houses of the cities of the Leuites are their possession among the children of Israel.

34 But the field of the suburbs of their cities may not be sold, for it is their perpetuall possession.

35 ¶ And if thy brother bee waxen poore, and †fallen in decay with thee, then thou shalt†relieue him, yea though he be a stranger, or a soiourner, that hee may liue with thee.

36 *Take thou no vsurie of him, or increase : but feare thy God, that thy brother may liue with thee.

37 Thou shalt not giue him thy money vpon vsurie, nor lend him thy victuals for increase.

38 I am the LORD your God, which brought you foorth out of the land of Egypt, to giue you the land of Canaan, and to be your God.

39 ¶ And *if thy brother that dwelleth by thee be waxen poore, and be sold vnto thee, thou shalt not †compell him to serue as a bond seruant.

40 But as an hired seruant, and as a soiourner he shall be with thee, and shall serue thee vnto the yere of Iubile.

41 And then shall hee depart from thee, both he and his children with him, and shall returne vnto his owne familie, and vnto the possession of his fathers shall he returne.

42 For they are my seruants, which I brought forth out of the land of Egypt : they shall not be sold †as bond men.

43 *Thou shalt not rule ouer him with rigour, but shalt feare thy God.

44 Both thy bondmen, and thy bondmaids, which thou shalt haue, shall be of the Heathen, that are round about you : of them shall ye buy bondmen and bondmaids.

45 Moreouer, of the children of the strangers that do soiourne among you, of them shall ye buy, and of their families that are with you, which they begat in your land : and they shalbe your possession.

46 And ye shall take them as an inheritance for your children after you, to inherite them for a possession, †they shal bee

‖ Or, one of the Leuites redeeme them.

† Hebr. his hand faileth
† Hebr. strengthen.

* Exod. 22.
25. deut. 23
19. pro. 28. 8
ezek. 18. 8
and 22. 12.

* Exo. 21. 2.
deut. 15. 12
ierem. 34.
14.
† Heb. serue thy selfe with him with the seruice, &c.

† Hebr. with the sale of a bondman.
* Ephe. 6. 9.
coloss. 4. 1.

† Hebr. ye. shall serue your selues with them.

Or, to bee ite cut off. ebr. for tting off.

Hebr. his and hath tained, ad found fficiencie.

Hebr. reemption elongeth nto it.

bee your bondmen for euer : but ouer your brethren the children of Israel, ye shall not rule one ouer another with rigour.

47 ¶ And if a soiourner or stranger † waxe rich by thee, and thy brother that dwelleth by him waxe poore, and sell himselfe vnto the stranger or soiourner by thee, or to the stocke of the strangers family :

48 After that he is sold, hee may be redeemed againe : one of his brethren may redeeme him.

49 Either his vncle, or his vncles sonne may redeeme him, or any that is nigh of kinne vnto him, of his family, may redeeme him : or if he be able, hee may redeeme himselfe.

50 And he shall reckon with him that bought him, from the yeere that he was sold to him, vnto the yeere of Iubile, and the price of his sale shalbe according vnto the number of yeeres, according to the time of an hired seruant shall it be with him.

51 If there be yet many yeeres behinde, according vnto them hee shall giue againe the price of his redemption, out of the money that hee was bought for.

52 And if there remaine but few yeeres vnto the yeere of Iubile, then he shall count with him, *and* according vnto his yeeres shall he giue him againe the price of his redemption.

53 And as a yeerely hired seruant shall he be with him : and *the other* shall not rule with rigour ouer him in thy sight.

54 And if hee be not redeemed ‖in these *yeeres*, then he shall goe out in the yeere of Iubile, *both* he, and his children with him.

55 For vnto me the children of Israel are seruants, they are my seruants whom I brought forth out of the land of Egypt : I *am* the Lord your God.

CHAP. XXVI.

1 Of Idolatry. 2 Religiousnes. 3 A blessing to them that keepe the Commandements. 14 A curse to those that breake them. 40 God promiseth to remember them that repent.

Ee shall make you * no Idoles nor grauen Image, neither reare you vp a ‖standing image, neither shall yee set vp any Image of stone in your land, to bow downe vnto it : For I *am* the Lord your God.

2 * Ye shal keepe my Sabbaths, and reuerence my Sanctuary : I *am* the Lord.

3 ¶ *If ye walke in my Statutes, and keepe my Commandements, and doe them ;

4 Then I will giue you raine in due season, and the land shall yeeld her increase, and the trees of the field shall yeeld their fruit.

5 And your threshing shall reach vnto the vintage, and the vintage shall reach vnto the sowing time : and yee shal eat your bread to the full, and *dwel in your land safely.

6 And I wil giue peace in the land, and ye shall lye downe, and none shall make you afraid : and I will †rid euill beasts out of the land, *neither shall the sword goe through your land.

7 And ye shall chase your enemies, and they shall fall before you by the sword.

8 And *fiue of you shal chase an hundred, and an hundred of you shall put ten thousand to flight : and your enemies shall fall before you by the sword.

9 For I wil haue respect vnto you, and make you fruitfull, and multiply you, & establish my couenant with you.

10 And yee shall eate old store, and bring forth the old, because of the new.

11 *And I will set my Tabernacle amongst you : and my soule shall not abhorre you.

12 *And I will walke among you, and will be your God, and ye shall be my people.

13 I am the Lord your God, which brought you forth out of the land of Egypt, that yee should not be their bondmen, & I haue broken the bandes of your yoke, and made you go vpright.

14 ¶ *But if ye will not hearken vnto me, and will not doe all these Commandements :

15 And if ye shall despise my Statutes, or if your soule abhorre my Iudgements, so that ye wil not doe all my Commaundements, *but* that yee breake my Couenant :

16 I also will doe this vnto you, I will euen appoint †ouer you terrour, consumption, and the burning ague, that shall consume the eyes, and cause sorrow of heart : and ye shall sow your seede

Marginal notes (left column)
† *Hebr. his hand obteine, &c.*

‖ *Or, by these meanes.*

* Exod. 20. 4. deut. 5. 8. and 16. 22. psal. 97. 7.

‖ *Or, pillar.*

Marginal notes (right column)
‖ *Or, figure stone. Heb a stone of picture.*

* Chap. 19. 30.

* Deut. 28. 1.

* Iob 11. 19.

† Heb. cau to cease.
* Iob 11. 19.

* Iosh. 23. 10.

* Ezech. 26.

* 2 Cor. 6. 16.

* Deut. 28. 15 lament 2. 17. mal 2. 2.

† Hebr. vp you.

seede in vaine, for your enemies shall eate it.

17 And I will set my face against you, and ye shall be slaine before your enemies: they that hate you shall reigne ouer you, and *ye shall flee when none pursueth you.

18 And if ye will not yet for all this hearken vnto me, then I will punish you seuen times more for your sinnes.

19 And I will breake the pride of your power, and I will make your heauen as yron, and your earth as brasse:

20 And your strength shall be spent in vaine: for your land shall not yeeld her increase, neither shall the trees of the land yeeld their fruits.

21 ¶ And if ye walke ||contrary vnto me, and will not hearken vnto mee, I will bring seuen times moe plagues vpon you, according to your sinnes.

22 I will also send wilde beasts among you, which shall rob you of your children, and destroy your cattell, and make you few in number, and your *high* wayes shall be desolate.

23 And if ye will not be reformed by these things, but will walke contrary vnto me:

24 * Then will I also walke contrary vnto you, and will punish you yet seuen times for your sinnes.

25 And I will bring a sword vpon you, that shall auenge the quarrell of *my* couenant: and when yee are gathered together within your cities, I wil send the pestilence among you, and ye shalbe deliuered into the hand of the enemie.

26 And when I haue broken the staffe of your bread, ten women shall bake your bread in one ouen, and they shall deliuer you your bread againe by weight: and ye shall eate, and not bee satisfied.

27 And if ye wil not for all this hearken vnto me, but walke contrary vnto mee,

28 Then I wil walke contrary vnto you also in fury, and I, euen I will chastise you seuen times for your sinnes.

29 * And ye shal eate the flesh of your sonnes, and the flesh of your daughters shall ye eate.

30 And I will destroy your high places, and * cut downe your images, and cast your carkeises vpon the carkeises of your idoles, and my soule shall abhorre you.

31 And I wil make your cities waste, and bring your sanctuaries vnto desolation, and I will not smell the sauour of your sweet odours.

32 And I will bring the land into desolation: and your enemies which dwel therein, shall be astonished at it.

33 And I will scatter you among the heathen, and will draw out a sword after you: and your land shall be desolate, and your cities waste.

34 Then shall the lande enioy her Sabbaths, as long as it lieth desolate, and yee be in your enemies land, euen then shall the land rest, and enioy her Sabbaths.

35 As long as it lieth desolate, it shall rest: because it did not rest in your Sabbaths, when ye dwelt vpon it.

36 And vpon them that are left aliue of you, I will send a faintnesse into their hearts in the lands of their enemies, and the sound of a †shaken leafe shall chase them, and they shall flee, as fleeing from a sword: and they shall fall, when none pursueth.

37 And they shall fall one vpon another, as it were before a sword, when none pursueth: and yee shall haue no power to stand before your enemies.

38 And yee shall perish among the Heathen, and the land of your enemies shall eate you vp.

39 And they that are left of you shall pine away in their iniquitie in your enemies lands, and also in the iniquities of their fathers shall they pine away with them.

40 If they shall confesse the iniquitie of their fathers, with their trespasse which they trespassed against me, and that also they haue walked contrary vnto me:

41 And *that* I also haue walked contrary vnto them, and haue brought them into the land of their enemies: if then their vncircumcised hearts bee humbled, and they then accept of the punishment of their iniquitie:

42 Then will I remember my couenant with Iacob, and also my couenant with Isaac, and also my couenant with Abraham will I remember, and I will remember the land.

43 The land also shalbe left of them, and shall enioy her Sabbaths, while she lieth desolate without them: and they shall accept of the punishment of their iniquitie: because, euen because they

Marginal notes:

ro. 28. 1.

*, at all entures h me, & erse 24.

Sam. 27. psal. 26.

eut. 28.

Chro. 7.

† *Heb. driuen.*

they despised my Iudgements, and because their soule abhorred my Statutes

44 And yet for all that, when they be in the land of their enemies, *I will not cast them away, neither will I abhorre them, to destroy them vtterly, and to breake my couenant with them: for I am the LORD their God.

45 But I wil for their sakes remember the couenant of their Ancestours, whom I brought forth out of the land of Egypt, in the sight of the Heathen, that I might be their God: I am the LORD.

46 These are the Statutes, and Iudgements, and Lawes which the LORD made betweene him and the children of Israel, in mount Sinai, by the hand of Moses.

* Deut. 4.
31. rom.
11. 26.

CHAP XXVII.

1 He that maketh a singular vow must bee the Lords. 2 The estimation of the person. 9 Of a beast giuen by vow. 14 Of a house. 16 Of a field and the redemption thereof. 28 No deuoted thing may be redeemed. 32 The tithe may not be changed.

Nd the LORD spake vnto Moses, saying,

2 Speake vnto the children of Israel, and say vnto them, When a man shal make a singular vow, the persons shall be for the LORD, by thy estimation.

3 And thy estimation shall be: Of the male from twentie yeeres old, euen vnto sixtie yeeres old: euen thy estimation shall be fiftie shekels of siluer, after the shekel of the Sanctuary.

4 And if it be a female, then thy estimation shall be thirtie shekels.

5 And if it be from fiue yeeres olde, euen vnto twentie yeeres old, then thy estimation shall be of the male twentie shekels, and for the female ten shekels.

6 And if it be from a moneth old, euen vnto fiue yeeres old, then thy estimation shall be of the male, fiue shekels of siluer, and for the female, thy estimation shall be three shekels of siluer.

7 And if it be from sixtie yeeres old, and aboue, if it be a male, then thy estimation shall be fifteene shekels, and for the female ten shekels.

8 But if he bee poorer then thy estimation, then he shall present himselfe before the Priest, and the Priest shall value him: according to his abilitie that

vowed, shall the Priest value him.

9 And if it be a beast whereof men bring an offering vnto the LORD, all that any man giueth of such vnto the LORD, shall be holy.

10 He shall not alter it, nor change it, a good for a bad, or a bad for a good: And if hee shall at all change beast for beast, then it, and the exchange thereof shall be holy.

11 And if it be any vncleane beast, of which they doe not offer a sacrifice vnto the LORD, then he shall present the beast before the Priest:

12 And the Priest shall value it, whether it be good or bad: as thou †valuest it who art the Priest: so shall it be.

13 But if hee will at all redeeme it, then he shall adde a fift part thereof vnto thy estimation.

14 ¶ And when a man shall sanctifie his house to be holy vnto the LORD, then the Priest shal estimate it, whether it be good or bad: as the Priest shall estimate it, so shall it stand.

15 And if he that sanctified it, will redeeme his house, then he shall adde the fift part of the money of thy estimation vnto it, and it shall be his.

16 And if a man shall sanctifie vnto the LORD some part of a field of his possession, then thy estimation shall be according to the seed thereof: ‖An Homer of barley seed shall be valued at fiftie shekels of siluer.

17 If hee sanctifie his field from the yeere of Iubile, according to thy estimation it shall stand.

18 But if hee sanctifie his field after the Iubile, then the Priest shall reckon vnto him the money, according to the yeeres that remaine, euen vnto the yeere of the Iubile, and it shall be abated from thy estimation.

19 And if he that sanctified the field, will in any wise redeeme it, then he shal adde the fift part of the money of thy estimation vnto it, and it shall be assured to him.

20 And if hee will not redeeme the field, or if he haue sold the field to another man, it shall not be redeemed any more.

21 But the field, when it goeth out in the Iubile, shall be holy vnto the LORD, as a field deuoted: the possession thereof shalbe the Priests.

22 And if a man sanctifie vnto the LORD a field which he hath bought, which

† Hebr. according
thy estim
on, O Pri
&c.

‖ Or, the
land of a
Homer, &

which is not of the fieldes of his possession :

23 Then the Priest shall reckon vnto him the worth of thy estimation, euen vnto the yeere of the Iubile, and hee shall giue thine estimation in that day, as a holy thing vnto the LORD.

24 In the yeere of the Iubile, the field shall returne vnto him of whom it was bought, euen to him to whom the possession of the land did belong.

25 And all thy estimations shall be according to the shekel of the Sanctuarie : *twentie Gerahs shall bee the shekel.

26 ¶ Onely the †firstling of the beasts which should be the LORDS firstling, no man shall sanctifie it, whether it bee oxe, or sheepe : It *is the LORDS.

27 And if *it be* of an vncleane beast, then hee shall redeeme it according to thine estimation, and shall adde a fifth part of it thereto : Or if it be not redeemed, then it shalbe sold according to thy estimation.

28 * Notwithstanding, no deuoted thing that a man shall deuote vnto the LORD, of all that he hath, both of man and beast, and of the field of his possession, shall be sold or redeemed : euery deuoted thing is most holy vnto the LORD.

29 None deuoted, which shalbe deuoted of men, shall be redeemed : but shall surely be put to death.

30 And all the tithe of the land, *whether* of the seed of the land, *or* of the fruit of the tree, is the LORDS : *it is* holy vnto the LORD.

31 And if a man will at all redeeme ought of his tithes, he shall adde thereto the fifth part thereof.

32 And concerning the tithe of the herde, or of the flocke, *euen* of whatsoeuer passeth vnder the rod, the tenth shalbe holy vnto the LORD.

33 He shall not search whether it be good or bad, neither shall he change it : and if he change it at all, then both it, and the change thereof, shall be holy ; it shall not be redeemed.

34 These *are* the Commandements which the LORD commanded Moses, for the children of Israel in mount Sinai.

Exod. 30.
, num. 3.
, ezech.
, 12.
*Hebr. first
rne, &c.*

Iosh. 6.

¶ THE FOVRTH BOOKE
of Moses, called Numbers.

CHAP. I.

1 God commaundeth Moses to number the people. 5 The Princes of the Tribes. 17 The number of euery Tribe. 47 The Leuites are exempted for the Seruice of the Lord.

And the LORD spake vnto Moses in the wildernesse of Sinai, in the Tabernacle of the Congregation, on the first *day* of the second moneth, in the second yeere, after they were come out of the land of Egypt, saying,

2 * Take yee the summe of all the Congregation of the children of Israel, after their families, by the house of their fathers, with the number of *their* names, euery male by their polle :

3 From twentie yeeres old and vpward, all that are able to goe foorth to warre in Israel : thou and Aaron shall number them by their armies.

4 And with you there shalbe a man of euery Tribe : euery one head of the house of his fathers.

5 ¶ And these *are* the names of the men that shall stand with you : of *the tribe of* Reuben, Elizur the sonne of Shedeur.

6 Of Simeon : Shelumiel the son of Zurishaddai.

7 Of Iudah : Nahshon, the sonne of Amminadab.

8 Of Issachar : Nethaneel, the sonne of Zuar.

Exod. 30.

9 Of

9 Of Zebulun : Eliab the sonne of Helon.

10 Of the children of Ioseph : of Ephraim, Elishama the sonne of Ammihud : of Manasseh, Gamaliel the sonne of Pedahzur.

11 Of Beniamin : Abidan, the sonne of Gideoni.

12 Of Dan : Ahiezer, the sonne of Ammishaddai.

13 Of Asher : Pagiel the sonne of Ocran.

14 Of Gad : Eliasaph, the sonne of Deuel.

15 Of Naphtali : Ahira the sonne of Enan.

16 These *were* the renowned of the Congregation, Princes of the tribes of their fathers, heads of thousands in Israel.

17 ¶ And Moses and Aaron tooke these men, which are expressed by *their* names.

18 And they assembled all the Congregation together on the first day of the second moneth, and they declared their pedegrees after their families, by the house of their fathers, according to the number of the names, from twenty yeres old and vpward by their polle.

19 As the LORD commaunded Moses, so he numbred them in the wildernesse of Sinai.

20 And the children of Reuben Israels eldest sonne, by their generations after their families, by the house of their fathers, according to the number of the names, by their polle, euery male from twenty yeeres old and vpward, all that were able to go forth to warre :

21 Those that were numbred of them, *euen* of the tribe of Reuben, *were* fourty and sixe thousand and fiue hundred.

22 ¶ Of the children of Simeon by their generations, after their families, by the house of their fathers, those that were numbred of them, according to the number of the names, by their polles, euery male from twenty yeeres old and vpward, all that were able to goe foorth to warre :

23 Those that *were* numbred of them, *euen* of the tribe of Simeon, *were* fiftie and nine thousand, and three hundred.

24 ¶ Of the children of Gad by their generations, after their families by the house of their fathers, according to the number of the names, from twenty

yeeres old and vpward, all that were able to goe foorth to warre :

25 Those that were numbred of them, *euen* of the tribe of Gad, *were* fourty and fiue thousand, sixe hundred and fiftie.

26 ¶ Of the children of Iudah by their generations, after their families by the house of their fathers, according to the number of the names, from twenty yeeres old and vpward, all that were able to goe foorth to warre :

27 Those that were numbred of them, *euen* of the tribe of Iudah, *were* threescore and fourteene thousand, and sixe hundred.

28 ¶ Of the children of Issachar, by their generations, after their families by the house of their fathers, according to the number of the names, from twenty yeres old and vpward, all that were able to goe foorth to warre :

29 Those that were numbred of them, *euen* of the tribe of Issachar, *were* fiftie and foure thousand, and foure hundred.

30 ¶ Of the children of Zebulun, by their generations, after their families, by the house of their fathers, according to the number of the names, from twenty yeres old and vpward, all that were able to goe foorth to warre :

31 Those that wece numbred of them, *euen* of the tribe of Zebulun, *were* fiftie and seuen thousand and foure hundred.

32 ¶ Of the children of Ioseph : *namely* of the children of Ephraim, by their generations, after their families, by the house of their fathers, according to the number of the names, from twenty yeres old and vpward, all that were able to goe foorth to warre :

33 Those that were numbred of them, *euen* of the tribe of Ephraim, *were* fourty thousand and fiue hundred.

34 ¶ Of the children of Manasseh by their generations, after their families, by the house of their fathers according to the number of the names, from twenty yeeres old and vpward, all that were able to go forth to warre :

35 Those that were numbred of them, *euen* of the tribe of Manasseh, *were* thirty and two thousand, and two hundred.

36 ¶ Of the children of Beniamin, by their generations, after their families, by the house of their fathers, according

ding to the number of the names from twenty yeeres old and vpward, all that were able to goe foorth to warre:

37 Those that were numbred of them, *euen* of the tribe of Beniamin, *were* thirtie and fiue thousand, and foure hundred.

38 ¶ Of the children of Dan, by their generations, after their families, by the house of their fathers, according to the number of the names, from twentie yeeres old and vpward, all that were able to goe forth to warre:

39 Those that were numbred of them, *euen* of the tribe of Dan, were threescore and two thousand, and seuen hundred.

40 ¶ Of the children of Asher, by their generations, after their families, by the house of their fathers, according to the number of the names, from twentie yeres old and vpward, all that were able to goe forth to warre:

41 Those that were numbred of them, *euen* of the tribe of Asher, *were* fourtie and one thousand, and fiue hundred.

42 ¶ Of the children of Naphtali, throughout their generations, after their families by the house of their fathers, according to the number of the names, from twentie yeeres olde and vpward, all that were able to goe forth to warre:

43 Those that were numbred of them, *euen* of the tribe of Naphtali, *were* fiftie and three thousand, and foure hundred.

44 These *are* those that were numbred, which Moses and Aaron numbred, and the Princes of Israel, being twelue men: each one was for the house of his fathers.

45 So were all those that were numbred of the children of Israel, by the house of their fathers, from twenty yeeres old and vpward, all that were able to goe forth to warre in Israel:

46 Euen all they, that were numbred, were six hundred thousand, and three thousand, and fiue hundred and fiftie.

47 ¶ But the Leuites after the tribe of their fathers, were not numbred among them.

48 For the LORD had spoken vnto Moses, saying,

49 Onely thou shalt not number the tribe of Leui, neither take the summe of them among the children of Israel.

50 But thou shalt appoint the Leuites ouer the Tabernacle of Testimonie, and ouer all the vessels thereof, and ouer all things that belong to it: they shall beare the Tabernacle, and all the vessels thereof, and they shall minister vnto it, and shall encampe round about the Tabernacle.

51 And when the Tabernacle setteth forward, the Leuites shall take it downe: and when the Tabernacle is to be pitched, the Leuites shall set it vp: and the stranger that commeth nigh, shall be put to death.

52 And the children of Israel shall pitch their tents euery man by his own campe, and euery man by his owne standerd, throughout their hostes.

53 But the Leuites shall pitch round about the Tabernacle of Testimonie, that there be no wrath vpon the Congregation of the children of Israel: and the Leuites shall keepe the charge of the Tabernacle of Testimonie.

54 And the children of Israel did according to all that the LORD commanded Moses, so did they.

CHAP. II.

1 The order of the Tribes in their tents.

A Nd the LORD spake vnto Moses, and vnto Aaron, saying,

2 Euery man of the children of Israel shall pitch by his owne standerd, with the ensigne of their fathers house: †farre off about the Tabernacle of the Congregation shall they pitch.   † *Heb. ouer against.*

3 And on the East side toward the rising of the Sunne, shall they of the standerd of the campe of Iudah pitch, throughout their armies: and Nahshon the sonne of Amminadab, *shall bee* captaine of the children of Iudah.

4 And his hoste, and those that were numbred of them, *were* threescore and fourteene thousand, and sixe hundred.

5 And those that doe pitch next vnto him, *shall be* the tribe of Issachar: and Nethaneel the sonne of Zuar, *shall bee* captaine of the children of Issachar.

6 And his hoste, and those that were numbred thereof, *were* fiftie and foure thousand, and foure hundred.

7 *Then* the tribe of Zebulun : and
Eliab

Eliab the sonne of Helon, *shalbe* captaine of the children of Zebulun.

8 And his hoste and those that were numbred thereof, *were* fiftie and seuen thousand, and foure hundred.

9 All that were numbred in the Campe of Iudah, were an hundred thousand, and fourescore thousand, and sixe thousand, and foure hundred, throughout their armies : these shall first set foorth.

10 ¶ On the Southside *shall be* the standerd of the Campe of Reuben, according to their armies : and the captaine of the children of Reuben shall be Elizur the sonne of Shedeur.

11 And his hoste, and those that were numbred thereof, *were* fourtie and sixe thousand, and fiue hundred.

12 And those which pitch by him, shall bee the tribe of Simeon, and the captaine of the children of Simeon *shall be* Shelumiel the sonne of Zurishaddai.

13 And his hoste, and those that were numbred of them, *were* fiftie and nine thousand, and three hundred.

14 Then the tribe of Gad : and the captaine of the sonnes of Gad *shall be* Eliasaph the sonne of Reuel.

15 And his hoste, and those that were numbred of them, *were* fourtie and fiue thousand, and sixe hundred and fiftie.

16 All that were numbred in the Campe of Reuben *were* an hundred thousand, and fiftie and one thousand, and foure hundred and fiftie throughout their armies : and they shall set foorth in the second ranke.

17 ¶ Then the Tabernacle of the Congregation shall set forward with the Campe of the Leuites, in the midst of the Campe: as they encampe, so shall they set forward, euery man in his place by their standerds.

18 ¶ On the West side shall bee the standerd of the Campe of Ephraim, according to their armies : and the captaine of the sonnes of Ephraim, *shall be* Elishama the sonne of Ammihud.

19 And his hoste, and those that were numbred of them, *were* fourtie thousand and fiue hundred.

20 And by him *shall be* the tribe of Manasseh : and the captaine of the children of Manasseh, shalbe Gamaliel the sonne of Pedahzur.

21 And his hoste, and those that

were numbred of them, *were* thirtie and two thousand, and two hundred.

22 Then the tribe of Beniamin : and the captaine of the sonnes of Beniamin, *shall bee* Abidan the sonne of Gideoni.

23 And his hoste, and those that were numbred of them, *were* thirtie and fiue thousand, and foure hundred.

24 All that were numbred of the Campe of Ephraim, *were* an hundred thousand, and eight thousand, and an hundred, throughout their armies : and they shall goe forward in the third ranke.

25 ¶ The standerd of the Campe of Dan *shall be* on the Northside by their armies : and the captaine of the children of Dan *shalbe* Ahiezer, the sonne of Ammishaddai.

26 And his hoste, and those that were numbred of them, *were* threescore and two thousand, and seuen hundred.

27 And those that encampe by him, shalbe the tribe of Asher : and the captaine of the children of Asher, *shalbe* Pagiel the sonne of Ocran.

28 And his hoste, and those that were numbred of them, *were* fourtie and one thousand, and fiue hundred.

29 ¶ Then the tribe of Naphtali : and the captaine of the children of Naphtali, *shall bee* Ahira the sonne of Enan.

30 And his hoste, and those that were numbred of them, *were* fiftie and three thousand, and foure hundred.

31 All they that were numbred in the Campe of Dan, *were* an hundred thousand, and fifty and seuen thousand, and sixe hundred : they shall goe hindmost with their standerds.

32 ¶ These *are* those which were numbred of the children of Israel, by the house of their fathers; all those that were numbred of the Campes throughout their hostes, *were* sixe hundred thousand, and three thousand, and fiue hundred and fiftie.

33 But the Leuites were not numbred among the children of Israel, as the LORD commanded Moses.

34 And the children of Israel did according to all that the LORD commanded Moses: so they pitched by their standerds, and so they set forward euery one after their families, according to the house of their fathers.

CHAP.

CHAP. III.

1 The sonnes of Aaron. 5 The Leuites are giuen to the Priests for the seruice of the Tabernacle, 11 in stead of the first borne. 14 The Leuites are numbred by their families. 21 The families, number and charge of the Gershonites, 27 Of the Kohathites, 33 Of the Merarites. 38 The place & charge of Moses & Aaron. 40 The first borne are freed by the Leuites. 44 The ouerplus are redeemed.

 Hese also are the generations of Aaron and Moses, in the day that the LORD spake with Moses in Mount Sinai.

Exod. 6.

2 And these are the names of the sonnes of Aaron : Nadab the * first borne, and Abihu, Eleazar and Ithamar.

3 These are the names of the sonnes of Aaron the Priests, which were anointed, † whom he consecrated to minister in the Priests office.

eb. whose nd he filled

Leuit. 10.
chap. 26.
1. chro.
2.

4 * And Nadab and Abihu died before the LORD, when they offered strange fire before the LORD in the wildernesse of Sinai, and they had no children : and Eleazar and Ithamar ministred in the Priests office in the sight of Aaron their father.

5 ¶ And the LORD spake vnto Moses, saying,

6 Bring the tribe of Leui neere, and present them before Aaron the Priest, that they may minister vnto him.

7 And they shall keepe his charge, and the charge of the whole Congregation before the Tabernacle of the Congregation, to doe the seruice of the Tabernacle.

8 And they shall keepe all the instruments of the Tabernacle of the Congregation, and the charge of the children of Israel, to doe the seruice of the Tabernacle.

9 And thou shalt giue the Leuites vnto Aaron and to his sonnes : they are wholly giuen vnto him out of the children of Israel.

10 And thou shalt appoint Aaron and his sonnes, and they shall waite on their priests office : and the stranger that commeth nigh , shall bee put to death.

11 And the LORD spake vnto Moses, saying,

12 And I, behold, I haue taken the Leuites from among the children of Israel, in stead of all the first borne that openeth the matrice among the children of Israel : therefore the Leuites shall be mine,

13 Because all the first borne are mine : * for on the day that I smote all the first borne in the land of Egypt, I halowed vnto mee all the first borne in Israel, both man, and beast, mine they shall be : I am the LORD.

* Exod. 13.
1. leuit. 27.
26. chap. 8.
16. luke 2.
23.

14 ¶ And the LORD spake vnto Moses, in the wildernesse of Sinai, saying,

15 Number the children of Leui, after the house of their fathers, by their families : euery male from a moneth old and vpward shalt thou number them.

16 And * Moses numbred them according to the † word of the LORD, as he was commanded.

* Gene. 46.
11. exod 6.
16. chap. 26
57. 1. chro.
6. 11.
† Hebr.
mouth.

17 And these were the sonnes of Leui, by their names : Gershon, and Kohath, and Merari.

18 And these are the names of the sonnes of Gershon, by their families : Libni, and Shimei.

19 And the sonnes of Kohath by their families : Amram , and Izehar , Hebron and Vzziel.

20 And the sonnes of Merari by their families : Mahli, and Mushi : these are the families of the Leuites, according to the house of their fathers.

21 Of Gershon was the familie of the Libnites, and the familie of the Shimites : these are the families of the Gershonites.

22 Those that were numbred of them , according to the number of all the males, from a moneth old and vpward, euen those that were numbred of them, were seuen thousand and fiue hundred.

23 The families of the Gershonites shal pitch behind the Tabernacle Westward.

24 And the chiefe of the house of the father of the Gershonites, shall be Eliasaph the sonne of Lael.

25 And the charge of the sonnes of Gershon, in the Tabernacle of the Congregation, shall be the Tabernacle, and the tent, the couering thereof, and the hanging for the doore of the Tabernacle of the Congregation :

26 And the hangings of the Court, and the curtaine for the doore of the court, which is by the Tabernacle, and by

by the Altar round about, and the cords of it, for all the seruice therof.

27 ¶ And of Kohath was the familie of the Amramites, and the familie of the Izeharites, and the familie of the Hebronites, and the familie of the Vzzielites : these are the families of the Kohathites.

28 In the number of all the males, from a moneth olde and vpward, were eight thousand, and sixe hundred, keeping the charge of the Sanctuary.

29 The families of the sonnes of Kohath, shall pitch on the side of the Tabernacle Southward.

30 And the chiefe of the house of the father of the families of the Kohathites shalbe Elizaphan the sonne of Vzziel.

31 And their charge shall be the Arke, and the Table, and the Candlesticke, and the altars, and the vessels of the Sanctuarie, wherewith they minister, and the hanging, and all the seruice thereof.

32 And Eleazar the sonne of Aaron the Priest, shall be chiefe ouer the chiefe of the Leuites, and haue the ouersight of them that keepe the charge of the Sanctuary.

33 ¶ Of Merari was the family of the Mahlites, and the family of the Mushites : these are the families of Merari.

34 And those that were numbred of them, according to the number of all the males from a moneth old & vpward, were sixe thousand and two hundred.

35 And the chiefe of the house of the father of the families of Merari, was Zuriel the sonne of Abihail : these shall pitch on the side of the Tabernacle Northwards.

† Heb. the office of the charge.

36 And † vnder the custody and charge of the sonnes of Merari, shall bee the boards of the Tabernacle, and the barres thereof, and the pillars thereof, and the sockets thereof, & all the vessels thereof, and all that serueth thereto :

37 And the pillars of the Court round about, and their sockets, and their pinnes, and their cords.

38 ¶ But those that encampe before the Tabernacle toward the East, euen before the Tabernacle of the Congregation Eastward, shall be Moses and Aaron, and his sonnes, keeping the charge of the Sanctuary, for the charge of the children of Israel : and the stranger that commeth nigh, shall be put to death.

39 All that were numbred of the Leuites, which Moses and Aaron numbred at the commaundement of the LORD, throughout their families, all the males from a moneth old and vpward, were twenty and two thousand.

40 ¶ And the LORD said vnto Moses, Number all the first borne of the males of the children of Israel, from a moneth old and vpward, and take the number of their names.

41 And thou shalt take the Leuites for me, (I am the LORD) in stead of all the first borne among the children of Israel, and the cattell of the Leuites, in stead of all the firstlings among the cattell of the children of Israel.

42 And Moses numbred as the LORD commanded him, all the first borne among the children of Israel.

43 And all the first borne males, by the number of names, from a moneth old & vpward, of those that were numbred of them, were twenty and two thousand, two hundred, and threescore and thirteene.

44 ¶ And the LORD spake vnto Moses, saying,

45 Take the Leuites in stead of all the first borne among the children of Israel, and the cattell of the Leuites in stead of their cattell, and the Leuites shalbe mine : I am the LORD.

46 And for those that are to be redeemed of the two hundred and threescore and thirteene, of the first borne of the children of Israel, which are more then the Leuites ;

47 Thou shalt euen take fiue shekels a piece, by the polle, after the shekel of the Sanctuary shalt thou take them ; * the shekel is twenty gerahs.

48 And thou shalt giue the money, wherewith the odde number of them is to be redeemed, vnto Aaron and to his sonnes.

49 And Moses tooke the redemption money, of them that were ouer and aboue them that were redeemed by the Leuites.

50 Of the first borne of the children of Israel tooke he the money ; a thousand, three hundred, and threescore and fiue shekels, after the shekel of the Sanctuary.

51 And Moses gaue the money of them that were redeemed, vnto Aaron and to his sonnes, according to the word

* Exod. 30
13. leuit.
27. 25.
chap. 18.
16. ezekl.
45. 12.

word of the LORD, as the LORD commanded Moses.

CHAP. IIII.

1 The age and time of the Leuites seruice. 4 The carriage of the Kohathites when the Priestes haue taken downe the Tabernacle. 16 The charge of Eleazar. 17 The office of the Priests. 21 The carriage of the Gershonites. 29 The carriage of the Merarites. 34 The number of the Kohathites, 38 of the Gershonites, 42 and of the Merarites.

ANd the LORD spake vnto Moses, and vnto Aaron, saying,

2 Take the summe of the sonnes of Kohath, from among the sonnes of Leui, after their families, by the house of their fathers.

3 From thirty yeeres old and vpward, euen vntill fifty yeres old, all that enter into the hoste, to doe the worke in the Tabernacle of the Congregation.

4 This *shall bee* the seruice of the sonnes of Kohath, in the Tabernacle of the Congregation, *about* the most Holy things.

5 ¶ And when the Campe setteth forward, Aaron shall come, and his sonnes, and they shall take downe the couering Vaile, and couer the Arke of Testimony with it:

6 And shall put thereon the couering of badgers skinnes, & shall spread ouer *it* a cloth wholly of blew, and shall put in the staues thereof.

7 And vpon the * table of Shewbread they shall spread a cloth of blew, and put thereon the dishes, and the spoones, and the bowles, and couers to || couer withall: and the continual bread shalbe thereon.

8 And they shall spread vpon them a clothe of scarlet, and couer the same with a couering of badgers skinnes, and shall put in the staues thereof.

9 And they shall take a cloth of blew, and couer the * candlesticke of the light, and his lampes, and his tongs, * and his snuffe dishes, and all the oyle vessels thereof, wherewith they minister vnto it.

10 And they shall put it, and all the vessels thereof, within a couering of badgers skinnes, and shall put *it* vpon a barre.

11 And vpon the golden Altar they shall spread a cloth of blew, and couer it

with a couering of badgers skinnes, and shall put to the staues thereof.

12 And they shall take all the instruments of ministery, wherewith they minister in the Sanctuary, and put them in a cloth of blew, and couer them with a couering of badgers skinnes, and shall put *them* on a barre.

13 And they shall take away the ashes from the Altar, and spread a purple cloth thereon:

14 And they shall put vpon it all the vessels thereof, wherewith they minister about it, *euen* the censers, the fleshhookes, and the shouels, and the || basons, all the vessels of the Altar: and they shall spread vpon it a couering of badgers skinnes, and put to the staues of it.

15 And when Aaron and his sonnes haue made an end of couering the Sanctuary, and all the vessels of the Sanctuary, as the campe is to set forward; after that, the sonnes of Kohath shall come to beare it: but they shal not touch any holy thing, lest they die. These things *are* the burden of the sonnes of Kohath in the Tabernacle of the Congregation.

16 ¶ And to the office of Eleazar the sonne of Aaron the Priest, *perteineth* the oile for the light, and the *sweet incense, and the dayly meat offering, and the * anoynting oyle, *and* the ouersight of all the Tabernacle, and of all that therein *is*, in the Sanctuary, and in the vessels thereof.

17 ¶ And the LORD spake vnto Moses, and vnto Aaron, saying,

18 Cut ye not off the tribe of the families of the Kohathites, from among the Leuites.

19 But thus doe vnto them, that they may liue, and not die: when they approche vnto the most Holy things, Aaron and his sonnes shall goe in, and appoint them euery one to his seruice, and to his burden.

20 But they shall not goe in to see when the holy things are couered, lest they die.

21 ¶ And the LORD spake vnto Moses, saying,

22 Take also the summe of the sonnes of Gershon, throughout the houses of their fathers, by their families:

23 From thirtie yeeres old and vpward, vntill fiftie yeeres old shalt thou num-

Marginal notes:

Exod. 25.

r, powre t withall.

Exod. 25.

Exod. 25.

|| *Or, bowles.*

* Exod. 30. 34.

* Exod. 30. 23.

† *Hebr. to warre the warfare.*

number them : all that enter in †to performe the seruice, to doe the worke in the Tabernacle of the Congregation.

24 This *is* the seruice of the families of the Gershonites, to serue, and for ‖ burdens.

‖ *Or, carriage.*

25 And they shall beare the curtaines of the Tabernacle, and the Tabernacle of the Congregation ; his couering, and the couering of the badgers skinnes that is aboue vpon it, and the hanging for the doore of the Tabernacle of the Congregation :

26 And the hangings of the Court, and the hanging for the doore of the gate of the Court which is by the Tabernacle, and by the Altar round about, and their cords, and all the instruments of their seruice, and all that is made for them : so shall they serue.

† *Hebr. mouth.*

27 At the † appointment of Aaron and his sonnes, shall be all the seruice of the sonnes of the Gershonites, in all their burdens, and in all their seruice : and yee shall appoint vnto them in charge all their burdens.

28 This *is* the seruice of the families of the sonnes of Gershon, in the Tabernacle of the Congregation : and their charge *shalbe* vnder the hande of Ithamar the sonne of Aaron the Priest.

29 ¶ As for the sonnes of Merari, thou shalt number them after their families, by the house of their fathers :

30 From thirty yeeres old and vpward, euen vnto fiftie yeeres old shalt thou number them, euery one that en-

† *Hebr. warfare.*

treth in to the † seruice, to doe the worke of the Tabernacle of the Congregation.

31 And this *is* the charge of their burden, according to all their seruice, in the Tabernacle of the Congregation, * the boards of the Tabernacle, and the barres thereof, and the pillars thereof, and sockets thereof :

* Exod. 26. 15.

32 And the pillars of the Court round about, and their sockets, and their pinnes, and their coards, with all their instruments, and with all their seruice : and by name yee shall reckon the instruments of the charge of their burden.

33 This *is* the seruice of the families of the sonnes of Merari, according to all their seruice in the Tabernacle of the Congregation, vnder the hand of Ithamar the sonne of Aaron the Priest.

34 ¶ And Moses and Aaron, and

the chiefe of the Congregation, numbred the sonnes of the Kohathites, after their families, and after the house of their fathers ;

35 From thirtie yeeres old and vpward, euen vnto fiftie yeeres old, euery one that entreth in to the seruice, for the worke in the Tabernacle of the Congregation.

36 And those that were numbred of them by their families, were two thousand, seuen hundred and fiftie.

37 These were they that were numbred of the families of the Kohathites ; all that might doe seruice in the Tabernacle of the Congregation, which Moses and Aaron did number, according to the commandement of the LORD, by the hand of Moses.

38 And those that were numbred of the sonnes of Gershon, throughout their families, and by the house of their fathers ;

39 From thirtie yeeres old and vpward, euen vnto fiftie yeeres old, euery one that entreth in to the seruice, for the worke in the Tabernacle of the Congregation :

40 Euen those that were numbred of them, throughout their families, by the houses of their fathers, were two thousand, and sixe hundred and thirtie.

41 These are they that were numbred of the families of the sonnes of Gershon, of all that might doe seruice in the Tabernacle of the Congregation, whom Moses and Aaron did number, according to the commandement of the LORD.

42 ¶ And those that were numbred of the families of the sonnes of Merari, throughout their families, by the house of their fathers ;

43 From thirtie yeeres old and vpward, euen vnto fiftie yeeres old, euery one that entreth in to the seruice, for the worke in the Tabernacle of the Congregation :

44 Euen those that were numbred of them after their families, *were* three thousand and two hundred.

45 These be those that were numbred of the families of the sonnes of Merari, whom Moses & Aaron numbred according to the word of the LORD by the hand of Moses.

46 All those that were numbred of the Leuites, whom Moses and Aaron, and the chiefe of Israel numbred, after their

their families, and after the house of their fathers:

47 From thirty yeeres old and vpward, euen vnto fifty yeeres old, euery one that came to doe the ſeruice of the miniſtery, and the ſeruice of the burden in the Tabernacle of the Congregation:

48 Euen thoſe that were numbred of them, were eight thouſand, and fiue hundred, and foureſcore.

49 According to the commandement of the LORD, they were numbred by the hand of Moſes, euery one according to his ſeruice, and according to his burden: Thus were they numbred of him, as the LORD commanded Moſes.

CHAP. V.

1 The vncleane are remoued out of the campe.
5 Reſtitution is to be made in treſpaſſes. 11 The triall of Iealouſie.

Nd the LORD ſpake vnto Moſes, ſaying,

2 Commaund the children of Iſrael, that they * put out of the campe euery leper, and euery one that hath an * iſſue, and whoſoeuer is defiled by the * dead:

3 Both male and female ſhal ye put out, without the campe ſhall yee put them, that they defile not their campes in the middeſt whereof I dwell.

4 And the children of Iſrael did ſo, and put them out, without the campe: as the LORD ſpake vnto Moſes, ſo did the children of Iſrael.

5 ¶ And the LORD ſpake vnto Moſes, ſaying,

6 Speake vnto the children of Iſrael, * When a man or woman ſhall commit any ſinne that men commit, to doe a treſpaſſe againſt the LORD, and that perſon be guiltie;

7 Then they ſhall confeſſe their ſinne, which they haue done: and hee ſhall recompenſe his treſpaſſe, * with the principall thereof, and adde vnto it the fifth part thereof, and giue it vnto him againſt whom he hath treſpaſſed.

8 But if the man haue no kinſman to recompenſe the treſpaſſe vnto, let the treſpaſſe be recompenſed vnto the LORD, euen to the Prieſt: beſide the ramme of the atonement, whereby an atonement ſhall be made for him.

9 And euery ‖ offering of all the holy things of the children of Iſrael, which they bring vnto the Prieſt, ſhall be his.

10 And euery mans halowed things ſhall be his: whatſoeuer any man giueth the Prieſt, it ſhall be * his.

11 ¶ And the LORD ſpake vnto Moſes, ſaying,

12 Speake vnto the children of Iſrael, and ſay vnto them, If any mans wife goe aſide, and commit a treſpaſſe againſt him;

13 And a man lye with her carnally, and it be hid from the eyes of her husband, and be kept cloſe, and ſhe be defiled, and there be no witneſſe againſt her, neither ſhe be taken with the maner;

14 And the ſpirit of ielouſie come vpon him, and he be ielous of his wife, and ſhee be defiled: or if the ſpirit of ielouſie come vpon him, and hee be ielous of his wife, and ſhe be not defiled:

15 Then ſhall the man bring his wife vnto the Prieſt, and he ſhall bring her offering for her, the tenth part of an Ephah of barley meale: hee ſhall powre no oyle vpon it, nor put frankincenſe thereon; for it is an offering of ielouſie, an offering of memoriall, bringing iniquitie to remembrance:

16 And the Prieſt ſhall bring her neere, and ſet her before the LORD.

17 And the Prieſt ſhall take holy water in an earthen veſſell, and of the duſt that is in the floore of the Tabernacle the Prieſt ſhall take, and put it into the water:

18 And the Prieſt ſhall ſet the woman before the LORD, and vncouer the womans head, and put the offering of memoriall in her hands, which is the Ielouſie offering: and the Prieſt ſhall haue in his hand the bitter water that cauſeth the curſe.

19 And the Prieſt ſhall charge her by an othe, and ſay vnto the woman, If no man haue lyen with thee, and if thou haſt not gone aſide to vncleanneſſe ‖ with another in ſtead of thy husband, be thou free from this bitter water that cauſeth the curſe.

20 But if thou haſt gone aſide to another in ſtead of thy husband, and if thou be defiled, and ſome man hath lien with thee beſide thine husband:

21 Then the Prieſt ſhall charge the woman with an othe of curſing, and the Prieſt ſhall ſay vnto the woman, The LORD make thee a curſe, and an othe

euit. 13.
euit. 15.
euit. 21.

euit. 6.

eui. 6. 5.

, heque
ring.

* Leuit. 10. 12.

‖ Or, being in the power of thy husband. Hebr. vnder thy husband.

† *Hebr. fall.*

othe among thy people, when the LORD doth make thy thigh to † rot, and thy belly to swell.

22 And this water that causeth the curse, shall go into thy bowels, to make *thy* belly to swell, and *thy* thigh to rot: and the woman shall say, Amen, Amen.

23 And the Priest shall write these curses in a booke, and hee shall blot *them* out with the bitter water:

24 And he shall cause the woman to drinke the bitter water, that causeth the curse: and the water that causeth the curse shall enter into her, *and become* bitter.

25 Then the Priest shall take the ielousie offering out of the womans hand, and shall waue the offering before the LORD, and offer it vpon the Altar.

26 And the Priest shal take an handfull of the offering, euen the memoriall thereof, and burne it vpon the Altar, and afterward shall cause the woman to drinke the water.

27 And when he hath made her to drinke the water, then it shall come to passe, that if shee be defiled, and haue done trespasse against her husband, that the water that causeth the curse, shall enter into her, *and become* bitter, and her belly shall swell, and her thigh shal rot: and the woman shalbe a curse among her people.

28 And if the woman be not defiled, but be cleane, then she shall be free, and shall conceiue seed.

29 This is the law of ielousies, when a wife goeth aside *to another* in stead of her husband, and is defiled:

30 Or when the spirit of ielousie commeth vpon him, and hee be ielous ouer his wife, and shall set the woman before the LORD, and the Priest shal execute vpon her all this law.

31 Then shall the man bee guiltlesse from iniquitie, and this woman shall beare her iniquitie.

CHAP. VI.

1 The Law of the Nazarites. 22 The forme of blessing the people.

Nd the LORD spake vnto Moses, saying,

2 Speake vnto the children of Israel, and say vnto them, When either man

or woman shall ‖ separate *themselues* to vow a vow of a Nazarite, to separate *themselues* vnto the LORD:

3 Hee shall separate himselfe from wine, and strong drinke, and shal drinke no vineger of wine, or vineger of strong drinke, neither shal he drinke any liquor of grapes, nor eate moist grapes, or dried.

4 All the dayes of his ‖ separation shall he eat nothing that is made of the † vine tree, from the kernels euen to the huske.

5 All the dayes of the vow of his separation, there shall no * rasour come vpon his head: vntill the dayes bee fulfilled in the which hee separateth himselfe vnto the LORD, he shall be holy, *and* shall let the lockes of the haire of his head grow.

6 All the dayes that he separateth himselfe vnto the LORD, hee shall come at no dead body.

7 Hee shall not make himselfe vncleane for his father, or for his mother, for his brother, or for his sister, when they die: because the † consecration of his God is vpon his head.

8 All the dayes of his separation he *is* holy vnto the LORD.

9 And if any man die very suddenly by him, and he hath defiled the head of his consecration, then he shall shaue his head in the day of his cleansing, on the seuenth day shall he shaue it.

10 And on the eight day he shal bring two turtles or two yong pigeons to the Priest, to the doore of the Tabernacle of the Congregation.

12 And the Priest shall offer the one for a sinne offering, and the other for a burnt offering, and make an atonement for him, for that hee sinned by the dead, and shall hallow his head that same day.

12 And hee shall consecrate vnto the LORD the dayes of his separation, and shall bring a lambe of the first yeere for a trespasse offering: but the dayes that were before shall be † lost, because his separation was defiled.

13 ¶ And this is the Lawe of the Nazarite: when the dayes of his separation are fulfilled, he shall be brought vnto the doore of the Tabernacle of the Congregation.

14 And he shall offer his offring vnto the LORD, one hee lambe of the first yeere without blemish, for a burnt offering,

‖ *Or, make themselues Nazarites.*

‖ *Or, Naze riteship.*

† *Heb. Vine of the wine.*

* *Iudg. 13. 5. 1. sam. &c. 11.*

† *Hebr. separation.*

† *Hebr. fal*

offering, and one ewe lambe of the first
yeere without blemish, for a sinne offering, and one lambe without blemish
for peace offerings,

15 And a basket of vnleauened bread,
cakes of fine flowre mingled with oyle,
and wafers of vnleauened bread anointed with oyle, and their meate offering,
and their drinke offerings.

16 And the Priest shall bring *them* before the Lᴏʀᴅ, and shall offer his
sinne offering, and his burnt offering.

17 And he shall offer the ramme for
a sacrifice of peace offerings vnto the
Lᴏʀᴅ, with the basket of vnleauened bread : the Priest shall offer also his
meate offering, and his drinke offering.

Acts 21.
4. 18 *And the Nazarite shal shaue the
head of his separation, at the doore of
the Tabernacle of the Congregation,
and shall take the haire of the head of
his separation, and put it in the fire
which is vnder the sacrifice of the peace
offerings.

19 And the Priest shall take the sodden shoulder of the ramme, and one vnleauened cake out of the basket, and
one vnleauened wafer, and shall put
them vpon the hands of the Nazarite,
after *the haire* of his separation is shauen.

Exod. 29.
7. 20 And the Priest shall waue them
*for a waue offring before the Lᴏʀᴅ :
this is holy for the Priest, with the
waue breast, and heaue shoulder : and
after that, the Nazarite may drinke
wine.

21 This *is* the Law of the Nazarite,
who hath vowed, and of his offering
vnto the Lᴏʀᴅ for his separation, besides that, that his hand shall get : according to the vow which he vowed, so he
must do after the law of his separation.

22 ¶ And the Lᴏʀᴅ spake vnto
Moses, saying,

23 Speake vnto Aaron, and vnto his
sonnes, saying, On this wise ye shall
blesse the children of Israel, saying vnto them :

24 The Lᴏʀᴅ blesse thee, and
keepe thee :

25 The Lᴏʀᴅ make his face shine
vpon thee, and be gracious vnto thee :

26 The Lᴏʀᴅ lift vp his countenance vpon thee, and giue thee peace.

27 And they shall put my Name
vpon the children of Israel, and I will
blesse them.

CHAP. VII.

1 The offering of the Princes at the dedication
of the Tabernacle. 10 Their seuerall offrings at the dedication of the Altar. 89 God
speaketh to Moses from the Mercie seat.

Nd it came to passe on the
day that Moses had fully
* set vp the Tabernacle,
and had anointed it, and
sanctified it, and all the instruments thereof, both the Altar, and
all the vessels thereof, and had anointed them, and sanctified them :   * Exod. 40.
18.

2 That the Princes of Israel, heads
of the house of their fathers, (who
were the Princes of the tribes, † and
were ouer them that were numbred)   † Heb. who
stood.
offered :

3 And they brought their offering
before the Lᴏʀᴅ, sixe couered wagons, and twelue oxen : a wagon for
two of the Princes, and for each one an
oxe, and they brought them before the
Tabernacle.

4 And the Lᴏʀᴅ spake vnto Moses, saying,

5 Take *it* of them, that they may be
to doe the seruice of the Tabernacle of
the Congregation, and thou shalt giue
them vnto the Leuites, to euery man
according to his seruice.

6 And Moses tooke the wagons,
and the oxen, and gaue them vnto the
Leuites.

7 Two wagons and foure oxen he
gaue vnto the sonnes of Gershon, according to their seruice.

8 And foure wagons and eight
oxen he gaue vnto the sonnes of Merari, according vnto their seruice, vnder
the hand of Ithamar the sonne of Aaron the Priest.

9 But vnto the sonnes of Kohath
he gaue none : because the seruice of the
Sanctuary belonging vnto them, *was
that* they should beare vpon their shoulders.

10 ¶ And the Princes offered for dedicating of the Altar, in the day that it
was anointed, euen the Princes offered
their offering before the Altar.

11 And the Lᴏʀᴅ said vnto Mo-
ses, They shall offer their offering eche
Prince on his day, for the dedicating of
the Altar.

12 ¶ And he that offered his offring
the first day, was Nahshon the sonne
of Amminadab, of the tribe of Iudah.

13 And

13 And his offering was one siluer charger, the weight thereof was an hundred and thirty *shekels*, one siluer bowle of seuentie shekels, after the shekel of the Sanctuary; both of them were full of fine flowre mingled with oile for a * meat offering:

Leuit. 2. 1.

14 One spoone of ten shekels of gold, full of incense:

15 One yong bullocke, one ramme, one lambe of the first yeere, for a burnt offering,

16 One kid of the goats for * a sinne offering:

Leuit. 4. 23.

17 And for a sacrifice of peace offerings, two oxen, fiue rammes, fiue hee goats, fiue lambes of the first yeere: this *was* the offering of Nahshon the sonne of Amminadab.

18 ¶ On the second day Nethaneel the sonne of Zuar, Prince of Issachar did offer.

19 He offered for his offering one siluer charger, the weight whereof was an hundred and thirtie *shekels*, one siluer bowle of seuenty shekels, after the shekel of the Sanctuary, both of them full of fine flowre mingled with oile, for a meat offering:

20 One spoone of gold of ten *shekels*, full of incense:

21 One yong bullocke, one ramme, one lambe of the first yeere for a burnt offering:

22 One kid of the goats for a sinne offering:

23 And for a sacrifice of peace offerings, two oxen, fiue rammes, fiue hee goats, fiue lambes of the first yeere: this *was* the offering of Nethaneel the sonne of Zuar.

24 ¶ On the third day Eliab the sonne of Helon, Prince of the children of Zebulun *did offer*.

25 His offering *was* one siluer charger, the weight whereof was an hundred and thirtie *shekels*, one siluer bowle of seuentie shekels, after the shekel of the Sanctuary, both of them full of fine flowre mingled with oile, for a meat offering:

26 One golden spoone of ten *shekels*, full of incense:

27 One yong bullocke, one ramme, one lambe of the first yeere for a burnt offering:

28 One kid of the goats for a sinne offering:

29 And for a sacrifice of peace offerings, two oxen, fiue rammes, fiue hee goats, fiue lambes of the first yeere: This *was* the offring of Eliab the sonne of Helon.

30 ¶ On the fourth day Elizur the sonne of Shedeur, Prince of the children of Reuben *did offer*.

31 His offering *was* one siluer charger of an hundred and thirty *shekels*, one siluer bowle of seuentie shekels, after the shekel of the Sanctuary, both of them full of fine flowre mingled with oyle, for a meat offering:

32 One golden spoone of tenne *shekels*, full of incense:

33 One yong bullocke, one ramme, one lambe of the first yeere for a burnt offering:

34 One kid of the goats for a sinne offering:

35 And for a sacrifice of peace offerings, two oxen, fiue rammes, fiue hee goats, fiue lambs of the first yere: This *was* the offering of Elizur the sonne of Shedeur.

36 ¶ On the fifth day Shelumiel the sonne of Zurishaddai Prince of the children of Simeon, *did offer*.

37 His offring *was* one siluer charger, the weight whereof was an hundred and thirtie *shekels*, one siluer bowle of seuentie shekels, after the shekel of the Sanctuary, both of them full of fine flowre, mingled with oyle, for a meate offering:

38 One golden spoone of ten *shekels*, full of incense:

39 One yong bullocke, one ramme, one lambe of the first yeere for a burnt offering:

40 One kidde of the goates for a sinne offering:

41 And for a sacrifice of peace offerings, two oxen, fiue rammes, fiue hee goates, fiue lambes of the first yeere: This *was* the offering of Shelumiel the sonne of Zurishaddai.

42 ¶ On the sixt day, Eliasaph the sonne of Deuel, Prince of the children of Gad, *offered*:

43 His offering *was* one siluer charger of the weight of an hundred and thirtie *shekels*, a siluer bowle of seuentie shekels, after the shekel of the Sanctuarie, both of them ful of fine flowre mingled with oyle, for a meate offering:

44 One golden spoone of ten *shekels*, full of incense:

45 One yong bullocke, one ramme, one

one lambe of the first yeere, for a burnt offering:

46 One kid of the goates for a sinne offering:

47 And for a sacrifice of peace offerings, two oxen, fiue rammes, fiue hee goates, fiue lambes of the first yeere. This *was* the offering of Eliasaph the sonne of Deuel.

48 ¶ On the seuenth day, Elishama the sonne of Ammiud, Prince of the children of Ephraim *offered*.

49 His offering *was* one siluer charger, the weight whereof was an hundred and thirtie *shekels*, one siluer bowle of seuentie shekels, after the shekel of the Sanctuarie, both of them full of fine flowre mingled with oile for a meat offering:

50 One golden spoone of ten *shekels*, full of incense:

51 One yong bullocke, one ramme, one lambe of the first yeere, for a burnt offering:

52 One kid of the goates for a sinne offering:

53 And for a sacrifice of peace offrings, two oxen, fiue rammes, fiue hee goats, fiue lambes of the first yeere. This *was* the offering of Elishama the sonne of Ammiud.

54 ¶ On the eight day *offered* Gamaliel the sonne of Pedazur, Prince of the children of Manasseh.

55 His offering *was* one siluer charger of an hundred and thirtie *shekels*, one siluer bowle of seuentie shekels, after the shekel of the Sanctuary, both of them full of fine flowre mingled with oile, for a meate offering:

56 One golden spoone of ten *shekels*, full of incense:

57 One yong bullocke, one ramme, one lambe of the first yeere, for a burnt offering:

58 One kid of the goates for a sinne offering:

59 And for a sacrifice of peace offerings, two oxen, fiue rammes, fiue hee goats, fiue lambes of the first yeere. This *was* the offering of Gamaliel the sonne of Pedazur.

60 ¶ On the ninth day, Abidan the sonne of Gideoni, prince of the children of Beniamin *offered*.

61 His offering *was* one siluer charger, the weight whereof was an hundred and thirtie *shekels*, a siluer bowle of seuentie shekels, after the shekel of the

Sanctuary, both of them full of fine flowre mingled with oyle, for a meate offering:

62 One golden spoone of ten *shekels*, full of incense:

63 One yong bullocke, one ramme, one lambe of the first yeere for a burnt offering:

64 One kid of the goats for a sinne offering:

65 And for a sacrifice of peace offerings, two oxen, fiue rammes, fiue hee goates, fiue lambes of the first yeere. This *was* the offering of Abidan, the sonne of Gideoni.

66 ¶ On the tenth day Ahiezer the sonne of Ammishaddai, Prince of the children of Dan *offered*.

67 His offring *was* one siluer charger, the weight whereof was an hundred and thirtie *shekels*, one siluer bowle of seuentie shekels, after the shekel of the Sanctuarie, both of them full of fine flowre mingled with oyle, for a meate offering:

68 One golden spoone of ten *shekels*, full of incense:

69 One yong bullocke, one ramme, one lambe of the first yeere, for a burnt offering:

70 One kid of the goates for a sinne offering:

71 And for a sacrifice of peace offerings, two oxen, fiue rammes, fiue hee goats, fiue lambes of the first yeere. This *was* the offering of Ahiezer the sonne of Ammishaddai.

72 ¶ On the eleuenth day, Pagiel the sonne of Ocran, Prince of the children of Asher *offered*.

73 His offering *was* one siluer charger, the weight whereof was an hundred and thirtie *shekels*, one siluer bowle of seuentie shekels, after the shekel of the Sanctuarie, both of them full of fine flowre mingled with oyle, for a meat offering:

74 One golden spoone of ten *shekels*, full of incense:

75 One yong bullocke, one ramme, one lambe of the first yeere for a burnt offering:

76 One kid of the goates for a sinne offering:

77 And for a sacrifice of peace offerings, two oxen, fiue rammes, fiue hee goats, fiue lambes of the first yeere. This *was* the offering of Pagiel the sonne of Ocran.

78 ¶ On

78 ¶ On the twelfth day, Ahira the sonne of Enan, Prince of the children of Naphtali, *offered.*

79 His offering *was* one siluer charger, the weight whereof was an hundred and thirtie *shekels*, one siluer bowle of seuentie shekels, after the shekel of the Sanctuary, both of them full of fine flowre mingled with oyle, for a meate offering:

80 One golden spoone of ten *shekels*, full of incense:

81 One yong bullocke, one ramme, one lambe of the first yeere for a burnt offering:

82 One kidde of the goats for a sinne offering:

83 And for a sacrifice of peace offrings, two oxen, fiue rammes, fiue hee goats, fiue lambs of the first yeere. This *was* the offering of Ahira the sonne of Enan.

84 This *was* the dedication of the Altar (in the day when it was annointed) by the Princes of Israel: twelue chargers of siluer, twelue siluer bowles, twelue spoones of gold:

85 Each charger of siluer *weighing* an hundred and thirtie *shekels*, each bowle seuentie: all the siluer vessels weighed two thousand and foure hundred *shekels*, after the shekel of the Sanctuary.

86 The golden spoones *were* twelue, full of incense, *weighing* ten *shekels* apiece, after the shekel of the Sanctuary: all the gold of the spoones, *was* an hundred and twentie *shekels*.

87 All the oxen for the burnt offering, *were* twelue bullocks, the rams twelue, the lambes of the first yeere twelue, with their meat offering: and the kids of the goats for sinne offering, twelue.

88 And all the oxen for the sacrifice of the peace offerings, *were* twenty and foure bullocks, the rammes sixtie, the hee goates sixtie, the lambes of the first yeere sixtie. This *was* the dedication of the Altar, after that it was anoynted.

89 And when Moses was gone into the Tabernacle of the Congregation, to speake with † him, then he heard the voyce of one speaking vnto him, from off the Mercie seat, that *was* vpon the Arke of Testimony from betweene the two Cherubims: and he spake vnto him.

† *i. God.*

CHAP. VIII.

1 How the lampes are to be lighted. 5 The consecration of the Leuites. 23 The age and time of their seruice.

Nd the Lord spake vnto Moses, saying,

2 Speake vnto Aaron, and say vnto him, When thou * lightest the lampes, the seuen lampes shall giue light, ouer against the candlesticke.

* Exod. 25. 37. and 40. 25.

3 And Aaron did so; he lighted the lampes therof, ouer against the candlestick, as the Lord * comanded Moses.

* Exod. 25. 31.

4 And this worke of the candlestick *was* of beaten gold, vnto the shaft thereof, vnto the flowres thereof was * beaten worke: according vnto the paterne which the Lord had shewed Moses, so he made the candlesticke.

* Exod. 25. 18.

5 ¶ And the Lord spake vnto Moses, saying,

6 Take the Leuites from among the children of Israel, and cleanse them.

7 And thus shalt thou doe vnto them, to cleanse them: sprinkle water of purifying vpon them, and † let them shaue all their flesh, and let them wash their clothes, and so make themselues cleane.

† *Hebr, let them cause rasortopass ouer, &c.*

8 Then let them take a yong bullocke with his meat offering, *euen* fine flowre mingled with oyle, and an other yong bullock shalt thou take for a sinne offering.

9 And thou shalt bring the Leuites before the Tabernacle of the Congregation; and thou shalt gather the whole assembly of the children of Israel together.

10 And thou shalt bring the Leuites before the Lord, and the children of Israel shall put their hands vpon the Leuites.

11 And Aaron shall † offer the Leuites before the Lord for an † offring of the children of Israel, that † they may execute the seruice of the Lord.

† *Heb, waue* † *Heb. waue offering.* † *Hebr. they may be to execute, &c*

12 And the Leuites shall lay their hands vpon the heads of the bullocks: and thou shalt offer the one for a sinne offering, and the other for a burnt offering vnto the Lord, to make an atonement for the Leuites.

13 And thou shalt set the Leuites before Aaron, and before his sonnes, and offer them for an offering vnto the Lord.

14 Thus

14 Thus shalt thou separate the Leuites from among the children of Israel : and the Leuites shalbe * mine.

hap. 3.

15 And after that, shall the Leuites goe in, to doe the seruice of the Tabernacle of the Congregation : and thou shalt clense them, and offer them for an offering.

16 For they are wholly giuen vnto me, from among the children of Israel : in stead of such as open euery wombe, *euen in stead of the first borne of all the children of Israel, haue I taken them vnto me.

hap. 3.
exod.
2. luke
23.

17 For all the first borne of the children of Israel, *are* mine, both man and beast : on the day that I smote euery first borne in the land of Egypt, I sanctified them for my selfe.

18 And I haue taken the Leuites for all the first borne of the children of Israel.

19 And I haue giuen the Leuites *as* a † gift to Aaron, and to his sonnes, from among the children of Israel, to do the seruice of the children of Israel, in the Tabernacle of the Congregation, and to make an atonement for the children of Israel : that there bee no plague among the children of Israel, when the children of Israel come nigh vnto the Sanctuarie.

Heb.giuen.

20 And Moses and Aaron, and all the Congregation of the children of Israel did to the Leuites according vnto all that the Lord commanded Moses, concerning the Leuites, so did the children of Israel vnto them.

21 And the Leuites were purified, and they washed their clothes : and Aaron offered them as an offering before the Lord, and Aaron made an atonement for them to cleanse them.

22 And after that, went the Leuites in, to do their seruice in the Tabernacle of the Congregation before Aaron and and before his sonnes : as the Lord had commanded Moses concerning the Leuites, so did they vnto them.

23 ¶ And the Lord spake vnto Moses, saying,

24 This *is it* that belongeth vnto the Leuites : from twentie and fiue yeeres old, and vpward, they shall goe in †to waite vpon the seruice of the Tabernacle of the Congregation.

Heb. to
warre the
warfare of
&c.

25 And from the age of fiftie yeeres they shall † cease waiting vpon the seruice thereof, and shall serue no more :

Hebr. re-
urne from
he warfare
ftheseruice

26 But shall minister with their brethren in the Tabernacle of the Congregation, to keepe the charge, and shall doe no seruice : thus shalt thou doe vnto the Leuites, touching their charge.

CHAP. IX.

1 The Passeouer is commanded againe. 6 A second Passeouer allowed for them that were vncleane or absent. 15 The cloude guideth the remouings & incampings of the Israelites.

Nd the Lord spake vnto Moses in the wilderdernesse of Sinai, in the first moneth of the second yeere, after they were come out of the land of Egypt, saying,

2 Let the children of Israel also keepe *the Passeouer, at his appointed season.

* Exod. 12.
1. &c. leuit.
23. 5. chap.
28. 16. deut.
16. 2.
† Hebr. be-
tweene the
two eue-
nings.

3 In the fourteenth day of this moneth † at euen, ye shall keepe it in his appointed season : according to all the rites of it, and according to all the ceremonies thereof shall ye keepe it.

4 And Moses spake vnto the children of Israel that they should keepe the Passeouer.

5 And they kept the Passeouer on the fourteenth day of the first moneth at Euen, in the wildernesse of Sinai : according to all that the Lord commanded Moses, so did the children of Israel.

6 ¶ And there were certaine men who were defiled by the dead body of a man , that they could not keepe the Passeouer on that day : and they came before Moses, and before Aaron on that day.

7 And those men said vnto him, We *are* defiled by the dead body of a man : wherefore are we kept backe, that wee may not offer an offring of the Lord in his appointed season among the children of Israel ?

8 And Moses saide vnto them, Stand still, and I will heare what the Lord wil command concerning you.

9 ¶ And the Lord spake vnto Moses, saying,

10 Speake vnto the children of Israel, saying, If any man of you, or of your posteritie shall be vncleane by reason of a dead body, or bee in a iourney afarre off, yet he shall keepe the Passeouer vnto the Lord.

11 The fourteenth day of the second moneth

moneth at Euen they shall keepe it, and eat it with vnleauened bread and bitter *herbes*.

*Exod. 12. 46. ioh. 19. 36.

12 They shall leaue none of it vnto the morning, nor breake any bone of it : * according to all the ordinances of the Passeouer they shall keepe it.

13 But the man that is cleane, and is not in a iourney, and forbeareth to keep the Passeouer, euen the same soule shall be cut off from his people, because hee brought not the offering of the Lord in his appointed season : that man shall beare his sinne.

14 And if a stranger shall soiourne among you, and will keepe the Passeouer vnto the Lord; according to the ordinance of the Passeouer, and according to the maner thereof, so shall he doe : * ye shall haue one ordinance, both for the stranger, and for him that was borne in the land.

*Exod. 12. 49.

15 ¶ And * on the day that the Tabernacle was reared vp, the cloud couered the Tabernacle, *namely* the Tent of the Testimony : and at Euen there was vpon the Tabernacle, as it were the appearance of fire, vntill the morning.

*Exod. 40. 34.

16 So it was alway : the cloud couered it *by day*, and the appearance of fire by night.

17 And when the cloud was taken vp from the Tabernacle, then after that, the children of Israel iourneyed, and in the place where the cloud abode, there the children of Israel pitched their tents.

18 At the commandement of the Lord the children of Israel iourneied, and at the commandement of the Lord they pitched : * as long as the cloud abode vpon the Tabernacle, they rested in the tents.

* 1. Corin. 10. 1.

19 And when the cloud † taried long vpon the Tabernacle many daies, then the children of Israel kept the charge of the Lord, and iourneyed not.

† Hebr. prolonged.

20 And so it was when the cloude was a few daies vpon the Tabernacle, according to the commandement of the Lord, they abode in their tents, and according to the commandement of the Lord, they iourneyed.

21 And so it was when the cloude † abode from Euen vnto the morning, and *that* the cloude was taken up in the morning, then they iourneyed : whether it was by day or by night that the

† Hebr. was.

cloude was taken vp, they iourneyed.

22 Or whether *it were* two dayes, or a moneth, or a yeere that the cloude taried vpon the Tabernacle, remayning thereon, the children of Israel *a-bode in their tents, and iourneyed not : but when it was taken vp, they iourneyed.

*Exod. 4 36. 37.

23 At the commandement of the Lord they rested in the tents, and at the commaundement of the Lord they iourneyed: they kept the charge of the Lord, at the commandement of the Lord by the hand of Moses.

CHAP. X.

Nd the Lord spake vnto Moses, saying, 2 Make thee two trumpets of siluer : of an whole piece shalt thou make them, that thou mayest vse them for the calling of the assembly, and for the iourneying of the campes.

3 And when they shall blow with them, all the assembly shall assemble themselues to thee, at the doore of the Tabernacle of the Congregation.

4 And if they blow *but* with one *trumpet*, then the Princes, *which are* heads of the thousands of Israel, shall gather themselues vnto thee.

5 When ye blow an alarme, then the campes that lie on the East parts, shall goe forward.

6 When you blow an alarme the second time, then the campes that lye on the Southside, shall take their iourney : they shall blow an alarme for their iourneys.

7 But when the Congregation is to be gathered together, you shal blow : but you shall not sound an alarme.

8 And the sonnes of Aaron the Priests shall blow with the trumpets; and they shalbe to you for an ordinance for euer throughout your generations.

9 And if ye goe to warre in your land, against the enemie that oppresseth you, then ye shall blow an alarme with the trumpets, and ye shalbe remembred before the Lord your God, and yee shalbe

shalbe saued from your enemies.

10 Also in the day of your gladnesse, and in your solemne dayes, and in the beginnings of your monethes, ye shall blow with the trumpets ouer your burnt offerings, and ouer the sacrifices of your peace offerings, that they may bee to you for a memoriall before your God: I *am* the Lord your God.

11 ¶ And it came to passe on the twentieth day of the second moneth, in the second yeere, that the cloude was taken vp from off the Tabernacle of the Testimony.

12 And the children of Israel tooke their iourneys out of the wildernesse of Sinai; and the cloud rested in the wildernesse of Paran.

13 And they first tooke their iourney, according to the commandement of the Lord, by the hand of Moses.

Chap. 2. 3. | 14 ¶ *In the first *place* went the standerd of the campe of the children of Iudah, according to their armies, and o-
Chap. 1. 7. | uer his hoste *was* * Nahshon the sonne of Amminadab.

15 And ouer the hoste of the tribe of the children of Issachar, *was* Nethaneel the sonne of Zuar.

16 And ouer the hoste of the tribe of the children of Zebulun, *was* Eliab the sonne of Helon.

17 And the Tabernacle was taken downe, and the sonnes of Gershon, and the sonnes of Merari set forward, bearing the Tabernacle.

18 ¶ And the standerd of the campe of Reuben set forward according to their armies: and ouer his hoste *was* Elizur the sonne of Shedeur.

19 And ouer the hoste of the tribe of the children of Simeon, *was* Shelumiel the sonne of Zurishaddai.

20 And ouer the hoste of the tribe of the children of Gad, *was* Eliasaph the sonne of Deuel.

Chap. 4. 4. | 21 And the Kohathites set forward,
*That is, | bearing the *Sanctuary, and *the* †other*
: Gersho- | did set vp the Tabernacle against they
tes,and the | came.
*erarites, |
e v. 17.* |

22 ¶ And the standerd of the campe of the children of Ephraim set forward, according to their armies, and ouer his hoste *was* Elishama the sonne of Ammiud.

23 And ouer the hoste of the tribe of the children of Manasseh *was* Gamaliel the sonne of Pedazur.

24 And ouer the hoste of the tribe of

the children of Beniamin, *was* Abidan the soune of Gideoni.

25 ¶ And the standerd of the campe of the children of Dan set forward, which was the rere-ward of all the campes throughout their hostes: and ouer his hoste *was* Ahiezer the sonne of Ammishaddai.

26 And ouer the hoste of the tribe of the children of Asher, *was* Pagiel the sonne of Ocran.

27 And ouer the hoste of the tribe of the children of Naphtali *was* Ahira the sonne of Enan.

28 † Thus were the iourneyings of the children of Israel, according to their armies, when they set forward. | † *Hebr.*
These.

29 ¶ And Moses said vnto Hobab the sonne of Raguel the Midianite Moses father in law, Wee are iourneying vnto the place of which the Lord said, I wil giue it you: come thou with vs, and we will doe thee good: for the Lord hath spoken good concerning Israel.

30 And he said vnto him, I will not goe, but I will depart to mine owne land, and to my kinred.

31 And he said, Leaue vs not, I pray thee, forasmuch as thou knowest how we are to encampe in the wilderuesse, and thou mayest bee to vs in stead of eyes.

32 And it shall bee if thou goe with vs, yea it shall be, that what goodnesse the Lord shall doe vnto vs, the same will we doe vnto thee.

33 ¶ And they departed from the Mount of the Lord three dayes iourney: and the Arke of the Couenant of the Lord went before them in the three dayes iourney, to search out a resting place for them.

34 And the cloude of the Lord *was* vpon them by day, when they went out of the campe.

35 And it came to passe when the Arke set forward, that Moses said, * Rise vp Lord, and let thine enemies be scattered, and let them that hate thee, flee before thee. | * Psal. 68.
1, 2.

36 And when it rested, he said, Returne, O Lord, vnto the †many thousands of Israel. | † *Hebr. ten*
thousand
thousands.

CHAP. XI.

1 The burning at Taberah quenched by Moses prayer. 4 The people lust for flesh, and loth Manna. 10 Moses complayneth of his charge.

charge. 16 God diuideth his burden vnto
seuentie Elders. 31 Quailes are giuen in
wrath at Kibroth-Hattaauah.

|| Or, were as it were complainers..
† Heb. it was euill in the eares of &c.

AND *when* the people || com-
plained, † it displeased the
LORD: and the LORD
heard it: and his anger
was kindled, and the fire
of the LORD burnt * among them,
and consumed *them that were* in the vttermost parts of the campe.

* Psal. 78. 21.

2 And the people cried vnto Moses,
and when Moses prayed vnto the
LORD, the fire † was quenched.

† Hebr. sunke.

3 And hee called the name of the
place || Taberah: because the fire of the
LORD burnt among them.

|| That is, a burning.

4 ¶ And the * mixt multitude that
was among them, † fell a lusting, and
the children of Israel † also wept a-
gaine, and said, * Who shal giue vs flesh
to eate?

* As Exod. 12. 38.
† Heb. lusted a lust.
† Hebr. returned and wept.
* 1. Cor. 10. 6.

5 We remember the fish which wee
did eate in Egypt freely: the cucumbers
and the melons, and the leekes, and the
onions, and the garlicke.
6 But now our soule is dried away,
there is nothing at all, besides this
Manna, before our eyes.
7 And * the Manna was as Coriander seed, and the † colour thereof as
the colour of Bdelium:

* Exod. 16. 14, 31.
† Hebr. eye of it, as the eye of.

8 *And* the people went about, and
gathered it, and ground it in milles, or
beat it in a morter, and baked it in pans,
and made cakes of it: and the taste of it
was as the taste of fresh oyle.
9 And when the dew fell vpon the
campe in the night, the Manna fell vpon it.
10 ¶ Then Moses heard the people
weepe throughout their families, euery
man in the doore of his tent, and the
anger of the LORD was kindled
greatly, Moses also was displeased.
11 And Moses said vnto the LORD,
Wherefore hast thou afflicted thy seruant? and wherefore haue I not found
fauour in thy sight, that thou layest the
burden of all this people vpon me?
12 Haue I conceiued all this people?
haue I begotten them, that thou shouldest say vnto me, Cary them in thy bosome (as a nursing father beareth the
sucking child) vnto the land which thou
swarest vnto their fathers?
13 Whence should I haue flesh to
giue vnto all this people? for they weep
vnto me, saying, Giue vs flesh, that we
may eate.
14 I am not able to beare all this
people alone, because it is too heauie for
mee.
15 And if thou deale thus with mee,
kill me, I pray thee out of hand, if I
haue found fauour in thy sight, and let
me not see my wretchednesse.
16 ¶ And the LORD said vnto Moses, Gather vnto me seuentie men, of
the Elders of Israel, whome thou
knowest to be the elders of the people,
and officers ouer them: and bring them
vnto the Tabernacle of the Congregation, that they may stand there with
thee.
17 And I will come downe and
talke with thee there, and I will take
of the spirit which is vpon thee, and wil
put *it* vpon them, and they shall beare
the burden of the people with thee, that
thou beare *it* not thy selfe alone.
18 And say thou vnto the people,
Sanctifie your selues against to morrow, and yee shall eate flesh: (for you
haue wept in the eares of the LORD,
saying, Who shall giue vs flesh to eate?
for it was well with vs in Egypt:)
therfore the LORD wil giue you flesh,
and ye shall eate.
19 Ye shall not eate one day, nor two
dayes, nor fiue dayes, neither ten dayes,
nor twentie dayes:
20 *But* euen a † whole moneth, vntill
it come out at your nostrels, and it bee
loathsome vnto you, because that yee
haue despised the LORD which is a-
mong you, and haue wept before him,
saying, Why came we foorth out of E-
gypt?

† Heb. moneth of dayes.

21 And Moses said, The people a-
mongst whome I *am*, *are* sixe hundred
thousand footmen, and thou hast said,
I will giue them flesh, that they may
eate a whole moneth.
22 Shall the flockes and the herds
be slaine for them to suffice them? or shal
all the fish of the sea bee gathered together for them, to suffice them?
23 And the LORD said vnto Moses, * Is the LORDS hand waxed
short? thou shalt see now whether my
word shall come to passe vnto thee, or
not.

* Esa. 50 and 59. 1

24 ¶ And Moses went out, and
tolde the people the wordes of the
LORD, and gathered the seuenty men
of the Elders of the people, and set
them

them round about the Tabernacle.

25 And the LORD came downe in a cloude, and spake vnto him, and tooke of the spirit that was vpon him, and gaue it vnto the seuentie Elders: and it came to passe that when the spirit rested vpon them, they prophesied, and did not cease.

26 But there remained two of the men in the campe, the name of the one *was* Eldad, & the name of the other Medad: and the Spirit rested vpon them, (and they were of them *that were* written, but went not out vnto the Tabernacle) and they prophesied in the campe.

27 And there ranne a yong man, and tolde Moses, and said, Eldad and Medad doe prophesie in the campe.

28 And Ioshua the sonne of Nun the seruant of Moses, one of his yong men, answered and said, My lord Moses, Forbid them.

29 And Moses said vnto him, Enuiest thou for my sake? Would God that all the LORDS people were Prophets, and that the LORD would put his Spirit vpon them.

30 And Moses gate him into the campe, he, and the Elders of Israel.

31 ¶ And there went forth a * winde from the LORD, and brought quailes from the sea, and let them fall by the campe, † as it were a dayes iourney on this side, and as it were a dayes iourney on the other side round about the campe, and as it were two cubits *high* vpon the face of the earth.

32 And the people stood vp all that day, and all *that* night, and all the next day, and they gathered the quailes: he that gathered least, gathered ten homers: and they spread *them* all abroad for themselues round about the campe.

33 And while the * flesh was yet betweene their teeth, yer it was chewed, the wrath of the LORD was kindled against the people, and the LORD smote the people with a very great plague.

34 And he called the name of that place, ‖ Kibroth-Hattaauah: because there they buried the people that lusted.

35 And the people iourneyed from Kibroth-Hattaauah, vnto Hazeroth: and † abode at Hazeroth.

CHAP. XII.

1 God rebuketh the sedition of Miriam and Aaron. 10 Miriams leprosie is healed at the

prayer of Moses. 14 God commandeth her to be shut out of the hoste.

ANd Miriam and Aaron spake against Moses, because of the ‖ Ethiopian woman, whom hee had married: for he had †married an Ethiopian woman.

2 And they said, Hath the LORD indeed spoken onely by Moses? Hath hee not spoken also by vs? And the LORD heard *it*.

3 (Now the man Moses was * very meeke, aboue all the men which were vpon the face of the earth.)

4 And the LORD spake suddenly vnto Moses, and vnto Aaron, and vnto Miriam, Come out ye three vnto the Tabernacle of the Congregation: and they three came out.

5 And the LORD came downe in the pillar of the cloude, and stood in the doore of the Tabernacle, and called Aaron and Miriam: and they both came foorth.

6 And hee saide, Heare now my words: If there be a Prophet among you, I the LORD will make my selfe knowen vnto him in a vision, *and* will speake vnto him in a dreame:

7 *My seruant Moses *is* not so, who *is* faithfull in all mine house.

8 With him will I speake * mouth to mouth euen apparantly, and not in darke speeches, and the similitude of the LORD shall hee behold: wherefore then were yee not afraid to speake against my seruant Moses?

9 And the anger of the LORD was kindled against them, and he departed.

10 And the cloud departed from off the Tabernacle, and behold, Miriam became leprous, *white* as snow: and Aaron looked vpon Miriam, and behold, she *was* leprous.

11 And Aaron said vnto Moses, Alas my lord, I beseech thee, lay not the sinne vpon vs, wherein we haue done foolishly, and wherein we haue sinned:

12 Let her not bee as one dead, of whom the flesh is halfe consumed, when he commeth out of his mothers wombe.

13 And Moses cryed vnto the LORD, saying, Heale her now, O God, I beseech thee.

14 ¶ And the LORD said vnto Moses, If her father had but spit in her

Marginal notes (left column):
Exod. 16. 3. psal. 78. 6.
Hebr. as ... were the way of a day.
* Psal. 78. 1.
*That is, The graues of lust.
* Hebr. they were in, &c.

Marginal notes (right column):
‖ Or, Cushite.
† Hebr. taken.
* Ecclu. 45. 4.
* Hebr. 3. 2.
* Exod. 33. 11.

* Leuit. 13.
46.

her face, should she not bee ashamed ſeuen dayes? let her be *shut out from the
campe seuen dayes, and after that let
her be receiued in againe.

15 And Miriam was shut out from
the campe seuen dayes : and the people
iourneied not, til Miriam was brought
in againe.

16 And afterward the people remoued from Hazeroth, and pitched in the
wildernesse of Paran.

CHAP XIII.

1 The names of the men who were sent to search
the land. 17 Their instructions. 21 Their
actes. 26 Their relation.

Nd the Lord spake
vnto Moses, saying,

2 Send thou men, that
they may search the lande
of Canaan, which I giue
vnto the children of Israel : of euery
tribe of their fathers shal ye send a man,
euery one a ruler among them.

3 And Moses by the commaundement of the Lord, sent them from
the wildernes of Paran : all those men
were heads of the children of Israel.

4 And these *were* their names. Of
the tribe of Reuben, Shammua the
sonne of Zaccur.

5 Of the tribe of Simeon, Shaphat the sonne of Hori.

6 Of the tribe of Iudah, Caleb the
sonne of Iephunneh.

7 Of the tribe of Issachar, Igal
the sonne of Ioseph.

8 Of the tribe of Ephraim, Oshea
the sonne of Nun.

9 Of the tribe of Beniamin, Palti
the sonne of Raphu.

10 Of the tribe of Zebulun, Gaddiel
the sonne of Sodi.

11 Of the tribe of Ioseph, *namely* of
the tribe of Manasseh, Gaddi the sonne
of Susi.

12 Of the tribe of Dan, Ammiel the
sonne of Gemalli.

13 Of the tribe of Asher, Sethur the
sonne of Michael.

14 Of the tribe of Naphtali, Nahbi
the sonne of Vophsi.

15 Of the tribe of Gad, Geuel the
sonne of Machi.

16 These are the names of the men
which Moses sent to spie out the land :
and Moses called Oshea the sonne of
Nun, Iehoshua.

17 ¶ And Moses sent them to spie
out the land of Canaan, and said vnto
them, Get you vp this *way* Southward, and goe vp into the mountaine :

18 And see the lande what it is, and
the people that dwelleth therein, whether they bee strong or weake, fewe or
many :

19 And what the lande is that they
dwell in, whether it be good or bad, and
what cities they bee that they dwell in,
whether in tents, or in strong holds :

20 And what the land *is*, whether it
be fat or leane, whether there be wood
therein, or not. And be ye of good courage, and bring of the fruit of the land :
(Now the time *was* the time of the first
ripe grapes)

21 ¶ So they went vp, and searched
the land, from the wildernesse of Zin,
vnto Rehob, as men come to Hamath.

22 And they ascended by the South,
and came vnto Hebron : where Ahiman, Sheshai, and Talmai, the children of Anak were : Now Hebron
was built seuen yeeres before Zoan in
Egypt.

23 *And they came vnto the ‖ brooke
of Eshcol, and cut downe from thence
a branch with one cluster of grapes, and
they bare it betweene two vpon a staffe,
and they brought of the pomegranates
and of the figs.

24 The place was called the ‖ brooke
‖ Eshcol, because of the cluster of grapes
which the children of Israel cut downe
from thence.

25 And they returned from searching of the land after fourty dayes.

26 ¶ And they went and came to
Moses, and to Aaron, and to all the
Congregation of the children of Israel
vnto the wildernesse of Paran, to Kadesh, and brought backe word vnto
them, and vnto all the Congregation,
and shewed them the fruit of the land.

27 And they told him, and said, We
came vnto the land whither thou sentest vs, & surely it floweth with * milke
and honie ; and this *is* the fruit of it.

28 Neuerthelesse, the people bee
strong that dwell in the land, and the cities are walled and very great : and
moreouer, we saw the children of Anak
there.

29 The Amalekites dwell in the
land of the South : and the Hittites,
and the Iebusites, and the Amorites
dwell in the mountaines : and the Canaanites

* Deut. 1.
24.
‖ Or, valley

‖ Or, valley
‖ i. a cluster
of grapes.

* Exod. 33
3.

naanites dwell by the sea, and by the coast of Iordane.

30 And Caleb stilled the people before Moses, and said, Let vs goe vp at once, and possesse it, for we are well able to ouercome it.

31 But the men that went vp with him, said, Wee be not able to goe vp against the people, for they are stronger then we.

32 And they brought vp an euill report of the land which they had searched, vnto the children of Israel, saying, The land through which we haue gone, to search it, *is* a land that eateth vp the inhabitants thereof, and all the people that we saw in it, *are* †men of a great stature.

Heb. men statures.

33 And there we saw the giants, the sonnes of Anak, *which come* of the giants: and wee were in our owne sight as grashoppers, and so wee were in their sight.

CHAP. XIIII.

1 The people murmure at the newes. 6 Ioshua and Caleb labour to stil them. 11 God threatneth them. 13 Moses perswadeth God and obtaineth pardon. 26 The murmurers are depriued of entring into the land. 36 The men who raised the euill report, die by a plague. 40 The people that would inuade the land against the wil of God, are smitten.

Nd all the Congregation lifted vp their voyce and cried; and the people wept that night.

2 And all the children of Israel murmured against Moses, and against Aaron: and the whole Congregation said vnto them, Would God that we had died in the land of Egypt, or would God we had died in this wildernesse.

3 And wherefore hath the Lord brought vs vnto this land, to fall by the sword, that our wiues, and our children should be a pray? were it not better for vs to returne into Egypt?

4 And they saide one to another, Let vs make a captaine, and let vs returne into Egypt.

5 Then Moses and Aaron fell on their faces before all the assembly of the Congregation of the children of Israel.

6 ¶ And Ioshua the sonne of Nun, and Caleb the sonne of Iephunneh, which were of them that searched the land, rent their clothes.

7 And they spake vnto all the company of the children of Israel, saying, The land which wee passed thorow to search it, *is* an exceeding good land.

8 If the Lord delight in vs, then he will bring vs into this land, and giue it vs, a land which floweth with milke and hony.

9 Onely rebell not yee against the Lord, neither feare yee the people of the land, for they are bread for vs: their †defence is departed from them, and the Lord *is* with vs: feare them not.

† *Hebr. shadow.*

10 But all the Congregation bade stone them with stones: and the glory of the Lord appeared in the Tabernacle of the Congregation, before all the children of Israel.

11 ¶ And the Lord said vnto Moses, How long will this people prouoke me? and how long will it bee, yer they beleeue me, for all the signes which I haue shewed among them?

12 I will smite them with the pestilence, and disinherite them, and will make of thee a greater nation, and mightier then they.

13 ¶ And * Moses said vnto the Lord, Then the Egyptians shall heare *it*, (for thou broughtest vp this people in thy might from among them:)

* Exod. 32. 12.

14 And they will tell it to the inhabitants of this land: *for* they haue heard that thou Lord *art* among this people, that thou Lord art seene face to face, and that *thy cloud standeth ouer them, and that thou goest before them, by day time in a pillar of a cloud, and in a pillar of fire by night.

* Exod. 13. 21.

15 ¶ Now if thou shalt kill all this people, as one man, then the nations which haue heard the fame of thee, will speake, saying,

16 Because the Lord was not *able to bring this people into the lande which he sware vnto them, therefore he hath slaine them in the wildernesse.

* Deut. 9. 28.

17 And now, I beseech thee, let the power of my Lord be great, according as thou hast spoken, saying,

18 The Lord is *long suffering, and of great mercie, forgiuing iniquitie and transgression, and by no meanes clearing *the guiltie*, *visiting the iniquity of the fathers vpon the children, vnto the third and fourth generation.

* Exod. 34. 6. psal. 103. 8.

* Exod. 20. 5. and 34. 7.

19 Pardon, I beseech thee, the iniquitie

‖ *Or, hither-*
to.

quitie of this people, according vnto the greatnesse of thy mercie, and as thou hast forgiuen this people, from Egypt, euen ‖vntill now.

20 And the Lord said, I haue pardoned, according to thy word.

21 But as truely as I liue, all the earth shalbe filled with the glory of the Lord.

22 Because all those men which haue seene my glory, and my miracles which I did in Egypt, and in the wildernesse, and haue tempted mee now these ten times, and haue not hearkened to my voice,

† *Hebr. if*
they see the
land.

23 † Surely they shall not see the land which I sware vnto their fathers, neither shall any of them that prouoked me, see it.

* Iosh. 14. 6.

24 But my seruant * Caleb, because hee had another spirit with him, (and hath followed mee fully) him will I bring into the land, whereinto he went, and his seed shall possesse it.

25 (Now the Amalekites, and the Canaanites dwelt in the valley) to morrow turne you and get you into the wildernesse, by the way of the Red sea.

26 ¶ And the Lord spake vnto Moses, and vnto Aaron, saying,

27 How long *shall I beare with* this euill congregation which murmure against mee? I haue heard the murmurings of the children of Israel, which they murmure against mee.

* Chap. 26.
65. and 32.
10.

28 Say vnto them, * As truely as I liue, saith the Lord, as ye haue spoken in mine eares, so will I doe to you:

* Deut. 1.
35.

29 Your carcases shall fall in this wildernesse, and all that were *numbred of you, according to your whole number from twentie yeeres old and vpward, which haue murmured against mee,

† *Heb. lifted*
vp my hand.

30 Doubtlesse ye shall not come into the land concerning which I †sware to make you dwell therein, saue Caleb the sonne of Iephunneh, and Ioshua the sonne of Nun.

31 But your little ones, which yee said should be a pray, them will I bring in, and they shall know the land which ye haue despised.

32 But as for you, your carkases, they shall fall in this wildernesse.

‖ *Or, feed.*

33 And your children shall ‖wander in the wildernes forty yeres, and beare your whoredomes, vntill your carkases be wasted in the wildernesse.

34 After the number of the dayes in which ye searched the land, *euen* *fortie dayes (each day for a yeere) shall yee beare your iniquities, *euen* forty yeeres, and yee shall know my ‖breach of promise.

* Ezech. 4.
6. psal. 95.
10.

‖ *Or, alte-*
ring of my
purpose.

35 I the Lord haue said, I will surely doe it vnto all this euill Congregation, that are gathered together against mee: in this wildernesse they shalbe consumed, & there they shall die.

36 And the men which Moses sent to search the land, who returned, and made all the Congregation to murmure against him, by bringing vp a slander vpon the land,

37 Euen those men that did bring vp the euill report vpon the land, * died by the plague, before the Lord.

* 1. Cor. 10
10. hebr. 3
10. iud. 5.

38 But Ioshua the sonne of Nun, and Caleb the sonne of Iephunneh, *which were* of the men that went to search the land, liued *still.*

39 And Moses told these sayings vnto all the children of Israel, and the people mourned greatly.

40 ¶ And they rose vp early in the morning, and gate them vp into the top of the mountaine, saying, Loe, we *be here, and will goe vp vnto the place which the Lord hath promised : for we haue sinned.

* Deut. 1.
41.

41 And Moses said, Wherefore now doe you transgresse the commaundement of the Lord? but it shall not prosper.

42 Goe not vp, for the Lord is not among you, that ye be not smitten before your enemies.

43 For the Amalekites, and the Canaanites *are* there before you, and yee shall fall by the sword, because yee are turned away from the Lord; therefore the Lord will not bee with you.

44 But they presumed to go vp vnto the hill top: neuertheles the Arke of the Couenant of the Lord, and Moses departed not out of the campe.

45 Then the Amalekites came downe, and the Canaanites which dwelt in that hill, and smote them, and *discomfited them, euen vnto Hormah.

* Deut. 1.
44.

CHAP. XV.

1 The law of the meat offering and the drinke offering. 13. 29 The stranger is vnder the same law. 17 The law of the first of the dough for a heaue offering. 22 The sacrifice for sinne

sinne of ignorance. 30 The punishment of presumption. 32 Hee that violated the Sabbath, is stoned. 37 The law of fringes.

Nd the LORD spake vnto Moses, saying,

2 * Speake vnto the children of Israel, and say vnto them, When ye be come into the land of your habitations, which I giue vnto you,

3 And will make an offering by fire vnto the LORD, a burnt offering or a sacrifice *in †performing a vow, or in a free will offering, or in your solemne feasts, to make a * sweet sauour vnto the LORD, of the herd or of the flocke :

4 Then * shall he that offereth his offering vnto the LORD, bring a meat offring of a tenth deale of flowre, mingled with the fourth part of an Hyn of oyle.

5 And the fourth part of an Hyn of wine for a drinke offring shalt thou prepare, with the burnt offering or sacrifice for one lambe.

6 Or for a ramme, thou shalt prepare for a meate offering two tenth deales of flowre mingled with the third part of an Hyn of oyle.

7 And for a drinke offering, thou shalt offer the third part of an Hyn of wine, for a sweete sauour vnto the LORD.

8 And when thou preparest a bullocke for a burnt offering, or for a sacrifice in performing a vow, or peace offerings vnto the LORD :

9 Then shall hee bring with a bullocke a meate offering of three tenth deales of flowre, mingled with halfe an Hyn of oyle.

10 And thou shalt bring for a drinke offering halfe an Hyn of wine, for an offering made by fire of a sweet sauour vnto the LORD.

11 Thus shall it be done for one bullocke, or for one ramme, or for a lambe, or a kidde.

12 According to the number that yee shall prepare, so shall yee doe to euery one, according to their number.

13 All that are borne of the countrey shall doe these things after this maner, in offering an offering made by fire of a sweet sauour, vnto the LORD.

14 And if a stranger soiourne with you, or whosoeuer bee among you in your generations, and will offer an offering made by fire of a sweete sauour

vnto the LORD : as ye doe, so hee shall doe.

15 * One ordinance shall be both for you of the Congregation, and also for the stranger that soiourneth with you, an ordinance for euer in your generations: as ye are, so shall the stranger bee, before the LORD.

16 One law, and one maner shall be for you, and for the stranger that soiourneth with you.

17 ¶ And the LORD spake vnto Moses, saying,

18 Speake vnto the children of Israel, and say vnto them, When ye come into the land whither I bring you,

19 Then it shall be that when ye eate of the bread of the land, yee shall offer vp an heaue offring vnto the LORD.

20 Ye shall offer vp a cake of the first of your dough, for an heaue offring : as ye doe the heaue offering of the threshing floore, so shall ye heaue it.

21 Of the first of your dough ye shal giue vnto the LORD, an heaue offering in your generations.

22 ¶ And if yee haue erred, and not obserued all these Commaundements which the LORD hath spoken vnto Moses,

23 Euen all that the LORD hath commanded you, by the hand of Moses from the day that the LORD commanded Moses, and henceforward among your generations :

24 Then it shalbe, if ought be committed by ignorance †without the knowledge of the Congregation, that all the Congregation shall offer one yong bullocke for a burnt offering, for a sweet sauour vnto the LORD, with his meate offering, and his drinke offering, according to the ‖manner, and one kid of the goats for a sinne offering.

25 And the Priest shall make an atonement for all the Congregation of the children of Israel, and it shal be forgiuen them, for it is ignorance : and they shall bring their offring, a sacrifice made by fire vnto the LORD, and their sinne offering before the LORD, for their ignorance.

26 And it shall bee forgiuen all the Congregation of the children of Israel, and the stranger that soiourneth among them, seeing all the people were in ignorance.

27 ¶ And * if any soule sinne through ignorance, then hee shall bring a shee goat

Leuit. 23.

Leuit. 22.
Ieb. sepa-ing.
Exod. 29.

Leuit. 2. 1.

* Exod. 12. 49. chap. 9. 14.

† Hebr. from the eyes.

‖ Or, ordinance.

* Leuit. 4. 27.

goat of the first yeere for a sinne offring.

28 And the Priest shall make an atonement for the soule that sinneth ignorantly, when he sinneth by ignorance before the LORD, to make an atonement for him, & it shalbe forgiuen him.

† *Hebr doeth.*

29 You shall haue one law for him that †sinneth through ignorance, *both for him* that is borne amongst the children of Israel, and for the stranger that soiourneth among them.

† *Hebr, with an high hand.*

30 ¶ But the soule that doeth ought †presumptuously, whether he be borne in the land, or a stranger, the same reprocheth the LORD : and that soule shall be cut off from among his people.

31 Because he hath despised the word of the LORD, and hath broken his commandement, that soule shall vtterly be cut off: his iniquitie shall be vpon him.

32 ¶ And while the children of Israel were in the wildernes, they found a man that gathered stickes vpon the Sabbath day.

33 And they that found him gathering sticks, brought him vnto Moses and Aaron, and vnto all the Congregation.

* *Leuit. 24. 12.*

34 And they put him * in ward, because it was not declared what should be done to him.

35 And the LORD said vnto Moses, The man shall bee surely put to death : all the Congregation shall stone him with stones without the campe.

36 And all the Cōgregation brought him without the campe, and stoned him with stones, and he died, as the LORD commanded Moses.

37 ¶ And the LORD spake vnto Moses, saying,

* *Deut. 22. 12. matth. 23. 5.*

38 Speake vnto the children of Israel, and bidde * them that they make them fringes in the borders of their garments, throughout their generations, and that they put vpon the fringe of the borders a ribband of blew.

39 And it shall bee vnto you for a fringe, that ye may looke vpon it, and remember all the commandements of the LORD, and doe them : and that ye seeke not after your owne heart, and your owne eyes, after which ye vse to goe a whoring :

40 That ye may remember, and doe all my commandements, and be holy vnto your God.

41 I *am* the LORD your God,

which brought you out of the land of Egypt, to bee your God : I *am* the LORD your God.

CHAP. XVI.

1 The rebellion of Korah, Dathan and Abiram, 23 Moses separateth the people from the rebels tents, 31 The earth swalloweth vp Korah, and a fire consumeth others. 36 The censers are reserued to holy vse. 41 Foureteene thousand and seuen hundred are slaine by a plague for murmuring against Moses and Aaron. 46 Aaron by incense stayeth the plague.

* *Chap. 3. ecclus. 45. 21. iu 11.*

NOw *Korah the sonne of Izhar, the sonne of Kohath, the sonne of Leui, and Dathan, and Abiram the sonnes of Eliab, and On the sonne of Peleth, sonnes of Reuben, tooke *men.*

2 And they rose vp before Moses, with certaine of the children of Israel, two hundred and fiftie Princes of the assembly, * famous in the Congregation, men of renowne.

* *Chap. 9.*

3 And they gathered themselues together against Moses, and against Aaron, and said vnto them, †Ye take too much vpon you, seeing all the Congregation are holy euery one of them, and the LORD is among them : wherfore then lift you vp your selues aboue the Congregation of the LORD?

† *Hebr. much for you.*

4 And when Moses heard it, he fell vpon his face.

5 And hee spake vnto Korah, and vnto all his company, saying, Euen to morrow the LORD will shew who *are* his, and who *is* holy, and will cause *him* to come neere vnto him : euen *him* whom he hath chosen, will he cause to come neere vnto him.

6 This doe : take you censers, Korah, and all his company :

7 And put fire therein, and put incense in them, before the LORD to morrow; And it shall be, *that* the man whom the LORD doeth choose, hee shall be holy : yee take too much vpon you, ye sonnes of Leui.

8 And Moses saide vnto Korah, Heare, I pray you, ye sonnes of Leui.

9 Seemeth it but a small thing vnto you, that the God of Israel hath separated you from the Congregation of Israel, to bring you neere to himselfe, to doe the seruice of the Tabernacle of the LORD, and to stand before the Con-

Congregation to minister vnto them?

10 And he hath brought thee neere *to him*, and all thy brethren the sonnes of Leui with thee : and seeke ye the Priesthood also?

11 For which cause both thou, and all thy company are gathered together against the LORD : and what is Aaron, that ye murmure against him?

12 ¶ And Moses sent to call Dathan and Abiram the sonnes of Eliab: which said, We will not come vp.

13 Is it a small thing that thou hast brought vs vp out of a land that floweth with milke and hony, to kill vs in the wildernesse, except thou make thy selfe altogether a prince ouer vs?

14. Moreouer, thou hast not brought vs into a land that floweth with milke and hony, or giuen vs inheritance of fields and vineyards : wilt thou †put out the eyes of these men? we will not come vp.

b. boare

15 And Moses was very wroth, and said vnto the LORD, * Respect not thou their offering : I haue not taken one asse from them, neither haue I hurt one of them.

n. 4. 4.

16 And Moses said vnto Korah, Be thou and all thy company before the LORD, thou, and they, and Aaron to morrow.

17 And take euery man his censer, and put incense in them, and bring yee before the LORD euery man his censer, two hundred and fiftie censers, thou also and Aaron, each *of you* his censer.

18 And they tooke euery man his censer, and put fire in them, and laide incense thereon, and stood in the doore of the Tabernacle of the Congregation with Moses and Aaron.

19 And Korah gathered all the Congregation against them, vnto the doore of the Tabernacle of the Congregation : and the glory of the LORD appeared vnto all the Congregation.

20 And the LORD spake vnto Moses, and vnto Aaron, saying,

21 Separate your selues from among this Congregation, that I may consume them in a moment.

22 And they fell vpon their faces, and said, O God, the God of the spirits of all flesh, shal one man sinne, and wilt thou be wroth with all the Congregation?

23 ¶ And the LORD spake vnto Moses, saying,

24 Speake vnto the Congregation, saying, Get you vp from about the tabernacle of Korah, Dathan, and Abiram.

25 And Moses rose vp, and went vnto Dathan and Abiram : and the Elders of Israel followed him.

26 And hee spake vnto the Congregation, saying, Depart, I pray you, from the tents of these wicked men, and touch nothing of theirs, lest ye be consumed in all their sinnes.

27 So they gate vp from the tabernacle of Korah, Dathan, and Abiram, on euery side: and Dathan and Abiram came out, and stood in the doore of their tents, and their wiues, & their sonnes, and their little children.

28 And Moses said, Hereby ye shall know that the LORD hath sent me to doe all these workes : for *I haue* not *done them* of mine owne mind.

29 If these men die † the common death of all men, or if they be visited after the visitation of all men, then the LORD hath not sent me :

30 But if the LORD †make a new thing, and the earth open her mouth, and swallow them vp, with all that appertaine vnto them, and they go downe quicke into the pit: then ye shall vnderstand that these men haue prouoked the LORD.

31 ¶ * And it came to passe as he had made an ende of speaking all these words, that the ground claue asunder that was vnder them :

32 And the earth opened her mouth, and swallowed them vp, and their houses, and all the men that appertained vnto Korah, and all their goods.

33 They, and all that appertained to them, went downe aliue into the pit, and the earth closed vpon them : and they perished from among the Congregation.

34 And all Israel that were round about them, fled at the crie of them: for they said, Lest the earth swallow vs vp *also.*

35 And there came out a fire from the LORD, and consumed the two hundred and fiftie men that offered incense.

36 ¶ And the LORD spake vnto Moses, saying,

37 Speake vnto Eleazar the sonne of Aaron the Priest, that he take vp the censers out of the burning, and scatter thou

† Hebr. as euery man dieth.

† Hebr. create a creature.

* Chap. 27. 3. deut. 11. 6. psal. 106. 17.

thou the fire yonder, for they are hallowed.

38 The censers of these sinners against their owne soules, let them make them broad plates for a couering of the Altar : for they offered them before the LORD, therefore they are hallowed, and they shall be a signe vnto the children of Israel.

39 And Eleazar the Priest tooke the brasen censers, wherewith they that were burnt had offered, and they were made broad *plates* for a couering of the Altar :

40 *To bee* a memoriall vnto the children of Israel, that no stranger, which is not of the seed of Aaron, come neere to offer incense before the LORD, that he be not as Korah, and as his company, as the LORD said to him by the hand of Moses.

41 ¶ But on the morrow, all the Congregation of the children of Israel murmured against Moses and against Aaron, saying, Ye haue killed the people of the LORD.

42 And it came to passe when the Congregation was gathered against Moses and against Aaron, that they looked toward the Tabernacle of the Congregation : and behold, the cloud couered it, and the glory of the LORD appeared.

43 And Moses and Aaron came before the Tabernacle of the Congregation.

44 ¶ And the LORD spake vnto Moses, saying,

45 Get you vp from among this Congregation, that I may consume them, as in a moment : and they fell vpon their faces.

46 ¶ And Moses said vnto Aaron, Take a censer, and put fire therein from off the Altar, and put on incense, and goe quickly vnto the Congregation, and make an atonement for them : for there is wrath gone out from the LORD; the plague is begun.

47 And Aaron tooke as Moses commanded, and ranne into the midst of the Congregation : and behold, the plague was begun among the people, and he put on incense, and made an atonement for the people.

48 And he stood betweene the dead and the liuing, and the plague was stayed.

49 Now they that died in the plague,

were fourteene thousand and seuen hundred, beside them that died about the matter of Korah.

50 And Aaron returned vnto Moses, vnto the doore of the Tabernacle of the Congregation; and the plague was stayed.

CHAP. XVII.

1 Aarons rod among all the rods of the Tribes onely flourisheth. 10 It is left for a monument against the rebels.

Nd the LORD spake vnto Moses, saying,

2 Speake vnto the children of Israel, and take of euery one of them a rod, according to the house of their fathers, of all their princes, according to the house of their fathers, twelue rods : write thou euery mans name vpon his rodde.

3 And thou shalt write Aarons name vpon the rod of Leui : for one rod shall be for the head of the house of their fathers.

4 And thou shalt lay them vp in the Tabernacle of the Congregation, before the Testimony, * where I will meet with you.

5 And it shall come to passe, that the mans rod whom I shall choose, shall blossome : and I will make to cease from mee the murmurings of the children of Israel, whereby they murmure against you.

6 ¶ And Moses spake vnto the children of Israel, and euery one of their Princes gaue him †a rod a piece, for each Prince one, according to their fathers houses, *euen* twelue rods : and the rod of Aaron was among their rods.

7 And Moses layd vp the rods before the LORD, in the Tabernacle of Witnesse.

8 And it came to passe that on the morrow Moses went into the Tabernacle of Witnesse, and behold, the rod of Aaron for the house of Leui was budded, and brought forth buds, and bloomed blossomes, and yeelded almonds.

9 And Moses brought out all the rods from before the LORD, vnto all the children of Israel : and they looked, and tooke euery man his rod.

10 ¶ And the LORD said vnto Moses, *Bring Aarons rod againe before the Testimony, to be kept for a token against the †rebels, and thou shalt quite

*Exod. 22.

† Hebr. a nod for o͡r Prince, e rod for or Prince.

* Hebr. 9

† Hebr. c. dren of re bellion.

quite take away their murmurings from me, that they die not.

11 And Moses did so: as the Lord commanded him, so did he.

12 And the children of Israel spake vnto Moses, saying, Behold, wee die, we perish, we all perish.

13 Whosoeuer commeth any thing neere vnto the Tabernacle of the Lord, shall die: Shall wee be consumed with dying?

CHAP. XVIII.

1 The charge of the Priests and Leuites. 9 The Priests portion. 21 The Leuites portion. 25 The heaue offering to the Priests out of the Leuites portion.

Nd the Lord sayd vnto Aaron, Thou and thy sonnes, and thy fathers house with thee, shall beare the iniquitie of the Sanctuary: and thou and thy sonnes with thee, shall beare the iniquitie of your Priesthood.

2 And thy brethren also of the tribe of Leui, the tribe of thy father, bring thou with thee, that they may be ioyned vnto thee, and minister vnto thee: but thou and thy sonnes with thee *shall minister* before the Tabernacle of Witnesse.

3 And they shall keepe thy charge, and the charge of all the Tabernacle: onely they shall not come nigh the vessels of the Sanctuarie, and the Altar, that neither they, nor you also die.

4 And they shall bee ioyned vnto thee, and keepe the charge of the Tabernacle of the Congregation, for all the seruice of the Tabernacle: and a stranger shall not come nigh vnto you.

5 And yee shall keepe the charge of the Sanctuary, and the charge of the Altar, that there be no wrath any more vpon the children of Israel.

6 And I, beholde, I haue *taken your brethren the Leuites from among the children of Israel: to you they are giuen as a gift for the Lord, to doe the seruice of the Tabernacle of the Congregation.

Chap. 3. 45.

7 Therefore thou and thy sonnes with thee, shall keepe your Priests office for euery thing of the Altar, and within the Vaile, and yee shall serue: I haue giuen your Priests office vnto you, as a seruice of gift: and the stranger that commeth nigh, shall bee put to death.

8 ¶ And the Lord spake vnto Aaron, Behold, I also haue giuen thee the charge of mine heaue offerings, of all the hallowed things of the children of Israel, vnto thee haue I giuen them by reason of the anointing, and to thy sonnes by an ordinance for euer.

9 This shall bee thine of the most holy things, *reserued* from the fire: euery oblation of theirs, euery meat offering of theirs, and euery sinne offering of theirs, and euery trespasse offering of theirs, which they shal render vnto me, shall be most holy for thee, and for thy sonnes.

10 In the most holy *place* shalt thou eate it, euery male shall eate it: it shall be holy vnto thee.

11 And this is thine: the heaue offering of their gift, with all the waue offrings of the children of Israel: I haue giuen them vnto thee, & to thy sonnes, and to thy *daughters with thee, by a statute for euer: euery one that is cleane in thy house, shall eate of it.

Leuit. 10 14.

12 All the †best of the oyle, and all the best of the wine, and of the wheat, the first fruits of them which they shall offer vnto the Lord, them haue I giuen thee.

Heb. fat.

13 And whatsoeuer is first ripe in the land, which they shall bring vnto the Lord, shall be thine, euery one that is cleane in thine house, shall eat of it.

14 *Euery thing deuoted in Israel, shall be thine.

Leuit. 27. 28.

15 Euery thing that openeth *the matrice in all flesh, which they bring vnto the Lord, whether it bee of men or beasts, shall be thine: Neuertheles the first borne of man shalt thou surely redeeme, and the firstling of vncleane beasts shalt thou redeeme.

Exod. 13. 2. & 22. 29. leuit. 27. 26 chap. 3. 13.

16 And those that are to be redeemed, from a moneth old shalt thou redeeme according to thine estimation, for the money of fiue shekels, after the shekel of the Sanctuary, *which is twentie gerahs.

Exod. 30. 13. leuit. 27 47. ezek. 45 12.

17 But the firstling of a cowe, or the firstling of a sheepe, or the firstling of a goat thou shalt not redeeme, they *are* holy: thou shalt sprinckle their blood vpon the Altar, and shalt burne their fat for an offering made by fire, for a sweet sauour vnto the Lord.

18 And the flesh of them shall bee thine: as the *waue breast, and as the right shoulder are thine.

Exod. 29. 26.

19 All

19 All the heaue offerings of the holy things, which the children of Israel offer vnto the LORD, haue I giuen thee and thy sonnes, and thy daughters with thee, by a statute for euer : it is a couenant of salt for euer , before the LORD vnto thee , and to thy seed with thee.

20 ¶ And the LORD spake vnto Aaron, Thou shalt haue no inheritance in their land, neither shalt thou haue any part among them: *I am thy part, and thine inheritance among the children of Israel.

* Deut. 10. 9. and 18. 2. iosh. 13. 14. 33. ezech. 44. 28.

21 And behold, I haue giuen the children of Leui all the tenth in Israel, for an inheritance, for their seruice which they serue, euen the seruice of the Tabernacle of the Congregation.

22 Neither must the children of Israel henceforth come nigh the Tabernacle of the Congregation, lest they beare sinne, †and die.

† Hebr. to die.

23 But the Leuites shall doe the seruice of the Tabernacle of the Congregation, and they shal beare their iniquitie: it shall be a statute for euer throughout your generations, that among the children of Israel they haue no inheritance.

24 But the tithes of the children of Israel which they offer as an heaue offering vnto the LORD, I haue giuen to the Leuites to inherite : therefore I haue said vnto them, Among the children of Israel they shall haue no inheritance.

25 ¶ And the LORD spake vnto Moses, saying,

26 Thus speake vnto the Leuites, and say vnto them, When ye take of the children of Israel the tithes, which I haue giuen you from them for your inheritance, then ye shal offer vp an heaue offering of it for the LORD, euen a tenth part of the tithe.

27 And this your heaue offering shall be reckoned vnto you, as though it were the corne of the threshing floore, and as the fulnesse of the wine presse.

28 Thus you also shal offer an heaue offering vnto the LORD of all your tithes which ye receiue of the children of Israel, and ye shall giue thereof the LORDS heaue offering to Aaron the Priest.

29 Out of all your gifts ye shal offer euery heaue offering of the LORD, of all the †best thereof, euen the hal-

† Hebr. fat.

lowed part thereof, out of it.

30 Therefore thou shalt say vnto them, When yee haue heaued the best thereof from it, then it shall be counted vnto the Leuites, as the encrease of the threshing floore, and as the encrease of the wine presse.

31 And ye shall eate it in euery place, ye and your houshold: for it is your reward for your seruice, in the Tabernacle of the Congregation.

32 And yee shall beare no sinne by reason of it, when ye haue heaued from it the best of it : neither shall ye pollute the holy things of the children of Israel, lest ye die.

CHAP. XIX.

1 The water of separation made of the ashes of a red heifer. 11 The law for the vse of it in purification of the vncleaue.

ANd the LORD spake vnto Moses , and vnto Aaron, saying,

2 This is the ordinance of the Law , which the LORD hath commaunded , saying, Speake vnto the children of Israel, that they bring thee a red heifer without spot, wherein is no blemish, and vpon which neuer came yoke.

3 And ye shall giue her vnto Eleazar the Priest, that hee may bring her *forth without the campe, and one shall slay her before his face.

* Hebr. 13. 11.

4 And Eleazar the Priest shall take of her blood with his finger, and *sprinkle of her blood directly before the Tabernacle of the Congregation seuen times.

* Heb. 9. 13.

5 And one shall burne the heifer in his sight : *her skinne, and her flesh, and her blood, with her doung, shall he burne.

* Exod. 29. 14. leuit. 4. 11, 12.

6 And the Priest shall take Cedarwood, and hysope, and scarlet, and cast it into the midst of the burning of the heifer.

7 Then the Priest shall wash his clothes, and hee shall bathe his flesh in water, and afterward he shall come into the campe, and the Priest shalbe vncleane vntill the euen.

8 And he that burneth her, shall wash his clothes in water, and bathe his flesh in water, and shall be vncleane vntill the Euen.

9 And a man that is cleane, shall gather

ther vp the ashes of the heifer, and lay them vp without the campe in a cleane place, and it shall bee kept for the Congregation of the children of Israel, for a water of separation : it *is* a purification for sinne.

10 And he that gathereth the ashes of the heifer, shall wash his clothes, and be vncleane vntil the Euen : and it shall be vnto the children of Israel, and vnto the stranger that soiourneth among them, for a statute for euer.

Heb. soule.

11 ¶ He that toucheth the dead body of any † man, shall bee vncleane seuen dayes.

12 He shall purifie himselfe with it on the third day, and on the seuenth day he shall be cleane : but if he purifie not himselfe the third day, then the seuenth day he shall not be cleane.

13 Whosoeuer toucheth the dead bodie of any man that is dead, and purifieth not himselfe, defileth the Tabernacle of the LORD, and that soule shall be cut off from Israel, because the water of separation was not sprinckled vpon him : he shall be vncleane, his vncleannesse *is* yet vpon him.

14 This *is* the law, when a man dieth in a tent; all that come into the tent, and all that *is* in the tent, shalbe vnclean seuen dayes.

15 And euery open vessel which hath no couering bound vpon it, is vncleane.

16 And whosoeuer toucheth one that is slaine with a sword in the open fields, or a dead body, or a bone of a man, or a graue, shall be vncleane seuen dayes.

Heb. Dust.
Heb. liuing waters shall giuen.

17 And for an vncleane person they shall take of the † ashes of the burnt heifer of purification for sinne, and *running water shall bee put thereto in a vessell :

18 And a cleane person shall take hysope, and dippe it in the water, and sprinckle *it* vpon the tent, and vpon all the vessels, and vpon the persons that were there, and vpon him that touched a bone, or one slaine, or one dead, or a graue.

19 And the cleane *person* shal sprinkle vpon the vncleane on the third day, and on the seuenth day : and on the seuenth day he shall purifie himselfe, and wash his clothes, and bathe himselfe in water, and shall be cleane at Euen.

20 But the man that shall bee vncleane, and shall not purifie himselfe, that soule shall bee cut off from among the Congregation : because he hath defiled the Sanctuary of the LORD, the water of separation hath not beene sprinkled vpon him, he *is* vncleane.

21 And it shall be a perpetuall statute vnto them, that he that sprinkleth the water of separation, shall wash his clothes : and he that toucheth the water of separation, shall be vncleane vntill Euen.

22 And whatsoeuer the vncleane person toucheth, shall be vncleane : and the soule that toucheth it, shall bee vncleane vntill Euen.

CHAP. XX.

1 The children of Israel come to Zin, where Miriam dieth. 2 They murmure for want of water. 7 Moses smiting the rocke bringeth forth water at Meribah. 14 Moses at Kadesh desireth passage thorow Edom, which is denied him. 22 At Mount Hor Aaron resigneth his place to Eleazar, and dieth.

Hen came the children of Israel, *euen* the whole Congregation, into the desert of Zin, in the first moneth : and the people abode in Kadesh, and Miriam died there, and was buried there.

2 And there was no water for the Congregation : and they gathered themselues together against Moses and against Aaron.

3 And the people chode with Moses, and spake, saying, Would God that we had died * when our brethren died before the LORD.

* Chap. 11. 33.

4 And * why haue yee brought vp the Congregation of the LORD into this wildernesse, that we and our cattell should die there?

* Exod. 17. 2.

5 And wherefore haue ye made vs to come vp out of Egypt, to bring vs in vnto this euil place? it *is* no place of seed, or of figges, or vines, or of pomegranates, neither is there any water to drinke.

6 And Moses and Aaron went from the presence of the assembly, vnto the doore of the Tabernacle of the congregation, and they fell vpon their faces : and the glory of the LORD appeared vnto them.

7 ¶ And the Lord spake vnto Moses, saying,

8 Take the rodde, and gather thou the assembly together, thou and Aaron thy

thy brother, and speake yee vnto the rocke before their eyes, and it shall giue foorth his water, and thou shalt bring foorth to them, water out of the rocke: so thou shalt giue the Congregation, and their beasts drinke.

9 And Moses tooke the rod from before the LORD, as he commanded him.

10 And Moses and Aaron gathered the Congregation together before the rocke, and hee said vnto them, Heare now, ye rebels; must we fetch you water out of this rocke?

11 And Moses lift vp his hand, and with his rod he smote the rocke twice: and the water came out abundantly, and the Congregation dranke, and their beasts *also.*

12 ¶ And the LORD spake vnto Moses and Aaron, Because ye beleeue *me not, to sanctifie me in the eyes of the children of Israel, therefore ye shall not bring this Congregation into the land which I haue giuen them.

* Psal. 106. 32. &c.
‖ *That is, strife.*

13 * This is the water of ‖ Meribah, because the children of Israel stroue with the LORD; and he was sanctified in them.

14 ¶ And Moses sent messengers from Kadesh, vnto the King of Edom; Thus saith thy brother Israel, Thou knowest all the trauaile that hath † befallen vs:

† *Hebr. found vs.*

15 How our fathers went downe into Egypt, and we haue dwelt in Egypt a long time: and the Egyptians vexed vs, and our fathers.

16 And when wee cryed vnto the LORD, he heard our voyce, and sent an Angel, and hath brought vs foorth out of Egypt: and behold, wee are in Kadesh, a citie in the vttermost of thy border.

17 Let vs passe, I pray thee, thorow thy countrey: we will not passe thorow the fields, or thorow the Vineyards, neither will we drinke of the water of the wells: wee will goe by the Kings *high*-way, we wil not turne to the right hand nor to the left, vntill wee haue passed thy borders.

18 And Edom said vnto him, Thou shalt not passe by me, lest I come out against thee with the sword.

19 And the children of Israel said vnto him, We will goe by the high-way: and if I and my cattell drinke of thy water, then I will pay for it: I will

onely (without *doing* any thing *else*) go thorow on my feet.

20 And he said, Thou shalt not goe thorow. And Edom came out against him with much people, and with a strong hand.

21 Thus Edom refused to giue Israel passage thorow his border: wherefore Israel turned away from him.

22 ¶ And the children of Israel, euen the whole Congregation, iourneyed from * Kadesh, and came vnto mount Hor.

* Chap. 33. 37.

23 And the LORD spake vnto Moses and Aaron in mount Hor, by the coast of the land of Edom, saying;

24 Aaron shall bee gathered vnto his people: for hee shall not enter into the land which I haue giuen vnto the children of Israel, because yee rebelled against my † word at the water of Meribah.

† *Hebr. mouth.*

25 * Take Aaron, and Eleazar his sonne, and bring them vp vnto mount Hor.

* Chap. 33. 38. deut. 32. 50.

26 And strippe Aaron of his garments, and put them vpon Eleazar his sonne, and Aaron shall be gathered *vnto his people,* and shall die there.

27 And Moses did as the LORD commaunded: and they went vp into mount Hor, in the sight of all the Congregation.

28 And Moses stripped Aaron of his garments, and put them vpon Eleazar his sonne, and * Aaron died there in the top of the mount: and Moses and Eleazar came downe from the mount.

* Deut. 10. 6. and 32. 50.

29 And when all the Congregation saw that Aaron was dead, they mourned for Aaron thirty dayes, *euen* all the house of Israel.

CHAP. XXI.

1 Israel with some losse destroy the Canaanites at Hormah. 4 The people murmuring are plagued with fiery serpents. 7 They repenting are healed by a brasen serpent. 10 Sundry iourneyes of the Israelites. 21 Sihon is ouercome, 33 and Og.

Nd when * king Arad the Canaanite, which dwelt in the South, heard tell that Israel came by the way of the spies, then hee fought against Israel, and tooke some of them prisoners.

* Chap. 33. 40.

2 And Israel vowed a vow vnto the

the LORD, and said, If thou wilt indeed deliuer this people into my hand, then I wil vtterly destroy their cities.

3 And the LORD hearkened to the voyce of Israel, and deliuered vp the Canaanites : and they vtterly destroyed them, and their cities, and hee called the name of the place ‖ Hormah.

4 ¶ And they iourneyed from mount Hor, by the way of the red sea, to compasse the land of Edom : and the soule of the people was much ‖ discouraged because of the way.

5 And the people spake against God and against Moses, Wherefore haue ye brought vs vp out of Egypt, to die in the wildernesse ? for there is no bread, neither is there any water, and our soule * loatheth this light bread.

6 And * the LORD sent fierie serpents among the people, and they bit the people, and much people of Israel died.

7 ¶ Therefore the people came to Moses, and said, We haue sinned : for wee haue spoken against the LORD, and against thee : pray vnto the LORD that hee take away the serpents from vs : and Moses prayed for the people.

8 And the LORD said vnto Moses, Make thee a fierie serpent, and set it vpon a pole : and it shall come to passe, that euery one that is bitten, when hee looketh vpon it, shall liue.

9 And * Moses made a serpent of brasse, and put it vpon a pole, and it came to passe, that if a serpent had bitten any man, when hee beheld the serpent of brasse, he liued.

10 ¶ And the children of Israel set forward, and * pitched in Oboth.

11 And they iourneyed from Oboth, and pitched at ‖ Iie-Abarim, in the wildernes which is before Moab, toward the Sunne rising.

12 ¶ From thence they remooued, and pitched in the valley of Zared.

13 From thence they remooued, and pitched on the other side of Arnon, which is in the wildernesse that commeth out of the coasts of the Amorites : for Arnon is the border of Moab, betweene Moab and the Amorites.

14 Wherefore it is said in the booke of the warres of the LORD, ‖ what he did in the Red sea, and in the brookes of Arnon,

15 And at the streame of the brookes that goeth downe to the dwelling of Ar, & † lieth vpon the border of Moab.

16 And from thence they went to Beer: that is the well whereof the LORD spake vnto Moses, Gather the people together, and I will giue them water.

17 ¶ Then Israel sang this song, † Spring vp O well, ‖ Sing ye vnto it :

18 The Princes digged the well, the nobles of the people digged it, by the direction of the Law-giuer, with their staues. And from the wildernesse they went to Mattanah :

19 And from Mattanah, to Nahaliel, and from Nahaliel to Bamoth :

20 And from Bamoth in the valley, that is in the † countrey of Moab, to the toppe of ‖ Pisgah, which looketh toward ‖ Ieshimon.

21 ¶ And Israel sent messengers vnto Sihon king of the Amorites, saying,

22 * Let me passe thorow thy land, we will not turne into the fields, or into the vineyards, we will not drinke of the waters of the well : but we will goe along by the kings high way, vntill wee be past thy borders.

23 * And Sihon would not suffer Israel to passe thorow his border : but Sihon gathered all his people together, and went out against Israel into the wildernes : and he came to Iahaz, and fought against Israel.

24 And * Israel smote him with the edge of the sword, and possessed his land from Arnon vnto Iabok, euen vnto the children of Ammon : for the border of the children of Ammon was strong.

25 And Israel tooke all these cities : and Israel dwelt in all the cities of the Amorites, in Heshbon, and in all the † villages thereof.

26 For Heshbon was the citie of Sihon the King of the Amorites, who had fought against the former King of Moab, and taken all his land out of his hand, euen vnto Arnon.

27 Wherefore they that speake in prouerbes, say, Come into Heshbon : let the citie of Sihon bee built and prepared.

28 For there is a fire gone out of Heshbon, a flame from the citie of Sihon : it hath consumed Ar of Moab, and the lordes of the high places of Arnon.

29 Woe to thee, Moab, thou art vndone, O people of * Chemosh : he hath giuen

*that is, vtterdestru-
on.*

*r, grieu. Hebr
rtened.*

*Chap.
6.
Wisd. 16.
5. 1. cor.
9.*

*. King. 18
ioh. 3. 14.*

Chap. 33

*r, heapes
Abarim.*

*Or, Vaheb
Suphah.*

† Heb. leaneth.

*† Heb. ascend
‖ Or, answere.*

*† Heb. field.
‖ Or, hill.
‖ Or, the
wildernesse.*

*Deut. 2.
27. iudges
11. 19.*

*Deut.
29. 7.*

*Iosh. 12. 2
psal. 135.
11. amos
2 9.*

*† Hebr.
daughters.*

*1. King. 11
7, 33.*

giuen his sonnes that escaped, and his daughters, into captiuitie vnto Sihon King of the Amorites.

30 We haue shot at them; Heshbon is perished euen vnto Dibon, and we haue layde them waste euen vnto Nophah, which *reacheth* vnto Medeba.

31 ¶ Thus Israel dwelt in the land of the Amorites.

32 And Moses sent to spy out Iaazer, and they tooke the villages thereof, and droue out the Amorites that *were* there.

33 ¶ *And they turned and went vp by the way of Bashan : and Og the King of Bashan went out against them, he, and all his people, to the battell at Edrei.

34 And the LORD said vnto Moses, Feare him not : for I haue deliuered him into thy hand, and all his people, and his land, and *thou shalt doe to him as thou didst vnto Sihon King of the Amorites, which dwelt at Heshbon.

35 So they smote him & his sonnes, and all his people, vntill there was none left him aliue, and they possessed his land.

CHAP. XXII.

1 Balaks first message for Balaam is refused. 15 His second message obtaineth him. 22 An Angel would haue slaine him, if his asse had not saued him. 36 Balak intertaineth him.

Nd the children of Israel set forward, and pitched in the plaines of Moab, on this side Iordane by Iericho.

2 ¶ And Balak the sonne of Zippor, saw all that Israel had done to the Amorites.

3 And Moab was sore afraid of the people, because they were many, and Moab was distressed, because of the children of Israel.

4 And Moab said vnto the elders of Midian; Now shall this company licke vp all that *are* round about vs, as the oxe licketh vp the grasse of the field. And Balak the sonne of Zippor, *was* King of the Moabites at that time.

5 *He sent messengers therefore vnto Balaam the sonne of Beor, to Pethor, which is by the riuer of the land of the children of his people, to call him, saying, Behold, there is a people come out from Egypt : beholde, they couer

the †face of the earth, and they abide ouer against me.

6 Come now therefore, I pray thee, curse mee this people, for they are too mightie for mee : peraduenture I shall preuaile, that we may smite them, and that I may driue them out of the land: for I wot that he whom thou blessest, is blessed, and hee whom thou cursest, is cursed.

7 And the elders of Moab, and the elders of Midian departed, with the rewards of diuination in their hand; and they came vnto Balaam, and spake vnto him the words of Balak.

8 And hee said vnto them, Lodge here this night, and I will bring you word againe as the LORD shal speake vnto mee : and the Princes of Moab abode with Balaam.

9 And God came vnto Balaam, and said, What men are these with thee?

10 And Balaam said vnto God, Balak the sonne of Zippor, King of Moab, hath sent vnto me, *saying;*

11 Behold, there is a people come out of Egypt, which couereth the face of the earth : Come now, curse me them; peraduenture †I shal be able to ouercome them, and driue them out.

12 And God saide vnto Balaam; Thou shalt not goe with them, thou shalt not curse the people: for they are blessed.

13 And Balaam rose vp in the morning, and said vnto the Princes of Balak, Get you into your land : for the LORD refuseth to giue mee leaue to goe with you.

14 And the Princes of Moab rose vp, and they went vnto Balak, and said, Balaam refuseth to come with vs.

15 ¶ And Balak sent yet againe Princes, moe, and more honourable then they.

16 And they came to Balaam, and said to him, Thus saith Balak the son of Zippor, †Let nothing, I pray thee, hinder thee from comming vnto me :

17 For I wil promote thee vnto very great honour, and I will do whatsoeuer thou saiest vnto me: Come therefore, I pray thee, curse me this people.

18 And Balaam answered and said vnto the seruants of Balak, *If Balak would giue me his house full of siluer and gold, I cannot goe beyond the word of the LORD my God, to doe lesse or more.

19 Now

* Deut. 3. 1. and 29. 7.

* Psal. 135. 11.

* Iosh. 24. 9.

† Hebr. ey

† Hebr. I shall preua in fighting gainst him

† Hebr. I not thou l ted from

* Chap. 2 13.

19 Now therefore, I, pray you, tarie yee also here this night, that I may know what the LORD will say vnto me more.

20 And God came vnto Balaam at night, and said vnto him, If the men come to call thee, rise vp, and goe with them : but yet the word which I shall say vnto thee, that shalt thou doe.

21 And Balaam rose vp in the morning, and sadled his asse, and went with the princes of Moab.

22 ¶ And Gods anger was kindled, because he went : and the Angel of the LORD stood in the way for an aduersarie against him : Now he was riding vpon his asse, and his two seruants *were* with him.

23 And * the Asse sawe the Angel of the LORD standing in the way, and his sword drawen in his hand : and the asse turned aside out of the way, and went into the field : and Balaam smote the asse, to turne her into the way.

2. Pet. 2. 5. Iude 11

24 But the Angel of the LORD stood in a path of the vineyards, a wall being on this side, & a wall on that side.

25 And when the asse saw the Angel of the LORD, she thrust her selfe vnto the wall, and crusht Balaams foote against the wall : and hee smote her againe.

26 And the Angel of the LORD went further, and stood in a narrowe place, where was no way to turne, either to the right hand, or to the left.

27 And when the asse sawe the Angel of the LORD, shee fell downe vnder Balaam, and Balaams anger was kindled, and hee smote the asse with a staffe.

28 And the LORD opened the mouth of the asse, and shee saide vnto Balaam, What haue I done vnto thee, that thou hast smitten mee these three times ?

29 And Balaam said vnto the asse, Because thou hast mocked mee : I would there were a sword in mine hand, for now would I kill thee.

30 And the asse said vnto Balaam, *Am* not I thine asse, † vpon which thou hast ridden || euer since I was thine, vnto this day ? was I euer wont to do so vnto thee ? And he said, Nay.

Hebr. who hast ridden vpon me.
|| *Or, euer since thou wast, &c.*

31 Then the LORD opened the eyes of Balaam, and hee saw the Angel of the LORD standing in the way, and his sword drawen in his hand : and hee bowed downe his head, and || fell flat on his face.

|| *Bowed himselfe.*

32 And the Angel of the LORD said vnto him, Wherefore hast thou smitten thine asse these three times ? Behold, I went out † to withstand thee, because *thy* way is peruerse before me.

† *Hebr. to be an aduersarie vnto thee*

33 And the asse saw me, and turned from me these three times : vnlesse shee had turned from me, surely now also I had slaine thee, and saued her aliue.

34 And Balaam said vnto the Angel of the LORD, I haue sinned : for I knew not that thou stoodest in the way against mee : Now therefore if it † displease thee, I will get mee backe againe.

† *Heb. be euill in thine eyes.*

35 And the Angel of the LORD said vnto Balaam, Goe with the men : but onely the word that I shall speake vnto thee, that thou shalt speake : So Balaam went with the princes of Balak.

36 ¶ And when Balak heard that Balaam was come, hee went out to meete him, vnto a citie of Moab, which *is* in the border of Arnon, which *is* in the vtmost coast.

37 And Balak said vnto Balaam, Did I not earnestly send vnto thee to call thee ? wherefore camest thou not vnto me ? Am I not able indeed to promote thee to honour ?

38 And Balaam saide vnto Balak, Loe, I am come vnto thee : haue I now any power at all to say any thing ? the worde that God putteth in my mouth, that shall I speake.

39 And Balaam went with Balak, and they came vnto || Kiriath-Huzoth.

|| *Or, a citie of streets.*

40 And Balak offered oxen, and sheepe, and sent to Balaam, and to the princes that *were* with him.

41 And it came to passe on the morrow, that Balak tooke Balaam, and brought him vp into the high places of Baal, that thence hee might see the vtmost part of the people.

CHAP. XXIII.

1.13.28 Balaks sacrifice. 7.18 Balaams parable.

And Balaam saide vnto Balak, Build me here seuen Altars, and prepare mee here seuen oxen, and seuen rammes.

2 And Balak did as Balaam had spoken, and Balak & Balaam offered on *euery* altar a bullocke and a ramme.

3 And

3 And Balaam said vnto Balak, Stand by thy burnt offring, and I wil goe : peraduenture the LORD will come to meete mee ; and whatsoeuer he sheweth me, I will tell thee. And ||he went *to* an high place.

|| Or, he went solitary.

4 And God met Balaam, and he said vnto him, I haue prepared seuen altars, and I haue offered vpon *euery* altar a bullocke and a ramme.

5 And the LORD put a word in Balaams mouth, and said, Returne vnto Balak, & thus thou shalt speake.

6 And he returned vnto him, and loe, he stood by his burnt sacrifice, hee, and all the Princes of Moab.

7 And he tooke vp his parable, and said, Balak the King of Moab hath brought mee from Aram, out of the mountaines of the East, *saying*, Come, curse me Iacob, and come, defie Israel.

8 How shall I curse, *whom* God hath not cursed ? or how shall I defie, *whom* the LORD hath not defied ?

9 For from the top of the rockes I see him, and from the hilles I behold him : loe, the people shall dwell alone, and shall not bee reckoned among the nations.

10 Who can count the dust of Iacob, and the number of the fourth part of Israel ? Let †mee die the death of the righteous, & let my last end be like his.

† Hebr. my soule, or my life.

11 And Balak saide vnto Balaam, What hast thou done vnto me? I tooke thee to curse mine enemies, and behold, thou hast blessed them altogether.

12 And he answered, and said, Must I not take heede to speake that which the LORD hath put in my mouth ?

13 And Balak said vnto him, Come, I pray thee, with me, vnto another place, from whence thou mayest see them : thou shalt see but the vtmost part of them, and shalt not see them all: and curse me them from thence.

14 ¶ And hee brought him into the fielde of Zophim, to the toppe of ||Pisgah, and built seuen altars, and offered a bullocke and a ramme on *euery* altar.

|| Or, the hill.

15 And he said vnto Balak, Stand here by thy burnt offering, while I meete *the* LORD yonder.

16 And the LORD met Balaam, and *put a word in his mouth, and saide, Goe againe vnto Balak, and say thus.

* Chap. 22. 35.

17 And when hee came to him, be-

hold, he stood by his burnt offring, and the Princes of Moab with him. And Balak said vnto him, What hath the LORD spoken ?

18 And he tooke vp his parable, and said, Rise vp Balak, & heare; hearken vnto me, thou sonne of Zippor :

19 God *is* not a man that he should lie, neither the sonne of man, that hee should repent : hath he said, and shall he not doe *it?* or, hath hee spoken, and shall he not make it good ?

20 Behold, I haue receiued *commandement* to blesse : and hee hath blessed, and I cannot reuerse it.

21 Hee hath not beheld iniquitie in Iacob, neither hath he seene peruersenesse in Israel : the LORD his God *is* with him, and the shoute of a King *is* among them.

22 * God brought them out of Egypt; he hath as it were the strength of an Vnicorne.

* Num. 24 6.

23 Surely there is no inchantment ||against Iacob, neither is there any diuination against Israel : according to this time it shalbe said of Iacob, and of Israel, What hath God wrought !

|| Or, in.

24 Beholde, the people shall rise vp as a great Lion, and lift vp himselfe as a yong Lion : hee shall not lie downe vntill he eate of the pray, and drinke the blood of the slaine.

25 ¶ And Balak said vnto Balaam, Neither curse them at all, nor blesse them at all.

26 But Balaam answered, and said vnto Balak, Told not I thee, saying, All that the LORD speaketh, that I must doe ?

27 ¶ And Balak saide vnto Balaam, Come, I pray thee, I will bring thee vnto another place, peraduenture it will please God, that thou mayest curse me them from thence.

28 And Balak brought Balaam vnto the top of Peor, that looketh toward Ieshimon.

29 And Balaam saide vnto Balak, Build mee here seuen altars, and prepare me here seuen bullocks, and seuen rammes.

30 And Balak did as Balaam had said, and offred a bullocke and a ramme on *euery* altar.

CHAP. XXIIII.

1 Balaam leauing diuinations, prophesieth the happinesse of Israel. 10 Balak in anger dismisseth

misseth him. 15 He prophesieth of the starre of Iacob, and the destruction of some nations.

Nd when Balaam sawe that it pleased the Lord to blesse Israel, hee went not, as at other * times to † seeke for inchantments, but hee set his face toward the wildernesse.

Chap. 23. 15.
*Heb. to the meeting of inchantments.

2 And Balaam lift vp his eyes, and he saw Israel abiding in his tents, according to their Tribes: and the Spirit of God came vpon him.

3 *And he tooke vp his parable, and said, Balaam the sonne of Beor hath said, and the man † whose eyes are open hath said:

Chap. 23.

*Heb. who had his eyes shut, but now open.

4 Hee hath said, *which* heard the words of God, which sawe the vision of the Almightie, falling *into a trance*, but hauing his eyes open:

5 How goodly are thy tents, O Iacob, *and* thy Tabernacles, O Israel!

6 As the valleyes are they spread forth, as gardens by the riuer side, as the trees of Lign-Aloes which the Lord hath planted, *and* as Cedar trees beside the waters.

7 He shall powre the water out of his buckets, and his seed *shall be* in many waters, and his King shall be higher then Agag, and his Kingdome shall be exalted.

8 God brought him forth out of Egypt, * he hath as it were the strength of an Vnicorne: he shall eate vp the nations his enemies, and shall breake their bones, and pierce *them* thorow with his arrowes.

Chap. 23.

9 * Hee couched, he lay downe as a Lyon, and as a great Lyon: who shal stirre him vp? Blessed *is* hee that blesseth thee, and cursed *is* hee that curseth thee.

Gen. 49.

10 ¶ And Balaks anger was kindled against Balaam, aud hee smote his hands together: and Balak said vnto Balaam, I called thee to curse mine enemies, and behold, thou hast altogether blessed *them* these three times.

11 Therefore now, flee thou to thy place: I thought to promote thee vnto great honour, but loe, the Lord hath kept thee backe from honour.

12 And Balaam said vnto Balak, Spake I not also to thy messengers which thou sentest vnto me, saying,

13 If Balak would giue mee his house full of siluer and gold, I cannot goe beyond the commandement of the Lord, to doe either good or bad of mine owne mind? *but* what the Lord saith, that will I speake.

14 And now beholde, I goe vnto my people: come therefore, and I will aduertise thee, what this people shall doe to thy people in the latter dayes.

15 ¶ And hee tooke vp his parable, and said, Balaam the sonne of Beor hath said, and the man *whose* eyes are open, hath said:

16 He hath said which heard the words of God, and knewe the knowledge of the most High, *which* sawe the vision of the Almightie, falling into a trance, but hauing his eyes open.

17 I shall see him, but not now: I shall behold him, but not nigh: There shall come a starre out of Iacob, and a Scepter shall rise out of Israel, and shall ‖ smite the corners of Moab, and destroy all the children of Sheth.

‖ Or, smite through the Princes of Moab.

18 And Edom shall bee a possession, Seir also shall be a possession for his enemies, and Israel shall doe valiantly.

19 Out of Iacob shall come he that shall haue dominion, and shall destroy him that remaineth of the citie.

20 ¶ And when he looked on Amalek, he tooke vp his parable, and sayd, Amalek *was* ‖ the first of the nations, but his latter end ‖ *shall bee*, that hee perish for euer.

‖ The first of the nations that warred against Israel, Exod. 17.
‖ Or, shalbe euen to destruction.

21 And hee looked on the Kenites, and tooke vp his parable, and saide, Strong is thy dwelling place, and thou puttest thy nest in a rocke:

22 Neuerthelesse, † the Kenite shall be wasted, ‖ vntil Asshur shal carie thee away captiue.

† Heb. Kain
‖ Or, how long shall it be ere Asshur carry thee away captiue.

23 And he tooke vp his parable, and said, Alas! who shall liue when God doeth this?

24 And shippes *shall come* from the coast of Chittim, and shal afflict Asshur, and shall afflict Eber, and hee also shall perish for euer.

25 And Balaam rose vp, and went and returned to his place: and Balak also went his way.

CHAP. XXV.

1 Israel at Shittim commit whoredome and Idolatrie. 6 Phinehas killeth Zimri and Cozbi. 10 God therefore giueth him an euerlasting Priesthood. 16 The Midianites are to be vexed.

And

* Chap. 33.
49.

Nd Israel abode in *Shittim, and the people begun to commit whoredome with the daughters of Moab.

2 And they called the people vnto the sacrifices of their gods: and the people did eate, and bowed downe to their gods.

3 And Israel ioyned himselfe vnto Baal-Peor: and the anger of the LORD was kindled against Israel.

* Deut. 4. 3.
iosh. 22. 17.

4 And the LORD said vnto Moses, *Take all the heads of the people, and hang them vp before the LORD against the Sunne, that the fierce anger of the LORD may be turned away from Israel.

5 And Moses said vnto the Iudges of Israel, Slay ye euery one his men, that were ioyned vnto Baal-Peor.

6 ¶ And behold, one of the children of Israel came and brought vnto his brethren a Midianitish woman, in the sight of Moses, and in the sight of all the Congregation of the children of Israel, who were weeping before the doore of the Tabernacle of the Congregation.

* Psal. 106.
30. 1. macc.
2. 45.

7 And *when Phinehas the sonne of Eleazar, the sonne of Aaron the Priest saw it, hee rose vp from amongst the Congregation, and tooke a iauelin in his hand.

8 And he went after the man of Israel into the tent, and thrust both of them thorow, the man of Israel, and the woman, thorow her belly: So the plague was stayed from the children of Israel.

* 1. Cor. 10.
8.

9 And *those that died in the plague, were twentie and foure thousand.

10 ¶ And the LORD spake vnto Moses, saying,

* Psal. 106.
30.

11 * Phinehas the sonne of Eleazar, the sonne of Aaron the Priest, hath turned my wrath away from the children of Israel, (while hee was zealous for my sake among them) that I consumed not the children of Israel in my ielousie.

* Ecclus.
45. 24. 1.
macc. 2. 54.

12 Wherefore say, * Behold, I giue vnto him my Couenant of peace.

13 And he shall haue it, and his seed after him, euen the Couenant of an euerlasting Priesthood, because he was zealous for his God, and made an atonement for the children of Israel.

14 Now the name of the Israelite that was slaine, euen that was slaine with the Midianitish woman, was Zimri the sonne of Salu, a Prince of †a chiefe house among the Simeonites.

† Heb. house
of a father.

15 And the name of the Midianitish woman that was slaine, was Cozbi, the daughter of Zur, hee was head ouer a people, and of a chiefe house in Midian.

16 ¶ And the LORD spake vnto Moses, saying,

17 *Vexe the Midianites, and smite them:

* Chap. 31.
2.

18 For they vexe you with their wiles, wherewith they haue beguiled you, in the matter of Peor, and in the matter of Cozbi, the daughter of a Prince of Midian their sister, which was slaine in the day of the plague, for Peors sake.

CHAP. XXVI.

1 The summe of all Israel is taken in the plaines of Moab. 52 The law of diuiding among them the inheritance of the land. 57 The families and number of the Leuites. 63 None were left of them which were numbred at Sinai, but Caleb and Ioshua.

Nd it came to passe after the plague, that the LORD spake vnto Moses, and vnto Eleazar the sonne of Aaron the Priest, saying,

2 Take the summe of all the Congregation of the children of Israel, *from twenty yeeres old and vpward, throughout their fathers house, all that are able to goe to warre in Israel.

* Chap. 1. 3

3 And Moses & Eleazar the Priest spake with them in the plaines of Moab by Iordane neere Iericho, saying,

4 Take the summe of the people from twenty yeeres old and vpward, as the LORD *commanded Moses, and the children of Israel which went foorth out of the land of Egypt.

* Chap. 1. 1

5 ¶ * Reuben the eldest sonne of Israel: the children of Reuben, Hanoch, of whom commeth the family of the Hanochites: of Pallu the family of the Palluites:

* Gene. 46.
8. exod. 6.
14. 1. chro.
5, 1.

6 Of Hesron the family of the Hesronites: of Carmi the family of the Carmites.

7 These are the families of the Reubenites: and they that were numbred of them, were fourtie and three thousand, and seuen hundred and thirtie.

8 And the sonnes of Pallu, Eliab.

9 And

9 And the sonnes of Eliab, Nemuel, and Dathan, and Abiram: this *is* that Dathan & Abiram, *which* were famous in the Congregation, who * stroue against Moses and against Aaron in the companie of Korah, when they stroue against the LORD:

* Chap. 16.

10 And the earth opened her mouth, and swallowed them vp together with Korah when that companie died, what time the fire deuoured two hundred and fiftie men : and they became a signe.

11 Notwithstanding, the children of Korah died not.

12 ¶ The sonnes of Simeon, after their families : Of Nemuel, the family of the Nemuelites : Of Iamin, the familie of the Iaminites : Of Iachin, the familie of the Iachinites :

13 Of Zerah, the familie of the Zarhites : Of Shaul, the familie of the Shaulites.

14 These *are* the families of the Simeonites, twentie and two thousand, and two hundred.

15 ¶ The children of Gad after their families : Of Zephon, the familie of the Zephonites : of Haggi the familie of the Haggites : of Shuni the familie of the Shunites.

16 Of Ozni, the familie of the Oznites : Of Eri the familie of the Erites.

17 Of Arod the familie of the Arodites : of Areli the familie of the Arelites.

18 These *are* the families of the children of Gad, according to those that were numbred of them, fourtie thousand and fiue hundred.

19 ¶ * The sonnes of Iudah, *were* Er and Onan : and Er and Onan died in the land of Canaan.

* Gen. 38. 2 &c. and 46. 12.

20 And the sonnes of Iudah after their families were : Of Shelah the familie of the Shelanites : Of Pharez the familie of the Pharzites : Of Zerah the familie of the Zarhites.

21 And the sonnes of Pharez were : Of Hesron the familie of the Hesronites : Of Hamul the familie of the Hamulites.

22 These *are* the families of Iudah according to those that were numbred of them, threescore and sixteene thousand and fiue hundred.

23 ¶ Of the sonnes of Issachar after their families : Of Tola the familie of the Tolaites : of Pua the familie of the Punites.

24 Of Iashub the familie of the Iashubites : of Shimron the familie of the Shimronites.

25 These *are* the families of Issachar according to those that were numbred of them, threescore and foure thousand, and three hundred.

26 ¶ Of the sonnes of Zebulun after their families, of Sered the familie of the Sardites : Of Elon the familie of the Elonites : of Iahleel the familie of the Iahleelites.

27 These *are* the families of the Zebulunites, according to those that were numbred of them, threescore thousand and fiue hundred.

28 ¶ The sonnes of Ioseph after their families, *were* Manasseh and Ephraim.

29 Of the sonnes of Manasseh : Of *Machir the familie of the Machirites : and Machir begate Gilead : Of Gilead *come* the familie of the Gileadites.

* Iosh. 17. 1

30 These *are* the sonnes of Gilead : Of Ieezer the family of the Ieezerites : Of Helek the familie of the Helekites.

31 And of Asriel the family of the Asrielites : and of Shechem the familie of the Shechemites.

32 And of Shemida the familie of the Shemidaites : and of Hepher the familie of the Hepherites.

33 ¶ And * Zelophehad the sonne of Hepher had no sonnes, but daughters : and the names of the daughters of Zelophehad, *were* Mahlah, and Noah, Hoglah, Milcah, and Tirzah.

* Chap. 27. 1.

34 These *are* the families of Manasseh, and those that were numbred of them, fiftie and two thousand and seuen hundred.

35 ¶ These *are* the sonnes of Ephraim, after their families : Of Shuthelah the familie of the Shuthalhites : Of Becher the familie of the Bachrites : Of Tahan the familie of the Tahanites.

36 And these *are* the sonnes of Shuthelah : Of Eran the familie of the Eranites.

37 These *are* the families of the sonnes of Ephraim, according to those that were numbred of them, thirtie and two thousand, and fiue hundred. These *are* the sonnes of Ioseph after their families.

38 ¶ The sonnes of Beniamin after their families : Of Bela the familie of the Belaites : Of Ashbel the familie of the

the Ashbelites: Of Ahiram the family of the Ahiramites:

39 Of Shupham the family of the Shuphamites: Of Hupham the family of the Huphamites.

40 And the sonnes of Bela were Ard and Naaman: *of Ard*, the family of the Ardites: *and* of Naaman the family of the Naamites.

41 These *are* the sonnes of Beniamin after their families; and they that were numbred of them, *were* fourty and fiue thousand, and sixe hundred.

42 ¶ These *are* the sonnes of Dan after their families: Of Shuham the family of the Shuhamites. These *are* the families of Dan, after their families.

43 All the families of the Shuhamites, according to those that were numbred of them, *were* three score and foure thousand, and foure hundred.

44 ¶ Of the children of Asher after their families: Of Iimna the family of the Iimnites: Of Iesui the family of the Iesuites: Of Beriah the family of the Beriites.

45 Of the sonnes of Beriah; of Heber the family of the Heberites: of Malchiel, the family of the Malchielites.

46 And the name of the daughter of Asher, was Sarah.

47 These *are* the families of the sonnes of Asher, according to those that were numbred of them; who were fiftie and three thousand, and foure hundred.

48 Of the sonnes of Naphtali, after their families, of Iahzeel the family of the Iahzeelites: Of Guni, the family of the Gunites:

49 Of Iezer, the family of the Iezerites: Of Shillem the family of the Shillemites.

50 These *are* the families of Naphtali, according to their families: and they that were numbred of them, were fourty and fiue thousand, and foure hundred.

51 These were the numbred of the children of Israel, sixe hundred thousand, and a thousand, seuen hundred and thirtie.

52 ¶ And the LORD spake vnto Moses, saying,

53 Vnto these the land shall be diuided for an inheritance, according to the number of names.

54 *To many thou shalt †giue the more inheritance, and to few thou shalt

†giue the lesse inheritance: to euery one shall his inheritance be giuen, according to those that were numbred of him.

55 Notwithstanding the land shall bee *diuided by lot: according to the names of the tribes of their fathers, they shall inherite.

56 According to the lot shall the possession thereof be diuided betweene many *and* few.

57 ¶ *And these *are* they that were numbred of the Leuites, after their families: Of Gershon, the family of the Gershonites: Of Kohath the family of the Kohathites: Of Merari the family of the Merarites.

58 These are the families of the Leuites: the family of the Libnites, the family of the Hebronites, the family of the Mahlites, the family of the Mushites, the family of the Korathites: and Kohath begate Amram.

59 And the name of Amrams wife was *Iochebed the daughter of Leui, whom *her mother* bare to Leui in Egypt: And shee bare vnto Amram, Aaron and Moses, and Miriam their sister.

60 And vnto Aaron was borne Nadab and Abihu, Eleazar and Ithamar.

61 And *Nadab and Abihu died, when they offered strange fire before the LORD.

62 And those that were numbred of them, were twenty and three thousand, all males from a moneth old and vpward: for they were not numbred among the children of Israel, because there was no inheritance giuen them among the children of Israel.

63 ¶ These are they that were numbred by Moses and Eleazar the Priest, who numbred the children of Israel in the plaines of Moab, by Iordane *neere* Iericho.

64 But among these there was not a man of them, whom Moses and Aaron the Priest numbred, when they numbred the children of Israel in the wildernesse of Sinai.

65 For the LORD had said of them, They *shall surely die in the wildernesse: and there was not left a man of them, saue Caleb the sonne of Iephunneh, and Ioshua the sonne of Nun.

CHAP. XXVII.

1 The daughters of Zelophehad sue for an inheritance.   6 The law of inheritances.   12 Moses

* Chap. 33. 54.
† Hebr. multiply his inheritance.

† Hebr. diminish his inheritance.
* Chap. 33. 54. Iosh. 11, 23. and 14. 2.
* Exod. 6. 16, 17, 18, 19.
* Exod. 2. 2. and 6. 20.
* Leuit. 10. 2. chap. 3. 4. 1. chro. 24. 2.
* Chap. 14. 28. 1. corin. 10. 5. 6.

12 Moses beeing told of his death, sueth for a successour. 18 Ioshua is appointed to succeed him.

 Hen came the daughters of *Zelophehad, the sonne of Hepher, the sonne of Gilead, the sonne of Machir, the sonne of Manasseh, of the families of Manasseh, the sonne of Ioseph ; and these are the names of his daughters : Mahlah, Noah, and Hoglah, and Milcah, and Tirzah.

* Chap. 26. 33. iosh. 17. 3.

2 And they stood before Moses, and before Eleazar the Priest, and before the Princes, and all the Congregation, by the doore of the Tabernacle of the Congregation, saying,

3 Our father *died in the wildernesse, and he was not in the company of them that gathered themselues together against the LORD in the company of Korah : but died in his owne sinne, and had no sonnes.

* Chap. 14. 35. and 26. 64, 65.

4 Why should the name of our father be †done away from among his family, because he hath no sonne ? Giue vnto vs therefore a possession among the brethren of our father

† Hebr. diminished.

5 And Moses brought their cause before the LORD.

6 ¶ And the LORD spake vnto Moses, saying,

7 The daughters of Zelophehad speake right : thou shalt surely giue them a possession of an inheritance among their fathers brethren, and thou shalt cause the inheritance of their father to passe vnto them.

8 And thou shalt speake vnto the children of Israel, saying, If a man die, and haue no sonne, then yee shall cause his inheritance to passe vnto his daughter.

9 And if he haue no daughter, then yee shall giue his inheritance vnto his brethren.

10 And if he haue no brethren, then yee shall giue his inheritance vnto his fathers brethren.

11 And if his father haue no brethren, then ye shall giue his inheritance vnto his kinseman that is next to him of his family, and hee shall possesse it: And it shall be vnto the children of Israel a statute of iudgement, as the LORD commanded Moses.

12 ¶ And the LORD saide vnto Moses, * Get thee vp into this mount Abarim, and see the land which I haue

* Deut. 32. 49.

giuen vnto the children of Israel.

13 And when thou hast seene it, thou also shalt be gathered vnto thy people, as *Aaron thy brother was gathered.

* Chap. 20. 14.

14 For ye *rebelled against my Commandement (in the desart of Zin, in the strife of the Congregation) to sanctifie me at the water, before their eyes : that is the *water of Meribah in Kadesh in the wildernesse of Zin.

* Chap. 20. 24.
* Exod. 17. 7.

15 ¶ And Moses spake vnto the LORD, saying,

16 Let the LORD, the God of the spirits of all flesh, set a man ouer the Congregation,

17 Which may goe out before them, and which may goe in before them, and which may lead them out, and which may bring them in, that the Congregation of the LORD bee not as sheepe which haue no shepheard.

18 ¶ And the LORD saide vnto Moses, Take thee Ioshua the sonne of Nun, a man in whom is the spirit, and lay thine hand vpon him.

19 And set him before Eleazar the Priest, and before all the Congregation: and giue him a charge in their sight.

20 And thou shalt put some of thine honour vpon him, that all the Congregation of the children of Israel may be obedient.

21 And he shall stand before Eleazar the Priest, who shall aske counsell for him, *after the iudgement of Vrim before the LORD : at his word shal they goe out, and at his word they shal come in, both he, and al the children of Israel with him, euen all the Congregation.

* Exod. 28. 30.

22 And Moses did as the LORD commanded him : and he tooke Ioshua and set him before Eleazar the Priest, and before all the Congregation.

23 And hee layd his handes vpon him, and gaue him a charge, as the LORD commaunded by the hand of Moses.

CHAP. XXVIII.

1 Offerings are to be obserued. 3 The continuall burnt offering. 9 The offering on the Sabbath, 11 on the New-moones, 16 at the Passeouer, 26 in the day of first fruits.

ANd the LORD spake vnto Moses, saying,

2 Command the children of Israel, and say vnto them, My offering, and my bread for my sacrifices, made by fire for

† *Hebr. a sauour of my rest.*

* *Exod. 29. 38.*

† *Heb. in a day.*

† *Hebr. betweene the twoeuenings*
* *Leuit. 2. 1.*
* *Exod. 29. 40.*

for a †sweet sauour vnto mee, shall yee obserue, to offer vnto me, in their due season.

3 And thou shalt say vnto them, * This is the offering made by fire, which ye shall offer vnto the Lord: Two lambes of the first yeere without spot † day by day, for a continuall burnt offering.

4 The one lambe shalt thou offer in the morning, and the other lambe shalt thou offer †at Euen.

5 And a tenth part of an Ephah of flowre for a * meate offering, mingled with the fourth part of an * Hyn of beaten oyle.

6 It is a continuall burnt offering which was ordeined in mount Sinai for a sweete sauour, a sacrifice made by fire vnto the Lord.

7 And the drinke offering thereof shall be the fourth part of an Hyn for the one lambe: in the holy place shalt thou cause the strong wine to bee powred vnto the Lord for a drinke offring.

8 And the other lambe shalt thou offer at Euen: as the meate offring of the morning, and as the drinke offering thereof, thou shalt offer it, a sacrifice made by fire of a sweet sauour vnto the Lord.

9 ¶ And on the Sabbath day, two lambes of the first yeere without spot, and two tenth deales of flowre for a meate offering mingled with oyle, and the drinke offering thereof.

10 This is the burnt offring of euery Sabbath, beside the continuall burnt offering, and his drinke offering.

11 ¶ And in the beginnings of your moneths, ye shall offer a burnt offering vnto the Lord: Two yong bullocks and one ramme, seuen lambs of the first yeere, without spot,

12 And three tenth deales of flowre for a meate offering, mingled with oyle, for one bullocke, and two tenth deales of flowre for a meat offering, mingled with oyle, for one ramme:

13 And a seuerall tenth deale of flowre mingled with oyle for a meate offering, vnto one lambe, for a burnt offering of a sweet sauour, a sacrifice made by fire vnto the Lord.

14 And their drinke offerings shal be halfe an Hin of wine vnto a bullocke, and the third part of an Hin vnto a ramme, and a fourth part of an Hin

vnto a lambe: This is the burnt offring of euery moneth, throughout the moneths of the yeere.

15 And one kidde of the goates for a sinne offering vnto the Lord shalbe offered, besides the continuall burnt offring and his drinke offering.

16 * And in the fourteenth day of the first moneth, is the Passeouer of the Lord.

17 And in the fifteenth day of this moneth is the feast: seuen dayes shall vnleauened bread be eaten.

18 In the * first day shall bee an holy conuocation, yee shall doe no maner of seruile worke therein.

19 But ye shall offer a sacrifice made by fire for a burnt offering vnto the Lord, two yong bullockes, and one ramme, and seuen lambes of the first yeere: they shall be vnto you without blemish.

20 And their meate offering shall be of flowre mingled with oyle: three tenth deales shall ye offer for a bullocke, and two tenth deales for a ramme.

21 A seuerall tenth deale shalt thou offer for euery lambe, throughout the seuen lambes:

22 And one goat for a sinne offering, to make an atonement for you.

23 Ye shal offer these beside the burnt offering in the morning, which is for a continuall burnt offering.

24 After this maner yee shall offer dayly throughout the seuen dayes, the meat of the sacrifice made by fire, of a sweet sauour vnto the Lord: it shal be offred beside the continuall burnt offring, and his drinke offering.

25 And on the seuenth day yee shall haue an holy conuocation: yee shall doe no seruile worke.

26 ¶ Also in the day of the first fruits when ye bring a new meat offering vnto the Lord, after your weekes bee out: ye shall haue an holy conuocation, ye shall doe no seruile worke.

27 But yee shall offer the burnt offering for a sweete sauour vnto the Lord, two yong bullockes, one ramme, seuen lambes of the first yeere.

28 And their meat offering of flowre mingled with oyle, three tenth deales vnto one bullocke, two tenth deales vnto one ramme,

29 A seuerall tenth deale vnto one lambe, thorowout the seuen lambes,

30 And one kidde of the goates, to make

* *Exod. 12. 18. leuit. 23. 5.*

* *Leuit. 23. 7.*

make an atonement for you.

31 Ye shall offer *them* besides the continuall burnt offering, and his meat offering, (they shall be vnto you without blemish) and their drinke offerings.

CHAP. XXIX.

1 The offering at the feast of Trumpets, 7 at the day of afflicting their soules, 13 and on the eight dayes of the feast of Tabernacles.

Nd in the seuenth moneth, on the first *day* of the moneth, ye shall haue an holy conuocation, yee shall doe no seruile worke : *it is a day of blowing the trumpets vnto you.

* Leuit. 23. 24.

2 And ye shall offer a burnt offering for a sweet sauour vnto the Lord, one yong bullocke, one ramme, and seuen lambes of the first yeere without blemish.

3 And their meat offering *shall be* of floure mingled with oyle, three tenth deales for a bullocke, *and* two tenth deales for a ramme :

4 And one tenth deale for one lambe thorowout the seuen lambes :

5 And one kidde of the goats for a sinne offering to make an atonement for you :

6 Beside the burnt offering of the moneth, and his meat offering, and the dayly burnt offering, and his meat offering, and their drinke offerings, according vnto their maner, for a sweet sauour, a sacrifice made by fire vnto the Lord.

7 ¶ And * ye shall haue on the tenth day of this seuenth moneth an holy conuocation ; and yee shall afflict your soules : yee shall not doe any worke *therein.*

* Leuit. 16. 29. and 23. 27.

8 But ye shall offer a burnt offering vnto the Lord for a sweet sauour, one yong bullock, one ramme, *and* seuen lambes of the first yeere, they shall bee vnto you without blemish.

9 And their meate offering shall be of floure mingled with oyle, three tenth deales to a bullocke, *and* two tenth deales to one ramme :

10 A seuerall tenth deale for one lambe, thorowout the seuen lambes ;

11 One kidde of the goats for a sinne offering, beside the sinne offering of atonement, and the continuall burnt offering, and the meat offering of it, and their drinke offerings.

12 ¶ And on the fifteenth day of the seuenth moneth, yee shall haue an holy conuocation, yee shall doe no seruile worke, and ye shall keepe a feast vnto the Lord seuen dayes.

13 And ye shall offer a burnt offring, a sacrifice made by fire, of a sweet sauour vnto the Lord, thirteene yong bullocks, two rammes, *and* fourteene lambes of the first yeere : They shall be without blemish.

14 And their meat offering *shall be* of floure mingled with oyle, three tenth deales vnto euery bullocke of the thirteene bullocks, two tenth deales to each ramme of the two rammes :

15 And a seuerall tenth deale to each lambe of the fourteene lambes :

16 And one kidde of the goats for a sinne offring, beside the continual burnt offering, his meate offering, and his drinke offering.

17 ¶ And on the second day *ye shal offer* twelue yong bullocks, two rammes, fourteene lambes of the first yeere without spot.

18 And their meat offring, and their drinke offerings for the bullockes, for the rammes, and for the lambes, *shall be* according to their number, after the maner :

19 And one kidde of the goats for a sinne offering, beside the continuall burnt offering, and the meate offering thereof, and their drinke offerings.

20 ¶ And on the third day eleuen bullocks, two rammes, fourteene lambs of the first yere without blemish.

21 And their meate offering, and their drinke offerings for the bullocks, for the rammes, and for the lambes, *shall be* according to their number after the maner :

22 And one goat for a sinne offering, beside the continuall burnt offering, and his meate offering, and his drinke offering.

23 ¶ And on the fourth day ten bullocks, two rammes, *and* fourteene lambs of the first yere without blemish.

24 Their meat offering, and their drinke offerings, for the bullocks, for the rammes, and for the lambes, *shall be* according to their number after the maner :

25 And one kidde of the goats for a sin offering, beside the continuall burnt offering, his meate offering, and his drinke offering.

26 ¶ And

26 ¶ And on the fift day, nine bullockes, two rammes, *and* fourteene lambes of the first yeere, without spot:

27 And their meat offring and their drinke offerings, for the bullockes, for the rammes, and for the lambes, *shall be* according to their number after the maner:

28 And one goate for a sinne offring, beside the continuall burnt offring, and his meate offering and his drinke offering.

29 ¶ And on the sixt day eight bullockes, two rammes, *and* fourteene lambes of the first yeere without blemish:

30 And their meat offring, and their drinke offerings, for the bullockes, for the rammes, and for the lambes, *shall be* according to their number, after the maner:

31 And one goat for a sinne offering, beside the continuall burnt offering, his meate offering and his drinke offering.

32 ¶ And on the seuenth day, seuen bullockes, two rammes, *and* fourteene lambes of the first yeere without blemish.

33 And their meate offring, and their drinke offerings, for the bullockes, for the rammes, and for the lambes, *shall be* according to their number, after the maner:

34 And one goat for a sinne offring, beside the continuall burnt offering, his meate offering, and his drinke offring.

* Leuit. 23. 36.

35 ¶ On the eight day, ye shall haue a *solemne assembly : ye shall do no seruile worke *therein:*

36 But ye shal offer a burnt offring, a sacrifice made by fire, of a sweet sauour vnto the Lord, one bullocke, one ramme, seuen lambes of the first yeere without blemish:

37 Their meate offering, and their drinke offrings, for the bullocke, for the ramme, and for the lambes *shall be* according to their number, after the maner:

38 And one goat for a sinne offering, beside the continuall burnt offring, and his meate offering, and his drinke offering.

¶ Or, offer.

39 These things ye shall ‖ doe vnto the Lord in your set feasts, besides your vowes, and your free will offerings, for your burnt offerings, and for your meate offerings, and for your drinke offerings, and for your peace offerings.

40 And Moses tolde the children of Israel, according to all that the Lord commanded Moses.

CHAP. XXX.

1 Vowes are not to be broken. 3 The exception of a maids vow, 6 Of a wiues, 9 Of a widowes, or her that is diuorced.

And Moses spake vnto the heads of the tribes, concerning the children of Israel, saying, This *is* the thing which the Lord hath commanded.

2 If a man vowe a vow vnto the Lord, or sweare an othe to bind his soule with a bond: he shall not †breake his word, hee shall doe according to all that proceedeth out of his mouth.

† Hebr. profane.

3 If a woman also vow a vow vnto the Lord, and binde *her selfe* by a bond, *being* in her fathers house in her youth;

4 And her father heare her vow, and her bond wherewith shee hath bound her soule, and her father shall holde his peace at her : then all her vowes shall stand, and euery bond wherewith shee hath bound her soule, shall stand.

5 But if her father disallow her in the day that he heareth; not any of her vowes or of her bonds, wherewith she hath bound her soule, shall stand: and the Lord shall forgiue her, because her father disallowed her.

6 And if she had at all an husband when †she vowed, or vttered ought out of her lips, wherewith shee bound her soule,

† Hebr. her vowes were vpon her.

7 And her husband heard *it*, and held his peace at her in the day that hee heard *it*: then her vowes shall stand, and her bonds wherewith shee bound her soule, shall stand.

8 But if her husband disallowe her on the day that he heard *it*, then he shall make her vowe which she vowed, and that which she vttered with her lippes wherewith shee bound her soule, of none effect, and the Lord shall forgiue her.

9 But euery vow of a widow, and of her that is diuorced, wherewith they haue bound their soules, shall stand against her.

10 And if she vowed in her husbands house, or bound her soule by a bond with an oath;

11 And

11 And her husband heard *it*, and held his peace at her, *and* disallowed her not : then all her vowes shall stand, and euery bond wherewith shee bound her soule, shall stand.

12 But if her husband hath vtterly made them voyd on the day hee heard *them :* then whatsoeuer proceeded out of her lips concerning her vowes, or concerning the bond of her soule, shall not stand : her husband hath made them voyd, and the LORD shal forgiue her.

13 Euery vow, and euery binding othe to afflict the soule, her husband may establish it, or her husband may make it voyd.

14 But if her husband altogether hold his peace at her, from day to day, then he establisheth all her vowes, or all her bonds which are vpon her : hee confirmeth them, because hee held his peace at her, in the day that hee heard *them*.

15 But if hee shall any wayes make *them* voyd after that he hath heard *them*, then he shall beare her iniquitie.

16 These *are* the statutes which the LORD commanded Moses betweene a man and his wife, betweene the father and his daughter, *being yet* in her youth, in her fathers house.

CHAP. XXXI.

1 The Midianites are spoyled, and Balaam slaine. 13 Moses is wroth with the officers, for sauing the women aliue. 19 How the souldiers with their captiues and spoile, are to be purified. 25 The proportion whereby the pray is to be diuided. 48 The voluntary oblation vnto the Treasury of the Lord.

Chap. 25. .

Chap. 27. .

ANd the LORD spake vnto Moses, saying,

2 * Auenge the children of Israel of the Midianites : afterward shalt thou * be gathered vnto thy people.

3 And Moses spake vnto the people, saying, Arme some of your selues vnto the warre, and let them goe against the Midianites, and auenge the LORD of Midian.

Hebr. a thousand of a -ibe, a thousand of a -ibe.

4 † Of euery tribe a thousand, throughout all the tribes of Israel, shall ye send to the warre.

5 So there were deliuered out of the thousands of Israel, a thousand of *euery* tribe, twelue thousand armed for warre.

6 And Moses sent them to the warre, a thousand of *euery* tribe, them and Phinehas the sonne of Eleazar the Priest, to the warre, with the holy instruments, and the trumpets to blow, in his hand.

7 And they warred against the Midianites, as the LORD commanded Moses, and they slew all the males.

8 And they slew the Kings of Midian, beside the rest of them that were slaine; *namely* * Eui, and Rekem, and Zur, and Hur, and Reba, fiue Kings of Midian; Balaam also the sonne of Beor they slew with the sword.

9 And the children of Israel tooke all the women of Midian captiues, and their little ones, and tooke the spoile of all their cattell, and all their flocks, and all their goods.

10 And they burnt all their cities wherein they dwelt, and all their goodly castles with fire :

11 And they tooke all the spoile, and all the pray, both of men and of beasts.

12 And they brought the captiues, and the pray, and the spoile vnto Moses and Eleazar the Priest, and vnto the Congregation of the children of Israel, vnto the campe at the plaines of Moab, which *are* by Iordan neere Iericho.

13 ¶ And Moses and Eleazar the Priest, and all the Princes of the Congregation went foorth to meete them without the campe.

14 And Moses was wroth with the officers of the hoste, *with* the captaines ouer thousands, and captaines ouer hundreds, which came from the † battel.

15 And Moses said vnto them, Haue ye saued all the women aliue ?

16 Behold, * these caused the children of Israel, through the * counsell of Balaam, to commit trespasse against the LORD in the matter of Peor, and there was a plague among the Congregation of the LORD.

17 Now therefore * kill euery male among the little ones, and kill euery woman that hath knowen man, by lying with † him.

18 But all the women children that haue not knowen a man by lying with him, keepe aliue for your selues.

19 And doe yee abide without the campe seuen dayes : whosoeuer hath killed any person, and * whosoeuer hath touched any slaine, purifie both your selues, and your captiues, on the third

* Iosh. 13. 21,

† *Hebr. hoste of warre.*

* Chap. 25. 2. 2. Pet. 2. 15.

* Iudg. 21. 11.

† *Hebr. a male.*

* Chap. 19. 11. &c.

third day, and on the seuenth day.

20 And purifie all *your* raiment; and all that is † made of skinnes, and all worke of goates *haire*, and all things made of wood.

† Hebr. in-strument or vessell of skinnes.

21 ¶ And Eleazar the Priest said vnto the men of warre which went to the battell, This *is* the ordinance of the law which the Lord commaunded Moses.

22 Onely the gold, and the siluer, the brasse, the yron, the tinne, and the lead,

23 Euery thing that may abide the fire, yee shall make it goe through the fire, and *it* shall be cleane: neuerthelesse, it shall be purified with the water of separation : and all that abideth not the fire, yee shall make goe through the water.

24 And ye shall wash your clothes on the seuenth day, and ye shalbe cleane, and afterward yee shall come into the campe.

25 ¶ And the Lord spake vnto Moses, saying,

26 Take the summe of the pray, † that was taken, both of man and of beast, thou and Eleazar the Priest, and the chiefe fathers of the Congregation :

† Hebr. of the captiuity

27 And diuide the pray into two parts, betweene them that tooke the warre vpon them, who went out to battell, and betweene all the Congregation.

28 And leuie a tribute vnto the Lord of the men of warre which went out to battell : one soule of fiue hundred, both of the persons, and of the beeues, and of the asses, and of the sheepe.

29 Take *it* of their halfe, and giue *it* vnto Eleazar the Priest, for an heaue offering of the Lord.

30 And of the children of Israels halfe, thou shalt take one portion of fiftie, of the persons, of the beeues, of the asses, and of the ‖ flockes, of all maner of beasts, and giue them vnto the Leuites, which keepe the charge of the Tabernacle of the Lord.

‖ Or, goats.

31 And Moses and Eleazar the Priest did as the Lord commanded Moses.

32 And the bootie *being* the rest of the pray which the men of war had caught, was six hundred thousand, and seuenty thousand, and fiue thousand sheepe,

33 And threescore and twelue thousand beeues,

34 And threescore and one thousand asses :

35 And thirtie and two thousand persons in all, of women that had not knowen man by lying with him.

36 And the halfe *which was* the portion of them that went out to warre, was in number three hundred thousand, and seuen and thirtie thousand, and fiue hundred sheepe.

37 And the Lords tribute of the sheepe was sixe hundred and threescore and fifteene.

38 And the beeues *were* thirtie and sixe thousand, of which the Lords tribute *was* threescore and twelue.

39 And the asses *were* thirtie thousand and fiue hundred, of which the Lords tribute *was* threescore and one.

40 And the persons *were* sixteene thousand, of which the Lords tribute *was* thirtie and two persons.

41 And Moses gaue the tribute *which was* the Lords heaue offering, vnto Eleazar the Priest, as the Lord commanded Moses.

42 And of the children of Israels halfe, which Moses diuided from the men that warred :

43 (Now the halfe that perteined vnto the Congregation, *was* three hundred thousand, and thirtie thousand, *and* seuen thousand, and fiue hundred sheepe :

44 And thirtie and sixe thousand beeues :

45 And thirtie thousand asses, and fiue hundred :

46 And sixteene thousand persons)

47 Euen of the children of Israels halfe, Moses tooke one portion of fiftie, both of man and of beast, and gaue them vnto the Leuites, which kept the charge of the Tabernacle of the Lord, as the Lord commanded Moses.

48 ¶ And the officers which were ouer thousands of the hoste, the captaines of thousands, and captaines of hundreds came neere vnto Moses.

49 And they said vnto Moses, Thy seruants haue taken the summe of the men of warre which are vnder our † charge, and there lacketh not one man of vs.

† Heb. h

50 Wee haue therefore brought an oblation for the Lord, what euerie man hath † gotten, of iewels of golde,

† Hebr. found.

eb. heaue
ring.

golde chaines, and bracelets, rings, earerings, and tablets, to make an atonement for our soules before the LORD.

51 And Moses and Eleazar the Priest tooke the gold of them : *euen* all wrought iewels.

52 And all the gold of the † offring that they offered vp to the LORD, of the captaines of thousands, and of the captaines of hundreds, was sixteene thousand, seuen hundred and fiftie shekels.

53 (*For* the men of warre had taken spoile, euery man for himselfe.)

54 And Moses and Eleazar the Priest tooke the gold of the captaines, of thousands, and of hundreds, and brought it into the Tabernacle of the Congregation, for a memoriall for the children of Israel before the LORD.

CHAP. XXXII.

1 The Reubenites and Gadites sue for their inheritance on that side Iorden. 6 Moses reproueth them. 16 They offer him conditions to his content. 33 Moses assigneth them the land. 39 They conquere it.

Ow the children of Reuben, and the children of Gad, had a very great multitude of cattell : and when they saw the land of Iazer, and the land of Gilead, that behold, the place was a place for cattell;

2 The children of Gad, and the children of Reuben, came and spake vnto Moses, and to Eleazar the Priest, and vnto the Princes of the Congregation, saying,

3 Ataroth, and Dibon, and Iazer, and Nimrah, and Heshbon, and Elealeh, and Shebam, and Nebo, and Beon,

4 *Euen* the countrey which the LORD smote before the Congregation of Israel, is a land for cattell, and thy seruants haue cattell.

5 Wherefore, said they, if wee haue found grace in thy sight, let this lande be giuen vnto thy seruants for a possession, *and* bring vs not ouer Iordane.

6 ¶ And Moses said vnto the children of Gad, and to the children of Reuben, Shall your brethren goe to warre, and shall ye sit here ?

debr.
rake.

7 And wherefore † discourage yee the heart of the children of Israel from going ouer into the lande, which the LORD hath giuen them ?

8 Thus did your fathers, when I sent them from Kadesh Barnea to see the land.

9 For * when they went vp vnto the valley of Eshcol, and saw the land, they discouraged the heart of the children of Israel, that they should not goe into the land which the LORD had giuen them.

10 And the LORDS anger was kindled the same time, and hee sware, saying,

11 Surely none of the men that came vp out of Egypt, * from twentie yeeres old and vpward, shall see the lande which I sware vnto Abraham, vnto Isaac, and vnto Iacob, because they haue not † wholly followed me :

12 Saue Caleb the sonne of Iephunneh the Kenezite, and Ioshua the sonne of Nun : for they haue wholly followed the LORD.

13 And the LORDS anger was kindled against Israel, and hee made them wander in the wildernesse fourty yeeres, vntill all the generation that had done euill in the sight of the LORD was consumed.

14 And beholde, ye are risen vp in your fathers stead, an increase of sinfull men, to augment yet the fierce anger of the LORD toward Israel.

15 For if yee turne away from after him, hee will yet againe leaue them in the wildernesse, and ye shall destroy all this people.

16 ¶ And they came neere vnto him, and said, Wee will build sheepfoldes here for our cattell, and cities for our litle ones.

17 But we our selues will goe ready armed before the children of Israel, vntill wee haue brought them vnto their place : and our litle ones shall dwell in the fenced cities, because of the inhabitants of the land.

18 Wee will not returne vnto our houses, vntill the children of Israel haue inherited euery man his inheritance :

19 For wee will not inherite with them on yonder side Iordane, or forward, because our inheritance is fallen to vs on this side Iordane Eastward.

20 ¶ And * Moses said vnto them, If ye will doe this thing, if ye will goe armed before the LORD to warre,

21 And

* Chap. 13.
24.

* Chap. 14.
28, 29.

† Heb. fulfilled after me.

* Iosh. 1.13

21 And will goe all of you armed o-uer Iordane before the LORD, vntill he hath driuen out his enemies from before him,

22 And the land bee subdued before the LORD: then afterward ye shall returne, and bee guiltlesse before the LORD, and before Israel; and this land shall be your possession before the LORD.

23 But if ye will not doe so, behold, yee haue sinned against the LORD: and bee sure your sinne will finde you out.

24 Build ye cities for your litle ones, and folds for your sheepe, and doe that which hath proceeded out of your mouth.

25 And the children of Gad, and the children of Reuben spake vnto Moses, saying, Thy seruants will doe as my lord commandeth.

26 Our little ones, our wiues, our flocks, and all our cattell shall be there in the cities of Gilead.

*Iosh. 4. 12.

27 But * thy seruants will passe o-uer, euery man armed for warre, before the LORD to battell, as my lord saith.

28 So concerning them Moses com-maunded Eleazar the Priest, and Io-shua the sonne of Nun, and the chiefe fathers of the tribes of the children of Israel:

29 And Moses said vnto them, If the children of Gad, and the children of Reuben will passe with you ouer Ior-dane, euery man armed to battell before the LORD, and the land shall be sub-dued before you, then ye shall giue them the land of Gilead for a possession:

30 But if they will not passe ouer with you armed, they shall haue posses-sions among you in the land of Ca-naan.

31 And the children of Gad, and the children of Reuben answered, saying, As the LORD hath said vnto thy ser-uants, so will we doe.

32 Wee will passe ouer armed before the LORD into the land of Canaan, that the possession of our inheritance on this side Iordane may be ours.

* Deut. 3.
12. Iosh. 13.
8. and 22 4.

33 And *Moses gaue vnto them, euen to the children of Gad, and to the chil-dren of Reuben, and vnto halfe the tribe of Manasseh the sonne of Ioseph, the kingdome of Sihon King of the Amorites, and the kingdome of Og King of Bashan, the land with the ci-

ties thereof, in the coastes, euen the cities of the countrey round about.

34 ¶ And the children of Gad built Dibon, and Ataroth, and Aroer,

35 And Atroth, Shophan, and Ia-azer, and Iogbehah,

36 And Bethnimrah, and Beth-haran, fenced cities : and foldes for sheepe.

37 And the children of Reuben built Heshbon, and Elealeh, and Kiria-thaim,

38 And Nebo, and Baalmeon (their names being changed) and Shibmah: and † gaue other names vnto the cities which they builded.

† Hebr. t
called by
names th
names of
cities.
* Gene. :
23.

39 And the children of * Machir, the sonne of Manasseh, went to Gilead, and tooke it, and dispossessed the Amo-rite which was in it.

40 And Moses gaue Gilead vnto Machir the sonne of Manasseh, and he dwelt therein.

* Deut.
14.

41 And * Iair the sonne of Manas-seh went and tooke the small townes thereof, and called them Hauoth-Iair.

42 And Nobah went and tooke Kenath, and the villages thereof, and called it Nobah, after his owne name.

CHAP. XXXIII.

1 Two and fourtie iourneyes of the Israelites.
50 The Canaanites are to be destroyed.

Hese are the iourneyes of the children of Israel, which went foorth out of the land of Egypt, with their armies, vnder the hand of Moses and Aaron.

2 And Moses wrote their goings out according to their iourneyes, by the commandement of the LORD : and these are their iourneyes according to their goings out.

* Exod.
37.

3 And they *departed from Rame-ses in the first moneth, on the fifteenth day of the first moneth : on the morrow after the Passeouer, the children of Is-rael went out with an high hand in the sight of all the Egyptians.

4 (For the Egyptians buried all their first borne, which the LORD had smitten among them : vpon their gods also the LORD executed iudge-ments.)

5 And the children of Israel remo-ued from Rameses, and pitched in Succoth.

6 And

Exod. 13. 6 And they departed from * Succoth, and pitched in Etham, which is in the edge of the wildernesse.

7 And they remoued from Etham, and turned againe vnto Pihahiroth, which is before Baal-zephon : and they pitched before Migdol.

Exod. 15. 8 And they departed from before Pihahiroth , and * passed thorow the midst of the sea, into the wildernes, and went three dayes iourney in the wildernesse of Etham, and pitched in Marah.

Exod. 15. 9 And they remoued from Marah, and * came vnto Elim, and in Elim were twelue fountaines of water, and three score and ten palme trees, and they pitched there.

10 And they remooued from Elim, and encamped by the red sea.

Exod. 16.1 11 And they remooued from the red sea, and encamped in the * wildernesse of Sin.

12 And they tooke their iourney out of the wildernesse of Sin, and encamped in Dophkah.

13 And they departed from Dophkah, and encamped in Alush.

Exod. 17.1 14 And they remoued from Alush, and encamped at * Rephidim , where was no water for the people to drinke.

Exod. 19.1 15 And they departed from Rephidim, and pitched in the *wildernesse of Sinai.

Chap. 11. 16 And they remoued from the desert of Sinai, and pitched * at || Kibroth Hattaauah.

**hat is,
e graues
ust.
Chap. 11.** 17 And they departed from Kibroth Hattaauah, and * encamped at Hazeroth.

18 And they departed from Hazeroth, and pitched in Rithmah.

19 And they departed from Rithmah , and pitched at Rimmon Parez.

20 And they departed from Rimmon Parez, and pitched in Libnah.

21 And they remoued from Libnah, and pitched at Rissah.

22 And they iourneyed from Rissah, and pitched in Kehelathah.

23 And they went from Kehelathah , and pitched in mount Shapher.

24 And they remoued from mount Shapher, and encamped in Haradah.

25 And they remooued from Haradah, and pitched in Makheloth.

26 And they remooued from Makheloth, and encamped at Tahath.

27 And they departed from Tahath, and pitched at Tarah.

28 And they remoued from Tarah, and pitched in Mithcah.

29 And they went from Mithcah, and pitched in Hashmonah.

30 And they departed from Hashmonah, and * encamped at Moseroth.   * Deu. 10. 6

31 And they departed from Moseroth, and pitched in Bene-Iaakan.

32 And they remooued from Bene-Iaakan, & encamped at Horhagidgad.

33 And they went from Horhagidgad, and pitched in Iotbathah.

34 And they remooued from Iotbathah, and encamped at Ebronah.

35 And they departed from Ebronah, and encamped at Ezion-gaber.

36 And they remoued from Eziongaber, and pitched in the * wildernes of Zin, which is Kadesh.   * Chap. 20. 1.

37 And they remooued from * Kadesh, and pitched in mount Hor, in the edge of the land of Edom.   * Chap. 20. 22.

38 And * Aaron the Priest went vp into mount Hor, at the commandement of the Lord, and died there in the fourtieth yeere, after the children of Israel were come out of the lande of Egypt, in the first day of the fift moneth.   * Chap. 20. 25. deut. 32. 50.

39 And Aaron was an hundred and twentie and three yeeres old, when hee died in mount Hor.

40 And * King Arad the Cananite (which dwelt in the South, in the land of Canaan) heard of the comming of the children of Israel.   * Chap. 21. 1, &c.

41 And they departed from mount * Hor, and pitched in Zalmonah.   * Cha. 21. 4

42 And they departed from Zalmonah, and pitched in Punon.

43 And they departed from Punon, and pitched in Oboth.

44 And they departed from Oboth, and pitched in || Iie-Abarim , in the border of Moab. || Or, heapes of Abarim.

45 And they departed from Iim, and pitched in Dibon Gad.

46 And they remoued from Dibon Gad, and encamped in Almon-Diblathaim.

47 And they remooued from Almon-Diblathaim , and pitched in the mountaines of Abarim, before Nebo.

48 And they departed from the mountaines of Abarim, and pitched in the plaines of Moab, by Iordan neere Iericho.

49 And they pitched by Iordane from Beth-Iesimoth, euen vnto || * Abel Shittim, in the plaines of Moab. || Or, the plaines of Shittim.   * Chap. 25. 1.

50 ¶ And

50 ¶ And the LORD spake vnto Moses, in the plaines of Moab by Iordane, neere Iericho, saying,

51 Speake vnto the children of Israel, and say vnto them, * When ye are passed ouer Iordane into the land of Canaan;

52 Then ye shall driue out all the inhabitants of the land from before you, and destroy all their pictures, and destroy all their molten images, and quite plucke downe all their high places.

53 And ye shall dispossesse *the inhabitants* of the land, and dwell therein : for I haue giuen you the land to possesse it.

54 And * ye shall diuide the land by lot, for an inheritance among your families, and to the moe ye shall †giue the more inheritance, and to the fewer yee shall †giue the lesse inheritance: euery mans inheritance shall bee in the place where his lot falleth, according to the tribes of your fathers, ye shall inherite.

55 But if ye will not driue out the inhabitants of the land from before you, then it shall come to passe that those which ye let remaine of them, shall be * prickes in your eyes, and thornes in your sides, and shal vexe you in the land wherein ye dwell.

56 Moreouer, it shall come to passe, that I shall do vnto you, as I thought to doe vnto them.

CHAP. XXXIIII.

1 The borders of the land. 16 The names of the men which shall diuide the land.

ANd the LORD spake vnto Moses, saying,

2 Command the children of Israel, and say vnto them, When ye come into the land of Canaan, (this *is* the land that shall fall vnto you for an inheritance, euen the land of Canaan, with the coasts thereof.)

3 Then * your South quarter shall be from the wildernesse of Zin, along by the coast of Edom, and your South border shall be the outmost coast of the salt Sea Eastward.

4 And your border shal turne from the South to the ascent of Akrabbim, and passe on to Zin : and the going foorth thereof shall be from the South to Kadesh-Barnea, and shall goe on to Hazar-Addar, and passe on to Azmon.

5 And the border shall fetch a compasse from Azmon vnto the riuer of Egypt, and the goings out of it shall be at the sea.

6 And as for the Westerne border, you shall euen haue the great sea for a border : this shall be your West border.

7 And this shall be your North border : from the great sea, you shall point out for you, mount Hor.

8 From mount Hor, ye shall point out *your border* vnto the entrance of Hamath : and the goings foorth of the border shall be to Zedad.

9 ¶ And the border shall goe on to Ziphron, and the goings out of it shall bee at Hazar Enan : this shall be your North border

10 And ye shall point out your East border, from Hazar Enan to Shepham.

11 And the coast shall goe downe from Shepham to Riblah, on the East side of Ain: and the border shall descend and shall reach vnto the †side of the sea of Chinnereth Eastward.

12 And the border shall goe downe to Iordane, and the goings out of it shall be at the salt sea : this shall be your land with the coastes thereof round about.

13 And Moses commanded the children of Israel, saying, This *is* the land which ye shall inherite by lot, which the LORD commanded to giue vnto the nine tribes, and to the halfe tribe.

14 * For the tribe of the children of Reuben, according to the house of their fathers, and the tribe of the children of Gad, according to the house of their fathers, haue receiued *their inheritance*, and halfe the tribe of Manasseh haue receiued their inheritance.

15 The two tribes, and the halfe tribe haue receiued their inheritance on this side Iordane neere Iericho, Eastward, toward the Sunne rising.

16 And the LORD spake vnto Moses, saying,

17 These *are* the names of the men which shall diuide the land vnto you : *Eleazar the Priest, and Ioshua the sonne of Nun.

18 And yee shall take one Prince of euery tribe, to diuide the land by inheritance.

19 And the names of the men *are* these: Of the tribe of Iudah, Caleb the sonne of Iephunneh.

20 And of the tribe of the children of

Marginal notes:
* Deut. 7. 2. iosh. 11. 12.
* Chap. 26. 53.
† Hebr. multiply his inheritance.
† Hebr. diminish his inheritance.
* Iosh. 23. 13. iudg. 2. 3.
* Iosh. 15. 1.
† Hebr. shoulder.
* Chap. 33. iosh. 2, 3.
* Iosh. 1 51.

of Simeon, Shemuel the sonne of Am-mihud.

21 Of the tribe of Beniamin, Elidad the sonne of Chislon.

22 And the Prince of the tribe of the children of Dan, Bukki the sonne of Iogli.

23 The Prince of the children of Io-seph: for the tribe of the children of Ma-nasseh, Hanniel the sonne of Ephod.

24 And the Prince of the tribe of the children of Ephraim, Kemuel the sonne of Shiphtan.

25 And the Prince of the tribe of the children of Zebulun, Elizaphan the sonne of Parnach.

26 And the Prince of the tribe of the children of Issachar, Paltiel the sonne of Azzan.

27 And the Prince of the tribe of the children of Asher, Ahihud the sonne of Shelomi.

28 And the Prince of the tribe of Naphtali, Pedahel the sonne of Ammihud.

29 These *are they* whom the LORD commaunded to diuide the inheritance vnto the children of Israel in the land of Canaan.

CHAP. XXXV.

1 Eight and fourtie Cities for the Leuites with their suburbs, and measure thereof. 6 Sixe of them are to be cities of refuge. 9 The lawes of murder. 31 No satisfaction for murder.

osh. 21.

ANd the LORD spake vnto Moses in the plaines of Moab by Iordane, neere Iericho, saying,

2 * Command the chil-dren of Israel, that they giue vnto the Leuites of the inheritance of their pos-session, cities to dwell in : and yee shall giue vnto the Leuites suburbs for the cities round about them.

3 And the cities shall they haue to dwell in, and the suburbs of them shall be for their cattell, and for their goods, and for all their beasts.

4 And the suburbs of the cities, which yee shall giue vnto the Leuites, *shall reach* from the wall of the citie, and outward, a thousand cubites round about.

5 And ye shall measure from with-out the city on the Eastside two thou-sand cubites, and on the Southside two thousand cubites, and on the Westside two thousand cubites, & on the North-side two thousand cubites : and the citie *shall be* in the midst; this shalbe to them the suburbs of the cities.

6 And among the cities which yee shal giue vnto the Leuites, there shalbe * sixe cities for refuge, which ye shall ap-point for the manslayer, that hee may flee thither : And to them ye shall †adde fourty and two cities.

7 *So* all the cities which ye shall giue to the Leuites, shall be fourty and eight cities : them *shall yee giue* with their sub-urbs.

8 And the cities which ye shal giue, *shalbe* of the possession of the children of Israel : from them that haue many ye shall giue many; but from them that haue few, ye shall giue few. Euery one shal giue of his cities vnto the Leuites, according to his inheritance which †he inheriteth.

9 ¶ And the LORD spake vnto Moses, saying,

10 Speake vnto the children of Is-rael, and say vnto them, * When ye bee come ouer Iordane, into the land of Canaan :

11 Then ye shall appoint you cities, to be cities of refuge for you ; that the slayer may flee thither which killeth a-ny person †at vnawares.

12 And they shall be vnto you cities for refuge from the auenger, that the man-slayer die not, vntill he stand be-fore the Congregation in iudgement.

13 And of these cities which ye shall giue, sixe cities shall ye haue for refuge.

14 Yee shall giue three cities on this side Iordane, and three cities shall yee giue in the land of Canaan, which shall be cities of refuge.

15 These sixe cities shall be a refuge, both for the children of Israel, and for the stranger, and for the soiourner a-mong them : that euery one that kil-leth any person vnawares, may flee thither.

16 * And if he smite him with an in-strument of Iron, (so that he die,) hee is a murderer : the murderer shall sure-ly be put to death.

17 And if he smite him †with throw-ing a stone, (wherewith hee may die) and he die, he is a murderer: the murde-rer shall surely be put to death.

18 Or if he smite him with an hand-weapon of wood, (wherewith he may die) and he die, hee is a murderer : the murderer

Marginal notes

* Deut. 4. 41. iosh. 20. 2. and 21. 3.
† Hebr. a-boue them ye shall giue.

† Hebr. they inherite.

* Deut. 19. 2. iosh. 20. 2.

† Hebr. by error.

* Exod. 21. 14.

† Hebr. with a stone of the hand.

murderer ſhall ſurely be put to death.

19 The reuenger of blood himſelfe ſhall ſlay the murtherer : when he meeteth him, he ſhall ſlay him.

* Deut. 19. 11.

20 * But if he thruſt him of hatred, or hurle at him by laying of waite that he die,

21 Or in enmitie ſmite him with his hand, that he die : hee that ſmote him ſhall ſurely be put to death, for hee is a murderer : the reuenger of blood ſhall ſlay the murderer, when hee meeteth him.

* Exod. 21. 13.

22 But if hee thruſt him ſuddenly * without enmitie, or haue caſt vpon him any thing without laying of wait,

23 Or with any ſtone wherewith a man may die, ſeeing him not, and caſt it vpon him, that he die, and was not his enemie, neither ſought his harme:

24 Then the Congregation ſhall iudge betweene the ſlayer, and the reuenger of blood, according to theſe iudgements.

25 And the Congregation ſhall deliuer the ſlayer out of the hand of the reuenger of blood, and the Congregation ſhal reſtore him to the city of his refuge, whither he was fled: and he ſhall abide in it vnto the death of the high Prieſt, which was annoynted with the holy oyle.

26 But if the ſlayer ſhall at any time come without the border of the citie of his refuge, whither he was fled :

27 And the reuenger of blood finde him without the borders of the citie of his refuge, and the reuenger of blood

† Hebr. no blood ſhalbe to him.

kill the ſlayer, he † ſhall not be guiltie of blood :

28 Becauſe he ſhould haue remained in the citie of his refuge, vntill the death of the high Prieſt : but after the death of the hie Prieſt, the ſlayer ſhal returne into the land of his poſſeſſion.

29 So theſe things ſhall be for a ſtatute of iudgment vnto you, thorowout your generations in al your dwellings.

30 Who ſo killeth any perſon, the murderer ſhall be put to death, by the

* Deut. 17. 6. and 19. 15. matt. 18 16. 2. cor. 13. 1. heb. 10. 28.

* mouth of witneſſes : but one witneſſe ſhall not teſtifie againſt any perſon, to cauſe him to die.

31 Moreouer, yee ſhall take no ſatisfaction for the life of a murderer, which

†Heb. faulty to die.

is † guiltie of death, but he ſhalbe ſurely put to death.

32 And yee ſhall take no ſatisfaction for him that is fled to the citie of his re-

fuge, that hee ſhould come againe to dwell in the land, vntil the death of the Prieſt.

33 So ye ſhall not pollute the lande wherein ye are : for blood, it defileth the

† Heb. the can be no piation fo the land.

land : and the † land cannot bee cleanſed of the blood that is ſhed therein, but by the blood of him that ſhed it.

34 Defile not therefore the lande which yee ſhall inhabite, wherein I dwell : for I the LORD dwell among the children of Iſrael.

CHAP. XXXVI.

1 The inconuenience of the inheritance of daughters, 5 is remedied by marying in their owne tribes, 7 leſt the inheritance ſhould be remoued from the tribe. 10 The daughters of Zelophehad marrie their fathers brothers ſonnes.

Nd the chiefe fathers of the families of the children of Gilead, the ſonne of Machir, the ſonne of Manaſſeh, of the families of the ſonnes of Ioſeph, came neere, and ſpake before Moſes, and before the Princes the chiefe fathers of the children of Iſrael.

* Chap. 1. ioſh. 1.

2 And they ſaid, * The LORD commanded my lord to giue the lande for an inheritance by lot to the children of Iſrael : and my lord was commanded by the LORD, to giue the inheritance of Zelophehad our brother, vnto his daughters.

† Heb. v whom th ſhall be.

3 And if they bee married to any of the ſonnes of the *other* tribes of the children of Iſrael, then ſhall their inheritance be taken from the inheritance of our fathers, and ſhall bee put to the inheritance of the tribe, † whereinto they are receiued: ſo ſhal it be taken from the lot of our inheritance.

4 And when the Iubile of the children of Iſrael ſhall be, then ſhall their inheritance be put vnto the inheritance of the tribe, whereunto they are received : So ſhal their inheritance be taken away from the inheritance of the tribe of our fathers.

5 And Moſes commanded the children of Iſrael, according to the worde of the LORD, ſaying, The tribe of the ſonnes of Ioſeph hath ſaid well.

6 This *is* the thing which the LORD doeth command concerning the daughters of Zelophehad, ſaying, Let

Hebr. be-iues.
Tob. 1. 9.

Let them †marry to whom they thinke best : *onely to the family of the tribe of their father shall they marry.

7 So shall not the inheritance of the children of Israel remooue from tribe to tribe : for euery one of the children of Israel shall †keepe himselfe to the inheritance of the tribe of his fathers.

Hebr. cleaue to e &c.

8 And euery daughter that possesseth an inheritance , in any tribe of the children of Israel , shall be wife vnto one of the family of the tribe of her father , that the children of Israel may enioy euery man the inheritance of his fathers.

9 Neither shall the inheritance remoue from one tribe to another tribe : but euery one of the tribes of the children of Israel , shall keepe himselfe to his owne inheritance.

10 Euen as the LORD commanded Moses, so did the daughters of Zelophehad.

11 * For Mahlah, Tirzah, and Hoglah, and Milcah, and Noah the daughters of Zelophehad, were married vnto their fathers brothers sonnes.

* Chap. 27. 1.

12 And they were married †into the families of the sonnes of Manasseh, the sonne of Ioseph, and their inheritance remained in the tribe of the family of their father.

† Hebr. to some that were of the families.

13 These *are* the commandements and the iudgements which the LORD commanded by the hand of Moses, vnto the children of Israel in the plaines of Moab, by Iordane, *neere* Iericho.

¶ THE FIFTH BOOKE OF
Moses, called Deuteronomie.

CHAP. I.

1 Moses speech in the end of the fortieth yeere, briefly rehearsing the story, 6 of Gods promise, 9 of giuing them officers, 19 of sending the spies to search the land, 34 of Gods anger for their incredulitie, 41 and disobedience.

Or, Zuph.

THESE *bee* the woordes which Moses spake vnto all Israel, on this side Iordane in the wildernes, in the plaine ouer against ‖the Red sea, betweene Paran, and Tophel, and Laban, and Hazeroth, and Dizahab.

2 (*There are* eleuen daies *iourney* from Horeb, by the way of mount Seir, vnto Kadesh-Barnea.)

3 And it came to passe in the fourtieth yeere, in the eleuenth moneth, on the first *day* of the moneth, that Moses spake vnto the children of Israel, according vnto all that the LORD had giuen him in commandement vnto them :

4 * After hee had slaine Sihon the King of the Amorites, which dwelt in Heshbon, and Og the King of Bashan, which dwelt at Astaroth, in Edrei.

* Num. 21. 24.

5 On this side Iordane, in the land of Moab, began Moses to declare this law, saying,

6 The LORD our God spake vnto vs in Horeb, saying, Ye haue dwelt long ynough in this mount :

7 Turne you , and take your iourney, and goe to the mount of the Amorites, and vnto †all *the places* nigh thereunto, in the plaine, in the hills, and in the vale, and in the South, and by the sea side, to the land of the Canaanites, and vnto Lebanon , vnto the great riuer, the riuer Euphrates.

† Hebr. all his neighbours.

8 Behold, I haue † set the land before you : Goe in, and possesse the land, which the LORD sware vnto your fathers, *Abraham, Isaac, and Iacob, to giue vnto them, and to their seed after them.

† Hebr. giuen.

* Gene. 15. 18. and 17. 7, 8.

9 ¶ And I spake vnto you at that time, saying, I am not able to beare you my selfe alone :

10 The

10 The Lord your God hath multiplied you, and beholde, you are this day as the starres of heauen for multitude.

11 (The Lord God of your fathers make you a thousand times so many moe as ye *are*, and blesse you as he hath promised you.)

12 How can I my selfe alone beare your cumbrance, and your burden, and your strife?

† Heb. giue.

13 † Take ye wise men, and vnderstanding, and knowen among your tribes, and I will make them rulers ouer you.

14 And ye answered me, and saide, The thing which thou hast spoken, is good *for vs* to doe.

15 So I tooke the chiefe of your tribes, wise men, and knowen, and

† Heb. gaue.

† made them heads ouer you, captaines ouer thousands, and captaines ouer hundreds, and captaines ouer fifties, and captaines ouer tennes, and officers among your tribes.

16 And I charged your Iudges at that time, saying, Heare *the causes* betweene your brethren, and *iudge righ-

* Ioh. 7. 24.

teously betweene euery man and his brother, & the stranger *that is* with him.

17 * Ye shall not † respect persons in

* Leuit. 19. 15. chap. 16 19. 1. sam. 16. 7. pro. 24. 23.
† Hebr. acknowledge faces.

iudgement, *but* you shall heare the small aswell as the great: you shall not bee afraid of the face of man, for the iudgment is Gods: and the cause that is too hard for you, bring it vnto me, and I will heare it.

18 And I commanded you at that time all the things which ye should doe.

19 ¶ And when wee departed from Horeb, we went through all that great and terrible wildernes, which you saw by the way of the mountaine of the Amorites, as the Lord our God commanded vs: and wee came to Kadesh Barnea.

20 And I said vnto you, Ye are come vnto the mountaine of the Amorites, which the Lord our God doth giue vnto vs.

21 Behold, the Lord thy God hath set the land before thee: Goe vp, *and* possesse *it*, as the Lord God of thy fathers hath said vnto thee: Feare not, neither be discouraged.

22 ¶ And ye came neere vnto mee euery one of you, and said, We will send men before vs, and they shall search vs out the land, and bring vs word againe,

by what way we must goe vp, and into what cities we shall come.

23 And the saying pleased mee well: and * I tooke twelue men of you, one of a tribe.

* Num. 13 3.

24 And * they turned and went vp into the mountaine, and came vnto the valley of Eshcol, and searched it out.

* Num. 13 24.

25 And they tooke of the fruit of the land in their handes, and brought it downe vnto vs, and brought vs worde againe, and said, It is a good lande which the Lord our God doeth giue vs.

26 Notwithstanding, ye would not goe vp, but rebelled against the commandement of the Lord your God.

27 And ye murmured in your tents and said, Because the Lord hated vs, he hath brought vs forth out of the land of Egypt, to deliuer vs into the hand of the Amorites, to destroy vs:

28 Whither shall wee goe vp? our brethren haue † discouraged our heart,

† Heb. melted.

saying, The people is greater and taller then we, the cities are great, and walled vp to heauen, and moreouer we haue seene the sonnes of the * Anakims there.

* Num. 1 29.

29 Then I said vnto you, Dread not, neither be afraid of them.

30 The Lord your God which goeth before you, he shall fight for you, according to all that hee did for you in Egypt before your eyes:

31 And in the wildernes, where thou hast seene how that the Lord thy God bare thee, as a man doth beare his sonne, in all the way that ye went, vntil ye came into this place.

32 Yet in this thing ye did not beleeue the Lord your God.

33 * Who went in the way before you

* Exod. 1 21.

to search you out a place to pitch your tents in, in fire by night, to shew you by what way ye should goe, and in a cloud by day.

34 And the Lord heard the voice of your words, and was wroth, and sware, saying,

35 * Surely there shall not one of

* Num. 29.

these men of this euill generation see that good land, which I sware to giue vnto your fathers:

36 Saue Caleb the sonne of Iephunneh, he shall see it, and to him will I giue the land that he hath troden vpon, and to his children, because hee hath † wholly followed the Lord.

† Heb. fulled to goe after.

37 * Also

* Num. 20.
12. and 27.
14.
* Chap. 3.
26. and 4.
21. and 34.
4.

37 * Also the LORD was angry with me for your sakes, saying, * Thou also shalt not goe in thither.

38 *But* Ioshua the sonne of Nun, which standeth before thee, he shall goe in thither. Encourage him: for he shall cause Israel to inherite it.

39 Moreouer, your litle ones, which ye said should be a pray, and your children, which in that day had no knowledge betweene good and euil, they shall goe in thither; and vnto them will I giue it, and they shall possesse it.

40 But as for you, turne ye, and take your iourney into the wildernesse, by the way of the Red sea.

* Num. 14.
40.

41 Then ye answered, and said vnto mee, * Wee haue sinned against the LORD, we will goe vp and fight, according to all that the LORD our God commanded vs. And when ye had girded on euery man his weapons of warre, yee were ready to goe vp into the hill.

42 And the LORD said vnto me, Say vnto them, Goe not vp, neither fight, for I am not among you: least ye be smitten before your enemies.

43 So I spake vnto you, and you would not heare, but rebelled against the commandement of the LORD, and † went presumptuously vp into the hill.

† Heb. you
were pre-
sumptuous
and went vp.

44 And the Amorites which dwelt in that mountaine, came out against you, and chased you, as Bees doe, and destroyed you in Seir, euen vnto Hormah.

45 And ye returned and wept before the LORD; but the LORD would not hearken to your voyce, nor giue eare vnto you.

46 So yee abode in Kadesh many dayes, according vnto the dayes that ye abode *there*.

CHAP. II.

1 The story is continued, that they were not to meddle with the Edomites, 9 nor with the Moabites, 17 nor with the Ammonites, 24 but Sihon the Amorite was subdued by them.

Hen we turned, and tooke our iourney into the wildernesse, by the way of the Red sea, as the LORD spake vnto mee: and wee compassed mount Seir many dayes.

2 And the LORD spake vnto me, saying,

3 Yee haue compassed this mountaine long enough: turne you Northward.

4 And commaund thou the people, saying, Ye are to passe through the coast of your brethren the children of Esau, which dwell in Seir, and they shall be afraid of you: take ye good heed vnto your selues therefore.

5 Meddle not with them, for I will not giue you of their land, † no not so much as a foote breadth, * because I haue giuen mount Seir vnto Esau for a possession.

† Hebr. euen
to the trea-
ding of the
sole of the
foote.
* Gene. 36.
8.

6 Ye shall buy meat of them for money, that ye may eat, and yee shall also buy water of them for money, that yee may drinke.

7 For the LORD thy God hath blessed thee, in all the workes of thy hand: hee knoweth thy walking thorow this great wildernesse: these fourtie yeres the LORD thy God hath bene with thee, thou hast lacked nothing.

8 And when we passed by from our brethren the children of Esau, which dwelt in Seir, thorow the way of the plaine from Elath, and from Ezion-Gaber, wee turned and passed by the way of the wildernesse of Moab.

9 And the LORD said vnto mee, ‖ Distresse not the Moabites, neither contend with them in battell: for I wil not giue thee of their land for a possession, because I haue giuen Ar vnto the children of Lot for a possession.

‖ Or, vse no
hostilitie a-
gainst Mo-
ab.

10 The Emims dwelt therein in times past, a people great, and many, and tall, as the Anakims:

11 Which also were accounted giants, as the Anakims, but the Moabites call them Emims.

12 * The Horims also dwelt in Seir beforetime, but the children of Esau †succeeded them when they had destroyed them from before them, & dwelt in their † stead, as Israel did vnto the land of his possession, which the LORD gaue vnto them.

* Gen. 36.
20.
† Hebr. in-
herited
them.
‖ Or, roome.

13 Now rise vp, *said I*, and get you ouer * the ‖ brooke Zered; and we went ouer the brooke Zered.

* Num. 21.
12.
‖ Or, valley.

14 And the space in which we came from Kadesh Barnea, vntill we were come ouer the brooke Zered, was thirtie and eight yeeres; vntill all the generation of the men of warre were wasted out from among the hoste, as the LORD sware vnto them.

15 For indeed the hand of the LORD was

was against them, to destroy them from among the hoste, vntill they were consumed.

16 ¶ So it came to passe, when all the men of warre were consumed and dead from among the people,

17 That the LORD spake vnto me, saying,

18 Thou art to passe ouer thorow Ar, the coast of Moab, this day.

19 And when thou commest nigh ouer against the children of Ammon, distresse them not, nor meddle with them: for I will not giue thee of the lande of the children of Ammon any possession, because I haue giuen it vnto the children of Lot for a possession:

20 (That also was accounted a land of Giants: giants dwelt therein in old time, and the Ammonites call them Zamzummims.

21 A people great, and many, and tall, as the Anakims: but the LORD destroyed them before them, and they succeeded them & dwelt in their stead:)

22 As he did to the children of Esau which dwelt in Seir, when he destroyed the Horims from before them, and they succeeded them, and dwelt in their stead euen vnto this day.

23 And the Auims which dwelt in Hazerim, euen vnto Azzah, the Caphtorims which came foorth out of Caphtor, destroyed them, and dwelt in their stead.

24 ¶ Rise ye vp, take your iourney, and passe ouer the riuer Arnon: Behold, I haue giuen into thy hand Sihon the Amorite king of Heshbon, and *† Heb. begin, possesse.* his land: †begin to possesse *it*, and contend with him in battell.

25 This day will I begin to put the dread of thee, and the feare of thee vpon the nations, *that are* vnder the whole heauen, who shall heare report of thee, and shall tremble, and be in anguish because of thee.

26 ¶ And I sent messengers out of the wildernesse of Kedemoth, vnto Sihon king of Heshbon, with wordes of peace, saying,

* Num. 21. 21, 22. 27 *Let me passe through thy land: I will goe along by the high way, I will neither turne vnto the right hand, nor to the left.

28 Thou shalt sell me meat for money, that I may eate, and giue me water for money that I may drinke: Only I will passe through on my feet:

29 As the children of Esau which dwell in Seir, and the Moabites which dwell in Ar, did vnto me, vntill I shall passe ouer Iordan, into the land which the LORD our God giueth vs.

30 But Sihon King of Heshbon would not let vs passe by him: for the LORD thy God hardened his spirit, and made his heart obstinate, that hee might deliuer him into thy hand, as *appeareth* this day.

31 And the LORD said vnto mee, Behold, I haue begun to giue Sihon and his land before thee: begin to possesse, that thou mayest inherit his land.

* Num. 21. 23. 32 *Then Sihon came out against vs, he & all his people to fight at Iahaz.

33 And the LORD our God deliuered him before vs, and wee smote him, and his sonnes, and all his people.

34 And we tooke all his cities at that time, and vtterly destroyed the †men, *† Heb. euecitie of men and women and litle ones.* and the women, and the litle ones of euery citie, we left none to remaine:

35 Onely the cattell wee tooke for a pray vnto our selues, and the spoyle of the cities, which we tooke:

36 From Aroer, which *is* by the brinke of the riuer of Arnon, and from the citie that *is* by the riuer euen vnto Gilead, there was not one citie too strong for vs: the LORD our God deliuered all vnto vs.

37 Onely vnto the land of the children of Ammon thou camest not, nor vnto any place of the riuer Iabbok, nor vnto the cities in the mountaines, nor vnto whatsoeuer the LORD our God forbade vs.

CHAP. III.

1 The story of the conquest of Og king of Bashan. 11 The bignes of his bed. 12 The distribution of those lands to the two tribes and halfe. 23 Moses prayer to enter into the land. 26 He is permitted to see it.

 Hen we turned, and went vp the way to Bashan: and *Og the King of Bashan came out against vs, hee, and all his people to ** Num. 21. 33, &c. cha 29. 7.* battell at Edrei.

2 And the LORD said vnto mee, Feare him not: for I will deliuer him, and all his people, and his land into thy hand, and thou shalt doe vnto him as thou didst vnto *Sihon king of the Amorites, which dwelt at Heshbon. ** Num. 21. 24.*

3 So the LORD our God deliuered

Num. 21.
3.

red into our hands * Og also the King of Bashan, and all his people : and wee smote him vntill none was left to him remayning.

4 And we tooke all his cities at that time, there was not a citie which wee tooke not from them; threescore cities, all the region of Argob, the kingdome of Og in Bashan.

5 All these cities were fenced with high walles, gates and barres, beside vnwalled townes a great many.

6 And we vtterly destroyed them, as we did vnto Sihon King of Heshbon, vtterly destroying the men, women, and children of euery citie.

7 But all the cattell, and the spoile of the cities, we tooke for a pray to our selues.

8 And we tooke at that time out of the hand of the two Kings of the Amorites, the land that was on this side Iordan, from the riuer of Arnon, vnto mount Hermon:

9 (*Which* Hermon the Sidonians call Syrion : and the Amorites call it Shenir.)

10 All the cities of the plaine, and all Gilead, and all Bashan, vnto Salchah, and Edrei, cities of the kingdome of Og in Bashan.

11 For onely Og King of Bashan remained of the remnant of giants ; behold, his bedsted was a bedsted of yron: is it not in Rabbath of the children of Ammon? Nine cubites was the length thereof, and foure cubites the breadth of it, after the cubite of a man.

12 And this land *which* we possessed at that time, from Aroer which *is* by the riuer Arnon, and halfe mount Gilead, and *the cities thereof, gaue I vnto the Reubenites, and to the Gadites.

Num. 32.
iosh. 13.
&c.

13 And the rest of Gilead, and all Bashan, *being* the kingdome of Og, gaue I vnto the halfe tribe of Manasseh : All the region of Argob with all Bashan, which was called the land of Giants.

14 Iair the sonne of Manasseh tooke all the countrey of Argob, vnto the coastes of Geshuri, and Maachathi ; and called them after his owne name, Bashan * Hauoth Iair, vnto this day.

Num. 32.

15 And I gaue Gilead vnto Machir.

16 And vnto the Reubenites, and vnto the Gadites, I gaue from Gilead, euen vnto the riuer Arnon, halfe the valley, and the border, euen vnto the

riuer Iabbok, which is the border of the children of Ammon:

17 The plaine also, and Iordan, and the coast *thereof,* from Chinnereth, euen vnto the sea of the plaine, *euen* the salt sea, vnder ‖ Ashdoth-Pisgah Eastward.

‖ *Or, vnder the springs of Pisgah, or the hill.*

18 ¶ And I commanded you at that time, saying, The Lord your God hath giuen you this land to possesse it: *ye shall passe ouer armed before your brethren the children of Israel, all *that are* †meet for the warre.

* Num. 32.
20.

†*Heb. sonnes of power.*

19 But your wiues, and your little ones, and your cattell (for I know that ye haue much cattel) shall abide in your cities, which I haue giuen you:

20 Vntill the Lord haue giuen rest vnto your brethren, as well as vnto you, and vntill they also possesse the land which the Lord your God hath giuen them beyond Iordan : and then shall ye *returne euery man vnto his possession, which I haue giuen you.

* Iosh. 22.
4.

21 ¶ And * I commanded Ioshua at that time, saying, Thine eyes haue seene all that the Lord your God hath done vnto these two Kings : so shal the Lord doe vnto all the kingdomes whither thou passest.

* Num. 27.
18.

22 Ye shall not feare them : for the Lord your God, he shal fight for you.

23 And I besought the Lord at that time, saying,

24 O Lord God, thou hast begun to shew thy seruant thy greatnesse, and thy mighty hand : for what God is there in heauen, or in earth, that can do according to thy workes, and according to thy might?

25 I pray thee let me goe ouer, and see the good land that is beyond Iordan, that goodly mountaine and Lebanon.

26 But the Lord * was wroth with me for your sakes, and would not heare mee : and the Lord said vnto me, Let it suffice thee, speake no more vnto me of this matter.

* Num. 20.
12. chap. 1.
37.

27 Get thee vp into the top of ‖ Pisgah, and lift vp thine eyes Westward, and Northward, and Southward, and Eastward, and beholde *it* with thine eyes : for thou shalt not goe ouer this Iordan.

‖ *Or, the hill.*

28 But charge Ioshua, and encourage him, and strengthen him : for hee shall goe ouer before this people, and he shall cause them to inherite the land which thou shalt see.

29 So

29 So we abode in the valley, ouer against Beth-Peor.

CHAP. IIII.

1 An Exhortation to obedience. 41 Moses appointeth the three Cities of refuge on that side Iordan.

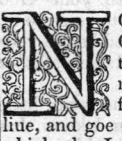

Nowe therefore hearken, O Israel, vnto the Statutes, and vnto the Iudgments which I teach you, for to do *them*, that ye may liue, and goe in and possesse the lande, which the LORD God of your fathers giueth you.

2 * Ye shall not adde vnto the word which I command you, neither shall you diminish *ought* from it, that ye may keepe the Commaundements of the LORD your God, which I command you.

* Chap. 12. 32. iosh. 1. 7 pro. 30. 6. reu. 22. 18.

3 Your eyes haue seene what the LORD did because of * Baal Peor: for all the men that followed Baal Peor, the LORD thy God hath destroyed them from among you.

* Num. 25. 4. &c.

4 But yee that did cleaue vnto the LORD your God, are aliue euery one of you this day.

5 Behold, I haue taught you Statutes, and Iudgements, euen as the LORD my God commanded me, that ye should do so, in the land whither ye goe to possesse it.

6 Keepe therefore, and doe *them;* for this *is* your wisedome and your vnderstanding in the sight of the nations, which shall heare all these statutes, and say, Surely this great nation is a wise and vnderstanding people.

7 For what nation *is there so* great, who hath God so nigh vnto them, as the LORD our God *is* in all things, that we call vpon him for?

8 And what nation *is there so* great, that hath Statutes and Iudgements *so* righteous, as all this Law which I set before you this day?

9 Onely take heed to thy selfe, and keepe thy soule diligently, lest thou forget the things which thine eyes haue seene, and lest they depart from thy heart all the dayes of thy life: but teach them thy sonnes, & thy sonnes sonnes:

10 *Specially*, the day that thou stoodst before the LORD thy God in Horeb, when the LORD said vnto mee, Gather me the people together, and I will make them heare my wordes, that they may learne to feare mee all the dayes that they shall liue vpon the earth, and that they may teach their children.

11 And ye came neere and stood vnder the mountaine, and the * mountaine burnt with fire vnto the † midst of heauen, with darkenes, cloudes, and thicke darkenesse.

* Exod. 19. 18.
† Heb. heart.

12 And the LORD spake vnto you out of the midst of the fire: ye heard the voyce of the words, but saw no similitude, † onely *ye heard* a voyce.

† Heb. saue a voyce.

13 And he declared vnto you his couenant, which he commanded you to performe, *euen* ten cõmandements, and he wrote them vpon two tables of stone.

14 ¶ And the LORD commanded me at that time, to teach you Statutes, and Iudgements, that yee might doe them in the land whither ye goe ouer to possesse it.

15 Take ye therfore good heed vnto your selues, (for ye saw no maner of similitude on the day *that* the LORD spake vnto you in Horeb, out of the midst of the fire)

16 Lest yee corrupt *your selues*, and make you a grauen image, the similitude of any figure, the likenes of male, or female,

17 The likenesse of any beast that *is* on the earth, the likenes of any winged foule that flieth in the aire,

18 The likenesse of any thing that creepeth on the ground, the likenesse of any fish that *is* in the waters beneath the earth:

19 And lest thou lift vp thine eyes vnto heauen, and when thou seest the sun, and the moone, and the starres, *euen* all the hoste of heauen, shouldest be driuen to worship them, and serue them, which the LORD thy God hath ‖ diuided vnto all nations vnder the whole heauen.

‖ Or, imparted.

20 But the LORD hath taken you, and brought you foorth out of the yron fornace, *euen* out of Egypt, to bee vnto him a people of inheritance, *as ye are* this day.

21 Furthermore, the LORD was angry with mee for your sakes, and sware that I should not goe ouer Iordan, and that I should not goe in vnto that good land which the LORD thy God giueth thee *for* an inheritance.

22 But I must die in this lande, I must not goe ouer Iordan: but ye shall goe ouer and possesse that good land.

23 Take

23 Take heed vnto your selues, lest ye forget the couenant of the LORD your God, which hee made with you, and make you a grauen image, *or* the likenes of any thing which the LORD thy God hath forbidden thee.

24 For the ** LORD thy God is a consuming fire, *euen* a iealous God.

* Chap. 9. 3.
ebr. 12.
9.

25 ¶ When thou shalt beget children, and childrens children, and shalt haue remained long in the land, and shal corrupt *your selues*, & make a grauen image, *or* the likenes of any thing, and shall doe euil in the sight of the LORD thy God, to prouoke him to anger:

26 I call heauen and earth to witnesse against you this day, that ye shall soone vtterly perish from off the land whereunto you goe ouer Iordan, to possesse it : yee shall not prolong *your* dayes vpon it, but shall vtterly bee destroyed.

27 And the LORD shall scatter you among the nations, and ye shall be left few in number among the heathen, whither the LORD shall lead you.

28 And there ye shall serue gods, the worke of mens hands, wood and stone, which neither see, nor heare, nor eate, nor smell.

29 But if from thence thou shalt seeke the LORD thy God, thou shalt finde him, if thou seeke him with all thy heart, and with all thy soule.

30 When thou art in tribulation, and all these things † are come vpon thee, euen in the latter dayes, if thou turne to the LORD thy God, and shalt be obedient vnto his voice:

Hebr.
aue found
ee.

31 (For the LORD thy God is a mercifull God) he will not forsake thee, neither destroy thee, nor forget the couenant of thy fathers, which he sware vnto them.

32 For aske now of the dayes that are past, which were before thee, since the day that God created man vpon earth, and *aske* from the one side of heauen vnto the other, Whether there hath bene *any such thing* as this great thing *is*, or hath bene heard like it ?

33 Did *euer* people heare the voyce of God speaking out of the midst of the fire, as thou hast heard, and liue ?

34 Or hath God assayed to goe and take him a nation from the midst of *another* nation, by temptations, by signes, and by wonders, and by warre, and by a mighty hand, and by a stretched out arme, and by great terrors, according to all that the LORD your God did for you in Egypt before your eyes ?

35 Vnto thee it was shewed, that thou mightest know, that the LORD hee is God; there is none else besides him.

36 Out of heauen hee made thee to heare his voice, that he might instruct thee : and vpon earth hee shewed thee his great fire, and thou heardest his words out of the midst of the fire.

37 And because he loued thy fathers, therefore he chose their seed after them, and brought thee out in his sight with his mightie power out of Egypt :

38 To driue out nations from before thee, greater and mightier then thou art, to bring thee in, to giue thee their land *for* an inheritance, as *it is* this day.

39 Know therefore this day, & consider it in thine heart, that the LORD hee is God in heauen aboue, and vpon the earth beneath : there is none else.

40 Thou shalt keepe therefore his Statutes, and his Commandements, which I command thee this day; that it may goe well with thee, and with thy children after thee, and that thou mayest prolong *thy* dayes vpon the earth, which the LORD thy God giueth thee, for euer.

41 ¶ Then Moses seuered three cities on this side Iordan, toward the Sunne rising:

42 That the slayer might flee thither, which should kill his neighbour vnawares, and hated him not in times past, and that fleeing vnto one of these cities he might liue :

43 *Namely*, * Bezer in the wildernesse, in the plaine countrey of the Reubenites; and Ramoth in Gilead of the Gadites; and Golan in Bashan, of the Manassites.

* Iosh. 20.
8.

44 ¶ And this *is* the Law which Moses set before the children of Israel :

45 These *are* the Testimonies, and the Statutes, and the Iudgements, which Moses spake vnto the children of Israel, after they came foorth out of Egypt;

46 On this side Iordan in the valley ouer against Beth-Peor, in the land of Sihon King of the Amorites, who dwelt at Heshbon, whom Moses and the children of Israel * smote, after they were come foorth out of Egypt.

* Num. 21.
24. chap. 1.
4.

47 And they possessed his land, and the

* Num. 21.
33. chap. 3.
3.

the land of * Og king of Bashan, two kings of the Amorites, *which* were on this side Iordan toward the sun rising,

48 From Aroer, which *is* by the banke of the riuer Arnon, euen vnto mount Sion, which *is* Hermon,

* Chap. 3.
17.

49 And all the plaine of this side Iordan Eastward, euen vnto the sea, of the plaine vnder the * springs of Pisgah.

CHAP. V.

1 The Couenant in Horeb. 6 The ten Commandements. 22 At the peoples request Moses receiueth the Law from God.

Nd Moses called all Israel, and sayd vnto them, Heare, O Israel, the Statutes and Iudgements which I speake in your eares this day, that ye may learne them,

† Heb. keepe
to doe them.
* Exod. 19.
5.

and † keepe and doe them.

2 * The Lord our God made a couenant with vs in Horeb.

3 The Lord made not this couenant with our fathers, but with vs: *euen* vs, who are all of vs here aliue this day.

4 The Lord talked with you, face to face, in the mount, out of the midst of the fire,

5 (I stood betweene the Lord and you, at that time, to shew you the word of the Lord: for ye were afraid by reason of the fire, and went not vp into the mount,) saying,

* Exod. 20.
2, &c. leuit.
26. 1. psal.
81. 10.
† Heb. seruants.

6 ¶ * I am the Lord thy God, which brought thee out of the lande of Egypt, from the house of † bondage.

7 Thou shalt haue none other gods before me.

8 Thou shalt not make thee any grauen image, *or any likenesse of any thing* that is in heauen aboue, or that is in the earth beneath, or that *is* in the waters beneath the earth.

* Exod. 34.
7.

9 Thou shalt not bow downe thy selfe vnto them, nor serue them: for * I the Lord thy God *am* a ielous God, visiting the iniquity of the fathers vpon the children, vnto the third and fourth generation of them that hate me,

* Ierem. 32.
18.

10 And * shewing mercy vnto thousands, of them that loue me, and keepe my commandements.

11 Thou shalt not take the name of the Lord thy God in vaine: for the Lord will not holde him guiltlesse that taketh his name in vaine.

12 Keepe the Sabbath day to sanctifie it, as the Lord thy God hath commanded thee.

13 Sixe dayes thou shalt labour, and doe all thy worke.

* Gen. 2. 2.
heb. 4, 4.

14 But the seuenth day *is* the * Sabbath of the Lord thy God: *in it* thou shalt not doe any worke, thou, nor thy sonne, nor thy daughter, nor thy man seruant, nor thy maid seruant, nor thine oxe, nor thine asse, nor any of thy cattel, nor thy stranger that *is* within thy gates, that thy man seruant and thy maid seruant may rest as well as thou.

15 And remember that thou wast a seruant in the land of Egypt, and that the Lord thy God brought thee out thence, through a mightie hand, and by a stretched out arme: Therefore the Lord thy God commaunded thee to keepe the Sabbath day.

16 ¶ Honour thy father and thy mother, as the Lord thy God hath commanded thee, that thy daies may be prolonged, and that it may goe well with thee, in the land which the Lord thy God giueth thee.

* Mat. 5. 2
* Luke 18.
20.

17 * Thou shalt not kill.

18 * Neither shalt thou commit adulterie.

* Rom. 13.

19 * Neither shalt thou steale.

20 Neither shalt thou beare false witnesse against thy neighbour.

* Rom. 7. 7

21 * Neither shalt thou desire thy neighbours wife, neither shalt thou couet thy neighbours house, his field, or his man seruant, or his maide seruant, his oxe, or his asse, or any thing that *is* thy neighbours.

22 ¶ These wordes the Lord spake vnto all your assembly in the mount out of the midst of the fire, of the cloud, and of the thicke darkenesse, *with* a great voice, and he added no more, and he wrote them in two Tables of stone, and deliuered them vnto me.

23 And it came to passe when yee heard the voice out of the midst of the darkenes (for the mountaine did burne with fire) that ye came neere vnto mee, *euen* all the heads of your tribes, and your elders.

24 And ye said, Behold, the Lord our God hath shewed vs his glory, and his greatnesse, and * we haue heard his voice out of the midst of the fire: wee haue seene this day that God doth talke with man, and * he liueth.

* Exod. 19
19.

* Chap. 4.
33.

25 Now therefore why should wee die?

Heb. adde heare.

die? for this great fire will consume vs. If we † heare the voyce of the Lord our God any more, then we shall die.

26 For who is there of all flesh that hath heard the voice of the liuing God, speaking out of the midst of the fire (as we *haue*) and liued?

27 Goe thou neere, and heare all that the Lord our God shall say; and speake thou vnto vs all that the Lord our God shall speake vnto thee, and *we will heare it, and doe it.

Exod. 20.

28 And the Lord heard the voice of your words, when ye spake vnto me, and the Lord said vnto me, I haue heard the voice of the wordes of this people, which they haue spoken vnto thee: they haue well said, all that they haue spoken.

29 O that there were such an heart in them, that they would feare me, and keepe my commandements alwayes, that it might bee well with them, and with their children for euer.

30 Goe, say to them, Get you into your tents againe.

31 But as for thee, stand thou here by me, and I will speake vnto thee all the Commandements, and the Statutes, and the Iudgements, which thou shalt teach them, that they may doe them in the land which I giue them to possesse it.

32 Ye shall obserue to doe therefore, as the Lord your God hath commanded you: you shall not turne aside to the right hand, or to the left.

33 Ye shall walke in all the wayes which the Lord your God hath commanded you, that ye may liue, and *that it may be* well with you, and that ye may prolong *your* dayes in the land which ye shall possesse.

CHAP. VI.

1 The end of the Law is obedience. 3 An exhortation thereto.

Hebr. passe er.

Ow these are the Commaundements, the Statutes, & the Iudgements, which the Lord your God commanded to teach you, that ye might doe *them* in the land whither ye † goe to possesse it:

2 That thou mightest feare the Lord thy God, to keepe all his Statutes, and his Commandements which I command thee; thou, and thy sonne,

and thy sonnes sonne, all the dayes of thy life: and that thy dayes may be prolonged.

3 ¶ Heare therefore, O Israel, and obserue to do *it*, that it may be wel with thee, and that ye may increase mightily, as the Lord God of thy fathers hath promised thee, in the land that floweth with milke and hony.

4 Heare, O Israel, the Lord our God *is* one Lord.

5 And *thou shalt loue the Lord thy God with all thine heart, and with all thy soule, and with all thy might.

Chap. 10. 12. mat. 22. 37. mar. 12. 30. luke 10. 27.
Chap. 11. 18.

6 And *these words which I command thee this day, shall bee in thine heart.

7 And thou shalt † teach them diligently vnto thy children, and shalt talke of them when thou sittest in thine house, and when thou walkest by the way, and when thou liest downe, and when thou risest vp.

† *Heb. whet or sharpen.*

8 And thou shalt binde them for a signe vpon thine hand, and they shalbe as frontlets betweene thine eyes.

9 And thou shalt write them vpon the posts of thy house, and on thy gates.

10 And it shall be when the Lord thy God shall haue brought thee into the land which hee sware vnto thy fathers, to Abraham, to Isaac, and to Iacob to giue thee, great and goodly cities, which thou buildedst not,

11 And houses full of all good things which thou filledst not, and welles digged which thou diggedst not, vineyards and oliue trees which thou plantedst not, *when thou shalt haue eaten and be full,

Chap. 8. 9, 10, &c.

12 *Then* beware lest thou forget the Lord which brought thee forth out of the land of Egypt, from the house of † bondage.

† *Heb. bondmen or seruants.*

13 Thou shalt *feare the Lord thy God, and serue him, & shalt sweare by his Name.

Chap. 10. 12, 20. and 13. 4.

14 Yee shall not goe after other gods, of the gods of the people which *are* round about you:

15 (For the Lord thy God is a ielous God among you) lest the anger of the Lord thy God bee kindled against thee, and destroy thee from off the face of the earth.

16 ¶ *Ye shal not tempt the Lord your God, * as yee tempted *him* in Massah.

Mat. 4. 7.
Exod. 17. 2.

17 You shall diligently keepe the Com-

Commandements of the LORD your God, and his Testimonies, and his Statutes, which he hath commanded thee.

18 And thou shalt doe that which *is* right and good in the sight of the LORD : that it may be well with thee, and that thou mayest goe in, and possesse the good land which the LORD sware vnto thy fathers;

19 To cast out all thine enemies from before thee, as the LORD hath spoken.

20 *And* when thy sonne asketh thee †in time to come, saying, What *meane* the Testimonies, & the Statutes, and the Iudgements, which the LORD our God hath commanded you?

21 Then thou shalt say vnto thy sonne, We were Pharaohs bondmen in Egypt, and the LORD brought vs out of Egypt with a mighty hand.

22 And the LORD shewed signes and wonders, great and † sore vpon E-gypt, vpon Pharaoh, and vpon all his houshold, before our eyes:

23 And hee brought vs out from thence, that hee might bring vs in, to giue vs the land which hee sware vnto our fathers.

24 And the LORD commanded vs to doe all these Statutes, to feare the LORD our God, for our good alwayes, that he might preserue vs aliue, as *it is* at this day.

25 And it shall be our righteousnes, if we obserue to doe all these Commandements, before the LORD our God, as he hath commanded vs.

CHAP. VII.

1 All communion with the Nations is forbidden, 4 for feare of Idolatrie, 6 for the holinesse of the people, 9 for the nature of God in his Mercie and Iustice, 17 for the assurednesse of victorie which God will giue ouer them.

Hen the *LORD thy God shall bring thee into the land whither thou goest to possesse it, and hath cast out many nations before thee, the *Hittites*, and the Girgashites, and the Amorites, and the Canaanites, and the Perizzites, and the Hiuites, and the Iebusites, seuen nations greater and mightier then thou:

2 And *when* the LORD thy God shall deliuer them before thee, thou

shalt smite them, and vtterly destroy them, * thou shalt make no couenant with them, nor shew mercy vnto them.

3 Neither shalt thou make marriages with them : thy daughter thou shalt not giue vnto his sonne, nor his daughter shalt thou take vnto thy sonne.

4 For they will turne away thy sonne from following mee, that they may serue other gods: so will the anger of the LORD be kindled against you, and destroy thee suddenly.

5 But thus shal ye deale with them; ye shall destroy their altars, and breake downe their † images, and cut downe their groues, and burne their grauen images with fire.

6 *For thou art an holy people vnto the LORD thy God: *the LORD thy God hath chosen thee to be a special people vnto himselfe, aboue all people that are vpon the face of the earth.

7 The LORD did not set his loue vpon you, nor choose you, because yee were moe in number then any people: (for ye were the fewest of all people,)

8 But because the LORD loued you, and because hee would keepe the othe which hee had sworne vnto your fathers, hath the LORD brought you out with a mighty hand, and redeemed you out of the house of bondmen, from the hand of Pharaoh king of Egypt.

9 Know therefore that the LORD thy God, he is God, the faithfull God, which keepeth Couenant and Mercy with them that loue him, and keepe his Commandements, to a thousand generations;

10 And repaieth them that hate him to their face, to destroy them: he wil not be slacke to him that hateth him, he will repay him to his face.

11 Thou shalt therefore keepe the Commandements, and the Statutes, and the Iudgements, which I command thee this day, to doe them.

12 ¶ Wherefore it shal come to passe, †if ye hearken to these iudgements, and keepe and do them : That the LORD thy God shall keepe vnto thee the Couenant and the Mercy which he sware vnto thy fathers.

13 And hee will loue thee, and blesse thee, and multiply thee : Hee will also blesse the fruit of thy wombe, and the fruit of thy land, thy corne, and thy wine, and thine oile, the encrease of thy kine,

† *Hebr. to morrow.*

† *Hebr. euil.*

* *Chap. 31. 3.*

* *Exod. 32. and 12.*

† *Hebr. s tues, or lars.*

* *Chap. 2. and 26 19.*
* *Exod. 5. 1. pet. 9.*

† *Hebr. b cause.*

kine, and the flockes of thy sheepe, in the land which hee sware vnto thy fathers to giue thee.

14 Thou shalt bee blessed aboue all people: *there shall not bee male or female barren among you or among your cattell.

15 And the Lord will take away from thee all sickenesse, and will put none of the * euill diseases of Egypt (which thou knowest) vpon thee: but will lay them vpon all them that hate thee.

16 And thou shalt consume all the people which the Lord thy God shall deliuer thee: thine eye shall haue no pitie vpon them, neither shalt thou serue their gods, for that *will be* a * snare vnto thee.

17 If thou shalt say in thine heart, These nations are moe then I, howe can I dispossesse them?

18 Thou shalt not be afraid of them: *but* shalt well remember, what the Lord thy God did vnto Pharaoh, and vnto all Egypt,

19 The great temptations which thine eyes sawe, and the signes and the wonders, and the mightie hand, and the stretched out arme, whereby the Lord thy God brought thee out: so shall the Lord thy God doe vnto all the people of whom thou art afraid.

20 * Moreouer, the Lord thy God will send the hornet among them, vntill they that are left and hide themselues from thee, be destroyed.

21 Thou shalt not bee affrighted at them: for the Lord thy God is among you, a mightie God, and terrible.

22 And the Lord thy God will †put out those nations before thee by litle and litle: thou mayest not consume them at once, lest the beastes of the field increase vpon thee.

23 But the Lord thy God shall deliuer them †vnto thee, and shall destroy them with a mightie destruction, vntill they be destroyed.

24 And he shall deliuer their kings into thine hand, and thou shalt destroy their name from vnder heauen: There shal no man be able to stand before thee, vntil thou haue destroyed them.

25 The grauen images of their gods * shall yee burne with fire: thou *shalt not desire the siluer or golde *that is* on them, nor take it vnto thee, lest thou bee snared therein: for it *is* an abominati-

on to the Lord thy God.

26 Neither shalt thou bring an abomination into thine house, lest thou bee a cursed thing like it: *but* thou shalt vtterly detest it, and thou shalt vtterly abhorre it, for * it is a cursed thing.

CHAP. VIII.

1 An exhortation to obedience in regard of Gods dealing with them.

Ll the commaundements which I commaund thee this day, shall yee obserue to doe, that yee may liue, and multiply, and goe in, and possesse the land which the Lord sware vnto your fathers.

2 And thou shalt remember all the way which the Lord thy God led thee these fourtie yeeres in the wildernesse, to humble thee, *and* to proue thee, to know what *was* in thine heart, whether thou wouldest keepe his commandements, or no.

3 And he humbled thee, and suffred thee to hunger, and fed thee with Manna, which thou knewest not, neither did thy fathers know: that he might make thee know, that man doth *not liue by bread onely, but by euery *word* that proceedeth out of the mouth of the Lord doth man liue.

4 *Thy raiment waxed not old vpon thee, neither did thy foote swell these fourtie yeeres.

5 Thou shalt also consider in thine heart, that as a man chasteneth his son, *so* the Lord thy God chasteneth thee.

6 Therefore thou shalt keepe the Commandements of the Lord thy God, to walke in his wayes, and to feare him.

7 For the Lord thy God bringeth thee into a good land, a lande of brookes of water, of fountaines, and depths that spring out of valleys and hilles,

8 A land of wheate, and barley, and vines, and fig trees, and pomegranats, a land of †oyle oliue, and hony,

9 A lande wherein thou shalt eate bread without scarcenes, thou shalt not lacke any thing in it: a lande whose stones *are* yron, and out of whose hils thou mayest digge brasse.

10 *When thou hast eaten and art full, then thou shalt blesse the Lord thy God, for the good lande which hee hath giuen thee.

11 Beware

Margin notes (left):
Exod. 23. &c.

Exod. 9. & 15.

Exod. 23.

Exod. 23. Iosh. 24

Hebr. *cke off.*

Hebr. be- *: thy* *e.*

hap. 12.

osh. 7. 1, 2. mac. 40.

Margin notes (right):
* Chap. 13. 17.

* Matt. 4. 4. luke 4. 4.

* Nehe. 9. 21.

† *Hebr. of oliue tree of oyle.*

* Chap. 6. 12. 13.

11 Beware that thou forget not the LORD thy God, in not keeping his Commandements, and his Iudgements, and his Statutes which I command thee this day:

12 Lest *when* thou hast eaten and art full, and hast built goodly houses, and dwelt *therein;*

13 And *when* thy heards and thy flocks multiply, and thy siluer and thy gold is multiplied, and all that thou hast is multiplied:

14 Then thine heart bee lifted vp, and thou forget the LORD thy God (which brought thee foorth out of the land of Egypt, from the house of bondage,

15 Who led thee through that great and terrible wildernesse, *wherein were* fierie serpents, and scorpions, & drought, where there was no water, * who brought thee foorth water out of the rocke of flint,

* Num. 20. 11.

16 Who fed thee in the wildernesse with * Manna, which thy fathers knew not, that hee might humble thee, and that hee might prooue thee, to doe thee good at thy latter end:)

* Exod. 16. 15.

17 And thou say in thine heart, My power, and the might of mine hand hath gotten me this wealth.

18 But thou shalt remember the LORD thy God: for *it is* he that giueth thee power to get wealth, that he may establish his Couenant, which he sware vnto thy fathers, as *it is* this day.

19 And it shalbe, if thou doe at all forget the LORD thy God, and walke after other gods, and serue them, and worship them; I testifie against you this day, that ye shall surely perish.

20 As the nations which the LORD destroyeth before your face, so shall yee perish; because ye would not be obedient vnto the voice of the LORD your God.

CHAP. IX.

1 Moses disswadeth them from the opinion of their owne righteousnesse, by rehearsing their seuerall rebellions.

 Eare, O Israel, thou art to passe ouer Iordan this day, to goe in, to possesse nations greater & mightier then thy selfe, Cities great, and fenced vp to heauen,

2 A people great and tall, the children of the Anakims, whom thou knowest, and *of whom* thou hast heard *say,* *Who can stand before the children of Anak?

* Num. 29.

3 Vnderstand therefore this day, that the LORD thy God *is* he, which goeth ouer before thee, as a * consuming fire: he shall destroy them, and he shall bring them downe before thy face: So shalt thou driue them out, and destroy them quickly, as the LORD hath said vnto thee.

* Chap. 4. 24. hebr. 29.

4 Speake not thou in thine heart, after that the LORD thy God hath cast them out from before thee, saying, For my righteousnesse the LORD hath brought mee in to possesse this land: but for the wickednesse of these nations, the LORD doeth driue them out from before thee.

5 Not for thy righteousnesse, or for the vprightnesse of thine heart, doest thou goe to possesse their land: But for the wickednesse of these nations the LORD thy God doeth driue them out from before thee, and that he may performe the word which the LORD sware vnto thy fathers, Abraham, Isaac and Iacob.

6 Vnderstand therefore, that the LORD thy God giueth thee not this good land to possesse it, for thy righteousnesse; for thou *art* a stiffe-necked people.

7 ¶ Remember *and* forget not, how thou prouokedst the LORD thy God to wrath in the wildernesse: from the day that thou didst depart out of the land of Egypt, vntill ye came vnto this place, yee haue bene rebellious against the LORD.

8 Also in Horeb yee prouoked the LORD to wrath, so that the LORD was angry with you, to haue destroyed you.

9 When I was gone vp into the mount, to receiue the Tables of stone, *euen* the Tables of the Couenant which the LORD made with you, then * I abode in the mount fortie dayes, and fortie nights, I neither did eate bread, nor drinke water:

* Exod. 18. and. 23.

10 * And the LORD deliuered vnto me two Tables of stone, written with the finger of God, and on them *was written* according to all the words which the LORD spake with you in the mount, out of the midst of fire, in the day of the assembly.

* Exod. 18.

11 And it came to passe at the end of fortie

fortie dayes, and fortie nights, *that* the LORD gaue mee the two Tables of stone, *euen* the Tables of the Couenant.

12 And the LORD said vnto mee, * Arise, get thee downe quickly from hence; for thy people which thou hast brought foorth out of Egypt, haue corrupted *themselues:* they are quickly turned aside out of the way which I commanded them; they haue made them a molten image.

13 Furthermore, the LORD spake vnto me, saying, I haue seene this people, and behold, it is a stifnecked people.

14 Let me alone, that I may destroy them, and blot out their name from vnder heauen : and I will make of thee a nation mightier and greater then they.

15 So I turned and came downe from the mount, and the mount burned with fire : and the two Tables of the Couenant were in my two hands.

16 And I looked, and behold, ye had sinned against the LORD your God, *and* had made you a molten calfe: ye had turned aside quickly out of the way which the LORD had commanded you.

17 And I tooke the two Tables, and cast them out of my two hands, and brake them before your eyes.

18 And I fell downe before the LORD, as at the first, fortie dayes and fortie nights, I did neither eate bread nor drinke water, because of all your sinnes which ye sinned, in doing wickedly in the sight of the LORD, to prouoke him to anger.

19 (For I was afraid of the anger, and whot displeasure wherewith the LORD was wroth against you, to destroy you.) But the LORD hearkned vnto me at that time also.

20 And the LORD was very angry with Aaron, to haue destroyed him : And I prayed for Aaron also the same time.

21 And I tooke your sinne, the calfe which ye had made, and burnt it with fire, and stamped it, *and* ground it very small, euen vntill it was as small as dust: and I cast the dust thereof into the brooke that descended out of the mount.

22 And at *Taberah, and at *Massah, and at *Kibroth-Hattaauah, ye prouoked the LORD to wrath.

23 Likewise when the LORD sent you from Kadesh Barnea, saying, Goe vp and possesse the land which I haue giuen you, then you rebelled against the commandement of the LORD your God, and ye beleeued him not, nor hearkened to his voyce.

24 You haue bin rebellious against the LORD, from the day that I knew you.

25 Thus I fell downe before the LORD fourtie dayes, and fourtie nights, as I fel downe *at the first*, because the LORD had said, he would destroy you.

26 I prayed therefore vnto the LORD, and said, O Lord GOD, destroy not thy people, and thine inheritance, which thou hast redeemed through thy greatnes, which thou hast brought foorth out of Egypt, with a mightie hand.

27 Remember thy seruants, Abraham, Isaac, and Iacob, looke not vnto the stubburnnesse of this people, nor to their wickednes, nor to their sinne :

28 Lest the land whence thou broughtest vs out, say, * Because the LORD was not able to bring them into the land which hee promised them, and because hee hated them, hee hath brought them out, to slay them in the wildernesse.

29 Yet they are thy people, and thine inheritance which thou broughtest out by thy mightie power, and by thy stretched out arme.

CHAP. X.

1 Gods mercie in restoring the two Tables, 6 in continuing the Priesthood, 8 in separating the tribe of Leui, 10 in hearkening vnto Moses his suit for the people. 12 An exhortation vnto obedience.

AT that time the LORD said vnto me, * Hew thee two Tables of stone, like vnto the first, and come vp vnto mee into the mount, and make thee an Arke of wood.

2 And I will write on the Tables the words that were in the first Tables which thou brakest, and thou shalt put them in the Arke.

3 And I made an Arke of Shittim wood, and hewed two Tables of stone like vnto the first, and went vp into the mount, hauing the two Tables in mine hand.

4 And he wrote on the Tables, according to the first writing, the tenne
+Com-

Kod. 32.

Num. 11.
Kod. 17.
um. 11.

* Num. 14. 16.

* Exod. 34. 1.

† *Hebr.*
words.

† Commandements, which the Lord spake vnto you in the mount, out of the midst of the fire, in the day of the assembly: and the Lord gaue them vnto me.

5 And I turned my selfe and came downe from the mount, and put the Tables in the Arke which I had made, and there they be, as the Lord commanded me.

6 ¶ And the children of Israel tooke their iourney from Beeroth, of the children of Iaakan, to * Mosera: * there Aaron died, and there he was buried, and Eleazar his sonne ministred in the Priests office in his stead.

* Num. 33. 30.
* Num. 20. 28.

7 From thence they iourneyed vnto Gudgodah, and from Gudgodah to Iotbath, a land of riuers of waters.

8 ¶ At that time the Lord separated the tribe of Leui, to beare the Arke of the Couenant of the Lord, to stand before the Lord, to minister vnto him, and to blesse in his Name, vnto this day.

* Num. 18. 20.

9 * Wherefore Leui hath no part nor inheritance with his brethren: the Lord is his inheritance, according as the Lord thy God promised him.

‖ *Or, fortie dayes.*

10 And I stayed in the mount, according to the ‖first time, fortie dayes, and fortie nights: and the Lord hearkened vnto mee at that time also, *and* the Lord would not destroy thee.

† *Hebr. goe in iourney.*

11 And the Lord said vnto me, Arise, †take *thy* iourney before the people, that they may goe in, and possesse the land which I sware vnto their fathers to giue vnto them.

12 ¶ And now Israel, what doeth the Lord thy God require of thee, but to feare the Lord thy God, to walke in all his waies, and to loue him, and to serue the Lord thy God, with all thy heart, and with all thy soule,

13 To keepe the Commandements of the Lord, and his Statutes, which I commaund thee this day for thy good?

14 Behold, the heauen, & the heauen of heauens *is* the Lords thy God, * the earth *also*, with all that therein is.

* Psal. 24. 1.

15 Onely the Lord had a delight in thy fathers, to loue them, and hee chose their seed after them, *euen* you, aboue all people, as *it is* this day.

16 Circumcise therefore the foreskin of your heart, and bee no more stiffenecked.

17 For the Lord your God is God of gods, and Lord of lords, a great God, a mighty, and a terrible, which *regardeth not persons, nor taketh reward.

* 2. Ch 19. 7. 1 34. 19. 10. 34. 2. 11. 2. 6. ep 6. 9. co 3. 25. 1. 1. 17.

18 He doeth execute the iudgement of the fatherlesse, and widow, and loueth the stranger, in giuing him food and raiment.

19 Loue yee therefore the stranger: for yee were strangers in the land of Egypt.

20 * Thou shalt feare the Lord thy God; him shalt thou serue, and to him shalt thou *cleaue, and sweare by his Name.

* Chap 13. ma 10. luk 8. * Chap 4.

21 He *is* thy praise, and he *is* thy God that hath done for thee these great and terrible things, which thine eyes haue seene.

22 Thy fathers went downe into Egypt * with threescore and ten persons: and now the Lord thy God hath made thee *as the starres of heauen, for multitude.

* Gene 27. exo 5. * Gene 5.

CHAP. XI.

1 An exhortation to obedience, 2 by their owne experience of Gods great works, 8 by promise of Gods great blessings, 16 and by threatnings. 18 A carefull study is required in Gods words. 26 The blessing and curse is set before them.

Herefore thou shalt loue the Lord thy God, and keepe his charge, and his Statutes, and his Iudgements, and his Commandements alway.

2 And know you this day : for *I speake* not with your children which haue not knowen, and which haue not seene the chastisement of the Lord your God, his greatnesse, his mighty hand, and his stretched out arme,

3 And his miracles, and his actes, which he did in the midst of Egypt, vnto Pharaoh the King of Egypt, and vnto all his land,

4 And what hee did vnto the army of Egypt, vnto their horses, and to their charets, how he made the water of the Red sea to ouerflow them as they pursued after you, and *how* the Lord hath destroyed them vnto this day,

5 And what hee did vnto you in the wildernesse, vntill yee came into this place,

6 And

Num. 16.
. and 27.
. psal. 106.
7.

6 And *what he did vnto Dathan, and Abiram, the sonnes of Eliab the sonne of Reuben: how the earth opened her mouth and swallowed them vp, and their housholds, and their tents, and all the ‖substance that ✝was in their possession in the middest of all Israel.

Or, liuing
substance
which fol-
lowed them.
Heb. was
their
et.

7 But your eyes haue seene all the great acts of the LORD, which he did.

8 Therefore shall yee keepe all the Commandements which I command you this day, that ye may be strong and goe in, and possesse the land whither ye goe to possesse it:

9 And that yee may prolong *your* dayes in the lande which the LORD sware vnto your fathers to giue vnto them, and to their seed, a land that floweth with milke and hony.

10 ¶ For the land whither thou goest in to possesse it, is not as the lande of Egypt from whence ye came out, where thou sowedst thy seed, and wateredst *it* with thy foot, as a garden of herbes:

11 But the lande whither ye goe to possesse it, *is* a lande of hilles and valleys, *and* drinketh water of the raine of heauen:

Heb. see-
eth.

12 A lande, which the LORD thy God ✝careth for: the eyes of the LORD thy God *are* always vpon it, from the beginning of the yeere, euen vnto the end of the yeere.

13 ¶ And it shall come to passe, if you shall hearken diligently vnto my Commandements which I command you this day, to loue the LORD your God, and to serue him with all your heart, and with all your soule;

14 That I will giue *you* the raine of your land in his due season, the first raine and the latter raine, that thou mayest gather in thy corne, and thy wine, and thine oyle.

Heb. giue.

15 And I will ✝send grasse in thy fields for thy cattell, that thou mayest eate and be full.

16 Take heede to your selues, that your heart be not deceiued, and ye turne aside, and serue other gods, and worship them:

17 And *then* the LORDS wrath be kindled against you, and hee shut vp the heauen, that there be no raine, and that the land yeeld not her fruit, and lest ye perish quickly from off the good land which the LORD giueth you.

18 ¶ Therefore shall ye lay vp these

my words in your heart, and in your soule, and *bind them for a signe vpon your hand, that they may bee as frontlets betweene your eyes.

* Chap. 6. 8

19 And *ye shal teach them your children, speaking of them, when thou sittest in thine house, and when thou walkest by the way, when thou liest downe, and when thou risest vp.

* Chap. 4.
10. & 6. 7.

20 And thou shalt write them vpon the doore posts of thine house, and vpon thy gates:

21 That your dayes may bee multiplied, and the dayes of your children, in the land which the LORD sware vnto your fathers to giue them, as the dayes of heauen vpon the earth.

22 ¶ For if ye shall diligently keepe all these Commaundements which I command you, to doe them, to loue the LORD your God, to walke in all his wayes, and to cleaue vnto him:

23 Then will the LORD driue out all these nations from before you, and ye shall possesse greater nations, and mightier then your selues.

24 * Euery place whereon the soles of your feet shall tread, shall be yours: from the wildernesse, and Lebanon, from the riuer, the riuer Euphrates, euen vnto the vttermost sea, shall your coast be.

* Iosh. 1. 3.

25 There shall no man bee able to stand before you: *for* the LORD your God shall lay the feare of you, and the dread of you vpon all the land that yee shall tread vpon, as hee hath said vnto you.

26 ¶ Behold, I set before you this day, a blessing and a curse:

27 *A blessing, if ye obey the Commandements of the LORD your God which I command you this day:

* Chap. 28.
2.

28 And a *curse, if ye will not obey the Commandements of the LORD your God, but turne aside out of the way, which I command you this day, to goe after other gods which yee haue not knowen.

* Chap. 28.
15.

29 And it shall come to passe when the LORD thy God hath brought thee in, vnto the land whither thou goest to possesse it, that thou shalt put *the blessing vpon mount Gerizim, and the curse vpon mount Ebal.

* Chap. 27.
13. iosh. 8.
33.

30 Are they not on the other side Iordan, by the way where the Sunne goeth downe, in the land of the Canaanites, which dwell in the champion ouer

uer against Gilgal, beside the plaines of Moreh?

31 For ye shall passe ouer Iordan, to goe in to possesse the land which the LORD your God giueth you, and ye shall possesse it, and dwell therein.

*Chap. 5. 32.

32 And yee shall obserue * to doe all the Statutes, and Iudgements, which I set before you this day.

CHAP. XII.

1 Monuments of Idolatrie are to be destroyed. 5 The place of Gods seruice is to be kept. 15. 23 Blood is forbidden. 17. 20. 26 Holy things must bee eaten in the Holy place. 19 The Leuite is not to be forsaken. 29 Idolatrie is not be inquired after.

Hese are the Statutes, and Iudgements, which ye shal obserue to do, in the land which the LORD God of thy fathers giueth thee to possesse it, all the dayes that yee liue vpon the earth.

*Chap. 7. 5.

‖ Or, inherite.

2 Yee shall vtterly destroy all the places, wherein the nations which yee shall ‖possesse, serued their gods, vpon the high mountaines, and vpon the hils, and vnder euery greene tree.

*Iudg. 2. 2. †Heb. break downe.

3 And * you shall †ouerthrow their altars, and breake their pillars, and burne their groues with fire, and you shall hew downe the grauen images of their gods, and destroy the names of them out of that place.

4 Yee shall not doe so vnto the LORD your God.

*1. King. 8. 29. 2. chro. 7. 12.

5 But vnto the place which the LORD your God shall * chuse out of all your tribes, to put his name there, *euen* vnto his habitation shall yee seeke, and thither thou shalt come:

6 And thither yee shall bring your burnt offrings, and your sacrifices, and your tithes, and heaue offrings of your hand, and your vowes, and your free wil offerings, and the firstlings of your heards, and of your flocks.

7 And there ye shall eate before the LORD your God, and yee shall reioyce in all that you put your hand vnto, ye and your housholds, wherein the LORD thy God hath blessed thee.

8 Ye shall not do after all the things that we doe here this day, euery man whatsoeuer *is* right in his owne eyes.

9 For yee are not as yet come to the rest, and to the inheritance which the LORD your God giueth you.

10 But when yee goe ouer Iordan, and dwel in the land which the LORD your God giueth you to inherite, and when he giueth you rest from all your enemies round about, so that ye dwell in safety:

11 Then there shall be a place which the LORD your God shall choose to cause his name to dwell there, thither shall ye bring all that I command you: your burnt offerings, and your sacrifices, your tithes, and the heaue offring of your hand, & all †your choice vowes, which ye vow vnto the LORD.

†Hebr. t choice of your vow

12 And yee shall reioyce before the LORD your God, ye and your sonnes and your daughters, and your men seruants, and your maid seruants, and the Leuite that is within your gates, forasmuch as *hee hath no part nor inheritance with you.

*Chap. 9.

13 Take heed to thy selfe, that thou offer not thy burnt offerings in euery place that thou seest:

14 But in the place which the LORD shal choose in one of thy tribes, there thou shalt offer thy burnt offerings, and there thou shalt do all that I command thee.

15 Notwithstanding, thou mayest kill and eate flesh in all thy gates, whatsoeuer thy soule lusteth after, according to the blessing of the LORD thy God which he hath giuen thee: the vncleane and the cleane may eate thereof, as of the Roe bucke, and as of the Hart.

16 *Onely ye shall not eat the blood: yee shall powre it vpon the earth as water.

*Chap. 23.

17 ¶ Thou mayest not eate within thy gates the tithe of thy corne, or of thy wine, or of thy oyle, or the firstlings of thy heards, or of thy flocke, nor any of thy vowes which thou vowest, nor thy free will offerings, or heaue offering of thine hand:

18 But thou must eate them before the LORD thy God, in the place which the LORD thy God shall choose, thou and thy sonne, and thy daughter, and thy man seruant, and thy maid seruant, and the Leuite that is within thy gates: and thou shalt reioyce before the LORD thy God, in all that thou puttest thine hands vnto.

19 *Take heed to thy selfe, that thou forsake not the Leuite, as †long as thou liuest vpon the earth.

*Chap. 27. ecch 7. 31. †Hebr. thy day

20 ¶ When

Gene. 28.
chap.
9.

20 ¶ When the LORD thy God shall enlarge thy border, * as hee hath promised thee , and thou shalt say, I will eate flesh (because thy soule longeth to eat flesh) thou mayest eat flesh whatsoeuer thy soule lusteth after.

21 If the place which the LORD thy God hath chosen to put his Name there, be too farre from thee, then thou shalt kill of thy herd and of thy flocke, which the LORD hath giuen thee, as I haue commaunded thee , and thou shalt eate in thy gates, whatsoeuer thy soule lusteth after.

22 Euen as the Roe bucke and the Hart is eaten, so thou shalt eate them: the vncleane and the cleane shall eate of them alike.

Heb. bee
sing.

23 Onely †be sure that thou eate not the blood : for the blood is the life, and thou mayest not eate the life with the flesh.

24 Thou shalt not eate it; thou shalt powre it vpon the earth as water.

25 Thou shalt not eate it, that it may goe well with thee, and with thy children after thee , when thou shalt doe that which is right in the sight of the LORD.

26 Onely thy holy things which thou hast , and thy vowes , thou shalt take, and goe vnto the place which the LORD shall chuse.

27 And thou shalt offer thy burnt offerings, the flesh and the blood, vpon the altar of the LORD thy God : and the blood of thy sacrifices shall be powred out vpon the altar of the LORD thy God, and thou shalt eate the flesh.

28 Obserue & heare all these words which I command thee, that it may go well with thee, and with thy children after thee for euer, when thou doest that which is good and right in the sight of the LORD thy God.

29 ¶ When the LORD thy God shall cut off the nations from before thee , whither thou goest to possesse them, and thou † succeedest them, and dwellest in their land :

Heb. inhe-
est or pos-
sessed them.

30 Take heede to thy selfe that thou be not snared †by following them, after that they be destroyed from before thee, and that thou enquire not after their gods , saying , How did these nations serue their gods ? euen so will I doe likewise.

Heb. after
em.

31 Thou shalt not doe so vnto the LORD thy God : for euery † abomi-

Heb. abo-
ination of
e.

nation to the LORD which hee hateth, haue they done vnto their gods : for euen their sonnes and their daughters they haue burnt in the fire to their gods.

32 What thing soeuer I command you, obserue to doe it : *thou shalt not adde thereto, nor diminish from it.

* Chap. 4. 2
iosh. 1. 7.
reue. 22. 18

CHAP. XIII.

1 Inticers to idolatrie, 6 how neere soeuer vnto thee, 9 are to be stoned vnto death. 12 Idolatrous cities are not to be spared.

IF there arise among you a prophet, or a dreamer of dreames, and giueth thee a signe, or a wonder :

2 And the signe or the wonder come to passe, whereof he spake vnto thee, saying, Let vs go after other gods (which thou hast not knowen) and let vs serue them :

3 Thou shalt not hearken vnto the words of that prophet, or that dreamer of dreames : for the LORD your God prooueth you , to know whether you loue the LORD your God with all your heart, and with all your soule.

4 Ye shall walke after the LORD your God, and feare him, and keepe his commandements, and obey his voyce, and you shall serue him, and * cleaue vnto him.

* Chap. 11.
20.

5 And that prophet or that dreamer of dreames shalbe put to death (because hee hath † spoken to turne you away from the LORD your God , which brought you out of the land of Egypt, and redeemed you out of the house of bondage, to thrust thee out of the way which the LORD thy God commanded thee to walke in) So shalt thou put the euill away from the midst of thee.

†Heb.spoken
reuolt a-
gainst the
Lord.

6 ¶ If thy brother, the sonne of thy mother, or thy sonne, or thy daughter, or the wife of thy bosome, or thy friend, which is as thine owne soule, entise thee secretly, saying , Let vs goe and serue other gods which thou hast not knowen, thou, nor thy fathers :

7 Namely of the gods of the people which are round about you, nigh vnto thee, or farre off from thee, from the one end of the earth, euen vnto the other end of the earth :

8 Thou shalt not consent vnto him nor hearken vnto him, neither shall thine eye pitie him, neither shalt thou
spare,

spare, neither shalt thou conceale him.

9 But * thou shalt surely kill him : Thine hand shall be first vpon him, to put him to death, and afterwards the hand of all the people.

10 And thou shalt stone him with stones, that hee die : because hee hath sought to thrust thee away from the LORD thy God, which brought thee out of the land of Egypt, from the house of † bondage.

11 And * all Israel shall heare, and feare, and shall doe no more any such wickednesse as this is, among you.

12 ¶ If thou shalt heare *say* in one of thy cities, which the LORD thy God hath giuen thee to dwell there, saying,

13 Certaine men, ‖ the children of Belial, are gone out from among you, and haue withdrawen the inhabitants of their citie, saying, Let vs goe & serue other gods, which ye haue not knowen :

14 Then shalt thou enquire and make search, and aske diligently : and behold, if *it be* trueth, *and* the thing certaine, *that* such abomination is wrought among you :

15 Thou shalt surely smite the inhabitants of that citie with the edge of the sword, destroying it vtterly, and all that is therein, and the cattell thereof, with the edge of the sword.

16 And thou shalt gather all the spoile of it, into the midst of the street thereof, and shalt burne with fire the citie, and all the spoile thereof euery whit, for the LORD thy God : and it shall be an heape for euer, it shall not bee built againe.

17 And there shall cleaue nought of the ‖ cursed thing to thine hand, that the LORD may turne from the fiercenesse of his anger, and shew thee mercy, and haue compassion vpon thee, and multiply thee, as he hath sworne vnto thy fathers ;

18 When thou shalt hearken to the voyce of the LORD thy God, to keepe all his Commaundements which I command thee this day, to doe that which is right in the eyes of the LORD thy God.

CHAP. XIIII.

1 Gods children are not to disfigure themselues in mourning. 3 What may, and what may not be eaten, 4 of beasts, 9 of fishes, 11 of foules. 21 That which dieth of it selfe, may not be eaten. 22 Tithes of diuine Seruice. 23 Tithes and firstlings of reioycing before the Lord. 28 The third yeeres tithe of Almes and Charitie.

Ee *are* the children of the LORD your God : * yee shall not cutte your selues, nor make any baldnesse betweene your eyes for the dead.

2 * For thou *art* an holy people vnto the LORD thy God, and the LORD hath chosen thee to be a peculiar people vnto himselfe, aboue all the nations that are vpon the earth.

3 ¶ Thou shalt not eate any abominable thing.

4 * These are the beasts which yee shall eate : the oxe, the sheepe, and the goat,

5 The Hart, and the Roe bucke, and the fallow deere, and the wilde goat, and the ‖ Pygarg, and the wilde oxe, and the chamois.

6 And euery beast that parteth the hoofe, and cleaueth the clift into two clawes, *and* cheweth the cud amongst the beasts : that ye shall eate.

7 Neuerthelesse these yee shall not eate, of them that chew the cud, or of them that diuide the clouen hoofe, *as* the camel, and the hare, and the cony : for they chew the cudde, but diuide not the hoofe, *therefore* they *are* vncleane vnto you.

8 And the swine, because it diuideth the hoofe, yet cheweth not the cud, it *is* vncleane vnto you : ye shall not eate of their flesh, nor touch their dead carkeise.

9 ¶ *These yee shall eate of all that *are* in the waters : all that haue finnes and scales shall ye eate :

10 And whatsoeuer hath not finnes and scales, ye may not eat : it *is* vncleane vnto you.

11 ¶ Of all cleane birds ye shall eate.

12 But these *are they* of which ye shall not eat : the Eagle, and the ossifrage, and the ospray,

13 And the glede, and the kite, and the vulture after his kinde,

14 And euery rauen after his kinde,

15 And the owle, & the night hawke, and the cuckow, and the hawke after his kinde,

16 The little owle, and the great owle, and the swanne,

17 And the pellicane, and the Geereagle, and the cormorant,

18 And

Marginal notes (left column):

* Chap. 17. 7.

† *Hebr. bondmen.*
* Chap. 17. 13.

‖ *Or, naughty men.*

‖ *Or, deuoted.*

Marginal notes (right column):

* Leuit. 19. 28.

* Chap. 7. 6. and 26. 18.

* Leuit. 1|
2.

‖ *Or, Bison,* Heb. Dishe|

* Leuit. 1|
9.

18 And the Storke, and the Heron after her kind, and the lapwing, and the *batte.

Leuit. 11.

19 And euery creeping thing that flyeth, is vncleane vnto you : they shall not be eaten.

20 *But* of all cleane foules ye may eat.

21 ¶ Ye shall not eate of any thing that dieth of it selfe : thou shalt giue it vnto the stranger that is in thy gates, that he may eate it, or thou mayest sell it vnto an alien : for thou *art* an holy people vnto the Lord thy God. *Thou shalt not seethe a kidde in his mothers milke.

Exod. 23. and 34.

22 Thou shalt truely tithe all the increase of thy seede, that the field bringeth forth yeere by yeere.

23 And thou shalt eate before the Lord thy God, in the place which he shall chuse to place his Name there, the tithe of thy corne , of thy wine, and of thine oyle , and the firstlings of thy herdes, *and* of thy flockes : that thou mayest learne to feare the Lord thy God alwayes.

24 And if the way bee too long for thee, so that thou art not able to carie it, *or* if the place be too farre from thee, which the Lord thy God shall chuse to set his name there, when the Lord thy God hath blessed thee :

25 Then shalt thou turne it into money, and binde vp the money in thine hand , and shalt goe vnto the place which the Lord thy God shal chuse.

26 And thou shalt bestow that money for whatsoeuer thy soule lusteth after, for oxen, or for sheepe, or for wine, or for strong drinke, or for whatsoeuer thy soule †desireth: and thou shalt eat there before the Lord thy God, and thou shalt reioyce, thou and thine houshold.

Heb. asketh hee.

chap. 12.

27 And *the Leuite that is within thy gates, thou shalt not forsake him : for he hath no part nor inheritance with thee.

28 ¶ At the end of three yeres thou shalt bring forth all the tithe of thine increase the same yeere, and shalt lay it vp within thy gates.

29 And the Leuite, because he hath no part nor inheritance with thee, and the stranger, and the fatherlesse, and the widowe which are within thy gates, shall come and shal eate, and be satisfied, that the Lord thy God may blesse thee , in all the worke of thine hande which thou doest.

CHAP. XV.

1 The seuenth yeere a yeere of release for the poore. 7 It must be no let of lending or giuing. 12 An Ebrew seruant, 16 except hee will not depart, must in the seuenth yeere goe foorth free and well furnished. 19 All firstlings males of the cattell are to bee sanctified vnto the Lord.

AT the end of *euery seuen yeeres thou shalt make a release.

2 And this is the maner of the release : Euery †creditour that lendeth ought vnto his neighbour , shall release it : hee shall not exact it of his neighbour, or of his brother, because it is called the Lords release.

3 Of a forreiner thou mayest exact it againe : but that which is thine with thy brother, thine hand shall release.

4 ‖ Saue when there shall bee no poore among you : for the Lord shal greatly blesse thee in the land which the Lord thy God giueth thee for an inheritance to possesse it :

5 Onely if thou carefully hearken vnto the voice of the Lord thy God, to obserue to doe all these commandements , which I commaund thee this day.

6 For the Lord thy God blesseth thee, as he promised thee, and *thou shalt lend vnto many nations, but thou shalt not borrow, and thou shalt reigne ouer many nations, but they shall not reigne ouer thee.

7 ¶ If there be among you a poore man of one of thy brethren within any of thy gates, in thy lande which the Lord thy God giueth thee, thou shalt not harden thy heart; nor shut thine hand from thy poore brother :

8 *But thou shalt open thine hand wide vnto him, and shalt surely lend him sufficient for his neede, in that which he wanteth.

9 Beware that there bee not a †thought in thy †wicked heart, saying, The seuenth yeere, the yeere of release is at hand, and thine eye be euill against thy poore brother, and thou giuest him nought, and hee crie vnto the Lord against thee, and it be sinne vnto thee.

10 Thou shalt surely giue him, and thine heart shall not bee grieued when thou giuest vnto him : because that for this thing the Lord thy God shall blesse

* Leuit. 25. 2, 4.

† Heb. master of the lending of his hand.

‖ Or, to the end that there be no poore among you.

* Chap. 28. 12.

* Mat. 5. 42 luke 6. 34.

† Heb. word.
† Heb. Belial

blesse thee in all thy workes, and in all that thou puttest thine hand vnto.

11 For the poore shall neuer cease out of the land: therefore I command thee, saying, Thou shalt open thine hand wide vnto thy brother, to thy poore, and to thy needy in the land.

*Exod. 21.
2. Iere. 34.
14.

12 ¶ *And *if thy brother, an Hebrew man, or an Hebrew woman, be sold vnto thee, and serue thee sixe yeres, then in the seuenth yeere thou shalt let him goe free from thee.

13 And when thou sendest him out free from thee, thou shalt not let him go away emptie:

14 Thou shalt furnish him liberally out of thy flocke, and out of thy floore, and out of thy wine presse, of that wherewith the LORD thy God hath blessed thee thou shalt giue vnto him.

15 And thou shalt remember that thou wast a bondman in the land of Egypt, and the LORD thy God redeemed thee: therefore I command thee this thing to day.

16 And it shall be if he say vnto thee, I will not goe away from thee, because he loueth thee, and thine house, because he is well with thee:

*Exod. 21.
6.

17 *Then thou shalt take an aule, and thrust it through his eare vnto the doore, and hee shall be thy seruant for euer: and also vnto thy mayd seruant thou shalt doe likewise.

18 It shall not seeme hard vnto thee when thou sendest him away free from thee: for hee hath bene worth a double hired seruant to thee, in seruing thee sixe yeeres: and the LORD thy God shall blesse thee in all that thou doest.

*Exod. 34.
19.

19 ¶ *All the firstling males that come of thy heard, and of thy flock, thou shalt sanctifie vnto the LORD thy God: thou shalt doe no worke with the firstling of thy bullocke, nor sheare the firstling of thy sheepe.

20 Thou shalt eate it before the LORD thy God yeere by yeere, in the place which the LORD shall choose, thou and thy houshold.

*. Leuit. 22.
20. cha. 17.
1. ecclus.
35. 12.

21 *And if there be any blemish therein; as if it be lame, or blinde, or haue any ill blemish, thou shalt not sacrifice it vnto the LORD thy God.

22 Thou shalt eate it within thy gates: the vncleane and the cleane person shall eat it alike, as the Roe bucke, and as the Hart.

*Chap. 12.
16, 23.

23 *Onely thou shalt not eate the

blood thereof: thou shalt powre it vpon the ground as water.

CHAP. XVI.

1 The feast of the Passeouer, 9 of Weekes, 13 of Tabernacles. 16 Euery male must offer, as he is able, at these three Feasts. 18 Of Iudges and Iustice. 22 Groues and Images are forbidden.

Bserue *the moneth of Abib, and keepe the Passeouer vuto the LORD thy God: for *in the moneth of Abib the LORD thy God brought thee foorth out of Egypt by night.

*Exod. 1
2. &c.

*Exod. 1
4.

2 Thou shalt therefore sacrifice the Passeouer vnto the LORD thy God, of the flocke and the heard, in the *place which the LORD shall choose to place his name there.

*Chap. 12
5.

3 *Thou shalt eat no leatuened bread with it: seuen dayes shalt thou eat vnleauened bread therewith, euen the bread of affliction, (for thou camest forth out of the land of Egypt in haste) that thou mayest remember the day when thou camest foorth out of the land of Egypt, all the dayes of thy life.

*Exod. 12
15.

4 *And there shall bee no leauened bread seene with thee in all thy coasts seuen dayes, neither shall there any thing of the flesh, which thou sacrificedst the first day at Euen, remaine all night, vntill the morning.

*Exod. 3
25.

5 Thou mayest not ‖ sacrifice the Passeouer within any of the gates, which the LORD thy God giueth thee.

‖ Or, kill.

6 But at the place which the LORD thy God shall choose to place his Name in, there thou shalt sacrifice the Passeouer at Euen, at the going downe of the Sunne, at the season that thou camest foorth out of Egypt.

7 And thou shalt roste and eate it in the place which the LORD thy God shall choose, and thou shalt turne in the morning, and goe vnto thy tents.

8 Sixe dayes thou shalt eate vnleauened bread, and on the seuenth day shall be a †solemne assembly to the LORD thy God: thou shalt doe no worke therein.

† Hebr. restraint.

9 ¶ *Seuen weekes shalt thou number vnto thee: beginne to number the seuen weekes, from such time as thou beginnest to put the sickle to the corne.

*Leuit. 23.
15.

10 And

10 And thou shalt keepe the feast of weekes vnto the LORD thy God with ‖ a tribute of a free will offering of thine hand, which thou shalt giue vnto the LORD thy God, according as the LORD thy God hath blessed thee.

Or, suffici-neie.

11 And thou shalt reioyce before the LORD thy God, thou, and thy sonne, and thy daughter, and thy man seruant and thy maid seruant, and the Leuite that is within thy gates, and the stranger, and the fatherlesse, and the widow, that *are* among you, in the place which the LORD thy God hath chosen to place his Name there.

12 And thou shalt remember that thou wast a bondman in Egypt: and thou shalt obserue & do these Statutes.

13 ¶ Thou shalt obserue the feast of Tabernacles seuen dayes, after that thou hast gathered in thy † corne, and thy wine.

Heb. floore nd thy wine resse.

14 And thou shalt reioice in thy feast, thou, and thy sonne, and thy daughter, and thy man seruant, and thy maid seruant, and the Leuite, the stranger, and the fatherlesse, and the widow, that *are* within thy gates.

15 Seuen dayes shalt thou keepe a solemne feast vnto the LORD thy God, in the place which the LORD shall chuse: because the LORD thy God shall blesse thee in all thy increase, and in all the workes of thine handes, therefore thou shalt surely reioyce.

Exod. 23. 4. and 34. 3.

16 ¶ * Three times in a yeere shal all thy males appeare before the LORD thy God, in the place which hee shall chuse: in the feast of Vnleauened bread, and in the feast of Weekes, and in the feast of Tabernacles: and they shal not appeare before the LORD * emptie.

Ecclus. 5. 4.
Heb. accor-ing to the ift of his and.

17 Euery man shall giue † as hee is able, according to the blessing of the LORD thy God, which he hath giuen thee.

18 ¶ Iudges and officers shalt thou make thee in all thy gates which the LORD thy God giueth thee throughout thy tribes: and they shall iudge the people with iust iudgement.

Exod. 23.
Or, matters

19 Thou shalt not wrest iudgement, thou shalt not respect persons, * neither take a gift: for a gift doth blind the eyes of the wise, and peruert the ‖ wordes of the righteous.

Heb. iu-tice, iustice.

20 That which is † altogether iust shalt thou followe, that thou mayest liue, and inherite the land which the LORD thy God giueth thee.

21 ¶ Thou shalt not plant thee a groue of any trees neere vnto the Altar of the LORD thy God, which thou shalt make thee:

22 * Neither shalt thou set thee vp any ‖ image, which the LORD thy God hateth.

* Leuit. 26. 1.
‖ Or, statue, or pillar.

CHAP. XVII.

1 The things sacrificed must bee sound. 2 Idolaters must bee slaine. 8 Hard controuersies are to bee determined by the Priests and Iudges. 12 The contemner of that Determination must die. 14 The election, 16 and duetie of a King.

THou shalt not sacrifice vnto the LORD thy God any bullocke, or ‖ sheepe wherein is blemish, *or* any euilfauourednes: for that is an abomination vnto the LORD thy God.

‖ Or, goat.

2 ¶ If there bee found among you within any of thy gates which the LORD thy God giueth thee, man or woman that hath wrought wickednes in the sight of the LORD thy God, in transgressing his couenant,

3 And hath gone and serued other gods, and worshipped them, either the Sunne, or Moone, or any of the hoste of heauen, which I haue not commanded,

4 And it be told thee, and thou hast heard *of it,* and inquired diligently, and behold, it *be* true, *and* the thing certaine, *that* such abomination is wrought in Israel:

5 Then shalt thou bring forth that man, or that woman (which haue committed that wicked thing) vnto thy gates, *euen* that man, or that woman, and shalt stone them with stones till they die.

6 * At the mouth of two witnesses, or three witnesses, shall he that is worthy of death, be put to death: but at the mouth of one witnesse he shall not bee put to death.

* Num. 35. 30. chap. 17. 6. & 19. 15. mat. 18. 16. iohn 8. 17. 2. cor. 13. 1. heb. 10. 28.

7 The hands of the witnesses shall be first vpon him, to put him to death, and afterward the hands of all the people: so thou shalt put the euil away from among you.

8 ¶ If there arise a matter too hard for thee in iudgement, betweene blood and blood, betweene plea and plea, and betweene stroke and stroke, being matters

ters of controuersie within thy gates:
then shalt thou arise, and get thee vp into the place, which the LORD thy
God shall choose;

9 And thou shalt come vnto the
Priests the Leuites, & vnto the Iudge
that shal be in those dayes, and enquire;
and they shall shew thee the sentence of
Iudgement.

10 And thou shalt doe according to
the sentence which they of that place
(which the LORD shall choose) shall
shew thee, and thou shalt obserue to do
according to all that they enforme thee:

11 According to the sentence of the
Law which they shall teach thee, and
according to the Iudgement which
they shall tell thee thou shalt doe : thou
shalt not decline from the Sentence
which they shall shew thee, to the right
hand, nor to the left.

† Hebr. not to hearken.

12 And the man that will doe presumptuously, † and will not hearken
vnto the Priest (that standeth to minister there before the LORD thy
God) or vnto the Iudge, euen that man
shall die, and thou shalt put away the
euill from Israel.

13 And all the people shal heare, and
feare, and doe no more presumptuously.

14 ¶ When thou art come vnto the
land which the LORD thy God gi-
ueth thee, and shalt possesse it, and shalt
dwell therein, and shalt say, I will set a
King ouer mee, like as all the nations
that *are* about me :

15 Thou shalt in any wise set *him*
King ouer thee, whom the LORD
thy God shall choose. *One* from among
thy brethren shalt thou set King ouer
thee : thou mayest not set a stranger o-
uer thee, which is not thy brother.

16 But he shall not multiply horses
to himselfe, nor cause the people to returne to Egypt, to the ende that hee
should multiply horses : for as much as
the LORD hath said vnto you, Yee
shall hencefoorth returne no more that
way.

17 Neither shall he multiply wiues
to himselfe, that his heart turne not a-
way : neither shall hee greatly multiply
to himselfe siluer and gold.

18 And it shall be when he sitteth vpon the Throne of his kingdome, that he
shall write him a copy of this Law in a
booke, out of *that which is* before the
Priests the Leuites.

19 And it shall be with him, and hee

shall reade therein all the dayes of his
life, that hee may learne to feare the
LORD his God, to keep all the words
of this Law, and these Statutes, to do
them :

20 That his heart bee not lifted vp
aboue his brethren, and that hee turne
not aside from the Commandement, to
the right hand, or to the left: to the end
that hee may prolong *his* dayes in his
kingdome, hee, and his children in the
midst of Israel.

CHAP. XVIII.

1 The Lord is the Priests and Leuites inheritance. 3 The Priests due. 6 The Leuites
portion. 9 The abominations of the Nations are to bee auoyded. 15 Christ the Prophet is to be heard. 20 The presumptuous
prophet is to die.

He Priests, the Leuites,
and all the tribe of Leui,
* shall haue no part nor inheritance with Israel :
they * shall eate the offerings of the LORD made by fire, and
his inheritance.

* Num. 1 20. chap. 10. 9.
* 1. Corin 9 13.

2 Therefore shall they haue no inheritance among their brethren : the
LORD *is* their inheritance, as he hath
said vnto them.

3 ¶ And this shalbe the Priests due
from the people, from them that offer a
sacrifice, whether it bee oxe or sheepe :
and they shall giue vnto the Priest the
shoulder, and the two cheekes, and the
maw.

4 The first fruit *also* of thy corne, of
thy wine, and of thy oyle, and the first
of the fleece of thy sheepe, shalt thou
giue him.

5 For the LORD thy God hath
chosen him out of all thy tribes, to stand
to minister in the Name of the LORD,
him, and his sonnes for euer.

6 ¶ And if a Leuite come from any
of thy gates out of all Israel, where he
soiourned, and come with all the desire
of his minde, vnto the place which the
LORD shall choose ;

7 Then hee shall minister in the
Name of the LORD his God, as all
his brethren the Leuites *doe*, which
stand there before the LORD.

8 They shall haue like portions to
eate, beside † that which commeth of the
sale of his patrimonie.

† Hebr. hi sales by the fathers.

9 ¶ When thou art come into the
land

land which the LORD thy God giueth thee, thou shalt not learne to doe after the abominations of those nations.

10 There shall not be found among you *any one* that maketh thy sonne, or his daughter *to passe thorow the fire, *or* that vseth diuination, *or* an obseruer of times, or an inchanter, or a witch,

11 * Or a charmer, or a consulter with familiar spirits, or a wyzard, or a * Necromancer.

12 For all that do these things, *are* an abomination vnto the LORD : and because of these abominations, the LORD thy God doth driue them out from before thee.

13 Thou shalt bee ‖ perfite with the LORD thy God.

14 For these nations which thou shalt ‖ possesse, hearkened vnto obseruers of times, and vnto diuiners : but as for thee, the LORD thy God hath not suffered thee so *to* doe.

15 ¶ * The LORD thy God will raise vp vnto thee a Prophet from the midst of thee, of thy brethren, like vnto me, vnto him ye shall hearken,

16 According to all that thou desiredst of the LORD thy God in Horeb, in the day of the assembly, saying, * Let mee not heare again the voice of the LORD my God, neither let mee see this great fire any more, that I die not.

17 And the LORD said vnto mee, They haue well *spoken* that which they haue spoken.

18 * I will raise them vp a Prophet from among their brethren, like vnto thee, and will put my wordes in his mouth, and hee shall speake vnto them all that I shall command him.

19 And it shall come to passe, that whosoeuer will not hearken vnto my words, which hee shall speake in my name, I will require *it* of him.

20 But the prophet which shall presume to speake a word in my name, which I haue not commanded him to speake, or that shall speake in the name of other gods, euen that prophet shall die.

21 And if thou say in thine heart, How shall wee know the word which the LORD hath not spoken?

22 When a prophet speaketh in the name of the LORD, if the thing follow not, nor come to passe, that *is* the thing which the LORD hath not spoken, *but* the prophet hath spoken it presumptuously : thou shalt not bee afraid of him.

CHAP. XIX.

1 The Cities of refuge. 4 The priuiledge thereof for the manslayer. 14 The landmarke is not to be remooued. 15 Two witnesses at the least. 16 The punishment of a false witnesse.

WHen the LORD thy God *hath cut off the nations, whose lande the LORD thy God giueth thee, and thou†succeedest them, and dwellest in their cities, and in their houses :

2 * Thou shalt separate three cities for thee in the midst of thy land, which the LORD thy God giueth thee to possesse it.

3 Thou shalt prepare thee a way, and diuide the coasts of thy land (which the LORD thy God giueth thee to inherit) into three parts, that euery slayer may flee thither.

4 ¶ And this is the case of the slayer which shall flee thither, that hee may liue : who so killeth his neighbour ignorantly, whom he hated not †in time past,

5 As when *a man* goeth into the wood with his neighbor, to hew wood, and his hand fetcheth a stroke with the axe to cut downe the tree, and the †head slippeth from the †helue, and †lighteth vpon his neighbour that he die, he shall flee vnto one of those cities, and liue :

6 Lest the auenger of the blood pursue the slaier, while his heart is hot, and ouertake him, because the way is long, and †slay him, whereas he was not worthy of death, in as much as hce hated him not †in time past.

7 Wherefore I command thee, saying, Thou shalt separate three cities for thee.

8 And if the LORD thy God enlarge thy coast (as he hath sworne vnto thy fathers) and giue thee all the lande which hee promised to giue vnto thy fathers :

9 (If thou shalt * keepe all these commandements to doe them, which I command thee this day, to loue the LORD thy God, and to walke euer in his wayes) *then shalt thou adde three cities moe for thee, beside these three:

10 That innocent blood be not shed in thy land which the LORD thy God giueth

Leuit. 18.

Leuit. 20.

. Sam. 7.

r, vpright sincere.

r, inherit

Koh. 1. 45 ts 3. 21. d 7. 37.

Exod. 20.

Iohn 1. . acts 3. &. 7. 37.

* Chap. 12. 29.

† Heb. inheritest, or possessest.

* Exod. 21. 13. num. 35 10. Iosh 20 2.

† Heb. from yesterday the third day.

† Heb. yron.
† Heb. wood.
† Heb. findeth.

† Heb. smite him in life.

† Heb. from yesterday, third day.

* Chap. 12. 20.

* Iosh. 20. 7

giueth thee for an inheritance, and so blood be vpon thee.

11 ¶ But if any man hate his neighbour and lie in wait for him, and rise vp against him, and smite him †mortally that hee die, and fleeth into one of these Cities:

12 Then the Elders of his citie shall send and fetch him thence, and deliuer him into the hand of the auenger of blood, that he may die.

13 Thine eye shall not pittie him, but thou shalt put away *the guilt of* innocent blood from Israel, that it may goe wel with thee.

14 ¶ Thou shalt not remooue thy neighbours *land*-marke, which they of old time haue set in thine inheritance, which thou shalt inherite, in the land that the LORD thy God giueth thee to possesse it.

15 ¶ *One witnesse shall not rise vp against a man for any iniquitie, or for any sinne, in any sinne that he sinneth: at the mouth of two witnesses, or at the mouth of three witnesses, shall the matter be stablished.

16 ¶ If a false witnes rise vp against any man to testifie ‖ against him *that which is* wrong:

17 Then both the men betweene whom the controuersie is, shall stand before the LORD, before the Priests, and the Iudges, which shall be in those dayes.

18 And the Iudges shall make diligent inquisition: and behold, if the witnesse be a false witnesse, *and* hath testified falsly against his brother:

19 *Then shall ye doe vnto him, as he had thought to haue done vnto his brother: so shalt thou put the euil away from among you.

20 And those which remaine shall heare, and feare, and shall henceforth commit no more any such euill among you.

21 And thine eye shall not pitie, *but* *life *shall goe* for life, eye for eye, tooth for tooth, hand for hand, foot for foot.

CHAP. XX.

1 The Priests exhortation to encourage the people to battell. 5 The officers proclamation who are to be dismissed from the warre. 10 How to vse the Cities that accept or refuse the proclamation of peace. 16 What Cities must bee deuoted. 19 Trees of mans meat must not be destroyed in the siege.

WHen thou goest out to battell against thine enemies, and seest horses and charets, *and* a people more then thou, be not afraid of them: for the LORD thy God *is* with thee, which brought thee vp out of the land of Egypt.

2 And it shall bee when ye are come nigh vnto the battell, that the Priest shall approach and speake vnto the people,

3 And shall say vnto them, Heare O Israel, you approach this day vnto battell against your enemies: let not your hearts †faint, feare not, and doe not †tremble, neither be ye terrified because of them.

4 For the LORD your God *is* hee that goeth with you, to fight for you against your enemies, to saue you.

5 ¶ And the Officers shall speake vnto the people, saying, What man is there that hath built a new house, and hath not dedicated it? let him goe and returne to his house, lest hee die in the battell, and an other man dedicate it.

6 And what man is hee that hath planted a Vineyard, and hath not yet †eaten of it? let him also go and returne vnto his house, lest he die in the battell, and an other man eate of it.

7 *And what man *is there* that hath betrothed a wife, and hath not taken her? let him goe and returne vnto his house, lest he die in battell, and another man take her.

8 And the Officers shall speake further vnto the people: and they shall say, *What man *is there* that is fearefull and faint hearted? let him goe and returne vnto his house, lest his brethrens heart †faint as well as his heart.

9 And it shall be when the Officers haue made an end of speaking vnto the people, that they shall make Captaines of the armies to †leade the people.

10 ¶ When thou commest nigh vnto a City to fight against it, then proclaime peace vnto it.

11 And it shall be, if it make thee answere of peace, and open vnto thee, then it shalbe *that* all the people that is found therein, shall be tributaries vnto thee, and they shall serue thee.

12 And if it will make no peace with thee, but will make warre against thee, then thou shalt besiege it.

13 And when the LORD thy God hath

Marginal notes

† Hebr. in life.

* Chap. 17. 6. hebr. 10. 28. numb. 35. 30. mat 18. 16. ioh. 8. 17. 2. cor. 13. 1. hebr. 10. 28.

‖ Or, falling away.

* Prou. 19. 5, 9. dan. 13. 62.

* Exod. 21. 23. leuit. 24. 20. mat. 5. 38.

† Hebr be tender.
† Hebr. mak haste.

† Heb. mad it common. See Leuit. 19. 23.
* Chap. 24. 5.

* Iudg. 7. 3

† Hebr. mel

† Hebr. to l in the head of the peopl

hath deliuered it into thine hands, thou shalt smite euery male thereof with the edge of the sword.

14 But the women, and the litle ones, and *the cattell, and all that is in the citie, *euen* all the spoile thereof, shalt thou †take vnto thy selfe, and thou shalt eate the spoile of thine enemies, which the Lord thy God hath giuen thee.

15 Thus shalt thou doe vnto all the cities which are very far off from thee, which are not of the cities of these nations.

16 But of the cities of these people which the Lord thy God doth giue thee for an inheritance, thou shalt saue aliue nothing that breatheth:

17 But thou shalt vtterly destroy them, *namely*, the Hittites, and the Amorites, the Canaanites, and the Perizzites, the Hiuites, and the Iebusites, as the Lord thy God hath commanded thee:

18 That they teach you not to do after all their abominations, which they haue done vnto their gods, so should ye sinne against the Lord your God.

19 ¶ When thou shalt besiege a citie a long time, in making warre against it to take it, thou shalt not destroy the trees thereof, by forcing an axe against them: for thou mayest eate of them, and thou shalt not cut them downe (‖ for the tree of the field is mans *life*) †to employ them in the siege.

20 Only the trees which thou knowest that they be not trees for meate, thou shalt destroy, and cut *them* downe, and thou shalt build bulwarkes against the city that maketh warre with thee, vntil †it be subdued.

CHAP. XXI.

1 The expiation of an vncertaine murder. 10 The vsage of a captiue taken to wife. 15 The first borne is not to be disinherited vpon priuate affection. 18 A stubburne sonne is to bee stoned to death. 22 The malefactour must not hang all night on a tree.

F one bee found slaine in the lande, which the Lord thy God giueth thee to possesse it, lying in the fielde, *and* it bee not knowen who hath slaine him:

2 Then thy Elders and thy Iudges shall come forth, and they shall measure vnto the cities which *are* round about him that is slaine.

3 And it shall be that the citie which is next vnto the slaine man, euen the Elders of that citie shall take an heifer which hath not bene wrought with, *and* which hath not drawen in the yoke.

4 And the Elders of that citie shall bring downe the heifer vnto a rough valley, which is neither eared nor sowen, and shall strike off the heifers necke there in the valley.

5 And the Priests the sonnes of Leui shall come neere (for them the Lord thy God hath chosen to minister vnto him, and to blesse in the Name of the Lord:) and by their †worde shall euery controuersie and euery stroke bee *tried*.

6 And all the Elders of that city that are next vnto the slaine man, shal wash their hands ouer the heifer that is beheaded in the valley.

7 And they shall answere, and say, Our hands haue not shedde this blood, neither haue our eyes seene *it*.

8 Be merciful, O Lord, vnto thy people Israel, whom thou hast redeemed, and lay not innocent blood †vnto thy people of Israels charge, and the blood shall be forgiuen them.

9 So shalt thou put away the *guilt of* innocent blood from among you, when thou shalt do that which is right in the sight of the Lord.

10 ¶ When thou goest forth to warre against thine enemies, and the Lord thy God hath deliuered them into thine hands, & thou hast taken them captiue,

11 And seest among the captiues a beautifull woman, and hast a desire vnto her, that thou wouldest haue her to thy wife:

12 Then thou shalt bring her home to thine house, and shee shall shaue her head, and ‖ pare her nailes.

13 And shee shall put the raiment of her captiuitie from off her, and shall remaine in thine house, and bewaile her father and her mother a full moneth: and after that, thou shalt go in vnto her and be her husband, and she shall be thy wife.

14 And it shall be if thou haue no delight in her, then thou shalt let her goe whither she will, but thou shalt not sell her at al for money, thou shalt not make merchandize of her, because thou hast humbled her.

15 ¶ If a man haue two wiues, one beloued and another hated, and they haue

* Iosh. 8. 2.

Heb. spoile

Or, for, O man the tree of the field is to be employed in the siege. Heb. to goe from before thee.

Hebr. it ome downe.

†Heb.mouth

†Heb. in the middest.

‖Or, suffer to grow. heb. make or dresse.

haue borne him children, *both* the beloued, and the hated: and if the first borne sonne be hers that was hated :

16 Then it shall be, when he maketh his sonnes to inherite that which hee hath, that he may not make the sonne of the beloued, first borne, before the sonne of the hated, *which is* indeed the first borne :

17 But hee shall acknowledge the sonne of the hated for the first borne, by giuing him a double portion of all †that hee hath : for hee is the beginning of his strength; the right of the first borne is his.

18 ¶ If a man haue a stubborne and rebellious sonne, which will not obey the voice of his father, or the voice of his mother, and that when they haue chastened him, wil not hearken vnto them :

19 Then shall his father and his mother lay hold on him, and bring him out vnto the Elders of his citie, and vnto the gate of his place :

20 And they shall say vnto the Elders of his citie, This our sonne *is* stubborne, and rebellious, hee will not obey our voice: he *is* a glutton, & a drunkard.

21 And all the men of his city shall stone him with stones, that hee die : so shalt thou put euill away from among you, and all Israel shall heare, & feare.

22 ¶ And if a man haue committed a sinne worthy of death, and he be to be put to death, and thou hang him on a tree :

23 His body shall not remaine all night vpon the tree, but thou shalt in any wise bury him that day : for * he that is hanged, is † accursed of God: that thy land be not defiled, which the LORD thy God giueth thee for an inheritance.

CHAP. XXII.

1 *Of humanitie toward brethren.* 5 *The sexe is to bee distinguished by apparell.* 6 *The dam is not to be taken with her yong ones.* 8 *The house must haue battlements.* 9 *Confusion is to be auoyded.* 12 *Fringes vpon the vesture.* 13 *The punishment of him that slandereth his wife.* 20. 22 *Of adulterie,* 25 *of rape,* 28 *and of fornication.* 30 *Incest.*

 Hou * shalt not see thy brothers oxe, or his sheepe go astray, and hide thy selfe from them : thou shalt in any case bring them againe vnto thy brother.

2 And if thy brother be not nigh vnto thee, or if thou know him not, then thou shalt bring it vnto thine owne house, and it shall be with thee, vntil thy brother seeke after it, and thou shalt restore it to him againe.

3 In like maner shalt thou do with his asse, and so shalt thou doe with his raiment : and with all lost thing of thy brothers which he hath lost, and thou hast found, shalt thou do likewise : thou mayest not hide thy selfe.

4 ¶ Thou shalt not see thy brothers asse or his oxe fall downe by the way, and hide thy selfe from them : thou shalt surely helpe him to lift them vp againe.

5 ¶ The woman shall not weare that which pertaineth vnto a man, neither shall a man put on a womans garment : for all that doe so, are abomination vnto the LORD thy God.

6 ¶ If a birds nest chance to be before thee in the way in any tree, or on the ground, whether they be yong ones, or egges, and the damme sitting vpon the yong, or vpon the egges, thou shalt not take the damme with the yong.

7 But thou shalt in any wise let the damme goe, and take the yong to thee, that it may be well with thee, and *that* thou mayest prolong *thy* dayes.

8 ¶ When thou buildest a new house, then thou shalt make a battlement for thy roofe, that thou bring not blood vpon thine house, if any man fall from thence.

9 ¶ Thou shalt not sow thy vineyard with diuers seeds : lest the † fruit of thy seed which thou hast sowen, and the fruit of thy Vineyard be defiled.

10 ¶ Thou shalt not plow with an oxe and an asse together.

11 ¶ * Thou shalt not weare a garment of diuers sorts, *as* of woollen, and linnen together.

12 ¶ Thou shalt make thee *fringes vpon the foure † quarters of thy vesture, wherewith thou couerest *thy selfe.*

13 ¶ If any man take a wife, and go in vnto her, and hate her,

14 And giue occasions of speach *against her*, and bring vp an euill name vpon her, and say, I tooke this woman, and when I came to her, I found her not a mayd :

15 Then shal the father of the damosell, and her mother take, and bring forth the tokens of the damosels virginitie.

† Hebr. that is found with him.

* Gal. 3. 13.
† Hebr. the curse of God.

* Exod. 23. 4.

† Hebr. fulnesse of the seed.

* Leuit. 19. 19.

* Num. 15 38.
† Hebr. wings.

nitie, vnto the Elders of the citie in the gate.

16 And the damosels father shall say vnto the Elders, I gaue my daughter vnto this man to wife, & he hateth her:

17 And loe, he hath giuen occasions of speech *against her*, saying, I found not thy daughter a maid: and yet these *are* the tokens of my daughters virginity; and they shall spread the cloth before the Elders of the citie.

18 And the Elders of that citie shall take that man, and chastise him.

19 And they shall amearse him in an hundred *shekels* of siluer, and giue them vnto the father of the damosell, because he hath brought vp an euill name vpon a virgine of Israel: and she shall be his wife, hee may not put her away all his dayes.

20 But if this thing be true, *and* the tokens of virginitie be not found for the damosel:

21 Then they shall bring out the damosell to the doore of her fathers house, and the men of her city shal stone her with stones that she die, because she hath wrought folly in Israel, to play the whore in her fathers house: so shalt thou put euill away from among you.

22 ¶ * If a man be found lying with a woman married to an husband, then they shall both of them die, *both* the man that lay with the woman, and the woman: so shalt thou put away euill from Israel.

23 ¶ If a damosell *that is* a virgin be betrothed vnto an husband, and a man find her in the citie, and lie with her:

24 Then yee shall bring them both out vnto the gate of that citie, and yee shall stone them with stones that they die; the damosel, because shee cried not, *being* in the citie; and the man, because he hath humbled his neighbours wife · so thou shalt put away euill from among you.

25 ¶ But if a man find a betrothed damosel in the field, and the man ‖force her, and lie with her: then the man only that lay with her, shall die.

26 But vnto the damosel thou shalt doe nothing, there is in the damosel no sinne worthy of death: for as when a man riseth against his neighbour, and slayeth him, euen so is this matter.

27 For he found her in the field, *and* the betrothed damosel cried, and there was none to saue her.

28 ¶ * If a man finde a damosel that is a virgin, which is not betrothed, and lay hold on her, and lie with her, and they be found:

29 Then the man that lay with her, shall giue vnto the damosels father fifty *shekels* of siluer, and she shalbe his wife, because he hath humbled her: he may not put her away all his dayes.

30 ¶ * A man shall not take his fathers wife, nor discouer his fathers skirt.

CHAP. XXIII.

1 Who may or may not enter into the Congregation. 9 Vncleannesse to bee auoided in the hoste. 15 Of the fugitiue seruant. 17 Of filthinesse. 18 Of abominable sacrifices. 19 Of vsury. 21 Of vowes. 24 Of trespasses.

 Ee that is wounded in the stones, or hath his priuie member cut off, shall not enter into the Congregation of the LORD.

2 A bastard shall not enter into the Congregation of the LORD: euen to his tenth generation shall he not enter into the Congregation of the LORD.

3 * An Ammonite, or Moabite shall not enter into the Congregation of the LORD, euen to their tenth generation shall they not enter into the Congregation of the LORD for euer,

4 Because they met you not with bread and with water in the way when ye came forth out of Egypt, and * because they hired against thee Balaam the son of Beor of Pethor of Mesopotamia, to curse thee.

5 Neuerthelesse, the LORD thy God would not hearken vnto Balaam: but the LORD thy God turned the curse into a blessing vnto thee, because the LORD thy God loued thee.

6 Thou shalt not seek their peace, nor their † prosperity all thy dayes for euer.

7 ¶ Thou shalt not abhorre an Edomite, for he is thy brother: thou shalt not abhorre an Egyptian, because thou wast a stranger in his land.

8 The children that are begotten of them, shal enter into the cōgregation of the LORD, in their third generation.

9 ¶ When the hoste goeth foorth against thine enemies, then keepe thee from euery wicked thing.

10 ¶ If there bee among you any man that is not cleane, by reason of vncleannesse that chanceth him by night, then

* Exod. 22. 16.

* Leuit. 18. 8.

* Nehem. 13. 1.

* Num. 22. 5, 6.

† Heb. good.

* Leuit. 20. 10.

Or, take strong hold of her.

then shall hee goe abroad out of the campe, hee shall not come within the campe.

† *Hebr. turneth toward.*

11 But it shalbe when euening †commeth on, he shall wash *himselfe* with water : and when the Sunne is downe, he shall come into the campe againe.

12 ¶ Thou shalt haue a place also without the campe, whither thou shalt goe foorth abroad.

13 And thou shalt haue a paddle vpon thy weapon : and it shall be when thou † wilt ease thy selfe abroad, thou shalt digge therewith, and shalt turne backe and couer that which commeth from thee.

† *Hebr. sittest downe.*

14 For the Lord thy God walketh in the midst of thy campe, to deliuer thee, and to giue vp thine enemies before thee : therefore shall thy campe be holy, that he see †no vncleane thing in thee, and turne away from thee.

† *Hebr. nakednesse of any thing.*

15 ¶ Thou shalt not deliuer vnto his master, the seruant which is escaped from his master vnto thee.

16 He shall dwell with thee, euen among you, in that place which he shall choose, in one of thy gates where it †liketh him best : thou shalt not oppresse him.

† *Hebr. is good for him.*

17 ¶ There shalbe no ‖ whore of the daughters of Israel, nor a Sodomite of the sonnes of Israel.

‖ *Or, Sodomitesse.*

18 Thou shalt not bring the hire of a whore, or the price of a dogge into the house of the Lord thy God for any vow : for euen both these are abomination vnto the Lord thy God:

19 ¶ *Thou shalt not lend vpon vsury to thy brother; vsury of money, vsury of victuals, vsury of any thing that is lent vpon vsury.

* *Exod. 22. 15. leuit. 25. 36. psal. 15. 5.*

20 Vnto a stranger thou maiest lend vpon vsury, but vnto thy brother thou shalt not lend vpon vsury : that the Lord thy God may blesse thee, in all that thou settest thine hand to, in the land whither thou goest to possesse it.

21 ¶ *When thou shalt vow a vow vnto the Lord thy God, thou shalt not slacke to pay it : for the Lord thy God will surely require it of thee; and it would be sinne in thee.

* *Eccles. 5. 3.*

22 But if thou shalt forbeare to vow, it shall be no sinne in thee.

23 That which is gone out of thy lippes, thou shalt keepe and performe; *euen* a freewill offering according as thou hast vowed vnto the Lord thy

God, which thou hast promised with thy mouth.

24 ¶ When thou commest into thy neighbors Vineyard, then thou mayest eate grapes thy fill, at thine owne pleasure, but thou shalt not put *any* in thy vessell.

25 When thou commest into the standing corne of thy neighbours, * then thou maiest plucke the eares with thine hand : but thou shalt not mooue a sickle vnto thy neighbours standing corne.

* *Matt. 12. 1. mar. 2. 23. luke 6. 1.*

CHAP. XXIIII.

1 Of diuorce.   5 A new maried man goeth not to warre.   6. 10 Of pledges.   7 Of manstealers.   8 Of leprosie.   14 The hire is to be giuen.   16 Of Iustice.   19 Of Charitie.

When * a man hath taken a wife and married her, and it come to passe that shee find no fauour in his eyes, because hee hath found some †vncleannesse in her : then let him write her a bill of † diuorcement, and giue *it* in her hand, and send her out of his house.

* *Matt. 5. 31. and 19. 7. mar. 10.*

† *Hebr. matter of nakednesse.*
† *Hebr. cutting off.*

2 And when shee is departed out of his house, she may goe and be another mans *wife.*

3 And *if* the latter husband hate her, and write her a bill of diuorcement, and giueth *it* in her hand, and sendeth her out of his house : Or if the latter husband die, which tooke her to be his wife,

4 Her former husband which sent her away, may not take her againe to be his wife, after that she is defiled : for that *is* abomination before the Lord, and thou shalt not cause the land to sinne, which the Lord thy God giueth thee for an inheritance.

5 ¶ * When a man hath taken a new wife, he shal not goe out to warre, neither †shall hee be charged with any businesse : *but* hee shall be free at home one yeere, and shall cheere vp his wife which he hath taken.

* *Chap. 2. 7.*
† *Hebr. not any thing shall passe vpon him.*

6 ¶ No man shall take the nether or the vpper milstone to pledge : for hee taketh *a mans* life to pledge.

7 ¶ If a man bee found stealing any of his brethren of the children of Israel, and maketh merchandize of him, or selleth him : then that thiefe shall die, and thou shalt put euill away from among you.

8 ¶ Take

8 ¶ Take heede, in * the plague of leprosie, that thou obserue diligently, and doe according to all that the Priests the Leuites shall teach you : as I commanded them, so ye shall obserue to doe.

Leuit. 13.

9 Remember what the Lord thy God did * vnto Miriam by the way, after that yee were come forth out of Egypt.

Num. 12.

10 ¶ When thou doest †lend thy brother any thing, thou shalt not goe into his house to fetch his pledge.

†Heb. lend the loane of any thing to &c.

11 Thou shalt stand abroad, and the man to whome thou doest lend, shall bring out the pledge abroad vnto thee.

12 And if the man be poore, thou shalt not sleepe with his pledge :

13 In any case thou shalt deliuer him the pledge againe when the Sun goeth downe, that he may sleepe in his owne raiment, and blesse thee: and it shall be righteousnesse vnto thee before the Lord thy God.

14 ¶ Thou shalt not oppresse an hired seruant *that is* poore and needy, *whether he be* of thy brethren, or of thy strangers that *are* in thy lande within thy gates.

Leuit. 19. tob. 4.

15 At his day * thou shalt giue *him* his hire, neither shall the Sun goe downe vpon it, for he is poore, and †setteth his heart vpon it, lest hee crie against thee vnto the Lord, and it bee sinne vnto thee.

Heb. hee setteth his soule vnto it.

16 * The fathers shall not bee put to death for the children, neither shall the children be put to death for the fathers : euery man shall be put to death for his owne sinne.

2. Kings 14. 6. 2. chr. 25. 4. ier. 31. 29. 30. ezek. 18. 20

17 ¶ Thou shalt not peruert the iudgement of the stranger, *nor* of the fatherles, nor take a widowes raiment to pledge.

18 But thou shalt remember that thou wast a bondman in Egypt, and the Lord thy God redeemed thee thence : therefore I command thee to doe this thing.

19 ¶ * When thou cuttest downe thine haruest in thy field, and hast forgot a sheafe in the field, thou shalt not go againe to fetch it : it shalbe for the stranger, for the fatherlesse, and for the widow : that the Lord thy God may blesse thee in all the worke of thine hands.

Leuit. 19. & 23. 22.

20 When thou beatest thine oliue tree thou shalt not †goe ouer the boughes againe : it shall be for the stranger, for the

†Heb. thou shalt not bough it after thee.

fatherlesse, and for the widow.

21 When thou gatherest the grapes of thy vineyard, thou shalt not gleane it †afterward, it shalbe for the stranger, for the fatherlesse, and for the widow.

†Heb. after thee.

22 And thou shalt remember that thou wast a bondman in the land of Egypt : therfore I command thee to doe this thing.

CHAP. XXV.

1 Stripes must not exceed fortie. 4 The Oxe is not to be musled. 5 Of raising seed vnto a brother. 11 Of the immodest woman. 13 Of vniust weights. 17 The memorie of Amalek is to be blotted out.

I F there bee a controuersie betweene men, and they come vnto iudgment, that *the Iudges* may iudge them, then they shall iustifie the righteous, and condemne the wicked.

2 And it shall be, if the wicked man be worthy to be beaten, that the Iudge shall cause him to lie downe, and to bee beaten before his face, according to his fault, by a certaine number.

3 * Fourtie stripes he may giue him, and not exceed : lest *if* he should exceede, and beate him aboue these, with many stripes, then thy brother should seeme vile vnto thee.

2. Cor. 11. 24.

4 ¶ * Thou shalt not mussell the oxe when he treadeth out *the corne.*

1. Cor. 9. 9 1. tim. 5. 18 †Hebr. thresheth.

5 ¶ * If brethren dwell together, and one of them die, and haue no child, the wife of the dead shall not marrie without, vnto a stranger : her ‖ husbands brother shall go in vnto her, and take her to him to wife, and performe the duetie of an husbands brother vnto her.

Matt. 22. 24. mar. 12. 19. luk. 20. 28. ‖Or, next kinseman.

6 And it shall be, that the first borne which she beareth, shall succeede in the name of his brother which is dead, that his name be not put out of Israel.

7 And if the man like not to take his ‖brothers wife, then let his brothers wife go vp to the gate, vnto the Elders, and say, * My husbands brother refuseth to raise vp vnto his brother a name in Israel : he will not performe the dutie of my husbands brother.

*‖Or, next kinsemans wife. * Ruth 3. 9.*

8 Then the Elders of his citie shall call him and speake vnto him : and if he stand *to it,* and say, I like not to take her :

9 Then shal his brothers wife come vnto him in the presence of the Elders, and loose his shooe from off his foote, and

and spit in his face, and shall answere, and say, So shall it bee done vnto that man that will not build vp his brothers house.

10 And his name shall bee called in Israel, the house of him that hath his shooe loosed.

11 ¶ When men striue together one with another, and the wife of the one draweth neere, for to deliuer her husband out of the hand of him that smiteth him, and putteth foorth her hand and taketh him by the secrets :

12 Then thou shalt cut off her hand, thine eye shall not pitie *her*.

13 ¶ Thou shalt not haue in thy bagge †diuers weights, a great, and a small.

† *Hebr. a stone and a stone.*

14 Thou shalt not haue in thine house +diuers measures, a great, and a small.

‖ *Hebr. an Ephah, and an Ephah.*

15 *But* thou shalt haue a perfect and iust weight, a perfect and iust measure shalt thou haue : that thy dayes may bee lengthened in the land which the LORD thy God giueth thee.

16 For all that doe such things, *and* all that doe vnrighteously, *are* an abomination vnto the LORD thy God.

. Exod. 17.
8.

17 ¶ * Remember what Amalek did vnto thee by the way, when ye were come foorth out of Egypt :

18 How he met thee by the way, and smote the hindmost of thee, *euen* all that were feeble behinde thee, when thou *wast* faint and weary; and he feared not God.

19 Therefore it shall bee when the LORD thy God hath giuen thee rest from all thine enemies round about, in the land which the LORD thy God giueth thee for an inheritance to possesse it; that thou shalt blot out the remembrance of Amalek from vnder heauen : thou shalt not forget *it*.

CHAP. XXVI.

1 The confession of him that offereth the basket of First fruits. 12 The prayer of him that giueth his third yeere Tithes. 16 The couenant betweene God and the people.

Nd it shall be when thou *art* come in vnto the land which the LORD giueth thee for an inheritance, and possessest it, and dwellest therein :

2 That thou shalt take of the first of all the fruit of the earth, which thou shalt bring of thy land that the LORD thy God giueth thee, and shalt put *it* in a basket, and shalt goe vnto the place which the LORD thy God shal choose to place his Name there .

3 And thou shalt goe vnto the Priest that shall be in those dayes, and say vnto him, I professe this day vnto the LORD thy God, that I am come vnto the countrey which the LORD sware vnto our fathers for to giue vs.

4 And the Priest shall take the basket out of thine hand, and set it downe before the Altar of the LORD thy God.

5 And thou shalt speake and say before the LORD thy God, A Syrian ready to perish *was* my father, and hee went downe into Egypt, and soiourned there with a few, and became there a nation, great, mighty, and populous.

6 And the Egyptians euil intreated vs, and afflicted vs, and layd vpon vs hard bondage.

7 And when wee cryed vnto the LORD God of our fathers, the LORD heard our voyce, and looked on our affliction, and our labour, and our oppression.

8 And the LORD brought vs foorth out of Egypt with a mightie hand, and with an out-stretched arme, and with great terriblenesse, and with signes, and with wonders.

9 And he hath brought vs into this place, and hath giuen vs this land, *euen* a land that floweth with milke and honie.

10 And now behold, I haue brought the First fruits of the land, which thou, O LORD, hast giuen mee : and thou shalt set it before the LORD thy God, and worship before the LORD thy God.

11 And thou shalt reioyce in euery good thing, which the LORD thy God hath giuen vnto thee, and vnto thine house, thou, and the Leuite, and the stranger that is among you.

12 ¶ When thou hast made an end of tithing all the tithes of thine increase, the third yeere, *which is* *the yeere of tything, and hast giuen *it* vnto the Leuite, the stranger, the fatherlesse, and the widow, that they may eate within thy gates, and be filled :

* Chap. 1
28.

13 Then thou shalt say before the LORD thy God, I haue brought away

away the hallowed things out of *mine* house, and also haue giuen them vnto the Leuite, and vnto the stranger, to the fatherlesse, and to the widow, according to all thy commandements, which thou hast commanded me : I haue not transgressed thy commandements, neither haue I forgotten *them.*

14 I haue not eaten thereof in my mourning, neither haue I taken away ought thereof for any vncleane *vse*, nor giuen ought thereof for the dead : *but* I haue hearkened to the voyce of the LORD my God, *and* haue done according to all that thou hast commaunded me.

15 * Looke downe from thy holy habitation, from heauen, and blesse thy people Israel, and the land which thou hast giuen vs, as thou swarest vnto our fathers, a land that floweth with milke and hony.

16 ¶ This day the LORD thy God hath commanded thee to doe these Statutes and Iudgements : thou shalt therefore keepe and doe them with all thine heart, and with all thy soule.

17 Thou hast auouched the LORD this day to be thy God, and to walke in his wayes, and to keepe his Statutes, and his Commaundements, and his Iudgements, and to hearken vnto his voice.

18 And * the LORD hath auouched thee this day to be his peculiar people, as he hath promised thee, and that *thou* shouldest keepe all his Commaundements :

19 And to make thee high aboue all nations which he hath made, in praise and in name, and in honour, and that thou mayest be an holy people vnto the LORD thy God, as he hath spoken.

CHAP. XXVII.

1 The people are commanded to write the Law vpon stones, 5 and to build an Altar of whole stones. 11 The Tribes diuided on Gerizzim and Ebal. 14 The curses pronounced on mount Ebal.

Nd Moses with the Elders of Israel commaunded the people, , saying, Keepe all the Commandements which I command you this day.

2 And it shall be on the day * when you shall passe ouer Iordan, vnto the land which the LORD thy God giueth

thee, that thou shalt set thee vp great stones, and plaister them with plaister.

3 And thou shalt write vpon them all the words of this Law when thou art passed ouer, that thou mayest goe in vnto the land which the LORD thy God giueth thee, a land that floweth with milke and hony, as the LORD God of thy fathers hath promised thee.

4 Therefore it shall be when ye bee gone ouer Iordan, that yee shall set vp these stones, which I command you this day, in mount Ebal, and thou shalt plaister them with plaister.

5 And there shalt thou build an Altar vnto the LORD thy God, an altar of stones : * thou shalt not lift vp any yron *toole* vpon them.

6 Thou shalt build the Altar of the LORD thy God of whole stones · and thou shalt offer burnt offerings theron vnto the LORD thy God.

7 And thou shalt offer peace offerings, and shalt eate there, and reioyce before the LORD thy God.

8 And thou shalt write vpon the stones all the words of this Law very plainely.

9 ¶ And Moses, and the Priestes the Leuites, spake vnto all Israel, saying, Take heed, and hearken O Israel, this day thou art become the people of the LORD thy God.

10 Thou shalt therefore obey the voyce of the LORD thy God, and doe his Commandements, and his Statutes which I command thee this day.

11 ¶ And Moses charged the people the same day, saying,

12 These shall stand vpon mount Gerizzim to blesse the people, when yee are come ouer Iordan : Simeon, and Leui, and Iudah, and Issachar, and Ioseph, and Beniamin.

13 And these shall stand vpon mount Ebal †to curse : Reuben, Gad, and Asher, and Zebulun, Dan, & Naphtali.

14 ¶ And * the Leuites shal speake, and say vnto all the men of Israel with a loud voyce :

15 Cursed *be* the man that maketh any grauen or molten image, an abomination vnto the LORD, the worke of the handes of the craftesman, and putteth *it* in a secret place : and all the people shall answere and say, Amen.

16 Cursed *be* he that setteth light by his father or his mother : and all the people shall say, Amen.

17 Cur-

Esa. 63. 15

Chap. 7. 6

Iosh. 4. 1.

* Exod. 20. 25. iosh. 8. 31.

† *Hebr. for a cursing.*

* Dan. 9. 11

17 Cursed *be* he that remooueth his neighbours land-marke: and all the people shall say, Amen.

18 Cursed *be* hee that maketh the blinde to wander out of the way: and all the people shall say, Amen.

19 Cursed *be* hee that peruerteth the iudgement of the stranger, fatherlesse, and widow: and all the people shall say, Amen.

20 Cursed *be* hee that lieth with his fathers wife, because he vncouereth his fathers skirt: and all the people shall say, Amen.

21 Cursed *be* hee that lieth with any maner of beast: and all the people shall say, Amen.

22 Cursed *be* hee that lieth with his sister, the daughter of his father, or the daughter of his mother: and all the people shall say, Amen.

23 Cursed *be* hee that lieth with his mother in law: and all the people shall say, Amen.

24 Cursed *be* hee that smiteth his neighbour secretly: and all the people shall say, Amen.

* Ezech. 22. 12.

25 *Cursed *be* he that taketh reward to slay an innocent person: and all the people shall say, Amen.

* Gal. 3. 10.

26 * Cursed *be* hee that confirmeth not all the words of this Law to doe them: and al the people shal say, Amen.

CHAP. XXVIII.

1 The blessings for Obedience. 15 The curses for disobedience.

* Leuit. 26. 3.

Nd it shall come to passe, *if thou shalt hearken diligently vnto the voyce of the LORD thy God, to obserue *and* to doe all his Commandements which I command thee this day; that the LORD thy God will set thee on high aboue all nations of the earth.

2 And all these blessings shall come on thee, and ouertake thee, if thou shalt hearken vnto the voice of the LORD thy God.

3 Blessed *shalt* thou *bee* in the citie, and blessed *shalt* thou *be* in the field.

4 Blessed *shall be* the fruit of thy body, and the fruit of thy ground, and the fruit of thy cattell, the increase of thy kine, and the flocks of thy sheepe.

|| Or, dough, or, kneading troughes.

5 Blessed *shall be* thy basket and thy †store.

6 Blessed *shalt* thou *bee* when thou commest in, and blessed *shalt* thou *bee* when thou goest out.

7 The LORD shall cause thine enemies that rise vp against thee, to bee smitten before thy face: they shall come out against thee one way, and flee before thee seuen wayes.

8 The LORD shall command the blessing vpon thee in thy ||store-houses, and in all that thou settest thine hand vnto, and he shall blesse thee in the land which the LORD thy God giueth thee.

|| Or, barne

9 The LORD shall establish thee an holy people vnto himselfe, as hee hath sworne vnto thee, if thou shalt keepe the Commaundements of the LORD thy God, and walke in his wayes.

10 And all people of the earth shall see, that thou art called by the Name of the LORD, and they shall bee afraid of thee.

11 And *the LORD shal make thee plenteous ||in goods, in the fruit of thy †body, and in the fruit of thy cattell, and in the fruit of thy ground, in the land which the LORD sware vnto thy fathers to giue thee.

* Chap. 30 9. etc.
|| Or, for good.
† Hebr. belly

12 The LORD shal open vnto thee his good treasure, the heauen to giue the raine vnto thy land in his season, and to blesse all the worke of thine hand: and *thou shalt lend vnto many nations, and thou shalt not borrow.

* Chap. 15. 6.

13 And the LORD shall make thee the head, and not the taile, and thou shalt be aboue onely, and thou shalt not be beneath: if that thou hearken vnto the Commandements of the LORD thy God, which I command thee this day, to obserue, and to doe *them:*

14 And thou shalt not go aside from any of the wordes which I command thee this day, to the right hand, or to the left, to goe after other gods, to serue them.

15 ¶ But it shal come to passe, *if thou wilt not hearken vnto the voyce of the LORD thy God, to obserue to doe all his Commandements and his Statutes, which I command thee this day, that all these curses shall come vpon thee, and ouertake thee.

* Leuit. 26. 14. lament. 2. 17. mala. 2. 2. baruc. 1. 20.

16 Cursed *shalt* thou *be* in the city, and cursed *shalt* thou *be* in the field.

17 Cursed *shall be* thy basket and thy store.

18 Cursed

18 Cursed *shalbe* the fruit of thy body, and the fruit of thy land, the increase of thy kine, and the flocks of thy sheepe.

19 Cursed *shalt* thou *bee* when thou commest in, and cursed *shalt* thou *bee* when thou goest out.

20 The Lord shall send vpon thee cursing, vexation, and rebuke, in all that thou settest thine hand vnto, †for to doe, vntill thou be destroyed, and vntill thou perish quickely, because of the wickednesse of thy doings, whereby thou hast forsaken me.

Heb. which thou wouldst doe.

21 The Lord shall make the pestilence cleaue vnto thee, vntill he haue consumed thee from off the land, whither thou goest to possesse it.

22 * The Lord shall smite thee with a consumption, and with a feuer, and with an inflammation, & with an extreme burning, and with the ‖ sword, and with blasting, and with mildewe: and they shall pursue thee vntill thou perish.

Leuit. 26.

Or, drought

23 And the heauen that is ouer thy head shall be brasse, and the earth that is vnder thee *shall be* yron.

24 The Lord shall make the raine of thy land powder & dust: from heauen shall it come downe vpon thee, vntill thou be destroyed.

25 The Lord shall cause thee to be smitten before thine enemies: thou shalt go out one way against them, and flee seuen wayes before them, and shalt be †remoued into all the kingdomes of the earth.

Heb. for a remouing.

26 And thy carkeise shalbe meat vnto all foules of the aire, and vnto the beasts of the earth, and no man shall fray *them* away.

27 The Lord wil smite thee with the botch of Egypt, and with the emerods, and with the scabbe, and with the itch, whereof thou canst not bee healed.

28 The Lord shall smite thee with madnesse, and blindnesse, and astonishment of heart.

29 And thou shalt grope at noone dayes, as the blind gropeth in darknes, and thou shalt not prosper in thy waies: and thou shalt be onely oppressed, and spoiled euermore, and no man shal saue thee.

30 Thou shalt betrothe a wife, and another man shall lie with her: thou shalt build an house, and thou shalt not dwell therein: *thou shalt plant a vine-

Deut. 20.

yard, and shalt not †gather the grapes thereof.

† Hebr. prophane, or vse it as common meat.

31 Thine oxe shall be slaine before thine eyes, and thou shalt not eat thereof: thine asse shall be violently taken away from before thy face, and †shal not be restored to thee: thy sheepe shall bee giuen vnto thine enemies, and thou shalt haue none to rescue *them*.

† Heb. shall not returne to thee, &c.

32 Thy sonnes, and thy daughters shall be giuen vnto another people, and thine eyes shal looke, and faile with longing for them al the day long: and there shall be no might in thine hand.

33 The fruit of thy land, and all thy labours, shall a nation which thou knowest not, eate vp: and thou shalt be onely oppressed and crushed alway:

34 So that thou shalt bee mad, for the sight of thine eyes which thou shalt see.

35 The Lord shall smite thee in the knees, and in the legges with a sore botch that cannot bee healed, from the sole of thy foot, vnto the top of thy head.

36 The Lord shal bring thee, and thy king which thou shalt set ouer thee, vnto a nation which neither thou, nor thy fathers haue knowen, and there shalt thou serue other gods, wood and stone.

37 And thou shalt become *an astonishment, a prouerbe, and a by-worde, among all nations whither the Lord shall leade thee.

* 1. King. 9 7. ier. 24. 9. and 25. 9.

38 *Thou shalt carie much seede out into the field, and shalt gather but litle in: for the locust shall consume it.

* Mica. 6. 15. agge. 1. 6.

39 Thou shalt plant vineyards and dresse *them*, but shalt neither drinke of the wine, nor gather *the grapes*: for the wormes shall eate them.

40 Thou shalt haue Oliue trees throughout al thy coasts, but thou shalt not anoint *thy selfe* with the oyle: for thine Oliue shall cast *his fruit*.

41 Thou shalt beget sonnes and daughters, but †thou shalt not enioy them: for they shall goe into captiuitie.

† Hebr. they shall not be thine.

42 All thy trees and fruit of thy land shall the locusts †consume.

‖ Or, possesse

43 The stranger that is within thee shall get vp aboue thee very high: and thou shalt come downe very low.

44 He shall lend to thee, and thou shalt not lend to him: he shall bee the head, and thou shalt be the taile.

45 Moreouer, all these curses shall come vpon thee, and shall pursue thee, and

and ouertake thee, til thou be destroied: because thou hearkenedst not vnto the voice of the Lord thy God, to keepe his Commandements, and his Statutes which he commanded thee.

46 And they shall be vpon thee for a signe, and for a wonder, and vpon thy seed for euer:

47 Because thou seruedst not the Lord thy God with ioyfulnesse, and with gladnesse of heart, for the aboundance of all things.

48 Therefore shalt thou serue thine enemies, which the Lord shall send against thee, in hunger, and in thirst, and in nakednesse, and in want of all things: and he shall put a yoke of iron vpon thy necke, vntill he haue destroyed thee.

49 The Lord shall bring a nation against thee from farre, from the end of the earth, *as swift* as the Eagle fleeth, a nation whose tongue thou † Heb. heare.   shalt not † vnderstand:

† Heb. strong of face.

50 A nation † of fierce countenance, which shal not regard the person of the old, nor shew fauour to the yong:

51 And hee shall eate the fruit of thy cattell, and the fruit of thy land, vntill thou be destroyed: which also shall not leaue thee *either* corne, wine, or oyle, *or* the increase of thy kine, or flockes of thy sheepe, vntill he haue destroyed thee.

52 And he shall besiege thee in all thy gates, vntill thy high and fenced walles come downe wherein thou trustedst throughout all thy land: and hee shall besiege thee in all thy gates, throughout all thy land which the Lord thy God hath giuen thee.

* Leuit. 26. 29. 2. king. 6. 29. Iam. 4. 10. baruc. 2. 3.
† Hebr. belly.

53 And * thou shalt eate the fruit of thine owne † body, the flesh of thy sonnes, and of thy daughters (which the Lord thy God hath giuen thee) in the siege, and in the straitnesse wherewith thine enemies shall distresse thee.

54 *So that* the man that is tender among you, and very delicate, his eye shalbe euill toward his brother, and toward the wife of his bosome, and towards the remnant of his children which he shall leaue:

55 So that he wil not giue to any of them of the flesh of his children whom he shall eate: because hee hath nothing left him in the siege, and in the straitnesse wherewith thine enemies shal distresse thee, in all thy gates.

56 The tender and delicate woman among you, which would not aduenture to set the sole of her foote vpon the ground, for delicatenesse and tendernesse, her eye shall be euill towards the husband of her bosome, and towards her sonne, and towards her daughter,

57 And towards her † yong one that † Hebr. af- ter-birth. cometh out from betweene her feete, and towards her children which shee shall beare: for shee shall eate them for want of all things secretly in the siege and straitnes, wherewith thine enemie shall distresse thee in thy gates.

58 If thou wilt not obserue to doe all the wordes of this Law that are written in this booke, that thou mayest feare this glorious and fearefull Name, The Lord Thy God:

59 Then the Lord wil make thy plagues wonderfull, and the plagues of thy seed, *euen* great plagues, and of long continuance, and sore sicknesses, and of long continuance.

60 Moreouer, hee will bring vpon thee all the diseases of Egypt, which thou wast afraid of, and they shal cleaue vnto thee.

61 Also euery sickenesse, and euery plague which is not written in the booke of this Law, them will the Lord † bring vpon thee, vntill thou † Hebr. cause to a- cend. be destroyed.

62 And ye shall be left few in number, whereas ye were * as the starres of heauen for multitude: because thou wouldest not obey the voyce of the Lord thy God. * Chap. 1 22.

63 And it shall come to passe, *that* as the Lord reioyced ouer you to doe you good, and to multiply you; so the Lord will reioyce ouer you to destroy you, and to bring you to nought; and ye shalbe plucked from off the land whither thou goest to possesse it.

64 And the Lord shall scatter thee among all people, from the *one* end of the earth, euen vnto the *other:* and there thou shalt serue other gods, which *neither* thou nor thy fathers haue knowen, *euen* wood and stone.

65 And among these nations shalt thou finde no ease, neither shall the sole of thy foote haue rest: but the Lord shall giue thee there a trembling heart, and failing of eyes, & sorrow of minde.

66 And thy life shall hang in doubt before thee, and thou shalt feare day and night, and shalt haue none assurance of thy life.

67 In

67 In the morning thou shalt say, Would God it were Euen : and at Euen thou shalt say, Would God it were morning, for the feare of thine heart wherewith thou shalt feare, and for the sight of thine eyes which thou shalt see.

68 And the LORD shall bring thee into Egypt againe, with ships, by the way whereof I spake vnto thee, Thou shalt see it no more againe : and there ye shall bee sold vnto your enemies for bondmen, and bondwomen, and no man shall buy *you*.

CHAP. XXIX.

1 Moses exhorteth them to obedience, by the memorie of the workes they haue seene. 10 All are presented before the Lord to enter into his Couenant. 18 The great wrath on him that flattereth himselfe in his wickednes. 29 Secret things belong vnto God.

Exod. 19.

THese *are* the woordes of the Couenant which the LORD commanded Moses to make with the children of Ifrael in the land of Moab, beside the Couenant which he made with them in Horeb.

2 ¶ And Moses called vnto all Israel, and said vnto them, *Yee haue seene all that the LORD did before your eyes in the land of Egypt vnto Pharaoh, and vnto all his seruants, and vnto all his land ;

3 The great temptations which thine eyes haue seene, the signes and those great miracles :

4 Yet the LORD hath not giuen you an heart to perceiue, and eyes to see, and eares to heare, vnto this day.

5 And I haue led you fourtie yeres in the wildernes : your clothes are not waxen old vpon you, and thy shooe is not waxen old vpon thy foot.

6 Ye haue not eaten bread, neither haue you drunke wine, or strong drink: that yee might knowe that I am the LORD your God.

7 And when yee came vnto this place, Sihon the king of Heshbon, and Og the King of Bashan, came out against vs vnto battell, and wee smote them.

8 And wee tooke their lande, and gaue it for an inheritance vnto the Reubenites, and to the Gadites, and to the halfe tribe of Manasseh.

Chap. 4. 6.
king. 2. 2.
ish. 1. 7.

9 *Keepe therefore the wordes of this Couenant and doe them, that yee may prosper in all that ye doe.

10 ¶ Ye stand this day all of you before the LORD your God : your captaines of your tribes, your Elders, and your officers, *with* all the men of Israel,

11 Your litle ones, your wiues, and thy stranger that is in thy campe, from the hewer of thy wood, vnto the drawer of thy water :

12 That thou shouldest † enter into Couenant with the LORD thy God, and into his othe which the LORD thy God maketh with thee this day .

13 That he may establish thee to day for a people vnto himselfe, and that hee may be vnto thee a God, as he hath said vnto thee, and as he hath sworne vnto thy fathers, to Abraham, to Isaac, and to Iacob.

14 Neither with you onely doe I make this couenant and this othe :

15 But with him that standeth here with vs this day before the LORD our God, and also with him that is not here with vs this day :

16 (For ye know how we haue dwelt in the land of Egypt, and how we came thorow the nations which ye passed by.

17 And ye haue seene their abominations, and their † idoles, wood, and stone, siluer, and gold, which were among them.)

18 Lest there should be among you man or woman, or familie, or tribe, whose heart turneth away this day frō the LORD our God, to goe *and* serue the gods of these nations : lest there should bee among you a root that beareth || gall and wormewood,

19 And it come to passe when he heareth the wordes of this curse, that hee blesse himselfe in his heart, saying, I shall haue peace, though I walke in the || imagination of mine heart, to adde † drunkennesse to thirst :

20 The LORD wil not spare him, but then the anger of the LORD, and his ielousie shall smoke against that man, and all the curses that are written in this booke shall lie vpon him, and the LORD shall blot out his name from vnder heauen.

21 And the LORD shall separate him vnto euill, out of all the tribes of Israel, according to all the curses of the Couenant, that † are written in this booke of the Law

22 So that the generation to come of

† *Heb. passe.*

† *Heb. donguie gods.*

|| *Or, a poisonfull herbe* Heb. *Rosh.*

|| *Or, stubbornnesse.*
† Heb. *the drunken to the thirstie*

† *Hebr. is written.*

of your children, that shall rise vp after you, and the stranger that shall come from a farre land, shall say, when they see the plagues of that land, and the sicknesses †which the LORD hath layd vpon it;

23 And that the whole land thereof is brimstone and salt, *and* burning, that it is not sowen, nor beareth, nor any grasse groweth therein, *like the ouerthrow of Sodome, and Gomorah, Admah, and Zeboim, which the LORD ouerthrew in his anger, and in his wrath:

24 Euen al nations shal say, *Wherefore hath the LORD done thus vnto this land? what *meaneth* the heat of this great anger?

25 Then men shall say, Because they haue forsaken the Couenant of the LORD God of their fathers, which he made with them when he brought them foorth out of the land of Egypt.

26 For they went and serued other gods, & worshipped them, gods whom they knew not, and †whom he had not giuen vnto them.

27 And the anger of the LORD was kindled against this land, to bring vpon it all the curses, that are written in this booke.

28 And the LORD rooted them out of their land, in anger and in wrath, and in great indignation, and cast them into another land, as *it is* this day.

29 The secret things *belong* vnto the LORD our God: but those things which are reuealed *belong* vnto vs, and to our children for euer, that wee may doe all the words of this Law.

CHAP. XXX.

1 Great mercies promised vnto the repentant. 11 The Commaundement is manifest. 15 Death and life are set before them.

And it shall come to passe when all these things are come vpon thee, the blessing, and the curse, which I haue set before thee, and thou shalt call *them* to minde among all the nations whither the LORD thy God hath driuen thee,

2 And shalt returne vnto the LORD thy God, and shalt obey his voyce according to all that I command thee this day, thou and thy children with al thine heart, and with all thy soule:

3 That then the LORD thy God will turne thy captiuitie, and haue compassion vpon thee, and wil returne and gather thee from all the nations whither the LORD thy God hath scattered thee.

4 *If any of thine be driuen out vnto the outmost parts of heauen, from thence will the LORD thy God gather thee, and from thence will he fetch thee.

5 And the LORD thy God will bring thee into the land which thy fathers possessed, and thou shalt possesse it: and he will doe thee good, and multiply thee aboue thy fathers.

6 And the LORD thy God will circumcise thine heart, and the heart of thy seed, to loue the LORD thy God with all thine heart, and with all thy soule, that thou mayest liue.

7 And the LORD thy God will put all these curses vpon thine enemies, and on them that hate thee, which persecuted thee.

8 And thou shalt returne and obey the voice of the LORD, and doe all his Commandements which I command thee this day.

9 *And the LORD thy God will make thee plenteous in euery worke of thine hand, in the fruit of thy body, and in the fruit of thy cattell, and in the fruit of thy land, for good: for the LORD will againe reioyce ouer thee for good, as he reioyced ouer thy fathers:

10 If thou shalt hearken vnto the voyce of the LORD thy God to keepe his Commandements, and his Statutes which are written in this booke of the Law, *and* if thou turne vnto the LORD thy God with all thine heart, and with all thy soule.

11 ¶ For this Commaundement which I command thee this day, it is not hidden from thee, neither is it farre off.

12 *It *is* not in heauen, that thou shouldest say, Who shal goe vp for vs to heauen, and bring it vnto vs, that wee may heare it, and doe it?

13 Neither *is* it beyond the sea, that thou shouldest say, Who shall goe ouer the sea for vs, and bring it vnto vs, that we may heare it, and doe it?

14 But the word is very nigh vnto thee, in thy mouth, and in thy heart, that thou mayest doe it.

15 ¶ See, I haue set before thee this day,

† *Hebr. wherewith the LORD hath made it sicke.*

* Gen. 19. 24, 25.

* 1. King. 9. 8. Iere. 22. 8.

† *Hebr. diuided: Or, who had not giuen to them any portion.*

* Nehe. 1. 9.

* Chap. 28 11.

* Rom. 10. 6. &c.

16 In that I command thee this day to loue the LORD thy God, to walke in his wayes, and to keepe his Commandements, and his Statutes, and his Iudgements, that thou maiest liue and multiply: and the LORD thy God shall blesse thee in the land, whither thou goest to possesse it.

17 But if thine heart turne away, so that thou wilt not heare, but shalt bee drawen away, and worship other gods and serue them:

18 I denounce vnto you this day, that ye shall surely perish, and that yee shall not prolong your dayes vpon the land, whither thou passest ouer Iordan, to goe to possesse it.

Chap. 4.
8. 19 * I call heauen and earth to record this day against you, that I haue set before you life and death, blessing and cursing: therefore choose life, that both thou and thy seed may liue:

20 That thou maiest loue the LORD thy God, and that thou mayest obey his voyce, and that thou mayest cleaue vnto him: for he is thy life, and the length of thy dayes, that thou mayest dwell in the land, which the LORD sware vnto thy fathers, to Abraham, to Isaac, and to Iacob, to giue them.

CHAP. XXXI.

1 Moses incourageth the people. 7 Hee incourageth Ioshua. 9 Hee deliuereth the Law vnto the Priests to reade it in the seuenth yere to the people. 14 God giueth a charge to Ioshua, 19 and a song to testifie against the people. 24 Moses deliuereth the booke of the Law to the Leuites to keepe. 28 Hee maketh a protestation to the Elders.

Nd Moses went & spake these wordes vnto all Israel.

2 And hee saide vnto them, I am an hundred and twentie yeeres old this day; I can no more goe out and come in: also the Num. 20.
2. chap. 3.
7. LORD hath said vnto mee, * Thou shalt not goe ouer this Iordan.

3 The LORD thy God, hee will goe ouer before thee, and he will destroy these nations from before thee, and thou shalt possesse them: and Ioshua, Num. 27.
4. hee shall goe ouer before thee, * as the LORD hath said.

4 And the LORD shall doe vnto them, as hee did to Sihon, and to Og

Kings of the Amorites, and vnto the land of them, whom he destroyed.

5 And * the LORD shall giue them * Chap. 7. 2. vp before your face, that ye may doe vnto them according vnto all the Commandements which I haue commanded you.

6 Be strong, and of a good courage, feare not, nor be afraid of them: for the LORD thy God, he it is that doeth goe with thee, he will not faile thee, nor forsake thee.

7 ¶ And Moses called vnto Ioshua, and said vnto him in the sight of all Israel, Bee strong, and of a good courage: for thou must goe with this people vnto the land, which the LORD hath sworne vnto their fathers to giue them; and thou shalt cause them to inherite it.

8 And the LORD, he it is that doth goe before thee, he will be with thee, hee will not faile thee, neither forsake thee: feare not, neither be dismayed.

9 ¶ And Moses wrote this Law, and deliuered it vnto the Priests the sonnes of Leui, which bare the Arke of the Couenant of the LORD, and vnto all the Elders of Israel.

10 And Moses commanded them, saying, At the end of euery seuen yeeres, in the solemnitie of the * yeere of release, * Chap. 15.
1. in the feast of Tabernacles,

11 When all Israel is come to appeare before the LORD thy God, in the place which hee shall choose; thou shalt reade this Law before all Israel, in their hearing.

12 Gather the people together, men, and women and children, and thy stranger that is within thy gates, that they may heare, and that they may learne, and feare the LORD your God, and obserue to doe all the wordes of this Law:

13 And that their children which haue not knowen any thing, may heare, and learne to feare the LORD your God, as long as yee liue in the land, whither ye goe ouer Iordan to possesse it.

14 ¶ And the LORD saide vnto Moses, Beholde, thy dayes approach that thou must die: call Ioshua, and present your selues in the Tabernacle of the Congregation, that I may giue him a charge. And Moses and Ioshua went and presented themselues in the Tabernacle of the Congregation.

15 And the LORD appeared in the Taber-

Tabernacle in a pillar of a cloud : and the pillar of the cloude stood ouer the doore of the Tabernacle.

16 ¶ And the LORD saide vnto Moses, Behold, thou shalt †sleepe with thy fathers, and this people wil rise vp, and goe a whoring after the gods of the strangers of the land whither they goe *to be* amongst them, and wil forsake me, and breake my couenant which I haue made with them.

† Hebr. lye downe.

17 Then my anger shall be kindled against them in that day , and I will forsake them , and I will hide my face from them, and they shall be deuoured, and many euils and troubles shall †befall them , so that they will say in that day, Are not these euils come vpon vs, because our God is not amongst vs ?

† Hebr. finde them.

18 And I will surely hide my face in that day, for all the euils which they shal haue wrought, in that they are turned vnto other gods.

19 Now therefore, write ye this song for you, and teach it the children of Israel : put it in their mouthes , that this song may be a witnesse for mee , against the children of Israel.

20 For when I shall haue brought them into the land which I sware vnto their fathers, that floweth with milke and hony ; and they shall haue eaten and filled themselues , and waxen fat ; then will they turne vnto other gods, and serue them, and prouoke me, and breake my couenant.

21 And it shall come to passe , when many euils and troubles are befallen them , that this song shall testifie †against them as a witnesse : for it shall not bee forgotten out of the mouthes of their seed : for I know their imagination which they †goe about euen now, before I haue brought them into the land, which I sware.

† Hebr. before.

† Hebr. doe.

22 ¶ Moses therefore wrote this song the same day, and taught it the children of Israel.

23 And he gaue Ioshua the sonne of Nun a charge , and said, * Bee strong, and of a good courage : for thou shalt bring the children of Israel into the land which I sware vnto them : and I will be with thee.

* Iosh. 1. 6.

24 ¶ And it came to passe when Moses had made an ende of writing the wordes of this Law in a booke, vntill they were finished,

25 That Moses commaunded the Leuites which bare the Arke of the Couenant of the LORD, saying,

26 Take this booke of the Law, and put it in the side of the Arke of the Couenant of the LORD your God, that it may bee there for a witnesse against thee.

27 For I know thy rebellion. and thy stiffe necke : Beholde, while I am yet aliue with you this day, yee haue bene rebellious against the LORD ; and how much more after my death ?

28 ¶ Gather vnto mee all the Elders of your tribes, and your Officers, that I may speake these words in their eares, and call heauen and earth to record against them.

29 For I know, that after my death yee will vtterly corrupt *your selues* , and turne aside from the *way* , which I haue commauded you : and euil wil befall you in the latter dayes , because yee wil doe euil in the sight of the LORD, to prouoke him to anger through the worke of your hands.

30 And Moses spake in the eares of al the Cōgregation of Israel the words of this song, vntill they were ended.

CHAP. XXXII.

1 Moses song, which setteth foorth Gods mercy and vengeance. 46 He exhorteth them to set their hearts vpon it. 48 God sendeth him vp to mount Nebo, to see the land, and die.

Giue eare, O yee heauens, and I will speake ; And heare, O earth, the words of my mouth.

2 My doctrine shall drop as the raine : my speach shall distill as the deaw, as the smal raine vpon the tender herbe, and as the showres vpon the grasse.

3 Because I wil publish the Name of the LORD : ascribe yee greatnesse vnto our God.

4 *He is* the rocke , his worke *is* perfect : for all his wayes *are* Iudgement : A God of trueth, and without iniquity, iust and right *is* he.

5 †They haue corrupted themselues, ‖their spot is not *the spot* of his children : *they are* a peruerse and crooked generation.

† Hebr. hath corr ted to hir selfe. ‖ Or, they are his child that is th blot

6 Doe ye thus requite the LORD, O foolish people , & vnwise ? Is not he thy Father *that* hath bought thee ? Hath he not made thee, and established thee ?

7 ¶ Remem-

Heb. gene-
tion and
neration.

7 ¶ Remember the dayes of olde, consider the yeeres of †many generations: aske thy father, and he will shewe thee, thy Elders, and they wil tell thee.

8 When the most High diuided to the nations their inheritance, when he separated the sonnes of Adam, hee set the bounds of the people according to the number of the children of Israel.

Heb. cord.

9 For the LORDS portion *is* his people: Iacob *is* the †lot of his inheritance.

r, com-
sed him
ut.

10 He found him in a desert land, and in the waste howling wildernesse: Hee ||ledde him about, he instructed him, hee kept him as the apple of his eye.

11 As an Eagle stirreth vp her nest, fluttereth ouer her yong, spreadeth abroad her wings, taketh them, beareth them on her wings:

12 *So* the LORD alone did leade him, and there was no strange God with him.

13 He made him ride on the high places of the earth, that he might eate the increase of the fields, and he made him to sucke hony out of the rocke, and oyle out of the flintie rocke,

14 Butter of kine, & milke of sheepe, with fat of lambes, and rammes of the breed of Bashan, & goats, with the fat of kidneis of wheat, and thou diddest drinke the pure blood of the grape.

15 ¶ But Iesurun waxed fat, and kicked: Thou art waxen fat, thou art growen thicke, thou art couered *with fatnes:* then he forsooke God *which* made him, and lightly esteemed the Rocke of his saluation.

16 They prouoked him to ielousie with strange *gods*, with abominations prouoked they him to anger.

r, which
e not
.

17 They sacrificed vnto deuils, ||not to God: to gods whom they knew not, to new *gods, that* came newly vp, whom your fathers feared not.

18 Of the Rocke that begate thee thou art vnmindfull, and hast forgotten God that formed thee.

r, despi-

19 And when the LORD saw *it*, he ||abhorred *them*, because of the prouoking of his sonnes, & of his daughters.

20 And he said, I will hide my face from them, I will see what their ende *shall be:* for they *are* a very froward generation, children in whom is no faith.

21 They haue mooued me to ielousie with *that which is* not god, they haue prouoked me to anger with their vanities: And *I will moue them to ielousie with *those which* are not a people, I will prouoke them to anger with a foolish nation.

22 For a fire is kindled in my anger, and ||shall burne vnto the lowest hell, and shall consume the earth with her increase, and set on fire the foundations of the mountaines.

23 I will heape mischiefes vpon them, I wil spend mine arrowes vpon them.

24 *They shall bee* burnt with hunger and deuoured with †burning heat, and with bitter destruction: I will also send the teeth of beasts vpon them, with the poison of serpents of the dust.

25 The sword without, and terrour †within shall †destroy both the yong man, and the virgin, the suckling *also* with the man of gray haires.

26 I said, I would scatter them into corners, I would make the remembrance of them to cease frō among men:

27 Were it not that I feared the wrath of the enemie, lest their aduersaries should behaue themselues strangely, *and* lest they should say, ||Our hande is high, and the LORD hath not done all this.

28 For they are a nation voide of counsel, neither is there any vnderstanding in them.

29 O that they were wise, that they vnderstood this, that they would consider their latter end.

30 How should *one chase a thousand, and two put ten thousand to flight, except their Rocke had sold them, and the LORD had shut them vp?

31 For their rocke is not as our Rocke, euen our enemies themselues being iudges.

32 For their vine is ||of the vine of Sodome, and of the fields of Gomorah: their grapes *are* grapes of gall, their clusters *are* bitter.

33 Their wine *is* the poison of dragons, and the cruell venime of Aspes.

34 Is not this laide vp in store with me, *and* sealed vp among my treasures?

35 To me belongeth *vengeance, and recompence, their foot shall slide in due time: for the day of their calamitie is at hand, and the things that shal come vpon them, make haste.

36 For the LORD shall iudge his people, and repent himselfe for his seruants, when he seeth that *their* †power is

Rom. 10. 9

|| Or, hath burned.
|| Or, hath consumed.

† Heb. burning coales.

† Heb. from the chambers.
† Heb. bereaue.

|| Or, our high hand and not the LORD hath done all this.

Iosh. 23. 10.

|| Or, is worse then the vine of Sodome. &c.

Ecclus. 28 1. rom. 12. 19. heb. 10. 30.

† Heb. hand.

is gone; and there is none shut vp, or left.

37 And he shall say, Where *are* their gods? their Rocke in whom they trusted;

38 Which did eat the fat of their sacrifices, & dranke the wine of their drinke offerings? let them rise vp and helpe you, *and* be †your protection.

† *Hebr. an hiding for you.*
* 1. Sam. 2. 6. tob. 13. 2. wisd. 16. 13.

39 See now, that I, *euen* I am he, and there is no god with mee; * I kill, and I make aliue : I wound, and I heale: neither is there any that can deliuer out of my hand.

40 For I lift vp my hand to heauen, and say, I liue for euer.

41 If I whet my glittering sword, and mine hand take holde on Iudgement, I will render vengeance to mine enemies, and will reward them that hate me.

42 I will make mine arrowes drunke with blood, (and my sword shal deuoure flesh) *and that* with the blood of the slaine, and of the captiues, from the beginning of reuenges vpon the enemie.

‖ *Or, praise his people ye nations. Or, sing ye.*
* Matt. 7. 6. rom. 15. 10.

43 ‖Reioyce, O *ye nations *with* his people, for he will auenge the blood of his seruants, and will render vengeance to his aduersaries, and wil be mercifull vnto his land, *and* to his people.

44 ¶ And Moses came and spake all the wordes of this song in the eares of the people, he and ‖Hoshea the sonne of Nun.

‖ *Or, Ioshua.*

45 And Moses made an end of speaking all these words to all Israel.

* Chap. 5. 6. and 11. 18.

46 And hee said vnto them, * Set your hearts vnto all the wordes which I testifie among you this day, which yee shall commaund your children to obserue to doe all the wordes of this Law.

47 For it *is* not a vaine thing for you : because it is your life, and through this thing yee shall prolong *your* dayes, in the land whither yee goe ouer Iordan to possesse it.

* Num. 27. 12.

48 And *the Lord spake vnto Moses that selfe same day, saying,

49 Get thee vp into this mountaine Abarim, vnto mount Nebo, which is in the land of Moab, that is ouer against Iericho, and behold the land of Canaan which I giue vnto the children of Israel for a possession :

50 And die in the mount whither thou goest vp, and bee gathered vnto

thy people, as *Aaron thy brother died in mount Hor, and was gathered vnto his people :

* Num. 20. 25, 28. and 33. 38.

51 Because *ye trespassed against me among the children of Israel, at the waters of ‖ Meribah Kadesh, in the wildernesse of Zin : because yee sanctified mee not in the midst of the children of Israel.

* Num. 20. 12, 13. and 27. 14.
‖ *Or, strife Kadesh.*

52 Yet thou shalt see the land before *thee*, but thou shalt not goe thither vnto the land which I giue the children of Israel.

CHAP. XXXIII.

1 *The Maiestie of God.* 6 *The blessings of the twelue Tribes.* 26 *The excellency of Israel.*

Nd this *is* the blessing, wherewith Moses the man of God blessed the children of Israel before his death.

2 And he said, The Lord came from Sinai, and rose vp from Seir vnto them, hee shined foorth from mount Paran, and hee came with ten thousands of Saints : from his Right hand *went* a †fierie Law for them.

† *Hebr. a fire of law.*

3 Yea hee loued the people; all his Saints *are* in thy hand : and they sate downe at thy feete; euery one shall receiue of thy wordes.

4 Moses commaunded vs a Law, euen the inheritance of the Congregation of Iacob.

5 And hee was King in Iesurun, when the heads of the people, *and* the Tribes of Israel were gathered together.

6 ¶ Let Reuben liue, and not die, and let *not* his men be few.

7 ¶ And this *is the blessing* of Iudah : and he said, Heare, Lord, the voice of Iudah, and bring him vnto his people : let his hands bee sufficient for him, and bee thou an helpe to him from his enemies.

8 ¶ And of Leui hee said, * *Let* thy Thummim and thy Vrim *be* with thy holy one, whom thou diddest prooue at Massah, *& with* whom thou didst striue at the waters of Meribah;

* Exod. 28. 30.

9 Who said vnto his father & to his mother, I haue not seene him, neither did hee acknowledge his brethren; nor knew his owne children : for they haue obserued thy word, and kept thy Couenant.

10 ‖They

‖ Or, let them
teach, &c.
‖ Or, let
them put
incense.
† Heb. at thy
nose.

10 ‖ They ſhal teach Iacob thy iudgments, and Iſrael thy Lawe : ‖ they
ſhall put incense † before thee, and whole
burnt ſacrifice vpon thine Altar.

11 Bleſſe, LORD, his ſubſtance, and
accept the worke of his handes, ſmite
thorow the loines of them that riſe a-
gainſt him, and of them that hate him,
that they riſe not againe.

12 ¶ And of Beniamin he ſaid, The
beloued of the LORD ſhall dwell in
ſafetie by him, and the LORD ſhall couer
him all the day long, and he ſhall dwell
betweene his ſhoulders.

* Gen. 49.
25.

13 ¶ And of Ioſeph he ſaid, *Bleſſed of the LORD be his land, for the
precious things of heauen, for the dew,
and for the deep that coucheth beneath;

14 And for the precious fruits brought
forth by the ſunne, and for the precious
things † put forth by the † moone,

† Heb. thruſt
forth.
† Hebr.
Moones.

15 And for the chiefe things of the ancient mountaines, and for the precious
things of the laſting hils,

16 And for the precious things of the
earth, and fulneſſe thereof, and for the
good will of him that dwelt in the buſh:
let the blessing come vpon the head of Ioſeph, and vpon the top of the head of
him that *was ſeparated frō his brethren.

* Gen. 49.
26.

17 His glory is like the firſtling of his
bullocke, & his hornes are like the hornes
of Vnicornes : with them he ſhall puſh
the people together, to the ends of the
earth : and they are the ten thouſands
of Ephraim, and they are the thouſands
of Manaſſeh.

18 ¶ And of Zebulun he ſaid, Reioyce, Zebulun, in thy going out ; and
Iſſachar, in thy tents.

19 They ſhall call the people vnto
the mountaine, there they ſhal offer ſacrifices of righteouſneſſe : for they ſhall
ſucke of the abundance of the ſeas, and
of treaſures hid in the ſand.

20 ¶ And of Gad he ſaid, Bleſſed be
he that enlargeth Gad : he dwelleth as
a lyon, and teareth the arme with the
crowne of the head.

21 And he prouided the firſt part for
himſelfe, becauſe there, in a portion of the
lawgiuer was he † ſeated, and hee came
with the heads of the people, he executed
the iuſtice of the LORD, and his iudgments with Iſrael.

Heb. ſieled.

22 ¶ And of Dan he ſaid, Dan is a
Lyons whelpe : hee ſhall leape from
Baſhan.

23 ¶ And of Naphtali he ſaid, O

Naphtali, ſatisfied with fauour, and full
with the bleſſing of the LORD : poſſeſſe thou the Weſt and the South.

24 ¶ And of Aſher hee ſaid, let A-
ſher be bleſſed with children, Let him
be acceptable to his brethren, and let
him dip his foot in oile.

25 Thy ‖ ſhooes ſhall bee yron and
braſſe, and as thy dayes, ſo ſhall thy
ſtrength bee.

‖ Or, vnder
thy ſhooes
ſhalbe yron.

26 ¶ There is none like vnto the
God of Ieſurun, who rideth vpon the
heauen in thy helpe, and in his excellencie on the ſkie.

27 The eternall God is thy refuge,
and vnderneath are the euerlaſting
armes : and he ſhall thruſt out the enemie from before thee, and ſhall ſay, Deſtroy them.

* Ier. 23. 6

28 *Iſrael then ſhall dwell in ſafetie alone : the fountaine of Iacob ſhalbe
vpon a land of corne and wine, alſo his
heauens ſhall drop downe deaw.

29 Happy art thou, O Iſrael : Who
is like vnto thee, O people! ſaued by the
LORD, the ſhield of thy helpe, and
who is the ſword of thy excellencie : and
thine enemies ‖ ſhal be found liars vnto
thee, and thou ſhalt tread vpon their
high places.

‖ Or, ſhal be
ſubdued.

CHAP. XXXIIII.

1 Moſes from Mount Nebo vieweth the lande.
5 He dieth there. 6 His buriall. 7 His age.
9 Thirty dayes mourning for him. 9 Ioſhua
succeedeth him. 10 The praiſe of Moſes.

ANd Moſes went vp from
the plaines of Moab, vnto
the mountaine of Nebo,
to the top of Piſgah, that
is ouer againſt Iericho :
and the LORD ſhewed him * all the
land of Gilead, vnto Dan,

‖ Or, Hill.

* Chap. 3.
27 2. mac.
2. 4.

2 And all Naphtali, and the lande
of Ephraim, and Manaſſeh, and all the
land of Iudah, vnto the vtmoſt ſea,

3 And the South, and the plaine of
the valley of Iericho, the citie of palme
trees vnto Zoar.

4 And the LORD ſaid vnto him,
*This is the land which I ſware vnto
Abraham, vnto Iſaac, and vnto Ia-
cob, ſaying, I will giue it vnto thy ſeed :
I haue cauſed thee to ſee it with thine
eyes, but thou ſhalt not go ouer thither.

* Gen. 12. 7
and 13. 15.

5 ¶ So Moſes the ſeruant of the
LORD died there in the land of Moab,
according to the word of the LORD.

6 And

6 And hee buried him in a valley in the land of Moab, ouer against Beth-Peor: but no man knoweth of his Sepulchre vnto this day

7 ¶ And Moses was an hundred and twentie yeeres olde when he died: his eye was not dimme, nor his †naturall force †abated.

† Hebr. moisture.
† Hebr. fled.

8 ¶ And the children of Israel wept for Moses in the plaines of Moab thirty dayes : So the dayes of weeping *and* mourning for Moses were ended.

9 ¶ And Ioshua the sonne of Nun *was* full of the Spirit of wisedome : for Moses had layd his handes vpon him, and the children of Israel hearkened vnto him, and did as the Lᴏʀᴅ commanded Moses.

10 ¶ And there arose not a Prophet since in Israel like vnto Moses, whom the Lᴏʀᴅ knew face to face :

11 In al the signes and the wonders which the Lᴏʀᴅ sent him to doe in the land of Egypt, to Pharaoh, and to all his seruants, and to all his land,

12 And in all that mighty hand, and in all the great terrour, which Moses shewed in the sight of all Israel.

¶ THE BOOKE OF
Ioshua.

CHAP. I.

1 The Lᴏʀᴅ appointeth Ioshua to succeede Moses. 3 The borders of the promised land. 5. 9 God promiseth to assist Ioshua. 8 He giueth him instructions. 10 He prepareth the people to passe ouer Iordan. 12 Ioshua putteth the two tribes and halfe in minde of their promise to Moses. 16 They promise him fealty.

Owe after the death of Moses the seruant of the Lᴏʀᴅ, it came to passe, that the Lᴏʀᴅ spake vnto Ioshua the sonne of Nun, Moses * minister, saying,

* Deut. 1. 38.

2 Moses my seruant is dead : now therefore arise, goe ouer this Iordan, thou, and all this people, vnto the land which I doe giue to them, *euen* to the children of Israel.

3 * Euery place that the sole of your foote shall tread vpon, that haue I giuen vnto you, as I said vnto Moses.

* Deut. 11. 24. chap. 14. 9.

4 From the wildernesse and this Lebanon, euen vnto the great Riuer, the riuer Euphrates, all the land of the Hittites, and vnto the great sea, toward the going downe of the Sunne, shalbe your coast.

5 There shall not any man be able to stand before thee all the dayes of thy life : as I was with Moses, *so* I will be with thee : * I will not faile thee, nor forsake thee.

* Heb. 13. 6.

6 * Bee strong, and of a good courage : for ‖ vnto this people shalt thou diuide for an inheritance the land which I sware vnto their fathers to giue them.

* Deut. 31. 23.
‖ Or, thou sholt cause this people to inherite the land, &c.

7 Onely bee thou strong, and very courageous, that thou mayest obserue to doe according to all the Law, which Moses my seruant commaunded thee : * turne not from it to the right hand, or to the left, that thou mayest ‖ prosper whither soeuer thou goest.

* Deu. 5. 32 and 28. 14.
‖ Or, doe wisely.

8 This booke of the Law shal not depart out of thy mouth, but thou shalt meditate therein day and night, that thou mayest obserue to doe according to all that is written therein : for then thou shalt make thy way prosperous, and then thou shalt ‖ haue good successe.

‖ Or, doe wisely.

9 Haue not I commanded thee ? be strong, and of a good courage, bee not afraid, neither be thou dismayed : for the Lᴏʀᴅ thy God *is* with thee, whither soeuer thou goest.

10 ¶ Then

10 ¶ Then Ioshua commanded the Officers of the people, saying,

11 Passe through the hoste, and command the people, saying, Prepare you victuals: for within three dayes ye shal passe ouer this Iordan, to goe in to possesse the land which the LORD your God giueth you, to possesse it.

12 ¶ And to the Reubenites, and to the Gadites, and to halfe the tribe of Manasseh, spake Ioshua, saying,

13 *Remember the word which Moses the seruant of the LORD commanded you, saying, The LORD your God hath giuen you rest, and hath giuen you this land:

14 Your wiues, your litle ones, and your cattell shall remaine in the lande which Moses gaue you on this side Iordan; but ye shall passe before your brethren † armed, all the mightie men of valour, and helpe them:

15 Vntill the LORD haue giuen your brethren rest, as *he hath giuen* you, and they also haue possessed the lande which the LORD your God giueth them · then yee shall returne vnto the land of your possession, and enioy it, which Moses the LORDS seruant gaue you on this side Iordan toward the Sunne rising.

16 ¶ And they answered Ioshua, saying, All that thou commandest vs, we will doe, and whither soeuer thou sendest vs, we will goe.

17 According as we hearkened vnto Moses in all things, so will we hearken vnto thee: onely the LORD thy God be with thee, as he was with Moses.

18 Whosoeuer he be that doth rebell against thy commandement, and will not hearken vnto thy words, in all that thou commandest him, he shall bee put to death: onely be strong, and of a good courage.

CHAP. II.

1 Rahab receiueth and concealeth the two spies sent from Shittim. 8 The couenant betweene her and them. 23 Their returne and relation.

Nd Ioshua the sonne of Nun sent out of Shittim two men, to spie secretly, saying, Go, view the land, euen Iericho: and they went, and *came into an harlots house, named Rahab, and † lodged there.

2 And it was told the king of Iericho, saying, Behold, there came men in hither to night, of the children of Israel, to search out the countrey.

3 And the king of Iericho sent vnto Rahab, saying, Bring forth the men that are come to thee, which are entred into thine house: for they bee come to search out all the countrey.

4 And the woman tooke the two men, and hid them, & said thus: There came men vnto mee, but I wist not whence they were:

5 And it came to passe *about the time* of shutting of the gate, when it was darke, that the men went out: whither the men went, I wote not: pursue after them quickely, for ye shall ouertake them.

6 But shee had brought them vp to the roofe of the house, and hid them with the stalkes of flaxe, which she had laid in order vpon the roofe.

7 And the men pursued after them the way to Iordan, vnto the foords: and assoone as they which pursued after them were gone out, they shut the gate.

8 ¶ And before they were laide downe, shee came vp vnto them vpon the roofe.

9 And she said vnto the men, I know that the LORD hath giuen you the land, and that your terrour is fallen vpon vs, and that all the inhabitants of the land † faint because of you.

10 For wee haue heard how the LORD *dried vp the water of the red Sea for you, when you came out of Egypt, and what you did vnto the two kings of the Amorites that *were* on the other side Iordan, *Sihon and Og, whom ye vtterly destroyed.

11 And assoone as we had heard *these things*, our hearts did melt, neither did there †remaine any more courage in any man, because of you: for the LORD your God, he is God in heauen aboue, and in earth beneath.

12 Now therfore, I pray you, sweare vnto me by the LORD, since I haue shewed you kindnesse, that ye will also shew kindnesse vnto my fathers house, and giue me a true token:

13 And that ye will saue aliue my father, and my mother, and my brethren, and my sisters, and all that they haue, and deliuer our liues from death.

14 And the men answered her, Our life † for yours, if yee vtter not this our businesse. And it shall bee when the LORD

---

* Num. 32 20.

* Heb. marshalled by fiue.

† Heb. melt.

* Exod. 14 21. chap. 4. 23.

* Num. 21 24.

† Heb. rose vp.

* Heb. 11. 31. iam. 2. 25.

† Heb. lay.

† Hebr. in stead of you to die.

LORD hath giuen vs the land, that wee will deale kindely and truely with thee.

15 Then ſhee let them downe by a coard thorow the window : for her house *was* vpon the towne wall, and she dwelt vpon the wall.

16 And she said vnto them, Get you to the mountaine, lest the pursuers meete you ; and hide your ſelues there three dayes, vntill the pursuers bee returned, and afterward may ye goe your way.

17 And the men said vnto her, Wee will bee blamelesse of this thine oath which thou hast made vs sweare :

18 Behold, when we come into the land, thou shalt binde this line of scarlet threed in the window which thou didst let vs downe by : and thou shalt †bring thy father and thy mother, and thy brethren, and all thy fathers houshold home vnto thee.   †*Hebr. gather.*

19 And it shall bee, that whosoeuer shall goe out of the doores of thy house into the street, his blood *shalbe* vpon his head, and wee will bee guiltlesse : and whosoeuer shall bee with thee in the house, his blood *shalbe* on our head, if *any* hand be vpon him.

20 And if thou vtter this our businesse, then we wilbe quit of thine oath which thou hast made vs to sweare.

21 And ſhee saide, According vnto your words, so be it. And she sent them away, & they departed : and she bound the scarlet line in the window.

22 And they went, and came vnto the mountaine, and abode there three dayes, vntill the pursuers were returned. And the pursuers sought *them* thorowout all the way, but found them not.

23 ¶ So the two men returned, and descended from the mountaine, and passed ouer, and came to Ioshua the ſonne of Nun, and told him all things that befell them.

24 And they saide vnto Ioshua, Truely the LORD hath deliuered into our hands all the land ; for euen all the inhabitants of the countrey doe †faint because of vs.   †*Hebr. melt.*

CHAP. III.

1 Ioshua commeth to Iordan. 2 The Officers instruct the people for the passage. 7 The LORD incourageth Ioshua. 9 Ioshua incourageth the people. 14 The waters of Iordan are diuided.

Nd Ioshua rose early in the morning, and they remooued from Shittim, and came to Iordan, hee and all the children of Iſrael, and lodged there before they paſſed ouer.

2 And it came to passe after three dayes, that the Officers went thorow the hoste ;

3 And they commanded the people, saying, When ye see the Arke of the Couenant of the LORD your God, and the Priests the Leuites bearing it, then yee shall remooue from your place, and goe after it.

4 Yet there shalbe a space betweene you and it, about two thousand cubites by measure : come not neere vnto it, that ye may know the way by which ye must goe : for yee haue not passed *this* way † heretofore.   †*Hebr. since yesterday & the third day.*

5 And Ioshua said vnto the people, * Sanctifie your ſelues : for to morrow the LORD wil do wōders among you.   * *Leuit. 20. 7. num. 11. 18. chap. 7. 13. 1. sam. 16. 5.*

6 And Ioshua spake vnto the Priests, saying, Take vp the Arke of the Couenant, and passe ouer before the people. And they tooke vp the Arke of the Couenant, and went before the people.

7 ¶ And the LORD saide vnto Ioshua, This day wil I begin to magnifie thee in the sight of all Israel, that they may know that * as I was with Moses, *so* I will be with thee.   * *Chap. 1. 5.*

8 And thou shalt commaund the Priests that beare the Arke of the Couenant, saying ; When ye are come to the brinke of the water of Iordan, yee shall stand still in Iordan.

9 ¶ And Ioshua said vnto the children of Israel, Come hither, and heare the words of the LORD your God.

10 And Ioshua saide, Hereby ye shall know that the liuing God is among you, and that he will without faile driue out from before you the Canaanites, and the Hittites, and the Hiuites, and the Perizzites, and Girgashites, and the Amorites, and the Iebusites.

11 Behold, the Arke of the Couenant, euen the Lord of all the earth, passeth ouer before you, into Iordan.

12 Now therefore take yee twelue men out of the Tribes of Israel, out of euery Tribe a man.

13 And

13 And it shall come to passe, assoone as the soles of the feete of the Priestes that beare the Arke of the LORD, the Lord of all the earth, shall rest in the waters of Iordan, *that* the waters of Iordan shall be cut off, *from* the waters that come downe from aboue: and they * shall stand vpon an heape.

14 ¶ And it came to passe when the people remooued from their tents, to passe ouer Iordan, and the Priests bearing the *Arke of the Couenant before the people;

15 And as they that bare the Arke were come vnto Iordan, and the feet of the Priestes that bare the Arke, were dipped in the brimme of the water, (for * Iordan ouerfloweth all his banks at the time of haruest)

16 That the waters which came downe from aboue, stood *and* rose vp vpon an heape very farre, from the city Adam, that *is* beside Zaretan: and those that came downe toward the sea of the plaine, *euen* the salt sea, failed, *and* were cut off: and the people passed ouer right against Iericho.

17 And the Priestes that bare the Arke of the Couenant of the LORD, stood firme on drie ground, in the midst of Iordan, and all the Israelites passed ouer on drie ground, vntill all the people were passed cleane ouer Iordan.

CHAP. IIII.

1 Twelue men are appointed to take twelue stones for a memoriall out of Iordan. 9 Twelue other stones are set vp in the middest of Iordan. 10. 19 The people passe ouer. 14 God magnifieth Ioshua. 20 The twelue stones are pitched in Gilgal.

Nd it came to passe when all the people were cleane passed * ouer Iordan, that the LORD spake vnto * Ioshua, saying,

2 Take you twelue men out of the people, out of euery tribe a man,

3 And command you them, saying, Take you hence out of the mids of Iordan, out of the place where the Priests feet stood firme, twelue stones, and yee shal cary them ouer with you, and leaue them in the lodging place where you shall lodge this night.

4 Then Ioshua called the twelue men, whom he had prepared of the children of Israel, out of euery tribe a man:

5 And Ioshua said vnto them, Passe ouer before the Arke of the LORD your God into the mids of Iordan, and take ye vp euery man of you a stone vpon his shoulder, according vnto the number of the tribes of the children of Israel:

6 That this may be a signe among you, *that* when your children aske their fathers †in time to come, saying, What meane you by these stones?

7 Then yee shall answere them, That the waters of Iordan were cut off before the Arke of the Couenant of the LORD, when it passed ouer Iordan, the waters of Iordan were cut off: and these stones shall bee for a memoriall vnto the children of Israel for euer.

8 And the children of Israel did so as Ioshua commanded, and tooke vp twelue stones out of the midst of Iordan, as the LORD spake vnto Ioshua, according to the number of the tribes of the children of Israel, and caried them ouer with them, vnto the place where they lodged, and laid them downe there.

9 And Ioshua set vp twelue stones in the midst of Iordan, in the place where the feet of the Priests which bare the Arke of the Couenant, stood: and they are there vnto this day.

10 ¶ For the Priests which bare the Arke, stood in the midst of Iordan, vntill euery thing was finished that the LORD commanded Ioshua to speake vnto the people, according to all that Moses commanded Ioshua : and the people hasted and passed ouer.

11 And it came to passe when all the people were cleane passed ouer, that the Arke of the LORD passed ouer, and the Priests in the presence of the people.

12 And *the children of Reuben, and the children of Gad, and halfe the tribe of Manasseh, passed ouer armed before the children of Israel, as Moses spake vnto them:

13 About fourty thousand ‖ prepared for war, passed ouer before the LORD vnto battell, to the plaines of Iericho.

14 ¶ On that day the LORD magnified Ioshua in the sight of all Israel, and they feared him, as they feared Moses all the dayes of his life.

15 And the LORD spake vnto Ioshua, saying,

16 Command the Priests that beare the

---

*Psal. 114. 3.

*Acts 7. 45

*1. Chron. 12. 15. ecclus. 24. 30.

*Deut. 27. 2.
*Chap. 3. 12.

† Heb. to morow.

*Num. 32. 27.

‖ Or, ready armed.

the Arke of the Testimony, that they come vp out of Iordan.

17 Ioſhua therefore commaunded the Priests, saying, Come yee vp out of Iordan.

18 And it came to paſſe when the Priests that bare the Arke of the Couenant of the LORD, were come vp out of the mids of Iordan, *and* the soles of the Priests feete were †lift vp vnto the dry land, that the waters of Iordan returned vnto their place, and †flowed ouer all his banks, as they did before.

†Hebr. plucked vp.

†Hebr. went.

19 ¶ And the people came vp out of Iordan on the tenth day of the first moneth, and encamped in Gilgal, in the East border of Iericho.

20 And those twelue stones which they tooke out of Iordan, did Ioſhua pitch in Gilgal.

21 And he spake vnto the children of Israel, saying, When your children shal aske their fathers †in time to come, saying, What meane these stones?

†Hebr. to morrow.

22 Then yee shall let your children know, saying, Israel came ouer this Iordan on dry land.

23 For the LORD your God dried vp the waters of Iordan from before you, vntill yee were passed ouer, as the LORD your God did to the Red sea, *which hee dried vp from before vs, vntill we were gone ouer:

*Exod. 14. 21.

24 That all the people of the earth might know the hand of the LORD, that it *is* mighty, that ye might feare the LORD your God †for euer.

†Hebr. all dayes.

CHAP. V.

1 The Canaanites are afraid. 2 Ioſhua renueth Circumcision. 10 The Passeouer is kept at Gilgal. 12 Manna ceaseth. 13 An Angel appeareth to Ioſhua.

A Nd it came to paſſe when all the Kings of the Amorites which were on the side of Iordan Westward, and all the Kings of the Canaanites, which were by the Sea, heard that the LORD had dried vp the waters of Iordan from before the children of Israel, vntil we were passed ouer, that their heart melted; neither was there spirit in them any more, because of the children of Israel.

2 ¶ At that time the LORD said vnto Ioſhua, *Make thee || sharpe kniues, and circumcise againe the children of Israel the second time.

*Exod. 4. 25.
§ Or, kniues of flints.

3 And Ioſhua made him sharpe kniues, and circumcised the children of Israel at || the hill of the foreskinnes.

||Or, Gibeah-hagraloth.

4 And this is the cause why Ioſhua did circumcise: all the people that came out of Egypt, that *were* males, *euen* all the men of warre, died in the wildernes by the way after·they came out of Egypt.

5 Now all the people that came out, were circumcised, but all the people that were borne in the wildernesse by the way, as they came foorth out of Egypt, *them* they had not circumcised.

6 For the children of Israel walked fourtie yeeres in the wildernesse, till all the people *that were* men of warre which came out of Egypt were consumed, because they obeyed not the voyce of the LORD, vnto whome the LORD sware that hee *would not shew them the land which the LORD sware vnto their fathers, that he would giue vs, a land that floweth with milke & honie.

*Num. 14. 23.

7 And their children, *whom* hee raised vp in their stead, them Ioſhua circumcised, for they were vncircumcised: because they had not circumcised them by the way.

8 And it came to paſſe †when they had done circumcising all the people, that they abode in their places in the campe, till they were whole.

†Heb. when the people had made an end to be circumcised.

9 And the LORD saide vnto Ioſhua, This day haue I rolled away the reproch of Egypt from off you: Wherefore the name of the place is called ||Gilgal vnto this day.

|| i. rolling.

10 ¶ And the children of Israel incamped in Gilgal, and kept the Passeouer, on the fourteenth day of the moneth at euen, in the plaines of Iericho.

11 And they did eate of the olde corne of the land, on the morrow after the Passeouer, vnleauened cakes, and parched *corne* in the selfe same day.

12 ¶ And the Manna ceased on the morrow after they had eaten of the old corne of the land, neither had the children of Israel Manna any more, but they did eate of the fruit of the land of Canaan that yeere.

13 ¶ And it came to paſſe when Ioſhua was by Iericho, that he lift vp his eyes, and looked, and beholde, there stood *a man ouer against him, with his sword dawen in his hand: and Ioſhua went vnto him, and said vnto him, Art thou for vs, or for our aduersaries?

*Exod. 23. 23.

14 And

‖ *Or, Prince.*

14 And he said, Nay, but *as* ‖ captaine of the hoste of the LORD am I now come. And Ioshua fell on his face to the earth, and did worship, and said vnto him, What saith my Lord vnto his seruant?

* Exod. 3. 5.
cts. 7. 33.

15 And the captaine of the LORDS hoste said vnto Ioshua, * Loose thy shooe from off thy foote, for the place whereon thou standest, is holy: And Ioshua did so.

CHAP. VI.

1 Iericho is shut vp. 2 God instructeth Ioshua how to besiege it. 12 The citie is compassed. 17 It must be accursed. 20 The walles fall downe. 22 Rahab is saued. 26 The builder of Iericho is cursed.

*Hebr. did
shut vp, and
was shut vp.*

OW Iericho † was straitly shut vp, because of the children of Israel : none went out, & none came in.

2 And the LORD said vnto Ioshua, See, I haue giuen into thine hand Iericho, and the King thereof, *and* the mighty men of valour.

3 And ye shall compasse the city, all *yee* men of warre, *and* goe round about the city once : thus shalt thou doe sixe dayes.

4 And seuen Priests shall beare before the Arke seuen trumpets of rams hornes : and the seuenth day yee shall compasse the city seuen times, and the Priests shall blow with the trumpets.

5 And it shall come to passe that when they make a long *blast* with the rammes-horne, *and* when ye heare the sound of the trumpet, all the people shall shout with a great shout: and the wall of the citie shall fall downe † flat, and the people shall ascend vp euery man straight before him.

*Hebr. vn-
er it.*

6 ¶ And Ioshua the sonne of Nun called the Priests, and said vnto them, Take vp the Arke of the Couenant, and let seuen Priests beare seuen trumpets of rammes-hornes, before the Arke of the LORD.

7 And he said vnto the people, Passe on, and compasse the city, and let him that is armed passe on before the Arke of the LORD.

8 ¶ And it came to passe when Ioshua had spoken vnto the people, that the seuen Priestes bearing the seuen trumpets of rammes hornes, passed on before the LORD, and blew with the

trumpets : and the Arke of the Couenant of the LORD followed them.

9 ¶ And the armed men went before the Priests that blew with the trumpets : and the † rereward came after the Arke, *the Priests* going on, and blowing with the trumpets.

† Heb. ga-
thering host

10 And Ioshua had commanded the people, saying, Ye shall not shout, nor † make any noise with your voice, neither shall any word proceed out of your mouth, vntill the day I bid you shoute, then shall ye shoute.

† Heb. make
your voyce
to be heard.

11 So the Arke of the LORD compassed the citie, going about *it* once : and they came into the campe, and lodged in the campe.

12 ¶ And Ioshua rose earely in the morning, and the Priests tooke vp the Arke of the LORD.

13 And seuen Priests bearing seuen trumpets of rammes hornes before the Arke of the LORD, went on continually, and blew with the trumpets : and the armed men went before them, but the rereward came after the Arke of the LORD, *the Priests* going on and blowing with the trumpets.

14 And the second day they compassed the citie once, and returned into the campe : so they did six dayes.

15 And it came to passe on the seuenth day, that they rose early about the dawning of the day, and compassed the citie after the same maner, seuen times : only on that day they compassed the citie seuen times.

16 And it came to passe at the seuenth time, when the Priests blewe with the trumpets, Ioshua said vnto the people, Shout, for the LORD hath giuen you the citie.

17 ¶ And the citie shalbe ‖ accursed, *euen* it, and all that *are* therein, to the LORD : onely Rahab the harlot shal liue, she, and all that *are* with her in the house, because * she hid the messengers that we sent.

‖ Or, deuo-
ted.

* Chap. 2. 4

18 And you, in any wise keepe your selues from the accursed thing, lest yee make your selues accursed, when yee take of the accursed thing, and make the campe of Israel a curse, and trouble it.

19 But all the siluer, and gold, and vessels of brasse and yron, are † consecrated vnto the LORD : they shall come into the treasurie of the LORD.

† Hebr.
holinesse.

20 So the people shouted when the Priests blew with the trumpets: and it came

came to passe when the people heard
the sound of the trumpet, and the people shouted with a great shout, that * the
wall fell downe † flat, so that the people went vp into the citie, euery man
straight before him, and they tooke the
citie.

* Heb. 11. 30.
† Hebr. vnder it.

21 And they vtterly destroyed all
that was in the city, both man and woman, yong and old, and oxe, and sheepe,
and asse, with the edge of the sword.

22 But Ioshua had said vnto the
two men that had spied out the countrey; Goe into the harlots house, and
bring out thence the woman and all
that she hath, * as ye sware vnto her.

* Chap. 2. 14. heb. 11. 31.

23 And the yong men that were
spies, went in, and brought out Rahab,
and her father, and her mother, and her
brethren, and all that she had: and they
brought out all her † kinred, and left
them without the campe of Israel.

† Hebr. families.

24 And they burnt the city with fire,
and all that was therein: onely the siluer & the gold, and the vessels of brasse
and of yron, they put into the Treasury
of the house of the Lord

25 And Ioshua saued Rahab the
harlot aliue, and her fathers houshold,
and all that she had: and she dwelleth
in Israel euen vnto this day, because
she hid the messengers which Ioshua
sent to spy out Iericho

26 ¶ And Ioshua adiured *them* at
that time, saying, * Cursed be the man
before the Lord, that riseth vp and
buildeth this city Iericho: he shall lay
the foundation therof in his first borne,
and in his yongest *sonne* shall hee set vp
the gates of it.

* 1. King. 16. 34.

27 So the Lord was with Io-
shua, and his fame was noised throughout all the countrey.

CHAP. VII.

1 The Israelites are smitten at Ai. 6 Ioshuas complaint. 10 God instructeth him what to doe. 16 Achan is taken by the Lot. 19 His confession. 22 Hee and all he had are destroyed in the valley of Achor.

BVt the children of Israel
committed a trespasse in
the accursed thing: for * A-
chan the sonne of Carmi,
the sonne of Zabdi, the
sonne of Zerah, of the tribe of Iudah,
tooke of the accursed thing: and the
anger of the Lord was kindled
against the children of Israel.

* Chap. 22. 20. 1. chron. 2. 7.

2 And Ioshua sent men from Iericho to Ai, which is beside Beth-auen,
on the East side of Bethel, and spake
vnto them, saying, Goe vp and view
the countrey And the men went vp,
and viewed Ai.

3 And they returned to Ioshua,
and said vnto him, Let not all the people goe vp: but let † about two or three
thousand men goe vp, and smite Ai,
and make not all the people to labour
thither, for they are but few.

† Heb. about 2000. men: or, about 3000. men.

4 So there went vp thither of the
people about three thousand men, and
they fled before the men of Ai.

5 And the men of Ai smote of them
about thirty and sixe men: for they chased them *from* before the gate euen vnto
Shebarim, and smote them in the ‖ going downe: Wherefore the hearts of
the people melted, & became as water.

‖ Or, in Morad.

6 ¶ And Ioshua rent his clothes,
and fell to the earth vpon his face, before the Arke of the Lord, vntill the
euentide, he and the Elders of Israel,
and put dust vpon their heads.

7 And Ioshua said, Alas, O Lord
God, wherefore hast thou at all
brought this people ouer Iordan, to
deliuer vs into the hand of the Amorites, to destroy vs? Would to God we
had bene content, and dwelt on the o-
ther side Iordan.

8 Oh Lord! what shall I say,
when Israel turneth their † backes before their enemies?

† Hebr neckes.

9 For the Canaanites, and all the
inhabitants of the land shall heare *of it*,
and shall enuiron vs round, and cut off
our name from the earth: and what
wilt thou doe vnto thy great Name?

10 ¶ And the Lord saide vnto
Ioshua, Get thee vp; wherefore † liest
thou thus vpon thy face?

† Heb. falles

11 Israel hath sinned, and they haue
also transgressed my Couenant which
I commaunded them: for they haue e-
uen taken of the accursed thing, and
haue also stollen, and dissembled also,
and they haue put it euen amongst their
owne stuffe.

12 Therefore the children of Israel
could not stand before their enemies;
but turned their backes before their enemies, because they were accursed: neither will I bee with you any more, except yee destroy the accursed from a-
mongst you

13 Vp,

13 Vp, sanctifie the people, and say, Sanctifie your selues against to morrow: for thus saith the LORD God of Israel, *There is* an accursed thing in the midst of thee, O Israel: thou canst not stand before thine enemies, vntill ye take away the accursed thing from among you.

14 In the morning therefore ye shal be brought, according to your tribes: and it shall be that the tribe which the LORD taketh, shall come according to the families *thereof*, and the familie which the LORD shall take, shal come by housholdes: and the housholdes which the LORD shall take, shal come man by man.

15 And it shalbe that he that is taken with the accursed thing, shall bee burnt with fire, he, and all that he hath: because he hath transgressed the couenant of the LORD, and because hee hath wrought ||folly in Israel.

|| Or, wickednesse.

16 ¶ So Ioshua rose vp earely in the morning, and brought Israel by their tribes, and the tribe of Iudah was taken.

17 And hee brought the familie of Iudah, and he tooke the familie of the Zarhites: and he brought the familie of the Zarhites, man by man, and Zabdi was taken.

18 And hee brought his houshold, man by man, and Achan the sonne of Carmi, the sonne of Zabdi, the sonne of Zerah, of the tribe of Iudah, was taken.

19 And Ioshua said vnto Achan, My sonne, giue, I pray thee, glory to the LORD God of Israel, and make confession vnto him, and tel me now, what thou hast done, hide it not from me.

20 And Achan answered Ioshua, and said, Indeed I haue sinned against the LORD God of Israel, and thus and thus haue I done.

21 When I saw among the spoiles a goodly Babylonish garment, and two hundred shekels of siluer, and a †wedge of gold of fiftie shekels weight, then I coueted them, and tooke them, and behold, they are hid in the earth in the midst of my tent, and the siluer vnder it.

†Heb.tongue

22 ¶ So Ioshua sent messengers, and they ran vnto the tent, and behold, it was hid in his tent, and the siluer vnder it.

23 And they tooke them out of the midst of the tent, and brought them vnto Ioshua, and vnto all the children of Israel, and †laid them out before the LORD.

† Heb. powred.

24 And Ioshua and all Israel with him tooke Achan the sonne of Zerah, and the siluer, and the garment, and the wedge of golde, and his sonnes, and his daughters, and his oxen, and his asses, and his sheepe, and his tent, and all that he had: and they brought them vnto the valley of Achor.

25 And Ioshua said, Why hast thou troubled vs? the LORD shall trouble thee this day. And all Israel stoned him with stones, and burned them with fire, after they had stoned them with stones.

26 And they raised ouer him a great heape of stones vnto this day: so the LORD turned from the fiercenesse of his anger: Wherefore the name of the place was called, The valley of ||Achor, vnto this day.

|| That is, trouble.

CHAP. VIII.

1 God incourageth Ioshua. 3 The stratageme whereby Ai was taken. 29 The king thereof is hanged. 30 Ioshua buildeth an Altar, 32 writeth the Lawe on stones, 33 propoundeth blessings and cursings.

A Nd the LORD said vnto Ioshua, *Feare not, neither be thou dismaid: take all the people of warre with thee, and arise, goe vp to Ai: See, I haue giuen into thy hand the king of Ai, and his people, and his citie, and his land.

* Deut. 1. 21. & 7. 18.

2 And thou shalt doe to Ai and her king, as thou diddest vnto * Iericho and her king: Onely the spoile thereof and *the cattell thereof shall ye take for a pray vnto your selues: lay thee an ambush for the citie, behind it.

*Chap. 6. 21

* Deut. 20 14.

3 ¶ So Ioshua arose, and all the people of warre, to goe vp against Ai: and Ioshua chose out thirtie thousand mighty men of valour, and sent them away by night:

4 And he commanded them, saying, Behold, ye shall lie in wait against the citie, *euen* behind the citie: goe not very farre from the citie, but be ye all ready:

5 And I, and all the people that are with mee, will approch vnto the citie: and it shall come to passe when they come out against vs, as at the first, that we will flee before them,

6 (For

6 (For they will come out after vs)
till we haue †drawen them from the citie; for they will say, They flee before
vs, as at the first : therefore we will flee
before them.

† Hebr. pul-led.

7 Then yee shall rise vp from the
ambush, and seise vpon the citie : for the
LORD your God will deliuer it into
your hand.

8 And it shall be when yee haue taken the citie, that ye shall set the citie on
fire : according to the commandement
of the LORD shall ye do. See, I haue
commanded you.

9 ¶ Ioshua therefore sent them
foorth, and they went to lie in ambush,
and abode betweene Bethel and Ai, on
the West side of Ai : but Ioshua lodged
that night among the people.

10 And Ioshua rose vp early in the
morning, and numbred the people, and
went vp; he, and the Elders of Israel,
before the people to Ai.

11 And all the people, *euen the people*
of warre that were with him, went vp,
and drew nigh, and came before the city,
and pitched on the North side of Ai :
now there was a valley betweene them
and Ai.

12 And he tooke about fiue thousand
men, and set them to lye in ambush betweene Bethel and Ai, on the West side
||of the citie.

|| Or, of Ai.

13 And when they had set the people,
euen all the hoste that was on the North
of the city, and their †liers in wait on the
West of the citie : Ioshua went th :
night into the midst of the valley.

† Hebr. their lyinginwait.

14 ¶ And it came to passe when the
King of Ai saw it, that they hasted, and
rose vp early, and the men of the citie
went out against Israel to battell, hee,
and all his people, at a time appointed,
before the plaine, but hee wist not that
there were liers in ambush against him
behind the city.

15 And Ioshua and all Israel made
as if they were beaten before them, and
fled by the way of the wildernesse.

16 And all the people that were in
Ai, were called together to pursue after
them : and they pursued after Ioshua,
and were drawen away from the city.

17 And there was not a man left in
Ai or Bethel, that went not out after
Israel : and they left the citie open, and
pursued after Israel.

18 And the LORD said vnto Ioshua, Stretch out the speare that is in
thy hand, toward Ai ; for I will giue it
into thine hand. And Ioshua stretched
out the speare that hee had in his hand,
toward the city.

19 And the ambush arose quickly
out of their place, and they ranne as
soone as he had stretched out his hand :
and they entred into the city, and tooke
it, and hasted, and set the citie on fire.

20 And when the men of Ai looked
behind them, they saw, and behold, the
smoke of the city ascended vp to heauen, and they had no †power to flee this
way or that way : and the people that
fled to the wildernesse, turned backe vpon the pursuers.

† Heb. hand.

21 And when Ioshua and all Israel saw that the ambush had taken the
city, and that the smoke of the city ascended, then they turned againe and slew
the men of Ai.

22 And the other issued out of the citie against them, so they were in the
midst of Israel ; some on this side, and
some on that side, and they smote them ;
so that they * let none of them remaine
or escape.

* Deut. 7. 2.

23 And the King of Ai they tooke a-
liue, and brought him to Ioshua.

24 And it came to passe when Israel had made an end of slaying all the
inhabitants of Ai, in the field, in the wildernesse wherein they chased them, and
when they were all fallen on the edge of
the sword, vntill they were consumed,
that all the Israelites returned vnto
Ai, and smote it with the edge of the
sword.

25 And so it was that all that fell
that day, both of men and women, *were*
twelue thousand, *euen* all the men of Ai.

26 For Ioshua drew not his hand
backe wherewith hee stretched out the
speare, vntill he had vtterly destroyed
all the inhabitants of Ai.

27 * Onely the cattell, and the spoile
of that city Israel tooke for a pray vnto
themselues, according vnto the word of
the LORD, which he * commaunded
Ioshua.

* Num. 31. 22, 26.

* Verse 2.

28 And Ioshua burnt Ai, and made
it an heape for euer, *euen* a desolation
vnto this day.

29 And the king of Ai he hanged on
a tree vntil euentide : and assoone as the
sunne was downe, Ioshua commaunded that they should take his carkeise
downe from the tree, and cast it at the
entring of the gate of the citie, and *raise
thereon

* Chap. 7. 25.

thereon a great heape of stones *that re-maineth* vnto this day.

30 ¶ Then Ioshua built an Altar vnto the LORD God of Israel in mount Ebal,

Exod. 20.
. deut.
. 5.

31 As Moses the seruant of the LORD commaunded the children of Israel, as it is written in the *booke of the Law of Moses, an Altar of whole stones, ouer which no man hath lift vp any yron : and they offred theron burnt offerings vnto the LORD, and sacrificed peace offerings.

32 ¶ And he wrote there vpon the stones a copie of the Lawe of Moses, which hee wrote in the presence of the children of Israel.

33 And all Israel, and their Elders, and Officers, and their Iudges, stood on this side the Arke, and on that side, before the Priests the Leuites, which bare the Arke of the Couenant of the LORD, aswell the stranger, as he that was borne among them : halfe of them ouer against mount Gerizim, and halfe of them ouer against mount Ebal, *as Moses the seruant of the LORD had commanded before, that they should blesse the people of Israel.

Deut. 11.
. & 27. 12

34 And afterward hee read all the words of the Law , the blessings and cursings, according to all that is written in the booke of the Law

35 There was not a word of all that Moses commanded , which Ioshua read not before all the Congregation of Israel, *with the women and the litle ones, and the strangers that †were conuersant among them

Deut. 31.
2.
Hebr.
alked.

CHAP. IX.

1 *The kings combine against Israel.* 3 *The Gibeonites by craft obtaine a League.* 16 *For which they are condemned to perpetual bondage.*

ANd it came to passe when all the kings which were on this side Iordan in the hilles, and in the valleys, and in all the coasts of the great sea , ouer against Lebanon, the Hittite, and the Amorite , the Canaanite, the Perizzite, the Hiuite, and the Iebusite heard *thereof*:

2 That gathered themselues together to fight with Ioshua , and with Israel, with one †accord.

Heb.mouth

3 ¶ And when the inhabitants of Gibeon heard what Ioshua had done vnto Iericho, and to Ai,

4 They did worke wilily, and went and made as if they had beene embassadours, and tooke old sackes vpon their asses, and wine-bottels, old, and rent, and bound vp,

5 And old shooes and clowted vpon their feet, & olde garments vpon them, and all the bread of their prouision was drie and mouldie.

6 And they went to Ioshua vnto the campe at Gilgal, and said vnto him, and to the men of Israel, Wee be come from a farre countrey : Now therefore make ye a league with vs.

7 And the men of Israel said vnto the Hiuites, Peraduenture yee dwell among vs, and how shall wee make a league with you ?

8 And they said vnto Ioshua, Wee *are* thy seruants. And Ioshua said vnto them, Who are ye ? and from whence come ye ?

9 And they said vnto him, From a very farre countrey thy seruants are come , because of the Name of the LORD thy God : for wee haue heard the fame of him, and all that hee did in Egypt,

10 And all that hee did to the two kings of the Amorites, that were beyond Iordan, to Sihon king of Heshbon, and to Og king of Bashan, which *was* at Ashtaroth.

11 Wherefore our Elders and all the inhabitants of our countrey, spake to vs, saying, Take victuals † with you for the iourney, and goe to meete them, and say vnto them, Wee *are* your seruants : therefore now make ye a league with vs.

† Hebr. in
your hand.

12 This our bread, wee tooke hote for our prouision out of our houses, on the day we came forth to goe vnto you : but now behold, it is dry, & it is mouldy.

13 And these bottels of wine which we filled, *were* new, and behold, they be rent : and these our garments, and our shooes are become old, by reason of the very long iourney.

14 And ||the men tooke of their victuals , and asked not counsell at the mouth of the LORD.

|| Or, they re-ceiued the
men by rea-son of their
victuals.

15 And Ioshua made peace with them, and made a league with them, to let them liue : and the princes of the Congregation sware vnto them.

16 ¶ And it came to passe at the end of

of three dayes, after they had made a league with them, that they heard that they *were* their neighbours, and that they dwelt among them.

17 And the children of Israel iourneyed, and came vnto their cities on the third day : now their cities were Gibeon, and Chephirah, and Beeroth, and Kiriath - iearim.

18 And the children of Israel smote them not, because the Princes of the Congregation had sworne vnto them by the LORD God of Israel : And all the Congregation murmured against the Princes.

19 But all the Princes said vnto all the Congregation, We haue sworne vnto them by the LORD God of Israel : now therefore we may not touch them.

20 This we will doe to them ; wee will euen let them liue, lest wrath be vpon vs, because of the oath which wee sware vnto them.

21 And the Princes said vnto them, Let them liue, (but let them bee hewers of wood, and drawers of water, vnto all the Congregation,) as the Princes had * promised them.

22 ¶ And Ioshua called for them, and he spake vnto them, saying, Wherefore haue ye beguiled vs, saying, We *are* very farre from you ? when ye dwell among vs.

23 Now therefore ye are cursed, and there shall † none of you bee freed from being bondmen, and hewers of wood, and drawers of water, for the house of my God.

24 And they answered Ioshua, and said, Because it was certainly told thy seruants, how that the LORD thy God * commanded his seruant Moses to giue you all the land, and to destroy all the inhabitants of the land from before you, therefore we were sore afraid of our liues because of you, and haue done this thing.

25 And now behold, we *are* in thine hand : as it seemeth good and right vnto thee to doe vnto vs, doe.

26 And so did he vnto them, and deliuered them out of the hand of the children of Israel, that they slew them not.

27 And Ioshua made them that day, hewers of wood, and drawers of water for the Congregation, and for the Altar of the LORD, euen vnto this day, in the place which he should choose.

Margin notes left column:
* Verse 15.

† Hebr. not be cut off from you.

* Deut. 7. 1.

CHAP. X.

1 Fiue Kings warre against Gibeon. 6 Ioshua rescueth it. 10 God fighteth against them with hailestones. 12 The Sunne and Moone stand still at the word of Ioshua. 16 The fiue Kings are murcd in a caue. 21 They are brought forth, 24 scornefully vsed, 26 and hanged. 28 Seuen Kings more are conquered. 43 Ioshua returneth to Gilgal.

Ow it came to passe when Adoni-zedek King of Ierusalem, had heard how Ioshua had taken Ai, and had vtterly destroyed it, (*as he had done to Iericho, and her King, so hee had done to * Ai, and her King) and how the inhabitants of Gibeon had made peace with Israel, and were among them,

2 That they feared greatly because Gibeon *was* a great citie, as † one of the royall cities, and because it *was* greater then Ai, and all the men thereof *were* mighty.

3 Wherefore Adoni-zedek King of Ierusalem, sent vnto Hoham King of Hebron, and vnto Piram, king of Iarmuth, and vnto Iaphia king of Lachish, and vnto Debir king of Eglon, saying,

4 Come vp vnto me, and helpe me, that we may smite Gibeon : for it hath made peace with Ioshua, and with the children of Israel.

5 Therefore the fiue Kings of the Amorites, the king of Ierusalem, the king of Hebron, the king of Iarmuth, the king of Lachish, the king of Eglon, gathered themselues together, and went vp, they, and all their hostes, and encamped before Gibeon, and made warre against it.

6 ¶ And the men of Gibeon sent vnto Ioshua to the campe to Gilgal, saying, Slacke not thy hand from thy seruants, come vp to vs quickly, and saue vs, and helpe vs : for all the kings of the Amorites that dwell in the mountaines, are gathered together against vs.

7 So Ioshua ascended from Gilgal, he, and all the people of warre with him, and all the mighty men of valour.

8 ¶ And the LORD said vnto Ioshua, Feare them not : for I haue deliuered them into thine hand ; there shall not a man of them stand before thee.

9 Ioshua therefore came vnto them suddenly,

Margin notes right column:
* Chap. 6. 15.
* Chap. 8. 3

† Hebr. citie of the kingdome.

suddenly, *and* went vp from Gilgal all night.

10 And the LORD discomfited them before Israel, and slewe them with a great slaughter at Gibeon, and chased them along the way that goeth vp to Bethoron, and smote them to Azekah and vnto Makkedah.

11 And it came to passe as they fled from before Israel, *and* were in the going downe to Bethoron, that the LORD cast downe great stones from heauen vpon them, vnto Azekah, and they died: they *were* moe which died with hailestones, then they whome the children of Israel slew with the sword.

Esa. 28. 21
cclus. 46. 4
Heb. bee
lent.

12 ¶ Then spake Ioshua to the LORD in the day when the LORD deliuered vp the Amorites before the children of Israel, and hee said in the sight of Israel, * Sunne, † stand thou still vpon Gibeon, and thou Moone in the valley of Aialon.

13 And the Sunne stood still, and the Moone stayed, vntill the people had a-uenged themselues vpō their enemies. Is not this written in the booke of ‖ Iasher? So the Sunne stood still in the midst of heauen, and hasted not to goe downe, about a whole day.

Or, the
pright?

14 And there was no day like that, before it, or after it, that the LORD hearkened vnto the voyce of a man: for the LORD fought for Israel.

15 ¶ And Ioshua returned, and all Israel with him, vnto the campe to Gilgal.

16 But these fiue kings fled, and hid themselues in a caue at Makkedah.

17 And it was told Ioshua, saying, The fiue kings are found hid in a caue at Makkedah.

18 And Ioshua said, Roule great stones vpon the mouth of the caue, and set men by it, for to keepe them.

Heb. cut off
he taile.

19 And stay you not, *but* pursue after your enemies, and † smite the hindmost of them, suffer them not to enter into their cities: for the LORD your God hath deliuered them into your hand.

20 And it came to passe when Io-shua and the children of Israel had made an end of slaying them with a ve-ry great slaughter, till they were con-sumed, that the rest *which* remained of them, entred into fenced cities.

21 And all the people returned to the campe to Ioshua at Makkedah in peace: none mooued his tongue against any of the children of Israel.

22 Then said Ioshua, Open the mouth of the caue, and bring out those fiue kings vnto me out of the caue.

23 And they did so, and brought forth those fiue kings vnto him out of the caue, the king of Ierusalem, the king of Hebron, the king of Iarmuth, the king of Lachish, *and* the king of Eglon.

24 And it came to passe when they brought out those kings vnto Ioshua, that Ioshua called for all the men of Israel, and saide vnto the captaines of the men of war which went with him, Come neere, put your feete vpon the neckes of these kings. And they came neere, and put their feet vpon the necks of them.

25 And Ioshua said vnto them, Feare not, nor be dismaid, bee strong, and of good courage: for thus shall the LORD doe to all your enemies against whom ye fight.

26 And afterward Ioshua smote them, and slew them, and hanged them on fiue trees: and they were hanging vpon the trees vntill the euening.

27 And it came to passe at the time of the going downe of the Sunne, *that* Ioshua commanded, and they * tooke them downe off the trees, and cast them into the caue, wherein they had beene hid, and laid great stones in the caues mouth, *which remain* vntil this very day.

* Deut. 21.
23. chap. 8.
29.

28 ¶ And that day Ioshua tooke Makkedah, and smote it with the edge of the sword, and the king thereof hee vtterly destroyed, them, and all the soules that were therein, he let none re-maine: and he did to the king of Mak-kedah, * as hee did vnto the king of Iericho.

* Chap. 6.
21.

29 Then Ioshua passed from Mak-kedah, and all Israel with him, vnto Libnah, and fought against Libnah.

30 And the LORD deliuered it also and the king thereof, into the hand of Israel, and he smote it with the edge of the sword, and all the soules that *were* therein: He let none remaine in it, but did vnto the king therof, as he did vnto the king of Iericho.

31 ¶ And Ioshua passed from Lib-nah and all Israel with him, vnto La-chish, and encamped against it, and fought against it.

32 And the LORD deliuered La-chish into the hande of Israel, which tooke it on the second day, and smote it with

with the edge of the sword, and all the ſoules that were therein, according to all that he had done to Libnah.

33 ¶ Then Horam king of Gezer, came vp to helpe Lachish, and Ioshua smote him and his people, vntill he had left him none remayning.

34 ¶ And from Lachish, Ioshua passed vnto Eglon, and all Israel with him, and they encamped against it, and fought against it.

35 And they tooke it on that day, and smote it with the edge of the sword, and all the ſoules that were therein he vtterly destroyed that day, according to all that he had done to Lachish.

36 And Ioshua went vp from Eglon, and all Israel with him, vnto Hebron, and they fought against it.

37 And they tooke it, and smote it with the edge of the sword, and the king thereof, and all the cities thereof, and all the ſoules that were therein, he left none remaining, according to all that he had done to Eglon: but destroyed it vtterly, and all the ſoules that were therein.

38 ¶ And Ioshua returned, and all Israel with him to Debir, and fought against it.

39 And hee tooke it, and the King thereof, and all the cities thereof, and they smote them with the edge of the sword, and vtterly destroyed all the ſoules that were therein, he left none remayning: as he had done to Hebron, so he did to Debir, and to the king thereof, as he had done also to Libnah, and to her king.

40 ¶ So Ioshua smote all the countrey of the hils, and of the South, and of the vale, and of the springs, and all their kings, hee left none remayning, but vtterly destroyed all that breathed, as the LORD God of Israel * commanded.

* Deut. 26. 16, 17.

41 And Ioshua smote them from Kadesh-Barnea, euen vnto Gaza, and all the countrey of Goshen, euen vnto Gibeon.

42 And all these Kings and their land did Ioshua take at one time: because the LORD God of Israel fought for Israel.

43 And Ioshua returned & al Israel with him, vnto the campe to Gilgal.

CHAP. XI.

1 Diuers Kings ouercome at the waters of Merom. 10 Hazor is taken and burnt. 16 All the countrey taken by Ioshua. 21 The Anakims cut off.

Nd it came to passe, when Iabin king of Hazor had heard those things, that hee sent to Iobab king of Madon, and to the king of Shimron, & to the king of Achshaph,

2 And to the kings that were on the North of the mountaines, and of the plaines South of Cinneroth, and in the valley, and in the borders of Dor, on the West;

3 And to the Canaanite on the East and on the West, and to the Amorite, and the Hittite, and the Perizzite, and the Iebusite in the mountaines, and to the Hiuite vnder Hermon in the land of Mizpeh.

4 And they went out, they and all their hostes with them, much people, euen as the sand that is vpon the Seashore in multitude, with horses and charets very many.

5 And when all these Kings were † met together, they came and pitched together at the waters of Merom, to fight against Israel.

† Hebr. assembled by appointment.

6 ¶ And the LORD saide vnto Ioshua, Be not afraid because of them: for to morrow about this time will I deliuer them vp al slaine before Israel: thou shalt hough their horses, and burne their charets with fire.

7 So Ioshua came, and all the people of warre with him, against them by the waters of Merom suddenly, and they fell vpon them.

8 And the LORD deliuered them into the hand of Israel, who smote them, and chased them vnto ‖ great Zidon, and vnto ‖ Misrephothmaim, and vnto the valley of Mizpeh Eastward, and they smote them, vntill they left them none remayning.

‖ Or, Zidon-Rabbah.
‖ Or, salt pits: Hebr. burning of waters.

9 And Ioshua did vnto them as the LORD bade him. hee houghed their horses, and burnt their charets with fire.

10 ¶ And Ioshua at that time turned backe, and tooke Hazor, and smote the king thereof with the sword: for Hazor beforetime was the head of all those kingdomes.

11 And they smote all the ſoules that were therein with the edge of the sword, vtterly destroying them: there was not † any left to breathe; and he burnt Hazor with fire.

† Hebr. any breath.

12 And

12 And all the cities of those kings, and all the kings of them, did Ioshua take, and smote them with the edge of the sword, *and* he vtterly destroied them, *as Moses the seruant of the LORD commanded.

Num. 33.
2. deut. 7.
and 20.
5, 17.

13 But as for the cities that stood still †in their strength, Israel burned none of them, saue Hazor onely; *that* did Io- shua burne.

Hebr. on eir heape.

14 And all the spoile of these cities, and the cattell, the children of Israel tooke for a pray vnto themselues: but euery man they smote with the edge of the sword, vntill they had destroyed them, neither left they any to breathe.

15 ¶ *As the LORD commanded Moses his seruant, so *did Moses com- mand Ioshua, and so did Ioshua: hee † left nothing vndone of all that the LORD commanded Moses.

Exod. 34.
Deut. 7. 2
Heb. he re- oued no- ing.

16 So Ioshua tooke all that land, the hilles, and all the South countrey, and all the land of Goshen, and the val- ley, and the plaine, and the mountaine of Israel, and the valley of the same:

17 *Euen* from the ||mount Halak, that goeth vp to Seir, vnto Baal-Gad, in the valley of Lebanon, vnder mount Hermon: and all their kings he tooke, and smote them, and slew them.

Or, the ooothe untaine.

18 Ioshua made warre a long time, with all those kings.

19 There was not a citie that made peace with the children of Israel, *saue the Hiuites the inhabitants of Gibeon; all *other* they tooke in battell.

Chap. 9. 3

20 For it was of the LORD to har- den their hearts, that they should come against Israel in battell, that he might destroy them vtterly, *&* that they might haue no fauour: but that hee might de- stroy them, as the LORD commanded Moses.

21 ¶ And at that time came Ioshua and cut off the Anakims from the mountaines, from Hebron, from De- bir, from Anab, and from all the moun- taines of Iudah, and from all the mountaines of Israel. Ioshua de- stroyed *them* vtterly with their cities.

22 There was none of the Anakims left in the land of the children of Israel: onely in Gaza, in Gath, and in Ashdod, there remained.

23 So Ioshua tooke the whole land according to all that the LORD saide vnto Moses, and Ioshua gaue it for an inheritance vnto Israel, * according to

Numb. 26

their diuisions by their tribes : and the land rested from warre.

CHAP. XII.

1 The two kings whose countreys Moses tooke and disposed of. 7 The one and thirty kings on the other side Iordan which Ioshua smote.

Ow these *are* the kings of the land, which the chil- dren of Israel smote, and possessed their land on the other side Iordan, to- ward the rising of the Sunne : from the riuer Arnon, vnto mount Hermon, and all the plaine on the East.

2 * Sihon king of the Amorites who dwelt in Heshbon, *and* ruled from A- roer, which *is* vpon the banke of the ri- uer of Arnon, and from the middle of the riuer, and from halfe Gilead vnto the riuer Iabbok, *which is* the border of the children of Ammon :

Num. 21 24. deu. 3. 6

3 And from the plaine, to the Sea of Cinneroth on the East, and vnto the sea of the plaine, *euen* the salt sea on the East, the way to Beth-Ieshimoth : and from the ||South, vnder ||* Ashdoth- Pisgah.

|| Or, Teman || Or, the springs of Pisgah, or the hill.

4 ¶ And the coast of Og king of Bashan, *which was* of the * remnant of the Giants, that dwelt at Ashtaroth, and at Edrei,

Deut. 3. 17. & 4. 49.
Deut. 3. 11. chap. 13. 12.

5 And reigned in mount Hermon, and in Salcah, and in all Bashan, vnto the border of the Geshurites, and the Maachathites, and halfe Gilead, the border of Sihon king of Heshbon.

6 Them did Moses the seruant of the LORD, and the children of Israel smite, and * Moses the seruant of the LORD gaue it for a possession vnto the Reubenites, and Gadites, and the halfe tribe of Manasseh.

Num. 32. 29. deut. 3. 12. chap. 13. 8.

7 ¶ And these are the kings of the countrey which Ioshua and the chil- dren of Israel smote on this side Ior- dan on the West, from Baal Gad in the valley of Lebanon, euen vnto * the mount Halak, that goeth vp to Seir, which Ioshua gaue vnto the tribes of Israel for a possession, according to their diuisions :

Chap. 11. 17.

8 In the mountaines and in the valleys, and in the plaines, and in the springs, and in the wildernesse, and in the South countrey : the Hittites, the Amorites, and the Canaanites, the Pe- rizzites, the Hiuites, and the Iebusites.
9 ¶ * The

* Chap. 6. 2.
* Chap. 8.
29.
* Chap. 10.
23.
* Chap. 10.
33.
* Chap. 10.
33.
* Chap. 10.
29.
* Chap. 10.
28.
‖ Or, Saron.
* Chap. 11.
10.
* Genes. 14.
1.

9 ¶ * The king of Iericho, one: the * king of Ai, which is beside Bethel, one:

10 * The king of Ierusalem, one : the king of Hebron, one:

11 The king of Iarmuth, one · the king of Lachis, one.

12 The king of Eglon, one: * the king of Gezer, one:

13 * The king of Debir, one : the king of Geder, one:

14 The king of Hormah one : the king of Arad, one:

15 * The king of Libnah, one : the king of Adullam, one:

16 * The king of Makkedah, one: the king of Bethel, one:

17 The king of Tappuah, one: the king of Hepher, one:

18 The king of Aphek, one: the king of ‖ Lasharon, one:

19 The king of Madon, one : * the king of Hazor, one:

20 The king of Shimron-Meron, one : the king of Achshaph, one:

21 The king of Taanach , one : the king of Megiddo, one:

22 The king of Kedesh, one : the king of Iokneam of Carmel, one:

23 The king of Dor, in the coast of Dor, one : the king of * the nations of Gilgal, one:

24 The king of Tirzah, one : all the kings thirtie and one.

CHAP. XIII.

1 The bounds of the land not yet conquered. 8 The inheritance of the two Tribes and halfe. 14. 33 The Lord and his sacrifices, are the inheritance of Leui. 15 The bounds of the inheritance of Reuben. 22 Balaam slaine. 24 The bounds of the inheritance of Gad, 29 and of the halfe tribe of Manasseh.

† Hebr. to possesse it.

Now Ioshua was old and stricken in yeeres, and the Lord saide vnto him; Thou art old, and stricken in yeres, and there remaineth yet very much land † to bee possessed.

2 This is the land that yet remaineth : all the borders of the Philistines, and all Geshuri,

3 From Sihor, which is before Egypt, euen vnto the borders of Ekron Northward, which is counted to the Canaanite : fiue lords of the Philistines ; the Gazathites, and the Ashdothites,

the Eshkalonites, the Gittites, and the Ekronites ; Also the Auites.

4 From the South, all the land of the Canaanites, and ‖ Mearah that is beside the Sidonians, vnto Aphek, to the borders of the Amorites:

5 And the land of the Giblites, and al Lebanon toward the Sunne rising, from Baal-Gad vnder mount Hermon, vnto the entring into Hamath.

6 All the inhabitants of the hill countrey, from Lebanon vnto Misrephothmaim , and all the Sidonians, them will I driue out from before the children of Israel : onely diuide thou it by lot vnto the Israelites, for an inheritance, as I haue commanded thee.

7 Now therefore, diuide this land for an inheritance vnto the nine tribes, and the halfe tribe of Manasseh,

8 With whom the Reubenites, and the Gadites haue receiued their inheritance, * which Moses gaue them , beyond Iordan Eastward , euen as Moses the seruant of the Lord gaue them :

9 From Aroer that is vpon the banke of the riuer Arnon, and the citie that is in the middest of the riuer, and all the plaine of Medeba vnto Dibon :

10 And all the cities of Sihon king of the Amorites, which reigned in Heshbon, vnto the border of the children of Ammon :

11 And Gilead, and the border of the Geshurites, and Maachathites, and all mount Hermon, and all Bashan vnto Salcah :

12 All the kingdome of Og in Bashan, which reigned in Ashtaroth and in Edrei, who remained of * the remnant of the giants : for these did Moses smite, and cast them out.

13 Neuerthelesse, the children of Israel expelled not the Geshurites, nor the Maachathites : but the Geshurites and the Maachathites dwel among the Israelites vntill this day

14 Onely vnto the tribe of Leui hee gaue none inheritance : the sacrifices of the Lord God of Israel made by fire, are their inheritance, as he said vnto them.

15 ¶ And Moses gaue vnto the tribe of the children of Reuben inheritance according to their families :

16 And their coast was from Aroer that is on the banke of the riuer Arnon, and the city that is in the midst of the riuer,

† Or, the caue.

* Num. 32.
33. deut. 3.
13. chap. 22.
4.

* Deut. 3.
11. chap.
12. 4.

uer, and all the plaine by Medeba.

17 Heshbon and all her cities that are in the plaine: Dibon, and ‖ Bamoth-Baal, and Beth-Baalmeon,

‖ Or, the gh places Baal, and use of Ba- meon.

18 And Iahazah, and Kedemoth, and Mephaath,

19 And Kiriathaim, and Sibmah, and Zareth-shahar, in the mount of the valley,

20 And Bethpeor, and * ‖ Ashdoth-Pisgah, and Beth-ieshimoth:

* Deut. 3.

‖ Or, springs Pisgah or hill.

21 And all the cities of the plaine, and all the kingdome of Sihon king of the Amorites, which reigned in Heshbon, whom Moses smote * with the princes of Midian, Eui, and Rekem, and Zur, and Hur, and Reba, which were dukes of Sihon, dwelling in the countrey.

* Num. 31.

22 ¶ Balaam also the sonne of Beor the ‖ Sooth-sayer did the children of Israel slay with the sword, among them that were slaine by them.

‖ Or, diuiner

23 And the border of the children of Reuben, was Iordan and the border *therof*: This was the inheritance of the children of Reuben after their families, the cities, and villages thereof.

24 And Moses gaue *inheritance* vnto the tribe of Gad, *euen* vnto the children of Gad, according to their families:

25 And their coast was Iazer, and all the cities of Gilead, and halfe the land of the children of Ammon, vnto Aroer that is before Rabbah:

26 And from Heshbon vnto Ramath-Mizpeh, and Betonim: and from Mahanaim vnto the border of Debir.

27 And in the valley, Beth-aram, and Beth-nimrah, and Succoth, and Zaphon the rest of the kingdome of Sihon king of Heshbon, Iordan, and *his* border, *euen* vnto the edge of the sea of Cinneroth, on the other side Iordan Eastward.

28 This is the inheritance of the children of Gad after their families: the cities and their villages.

29 ¶ And Moses gaue *inheritance* vnto the halfe tribe of Manasseh: and *this* was *the possession* of the halfe tribe of Manasseh, by their families.

30 And their coast was frō Mahanaim all Bashan, all the kingdome of Og king of Bashan, and all the townes of Iair, which are in Bashan, threescore cities:

31 And halfe Gilead, and Ashtaroth, and Edrei, cities of the kingdom of Og in Bashan, *were perteining* vnto the children of Machir the sonne of Manasseh, *euen* to the one halfe of the * children of Machir by their families.

* Num. 32. 39.

32 These are the *countreyes* which Moses did distribute for inheritance in the plaines of Moab, on the other side Iordan by Iericho Eastward.

33 * But vnto the tribe of Leui Moses gaue not *any* inheritance: the Lord God of Israel was their inheritance, * as he said vnto them.

* Chap. 18. 7.

* Num. 18. 20.

CHAP. XIIII.

1 The nine tribes and a halfe are to haue their inheritance by lot. 6 Caleb by priuiledge obtaineth Hebron.

AND these *are the countreys* which the children of Israel inherited in the lande of Canaan, * which Eleazar the Priest, & Ioshua the sonne of Nun, and the heads of the fathers of the tribes of the children of Israel distributed for inheritance to them

* Num. 34. 17.

2 * By lot *was* their inheritance, as the Lord commanded by the hande of Moses, for the nine tribes, and for the halfe tribe.

* Num. 26 55. & 33. 54.

3 For Moses had giuen the inheritance of two tribes and an halfe tribe, on the other side Iordan: but vnto the Leuites hee gaue none inheritance among them.

4 For the children of Ioseph were two tribes, Manasseh and Ephraim: therefore they gaue no part vnto the Leuites in the land, saue cities to dwell *in*, with their suburbs for their cattell, and for their substance.

5 * As the Lord commaunded Moses, so the children of Israel did, and they diuided the land.

* Num. 35 2. chap. 21. 2.

6 ¶ Then the children of Iudah came vnto Ioshua in Gilgal: and Caleb the sonne of Iephunneh the Kenezite, said vnto him, Thou knowest the thing that the Lord said vnto Moses the man of God concerning me and thee, in Kadesh Barnea.

7 Fourtie yeeres olde *was* I when Moses the seruant of the Lord sent me from Kadesh Barnea, to espie out the land, and I brought him worde againe, as it was in mine heart.

8 Neuerthelesse, my brethren that went vp with me, made the heart of the people

* Num. 14. 24.
people melt: but I wholly *followed the LORD my God.

9 And Moses sware on that day, saying, Surely the land whereon thy feet haue troden, shall be thine inheritance, and thy childrens for euer, because thou hast wholly followed the LORD my God.

10 And now beholde, the LORD hath kept me aliue, as he said, these forty and fiue yeres, euen since the LORD spake this word vnto Moses, while the children of Israel † wandered in the wildernesse: and now loe, I am this day fourescore and fiue yeeres old.

† Hebr. walked.

* Ecclus. 46. 9.
11 *As yet I am as strong this day, as I was in the day that Moses sent mee: as my strength was then, euen so is my strength now, for warre, both to goe out and to come in.

12 Now therefore giue mee this mountaine, whereof the LORD spake in that day, (for thou heardest in that day how the Anakims were there, and that the cities were great and fenced)if so be the LORD will be with me, then I shall bee able to driue them out, as the LORD said.

13 And Ioshua blessed him, and gaue vnto Caleb the sonne of Iephunneh, Hebron for an inheritance.

* Chap. 21. 12. 1. macc. 2. 56.
14 *Hebron therefore became the inheritance of Caleb the sonne of Iephunneh the Kenezite vnto this day: because that hee wholly followed the LORD God of Israel.

* Chap. 15. 13.
15 And *the name of Hebron before, was Kiriath-Arba, which Arba was a great man among the Anakims: and the land had rest from warre.

CHAP. XV.

1 The borders of the lot of Iudah. 13 Calebs portion and conquest. 16 Othniel for his valour, hath Achsah Calebs daughter to wife. 18 Shee obtaineth a blessing of her father. 21 The Cities of Iudah. 63 The Iebusites not conquered.

* Num. 34. 3.

* Num. 33. 36.
THis then was the lot of the tribe of the children of Iudah by their families, *euen to the border of Edom; the * wildernesse of Zin Southward, was the vttermost part of the South coast:

2 And their South border was from the shore of the salt sea, from the †bay that looketh Southward.

† Hebr. tongue.

3 And it went out to the Southside to ‖ Maalehacrabbim, and passed along to Zin, and ascended vp on the Southside vnto Kadesh-Barnea: and passed along to Hezron, and went vp to Adar, and fetched a compasse to Karkaa.

‖ Or, the going vp to Acrabbim.

4 From thence it passed toward Azmon, and went out vnto the riuer of Egypt, and the goings out of that coast were at the sea: this shalbe your South coast.

5 And the East border was the salt Sea, euen vnto the end of Iordan: and their border in the North quarter, was from the bay of the sea, at the vttermost part of Iordan.

6 And the border went vp to Bethhogla, and passed along by the North of Beth-arabah, and the border went vp to the stone of Bohan the sonne of Reuben.

7 And the border went vp toward Debir from the valley of Achor, and so Northward, looking toward Gilgal, that is before the going vp to Adummim, which is on the Southside of the riuer and the border passed towards the waters of Enshemesh, and the goings out thereof were * at En-Rogel.

* 1. King. 9.

8 And the border went vp by the valley of the sonne of Hinnom, vnto the South side of the Iebusite, the same is Ierusalem: and the border went vp to the top of the mountaine, that lieth before the valley of Hinnom, Westward, which is at the end of the valley of the giants, Northward.

9 And the border was drawen from the top of the hill vnto the fountaine of the water of Nephtoah, and went out to the cities of mount Ephron, and the border was drawen to Baalah, which is Kiriath-iearim.

10 And the border compassed from Baalah Westward vnto mount Seir, and passed along vnto the side of mount Iearim, (which is Chesalon) on the North side, and went downe to Bethshemesh, and passed on to Timnah.

11 And the border went out vnto the side of Ekron Northward: and the border was drawen to Shicron, and passed along to mount Baalah, and went out vnto Iabneel, and the goings out of the border were at the sea.

12 And the West border was to the great sea, and the coast therof: this is the coast of the children of Iudah round about, according to their families.

13 ¶ And

13 ¶ And vnto Caleb the sonne of Iephunneh, he gaue a part among the children of Iudah, according to the cōmandement of the LORD to Ioshua, *euen* * ||the citie of Arba the father of Anak, which *citie* is Hebron.

*Chap. 14. 15.
|| Or, Kiriath-arba.
* Iudg. 1. 10

14 And Calebdroue thence *the three sonnes of Anak, Sheshai, and Ahiman, and Talmai, the children of Anak.

15 And he went vp thence to the inhabitants of Debir : and the name of Debir before was Kiriath-Sepher.

16 ¶ And Caleb said, He that smiteth Kiriath-Sepher, and taketh it, to him will I giue Achsah my daughter to wife.

17 And Othniel the sonne of Kenaz, the brother of Caleb, tooke it : and hee gaue him Achsah his daughter to wife.

18 And it came to passe as shee came *vnto him*, that she moued him to aske of her father a field, and she lighted off her asse ; and Caleb said vnto her, What wouldest thou ?

19 Who answered, Giue mee a blessing ; for thou hast giuen mee a Southland, giue me also springs of water ; and he gaue her the vpper springs, and the nether springs.

20 This *is* the inheritance of the tribe of the children of Iudah according to their families.

21 And the vttermost cities of the tribe of the children of Iudah toward the coast of Edom Southward, were Kabzeel, and Eder, and Iagur,

22 And Kinah, and Dimonah, and Adadah,

23 And Kedesh, and Hazor, and Ithnan,

24 Ziph, and Telem, and Bealoth,

25 And Hazor, Hadattah, and Kerioth : *and* Hezron, which is Hazor,

26 Amam, and Shema, and Moladah,

27 And Hazar-Gaddah, and Heshmon, and Beth-palet,

28 And Hazarshual, and Beersheba, and Biziothiah,

29 Baalah, and Iim, and Azem,

30 And Eltolad, and Chesil, and Hormah,

31 And Ziklag, and Madmannah, and Sansannah,

32 And Lebaoth, and Shilhim, and Ain, and Rimmon : all the cities *are* twentie and nine, with their villages.

33 *And* in the valley, Esthaol, and Zoreah, and Ashnah,

34 And Zanoah, and Engannim, Tappuah, and Enam,

35 Iarmuth, and Adullam, Socoh, and Azekah,

36 And Sharaim, and Adithaim, and Gederah, || and Gederothaim : fourteene cities with their villages.

|| Or, or.

37 Zenam, and Hadashah, & Migdalgad,

38 And Dileam, and Mizpeh, and Ioktheel,

39 Lachish, and Bozkath, & Eglon,

40 And Cabbon, and Lahmam, and Kithlish,

41 And Gederoth, Beth-dagon, and Naamah, and Makkedah : sixteene cities with their villages.

42 Lebnah, and Ether, and Ashan,

43 And Iiphta, and Ashnah, and Nezib,

44 And Keilah, and Achzib, and Mareshah : nine cities with their villages.

45 Ekron with her townes, and her villages.

46 From Ekron euen vnto the sea, all that lay † neere Ashdod, with their villages.

† Hebr. by the place of.

47 Ashdod with her townes and her villages, Gaza with her townes and her villages, vnto the riuer of Egypt, and the great sea and the border *thereof*.

48 ¶ And in the mountaines, Shamir, and Iattir, and Socoh,

49 And Dannah, & Kiriath-Sannath, which is Debir,

50 And Anab, and Ashtemoh, and Anim,

51 And Goshen, and Holon, and Giloh : eleuen cities with their villages.

52 Arab, and Dumah, and Eshean,

53 And ||Ianum, and Beth-tappuah, and Aphekah,

|| Or, Ianus.

54 And Humtah, and *Kiriatharba (which is Hebron) and Zior, nine cities with their villages.

* Chap. 14. 15.

55 Maon, Carmel, and Ziph, and Iuttah,

56 Ind Iezreel, and Iokdeam, and Zanoah,

57 Cain, Gibbeah, and Timnah : ten cities with their villages.

58 Halhul, Beth-zur, and Gedor,

59 And Maarah, and Bethanoth, & Eltekon : six cities with their villages.

60 Kiriath-baal, which *is* Kiriathiearim, and Rabbah : two cities with their villages.

61 ¶ In

61 ¶ In the wildernesse, Beth-ara-bah, Middin, and Secacah,

62 And Nibshan, and the city of Salt, and Engedi: sixe cities with their villages.

63 As for the Iebusites the inhabitants of Ierusalem, the children of Iudah could not driue them out: but the Iebusites dwell with the children of Iudah at Ierusalem vnto this day.

CHAP. XVI.

1 The generall borders of the sonnes of Ioseph. 5 The border of the inheritance of Ephraim. 10 The Canaanites not conquered.

Nd the lot of the children of Ioseph †fell from Iordan by Iericho, vnto the water of Iericho on the East, to the wildernesse that goeth vp from Iericho throughout mount Bethel;

† Hebr. went foorth.

2 And goeth out from Bethel to *Luz, and passeth along vnto the borders of Archi, to Ataroth,

* Iudg. 1. 26.

3 And goeth downe Westward, to the coast of Iaphleti, vnto the coast of Bethoron the nether, and to Gezer: and the goings out thereof are at the Sea.

4 So the children of Ioseph, Manasseh, and Ephraim, tooke their inheritance.

5 ¶ And the border of the children of Ephraim according to their families, was thus: euen the border of their inheritance on the East side was Ataroth-Addar, vnto Bethoron the vpper.

6 And the border went out toward the Sea, to Michmethah on the Northside, and the border went about Eastward vnto Taanath Shiloh, and passed by it on the East to Ianohah:

7 And it went downe from Ianohah to Ataroth and to Naarath, and came to Iericho, and went out at Iordane.

8 The border went out from Tappuah Westward vnto the riuer Kanah: and the goings out thereof were at the Sea. This is the inheritance of the tribe of the children of Ephraim by their families.

9 And the separate cities for the children of Ephraim were among the inheritance of the children of Manasseh, all the cities with their villages.

10 And they draue not out the Ca-naanites that dwelt in Gezer: but the Canaanites dwell among the Ephramites vnto this day, and serue vnder tribute.

CHAP. XVII

1 The lot of Manasseh. 8 His coast. 12 The Canaanites not driuen out. 14 The children of Ioseph obtaine another lot.

Here was also a lot for the tribe of Manasseh; (*for hee was the first borne of Ioseph) to wit, for Machir the first borne of Manasseh the father of Gilead: because he was a man of warre, therefore hee had Gilead and Bashan.

* Gene. 41. 51. and 46. 20. and 50. 23. num. 32. 39.

2 There was also a lot for * the rest of the children of Manasseh by their families; for the children of Abiezer, and for the children of Helek, and for the children of Asriel, and for the children of Shechem, and for the children of Hepher, and for the children of Shemida: these were the male children of Manasseh, the sonne of Ioseph by their families.

* Num. 26 29.

3 ¶ But * Zelophehad the sonne of Hepher, the sonne of Gilead, the sonne of Machir, the sonne of Manasseh, had no sonnes but daughters: And these are the names of his daughters, Mahlah, and Noah, Hoglah, Milcah, and Tirzah.

* Num. 26 33. and 27 1. and 36.

4 And they came neere before Eleazar the Priest, and before Ioshua the sonne of Nun, and before the Princes, saying, The LORD commanded Moses to giue vs an inheritance among our brethren: therefore according to the commaundement of the LORD, hee gaue them an inheritance among the brethren of their father.

5 And there fel ten portions to Manasseh, beside the land of Gilead and Bashan, which were on the other side Iordan;

6 Because the daughters of Manasseh had an inheritance among his sonnes: and the rest of Manassehs sonnes had the land of Gilead.

7 ¶ And the coast of Manasseh was from Asher to Michmethah, that lieth before Shechem, and the border went along on the right hand, vnto the inhabitants of Entappuah.

8 Now Manasseh had the land of Tappuah: but Tappuah on the border

‖ Or, brooke of reeds.

9 And the coast descended vnto the ‖ riuer Kanah, Southward of the riuer: these cities of Ephraim *are* among the cities of Manasseh: the coast of Manasseh also *was* on the North side of the riuer, and the outgoings of it were at the Sea

10 Southward *it was* Ephraims, and Northward *it was* Manassehs, and the sea is his border, and they met together in Asher on the North, and in Issachar on the East.

11 And Manasseh had in Issachar and in Asher, Bethshean & her townes, and Ibleam and her townes, and the inhabitants of Dor and her townes, and the inhabitants of Endor and her townes, and the inhabitants of Taanach and her townes, and the inhabitants of Megiddo and her townes, euen three countreyes.

12 Yet the children of Manasseh could not driue out *the inhabitants* of those cities, but the Canaanites would dwell in that land.

13 Yet it came to passe when the children of Israel were waxen strong, that they put the Canaanites to tribute: but did not vtterly driue them out.

14 And the children of Ioseph spake vnto Ioshua, saying, Why hast thou giuen me *but* one lot and one portion to inherit, seeing I am a great people, forasmuch as the LORD hath blessed me hitherto?

15 And Ioshua answered them, If thou be a great people, then get thee vp to the wood *countrey*, and cut downe for thy selfe there in the land of the Perizzites, and of the ‖ giants, if mount Ephraim be too narrow for thee.

‖ Or, Rephaims.

16 And the children of Ioseph saide, The hill is not enough for vs: and all the Canaanites that dwell in the lande of the valley, haue charets of yron, both they who *are* of Bethshean and her townes, and they who *are* of the valley of Iezreel.

17 And Ioshua spake vnto the house of Ioseph, *euen* to Ephraim, and to Manasseh, saying, Thou art a great people, and hast great power: Thou shalt not haue one lot *onely*.

18 But the mountaine shalbe thine, for it is a wood, and thou shalt cut it downe: and the outgoings of it shalbe thine: for thou shalt driue out the Cana-

anites, though they haue yron charets, *and* though they *be* strong.

CHAP. XVIII.

1 The Tabernacle is set vp at Shiloh. 2 The remainder of the land is described, and diuided into seuen parts. 10 Ioshua diuideth it by lot. 11 The lot and border of Beniamin. 21 Their cities.

And the whole Congregation of the children of Israel assembled together at Shiloh, & set vp the Tabernacle of the Congregation there, and the land was subdued before them.

2 And there remained among the children of Israel seuen tribes, which had not yet receiued their inheritance.

3 And Ioshua said vnto the children of Israel, How long are you slacke to goe to possesse the lande which the LORD God of your fathers hath giuen you?

4 Giue out from among you three men, for *each* tribe: and I will send them, and they shall rise, & goe through the land, and describe it according to the inheritance of them, and they shal come *againe* to me.

5 And they shall diuide it into seuen parts: Iudah shall abide in their coast on the South, and the house of Ioseph shall abide in their coasts on the North.

6 Ye shall therfore describe the land *into* seuen parts, and bring *the description* hither to me: that I may cast lots for you here before the LORD our God.

7 But the Leuites haue no part among you, for the Priesthood of the LORD *is* their inheritance: and Gad and Reuben, and halfe the tribe of Manasseh, haue receiued their inheritance beyond Iordan on the East, which Moses the seruant of the LORD gaue them.

8 ¶ And the men arose, and went away: and Ioshua charged them that went to describe the land, saying, Goe, and walke through the land, & describe it, and come againe to me, that I may here cast lots for you, before the LORD in Shiloh.

9 And the men went, and passed thorow the land, and described it by cities, into seuen parts in a booke, and came *againe* to Ioshua to the hoste at Shiloh.

10 ¶ And

10 ¶ And Ioshua cast lots for them in Shiloh, before the Lᴏʀᴅ : and there Ioshua diuided the land vnto the children of Israel according to their diuisions.

11 ¶ And the lot of the tribe of the children of Beniamin came vp according to their families : and the coast of their lot came foorth betweene the children of Iudah, and the children of Ioseph.

12 And their border on the North-side was from Iordan, and the border went vp to the side of Iericho, on the North side, and went vp through the mountaines Westward, and the goings out thereof were at the wildernesse of Beth-auen.

13 And the border went ouer from thence toward Luz, to the side of Luz, (which is Bethel) Southward, and the border descended to Ataroth-Adar, neere the hill that *lieth* on the South side of the nether Beth-horon.

14 And the border was drawen *thence*, and compassed the corner of the Sea Southward, from the hill that *lieth* before Beth-horon Southward: and the goings out thereof were at Kiriath-baal (which is Kiriath-iearim) a city of the children of Iudah : This was the West quarter.

15 And the South quarter was from the end of Kiriath-iearim, & the border went out on the West, and went out to the well of waters of Nephtoah.

16 And the border came downe to the end of the mountaine, that *lieth* before the valley of the sonne of Hinnom, *and* which is in the valley of the Giants on the North, and descended to the valley of Hinnom to the side of Iebusi on the South, and descended to En-Rogel,

17 And was drawen frō the North, and went foorth to Enshemesh, and went foorth toward Geliloth, which is ouer against the going vp of Adummim, and descended to *the stone of Bohan the sonne of Reuben,

*Chap. 15. 6.

18 And passed along toward the side ouer against Arabah Northward, and went downe vnto ‖Arabah.

‖ Or, the plaine.

19 And the border passed along to the side of Beth-hoglah Northward: and the outgoings of the border were at the North †bay of the salt Sea at the South end of Iordane : This *was* the South coast.

† Hebr. tongue.

20 And Iordane was the border of

it on the East side : this *was* the inheritance of the children of Beniamin, by the coasts thereof round about, according to their families.

21 Now the cities of the tribe of the children of Beniamin according to their families, were Iericho, and Bethhoglah, and the valley of Keziz,

22 And Betharabah, and Zemaraim, and Bethel,

23 And Auim, and Parah, and Ophrah,

24 And Chephar-Haammonai, and Ophni, and Gaba, twelue cities with their villages

25 Gibeon, and Ramah, and Beeroth,

26 And Mizpeh, and Chephirah, and Mozah,

27 And Rekem, and Irpeel, and Taralah,

28 And Zela, Eleph, and Iebusi, (which is Ierusalem) Gibeath, *and* Kiriath, foureteene cities with their villages. This is the inheritance of the children of Beniamin according to their families.

CHAP. XIX.

1 The lot of Simeon, 10 Of Zebulun, 17 Of Issachar, 24 Of Asher, 32 Of Naphtali, 40 Of Dan. 46 The children of Israel giue an inheritance to Ioshua.

Nd the second lot came foorth to Simeon, *euen* for the tribe of the children of Simeon according to their families : and their inheritance was within the inheritance of the children of Iudah.

2 And they had in their inheritance Beer-sheba, or Sheba, and Moladah,

3 And Hazarshual, and Balah, and Azem,

4 And Eltolad, and Bethul, and Hormah,

5 And Ziklag, and Beth-marcaboth, and Hazar-susah,

6 And Beth-lebaoth, and Sharuhen : thirteene cities and their villages.

7 Ain, Remmon, and Ether, and Ashan : foure cities and their villages,

8 And all the villages that were round about these cities, to Baalath-Beer, Ramath of the South : This is the inheritance of the tribe of the children of Simeon according to their families.

9 Out

9 Out of the portion of the children of Iudah *was* the inheritance of the children of Simeon : for the part of the children of Iudah was too much for them : therefore the children of Simeon had their inheritance within the inheritance of them.

10 ¶ And the third lot came vp for the children of Zebulun, according to their families : and the border of their inheritance was vnto Sarid.

11 And their border went vp toward the Sea, and Maralah, and reached to Dabbasheth, and reached to the riuer that *is* before Iokneam,

12 And turned from Sarid Eastward, toward the Sunne rising, vnto the border of Chisloth Tabor, and then goeth out to Daberath, and goeth vp to Iaphia,

13 And from thence passeth on along on the East to Gittah-Hepher, to Ittah-Kazin, and goeth out to Remmon || Methoar to Neah.

| Or, which is drawen.

14 And the border compasseth it on the North side to Hannathon : and the outgoings thereof are in the valley of Iiphthah-el.

15 And Kattath, and Nahallal, and Shimron, and Idalah, and Bethlehem : twelue cities with their villages.

16 This *is* the inheritance of the children of Zebulun according to their families, these cities with their villages.

17 ¶ *And* the fourth lot came out to Issachar for the children of Issachar according to their families.

18 And their border was toward Izreel, and Chesulloth, and Shunem,

19 And Hapharaim, and Shion, and Anaharath,

20 And Rabbith, and Kishion, and Abez,

21 And Remeth, and Engannim, and Enhaddah, and Bethpazzez.

22 And the coast reacheth to Tabor, and Shahazimath, and Bethshemesh, and the outgoings of their border were at Iordan, sixteene cities with their villages.

23 This is the inheritance of the tribe of the children of Issachar according to their families, the cities, and their villages.

24 ¶ And the fift lot came out for the tribe of the children of Asher according to their families.

25 And their border was Helkath, and Hali, and Beten, and Achshaph,

26 And Alammelech, and Amad, and Misheal, and reacheth to Carmel westward, and to Shihor-Libnath,

27 And turneth toward the Sunne rising to Beth-dagon, and reacheth to Zebulun, and to the valley of Iiphthah-el toward the Northside of Bethemek, and Neiel, and goeth out to Cabul on the left hand,

28 And Hebron, and Rehob, and Hammon, and Kanah, *euen* vnto great Zidon :

29 And *then* the coast turneth to Ramah, and to the strong citie † Tyre, and the coast turneth to Hosah : and the outgoings thereof are at the Sea from the coast to Achzib.

† Heb. Tzor.

30 Ummah also, and Aphek, and Rehob : twentie and two cities with their villages.

31 This is the inheritance of the tribe of the children of Asher according to their families, these cities with their villages.

32 ¶ The sixt lot came out to the children of Naphtali : euen for the children of Naphtali according to their families.

33 And their coast was from Heleph, from Allon to Zaanannim, and Adami, Nekeb, and Iabneel vnto Lakum : and the outgoings thereof were at Iordan.

34 And then the coast turneth westward to Aznoth-Tabor, and goeth out from thence to Hukkok, and reacheth to Zebulun on the Southside, and reacheth to Asher on the Westside, and to Iudah vpon Iordan toward the Sun rising.

35 And the fenced cities are Ziddim, Zer, and Hammath, Rakkath, and Cinnereth,

36 And Adamah, and Ramah, and Hazor,

37 And Kedesh, and Edrei, and Enhazor,

38 And Iron, and Migdal-el, Horem, and Bethanah, and Bethshemesh, nineteene cities with their villages.

39 This *is* the inheritance of the tribe of the children of Naphtali according to their families, the cities and their villages.

40 ¶ And the seuenth lot came out for the tribe of the children of Dan according to their families :

41 And the coast of their inheritance was Zorah, and Eshtaol, and Irshemesh,

42 And

42 And Shaalabbin, and Aiialon, and Iethlah,

43 And Elon, and Thimnathah, and Ekron,

44 And Eltekeh, and Gibbethon, and Baalah,

45 And Iehud, and Bene-berak, and Gath-rimmon,

46 And Meiarkon, and Rakkon, with the border ||before ||Iapho.

‖ *Or, ouer against.*
‖ *Or, Ioppa, Acts. 9. 36.*

47 And the coast of the children of Dan went out *too little* for them : therefore the children of Dan went vp to fight against Leshem, and tooke it, and smote it with the edge of the sword, and possessed it, and dwelt therein, and called Leshem, * Dan, after the name of Dan their father.

* Iudg. 18. 29.

48 This is the inheritance of the tribe of the children of Dan according to their families, these cities with their villages.

49 ¶ When they had made an end of diuiding the land for inheritance by their coasts, the children of Israel gaue an inheritance to Ioshua the sonne of Nun among them :

50 According to the word of the LORD, they gaue him the citie which he asked, euen * Timnath-Serah in mount Ephraim : and he built the citie, and dwelt therein.

* Chap. 24. 30.

51 * These are the inheritances which Eleazar the Priest, and Ioshua the sonne of Nun, and the heads of the fathers of the tribes of the children of Israel, diuided for an inheritance by lot, in Shiloh before the LORD, at the doore of the Tabernacle of the Congregation : so they made an end of diuiding the countrey.

* Num. 34. 17.

CHAP. XX.

1 God commandeth, 7 and the children of Israel appoint the sixe cities of Refuge.

He LORD also spake vnto Ioshua, saying,

2 Speake to the children of Israel, saying, * Appoint out for you cities of refuge, whereof I spake vnto you by the hand of Moses :

* Exod. 21. 13. num. 35. 6, 11. 14. deut. 19. 2.

3 That the slayer that killeth any person vnawares *and* vnwittingly, may flee thither : and they shall be your refuge from the auenger of blood.

4 And when he that doeth flee vnto one of those cities, shall stand at the en-

tring of the gate of the city, and shall declare his cause in the eares of the Elders of that citie; they shall take him into the citie vnto them, and giue him a place, that he may dwell among them.

5 And if the auenger of blood pursue after him, then they shal not deliuer the slayer vp into his hand : because hee smote his neighbour vnwittingly, and hated him not beforetime.

6 And hee shall dwell in that citie, vntill he stand before the Congregation for iudgement, *and* * vntill the death of the high Priest that shall bee in those dayes: then shall the slayer returne, and come vnto his owne city, and vnto his owne house, vnto the citie from whence he fled.

* Num. 35. 25.

7 ¶ And they †appointed Kedesh in Galilee, in mount Naphtali, and Shechem in mount Ephraim, and Kiriath-arba (which is Hebron) in the mountaine of Iudah.

† *Hebr. sanctified.*

8 And on the other side Iordan by Iericho Eastward, they assigned * Bezer in the wildernesse vpon the plaine, out of the tribe of Reuben, and Ramoth in Gilead out of the tribe of Gad, and Golan in Bashan out of the tribe of Manasseh.

* Deut. 4. 43. 1. chro. 6. 78.

9 These were the cities appointed for all the children of Israel, and for the stranger that soiourneth among them, that whosoeuer killeth any person at vnawares might flee thither, & not die by the hand of the auenger of blood, vntill he stood before the Congregation.

CHAP. XXI.

1 Eight and fortie cities giuen by lot, out of the other tribes, vnto the Leuites. 43 God gaue the land, and rest vnto the Israelites, according to his promise.

Hen came neere the heads of the fathers of the Leuites vnto Eleazar the Priest, and vnto Ioshua the sonne of Nun, and vnto the heads of the fathers of the tribes of the children of Israel.

2 And they spake vnto them at Shiloh in the land of Canaan, saying, * The LORD commaunded by the hand of Moses, to giue vs Cities to dwell in, with the suburbs thereof for our cattell.

* Num. 35. 2.

3 And the children of Israel gaue vnto the Leuites out of their inheritance

tance at the commandement of the LORD, these cities and their suburbs.

4 And the lot came out for the families of the Kohathites : and the children of Aaron the Priest, *which were* of the Leuites, had by lot out of the tribe of Iudah, and out of the tribe of Simeon, and out of the tribe of Beniamin, thirteene cities.

5 And the rest of the children of Kohath *had* by lot, out of the families of the tribe of Ephraim, and out of the tribe of Dan, and out of the halfe tribe of Manasseh, ten cities.

6 And the children of Gershon *had* by lot out of the families of the tribe of Issachar, and out of the tribe of Asher, and out of the tribe of Naphtali, and out of the halfe tribe of Manasseh in Bashan, thirteene cities.

7 The children of Merari by their families, *had* out of the tribe of Reuben, and out of the tribe of Gad, and out of the tribe of Zebulun, twelue cities.

8 And the children of Israel gaue by lot vnto the Leuites these cities with their suburbs, as the LORD commanded by the hand of Moses.

9 ¶ And they gaue out of the tribe of the children of Iudah, and out of the tribe of the children of Simeon, these cities which are *here* †mentioned by name,

† Hebr.
called.

10 Which the children of Aaron being of the families of the Kohathites, who were of the children of Leui, had : (for theirs was the first lot.)

|Or, Kiri-
ith-arbah.

11 And they gaue them ‖ the citie of Arbah the father of Anak (*which citie* is Hebron) in the hill countrey of Iudah, with ẏ suburbs thereof round about it.

* Chap. 14
4. 1. chro.
5. 56.

12 But the fields of the citie, and the villages thereof, gaue they to * Caleb the sonne of Iephunneh, for his possession.

13 ¶ Thus they gaue to the children of Aaron the Priest Hebron with her suburbs *to bee* a citie of refuge for the slayer, and Libnah with her suburbs,

14 And Iattir with her suburbs, and Eshtemoa with her suburbs :

15 And Holon with her suburbs, and Debir with her suburbs :

16 And Ain with her suburbs, and Iuttah with her suburbs, and Beth-shemesh with her suburbs, nine cities out of those two tribes.

17 And out of the tribe of Beniamin, Gibeon with her suburbs, Geba with her suburbs,

18 Anathoth with her suburbs, and Almon with her suburbs, foure cities.

19 All the cities of the children of Aaron the Priests, were thirteene cities with their suburbs.

20 ¶ And the families of the children of Kohath the Leuites, which remained of the children of Kohath, euen they had the cities of their lot out of the tribe of Ephraim.

21 For they gaue them Shechem with her suburbs in mount Ephraim, *to be* a citie of refuge for the slayer : and Gezer with her suburbs,

22 And Kibzaim with her suburbs, and Beth-horon with her suburbs, foure cities.

23 And out of the tribe of Dan, Eltekeh with her suburbs, Gibethon with her suburbs,

24 Aijalon with her suburbs, Gathrimmon, with her suburbs : foure cities.

25 And out of the halfe tribe of Manasseh, Tanach with her suburbs, and Gathrimmon with her suburbs, two cities.

26 All the cities were ten with their suburbs, for the families of the children of Kohath that remained.

27 ¶ And vnto the children of Gershon of the families of the Leuites, out of the *other* halfe tribe of Manasseh, *they gaue* Golan in Bashan, with her suburbs, *to be* a citie of refuge for the slayer : and Beeshterah with her suburbs, two cities.

28 And out of the tribe of Issachar, Kishon with her suburbs, Dabareh with her suburbs,

29 Iarmuth with her suburbs, Engannim with her suburbs, foure cities.

30 And out of the tribe of Asher Mishal with her suburbs, Abdon with her suburbs,

31 Helkah with her suburbs, and Rehob with her suburbs, foure cities.

32 And out of the tribe of Naphtali, Kedesh in Galilee with her suburbs, *to be* a citie of refuge for the slayer, and Hammoth-dor with her suburbs, and Kartan with her suburbs, three cities.

33 All the cities of the Gershonites according to their families *were* thirteene cities with their suburbs.

34 ¶ And vnto the families of the children of Merari the rest of the Leuites, out of the tribe of Zebulun, Iokneam, with her suburbs, and Kar-

Kartah with her suburbs,

35 Dimnah with her suburbs, Nahalal with her suburbs, foure cities.

36 And out of the tribe of Reuben, Bezer with her suburbs, and Iahazah with her suburbs,

37 Kedemoth with her suburbs, and Mephaath with her suburbs, foure cities.

38 And out of the tribe of Gad, Ramoth in Gilead with her suburbs, *to be* a city of refuge for the slayer; and Mahanaim with her suburbs,

39 Heshbon with her suburbs, Iazer with her suburbs, foure cities in all.

40 So all the cities for the children of Merari by their families, which were remayning of the families of the Leuites, *were by* their lot, twelue cities.

41 All the cities of the Leuites within the possession of the children of Israel, were fourty and eight cities, with their suburbs.

42 These cities were euery one with their suburbs round about them: thus were all these cities.

43 ¶ And the LORD gaue vnto Israel all the land which hee sware to giue vnto their fathers: and they possessed it, and dwelt therein.

44 And the LORD gaue them rest round about, according to all that he sware vnto their fathers, and there stood not a man of all their enemies before them: the LORD deliuered all their enemies into their hand.

*Chap. 23. 14, 15.

45 * There failed not ought of any good thing which the LORD had spoken vnto the house of Israel: all came to passe.

CHAP. XXII.

1 The two Tribes and halfe with a blessing are sent home. 9 They build the Altar of testimony, in their iourney. 11 The Israelites are offended thereat. 21 They giue them good satisfaction.

Hen Ioshua called the Reubenites, and the Gadites, and the halfe tribe of Manasseh,

2 And said vnto them, Yee haue kept all that Moses the seruant of the LORD commanded you, and haue obeyed my voyce in all that I commanded you.

3 Yee haue not left your brethren these many dayes vnto this day, but

haue kept the charge of the commandement of the LORD your God.

4 And now the LORD your God hath giuen rest vnto your brethren, as hee promised them: therefore now returne yee, and get yee vnto your tents, and vnto the land of your possession, * which Moses the seruant of the LORD gaue you on the other side Iordane.

*Num. 32. 33. chap. 13. 8.

5 But take diligent heed, to doe the Commandement and the Law, which Moses the seruant of the LORD charged you, * to loue the LORD your God, and to walke in all his wayes, and to keepe his Commaundements, and to cleaue vnto him, and to serue him with all your heart, and with all your soule.

*Deut. 10. 12.

6 So Ioshua blessed them, and sent them away: and they went vnto their tents.

7 ¶ Now to the *one* halfe of the tribe of Manasseh Moses had giuen *possession* in Bashan: but vnto the *other* halfe therof gaue Ioshua among their brethren on this side Iordane Westward. And when Ioshua sent them away also vnto their tents, then hee blessed them,

8 And he spake vnto them, saying; Returne with much riches vnto your tents, and with very much cattell, with siluer and with gold, and with brasse, and with iron, and with very much raiment: Diuide the spoile of your enemies with your brethren.

9 ¶ And the children of Reuben, and the children of Gad, and the halfe tribe of Manasseh returned, and departed from the children of Israel out of Shiloh which *is* in the land of Canaan, to goe vnto the countrey of Gilead, to the land of their possession, whereof they were possessed, according to the word of the LORD by the hand of Moses.

10 ¶ And when they came vnto the borders of Iordan, that *are* in the land of Canaan, the children of Reuben, and the children of Gad, and the halfe tribe of Manasseh built there an altar by Iordan, a great altar to see to.

11 ¶ And the children of Israel heard say, Behold, the children of Reuben, and the children of Gad, and the halfe tribe of Manasseh, haue built an altar ouer against the land of Canaan, in the borders of Iordan, at the passage of the children of Israel.

12 And

12 And when the children of Israel heard of it, the whole Congregation of the children of Israel gathered themselues together at Shiloh, to goe vp to warre against them.

13 And the children of Israel sent vnto the children of Reuben, and to the children of Gad, and to the halfe tribe of Manasseh into the lande of Gilead, Phinehas the son of Eleazar the Priest,

14 And with him ten princes, of ech †chiefe house a prince, throughout all the tribes of Israel, and each one was an head of the house of their fathers, among the thousands of Israel.

Heb. house of the father.

15 ¶ And they came vnto the children of Reuben, and to the children of Gad, and to the halfe tribe of Manasseh vnto the land of Gilead, and they spake with them, saying,

16 Thus saith the whole Congregation of the Lord, What trespasse is this that ye haue committed against the God of Israel, to turne away this day from following the Lord, in that ye haue builded you an altar, that yee might rebell this day against the Lord?

17 Is the iniquitie *of Peor too little for vs, from which we are not cleansed vntil this day, (although there was a plague in the Congregation of the Lord)

Num. 25.

18 But that ye must turne away this day from following the Lord? and it will be, *seeing* yee rebell to day against the Lord, that to morrow he will be wroth with the whole Congregation of Israel.

19 Notwithstanding, if the lande of your possession be vncleane, then passe yee ouer vnto the land of the possession of the Lord, wherein the Lords Tabernacle dwelleth, and take possession among vs: but rebell not against the Lord, nor rebell against vs, in building you an altar, beside the Altar of the Lord our God.

20 Did not Achan the sonne of Zerah commit a trespasse in the accursed thing, and wrath fell on *all the Congregation of Israel? and that man perished not alone in his iniquitie.

Chap. 7. , 5.

21 ¶ Then the children of Reuben, and the children of Gad, and the halfe tribe of Manasseh, answered and saide vnto the Heads of the thousands of Israel,

22 The Lord God of gods, the Lord God of gods, hee knoweth, and Israel he shall know, if *it bee* in rebellion, or if in transgression against the Lord, (saue vs not this day,)

23 That wee haue built vs an altar to turne from following the Lord, or if to offer thereon burnt offering, or meat offering, or if to offer peace offerings thereon, let the Lord himselfe require *it;*

24 And if we haue not rather done it for feare of this thing, saying, †In time to come your children might speake vnto our children, saying, What haue you to doe with the Lord God of Israel?

† Hebr. to morrow.

25 For the Lord hath made Iordan a border betweene vs and you, yee children of Reuben, and children of Gad, yee haue no part in the Lord: so shal your children make our children cease from fearing the Lord:

26 Therefore we said, Let vs now prepare to build vs an altar, not for burnt offering, nor for sacrifice,

27 But that it may bee *a witnesse betweene vs and you, and our generations after vs, that we might do the seruice of the Lord before him with our burnt offrings, and with our sacrifices, and with our peace offerings, that your children may not say to our children in time to come, Ye haue no part in the Lord.

* Gen. 31. 48. chap. 24 27. ver. 34.

28 Therefore said we, that it shalbe, when they should so say to vs, or to our generations in time to come, that wee may say *againe,* Beholde the paterne of the altar of the Lord, which our fathers made, not for burnt offrings, nor for sacrifices, but it *is* a witnes betweene vs and you.

29 God forbid that we should rebell against the Lord, and turne this day from following the Lord, to build an altar for burnt offerings, for meate offerings, or for sacrifices, besides the Altar of the Lord our God that *is* before his Tabernacle.

30 ¶ And when Phinehas the Priest and the Princes of the Congregation, and Heads of the thousands of Israel which were with him, heard the words that the children of Reuben and the children of Gad, and the children of Manasseh spake, †it pleased them.

† Hebr. it was good in their eyes.

31 And Phinehas the sonne of Eleazar the Priest said vnto the children of Reuben, and to the children of Gad, and to the children of Manasseh, This day we

we perceiue that the LORD is among vs, because ye haue not committed this trespasse against the LORD: †now ye haue deliuered the children of Israel out of the hand of the LORD.

32 ¶ And Phinehas the sonne of Eleazar the Priest, and the Princes, returned from the children of Reuben, and from the children of Gad, out of the land of Gilead, vnto the land of Canaan, to the children of Israel, & brought them word againe.

33 And the thing pleased the children of Israel, and the children of Israel blessed God, and did not intend to goe vp against them in battel, to destroy the land wherein the children of Reuben and Gad dwelt.

34 And the children of Reuben, and the children of Gad called the altar ‖Ed: for it shall bee a witnesse betweene vs, that the LORD is God.

CHAP. XXIII.

1 Ioshuas exhortation before his death, 3 by former benefits, 5 by promises, 11 and by threatnings.

And it came to passe, a long time after that the LORD had giuen rest vnto Israel from all their enemies round about, that Ioshua waxed old, and †stricken in age.

2 And Ioshua called for all Israel, and for their Elders, & for their Heads, and for their Iudges, and for their Officers, and said vnto them; I am old, and stricken in age.

3 And yee haue seene all that the LORD your God hath done vnto all these nations, because of you; for the * LORD your God is hee that hath fought for you.

4 Behold, I haue diuided vnto you by lot these nations that remaine, to bee an inheritance for your tribes, from Iordan, with all the nations that I haue cut off, euen vnto the great Sea †Westward.

5 And the LORD your God, hee shall expell them from before you, and driue them from out of your sight, & ye shall possesse their land, as the LORD your God hath promised vnto you.

6 Be ye therefore very courageous to keepe and to doe all that is written in the booke of the Law of Moses, *that yee turne not aside therefrom, to the

right hand, or to the left,

7 That yee come not among these nations, these that remaine amongst you, neither * make mention of the name of their gods, nor cause to sweare by them, neither serue them, nor bow your selues vnto them.

8 ‖ But cleaue vnto the LORD your God, as yee haue done vnto this day.

9 ‖ For the LORD hath driuen out from before you, great nations, and strong: But as for you, no man hath beene able to stand before you vnto this day.

10 * One man of you shall chase a thousand: for the LORD your God, he it is that fighteth for you, as hee hath promised you.

11 Take good heed therefore vnto your †selues, that ye loue the LORD your God.

12 Else, if ye do in any wise go backe, and cleaue vnto the remnant of these nations, euen these that remaine among you, and shall make marriages with them, and goe in vnto them, and they to you:

13 Know for a certainety, that the LORD your God will no more driue out any of these nations from before you: *but they shalbe snares and traps vnto you, and scourges in your sides, and thornes in your eyes, vntill yee perish from off this good land which the LORD your God hath giuen you.

14 And behold, this day I am going the way of all the earth, and ye know in all your hearts, and in all your soules, that *not one thing hath failed of all the good things which the LORD your God spake concerning you; all are come to passe vnto you, and not one thing hath failed thereof.

15 Therefore it shall come to passe, that as all good things are come vpon you, which the LORD your God promised you : so shall the LORD bring vpon you all euill things, vntill he haue destroyed you from off this good land which the LORD your God hath giuen you.

16 When yee haue transgressed the Couenant of the LORD your God, which hee commaunded you, and haue gone and serued other gods, and bowed your selues to them : then shall the anger of the LORD bee kindled against you, and yee shall perish quickly from

Marginal notes

† Hebr. Then.

‖ That is, a witnesse.

† Heb. come into dayes.

* Exod. 14. 4.

† Hebr. at the Sunne set.

* Deut. 5. 32. and 28. 14.

* Psal. 16.

‖ Or, for if you will cleaue, &c

‖ Or, then the LORD will driue.

* Leuit. 26 8. deut. 32 30.

†Heb. soule

* Exod. 23 33. numb. 33. 55. deu 7. 16.

* Chap. 21 45.

from off the good land which hee hath giuen vnto you.

CHAP. XXIIII.

1 Ioshua assembleth the tribes at Shechem. 2 A briefe historie of Gods benefits from Terah. 14 He reneweth a couenant betweene them and God. 26 A stone the witnesse of the couenant. 29 Ioshuas age, death and buriall. 32 Iosephs bones are buried. 33 Eleazar dieth.

Nd Ioshua gathered all the Tribes of Israel to Shechem, and called for the Elders of Israel, and for their Heads, and for their Iudges, and for their Officers, and they presented themselues before God.

2 And Ioshua said vnto all the people, Thus saith the LORD God of Israel, * Your fathers dwelt on the other side of the flood in old time, *euen* Terah the father of Abraham, and the father of Nachor: and they serued other gods.

3 And I tooke your father Abraham frō the other side of the flood, and led him throughout all the land of Canaan, and multiplied his seed, and * gaue him Isaac.

4 And I gaue vnto Isaac, * Iacob and Esau: & I gaue vnto * Esau mount Seir, to possesse it : * but Iacob and his children went downe into Egypt.

5 * I sent Moses also and Aaron, and I plagued Egypt, according to that which I did amongst them : and afterward, I brought you out.

6 And I * brought your fathers out of Egypt: and you came vnto the sea, and the Egyptians pursued after your fathers with charets and horsemen vnto * the red sea.

7 And when they cried vnto the LORD, hee put darkenesse betweene you and the Egyptians, and brought the sea vpon them, and couered them, and your eyes haue seene what I haue done in Egypt, and ye dwelt in the wildernes a long season.

8 And I brought you into the land of the Amorites, which dwelt on the other side Iordan : * and they fought with you, and I gaue them into your hand, that ye might possesse their land, and I destroyed them from before you.

9 Then Balak the sonne of Zippor king of Moab, arose and warred against Israel, and * sent and called Balaam the sonne of Beor to curse you :

10 But I would not hearken vnto Balaam, therefore he blessed you still : so I deliuered you out of his hand.

11 And ye went ouer Iordan, and came vnto Iericho : and the men of Iericho fought against you, the Amorites, and the Perizzites, & the Canaanites, and the Hittites, and the Girgashites, the Hiuites, and the Iebusites, and I deliuered them into your hand.

12 And * I sent the hornet before you, which draue them out from before you, *euen* the two kings of the Amorites : *but* not with thy sword, nor with thy bow.

13 And I haue giuen you a land for which ye did not labour, & cities which ye built not, and yee dwell in them : of the vineyards and Oliue-yards which ye planted not, doe ye eate.

14 ¶ Now therefore, feare the LORD, and serue him in sinceritie, and in trueth, and put away the gods which your fathers serued on the other side of the flood, and in Egypt : and serue yee the LORD.

15 And if it seeme euill vnto you to serue the LORD, choose you this day whome you will serue, whether the gods which your fathers serued that were on the other side of the flood, or the gods of the Amorites, in whose lande ye dwell : but as for mee and my house, we will serue the LORD.

16 And the people answered and said, God forbid that wee should forsake the LORD, to serue other gods.

17 For the LORD our God, he *it is* that brought vs vp and our fathers out of the land of Egypt, from the house of bondage, & which did those great signes in our sight, and preserued vs in all the way wherein we went, and among all the people through whom we passed.

18 And the LORD draue out from before vs all the people, euen the Amorites which dwelt in the land : *therefore* will we also serue the LORD, for he is our God.

19 And Ioshua said vnto the people, Ye cannot serue the LORD : for hee is an holy God : he is a ielous God, he will not forgiue your transgressions nor your sinnes.

20 If yee forsake the LORD, and serue strange gods, * then he will turne, and doe you hurt, and consume you, after that he hath done you good.

21 And the people said vnto Ioshua, Nay,

Marginal notes

* Gen. 11.
11. iudit. 5.
5, 7.

* Gen. 21. 2

* Gen. 25.
*6.
* Gen. 36. 8
* Gen. 46. 6

* Exo. 3. 10

* Exod. 12.
*7.

* Exod. 14.
*.

* Num. 21
*3.

* Num. 22.
3. deut. 23. 4

* Exod. 23.
28. deut. 7.
20.

* Chap. 23.
15.

Nay, but we will serue the Lord.

22 And Ioshua said vnto the people, Yee are witnesses against your selues, that yee haue chosen you the Lord, to serue him. And they said, *We are* witnesses.

23 Now therefore put away, *said he,* the strange gods which are among you, and encline your heart vnto the Lord God of Israel.

24 And the people saide vnto Ioshua; The Lord our God will we serue, and his voice will we obey.

25 So Ioshua made a couenant with the people that day, and set them a Statute, & an Ordinance in Shechem.

26 ¶ And Ioshua wrote these words in the booke of the Law of God, and tooke a great stone, and set it vp there, vnder an oake, that was by the Sanctuary of the Lord.

27 And Ioshua saide vnto all the people, Behold, this stone shalbe a witnesse vnto vs; for it hath heard all the words of the Lord which hee spake vnto vs; it shall be there for a witnesse vnto you, lest ye deny your God.

28 So Ioshua let the people depart, euery man vnto his inheritance.

29 ¶ And it came to passe after these things, that Ioshua the sonne of Nun the seruant of the Lord died, being an hundred and ten yeeres old.

30 And they buried him in the border of his inheritance in *Timnath-Serah, which *is* in mount Ephraim, on the North side of the hill of Gaash.

31 And Israel serued the Lord all the dayes of Ioshua, & all the dayes of the Elders that †ouerliued Ioshua, and which had knowen al the works of the Lord, that he had done for Israel.

32 ¶ And *the bones of Ioseph, which the children of Israel brought vp out of Egypt, buried they in Shechem, in a parcell of ground which Iacob bought of *the sonnes of Hamor the father of Shechem, for an hundred ‖pieces of siluer; and it became the inheritance of the children of Ioseph.

33 And Eleazar the sonne of Aaron died, and they buried him in a hill that pertained to Phinehas his son, which was giuen him in mount Ephraim.

*Chap. 19.
50. iudg. 2.
9

† *Hebr. pro*
longed their
dayes after
Ioshua.

* Gen. 50.
25. exod.
13. 19.

* Gene. 33.
19.

‖ *Or, lambs*

¶ THE BOOKE OF
Iudges.

CHAP. I.

1 The actes of Iudah and Simeon. 4 Adoni-bezek iustly requited. 8 Hierusalem taken. 10 Hebron taken. 11 Othniel hath Achsah to wife for taking of Debir. 16 The Kenites dwel in Iudah. 17 Hormah, Gaza, Askelon and Ekron taken. 21 The acts of Beniamin. 22 Of the house of Ioseph, who take Bethel. 30 Of Zebulun. 31 Of Asher. 33 Of Naphtali. 34 Of Dan.

OW after the death of Ioshua, it came to passe, that the children of Israel asked the Lord, saying, Who shal goe vp for vs against the Canaanites first, to fight against them?

2 And the Lord sayd, Iudah shall goe vp : Behold, I haue deliuered the land into his hand.

3 And Iudah saide vnto Simeon his brother, Come vp with me into my lot, that wee may fight against the Canaanites, and I likewise will goe with thee into thy lot. So Simeon went with him.

4 And Iudah went vp, and the Lord deliuered the Canaanites and the Perizzites into their hand : and they slew of them in Bezek ten thousand men.

5 And they found Adoni-bezek in Bezek : and they fought against him, and they slew the Canaanites, and the Perizzites.

6 But Adoni-bezek fled, and they pursued after him, and caught him, and cut off his thumbes, and his great toes.

7 And

Hebr. the numbes of their hands and of their seete.
Or, gleaned

7 And Adoni-bezek said, Three-score & ten kings, hauing † their thumbs and their great toes cut off, ‖ gathered *their meate* vnder my table: as I haue done, so God hath requited mee, and they brought him to Ierusalem, and there he died.

8 (Now the children of Iudah had fought against Ierusalem, and had taken it, and smitten it with the edge of the sword, and set the citie on fire)

Iosh. 10.
5. and 11.
5. and 15.
8.

9 ¶ * And afterward the children of Iudah downe to fight against the Canaanites that dwelt in the moū-taine, & in the South, and in the ‖valley.

Or, lowe countrey.

10 And Iudah went against the Ca-naanites that dwelt in Hebron (nowe the name of Hebron before *was* * Kiri-ath-arba) and they slew Sheshai, and Ahiman, and Talmai.

Iosh. 15.
8.

11 And from thence he went against the inhabitants of Debir, (& the name of Debir before was Kiriath-sepher)

12 And Caleb said, Hee that smiteth Kiriath-sepher, and taketh it, to him will I giue Achsah my daughter to wife.

13 And Othniel the sonne of Kenaz Calebs yonger brother tooke it: and he gaue him Achsah his daughter to wife.

14 And it came to passe when shee came *to him*, that she moued him to aske of her father a field : and shee lighted from off her asse, and Caleb said vnto her, What wilt thou?

15 And she said vnto him, Giue me a blessing: for thou hast giuen mee a South land, giue me also springs of wa-ter. And Caleb gaue her the vpper springs, and the nether springs.

16 ¶ And the children of the Kenite, Moses father in law, went vp out of the citie of palme trees, with the chil-dren of Iudah into the wildernesse of Iudah, which *lieth* in the South of A-rad, and they went and dwelt among the people.

17 And Iudah went with Simeon his brother, and they slew the Canaa-nites that inhabited Zephath, and vt-terly destroyed it, (and the name of the * citie was called Hormah.)

Num. 21.

18 Also Iudah tooke Gaza with the coast thereof, and Askelon with the coast thereof, and Ekron with the coast thereof.

19 And the LORD was with Iu-dah, and hee ‖draue out *the inhabitants* of the mountaine, but could not driue out

Or, he pos-essed the mountaine.

the inhabitants of the valley, because they had charets of yron.

20 And they gaue Hebron vnto Ca-leb, * as Moses saide: and hee expelled thence the three sonnes of Anak.

* Num. 14.
24. Iosh. 14
13. & 15.
14.

21 And the children of Beniamin did not driue out the Iebusites that inhabi-ted Ierusalem : but the Iebusites dwel with the children of Beniamin in Ie-rusalem, vnto this day.

22 ¶ And the house of Ioseph, they also went vp against Bethel : and the LORD was with them.

23 And the house of Ioseph sent to descrie Bethel (now the name of the ci-tie before was * Luz)

* Gen. 28.
19.

24 And the spies sawe a man come forth out of the citie, and they said vnto him, Shew vs, wee pray thee, the en-trance into the citie, and * we will shew thee mercie.

* Iosh. 2. 14

25 And when hee shewed them the entrance into the citie, they smote the ci-tie with the edge of the sword: but they let goe the man and all his familie.

26 And the man went into the lande of the Hittites, and built a citie, and cal-led the name thereof Luz : which is the name thereof vnto this day.

27 ¶ * Neither did Manasseh driue out *the inhabitants* of Bethshean, and her townes, nor Taanach and her townes, nor the inhabitants of Dor, and her townes, nor the inhabitants of Ible-am, and her townes, nor the inhabi-tants of Megiddo, and her townes : but the Canaanites would dwel in that land.

* Iosh. 17.
11, 12.

28 And it came to passe when Israel was strong, that they put the Canaa-nites to tribute; and did not vtterly driue them out.

29 ¶ * Neither did Ephraim driue out the Canaanites that dwelt in Ge-zer : but the Canaanites dwelt in Ge-zer among them.

* Iosh. 16.
10.

30 ¶ Neither did Zebulun driue out the inhabitants of Kitron, nor the in-habitants of Nahalol : but the Canaa-nites dwelt among them, and became tributaries.

31 ¶ Neither did Asher driue out the inhabitants of Accho, nor the inhabi-tants of Zidon, nor of Ahlab, nor Ach-zib, nor Helbath, nor Aphik, nor of Rehob :

32 But the Asherites dwelt among the Canaanites, the inhabitants of the land : for they did not driue them out.

33 ¶ Nei-

33 ¶ Neither did Naphtali driue out the inhabitants of Bethſhemeſh, nor the inhabitants of Bethanath, but hee dwelt among the Canaanites, the inhabitants of the land: neuertheleſſe, the inhabitants of Bethſhemeſh, and of Bethanath, became tributaries vnto them.

34 And the Amorites forced the children of Dan into the mountaine: for they would not ſuffer them to come downe to the valley.

35 But the Amorites would dwell in mount Heres in Aiialon, & in Shaalbim: yet the hand of the houſe of Ioſeph †preuailed, ſo that they became tributaries.

† Hebr. was heauy.

36 And the coaſt of the Amorites was from ‖the going vp to Akrabbim, from the rocke, and vpward.

‖ Or, Maale-Akrabbim.

CHAP. II.

1 An Angel rebuketh the people at Bochim. 6 The wickedneſſe of the new generation after Ioſhua. 14 Gods anger and pitie towards them. 20 The Canaanites are left to proue Israel.

And an ‖ Angel of the LORD came vp from Gilgal to Bochim, and ſaid, I made you to goe vp out of Egypt, and haue brought you vnto the land which I ſware vnto your fathers, and I ſaid, I will neuer breake my Couenant with you.

‖ Or, meſſenger.

2 And * yee ſhall make no league with the inhabitants of this land, * you ſhal throw downe their altars. But ye haue not obeyed my voyce; Why haue ye done this?

* Deut. 7. 2.
* Deut. 12. 3.

3 Wherefore I also ſaid, I will not driue them out from before you: but they ſhalbe * as thornes in your ſides, and their gods ſhalbe a * ſnare vnto you.

* Ioſh. 23. 13.
* Exod. 23. 33. and 34. 12.

4 And it came to paſſe when the Angel of the LORD ſpake theſe words vnto all the children of Israel, that the people lift vp their voice, and wept.

5 And they called the name of that place * Bochim: and they ſacrificed there vnto the LORD.

* That is, weepers.

6 ¶ And when Ioſhua had let the people goe, the children of Israel went euery man vnto his inheritance, to poſſeſſe the land.

7 And the people ſerued the LORD all the dayes of Ioſhua, and all the dayes of the Elders that † outliued Ioſhua, who had ſeene all the great workes of the LORD, that hee did for Israel.

† Hebr. prolonged dayes after Ioſhu.

8 And Ioſhua the ſonne of Nun, the ſeruant of the LORD died, being an hundred and ten yeeres old.

9 And they buried him in the border of his inheritance in Timnath-Heres, in the mount of Ephraim, on the North ſide of the hill Gaaſh.

10 And also all that generation were gathered vnto their fathers: and there aroſe another generation after them, which knew not the LORD, nor yet the woorkes which hee had done for Israel.

11 ¶ And the children of Israel did euil in the ſight of the LORD, and ſerued Baalim:

12 And they forſooke the LORD God of their fathers, which brought them out of the land of Egypt, and followed other gods, of the gods of the people that were round about them, and bowed themſelues vnto them, and prouoked the LORD to anger.

13 And they forſooke the LORD, and ſerued Baal and Aſhtaroth.

14 ¶ And the anger of the LORD was hote againſt Israel, and he deliuered them into the hands of ſpoilers that ſpoiled them, and *he ſold them into the hands of their enemies round about, ſo that they could not any longer ſtand before their enemies.

* Psal. 44. 12. iſa. 50. 1.

15 Whither ſoeuer they went out, the hand of the LORD was againſt them for euill, as the LORD had ſaid, and *as the LORD had ſworne vnto them: and they were greatly diſtreſſed.

* Leuit. 26 deut. 28.

16 ¶ Neuerthelesse, the LORD rayſed vp Iudges, which † deliuered them out of the hand of thoſe that ſpoyled them.

† Hebr. ſaued.

17 And yet they would not hearken vnto their Iudges, but they went a whoring after other gods, and bowed themſelues vnto them: they turned quickly out of the way, which their fathers walked in, obeying the Commandements of the LORD; but they did not ſo.

18 And when the LORD raiſed them vp Iudges, then the LORD was with the Iudge, and deliuered them out of the hand of their enemies, all the dayes of the Iudge (for it repented the LORD, becauſe of their gronings by reason

reason of them that oppressed them, and vexed them:)

* Chap. 3. 2. Or, were orrupt.

19 And it came to passe * when the Iudge was dead, that they returned, and ‖ corrupted themselues more then their fathers, in following other gods, to serue them, and to bow downe vnto them: † they ceased not from their owne doings, nor from their stubborne way.

Hebr. they t nothing all of their.

20 ¶ And the anger of the Lord was hote against Israel, and he said, Because that this people hath transgressed my Couenant which I commanded their fathers, and haue not hearkened vnto my voice:

21 I also will not henceforth driue out any from before them of the nations which Ioshua left when he died:

22 That through them I may proue Israel, whether they will keepe the way of the Lord, to walke therein, as their fathers did keepe it, or not.

Or, suffred.

23 Therefore the Lord ‖ left those nations, without driuing them out hastily, neither deliuered he them into the hand of Ioshua.

CHAP. III.

1 The nations which were left to prooue Israel. 6 By communion with them they commit idolatrie. 8 Othniel deliuereth them from Chushan-Rishathaim. 12 Ehud from Eglon. 31 Shamgar from the Philistines.

Ow these are the nations which the Lord left, to prooue Israel by them, (euen as many of Israel as had not knowen all the warres of Canaan;

2 Onely that the generations of the children of Israel might know to teach them warre, at the least such as before knew nothing thereof:)

3 Namely fiue lords of the Philistines, and all the Canaanites, and the Sidonians, and the Hiuites that dwelt in mount Lebanon, from mount Baal-Hermon, vnto the entring in of Hamath.

4 And they were to prooue Israel by them, to know whether they would hearken vnto the Commaundements of the Lord, which hee commaunded their fathers by the hand of Moses.

5 ¶ And the children of Israel dwelt among the Canaanites, Hittites, and Amorites, and Perizzites, and Hiuites, and Iebusites,

6 And they tooke their daughters to be their wiues, and gaue their daughters to their sonnes, and serued their gods.

7 And the children of Israel did euill in the sight of the Lord, and forgate the Lord their God, and serued Baalim, and the groues.

8 ¶ Therefore the anger of the Lord was hote against Israel, and he sold them into the hand of Chushan-Rishathaim king of † Mesopotamia: and the children of Israel serued Chushan-Rishathaim eight yeeres.

† Hebr. Aram-naharaim.

9 And when the children of Israel cryed vnto the Lord, the Lord raised vp a † deliuerer to the children of Israel, who deliuered them, euen Othniel the sonne of Kenaz, Calebs yonger brother.

† Hebr. sauiour.

10 And the Spirit of the Lord † came vpon him, and he iudged Israel, and went out to warre, & the Lord deliuered Chushan-Rishathaim king of † Mesopotamia into his hand; and his hand preuailed against Chushan-Rishathaim.

† Hebr. was.

† Hebr. Aram.

11 And the land had rest forty yeres: and Othniel the sonne of Kenaz died.

12 ¶ And the children of Israel did euill againe in the sight of the Lord: and the Lord strengthened Eglon the king of Moab against Israel, because they had done euill in the sight of the Lord.

13 And hee gathered vnto him the children of Ammon, and Amalek, and went and smote Israel, and possessed the city of Palme-trees.

14 So the children of Israel serued Eglon the King of Moab eighteene yeeres.

15 But when the children of Israel cried vnto the Lord, the Lord raised them vp a deliuerer, Ehud the sonne of Gera, ‖ a Beniamite, a man ‖ left handed: and by him the children of Israel sent a Present vnto Eglon the king of Moab.

‖ Or, the sonne of Iemini.

† Hebr. shut of his right hand.

16 But Ehud made him a dagger (which had two edges) of a cubite length, and he did gird it vnder his raiment, vpon his right thigh,

17 And he brought the present vnto Eglon king of Moab: and Eglon was a very fat man.

18 And when he had made an end to offer the Present, he sent away the people that bare the Present.

19 But

19 But hee himselfe turned againe from the ‖ quarries that were by Gilgal, and said, I haue a secret errand vnto thee, O king: who said, Keepe silence. And all that stood by him, went out from him.

† Or, grauen images.

20 And Ehud came vnto him, and he was sitting in † a Summer parlour, which hee had for himselfe alone: And Ehud said, I haue a message from God vnto thee. And he arose out of *his* seat.

† Heb. a parlour of cooling.

21 And Ehud put forth his left hand, and tooke the dagger from his right thigh, and thrust it into his belly.

22 And the haft also went in after the blade: and the fatte closed *vpon* the blade, so that hee could not drawe the dagger out of his belly, and the ‖ dirt came out.

‖ Or, it came out at the fundament.

23 Then Ehud went forth through the porche, and shut the doores of the parlour vpon him, and locked them.

24 When he was gone out, his seruants came, and when they saw, that behold, the doores of the parlour were locked, they said, Surely he ‖ couereth his feet in his Summer chamber.

‖ Or, doth hiseasement.

25 And they taried till they were ashamed: and behold, he opened not the doores of the parlour, therefore they tooke a key, and opened *them*: and behold, their lord was fallen downe dead on the earth.

26 And Ehud escaped while they taried: and passed beyond the quarries, and escaped vnto Seirath.

27 And it came to passe when hee was come, that hee blew a trumpet in the mountaine of Ephraim, and the children of Israel went downe with him from the mount, & he before them.

28 And hee said vnto them, Follow after me: for the LORD hath deliuered your enemies the Moabites into your hand. And they went downe after him, and tooke the foords of Iordan toward Moab, and suffered not a man to passe ouer.

29 And they slewe of Moab at that time about ten thousand men, all † lusty, and all men of valour, and there escaped not a man.

† Heb. fat.

30 So Moab was subdued that day vnder the hand of Israel: and the land had rest fourescore yeeres.

31 ¶ And after him was Shamgar the sonne of Anath, which slew of the Philistines six hundred men with an oxe goad, and he also deliuered Israel.

CHAP. IIII.

1 Deborah and Barak deliuer them from Iabin and Sisera. 18 Iael killeth Sisera.

And the children of Israel againe did euil in the sight of the LORD, when Ehud was dead.

2 And the LORD sold them into the hande of Iabin king of Canaan: that reigned in Hazor, the captaine of whose host was Sisera, which dwelt in Harosheth of the Gentiles.

3 And the children of Israel cried vnto the LORD : for he had nine hundred charets of yron : and twentie yeres hee mightily oppressed the children of Israel.

4 ¶ And Deborah a prophetesse, the wife of Lapidoth, shee iudged Israel at that time.

5 And shee dwelt vnder the palme tree of Deborah, betweene Ramah and Bethel in mount Ephraim: and the children of Israel came vp to her for iudgement.

6 And shee sent and called Barak the sonne of Abinoam, out of Kedesh-Naphtali, and said vnto him, Hath not the LORD God of Israel commaunded, *saying*, Goe, and drawe toward mount Tabor, and take with thee ten thousand men of the children of Naphtali, and of the children of Zebulun ?

7 And I wil draw vnto thee to the * riuer Kishon, Sisera the captaine of Iabins army, with his charets, and his multitude, and I will deliuer him into thine hand.

* Psal. 83. 9, 10.

8 And Barak said vnto her, If thou wilt goe with me, then I wil goe : but if thou wilt not goe with mee, then I will not goe.

9 And she said, I wil surely go with thee, notwithstanding the iourney that thou takest, shal not be for thine honor: for the LORD shall sell Sisera into the hand of a woman. And Deborah arose, & went with Barak to Kedesh.

10 ¶ And Barak called Zebulun, and Naphtali to Kedesh, and he went vp with ten thousand men at his feete : and Deborah went vp with him.

11 Now Heber the Kenite, which was of the children of *Hobab the father in law of Moses, had seuered himselfe from the Kenites, and pitched his tent vnto the plaine of Zaanaim, which is by Kedesh.

* Numb. 1 29.

12 And

Hebr. ga-
ered by cry
procla-
ation.

12 And they shewed Sisera, that Barak the sonne of Abinoam was gone vp to mount Tabor.

13 And Sisera † gathered together all his charets, euen nine hundred charets of iron, and al the people that were with him, from Harosheth of the Gentiles, vnto the riuer of Kishon.

14 And Deborah said vnto Barak, Vp, for this *is* the day in which the LORD hath deliuered Sisera into thine hand : Is not the LORD gone out before thee ? so Barak went downe from mount Tabor, and ten thousand men after him.

Psal. 83.

15 And the * LORD discomfited Sisera, and all his charets, and all his hoste with the edge of the sword, before Barak : so that Sisera lighted downe off his charet, and fled away on his feet.

16 But Barak pursued after the charets, and after the hoste vnto Harosheth of the Gentiles, and all the host of Sisera fell vpon the edge of the sword; *and* there was not † a man left.

Hebr. vnto
e.

17 Howbeit Sisera fled away on his feet, to the tent of Iael the wife of Heber the Kenite : for there was peace betweene Iabin the king of Hazor, and the house of Heber the Kenite.

18 ¶ And Iael went out to meete Sisera, and said vnto him, Turne in, my lord, turne in to me, feare not. And when hee had turned in vnto her, into the tent, shee couered him with a ‖ mantle.

Or, rugge,
blanket.

19 And he said vnto her, Giue me, I pray thee, a litle water to drinke, for I am thirstie. And she opened *a bottle of milke, and gaue him drinke, and couered him.

Chap. 5.

20 Againe he said vnto her, Stand in the doore of the tent, and it shall bee when any man doeth come and enquire of thee and say, Is there any man here ? that thou shalt say, No.

Hebr. put.

21 Then Iael Hebers wife, † tooke a naile of the tent, and tooke an hammer in her hand, and went softly vnto him, and smote the naile into his temples, and fastened it into the ground : (for he was fast asleepe, and weary ;) so he died.

22 And behold, as Barak pursued Sisera, Iael came out to meet him, and said vnto him, Come, and I will shew thee the man whom thou seekest. And when he came into her *tent*, behold, Sisera lay dead, and the naile *was* in his temples.

23 So God subdued on that day, Iabin the king of Canaan, before the children of Israel.

24 And the hand of the children of Israel † prospered, & preuailed against Iabin the king of Canaan, vntill they had destroyed Iabin king of Canaan.

† Hebr. go-
ing, went
and was
hard.

CHAP. V.

1 The Song of Deborah and Barak.

Hen sang Deborah, and Barak the son of Abinoam, on that day, saying,

2 Praise ye the LORD, for the auenging of Israel, when the people willingly offered themselues.

3 Heare, O ye kings, giue eare, O ye Princes : I, *euen* I will sing vnto the LORD, I wil sing *praise* to the LORD God of Israel.

4 LORD, * when thou wentest out of Seir, when thou marchedst out of the field of Edom, the earth trembled, and the heauens dropped, the clouds also dropped water.

* Deut. 4.
11.

5 * The mountaines † melted from before the LORD, *euen* * that Sinai, from before the LORD God of Israel.

6 In the dayes of * Shamgar the son of Anath, in the dayes of * Iael, the high wayes were vnoccupied, and the † traueilers walked thorow † by-wayes.

* Psal. 97.5.
† Hebr.
flowed.
* Exod. 19.
18.
* Chap. 3.
31.
* Chap. 4.
18.
† Hebr. wal-
kers of paths.
† Hebr.
crooked
wayes.

7 *The inhabitants* of the villages ceased, they ceased in Israel, vntill that I Deborah arose, that I arose a mother in Israel.

8 They chose new gods ; then was warre in the gates : was there a shield or speare seene among fourtie thousand in Israel ?

9 My heart is toward the gouernours of Israel, that offered themselues willingly among the people : Blesse ye the LORD.

10 ‖ Speake yee that ride on white asses, yee that sit in Iudgement, and walke by the way.

‖ Or, medi-
tate.

11 *They that are deliuered* from the noise of Archers in the places of drawing water ; there shall they rehearse the righteous acts of the LORD, *euen* the †righteous acts *towards the inhabitants* of his villages in Israel : then shall the people of the LORD goe downe to the gates.

12 Awake,

† Hebr. righ-
teousnesses
of the Lord.

12 Awake, awake Deborah: awake, awake, vtter a song: arise Barak, and leade thy captiuitie captiue, thou sonne of Abinoam.

13 Then hee made him that remaineth, haue dominion ouer the Nobles among the people: the LORD made me haue dominion ouer the mightie.

14 Out of Ephraim was there a roote of them against Amalek, after thee Beniamin, among thy people: Out of Machir came downe gouernours, †and out of Zebulun they that †handle the pen of the writer.

15 And the princes of Issachar *were* with Deborah: euen Issachar, and also Barak, he was sent on †foot into the valley: ‖ for the diuisions of Reuben, *there were* great †thoughts of heart.

16 Why abodest thou among the sheepefolds, to heare the bleatings of the flocks? ‖ *for* the diuisions of Reuben *there were* great searchings of heart.

17 Gilead abode beyond Iordan: and why did Dan remaine in ships? Asher continued on the sea ‖ shore, and abode in his ‖ breaches.

18 Zebulun and Naphtali *were* a people that †ieoparded their liues vnto the death, in the high places of the field.

19 The kings came *and* fought, then fought the kings of Canaan in Taanach by the waters of Megiddo, they tooke no gaine of money.

20 They fought from heauen, the starres in their †courses fought against Sisera.

21 The riuer of Kishon swept them away, that ancient riuer, the riuer Kishon: O my soule, thou hast troden downe strength.

22 Then were the horse hoofes broken, by the meanes of the ‖ pransings, the pransings of their mightie ones.

23 Curse ye Meroz (said the Angel of the LORD) curse ye bitterly the inhabitants thereof: because they came not to the helpe of the LORD, to the helpe of the LORD against the mighty.

24 Blessed aboue women shal Iael the wife of Heber the Kenite be, blessed shall she be aboue women in the tent.

25 He asked water, *and* she gaue him milke, shee brought foorth butter in a lordly dish.

26 Shee put her hand to the naile, and her right hand to the workemens hammer: and with the hammer shee †smote Sisera, shee smote off his head,

when she had pearsed & striken through his temples.

27 †At her feete he bowed, he fell, he lay downe: at her feet he bowed, he fell; where he bowed, there he fel down †dead.

28 The mother of Sisera looked out at a window, and cried through the lattesse, Why is his charet so long in comming? Why tarie the wheeles of his charets?

29 Her wise ladies answered her, yea she returned †answere to her selfe,

30 Haue they not sped? haue they *not* diuided the pray †to euery man a damosell or two? To Sisera a pray of diuers colours, a pray of diuers colours, of needle worke, of diuers colours of needle worke on both sides, meet †for the necks of *them that take* the spoile?

31 So let all thine enemies perish, O LORD: but *let* them that loue him, *be* as the Sunne when he goeth foorth in his might. And the land had rest fourtie yeeres.

CHAP. VI.

1 The Israelites for their sinne are oppressed by Midian. 8 A prophet rebuketh them. 11 An Angel sendeth Gideon for their deliuerance. 17 Gideons Present is consumed with fire. 24 Gideon destroyeth Baals altar, and offreth a sacrifice vpon the altar Iehouah-shalom. 28 Ioash defendeth his son, & calleth him Ierubbaal. 33 Gideons armie. 36 Gideons signes.

AND the children of Israel did euill in the sight of the LORD: and the LORD deliuered them into the hande of Midian seuen yeeres.

2 And the hand of Midian †preuailed against Israel: *and* because of the Midianites, the children of Israel made them the dennes which *are* in the mountaines, and caues, & strong holds.

3 And *so* it was when Israel had sowen, that the Midianites came vp, & the Amalekites, & the children of the East, euen they came vp against them,

4 And they encamped against them, and destroyed the encrease of the earth, till thou come vnto Gaza, and left no sustenance for Israel, neither ‖ sheepe, nor oxe, nor asse.

5 For they came vp with their cattell and their tents, and they came as Grashoppers for multitude, for both they and their camels were without number:

Marginal notes (left column):

† Heb. drawe with the pen, &c.

† Hebr. his feete.
‖ Or, in the diuisions, &c.
† Hebr. impressions.
‖ Or, in.

‖ Or, port.
‖ Or, creeks.

† Heb. exposed to reproch.

† Heb. paths.

‖ Or, tramplings, or plungings.

† Heb. hammered.

Marginal notes (right column):

† Hebr. betweene.

† Heb. destroyed.

† Heb. word.

† Heb. to head of a man.

† Hebr. fo the neckes of the spoile

† Heb. was strong.

‖ Or, goate

number : and they entred into the land to destroy it.

6 And Israel was greatly impoue-rished, because of the Midianites, and the children of Israel cryed vnto the LORD.

7 ¶ And it came to passe when the children of Israel cryed vnto the LORD, because of the Midianites,

8 That the LORD sent †a Pro-phet vnto the children of Israel, which said vnto them ; Thus saith the LORD God of Israel, I brought you vp from Egypt, and brought you foorth out of the house of bondage,

9 And I deliuered you out of the hand of the Egyptians, and out of the hand of al that oppressed you, and draue them out from before you, and gaue you their land :

10 And I said vnto you, I am the LORD your God, *feare not the gods of the Amorites in whose land ye dwel: But ye haue not obeyed my voice.

11 ¶ And there came an Angel of the LORD, and sate vnder an Oake which was in Ophrah, that pertained vn-to Ioash the Abi-Ezrite: and his sonne *Gideon threshed wheat by the wine-presse, †to hide it from the Midianites.

12 And the Angel of the LORD appeared vnto him, and said vnto him, The LORD is with thee, thou migh-tie man of valour.

13 And Gideon said vnto him, Oh my Lord, if the LORD bee with vs, why then is all this befallen vs ? and where be all his miracles which our fa-thers tolde vs of, saying, Did not the LORD bring vs vp from Egypt? but now the LORD hath forsaken vs, and deliuered vs into the hands of the Mi-dianites.

14 And the LORD looked vpon him, and said, Goe in this thy might, and thou shalt saue Israel from the hand of the Midianites : haue not I sent thee ?

15 And hee said vnto him, Oh my lord, wherewith shall I saue Israel ? behold, ||my family is poore in Manas-seh, and I am the least in my fathers house.

16 And the LORD said vnto him, Surely I will be with thee, and thou shalt smite the Midianites, as one man.

17 And he said vnto him, If now I haue found grace in thy sight, then shew me a signe, that thou talkest with me.

18 Depart not hence , I pray thee, vntill I come vnto thee, and bring forth my ||Present, and set it before thee. And hee saide, I will tary vntill thou come againe.

19 ¶ And Gideon went in, and made ready †a kid, and vnleauened cakes of an Ephah of floure : the flesh he put in a basket, and he put the broth in a pot, and brought it out vnto him vnder the oake, and presented it.

20 And the Angel of God sayd vn-to him, Take the flesh, and the vnleaue-ned cakes , and lay them vpon this rocke, and powre out the broth. And he did so.

21 ¶ Then the Angel of the LORD put foorth the end of the staffe that was in his hand, and touched the flesh, and the vnleauened cakes, and there rose vp fire out of the rocke, and consumed the flesh and the vnleauened cakes : then the Angel of the LORD departed out of his sight.

22 And when Gideon perceiued that hee was an Angel of the LORD, Gi-deon said, Alas, O Lord GOD : *for because I haue seene an Angel of the LORD face to face.

23 And the LORD said vnto him, Peace be vnto thee, feare not, thou shalt not die.

24 Then Gideon built an Altar there vnto the LORD, and called it ||Iehouah-shalom: vnto this day it is yet in Ophrah, of the Abi-Ezrites.

25 ¶ And it came to passe the same night, that the LORD said vnto him, Take thy fathers yong bullocke, ||euen the second bullocke of seuen yeeres old, and throw downe the altar of Baal that thy father hath, and cut downe the groue that is by it :

26 And builde an Altar vnto the LORD thy God vpon the top of this †rocke, in ||the ordered place, and take the second bullocke , and offer a burnt sacrifice with the wood of the groue, which thou shalt cut downe.

27 Then Gideon tooke ten men of his seruants, and did as the LORD had said vnto him: And so it was be-cause hee feared his fathers houshold, and the men of the city, that he could not doe it by day , that hee did it by night.

28 ¶ And when the men of the citie arose earely in the morning, behold, the altar of Baal was cast downe, and the groue

---

Marginal notes:

||Or, meat offering.

† Hebr. a kid of the goates.

ebr. a , a Pro-t.

King. 35, 36. m. 10. 2.

eb. 11. alled eon. ebr. to se it to

my sand is neanest.

*Exod. 33. 20. chap. 13, 22.

||That is, The Lord send peace.

||Or, and.

† Hebr. strong place. ||Or, in an orderly ma-ner.

groue was cut downe that *was* by it, and the second bullocke was offered vpon the altar that was built.

29 And they said one to another, Who hath done this thing? And when they enquired and asked, they said, Gideon the sonne of Ioash hath done this thing.

30 Then the men of the citie said vnto Ioash, Bring out thy sonne, that he may die : because he hath cast downe the altar of Baal, and because hee hath cut downe the groue that *was* by it.

31 And Ioash said vnto all that stood against him, Will ye pleade for Baal? will ye saue him? He that will plead for him, let him be put to death whilest *it is yet* morning: if he be a god, let him plead for himselfe, because one hath cast down his altar.

32 Therefore on that day hee called him Ierubbaal, saying, Let Baal plead against him, because *hee* hath throwen downe his altar.

33 ¶ Then all the Midianites, and the Amalekites, and the children of the East were gathered together, and went ouer, and pitched in the valley of Iezreel.

† *Hebr. clothed.*
* *Num. 10. 3. chap. 3. 27.*
† *Heb. was called after him.*

34 But the Spirit of the LORD †came vpon Gideon, and hee *blewe a trumpet, and Abiezer †was gathered after him.

35 And he sent messengers throughout all Manasseh, who also was gathered after him, and hee sent messengers vnto Asher, and vnto Zebulun, and vnto Naphtali, and they came vp to meete them.

36 ¶ And Gideon said vnto God, If thou wilt saue Israel by mine hand, as thou hast said,

37 Beholde, I will put a fleece of wooll in the floore : *and* if the deaw be on the fleece onely, and it bee drie vpon all the earth *beside*, then shall I know that thou wilt saue Israel by my hande, as thou hast said.

38 And it was so : for he rose vp early on the morrow, and thrust the fleece together, and wringed the deaw out of the fleece, a bowle full of water.

* *Gen. 18. 32.*

39 And Gideon said vnto God, * Let not thine anger be hote against me, and I will speake but this once : Let mee prooue, I pray thee, but this once with the fleece. Let it now be drie onely vpon the fleece, and vpon all the ground let there be deaw.

40 And God did so that night : for it was drie vpon the fleece onely, and there was deaw on all the ground.

CHAP. VII.

1 Gideons armie of two and thirtie thousand is brought to three hundred. 9 He is encouraged by the dreame and interpretation of the barley cake. 16 His stratageme of trumpets and lampes in pitchers. 24 The Ephraimites take Oreb and Zeeb.

THen Ierubbaal (who is Gideon) and all the people that were with him, rose vp early, and pitched beside the well of Harod: so that the hoste of the Midianites were on the North side of them by the hill of Moreh, in the valley.

2 And the LORD said vnto Gideon, The people that are with thee, *are* too many for me to giue the Midianites into their handes, lest Israel vaunt themselues against mee, saying, Mine owne hand hath saued me.

* *Deut. 20. 1. mac. 3. 4*

3 Now therefore go to, proclaime in the eares of the people, saying, *Whosoeuer is fearefull and afraid, let him returne and depart earely from mount Gilead : and there returned of the people twentie and two thousand, & there remained ten thousand.

4 And the LORD said vnto Gideon, The people *are* yet too many: bring them downe vnto the water, and I will trie them for thee there: and it shall bee that of whome I say vnto thee, This shall goe with thee, the same shall goe with thee : and of whomsoeuer I say vnto thee, This shal not goe with thee, the same shall not goe.

5 So he brought downe the people vnto the water : and the LORD sayd vnto Gideon, Euery one that lappeth of the water with his tongue as a dog lappeth, him shalt thou set by himselfe, likewise euery one that boweth downe vpon his knees to drinke.

6 And the number of them that lapped *putting* their hand to their mouth, were three hundred men: but all the rest of the people bowed downe vpon their knees to drinke water.

7 And the LORD said vnto Gideon, By the three hundred men that lapped, will I saue you, and deliuer the Midianites into thine hand : and let all the *other* people goe euery man vnto his place.

8 So

8 So the people tooke victuals in their hand, and their trumpets: and he sent all *the rest of* Israel, euery man vnto his tent, and reteined those three hundred men: and the hoste of Midian was beneath him in the valley.

9 ¶ And it came to passe the same night, that the LORD sayd vnto him, Arise, get thee downe vnto the hoste, for I haue deliuered it into thine hand.

10 But if thou feare to goe downe, goe thou with Phurah thy seruant downe to the hoste.

11 And thou shalt heare what they say, and afterward shall thine handes be strengthened to goe downe vnto the hoste. Then went hee downe, with Phurah his seruant, vnto the outside of the ‖armed men, that were in the hoste.

‖Or, rankes fiue.

12 And the Midianites, and the Amalekites, and *all the children of the East, lay along in the valley like grashoppers for multitude, and their camels were without number, as the sand by the Sea side for multitude.

*Chap. 6.

13 And when Gideon was come, beholde, there was a man that tolde a dreame vnto his fellow, and sayd, Behold, I dreamed a dreame, and loe, a cake of Barley bread tumbled into the hoste of Midian, and came vnto a tent, and smote it that it fell, and ouerturned it, that the tent lay along.

14 And his fellow answered, and said, This is nothing els saue the sword of Gideon the sonne of Ioash, a man of Israel: *for* into his hand hath God deliuered Midian, and all the hoste.

15 ¶ And it was *so*, when Gideon heard the telling of the dreame, and †the interpretation thereof, that hee worshipped, and returned into the host of Israel, and sayd, Arise, for the LORD hath deliuered into your hand the host of Midian.

†Hebr. the breaking thereof.

16 And he diuided the three hundred men into three companies, and hee put a †trumpet in euery mans hand, with empty pitchers, and ‖lampes within the pitchers,

†Hebr. trumpets in the hand of all of them.
‖Or, firebrands: or torches.

17 And hee said vnto them, Looke on mee, and doe likewise; and beholde, when I come to the outside of the campe, it shall be that as I doe, so shall ye doe.

18 When I blow with a trumpet, I and all that are with mee, then blow ye the trumpets also on euery side of all the campe, and say, *The sword* of the LORD, and of Gideon.

19 ¶ So Gideon and the hundred men that were with him, came vnto the outside of the campe, in the beginning of the middle watch, and they had but newly set the watch, and they blew the trumpets, and brake the pitchers that were in their hands.

20 And the three companies blew the trumpets, and brake the pitchers, and held the lampes in their left hands, and the trumpets in their right hands to blow *withall*: and they cryed, The sword of the LORD, and of Gideon.

21 And they stood euery man in his place, round about the campe: and all the host ranne, and cried, and fled.

22 And the three hundred blew the trumpets, and *the LORD set euery mans sword against his fellow, euen throughout all the host: and the host fled to Beth-shittah, ‖in Zererath, and to the †border of Abel Meholah, vnto Tabbath.

*Esay 9. 4.
‖Or, towards.
†Hebr. lip.

23 And the men of Israel gathered themselues together out of Naphtali, and out of Asher, and out of all Manasseh, and pursued after the Midianites.

24 ¶ And Gideon sent messengers throughout all mount Ephraim, saying; Come downe against the Midianites, and take before them the waters vnto Beth-barah, and Iordan. Then all the men of Ephraim gathered themselues together, and tooke the waters vnto Beth-barah, and Iordane.

25 And they tooke *two Princes of the Midianites, Oreb, and Zeeb; and they slew Oreb vpon the rocke Oreb, and Zeeb they slew at the winepresse of Zeeb, and pursued Midian, and brought the heads of Oreb and Zeeb, to Gideon on the other side Iordan.

*Psal. 83. 11. esa. 10. 26.

CHAP. VIII.

1 Gideon pacifieth the Ephraimites. 4 Succoth and Penuel refuse to relieue Gideons army. 10 Zebah and Zalmunna are taken. 13 Succoth and Penuel are destroyed. 17 Gideon reuengeth his brethrens death on Zebah and Zalmunna. 22 Hee refuseth gouernment. 24 His Ephod cause of Idolatry. 22 Midian subdued. 29 Gideons children, and death. 33 The Israelites idolatry, and ingratitude.

And

† Hebr. what thing is this, thou-hast done vnto vs?

† Hebr. strongly.

A Nd the men of Ephraim said vnto him, † Why hast thou serued vs thus, that thou calledst vs not when thou wentest to fight with the Midianites? And they did chide with him † sharpely.

2 And he said vnto them, What haue I done now in comparison of you? Is not the gleaning of the grapes of Ephraim better then the vintage of Abiezer?

† Heb. spirit.

3 God hath deliuered into your hands the princes of Midian, Oreb and Zeeb: and what was I able to doe in comparison of you? then their † anger was abated toward him, when he had said that.

4 ¶ And Gideon came to Iordan, *and* passed ouer, hee, and the three hundred men that *were* with him, faint, yet pursuing *them*.

5 And he said vnto the men of Succoth, Giue, I pray you, loaues of bread vnto the people that follow me, for they *bee* faint, and I am pursuing after Zebah and Zalmunna, kings of Midian.

6 ¶ And the princes of Succoth said, Are the hands of Zebah and Zalmunna now in thine hands, that wee should giue bread vnto thine armie?

7 And Gideon said, Therfore when the LORD hath deliuered Zebah and Zalmunna into mine hand, then I wil *† Heb. thresh* † teare your flesh with the thornes of the wildernesse, and with briers.

8 ¶ And he went vp thence to Penuel, and spake vnto them likewise: and the men of Penuel answered him, as the men of Succoth had answered him.

9 And he spake also vnto the men of Penuel, saying, When I come againe in peace, I will breake downe this towre.

10 ¶ Now Zebah and Zalmunna *were* in Karkor, and their hostes with them, about fifteene thousand men, all that were left of all the hosts of the children of the East: for there fell ‖ an hundred and twentie thousand men that drew sword.

‖ Or, an hundreth and twenty thousand, euery one drawing a sword.

11 ¶ And Gideon went vp by the way of them that dwelt in tents, on the East of Nobah, and Iogbehah, and smote the host: for the host was secure.

12 And when Zebah and Zalmunna fled, he pursued after them, and took the two kings of Midian, Zebah, and *† Heb. terrified.* Zalmunna, & † discomfited all the host.

13 ¶ And Gideon the sonne of Ioash

returned from battel before the Sunne was vp,

14 And caught a yong man of the men of Succoth, and enquired of him: and he † described vnto him the princes *† Heb. wr* of Succoth and the elders thereof, euen threescore and seuenteene men.

15 And he came vnto the men of Succoth, and said, Behold Zebah and Zalmunna, with whom ye did vpbraid me, saying, Are the handes of Zebah and Zalmunna now in thine hand, that we should giue bread vnto thy men that *are* wearie?

16 And hee tooke the Elders of the citie, and thornes of the wildernes, and briers, and with them hee † taught the *† Heb. m to know.* men of Succoth.

17 And he beat downe the towre of * Penuel, and slew the men of the citie. ** 1. King 25.*

18 ¶ Then said he vnto Zebah and Zalmunna, What maner of men were they whom ye slew at Tabor? And they answered, As thou art, so *were* they, ech one † resembled the children of a king. *† Heb. according to the forme, &*

19 And hee said, They were my brethren, euen the sonnes of my mother: as the LORD liueth, if yee had saued them aliue, I would not slay you.

20 And he said vnto Iether his first borne, Vp, *and* slay them: but the youth drew not his sword: for he feared, because he was yet a youth.

21 Then Zebah and Zalmunna said, Rise thou, and fall vpon vs: for as the man *is*, so *is* his strength. And Gideon arose, and slewe Zebah and Zalmunna, & tooke away the ‖ornaments that *were* on their camels neckes. *‖ Or, ornaments like the moone*

22 ¶ Then the men of Israel saide vnto Gideon, Rule thou ouer vs, both thou, and thy sonne, & thy sonnes sonne also: for thou hast deliuered vs from the hand of Midian.

23 And Gideon said vnto them, I will not rule ouer you, neither shall my sonne rule ouer you: the LORD shall rule ouer you.

24 ¶ And Gideon said vnto them, I would desire a request of you, that you would giue me euery man the earerings of his pray. For they had golden eare-rings, because they were Ishmaelites.

25 And they answered, We will willingly giue *them*. And they spread a garment, and did cast therein, euery man the earerings of his pray.

26 And the weight of the golden eare-

Or, sweete
iewels.

eare-rings that hee requested, was a thousand and seuen hundred *shekels* of gold, beside ornaments, and ||collars, & purple raiment that *was* on the kings of Midian, and beside the chaines that *were* about their camels necks.

27 And Gideon made an Ephod thereof, and put it in his citie, *euen* in Ophrah: and all Israel went thither a whoring after it; which thing became a snare vnto Gideon, and to his house.

28 ¶ Thus was Midian subdued before the children of Israel; so that they lifted vp their heads no more: and the countrey was in quietnesse fourtie yeeres, in the dayes of Gideon.

29 ¶ And Ierubbaal the sonne of Ioash went & dwelt in his owne house.

Heb. going
out of his
nigh.

30 And Gideon had threescore and ten sonnes †of his body begotten: for he had many wiues.

31 And his concubine that was in Shechem, shee also bare him a sonne,

Heb. set.

whose name he †called Abimelech.

32 ¶ And Gideon the sonne of Ioash died, in a good olde age, and was buried in the sepulchre of Ioash his father, in Ophrah of the Abi-Ezrites.

33 And it came to passe as soone as Gideon was dead, that the children of Israel turned againe, and went a whoring after Baalim, and made Baal-Berith their god.

34 And the children of Israel remembred not the LORD their God, who had deliuered them out of the hands of all their enemies, on euery side:

35 Neither shewed they kindnesse to the house of Ierubbaal, *namely* Gideon, according to all the goodnesse which he had shewed vnto Israel.

CHAP. IX.

1 Abimelech by conspiracie with the Sheche-mites, and murder of his brethren, is made King. 7 Iotham by a parable rebuketh them and foretelleth their ruine. 22 Gaal conspireth with the Shechemites against him. 30 Zebul reuealeth it. 34 Abimelech ouercommeth them, and soweth the citie with salt. 46 Hee burneth the holde of the god Berith. 50 At Thebez he is slaine by a piece of a milstone. 56 Iothams curse is fulfilled.

Nd Abimelech the sonne of Ierubbaal went to Shechem, vnto his mothers brethren, and communed with them, and with all the family of the house of his mothers father, saying;

2 Speake, I pray you, in the eares of all the men of Shechem; †Whether is better for you, either that all the sonnes of Ierubbaal (which are threescore and ten persons) reigne ouer you, or that one reigne ouer you? Remember also, that I am your bone, and your flesh.

† Heb. What
is good? whe-
ther &c.

3 And his mothers brethren spake of him in the eares of all the men of Shechem, all these wordes, and their hearts inclined to †follow Abimelech: for they said, He is our brother.

† Heb. after.

4 And they gaue him threescore and ten *pieces* of siluer, out of the house of Baal-Berith, wherewith Abimelech hired vaine & light persons, which followed him.

5 And hee went vnto his fathers house at Ophrah, and slewe his brethren the sonnes of Ierubbaal, *being* threescore and tenne persons, vpon one stone: notwithstanding, yet Iotham the youngest sonne of Ierubbaal was left; for he hid himselfe.

6 And all the men of Shechem gathered together, and all the house of Millo, and went, and made Abimelech King, ||by the plaine of the pillar that *was* in Shechem.

|| Or, by the
oke of the
pillar. See
Iosh. 24.
26.

7 ¶ And when they told *it* to Iotham, he went and stood in the top of mount Gerizim, and lift vp his voice, and cried, and said vnto them, Hearken vnto mee, you men of Shechem, that God may hearken vnto you.

8 The trees went foorth on a time to annoint a King ouer them, and they said vnto the Oliue tree, Reigne thou ouer vs.

9 But the Oliue tree saide vnto them, Should I leaue my fatnesse, wherewith by mee they honour God and man, and ||goe to bee promoted ouer the trees?

|| Or, goe vp
and downe
for other
trees.

10 And the trees said to the Figge tree, Come thou, and reigne ouer vs.

11 But the Figge tree saide vnto them, Should I forsake my sweetenesse, and my good fruit, and goe to be promoted ouer the trees?

12 Then saide the trees vnto the Vine, Come thou, *and* reigne ouer vs.

13 And the Vine said vnto them, Should I leaue my wine, which cheareth God and man, and goe to bee promoted ouer the trees?

14 Then

‖ Or, thistle.

14 Then said all the trees vnto the ‖ Bramble, Come thou, and reigne o-uer vs.

15 And the Bramble said vnto the trees, If in trueth ye anoint me King ouer you, then come, *and* put your trust in my shadow : and if not, let fire come out of the Bramble, and deuoure the Cedars of Lebanon.

16 Now therefore, if yee haue done truely and sincerely, in that yee haue made Abimelech King, and if yee haue dealt well with Ierubbaal, and his house, and haue done vnto him according to the deseruing of his hands :

† Heb. cast his life.

17 (For my father fought for you, aud †aduentured his life farre, and de-liuered you out of the hand of Midian :

18 And yee are risen vp against my fathers house this day, and haue slaine his sonnes, threescore and ten persons, vpon one stone, and haue made Abime-lech the sonne of his maidseruant, king ouer the men of Shechem, because he is your brother.)

19 If yee then haue dealt truely and sincerely with Ierubbaal, and with his house this day, *then* reioyce yee in Abi-melech, aud let him also reioyce in you.

20 But if not, let fire come out from Abimelech, aud deuoure the men of Shechem and the house of Millo : and let fire come out from the men of She-chem, and from the house of Millo, and deuoure Abimelech.

21 And Iotham ran away, and fled, and went to Beer, and dwelt there for feare of Abimelech his brother.

22 ¶ When Abimelech had reigned three yeeres ouer Israel,

23 Then God sent an euill spirit be-tweene Abimelech & the men of She-chem : and the men of Shechem dealt treacherously with Abimelech :

24 That the crueltie done to the threescore and ten sonnes of Ierubbaal might come, and their blood be laid vp-on Abimelech their brother which slew them, and vpon the men of Shechem which †aided him in the killing of his brethren.

† Hebr. strengthened his hands to kill.

25 And the men of Shechem set ly-ers in wait for him in the toppe of the mountaines, and they robbed all that came along that way by them : and it was told Abimelech.

26 And Gaal the sonne of Ebed came with his brethren, and went ouer to Shechem : and the men of Shechem put their confidence in him.

27 And they went out into the fields, and gathered their vineyards, and trode *the* grapes, and made ‖merry, and went into the house of their god, and did eate and drinke, and cursed Abime-lech.

‖ Or, song

28 And Gaal the sonne of Ebed said, Who is Abimelech, and who is She-chem, that we should serue him? Is not he the sonne of Ierubbaal? and Zebul his officer? serue the men of Hamor the father of Shechem ' for why should we serue him?

29 And would to God this people were vnder my hand ; then would I re-moue Abimelech. And he said to Abi-melech, Increase thine armie and come out.

30 ¶ And when Zebul the ruler of the citie heard the wordes of Gaal the sonne of Ebed, his anger was ‖kindled.

‖ Or, hote

31 And he sent messengers vnto Abi-melech †priuily, saying, Behold, Gaal the sonne of Ebed, and his brethren, be come to Shechem, and behold, they for-tifie the citie against thee.

† Heb. or tily, or to Tormah.

32 Now therefore vp by night, thou and the people that is with thee, and lie in wait in the field.

33 And it shalbe, that in the morning assoone as the Sunne is vp, thou shalt rise earely, and set vpon the citie : and behold, *when* he and the people that is with him, come out against thee, then mayest thou doe to them †as thou shalt finde occasion.

† Hebr. thine har shall fin.

34 ¶ And Abimelech rose vp, and all the people that were with him, by night, and they laid wait against She-chem in foure companies.

35 And Gaal the sonne of Ebed went out, and stood in the entring of the gate of the citie : and Abimelech rose vp, and the people that were with him, from ly-ing in waite.

36 And when Gaal saw the people, he said to Zebul, Behold, there come people downe frō the top of the moun-taines. And Zebul saide vnto him, Thou seest the shadow of the moun-taines, as *if they were* men.

37 And Gaal spake againe, and said, See, there come people downe by the †middle of the land, and another com-panie come along by the plaine of ‖Me-onenim.

† Heb. na
‖ Or, the garders times.

38 Then said Zebul vnto him, Where is now thy mouth, *wherwith* thou saidst, Who

Who is Abimelech, that wee should serue him? Is not this the people that thou hast despised? Goe out, I pray now, and fight with them.

39 And Gaal went out before the men of Shechem, and fought with Abimelech.

40 And Abimelech chased him, and hee fledde before him, and many were ouerthrowen and wounded, euen vnto the entring of the gate.

41 And Abimelech dwelt at Arumah: and Zebul thrust out Gaal and his brethren, that they should not dwell in Shechem.

42 And it came to passe on the morrow, that the people went out into the field, and they tolde Abimelech.

43 And he tooke the people, and diuided them into three companies, and laide waite in the field, and looked, and behold, the people were come forth out of the citie, and he rose vp against them, and smote them.

44 And Abimelech, and the companie that *was* with him, rushed forward, and stood in the entring of the gate of the citie: and the two other companies ranne vpon all the people that *were* in the fields, and slew them.

45 And Abimelech fought against the citie all that day, and he tooke the citie, and slewe the people that was therein, and beat downe the citie, and sowed it with salt.

46 ¶ And when all the men of the tower of Shechem heard that, they entred into an holde of the house of the god Berith.

47 And it was told Abimelech, that all the men of the towre of Shechem were gathered together.

48 And Abimelech gate him vp to mount Zalmon, hee and all the people that *were* with him, & Abimelech tooke an axe in his hand, and cut downe a bough from the trees, and tooke it, and laide *it* on his shoulder, and said vnto the people that *were* with him, What ye haue seene †me doe, make haste, and doe as I *haue done.*

Heb. I aue done.

49 And all the people likewise cut downe euery man his bough, and followed Abimelech, and put them to the holde, and set the holde on fire vpon them: so that all the men of the towre of Shechem died also, about a thousand men and women.

50 ¶ Then went Abimelech to Thebez, and encamped against Thebez, and tooke it.

51 But there was a strong towre within the city, and thither fled all the men and women, and all they of the citie, and shut it to them, and gate them vp to the top of the towre.

52 And Abimelech came vnto the towre, and fought against it, and went hard vnto the doore of the towre, to burne it with fire.

53 And a certaine woman * cast a piece of a milstone vpon Abimelechs head, and all to brake his scull.

* 2. Sam. 11. 21.

54 Then hee called hastily vnto the young man his armour-bearer, and said vnto him, Draw thy sword, and slay me, that men say not of me, A woman slewe him: and his young man thrust him through, and he died.

55 And when the men of Israel saw that Abimelech was dead, they departed euery man vnto his place.

56 ¶ Thus God rendred the wickednesse of Abimelech which hee did vnto his father, in slaying his seuentie brethren.

57 And all the euill of the men of Shechem, did God render vpon their heads: and vpon them came the curse of Iotham the sonne of Ierubbaal.

CHAP. X.

1 Tola iudgeth Israel in Shamir. 3 Iair, whose thirtie sonnes had thirtie cities. 6 The Philistines and Ammonites oppresse Israel. 10 In their miserie, God sendeth them to their false gods. 15 Vpon their repentance, hee pitieth them.

Nd after Abimelech, there arose to ‖defend Israel, Tola the sonne of Puah, the sonne of Dodo, a man of Issachar, and he dwelt in Shamir in mount Ephraim.

‖Or, deliuer. Heb. saue.

2 And he iudged Israel twenty and three yeeres, and died, and was buried in Shamir.

3 ¶ And after him arose Iair a Gileadite, and iudged Israel twentie and two yeeres.

4 And hee had thirtie sonnes that rode on thirtie asse-colts, and they had thirtie cities, which are called ‖Hauoth-Iair vnto this day, which are in the land of Gilead.

‖Or, the villages of Iair

5 And Iair died, and was buried in Camon.

6 ¶ And

* Chap. 2.
11. and 3. 7.
and 4. 1. &
6. 1. &. 13. 1
* Chap. 2.
13.

6 ¶ And *the children of Israel did euill againe in the sight of the Lord, and serued Baalim and *Ashtaroth, and the gods of Syria, and the gods of Zidon, and the gods of Moab, and the gods of the children of Ammon, and the gods of the Philistines, and forsooke the Lord, and serued not him.

7 And the anger of the Lord was hot agaiust Israel, and hee solde them into the hands of the Philistines, and into the hands of the children of Ammon.

† Hebr.
crushed.

8 And that yere they vexed and †oppressed the children of Israel: eighteene yeeres, all the children of Israel that were on the other side Iordan, in the land of the Amorites, which is in Gilead.

9 Moreouer, the children of Ammon passed ouer Iordan, to fight also against Iudah, and against Beniamin, and against the house of Ephraim ; so that Israel was sore distressed.

10 ¶ And the children of Israel cried vnto the Lord, saying, Wee haue sinned against thee, both because wee haue forsaken our God, and also serued Baalim.

11 And the Lord said vnto the children of Israel, Did not I deliuer you from the Egyptians, and from the Amorites, from the children of Ammon, and from the Philistines ?

12 The Zidonians also and the Amalekites, and the Maonites did oppresse you, and ye cried to me, and I deliuered you out of their hand.

* Deut. 32.
15. ierem. 2.
13.

13 *Yet ye haue forsaken me, and serued other gods : wherefore I will deliuer you no more.

14 Go, and cry vnto the gods which ye haue chosen, let them deliuer you in the time of your tribulation.

15 ¶ And the children of Israel said vnto the Lord, We haue sinned, doe

† Hebr. is
good in thine
eyes.

thou vnto vs whatsoeuer †seemeth good vnto thee, deliuer vs onely, wee pray thee, this day.

† Hebr. gods
of strangers.

16 And they put away the †strange gods from among them, and serued the Lord · and his soule †was grieued

† Hebr. was
shortened.

for the misery of Israel.

† Hebr. cried
together.

17 Then the children of Ammon were †gathered together, and encamped in Gilead : and the children of Israel assembled themselues together, and encamped in Mizpeh.

18 And the people and Princes of Gi-

lead, said one to another, What man is hee that will begin to fight against the children of Ammon? he shall *be Head ouer all the inhabitants of Gilead.

* Chap. 11
6.

CHAP. XI.

1 The Couenant betweene Iephthah and the Gileadites, that hee should be their head. 12 The treaty of peace betweene him and the Ammonites is in vaine. 29 Iephthahs vow. 32 His conquest of the Ammonites. 34 He performeth his vow on his daughter.

N Ow *Iephthah the Gileadite was a mightie man of valour, and he was the sonne of † an harlot : and Gilead begate Iephthah.

* Hebr. 1
32. called
Iephte.

† Hebr. a u
man, an ha
lot.

2 And Gileads wife bare him sonnes, and his wiues sonnes grew vp, and they thrust out Iephthah, and said vnto him, Thou shalt not inherite in our fathers house, for thou art the son of a strange woman.

3 Then Iephthah fled †from his brethren, and dwelt in the land of Tob: and there were gathered vaine men to Iephthah, and went out with him.

† Hebr. fro
the face.

4 ¶ And it came to passe, †in processe of time, that the children of Ammon made warre against Israel.

† Hebr. aft
dayes.

5 And it was so, that when the children of Ammon made war against Israel, the Elders of Gilead went to fetch Iephthah out of the land of Tob,

6 And they said vnto Iephthah, Come and bee our Captaine, that wee may fight with the children of Ammon.

7 And Iephthah said vnto the Elders of Gilead, Did not ye hate me, and expell me out of my fathers house? And why are ye come vnto mee now when ye are in distresse ?

8 And the Elders of Gilead said vnto Iephthah, Therefore we turne againe to thee now, that thou mayest go with vs, and fight against the children of Ammon, and bee our head ouer all the inhabitants of Gilead.

9 And Iephthah said vnto the Elders of Gilead, If ye bring me home againe to fight against the children of Ammon, and the Lord deliuer them before me ; shall I be your Head ?

10 And the Elders of Gilead said vnto Iephthah, The Lord †be witnes betweene vs, if we doe not so according to thy words.

† Hebr. be
the hearer
betweene
vs.

11 Then Iephthah went with the Elders

ders of Gilead, and the people made him head and captaine ouer them: and Iephthah vttered all his words before the LORD in Mizpeh.

12 ¶ And Iephthah sent messengers vnto the king of the children of Ammon, saying, What hast thou to do with me, that thou art come against mee to fight in my land?

13 And the king of the children of Ammon answered vnto the messengers of Iephthah; * Because Israel tooke away my land when they came vp out of Egypt, from Arnon euen vnto Iabbok, and vnto Iordan: now therfore restore those *lands* againe peaceably.

14 And Iephthah sent messengers againe vnto the king of the children of Ammon:

15 And said vnto him, Thus saith Iephthah; * Israel tooke not away the land of Moab, nor the land of the children of Ammon:

16 But when Israel came vp from Egypt, and walked through the wildernesse, vnto the red sea, and came to Kadesh;

17 Then * Israel sent messengers vnto the king of Edom saying, Let me, I pray thee, passe through thy land. But the king of Edom would not hearken *thereto:* And in like maner they sent vnto the king of Moab: but hee would not *consent:* & Israel abode in Kadesh.

18 Then they went along through the wildernes, and compassed the land of Edom, and the land of Moab, and came by the Eastside of the land of Moab, and pitched on the other side of Arnon, * but came not within the border of Moab: for Arnon *was* the border of Moab.

19 And * Israel sent messengers vnto Sihon king of the Amorites, the king of Heshbon, and Israel said vnto him, Let vs passe, we pray thee, thorow thy land, vnto my place.

20 But Sihon trusted not Israel, to passe through his coast: but Sihon gathered all his people together, and pitched in Iahaz, and fought against Israel.

21 And the LORD God of Israel deliuered Sihon and all his people into the hand of Israel, and they smote them: so Israel possessed all the land of the Amorites, the inhabitants of that countrey.

22 And they possessed * all the coasts of the Amorites, from Arnon euen vnto Iabbok, and from the wildernesse euen vnto Iordan.

23 So nowe the LORD God of Israel hath dispossessed the Amorites from before his people Israel, and shouldest thou possesse it?

24 Wilt not thou possesse that which Chemosh thy god giueth thee to possesse? so whomsoeuer the LORD our God shal driue out from before vs, them will we possesse.

25 * And now, art thou any thing better then Balak the sonne of Zippor king of Moab? Did hee euer striue against Israel, or did hee euer fight against them,

26 While Israel dwelt in Heshbon, and her townes, and in Aroer, and her townes, and in all the cities that bee along by the coasts of Arnon, three hundred yeeres? Why therefore did yee not recouer them within that time?

27 Wherefore, I haue not sinned against thee, but thou doest me wrong to warre against mee: the LORD the Iudge, bee Iudge this day betweene the children of Israel, and the children of Ammon.

28 Howbeit, the king of the children of Ammon hearkened not vnto the words of Iephthah which hee sent him.

29 ¶ Then the Spirit of the LORD came vpon Iephthah, and he passed ouer Gilead and Manasseh, and passed ouer Mizpeh of Gilead, and from Mizpeh of Gilead hee passed ouer vnto the children of Ammon.

30 And Iephthah vowed a vowe vnto the LORD, and said, If thou shalt without faile deliuer the children of Ammon into mine hands,

31 Then it shall be, that † whatsoeuer commeth forth of the doores of my house to meete me, when I returne in peace from the children of Ammon, shall surely be the LORDS, ‖ and I will offer it vp for a burnt offering.

32 ¶ So Iephthah passed ouer vnto the children of Ammon to fight against them, and the LORD deliuered them into his hands.

33 And hee smote them from Aroer, euen till thou come to Minnith, *euen* twentie cities, and vnto the ‖ plaine of the vineyards, with a very great slaughter: thus the children of Ammon

Num. 21.

Deut. 2. 9.

Num. 20.

Num. 22. and 22.

Deut. 2.

* Deut. 2. 36.

* Num. 22. 2. deut. 23. 4. iosh. 24. 9

† Hebr. that which commeth forth shall come forth.

‖ Or, *I will offer it, &c.*

‖ Or, *Abel.*

mon were subdued before the children of Israel.

34 ¶ And Iephthah came to Mizpeh vnto his house, and beholde, his daughter came out to meete him with timbrels and with dances, and she was his onely childe: ‖beside her he had neither sonne nor daughter.

Or, he had not of his owne either sonne or daughter. Heb. of himselfe.

35 And it came to passe when he saw her, that he rent his clothes, and said, Alas, my daughter, thou hast brought me very low, and thou art one of them that trouble me: for I haue opened my mouth vnto the LORD, and I cannot goe backe.

36 And she said vnto him, My father, *if* thou hast opened thy mouth vnto the LORD, doe to me according to that which hath proceeded out of thy mouth; forasmuch as the LORD hath taken vengeance for thee of thine enemies, euen of the children of Ammon.

37 And she said vnto her father, Let this thing be done for me: Let me alone two moneths, that I may †goe vp and downe vpon the mountaines, and bewaile my virginitie, I, and my fellowes.

†Heb. Goe, and goe downe.

38 And he said, Goe. And he sent her away *for* two moneths, and shee went with her companions, and bewailed her virginitie vpon the mountaines.

39 And it came to passe at the ende of two moneths that shee returned vnto her father, who did with her *according* to his vow which he had vowed: and she knew no man: & it was a ‖custome in Israel,

‖Or, ordinance.

40 *That* the daughters of Israel went †yeerely ‖to lament the daughter of Iephthah the Gileadite foure dayes in a yeere.

†Heb. from yeere to yere. ‖Or, to talke with.

CHAP. XII.

1 The Ephraimites quarrelling with Iephthah, and discerned by Shibboleth, are slaine by the Gileadites. 7 Iephthah dieth. 8 Ibzan, who had thirtie sonnes and thirtie daughters, 11 and Elon, 13 and Abdon who had fourtie sonnes, and thirtie nephewes, iudged Israel.

And the men of Ephraim †gathered themselues together, and went Northward, & said vnto Iephthah, Wherefore passedst thou ouer to fight against the children of Ammon, and didst not call vs to goe with thee ? Wee will burne thine house vpon thee with fire.

†Hebr. were called.

2 And Iephthah saide vnto them, I and my people were at great strife with the children of Ammon : and when I called you, ye deliuered me not out of their hands.

3 And when I sawe that ye deliuered *me* not, I put my life in my handes, and passed ouer against the children of Ammon, and the LORD deliuered them into my hand : Wherfore then are ye come vp vnto me this day, to fight against me ?

4 Then Iephthah gathered together all the men of Gilead, and fought with Ephraim : and the men of Gilead smote Ephraim, because they said, Yee Gileadites are fugitiues of Ephraim, among the Ephraimites and among the Manassites.

5 And the Gileadites tooke the passages of Iordan before the Ephraimites : and it was so that when those Ephraimites which were escaped saide, Let me go ouer, that the men of Gilead said vnto him, Art thou an Ephraimite? If he said, Nay :

6 Then said they vnto him, Say now, Shibboleth : and he said, Sibboleth : for hee could not frame to pronounce it right. Then they tooke him, and slewe him at the passages of Iordan : and there fell at that time of the Ephraimites, fourtie & two thousand.

7 And Iephthah iudged Israel sixe yeeres : then died Iephthah the Gileadite, and was buried in *one of* the cities of Gilead.

8 ¶ And after him Ibzan of Bethlehem iudged Israel.

9 And hee had thirtie sonnes, and thirtie daughters, whome hee sent abroad, and tooke in thirtie daughters from abroad for his sonnes. And hee iudged Israel seuen yeeres.

10 Then died Ibzan, and was buried at Bethlehem.

11 ¶ And after him, Elon, a Zebulonite iudged Israel, and he iudged Israel ten yeeres.

12 And Elon the Zebulonite died, and was buried in Aiialon in the countrey of Zebulun.

13 ¶ And after him, Abdon, the sonne of Hillel a Pirathonite iudged Israel.

14 And he had fourty sonnes, and thirtie †nephewes, that rode on threescore and ten asse-colts : and he iudged Israel eight yeeres,

†Heb. sonnes sonnes.

15 And

15 And Abdon the ſonne of Hillel the Pirathonite died, and was buried in Pirathon in the land of Ephraim, in the mount of the Amalekites.

CHAP. XIII.

1 Israel is in the hand of the Philistines. 2 An Angel appeareth to Manoahs wife. 8 The Angel appeareth to Manoah. 15 Manoahs sacrifice, whereby the Angel is discoured. 24 Samson is borne.

ebr. ad-
to com-
, &c.
hap. 2.
and 3. 7.
4. 1.
6. 1. and
6.

And the children of Iſrael † * did euill againe in the ſight of the LORD, and the LORD deliuered them into the hand of the Philiſtines forty yeeres.

2 ¶ And there was a certaine man of Zorah, of the family of the Danites, whoſe name was Manoah, and his wife was barren, and bare not.

Xum. 6.
.

3 And the Angel of the LORD appeared vnto the woman, and ſaid vnto her, Behold now, thou art barren, and beareſt not : but thou ſhalt conceiue and beare a ſonne.

4 Now therefore beware * I pray thee, and drinke not wine, nor ſtrong drinke, and eat not any vncleane thing.

Jum. 6. 5.
sam. 1.

5 For loe, thou ſhalt conceiue, and beare a ſonne, and * no raſor ſhall come on his head : for the child ſhall be a Nazarite vnto God from the wombe : and he ſhall begin to deliuer Iſrael out of the hand of the Philiſtines.

6 ¶ Then the woman came, and told her husband, ſaying ; A man of God came vnto mee, and his countenance was like the countenance of an Angel of God, very terrible : but I asked him not whence he was, neither told he me his name :

7 But he ſaid vnto mee, Behold, thou ſhalt conceiue and beare a ſonne; and now, drinke no wine nor ſtrong drinke, neither eate any vncleane thing: for the childe ſhal be a Nazarite to God, from the wombe, to the day of his death.

8 ¶ Then Manoah entreated the LORD, and ſaid, O my LORD, let the man of God which thou didſt ſend, come againe vnto vs, & teach vs what we ſhall do vnto the childe that ſhall be borne.

9 And God hearkened to the voyce of Manoah ; and the Angel of God came againe vnto the woman as ſhee ſate in the field : But Manoah her husband was not with her.

10 And the woman made haſte, and ranne, and ſhewed her husband, and ſaid vnto him ; Behold, the man hath appeared vnto me, that came vnto me the other day.

11 And Manoah aroſe, and went after his wife, and came to the man, and ſaid vnto him, Art thou the man that ſpakeſt vnto the woman ? And he ſaid, I am.

12 And Manoah ſaid, Now let thy words come to paſſe : † How ſhall wee order the childe, and ‖ how ſhall we doe vnto him ?

† Hebr. what
shall be the
maner of
the, &c.
‖ Or, what
shall he doe?
Hebr. What
shall be his
worke ?

13 And the Angel of the LORD ſaid vnto Manoah, Of all that I ſaid vnto the woman, let her beware.

14 She may not eate of any thing that commeth of the Vine, neither let her drinke wine or ſtrong drinke, nor eat any vncleane thing: all that I commanded her, let her obſerue.

15 ¶ And Manoah ſaide vnto the Angel of the LORD, I pray thee let vs deteine thee, vntill wee ſhall haue made ready a kid † for thee.

† Hebr. be-
fore thee.

16 And the Angel of the LORD ſaid vnto Manoah, Though thou deteine mee, I will not eat of thy bread : and if thou wilt offer a burnt offering, thou muſt offer it vnto the LORD : for Manoah knew not that he was an Angel of the LORD.

17 And Manoah ſaid vnto the Angel of the LORD, What is thy name, that when thy ſayings come to paſſe, we may doe thee honour ?

18 And the Angel of the LORD ſaid vnto him, Why askeſt thou thus after my name, ſeeing it is ‖ ſecret ?

‖ Or, won-
derfull.

19 So Manoah tooke a kid, with a meat offering, and offered it vpon a rocke vnto the LORD : and the Angel did wonderouſly, and Manoah and his wife looked on.

20 For it came to paſſe, when the flame went vp toward heauen from off the altar, that the Angel of the LORD aſcended in the flame of the altar : and Manoah and his wife looked on it, and fell on their faces to the ground.

21 (But the Angel of the LORD did no more appeare to Manoah and to his wife :) then Manoah knewe that he was an Angel of the LORD.

22 And Manoah ſaid vnto his wife, * We

* Exod. 33.
20. chap. 6.
22.

* Wee shall surely die, because wee haue seene God.

23 But his wife said vnto him, If the LORD were pleased to kill vs, he would not haue receiued a burnt offering and a meat offering at our hands, neither would hee haue shewed vs all these things, nor would as at this time haue told vs *such things* as these.

24 ¶ And the woman bare a sonne, and called his name Samson: and the child grew, & the LORD blessed him.

25 And the Spirit of the LORD beganne to mooue him at times in the campe of Dan, betweene Zorah and Eshtaol.

CHAP. XIIII.

1 Samson desireth a wife of the Philistines. 2 In his iourney hee killeth a Lion. 8 In a second iourney hee findeth hony in the carkeis. 10 Samsons marriage feast. 12 His riddle by his wife is made knowen. 19 He spoileth thirtie Philistines. 20 His wife is married to another.

And Samson went down to Timnath, and sawe a woman in Timnath, of the daughters of the Philistines.

2 And hee came vp, and told his father and his mother, and said, I haue seene a woman in Timnath, of the daughters of the Philistines: nowe therefore get her for me to wife.

3 Then his father and his mother said vnto him, Is there neuer a woman among the daughters of thy brethren, or among all my people, that thou goest to take a wife of the vncircumcised Philistines? And Samson said vnto his father, Get her for me, for †shee pleaseth me well.

† Heb. she is
right in mine
eyes.

4 But his father and his mother knew not that it was of the LORD, that hee sought an occasion against the Philistines: for at that time the Philistines had dominion ouer Israel.

5 ¶ Then went Samson downe, and his father & his mother, to Timnath, and came to the vineyards of Timnath: and behold, a young Lion roared †against him.

† Hebr. in
meeting
him.

6 And the Spirit of the LORD came mightily vpon him, and hee rent him as he would haue rent a kid, and he had nothing in his hand: but hee told not his father or his mother what hee had done.

7 And hee went downe and talked with the woman, and she pleased Samson well.

8 ¶ And after a time hee returned to take her, and he turned aside to see the carkeis of the Lion: and beholde, there was a swarme of Bees, and honie in the carkeis of the Lion

9 And hee tooke thereof in his handes, and went on eating, and came to his father and mother, and hee gaue them, and they did eate: but he told not them that he had taken the hony out of the carkeis of the Lion.

10 ¶ So his father went downe vnto the woman, and Samson made there a feast: for so vsed the young men to doe.

11 And it came to passe when they saw him, that they brought thirtie companions to be with him.

12 ¶ And Samson said vnto them, I will now put foorth a riddle vnto you: if you can certeinly declare it me, within the seuen dayes of the feast, and finde it out, then I will giue you thirtie ‖ sheetes, and thirtie change of garments:

‖ Or, sh

13 But if ye cannot declare it me, then shall yee giue me thirtie sheetes, and thirtie change of garments. And they said vnto him, Put foorth thy riddle, that we may heare it.

14 And hee said vnto them, Out of the eater came foorth meate, and out of the strong came foorth sweetnesse. And they could not in three dayes expound the riddle.

15 And it came to passe on the seuenth day, that they said vnto Samsons wife, Entice thy husband, that hee may declare vnto vs the riddle, lest we burne thee and thy fathers house with fire: Haue yee called vs, † to take that wee haue? is it not so?

† Heb. t
sesse vs
impoue
vs?

16 And Samsons wife wept before him, and said, Thou doest but hate me, and louest me not: thou hast put foorth a riddle vnto the children of my people, and hast not tolde *it* me And hee said vnto her, Behold, I haue not tolde *it* my father nor my mother, and shall I tell *it* thee?

17 And shee wept before him ‖ the seuen dayes, while the feast lasted: and it came to passe on the seuenth day, that he tolde her, because shee lay sore vpon him: and she tolde the riddle to the children of her people.

‖ Or, th
of the s
dayes,

18 And

18 And the men of the city said vnto him on the seuenth day before the sunne went downe, What is sweeter then honie? and what is stronger then a Lion? And he said vnto him, If ye had not plowed with my heifer, yee had not found out my riddle.

19 ¶ And the Spirit of the LORD came vpon him, and hee went downe to Ashkelon, and slewe thirtie men of them, and tooke their ||spoile, and gaue change of garments vnto them which expounded the riddle, and his anger was kindled, and hee went vp to his fathers house.

Or, apparel.

20 But Samsons wife was *giuen* to his companion, whom hee had vsed as his friend.

CHAP. XV.

1 Samson is denied his wife. 3 He burneth the Philistines corne with foxes and firebrands. 6 His wife and her father are burnt by the Philistines. 7 Samson smiteth them hip and thigh. 9 He is bound by the men of Iudah and deliuered to the Philistines. 14 Hee killeth them with a iawbone. 18 God maketh the fountaine En-hakkore for him in Lehi.

BVt it came to passe within a while after, in the time of wheat haruest, that Samson visited his wife with a kid, and he said, I will goe in to my wife into the chamber. But her father would not suffer him to goe in.

2 And her father saide, I verily thought that thou haddest vtterly hated her, therfore I gaue her to thy companion : is not her younger sister fairer then she? †take her, I pray thee, in stead of her.

† *Heb. let her be thine.*

3 ¶ And Samson said concerning them, ||Now shal I be more blamelesse then the Philistines, though I do them a displeasure.

¶ *Or, now shall I bee blamelesse from the Philistines, though, &c.*
|| *Or, torches.*

4 And Samson went and caught three hundred foxes, and tooke ||firebrands, and turned taile to taile, and put a firebrand in the midst betweene two tailes.

5 And when hee had set the brands on fire, he let them goe into the standing corne of the Philistines, and burnt vp both the shockes, and also the standing corne, with the vineyards *and* oliues.

6 ¶ Then the Philistines saide, Who hath done this? and they answered, Samson the sonne in law of the Timnite, because hee had taken his wife, and giuen her to his companion. And the Philistines came vp, and burnt her and her father with fire.

7 ¶ And Samson said vnto them, Though ye haue done this, yet will I be auenged of you, and after that, I wil cease.

8 And he smote them hip and thigh, with a great slaughter ; and hee went down and dwelt in the top of the rocke Etam.

9 ¶ Then the Philistines went vp, and pitched in Iudah, and spread themselues in Lehi.

10 And the men of Iudah said, Why are ye come vp against vs? and they answered, To bind Samson are we come vp, to doe to him, as he hath done to vs.

11 Then three thousand men of Iudah †went to the top of the rocke Etam, and sayd to Samson ; Knowest thou not that the Philistines are rulers ouer vs? What *is* this *that* thou hast done vnto vs? And he said vnto them, As they did vnto me, so haue I done vnto them.

† *Heb. went downe.*

12 And they said vnto him, Wee are come downe to binde thee, that we may deliuer thee into the hand of the Philistines. And Samson said vnto them, Sweare vnto me, that yee will not fall vpon me your selues.

13 And they spake vnto him, saying ; No : but wee will binde thee fast, and deliuer thee into their hand : but surely we will not kill thee. And they bound him with two new cordes, and brought him vp from the rocke.

14 ¶ And when he came vnto Lehi, the Philistines shouted against him : and the Spirit of the LORD came mightily vpon him, and the cordes that were vpon his armes became as flaxe that was burnt with fire, & his bands †loosed from off his hands.

† *Hebr. were melted.*
† *Heb. moist.*

15 And he found a †new iawbone of an asse, and put foorth his hand, and tooke it, and slewe a thousand men therewith.

16 And Samson said, With the iawbone of an asse, †heapes vpon heapes, with the iaw of an asse haue I slaine a thousand men.

† *Heb. an heape, two heapes.*

17 And it came to passe when he had made an end of speaking, that hee cast away the iaw bone out of his hand, and called that place ||Ramath-Lehi.

18 ¶ And hee was sore athirst, and called on the LORD, and said, Thou hast

|| *That is, The lifting vp of the iaw-bone, or, casting away of the iaw-bone.*

hast giuen this great deliuerance into the hand of thy seruant : and now shall I die for thirst, and fall into the hand of the vncircumcised ?

19 But God claue an hollow place that was in ||the iawe, and there came water thereout, & when he had drunke, his spirit came againe, and he reuiued : wherefore hee called the name thereof ||En-hakkore, which is in Lehi, vnto this day :

20 And he iudged Israel in the dayes of the Philistines twentie yeeres.

marginal: || Or, Lehi.

marginal: || That is, the well of him that called or cried.

CHAP. XVI.

1 Samson at Gaza escapeth, and carieth away the gates of the city. 4 Delilah corrupted by the Philistines, entiseth Samson. 6 Thrise she is deceiued. 15 At last shee ouercommeth him. 21 The Philistines take him, and put out his eyes. 22 His strength renewing, hee pulleth downe the house vpon the Philistines, and dieth.

Hen went Samson to Gaza, and saw there †an harlot, and went in vnto her. 2 *And it was told* the Gazites, saying, Samson is come hither. And they compassed *him* in, and layd wait for him all night in the gate of the citie, and were †quiet all the night, saying, In the morning when it is day, we shall kill him.

3 And Samson lay till midnight, and arose at midnight, and tooke the doores of the gate of the city, and the two posts, and went away with them, †barre and all, and put them vpon his shoulders, and caried them vp to the toppe of an hill that is before Hebron.

4 ¶ And it came to passe afterward, that he loued a woman in the valley ||of Sorek, whose name was Delilah.

5 And the lords of the Philistines came vp vnto her, and said vnto her, Entice him, and see wherein his great strength *lieth*, and by what meanes we may preuaile against him, that we may bind him, to ||afflict him : and we will giue thee euery one of vs, eleuen hundreth *pieces* of siluer.

6 ¶ And Delilah said to Samson, Tel me, I pray thee, wherein thy great strength *lyeth*, and wherewith thou mightest be bound, to afflict thee.

7 And Samson said vnto her, If they binde mee with seuen ||greene withs, that were neuer dried, then shall

marginal: † Heb. a woman an harlot.

marginal: † Heb. silent.

marginal: † Heb. with the barre.

marginal: || Or, by the brooke.

marginal: || Or, humble.

marginal: || Or, newe coards. heb. moist.

I be weake, and be as †another man.

8 Then the lords of the Philistines brought vp to her her seuen greene withs, which had not bene dried, & she bound him with them.

9 Now there were men lying in wait, abiding with her in the chamber : and she said vnto him, The Philistines *be* vpon thee, Samson. And he brake the withs, as a threed of tow is broken, when it †toucheth the fire : so his strength was not knowen.

10 And Delilah said vnto Samson, Behold, thou hast mocked me, and told mee lies : now tell mee, I pray thee, wherewith thou mightest be bound.

11 And he said vnto her, If they bind me fast with newe ropes †that neuer were occupied, then shall I bee weake, and be as another man.

12 Delilah therfore tooke new ropes, and bound him therewith, and said vnto him, The Philistines *be* vpon thee, Samson. (And there were liers in wait abiding in the chamber.) and hee brake them from off his armes, like a threed.

13 And Delilah said vnto Samson, Hitherto thou hast mocked me, and told me lies : tell me wherewith thou mightest be bound. And he said vnto her, If thou weauest the seuen lockes of my head with the web.

14 And she fastened it with the pinne, and said vnto him, The Philistines *be* vpon thee, Samson. And hee awaked out of his sleepe, and went away with the pinne of the beame, & with the web.

15 ¶ And shee said vnto him, How canst thou say, I loue thee, when thine heart is not with mee ? Thou hast mocked mee these three times, and hast not told me wherin thy great strength *lieth*.

16 And it came to passe, when she pressed him daily with her wordes, and vrged him, *so* that his soule was †vexed vnto death,

17 That he told her all his heart, and said vnto her, There hath not come a rasor vpon mine head : for I *haue* bene a Nazarite vnto God from my mothers wombe : If I bee shauen, then my strength will goe from me, and I shall become weake, and bee like any *other* man.

18 And when Delilah saw that he had told her all his heart, she sent and called for the Lords of the Philistines, saying, Come vp this once, for hee hath shewed me all his heart. Then the lords of the Phili-

marginal: † Heb. one.

marginal: † Heb. smelleth.

marginal: † Heb. wher with worke hath not bin done.

marginal: † Heb. shortned.

Philistines came vp vnto her, & brought money in their hand.

19 And she made him sleepe vpon her knees, and she called for a man, and she caused him to shaue off the seuen lockes of his head, and she began to afflict him, and his strength went from him.

20 And she said, The Philistines be vpon thee, Samson. And hee awoke out of his sleepe, and said, I will go out as at other times before, and shake my selfe. And he wist not that the LORD was departed from him.

21 ¶ But the Philistines tooke him and †put out his eyes, and brought him downe to Gaza, and bound him with fetters of brasse, and he did grind in the prison house.

Hebr. boaed out.

22 Howbeit, the haire of his head began to grow againe, || after he was shauen.

Or, as when ç was shaaen.

23 Then the lords of the Philistines gathered them together, for to offer a great sacrifice vnto Dagon their god, and to reioyce: for they said, Our god hath deliuered Samson our enemy into our hand.

24 And when the people saw him, they praised their god: for they said, Our god hath deliuered into our hands our enemy, and the destroyer of our countrey, †which slew many of vs.

Hebr. and who multiplied our slaine.

25 And it came to passe when their hearts were merry, that they said, Call for Samson, that hee may make vs sport. And they called for Samson out of the prison house, and he made †them sport, and they set him betweene the pillars.

Hebr. before them.

26 And Samson said vnto the lad that held him by the hand, Suffer mee, that I may feele the pillars whereupon the house standeth, that I may leane vpon them.

27 Now the house was full of men and women, and all the lords of the Philistines *were* there: and *there were* vpon the roofe about three thousand men and women, that behelde while Samson made sport.

28 And Samson called vnto the LORD, and said, O Lord GOD, remember me, I pray thee, & strengthen mee, I pray thee, onely this once, O God, that I may be at once auenged of the Philistines, for my two eyes.

29 And Samson tooke hold of the two middle pillars, vpon which the house stood, and || on which it was borne

Or, he leaed on them.

vp, of the one with his right hand, and of the other with his left.

30 And Samson said, Let †me die with the Philistines: & he bowed himselfe with *all his* might: and the house fel vpon the lords, and vpon all the people that were therein: so the dead which he slew at his death, were moe, then they which he slew in his life.

†*Hebr. my soule.*

31 Then his brethren, and all the house of his father, came downe, and tooke him, and brought *him* vp, and buried him betweene Zorah and Eshtaol, in the burying place of Manoah his father: and hee iudged Israel twentie yeeres.

CHAP. XVII.

1 Of the money that Micah first stole, then restored, his mother maketh Images, 5 and hee hireth a Leuite to be his Priest.

ANd there was a man of mount Ephraim, whose name was Micah.

2 And he said vnto his mother, The eleuen hundred *shekels* of siluer, that were taken from thee, about which thou cursedst, and spakest of also in mine eares, behold, the siluer *is* with mee, I tooke it. And his mother said, Blessed be thou of the LORD, my sonne.

3 And when hee had restored the eleuen hundred *shekels* of siluer to his mother, his mother said, I had wholly dedicated the siluer vnto the LORD, from my hand, for my sonne, to make a grauen image and a molten image: now therefore I will restore it vnto thee.

4 Yet hee restored the money vnto his mother, and his mother tooke two hundred *shekels* of siluer, and gaue them to the founder, who made thereof a grauen image and a molten image, and they were in the house of Micah.

5 And the man Micah had an house of gods, and made an * Ephod, and * Teraphim, and †consecrated one of his sonnes, who became his Priest.

6 *In those dayes *there was* no king in Israel, but euery man did that which was right in his owne eyes.

*Chap. 8.
27.
*Gen. 31.
19. ose. 3. 4
†*Hebr. filled the hand.*
*Chap. 18.
1. and 21.
25.*

7 ¶ And there was a young man out of Bethlehem Iudah, of the family of Iudah, who was a Leuite, and he soiourned there.

8 And the man departed out of the citie

citie from Bethlehem Iudah, to ſo-
iourne where he could finde *a place:* and
he came to mount Ephraim to the houſe
of Micah, †as he iourneyed.

† Heb. in ma-king his way.

9 And Micah ſaid vnto him, Whence
commeſt thou? And he ſaid vnto him,
I am a Leuite, of Bethlehem Iudah,
and I goe to ſoiourne where I may
finde *a place.*

10 And Micah ſaid vnto him, Dwell
with me, and be vnto me a father and
a Prieſt, and I will giue thee ten *ſhekels*
of ſiluer by the yeere, and ‖a ſuite of apparell, and thy victuals. So the Leuite went in.

‖ Or, a dou-ble ſuit, &c. Heb. an or-der of gar-ments.

11 And the Leuite was content to
dwell with the man, and the yong man
was vnto him as one of his ſonnes.

12 And Micah conſecrated the Leuite, and the young man became his
Prieſt, and was in the houſe of Micah.

13 Then ſaid Micah, Now know
I that the LORD will doe me good,
ſeeing I haue a Leuite to my Prieſt.

CHAP. XVIII.

1 The Danites ſend fiue men to ſeeke out an inheritance. 3 At the houſe of Micah they conſult with Ionathan, and are incouraged in
their way. 7 They ſearch Laiſh, and bring
backe newes of good hope. 11 Sixe hundred
men are ſent to ſurprize it. 14 In the way
they robbe Micah of his Prieſt and his conſe-
crate things. 27 They win Laiſh and call it
Dan. 30 They ſet vp Idolatrie, wherein Ionathan inherited the Prieſthood.

* Chap. 17. 6. and 21. 25.

IN *thoſe dayes *there was*
no king in Iſrael: and in
thoſe daies the tribe of the
Danites ſought them an
inheritance to dwel in: for
vnto that day, *all* their inheritance had
not fallen vnto them, among the tribes
of Iſrael.

2 And the children of Dan ſent of
their family, fiue men from their coaſts,
†men of valour, from Zorah, and
from Eſhtaol, to ſpy out the land, and
to ſearch it, and they ſaid vnto them,
Goe, ſearch the land: Who when they
came to mount Ephraim, to the houſe
of Micah, they lodged there.

† Hebr. ſonnes.

3 When they *were* by the houſe of
Micah, they knew the voice of the yong
man the Leuite: and they turned in
thither, & ſaid vnto him, Who brought
thee hither? And what makeſt thou in
this place? and what haſt thou here?

4 And hee ſaid vnto them, Thus
and thus dealeth Micah with me, and
hath hired me, and I am his Prieſt.

5 And they ſayd vnto him, Aske
counſell, we pray thee, of God, that we
may know, whether our way which
we goe, ſhall be proſperous.

6 And the Prieſt ſaid vnto them,
Goe in peace: before the LORD *is* your
way wherein ye goe.

7 ¶ Then the fiue men departed,
and came to Laiſh, and ſaw the people
that were therein, how they dwelt
careleſſe, after the maner of the Zidonians, quiet and ſecure, and there was
no † magiſtrate in the land that might
put them to ſhame in any thing, and
they *were* farre from the Zidonians,
and had no buſineſſe with any man.

† Heb. poſſe-ſour, or heire of reſtraine

8 And they came vnto their brethren to Zorah, and Eſhtaol: and
their brethren ſaid vnto them, What
ſay yee?

9 And they ſaid, Ariſe, that we may
goe vp againſt them: for we haue ſeene
the land, and behold, it *is* very good: and
are ye ſtill? Bee not ſlothfull to goe, *and*
to enter to poſſeſſe the land.

10 When ye goe, ye ſhall come vnto a
people ſecure, and to a large land: for
God hath giuen it into your handes: a
place where there is no want of any
thing, that *is* in the earth.

11 ¶ And there went from thence of
the family of the Danites out of Zorah, and out of Eſhtaol, ſixe hundred
men, †appoynted with weapons of
warre.

† Heb. gir-ded.

12 And they went vp, and pitched in
Kiriath-iearim, in Iudah: Wherefore
they called that place Mahaneh-Dan,
vnto this day: behold, *it is* behinde Kiriath-iearim.

13 And they paſſed thence vnto
mount Ephraim, and came vnto the
houſe of Micah.

14 ¶ Then anſwered the fiue men
that went to ſpie out the countrey of
Laiſh, and ſaide vnto their brethren,
Doe ye know that there is in theſe houſes an Ephod, and Teraphim, and a
grauen image, and a molten image?
Now therefore conſider what ye haue
to doe.

15 And they turned thitherward, and
came to the houſe of the yong man the
Leuite, *euen* vnto the houſe of Micah,
and † ſaluted him.

† Heb. aſk him of pe

16 And the ſix hundred men appointed

ted with their weapons of war, which were of the children of Dan, stood by the entring of the gate.

17 And the fiue men that went to spie out the land, went vp *and* came in thither, *and* tooke the grauen image, and the Ephod, and the Teraphim, and the molten image: and the Priest stood in the entring of the gate, with the sixe hundreth men that were appointed with weapons of warre.

18 And these went into Micahs house, and fetched the carued image, the Ephod, and the Teraphim, and the molten image: then said the Priest vnto them, What doe ye?

19 And they said vnto him, Hold thy peace, lay thine hand vpon thy mouth, and goe with vs, and bee to vs a father and a Priest: Is it better for thee to bee a Priest vnto the house of one man, or that thou be a Priest vnto a tribe and a family in Israel?

20 And the Priests heart was glad, and he tooke the Ephod, and the Teraphim, and the grauen image, and went in the middest of the people.

21 So they turned, and departed, and put the little ones, and the cattell, and the cariage before them.

22 ¶ *And* when they were a good way from the house of Micah, the men that were in the houses neere to Micahs house, were gathered together, and ouertooke the children of Dan.

23 And they cried vnto the children of Dan: and they turned their faces, and said vnto Micah, What aileth thee, † that thou commest with such a company?

Heb. that thou art gathered together?

24 And he said, Yee haue taken away my gods which I made, and the Priest, and ye are gone away: and what haue I more? and what is this that yee say vnto me, What aileth thee?

25 And the children of Dan said vnto him, Let not thy voyce bee heard among vs, lest † angry fellowes run vpon thee, and thou lose thy life, with the liues of thy houshold.

Heb. bitter of soule.

26 And the children of Dan went their way: and when Micah sawe that they were too strong for him, he turned and went backe vnto his house.

27 And they tooke the things which Micah had made, and the Priest which hee had, and came vnto Laish, vnto a people that were at quiet, and secure, and they smote them with the edge of the sword, and burnt the citie with fire.

28 And there was no deliuerer, because it was farre from Zidon, and they had no businesse with any man: and it was in the valley that *lieth* by Beth-rehob, and they built a citie, and dwelt therein.

29 And they called the name of the * city, Dan, after the name of Dan their father, who was borne vnto Israel: howbeit the name of the citie was Laish at the first.

Iosh. 19. 47.

30 ¶ And the children of Dan set vp the grauen image: and Ionathan the sonne of Gershom, the sonne of Manasseh, hee and his sonnes, were Priests to the tribe of Dan, vntill the day of the captiuitie of the land.

31 And they set them vp Micahs grauen image, which hee made, all the time that the house of God was in Shiloh.

CHAP. XIX.

1 A Leuite goeth to Bethlehem to fetch home his wife. 16 An old man entertaineth him at Gibeah. 22 The Gibeonites abuse his concubine to death. 29 He diuideth her into twelue pieces to send them to the twelue tribes.

ND it came to passe in those dayes, * when there *was* no King in Israel, that there was a certaine Leuite soiourning on the side of mount Ephraim, who tooke to him † a concubine out of Bethlehem Iudah.

Chap. 17. 6. and 18. 1 and 21. 25.

† Heb. a woman a concubine, or a wife a concubine.

2 And his concubine played the whore against him, and went away from him vnto her fathers house to Bethlehem Iudah, and was there ‖ foure whole moneths.

‖ Or, a yeere and foure moneths. Heb. dayes, foure moneths.

3 And her husband arose, and went after her to speake † friendly vnto her, and to bring her againe, hauing his seruant with him, and a couple of asses: and shee brought him into her fathers house, and when the father of the damsell saw him, he reioyced to meet him.

† Heb. to her heart.

4 And his father in law, the damosels father, reteined him, and hee abode with him three dayes: so they did eate and drinke, and lodged there.

5 ¶ And it came to passe on the fourth day, when they arose earely in the morning, that he rose vp to depart: and the damosels father saide vnto his sonne in lawe, † Comfort thine heart with a morsell of bread, and afterward goe your way.

† Heb. strengthen.

6 And

6 And they sate downe, and did eat and drinke both of them together: for the damosels father had saide vnto the man, Be content, I pray thee, and tary all night, and let thine heart be merrie.

7 And when the man rose vp to depart, his father in law vrged him: therfore he lodged there againe.

8 And hee arose early in the morning on the fift day to depart, and the damosels father sayd, Comfort thine heart, I pray thee. And they taried † vntill after noone, and they did eate both of them.

9 And when the man rose vp to depart, hee and his concubine, and his seruant; his father in law, the damsels father, said vnto him, Behold, now the day † draweth towardes euening, I pray you tarie all night: behold, † the day groweth to an ende, lodge heere, that thine heart may be merrie; and to morrow get you early on your way, that thou mayest goe † home.

10 But the man would not tary that night, but he rose vp and departed, and came † ouer against Iebus (which is Ierusalem:) and *there were* with him two asses sadled, his concubine also *was* with him.

11 And when they *were* by Iebus, the day was farre spent, and the seruant said vnto his master, Come, I pray thee, and let vs turne in into this citie of the Iebusites, and lodge in it.

12 And his master said vnto him, We will not turne aside hither into the citie of a stranger, that is not of the children of Israel, we wil passe ouer to Gibeah.

13 And hee sayde vnto his seruant, Come, and let vs draw neere to one of these places to lodge all night, in Gibeah, or in Ramah.

14 And they passed on and went their way, and the sunne went downe vpon them *when they were* by Gibeah, which *belongeth* to Beniamin.

15 And they turned aside thither, to go in *and* to lodge in Gibeah: and when he went in, he sate him downe in a street of the citie: for there was no man that tooke them into his house to lodging.

16 ¶ And behold, there came an olde man from his worke out of the field at euen, which was also of mount Ephraim; and hee soiourned in Gibeah, but the men of the place were Beniamites.

17 And when he had lift vp his eyes, he saw a wayfaring man in the streete

of the citie: and the old man said, Whither goest thou? and whence commest thou?

18 And he said vnto him, We are passing from Bethlehem Iudah, toward the side of mount Ephraim, from thence am I: and I went to Bethlehem Iudah, but I am *now* going to the house of the LORD, and there is no man that † receiueth me to house.

19 Yet there is both straw and prouender for our asses, and there is bread and wine also for me and for thy handmaid, and for the young man *which is* with thy seruants: there is no want of any thing.

20 And the olde man said, Peace be with thee; howsoeuer, let all thy wants *lie* vpon me; only lodge not in the street.

21 So he brought him into his house, and gaue prouender vnto the asses: and they washed their feet, and did eate and drinke.

22 ¶ Now as they were making their hearts merrie, behold, the men of the citie, certaine sonnes of Belial, beset the house round about, *and* beat at the doore, and spake to the master of the house, the olde man, saying; Bring foorth the man that came into thine house, that we may know him.

23 And *the man, the master of the house, went out vnto them, and said vnto them, Nay my brethren, nay, I pray you doe not so wickedly; seeing that this man is come into mine house, doe not this folly.

24 Behold, *here is* my daughter, a maiden, and his concubine, them I wil bring out now, and humble yee them, and doe with them what seemeth good vnto you: but vnto this man doe not † so vile a thing.

25 But the men would not hearken to him: so the man tooke his concubine, and brought her foorth vnto them, and they knew her, and abused her all the night vntill the morning: and when the day began to spring, they let her goe.

26 Then came the woman in the dawning of the day, and fell downe at the doore of the mans house, where her lord was, till it was light.

27 And her lord rose vp in the morning, & opened the doores of the house, and went out to goe his way: and behold, the woman his concubine was fallen downe at the doore of the house, and her hands *were* vpon the threshold.

28 And

† *Heb. till the day declined.*

† *Heb. is weake.*

† *Heb. it is the pitching time of the day.*

† *Heb. to thy tent.*

† *Heb. to ouer against Iebus.*

† *Hebr. gathereth.*

* Genes. 19. 6.

† *Hebr. the matter of this folly.*

28 And he said vnto her, Vp, and let vs be going. But none answered : then the man tooke her *vp* vpon an asse, and the man rose vp, and gate him vnto his place.

29 ¶ And when he was come into his house, hee tooke a knife, and layd hold on his concubine, and diuided her, *together* with her bones, into twelue pieces, and sent her into all the coasts of Israel.

30 And it was so that all that saw it, said, There was no such deed done nor seene, from the day that the children of Israel came vp out of the land of E-gypt, vnto this day : consider of it, take aduise, and speake *your mindes.*

CHAP. XX.

1 The Leuite in a generall assembly declareth his wrong. 8 The decree of the assembly. 12 The Beniamites being cited, make head against the Israelites. 18 The Israelites in two battels loose fourty thousand. 26 They destroy by a stratageme all the Beniamites, except six hundred.

Hen all the children of Is-rael went out, and the Congregation was ga-thered together as one man, from Dan euen to Beer-sheba, with the land of Gilead, vnto the LORD in Mizpeh.

2 And the chiefe of al the people, *euen* of all the tribes of Israel, presented themselues in the assembly of the peo-ple of God, foure hundred thousand footmen that drew sword.

3 (Now the children of Beniamin heard that the children of Israel were gone vp to Mizpeh.) Then said the chil-dren of Israel, Tell vs, how was this wickednesse ?

Heb. the an the Le-te. 4 And †the Leuite the husband of the woman that was slaine, answered and said, I came into Gibeah that *be-longeth* to Beniamin, I and my concu-bine, to lodge.

5 And the men of Gibeah rose a-gainst me, and beset the house round a-bout vpon me by night, and thought to haue slaine mee, *and* my concubine haue *Heb. hum-ed.* they †forced that she is dead.

6 And I tooke my concubine, and cut her in pieces, and sent her through-out all the countrey of the inheritance of Israel : for they haue committed lewdnesse and folly in Israel.

7 Behold, ye are all children of Is-rael, giue here your aduise and counsell.

8 ¶ And all the people arose as one man, saying, We will not any *of vs* goe to his tent, neither will wee any *of vs* turne into his house :

9 But now, this *shall bee* the thing which we will doe to Gibeah, *we will goe vp* by lot against it :

10 And we wil take ten men of a hun-dred throughout all the tribes of Is-rael, and an hundred of a thousand, and a thousand out of ten thousand, to fetch victuall for the people, that they may doe, when they come to Gibeah of Ben-iamin, according to all the folly that they haue wrought in Israel.

11 So all the men of Israel were ga-thered against the citie, †knit together as one man. †*Hebr. fel-lowes.*

12 ¶ And the tribes of Israel sent men thorow all the tribe of Beniamin, saying, What wickednesse is this that is done among you ?

13 Now therfore deliuer vs the men, the children of Belial which *are* in Gi-beah, that wee may put them to death, and put away euill from Israel : but the children of Beniamin would not hearken to the voice of their brethren the children of Israel.

14 But the children of Beniamin gathered themselues together out of the cities, vnto Gibeah, to goe out to battell against the children of Israel.

15 And the children of Beniamin were numbred at that time out of the cities, twentie and sixe thousand men that drew sword, beside the inhabitants of Gibeah, which were numbred seuen hundred chosen men.

16 Among all this people *there were* seuen hundred chosen men * left han-ded, euery one could sling stones at an haire *breadth,* and not misse. * Chap. 3. 15.

17 And the men of Israel, beside Beniamin, were numbred foure hun-dred thousand men that drewe sword ; all these *were* men of warre.

18 ¶ And the children of Israel a-rose, and went vp to the house of God, and asked counsell of God, and saide, Which of vs shall goe vp first to the bat-tell against the children of Beniamin ? And the LORD said, Iudah shall *goe vp* first.

19 And the children of Israel rose vp in the morning, and encamped a-gainst Gibeah.

20 And

20 And the men of Israel went out to battell against Beniamin, and the men of Israel put themselues in aray to fight against them at Gibeah.

21 And the children of Beniamin came forth out of Gibeah, and destroied downe to the ground of the Israelites that day, twenty & two thousand men.

22 And the people the men of Israel incouraged themselues, & set their battel againe in aray, in the place where they put themselues in aray the first day.

23 (And the children of Israel went vp and wept before the LORD vntill Euen, and asked counsel of the LORD, saying, Shall I goe vp againe to battell against the children of Beniamin my brother? And the LORD saide, Goe vp against him.)

24 And the children of Israel came neere against the children of Beniamin, the second day.

25 And Beniamin went foorth against them out of Gibeah the second day, & destroyed down to the ground of the children of Israel againe, eighteene thousand men, all these drew the sword.

26 ¶ Then all the children of Israel, and all the people went vp, and came vnto the house of God, and wept, and sate there before the LORD, and fasted that day vntill Euen, and offered burnt offerings, and peace offerings before the LORD.

27 And the children of Israel enquired of the LORD, (for the Arke of ŷ couenant of God *was* there in those daies,

28 And Phinehas the sonne of Eleazar the sonne of Aaron stood before it in those dayes.) saying; Shall I yet againe goe out to battel against the children of Beniamin my brother, or shall I cease? And the LORD said, Goe vp; for to morrow I will deliuer them into thine hand.

29 And Israel set lyers in waite round about Gibeah.

30 And the children of Israel went vp against the children of Beniamin on the third day, and put themselues in aray against Gibeah, as at other times.

31 And the children of Beniamin went out against the people, *and* were drawen away from the citie, and they began to † smite of the people *and* kill as at other times, in the high wayes, of which one goeth vp to ‖ the house of God, and the other to Gibeah in the field, about thirtie men of Israel.

32 And the children of Beniamin said, They are smitten downe before vs, as at the first: But the children of Israel said, Let vs flee, and draw them from the citie, vnto the high wayes.

33 And all the men of Israel rose vp out of their place, and put themselues in aray at Baal Tamar: and the lyers in waite of Israel came foorth out of their places, euen out of the medowes of Gibeah.

34 And there came against Gibeah ten thousand chosen men, out of all Israel, and the battell was sore: but they knew not that euill was neere them.

35 And the LORD smote Beniamin before Israel, and the children of Israel destroyed of the Beniamites that day, twentie and fiue thousand, and an hundred men; all these drew the sword.

36 So the children of Beniamin saw that they were smitten: for the men of Israel gaue place to the Beniamites, because they trusted vnto the lyers in wait, which they had set beside Gibeah.

37 And the liers in wait hasted, and rushed vpon Gibeah, and the liers in wait ‖ drew *themselues* along, and smote all the citie with the edge of the sword.

38 Nowe there was an appointed ‖ signe between the men of Israel † and the liers in wait, that they should make a great † flame with smoke rise vp out of the citie.

39 And when the men of Israel retired in the battell, Beniamin began to † smite and kill of the men of Israel about thirtie persons; for they saide, Surely they are smitten downe before vs, as *in* the first battell.

40 But when the flame began to arise vp out of the citie, with a pillar of smoke, the Beniamites looked behind them, and behold, the † flame of the citie ascended vp to heauen.

41 And when the men of Israel turned againe, the men of Beniamin were amased; for they saw that euill † was come vpon them.

42 Therefore they turned *their backs* before the men of Israel, vnto ŷ way of the wildernes, but the battel ouertooke them: & them which came out of the cities, they destroyed in the midst of them.

43 *Thus* they inclosed the Beniamites round about, *and* chased them, and trode them downe ‖ with ease † ouer against Gibeah toward the sunne rising.

44 And there fell of Beniamin eighteene

‖ Or, made a long sou with the trumpet.
† Or, time.
† Heb. wil
† Heb. eleu tion.
† Hebr. to smite the wounded.
† Heb. the whole consumption.
† Heb. tou ched them.
‖ Or, from Menuchah &c.
† Heb. vnt oueragain

eighteene thousand men; all these *were* men of valour.

45 And they turned and fled toward the wildernesse vnto the rocke of Rimmon: and they gleaned of them in the high wayes fiue thousand men: and pursued hard after them vnto Gidom, and slew two thousand men of them.

46 So that all which fell that day of Beniamin, were twentie and fiue thousand men that drew the sword; all these *were* men of valour.

Chap. 21. 47 * *But* six hundred men turned and fledde to the wildernesse vnto the rocke Rimmon, and abode in the rocke Rimmon foure moneths.

48 And the men of Israel turned againe vpon the children of Beniamin, and smote them with the edge of the sword, as well the men of euery citie, as *Heb. was nnd.* the beast, and all that † came to hand : *Heb. were nnd.* also they set on fire all the cities that † they came to.

CHAP. XXI.

1 The people bewaile the desolation of Beniamin. 8 By the destruction of Iabesh Gilead they prouide them foure hundred wiues. 16 They aduise them to surprise the virgines that daunced at Shiloh.

Owe the men of Israel had sworne in Mizpeh, saying, There shall not any of vs giue his daughter vnto Beniamin to wife.

2 And the people came to the house of God, and abode there till euen before God, and lift vp their voices, and wept sore :

3 And said, O LORD God of Israel, why is this come to passe in Israel, that there should bee to day one tribe lacking in Israel?

4 And it came to passe on the morrow, that the people rose early, and built there an Altar, and offered burnt offerings, and peace offerings.

5 And the children of Israel sayd, Who *is there* among all the tribes of Israel, that came not vp with the congregation vnto the LORD? for they had made a great oath concerning him that came not vp to the LORD to Mizpeh, saying, He shall surely be put to death.

6 And the children of Israel repented them for Beniamin their brother, and said, There is one tribe cut off from Israel this day :

7 How shall wee doe for wiues for them that remaine, seeing wee haue sworne by the LORD, that wee will not giue them of our daughters to wiues?

8 ¶ And they said, What one *is there* of the tribes of Israel, that came not vp to Mizpeh to the LORD? And beholde, there came none to the campe from Iabesh Gilead to the assembly.

9 For the people were numbred, and behold, there were none of the inhabitants of Iabesh Gilead there.

10 And the congregation sent thither twelue thousand men of the valiantest, and commaunded them, saying, Goe, and smite the inhabitants of Iabesh Gilead with the edge of the sword, with the women and the children.

11 And this *is* the thing that yee shall doe, * Yee shall vtterly destroy euery male, and euery woman that hath † lien by man. *Num. 31. 17.* *† Heb. knoweth the lying with man.*

12 And they found among the inhabitants of Iabesh Gilead, foure hundred † yong virgins that had knowen no man, by lying with any male : and they brought them vnto the campe to Shiloh, which *is* in the land of Canaan. *† Hebr. yong women virgins.*

13 And the whole Congregation sent *some* † to speake to the children of Beniamin that *were* in the rocke Rimmon, and to ‖ call peaceably vnto them. *† Hebr. and spake and called.* *‖ Or, proclaime peace.*

14 And Beniamin came againe at that time, and they gaue them wiues which they had saued aliue of the women of Iabesh Gilead: and yet so they sufficed them not.

15 And the people repented them for Beniamin, because that the LORD had made a breach in the tribes of Israel.

16 ¶ Then the Elders of the Congregation said, How shall we doe for wiues for them that remaine? seeing the women are destroyed out of Beniamin.

17 And they said, There must be an inheritance for them that bee escaped of Beniamin, that a tribe be not destroyed out of Israel.

18 Howbeit wee may not giue them wiues of our daughters. For the children of Israel haue sworne, saying, Cursed be he that giueth a wife to Beniamin.

19 Then they said, Behold, *there is a* feast of the LORD in Shiloh † yerely, *in a place* which *is* on the Northside of Bethel on the ‖East side ‖ of the hie way that *† Heb. from yeere to yeere.* *‖ Or, towards the Sunne rising.* *‖ Or, on.*

that goeth vp from Bethel to She-chem, and on the South of Lebanon.

20 Therefore they commanded the children of Beniamin, saying, Goe and lie in wait in the vineyards.

21 And see, and behold, if the daughters of Shiloh come out to daunce in daunces, then come yee out of the vineyards, and catch you euery man his wife of the daughters of Shiloh, and goe to the land of Beniamin.

22 And it shall bee when their fathers or their brethren come vnto vs to complaine, that we will say vnto them, ‖ Bee fauourable vnto them for our sakes : because we reserued not to each man his wife in the warre : for yee did

‖ Or, gratifie vs in them.

not giue vnto them at this time, that you should be guiltie.

23 And the children of Beniamin did so, and tooke them wiues according to their number, of them that daunced, whome they caught : and they went and returned vnto their inheritance, and repaired the cities, and dwelt in them.

24 And the children of Israel departed thence at that time, euery man to his tribe, and to his family, and they went out from thence euery man to his inheritance.

25 *In those dayes there was no King in Israel : euery man did that which was right in his owne eyes.

* Cnap. 1 6. and 18. 1. and 19.

¶ THE BOOKE OF
Ruth.

CHAP. I.

1 Elimelech driuen by famine into Moab, dieth there. 4 Mahlon and Chilion, hauing married wiues of Moab, die also. 6 Naomi returning homeward, 8 disswadeth her two daughters in law from going with her. 14 Orpah leaueth her, but Ruth with great constancie accompanieth her. 19 They two come to Bethlehem, where they are gladly receiued.

Owe it came to passe in the dayes when ẙ Iudges † ruled, that there was a famine in the land : and a certaine man of Bethlehem Iudah, went to soiourne in the countrey of Moab, he, and his wife, and his two sonnes.

† Hebr. iudged.

2 And the name of the man *was* Elimelech, and the name of his wife, Naomi, and the name of his two sonnes, Mahlon, and Chilion, Ephrathites of Bethlehem Iudah : and they came into the countrey of Moab, and † continued there.

†Hebr.were.

3 And Elimelech Naomies hus-

band died, and shee was left, and her two sonnes ;

4 And they tooke them wiues of the women of Moab : the name of the one *was* Orpah, and the name of the other Ruth : and they dwelled there about ten yeeres.

5 And Mahlon and Chilion died also both of them, and the woman was left of her two sonnes, and her husband.

6 ¶ Then shee arose with her daughters in law, that shee might returne from the countrey of Moab : for shee had heard in the countrey of Moab, how that the LORD had visited his people, in giuing them bread.

7 Wherefore she went foorth out of the place where she was, and her two daughters in law with her : and they went on the way to returne vnto the land of Iudah.

8 And Naomi said vnto her two daughters in law, Goe, returne each to her mothers house : the LORD deale kindly with you, as ye haue dealt with the dead, and with me.

9 The LORD graunt you, that you may finde rest each *of you* in the house of her husband. Then she kissed them,

them, and they lift vp their voyce and wept.

10 And they said vnto her, Surely wee will returne with thee, vnto thy people.

11 And Naomi said, Turne againe, my daughters : why will you goe with mee? Are there yet any moe sonnes in my wombe, that they may be your husbands?

12 Turne againe, my daughters, go *your way*, for I am too old to haue an husband : if I should say, I haue hope, if I should || haue a husband also to night, and should also beare sonnes :

Or, if I were with an husband.
Heb. hope.

13 Would ye †tary for them till they were growen? would ye stay for them from hauing husbands? nay my daughters : for †it grieueth me much for your sakes, that the hand of the Lord is gone out against me.

Hebr. I haue much bitternes.

14 And they lift vp their voyce, and wept againe : and Orpah kissed her mother in law, but Ruth claue vnto her.

15 And she said, Behold, thy sister in law is gone backe vnto her people, and vnto her gods : returne thou after thy sister in law.

Or, be not against me.

16 And Ruth said, || Intreate mee not to leaue thee, *or* to returne from following after thee : for whither thou goest, I will goe ; and where thou lodgest, I will lodge : thy people shall be my people, and thy God my God :

17 Where thou diest, wil I die, and there will I bee buried : the Lord doe so to me, and more also, if *ought* but death part thee and me.

18 When shee sawe that shee †was stedfastly minded to goe with her, then shee left speaking vnto her.

Hebr. strengthened her selfe.

19 ¶ So they two went vntill they came to Bethlehem : And it came to passe when they were come to Bethlehem, that all the citie was mooued about them, and they said, Is this Naomi?

20 And she said vnto them, Call me not || Naomi ; call mee || Mara : for the Almightie hath dealt very bitterly with me.

That is, pleasant.
That is, bitter.

21 I went out full, and the Lord hath brought me home againe emptie : Why then call ye me Naomi, seeing the Lord hath testified against me, and the Almighty hath afflicted me?

22 So Naomi returned, and Ruth the Moabitesse her daughter in law with her, which returned out of the countrey of Moab : and they came to Bethlehem, in the beginning of barley haruest.

CHAP. II.

1 Ruth gleaneth in the fields of Boaz. 4 Boaz taking knowledge of her, 8 sheweth her great fauour. 18 That which she got, shee carieth to Naomi.

Nd Naomi had a kinseman of her husbands, a mighty man of wealth, of the familie of Elimelech, and his name was Boaz.

2 And Ruth the Moabitesse saide vnto Naomi, Let me now goe to the field, and gleane eares of corne after *him*, in whose sight I shall finde grace. And shee saide vnto her, Goe, my daughter.

3 And she went, and came, and gleaned in the field after the reapers : and her †happe was to light on a part of the fielde *belonging* vnto || Boaz, who *was* of the kinred of Elimelech.

† Heb. happe happened.
|| Called Mat. 1. 5. Booz.

4 ¶ And behold, Boaz came from Bethlehem, and said vnto the reapers, The Lord *bee* with you ; and they answered him, The Lord blesse thee.

5 Then said Boaz vnto his seruant, that was set ouer the reapers, Whose damosell *is* this?

6 And the seruaunt that was set ouer the reapers, answered and said, It is the Moabitish damosell that came backe with Naomi out of the countrey of Moab :

7 And she said, I pray you, let mee gleane and gather after the reapers amongst the sheaues : so shee came, and hath continued euen from the morning vntill now, *that* she taried a little in the house.

8 Then said Boaz vnto Ruth, Hearest thou not, my daughter? Goe not to gleane in another field, neither goe from hence, but abide here fast by my maidens.

9 Let thine eyes be on the field that they doe reape, and go thou after them : Haue I not charged the young men, that they shall not touch thee? and when thou art athirst, goe vnto the vessels, and drinke of that which the yong men haue drawen.

10 Then she fel on her face, and bowed her selfe to the ground, and said vnto him,

him, Why haue I found grace in thine eyes, that thou shouldest take knowledge of me, seeing I am a stranger?

11 And Boaz answered and said vnto her, It hath fully bene shewed me, all that thou hast done vnto thy mother in law since the death of thine husband: and *how* thou hast left thy father and thy mother, and the land of thy natiuitie, and art come vnto a people, which thou knewest not heretofore.

12 The Lord recompense thy worke, and a full reward be giuen thee of the Lord God of Israel, vnder whose wings thou art come to trust.

‖ *Or, I finde fauour.*
13 Then she said, ‖ Let me finde fauour in thy sight, my lord, for that thou hast comforted mee, and for that thou † *Heb. to the heart.* hast spoken †friendly vnto thine handmaid, though I be not like vnto one of thy hand-maidens.

14 And Boaz sayde vnto her, At meale time come thou hither, and eate of the bread, and dip thy morsell in the vineger: and shee sate beside the reapers: and he reached her parched corne, and she did eate, and was sufficed, and left.

15 And when shee was risen vp to gleane, Boaz commanded his young men, saying, Let her gleane euen a† *Heb. shame her not.*mong the sheaues, & †reproch her not.

16 And let fall also *some* of the handfuls of purpose for her, and leaue them that she may gleane *them*, and rebuke her not.

17 So she gleaned in the field vntill euen, and beat out that she had gleaned: and it was about an Ephah of barley.

18 ¶ And shee tooke *it* vp, and went into the citie: and her mother in lawe saw what shee had gleaned; and shee brought foorth, and gaue to her that she had reserued, after she was sufficed.

19 And her mother in law said vnto her, Where hast thou gleaned to day? and where wroughtest thou? blessed be hee that did take knowledge of thee. And shee shewed her mother in lawe with whom shee had wrought, and said, The mans name with whom I wrought to day, is Boaz.

20 And Naomi said vnto her daughter in law, Blessed be he of the Lord, who hath not left off his kindnesse to the liuing and to the dead. And Naomi said vnto her, The man is neere of kin ‖ *Or, one that hath right to redeeme.* vnto vs, ‖one of our next kinsemen.

21 And Ruth the Moabitesse said,

He said vnto me also, Thou shalt keepe fast by my yong men, vntill they haue ended all my haruest.

22 And Naomi said vnto Ruth her daughter in law, It is good, my daughter, that thou goe out with his mai‖ *Or, fall vp on thee.*dens, that they ‖meete thee not in any other field.

23 So shee kept fast by the maidens of Boaz to gleane, vnto the end of barley haruest, and of wheat haruest, and dwelt with her mother in law.

CHAP. III.

1 By Naomi her instruction, 5 Ruth lieth at Boaz his feete. 8 Boaz acknowledgeth the right of a kinseman. 14 He sendeth her away with six measures of barley.

Hen Naomi her mother in law said vnto her, My daughter, shal I not seeke rest for thee, that it may be well with thee?

2 And now is not Boaz of our kinred, with whose maidens thou wast? Behold, he winnoweth barley to night in the threshing floore.

3 Wash thy selfe therefore, and annoint thee, and put thy raiment vpon thee, and get thee downe to the floore: *but* make not thy selfe knowen vnto the man, vntill hee shall haue done eating and drinking.

4 And it shall be when hee lieth downe, that thou shalt marke the place where hee shall lie, and thou shalt goe ‖ *Or, lift vp the clothes that are on his feete.*in, and ‖vncouer his feete, and lay thee downe, and he will tell thee what thou shalt doe.

5 And shee said vnto her, All that thou sayest vnto me, I will doe.

6 ¶ And she went downe vnto the floore, and did according to all that her mother in law bade her.

7 And when Boaz had eaten and drunke, and his heart was merrie, hee went to lie downe at the ende of the heape of corne: and she came softly, and vncouered his feet, and laid her downe.

8 ¶ And it came to passe at midnight, that the man was afraid, and ‖ *Or, tooke holde on.*‖turned himselfe: and behold, a woman lay at his feete.

9 And hee said, Who *art* thou? And she answered, I *am* Ruth thine handmaid: spread therefore thy skirt ouer ‖ *Or, one that hath right to redeeme.*thine handmaid, for thou *art* ‖a neare kinseman.

10 And

10 And hee said, Blessed be thou of the LORD, my daughter : *for* thou hast shewed more kindnesse in the latter ende, then at the beginning, in as much as thou followedst not yong men, whether poore, or rich.

Heb. gate.

11 And now my daughter, feare not, I will doe to thee all that thou requirest : for all the † citie of my people doeth know, that thou art a vertuous woman.

12 And now it is true, that I am *thy* neare kinseman : howbeit there is a kinseman nearer then I.

13 Tary this night, and it shall be in the morning, that if hee will performe vnto thee the part of a kinseman, well, let him doe the kinsemans part ; but if hee will not doe the part of a kinseman to thee, then will I doe the part of a kinseman to thee, as the LORD liueth : lie downe vntill the morning.

14 ¶ And shee lay at his feete vntill the morning : and she rose vp before one could know another. And he said, Let it not be knowen, that a woman came into the floore.

Or, sheete, or, apron.

15 Also he said, Bring the ‖ vaile that thou hast vpon thee, and holde it. And when she helde it, he measured sixe *measures* of barley, and laide it on her : and he went into the citie.

16 And when shee came to her mother in law, she said, Who *art* thou, my daughter? and she tolde her all that the man had done to her.

17 And she said, These sixe *measures* of barley gaue he me, for he said to me, Go not emptie vnto thy mother in law.

18 Then said she, Sit still, my daughter, vntill thou know how the matter will fall : for the man will not be in rest, vntil he haue finished the thing this day.

CHAP. IIII.

1 Boaz calleth into iudgment the next kinseman. 6 He refuseth the redemption according to the maner in Israel. 9 Boaz buyeth the inheritance. 11 He marrieth Ruth. 13 She beareth Obed the grandfather of Dauid. 18 The generation of Pharez.

THen went Boaz vp to the gate, and sate him downe there : and beholde, the kinseman of whome Boaz spake, came by, vnto whom he said, Ho, such a one : turne aside, sit downe here. And hee turned aside, and sate downe.

2 And hee tooke ten men of the Elders of the citie, and said, Sit ye downe here. And they sate downe.

3 And he said vnto the kinseman : Naomi that is come againe out of the countrey of Moab, selleth a parcell of land, which was our brother Elimelechs.

4 And † I thought to aduertise thee, saying, Buy *it* before the inhabitants, and before the Elders of my people. If thou wilt redeeme *it*, redeeme *it*, but if thou wilt not redeeme *it*, then tell mee, that I may know : for there is none to redeeme *it*, besides thee, and I *am* after thee. And he said, I will redeeme *it*.

† Heb. I said I wil reueale in thine eare.

5 Then said Boaz, What day thou buyest the field of the hand of Naomi, thou must buy *it* also of Ruth the Moabitesse, the wife of the dead, to raise vp the name of the dead vpon his inheritance.

6 ¶ And the kinseman said, I cannot redeeme *it* for my selfe, lest I marre mine owne inheritance : redeeme thou my right to thy selfe, for I cannot redeeme *it*.

7 * Now this was *the maner* in former time in Israel, concerning redeeming and concerning changing, for to confirme all things : a man plucked off his shooe, and gaue *it* to his neighbour: and this *was* a testimonie in Israel.

* Deut. 25. 7, 9.

8 Therfore the kinseman said vnto Boaz, Buy *it* for thee : so he drew off his shooe.

9 ¶ And Boaz saide vnto the Elders, and vnto all the people, Ye *are* witnesses this day, that I haue bought all that was Elimelechs, and all that was Chilions, and Mahlons, of the hande of Naomi.

10 Moreouer, Ruth the Moabitesse, the wife of Mahlon, haue I purchased to be my wife, to raise vp the name of the dead vpon his inheritance, that the name of the dead be not cut off from among his brethren, and from the gate of his place : ye *are* witnesses this day.

11 And all the people that were in the gate, and the Elders said, *Wee are* witnesses : The LORD make the woman that is come into thine house, like Rachel and like Leah, which two did build the house of Israel : and ‖ do thou worthily in Ephratah, and † bee famous in Bethlehem.

‖ Or, get thee riches or power.
† Hebr. proclaime thy name.
* Gen. 38. 29. 1. chro. 2. 4. matt. 1. 3.

12 And let thy house be like the house of Pharez, (* whom Tamar bare vnto

to Iudah) of the seed which the Lord shall giue thee of this yong woman.

13 ¶ So Boaz tooke Ruth, and she was his wife: and when he went in vnto her, the Lord gaue her conception, and she bare a sonne.

14 And the women said vnto Naomi, Blessed be the Lord which hath not †left thee this day without a ‖kinseman, that his name may bee famous in Israel :

15 And he shalbe vnto thee a restorer of *thy* life, and †a nourisher of †thine old age : for thy daughter in law which loueth thee, which is better to thee then seuen sonnes, hath borne him.

16 And Naomi tooke the childe, and

† Hebr. caused to cease vnto thee
‖ Or, redeemer.

† Hebr. to nourish.
† Heb. thy gray haires.

laid it in her bosome, and became nurse vnto it.

17 And the women her neighbours gaue it a name, saying, There is a sonne borne to Naomi, and they called his name Obed : hee *is* the father of Iesse the father of Dauid.

18 ¶ Now these are the generations of Pharez : *Pharez begate Hezron,

19 And Hezron begate Ram, and Ram begate Amminadab,

20 And Amminadab begate Nahshon, and Nahshon begate ‖Salmon,

21 And Salmon begate Boaz, and Boaz begate Obed,

22 And Obed begat Iesse, and Iesse begate Dauid.

** 1. Chron 2. 4. matt 1. 3.*

‖ Or, Salmah.

¶ THE FIRST BOOKE

of Samuel, otherwise called, The

first Booke of the Kings.

CHAP. I.

1 Elkanah a Leuite hauing two wiues, worshippeth yeerely at Shiloh. 4 Hee cherisheth Hannah, though barren, and prouoked by Peninnah. 9 Hannah in griefe, prayeth for a childe. 12 Eli first rebuking her, afterwards blesseth her. 19 Hannah hauing borne Samuel, stayeth at home till he be weaned. 24 She presenteth him, according to her vow, to the Lord.

Ow there was a certaine man of Ramathaim Zophim, of mount Ephraim, & his name was Elkanah, the sonne of Ieroham, the sonne of Elihu, the sonne of Tohu, the sonne of Zuph, an Ephrathite ;

2 And he had two wiues, the name of the one *was* Hannah, and the name of the other Peninnah : and Peninnah had children, but Hannah had no children.

3 And this man went vp out of his citie * †yeerely, to worship and to sacrifice vnto the Lord of hostes in Shiloh ; and the two sonnes of Eli, Hophni, and Phinehas, the Priests of the Lord, *were* there.

4 ¶ And when the time was, that Elkanah offered, he gaue to Peninnah his wife, and to all her sonnes, and her daughters, portions.

5 But vnto Hannah he gaue ‖a worthy portion : (for he loued Hannah, but the Lord had shut vp her wombe.

6 And her aduersary also †prouoked her sore, for to make her fret, because the Lord had shut vp her wombe.)

7 And *as* he did so yeere by yeere, ‖ when she went vp to the house of the Lord, so she prouoked her ; therefore she wept, and did not eat.

8 Then said Elkanah her husband to her, Hannah, why weepest thou ? and why eatest thou not ? and why is thy heart grieued ? Am not I better to thee, then ten sonnes ?

9 ¶ So Hannah rose vp after they had eaten in Shiloh, and after they had drunke,

** Deut. 16.*
† Hebr. f yeere to yeere.

‖ Or, a double po tion.

† Hebr. a gred her.

‖ Or, fron the time that she, Hebr. fr her going

drunke; (now Eli the Priest sate vpon a seat by a poste of the Temple of the LORD.)

10 And shee was †in bitternesse of soule, and prayed vnto the LORD, and wept sore.

11 And she vowed a vow, and said, O LORD of hostes, if thou wilt indeed looke on the affliction of thine handmayd, and remember me, and not forget thine handmayd, but wilt giue vnto thine handmayd †a man childe, then I will giue him vnto the LORD all the dayes of his life, and *there shall no rasor come vpon his head.

12 And it came to passe as she †continued praying before the LORD, that Eli marked her mouth.

13 Now Hannah, shee spake in her heart, onely her lippes mooued, but her voice was not heard: therefore Eli thought she had beene drunken.

14 And Eli said vnto her, How long wilt thou be drunken? put away thy wine from thee.

15 And Hannah answered, and said, No, my lord, I am a woman †of a sorrowfull spirit: I haue drunke neither wine nor strong drinke, but haue powred out my soule before the LORD.

16 Count not thine handmaid for a daughter of Belial: for out of the abundance of my ||complaint and griefe, haue I spoken hitherto.

17 Then Eli answered, and said, Goe in peace: and the God of Israel grant thee thy petition, that thou hast asked of him.

18 And she said, Let thine handmaid finde grace in thy sight. So the woman went her way, and did eate, and her countenance was no more sad.

19 ¶ And they rose vp in the morning early, and worshipped before the LORD, and returned, and came to their house to Ramah: and Elkanah knewe Hannah his wife, and the LORD remembred her.

20 Wherefore it came to passe when the †time was come about, after Hannah had conceiued, that shee bare a sonne, and called his name ||Samuel, saying; Because I haue asked him of the LORD.

21 And the man Elkanah, and all his house, went vp to offer vnto the LORD the yeerely sacrifice, and his vowe.

22 But Hannah went not vp; for shee said vnto her husband, I will not goe vp vntill the childe be weaned, and then I will bring him, that he may appeare before the LORD, and there abide for euer.

23 And Elkanah her husband said vnto her, Do what seemeth thee good, tary vntill thou haue weaned him, only the LORD establish his word: so the woman abode, and gaue her sonne sucke vntill she weaned him.

24 ¶ And when shee had weaned him, shee tooke him vp with her, with three bullocks, and one Ephah of floure, and a bottle of wine, and brought him vnto the house of the LORD in Shiloh: and the childe was young.

25 And they slew a bulloeke, and brought the childe to Eli.

26 And she said, Oh my lord, as thy soule liueth, my lord, I am the woman, that stood by thee heere, praying vnto the LORD.

27 For this childe I prayed, and the LORD hath giuen me my petition, which I asked of him:

28 Therefore also I haue ||lent him to the LORD as long as hee liueth, ||he shall be lent to the LORD. And he worshipped the LORD there

CHAP. II.

1 Hannahs song in thankefulnesse. 12 The sinne of Elies sonnes. 18 Samuels ministerie. 20 By Elies blessing, Hannah is more fruitfull. 22 Eli reproueth his sonnes. 28 A prophecie against Elies house.

Nd Hannah prayed, and said, My heart reioyceth in the LORD, mine horne is exalted in the LORD: my mouth is inlarged ouer mine enemies: because I reioyce in thy saluation.

2 There is none holy as the LORD: for there is none beside thee: neither is there any Rocke like our God.

3 Talke no more so exceeding proudly, let not †arrogancie come out of your mouth: for the LORD is a God of knowledge, and by him actions are weighed.

4 The bowes of the mightie men are broken, and they that stumbled are girt with strength.

5 They that were full, haue hired out themselues for bread: and they that were hungry, ceased: so that the barren hath

---

Side notes (left column):

Hebr. bitter of soule.

Hebr. seed men.

Num. 6. 5.
Iudg. 13. 5.

Hebr. multiplied to pray.

Hebr. hard spirit.

Or, meditation.

Hebr. return of dayes.

That is, asked of God.

Side notes (right column):

|| Or, returned him, whom I haue obtained by petition to the LORD.
|| Or, hee whom I haue obtained by petition, shalbe returned.

† Hebr. hard.

* Deut. 32.
39. wisd.
16. 13. tob.
13. 2.

hath borne seuen, and she that hath many children, is waxed feeble.

6 * The Lord killeth and maketh aliue, he bringeth downe to the graue, and bringeth vp.

7 The Lord maketh poore, and maketh rich : he bringeth low, and lifteth vp.

* Psal. 113.
7.

8 He *raiseth vp the poore out of the dust, *and* lifteth vp the begger from the dunghill, to set *them* among princes, and to make them inherit the throne of glory : for the pillars of the earth *are* the Lords, and hee hath set the world vpon them.

9 He will keepe the feet of his saints, and the wicked shall bee silent in darkenesse; for by strength shall no man preuaile.

* Chap. 7.
10.

10 The aduersaries of the Lord shalbe broken to pieces : *out of heauen shal he thunder vpon them : the Lord shall iudge the ends of the earth, and he shal giue strength vnto his king, and exalt the horne of his Anointed.

11 And Elkanah went to Ramah to his house, and the child did minister vnto the Lord before Eli the Priest.

12 ¶ Now the sonnes of Eli were sonnes of Belial, they knewe not the Lord.

13 And the priests custome with the people *was, that* when any man offred sacrifice, the priestes seruant came, while the flesh was in seething, with a flesh-hooke of three teeth in his hand,

14 And he strooke *it* into the panne, or kettle, or caldron, or pot : all that the flesh - hooke brought vp, the priest tooke for himselfe : so they did in Shiloh vnto all the Israelites that came thither.

15 Also before they burnt the fat, the priests seruant came, & said to the man that sacrificed, Giue flesh to roste for the priest, for he wil not haue sodden flesh of thee, but raw.

† Hebr. as
on the day.

16 And if any man said vnto him, Let them not faile to burne the fat †presently, and then take *as much* as thy soule desireth : then hee would answere him, Nay, but thou shalt giue it mee now : and if not, I will take it by force.

17 Wherefore the sinne of the yong men was very great before the Lord : for men abhorred the offering of the Lord.

* Exod. 28.
4.

18 ¶ But Samuel ministred before the Lord, being a child, *girded with a linnen Ephod.

19 Moreouer, his mother made him a litle coate, and brought *it* to him from yeere to yeere, when she came vp with her husband, to offer the yeerely sacrifice.

20 ¶ And Eli blessed Elkanah, and his wife, and said, The Lord giue thee seed of this woman, for the ‖loane which is lent to the Lord. And they went vnto their owne home.

‖ Or, petiti
which hee
asked, &c

21 And the Lord visited Hannah, so that shee conceiued, and bare three sonnes, and two daughters : and the child Samuel grew before the Lord.

22 ¶ Now Eli was very olde, and heard all that his sonnes did vnto all Israel, and how they lay with the women that †assembled at the doore of the Tabernacle of the Congregation.

† Hebr. as
sembled by
troupes.

23 And he said vnto them, Why doe ye such things? for ‖ I heare of your euil dealings, by all this people.

‖ Or, I hea
euill word
of you.

24 Nay my sonnes : for it is no good report that I heare ; yee make the Lords people to ‖transgresse.

‖ Or, to cr
out.

25 If one man sinne against another, the Iudge shall iudge him : but if a man sinne against the Lord, who shall intreat for him ? Notwithstanding they hearkened not vnto the voice of their father, because the Lord would slay them.

26 (And the child Samuel grew on, and was in fauour, both with the Lord, and also with men.)

27 ¶ And there came a man of God vnto Eli, and saide vnto him, Thus saith the Lord, Did I plainely appeare vnto the house of thy father, when they were in Egypt in Pharaohs house ?

28 And did I chuse him out of all the tribes of Israel, to be my Priest, to offer vpon mine altar, to burne incense, to weare an Ephod before mee ? and *did I giue vnto the house of thy father, all the offerings made by fire of the children of Israel ?

* Leuit. 1
14.

29 Wherefore kicke ye at my sacrifice, and at mine offering, which I haue commaunded *in my* habitation, and honourest thy sonnes aboue mee, to make your selues fat with the chiefest of all the offrings of Israel my people ?

30 Wherefore the Lord God of Israel saith, I sayd indeede, *that* thy house, & the house of thy father should walke before me for euer : but now the Lord saith, Be it farre from mee ;
for

for them that honour me, I will honour, and they that despise me, shall be lightly esteemed.

31 Behold, the dayes come, that I will cut off thine arme, and the arme of thy fathers house, that there shall not be an old man in thine house.

^{‖ Or, the affliction of the Tabernacle, for all the wealth which God would haue giuen Israel.}

32 And thou shalt see ‖an enemie *in my* habitation, in all the wealth which God shall giue Israel, and there shall not bee an olde man in thine house for euer.

33 And the man of thine, *whom* I shall not cut off from mine Altar, *shall be* to consume thine eyes, and to grieue thine heart: and all the increase of thine house shall die † in the floure of their age.

^{† Heb. men.}

34 And this shall bee a signe vnto thee, that shall come vpon thy two sonnes, on Hophni and Phinehas : in one day they shall die both of them.

35 And I will raise me vp a faithfull Priest, that shall doe according to *that which is* in my heart and in my mind, and I will build him a sure house, and hee shall walke before mine Anointed for euer.

36 And it shall come to passe, that euery one that is left in thine house, shal come *and* crouch to him for a piece of siluer, and a morsel of bread, and shall say, † Put me (I pray thee) into ‖one of the Priests offices, that I may eat a piece of bread.

^{† Heb. ioyne.
‖ Or, Somewhat about the Priesthood.}

CHAP. III.

1 How the word of the Lord was first reuealed to Samuel. 11 God telleth Samuel the destruction of Elies house. 15 Samuel, though loth, telleth Eli the vision. 19 Samuel groweth in credit.

And the child Samuel ministred vnto the LORD before Eli : and the word of the LORD was precious in those daies, there was no open vision.

2 And it came to passe at that time, when Eli was layd downe in his place, and his eyes beganne to waxe dimme, that he could not see,

3 And yer the lampe of God went out in the Temple of the LORD, where the Arke of God was, and Samuel was layd downe *to sleepe*,

4 That the LORD called Samuel, and he answered, Here am I.

5 And he ranne vnto Eli, and sayd,

Here am I, for thou calledst me. And he said, I called not; lie downe againe. And he went and lay downe.

6 And the LORD called yet againe, Samuel. And Samuel arose, and went to Eli, and said, Here am I, for thou diddest call me. And he answered, I called not, my sonne; lie downe againe.

7 ‖ Now Samuel did not yet know the LORD, neither was the word of the LORD yet reuealed vnto him.

^{‖ Or, thus did Samuel, before he knew the LORD; and before the word of the LORD was reuealed vnto him.}

8 And the LORD called Samuel againe the third time. And hee arose, and went to Eli, and said, Here am I, for thou diddest call me. And Eli perceiued that the LORD had called the childe.

9 Therefore Eli said vnto Samuel, Go, lie downe, & it shal be, if he call thee, that thou shalt say, Speake LORD, for thy seruant heareth. So Samuel went, and lay downe in his place.

10 And the LORD came, and stood and called as at other times, Samuel, Samuel. Then Samuel answered, Speake, for thy seruant heareth.

11 ¶ And the LORD sayd to Samuel, Behold, I will doe a thing in Israel, at which, both the eares of * euery one that heareth it, shall tingle.

^{* 2. Kin. 21. 12.}

12 In that day, I will performe against Eli, all things which I haue spoken concerning his house : † when I begin, I will also make an end.

^{† Hebr. beginning and ending.}

13 ‖*For I haue tolde him, that I will iudge his house for euer, for the iniquitie which hee knoweth : because his sonnes made themselues ‖vile, and he † restrained them not.

^{‖ Or, and I will tell him, &c.
* Chap. 2. 29, 30, 31, &c.
‖ Or, accursed.
† Heb. frowned not vpon them.}

14 And therefore I haue sworne vnto the house of Eli, that the iniquitie of Elies house shall not be purged with sacrifice, nor offering for euer.

15 ¶ And Samuel lay vntill the morning, and opened the doores of the house of the LORD : and Samuel feared to shew Eli the vision.

16 Then Eli called Samuel, and said, Samuel my sonne. And he answered, Here am I.

17 And he said, What *is* the thing that the LORD hath said vnto thee? I pray thee hide it not from mee : God doe so to thee, and † more also, if thou hide *any* ‖thing from me, of all the things that hee said vnto thee.

^{† Hebr. so adde.
‖ Or, word.}

18 And Samuel tolde him † euery whit, and hid nothing from him. And hee

^{† Heb all the things, or words.}

he said, It *is* the LORD : Let him doe what seemeth him good.

19 ¶ And Samuel grew, and the LORD was with him, and did let none of his words fall to the ground.

20 And all Israel from Dan euen to Beer-sheba, knew that Samuel was ‖ established to bee a Prophet of the LORD.

21 And the LORD appeared againe in Shiloh : for the LORD reueiled himselfe to Samuel in Shiloh, by the word of the LORD.

‖ *Or, faithfull.*

CHAP. IIII.

1 The Israelites are ouercome by the Philistines at Aben-Ezer. 3 They fetch the Arke, vnto the terrour of the Philistines. 10 They are smitten againe, the Arke taken, Hophni and Phinehas are slaine. 12 Eli at the newes, falling backward, breaketh his necke. 19 Phinehas wife, discouraged in her trauaile with Ichabod, dieth.

ANd the word of Samuel ‖ came to all Israel. Now Israel went out against the Philistines to battell, and pitched beside Ebenezer : and the Philistines pitched in Aphek.

‖ *Or, came to passe: Hebr. was.*

2 And the Philistines put themselues in aray against Israel : and when † they ioyned battell, Israel was smitten before the Philistines : and they slew of † the armie in the field, about foure thousand men.

† *Hebr. the battell was spread.*
† *Hebr. the aray.*

3 ¶ And when the people were come into the campe, the Elders of Israel said, Wherefore hath the LORD smitten vs to day before the Philistines ? Let vs † fetch the Arke of the Couenant of the LORD out of Shiloh vnto vs, that when *it* commeth among vs, *it* may saue vs out of the hand of our enemies.

† *Hebr. take vnto vs.*

4 So the people sent to Shiloh, that they might bring from thence the Arke of the Couenant of the LORD of hostes, which dwelleth *betweene* the Cherubims : and the two sonnes of Eli, Hophni, and Phinehas *were* there, with the Arke of the Couenant of God.

5 And when the Arke of the Couenant of the LORD came into the campe, all Israel shouted with a great shout, so that the earth rang againe.

6 And when the Philistines heard the noise of the shout, they said, What meaneth the noise of this great shout in the campe of the Hebrewes ? And they vnderstood, that the Arke of the LORD was come into the campe.

7 And the Philistines were afraid, for they saide, God is come into the campe. And they said, Woe vnto vs: for there hath not bene such a thing † heretofore.

† *Hebr. yesterday, or the third day.*

8 Woe vnto vs : who shall deliuer vs out of the hand of these mightie Gods ? these are the Gods that smote the Egyptians with all the plagues in the wildernesse.

9 Bee strong, and quit your selues like men, O ye Philistines, that yee be not seruants vnto the Hebrewes, *as they haue bene to you: † quit your selues like men, and fight.

* Iudg. 13. 1.
† *Hebr. Be men.*

10 ¶ And the Philistines fought, and Israel was smitten, and they fled euery man into his tent : and there was a very great slaughter, for there fell of Israel thirtie thousand footmen.

11 And the Arke of God was taken, and the two sonnes of Eli, Hophni and Phinehas † were slaine.

† *Hebr. died.*

12 ¶ And there ran a man of Beniamin out of the army, and came to Shiloh the same day with his clothes rent, and with earth vpon his head.

13 And when hee came, loe, Eli sate vpon a seat by the way side, watching : for his heart trembled for the Arke of God. And when the man came into the citie, and told it, all the city cried out.

14 And when Eli heard the noise of the crying, hee said ; What meaneth the noise of this tumult ? And the man came in hastily, and told Eli.

15 Now Eli was ninetie and eight yeeres old, and *his eyes † were dimme, that he could not see.

* Chap. 3. 2.
† *Hebr. stood.*

16 And the man said vnto Eli, I am he, that came out of the army, and I fled to day out of the army. And he said, What † is there done, my sonne ?

† *Hebr. is the thing.*

17 And the messenger answered, and said, Israel is fled before the Philistines, and there hath bene also a great slaughter among the people, and thy two sonnes also, Hophni & Phinehas, are dead, and the Arke of God is taken.

18 And it came to passe when hee made mention of the Arke of God, that he fell from off the seat backward by the side of the gate, and his necke brake, and hee died : for he was an old man, and heauie, and hee had iudged Israel fortie yeeres.

19 ¶ And

‖ *Or, to crie out.*

19 ¶ And his daughter in law Phinehas wife was with childe *neere* ‖to be deliuered : and when shee heard the tidings that the Arke of God was taken, and that her father in law, and her husband were dead , shee bowed her selfe

† *Hebr. were turned.*

and traueyled; for her paines † came vpon her.

20 And about the time of her death, the women that stood by her, said vnto her : Feare not , for thou hast borne a sonne. But she answered not, †neither

† *Heb. set not her heart*

did she regard *it.*

‖ *That is, where is the glory?*

‖ *Or, there is no glory.*

21 And she named the childe ‖Ichabod , saying, ‖ The glory is departed from Israel, (because the Arke of God was taken, and because of her father in law and her husband.)

22 And she said, The glory is departed from Israel : for the Arke of God is taken.

CHAP. V.

1 The Philistines hauing brought the Arke into Ashdod, set it in the house of Dagon. 3 Dagon is smitten downe and cut in pieces, and they of Ashdod smitten with Emerods. 8 So God dealeth with them of Gath, when it was brought thither : 10 and so with them of Ekron when it was brought thither.

Nd the Philistines tooke the Arke of God , and brought it from Ebenezer vnto Ashdod.

2 When the Philistines tooke the Arke of God, they brought it into the house of Dagon, and set it by Dagon

3 ¶ And when they of Ashdod arose earely on the morrow, behold, Dagon was fallen vpon his face to the earth, before the Arke of the Lord· and they tooke Dagon , and set him in his place againe.

4 And when they arose earely on the morrow morning, behold, Dagon was fallen vpon his face to the ground, before the Arke of the Lord : and the head of Dagon, and both the palmes of his hands were cut off vpon the threshold, only ‖the stumpe of Dagon was

‖ *Or, the filthy part.*

left to him.

5 Therefore neither the priests of Dagon, nor any that come into Dagons house ; tread on the threshold of Dagon in Ashdod vnto this day

6 But the hand of the Lord was heauy vpon them of Ashdod, and he de-

* *Psal. 78. 66.*

stroyed them, and smote them with *E-

merods, *euen* Ashdod, and the coastes thereof.

7 And when the men of Ashdod saw that *it was* so, they said, The Arke of the God of Israel shall not abide with vs : for his hand is sore vpon vs, and vpon Dagon our god.

8 They sent therefore , and gathered all the lords of the Philistines vnto them, and said, What shall we doe with the Arke of the God of Israel ? And they answered, Let the Arke of the God of Israel bee caried about vnto Gath. And they caried the Arke of the God of Israel about *thither.*

9 And it was so, that after they had caried it about, the hand of the Lord was against the citie with a very great destruction : and hee smote the men of the citie both small and great, and they had Emerods in their secret parts.

10 ¶ Therfore they sent the Arke of God to Ekron : and it came to passe as the Arke of God came to Ekron, that the Ekronites cried out, saying, They haue brought about the Arke of the God of Israel to vs, to slay vs, and our people.

11 So they sent and gathered together all the lords of the Philistines, and said , Send away the Arke of the God of Israel, and let it goe againe to his owne place, that it slay vs not, and our people : for there was a deadly destruction throughout all the citie : The hand of God was very heauy there.

12 And the men that died not , were smitten with the Emerods : and the cry of the citie went vp to heauen.

CHAP. VI.

1 After seuen moneths the Philistines take counsell, how to send backe the Arke. 10 They bring it on a new cart with an offering vnto Bethshemesh. 19 The people are smitten for looking into the Arke. 21 They send to them of Kiriath-iearim to fetch it.

ND the Arke of the Lord was in the country of the Philistines seuen moneths.

2 And the Philistines called for the priests and the diuiners, saying, What shall we doe to the Arke of the Lord ? Tell vs wherewith we shall send it to his place ?

3 And they said, If yee send away the Arke of the God of Israel, send it not

not empty : but in any wise returne him a trespasse offring: then ye shall be healed, and it shall be knowen to you, why his hand is not remooued from you.

4 Then said they, What *shall be* the trespasse offring, which wee shall returne to him? They answered, Fiue golden Emerods, and fiue golden mice, *according to* the number of the lordes of the Philistines : for one plague was on †you all, and on your lords.

† Heb. them.

5 Wherefore ye shall make images of your Emerodes, and images of your Mice, that marre the land, and ye shall giue glory vnto the God of Israel : peraduenture hee will lighten his hand from off you, and from off your gods, and from off your land.

6 Wherefore then doe yee harden your hearts, as the Egyptians and Pharaoh hardened their hearts? when he had wrought ‖wonderfully among them, * did they not let †the people goe, and they departed?

‖ Or, reproachfully.
＊ Exod. 12. 31.
† Heb. them.

7 Now therefore make a new cart, and take two milch-kine, on which there hath come no yoke, and tie the kine to the cart, and bring the calues home from them.

8 And take the Arke of the Lord, and lay it vpon the cart, and put the iewels of golde, which ye returne him for a trespasse offering, in a coffer by the side thereof, and send it away, that it may goe.

9 And see, if it goeth vp by the way of his owne coast to Bethshemesh, then ‖he hath done vs this great euill : but if not, then wee shall know that it is not his hand that smote vs ; it *was* a chance *that* happened to vs.

‖ Or, it.

10 ¶ And the men did so : and tooke two milch-kine, and tied them to the cart, and shut vp their calues at home.

11 And they layde the Arke of the Lord vpon the cart, and the coffer, with the mice of golde, and the images of their Emerods.

12 And the kine tooke the straight way to the way of Bethshemesh, and went along the high way, lowing as they went, and turned not aside to the right hand, or to the left : and the lords of the Philistines went after them, vnto the border of Bethshemesh.

13 And they of Bethshemesh were reaping their wheat haruest in the valley : and they lifted vp their eyes, and saw the Arke, and reioyced to see *it.*

14 And the cart came into the field of Ioshua a Bethshemite, & stood there, where there *was* a great stone : and they claue the wood of the cart, and offered the kine, a burnt offering vnto the Lord.

15 And the Leuites tooke downe the Arke of the Lord, and the coffer that *was* with it, wherein the iewels of golde *were*, and put them on the great stone : And the men of Bethshemesh offered burnt offrings, and sacrificed sacrifices the same day vnto the Lord.

16 And when the fiue lordes of the Philistines had seene *it*, they returned to Ekron the same day.

17 And these are the golden Emerods which the Philistines returned for a trespasse offering vnto the Lord ; for Ashdod one, for Gaza one, for Askelon one, for Gath one, for Ekron one.

18 And the golden Mice *according to* the number of all the cities of the Philistines, *belonging* to the fiue lordes, both of fenced cities, and of countrey villages, euen vnto the ‖great *stone of* Abel, whereon they set downe the Arke of the Lord ; *which stone remaineth* vnto this day, in the field of Ioshua the Bethshemite.

‖ Or, great stone.

19 ¶ And he smote the men of Bethshemesh, because they had looked into the Arke of the Lord, euen he smote of the people fiftie thousand, and threescore and tenne men : and the people lamented, because the Lord had smitten *many* of the people with a great slaughter.

20 And the men of Bethshemesh said, Who is able to stand before this holy Lord God? and to whom shal he goe vp from vs?

21 ¶ And they sent messengers to the inhabitants of Kiriath-iearim, saying, The Philistines haue brought againe the Arke of the Lord ; come ye downe, and fetch it vp to you.

CHAP. VII.

1 They of Kiriath-iearim bring the Arke into the house of Abinadab, and sanctifie Eleazar his sonne to keepe it. 2 After twentie yeeres 3 The Israelites, by Samuels meanes, solemnly repent at Mizpeh. 7 While Samuel prayeth and sacrificeth, the Lord discomfiteth the Philistines by thunder, at Eben-ezer. 13 The Philistines are subdued. 15 Samuel peaceably and religiously iudgeth Israel.

And

ANd the men of Kiriath-iearim came, and fetcht vp the Arke of the LORD, and brought it into the house of Abinadab in the hill, and sanctified Eleazar his sonne, to keepe the Arke of the LORD.

2 And it came to passe while the Arke abode in Kiriath-iearim, that the time was long: for it was twentie yeeres: and all the house of Israel lamented after the LORD.

3 ¶ And Samuel spake vnto all the house of Israel, saying, If ye doe returne vnto the LORD with all your hearts, *then* *put away the strange gods, and *Ashtaroth from among you, and prepare your hearts vnto the LORD, and *serue him onely: & he will deliuer you out of the hand of the Philistines.

* Iosh. 24. 15, 23.
* Iudg. 2. 13.
* Deut. 6. 4. matt. 4. 10. luke 4. 8.

4 Then the children of Israel did put away *Baalim, and Ashtaroth, and serued the LORD onely.

* Iudg. 2. 11.

5 And Samuel said, Gather all Israel to Mizpeh, and I will pray for you vnto the LORD.

6 And they gathered together to Mizpeh, and drew water, and powred it out before the LORD, and fasted on that day, aud said there, We haue sinned against the LORD. And Samuel iudged the children of Israel in Mizpeh.

7 And when the Philistines heard that the children of Israel were gathered together to Mizpeh, the lords of the Philistines went vp against Israel: and when the children of Israel heard *it*, they were afraid of the Philistines.

8 And the children of Israel said to Samuel, †Cease not to crie vnto the LORD our God for vs, that he will saue vs out of the hand of the Philistines.

† *Heb. be not silent from vs from crying.*

9 ¶ And Samuel tooke a sucking lambe, and offered it for a burnt offering wholly vnto the LORD; and Samuel cried vnco the LORD for Israel, and the LORD ‖heard him.

‖ *Or, answered.*

10 And as Samuel was offering vp the burnt offering, the Philistines drewe neere to battell against Israel: but the LORD thundred with a great thunder on that day vpon the Philistines, and discomfited them, and they were smitten before Israel.

11 And the men of Israel went out of Mizpeh, and pursued the Philistines, and smote them, vntill *they came* vnder Bethcar.

12 Then Samuel tooke a stone, and set it betweene Mizpeh and Shen, and called the name of it ‖Eben-Ezer, saying, Hitherto hath the LORD helped vs.

‖ That is, *the stone of helpe.*

13 ¶ So the Philistines were subdued, and they came no more into the coast of Israel: and the hand of the LORD was against the Philistines, all the dayes of Samuel.

14 And the cities which the Philistines had taken from Israel, were restored to Israel, from Ekron euen vnto Gath, and the coasts thereof did Israel deliuer out of the hands of the Philistines: and there was peace betweene Israel and the Amorites.

15 And Samuel iudged Israel all the dayes of his life.

16 And he went from yeere to yeere †in circuit to Bethel, and Gilgal, and Mizpeh, and iudged Israel in all those places.

† *Heb. and he circuited.*

17 And his returne *was* to Ramah: for there *was* his house: and there hee iudged Israel, and there hee built an altar vnto the LORD.

CHAP. VIII.

1 By occasion of the ill gouernment of Samuels sonnes, the Israelites aske a King. 6 Samuel praying in griefe is comforted by God. 10 Hee telleth the manner of a King. 19 God willeth Samuel to yeeld vnto the importunitie of the people.

ANd it came to passe, when Samuel was old, that he made his sonnes Iudges ouer Israel.

2 Now the name of his first borne was Ioel, and the name of his second, Abiah: *they were* Iudges in Beer-sheba.

3 And his sonnes walked not in his wayes, but turned aside after lucre, and *tooke bribes, & peruerted iudgement.

* Deut. 16. 19.

4 Then all the Elders of Israel gathered themselues together, and came to Samuel vnto Ramah,

5 And said vnto him, Behold, thou art olde, and thy sonnes walke not in thy wayes: now *make vs a King to iudge vs, like all the nations.

* Ose. 13. 10 acts 13. 21.

6 ¶ But the thing †displeased Samuel, when they said, Giue vs a King to iudge vs: and Samuel prayed vnto the LORD.

† *Heb. was euill in the eyes of Samuel.*

7 And the LORD said vnto Samuel,

muel, Hearken vnto the voyce of the people in all that they say vnto thee : for they haue not reiected thee, but they haue reiected mee, that I should not reigne ouer them.

8 According to all the works which they haue done since the day that I brought them vp out of Egypt euen vnto this day, wherewith they haue forsaken me, and serued other gods : so doe they also vnto thee.

9 Nowe therefore ||hearken vnto their voyce : ||howbeit, yet protest solemnly vnto them, and shew them the maner of the King that shall reigne ouer them.

10 ¶ And Samuel told all the words of the LORD vnto the people, that asked of him a King.

11 And hee sayd, This will be the maner of the king that shall reigne ouer you : Hee will take your sonnes, and appoint *them* for himselfe for his charets, and to bee his horsemen, and *some* shall runne before his charets.

12 And hee will appoint him Captaines ouer thousands, and captaines ouer fifties, and *will set them* to eare his ground, and to reape his haruest, and to make his instruments of warre, and instruments of his charets.

13 And he will take your daughters to be confectionaries, and to be cookes, and to be bakers.

14 And he will take your fields, and your vineyards, and your oliue-yards, *euen* the best *of them*, and giue *them* to his seruants.

15 And he will take the tenth of your seed, and of your vineyards, and giue to his †officers, and to his seruants.

16 And hee will take your men seruants, and your mayd seruants, and your goodliest young men, and your asses, and put them to his worke.

17 Hee will take the tenth of your sheepe, and ye shall be his seruants.

18 And ye shall cry out in that day, because of your king which ye shal haue chosen you ; and the LORD will not heare you in that day.

19 ¶ Neuerthelesse, the people refused to obey the voyce of Samuel ; and they said, Nay, but we wil haue a King ouer vs :

20 That we also may be like all the nations, and that our King may iudge vs, and goe out before vs, and fight our battels.

‡ Or, obey.

‡ Or, notwithstanding, when thou hast solemnly protested against them, then thou shalt shew, &c.

† Heb. Eunuches.

21 And Samuel heard all the words of the people, and he rehearsed them in the eares of the LORD.

22 And the LORD said to Samuel, Hearken vnto their voyce, and make them a King. And Samuel said vnto the men of Israel, Goe yee euery man vuto his citie.

CHAP. IX.

1 Saul despairing to finde his fathers asses, 6 by the counsell of his seruaunt, 11 and direction of young maidens, 15 according to Gods reuelation, 18 commeth to Samuel. 19 Samuel entertaineth Saul at the feast. 25 Samuel after secret communication, bringeth Saul on his way.

Ow there was a man of Beniamin, whose name was * Kish, the sonne of Abiel, the sonne of Zeror, the sonne of Bechorath, the sonne of Aphiah, a ||Beniamite, a mighty man of ||power.

2 And he had a sonne, whose name was Saul, a choice young man, and a goodly : and *there was* not among the children of Israel a goodlier person then hee : from his shoulders and vpward, *hee was* higher then any of the people.

3 And the asses of Kish, Sauls father, were lost ; and Kish said to Saul his sonne, Take nowe one of the seruants with thee, and arise, goe seeke the asses.

4 And he passed thorow mount Ephraim, and passed thorow the land of Shalisha, but they found *them* not : then they passed thorow the land of Shalim, and *there* they were not : and hee passed thorow the land of the Beniamites, but they found *them* not.

5 *And* when they were come to the land of Zuph, Saul said to his seruant that was with him, Come, and let vs returne, lest my father leaue *caring* for the asses, and take thought for vs.

6 And hee said vnto him, Behold now, *there is* in this citie a man of God, and he is an honourable man ; all that he saith, commeth surely to passe : Now let vs goe thither ; peraduenture he can shew vs our way that we should goe.

7 Then said Saul to his seruaunt, But behold, *if* we goe, what shall wee bring the man ? for the bread † is spent in our vessels, and there is not a present to bring

* Chap. 14. 51. 1. chro. 8. 33.

‡ Or, the sonne of a man of Iemini.

‡ Or, substance.

† Hebr is gone out of &c.

† *Hebr. is with vs?*

† *Hebr. there is found in my hand.*

† *Hebr. thy word is good.*

† *Hebr. in the ascent of the citie.*

‖ *Or, feast.*

† *Heb. to day.*

* Chap. 15. 1. acts. 13. 21.
† *Heb. reueiled the eare of Samuel.*

† *Hebr. restraine in.*

bring to the man of God : What † haue wee ?

8 And the seruant answered Saul againe, and said, † Behold, I haue here at hand the fourth part of a shekel of siluer; that wil I giue to the man of God, to tell vs our way.

9 (Beforetime in Israel, when a man went to enquire of God, thus he spake ; Come, and let vs go to the Seer : for he that is now *called* a Prophet, was beforetime called a Seer.)

10 Then said Saul to his seruant, † Wel said, come, let vs go: so they went vnto the city where the man of God *was.*

11 ¶ And as they went vp † the hill to the city, they found yong maydens going out to draw water, and said vnto them, Is the Seer here ?

12 And they answered them, and said, He is: behold, *he is* before you, make haste now : for he came to day to the citie; for there is ‖ a sacrifice of the people to day in the high place.

13 Assoone as ye be come into the citie, ye shall straightway finde him, before he goe vp to the high place to eate: for the people will not eate vntill hee come, because he doth blesse the sacrifice, *and* afterwards they eat that be bidden: Now therefore get you vp, for † about this time ye shall finde him.

14 And they went vp into the citie : and when they were come into the citie, behold, Samuel came out against them, for to goe vp to the hie place.

15 ¶ * Now the LORD had † told Samuel in his eare a day before Saul came, saying,

16 To morrow about this time I will send thee a man out of the land of Beniamin, and thou shalt anoynt him to be Captaine ouer my people Israel, that he may saue my people out of the hand of the Philistines: for I haue looked vpon my people, because their cry is come vnto me.

17 And when Samuel saw Saul, the LORD said vnto him, Behold the man whom I spake to thee of : this same shall † reigne ouer my people.

18 Then Saul drew neere to Samuel in the gate, and said, Tell me, I pray thee, where the Seers house is.

19 And Samuel answered Saul, and said, I am the Seer: Goe vp before me vnto the high place, for ye shall eate with me to day, and to morrow I will let thee goe, and will tell thee all

that is in thine heart.

20 And as for thine asses that were lost † three dayes agoe, set not thy minde on them, for they are found : And on whom is all the desire of Israel ? is it not on thee, & on all thy fathers house?

21 And Saul answered, and said, Am not I a Beniamite, of the smallest of the tribes of Israel ? and my family the least of all the families of the tribe of Beniamin ? Wherefore then speakest thou † so to me ?

22 And Samuel tooke Saul, and his seruant, and brought them into the parlour, & made them sit in the chiefest place among them that were bidden, which were about thirtie persons.

23 And Samuel said vnto the cooke, Bring the portion which I gaue thee, of which I said vnto thee, Set it by thee.

24 And the cooke took vp the shoulder, and that which was vpon it, and set it before Saul, and *Samuel* said, Behold, that which is ‖ left, set *it* before thee, *and* eate : for vnto this time hath it bene kept for thee, *since* I said I haue inuited the people : So Saul did eat with Samuel that day.

25 ¶ And when they were come downe from the high place into the citie, *Samuel* communed with Saul vpon the top of the house.

26 And they arose early: and it came to passe about the spring of the day, that Samuel called Saul to the top of the house, saying, Vp, that I may send thee away : And Saul arose, and they went out both of them, hee and Samuel, abroad.

27 And *as* they were going downe to the end of the city, Samuel said to Saul, Bid the seruant passe on before vs, (and he passed on) but stand thou still † a while, that I may shew thee the word of God.

† *Hebr. to day three dayes.*

† *Hebr. according to this word?*

‖ *Or, reserued.*

† *Hebr. to day.*

CHAP. X.

1 Samuel anoynteth Saul. 2 Hee confirmeth him by prediction of three signes. 9 Sauls heart is changed, and he prophecieth. 14 He concealeth the matter of the kingdome from his vncle. 17 Saul is chosen at Mizpeh by lot. 26 The different affections of his subiects.

Hen Samuel tooke a viall of oile, and powred *it* vpon his head, & kissed him, and said, *Is it* not because the LORD hath anoynted thee to be captain ouer his inheritance?
2 When

* Gen. 35.
20.

† Heb. the
businesse.

† Heb. aske
thee of peace

† Heb. and it
shall come to
passe that
when these
signes &c.
† Heb. do for
thee as thine
hand shall
finde.

* Chap. 13.
8.

† Heb. shoul-
der.
† Heb. tur-
ned.

† Heb. A
man to his
neighbour.
* Chap. 19.
24.
† Heb. from
thence.

2 When thou art departed from me to day, then thou shalt find two men by * Rachels sepulchre in the border of Beniamin, at Zelzah: and they will say vnto thee, The asses which thou wentest to seeke, are found: and loe, thy father hath left † the care of the asses, and sorroweth for you, saying, What shall I doe for my sonne?

3 Then shalt thou goe on forward from thence, and thou shalt come to the plaine of Tabor, and there shall meete thee three men, going vp to God to Bethel, one carying three kids, and another carying three loaues of bread, and another carying a bottle of wine.

4 And they will † salute thee, and giue thee two *loaues* of bread, which thou shalt receiue of their hands.

5 After that thou shalt come to the hill of God, where is the garison of the Philistines: and it shall come to passe when thou art come thither to the citie, that thou shalt meet a company of prophets comming downe from the high place, with a psalterie, and a tabret, and a pipe, and a harpe before them, and they shall prophecie.

6 And the Spirit of the LORD will come vpon thee, and thou shalt prophecie with them, and shalt be turned into another man.

7 And † let it be when these signes are come vnto thee, † that thou doe as occasion serue thee, for God is with thee.

8 And thou shalt goe downe before me to Gilgal, and behold, I will come downe vnto thee, to offer burnt offerings, *and* to sacrifice sacrifices of peace offerings: * seuen dayes shalt thou tarie, till I come to thee, and shew thee what thou shalt doe.

9 ¶ And it was so that when he had turned his † backe to go from Samuel, God † gaue him another heart: and all those signes came to passe that day.

10 And when they came thither to the hill, behold, a company of the prophets met him, and the spirit of God came vpon him, and hee prophesied among them.

11 And it came to passe when all that knew him beforetime, saw, that behold, hee prophesied among the prophets, then the people said † one to another, What is this that is come vnto the sonne of Kish? * Is Saul also among the prophets?

12 And one † of the same place an-

swered, and sayd, But who is their father? Therefore it became a prouerbe, Is Saul also among the Prophets?

13 And when he had made an end of prophesying, he came to the high place.

14 ¶ And Sauls vncle saide vnto him, and to his seruant, Whither went ye? And he said, To seeke the asses: and when we saw that *they were* no where, we came to Samuel.

15 And Sauls vncle said, Tell me, I pray thee, what Samuel said vnto you.

16 And Saul sayd vnto his vncle; He told vs plainely that the asses were found. But of the matter of the kingdome, whereof Samuel spake, he told him not.

17 ¶ And Samuel called the people together vnto the LORD to Mizpeh;

18 And said vnto the children of Israel, Thus saith the LORD God of Israel, I brought vp Israel out of Egypt, and deliuered you out of the hand of the Egyptians, and out of the hand of all kingdomes, *and* of them that oppressed you.

19 And ye haue this day reiected your God, who himselfe saued you out of all your aduersities & your tribulations: and ye haue said vnto him, *Nay*, but set a king ouer vs. Now therefore present your selues before the LORD by your tribes, and by your thousands.

20 And when Samuel had caused all the tribes of Israel to come neere, the tribe of Beniamin was taken.

21 When he had caused the tribe of Beniamin to come neere by their families, the familie of Matri was taken, and Saul the sonne of Kish was taken: and when they sought him, he could not be found.

22 Therefore they enquired of the LORD further, if the man should yet come thither: and the LORD answered, Behold, hee hath hid himselfe among the stuffe.

23 And they ranne, and fetched him thence, and when he stood among the people, he was higher then any of the people, from the shoulders & vpward.

24 And Samuel said to all the people, See ye him whome the LORD hath chosen, that there is none like him among all the people? And all the people shouted, and saide, † God saue the King.

25 Then Samuel tolde the people the

† Heb. let
the king liue

the maner of the kingdome, and wrote it in a booke, and layd it vp before the LORD, and Samuel sent all the people away, euery man to his house.

26 ¶ And Saul also went home to Gibeah, and there went with him a band of men, whose hearts God had touched.

27 But the children of Belial sayd, Howe shall this man saue vs? and they despised him, and brought him no presents: but ‖he held his peace.

Or, he was, s though he id beene eafe.

CHAP. XI.

1 Nahash offereth them of Iabesh Gilead a reprochfull condition. 4 They send messengers and are deliuered by Saul. 12 Saul thereby is confirmed, and his kingdome renewed.

Hen Nahash the Ammonite came vp, and encamped against Iabesh Gilead: and all the men of Iabesh sayde vnto Nahash, Make a couenant with vs, and we will serue thee.

2 And Nahash the Ammonite answered them, On this condition will I make a couenant with you, that I may thrust out all your right eyes, and lay it for a reproch vpon all Israel.

3 And the Elders of Iabesh sayd vnto him, †Giue vs seuen daies respite, that we may send messengers vnto all the coasts of Israel: and then, if there be no man to saue vs, we will come out to thee.

Hebr. forbeare vs.

4 ¶ Then came the messengers to Gibeah of Saul, and told the tidings in the eares of the people: and all the people lift vp their voyces, and wept.

5 And behold, Saul came after the herd out of the field, and Saul sayd, What aileth the people that they weep? and they told him the tidings of the men of Iabesh.

6 And the Spirit of God came vpon Saul, when he heard those tydings, and his anger was kindled greatly.

7 And he tooke a yoke of oxen, and hewed them in pieces, and sent them throughout all the coasts of Israel by the hands of messengers, saying, Whosoeuer commeth not foorth after Saul and after Samuel, so shall it bee done vnto his oxen: and the feare of the LORD fell on the people, and they came out †with one consent.

Heb. as one man.

8 And when he numbred them in Bezek, the children of Israel were three hundred thousand, and the men of Iudah thirty thousand.

9 And they said vnto the messengers that came, Thus shall yee say vnto the men of Iabesh Gilead, To morrow by that time the sunne be hote, ye shal haue ‖helpe. And the messengers came, and shewed it to the men of Iabesh, and they were glad.

‖ *Or, deliuerance.*

10 Therfore the men of Iabesh said, To morrow wee will come out vnto you, and ye shall doe with vs all that seemeth good vnto you.

11 And it was so on the morrow, that Saul put the people in three cōpanies, and they came into the midst of the host in the morning watch, and slewe the Ammonites, vntill the heat of the day: and it came to passe, that they which remained were scattered, so that two of them were not left together.

12 ¶ And the people said vnto Samuel, Who is he that said, Shall Saul reigne ouer vs? bring the men, that we may put them to death.

13 And Saul said, There shall not a man be put to death this day: for to day the LORD hath wrought saluation in Israel.

14 Then said Samuel to the people, Come, and let vs goe to Gilgal, and renew the kingdome there.

15 And all the people went to Gilgal, and there they made Saul King before the LORD in Gilgal: and there they sacrificed sacrifices of peace offerings before the LORD: and there Saul and all the men of Israel reioyced greatly.

CHAP. XII.

1 Samuel testifieth his integritie. 6 Hee reproueth the people of ingratitude. 16 He terrifieth them with thunder in haruest time. 20 He comforteth them in Gods mercy.

ND Samuel saide vnto all Israel, Beholde, I haue hearkned vnto your voice in all that ye said vnto mee, and haue made a King ouer you.

2 And now behold, the King walketh before you: and I am olde, and gray headed, and behold, my sonnes are with you: and I haue walked before you from my childhood vnto this day.

3 Behold, *here I *am*, witnesse against*

* *Ecclus. 46. 19.*

gainst me before the LORD, and before his Anoynted: Whose oxe haue I taken? or whose asse haue I taken? or whom haue I defrauded? whom haue I oppressed? or of whose hand haue I receiued any † bribe ‖ to blinde mine eyes therewith? and I will restore it you.

† Hebr. ransome.
‖ Or, that I should hide mine eyes at at him.

4 And they said, Thou hast not defrauded vs, nor oppressed vs, neither hast thou taken ought of any mans hand.

5 And hee said vnto them, The LORD is witnesse against you, and his Anointed is witnesse this day, that ye haue not found ought in my hand: And they answered, He is witnesse.

6 ¶ And Samuel said vnto the people, It is the LORD that ‖ aduanced Moses and Aaron, and that brought your fathers vp out of the land of Egypt.

‖ Or, made.

7 Now therefore stand still, that I may reason with you before the LORD, of all the † righteous acts of the LORD, which he did † to you and your fathers.

† Hebr. righteousnesses, Or, benefits.
† Heb. with.
* Gen. 46. 5, 6.

8 * When Iacob was come into Egypt, and your fathers cried vnto the LORD, then the LORD * sent Moses and Aaron, which brought foorth your fathers out of Egypt, and made them dwell in this place.

* Exod. 4. 16.

9 And when they forgat the LORD their God, * he sold them into the hand of Sisera captaine of the hoste of Hazor, and into the hand of the Philistines, and into the hand of the king of Moab, and they fought against them.

* Iudg. 4. 2.

10 And they cried vnto the LORD, and said, Wee haue sinned, because we haue forsaken the LORD, and haue serued Baalim and Ashtaroth : but now deliuer vs out of the hand of our enemies, and we will serue thee.

11 And the LORD sent Ierubbaal, and Bedan, and * Iephthah, and Samuel, and deliuered you out of the hand of your enemies on euery side, and yee dwelled safe.

* Iudg. 11. 1.

12 And when ye saw that Nahash the king of the children of Ammon came against you, ye said vnto me, Nay, but a King shall reigne ouer vs, when the LORD your God was your King.

13 Now therefore, behold the King whom yee haue chosen, and whom yee haue desired: and behold, the LORD hath set a King ouer you.

14 If ye will feare the LORD, and serue him, and obey his voice, and not rebell against the † Commandement of the LORD, then shall both ye and also the King that reigneth ouer you, † continue following the LORD your God.

† Hebr. mouth.
† Hebr. be after.

15 But if ye wil not obey the voice of the LORD, but rebel against the Commandement of the LORD, then shall the hand of the LORD be against you, as it was against your fathers.

16 ¶ Now therefore stand and see this great thing which the LORD will doe before your eyes.

17 Is it not wheat haruest to day? I will call vnto the LORD, and hee shall send thunder and raine, that ye may perceiue and see that your wickednesse is great, which ye haue done in the sight of the LORD, in asking you a King.

18 So Samuel called vnto the LORD, and the LORD sent thunder and raine that day : and all the people greatly feared the LORD and Samuel.

19 And all the people said vnto Samuel, Pray for thy seruants vnto the LORD thy God, that we die not : for we haue added vnto all our sinnes, this euil, to aske vs a King.

20 ¶ And Samuel saide vnfo the people, Feare not : (ye haue done al this wickednesse, yet turne not aside from following the LORD, but serue the LORD with all your heart :

20 And turne ye not aside, for then should ye goe after vaine things, which cannot profit, nor deliuer, for they are vaine.)

22 For the LORD wil not forsake his people, for his great Names sake : because it hath pleased the LORD to make you his people.

23 Moreouer, as for me, God forbid that I should sin against the LORD, † in ceasing to pray for you : but I will teach you the good and the right way.

† Hebr. from ceasing.

24 Onely feare the LORD, and serue him in trueth with all your heart : for consider ‖ how great things he hath done for you.

‖ Or, what great thir &c.

25 But if yee shall still doe wickedly, yee shall be consumed, both yee and your King.

CHAP. XIII.

stines great hoste. 6 The distresse of the Israelites. 8 Saul weary of staying for Samuel, sacrificeth. 11 Samuel reproueth him. 17 The three spoiling bands of the Philistines. 19 The policie of the Philistines, to suffer no Smith in Israel.

† Hebr. the sonne of one yeere in his reigning.

SAul †reigned one yeere, and when he had reigned two yeeres ouer Israel,

2 Saul chose him three thousand men of Israel : *whereof* two thousand were with Saul in Michmash, and in mount Bethel, and a thousand were with Ionathan in Gibeah of Beniamin : and the rest of the people he sent euery man to his tent.

‖ Or, the hill.

3 And Ionathan smote the garison of the Philistines that *was* in ‖Geba, and the Philistines heard *of it*: and Saul blew the trumpet thorowout all the land, saying, Let the Hebrewes heare.

† Hebr. did stinke.

4 And all Israel heard say, that Saul had smitten a garison of the Philistines, and that Israel also †was had in abomination with the Philistines: and the people were called together after Saul to Gilgal.

5 ¶ And the Philistines gathered themselues together, to fight with Israel, thirtie thousand charets, and sixe thousand horsemen, and people as the sand which is on the sea shore in multitude, and they came vp, and pitched in Michmash, Eastward from Beth-auen.

6 When the men of Israel saw that they were in a strait : (for the people were distressed:) then the people did hide themselues in caues, and in thickets, and in rocks, and in high places, and in pits.

7 And *some* of the Hebrewes went ouer Iordane, to the land of Gad and Gilead; as for Saul, he *was* yet in Gilgal, and all the people †followed him trembling.

† Hebr. trembled after him.
* Chap. 10. 8.

8 ¶ *And he taried seuen dayes, according to the set time that Samuel *had appointed:* but Samuel came not to Gilgal, and the people were scattered from him.

9 And Saul said, Bring hither a burnt offring to me, and peace offrings. And he offered the burnt offering.

10 And it came to passe that assoone as he had made an end of offering the burnt offering, behold, Samuel came, and Saul went out to meete him, that he might †salute him.

† Heb. blesse him.

11 ¶ And Samuel said, What hast thou done? And Saul said, Because I sawe that the people were scattered from me, and that thou camest not within the dayes appointed, and that the Philistines gathered themselues together to Michmash:

12 Therfore said I, The Philistines will come downe now vpon me to Gilgal, and I haue not †made supplication vnto the LORD: I forced my selfe therefore, and offered a burnt offering.

† Hebr. intreated the face.

13 And Samuel said to Saul, Thou hast done foolishly: thou hast not kept the commandement of the LORD thy God, which hee commanded thee: for now would the LORD haue established thy kingdome vpon Israel for euer.

14 But now thy kingdome shall not continue: the LORD hath sought him a man after his owne heart, and the LORD hath commanded him to bee captaine ouer his people, because thou hast not kept that which the LORD commanded thee.

15 And Samuel arose, and gate him vp from Gilgal, vnto Gibeah of Beniamin, and Saul numbred the people that were †present with him, about sixe hundred men.

† Heb. found

16 And Saul and Ionathan his sonne, and the people that were present with them, abode in Gibeah of Beniamin : but the Philistines encamped in Michmash.

17 ¶ And the spoilers came out of the campe of the Philistines, in three companies: one company turned vnto the way that leadeth to Ophrah, vnto the land of Shual.

18 And another company turned the way to Bethoron : and another companie turned to the way of the border, that looketh to the valley of Zeboim toward the wildernesse.

19 ¶ Now there was no smith found thorowout all the land of Israel : for the Philistines said, Lest the Hebrewes make them swords or speares.

20 But all the Israelites went downe to the Philistines, to sharpen euery man his share and his coulter, and his axe, and his mattocke.

21 Yet they had a †file for the mattocks, and for the coulters, and for the forkes, and for the axes, and †to sharpen the goads.

† Hebr. a file with mouthes.
† Heb. to set.

22 So

22 So it came to passe in the day of battell, that there was neither sword nor speare found in the hand of any of the people that were with Saul and Ionathan : but with Saul & with Ionathan his sonne was there found.

¹ Or, standing campe.

23 And the ‖garison of the Philistines went out to the passage of Michmash.

CHAP. XIIII.

1 Ionathan, vnwitting to his father, the Priest, or the people, goeth and miraculously smiteth the Philistines garrison. 15 A diuine terrour maketh them beate themselues. 17 Saul not staying the Priests answere, setteth on them. 21 The captiuated Hebrewes, and the hidden Israelites, ioyne against them. 24 Sauls vnaduised adiuration, hindreth the victory. 32 Hee restraineth the people from eating blood. 35 He buildeth an Altar. 36 Ionathan taken by lot, is saued by the people. 47 Sauls strength and family.

‖ Or, there was a day.

Ow ‖ it came to passe vpon a day, that Ionathan the sonne of Saul said vnto the yong man that bare his armour, Come, and let vs goe ouer to the Philistines garison, that is on the other side: but hee told not his father.

2 And Saul taried in the vttermost part of Gibeah, vnder a Pomegranate tree, which is in Migron: and the people that were with him, were about sixe hundred men:

* Chap. 4. 21.

3 And Ahiah the sonne of Ahitub, *Ichabods brother, the sonne of Phinehas, the sonne of Eli, the LORDs Priest in Shiloh, wearing an Ephod: and the people knew not that Ionathan was gone.

4 ¶ And betweene the passages, by which Ionathan sought to go ouer vnto the Philistines garison, there was a sharpe rocke on the one side, and a sharp rocke on the other side: and the name of the one was Bozez, and the name of the other Seneh.

† Heb. tooth.

5 The †forefront of the one was situate Northward ouer against Michmash, and the other Southward ouer against Gibeah.

6 And Ionathan said to the young man that bare his armour, Come, and let vs goe ouer vnto the garison of these vncircumcised; it may be that the LORD will worke for vs: for there is no restraint to the LORD, * to saue by many, or by few.

* 2. Chron. 14. 11.

7 And his armour bearer sayd vnto him, Doe all that is in thine heart: turne thee, behold, I am with thee, according to thy heart.

8 Then said Ionathan, Behold, we will passe ouer vnto these men, and we will discouer our selues vnto them.

9 If they say thus vnto vs, †Tary vntill we come to you : then wee will stand still in our place, and will not goe vp vnto them.

† Heb. be still.

10 But if they say thus, Come vp vnto vs: then we will goe vp; for *the LORD hath deliuered them into our hand: and this shall be a signe vnto vs.

* 1. Macc. 4. 30.

11 And both of them discouered themselues vnto the garison of the Philistines : and the Philistines sayd, Behold, the Hebrewes come foorth out of the holes, where they had hid themselues.

12 And the men of the garison answered Ionathan and his armour bearer, and said, Come vp to vs, and wee will shew you a thing. And Ionathan said vnto his armour bearer, Come vp after me; for the LORD hath deliuered them into the hand of Israel.

13 And Ionathan climed vp vpon his hands, and vpon his feete, and his armour bearer after him: and they fell before Ionathan; and his armour bearer slew after him.

14 And that first slaughter which Ionathan and his armour-bearer made, was about as it were twentie men, within as it were ‖an halfe acre of land, which a yoke of oxen might plow.

‖ Or, halfe furrow of acre of lan

15 And there was trembling in the hoste, in the field, and among all the people : the garison and the spoilers, they also trembled, and the earth quaked: so it was †a very great trembling.

† Hebr. a trembling of God.

16 And the watchmen of Saul in Gibeah of Beniamin looked : and behold, the multitude melted away, and they went on beating downe one another.

17 Then said Saul vnto the people that were with him, Number now, and see who is gone from vs. And when they had numbred, behold, Ionathan and his armour bearer were not there.

18 And Saul said vnto Ahiah, Bring hither the Arke of God: (for the Arke of God was at that time with the children of Israel.)

19 ¶ And it came to passe while Saul talked

‖ Or, tumult.

† Heb. were
cryed toge-
ther.
* Iudg. 7.
22. 2. chro.
20. 23.

talked vnto the Priest, that the ‖noise that was in the hoste of the Philistines went on, and increased: And Saul said vnto the Priest, Withdraw thine hand.

20 And Saul and all the people that were with him †assembled themselues, and they came to the battel, and behold, *euery mans sword was against his fellow, *and there was* a very great discomfiture.

21 Moreouer, the Hebrewes *that* were with the Philistines before that time, which went vp with them into the campe *from the countrey* round about; euen they also *turned* to be with the Israelites, that *were* with Saul and Ionathan.

22 Likewise all the men of Israel, which had hid themselues in mount Ephraim, *when* they heard that the Philistines fled, euen they also followed hard after them in the battell.

23 So the LORD saued Israel that day: and the battell passed ouer vnto Beth-auen.

24 ¶ And the men of Israel were distressed that day; for Saul had adiured the people, saying, Cursed bee the man that eateth any foode vntill euening, that I may be auenged on mine enemies: so none of the people tasted any food.

25 And all *they of* the, land came to a wood, and there was honie vpon the ground.

26 And when the people were come into the wood, behold, the honie dropped, but no man put his hand to his mouth: for the people feared the oath.

27 But Ionathan heard not when his father charged the people with the oath; wherefore he put foorth the ende of the rodde that *was* in his hand, and dipt it in an hony combe, and put his hand to his mouth, and his eyes were enlightened.

28 Then answered one of the people, and said, Thy father straitly charged the people with an oath, saying, Cursed be the man that eateth any food this day. And the people were ‖faint.

‖ Or, wearie.

29 Then said Ionathan, My father hath troubled the land: see, I pray you, how mine eyes haue beene enlightened, because I tasted a little of this honie:

30 How much more, if haply the people had eaten freely to day of the spoile of their enemies which they found? for had there not beene now a much greater slaughter among the Philistines?

31 And they smote the Philistines that day from Michmash to Aiialon: and the people were very faint.

32 And the people flewe vpon the spoile, and tooke sheepe, and oxen, and calues, and slew them on the ground, and the people did eate them *with the blood.

33 ¶ Then they tolde Saul, saying, Behold, the people sinne against the LORD, in that they eate with the blood. And he said, Yee haue ‖transgressed: roule a great stone vnto mee this day.

34 And Saul said, Disperse your selues among the people, and say vnto them, Bring me hither euery man his oxe, and euery man his sheepe, and slay *them* here, and eat, and sinne not against the LORD in eating with the blood. And all the people brought euery man his oxe †with him that night, and slew *them* there.

35 And Saul built an altar vnto the LORD: †the same was the first altar that he built vnto the LORD.

36 ¶ And Saul saide, Let vs goe downe after the Philistines by night, and spoile them vntil the morning light, and let vs not leaue a man of them. And they said, Do whatsoeuer seemeth good vnto thee. Then said the priest, Let vs draw neere hither vnto God.

37 And Saul asked counsell of God, Shall I goe downe after the Philistines? Wilt thou deliuer them into the hand of Israel? But he answered him not that day.

38 And Saul said, Draw yee neere hither *all the †chiefe of the people: and know and see, wherein this sinne hath beene this day.

39 For as the LORD liueth, which saueth Israel, though it bee in Ionathan my sonne, he shall surely die: But *there was* not a man among all the people that answered him.

40 Then said he vnto all Israel, Be ye on one side, and I, and Ionathan my sonne will be on the other side. And the people said vnto Saul, Doe what seemeth good vnto thee.

41 Therefore Saul saide vnto the LORD God of Israel, ‖Giue a perfect *lot.* And Saul and Ionathan were taken: but the people †escaped.

42 And Saul said, Cast *lots* betweene me

* Leuit. 7.
26. and 19.
26. deut.
12. 16.

‖ Or, dealt
treache-
rously.

† Heb. in his
hand.

† Hebr. that
Altar he be-
ganne to
build vnto
the LORD.

* Iudg. 20.2
† Heb. cor-
ners.

‖ Or, shew
the innocent.

† Heb. went
forth.

me and Ionathan my sonne. And Ionathan was taken.

43 Then Saul said to Ionathan, Tell me what thou hast done. And Ionathan tolde him, and saide, I did but taste a litle hony with the end of the rodde that *was* in mine hand, *and* loe, I must die.

44 And Saul answered, God do so, and more also : for thou shalt surely die, Ionathan.

45 And the people said vnto Saul, Shall Ionathan die, who hath wrought this great saluation in Israel ? God forbid : as the LORD liueth, there shal not one haire of his head fall to the ground : for hee hath wrought with God this day. So the people rescued Ionathan, that hee died not.

46 Then Saul went vp from following the Philistines : and the Philistines went to their owne place.

47 ¶ So Saul tooke the kingdom ouer Israel, and fought against all his enemies on euery side, against Moab, and against the children of Ammon, and against Edom, and against the kings of Zobah, and against the Philistines : and whithersoeuer hee turned himselfe, he vexed *them*.

48 And he ‖gathered an hoste, and smote the Amalekites, and deliuered Israel out of the handes of them that spoiled them.

‖ *Or, wroght mightily*

49 Now the sonnes of Saul, *were* Ionathan, and Ishui, and Melchishua : and the names of his two daughters *were these :* the name of the first borne Merab, and the name of the yonger Michal :

50 And the name of Sauls wife *was* Ahinoam, the daughter of Ahimaaz, and the name of the captaine of his host *was* Abner, the sonne of Ner, Sauls vncle.

51 And Kish *was* the father of Saul, and Ner the father of Abner *was* the sonne of Abiel.

52 And there was sore warre against the Philistines, all the dayes of Saul : and when Saul saw any strong man, or any valiant man, he tooke him vnto him.

CHAP. XV.

1 Samuel sendeth Saul to destroy Amalek. 6 Saul fauoureth the Kenites. 8 Hee fpareth Agag and the best of the spoile. 10 Samuel denounceth vnto Saul commending and excusing himselfe, Gods reiection of him for his disobedience. 24 Sauls humiliation. 32 Samuel killeth Agag. 34 Samuel and Saul part.

Amuel also saide vnto Saul, *The LORD sent me to annoint thee to bee king ouer his people, ouer Israel : nowe therefore hearken thou vnto the voyce of the words of the LORD.

* Chap. 9. 16.

2 Thus saith the LORD of hosts, I remember that which Amalek did to Israel, *how he laid *wait* for him in the way when he came vp from Egypt.

* Exod. 17. 8. num. 24. 20.

3 Now goe, and smite Amalek, and vtterly destroy all that they haue, and spare them not; but slay both man and woman, infant and suckling, oxe and sheepe, camell and asse.

4 And Saul gathered the people together, and numbred them in Telaim, two hundred thousand footmen, and ten thousand men of Iudah.

5 And Saul came to a citie of Amalek, and ‖laid waite in the valley.

‖ *Or, fought*

6 ¶ And Saul saide vnto the Kenites, Goe, depart, get you downe from among the Amalekites, lest I destroy you with them : for yee shewed kindnesse to all the children of Israel when they came vp out of Egypt. So the Kenites departed from among the Amalekites.

7 And Saul smote the Amalekites from Hauilah, *vntill* thou commest to Shur, that *is* ouer against Egypt.

8 And hee tooke Agag the king of the Amalekites aliue, and vtterly destroyed all the people with the edge of the sword.

9 But Saul and the people spared Agag, and the best of the sheepe, and of the oxen, and of the ‖fatlings, and the lambes, and all that was good, and would not vtterly destroy them : but euery thing that was vile, and refuse, that they destroyed vtterly.

‖ *Or, of the second sort*

10 ¶ Then came the word of the LORD vnto Samuel, saying ;

11 It repenteth me that I haue set vp Saul to be king : for hee is turned backe from following me, and hath not performed my commandements. And it grieued Samuel ; and he cried vnto the LORD all night.

12 And when Samuel rose early to meet Saul in the morning, it was tolde Samuel, saying, Saul came to Carmel, and behold, he set him vp a place, and is gone

gone about, and passed on, and gone downe to Gilgal.

13 And Samuel came to Saul, and Saul said vnto him, Blessed be thou of the Lord: I haue performed the commandement of the Lord.

14 And Samuel said, What meaneth then this bleating of the sheepe in mine eares, and the lowing of the oxen which I heare?

15 And Saul sayde, They haue brought them from the Amalekites: for the people spared the best of the sheepe, and of the oxen, to sacrifice vnto the Lord thy God, and the rest we haue vtterly destroyed.

16 Then Samuel sayd vnto Saul, Stay, and I will tell thee what the Lord hath said to mee this night. And he said vnto him, Say on.

17 And Samuel said, When thou wast litle in thine owne sight, wast thou not made the Head of the tribes of Israel, and the Lord anointed thee King ouer Israel?

18 And the Lord sent thee on a iourney, and said, Goe, and vtterly destroy the sinners the Amalekites, and fight against them, vntill †they be consumed.

Heb. they onsume hem.

19 Wherefore then didst thou not obey the voice of the Lord, but didst flie vpon the spoile, and didst euill in the sight of the Lord?

20 And Saul said vnto Samuel; Yea, I haue obeyed the voice of the Lord, and haue gone the way which the Lord sent me, and haue brought Agag the king of Amalek, and haue vtterly destroyed the Amalekites.

21 But the people tooke of the spoile, sheepe and oxen, the chiefe of the things which should haue bene vtterly destroyed, to sacrifice vnto the Lord thy God in Gilgal.

22 And Samuel saide, Hath the Lord *as great* delight in burnt offerings and sacrifices, as in obeying the voice of the Lord? Behold, *to obey, is* better then sacrifice: *and* to hearken, then the fat of rammes.

Eccles. 17. ose. 6. matt. 9. 3. and 12.

23 For rebellion *is as* the sin of †witchcraft, and stubburnnesse *is as* iniquitie and idolatrie: because thou hast reiected the word of the Lord, he hath also reiected thee from *being* king.

Heb. diuination.

24 ¶ And Saul said vnto Samuel, I haue sinned: for I haue transgressed the Commandement of the Lord,

and thy wordes; because I feared the people, and obeyed their voice.

25 Now therefore, I pray thee, pardon my sinne, and turne againe with me, that I may worship the Lord.

26 And Samuel said vnto Saul, I will not returne with thee: for thou hast reiected the word of the Lord, and the Lord hath reiected thee from being king ouer Israel.

27 And as Samuel turned about to goe away, he laid hold vpon the skirt of his mantle, and it rent.

28 And Samuel said vnto him, The Lord hath rent the kingdome of Israel from thee this day, and hath giuen it to a neighbour of thine, *that is* better then thou.

29 And also the ‖strength of Israel will not lie, nor repent: for he is not a man that he should repent.

‖ *Or, eternitie: or, victory.*

30 Then he said, I haue sinned; *yet* honour me now, I pray thee, before the Elders of my people, and before Israel, and turne againe with me, that I may worship the Lord thy God.

31 So Samuel turned againe after Saul, and Saul worshipped the Lord.

32 ¶ Then said Samuel, Bring you hither to me Agag the king of the Amalekites: and Agag came vnto him delicately. And Agag said, Surely the bitternesse of death is past.

33 And Samuel said, *As thy sword hath made women childlesse, so shall thy mother bee childlesse among women. And Samuel hewed Agag in pieces before the Lord in Gilgal.

* *Exod. 17. 11. num. 14. 45.*

34 ¶ Then Samuel went to Ramah, and Saul went vp to his house to Gibeah of Saul.

35 And Samuel came no more to see Saul vntill the day of his death: neuerthelesse, Samuel mourned for Saul: and the Lord repented that he had made Saul king ouer Israel.

CHAP. XVI.

1 Samuel sent by God, vnder pretence of a sacrifice, commeth to Bethlehem. 6 His humane iudgement is reprooued. 11 He anointeth Dauid. 15 Saul sendeth for Dauid to quiet his euill spirit.

Nd the Lord said vnto Samuel, How long wilt thou mourne for Saul, seeing I haue reiected him from reigning ouer Israel?

Israel? Fill thine horne with oile, and goe, I will send thee to Iesse the Bethlehemite: for I haue prouided mee a King among his sonnes.

2 And Samuel said, How can I goe? if Saul heare *it*, he will kill mee. And the LORD said, Take an heifer †with thee, and say, I am come to sacrifice to the LORD.

† *Hebr. in thine hand.*

3 And call Iesse to the sacrifice, and I will shew thee what thou shalt doe: and thou shalt anoynt vnto mee *him* whom I name vnto thee.

4 And Samuel did that which the LORD spake, and came to Bethlehem: and the elders of the towne trembled at his †comming, and said, Commest thou peaceably?

† *Hebr. meeting.*

5 And hee said, Peaceably: I am come to sacrifice vnto the LORD: sanctifie your selues, and come with me to the sacrifice: and he sanctified Iesse, and his sonnes, and called them to the sacrifice.

6 ¶ And it came to passe when they were come, that he looked on Eliab, and said, Surely the LORDS anointed is before him.

7 But the LORD said vnto Samuel, Looke not on his countenance, or on the height of his stature, because I haue refused him: for *the LORD seeth* not, as man seeth; For man looketh on the †outward appearance, but the LORD looketh on the *heart.

† *Hebr. eyes.*
* 1. Chron.
28. 9. psal.
7. 9. ierem.
11. 20. and
17. 10. and
20. 12.

8 Then Iesse called Abinadab, and made him passe before Samuel: and he said, Neither hath the LORD chosen this.

9 Then Iesse made Shammah to passe by: and he said, Neither hath the LORD chosen this.

10 Againe Iesse made seuen of his sonnes to passe before Samuel; and Samuel said vnto Iesse, The LORD hath not chosen these.

11 And Samuel saide vnto Iesse, Are here all *thy* children? And he said, There remaineth yet the yongest, and behold, he keepeth the sheepe. And Samuel said vnto Iesse, *Send, and fetch him: for we will not sit †downe, till hee come hither.

* 2. Sam. 7.
8. psal. 78.
71.
† *Heb. round.*

12 And he sent, and brought him in: now he *was* ruddy, *and* withal †of a beautifull countenance, and goodly to looke to: And the LORD said, Arise, anoint him: for this *is* he.

† *Hebr. faire of eyes.*

13 Then Samuel tooke the horne of oile, and annointed him in the midst of his brethren: and the Spirit of the LORD came vpon Dauid, from that day forward: So Samuel rose vp and went to Ramah.

14 ¶ But the spirit of the LORD departed from Saul, and an euil spirit from the LORD ||troubled him.

|| *Or, terrified.*

15 And Sauls seruants said vnto him, Behold now, an euill spirit from God troubleth thee.

16 Let our lord now command thy seruants *which are* before thee, to seeke out a man, who *is* a cunning player on an harpe: and it shall come to passe when the euill spirit from God is vpon thee, that hee shall play with his hand, and thou shalt be well.

17 And Saul said vnto his seruants, Prouide mee now a man, that can play well, and bring him to me.

18 Then answered one of the seruants, and said, Behold, I haue seene a sonne of Iesse the Bethlehemite, that is cunning in playing, and a mighty valiant man, and a man of warre, and prudent in ||matters, and a comely person, and the LORD is with him.

|| *Or, speech*

19 ¶ Wherefore Saul sent messengers vnto Iesse, and said, Send me Dauid thy sonne, which *is* with the sheepe.

20 And Iesse tooke an asse *laden* with bread, and a bottle of wine, and a kid, and sent *them* by Dauid his sonne vnto Saul.

21 And Dauid came to Saul, and stood before him: and hee loued him greatly, and hee became his armour bearer.

22 And Saul sent to Iesse, saying, Let Dauid, I pray thee, stand before me: for hee hath found fauour in my sight.

23 And it came to passe, when the *euill* spirit from God was vpon Saul, that Dauid tooke an harpe, and played with his hand: So Saul was refreshed, and was well, and the euill spirit departed from him.

CHAP. XVII.

1 The armies of the Israelites, and Philistines beeing readie to battell, 4 Goliath commeth proudly forth, to chalenge a combate. 12 Dauid sent by his father to visit his brethren, taketh the chalenge. 28 Eliab chideth him. 30 He is brought to Saul. 32 He sheweth the reason of his confidence. 38 Without

Without armour, armed by faith, he ſlayeth the Giant. 55 Saul taketh notice of Dauid.

Ow the Philiſtines gathered together their armies to battell, and were gathered together at Shochoh, which *belongeth* to Iudah, and pitched betweene Shochoh and Azekah, in ‖Ephes-Dammim.

2 And Saul and the men of Israel were gathered together, and pitched by the valley of Elah, and †set the battell in aray against the Philiſtines.

3 And the Philiſtines ſtood on a mountaine on the one ſide, and Israel ſtood on a mountaine on the other ſide: and there *was* a valley betweene them.

4 ¶ And there went out a champion out of the campe of the Philiſtines, named Goliath of Gath : whoſe height *was* ſixe cubites and a ſpan.

5 And *he had* an helmet of braſſe vpon his head, and he was †armed with a coate of male : and the weight of the coat was fiue thouſand ſhekels of braſſe.

6 And *he had* greaues of braſſe vpon his legs, and a ‖target of braſſe betweene his ſhoulders.

7 And the ſtaffe of his ſpeare was like a weauers beame, and his ſpeares head *weighed* ſixe hundred ſhekels of yron; and one bearing a ſhield, went before him.

8 And hee ſtood and cried vnto the armies of Israel, and ſaid vnto them, Why are yee come out to ſet your battell in aray? am not I a Philiſtine, and you ſeruants to Saul? chuſe you a man for you, and let him come downe to me.

9 If he be able to fight with mee, and to kill me, then will we be your ſeruants : but if I preuaile againſt him, and kill him, then ſhall yee be our ſeruants, and ſerue vs.

10 And the Philiſtine ſaid, I defie the armies of Israel this day ; giue me a man, that we may fight together.

11 When Saul and all Israel heard thoſe words of the Philiſtine, they were diſmayed, and greatly afraid.

12 ¶ Now Dauid *was* *the ſonne of that Ephrathite of Bethlehem Iudah, whoſe name was Ieſſe, and hee had eight ſonnes : and the man went among men for an old man in the dayes of Saul.

13 And the three eldest ſonnes of Ieſſe went, *and* followed Saul to the battell : and the names of his three ſonnes that went to the battell, *were*, Eliab the first borne, and next vnto him, Abinadab, and the third, Shammah.

14 And Dauid was the yongeſt : and the three eldeſt followed Saul.

15 But Dauid went, and returned from Saul, to feed his fathers ſheepe at Bethlehem.

16 And the Philiſtine drewe neere, morning and euening, and preſented himſelfe forty dayes.

17 And Ieſſe ſaid vnto Dauid his ſonne, Take now for thy brethren an ephah of this parched corne, and theſe ten loaues, and run to the campe to thy brethren.

18 And carie theſe ten †cheeſes vnto the †Captaine of *their* thouſand, and looke how thy brethren fare, and take their pledge.

19 Now Saul, and they, and all the men of Israel *were* in the valley of Elah, fighting with the Philiſtines.

20 ¶ And Dauid roſe vp earely in the morning, and left the ſheepe with a keeper, and tooke, and went, as Ieſſe had commanded him ; and he came to the ‖trench, as the hoſt was going forth to ‖the fight, and ſhouted for the battell.

21 For Israel and the Philiſtines had put the battel in aray, army againſt armie.

22 And Dauid left † his cariage in the hand of the keeper of the cariage, and ranne into the armie, and came and †ſaluted his brethren.

23 And as he talked with them, behold, there came vp the champion (the Philiſtine of Gath, Goliath by name) out of the armies of the Philiſtines, and ſpake according to the ſame words: and Dauid heard *them*.

24 And all the men of Israel, when they ſaw the man, fled †from him, and were ſore afraid.

25 And the men of Israel ſaid, Haue yee ſeene this man that is come vp? Surely to defie Israel is he come vp : and it ſhall be that the man who killeth him, the king wil enrich him with great riches, and *will giue him his daughter, and make his fathers houſe free in Israel.

26 And Dauid ſpake to the men that ſtood by him, ſaying ; What ſhall bee done to the man that killeth this Philiſtine, and taketh away the reproch from Israel? for who is this vncircumciſed

Marginal notes:

Or, the coaſt of Dammim.

Heb. ranged the battell.

Heb. cloathed.

Or, gorget.

Chap, 16. 1.

† Heb. cheeſes of milke.

† Heb. captaine of a thouſand.

‖ Or, place of the cariage.
‖ Or, battell ray, or place of fight.

† Hebr. the veſſels from vpon him.

† Heb. asked his brethren of peace.

† Heb. from his face.

* Ioſh. 15. 16.

cumcised Philistine, that he should defie the armies of the liuing God?

27 And the people answered him after this maner, saying, So shall it be done to the man that killeth him.

28 ¶ And Eliab his eldest brother heard when he spake vnto the men, and Eliabs anger was kindled against Dauid, and he said, Why camest thou down hither? and with whom hast thou left those few sheepe in the wildernesse? I know thy pride, and the naughtinesse of thine heart ; for thou art come downe, that thou mightest see the battell.

29 And Dauid saide, What haue I now done? Is there not a cause?

30 ¶ And hee turned from him towards another, and spake after the same † maner : and the people answered him againe after the former maner. †Hebr. word.

31 And when the words were heard which Dauid spake, they rehearsed them before Saul : and he †sent for him. †Heb. tooke him.

32 ¶ And Dauid said to Saul, Let no mans heart faile, because of him : thy seruant will goe and fight with this Philistine.

33 And Saul said to Dauid, Thou art not able to goe against this Philistine, to fight with him : for *thou art but a* youth, and he a man of warre from his youth.

34 And Dauid said vnto Saul, Thy seruant kept his fathers sheepe, and there came a Lyon, and a Beare, and tooke a ‖lambe out of the flocke : ‖ Or, kid.

35 And I went out after him, and smote him, and deliuered *it* out of his mouth : and when he arose against me, I caught him by his beard, and smote him, and slew him.

36 Thy seruant slew both the Lyon and the Beare : and this vncircumcised Philistine shall be as one of them, seeing he hath defied the armies of the liuing God.

37 Dauid saide moreouer, The LORD that deliuered me out of the paw of the Lyon, and out of the pawe of the Beare, he will deliuer me out of the hand of this Philistine. And Saul said vnto Dauid, Goe, and the LORD be with thee.

38 ¶ And Saul †armed Dauid with his armour, and hee put an helmet of brasse vpon his head, also he armed him with a coat of male. †Heb. cloathed, &c. with his cloathes.

39 And Dauid girded his sword vpon his armour, and he assayed to goe,

for he had not proued *it* : and Dauid said vnto Saul, I cannot goe with these : for I haue not proued *them*. And Dauid put them off him.

40 And hee tooke his staffe in his hand, and chose him fiue smoothe stones out of the ‖brooke, and put them in a shepheards †bag which he had, euen in a scrip, and his sling was in his hande, and he drew neere to the Philistine. ‖ Or, valle †Heb. ves sell.

41 And the Philistine came on and drew neere vnto Dauid, and the man that bare the shield, *went* before him.

42 And when the Philistine looked about, and saw Dauid, hee disdained him : for he was *but* a youth, and ruddy, and of a faire countenance.

43 And the Philistine said vnto Dauid, Am I a dog, that thou commest to me with staues? and the Philistine cursed Dauid by his gods.

44 And the Philistine said to Dauid, Come to me, and I will giue thy flesh vnto the foules of the aire, and to the beasts of the field.

45 Then said Dauid to the Philistine, Thou commest to mee with a sword, and with a speare, and with a shield : but I come to thee in the Name of the LORD of hostes, the God of the armies of Israel, whom thou hast defied.

46 This day wil the LORD †deliuer thee into mine hand, and I will smite thee, and take thine head from thee, and I wil giue the carkeises of the host of the Philistines this day vnto the foules of the aire, and to the wild beasts of the earth, that all the earth may know that there is a God in Israel. †Hebr. shu thee vp.

47 And all this assembly shal know that the LORD saueth not with sword & speare (for the battell is the LORDS) and he will giue you into our hands.

48 And it came to passe when the Philistine arose, and came, and drewe nigh to meet Dauid, that Dauid hasted, and ran toward the armie to meete the Philistine.

49 And Dauid put his hande in his bag, and tooke thence a stone, and slang it, & smote the Philistine in his forehead, that the stone sunke into his forehead, and he fell vpon his face to the earth.

50 So * Dauid preuailed ouer the Philistine with a sling and with a stone, and smote the Philistine, and slew him, but there was no sword in the hande of Dauid. * Ecclus. 47. 4. 1. macc. 4. 30

51 There-

51 Therefore Dauid ran and stood vpon the Philistine, and tooke his sword, and drewe it out of the sheath thereof, and slew him, and cut off his head therewith. And when the Philistines sawe their champion was dead, they fled.

52 And the men of Israel, and of Iudah arose, and shouted, and pursued the Philistines, vntill thou come to the valley, and to the gates of Ekron: and the wounded of the Philistines fell downe by the way to Shaaraim, euen vnto Gath, and vnto Ekron.

53 And the children of Israel returned from chasing after the Philistines, and they spoiled their tents.

54 And Dauid tooke the head of the Philistine, and brought it to Ierusalem, but he put his armour in his tent.

55 ¶ And when Saul sawe Dauid goe forth against the Philistine, he sayd vnto Abner the captaine of the hoste, Abner, whose sonne is this youth? And Abner said, *As* thy soule liueth, O king, I cannot tell.

56 And the king said, Enquire thou whose sonne the stripling is.

57 And as Dauid returned from the slaughter of the Philistine, Abner tooke him, & brought him before Saul, with the head of the Philistine in his hand.

58 And Saul saide to him, Whose sonne art thou, *thou* yong man? And Dauid answered, I am the sonne of thy seruant Iesse, the Bethlehemite.

C H A P. XVIII.

1 Ionathan loueth Dauid. 5 Saul enuieth his praise, 10 Seeketh to kill him in his furie, 12 Feareth him for his good successe, 17 Offereth him his daughters for a snare. 22 Dauid perswaded to be the Kings sonne in law, giueth two hundred foreskinnes of the Philistines for Michals dowrie. 28 Sauls hatred, and Dauids glory increaseth.

Nd it came to passe when hee made an ende of speaking vnto Saul, that the soule of Ionathan was knit with the soule of Dauid, and Ionathan loued him as his owne soule.

2 And Saul tooke him that day, and would let him go no more home to his fathers house.

3 Then Ionathan and Dauid made a couenant, because he loued him as his owne soule.

4 And Ionathan stript himselfe of the robe that *was* vpon him, and gaue it to Dauid, and his garments, euen to his sword, and to his bow, and to his girdle.

5 ¶ And Dauid went out, whither soeuer Saul sent him, and ‖ behaued himselfe wisely: and Saul set him ouer the men of warre, and he was accepted in the sight of all the people, and also in the sight of Sauls seruants.

6 And it came to passe as they came when Dauid was returned from the slaughter of the ‖ Philistine, that the women came out of all cities of Israel, singing and dancing, to meete king Saul, with tabrets, with ioy, and with †instruments of musicke.

7 And the women answered one another as they played, and said, *Saul hath slaine his thousands, and Dauid his ten thousands.

8 And Saul was very wroth, and the saying † displeased him, and he sayd, They haue ascribed vnto Dauid tenne thousands, and to me they haue ascribed *but* thousands: and *what* can he haue more, but the kingdome?

9 And Saul eyed Dauid from that day, and forward.

10 ¶ And it came to passe on the morrow, that the euill spirit from God came vpon Saul, and he prophecied in the midst of the house: and Dauid played with his hand, as at other times: and *there was* a iauelin in Sauls hand.

11 And Saul cast the iauelin; for hee said, I will smite Dauid euen to the wall with it: and Dauid auoided out of his presence twice.

12 ¶ And Saul was afraid of Dauid, because the LORD was with him, and was departed from Saul.

13 Therefore Saul remooued him from him, and made him his captaine ouer a thousand, and hee went out and came in before the people.

14 And Dauid ‖ behaued himselfe wisely in all his wayes; & the LORD *was* with him.

15 Wherefore when Saul saw that hee behaued himselfe very wisely, hee was afraid of him.

16 But all Israel and Iudah loued Dauid, because hee went out and came in before them.

17 ¶ And Saul said to Dauid, Behold, my elder daughter Merab, her will I giue thee to wife: onely be thou †valiant

‖ *Or, prospered.*

‖ *Or, Philistines.*

† *Heb. three stringed instruments.*
* Chap. 21. 11: and 29. 5. ecclus. 47. 6.

† *Hebr. was euill in his eyes.*

‖ *Or, prospered.*

† *Hebr. a sonne of valour.*

†valiant for me, and fight the LORDS battels: for Saul said, Let not mine hand be vpon him, but let the hand of the Philistines be vpon him.

18 And Dauid said vnto Saul, Who am I? and what is my life, *or* my fathers family in Israel, that I should be sonne in law to the king?

19 But it came to passe at the time when Merab Sauls daughter should haue beene giuen to Dauid, that shee was giuen vnto Adriel the Meholathite to wife.

20 And Michal Sauls daughter loued Dauid: and they tolde Saul, and the thing †pleased him.

† *Hebr. was right in his eyes.*

21 And Saul said, I will giue him her, that she may be a snare to him, and that the hand of the Philistines may be against him. Wherefore Saul said to Dauid, Thou shalt this day be my sonne in law, in *the one of* the twaine.

22 ¶ And Saul commanded his seruants, *saying*, Commune with Dauid secretly, and say, Behold, the king hath delight in thee, and all his seruants loue thee: now therefore be the kings sonne in law.

23 And Sauls seruants spake those wordes in the eares of Dauid: And Dauid said, Seemeth it to you a light thing to be a kings sonne in law, seeing that I am a poore man, and lightly esteemed?

24 And the seruants of Saul tolde him, saying; †On this manner spake Dauid.

† *Hebr. according to these woras.*

25 And Saul said, Thus shall yee say to Dauid, The King desireth not *any* dowrie, but an hundred foreskinnes of the Philistines, to be auenged of the kings enemies. But Saul thought to make Dauid fal by the hand of the Philistines.

26 And when his seruants told Dauid these wordes, it pleased Dauid well to be the kings sonne in lawe: and the dayes were not †expired.

† *Hebr. fulfilled.*

27 Wherefore Dauid arose, hee and his men, and slew of the Philistines two hundred men, and Dauid brought their foreskinnes, and they gaue them in full tale to the king, that hee might be the kings sonne in law: and Saul gaue him Michal his daughter to wife.

28 ¶ And Saul saw and knew that the LORD was with Dauid, and that Michal Sauls daughter loued him.

29 And Saul was yet the more a-fraid of Dauid; and Saul became Dauids enemie continually.

30 Then the Princes of the Philistines went foorth: and it came to passe after they went foorth, *that* Dauid behaued himselfe more wisely then all the seruants of Saul, so that his name was †much set by.

† *Hebr. precious.*

CHAP. XIX.

1 Ionathan discloseth his fathers purpose to kill Dauid. 4 Hee perswadeth his father to reconciliation. 8 By reason of Dauids good successe in a new warre, Sauls malicious rage breaketh out against him. 12 Michal deceiueth her father with an image in Dauids bed. 18 Dauid commeth to Samuel in Naioth. 20 Sauls messengers sent to take Dauid, 22 and Saul himselfe, prophesie.

 Nd Saul spake to Ionathan his sonne, and to all his seruants, that they should kill Dauid.

2 But Ionathan Sauls sonne delighted much in Dauid, and Ionathan told Dauid, saying, Saul my father seeketh to kill thee: Now therefore, I pray thee, take heed to thy selfe vntill the morning, and abide in a secret place, and hide thy selfe:

3 And I will goe out and stand beside my father in the field where thou art, and I will commune with my father of thee, and what I see, that I will tell thee.

4 ¶ And Ionathan spake good of Dauid vnto Saul his father, and said vnto him, Let not the King sinne against his seruant, against Dauid: because hee hath not sinned against thee, and because his workes *haue bene* to thee ward very good.

5 For he did put his *life in his hand, and slew the Philistine, & the LORD wrought a great saluation for all Israel: thou sawest *it*, and didst reioyce: Wherefore then wilt thou sinne against innocent blood, to slay Dauid without a cause?

* Iudg. 9. 17. and 12. 3. chap. 28. 21. psalm. 119. 109.

6 And Saul hearkened vnto the voyce of Ionathan; and Saul sware, As the LORD liueth, he shall not be slaine.

7 And Ionathan called Dauid, and Ionathan shewed him all those things: and Ionathan brought Dauid to Saul, and he was in his presence, as †in times past.

† *Hebr. yesterday, third day.*

8 ¶ And

8 ¶ And there was warre againe, and Dauid went out, and fought with the Philistines, and slew them with a great slaughter, & they fled from †him.

*Heb. his face.

9 And the euill spirit from the LORD was vpon Saul, as he sate in his house with his iauelin in his hand: and Dauid played with *his* hand.

10 And Saul sought to smite Dauid euen to the wall, with the iauelin: but hee slipt away out of Sauls presence, and he smote the iauelin into the wall: and Dauid fled, and escaped that night.

11 Saul also sent messengers vnto Dauids house, to watch him, and to slay him in the morning: and Michal Dauids wife tolde him, saying, If thou saue not thy life to night, to morrow thou shalt be slaine.

12 ¶ So Michal let Dauid downe thorow a window: and hee went and fled, and escaped.

13 And Michal tooke an image, and laid *it* in the bedde, and put a pillow of goats haire for his bolster, and couered it with a cloth.

14 And when Saul sent messengers to take Dauid, she said, He is sicke.

15 And Saul sent the messengers *againe* to see Dauid, saying, Bring him vp to me in the bedde, that I may slay him.

16 And when the messengers were come in, behold, *there was* an image in the bed, with a pillow of goates haire for his bolster.

17 And Saul said vnto Michal, Why hast thou deceiued me so, and sent away mine enemie, that he is escaped? And Michal answered Saul, Hee said vnto me, Let mee goe; Why should I kill thee?

18 ¶ So Dauid fledde, and escaped, and came to Samuel to Ramah, and told him all that Saul had done to him: and hee and Samuel went, and dwelt in Naioth.

19 And it was told Saul, saying, Behold, Dauid *is* at Naioth in Ramah.

20 And Saul sent messengers to take Dauid: and when they sawe the company of the Prophets prophecying, and Samuel standing *as* appointed o-uer them, the Spirit of God was vpon the messengers of Saul, and they also prophecied.

21 And when it was tolde Saul, he sent other messengers, and they prophe-cied likewise: and Saul sent messen-gers againe the third time, and they prophecied also.

22 Then went hee also to Ramah, and came to a great well that *is* in Se-chu: and he asked, and said, Where are Samuel and Dauid? And one said, Be-hold, they be at Naioth in Ramah.

23 And hee went thither to Naioth in Ramah: and the Spirit of God was vpon him also, and he went on and pro-phecied vntill hee came to Naioth in Ramah:

24 And he stript off his clothes also, and prophecied before Samuel in like manner, and †lay downe naked all that day, and all that night: wherefore they say, *Is Saul also among the Pro-phets?

†Heb. fell.

*Chap. 10. 11.

CHAP. XX.

ANd Dauid fled from Nai-oth in Ramah, and came and said before Ionathan, What haue I done? what *is* mine iniquity? and what *is* my sinne before thy father, that he see-keth my life?

2 And he said vnto him, God forbid, thou shalt not die; beholde, my father will doe nothing, either great or small, but that he will †shew it me: and why should my father hide this thing from me? it *is* not so.

†Heb. vnco-uer mine eare.

3 And Dauid sware moreouer, and said, Thy father certeinly knoweth that I haue found grace in thine eyes, and he sayth, Let not Ionathan know this, lest he be grieued: but truely, *as* the LORD liueth, and *as* thy soule liueth, there *is* but a step betweene me & death.

4 Then said Ionathan vnto Da-uid, ‖ Whatsoeuer thy soule †desireth, I will euen doe *it* for thee.

‖ Or, Say, what is thy mind, and I will doe, &c. †Heb. spea-keth, or thin-keth.

5 And Dauid said vnto Ionathan, Behold, to morrow *is* the new moone, and I should not faile to sit with the king at meate: but let me goe, that I may hide my selfe in the fields vnto the third day at euen.

6 If thy father at all misse me, then say, Dauid earnestly asked *leaue* of me that he might runne to Bethlehem his citie:

‖ Or, feast.

citie: for *there is* a yeerely ‖ sacrifice there for all the family.

7 If he say thus, *It is* well, thy seruant shall haue peace: but if he be very wroth, then be sure that euill is determined by him.

8 Therefore thou shalt deale kindly with thy seruant, for *thou hast brought thy seruant into a couenant of the LORD with thee: notwithstanding, if there be in me iniquitie, slay me thy selfe: for why shouldest thou bring me to thy father?

* Chap. 18. 3. and 23. 18.

9 And Ionathan said, Farre be it from thee: for if I knew certainely that euill were determined by my father to come vpon thee, then would not I tell it thee?

10 Then said Dauid to Ionathan, Who shall tell me? or what *if* thy father answere thee roughly?

11 ¶ And Ionathan said vnto Dauid, Come, and let vs goe out into the field. And they went out both of them into the field.

12 And Ionathan said vnto Dauid, O LORD God of Israel, when I haue †sounded my father, about to morrow any time, *or* the third day, and behold, *if* there be good toward Dauid, and I then send not vnto thee, and †shew it thee;

† Heb. searched.

† Heb. vncouer thine eare.

13 The LORD doe so and much more to Ionathan: but if it please my father to doe thee euill, then I wil shew it thee, and send thee away, that thou mayest goe in peace, and the LORD be with thee, as hee hath beene with my father.

14 And thou shalt not onely while yet I liue, shew me the kindnesse of the LORD, that I die not:

15 But *also* thou shalt not cut off thy kindnesse from my house for euer: no not when the LORD hath cut off the enemies of Dauid, euery one from the face of the earth.

16 So Ionathan †made *a couenant* with the house of Dauid, *saying*, Let the LORD euen require *it* at the hande of Dauids enemies.

† Heb. cut.

17 And Ionathan caused Dauid to sweare againe, ‖ because he loued him: for he loued him as he loued his owne soule.

‖ Or, by his loue towards him.

18 Then Ionathan said to Dauid, To morrow *is* the newe moone: and thou shalt be missed, because thy seat wil be †emptie.

†Heb.missed.

19 And when thou hast stayed three dayes, then thou shalt goe downe ‖ quickly, and come to the place where thou diddest hide thy selfe, †when the businesse was in hand, and shalt remaine by the stone ‖ Ezel.

‖ Or, diligently. H greatly.
† Heb. in day of the businesse.

20 And I will shoot three arrowes on the side *thereof*, as though I shot at a marke.

21 And behold, I will send a ladde, *saying*, Goe, find out the arrowes. If I expresly say vnto the lad, Behold, the arrowes *are* on this side of thee, take them: then come thou, for there is peace to thee, and †no hurt, *as* the LORD liueth.

‖ Or, that sheweth th way.

† Heb. no any thing.

22 But if I say thus vnto the yong man, Behold, the arrowes *are* beyond thee: goe thy way, for the LORD hath sent thee away.

23 And as touching the matter which thou and I haue spoken of, behold, the LORD *be* betweene thee and mee for euer.

24 ¶ So Dauid hid himselfe in the field: and when the newe moone was come, the king sate him downe to eate meate.

25 And the king sate vpon his seate, as at other times, *euen* vpon a seate by the wall: and Ionathan arose, and Abner sate by Sauls side, and Dauids place was emptie.

26 Neuerthelesse, Saul spake not any thing that day: for hee thought, Some thing hath befallen him, hee is not cleane; surely he is not cleane.

27 And it came to passe on the morrow *which was* the second day of the moneth, that Dauids place was emptie: and Saul said vnto Ionathan his sonne, Wherefore commeth not the sonne of Iesse to meat, neither yesterday nor to day?

28 And Ionathan answered Saul, Dauid earnestly asked *leaue* of me, *to goe* to Bethlehem.

29 And he said, Let me goe, I pray thee, for our familie hath a sacrifice in the citie, and my brother, hee hath commanded mee *to be there*: and now if I haue found fauour in thine eyes, let me get away, I pray thee, and see my brethren: Therefore he commeth not vnto the kings table.

30 Then Sauls anger was kindled against Ionathan, and hee said vnto him, ‖ Thou sonne of the peruerse rebellious *woman*, doe not I know that thou hast

‖ Or, thou peruerse rebell. He sonne of pe uerse rebe lion.

hast chosen the sonne of Iesse to thine owne confusion, and vnto the confusion of thy mothers nakednesse?

31 For as long as the sonne of Iesse liueth vpon the ground, thou shalt not be stablished, nor thy kingdome: wherefore now send and fetch him vnto mee, for he †shall surely die.

† Heb. is the sonne of death.

32 And Ionathan answered Saul his father, and said vnto him, Wherefore shall hee be slaine? what hath hee done?

33 And Saul cast a iauelin at him to smite him, whereby Ionathan knewe that it was determined of his father to slay Dauid.

34 So Ionathan arose from the table in fierce anger, and did eate no meat the second day of the moneth: for hee was grieued for Dauid, because his father had done him shame.

35 ¶ And it came to passe in the morning, that Ionathan went out into the field, at the time appointed with Dauid, and a little ladde with him.

36 And he said vnto his lad, Runne, finde out now the arrowes which I shoote. And as the ladde ranne, he shot an arrow †beyond him.

† Hebr. to passe ouer him.

37 And when the ladde was come to the place of the arrow, which Ionathan had shot, Ionathan cryed after the ladde, and said, Is not the arrow beyond thee?

38 And Ionathan cryed after the ladde, Make speed, haste, stay not. And Ionathans ladde gathered vp the arrowes, and came to his master.

39 But the lad knew not any thing: onely Ionathan and Dauid knew the matter.

40 And Ionathan gaue his †artillery vnto †his ladde, and said vnto him, Goe, cary *them* to the citie.

† Heb. instruments.
† Hebr. that was his.

41 ¶ And assoone as the ladde was gone, Dauid arose out of *a place* toward the South, and fell on his face to the ground, and bowed himselfe three times: and they kissed one another, and wept one with another, vntill Dauid exceeded.

42 And Ionathan said to Dauid, Goe in peace, ‖forasmuch as wee haue sworne both of vs in the Name of the Lord, saying; The Lord be betweene me and thee, and betweene my seede and thy seede for euer. And hee arose, and departed: and Ionathan went into the citie.

‖ Or, The Lord be witnesse of that which, &c.

CHAP. XXI.

1 Dauid at Nob, obtaineth of Ahimelech hallowed bread. 7 Doeg was present. 8 Dauid taketh Goliaths sword. 10 Dauid at Gath faineth himselfe madde.

Hen came Dauid to Nob, to Ahimelech the Priest, and Ahimelech was afraide at the meeting of Dauid, and said vnto him, Why *art* thou alone, and no man with thee?

2 And Dauid said vnto Ahimelech the Priest, The king hath commanded me a businesse, and hath said vnto me, Let no man know any thing of the businesse whereabout I send thee, and what I haue commanded thee: and I haue appointed *my* seruants to such and such a place.

3 And therefore what is vnder thine hand? giue me fiue loaues of bread in mine hand, or what there is †present.

† Heb. found.

4 And the Priest answered Dauid, and said, There is no common bread vnder mine hand, but there is *hallowed bread: if the young men haue kept themselues at least from women.

** Exod. 25. 30. leuit. 24. 5. matt. 12. 4.*

5 And Dauid answered the Priest, and said vnto him, Of a trueth women haue beene kept from vs about these three dayes, since I came out, and the vessels of the young men are holy, ‖yea, though it were sanctified this day in the vessell.

‖ Or, especially whe this day there is other sanctified in the vessell.

6 So the Priest gaue him hallowed *bread;* for there was no bread there, but the Shewbread that was taken from before the Lord, to put hote bread in the day when it was taken away.

7 Now a certaine man of the seruants of Saul *was* there that day, detained before the Lord, and his name *was* Doeg an Edomite, the chiefest of the heardmen that *belonged* to Saul.

8 ¶ And Dauid said vnto Ahimelech, And is there not here vnder thine hand speare or sword? for I haue neither brought my sword nor my weapons with mee, because the kings businesse required haste.

9 And the Priest said, The sword of Goliath the Philistine, whome thou slewest in *the valley of Elah, behold, it is heere wrapt in a cloth behinde the Ephod: if thou wilt take that, take it; for there is no other saue that, here. And Dauid

** Chap. 17. 2.*

Dauid saide, There is none like that, giue it me.

10 ¶ And Dauid arose, and fled that day, for feare of Saul, and went to Achish, the king of Gath.

11 And the seruants of Achish sayd vnto him, Is not this Dauid the king of the land? Did they not sing one to another of him in daunces, saying, *Saul hath slaine his thousands, and Dauid his ten thousands?

* Chap. 18. 7. and 29. 5. ecclus. 47. 6.

12 And Dauid layd vp these wordes in his heart, and was sore afraid of Achish the king of Gath.

13 And he changed his behauiour before them, and fained himselfe mad in their hands, and ||scrabled on the doores of the gate, and let his spittle fall downe vpon his beard.

|| Or, made markes.

14 Then saide Achish vnto his seruants, Loe, you see the man ||is mad: wherefore then haue yee brought him to mee?

|| Or, playeth the mad-man.

15 Haue I need of mad-men, that ye haue brought this fellow to play the mad-man in my presence? Shall this fellow come into my house?

CHAP. XXII.

1 Companies resort vnto Dauid at Adullam. 3 At Mizpeh he commendeth his parents vnto the King of Moab. 5 Admonished by Gad, hee commeth to Hareth. 6 Saul going to pursue him, complaineth of his seruants vnfaithfulnesse. 9 Doeg accuseth Ahimelech. 11 Saul cōmandeth to kil the Priests. 17 The footmen refusing, Doeg executeth it. 20 Abiathar escaping, bringeth Dauid the newes.

Dauid therefore departed thence, and escaped to the caue Adullam: and when his brethren, and all his fathers house heard it, they went downe thither to him.

2 And euery one that was in distresse, and euery one that † was in debt, and euery one that was † discontented, gathered themselues vnto him, and he became a captaine ouer them: and there were with him about foure hundred men.

† Hebr. had a creditour.
† Hebr. bitter of soule.

3 ¶ And Dauid went thence to Mizpeh of Moab; and he said vnto the king of Moab, Let my father, and my mother, I pray thee, come foorth, and be with you, till I know what God will doe for me.

4 And he brought them before the king of Moab: and they dwelt with him all the while that Dauid was in the hold.

5 ¶ And the Prophet Gad said vnto Dauid, Abide not in the hold; depart, and get thee into the land of Iudah. Then Dauid departed, and came into the forrest of Hareth.

6 ¶ When Saul heard that Dauid was discouered, and the men that were with him; (now Saul abode in Gibeah vnder a ||tree in Ramah, hauing his speare in his hand, and all his seruants were standing about him.)

||Or, groue in a hie place.

7 Then Saul saide vnto his seruants that stood about him, Heare now, ye Beniamites: Will the sonne of Iesse giue euery one of you fields, and Vineyards, and make you all captaines of thousands, and captaines of hundreds:

8 That all of you haue conspired against me, and there is none that † sheweth mee, that my sonne hath made a league with the sonne of Iesse, and there is none of you that is sorry for me, or sheweth vnto me that my sonne hath stirred vp my seruant against me, to lye in wait, as at this day?

† Hebr. vncouereth mine eare.

9 ¶ Then answered Doeg the Edomite, (which was set ouer the seruants of Saul) and saide, I saw the sonne of Iesse comming to Nob, to Ahimelech the sonne of Ahitub.

10 And hee enquired of the LORD for him, and gaue him victuals, and gaue him the sword of Goliath the Philistine.

11 Then the king sent to call Ahimelech the Priest, the sonne of Ahitub, and all his fathers house, the Priests that were in Nob: and they came all of them to the king.

12 And Saul said, Heare now thou sonne of Ahitub: and hee answered, † Here I am, my lord.

† Hebr. behold me.

13 And Saul saide vnto him, Why haue ye conspired against me, thou and the sonne of Iesse, in that thou hast giuen him bread, and a sword, and hast enquired of God for him, that he should rise against mee, to lye in waite, as at this day?

14 Then Ahimelech answered the king, and said, And who is so faithfull among all thy seruants, as Dauid, which is the kings sonne in law, and goeth at thy bidding, and is honourable in thine house?

15 Did I then beginne to enquire of God

*ebr. litle
great.

God for him? be it farre from mee: let not the king impute any thing vnto his seruant, *nor* to all the house of my father : for thy seruant knew nothing of all this, †lesse or more.

16 And the king saide, Thou shalt surely die, Ahimelech, thou, and all thy fathers house.

*, guard.
b. the
ners.

17 ¶ And the king said vnto the ||footmen that stood about him, Turne and slay the Priests of the LORD, because their hand also *is* with Dauid, and because they knew when he fled, and did not shew it to mee. But the seruants of the king would not put foorth their hand to fall vpon the Priestes of the LORD.

18 And the king said to Doeg, Turne thou and fall vpon the Priests. And Doeg the Edomite turned, and hee fell vpon the Priests, and slew on that day foure score and fiue persons, that did weare a linnen Ephod.

19 And Nob the citie of the Priests smote he with the edge of the sword, both men and women, children and sucklings, and oxen and asses, and sheepe, with the edge of the sword.

20 ¶ And one of the sonnes of Ahimelech, the sonne of Ahitub, named Abiathar, escaped and fled after Dauid :

21 And Abiathar shewed Dauid that Saul had slaine the LORDS Priests.

22 And Dauid said vnto Abiathar, I knew *it* that day, when Doeg the Edomite was there, that he would surely tell Saul : I haue occasioned *the death* of all the persons of thy fathers house.

23 Abide thou with me, feare not : for he that seeketh my life, seeketh thy life : but with me thou shalt bee in safegard.

CHAP. XXIII.

1 *Dauid enquiring of the Lord by Abiathar, rescueth Keilah.* 7 *God shewing him the comming of Saul and the trecherie of the Keilites, he escapeth from Keilah.* 14 *In Ziph Ionathan commeth and comforteth him.* 19 *The Ziphites discouer him to Saul.* 25 *At Maon he is rescued from Saul by the inuasion of the Philistines.* 29 *He dwelleth at En-gedi.*

Hen they told Dauid, saying, Beholde, the Philistines fight against Keilah, and they rob the threshing floores.

2 Therefore Dauid enquired of the LORD, saying, Shall I go and smite these Philistines? And the LORD said vnto Dauid, Goe, and smite the Philistines, and saue Keilah.

3 And Dauids men said vnto him, Behold, we be afraid here in Iudah : how much more then if wee come to Keilah against the armies of the Philistines?

4 Then Dauid enquired of the LORD yet againe : And the LORD answered him, and said, Arise, go down to Keilah : for I will deliuer the Philistines into thine hand.

5 So Dauid and his men went to Keilah, and fought with the Philistins, and brought away their cattell, and smote them with a great slaughter : so Dauid saued the inhabitants of Keilah.

6 And it came to passe when Abiathar the sonne of Ahimelech * fled to Dauid to Keilah, *that* hee came downe *with* an Ephod in his hand.

* Chap. 22.
20.

7 ¶ And it was told Saul that Dauid was come to Keilah : and Saul said, God hath deliuered him into mine hand : for he is shut in, by entring into a towne that hath gates and barres.

8 And Saul called all the people together to warre, to goe downe to Keilah, to besiege Dauid, and his men.

9 ¶ And Dauid knewe that Saul secretly practised mischiefe against him, and hee said to Abiathar the Priest, Bring hither the Ephod.

10 Then saide Dauid, O LORD God of Israel, thy seruant hath certainly heard that Saul seeketh to come to Keilah, to destroy the citie for my sake.

11 Will the men of Keilah deliuer me vp into his hande? will Saul come downe, as thy seruant hath heard, O LORD God of Israel? I beseech thee tell thy seruant. And the LORD said, He will come downe.

12 Then said Dauid, Will the men of Keilah †deliuer me, and my men, into the hand of Saul? And the LORD said, They will deliuer thee vp.

† Hebr. shut
vp.

13 ¶ Then Dauid and his men, *which were* about sixe hundred, arose, and departed out of Keilah, and went whithersoeuer they could goe : and it was told Saul that Dauid was escaped from Keilah, and hee forbare to goe foorth.

14 And Dauid abode in the wildernesse

nesse in strong holds, and remained in a mountaine in the wildernes of Ziph : and Saul sought him euery day, but God deliuered him not into his hand.

15 And Dauid saw that Saul was come out to seeke his life : and Dauid *was* in the wildernes of Ziph in a wood.

16 ¶ And Ionathan Sauls sonne arose, & went to Dauid into the wood, and strengthened his hand in God.

17 And he said vnto him, Feare not; for the hand of Saul my father shall not finde thee, and thou shalt be king o-uer Israel, and I shall be next vnto thee . and that also Saul my father knoweth.

18 And they two made a couenant before the LORD : and Dauid abode in the wood, and Ionathan went to his house.

19 ¶ Then came vp the Ziphites to Saul to Gibeah, saying, Doth not Da-uid hide himselfe with vs in strong holds in the wood, in the hill of Hachi-lah, which *is* †on the South of ||Ieshi-mon?

† Hebr. on the right hand.
|| Or, the wil-dernesse?

20 Now therefore, O king, come downe according to all the desire of thy soule to come downe, and our part shall be to deliuer him into the kings hand.

21 And Saul said, Blessed *be* yee of the LORD, for yee haue compassion on me.

22 Goe, I pray you, prepare yet, and know, and see his place where his †haunt is, *and* who hath seene him there : for it is told mee that he dealeth very subtilly.

† Heb. foote shalbe.

23 See therefore, and take know-ledge of all the lurking places where he hideth himselfe, and come ye againe to me with the certainty, and I will goe with you : and it shall come to passe, if he be in the land, that I will search him out throughout all the thousands of Iudah.

24 And they arose, & went to Ziph before Saul : but Dauid and his men *were* in the wildernesse of Maon, in the plaine on the South of Ieshimon.

25 Saul also and his men went to seeke *him*, and they told Dauid : where-fore he came downe into a rocke, and a-bode in the wildernesse of Maon : and when Saul heard that, he pursued af-ter Dauid in the wildernes of Maon.

26 And Saul went on this side of the mountaine, and Dauid and his men on that side of the mountaine : and Da-uid made haste to get away for feare of Saul : for Saul and his men compassed Dauid and his men round about to take them.

27 ¶ But there came a messenger vnto Saul, saying, Haste thee, and come : for the Philistines haue †inuaded the land.

† Hebr. spread th selues v. &c.

28 Wherefore Saul returned from pursuing after Dauid, & went against the Philistines ; therefore they called that place ||Sela-Hammahlekoth.

|| That is the rock diuision.

29 ¶ And Dauid went vp from thence, and dwelt in strong holds at En-gedi.

CHAP. XXIIII.

1 Dauid in a caue at Engedi, hauing cut off Sauls skirt, spareth his life. 8 Hee sheweth thereby his innocencie. 16 Saul acknow-ledging his fault, taketh an oath of Dauid, and departeth.

Nd it came to passe when Saul was returned from †folowing the Philistines, that it was told him, say-ing, Behold, Dauid is in the wildernesse of En-gedi.

† Heb. o

2 Then Saul tooke three thousand chosen men out of all Israel, and went to seeke Dauid and his men vpon the rockes of the wilde goates.

3 And hee came to the sheepe coates by the way, where *was* a caue, and Saul went in to couer his feete : and Dauid and his men remained in the sides of the caue.

4 And the men of Dauid sayd vnto him, Beholde the day of which the LORD sayd vnto thee, Behold, I wil deliuer thine enemy into thine hand, that thou mayest doe to him as it shall seeme good vnto thee. Then Dauid a-rose, and cut off the skirt of † Sauls robe priuily.

† Hebr. robe, w' was Sau

5 And it came to passe afterward, that Dauids heart smote him, because he had cut off Sauls skirt.

6 And hee sayd vnto his men, The LORD forbid that I should doe this thing vnto my master the LORDs Anoynted, to stretch forth mine hand a-gainst him, seeing he *is* the Anoynted of the LORD.

7 So Dauid †stayed his seruants with these wordes, and suffered them not to rise against Saul : but Saul rose vp out of the caue, and went on *his* way.

† Hebr. off.

8 Dauid also rose afterward, and went

went out of the caue, and cryed after Saul, saying, My lord the king. And when Saul looked behinde him, Dauid stouped with his face to the earth, and bowed himselfe.

9 ¶ And Dauid said to Saul, Wherfore hearest thou mens words, saying, Behold, Dauid seeketh thy hurt?

10 Behold, this day thine eyes haue seene, how that the LORD had deliuered thee to day into mine hand in the caue: and some bade *me* kill thee, but *mine eye* spared thee, and I said, I will not put foorth mine hand against my lord, for hee *is* the LORDS Anointed.

11 Moreouer my father, See, yea see the skirt of thy robe in my hand for in that I cut off the skirt of thy robe, and killed thee not, know thou and see, that there is neither euill nor transgression in mine hand, and I haue not sinned against thee; yet thou huntest my soule, to take it.

12 The LORD iudge betweene me and thee, and the LORD auenge me of thee: but mine hand shall not be vpon thee.

13 As saith the prouerbe of the ancients, Wickednesse proceedeth from the wicked: but mine hand shall not be vpon thee.

14 After whom is the king of Israel come out? after whom doest thou pursue? After a dead dogge, after a flea.

15 **Heb. iudge** The LORD therfore be Iudge, and iudge betweene me and thee, and see, and plead my cause, and †deliuer me out of thine hand.

16 ¶ And it came to passe when Dauid had made an ende of speaking these words vnto Saul, that Saul said, Is this thy voice, my sonne Dauid? And Saul lift vp his voice, and wept.

17 And he said to Dauid, Thou art more righteous then I: for thou hast rewarded mee good, whereas I haue rewarded thee euill.

18 And thou hast shewed this day how that thou hast dealt well with me: forasmuch as when the LORD had †deliuered me into thine hand, thou killedst me not.

Heb. shut vp.

19 For if a man finde his enemie, will hee let him goe well away? wherefore the LORD reward thee good, for that thou hast done vnto me this day.

20 And now behold, I know well that thou shalt surely be King, and that

the kingdome of Israel shall be establi-shed in thine hand.

21 Sweare now therefore vnto me by the LORD, that thou wilt not cut off my seede after mee, and that thou wilt not destroy my name out of my fathers house.

22 And Dauid sware vnto Saul, and Saul went home: but Dauid and his men gate them vp vnto the holde.

CHAP. XXV.

1 Samuel dieth. 2 Dauid in Paran sendeth to Nabal. 10 Prouoked by Nabals churlish-nesse, hee mindeth to destroy him. 14 Abigail vnderstanding thereof, 18 taketh a pre-sent, 23 and by her wisedome 32 pacifi-eth Dauid. 36 Nabal hearing thereof, di-eth. 39 Dauid taketh Abigail and Ahinoam to be his wiues. 44 Michal is giuen to Phalti.

* Chap. 28. 3. ecclus. 46. 13, 20.

ANd *Samuel died, and all the Israelites were ga-thered together, and la-mented him, and buried him in his house at Ra-mah. And Dauid arose, & went downe to the wildernesse of Paran.

2 And there *was* a man in Maon, whose ‖ possessions *were* in Carmel, and the man *was* very great, and hee had three thousand sheepe, and a thousand goates: and he was shearing his sheepe in Carmel.   ‖*Or, busines.*

3 Now the name of the man *was* Nabal, and the name of his wife, Abi-gail: and shee *was* a woman of good vn-derstanding, and of a beautifull counte-nance: but the man *was* churlish and euill in his doings, and hee *was* of the house of Caleb.

4 ¶ And Dauid heard in the wilder-nesse, that Nabal did sheare his sheepe.

5 And Dauid sent out ten yong men, and Dauid said vnto the young men, Get you vp to Carmel, and goe to Na-bal, and †greete him in my name;

† *Heb. aske him in my name, of peace.*

6 And thus shall ye say to him that liueth *in prosperitie*, Peace *be* both to thee, and peace *be* to thine house, and peace *be* vnto all that thou hast.

7 And now, I haue heard that thou hast shearers: now thy shepheards which were with vs, wee †hurt them not, neither was there ought missing vnto them, all the while they were in Carmel.   † *Heb. sha-med.*

8 Aske thy yong men, and they will shew thee: wherefore let the yong men finde

† Heb. re-sted.

finde fauour in thine eyes: (for we come in a good day) giue, I pray thee, whatsoeuer commeth to thine hand, vnto thy seruants, and to thy sonne Dauid.

9 And when Dauids yong men came, they spake to Nabal according to all those words in the name of Dauid, and † ceased.

10 ¶ And Nabal answered Dauids seruants, and said, Who is Dauid? and who is the sonne of Iesse? There bee many seruants now a daies that breake away euery man from his master.

† Hebr. slaughter.

11 Shall I then take my bread and my water, and my † flesh that I haue killed for my shearers, and giue it vnto men, whom I know not whence they bee?

12 So Dauids yong men turned their way, and went againe, and came and told him all those sayings.

13 And Dauid said vnto his men, Gird you on euery man his sword. And they girded on euery man his sword, and Dauid also girded on his sword: and there went vp after Dauid about foure hundred men, and two hundred abode by the stuffe.

14 ¶ But one of the yong men told Abigail Nabals wife, saying, Behold, Dauid sent messengers out of the wildernesse to salute our master: and † he railed on them.

† Hebr. flew vpon them.
† Heb. sha-med.

15 But the men were very good vnto vs, and we were not † hurt, neither missed we any thing as long as wee were conuersant with them, when we were in the fields.

16 They were a wall vnto vs both by night and day, all the while we were with them keeping sheepe.

17 Now therefore know and consider what thou wilt doe: for euill is determined against our master, and against all his houshold: for he is such a sonne of Belial, that a man cannot speake to him.

18 ¶ Then Abigail made haste, and tooke two hundred loaues, and two bottles of wine, and fiue sheepe readie dressed, and fiue measures of parched corne, and an hundred ||clusters of raisins, and two hundred cakes of figges, and laid them on asses.

|| Or, lumps.

19 And she said vnto her seruants, Goe on before me, behold, I come after you: but she told not her husband Nabal.

20 And it was so as she rode on the asse, that she came downe by the couert of the hill, and behold, Dauid and his men came downe against her, and she met them.

21 (Now Dauid had said, Surely in vaine haue I kept all that this fellow hath in the wildernesse, so that nothing was missed of all that pertained vnto him: and he hath requited me euil for good.

22 So and more also doe God vnto the enemies of Dauid, if I leaue of all that pertaine to him by the morning light, any that pisseth against the wall.)

23 And when Abigail saw Dauid, she hasted, and lighted off the asse, and fell before Dauid on her face, and bowed her selfe to the ground,

24 And fell at his feet, and said, Vpon me, my lord, vpon me let this iniquitie be, and let thine handmaid, I pray thee, speake in thine † audience, and heare the words of thine handmaid.

† Heb. eare.

25 Let not my lord, I pray thee, † regard this man of Belial, euen Nabal: for as his name is, so is he: Nabal is his name, and folly is with him: But I thine handmaid saw not the yong men of my lord, whom thou didst send.

† Heb. lay to his heart.

26 Now therefore, my lord, as the LORD liueth, and as thy soule liueth, seeing the LORD hath withholden thee from comming to shed blood, and from † auenging thy selfe with thine owne hand: now let thine enemies and they that seeke euill to my lord, bee as Nabal.

† Hebr. sauing thy selfe.

27 And now this ||blessing which thine handmaid hath brought vnto my lord, let it euen be giuen vnto the yong men that †follow my lord.

|| Or, prese
† Heb. wal at the feet &c.

28 I pray thee, forgiue the trespasse of thine handmaide: for the LORD will certainely make my lord a sure house, because my lord fighteth the battels of the LORD, and euill hath not bene found in thee all thy dayes.

29 Yet a man is risen to pursue thee, and to seeke thy soule: but the soule of my lord shall be bound in the bundle of life with the LORD thy God, and the soules of thine enemies, them shall he sling out, † as out of the middle of a sling.

† Heb. in th midst of th bought of a sling.

30 And it shall come to passe when the LORD shal haue done to my lord, according to all the good that hee hath spoken concerning thee, and shall haue appointed thee ruler ouer Israel;

31 That

Hebr. no ggering: stumng.

31 That this shall bee no †griefe vnto thee, nor offence of heart vnto my lord, either that thou hast shed blood causelesse, or that my lord hath auenged himselfe: But when the Lord shall haue dealt well with my lord, then remember thine handmayd.

32 ¶ And Dauid sayd to Abigail, Blessed *be* the Lord God of Israel, which sent thee this day to meet me.

33 And blessed bee thy aduice, and blessed be thou, which hast kept me this day from comming to shed blood, and from auenging my selfe with mine owne hand.

34 For in very deed, as the Lord God of Israel liueth, which hath kept mee backe from hurting thee, except thou hadst hasted and come to meet me, surely there had not bene left vnto Nabal, by the morning light, any that pisseth against the wall.

35 So Dauid receiued of her hand that which shee had brought him, and sayd vnto her, Goe vp in peace to thine house; See, I haue hearkened to thy voyce, and haue accepted thy person.

36 ¶ And Abigail came to Nabal, and behold, he held a feast in his house like the feast of a king; & Nabals heart *was* merry within him, for hee *was* very drunken: wherefore shee tolde him nothing, lesse or more, vntill the morning light.

37 But it came to passe in the morning, when the wine was gone out of Nabal, and his wife had told him these things, that his heart died within him, and he became *as* a stone.

38 And it came to passe about ten dayes *after*, that the Lord smote Nabal, that he died.

39 ¶ And when Dauid heard that Nabal was dead, he said, Blessed *be* the Lord, that hath pleaded the cause of my reproch from the hand of Nabal, and hath kept his seruant from euil: for the Lord hath returned the wickednesse of Nabal vpon his owne head. And Dauid sent, and communed with Abigail, to take her to wife.

40 And when the seruants of Dauid were come to Abigail to Carmel, they spake vnto her, saying, Dauid sent vs vnto thee, to take thee to him to wife.

41 And shee arose, and bowed her selfe on her face to the earth, and sayd, Beholde, *let* thine handmayd *bee* a seruant to wash the feet of the seruants of my lord.

42 And Abigail hasted, and rose, and rode vpon an asse, with fiue damosels of hers that went †after her; and she went after the messengers of Dauid, and became his wife.

43 Dauid also tooke Ahinoam *of Iezreel, and they were also both of them his wiues.

44 ¶ But Saul had giuen *Michal his daughter, Dauids wife, to Phalti the sonne of Laish, which *was* of Gallim.

† *Hebr. at her feet.*

* Iosh. 15 56.

* 2. Sam. 3. 14, 15.

CHAP. XXVI.

1 Saul by the discouery of the Ziphites, commeth to Hachilah against Dauid. 4 Dauid comming into the trench, stayeth Abishai from killing Saul, but taketh his speare and cruse. 13 Dauid reprooueth Abner. 18 and exhorteth Saul. 21 Saul acknowledgeth his sinne.

And the Ziphites came vnto Saul to Gibeah, saying, *Doeth not Dauid hide himselfe in the hill of Hachilah, *which is* before Ieshimon?

2 Then Saul arose, and went downe to the wildernesse of Ziph, hauing three thousand chosen men of Israel with him, to seeke Dauid in the wildernesse of Ziph.

3 And Saul pitched in the hill of Hachilah, which *is* before Ieshimon by the way: but Dauid abode in the wildernesse, and he saw that Saul came after him into the wildernesse.

4 Dauid therefore sent out spies, and vnderstood that Saul was come in very deed.

5 ¶ And Dauid arose, and came to the place where Saul had pitched: and Dauid beheld the place where Saul lay, and *Abner the sonne of Ner the captaine of his hoste: and Saul lay in the ||trench, and the people pitched round about him.

6 Then answered Dauid, and sayd to Ahimelech the Hittite, and to Abishai the sonne of Zeruiah brother to Ioab, saying, Who will goe downe with me to Saul to the campe? And Abishai sayd, I will goe downe with thee.

7 So Dauid and Abishai came to the people by night, and behold, Saul lay sleeping within the trench, and his speare stucke in the ground at his bolster:

* Chap. 23. 19.

* Chap. 14. 50. and 17. 55. 1 *Or, midst of his carriages.*

ster : but Abner and the people lay round about him.

8 Then said Abishai to Dauid, God hath † deliuered thine enemie into thine hand this day : now therefore let mee smite him, I pray thee, with *the* speare, euen to the earth at once, and I will not *smite* him the second time.

9 And Dauid sayd to Abishai, Destroy him not : for who can stretch forth his hand against the Lords Anointed, and be guiltlesse ?

10 Dauid said furthermore, As the Lord liueth, the Lord shal smite him, or his day shall come to die, or hee shall descend into battell, and perish.

11 The Lord forbid that I should stretch foorth mine hand against the Lords Anointed : but I pray thee, take thou now the speare that is at his bolster, and the cruse of water, and let vs goe.

12 So Dauid tooke the speare and the cruse of water from Sauls bolster, and they gate them away, and no man saw it , nor knew it , neither awaked : for they were all asleepe, because a deepe sleepe *from* the Lord was fallen vpon them.

13 ¶ Then Dauid went ouer to the other side, and stood on the toppe of an hill afarre off (a great space being betweene them :)

14 And Dauid cryed to the people, and to Abner the sonne of Ner, saying, Answerest thou not, Abner ? Then Abner answered, and sayd, Who *art* thou *that* cryest to the King ?

15 And Dauid said to Abner, *Art* not thou a valiant man ? and who *is* like to thee in Israel ? Wherefore then hast thou not kept thy lord the king ? for there came one of the people in, to destroy the king thy lord.

16 This thing *is* not good that thou hast done : as the Lord liueth, ye are † worthy to die, because yee haue not kept your master the Lords Anointed : and now see where the Kings speare is , and the cruse of water that was at his bolster.

17 And Saul knew Dauids voyce, and said, Is this thy voice, my sonne Dauid ? And Dauid saide, It is my voice, my lord, O king.

18 And he said, Wherefore doeth my lord thus pursue after his seruant ? for what haue I done ? or what euill is in mine hand ?

19 Now therefore , I pray thee, let my lord the king heare the words of his seruant : If the Lord haue stirred thee vp against mee, let him † accept an offering : but if they *be* the children of men, cursed *be* they before the Lord: for they haue driuen me out this day from † abiding in the inheritance of the Lord, saying, Goe serue other gods.

20 Now therefore, let not my blood fall to the earth before the face of the Lord : for the king of Israel is come out to seeke a flea, as when one doeth hunt a partridge in the mountaines

21 ¶ Then said Saul, I haue sinned : Returne, my sonne Dauid, for I will no more doe thee harme; because my soule was precious in thine eyes this day : behold, I haue played the foole, and haue erred exceedingly.

22 And Dauid answered, and sayd, Behold the kings speare, and let one of the yong men come ouer and fetch it.

23 The Lord render to euery man his righteousnesse , and his faithfulnesse : for the Lord deliuered thee into my hand to day, but I would not stretch foorth mine hand against the Lords Anointed

24 And behold, as thy life was much set by this day in mine eyes: so let my life bee much set by in the eyes of the Lord, and let him deliuer me out of all tribulation

25 Then Saul said to Dauid, Blessed be thou, my sonne Dauid: thou shalt both doe great *things*, and also shalt still preuaile. So Dauid went on his way, and Saul returned to his place.

CHAP XXVII.

1 Saul hearing Dauid to be in Gath, seeketh no more for him: 5 Dauid beggeth Ziklag of Achish. 8 Hee inuading other countreys, perswadeth Achish he fought against Iudah.

AND Dauid sayd in his heart, I shall now † perish one day by the hand of Saul : there is nothing better for me, then that I should speedily escape into the land of the Philistines; and Saul shal despaire of me, to seeke me any more in any coast of Israel : so shall I escape out of his hand.

2 And Dauid arose, and hee passed ouer with the six hundred men that

were

---

† *Heb. shut vp.*

† *Heb. the sonnes of death.*

† *Heb. sm*

† *Heb. cle uing.*

† *Hebr. consume*

were with him, vnto Achish the sonne of Maoch king of Gath.

3 And Dauid dwelt with Achish at Gath, he, and his men, euery man with his houshold, *euen* Dauid with his two wiues, Ahinoam the Iezreelitesse, and Abigail the Carmelitesse Nabals wife.

4 And it was told Saul, that Dauid was fled to Gath, and he sought no more againe for him.

5 ¶ And Dauid said vnto Achish, If I haue now found grace in thine eyes, let them giue mee a place in some towne in the countrey, that I may dwel there : for why should thy seruant dwell in the royall citie with thee ?

6 Then Achish gaue him Ziklag that day : wherfore Ziklag pertaineth vnto the kings of Iudah vnto this day.

7 And †the time that Dauid dwelt in the countrey of the Philistines, was †a full yeere, and foure moneths.

8 ¶ And Dauid and his men went vp and inuaded the Geshurites, and the ‖ Gezrites, and the Amalekites : for those *nations* were of old the inhabitants of the land, as thou goest to Shur, e-uen vnto the land of Egypt.

9 And Dauid smote the land, and left neither man nor woman aliue, and tooke away the sheepe, and the oxen, and the asses, and the camels, and the apparell, and returned, and came to A-chish.

10 And Achish said, ‖ Whither haue ye made a rode to day? And Dauid said, Against the South of Iudah, and a-gainst the South of the Ierahmee-lites, and against the South of the Ke-nites.

11 And Dauid saued neither man nor woman aliue, to bring *tidings* to Gath, saying, Lest they should tell on vs, saying, So did Dauid, and so will be his maner, all the while he dwelleth in the countrey of the Philistines.

12 And Achish beleeued Dauid, say-ing, Hee hath made his people Israel †vtterly to abhorre him, therefore hee shall be my seruant for euer.

CHAP. XXVIII.

1 Achish putteth confidence in Dauid. 3 Saul hauing destroyed the witches, 4 and now in his feare forsaken of God, 7 seeketh to a witch. 9 The witch, encouraged by Saul, raiseth vp Samuel. 15 Saul hearing his ruine, fainteth. 21 The woman with his seruants refresh him with meate.

 ND it came to passe in those dayes, that the Phi-listines gathered their ar-mies together for war-fare, to fight with Israel : And Achish said vnto Dauid, Knowe thou assuredly, that thou shalt goe out with me to battell, thou, and thy men.

2 And Dauid said to Achish, Surely thou shalt know what thy seruant can doe. And Achish said to Dauid, Ther-fore will I make thee keeper of mine head for euer.

3 ¶ Now *Samuel was dead, and all Israel had lamented him, and buri-ed him in Ramah, euen in his owne ci-tie : and Saul had put away those that had familiar spirits, and the wyzards, out of the land.

4 And the Philistines gathered themselues together, and came and pit-ched in Shunem : and Saul gathered all Israel together, and they pitched in Gilboa.

5 And when Saul saw the hoste of the Philistines, he was afraid, and his heart greatly trembled.

6 And when Saul enquired of the LORD, the LORD answered him not, neither by dreames, nor by Vrim, nor by Prophets.

7 ¶ Then said Saul vnto his ser-uants, Seeke me a woman that hath a familiar spirit, that I may goe to her, and enquire of her. And his seruant said to him, Beholde, *there is* a woman that hath a familiar spirit at Endor.

8 And Saul disguised himselfe, and put on other raiment, and hee went, and two men with him, and they came to the woman by night, and he said, I pray thee diuine vnto me by the famili-ar spirit, and bring me *him* vp whom I shall name vnto thee.

9 And the woman saide vnto him, Beholde, thou knowest what Saul hath done, how hee hath cut off those that haue familiar spirits, and the wy-zards out of the land : wherefore then layest thou a snare for my life, to cause me to die ?

10 And Saul sware to her by the LORD, saying, As the LORD liueth, there shall no punishment happen to thee for this thing.

11 Then said the woman, Whome shall I bring vp vnto thee? and he said, Bring me vp Samuel.

12 And when the woman saw Sa-muel,

Heb. the number of dayes.
Hebr. a eere of dayes.

*Or, Ger-*ites.

Or, did you ot make a ode, &c

Hebr. to tinke.

* Chap. 25. 1.

muel, she cried with a lowd voyce; and the woman spake to Saul, saying, Why hast thou deceiued me? for thou *art* Saul.

13 And the king sayd vnto her, Be not afraid: for what sawest thou? And the woman said vnto Saul, I saw gods ascending out of the earth.

† *Hebr. what is his forme?*

14 And he said vnto her, † What forme is he of? And she said, An old man commeth vp, and he is couered with a mantle. And Saul perceiued that it was Samuel, and hee stouped with his face to the ground, and bowed himselfe.

15 ¶ And Samuel said to Saul, Why hast thou disquieted me, to bring me vp? And Saul answered, I am sore distressed; for the Philistins make war against me, and God is departed from me, and answereth me no more, neither † by Prophets, nor by dreames: therefore I haue called thee, that thou mayst make knowen vnto me, what I shall doe.

† *Hebr. by the hand of Prophets.*

16 Then said Samuel, Wherefore then doest thou aske of mee, seeing the LORD is departed from thee, and is become thine enemy?

‖ *Or, for himselfe.*
* *Chap. 15. 28.*
† *Hebr. mine hand.*

17 And the LORD hath done ‖ to him, * as hee spake by † mee: for the LORD hath rent the kingdome out of thine hand, and giuen it to thy neighbour, *euen* to Dauid:

18 Because thou obeiedst not the voice of the LORD, nor executedst his fierce wrath vpon Amalek, therefore hath the LORD done this thing vnto thee this day.

19 Moreouer, the LORD will also deliuer Israel with thee, into the hand of the Philistines: and to morrow *shalt* thou and thy sonnes *bee* with mee: the LORD also shall deliuer the hoste of Israel into the hand of the Philistines.

† *Hebr. made haste and fell with the fulnesse of his stature.*

20 Then Saul † fell straightway all along on the earth, and was sore afraid, because of the words of Samuel, & there was no strength in him: for he had eaten no bread all the day, nor al the night.

21 ¶ And the woman came vnto Saul, and saw that he was sore troubled, and sayd vnto him, Behold, thine handmayd hath obeyed thy voice, and I haue put my life in my hand, and haue hearkened vnto thy words which thou spakest vnto me.

22 Now therefore, I pray thee, hearken thou also vnto the voyce of thine handmaid, & let me set a morsel of bread before thee; & eat, that thou mayest haue strength, when thou goest on thy way.

23 But hee refused, and said, I will not eate. But his seruants together with the woman compelled him, and he hearkened vnto their voyce: so he arose from the earth, & sate vpon the bed.

24 And the woman had a fat calfe in the house, and she hasted, and killed it, and tooke flower and kneaded *it*, and did bake vnleauened bread thereof.

25 And she brought *it* before Saul, and before his seruants, and they did eate: then they arose vp, and went away that night.

CHAP. XXIX.

1 Dauid marching with the Philistines, 3 is disalowed by their Princes. 6 Achish dismisseth him with commendations of his fidelity.

NOw the Philistines gathered together all their armies to Aphek: and the Israelites pitched by a fountaine which *is* in Iezreel.

2 And the lords of the Philistines passed on by hundreds, and by thousands: but Dauid and his men passed on in the rere-ward with Achish.

3 Then said the princes of the Philistines, What *doe* these Hebrewes *here?* And Achish said vnto the princes of the Philistines, *Is* not this Dauid the seruant of Saul the king of Israel, which hath bene with me these dayes, or these yeeres, and I haue found no fault in him since he fell *vnto me*, vnto this day?

4 And the princes of the Philistines were wroth with him, and the princes of the Philistines said vnto him, * Make this fellow returne, that he may goe againe to his place which thou hast appointed him, and let him not go downe with vs to battel, lest in the battell he be an aduersary to vs: for wherewith should hee reconcile himselfe vnto his master? should it not be with the heads of these men?

* *1. Chro 12. 19.*

5 *Is* not this Dauid, of whom they sang one to another in daunces, saying, * Saul slew his thousands, and Dauid his ten thousands?

* *Chap. 7. and 21 11.*

6 ¶ Then Achish called Dauid, and said vnto him, Surely, as the LORD liueth, thou hast bene vpright, and thy going out and thy comming in with me in the hoste is good in my sight: for I haue not found euil in thee, since the day of thy comming vnto me vnto this day: neuertheles, the † lords fauour thee not.

† *Hebr. t art not g in the eye the lords.*

7 Wherefore now returne and goe in

Hebr. doe
not euill in
the eyes of
the lords.

Hebr. be-
fore thee.

†Heb. bitter.

in peace, that thou †displease not the lords of the Philistines.

8 ¶ And Dauid said vnto Achish, But what haue I done? and what hast thou found in thy seruant so long as I haue bene †with thee vnto this day, that I may not goe fight against the enemies of my lord the king?

9 And Achish answered, and said to Dauid, I know that thou *art* good in my sight, as an Angel of God: notwithstanding the Princes of the Philistines haue said, Hee shall not goe vp with vs to the battell.

10 Wherfore now rise vp early in the morning, with thy masters seruants that are come with thee: and assoone as yee be vp early in the morning, and haue light, depart.

11 So Dauid and his men rose vp early to depart in the morning, to returne into the land of the Philistines; and the Philistines went vp to Iezreel.

CHAP. XXX.

1 The Amalekites spoile Ziklag. 4 Dauid asking counsell, is encouraged by God to pursue them. 11 By the meanes of a reuiued Egyptian, he is brought to the enemies, and recouereth all the spoile. 22 Dauids law to diuide the spoile equally betweene them that fight, and them that keepe the stuffe. 26 He sendeth presents to his friends.

Nd it came to passe when Dauid and his men were come to Ziklag on the third day, that the Amalekites had inuaded the South and Ziklag, and smitten Ziklag, and burnt it with fire:

2 And had taken the women captiues, that *were* therein; they slewe not any either great or smal, but caried *them* away, and went on their way.

3 ¶ So Dauid and his men came to the citie, and beholde, it was burnt with fire, and their wiues, and their sonnes, and their daughters were taken captiues.

4 Then Dauid and the people that were with him, lift vp their voice, and wept, vntill they had no more power to weepe.

5 And Dauids two wiues were taken captiues, Ahinoam the Iezreelitesse, and Abigail the wife of Nabal the Carmelite.

6 And Dauid was greatly distres-

sed: for the people spake of stoning him, because the soule of all the people was †grieued, euery man for his sonnes, and for his daughters: but Dauid encouraged himselfe in the LORD his God.

7 And Dauid said to Abiathar the Priest Ahimelechs sonne, I pray thee, bring mee hither the Ephod: and Abiathar brought thither the Ephod to Dauid.

8 And Dauid enquired at the LORD, saying; Shall I pursue after this troupe? shall I ouertake them? And he answered him, Pursue, for thou shalt surely ouertake *them*, and without faile recouer *all*.

9 So Dauid went, hee, and the sixe hundred men that *were* with him, and came to the brooke Besor, where those that were left behinde, stayed.

10 But Dauid pursued, he and foure hundred men: (for two hundred abode behinde, which were so faint that they could not goe ouer the brooke Besor.)

11 ¶ And they found an Egyptian in the field, and brought him to Dauid, and gaue him bread, and he did eate, and they made him drinke water.

12 And they gaue him a piece of a cake of figges, and two clusters *of raisins:* and when hee had eaten, his spirit came againe to him: for hee had eaten no bread, nor drunke any water, three dayes and three nights.

13 And Dauid sayde vnto him, To whome *belongest* thou? and whence *art* thou? And he said, I am a yong man of Egypt, seruant to an Amalekite, and my master left me, because three dayes agone I fell sicke.

14 Wee made an inuasion *vpon* the South of the Cherethites, and vpon the *coast* which *belongeth* to Iudah, and vpon the South of Caleb, and wee burnt Ziklag with fire.

15 And Dauid sayde to him, Canst thou bring me downe to this company? And he said, Sweare vnto me by God, that thou wilt neither kill me, nor deliuer mee into the handes of my master, and I will bring thee downe to this company.

16 ¶ And when he had brought him downe, behold, they *were* spread abroad vpon all the earth, eating and drinking, and dauncing, because of all the great spoile that they had taken out of the land of the Philistines, and out of the land of Iudah.

17 And

† Heb. their morrow.

17 And Dauid smote them from the twilight, euen vnto the euening of † the next day: and there escaped not a man of them, saue foure hundred yong men which rode vpon camels, and fled.

18 And Dauid recouered all that the Amalekites had caried away: and Dauid rescued his two wiues.

19 And there was nothing lacking to them, neither small nor great, neither sonnes nor daughters, neither spoile, nor any thing that they had taken to them: Dauid recouered all.

20 And Dauid tooke all the flockes, and the herds, which they draue before those other cattell, and said, This is Dauids spoile.

21 ¶ And Dauid came to the two hundred men which were so faint that they could not follow Dauid, whome they had made also to abide at the brook Besor: and they went forth to meet Dauid, and to meete the people, that were with him; and when Dauid came neere to the people, he ‖saluted them.

‖ Or, asked them howe they did.
† Heb. men.

22 Then answered all the wicked men, and men of Belial, of †those that went with Dauid, and said, Because they went not with vs, we wil not giue them ought of the spoile, that wee haue recouered, saue to euery man his wife and his children, that they may leade them away, and depart.

23 Then said Dauid, Ye shall not do so, my brethren, with that which the LORD hath giuen vs, who hath preserued vs, and deliuered the companie that came against vs, into our hand.

24 For who will hearken vnto you in this matter? But as his part is that goeth downe to the battell, so shall his part bee that tarieth by the stuffe: they shall part alike.

† Heb. and forward.

25 And it was so from that day †forward, that he made it a statute, and an ordinance for Israel, vnto this day.

26 ¶ And when Dauid came to Ziklag, hee sent of the spoile vnto the Elders of Iudah, euen to his friends, (saying, Behold a †Present for you, of the spoile of the enemies of the LORD)

† Heb. blessing.

27 To them which were in Bethel, and to them which were in South Ramoth, and to them which were in Iattir,

28 And to them which were in Aroer, and to them which were in Siphmoth, and to them which were in Eshtemoa,

29 And to them which were in Rachal, and them which were in the cities of the Ierahmeelites, and to them which were in the cities of the Kenites,

30 And to them which were in Hormah, and to them which were in Chorashan, and to them which were in Athach,

31 And to them which were in Hebron, and to all the places where Dauid himselfe and his men were wont to haunt.

CHAP. XXXI.

1 Saul hauing lost his armie, and his sonnes slaine, he and his armour bearer kill themselues. 7 The Philistines possesse the forsaken townes of the Israelites. 8 They triumph ouer the dead carkeises. 11 They of Iabesh Gilead, recouering the bodies by night, burne them at Iabesh, and mournfully burie their bones.

* 1. Chro 10. 1.

Owe *the Philistines fought against Israel: and the men of Israel fled from before the Philistines, and fell downe ‖slaine in mount Gilboa.

‖ Or, wounded.

2 And the Philistines followed hard vpon Saul, and vpon his sonnes, and the Philistines slewe Ionathan, and Abinadab, and Malchishua, Sauls sonnes.

3 And the battell went sore against Saul, and the †archers †hit him, and he was sore wounded of the archers.

† Heb. sh ters, men with bow
† Heb. fo him.

4 Then said Saul vnto his armour bearer, Draw thy sword, and thrust me through therewith, lest these vncircumcised come and thrust me through, and ‖abuse mee. But his armour bearer would not, for he was sore afraid: therfore Saul tooke a sword, & fell vpon it.

‖ Or, moc me.

5 And when his armour bearer saw that Saul was dead, he fell likewise vpon his sword, and died with him.

6 So Saul died, and his three sons, and his armour bearer, and all his men that same day together.

7 ¶ And when the men of Israel that were on the other side of the valley, and they that were on the other side Iordane, saw that the men of Israel fled, and that Saul and his sonnes were dead, they forsooke the cities and fled, and the Philistines came and dwelt in them.

8 And it came to passe on the morrow when the Philistines came to strip the slaine, that they found Saul, and his three sons fallen in mount Gilboa.

9 And they cut off his head, and stripped

stripped off his armour, and sent into the land of the Philistines round about to publish *it in* the house of their idoles, and among the people.

10 And they put his armour in the house of Ashtaroth : and they fastened his body to the wall of Bethshan.

Or, concerning him.

11 ¶ And when the inhabitants of Iabesh Gilead heard ‖ of that which the

Philistines had done to Saul :

12 All the valiant men arose, and went all night, and tooke the body of Saul, and the bodies of his sonnes from the wall of Bethshan, and came to Iabesh, and *burnt them there.

*Iere. 34. 5.

13 And they tooke their bones, and *buried *them* vnder a tree at Iabesh, and fasted seuen dayes.

*2. Sam. 2. 4.

¶ THE SECOND BOOKE
of Samuel, otherwiſe called, The
second Booke of the Kings.

CHAP. I.

1 The Amalekite, who brought tidings of the ouerthrow, and accused himselfe of Sauls death, is slaine. 17 Dauid lamenteth Saul and Ionathan with a song.

Ow it came to passe after ỹ death of Saul, when Dauid was returned from *the slaughter of the Amalekites, and Dauid had abode two daies in Ziklag,

*1. Sam. ○. 17.

2 It came euen to passe on the third day, that behold, a man came out of the campe from Saul, with his clothes rent, and earth vpon his head : and so it was when he came to Dauid, that hee fell to the earth, and did obeysance.

3 And Dauid said vnto him, From whence commest thou? And he said vnto him, Out of the campe of Israel am I escaped.

Heb. what ○as &c.

4 And Dauid said vnto him, †How went the matter? I pray thee, tell mee. And he answered, That the people are fled from the battell, and many of the people also are fallen and dead, and Saul and Ionathan his sonne are dead also.

5 And Dauid said vnto the yong man that told him, How knowest thou

that Saul and Ionathan his sonne be dead?

6 And the yong man that told him, said, As I happened by chance vpon mount Gilboa, behold, Saul leaned vpon his speare : and loe, the charets and horsemen followed hard after him.

7 And when he looked behind him, he saw me, and called vnto mee : and I answered, †Here am I.

†*Hebr. behold me.*

8 And hee said vnto mee, Who *art* thou? and I answered him, I *am* an Amalekite.

9 He said vnto me againe, Stand, I pray thee, vpon me, and slay me : for ‖ anguish is come vpon mee, because my life *is* yet whole in me.

‖*Or, my coat of male, (or, my embroidered coat) hindereth mee, that my, &c.*

10 So I stood vpon him, and slew him, because I was sure that hee could not liue after that hee was fallen : And I tooke the crowne that *was* vpon his head, and the bracelet that *was* on his arme, and haue brought them hither vnto my lord.

11 Then Dauid tooke hold on his clothes, and *rent them, and likewise all the men that *were* with him.

*Chap. 3. 31. and 13. 31.

12 And they mourned and wept, and fasted vntill Euen, for Saul and for Ionathan his sonne, and for the people of the Lord, and for the house of Israel, because they were fallen by the sword.

13 ¶ And Dauid said vnto the yong man that told him, Whence *art* thou? And

And he answered, I am the sonne of a stranger, an Amalekite.

*Psal. 105. 15.

14 And Dauid said vnto him, *How wast thou not afraid to stretch foorth thine hand, to destroy the Lords Anointed?

15 And Dauid called one of the yong men, and sayd, Goe neere, and fall vpon him. And hee smote him, that hee dyed.

16 And Dauid said vnto him, Thy blood be vpon thy head: for thy mouth hath testified against thee, saying, I haue slaine the Lords Annoynted.

17 ¶ And Dauid lamented with this lamentation ouer Saul, and ouer Ionathan his sonne:

*Iosh. 10. 13.
‖ Or, of the vpright.

18 (Also hee bade them teach the children of Iudah the vse of the bow: behold, it is written *in the booke ‖of Iasher.)

19 The beauty of Israel is slaine vpon thy high places: how are the mightie fallen!

*Micah 1. 10.

20 *Tell it not in Gath, publish it not in the streetes of Askelon: lest the daughters of the Philistines reioyce, lest the daughters of the vncircumcised triumph.

21 Yee mountaines of Gilboa, let there bee no dewe, neither let there be raine vpon you, nor fields of offerings: for there the shield of the mightie is vilely cast away, the shield of Saul, as though hee had not beene annointed with oile.

22 From the blood of the slaine, from the fat of the mightie, the bow of Ionathan turned not backe, and the sword of Saul returned not emptie.

† Or, sweet.

23 Saul and Ionathan were louely and ‖pleasant in their liues, and in their death they were not diuided: they were swifter then Eagles, they were stronger then Lions.

24 Yee daughters of Israel, weepe ouer Saul, who clothed you in scarlet, with other delights, who put on ornaments of golde vpon your apparell.

25 How are the mightie fallen in the midst of the battell! O Ionathan, thou wast slaine in thine high places.

26 I am distressed for thee, my brother Ionathan, very pleasant hast thou beene vnto mee: thy loue to mee was wonderfull, passing the loue of women.

27 How are the mightie fallen, and the weapons of warre perished!

CHAP. II.

1 Dauid by Gods direction, with his companie goeth vp to Hebron, where he is made King of Iudah. 5 He commendeth them of Iabesh Gilead, for their kindnesse to Saul. 8 Abner maketh Ishbosheth king of Israel. 12 A mortall skirmish betweene twelue of Abners, and twelue of Ioabs men. 18 Asahel is slaine. 25 At Abners motion Ioab soundeth a retreat. 32 Asahels buriall.

ANd it came to passe after this, that Dauid enquired of the Lord, saying, Shall I goe vp into any of the Cities of Iudah? And the Lord said vnto him, Goe vp. And Dauid said, Whither shall I goe vp? And he said, Vnto Hebron.

2 So Dauid went vp thither, and his two wiues also, Ahinoam the Iezreelitesse, and Abigail Nabals wife the Carmelite.

3 And his men that were with him, did Dauid bring vp, euery man with his houshold: and they dwelt in the cities of Hebron.

*1. Macc 2. 57.

4 And *the men of Iudah came, and there they anointed Dauid king ouer the house of Iudah: and they tolde Dauid, saying; That *the men of Iabesh Gilead were they that buried Saul.

*1. Sam. 31. 13.

5 ¶ And Dauid sent messengers vnto the men of Iabesh Gilead, and said vnto them, Blessed be ye of the Lord, that ye haue shewed this kindnesse vnto your lord, euen vnto Saul, and haue buried him.

6 And now the Lord shewe kindnesse and trueth vnto you: and I also will requite you this kindnesse, because ye haue done this thing.

† Heb. be the sonne of valour.

7 Therefore now let your handes be strengthened, and †be ye valiant: for your master Saul is dead, and also the house of Iudah haue anointed me king ouer them.

† Heb. the hoste who was Saul.

8 ¶ But Abner the sonne of Ner, captaine of †Sauls hoste, tooke Ishbosheth the sonne of Saul, and brought him ouer to Mahanaim.

9 And hee made him king ouer Gilead, and ouer the Ashurites, and ouer Iezreel, and ouer Ephraim, and ouer Beniamin, and ouer all Israel.

10 Ishbosheth Sauls sonne was fortie yeeres olde when he began to reigne ouer Israel, and reigned two yeres: but the house of Iudah followed Dauid.

11 (And

Heb. num-
er of dayes.

11 (And the †time that Dauid was King in Hebron ouer the house of Iudah, *was* seuen yeeres, and sixe moneths)

12 ¶ And Abner the sonne of Ner, and the seruants of Ishbosheth the sonne of Saul, went out from Mahanaim, to Gibeon.

13 And Ioab the sonne of Zeruiah, and the seruants of Dauid went out,

Heb. them
gether.

and met †together by the poole of Gibeon: and they sate downe, the one on the one side of the poole, and the other on the other side of the poole.

14 And Abner said to Ioab, Let the yong men now arise, and play before vs: and Ioab saide, Let them arise.

15 Then there arose and went ouer by number twelue of Beniamin, which *pertained* to Ishbosheth the sonne of Saul, and twelue of the seruants of Dauid.

16 And they caught euery one his fellow by the head, and *thrust* his sword in his fellowes side, so they fell downe together: Wherfore that place was called

That is,
e field of
rong men.

‖Helkath-hazzurim, which is in Gibeon.

17 And there was a very sore battell that day: and Abner was beaten, and the men of Israel, before the seruants of Dauid.

18 ¶ And there were three sonnes of Zeruiah there, Ioab, and Abishai, and

Heb. of his
eete..

Asahel: and Asahel *was as* light †of foot

Heb. as one
the Roes
at is in the
eld.

†as a wilde Roe.

19 And Asahel pursued after Abner, and in going he turned not to the right

Heb. from
fter Ab-
er.

hand nor to the left from †following Abner.

20 Then Abner looked behind him, and said, Art thou Asahel? And he answered, I *am*.

21 And Abner said to him, Turne thee aside to thy right hand, or to thy left, and lay thee holde on one of the

Or, spoile.

yong men, and take thee his ‖armour. But Asahel would not turne aside from following of him.

22 And Abner said againe to Asahel, Turne thee aside from following me: Wherefore should I smite thee to the ground? how then should I holde vp my face to Ioab thy brother?

23 Howbeit hee refused to turne aside: wherefore Abner with the hinder ende of the speare smote him vnder the fift *ribbe*, that the speare came out behinde him, and hee fell downe there, and died

in the same place: and it came to passe, that as many as came to the place where Asahel fell downe and died, stood still.

24 Ioab also and Abishai pursued after Abner: and the Sunne went downe when they were come to the hill of Ammah, that *lieth* before Giah by the way of the wildernesse of Gibeon.

25 ¶ And the children of Beniamin gathered themselues together after Abner, and became one troupe, and stood on the top of an hill.

26 Then Abner called to Ioab, and said, Shall the sword deuoure for euer? Knowest thou not that it wil be bitternesse in the latter end? How long shall it bee then, yer thou bid the people returne from following their brethren?

27 And Ioab said, As God liueth, vnlesse thou hadst spoken, surely then †in the morning the people had ‖gone vp euery one from following his brother.

† Heb. from
the morning.
‖Or, gone
away.

28 So Ioab blew a trumpet, and all the people stood still, and pursued after Israel no more, neither fought they any more.

29 And Abner and his men walked all that night thorow the plaine, and passed ouer Iordane, and went thorow all Bithron, and they came to Mahanaim.

30 And Ioab returned from folowing Abner; and when he had gathered all the people together, there lacked of Dauids seruants nineteene men, and Asahel.

31 But the seruants of Dauid had smitten of Beniamin and of Abners men, *so that* three hundred and threescore men died.

32 ¶ And they tooke vp Asahel, and buried him in the sepulchre of his father which *was* in Bethlehem: and Ioab and his men went all night, and they came to Hebron at breake of day.

CHAP. III.

1 During the warre Dauid still waxeth stronger. 2 Sixe sonnes were borne to him in Hebron. 6 Abner displeased with Ishbosheth, 12 reuolteth to Dauid. 13 Dauid requireth a condition to bring him his wife Michal. 17 Abner hauing communed with the Israelites, is feasted by Dauid, and dismissed. 22 Ioab returning from battell, is displeased with the king, and killeth Abner. 28 Dauid curseth Ioab, 31 and mourneth for Abner.

Now

Ow there was long war betweene the house of Saul, and the house of Dauid: but Dauid waxed stronger and stronger, and the house of Saul waxed weaker and weaker.

2 ¶ And vnto Dauid were sonnes borne in Hebron: and his first borne was Amnon, of Ahinoam the Iezreelitesse.

3 And his second, Chileab, of Abigail the wife of Nabal the Carmelite: and the third, Absalom the sonne of Maacah, the daughter of Talmai king of Geshur;

4 And the fourth, Adoniiah the son of Haggith: and the fifth, Shephatiah the sonne of Abital;

5 And the sixth, Ithream by Eglah Dauids wife: these were borne to Dauid in Hebron.

6 ¶ And it came to passe while there was warre between the house of Saul and the house of Dauid, that Abner made himselfe strong for the house of Saul.

7 And Saul had a concubine, whose name *was* *Rizpah, the daughter of Aiah: and *Ishbosheth* saide to Abner, Wherefore hast thou gone in vnto my fathers concubine?

8 Then was Abner very wroth for the words of Ishbosheth, and said, *Am* I a dogs head, which against Iudah doe shew kindnesse this day vnto the house of Saul thy father, to his brethren, and to his friends, and haue not deliuered thee into the hand of Dauid, that thou chargest mee to day with a fault concerning this woman?

9 So doe God to Abner, and more also, except, as the LORD hath sworne to Dauid, euen so I doe to him:

10 To translate the kingdome from the house of Saul, and to set vp the throne of Dauid ouer Israel, and ouer Iudah, from Dan euen to Beer-sheba.

11 And he could not answere Abner a word againe, because he feared him.

12 ¶ And Abner sent messengers to Dauid on his behalfe, saying, Whose *is* the land? saying *also*, Make thy league with me, and behold, my hand *shall bee* with thee, to bring about all Israel vnto thee.

13 ¶ And he said, Well, I will make a league with thee: but one thing I require of thee, †that is, Thou shalt not see my face, except thou first bring Michal Sauls daughter, when thou commest to see my face.

14 And Dauid sent messengers to Ishbosheth Sauls sonne, saying, Deliuer mee my wife Michal, which I espoused to mee for *an hundred foreskinnes of the Philistines.

15 And Ishbosheth sent, and tooke her from her husband, *euen* from *Phaltiel the sonne of Laish.

16 And her husband went with her †along weeping behinde her to Bahurim: then said Abner vnto him, Goe, returne. And he returned.

17 ¶ And Abner had communication with the Elders of Israel, saying, Yee sought for Dauid †in times past, to be king ouer you.

18 Now then doe *it*, for the LORD hath spoken of Dauid, saying, By the hand of my seruant Dauid I will saue my people Israel out of the hand of the Philistines, and out of the hand of all their enemies.

19 And Abner also spake in the eares of Beniamin; and Abner went also to speake in the eares of Dauid in Hebron, all that seemed good to Israel, and that seemed good to the whole house of Beniamin.

20 So Abner came to Dauid to Hebron, and twenty men with him: and Dauid made Abner, and the men that *were* with him, a feast.

21 And Abner said vnto Dauid, I will arise, and goe, and will gather all Israel vnto my lord the king, that they may make a league with thee, and that thou mayest raigne ouer all that thine heart desireth And Dauid sent Abner away, and he went in peace.

22 ¶ And behold, the seruants of Dauid, and Ioab came from *pursuing* a troupe, and brought in a great spoile with them: (but Abner *was* not with Dauid in Hebron, for he had sent him away, and he was gone in peace.)

23 When Ioab and all the host that *was* with him, were come, they told Ioab, saying, Abner the sonne of Ner came to the king, and he hath sent him away, and he is gone in peace.

24 Then Ioab came to the king, and said, What hast thou done? behold, Abner came vnto thee, why is it that thou hast sent him away, & he is quite gone?

25 Thou knowest Abner the sonne of Ner, that he came to deceiue thee, and to know thy going out, and thy comming

*Chap. 21. 10.

†Hebr. saying.

* 1. Sam. 18. 25, 27.

* 1. Sam. 44. Phalti

† Hebr. going, and weeping.

† Hebr. b yesterday and the third day

ming in, & to know all that thou doest.

26 And when Ioab was come out from Dauid, hee sent messengers after Abner, which brought him againe from the well of Siriah; but Dauid knew it not.

27 And when Abner was returned to Hebron, * Ioab tooke him aside in the gate to speake with him ||quietly: and smote him there vnder the fift ribbe, that he died, for the blood of * Asahel his brother.

28 ¶ And afterward when Dauid heard it, hee said, I and my kingdome are guiltlesse before the LORD for euer, from the †blood of Abner the sonne of Ner:

29 Let it rest on the head of Ioab, and on all his fathers house, & let there not †faile from the house of Ioab one that hath an issue, or that is a leper, or that leaneth on a staffe, or that falleth on the sword, or that lacketh bread.

30 So Ioab and Abishai his brother slew Abner, because he had slaine their brother * Asahel at Gibeon in the battell.

31 ¶ And Dauid said to Ioab, and to all the people that were with him, Rent your clothes, and girde you with sackecloth, and mourne before Abner. And king Dauid himselfe followed the †biere.

32 And they buried Abner in Hebron, and the king lift vp his voice, and wept at the graue of Abner; and all the people wept.

33 And the king lamented ouer Abner, and said, Died Abner as a foole dieth?

34 Thy hands were not bound, nor thy feete put into fetters: as a man falleth before †wicked men, so fellest thou. And all the people wept againe ouer him.

35 And when all the people came to cause Dauid to eate meate while it was yet day, Dauid sware, saying, So doe God to mee, and more also, if I taste bread or ought else, till the Sunne be downe.

36 And all the people tooke notice of it, and it †pleased them: as whatsoeuer the King did, pleased all the people.

37 For all the people, and all Israel vnderstood that day, that it was not of the King to slay Abner the sonne of Ner.

38 And the King said vnto his seruants, Knowe yee not that there is a prince and a great man fallen this day in Israel?

39 And I am this day †weake, though anointed King, and these men the sonnes of Zeruiah be too hard for me: the LORD shall reward the doer of euill, according to his wickednesse.

CHAP. IIII.

1 The Israelites being troubled at the death of Abner, 2 Baanah and Rechab slay Ishbosheth, and bring his head to Hebron. 9 Dauid causeth them to be slaine, and Ishboshets head to be buried.

AND when Sauls sonne heard that Abner was dead in Hebron, his hands were feeble, and all the Israelites were troubled.

2 And Sauls sonne had two men that were captaines of bands: the name of the one was Baanah, and the name of the †other Rechab, the sonnes of Rimmon a Beerothite, of the children of Beniamin: (for Beeroth also was reckoned to Beniamin:

3 And the Beerothites fled to Gittaim, and were soiourners there vntill this day.)

4 And Ionathan, Sauls sonne, had a sonne that was lame of his feete, and was fiue yeeres olde when the tidings came of Saul and Ionathan out of Iezreel, and his nource tooke him vp, and fled: and it came to passe as she made haste to flee, that hee fell, and became lame, and his name was Mephibosheth.

5 And the sonnes of Rimmon the Beerothite, Rechab and Baanah, went, and came about the heat of the day to the house of Ishbosheth, who lay on a bed at noone.

6 And they came thither into the midst of the house, as though they would haue fetched wheat, and they smote him vnder the fift rib, and Rechab and Baanah his brother escaped.

7 For when they came into the house, hee lay on his bedde in his bedchamber, and they smote him, and slew him, and beheaded him, and tooke his head, and gate them away thorow the plaine all night.

8 And they brought the head of Ishbosheth vnto Dauid to Hebron, and said to the King, Behold the head of

---

Marginal notes (left column):

* 1. King.
*. 5.
Or, peaceably.
* Chap. 2.
3.

* Heb. bloods

* Heb. be cut off.

* Chap. 2.
23.

* Heb. bed.

† Heb. children of iniquitie.

† Heb. was good in their eyes.

Marginal notes (right column):

† Heb. tender.

† Heb. second.

of Ishbosheth the sonne of Saul, thine enemie, which sought thy life, and the LORD hath auenged my lord the king this day of Saul and of his seed.

9 ¶ And Dauid answered Rechab and Baanah his brother, the sonnes of Rimmon the Beerothite, and said vnto them, *As* the LORD liueth, who hath redeemed my soule out of all aduersitie,

10 When *one told me, saying, Behold, Saul is dead, (†thinking to haue brought good tidings) I tooke hold of him, and slew him in Ziklag, ||who *thought* that I would haue giuen him a reward for his tidings:

* Chap. 1
15.
† Heb. hee
was in his
owne eyes as
a bringer,
&c.
¶ Or, which
was the re-
ward I gaue
him for his
tidings.

11 How much more, when wicked men haue slaine a righteous person, in his owne house, vpon his bed? Shall I not therefore now require his blood of your hand, and take you away from the earth?

12 And Dauid commanded his yong men, and they slew them, and cut off their hands and their feete, and hanged them vp ouer the poole in Hebron: but they tooke the head of Ishbosheth, and buried *it* in the *sepulchre of Abner, in Hebron.

* Chap. 3.
34.

CHAP. V.

1 The tribes come to Hebron to annoint Dauid ouer Israel. 4 Dauids age. 6 Hee taking Zion from the Iebusites dwelleth in it. 11 Hiram sendeth to Dauid. 13 Eleuen sonnes are borne to him in Ierusalem. 17 Dauid directed by God smiteth the Philistines at Baal Perazim, 22 and againe at the Mulberie trees.

* 1. Chron.
11. 1.

THen *came all the tribes of Israel to Dauid vnto Hebron, and spake, saying, Behold, we are thy bone, and thy flesh.

2 Also in time past when Saul was king ouer vs, thou *wast hee* that leddest out and broughtest in Israel: and the LORD said to thee, *Thou shalt feed my people Israel, and thou shalt bee a captaine ouer Israel.

* Psal. 78.
71.

3 So all the Elders of Israel came to the King to Hebron, and King Dauid made a league with them in Hebron before the LORD: and they anointed Dauid King ouer Israel.

4 ¶ Dauid was thirtie yeeres old when he began to reigne, *and* he reigned fourtie yeeres.

5 In Hebron he reigned ouer Iudah *seuen yeeres, and six moneths: and in Ierusalem he reigned thirty and

* Chap. 2. 11

three yeres ouer all Israel and Iudah.

6 ¶ And the king and his men went to Ierusalem, vnto the Iebusites, the inhabitants of the land: which spake vnto Dauid, saying, Except thou take away the blind and the lame, thou shalt not come in hither: || Thinking, Dauid cannot come in hither.

|| Or, saying
Dauid shal
not &c.

7 Neuerthelesse, Dauid tooke the strong hold of Zion: the same *is* the citie of Dauid.

8 And Dauid said on that day, Whosoeuer getteth vp to the gutter, and smiteth the Iebusites, and the lame, and the blind, *that are* hated of Dauids soule, *heshallbechiefeandcaptaine:||Wherefore they said, The blind and the lame shall not come into the house.

* 1. Chron.
11. 6.
|| Or, becaus
they had sai
euen the
blind & the
lame, He
shal not com
into the
house.

9 So Dauid dwelt in the fort, and called it the citie of Dauid, and Dauid built round about, from Millo and inward.

10 And Dauid †went on, and grew great, and the LORD God of hosts was with him.

† Heb. went
going and
growing.

11 ¶ And *Hiram king of Tyre sent messengers to Dauid, and Cedar trees, and carpenters, and †Masons: and they built Dauid an house.

* 1. Chron.
14. 1.
† Hebr. hew
ers of the
stone of the
wall.

12 And Dauid perceiued that the LORD had established him King ouer Israel, and that he had exalted his kingdome for his people Israels sake.

13 ¶ And *Dauid tooke him mo concubines and wiues out of Ierusalem, after he was come from Hebron, and there were yet sonnes and daughters borne to Dauid.

* 1. Chron.
3. 9.

14 And *these *be* the names of those that *were* borne vnto him in Ierusalem, Shammua, & Shobab, and Nathan, and Solomon:

15 Ibhar also, and Elishua, and Nepheg, and Iaphia,

16 And Elishama, and Eliada, and Eliphalet.

* 1. Chron.
3. 5.

17 ¶ *But when the Philistines heard that they had anointed Dauid King ouer Israel, all the Philistines came vp to seeke Dauid, and Dauid heard *of it*, and went downe to the hold.

* 1. Chron.
11. 16.
and 14. 8.

18 The Philistines also came, and spred themselues in the valley of Rephaim.

19 And Dauid enquired of the LORD, saying, Shall I goe vp to the Philistines? wilt thou deliuer them into mine hand? And the LORD said vnto Dauid, Goe vp: for I will doubtlesse

sa. 28.

lesse deliuer the Philistines into thine hand.

20 And *Dauid came to Baal-Perazim, and Dauid smote them there, and said, The LORD hath broken foorth vpon mine enemies before me, as the breach of waters. Therefore he called the name of that place, ||Baal-Perazim.

nat is, plaine of uches.

21 And there they left their images, and Dauid and his men *||burnt them.

Chron. 12. , tooke n away.

22 ¶ And the Philistines came vp yet againe, and spread themselues in the valley of Rephaim.

23 And when Dauid enquired of the LORD, he said, Thou shalt not goe vp : but fetch a compasse behinde them, and come vpon them ouer against the Mulbery trees.

24 And let it be when thou hearest the sound of a going in the tops of the mulbery trees, that then thou shalt bestirre thy selfe : for then shal the LORD goe out before thee, to smite the host of the Philistines.

25 And Dauid did so, as the LORD had commaunded him ; and smote the Philistines from Geba, vntil thou come to Gazer.

CHAP. VI.

1 Dauid fetcheth the Arke from Kiriath-iearim on a new cart. 6 Vzzah is smitten at Perez-Vzzah. 9 God blesseth Obed-Edom for the Arke. 12 Dauid bringing the Arke into Zion with sacrifices, daunceth before it, for which Michol despiseth him. 17 Hee placeth it in a tabernacle with great ioy and feasting. 20 Michal reprouing Dauid for his religious ioy, is childlesse to her death.

Chro. 5, 6.

Gaine, Dauid gathered together all the chosen men of Israel, thirtie thousand :

2 And *Dauid arose and went with all the people that were with him, from Baale of Iudah, to bring vp from thence the Arke of God, || whose Name is called by the Name of the LORD of hostes, that dwelleth betweene the Cherubims.

r, at ich the me, euen Name of LORD hosts was ed vpon. heb. made -ide. r, the hill.

3 And they †set the Arke of God vpon a new cart, and brought it out of the house of Abinadab that was in ||Gibeah: and Vzzah and Ahio the sonnes of Abinadab, draue the new cart.

Sam. 7.

4 And they brought it out of *the house of Abinadab which was at Gibeah, †accompanying the Arke of God; and Ahio went before the Arke.

5 And Dauid and all the house of Israel played before the LORD on all manner of instruments made of Firrewood, euen on harpes, and on Psalteries, and on timbrels, and on cornets, and on cimbals.

6 ¶ And *when they came to Nachons threshing floore, Vzzah put forth his hand to the Arke of God, and tooke hold of it, for the oxen ||shooke it.

7 And the anger of the LORD was kindled against Vzzah, and God smote him there for his ||errour, and there he died by the Arke of God.

8 And Dauid was displeased, because the LORD had †made a breach vpon Vzzah : And hee called the name of the place, ||Perez-Vzzah to this day.

9 And Dauid was afraide of the LORD that day, and said, How shall the Arke of the LORD come to me ?

10 So Dauid would not remoue the Arke of the LORD vnto him into the citie of Dauid : but Dauid caried it aside into the house of Obed Edom, the Gittite.

11 And the Arke of the LORD continued in the house of Obed Edom the Gittite, three moneths : and the LORD blessed Obed Edom, and all his household.

12 ¶ And it was told king Dauid, saying, *The LORD hath blessed the house of Obed Edom, and all that pertained vnto him, because of the Arke of God. So Dauid went, and brought vp the Arke of God, from the house of Obed Edom, into the citie of Dauid, with gladnesse.

13 And it was so, that when they that bare the Arke of the LORD, had gone six paces, hee sacrificed oxen and fatlings.

14 And Dauid daunced before the LORD with all his might, and Dauid was girded with a linnen Ephod.

15 So Dauid and all the house of Israel brought vp the Arke of the LORD with shouting, and with the sound of the trumpet.

16 And as the Arke of the LORD came into the citie of Dauid, Michal Sauls daughter looked through a window, and saw king Dauid leaping and dauncing before the LORD, and she despised him in her heart.

17 ¶ And

† Hebr. with.

ⁿ 1. Chron. 13. 9.

|| Or, stumbled.

|| Or, rashnesse.

† Hebr. broken.

|| That is, The breach of Vzzah.

* 1. Chron. 13. 25.

17 ¶ And they brought in the Arke of the LORD, and set it in his place, in the midst of the Tabernacle that Dauid had †pitched for it : and Dauid offered burnt offerings, and peace offrings before the LORD.

18 And assoone as Dauid had made an end of offering burnt offerings and peace offerings, *hee blessed the people in the Name of the LORD of hostes.

19 And hee dealt among all the people, euen among the whole multitude of Israel, as well to the women as men, to euery one a cake of bread, and a good piece of flesh, and a flagon of wine: so all the people departed euery one to his house.

20 ¶ Then Dauid returned to blesse his houshold : and Michal the daughter of Saul came out to meete Dauid, and said, How glorious was the King of Israel to day, who vncouered himselfe to day in the eyes of the handmaids of his seruants, as one of the vaine fellowes ‖shamelessely vncouereth himselfe!

21 And Dauid said vnto Michal, It was before the LORD, which chose me before thy father, & before all his house, to appoint me ruler ouer the people of the LORD, ouer Israel : therefore will I play before the LORD.

22 And I will yet be more vile then thus, and will be base in mine owne sight : and ‖of the maid seruants which thou hast spoken of, of them shall I be had in honour.

23 Therefore Michal the daughter of Saul had no childe vnto the day of her death.

CHAP. VII.

1 Nathan first approouing the purpose of Dauid to build God an house, 4 after by the word of God forbiddeth him. 12 He promiseth him benefites and blessings in his seede. 18 Dauids prayer and thankesgiuing.

AND it came to passe, *when the King sate in his house, and the LORD had giuen him rest round about frō all his enemies;

2 That the king said vnto Nathan the Prophet, See now, I dwell in an house of Cedar, but the Arke of God dwelleth within curtaines.

3 And Nathan sayde to the King,

Go, doe all that is in thine heart : for the LORD is with thee.

4 ¶ And it came to passe that night, that the word of the LORD came vnto Nathan, saying ;

5 Goe and tell †my seruant Dauid, Thus sayth the LORD, Shalt thou build me an house for me to dwell in?

6 Whereas I haue not dwelt in any house, since the time that I brought vp the children of Israel out of Egypt, euen to this day, but haue walked in a tent and in a tabernacle.

7 In all the places wherein I haue walked with all the children of Israel, spake I a word with ‖any of the tribes of Israel, whome I commanded to feede my people Israel, saying, Why build ye not me an house of Cedar?

8 Now therefore so shalt thou say vnto my seruant Dauid ; Thus sayth the LORD of hostes, *I tooke thee from the sheepe-cote, †from following the sheepe, to be ruler ouer my people, ouer Israel.

9 And I was with thee whithersoeuer thou wentest, and haue cut off all thine enemies †out of thy sight, and haue made thee a great name, like vnto the name of the great men that are in the earth.

10 (Moreouer I will appoint a place for my people Israel, and will plant them, that they may dwell in a place of their owne, and mooue no more : neither shall the children of wickednesse afflict them any more, as beforetime,

11 And as since the time that I commanded Iudges to bee ouer my people Israel, and haue caused thee to rest from all thine enemies :) Also the LORD telleth thee, that he will make thee an house.

12 ¶ And *when thy dayes be fulfilled, and thou shalt sleepe with thy fathers, I will set vp thy seede after thee, which shall proceede out of thy bowels, and I will establish his kingdome.

13 *Hee shall build an house for my Name, and I will stablish the throne of his kingdome for euer.

14 *I will be his father, and he shall be my sonne: *if hee commit iniquitie, I will chasten him with the rodde of men, and with the stripes of the children of men.

15 But my mercie shall not depart away from him, as I tooke it from Saul, whom I put away before thee.

16 And

† Heb. stret-ched.

* 1. Chron. 16. 2.

‖ Or, openly.

‖ Or, of the handmaids of my seruants.

* 1. Chron. 17. 2.

† Heb. seruant Dauid.

‖ In the Chro. 1 any of Iudges

* 1. Sa 12. psa 70. † Heb. after.

† Heb. thy fac

* 1. K 8. 20.

* 1. K 5. 5. a 12. 1. 22. 10.

* Heb * Psa 31, 32.

16 And thine house, and thy kingdome shall be stablished for euer before thee: thy throne shall bee stablished for euer.

17 According to all these words, and according to all this vision, so did Nathan speake vnto Dauid.

18 ¶ Then went king Dauid in, and sate before the LORD, and hee said, Who *am* I, O Lord GOD? and what *is* my house, that thou hast brought me hitherto?

19 And this was yet a small thing in thy sight, O Lord GOD: but thou hast spoken also of thy seruants house for a great while to come, and *is* this the †maner of man, O Lord GOD?

Heb. Law.

20 And what can Dauid say more vnto thee? for thou, Lord GOD, knowest thy seruant.

21 For thy words sake, and according to thine owne heart hast thou done all these great things, to make thy seruant know *them.*

22 Wherefore thou art great, O Lord GOD: for *there is* none like thee, neither *is there* any God beside thee, according to all that we haue heard with our eares.

Deut. 4. 7

23 And * what one nation in the earth *is* like thy people, *euen* like Israel, whom God went to redeeme for a people to himselfe, & to make him a name and to doe for you great things, and terrible, for thy lande, before thy people which thou redeemedst to thee from Egypt, *from* the nations, and their gods?

24 For thou hast confirmed to thy selfe thy people Israel *to be* a people vnto thee for euer: and thou, LORD art become their God.

25 And now, O LORD God, the word that thou hast spoken, concerning thy seruant, and concerning his house, establish *it* for euer, and doe as thou hast said.

26 And let thy name bee magnified for euer, saying, The LORD of hosts *is* the God ouer Israel: and let the house of thy seruant Dauid bee established before thee.

Heb. opened the eare.

27 For thou, O LORD of hostes, God of Israel, hast †reuealed to thy seruant, saying, I will build thee an house: therfore hath thy seruant found in his heart to pray this prayer vnto thee.

Ioh. 17. 7.

28 And now, O Lord GOD, (thou art that God, and *thy words be true,

and thou hast promised this goodnesse vnto thy seruant.)

29 Therefore now †let it please thee to blesse the house of thy seruant, that it may continue for euer before thee: for thou, O Lord GOD, hast spoken *it,* and with thy blessing let the house of thy seruant be blessed for euer.

† Heb. bee thou pleased and blesse.

CHAP. VIII.

1 Dauid subdueth the Philistines and the Moabites. 3 He smiteth Hadadezer, and the Syrians. 9 Toi sendeth Ioram with Presents to blesse him. 11 The Presents and the spoile Dauid dedicateth to God. 14 He putteth garisons in Edom. 16 Dauids officers.

Nd * after this it came to passe, that Dauid smote the Philistines, and subdued them: and Dauid tooke ‖Metheg-Ammah out of the hand of the Philistines.

* 1. Chron. 18. 1. &c. psal. 60. 2.

‖ Or, the bridle of Ammah.

2 And he smote Moab, and measured them with a line, casting them downe to the ground: euen with two lines measured he, to put to death, and with one full line to keepe aliue: and so the Moabites became Dauids seruants, *and* brought gifts.

3 ¶ Dauid smote also Hadadezer the sonne of Rehob, king of Zobah, as he went to recouer his border at the riuer Euphrates.

4 And Dauid tooke ‖from him a thousand ‖*charets*, and seuen hundred horsemen, and twentie thousand footemen: and Dauid houghed all the charet *horses*, but reserued of them *for* an hundred charets.

‖ Or, of his.
‖ As 1. Chr. 18. 4.

5 And when the Syrians of Damascus came to succour Hadadezer king of Zobah, Dauid slew of the Syrians two and twentie thousand men.

6 Then Dauid put garisons in Syria of Damascus: And the Syrians became seruants to Dauid, *and* brought gifts: and the LORD preserued Dauid whithersoeuer he went.

7 And Dauid tooke the shields of gold that were on the seruants of Hadadezer, and brought them to Ierusalem.

8 And from Betah and from Berothai, cities of Hadadezer, King Dauid tooke exceeding much brasse.

9 ¶ When Toi king of Hamath heard that Dauid had smitten all the hoste of Hadadezer,

10 Then

† *Hebr. aske*
him of peace.

† *Hebr. was*
a man of
warres with.
† *Hebr. in*
his hand
were.

† *Hebr. his*
smiting.

‖ *Or, re-*
membran-
cer, or wri-
ter of Chro-
nicles.
‖ *Or, secre-*
tary.
* 1. Chron.
18. 17.

‖ *Or, Prin-*
ces.

10 Then Toi sent Ioram his sonne vnto king Dauid to †salute him, and to blesse him, because hee had fought against Hadadezer, and smitten him: (for Hadadezer †had warres with Toi) and *Ioram* †brought with him vessels of siluer, and vessels of gold, and vessels of brasse;

11 Which also king Dauid did dedicate vnto the LORD, with the siluer and gold that he had dedicate of all nations which he subdued ·

12 Of Syria, and of Moab, and of the children of Ammon, and of the Philistines, & of Amalek, and of the spoile of Hadadezer sonne of Rehob king of Zobah.

13 And Dauid gate *him* a name when he returned from †smiting of the Syrians in the valley of salt, *being* eighteene thousand *men*.

14 ¶ And he put garrisons in Edom; thorowout all Edom put he garrisons, and all they of Edom became Dauids seruants : and the LORD preserued Dauid whithersoeuer he went.

15 And Dauid reigned ouer all Israel, and Dauid executed iudgement and iustice vnto all his people.

16 And Ioab the sonne of Zeruiah *was* ouer the host, and Iehoshaphat the sonne of Ahilud *was* ‖ Recorder.

17 And Zadok the sonne of Ahitub, and Ahimelech the sonne of Abiathar, *were* the Priests, and Seraiah *was* the ‖ scribe.

18 * And Benaiah the sonne of Iehoiada was *ouer* both the Cherethites, and the Pelethites, and Dauids sonnes were ‖ chiefe rulers.

CHAP. IX.

1 Dauid by Ziba, sendeth for Mephibosheth.
7 For Ionathans sake he intertaineth him at
his table, and restoreth him all that was Sauls.
9 He maketh Ziba his farmour.

Nd Dauid said, Is there yet any that is left of the house of Saul, that I may shew him kindnesse for Ionathans sake?

2 And there was of the house of Saul, a seruant whose name was Ziba : and when they had called him vnto Dauid, the king said vnto him, *Art* thou Ziba? And he said, Thy seruant *is* he.

3 And the king said, Is there not yet any of the house of Saul, that I

may shew the kindnesse of God vnto him ? and Ziba said vnto the king, Ionathan hath yet a sonne, which is * lame on his feete.

4 And the king saide vnto him, Where *is* hee? and Ziba said vnto the king, Behold, he *is* in the house of Machir the sonne of Ammiel, in Lodebar.

5 ¶ Then king Dauid sent, and fet him out of the house of Machir the son of Ammiel, from Lodebar.

6 Now when Mephibosheth the sonne of Ionathan the sonne of Saul, was come vnto Dauid, hee fell on his face, and did reuerence : and Dauid said, Mephibosheth ! And he answered, Behold thy seruant.

7 ¶ And Dauid saide vnto him, Feare not, for I will surely shew thee kindnesse, for Ionathan thy fathers sake, and will restore thee all the land of Saul thy father, and thou shalt eate bread at my table continually.

8 And hee bowed himselfe, and saide, What *is* thy seruant, that thou shouldest looke vpon such a dead dogge as I *am?*

9 ¶ Then the king called to Ziba Sauls seruant, and said vnto him, I haue giuen vnto thy masters sonne all that pertained to Saul, and to all his house.

10 Thou therefore and thy sonnes, and thy seruants, shall till the land for him, and thou shalt bring in *the fruits*, that thy masters sonne may haue food to eate : but Mephibosheth thy masters sonne shall eat bread alway at my table. Now Ziba had fifteene sonnes, and twenty seruants.

11 Then saide Ziba vnto the king, According to all that my lord the king hath commanded his seruant, so shall thy seruant doe : as for Mephibosheth, *said the King*, he shall eate at my table, as one of the kings sonnes.

12 And Mephibosheth had a yong sonne whose name *was* Micha : and all that dwelt in the house of Ziba, *were* seruants vnto Mephibosheth.

13 So Mephibosheth dwelt in Ierusalem : for hee did eate continually at the kings table, and was lame on both his feete.

CHAP. X.

1 Dauids messengers sent to comfort Hanun
the sonne of Nahash, are villenously intreated. 6 The Ammonites, strengthened by the
Syrians,

* Chap. 4.
4.

Syrians, are ouercome by Ioab and Abishai. 15 Shobach making a new supply of the Syrians at Helam, is slaine by Dauid.

Nd it came to passe, after this, that the *king of the children of Ammon died, and Hanun his sonne reigned in his stead.

1. Chron. 1.

2 Then said Dauid, I will shewe kindnes vnto Hanun the sonne of Nahash, as his father shewed kindnes vnto me. And Dauid sent to comfort him by the hand of his seruants, for his father: and Dauids seruants came into the land of the children of Ammon.

3 And the princes of the children of Ammon saide vnto Hanun their lord, † Thinkest thou that Dauid doeth honour thy father, that he hath sent comforters vnto thee? Hath not Dauid rather sent his seruants vnto thee, to search the citie, and to spie it out, and to ouerthrow it?

Hebr. in ine eyes th Da. d?

4 Wherefore Hanun tooke Dauids seruants, and shaued off the one halfe of their beards, and cut off their garments in the middle, *euen* to their buttocks, and sent them away.

5 When they told *it* vnto Dauid, he sent to meet them, because the men were greatly ashamed: and the King saide, Tarie at Iericho vntill your beards be growen, *and* then returne.

6 ¶ And when the children of Ammon saw that they stanke before Dauid, the children of Ammon sent, and hired the Syrians of Beth-Rehob, and the Syrians of Zoba, twentie thousand footmen, and of king Maacah, a thousand men, and of Ishtob twelue thousand men.

7 And when Dauid heard of it, he sent Ioab, and all the hoste of the mightie men.

8 And the children of Ammon came out, and put the battell in aray at the entring in of the gate: and the Syrians of Zoba and of Rehob, and Ishtob, and Maacah, *were* by themselues in the field.

9 When Ioab saw that the front of the battell was against him, before and behind, he chose of all the choise men of Israel, and put them in aray against the Syrians.

10 And the rest of the people he deliuered into the hand of Abishai his brother, that he might put them in aray against the children of Ammon.

11 And he said, If the Syrians bee too strong for me, then thou shalt helpe me: but if the children of Ammon bee too strong for thee, then I will come and helpe thee.

12 Be of good courage, and let vs play the men, for our people, and for the cities of our God: and the LORD doe that which seemeth him good.

13 And Ioab drew nigh, and the people that *were* with him, vnto the battell against the Syrians: and they fled before him.

14 And when the children of Ammon saw that the Syrians were fledde, then fled they also before Abishai, and entred into the citie: so Ioab returned from the children of Ammon, and came to Ierusalem.

15 ¶ And when the Syrians sawe that they were smitten before Israel, they gathered themselues together.

16 And Hadarezer sent, and brought out the Syrians that *were* beyond the riuer, and they came to Helam, and Shobach the captaine of the hoste of Hadarezer *went* before them.

17 And when it was told Dauid, he gathered all Israel together, and passed ouer Iordane, and came to Helam: and the Syrians set themselues in aray against Dauid, and fought with him.

18 And the Syrians fled before Israel, and Dauid slew *the men* of seuen hundred charets of the Syrians, and fourtie thousand horsemen, and smote Shobach the captaine of their hoste, who died there.

19 And when all the kings that were seruants to Hadarezer sawe, that they were smitten before Israel, they made peace with Israel, and serued them: so the Syrians feared to helpe the children of Ammon any more.

CHAP. XI.

1 While Ioab besieged Rabbah, Dauid committeth adulterie with Bath-sheba. 6 Vriah sent for by Dauid to couer the adulterie, would not goe home neither sober nor drunken. 14 Hee carieth to Ioab the letter of his death. 18 Ioab sendeth the newes thereof to Dauid. 26 Dauid taketh Bath-sheba to wife.

Nd it came to passe, that †after the yeere was expired, at the time when kings goe foorth *to battell,* that *Dauid sent Ioab and his seruants with him, and all Israel;

† *Heb. at the returne of the yeere.*

* *1. Chron. 20. 1.*

rael; and they destroyed the children of Ammon, and besieged Rabbah : but Dauid taried still at Ierusalem.

2 ¶ And it came to passe in an euening tide, that Dauid arose from off his bed, and walked vpon the roofe of the kings house : and from the roofe he saw a woman washing her selfe; and the woman was very beautifull to looke vpon.

3 And Dauid sent and enquired after the woman: and one said, Is not this Bath-sheba the daughter of Eliam, the wife of Vriah the Hittite?

4 And Dauid sent messengers, and tooke her, and shee came in vnto him, and he lay with her, (|| for she was *purified from her vncleannesse) and shee returned vnto her house.

‡ Or, and whē she had purified her selfe, &c. she returned.
* Leuit. 15. 19. and 18. 19.

5 And the woman conceiued, and sent and tolde Dauid, and said, I am with childe.

6 ¶ And Dauid sent to Ioab, saying, Send me Vriah the Hittite. And Ioab sent Vriah to Dauid.

7 And when Vriah was come vnto him, Dauid demanded of him †how Ioab did, and how the people did, and how the warre prospered.

† Heb. of the peace of &c.

8 And Dauid said to Vriah, Goe downe to thy house, and wash thy feete. And Vriah departed out of the Kings house, and there †followed him a messe of meat from the king.

† Heb. went out after him.

9 But Vriah slept at the doore of the kings house, with all the seruants of his lord, and went not downe to his house.

10 And when they had tolde Dauid, saying, Vriah went not downe vnto his house, Dauid said vnto Vriah, Camest thou not from thy iourney? why then diddest thou not goe downe vnto thine house?

11 And Vriah said vnto Dauid, The Arke, and Israel, and Iudah abide in tents, and my lord Ioab, and the seruants of my lord are encamped in the open fields; shall I then goe into mine house, to eate and to drinke, and to lie with my wife? As thou liuest, and as thy soule liueth, I will not doe this thing.

12 And Dauid said to Vriah, Tary here to day also, and to morow I will let thee depart. So Vriah abode in Ierusalem that day, and the morrow.

13 And when Dauid had called him, hee did eate and drinke before him, and he made him drunke: and at euen hee went out to lie on his bed with the seruants of his lord, but went not downe to his house.

14 ¶ And it came to passe in the morning, that Dauid wrote a letter to Ioab, and sent it by the hand of Vriah.

15 And he wrote in the letter, saying, Set yee Vriah in the forefront of the †hottest battel, and retire ye †from him, that he may be smitten, and die.

† Heb. str
† Heb. fr after him

16 And it came to passe when Ioab obserued the citie, that he assigned Vriah vnto a place where hee knewe that valiant men were.

17 And the men of the city went out, and fought with Ioab: and there fell some of the people of the seruants of Dauid, and Vriah the Hittite died also.

18 ¶ Then Ioab sent, and tolde Dauid all the things concerning the warre :

19 And charged the messenger, saying, When thou hast made an ende of telling the matters of the warre vnto the King ;

20 And if so be that the kings wrath arise, and hee say vnto thee, Wherefore approched ye so nigh vnto the city when yee did fight? Knew yee not that they would shoot from the wall?

21 Who smote *Abimelech the sonne of Ierubbesheth? Did not a woman cast a piece of a milstone vpon him from the wall, that he died in Thebez? why went ye nigh the wall? Then say thou, Thy seruant Vriah the Hittite is dead also.

* Iudg. 53.

22 ¶ So the messenger went, and came and shewed Dauid all that Ioab had sent him for.

23 And the messenger said vnto Dauid, Surely the men preuailed against vs, and came out vnto vs into the field, and we were vpon them euen vnto the entring of the gate.

24 And the shooters shot from off the wall vpon thy seruants, and some of the Kings seruants be dead, and thy seruant Vriah the Hittite is dead also.

25 Then Dauid said vnto the messenger, Thus shalt thou say vnto Ioab, Let not this thing †displease thee: for the sword deuoureth †one as well as another : Make thy battell more strong against the citie, and ouerthrow it: and encourage thou him.

† Heb. b euill int eyes.
† Heb. s and such

26 ¶ And when the wife of Vriah heard that Vriah her husband was dead,

dead, she mourned for her husband.

27 And when the mourning was past, Dauid sent, and fet her to his house, and she became his wife, and bare him a sonne: but the thing that Dauid had done, †displeased the Lord.

Heb. was euill in the ies of.

CHAP. XII.

1 Nathans parable of the Ewe lambe, causeth 'Dauid to be his owne Iudge. 7 Dauid, reproued by Nathan, confesseth his sinne and is pardoned. 15 Dauid mourneth and prayeth for the childe, while it liued. 24 Salomon is borne and named Iedidiah. 26 Dauid taketh Rabbah, and tortureth the people thereof.

Nd the Lord sent Nathan vnto Dauid: and he came vnto him, and said vnto him, There were two men in one citie; the one rich, and the other poore.

2 The rich *man* had exceeding many flockes and herds.

3 But the poore *man* had nothing saue one litle ewe lambe, which he had bought and nourished vp: and it grew vp together with him, and with his children, it did eate of his owne †meate, and dranke of his owne cup, and lay in his bosome, and was vnto him as a daughter.

Heb. morsell.

4 And there came a traueller vnto the rich man, and he spared to take of his owne flocke, and of his owne herd, to dresse for the wayfaring man that was come vnto him, but tooke the poore mans lambe, and dressed it for the man that was come to him.

5 And Dauids anger was greatly kindled against the man, and he said to Nathan, As the Lord liueth, the man that hath done this thing, ‖shall surely die.

Or, is worthy to die.

6 And he shall restore the Lambe *fourefold, because he did this thing, aud because he had no pittie.

Exo.22. 1

7 ¶ And Nathan said to Dauid, Thou art the man: thus saith the Lord God of Israel, I *anointed thee king ouer Israel, and I deliuered thee out of the hand of Saul,

Sam. 16. 3.

8 And I gaue thee thy Masters house, and thy Masters wiues into thy bosome, and gaue thee the house of Israel and of Iudah, and if that had bene too litle, I would moreouer haue giuen vnto thee such and such things.

9 Wherefore hast thou despised the commandement of the Lord, to doe euill in his sight? thou hast killed Vriah the Hittite with the sword, and hast taken his wife to be thy wife, and hast slaine him with the sword of the children of Ammon.

10 Now therefore the sword shall neuer depart from thine house; because thou hast despised me, and hast taken the wife of Vriah the Hittite, to be thy wife.

11 Thus saith the Lord, Behold, I will raise vp euill against thee out of thine owne house, and I will *take thy wiues before thine eyes, and giue *them* vnto thy neighbour, and he shall lie with thy wiues in the sight of this Sunne.

Deut. 28. 30. chap. 16. 22.

12 For thou diddest *it* secretly: but I will do this thing before all Israel, and before the Sunne.

13 And Dauid saide vnto Nathan, *I haue sinned against the Lord. And Nathan saide vnto Dauid, The Lord also hath put away thy sinne, thou shalt not die.

Ecclus. 47. 11.

14 Howbeit, because by this deede thou hast giuen great occasion to the enemies of the Lord to blaspheme, the childe also that is borne vnto thee, shall surely die.

15 ¶ And Nathan departed vnto his house: and the Lord strake the childe that Vriahs wife bare vnto Dauid, and it was very sicke.

16 Dauid therfore besought God for the childe, and Dauid †fasted, and went in, and lay all night vpon the earth.

†*Heb. fasted a fast.*

17 And the Elders of his house arose, *and went* to him, to raise him vp from the earth: but he would not, neither did he eate bread with them.

18 And it came to passe on the seuenth day, that the childe died: and the seruants of Dauid feared to tell him that the child was dead: for they saide, Behold, while the childe was yet aliue, we spake vnto him, and he would not hearken vnto our voice: how will he then †vexe himselfe, if we tell him that the childe is dead?

†*Heb. doe hurt.*

19 But when Dauid saw that his seruants whispered, Dauid perceiued that the childe was dead: therefore Dauid said vnto his seruants, Is the child dead? and they said, He is dead.

20 Then Dauid arose from the earth and washed, and anointed *himselfe*, and changed

changed his apparell, and came into the house of the LORD, and worshipped: then hee came to his owne house, and when he required, they set bread before him, and he did eate.

21 Then said his seruants vnto him, What thing *is* this that thou hast done? thou didst fast and weepe for the childe, while it was aliue, but when the childe was dead, thou didst rise and eat bread.

22 And he said, While the child was yet aliue, I fasted and wept: for I said, Who can tell, *whether* God will be gracious to me, that the child may liue?

23 But now hee is dead, Wherefore should I fast? Can I bring him backe againe? I shall goe to him, but he shall not returne to me.

24 ¶ And Dauid comforted Bathsheba his wife, and went in vnto her, and lay with her: and *she bare a sonne, and he called his name Solomon, and the LORD loued him.

a Matt. 1. 6.

25 And hee sent by the hand of Nathan the Prophet, and * hee called his name ‖Iedidiah, because of the LORD.

b 1. Chron. 22. 9.
† That is, *Beloued of the Lord.*

26 ¶ And Ioab fought against Rabbah of the children of Ammon, and tooke the royall citie.

27 And Ioab sent messengers to Dauid, and said, I haue fought against Rabbah, and haue taken the citie of waters.

28 Now therefore, gather the rest of the people together, and encampe against the citie, and take it: lest I take the citie, and † it be called after my name.

† Hebr. *my name be called vpon it.*

29 And Dauid gathered all the people together, and went to Rabbah, and fought against it, and tooke it.

30 *And he tooke their kings crowne from off his head (the weight whereof *was* a talent of gold, with the precious stones) and it was *set* on Dauids head, and he brought forth the spoile of the citie † in great abundance.

c 1. Chron. 20. 2.

† Hebr. *very great.*

31 And he brought foorth the people that *were* therein, and put *them* vnder sawes, and vnder harrowes of yron, and vnder axes of yron, and made them passe through the bricke-kilne: And thus did he vnto all the cities of the children of Ammon. So Dauid and all the people returned vnto Ierusalem.

CHAP. XIII.

1 Amnon louing Tamar, by Ionadabs counsell faining himselfe sicke, rauisheth her. 15 Hee hateth her, and shamefully turneth her a-way. 19 Absalom entertaineth her, and concealeth his purpose. 23 At a sheepe-shearing, among all the Kings sonnes, hee killeth Amnon. 30 Dauid grieuing at the newes is comforted by Ionadab. 37 Absalom flieth to Talmai at Geshur.

Nd it came to passe after this, that Absalom the sonne of Dauid had a faire sister, whose name *was* Tamar : and Amnon the sonne of Dauid loued her.

2 And Amnon was so vexed, that he fell sicke for his sister Tamar: for she was a virgine, and † Amnon thought it hard for him to doe any thing to her.

† Heb. *it w maruelous or hidden the eyes of Amnon.*

3 But Amnon had a friend, whose name *was* Ionadab, the sonne of Shimeah, Dauids brother: and Ionadab *was* a very subtill man.

4 And he saide vnto him, Why *art* thou, being the Kings sonne, † leane † from day to day? Wilt thou not tel me? and Amnon said vnto him, I loue Tamar my brother Absaloms sister.

† Heb. *thir*
† Heb. *morning by morning.*

5 And Ionadab said vnto him, Lay thee downe on thy bed, and make thy selfe sicke: and when thy father commeth to see thee, say vnto him, I pray thee, let my sister Tamar come, and giue me meat, and dresse the meat in my sight, that I may see *it*, and eate *it* at her hand.

6 ¶ So Amnon lay downe, and made himselfe sicke: and when the king was come to see him, Amnon said vnto the king, I pray thee, let Tamar my sister come, & make me a couple of cakes in my sight, that I may eat at her hand.

7 Then Dauid sent home to Tamar, saying, Goe now to thy brother Amnons house, and dresse him meat.

8 So Tamar went to her brother Amnons house (and hee was laide downe) and she tooke ‖flowre, and kneaded *it*, and made cakes in his sight, and did bake the cakes.

‖ Or, *paste*

9 And she tooke a pan, and powred *them* out before him, but hee refused to eate: and Amnon said, Haue out all men from mee : And they went out euery man from him

10 And Amnon saide vnto Tamar, Bring the meate into the chamber, that I may eate of thine hand. And Tamar tooke the cakes which shee had made, and brought *them* into the chamber to Amnon her brother.

11 And when shee had brought *them* vnto

vnto him to eate, hee tooke hold of her, and said vnto her, Come lye with mee, my sister.

12 And she answered him, Nay, my brother, doe not † force me: for * † no such thing ought to bee done in Israel; doe not thou this folly.

13 And I, whither shall I cause my shame to goe? and as for thee, thou shalt be as one of the fooles in Israel: now therefore, I pray thee, speake vnto the king, for he will not withhold me from thee.

14 Howbeit hee would not hearken vnto her voice, but being stronger then shee, forced her, and lay with her.

15 ¶ Then Amnon hated her † exceedingly, so that the hatred wherwith he hated her, was greater then the loue wherewith hee had loued her: And Amnon said vnto her, Arise, be gone.

16 And she said vnto him, There is no cause: this euill in sending me away, is greater then the other that thou diddest vnto me: But he would not hearken vnto her.

17 Then hee called his seruant that ministred vnto him, and said, Put now this *woman* out from mee, and bolt the doore after her.

18 And shee had a garment of diuers colours vpon her: for with such robes were the Kings daughters, that were virgins, apparelled. Then his seruant brought her out, and bolted the doore after her.

19 ¶ And Tamar put ashes on her head, and rent her garment of diuers colours that was on her, and layde her hand on her head, and went on, crying.

20 And Absalom her brother sayde vnto her, Hath Amnon thy brother beene with thee? But holde nowe thy peace, my sister: he is thy brother, † regard not this thing. So Tamar remained † desolate in her brother Absaloms house.

21 ¶ But when King Dauid heard of all these things, he was very wroth.

22 And Absalom spake vnto his brother Amnon neither good nor bad: for Absalom hated Amnon, because he had forced his sister Tamar.

23 ¶ And it came to passe after two full yeeres, that Absalom had sheepe-shearers in Baal-Hazor, which is beside Ephraim: and Absalom inuited all the kings sonnes.

24 And Absalom came to the King,

and said, Behold now, thy seruant hath sheepe-shearers, Let the King, I beseech thee, and his seruants, goe with thy seruant.

25 And the King sayde to Absalom, Nay, my sonne, let vs not all now goe, lest we be chargeable vnto thee. And he pressed him: howbeit he would not goe, but blessed him.

26 Then said Absalom, If not, I pray thee, let my brother Amnon goe with vs. And the King said vnto him, Why should he goe with thee?

27 But Absalom pressed him, that he let Amnon and all the kings sonnes goe with him.

28 ¶ Now Absalom had commanded his seruants, saying, Marke yee now when Amnons heart is merrie with wine, and when I say vnto you, Smite Amnon, then kill him, feare not: ‖ haue not I commanded you? be couragious, and be † valiant.

29 And the seruants of Absalom did vnto Amnon as Absalom had commanded: then all the Kings sonnes arose, and euery man † gate him vp vpon his mule, and fled.

30 ¶ And it came to passe while they were in the way, that tidings came to Dauid, saying, Absalom hath slaine all the Kings sonnes, and there is not one of them left.

31 Then the king arose, and tare his garments, and lay on the earth: and all his seruants stoode by with their clothes rent.

32 And Ionadab the sonne of Shimeah Dauids brother, answered and said, Let not my lord suppose that they haue slaine all the yong men the Kings sonnes; for Amnon onely is dead: for by the † appointment of Absalom this hath beene ‖ determined, from the day that he forced his sister Tamar.

33 Now therefore let not my lord the King take the thing to his heart, to thinke that all the Kings sonnes are dead: for Amnon onely is dead.

34 But Absalom fled: and the yong man that kept the watch, lift vp his eyes, and looked, and behold, there came much people by the way of the hill side behind him.

35 And Ionadab said vnto the king, Behold, the kings sonnes come: † as thy seruant said, so it is.

36 And it came to passe assoone as hee had made an ende of speaking, that behold,

† Heb. humble me.
* Leuit. 18. 9.
† Heb. It ought not so to be done.

† Heb. with great hatred greatly.

† Heb. set not thine heart.
† Heb. and desolate.

† Or, will you not, since I haue commanded you?
† Heb. sonnes of valour.

† Heb. rode.

† Heb. mouth
‖ Or, setled.

† Heb. according to the word of thy seruant.

behold, the kings sonnes came, and lift vp their voice, and wept; and the King also and all his seruants wept †very sore.

† Hebr. with a great weeping greatly.

37 ¶ But Absalom fled, and went to Talmai the sonne of ||Ammihud king of Geshur : and *Dauid* mourned for his sonne euery day.

|| Or, Ammihur.

38 So Absalom fled, and went to Geshur, and was there three yeeres.

39 And *the soule of* king Dauid ||longed to goe foorth vnto Absalom : for he was comforted concerning Amnon, seeing he was dead.

|| Or, was consumed.

CHAP. XIIII.

1 Ioab, suborning a widow of Tekoah, by a parable to incline the Kings heart to fetch home Absalom, bringeth him to Hierusalem. 25 Absaloms beautie, haire, and children. 28 After two yeres, Absalom by Ioab is brought into the Kings presence.

Ow Ioab the sonne of Zeruiah, perceiued that the kings heart *was* toward Absalom.

2 And Ioab sent to Tekoah, and fetcht thence a wise woman, and said vnto her, I pray thee, faine thy selfe to be a mourner, and put on now mourning apparel, and anoint not thy selfe with oile, but be as a woman that had a long time mourned for the dead:

3 And come to the king, and speake on this maner vnto him : so Ioab put the words in her mouth.

4 ¶ And when the woman of Tekoah spake to the king, shee fell on her face to the ground, and did obeysance, and said, †Helpe, O king.

† Hebr. saue.

5 And the king said vnto her, What aileth thee? And she answered, I am indeed a widow woman, and mine husband is dead.

6 And thy handmayd had two sonnes, and they two stroue together in the field, and there was †none to part them, but the one smote the other, and slew him.

† Hebr. no deliuerer betweene them.

7 And behold, the whole family is risen against thine handmayd, and they said, Deliuer him that smote his brother, that we may kill him, for the life of his brother whom he slew, and we will destroy the heire also : and so they shall quench my cole which is left, and shall not leaue to my husband *neither* name nor remainder †vpon the earth.

† Hebr. vpon the face of the earth.

8 And the king saide vnto the woman, Goe to thine house, and I will giue charge concerning thee.

9 And the woman of Tekoah said vnto the king, My lord, O king, the iniquitie *bee* on mee, and on my fathers house : and the king and his throne *bee* guiltlesse.

10 And the king said, Whosoeuer saith *ought* vnto thee, bring him to mee, and he shall not touch thee any more.

11 Then said she, I pray thee, let the king remember the LORD thy God, †that thou wouldest not suffer the reuengers of blood to destroy any more, lest they destroy my sonne. And he said, As the LORD liueth, there shall not one haire of thy sonne fall to the earth.

† Hebr. that the reuenger of blood doe not multiply to destroy.

12 Then the woman said, Let thine handmayd, I pray thee, speake one word vnto my lord the king. And hee said, Say on.

13 And the woman said, Wherefore then hast thou thought such a thing against the people of God? For the king doeth speake this thing as one which is faulty, in that the king doeth not fetch home againe his banished.

14 For we must needs die, and are as water spilt on the ground, which cannot bee gathered vp againe : ||neither doeth God respect any person, yet doeth he deuise meanes, that his banished bee not expelled from him.

|| Or, because God hath not taken away his life, he hath also deuised meanes, &c.

15 Now therefore that I am come to speake of this thing vnto my lord the king, *it is* because the people haue made me afraid : and thy handmayd said, I will now speake vnto the king; it may bee that the king will performe the request of his handmayd.

16 For the king wil heare, to deliuer his handmayd out of the hand of the man *that would* destroy mee, and my sonne together out of the inheritance of God :

17 Then thine handmayd said, The word of my lord the king shall now be †comfortable : for as an Angel of God, so *is* my lord the king †to discerne good and bad : therfore the LORD thy God will be with thee.

† Hebr. for rest.
† Hebr. to heare.

18 Then the king answered and said vnto the woman, Hide not from me, I pray thee, the thing that I shall aske thee. And the woman said, Let my lord the king now speake.

19 And the king said, Is not the hand

hand of Ioab with thee in all this?
And the woman answered and said, As
thy soule liueth, my lord the king, none
can turne to the right hand or to the left
from ought that my lord the king hath
spoken : for thy seruant Ioab, hee bade
me, and he put all these wordes in the
mouth of thine handmaid :

20 To fetch about this forme of
speech hath thy seruant Ioab done this
thing: and my lord *is* wise, according to
the wisedome of an Angel of God, to
know all things that *are* in the earth.

21 ¶ And the king said vnto Ioab,
Behold now, I haue done this thing:
goe therefore, bring the yong man Absalom againe.

† Heb. bles-
sed.

22 And Ioab fell to the ground on
his face, & bowed himselfe, and † thanked the king : and Ioab said, To day thy
seruant knoweth that I haue found
grace in thy sight, my lord O king, in
that the king hath fulfilled the request of
‖his seruant.

‖ Or, thy.

23 So Ioab arose, and went to Geshur, & brought Absalom to Ierusalem.

24 And the king said, Let him turne
to his owne house, & let him not see my
face. So Absalom returned to his owne
house, and sawe not the kings face.

† Heb. and
as Absa-
lom there
was not a
beautifull
man in all
Israel, to
praise
greatly.

25 ¶ † But in all Israel there was
none to be so much praised as Absalom,
for his beautie : from the sole of his foot
euen to the crowne of his head, there
was no blemish in him.

26 And when he polled his head, (for
it was at euery yeres end that he polled
it : because *the haire* was heauy on him,
therefore he polled it) hee weighed the
haire of his head at two hundred shekels after the kings weight.

27 And vnto Absalom there were
borne three sonnes, and one daughter,
whose name *was* Tamar : shee was a
woman of a faire countenance.

28 ¶ So Absalom dwelt two full
yeeres in Ierusalem, and saw not the
kings face.

29 Therefore Absalom sent for Ioab, to haue sent him to the king, but hee
would not come to him : and when hee
sent againe the second time, hee would
not come.

† Heb. neere
my place.

30 Therefore hee said vnto his seruants, See, Ioabs field is † neere mine,
and he hath barley there: goe, and set it
on fire : and Absaloms seruants set the
field on fire.

31 Then Ioab arose, and came to
Absalom vnto his house, and said vnto
him, Wherefore haue thy seruants set
my field on fire?

32 And Absalom answered Ioab,
Behold, I sent vnto thee, saying, come
hither, that I may send thee to the king
to say, Wherefore am I come from Geshur? It had bene good for mee *to haue
bene* there still : now therefore let me see
the kings face : and if there bee any iniquitie in me, let him kill me.

33 So Ioab came to the King, and
told him : and when hee had called for
Absalom, he came to the king, and bowed himselfe on his face to the ground before the king, and the King kissed Absalom.

CHAP. XV.

1 Absalom, by faire speeches and courtesies,
stealeth the hearts of Israel. 7 Vnder pretence
of a vow he obtaineth leaue to go to Hebron.
10 He maketh there a great conspiracie. 13
Dauid vpon the newes fleeth from Ierusalem.
19 Ittai would not leaue him. 24 Zadok and
Abiathar are sent backe with the Arke. 30
Dauid and his companie go vp mount Oliuet
weeping. 31 He curseth Ahithophels counsel.
32 Hushai is sent backe with instructions.

Nd it came to passe after
this, that Absalom prepa-
red him charets and hor-
ses, and fiftie men to runne
before him.

2 And Absalom rose vp earely, and
stood beside the way of the gate: and it
was so, that when any man that had a
controuersie, † came to the king for iudgment, then Absalom called vnto him,
and said, Of what citie *art* thou? And
he said, Thy seruant *is* of one of the
tribes of Israel.

† Hebr. to
come.

3 And Absalom said vnto him, See,
thy matters *are* good & right, but there
is ‖no man deputed of the king to heare
thee.

‖ Or, none
will heare
you from the
king down-
ward.

4 Absalom said moreouer, Oh that
I were made Iudge in the land, that
euery man which hath any suit or cause,
might come vnto me, and I would do
him iustice.

5 And it was so, that when any man
came nigh to him, to doe him obeisance,
he put foorth his hand, and tooke him,
and kissed him.

6 And on this maner did Absalom
to all Israel, that came to the King for
iudgement: so Absalom stole the hearts
of the men of Israel.

7 ¶ And

7 ¶ And it came to passe after four-tie yeeres, that Absalom said vnto the king, I pray thee, let mee goe and pay my vow which I haue vowed vnto the LORD in Hebron.

8 For thy seruant vowed a vowe while I abode at Geshur in Syria, say-ing, If the LORD shall bring mee a-gaine in deed to Ierusalem, then I will serue the LORD.

9 And the king said vnto him, Goe in peace. So he arose, and went to He-bron.

10 ¶ But Absalom sent spies tho-rowout all the tribes of Israel, saying, As soone as yee heare the sound of the trumpet, then yee shall say, Absalom reigneth in Hebron.

11 And with Absalom went two hundred men out of Ierusalem, that were called, and they went in their sim-plicitie, and they knew not any thing.

12 And Absalom sent for Ahithophel the Gilonite, Dauids counseller, from his citie, euen from Giloh, while he offe-red sacrifices : and the conspiracie was strong, for the people encreased conti-nually with Absalom.

13 ¶ And there came a messenger to Dauid, saying, The hearts of the men of Israel are after Absalom.

14 And Dauid said vnto all his ser-uants that were with him at Ierusa-lem, Arise, and let vs flee; for wee shall not else escape from Absalom : make speede to depart, lest hee ouertake vs † Heb. thrust suddenly, and † bring euill vpon vs, and smite the city with the edge of the sword.

15 And the kings seruants said vnto the king, Behold, thy seruants are readie to doe whatsoeuer my lord the king shall † Heb. chuse. † appoint.

16 And the king went foorth, and all † Heb. at his his houshold † after him : and the King feete. left tenne women, which were concu-bines, to keepe the house.

17 And the king went forth, and all the people after him, and taried in a place that was farre off.

18 And all his seruants passed on be-side him : and all the Cherethites, and all the Pelethites, and all the Gittites, sixe hundred men, which came after him from Gath, passed on before the king.

19 ¶ Then said the king to Ittai the Gittite, Wherefore goest thou also with vs ? Returne to thy place, and abide with the King : for thou art a stranger, and also an exile.

20 Whereas thou camest but yester-day, should I this day † make thee goe † Heb. mak vp and downe with vs ? Seeing I goe thee wander whither I may, returne thou, and take in going ? backe thy brethren : mercie and trueth be with thee.

21 And Ittai answered the King, and said, As the LORD liueth, and as my lord the king liueth, surely in what place my lord the king shall be, whether in death or life, euen there also will thy seruant be.

22 And Dauid said to Ittai, Goe, and passe ouer. And Ittai the Gittite passed ouer, and all his men, and all the little ones that were with him.

23 And all the countrey wept with a loude voice, and all the people passed ouer : the King also himselfe passed o-uer the brooke || Kidron, and all the peo-|| Called Ioh ple passed ouer, toward the way of the 18. 1. Ce-wildernesse. dron.

24 ¶ And loe, Zadok also, and all the Leuites were with him, bearing the Arke of the Couenant of God, and they set downe the Arke of God ; and Abia-thar went vp, vntill all the people had done passing out of the citie.

25 And the King said vnto Zadok, Cary backe the Arke of God into the ci-tie : if I shall finde fauour in the eyes of the LORD, he wil bring me againe, and shew me both it, and his habitation.

26 But if he thus say, I haue no de-light in thee : beholde, here am I, let him doe to me, as seemeth good vnto him.

27 The king said also vnto Zadok the Priest, * Art not thou a Seer ? Re-* 1. Sam. turne into the citie in peace, and your 9. 9. two sonnes with you, Ahimaaz thy sonne, and Ionathan the sonne of A-biathar.

28 See, I will tarie in the plaine of the wildernesse, vntill there come word from you to certifie me.

29 Zadok therefore and Abiathar caried the Arke of God againe to Ieru-salem ; and they taried there.

30 ¶ And Dauid went vp by the ascent of mount Oliuet, † and wept as † Heb. goin he went vp, and had his head couered, vp and wee and he went barefoote, and all the peo-ping. ple that was with him, couered euery man his head, and they went vp, wee-ping as they went vp.

31 ¶ And one tolde Dauid, saying, Ahithophel is among the conspirators with Absalom. And Dauid sayde, O LORD, I pray thee turne the counsell of

of Ahithophel into foolishnesse.

32 ¶ And it came to passe, that *when* Dauid was come to the top *of the mount*, where he worshipped God, behold, Hushai the Archite came to meet him, with his coat rent, and earth vpon his head:

33 Vnto whom Dauid said, If thou passest on with me, then thou shalt be a burden vnto me.

34 But if thou returne to the citie, and say vnto Absalom, I wil be thy seruant, O king : *as I haue bene* thy fathers seruant hitherto, so will I now also be thy seruant : then mayest thou for mee defeat the counsell of Ahithophel.

35 And *hast thou* not there with thee Zadok , and Abiathar the Priests ? therefore it shall be, that what thing soeuer thou shalt heare out of the kings house, thou shalt tell *it* to Zadok and Abiathar the Priests.

36 Behold, *they haue* there with them their two sonnes, Ahimaaz Zadoks *sonne*, and Ionathan Abiathars *sonne :* and by them ye shall send vnto me euery thing that ye can heare.

37 So Hushai Dauids friend came into the citie, and Absalom came into Ierusalem.

CHAP. XVI.

1 Ziba by presents and false suggestions, obtaineth his masters inheritance. 5 At Bahurim Shimei curseth Dauid. 9 Dauid with patience abstaineth, and restraineth others from reuenge. 15 Hushai insinuateth himselfe into Absaloms counsaile. 20 Ahithophels counsaile.

And when Dauid was a little past the top *of the hill*, Beholde , Ziba the seruant of Mephibosheth met him with a couple of asses sadled, and vpon them two hundred *loaues* of bread , and an hundred bunches of raisins, and an hundred of summer fruits, and a bottell of wine.

2 And the King saide vnto Ziba, What meanest thou by these ? And Ziba saide, The asses bee for the kings houshold to ride on, and the bread and summer fruit for the yong men to eate, and the wine, that such as be faint in the wildernesse, may drinke.

3 And the king said, And where is thy masters sonne ? and Ziba said vnto the king, Behold, he abideth at Ierusalem : for hee said, To day shall the house of Israel restore mee the kingdome of my father.

4 Then said the king to Ziba, Behold, thine are all that pertained vnto Mephibosheth. And Ziba saide, † I humbly beseech thee *that* I may finde grace in thy sight, my lord, O king.

5 ¶ And when king Dauid came to Bahurim, behold, thence came out a man of the family of the house of Saul, whose name was Shimei the sonne of Gera: ‖ hee came foorth, and cursed still as he came.

6 And he cast stones at Dauid, and at all the seruants of king Dauid : and all the people, and all the mighty men were on his right hand, and on his left.

7 And thus said Shimei when hee cursed, Come out, come out thou † bloody man, and thou man of Belial :

8 The Lord hath returned vpon thee all the blood of the house of Saul, in whose stead thou hast raigned, and the Lord hath deliuered the kingdome into the hand of Absalom thy sonne : and † behold, thou *art taken* to thy mischiefe, because thou *art* a bloody man.

9 ¶ Then said Abishai the sonne of Zeruiah vnto the king, Why should this *dead dogge curse my lord the king ? let mee goe ouer, I pray thee, and take off his head.

10 And the king said, What haue I to doe with you, ye sonnes of Zeruiah ? So let him curse, because the Lord hath said vnto him, Curse Dauid. Who shall then say, Wherefore hast thou done so ?

11 And Dauid said to Abishai, and to all his seruants, Beholde, my sonne which came foorth of my bowels, seeketh my life : how much more now *may* this Beniamite *doe it ?* let him alone, and let him curse : for the Lord hath bidden him.

12 It may bee that the Lord will looke on mine ‖ affliction, and that the Lord will requite good for his cursing this day.

13 And as Dauid and his men went by the way, Shimei went along on the hilles side ouer against him, and cursed as hee went, and threw stones at him, and † cast dust.

14 And the king, and all the people that were with him, came weary, and refreshed themselues there.

15 ¶ And Absalom and al the people the

† *Hebr.* I doe obeysance.

‖ *Or, he still came foorth and cursed.*

† *Hebr. man of blood.*

† *Hebr. behold thee in thy euill.*

1. Sam. 24. 15. chap. 3. 8.

‖ *Or, teares, Hebr. eye.*

† *Hebr. dusted him with dust.*

the men of Israel, came to Ierusalem, and Ahithophel with him.

16 And it came to passe when Hushai the Archite, Dauids friend, was come vnto Absalom, that Hushai said vnto Absalom, †God saue the king, God saue the king.

† *Heb. let the king liue.*

17 And Absalom said to Hushai, *Is* this thy kindnesse to thy friend? Why wentest thou not with thy friend?

18 And Hushai said vnto Absalom, Nay, but whom the LORD and this people, and all the men of Israel chuse, his will I bee, and with him will I abide.

19 And againe, whom should I serue? should I not *serue* in the presence of his sonne? as I haue serued in thy fathers presence, so will I be in thy presence.

20 ¶ Then said Absalom to Ahithophel, Giue counsell among you what we shall doe.

21 And Ahithophel said vnto Absalom, Goe in vnto thy fathers concubines, which he hath left to keepe the house, and all Israel shall heare that thou art abhorred of thy father, then shall the hands of all that are with thee be strong.

22 So they spread Absalom a tent vpon the top of the house, and Absalom went in vnto his fathers concubines, in the sight of all Israel.

23 And the counsell of Ahithophel which he counselled in those dayes, was as if a man had enquired at the †Oracle of God: so *was* all the counsell of Ahithophel, both with Dauid and with Absalom.

Heb. word.

CHAP. XVII.

1 Ahithophels counsell is ouerthrowen by Hushais, according to Gods appointment. 15 Secret intelligence is sent vnto Dauid. 23 Ahithophel hangeth himselfe. 25 Amasa is made captaine. 27 Dauid at Mahanaim is furnished with prouision.

MOreouer Ahithophel said vnto Absalom, Let mee nowe chuse out twelue thousand men, and I will arise and pursue after Dauid this night.

2 And I wil come vpon him while hee is wearie and weake handed, and wil make him afraid: and all the people that are with him shall flee, and I will smite the king onely.

3 And I wil bring backe all the people vnto thee: the man whom thou seekest *is* as if all returned: so all the people shall be in peace.

4 And the saying †pleased Absalom well, and all the Elders of Israel.

† *Hebr. we right in the eyes of &c.*

5 Then said Absalom, Call now Hushai the Archite also, and let vs heare likewise †what he saith.

† *Hebr. wh is in his mouth.*

6 And when Hushai was come to Absalom, Absalom spake vnto him, saying, Ahithophel hath spoken after this maner: shall we doe after his †saying? if not, speake thou.

† *Heb. wor*

7 And Hushai said vnto Absalom, The counsell that Ahithophel hath †giuen, *is* not good at this time.

† *Heb. cou selled.*

8 For, (said Hushai,) thou knowest thy father and his men, that they *bee* mightie men, and they *be* †chafed in their minds, as a beare robbed of her whelps in the field: and thy father *is* a man of warre, and will not lodge with the people.

† *Heb. bitt of soule.*

9 Behold, he is hid now in some pit, or in some *other* place: and it wil come to passe when some of them bee †ouerthrowen at the first, that whosoeuer heareth it, wil say, There is a slaughter among the people that followe Absalom.

† *Heb. fal len.*

10 And he also *that is* valiant, whose heart *is* as the heart of a Lyon, shall vtterly melt: for all Israel knoweth that thy father is a mightie man, and they which be with him *are* valiant men.

11 Therefore I counsell, that all Israel be generally gathered vnto thee, from Dan euen to Beer-sheba, as the sand *that is* by the sea for multitude, and †that thou goe to battell in thine owne person.

† *Heb. the thy face o presence &c.*

12 So shall wee come vpon him in some place where he shall be found, and we will light vpon him as the dew falleth on the ground: and of him and of all the men that *are* with him, there shall not be left so much as one.

13 Moreouer, if hee be gotten into a citie, then shall all Israel bring ropes to that city, and we will draw it into the riuer, vntill there be not one small stone found there.

14 And Absalom and all the men of Israel said, The counsell of Hushai the Archite, *is* better then the counsell of Ahithophel: For the LORD had †appointed to defeate the good counsell of Ahitho-

† *Heb. co manded.*

Ahithophel, to the intent that the Lord might bring euill vpon Absalom.

15 ¶ Then said Hushai vnto Zadok and to Abiathar the Priestes, Thus and thus did Ahithophel counsell Absalom and the Elders of Israel, and thus and thus haue I counselled.

16 Now therefore send quickly, and tell Dauid, saying, Lodge not this night in the plaines of the wildernes, but speedily passe ouer, lest the King be swallowed vp, and all the people that are with him.

17 Now Ionathan and Ahimaaz stayed by En-rogel : (for they might not be seene to come into the citie) and a wench went and tolde them : and they went, and tolde king Dauid.

18 Neuerthelesse, a ladde saw them, and tolde Absalom : but they went both of them away qnickely, and came to a mans house in Bahurim, which had a Well in his court, whither they went downe.

19 And the woman tooke and spread a couering ouer the welles mouth, and spread ground corne thereon ; and the thing was not knowen.

20 And when Absaloms seruants came to the woman to the house, they said, Where is Ahimaaz and Ionathan? And the woman said vnto them, They be gone ouer the brooke of water. And when they had sought, and could not finde them, they returned to Ierusalem.

21 And it came to passe after they were departed, that they came vp out of the Well, and went and tolde king Dauid, and said vnto Dauid, Arise, and passe qnickely ouer the water : for thus hath Ahithophel counselled against you.

22 Then Dauid arose, and all the people that were with him, and they passed ouer Iordane : by the morning light there lacked not one of them that was not gone ouer Iordane.

† Heb. done.

23 ¶ And when Ahithophel sawe that his counsell was not †followed, he sadled his asse, and arose, and gate him home to his house, to his citie, and †put his houshold in order, and hanged himselfe, and died, and was buried in the sepulchre of his father.

† Heb. gaue charge concerning his house.

24 Then Dauid came to Mahanaim : and Absalom passed ouer Iordane, he and all the men of Israel with him.

25 ¶ And Absalom made Amasa captaine of the hoste in stead of Ioab : which Amasa was a mans sonne whose name was Ithra an Israelite, that went in to Abigail the daughter of Nahash, sister to Zeruiah Ioabs mother.

26 So Israel and Absalom pitched in the land of Gilead.

27 ¶ And it came to passe when Dauid was come to Mahanaim, that Shobi the sonne of Nahash of Rabbah of the children of Ammon, and Machir the sonne of Ammiel of Lodebar, and Barzillai the Gileadite, of Rogelim,

28 Brought beds, and ‖basins, and earthen vessels, and wheat, and barley, and floure, and parched corne, & beanes, and lentiles, and parched pulse,

‖ Or, cups.

29 And honie, and butter, and sheepe, and cheese of kine for Dauid, and for the people that were with him, to eate : for they said, The people is hungrie, and wearie, and thirstie in the wildernesse.

CHAP. XVIII.

1 Dauid viewing the armies in their march, giueth them charge of Absalom. 6 The Israelites are sore smitten in the wood of Ephraim. 9 Absalom hanging in an Oke, is slaine by Ioab, and cast into a pit. 18 Absaloms place. 19 Ahimaaz and Cushi bring tidings to Dauid. 33 Dauid mourneth for Absalom.

And Dauid numbred the people that were with him, and set captaines of thousands, and captaines of hundreds ouer them.

2 And Dauid sent forth a third part of the people vnder the hand of Ioab, and a third part vnder the hand of Abishai the sonne of Zeruiah Ioabs brother, and a third part vnder the hand of Ittai the Gittite : and the king said vnto the people, I will surely goe foorth with you my selfe also.

3 But the people answered, Thou shalt not goe foorth : for if we flee away, they will not care for vs, neither if halfe of vs die will they †care for vs : but now thou art †worth ten thousand of vs : therefore now it is better that thou †succour vs out of the citie.

† Heb. set their heart on vs.
† Heb. as ten thousand of vs.
† Heb. be to succour.

4 And the King sayde vnto them, What seemeth you best, I will doe. And the King stood by the gate side, and all the people came out by hundreds, and by thousands.

5 And the king commanded Ioab, and

and Abishai, and Ittai, saying, *Deale* gently for my sake with the yong man, *euen* with Absalom. And all the people heard when the king gaue all the captaines charge concerning Absalom.

6 ¶ So the people went out into the field against Israel : and the battell was in the wood of Ephraim,

7 Where the people of Israel were slaine before the seruants of Dauid, and there was there a great slaughter that day of twenty thousand *men*.

8 For the battell was there scattered ouer the face of all the countrey : and the wood †deuoured more people that day, then the sword deuoured.

9 ¶ And Absalom met the seruants of Dauid ; and Absalom rode vpon a mule, and the mule went vnder the thicke boughs of a great Oke, and his head caught hold of the Oke, and hee was taken vp betweene the heauen and the earth, and the mule that *was* vnder him, went away.

10 And a certaine man saw *it*, and told Ioab, and said, Behold, I saw Absalom hanged in an Oke.

11 And Ioab said vnto the man that told him, And behold; thou sawest *him*, and why didst thou not smite him there to the ground, and I would haue giuen thee tenne *shekels* of siluer, and a girdle ?

12 And the man saide vnto Ioab, Though I should †receiue a thousand *shekels* of siluer in mine hand, *yet* would I not put foorth mine hand against the Kings sonne : for in our hearing the King charged thee, and Abishai, and Ittai, saying, †Beware that none *touch* the yong man Absalom.

13 Otherwyse, I should haue wrought falshood against mine *owne* life : for there is no matter hid from the King, and thou thy selfe wouldest haue set thy selfe against *me*.

14 Then said Ioab, I may not tary thus †with thee. And hee tooke three darts in his hand, and thrust them thorow the heart of Absalom, while hee was yet aliue in the †midst of the Oke.

15 And ten yong men that bare Ioabs armour, compassed about and smote Absalom, and slew him.

16 And Ioab blew the trumpet, and the people returned from pursuing after Israel : for Ioab helde backe the people.

17 And they tooke Absalom, and

cast him into a great pit in the wood, and layd a very great heape of stones vpon him : and all Israel fled euery one to his tent.

18 ¶ Now Absalom in his life time had taken and reared vp for himselfe a pillar, which *is* in *the Kings dale : for hee said, I haue no sonne to keepe my name in remembrance : And hee called the pillar after his owne name, and it is called vnto this day, Absaloms place.

19 ¶ Then said Ahimaaz the sonne of Zadok, Let mee now runne, and beare the King tidings, how that the LORD hath †auenged him of his enemies.

20 And Ioab said vnto him, Thou shalt not †beare tidings this day, but thou shalt beare tidings another day : but this day thou shalt beare no tidings, because the Kings sonne is dead.

21 Then said Ioab to Cushi, Goe tell the King what thou hast seene. And Cushi bowed himselfe vnto Ioab, and ranne.

22 Then said Ahimaaz the sonne of Zadok yet againe to Ioab, But †howsoeuer, let mee, I pray thee, also runne after Cushi. And Ioab said, Wherefore wilt thou runne, my sonne, seeing that thou hast no tidings ||ready ?

23 But howsoeuer, (*said he*) let mee runne : And hee said vnto him, Runne. Then Ahimaaz ranne by the way of the plaine, and ouerranne Cushi.

24 And Dauid sate betweene the two gates : and the watchman went vp to the roofe ouer the gate vnto the wall, and lift vp his eyes, and looked, and behold, a man running alone.

25 And the watchman cried, and told the King. And the king said, If he *bee* alone, *there is* tidings in his mouth. And he came apace, and drew neere.

26 And the watchman saw another man running, and the watchman called vnto the porter, and said, Behold, *another* man running alone. And the King said, He also bringeth tidings.

27 And the watchman said, †Mee thinketh the running of the foremost is like the running of Ahimaaz the sonne of Zadok. And the King said, Hee *is* a good man, and commeth with good tidings.

28 And Ahimaaz called, and said vnto the King, ||All is well. And hee fell downe to the earth vpon his face before the King, and saide, Blessed *bee* the
                                                            LORD

Hebr. multiplied to deuoure.

†Heb. weigh vpon mine hand.

†Hebr. beware whosoeuer ye be, of &c.

†Hebr. before thee.

†Heb. heart.

*Gene. 14. 17.

†Hebr. iudged him from the hand &c.

†Hebr. bo man of tidings.

†Hebr. be what may.

|| Or, conuenient.

†Hebr. I see the running.

|| Or, peace be to thee Hebr. pea

eb. shut

ebr. Is
re peace?

ebr. ti-
ngs is
night.

LORD thy God which hath †deliue-red vp the men that lift vp their hande against my lord the King.

29 And the king said , † Is the yong man Absalom safe? And Ahimaaz an-swered, When Ioab sent the kings ser-uant, and *me* thy seruant, I saw a great tumult, but I knew not what *it was*.

30 And the king said *vnto him,* Turne aside *and* stand here. And hee turned a-side, and stood still.

31 And behold, Cushi came, and Cushi said, † Tidings my lord the king: for the LORD hath auenged thee this day of all them that rose vp against thee.

32 And the king said vnto Cushi, Is the yong man Absalom safe? And Cu-shi answered , The enemies of my lord the king, and all that rise against thee to doe *thee* hurt, be as that yong man is.

33 ¶ And the king was much moued, and went vp to the chamber ouer the gate, and wept: and as he went, thus hee said , O my sonne Absalom , my sonne, my sonne Absalom : would God I had died for thee , O Absalom , my sonne, my sonne.

CHAP. XIX.

1 Ioab causeth the king to cease his mourning. 9 The Israelites are earnest to bring the king backe. 11 Dauid sendeth to the Priests to in-cite them of Iudah. 18 Shimei is pardoned. 24 Mephibosheth excused. 32 Barzillai dis-missed, Chimham his sonne is taken into the Kings familie. 41 The Israelites expostulate with Iudah for bringing home the King without them.

Nd it was told Ioab, Be-holde , the king weepeth and mourneth for Absa-lom.

2 And the †victorie that day was turned into mourning vnto all the people : for the people heard say that day, how the king was grieued for his sonne.

3 And the people gate them by stealth that day into the citie, as people beeing ashamed steale away when they flee in battell.

4 But the king couered his face, and the king cried with a loud voyce, O my sonne Absalom, O Absalom my sonne, my sonne.

5 And Ioab came into the house to the king, and said, Thou hast shamed this day the faces of all thy seruants,

Ieb. sal-
tion or de-
erance.

which this day haue saued thy life, and the liues of thy sonnes, & of thy daugh-ters, and the liues of thy wiues , and the liues of thy concubines,

6 † In that thou louest thine ene-mies, and hatest thy friends ; for thou hast declared this day, †that thou re-gardest neither princes , nor seruants : for this day I perceiue, that if Absalom had liued, and all we had died this day, then it had pleased thee well.

7 Now therefore arise, goe foorth, and speake †comfortably vnto thy ser-uants : for I sweare by the LORD, if thou goe not forth, there wil not tarie one with thee this night, and that will be worse vnto thee then all the euill that befell thee from thy youth vntill now.

8 Then the King rose , and sate in the gate: and they told vnto all the peo-ple, saying, Behold, the king doth sit in the gate : and all the people came before the king : for Israel had fled euery man to his tent.

9 ¶ And all the people were at strife throughout all the tribes of Israel, say-ing, The king saued vs out of the hand of our enemies, and he deliuered vs out of the hand of the Philistines, and now he is fled out of the land for Absalom.

10 And Absalom whom wee anoin-ted ouer vs, is dead in battell : nowe therefore why †speake ye not a word of bringing the king backe?

11 ¶ And King Dauid sent to Za-dok and to Abiathar the priests, saying, Speake vnto the Elders of Iudah, saying, Why are ye the last to bring the king backe to his house? (seeing the speech of all Israel is come to the king, euen to his house.)

12 Yee *are* my brethren, Yee *are* my bones and my flesh : wherfore then are ye the last to bring backe the king?

13 And say ye to Amasa: *Art* thou not of my bone, and of my flesh? God do so to me, and more also, if thou be not cap-taine of the hoste before me continually in the roome of Ioab.

14 And he bowed the heart of all the men of Iudah, euen as *the heart* of one man, so that they sent *this word* vnto the King, Returne thou and all thy ser-uants.

15 So the King returned, and came to Iordan : and Iudah came to Gilgal, to goe to meet the King, to conduct the king ouer Iordane.

16 ¶ And *Shimei the sonne of
Gera,

† *Heb. by lo-*
uing, &c.
† *Heb. that*
princes or
seruants are
not to thee.

† *Heb. to the*
heart of thy
seruants.

† *Heb are ye*
silent?

* *1 King.*
2. 8.

Gera, a Beniamite, which *wass* of Bahurim, hasted, & came downe with the
men of Iudah, to meet King Dauid.

* Chap.
16. 1.

17 And there *were* a thousand men of
Beniamin with him, and *Ziba the seruant of the house of Saul, and his fifteene sonnes and his twenty seruants
with him, and they went ouer Iordane
before the King.

18 And there went ouer a ferry-boat
to cary ouer the kings houshold, and to
doe †what he thought good : and Shimei the sonne of Gera fell downe before the king as he was come ouer Iordane ;

† Heb. the
good in his
eyes.

19 And said vnto the king, Let not
my lord impute iniquitie vnto me, neither do thou remember that which thy
seruant did peruersly the day that my
lord the king *went out of Ierusalem,
that the king should take it to his heart.

* Chap. 16.
13.

20 For thy seruant doeth know that
I haue sinned : therefore behold, I am
come the first this day of all the house of
Ioseph, to goe downe to meete my lord
the king.

21 But Abishai the sonne of Zeruiah
answered, and sayd, Shall not Shimei
be put to death for this, because hee cursed the LORDS Anointed?

22 And Dauid said, What haue I to
doe with you, yee sonnes of Zeruiah,
that yee should this day be aduersaries
vnto me? shall there any man be put to
death this day in Israel? for doe not I
know, that I *am* this day King ouer
Israel?

23 Therfore the king said vnto Shimei, Thou shalt not die : and the King
sware vnto him.

24 ¶ And Mephibosheth the sonne
of Saul came downe to meet the king,
and had neither dressed his feete, nor
trimmed his beard, nor washed his
clothes, from the day the King departed, vntill the day hee came againe in
peace.

25 And it came to passe when he was
come to Ierusalem to meete the King,
that the King sayd vnto him, Wherefore wentest not thou with me, Mephibosheth?

26 And hee answered, My lord O
king, my seruant deceiued mee ; for thy
seruant sayd, I will saddle me an asse
that I may ride thereon, and goe to the
king, because thy seruant is lame :

* Chap.
16. 3.

27 And *hee hath slandered thy seruant vnto my lord the king, but my lord

the King *is* as an Angel of God : doe
therefore what *is* good in thine eyes.

28 For all of my fathers house were
but †dead men before my lord the king:
yet diddest thou set thy seruant among
them that did eate at thine owne table:
what right therefore haue I yet to crie
any more vnto the king?

† Heb. me
of death.

29 And the king said vnto him, Why
speakest thou any more of thy matters?
I haue said, Thou and Ziba diuide
the land.

30 And Mephibosheth said vnto the
king, Yea, let him take all, forasmuch
as my lorde the king is come againe in
peace vnto his owne house.

31 ¶ And Barzillai the Gileadite
came downe from Rogelim, and went
ouer Iordane with the king, to conduct
him ouer Iordane.

32 Now Barzillai was a very aged
man, *euen* fourescore yeeres olde, and
*he had prouided the king of sustenance
while he lay at Mahanaim : for he *was* a
very great man.

* Chap. 1
27.

33 And the king said vnto Barzillai,
Come thou ouer with me, and I will
feede thee with me in Ierusalem.

34 And Barzillai sayde vnto the
king, †How long haue I to liue, that I
should goe vp with the King vnto Ierusalem?

† How ma
dayes are
yeeres of
life?

35 I *am* this day fourescore yeeres
olde : *and* can I discerne betweene good
and euill? Can thy seruant taste what
I eate, or what I drinke? can I heare
any more the voice of singing men and
singing women? wherfore then should
thy seruant bee yet a burden vnto my
lord the king?

36 Thy seruant will goe a little way
ouer Iordane with the king : and why
should the king recompense it me with
such a reward?

37 Let thy seruant, I pray thee,
turne backe againe, that I may die in
mine owne citie, and *be* buried by the
graue of my father, and of my mother :
but behold thy seruant Chimham, let
him go ouer with my lord the king, and
doe to him what shall seeme good vnto
thee.

38 And the king answered, Chimham shal goe ouer with me, and I will
doe to him that which shall seeme good
vnto thee : and whatsoeuer thou shalt
†require of me, that will I doe for thee.

† Heb. chu

39 And all the people went ouer
Iordane   and when the king was come
                                        ouer,

ouer, the king kissed Barzillai, and blessed him, and he returned vnto his owne place.

40 Then the King went on to Gilgal, and Chimham went on with him: and all the people of Iudah conducted the king, and also halfe the people of Israel.

41 ¶ And behold, all the men of Israel came to the king, and said vnto the king, Why haue our brethren the men of Iudah stollen thee away, and haue brought the King and his houshold, and all Dauids men with him, ouer Iordane?

42 And all the men of Iudah answered the men of Israel, Because the king is neere of kinne to vs: wherefore then be ye angrie for this matter? Haue we eaten at all of the kings cost? or hath he giuen vs any gift?

43 And the men of Israel answered the men of Iudah, and said, Wee haue ten parts in the king, and we haue also more *right* in Dauid then yee: why then did yee † despise vs, that our aduice should not be first had in bringing backe our king? And the wordes of the men of Iudah were fiercer then the words of the men of Israel.

CHAP. XX.

1 By occasion of the quarrell, Sheba maketh a party in Israel. 3 Dauids ten concubines are shut vp in perpetual prison. 4 Amasa made captaine ouer Iudah, is slaine by Ioab. 14 Ioab pursueth Sheba vnto Abel. 16 A wise woman saueth the citie by Shebaes head. 23 Dauids Officers.

Nd there happened to bee there a man of Belial, whose name *was* Sheba the sonne of Bichri, a Beniamite, & hee blew a trumpet, and said, Wee haue no part in Dauid, neither haue we inheritance in the sonne of Iesse: euery man to his tents, O Israel.

2 So euery man of Israel went vp from after Dauid, *and* followed Sheba the sonne of Bichri: but the men of Iudah claue vnto their king, from Iordane euen to Ierusalem.

3 ¶ And Dauid came to his house at Ierusalem, and the king tooke the ten women his *concubines, whom he had left to keep the house, and put them in †ward, and fed them, but went not in

vnto them: so they were †shut vp vnto the day of their death, †liuing in widowhood.

4 ¶ Then said the king to Amasa, †Assemble me the men of Iudah within three dayes, and be thou here present.

5 So Amasa went to assemble the men of Iudah; but hee taried longer then the set time which he had appointed him.

6 And Dauid said to Abishai, Now shall Sheba the sonne of Bichri doe vs more harme then did Absalom: take thou thy lords seruants, and pursue after him, lest he get him fenced cities, and †escape vs.

7 And there went out after him Ioabs men, and the *Cherethites, and the Pelethites, and all the mighty men: and they went out of Ierusalem, to pursue after Sheba the sonne of Bichri.

8 When they *were* at the great stone which *is* in Gibeon, Amasa went before them: and Ioabs garment that he had put on, was girded vnto him, and vpon it a girdle *with* a sword fastned vpon his loynes in the sheath thereof, and as hee went forth, it fell out.

9 And Ioab saide to Amasa, Art thou in health, my brother? And Ioab tooke Amasa by the beard with the right hand to kisse him.

10 But Amasa tooke no heed to the sword that *was* in Ioabs hand: so hee smote him therewith in the fifth *rib*, and shed out his bowels to the ground, and †strake him not againe, and he died: so Ioab and Abishai his brother pursued after Sheba the sonne of Bichri.

11 And one of Ioabs men stood by him, and said, He that fauoureth Ioab, and hee that *is* for Dauid, *let him goe* after Ioab.

12 And Amasa wallowed in blood in the mids of the high way: and when the man saw that all the people stood still, he remoued Amasa out of the high way into the field, and cast a cloth vpon him, when hee saw that euery one that came by him, stood still.

13 When he was remoued out of the high way, all the people went on after Ioab, to pursue after Sheba the sonne of Bichri.

14 ¶ And hee went thorow all the tribes of Israel vnto Abel, and to Bethmaachah, and all the Berites: and they were gathered together, and went also after him.

15 And

† *Hebr.* bound.
† *Hebr. in widowhood of life.*
† *Hebr. call.*

† *Hebr. deliuer himselfe from our eyes.*
* Chap. 8. 18.

† *Hebr. doubled not his stroke.*

ꞔr. set ꞓ light.

ꞔr. 16.

ꞔr. a ꞓ of ꞓ.

15 And they came and besieged him in Abel of Bethmaachah, and they cast vp a banke against the citie, and ‖it stood in the trench : and all the people that *were* with Ioab, † battered the wall, to throw *it* downe.

‖ Or, *it stood against the outmost wall*

† *Heb. marred to throw downe.*

16 ¶ Then cried a wise woman out of the citie, Heare, heare ; say, I pray you, vnto Ioab, Come neere hither, that I may speake with thee.

17 And when he was come neere vnto her, the woman said, *Art* thou Ioab? And he answered, I *am* he: Then shee said vnto him, Heare the words of thine handmaid. And he answered, I doe heare.

18 Then she spake, saying, ‖They were wont to speake in old time, saying, They shall surely aske counsell at Abel. and so they ended *the matter.*

‖ Or, *They plainly spake in the beginning, saying, surely they will aske of Abel; and so make an end*

19 I *am* one of them that are peaceable *and* faithfull in Israel: thou seekest to destroy a citie, and a mother in Israel : Why wilt thou swallow vp the inheritance of the LORD?

20 And Ioab answered and saide, Farre be it, farre be it from me, that I should swallow vp or destroy.

21 The matter is not so : but a man of mount Ephraim (Sheba the sonne of Bichri †by name) hath lift vp his hand against the king, *euen* against Dauid: deliuer him onely, and I will depart from the city. And the woman said vnto Ioab, Behold, his head shall be throwen to thee ouer the wall.

† *Heb. by his name.*

22 Then the woman went vnto all the people in her wisedome, and they cut off the head of Sheba the sonne of Bichri, and cast *it* out to Ioab: and hee blew a trumpet, and they †retired from the citie, euery man to his tent: & Ioab returned to Ierusalem vnto the king.

† *Heb. were scattered.*

23 ¶ Now *Ioab *was* ouer all the hoste of Israel, and Benaiah the sonne of Iehoiada *was* ouer the Cherethites, and ouer the Pelethites.

* Chap. 8. 16.

24 And Adoram *was* ouer the tribute, and Iehoshaphat the sonne of Ahilud *was* ‖Recorder.

25 And Sheua *was* scribe, and Zadok, and Abiathar *were* the Priests.

‖ Or, re-membrancer

26 And Ira also the Iairite, was ‖ a chiefe ruler about Dauid.

‖ Or, a prince.

CHAP. XXI.

1 The three yeeres famine for the Gibeonites, cease, by hanging seuen of Sauls sonnes. 10 Rizpahs kindnes vnto the dead. 12 Dauid burieth the bones of Saul and Ionathan in his fathers sepulchre. 15 Foure battels against the Philistines, wherein foure valiants of Dauid slay foure gyants.

THen there was a famine in the dayes of Dauid three yeeres, yeere after yeere, and Dauid †enquired of the LORD. And the LORD answered, *It is* for Saul, and for *his* bloodie house, because he slew the Gibeonites.

† *Heb.so the face*

2 And the king called the Gibeonites, and said vnto them, (now the Gibeonites were not of the children of Israel, but *of the remnant of the Amorites, and the children of Israel had sworne vnto them : and Saul sought to slay them, in his zeale to the children of Israel and Iudah)

* Iosh. 16, 17.

3 Wherefore Dauid said vnto the Gibeonites, What shall I doe for you ? and wherwith shall I make the atonement, that ye may blesse the inheritance of the LORD?

4 And the Gibeonites saide vnto him, ‖We will haue no siluer nor golde of Saul, nor of his house, neither for vs shalt thou kill any man in Israel. And he said, What you shall say, *that* will I doe for you.

‖ Or, *It not silu gold tha haue to with Sa his hous taines if vs to kil*

5 And they answered the king, The man that consumed vs, and that ‖deuised against vs, *that* we should be destroied from remaining in any of the coasts of Israel,

‖ Or, cu off.

6 Let seuen men of his sonnes bee deliuered vnto vs, and wee will hang them vp vnto the LORD in Gibeah of Saul, ‖*whome* the LORD did chuse. And the king said, I will giue *them.*

‖ Or, che of the L

7 But the king spared Mephibosheth the sonne of Ionathan the sonne of Saul, because of the *LORDS othe that was betweene them, betweene Dauid, and Ionathan the sonne of Saul.

* 1. San 3. and 2 42.

8 But the king tooke the two sons of Rizpah the daughter of Aiah, whom she bare vnto Saul, Armoni and Mephibosheth, and the fiue sonnes of ‖ Michal the daughter of Saul, whome she † brought vp for Adriel the sonne of Barzillai the Meholathite.

‖ Or, M chals si † Heb. to Adri

9 And hee deliuered them into the hands of the Gibeonites, and they hanged them in the hill before the LORD : and they fell all seuen together, and were put to death in the dayes of haruest,

uest, in the first *dayes*, in the beginning of barley harueſt.

10 ¶ And *Rizpah the daughter of Aiah tooke ſackecloth, and ſpread it for her vpon the rocke, from the beginning of harueſt, vntill water dropped vpon them out of heauen, and ſuffered neither the birds of the aire to reſt on them by day, nor the beaſtes of the fielde by night.

11 And it was tolde Dauid what Rizpah the daughter of Aiah the concubine of Saul had done.

12 ¶ And Dauid went and tooke the bones of Saul, and the bones of Ionathan his ſonne from the men of Iabeſh Gilead, which had ſtollen them from the ſtreet of Bethſhan where the *Philiſtines had hanged them, when the Philiſtines had ſlaine Saul in Gilboa.

13 And hee brought vp from thence the bones of Saul, and the bones of Ionathan his ſonne, and they gathered the bones of them that were hanged.

14 And the bones of Saul and Ionathan his ſonne buried they in the countrey of Beniamin in Zelah, in the ſepulchre of Kiſh his father: and they perfourmed all that the king commanded: and after that, God was entreated for the land.

15 ¶ Moreouer, the Philiſtines had yet warre againe with Iſrael, and Dauid went down, and his ſeruants with him, and fought againſt the Philiſtines, and Dauid waxed faint.

16 And Iſhbi-benob which *was* of the ſonnes of ‖the gyant, (the weight of whoſe †ſpeare weighed three hundred ſhekels of braſſe in weight) he being girded with a new *ſword*, thought to haue ſlaine Dauid.

17 But Abiſhai the ſonne of Zeruiah ſuccoured him, and ſmote the Philiſtine, and killed him. Then the men of Dauid ſware vnto him, ſaying, Thou ſhalt goe no more out with vs to battell, that thou quench not the ‖light of Iſrael.

18 *And it came to paſſe after this, that there was againe a battell with the Philiſtines at Gob: then Sibbechai the Huſhathite ſlew Saph, which *was* of the ſonnes of ‖the Gyant.

19 And there was againe a battell in Gob, with the Philiſtines, where Elhanan the ſonne of Iaare-Oregim a Bethlehemite, ſlewe *the brother of Go-

liath the Gittite, the ſtaffe of whoſe ſpeare *was* like a weauers beame.

20 And there was yet a battell in Gath, where was a man of *great* ſtature, that had on euery hand ſix fingers, and on euery foote ſixe toes, foure and twenty in number, and he alſo was borne to ‖the Gyant.

21 And when he ‖defied Iſrael, Ionathan the ſonne of *Shimea the brother of Dauid, ſlew him.

22 Theſe foure were borne to the Gyant in Gath, and fell by the hand of Dauid, and by the hand of his ſeruants.

CHAP. XXII.

A Psalme of thankesgiuing for Gods powerfull deliuerance, and manifold blessings.

Nd Dauid ſpake vnto the LORD the wordes of this ſong, in the day *that* the LORD had deliuered him out of the hand of all his enemies, and out of the hand of Saul.

2 And he ſaid, *The LORD *is* my rocke and my fortreſſe, and my deliuerer:

3 The God of my rocke, in him will I truſt: hee *is* my ſhield, and the horne of my ſaluation, my high tower, and my refuge, my Sauiour; thou ſaueſt me from violence.

4 I will call on the LORD, who is worthy to be praiſed: ſo ſhall I be ſaued from mine enemies.

5 When the ‖waues of death compaſſed me: the floods of †vngodly men made me afraid.

6 The ‖ſorowes of Hell compaſſed me about: the ſnares of death preuented me.

7 In my diſtreſſe I called vpon the LORD, and cryed to my God, and hee did heare my voice out of his Temple, and my crie *did enter* into his eares.

8 Then the earth ſhooke and trembled: the foundations of heauen mooued and ſhooke, becauſe hee was wroth.

9 There went vp a ſmoake †out of his noſtrils, and fire out of his mouth deuoured: coales were kindled by it.

10 Hee bowed the heauens alſo and came downe: and darkeneſſe *was* vnder his feete.

11 And

hap. 3. 7.

Sam.
0.

, Rapha.
eb. the
fe, or the
d.

eb. can-
or lampe

Chron.
4.

r, Rapha.

See 1.
ro. 20. 5.

‖ *Or, Rapha.*
‖ *Or, repro-
ched.*
* 1. Sam.
16. 9.

**Psal.* 18. 2.
&c.

‖ *Or, pangs.*
† *Heb. Be-
lial.*

‖ *Or, coards.*

† *Heb. by.*

11 And he rode vpon a Cherub, and did flie: and hee was seene vpon the wings of the winde.

12 And hee made darkenesse pauilions round about him, † darke waters, *and* thicke clouds of the skies.

† Hebr. binding of waters.

13 Through the brightnesse before him, were coales of fire kindled.

14 The LORD thundred from heauen: and the most high vttered his voice.

15 And he sent out arrowes, and scattered them; lightning, and discomfited them.

16 And the channels of the Sea appeared, the foundations of the world were discouered, at the rebuking of the LORD, at the blast of the breath of his nostrils.

17 He sent from aboue, he tooke me: he drew me out of ||many waters.

|| Or, great.

18 He deliuered me from my strong enemy, *and* from them that hated mee: for they were too strong for me.

19 They preuented me in the day of my calamitie : but the LORD was my stay.

20 Hee brought me forth also into a large place: he deliuered me, because hee delighted in me.

21 The LORD rewarded mee according to my righteousnesse: according to the cleannesse of my hands, hath hee recompensed me.

22 For I haue kept the wayes of the LORD, and haue not wickedly departed from my God.

23 For all his iudgements *were* before me : and as for his Statutes, I did not depart from them.

24 I was also vpright †before him: and haue kept my selfe from mine iniquitie.

† Hebr. to him.

25 Therefore the LORD hath recompensed me, according to my righteousnesse : according to my cleannesse † in his eye sight.

† Hebr. before his eyes.

26 With the merciful thou wilt shew thy selfe mercifull, *and* with the vpright man thou wilt shew thy selfe vpright.

27 With the pure thou wilt shew thy selfe pure : and with the froward, thou wilt ||shew thy selfe vnsauoury.

|| Or, wrestle. ps. 18. 27.

28 And the afflicted people thou wilt saue: but thine eyes *are* vpon the hautie, *that* thou mayest bring *them* downe.

29 For thou *art* my ||lampe, O LORD : and the LORD wil lighten my darkenesse.

|| Or, candle.

|| Or, broken a troupe.

30 For by thee I haue ||run through a troupe: by my God haue I leaped ouer a wall.

|| Or, re

31 As for God, his way is perfect, the word of the LORD is ||tried: he is a buckler to all them that trust in him.

32 For who *is* God, saue the LORD? and who *is* a rocke, saue our God?

33 God is my strength *and* power: and he † maketh my way perfect.

† Hebr. deth, or loose th.
† Heb. e leth.

34 Hee † maketh my feet like hindes *feet* : and setteth mee vpon my high places.

35 He teacheth my hands † to warre: so that a bow of steele is broken by mine armes.

† Hebr. the war

36 Thou hast also giuen mee the shield of thy saluation : and thy gentlenesse † hath made me great.

† Hebr. tiplied

37 Thou hast enlarged my steps vnder me : so that my † feet did not slip.

† Hebr. cles.

38 I haue pursued mine enemies, and destroyed them : and turned not againe vntill I had consumed them.

39 And I haue consumed them and wounded them, that they could not arise : yea, they are fallen vnder my feet.

40 For thou hast girded mee with strength to battel: them that rose vp against me, hast thou † subdued vnder me.

† Hebr. sed to b

41 Thou hast also giuen mee the necks of mine enemies, that I might destroy them that hate me.

42 They looked, but there was none to saue : *euen* vnto the LORD, but he answered them not.

43 Then did I beat them as small as the dust of the earth : I did stampe them as the myre of the street, *and* did spread them abroad.

44 Thou also hast deliuered mee from the striuings of my people, thou hast kept mee *to be* head of the heathen: a people which I knew not, shall serue me.

45 †Strangers shall ||submit themselues vnto me : as soone as they heare, they shall be obedient vnto me.

† Heb. so of the st ger.
|| Or, yee fained dience. lye.

46 Strangers shall fade away : and they shall bee afraid out of their close places.

47 The LORD liueth, and blessed *be* my rocke: and exalted be the God of the rocke of my saluation.

48 It *is* God that † auengeth mee, and *that* bringeth downe the people vnder me :

† Hebr. g ueth auen ment for

49 And that bringeth me forth from mine enemies : thou also hast lifted mee

vp

om. 15. 9

vp on high aboue them that rose vp a-
gainst me : thou hast deliuered me from
the violent man.

50 Therefore I will giue thankes
vnto thee, O LORD, among *the heathen : and I will sing praises vnto thy
Name.

51 He is the towre of saluation for his
king : and sheweth mercy to his Anointed, vnto Dauid, and *to his seede for
euermore.

1a. 7. 13

C H A P. XXIII.

1 Dauid in his last words, professeth his faith in
Gods promises to be beyond sence or experience. 6 The different state of the wicked.
8 A catalogue of Dauids mightie men.

Owe these bee the last
words of Dauid : Dauid
the sonne of Iesse saide,
and the man who was
raised vp on high, the A-
nointed of the God of Iacob, and the
sweet Psalmist of Israel, said,

2 The spirit of the LORD spake
by me, and his word *was in my tongue.

3 The God of Israel said, the Rocke
of Israel spake to me : ‖he that ruleth
ouer men must be iust, ruling in the feare
of God :

4 And he shall be as the light of the
morning, when the Sunne riseth, euen a
morning, without cloudes; as the tender
grasse springing out of the earth by cleare
shining after raine :

5 Although my house be not so with
God : yet he hath made with mee an e-
uerlasting couenant, ordred in al things
and sure : for this is all my saluation, and
all my desire, although he make it not to
grow.

6 ¶ But the sonnes of Belial shall bee
all of them as thornes thrust away, because they cannot be taken with hands,

7 But the man that shal touch them,
must be †fenced with yron, and the staffe
of a speare, and they shall bee vtterly
burnt with fire in the same place.

8 ¶ These be the names of the mightie men whome Dauid had : ‖The
Tachmonite that sate in the seat, chiefe
among the captaines, (the same was A-
dino the Eznite:) ‖hee lift vp his speare a-
gainst eight hundred, †whom he slew at
one time.

9 And after him was *Eleazar the
sonne of Dodo the Ahohite, one of the
three mightie men with Dauid, when
they defied the Philistines that were

r, be thou
er, &c.

eb. filled.

x, Ioshe-
sebet the
chmonite
d of the
ee.
e 1. chr.
11.
eb.slaine.

. Chron.
12.

there gathered together to battell, and
the men of Israel were gone away.

10 He arose, and smote the Philistines
vntill his hand was wearie, and his
hand claue vnto the sword : and the
LORD wrought a great victorie that
day, and the people returned after him
onely to spoile.

11 And after him was *Shammah
the sonne of Agee the Hararite : and the
Philistines were gathered together
‖into a troupe, where was a piece of
ground full of lentiles : and the people
fled from the Philistines.

12 But hee stood in the midst of the
ground, and defended it, and slewe the
Philistines : and the LORD wrought
a great victorie.

13 And ‖three of the thirtie chiefe
went downe and came to Dauid in the
haruest time, vnto the caue of Adullam :
and the troupe of the Philistines pitched in the valley of Rephaim.

14 And Dauid was then in an holde,
and the garison of the Philistines was
then in Bethlehem.

15 And Dauid longed, and said, Oh
that one would giue mee drinke of the
water of the well of Bethlehem which
is by the gate.

16 And the three mightie men brake
through the host of the Philistines, and
drew water out of the Well of Bethlehem, that was by the gate, and tooke it,
and brought it to Dauid : neuerthelesse
he would not drinke thereof, but powred it out vnto the LORD.

17 And he said, Be it farre from me,
O LORD, that I should doe this : is
not this the blood of the men that went
in ieopardie of their liues ? therefore he
would not drinke it. These things did
these three mightie men.

18 And *Abishai the brother of Ioab,
the sonne of Zeruiah, was chiefe a-
mong three, and he lift vp his speare a-
gainst three hundred, †and slew them, and
had the name among three.

19 Was hee not most honourable of
three ? therefore he was their captaine :
howbeit, hee attained not vnto the first
three.

20 And Benaiah the sonne of Iehoiada the sonne of a valiant man, of
Kabzeel, †who had done many actes,
he slew two ‖lion-like men of Moab :
hee went downe also, and slewe a
Lyon in the middest of a pit in time of
snow.

21 And

*1. Chron.
11. 27.

‖Or, for for-
raging.

‖Or, the
three cap-
taines ouer
the thirtie.

*1. Chron.
11. 20.

†Heb.slaine.

†Heb. great
of acts.
†Hebr. lion
of God.

† Heb. a man
of counte-
nance or
sight: called
1. Chro. 11.
23. a man of
great sta-
ture.

21 And he slew an Egyptian †a good-ly man: and the Egyptian had a speare in his hand; but he went downe to him with a staffe, and plucked the speare out of the Egyptians hand, and slewe him with his owne speare.

22 These things did Benaiah the sonne of Iehoiada, and had the name among three mightie men.

‖ Or, honou-
rable among
the thirtie.

23 Hee was ‖more honourable then the thirtie, but hee attained not to the *first* three: and Dauid set him ouer his ‖guard.

‖ Or, Coun-
cil: Heb. at
his command
* Chap. 2.
18.

24 *Asahel the brother of Ioab *was* one of the thirtie: Elhanan the sonne of Dodo of Bethlehem,

25 Shammah the Harodite, Elika the Harodite,

* 1. Chron.
11. 27.

26 Helez the * Paltite, Ira the sonne of Ikkesh the Tekoite,

27 Abiezer the Anethothite, Mebunnai the Hushathite,

28 Zalmon the Ahohite, Maharai the Netophathite,

29 Heleb the sonne of Baanah, a Netophathite, Ittai the sonne of Ribai out of Gibeah of the children of Beniamin.

‖ Or, valleys.

30 Benaiah the Pirathonite, Hiddai of the ‖brookes of Gaash,

31 Abialbon the Arbathite, Azmaueth the Barhumite,

32 Elihaba the Shaalbonite: of the sonnes of Iashen, Ionathan,

33 Shammah the Hararite, Ahiam the sonne of Sharar the Hararite,

34 Eliphelet the sonne of Ahasbai, the sonne of the Maachathite, Eliam the sonne of Ahithophel the Gilonite,

35 Hezrai the Carmelite, Paarai the Arbite,

36 Igal the sonne of Nathan of Zobah, Bani the Gadite,

37 Zelek the Ammonite, Naharai the Berothite, armour-bearer to Ioab the sonne of Zeruiah,

38 Ira an Ithrite, Gareb an Ithrite,

39 Vriah the Hittite: thirtie and seuen in all.

CHAP. XXIIII.

1 Dauid tempted by Satan, forceth Ioab to number the people. 5 The captaines in nine moneths and twentie dayes, bring the muster of eleuen thousand fighting men. 10 Dauid hauing three plagues propounded by Gad, repenteth, and chuseth the three dayes pestilence. 15 After the death of threescore

and ten thousand, Dauid by repentance preuenteth the destruction of Ierusalem. 18 Dauid, by Gads direction purchaseth Araunahs threshing-floore, where hauing sacrificed, the plague stayeth.

AND againe the anger of the LORD was kindled against Israel, and ‖hee mooued Dauid against them, to say, Goe, number Israel and Iudah.

‖ Satan.
1. Chron.
21. 1.

2 For the king said to Ioab the captaine of the hoste, which *was* with him, ‖Goe now through all the tribes of Israel, from Dan euen to Beer-sheba, and number ye the people, that I may know the number of the people.

‖ Or, com
passe.

3 And Ioab sayde vnto the King, Now the LORD thy God adde vnto the people (how many soeuer they be) an hundred folde, and that the eyes of my lorde the king may see it: but why doeth my lord the king delight in this thing?

4 Notwithstanding, the kings word preuailed against Ioab, and against the captaines of the hoste: and Ioab and the captaines of the host went out from the presence of the king, to number the people of Israel.

5 ¶ And they passed ouer Iordane, and pitched in Aroer, on the right side of the citie that *lieth* in the midst of the ‖riuer of Gad, and toward Iazer.

‖ Or, val

6 Then they came to Gilead, and to the ‖land of Tahtim-Hodshi: and they came to Dan-Iaan, and about to Zidon,

‖ Or, ne
land nev
nhabite

7 And came to the strong holde of Tyre, and to all the cities of the Hiuites, and of the Canaanites. and they went out to the South of Iudah, *euen* to Beer-sheba.

8 So when they had gone through all the land, they came to Ierusalem at the ende of nine moneths, and twentie dayes.

9 And Ioab gaue vp the summe of the number of the people vnto the king, and there were in Israel eight hundred thousand valiant men that drewe the sword: and the men of Iudah were fiue hundred thousand men.

10 ¶ And Dauids heart smote him, after that hee had numbred the people: and Dauid sayde vnto the LORD, I haue sinned greatly in that I haue done: and nowe I beseech thee, O LORD, take away the iniquitie of thy

thy seruant, for I haue done very foolishly.

11 For when Dauid was vp in the morning, the word of the LORD came vnto the Prophet Gad Dauids Seer, saying,

12 Goe and say vnto Dauid, Thus saith the LORD, I offer thee three things; chuse thee one of them, that I may doe it vnto thee.

13 So Gad came to Dauid, and told him, and said vnto him, Shall seuen yeeres of famine come vnto thee in thy land? or wilt thou flee three moneths before thine enemies, while they pursue thee? or that there be three dayes pestilence in thy land? Now aduise, and see what answere I shall returne to him that sent me.

14 And Dauid saide vnto Gad, I am in a great strait : let vs fall now into the hand of the LORD (for his mercies are ‖great,) and let me not fall into the hand of man.

Or, many.

15 ¶ So the LORD sent a pestilence vpon Israel, from the morning, euen to the time appointed : and there died of the people from Dan euen to Beersheba, seuentie thousand men.

16 And when the Angel stretched out his hand vpon Ierusalem to destroy it, *the LORD repented him of the euill, and said to the Angel that destroyed the people, It is ynough : stay now thine hand. And the Angel of the LORD was by the threshing place of Araunah the Iebusite.

1. Sam.
5. 11.

17 And Dauid spake vnto the LORD when he saw the Angel that smote the people, and said, Loe, I haue sinned, and I haue done wickedly : but these sheepe, what haue they done? Let thine hand, I pray thee, be against mee,

and against my fathers house.

18 ¶ And Gad came that day to Dauid, and said vnto him, Goe vp, reare an Altar vnto the LORD, in the threshing floore of Araunah the Iebusite.

19 And Dauid, according to the saying of Gad, went vp, as the LORD commanded.

20 And Araunah looked, and saw the King and his seruants comming on toward him : and Araunah went out, and bowed himselfe before the King on his face vpon the ground.

21 And Araunah said, Wherefore is my lord the King come to his seruant? and Dauid saide, To buy the threshing floore of thee, to build an Altar vnto the LORD, that the plague may be stayed from the people.

22 And Araunah said vnto Dauid, Let my lord the King take and offer vp what seemeth good vnto him : Beholde, *here be* oxen for burnt sacrifice, and threshing instruments, and *other* instruments of the oxen for wood.

23 All these things did Araunah, *as* a king, giue vnto the King : and Araunah saide vnto the King, The LORD thy God accept thee.

24 And the King said vnto Araunah, Nay, but I will surely buy it of thee at a price : neither will I offer burnt offerings vnto the LORD my God, of that which doeth cost mee nothing. So Dauid bought the threshing floore, and the oxen, for fiftie shekels of siluer.

25 Aud Dauid built there an Altar vnto the LORD, and offered burnt offerings, and peace offerings : so the LORD was intreated for the land, and the plague was stayed from Israel.

¶ THE

¶ THE FIRST BOOKE OF
the Kings, commonly called The
third Booke of the Kings.

CHAP. I.

1 Abishag cherisheth Dauid in his extreame age. 5 Adonijah, Dauids dearling, vsurpeth the kingdome. 11 By the counsel of Nathan, 15·Bath-sheba moueth the king, 22 and Nathan secondeth her. 28 Dauid reneweth his oath to Bath-sheba. 32 Salomon by Dauids appointment, beeing annointed King by Zadok and Nathan, the people triumph. 41 Ionathan, bringing these newes, Adoniiahs guests flie. 50 Adonijah flying to the hornes of the Altar, vpon his good behauiour is dismissed by Solomon.

 Ow King Dauid was olde, *and* †striken in yeeres, and they couered him with clothes, but hee gate no heate.

2 Wherefore his seruants said vnto him, †Let there be sought for my lord the king †a yong virgin, and let her stand before the King, and let her †cherish him, and let her lie in thy bosome, that my lord the King may get heate.

3 So they sought for a faire damosel throughout all the coasts of Israel, and found Abishag a Shunammite, and brought her to the King.

4 And the damosell was very faire, and cherished the king, and ministred to him : but the king knew her not.

5 ¶ Then Adoniiah the sonne of Haggith exalted himselfe, saying, I wil †be king : And he prepared him charets and horsemen, and fiftie men to runne before him.

6 And his father had not displeased him †at any time, in saying, Why hast thou done so ? And hee also *was* a very goodly man, and *his mother* bare him after Absalom.

7 And hee †conferred with Ioab the sonne of Zeruiah, and with Abiathar the Priest : and they following Adoniiah, †helped *him.*

8 But Zadok the Priest, and Benaiah the sonne of Iehoiada, and Nathan the Prophet, and Shimei, and Rei, and the mightie men which *belonged* to Dauid, were not with Adoniiah.

9 And Adoniiah slew sheepe, and oxen, and fat cattell, by the stone of Zoheleth, which *is* by ||En-Rogel, and called all his brethren the kings sonnes, and all the men of Iudah the kings seruants.

10 But Nathan the Prophet, and Benaiah, and the mightie men, and Solomon his brother he called not.

11 ¶ Wherefore Nathan spake vnto Bath-sheba the mother of Solomon, saying, Hast thou not heard that Adoniiah the son of *Haggith doth reigne, and Dauid our lord knoweth *it* not ?

12 Now therefore come, let mee, I pray thee, giue thee counsell, that thou mayest saue thine owne life, and the life of thy sonne Solomon.

13 Goe, and get thee in vnto King Dauid, and say vnto him, Diddest not thou, my lord, O king, sweare vnto thine handmaid, saying, Assuredly Solomon thy sonne shall reigne after mee, and he shall sit vpon my throne ? why then doth Adoniiah reigne ?

14 Beholde, while thou yet talkest there with the king, I also will come in after thee, and †confirme thy words.

15 ¶ And Bath-sheba went in vnto the King into the chamber : and the king was very olde, and Abishag the Shunammite ministred vnto the king.

16 And Bathsheba bowed, and did obeysance vnto the king : and the king said, †What wouldest thou ?

17 And she said vnto him, My lord, thou

Marginal notes (left column):
† *Hebr. entred into dayes.*
† *Heb. let them seeke.*
† *Hebr. a damsell, a virgine.*
† *Heb. be a cherisher vnto him.*
† *Heb. reigne*
† *Heb. from his dayes.*

Marginal notes (right column):
† *Heb. his words were with Ioab*
† *Heb. helped after Adonijah.*
‖ *Or, the well Rogel*
* 2. Sam 3. 4.
† *Heb. fill*
† *Heb. what to thee ?*

thou swarest by the LORD thy God vnto thine handmaid, *saying*, Assuredly Solomon thy sonne shall reigne after me, and he shall sit vpon my throne:

18 And now behold, Adoniiah reigneth; and now my lord the king, thou knowest *it* not.

19 And he hath slaine oxen, and fat cattell, and sheepe in abundance, and hath called all the sonnes of the king, and Abiathar the Priest, and Ioab the captaine of the hoste: but Solomon thy seruant hath he not called.

20 And thou, my lord O king, the eyes of all Israel *are* vpon thee, that thou shouldest tell them who shall sit on the throne of my lord the king after him.

21 Otherwise it shall come to passe, when my lord the king shal sleepe with his fathers, that I and my sonne So- *Hebr. sin-* lomon shall be counted †offenders. *ners.*

22 ¶ And loe, while shee yet talked with the king, Nathan the Prophet also came in.

23 And they tolde the king, saying, Beholde Nathan the Prophet. And when hee was come in before the king, he bowed himselfe before the king with his face to the ground.

24 And Nathan said, My lord O king, hast thou said, Adoniiah shall reigne after mee, and hee shall sit vpon my throne?

25 For hee is gone downe this day, and hath slaine oxen, and fat cattel, and sheepe in abundance, and hath called all the kings sonnes, and the captaines of the host, and Abiathar the Priest : and behold, they eate and drinke before him, and say, † God saue king Adoniiah.

Hebr. Let- 26 But me, *euen* me thy seruant, and *ing Ado-* Zadok the Priest, and Benaiah the *niiah liue.* sonne of Iehoiada, and thy seruant Solomon hath he not called.

27 Is this thing done by my lord the king, and thou hast not shewed it vnto thy seruant, who should sit on the throne of my lord the king, after him?

28 ¶ Then king Dauid answered, and said, Call me Bathsheba. And she *Hebr. be-* came †into the kings presence, and stood *'ore the* before the king. *'ing.*

29 And the king sware, and said, As the LORD liueth, that hath redeemed my soule out of all distresse,

30 Euen as I sware vnto thee by the LORD God of Israel, saying, Assuredly Solomon thy sonne shall reigne

after me, and he shall sit vpon my throne in my stead; euen so wil I certainly doe this day.

31 Then Bathsheba bowed with *her* face to the earth, and did reuerence to the king, and said, Let my lord king Dauid liue for euer.

32 ¶ And king Dauid said, Call me Zadok the Priest, and Nathan the Prophet, and Benaiah the sonne of Iehoiada. And they came before the king.

33 The king also saide vnto them, Take with you the seruants of your lord, and cause Solomon my sonne to ride vpon †mine owne mule, and bring *† Heb. which* him downe to Gihon. *belongeth to me.*

34 And let Zadok the Priest, and Nathan the Prophet, anoint him there King ouer Israel · and blow ye with the trumpet, and say, God saue King Solomon.

35 Then ye shall come vp after him, that hee may come and sit vpon my throne; for he shall be king in my stead: and I haue appointed him to be ruler ouer Israel, and ouer Iudah.

36 And Benaiah the sonne of Iehoiada answered the King, and said, Amen : The LORD God of my lord the king say so too.

37 As the LORD hath bene with my lord the King, euen so be he with Solomon, and make his throne greater then the throne of my lord King Dauid.

38 So Zadok the Priest, and Nathan the Prophet, and Benaiah the sonne of Iehoiada, and the Cherethites, and the Pelethites went downe, and caused Solomon to ride vpon King Dauids mule, and brought him to Gihon.

39 And Zadok the Priest tooke an horne of oile out of the Tabernacle, and anointed Solomon : and they blew the trumpet, and all the people said, God saue King Solomon.

40 And all the people came vp after him, and the people piped with ‖pipes, *‖ Or, flutes.* and reioyced with great ioy, so that the earth rent with the sound of them.

41 ¶ And Adoniiah and all the ghests that *were* with him, heard it as they had made an end of eating : and when Ioab heard the sound of the trumpet, hee said, Wherefore *is* this noise of the citie, being in an vproare?

42 And while hee yet spake, behold, Ionathan the sonne of Abiathar the Priest

Priest came, and Adoniiah sayde vnto him, Come in, for thou art a valiant man, and bringest good tidings.

43 And Ionathan answered, and said to Adoniiah, Verily our lorde king Dauid hath made Solomon king.

44 And the king hath sent with him Zadok the Priest, and Nathan the Prophet, and Benaiah the sonne of Iehoiada, and the Cherethites, and the Pelethites, and they haue caused him to ride vpon the kings mule.

45 And Zadok the Priest, and Nathan the Prophet haue anointed him king in Gihon : and they are come vp from thence reioycing, so that the citie rang againe : this is the noyse that yee haue heard.

46 And also Solomon sitteth on the throne of the kingdome.

47 And moreouer, the kings seruants came to blesse our lorde king Dauid, saying, God make the name of Solomon better then thy name, and make his throne greater then thy throne. And the king bowed himselfe vpon the bed.

48 And also thus sayde the King, Blessed *be* the LORD God of Israel, which hath giuen *one* to sit on my throne this day, mine eyes euen seeing *it*.

49 And all the guests that were with Adoniiah, were afraid, and rose vp, and went euery man his way.

50 ¶ And Adoniiah feared because of Solomon, and arose, and went, and caught hold on the hornes of the Altar.

51 And it was tolde Solomon, saying, Behold, Adoniiah feareth King Solomon : for loe, he hath caught hold on the hornes of the Altar, saying, Let King Solomon sweare vnto mee to day, that hee will not slay his seruant with the sword.

52 And Solomon sayd, If hee will shewe himselfe a worthy man, there shall not an haire of him fall to the earth : but if wickednesse shall be found in him, he shall die.

53 So king Solomon sent, and they brought him downe from the Altar, and hee came and bowed himselfe to king Solomon : and Solomon sayde vnto him, Goe to thine house.

CHAP. II.

1 Dauid hauing giuen a charge to Solomon, 3 of religiousnesse, 5 of Ioab, 7 of Barzillai, 8 of Shimei, 10 dieth. 12 Solomon succeedeth. 13 Adoniiah, mouing Bath-sheba

to sue vnto Solomon for Abishag, is put to death. 26 Abiathar hauing his life giuen him, is depriued of the Priesthood. 28 Ioab fleeing to the hornes of the Altar, is there slaine. 35 Benaiah is put in Ioabs roume, and Zadok in Abiathars. 36 Shimei confined to Ierusalem, by occasion of going thence to Gath, is put to death.

Ow the dayes of Dauid drew nigh, that he should die, and he charged Solomon his sonne, saying ;

2 I goe the way of all the earth : be thou strong therefore, and shew thy selfe a man.

3 And keepe the charge of the LORD thy God, to walke in his wayes, to keepe his Statutes, *and* his Commandements, & his Iudgements, and his Testimonies, as it is written in the Law of Moses, that thou mayest *‖prosper in all that thou doest, and whithersoeuer thou turnest thy selfe :

4 That the LORD may continue his word which hee spake concerning me, saying, If thy children take heede to their way, to walke before mee in trueth, with all their heart, and with all their soule, * there shall not †faile thee (sayd hee) a man on the throne of Israel.

5 Moreouer thou knowest also what Ioab the sonne of Zeruiah did to mee, *and* what he did to the two captaines of the hostes of Israel, vnto * Abner the sonne of Ner, and vnto * Amasa the sonne of Iether, whom hee slewe, and †shed the blood of warre in peace, and put the blood of warre vpon his girdle that *was* about his loynes, and in his shooes that *were* on his feet.

6 Doe therefore according to thy wisedome, and let not his hoare head goe downe to the graue in peace.

7 But shewe kindnesse vnto the sonnes of * Barzillai the Gileadite, and let them be of those that eate at thy table : for so they came to me when I fled because of Absalom thy brother.

8 And behold, thou *hast* with thee * Shimei the sonne of Gera, a Beniamite of Bahurim, which cursed mee with a †grieuous curse, in the day when I went to Mahanaim : but hee came downe to meete me at Iordane, and I sware to him by the LORD, saying, *I will not put thee to death with the sword.

9 Nowe therefore holde him not guiltlesse :

*Deut. 9. Iosh. 1.
‖ Or, doe wisely.

* 2. Sam. 7. 12.
† Heb. be cut off fr thee from the thron

* 2. Sam. 27.
* 2. Sam 20. 10.
† Heb. pi

* 2. Sam 19. 31.

* 2. Sam 16. 5.
† Heb. str

* 2. Sam 19. 23.

guiltlesse : for thou *art* a wise man, and knowest what thou oughtest to doe vnto him, but his hoare head bring thou downe to the graue with blood.

10 So * Dauid slept with his fathers, and was buried in the citie of Dauid.

11 And the dayes that Dauid *raigned ouer Israel, *were* fourty yeeres : seuen yeeres raigned hee in Hebron, and thirty and three yeeres raigned hee in Ierusalem.

12 ¶ * Then sate Solomon vpon the throne of Dauid his father, and his kingdome was established greatly.

13 ¶ And Adoniiah the sonne of Haggith came to Bathsheba the mother of Solomon, and she said, Commest thou peaceably ? And he said, Peaceably.

14 He said moreouer, I haue somewhat to say vnto thee. And she saide, Say on.

15 And he said, Thou knowest that the kingdome was mine, and that all Israel set their faces on me, that I should raigne : howbeit the kingdome is turned about, and is become my brothers : for it was his from the Lord.

16 And now I aske one petition of thee, † deny me not. And she saide vnto him, Say on.

17 And hee saide, Speake, I pray thee, vnto Solomon the king (for hee will not say thee nay) that he giue me Abishag the Shunammite to wife.

18 And Bathsheba said, Wel, I will speake for thee vnto the king.

19 ¶ Bathsheba therefore went vnto king Solomon, to speake vnto him for Adoniiah : and the king rose vp to meete her, and bowed himselfe vnto her, and sate downe on his throne, and caused a seate to bee set for the Kings mother, and she sate on his right hand.

20 Then she said, I desire one small petition of thee, I pray thee say me not nay : and the King said vnto her, Aske on, my mother, for I will not say thee nay.

21 And she saide, Let Abishag the Shunammite be giuen to Adoniiah thy brother to wife.

22 And king Solomon answered, and said vnto his mother, And why doest thou aske Abishag the Shunammite for Adoniiah ? Aske for him the kingdome also (for he *is* mine elder brother) euen for him, and for Abiathar the Priest, & for Ioab the sonne of Zeruiah.

23 Then king Solomon sware by the Lord, saying, God doe so to me, and more also, if Adoniiah haue not spoken this word against his owne life.

24 Now therefore as the Lord liueth, which hath established mee, and set mee on the throne of Dauid my father, and who hath made me an house as he *promised, Adoniiah shall be put to death this day.

25 And king Solomon sent by the hand of Benaiah the sonne of Iehoiada, and he fell vpon him that he died.

26 ¶ And vnto Abiathar the Priest saide the King, Get thee to Anathoth, vnto thine own fields, for thou *art* † worthy of death : but I will not at this time put thee to death, because thou barest the arke of the Lord God before Dauid my father, and because thou hast bene afflicted in all wherein my father was afflicted.

27 So Solomon thrust out Abiathar from beeing Priest vnto the Lord : that hee might *fulfill the word of the Lord, which hee spake concerning the house of Eli in Shiloh.

28 ¶ Then tidings came to Ioab (for Ioab had turned after Adoniiah, though hee turned not after Absalom) and Ioab fled vnto the Tabernacle of the Lord, and caught hold on the hornes of the Altar.

29 And it was told king Solomon that Ioab was fled vnto the Tabernacle of the Lord, and behold, hee *is* by the Altar : Then Solomon sent Benaiah the sonne of Iehoiada, saying, Goe fall vpon him.

30 And Benaiah came to the Tabernacle of the Lord, and said vnto him, Thus saith the king, Come foorth. And he said, Nay, but I will die heere. And Benaiah brought the king word againe, saying, Thus said Ioab, and thus he answered me.

31 And the king saide vnto him, Doe as he hath said, and fall vpon him, and bury him, that thou mayest take away the innocent blood which Ioab shed, from mee, and from the house of my father.

32 And the Lord shall returne his blood vpon his owne head, who fell vpon two men, more righteous and better then hee, and slew them with the sword, my father Dauid not knowing thereof, *to wit*, * Abner the sonne of Ner, captaine of the hoste of Israel, and
* Amasa

Act 2.
. and 13.
.

2. Sam. 5. 4
chron. 29
, 27.

2. Chron.
. 23.

Heb. turne
ot away
y face.

* 2. Sam. 7.
12, 13.

† Heb. a man
of death.

* 1. Sam. 2.
31, 35.

* 2. Sam.
3. 27.

* 2. Sam. 20. 10.

* Amasa the sonne of Iether, captaine of the hoste of Iudah.

33 Their blood shall therefore returne vpon the head of Ioab, and vpon the head of his seed for euer : but vpon Dauid, and vpon his seede, and vpon his house, and vpon his throne, shall there bee peace for euer from the LORD.

34 So Benaiah the sonne of Iehoiada went vp, and fell vpon him, and slewe him, and hee was buried in his owne house in the wildernesse.

35 ¶ And the king put Benaiah the sonne of Iehoiada in his roome ouer the hoste, and Zadok the Priest did the king put in the roume of Abiathar.

36 ¶ And the king sent, and called for Shimei, and said vnto him, Build thee an house in Ierusalem, and dwell there, and goe not forth thence any whither.

37 For it shall be, that on the day thou goest out, & passest ouer the brooke Kidron, thou shalt know for certaine, that thou shalt surely die : thy blood shal be vpon thine owne head.

38 And Shimei said vnto the King, The saying *is* good : as my lord the king hath said, so will thy seruant doe. And Shimei dwelt in Ierusalem many dayes.

39 And it came to passe at the end of three yeeres, that two of the seruants of Shimei ranne away vnto Achish sonne of Maachah king of Gath : and they told Shimei, saying, Beholde, thy seruants *be* in Gath.

40 And Shimei arose, and sadled his asse, and went to Gath to Achish, to seeke his seruants : and Shimei went and brought his seruants from Gath.

41 And it was told Solomon, that Shimei had gone from Ierusalem to Gath, and was come againe.

42 And the king sent and called for Shimei, and said vnto him, Did I not make thee to sweare by the LORD, and protested vnto thee, saying, Know for a certaine, that on the day thou goest out, and walkest abroad any whither, that thou shalt surely die? And thou saidest vnto me, The word *that* I haue heard, *is* good.

43 Why then hast thou not kept the Oath of the LORD, and the commandement that I haue charged thee with?

44 The king said moreuer to Shi-

mei, Thou knowest all the wickednesse which thine heart is priuie to, that thou diddest to Dauid my father : therefore the LORD shall returne thy wickednesse vpon thine owne head.

45 And king Salomon *shall be* blessed, and the throne of Dauid shall bee established before the LORD for euer.

46 So the king commaunded Benaiah the sonne of Iehoiada, which went out, and fell vpon him, that he died, and the * kingdome was established in the hand of Solomon.

* 2. Chron. 1. 1.

CHAP. III.

1 Solomon marieth Pharaohs daughter. 2 Hie places being in vse, Solomon sacrificeth at Gibeon. 5 Solomon at Gibeon, in the choice which God gaue him, preferring wisedome, obtaineth wisedome, riches, and honour. 16 Solomons iudgement betweene the two harlots, maketh him renowmed.

AND * Solomon made affinitie with Pharaoh king of Egypt, and tooke Pharaohs daughter, and brought her into the citie of Dauid, vntill he had made an end of building his owne house, and the house of the LORD, and the wall of Ierusalem round about.

* Chap. 7. (

2 Only the people sacrificed in high places, because there was no house built vnto the Name of the LORD vntill those dayes.

3 And Solomon loued the LORD, walking in the statutes of Dauid his father : onely he sacrificed and burnt incense in high places.

4 And the king went to Gibeon to sacrifice there, for that was the great high place : a thousand burnt offerings did Solomon offer vp on that Altar.

5 ¶ In Gibeon the LORD appeared to Solomon in a dreame by night : and God sayd, Aske what I shall giue thee

6 And Solomon said, Thou hast shewed vnto thy seruant Dauid my father great ||mercy, according as he walked before thee in trueth, and in righteousnesse, and in vprightnesse of heart with thee, and thou hast kept for him this great kindnesse, that thou hast giuen him a sonne to sit on his throne, as *it is* this day.

|| Or, bount

7 And now, O LORD my God, thou hast made thy seruant King in stead

stead of Dauid my father : and I am but a litle childe : I know not how to goe out or come in.

8 And thy seruant is in the midst of thy people which thou hast chosen, a great people, that cannot be numbred, nor counted for multitude.

9 *Giue therefore thy seruant an †vnderstanding heart, to iudge thy people, that I may discerne betweene good and bad : for who is able to iudge this thy so great a people?

10 And the speach pleased the LORD, that Solomon had asked this thing.

11 And God said vnto him, Because thou hast asked this thing, and hast not asked for thy selfe †long life, neither hast asked riches for thy selfe, nor hast asked the life of thine enemies, but hast asked for thy selfe vnderstanding †to discerne iudgement;

12 Behold, I haue done according to thy word : loe, I haue giuen thee a wise and an vnderstanding heart, so that there was none like thee before thee, neither after thee shall any arise like vnto thee.

13 And I haue also *giuen thee that which thou hast not asked, both riches, and honour : so that there ‖shall not be any among the Kings like vnto thee, all thy dayes.

14 And if thou wilt walke in my wayes, to keepe my Statutes and my Commandements, *as thy father Dauid did walke, then I will lengthen thy dayes.

15 And Solomon awoke, and behold, it was a dreame: and he came to Ierusalem, and stood before the Arke of the Couenant of the LORD, and offered vp burnt offerings, and offered peace offerings, and made a feast to all his seruants.

16 ¶ Then came there two women that were harlots, vnto the king, and stood before him.

17 And the one woman said, O my lord, I and this woman dwell in one house, and I was deliuered of a childe, with her in the house.

18 And it came to passe the third day after that I was deliuered, that this woman was deliuered also : and wee were together ; there was no stranger with vs in the house, saue we two in the house.

19 And this womans childe died in the night : because she ouerlaid it.

20 And shee arose at midnight, and tooke my sonne from beside me, while thine handmaid slept, and layd it in her bosome, and layd her dead childe in my bosome.

21 And when I rose in the morning to giue my childe sucke, behold, it was dead : but when I had considered it in the morning, beholde, it was not my sonne, which I did beare.

22 And the other woman said, Nay, but the liuing is my sonne, and the dead is thy sonne : And this said, No, but the dead is thy sonne, and the liuing is my sonne. Thus they spake before the king.

23 Then said the King, The one saith, This is my sonne, that liueth, and thy sonne is the dead: and the other saith Nay : but thy sonne is the dead, and my sonne is the liuing.

24 And the King said, Bring mee a sword. And they brought a sword before the king :

25 And the king said, Diuide the liuing childe in two, and giue halfe to the one, and halfe to the other.

26 Then spake the woman whose the liuing childe was, vnto the king, (for her bowels †yerned vpon her sonne) and she said, O my lord, giue her the liuing childe, and in no wise slay it : But the other said ; Let it be neither mine nor thine, but diuide it.

27 Then the King answered and said, Giue her the liuing child, and in no wise slay it: she is the mother thereof.

28 And all Israel heard of the Iudgement which the king had iudged, and they feared the King : for they saw that the wisedome of God was †in him, to doe Iudgement.

CHAP. IIII.

1 Solomons Princes. 7 His twelue Officers for prouision. 20. 24 The peace and largenesse of his kingdome. 22 His daily prouision. 26 His stables. 29 His wisedome.

SO King Solomon was king ouer all Israel.

2 And these were the Princes which he had, Azariah the sonne of Zadok, ‖the Priest,

3 Elihoreph, and Ahiah the sonnes of Shisha, ‖Scribes : Iehoshaphat the sonne of Ahilud the ‖Recorder.

4 And Benaiah the sonne of Iehoiada was ouer the host : And Zadok and

---

Margin notes left column:

2. Chron. 10.
Hebr. hearing.

Hebr. madayes.

Hebr. to are.

Matth. 6.
wisd. 7.

or, hath t bene.

Chap. 15.

Margin notes right column:

† Hebr. were hot.

† Hebr. in the midst of him.

‖ Or, the chiefe Officer.
‖ Or, Secretaries.
‖ Or, remembrancer.

and Abiathar *were* the Priests:

5 And Azariah the sonne of Nathan *was* ouer the officers: and Zabud the sonne of Nathan *was* principall officer, *and* the kings friend.

6 And Ahishar was ouer the houshold: and *Adoniram the sonne of Abda was ouer the ‖ tribute.

*Chap. 5.
14.
‖ Or, leuie.*

7 ¶ And Solomon had twelue officers ouer all Israel, which prouided victuals for the king and his houshold: each man his moneth in a yeere made prouision.

8 And these are their names: ‖ the sonne of Hur in mount Ephraim,

‖ Or, Benhur.

9 The ‖sonne of Dekar in Makaz, and in Shaalbim, and Bethshemesh, and Elon-Bethhanan.

‖ Or, Ben-Dekar.

10 The ‖sonne of Heseb in Aruboth, *to him pertained* Sochoh, and all the land of Hepher:

‖ Or, Ben-Heseb.

11 The ‖sonne of Abinadab in all the region of Dor, which had Taphath the daughter of Solomon to wife:

‖ Or, Ben-Abinadab.

12 Baana the sonne of Ahilud, *to him pertained* Taanach and Megiddo, and all Beth-shean, which *is* by Zartanah beneath Iezreel, from Beth-shean to Abel-Meholah, euen vnto *the place that is* beyond Iokneam:

13 The ‖sonne of Geber in Ramoth Gilead, to him *pertained* the townes of Iair the sonne of Manasseh, which *are* in Gilead: to him *also pertained* the region of Argob, which *is* in Bashan, threescore great cities, with walles, and brasen barres.

‖ Or, Ben-Geber.

14 Ahinadab the sonne of Iddo *had* ‖Mahanaim.

‖ Or, to Mahanaim.

15 Ahimaaz *was* in Naphtali; he also tooke Basmath the daughter of Solomon to wife:

16 Baanah the sonne of Hushai *was* in Asher and in Aloth:

17 Iehoshaphat the sonne of Paruah in Issachar:

18 Shimei the sonne of Elah in Beniamin:

19 Geber the sonne of Vri *was* in the countrey of Gilead, *in* the countrey of Sihon king of the Amorites, and of Og king of Bashan; and hee *was* the onely officer which *was* in the land.

20 ¶ Iudah and Israel *were* many, as the sand which is by the sea in multitude, eating and drinking and making merrie.

21 And *Solomon reigned ouer all kingdoms from the riuer vnto the land

*Ecclus.
47. 15.*

of the Philistines, and vnto the border of Egypt: they brought presents, and serued Solomon all the dayes of his life.

22 ¶ And Solomons †prouision for one day, was thirtie measures of fine floure, and threescore †measures of meale,

†*Heb. bread*
†*Heb. Cors*

23 Ten fat oxen, and twentie oxen out of the pastures, and an hundred sheepe, beside Harts, and Roe-buckes, and fallow Deere, and fatted foule.

24 For he had dominion ouer all *the region* on this side the Riuer, from Tiphsah euen to Azzah ouer all the kings on this side the Riuer: and he had peace on all sides round about him.

25 And Iudah and Israel dwelt †safely, euery man vnder his Vine, and vnder his Figtree, from Dan euen to Beer-sheba, all the dayes of Solomon.

†*Heb. confidently.*

26 ¶ And *Solomon had fourtie thousand stalles of horses for his charets, and twelue thousand horsemen.

*2. Chron
9. 25.*

27 And those officers prouided victuall for king Solomon, and for all that came vnto king Solomons table, euery man in his moneth: they lacked nothing.

28 Barley also and straw for the horses and ‖dromedaries, brought they vnto the place where the officers were, euery man according to his charge.

‖ Or, mule,
or swift
beasts.

29 ¶ And *God gaue Solomon wisdome, and vnderstanding, exceeding much, and largenesse of heart, euen as the sand that *is* on the sea shoare.

*Ecclus.
47. 14, 15,
16.*

30 And Solomons wisedome excelled the wisedome of all the children of the East countrey, and all the wisedome of Egypt.

31 For hee was wiser then all men; then Ethan the Ezrahite, and Heman, and Chalcol, and Darda the sonnes of Mahol: and his fame was in all nations round about.

32 And he spake three thousand prouerbes: and his songs were a thousand and fiue.

33 And hee spake of trees, from the Cedar tree that *is* in Lebanon, euen vnto the Hyssope that springeth out of the wall: hee spake also of beasts, and of foule, and of creeping things, and of fishes.

34 And there came of all people to heare the wisedome of Solomon, from all kings of the earth, which had heard of his wisedome.

C H A P.

CHAP. V.

1 Hiram sending to congratulate Solomon, is certified of his purpose to build the Temple, and desired to furnish him with timber thereto. 7 Hiram blessing God for Solomon, and requesting food for his family, furnisheth him with trees. 13 The number of Solomons workemen and labourers.

Nd Hiram king of Tyre sent his seruants vnto Solomon : (for hee had heard that they had anointed him King in the roume of his father,) for Hiram was euer a louer of Dauid.

*1.Chro. 2.3.

2 And * Solomon sent to Hiram, saying,

3 Thou knowest how that Dauid my father could not build an house vnto the Name of the LORD his God, for the warres which were about him on euery side, vntill the LORD put them vnder the soles of his feet.

4 But now the LORD my God hath giuen me rest on euery side, so that there is neither aduersary, nor euill occurrent.

† Hebr. say. * 2. Sam 7. 13. 1. chro. 22. 10.

5 And behold, I †purpose to build an house vnto the Name of the LORD my God, *as the LORD spake vnto Dauid my father, saying, Thy sonne, whom I will set vpon thy throne in thy roume, he shall build an house vnto my Name.

6 Now therefore command thou, that they hew me Cedar trees out of Lebanon, and my seruants shall bee with thy seruants: and vnto thee will I giue hire for thy seruants, according to all that thou shalt †appoint : for thou knowest that *there is* not among vs, any that can skill to hew timber, like vnto the Sidonians.

‡ Hebr. say.

7 ¶ And it came to passe when Hiram heard the wordes of Solomon, that hee reioyced greatly, and said, Blessed be the LORD this day, which hath giuen vnto Dauid a wise sonne ouer this great people.

† Hebr. heard.

8 And Hiram sent to Solomon, saying, I haue †considered the things which thou sentest to me for: *and* I will doe all thy desire concerning timber of Cedar, and concerning timber of firre.

9 My seruants shall bring *them* downe from Lebanon vnto the Sea : and I wil conuey them by sea in flotes, vnto the place that thou shalt †appoint

† Hebr. send.

me, and will cause them to be discharged there, and thou shalt receiue *them:* and thou shalt accomplish my desire, in giuing food for my houshold.

10 So Hiram gaue Solomon Cedar trees, and Firre trees, *according* to all his desire.

11 And Solomon gaue Hiram twentie thousand †measures of wheate for food to his houshold, and twentie measures of pure oile : thus gaue Solomon to Hiram yeere by yeere.

† Heb. Cors.

12 And the LORD gaue Solomon wisedome, *as hee promised him : and there was peace betweene Hiram and Solomon, and they two made a league together.

* Cha. 3. 12

13 ¶ And King Solomon raised a †leuie out of all Israel, and the leuie was thirtie thousand men.

† Heb. tribute of men.

14 And hee sent them to Lebanon, ten thousand a moneth by courses : a moneth they were in Lebanon, *and* two moneths at home : and * Adoniram *was* ouer the leuie.

* Chap. 4. 6.

15 And Solomon had threescore and ten thousand that bare burdens, and fourescore thousand hewers in the mountaines :

16 Besides the chiefe of Solomons officers which *were* ouer the worke, three thousand and three hundred, which ruled ouer the people that wrought in the worke.

17 And the king commanded, and they brought great stones, costly stones, *and* hewed stones, to lay the foundation of the house.

18 And Solomons builders, and Hirams builders, did hewe them, and the ‖stone squarers : so they prepared timber and stones to build the house.

‖ Or, Giblites, as Ezek. 27. 9.

CHAP. VI.

1 The building of Solomons Temple. 5 The chambers thereof. 11 Gods promise vnto it. 15 The sieling and adorning of it: 23 The Cherubims. 31 The doores. 36 The court. 37 The time of building it.

Nd *it came to passe in the foure hundred and fourescore yeere after the children of Israel were come out of the land of Egypt, in the fourth yere of Solomons reigne ouer Israel, in the moneth Zif, which *is* the second moneth, that he †began to build the house of the LORD.

2. Chron. 3. 1.

† Heb. built.

2 And

2 And the house which king Solomon built for the LORD, the length thereof *was* threescore cubites, and the breadth thereof twentie cubits, and the height thereof thirtie cubites.

3 And the porch before the Temple of the house : twentie cubites *was* the length thereof, according to the breadth of the house, and tenne cubites *was* the breadth thereof before the house.

4 And for the house he made ‖ windowes of narrow lights.

‖ Or, *windowes broad within* and *narrowwithout:or,skewed and closed.*
‖ Or, *vpon, or ioyning to.*
† Heb. *floores*
† Heb. *ribs.*

5 ¶ And ‖against the wall of the house he built †chambers round about, *against* the walles of the house round about, *both* of the Temple and of the Oracle : and hee made †chambers round about.

6 The nethermost chamber *was* fiue cubites broad, and the middle *was* sixe cubites broad, and the third *was* seuen cubites broad : for without *in the wall* of the house hee made †narrowed rests round about, that *the beames* should not bee fastened in the walles of the house.

† Heb. *narrowings, or, rebatements.*

7 And the house when it was in building, was built of stone, made ready before it was brought thither : so that there was neither hammer nor axe, nor any toole of yron heard in the house, while it was in building.

8 The doore for the middle chamber *was* in the right †side of the house : and they went vp with winding staires into the middle *chamber*, and out of the middle into the third.

† Heb. *shoulder.*

9 So he built the house and finished it : and couered the house ‖with beams and boards of Cedar.

10 And then hee built chambers against all the house, fiue cubites high : and they rested on the house with timber of Cedar.

‖ Or, *the vault beams and the sielings with Cedar.*

11 ¶ And the word of the LORD came to Solomon, saying ;

12 Concerning this House which thou art in building, if thou wilt walke in my Statutes, and execute my Iudgments, and keepe all my Commandements to walke in them : then will I performe my word with thee, *which I spake vnto Dauid thy father.

* 2. Sam. 7. 13. 1. chro. 22. 10.

13 And I will dwell among the children of Israel, and will not forsake my people Israel.

14 So Solomon built the house, and finished it.

15 And hee built the walles of the house within with boards of Cedar, both the floore of the house, and the walles of the sieling : and hee couered *them* on the inside with wood, and couered the floore of the house with plankes of firre.

‖ Or, *from the floore of the house vnto the walles, &c.* And so ver. 16.

16 And hee built twentie cubites on the sides of the house, both the floore, and the walles with boards of Cedar : he euen built *them* for it within, *euen* for the Oracle, *euen* for the most holy place.

17 And the house, that is, the Temple before it, was fortie cubites *long*.

18 And the Cedar of the house within was carued with ‖knops, and †open flowres : all *was* Cedar, there was no stone seene.

‖ Or, *gourds* † Heb. *openings of flowres.*

19 And the Oracle he prepared in the house within, to set there the Arke of the Couenant of the LORD.

20 And the Oracle in the forepart, was twenty cubits in length and twentie cubites in breadth, and twentie cubites in the height thereof : and hee ouerlayd it with †pure golde, and so couered the Altar *which was* of Cedar.

† Heb. *shut vp.*

21 So Solomon ouerlayd the house within with pure golde : and he made a partition, by the chaines of golde before the Oracle, and he ouerlaid it with gold.

22 And the whole house he ouerlaid with golde vntill he had finished all the house : also the whole Altar that *was* by the Oracle he ouerlaide with golde.

23 ¶ And within the Oracle he made two Cherubims of ‖Oliue tree, *each* ten cubites high.

‖ Or, *oylie.* Heb. *trees of oyle.*

24 And fiue cubits *was* the one wing of the Cherub, and fiue cubits the other wing of the Cherub : from the vttermost part of the one wing, vnto the vttermost part of the other, were ten cubites.

25 And the other Cherub was tenne cubites : both the Cherubims were of one measure, and one size.

26 The height of the one Cherub *was* ten cubites, and so *was it* of the other Cherub.

27 And he set the Cherubims within the inner house : and *‖they stretched foorth the wings of the Cherubims, so that the wing of the one touched the *one* wall, and the wing of the other Cherub touched the other wall : & their wings touched one another in the midst of the house.

* Exod. 25. 20.
‖ Or, *the Cherubims stretched foot fo their wings.*

28 And he ouerlayd the Cherubims with golde.

29 And hee carued all the walles of the

the house round about with carued figures of Cherubims, and palme trees, and †open flowers, within & without.

† Heb. openings of flowers.

30 And the floore of the house hee ouerlayed with gold, within and without.

31 ¶ And for the entring of the Oracle he made doores of Oliue tree: the lintell *and* side posts *were* ‖ a fifth part *of the wall.*

‖ Or, fiue square.

32 The ‖two doores also *were* of Oliue tree, and he carued vpon them carvings of Cherubims, and palme trees, and †open flowers, and ouerlayd *them* with gold, and spread gold vpon the Cherubims, and vpon the palme trees.

‖ Or, leaues of the doores.

† Hebr. openings of flowers.

33 So also made hee for the doore of the Temple postes of Oliue tree ‖ a fourth part *of the wall.*

‖ Or, foure square.

34 And the two doores *were* of firre tree: the two leaues of the one doore *were* folding, and the two leaues of the other doore *were* folding.

35 And he carued *thereon* Cherubims, and palme trees, and open flowers: and couered *them* with gold, fitted vpon the carued worke.

36 ¶ And hee built the inner Court with three rowes of hewed stone, and a row of Cedar beames.

37 ¶ In the fourth yeere was the foundation of the house of the LORD layd, in the moneth Zif.

38 And in the eleuenth yeere in the moneth Bul (which *is* the eight moneth) was the house finished ‖throughout all the parts therof, and according to all the fashion of it: So was he seuen yeeres in building it.

‖ Or, with all the appurtenances therof, and with all the ordinances therof.

CHAP. VII.

1 The building of Solomons house. 2 Of the house of Lebanon. 6 Of the porch of pillars. 7 Of the porch of Iudgement. 8 Of the house for Pharaohs daughter. 13 Hirams worke of the two pillars. 23 Of the molten Sea. 27 Of the ten bases. 38 Of the ten lauers, 40 And all the vessels.

* Chap. 9. 10.

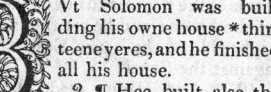**B**Vt Solomon was building his owne house *thirteene yeres, and he finished all his house.

2 ¶ Hee built also the house of the forrest of Lebanon; the length thereof *was* a hundred cubites, and the breadth thereof fiftie cubites, and the height thereof thirtie cubites, vpon foure rowes of Cedar pillars,

with Cedar beames vpon the pillars.

3 And it *was* couered with Cedar aboue vpon the †beames, that *lay* on fortie fiue pillars, fifteene in a row.

† Heb. ribs.

4 And *there were* windowes in three rowes, and †light *was* against light *in* three rankes.

† Hebr. sight against sight.

5 And all the ‖doores and postes were square, with the windowes: and light *was* against light *in* three rankes.

‖ Or, spaces and pillars were square in prospect.

6 ¶ And he made a porch of pillars, the length thereof *was* fiftie cubites, and the breadth thereof thirtie cubites: and the porch was ‖before them: and the *o-ther* pillars, and the thicke beame were ‖before them.

‖ Or, according to them.

‖ Or, according to them.

7 ¶ Then hee made a porch for the throne where he might iudge, euen the porch of Iudgement: and it was couered with Cedar from †one side of the floore to the other.

† Hebr. from floore to floore.

8 ¶ And his house where he dwelt, *had* another court within the porch, *which* was of the like worke: Solomon made also an house for Pharaohs daughter, (*whom he had taken *to wife*) like vnto this porch.

* Chap. 3. 1.

9 All these were of costly stones, according to the measures of hewed stones, sawed with sawes, within and without, euen from the foundation vnto the coping, and so on the outside toward the great court.

10 And the foundation *was* of costly stones, *euen* great stones; stones of ten cubites, and stones of eight cubites.

11 And aboue were costly stones (after the measures of hewed stones) and Cedars.

12 And the great court round about, was with three rowes of hewed stones, and a row of Cedar beames, both for the inner court of the house of the LORD, and for the porch of the house.

13 ¶ And king Solomon sent and fet Hiram out of Tyre.

14 Hee was †a widowes sonne of the tribe of Naphtali, and his father *was* a man of Tyre, a worker in brasse, and he was filled with wisedome, and vnderstanding, and cunning to worke all workes in brasse: and hee came to king Solomon, and wrought all his worke.

† Hebr. the sonne of a widow woman.

15 For †he cast two pillars of brasse of eighteene cubites high a piece: and a line of twelue cubites did compasse either of them about.

† Hebr. fashioned.

16 And hee made two Chapiters of molten brasse, to set vpon the tops of the

the pillars: the height of the one chapiter *was* fiue cubites, and the height of the other chapiter *was* fiue cubites:

17 And nets of checker worke, *and* wreathes of chaine worke, for the chapiters which *were* vpon the top of the pillars: seuen for the one chapiter, and seuen for the other chapiter.

18 And he made the pillars, and two rowes round about vpon the one networke, to couer the chapiters that *were* vpon the top, with pomegranates: and so did he for the other chapiter.

19 And the chapiters that *were* vpon the top of the pillars, *were* of lillie worke in the porch, foure cubites.

20 And the chapiters vpon the two pillars *had pomegranates* also, aboue, ouer against the belly which was by the networke: and the pomegranates were two hundred in rowes round about, vpon the other chapiter.

21 *And he set vp the pillars in the porch of the temple: and hee set vp the right pillar, and called the name therof ‖ Iachin: and he set vp the left pillar, and called the name thereof ‖ Boaz.

22 And vpon the top of the pillars *was* lillie worke: so was the worke of the pillars finished.

23 ¶ And he made a moulten Sea, ten cubites † from the one brim to the other: *it was* round all about, & his height was fiue cubits: and a line of thirtie cubites did compasse it round about.

24 And vnder the brimme of it round about *there were* knops compassing it, ten in a cubite, *compassing the sea round about: the knops were cast in two rowes, when it was cast.

25 It stood vpon twelue oxen, three looking toward the North, and three looking toward the West, and three looking toward the South, and three looking toward the East: and the Sea *was* set aboue vpon them, and all their hinder parts *were* inward.

26 And it was an hand breadth thicke, and the brimme thereof was wrought like the brim of a cup, with flowres of lillies: it contained two thousand Baths.

27 ¶ And he made ten bases of brasse; foure cubites *was* the length of one base, and foure cubites the breadth thereof, and three cubites the height of it.

28 And the worke of the bases was on this *maner:* they had borders, and the borders *were* betweene the ledges:

29 And on the borders that *were* betweene the ledges *were* lyons, oxen, and Cherubims: and vpon the ledges there was a base aboue: and beneath the lyons and oxen were certaine additions made of thinne worke.

30 And euery base had foure brasen wheeles, and plates of brasse: and the foure corners therof had vndersetters: vnder the lauer were vndersetters molten, at the side of euery addition.

31 And the mouth of it within the chapiter, and aboue, was a cubite: but the mouth thereof was round *after* the worke of the base, a cubite and an halfe: and also vpon the mouth of it were grauings with their borders, foure square not round.

32 And vnder the borders were foure wheeles: & the axletrees of the wheeles *were* † ioyned to the base, and the height of a wheele *was* a cubite and halfe a cubite.

33 And the worke of the wheeles *was* like the worke of a charet wheele: their axletrees and their naues, and their felloes, and their spokes *were* all molten.

34 And *there were* foure vndersetters to the foure corners of one base: and the vndersetters *were* of the very base it selfe.

35 And in the top of the base *was there* a round compasse of halfe a cubite high: and on the top of the base the ledges thereof, and the borders thereof *were* of the same.

36 For on the plates of the ledges thereof, and on the borders thereof, he graued Cherubims, lions, and palme trees, according to the † proportion of euery one, and additions round about.

37 After this maner he made the ten bases: all of them had one casting, one measure, and one size.

38 ¶ Then made hee ten lauers of brasse: one lauer conteined fourtie baths: *and* euery lauer was foure cubites, *and* vpon euery one of the ten bases, one lauer.

39 And he put fiue bases on the right † side of the house, and fiue on the left side of the house: and he set the Sea on the right side of the house Eastward, ouer against the South.

40 ¶ And Hiram made the lauers, and the shouels, and the basons: So Hiram made an ende of doing all the worke that hee made King Solomon, for the house of the LORD.

41 The two pillars, and the *two* bowles

* 2. Chr. 3. 17.

‖ That is, he shall establish.
‖ That is, in it is strength

† Heb. from his brimme, to his brim.

* 2. Chron. 4. 3.

† Heb. in the base.

† Heb. nakednesse.

† Heb. shoulder.

bowles of the chapiters that *were* on the top of the two pillars: and the two networkes, to couer the two bowles of the chapiters which were vpon the top of the pillars:

42 And foure hundred Pomegranates for the two networkes, *euen* two rowes of Pomegranates for one networke, to couer the two bowles of the chapiters that *were* † vpon the pillars:

43 And the ten bases, and ten lauers on the bases.

44 And one Sea, and twelue oxen vnder the Sea.

45 And the pots, and the shouels, and the basons: and all these vessels which Hiram made to King Solomon, for the house of the LORD, *were* of †bright brasse.

46 In the plaine of Iordane did the king cast them †in the clay ground, betweene Succoth and Zarthan.

47 And Solomon left all the vessels *vnweighed,* †because they were exceeding many: neither was the weight of the brasse †found out.

48 And Solomon made all the vessels that *pertained* vnto the house of the LORD: the Altar of gold, and the table of gold, whereupon the Shewbread *was*:

49 And the candlesticks of pure gold, fiue on the right *side,* and fiue on the left, before the Oracle, with the flowers, and the lampes, and the tongs of gold,

50 And the boules, and the snuffers, and the basons, & the spoones, and the †censers of pure gold: and the hindges of gold, *both* for the doores of the inner house the most Holy place, *and* for the doores of the house, *to wit,* of the temple.

51 So was ended all the worke that king Solomon made for the house of the LORD: and Solomon brought in the †things * which Dauid his father had dedicated, *euen* the siluer, and the gold, & the vessels did he put among the treasures of the house of the LORD.

CHAP. VIII.

1 The feast of the dedication of the Temple. 12. and 54. Solomons blessing. 22 Solomons prayer. 62 His sacrifice of peace offrings.

THen *Solomon assembled the Elders of Israel, and all the heads of the tribes, the †chiefe of the fathers of the children of Israel,

vnto king Solomon in Ierusalem, that they might bring vp the Arke of the Couenant of the LORD, out of the citie of Dauid, which is Zion.

2 And all the men of Israel assembled themselues vnto king Solomon, at the feast, in the moneth Ethanim, which *is* the seuenth moneth.

3 And all the Elders of Israel came, and the Priests tooke vp the Arke.

4 And they brought vp the Arke of the LORD, and the Tabernacle of the Congregation, and all the holy vessels that *were* in the Tabernacle, euen those did the Priests & the Leuites bring vp.

5 And king Solomon, and all the Congregation of Israel, that were assembled vnto him, *were* with him before the Arke, sacrificing sheepe, and oxen, that could not bee told nor numbred for multitude.

6 And the Priests brought in the Arke of the Couenant of the LORD vnto his place, into the Oracle of the house to the most holy place, euen vnder the wings of the Cherubims.

7 For the Cherubims spread forth *their* two wings ouer the place of the Arke, and the Cherubims couered the Arke, and the staues thereof aboue.

8 And they drew out the staues, that the †ends of the staues were seene out in the ‖Holy place before the Oracle, and they were not seene without: and there they are vnto this day.

9 There was nothing in the Arke, * saue the two Tables of stone, which Moses put there at Horeb, ‖when the LORD made *a Couenant* with the children of Israel, when they came out of the land of Egypt.

10 And it came to passe when the Priests were come out of the holy place, that the cloud * filled the house of the LORD;

11 So that the Priests could not stand to minister, because of the cloud: for the glory of the LORD had filled the house of the LORD.

12 ¶ Then spake Solomon; The LORD * said that hee would dwell in the thicke darkenesse.

13 I haue surely built thee an house to dwel in, a setled place for thee to abide in for euer.

14 And the King turned his face about, and blessed all the Congregation of Israel: (and all the Congregation of Israel stood.)

15 And

Marginal notes (left column):

† Hebr. vpon the face.

† Hebr. made bright, or scoured.
† Hebr. in the thicknesse of the ground.

† Hebr. for the exceeding multitude.
†Hebr. searched.

† Heb. ashpans.

† Heb. things of Dauid.
* 2. Chron. 5. 1.

* 2. Chron. 5. 2.

† Hebr. Princes.

Marginal notes (right column):

† Heb. heads.
‖ Or, Arke, as 2. Chron. 5. 9.

* Deut. 10. 5.
‖ Or, where.

* Exod. 40. 34.

* 2. Chro 6. 1.

15 And he said, Blessed *be* the LORD God of Israel, which spake with his mouth vnto Dauid my father, and hath with his hand fulfilled *it*, saying;

16 Since the day that I brought foorth my people Israel out of Egypt, I chose no citie out of all the tribes of Israel to build an house that my Name might be therein; but I chose * Dauid to be ouer my people Israel.

* 2. Sam. 7. 8.

17 And it was in the heart of Dauid my father, to builde an house for the Name of the LORD God of Israel.

18 And the LORD sayd vnto Dauid my father, Whereas it was in thine heart to build an house vnto my Name, thou diddest well that it was in thine heart.

19 Neuerthelesse, thou shalt not build the house, but thy sonne that shall come foorth out of thy loynes, hee shall build the house vnto my Name.

20 And the LORD hath perfourmed his word that he spake, and I am risen vp in the roume of Dauid my father, and sit on the throne of Israel, as the LORD promised, and haue built an House for the Name of the LORD God of Israel.

21 And I haue set there a place for the Arke, wherein *is* the Couenant of the LORD, which he made with our fathers, when he brought them out of the land of Egypt.

22 ¶ And Solomon stood before * the Altar of the LORD, in the presence of all the Congregation of Israel, and spread foorth his handes toward heauen:

* 2. Chron. 6. 13.

23 And hee said, * LORD God of Israel, *there is* no God like thee, in heauen aboue, or on earth beneath, who keepest couenant and mercy with thy seruants, that walke before thee with all their heart:

* 2. Macc. 2. 8.

24 Who hast kept with thy seruant Dauid my father that thou promisedst him: thou spakest also with thy mouth, and hast fulfilled it with thine hand, as *it is* this day.

25 Therefore now LORD God of Israel, keepe with thy seruant Dauid my father, that thou promisedst him, saying; *†There shall not faile thee a man in my sight to sit on the Throne of Israel; †so that thy children take heede to their way, that they walke before me as thou hast walked before me:

* Chap. 2. 4. 2. Sam. 7. 12.
† Heb. there shall not be cut off vnto thee a man from my sight.
† Heb. onely if.

26 And now, O God of Israel, let thy worde (I pray thee) bee verified, which thou spakest vnto thy seruant Dauid my father.

27 But will God indeede dwell on the earth? Behold, the heauen, and heauen of heauens cannot conteine thee: how much lesse this House that I haue builded?

28 Yet haue thou respect vnto the prayer of thy seruant, and to his supplication, O LORD my God, to hearken vnto the crie and to the prayer, which thy seruant prayeth before thee to day:

29 That thine eyes may be open toward this house, night and day, *euen* toward the place of which thou hast said, * My Name shall be there: that thou mayest hearken vnto the prayer which thy seruant shall make ‖towards this place.

* Deut. 12. 11.
‖ Or, in this place.

30 And hearken thou to the supplication of thy seruant, and of thy people Israel, when they shall pray ‖towards this place: and heare thou in heauen thy dwelling place, and when thou hearest, forgiue.

‖ Or, in this place.

31 ¶ If any man trespasse against his neighbour, †and an oath be laid vpon him to cause him to sweare, and the oath come before thine Altar in this house:

† Heb. and he require an oath of him.

32 Then heare thou in heauen, and doe, and iudge thy seruants, condemning the wicked to bring his way vpon his head, and iustifying the righteous, to giue him according to his righteousnesse.

33 ¶ When thy people Israel bee smitten downe before the enemie, because they haue sinned against thee, and shall turne againe to thee, and confesse thy Name, and pray, and make supplication vnto thee ‖in this house:

‖ Or, towards.

34 Then heare thou in heauen, and forgiue the sinne of thy people Israel, and bring them againe vnto the land, which thou gauest vnto their fathers.

35 ¶ When heauen is shut vp, and there is no raine, because they haue sinned against thee: if they pray towards this place, and confesse thy Name, and turne from their sinne, when thou afflictest them:

36 Then heare thou in heauen, and forgiue the sinne of thy seruants, and of thy people Israel, that thou teach them the good way wherein they should walke, and giue raine vpon thy land which

which thou hast giuen to thy people for an inheritance.

37 ¶ If there be in the land famine, if there be pestilence, blasting, mildew, locust, *or* if there be caterpiller : if their enemy besiege them in the land of their ||cities, whatsoeuer plague, whatsoeuer sicknes *there be* ;

|| Or, iuris-diction.

38 What prayer and supplication soeuer be made by any man, *or* by all thy people Israel, which shall know euery man the plague of his owne heart, and spread forth his handes towards this house :

39 Then heare thou in heauen thy dwelling place, and forgiue, and do, and giue to euery man according to his wayes, whose heart thou knowest ; (for thou, *euen* thou onely knowest the hearts of all the children of men,)

40 That they may feare thee all the dayes that they liue, in the land which thou gauest vnto our fathers.

41 Moreouer, concerning a stranger that is not of thy people Israel, but commeth out of a farre countrey, for thy Names sake ;

42 (For they shall heare of thy great Name, and of thy strong hand, and of thy stretched out arme) when hee shall come and pray towards this house :

43 Heare thou in heauen thy dwelling place, and doe according to all that the stranger calleth to thee for : that all people of the earth may know thy Name, to feare thee, as *doe* thy people Israel, and that they may know that †this house which I haue builded, is called by thy Name.

† Hebr. thy Name is called vpon this house.

44 ¶ If thy people goe out to battell against their enemie, whithersoeuer thou shalt send them, and shall pray vnto the LORD †toward the city which thou hast chosen, and *toward* the house that I haue built for thy Name :

† Hebr. the way of the citie.

45 Then heare thou in heauen their prayer & their supplication, and mainteine their ||cause.

|| Or, right.

46 If they sinne against thee, (*for there is no man that sinneth not,) and thou be angry with them, and deliuer them to the enemy, so that they cary them away captiues, vnto the land of the enemy, farre or neere ;

* 2. Chron. 6. 36. ec-cles. 7. 22. 1. iohn 1. 8, 10.

47 *Yet* if they shall †bethinke themselues, in the land whither they were caried captiues, and repent, and make supplication vnto thee in the land of them that caried them captiues, saying,

† Heb. bring backe to their heart.

Wee haue sinned, and haue done peruersly, we haue committed wickednes ;

48 And so returne vnto thee with all their heart, and with all their soule, in the land of their enemies, which led them away captiue, and pray vnto thee toward their land, which thou gauest vnto their fathers, the city which thou hast chosen, and the house which I haue built for thy Name :

49 Then heare thou their prayer and their supplication in heauen thy dwelling place, and mainteine their ||cause,

|| Or, right.

50 And forgiue thy people that haue sinned against thee, and all their transgressions, wherein they haue transgressed against thee, and giue them compassion before them who caried them captiue, that they may haue compassion on them :

51 For they *bee* thy people and thine inheritance, which thou broughtest foorth out of Egypt, from the mids of the furnace of iron :

52 That thine eyes may be open vnto the supplication of thy seruant, and vnto the supplication of thy people Israel, to hearken vnto them in all that they call for vnto thee.

53 For thou didst separate them from among all the people of the earth, to be thine inheritance, as thou spakest by the hand of Moses thy seruant, when thou *broughtest our fathers out of E-gypt, O Lord GOD.

* Exod. 19. 6.

54 And it was so, that when Solomon had made an end of praying vnto this prayer and supplication vnto the LORD, he arose from before the Altar of the LORD, from kneeling on his knees, with his handes spread vp to heauen.

55 And he stood, and blessed all the Congregation of Israel, with a lowd voice, saying;

56 Blessed *be* the LORD, that hath giuen rest vnto his people Israel, according to all that he promised : there hath not †failed one word of all his good promise, which he promised by the hand of Moses his seruant.

† Heb. fallen.

57 The LORD our God be with vs, as he was with our fathers : let him not leaue vs, nor forsake vs :

58 That hee may encline our hearts vnto him, to walke in all his wayes, and to keepe his Commaundements, and his Statutes, and his Iudgements

ments which hee commaunded our fathers.

59 And let these my wordes wherewith I haue made supplication before the Lord, be nigh vnto the Lord our God, day and night, that hee maintaine the cause of his seruant, and the cause of his people Israel †at all times, as the matter shall require:

60 That all the people of the earth may know that the Lord is God: *and that* there is none else.

61 Let your heart therefore be perfect with the Lord your God, to walke in his Statutes, and to keepe his Commandements, as at this day.

62 ¶ And *the king, and all Israel with him, offered sacrifice before the Lord.

63 And Solomon offered a sacrifice of peace offerings, which he offered vnto the Lord, two and twentie thousand oxen, and an hundred and twentie thousand sheepe: so the king and all the children of Israel dedicated the house of the Lord.

64 The same day did the king hallow the middle of the Court that was before the house of the Lord: for there hee offered burnt offerings, and meat offerings, and the fat of the peace offerings: because *the brasen Altar that *was* before the Lord, *was* too little to receiue the burnt offerings, and meat offerings, and the fat of the peace offerings.

65 And at that time Solomon held a feast, and all Israel with him, a great Congregation, from the entring in of Hamath, vnto the riuer of Egypt, before the Lord our God, seuen dayes and seuen dayes, *euen* fourteene dayes.

66 On the eight day he sent the people away: and they ‖ blessed the King, and went vnto their tents ioyfull, and glad of heart, for all the goodnesse that the Lord had done for Dauid his seruant, and for Israel his people.

CHAP. IX.

And *it came to passe, when Solomon had finished the building of the house of the Lord, and the kings house, and all Solomons desire which hee was pleased to doe,

2 That the Lord appeared to Solomon the second time, *as hee had appeared vnto him at Gibeon.

3 And the Lord said vnto him, I haue heard thy prayer and thy supplication that thou hast made before me: I haue hallowed this house which thou hast built, *to put my Name there for euer, and mine eyes and mine heart shall be there perpetually.

4 And if thou wilt walke before me, as Dauid thy father walked, in integritie of heart, and in vprightnesse, to doe according to all that I haue commanded thee, *and* wilt keepe my Statutes, and my Iudgements:

5 Then I will establish the throne of thy kingdome vpon Israel for euer, *as I promised to Dauid thy father, saying, There shall not faile thee a man vpon the throne of Israel.

6 *But* if you shall at all turne from following me, you or your children, and will not keepe my Commandements, *and* my Statutes, which I haue set before you, but goe and serue other gods, and worship them:

7 Then will I cut off Israel out of the land which I haue giuen them; and this house which I haue hallowed *for my Name, will I cast out of my sight, and Israel shall bee a prouerbe, and a by-word among all people:

8 And at this house *which* is high, euery one that passeth by it, shalbe astonished, and shall hisse, and they shal say, *Why hath the Lord done thus vnto this land, and to this house?

9 And they shall answere, Because they forsooke the Lord their God, who brought forth their fathers out of the land of Egypt, and haue taken hold vpon other gods, and haue worshipped them, and serued them: therefore hath the Lord brought vpon them all this euill.

10 ¶ And *it came to passe at the end of twentie yeeres, when Solomon had built the two houses, the house of the Lord, and the Kings house,

11 (Now Hiram the king of Tyre had furnished Solomon with Cedar trees,

---

Marginal notes (left column):

† Heb. the thing of a day in his day.

* 2. Chron. 7. 4.

* 2. Chron. 7. 7.

‖ Or, thanked.

Marginal notes (right column):

* 2. Chron. 7. 11.

* Chap. 3. 5.

* Cha. 8. 29

* 2. Sam. 7. 12. 1. chro. 22. 10.

* Ier. 7. 14.

* Deut. 29. 24. ierem. 22. 8.

* 2. Chron. 8. 1.

trees, and firre trees, and with golde according to al his desire) that then Solomon gaue Hiram twentie cities in the land of Galile.

12 And Hiram came out from Tyre to see the cities which Solomon had giuen him, and they †pleased him not.

† Heb. were not right in his eyes.

13 And he said, What cities *are* these which thou hast giuen me, my brother? And he called them the land of ‖Cabul vnto this day.

‖ That is, displeasing or, dirtie.

14 And Hiram sent to the king sixe score talents of gold.

15 ¶ And this *is* the reason of the leuie which king Solomon raised, for to build the house of the LORD, and his owne house, and Millo, and the wall of Ierusalem, and Hazor, and Megiddo, and Gezer.

16 *For* Pharaoh king of Egypt had gone vp, and taken Gezer, and burnt it with fire, and slaine the Canaanites that dwelt in the citie, and giuen it for a present vnto his daughter Solomons wife.

17 And Solomon built Gezer, and Beth - horon the nether,

18 And Baalath, and Tadmor in the wildernesse, in the land.

19 And all the cities of store that Solomon had, and cities for his charets, and cities for his horsemen, and †that which Solomon desired to build in Ierusalem, and in Lebanon, and in all the land of his dominion.

† Heb. the desire of Solomon which he desired.

20 *And* all the people that were left of the Amorites, Hittittes, Perizzites, Hiuites, and Iebusites, which were not of the children of Israel,

21 Their children that were left after them in the land, whom the children of Israel also were not able vtterly to destroy, vpon those did Solomon leuie a tribute of bond-seruice vnto this day.

22 But of the children of Israel did Solomon *make no bondmen : but they *were* men of warre, and his seruants, and his princes, and his captaines, and his rulers of his charets, and his horsemen.

* Leuit. 25. 39.

23 These *were* the chiefe of the officers that *were* ouer Solomons worke, fiue hundred and fiftie, which bare rule ouer the people that wrought in the worke.

24 ¶ But *Pharaohs daughter came vp out of the citie of Dauid, vnto her house which Solomon had built for her : then did he build Millo.

* 2. Chron. 8. 11.

25 ¶ And three times in a yeere did Solomon offer burnt offerings, and peace offerings vpon the Altar which he built vnto the LORD, and he burnt incense †vpon the altar that *was* before the LORD : so he finished the house.

† Hebr. vpon it.

26 ¶ And king Solomon made a nauie of ships in Ezion Geber, which *is* beside Eloth, on the †shoare of the red sea, in the land of Edom.

† Heb. lip.

27 And Hiram sent in the nauie his seruants, shipmen that had knowledge of the Sea, with the seruants of Solomon.

28 And they came to Ophir, and fet from thence gold foure hundred and twentie talents, and brought *it* to king Solomon.

CHAP. X.

1 *The Queene of Sheba admireth the wisdome of Solomon.* 14 *Solomons gold.* 16 *His targets.* 18 *The throne of Iuorie.* 21 *His vessels.* 24 *His presents.* 26 *His chariots and horse.* 28 *His tribute.*

ANd when the *Queene of Sheba heard of the fame of Solomon, concerning the Name of the LORD; shee came to prooue him with hard questions.

* 2. Chron. 9. 1. mat. 12 42. luke 11. 31.

2 And she came to Ierusalem with a very great traine, with camels that bare spices, and very much gold, and precious stones : and when shee was come to Solomon, she communed with him, of all that was in her heart.

3 And Solomon tolde her all her †questions : there was not any thing hid from the king, which hee told her not.

† Heb. words

4 And when the Queene of Sheba had seene all Solomons wisedome, and the house that he had built,

5 And the meat of his table, and the sitting of his seruants, and the †attendance of his ministers, and their apparell, and his ‖ cup-bearers, and his ascent by which hee went vp vnto the house of the LORD : there was no more spirit in her.

† Heb. standing.
‖ Or, Butlers

6 And she said to the king, It was a true †report that I heard in mine owne land, of thy ‖actes and of thy wisedome.

† Heb. word.
‖ Or, sayings

7 Howbeit, I beleeued not the words, vntill I came and mine eyes had seene *it:* and beholde, the halfe was not told me: †thy wisedom and prosperitie exceedeth the fame which I heard.

† Heb. thou hast added wisedome and goodnes to the fame.

8 Happie

8 Happie *are* thy men, happy *are* these thy seruants, which stand continually before thee, *and* that heare thy wisedom.

9 Blessed be the LORD thy God which delighted in thee, to set thee on the throne of Israel; because the LORD loued Israel for euer, therefore made he thee King, to doe iudgement and iustice.

10 And she gaue the king an hundred and twentie talents of gold, and of spices very great store, & precious stones: there came no more such abundance of spices, as these, which the Queene of Sheba gaue to king Solomon.

11 And the nauie also of Hiram that brought gold from Ophir, brought in from Ophir, great plentie of Almug trees, and precious stones.

12 And the king made of the Almug trees, ||pillars for the house of the LORD, and for the Kings house, Harpes also and Psalteries for singers: there came no such *Almug trees, nor were seene vnto this day.

13 And king Solomon gaue vnto the Queene of Sheba, al her desire *whatsoeuer* she asked, besides that which Solomon gaue her †of *his* royall bountie: so she turned and went to her owne countrey, she and her seruants.

14 ¶ Now the weight of gold that came to Solomon in one yere, was six hundred, threescore & six talents of gold,

15 Besides *that he had* of the merchant men, and of the traffique of the spice-merchants, and of all the kings of Arabia, and of the ||gouernours of the countrey.

16 ¶ And king Solomon made two hundred targets of beaten golde: sixe hundred *shekels* of golde went to one target.

17 And *he made* three hundred shields of beaten gold, three pound of gold went to one shield; and the king put them in the *house of the forrest of Lebanon.

18 ¶ Moreouer the king made a great throne of yuorie, and ouerlaide it with the best gold.

19 The throne *had* six steps, and the top of the throne *was* round †behind: and *there were* †stayes on either side on the place of the seate, and two lyons stood beside the stayes.

20 And twelue lions stood there on the one side and on the other vpon the sixe steps: there was not †the like made in any kingdome.

Marginal notes left column:
||Or, railes. Heb. *a prop.*
*2. Chron. 9. 10
†Hebr. *according to the hand of king Solomon.*
||Or, *Captaines.*
*Chap. 7. 2
†Heb. *on the hinder part thereof.*
†Heb. *hands.*
†Heb. *so.*

21 ¶ And all king Solomons drinking vessels *were* of gold, and all the vessels of the house of the forrest of Lebanon *were* of pure gold, ||none were of siluer, it was nothing accounted of in the dayes of Solomon.

22 For the king *had* at sea a nauie of Tharshish, with the nauie of Hiram: once in three yeeres came the nauie of Tharshish, bringing golde and siluer, || yuorie, and apes, and peacocks.

23 So king Solomon exceeded all the kings of the earth, for riches and for wisedome.

24 ¶ And all the earth †sought to Solomon, to heare his wisedom which God had put in his heart.

25 And they brought euery man his present, vessels of siluer, and vessels of gold, and garments, and armour, and spices, horses, and mules, a rate yeere by yeere.

26 ¶ And Solomon gathered together *charets and horsemen. And hee had a thousand and foure hundred charets, and twelue thousand horsemen, whom he bestowed in the cities for charets, and with the king at Ierusalem.

27 And the king †made siluer *to be* in Ierusalem as stones, and Cedars made he *to be* as the Sycomore trees, that *are* in the vale for abundance.

28 ¶ *†And Solomon had horses brought out of Egypt, and linen yarne: the kings merchants receiued the linen yarne at a price.

29 And a charet came vp and went out of Egypt for sixe hundred *shekels* of siluer, and an horse for an hundred and fiftie: and so for all the kings of the Hittites, and for the kings of Syria, did they bring *them* out †by their meanes.

Marginal notes right column:
||Or, there was no siluer in them.
||Or, Elephants teet
†Heb. *sought the face of.*
*2. Chron. 1. 14.
†Heb. *gaue*
2. Chron. 1. 16. & 9. 28.
†Heb. *and the going forth of the horses which was Solomons.*
†Hebr. *by their hand*

CHAP. XI.

1 Solomons wiues and concubines. 4 In his old age they draw him to idolatry. 9 God threatneth him. 14 Solomons aduersaries were Hadad, who was intertained in Egypt, 23 Rezon who reigned in Damascus, 26 And Ieroboam, to whom Ahiiah prophesied. 41 Solomons actes, reigne, and death: Rehoboam succeedeth him.

Vt King Solomon loued *many strange women, (|| together with ȳ daughter of Pharaoh) women of the Moabites, Ammonites, Edomites, Sidonians & Hittites:

*Deut. 17 17. ecclus. 49. 19.
||Or, beside

2 Of

2 Of the nations concerning which the Lord said vnto the children of Israel, * Yee shall not goe in to them, neither shall they come in vnto you, *for* surely they will turne away your heart after their gods : Solomon claue vnto these in loue.

3 And he had seuen hundred wiues, Princesses, and three hundred concubines : and his wiues turned away his heart.

4 For it came to passe when Solomon was old, that his wiues turned away his heart after other gods : and his heart was not perfect with the Lord his God, as *was* the heart of Dauid his father.

5 For Solomon went after * Ashtoreth the goddesse of the Zidonians, and after Milcom the abomination of the Amorites.

6 And Solomon did euill in the sight of the Lord, and † went not fully after the Lord, as *did* Dauid his father.

7 Then did Solomon build an hie place for Chemosh the abomination of Moab, in the hill that *is* before Ierusalem, and for Molech the abomination of the children of Ammon.

8 And likewise did hee for all his strange wiues, which burnt incense and sacrificed vnto their gods.

9 ¶ And the Lord was angry with Solomon, because his heart was turned from the Lord God of Israel * which had appeared vnto him twise,

10 And * had commaunded him concerning this thing, that hee should not goe after other gods : but hee kept not that which the Lord commanded.

11 Wherefore the Lord said vnto Solomon ; Forasmuch as this † is done of thee, and thou hast not kept my Couenant, and my Statutes which I haue commanded thee, * I wil surely rend the kingdome from thee, and will giue it to thy seruant.

12 Notwithstanding in thy dayes I wil not doe it, for Dauid thy fathers sake : *but* I wil rend it out of the hand of thy sonne.

13 Howbeit, I wil not rend away all the kingdome : *but* wil giue one tribe to thy sonne, for Dauid my seruants sake, and for Ierusalems sake, which I haue chosen.

14 ¶ And the Lord stirred vp an aduersary vnto Solomon, Hadad the Edomite : hee *was* of the kings seed in Edom.

15 * For it came to passe when Dauid was in Edom, and Ioab the captaine of the host was gone vp to bury the slaine, after he had smitten euery male in Edom :

16 (For sixe moneths did Ioab remaine there with all Israel, vntil hee had cut off euery male in Edom.)

17 That Hadad fled, he and certaine Edomites of his fathers seruants with him, to goe into Egypt : Hadad being yet a litle childe.

18 And they arose out of Midian, and came to Paran, and they tooke men with them out of Paran, and they came to Egypt, vnto Pharaoh king of Egypt, which gaue him an house, and appointed him vitailes, and gaue him land.

19 And Hadad found great fauour in the sight of Pharaoh, so that he gaue him to wife the sister of his owne wife, the sister of Tahpenes the Queene.

20 And the sister of Tahpenes bare him Genubath his sonne, whom Tahpenes weaned in Pharaohs house : and Genubath was in Pharaohs houshold among the sonnes of Pharaoh.

21 And when Hadad heard in Egypt that Dauid slept with his fathers, and that Ioab the captaine of the host was dead, Hadad said to Pharaoh, † Let me depart, that I may go to mine owne countrey.

22 Then Pharaoh said vnto him, But what hast thou lacked with mee, that, behold, thou seekest to goe to thine owne countrey ? And hee answered, † Nothing : Howbeit, let mee goe in any wise.

23 ¶ And * God stirred him vp *another* aduersary : Rezon, the sonne of Eliadah, which fled from his lord Hadadezer king of Zobah :

24 And he gathered men vnto him, and became captaine ouer a band, when Dauid slew them *of Zobah* : and they went to Damascus, and dwelt therein, and reigned in Damascus.

25 And he was an aduersarie to Israel all the dayes of Solomon, beside the mischiefe that Hadad *did* : and he abhorred Israel, and reigned ouer Syria.

26 ¶ And * Ieroboam the sonne of Nebat, an Ephrathite of Zereda, Solomons seruant, (whose mothers name *was*

ᴋod. 34.

ᴊdg. 2.

ᴇbr. ful-
d not af-

ʜap. 3.

ʜap. 6.

ᴇbr. is
ι thee.

ʜap. 12.

* 2. Sam. 8.
14.

† Heb. send
me away.

† Heb. Not.

* 2. Sam. 8.
3. and 10.
18.

* 2. Chron.
13. 6.

† *Hebr. clo-sed.*

was Zeruah a widow woman) euen he lift vp *his* hand against the king.

27 And this *was* the cause that hee lift vp *his* hand against the king : Solomon built Millo, *and* †repaired the breaches of the citie of Dauid his father.

† *Heb. did worke.*

28 And the man Ieroboam *was* a mightie man of valour : and Solomon seeing the young man that he †was industrious, hee made him ruler ouer all the †charge of the house of Ioseph.

† *Hebr. burden.*

29 And it came to passe at that time when Ieroboam went out of Ierusalem, that the Prophet Ahiiah the Shilonite found him in the way : and hee had clad himselfe with a new garment ; and they two were alone in the field.

30 And Ahiiah caught the new garment that *was* on him, and rent it in twelue pieces.

31 And he said to Ieroboam, Take thee tenne pieces : for thus sayth the Lord the God of Israel, Behold, I will rent the kingdome out of the hand of Solomon, and will giue ten tribes to thee :

32 (But hee shall haue one tribe, for my seruant Dauids sake, and for Ierusalems sake, the citie which I haue chosen out of all the tribes of Israel :)

33 Because that they haue forsaken mee, and haue worshipped Ashtaroth the goddesse of the Zidonians, Chemosh the god of the Moabites, and Milcom the god of the children of Ammon, and haue not walked in my wayes, to doe that which is right in mine eyes, and *to keepe* my Statutes, and my Iudgements, as *did* Dauid his father.

34 Howbeit, I will not take the whole kingdome out of his hand : but I will make him Prince all the dayes of his life, for Dauid my seruants sake, whom I chose, because hee kept my Commandemeuts and my Statutes :

* *Chap. 12. 15.*

35 But *I will take the kingdome out of his sonnes hand, and will giue it vnto him, *euen* ten tribes.

36 And vnto his sonne will I giue one tribe, that Dauid my seruant may haue a †light alway before me in Ierusalem, the citie which I haue chosen me to put my Name there.

† *Heb. lampe or candle.*

37 And I will take thee, and thou shalt reigne according to all that thy soule desireth, and shalt be King ouer Israel.

38 And it shall be, if thou wilt hearken vnto all that I command thee, and

wilt walke in my wayes, and doe that is right in my sight, to keepe my Statutes and my Commandements, as Dauid my seruant did ; that I will be with thee, and build thee a sure house, as I built for Dauid, and will giue Israel vnto thee.

39 And I will for this afflict the seed of Dauid, but not for euer.

40 Solomon sought therefore to kill Ieroboam, and Ieroboam arose, and fledde into Egypt, vnto Shishak king of Egypt, and was in Egypt vntill the death of Solomon.

41 ¶ And the rest of the ‖actes of Solomon, and all that he did, and his wisedome, are they not written in the booke of the actes of Solomon ?

‖ *Or, word or things.*

42 And the †time that Solomon reigned in Ierusalem, ouer all Israel, *was* *fourtie yeeres.

† *Heb. day*

* *2. Chron. 9. 30.*

43 And Solomon slept with his fathers, and was buried in the citie of Dauid his father : and *Rehoboam his sonne reigned in his stead.

* *Mat. 1. called Roboam.*

CHAP. XII.

1 *The Israelites assembled at Shechem to crowne Rehoboam, by Ieroboam make a suite of relaxation vnto him.* 6 *Rehoboam refusing the olde mens counsell, by the aduice of young men, answereth them roughly.* 16 *Ten tribes reuolting, kill Adoram, and make Rehoboam to flee.* 21 *Rehoboam raising an armie, is forbidden by Shemaiah.* 25 *Ieroboam strengtheneth himselfe by cities,* 26 *and by the idolatrie of the two calues.*

ND *Rehoboam went to Shechem : for all Israel were come to Shechem to make him king.

* *2. Chron. 10. 1.*

2 And it came to passe when Ieroboam the sonne of Nebat, who was yet in * Egypt, heard of it (for hee was fled from the presence of king Solomon, and Ieroboam dwelt in Egypt :)

* *Chap. 40.*

3 That they sent, and called him : and Ieroboam and all the Congregation of Israel came, and spake vnto Rehoboam, saying ;

4 Thy father made our *yoke grieuous : now therefore, make thou the grieuous seruice of thy father, and his heauy yoke which he put vpon vs, lighter, and we will serue thee.

* *Chap. 4*

5 And hee said vnto them, Depart yet for three daies, then come againe to me.

me. And the people departed.

6 ¶ And king Rehoboam consulted with the old men that stood before Solomon his father, while he yet liued, and said, How doe you aduise, that *I* may answere this people?

7 And they spake vnto him, saying, If thou wilt be a seruant vnto this people this day, and wilt serue them, and answere them, and speake good words to them, then they will be thy seruants for euer.

8 But hee forsooke the counsell of the old men, which they had giuen him, and consulted with the yong men, that were growen vp with him, *and* which stood before him.

9 And hee said vnto them, What counsell giue ye, that we may answere this people, who haue spoken to mee, saying, Make the yoke which thy father did put vpon vs, lighter?

10 And the young men that were growen vp with him, spake vnto him, saying, Thus shalt thou speake vnto this people that spake vnto thee, saying, Thy father made our yoke heauy, but make thou it lighter vnto vs; thus shalt thou say vnto them, My litle *finger* shall bee thicker then my fathers loynes.

11 And now whereas my father did lade you with a heauy yoke, I wil adde to your yoke: my father hath chastised you with whippes, but I will chastise you with scorpions.

12 ¶ So Ieroboam and all the people came to Rehoboam the third day, as the king had appointed, saying, Come to me againe the third day.

13 And the king answered the people †roughly, and forsooke the old mens counsell that they gaue him:

Heb. hard-ly.

14 And spake to them after the counsell of the young men, saying, My father made your yoke heauy, and I will adde to your yoke; my father *also* chastised you with whips, but I will chastise you with scorpions.

15 Wherefore the king hearkened not vnto the people: for the cause was from the LORD, that hee might performe his saying, which the LORD spake by *Ahiiah the Shilonite vnto Ieroboam the sonne of Nebat.

* Chap. 11. 1.

16 ¶ So when all Israel saw that the king hearkned not vnto them, the people answered the king, saying, What portion haue we in Dauid? nei-

ther *haue we* inheritance in the sonne of Iesse: to your tents, O Israel: nowe see to thine owne house, Dauid. So Israel departed vnto their tents.

17 But as for the children of Israel which dwelt in the cities of Iudah, Rehoboam reigned ouer them.

18 Then king Rehoboam sent Adoram, who *was* ouer the tribute, and all Israel stoned him with stones that hee died: therefore king Rehoboam †made speed to get him vp to his charet, to flee to Ierusalem.

†*Heb. streng-thened him-selfe.*

19 So Israel ‖rebelled against the house of Dauid vnto this day.

‖ *Or, fell a-way.*

20 And it came to passe when all Israel heard that Ieroboam was come againe, that they sent and called him vnto the Congregation, and made him king ouer all Israel: there was none that followed the house of Dauid, but the tribe of Iudah *onely.

* Chap. 11. 13.

21 ¶ And when Rehoboam was come to Ierusalem, hee assembled all the house of Iudah, with the tribe of Beniamin, an hundred and fourescore thousand chosen men which were warriers, to fight against the house of Israel, to bring the kingdome againe to Rehoboam the sonne of Solomon.

22 But *the word of God came vnto Shemaiah, the man of God, saying,

* 2. Chron. 11. 2.

23 Speake vnto Rehoboam the sonne of Solomon king of Iudah, and vnto all the house of Iudah and Beniamin, and to the remnant of the people, saying,

24 Thus saith the LORD, Ye shall not goe vp, nor fight against your brethren the children of Israel: returne euery man to his house, for this thing is from me. They hearkened therefore to the word of the LORD, and returned to depart, according to the word of the LORD.

25 ¶ Then Ieroboam built Shechem in mount Ephraim, and dwelt therein, and went out from thence, and built Penuel.

26 And Ieroboam said in his heart, Now shall the kingdome returne to the house of Dauid:

27 If this people goe vp, to doe sacrifice in the house of the LORD at Ierusalem, then shall the heart of this people turne againe vnto their lorde, *euen* vnto Rehoboam king of Iudah, and they shall kill mee, and goe againe to Rehoboam king of Iudah.

28 Where-

28 Whereupon the king tooke counsell, and made two calues of gold, and said vnto them, It is too much for you to goe vp to Ierusalem : *Behold thy gods, O Israel, which brought thee vp out of the land of Egypt.

* Exod. 32. 8.

29 And he set the one in Bethel, and the other put he in Dan.

30 And this thing became a sinne: for the people went *to worship* before the one, *euen* vnto Dan.

31 And he made an house of hie places, and made priests of the lowest of the people, which were not of the sonnes of Leui.

32 And Ieroboam ordeined a feast in the eight moneth, on the fifteenth day of the moneth, like vnto the feast that *is* in Iudah, and he ||offered vpon the altar (so did he in Bethel,) ||sacrificing vnto the calues that he had made: and he placed in Bethel the priests of the high places which he had made.

|| Or, went vp to the altar &c.
|| Or to sacrifice.

33 So hee || offered vpon the altar, which hee had made in Bethel, the fifteenth day of the eighth moneth, euen in the moneth which he had deuised of his owne heart: and ordeined a feast vnto the children of Israel, and he offered vpon the altar, †and burnt incense.

| Or, went vp to the altar &c.

† Hebr. to burne incense.

CHAP. XIII.

1 Ieroboams hand, that offered violence to him that prophesied against his altar at Bethel, withereth, 6 and at the prayer of the Prophet is restored. 7 The Prophet, refusing the kings intertainment, departeth from Bethel. 11 An old Prophet, seducing him, bringeth him backe. 20 He is reproued by God, 23 slaine by a Lion, 26 buried by the old Prophet, 31 Who confirmeth his prophecie. 33 Ieroboams obstinacie.

Nd behold, there came a man of God out of Iudah by the word of the LORD vnto Bethel : and Ieroboam stood by the altar to ||burne incense.

| Or, to offer.

2 And hee cried against the altar in the word of the LORD, and said, O altar, altar, thus saith the LORD, Behold, a child shalbe borne vnto the house of Dauid, *Iosiah by name, and vpon thee shall he offer the priests of the high places that burne incense vpon thee, and mens bones shall bee burnt vpon thee.

* 2. King. 23. 17.

3 And he gaue a signe the same day,

saying, This is the signe which the LORD hath spoken : Behold, the altar shall be rent, and the ashes that are vpon it, shalbe powred out.

4 And it came to passe when king Ieroboam heard the saying of the man of God, which had cried against the altar in Bethel, that he put forth his hand from the altar, saying, Lay hold on him : And his hand which hee put foorth against him, dried vp, so that hee could not pull it in againe to him.

5 The altar also was rent, and the ashes powred out from the altar, according to the signe which the man of God had giuen by the word of the LORD.

6 And the king answered, and said vnto the man of God, Intreat now the face of the LORD thy God, and pray for mee, that my hand may be restored mee againe. And the man of God besought † the LORD, and the kings hand was restored againe, and became as it was before.

† Hebr. th face of th LORD.

7 And the king said vnto the man of God, Come home with mee, and refresh thy selfe, and I wil giue thee a reward.

8 And the man of God said vnto the king, If thou wilt giue mee halfe thine house, I will not goe in with thee, neither will I eat bread, nor drinke water in this place :

9 For so was it charged mee by the word of the LORD, saying, Eate no bread, nor drinke water, nor turne againe by the same way that thou camest.

10 So he went another way, and returned not by the way that hee came to Bethel.

11 ¶ Now there dwelt an old Prophet in Bethel, and his sonne came and told him all the workes that the man of God had done that day in Bethel : the words which hee had spoken vnto the king, them they tolde also to their father.

12 And their father said vnto them, What way went he? for his sonnes had seene what way the man of God went, which came from Iudah.

13 And hee saide vnto his sonnes, Saddle me the asse. So they sadled him the asse, and he rode thereon,

14 And went after the man of God, and found him sitting vnder an oke; and he said vnto him, Art thou the man of God that camest from Iudah? And he said, I *am.*

15 Then

15 Then hee said vnto him, Come home with me, and eate bread.

16 And he said, I may not returne with thee, nor goe in with thee : neither will I eat bread, nor drinke water with thee in this place.

17 For †it was said to mee by the word of the LORD, Thou shalt eate no bread, nor drinke water there, nor turne againe to go by the way that thou camest.

† Hebr. a word was.

18 He said vnto him, I *am* a prophet also as thou *art*, and an angel spake vnto me by the word of the LORD, saying, Bring him backe with thee into thine house, that he may eat bread, and drinke water : *But* he lied vnto him.

19 So he went backe with him, and did eate bread in his house, and dranke water.

20 ¶ And it came to passe as they sate at the table, that the word of the LORD came vnto the prophet that brought him backe :

21 And he cried vnto the man of God that came from Iudah, saying, Thus saith the LORD, Forasmuch as thou hast disobeied the mouth of the LORD, and hast not kept the commandement which the LORD thy God commanded thee,

22 But camest backe, and hast eaten bread, and drunke water, in the place, of the which the LORD did say to thee, Eate no bread, and drinke no water; thy carcaise shall not come vnto the sepulchre of thy fathers.

23 ¶ And it came to passe after he had eaten bread, and after hee had drunke, that he sadled for him the asse, *to wit*, for the Prophet, whome hee had brought backe.

24 And when he was gone, a lyon met him by the way, and slew him : and his carcaise was cast in the way, and the asse stood by it, the lyon also stood by the carcaise.

25 And beholde, men passed by, and saw the carcaise cast in the way, and the lyon standing by the carcaise : and they came and told it in the citie where the old prophet dwelt.

26 And when the prophet that brought him back from the way, heard *thereof*, he said, It is the man of God, who was disobedient vnto the word of the LORD : therefore the LORD hath deliuered him vnto the lion, which hath †torne him, and slaine him, accor-

Heb. broen.

ding to the word of the LORD, which he spake vnto him.

27 And he spake to his sonnes, saying, Saddle me the asse : and they sadled *him*.

28 And he went and found his carcaise cast in the way, and the asse and the lyon standing by the carcaise : the lyon had not eaten the carcaise, nor †torne the asse.

† Heb. broken.

29 And the prophet tooke vp the carcaise of the man of God, and laid it vpon the asse, and brought it backe : and the old prophet came to the city, to mourne, and to burie him.

30 And hee laid his carcaise in his owne graue, and they mourned ouer him, *saying*, Alas my brother.

31 And it came to passe after hee had buried him, that he spake to his sonnes, saying, When I am dead, then bury me in the sepulchre, wherein the man of God is buried, lay my bones beside his bones.

32 For the saying which hee cried by the word of the LORD against the altar in Bethel, and against all the houses of the high places which *are* in the cities of Samaria, shall surely come to passe.

33 ¶ After this thing, Ieroboam returned not from his euill way, but †made againe of the lowest of the people priests of the high places : whosoeuer would, he †consecrated him, and he became one of the priests of the high places.

† Heb. returned and made.
† Heb. filled his hand.

34 And this thing became sinne vnto the house of Ieroboam, euen to cut it off, and to destroy it from off the face of the earth.

CHAP. XIIII.

1 Abijah being sicke, Ieroboam sendeth his wife disguised with Presents to the prophet Ahijah at Shiloh. 5 Ahijah forewarned by God, denounceth Gods iudgement. 17 Abijah dieth and is buried. 19 Nadab succeedeth Ieroboam. 21 Rehoboams wicked reigne. 25 Shishak spoileth Ierusalem. 29 Abiiam succeedeth Rehoboam.

AT that time Abiiah the sonne of Ieroboam fell sicke.

2 And Ieroboam said to his wife, Arise, I pray thee, and disguise thy selfe, that thou be not knowen to be the wife of Ieroboam : and get thee to Shiloh : Behold, there

Heb. broen.

there *is* Ahiiah the Prophet, which told mee that * I should *be* king ouer this people.

* Chap. 11. 31.

† *Heb. in thine hand.*

‖ *Or, cakes.*

‖ *Or, bottle.*

3 And take † with thee ten loaues, and ‖ cracknels, and a ‖ cruse of honie, and goe to him: he shall tell thee what shall become of the childe.

4 And Ieroboams wife did so, and arose, and went to Shiloh, and came to the house of Ahiiah: but Ahiiah could not see, for his eyes † were set by reason of his age.

† *Heb. stood for hoarines.*

5 ¶ And the Lord said vnto Ahiiah, Behold, the wife of Ieroboam commeth to aske a thing of thee for her sonne, for hee is sicke: thus and thus shalt thou say vnto her: for it shall be when shee commeth in, that shee shall faine her selfe to be another woman.

6 And it was so, when Ahiiah heard the sound of her feet, as she came in at the doore, that hee said, Come in, thou wife of Ieroboam, why fainest thou thy selfe to be another? for I am sent to thee with † heauie *tidings*.

† *Heb. hard.*

7 Goe, tell Ieroboam, Thus saith the Lord God of Israel, Forasmuch as I exalted thee from among the people, and made thee prince ouer my people Israel,

8 And rent the kingdome away from the house of Dauid, and gaue it thee: and *yet* thou hast not beene as my seruant Dauid, who kept my Commandements, and who followed mee with all his heart, to doe that onely which was right in mine eyes,

9 But hast done euill aboue all that were before thee: for thou hast gone and made thee other gods, and molten images, to prouoke me to anger, and hast cast me behinde thy backe:

* 1. King. 15. 29.

10 Therefore behold, * I will bring euill vpon the house of Ieroboam, and will cut off from Ieroboam, * him that pisseth against the wall, *and* him that *is* shut vp and left in Israel, and will take away the remnant of the house of Ieroboam, as a man taketh away dung, till it be all gone.

* Chap. 21. 21. 2. king. 9. 8.

11 Him that dieth of Ieroboam in the citie, shall the dogs eate: and him that dieth in the field, shall the foules of the aire eate: for the Lord hath spoken *it*.

12 Arise thou therefore, get thee to thine owne house: and when thy feete enter into the citie, the child shall die.

13 And all Israel shall mourne for him, and bury him: for he onely of Ieroboam shal come to the graue, because in him there is found some good thing toward the Lord God of Israel, in the house of Ieroboam.

14 Moreouer, the Lord shall raise him vp a king ouer Israel, who shal cut off the house of Ieroboam that day: but what? euen now.

15 For the Lord shall smite Israel, as a reede is shaken in the water, and hee shall root vp Israel out of this good land, which hee gaue to their fathors, and shall scatter them beyond the Riuer, because they haue made their groues, prouoking the Lord to anger.

16 And hee shall giue Israel vp, because of the sinnes of Ieroboam, who did sinne, & who made Israel to sinne.

17 ¶ And Ieroboams wife arose, and departed, and came to Tirzah: *and* when shee came to the threshold of the doore, the child died.

18 And they buried him, and all Israel mourned for him, according to the word of the Lord, which hee spake by the hand of his seruant Ahiiah the Prophet.

19 And the rest of the actes of Ieroboam, how hee warred, and how hee reigned, behold, they *are* written in the booke of the Chronicles of the kings of Israel.

20 And the dayes which Ieroboam reigned, *were* two and twentie yeeres: and he † slept with his fathers, and Nadab his sonne reigned in his stead.

† *Heb. le downe.*

21 ¶ And Rehoboam the sonne of Solomon reigned in Iudah: * Rehoboam *was* fourtie and one yeeres olde when he began to reigne, and hee reigned seuenteene yeeres in Ierusalem, the citie which the Lord did chuse out of all the tribes of Israel, to put his Name there: and his mothers name was Naamah an Ammonitesse.

* 2. Chro 12. 13.

22 And Iudah did euill in the sight of the Lord, and they prouoked him to iealousie with their sinnes which they had committed, aboue all that their fathers had done.

23 For they also built them high places, and ‖ images, and groues on euery high hill, and vnder euery greene tree.

‖ *Or, sta ding ime or statu*

24 And there were also Sodomites in the land, *and* they did according to all the abominations of the nations which the

the LORD cast out before the children of Israel.

25 ¶ And it came to passe in the fift yeere of king Rehoboam, *that* Shishak king of Egypt came vp against Ierusalem :

26 And he tooke away the treasures of the house of the LORD, and the treasures of the kings house, hee euen tooke away all : and he tooke away all the shields of gold *which Solomon had made.

Chap. 10.

27 And king Rehoboam made in their stead brasen shields, and committed them vnto the hands of the chiefe of the †guard, which kept the doore of the kings house.

†Heb. run-ners.

28 And it was so, when the king went into the house of the LORD, that the guard bare them, and brought them backe into the guard-chamber.

29 ¶ Nowe the rest of the actes of Rehoboam, and all that hee did, are they not written in the booke of the Chronicles of the kings of Iudah ?

30 And there was warre betweene Rehoboam and Ieroboam all *their* dayes.

31 And Rehoboam slept with his fathers, and was buried with his fathers in the city of Dauid : and his mothers name was Naamah an Ammonitesse. And Abijam his sonne reigned in his stead.

CHAP. XV.

1 Abiiams wicked reigne. 7 Asa succeedeth him. 9 Asas good reigne. 16 The warre betweene Baasha and him, causeth him to make a league with Benhadad. 23 Iehoshaphat succeedeth Asa. 25 Nadabs wicked reigne. 27 Baasha conspiring against him executeth Ahiiahs prophecy. 31 Nadabs acts and death. 33 Baashas wicked reigne.

. Chro. 22.

Owe in the eighteenth yeere of king *Ieroboam the sonne of Nebat, reigned Abiiam ouer Iudah.

2 Three yeeres reigned hee in Ierusalem : and his mothers name *was* Maachah, the daughter of Abishalom.

3 And he walked in all the sinnes of his father, which hee had done before him : and his heart was not perfect with the LORD his God, as the heart of Dauid his father.

4 Neuerthelesse, for Dauids sake did the LORD his God giue him a ‖lampe in Ierusalem, to set vp his sonne after him, and to establish Ierusalem :

‖Or, candle.

5 Because Dauid did that which *was* right in the eies of the LORD, and turned not aside from any thing that he commanded him all the daies of his life, *saue onely in the matter of Vriiah the Hittite.

* 2. Sam. 11 4. and 12. 9.

6 And there was warre betweene Rehoboam and Ieroboam all the dayes of his life.

7 Now the rest of the actes of Abiiam, and all that hee did, are they not written in the *booke of the Chronicles of the Kings of Iudah ? And there was warre betweene Abiiam and Ieroboam.

* 2. Chron. 13. 3.

8 And Abiiam slept with his fathers, and they buried him in the citie of Dauid : and Asa his sonne reigned in his stead.

9 ¶ And *in the twentieth yeere of Ieroboam king of Israel, reigned Asa ouer Iudah.

* 2. Chron. 14. 1.

10 And forty and one yeeres reigned hee in Ierusalem : and his ‖mothers name *was* Maachah, the daughter of Abishalom.

‖ That is, grandmother.

11 And Asa did that which *was* right in the eies of the LORD, as did Dauid his father.

12 And hee tooke away the Sodomites out of the land, and remooued all the idoles that his fathers had made.

13 And also *Maachah his mother, euen her hee remoued from *being* Queene, because she had made an idole in a groue, and Asa †destroyed her idole, and burnt *it* by the brooke Kidron.

* 2. Chron. 15. 16.

† Heb. cut off.

14 But the high places were not remooued : neuerthelesse, Asa his heart was perfect with the LORD all his dayes.

15 And he brought in the †things which his father had dedicated, and the things which himselfe had dedicated, into the house of the LORD, siluer, and gold, and vessels.

† Heb. holy.

16 ¶ And there was war betweene Asa and Baasha King of Israel all their dayes.

17 And Baasha king of Israel went vp against Iudah, and built Ramah, that he might not suffer any to goe out or come in to Asa king of Iudah.

18 Then

18 Then Asa tooke all the siluer and the golde that *were* left in the treasures of the house of the LORD, and the treasures of the kings house, and deliuered them into the hand of his seruants: and king Asa sent them to * Benhadad the sonne of Tabrimon, the sonne of Hezion king of Syria, that dwelt at Damascus, saying,

*2. Chron. 16. 2.

19 *There is* a league betweene me and thee, *and* betweene my father and thy father: behold, I haue sent vnto thee a present of siluer and gold; come and breake the league with Baasha king of Israel, that he may †depart from me.

† Hebr. goe vp.

20 So Benhadad hearkened vnto king Asa, and sent the captaines of the hosts, which he had, against the cities of Israel, and smote Iion, and Dan, and Abel-Bethmaachah, and all Cinneroth, with all the land of Naphtali.

21 And it came to passe when Baasha heard *thereof,* that hee left off building of Ramah, and dwelt in Tirzah.

22 Then king Asa made a Proclamation throughout all Iudah, (none *was* †exempted:) and they tooke away the stones of Ramah, and the timber thereof wherewith Baasha had builded, and king Asa built with them Geba of Beniamin, and Mizpah.

† Hebr. free.

23 The rest of all the acts of Asa, and all his might, and all that he did, and the cities which hee built, are they not written in the booke of the Chronicles of the Kings of Iudah? Neuerthelesse in the time of his old age, hee was diseased in his feete.

24 And Asa slept with his fathers, and was buried with his fathers, in the citie of Dauid his father: and *Iehoshaphat his sonne reigned in his stead.

* Matth 1. 8. called Iosaphat.

25 ¶ And Nadab the sonne of Ieroboam †began to reigne ouer Israel, in the second yeere of Asa king of Iudah, and reigned ouer Israel two yeeres.

† Hebr. reigned.

26 And he did euill in the sight of the LORD, and walked in the way of his father, and in his sinne wherewith hee made Israel to sinne.

27 ¶ And Baasha the sonne of Ahiiah, of the house of Issachar, conspired against him, and Baasha smote him at Gibbethon, which belongeth to the Philistines, (for Nadab and all Israel layd siege to Gibbethon,)

28 Euen in the third yeere of Asa king of Iudah, did Baasha slay him, and reigned in his stead.

29 And it came to passe when hee raigned, that he smote all the house Ieroboam, hee left not to Ieroboam any that breathed, vntill hee had destroyed him, according vnto *the saying of the LORD, which hee spake by his seruant Ahiiah the Shilonite:

*Chap. 14 10.

30 Because of the sinnes of Ieroboam which he sinned, and which hee made Israel sinne, by his prouocation wherewith he prouoked the LORD God of Israel to anger.

31 ¶ Now the rest of the acts of Nadab, and all that hee did, are they not written in the booke of the Chronicles of the Kings of Israel?

32 And there was warre betweene Asa and Baasha king of Israel al their dayes.

33 In the third yeere of Asa King of Iudah, began Baasha the sonne of Ahiiah to reigne ouer all Israel in Tirzah; twentie and foure yeeres.

34 And hee did euill in the sight of the LORD, and walked in the way of Ieroboam, and in his sinne wherewith he made Israel to sinne.

CHAP. XVI.

1. 7 Iehus prophesie against Baasha. 5 Elah succeedeth him. 8 Zimri conspiring against Elah, succeedeth him. 11 Zimri executeth Iehus prophesie. 15 Omri made King by the souldiers, forceth Zimri desperatly to burne himselfe. 21 The kingdome being diuided, Omri preuaileth against Tibni. 23 Omri buildeth Samaria. 25 His wicked reigne. 27 Ahab succeedeth him. 29 Ahabs most wicked reigne. 34 Ioshuas curse vpon Hiel the builder of Iericho.

THen the word of the LORD came to Iehu the sonne of Hanani, against Baasha, saying,

2 Forasmuch as I exalted thee out of the dust, and made thee Prince ouer my people Israel, and thou hast walked in the way of Ieroboam, and hast made my people Israel to sinne, to prouoke mee to anger with their sinnes:

3 Behold, I will take away the posteritie of Baasha, and the posteritie of his house: and will make thy house like *the house of Ieroboam the sonne of Nebat.

*Chap.) 29.

4 *Him

* Chap. 14.
11.

4 *Him that dieth of Baasha in the citie, shall the dogs eate: and him that dieth of his in the fields, shall the foules of the aire eate.

* 2. Chron.
16. 1.

5 Now the rest of the actes of Baasha, and what he did, and his might, are they not written in the *booke of the Chronicles of the kings of Israel?

6 So Baasha slept with his fathers, and was buried in Tirzah, and Elah his sonne reigned in his stead.

7 And also by the hand of the prophet Iehu the sonne of Hanani, came the word of the LORD against Baasha, and against his house, euen for all the euill that hee did in the sight of the LORD, in prouoking him to anger with the worke of his hands, in being like the house of Ieroboam, and because he killed him.

8 ¶ In the twentieth and sixt yeere of Asa king of Iudah, began Elah the sonne of Baasha to reigne ouer Israel in Tirzah, two yeeres.

9 And his seruant Zimri (captaine of halfe his charets) conspired against him as he was in Tirzah drinking himselfe drunke in the house of Arza †steward of his house in Tirzah.

*Heb. which
was ouer.*

10 And Zimri went in and smote him, and killed him, in the twentie and seuenth yeere of Asa king of Iudah, and reigned in his stead.

11 ¶ And it came to passe when hee began to reigne, assoone as hee sate on his throne, that he slew all the house of Baasha: hee left him not one that pisseth against a wall, ‖neither of his kinsfolkes, nor of his friends.

*Or, both
is kinsemen
and his
friends.*

12 Thus did Zimri destroy all the house of Baasha, according to the word of the LORD, which he spake against Baasha †by Iehu the prophet,

*Heb. by the
and of.*

13 For all the sinnes of Baasha and the sinnes of Elah his sonne, by which they sinned, and by which they made Israel to sinne, in prouoking the LORD God of Israel to anger with their vanities.

14 Now the rest of the actes of Elah, and all that he did, are they not written in the booke of the Chronicles of the kings of Israel?

15 ¶ In the twentie and seuenth yeere of Asa king of Iudah, did Zimri reigne seuen dayes in Tirzah: and the people were encamped against Gibbethon which *belonged* to the Philistines.

16 And the people that were encamped, heard say, Zimri hath conspired, and hath also slaine the king: Wherfore all Israel made Omri the captaine of the hoste, king ouer Israel that day, in the campe.

17 And Omri went vp from Gibbethon, and all Israel with him, and they besieged Tirzah.

18 And it came to passe when Zimri saw that the citie was taken, that hee went into the palace of the kings house, and burnt the kings house ouer him with fire, and died,

19 For his sinnes which he sinned in doing euill in the sight of the LORD, in walking in the way of Ieroboam, and in his sinne which he did, to make Israel sinne.

20 Now the rest of the acts of Zimri, and his treason that hee wrought, are they not written in the booke of the Chronicles of the kings of Israel?

21 ¶ Then were the people of Israel diuided into two parts: halfe of the people followed Tibni the sonne of Ginath, to make him king: and halfe followed Omri.

22 But the people that followed Omri preuailed against the people that followed Tibni the sonne of Ginath: so Tibni died, and Omri reigned.

23 ¶ In the thirtie and one yeere of Asa king of Iudah, began Omri to reigne ouer Israel twelue yeeres: sixe yeeres reigned he in Tirzah.

24 And hee bought the hill Samaria of Shemer, for two talents of siluer, and built on the hill, and called the name of the citie which hee built, after the name of Shemer, owner of the hill, †Samaria.

*† Heb. Sho-
meron.*

25 ¶ But Omri wrought euil in the eyes of the LORD, and did worse then all that *were* before him.

26 For he walked in all the way of Ieroboam the son of Nebat, and in his sinne wherewith hee made Israel to sinne, to prouoke the LORD God of Israel to anger with their vanities.

27 Now the rest of the acts of Omri, which he did, and his might that he shewed, are they not written in the booke of the Chronicles of the kings of Israel?

28 So Omri slept with his fathers, and was buried in Samaria, and Ahab his sonne reigned in his stead.

29 ¶ And in the thirtie and eight yeere of Asa king of Iudah, began Ahab

Ahab the sonne of Omri to reigne ouer Israel, and Ahab the sonne of Omri reigned ouer Israel in Samaria, twentie and two yeeres.

30 And Ahab the sonne of Omri did euill in the sight of the Lord, aboue all that *were* before him.

† *Heb. was it a light thing?* &c.

31 And it came to passe, † as if it had beene a light thing for him to walke in the sinnes of Ieroboam the sonne of Nebat; that hee tooke to wife Iezebel the daughter of Ethbaal king of the Zidonians, and went and serued Baal, and worshipped him.

32 And hee reared vp an Altar for Baal, in the house of Baal, which hee had built in Samaria.

33 And Ahab made a groue, and Ahab did more to prouoke the Lord God of Israel to anger, then all the kings of Israel that were before him.

* Iosh. 6. 26.

34 ¶ In his dayes did Hiel the Bethelite build Iericho: he laid the foundation therof in Abiram his first borne, and set vp the gates thereof in his yongest sonne Segub, * according to the word of the Lord, which hee spake by Ioshua the sonne of Nun.

CHAP. XVII.

1 Elijah hauing prophecied against Ahab, is sent to Cherith, where the rauens feed him. 8 He is sent to the widow of Zarephath. 17 Hee raiseth the widowes sonne. 24 The woman beleeueth him.

† *Heb. Eliiahu. Luke 4. 25. he is called Elias.* * Ecclus. 48. 3. iames 5. 17.

ANd † Eliiah the Tishbite, who was of the inhabitants of Gilead, said vnto Ahab, * As the Lord God of Israel liueth, before whome I stand, there shall not be deaw nor raine these yeres, but according to my word.

2 And the worde of the Lord came vnto him, saying,

3 Get thee hence, and turne thee Eastward, and hide thy selfe by the brooke Cherith, that *is* before Iordane.

4 And it shall bee, *that* thou shalt drinke of the brooke, and I haue commanded the rauens to feed thee there.

5 So hee went, and did according vnto the word of the Lord: for hee went and dwelt by the brooke Cherith, that *is* before Iordane.

6 And the rauens brought him bread and flesh in the morning, and bread and flesh in the euening: and hee dranke of the brooke.

7 And it came to passe † after a while, that the brooke dryed vp, because there had beene no raine in the land.

† *Heb. at the end of dayes*

8 ¶ And the word of the Lord came vnto him, saying,

9 Arise, get thee to * Zarephath, which *belongeth* to Zidon, and dwell there: behold, I haue commaunded a widow woman there to sustaine thee.

* Luke 4. 26. called Sarepta.

20 So he arose, and went to Zarephath: and when he came to the gate of the citie, behold, the widow woman was there gathering of stickes: and he called to her, and said, Fetch me, I pray thee, a little water in a vessell, that I may drinke.

11 And as shee was going to fetch it, he called to her, and said, Bring mee, I pray thee, a morsell of bread in thine hand.

12 And she said, As the Lord thy God liueth, I haue not a cake, but an handfull of meale in a barrell, and a little oyle in a cruse: and behold, I am gathering two stickes, that I may goe in, and dresse it for me and my sonne, that we may eate it, and die.

13 And Eliiah said vnto her, Feare not, goe, *and* doe as thou hast said: but make mee thereof a little cake first, and bring it vnto mee, and after make for thee, and for thy sonne.

14 For thus saith the Lord God of Israel, The barrell of meale shall not waste, neither shall the cruse of oile faile, vntill the day *that* the Lord † sendeth raine vpon the earth.

† *Heb. giueth.*

15 And shee went, and did according to the saying of Eliiah: and she, and he, and her house did eate ‖ *many* dayes.

‖ *Or, a full yeere.*

16 *And* the barrell of meale wasted not, neither did the cruse of oyle faile, according to the word of the Lord, which he spake † by Eliiah.

† *Heb. by hand of.*

17 ¶ And it came to passe after these things, *that* the sonne of the woman, the mistresse of the house, fell sicke, and his sickenesse was so sore, that there was no breath left in him.

18 And shee sayd vnto Eliiah, What haue I to doe with thee? O thou man of God! Art thou come vnto me to call my sinne to remembrance, and to slay my sonne?

19 And he said vnto her, Giue me thy sonne. And he tooke him out of her bosome, and caried him vp into a loft, where he abode, and laide him vpon his owne bed.

20 And

20 And hee cried vnto the Lord, and said, O Lord my God, hast thou also brought euill vpon the widow, with whom I soiourne, by slaying her sonne?

21 And he †stretched himselfe vpon the child three times, and cried vnto the Lord, and said; O Lord my God, I pray thee, let this childes soule come †into him againe.

22 And the Lord heard the voice of Eliiah, and the soule of the child came into him againe, and he reuiued.

23 And Eliiah tooke the childe, and brought him downe out of the chamber into the house, and deliuered him vnto his mother. and Eliiah said, See, thy sonne liueth.

24 ¶ And the woman said to Eliiah, Now by this I know, that thou art a man of God, and that the word of the Lord in thy mouth is trueth.

CHAP. XVIII.

1 In the extremitie of famine Eliiah sent to Ahab, meeteth good Obadiah. 9 Obadiah bringeth Ahab to Eliiah. 17 Eliiah reprouing Ahab, by fire from heauen conuinceth Baals prophets. 41 Eliiah by prayer obtaining raine, followeth Ahab to Iezreel.

Nd it came to passe *after* many daies, that the word of the Lord came to Eliiah in the third yeere, saying, Goe shewe thy selfe vnto Ahab, and I will send raine vpon the earth.

2 And Eliiah went to shew himselfe vnto Ahab, and *there was* a sore famine in Samaria.

3 And Ahab called †Obadiah which *was* †the gouernour of his house: (now Obadiah feared the Lord greatly:

4 For it was so, when †Iezebel cut off the Prophets of the Lord, that Obadiah tooke an hundred Prophets, and hid them by fiftie in a caue, and fed them with bread and water.)

5 And Ahab said vnto Obadiah, Goe into the land, vnto all fountaines of water, and vnto all brookes: peraduenture we may finde grasse to saue the horses and mules aliue, that we †leese not all the beasts.

6 So they diuided the land betweene them to passe throughout it: Ahab went one way by himselfe, and Obadiah went another way by himself.

7 ¶ And as Obadiah was in the way, behold, Eliiah met him: and hee knew him, and fell on his face, and said; *Art* thou that my lord Eliiah?

8 And he answered him, I am: goe, tell thy lord, Behold, Eliiah *is here.*

9 And he said, What haue I sinned, that thou wouldest deliuer thy seruant into the hand of Ahab, to slay mee?

10 As the Lord thy God liueth, there is no nation or kingdome, whither my lord hath not sent to seeke thee: and when they said, He is not *there*, hee tooke an oath of the kingdome and nation, that they found thee not.

11 And now thou sayest, Goe, tell thy lord, Behold, Eliiah *is here.*

12 And it shall come to passe, *as soone* as I am gone from thee, that the spirit of the Lord shall cary thee whither I know not; and so when I come and tell Ahab, and he cannot finde thee, he shall slay mee, but I thy seruant feare the Lord from my youth.

13 Was it not told my lord, what I did when Iezebel slew the Prophets of the Lord? how I hid an hundred men of the Lords Prophets, by fiftie in a caue, and fedde them with bread and water?

14 And now thou sayest, Goe, tell thy lord, Behold, Eliiah *is here*; and hee shall slay me.

15 And Eliiah said, As the Lord of hostes liueth, before whom I stand, I will surely shew my selfe vnto him to day.

16 So Obadiah went to meete Ahab, and told him: and Ahab went to meete Eliiah.

17 ¶ And it came to passe when Ahab saw Eliiah, that Ahab saide vnto him, Art thou hee that troubleth Israel?

18 And hee answered, I haue not troubled Israel, but thou and thy fathers house, in that yee haue forsaken the Commandements of the Lord, and thou hast followed Baalim.

19 Now therefore send, *and* gather to mee all Israel vnto mount Carmel, and the prophets of Baal foure hundred and fiftie, and the prophets of the groues foure hundred, which eate at Iezebels table.

20 So Ahab sent vnto all the children of Israel, and gathered the prophets together vnto mount Carmel.

21 And

† Hebr. measured.

† Hebr. into his inward parts.

† Hebr. Obadiahu.
† Hebr. ouer his house.

† Hebr. Izebel.

† Hebr. that we cut not off our selues from the beasts.

21 And Eliiah came vnto all the people, and said, How long halt yee betweene two ||opinions? If the LORD bee God, follow him: but if Baal, *then* follow him: and the people answered him not a word.

22 Then said Eliiah vnto the people, I, *euen* I onely remaine a Prophet of the LORD: but Baals prophets *are* foure hundred and fiftie men.

23 Let them therefore giue vs two bullocks, and let them chuse one bullocke for themselues, and cut it in pieces, and lay it on wood, and put no fire vnder: and I will dresse the other bullocke, and lay *it* on wood, and put no fire vnder.

24 And call ye on the name of your gods, and I will call on the Name of the LORD: and the God that answereth by fire, let him be God. And all the people answered, and said, †It is well spoken.

25 And Eliiah said vnto the prophets of Baal, Chuse you one bullocke for yourselues, and dresse *it* first, for yee *are* many: and call on the name of your gods, but put no fire vnder.

26 And they took the bullocke which was giuen them, and they dressed *it*, and called on the name of Baal from morning, euen vntil noone, saying, O Baal, ||heare vs. But there was no voyce, nor any that ||answered: And they ||leapt vpon the altar which was made.

27 And it came to passe at noone, that Eliiah mocked them, and said, Crie †aloud: for he *is* a god, either||he is talking, or he †is pursuing, or hee is in a iourney, *or* peraduenture he sleepeth, and must be awaked.

28 And they cried loud, and cut themselues after their maner, with kniues, and lancers, till †the blood gushed out vpon them.

29 And it came to passe when midday was past, and they prophesied vntil the *time* of the †offering of the *euening* sacrifice; *that there was* neither voice, nor any to answere, nor †any that regarded.

30 And Eliiah said vnto all the people, Come neere vnto me. And all the people came neere vnto him. And he repaired the Altar of the LORD that was broken downe.

31 And Eliiah tooke twelue stones, according to the number of the tribes of the sonnes of Iacob, vnto whome the word of the LORD came, saying,

* Israel shall bee thy name.

32 And with the stones hee built an altar in the Name of the LORD, and hee made a trench about the altar, as great as would containe two measures of seed.

33 And he put the wood in order, and cut the bullocke in pieces, and laide him on the wood, and said, Fill foure barrels with water, and powre it on the burnt sacrifice, and on the wood.

34 And hee said, Doe it the second time. And they did it the second time. And he said, Doe it the third time. And they did it the third time.

35 And the water †ran round about the altar, and hee filled the trench also with water

36 And it came to passe at the time of the offering of the *euening* sacrifice, that Eliiah the prophet came neere and said, LORD God of Abraham, Isaac, and of Israel, Let it bee knowen this day that thou *art* God in Israel, and *that* I *am* thy seruant, and *that* I haue done all these things at thy word.

37 Heare me, O LORD, heare me, that this people may know that thou *art* the LORD God, and *that* thou hast turned their heart backe againe.

38 Then the fire of the LORD fell, and consumed the burnt sacrifice, and the wood, and the stones, and the dust, and licked vp the water that *was* in the trench.

39 And when all the people sawe it, they fell on their faces: and they saide, The LORD, he *is* the God, the LORD, he *is* the God.

40 And Eliiah saide vnto them, ||Take the prophets of Baal, let not one of them escape: And they tooke them, and Eliiah brought them downe to the brooke Kishon, and slewe them there.

41 ¶ And Eliiah said vnto Ahab, Get thee vp, eate and drinke, for there *is* ||a sound of abundance of raine.

42 So Ahab went vp to eate and to drinke, and Eliiah went vp to the top of Carmel, and he cast himselfe downe vpon the earth, and put his face betweene his knees,

43 And said to his seruant, Goe vp now, looke toward the Sea. And hee went vp, and looked, and saide, *There is* nothing. And he said, Goe againe seuen times.

44 And it came to passe at the seuenth

Marginal notes

|| Or, *thoughts*.

† Hebr. *the word is good*.

|| Or, *answere*.
|| Or, *heard*.
|| Or, *leaped vp & downe at the altar*.

† Heb. *with a great voice*.
|| Or, *he meditateth*.
† Heb. *hath a pursuit*.

† Hebr. *powred out blood vpon them*.

† Hebr. *ascending*.

† Hcb. *attention*.

* Gen. 32. 28. 2. king 17. 34.

† Heb. *we*...

|| Or, *apprehend*.

|| Or, *a sound of a noise of raine*.

uenth time, that he said, Behold, there
ariseth a little cloud out of the Sea, like
a mans hand. And he said, Goe vp, say
vnto Ahab, †Prepare *thy charet*, and
get thee downe, that the raine stop thee
not.

Heb. tie,
binde.

45 And it came to passe in the meane
while, that the heauen was blacke with
cloudes and winde, and there was a
great raine : and Ahab rode and went
to Iezreel.

46 And the hand of the LORD
was on Eliiah ; and hee girded vp his
loynes, and ranne before Ahab, †to the
entrance of Iezreel.

Heb. till
ou come
Iezreel.

CHAP. XIX.

1 Eliiah threatned by Iezebel, fleeth to Beer-
sheba, 4 In the wildernesse being wearie of
his life, is comforted by an Angel. 9 At Horeb God appeareth vnto him, sending him to
anoint Hazael, Iehu, and Elisha. 19 Elisha
taking leaue of his friends, followeth Elijah.

ND Ahab told Iezebel
all that Eliiah had done,
and withall, how hee had
slaine all the Prophets
with the sword.

2 Then Iezebel sent a messenger
vnto Eliiah, saying; So let the gods do
to me, and more also, if I make not thy
life as the life of one of them, by to morrow about this time.

3 And when he saw *that*, hee arose,
and went for his life, and came to Beer-
sheba, which *belongeth* to Iudah, and
left his seruant there.

4 ¶ But he himselfe went a dayes
iourney into the wildernesse, and came
and sate downe vnder a Iuniper tree :
and hee requested †for himselfe that hee
might die, and sayd, *It is* enough, now
O LORD, take away my life : for I
am not better then my fathers.

Heb. for
s life.

5 And as hee lay and slept vnder a
Iuniper tree, behold then, an Angel
touched him, and sayd vnto him, Arise,
and eate.

6 And he looked, and behold, there
was a cake baken on the coales, and a
cruse of water at his † head : and hee did
eate and drinke, and laide him downe
againe.

Heb. bol-
er.

7 And the Angel of the LORD
came againe the second time, and touched him, and sayd, Arise, *and* eate, because the iourney *is* too great for thee.

8 And hee arose, and did eate and

drinke, and went in the strength of that
meate fourtie dayes and fourtie nights,
vnto Horeb the mount of God.

9 ¶ And he came thither vnto a caue,
and lodged there, and behold, the word
of the LORD *came* to him, and he said
vnto him, What doest thou here, E-
liiah ?

10 And hee sayd, I haue beene very
iealous for the LORD God of hostes :
for the children of Israel haue forsaken
thy Couenant, throwen downe thine
Altars, and slaine thy Prophets with
the sword : and *I, euen* I onely am
left, and they seeke my life, to take it a-
way.

*Rom.11.3.

11 And he sayd, Goe forth, and stand
vpon the mount before the LORD.
And beholde, the LORD passed by,
and a great and strong winde rent the
mountaines, and brake in pieces the
rockes, before the LORD; *but* the
LORD *was* not in the winde : and after the winde an earthquake, *but* the
LORD *was* not in the earthquake.

12 And after the earthquake, a fire,
but the LORD *was* not in the fire : and
after the fire, a still small voice.

13 And it was so, when Eliiah heard
it, that he wrapped his face in his mantle, and went out, and stood in the entring in of the caue : and behold, *there*
came a voice vnto him, and sayd, What
doest thou here, Eliiah ?

14 And he sayd, I haue beene very
iealous for the LORD God of hostes,
because the children of Israel haue forsaken thy Couenant, throwen downe
thine Altars, and slaine thy Prophets
with the sword, and I, *euen* I onely
am left, and they seeke my life, to take it
away.

15 And the LORD sayd vnto him,
Goe, returne on thy way to the wildernesse of Damascus : and when thou
commest, anoint Hazael to be King o-
uer Syria.

16 And Iehu the sonne of Nimshi
shalt thou anoint to bee king ouer Israel : and *Elisha the sonne of Shaphat of Abel Meholah, shalt thou annoint to be Prophet in thy roume.

*Luk. 4. 27
called Eli-
seus.

17 And *it shall come to passe, that
him that escapeth the sword of Hazael,
shall Iehu slay : and him that escapeth
from the sword of Iehu, shall Elisha
slay.

*2. King.
9. 1, 3, ec-
clus. 48. 6.

18 *Yet ||I haue left *me* seuen thou-
sand in Israel, all the knees which
haue

*Rom.
11. 4.
||*Or, I will*
leaue.

haue not bowed vnto Baal, and euery mouth which hath not kissed him.

19 ¶ So hee departed thence and found Elisha the sonne of Shaphat, who was plowing with twelue yoke of oxen before him, and hee with the twelfth : and Eliiah passed by him, and cast his mantle vpon him.

20 And he left the oxen, and ranne after Eliiah, and said, Let mee, I pray thee, kisse my father and my mother, and then I wil follow thee : and he said vnto him, † Goe backe againe; for what haue I done to thee ?

† Hebr. goe returne.

21 And he returned backe from him, and tooke a yoke of oxen, & slew them, and boyled their flesh with the instruments of the oxen, and gaue vnto the people, and they did eat : then he arose, and went after Eliiah, and ministred vnto him.

CHAP. XX.

1 Benhadad not content with Ahabs hommage, besiegeth Samaria. 13 By the direction of a Prophet, the Syrians are slaine. 22 As the Prophet forewarned Ahab, the Syrians trusting in the valleys, come against him in Aphek. 28 By rhe word of the Prophet, and Gods iudgment, the Syrians are smitten againe. 31 The Syrians submitting themselues, Ahab sendeth Benhadad away with a couenant. 35 The Prophet vnder the parable of a prisoner, making Ahab to iudge himselfe, denounceth Gods iudgement against him.

And Benhadad the King of Syria gathered all his hoste together, and *there were* thirtie and two kings with him, and horses, and charets : and hee went vp and besieged Samaria, and warred against it.

2 And hee sent messengers to Ahab king of Israel, into the city, and saide vnto him, Thus saith Benhadad,

3 Thy siluer and thy gold is mine, thy wiues also, and thy children, *euen* the goodliest, are mine.

4 And the king of Israel answered, and said, My lord O king, according to thy saying, I *am* thine, and all that I haue.

5 And the messengers came againe, and saide, Thus speaketh Benhadad, saying, Although I haue sent vnto thee, saying, Thou shalt deliuer me thy siluer, and thy gold, and thy wiues, and thy children :

6 Yet I will send my seruants vnto thee to morrow about this time, and they shall search thine house, and the houses of thy seruants ; and it shall be, that whatsoeuer is †pleasant in thine eies, they shall put *it* in their hand, and take *it* away.

† Heb. desrable.

7 Then the king of Israel called all the Elders of the land, and saide ; Marke, I pray you, and see how this *man* seeketh mischiefe: for hee sent vnto me for my wiues, and for my children, and for my siluer, and for my gold, and †I denied him not.

† Heb. I knot backe from him

8 And all the Elders, and all the people said vnto him ; Hearken not *vnto him,* nor consent.

9 Wherefore hee said vnto the messengers of Benhadad, Tell my lord the king, All that thou diddest send for to thy seruant at the first, I will doe : but this thing I may not doe. And the messengers departed, and brought him word againe.

10 And Benhadad sent vnto him, and said, The gods doe so vnto me and more also, if the dust of Samaria shall suffice for handfuls for all the people that †follow me.

† Heb. army feete.

11 And the king of Israel answered, and said, Tell *him,* Let not him that girdeth on *his harnesse,* boast himselfe, as he that putteth it off.

12 And it came to passe, when *Benhadad* heard this †message (as hee was drinking, he and the kings in the ‖pauilions) that hee said vnto his seruants, ‖Set *yourselues in aray.* And they set *themselues in aray* against the citie.

† Heb. w
‖ Or, Te
‖ Or, pla the engi and they placed er gines.
† Heb. ap ched.

13 ¶ And behold, there †came a Prophet vnto Ahab king of Israel, saying, Thus saith the Lord, Hast thou seene all this great multitude ? behold, I will deliuer it into thine hand this day, and thou shalt knowe that I am the Lord.

14 And Ahab saide, By whom ? and he saide, Thus saith the Lord, *Euen* by the ‖young men of the Princes of the prouinces: Then he said, Who shall †order the battell ? And hee answered, Thou.

‖ Or, ser uants.
† Heb. B or, tie.

15 Then he numbred the young men of the Princes of the prouinces, and they were two hundred and thirty two : and after them hee numbred all the people, *euen* all the children of Israel, *being* seuen thousand.

16 And they went out at noone : But Benhadad

Benhadad was drinking himselfe drunke in the pauilions, hee and the kings, the thirty and two kings that helped him.

17 And the young men of the Princes of the Prouinces went out first, and Benhadad sent out, and they told him, saying, There are men come out of Samaria.

18 And he said, Whether they be come out for peace, take them aliue: or whether they be come out for warre, take them aliue.

19 So these yong men of the princes of the prouinces, came out of the citie, and the armie which followed them:

20 And they slew euery one his man: and the Syrians fled, and Israel pursued them: and Benhadad the king of Syria escaped on an horse, with the horsemen.

21 And the king of Israel went out, and smote the horses and charets, and slewe the Syrians with a great slaughter.

22 ¶ And the Prophet came to the king of Israel, and said vnto him, Goe, strengthen thy selfe, and marke and see what thou doest: for at the returne of the yeere, the king of Syria will come vp against thee.

23 And the seruants of the King of Syria said vnto him, Their gods *are* gods of the hilles, therefore they were stronger then wee: but let vs fight against them in the plaine, and surely we shall be stronger then they.

24 And doe this thing, Take the kings away, euery man out of his place, and put captaines in their roumes.

Heb. that vas fallen.

25 And number thee an armie, like the armie †that thou hast lost, horse for horse, and charet for charet: and wee will fight against them in the plaine, *and* surely wee shall be stronger then they. And hee hearkened vnto their voice, and did so.

26 And it came to passe at the returne of the yeere, that Benhadad numbred the Syrians, and went vp to Aphek,

† Heb. to the warre with Israel.

†to fight against Israel.

27 And the children of Israel were numbred, and ‖were all present, and went against them: and the children of Israel pitched before them, like two little flockes of kids: but the Syrians filled the countrey.

‖ Or, were victualled.

28 ¶ And there came a man of God, and spake vnto the king of Israel, and

sayd, Thus sayth the LORD, Because the Syrians haue sayde, The LORD *is* God of the hilles, but hee *is* not God of the valleys: therefore will I deliuer all this great multitude into thine hand, *and* yee shall know that I am the LORD.

29 And they pitched one ouer against the other seuen daies, and so it was, that in the seuenth day the battell was ioyned: and the children of Israel slewe of the Syrians an hundred thousand footmen in one day.

30 But the rest fled to Aphek, into the citie, and there a wall fell vpon twentie and seuen thousand of the men that were left: and Benhadad fled, and came into the citie, ‖into an inner chamber.

‖ Or, from chamber to chamber. Heb. into a chamber within a chamber.

31 ¶ And his seruants said vnto him, Behold now, wee haue heard that the kings of the house of Israel are mercifull kings: let vs, I pray thee, put sackcloth on our loines, and ropes vpon our heads, and goe out to the king of Israel; peraduenture he will saue thy life.

32 So they girded sackcloth on their loynes, and *put* ropes on their heads, and came to the king of Israel, and said, Thy seruant Benhadad saith, I pray thee, let me liue. And he said, Is he yet aliue? he *is* my brother.

33 Now the men did diligently obserue whether any thing would come from him, and did hastily catch *it*: and they saide, Thy brother Benhadad. Then he said, Goe ye, bring him: then Benhadad came forth to him: and hee caused him to come vp into the charet.

34 And *Benhadad* said vnto him, The cities which my father tooke from my father, I will restore, and thou shalt make streets for thee in Damascus, as my father made in Samaria. Then, *said Ahab*, I will send thee away with this couenant. So he made a couenant with him, and sent him away.

35 ¶ And a certaine man of the sonnes of the Prophets, saide vnto his neighbour in the word of the LORD, Smite me, I pray thee. And the man refused to smite him.

36 Then said he vnto him, Because thou hast not obeyed the voyce of the LORD, beholde, assoone as thou art departed from me, a lyon shall slay thee. And assoone as hee was departed from him, a lyon found him, and slew him.

37 Then he found another man, and said, Smite me, I pray thee. And the man

† *Hebr. smi-*
ting and
wounding.

man smote him, so that in †smiting hee wounded *him.*

38 So the prophet departed, and waited for the king by the way, and disguised himselfe with ashes vpon his face.

39 And as the king passed by, he cried vnto the king : and he saide, Thy seruant went out into the mids of the battell, and behold, a man turned aside, and brought a man vnto me, and said, Keep this man : if by any meanes he be missing, then shall thy life be for his life, or else thou shalt †pay a talent of siluer.

† *Heb. weigh*

40 And as thy seruant was busie here and there, †he was gone. And the king of Israel saide vnto him, So *shall* thy iudgement *bee*, thy selfe hast discided *it.*

† *Heb. hee*
was not.

41 And he hasted, and tooke the ashes away from his face, and the king of Israel discerned him that hee *was* of the Prophets.

42 And hee said vnto him, Thus saith the Lord, * Because thou hast let goe out of *thy* hand, a man whom I appointed to vtter destruction, therfore thy life shall goe for his life, and thy people for his people.

* Chap. 22.
48.

43 And the king of Israel went to his house, heauie, and displeased, and came to Samaria.

CHAP. XXI.

1 Ahab being denied Naboths vineyard, is grieued. 5 Iezebel writing letters against Naboth, he is condemned of blasphemie. 15 Ahab taketh possession of the vineyard. 17 Eliiah denounceth iudgements against Ahab and Iezebel. 25 Wicked Ahab repenting, God deferreth the iudgement.

Nd it came to passe after these things, that Naboth the Iezreelite had a vineyard, which *was* in Iezreel, hard by the palace of Ahab king of Samaria

2 And Ahab spake vnto Naboth, saying, Giue me thy vineyard, that I may haue it for a garden of herbes, because it *is* neere vnto my house, and I will giue thee for it a better vineyard then it : *or* if it †seeme good to thee, I will giue thee the worth of it in money.

† *Hebr. he*
good in thine
eyes.

3 And Naboth said to Ahab, The Lord forbid it mee, that I should giue the inheritance of my fathers vnto thee

4 And Ahab came into his house, heauie, and displeased, because of the word which Naboth the Iezreelite had spoken to him : for he had saide, I will not giue thee the inheritance of my fathers : and he laid him downe vpon his bed, and turned away his face, and would eate no bread.

5 ¶ But Iezebel his wife came to him, and said vnto him, Why is thy spirit so sad, that thou eatest no bread ?

6 And he said vnto her, Because I spake vnto Naboth the Iezreelite, and said vnto him, Giue mee thy vineyard for money, or else if it please thee, I will giue thee *another* vineyard for it : And he answered, I wil not giue thee my vineyard.

7 And Iezebel his wife saide vnto him, Doest thou now gouerne the kingdome of Israel ? Arise, *and* eate bread, and let thine heart bee merrie : I will giue thee the vineyard of Naboth the Iezreelite.

8 So shee wrote letters in Ahabs name, and sealed *them* with his seale, and sent the letters vnto the Elders, and to the Nobles that were in his citie dwelling with Naboth.

9 And she wrote in the letters, saying, Proclaime a fast, and set Naboth † on high among the people :

† *Heb. in t*
top of the
people.

10 And set two men, sonnes of Belial before him, to beare witnes against him, saying, Thou diddest blaspheme God and the king : and then carie him out, and stone him that he may die.

11 And the men of his citie, *euen* the Elders and the Nobles who were the inhabitants in his citie, did as Iezebel had sent vnto them, *and* as it was written in the letters which she had sent vnto them.

12 They proclaimed a fast, and set Naboth on high among the people.

13 And there came in two men, children of Belial, and sate before him : and the men of Belial witnessed against him, euen against Naboth, in the presence of the people, saying, Naboth did blaspheme God and the king. Then they caried him foorth out of the citie, and stoned him with stones, that hee died.

14 Then they sent to Iezebel, saying, Naboth is stoned, and is dead.

15 ¶ And it came to passe when Iezebel heard that Naboth was stoned and was dead, that Iezebel said to Ahab,

hab, Arise, take possession of the Vineyard of Naboth the Iezreelite, which hee refused to giue thee for money : for Naboth is not aliue, but dead.

16 And it came to passe when Ahab heard that Naboth was dead, that Ahab rose vp to goe downe to the Vineyard of Naboth the Iezreelite, to take possession of it.

17 ¶ And the word of the LORD came to Eliiah the Tishbite, saying,

18 Arise, goe downe to meet Ahab king of Israel, which *is* in Samaria: behold, hee *is* in the Vineyard of Naboth, whither he is gone downe to possesse it.

19 And thou shalt speake vnto him, saying, Thus saith the LORD, Hast thou killed, and also taken possession? And thou shalt speake vnto him, saying, Thus saith the LORD; In the place where dogs licked the blood of Naboth, shall dogges licke thy blood, euen thine.

20 And Ahab said to Eliiah, Hast thou found me, O mine enemie? And he answered, I haue found *thee*: because thou hast sold thy selfe to worke euill in the sight of the LORD.

Chap. 14.
, 2. king.
6.
1. Sam.
, 22.
Chap. 14.

21 Behold, *I will bring euill vpon thee, and will take away thy posteritie, and will cut off from Ahab *him that pisseth against the wall, and *him that is shut vp, and left in Israel.

Chap. 15.

Chap. 16.

22 And will make thine house like the house of *Ieroboam the sonne of Nebat, and like the house of *Baasha the sonne of Ahiiah, for the prouocation wherewith thou hast prouoked *mee* to anger, and made Israel to sinne.

King. 9.

Or, ditch.

23 And *of Iezebel also spake the LORD, saying, The dogs shall eate Iezebel by the ‖ wall of Iezreel.

24 Him that dieth of Ahab in the citie, the dogs shall eate : and him that dieth in the field, shall the foules of the aire eat.

25 ¶ But there was none like vnto Ahab, which did sell himselfe to worke wickednesse in the sight of the LORD, whom Iezebel his wife ‖ stirred vp.

Or, incited.

26 And hee did very abominably in following Idoles, according to all things as did the Amorites, whom the LORD cast out before the children of Israel.

27 And it came to passe when Ahab heard those wordes, that hee rent his clothes, and put sackecloth vpon his flesh, and fasted, and lay in sackcloth, and went softly.

28 And the word of the LORD came to Eliiah the Tishbite, saying,

29 Seest thou how Ahab humbleth himselfe before mee? because hee humbleth himselfe before mee, I will not bring the euill in his dayes: *but* in his sonnes dayes will I bring the euill vpon his house.

CHAP. XXII.

1 Ahab seduced by false prophets, according to the word of Micaiah, is slaine at Ramoth Gilead. 37 The dogges licke vp his blood, and Ahaziah succeedeth him. 41 Iehoshaphats good reigne, 45 his acts. 50 Iehoram succeedeth him. 51 Ahaziahs euil reigne.

 Nd *they continued three yeeres without warre betweene Syria and Israel.

* 1. Chron.
18. 1, &c.

2 And it came to passe on the third yere, that Iehoshaphat the King of Iudah came downe to the king of Israel.

3 (And the king of Israel said vnto his seruants, Know ye that Ramoth in Gilead is ours, and wee be †still, *and* take it not out of the hand of the king of Syria?)

† Hebr. silent from taking it.

4 And hee said vnto Iehoshaphat, Wilt thou goe with me to battel to Ramoth Gilead? And Iehoshaphat said to the king of Israel, *I am as thou art*, my people as thy people, my horses as thy horses.

* 2. King. 3.
7.

5 And Iehoshaphat said vnto the king of Israel, Enquire, I pray thee, at the word of the LORD to day.

6 Then the king of Israel gathered the prophets together about foure hundred men, and said vnto them, Shall I goe against Ramoth Gilead to battell, or shall I forbeare? And they said, Goe vp, for the LORD shall deliuer it into the hand of the king.

7 And Iehoshaphat said, *Is* there not here a Prophet of the LORD besides, that we might enquire of him?

8 And the king of Israel said vnto Iehoshaphat, There is yet one man, (Micaiah the sonne of Imlah) by whom we may enquire of the LORD; but I hate him, for he doth not prophesie good concerning me, but euill. And Iehoshaphat said, Let not the King say so.

9 Then the king of Israel called an

‖ Or, Eunuch.

an ‖Officer, and said, Hasten *hither* Micaiah the sonne of Imlah.

10 And the King of Israel and Iehoshaphat the King of Iudah sate each on his throne, hauing put on their robes, in a †voyd place in the entrance of the gate of Samaria, and all the Prophets prophecied before them.

†Heb. floore.

11 And Zedekiah the sonne of Chenaanah made him hornes of yron : and he sayd, Thus saith the LORD, With these shalt thou push the Syrians, vntill thou haue consumed them.

12 And all the Prophets prophecied so, saying ; Goe vp to Ramoth Gilead, and prosper : for the LORD shall deliuer *it* into the kings hand.

13 And the messenger that was gone to call Micaiah, spake vnto him, saying, Behold now, the words of the prophets *declare* good vnto the King with one mouth : let thy word, I pray thee, bee like the word of one of them, and speake *that which is* good.

14 And Micaiah sayde, As the LORD liueth, what the LORD saith vnto me, that will I speake.

15 ¶ So he came to the king, and the king sayd vnto him, Micaiah, shall wee goe against Ramoth Gilead to battell, or shall we forbeare ? And he answered him, Go, and prosper : for the LORD shall deliuer *it* into the hand of the king.

16 And the king said vnto him, How many times shall I adiure thee, that thou tell me nothing but that which is true, in the Name of the LORD ?

17 And hee sayd, I saw all Israel scattered vpon the hilles, as sheepe that haue not a shepheard. And the LORD said, These haue no master, let them returne euery man to his house in peace.

18 And the King of Israel said vnto Iehoshaphat, Did I not tell thee, that he would prophecie no good concerning me, but euill ?

19 And he said, Heare thou therefore the word of the LORD : I sawe the LORD sitting on his Throne, and all the hoste of heauen standing by him, on his right hand and on his left.

‖ Or, deceiue.

20 And the LORD said, Who shall ‖perswade Ahab, that hee may goe vp and fall at Ramoth Gilead ? And one sayd on this manner, and another said on that manner.

21 And there came forth a spirit, and stood before the LORD, and said, I will perswade him.

22 And the LORD said vnto him, Wherewith ? And hee sayd, I will goe foorth, and I will be a lying spirit in the mouth of all his prophets. And he said, Thou shalt perswade him, and preuaile also : Goe forth, and doe so.

23 Now therfore behold, the LORD hath put a lying spirit in the mouth of all these thy prophets, and the LORD hath spoken euill concerning thee.

24 But Zedekiah the sonne of Chenaanah went neere, and smote Micaiah on the cheeke, and said, *Which way* went the Spirit of the LORD from me, to speake vnto thee ?

* 2. Chro 18. 23.

25 And Micaiah sayde, Beholde, thou shalt see in that day, when thou shalt goe ‖into an inner chamber, to hide thy selfe.

‖ Or, from chamber to chamber. Heb. cha ber in a chamber.

26 And the King of Israel sayde, Take Micaiah, and cary him backe vnto Amon the gouernour of the citie, and to Ioash the kings sonne :

27 And say, Thus sayth the King, Put this fellow in the prison, and feede him with bread of affliction, and with water of afflictiō, vntill I come in peace.

28 And Micaiah saide, If thou returne at all in peace, the LORD hath not spoken by me. And he said, Hearken, O people, euery one of you.

29 So the King of Israel, and Iehoshaphat the king of Iudah, went vp to Ramoth Gilead.

30 And the king of Israel said vnto Iehoshaphat, ‖I wil disguise my selfe, & enter into the battell, but put thou on thy robes. And the King of Israel disguised himselfe, & went into the battell.

‖ Or, whe he was to guise hir selfe and ter into battell.

31 But the King of Syria commanded his thirtie and two Captaines that had rule ouer his charets, saying, Fight neither with small nor great, saue only with the king of Israel.

32 And it came to passe, when the captaines of the charets saw Iehoshaphat, that they said, Surely it is the king of Israel. And they turned aside to fight against him : and Iehoshaphat cryed out.

33 And it came to passe, when the captaines of the charets perceiued that it was not the king of Israel, that they turned backe from pursuing him.

34 And a certaine man drew a bow †at a venture, and smote the king of Israel betweene the †ioynts of the harnesse : wherefore hee sayd vnto the driuer of his charet, Turne thine hand, and

† Heb. in simplicit † Heb. io. and the brestplat

and cary me out of the hoste, for I am †wounded.

35 And the battell †increased that day : and the king was stayed vp in his charet against the Syrians, and died at euen : and the blood ranne out of the wound, into the †mids of the charet.

36 And there went a proclamation throughout the hoste, about the going downe of the Sunne, saying, Euery man to his citie, and euery man to his owne countrey.

37 ¶ So the King died, and †was brought to Samaria, and they buried the king in Samaria.

38 And one washed the charet in the poole of Samaria, and the dogges licked vp his blood, and they washed his armour, according *vnto the word of the LORD which he spake.

39 Now the rest of the actes of Ahab, and all that he did, and the Iuory house which he made, and all the cities that he built, *are* they not written in the booke of the Chronicles of the Kings of Israel ?

40 So Ahab slept with his fathers, and Ahaziah his sonne reigned in his stead.

41 ¶ And *Iehoshaphat the sonne of Asa began to reigne ouer Iudah in the fourth yeere of Ahab King of Israel.

42 Iehoshaphat *was* thirtie and fiue yeeres olde when hee began to reigne, and he reigned twentie and fiue yeeres in Ierusalem : and his mothers name *was* Azubah the daughter of Shilhi.

43 And he walked in all the wayes of Asa his father, hee turned not aside from it, doing that which was right in the eyes of the LORD : neuerthelesse,

the high places were not taken away : *for* the people offered and burnt incense yet in the high places.

44 And Iehoshaphat made peace with the king of Israel.

45 Now the rest of the actes of Iehoshaphat, and his might that hee shewed, and how he warred, are they not written in the booke of the Chronicles of the Kings of Iudah ?

46 And the remnant of the Sodomites which remained in the dayes of his father Asa, he tooke out of the land.

47 There was then no king in Edom : a deputie *was* king.

48 Iehoshaphat ||made shippes of Tharshish to goe to Ophir for golde : but they went not, for the shippes were broken at Ezion Geber.

49 Then said Ahaziah the sonne of Ahab vnto Iehoshaphat, Let my seruants goe with thy seruants in the ships : But Iehoshaphat would not.

50 ¶ And Iehoshaphat slept with his fathers, and was buried with his fathers in the citie of Dauid his father : and Iehoram his sonne reigned in his stead.

51 ¶ Ahaziah the sonne of Ahab began to reigne ouer Israel in Samaria the seuenteenth yeere of Iehoshaphat king of Iudah, and reigned two yeres ouer Israel.

52 And he did euill in the sight of the LORD, and walked in the way of his father, and in the way of his mother, and in the way of Ieroboam the sonne of Nebat, who made Israel to sinne.

53 For he serued Baal, and worshipped him, and prouoked to anger the LORD God of Israel, according vnto all that his father had done.

¶ THE

Marginal notes (left):
†eb. made ... ‖eb. as- ded.
†eb. bo- ...e.
‖eb. came.
hap. 21.
Chron. 31.

Marginal notes (right):
‖ Or, had ten ships.

¶ THE SECOND BOOKE

of the Kings, commonly called, The

fourth Booke of the Kings.

CHAP. I.

1 Moab rebelleth. 2 Ahaziah, sending to Baal-zebub, hath his iudgement by Eliiah. 5 Eliiah twise bringeth fire from heauen vpon them whom Ahaziah sent to apprehend him. 13 He pitieth the third captaine, and incouraged by an Angel, telleth the King of his death. 17 Iehoram succeedeth Ahaziah.

*Chap. 3. 5.

THen Moab rebelled against Israel, *after the death of Ahab.

2 And Ahaziah fel downe thorow a lattesse in his vpper chamber that *was* in Samaria, and was sicke: and he sent messengers, and said vnto them, Goe, enquire of Baalzebub the god of Ekron, whether I shal recouer of this disease.

3 But the Angel of the LORD said to Eliiah the Tishbite, Arise, goe vp to meete the messengers of the king of Samaria, and say vnto them, *Is* it not because there is not a God in Israel, *that* ye goe to enquire of Baalzebub the god of Ekron?

† Heb. the bed, whither thou art gone vp,thou shalt not come downe from it.

4 Now therefore, thus sayeth the LORD, †Thou shalt not come downe from that bed on which thou art gone vp, but shalt surely die. And Eliiah departed.

5 ¶ And when the messengers turned backe vnto him, he said vnto them, Why are ye now turned backe?

6 And they said vnto him, There came a man vp to meet vs, and said vnto vs, Goe, turne againe vnto the king that sent you, and say vnto him, Thus saith the LORD, *Is* it not because there is not a God in Israel, *that* thou sendest to enquire of Baalzebub the god of Ekron? therefore thou shalt not come downe from that bedde on which thou art gone vp, but shalt surely die.

7 And hee said vnto them, †What maner of man *was he* which came vp to meet you, and told you these words?

† Heb. was the ner of man?

8 And they answered him, He was an hairy man, and girt with a girdle of leather about his loynes: and he said, It *is* Eliiah the Tishbite.

9 Then the King sent vnto him a captaine of fiftie, with his fiftie: and he went vp to him, (and behold, he sate on the top of an hill) and hee spake vnto him, Thou man of God, the king hath said, Come downe.

10 And Eliiah answered, and said to the captaine of fiftie, If I *be* a man of God, then let fire come downe from heauen, and consume thee and thy fiftie. And there came downe fire from heauen, and consumed him and his fiftie.

11 Againe also hee sent vnto him another captaine of fiftie, with his fiftie: And hee answered, and said vnto him, O man of God, Thus hath the king said, Come downe quickly.

12 And Eliiah answered, and saide vnto them, If I *be* a man of God, let fire come downe from heauen, and consume thee, and thy fiftie. And the fire of God came downe from heauen, and consumed him, and his fiftie.

13 ¶ And hee sent againe a captaine of the third fiftie, with his fiftie: and the third captaine of fiftie went vp, and came and †fell on his knees before Eliiah, and besought him, and saide vnto him, Oh man of God, I pray thee, let my life, and the life of these fiftie thy seruants, be precious in thy sight.

† Hebr. bowed.

14 Behold, there came fire downe from heauen, and burnt vp the two captaines of the former fifties, with their fifties: Therefore let my life now be precious in thy sight.

15 And

15 And the Angel of the LORD said vnto Elijah, Goe downe with him, be not afraid of him. And he arose, and went downe with him vnto the king.

16 And he said vnto him, Thus saith the LORD, Forasmuch as thou hast sent messengers to enquire of Baalzebub the god of Ekron (*is* it not because there is no God in Israel, to enquire of his word?) therefore thou shalt not come downe off that bed on which thou art gone vp, but shalt surely die

17 ¶ So he died, according to the worde of the LORD 'which Eliiah had spoken: and Iehoram reigned in his stead, in the second yeere of Iehoram the sonne of Iehoshaphat king of Iudah, because he had no sonne.

18 Now the rest of the actes of Ahaziah, which hee did, are they not written in the booke of the Chronicles of the kings of Israel?

CHAP. II

1 Elijah, taking his leaue of Elisha, with his mantle diuideth Iordan, 9 and granting Elisha his request, is taken vp by a fierie charet into heauen. 12 Elisha, diuiding Iordan with Elijahs mantle, is acknowledged his successor. 16 The young prophets, hardly obtaining leaue to seeke Elijah, could not finde him. 19 Elisha with salt, healeth the vnwholesome waters. 23 Beares destroy the children that mocked Elisha.

 Nd it came to passe when the LORD would take vp Elijah into heauen by a whirlewinde, that Elijah went with Elisha from Gilgal

2 And Elijah said vnto Elisha, Tarie here, I pray thee for the LORD hath sent me to Bethel : and Elisha said vnto him, As the LORD liueth, and as thy soule liueth, I wil not leaue thee. So they went downe to Bethel.

3 And the sonnes of the Prophets that *were* at Bethel, came foorth to Elisha, and said vnto him, Knowest thou that the LORD will take away thy master from thy head to day? And he said, Yea, I know *it*, hold you your peace.

4 And Elijah said vnto him, Elisha, tarie here, I pray thee: for the LORD hath sent me to Iericho: And hee said, As the LORD liueth, and as thy soule liueth, I will not leaue thee. So they came to Iericho.

5 And the sonnes of the Prophets that *were* at Iericho came to Elisha, and said vnto him, Knowest thou that the LORD will take away thy master from thy head to day? and hee answered, Yea, I knowe *it*, holde you your peace.

6 And Elijah said vnto him, Tarie, I pray thee, here : for the LORD hath sent me to Iordan And he said, As the LORD liueth, and as thy soule liueth, I will not leaue thee. And they two went on.

7 And fiftie men of the sonnes of the Prophets went, and stood † to view afarre off : and they two stood by Iordan.

† Hebr. in sight, or ouer against.

8 And Elisha tooke his mantle, and wrapt it together, and smote the waters, and they were diuided hither and thither, so that they two went ouer on drie ground

9 ¶ And it came to passe when they were gone ouer, that Elijah said vnto Elisha, Aske what I shall doe for thee, before I be taken away from thee. And Elisha said, I pray thee, let a double portion of thy spirit be vpon me.

10 And hee said, † Thou hast asked a hard thing: *neuerthelesse*, if thou see me, *when I am* taken from thee, it shall be so vnto thee: but if not, it shall not be *so*.

† Hebr. thou hast done hard in asking.

11 And it came to passe as they still went on and talked, that beholde, *there appeared* a charet of fire, and horses of fire, and parted them both asunder, and * Elijah went vp by a whirlewind into heauen.

* Ecclus. 48 9. 1. mac. 2. 58.

12 ¶ And Elisha saw *it*, and he cried, * My father, my father, the charet of Israel, and the horsemen thereof. And he saw him no more : and he tooke hold of his owne cloathes, and rent them in two pieces.

* Chap. 13. 14.

13 He tooke vp also the mantle of Elijah that fell from him, and went back, and stood by the † banke of Iordan.

† Hebr. lip.

14 And he tooke the mantle of Eliiah that fell from him, and smote the waters, and said, Where is the LORD God of Elijah? and when hee also had smitten the waters, they parted hither and thither : and Elisha went ouer.

15 And when the sonnes of the Prophets which *were* * to view at Iericho, saw him, they said, The spirit of Elijah doth rest on Elisha : And they came to meet him, and bowed themselues to the ground before him.

* Verse 7.

16 ¶ And

16 ¶ And they said vnto him, Behold now, there bee with thy seruants fiftie †strong men, let them goe, we pray thee, and seeke thy master : lest peraduenture the Spirit of the LORD hath taken him vp, and cast him vpon †some mountaine, or into some valley. And he said, Ye shall not send

† *Hebr. sonnes of strength.*

† *Hebr. one of the mountaines.*

17 And when they vrged him, till he was ashamed, he said, Send They sent therefore fiftie men, and they sought three dayes, but found him not.

18 And when they came againe to him (for he taried at Iericho) hee said vnto them, Did I not say vnto you, Goe not?

19 ¶ And the men of the city said vnto Elisha, Behold, I pray thee, the situation of this city *is* pleasant, as my lord seeth : but the water *is* nought, and the ground †barren.

† *Hebr. causing to miscary.*

20 And hee said, Bring mee a new cruse, and put salt therein. And they brought it to him

21 And he went forth vnto the spring of the waters, and cast the salt in there, and said, Thus saith the LORD, I haue healed these waters; there shall not be from thence any more death, or barren *land.*

22 So the waters were healed vnto this day, according to the saying of Elisha, which he spake.

23 ¶ And he went vp from thence vnto Bethel : and as hee was going vp by the way, there came foorth little children out of the citie, and mocked him, and said vnto him, Goe vp thou bald head, Goe vp thou bald head.

24 And hee turned backe, and looked on them, and cursed them in the Name of the LORD : and there came foorth two shee Beares out of the wood, and tare fortie and two children of them.

25 And hee went from thence to mount Carmel, and from thence he returned to Samaria.

CHAP. III.

Ow Iehoram the sonne of Ahab began to reigne ouer Israel in Samaria, the eighteenth yere of Iehoshaphat king of Iudah, and reigned twelue yeeres.

2 And he wrought euill in the sight of the LORD, but not like his father and like his mother; for hee put away the †image of Baal that his father had made.

† *Hebr. statue.*

3 Neuerthelesse, hee cleaued vnto the sinnes of Ieroboam the sonne of Nebat, which made Israel to sinne; he departed not therefrom.

4 ¶ And Mesha king of Moab was a sheepe-master, and rendred vnto the king of Israel an hundred thousand lambes, and an hundred thousand rammes, with the wooll.

5 But it came to passe when *Ahab was dead, that the king of Moab rebelled against the king of Israel.

" Chap. 1.

6 ¶ And king Iehoram went out of Samaria the same time, and numbred all Israel.

7 And he went, and sent to Iehoshaphat the King of Iudah, saying, The king of Moab hath rebelled against mee : Wilt thou goe with mee against Moab to battell? and he said, I will goe vp : *I am as thou art, my people as thy people, *and* my horses as thy horses.

* 1. Ki 22. 4.

8 And he said, Which way shall we goe vp? And he answered, The way through the wildernesse of Edom.

9 So the king of Israel went, and the king of Iudah, and the king of Edom : and they fetch a compasse of seuen dayes iourney : and there was no water for the hoste, and for the cattell †that followed them.

† *Hebr. their fe*

10 And the king of Israel said, Alas, that the LORD hath called these three kings together, to deliuer them into the hand of Moab.

11 But Iehoshaphat said, *Is* there not here a Prophet of the LORD, that we may enquire of the LORD by him? And one of the king of Israels seruants answered, and said, Here *is* Elisha the sonne of Shaphat, which powred water on the hands of Eliiah.

12 And Iehoshaphat saide, The word of the LORD is with him. So the king of Israel, & Iehoshaphat, and the king of Edom went downe to him.

13 And Elisha saide vnto the king of Israel,

Israel, What haue I to doe with thee? Get thee to the prophets of thy father, and to the prophets of thy mother. And the king of Israel said vnto him, Nay: for the LORD hath called these three kings together, to deliuer them into the hand of Moab.

14 And Elisha said, As the LORD of hostes liueth, before whom I stand, Surely were it not that I regard the presence of Iehoshaphat the King of Iudah, I would not looke toward thee, nor see thee.

15 But now bring me a minstrell. And it came to passe when the minstrell played, that the hand of the LORD came vpon him.

16 And hee sayde, Thus sayth the LORD, Make this valley full of ditches.

17 For thus sayth the LORD, Yee shall not see winde, neither shall ye see raine, yet that valley shall be filled with water, that ye may drinke, both ye, and your cattell, and your beasts.

18 And this is but a light thing in the sight of the LORD, he will deliuer the Moabites also into your hand.

19 And ye shall smite euery fenced citie, and euery choice citie, and shall fell euery good tree, and stop all welles of *Heb. grieue* water, and †marre euery good piece of land with stones.

20 And it came to passe in the morning when the meate offering was offered, that behold, there came water by the way of Edom, and the countrey was filled with water.

21 ¶ And when all the Moabites heard that the kings were come vp to *Heb. were yed toge- er.* fight against them, they †gathered all *Heb. gird mselfe th a gir- e.* that were able to †put on armour, and vpward, and stood in the border.

22 And they rose vp early in the morning, and the Sunne shone vpon the water, and the Moabites sawe the water on the other side as red as blood.

23 And they said, This *is* blood: the *Heb. de- royed.* kings are surely †slaine, aud they haue smitten one another: now therefore, Moab, to the spoile.

24 And when they came to the campe of Israel, the Israelites rose vp and smote the Moabites, so that they fledde *Or, they note in it, wen smi- ng.* before them: but ‖they went forward smiting the Moabites, euen in *their* countrey.

25 And they beat downe the cities, and on euery good piece of land cast euery man his stone, and filled it, and they stopped all the welles of water, and felled all the good trees: †onely in Kirharaseth left they the stones thereof: howbeit the slingers went about *it*, and smote it. †*Heb. vntill he left the stones thereof in Kirharaseth.*

26 ¶ And when the king of Moab sawe that the battell was too sore for him, he tooke with him seuen hundred men that drewe swordes, to breake thorow euen vnto the king of Edom. but they could not.

27 Then hee tooke his eldest sonne that should haue reigned in his stead, and offered him for a burnt offering vpon the wall: and there was great indignation against Israel, and they departed from him, and returned to their owne land.

CHAP. IIII.

1 Elisha multiplieth the widowes oyle. 8 Hee giueth a sonne to the good Shunammite. 18 Hee raiseth againe her dead sonne. 38 At Gilgal hee healeth the deadly pottage. 42 Hee satisfieth an hundred men with twentie loaues.

Ow there cryed a certaine woman of the wiues of the sonnes of the Prophets vnto Elisha, saying, Thy seruant my husband is dead, and thou knowest that thy seruant did feare the LORD: and the creditour is come to take vnto him my two sonnes to be bondmen.

2 And Elisha said vnto her, What shall I doe for thee? Tell mee, what hast thou in the house? And shee sayd, Thine handmaid *hath* not any thing in the house, saue a pot of oyle.

3 Then hee said, Goe, borrow thee vessels abroad, of all thy neighbours; *euen* emptie vessels, ‖borrow not a few. ‖*Or, scant not.*

4 And when thou art come in, thou shalt shut the doore vpon thee, and vpon thy sonnes, and shalt powre out into all those vessels, and thou shalt set aside that which is full.

5 So shee went from him, and shut the doore vpon her, & vpon her sonnes: who brought *the vessels* to her, and shee powred out.

6 And it came to passe, when the vessels were full, that shee said vnto her sonne, Bring me yet a vessell. And hee said vnto her, *There is* not a vessel more. And the oyle stayed.

7 Then|

‖ Or, credi-
tour.

† Heb. there
was a day.

† Heb. laid
hold on him.

7 Then she came, and told the man of God: and he said, Goe, sell the oyle, and pay thy ‖debt, and liue thou and thy children of the rest.

8 ¶ Aud †it fell on a day, that Elisha passed to Shunem, where was a great woman; and shee †constrained him to eate bread: And so it was, that as oft as he passed by, hee turned in thither to eate bread.

9 And shee said vnto her husband, Behold now, I perceiue that this is an holy man of God, which passeth by vs continually.

10 Let vs make a litle chamber, I pray thee, on the wall, and let vs set for him there a bed, and a table, and a stoole, and a candlesticke: and it shall be when he commeth to vs, that hee shall turne in thither.

11 And it fell on a day that hee came thither, and hee turned into the chamber, and lay there.

12 And he said to Gehazi his seruant, Call this Shunammite. And when hee had called her, she stood before him.

13 And he said vnto him, Say, now vnto her, Behold, thou hast beene carefull for vs with all this care; What is to be done for thee? Wouldest thou be spoken for to the king, or to the captaine of the hoste? And she answered, I dwell among mine owne people.

14 And he said, What then is to bee done for her? And Gehazi answered, Verily she hath no child, and her husband is old.

15 And he said, Call her. And when he had called her, she stood in the doore.

* Gen. 18.
10.
† Heb. set
time.

16 And he said, * About this †season, according to the time of life, thou shalt imbrace a sonne. And she said, Nay my lord, thou man of God, doe not lie vnto thine handmaid.

17 And the woman conceiued, and bare a sonne at that season, that Elisha had said vnto her, according to the time of life.

18 ¶ And when the child was growen, it fell on a day that hee went out to his father, to the reapers.

19 And he said vnto his father, My head, my head: and he said to a ladde, Carie him to his mother.

20 And when he had taken him, and brought him to his mother, hee sate on her knees till noone, and then died.

21 And she went vp, and laid him on the bed of the man of God, and shut the doore vpon him, and went out.

22 And she called vnto her husband, and said, Send me, I pray thee, one of the yong men, and one of the asses, that I may runne to the man of God, and come againe.

23 And he said, Wherefore wilt thou goe to him to day? it is neither newe moone nor Sabbath And shee said, It shalbe †well.

24 Then she sadled an asse, and said to her seruant, Driue, and goe forward: †slacke not thy riding for mee, except I bid thee.

25 So she went, and came vnto the man of God to mount Carmel: and it came to passe when the man of God saw her afarre off, that hee said to Gehazi his seruant, Behold, yonder is that Shunammite:

26 Runne now, I pray thee, to meet her, and say vnto her, Is it wel with thee? is it wel with thy husband? is it wel with the child? And she answered, It is well.

27 And when shee came to the man of God to the hill, shee caught †him by the feet: but Gehazi came neere to thrust her away. And the man of God saide, Let her alone, for her soule is †vexed within her; and the LORD hath hid it from me, and hath not told me.

28 Then shee said, Did I desire a sonne of my LORD? did I not say, Doe not deceiue me?

29 Then he said to Gehazi, Gird vp thy loines, and take my staffe in thine hand, and goe thy way: if thou meete any man, salute him not: and if any salute thee, answere him not againe: and lay my staffe vpon the face of the childe.

30 And the mother of the childe said, As the LORD liueth, and as thy soule liueth, I will not leaue thee. And he arose, and followed her.

31 And Gehazi passed on before them, and laid the staffe vpon the face of the child, but there was neither voyce, nor †hearing: wherefore he went againe to meete him, and tolde him, saying, The child is not awaked.

32 And when Elisha was come into the house, behold, the child was dead, and laid vpon his bed.

33 He went in therefore, and shut the doore vpon them twaine, and prayed vnto the LORD.

34 And he went vp, and lay vpon the child, and put his mouth vpon his mouth, and his eyes vpon his eyes, and his

† Heb. pe

† Heb. r
straine
for me t
ride.

† Heb. t
feete.

† Heb.

† Heb.
tion.

his hands vpon his hands, and he stretched himselfe vpon the child, and the flesh of the child waxed warme.

35 Then he returned, and walked in the house †to and fro, and went vp, and stretched himselfe vpon him : and the child neesed seuen times, and the child opened his eyes.

36 And hee called Gehazi, and said, Call this Shunammite. So hee called her : and when shee was come in vnto him, he said, Take vp thy sonne.

37 Then she went in, and fell at his feet, and bowed her selfe to the ground, and tooke vp her sonne, and went out.

38 ¶ And Elisha came againe to Gilgal, and there was a dearth in the land, and the sonnes of the Prophets *were* sitting before him : and hee said vnto his seruant, Set on the great pot, and seethe pottage for the sonnes of the Prophets.

39 And one went out into the field to gather herbes, and found a wild vine, and gathered thereof wilde gourds his lap full, and came and shred them into the pot of pottage : for they knew *them* not.

40 So they powred out for the men to eat: and it came to passe as they were eating of the pottage, that they cried out, and said, O thou man of God, *there is* death in the pot. And they could not eate *thereof.*

41 But he said, Then bring meale. And he cast *it* into the pot : And he said, Powre out for the people, that they may eat. And there was no †harme in the pot.

42 ¶ And there came a man from Baal-Shalisha, and brought the man of God bread of the first fruits, twentie loaues of barley, and full eares of corne †in the huske thereof : and he said, Giue vnto the people, that they may eate.

43 And his seruitour saide, What should I set this before an hundred men? He said againe, Giue the people, that they may eate : for thus saith the LORD, *They shall eate, and shall leaue *thereof.*

44 So he set *it* before them, and they did eate, and left *thereof,* according to the word of the LORD.

CHAP. V.

him some of the earth. 20 Gehazi, abusing his masters name vnto Naaman, is smitten with leprosie.

Ow Naaman captaine of the host of the king of Syria, was a great man †with his master, and ‖honourable, because by him the LORD had giuen ‖deliuerance vnto Syria : He was also a mighty man in valour, *but he was* a leper.

2 And the Syrians had gone out by companies, and had brought away captiue out of the land of Israel a litle maid, & she †waited on Naamans wife.

3 And shee saide vnto her mistresse, Would God my lord *were* †with the Prophet that *is* in Samaria, for hee would †recouer him of his leprosie.

4 And one went in, and tolde his lord, saying, Thus and thus said the mayd that *is* of the land of Israel.

5 And the king of Syria said, Goe to, Goe, and I will send a letter vnto the king of Israel. And hee departed, and tooke †with him ten talents of siluer, and sixe thousand *pieces* of gold, and ten changes of raiment.

6 And hee brought the letter to the king of Israel, saying, Now when this letter is come vnto thee, behold, I haue *therewith* sent Naaman my seruant to thee, that thou mayest recouer him of his leprosie.

7 And it came to passe when the king of Israel had read the letter, that he rent his clothes, and said, *Am* I God, to kill and to make aliue, that this man doeth send vnto me, to recouer a man of his leprosie? Wherefore consider, I pray you, and see how he seeketh a quarrell against me.

8 ¶ And it was so when Elisha the man of God had heard, that the king of Israel had rent his clothes, that he sent to the king, saying, Wherefore hast thou rent thy clothes? Let him come now to mee, and he shall know that there is a Prophet in Israel.

9 So Naaman came with his horses, and with his charet, and stood at the doore of the house of Elisha.

10 And Elisha sent a messenger vnto him, saying, Goe and wash in Iordane seuen times, and thy flesh shall come againe to thee, and thou shalt be cleane.

11 But Naaman was wroth, and went away, and saide, Beholde, †I thought, He will surely come out to me and

Marginal notes

eb. once ier, and e thither.

† *Hebr. before.*
‖ *Or, gracious. Hebr. lifted vp, or accepted in countenance.*
‖ *Or, victory.*

† *Hebr. was before.*

† *Hebr. before.*

† *Hebr. gather in.*

† *Hebr. in his hand.*

Hebr. euil ng.

r, in his ip, or gar-ent.

ohn 6.

† *Hebr. said. Or, I said with my selfe, He will surely come out &c.*

† Hebr. mooue vp and downe.

‖ Or, A-mana.

and stand, and call on the Name of the LORD his God, †and strike his hand ouer the place, and recouer the leper

12 Are not ‖Abana and Pharpar, ri-uers of Damascus, better then all the waters of Israel? May I not wash in them, and be cleane? So he turned, and went away in a rage.

13 And his seruants came neere and spake vnto him, and said, My father, If the Prophet had bid thee do some great thing, wouldest thou not haue done it? How much rather then, when hee saith to thee, Wash and be cleane?

* Luke 4. 27.

14 Then went he downe, and dip-ped himselfe seuen times in Iordan, ac-cording to the saying of the man of God: and his flesh came againe like vnto the flesh of a litle childe, and *he was cleane.

15 ¶ And he returned to the man of God, he and all his company, and came, and stood before him: and he said, Be-hold, now I know that there is no God in all the earth, but in Israel: now therefore, I pray thee, take a blessing of thy seruant.

16 But he said, As the LORD li-ueth, before whom I stand, I will re-ceiue none. And hee vrged him to take it, but he refused.

17 And Naaman said, Shall there not then, I pray thee, be giuen to thy seruant two mules burden of earth? for thy seruant wil henceforth offer nei-ther burnt offering, nor sacrifice vnto other gods, but vnto the LORD.

18 In this thing the LORD par-don thy seruant, that when my master goeth into the house of Rimmon to worship there, and hee leaneth on my hand, and I bow my selfe in the house of Rimmon: when I bow downe my selfe in the house of Rimmon, the LORD pardon thy seruant in this thing

19 And he said vnto him, Go in peace. So he departed from him, †a litle way.

† Hebr. a litle piece of ground.

20 ¶ But Gehazi the seruant of E-lisha the man of God, said, Behold, my master hath spared Naaman this Sy-rian, in not receiuing at his hands that which hee brought: but as the LORD liueth, I wil runne after him, and take somewhat of him.

21 So Gehazi followed after Naa-man: and when Naaman saw him running after him, hee lighted downe from the charet to meet him, and said,

† Hebr. Is there peace?

† Is all well?

22 And he said, All is well: my ma-ster hath sent me, saying, Behold, euen now there be come to mee from mount Ephraim two yong men, of the sonnes of the Prophets: Giue them, I pray thee, a talent of siluer, and two changes of garments.

23 And Naaman said, Bee content, take two talents: and hee vrged him, and bound two talents of siluer in two bags, with two changes of garments, and layde them vpon two of his ser-uants, and they bare them before him.

‖ Or, see place.

24 And when he came to the ‖towre, he tooke them from their hand, and be-stowed them in the house, and hee let the men goe, and they departed.

25 But he went in, and stood before his master: and Elisha said vnto him, Whence commest thou, Gehazi? And hee said, Thy seruant went †no whither

† Hebr. hither o thither

26 And he said vnto him, Went not mine heart with thee, when the man tur-ned againe from his charet to meete thee? Is it a time to receiue money, and to receiue garments, and Oliue yards, and Vineyards, and sheepe, and oxen, and men seruants, and mayd seruants?

27 The leprosie therefore of Naa-man shall cleaue vnto thee, and vnto thy seede for euer: And hee went out from his presence a leper as white as snow.

CHAP VI.

1 Elisha giuing leaue to the yong Prophets to inlarge their dwellings, causeth yron to swim. 8 Hee discloseth the king of Syria his coun-sell. 13 The armie which was sent to Do-than to apprehend Elisha, is smitten with blindnesse: 19 Being brought into Sama-ria, they are dismissed in peace. 24 The fa-mine in Samaria, causeth women to eate their owne children. 30 The king sendeth to slay Elisha.

Nd the sonnes of the Pro-phets saide vnto Elisha, Beholde now, the place where wee dwell with thee, is too strait for vs:

2 Let vs goe, wee pray thee, vnto Iordane, and take thence euery man a beame, and let vs make vs a place there where we may dwell. And hee answe-red, Goe ye.

3 And one said, Be content, I pray thee, and goe with thy seruants. And he answered, I will goe.

4 So hee went with them: and when

when they came to Iordane, they cut downe wood.

5 But as one was felling a beame, the †axe head fell into the water : and hee cryed, and sayd, Alas master, for it was borrowed.

Heb. yron.

6 And the man of God said, Where fell it ? and hee shewed him the place : and he cut downe a sticke, and cast it in thither, and the yron did swimme.

7 Therefore said he, Take it vp to thee : And hee put out his hand, and tooke it.

8 ¶ Then the king of Syria warred against Israel, and tooke counsell with his seruants, saying, In such and such a place *shall be* my ‖campe.

r, encam-'g.

9 And the man of God sent vnto the king of Israel, saying, Beware that thou passe not such a place; for thither the Syrians are come downe.

10 And the king of Israel sent to the place which the man of God tolde him, and warned him of, and saued himselfe there, not once nor twise.

11 Therefore the heart of the king of Syria was sore troubled for this thing, and he called his seruants, and said vnto them, Will ye not shewe me which of vs *is* for the king of Israel ?

12 And one of his seruants sayde, †None, my lord O king ; but Elisha the Prophet, that is in Israel, telleth the king of Israel, the wordes that thou speakest in thy bed-chamber.

Heb. No.

13 ¶ And he said, Goe and spie where he *is*, that I may send and fetch him. And it was tolde him, saying, Behold, he *is* in Dothan.

14 Therefore sent he thither horses, and charets, and a †great hoste : and they came by night, and compassed the citie about.

Heb. hea-.

15 And when the ‖seruant of the man of God was risen early and gone forth, behold, an host compassed the citie, both with horses and charets : and his seruant said vnto him, Alas my master, how shall we doe ?

r, mini-r.

16 And he answered, Feare not : for * they that *be* with vs, *are* moe then they that *be* with them.

. Chron.
. 7.

17 And Elisha prayed, and sayde, LORD, I pray thee, open his eyes that he may see. And the LORD opened the eyes of the young man, and hee saw : and behold, the mountaine *was* full of horses, and charets of fire round about Elisha.

18 And when they came downe to him, Elisha prayed vnto the LORD, and said, Smite this people, I pray thee, with blindnesse. And hee smote them with blindnesse, according to the word of Elisha.

19 ¶ And Elisha saide vnto them, This *is* not the way, neither *is* this the citie : †follow me, and I will bring you to the man whom ye seeke. But hee led them to Samaria.

† Heb. come ye after me.

20 And it came to passe when they were come into Samaria, that Elisha said, LORD, open the eyes of these men, that they may see. And the LORD opened their eyes, and they saw, and beholde, *they were* in the mids of Samaria.

21 And the king of Israel saide vnto Elisha, when he saw them, My father, shall I smite *them*? shall I smite *them*?

22 And he answered, Thou shalt not smite *them* : wouldest thou smite those whom thou hast taken captiue with thy sword, and with thy bow ? set bread and water before them, that they may eate, and drinke, and go to their master.

23 And hee prepared great prouision for them, and when they had eaten and drunke, hee sent them away, and they went to their master : so the bands of Syria came no more into the lande of Israel.

24 ¶ And it came to passe after this, that Benhadad king of Syria gathered all his hoste, and went vp, and besieged Samaria.

25 And there was a great famine in Samaria : and behold, they besieged it, vntill an asses head was *solde* for fourescore *pieces* of siluer, and the fourth part of a kab of doues doung for fiue *pieces* of siluer.

26 And as the king of Israel was passing by vpon the wall, there cried a woman vnto him, saying, Helpe, my lord, O king.

27 And he said, ‖If the LORD do not helpe thee, whence shall I helpe thee ? out of the barne floore, or out of the wine presse ?

‖ Or, Let not the Lord saue thee.

28 And the king said vnto her, What aileth thee ? And shee answered, This woman said vnto me, Giue thy sonne, that we may eate him to day, and wee will eate my sonne to morrow.

29 So *we boyled my sonne, and did eate him : and I saide vnto her on the †next day, Giue thy sonne, that we may eate

* Deut. 28. 53.
† Heb. other.

eate him : and she hath hid her sonne.

30 ¶ And it came to passe when the king heard the words of the woman, that he rent his clothes, and hee passed by vpon the wall, and the people looked, and behold, hee had sackcloth within, vpon his flesh.

31 Then he said, God doe so, and more also to mee, if the head of Elisha the sonne of Shaphat, shall stand on him this day.

32 But Elisha sate in his house (and the elders sate with him) and the king sent a man from before him: but yer the messenger came to him, hee said to the Elders, See yee how this sonne of a murderer hath sent to take away mine head? Looke when the messenger commeth, shut the doore, and hold him fast at the doore : Is not the sound of his masters feete behind him?

33 And while hee yet talked with them, beholde, the messenger came downe vnto him : and he said, Behold, this euill is of the LORD, what should I waite for the LORD any longer?

CHAP. VII.

1 Elisha prophecieth incredible plenty in Samaria. 3 Foure Lepers venturing on the host of the Syrians, bring tydings of their flight. 22 The king finding by spies the newes to be true, spoileth the tents of the Syrians. 17 The Lord, who would not beleeue the prophecie of plenty, hauing the charge of the gate, is troden to death in the presse.

HenElisha said, Heare yee the word of the LORD, Thus saith the LORD, To morrowe about this time shal a measure of fine flower be sold for a shekell, and two measures of barley for a shekel, in the gate of Samaria.

† Heb. a Lord which belonged to the King, leaning vpon his hand.

2 Then †a lord on whose hand the king leaned, answered the man of God, and said, Behold, if the LORD would make windowes in heauen, might this thing bee? and he saide, Behold, thou shalt see it with thine eies, but shalt not eate thereof.

3 ¶ And there were foure leprous men at the entring in of the gate : and they saide one to another, Why sit wee here vntill we die?

4 If we say, We will enter into the citie, then the famine is in the citie, and wee shall die there : and if we sit still here, we die also. Now therefore come,

and let vs fall vnto the host of the Syrians : if they saue vs aliue, we shall liue; and if they kill vs, we shall but die.

5 And they rose vp in the twilight, to goe vnto the campe of the Syrians : and when they were come to the vttermost part of the campe of Syria, behold, there was no man there.

6 For the LORD had made the host of the Syrians to heare a noise of charets, and a noise of horses, euen the noise of a great host : and they said one to another, Loe, the king of Israel hath hired against vs the kings of the Hittites, and the kings of the Egyptians, to come vpon vs.

7 Wherefore they arose and fled in the twilight, and left their tents, and their horses, and their asses, euen the campe as it was, and fled for their life.

8 And when these lepers came to the vttermost part of the campe, they went into one tent, and did eate, and drinke, and carried thence siluer, and gold, and raiment, and went and hid it, and came againe, and entred into another tent, and carried thence also, and went and hid it.

9 Then they said one to another, We doe not well : this day is a day of good tydings, and we hold our peace : if we tarie till the morning light, †some mischiefe will come vpon vs : nowe therefore come, that we may goe, and tell the kings houshold.

† Heb. u shall finde nishmen

10 So they came, and called vnto the porter of the citie : and they told them, saying; We came to the campe of the Syrians, and behold, there was no man there, neither voice of man, but horses tyed, and asses tyed, and the tents as they were.

11 And hee called the porters, and they told it to the kings house within.

12 ¶ And the king arose in the night, and said vnto his seruants, I will now shew you what the Syrians haue done to vs : They know that we be hungrie, therefore are they gone out of the camp, to hide themselues in the field, saying; When they come out of the citie, we shal catch them aliue, and get into the citie.

13 And one of his seruants answered, and said, Let some take, I pray thee, fiue of the horses that remaine, which are left †in the citie: (behold, they are as all the multitude of Israel that are left in it : behold, I say, they are euen as all the multitude of the Israelites

† Heb. in

lites that are consumed) and let vs send, and see.

14 They tooke therefore two charet horses, and the king sent after the hoste of the Syrians, saying, Goe, and see.

15 And they went after them vnto Iordane, and loe, all the way was full of garments, and vessels, which the Syrians had cast away in their haste : and the messengers returned, and told the king.

16 And the people went out, and spoiled the tents of the Syrians : So a measure of fine flowre was *sold* for a shekell, and two measures of barley for a shekel, according to the word of the Lord.

17 ¶ And the king appointed the lord on whose hand he leaned, to haue the charge of the gate : and the people trode vpon him in the gate, and he died, as the man of God had said, who spake when the king came downe to him.

18 And it came to passe, as the man of God had spoken to the king, saying, Two measures of barley for a shekel, and a measure of fine flowre for a shekel, shalbe to morrow about this time, in the gate of Samaria :

19 And that lord answered the man of God, and said, Now behold, if the Lord should make windowes in heauen, might such a thing be? And he said, Behold, thou shalt see it with thine eyes, but shalt not eate thereof.

20 And so it fell out vnto him : for the people trode vpon him in the gate, and he died.

CHAP. VIII.

1 The Shunammite, hauing left her countrey seuen yeeres, to auoide the forewarned famine, for Elishas miracle sake, hath her land restored by the king. 7 Hazael being sent with a present by Benhadad to Elisha at Damascus, after he had heard the prophesie, killeth his master, and succeedeth him. 16 Iehorams wicked reigne in Iudah. 20 Edom and Libnah reuolt. 23 Ahaziah succeedeth Iehoram. 25 Ahaziahs wicked reigne. 28 He visiteth Iehoram wounded, at Iezreel.

Chap.
35.

Hen spake Elisha vnto the woman (*whose sonne he had restored to life) saying, Arise, and goe thou and thine housholde, and soiourne whersoeuer thou canst soiourne : for the Lord hath called for a famin, and it shall also come vpon the land seuen yeeres.

2 And the woman arose, and did after the saying of the man of God : and she went with her housholde, and soiourned in the land of the Philistines seuen yeeres.

3 And it came to passe at the seuen yeeres ende, that the woman returned out of the land of the Philistines : and she went foorth to crie vnto the king for her house, and for her land.

4 And the king talked with Gehazi the seruant of the man of God, saying, Tell mee, I pray thee, all the great things that Elisha hath done.

5 And it came to passe as he was telling the King how hee had restored a dead body to life, that behold, the woman whose sonne he had restored to life, cryed to the King for her house and for her land. And Gehazi said, My lord O king, this *is* the woman, and this *is* her sonne, whom Elisha restored to life.

6 And when the king asked the woman, shee tolde him. So the King appointed vnto her a certaine ||officer, saying, Restore all that was hers, and all the fruites of the field, since the day that she left the land, euen till now.

7 ¶ And Elisha came to Damascus, and Benhadad the king of Syria was sicke, and it was tolde him, saying, The man of God is come hither.

8 And the king said vnto Hazael, Take a present in thine hand, and goe meete the man of God, and enquire of the Lord by him, saying, Shall I recouer of this disease?

9 So Hazael went to meete him, and tooke a present †with him, euen of euery good thing of Damascus, fourtie camels burden, and came, and stood before him, and said, Thy sonne Benhadad king of Syria hath sent me to thee, saying, Shall I recouer of this disease?

10 And Elisha said vnto him, Goe, say vnto him, Thou mayest certeinly recouer : howbeit, the Lord hath shewed me, that he shall surely die.

11 And hee setled his countenance †stedfastly, vntill he was ashamed : and the man of God wept.

12 And Hazael said, Why weepeth my lord? And he answered, Because I know the euill that thou wilt doe vnto the children of Israel : their strong holds wilt thou set on fire, and their young men wilt. thou slay with the sword, and wilt dash their children, and rip vp their women with childe.

13 And

‖ *Or, Eunuch.*

† *Heb. in his hand.*

† *Heb. and set it.*

13 And Hazael said, But what, *is* thy seruant a dogge, that he should doe this great thing? And Elisha answered, The LORD hath shewed mee that thou *shalt be* king ouer Syria.

14 So he departed from Elisha, and came to his master, who saide to him, What said Elisha to thee? and hee answered, He told me that thou shouldst surely recouer

15 And it came to passe on the morrow, that he tooke a thicke cloth, and dipt it in water, and spread *it* on his face, so that he died, and Hazael reigned in his stead.

* 2. Chron. 21. 4.
† Hebr. reigned.

16 ¶ And in the fifth yeere of Ioram the sonne of Ahab king of Israel, Iehoshaphat *being* then king of Iudah, * Iehoram the sonne of Iehoshaphat king of Iudah †began to reigne

17 Thirtie and two yeeres old was he when he began to reigne, and hee reigned eight yeeres in Ierusalem.

18 And he walked in the way of the kings of Israel, as did the house of Ahab : for the daughter of Ahab was his wife, and hee did euill in the sight of the LORD.

* 2. Sam. 7. 13.
† Hebr. candle, or lampe

19 Yet the LORD would not destroy Iudah, for Dauid his seruants sake, * as hee promised to giue to him alway a †light, and to his children.

20 ¶ In his dayes Edom reuolted from vnder the hand of Iudah, and made a king ouer themselues.

21 So Ioram went ouer to Zair, and all the charets with him, and hee rose by night, and smote the Edomites, which compassed him about : and the captaines of the charets, and the people fled into their tents.

22 Yet Edom reuolted from vnder the hand of Iudah vnto this day. Then Libnah reuolted at the same time.

23 And the rest of the actes of Ioram, and all that hee did, are they not written in the booke of the Chronicles of the kings of Iudah?

24 And Ioram slept with his fathers, and was buried with his fathers in the citie of Dauid : And * Ahaziah his sonne reigned in his stead

* 2. Chron. 22. 1.

25 ¶ In the twelfth yeere of Ioram the sonne of Ahab, king of Israel, did Ahaziah, the sonne of Iehoram king of Iudah, begin to reigne.

26 Two and twentie yeeres old *was* Ahaziah when he began to reigne, and he reigned one yeere in Ierusalem, and his mothers name *was* Athaliah the daughter of Omri king of Israel.

27 And he walked in the way of the house of Ahab, and did euill in the sight of the LORD, as *did* the house of Ahab : for hee *was* the sonne in law of the house of Ahab

28 ¶ And he went with Ioram the sonne of Ahab, to the warre against Hazael king of Syria in Ramoth Gilead, and the Syrians wounded Ioram.

29 And king Ioram went backe to be healed in Iezreel, of the woundes †which the Syrians †had giuen him at Ramah, when hee fought against Hazael king of Syria : And Ahaziah the son of Iehoram king of Iudah, went downe to see Ioram the sonne of Ahab in Iezreel, because he was sicke.

† Hebr. wherew the Syri had wou ded.
† Hebr. wounde

CHAP. IX.

1 Elisha sendeth a yong Prophet with instructions to annoint Iehu at Ramoth Gilead. 4 The Prophet hauing done his message, flieth. 11 Iehu being made king by the souldiers, killeth Ioram in the field of Naboth. 27 Ahaziah is slaine at Gur, and buried at Ierusalem. 30 Proud Iezebel is throwen downe out of a window, and eaten by dogs

Nd Elisha the Prophet called one of the childreu of the Prophets, and said vnto him, Gird vp thy loines, and take this boxe of oile in thine hand, and goe to Ramoth Gilead.

2 And when thou commest thither, looke out there Iehu the sonne of Iehoshaphat, the sonne of Nimshi, and goe in, and make him arise vp from among his brethren, and carie him to an †inner chamber

3 Then * take the boxe of oile, and powre it on his head, and say, Thus saith the LORD, I haue anointed thee king ouer Israel : then open the doore, and flee, and tary not.

4 ¶ So the yong man, *euen* the yong man the Prophet, went to Ramoth Gilead :

5 And when hee came, behold, the captaines of the host were sitting ; and hee said, I haue an errand to thee, O captaine : And Iehu said, Vnto which of all vs? And he said, To thee, O captaine.

6 And hee arose, and went into the house,

† Heb. ch ber in a chamber
* 1. Kir 19. 16.

house, and hee powred the oyle on his head, and said vnto him, Thus sayth the LORD God of Israel, I haue anoynted thee king ouer the people of the LORD, *euen* ouer Israel.

7 And thou shalt smite the house of Ahab thy master, that I may auenge the blood of my seruants the Prophets, and the blood of all the seruants of the LORD, *at the hand of Iezebel.

8 For the whole house of Ahab shal perish, and *I will cut off from Ahab, him that pisseth against the wall, and him that is shut vp and left in Israel.

9 And I will make the house of A-hab, like the house of *Ieroboam the sonne of Nebat, and like the house of *Baasha the sonne of Ahiiah.

10 And the dogges shal eate Iezebel in the portion of Iezreel, and there shal be none to burie *her. And he opened the doore, and fled.

11 ¶ Then Iehu came foorth to the seruants of his lord, and *one* said vnto him, Is all well? wherefore came this madde fellow to thee? And he said vn-to them, Yee know the man, and his communication.

12 And they said, *It is* false, tell vs now: And hee sayde, Thus and thus spake he to me, saying, Thus saith the LORD, I haue anoynted thee King ouer Israel.

13 Then they hasted, and tooke eue-ry man his garment, and put it vnder him on the top of the staires, and blewe with trumpets, saying, Iehu †is king.

14 So Iehu the sonne of Iehosha-phat, the sonne of Nimshi, conspired a-gainst Ioram: (now Ioram had kept Ramoth Gilead, hee, and all Israel, be-cause of Hazael king of Syria:

15 But *king †Ioram was retur-ned to bee healed in Iezreel, of the wounds which the Syrians had †gi-uen him, when he fought with Hazael king of Syria.) And Iehu said, If it be your minds, then †let none goe forth *nor* escape out of the citie, to goe to tell *it* in Iezreel.

16 So Iehu rode in a chariot, and went to Iezreel, (for Ioram lay there:) and Ahaziah king of Iudah was come downe to see Ioram.

17 And there stood a watchman on the towre in Iezreel, and hee spied the company of Iehu as he came, and said, I see a companie. And Ioram sayd, Take an horseman, and send to meete

them, and let him say, *Is it* peace?

18 So there went one on horsebacke to meete him, and said, Thus sayth the king, *Is it* peace? And Iehu said, What hast thou to doe with peace? turne thee behinde me. And the watchman tolde, saying, The messenger came to them, but he commeth not againe.

19 Then he sent out a second on horse-backe, which came to them, and sayd, Thus sayth the king, *Is it* peace? And Iehu answered, What hast thou to doe with peace? turne thee behinde me.

20 And the watchman tolde, saying, He came euen vnto them, and commeth not againe: and the ‖driuing is like the driuing of Iehu the sonne of Nimshi; for he driueth †furiously.

21 And Ioram said, †Make readie. And his charet was made ready. And Ioram king of Israel, and Ahaziah king of Iudah, went out, each in his charet, and they went out against Ie-hu, and †met him in the portion of Na-both the Iezreelite.

22 And it came to passe when Io-ram saw Iehu, that hee said, *Is it* peace, Iehu? And he answered, What peace, so long as the whoredomes of thy mo-ther Iezebel, and her witchcrafts *are so* many?

23 And Ioram turned his hand, and fled, and said to Ahaziah, There is trea-chery, O Ahaziah.

24 And Iehu †drew a bowe with his full strength, and smote Iehoram betweene his armes, and the arrow went out at his heart, and hee †sunke downe in his charet.

25 Then said *Iehu* to Bidkar his cap-taine, Take vp, *and* cast him in the por-tion of the field of Naboth the Iezree-lite: for remember, how that when I and thou rode together after Ahab his father, the LORD laide this burden vpon him.

26 *Surely I haue seene yesterday the †blood of Naboth, and the blood of his sonnes, sayd the LORD, and I will requite thee in this ‖plat, sayth the LORD. Now therefore take *and* cast him into the plat *of ground*, according to the word of the LORD.

27 ¶ But when Ahaziah the king of Iudah saw *this*, hee fled by the way of the garden house: and Iehu follow-ed after him, and said, Smite him also in the charet; *and they did so*, at the going vp to Gur, which is by Ibleam: And hee

1. Kings
. 15.

1. Kings
. 10. and
. 21.

1. Kings
. 10. and
. 22.
1. Kings
. 3.

Heb. reig-
eth.

Cha. 8. 29
Heb. Ieho-
um.
Heb. smote

Heb. let no
scaper goe,
'c.

‡ Or, mar-
ching.

† Heb. in
madnesse.
† Heb. bind.

† Heb. found

† Heb. filled
his hand
with a bow.

† Heb. bow-
ed.

*. 1. Kings
21. 29.
† Heb. bloods

‖Or, portion.

hee fled to Megiddo, and died there.

28 And his seruants caried him in a charet to Ierusalem, and buried him in his sepulchre with his fathers, in the citie of Dauid.

29 And in the eleuenth yeere of Ioram the sonne of Ahab, began Ahaziah to reigne ouer Iudah.

30 ¶ And when Iehu was come to Iezreel, Iezebel heard *of it*, and shee †painted her face, and tyred her head, and looked out at a window.

† Heb. put her eyes in painting.

31 And as Iehu entred in at the gate, she said, Had Zimri peace, who slew his master?

32 And he lift vp his face to the window, and said, Who is on my side, who? And there looked out to him two *or* three ‖ Eunuches.

‖ Or, chamberlaines.

33 And he said, Throw her downe. So they threw her downe, and *some* of her blood was sprinkled on the wall, and on the horses: and he trode her vnder foote.

34 And when he was come in, hee did eate and drinke, and saide, Goe, see now this cursed *woman*, and burie her: for she *is* a kings daughter.

35 And they went to burie her, but they found no more of her then the skul, and the feete, & the palmes of *her* hands.

36 Wherefore they came againe, and told him: and he said, This *is* the word of the LORD, which he spake †by his seruant Elijah the Tishbite, saying, *In the portion of Iezreel shall dogs eate the flesh of Iezebel:

† Heb. by the hand of.
* 1. King. 21. 23.

37 And the carkeise of Iezebel shall be as doung vpon the face of the field in the portion of Iezreel, *so* that they shall not say, This *is* Iezebel.

CHAP. X.

1 Iehu by his letters causeth seuentie of Ahabs children to be beheaded. 8 He excuseth the facte by the prophecie of Elijah. 12 At the shearing house he slayeth two and fourtie of Ahaziahs brethren. 15 Hee taketh Iehonadab into his company. 18 By subtiltie hee destroyeth all the worshippers of Baal. 29 Iehu followeth Ieroboams sinnes. 32 Hazael oppresseth Israel. 34 Iehoahaz succeedeth Iehu.

AND Ahab had seuentie sonnes in Samaria: and Iehu wrote letters, and sent to Samaria vnto the rulers of Iezreel, to the Elders, and to †them that brought vp Ahabs *children*, saying,

† Heb. nourishers.

2 Now assoone as this letter commeth to you, seeing your masters sons *are* with you, and there *are* with you charets and horses, a fenced citie also, and armour:

3 Looke euen out the best and meetest of your masters sonnes, and set *him* on his fathers throne, and fight for your masters house.

4 But they were exceedingly afraid, and said, Behold, two kings stood not before him: how then shall we stand?

5 And he that *was* ouer the house, and he that *was* ouer the citie, the elders also, and the bringers vp *of the children*, sent to Iehu, saying, Wee are thy seruants, and will doe all that thou shalt bid vs, we will not make any king: doe thou *that which is* good in thine eyes.

6 Then he wrote a letter the second time to them, saying, If yee *be* †mine, and if ye will hearken vnto my voyce, take ye the heads of the men your masters sonnes, and come to me to Iezreel by to morow this time: (now the kings sonnes being seuenty persons, *were* with the great men of the city, which brought them vp.)

† Heb. for me.

7 And it came to passe when the letter came to them, that they tooke the kings sonnes, and slewe seuentie persons, and put their heads in baskets, and sent him *them* to Iezreel.

8 ¶ And there came a messenger, and tolde him, saying, They haue brought the heads of the kings sonnes. And he said, Lay ye them in two heaps at the entring in of the gate, vntill the morning.

9 And it came to passe in the morning, that he went out, & stood, and said to all the people, Ye *be* righteous: behold, I conspired against my master, and slew him: But who slew all these?

10 Know now, that there shall fall vnto the earth nothing of the worde of the LORD, which the LORD spake concerning the house of Ahab: for the LORD hath done *that* which he spake *†by his seruant Elijah.

* 1. King. 21. 29.
† Heb. by the hand of.

11 So Iehu slew all that remained of the house of Ahab, in Iezreel, and all his great men, and his ‖kinsefolkes, and his priests, vntill he left him none remaining.

‖ Or, acquaintance

12 ¶ And hee arose, and departed, and came to Samaria: And *as* he was at the †shearing house in the way,

13 Iehu †met with the brethren of Aha-

† Heb. house of shepheards binding sheepe.
† Heb. foun

*Hebr. to
the peace of
&c.*

Ahaziah king of Iudah, and said, Who *are* ye? And they answered, Wee *are* the brethren of Ahaziah, and we go downe †to salute the children of the King, and the children of the Queene.

14 And hee said, Take them aliue. And they tooke them aliue, and slew them at the pit of the shearing house, *euen* two and fourty men; neither left he any of them.

*Hebr.
mind.*

*Hebr.
blessed.*

15 ¶ And when hee was departed thence, he †lighted on Iehonadab the sonne of Rechab, *comming* to meet him: and he †saluted him, & said to him, Is thine heart right, as my heart *is* with thy heart? And Iehonadab answered, It is: If it be, giue mee thine hand. And hee gaue him his hand, and hee tooke him vp to him into the charet.

16 And he said, Come with me, and see my zeale for the Lord: so they made him ride in his charet.

17 And when he came to Samaria, he slew all that remained vnto Ahab in Samaria, till he had destroyed him, according to the saying of the Lord, which he spake to Eliah.

18 ¶ And Iehu gathered all the people together, and said vnto them, Ahab serued Baal a litle, *but* Iehu shall serue him much.

19 Now therefore, call vnto me all the prophets of Baal, all his seruants, and all his priests, let none be wanting: for I haue a great sacrifice *to doe* to Baal; whosoeuer shall be wanting, he shall not liue. But Iehu did *it* in subtilitie, to the intent that hee might destroy the worshippers of Baal.

*Hebr. san-
ctifie.*

20 And Iehu said, †Proclaime a solemne assembly for Baal. And they proclaimed *it.*

21 And Iehu sent through all Israel, and all the worshippers of Baal came, so that there was not a man left that came not: and they came into the house of Baal; and the house of Baal was ‖full from one end to another.

*Or, so full,
that they
ood mouth
to mouth.*

22 And he said vnto him that was ouer the vestrie, Bring forth vestments for all the worshippers of Baal. And he brought them forth vestments.

23 And Iehu went, and Iehonadab the sonne of Rechab into the house of Baal, and said vnto the worshippers of Baal, Search, and looke that there be here with you none of the seruants of the Lord, but the worshippers of Baal onely.

24 And when they went in to offer sacrifices, and burnt offerings, Iehu appointed fourescore men without, and said, If any of the men whom I haue brought into your hands, escape, hee that letteth him goe, his life *shall be* for the life of him.

25 And it came to passe assoone as hee had made an end of offering the burnt offering, that Iehu saide to the guard, and to the captaines, Goe in, *and* slay them, let none come foorth. And they smote them with the †edge of the sword, and the guard, and the captaines cast them out, and went to the citie of the house of Baal.

*† Hebr.
the mouth.*

26 And they brought foorth the †I-mages out of the house of Baal, and burnt them.

*† Hebr. sta-
tues.*

27 And they brake downe the image of Baal, and brake downe the house of Baal, and made it a draughthouse, vnto this day.

28 Thus Iehu destroyed Baal out of Israel.

29 ¶ Howbeit, *from* the sinnes of Ie-roboam the sonne of Nebat, who made Israel to sinne, Iehu departed not from after them, *to wit*, the golden calues that *were* in Bethel, and that *were* in Dan.

30 And the Lord said vnto Iehu, Because thou hast done well in executing that which is right in mine eyes, *and* hast done vnto the house of Ahab according to all that *was* in mine heart, thy children of the fourth *generation*, shal sit on the throne of Israel.

31 But Iehu †tooke no heede to walke in the Law of the Lord God of Israel, with all his heart: *for* he departed not from the sinnes of Iero-boam, which made Israel to sinne.

*† Hebr. ob-
serued not.*

32 ¶ In those dayes the Lord began †to cut Israel short: and Hazael smote them in all the coasts of Israel:

*† Hebr. to
cut off the
ends.*

33 From Iordan †Eastward, all the land of Gilead, the Gadites, and the Reubenites, and the Manassites, from Aroer, (which *is* by the riuer Arnon) ‖euen Gilead and Bashan.

*† Hebr. to-
ward the ri-
sing of the
Sunne.*

*‖ Or, euen to
Gilead and
Bashan.*

34 Now the rest of the acts of Ie-hu, and all that he did, & all his might, are they not written in the booke of the Chronicles of the kings of Israel?

35 And Iehu slept with his fathers, and they buried him in Samaria, and Iehoahaz his sonne reigned in his stead.

36 And

36 And † the time that Iehu reigned ouer Israel in Samaria, *was* twentie and eight yeeres.

CHAP XI.

1 Iehoash, being saued by Iehosheba his aunt from Athaliahs massacre of the seed royall, is hid six yeeres in the house of God. 4 Iehoiada giuing order to the captaines, in the seuenth yeere anointeth him King. 13 Athaliah is slaine. 17 Iehoiada restoreth the worship of God.

* 2. Chron.
22. 10.

† Heb. seede
of the king-
dome.

A Nd when * Athaliah the mother of Ahaziah sawe that her sonne was dead, she arose, and destroyed all the † seed royall

2 But Iehosheba the daughter of king Ioram, sister of Ahaziah, tooke Ioash the sonne of Ahaziah, and stale him from among the Kings sonnes which were slaine, and they hid him, *euen* him and his nurse in the bed-chamber from Athaliah, so that he was not slaine.

3 And he was with her hidde in the House of the LORD, sixe yeeres : and Athaliah did reigne ouer the land.

* 2. Chron.
23. 1.

4 ¶ And * the seuenth yeere Iehoiada sent and fet the rulers ouer hundreds, with the captains, and the guard, and brought them to him into the house of the LORD, and made a couenant with them, and tooke an othe of them in the house of the LORD, and shewed them the Kings sonne.

5 And he commanded them, saying, This *is* the thing that yee shall doe ; A third part of you that enter in on the Sabbath, shall euen be keepers of the watch of the kings house :

6 And a third part *shall be* at the gate of Sur, and a third part at the gate behinde the guard : so shall yee keepe the watch of the house. ||that it be not broken downe.

|| Or, from
breaking vp.

|| Or, compa-
nies. Heb.
hands.

7 And two ||parts of all you, that goe foorth on the Sabbath, *euen* they shall keepe the watch of the house of the LORD about the King.

8 And yee shall compasse the King round about, euery man with his weapons in his hand : and he that commeth within the ranges, let him bee slaine : and be yee with the king, as hee goeth out, and as he commeth in.

9 And the captaines ouer the hundreds did according to all things that Iehoiada the Priest commanded : and they tooke euery man his men that were to come in on the Sabbath, with them that should goe out on the Sabbath, and came to Iehoiada the Priest.

10 And to the captaines ouer hundreds, did the Priest giue king Dauids speares and shields, that were in the Temple.

11 And the guard stood, euery man with his weapons in his hand, round about the king, from the right † corner of the Temple, to the left corner of the Temple, *along* by the Altar and the Temple.

† Heb. ſho▸
der.

12 And he brought foorth the kings sonne, and put the crowne vpon him, and *gaue him* the Testimonie, and they made him King, and anointed him, and they clapt their hands, and said, † God saue the King.

† Heb. let
the king
liue.

13 ¶ And when Athaliah heard the noise of the guard, *and* of the people, she came to the people, into the Temple of the LORD.

14 And when shee looked, behold, the king stood by a pillar, as the maner was, and the Princes, and the trumpetters by the King, and all the people of the land reioyced, and blew with trumpets : and Athaliah rent her clothes, and cryed, Treason, treason.

15 But Iehoiada the Priest commanded the captaines of the hundreds, the officers of the hoste, and sayde vnto them, Haue her foorth without the ranges ; and him that followeth her, kill with the sword : for the Priest had sayd, Let her not be slaine in the house of the LORD.

16 And they laid hands on her, and she went by the way, by the which the horses came into the kings house, and there was she slaine.

17 ¶ And Iehoiada made a couenant betweene the LORD and the king, and the people, that they should be the LORDS people ; betweene the king also and the people.

18 And all the people of the land went into the house of Baal, and brake it down, his altars, and his images brake they in pieces throughly, and slew Mattan the priest of Baal before the altars : and the Priest appointed † officers ouer the house of the LORD

† Heb. offi▸

19 And hee tooke the rulers ouer hundreds, and the captaines, and the guard, and all the people of the land, and

and they brought downe the king from the house of the LORD, and came by the way of the gate of the guard, to the kings house, and he sate on the throne of the kings.

20 And all the people of the land reioyced, and the citie was in quiet, and they slew Athaliah with the sword, *beside* the kings house.

21 Seuen yeeres old was Iehoash when he began to reigne.

CHAP. XII.

1 Iehoash reigneth well all the dayes of Iehoiada. 4 Hee giueth order for the repaire of the Temple. 17 Hazael is diuerted from Ierusalem by a present of the halowed treasures. 19 Iehoash being slaine by his seruants, Amaziah succeedeth him.

margin: Chron. 1.

IN * the seuenth yeere of Iehu, Iehoash began to reigne, and fourtie yeeres reigned he in Ierusalem, and his mothers name *was* Zibiah of Beersheba.

2 And Iehoash did that which *was* right in the sight of the LORD all his dayes, wherein Iehoiada the Priest instructed him.

3 But the high places were not taken away: the people still sacrificed, and burnt incense in the high places.

margin: r, holy ngs. Heb. inesses.

4 ¶ And Iehoash said to the priests, All the money of the ‖ dedicated things that is brought into the house of the LORD, euen the money of euery one that passeth *the account*, † the money that euery man is set at, *and* all the money that † commeth into any mans heart, to bring into the house of the LORD,

margin: Heb. the ney of the les of his imation. Ieb. ascenth vpon : heart of nan.

5 Let the priests take *it* to them, euery man of his acquaintance, and let them repaire the breaches of the house, wheresoeuer any breach shalbe found.

6 But it was so *that* † in the three and twentieth yeere of king Iehoash, the priests had not repaired the breaches of the house.

margin: Heb. in the entieth ere, and rd yeere.

7 Then king Iehoash called for Iehoiada the priest, and the *other* priests, and saide vnto them, Why repaire ye not the breaches of the house? now therefore receiue no more money of your acquaintance, but deliuer it for the breaches of the house.

8 And the priests consented to receiue no more money of the people, neither to repaire the breaches of the house.

9 But Iehoiada the priest tooke a chest, and bored a hole in the lid of it, and set it beside the Altar, on the right side, as one commeth into the house of the LORD, and the priests that kept the † doore, put therin all the money that was brought into the house of the LORD.

margin: † Heb. threshold.

10 And it was so when they saw that *there was* much money in the chest, that the kings ‖ scribe, and the high priest came vp, and they † put vp in bags and told the money that was found in the house of the LORD.

margin: ‖ Or, secretarie. † Heb. bound vp.

11 And they gaue the money, being told, into the handes of them that did the worke, that had the ouersight of the house of the LORD: and they † laid it out to the carpenters and builders, that wrought vpon the house of the LORD,

margin: † Hebr. brought it foorth.

12 And to Masons, and hewers of stone, and to buy timber, and hewed stone to repaire the breaches of the house of the LORD, and for all that † was laid out for the house to repaire *it*.

margin: † Heb. went forth.

13 Howbeit, there were not made for the house of the LORD, bowles of siluer, snuffers, basons, trumpets, any vessels of gold, or vessels of siluer, of the money that was brought into the house of the LORD:

14 But they gaue that to the workemen, and repaired therewith the house of the LORD.

15 Moreouer, they reckned not with the men, into whose hand they deliuered the money to be bestowed on workmen: for they dealt faithfully.

16 The trespasse money, and sinnemoney was not brought into the house of the LORD: it was the Priests.

17 ¶ Then Hazael king of Syria went vp, and fought against Gath, and tooke it: and Hazael set his face to goe vp to Ierusalem.

18 And Iehoash king of Iudah tooke all the hallowed things that Iehoshaphat, and Iehoram, and Ahaziah his fathers, kings of Iudah had dedicate, and his owne hallowed things, and all the gold that was found in the treasures of the house of the LORD, and in the kings house, and sent it to Hazael king of Syria, and hee † went away from Ierusalem.

margin: † Heb. went vp.

19 ¶ And the rest of the actes of Iehoash, and all that he did, are they not written in the booke of the Chronicles of the kings of Iudah?

20 And

20 And his seruants arose, and made a conspiracie, and slew Iehoash in ||the house of Millo, which goeth downe to Silla.

|| Or, Beth-Millo.

21 For Iozachar the sonne of Shimeath, and Iehozabad the sonne of Shomer, his seruants, smote him, and he died; and they buried him with his fathers in the citie of Dauid, and Amaziah his sonne reigned in his stead.

CHAP. XIII

1 Iehoahaz his wicked reigne. 3 Iehoahaz oppressed by Hazael, is relieued by prayer. 8 Ioash succeedeth him. 10 His wicked reigne. 12 Ieroboam succeedeth him. 14 Elisha dying prophecieth to Ioash three victories ouer the Syrians. 20 The Moabites inuading the land, Elishas bones raise vp a dead man. 22 Hazael dying, Ioash getteth three victories ouer Benhadad.

† Heb. in the twentieth yeere and third yeere.

IN †the three and twentieth yeere of Ioash the sonne of Ahaziah king of Iudah, Iehoahaz the sonne of Iehu beganne to reigne ouer Israel in Samaria, *and reigned* seuenteene yeeres.

2 And hee did that which *was* euill in the sight of the Lord, and †followed the sinnes of Ieroboam the sonne of Nebat, which made Israel to sinne, he departed not there from.

† Heb. walked after.

3 ¶ And the anger of the Lord was kindled against Israel, and hee deliuered them into the hand of Hazael king of Syria, and into the hand of Benhadad the sonne of Hazael, all *their* dayes

4 And Iehoahaz besought the Lord, and the Lord hearkened vnto him: for hee saw the oppression of Israel, because the king of Syria oppressed them.

5 (And the Lord gaue Israel a sauiour, so that they went out from vnder the hand of the Syrians: and the children of Israel dwelt in their tents †as before-time.

† Heb. as yesterday, and third day.

6 Neuerthelesse, they departed not from the sinnes of the house of Ieroboam, who made Israel sinne, but †walked therein: and there †remained the groue also in Samaria.)

† Heb. hee walked.
† Heb. stood.

7 Neither did he leaue of the people to Iehoahaz, but fiftie horsemen, and tenne charets, and tenne thousand footmen: for the king of Syria had destroyed them, and had made them like the dust by threshing.

8 ¶ Nowe the rest of the actes of Iehoahaz, and all that he did, and his might, are they not written in the booke of the Chronicles of the kings of Israel?

9 And Iehoahaz slept with his fathers, and they buried him in Samaria, and Ioash his sonne reigned in his stead.

10 ¶ In the thirty and seuenth yeere of Ioash king of Iudah, beganne Iehoash the sonne of Iehoahaz to reigne ouer Israel in Samaria, *and reigned* sixteene yeeres.

11 And hee did that which *was* euill in the sight of the Lord; hee departed not from all the sinnes of Ieroboam the sonne of Nebat, who made Israel sinne: *but* hee walked therein.

12 And the rest of the actes of Ioash, and all that hee did, and his might, wherewith hee fought against Amaziah king of Iudah, are they not written in the booke of the chronicles of the kings of Israel?

13 And Ioash slept with his fathers, and Ieroboam sate vpon his throne: and Ioash was buried in Samaria with the kings of Israel.

14 ¶ Nowe Elisha was fallen sicke, of his sicknesse whereof he died, and Ioash the king of Israel came downe vnto him, and wept ouer his face, and said, O my father, my father, the charet of Israel, and the horsemen thereof

15 And Elisha said vnto him, Take bowe and arrowes. And he tooke vnto him bowe and arrowes.

16 And he said to the king of Israel, † Put thine hand vpon the bowe. And he put his hand *vpon it:* and Elisha put his hands vpon the kings hands.

† Heb. mak thine hand to ride.

17 And he sayd, Open the window Eastward. And hee opened *it.* Then Elisha sayd, Shoote. And he shot. And he said; The arrowe of the Lords deliuerance, and the arrowe of deliuerance from Syria: for thou shalt smite the Syrians in Aphek, till thou haue consumed *them.*

18 And he sayd, Take the arrowes. And he tooke *them.* And hee said vnto the king of Israel, Smite vpon the ground. And he smote thrise, and stayed.

19 And the man of God was wroth with him, and saide, Thou shouldest haue

haue smitten fiue or sixe times, then haddest thou smitten Syria till thou haddest consumed *it* : whereas now thou shalt smite Syria *but* thrice.

20 ¶ And Elisha died, and they buried him : And the bands of the Moabites inuaded the land at the comming in of the yeere.

21 And it came to passe as they were burying a man, that behold, they spyed a band *of men*, and they cast the man into the sepulchre of Elisha : and when the man † was let downe, and touched the bones of Elisha, *he reuiued, and stood vp on his feete.

22 ¶ But Hazael king of Syria, oppressed Israel all the dayes of Iehoahaz.

23 And the LORD was gracious vnto them, and had compassion on them, and had respect vnto them, because of his couenant with Abraham, Isaac, and Iacob, and would not destroy them, neither cast hee them from his †presence as yet.

24 So Hazael the king of Syria dyed, and Benhadad his sonne reigned in his stead.

25 And Iehoash the sonne of Iehoahaz †tooke againe out of the hand of Benhadad the sonne of Hazael, the cities which he had taken out of the hand of Iehoahaz his father, by warre : three times did Ioash beat him, and recouered the cities of Israel.

CHAP. XIIII.

1 Amaziah his good reigne. 5 His iustice on the murderers of his father. 7 His victory ouer Edom. 8 Amaziah prouoking Iehoash, is ouercome and spoiled. 15 Ieroboam succeedeth Iehoash. 17 Amaziah slaine by a conspiracie. 21 Azariah succeedeth him. 23 Ieroboams wicked reigne. 28 Zachariah succeedeth him.

IN the second yeere of Ioash sonne of Iehoahaz king of Israel, reigned *Amaziah the sonne of Ioash king of Iudah.

2 Hee was twentie and fiue yeeres olde when he began to reigne, and reigned twentie and nine yeeres in Ierusalem : and his mothers name *was* Iehoaddan of Ierusalem.

3 And he did that which *was* right in the sight of the LORD, yet not like Dauid his father : hee did according to all things as Ioash his father did.

4 Howbeit, the high places were not taken away : as yet the people did sacrifice, and burnt incense on the high places.

5 ¶ And it came to passe assoone as the kingdome was confirmed in his hand, that he slew his seruants *which had slaine the king his father.

6 But the children of the murderers he slew not, according vnto that which is written in the booke of the Law of Moses, wherein the LORD commanded, saying, *The fathers shal not be put to death for the children, nor the children be put to death for the fathers : but euery man shall be put to death for his owne sinne.

7 He slew of Edom in the valley of salt, ten thousand, and tooke ||Selah by warre, and called the name of it, Ioktheel, vnto this day.

8 ¶ Then Amaziah sent messengers to Iehoash the sonne of Iehoahaz sonne of Iehu king of Israel, saying, Come, let vs looke one another in the face.

9 And Iehoash the king of Israel sent to Amaziah king of Iudah, saying, The thistle that *was* in Lebanon, sent to the Cedar that *was* in Lebanon, saying, Giue thy daughter to my sonne to wife. And there passed by a wilde beast that *was* in Lebanon, and trode downe the thistle.

10 Thou hast indeed smitten Edom, and thine heart hath lifted thee vp : glory *of this*, and tary †at home : for why shouldest thou meddle to *thy* hurt, that thou shouldest fall, *euen* thou, and Iudah with thee?

11 But Amaziah would not heare : therefore Iehoash king of Israel went vp, and hee, and Amaziah king of Iudah, looked one another in the face at Bethshemesh, which *belongeth* to Iudah.

12 And Iudah †was put to the worse before Israel, and they fled euery man to their tents.

13 And Iehoash king of Israel tooke Amaziah king of Iudah, the sonne of Iehoash the sonne of Ahaziah at Bethshemesh, and came to Ierusalem, and brake downe the wall of Ierusalem, from the gate of Ephraim, vnto the corner gate, foure hundred cubites.

14 And he tooke all the golde and siluer, and all the vessels that were found in the house of the LORD, and in the trea-

treasures of the kings house, and hostages, and returned to Samaria.

15 ¶ Now the rest of the acts of Iehoash which he did, and his might, and how he fought with Amaziah king of Iudah, are they not written in the booke of the Chronicles of the kings of Israel?

16 And Iehoash slept with his fathers, and was buried in Samaria, with the kings of Israel, and Ieroboam his sonne reigned in his stead.

17 ¶ And Amaziah the sonne of Ioash king of Iudah, liued after the death of Iehoash sonne of Iehoahaz king of Israel, fifteene yeeres.

18 And the rest of the acts of Amaziah, are they not written in the booke of the Chronicles of the kings of Iudah?

*2. Chron. 25. 27.

19 Now *they made a conspiracie against him in Ierusalem: and he fled to Lachish, but they sent after him to Lachish, and slew him there.

20 And they brought him on horses, and he was buried at Ierusalem with his fathers, in the city of Dauid.

*2. Chron. 26. 1. He is called Vz-ziah.

21 ¶ And all the people of Iudah tooke *Azariah (which was sixteene yeeres old) and made him king in stead of his father Amaziah.

22 He built Elath, and restored it to Iudah, after that the king slept with his fathers.

23 ¶ In the fifteenth yeere of Amaziah the sonne of Ioash king of Iudah, Ieroboam the sonne of Ioash king of Israel began to raigne in Samaria, and raigned forty and one yeeres:

24 And hee did that which was euill in the sight of the LORD · hee departed not from all the sinnes of Ieroboam the sonne of Nebat, who made Israel to sinne.

25 Hee restored the coast of Israel, from the entring of Hamath, vnto the sea of the plaine, according to the word of the LORD God of Israel, which *Matth. 12. 39, 40. called Ionas. he spake by the hand of his seruant *Ionah, the sonne of Amittai the Prophet, which was of Gath Hepher.

26 For the LORD saw the affliction of Israel, that it was very bitter: for there was not any shut vp, nor any left, nor any helper for Israel.

27 And the LORD said not, that hee would blot out the name of Israel from vnder heauen: but he saued them by the hand of Ieroboam the sonne of Ioash.

28 ¶ Now the rest of the actes of Ieroboam, and all that he did, and his might, how he warred, and how he recouered Damascus and Hamath, which belonged to Iudah, for Israel, are they not written in the booke of the Chronicles of the kings of Israel?

29 And Ieroboam slept with his fathers, euen with the kings of Israel, and Zachariah his sonne reigned in his stead.

CHAP. XV.

1 Azariah his good reigne. 5 He dying a Leper, Iotham succeedeth. 8 Zachariah, the last of Iehu his generation, reigning ill, is slaine by Shallum. 13 Shallum reigning a moneth, is slaine by Menahem. 16 Menahem strengtheneth himselfe by Pul. 21 Pekahiah succeedeth him. 23 Pekahiah is slaine by Pekah. 27 Pekah is oppressed by Tiglath Pileser, and slaine by Hoshea. 32 Iothams good reigne. 36 Ahaz succeedeth him.

IN the twenty and seuenth yeere of Ieroboam king of Israel, began Azariah sonne of Amaziah king of Iudah to reigne.

2 Sixteene yeeres old was he when he began to reigne, and he reigned two and fifty yeeres in Ierusalem: and his mothers name was Iecholiah of Ierusalem.

3 And he did that which was right in the sight of the LORD, according to all that his father Amaziah had done;

4 Saue that the high places were not remoued: the people sacrificed, and burnt incense still on the high places.

5 ¶ And the LORD smote the king, so that hee was a Leper vnto the day of his death, and dwelt in a seuerall house, and Iotham the kings sonne was ouer the house, iudging the people of the land.

6 And the rest of the actes of Azariah, and all that hee did, are they not written in the booke of the Chronicles of the kings of Iudah?

7 So Azariah slept with his fathers, and they buried him with his fathers in the city of Dauid, and Iotham his sonne reigned in his stead.

8 ¶ In the thirty and eight yeere of Azariah king of Iudah, did Zachariah the sonne of Ieroboam reigne ouer Israel in Samaria six moneths.

9 And hee did that which was euil in the

the sight of the LORD, as his fathers had done : he departed not from the sinnes of Ieroboam the sonne of Nebat, who made Israel to sinne.

10 And Shallum the sonne of Iabesh, conspired against him, and smote him before the people , and slewe him, and reigned in his stead.

11 And the rest of the actes of Zachariah, beholde, they are written in the booke of the chronicles of the kings of Israel.

Chap. 10.

12 This was *the word of the LORD which he spake vnto Iehu, saying, Thy sonnes shall sit on the throne of Israel, vnto the fourth generation. And so it came to passe.

Matth. 1. called O- as. Hebr. a oneth of ayes.

13 ¶ Shallum the sonne of Iabesh began to reigne in the nine and thirtieth yeere of *Vzziah king of Iudah, and he reigned †a full moneth in Samaria.

14 For Menahem the sonne of Gadi, went vp from Tirzah, and came to Samaria, and smote Shallum the sonne of Iabesh, in Samaria, and slew him, and reigned in his stead.

15 And the rest of the actes of Shallum, and the conspiracy which he made, behold, they are written in the booke of the chronicles of the kings of Israel.

16 ¶ Then Menahem smote Tiphsah, and all that were therein, and the coasts thereof from Tirzah : because they opened not to him, therfore he smote it, and all the women therein that were with child, he ript vp.

17 In the nine and thirtieth yeere of Azariah king of Iudah, began Menahem the sonne of Gadi to reigne ouer Israel, and reigned tenne yeres in Samaria.

18 And he did that which was euill in the sight of the LORD : hee departed not all his dayes from the sinnes of Ieroboam the sonne of Nebat, who made Israel to sinne.

* 1. Chron. 5. 26.

19 *And Pul the king of Assyria came against the land : and Menahem gaue Pul a thousand talents of siluer, that his hand might be with him, to confirm the kingdome in his hand.

† Heb. cau- sed to come forth.

20 And Menahem †exacted the mony of Israel, euen of all the mightie men of wealth, of each man fiftie shekels of siluer, to giue to the king of Assyria : so the king of Assyria turned backe, and stayed not there in the land.

21 ¶ And the rest of the acts of Me-

nahem, and all that he did, are they not written in the booke of the Chronicles of the kings of Israel ?

22 And Menahem slept with his fathers, and Pekahiah his sonne reigned in his stead.

23 ¶ In the fiftieth yere of Azariah king of Iudah, Pekahiah the sonne of Menahem began to reigne ouer Israel in Samaria, and reigned two yeeres.

24 And he did that which was euill in the sight of the LORD, hee departed not from the sinnes of Ieroboam the sonne of Nebat, who made Israel to sinne.

25 But Pekah the sonne of Remaliah, a captaine of his, conspired against him, and smote him in Samaria, in the palace of the kings house , with Argob, and Arieh, and with him fiftie men of the Gileadites : and hee killed him, and reigned in his roume.

26 And the rest of the actes of Pekahiah, and all that he did, beholde, they are written in the booke of the chronicles of the kings of Israel.

27 ¶ In the two and fiftieth yeere of Azariah king of Iudah, Pekah the sonne of Remaliah began to reigne ouer Israel in Samaria , and reigned twentie yeeres.

28 And he did that which was euill in the sight of the LORD, hee departed not from the sinnes of Ieroboam the sonne of Nebat, who made Israel to sinne.

29 In the dayes of Pekah king of Israel, came Tiglath Pileser king of Assyria, and tooke Iion, and Abel-Beth - maachah, and Ianoah, and Kedesh, and Hazor, and Gilead, and Galilee, all the land of Naphtali, and caried them captiue to Assyria.

30 And Hoshea the sonne of Elah, made a conspiracie against Pekah the sonne of Remaliah, and smote him, and slew him, and reigned in his stead, in the twentieth yeere of Iotham the sonne of Vzziah.

31 And the rest of the actes of Pekah, and all that he did, behold, they are written in the booke of the Chronicles of the kings of Israel.

* 2. Chron. 27. 1.

32 ¶ *In the second yeere of Pekah the sonne of Remaliah king of Israel, began Iotham the sonne of Vzziah king of Iudah to reigne.

33 Fiue and twentie yeeres olde was he when he began to reigne, and hee
           reigned

reigned sixteene yeeres in Ierusalem : and his mothers name *was* Ierusha, the daughter of Zadok.

34 And he did that *which was* right in the sight of the LORD : hee did according to all that his father Vzziah had done.

35 ¶ Howbeit, the high places were not remoued : the people sacrificed and burnt incense still in the high places : He built the higher gate of the house of the LORD

36 ¶ Now the rest of the actes of Iotham, and all that hee did, are they not written in the booke of the Chronicles of the kings of Iudah?

37 (In those dayes the LORD began to send against Iudah, Rezin the king of Syria, and Pekah the sonne of Remaliah)

38 And Iotham slept with his fathers, and was buried with his fathers in the citie of Dauid his father, and Ahaz his sonne reigned in his stead.

CHAP. XVI.

1 Ahaz his wicked reigne. 5 Ahaz assailed by Rezin and Pekah, hireth Tiglath Pileser against them. 10 Ahaz sending a paterne of an Altar from Damascus to Vrijah, diuerteth the brasen Altar to his owne deuotion. 17 Hee spoileth the Temple. 19 Hezekiah succeedeth him.

* 2. Chron. 28. 1.

IN * the seuenteenth yeere of Pekah the sonne of Remaliah, Ahaz the sonne of Iotham King of Iudah began to reigne.

2 Twentie yeeres olde *was* Ahaz when hee began to reigne, and reigned sixteene yeeres in Ierusalem, and did not that *which was* right in the sight of the LORD his God, like Dauid his father.

3 But hee walked in the way of the kings of Israel, yea & made his sonne to passe through the fire, according to the abominations of the heathen, whom the LORD cast out from before the children of Israel

4 And hee sacrificed and burnt incense in the high places, and on the hils, and vnder euery greene tree.

* Isa 7. 1.

5 ¶ * Then Rezin king of Syria, and Pekah sonne of Remaliah king of Israel, came vp to Ierusalem to warre : and they besieged Ahaz, but could not ouercome him.

6 At that time Rezin king of Syria, recouered Elath to Syria, & draue the Iewes from Elath. and the Syrians came to Elath, and dwelt there vnto this day.

7 So Ahaz sent messengers to Tiglath Pileser king of Assyria, saying, I *am* thy seruant, and thy sonne : come vp, and saue me out of the hand of the king of Syria, and out of the hand of the king of Israel, which rise vp against me.

8 And Ahaz tooke the siluer and gold that was found in the house of the LORD, and in the treasures of the kings house, and sent it *for* a present to the king of Assyria.

9 And the king of Assyria hearkened vnto him : for the king of Assyria went vp against Damascus, and tooke it, and caried *the people of* it captiue to Kir, and slew Rezin

10 ¶ And King Ahaz went to † Damascus, to meete Tiglath Pileser king of Assyria, and saw an altar that *was* at Damascus : and king Ahaz sent to Vriiah the Priest the fashion of the altar, and the paterne of it, according to all the workemanship thereof.

† Heb. Damesek.

11 And Vriiah the Priest built an altar : according to all that king Ahaz had sent from Damascus, so Vriiah the Priest made *it*, against king Ahaz came from Damascus.

12 And when the king was come from Damascus, the King saw the altar : and the King approched to the altar, and offered thereon.

13 And he burnt his burnt offering, and his meate offering, and powred his drinke offering, and sprinkled the blood of † his peace offerings vpon the altar.

† Heb. whic were his.

14 And hee brought also the brasen altar which was before the LORD, from the forefront of the house, from betweene the altar and the house of the LORD, and put it on the North side of the altar.

15 And king Ahaz commanded Vriiah the Priest, saying, Vpon the great altar, burne the morning burnt offering, and the euening meate offering, and the Kings burnt sacrifice, and his meate offering, with the burnt offering of all the people of the land, and their meate offering, and their drinke offerings, and sprinkle vpon it all the blood of the burnt offering, and all the blood of the sacrifice : and the brasen altar shall be for me to enquire *by*.

16 Thus

16 Thus did Vriiah the Priest, according to all that king Ahaz commaunded.

17 ¶ And king Ahaz cut off the borders of the bases, and remooued the lauer from off them, and tooke downe the sea from off the brasen oxen that were vnder it, and put it vpon a pauement of stones :

18 And the couert for the Sabbath that they had built in the house, and the kings entry without, turned hee from the house of the LORD, for the king of Assyria.

19 ¶ Now the rest of the actes of Ahaz, which he did, are they not written in the booke of the Chronicles of the kings of Iudah ?

20 And Ahaz slept with his fathers, and was buried with his fathers in the city of Dauid, and Hezekiah his sonne reigned in his stead.

CHAP. XVII.

1 Hoshea his wicked reigne. 3 Being subdued by Shalmaneser, hee conspireth against him with So King of Egypt. 5 Samaria for their sinnes, is captiuated. 24 The strange nations, which were transplanted in Samaria, beeing plagued with Lions, make a mixture of Religions.

IN the twelfth yeere of Ahaz, king of Iudah, began Hoshea the sonne of Elah to reigne in Samaria, ouer Israel nine yeeres.

2 And hee did that *which was* euill in the sight of the LORD, but not as the kings of Israel that were before him.

3 ¶ Against him came vp Shalmaneser king of Assyria, and Hoshea became his seruant, and †gaue him ||presents.

> Hebr. ren-red.
> Or, tribute.

4 And the king of Assyria found conspiracie in Hoshea : for hee had sent messengers to So king of Egypt, and brought no present to the king of Assyria, as *he had done* yeere by yeere : therefore the king of Assyria shut him vp, and bound him in prison.

5 ¶ Then the king of Assyria came vp thorowout all the land, and went vp to Samaria, and besieged it three yeres.

> * Chap. 18.
> 0.

6 ¶ *In the ninth yeere of Hoshea, the king of Assyria tooke Samaria, and caried Israel away into Assyria, and placed them in Halah, and in Habor *by* the riuer of Gozan, and in the cities of the Medes.

7 For so it was, that the children of Israel had sinned against the LORD their God, which had brought them vp out of the land of Egypt, from vnder the hand of Pharaoh king of Egypt, and had feared other gods,

8 And walked in the statutes of the heathen, (whom the LORD cast out from before the children of Israel) and of the kings of Israel, which they had made.

9 And the children of Israel did secretly those things that were not right, against the LORD their God : and they built them high places in all their cities, from the tower of the watchmen, to the fenced city.

10 And they set them vp †images, and groues in euery high hill, and vnder euery greene tree.

> † Heb. statues.

11 And there they burnt incense in all the high places, as did the heathen whom the LORD caried away before them, and wrought wicked things to prouoke the LORD to anger.

12 For they serued idoles, whereof the LORD had said vnto them, *Yee shall not doe this thing.

> * Deut. 4. 19.

13 Yet the LORD testified against Israel, and against Iudah, †by all the Prophets, *and by* all the Seers, saying, *Turne ye from your euill wayes, and keepe my commandements, and my statutes, according to all the law which I commanded your fathers, and which I sent to you by my seruants the Prophets.

> † Heb. by the hand of all.
> * Ierem. 18. 11. and 25. 5. & 35. 15.

14 Notwithstanding, they would not heare, but *hardened their neckes, like to the necke of their fathers, that did not beleeue in the LORD their God.

15 And they reiected his Statutes, and his Couenant that hee made with their fathers, and his Testimonies which he testified against them, and they followed vanitie, and became vaine, and went after the heathen that were round about them, concerning whom the LORD had charged them, that they should not doe like them.

16 And they left all the Commandements of the LORD their God, and *made them molten images, *euen* two calues, and made a groue, and worshiped all the hoste of heauen, and serued Baal.

> * Exod. 32. 8. 1. king. 12. 28.

17 And they caused their sonnes and their daughters to passe through the fire,

fire, and vsed diuination, and inchantments, and sold themselues to doe euill in the sight of the LORD, to prouoke him to anger.

18 Therefore the LORD was very angry with Israel, and remoued them out of his sight, there was none left, but the tribe of Iudah onely.

19 Also Iudah kept not the Commandements of the LORD their God, but walked in the Statutes of Israel which they made.

20 And the LORD reiected all the seed of Israel, and afflicted them, and deliuered them into the hand of spoilers, vntill he had cast them out of his sight.

21 For he rent Israel from the house of Dauid, and they made Ieroboam the sonne of Nebat king, and Ieroboam draue Israel from following the LORD, and made them sinne a great sinne.

22 For the children of Israel walked in al the sinnes of Ieroboam which he did, they departed not from them:

23 Vntill the LORD remoued Israel out of his sight, as hee had said by all his seruants the Prophets: so was Israel caried away out of their owne land to Assyria, vnto this day.

24 ¶ And the King of Assyria brought men from Babylon, and from Cuthah, and from Aua, and from Hamath, and from Sepharuaim, and placed *them* in the cities of Samaria, in stead of the children of Israel: and they possessed Samaria, and dwelt in the cities thereof.

25 And so it was at the beginning of their dwelling there, *that* they feared not the LORD; therefore the LORD sent Lions among them, which slew some of them.

26 Wherefore they spake to the king of Assyria, saying, The nations which thou hast remoued, and placed in the cities of Samaria, know not the maner of the God of the land: therfore hee hath sent Lions among them, and beholde, they slay them, because they know not the maner of the God of the land.

27 Then the king of Assyria commanded, saying, Carie thither one of the priests whom ye brought from thence, and let them goe and dwell there, and let him teach them the maner of the God of the land.

28 Then one of the priests whom

they had caried away from Samaria, came and dwelt in Bethel, and taught them howe they should feare the LORD.

29 Howbeit, euery nation made gods of their owne, and put them in the houses of the high places which the Samaritanes had made, euery nation in their cities wherein they dwelt:

30 And the men of Babylon made Succoth-Benoth, and the men of Cuth made Nergal, and the men of Hamath made Ashima:

31 And the Auites made Nibhaz and Tartak: and the Sepharuites burnt their children in fire to Adrammelech, and Anammelech, the gods of Sepharuaim.

32 So they feared the LORD, and made vnto themselues of the lowest of them priests of the high places, which sacrificed for them in the houses of the high places.

33 * They feared the LORD, and serued their owne gods, after the maner of the nations ǁwhom they caried away from thence.

34 Vnto this day they doe after the former maners: they feare not the LORD, neither doe they after their Statutes, or after their Ordinances, or after the Law and Commaundement which the LORD commaunded the children of Iacob, *whom hee named Israel,

35 With whom the LORD had made a Couenant, and charged them, saying, * Yee shall not feare other gods, nor bow your selues to them, nor serue them, nor sacrifice to them:

36 But the LORD, who brought you vp out of the land of Egypt, with great power, and a stretched out arme, him shall ye feare, and him shall ye worship, and to him shall ye doe sacrifice.

37 And the Statutes, and the Ordinances, and the Law, and the Commandement which he wrote for you, ye shall obserue to doe for euermore, and ye shall not feare other gods:

38 And the Couenant that I haue made with you, ye shall not forget, neither shall ye feare other gods.

39 But the LORD your God yee shall feare, and he shall deliuer you out of the hand of all your enemies.

40 Howbeit, they did not hearken, but they did after their former maner.

41 So these nations feared the LORD,

* Sophan.
5.

‖ Or, who caried them away from thence.

* Gen. 32. 28. 1. king. 18. 31.

* Iudg. 6. 10.

LORD, and serued their grauen images, both their children, and their childrens children : as did their fathers, so doe they vnto this day.

CHAP. XVIII.

1 Hezekiah his good reigne. 4 He destroyeth idolatrie, and prospereth. 9 Samaria is caried captiue for their sins. 13 Sennacherib inuading Iudah, is pacified by a tribute. 17 Rabshakeh sent by Sennacherib againe, reuileth Hezekiah, and by blasphemous perswasions, solliciteth the people to reuolt.

NOw it came to passe in the third yere of Hoshea sonne of Elah king of Israel, *that* * Hezekiah the sonne of Ahaz king of Iudah, began to reigne.

2 Twentie and fiue yeeres old was he when hee began to reigne, and hee reigned twentie and nine yeeres in Ierusalem : His mothers name also *was* Abi, the daughter of Zachariah.

3 And he did that which *was* right in the sight of the LORD, according to all that Dauid his father did.

4 ¶ He remooued the high places, and brake the †images, and cut downe the groues, and brake in pieces the * brasen serpent that Moses had made : for vnto those dayes the children of Israel did burne incense to it : and he called it Nehushtan.

5 He trusted in the LORD God of Israel, so that after him was none like him among all the kings of Iudah, nor *any* that were before him.

6 For he claue to the LORD, *and* departed not †from following him, but kept his commandements, which the LORD commanded Moses.

7 And the LORD was with him, *and* hee prospered whithersoeuer hee went forth : and he rebelled against the king of Assyria, and serued him not.

8 He smote the Philistines euen vnto †Gaza, and the borders thereof, from the towre of the watchmen to the fenced cities.

9 ¶ And * it came to passe in the fourth yeere of king Hezekiah, (which was the seuenth yeere of Hoshea, sonne of Elah king of Israel) that Shalmaneser king of Assyria came vp against Samaria, and besieged it.

10 And at the end of three yeeres they tooke it : *euen* in the sixt yeere of Hezekiah (that is * the ninth yeere of Hoshea king of Israel) Samaria was taken.

11 And the king of Assyria did carie away Israel vnto Assyria, and put them in Halah and in Habor *by* the riuer of Gozan, & in the cities of the Medes :

12 Because they obeyed not the voice of the LORD their God, but transgressed his Couenant, *and* all that Moses the seruant of the LORD commanded, and would not heare *them*, nor doe *them*.

13 ¶ Now * in the fourteenth yeere of king Hezekiah, did †Sennacherib king of Assyria come vp against all the fenced cities of Iudah, and tooke them.

14 And Hezekiah king of Iudah sent to the king of Assyria to Lachish, saying, I haue offended, returne from me : that which thou puttest on me, wil I beare. And the king of Assyria appointed vnto Hezekiah king of Iudah, three hundred talents of siluer, and thirtie talents of gold.

15 And Hezekiah gaue *him* all the siluer that was found in the house of the LORD, and in the treasures of the kings house.

16 At that time did Hezekiah cut off *the gold from* the doores of the temple of the LORD, and *from* the pillars which Hezekiah king of Iudah had ouerlaid, and gaue †it to the king of Assyria.

17 ¶ And the king of Assyria sent Tartan and Rabsaris, and Rabshakeh, from Lachish to king Hezekiah, with a †great hoste against Ierusalem : and they went vp, and came to Ierusalem · and when they were come vp, they came and stood by the conduit of the vpper poole, which *is* in the high way of the fullers field.

18 And when they had called to the king, there came out to them Eliakim the sonne of Helkiah, which *was* ouer the houshold, and Shebna the ‖Scribe, and Ioah the sonne of Asaph the Recorder.

19 And Rabshakeh said vnto them, Speake yee now to Hezekiah, Thus saith the great king, the king of Assyria, What confidence *is* this wherein thou trustest ?

20 Thou ‖sayest, (but *they are but* †vaine words) ‖*I haue* counsell and strength for the warre : now on whom doest thou trust, that thou rebellest against me ?

21 Now behold, thou †trustest vpon the staffe of this bruised reed, *euen* vpon Egypt,

---

Marginal notes (left column):

2. Chron. 27. and 1. hee called Elias, Mat. 9.

*Heb. statues. Numb. 8.

*Heb. from after him.

Heb. Azah. !

Cha. 17. 3

Cha. 17. 6

Marginal notes (right column):

* 2. Chron. 32. 1. esa. 36. 1. ecclu. 48. 18. †Heb. Sancherib.

† Heb. them.

† Heb. heauy

‖ Or, Secretarie.

‖ Or, talkest. † Heb. word of the lips. ‖ Or, but counsell and strength are for the war.

† Heb. trustest thee.

Egypt, on which if a man leane, it will goe into his hand, and pierce it : so *is* Pharaoh king of Egypt vnto all that trust on him.

22 But if ye say vnto me, We trust in the Lord our God : *is* not that hee whose high places, and whose altars Hezekiah hath taken away, and hath said to Iudah and Ierusalem, Ye shall worship before this altar in Ierusalem ?

23 Now therefore, I pray thee, giue ‖pledges to my lord the king of Assyria, and I will deliuer thee two thousand horses, if thou be able on thy part to set riders vpon them.

24 How then wilt thou turne away the face of one captaine of the least of my masters seruants, and put thy trust on Egypt for charets and for horsemen ?

25 Am I now come vp without the Lord against this place, to destroy it ? The Lord sayd to me, Goe vp against this land, and destroy it.

26 Then said Eliakim the sonne of Hilkiah, and Shebna, and Ioah, vnto Rabshakeh, Speake, I pray thee, to thy seruants in the Syrian language, (for wee vnderstand *it*) and talke not with vs in the Iewes language, in the eares of the people that *are* on the wall.

27 But Rabshakeh sayd vnto them, Hath my master sent me to thy master, and to thee, to speake these wordes? hath he not *sent me* to the men which sit on the wall, that they may eate their owne doung, and drinke their †owne pisse with you?

28 Then Rabshakeh stood and cried with a loude voice in the Iewes language, and spake, saying, Heare the word of the great king, the king of Assyria.

29 Thus sayth the king, Let not Hezekiah deceiue you, for he shall not be able to deliuer you out of his hand :

30 Neither let Hezekiah make you trust in the Lord, saying, The Lord will surely deliuer vs, and this city shall not bee deliuered into the hand of the king of Assyria.

31 Hearken not to Hezekiah: for thus sayth the king of Assyria, ‖Make *an a-greement* with me by a present, and come out to me, and then eate yee euery man of his owne vine, and euery one of his figge tree, and drinke yee euery one the waters of his ‖cisterne :

32 Vntill I come and take you a-

Margin left:
‖ *Or, hosta-ges.*

† *Heb. the water of their feete?*

‖ *Or, seeke my fauour. Heb. make with me a blessing.*

‖ *Or, pit.*

way to a land like your owne land, a land of corne and wine, a land of bread and vineyards, a land of oile Oliue, and of honie, that yee may liue, and not die: and hearken not vnto Hezekiah, when hee ‖perswadeth you, saying, The Lord will deliuer vs.

33 Hath any of the gods of the nations deliuered at all his land out of the hand of the king of Assyria ?

34 Where *are* the gods of Hamath, and of Arpad ? where *are* the gods of Sephãruaim, Hena, and Iuah? haue they deliuered Samaria out of mine hand ?

35 Who *are* they among all the gods of the countreys, that haue deliuered their countrey out of mine hand, that the Lord should deliuer Ierusalem out of mine hand?

36 But the people helde their peace, and answered him not a word : for the kings commaundement was, saying, Answere him not.

37 Then came Eliakim the sonne of Hilkiah, which *was* ouer the houshold, and Shebna the Scribe, and Ioah the sonne of Asaph the Recorder, to Hezekiah with *their* clothes rent, and tolde him the words of Rabshakeh.

Margin right:
‖ *Or, dece-ueth.*

CHAP. XIX.

1 Hezekiah mourning, sendeth to Esay to pray for them. 6 Esay comforteth them. 8 Sennacherib going to encounter Tirhakah, sendeth a blasphemous letter to Hezekiah. 14 Hezekiah his prayer. 20 Esay his prophecie of the pride and destruction of Sennacherib, and the good of Zion. 35 An Angel slayeth the Assyrians. 36 Sennacherib is slaine at Nineueh by his owne sonnes.

A Nd * it came to passe when King Hezekiah heard *it*, that hee rent his clothes, and couered himselfe with sackecloth, and went into the house of the Lord.

2 And hee sent Eliakim, which *was* ouer the houshold, and Shebna the Scribe, and the Elders of the Priests, couered with sackcloth, to Esai the Prophet the sonne of Amoz.

3 And they sayd vnto him, Thus sayth Hezekiah, This day *is* a day of trouble, and of rebuke, and ‖blasphemie : for the children are come to the birth, and *there is* not strength to bring foorth.

Margin right:
* *Esal. 37.*

‖ *Or, proue-cation.*

4 It

4 It may be, the LORD thy God will heare all the words of Rabshakeh whome the king of Assyria his master hath sent to reproch the liuing God, and will reproue the wordes which the LORD thy God hath heard: wherefore lift vp *thy* prayer for the remnant that are †left.

*Heb. found

5 So the seruants of king Hezekiah came to Isaiah.

Luke 3. 4. lled E-ias.

6 ¶ And *Isaiah said vnto them, Thus shal ye say to your master, Thus saith the LORD, Be not afraid of the wordes which thou hast heard, with which the seruants of the king of Assyria haue blasphemed me.

7 Behold, I will send a blast vpon him, and he shall heare a rumour, and shall returne to his owne land, and I will cause him to fall by the sword in his owne land.

8 ¶ So Rabshakeh returned, and found the king of Assyria warring against Libnah: for hee had heard that he was departed from Lachish.

9 And when he heard say of Tirhakah king of Ethiopia, Behold, hee is come out to fight against thee: hee sent messengers againe vnto Hezekiah, saying,

10 Thus shall ye speake to Hezekiah king of Iudah, saying, Let not thy God in whome thou trustest, deceiue thee, saying, Ierusalem shall not be deliuered into the hande of the king of Assyria.

11 Behold, thou hast heard what the kings of Assyria haue done to all lands, by destroying them vtterly: and shalt thou be deliuered?

12 Haue the gods of the nations deliuered them which my fathers haue destroyed? *As* Gozan, and Haran, and Rezeph, and the children of Eden which *were* in Thelasar?

13 Where is the king of Hamath, and the king of Arpad, and the king of the citie of Sepharuaim, of Hena, and Iuah?

14 ¶ And Hezekiah receiued the letter of the hand of the messengers, and read it: and Hezekiah went vp into the house of the LORD, and spread it before the LORD.

15 And Hezekiah prayed before the LORD, and said, O LORD God of Israel, which dwellest *between* the Cherubims, thou art the God, *euen* thou alone, of all the kingdomes of the earth, thou hast made heauen and earth.

16 LORD, bow downe thine eare, and heare: open, LORD, thine eyes, and see: and heare the words of Sennacherib which hath sent him to reproch the liuing God.

17 Of a trueth, LORD, the kings of Assyria haue destroyed the nations and their lands,

18 And haue †cast their gods into the fire: for they *were* no gods, but the worke of mens hands, wood and stone: therfore they haue destroyed them.

† Heb. giuen

19 Now therefore, O LORD our God, I beseech thee, saue thou vs out of his hand, that all the kingdoms of the earth may know, that thou art the LORD God, *euen* thou onely.

20 ¶ Then Isaiah the sonne of Amoz sent to Hezekiah, saying, Thus saith the LORD God of Israel, That which thou hast prayed to mee against Sennacherib king of Assyria, I haue heard.

21 This *is* the word that the LORD hath spoken concerning him, The Virgin, the daughter of Zion hath despised thee, *and* laughed thee to scorne, the daughter of Ierusalem hath shaken her head at thee.

22 Whome hast thou reproched and blasphemed? and against whome hast thou exalted *thy* voyce, and lift vp thine eyes on high? *euen* against the Holy One of Israel.

23 †By thy messengers thou hast reproched the Lord, and hast said, With the multitude of my charets, I am come vp to the height of the mountaines, to the sides of Lebanon, and will cut downe †the tall cedar trees thereof, *and* the choice firre trees thereof: and I will enter into the lodgings of his borders, *and into* the ||forrest of his Carmel.

† Heb. by the hand of.

† Heb. the talnesse, &c.

|| Or, the forrest and his fruitful field

24 I haue digged & drunke strange waters, and with the sole of my feete haue I dried vp all the riuers of ||besieged places.

|| Or, fenced

25 ||Hast thou not heard long agoe, how I haue done it, *and* of ancient times that I haue formed it? now haue I brought it to passe, that thou shouldest be to lay waste fenced cities into ruinous heapes.

|| Or, hast thou not heard how I haue made it long agoe, and formed it of ancient times? should I now bring it to be laide waste, and fenced cities to be ruinous heapes? † Heb. short of hand.

26 Therefore their Inhabitants were †of small power, they were dismayed and confounded, they were *as* the grasse of the field, and *as* the greene herbe,

herbe, *as* the graſſe on the houſe tops, and as *corne* blaſted before it be growen vp.

27 But I know thy ‖ abode , and thy going out, and thy comming in, and thy rage against me.

28 Becauſe thy rage against me, and thy tumult is come vp into mine eares, therefore I will put my hooke in thy noſe, and my bridle in thy lips , and I will turne thee backe by the way by which thou cameſt.

29 And this *ſhalbe* a ſigne vnto thee, Yee ſhall eate this yeere ſuch things as grow of themſelues, and in the ſecond yeere that which ſpringeth of the ſame, and in the third yeere ſow ye and reape, and plant Vineyards , and eate the fruits thereof.

30 And †the remnant that is eſcaped of the houſe of Iudah, ſhall yet againe take root downeward, and beare fruit vpward.

31 For out of Ieruſalem ſhall goe forth a remnant, and †they that eſcape out of mount Zion : the zeale of the LORD of hoſtes ſhall doe this.

32 Therefore thus ſaith the LORD concerning the king of Aſſyria, He ſhall not come into this city, nor ſhoot an arrow there, nor come before it with ſhield, nor caſt a banke against it :

33 By the way that hee came, by the ſame ſhal he returne, and ſhal not come into this city, ſaith the LORD.

34 For I will defend this citie, to ſaue it, for mine owne ſake, and for my ſeruant Dauids ſake.

35 ¶ And *it came to paſſe that night, that the Angel of the LORD went out, and ſmote in the campe of the Aſſyrians, an hundred foure ſcore and fiue thouſand : and when they aroſe early in the morning, behold, they *were* all dead corpſes.

36 So Sennacherib king of Aſſyria departed, and went and returned, and dwelt at Nineueh.

37 And it came to paſſe as hee was worſhiping in the houſe of Niſroch his god, that Adramelech, and Sharezer his ſonnes, ſmote him with the ſword: and they eſcaped into the land of †Armenia, and Eſarhaddon his ſonne reigned in his ſtead.

CHAP. XX.

1 Hezekiah hauing receiued a meſſage of death, by prayer hath his life lengthned. 8 The

Sunne goeth tenne degrees backward, for a ſigne of that promiſe. 12 Berodach Baladan ſending to viſite Hezekiah , becauſe of the wonder, hath notice of his treaſures. 14 Iſaiah vnderſtanding thereof , foretelleth the Babylonian captiuitie. 20 Manaſſeh ſucceedeth Hezekiah.

IN thoſe dayes *was Hezekiah ſicke vnto death: and the Prophet Iſaiah the ſonne of Amos came to him, and ſaide vnto him, Thus ſaith the LORD , †Set thine houſe in order : for thou ſhalt die, and not liue.

2 Then hee turned his face to the wall , and prayed vnto the LORD, ſaying ;

3 I beſeech thee , O LORD, remember now how I haue walked before thee in trueth , and with a perfect heart , and haue done that which is good in thy ſight : and Hezekiah wept †ſore.

4 And it came to paſſe afore Iſaiah was gone out into the middle ‖court, that the word of the LORD came to him, ſaying ;

5 Turne againe , and tell Hezekiah the captaine of my people, Thus ſaith the LORD, the God of Dauid thy father, I haue heard thy prayer, I haue ſeene thy teares : behold , I will heale thee; on the third day thou ſhalt goe vp vnto the houſe of the LORD.

6 And I will adde vnto thy dayes fifteene yeeres, and I will deliuer thee, and this city, out of the hand of the king of Aſſyria, and I will defend this citie for mine owne ſake, and for my ſeruant Dauids ſake.

7 And Iſaiah ſaid, Take a lumpe of figs. And they tooke and layd *it* on the boile, and he recouered.

8 ¶ And Hezekiah ſaid vnto Iſaiah , What *ſhall bee* the ſigne that the LORD wil heale me, and that I ſhall goe vp into the houſe of the LORD the third day ?

9 And Iſaiah ſaid, This ſigne ſhalt thou *haue* of the LORD , that the LORD will doe the thing that hee hath ſpoken : ſhall the ſhadow goe forward ten degrees, or *goe backe tenne degrees ?

10 And Hezekiah anſwered, It is a light thing for the ſhadow to goe downe tenne degrees : nay, but let the ſhadow returne backward tenne degrees.

11 And

‖ *Or, ſitting.*

† *Hebr. the eſcaping of the houſe of Iudah that remaineth.*

† *Hebr. the eſcaping.*

* *Iſa. 37. 36. tob. 1. 21. ecclus. 48. 24. 1. macc. 7. 41. 2. macc. 8. 19.*

† *Hebr. A-rarat.*

* 2. Chro 32. 24. iſa 38. 1.

† Hebr. g charge co cerning th houſe.

† Hebr. u a great u ping. ‖ Or, city

* Ecclus, 48. 24. iſa 38. 8.

11 And Isaiah the Prophet cryed vnto the LORD, and he brought the shadow tenne degrees backeward, by which it had gone downe in the †diall of Ahaz.

12 ¶ *At that time Berodach-Baladan the sonne of Baladan King of Babylon, sent letters and a present vnto Hezekiah : for he had heard that Hezekiah had beene sicke.

13 And Hezekiah hearkened vnto them, and shewed them the house of his ‖ precious things, the siluer, and the golde, and the spices, and the precious oyntment, and all the house of his ‖ armour, and all that was found in his treasures : there was nothing in his house, nor in all his dominion, that Hezekiah shewed them not.

14 ¶ Then came Isaiah the Prophet vnto King Hezekiah, and sayde vnto him, What sayd these men? and from whence came they vnto thee? And Hezekiah sayde, They are come from a farre countrey, euen from Babylon.

15 And he said, What haue they seene in thine house? And Hezekiah answered, All the things that are in mine house haue they seene : there is nothing among my treasures, that I haue not shewed them.

16 And Isaiah said vnto Hezekiah, Heare the word of the LORD.

17 Behold, the dayes come, that all that is in thine house, and that which thy fathers haue layde vp in store vnto this day, *shall be caried vnto Babylon : nothing shall be left, sayth the LORD.

18 And of thy sonnes that shall issue from thee, which thou shalt beget, shall they take away, and they shall bee Eunuches in the palace of the king of Babylon.

19 Then said Hezekiah vnto Isaiah, Good is the word of the LORD which thou hast spoken. And he said, ‖Is it not good, if peace and trueth be in my dayes?

20 ¶ And the rest of the actes of Hezekiah, and all his might, and how hee made a poole and a conduit, & brought water into the city, are they not written in the booke of the Chronicles of the Kings of Iudah?

21 And Hezekiah slept with his fathers, and Manasseh his sonne reigned in his stead.

Heb. deſcẽſ.
Iſal. 39. 1.
r, spicery.
r, iewels.
eb. vessels.
Chap. 24.
s. & 25. 13
re. 27. 19.
Or, shall
here not be
eace and
rueth? &c.

CHAP. XXI.

1 Manasseh his reigne. 3 His great idolatrie. 10 His wickednesse causeth prophecies against Iudah. 17 Amon succeedeth him. 19 Amons wicked reigne. 23 Hee being slaine by his seruants, and those murderers slaine by the people, Iosiah is made King.

Anasseh *was twelue yeres olde when hee beganne to reigne, and reigned fiftie and fiue yeeres in Ierusalem : and his mothers name was Hephzibah.

2 And hee did that which was euill in the sight of the LORD, after the abominations of the heathen, whom the LORD cast out before the children of Israel.

3 For he built vp againe the high places, *which Hezekiah his father had destroyed, and hee reared vp altars for Baal, and made a groue, as did Ahab king of Israel, and worshipped all the hoste of heauen, and serued them.

4 And *he built altars in the house of the LORD, of which the LORD sayd, *In Ierusalem will I put my Name.

5 And he built altars for all the host of heauen, in the two courts of the house of the LORD.

6 And he made his sonne passe thorow the fire, and obserued times, and vsed enchantments, and dealt with familiar spirits, and wizards : he wrought much wickednesse in the sight of the LORD, to prouoke him to anger.

7 And he set a grauen image of the groue that he had made, in the house, of which the LORD said to Dauid, and to Solomon his sonne, *In this house and in Ierusalem, which I haue chosen out of all tribes of Israel, wil I put my Name for euer:

8 Neither will I make the feete of Israel mooue any more out of the land, which I gaue their fathers : onely if they will obserue to doe according to all that I haue commanded them, and according to all the Law, that my seruant Moses commanded them.

9 But they hearkened not : and Manasseh seduced them to doe more euill then did the nations, whome the LORD destroyed before the children of Israel.

10 ¶ And the LORD spake by his seruants the Prophets, saying,

11 *Be-

* 2. Chron. 33. 1.
* Cha. 18. 4.
* Iere. 32. 34.
* 2. Sam. 7. 13.
* 1. King. 8. 29. and 9. 3. chap. 23. 27.

11 *Because Manasseh king of Iudah hath done these abominations, *and* hath done wickedly aboue all that the Amorites did, which *were* before him, and hath made Iudah also to sinne with his idoles:

12 Therefore thus saith the LORD God of Israel, Behold, I am bringing *such* euill vpon Ierusalem and Iudah, that whosoeuer heareth of it, both *his eares shall tingle.

13 And I will stretch ouer Ierusalem the line of Samaria, and the plummet of the house of Ahab: and I will wipe Ierusalem as a man wipeth a dish, †wiping it and turning *it* vpside downe.

14 And I will forsake the remnant of mine inheritance, and deliuer them into the hand of their enemies, and they shall become a pray and a spoile to all their enemies,

15 Because they haue done that *which was* euill in my sight, and haue prouoked me to anger since the day their fathers came forth out of Egypt, euen vnto this day.

16 Moreouer, Manasseh shed innocent blood very much, till he had filled Ierusalem †from one end to another, beside his sinne wherwith he made Iudah to sinne, in doing that *which was* euill in the sight of the LORD.

17 ¶ Now the rest of the actes of Manasseh, and all that he did, and his sinne that he sinned, are they not written in the booke of the Chronicles of the kings of Iudah?

18 And *Manasseh slept with his fathers, and was buried in the garden of his owne house, in the garden of Vzza: and Amon his sonne reigned in his stead.

19 ¶ Amon was twentie and two yeres old when he began to reigne, and he reigned two yeeres in Ierusalem: and his mothers name *was* Meshullemeth, the daughter of Haruz of Iotbah.

20 And he did that *which was* euill in the sight of the LORD, as his father Manasseh did.

21 And he walked in all the wayes that his father walked in, and serued the idoles that his father serued, and worshipped them:

22 And he forsooke the LORD God of his fathers, and walked not in the way of the LORD.

23 ¶ And the seruants of Amon conspired against him, and slew the king in his owne house.

24 And the people of the land slew al them that had conspired against king Amon, and the people of the land made Iosiah his sonne king in his stead.

25 Now the rest of the acts of Amon, which he did, are they not written in the booke of the chronicles of the kings of Iudah?

26 And he was buried in his sepulchre, in the garden of Vzza, and *Iosiah his sonne reigned in his stead.

CHAP. XXII.

1 Iosiah his good reigne. 3 He taketh care for the repaire of the Temple. 8 Hilkiah hauing found a booke of the Lawe, Iosiah sendeth to Huldah to enquire of the Lord. 15 Huldah prophesieth destruction of Ierusalem, but respite thereof in Iosiahs time.

Osiah *was eight yeeres old when hee beganne to reigne, and hee reigned thirtie and one yeeres in Ierusalem: and his mothers name *was* Iedidah, the daughter of Adaiah of Boscath.

2 And he did that *which was* right in the sight of the LORD, and walked in all the wayes of Dauid his father, and turned not aside to the right hand, or to the left.

3 ¶ And it came to passe in the eighteenth yeere of king Iosiah, that the king sent Shaphan the sonne of Azaliah, the sonne of Meshullam the Scribe to the house of the LORD, saying,

4 Goe vp to Hilkiah the high priest, that he may summe the siluer which is brought into the house of the LORD, which the keepers of the †doore haue gathered of the people.

5 And let them deliuer it into the hand of the doers of the worke, that haue the ouersight of the house of the LORD: and let them giue it to the doers of the worke, which is in the house of the LORD, to repaire the breaches of the house,

6 Vnto carpenters, and builders, and masons, and to buy timber and hewen stone, to repaire the house.

7 Howbeit, there was no reckoning made with them, of the money that was deliuered into their hand, because they dealt faithfully.

8 ¶ And

Margin notes
* Iere. 15. 4

*. 1 Sam. 3. 11.

† Heb. he wipeth and turneth it vpon the face thereof.

† Heb. from mouth to mouth.

* 2. Chron. 33. 20.

* Mat. 1. 1 called Iosias.

* 2. Chron. 34. 1.

† Heb. threshold.

8 ¶ And Hilkiah the high Priest said vnto Shaphan the Scribe, I haue found the booke of the Law in the house of the LORD. And Hilkiah gaue the booke to Shaphan, and he read it.

9 And Shaphan the Scribe came to the king, and brought the king word againe, and said, Thy seruants haue †gathered the money that was found in the house, and haue deliuered it into the hand of them that doe the worke, that haue the ouersight of the house of the LORD.

*Hebr. mel-
sd.*

10 And Shaphan the Scribe shewed the king, saying, Hilkiah the Priest hath deliuered mee a booke : and Shaphan read it before the king.

11 And it came to passe when the king had heard the words of the booke of the Law, that he rent his clothes.

12 And the king commanded Hilkiah the Priest, and Ahikam the sonne of Shaphan, and Achbor the sonne of Michaiah, and Shaphan the Scribe, and Asahiah a seruant of the Kings, saying,

13 Goe yee, enquire of the LORD for me, and for the people, and for all Iudah, concerning the wordes of this booke that is found : for great *is* the wrath of the LORD that is kindled against vs, because our fathers haue not hearkened vnto the woordes of this booke, to doe according vnto all that which is written concerning vs.

14 So Hilkiah the Priest, and Ahikam, and Achbor, and Shaphan, and Asahiah, went vnto Huldah the Prophetesse, the wife of Shallum the sonne *of* Tikuah, the sonne of Harhas, keeper of the †wardrobe : now she dwelt in Ierusalem in ‖the colledge : And they communed with her.

*Hebr. gar-
nents.
Or, in the
ccond part.*

15 ¶ And she said vnto them, Thus saith the LORD God of Israel, Tell the man that sent you to me ;

16 Thus saith the LORD, Behold, I will bring euill vpon this place, and vpon the inhabitants thereof, *euen* all the words of the booke which the king of Iudah hath read.

17 Because they haue forsaken me, and haue burnt incense vnto other gods, that they might prouoke mee to anger with all the woorkes of their handes : therefore my wrath shall bee kindled against this place, and shall not be quenched.

18 But to the king of Iudah which sent you to enquire of the LORD, Thus shall yee say to him, Thus saith the LORD God of Israel, as touching the woordes which thou hast heard :

19 Because thine heart was tender, and thou hast humbled thy selfe before the LORD, when thou heardest what I spake against this place, and against the inhabitants thereof, that they should become a desolation and a curse, and hast rent thy cloathes, and wept before me ; I also haue heard *thee*, saith the LORD.

20 Behold therefore, I will gather thee vnto thy fathers, and thou shalt be gathered into thy graue in peace, and thine eyes shal not see all the euil which I will bring vpon this place. And they brought the king word againe.

CHAP. XXIII.

1 Iosiah causeth the booke to bee read in a solemne assembly. 3 He reneweth the Couenant of the LORD. 4 He destroyeth idolatry. 15 He burnt dead mens bones vpon the altar of Bethel, as was foreprophesied. 21 He kept a most solemne Passeouer. 24 He put away witches, and all abomination. 26 Gods finall wrath against Iudah. 29 Iosiah prouoking Pharaoh Nechoh, is slaine at Megiddo. 31 Iehoahaz succeeding him, is imprisoned by Pharaoh Nechoh, who made Ioiakim king. 36 Ioiakim his wicked reigne.

ANd *the king sent, and they gathered vnto him all the Elders of Iudah, and of Ierusalem.

* 2. Chron.
34. 30.

2 And the king went vp into the house of the LORD, and all the men of Iudah, and all the inhabitants of Ierusalem with him, and the Priestes, and the Prophets, and all the people † both small and great : and he read in their eares all the wordes of the booke of the Couenant which was found in the house of the LORD

† *Hebr. from
small euen
vnto great.*

3 ¶ And the King stood by a pillar, and made a Couenant before the LORD, to walke after the LORD, and to keepe his Commaundements, and his Testimonies, & his Statutes, with all *their* heart, and all *their* soule, to performe the words of this Couenant, that were written in this booke : and all the people stood to the Couenant.

4 And the king commanded Hilkiah the

the high Priest, and the priests of the second order, and the keepers of the doore to bring forth out of the Temple of the LORD all the vessels that were made for Baal, and for the groue, and for all the hoste of heauen : and he burnt them without Ierusalem in the fields of Kidron, and caried the ashes of them vnto Bethel.

5 And hee † put downe the † idolatrous priests whome the kings of Iudah had ordeined to burne incense in the high places, in the cities of Iudah and in the places round about Ierusalem : them also that burnt incense vnto Baal, to the Sunne, and to the Moone, and to the ‖ Planets, and to all the hoste of heauen.

† Heb. caused to cease.
† Heb. Chemarim.

‖ Or, twelue signes or constellations.

6 And he brought out the * groue from the house of the LORD, without Ierusalem, vnto the brooke Kidron, and burnt it at the brooke Kidron, and stampt it small to powder, and cast the powder thereof vpon the graues of the children of the people.

* Cha. 21. 7.

7 And he brake downe the houses of the Sodomites that were by the house of the LORD, where the women woue † hangings for the groue.

† Heb. houses.

8 And he brought all the priests out of the cities of Iudah, and defiled the high places where the priests had burnt incense, from Geba to Beersheba, and brake downe the hie places of the gates that were in the entring in of the gate of Ioshua the gouernour of the citie, which were on a mans left hand at the gate of the citie.

9 Neuerthelesse, the priests of the high places came not vp to the Altar of the LORD in Ierusalem, but they did eate of the vnleauened bread among their brethren.

10 And he defiled Topheth which is in the valley of the children of Hinnom, that no man might make his sonne or his daughter to passe through the fire to Molech.

11 And he tooke away the horses that the kings of Iudah had giuen to the Sunne, at the entring in of the house of the LORD, by the chamber of Nathanmelech the ‖ chamberlaine, which was in the suburbs, and burnt the charets of the Sunne with fire,

‖ Or, Eunuch, or Officer.

12 And the altars that were on the top of the vpper chamber of Ahaz, which the kings of Iudah had made, and the altars which * Manasseh had

* Cha. 21. 5

made in the two courts of the house of the LORD, did the king beat downe, and ‖ brake them downe from thence, and cast the dust of them into the brooke Kidron.

‖ Or, ran from thence

13 And the high places that were before Ierusalem, which were on the right hand of the ‖ mount of corruption, which * Solomon the king of Israel had builded for Ashtoreth, the abomination of the Zidonians, and for Chemosh the abomination of the Moabites, and for Milchom the abomination of the children of Ammon, did the king defile.

‖ That is, t mount of C liues.
* 1. King. 11. 7.

14 And he brake in pieces the † images, and cut downe the groues, and filled their places with the bones of men.

† Heb. statues.

15 ¶ Moreouer the altar that was at Bethel, and the high place which Ieroboam the sonne of Nebat, who made Israel to sinne, had made, both that altar, and the high place he brake downe, and burnt the high place, and stampt it small to powder, and burnt the groue.

16 And as Iosiah turned himselfe, he spied the sepulchres that were there in the mount, and sent, & tooke the bones out of the sepulchres, and burnt them vpon the altar, and polluted it, according to the * word of the LORD which the man of God proclaimed, who proclaimed these words.

* 1. King. 13. 2.

17 Then hee said, What title is that that I see? and the men of the city told him, It is the sepulchre of the man of God, which came from Iudah, and proclaimed these things that thou hast done against the altar of Bethel.

18 And he said, Let him alone : let no man moue his bones: so they let his bones † alone, with the bones of the Prophet that came out of Samaria.

† Hebr. to escape.

19 And all the houses also of the hie places that were in the cities of Samaria, which the kings of Israel had made to prouoke the LORD to anger, Iosiah tooke away, and did to them according to all the actes that hee had done in Bethel.

20 And he ‖ slew all the priests of the high places that were there, vpon the altars, and burnt mens bones vpon them, and returned to Ierusalem.

‖ Or sacrificed.

21 ¶ And the King commanded all the people saying, * Keepe the Passeouer vnto the LORD your God, * as it is written in this booke of the Couenant.

* 2. Chron. 35. 1. 1. esd 1. 1.
* Exo. 12. 3 deut. 16. 2.

22 Surely

22 Surely there was not holden such a Passeouer, from the daies of the Iudges that iudged Israel, nor in all the dayes of the kings of Israel, nor of the kings of Iudah:

23 But in the eighteenth yeere of king Iosiah, *wherein* this Passeouer was holden to the LORD in Ierusalem.

24 ¶ Moreouer the *workers* with familiar spirits, and the wizards, and the ||images, and the idoles, and all the abominations that were spied in the land of Iudah, and in Ierusalem, did Iosiah put away, that he might performe the wordes of *the lawe, which were written in the booke that Hilkiah the priest found in the house of the LORD.

|| Or, Tera- ohim.

* Leuit. 20. 27. deut. 18. 11.

25 And like vnto him was there no king before him, that turned to the LORD with all his heart, and with all his soule, and with all his might, according to all the Law of Moses, neither after him arose there *any* like him.

26 ¶ Notwithstanding, the LORD turned not from the fiercenesse of his great wrath, wherwith his anger was kindled against Iudah, because of all the †prouocations that Manasseh had prouoked him withall.

† Heb. an- gers.

27 And the LORD said, I will remoue Iudah also out of my sight, as I haue remoued Israel, and will cast off this citie Ierusalem, which I haue chosen, and the house of which I sayd, *My name shall be there.

* 1. King. 8. 29. & 9. 3. Chap. 21. 7.

28 Now the rest of the actes of Iosiah, and all that hee did, are they not written in the booke of the chronicles of the kings of Iudah?

29 ¶ *In his dayes, Pharaoh Nechoh king of Egypt, went vp against the king of Assyria to the riuer Euphrates: and king Iosiah went against him, and hee slew him at Megiddo, when he had seene him.

* 2. Chron. 35. 20.

30 And his seruants caried him in a charet dead from Megiddo, & brought him to Ierusalem, and buried him in his owne sepulchre: and *the people of the land tooke Iehoahaz the sonne of Iosiah, and anointed him, and made him king in his fathers stead.

* 2. Chron. 36. 1.

31 ¶ Iehoahaz *was* twenty and three yeeres olde when he beganne to reigne, and hee reigned three moneths in Ierusalem: and his mothers name *was* Hamital, the daughter of Ieremiah, of Libnah.

32 And hee did that *which was* euill in the sight of the LORD, according to all that his fathers had done.

33 And Pharaoh Nechoh put him in bandes at Riblah in the land of Hamath, ||that he might not reigne in Ierusalem, and †put the land to a tribute of an hundred talents of siluer, and a talent of golde.

|| *Or, because he reigned.*
† *Heb. set a mulct vpon the land.*

34 And Pharaoh Nechoh made Eliakim the sonne of Iosiah king, in the roume of Iosiah his father, and turned his name to *Iehoiakim, and tooke Iehoahaz away: and hee came to Egypt, and died there.

* Matth. 1. 12. *called Iakim.*

35 And Iehoiakim gaue the siluer, and the golde to Pharaoh, but he taxed the land to giue the money according to the commandement of Pharaoh: hee exacted the siluer and the golde of the people of the land, of euery one according to his taxation, to giue *it* vnto Pharaoh Nechoh.

36 ¶ Iehoiakim *was* twentie and fiue yeere olde when he began to reigne, and he reigned eleuen yeeres in Ierusalem: and his mothers name was Zebudah, the daughter of Pedaiah of Rumah.

37 And he did that *which was* euill in the sight of the LORD, according to all that his fathers had done.

CHAP. XXIIII.

1 Iehoiakim, first subdued by Nebuchadnezzar, then rebelling against him, procureth his owne ruine. 5 Iehoiachin succeedeth him. 7 The King of Egypt is vanquished by the King of Babylon. 8 Iehoiachin his euill reigne. 10 Ierusalem is taken and carried captiue into Babylon. 17 Zedekiah is made King, and reigneth ill, vnto the vtter destruction of Iudah.

IN his dayes Nebuchadnezzar king of Babylon came vp, and Iehoiakim became his seruant three yeeres: then hee turned and rebelled against him.

2 And the LORD sent against him bands of the Chaldees, and bandes of the Syrians, and bandes of the Moabites, and bands of the children of Ammon, and sent them against Iudah to destroy it, *according to the word of the LORD, which hee spake †by his seruants the Prophets.

* Chap. 20. 17. and 23. 27.
† *Heb. by the hand of.*

3 Surely at the commandement of the

the LORD came *this* vpon Iudah, to remooue *them* out of his sight, for the sinnes of Manasseh, according to all that he did:

4 And also for the innocent blood that hee shedde: (for hee filled Ierusalem with innocent blood) which the LORD would not pardon.

5 ¶ Nowe the rest of the actes of Iehoiakim, and all that he did, *are they* not written in the booke of the Chronicles of the Kings of Iudah?

6 So Iehoiakim slept with his fathers: and Iehoiachin his sonne reigned in his stead.

7 And the king of Egypt came not againe any more out of his land: for the King of Babylon had taken from the riuer of Egypt, vnto the riuer Euphrates, all that pertained to the King of Egypt.

8 ¶ Iehoiachin was eighteene yeres old when he began to reigne, & he reigned in Ierusalem three moneths: & his mothers name *was* Nehushta the daughter of Elnathan, of Ierusalem.

9 And hee did that *which was* euill in the sight of the LORD, according to all that his father had done.

* Dan. 1. 1.

10 ¶ * At that time the seruants of Nebuchadnezzar King of Babylon came vp against Ierusalem, and the citie † was besieged.

† Heb. came into siege.

11 And Nebuchadnezzar king of Babylon came against the citie, and his seruants did besiege it.

12 And Iehoiachin the King of Iudah went out to the king of Babylon, hee, and his mother, and his seruants, and his princes, and his ||officers: and the king of Babylon tooke him in the eight yeere of his reigne.

|| Or, Eunuches.

13 *And hee caried out thence all the treasures of the house of the LORD, and the treasure of the kings house, and cut in pieces all the vessels of gold which Solomon King of Israel had made in the Temple of the LORD, as the LORD had said.

* Chap. 20. 17. esa. 39. 6

14 And hee caried away all Ierusalem, and all the princes, & all the mighty men of valour, *euen* tenne thousand captiues, and all the craftsmen, and smiths: none remained, saue the poorest sort of the people of the land.

15 And *he caried away Iehoiachin to Babylon, and the kings mother, and the kings wiues, and his ||officers, and the mighty of the land, those caried hee

* 2. Chron. 36. 10. esth. 2. 6.
|| Or, Eunuches.

into captiuitie, from Ierusalem to Babylon.

16 And all the men of might, *euen* seuen thousand, and craftsmen, & smiths a thousand, all that were strong and apt for warre, euen them the king of Babylon brought captiue to Babylon.

17 ¶ And *the king of Babylon made Mattaniah his fathers brother king in his stead, and changed his name to Zedekiah.

* Iere. 37. and 52. 1

18 Zedekiah *was* twentie and one yeeres olde when hee began to reigne, *and* he reigned eleuen yeeres in Ierusalem: and his mothers name *was* Hamutal, the daughter of Ieremiah of Libnah.

19 And hee did that *which was* euill in the sight of the LORD, according to all that Iehoiachin had done.

20 For through the anger of the LORD it came to passe in Ierusalem and Iudah, vntill he had cast them out from his presence, that Zedekiah rebelled against the king of Babylon.

CHAP. XXV.

1 Ierusalem is besieged. 4 Zedekiah taken, his sonnes slaine, his eyes put out. 8 Nabuzaradan defaceth the city, carieth the remnant, except a few poore labourers, into captiuitie, 13 Spoileth and carieth away the treasures. 18 The Nobles are slaine at Riblah. 22 Gedaliah, who was set ouer them that remained, being slaine, the rest flee into Egypt. 27 Euilmerodach aduanceth Iehoiachin in his court.

 Nd it came to passe *in the ninth yeere of his reigne, in the tenth moneth, in the tenth *day* of the moneth, that Nebuchadnezzar king of Babylon came, hee, and all his hoste, against Ierusalem, and pitched against it, and they built fortes against it, round about.

* Iere. 39. and 52. 4.

2 And the citie was besieged vnto the eleuenth yeere of king Zedekiah.

3 And on the ninth *day* of the *fourth moneth, the famine preuailed in the city, and there was no bread for the people of the land.

* Iere. 52.

4 ¶ And the citie was broken vp, and all the men of warre *fled* by night, by the way of the gate, betweene two walles, which *is* by the kings garden, (now the Caldees *were* against the citie round about) and *the King* went the way toward the plaine.

5 And

5 And the army of the Caldees purſued after the King, and ouertooke him in the plaines of Iericho : and all his armie were ſcattered from him.

6 So they tooke the King, and brought him vp to the King of Babylon, to Riblah, and they gaue †iudgement vpon him.

7 And they ſlew the ſonnes of Zedekiah before his eyes, and †put out the eyes of Zedekiah, and bound him with fetters of braſſe, and carried him to Babylon.

8 ¶ And in the fifth moneth, on the ſeuenth *day* of the moneth (which is the nineteenth yeere of King Nebuchadnezzar King of Babylon) came Nebuzaradan ||captaine of the guard, a ſeruant of the king of Babylon, vnto Ieruſalem :

9 And hee burnt the houſe of the LORD, and the kings houſe, and all the houſes of Ieruſalem, and euery great mans houſe burnt he with fire.

10 And all the army of the Caldees that were with the captaine of the guard, brake downe the walles of Ieruſalem round about.

11 Now the reſt of the people that were left in the citie, and the †fugitiues that fell away to the king of Babylon, with the remnant of the multitude, did Nebuzaradan the captaine of the guard cary away.

12 But the captaine of the guard left of the poore of the land, to be Vine-dreſſers, and husbandmen.

13 And *the pillars of braſſe that *were* in the houſe of the LORD, and the baſes, and the braſen ſea that *was* in the houſe of the LORD, did the Caldees breake in pieces, and caried the braſſe of them to Babylon.

14 And the pots, and the ſhouels, and the ſnuffers, and the ſpoones, and all the veſſels of braſſe wherewith they miniſtred, tooke they away.

15 And the fire-pans, and the bowles, & ſuch things as were of golde, *in* golde, and of ſiluer, *in* ſiluer, the captaine of the guard tooke away.

16 The two pillars, †one ſea, and the baſes which Solomon had made for the houſe of the LORD, the braſſe of al theſe veſſels was without weight.

17 *The height of the one pillar was eighteene cubits, and the chapiter vpon it was braſſe : and the height of the chapiter three cubites ; and the wreathen

worke, and pomegranates vpon the chapiter round about, all of braſſe : and like vnto theſe had the ſecond pillar with wreathen worke.

18 ¶ And the captaine of the guard, tooke Seraiah the chiefe Prieſt, and Zephaniah the ſecond Prieſt, and the three keepers of the †doore.

19 And out of the citie hee tooke an ||Officer, that was ſet ouer the men of warre, and fiue men of them that †were in the kings preſence, which were found in the citie, and the ||principall Scribe of the hoſte, which muſtered the people of the land, and threeſcore men of the people of the land that were found in the citie.

20 And Nebuzaradan captaine of the guard tooke theſe, and brought them to the king of Babylon, to Riblah.

21 And the King of Babylon ſmote them, and ſlew them at Riblah in the land of Hamath : ſo Iudah was caried away out of their land.

22 ¶ And as for the people that remained in the land of Iudah, whom Nebuchadnezzar King of Babylon had left, euen ouer them he made Gedaliah the ſonne of Ahikam, the ſonne of Shaphan, ruler.

23 And when all the *captaines of the armies, they, and their men, heard that the King of Babylon had made Gedaliah gouernour, there came to Gedaliah to Miſpah, euen Ishmael the ſonne of Nethaniah, and Iohanan the ſonne of Careah, and Seraiah the ſonne of Tanhumeth the Netophathite, and Iaazaniah the ſonne of a Maachathite, they, and their men.

24 And Gedaliah ſware to them and to their men, and ſaid vnto them, Feare not to be the ſeruants of the Caldees : dwell in the land, and ſerue the King of Babylon ; and it ſhall bee well with you.

25 But it came to paſſe in the ſeuenth moneth, that Ishmael the ſonne of Nethaniah, the ſonne of Elishama, of †the ſeed royal, came, and ten men with him, and *ſmote Gedaliah, that he died, and the Iewes, and the Caldees that were with him at Mizpah.

26 And all the people both ſmall and great, and the captaines of the armies aroſe, and came to Egypt : for they were afraid of the Caldees.

27 ¶ And it came to paſſe in the ſeuen and

Marginal notes (left column):
· Hebr. ſpake †udgement with him.

· Heb. made ⸳linde.

‡ Or, chiefe Marſhall.

‡ Hebr. fal⸳len away.

* Chap. 20. 17. Iere. 27. ‡‡.

* 1. King. 7. 15. Iere. 52. 21.

† Hebr. the one ſea.

* 1. King. 7. 15. Iere. 52. 21.

Marginal notes (right column):
† Hebr. threſhold.

|| Or, Eunuch.
† Hebr. ſaw the Kings face.
|| Or, ſcribe of the captaine of the hoſte.

* Iere. 40. 3, 9.

* Iere. 40. 7.

† Hebr. of the king-dome.
* Iere. 41. 2.

and thirtieth yeere of the captiuitie of Iehoiachin king of Iudah, in the twelfth moneth, on the seuen and twentieth *day* of the moneth, that Euilmerodach king of Babylon, in the yeere that he began to reigne, did lift vp the head of Iehoiachin king of Iudah out of prison.

28 And he spake †kindly to him, and

† *Heb. good things with him.*

set his throne aboue the throne of the kings that *were* with him in Babylon,

29 And changed his prison garments: and he did eate bread continually before him all the dayes of his life.

30 And his allowance *was* a continuall allowance giuen him of the king, a dayly rate for euery day, all the dayes of his life.

¶ THE FIRST BOOKE

of the Chronicles.

CHAP. I.

1 Adams line to Noah. 5 The sonnes of Iapheth. 8 The sonnes of Ham. 17 The sonnes of Shem. 24 Shems line to Abraham. 29 Ishmaels sonnes. 32 The sonnes of Keturah. 34 The posteritie of Abraham by Esau. 43 The Kings of Edom. 51 The Dukes of Edom.

* Gen. 5. 3, 9.

Dam, * Sheth, Enosh,

2 Kenan, Mahalaleel, Iered,

3 Henoch, Methushelah, Lamech,

4 Noah, Shem, Ham, & Iapheth.

* Gen. 10. 2

5 ¶ * The sonnes of Iapheth: Gomer, and Magog, and Madai, and Iauan, and Tubal, and Meshech, and Tiras.

6 And the sonnes of Gomer: Ashchenaz, and ‖ Riphath, and Togarmah.

‖ *Or, Diphath, as it is in some copies.*

‖ *Or, Rodanim, accorning to some copies.*

7 And the sonnes of Iauan: Elishah, and Tarshish, Kittim, and ‖ Dodanim.

8 ¶ The sonnes of Ham: Cush, and Mizraim, Put, and Canaan.

9 And the sonnes of Cush: Siba, and Hauilah, and Sabta, and Raamah, and Sabtecha: and the sonnes of Raamah: Sheba, and Dedan.

* Gen. 10. 8

10 And Cush * begate Nimrod: hee began to be mightie vpon the earth.

11 And Mizraim begate Ludim, and

Anamim, and Lehabim, and Naphtuhim,

12 And Pathrusim, and Casluhim (of whome came the Philistines) and * Caphthorim.

* Deut. 2. 23.

13 And Canaan begate Zidon his first borne, and Heth.

14 The Iebusite also, and the Amorite, and the Girgashite,

15 And the Hiuite, and the Arkite, and the Sinite,

16 And the Aruadite, and the Zemarite, and the Hamathite.

17 ¶ The sonnes of * Shem: Elam, and Asshur, and Arphaxad, and Lud, and Aram, and Vz, & Hul, and Gether, and ‖ Meshech.

* Gen. 10. 23. & 11. 10.

‖ *Or, Mash gen. 10. 23*

18 And Arphaxad begate Shelah, and Shelah begate Eber.

19 And vnto Eber were borne two sonnes: the name of the one *was* ‖ Peleg, (because in his dayes the earth was diuided) and his brothers name *was* Ioktan.

‖ *That is, uision.*

20 And * Ioktan begate Almodad, and Sheleph, and Hazermaueth, and Ierah,

* Gen. 10. 26.

21 Hadoram also, and Vzal, and Diklah,

22 And Ebal, and Abimael, and Sheba,

23 And Ophir, and Hauilah, and Iobab: all these *were* the sonnes of Ioktan.

24 ¶ * Shem, Arphaxad, Shelah,

* Luke 3. * Gen. 11. 15.

25 * Eber, Peleg, Rehu,

26 Serug, Nahor, Terah,

27 * Abram,

27 *Abram, the same is Abraham.

28 The sonnes of Abraham : *Isaac, and *Ishmael.

29 ¶ These are their generations: The *first-borne of Ishmael, Nebaioth, then Kedar, and Adbeel, and Mibsam,

30 Mishma, and Dumah, Massa, ||Hadad, and Tema,

31 Ietur, Naphish, and Kedemah. These are the sonnes of Ishmael.

32 ¶ Now the sonnes of Keturah, Abrahams Concubine : she bare Zimran, and Iokshan, and Medan, and Midian, and Ishbak, and Shuah. And the sonnes of Iokshan, Sheba, and Dedan.

33 And the sonnes of Midian : Ephah, and Ephar, and Henoch, and Abida, and Eldaah. All these are the sonnes of Keturah.

34 And Abraham begate Isaac. The sonnes of Isaac : Esau, and Israel.

35 ¶ The sonnes of *Esau : Eliphaz, Reuel, and Ieush, and Iaalam, and Korah.

36 The sonnes of Eliphaz : Teman, and Omar, ||Zephi, and Gatam, Kenaz, and Timna, and Amalek.

37 The sonnes of Reuel : Nahath, Zerah, Shammah, and Mizzah.

38 And the sonnes of Seir : Lotan, and Shobal, and Zibeon, and Anah, and Dishon, and Ezer, and Dishan.

39 And the sonnes of Lotan : Hori, and ||Homam : and Timna was Lotans sister.

40 The sonnes of Shobal : ||Alian, and Manahath, and Ebal, ||Shephi, and Onam. And the sonnes of Zibeon : Aiah, and Anah.

41 The sonnes of Anah : *Dishon. And the sonnes of Dishon : ||Amram, and Eshban, and Ithran, and Cheran.

42 The sonnes of Ezer : Bilham, and Zauan, and ||Iakan. The sonnes of Dishon : Vz, and Aran.

43 ¶ Now these are the *kings that reigned in the land of Edom, before any king reigned ouer the children of Israel. Bela the sonne of Beor; and the name of his citie, was Dinhabah.

44 And when Bela was dead, Iobab the sonne of Zerah of Bosrah, reigned in his stead.

45 And when Iobab was dead, Husham of the land of the Temanits, reigned in his stead.

46 And when Husham was dead, Hadad the sonne of Bedad (which smote Midian in the field of Moab) reigned in his stead : and the name of his citie was Auith.

47 And when Hadad was dead, Samlah of Masrekah, reigned in his stead.

48 And when Samlah was dead, Shaul of Rehoboth *by the riuer, reigned in his stead.

49 And when Shaul was dead, Baal-hanan the sonne of Achbor, reigned in his stead.

50 And when Baal-hanan was dead, ||Hadad reigned in his stead : and the name of his citie was ||Pai : and his wiues name was Mehetabel the daughter of Matred, the daughter of Mezahab.

51 ¶ Hadad dyed also. And the *Dukes of Edom were : Duke Timnah, Duke Aliah, Duke Ietheth,

52 Duke Aholibamah, Duke Elah, Duke Pinon,

53 Duke Kenaz, Duke Teman, Duke Mibzar,

54 Duke Magdiel, Duke Iram. These are the Dukes of Edom.

CHAP. II.

1 The sonnes of Israel. 3 The posteritie of Iudah by Tamar. 13 The children of Iesse. 18 The posteritie of Caleb the sonne of Hesron. 21 Hesrons posteritie by the daughter of Machir. 25 Ierahmeels posteritie. 34 Sheshans posteritie. 42 another branch of Calebs posteritie. 50 The posteritie of Caleb the sonne of Hur.

These are the sonnes of ||Israel : *Reuben, Simeon, Leui, and Iudah, Issachar, and Zebulun,

2 Dan, Ioseph, and Beniamin, Naphtali, Gad, and Asher.

3 ¶ The sonnes of *Iudah : Er, and Onan, and Shelah. Which three were borne vnto him, of the daughter of Shua the Canaanites. And Er the first-borne of Iudah, was euill in the sight of the Lord, and he slue him.

4 And *Tamar his daughter-in law bare him Pharez, and Zerah. All the sonnes of Iudah were fiue.

5 The sonnes of *Pharez : Hezron, and Hamul.

6 And the sonnes of Zerah : ||Zimri, *and Ethan, and Heman, and Calcol, and ||Dara. Fiue of them in all.

7 And

* Gen. 17. 5
* Gen. 21. 2, 3.
* Gen. 16. 11.
* Gen. 25. 13, to 17.
|| Or, Hadar, Gen. 25. 14
* Gen. 36. 9, 10.
|| Or, Zepho, Gen. 36. 12
|| Or, Heman, Gen. 36. 22.
|| Or, Aluan, Gen. 36. 23
|| Or, Sepho, Gen. 36. 23
* Chap. 2. 31.
|| Or Hemdan, Gen. 36. 26.
|| Or Akan, Gen. 36. 27
* Gen. 36. 31.
* Gen. 36. 37.
|| Or, Hadar, Gen. 36. 39
|| Or, Pau, Gen. 36. 39
* Gen. 36. 40.
|| Or, Iacob.
* Gen. 29. 32. & 30. 5. & 35. 18; 22. & 46. 8. &c.
* Gen. 38. 3. & 46. 12.
* Gen. 38. 2.
* Gen. 38. 29, 30. Mat. 1. 3.
* Ruth. 4. 18.
|| Or, Zabdi, Iosh. 7. 1.
* 1. Kin. 4. 31.
|| Or, Darda.

‖ Or, Achan.

* Iosh. 6. 19. and 7. 1, 25.

‖ Or, Aram. Mat. 1. 3. ‖ Or, Caleb. ver. 18. * Ruth. 4. 19.

* 1. Sam. 16. 6.

‖ Or, Shamma, 1. Sam. 16. 9.

* Exod. 31. 2.

† Heb. tooke.

* Num. 32. 41. deut. 3. 14. iosh. 13. 30.

* Chap. 11. 41.

7 And the sonnes of Carmi : ‖ Achar, the troubler of Israel, who transgressed in the thing * accursed.

8 And the sonnes of Ethan : Azariah.

9 The sonnes also of Hezron, that were borne vnto him : Ierahmeel, and ‖ Ram, and ‖ Chelubai.

10 And Ram * begate Aminadab, and Aminadab begat Nahshon, prince of the children of Iudah.

11 And Nahshon begate Salma, and Salma begate Boaz.

12 And Boaz begate Obed, and Obed begate Iesse.

13 ¶ * And Iesse begate his firstborne Eliab, and Abinadab the second, and ‖ Shimma the third,

14 Nathanael the fourth, Raddai the fifth,

15 Ozem the sixth, Dauid the seuenth :

16 Whose sisters were Zeruiah, and Abigail. And the sonnes of Zeruiah : Abishai, and Ioab, and Asahel, three.

17 And Abigail bare Amasa. And the father of Amasa, was Iether the Ishmeelite.

18 ¶ And Caleb the sonne of Hezron, begate children of Azubah his wife, and of Ierioth : her sonnes are these : Iesher, Shobab, and Ardon.

19 And when Azubah was dead, Caleb tooke vnto him Ephrath, which bare him Hur.

20 And Hur begate Vri, and Vri begate * Bezaleel.

21 ¶ And afterward Hezron went in to the daughter of Machir, the father of Gilead, whom hee ‖ married when he was threescore yeeres old, and she bare him Segub.

22 And Segub begate Iair, who had three and twenty cities in the land of Gilead:

23 * And he tooke Geshur, and Aram, with the townes of Iair, from them, with Kenath, and the townes thereof, euen threescore cities. All these belonged to the sonnes of Machir, the father of Gilead.

24 And after that Hezron was dead in Caleb Ephratah, then Abiah Hezrons wife, bare him Ashur, the father of Tekoa.

25 ¶ And the sonnes of Ierahmeel the first-borne of Hezron, were Ram the first-borne, and Bunah, and Oren, and Ozen, and Ahiiah.

26 Ierahmeel had also an other wife, whose name was Atarah, she was the mother of Onam.

27 And the sonnes of Ram the firstborne of Ierahmeel, were Maaz, and Iamin, and Ekar.

28 And the sonnes of Onam were, Shammai, and Iada. And the sonnes of Shammai : Nadab, and Abishur.

29 And the name of the wife of Abishur was Abihail, and shee bare him Ahban, and Molid.

30 And the sonnes of Nadab : Seled, and Appaim. But Seled died without children.

31 And the sonnes of Appaim, Ishi : and the sonnes of Ishi, Sheshan : and the children of Sheshan, Ahlai.

32 And the sonnes of Iada the brother of Shammai, Iether, and Ionathan : and Iether died without children.

33 And the sonnes of Ionathan, Peleth, and Zaza. These were the sonnes of Ierahmeel.

34 ¶ Now Sheshan had no sonnes, but daughters : and Sheshan had a seruant, an Egyptian, whose name was Iarha.

35 And Sheshan gaue his daughter to Iarha his seruant to wife, and she bare him Attai.

36 And Attai begate Nathan, and Nathan begate * Zabad,

37 And Zabad begate Ephlal, and Ephlal begate Obed,

38 And Obed begate Iehu, and Iehu begate Azariah,

39 And Azariah begate Helez, and Helez begate Eleasah,

40 And Eleasah begate Sisamai, and Sisamai begate Shallum,

41 And Shallum begate Iekamiah, and Iekamiah begate Elishama.

42 ¶ Now the sonnes of Caleb the brother of Ierahmeel were, Mesha his first-borne, which was the father of Ziph : and the sonnes of Maresha the father of Hebron.

43 And the sonnes of Hebron : Korah, and Tappuah, and Rekem, and Shema.

44 And Shema begat Raham, the father of Iorkoam : and Rekem begate Shammai.

45 And the sonne of Shammai was Maon : and Maon was the father of Beth-zur.

46 And Ephah Calebs concubine bare

bare Haran, and Moza, and Gazez: and Haran begate Gazez.

47 And the sonnes of Iahdai : Regem, and Iotham, and Geshan, and Pelet, and Ephah, and Shaaph.

48 Maacha Calebs concubine, bare Sheber, and Tirhanah.

49 Shee bare also Shaaph the father of Madmannah, Sheua the father of Machbenah, & the father of Gibea : And the daughter of Caleb *was Achsah.

50 ¶ These were the sonnes of Caleb, the sonne of Hur, the first borne of Ephratah : Shobal the father of Kiriath-iearim,

51 Salma the father of Bethlehem : Hareph the father of Beth-gader.

52 And Shobal the father of Kiriath-iearim, had sonnes, ||Haroe, and ||halfe of the Manahethites.

53 And the families of Kiriath-iearim, the Ithrites, and the Puhites, and the Shumathites, and the Mishraites : of them came the Zareathites, and the Eshtaulites.

54 The sonnes of Salmah : Bethlehem, and the Netophathites, ||Ataroth, the house of Ioab, and halfe of the Manahethites, the Zorites.

55 And the families of the Scribes, which dwelt at Iabez : the Tirathites, the Shimeathites, and Suchathites. These are the *Kenites that came of Hemath, the father of the house of *Rechab.

CHAP. III.

1 The sonnes of Dauid. 10 His line to Zedekiah. 17 The successors of Ieconiah.

Ow these were the sonnes of Dauid, which were borne vnto him in Hebron. The first borne *Amnon, of Ahinoam the *Iesreelitesse : the second ||Daniel, of Abigail the Carmelitesse :

2 The third, Absalom the sonne of Maacha, the daughter of Talmai king of Geshur : the fourth, Adoniah the sonne of Haggith :

3 The fifth, Shephatia of Abital : the sixth, Ithream by * Eglah his wife.

4 These sixe were borne vnto him in Hebron, and there hee reigned seuen yeeres, and sixe moneths : and in Ierusalem he reigned thirty and three yeres.

5 *And these were borne vnto him in Ierusalem. ||Shimea, and Shobab,

and Nathan, and Solomon, foure, of ||Bathshua the daughter of ||Ammiel.

6 Ibhar also, and ||Elishama, and Eliphelet,

7 And Noga, and Nepheg, and Iaphia,

8 And Elishama, and ||Eliada, and Eliphelet, nine.

9 These were all the sonnes of Dauid: beside the sonnes of the concubines, and Tamar *their sister.

10 ¶ And Solomons sonne was *Rehoboam : ||Abia his sonne : Asa his son: Iehoshaphat his sonne :

11 Ioram his sonne : ||Ahaziah his sonne : Ioash his sonne :

12 Amaziah his sonne : ||Azariah his sonne : Iotham his sonne :

13 Ahaz his sonne : Hezekiah his sonne : Manasseh his sonne :

14 Amon his sonne : Iosiah his sonne.

15 And the sonnes of Iosiah were : the first borne ||Iohanan, the second ||Ioakim, the third ||Zedekiah, the fourth Sallum.

16 And the sonnes of *Ioakim : ||Ieconiah his sonne, ||Zedekiah his sonne.

17 ¶ And the sonnes of ||Ieconiah, Assir, †Salathiel *his sonne,

18 Malchiram also, and Pedaiah, and Shenazar, Iecamiah, Hosama, and Nedabiah.

19 And the sonnes of Pedaiah were : Zerubbabel, and Shimei : And the sonne of Zerubbabel, Meshullam, and Hananiah, and Shelomith their sister.

20 And Hazubah, and Ohel, and Berechiah, & Hasadiah, Iushabhesed, fiue.

21 And the sonnes of Hananiah, Pelatiah, and Iesaiah : the sonnes of Rephaiah, the sons of Arnan, the sonnes of Obadiah, the sonnes of Sechaniah.

22 And the sonnes of Sechaniah, Semaiah : and the sonnes of Semaiah, Hattush, and Igeal, and Bariah, and Neariah, and Shaphat, sixe.

23 And the sonnes of Neariah : Elioenai, and †Hezekiah, and Azrikam, three.

24 And the sonnes of Elioenai, were : Hodaiah, and Eliashib, and Pelaiah, and Akkub, and Iohanan, and Dalaiah, and Anani, seuen.

CHAP. IIII.

1.11 The posteritie of Iudah by Caleb the sonne of Hur. 5 Of Ashur the posthumus son of Hezron.

Side notes (left column):

* Iosh. 15. 7.

|| Or, Reaiah, chap. 4. 2.
|| Or, halfe of the Menuchites, Or Hatsihammenuchoth.

|| Or, Atarites, or, crownes of the house of Ioab.

* Iud. 1. 16

* Ier. 35. 2.

* 2. Sam. 3. 2
* Iosh. 15. 56.
|| Or, Chileab, 2. sam. 3. 3

* 2. Sam. 3. 5

* 2. Sam. 5. 14.
|| Or, Shammua, 2. Sam. 5. 14.

Side notes (right column):

|| Or, Bethsabe, 2. Sam. 11. 13.
|| Or, Eliam, 2. Sam. 11. 3
|| Or, Elishua 2. Sam. 5. 15

|| Or, Beliada, 1. Chro. 14. 7.

* 2. Sam. 13. 1.
* 1. King. 11 43. & 15. 8
|| Or, Abiam, 15. 1
|| Or, Azariah, 2. chr. 22. 6. & 21. 17.
|| Or, Vzziah 2. king. 15. 30.

|| Or, Ioachaz, 2. king. 23. 30.
|| Or, Eliakim, 2. king. 23. 34.
|| Or, Mathania, 2. kin. 24. 17.
* Mat. 1. 11.
|| Or, Iehoiachin, 2. king. 24. 6.
|| Or, Coniah, ier. 22. 24.
† Heb. Shealtiel.
* 2. King. 24. 17. being his vncle.
* Mat. 1. 12

† Heb. Hiskijah.

ron. 9 Of Iabez, and his prayer. 21 The posteritie of Shelah. 24 The posteritie and cities of Simeon. 39 Their conquest of Gedor, and of the Amalekites in mount Seir.

* Gen. 38. 29. and 46. 12.
‖ Or, Chelubai, Chap. 2. 9. or Caleb, Chap. 2. 18.
‖ Or, Haroe, Chap. 2. 52.

THE sonnes of Iudah : * Pharez , Hezron , and ‖ Carmi , and Hur, and Shobal.

2 And ‖ Reaiah , the son of Shobal, begate Iahath and Iahath begate Ahumai, & Lahad. These are the families of the Zorathites.

3 And these *were* of the father of Etam : Iezreel & Ishma, and Idbash : and the name of their sister *was* Hazelelponi.

4 And Penuel the father of Gedor, and Ezer the father of Hushah. These *are* the sonnes of Hur, the first borne of Ephratah, the father of Bethlehem.

* Cha. 2. 24.

5 ¶ And * Ashur the father of Tekoa, had two wiues : Helah, & Naarah.

6 And Naarah bare him Ahusam, and Hepher, and Temeni, and Ahashtari. These *were* the sonnes of Naarah.

7 And the sonnes of Helah *were* : Zereth, and Zoar, and Ethnan.

8 And Coz begate Anub, and Zobebah, and the families of Aharhel, the sonne of Harum.

‖ That is, sorrowfull.

9 ¶ And Iabez was more honourable then his brethren : and his mother called his name ‖ Iabez , saying , Because I bare him with sorrow.

† Heb. If thou wilt, &c.

† Heb. doe me.

10 And Iabez called on the God of Israel , saying , † Oh that thou wouldest blesse mee indeede, and enlarge my coast , and that thine hand might bee with me, and that thou wouldest † keepe mee from euill , that it may not grieue me. And God granted him that which he requested.

11 ¶ And Chelub the brother of Shuah, begate Mehir , which *was* the father of Eshton.

‖ Or, the city of Nahash.

12 And Eshton begate Beth-rapha, and Paseah, and Tehinnah the father of ‖ Ir-nahash. These *are* the men of Rechah.

13 And the sonnes of Kenaz : Othniel, and Saraia : and the sonnes of Othniel, ‖ Hathath.

‖ Or, Hathath, and Meonothai, who begate &c.
‖ Or, inhabitants of the valley.
‖ That is, craftesmen.
‖ Or, Vknaz.

14 And Meonothai begate Ophrah : and Seraiah begate Ioab, the father of the ‖ valley of ‖ Charasim , for they were craftesmen.

15 And the sonnes of Caleb the sonne of Iephunneh : Iru, Elah, and Naam, and the sonnes of Elah, ‖euen Kenaz.

16 And the sonnes of Iehaleleel :

Ziph, and Ziphah, Tiria, and Asareel.

17 And the sonnes of Ezra *were* : Iether, and Mered, and Epher, and Ialon : and she bare Miriam, and Shammai, & Ishbah the father of Eshtemoa.

‖ Or, the Iewesse.

18 And his wife ‖ Iehudiiah bare Iered the father of Gedor, and Heber the father of Socho, and Iekuthiel the father of Zanoah. And these are the sonnes of Bithiah the daughter of Pharaoh, which Mered tooke.

‖ Or, Iehudiiah, mentioned before.

19 And the sonnes of his wife ‖ Hodiah, the sister of Naham the father of Keilah, the Garmite , and Eshtemoa the Maachathite.

20 And the sonnes of Simeon *were* : Amnon, and Rinnah, Ben-hanan, and Tilon. And the sonnes of Ishi *were* : Zoheth, and Ben-zoheth.

* Gen. 38. 1, 5.

21 ¶ The sonnes of Shelah * the sonne of Iudah *were* : Er the father of Lecah, and Laadah the father of Mareshah, and the families of the house of them that wrought fine linnen, of the house of Ashbea.

22 And Iokim, and the men of Chozeba, and Ioash, and Saraph , who had the dominion in Moab, & Iashubi Lehem. And these are ancient things.

23 These *were* the Potters, and those that dwelt amongst plants and hedges. There they dwelt with the king for his worke.

‖ Or, Iemuel, Gen. 46. 10. Exod. 6. 15.

24 ¶ The sonnes of Simeon *were* : ‖ Nemuel, and Iamin, Iarib, Zerah, *and* Shaul :

25 Shallum his sonne : Mibsam his sonne : Mishma his sonne.

26 And the sonnes of Mishma : Hamuel his sonne , Zacchur his sonne, Shimei his sonne.

27 And Shimei *had* sixteene sonnes, and six daughters, but his brethren had not many children, neither did all their family multiply † like to the children of Iudah.

† Heb. vnto.

* Iosh. 19.

28 And they dwelt at * Beer-sheba, and Moladah, and Hazar-shual,

29 And at ‖ Bilha, and at Ezem, and at ‖ Tolad,

‖ Or, Bela, Iosh. 19. 3.
‖ Or, Eltolad, Ios. 19.

30 And at Bethuel, and at Hormah, and at Ziklag,

31 And at Beth - marcaboth , and ‖ Hazar- Susim, and at Bethbirei, and at Shaaraim. These were their cities, vnto the reigne of Dauid.

‖ Or, Hazar Susa, Iosh. 19. 5.

32 And their villages *were* : ‖ Etam, and Ain, Rimmon, and Tochen, and Ashan, fiue cities.

‖ Or, Ether Iosh. 19. 7.

33 And

‖ Or, Baa-
ath-Beer,
Iosh. 19. 8.
‖ Or, as they
diuided
themselues
by nations a-
mong them.

33 And all their villages that *were* round about the same cities, vnto ‖ Baal. These were their habitations, and their ‖genealogie:

34 And Meshobab, and Iamlech, and Ioshah the sonne of Amashiah,

35 And Ioel, and Iehu the sonne of Iosibia, the sonne of Seraia, the sonne of Asiel,

36 And Elioenai, and Iaakobah, and Iesohaiah, and Asaiah, and Adiel, and Iesimiel, and Benaiah,

37 And Ziza the sonne of Shiphi, the sonne of Allon, the sonne of Iedaia, the sonne of Shimri, the sonne of Shemaiah.

Hebr. com-
ning.

38 These †mentioned by *their* names, *were* Princes in their families, and the house of their fathers increased greatly.

39 ¶ And they went to the entrance of Gedor, euen vnto the East side of the valley, to seeke pasture for their flocks.

40 And they found fat pasture and good, and the land *was* wide, and quiet, and peaceable: for *they* of Ham had dwelt there of old.

41 And these written by name, came in the dayes of Hezekiah king of Iudah, and smote their tents, and the habitations that were found there, and destroyed them vtterly vnto this day, and dwelt in their roomes: because *there was* pasture there for their flocks.

42 And *some* of them, *euen* of the sonnes of Simeon, fiue hundred men, went to mount Seir, hauing for their captaines Pelatiah, and Neariah, and Rephaiah, and Vzziel, the sonnes of Ishi.

43 And they smote the rest of the Amalekites that were escaped, and dwelt there vnto this day.

CHAP. V.

1 The line of Reuben (who lost his birthright) vnto the captiuitie. 9 Their habitation and conquest of the Hagarites. 11 The chiefe men, and habitations of Gad. 18 The number and conquest of Reuben, Gad, and the halfe of Manasseh. 23 The habitations and chiefe men of that halfe tribe. 25 Their captiuitie for their sinne.

* Gen. 35.
22. and 49.
4.

OW the sonnes of Reuben the first borne of Israel, (for *hee was* the first borne, but, forasmuch as he defiled his fathers bed, his birthright was giuen vnto the sonnes of Ioseph the sonne of Israel: and the genealogie is not to be reckoned after the birthright.

2 For *Iudah preuailed aboue his brethren, and of him came the *chiefe ‖rulers, but the birthright was *Iosephs.

3 The *sonnes, *I say,* of Reuben the first borne of Israel were: Hanoch, and Pallu, Ezron, and Carmi.

4 The sonnes of Ioel: Shemaiah his sonne: Gog his sonne: Shimei his sonne:

5 Micah his son: Reaia his sonne: Baal his sonne.

6 Beerah his sonne: whom ‖ Tilgath-pilneser king of Assyria, carried away *captiue:* He *was* Prince of the Reubenites.

7 And his brethren by their families (when the genealogie of their generations was reckoned) *were* the chiefe, Ieiel, and Zechariah,

8 And Bela the sonne of Azah, the sonne of ‖Shema, the sonne of Ioel, who dwelt in *Aroer, euen vnto Nebo, and Baalmeon.

9 And Eastward he inhabited vnto the entring in of the wildernes, from the riuer Euphrates: because their cattell were multiplied in the land of Gilead.

10 And in the dayes of Saul, they made warre with the Hagarites, who fell by their hand: and they dwelt in their tents †throughout all the East *land* of Gilead.

11 ¶ And the children of Gad dwelt ouer against them, in the land of *Bashan vnto Salchah.

12 Ioel the chiefe, and Shapham the next: and Iaanai, and Shaphat in Bashan.

13 And their brethren of the house of their fathers, *were:* Michael, and Meshullam, and Sheba, and Iorai, and Iachan, and Zia, and Heber, seuen.

14 These are the children of Abihail the sonne of Huri, the sonne of Iaroah, the sonne of Gilead, the sonne of Michael, the sonne of Ieshishai, the sonne of Iahdo, the sonne of Buz:

15 Ahi the sonne of Abdiel, the sonne of Guni, chiefe of the house of their fathers.

16 And they dwelt in Gilead in Bashan, and in her townes, and in all the Suburbs of *Sharon, vpon †their borders.

* Gen. 49.
9, 10.
* Mich. 5. 2.
matth. 2. 6.
‖ Or, Prince.

* Gen. 46.
9. exod. 6.
14. num. 26.
5.

‖ Or, Tig-
lath-pilne-
ser, 2. king.
15. 29. and
16. 7.

‖ Or, Shema-
iah, ver. 4.
* Iosh. 13.
15, 16.

† Hebr. vpon
all the face
of the East.
* Iosh. 13.
11.

* Chap. 27.
29.
† Hebr. their
goings forth.

17 All these were reckoned by genealogies in the dayes of Iotham *king of Iudah, and in the dayes of Ieroboam king of Israel.

2. Kings 15. 5, 32.

18 ¶ The sonnes of Reuben, and the Gadites, and halfe the tribe of Manasseh, of † valiant men, men able to beare buckler and sword, and to shoote with bow, and skilfull in warre, *were* foure and fourtie thousand, seuen hundred and threescore, that went out to the warre.

† Heb. sons of valour.

19 And they made warre with the Hagarites, with *Ietur, and Nephish, and Nodab.

Gen. 25. 15.

20 And they were helped against them, and the Hagarites were deliuered into their hand, and all that *were* with them: for they cried to God in the battell, and he was intreated of them, because they put their trust in him.

21 And they †tooke away their cattell: of their camels fiftie thousand, and of sheepe two hundred and fiftie thousand, and of asses two thousand, and of †men an hundred thousand.

† Heb. led captiue.

† Heb. soules of men, as num. 31. 35.

22 For there fell downe many slaine, because the warre *was* of God. And they dwelt in their steads vntil the captiuity.

23 ¶ And the children of the halfe tribe of Manasseh dwelt in the lande : they increased from Bashan vnto Baal-hermon, and Senir, and vnto mount Hermon.

24 And these *were* the heads of the house of their fathers, euen Epher, and Ishi, & Eliel, and Azriel, and Ieremiah, and Hodauiah, and Iahdiel, mightie men of valour, †famous men, & heads of the house of their fathers.

† Hebr. men of names.

25 ¶ And they transgressed against the God of their fathers, and went *a whoring after the Gods of the people of the land, whome God destroyed before them.

2. King. 17. 7.

26 And the God of Israel stirred vp the spirit of * Pul king of Assyria, and the spirit of Tilgath-pilneser king of Assyria, and he caried them away (euen the Reubenites, and the Gadites, and the halfe tribe of Manasseh:) & brought them vnto *Halah, and Habor, and Hara, and to the riuer Gozan, vnto this day.

2. Kings 15. 19.

2. King. 17. 6.

CHAP. VI.

1 The sonnes of Leui. 4 The line of the Priests vnto the captiuitie. 16 The families of Gershom, Merari, and Kohath. 49 The office of Aaron and his line vnto Ahimaaz. 54 The cities of the Priests and Leuites.

THe sonnes of Leui : *‖ Gershon, Kohath & Merari.

2 And the sonnes of Kohath : Amram, Izahar, & Hebron, & Vzziel.

Gen. 46. 11. exod. 6. 17.
‖ Or, Gershom, ver. 1.

3 And the children of Amram : Aaron, and Moses, and Miriam. The sonnes also of Aaron : *Nadab, and Abihu, Eleazar, and Ithamar.

Leuit. 10. 1.

4 ¶ Eleazar begate Phinehas, Phinehas begate Abishua.

5 And Abishua begate Bukki, and Bukki begate Vzzi,

6 And Vzzi begate Zerahiah, and Zerahiah begate Meraioth,

7 Meraioth begate Amariah, and Amariah begate Ahitub,

8 And *Ahitub begate Zadok, and Zadok begate Ahimaaz,

2. Sam. 1 27.

9 And Ahimaaz begate Azariah, and Azariah begate Iohanan,

10 And Iohanan begate Azariah, (hee it *is* that executed the Priests office, in †the *temple that Solomon built in Ierusalem)

† Hebr. in the house.
2. Chron. 3. 1. king. (

11 And Azariah begate Amariah, and Amariah begate Ahitub,

12 And Ahitub begate Zadok, and Zadok begate ‖Shallum,

‖ Or, Meshullam. 1. chro. 9. 1

13 And Shallum begate Hilkiah, and Hilkiah begate Azariah,

14 And Azariah begate * Seraiah, and Seraiah begate Iehozadak,

Nehem. 11. 11.

15 And Iehozadak went *into captiuitie,* *when the LORD caried away Iudah and Ierusalem by the hand of Nebuchad-nezzar.

2. Kings 25. 18.

16 ¶ The sonnes of Leui : *‖ Gershom, Kohath, and Merari.

Exod. 6. 17.
‖ Or, Gershon, ver. 1.

17 And these *be* the names of the sonnes of Gershom : Libni, & Shimei.

18 And the sonnes of Kohath *were :* Amram, and Izhar, and Hebron, and Vzziel.

19 The sonnes of Merari : Mahli, and Mushi. And these *are* the families of the Leuites, according to their fathers.

20 Of Gershom : Libni his sonne, Iahath his sonne, * Zimmah his sonne,

Vers. 42.

21 ‖Ioah his sonne, ‖Iddo his sonne, Zerah his sonne, Ieaterai his sonne,

‖ Or, Ethan ver. 2.
‖ Or, Adaia ver. 41.

22 The sonnes of Kohath : ‖Amminadab his sonne, Korah his sonne, Assir his sonne,

‖ Or, Izahar, ver. 2, 18.

23 Elkanah

23 Elkanah his sonne, and Ebiasaph his sonne, and Assir his sonne,

24 Tahath his sonne, Vriel his sonne, Vzziah his sonne, and Shaul his sonne.

See 35. & 6. verses.

25 And the sonnes of Elkanah : * Amasai, and Ahimoth.

Or Zuph, . Sam. 1. 1.

26 As for Elkanah : the sonnes of Elkanah, ||Zophai his sonne, and Nahath his sonne,

27 Eliab his sonne, Ieroham his sonne, Elkanah his sonne.

Called also Ioel, ver. 33. § 1. Sam. . 2.

28 And the sonnes of Samuel : the first borne ||Vashni, and Abiah.

29 The sonnes of Merari : Mahli, Libni his sonne, Shimei his sonne, Vzza his sonne,

30 Shimea his sonne, Haggiah his sonne, Asaiah his sonne.

Chap. 16. 1.

31 And these *are they*, whom Dauid set ouer the seruice of song in the house of the Lord, after that the * Arke had rest.

32 And they ministred before the dwelling place of the Tabernacle of the Congregation, with singing, vntill Solomon had built the house of the LORD in Ierusalem : and then they waited on their office, according to their order.

Heb. stood.

33 And these are they that †waited with their children of the sonnes of the Kohathites, Heman a singer : the sonne of Ioel, the sonne of Shemuel,

34 The sonne of Elkanah, the sonne of Ieroham, the sonne of Eliel, the sonne of Toah,

35 The sonne of Zuph, the sonne of Elkanah, the sonne of Mahath, the sonne of Amasai,

36 The sonne of Elkanah, the sonne of Ioel, the sonne of Azariah, the sonne of Zephaniah,

37 The sonne of Tahath, the sonne of Assir, the sonne of *Ebiasaph, the sonne of Korah,

Exod. 6. 24.

38 The sonne of Izhar, the sonne of Kohath, the sonne of Leui, the sonne of Israel.

39 And his brother Asaph (who stood on his right hand) *euen* Asaph the sonne of Berachiah, the sonne of Shimea,

40 The sonne of Michael, the sonne of Baasiah, the sonne of Melchiah,

41 The sonne of Ethni, the sonne of Zerah, the sonne of Adaiah,

42 The sonne of Ethan, the sonne of Zimmah, the sonne of Shimei,

43 The sonne of Iahath, the sonne

of Gershom, the sonne of Leui.

44 And their brethren the sonnes of Merari, *stood* on the left hand: Ethan the sonne of ||Kishi, the sonne of Abdi, the sonne of Malluch,

||Or, Kushaiah, chap. 15. 17.

45 The sonne of Hashabiah, the sonne of Amaziah, the sonne of Hilkiah,

46 The sonne of Amzi, the sonne of Bani, the sonne of Shamer,

47 The sonne of Mahli, the sonne of Mushi, the sonne of Merari, the sonne of Leui.

48 Their brethren also the Leuits were appointed vnto all maner of seruice of the Tabernacle of the house of God.

49 ¶ But Aaron, and his sonnes offered *vpon the altar of the burnt offering, and * on the altar of incense, *and were appointed* for all the worke of the place most holy, and to make an atonement for Israel, according to all that Moses the seruant of God had commaunded.

* Leuit. 1. 9.
* Exod. 30. 7.

50 And these *are* the sonnes of Aaron : Eleazar his sonne, Phinehas his sonne, Abishua his sonne,

51 Bukki his sonne, Vzzi his sonne, Zerahiah his sonne,

52 Meraioth his sonne, Amariah his sonne, Ahitub his sonne,

53 Zadok his sonne, Ahimaaz his sonne.

54 ¶ Now these *are* their dwelling places, throughout their castels in their coasts, of the sonnes of Aaron, of the families of the Kohathites : for theirs was the lot.

55 And they gaue them Hebron in the land of Iudah, and the suburbes thereof round about it.

56 But the fields of the citie, and the villages thereof, they gaue to Caleb the sonne of Iephunneh.

57 And to the sonnes of Aaron they gaue the cities of Iudah, namely Hebron the citie of refuge, and Libna with her suburbes, and Iattir and Eshtemoa, with their suburbes,

58 And ||Hilen with her suburbes, Debir with her suburbes,

||Or Holon, Iosh. 21. 15.

59 And ||Ashan with her suburbes, and Beth-shemesh with her suburbes.

||Or Ain, Iosh. 21. 16.

60 And out of the tribe of Beniamin, Geba with her suburbes, and ||Alemeth with her suburbes, Anathoth with her suburbes. All their cities throughout their families *were* thirteene cities.

||Or Almon, Iosh. 21. 18.

61 And

61 And vnto the sonnes of Kohath, which were left of the family of that tribe, *were cities giuen* out of the halfe tribe, *namely* out of the halfe *tribe* of Manasseh, by *lot, ten cities.

* Iosh. 21. 5

62 And to the sonnes of Gershom throughout their families, out of the tribe of Issachar, and out of the tribe of Asher, and out of the tribe of Naphtali, and out of the tribe of Manasseh in Bashan, thirteene cities.

63 Vnto the sonnes of Merari *were giuen* by lot, throughout their families, out of the tribe of Reuben, and out of the tribe of Gad, and out of the tribe of Zebulun, * twelue cities.

* Iosh. 21. 7, 34.

64 And the children of Israel gaue to the Leuites these cities, with their suburbs.

65 And they gaue by lot, out of the tribe of the children of Iudah, and out of the tribe of the children of Simeon, and out of the tribe of the children of Beniamin, these cities, which are called by *their* names.

66 And the *residue* of the families of the sonnes of Kohath, had cities of their coasts, out of the tribe of Ephraim.

* Iosh. 21. 21.

67 * And they gaue vnto them *of* the cities of refuge, Shechem in mount Ephraim, with her suburbs: *they gaue* also Gezer with her suburbs,

68 And Iokmeam with her suburbs, & Beth-horon with her suburbs,

69 And Aialon with her suburbs, and Gath-rimmon with her suburbs.

70 And out of the halfe tribe of Manasseh, Aner with her suburbs, and Bileam with her suburbs, for the family of the remnant of the sonnes of Kohath.

71 Vnto the sonnes of Gershom, *were giuen* out of the family of the halfe tribe of Manasseh, Golan in Bashan with her suburbs, and Ashtaroth with her suburbs.

72 And out of the tribe of Issachar, Kedesh with her suburbs, Daberath with her suburbs,

73 And Ramoth with her suburbs, and Anem with her suburbs.

74 And out of the tribe of Asher, Mashal with her suburbs, and Abdon with her suburbs,

75 And Hukok with her suburbs, and Rehob with her suburbs.

76 And out of the tribe of Naphtali, Kedesh in Galilee, with her suburbs, and Hammon with her subnrbs, and Kiriathaim with her suburbs.

77 Vnto the rest of the children of Merari *were giuen* out of the tribe of Zebulun, Rimmon with her suburbs, Tabor with her suburbs.

78 And on the other side Iorden by Iericho, on the East side of Iorden, *were giuen them* out of the tribe of Reuben, ‖ Bezer in the wildernesse with her suburbs, & Iahzah with her suburbs,

‖ *Or, Bozor* Iosh. 21. 38

79 Kedemoth also with her suburbs, & Mephaath with her suburbs.

80 And out of the tribe of Gad, Ramoth in Gilead with her suburbs, and Mahanaim with her suburbs,

81 And Heshbon with her suburbs, and Iazer with her suburbs.

CHAP. VII.

1 The sonnes of Issachar, 6 Of Beniamin, 13 Of Naphtali, 14 Of Manasseh, 20, 24 And of Ephraim. 21 The calamitie of Ephraim by the men of Gath. 23 Beriah is borne. 28 Ephraims habitations. 30 The sonnes of Asher.

NOw the sonnes of Issachar *were*, *Tola, and Puah, Iashub, and Shimron, foure.

* Gen. 46. 13. num. 26. 23.

2 And the sonnes of Tola : Vzzi, and Rephaiah, and Ieriel, and Iahmai, and Iibsam, and Shemuel, heads of their fathers house, *to wit,* of Tola, *they were* valiant men of might in their generations, * whose number *was* in the dayes of Dauid two and twentie thousand and sixe hundred.

* 2. Sam. 24 1, 2.

3 And the sonnes of Vzzi, Izrahiah : and the sonnes of Izrahiah, Michael, and Obadiah, and Ioel, Ishiah, fiue : all of them chiefe men.

4 And with them, by their generations, after the house of their fathers, *were* bands of souldiers for warre, sixe and thirtie thousand men : for they had many wiues and sonnes.

5 And their brethren among all the families of Issachar, *were* men of might, reckoned in all by their genealogies, fourescore and seuen thousand.

6 ¶ *The sonnes* of * Beniamin : Bela, and Becher, and Iediael, three.

* Gen 46. 21.

7 And the sonnes of Bela : Ezbon, and Vzzi, and Vzziel, and Ierimoth, and Iri, fiue, heads of the house of *their* fathers, mightie men of valour, and were reckoned by their genealogies, twentie and two thousand, and thirtie and foure.

8 And the sonnes of Becher : Zemira,

mira, and Ioash, and Eliezer, and Elioenai, and Omri, and Ierimoth, and Abiah, and Anathoth, and Alameth. All these *are* the sonnes of Becher.

9 And the number of them, after their genealogie by their generations, heads of the house of their fathers, mightie men of valour, *was* twentie thousand and two hundred.

10 The sonnes also of Iediael, Bilhan: and the sonnes of Bilhan, Ieush, and Beniamin, and Ehud, and Chenaanah, and Zethan, and Tharshish, and Ahishahar.

11 All these the sonnes of Iediael, by the heads of their fathers, mighty men of valour, *were* seuenteene thousand and two hundred souldiers, fit to goe out for warre *and* battaile.

*r, Iri,
rs. 7.
*r, Ahi-
m. num.
. 38.

12 Shuppim also, and Huppim, the children of || Ir, *and* Hushim, the sonnes of || Aher.

13 ¶ The sonnes of Naphtali, Iahziel, and Guni, and Iezer, and Shallum, the sonnes of Bilhah.

14 ¶ The sonnes of Manasseh: Ashriel, whom shee bare (*but* his concubine the Aramitesse, bare Machir the father of Gilead.

15 And Machir tooke to wife *the sister* of Huppim and Shuppim, whose sisters name was Maachah) and the name of the second *was* Zelophehad : and Zelophehad had daughters.

16 And Maachah the wife of Machir bare a sonne, and shee called his name Peresh, and the name of his brother *was* Sheresh, and his sonnes *were* Vlam and Rakem.

1. Sam. 12
.

17 And the sonnes of Vlam, * Bedan. These *were* the sonnes of Gilead, the sonne of Machir, the sonne of Manasseh.

18 And his sister Hammoleketh bare Ishad, and Abiezer, and Mahalah.

19 And the sonnes of Shemida *were* : Ahian, and Shechem, and Likhi, and Aniam.

20 ¶ And the sonnes of Ephraim : Shuthelah: and Bered his sonne, and Tahath his sonne, and Eladah his sonne, and Tahath his sonne,

21 ¶ And Zabad his sonne, and Shuthelah his sonne, and Ezer, and Elead, whom the men of Gath, that were borne in that land slewe, because they came downe to take away their cattell.

22 And Ephraim their father mourned many dayes, and his brethren came

to comfort him.

23 ¶ And when hee went in to his wife, shee conceiued and bare a sonne, and he called his name, Beriah, because it went euill with his house.

24 (And his daughter was Sherah, who built Bethoron the nether, and the vpper, and Vzzen Sherah.)

25 And Rephah *was* his sonne, also Rezeph, and Telah his sonne, and Tahan his sonne,

26 Laadan his sonne, Amihud his sonne, Elishama his sonne,

27 || Non his sonne, Iehoshua his sonne.

28 ¶ And their possessions and habitations *were*, Bethel, and the townes thereof, and Eastward * Naaran, and Westward Gezer with the † townes thereof, Shechem also and the townes thereof, vnto ||Gaza and the townes thereof.

29 And by the borders of the children of * Manasseh, Bethshean and her townes, Taanach and her townes, * Megiddo and her townes, Dor and her townes. In these dwelt the children of Ioseph the sonne of Israel.

30 ¶ *The sonnes of Asher : Imnah, and Isuah, and Ishuai, and Beriah, and Serah their sister.

31 And the sonnes of Beriah : Heber, and Malchiel, who *is* the father of Birzauith.

32 And Heber begate Iaphlet, and Shomer, and Hotham, and Shuah their sister.

33 And the sonnes of Iaphlet : Pasach, and Bimhal, and Ashuath. These *are* the children of Iaphlet.

34 And the sonnes of Shamer : Ahi, and Rohgah, Iehubbah, and Aram.

35 And the sonne of his brother, Helem : Zophah, and Imna, and Shelesh, and Amal.

36 The sonnes of Zophah : Suah, and Harnepher, and Shual, and Beri, and Imrah :

37 Bezer, and Hod, and Shamma, and Shilshah, and Ithran, and Beera.

38 And the sonnes of Iether : Iephunneh, and Pispa, and Ara.

39 And the sonnes of Vlla : Arah, and Haniel, and Rezia.

40 All these *were* the children of Asher, heads of their fathers house, choice *and* mightie men of valour, chiefe of the princes. And the number throughout the genealogie of them, that were apt to

|| Or, Nun.
numb. 13, 9.

* Iosh. 16. 7
† Hebr.
daughters.
|| Or, A-
dassa, 1.
mac. 7. 45.

* Iosh. 17. 7

* Iosh. 17.
11.

* Gen. 46.
17.

to the warre *and* to battell, was twentie and sixe thousand men.

CHAP. VIII.

1 *The sonnes and chiefe men of Beniamin.* 33 *The stocke of Saul and Ionathan.*

Gene. 46.
21. num. 26.
38.

NOw Beniamin begate *Bela his first borne, Ashbel the second, and Aharah the third,

2 Nohah the fourth, and Rapha the fifth.

Or, Ard,
Gen. 46. 21.

3 And the sonnes of Bela *were:* ||Addar, and Gera, and Abihud,

4 And Abishua, and Naaman, and Ahoah,

Or, Shu-
pham, Num.
26. 39.

5 And Gera, and ||Shephuphan, and Huram.

6 And these are the sonnes of Ehud: these are the heads of the fathers of the inhabitants of Geba, and they re-

Chap. 2.
52.

moued them to *Manahath:

7 And Naaman, and Ahiah, and Gera, he remooued them, and begate Vzza, and Ahihud.

8 And Shaharaim begate *children* in the countrey of Moab. After hee had sent them away: Hushim, and Baara were his wiues.

9 And he begat of Hodesh his wife, Iobab, and Zibia, and Mesha, and Malcham,

10 And Ieuz, and Shachia, and Mirma. These *were* his sonnes, heads of the fathers.

11 And of Hushim he begate Ahitub, and Elpaal.

12 The sonnes of Elpaal: Eber, and Misham, & Shamed, who built Ono, and Lod with the townes thereof.

13 Beriah also and Shema, who *were* heads of the fathers of the inhabitants of Aialon, who droue away the inhabitants of Gath.

14 And Ahio, Shashak, and Ierimoth,

15 And Zebadiah, & Arad, & Ader,

16 And Michael, and Ispah, and Ioha the sonnes of Beriah,

17 And Zebadiah, and Meshullam, and Hezeki, and Heber,

18 Ishmerai also, and Iezliah, and Iobab the sonnes of Elpaal.

19 And Iakim, and Zichri, & Zabdi,

20 And Elienai, and Zilthai, & Eliel,

21 And Adaiah, and Beraiah, and Shimrath, the sonnes of ||Shimhi,

Or, Shema,
vers. 13.

22 And Ishpan, and Heber, & Eliel,

23 And Abdon, and Zichri, and Hanan,

24 And Hananiah, and Elam, and Antothiiah,

25 And Iphedeiah, and Penuel, the sonnes of Shashak,

26 And Shamsherai, and Shehariah, and Athaliah,

27 And Iaresiah, and Eliah, and Zichri the sonnes of Ieroham.

28 These *were* heads of the fathers, by their generations, chiefe *men.* These dwelt in Ierusalem.

Called
hieI, 1. C
9. 35.
Chap.
35.

29 And at Gibeon *dwelt* the ||father of Gibeon, (whose *wiues name was* Maachah:)

30 And his first borne sonne Abdon, and Zur, and Kish, and Baal, & Nadab,

Or, Za
riah, 1.
9. 37.

31 And Gidor, & Ahio, and ||Zacher,

Or, Shi
meam, c
38.
1. Sam.
51.

32 And Mikloth begate ||Shimeah. And these also dwelt with their brethren in Ierusalem, ouer against them.

33 ¶ And *Ner begate Kish, and Kish begate Saul, and Saul begate Ionathan, and Malchishua, and Abinadab, and ||Eshbaal.

Or, Ish
sheth, 2.
Sam. 2.
Or, Me
phiboshe
2. Sam.

34 And the sonne of Ionathan *was* ||Meribbaal, and Meribbaal begate Micah.

Or, Ta
rea, c. 9.

35 And the sonnes of Micah *were* Pithon, and Melech, and ||Tarea, and Ahaz.

36 And Ahaz begat Iehoadah, and Iehoadah begate Alemeth, and Asmaueth, and Zimri, and Zimri begate Moza,

37 And Moza begate Binea: Rapha *was* his sonne, Elasa his sonne, Azel his sonne:

38 And Azel *had* sixe sonnes, whose names *are* these, Azrikam, Bocheru, and Ishmael, and Sheariah, and Obadiah, and Hanan. All these *were* the sonnes of Azel.

39 And the sonnes of Eshek his brother *were* Vlam his first-borne, Iehush the second, and Eliphelet the third.

40 And the sonnes of Vlam were mighty men of valour, archers, and had many sonnes, and sonnes sonnes, an hundred and fiftie. All these are of the sonnes of Beniamin.

CHAP. IX.

1 *The originall of Israels and Iudahs genealogies.* 2 *The Israelites,* 10 *the Priests,* 14 *and the Leuites, with Nethinims which dwelt in Ierusalem.* 27 *The charge of certaine Leuites.* 35 *The stocke of Saul and Ionathan.*

So

O all Israel were reckoned by genealogies, & behold, they were written in the booke of the Kings of Israel and Iudah, *who* were caried away to Babylon for their transgression.

2 ¶ Now the first inhabitants *that dwelt* in their possessions, in their cities, *were* the Israelites, the Priests, Leuits, and the Nethinims.

3 And in *Ierusalem dwelt of the children of Iudah, and of the children of Beniamin, and of the children of Ephraim, and Manasseh.

4 Vthai the sonne of Amihud, the sonne of Omri, the sonne of Imri, the sonne of Bani, of the children of Pharez the sonne of Iudah.

5 And of the Shilonites : Asaiah the first borne, and his sonnes.

6 And of the sonnes of Zerah : Ieuel, and their brethren, sixe hundred and ninetie.

7 And of the sonnes of Beniamin : Sallu the sonne of Meshullam, the sonne of Hodauiah, the sonne of Hasenuah :

8 And Ibneiah the sonne of Ieroham, and Elah the sonne of Vzzi, the sonne of Michri, and Meshullam the sonne of Shephatiah, the sonne of Reuel, the sonne of Ibniiah,

9 And their brethren, according to their generations, nine hundred and fiftie and sixe. All these men *were* chiefe of the fathers in the house of their fathers.

10 ¶ And of the Priests : Iedaiah, and Iehoiarib, and Iachin,

11 And Azariah the sonne of Hilkiah, the sonne of Meshullam, the sonne of Zadok, the sonne of Meraioth, the sonne of Ahitub the ruler of the house of God.

12 And Adaiah the sonne of Ieroham, the sonne of Passhur, the sonne of Malchiiah, and Maasia the sonne of Adiel, the sonne of Iahzerah, the sonne of Meshullam, the sonne of Meshillemith, the sonne of Immer.

13 And their brethren, heads of the house of their fathers, a thousand, and seuen hundred and threescore, very †able men for the worke of the seruice of the house of God.

14 And of the Leuites : Shemaiah the sonne of Hasshub, the sonne of Azrikam, the sonne of Hashabiah, of the sonnes of Merari.

15 And Bakbakkar, Heresh, and Galal : and Mattaniah the sonne of Micah, the sonne of Zichri, the sonne of Asaph.

16 And Obadiah the sonne of Shemaiah, the sonne of Galal, the sonne of Ieduthun : and Berechiah the sonne of Asa, the sonne of Elkanah, that dwelt in the villages of the Netophathites.

17 And the Porters *were* Shallum, and Akkub, and Talmon, and Ahiman, and their brethren : Shallum *was* the chiefe.

18 (Who hitherto *waited* in the kings gate Eastward) they were Porters in the companies of the children of Leui.

19 And Shallum the sonne of Kore, the sonne of Ebiasaph, the sonne of Korah, and his brethren (of the house of his father) the Korahites, *were* ouer the worke of the seruice, keepers of the †gates of the Tabernacle : and their fathers being ouer the hoste of the LORD, *were* keepers of the entrie.

20 And Phinehas the sonne of Eleazar was the ruler ouer them in time past, *and* the LORD *was* with him.

21 *And* Zechariah the sonne of Meshelemiah, *was* porter of the doore of the Tabernacle of the Congregation.

22 All these which were chosen to be porters in the gates, *were* two hundred and twelue. These were reckoned by their genealogie in their villages : whom Dauid and Samuel the Seer, †did ordeine in their ‖set office.

23 So they and their children *had* the ouersight of the gates of the house of the LORD, *namely*, the house of the Tabernacle, by wards.

24 In foure quarters were the porters : toward the East, West, North, and South.

25 And their brethren, *which were* in their villages, *were* to come after seuen dayes, from time to time with them.

26 For these Leuites, the foure chiefe porters, were in their ‖set office, and were ouer the ‖chambers and treasuries of the house of God.

27 ¶ And they lodged round about the house of God, because the charge was vpon them, and the opening thereof euery morning, perteined to them.

28 And *certaine* of them had the charge of the ministring vessels, that they should †bring them in and out by tale.

29 *Some* of them also *were* appointed to ouersee the vessels, and all the ‖instruments of the Sanctuarie, and the fine

Marginal notes (left):
ehem.

Heb. migh-men of lour.

Marginal notes (right):
† Heb. thresholds.

† Heb. founded.
‖ Or, trust.

‖ Or, trust.
‖ Or, storehouses.

† Heb. bring them in by tale, and carie them out by tale.
‖ Or, vessels.

fine floure, and the wine, and the oyle, and the frankincense, and the spices.

30 And *some* of the sonnes of the Priests made * the oyntment of the spices.

* Exod. 30. 23.

31 And Mattithiah, one of the Leuites (who was the first borne of Shallum the Korahite) had the ||set office ouer the things that were made ||in the pannes.

|| Or, trust.

|| Or, on flat plates, or, slices.

32 And *other* of their brethren of the sonnes of the Kohathites, *were* ouer the † Shew-bread to prepare *it* euery Sabbath.

† Heb. bread of ordering.

33 And these *are* the singers, chiefe of the fathers of the Leuites, who *remayning* in the chambers, *were* free: for † they were imployed in that worke, day and night.

† Hebr. vpon them.

34 These chiefe fathers of the Leuites, were chiefe throughout their generations ; these dwelt at Ierusalem.

35 ¶ And in Gibeon dwelt the father of Gibeon, Iehiel, whose wiues name *was* * Maacha :

ᵃ Chap. 8. 29.

36 And his first borne sonne Abdon, then Zur, and Kish, and Baal, and Ner, and Nadab,

37 And Gedor, and Ahio, and Zechariah, and Mikloth.

38 And Mikloth begate Shimeam: and they also dwelt with their brethren at Ierusalem, ouer against their brethren.

39 * And Ner begat Kish, and Kish begate Saul, and Saul begate Ionathan, and Malchishua, and Abinadab, and Eshbaal.

* I. Chro. 8. 33.

40 And the sonne of Ionathan was Meribbaal : and Meribbaal begate Micah.

41 And the sonnes of Micah were Pithon, and Melech, and Tahrea, *and Ahaz*.

* Chap. 8. 35.

42 And Ahaz begate Iarah, and Iarah begate Alemeth, & Azmaueth, and Zimri : and Zimri begate Moza,

43 And Moza begate Binea : and Rephaiah his son, Eleasah his sonne, Azel his sonne.

44 And Azel had six sonnes, whose names are these : Azrikam, Bocheru, and Ismael, and Sheariah, and Obadiah, and Hanan. These *were* the sonnes of Azel.

CHAP. X.

1 Sauls ouerthrow and death. 8 The Philistines triumph ouer Saul. 11 The kindnes of

Iabesh Gilead, towards Saul and his sonnes. 13 Sauls sinne for which the kingdome was translated from him to Dauid.

Owe * the Philistines fought against Israel, and the men of Israel fled from before the Philistines, and fell downe ||slaine in mount Gilboa.

* 1. Sam 1, 2.

|| Or, wo ded.

2 And the Philistines followed hard after Saul, and after his sonnes, and the Philistines slew Ionathan, and ||Abinadab, and Malchishua, the sonnes of Saul.

|| Or, Ie 1. Sam. 49.

3 And the battell went sore against Saul, and the † archers † hit him, and he was wounded of the archers.

† Hebr. ters wi bowes. † Hebr him. -

4 Then saide Saul to his armour bearer, Draw thy sword, and thrust me through therewith, lest these vncircumcised come, and ||abuse mee : but his armour bearer would not, for he was sore afraid. So Saul tooke a sword, and fell vpon it.

|| Or, m me.

5 And when his armour bearer saw that Saul was dead, hee fell likewise on the sword, and died.

6 So Saul died, and his three sonnes, and all his house died together.

7 And when all the men of Israel that *were* in the valley, saw that they fled, and that Saul and his sonnes were dead : then they forsooke their cities, and fled, and the Philistines came and dwelt in them.

8 ¶ And it came to passe on the morrow, when the Philistines came to strip the slaine, that they found Saul and his sonnes fallen in mount Gilboa.

9 And when they had stripped him, they tooke his head, and his armour, and sent into the land of the Philistines round about, to cary tidings vnto their idoles, and to the people.

10 And they put his armour in the house of their gods, and fastened his head in the temple of Dagon.

11 ¶ And when all Iabesh Gilead heard all that the Philistines had done to Saul :

12 They arose, all the valiant men, and tooke away the body of Saul, and the bodies of his sonnes, and brought them to Iabesh, and buried their bones vnder the oke in Iabesh, and fasted seuen dayes.

13 ¶ So Saul died for his transgression which hee † committed against the LORD, *euen* against the word of the LORD

† Heb. gressed * 1. Sa 23.

Lord which he kept not, and also for asking *counsel* of one that had a familiar spirit, *to enquire *of it*:

14 And enquired not of the Lord: therefore he slew him, and turned the kingdome vnto Dauid the sonne of †Iesse.

CHAP. XI.

1 Dauid by a generall consent is made king at Hebron. 4 Hee winneth the castle of Sion from the Iebusites, by Ioabs valour. 10 A catalogue of Dauids mightie men.

Hen *all Israel gathered themselues to Dauid vn-Hebron, saying, Behold, wee *are* thy bone and thy flesh.

2 And moreouer †in time past, euen *when* Saul was king, thou *wast he* that leddest out and broughtest in Israel: and the Lord thy God said vnto thee, Thou shalt ||feede my people Israel, and thou shalt be ruler ouer my people Israel.

3 Therefore came all the Elders of Israel to the king to Hebron, and Dauid made a couenant with them in Hebron before the Lord, and they annointed Dauid king ouer Israel, according to the word of the Lord, †by *Samuel.

4 ¶ And Dauid & all Israel, *went to Ierusalem, which *is* Iebus, where the Iebusites *were* the inhabitants of the land.

5 And the inhabitants of Iebus said to Dauid, Thou shalt not come hither. Neuerthelesse Dauid tooke the castle of Zion, which *is* the citie of Dauid.

6 And Dauid said, Whosoeuer smiteth the Iebusites first, shall be †chiefe, and captaine. So Ioab the sonne of Zeruiah went first vp, and was chiefe.

7 And Dauid dwelt in the castell: therefore they called †it the citie of Dauid.

8 And he built the citie round about, euen from Millo round about : and Ioab †repaired the rest of the citie.

9 So Dauid †waxed greater and greater : for the Lord of hostes *was* with him.

10 ¶ *These also *are* the chiefe of the mightie men, whom Dauid had, who ||strenthened themselues with him in his kingdome, *and* with all Israel, to make him king according to the word of the Lord, concerning Israel.

11 And this *is* the number of the mightie men, whom Dauid had : Iashobeam ||an Hachmonite, the chiefe of the captaines : he lift vp his speare against three hundred, slaine *by him* at one time.

12 And after him *was* Eleazar the sonne of Dodo the Ahohite, who was one of the three mighties.

13 He was with Dauid at ||Pasdammim ; and there the Philistines were gathered together to battell ; where was a parcell of ground full of barley, and the people fled from before the Philistines.

14 And they ||set themselues in the middest of that parcell, and deliuered it, and slue the *Philistines, & the Lord saued them by a great ||deliuerance.

15 ¶ Now ||three of the thirtie captaines, went downe to the rocke of Dauid, into the caue of Adullam, and the host of the Philistines encamped in the valley of Rephaim.

16 And Dauid *was* then in the hold, and the Philistines garison *was* then at Bethlehem.

17 And Dauid longed and said, Oh that one would giue me drinke of the water of the well of Bethlehem, that *is* at the gate.

18 And the three brake through the host of the Philistines, and drew water out of the well of Bethlehem, that *was* by the gate, and tooke *it* and brought *it* to Dauid. But Dauid would not drink of it, but powred it out to the Lord,

19 And said, My God forbid it mee, that I should doe this thing. Shall I drinke the blood of these men, †that haue put their liues in ieopardie ? for with *the ieopardie of* their liues, they brought it : therfore he would not drink it. These things did these three mightiest.

20 ¶ And Abishai the brother of Ioab, he was chiefe of the three. For lifting vp his speare against three hundred, he slew *them*, and had a name among the three.

21 *Of the three, hee was more honourable then the two, for he was their captaine ; howbeit, he attained not to the *first* three.

22 Benaiah the sonne of Iehoiada, the sonne of a valiant man of Kabzeel, †who had done many acts : he slue two Lyon-like men of Moab, also he went downe and slue a Lyon in a pit in a snowy day.

23 And

.Sam. 28.

Heb. Isai.

2. Sam. 5.

Heb. both sterday ad the third ay.

Or, rule.

Heb. by the nd of.
1. Sam. 16.
.
2. Sam. 5. 6

Heb. head.

That is, ion, 2. Sam 7.

Heb. reuied.
Heb. wēht going and creasing.

2. Sam. 23.

Or, held rongly with im.

|| Or, Sonne of Hach-moni.

|| Or, Ephes-dammim, 1. Sam. 17. 1

|| Or, stood.

* 2. Sam. 23 13.
|| Or, salua-tion.
|| Or, three captaines ouer the thirtie.

† Heb. with their liues?

* 2. Sam. 23. 19. &c.

† Heb. great of deeds.

†Heb. a man of measure.

23 And he slue an Egyptian, †a man of *great* stature, fiue cubits high, and in the Egyptians hand *was* a speare like a weauers beame: and he went downe to him with a staffe, and pluckt the speare out of the Egyptians hand, and slue him with his owne speare.

24 These things did Benaiah the sonne of Iehoiada, and had the name among the three mighties.

25 Behold, hee was honourable among the thirtie, but attained not to the *first* three: and Dauid set him ouer his guard.

26 ¶ Also the valiant men of the armies *were* Asahel the brother of Ioab, Elhanan the sonne of Dodo of Bethlehem.

‖ Or, Harodite, 2. Sam. 23. 25.

27 Shammoth the ‖ Harorite, Helez the Pelonite,

28 Ira the sonne of Ikkesh the Tekoite, Abiezer the Antothite,

29 Sibbecai the Hushathite, Ilai the Ahohite,

30 Maharai the Netophathite, Heled the sonne of Baanah the Netophathite,

31 Ithai the sonne of Ribai of Gibeah, *that perteined* to the children of Beniamin, Benaiah the Pirathonite,

32 Hurai of the brookes of Gaash, Abiel the Arbathite,

33 Azmaueth the Baharumite, Elihaba the Shaalbonite,

34 The sonnes of Hashem the Gizonite: Ionathan the sonne of Shageh the Hararite,

35 Ahiham the sonne of Sacar the Hararite, Eliphal the sonne of Vr,

36 Hepher the Mecherathite, Ahiah the Pelonite,

37 Hezro the Carmelite, Naarai the sonne of Ezbai,

38 Ioel the brother of Nathan, Mibhar the ‖ sonne of Haggeri,

‖ Or, the Haggerite.

39 Zelek the Ammonite, Naharai the Berothite, the armour bearer of Ioab the sonne of Zeruiah,

40 Ira the Ithrite, Gareb the Ithrite,

41 Vriah the Hittite, Zabad the sonne of Ahlai,

42 Adina the sonne of Shiza the Reubenite, a captaine of the Reubenites, and thirtie with him,

43 Hanan the sonne of Maacah, and Ioshaphat the Mithnite,

44 Vzzia the Ashterathite, Shama and Iehiel the sonnes of Hothan the Aroerite,

45 Iediael the ‖ sonne of Zimri, and Ioha his brother, the Tizite,

‖ Or, Zimrite.

46 Eliel the Mahauite, and Ieribai, and Ioshauiah the sonnes of Elnaan, and Ithmah the Moabite,

47 Eliel, and Obed, and Iasiel the Mesobaite.

CHAP XII.

1 The companies that came to Dauid at Ziklag.
23 The armies that came to him at Hebron.

* 1. Sam 27. 1.
†Heb. be yet shut

Ow *these are they* that came to Dauid to Ziklag †while hee yet kept himselfe close, because of Saul the sonne of Kish: and they *were* among the mighty men, helpers of the warre.

2 They were armed with bowes, and could vse both the right hand and the left, in *hurling* stones, and *shooting* arrowes out of a bow, *euen* of Sauls brethren of Beniamin.

3 The chiefe *was* Ahiezer, then Ioash the sonnes of ‖ Shemaah the Gibeathite, and Ieziel, and Pelet, the sonnes of Azmaueth, and Berachah, and Iehu the Antothite,

‖ Or, Hamaa.

4 And Ismaiah the Gibeonite, a mightie man among the thirtie, and ouer the thirtie, and Ieremiah, and Iahaziel, and Iohanan, and Iosabad the Gederathite,

5 Eleuzai, and Ierimoth, and Bealiah, and Shemariah, and Shephatiah the Haruphite,

6 Elkanah, and Iesiah, and Azariel, and Ioezer, and Iashobeam, the Korhites,

7 And Ioelah, and Zebadiah the sonnes of Ieroam of Gedor.

8 And of the Gadites there separated themselues vnto Dauid, into the hold to the wildernesse, men of might, *and* men †of warre, fit for the battel, that could handle shield and buckler, whose faces *were* like the faces of Lyons, and were †as swift as the Roes vpon the mountaines:

†Heb. of hoste.

†Heb. as Roes vpon the mountaines to make haste.

9 Ezer the first, Obadiah the second, Eliab the third,

10 Mashmannah the fourth, Ieremiah the fift,

11 Atthai the sixt, Eliel the seuenth,

12 Iohanan the eighth, Elzabad the ninth,

13 Ieremiah the tenth, Machbanai the eleuenth.

14 These *were* of the sonnes of Gad, captaines

*r, one that
as least
uld resist
a hundred,
nd the grea-
st a thou-
nd.

Heb. filled
er.
Iosh. 3. 15.

Heb. before
em.

Heb. be one

Or, vio-
nce.

Heb. the
pirit clo-
ed Ama-
i.

1. Sam.
9. 4.
Heb. on our
eads.

Or, with a
and.

Or, cap-
taines, or,
nen,
Heb. heads.

Or, prepa-
red.

captaines of the hoste : ||one of the least was ouer an hundred, and the greatest, ouer a thousand.

15 These *are* they that went ouer Iorden in the first moneth, when it had †ouerflowen all his *bankes, and they put to flight all them of the valleis, *both* toward the East, and toward the West.

16 And there came of the children of Beniamin, and Iudah, to the hold vnto Dauid.

17 And Dauid went out †to meete them, and answered and sayd vnto them : If yee bee come peaceably vnto me to helpe me, mine heart shall †be knit vnto you : but if yee be come to betray me to mine enemies, seeing there is no ||wrong in mine hands : the God of our fathers looke thereon, and rebuke *it*.

18 Then †the spirit came vpon Amasai, *who was* chiefe of the captaines, *and he sayd*, Thine *are we*, Dauid, and on thy side, thou sonne of Iesse : Peace, peace be vnto thee, and peace be to thine helpers ; for thy God helpeth thee. Then Dauid receiued them, and made them captaines of the band.

19 And there fell some of Manasseh to Dauid, when he came with the Philistines against Saul to battell, but they helped them not. For the Lords of the Philistines, vpon aduisement, sent him away, saying, *Hee will fall to his master Saul, †to *the ieopardie of* our heads.

20 As he went to Ziklag, there fell to him of Manasseh, Adnah, and Iozabad, and Iediel, and Michael, and Iozabad, and Elihu, and Zilthai, captaines of the thousands that *were* of Manasseh.

21 And they helped Dauid ||against the band *of the Rouers :* for they *were* all mighty men of valour, and were captaines in the hoste.

22 For at *that* time day by day, there came to Dauid to helpe him, vntill it was a great hoste, like the hoste of God.

23 ¶ And these are the numbers of the ||bands, *that* were ready armed to the warre, and came to Dauid to Hebron, to turne the kingdome of Saul to him, according to the word of the Lord.

24 The children of Iudah that bare shield, and speare, *were* sixe thousand, and eight hundred, readie ||armed to the warre.

25 Of the children of Simeon, mighty men of valour for the warre, seuen thousand and one hundred.

26 Of the children of Leui, foure thousand and sixe hundred.

27 And Iehoiada was the leader of the Aaronits, and with him *were* three thousand, and seuen hundred.

28 And Zadok, a young man mightie of valour, and of his fathers house twentie and two captaines.

29 And of the children of Beniamin the †kinred of Saul three thousand : for hitherto †the greatest part of them had kept the ward of the house of Saul.

30 And of the children of Ephraim, twentie thousand, and eight hundred, mightie men of valour, †famous throughout the house of their fathers.

31 And of the halfe tribe of Manasseh, eighteene thousand, which were expressed by name, to come and make Dauid king.

32 And of the children of Issachar, which were men that had vnderstanding of the times, to know what Israel ought to doe : the heads of them were two hundred, and all their brethren were at their commandement.

33 Of Zebulun, such as went foorth to battell, ||expert in warre, with all instruments of warre, fifty thousand, which could ||keepe ranke : They *were* †not of double heart.

34 And of Naphtali a thousand captaines, and with them, with shield and speare, thirtie and seuen thousand.

35 And of the Danites, expert in war, twentie and eight thousand, and sixe hundred.

36 And of Asher, such as went foorth to battell, ||expert in warre, fourtie thousand.

37 And on the other side of Iorden, of the Reubenites, & the Gadites, and of the halfe tribe of Manasseh, with all maner of instruments of warre for the battell, an hundred and twentie thousand.

38 All these men of warre, that could keepe ranke, came with a perfect heart to Hebron, to make Dauid king ouer all Israel : and all the rest also of Israel, *were* of one heart to make Dauid king.

39 And there they were with Dauid three dayes, eating and drinking : for their brethren had prepared for them.

40 Moreouer, they that were nigh them, euen vnto Issachar, and Zebulun,

† Heb. bre-
thren.
† Heb. a
multitude of
them.

† Heb. men
of names.

||Or, rangers
of battell, or
ranged in
battell.
||Or, set the
battell in a-
ray.
† Heb. with-
out a heart
and a heart.

||Or, keeping
their ranke.

lun, and Naphtali brought bread on asses, and on camels, and on mules, and on oxen, *and* ||meat, meale, cakes of figs, and bunches of raisins, and wine, and oyle, and oxen, and sheepe abundantly: for there *was* ioy in Israel.

|| Or, vitaile of meale.

CHAP. XIII.

1 Dauid fetcheth the Arke with great solemnitie from Kiriath-iearim. 9 Vzza being smitten, the Arke is left at the house of Obed-Edom.

Nd Dauid consulted with the captaines of thousands, and hundreds, *and* with euery leader.

2 And Dauid said vnto all the Congregation of Israel, If it *seeme* good vnto you, and that it *be* of the LORD our God, †let vs send abroad vnto our brethren euery where, that are left in all the land of Israel, and with them also to the Priests and Leuites which *are* in †their cities *and* suburbs, that they may gather themselues vnto vs.

† Hebr. let vs breake foorth and send.

† Hebr. in the cities of their suburbs.

3 And let vs †bring againe the Arke of our God to vs: for wee enquired not at it in the dayes of Saul.

† Heb. bring about.

4 And all the Congregation saide, that they would doe so: for the thing was right in the eyes of all the people.

5 So *Dauid gathered all Israel together, from Shihor of Egypt, euen vnto the entring of Hemath, to bring the Arke of God from Kiriath-iearim.

* 1. Sam. 7. 1. 2. sam. 6. 2.

6 And Dauid went vp, and all Israel, to * Baalah, that is, to Kiriath-iearim, which *belonged* to Iudah, to bring vp thence the Arke of God the LORD, that dwelleth betweene the Cherubims, whose name is called on *it*.

* Iosh. 16. 9.

7 And they †caried the Arke of God in a new cart, out of the house of Abinadab: and Vzza, and Ahio draue the cart.

† Heb. made the Arke to ride.

8 And Dauid and all Israel played before God with all *their* might, and with †singing, and with harpes, and with psalteries, and with tymbrels, and with cymbals, and with trumpets.

† Heb. songs.

9 ¶ And when they came vnto the threshing floore of ||Chidon, Vzza put foorth his hand to hold the Arke, for the oxen ||stumbled.

|| Called Nachon, 2. Sam. 6. 6.

|| Or, shooke it.

10 And the anger of the LORD was kindled against Vzza, and hee smote him, because hee put his hand to the *Arke: and there he died before God.

* Num. 4. 15.

11 And Dauid was displeased, be-

cause the LORD had made a breach vpon Vzza; wherefore that place is called † Perez-Vzza, to this day.

† Heb. breach of Vzza.

12 And Dauid was afraide of God that day, saying, How shall I bring the Arke of God home to me?

13 So Dauid †brought not the Arke home to himselfe to the city of Dauid, but caried it aside into the house of Obed-Edom the Gittite.

† Hebr. remooued.

14 And the Arke of God remained with the family of Obed-Edom in his house three moneths. And the LORD blessed * the house of Obed-Edom, and all that he had.

* As chap 26. 5.

CHAP. XIIII.

1 Hirams kindnesse to Dauid. 2 Dauids felicitie in people, wiues and children. 8 His two victories against the Philistines.

Ow *Hiram king of Tyre sent messengers to Dauid, and timber of Cedars, with masons, and carpenters to build him an house.

* 2. Sam. 11. &c.

2 And Dauid perceiued that the LORD had confirmed him king ouer Israel, for his kingdome was lift vp on high, because of his people Israel.

3 ¶ And Dauid tooke †moe wiues at Ierusalem: and Dauid begate moe sonnes and daughters.

† Hebr. ye

4 Now these *are* the names of *his* children which hee had in Ierusalem: Shammua, and Shobab, Nathan, and Solomon,

5 And Ibhar, and Elishua, and Elpalet,

6 And Noga, and Nepheg, and Iaphia,

7 And Elishama, and ||Beeliada, and Elpalet.

|| Or, Eliada 2. Sam. 5. 16.

8 ¶ And when the Philistines heard that * Dauid was anoynted king ouer all Israel, all the Philistines went vp to seeke Dauid: and Dauid heard *of it*, and went out against them.

2. Sam. 5. 17.

9 And the Philistines came & spread themselues in the valley of Rephaim.

10 And Dauid enquired of God, saying, Shall I goe vp against the Philistines? and wilt thou deliuer them into mine hand? And the LORD said vnto him, Go vp, for I will deliuer them into thine hand.

11 So they came vp to Baal-Perazim, and Dauid smote them there. Then Dauid said, God hath broken in vpon

Ieb. that a place of eaches.

2. Sam. 5.

vpon mine enemies by mine hand, like the breaking foorth of waters: therefore they called the name of that place, †Baal-Perazim.

12 And when they had left their gods there, Dauid gaue a commandement, and they were burnt with fire.

13 And the Philistines yet againe spread themselues abroad in the valley.

14 Therfore Dauid enquired againe of God, and God said vnto him, Goe not vp after them, turne away from them, *and come vpon them ouer against the mulbery trees.

15 And it shall bee, when thou shalt heare a sound of going in the tops of the mulbery trees, *that* then thou shalt goe out to battaile: for God is gone foorth before thee, to smite the hoste of the Philistines.

16 Dauid therefore did as God commanded him: and they smote the hoste of the Philistines from Gibeon euen to Gazer.

17 And the fame of Dauid went out into all lands, and the LORD brought the feare of him vpon all nations.

CHAP. XV.

1 *Dauid hauing prepared a place for the Arke, ordereth the Priestes and Leuites to bring it from Obed-Edom.* 25 *Hee perfourmeth the solemnitie thereof with great ioy.* 29 *Michal despiseth him.*

Heb. It is not to cary the Arke of God, but for the Leuites. Num. 4. , 15.

Nd *Dauid* made him houses in the citie of Dauid, and prepared a place for the Arke of God, and pitched for it a tent.

2 Then Dauid sayd, †None ought to carie the *Arke of God, but the Leuites: for them hath the LORD chosen to cary the Arke of God, and to minister vnto him for euer.

3 And Dauid gathered all Israel together to Ierusalem, to bring vp the Arke of the LORD vnto his place, which hee had prepared for it.

4 And Dauid assembled the children of Aaron, and the Leuites.

5 Of the sonnes of Kohath : Vriel the chiefe, and his ||brethren an hundred and twentie.

Or, kinsemen.

6 Of the sonnes of Merari : Asaiah the chiefe, and his brethren two hundred and twentie.

7 Of the sonnes of Gershom: Io-

el the chiefe, and his brethren an hundred and thirtie.

8 Of the sonnes of Elizaphan : Shemaiah the chiefe, and his brethren two hundred.

9 Of the sonnes of Hebron : Eliel the chiefe, and his brethren fourescore.

10 Of the sonnes of Vzziel : Amminadab the chiefe, and his brethren an hundred and twelue.

11 And Dauid called for Zadok and Abiathar the Priests, and for the Leuites, for Vriel, Asaiah and Ioel, Shemaiah, and Eliel, and Amminadab,

12 And said vnto them, Yee *are* the chiefe of the fathers of the Leuites: sanctifie your selues *both* yee and your brethren, that you may bring vp the Arke of the LORD God of Israel, vnto *the place that* I haue prepared for it.

13 For because ye *did it* not at the first, the LORD our God made a breach vpon vs, for that we sought him not after the due order.

14 So the Priestes and the Leuites sanctified themselues to bring vp the Arke of the LORD God of Israel.

15 And the children of the Leuites bare the Arke of God vpon their shoulders, with the staues thereon, as *Moses commanded, according to the word of the LORD.

16 And Dauid spake to the chiefe of the Leuites, to appoint their brethren *to be* the singers with instruments of musicke, Psalteries, and Harpes, and Cymbales, sounding, by lifting vp the voice with ioy.

17 So the Leuites appointed *Heman the sonne of Ioel : and of his brethren, *Asaph the sonne of Berechiah : and of the sonnes of Merari their brethren, *Ethan the sonne of Kushaiah.

18 And with their brethren of the second degree, Zachariah, Ben, and Iaziel, & Shemiramoth, and Iehiel, and Vnni, Eliab, and Benaiah, and Maasiah, and Mattithiah, and Eliphaleh, and Mikniah, and Obed Edom, and Iehiel the Porters.

19 So the Singers, Heman, Asaph, and Ethan, were *appointed* to sound with cymbales of brasse.

20 And Zachariah, and Aziel, and Shemiramoth, and Iehiel, and Vnni, and Eliab, and Maasiah, and Benaiah, with Psalteries on Alamoth.

21 And Mattithiah, and Eliphaleh, and

*Exod. 25. 14.

*Chap. 6. 33.

*Vers. 39.

*Vers. 44.

‖ Or, on the
eight to o-
uersee.
‖ Or, was for
the cariage:
he instructed
about the
cariage.
† Heb. lifting
vp.

and Mikniah, and Obed Edom, and
Ieiel, and Azzaziah, with harpes on
the ‖ Sheminith to excell.

22 And Chenaniah chiefe of the Leuites ‖ was for † song: he instructed about
the song, because he was skilfull.

23 And Berechiah, and Elkanah
were doore keepers for the Arke.

24 And Shebaniah, and Iehoshaphat, and Nathaneel, and Amasai, and
Zachariah, and Benaiah, and Eliezer
the priests, did blow with the trumpets
before the Arke of God : and Obed E-
dom, and Iehiah were doore keepers
for the Arke.

* 2. Sam. 6.
12, 13. &c.

25 ¶ So * Dauid and the Elders of
Israel, and the captaines ouer thousands, went to bring vp the Arke of the
couenant of the Lord, out of the
house of Obed Edom with ioy.

26 And it came to passe when God
helped the Leuites that bare the Arke
of the couenant of the Lord, that
they offered seuen bullocks, and seuen
rammes.

27 And Dauid was clothed with a
robe of fine linnen, and all the Leuites
that bare the Arke, and the singers, and

‖ Or, cariage

Chenaniah the master of the ‖ song,
with the singers. Dauid also had vpon
him, an Ephod of linnen.

28 Thus all Israel brought vp the
Arke of the Couenant of the Lord
with shouting, and with sound of the
cornet, and with trumpets, and with
cymbals, making a noise with psalteries and harpes.

29 ¶ And it came to passe as the Arke
of the couenant of the Lord came
to the citie of Dauid, that Michal the
daughter of Saul looking out at a window, saw King Dauid dauncing and
playing : and shee despised him in her
heart.

CHAP. XVI.

1 Dauids festiuall sacrifice. 4 Hee ordereth a
Quire to sing Thanksgiuing. 7 The Psalme
of Thankesgiuing. 37 He appointeth Ministers, Porters, Priests and Musitians, to attend
continually on the Arke.

* 2. Sam. 6.
17.

 O * they brought the Arke
of God, and set it in the
midst of the tent that Dauid had pitched for it: and
they offered burnt sacrifices, and peace offerings before God.

2 And when Dauid had made an

end of offering the burnt offerings, and
the peace offrings, he blessed the people
in the name of the Lord.

3 And hee dealt to euery one of Israel, both man and woman, to euery
one a loafe of bread, and a good piece of
flesh, and a flagon of wine.

4 ¶ And he appointed certaine of the
Leuites to minister before the Arke of
the Lord, and to record, and to
thanke and praise the Lord God of
Israel,

5 Asaph the chiefe, and next to him
Zachariah, Ieiel, and Shemiramoth,
and Iehiel, and Mattithiah, and E-
liab, and Benaiah, and Obed Edom:
and Ieiel †with Psalteries and with
harpes: but Asaph made a sound with
cymbals.

† Heb. wi
instrumer
of Psalte-
ries,& har

6 Benaiah also and Iahaziel the
Priestes, with trumpets continually
before the Arke of the Couenant of
God.

7 ¶ Then on that day, Dauid deliuered first this Psalme to thanke the
Lord, into the hand of Asaph and
his brethren:

8 * Giue thankes vnto the Lord,
call vpon his name, make knowen his
deeds among the people.

* Psal. 10.
1.

9 Sing vnto him, sing psalmes vnto him, talke you of all his wonderous
workes.

10 Glory yee in his holy Name, let
the heart of them reioyce that seeke the
Lord.

11 Seeke the Lord, and his
strength, seeke his face continually.

12 Remember his marueilous works
that he hath done, his wonders, and
the iudgements of his mouth,

13 O ye seed of Israel his seruant, ye
children of Iacob his chosen ones.

14 He is the Lord our God, his
iudgements are in all the earth.

15 Be ye mindfull alwayes of his
Couenant : the worde which hee commanded to a thousand generations:

16 Euen of the * Couenant which hee
made with Abraham, and of his othe
vnto Isaac:

* Gen. 17.
and 26. 3.
& 28. 13.

17 And hath confirmed the same to
Iacob for a lawe, and to Israel for an
euerlasting Couenant,

18 Saying, vnto thee will I giue
the land of Canaan, the †lot of your inheritance.

† Heb. the
coard.
† Heb. me
of number
* Gen. 34.
30.

19 When ye were but †few, * euen a
few, and strangers in it:

20 And

20 And when they went from nation to nation, and from *one* kingdome to another people:

Gen. 12. 7. and 0. 3.
21 Hee ſuffered no man to doe them wrong: yea, hee *reproued kings for their ſakes,

22 *Saying,* *Touch not mine anointed, and doe my Prophets no harme.

Pſal. 96. 1.
23 *Sing vnto the Lᴏʀᴅ all the earth: ſhew foorth from day to day his ſaluation.

24 Declare his glory among the heathen: his marueilous workes among all nations.

25 For great *is* the Lᴏʀᴅ, and greatly to be praiſed: he alſo *is* to be feared aboue all gods.

Leu. 19. 4
26 For all the gods *of the people *are* idoles: but the Lᴏʀᴅ made the heauens.

27 Glory and honour *are* in his preſence: ſtrength and gladneſſe *are* in his place.

28 Giue vnto the Lᴏʀᴅ, yee kinreds of the people: giue vnto the Lᴏʀᴅ glory and ſtrength.

29 Giue vnto the Lᴏʀᴅ the glory *due* vnto his Name: bring an offering, and come before him, worſhip the Lᴏʀᴅ in the beautie of holineſſe.

30 Feare before him all the earth: the world alſo ſhall be ſtable, that it be not mooued.

31 Let the heauens be glad, and let the earth reioyce: and let men ſay among the nations, The Lᴏʀᴅ reigneth.

32 Let the ſea roare, and the fulneſſe thereof: let the fieldes reioyce, and all that *is* therein.

33 Then ſhall the trees of the wood ſing out at the preſence of the Lᴏʀᴅ, becauſe hee commeth to iudge the earth.

* Pſa. 107.1 and 118. 1. and 136. 1.
34 *O giue thanks vnto the Lᴏʀᴅ, for hee *is* good: for his mercy endureth for euer.

35 And ſay yee, Saue vs, O God of our ſaluation, and gather vs together, and deliuer vs from the heathen, that we may giue thanks to thy holy Name, *and* glory in thy praiſe.

* Deut. 27. 15.
36 Bleſſed *be* the Lᴏʀᴅ God of Iſrael for euer and euer: and all *the people ſaide, Amen, and praiſed the Lᴏʀᴅ.

37 ¶ So hee left there before the Arke of the couenant of the Lᴏʀᴅ,

Aſaph and his brethren, to miniſter before the Arke continually, as euery dayes worke required:

38 And Obed Edom with their brethren, threeſcore and eight: Obed Edom alſo the ſonne of Ieduthun, and Hoſah to be porters:

39 And Zadok the Prieſt, and his brethren the Prieſts, before the Tabernacle of the Lᴏʀᴅ, in the high place that *was* at Gibeon,

† Heb. in the morningand in the euening.
40 To offer burnt offerings vnto the Lᴏʀᴅ, vpon the Altar of the burnt offering continually † morning and euening, and *to doe* according to all that is written in the Lawe of the Lᴏʀᴅ, which hee commanded Iſrael:

41 And with them Heman and Ieduthun, and the reſt that were choſen, who were expreſſed by name, to giue thankes to the Lᴏʀᴅ, becauſe his mercy *endureth* for euer.

† Heb. for the gate.
42 And with them Heman and Ieduthun with trumpets and cymbales, for thoſe that ſhould make a ſound, and with muſicall inſtruments of God: and the ſonnes of Ieduthun were † Porters.

43 And all the people departed euery man to his houſe, and Dauid returned to bleſſe his houſe.

CHAP. XVII.

1 Nathan firſt approuoing the purpoſe of Dauid, to build God an houſe, 3 after by the word of God forbiddeth him. 11 Hee promiſeth him bleſſings and benefits in his ſeed. 16 Dauids prayer and thankeſgiuing.

* 2. Sam. 7. 1, &c.

Ow *it came to paſſe, as Dauid ſate in his houſe, that Dauid ſayde to Nathan the Prophet, Loe, I dwell in an houſe of Cedars, but the Arke of the Couenant of the Lᴏʀᴅ *remaineth* vnder curtaines.

2 Then Nathan ſayd vnto Dauid, Doe all that is in thine heart, for God *is* with thee.

3 ¶ And it came to paſſe the ſame night, that the word of God came to Nathan, ſaying,

4 Goe and tell Dauid my ſeruant, Thus ſaith the Lᴏʀᴅ, Thou ſhalt not build me an houſe to dwell in.

5 For I haue not dwelt in a houſe ſince the day that I brought vp Iſrael, vnto

† *Heb. haue bene.*

vnto this day, but † haue gone from tent to tent, and from one Tabernacle *to a-nother.*

6 Wheresoeuer I haue walked with all Israel, spake I a word to any of the Iudges of Israel (whom I comman-ded to feed my people) saying, Why haue ye not built me an house of Cedars?

7 Now therefore thus shalt thou say vnto my seruant Dauid, Thus saith the LORD of hosts, I tooke thee from the *Sheep-*coat, *euen* † from folowing the sheep, that thou shouldest be ruler ouer my people Israel:

† *Heb. from after.*

8 And I haue bene with thee whi-thersoeuer thou hast walked, and haue cut off all thine enemies from before thee, and haue made thee a name, like the name of the great men that *are* in the earth.

9 Also I will ordeine a place for my people Israel, and will plant them, and they shall dwell in their place, and shall be moued no more: neither shal the chil-dren of wickednesse waste them any more (as at the beginning,

10 And since the time that I com-manded Iudges *to bee* ouer my people Israel.) Moreouer, I will subdue all thine enemies. Furthermore I tel thee, that the LORD will build thee an house.

11 ¶ And it shall come to passe, when thy dayes be expired, that thou must go *to be* with thy fathers, that I will raise vp thy seed after thee, which shall bee of thy sonnes, and I wil stablish his king-dome.

12 He shall build me an house, and I will stablish his throne for euer.

* 2. King. 9. 14.

13 I * will be his father, and he shall be my sonne, and I will not take my mercie away from him, as I tooke it from *him* that was before thee.

14 But I will settle him in mine house, and in my kingdom for euer, and his throne shall bee established for euer-more.

15 According to all these words, and according to all this vision, so did Na-than speake vnto Dauid.

16 ¶ And Dauid the king came, and sate before the LORD, and said, Who am I, O LORD God, and what *is* mine house, that thou hast brought mee hitherto?

17 And *yet* this was a small thing in thine eyes, O God: for thou hast *also* spo-ken of thy seruants house, for a great

while to come, and hast regarded mee according to the estate of a man of high degree, O LORD God.

18 What can Dauid *speake* more to thee for the honour of thy seruant? for thou knowest thy seruant.

19 O LORD, for thy seruants sake, and according to thine owne heart, hast thou done all this greatnesse in making knowen all these † great things.

† *Heb. grea-nesses.*

20 O LORD, *there is* none like thee neither *is there* any God besides thee, ac-cording to all that we haue heard with our eares.

21 And what one nation in the earth *is* like thy people Israel, whome God went to redeeme *to be* his owne people, to make thee a name of greatnesse and terriblenesse, by driuing out nations from before thy people whom thou hast redeemed out of Egypt?

22 For thy people Israel didst thou make thine owne people for euer, and thou, LORD, becamest their God.

23 Therefore now LORD, let the thing that thou hast spoken concerning thy seruant, and concerning his house, be established for euer, and doe as thou hast said.

24 Let it euen bee established, that thy name may bee magnified for euer, saying, The LORD of hosts *is* the God of Israel, *euen* a God to Israel: and let the house of Dauid thy seruant be e-stablished before thee.

25 For thou, O my God, † hast tolde thy seruant that thou wilt build him an house: therefore thy seruant hath found *in his heart* to pray before thee.

† *Heb. has reuealed th eare of thy seruant.*

26 And now, LORD (thou art God, and hast promised this goodnesse vnto thy seruant.)

27 Now therefore ‖ let it please thee to blesse the house of thy seruant, that it may bee before thee for euer: for thou blessest, O LORD, and it *shalbe* blessed for euer.

‖ *Or, it hat pleased the*

CHAP. XVIII.

1 Dauid subdueth the Philistines and the Moa-bites. 3 He smiteth Hadadezer and the Syri-ans. 9 Tou sendeth Hadoram with presents to blesse Dauid. 11 The presents & the spoile, Dauid dedicateth to God. 13 He putteth ga-risons in Edom. 14 Dauids officers.

 Ow after this, *it came to passe, that Dauid smote the Philistines & subdued them, and tooke Gath, and her townes,

* 2. Sam. 1. &c.

townes out of the hand of the Philistines.

2 And he smote Moab, and the Moabites became Dauids seruants, *and* brought gifts.

3 ¶ And Dauid smote ‖ Hadarezer king of Zobah vnto Hamath, as hee went to stablish his dominion by the riuer Euphrates.

4 And Dauid tooke from him a thousand charets, and seuen thousand horsemen, and twentie thousand footmen: Dauid also houghed all the charet *horses*, but reserued of them an hundred charets.

5 And when the Syrians of † Damascus came to helpe Hadarezer king of Zobah, Dauid slew of the Syrians two and twentie thousand men.

6 Then Dauid put *garisons* in Syria Damascus, and the Syrians became Dauids seruants, and brought giftes. Thus the LORD preserued Dauid, whithersoeuer he went.

7 And Dauid tooke the shields of golde that were on the seruants of Hadarezer, & brought them to Ierusalem.

8 Likewise from ‖ Tibhath, and from Chun, cities of Hadarezer, broght Dauid very much brasse, wherewith * Solomon made the brasen Sea, and the pillars, and the vessels of brasse.

9 ¶ Now when ‖ Tou king of Hamath heard how Dauid had smitten all the hoste of Hadarezer king of Zobah:

10 Hee sent ‖Hadoram his sonne to king Dauid, ‖to enquire of his welfare, and to †congratulate him, because hee had fought against Hadarezer, and smitten him (for Hadarezer †had warre with Tou) and *with him* all manner of vessels of golde and siluer, and brasse.

11 ¶ Them also king Dauid dedicated vnto the LORD, with the siluer and the golde that he brought from all *these* nations: from Edom, and from Moab, and from the children of Ammon, and from the Philistines, and from Amalek.

12 Moreouer, Abishai the sonne of Zeruiah, slew of the Edomites in the valley of salt, eighteene thousand.

13 ¶ And he put garisons in Edom, and all the Edomites became Dauids seruants. Thus the LORD preserued Dauid whithersoeuer he went.

14 ¶ So Dauid reigned ouer all Israel, and executed iudgement and iustice

among all his people.

15 And Ioab the sonne of Zeruiah *was* ouer the hoste, and Iehoshaphat the sonne of Ahilud, ‖Recorder.

16 And Zadok the sonne of Ahitub, and ‖Abimelech the sonne of Abiathar, *were* the Priests, and ‖Shausha *was* Scribe.

17 And Benaiah the sonne of Iehoiada *was* ouer the Cherethites, and the Pelethites: and the sonnes of Dauid *were* †chiefe about the king.

CHAP. XIX.

1 Dauids messengers sent to comfort Hanun the sonne of Nahash, are villanously intreated. 6 The Ammonites strengthened by the Syrians, are ouercome by Ioab and Abishai. 16 Shophach making a new supply of the Syrians, is slaine by Dauid.

Now * it came to passe after this, that Nahash the King of the children of Ammon dyed, & his sonne reigned in his stead.

2 And Dauid sayde, I will shewe kindnesse vnto Hanun the sonne of Nahash, because his father shewed kindnesse to mee. And Dauid sent messengers to comfort him concerning his father. So the seruants of Dauid came into the land of the children of Ammon, to Hanun, to comfort him.

3 But the Princes of the children of Ammon sayde to Hanun, †Thinkest thou that Dauid doeth honour thy father, that he hath sent comforters vnto thee? Are not his seruants come vnto thee for to search, and to ouerthrow, and to spie out the land?

4 Wherefore Hanun tooke Dauids seruants, and shaued them, and cut off their garments in the middest, hard by their buttockes, and sent them away.

5 Then there went certeine, and told Dauid, how the men were serued, and hee sent to meet them (for the men were greatly ashamed) and the King sayde, Tary at Iericho vntill your beards be growen, *and* then returne.

6 ¶ And when the children of Ammon sawe, that they had made themselues †odious to Dauid; Hanun and the children of Ammon sent a thousand talents of siluer, to hire them charets and horsemen out of Mesopotamia, and out of Syria-Maachah, and out of Zobah.

7 So

Or, Hadarezer in am.

Heb. Darmesek.

Called in the booke of Sam. Beta and Berothai.
1. King. 7.
23. and 2.
Chro. 4. 15.
Or, Toi, 2.
Sam. 8. 9.

Or, Ioram,
2. *Sam. 8.*
10.
Or, to salute.
Heb. to blesse.
Heb. was the man of warres.

‖ *Or, Remembrancer.*
‖ *Called Ahimelech in Sam.*
‖ *Called Saraia in Sam. and Sisa, 1. King. 4. 2.*

† *Heb. at the hand of the King.*

* 2. Sam. 10 ver. 1, &c.

† *Heb. In thine eyes doeth Dauid, &c.*

† *Heb. to stinke.*

7 So they hired thirtie and two thousand charets, and the king of Maachah and his people, who came and pitched before Medeba. And the children of Ammon gathered themselues together from their cities, and came to battaile.

8 And when Dauid heard *of it*, hee sent Ioab, and all the host of the mightie men.

9 And the children of Ammon came out, and put the battell in aray before the gate of the citie, and the kings that were come, *were* by themselues in the field.

10 Now when Ioab saw that †the battell was set against him, before and behinde : hee chose out of all the ||choice of Israel, and put them in aray against the Syrians.

11 And the rest of the people hee deliuered vnto the hand of †Abishai his brother, and they set themselues in aray against the children of Ammon.

12 And he said, If the Syrians bee too strong for me, then thou shalt helpe me : but if the children of Ammon be too strong for thee, then I wil helpe thee.

13 Be of good courage, and let vs behaue our selues valiantly for our people, and for the Cities of our God : and let the LORD do that *which is* good in his sight.

14 So Ioab and the people that *were* with him, drew nigh before the Syrians, vnto the battell; and they fled before him.

15 And when the children of Ammon saw that the Syrians were fled, they likewise fled before Abishai his brother, and entred into the city. Then Ioab came to Ierusalem.

16 ¶ And when the Syrians saw that they were put to the worse before Israel, they sent messengers, and drew forth the Syrians, that *were* beyond the ||Riuer : and ||Shophach the captaine of the hoste of Hadarezer, *went* before them.

17 And it was tolde Dauid, and hee gathered all Israel, and passed ouer Iordane, and came vpon them, and set *the battell* in aray against them : so when Dauid had put the battell in aray against the Syrians, they fought with him.

18 But the Syrians fled before Israel, and Dauid slew of the Syrians seuen thousand men, *which fought* in cha-

Marginal notes left column:
† *Hebr. the face of the battell was.*
‖ *Or, yong men.*

† *Hebr. Abishai.*

‖ *i. Euphrates.*
‖ *Or, Shobach, 2. sam. 10. 16.*

rets, and fourty thousand footmen, and killed Shophach the captaine of the hoste.

19 And when the seruants of Hadarezer saw that they were put to the worse before Israel, they made peace with Dauid, and became his seruants : neither would the Syrians helpe the children of Ammon any more.

CHAP. XX.

1 Rabbah is besieged by Ioab, spoiled by Dauid, and the people thereof tortured. 4 Three giants are slaine in three seuerall ouerthrowes of the Philistines.

Nd *it came to passe, that †after the yeere was expired, at the time that kings goe out *to battell*, Ioab led forth the power of the armie, and wasted the countrey of the children of Ammon, and came and besieged Rabbah (but Dauid taried at Ierusalem,) and Ioab smote Rabbah, and destroyed it.

2 And Dauid *tooke the crowne of *their king* from off his head, and found it †to weigh a talent of gold, and *there were* precious stones in it, and it was set vpon Dauids head; and hee brought also exceeding much spoile out of the city.

3 And hee brought out the people that *were* in it, and cut them with sawes, and with harrowes of yron, and with axes : euen so dealt Dauid with all the cities of the children of Ammon. And Dauid and all the people returned to Ierusalem.

4 ¶ And it came to passe after this, *that there ||arose warre at ||Gezer with the Philistines, at which time Sibbechai the Hushathite, slew Sippai, that was of the children of ||the giant : and they were subdued.

5 And there was warre againe with the Philistines, and Elhanan the sonne of ||Iair, slew Lahmi the brother of Goliath the Gittite, whose spearestaffe was like a weauers beame.

6 And yet againe *there was warre at Gath, where was a man †of *great* stature, whose fingers and toes *were* foure and twentie, sixe *on each hand*, and sixe *on each foot*. And he also was †the sonne of the giant.

7 But when he ||defied Israel, Ionathan the sonne of ||Shimea Dauids brother, slew him.

8 These

Marginal notes right column:
* 2. Sam. [?] 1.
† *Hebr. at the returne of the yeere.*

* 2. Sam. [?] 26.
† *Hebr. the weight of.*

* 2. Sam. [?] 18.
‖ *Or, continued, Het stood.*
‖ *Or, Gob.*
‖ *Or, Raph.*

‖ *Called at Iaare-oregim, 2. sa. 21. 19.*
* 2. Sam. [?] 20.
† *Hebr. a man of m[...] sure.*
† *Hebr. borne to the giant or, Rapha.*
‖ *Or, reproched.*
‖ *Called Shammah, 1. Sam. 16 [?] 9.*

8 These were borne vnto the Giant in Gath, and they fell by the hand of Dauid, and by the hand of his ſeruants.

CHAP. XXI.

1 Dauid tempted by Satan, forceth Ioab to number the people. 5 The number of the people being brought, Dauid repenteth of it. 9 Dauid hauing three plagues propounded by Gad, chuſeth the peſtilence. 14 After the death of 70000, Dauid by repentance preuenteth the deſtruction of Ieruſalem. 18 Dauid by Gads direction, purchaſeth Ornans threſhing floore, where hauing built an Altar, God giueth a ſigne of his fauour by fire, and ſtayeth the plague. 28 Dauid ſacrificeth there, being reſtrained from Gibeon by feare of the Angel.

Sam. 24. &c.

ANd * Satan ſtoode vp againſt Israel, and prouoked Dauid to number Israel.

2 And Dauid ſaide to Ioab, and to the rulers of the people, Goe, number Israel from Beer-ſheba euen to Dan: and bring the number of them to me, that I may know it.

3 And Ioab anſwered, The Lord make his people an hundred times ſo many moe as they bee: but, my lord the king, are they not al my lords ſeruants? why then doeth my lord require this thing? why will hee bee a cauſe of treſpaſſe to Israel?

4 Neuertheleſſe, the kings word preuailed againſt Ioab: wherefore Ioab departed, and went throughout all Israel, and came to Ieruſalem.

5 ¶ And Ioab gaue the ſumme of the number of the people vnto Dauid: and all they of Israel were a thouſand thouſand, and an hundred thouſand men that drew ſword: and Iudah was foure hundred threeſcore and ten thouſand men, that drew ſword.

6 But Leui and Beniamin counted hee not among them: for the kings word was abominable to Ioab.

7 † And God was diſpleaſed with this thing, therefore he ſmote Israel.

8 And Dauid ſaide vnto God, *I haue ſinned greatly, becauſe I haue done this thing: but uow, I beſeech thee, doe away the iniquitie of thy ſeruant, for I haue done very fooliſhly.

9 ¶ And the Lord ſpake vnto Gad, Dauids Seer, ſaying,

10 Goe and tell Dauid, ſaying, Thus ſaith the Lord, I †offer thee three things, chooſe thee one of them, that I may doe it vnto thee.

11 So Gad came to Dauid, and ſaid vnto him, Thus ſaith the Lord, †Chooſe thee

12 Either three yeeres famine, or three moneths to bee deſtroyed before thy foes (while that the ſword of thine enemies ouertaketh thee) or elſe three dayes the ſword of the Lord, euen the peſtilence in the land, and the Angel of the Lord deſtroying throughout all the coaſts of Israel. Now therefore aduiſe thy ſelfe, what word I ſhall bring againe to him that ſent me.

13 And Dauid ſaid vnto Gad, I am in a great ſtrait. Let mee fall now into the hand of the Lord (for very ‖great are his mercies,) but let me not fall into the hand of man.

14 ¶ So the Lord ſent peſtilence vpon Israel: and there fell of Israel, ſeuentie thouſand men.

15 And God ſent an *Angel vnto Ieruſalem to deſtroy it: and as he was deſtroying, the Lord beheld, and he repented him of the euill, and ſaid to the Angel that deſtroyed, It is ynough, ſtay now thine hand. And the Angel of the Lord ſtood by the threſhing floore of ‖Ornan the Iebuſite.

16 And Dauid lift vp his eyes, and ſaw the Angel of the Lord ſtand betweene the earth and the heauen, hauing a drawen ſword in his hand ſtretched out ouer Ieruſalem. Then Dauid and the Elders of Israel, who were clothed in ſackecloth, fell vpon their faces.

17 And Dauid ſaid vnto God, Is it not I that commanded the people to be numbred? euen I it is that haue ſinned, and done euill indeed, but as for theſe ſheepe, what haue they done? Let thine hand, I pray thee, O Lord my God, be on me, and on my fathers houſe, but not on thy people, that they ſhould bee plagued.

18 ¶ Then the *Angel of the Lord commanded Gad to ſay to Dauid, that Dauid ſhould goe vp and ſet vp an Altar vnto the Lord, in the threſhing floore of Ornan the Iebuſite.

19 And Dauid went vp at the ſaying of Gad, which he ſpake in the Name of the Lord.

20 ‖And Ornan turned backe and ſaw the Angel, and his foure ſonnes with

† Hebr. ſtretch out.

† Hebr. take to thee.

‖ Or, many.

* 2. Sam. 24. 16.

‖ Or, Araunah. 2. sam. 24. 18.

* 2. Chron. 3. 1.

‖ Or, when Ornan turned backe, and ſaw the Angel, then he and his foure ſonnes with him, hid themſelues.

And it was euill in the eyes of the LORD concerning this thing. * 2. Sam. 24. 10.

with him, hid themselues. Now Ornan was threshing wheat.

21 And as Dauid came to Ornan, Ornan looked and saw Dauid, and went out of the threshing floore, and bowed himselfe to Dauid with his face to the ground.

22 Then Dauid saide to Ornan, † Grant mee the place of *this* threshing floore, that I may build an Altar therein vnto the Lord: thou shalt grant it mee for the full price, that the plague may be stayed from the people.

† Heb. giue.

23 And Ornan saide vnto Dauid, Take *it* to thee, and let my lord the king do that which *is* good in his eyes. Loe, I giue *thee* the oxen *also* for burnt offerings, and the threshing instruments for wood, and the wheat for the meate offering, I giue it all.

24 And king Dauid said to Ornan; Nay, but I wil verily buy it for the full price: for I will not take that which *is* thine for the Lord, nor offer burnt offerings without cost.

25 So *Dauid gaue to Ornan for the place, sixe hundred shekels of gold by weight.

* 2. Sam. 24. 24.

26 And Dauid built there an Altar vnto the Lord, and offered burnt offerings, and peace offerings, and called vpon the Lord, and hee answered him from heauen by fire vpon the Altar of burnt offering.

27 And the Lord commaunded the Angel, and hee put vp his sword againe into the sheath thereof.

28 ¶ At that time, when Dauid saw that the Lord had answered him in the threshing floore of Ornan the Iebusite, then he sacrificed there.

29 For the tabernacle of the Lord which Moses made in the wildernesse, and the Altar of the burnt offering *were* at that season, in the high place at * Gibeon:

* Chap. 16. 39. 2. Chro. 1. 3. 1. king. 3. 4.

30 But Dauid could not goe before it to euquire of God; for he was afraid, because of the sword of the Angel of the Lord.

CHAP. XXII.

1 Dauid foreknowing the place of the Temple, prepareth abundance for the building of it. 6 Hee instructeth Solomon in Gods promises, and his duety in building the Temple. 17 He chargeth the Princes to assist his sonne.

Hen Dauid said, This is the house of the Lord God, and this *is* the Altar of the burnt offering for Israel.

2 And Dauid commanded to gather together the strangers that *were* in the land of Israel: and hee set masons to hew wrought stones to build the house of God.

3 And Dauid prepared yron in abundance for the nailes for the doores of the gates, and for the ioynings, and brasse in abundance without weight;

4 Also Cedar trees in abundance: for the Zidonians, and they of Tyre, brought much Cedar wood to Dauid.

5 And Dauid said, * Solomon my sonne *is* yong and tender, and the house *that is* to be builded for the Lord, *must be* exceeding magnificall, of fame and of glory throughout all countreys: I will *therefore* now make preparation for it. So Dauid prepared abundantly before his death.

* Chap. 1.

6 ¶ Then hee called for Solomon his sonne, and charged him to build an house for the Lord God of Israel.

7 And Dauid saide to Solomon; My sonne, as for me, it was in my mind to build an house vnto the Name of the Lord my God.

8 But the word of the Lord came to mee, saying, * Thou hast shed blood abundantly, and hast made great warres: thou shalt not build an house vnto my Name, because thou hast shed much blood vpon the earth in my sight.

* Chap. 2 3. 2. sam 13.

9 Behold, a sonne shall bee borne to thee, who shall be a man of rest, and I will giue him rest from all his enemies round about: for his name shalbe ‖ Solomon, and I wil giue peace and quietnesse vnto Israel in his dayes.

‖ That is peaceable

10 Hee shall build an house for my Name, and he shal be my sonne, and I *will be* his father, and I will establish the throne of his kingdome ouer Israel for euer.

11 Now my sonne, The Lord be with thee, and prosper thou, and build the house of the Lord thy God, as he hath said of thee.

12 Onely the Lord giue thee wisedome and vnderstanding, and giue thee charge concerning Israel, that thou mayest keepe the Law of the Lord thy God.

13 Then shalt thou prosper, if thou takest

takeſt heed to fulfill the Statutes and Iudgements which the LORD charged Moſes with, concerning Israel: be ſtrong, and of good courage, dread not, nor be diſmayed.

14 Now beholde, ‖in my trouble I haue prepared for the house of the LORD an hundred thousand talents of gold, and a thousand thousand talents of ſiluer, and of braſſe and yron without * weight: (for it is in abundance) timber also and ſtone haue I prepared, and thou mayeſt adde thereto.

15 Moreouer, *there are* workmen with thee in abundance, hewers, and ‖workers of ſtone and timber, and all maner of cunning men for euery maner of worke:

16 Of the gold, the ſiluer, and the braſſe, and the yron, *there is* no number. Arise therefore, and be doing, and the LORD be with thee.

17 ¶ Dauid also commanded all the Princes of Israel to helpe Solomon his ſonne, *saying,*

18 *Is* not the LORD your God with you? and hath he *not* giuen you reſt on euery ſide? for he hath giuen the inhabitants of the land into mine hand, and the land is subdued before the LORD, and before his people.

19 Now ſet your heart and your ſoule to ſeeke the LORD your God: arise therfore, and build ye the Sanctuary of the LORD God, to bring the Arke of the Couenant of the LORD, & the holy veſſels of God, into the house that is to be built to the Name of the LORD.

CHAP. XXIII.

1 Dauid in his old age maketh Solomon King. 2 The number and diſtribution of the Leuites 7 The families of the Gerſhonites. 12 The ſonnes of Kohath. 21 The ſonnes of Merari. 24 The office of the Leuites.

S O *when Dauid was old and full of dayes, he made Solomon his ſonne king ouer Israel.

2 ¶ And he gathered together all the Princes of Israel, with the Prieſts and the Leuites.

3 Now the Leuites were numbred from the age of thirtie * yeeres and vpward: and their number, by their polles, man by man, was thirtie and eight thousand.

4 Of which, twentie and foure

thousand *were* ‖ to ſet forward the work of the house of the LORD: and sixe thousand *were* Officers and Iudges.

5 Moreouer, foure thousand *were* porters, and foure thousand praised the LORD with the inſtruments which I made (*said Dauid*) to praise *therewith.*

6 And *Dauid diuided them into †courses among the ſonnes of Leui, *namely* Gerſhon, Kohath, and Merari.

7 ¶ Of the * Gerſhonites *were* ‖Laadan, and Shimei.

8 The ſonnes of Laadan, the chiefe *was* Iehiel, and Zetham, and Ioel, three.

9 The ſonnes of Shimei: Shelomith, and Haziel, and Haran, three. These *were* the chiefe of the fathers of Laadan.

10 And the ſonnes of Shimei *were*: Iahath, ‖Zina, and Ieuſh, and Beriah. These foure *were* the ſonnes of Shimei.

11 And Iahath was the chiefe, and Ziza the second: but Ieuſh and Beriah †had not many ſonnes: therefore they were in one reckoning, according to *their* fathers house.

12 ¶ The ſonnes of Kohath: Amram, Izhar, Hebron, and Vzziel, foure.

13 The ſonnes of * Amram: Aaron and Moses: and * Aaron was ſeparated, that he should ſanctifie the moſt holy things, he and his ſonnes for euer, to burne *incense* before the LORD, to miniſter vnto him, and to bleſſe in his Name for euer.

14 *Now concerning Moſes the man of God, his ſonnes were named of the tribe of Leui.

15 The ſonnes of Moſes *were*: * Gerſhom and Eliezer.

16 Of the ſonnes of Gerſhom Shebuel *was* the chiefe.

17 And the ſonnes of Eliezer *were*: * Rehabiah ‖the chiefe. And Eliezer had none other ſonnes: but the ſonnes of Rehabiah †were very many.

18 Of the ſonnes of Izhar, Shelomith the chiefe.

19 Of the ſonnes of Hebron, Ieriah the firſt, Amariah the second, Iahaziel the third, and Iekamiam the fourth.

20 Of the ſonnes of Vzziel: Michah the firſt, and Iesiah the second.

21 ¶ The ſonnes of Merari: Mahli and Muſhi. The ſonnes of Mahli: Eleazar and Kiſh.

22 And Eleazar died, and had no ſonnes

Marginal notes

, in my ertie.

s Ver. 3.

hat is, aſons and rpenters.

hap. 28.

ſum. 4. 3.

‖ Or, to o-uorſee.

* Exod. 6. 16 1. chro. 6. 1. &c. 2. chro. 8. 14. and 29. 25.
† Heb. diuiſions.
* Chap. 26. 21.
‖ Or, Libni, chap. 6. 17.

‖ Or, Ziza, ver. 11.

† Heb. did not multiply ſonnes.

* Exo. 6. 20.
* Exod. 28. heb. 5. 4.

* Exo. 2. 22.

* Exo.18.3, 4

* Chap. 26. 25.
‖ Or, the first
† Heb. were highly multiplied.

‖ *Or, kinse-*
men.

sonnes but daughters : and their ‖brethren the sonnes of Kish tooke them.

23 The sonnes of Mushi : Mahli, and Eder, and Ierimoth, three.

* Num. 10.
24.

24 ¶ These *were* the sonnes of *Leui after the house of their fathers, euen the chiefe of the fathers, as they were counted by number of names by their polles, that did the worke for the seruice of the house of the Lord, from the age of *twentie yeeres and vpward.

* Num. 1. 3.

‖ *Or, and he dwelleth in Ierusalem, &c.*

25 For Dauid sayd, The Lord God of Israel hath giuen rest vnto his people, ‖*that* they may dwell in Ierusalem for euer.

26 And also vnto the Leuites : they shall no *more* cary the Tabernacle, nor any vessels of it for the seruice thereof.

† *Heb. number.*

27 For by the last words of Dauid, the Leuites *were* †numbred from twentie yeeres olde, and aboue :

† *Heb. their station was at the hand of the sonnes of Aaron.*

28 Because †their office *was* to wait on the sonnes of Aaron, for the seruice of the house of the Lord, in the courts, and in the chambers, and in the purifying of all holy things, and the worke of the seruice of the house of God :

* Chap. 9.
29, &c.
leuit. 6. 21.

29 Both for the * shew-bread, and for the fine floure for meat offering, and for the vnleauened cakes, and for *that which is baked* in the ‖panne, and for *that which* is fried, and for all maner of measures and size :

‖ *Or, flat plate.*

30 And to stand euery morning to thanke and praise the Lord, and likewise at Euen :

31 And to offer all burnt sacrifices vnto the Lord in the Sabbaths, in the new moones, and on the set feasts, by number, according to the order commanded vnto them continually before the Lord :

32 And that they should keepe the charge of the Tabernacle of the Congregation, and the charge of the holy place, and the charge of the sonnes of Aaron their brethren, in the seruice of the house of the Lord.

CHAP. XXIIII.

1 *The diuisions of the sonnes of Aaron by lot into foure and twenty orders.* 20 *The Kohathites,* 27 *and the Merarites diuided by lot.*

* Leui. 10. 4

NOw *these* are the diuisions of the sonnes of Aaron. * The sonnes of Aaron : Nadab and Abihu, Eleazar and Ithamar.

* Num. 3.
and 26. 60.

2 But Nadab and Abihu died * before their father, and had no children : Therefore Eleazar and Ithamar executed the Priests office.

3 And Dauid distributed them, both Zadok of the sonnes of Eleazar, and Ahimelech of the sonnes of Ithamar, according to their offices in their seruice.

4 And there were moe chiefe men found of the sonnes of Eleazar, then of the sonnes of Ithamar : and *thus* were they diuided. Among the sonnes of Eleazar there were sixteene chiefe men of the house of their fathers, and eight among the sonnes of Ithamar according to the house of their fathers.

5 Thus were they diuided by lot, one sort with another ; for the gouernours of the Sanctuarie, and gouernours of the house of God, were of the sonnes of Eleazar, and of the sonnes of Ithamar.

6 And Shemaiah the sonne of Nathanael the Scribe, *one* of the Leuites, wrote them before the King and the Princes, and Zadok the Priest, and Ahimelech the sonne of Abiathar, and *before* the chiefe of the fathers of the priests and Leuites : one †principall houshold being taken for Eleazar, and one taken for Ithamar.

† *Heb. hou of the fathe*

7 Now the first lot came foorth to Iehoiarib : the second to Iedaiah,

8 The third to Harim, the fourth to Seorim,

9 The fifth to Malchiiah, the sixth to Miiamin,

10 The seuenth to Hakkoz, the eight to * Abiiah,

* Luk. 1. 5

11 The ninth to Ieshua, the tenth to Shecaniah,

12 The eleuenth to Eliashib, the twelfth to Iakim,

13 The thirteenth to Huppah, the fourteenth to Ieshebeab,

14 The fifteenth to Bilgah, the sixteenth to Immer,

15 The seuenteenth to Hezir, the eighteenth to Aphses,

16 The ninteenth to Pethahiah, the twentieth to Iehezekel,

17 The one and twentieth to Iachin, the two and twentieth to Gamul,

18 The three and twentieth to Delaiah, the foure and twentieth to Maaziah.

19 These *were* the orderings of them in their seruice to come into the house of the Lord according to their maner, vnder

vnder Aaron their father, as the LORD God of Israel had commanded him.

20 ¶ And the rest of the sonnes of Leui *were* these: of the sons of Amram, Shubael : of the sonnes of Shubael, Iedeiah.

21 Concerning Rehabiah, of the sons of Rehabiah, the first *was* Isshiah.

22 Of the Izharites, Shelomoth : of the sonnes of Shelomoth, Iahath.

chap. 23.
and 26.

23 And the sonnes *of* * *Hebron,* Ieriah *the first,* Amariah the second, Iahaziel the third, Iekameam the fourth.

24 Of the sonnes of Vzziel, Michah : of the sonnes of Michah, Shamir.

25 The brother of Michah *was* Isshiah : of the sonnes of Isshiah, Zechariah.

26 The sonnes of Merari *were* Mahli and Mushi : the sonnes of Iaaziah, Beno.

27 ¶ The sonnes of Merari by Iaaziah, Beno, and Shoham, and Zaccur, and Ibri.

28 Of Mahli *came* Eleazar, who had no sonnes.

29 Concerning Kish : the sonne of Kish was Ierahmeel.

30 The sonnes also of Mushi, Mahli, and Eder, and Ierimoth. These *were* the sonnes of the Leuites after the house of their fathers.

31 These likewise cast lots ouer against their brethren the sonnes of Aaron, in the presence of Dauid the King, and Zadok and Ahimelech, and the chiefe of the fathers of the priests and Leuites, euen the principall fathers ouer against their yonger brethren.

CHAP. XXV.

1 The number & offices of the singers. 8 Their diuision by lot, into foure and twentie orders.

Oreouer Dauid and the captaines of the hoste separated to the seruice of the sonnes of Asaph, and of Heman, and of Ieduthun, who should prophesie with harps, with psalteries, and with cymbals : and the number of the workmen, according to their seruice, was :

2 Of the sonnes of Asaph : Zaccur, and Ioseph, and Nethaniah, and Asarelah, the sonnes of Asaph vnder the hands of Asaph, which prophesied † according to the order of the king.

Otherwise
alled Iesha-
elah, v. 14.
Heb. by the
and of the
ing.

3 Of Ieduthun : the sonnes of Ieduthun, Gedaliah, and || Zeri, and Ieshaiah, Hashabiah, and Mattithiah, ||sixe, vnder the handes of their father Ieduthun, who prophesied with a harpe, to giue thankes and to praise the LORD.

|| *Or, Izri,*
ver. 11.

|| *With Shi-*
mei mentio-
ned ver. 17.

4 Of Heman : the sonnes of Heman, Bukkiah, Mattaniah, || Vzziel, ||Shebuel, and Ierimoth, Hananiah, Hanani, Eliatha, Giddalti, and Romamti-Ezer, Ioshbekashah, Mallothi, Hothir, *and* Mahazioth :

|| *Or, Aza-*
reel, ver. 18.
|| *Or, Shuba-*
el, ver. 20.

5 All these were the sonnes of Heman the kings Seer in the ||wordes of God, to lift vp the horne. And God gaue to Heman fourteene sonnes and three daughters

|| *Or, mat-*
ters.

6 All these were vnder the hands of their father, for song *in* the house of the LORD with cymbals, psalteries and harpes, for the seruice of the house of God, † according to the kings order, to Asaph, Ieduthun, and Heman.

† *Heb. by the*
hands of the
King.

7 So the number of them, with their brethren that were instructed in the songs of the LORD, *euen* all that were cunning, *was* two hundred, foure score and eight.

8 ¶ And they cast lots ward against *ward,* as well the small as the great, the teacher as the scholler

9 Now the first lot came foorth for Asaph to Ioseph, the second to Gedaliah, who with his brethren and sonnes *were* twelue :

10 The third to Zaccur, *he,* his sons, and his brethren *were* twelue :

11 The fourth to Izri, *he,* his sonnes and his brethren *were* twelue :

12 The fift to Nethaniah, *hee,* his sonnes and his brethren *were* twelue :

13 The sixt to Bukkiah, *he,* his sons and his brethren *were* twelue.

14 The seuenth to Iesharelah, *hee,* his sonnes & his brethren *were* twelue :

15 The eight to Ieshaiah, *hee,* his sonnes and his brethren, *were* twelue :

16 The ninth to Mattaniah, *he,* his sonnes and his brethren *were* twelue :

17 The tenth to Shimei, *he,* his sons and his brethren *were* twelue :

18 The eleuenth to Azareel, *hee,* his sonnes and his brethren *were* twelue.

19 The twelfth to Hashabiah, *he,* his sonnes and his brethren, *were* twelue :

20 The thirteenth to Shubael, *hee,* his sonnes and his brethren *were* twelue :

21 The fourteenth to Mattithiah, *he,*

hee, his sonnes and his brethren, *were* twelue.

22 The fifteenth to Ierimoth, *hee,* his sonnes & his brethren, *were* twelue:

23 The sixteenth to Hananiah, *hee,* his sonnes & his brethren, *were* twelue:

24 The seuenteenth to Ioshbeka-shah, *he,* his sonnes and his brethren, *were* twelue:

25 The eighteenth to Hanani: *hee,* his sonnes & his brethren, *were* twelue:

26 The nineteenth to Mallothi, *hee,* his sonnes & his brethren, *were* twelue:

27 The twentieth to Eliathah, *hee,* his sonnes & his brethren, *were* twelue:

28 The one and twentieth to Ho-thir, *he,* his sonnes and his brethren *were* twelue.

29 The two and twentieth to Gid-dalti, *hee,* his sonnes and his brethren, *were* twelue.

30 The three and twentieth to Ma-hazioth, *he,* his sonnes and his brethren, *were* twelue.

31 The foure and twentieth to Ro-mamti-Ezer, *he,* his sonnes and his bre-thren, *were* twelue.

CHAP. XXVI.

1 The diuisions of the porters. 13 The gates as-signed by lot. 20 The Leuites that had charge of the treasures. 29 Officers and Iudges.

||Or, Shele-miah, ver. 14.|| Concerning the diuisions of the porters: of the Kor-hites *was* ||Meshelemiah the sonne of Kore, of the ||Or, Abia-saph, chap.9. 19. & 6. 37. sonnes of ||Asaph.

2 And the sonnes of Meshelemiah *were* Zechariah the first borne, Iediael the second, Zebadiah the third, Iath-niel the fourth,

3 Elam the fifth, Iehohanan the sixth, Elioenai the seuenth.

4 Moreouer the sonnes of Obed-E-dom *were* Shemaiah the first borne, Ie-hozabad the second, Ioah the thirde, and Sacar the fourth, and Nethaneel the fifth.

5 Ammiel the sixth, Issachar the se-uenth, Peulthai the eighth : for God ||That is, Obed-E-dom, as chap. 13. 14. blessed ||him.

6 Also vnto Shemaiah his sonne were sonnes borne, that ruled through-out the house of their father : for they *were* mighty men of valour.

7 The sonnes of Shemaiah : Oth-ni, and Rephael, and Obed, Elza-bad, whose brethren were strong men ;

Elihu, and Semachiah.

8 All these of the sonnes of Obed-Edom : they and their sonnes and their brethren, able men for strength for the seruice, *were* threescore and two of O-bed-Edom.

9 And Meshelemiah *had* sonnes and brethren, strong men, eighteene.

10 Also Hosah of the children of Me-rari, had sonnes : Simri the chiefe, (for *though* he was not the first borne, yet his father made him the chiefe)

11 Hilkiah the second, Tebaliah the thirde, Zechariah the fourth : all the sonnes and brethren of Hosah, *were* thir-teene.

12 Among these were the diuisions of the porters, *euen* among the chiefe men, hauing wards one against an-other, to minister in the house of the LORD.

13 ¶ And they cast lots ||as well the small as the great, according to the house of their fathers for euery gate. ||Or, aswe for the sm as for the great.

14 And the lot Eastward fel to ||She-lemiah ; then for Zechariah his sonne (a wise counseller :) they cast lots, and his lot came out Northward. ||Called M shelemiah ver. 1.

15 To Obed - Edom Southward, and to his sonnes, the house of † A-suppim. †Hebr. ga therings.

16 To Shuppim and Hosa, *the lot came foorth* Westward with the gate Shallecheth, by the causey of the going ||vp, ward against ward.

17 Eastward *were* sixe Leuites, Northward foure a day, Southward foure a day, and toward Asuppim two *and* two. ||See 1. ki 10. 4. 2. c 9. 4, 11.

18 And Parbar Westward, foure at the causey, *and* two at Parbar.

19 These *are* the diuisions of the por-ters among the sonnes of Kore, and a-mong the sonnes of Merari.

20 ¶ And of the Leuites, Ahiiah *was* ouer the treasures of the house of God, and ouer the treasures of the † dedicate things. †Heb. ho things.

21 As concerning the sonnes of ||La-adan : the sonnes of the Gershonite Laadan, hiefe fathers ; *euen* of Laadan the Gershonite, *were* ||Iehieli. ||Or, Lib chap. 6. 1

22 The sonnes of Iehieli, Zetham and Ioel his brother, *which were* ouer the treasures of the house of the LORD. ||Or, Iehie chap. 23.

23 Of the Amramites, *and* the Iz-harites, the Hebronites, *and* the Vz-zielites :

24 And Shebuel the sonne of Ger-shom,

shom, the sonne of Moses, *was* ruler of the treasures.

25 And his brethren by Eliezer: Rehabiah his sonne, and Ieshaiah his sonne, and Ioram his sonne, and Zichri his sonne, & Shelomith his sonne.

26 Which Shelomith and his brethren, were ouer all the treasures of the dedicate things, which Dauid the king and the chiefe fathers, the captaines ouer thousands and hundreds, and the captaines of the hoste had dedicated.

27 † Out of the spoyles wonne in battels, did they dedicate to maintaine the house of the LORD. *eb. out of battels spoiles.*

28 And all that Samuel the Seer, and Saul the sonne of Kish, and Abner the sonne of Ner, and Ioab the sonne of Zeruiah had dedicated, and whosoeuer had dedicated any thing, it *was* vnder the hand of Shelomith and of his brethren.

29 ¶ Of the Izharites, Chenaniah and his sonnes, *were* for the outward busines ouer Israel, for officers and Iudges.

30 *And* of the Hebronits, Hashabiah and his brethren, men of valour, a thousand and seuen hundred, *were* †officers among them of Israel on this side Iorden westward, in all busines of the LORD, and in the seruice of the king. *eb. ouer charge.*

31 Among the Hebronites *was* Ieriiah the chiefe, *euen* among the Hebronits, according to the generations of his fathers: in the fourtieth yeere of the reigne of Dauid, they were sought for, and there were found among them mightie men of valour, at Iazer of Gilead.

32 And his brethren, men of valour, were two thousand and seuen hundred chiefe fathers, whom King Dauid made rulers ouer the Reubenites, the Gadites, & the halfe tribe of Manasseh, for euery matter perteining to God, and †affaires of the king. *eb. thing.*

CHAP. XXVII.

1 The twelue Captaines, for euery seuerall moneth. 16 The Princes of the twelue Tribes. 23 The numbring of the people is hindered. 25 Dauids seuerall Officers.

Owe the children of Israel after their number, *to wit*, the chiefe fathers and captaines of thousands and hundreds, and their officers that serued the king in any matter of the courses, which came in, and went out moneth by moneth, throughout all the moneths of the yeare, of euery course *were* twentie and foure thousand.

2 Ouer the first course for the first moneth *was* Iashobeam the sonne of Zabdiel, and in his course *were* twentie and foure thousand.

3 Of the children of Perez, *was* the chiefe of all the captaines of the host, for the first moneth.

4 And ouer the course of the second moneth *was* ‖ Dodai an Ahohite, and of his course was Mikloth also the ruler: In his course *likewise were* twentie and foure thousand. *‖ Or, Dodo. 2 Sam. 23. 9.*

5 The third captaine of the host for the third month *was* Benaiah the sonne of Iehoiada a ‖chiefe priest, and in his course *were* twenty and foure thousand. *‖ Or, principall officer.*

6 This *is that* Benaiah, *who was* *mightie among the thirtie, and aboue the thirty: and in his course *was* Amizabad his sonne. ** 2. Sam. 23. 20. 22. 23. & 1. Chron. 11. 24.*

7 The fourth *captaine* for the fourth moneth *was* Asahel the brother of Ioab, and Zebadiah his sonne after him: and in his course *were* twentie and foure thousand.

8 The fifth *captaine* for the fifth moneth, *was* Shamhuth the Izrahite: and in his course *were* twentie and foure thousand.

9 The sixt *captaine* for the sixt moneth, *was* Ira the son of Ikkesh the Tekoite: and in his course *were* twentie and foure thousand.

10 The seuenth *captaine* for the seuenth moneth *was* Helez the Pelonite, of the children of Ephraim: and in his course *were* twentie and foure thousand.

11 The eighth *captaine* for the eighth moneth, *was* Sibbecai the Hushathite, of the Zarhites: and in his course *were* twentie and foure thousand.

12 The ninth *captaine* for the ninth moneth, *was* Abiezer the Anetothite, of the Beniamites: and in his course *were* twentie and foure thousand.

13 The tenth *captaine* for the tenth moneth, *was* Maharai the Netophathite, of the Zarhites: and in his course *were* twentie and foure thousand.

14 The eleuenth *captaine* for the eleuenth moneth *was* Benaiah the Pirathonite, of the children of Ephraim: and in his course *were* twenty and foure thousand.

15 The

‖ *Or, Heled, Chap.* 11. 30

15 The twelfth *captaine* for the twelfth moneth, *was* ‖ Heldai the Netophathite, of Othniel : and in his course *were* twentie and foure thousand.

16 ¶ Furthermore, ouer the tribes of Israel : The Ruler of the Reubenites *was* Eliezer the sonne of Zichri : of the Simeonites, Shephatiah the sonne of Maachah.

17 Of the Leuites : Hashabiah the sonne of Kemuel ; of the Aaronites, Zadok.

18 Of Iudah, Elihu, *one* of the brethren of Dauid : of Issachar, Omri the sonne of Michael.

19 Of Zebulun, Ishmaiah the son of Obadiah : of Naphtali, Ierimoth the sonne of Azriel.

20 Of the children of Ephraim, Hoshea the sonne of Azazziah : of the halfe tribe of Manasseh, Ioel the sonne of Pedaiah.

21 Of the halfe tribe of Manasseh in Gilead, Iddo the sonne of Zechariah : of Beniamin, Iaasiel the son of Abner.

22 Of Dan, Azariel the sonne of Ieroham. These *were* the princes of the tribes of Israel.

23 ¶ But Dauid tooke not the number of them from twentie yeeres olde and vnder : because the LORD had said, hee would increase Israel like to the starres of the heauens.

* 1. Chron. 21. 7. 2. sam. 24. 5. &c.
† *Heb.* ascended.

24 Ioab the sonne of Zeruiah began to number, * but he finished not, because there fell wrath for it against Israel, neither † was the number put in the account of the Chronicles of King Dauid.

25 ¶ And ouer the Kings treasures, *was* Azmaueth the sonne of Adiel : and ouer the store-houses in the fields, in the cities, and in the villages, and in the castles, *was* Iehonathan the sonne of Vzziah.

26 And ouer them that did the worke of the field, for tillage of the ground, *was* Ezri the sonne of Chelub.

† *Heb. ouer that which was of the vineyards.*

27 And ouer the Vineyards, *was* Shimei the Ramathite : † ouer the increase of the vineyards for the wine cellars, was Sabdi the Ziphmite.

28 And ouer the Oliue trees, and the Sycomore trees that *were* in the lowe plaines, *was* Baal-hanan the Gederite : and ouer the cellars of oyle *was* Ioash.

29 And ouer the herdes that fed in Sharon, *was* Shetrai the Sharonite : and ouer the herds that *were* in the val-

leys, *was* Shaphat the sonne of Adlai.

30 Ouer the camels also, *was* Obil the Ishmaelite : and ouer the Asses, *was* Iehdeiah the Meronothite.

31 And ouer the flockes, *was* Iaziz the Hagerite. All these *were* the rulers of the substance which *was* king Dauids.

32 Also Ionathan Dauids vncle, was a counseller, a wise man, and a ‖ Scribe : and Iehiel the ‖ sonne of Hachmoni, *was* with the kings sonnes.

‖ *Or, se tarie.*
‖ *Or, H monite.*

33 And Ahitophel *was* the kings counseller, and Hushai the Archite, *was* the kings companion.

34 And after Ahitophel, *was* Iehoiada the sonne of Benaiah, and Abiathar : and the general of the Kings armie *was* Ioab.

CHAP. XXVIII

1 Dauid in a solemne assembly, hauing declared Gods fauour to him, and promise to his sonne Solomon, exhorteth them to feare God. 9. 20 Hee encourageth Solomon to build the Temple. 11 He giueth him paternes for the forme, and gold and siluer for the materials.

ND Dauid assembled all the Princes of Israel, the Princes of the tribes, and the captains of the companies that ministred to the king by course : and the captaines ouer the thousands, and captaines ouer the hundreds, and the stewards ouer all the substance and ‖ possession of the King, and of his sonnes, with the ‖ officers, and with the mightie men, and with all the valiant men, vnto Ierusalem.

‖ *Or, ca*
‖ *Or, E*
nuches.

2 Then Dauid the king stood vp vpon his feete, and said, Heare me, my brethren, and my people : As for me, I had in mine heart to builde an house of rest for the Arke of the Couenant of the LORD, and for the * footestoole of our God, & had made ready for the building.

* 2. Sa
5. 13. 1.
5. 5. 1.
22. 8.

3 But God said vnto me, Thou shalt not builde an house for my Name, because thou *hast been* a man of warre, and hast shed † blood

† *Heb.*

4 Howbeit, the LORD God of Israel chose me before all the house of my father, to be king ouer Israel for euer : for he hath chosen * Iudah to be the ruler ; & of the house of Iudah, the house of my father ; and among the sonnes of my father, he liked me to make *me* king ouer all Israel.

Gen. 49.
1. sam.
13. psal.
67

5 * And of all my sonnes (for the LORD hath giuen me many sonnes) hee

* Cha.

hee hath chosen Solomon my sonne, to sit vpon the throne of the kingdome of the Lord ouer Israel.

6 And he said vnto me, * Solomon thy sonne, hee shall build my house and my courts : for I haue chosen him to be my sonne, and I will be his father.

7 Moreouer, I will establish his kingdome for euer, if he be † constant to do my commandements and my iudgements, as at this day.

8 Now therefore in the sight of all Israel, the congregation of the Lord, and in the audience of our God, keepe, and seeke for all the commandements of the Lord your God, that ye may possesse this good land, and leaue it for an inheritance for your children after you, for euer.

9 ¶ * And thou, Solomon my sonne, know thou the God of thy father, and serue him with a perfite heart, and with a willing minde : for the Lord searcheth all hearts, and vnderstandeth all the imaginations of the thoughts : if thou seeke him, he will be found of thee, but if thou forsake him, he will cast thee off for euer.

10 Take heed now, for the Lord hath chosen thee to builde an house for the Sanctuarie : be strong, and doe it.

11 ¶ Then Dauid gaue to Solomon his sonne the paterne of the porch, and of the houses thereof, and of the treasuries thereof, and of the vpper chambers thereof, and of the inner parlours thereof, and of the place of the Mercie-seate.

12 And the paterne † of all that hee had by the spirit, of the courts of the house of the Lord, and of all the chambers round about, of the treasuries of the house of God, and of the treasuries of the dedicate things :

13 Also for the courses of the Priests and the Leuites, & for all the worke of the seruice of the house of the Lord, and for all the vessels of seruice in the house of the Lord.

14 Hee gaue of golde by weight, for things of golde, for all instruments of all manner of seruice : siluer also for all instruments of siluer, by weight, for all instruments of euery kinde of seruice :

15 Euen the weight for the Candlestickes of golde, and for their lampes of golde, by weight for euery candlesticke, and for the lampes thereof : and for the Candlestickes of siluer by weight, both

for the Candlesticke and also for the lampes thereof, according to the vse of euery candlesticke.

16 And by weight hee gaue golde for the tables of shew-bread, for euery table, and likewise siluer for the tables of siluer.

17 Also pure golde for the flesh-hookes, and the bowles, and the cups : and for the golden basins hee gaue golde by weight, for euery basin; and likewise siluer by weight, for euery basin of siluer.

18 And for the Altar of incense, refined golde by weight; and gold for the paterne of the charet of the * Cherubims, that spread out their wings, and couered the Arke of the Couenant of the Lord.

19 All this, sayd Dauid, the Lord made mee vnderstand in writing by his hand vpon mee, euen all the workes of this paterne.

20 And Dauid said to Solomon his sonne, Be strong, and of good courage, and doe it: feare not, nor be dismayed, for the Lord God, euen my God, will be with thee; he will not faile thee, nor forsake thee, vntill thou hast finished all the worke for the seruice of the house of the Lord.

21 And behold, the courses of the Priests and the Leuites, euen they shall be with thee for all the seruice of the house of God, and there shall be with thee for all manner of workemanship, euery willing skilfull man, for any manner of seruice : also the Princes and all the people will bee wholly at thy commandement.

CHAP. XXIX.

1 Dauid by his example and intreatie, 6 causeth the Princes and people to offer willingly. 10 Dauids thankesgiuing and prayer. 20 The people hauing blessed God and sacrificed, make Solomon King. 26 Dauids reigne and death.

Vrthermore, Dauid the King said vnto all the congregation, Solomon my sonne, whome alone God hath chosen, is yet * young and tender, and the worke is great : for the palace is not for man, but for the Lord God.

2 Now I haue prepared with all my might for the house of my God, the gold

Sam. 7.
2. chro.

eb. strong

Sam. 16.
sal. 139.
nd 7. 9.
. 11. 20.
17. 10.
20. 12.

eb. of all
t was
h him.

*1. Sam. 4. 4
1. king. 6.
23, &c.

*Cha. 22. 5.

gold for *things to be made* of gold, the siluer for *things* of siluer, and the brasse for
things of brasse, the yron for *things* of y-
ron, and wood for *things* of wood, onix
stones, and stones to be set, glistering
stones, and of diuers colours, and all
maner of precious stones, and marble
stones in abundance.

3 Moreouer, because I haue set my
affection to the house of my God, I
haue of mine owne proper good, of gold
and siluer, *which* I haue giuen to the
house of my God, ouer & aboue all that
I haue prepared for the holy house:

4 *Euen* three thousand talents of
gold, of the gold of *Ophir, and seuen
thousand talents of refined siluer, to o-
uerlay the walles of the houses withall.

5 The gold for *things* of golde, and
the siluer for *things* of siluer, and for all
maner of worke *to be made* by the hands
of Artificers. And who then is willing
†to consecrate his seruice this day vnto
the Lord?

6 ¶ Then the chiefe of the fathers
and Princes of the tribes of Israel, and
the captaines of thousands and of hundreds, with the rulers ouer the Kings
worke, offered willingly,

7 And gaue for the seruice of the
house of God, of gold fiue thousand talents, and ten thousand drammes: and
of siluer, ten thousand talents: and of
brasse, eighteene thousand talents: and
one hundred thousand talents of yron.

8 And they with whom precious
stones were found, gaue them to the
treasure of the house of the Lord, by
the hand of Iehiel the Gershonite.

9 Then the people reioyced, for that
they offred willingly, because with perfect heart they offered willingly to the
Lord: and Dauid the King also reioyced with great ioy.

10 ¶ Wherefore Dauid blessed the
Lord before all the Congregation:
and Dauid saide, Blessed *bee* thou,
Lord God of Israel our father, for
euer and euer.

11 Thine, O Lord, *is* the greatnes, and the power, and the glory, & the
victorie, and the maiestie: for all *that is* in
the heauen & in the earth, *is thine*: thine
is *the kingdome, O Lord, and thou
art exalted as head aboue all.

12 Both riches, and honour come of
thee, and thou reignest ouer all, and in
thine hand *is* power and might, and in

thine hand *it is* to make great, and to
giue strength vnto all.

13 Now therefore, our God, wee
thanke thee, and praise thy glorious
Name.

14 But who *am* I, and what *is* my
people, that we should †be able to offer
so willingly after this sort? for all things
come of thee, and of †thine owne haue
we giuen thee.

15 For we *are* strangers before thee,
and soiourners, as *were* all our fathers:
*Our dayes on the earth *are* as a shadow, and there *is* none †abiding.

16 O Lord our God, all this store
that we haue prepared to build thee an
house for thine holy Name, commeth of
thine hand, and *is* all thine owne.

17 I know also, my God, that thou
*triest the heart, and hast pleasure in vp-
rightnesse. As for me, in the vprightnes
of mine heart I haue willingly offered
all these things: and now haue I seene
with ioy, thy people which are †present
here, to offer willingly vnto thee.

18 O Lord God of Abraham,
Isaac and of Israel our fathers, keepe
this for euer in the imagination of the
thoughts of the heart of thy people, and
‖prepare their heart vnto thee:

19 And giue vnto Solomon my sonne
a perfect heart to keepe thy Commaundements, thy testimonies, and thy statutes, and to doe all *these things*, and to
build the pallace, *for* the which I haue
made prouision.

20 ¶ And Dauid said to all the Congregation: Nowe blesse the Lord
your God. And all the Congregation
blessed the Lord God of their fathers, and bowed downe their heads,
and worshipped the Lord, and the
King.

21 And they sacrificed sacrifices vnto
the Lord, & offered burnt offerings
vnto the Lord on the morrow after
that day, euen a thousand bullockes, a
thousand rams, *and* a thousand lambes,
with their drinke offerings, and sacrifices in abundance for all Israel:

22 And did eate and drinke before
the Lord on that day with great
gladnesse, and they made Solomon the
sonne of Dauid King the second time,
and *anointed *him* vnto the Lord to
be the chiefe gouernour, and Zadok to
be Priest.

23 Then Solomon sate on the
throne of the Lord, as king in stead
of

Margin notes

*1. king. 9.
28.

† *Hebr. to fill
his hand.*

*Mat. 6. 13
1. tim. 1. 17.
apoc. 5. 13.

† *Hebr. r
taine or
tainstren*

† *Hebr. c
thine har*

* Psal. 39
and 90. 9
heb. 11.
1. pet. 2.
† *Hebr. e
pectation*

* Cha. 28
1. Sam. 16

† *Heb. fo*

‖ *Or, stabi*

1. King.
33.

24 And all the princes and the mightie men, and all the sonnes likewise of king Dauid, †submitted themselues vnto Solomon the King.

*Heb. gaue hand vn- Solomon.

25 And the LORD magnified Solomon exceedingly in the sight of all Israel, and *bestowed vpon him such royal maiestie, as had not bene on any king before him in Israel.

King. 3. 2. chro. 2. eccles. 9.

26 ¶ Thus Dauid the sonne of Iesse, reigned ouer all Israel.

27 And the time that he reigned ouer Israel, was fourtie yeeres. Seuen yeeres reigned hee in Hebron, and thirtie and three yeeres reigned hee in Ierusalem.

28 And he died in a good old age, full of dayes, riches and honour : and Solomon his sonne reigned in his stead.

29 Now the acts of Dauid the King first and last, behold, they are written in the ‖booke of Samuel the Seer, and in the †booke of Nathan the Prophet, and in the booke of Gad the Seer,

30 With all his reigne and his might, and the times that went ouer him, and ouer Israel, and ouer all the kingdomes of the countreys.

‖Or, historie.
†Hebr. words.

¶ THE SECOND BOOKE

of the Chronicles.

CHAP. I.

1 The solemne offering of Solomon at Gibeon. 7 Solomons choise of wisdome is blessed by God. 13 Solomons strength and wealth.

Nd Solomon the sonne of Dauid was strengthned in his kingdome, *and the LORD his God was with him, & magnified him exceedingly.

* King. 2.

2 Then Solomon spake vnto all Israel, to the captaines of thousands, and of hundreds, and to the Iudges, and to euery gouernour in all Israel, the chiefe of the fathers.

3 So Solomon and all the Congregation with him, went to the high place that was at *Gibeon, for there was the Tabernacle of the Congregation of God, which Moses the seruant of the LORD had made in the wildernesse.

. King. 3. 1. Chro. . 39. d 21. 29.

4 *But the Arke of God had Dauid brought vp from Kiriath-iearim, to the place which Dauid had prepared for it : for he had pitched a tent for it at Ierusalem.

. Sam 6. 17.

5 Moreouer *the brasen Altar that

Exod. 38.

Bezaleel the sonne of Vri, the sonne of Hur, had made, ‖hee put before the Tabernacle of the LORD : and Solomon and the Congregation sought vnto it.

‖Or, was there.

6 And Solomon went vp thither to the brasen Altar before the LORD, which was at the Tabernacle of the Congregation, and offered a thousand burnt offerings vpon it.

7 ¶ In that night did God appeare vnto Solomon, and saide vnto him ; Aske what I shall giue thee.

8 And Solomon saide vnto God, Thou hast shewed great mercy vnto Dauid my father, and hast made *me to reigne in his stead :

* 1. Chro. 28. 5.

9 Now, O LORD God, let thy promise vnto Dauid my father be established : *for thou hast made mee King ouer a people, †like the dust of the earth in multitude.

* 1. King. 3. 9.
† Heb. much as the dust of the earth.

10 Giue *mee now wisedome and knowledge, that I may goe out and come in before this people. For who can iudge this thy people, that is so great ?

* 1. King. 3. 11, 12. num. 27. 17.

11 And God said to Solomon, Because this was in thine heart, and thou hast not asked riches, wealth, or honour, nor the life of thine enemies, neither yet hast asked long life ; but hast asked

asked wisedome and knowledge for thy selfe, that thou mayest iudge my people, ouer whom I haue made thee King:

12 Wisedome and knowledge is granted vnto thee, and I will giue thee riches, and wealth, and honour, such as *none of the kings haue had, that haue beene before thee, neither shall there any after thee haue the like.

* 1. Chron. 29. 25. eccles. 2. 9. 2. chro. 9. 22.

13 ¶ Then Solomon came *from his iourney* to the high place that *was* at Gibeon, to Ierusalem, from before the Tabernacle of the Congregation, and reigned ouer Israel.

14 * And Solomon gathered charets and horsemen : and hee had a thousand and foure hundred charets, and twelue thousand horsemen, which he placed in the charet - cities, and with the King at Ierusalem.

* 1. King. 10. 26. &c. and 4. 26.

15 * And the King † made siluer and gold at Ierusalem *as* plenteous as stones, and Cedar trees made hee as the Sycomore trees, that *are* in the vale for abundance.

* 1. King. 10. 26. 2. chro. 9. 27, 28. † Heb. gaue.

16 * And † Solomon had horses brought out of Egypt, and linen yarne: the Kings merchants receiued the linnen yarne at a price.

* 1. King. 10. 28. 2. chro. 9. 28. † Heb. the going foorth of the horses which was Solomons.

17 And they fetcht vp and brought foorth out of Egypt, a charet for sixe hundred shekels of siluer, and an horse for an hundred and fiftie: and so brought they out horses for all the kings of the Hittites, and for the kings of Syria, †by their meanes.

† Heb. by their hand.

CHAP. II.

1 and 17 Solomons labourers for the building of the Temple. 3 His embassage to Huram for workemen and prouision of stuffe. 11 Huram sendeth him a kinde answere.

AND Solomon determined to build an house for the Name of the LORD, and an house for his kingdome.

2 And Solomon told out threescore and tenne thousand men to beare burdens, and fourescore thousand to hewe in the mountaine, and three thousand and six hundred to ouersee them.

3 ¶ And Solomon sent to ||Huram the king of Tyre, saying, As thou diddest deale with Dauid my father, and diddest send him Cedars to builde him an house to dwell therein, *euen so deale with me.*

|| Or, Hiram, 1. King. 5. 1.

4 Behold, I build an house to the name of the LORD my God, to dedicate *it* to him, and to burne before him †sweet incense, and for the continuall shew-bread, and for the burnt offrings morning and euening, on the Sabbaths, and on the new Moones, and on the solemne feasts of the LORD our God. This *is an ordinance* for euer to Israel.

† Heb. incense of ces.

5 And the house which I build, *is* great: for great *is* our God aboue all gods.

6 *But who †is able to build him an house, seeing the heauen, and heauen of heauens cannot conteine him? who am I then that I should build him an house? saue onely to burne sacrifice before him?

* 1. King 27. 2. ch 6. 18. † Heb. h retained obtained strength.

7 Send me now therefore a man, cunning to worke in gold and in siluer, and in brasse, and in yron, and in purple and crimson, and blew, and that can skil to †graue, with the cunning men that *are* with me in Iudah, and in Ierusalem, whome Dauid my father did prouide.

† Heb. to graue g uings.

8 Send me also Cedar trees, firre trees, and ||Algume trees, out of Lebanon : (for I know that thy seruants can skill to cut timber in Lebanon) and behold, my seruants *shalbe* with thy seruants,

|| Or, Almuggim, Kin. 10.

9 Euen to prepare me timber in abundance : for the house which I am about to build, shalbe †wonderfull great.

† Heb. g and won full.

10 And behold, I will giue to thy seruants the hewers that cut timber, twentie thousand measures of beaten wheat, and twentie thousand measures of barley, and twentie thousand baths of wine, and twentie thousand baths of oyle.

11 ¶ Then Huram the king of Tyre answered in writing, which hee sent to Solomon : Because the LORD hath loued his people, hee hath made thee King ouer them.

12 Huram said moreouer, Blessed *be* the LORD God of Israel that made heauen and earth, who hath giuen to Dauid the King a wise sonne, †indued with prudence and vnderstanding, that might build an house for the LORD, and an house for his kingdome.

† Heb. kr ing prud and und standing

13 And now I haue sent a cunning man (indued with vnderstanding) of Huram my fathers:

14 The sonne of a woman of the daugh-

daughters of Dan, and his father *was* a man of Tyre, skilfull to worke in golde and in siluer, in brasse, in yron, in stone and in timber, in purple, in blew, and in fine linen, and in crimson : also to graue any maner of grauing, and to find out euery deuice which shall be put to him, with thy cunning men, and with the cunning men of my lord Dauid thy father.

15 Now therefore the wheate and the barley, the oyle and the wine, which my lord hath spoken of, let him send vnto his seruants :

16 And wee will cut wood out of Lebanon, †as much as thou shalt need, and wee will bring it to thee in flotes by sea to †Ioppa, and thou shalt carie it vp to Ierusalem.

17 ¶ * And Solomon numbred all †the strangers that *were* in the lande of Israel, after the numbring wherewith Dauid his father had numbred them : and they were found an hundred and fiftie thousand, and three thousand and sixe hundred.

18 And he set *threescore and ten thousand of them *to be* bearers of burdens, and fourescore thousand *to be* hewers in the mountaine, and three thousand and sixe hundred ouerseers to set the people a worke.

CHAP. III.

1 The place, and time of building the Temple. 3 The measure and ornaments of the house. 11 The Cherubims. 14 The vaile and pillars.

THen *Solomon began to build the house of the LORD at Ierusalem in Mount Moriah, ‖where the LORD appeared vnto Dauid his father, in the place that Dauid had prepared in the threshing floore of ‖Ornan the Iebusite.

2 And he began to build in the second *day* of the second moneth, in the fourth yeere of his reigne.

3 ¶ Now these *are the things* *wherein Solomon was †instructed for the building of the house of God. The length by cubites after the first measure *was* threescore cubites, and the breadth twentie cubites.

4 And the *porch that *was* in the front *of the house,* the length *of it* was atcording to the breadth of the house, twentie cubites, and the height *was* an hundred and

twenty : and he ouerlaid it within, with pure gold.

5 And the greater house hee sieled with firre tree, which he ouerlaid with fine gold, and set thereon palme trees and chaines.

6 And he †garnished the house with precious stones for beautie, and the gold *was* gold of Paruaim.

7 Hee ouerlaid also the house, the beames, the postes and the wals thereof, and the doores thereof with gold, and graued Cherubims on the walles.

8 And he made the most holy house, the length whereof was, according to the breadth of the house, twenty cubits, and the breadth thereof twentie cubits : and he ouerlaid it with fine gold *amounting* to sixe hundred talents.

9 And the weight of the nailes was fiftie shekels of gold : and he ouerlaide the vpper chambers with gold.

10 And in the most holy place hee made two Cherubims of ‖image work, and ouerlaid them with gold.

11 ¶ And the wings of the Cherubims *were* twentie cubites long : *one* wing of the one *Cherub was* fiue cubites, reaching to the wall of the house : and the other wing was likewise fiue cubites, reaching to the wing of the other Cherub :

12 And *one* wing of the other Cherub was fiue cubites, reaching to the wall of the house : and the other wing was fiue cubites also, ioyning to the wing of the other Cherub.

13 The wings of these Cherubims spread themselues forth twentie cubits : and they stood on their feet, and their faces *were* ‖inward.

14 ¶ And he made the *vaile of blue and purple, and crimson, and fine linen, and †wrought Cherubims thereon.

15 Also hee made before the house, *two pillars of thirtie and fiue cubites †high, and the chapiter that was on the top of each of them, was fiue cubites.

16 And he made chaines, *as* in the Oracle, and put *them* on the heads of the pillars, and made an hundred pomegranates, and put *them* on the chaines.

17 And he *reared vp the pillars before the temple, one on the right hand, and the other on the left, and called the name of that on the right hand, ‖Iachin, and the name of that on the left, ‖Boaz.

CHAP.

Heb. according to all thy need.
Heb. Iapho

As Ver. 3. Hebr. the men the strangers.

As it is ver.

1. Kin. 6.1, &c.

Or, which was seene of Dauid his father.

Or, Araunah, 2. Sam. 24. 18. 1. chr. 21. 18.

*1. King. 6.2.
†Heb. founded.*

1. King. 6.3.

†*Heb. couered.*

‖*Or, (as some thinke) of moouable worke.*

‖*Or, toward the house.*
Mat. 27. 51

†*Heb. caused to ascend*

†*Ier. 52. 21
1. king. 7. 15
†Hebr. long.*

1. King. 7. 21.

‖*That is, he shal establish*
†*That is, in it is strength*

CHAP. IIII.

1 The Altar of brasse. 2 The molten Sea vpon twelue oxen. 6 The ten lauers, candlesticks, and tables. 9 The Courts & the instruments of brasse. 19 The instruments of gold.

Oreouer he made an Altar of brasse, twentie cubites the length thereof, and twentie cubites the breadth thereof, and ten cubites the height therof.

2 ¶ * Also he made a molten Sea of ten cubites, †from brim to brim, round in compasse, and fiue cubites the height thereof, and a line of thirtie cubites did compasse it round about.

3 * And vnder it *was* the similitude of oxen, which did compasse it round about: tenne in a cubite compassing the Sea round about. Two rowes of oxen *were* cast, when it was cast.

4 It stood vpon twelue oxen: three looking toward the North, and three looking toward the West, and three looking toward the South, and three looking toward the East: and the Sea *was* set aboue vpon them, and all their hinder parts *were* inward.

5 And the thicknes of it *was* an hand breadth, & the brim of it like the worke of the brim of a cup, ‖with flowers of Lillies: *and* it receiued *and* held three thousand baths.

6 ¶ He made also ten Lauers, and put fiue on the right hand, and fiue on the left, to wash in them: such things as they offered for the †burnt offring, they washed in them, but the Sea was for the Priests to wash in.

7 And hee made ten candlesticks of gold according to their forme, and set *them* in the Temple, fiue on the right hand, and fiue on the left.

8 He made also ten tables, and placed *them* in the Temple, fiue on the right side, and fiue on the left: and hee made an hundred ‖basens of gold.

9 ¶ Furthermore, hee made the court of the Priests, and the great court, and doores for the court, and ouerlayd the doores of them with brasse.

10 And he set the Sea on the rightside of the East end, ouer against the South.

11 And Huram made the pots, and the shouels, and the ‖basens, and Huram †finished the worke that he was to make for King Solomon for the house of God:

12 *To wit*, the two pillars, and the pommels, and the chapiters, which *were* on the top of the two pillars, and the two wreathes to couer the two pommels of the chapiters, which *were* on the top of the pillars:

13 And foure hundred Pomegranats on the two wreathes: two rowes of Pomegranats on each wreath, to couer the two pommels of the chapiters, which *were* †vpon the pillars.

14 He made also bases; and ‖lauers made he vpon the bases.

15 One Sea, & twelue oxen vnder it.

16 The pots also, and the shouels, and the fleshhookes, and all their instruments, did Huram his father make to King Solomon for the house of the Lord, of †bright brasse.

17 In the plaine of Iordan did the King cast them, in the †clay-ground, betweene Succoth and Zeredathah.

18 Thus Solomon made all these vessels in great abundance: for the weight of the brasse could not be found out.

19 ¶ And Solomon made all the vessels, that *were* for the house of God, the golden Altar also, and the tables whereon the Shew-bread *was* set.

20 Moreouer the candlesticks with their lampes, that they should burne after the maner, before the Oracle, of pure gold:

21 And the flowers, and the lamps, and the tongs *made he* of golde, *and* that †perfect gold.

22 And the snuffers, and the ‖basens, and the spoones, and the censers, of pure gold. And the entry of the house, the inner doores thereof for the most Holy place, and the doores of the house of the Temple, *were* of gold.

CHAP. V.

1 The dedicated treasures. 2 The solemne induction of the Arke into the oracle. 11 God being praised, giueth a visible signe of his fauour.

Hus al the worke that Solomon made for the house of the Lord, was finished: * & Solomon brought in all the things that Dauid his father had dedicated; and the siluer, and the gold, and all the instruments, put he among the treasures of the house of God.

2 ¶ * Then Solomon assembled the

Marginal notes

* 1. King. 7. 23. &c.
† Hebr. from his brim, to his brim.

* 1. King. 7. 24.

‖ Or, like a Lillie flower.

† Hebr. the worke of burnt offering.

‖ Or, bowles.

‖ Or, bowles.
† Hebr. finished to make.

† Hebr. vpon the face.
‖ Or, caldrons.

† Heb. made bright, or scoured.
† Heb. thicknesses of the ground.

† Hebr. perfections of gold.
‖ Or, bowles.

* 1. King. 5¹.

* 1. King. 1. &c.

the Elders of Israel, and all the heads of the Tribes, the chiefe of the fathers of the children of Israel vnto Ierusalem, to bring vp the Arke of the Couenant of the LORD, out of the citie of Dauid, which is Zion.

3 Wherefore all the men of Israel assembled themselues vnto the king in the feast, which was in the seuenth moneth.

4 And all the Elders of Israel came, and the Leuites tooke vp the Arke.

5 And they brought vp the Arke, and the tabernacle of the Congregation, and all the holy vessels that were in the tabernacle, these did the Priests and the Leuites bring vp.

6 Also king Solomon and all the congregation of Israel that were assembled vnto him before the Arke, sacrificed sheepe and oxen, which could not be told nor numbred for multitude.

7 And the priests brought in the Arke of the Couenant of the LORD vnto his place, to the Oracle of the house, into the most holy place, euen vnder the wings of the Cherubims:

8 For the Cherubims spread foorth their wings ouer the place of the Arke, and the Cherubims couered the Arke and the staues thereof, aboue.

9 And they drew out the staues of the Arke, that the ends of the staues were seene from the Arke before the Oracle, but they were not seene without. And there ||it is vnto this day.

10 There was nothing in the Arke saue the two tables which Moses *put therein at Horeb, || when the LORD made a couenant with the children of Israel, when they came out of Egypt.

11 ¶ And it came to passe when the Priests were come out of the holy place (for all the priests that were †present were sanctified, and did not then wait by course)

12 *Also the Leuites which were the singers, all of them of Asaph, of Heman, of Ieduthun, with their sonnes and their brethren, being arayed in white linnen hauing cymbals, and psalteries, and harpes, stood at the East end of the altar, and with them an hundred and twentie Priests, sounding with trumpets:)

13 It came euen to passe, as the trumpetters and singers were as one, to make one sound to be heard in praising

and thanking the LORD: and when they lift vp their voyce with the trumpets, and cymbals, and instruments of musicke, and praised the LORD, saying, * For he is good, for his mercie endureth for euer: that then the house was filled with a cloude, euen the house of the LORD.

14 So that the Priests could not stand to minister, by reason of the cloud: for the glory of the LORD had filled the house of God.

CHAP. VI.

1 Solomon hauing blessed the people, blesseth God. 12 Solomons prayer in the consecration of the Temple, vpon the brasen scaffold.

THen *said Solomon, The LORD hath said that he would dwell in the *thicke darkenesse.

2 But I haue built an house of habitation for thee, and a place for thy dwelling for euer.

3 And the King turned his face and blessed the whole Congregation of Israel, (and all the Congregation of Israel stood)

4 And he said, Blessed be the LORD God of Israel, who hath with his handes fulfilled that which he spake with his mouth to my father Dauid, saying,

5 Since the day that I brought foorth my people out of the land of Egypt, I chose no citie among all the tribes of Israel to builde an house in, that my Name might be there, neither chose I any man to be a ruler ouer my people Israel:

6 But I haue chosen Ierusalem, that my name might be there, and haue chosen Dauid to be ouer my people Israel.

7 Now *it was in the heart of Dauid my father to build an house for the Name of the LORD God of Israel.

8 But the LORD said to Dauid my father : Forasmuch as it was in thine heart to builde an house for my Name, thou diddest well in that it was in thine heart.

9 Notwithstanding thou shalt not build the house, but thy sonne which shall come foorth out of thy loynes, he shall build the house for my Name.

10 The LORD therefore hath performed his word that he hath spoken: for

|| Or, they are there, as 1. king. 8. 8.

* Deut. 10. 2, 5.
|| Or, where.

† Hsb. found

* 1. Chron. 24. 5.

* Psal. 136.

* 1. King. 8. 12, &c.
* Leuit. 16. 2.

* 2. Sam. 7. 2. 1. chro. 28. 2.

for I am risen vp in the roome of Dauid my father, and am set on the throne of Israel, as the LORD promised, and haue built the house for the Name of the LORD God of Israel.

11 And in it haue I put the Arke, wherein *is* the Couenant of the LORD, that hee made with the children of Israel.

12 ¶ And he stood before the Altar of the LORD, in the presence of all the Congregation of Israel, and spread foorth his hands :

13 (For Solomon had made a brasen scaffold of fiue cubites †long, and fiue cubites broad, and three cubites high, and had set it in the midst of the Court, and vpon it hee stood, and kneeled downe vpon his knees before all the Congregation of Israel, and spread foorth his hands towards heauen.)

14 And said, O LORD God of Israel, *there is no God* like thee in the heauen, nor in the earth, which keepest couenant, and *shewest* mercy vnto thy seruants, that walke before thee with all their hearts,

15 Thou which hast kept with thy seruant Dauid my father, that which thou hast promised him : and spakest with thy mouth, and hast fulfilled it with thine hand, as it is this day.

16 Now therefore, O LORD God of Israel, keepe with thy seruant Dauid my father, that which thou hast promised him, saying, *There shall not †faile thee a man in my sight, to sit vpon the throne of Israel : *yet so, that thy children take heede to their way, to walke in my Law, as thou hast walked before me.

17 Now then, O LORD God of Israel, let thy word be verified, which thou hast spoken vnto thy seruant Dauid.

18 (But wil God in very deed dwell with men on the earth? *Behold, heauen, and the heauen of heauens cannot conteine thee : how much lesse this house which I haue built?)

19 Haue respect therfore to the prayer of thy seruant, and to his supplication, O LORD my God, to hearken vnto the cry, and the prayer which thy seruant prayeth before thee :

20 That thine eyes may bee open vpon this house day and night, vpon the place whereof thou hast saide, that thou wouldest put thy Name there, to hearken vnto the prayer, which thy seruant prayeth ‖towards this place.

21 Hearken therefore vnto the supplications of thy seruant, and of thy people Israel, which they shall †make towards this place : heare thou from thy dwelling place, euen from heauen ; and when thou hearest, forgiue.

22 ¶ If a man sinne against his neighbour, †and an oath be layd vpon him, to make him sweare, and the oath come before thine Altar in this house :

23 Then heare thou from heauen, and doe, and iudge thy seruants by requiting the wicked, by recompensing his way vpon his owne head, and by iustifying the righteous, by giuing him according to his righteousnesse.

24 ¶ And if thy people Israel †be put to the worse before the enemy, because they haue sinned against thee, and shall returne and confesse thy Name, and pray and make supplication before thee ‖in this house :

25 Then heare thou from the heauens, and forgiue the sinne of thy people Israel, and bring them againe vnto the land which thou gauest to them, and to their fathers.

26 ¶ When the *heauen is shut vp, and there is no raine, because they haue sinned against thee : *yet* if they pray towards this place, and confesse thy Name, and turne from their sinne, when thou doest afflict them :

27 Then heare thou from heauen, and forgiue the sinne of thy seruants, and of thy people Israel ; when thou hast taught them the good way, wherein they should walke, and send raine vpon the land, which thou hast giuen vnto thy people for an inheritance.

28 ¶ If there *be dearth in the land, if there be pestilence, if there be blasting, or mil-dew, locusts or caterpillers ; if their enemies besiege them in the †cities of their land : whatsoeuer sore, or whatsoeuer sicknesse there *be* :

29 *Then* what prayer, *or* what supplication soeuer shall bee made of any man, or of all thy people Israel, when euery one shal know his owne sore and his owne griefe, and shall spread foorth his hands ‖in this house :

30 Then heare thou from heauen thy dwelling place, and forgiue, and render vnto euery man according vnto all his wayes, whose heart thou knowest (for thou onely *knowest the hearts of

---

Marginal notes

† Hebr. the length thereof, &c.

* Exod. 15. 11.

* 2. Sam. 7. 12. 1. king. 2. 4. and 6. 12.
† Heb. there shall not a man be cut off.
* Psal. 132. 12.

* Chap. 2. 6. esay 66. 1. acts. 7. 49.

‖ Or, in this place.

† Heb. pra.

† Hebr. and he require an oath of him.

‖ Or, bee smitten.

‖ Or, toward

* 1. King. 17. 1.

* Chap. 20. 9.
† Hebr. in the land of their gates.

‖ Or, toward this house.

* 1. Chron. 28. 9.

*Hebr. all
e dayes
hich.*

*Hebr. vpon
e face of
e land.*

*Iohn 12.
. acts. 8.*

of the children of men :)

31 That they may feare thee, to walke in thy waies †so long as they liue †in the land which thou gauest vnto our fathers.

32 ¶ Moreouer concerning the stranger *which is not of thy people Israel, but is come from a farre countrey for thy great Names sake, & thy mightie hand, and thy stretched out arme : if they come and pray in this house:

*Heb. thy
'ame is cal-
d vpon this
use.*

33 Then heare thou from the heauens, euen from thy dwelling place, and doe according to all that the stranger calleth to thee for; that all people of the earth may know thy Name, and feare thee, as doeth thy people Israel, and may know that † this house which I haue built, is called by thy Name.

34 If thy people goe out to warre against their enemies by the way that thou shalt send them, and they pray vnto thee toward this citie which thou hast chosen, and the house which I haue built for thy Name:

Or, right.

35 Then heare thou from the heauens their prayer and their supplication, and maintaine their ‖cause.

*Prou. 20. 9.
cles. 7. 21.
ames 3. 2.
iohn 1. 8.*

*Heb. they
rat take
rem cap-
ues cary
rem away.*

*Heb. bring
rack to their
eart.*

36 If they sinne against thee (for *there is* * no man which sinneth not) and thou be angry with them, and deliuer them ouer before their enemies, and † they cary them away captiues vnto a land far off or neere:

37 Yet *if* they †bethinke themselues in the land whither they are caried captiue, and turne and pray vnto thee in the land of their captiuitie, saying, Wee haue sinned, we haue done amisse, and haue dealt wickedly:

38 If they returne to thee with all their heart, and with all their soule, in the land of their captiuitie, whither they haue caried them captiues, and pray toward their land which thou gauest vnto their fathers, and *toward* the citie which thou hast chosen, and toward the house which I haue built for thy Name:

Or, right.

39 Then heare thou from the heauens, *euen* from thy dwelling place, their prayer and their supplications, and maintaine their ‖cause, and forgiue thy people, which haue sinned against thee.

*Heb. to the
rayer of this
place.*

40 Now, my God, let (I beseech thee) thine eyes bee open, and let thine eares be attent †vnto the prayer *that is made* in this place.

41 Now *therefore arise, O LORD God, into thy resting place, thou, and the Arke of thy strength : Let thy Priests, O LORD God, be clothed with saluation, and let thy Saints reioyce in goodnesse.

*Psal. 132. 9

42 O LORD God, turne not away the face of thine anointed : remember the mercies of Dauid thy seruant.

CHAP. VII.

1 God hauing giuen testimonie to Solomons prayer by fire from heauen, and glory in the Temple, the people worship him. 4 Solomons solemne sacrifice. 8 Solomon hauing kept the feast of Tabernacles and the feast of the Dedication of the Altar, dismisseth the people. 12 God appearing to Solomon, giueth him promises vpon condition.

Ow when Solomon had made an ende of praying, the *fire came downe from heauen, and consumed the burnt offering, and the sacrifices, and the glory of the LORD filled the house.

*1. King. 8.
54, &c. le-
uit. 9. 24.

2 And the Priests could not enter into the house of the LORD, because the glory of the LORD had filled the LORDS house.

3 And when all the children of Israel saw how the fire came downe, and the glory of the LORD vpon the house, they bowed themselues with their faces to the ground vpon the pauement, and worshipped, and praised the LORD, *saying*, For hee *is* good, for his mercy *endureth* for euer.

4 ¶ Then the King and all the people, offered sacrifices before the LORD.

5 And King Solomon offered a sacrifice of twentie and two thousand oxen, and an hundred and twentie thousand sheepe. So the King and all the people, dedicated the house of God.

6 *And the Priests waited on their offices : the Leuites also with instruments of musicke of the LORD, which Dauid the King had made to praise the LORD, because his mercy *endureth* for euer, when Dauid praised †by their ministerie : and the Priests sounded trumpets before them, and all Israel stood.

*1. Chron.
16. 16.

†Heb. by
their hand.

7 Moreouer, Solomon hallowed the middle of the Court, that *was* before the house of the LORD : for there hee offered burnt offerings, and the fat of the peace offerings, because the brasen
altar

Altar which Solomon had made, was not able to receiue the burnt offerings, and the meat offerings, and the fat.

8 ¶ Also at the same time Solomon kept the feast seuen dayes, and all Israel with him, a very great Congregation, from the entring in of Hamath, vnto the * Riuer of Egypt.

9 And in the eight day they made †a solemne assembly : for they kept the dedication of the Altar seuen dayes, and the feast seuen dayes.

10 And on the three and twentieth day of the seuenth moneth, he sent the people away into their tents, glad and merry in heart for the goodnesse that the Lord had shewed vnto Dauid, and to Solomon, and to Israel his people.

11 Thus * Solomon finished the house of the Lord, and the Kings house : and all that came into Solomons heart to make in the house of the Lord, and in his owne house, hee prosperously effected.

12 ¶ And the Lord appeared to Solomon by night, and said vnto him, I haue heard thy prayer, * and haue chosen this place to my selfe for an house of sacrifice.

13 If I shut vp heauen that there bee no raine, or if I command the locusts to deuoure the land, or if I send pestilence among my people :

14 If my people †which are called by my Name, shall humble themselues and pray, and seeke my face, and turne from their wicked wayes : then will I heare from heauen, and will forgiue their sinne, and will heale their land.

15 Now mine eyes shalbe open, and mine * eares attent †vnto the prayer that is made in this place.

16 For now haue * I chosen, & sanctified this house, that my Name may be there for euer : and mine eyes and mine heart shalbe there perpetually.

17 And as for thee, if thou wilt walke before me, as Dauid thy father walked, and doe according to all that I haue commanded thee, and shalt obserue my Statutes, and my Iudgements :

18 Then wil I stablish the throne of thy kingdome, according as I haue couenanted with Dauid thy father, saying, *† There shall not faile thee a man to be ruler in Israel.

19 * But if yee turne away and forsake my Statutes and my Commandements which I haue set before you, and shall goe and serue other gods, and worship them :

20 Then will I plucke them vp by the roots out of my land which I haue giuen them, and this house which I haue sanctified for my Name, wil I cast out of my sight, and will make it to be a prouerbe, and a by-word among all nations.

21 And this house which is high, shall be an astonishment to euery one that passeth by it ; so that hee shall say ; * Why hath the Lord done thus vnto this land, and vnto this house ?

22 And it shalbe answered, Because they forsooke the Lord God of their fathers, which brought them forth out of the land of Egypt, and layd hold on others gods, and worshipped them, aud serued them : Therefore hath hee brought all this euil vpon them.

CHAP. VIII.

1 Solomons buildings. 7 The Gentiles which were left, Solomon made tributaries, but the Israelites, rulers. 11 Pharaohs daughter remoueth to her house. 12 Solomons yeerely solemne sacrifices. 14 Hee appointeth the Priests and Leuites to their places. 17 The Nauie fetcheth gold from Ophir.

Nd *it came to passe (at the end of twentie yeeres, wherein Solomon had built the house of the Lord, & his own house)

2 That the cities which Huram had restored to Solomon, Solomon built them, and caused the children of Israel to dwell there.

3 And Solomon went to Hamath Zobah, and preuailed against it.

4 And he built Tadmor in the wildernesse, and all the store-cities, which he built in Hamath.

5 Also he built Beth-horon the vpper, and Beth-horon the nether, fensed cities with walles, gates and barres :

6 And Baalath, and all the store-cities that Solomon had, and all the charet-cities, and the cities of the horsemen, and †all that Solomon desired to build in Ierusalem, and in Lebanon, and throughout all the land of his dominion.

7 ¶ As for all the people that were left of the Hittites, and the Amorites, and

* Iosh. 13. 3.
† Hebr. a restraint.

* 1. King. 9. 1. &c.

* Deut 12. 5.

† Hebr. vpon whom my Name is called.

* Chap. 6. 40.
† Heb. to the prayer of this place.
* Chap. 6. 6.

* Chap. 6. 16.
† Hebr. there shall not be cut off to thee.
* Leuit. 26. 14. deut. 28. 15.

* Deut. 29 24, iere. 22 8, 9.

* 1. King. 10, &c.

† Hebr. all the desire of Solomon, which he desired to build.

and the Perizzites, and the Hiuites, and the Iebusites, which were not of Israel :

8 But of their children, who were left after them in the land, whom the children of Israel consumed not ; them did Solomon make to pay tribute, vntill this day.

9 But of the children of Israel did Solomon make no seruants for his worke : but they were men of warre, and chiefe of his captaines, and captaines of his charets and horsemen.

10 And these *were* the chiefe of king Solomons officers, euen two hundred and fifty, that bare rule ouer the people.

*1. King.
3. 1. & 7. 8.

11 ¶ And Solomon *brought vp the daughter of Pharaoh out of the citie of Dauid, vnto the house that he had built for her : for hee said, My wife shall not dwell in the house of Dauid king of Israel, because the *places* are †holy, whereunto the Arke of the Lord hath come.

*Heb. holinesse.

12 ¶ Then Solomon offered burnt offerings vnto the Lord on the Altar of the Lord, which he had built before the porch :

*Exod. 29.
23.

13 Euen after a certaine rate euery *day, offering according to the commandement of Moses, on the Sabbaths, and on the new Moones, and on the solemne Feasts *three times in the yeere, *euen* in the feast of Vnleauened bread, and in the feast of Weekes, and in the feast of Tabernacles.

*Exod. 23.
14. deut.
16. 16.

14 ¶ And he appointed, according to the order of Dauid his father, the *courses of the Priests to their seruice, and the Leuites to their charges, to praise and minister before the Priests, as the duety of euery day required : the *porters also by their courses, at euery gate : for †so had Dauid the man of God commanded.

*1. Chron.
24. 1.

*1. Chron.
9. 17.
†Heb. so was
the commandement of
Dauid the
man of God.

15 And they departed not from the commandement of the King vnto the Priests and Leuites, concerning any matter, or concerning the treasures.

16 Now all the worke of Solomon was prepared vnto the day of the foundation of the house of the Lord, and vntill it was finished : *so* the house of God was perfected.

17 ¶ Then went Solomon to Ezion Geber, and to || Eloth, at the sea side in the land of Edom.

||Or, Elath,
deut. 2. 8.

18 And Huram sent him by the hands of his seruants, shippes, and seruants that had knowledge of the sea ; and they went with the seruants of Solomon to Ophir, and tooke thence foure hundred and fiftie talents of golde, and brought *them* to king Solomon.

CHAP. IX.

1 The Queene of Sheba admireth the wisedome of Solomon. 13 Solomons golde, 15 His Targets. 17 The throne of Iuory. 20 His vessels. 23 His presents. 25 His chariots and horse. 26 His tributes. 29 His reigne and death.

And *when the Queene of Sheba heard of the fame of Solomon, shee came to prooue Solomon with hard questions at Ierusalem, with a very great companie, and camels that bare spices, and golde in abundance, and precious stones : and when she was come to Solomon, shee communed with him of all that was in her heart.

*1. King.
10. 1, &c.
mat. 12. 42.
luke 11. 31.

2 And Solomon tolde her all her questions : and there was nothing hid from Solomon, which he told her not.

3 And when the Queene of Sheba had seene the wisedome of Solomon, and the house that he had built,

4 And the meate of his table, and the sitting of his seruants, and the attendance of his ministers, and their apparell, his || cup-bearers also, and their apparell, and his ascent, by which hee went vp into the house of the Lord; there was no more spirit in her.

||Or, butlers

5 And she said to the King, It *was* a true †report which I heard in mine owne land, of thine || actes, and of thy wisedome :

†Heb. word.
||Or, sayings

6 Howbeit, I beleeued not their wordes, vntill I came, and mine eyes had seene *it :* and behold, the one halfe of the greatnesse of thy wisedome was not tolde mee : *for* thou exceedest the fame that I heard.

7 Happy *are* thy men, and happy *are* these thy seruants, which stand continually before thee, and heare thy wisedome.

8 Blessed be the Lord thy God, which delighted in thee to set thee on his throne, to be King for the Lord thy God : because thy God loued Israel, to establish them for euer, therefore made hee thee King ouer them, to doe iudgement and iustice.

9 And

9 And she gaue the king an hundred and twentie talents of gold, and of spices great abundance, & precious stones : neither was there any such spice as the Queene of Sheba gaue King Solomon.

10 And the seruants also of Huram, and the seruants of Solomon, which brought gold from Ophir, brought Algume trees and, precious stones.

11 And the king made *of* the Algume trees, †terrises to the house of the Lord, and to the kings palace, and harpes and psalteries for singers : and there were none such seene before in the land of Iudah.

‖Or, staires: Heb. high wayes.

12 And King Solomon gaue to the Queene of Sheba, all her desire, whatsoeuer she asked, besides that which she had brought vnto the king : So she turned, and went away to her owne land, she, and her seruants.

13 ¶ Now the weight of gold that came to Solomon in one yeere, was sixe hundred and threescore and sixe talents of gold :

14 Besides that which chapmen and merchants brought : and all the kings of Arabia, and ‖gouernours of the countrie, brought gold and siluer to Solomon.

‖Or, captaines.

15 ¶ And king Solomon made two hundred targets of beaten gold : sixe hundred *shekels* of beaten gold went to one target.

16 And three hundred shields *made he* of beaten gold : three hundred *shekels* of gold went to one shield : and the king put them in the house of the forrest of Lebanon.

17 Moreouer the king made a great throne of yuorie, and ouerlaid it with pure gold.

18 And *there were* sixe steps to the throne, with a footstoole of gold, *which were* fastened to the throne, and †stayes on each side of the sitting place, and two lyons standing by the stayes

† Heb. hands

19 And twelue lyons stood there on the one side and on the other, vpon the sixe steps. There was not the like made in any kingdome.

20 ¶ And all the drinking vessels of King Solomon *were* of gold, and all the vessels of the house of the forrest of Lebanon *were* of †pure gold : ‖none *were* of siluer; it was *not* any thing accounted of in the dayes of Solomon.

† Heb. shut vp.
‖ Or, there was no siluer in them.

21 For the kings ships went to Tarshish with the seruants of Huram : euerie three yeeres once came the ships of Tarshish bringing golde, and siluer, ‖yuorie, and apes, and peacocks.

‖ Or, elephants tee

22 And king Solomon passed all the kings of the earth in riches and wisedome.

23 ¶ And all the kings of the earth sought the presence of Solomon, to heare his wisedome, that God had put in his heart.

24 And they brought euery man his present, vessels of siluer, and vessels of gold, and raiment, harnesse, and spices, horses, and mules, a rate yeere by yeere.

25 ¶ And Solomon *had foure thousand stalles for horses, and charets, and twelue thousand horsemen, whom hee bestowed in the charet cities, and with the king at Ierusalem.

* 1. King. 26.

26 ¶ And hee reigned ouer all the kings, *from the ‖riuer, euen vnto the land of the Philistines, and to the border of Egypt.

* Gen. 15. 18.
‖ That is, Euphrates

27 And the king †made siluer in Ierusalem as stones, and cedar trees made he as the Sycomore trees, that *are* in the low plaines, in abundance.

† Heb. gau

28 *And they brought vnto Solomon horses out of Egypt, and out of all lands.

* 1. King. 28. and 2. chron. 1. 1

29 ¶ Now the rest of the *actes of Solomon first and last, *are* they not written in the †booke of Nathan the Prophet, and in the prophesie of Ahiiah the Shilonite, and in the visions of *Iddo the Seer, against Ieroboam the sonne of Nebat ?

* 1. King. 41.
† Heb. word
* Chap. 12. 15.

30 And Solomon reigned in Ierusalem ouer all Israel, fourtie yeeres

31 And Solomon slept with his fathers, and hee was buried in the citie of Dauid his father, and Rehoboam his sonne reigned in his stead.

CHAP. X.

1 The Israelites assembled at Shechem to crowne Rehoboam, by Ieroboam make a suite of relaxation vnto him. 6 Rehoboam, refusing the old mens counsell, by the aduice of yong men, answereth them roughly. 16 Tenne Tribes reuolting, kill Hadoram, and make Rehoboam to flie.

AND *Rehoboam went to Shechem : for to Shechem were all Israel come to make him king.

1. King 12. 1, &c.

2 And it came to passe when Ieroboam the sonne of Nebat (who

(who *was* in Egypt, whither hee had fled from the presence of Solomon the king) heard it, that Ieroboam returned out of Egypt.

3 And they sent and called him. So Ieroboam and all Israel came, and spake to Rehoboam, saying,

4 Thy father made our yoke grieuous, nowe therefore ease thou somewhat the grieuous seruitude of thy father, and his heauy yoke that he put vpon vs, and we will serue thee.

5 And hee said vnto them, Come againe vnto me after three dayes. And the people departed.

6 ¶ And king Rehoboam tooke counsell with the old men that had stood before Solomon his father, while hee yet liued, saying, What counsell giue ye *me*, to returne answere to this people?

7 And they spake vnto him, saying, If thou bee kinde to this people, and please them, and speake good words to them, they will be thy seruants for euer.

8 But he forsooke the counsell which the old men gaue him, and tooke counsell with the yong men, that were brought vp with him, that stood before him.

9 And he said vnto them, What aduice giue ye, that wee may returne answere to this people, which haue spoken to me, saying, Ease vpon vs the yoke that thy father did put vpon vs?

10 And the yong men that were brought vp with him, spake vnto him, saying, Thus shalt thou answere the people that spake vnto thee, saying, Thy father made our yoke heauy, but make thou it somewhat lighter for vs: thus shalt thou say vnto them, My litle finger shall be thicker then my fathers loynes.

† *Heb. laded.*

11 For where as my father † put a heauy yoke vpon you, I will put more to your yoke: my father chastised you with whips, but I *will chastise you* with scorpions.

12 So Ieroboam and all the people came to Rehoboam on the third day, as the King bade, saying, Come againe to me on the third day

13 And the king answered them roughly, and king Rehoboam forsooke the counsell of the old men,

14 And answered them after the aduice of the yong men, saying, My father made your yoke heauy, but I will adde thereto: my father chastised you

with whips, but I *will chastise you* with scorpions.

15 So the king hearkened not vnto the people, for the cause was of God, that the Lord might performe his word, which he spake by the *hand of Ahijah the Shilonite to Ieroboam the sonne of Nebat.

* 1. King. 11 29.

16 ¶ And when all Israel *sawe* that the king would not hearken vnto them, the people answered the king saying, What portion *haue* wee in Dauid? and wee *haue* none inheritance in the sonne of Iesse: Euery man to your tents, O Israel: and now Dauid, see to thine owne house. So all Israel went to their tents.

17 But as for the children of Israel that dwelt in the cities of Iudah, Rehoboam reigned ouer them.

18 Then king Rehoboam sent Hadoram that *was* ouer the tribute, and the children of Israel stoned him with stones, that he died: but king Rehoboam †made speed to get him vp to his charet, to flee to Ierusalem.

† *Heb streng-thened him-selfe.*

19 And Israel rebelled against the house of Dauid vnto this day.

CHAP. XI.

A Nd *when Rehoboam was come to Ierusalem, he gathered of the house of Iudah and Beniamin, an hundred and fourescore thousand chosen *men*, which were warriers, to fight against Israel, that hee might bring the kingdome againe to Rehoboam.

* 1. King. 12 21, &c.

2 But the worde of the Lord came to Shemaiah the man of God, saying,

3 Speake vnto Rehoboam the son of Solomon, king of Iudah, and to all Israel in Iudah & Beniamin, saying,

4 Thus saith the Lord; Ye shall not goe vp, nor fight against your brethren: returne euery man to his house, for this thing is done of me. And they obeyed the words of the Lord, and returned from going against Ieroboam.

5 ¶ And

5 ¶ And Rehoboam dwelt in Ierusalem, and built cities for defence in Iudah.

6 He built euen Bethlehem, and Etam, and Tekoa,

7 And Bethzur, and Shoco, and Adullam,

8 And Gath, and Maresha, and Ziph,

9 And Adoraim, and Lachish, and Azekah,

10 And Zorah, and Aialon, and Hebron, which *are* in Iudah and in Beniamin, fenced cities.

11 And he fortified the strong holds, and put captaines in them, and store of vitaile, and of oyle and wine.

12 And in euery seuerall citie he put shields and speares, and made them exceeding strong, hauing Iudah and Beniamin on his side.

13 ¶ And the Priests and the Leuites that *were* in all Israel, † resorted to him out of all their coasts.

† Hebr. presented themselues to him.

14 For the Leuites left their suburbs, and their possession, and came to Iudah and Ierusalem : for Ieroboam * and his sonnes had cast them off from executing the Priests office vnto the Lord

* Chap. 13. 9.

15 And hee ordeined him priests for the high places, and for the deuils, and for the calues which he had made.

16 And after them out of all the tribes of Israel, such as set their hearts to seeke the Lord God of Israel, came to Ierusalem, to sacrifice vnto the Lord God of their fathers.

17 So they strengthened the kingdome of Iudah, and made Rehoboam the sonne of Solomon strong, three yeeres : for three yeeres they walked in the way of Dauid and Solomon.

18 ¶ And Rehoboam tooke him Mahalath the daughter of Ierimoth the sonne of Dauid to wife, *and* Abihail the daughter of Eliab the son of Iesse :

19 Which bare him children, Ieush, and Shamariah, and Zaham.

20 And after her, hee tooke * Maacah the daughter of Absalom, which bare him Abiiah, and Atthai, and Ziza, and Shelomith

* 1. King. 15. 2.

21 And Rehoboam loued Maacah the daughter of Absalom, aboue all his wiues and his concubines : for he tooke eighteene wiues, and threescore concubines, and begate twentie and eight sonnes, and threescore daughters.

22 And Rehoboam made Abiiah the sonne of Maacah the chiefe, to be ruler among his brethren: for *he thought* to make him king.

23 And he dealt wisely, and dispersed of all his children throughout all the countries of Iudah and Beniamin, vnto euery fenced citie: and hee gaue them vitaile in abundance : and hee desired †many wiues.

† Hebr. a multitude of wiues.

CHAP. XII.

1 Rehoboam forsaking the Lord, is punished by Shishak. 5 He and the Princes repenting at the preaching of Shemaiah, are deliuered from destruction, but not from spoile. 13 The reigne and death of Rehoboam.

And it came to passe when Rehoboam had established the kingdome, and had strengthened himselfe, hee forsooke the Law of the Lord, and all Israel with him.

2 And it came to passe, that in the fifth yere of Rehoboam, Shishak king of Egypt came vp against Ierusalem, (*because they had transgressed against the Lord)

* 1. King. 14. 24. and 25.

3 With twelue hundred charets, and threescore thousand horsemen : and the people *were* without number that came with him out of Egypt : the Lubims, the Sukkiims, & the Ethiopians.

4 And hee tooke the fenced cities which *perteined* to Iudah, and came to Ierusalem.

5 ¶ Then came Shemaiah the prophet to Rehoboam, and to the Princes of Iudah that were gathered together to Ierusalem because of Shishak, and said vnto them, Thus saith the Lord, Ye haue forsaken me, and therfore haue I also left you in the hand of Shishak.

6 Whereupon, the Princes of Israel, and the king humbled themselues; and they saide, The Lord *is* righteous.

7 And when the Lord saw that they humbled themselues, the word of the Lord came to Shemaiah, saying, They haue humbled themselues, *therefore* I will not destroy them, but I will grant them ‖ some deliuerance, and my wrath shall not bee powred out vpon Ierusalem, by the hand of Shishak.

‖ Or, a litle while.

8 Neuerthelesse they shalbe his seruants,

uants, that they may know my seruice, and the seruice of the kingdomes of the countreys.

9 So Shishak king of Egypt came vp against Ierusalem, and tooke away the treasures of the house of the LORD, and the treasures of the kings house, hee tooke all: he caried away also the shields of gold, which Solomon had * made.

10 In stead of which, king Rehoboam made shields of brasse, and committed *them* to the hands of the chiefe of the guard, that kept the entrance of the Kings house.

11 And when the king entred into the house of the LORD, the guard came and fet them, and brought them againe into the guard-chamber.

12 And when he humbled himselfe, the wrath of the LORD turned from him, that hee would not destroy *him* altogether; ||and also in Iudah things went well.

13 ¶ So king * Rehoboam strengthened himselfe in Ierusalem, and reigned: for Rehoboam *was* one and fourty yeeres olde when hee began to reigne, and he reigned seuenteene yeeres in Ierusalem, the citie which the LORD had chosen out of all the tribes of Israel, to put his Name there: and his mothers name *was* Naamah an Ammonitesse

14 And hee did euill, because hee ||prepared not his heart to seeke the LORD.

15 Now the acts of Rehoboam first and last, are they not written in the †booke of Shemaiah the Prophet, and of Iddo the Seer, concerning genealogies? and *there were* warres betweene Rehoboam & Ieroboam continually.

16 And Rehoboam slept with his fathers, and was buried in the citie of Dauid, and Abiiah his sonne reigned in his stead.

CHAP. XIII.

1 Abiiah succeeding, maketh warre against Ieroboam. 4 Hee declareth the right of his cause. 13 Trusting in God, hee ouercommeth Ieroboam. 21 The wiues and children of Abiiah.

Owe *in the eighteenth yeere of king Ieroboam, began Abiiah to reigne ouer Iudah.

2 He reigned three yeres in Ierusalem: (his mothers name also *was* Michaiah the daughter of Vriel of Gibea:) and there was warre between Abiiah and Ieroboam.

3 And Abiiah †set the battel in aray with an army of valiant men of warre, euen foure hundred thousand chosen men: Ieroboam also set the battell in aray against him with eight hundred thousand chosen men, being mightie men of valour.

4 ¶ And Abiiah stood vp vpon mount Zemaraim, which *is* in mount Ephraim, and sayde, Heare mee thou Ieroboam, and all Israel:

5 Ought you not to know, that the LORD God of Israel gaue the kingdome ouer Israel to Dauid for euer, *euen* to him and to his sonnes by a couenant of salt?

6 Yet Ieroboam the sonne of Nebat, the seruant of Solomon the sonne of Dauid, is risen vp, and hath * rebelled against his LORD

7 And there are gathered vnto him vaine men the children of Belial, and haue strengthened themselues against Rehoboam the sonne of Solomon, when Rehoboam was young, & tender hearted, and could not withstand them.

8 And now ye thinke to withstand the kingdome of the LORD, in the hand of the sonnes of Dauid, and ye *be* a great multitude, and *there are* with you golden calues, which Ieroboam * made you for gods.

9 * Haue yee not cast out the Priests of the LORD the sonnes of Aaron, and the Leuites, and haue made you priests after the maner of the nations of *other* lands? so that whosoeuer commeth to † consecrate himselfe with a young bullocke and seuen rammes, the same may be a priest of *them* that are no gods.

10 But as for vs, the LORD *is* our God, and wee haue not forsaken him, and the Priests *which* minister vnto the LORD, *are* the sonnes of Aaron, and the Leuites *waite* vpon *their* businesse.

11 * And they burne vnto the LORD euery morning, and euery euening, burnt sacrifices and sweete incense: the *shew*-bread also *set they* in order vpon the pure table, and the Candlesticke of golde with the lampes therof, to burne euery euening: for we keepe the charge of the LORD our God, but yee haue forsaken him.

12 And

Marginal notes

* Cha. 9. 15

|| Or, and yet in Iudah there were good things.
* 1. King. 14. 21.

|| Or, fixed.

† Heb. words

* 1. King. 15. 1, &c.

† Heb. bound together.

* 1. King 11. 26.

* 1. King. 12. 28.
* Chap. 11 14.

† Heb. to fill his hand.

* Chap. 2. 4.

* Leu. 24. 6.

12 And behold, God *himselfe is* with vs for *our* captaine, and his Priests with sounding trumpets to cry alarme against you : O children of Israel, fight ye not against the Lord God of your fathers, for you shall not prosper.

13 ¶ But Ieroboam caused an ambushment to come about behinde them: so they were before Iudah, and the ambushment *was* behind them.

14 And when Iudah looked backe, behold, the battel *was* before and behind; and they cried vnto the Lord, and the Priests sounded with the trumpets.

15 Then the men of Iudah gaue a shout : and as the men of Iudah shouted, it came to passe that God smote Ieroboam and all Israel, before Abiiah and Iudah.

16 And the children of Israel fled before Iudah : and God deliuered them into their hand.

17 And Abiiah and his people slew them with a great slaughter : so there fel downe slaine of Israel, fiue hundred thousand chosen men.

18 Thus the children of Israel were brought vnder at that time, and the children of Iudah preuailed, because they relied vpon the Lord God of their fathers.

19 And Abiiah pursued after Ieroboam, & tooke cities from him, Beth-el with the townes thereof, and Ieshanah with the townes thereof, and Ephrain with the townes thereof.

20 Neither did Ieroboam recouer strength againe in the dayes of Abiiah: and the Lord strooke him, & he died.

21 ¶ But Abiiah waxed mighty, and married fourteene wiues, and begate twentie and two sonnes, and sixteene daughters.

22 And the rest of the acts of Abiiah, and his waies, and his sayings, *are* written in the ‖story of the Prophet *Iddo.

* *Or, commentary.*
* *Chap. 12. 5.*

CHAP. XIIII.

1 Asa succeeding destroieth idolatry. 6 Hauing peace, he strengtheneth his kingdome with forts and armies. 9 Calling on God, he ouerthroweth Zerah, and spoileth the Ethiopians.

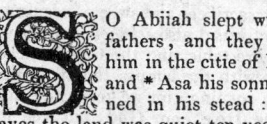

SO Abiiah slept with his fathers, and they buried him in the citie of Dauid, and *Asa his sonne reigned in his stead : in his dayes the land was quiet ten yeeres.

* *1. King. 15. 8. &c.*

2 And Asa did that *which was* good and right in the eyes of the Lord his God.

3 For hee tooke away the altars of the strange gods, and the high places, and brake downe the †images, and cut downe the groues :

† *Hebr. statues.*

4 And commanded Iudah to seeke the Lord God of their fathers, and to do the Law, and the Commandement.

5 Also he tooke away out of all the cities of Iudah, the high places and the †images : and the kingdome was quiet before him.

† *Hebr. Sun images.*

6 ¶ And hee built fenced cities in Iudah ; for the land had rest, and hee had no warre in those yeeres ; because the Lord had giuen him rest.

7 Therefore hee said vnto Iudah, Let vs build these cities, & make about them walles, and towers, gates and barres, while the land *is* yet before vs : because wee haue sought the Lord our God, wee haue sought *him*, and hee hath giuen vs rest on euery side : so they built, and prospered.

8 And Asa had an armie *of men* that bare targets and speares, out of Iudah three hundred thousand, and out of Beniamin, that bare shields and drew bowes, two hundred and fourescore thousand : all these *were* mighty men of valour.

9 ¶ *And there came out against them Zerah the Ethiopian, with an host of a thousand thousand, and three hundred charets, and came vnto Mareshah.

* *Chap. 16. 8.*

10 Then Asa went out against him, and they set the battel in aray in the valley of Zephathah at Mareshah.

11 And Asa cried vnto the Lord his God, and said, Lord, it *is* *nothing with thee to helpe, whether with many, or with them that haue no power. Helpe vs, O Lord our God, for we rest on thee, and in thy Name wee goe against this multitude : O Lord thou art our God, let not ‖man preuaile against thee.

* *1. Sam. 6.*

‖ *Or, mortal man.*

12 So the Lord smote the Ethiopians before Asa, and before Iudah, and the Ethiopians fled.

13 And Asa and the people that *were* with him, pursued them vnto Gerar : and the Ethiopians were ouerthrown, that they could not recouer themselues, for they were † destroyed before the Lord, and before his hoste, and they caried away very much spoile.

† *Hebr. broken.*

14 And they smote all the cities round

round about Gerar, for the feare of the LORD came vpon them: and they spoiled all the cities, for there was exceeding much spoile in them.

15 They smote also the tents of cattell, and caried away sheepe and camels inabundance, and returned to Ierusalem.

CHAP. XV.

1 Asa with Iudah and many of Israel, moued by the prophesie of Azariah the sonne of Oded, make a solemne couenant with God. 16 He putteth downe Maachah his mother, for her idolatry. 18 He bringeth dedicate things into the house of God, and enioyeth a long peace.

A ND the Spirit of God came vpon Azariah the sonne of Oded.

Heb. before Asa.

2 And he went out †to meet Asa, and said vnto him, Heare ye me, Asa, and all Iudah, and Beniamin, The LORD *is* with you, while yee be with him: and if yee seeke him, he will be found of you: but if ye forsake him, he will forsake you.

3 Now for a long season Israel *hath bene* without the true God, and without a teaching priest, and without law.

4 But when they in their trouble did turne vnto the LORD God of Israel, and sought him, hee was found of them.

5 And in those times *there was* no peace to him that went out, nor to him that came in, but great vexations *were* vpon all the inhabitants of the countreys.

† Hebr. beaten in pieces.

6 And nation was †destroyed of nation, and citie of citie: for God did vexe them with all aduersitie.

7 Be ye strong therefore, and let not your hands bee weake: for your worke shall be rewarded.

8 And when Asa heard these words, and the prophesie of Oded the prophet, he tooke courage, and put away the †abominable idoles out of all the lande of Iudah and Beniamin, and out of the cities which hee had taken from mount Ephraim, and renewed the Altar of the LORD, that *was* before the porch of the LORD.

† Heb. abominations.

9 And he gathered all Iudah and Beniamin, and the strangers with them out of Ephraim and Manasseh, and out of Simeon: (for they fell to him out of Israel in abundance when they saw that the LORD his God *was* with him.)

10 So they gathered themselues together at Ierusalem, in the third moneth, in the fifteenth yeere of the reigne of Asa.

11 And they offered vnto the LORD †the same time, of the spoile *which* they had brought, seuen hundred oxen, and seuen thousand sheepe.

† Heb. in that day.

12 And they entred into a couenant to seeke the LORD God of their fathers, with all their heart and with all their soule:

13 That whosoeuer would not seeke the LORD God of Israel, *should be put to death, whether small or great, whether man or woman.

Deut. 13. 9

14 And they sware vnto the LORD with a loud voice, and with shouting, and with trumpets, and with cornets.

15 And all Iudah reioyced at the oath: for they had sworne with all their heart, & sought him with their whole desire, and he was found of them: and the LORD gaue them rest round about.

16 ¶ And also concerning *Maachah the mother of Asa the king, he remoued her from beeing Queene, because she had made an †idole in a groue: and Asa cut downe her idole, and stamped *it*, and burnt *it* at the brooke Kidron.

*1. King. 15. 13.

† Heb. horror

17 But the high places were not taken away out of Israel: neuerthelesse the heart of Asa was perfect all his dayes.

18 ¶ And he brought into the house of God the things that his father had dedicated, and that he himselfe had dedicated, siluer, and gold, and vessels.

19 And there was no *more* warre vnto the fiue and thirtieth yeere of the reigne of Asa.

CHAP. XVI.

1 Asa, by the aide of the Syrians, diuerteth Baasha from building of Ramah. 7 Being reproued thereof by Hanani, he putteth him in prison. 11 Among his other actes in his disease he seeketh not to God, but to the Physitians. 13 His death and buriall.

I N *the sixe and thirtieth yeere of the reigne of Asa, Baasha king of Israel came vp against Iudah, and built Ramah, to the intent that hee might let none goe out or come in to Asa king of Iudah.

*1. Kings 15. 17.

2 Then

2 Then Asa brought out siluer and golde out of the treasures of the house of the Lord, and of the kings house, and sent to Benhadad King of Syria that dwelt at †Damascus, saying;

† *Heb. Darmesek.*

3 *There is* a league betweene me and thee, as *there was* betweene my father and thy father: beholde, I haue sent thee siluer and golde, goe, breake thy league with Baasha king of Israel, that he may depart from me.

4 And Benhadad hearkened vnto king Asa, and sent the captaines of †his armies against the cities of Israel, and they smote Iion, and Dan, and Abel-maim, & all the store-cities of Naphtali.

† *Heb. which were his.*

5 And it came to passe, when Baasha heard *it*, that hee left off building of Ramah, and let his worke cease.

6 Then Asa the king tooke all Iudah, and they caried away the stones of Ramah, and the timber thereof, wherewith Baasha was a building, and hee built therewith Geba and Mizpah.

7 ¶ And at that time Hanani the Seer came to Asa king of Iudah, and said vnto him, Because thou hast relyed on the king of Syria, and not relyed on the Lord thy God, therefore is the hoste of the king of Syria escaped out of thine hand.

8 Were * not the Ethiopians and the Lubims a †huge hoste, with very many charets and horsemen? Yet because thou diddest relie on the Lord, he deliuered them into thine hand.

* *Cha. 14. 9.*
† *Heb. in abundance.*

9 For the eyes of the Lord run to and fro throughout the whole earth, ‖to shewe himselfe strong in the behalfe of *them*, whose heart is perfite towards him. Herein thou hast done foolishly; therefore, from hencefoorth thou shalt haue warres.

‖ *Or, strongly to holde with them, &c.*

10 Then Asa was wroth with the Seer, and put him in a prison-house; for he was in a rage with him because of this thing. And Asa†oppressed some of the people the same time.

† *Heb. crushed.*

11 ¶ And behold, the actes of Asa first and last, lo, they *are* written in the booke of the Kings of Iudah and Israel.

12 And Asa in the thirtie and ninth yeere of his reigne, was diseased in his feete, vntill his disease *was* exceeding *great:* yet in his disease hee sought not to the Lord, but to the Physicians.

13 ¶ And Asa slept with his fathers, and died in the one and fourtieth yeere of his reigne.

14 And they buried him in his owne sepulchres which he had †made for himselfe in the citie of Dauid, and laide him in the bed, which was filled with sweet odours, and diuers kindes *of spices* prepared by the Apothecaries arte: & they made a very great burning for him.

† *Heb. digged.*

CHAP. XVII.

1 Iehoshaphat succeeding Asa, reigneth well, and prospereth. 7 He sendeth Leuites with the Princes to teach Iudah. 10 His enemies being terrified by God, some of them bring him presents and tribute. 12 His greatnesse, captaines and armies.

AND * Iehoshaphat his sonne reigned in his stead, and strengthened himselfe against Israel.

* *1. King. 15. 24.*

2 And he placed forces in all the fenced cities of Iudah, and set garisons in the land of Iudah, and in the cities of Ephraim, which Asa his father had taken.

3 And the Lord was with Iehoshaphat, because hee walked in the first wayes of his father Dauid, and sought not vnto Baalim:

4 But sought to the Lord God of his father, and walked in his commandements, and not after the doings of Israel:

5 Therefore the Lord stablished the kingdome in his hand, and all Iudah †brought to Iehoshaphat presents, and he had riches and honour in abundance.

† *Heb. gaue*

6 And his heart was ‖lift vp in the wayes of the Lord: moreouer hee tooke away the high places and groues out of Iudah.

‖ *That is, was encouraged.*

7 ¶ Also in the third yeere of his reigne, hee sent to his princes, *euen* to Benhail, and to Obadiah, and to Zechariah, and to Nethaneel, and to Michaiah, to teach in the cities of Iudah:

8 And with them *hee sent* Leuites, *euen* Shemaiah, and Nethaniah, and Zebadiah, and Asahel, and Shemiramoth, and Iehonathan, and Adoniiah, and Tobiiah, and Tob-adoniiah, Leuites: and with them, Elishama and Iehoram, Priests.

9 And they taught in Iudah, and *had* the book of the Law of the Lord with them, and went about throughout all the cities of Iudah, and taught the people.

10 ¶ And

Heb. was.

10 ¶ And the feare of the LORD †fell vpon all the kingdomes of the lands that *were* round about Iudah, so that they made no warre against Iehoshaphat.

11 Also *some* of the Philistines brought Iehoshaphat presents, and tribute siluer, and the Arabians brought him flocks, seuen thousand and seuen hundred rammes, and seuen thousand and seuen hundred he goats.

Or, palaces

12 ¶ And Iehoshaphat waxed great exceedingly, and he built in Iudah ||castles, and cities of store.

13 And he had much businesse in the cities of Iudah : and the men of warre, mightie men of valour, *were* in Ierusalem.

14 And these *are* the numbers of them according to the house of their fathers: Of Iudah, the captaines of thousands, Adnah the chiefe, and with him mighty men of valour, three hundred thousand.

Heb. at his hand.

15 And †next to him *was* Iehohanan the captaine, and with him two hundred and fourescore thousand.

16 And next him was Amasiah the sonne of Zichri, who willingly offered himselfe vnto the LORD, and with him two hundred thousand mightie men of valour.

17 And of Beniamin, Eliada a mightie man of valour, and with him, armed men with bow and shield two hundred thousand.

18 And next him *was* Iehoshabad, and with him an hundred and foure score thousand, ready prepared for the warre.

19 These waited on the king, besides those whom the king put in the fenced cities throughout all Iudah.

CHAP. XVIII.

1 Iehoshaphat ioyned in affinitie with Ahab, is perswaded to goe with him against Ramoth Gilead. 4 Ahab seduced by false prophets, according to the worde of Micaiah is slaine there.

* 1. King. 22 2.

† Heb. at the end of yeeres.

NOw Iehoshaphat had riches and honour in abundance, and ioyned affinitie with Ahab.

2 ** And †after *certaine* yeeres, he went downe to Ahab to Samaria : and Ahab killed sheepe and oxen for him in abundance, and for the people that he had with him, and perswa-

ded him to goe vp with him to Ramoth Gilead.

3 And Ahab king of Israel said vnto Iehoshaphat king of Iudah, Wilt thou goe with me to Ramoth Gilead? And he answered him, I *am* as thou *art*, and my people as thy people, and *we will be* with thee in the warre.

4 ¶ And Iehoshaphat saide vnto the king of Israel, Enquire, I pray thee, at the word of the LORD to day.

5 Therefore the king of Israel gathered together of prophets foure hundred men, and said vnto them, Shal we goe to Ramoth Gilead to battel, or shal I forbeare? And they said, Goe vp, for God will deliuer *it* into the kings hand.

6 But Iehoshaphat saide, *Is* there not here a Prophet of the LORD †besides, that we might enquire of him?

† Heb. yet or more.

7 And the king of Israel said vnto Iehoshaphat, *There is* yet one man, by whom we may enquire of the LORD: but I hate him, for he neuer prophesied good vnto me, but alwayes euill: the same *is* Micaiah the sonne of Iimla. And Iehoshaphat saide, Let not the king say so.

8 And the king of Israel called for one of his || officers, and saide, †Fetch quickly Micaiah the sonne of Iimla.

|| Or, Eunuches.
† Heb. hasten

9 And the king of Israel and Iehoshaphat king of Iudah sate, either of them on his throne, clothed in their robes, and they sate in a ||voide place at the entring in of the gate of Samaria, and all the prophets prophesied before them.

|| Or, floore.

10 And Zedekiah the sonne of Chenaanah, had made him hornes of yron, and said, Thus saith the LORD, With these thou shalt push Syria, vntil †they be consumed.

† Hebr. thou consume them.

11 And all the prophets prophesied so, sayiug, Goe vp to Ramoth Gilead, and prosper · for the LORD shall deliuer *it* into the hand of the king.

12 And the messenger that went to call Micaiah, spake to him, saying, Behold, the words of the prophets *declare* good to the king †with one assent: let thy word therefore, I pray thee, be like one of theirs, and speake thou good.

† Heb. with one mouth.

13 And Micaiah said, As the LORD liueth, euen what my God saith, that will I speake

14 And when hee was come to the king, the king sayd vnto him, Micaiah, shall we goe to Ramoth Gilead to battell,

tell, or shall I forbeare? and he sayd, Goe yee vp, and prosper, and they shall be deliuered into your hand.

15 And the king sayd to him, Howe many times shall I adiure thee, that thou say nothing but the truth to me, in the name of the LORD?

16 Then he sayd, I did see all Israel scattered vpon the mountaines, as sheepe that haue no shepheard: and the LORD sayd, These haue no master, let them returne *therefore*, euery man to his house in peace.

17 (And the king of Israel sayd to Iehoshaphat, Did I not tell thee, *that* hee would not prophesie good vnto mee, ‖ but euill?)

¹ Or, but for euill.

18 Againe he sayd; Therefore heare the word of the LORD : I sawe the LORD sitting vpon his throne, and all the hoste of heauen standing on his right hand, and *on* his left.

19 And the LORD sayd, Who shall entise Ahab king of Israel, that hee may goe vp and fall at Ramoth Gilead? And one spake, saying after this maner, and another saying after that maner.

* Iob. 1. 6.

20 Then there came out a *spirit, and stood before the LORD, and sayd, I will entise him. And the LORD sayd vnto him, Wherewith?

21 And hee sayd, I will goe out, and be a lying spirit in the mouth of all his prophets. And the LORD sayd, Thou shalt entise *him*, and thou shalt also preuaile : goe out, and doe *euen* so.

22 Nowe therefore behold, the LORD hath put a lying spirit in the mouth of these thy prophets, and the LORD hath spoken euill against thee.

23 Then Zedekiah the sonne of Chenaanah, came neere, and smote Micaiah vpon the cheeke, and sayd, Which way went the spirit of the LORD from mee, to speake vnto thee?

24 And Micaiah sayd, Behold, thou shalt see on that day, when thou shalt goe ‖into an inner chamber to hide thy selfe.

¹ Or, from chamber to chamber: Heb. chamber in a chamber.

25 Then the king of Israel sayd, Take yee Micaiah, and carie him backe to Amon the gouernour of the citie, and to Ioash the kings sonne.

26 And say, Thus saith the king, Put this fellow in the prison, and feede him with bread of affliction, and with water of affliction, vntill I returne in peace.

27 And Micaiah sayd, If thou certainly returne in peace, then hath not the LORD spoken by mee. And hee sayd, Hearken all yee people.

28 So the king of Israel, and Iehoshaphat the king of Iudah, went vp to Ramoth Gilead.

29 And the king of Israel sayd vnto Iehoshaphat, I will disguise my selfe, and will goe to the battell, but put thou on thy robes. So the king of Israel disguised himselfe, and they went to the battell.

30 Now the king of Syria had commaunded the captaines of the charets that *were* with him, saying, Fight ye not with small or great, saue onely with the king of Israel.

31 And it came to passe when the captaines of the charets saw Iehoshaphat, that they sayd, It is the king of Israel : therefore they compassed about him to fight. But Iehoshaphat cryed out, and the LORD helped him, and God moued them *to depart* from him.

32 For it came to passe, that when the captaines of the charets perceiued that it was not the king of Israel, they turned backe againe †from pursuing him.

† Heb. fro after him

33 And a *certaine* man drew a bowe †at a venture, and smote the king of Israel †betweene the ioints of the harnesse : therefore hee sayd to his charetman, Turne thine hand, that thou mayest carie me out of the hoste, for I am †wounded.

† Heb. in simplicitie
† Heb. betweene the ioints and betweene brestplate.
† Heb. made sicke.

34 And the battell increased that day: howbeit the king of Israel stayed *himselfe* vp in his charet against the Syrians, vntill the Euen : and about the time of the sunne going downe, hee dyed.

CHAP. XIX.

1 Iehoshaphat, reproued by Iehu, visiteth his kingdome. 5 His instructions to the Iudges, 8 To the Priests and Leuites.

Nd Iehoshaphat the king of Iudah returned to his house in peace to Ierusalem

2 And Iehu the sonne of Hanani the seer, went out to meete him, and sayd to king Iebōshaphat, Shouldest thou helpe the vngodly, and loue them that hate the LORD? Therefore *is* wrath vpon thee from before the LORD.

3 Neuerthelesse,

* Chap. 17.
4, 6.

3 Neuerthelesse, there *are good things found in thee, in that thou hast taken away the groues out of the land, and hast prepared thine heart to seeke God.

4 And Iehoshaphat dwelt at Ierusalem : and †hee went out againe through the people, from Beer-sheba to mount Ephraim, and brought them backe vnto the Lord God of their fathers.

* Hebr. he returned and went out.

5 ¶ And he set Iudges in the land, throughout all the fenced cities of Iudah, city by city,

6 And said to the Iudges, Take heed what ye doe : for yee iudge not for man, but for the Lord, who is with you †in the iudgement.

7 Wherefore now, let the feare of the Lord be vpon you, take heed and doe it: for there is no *iniquitie with the Lord our God, nor respect of persons, nor taking of gifts.

* Hebr. in the matter of iudgement.

* Deut. 10. 17. iob 34. 19. act. 10. 34. rom. 2. 11. Col. 2. 6. 1. pet. 1. 17.

8 ¶ Moreouer in Ierusalem did Iehoshaphat set of the Leuites, and of the Priests, and of the chiefe of the fathers of Israel, for the iudgement of the Lord, and for controuersies, when they returned to Ierusalem.

9 And hee charged them, saying, Thus shall yee doe in the feare of the Lord faithfully, and with a perfect heart.

10 And what cause soeuer shal come to you of your brethren that dwell in their cities, betweene blood and blood, betweene Law and Commandement, Statutes and Iudgements, yee shall euen warne them that they trespasse not against the Lord, and so wrath come vpon you, and vpon your brethren: this doe, & ye shall not trespasse.

11 And behold, Amariah the chiefe Priest is ouer you in all matters of the Lord, and Zebadiah the sonne of Ishmael, the ruler of the house of Iudah, for all the Kings matters : Also the Leuites shall be officers before you. †Deale couragiously, and the Lord shalbe with the good.

† Hebr. take courage and doe:

CHAP. XX.

I T came to passe after this also, that the children of Moab, and the children of Ammon, and with them, other beside the Ammonites, came against Iehoshaphat to battell.

2 Then there came some that tolde Iehoshaphat, saying, There commeth a great multitude against thee from beyond the Sea on this side Syria, and behold, they bee in Hazazon-Tamar, which is En-gedi.

3 And Iehoshaphat feared, and set †himselfe to seeke the Lord, and proclaimed a fast throughout all Iudah.

† Hebr. his faee.

4 And Iudah gathered themselues together, to aske helpe of the Lord : euen out of all the cities of Iudah they came to seeke the Lord.

5 ¶ And Iehoshaphat stood in the Congregation of Iudah and Ierusalem, in the house of the Lord before the new Court,

6 And said, O Lord God of our fathers, art not thou God in heauen? and rulest not thou ouer all the kingdoms of the heathen.? and in thine hand is there not power and might, so that none is able to withstand thee?

7 Art not thou our God, †who didst driue out the inhabitants of this land before thy people Israel, and gauest it to the seed of Abraham thy friend for euer?

† Heb. thou.

8 And they dwelt therein, and haue built thee a Sanctuarie therein for thy Name, saying,

9 *If, when euill commeth vpon vs, as the sword, iudgement, or pestilence, or famine, wee stand before this house, and in thy presence (for thy Name is in this house) and cry vnto thee in our affliction, then thou wilt heare & helpe.

* Chap. 6. 28. 1. king. 8. 37.

10 And now behold, the children of Ammon, and Moab, and mount Seir, whom thou *wouldest not let Israel inuade, when they came out of the land of Egypt, but they turned from them, and destroyed them not:

* Deut. 2. 9.

11 Beholde, I say, how they reward vs, to come to cast vs out of thy possession, which thou hast giuen vs to inherit.

12 O our God, wilt thou not iudge them? for wee haue no might against this

this great company that commeth against vs? neither know wee what to doe; but our eyes *are* vpon thee.

13 And all Iudah stood before the LORD, with their litle ones, their wiues and their children.

14 ¶ Then vpon Iahaziel the sonne of Zechariah, the sonne of Benaiah, the sonne of Iehiel, the sonne of Mattaniah, a Leuite of the sons of Asaph, came the Spirit of the LORD in the midst of the Congregation:

15 And he said, Hearken yee, all Iudah, and ye inhabitants of Ierusalem, and thou king Iehoshaphat, Thus sayth the LORD vnto you; Be not afraid, nor dismayed by reason of this great multitude; for the battell *is* not yours, but Gods.

16 To morrow goe ye downe against them : behold, they come vp by the † cliffe of Ziz, and ye shall finde them at the end of the ‖ brooke, before the wildernesse of Ieruel.

† Heb. ascent.
‖ Or, valley.

17 Yee shall not *neede* to fight in this *battell*; set your selues, stand yee *still*, and see the saluation of the LORD with you, O Iudah and Ierusalem : feare not, nor be dismayed; to morow goe out against them, for the LORD *will bee* with you.

18 And Iehoshaphat bowed his head, with his face to the ground : and all Iudah, and the inhabitants of Ierusalem, fell before the LORD, worshipping the LORD.

19 And the Leuites, of the children of the Kohathites, and of the children of the Korhites, stood vp to praise the LORD God of Israel, with a loude voice on high.

20 ¶ And they rose early in the morning, and went foorth into the wildernesse of Tekoa : and as they went forth, Iehoshaphat stood and said, Heare me, O Iudah, and yee inhabitants of Ierusalem ; *Beleeue in the LORD your God, so shall you be established; beleeue his Prophets, so shall yee prosper.

* Isai. 7. 9.

21 And when he had consulted with the people, he appointed Singers vnto the LORD, and † that should praise the beautie of holinesse, as they went out before the armie ; and to say, Praise the LORD, for his mercy *endureth* for euer.

† Heb. praisers.

22 ¶ † And when they beganne † to sing and to praise, the LORD set ambushments against the children of Ammon, Moab, and mount Seir, which

† Heb. and in the time that they, &c.
† Heb. in singing and praise.

were come against Iudah, and ‖ they were smitten.

‖ Or, they smote one another.

23 For the children of Ammon and Moab, stood vp against the inhabitants of mount Seir, vtterly to slay and destroy *them* : and when they had made an end of the inhabitants of Seir, euery one helped † to destroy another.

† Heb. for the destruction.

24 And when Iudah came toward the watch-tower in the wildernesse, they looked vnto the multitude, and behold, they *were* dead bodies fallen to the earth, and † none escaped.

† Heb. there was not an escaping.

25 And when Iehoshaphat and his people came to take away the spoile of them, they found among them in abundance both riches with the dead bodies, and precious iewels (which they stript off for themselues) more then they could cary away : and they were three dayes in gathering of the spoile, it was so much.

26 ¶ And on the fourth day they assembled themselues in the valley of ‖ Berachah ; for there they blessed the LORD : therfore the name of the same place was called the valley of Berachah vnto this day.

‖ That is, blessing.

27 Then they returned, euery man of Iudah and Ierusalem, and Iehoshaphat in the † forefront of them, to go againe to Ierusalem with ioy : for the LORD had made them to reioyce ouer their enemies.

† Heb. head.

28 And they came to Ierusalem with Psalteries, and harpes, and trumpets, vnto the house of the LORD.

29 And the feare of God was on all the kingdoms of *those* countreys, when they had heard that the LORD fought against the enemies of Israel.

30 So the Realme of Iehoshaphat was quiet ; for his God gaue him rest round about.

31 ¶ *And Iehoshaphat reigned ouer Iudah : Hee *was* thirtie and fiue yeeres olde when hee began to reigne, and he reigned twentie and fiue yeeres in Ierusalem : and his mothers name *was* Azubah the daughter of Shilhi.

* 1. King. 22. 41, &c.

32 And he walked in the way of Asa his father, and departed not from it, doing that which *was* right in the sight of the LORD.

33 Howbeit the high places were not taken away : for as yet the people had not prepared their hearts vnto the God of their fathers.

34 Now the rest of the actes of Iehoshaphat

Heb. words.
* 1. Kings
6. 1.
Heb. was
made to as-
cend.

hoshaphat first and last, behold, they are written in the †booke of Iehu the sonne of Hanani; *who †is mentioned in the booke of the Kings of Israel.

35 ¶ And after this did Iehoshaphat king of Iudah ioine himselfe with Ahazia king of Israel, who did very wickedly:

36 And he ioyned himselfe with him to make ships to goe to Tarshish : and they made the ships in Ezion-Geber.

37 Then Eliezer the sonne of Dodauah of Mareshah, prophesied against Iehoshaphat, saying; Because thou hast ioyned thy selfe with Ahaziah, the LORD hath broken thy workes · and the ships were broken, that they were not able to goe to Tarshish.

CHAP. XXI.

1 Iehoram succeeding Iehoshaphat, slayeth his brethren. 5 His wicked reigne. 8 Edom and Libnah reuolt. 12 The prophecie of Eliiiah against him in writing. 16 Philistines and Arabians oppresse him. 18 His incurable disease, infamous death, and buriall.

* 1. King.
22. 50.

Ow *Iehoshaphat slept with his fathers, and was buried with his fathers in the citie of Dauid : and Iehoram his sonne reigned in his stead.

2 And he had brethren the sonnes of Iehoshaphat, Azariah, and Iehiel, and Zechariah, and Azariah, and Michael, and Shephatiah : All these were the sonnes of Iehoshaphat king of Israel.

3 And their father gaue them great giftes of siluer and of golde, and of precious things, with fenced cities in Iudah : but the kingdome gaue hee to Iehoram, because he was the first borne.

* 2. King. 8.
16, 17.

4 Now *when Iehoram was risen vp to the kingdome of his father, he strengthened himselfe, and slew all his brethren with the sword, and diuers also of the Princes of Israel.

5 ¶ Iehoram was thirtie and two yeeres olde when hee began to reigne, and hee reigned eight yeeres in Ierusalem.

6 And he walked in the way of the kings of Israel, like as did the house of Ahab : for hee had the daughter of *Ahab to wife : and he wrought that which was euill in the eyes of the LORD.

* Cha. 22. 2.

7 Howbeit the LORD would not

destroy the house of Dauid, because of the couenant that hee had made with Dauid, and as hee promised, to giue a †light to him and to his *sons for euer.

8 ¶ In his dayes the Edomites reuolted from vnder the †dominion of Iudah, and made themselues a king.

9 Then Iehoram *went forth with his Princes, and all his charets with him: and he rose vp by night, and smote the Edomites which compassed him in, and the captaines of the charets.

10 So the Edomites reuolted from vnder the hand of Iudah vnto this day. The same time also did Libnah reuolt from vnder his hand, because he had forsaken the LORD God of his fathers.

11 Moreouer, he made high places in the mountaines of Iudah, and caused the inhabitants of Ierusalem to commit fornication, and compelled Iudah thereto.

12 ¶ And there came a writing to him from Eliiah the Prophet, saying, Thus saith the LORD God of Dauid thy father, Because thou hast not walked in the wayes of Iehoshaphat thy father, nor in the wayes of Asa king of Iudah :

13 But hast walked in the way of the kings of Israel, and hast made Iudah and the inhabitants of Ierusalem to goe a whoring, like to the whoredomes of the house of Ahab, and also hast slaine thy brethren of thy fathers house, which were better then thy selfe :

14 Behold, with a †great plague wil the LORD smite thy people, and thy children, and thy wiues, and all thy goods.

15 And thou shalt haue great sicknesse by disease of thy bowels, vntil thy bowels fall out, by reason of the sickenesse day by day.

16 ¶ Moreouer, the LORD stirred vp against Iehoram the spirit of the Philistines, and of the Arabians, that were neere the Ethiopians.

17 And they came vp into Iudah, and brake into it, and †caried away all the substance that was found in the kings house, and his sonnes also and his wiues; so that there was neuer a sonne left him, saue ||Iehoahaz, the yongest of his sonnes.

18 ¶ And after all this, the LORD smote him in his bowels, with an incurable disease.

† Heb. lamp,
or candle.
* 2. Sam. 8.
1. king. 11.
36. 2. king.
8. 19. psal.
132. 11, &c.
* 2. King.
8. 21.

† Heb. a
great stroke.

† Heb. caried
captiue.

|| Or, Aha-
ziah, chap.
22. 1. or, A-
zariah, ver.
6.

19 And

19 And it came to paſſe, that in proceſſe of time, after the end of two yeres, his bowels fell out by reaſon of his sickeneſſe : so hee dyed of sore diseases. And his people made no burning for him, like the burning of his fathers.

20 Thirtie and two yeeres old was he when he began to reigne, and he reigned in Ieruſalem eight yeeres, and departed †without being desired : howbeit, they buried him in the citie of Dauid, but not in the sepulchres of the kings.

† Heb. without desire.

CHAP. XXII.

1 Ahaziah succeeding, reigneth wickedly. 5 In his confederacie with Ioram the sonne of Ahab, he is slaine by Iehu. 10 Athaliah destroying all the seed royall, saue Ioash, whō Iehoshabeath his aunt hid, vsurpeth the kingdom.

*2. King. 8. 24, &c.

Nd *the inhabitants of Ieruſalem made Ahaziah his yongeſt sonne, king in his ſtead : for the band of men that came with the Arabians to the campe, had slaine all the *eldest. So Ahaziah the sonne of Iehoram king of Iudah reigned.

*Chap. 21. 17.

2 Fourtie and two yeeres old was Ahaziah, when he began to reigne, and he reigned one yeere in Ieruſalem : his mothers name also was *Athaliah the daughter of Omri.

*Chap. 21. 6

3 Hee also walked in the wayes of the house of Ahab : for his mother was his counseller to doe wickedly.

4 Wherefore he did euill in the sight of the LORD, like the house of Ahab : for they were his counsellers after the death of his father, to his destruction.

5 ¶ He walked also after their counsell, and went with Iehoram the sonne of Ahab king of Israel, to warre against Hazael king of Syria at Ramoth Gilead : and the Syrians smote Ioram.

6 And he returned to bee healed in Iezreel, because of the wounds †which were giuen him at Ramah when hee fought with Hazael king of Syria. And ‖Azariah the sonne of Iehoram king of Iudah, went downe to see Iehoram the sonne of Ahab at Iezreel, because he was sicke.

† Heb. wherwith they wounded him.
‖ Otherwise called Ahaziah, ver. 1. & Iehoahaz chap. 21. 17.

7 And †the destruction of Ahaziah was of God by comming to Ioram : For when he was come, hee went out with Iehoram against Iehu the sonne of Nimshi, *whome the LORD had

† Hebr. treading downe.

*2. King. 9. 7.

anointed to cut off the house of Ahab.

8 And it came to paſſe, that when Iehu was executing iudgement vpon the house of Ahab, and found the princes of Iudah, and the sonnes of the brethren of Ahaziah, that ministred to Ahaziah, he slew them.

9 *And he sought Ahaziah : and they caught him (for he was hid in Samaria) and brought him to Iehu : and when they had slaine him, they buried him : because, said they, hee is the sonne of Iehoshaphat, who sought the LORD with all his heart. So the house of Ahaziah had no power to keepe still the kingdome.

*2. Kings 9. 27.

10 ¶ *But when Athaliah the mother of Ahaziah, sawe that her sonne was dead, shee arose, and destroyed all the seed royall of the house of Iudah.

*2. Kings 11. 1.

11 But Iehoshabeath the daughter of the king, tooke Ioash the sonne of Ahaziah, and stole him from among the kings sonnes, that were slaine, and put him and his nurse in a bed chamber. So Iehoshabeath the daughter of king Iehoram, the wife of Iehoiada the priest (for she was the sister of Ahaziah) hid him from Athaliah, so that she slew him not.

12 And he was with them hid in the house of God six yeeres, and Athaliah reigned ouer the land.

CHAP. XXIII.

1 Iehoiada hauing set things in order, maketh Ioash king. 12 Athaliah is slaine. 16 Iehoiada restoreth the worship of God.

Nd *in the seuenth yeere Iehoiada strengthened himselfe, and tooke the captaines of hundreds, Azariah the sonne of Ieroham, and Ishmael the sonne of Iehohanan, and Azariah the sonne of Obed, and Maasiah the sonne of Adaiah, and Elishaphat the sonne of Zichri, into couenant with him.

*2. Kings 11. 4, &c.

2 And they went about in Iudah, and gathered the Leuites out of all the cities of Iudah, and the chiefe of the fathers of Israel, and they came to Ierusalem.

3 And all the Congregation made a couenant with the king in the house of God : and he said vnto them, Beholde, the kings sonne shall reigne, as the LORD hath *said of the sonnes of Dauid.

*2. Sam. 11
12.-1. kings 2. 4. and 9. 5
2. chr. 6. 16. and 7. 18.

4 This

4 This *is* the thing that yee shall doe, A third part of you entring on the Sabbath, of the priests and of the Leuites, *shalbe* porters of the † doores.

Hebr. thre-holds.

5 And a thirde part shall bee at the kings house, and a third part at the gate of the foundation : and all the people *shall be* in the Courts of the house of the LORD.

6 But let none come into the house of the LORD, saue the Priests, & they that minister of the Leuites, they shall go in, for they *are* holy : but all the people shall keepe the watch of the LORD.

7 And the Leuites shall compasse the king round about, euery man with his weapons in his hand, and whoso-euer else commeth into the house, hee shalbe put to death : but be you with the King when he commeth in, and when he goeth out.

8 So the Leuites and all Iudah did according to all things that Iehoiada the Priest had commanded : and tooke euery man his men that were to come in on the Sabbath, with them that were to goe *out* on the Sabbath : for Iehoiada the Priest dismissed not the courses.

9 Moreouer, Iehoiada the Priest deliuered to the captaines of hundreds, speares and bucklers, and shields, that had bene King Dauids, which *were* in the house of God.

Hebr. shoulder.
Heb. house.

10 And hee set all the people (euery man hauing his weapon in his hand) from the right † side of the † Temple, to the left side of the Temple, along by the Altar and the Temple, by the King, round about.

11 Then they brought out the kings sonne, and put vpon him the Crowne, and *gaue him* the Testimony, and made him King : and Iehoiada and his sonnes anointed him, and said, † God saue the King.

Deut. 17. 18.
† Hebr. Let the King liue.

12 ¶ Now when Athaliah heard the noise of the people running and praising the King ; she came to the people into the house of the LORD.

13 And she looked, and behold, the king stood at his pillar, at the entring in, and the Princes, and the trumpets by the King : and all the people of the land reioyced, and sounded with trum-pets ; also the singers with instruments of musicke ; and such as taught to sing praise. Then Athaliah rent her clothes, and said, † Treason, treason.

† Hebr. con-spiracie.

14 Then Iehoiada the Priest brought out the captaines of hundreds, that were set ouer the host, and said vn-to them, Haue her foorth of the ranges : and who so followeth her, let him bee slaine with the sword. For the Priest said ; Slay her not in the house of the LORD.

15 So they layd handes on her, and when shee was come to the entring of the horse gate, by the kings house, they slew her there.

16 ¶ And Iehoiada made a coue-nant betweene him, and betweene all the people, and betweene the king, that they should be the LORDS people.

17 Then all the people went to the house of Baal, and brake it downe, and brake his altars and his images in pie-ces, and slew * Mattan the priest of Baal before the altars.

Deut. 13. 13. 9.

18 Also Iehoiada appointed the of-fices of the house of the LORD by the hand of the Priests the Leuites, whom Dauid had * distributed in the house of the LORD, to offer the burnt offrings of the LORD, as it is written in the * Law of Moses, with reioycing and with singing, *as it was ordeined* † by Dauid.

1. Chro. 24. 1.
Num. 28. 2.
† Hebr. by the hands of Dauid.
1. Chro. 26. 1. &c.

19 And he set the * porters at the gates of the house of the LORD, that none which was vncleane in any thing, should enter in.

20 And hee tooke the captaines of hundreds, and the nobles, and the go-uernours of the people, and all the peo-ple of the land, and brought downe the king from the house of the LORD : and they came through the high gate into the kings house, and set the king vpon the throne of the kingdome.

21 And all the people of the land re-ioyced, and the city was quiet, after that they had slaine Athaliah w̓ the sword.

CHAP. XXIIII.

Oash *was* seuen yeeres old when he beganne to reigne ; and he reigned for-tie yeeres in Ierusalem : his mothers name also

2. Kin. 12. 1. &c.

was

was Zibiah, of Beer-sheba.

2 And Ioash did that which *was* right in the sight of the LORD, all the dayes of Iehoiada the Priest.

3 And Iehoiada tooke for him two wiues, and he begat sonnes and daughters.

4 ¶ And it came to passe after this that Ioash was minded † to repaire the house of the LORD.

† *Heb. to renew.*

5 And hee gathered together the priests and the Leuites, and saide to them, Go out vnto the cities of Iudah, and gather of all Israel money to repaire the house of your God from yeere to yere, and see that ye haste the matter: howbeit the Leuites hastened *it* not.

6 And the king called for Iehoiada the chiefe, and saide vnto him, Why hast thou not required of the Leuites to bring in out of Iudah and out of Ierusalem, the collection, *according to the commandement* of * Moses the seruant of the LORD, and of the Congregation of Israel, for the tabernacle of Witnesse?

* *Exod. 30. 12, 13, 14.*

7 For the sonnes of Athaliah that wicked woman, had broken vp the house of God, and also all the dedicate things of the house of the LORD, did they bestow vpon Baalim.

8 And at the kings commandement they made a chest, and set it without, at the gate of the house of the LORD.

9 And they made † a proclamation through Iudah & Ierusalem, to bring in to the LORD, the collection that Moses the seruant of God *laid* vpon Israel in the wildernesse.

† *Hebr. a voice.*

10 And all the Princes and all the people reioyced, and brought in, and cast into the chest, vntill they had made an ende.

11 Now it came to passe that at what time the chest was brought vnto the kings office, by the hand of the Leuites: and when they sawe that *there was* much money : the kings Scribe, and the high priests officer, came and emptied the chest, and tooke it, and caried it to his place againe. Thus they did day by day, and gathered money in abundance.

12 And the king and Iehoiada gaue it to such as did the worke of the seruice of the house of the LORD, and hired Masons and carpenters to repaire the house of the LORD, and also such as wrought yron and brasse to mend the house of the LORD.

13 So the workemen wrought, and

† the worke was perfected by them : and they set the house of God in his state, and strengthened it.

† *Hebr. the healing went vp vpon the worke.*

14 And when they had finished *it*, they brought the rest of the money before the king and Iehoiada, whereof were made vessels for the house of the LORD, euen vessels to minister and to ‖ offer withall, and spoones, and vessels of golde and siluer : and they offered burnt offerings in the house of the LORD continually, all the dayes of Iehoiada.

‖ *Or, pestils.*

15 ¶ But Iehoiada waxed old, and was full of dayes when hee died : an hundred and thirtie yeeres olde *was hee* when hee died.

16 And they buried him in the citie of Dauid among the kings, because he had done good in Israel, both towards God, and towards his house.

17 Now after the death of Iehoiada, came the Princes of Iudah, and made obeysance to the king : then the king hearkened vnto them.

18 And they left the house of the LORD God of their fathers, and serued groues and idols : and wrath came vpon Iudah and Ierusalem for this their trespasse.

19 Yet hee sent prophets to them to bring them againe vnto the LORD, and they testified against them : but they would not giue eare.

20 And the spirit of God † came vpon Zechariah the sonne of Iehoiada the priest, which stood aboue the people, and said vnto them : Thus saith God, Why transgresse yee the commandements of the LORD, that yee cannot prosper? because yee haue forsaken the LORD, he hath also forsaken you.

† *Heb. clothed.*

21 And they conspired against him, and stoned him with stones at the commandement of the king, in the court of the house of the LORD.

22 Thus Ioash the king remembred not the kindnesse which Iehoiada his father had done to him, but slew his sonne : and when he died, he said, The LORD looke vpon *it*, and require *it*.

23 ¶ And it came to passe † at the end of the yeere, that the hoste of Syria came vp against him : and they came to Iudah and Ierusalem, and destroyed all the Princes of the people from among the people, and sent all the spoile of them vnto the king of † Damascus.

† *Heb. in the reuolution of the yeere.*

† *Heb. Darmesek.*

24 For the armie of the Syrians came

came with a small companie of men, and the LORD deliuered a very great hoste into their hand, because they had forsaken the LORD God of their fathers : so they executed iudgement against Ioash.

25 And when they were departed from him (for they left him in great diseases) his owne seruants conspired against him, for the blood of the sonnes of Iehoiada the Priest, and slewe him on his bed, and he died : and they buried him in the citie of Dauid, but they buried him not in the sepulchres of the Kings.

26 And these are they that conspired against him ; ‖Zabad the sonne of Shimeah an Ammonitesse, and Iehozabad the sonne of ‖Shimrith a Moabitesse.

27 ¶ Now concerning his sonnes, and the greatnesse of the burdens laide vpon him, and the †repairing of the house of God, behold, they are written in the ‖story of the booke of the Kings. And Amaziah his sonne reigned in his stead.

CHAP. XXV.

1 Amaziah beginneth to reigne well. 3 Hee executeth iustice on the traitours. 5 Hauing hired an armie of Israelites against the Edomites, at the word of a Prophet, he loseth the hundred talents, and dismisseth them. 11 He ouerthroweth the Edomites. 10. 13 The Israelites discontented with their dismission, spoile as they returne home. 14 Amaziah proud of his victory, serueth the gods of Edom, and despiseth the admonitions of the Prophet. 17 Hee prouoketh Ioash to his ouerthrow. 25 His reigne. 27 Hee is slaine by conspiracie.

Amaziah *was twentie and fiue yeeres olde when hee began to reigne, and hee reigned twentie and nine yeeres in Ierusalem, and his mothers name was Iehoadan of Ierusalem.

2 And hee did that which was right in the sight of the LORD, but not with a perfite heart.

3 ¶ Now it came to passe when the kingdome was †established to him, that he slew his seruants, that had killed the king his father.

4 But hee slewe not their children, but did as it is written in the Law in the booke of Moses, where the LORD

commanded, saying, *The fathers shall not die for the children, neither shall the children die for the fathers ; but euery man shall die for his owne sinne.

5 ¶ Moreouer, Amaziah gathered Iudah together, and made them Captaines ouer thousands, and captaines ouer hundreds, according to the houses of their fathers, throughout all Iudah and Beniamin : And he numbred them from twentie yeeres olde and aboue, and found them three hundred thousand choice men, able to goe foorth to warre, that could handle speare and shield.

6 Hee hired also an hundred thousand mightie men of valour, out of Israel, for an hundred talents of siluer.

7 But there came a man of God to him, saying, O king, let not the armie of Israel goe with thee : for the LORD is not with Israel, to wit, with all the children of Ephraim.

8 But if thou wilt goe, doe it, bee strong for the battell : God shall make thee fall before the enemy : for God hath power to helpe, and to cast downe.

9 And Amaziah said to the man of God, But what shall wee doe for the hundred talents which I haue giuen to the †armie of Israel ? And the man of God answered, The LORD is able to giue thee much more then this.

10 Then Amaziah separated them, to wit, the armie that was come to him out of Ephraim, to goe †home againe. Wherfore their anger was greatly kindled against Iudah, and they returned home in †great anger.

11 ¶ And Amaziah strengthened himselfe, and ledde foorth his people, and went to the valley of salt, and smote of the children of Seir, ten thousand.

12 And other ten thousand left aliue, did the children of Iudah cary away captiue, and brought them vnto the top of the rocke, and cast them downe from the top of the rocke, that they all were broken in pieces.

13 ¶ But the †souldiers of the army which Amaziah sent backe, that they should not goe with him to battell, fell vpon the cities of Iudah, from Samaria euen vnto Beth-horon, and smote three thousand of them, and took much spoile.

14 ¶ Now it came to passe, after that Amaziah was come from the slaughter of the Edomites, that hee brought

‖ Or, Iozachar, 2. king. 12. 21.
‖ Or, Shomer.

† Heb. founding.

‖ Or, Commentarie.

* 2. King. 14. 1, &c.

† Heb. confirmed vpon him.

* Deut. 24. 16. 2. king. 14. 6. iere. 31. 30. ezek. 18. 20.

† Heb. band.

† Heb. to their place.

† Heb. in heat of anger.

† Heb. the sonnes of the band.

brought the gods of the children of Seir, and set them vp to be his gods, and bowed down himselfe before them, and burned incense vnto them.

15 Wherfore the anger of the LORD was kindled against Amaziah, and hee sent vnto him a Prophet, which said vnto him, Why hast thou sought after the gods of the people, which could not deliuer their owne people out of thine hand?

16 And it came to passe as hee talked with him, that *the king* said vnto him, Art thou made of the Kings counsell? forbeare; why shouldest thou be smitten? Then the Prophet forbare, and said, I know that God hath †determined to destroy thee, because thou hast done this, and hast not hearkened vnto my counsell.

† *Heb. counselled.*

17 ¶ Then Amaziah king of Iudah tooke aduice, and sent to Ioash the sonne of Iehoahaz the sonne of Iehu, king of Israel, saying, Come, let vs see one another in the face.

* *2. King. 14. 8, 9.*

18 * And Ioash king of Israel sent to Amaziah king of Iudah, saying, The ‖thistle that *was* in Lebanon, sent to the Cedar that *was* in Lebanon, saying, Giue thy daughter to my sonne to wife: and there passed by a †wild beast that *was* in Lebanon, and trode downe the thistle.

‖ *Or, furre bush, or thorne.*

† *Hebr. a beast of the field.*

19 Thou sayest, Loe, thou hast smitten the Edomites, and thine heart lifteth thee vp to boast. Abide now at home, why shouldest thou meddle to *thine* hurt, that thou shouldest fall, *euen* thou, and Iudah with thee?

20 But Amaziah would not heare: for it *came* of God, that he might deliuer them into the hand *of their enemies*, because they sought after the gods of Edom.

21 So Ioash the King of Israel went vp, and they saw one another in the face, *both* hee and Amaziah King of Iudah at Beth-shemesh, which *belongeth* to Iudah.

22 And Iudah was †put to the worse before Israel, and they fled euery man to his tent.

† *Hebr. smitten.*

23 And Ioash the king of Israel tooke Amaziah king of Iudah the son of Ioash, the son of Ioahaz, at Beth-shemesh, and brought him to Ierusalem, and brake downe the wall of Ierusalem, from the gate of Ephraim to †the corner gate, foure hundred cubits.

† *Hebr. the gate of it that looketh.*

24 And *hee tooke* all the gold and the siluer, and all the vessels that were found in the house of God with Obed-Edom, and the treasures of the kings house, the hostages also, and returned to Samaria.

25 ¶ And Amaziah the sonne of Ioash King of Iudah liued after the death of Ioash sonne of Iehoahaz king of Israel, fifteene yeeres.

26 Now the rest of the acts of Amaziah, first and last, behold, *are* they not written in the booke of the Kings of Iudah and Israel?

27 ¶ Now after the time that Amaziah did turne away †from following the LORD, they †made a conspiracie against him in Ierusalem, and he fled to Lachish: but they sent to Lachish after him, and slew him there.

† *Heb. from after.*
† *Hebr. conspired a conspiracie.*

28 And they brought him vpon horses, and buried him with his fathers in the citie of ‖Iudah.

‖ *That is, the citie of Dauid, as it is 2. king. 14. 20.*

CHAP. XXVI.

1 Vzziah succeeding, and reigning well in the dayes of Zechariah, prospereth. 16 Waxing proud, he inuadeth the Priests office, and is smitten with leprosie. 22 Hee dieth, and Iotham succeedeth him.

Hen all the people of Iudah * tooke ‖ Vzziah, who *was* sixteene yeeres old, and made him King in the roome of his father Amaziah.

* *2. King. 14. 21. and 15. 1.*
‖ *Or, Azariah.*

2 He built Eloth, and restored it to Iudah: after that the King slept with his fathers.

3 Sixteene yeeres old *was* Vzziah, when he began to reigne, and he reigned fiftie and two yeeres in Ierusalem: his mothers name also *was* Iecoliah of Ierusalem.

4 And hee did that which *was* right in the sight of the LORD, according to all that his father Amaziah did.

5 And hee sought God in the dayes of Zechariah, who had vnderstanding †in the visions of God: and as long as he sought the LORD, God made him to prosper.

† *Hebr. in the seeing of God.*

6 And hee went foorth and warred against the Philistines, & brake downe the wall of Gath, and the wall of Iabneh, and the wall of Ashdod, and built cities ‖about Ashdod, and among the Philistines.

‖ *Or, in the countrey of Ashdod.*

7 And

7 And God helped him against the Philistines, and against the Arabians, that dwelt in Gur - baal, and the Mehunims.

8 And the Ammonites gaue gifts to Vzziah, and his name †spread abroad euen to the entring in of Egypt : for hee strengthened himſelfe exceedingly.

9 Moreouer Vzziah built towers in Ierusalem at the corner gate, and at the valley gate, and at the turning *of the* wall, and ‖fortified them.

10 Also he built towers in the desert, and ‖ digged many welles, for hee had much cattell, both in the low countrey, and in the plaines : husbandmen *also*, and vine dressers in the mountaines, and in ‖Carmel : for hee loued †husbandrie.

11 Moreouer, Vzziah had an host of fighting men, that went out to warre by bands, according to the number of their account, by the hand of Ieiel the Scribe, and Maasiah the ruler, vnder the hand of Hananiah, *one* of the kings captaines.

12 The whole number of the chiefe of the fathers of the mightie men of valour, *were* two thousand and sixe hundred.

13 And vnder their hand *was* †an armie, three hundred thousand, and seuen thousand, and fiue hundred, that made warre with mightie power, to helpe the king against the enemie.

14 And Vzziah prepared for them throughout all the hoste , shields, and speares, and helmets, and habergions, and bowes, and † slings *to cast* stones.

15 And hee made in Ierusalem engines inuented by cunning men, to bee on the towers, & vpon the bulwarks, to shoote arrowes and great stones withall : and his name †spread farre abroad, for he was marueilously helped, till he was strong.

16 ¶ But when he was strong, his heart was lifted vp to *his* destruction : for he transgressed against the LORD his God , and went into the temple of the LORD, to burne incense vpon the altar of incense.

17 And Azariah the priest went in after him , and with him fourescore priests of the LORD, that were valiant men.

18 And they withstood Vzziah the king, and said vnto him, It *perteineth not vnto thee, Vzziah, to burne incense

vnto the LORD , but to the *priestes the sonnes of Aaron, that are consecrated to burne incense. Goe out of the Sanctuarie ; for thou hast trespassed, neither shall it *be* for thine honour from the LORD God.

19 Then Vzziah was wroth , and *had* a censer in his hand, to burne incense, and while he was wroth with the priests, the leprosie euen rose vp in his forehead, before the priests, in the house of the LORD, from beside the incense altar.

20 And Azariah the chiefe priest, and all the priests looked vpon him, and behold, he was leprous in his forehead, and they thrust him out from thence, yea himselfe *hasted also to go out, because the LORD had smitten him.

21 *And Vzziah the king was a leper vnto the day of his death, and dwelt in a *seuerall house being a leper, for he was cut off from the house of the LORD : and Iotham his sonne *was* ouer the kings house, iudging the people of the land.

22 ¶ Now the rest of the actes of Vzziah first and last, did Isaiah the prophet the sonne of Amoz write.

23 So Vzziah slept with his fathers, and they buried him with his fathers in the field of the buriall *which belonged* to the kings : for they saide, He *is* a leper : And Iotham his sonne reigned in his stead.

CHAP. XXVII.

1 Iotham reigning well, prospereth. 5 He subdueth the Ammonites. 7 His reigne. 9 Ahaz succeedeth him.

Iotham *was twenty and fiue yeeres olde, when hee began to reigne , and hee reigned sixteene yeeres in Ierusalem : his mothers name also *was* Ierushah, the daughter of Zadok.

2 And he did that which *was* right in the sight of the LORD, according to all that his father Vzziah did : howbeit hee entred not into the temple of the LORD. And the people did yet corruptly.

3 He built the high gate of the house of the LORD, and on the wall of ‖ Ophel, he built much.

4 Moreouer hee built cities in the mountaines of Iudah, and in the forrests he built castles and towers.

5 ¶ He

Marginal notes

* Heb. went.

‖ Or, repaired.

‖ Or, cut out many ciſternes.

‖ Or, fruitfull fields.
† Hebr. ground.

† Hebr. the power of an armie.

† Heb. stones of slings.

† Heb. went foorth.

*Num. 18. 7

* Exo. 30. 7

* As Ester 6 12.

* 2. Kings 15. 5.

* Leuit. 13. 46.
† Heb. free.

* 2. Kings 15. 32.

‖ Or, the tower.

5 ¶ He fought also with the king of the Ammonites, and preuailed against them. And the children of Ammon gaue him the same yeere an hundred talents of siluer, and ten thousand measures of wheate, and tenne thousand of barley. † So much did the children of Ammon pay vnto him, both the second yeere, and the third.

† Heb. much.

6 So Iotham became mightie, because he ‖ prepared his wayes before the LORD his God.

‖ Or, establi- shed.

7 ¶ Now the rest of the actes of Iotham, and all his warres, and his wayes, lo, they are written in the booke of the Kings of Israel and Iudah.

8 Hee was fiue and twentie yeeres olde when he began to reigne, and reigned sixteene yeeres in Ierusalem.

9 ¶ And Iotham slept with his fathers, and they buried him in the city of Dauid: and Ahaz his sonne reigned in his stead.

CHAP. XXVIII.

1 Ahaz reigning very wickedly, is greatly afflicted by the Syrians. 6 Iudah being captiuated by the Israelites, is sent home by the counsell of Oded the Prophet. 16 Ahaz sending for aide to Assyria, is not helped thereby. 22 In his distresse, he groweth more idolatrous. 26 He dying, Hezekiah succeedeth him.

* 2. King. 16. 2.

Haz * was twentie yeeres olde when hee beganne to reigne, and he reigned sixteene yeres in Ierusalem: but hee did not that which *was* right in the sight of the LORD, like Dauid his father.

2 For he walked in the wayes of the Kings of Israel, and made also molten images for Baalim.

‖ Or, offered sacrifice.

3 Moreouer, he ‖ burnt incense in the valley of the sonne of Hinnom, & burnt *** his children in the fire, after the abominations of the heathen, whome the LORD had cast out before the children of Israel.

* Leuit. 18. 21.

4 Hee sacrificed also, and burnt incense in the high places, and on the hils, and vnder euery greene tree.

5 Wherefore the LORD his God deliuered him into the hand of the king of Syria, and they smote him, and caried away a great multitude of them captiues, and brought them to † Damascus: And he was also deliuered into the hand of the king of Israel, who smote

† Heb. Dar- mesek.

him wich a great slaughter.

6 ¶ For Pekah the sonne of Remaliah slew in Iudah an hundred & twentie thousand in one day, which were all † valiant men: because they had forsaken the LORD God of their fathers.

† Heb. sonne of valour.

7 And Zichri a mightie man of Ephraim, slue Maaseiah the kings sonne, and Azrikam the gouernour of the house, and Elkanah that was † next to the King.

† Heb. the second to the King.

8 And the children of Israel caried away captiue of their brethren, two hundred thousand, women, sonnes and daughters, and tooke also away much spoile from them, and brought the spoile to Samaria.

9 But a Prophet of the LORD was there, whose name was Oded: and hee went out before the hoste that came to Samaria, and said vnto them, Behold, because the LORD God of your fathers was wroth with Iudah, he hath deliuered them into your hand, and yee haue slaine them in a rage *that* reacheth vp vnto heauen.

10 And now ye purpose to keepe vnder the children of Iudah and Ierusalem for bondmen, and bondwomen vnto you: *But* are there not with you, euen with you, sinnes against the LORD your God?

11 Now heare me therefore, and deliuer the captiues againe, which ye haue taken captiue of your brethren: for the fierce wrath of God *is* vpon you.

12 Then certeine of the heads of the children of Ephraim, Azariah the sonne of Iohanan, Berechiah the sonne of Meshillemoth, and Iehizkiah the son of Shallum, and Amasa the sonne of Hadlai, stood vp against them that came from the warre,

13 And said vnto them, Ye shall not bring in the captiues hither: for whereas wee haue offended against the LORD *already*, ye intend to adde more to our sinnes and to our trespasse: for our trespasse is great, and *there is* fierce wrath against Israel.

14 So the armed men left the captiues, and the spoile before the Princes, and all the congregation.

15 And the men which were expressed by name, rose vp and tooke the captiues, aud with the spoile clothed all that were naked among them, and arayed them, and shod them, and gaue them to eate and to drinke, and anointed

* Deut. 34. 3.

ted them, and caried all the feeble of them vpon asses, and brought them to Iericho, * the city of palme-trees, to their brethren: then they returned to Samaria.

16 ¶ At that time did king Ahaz send vnto the kings of Assyria to helpe him.

17 For againe the Edomites had come and smitten Iudah, and caried a-way † captiues.

† Hebr. a captiuitie.

18 The Philistines also had inuaded the cities of the low-countrey, and of the South of Iudah, and had taken Beth-shemesh, and Aialon, and Gede-roth, and Shocho with the villages thereof, and Timnah with the villages thereof, Gimzo also, and the villages thereof: and they dwelt there.

19 For the LORD brought Iudah low, because of Ahaz king of Israel; for he made Iudah naked, and transgres-sed sore against the LORD.

20 And Tilgath-Pilneser king of Assyria came vnto him, and distressed him, but strengthened him not.

21 For Ahaz tooke away a portion out of the house of the LORD, and out of the house of the King, and of the Princes, and gaue it vnto the King of Assyria: but he helped him not.

22 ¶ And in the time of this distresse did hee trespasse yet more against the LORD: This is that king Ahaz.

23 For he sacrificed vnto the gods of † Damascus, which smote him: and he said, Because the gods of the kings of Syria helpe them, therefore will I sa-crifice to them, that they may helpe me: but they were the ruine of him, and of all Israel.

† Heb. Dar-mesek.

24 And Ahaz gathered together the vessels of the house of God, and cut in pieces the vessels of the house of God, and shut vp the doores of the house of the LORD, and hee made him altars in euery corner of Ierusalem.

25 And in euery seuerall city of Iu-dah hee made high places to ‖burne in-cense vnto other gods, and prouoked to anger the LORD God of his fa-thers.

‖Or, to offer.

26 ¶ Now the rest of his acts, and of all his wayes, first and last, behold, they are written in the booke of the kings of Iudah and Israel.

27 And Ahaz slept with his fa-thers, and they buried him in the citie, euen in Ierusalem: but they brought him not into the sepulchres of the kings of Israel: and Hezekiah his sonne reig-ned in his stead.

CHAP. XXIX.

1 Hezekiah his good reigne. 3 He restoreth Religion. 5 He exhorteth the Leuites. 12 They sanctifie themselues, and cleanse the house of God. 20 Hezekiah offereth so-lemne sacrifices, wherein the Leuites were more forward then the Priests.

 Ezekiah *began to reigne when hee was fiue and twentie yeeres old, and he reigned nine and twentie yeeres in Ierusalem: and his mothers name was Abiiah the daughter of Zechariah.

* 2. King. 18. 1.

2 And hee did that which was right in the sight of the LORD, according to all that Dauid his father had done.

3 ¶ He, in the first yere of his reigne, in the first moneth, opened the doores of the house of the LORD, and repai-red them.

4 And hee brought in the Priests, and the Leuites, and gathered them together into the East street,

5 And said vnto them, Heare me, ye Leuites, sanctifie now your selues, and sanctifie the house of the LORD God of your fathers, and cary foorth the fil-thinesse out of the holy place.

6 For our fathers haue trespassed, and done that which was euill in the eyes of the LORD our God, and haue forsaken him, and haue turned away their faces from the habitation of the LORD, and †turned their backs.

† Hebr. gi-uen the necke.

7 Also they haue shut vp the doores of the Porch, and put out the lampes, and haue not burnt incense, nor offered burnt offerings in the holy place, vnto the God of Israel.

8 Wherfore the wrath of the LORD was vpon Iudah and Ierusalem, and he hath deliuered them to †trouble, to astonishment, and to hissing, as yee see with your eyes.

† Hebr. com-motion.

9 For loe, our fathers haue fallen by the sword, and our sonnes and our daughters, and our wiues, are in capti-uitie for this.

10 Now it is in mine heart to make a couenant with the LORD God of Is-rael, that his fierce wrath may turne a-way from vs.

11 My sonnes, ‖bee not now negli-gent:

‖ Or, be not now decei-ued.

gent : for the LORD hath *chosen you to stand before him, to serue him, and that you should minister vnto him, and ||burne incense.

12 ¶ Then the Leuites arose, Mahath the sonne of Amashai, and Ioel the sonne of Azariah, of the sonnes of the Kohathites: and of the sonnes of Merari, Kish the sonne of Abdi, and Azariah the sonne of Iahalelel : and of the Gershonites Ioah, the sonne of Zimmah, and Eden the sonne of Ioah:

13 And of the sonnes of Elizaphan, Shimri, and Iehiel : and of the sonnes of Asaph, Zechariah and Mattaniah :

14 And of the sonnes of Heman, Iehiel, and Shimei : and of the sonnes of Ieduthun, Shemaiah and Vzziel.

15 And they gathered their brethren, and sanctified themselues, and came according to the commandement of the king, || by the words of the LORD, to cleanse the house of the LORD.

16 And the priests went into the inner part of the house of the LORD, to cleanse it, and brought out all the vncleannes that they found in the temple of the LORD, into the court of the house of the LORD. And the Leuites tooke it, to carie it out abroad into the brooke Kidron.

17 Now they began on the first day of the first moneth to sanctifie, and on the eight day of the moneth, came they to the porch of the LORD. So they sanctified the house of the LORD in eight dayes, and in the sixteenth day of the first moneth, they made an end.

18 Then they went in to Hezekiah the king, and said, We haue cleansed all the house of the LORD, and the altar of burnt offering, with all the vessels thereof, and the shew-bread table, with all the vessels thereof.

19 Moreouer all the vessels which king Ahaz in his reigne did cast away in his transgression, haue we prepared and sanctified, and behold, they are before the altar of the LORD.

20 ¶ Then Hezekiah the king rose earely, and gathered the rulers of the citie, and went vp to the house of the LORD.

21 And they brought seuen bullocks and seuen rammes, and seuen lambes, and seuen hee goats for a *sinne offring for the kingdome, and for the Sanctuarie, and for Iudah : and he commaunded the priests the sonnes of Aaron to offer them on the Altar of the LORD.

22 So they killed the bullockes, and the priestes receiued the blood, and *sprinkled it on the altar: likewise when they had killed the rams, they sprinkled the blood vpon the altar : they killed also the lambes, and they sprinkled the blood vpon the altar.

23 And they brought †foorth the hee goats for the sinne offering, before the king and the congregation, and laide their *hands vpon them :

24 And the priests killed them, and they made reconciliation with their blood vpon the altar, to make an atonement for all Israel : for the king commanded that the burnt offring and the sin offering should be made for all Israel.

25 *And hee set the Leuites in the house of the LORD with cymbals, with psalteries, and with harpes, according to the commandement of Dauid, and of Gad the kings Seer, and Nathan the prophet : for so was the commandement †of the LORD †by his prophets.

26 And the Leuites stood with the instruments of Dauid, and the priestes with the trumpets.

27 And Hezekiah commaunded to offer the burnt offering vpon the altar : and †when the burnt offering began, the song of the LORD began also with the trumpets, and with the †instruments ordeined by Dauid king of Israel.

28 And all the congregation worshipped, and the †singers sang, and the trumpetters sounded : and all this continued vntill the burnt offering was finished.

29 And when they had made an end of offering, the king and all that were †present with him, bowed themselues and worshipped.

30 Moreouer Hezekiah the king and the Princes, commanded the Leuites to sing praise vnto the LORD, with the words of Dauid, and of Asaph the Seer : and they sang praises with gladnes, and they bowed their heads and worshipped.

31 Then Hezekiah answered and said, Now ye haue †consecrated your selues vnto the LORD : come neere and bring sacrifices, and thanke-offerings into the house of the LORD. And the congregation brought in sacrifices, and thank-offrings, and as many as were of a free heart, burnt offerings.

32 And

---

*Num. 8. 14 and 18. 2, 6.

‖ Or, offer sacrifice.

‖ Or, in the busines of the Lord.

* Leuit. 4. 14.

* Leuit. 8. 14, 15, 16, 9. 21.

† Heb. nee

* Leuit. 4. 15.

* 1. Chro. 4. and 25.

† Heb. by hand of th Lord.
† Heb. by hand of.

† Heb. in time.

† Heb. ha of instruments.

† Heb. so

† Heb. for

‖ Or, fille your han

32 And the number of the burnt offerings which the congregation brought, *was* threescore and ten bullockes, an hundred rammes, *and* two hundred lambs : all these *were* for a burnt offring to the LORD.

33 And the consecrated things *were*, sixe hundred oxen, and three thousand sheepe.

34 But the Priests were too few, so that they could not flay all the burnt offerings : wherefore their brethren the Leuites † did helpe them, till the worke was ended, and vntill the *other* Priestes had sanctified themselues : for the Leuites *were* more vpright in heart, to sanctifie themselues, then the Priests.

Heb.streng- *'hened them*

35 And also the burnt offerings *were* in abundance, with the fat of the peace offerings, & the drinke offrings, for *euery* burnt offering. So the seruice of the house of the LORD was set in order.

36 And Hezekiah reioyced, and all the people, that God had prepared the people : for the thing was *done* suddenly.

CHAP. XXX.

1 Hezekiah proclaimeth a solemne Passeouer on the second moneth, for Iudah and Israel.
13 The assembly hauing destroyed the altars of idolatry, keepe the feast fourteene dayes.
27 The Priests and Leuites blesse the people.

AND Hezekiah sent to all Israel and Iudah, and wrote letters also to Ephraim and Manasseh, that they should come to the house of the LORD at Ierusalem, to keepe the Passeouer vnto the LORD God of Israel.

2 For the king had taken counsell, and his Princes, and all the congregation in Ierusalem, to keepe the Passeouer in the second *moneth.

* Num. 19. 11.

3 For they could not keepe it at that time, because the Priests had not sanctified themselues sufficiently, neither had the people gathered themselues together to Ierusalem.

4 And the thing † pleased the king, and all the Congregation.

† Heb. was right in the eyes of the King.

5 So they established a decree, to make proclamation throughout all Israel, from Beersheba euen to Dan, that they should come to keepe the Passeouer vnto the LORD God of Israel at Ierusalem : for they had not done *it* of a long *time in such sort*, as it was written.

6 So the Postes went with the letters †from the King and his Princes, throughout all Israel and Iudah, and according to the commandement of the king, saying; Yee children of Israel, turne againe vnto the LORD God of Abraham, Isaac and Israel, and hee wil returne to the remnant of you, that are escaped out of the hand of the kings of Assyria.

† Heb. from the hand.

7 And be not ye like your fathers, and like your brethren, which trespassed against the LORD God of their fathers, *who* therefore gaue them vp to desolation, as ye see.

8 Now †be yee not stiffe-necked as your fathers were, *but* † yeeld your selues vnto the LORD, and enter into his Sanctuarie, which he hath sanctified for euer : and serue the LORD your God, that the fiercenesse of his wrath may turne away from you.

† Harden not your neckes.
† Heb. giue the hand.

9 For if yee turne againe vnto the LORD, your brethren and your children shall *finde* compassion before them that leade them captiue, so that they shall come againe into this land : for the LORD your God *is* gracious and * mercifull, and will not turne away *his* face from you, if ye returne vnto him.

* Exo. 34. 5.

10 So the Posts passed from citie to citie, through the countrey of Ephraim and Manasseh, euen vnto Zebulun : but they laughed them to scorne, and mocked them.

11 Neuerthelesse, diuers of Asher, and Manasseh, and of Zebulun, humbled themselues, and came to Ierusalem.

12 Also in Iudah, the hand of God was to giue them one heart to doe the commandement of the king and of the Princes, by the word of the LORD.

13 ¶ And there assembled at Ierusalem much people, to keepe the feast of vnleauened bread in the second moneth, a very great congregation.

14 And they arose and tooke away the *altars that *were* in Ierusalem, and all the altars for incense tooke they away, and cast *them* into the brooke Kidron.

* Chap. 28. 24.

15 Then they killed the Passeouer on the fourteenth *day* of the second moneth : and the Priests and the Leuites were ashamed, and sanctified themselues, and brought in the burnt offerings into the house of the LORD.

16 And they stood in †their place after

† Heb. their standing.

ter their maner, according to the Law of Moses the man of God : The priests sprinckled the blood, *which they receiued* of the hand of the Leuites.

17 For there were many in the Congregation that were not sanctified : therefore the Leuites had the charge of the killing of the Passeouers for euery one that was not cleane, to sanctiſie *them* vnto the LORD.

18 For a multitude of the people, *euen* many of Ephraim and Manasseh, Issachar and Zebulun, had not cleansed themselues : yet did they eate the Passeouer otherwise then it was written. But Hezekiah prayed for them, saying; The good LORD pardon euery one,

19 That prepareth his heart to seeke God, the LORD God of his fathers, though hee be not *cleansed* according to the purification of the Sanctuary.

20 And the LORD hearkened to Hezekiah, and healed the people.

† *Heb. found.*

21 And the children of Israel that were †present at Ierusalem, kept the feast of vnleauened bread seuen dayes with great gladnesse : and the Leuites and the Priests praised the LORD day by day, *singing* with †lowd instruments vnto the LORD.

† *Hebr. instruments of strength.*
† *Hebr. to the heart of all &c.*

22 And Hezekiah spake †comfortably vnto all the Leuites, that taught the good knowledge of the LORD : and they did eate throughout the feast, seuen dayes, offering peace-offerings, and making confession to the LORD God of their fathers.

23 And the whole assembly tooke counsel to keepe other seuen dayes : and they kept *other* seuen dayes with gladnesse.

24 For Hezekiah king of Iudah †did giue to the Congregation, a thousand bullockes, and seuen thousand sheep: and the Princes gaue to the Congregation a thousand bullocks, and ten thousand sheepe, and a great number of Priests sanctified themselues.

† *Heb. lifted vp or offred.*

25 And all the Congregation of Iudah, with the Priests and the Leuites, and al the Congregation that came out of Israel, and the strangers that came out of the land of Israel, and that dwelt in Iudah, reioyced.

26 So there was great ioy in Ierusalem : for since the time of Solomon the sonne of Dauid King of Israel, *there was* not the like in Ierusalem.

27 ¶ Then the Priests the Leuites

---

arose, and blessed the people : and their voice was heard, and their prayer came vp to †his holy dwelling place, *euen* vnto heauen.

† *Hebr. the habitation of his holinesse*

CHAP. XXXI.

1 The people is forward in destroying idolatry. 2 Hezekiah ordereth the courses of the priests and Leuites, and prouideth for their worke and maintenance. 5 The peoples forwardnesse in offerings and tithes. 11 Hezekiah appointeth officers to dispose of the tithes. 20 The sinceritie of Hezekiah.

 Ow when all this was finished, all Israel that were †present, went out to the cities of Iudah, and *brake the †images in pieces, and cut downe the groues, and threw downe the high places and the altars out of all Iudah and Beniamin, in Ephraim also and Manasseh, †vntill they had vtterly destroyed them all. Then all the children of Israel returned euery man to his possession into their owne cities.

† *Heb. found*
* 2. King. 18. 4.
† *Hebr. statues.*
† *Heb. vntil to make an end.*

2 ¶ And Hezekiah appointed the courses of the Priests and the Leuites after their courses, euery man according to his seruice, the Priests and Leuites for burnt offerings, and for peace offerings, to minister and to giue thankes, and to praise in the gates of the tents of the LORD.

3 *He appointed* also the kings portion of his substance, for the burnt offrings, *to wit*, for the morning and euening burnt offrings; and the burnt offrings for the Sabbaths, and for the New-moones, and for the set feasts, as it *is* written in the Law *of the LORD.

* Num. 28.

4 Moreouer, he commaunded the people that dwelt in Ierusalem, to giue the portion of the Priests, and the Leuites, that they might be incouraged in the Law of the LORD.

5 ¶ And assoone as the commaundement †came abroad, the children of Israel brought in abundance the first fruits of corne, wine and oile, & ‖hony, and of all the increase of the field, and the tithe of all things brought they in abundantly.

† *Hebr. brought foorth.*
‖ *Or, dates.*

6 And concerning the children of Israel and Iudah, that dwelt in the cities of Iudah, they *also* brought in the tithes of oxen and sheepe, and the tithe of holy *things, which were consecrated

* Leuit. 27. 30. deu. 14. 28.

ted vnto the Lord their God, *and* layd *them* †by heapes.

† *Heb. heapes heapes*

7 In the third moneth they began to lay the foundation of the heapes, and finished *them* in the seuenth moneth.

8 And when Hezekiah and the princes came, and saw the heapes, they blessed the Lord, and his people Israel.

9 Then Hezekiah questioned with the priests and the Leuites concerning the heapes.

10 And Azariah the chiefe priest of the house of Zadok, answered him & said: Since *the* people began to bring the offerings into the house of the Lord, wee haue had enough to eate, and haue left plentie: for the Lord hath blessed his people; and that which is left, *is* this great store.

11 ¶ Then Hezekiah commanded to prepare ‖chambers in the house of the Lord, and they prepared *them*,

‖ *Or, store-houses.*

12 And brought in the offerings and the tithes, and the dedicate things, faithfully: ouer which Cononiah the Leuite *was* ruler, and Shimei his brother was the next.

13 And Iehiel, and Azariah, and Nahath, and Asahel, and Ierimoth, and Iozabad, and Eliel, and Ismachiah, and Mahath, and Benaiah *were* ouerseers †vnder the hande of Cononiah, and Shimei his brother, at the commandement of Hezekiah the king, and Azariah the ruler of the house of God.

† *Heb. at the hand.*

14 And Kore the sonne of Immah the Leuite the porter toward the East, *was* ouer the free will offerings of God, to distribute the oblations of the Lord, and the most holy things.

15 And †next him *were* Eden, and Miniamin, and Ieshua, and Shemaiah, Amariah, and Shechaniah, in the cities of the priests, in *their* ‖set office, to giue to their brethren by courses, as wel to the great as to the small:

† *Heb. at his hand.*

‖ *Or, trust.*

16 Beside their genealogie of males, from three yeeres old and vpward, *euen* vnto euery one that entreth into the house of the Lord, his dayly portion for their seruice in their charges, according to their courses:

17 Both to the genealogie of the priests by the house of their fathers, and the Leuites from twenty yeeres olde and vpward, in their charges by their courses:

18 And to the genealogie of all their litle ones, their wiues, and their sonnes, and their daughters, through all the congregation: for in their ‖set office they sanctified themselues in holinesse.

‖ *Or, trust.*

19 Also of the sonnes of Aaron the priests, which *were* in the fields of the suburbs of their cities, in euery seuerall citie, the men that *were* expressed by name, to giue portions to all the males among the priests, and to all that were reckoned by genealogies, among the Leuites.

20 ¶ And thus did Hezekiah throughout al Iudah, and wrought that which *was* good and right, and trueth before the Lord his God.

21 And in euery worke that he began in the seruice of the house of God, and in the law, and in the commandements to seeke his God, he did *it* with all his heart, and prospered.

CHAP. XXXII.

1 Sennacherib inuading Iudah, Hezekiah fortifieth himselfe and encourageth his people. 9 Against the blasphemies of Sennacherib by message and letters, Hezekiah & Isaiah pray. 21 An Angel destroyeth the hoste of the Assyrians, to the glory of Hezekiah. 24 Hezekiah praying in his sickenes, God giueth him a signe of recouerie. 25 He waxing proud, is humbled by God. 27 His wealth and works. 31 His errour in the embassage of Babylon. 32 He dying, Manasseh succeedeth him.

After *these things and the establishment *therof*, Sennacherib king of Assyria came, and entred into Iudah, & encamped against the fenced cities, and thought †to winne them for himselfe.

* *2. king. 18. 13, &c. esai. 36. 1, &c.*

† *Hebr. to breake them vp.*

2 And when Hezekiah sawe that Sennacherib was come, and that †hee was purposed to fight against Ierusalem,

† *Heb. his face was to warre.*

3 He tooke counsel with his princes, and his mightie men, to stop the waters of the fountaines, which *were* without the citie: and they did helpe him.

4 So there was gathered much people together, who stopt all the fountaines, and the brooke that †ranne through the midst of the land, saying, Why should the kings of Assyria come, and finde much water?

† *Heb. ouer-flowed.*

5 Also he strengthened himselfe, and built vp all the wall that was broken, and raised *it* vp to the towers, and another

ther wall without, and prepared Millo in the citie of Dauid, and made ||darts and shields in abundance.

Or, swords, or weapons.

6 And hee set captaines of warre o-uer the people, and gathered them to-gether to him in the streete of the gate of the city, and spake †comfortably to them, saying;

† Heb. hee spake to their heart.

7 Be strong and couragious, be not afraid nor dismayed for the king of As-syria, nor for all the multitude that *is* with him : for there *bee* moe with vs, then with him.

8 *With him *is* an arme of flesh, but with vs *is* the LORD our God to helpe vs, and to fight our battels. And the people †rested themselues vpon the words of Hezekiah king of Iudah.

* Iere. 17. 5.

† Heb. lea-ned.

9 ¶ *After this did Sennacherib king of Assyria send his seruants to Ie-rusalem (but he *himselfe laide siege* against Lachish, and all his †power with him) vnto Hezekiah king of Iudah, and vn-to all Iudah that *were* at Ierusalem, saying;

* 2. King. 18. 17.

† Heb. do-minion.

10 Thus sayth Sennacherib king of Assyria, Whereon doe ye trust, that yee abide ||in the siege in Ierusalem?

|Or, in the strong hold.

11 Doeth not Hezekiah perswade you to giue ouer your selues to die by fa-mine and by thirst, saying, The LORD our God shall deliuer vs out of the hand of the king of Assyria?

12 Hath not the same Hezekiah ta-ken away his high places, and his al-tars, and commanded Iudah and Ie-rusalem, saying; Yee shall worship be-fore one altar, & burne incense vpon it?

13 Know ye not what I and my fa-thers haue done vnto all the people of *other* lands? were the gods of the nati-ons of those landes any wayes able to deliuer their lands out of mine hand?

14 Who *was there* among all the gods of those nations, that my fathers vtter-ly destroyed, that could deliuer his peo-ple out of mine hand, that your God should bee able to deliuer you out of mine hand?

15 Now therefore let not Hezekiah deceiue you, nor perswade you on this manner, neither yet beleeue him : for no god of any nation or kingdome was a-ble to deliuer his people out of mine hand, & out of the hand of my fathers: how much lesse shall your God deliuer you out of mine hand?

16 And his seruants spake yet *more* against the LORD God, and against

his seruant Hezekiah.

17 Hee wrote also letters to raile on the LORD God of Israel, & to speake against him, saying, As the gods of the nations of *other* lands haue not deliue-red their people out of mine hand : so shall not the God of Hezekiah deliuer his people out of mine hand.

18 Then they cryed with a loude voice in the Iewes speech vnto the peo-ple of Ierusalem that were on the wal, to affright them, and to trouble them, that they might take the city.

19 And they spake against the God of Ierusalem, as against the gods of the people of the earth *which were* the worke of the hands of man.

20 For this *cause* Hezekiah the king, and the Prophet Isaiah the sonne of Amoz, prayed and cryed to heauen.

21 ¶ *And the LORD sent an An-gel, which cut off all the mightie men of valour, and the leaders and captains in the campe of the king of Assyria : so hee returned with shame of face to his owne land. And when ʾhee was come into the house of his god, they that came foorth of his owne bowels, †slew him there with the sword.

* 2. King 19. 35, &

† Heb. m him fall.

22 Thus the LORD saued Heze-kiah, and the inhabitants of Ierusa-lem, from the hand of Sennacherib the king of Assyria, and from the hand of all *other*, and guided them on euery side.

23 And many brought gifts vnto the LORD to Ierusalem, and †presents to Hezekiah king of Iudah : so that hee was magnified in the sight of all nati-ons, from thenceforth.

† Heb. pr tious thin

24 ¶ *In those dayes Hezekiah was sicke to the death, and prayed vnto the LORD : and he spake vnto him, and he ||gaue him a signe.

* 2. King 1. isai. 3

| Or, wro a miracle for him.

25 But Hezekiah rendred not againe, according to the benefit done vnto him: for his heart was lifted vp, therefore there was wrath vpon him, and vpon Iudah and Ierusalem.

26 Notwithstanding, Hezekiah hum-bled himselfe for †the pride of his heart, (*both* hee and the inhabitants of Ieru-salem) so that the wrath of the LORD came not vpon them in the dayes of He-zekiah.

† Heb. th lifting vp

27 ¶ And Hezekiah had exceeding much riches, and honour : and he made himselfe treasuries for siluer, and for golde, and for precious stones, and for
spices,

† Hebr. in-
struments of
desire.

spices, and for shields, and for all maner of † pleasant iewels;

28 Store-houses also for the increase of corne, and wine and oile; and stalles for all maner of beasts, and coates for flocks.

29 Moreouer, hee prouided him cities, and possessions of flockes & heards in abundance: for God had giuen him substance very much.

30 This same Hezekiah also stopped the vpper water - course of Gihon, and brought it straight downe to the West-side of the City of Dauid. And Hezekiah prospered in all his workes.

† Hebr. in-
terpreters.
* 2. King.
20. 12. isa.
39. 1.

31 ¶ Howbeit, in *the businesse* of the † Embassadours of the Princes of Babylon, who *sent vnto him to enquire of the wonder that was done in the land, God left him, to try him, that he might know all that was in his heart.

† Hebr. kind-
nesses.

32 ¶ Now, the rest of the acts of Hezekiah, and his † goodnesse, behold, they are written in the vision of Isaiah the Prophet, the sonne of Amoz, *and* in the booke of the kings of Iudah and Israel.

‖ Or, highest.

33 And Hezekiah slept with his fathers, and they buried him in the ‖ chiefest of the Sepulchres of the sonnes of Dauid: and all Iudah and the inhabitants of Ierusalem did him honour at his death: and Manasseh his sonne reigned in his stead.

CHAP. XXXIII.

1 Manasseh his wicked reigne. 3 Hee setteth vp idolatry, and would not be admonished. 11 He is caried into Babylon. 12 Vpon his prayer to God hee is released, and putteth downe idolatry. 18 His acts. 20 Hee dying, Amon succeedeth him. 21 Amon reigning wickedly is slaine by his seruants. 25 The murtherers beeing slaine, Iosiah succeedeth him.

* 2. King.
21. 1. &c.

Manasseh *was twelue yeeres old when he began to reigne, and he reigned fiftie and fiue yeres in Ierusalem:

* Deut. 18.
9.

2 But did that which *was* euil in the sight of the Lord, like vnto the abominations of the heathen, *whom the Lord had cast out before the children of Israel.

† Hebr. hee
returned
and built.
* 2. King.
18. 4.

3 ¶ For † hee built againe the high places, which Hezekiah his father had *broken downe, and he reared vp altars for Baalim, and made groues, and

worshipped all the host of heauen, and serued them.

4 Also hee built altars in the house of the Lord, whereof the Lord had saide, *In Ierusalem shall my Name be for euer.

* Deut. 12.
11. 1. king.
8. 29. and
9. 3. 2. chro.
6. 6. and 7.
16.

5 And he built altars for all the host of heauen, in the two Courts of the house of the Lord.

6 And he caused his children to passe through the fire in the valley of the son of Hinnom: also he obserued times, and vsed inchantments, and vsed witchcraft, and dealt with a familiar spirit, and with wizards: he wrought much euill in the sight of the Lord, to prouoke him to anger.

7 And hee set a carued image (the idole which he had made) in the house of God, of which God had said to Dauid, and to Solomon his sonne: in *this house, and in Ierusalem which I haue chosen before all the tribes of Israel, will I put my Name for euer.

* Psal. 132.
14.

8 Neither will I any more remoue the foot *of Israel from out of the land which I haue appointed for your fathers; so that they will take heed to doe all that I haue commanded them, according to the whole Law, and the statutes, and the ordinances by the hand of Moses.

* 2. Sam. 7.
10.

9 So Manasseh made Iudah, and the inhabitants of Ierusalem to erre, *and* to doe worse then the heathen, whom the Lord had destroyed before the children of Israel.

10 And the Lord spake to Manasseh, and to his people: but they would not hearken.

11 ¶ Wherfore the Lord brought vpon them the captaines of the host † of the king of Assyria, which took Manasseh among the thornes, & bound him with ‖ fetters, & caried him to Babylon.

† Heb. which
were the
kings.
‖ Or, chaines.

12 And when hee was in affliction, he besought the Lord his God, and humbled himselfe greatly before the God of his fathers,

13 And prayed vnto him, and he was intreated of him, and heard his supplication, and brought him againe to Ierusalem into his kingdome. Then Manasseh knew that the Lord hee *was* God.

14 Now after this, hee built a wall without the citie of Dauid, on the Westside of Gihon, in the valley, euen to the entring in at the fish-gate, and compassed

‖ *Or, the tower.*

sed about ‖Ophel, and raised it vp a very great height , and put captaines of warre in all the fenced cities of Iudah.

15 And hee tooke away the strange gods and the idol out of the house of the Lord, and all the altars that he had built in the mount of the house of the Lord, and in Ierusalem, and cast *them* out of the citie.

16 And hee repaired the altar of the Lord, and sacrificed thereon peace offerings, and thanke offerings, and commaunded Iudah to serue the Lord God of Israel.

17 Neuerthelesse , the people did sacrifice still in the high places, *yet* vnto the Lord their God only.

18 ¶ Nowe the rest of the actes of Manasseh, & his prayer vnto his God, and the words of the seers that spake to him in the name of the Lord God of Israel, behold , they are *written* in the booke of the kings of Israel :

19 His prayer also, and how *God* was intreated of him, and all his sinne, and his trespasse, and the places wherein he built high places, and set vp groues and grauen images before hee was humbled : behold, they are written among the sayings of ‖the Seers.

‖ *Or, Hosai.*

20 ¶ So Manasseh slept with his fathers, and they buried him in his owne house : and Amon his sonne reigned in his stead.

* 2. Kin. 21. 19. &c.

21 ¶ *Amon was two and twentie yeeres old, when he beganne to reigne, and reigned two yeares in Ierusalem.

22 But he did that which *was* euill in the sight of the Lord, as did Manasseh his father : for Amon sacrificed vnto all the carued images, which Manasseh his father had made, and serued them ;

† *Heb. multiplied trespasse.*

23 And humbled not himselfe before the Lord, as Manasseh his father had humbled himselfe : but Amon † trespassed more and more.

24 And his seruants conspired against him , and slew him in his owne house.

25 ¶ But the people of the land slew all them that had conspired against king Amon, and the people of the land made Iosiah his sonne , king in his stead.

CHAP. XXXIIII.

1 Iosiah his good reigne. 3 He destroyeth Idolatry. 8 Hee taketh order for the repaire of the Temple. 14 Hilkiah hauing found a booke of the Law, Iosiah sendeth to Huldah to inquire of the Lord. 23 Huldah prophecieth destruction of Ierusalem, but respit therof in Iosiahs time. 29 Iosiah causing it to be read in a solemne assembly , reneweth the couenant with God.

* 2. Kin. 22. 1. &c.

I* Osiah *was* eight yeeres old when hee beganne to reigne , and he reigned in Ierusalem one and thirty yeeres.

2 And he did that which *was* right in the sight of the Lord, and walked in the wayes of Dauid his father, and declined *neither* to the right hand nor to the left.

3 ¶ For in the eight yeare of his reigne, while he was yet young, hee beganne to seeke after the God of Dauid his father : and in the twelfth yeere hee beganne to *purge Iudah and Ierusalem from the high places and the groues, and the carued images, and the molten images.

* 1. Kin. 13. 2.

4 *And they brake downe the altars of Baalim in his presence, and ‖ the images that were on high aboue them, he cut downe , and the groues, and the carued images, and the molten images he brake in peeces, and made dust of *them*, and strowed *it* vpon the † graues of them, that had sacrificed vnto them.

* Leuit. 26. 30.
‖ *Or, sun-Images.*

† *Heb. face of the graues.*

5 And hee burnt the bones of the priests vpon their altars, and cleansed Iudah and Ierusalem.

6 And *so did he* in the cities of Manasseh , and Ephraim , and Simeon, euen vnto Naphtali, with their ‖ mattockes, round about.

‖ *Or, maules.*

7 And when he had broken downe the altars and the groues, and had beaten the grauen images † into pouder, and cut downe all the idoles throughout all the land of Israel, hee returned to Ierusalem.

† *Heb. to make pouder.*

8 ¶ Now in the eighteenth yeere of his reigne, when hee had purged the land, and the house ; he sent Shaphan the sonne of Azaliah, and Maasiah the gouernour of the citie, and Ioah the sonne of Ioahaz the recorder , to repaire the house of the Lord his God.

9 And when they came to Hilkiah the high priest, they deliuered the money that was brought into the house of God , which the Leuites that kept the doores,

doores, had gathered of the hand of Manasseh, and Ephraim, and of all the remnant of Israel, and of all Iudah, and Beniamin, and they returned to Ierusalem.

10 And they put *it* in the hand of the workemen that had the ouersight of the house of the LORD, and they gaue it to the workemen that wrought in the house of the LORD, to repaire and mend the house.

Or, to raf- ter.

11 Euen to the artificers and builders gaue they it, to buy hewen stone, and timber for couplings, and ||to floore the houses, which the kings of Iudah had destroyed.

12 And the men did the worke faithfully, and the ouerseers of them *were* Iahath, and Obadiah, the Leuites, of the sonnes of Merari, and Sechariah, and Meshullam, of the sonnes of the Kohathites, to set *it* forward : and *o-ther* of the Leuites, all that could skill of instruments of musicke.

13 Also they *were* ouer the bearers of burdens, and *were* ouerseers of all that wrought the worke in any manner of seruice : and of the Leuites *there were* Scribes, and officers, and porters.

* 2. Kings 22. 8, &c.
† Heb. by the hand of.

14 ¶ And when they brought out the money that was brought into the house of the LORD, Hilkiah the priest * found a booke of the lawe of the LORD, *giuen* † by Moses.

15 And Hilkiah answered and saide to Shaphan the scribe : I haue found the booke of the law in the house of the LORD. And Hilkiah deliuered the booke to Shaphan :

16 And Shaphan caried the booke to the king, and brought the king word backe againe, saying, All that was committed † to thy seruants, they doe *it*.

† Heb. to the hand of.
† Heb. pow- red out, or melted.

17 And they haue † gathered toge- ther the money that was found in the house of the LORD, and haue deliue- red it into the hand of the ouerseers, and to the hand of the workemen.

18 Then Shaphan the scribe tolde the king, saying, Hilkiah the priest giuen me a booke. And Shaphan read † it before the king.

† Heb. in it.

19 And it came to passe when the king had heard the words of the lawe, that he rent his clothes.

20 And the king commanded Hilki- ah, and Ahikam the sonne of Sha- phan, and ||Abdon the sonne of Micah, and Shaphan the scribe, and Asaiah a

|| Or, Ach- bor, 2. kings 22. 12.

seruant of the kings, saying,

21 Goe, enquire of the LORD for me, and for them that are left in Israel and in Iudah, concerning the wordes of the booke that is found : for great is the wrath of the LORD that is pow- red out vpon vs, because our fathers haue not kept the word of the LORD, to doe after all that is written in this booke.

22 And Hilkiah and they that the king had *appointed* went to Huldah the prophetesse, the wife of Shallum the sonne of Tikuath, the sonne of ||Has- rah, keeper of the † wardrobe (now she dwelt in Ierusalem in the ||colledge,) and they spake to her to that *effect*.

|| Or, Har- has, 2. kings 22. 14.
† Heb. gar- ments.
|| Or, in the schoole, or in the second part.

23 ¶ And she answered them, Thus saith the LORD God of Israel : Tell ye the man that sent you to me,

24 Thus saith the LORD, behold, I will bring euill vpon this place, and vpon the inhabitants thereof, *euen* all the curses that are written in the booke which they haue read before the king of Iudah :

25 Because they haue forsaken mee, and haue burned incense vnto other gods, that they might prouoke mee to anger with all the workes of their hands, therefore my wrath shall bee powred out vpon this place, and shall not be quenched.

26 And as for the king of Iudah, who sent you to enquire of the LORD, so shal ye say vnto him : Thus saith the LORD God of Israel, *concerning* the words which thou hast heard :

27 Because thine heart was tender, and thou didst humble thy selfe before God, when thou heardest his words against this place, and against the inha- bitants thereof, and humbledst thy selfe before me, and diddest rend thy clothes, and weepe before me, I haue euen heard thee also, saith the LORD.

28 Behold, I will gather thee to thy fathers, and thou shalt bee gathered to thy graue in peace, neither shall thine eyes see all the euill that I will bring vpon this place, and vpon the inhabi- tants of the same. So they brought the king word againe.

29 ¶ * Then the king sent, and ga- thered together all the Elders of Iu- dah and Ierusalem.

* 2. Kings 23. 1.

30 And the king went vp into the house of the LORD, and all the men of Iudah, and the inhabitants of Ie- rusalem,

† Heb. from great euen to small.

rusalem, and the priests and the Leuites, and all the people † great and small: and he read in their eares all the words of the booke of the couenant, that was found in the house of the LORD.

31 And the King stood in his place, & made a Couenant before the LORD, to walke after the LORD, and to keepe his Commandements, and his Testimonies, and his Statutes, with all his heart, & with all his soule, to performe the words of the Couenant which are written in this booke.

† Heb. found

32 And he caused all that were † present in Ierusalem and Beniamin, to stand to it. And the inhabitants of Ierusalem did according to the couenant of God, the God of their fathers.

33 And Iosiah tooke away all the abominations out of all the countreys that perteined to the children of Israel, and made all that were present in Israel to serue, euen to serue the LORD their God. And all his dayes they departed not † from folowing the LORD the God of their fathers.

† Heb. from after.

CHAP. XXXV.

1 Iosiah keepeth a most solemne Passeouer. 20 Hee prouoking Pharaoh Nechoh, is slaine at Megiddo. 25 Lamentations for Iosiah.

* 2. King. 23. 21, 22.

* Exo. 12. 6.

MOreouer * Iosiah kept a Passeouer vnto ỹ LORD in Ierusalem : and they killed the Passeouer on the fourteenth *day of the first moneth.

2 And hee set the Priestes in their charges, and encouraged them to the seruice of the house of the LORD,

3 And said vnto the Leuites, that taught all Israel, which were holy vnto the LORD, Put the holy Arke in the house, which Solomon the sonne of Dauid king of Israel did build; it shall not be a burden vpon your shoulders: serue now the LORD your God, and his people Israel.

4 And prepare your selues by the houses of your fathers, after your courses, according to the *writing of Dauid king of Israel, and according to the *writing of Solomon his sonne.

5 And stand in the holy place according to the diuisions of the †families of the fathers of your †brethren the people, and after the diuision of the families of the Leuites.

* 1. Chron. 9. 10. and chap. 23, 24. 25, and 26.
* 2. Chron. 8. 14.
† Heb. the house of the fathers.
† Heb. the sonnes of the people.

6 So kill the Passeouer, and sanctifie your selues, and prepare your brethren, that they may doe according to the word of the LORD, by the hand of Moses.

7 And Iosiah †gaue to the people, of the flocke, lambes and kiddes, all for the Passeouer - offerings, for all that were present, to the number of thirtie thousand, and three thousand bullocks: these were of the kings substance.

† Heb. offred

8 And his Princes † gaue willingly vnto the people, to the Priests and to the Leuites : Hilkiah, and Zachariah, and Iehiel, rulers of the house of God, gaue vnto the Priests for the Passeouer-offerings, two thousand and sixe hundred small cattell, and three hundred oxen.

† Heb. offred

9 Conaniah also, and Shemaiah, and Nethaneel, his brethren, & Hashabiah, and Iehiel, and Ioshabad chiefe of the Leuites, †gaue vnto the Leuites for Passeouer-offerings, fiue thousand small cattell, and fiue hundred oxen.

† Heb. offred

10 So the seruice was prepared, and the Priests stood in their place, and the Leuites in their courses, according to the kings commandement.

11 And they killed the Passeouer, and the Priestes sprinckled the blood from their handes, and the Leuites * flayed them.

* See Chap. 29. 34.

12 And they remooued the burnt offerings, that they might giue according to the diuisions of the families of the people, to offer vnto the LORD, as it is written in the booke of Moses : and so did they with the oxen.

13 And they * rosted the Passeouer with fire, according to the ordinance : but the other holy offerings sod they in pots, and in cauldrons, and in pannes, and † diuided them speedily among all the people.

* Exod. 12. 8, 9.

† Heb. made them runne

14 And afterward they made ready for themselues, and for the Priests : because the Priests the sonnes of Aaron were busied in offring of burnt offrings, and the fat vntill night : therefore the Leuites prepared for themselues, and for the Priests the sonnes of Aaron.

15 And the singers the sonnes of Asaph, were in their †place according to the *commandement of Dauid, and Asaph, and Heman, and Ieduthun the kings Seer : and the Porters *waited at euery gate : they might not depart from their seruice ; for their brethren the Leuites prepared for them.

† Heb. station
* 1. Chron. 25. 1, &c.
* 1. Chron. 9. 17. and 26. 14.

16 So

16 So all the seruice of the Lord was prepared the same day, to keepe the Passeouer, and to offer burnt offerings vpon the altar of the Lord, according to the commaundement of king Iosiah.

17 And the children of Israel that were †present, kept the Passeouer at that time, and the feast of vnleauened bread seuen dayes.

Heb. found.

18 And there was no Passeouer like to that, kept in Israel, from the dayes of Samuel the Prophet : neither did all the Kings of Israel keepe such a Passeouer, as Iosiah kept, and the Priests and the Leuites, and all Iudah and Israel that were present, and the inhabitants of Ierusalem.

19 In the eighteenth yeere of the reigne of Iosiah, was this Passeouer kept.

20 ¶ *After all this, when Iosiah had prepared the † Temple, Necho king of Egypt came vp to fight against Carchemish by Euphrates : and Iosiah went out against him.

2. King. 23. 29.
Heb. house.

21 But hee sent Embassadours to him, saying, What haue I to doe with thee, thou king of Iudah? *I come* not against thee this day, but against the house, †wherewith I haue warre : for God commaunded mee to make haste : forbeare thee from *medling* with God, who *is* with mee, that hee destroy thee not.

Hebr. the house of my warre.

22 Neuerthelesse Iosiah would not turne his face from him, but disguised himselfe that he might fight with him, and hearkened not vnto the wordes of Necho from the mouth of God, and came to fight in the valley of Megiddo.

23 And the archers shot at king Iosiah : and the King saide to his seruants, Haue mee away, for I am †sore wounded.

Hebr. made sicke.

24 His seruants therefore tooke him out of that charet, and put him in the second charet that hee *had :* and they brought him to Ierusalem, and hee died, and was buried ||in *one of the* Sepulchres of his fathers. And *all Iudah and Ierusalem mourned for Iosiah.

Or, among the sepulchres.
Zach. 12. 1.

25 ¶ And Ieremiah lamented for Iosiah, and all the singing men and the singing women spake of Iosiah in their lamentations to this day, and made them an ordinance in Israel ; and behólde, they are written in the Lamentations.

26 Now the rest of the acts of Iosiah, and his †goodnes, according to that which *was* written in the Law of the Lord,

† Hebr. kindnesses.

27 And his deedes first and last ; behold, they *are* written in the booke of the kings of Israel and Iudah.

CHAP. XXXVI.

1 Iehoahaz succeeding, is deposed by Pharaoh, and caried into Egypt. 5 Iehoiakim raigning ill, is caried bound into Babylon. 9 Iehoiachin succeeding reigneth ill, and is brought into Babylon. t1 Zedekiah succeeding reigneth ill, and despiseth the Prophets, and rebelleth against Nebuchadnezzar. 14 Ierusalem for the sinnes of the Priests and people, is wholely destroyed. 22 The proclamation of Cyrus.

Hen *the people of the land tooke Iehoahaz the son of Iosiah, and made him King in his fathers stead in Ierusalem.

2. King. 23. 30. &c.

2 Iehoahaz *was* twentie and three yeeres old, when hee began to reigne, and hee reigned three moneths in Ierusalem.

3 And the king of Egypt †put him downe at Ierusalem, and †condemned the land in an hundred talents of siluer, and a talent of gold.

† Hebr. remooued him.
† Hebr. mulcted.

4 And the king of Egypt made Eliakim his brother, king ouer Iudah and Ierusalem ; and turned his name to Iehoiakim. And Necho tooke Iehoahaz his brother, and caried him to Egypt.

5 ¶ Iehoiakim *was* twentie and fiue yeres old when he began to reigne, and he reigned eleuen yeeres in Ierusalem : and hee did that which *was* euill in the sight of the Lord his God.

6 Against him came vp Nebuchadnezzar King of Babylon, and bound him in ||fetters to cary him to Babylon.

Or, chaines.

7 * Nebuchadnezzar also caried of the vessels of the house of the Lord to Babylon, and put them in his temple at Babylon.

2. King. 24. 13. dan. 1. 1, 2.

8 Now the rest of the acts of Iehoiakim, and his abominations which he did, and that which *was* found in him, behold, they are written in the booke of the Kings of Israel and Iudah : and ||Iehoiachin his sonne reigned in his stead.

Or, Ieconiah, 1. chro. 3. 16. or, Coniah, ier. 22. 24.
2. King. 24. 8.

9 ¶ * Iehoiachin *was* eight yeeres old when hee began to reigne, and hee reigned

reigned three moneths and ten dayes in Ierusalem, and hee did that which *was* euill in the sight of the LORD.

10 And †when the yeere was expired, King Nebuchadnezzar sent, and brought him to Babylon, with the † goodly vessels of the house of the LORD, and made ‖ Zedekiah his brother, king ouer Iudah and Ierusalem.

11 ¶ *Zedekiah *was* one and twentie yeres old, when he began to reigne, and reigned eleuen yeeres in Ierusalem.

12 And hee did that which *was* euill in the sight of the LORD his God, *and* humbled not himselfe before Ieremiah the Prophet, *speaking* from the mouth of the LORD.

13 And he also rebelled against king Nebuchadnezzar, who had made him sweare by God: but he stiffened his necke, and hardened his heart from turning vnto the LORD God of Israel.

14 ¶ Moreouer all the chiefe of the priests, and the people transgressed very much, after all the abominations of the heathen, and polluted the house of the LORD which hee had hallowed in Ierusalem.

15 *And the LORD God of their fathers sent to them † by his messengers, rising vp ‖ betimes, and sending: because he had compassion on his people, and on his dwelling place:

16 But they mocked the messengers of God, and despised his wordes, and misused his prophets, vntill the wrath of the LORD arose against his people, till there was no † remedie.

17 * Therefore hee brought vpon them the king of the Caldees, who slew their yong men with the sword, in the house of their sanctuarie, and had no compassion vpon yong man or maiden, olde man, or him that stouped for age: he gaue *them* all into his hand.

18 And all the vessels of the house of God great and small, and the treasures of the house of the LORD, and the treasures of the king, and of his princes: all *these* he brought to Babylon.

19 And they burnt the house of God, and brake downe the wall of Ierusalem, and burnt all the palaces thereof with fire, and destroyed all the goodly vessels thereof.

20 And † them that had escaped from the sword, caried he away to Babylon: where they were seruants to him and his sonnes, vntill the reigne of the kingdome of Persia:

21 To fulfill the word of the LORD by the mouth of *Ieremiah, vntill the land *had enioyed her Sabbaths: *for* as long as shee lay desolate, shee kept Sabbath, to fulfill threescore and tenne yeeres.

22 ¶ *Now in the first yeere of Cyrus king of Persia (that the word of the LORD spoken by the mouth of *Ieremiah, might bee accomplished) the LORD stirred vp the spirit of Cyrus king of Persia, that hee made a proclamation throughout all his kingdome, and *put it* also in writing, saying,

23 Thus saith Cyrus king of Persia, All the kingdomes of the earth hath the LORD God of heauen giuen mee, and he hath charged me to build him an house in Ierusalem, which *is* in Iudah: Who *is there* among you of all his people? the LORD his God *be* with him, and let him goe vp.

Marginal notes left column:
† *Hebr. at the returne of the yeere.*
† *Heb. vessels of desire.*
‖ *Or, Mattaniah, 2.kin. 24. 17. ier. 37. 1.*
* *Ier. 52. 1, &c. 2. king 24. 18.*
* *Ier. 25. 3. and 35. 15.*
† *Heb. by the hand of his messengers.*
‖ *That is, continually and carefully*
† *Heb. healing.*
* *2. Kings 25. 1, &c.*

Marginal notes right column:
† *Heb. the remainder from the sword.*
* *Ier. 25. 9. 12. & 29. 10.*
* *Leuit. 26. 34. and 35. and 43.*
* *Ezra 1. 1.*
* *Ier. 25. 13. and 29. 10.*

¶ EZRA.

¶ EZRA.

CHAP. I.

1 The Proclamation of Cyrus for the building of the Temple. 5 The people prouide for the returne. 7 Cyrus restoreth the vessels of the Temple to Sheshbazzar.

OW in the first yeere of Cyrus King of Persia, (that the word of the LORD * by the mouth of Ieremiah, might be fulfilled) ẙ LORD stirred vp the spirit of Cyrus king of Persia, that he † made a proclamation throughout all his kingdome, and *put it* also in writing, saying;

2 Thus sayth Cyrus king of Persia, The LORD God of heauen hath giuen mee all the kingdomes of the earth, and he hath * charged me to build him an house at Ierusalem, which *is* in Iudah.

3 Who *is* there among you of all his people? his God be with him, and let him goe vp to Ierusalem, which is in Iudah, and build the house of the LORD God of Israel (He *is* the God) which *is* in Ierusalem.

4 And whosoeuer remaineth in a-ny place where hee soiourneth, let the men of his place † helpe him with siluer, and with golde, and with goods, and with beasts, besides the free-will offe-ring for the house of God that is in Ie-rusalem.

5 ¶ Then rose vp the chiefe of the fathers of Iudah and Beniamin, and the Priests, and the Leuites, with all *them* whose spirit God had raised to goe vp, to build the house of the LORD which is in Ierusalem.

6 And all they that *were* about them, ‖strengthened their hands with vessels of siluer, with golde, with goods, and with beasts, and with precious things; besides all *that* was willingly offered.

7 ¶ Also Cyrus the king brought foorth the vessels of the house of the LORD, * which Nebuchadnezzar had brought foorth out of Ierusalem, and had put them in the house of his gods:

8 Euen those did Cyrus king of Persia bring foorth, by the hand of Mithre-dath the treasurer, and numbred them vnto * Sheshbazzar the Prince of Iu-dah.

9 And this *is* the number of them: thirtie chargers of golde, a thousand chargers of siluer, nine and twentie kniues:

10 Thirtie basins of golde: siluer ba-sins of a second sort, foure hundred and ten: *and* other vessels a thousand.

11 All the vessels of golde and of sil-uer, *were* fiue thousand and foure hun-dred. All *these* did Sheshbazzar bring vp with *them of* † the captiuitie, that were brought vp from Babylon vnto Ierusalem.

CHAP. II.

1 The number that returne, of the people, 36 of the Priests, 40 of the Leuites, 43 of the Nethinims, 55 of Solomons seruants, 62 of the Priests which could not shewe their pedi-gree. 64 The whole number of them, with their substance. 68 Their oblations.

ow * these *are* the children of the prouince, that went vp out of the captiuitie, of those which had beene ca-ried away, whom Nebu-chadnezzar the King of Babylon had caried away vnto Babylon, and came againe vnto Ierusalem and Iudah, euery one vnto his citie;

2 Which came with Zerubbabel, Ieshua, Nehemiah, ‖ Saraiah, Ree-laiah, Mordecai, Bilshan, Mispar, Bi-guai, Rehum, Baanah: The number of the men of the people of Israel.

3 The children of Parosh, two thou-sand, an hundred seuentie and two.

4 The children of Shephatiah, three hundred seuentie and two.

5 The

Margin notes (right column)
* 2. Kings 24. 13. 2. chr. 36. 7.

* See Chap. 5. 14.

† *Hebr. the transporta-tion.*

* Nehem. 7. 6, &c.

‖*Or, Azari-ah, nehe. 7.7.*

Margin notes (left column)
ron. ere. and

au-uice .

4. 28. 13.

tif

is, them.

5 The children of Arah, seuen hundred, seuentie and fiue.

6 The children of * Pahath-Moab, of the children of Ieshua and Ioab, two thousand, eight hundred and twelue.

7 The children of Elam, a thousand, two hundred fiftie and foure.

8 The children of Zattu, nine hundred fourtie and fiue.

9 The children of Zaccai, seuen hundred and threescore.

10 The children of ‖ Bani, sixe hundred, fourtie and two.

11 The children of Bebai, sixe hundred, twentie and three.

12 The children of Azgad, a thousand, two hundred, twentie and two.

13 The children of Adonikam, sixe hundred, sixtie and sixe.

14 The children of Biguai, two thousand fiftie and sixe.

15 The children of Adin, foure hundred, fiftie and foure.

16 The children of Ater of Hezekiah, ninetie and eight.

17 The children of Bezai, three hundred twenty and three.

18 The children of ‖ Iorah, an hundred and twelue.

19 The children of Hashum, two hundred twentie and three.

20 The children of ‖ Gibbar, ninetie and fiue.

21 The children of Bethlehem, an hundred twentie and three.

22 The children of Netophah, fiftie and sixe.

23 The men of Anathoth, an hundred twentie and eight.

24 The children of ‖ Azmaueth, fortie and two.

25 The children of Kiriath - arim, Chephirah, and Beeroth, seuen hundred, and fourtie and three.

26 The children of Ramah and Gaba, sixe hundred, twentie and one.

27 The men of Michmas, an hundred, twentie and two.

28 The men of Bethel and Ai, two hundred, twentie and three.

29 The children of Nebo, fiftie and two.

30 The children of Magbish, an hundred fiftie and sixe.

31 The children of the other * Elam, a thousand, two hundred, fiftie and foure.

32 The children of Harim, three hundred and twentie.

Left margin notes

* Nehem. 7. 10.

‖ Or, Binnui, nehem. 7. 15.

‖ Or, Hariph, nehem. 7. 24.

‖ Or, Gibeon, nehem. 7. 25.

‖ Or, Beth-Asmaueth, Nehe. 7. 28.

* See ver. 7.

---

33 The children of Lod ‖ Hadid, and Ono, seuen hundred, twentie and fiue.

34 The children of Iericho, three hundred fourtie and fiue.

35 The children of Senaah, three thousand and sixe hundred and thirtie.

36 ¶ The Priests. The children of * Iedaiah, of the house of Ieshua, nine hundred, seuentie and three.

37 The children of * Immer, a thousand, fiftie and two.

38 The children of * Pashur, a thousand, two hundred, fourtie and seuen.

39 The children of * Harim, a thousand and seuenteene.

40 ¶ The Leuites. The children of Ieshua, and Kadmiel, of the children of ‖ Hodauia, seuentie and foure.

41 ¶ The singers. The children of Asaph, an hundred twentie and eight.

42 ¶ The children of the porters. The children of Shallum, the children of Ater, the children of Talmon, the children of Akkub, the children of Hatita, the children of Shobai, in all, an hundred thirtie and nine.

43 ¶ The Nethinims. The children of Ziha, the children of Hasupha, the children of Tabbaoth,

44 The children of Keros, the children of Siaha, the children of Padon,

45 The children of Lebanah, the children of Hagabah, the children of Akkub,

46 The children of Hagab, the children of ‖ Shalmai, the children of Hanan.

47 The children of Giddel, the children of Gahar, the children of Reaiah,

48 The children of Rezin, the children of Nekoda, the children of Gazzam,

49 The children of Vzza, the children of Paseah, the children of Besai,

50 The children of Asnah, the children of Mehunim, the children of Nephushim,

51 The children of Bakbuk, the children of Hakupha, the children of Harhur,

52 The children of ‖ Bazluth, the children of Mehida, the children of Harsha,

53 The children of Barkos, the children of Sisera, the children of Thamah,

54 The children of Neziah, the children of Hatipha,

55 ¶ The

Right margin notes

‖ Or, F as it i some c

* 1. C 24. 7.

* 1. C 24. 14.

* 1. C 12.

* 1 C 24. 8.

‖ Or, chap. called Hoder nehem

‖ Or, S lat.

‖ Or, S lith, i hem.

55 ¶ The children of Solomons seruants. The children of Sotai, the children of Sophereth, the children of ‖ Peruda,

Or, Perida,
n Nehem.

56 The children of Iaalah, the children of Darkon, the children of Giddel,

57 The children of Shephatiah, the children of Hattil, the children of Pochereth of Zebaim, the children of ‖ Ami.

Or, Amon,
Nehem.
Iosh. 9.
, 27.
chro. 9. 2.
1. King. 9.

58 All the *Nethinims, and the children of * Solomons seruants, were three hundred ninetie and two.

59 And these were they which went vp from Tel-melah, Tel-Harsa, Cherub, Addan, and Immer: but they could not shewe their fathers house, and their ‖seed, whether they were of Israel.

Or, pede-
ee.

60 The children of Delaiah, the children of Tobiah, the children of Nekoda : sixe hundred fiftie and two.

61 ¶ And of the children of the priests: the children of Habaiah, the children of Koz, the children of Barzillai, (which tooke a wife of the daughters of * Barzillai the Gileadite, and was called after their name.)

. Sam. 17

62 These sought their register among those that were reckoned by genealogie, but they were not found : therefore were they †as polluted, put from the priesthood.

Keb. they
repolluted
om the
esthood.
r, gouer-
ur.

63 And the ‖ Tirshatha said vnto them, that they should not eate of the most holy things, till there stood vp a priest with * Vrim & with Thummim.

Exod. 28.

64 ¶ The whole Congregation together, was fourtie and two thousand, three hundred and threescore :

65 Beside their seruants and their maids, of whom there were seuen thousand, three hundred thirtie and seuen : and there were among them two hundred singing men, and singing women.

66 Their horses were seuen hundred, thirtie and sixe : their mules, two hundred fourtie and fiue :

67 Their camels, foure hundred, thirty and fiue : their asses, sixe thousand, seuen hundred and twentie.

68 ¶ And some of the chiefe of the fathers, when they came to the house of the Lord which is at Ierusalem, offered freely for the house of God, to set it vp in his place :

69 They gaue after their abilitie, vnto the * treasure of the worke, threescore and one thousand drammes of golde, and fiue thousand pound of siluer, and one hundred priests garments.

Chron.
20.

70 So the priests and the Leuites, and some of the people, and the singers, and the porters, and the Nethinims, dwelt in their cities, and all Israel in their cities.

CHAP. III.

1 The Altar is set vp. 4 Offerings frequented. 7 Workmen prepared. 8 The foundations of the Temple are laid in great ioy & mourning.

ND when the seuenth moneth was come, and the children of Israel were in the cities: the people gathered themselues together, as one man to Ierusalem.

2 Then stood vp ‖ Ieshua the sonne of Iozadak, & his brethren the priests, and *Zerubbabel the sonne of * Shealtiel, and his brethren, and builded the Altar of the God of Israel, to offer burnt offrings thereon, as it is * written in the law of Moses the man of God.

‖ Or, Iosua.
Hagge 1. 1.
* Matth. 1.
12. and luke
3. 27. called
Zorobabel.
* Matth. 1.
12. and luke
3. 27. called
Salathiel.
* Deut. 12. 5.

3 And they set the altar vpon his bases, (for feare was vpon them, because of the people of those countreys) and they offered burnt offerings thereon vnto the Lord, euen burnt offerings, morning and euening.

4 They kept also the feast of tabernacles, *as it is written, and *offred the dayly burnt offrings, by number, according to the custome, †as the duetie of euery day required :

* Num. 29.
12.
* Exod. 23.
16.
† Hebr. the
matter of the
day in his
day.

5 And afterward offered the continuall burnt offering, both of the new moones, and of all the set feasts of the Lord, that were consecrated, and of euery one that willingly offred, offered a free will offering vnto the Lord.

6 From the first day of the seuenth moneth, began they to offer burnt offerings vnto the Lord : but the †foundation of the temple of the Lord was not yet laid.

† Hebr. the
Temple of
the Lord
was not yet
founded.

7 They gaue money also vnto the masons, and to the ‖carpenters, and meate, and drinke, and oyle, vnto them of Zidon, and to them of Tyre, to bring Cedar trees from Lebanon to the sea of * Ioppa : according to the grant that they had of Cyrus king of Persia.

‖ Or, worke-
men.

* Acts 9. 3.

8 ¶ Now in the second yere of their comming vnto the house of God at Ierusalem, in the second moneth, began Zerubbabel the sonne of Shealtiel, and Ieshua the sonne of Iozadak, and the

the remnant of their brethren, the Priests and the Leuites, and all they that were come out of the captiuitie vnto Ierusalem: and appointed the Leuites, from twentie yeeres olde and vpward, to set forward the worke of the house of the LORD.

9 Then stood Ieshua, *with* his sons and his brethren, Kadmiel and his sonnes, the sonnes of ‖ Iudah †together, to set forward the workemen in the house of God: the sonnes of Henadad, with their sonnes and their brethren the Leuites.

‖ Or, Hodauiah, Chap. 2. 40.
†Heb. as one.

10 And when the builders laide the foundation of the Temple of the LORD, they set the Priests in their apparell with Trumpets, and the Leuites the sonnes of Asaph, with Cymbales, to praise the LORD, after the * ordinance of Dauid king of Israel.

* 1. Chro. 6. 31. and cha. 16. 7. and 25, 1.

11 And they sung together by course, in praising, and giuing thanks vnto the LORD; Because hee is good, for his mercy endureth for euer towards Israel. And all the people shouted with a great shoute, when they praised the LORD; because the foundation of the house of the LORD was laide.

12 But many of the Priests and Leuites, and chiefe of the fathers, who *were* ancient men, that had seene the first house; when the foundation of this house was laide before their eyes, wept with a loude voice, and many shouted aloude for ioy:

13 So that the people could not discerne the noyse of the shout of ioy, from the noyse of the weeping of the people: for the people shouted with a loude shout, and the noyse was heard a-farre off.

CHAP. IIII.

1 The aduersaries, being not accepted in the building of the Temple with the Iewes, endeauour to hinder it. 7 Their Letter to Artaxerxes. 17 The decree of Artaxerxes. 23 The building is hindred.

† Hebr. the sonnes of the transportation.

Ow when the aduersaries of Iudah and Beniamin, heard that † the children of the captiuitie builded the Temple vnto the LORD God of Israel:

2 Then they came to Zerubbabel, and to the chiefe of the fathers, and said vnto them, Let vs build with you, for wee seeke your God, as yee *doe*, and we

doe sacrifice vnto him, since the dayes of Esar-Haddon king of Assur, which brought vs vp hither.

3 But Zerubbabel and Ieshua, and the rest of the chiefe of the fathers of Israel, said vnto them, You haue nothing to doe with vs, to build an house vnto our God, but we our selues together will build vnto the LORD God of Israel, as king Cyrus the King of Persia hath commanded vs.

4 Then the people of the land weakened the handes of the people of Iudah, and troubled them in building,

5 And hired counsellers against them, to frustrate their purpose, all the dayes of Cyrus king of Persia, euen vntill the reigne of Darius king of Persia.

6 And in the reigne of † Ahasuerus, in the beginning of his reigne, wrote they vnto him an accusation against the inhabitants of Iudah and Ierusalem.

† Heb. Ahueros

7 ¶ And in the dayes of Artaxerxes wrote ‖ Bishlam, Mithredath, Tabeel, and the rest of their † companions, vnto Artaxerxes king of Persia; and the writing of the letter *was* written in the Syrian tongue, and interpreted in the Syrian tongue.

‖ Or, in peace.
† Heb. ties.

8 Rehum the Chancellour, and Shimshai the ‖ Scribe, wrote a letter against Ierusalem, to Artaxerxes the king, in this sort:

‖ Or, Setarie.

9 Then, *wrote* Rehum the Chancellour, and Shimshai the Scribe, and the rest of their †companions; the Dinaites, the Apharsathkites, the Tarpelites, the Apharsites, the Archeuites, the Babylonians, the Susanchites, the Dehauites, *and* the Elamites,

‖ Chalcieties.

10 And the rest of the nations whom the great and noble Asnappar brought ouer, and set in the cities of Samaria, and the rest that *are* on this side the Riuer, †and at such a time.

11 ¶ This *is* the copy of the Letter, that they sent vnto him, *euen* vnto Artaxerxes the king: Thy seruants on this side the Riuer, and at such a time,

† Chaeneth.

12 Be it knowen vnto the king, that the Iewes which came vp from thee to vs, are come vnto Ierusalem, building the rebellious and the bad citie, and haue ‖ set vp the walles thereof, and †ioyned the foundations.

‖ Or,
† Cho ed to

13 Be it knowen now vnto the king, that if this city be builded, and the wals set vp againe, then will they not † pay tolle, tribute, and custome, and so thou shalt

† Cho

shalt endammage the || reuenue of the
kings.
14 Now because we † haue maintenance *from the Kings* palace, and it was
not meete for vs to see the kings dishonour: therefore haue we sent, and certified the king,
15 That search may be made in the
booke of the Records of thy fathers: so
shalt thou finde in the booke of the Records, and know, that this City *is* a rebellious city, and hurtfull vnto Kings
and prouinces, and that they haue † moued sedition † within the same of olde
time: for which cause was this citie destroyed.
16 We certifie the king, that if this citie be builded *againe*, & the walles thereof
set vp: by this meanes, thou shalt haue
no portion on this side the Riuer.
17 ¶ *Then* sent the king an answere
vnto Rehum the Chancellour, and to
Shimshai the scribe, and to the rest of
their † companions, that dwell in Samaria, and vnto the rest beyond the Riuer, Peace, and at such a time.
18 The letter, which ye sent vnto vs,
hath bene plainly read before me.
19 And † I commaunded, and search
hath bene made, and it is found, that
this citie of old time hath † made insurrection against Kings, and that rebellion & sedition haue bene made therein.
20 There haue bene mighty Kings
also ouer Ierusalem, which haue ruled ouer all *countreys* beyond the Riuer,
and tolle, tribute, and custome, was
payd vnto them.
21 † Giue ye now commandement,
to cause these men to cease, and that this
citie be not builded, vntill *another* commandement shall be giuen from me.
22 Take heed now that ye faile not
to doe this: why should damage grow
to the hurt of the kings?
23 ¶ Now when the copy of King
Artaxerxes letter was read before Rehum and Shimshai the scribe, and their
companions, they went vp in haste to
Ierusalem, vnto the Iewes, and made
them to cease, by † force and power.
24 Then ceased the woorke of the
house of the God, which *is* at Ierusalem. So it ceased, vnto the second yeere
of the reigne of Darius king of Persia.

...ngth. *...al. we ...salted the salt ...palace.* *...d. made.* *...ald. in ...midst ...eof.* *...al, so...es.* *...ald. by ...a decree ...t.* *...ald. lif... ...p it* *...al. make ...cree.* *...hald. by ...ne and ...er.*

CHAP. V.

1 Zerubbabel and Shealtiel, incited by Haggai and Zacharie, set forward the building of the Temple. 3 Tatnai and Shether-Boznai could not hinder the Iewes. 6 Their letter to Darius against the Iewes.

THen the Prophets, * Hag-
gai the Prophet, and Ze-
chariah the sonne of Id-
do, prophesied vnto the
Iewes that *were* in Iu-
dah and Ierusalem, in the Name of
the God of Israel, *euen* vnto them.
2 Then rose vp Zerubbabel the
sonne of Shealtiel, and Ieshua the
sonne of Iozadak, and began to build
the house of God which *is* at Ierusalem: and with them *were* the Prophets
of God helping them.
3 ¶ At the same time came to them
Tatnai, gouernour on this side the Riuer, and Shethar-Boznai, and their
companions, and said thus vnto them;
Who hath commaunded you to build
this house, and to make vp this wall?
4 Then said wee vnto them after
this maner, What are the names of the
men † that make this building?
5 But the eye of their God was vpon the Elders of the Iewes, that they
could not cause them to cease, till the
matter came to Darius: and then they
returned answere by letter concerning
this *matter*.
6 ¶ The copy of the letter that Tatnai, gouernour on this side the Riuer,
and Shethar-Boznai, and his companions the Apharsachites, which *were*
on this side the Riuer, sent vnto Darius the King:
7 They sent a letter vnto him,
† wherein was written thus: Vnto Darius the king, all peace.
8 Be it knowen vnto the king, that
we went into the prouince of Iudea, to
the house of the great God, which is
builded with † great stones, & timber is
laied in the wals, and this worke goeth
fast on, and prospereth in their hands.
9 Then asked we those Elders, *and*
said vnto them thus, Who commanded
you to build this house, and to make vp
these walles?
10 We asked their names also, to certifie thee, that we might write the names
of the men that were the chiefe of them.
11 And thus they returned vs answere, saying, We are the seruants of
the God of heauen and earth, and build
the house that was builded these many
yeeres agoe, which a great King of Israel builded, * and set vp.

12 But

* Agge. 1. 1. zach. 1. 1.

† *Chald. that build this building.*

† *Chald. in the midst whereof.*

† *Chald. stones of ro-ling.*

* 1. King. 6. 1.

12 But after that our fathers had prouoked the God of heauen vnto wrath : he gaue them into the hande of * Nebuchadnezzar the king of Babylon, the Caldean, who destroyed this house, and caried the people away into Babylon.

13 But in the first yere of * Cyrus the king of Babylon, *the same* king Cyrus made a decree to build this house of God.

14 And the vessels also of golde and siluer of the house of God, which Nebuchadnezzar tooke out of the Temple that *was* in Ierusalem, and brought them into the temple of Babylon, those did Cyrus the king take out of the temple of Babylon, and they were deliuered vnto one, * whose name *was* Sheshbazzar, whome he had made ‖ gouernour :

15 And said vnto him, Take these vessels, goe, carie them into the temple that is in Ierusalem, and let the house of God be builded in his place.

16 Then came the same Sheshbazzar, *and* laid the foundation of the house of God, which *is* in Ierusalem. And since that time, euen vntill now, hath it bin in building, & *yet* it is not finished.

17 Now therefore, if it *seeme* good to the king, let there be search made in the kings treasure house which *is* there at Babylon, whether it be *so* that a decree was made of Cyrus the king, to build this house of God at Ierusalem : and let the king send his pleasure to vs concerning this matter.

CHAP. VI.

1 Darius finding the decree of Cyrus, maketh a new decree for the aduancement of the building. 13 By the helpe of the enemies, and the directions of the prophets, the Temple is finished. 16 The feast of the Dedication is kept. 19 And the Passeouer.

Hen Darius the King made a decree, and search was made in the house of the † rolles, where the treasures were † laide vp in Babylon.

2 And there was found at ‖ Achmetha, in the palace that *is* in the prouince of the Medes, a rolle, and therein was a record thus written :

3 In the first yeere of Cyrus the king, the *same* Cyrus the king made a decree concerning the house of God at Ie-

rusalem : Let the house be builded, the place where they offered sacrifices, and let the foundations thereof be strongly laid, the height therof threescore cubits, and the breadth thereof threescore cubites :

4 *With* three rowes of great stones, and a row of new timber : and let the expences bee giuen out of the kings house.

5 And also let the golden, and siluer vessels of the house of God, which Nebuchadnezzar tooke foorth out of the temple which *is* at Ierusalem, and brought vnto Babylon, be restored, and †brought againe vnto the temple which *is* at Ierusalem, *euery one* to his place, and place *them* in the house of God.

6 Now *therefore* Tatnai, gouernour beyond the riuer, Shethar‑Boznai, and †your companions the Apharsachites, which *are* beyond the riuer, be ye farre from thence :

7 Let the worke of this house of God alone, let the gouernour of the Iewes, and the elders of the Iewes, build this house of God in his place.

8 Moreouer †I make a decree, what ye shall doe to the Elders of these Iewes, for the building of this house of God : that of the kings goods, euen of the tribute beyond the riuer, forthwith expences be giuen vnto these men, that they be not †hindered.

9 And that which they haue need of, both yong bullocks, and rammes, and lambes, for the burnt offerings of the God of heauen, wheat, salt, wine, and oyle, according to the appoyment of the priests which *are* at Ierusalem, let it be giuen them, day by day without faile :

10 That they may offer sacrifices †of sweet sauours vnto the God of heauen, and pray for the life of the king, and of his sonnes.

11 Also I haue made a decree, that whosoeuer shall alter this word, let timber be pulled down from his house, and being set vp, let him bee †hanged thereon, and let his house bee made a doung hill for this.

12 And the God that hath caused his name to dwell there, destroy all kings and people that shall put to their hand, to alter *and* to destroy this house of God which *is* at Ierusalem. I Darius haue made a decree, let it be done with speed.

13 ¶ Then Tatnai gouernour on this side the riuer, Shethar‑Boznai, & their com-

* 2. Kings 24. 2. and 25. 8.

* Ezra. 1. 1.

* Ezra 1. 18 and 6. 5.
‖ Or, deputy.

† Chalde, bookes.
† Chalde, made to descend.
‖ Or, Echatana, or in a coffer.

† Cha

† Che their ties.

† Che me a is me

† Ch made cease

† Ch rest.

† Ch him stro

companions, according to that which Darius the king had sent, so they did speedily.

14 And the elders of the Iewes builded, and they prospered, through the prophecying of Haggai the Prophet, and Zechariah the sonne of Iddo, and they builded, and finished it, according to the commandement of the God of *Israel, and according to the † commandement of Cyrus and Darius, and Artaxerxes king of Persia.

15 And this honse was finished on the third day of the month Adar, which was in the sixt yere of the reigne of Darius the king.

16 ¶ And the children of Israel, the Priests and the Leuites, and the rest of †the children of the captiuitie, kept the dedicatiõ of this house of God, with ioy,

17 And offered at the dedication of this house of God, an hundred bullockes, two hundred rammes, foure hundred lambes; and for a sinne offering for all Israel, twelue hee goates, according to the number of the tribes of Israel.

18 And they set the Priests in their diuisions, and the Leuites in their courses, for the seruice of God, which *is at Ierusalem, † * as it is written in the booke of Moses.

19 And the children of the captiuitie kept the Passeouer, vpon the fourteenth *day* of the first moneth:

20 For the Priestes and the Leuites were purified together, all of them *were* pure, and killed the Passeouer for all the children of the captiuitie, and for their brethren the Priests, and for themselues.

21 And the children of Israel, which were come againe out of captiuitie, and all such as had separated themselues vnto them, from the filthinesse of the heathen of the land, to seeke the Lord God of Israel, did eate,

22 And kept the feast of vnleauened bread seuen dayes, with ioy: for the Lord had made them ioyfull, and turned the heart of the king of Assyria vnto them, to strengthen their handes in the worke of the house of God, the God of Israel.

CHAP. VII.

1 Ezra goeth vp to Ierusalem. 11 The gracious commission of Artaxerxes to Ezra. 27 Ezra blesseth God for his fauour.

Ow after these things, in the reigne of Artaxerxes king of Persia, Ezra the son of Seraiah, the sonne of Azariah, the sonne of Hilkiah,

2 The sonne of Shallum, the sonne of Zadok, the sonne of Ahitub,

3 The sonne of Amariah, the sonne of Azariah, the sonne of Meraioth,

4 The sonne of Zeraiah, the sonne of Vzzi, the sonne of Bukki,

5 The sonne of Abishua, the sonne of Phinehas, the sonne of Eleazar, the sonne of Aaron the chiefe Priest:

6 This Ezra went vp from Babylon, and hee *was* a ready Scribe in the law of Moses, which the Lord God of Israel had giuen: and the king granted him all his request, according to the hand of the Lord his God vpon him.

7 And there went vp *some* of the children of Israel, and of the Priests, and the Leuites, and the Singers, and the Porters, and the Nethinims, vnto Ierusalem, in the seuenth yeere of Artaxerxes the king.

8 And he came to Ierusalem in the fifth moneth, which *was* in the seuenth yeere of the king.

9 For vpon the first *day* of the first moneth, † began he to go vp frõ Babylon, and on the first *day* of the fifth moneth, came he to Ierusalem, according to the good hand of his God vpon him.

10 For Ezra had prepared his heart to seeke the Law of the Lord, and to doe *it*, and to teach in Israel, Statutes and Iudgements.

11 ¶ Now this *is* the copy of the letter that the king Artaxerxes gaue vnto Ezra the Priest, the Scribe, *euen* a Scribe of the words of the commandements of the Lord, and of his Statutes to Israel.

12 Artaxerxes king of kings, ‖ Vnto Ezra the Priest, a Scribe of the Law of the God of heauen, Perfect *peace*, and at such a time.

13 I make a decree, that all they of the people of Israel, and of his Priests, and Leuites in my Realme, which are minded of their owne free-will to goe vp to Ierusalem, goe with thee.

14 Forasmuch as thou art sent † of the king, and of his * seuen counsellers, to enquire concerning Iudah and Ierusalem, according to the Lawe of thy God, which *is* in thine hand;

15 And

Chald. Decree.

Chald. the ˜onnes of the ˜ransportaˉion.

Chald. acˉrding to ˜e writing. Num. 3. 6. ˉnd 8. 9.

† He was the foundation of the going vp.

‖ Or, to Ezra the Priest a perfit Scribe of the Lawe of the God of heauen, Peace, &c.

† Chal. from before the King. * Esth. 1. 14.

15 And to cary the siluer and gold, which the king and his counsellers haue freely offered vnto the God of Israel, whose habitation *is* in Ierusalem.

*Chap. 8. 25.

16 * And all the siluer and gold, that thou canst find in all the prouince of Babylon, with the free-will offering of the people, and of the priests, offering willingly for the house of their God, which *is* in Ierusalem:

17 That thou maiest buy speedily with this money, bullockes, rammes, lambes, with their meate offerings, and their drinke offerings, and offer them vpon the altar of the house of your God, which *is* in Ierusalem.

18 And whatsoeuer shall seeme good to thee, and to thy brethren, to doe with the rest of the siluer and gold; that doe, after the will of your God.

19 The vessels also that are giuen thee, for the seruice of the house of thy God, those deliuer thou before the God of Ierusalem.

20 And whatsoeuer more shall be needfull for the house of thy God, which thou shalt haue occasion to bestowe; bestowe it out of the kings treasure house.

21 And I, *euen* I Artaxerxes the king, doe make a decree to all the treasurers which *are* beyond the riuer, that whatsoeuer Ezra the priest, the scribe of the law of the God of heauen, shall require of you, it be done speedily,

† Chald: Cores.

22 Vnto an hundred talents of siluer, and to an hundred † measures of wheate, and to an hundred bathes of wine, and to an hundred bathes of oyle, and salt, without prescribing *how much.*

† Heb. what-soeuer is of the decree.

23 † Whatsoeuer is commanded by the God of heauen, let it be diligently done, for the house of the God of heauen: for why should there be wrath against the realme of the king and his sonnes?

24 Also we certifie you, that touching any of the priests, and Leuites, singers, porters, Nethinims, or ministers of this house of God, it shall not be lawfull to impose tolle, tribute, or custome vpon them.

25 And thou, Ezra, after the wisdome of thy God, that *is* in thine hand, set magistrates and iudges, which may iudge all the people, that *are* beyond the riuer, all such as know the lawes of thy God, and teach yee them that knowe *them* not.

26 And whosoeuer will not doe the law of thy God, and the law of the king, let iudgement be executed speedily vpon him, whether it be vnto death, or to † banishment, or to confiscation of goods, or to imprisonment.

† Chald. to rooting ou

27 ¶ Blessed *be* the LORD God of our fathers, which hath put *such a thing* as this, in the kings heart, to beautifie the house of the LORD which *is* in Ierusalem:

28 And hath extended mercy vnto me, before the king and his counsellers, and before all the kings mighty princes, and I was strengthned as the hand of the LORD my God *was* vpon me, and I gathered together out of Israel, chiefe men to goe vp with me.

CHAP. VIII.

1 The companions of Ezra, who returned from Babylon. 15 He sendeth to Iddo for ministers for the Temple. 21 He keepeth a fast. 24 He committeth the treasures to the custodie of the Priests. 31 From Ahaua they come to Ierusalem. 33 The treasure is weighed in the Temple. 36 The commission is deliuered.

These *are* now the chiefe of their fathers, and *this is* the genealogie of them that went vp with mee from Babylon, in the reigne of Artaxerxes the king.

2 Of the sonnes of Phinehas, Gershom: of the sonnes of Ithamar, Daniel: of the sonnes of Dauid, Hattush.

3 Of the sonnes of Shechaniah, of the sonnes of Pharosh, Zechariah, and with him were reckoned, by genealogie of the males, an hundred and fiftie.

4 Of the sonnes of Pahath-Moab, Elihoenai the sonne of Zerahiah: and with him, two hundred males.

5 Of the sonnes of Shechaniah, the sonne of Iahaziel, and with him three hundred males.

6 Of the sonnes also of Adin, Ebed the sonne of Ionathan, and with him fiftie males.

7 And of the sonnes of Elam, Ieshaiah the sonne of Athaliah, and with him seuentie males.

8 And of the sonnes of Shephatiah, Zebadiah the sonne of Michael, and with him fourescore males.

9 Of the sonnes of Ioab, Obadiah the sonne of Iehiel: and with him two hundred and eighteene males.

10 And

10 And of the sonnes of Shelomith, the sonne of Iosiphiah, and with him an hundred and threescore males.

11 And of the sonnes of Bebai, Zechariah the sonne of Bebai, and with him twenty and eight males.

12 And of the sonnes of Azgad, Iohanan || the sonne of Hakkatan, and with him an hundred and ten males.

Or, the yongest son.

13 And of the last sonnes of Adonikam, whose names *are* these : Eliphelet, Iehiel, and Shemaiah, and with them threescore males.

14 Of the sonnes also of Biguai, Vthai, and || Zabbud, and with them seuentie males.

Or, Zacnur, as some read.

15 ¶ And I gathered them together to the riuer, that runneth to Ahaua, and there || abode wee in tents three dayes : and I viewed the people, and the Priests, and found there none of the sonnes of Leui.

Or, pitched.

16 Then sent I for Eliezer, for Ariel, for Shemaiah, and for Elnathan, and for Iarib, and for Elnathan, and for Nathan, and for Zechariah, and for Meshullam, chiefe men; also for Iarib, and for Elnathan, men of vnderstanding.

17 And I sent them with commandement vnto Iddo the chiefe at the place Casiphia, and I || told them what they should say vnto Iddo, *and* to his brethren the Nethinims, at the place Casiphia, that they should bring vnto vs ministers for the house of our God.

Hebr. I put words in their mouth.

18 And by the good hand of our God vpon vs, they brought vs a man of vnderstanding, of the sonnes of Mahli the sonne of Leui, the sonne of Israel, and Sherebiah, with his sonnes, and his brethren, eighteene.

19 And Hashabiah, and with him Ieshaiah of the sonnes of Merari, his brethren, and their sonnes, twentie.

20 * Also of the Nethinims, whom Dauid, and the Princes had appointed for the seruice of the Leuites, two hundred and twentie Nethinims : all of them were expressed by name.

See Chap. 43.

21 ¶ Then I proclaimed a fast there, at the riuer Ahaua, that we might afflict our selues before our God, to seeke of him a right way for vs, and for our little ones, and for all our substance.

22 For I was ashamed to require of the king a band of souldiers and horsmen, to helpe vs against the enemie in the way : because wee had spoken vnto the king, saying, The hand of our God *is* vpon all them for good, that seeke him, but his power and his wrath is against all them that forsake him.

23 So we fasted, and besought our God for this, and hee was intreated of vs.

24 ¶ Then I separated twelue of the chiefe of the Priests, Sherebiah, Hashabiah, and ten of their brethren with them,

25 And weighed vnto them the siluer and the gold, and the vessels, *euen* the offering of the house of our God, which the king and his counsellours, and his lords, and all Israel there present, had offered :

26 I euen weighed vnto their hand, sixe hundred and fifty talents of siluer, and siluer vessels an hundred talents, and of gold an hundred talents :

27 Also twenty basons of gold, of a thousand drammes, and two vessels of † fine copper, † precious as gold.

† Hebr. yellow or shining brasse.
† Hebr. desireable.

28 And I said vnto them, Yee are holy vnto the LORD, the vessels are holy also, and the siluer and the gold *are* a free-will offring vnto the LORD God of your fathers.

29 Watch ye, and keepe *them*, vntill yee weigh *them* before the chiefe of the Priests, and the Leuites, and chiefe of the fathers of Israel at Ierusalem, in the chambers of the house of the LORD.

30 So tooke the Priests and the Leuites the weight of the siluer and the gold, and the vessels, to bring *them* to Ierusalem, vnto the house of our God.

31 ¶ Then wee departed from the riuer of Ahaua, on the twelfth *day* of the first moneth, to goe vnto Ierusalem ; and the hand of our God was vpon vs, and hee deliuered vs from the hand of the enemie, and of such as lay in wait by the way.

32 And we came to Ierusalem, and abode there three dayes.

33 ¶ Now on the fourth day was the siluer and the gold, and the vessels weighed in the house of our God, by the hand of Meremoth the sonne of Vriah the Priest, and with him *was* Eleazar the sonne of Phinehas, and with them *was* Iozabad the sonne of Ieshua, and Noadiah the sonne of Binnui, Leuites :

34 By number, *and* by weight of euery

uery one : and all the weight was written at that time.

35 *Also* the children of those that had bene caried away which were come out of the captiuitie, offered burnt offrings vnto the God of Israel, twelue bullocks for all Israel, ninetie and sixe rammes, seuentie and seuen lambes, twelue hee goates for a sinne offering : All *this was* a burnt offering vnto the LORD.

36 ¶ And they deliuered the Kings commissions vnto the kings lieuteuants, and to the gouernours on this side the riuer, and they furthered the people, and the house of God.

CHAP. IX.

1 Ezra mourneth for the affinitie of the people with strangers. 5 He prayeth vnto God with confession of sinnes.

Owe when these things were done, the Princes came to me, saying, The people of Israel, and the priests and the Leuites, haue not separated themselues from the people of the lands, *doing* according to their abominations, *euen* of the Canaanites, the Hittites, the Perizzites, the Iebusites, the Ammonites, the Moabites, the Egyptians, and the Amorites.

2 For they haue taken of their daughters for themselues, and for their sonnes : so that the holy seed haue mingled themselues with the people of *those* lands, yea the hand of the princes and rulers hath bin chiefe in this trespasse.

3 And when I heard this thing, I rent my garment and my mantle, and pluckt off the haire of my head, and of my beard, and sate downe astonied.

4 Then were assembled vnto me euery one that trembled at the words of the God of Israel, because of the transgression of those that had bene caried away, and I sate astonied, vntill the euening sacrifice.

5 ¶ And at the euening sacrifice, I *‖ Or, afflicti-* arose vp from my ‖heauinesse, and ha- *on.* uing rent my garment and my mantle, I fell vpon my knees, and spread out my hands vnto the LORD my God,

6 And said, O my God, I am ashamed, and blush to lift vp my face to thee, my God : for our iniquities are increa- *‖ Or, guilti-* sed ouer our head, and our ‖trespasse is *nesse.*

growen vp vnto the heauens.

7 Since the dayes of our fathers, *haue* wee *beene* in a great trespasse vnto this day, & for our iniquities haue we, our kings and our priests, bin deliuered into the hand of the kings of the lands, to the sword, to captiuitie, and to a spoile, and to confusion of face, as *it is* this day.

8 And now for a † litle space grace *† Hebr.* hath bene shewed from the LORD our *ment.* God, to leaue vs a remnant to escape, and to giue vs ‖ a ‖ naile in his holy *‖ Or, a p* place, that our God may lighten our *‖ That i* eyes, and giue vs a litle reuiuing in our *constant* bondage : *sure ab*

9 For wee *were* bondmen, yet our God hath not forsaken vs in our bondage, but hath extended mercie vnto vs in the sight of the kings of Persia, to giue vs a reuiuing to set vp the house of our God, and † to repaire the desolati- *† Heb.* ons thereof, and to giue vs a wall in *vp.* Iudah and in Ierusalem.

10 And now, O our God, what shal we say after this ? for we haue forsaken thy commandements,

11 Which thou hast commanded by † thy seruants the prophets, saying, *† Heb. th* *The land vnto which ye go to possesse *hand of* it, is an vncleane land, with the filthi- *seruant* nesse of the people of the lands, with *＊ Exod* their abominations, which haue filled it *32. deu* † from one end to another, with their *† Heb. f* vncleannesse. *mouth t* *mouth.*

12 Nowe therefore giue not your daughters vnto their sonnes, neither take their daughters vnto your sonnes, nor seeke their peace or their wealth for euer : that ye may bee strong, and eate the good of the land, and leaue *it* for an inheritance to your children for euer.

13 And after all that is come vpon vs, for our euill deeds, and for our great trespasse, seeing that thou, our God, † hast punished vs lesse, then our iniqui- *† Heb.* ties *deserue*, and hast giuen vs *such* deli- *withhel* uerance as this. *neath o* *iniquit*

14 Should wee againe breake thy commandements, and ioyne in affinitie with the people of these abominations? wouldest thou not be angry with vs, til thou haddest consumed vs, so that there should be no remnant, nor escaping ?

15 O LORD God of Israel, thou *art* righteous, for wee remaine yet escaped, as *it is* this day : Behold, we *are* before thee in our trespasses : for wee can not stand before thee, because of this.
CHAP.

CHAP. X.

1 Shechaniah encourageth Ezra to reforme the strange mariages. 6 Ezra mourning, assembleth the people. 9 The people at the exhortation of Ezra, repent and promise amendment. 15 The care to performe it. 18 The names of them who had maried strange wiues.

Hebr. wept great weeping.

NOw when Ezra had praied, and when he had confessed, weeping, and casting himselfe downe before the house of God, there assembled vnto him out of Israel, a very great congregation of men, and women, and children : for the people †wept very sore.

2 And Shechaniah the sonne of Iehiel, *one* of the sonnes of Elam, answered and said vnto Ezra, Wee haue trespassed against our God, and haue taken strange wiues, of the people of the land : yet now there is hope in Israel concerning this thing.

Hebr. to bring forth.

3 Now therefore let vs make a couenant with our God, †to put away all the wiues, & such as are borne of them, according to the counsell of my lord, and of those that tremble at the commandement of our God, and lee it be done according to the Law.

4 Arise, for this matter *belongeth* vnto thee, wee also *will be* with thee : be of good courage, and doe *it.*

5 Then arose Ezra, and made the chiefe Priests, the Leuites, and all Israel to sweare, that they should doe according to this word : and they sware.

6 ¶ Then Ezra rose vp from before the house of God, and went into the chamber of Iohanan, the sonne of Eliashib : and *when* hee came thither, hee did eate no bread, nor drinke water : for hee mourned because of the transgression of them that had bene caried away.

7 And they made Proclamation throughout Iudah and Ierusalem, vnto all the children of the captiuitie, that they should gather themselues together vnto Ierusalem ;

eb. deuo-

8 And that whosoeuer would not come within three dayes, according to the counsell of the Princes, and the Elders, all his substance should be †forfeited, and himselfe separated from the congregation of those that had beene caried away.

9 ¶ Then all the men of Iudah and Beniamin, gathered themselues together vnto Ierusalem, within three dayes : it *was* the ninth moneth, on the twentieth *day* of the moneth, and all the people sate in the streete of the house of God, trembling because of *this* matter, and for †the great raine.

† Hebr. the showres.

10 And Ezra the Priest stood vp, and said vnto them, Yee haue transgressed, and †haue taken strange wiues, to encrease the trespasse of Israel.

† Hebr. haue caused to dwel, or haue brought backe.

11 Now therefore make confession vnto the LORD God of your fathers, and doe his pleasure : and separate your selues from the people of the land, and from the strange wiues.

12 Then all the congregation answered, and said with a loude voice, As thou hast said, so must we doe :

13 But the people are many, and it *is* a time of much raine, and we are not able to stand without ; neither is this a worke of one day or two : for ‖wee are many that haue transgressed in this thing.

‖ Or, wee haue greatly offended in this thing.

14 Let now our rulers of all the congregation stand, and let all them which haue taken strange wiues in our cities, come at appointed times, & with them the Elders of euery citie, and the Iudges thereof ; vntill the fierce wrath of our God ‖for this matter, be turned from vs.

‖ Or, till this matter be dispatched.

15 ¶ Onely Ionathan the sonne of Asahel, and Iahaziah the sonne of Tikuah, †were employed about this matter : and Meshullam, and Shabbethai the Leuite, helped them.

† Heb. stooc.

16 And the children of the captiuitie did so : and Ezra the Priest, *with* certaine chiefe of the fathers, after the house of their fathers, and all of them by *their* names, were separated, and sate downe in the first day of the tenth moneth to examine the matter.

17 And they made an ende, with all the men that had taken strange wiues, by the first day of the first moneth.

18 ¶ And among the sonnes of the Priestes, there were found that had taken strange wiues : namely, of the sons of Ieshua the sonne of Iozadak, and his brethren, Maasiah, and Eliezer, and Iarib, and Gedaliah.

19 And they gaue their hands, that they would put away their wiues : and being guiltie, *they offered* a ramme of the flocke for their trespasse.

20 And of the sonnes of Immer, Hanani, and Zebadiah :

21 And

*17

21 And of the sonnes of Harim, Maasiah, and Eliiah, and Shemaiah, and Iehiel, and Vzziah.

22 And of the sonnes of Pashur: Elioenai, Maasiah, Ishmael, Nethaneel, Iozabad and Elasah.

23 Also of the Leuites: Iozabad, and Shimei, and Kelaiah (the same is Kelitah) Pethahiah, Iudah, and Eliezer.

24 Of the singers also, Eliashib; and of the porters, Shallum, and Telem, and Vri.

25 Moreouer of Israel, of the sonnes of Parosh, Ramiah, and Iesiah, and Málchiah, and Miamin, and Eleazar, and Malchijah, and Benaiah.

26 And of the sonnes of Elam: Mattaniah, Zechariah, and Iehiel, and Abdi, and Ieremoth, and Eliah.

27 And of the sonnes of Zattu: Elioenai, Eliashib, Mattaniah, and Ieremoth, and Zabad, and Aziza.

28 Of the sonnes also of Bebai: Iehohanan, Hananiah, Zabbai, & Athlai.

29 And of the sonnes of Bani: Meshullam, Malluch, and Adaiah, Iashub, and Sheal, and Ramoth.

30 And of the sonnes of Pahath Moab: Adna, aud Chelal, Benaiah,

Maasiah, Mattaniah, Bezaleel, and Binnui, and Manasseh.

31 And of the sonnes of Harim: Eliezer, Ishiiah, Malchiah, Shemaiah, Shimeon,

32 Beniamin, Malluch, and Shemariah.

33 Of the sonnes of Hashum: Mattenai, Mattatha, Zabad, Eliphelet, Ieremai, Manasseh, and Shimei.

34 Of the sonnes of Bani: Maadai, Amram, and Vel,

35 Benaiah, Bedaiah, Chelluh,

36 Vaniah, Meremoth, Eliashib,

37 Mattaniah, Mattenai, and Iaasau,

38 And Bani, and Bennui, Shimei,

39 And Shelemiah, and Nathan, and Adaiah,

40 || Machnadebai, Shashai, Sharai,

41 Azareel, and Shelemiah, Shemariah,

42 Shallum, Amariah, and Ioseph.

43 Of the sonnes of Nebo, Iehiel, Mattithiah, Zabad, Zebina, Iadau, and Ioel, Benaiah.

44 All these had taken strange wiues: and some of them had wiues, by whom they had children.

|| Or, Machadebai, cording to some cop

¶THE BOOKE OF
Nehemiah.

CHAP. I.

1 Nehemiah, vnderstanding by Hañani, the misery of Ierusalem, mourneth, fasteth and prayeth. 5 His prayer.

He words of Nehemiah the sonne of Hachaliah. And it came to passe in the moneth Chisleu, in the twentieth yeere, as I was in Shushan the palace;

2 That Hanani, one of my brethren came, he and certaine men of Iudah, and

I asked them concerning the Iewes that had escaped, which were left of the captiuitie, and concerning Ierusalem.

3 And they said vnto me, The remnant that are left of the captiuitie there in the prouince, are in great affliction and reproch: the wall of Ierusalem also * is broken downe, and the gates thereof are burnt with fire.

4 ¶ And it came to passe when I heard these words, that I sate downe and wept, and mourned certaine dayes, and fasted, and prayed before the God of heauen,

5 And said, I beseech thee, * O LORD God of heauen, the great and terrible

* 2. Kin 9.

* Dan.

terrible God, that keepeth couenant and mercie for them that loue him, and obserue his commandements:

6 Let thine eare now be attentiue, and thine eyes open, that thou mayest heare the prayer of thy seruant, which I pray before thee now, day and night, for the children of Israel thy seruants, and confesse the sinnes of the children of Israel, which wee haue sinned against thee: both I, and my fathers house haue sinned.

7 We haue dealt very corruptly against thee, and haue not kept the commandements, nor the statutes, nor the iudgements, which thou commandedst thy seruant Moses.

8 Remember, I beseech thee, the word that thou commandedst thy seruant Moses, saying, *If yee transgresse, I will scatter you abroad among the nations:

9 But if ye turne vnto me, and keepe my commandements, and doe them: *though there were of you cast out vnto the vttermost part of the heauen, yet will I gather them from thence, and will bring them vnto the place that I haue chosen, to set my Name there.

10 Now these are thy seruants, and thy people, whom thou hast redeemed by thy great power, and by thy strong hand.

11 O Lord, I beseech thee, let now thine eare be attentiue to the prayer of thy seruant, and to the prayer of thy seruants, who desire to feare thy name: and prosper, I pray thee, thy seruant this day, and grant him mercie in the sight of this man. For I was the kings cup-bearer.

CHAP. II.

1 Artaxerxes vnderstanding the cause of Nehemiahs sadnesse, sendeth him with letters and commission to Ierusalem. 9 Nehemiah, to the griefe of the enemies, commeth to Ierusalem. 12 Hee vieweth secretly the ruines of the walles. 17 He inciteth the Iewes to build in despite of the enemies.

Nd it came to passe, in the moneth Nisan, in the twentieth yeere of Artaxerxes the king, that wine was before him: and I tooke vp the wine, and gaue it vnto the King: now I had not bene beforetime sad in his presence.

2 Wherefore the king said vnto me, Why is thy countenance sadde, seeing thou art not sicke? this is nothing else but sorrow of heart. Then I was very sore afraid,

3 And said vnto the king, Let the king liue for euer: why should not my countenance be sad, when the city, the place of my fathers Sepulchres, lyeth waste, and the gates thereof are consumed with fire?

4 Then the king said vnto me, For what doest thou make request? So I prayed to the God of heauen.

5 And I said vnto the king, If it please the king, and if thy seruant haue found fauour in thy sight, that thou wouldest send me vnto Iudah vnto the City of my fathers sepulchres, that I may build it.

6 And the king saide vnto mee (the †Queene also sitting by him) For how long shall thy iourney bee? and when wilt thou returne? So it pleased the king to send me, and I set him a time.

7 Moreouer I saide vnto the king, If it please the king, let letters be giuen mee to the gouernours beyond the Riuer, that they may conuey me ouer, till I come into Iudah;

8 And a letter vnto Asaph the keeper of the kings forrest, that he may giue me timber to make beames for the gates of the palace which appertained to the house, and for the wall of the Citie, and for the house that I shall enter into: And the king granted me, according to the good hand of my God vpon me.

9 ¶ Then I came to the gouernours beyond the riuer, and gaue them the kings letters: (now the king had sent captaines of the army, and horsemen with me.)

10 When Sanballat the Horonite, and Tobiah the seruant, the Ammonite, heard of it, it grieued them exceedingly, that there was come a man, to seeke the welfare of the children of Israel.

11 So I came to Ierusalem; and was there three dayes.

12 ¶ And I arose in the night, I, and some few men with mee, neither tolde I any man what God had put in my heart to doe at Ierusalem: neither was there any beast with mee, saue the beast that I rode vpon.

13 And I went out by night, by the gate of the valley, euen before the dragon

---

ut. 4.
.c.

ut. 30.

† Hebr. wife.

gon well, and to the doung-port, and viewed the walls of Ierusalem, which were broken downe, and the gates thereof were consumed with fire.

14 Then I went on to the gate of the fountaine, and to the kings poole: but there was no place for the beast that was vnder me, to passe.

15 Then went I vp in the night by the brooke, and viewed the wall, and turned backe, and entred by the gate of the valley, and *so* returned.

16 And the rulers knew not whither I went, or what I did, neither had I as yet tolde it to the Iewes, nor to the Priests, nor to the nobles, nor to the rulers, nor to the rest that did the worke.

17 ¶ Then said I vnto them, Yee see the distresse that we are in, how Ierusalem lieth waste, and the gates therof are burnt with fire: come, and let vs builde vp the wall of Ierusalem, that we be no more a reproch.

18 Then I told them of the hand of my God, which was good vpon me; as also the kings wordes that he had spoken vnto me. And they said, Let vs rise vp and builde. So they strengthened their hands for this good *worke.*

19 But when Sanballat the Horonite, and Tobiah the seruant the Ammonite, and Geshem the Arabian heard it, they laughed vs to scorne, and despised vs, and said, What is this thing that yee doe? will ye rebell against the king?

20 Then answered I them, and said vnto them, The God of heauen, he will prosper vs, therefore wee his seruants will arise and build: But you haue no portion, nor right, nor memoriall in Ierusalem.

CHAP. III.

1 The names and order of them that builded the wall.

HEn Eliashib the hie priest, rose vp with his brethren the Priests, and they built the sheepe-gate, they sanctified it, & set vp the doores of it, euen vnto the towre of Meah they sanctified it, vnto the towre of *Hananeel.

2 And †next vnto him builded the men of Iericho: and next to them builded Zaccur the sonne of Imri.

3 But the fish-gate did the sonnes of Hassenaah build, who also laide the beames thereof, and set vp the doores

* Iere. 3. 38.

† Hebr. at his hand.

thereof, the locks therof, and the barres thereof.

4 And next vnto them repaired Merimoth the son of Vriah, the sonne of Koz: and next vnto them repaired Meshullam the sonne of Berechiah, the sonne of Meshezabeel: and next vnto them repaired Zadok the sonne of Baana.

5 And next vnto them, the Tekoites repaired; but their nobles put not their neckes to the worke of their LORD.

6 Moreouer the olde gate repaired Iehoiada the sonne of Paseah, and Meshullam the sonne of Besodaiah; they laid the beames thereof, and set vp the doores thereof, and the lockes thereof, and the barres thereof.

7 And next vnto them repaired Melatiah the Gibeonite, and Iadon the Meronothite, the men of Gibeon, and of Mizpah, vnto the throne of the gouernour on this side the Riuer.

8 Next vnto him repaired Vzziel the sonne of Harhaiah, of the goldsmiths: next vnto him also repaired Hananiah, the sonne of *one of* the Apothecaries, and they ‖ fortified Ierusalem vnto the broad wall.

9 And next vnto them repaired Rephaiah the sonne of Hur, the ruler of the halfe part of Ierusalem.

10 And next vnto them repaired Iedaiah the sonne of Harumaph, euen ouer against his house: and next vnto him repaired Hattush the sonne of Hashabniah.

11 Malchiiah the sonne of Harim, and Hashub the son of Pahath-Moab, repaired the †other piece, & the towre of the furnaces.

12 And next vnto him repaired Shallum the sonne of Halloesh the ruler of the halfe part of Ierusalem, hee, and his daughters.

13 The valley-gate repaired Hanun, and the inhabitants of Zanoah; they built it, and set vp the doores thereof, the lockes therof, and the bars thereof, and a thousand cubits on the wall, vnto the doung-gate.

14 But the doung-gate repaired Malchiah the sonne of Rechab, the ruler of part of Beth-haccerem: hee built it, and set vp the doores thereof, the lockes thereof, and the barres thereof.

15 But the gate of the fountaine repaired Shallum the sonne of Col-hozeh, the ruler of part of Mizpah: hee built

‖ Or, le rusale to the wall.

† Hebr cond m sure.

built it, and couered it, and set vp the doores thereof, the lockes thereof, and the barres thereof, and the wall of the poole of * Siloah by the kings garden, and vnto the staires that goe downe from the citie of Dauid.

16 After him repaired Nehemiah the sonne of Azbuk, the ruler of the halfe part of Beth-zur, vnto the *place* ouer against the sepulchres of Dauid, and to the poole that was made, * and vnto the house of the mightie.

17 After him repaired the Leuites, Rehum the sonne of Bani : next vnto him repaired Hashabiah the ruler of the halfe part of Keilah in his part.

18 After him repaired their brethren, Bauai, the sonne of Henadad the ruler of the halfe part of Keilah.

19 And next to him repaired Ezer the sonne of Ieshua, the ruler of Mizpah, another piece, ouer against the going vp to the armorie, at the turning *of the wall.*

20 After him Baruch the sonne of ‖ Zabbai, earnestly repaired the other piece, from the turning of *the wall* vnto the doore of the house of Eliashib the high Priest.

21 After him repaired Merimoth the sonne of Vriiah, the sonne of Koz, another piece, from the doore of the house of Eliashib, euen to the end of the house of Eliashib.

22 And after him repaired the Priests, the men of the plaine.

23 After him repaired Beniamin, and Hashub, ouer against their house : after him repaired Azariah the sonne of Maaseiah, the sonne of Ananiah, by his house.

24 After him repaired Binnui the sonne of Henadad, another piece from the house of Azariah, vnto the turning *of the wall,* euen vnto the corner.

25 Palal the sonne of Vzai, ouer against the turning of *the wall,* and the tower which lyeth out, from the kings hie house, that was by the * court of the prison : after him, Pedaiah the sonne of Parosh.

26 Moreouer the Nethinims dwelt in * ‖ Ophel, vnto *the place* ouer against the water gate, toward the East, and the tower that lieth out.

27 After them the Tekoites repaired another piece, ouer against the great tower that lieth out, euen vnto the wall of Ophel.

28 From aboue the horsegate repaired the Priests, euery one ouer against his house.

29 After them repaired Zadok the sonne of Immer, ouer against his house : after him repaired also Shemaiah, the son of Shechaniah, the keeper of the East-gate.

30 After him repaired Hananiah the sonne of Shelemiah, and Hanun the sixth sonne of Zalaph, another piece : after him repaired Meshullam, the sonne of Berechiah ouer against his chamber.

31 After him repaired Malchiah, the goldsmiths sonne, vnto the place of the Nethinims, and of the merchants, ouer against the gate Miphkad, and to the going vp of the ‖corner.

32 And betweene the going vp of the corner vnto the sheepe-gate, repaired the gold-smithes and the merchants.

CHAP. IIII.

1 While the enemies scoffe, Nehemiah prayeth and continueth the worke. 7 Vnderstanding the wrath and secrets of the enemy, hee setteth a watch. 13 Hee armeth the labourers, 19 and giueth military precepts.

Vt it came to passe, that when Sanballat heard, that we builded the wall, he was wroth, and tooke great indignation, and mocked the Iewes.

2 And he spake before his brethren, and the army of Samaria, and said, What doe these feeble Iewes? wil they †fortifie themselues? will they sacrifice? wil they make an end in a day? wil they reuiue the stones, out of the heapes of the rubbish, which are burnt?

3 Now Tobiah the Ammonite *was* by him, and he said, Euen that which they build, if a foxe goe vp, he shall euen breake downe their stone wall.

4 Heare, O our God, for we are †despised : and turne their reproch vpon their owne head, and giue them for a pray, in the land of captiuitie.

5 And couer not their iniquitie, and let not their sinne bee blotted out from before thee : for they haue prouoked *thee* to anger before the builders.

6 So built we the wall, and all the wall was ioyned together vnto the halfe therof : for the people had a minde to worke.

7 ¶ But

Marginal notes (left):
‖n 9. 7.
King.
.
Zac.
re. 32.
Chron.
3.
, the
er.

Marginal notes (right):
‖ Or, corner chamber.

† Hebr. leaue to themselues.

† Hebr. despight.

7 ¶ But it came to passe that when Sanballat and Tobiah, and the Arabians, and the Ammonites, and the Ashdodites, heard that the walles of Ierusalem †were made vp, and that the breaches began to bee stopped, then they were very wroth,

† Hebr. ascended.

8 And conspired all of them together, to come *and* to fight against Ierusalem, and †to hinder it.

† Hebr. to make an errour to it.

9 Neuertheles, we made our prayer vnto our God, and set a watch against them, day and night, because of them.

10 And Iudah said, The strength of the bearers of burdens is decayed, and *there is* much rubbish, so that we are not able to build the wall.

11 And our aduersaries said, They shall not know, neither see, till wee come in the midst among them, and slay them, and cause the worke to cease.

12 And it came to passe that when the Iewes which dwelt by them, came, they said vnto vs ten times, || From all places, whence yee shall returne vnto vs, *they will be vpon you.*

‖ Or, that from all places ye must returne to vs.

13 ¶ Therefore set I †in the lower places behind the wall, *and* on the higher places, I euen set the people, after their families, with their swords, their speares, and their bowes.

† Heb. from the lower parts of the place, &c.

14 And I looked, and rose vp, and said vnto the Nobles, and to the rulers, and to rest of the people, Bee not ye afraid of them : Remember the Lord which is great and terrible, and fight for your brethren, your sonnes and your daughters, your wiues & your houses.

15 And it came to passe when our enemies heard that it was knowen vnto vs, and God had brought their counsell to nought, that we returned all of vs to the wall, euery one vnto his worke.

16 And it came to passe from that time forth, that the halfe of my seruants wrought in the worke, and the other halfe of them held both the speares, the shields and the bowes, and the habergeons, and the rulers *were* behind all the house of Iudah.

17 They which builded on the wall, and they that bare burdens, with those that laded, *euery one* with one of his hands wrought *in* the worke, and with the other *hand* held a weapon.

18 For the builders, euery one had his sword girded †by his side, and *so* builded : and he that sounded the trumpet *was* by mee.

† Heb. on his loynes.

19 ¶ And I said vnto the Nobles, and to the rulers, and to the rest of the people, The worke *is* great and large, and wee are separated vpon the wall, one farre from another :

20 In what place therefore ye heare the sound of the trumpet, resort ye thither vnto vs : our God shal fight for vs.

21 So wee laboured in the worke : and halfe of them held the speares, from the rising of the morning, til the starres appeared.

22 Likewise at the same time said I vnto the people, Let euery one, with his seruant, lodge within Ierusalem, that in the night they may be a guard to vs, and labour on the day.

23 So neither I, nor my brethren, nor my seruants, nor the men of the guard which followed me, none of vs put off our clothes, || *sauing that* euery one put them off for washing.

‖ Or, euery one we with hi weapon water.

CHAP. V.

1 The Iewes complaine of their debt, morgage, and bondage. 6 Nehemiah rebuketh the vsurers, and causeth them to make a couenant of restitution. 14 Hee forbeareth his owne allowance, and keepeth hospitalitie.

ANd there was a great crie of the people, and of their wiues, against their brethren the Iewes.

2 For there were that said, We, our sonnes, and our daughters are many : therefore wee take vp corne *for them,* that we may eat, and liue.

3 Some also there were that saide, We haue morgaged our landes, vineyards and houses, that we might buy corne, because of the dearth.

4 There were also that said, Wee haue borrowed money for the kings tribute, *and that vpon* our lands and vineyards.

5 Yet now our flesh *is* as the flesh of our brethren, our children as their children : and loe, wee bring into bondage our sonnes and our daughters, to bee seruants, and some of our daughters are brought vnto bondage *already,* neither is it in our power *to redeeme them :* for other men *haue* our lands and vineyards.

6 ¶ And I was very angry, when I heard their crie, and these words.

7 Then †I consulted with my selfe, and I rebuked the Nobles, and the rulers,

† Heb. heart c ted in

lers, and said vnto them, You exact v-surie, euery one of his brother. And I set a great assembly against them :

8 And I said vnto them, We, after our abilitie, haue * redeemed our brethren the Iewes, which were sold vnto the heathen; and will you euen sell your brethren ? or shall they be sold vnto vs ? Then held they their peace, and found nothing to answere.

9 Also I said, It is not good that yee doe : ought yee not to walke in the feare of our God, because of the reproch of the heathen our enemies ?

10 I likewise, and my brethren, and my seruants, might exact of them money and corne : I pray you let vs leaue off this vsurie.

11 Restore, I pray you, to them, euen this day, their lands, their vineyards, their oliue - yards, and their houses, also the hundreth part of the money, and of the corne, the wine, and the oyle, that ye exact of them.

12 Then said they, Wee will restore them, and will require nothing of them; so will we doe, as thou sayest. Then I called the Priests, and tooke an oath of them, that they should doe according to this promise.

13 Also I shooke my lap, and said, So God shake out euery man from his house, and from his labour, that performeth not this promise, euen thus be he shaken out, and †emptied. And all the Congregation said, Amen, and praised the LORD. And the people did according to this promise.

14 ¶ Moreouer, from the time that I was appointed to be their gouernor in the land of Iudah, from the twentieth yeere euen vnto the two and thirtieth yere of Artaxerxes the king, that is, twelue yeres, I and my brethren, haue not eaten the bread of the gouernour :

15 But the former gouernours that had bene before me, were chargeable vnto the people, and had taken of them bread, and wine, beside fourtie shekels of siluer, yea euen their seruants bare rule ouer the people : but so did not I, because of the feare of God.

16 Yea also I continued in the worke of this wall, neither bought wee any land : and all my seruants were gathered thither vnto the worke.

17 Moreouer, there were at my table, an hundred and fiftie of the Iewes and rulers, besides those that came vn-

to vs from among the heathen that are about vs.

18 Now that which was prepared for me daily, was one oxe, and sixe choice sheepe, also foules were prepared for mee, and once in ten dayes, store of all sorts of wine : yet for all this required not I the bread of the gouernour, because the bondage was heauy vpon this people.

19 * Thinke vpon mee, my God, for good, according to all that I haue done for this people.

CHAP. VI.

1 Sanballat practiseth by craft, by rumours, by hired prophecies, to terrifie Nehemiah. 15 The worke is finished to the terrour of the enemies. 17 Secret intelligence passeth betweene the enemies, and the nobles of Iudah.

OW it came to passe when Sanballat, and Tobiah, and Geshem the Arabian, and the rest of our enemies heard, that I had builded the wall, and that there was no breach left therein : (though at that time I had not set vp the doores vpon the gates,)

2 That Sanballat, and Geshem sent vnto me, saying, Come, let vs meet together in some one of the villages in the plaine of Ono : But they thought to doe me mischiefe.

3 And I sent messengers vnto them, saying, I am doing a great worke, so that I can not come down : why should the worke cease, whilest I leaue it, and come downe to you ?

4 Yet they sent vnto me foure times, after this sort : and I answered them after the same maner.

5 Then sent Sanballat his seruant vnto me, in like manner, the fifth time, with an open letter in his hand :

6 Wherein was written; It is reported among the heathen, and ‖ Gashmu sayth it, that thou and the Iewes thinke to rebell : for which cause thou buildest the wall, that thou mayest be their King, according to these words.

7 And thou hast also appointed Prophets to preach of thee at Ierusalem, saying, There is a King in Iudah. And now shall it be reported to the king, according to these wordes. Come now therefore, and let vs take counsell together.

8 Then

*Deut. 25.

† empty
id.

* Chap. 13. 22.

‖ Or, Geshem, ver. 2.

8 Then I sent vnto him, saying, There are no such things done as thou sayest, but thou feignest them out of thine owne heart.

9 For they all made vs afraid, saying, Their handes shall be weakened from the worke that it bee not done. Now therefore, *O God*, strengthen my hands.

10 Afterward I came vnto the house of Shemaiah the sonne of Delaiah, the sonne of Mehetabel, who *was* shut vp, and he said, Let vs meet together in the house of God, within the Temple, and let vs shut the doores of the Temple; for they will come to slay thee, yea in the night wil they come to slay thee.

11 And I said, Should such a man as I, flee? and who is there, that being as I am, would goe into the Temple to saue his life? I will not goe in.

12 And loe, I perceiued that God had not sent him, but that he pronounced this prophecie against mee: for Tobiah, and Sanballat had hired him.

13 Therefore *was* hee hired, that I should be afraid, and doe so, and sinne, and that they might haue *matter* for an euill report, that they might reproch mee.

14 My God, thinke thou vpon Tobiah, and Sanballat, according to these their workes, and on the prophetesse Noadiah, and the rest of the prophets, that would haue put me in feare.

15 ¶ So the wall was finished, in the twentie and fifth day of *the moneth* Elul, in fiftie and two dayes.

16 And it came to passe that when all our enemies heard thereof, and all the heathen, that *were* about vs, saw *these things*, they were much cast downe in their owne eyes: for they perceiued that this worke was wrought of our God.

17 ¶ Moreouer, in those dayes the nobles of Iudah †sent many letters vnto Tobiah, and *the letters* of Tobiah came vnto them.

† *Hebr. multiplied letters passing to Tobiah.*

18 For *there were* many in Iudah sworne vnto him: because hee was the sonne in law of Shechaniah the sonne of Arah, and his sonne Iohanan had taken the daughter of Meshullam, the sonne of Berechiah.

19 Also they reported his good deeds before me, and vttered my ‖ wordes to him: *and* Tobiah sent letters to put me in feare.

‖ *Or, matters.*

CHAP. VII.

1 Nehemiah committeth the charge of Ierusalem to Hanani and Hananiah. 5 A register of the genealogie of them which came at the first out of Babylon, 9 of the people, 39 of the Priests. 43 of the Leuites. 46 of the Nethinims. 57 of Solomons seruants. 63 and of the Priests which could not find their pedegree. 66 The whole number of them, with their substance. 70 Their oblations.

Ow it came to passe when the wall was built, and I had set vp the doores; and the porters, and the singers, and the Leuites were appointed,

2 That I gaue my brother Hanani, and Hananiah the ruler of the palace, charge ouer Ierusalem (for hee was a faithfull man, and feared God aboue many.)

3 And I said vnto them; Let not the gates of Ierusalem be opened, vntill the Sunne bee hot; and while they stand by, let them shut the doores, and barre them. And appoint watches of the inhabitants of Ierusalem, euery one in his watch, and euery one to bee ouer against his house.

4 Now the city *was* †large and great, but the people *were* few therein, and the houses were not builded.

† *Hebr. broad ces.*

5 ¶ And my God put into mine heart, to gather together the nobles, and the rulers, & the people, that they might be reckoned by genealogie. And I found a register of the genealogie of them which came vp at the first, and found written therein;

6 * These *are* the children of the prouince, that went vp out of the captiuitie, of those that had beene caried away whom Nebuchadnezzar the King of Babylon had caried away, and came againe to Ierusalem and to Iudah, euery one vnto his citie:

* *Ezra &c.*

7 Who came with Zerubbabel, Ieshua, Nehemiah, ‖ Azariah, Raamiah, Nahamani, Mordecai, Bilshan, Mispereth, Biguai, Nahum, Baanah. The number, *I say*, of the men of the people of Israel, *was this:*

‖ *Or, Siah.*

8 The children of Parosh, two thousand, an hundred, seuentie and two.

9 The children of Shephatiah, three hundred, seuentie and two.

10 The children of Arah, sixe hundred, fiftie and two.

11 The

11 The children of Pahath-Moab, of the children of Ieshua, and Ioab, two thousand, and eight hundred, *and* eighteene.

12 The children of Elam, a thousand, two hundred, fiftie and foure.

13 The children of Zattu, eight hundred fourtie and fiue.

14 The children of Zaccai, seuen hundred and threescore.

ani. 15 The children of ‖ Binnui, sixe hundred, fourty and eight.

16 The children of Bebai, sixe hundred, twentie and eight.

17 The children of Azgad, two thousand, three hundred, twentie and two.

18 The children of Adonikam, sixe hundred, threescore and seuen.

19 The children of Biguai, two thousand, threescore and seuen.

20 The children of Adin, sixe hundred, fiftie and fiue.

21 The children of Ater of Hezekiah, ninetie and eight.

22 The children of Hashum, three hundred, twentie and eight.

23 The children of Bezai, three hundred twentie and foure.

rd. 24 The children of ‖ Hariph, an hundred and twelue.

ibbar. 25 The children of ‖ Gibeon, ninetie and fiue.

26 The men of Bethlehem, and Netophah, an hundred, fourescore and eight.

27 The men of Anathoth, an hundred, twentie and eight.

zma- 28 The men of ‖ Bethazmaueth, fourtie and two.

Kiri- 29 The men of ‖ Kiriath-iearim, *m.* Chephirah and Beeroth, seuen hundred fourtie and three.

30 The men of Ramah and Geba, sixe hundred, twentie and one.

31 The men of Michmash, an hundred and twenty and two.

32 The men of Bethel and Ai, an hundred, twentie and three.

33 The men of the other Nebo, fiftie and two.

er.12. 34 The children of the other * Elam, a thousand, two hundred, fiftie & foure.

35 The children of Harim, three hundred and twentie.

36 The children of Iericho, three hundred, fourtie and fiue.

37 The children of Lod, Hadid, and Ono, seuen hundred, twentie and one.

38 The children of Senaa, three

thousand, nine hundred, and thirty.

39 ¶ The Priests. The children of * Iedaia, of the house of Ieshua, nine hundred, seuentie and three.   *1. Chro. 24. 7.*

40 The children of Immer, a thousand, fifty and two.

41 The children of Pashur, a thousand, two hundred, fourtie and seuen.

42 The children of Harim, a thousand, *and* seuenteene.

43 ¶ The Leuites. The children of Ieshua, of Kadmiel, *and* of the children of ‖ Hodeuah, seuentie and foure.   ‖ *Or, Hodauiah, Ezra 2. 4. Or, Iudah, Ezra 3. 9*

44 ¶ The singers. The children of Asaph, an hundred, fourtie and eight.

45 ¶ The porters. The children of Shallum, the children of Ater, the children of Talmon, the children of Akkub, the children of Hatita, the children of Shobai, an hundred, thirtie and eight.

46 ¶ The Nethinims. The children of Ziha, the children of Hashupha, the children of Tabaoth,

47 The children of Keros, the children of Sia, the children of Padon,

48 The children of Lebana, the children of Hagaba, the children of Shalmai,

49 The children of Hanan, the children of Giddel, the children of Gahar,

50 The children of Reaiah, the children of Rezin, the children of Nekoda,

51 The children of Gazzam, the children of Vzza, the children of Phaseah,

52 The children of Besai, the children of Meunim, the children of Nephishesim,

53 The children of Bakbuk, the children of Hakupha, the children of Harhur,

54 The children of Baslith, the children of Mehida, the children of Harsha,

55 The children of Barkos, the children of Sisera, the children of Tamah,

56 The children of Neziah, the children of Hatipha.

57 ¶ The children of Solomons seruants: The children of Sotai, the children of Sophereth, the children of Perida,

58 The children of Iaala, the children of Darkon, the children of Giddel,

59 The children of Shephatiah, the children of Hattil, the children of Pochereth Zebaim, the children of ‖ Amon.   ‖ *Or, Ami.*

60 All the Nethinims, and the children of Solomons seruants, *were* three hundred ninetie and two.

61 * And these were they which went   * *Ezra. 2. 43.*

vp

vp also from Tel-Melah, Tel-Hare-sha, Cherub, Addon, and Immer : but they could not shewe their fathers house, nor their ‖seede, whether they *were* of Israel.

‖ Or, pedegree.

62 The children of Delaiah, the children of Tobiah, the children of Neko-da, sixe hundred fourtie and two.

63 ¶ And of the priests: the children of Habaiah, the children of Koz, the children of Barzillai, which tooke *one* of the daughters of Barzillai the Gileadite to wife, and was called after their name.

64 These sought their register, *among* those that were reckoned by gene-alogie, but it was not found : therfore were they, as polluted, put from the priesthood.

‖ Or, the gouernour.

65 And ‖ the Tirshatha said vnto them, that they should not eate of the most holy things, till there stood *vp* a priest with Vrim and Thummim.

66 ¶ The whole congregation to-gether, *was* fourtie and two thousand, three hundred and threescore :

67 Beside their man seruants, and their maid seruants, of whome *there were* seuen thousand, three hundred, thirtie and seuen : and they had two hundred fourtie and fiue singing men and singing women.

68 Their horses, seuen hundred, thirtie and sixe : their mules, two hundred fourtie and fiue :

69 *Their* camels, foure hundred thirtie and fiue : sixe thousand, seuen hundred and twentie asses.

† Hebr. part.

70 ¶ And †some of the chiefe of the fathers, gaue vnto the worke : The Tirshatha gaue to the treasure, a thousand drammes of gold, fiftie basons, fiue hundred and thirtie priests garments.

71 And *some* of the chiefe of the fathers gaue to the treasure of the worke twentie thousand drammes of golde, and two thousand and two hundred pound of siluer.

72 And that which the rest of the people gaue, *was* twentie thousand drammes of gold, and two thousand pound of siluer, and threescore and seuen priests garments.

73 So the priests, and the Leuites, and the porters, and the singers, and *some* of the people, and the Nethinims, and all Israel, *dwelt* in their cities : And when the seuenth moneth came, the children of Israel were in their cities.

CHAP. VIII.

Nd all the people gathe-red themselues together, as one man, into the street that *was* before the water gate, * and they spake vnto Ezra the scribe, to bring the booke of the Law of Moses, which the Lord had commanded to Israel.

* Ezra 3. and 7. 6.

2 And Ezra the priest brought the Law before the Congregation, both of men and women, and all †that could heare with vnderstanding, vpon the first day of the seuenth moneth.

† Heb. that vnderstoo in hearing

3 And hee read therein before the street that *was* before the water gate, †from the morning vntill midday, be-fore the men and the women, and those that could vnderstand : And the eares of all the people were *attentiue* vnto the booke of the law.

† Heb. fr the light.

4 And Ezra the scribe, stood vpon a †pulpit of wood, which they had made for the purpose, and beside him stood Mattithiah, and Shema, and Anaiah, and Vrijah, and Hilkiah, and Maase-iah, on his right hand : and on his left hand, Pedaiah, and Mishael, and Mal-chiah, and Hashum, and Hashbadana, Zechariah, and Meshullam.

† Heb. to of wood.

5 And Ezra opened the booke in the †sight of all the people (for hee was a-boue al the people) and when he opened it, all the people stood vp :

† Hebr. c

6 And Ezra blessed the Lord the great God : and al the people answered, Amen, Amen, with lifting vp their hands : and they bowed their heads, and worshipped the Lord, with their faces to the ground.

7 Also Ieshua and Bani, and She-rebiah, Iamin, Akkub, Shabbethai, Hodijah, Maaseiah, Kelita, Azariah, Iozabad, Hanan, Pelaiah, and the Le-uites, caused the people to vnderstand the law : and the people *stood* in their place.

8 So they read in the booke, in the Law of God distinctly, and gaue the sense, and caused *them* to vnderstand the reading.

9 ¶ And Nehemiah, which is the ‖ Tirshatha, and Ezra the Priest the Scribe, and the Leuites that taught the

‖ Or, th uernou

the people, said vnto all the people,
This day is holy vnto the LORD
your God, mourne not, nor weepe: for
all the people wept, when they heard
the words of the Law.

10 Then hee sayd vnto them, Goe
your way, eat the fat, & drinke the sweet,
and send portions vnto them, for whom
nothing is prepared : for this day is holy vnto our LORD : neither be ye sory, for the ioy of the LORD is your
strength.

11 So the Leuites stilled all the people, saying, Holde your peace, for the
day is holy, neither be ye grieued.

12 And all the people went their
way to eate, and to drinke, and to send
portions, and to make great mirth, because they had vnderstood the wordes
that were declared vnto them.

13 ¶ And on the second day were gathered together the chiefe of the fathers
of all the people, the Priestes and the
Leuites, vnto Ezra the Scribe, euen
‖ to vnderstand the wordes of the
Law.

14 And they found written in the
Law whith the LORD had commanded †by Moses, that the children of Israel should dwell in * boothes, in the
feast of the seuenth moneth :

15 And that they should publish and
proclaime in all their cities, and in Ierusalem, saying, Goe foorth vnto the
mount, and fetch Oliue branches, and
Pine branches, and Myrtle branches,
and Palme branches, and branches of
thicke trees, to make boothes, as it is
written.

16 So the people went foorth, and
brought *them*, and made themselues
boothes, euery one vpon the roofe of
his house, and in their courts, and in
the courts of the house of God, and in
the streete of the water-gate, and in the
streete of the gate of Ephraim.

17 And all the congregation of them
that were come againe out of the captiuitie, made boothes, and sate vnder the
boothes : for since the dayes of Ieshua
the sonne of Nun, vnto that day, had
not the children of Israel done so : and
there was very great gladnesse.

18 Also day by day from the first day
vnto the last day, he read in the booke
of the Law of God : and they kept the
feast seuen dayes, and on the eight day
was †a solemne assembly according vnto the maner.

ɥat
ıght
ɪt in
rds of
ɯ.

by the
of.
ɪt. 23.
ɪt.

a re-
.

CHAP. IX.

1 A solemne Fast, and repentance of the people. 4 The Leuites make a religious confession of Gods goodnes, and their wickednes.

Ow in the * twentie and
fourth day of this mo-
neth, the children of Israel were assembled with fasting, & with sackclothes,
and earth vpon them.

2 And the seede of Israel separated
themselues from all † strangers, and
stood and confessed their sinnes, and the
iniquities of their fathers.

3 And they stood vp in their place,
and read in the booke of the Law of
the LORD their God, *one* fourth part
of the day, and *another* fourth part they
confessed and worshipped the LORD
their God.

4 ¶ Then stoode vp, vpon the
‖ staires of the Leuites, Ieshua and
Bani, Kadmiel, Shebaniah, Bunni,
Sherebiah, Bani, *and* Chenani, and
cryed with a loude voice vnto the
LORD their God.

5 Then the Leuites, Ieshua and
Kadmiel, Bani, Hashabniah, Sherebiah, Hodiiah, Shebaniah, *and* Pethahiah, sayde, Stand vp, *and* blesse the
LORD your God for euer and euer,
and blessed bee thy glorious Name,
which is exalted aboue all blessing and
praise.

6 Thou, *euen* thou art LORD a-
lone, *thou hast made heauen, the heauen of heauens, with all their hoste, the
earth, and all things that *are* therein,
the seas, and all that *is* therin, and thou
preseruest them all, and the hoste of heauen worshippeth thee.

7 Thou art the LORD the God,
who diddest choose * Abram, and
broughtest him forth out of Vr of the
Caldees, and gauest him the name of
Abraham :

8 And foundest his heart *faithfull
before thee, & madest a *couenant with
him, to giue the land of the Canaanites,
the Hittites, the Amorites, and the Perizzites, and the Iebusites, and the Girgashites, to giue *it, I say,* to his seed, and
hast performed thy words, for thou *art*
righteous,

9 *And didst see the affliction of our
fathers in Egypt, and heardest their cry
by the red Sea,

10 And shewedst signes * and wonders

* Chap. 8. 2

† Heb. stra͠ge
children.

‖ Or, scaf-
fold.

* Gen. 1. 1.

* Gen. 11.
31. and 12.
1. & 17. 5.

* Gen. 15. 6.
* Gen. 12.
17. and 15.
18. & 17. 9.

* Exod. 3. 7.
and 14. 19.

* Exod. 7. 8,
9, 10, 12, &
14. chapters

ders vpon Pharaoh, and on all his seruants, and on all the people of his land: for thou knewest that they dealt proudlie against them: so didst thou get thee a name, as *it is* this day.

* Exod. 14. 22.

11 * And thou didst diuide the sea before them, so that they went through the midst of the sea on the drie land, and their persecutours thou threwest into the deepes, as a stone into the mightie * waters.

* Exod. 15. 10.
* Exod. 13. 21.

12 Moreouer thou * leddest them in the day by a cloudy pillar, and in the night, by a pillar of fire, to giue them light in the way wherin they should go.

* Exod. 20. 1 and 19. 20.

13 Thou * camest downe also vpon mount Sinai, and spakest with them from heauen, and gauest them right iudgements, and †true lawes, good statutes and commandements:

† Heb. lawes of trueth.

14 And madest knowen vnto them thy holy Sabbath, and commandedst them precepts, statutes, and lawes, by the hand of Moses thy seruant:

* Exod. 16. 15. & 17. 6. num. 20. 9.

15 And * gauest them bread from heauen for their hunger, and broughtest forth water for them out of the rocke, for their thirst, and promisedst them

* Deut. 1. 8
† Heb. which thou hadst lift vp thine hand to giue them.

that they should * goe in to possesse the land, †which thou hadst sworne to giue them.

16 But they and our fathers dealt proudly, aud hardened their necks, and hearknd not to thy commandements:

17 And refused to obey, neither were mindful of the wonders that thou didst among them: but hardened their necks,

* Num. 14. 4.

and in their rebellion appointed * a captaine to returne to their bondage: but

† Heb. a god of pardons.

thou *art* †a God ready to pardon, gracious and mercifull, slow to anger, and of great kindnes, & forsookest them not.

* Exo. 32. 4

18 Yea * when they had made them a molten calfe, and said, This *is* thy God, that brought thee vp out of Egypt, and had wrought great prouocations:

19 Yet thou, in thy manifold mercies, forsookest them not in the wildernesse:

* Exod. 13. 22. num. 14 14. 1. cor. 10. 1.

the * pillar of the cloude departed not from them by day, to leade them in the way, neither the pillar of fire by night, to shew them light, and the way wherin they should goe.

* Num. 11. 17.

20 Thou gauest also thy * good spirit, to instruct them, and withheldest

* Exod. 16. 15. & 17. 6. iosh. 3. 12.

not thy * Manna from their mouth, and gauest them water for their thirst.

21 Yea fourtie yeeres diddest thou sustaine them in the wildernesse, so that

they lacked nothing; their * clothes waxed not old, and their feet swelled not.

* De

22 Moreouer, thou gauest them kingdomes and nations, and diddst diuide them into corners: so they possessed the land of * Sihon, and the land of the king of Heshbon, and the land of Og king of Bashan.

* Nu 21, &

23 Their children also multipliedst thou as the starres of heauen, and broughtest them into the land, concerning which thou hadst promised to their fathers, that they should goe in to possesse *it.*

24 So the children went in, and possessed the land, and thou subduedst before them the inhabitants of the lande, the Canaanites, and gauest them into their hands, with their kings, and the people of the land, that they might doe with them, †as they would.

† He ding will.

25 And they tooke strong cities, and a fat land, and possessed houses ful of all goods, ‖ welles digged, vineyards, and Oliue yards, and †fruit trees in abundance: So they did eat and were filled, and became fat, and delighted themselues in thy great goodnesse.

‖Ore
† He of fr

26 Neuerthelesse, they were disobedient, and rebelled against thee, and cast thy law behind their backes, and slewe thy * prophets, which testified against them to turne them to thee, and they wrought great prouocations.

* 1. 20.

27 Therefore thou deliueredst them into the hande of their enemies, who vexed them, & in the time of their trouble, when they cried vnto thee, thou heardest them from heauen: and according to thy manifold mercies, thou gauest them sauiours, who saued them out of the hand of their enemies.

28 But after they had rest, †they did euill againe before thee: therefore leftest thou them in the hand of their enemies, so that they had the dominion ouer them: yet when they returned and cried vnto thee, thou heardest them from heauen, and many times didst thou deliuer them, according to thy mercies:

† H rett doe

29 And testifiedst against them, that thou mightest bring them againe vnto thy lawe: yet they dealt proudly, and hearkened not vnto thy commaundements, but sinned against thy iudgements, (which if a man doe, he shal liue in them) †and withdrew the shoulder, and hardened their necke, and would not heare.

† H gat dr sho

30 Yet

30 Yet many yeres diddest thou †forbeare them, and testifiedst *against them by thy Spirit † in thy Prophets : yet would they not giue eare : therefore gauest thou them into the hand of the people of the lands.

31 Neuerthelesse, for thy great mercies sake, thou diddest not vtterly consume them, nor forsake them ; for thou art a gracious and mercifull God.

32 Now therefore, our God, the great, the *mightie, and the terrible God, who keepest couenant and mercie : let not all the †trouble seeme little before thee, † that hath come vpon vs, on our Kings, on our Princes, & on our Priests, and on our Prophets, & on our fathers, & on al thy people, since the time of the Kings of Assyria, vnto this day.

33 Howbeit, thou art iust in all that is brought vpon vs, for thou hast done right, but we haue done wickedly :

34 Neither haue our kings, our Princes, our Priests, nor our fathers kept thy Law, nor hearkened vnto thy Commandements, and thy Testimonies, wherewith thou didst testifie against them.

35 For they haue not serued thee in their kingdome, and in thy great goodnesse that thou gauest them, and in the large and fat land which thou gauest before them, neither turned they from their wicked workes.

36 Behold, we are seruants this day ; and for the land that thou gauest vnto our fathers, to eat the fruit thereof, and the good thereof, behold, wee are seruants in it.

37 And it yeeldeth much increase vnto the kings, whom thou hast set ouer vs, because of our sinnes : also they haue dominion ouer our bodies, and ouer our cattell, at their pleasure ; and wee are in great distresse.

38 And because of all this, wee make a sure couenant, and write it, and our Princes, Leuites, and Priestes, †seale vnto it.

CHAP. X.

1 The names of them that sealed the couenant. 29 The points of the couenant.

Ow those † that sealed were, Nehemiah ‖ the Tirshatha the sonne of Hachaliah, and Zidkiiah,

2 Seraiah, Azariah, Ieremiah,

3 Pashur, Amariah, Malchiah,

4 Hattush, Shebaniah, Malluch,

5 Harim, Merimoth, Obadiah,

6 Daniel, Ginnethon, Baruch,

7 Meshullam, Abiiah, Miiamin,

8 Maaziah, Bilgai, Shemaiah : these were the Priests.

9 And the Leuites : both Ieshua the sonne of Azaniah, Binnui, of the sonnes of Henadad, Kadmiel ;

10 And their brethren, Shebaniah, Hodiiah, Kelita, Pelaiah, Hanan,

11 Micah, Rehob, Hashabiah,

12 Zaccur, Sherebiah, Shebaniah,

13 Hodiiah, Bani, Beninu,

14 The chiefe of the people. Parosh, Pahath-Moab, Elam, Zatthu, Bani,

15 Bunni, Azgad, Bebai,

16 Adoniiah, Biguai, Adin,

17 Ater, Hizkiiah, Azzur,

18 Hodiah, Hashum, Bezai,

19 Hariph, Anathoth, Nebai,

20 Magpiash, Meshullam, Hezir,

21 Meshezabeel, Zadok, Iaddua,

22 Pelatiah, Hanan, Anaiah,

23 Hoshea, Hananiah, Hashub,

24 Hallohesh, Pileha, Shobek,

25 Rehum, Hashabnah, Maaseiah,

26 And Ahiiah, Hanan, Anan,

27 Malluch, Harim, Baanah.

28 ¶ * And the rest of the people, the Priests, the Leuites, the Porters, the singers, the Nethinims, and all they that had separated themselues from the people of the lands, vnto the Law of God, their wiues, their sonnes, and their daughters, euery one hauing knowledge, and hauing vnderstanding.

29 They claue to their brethren their nobles, and entred into a curse, and into an oath to walke in Gods law, which was giuen † by Moses the seruant of God, and to obserue and doe all the commandements of the LORD our Lord, and his Iudgements, and his statutes :

30 And that we would not giue *our daughters vnto the people of the land, nor take their daughters for our sonnes.

31 * And if the people of the land bring ware or any victuals on the Sabbath day, to sell, that we would not buy it of them on the Sabbath, or on the holyday, and that wee would leaue the seuenth yeere, and the * exaction of † euerie debt.

32 Also we made ordinances for vs, to

Marginal notes

* Ezr. 2. & 3

† Heb. by the hand of.

* Exo. 34. 16 deut. 7. 3.

* Exod. 20. 10. leui. 23. 12. nehem. 13. 23.

* Deut. 15. 2 leuit. 25. 4. † Heb. euery hand.

to charge our selues yeerely, with the third part of a shekel, for the seruice of the house of our God,

33 For the shew-bread, and for the continuall meate-offering, and for the continuall burnt offering, of the Sabbaths, of the new moones, for the setfeastes, and for the holy things, and for the sin-offerings, to make an atonement for Israel, and for all the worke of the house of our God.

34 And we cast the lots among the priests, the Leuites, and the people, for the wood offering, to bring it into the house of our God, after the houses of our fathers, at times appointed, yeere by yeere, to burne vpon the altar of the LORD our God, as it is written in the *law:

* See num.
28. & 29.
chap. and
Exod. 23.
19. and Leuit. 19. 23.

35 And to bring the first fruits of our ground, and the first fruites of all fruit of all trees, yeere by yeere, vnto the house of the LORD.

36 Also the first-borne of our sonnes, and of our cattell (as it is written * in the lawe) and the firstlings of our heards, and of our flockes, to bring to the house of our God, vnto the priests that minister in the house of our God:

* Exod. 13.
2. Leuit. 23.
17. num.
15. 19. and
18. 12. &c.

37 And that we should bring the first fruits of our dough, and our offerings, and the fruit of all maner of trees, of wine and of oile, vnto the priests, to the chambers of the house of our God, and the tithes of our ground vnto the Leuites, that the same Leuites might haue the tithes, in all the cities of our tillage.

38 And the priest the sonne of Aaron, shall be with the Leuites, * when the Leuites take tithes, and the Leuites shal bring vp the tithe of the tithes vnto the house of our God, to the chambers into the treasure house.

* Num. 18.
26.

39 For the children of Israel, and the children of Leui, shall bring the offering of the corne, of the new wine, and the oyle, vnto the chambers, where are the vessels of the sanctuarie, and the priests that minister, and the porters, and the singers, and we will not forsake the house of our God.

CHAP. XI.

1 The rulers, voluntary men, and the tenth man chosen by Lot, dwell at Ierusalem. 3 A catalogue of their names. 20 The residue dwell in other cities.

Nd the rulers of the people dwelt at Ierusalem: the rest of the people also cast lots, to bring one of tenne, to dwell in Ierusalem, the holy citie, and nine parts to dwell in other cities.

2 And the people blessed all the men, that willingly offered themselues, to dwell at Ierusalem.

3 ¶ Now these are the chiefe of the prouince that dwelt in Ierusalem: but in the cities of Iudah dwelt euerie one in his possession in their cities, to wit, Israel, the priests, and the Leuites, and the Nethinims, and the children of Solomons seruants.

4 And at Ierusalem dwelt certaine of the children of Iudah, and of the children of Beniamin. Of the children of Iudah: Athaiah the sonne of Vzziah, the sonne of Zechariah, the sonne of Amariah, the sonne of Shephatiah, the sonne of Mahalaleel, of the children of Perez.

5 And Maaseiah the sonne of Baruch the sonne of Col-Hozeh, the sonne of Hazaiah the sonne of Adaiah, the sonne of Ioiarib, the sonne of Zechariah, the sonne of Shiloni.

6 All the sonnes of Perez that dwelt at Ierusalem, were foure hundred threescore and eight valiant men.

7 And these are the sonnes of Beniamin: Sallu the sonne of Meshullam, the sonne of Ioed, the sonne of Pedaiah, the sonne of Kolaiah, the sonne of Maaseiah, the sonne of Ithiel, the sonne of Iesaiah.

8 And after him Gabai, Sallai, nine hundred twentie and eight.

9 And Ioel the sonne of Zichri was their ouerseer: and Iudah the sonne of Senuah, was second ouer the city.

10 Of the Priests: Iedaiah the sonne of Ioiarib, Iachin;

11 Seraiah the sonne of Hilkiah, the sonne of Meshullam, the sonne of Zadok, the sonne of Meraioth, the sonne of Ahitub, was the ruler of the house of God.

12 And their brethren that did the worke of the house, were eight hundred twentie and two: and Adaiah the sonne of Ieroham, the sonne of Pelaliah, the sonne of Amzi, the sonne of Zechariah, the sonne of Pashur, the sonne of Malchiah,

13 And

13 And his brethren, chiefe of the fathers, two hundred fourty and two : and Amashai the sonne of Azareel, the sonne of Ahasai, the sonne of Meshilemoth, the sonne of Immer.

14 And their brethren mighty men of valour, an hundred twenty and eight; and their ouerseer was Zabdiel, ‖ the sonne of *one of* the great men.

Or, the sonne of Haggedolim.

15 Also of the Leuites : Shemaiah the sonne of Hashub, the sonne of Azrikam, the sonne of Hashabiah, the sonne of Bunni.

16 And Shabbethai, and Iozabad, of the chiefe of the Leuits, † had the ouersight of the outward businesse of the house of God.

Hebr. were ouer.

17 And Mattaniah the sonne of Micha, the sonne of Zabdi, the sonne of Asaph, was the principall to beginne the thankesgiuing in prayer : and Bakbukiah the second among his brethren, and Abda the sonne of Shammua, the sonne of Galal, the sonne of Ieduthun.

18 All the Leuites in the holy City, were two hundred, fourescore and foure.

19 Moreouer, the porters, Akkub, Talmon, and their brethren that kept † the gates, were an hundred seuenty and two.

Hebr. at the gates.

20 ¶ And the residue of Israel, of the Priests and the Leuites, were in all the cities of Iudah, euery one in his inheritance.

21 *But the Nethinims dwelt in ‖ Ophel : and Ziha, and Gispa were ouer the Nethinims.

See Chap. 26.
‖ Or, the tower.

22 The ouerseer also of the Leuites at Ierusalem, was Vzzi the sonne of Bani, the son of Hashabiah, the sonne of Mattaniah, the sonne of Micha: Of the sonnes of Asaph, the singers were ouer the businesse of the house of God.

23 For it was the kings commandement concerning them, that ‖ a certaine portion should be for the singers, due for euery day.

‖ Or, a sure ordinance.

24 And Pethahiah the sonne of Meshezabel, of the children of Zerah the sonne of Iudah, was at the kings hand in all matters concerning the people.

25 And for the villages, with their fields, some of the children of Iudah dwelt at Kiriath-arba, and in the villages thereof; and at Dibon, and in the villages thereof, and at Iekabzeel, and in the villages thereof:

26 And at Ieshua, and at Moladah, and at Beth-phelet,

27 And at Hazer - Shual, and at Beer-sheba, and in the villages thereof:

28 And at Ziglag, and at Mekonah, and in the villages thereof:

29 And at En-Rimmon, and at Zareah, and at Iarmuth,

30 Zanoah, Adullam, and in their villages, at Lachish, and the fieldes thereof: at Azekah, and in the villages thereof. And they dwelt from Beersheba, vnto the valley of Hinnom.

31 The children also of Beniamin, ‖ from Geba, dwelt ‖ at Michmash, and Aiia, and Beth-el, and in their villages:

‖ Or, of Geba.
‖ Or, to Michmash.

32 And at Anathoth, Nob, Ananiah,

33 Hazor, Ramah, Gittaim,

34 Hadid, Zeboim, Neballat,

35 Lod, and Ono, the valley of craftes-men.

36 And of the Leuites, were diuisions in Iudah, and in Beniamin.

CHAP. XII.

1 The Priests, 8 and the Leuites which came vp with Zerubbabel. 10 The succession of hie Priests. 22 Certaine chiefe Leuites. 27 The solemnitie of the dedication of the walls. 44 The offices of Priests and Leuites appointed in the Temple.

 Ow these are the *Priests and the Leuits that went vp with Zerubbabel the sonne of Shealtiel, and Ieshua : Seraiah, Ieremiah, Ezra,

* Ezra 2. 1.

2 Amariah, ‖ Malluch, Hattush,

3 ‖ Shecaniah, ‖ Rehum, ‖ Merimoth,

4 Iddo, ‖ Ginnetho, Abiiah,

5 ‖ Miamin, ‖ Madiah, Bilgah,

6 Shemaiah, & Ioiarib, Iedaiah,

7 ‖ Sallu, Amok, Hilkiah, Iedaiah: these were the chiefe of the Priests, and of their brethren in the dayes of Ieshua.

‖ Or, Melicu, ver. 14.
‖ Or, Sebaniah, ver. 14.
‖ Or, Harim, ver. 15.
‖ Or, Meraioth, ver. 15.
‖ Or, Ginnethon, ver. 16.
‖ Or, Miniamin, ver. 17.
‖ Or, Moadiah, ver. 17.
‖ Or, Sallai, ver. 20.

8 Moreouer the Leuites : Ieshua, Binnui, Kadmiel, Sherebiah, Iudah, and Mattaniah, which was ouer the ‖ thankesgiuing, he and his brethren.

‖ That is, the Psalmes of thankesgiuing.

9 Also Bakbukiah, and Vnni; their brethren, were ouer against them in the watches.

10 ¶ And Ieshua begate Ioiakim, Ioiakim also begate Eliashib, and Eliashib begate Ioiada,

11 And Ioiada begate Ionathan, and Ionathan begate Iaddua.

12 And in the dayes of Ioiakim, were Priests the chiefe of the fathers: of

of Seraiah, Meraiah: of Ieremiah, Hananiah:

13 Of Ezra, Meshullam: of Amariah, Iehohanan:

14 Of Melicu, Ionathan : of Shebaniah, Ioseph :

15 Of Harim, Adna : of Meraioth, Helkai :

16 Of Iddo, Zecharıah : of Ginnethon, Meshullam :

17 Of Abijah, Zichri : of Miniamin, of Moadiah, Piltai :

18 Of Bilgah, Shammua : of Shemaiah, Iehonathan :

19 And of Ioiarib, Mattenai: of Iedaiah, Vzzi :

20 Of Sallai, Kallai : of Amok, Eber :

21 Of Hilkiah, Hashabiah : of Iedaiah, Nethanael

22 ¶ The Leuites in the dayes of Eliashib, Ioiada, and Iohanan, and Iaddua, *were* recorded chiefe of the fathers : also the Priests, to the reigne of Darius the Persian.

23 The sonnes of Leui, the chiefe of the fathers, *were* written in the booke *1. Chro. 9.* of the * Chronicles, euen vntill the dayes of Iohanan the sonne of Eliashib.

24 And the chiefe of the Leuites : Hashabiah, Sherebiah, and Ieshua the sonne of Kadmiel, with their brethren ouer against them, to praise *and* to giue thankes, according to the commandement of Dauid the man of God, ward ouer against ward.

25 Mattaniah, and Bakbukiah, Obadiah, Meshullam, Talmon, Akkub, *were* porters keeping the ward, at ‖ *Or, treasuries, or assemblies.* the ‖thresholds of the gates.

26 These were in the dayes of Ioiakim, the sonne of Ieshua, the sonne of Iozadak, and in the dayes of Nehemiah the gouernour, and of Ezra the Priest, the Scribe.

27 ¶ And at the dedication of the wall of Ierusalem, they sought the Leuites out of all their places, to bring them to Ierusalem, to keepe the dedication with gladnesse, both with thankesgiuings and with singing, *with* cymbals, psalteries, and with harpes.

28 And the sonnes of the Singers gathered themselues together, both out of the plaine countrey round about Ierusalem, and from the villages of Netophathi.

29 Also from the house of Gilgal, and out of the fields of Geba, and Az-

maueth: for the Singers had builded them villages round about Ierusalem.

30 And the Priests and the Leuites purified themselues, and purified the people, and the gates, and the wall.

31 Then I brought vp the princes of Iudah vpon the wall, and appointed two great *companies of them* that gaue thankes, *whereof one* went on the right hand vpon the wall toward the doung-gate :

32 And after them went Hoshaiah, and halfe of the Princes of Iudah,

33 And Azariah, Ezra, and Meshullam,

34 Iudah, and Beniamin, and Shemaiah, and Ieremiah,

35 And *certaine* of the Priests sonnes with trumpets: *namely,* Zechariah the sonne of Ionathan, the sonne of Shemaiah, the sonne of Mattaniah, the sonne of Michaiah, the sonne of Zaccur, the sonne of Asaph :

36 And his brethren, Shemaiah, and Asarael, Milalai, Gilalai, Maai, Nethanael, and Iudah, Hanani, with the musicall instruments of Dauid the man of God ; and Ezra the Scribe before them.

37 And at the fountaine-gate, which was ouer against them, they went vp by the staires of the citie of Dauid, at the going vp of the wall, aboue the house of Dauid, euen vnto the water-gate, Eastward.

38 And the other *company* of them that gaue thankes, went ouer against them, and I after them, and the halfe of the people vpon the wall, from beyond the towre of the fornaces, euen vnto the broad wall,

39 And from aboue the gate of Ephraim, and aboue the olde gate, and aboue the fish-gate, and the towre of Hananeel, and the towre of Meah, euen vnto the sheepegate; and they stood still in the prison gate.

40 So stood the two companies of them that gaue thankes in the house of God, and I, and the halfe of the rulers with me :

41 And the Priests : Eliakim, Maaseiah, Miniamin, Michaiah, Elioenai, Zachariah, *and* Hananiah with trumpets :

42 And Maaseiah, and Shemaiah, and Eleazar, and Vzzi, and Iehohanan, and Malchiiah, and Elam, and Ezer. And the Singers † sang loud, with *† Heb. their v‥ to be h‥* Iezra-

43 Also that day they offered great ſacrifices, and reioyced; for God had made them reioyce with great ioy: the wiues alſo and the children reioyced: ſo that the ioy of Ieruſalem was heard euen afarre off.

44 ¶ And at that time were ſome appointed ouer the chambers for the treaſures, for the offerings, for the firſt fruits, and for the tithes, to gather into them out of the fields of the cities the portions of the ‖law for the prieſts and Leuites: †for Iudah reioyced for the Prieſts, & for the Leuites †that waited.

45 And both the ſingers and the porters kept the ward of their God, and the ward of the purification, *according to the commandement of Dauid, and of Solomon his ſonne.

46 For in the dayes of Dauid *and Aſaph of old, there were chiefe of the ſingers, and ſongs of praiſe and thankſgiuing vnto God.

47 And all Iſrael in the dayes of Zerubbabel, and in the dayes of Nehemiah, gaue the portions of the ſingers, and the porters, euery day his portion, and they ‖ſanctified holy things vnto the Leuites, * and the Leuites ſanctified them vnto the children of Aaron.

CHAP. XIII.

1 Vpon the reading of the Law, ſeparation is made from the mixed multitude. 4 Nehemiah at his returne, cauſeth the chambers to bee cleanſed. 10 He reformeth the offices in the houſe of God. 15 The violation of the Sabbath, 23 & the mariages with ſtrange wiues.

O N that day †they read in the *booke of Moſes in the †audience of the people, and therein was found written, that the Ammonite and the Moabite ſhould not come into the Congregation of God for euer.

2 *Becauſe they met not the children of Iſrael with bread, and with water, but hired Balaam againſt them, that he ſhould curſe them: howbeit our God turned the curſe into a bleſſing.

3 Now it came to paſſe when they had heard the law, that they ſeparated from Iſrael all the mixed multitude.

4 ¶ And before this Eliaſhib the prieſt †hauing the ouerſight of the chamber of the houſe of our God, was allied vnto Tobiah:

5 And hee had prepared for him a great chamber, where aforetime they laid the meat offrings, the frankincenſe and the veſſels, and the tithes of the corne, the new wine, and the oile, which was †commanded to be giuen to the Leuites, and the ſingers, and the porters, and the offerings of the prieſts.

6 But in all this time was not I at Ieruſalem: for in the two and thirtieth yeere of Artaxerxes king of Babylon, came I vnto the king, and †after certaine dayes, ‖obtained I leaue of the King:

7 And I came to Ieruſalem, and vnderſtood of the euil that Eliaſhib did for Tobiah, in preparing him a chamber in the courts of the houſe of God.

8 And it grieued me ſore, therefore I caſt foorth all the houſhold ſtuffe of Tobiah out of the chamber:

9 Then I commanded, and they cleanſed the chambers, and thither brought I againe the veſſels of the houſe of God, with the meate offering, and the frankincenſe.

10 ¶ And I perceiued that the portions of the Leuites had not beene giuen them: for the Leuites and the ſingers that did the worke, were fled euery one to his field.

11 Then contended I with the rulers, and ſaid, Why is the houſe of God forſaken? And I gathered them together, and ſet them in their †place.

12 Then brought all Iudah the tithe of the corne, and the new wine, and the oyle, vnto the ‖treaſuries.

13 And I made treaſurers ouer the treaſuries, Shelemiah the prieſt, and Zadok the ſcribe, and of the Leuites, Pedaiah: and †next to them was Hanan the ſonne of Zaccur, the ſonne of Mattaniah: for they were counted faithfull, and †their office was to diſtribute vnto their brethren.

14 *Remember me, O my God, concerning this, and wipe not out my †good deeds, that I haue done for the houſe of my God, and for the ‖offices thereof.

15 ¶ In thoſe dayes ſawe I in Iudah, ſome treading wine preſſes on the Sabbath, and bringing in ſheaues, and lading aſſes, as alſo wine, grapes, and figs, and all maner of burdens, which they brought into Ieruſalem on the Sabbath day: and I teſtified againſt them in the day wherein they ſolde victuals.

16 There

Marginal notes

s, ap-
by
for
of

that

ron.
25.

ron.
&c.

is, ſet
. 18.

there
ad.
a. 22.
23. 3
eares

. 22.
. 24. 9

being
er.

† Hebr. the commandement of the Leuites.

† Heb. at the end of daies.
‖ Or, I earneſtly requeſted.

† Heb. ſtanding.

‖ Or, ſtorehouſes.

† Hebr. at their hand.

† Heb. it was vpon them.

* Verſe 22.
† Heb. kindneſſes.

‖ Or, obſeruations.

16 There dwelt men of Tyre also therein, which brought fish and all maner of ware, and solde on the Sabbath vnto the children of Iudah, and in Ierusalem.

17 Then I contended with the Nobles of Iudah, and sayd vnto them, What euill thing is this that ye doe, and profane the Sabbath day?

18 Did not your fathers thus, and did not our God bring all this euill vpon vs, and vpon this citie? yet ye bring more wrath vpon Israel, by profaning the Sabbath.

19 And it came to passe, that when the gates of Ierusalem beganne to be darke before the Sabbath, I commanded that the gates should be shut, and charged that they should not be opened till after the Sabbath : and some of my seruants set I at the gates, *that* there should no burden be brought in on the Sabbath day.

20 So the merchants, and sellers of all kinde of ware, lodged without Ierusalem once or twice.

21 Then I testified against them, and said vnto them, Why lodge yee †about the wall? If ye doe *so* againe, I will lay hands on you. From that time forth came they no *more* on the Sabbath.

22 And I commanded the Leuites, that they should cleanse themselues, and that they should come and keepe the gates, to sanctifie the Sabbath day: Remember me, O my God, *concerning* this also, and spare me, according to the ‖greatnesse of thy mercie.

23 ¶ In those dayes also sawe I

Iewes *that* †had maried wiues of Ashdod, of Ammon, *and* of Moab :

24 And their children spake halfe in the speech of Ashdod, and †could not speake in the Iewes language, but according to the language †of ech people.

25 And I contended with them, and ‖ cursed them, and smote certeine of them, and pluckt off their haire, and made them sweare by God, *saying*, Yee shall not giue your daughters vnto their sonnes, nor take their daughters vnto your sonnes, or for your selues.

26 Did not Solomon king of Israel sinne by these things? yet among many nations was there no king like him, who was beloued of his God, and God made him king ouer all Israel : *neuerthelesse, euen him did outlandish women cause to sinne.

27 Shall wee then hearken vnto you, to doe all this great euill, to transgresse against our God, in marrying strange wiues?

28 And *one* of the sonnes of Ioiada, the sonne of Eliashib the high Priest, *was* sonne in law to Sanballat the Horonite : therfore I chased him from me.

29 Remember them, O my God, †because they haue defiled the Priesthood, and the couenant of the Priesthood, and of the Leuites.

30 Thus cleansed I them from all strangers, and appointed the wards of the Priests and the Leuites, euery one in his businesse :

31 And for the wood-offering, at times appointed, and for the first fruits. Remember me, O my God, for good.

---

† *Heb. before the wall.*

‖ *Or, multitude.*

† *Heb. made to dwell with them.*

† *Heb. discerne not to speake.*

† *Heb. of people and people.*

‖ *Or, reuiled them.*

* 1. K[ings] 1[1], &c.

† *Heb. defiling.*

¶ THE

¶ THE BOOKE OF

Esther.

CHAP. I.

1 Ahasuerus maketh royall feasts. 10 Vasthi, sent for, refuseth to come. 13 Ahasuerus, by the counsell of Memucan, maketh the decree of mens soueraigntie.

Ow it came to passe in the dayes of Ahasuerus, (this *is* Ahasuerus which reigned from India, euen vnto Ethiopia, ouer an hundred, and seuen and twentie prouinces.)

2 *That* in those dayes, when the King Ahasuerus sate on the throne of his kingdome, which was in Shushan the palace :

3 In the third yeere of his reigne, he made a feast vnto all his Princes, and his seruants, the power of Persia and Media, the Nobles and Princes of the prouinces being before him.

4 When he shewed the riches of his glorious kingdome, and the honour of his excellent maiestie, many dayes, *euen* an hundred and fourescore dayes.

5 And when these dayes were expired, the king made a feast vnto all the people that were †present in Shushan the palace, both vnto great and small, seuen dayes, in the court of the garden of the kings palace,

6 *Where were* white, greene and ‖blew *hangings*, fastened with cords of fine linnen, and purple, to siluer rings, and pillers of marble : the beds *were* of gold and siluer, vpon a pauement of ‖red, and blewe, and white, and blacke marble.

7 And they gaue *them* drinke in vessels of gold, (the vessels being diuers one from another) and †royall wine in abundance, according to the †state of the king.

8 And the drinking *was* according to the law, none did compell : for the king had appointed to all the officers of his house, that they should doe according to euery mans pleasure.

9 Also Vasthi the Queene made a feast for the women, *in* the royall house which *belonged* to king Ahasuerus.

10 ¶ On the seuenth day, when the heart of the King was merry with wine, he commanded Mehuman, Biztha, Harbona, Bigtha, and Abagtha, Zethar, and Carcas, the seuen ‖chamberlens that serued in the presence of Ahasuerus the king,

11 To bring Vasthi the Queene before the king, with the Crowne royall, to shew the people, and the Princes her beautie: for she *was* †faire to looke on.

12 But the Queene Vasthi refused to come at the Kings commandement † by his chamberlens : therefore was the King very wroth, and his anger burned in him.

13 ¶ Then the king saide to the wise men, which knew the times (for so *was* the Kings maner towards all that knew law, and iudgement:

14 And the next vnto him, *was* Carshena, Shethar, Admatha, Tarshis, Meres, Marsena, *and* Memucan, the seuen * Princes of Persia, and Media, which saw the Kings face, *and* which sate the first in the kingdome.)

15 †What • shall wee doe vnto the Queene Vasthi, according to law, because she hath not performed the commandement of the king Ahasuerus, by the chamberlens ?

16 And Memucan answered before the king and the Princes ; Vasthi the Queene hath not done wrong to the king onely, but also to all the Princes, and to all the people that *are* in all the pro-

---

Side notes (right column):

† Heb. according to the hand of the king.

‖ Or, Eunuches.

† Hebr. good of countenance.

† Hebr. which was by the hand of his Eunuches.

* Ezra. 7. 14.

† Hebr. what to doe?

Side notes (left column):

‖ violet.

‖ of porphyre, and marble, one of colour.

† Hebr. wine of the kingdome.

prouinces of the king Ahasuerus.

17 For *this* deed of the queene shall come abroad vnto all women, so that they shal despise their husbands in their eyes, when it shall bee reported ; The king Ahasuerus commanded Vasthi the queene to be brought in before him, but she came not.

18 *Likewise* shall the Ladies of Persia and Media say this day vnto all the kings princes, which haue heard of the deed of the Queene. Thus *shall there arise* too much contempt and wrath.

19 †If it please the king, let there go a royall commandement †from him, and let it bee written among the lawes of the Persians, and the Medes, †that it be not altered, that Vasthi come no more before king Ahasuerus, and let the king giue her royall estate †vnto another that is better then she.

20 And when the kings decree, which he shal make, shalbe published throughout all his empire, (for it is great :) all the wiues shall giue to their husbands honour, both to great and small.

21 And the saying †pleased the king and the princes, and the king did according to the word of Memucan :

22 For he sent letters into all the kings prouinces, into euery prouince, according to the writing thereof, and to euery people after their language, that euery man should beare rule in his owne house, and †that *it* should be published according to the language of euerie people.

CHAP. II.

1 *Out* of the choise of virgines, a Queene is to be chosen. 5 Mordecai the nursing father of Esther. 8 Esther is preferred by Hegai before the rest. 12 The maner of purification, & going in to the king. 15 Esther best pleasing the king, is made Queene. 21 Mordecai discouering a treason, is recorded in the Chronicles.

AFter these things, when the wrath of king Ahasuerus was appeased , hee remembred Vasthi, and what shee had done, and what was decreed against her.

2 Then saide the kings seruants, that ministred vnto him, Let there bee faire yong virgins sought for the king:

3 And let the king appoint officers in all the prouinces of his kingdome, that they may gather together all the faire yong virgins vnto Shushan the palace, to the house of the women †vnto the custodie of ||Hege the kings chamberlaine, keeper of the women, and let their things for purification bee giuen *them* :

4 And let the maiden which pleaseth the king, bee Queene in stead of Vasthi. And the thing pleased the king, and he did so.

5 ¶ *Now* in Shushan the palace, there was a certaine Iew, whose name *was* Mordecai, the sonne of Iair, the sonne of Shimei, the sonne of Kish, a Beniamite.

6 *Who had bene caried away from Ierusalem, with the captiuitie which had bene caried away with Ieconiah king of Iudah, whom Nebuchadnezzar the King of Babylon had caried away.

7 And hee †brought vp Hadassah (that is Esther) his vncles daughter, for she had neither father nor mother, and the maid was †faire and beautiful, whom Mordecai (when her father and mother were dead) tooke for his owne daughter.

8 ¶ So it came to passe, when the kings commandement and his decree was heard, and when many maidens were gathered together vnto Shushan the palace, to the custodie of Hegai, that Esther was brought *also* vnto the kings house, to the custodie of Hegai, keeper of the women.

9 And the maiden pleased him, and she obtained kindnesse of him, and hee speedily gaue her her things for purification , with †such things as belonged to her, and seuen maidens, which were meet to be giuen her, out of the Kings house, and †hee preferred her and her maids, vnto the best *place* of the house of the women.

10 Esther had not shewed her people, nor her kinred : for Mordecai had charged her, that she should not shew *it*.

11 And Mordecai walked euery day before the court of the womens house, †to know how Esther did, and what should become of her.

12 ¶ Now when euery maids turne was come, to goe in to King Ahasuerus, after that shee had bene twelue moneths, according to the maner of the women (for so were the dayes of their purifications accomplished, *to wit*, sixe moneths with oile of myrrhe, and sixe

moneths

† *Heb. if it be good with the king.*
† *Heb. from before him.*
† *Heb. that it passe not away.*

† *Hebr. vnto her companion.*

† *Heb. was good in the eyes of the king.*

† *Hebr. that one should publish it according to the language of his people.*

† *the*
‖ *Or ver.*

2. 15. 1 and 36. 1

† *He rish*

† *He of ſo and coun*

† *He port*

† *He char*

† *He know peac*

moneths with sweet odours, and with *other* things for the purifying of the women.)

13 Then thus came euery maiden vnto the king, whatsoeuer she desired, was giuen her, to goe with her out of the house of the women, vnto the kings house.

14 In the euening she went, and on the morrowe she returned into the second house of the women, to the custodie of Shaashgaz the kings chamberlen, which kept the concubines : shee came in vnto the king no more, except the king delighted in her, and that shee were called by name.

15 ¶ Now when the turne of Esther, the daughter of Abihail, the vncle of Mordecai (who had taken her for his daughter) was come, to goe in vnto the king : she required nothing, but what Hegai the kings chamberlen the keeper of the women, appointed : And Esther obtained fauour in the sight of all them that looked vpon her.

16 So Esther was taken vnto king Ahasuerus, into his house royall, in the tenth moneth (which *is* the moneth Tebeth) in the seuenth yeere of his reigne.

17 And the king loued Esther aboue all the women, and she obtained grace and ||fauour †in his sight, more then all the virgins ; so that hee set the royall crowne vpon her head, and made her queene, in stead of Vasthi.

18 Then the king made a great feast vnto all his princes and his seruants, *euen* Esthers feast, and hee made a †release to the prouinces, and gaue gifts, according to the state of the king.

19 And when the virgins were gathered together the second time, then Mordecai sate in the kings gate.

20 Esther had not *yet* shewed her kindred, nor her people, as Mordecai had charged her : For Esther did the commandement of Mordecai, like as when she was brought vp with him.

21 ¶ In those dayes, (while Mordecai sate in the kings gate) two of the kings chamberlens, ||Bigthan and Teresh, of those which kept †the doore, were wroth, and sought to lay hand on the king Ahasuerus :

22 And the thing was knowen to Mordecai, who told it vnto Esther the Queene, and Esther certified the king thereof, in Mordecais name.

23 And when inquisition was made

of the matter, it was found out ; therfore they were both hanged on a tree : and it was written in the booke of the chronicles before the king.

CHAP. III.

1 Haman aduanced by the king, and despised by Mordecai, seeketh reuenge vpon all the Iewes. 7 Hee casteth Lots. 8 Hee obtaineth by calumniation, a Decree of the king, to put the Iewes to death.

Fter these things did king Ahasuerus promote Haman, the sonne of Amedatha the Agagite, and aduanced him, and set his seate aboue all the princes that *were* with him.

2 And all the kings seruants, that *were* in the kings gate, bowed, and reuerenced Haman, for the king had so commanded concerning him : but Mordecai bowed not, nor did *him* reuerence.

3 Then the kings seruants, which *were* in the kings gate, sayd vnto Mordecai, Why transgressest thou the kings commandement ?

4 Now it came to passe, when they spake daily vnto him, and he hearkened not vnto them ; that they told Haman, to see whether Mordecai his matters would stand, for he had told them that he *was* a Iewe.

5 And when Haman saw that Mordecai bowed not, nor did him reuerence, then was Haman full of wrath.

6 And hee thought scorne to lay hands on Mordecai alone, for they had shewed him the people of Mordecai : wherefore Haman sought to destroy all the Iewes, that *were* throughout the whole kingdome of Ahasuerus, euen the people of Mordecai.

7 ¶ In the first moneth (that is, the moneth Nisan) in the twelfth yeere of king Ahasuerus, they cast Pur, that *is*, the lot, before Haman, from day to day, and from moneth to moneth, *to* the twelfth moneth, that *is* the moneth Adar.

8 ¶ And Haman saide vnto king Ahasuerus : There is a certaine people scattered abroad, and dispersed among the people, in all the prouinces of thy kingdome, and their lawes *are* diuerse from all people, neither keepe they the kings lawes ; therefore it *is* not †for the kings profit to suffer them.

9 If

, kind-
. be-
him.

5. rest.

Big-
chap.
. the
old.

† *Heb. meete*
or, equall.

9 If it please the king, let it be written, †that they may be destroyed: and I will †pay ten thousand talents of siluer to the handes of those that haue the charge of the businesse, to bring *it* into the kings treasuries.

10 And the king tooke his ring from his hand, and gaue it vnto Haman the sonne of Ammedatha the Agagite, the Iewes ||enemie.

11 And the king saide vnto Haman, The siluer *is* giuen to thee, the people also, to doe with them, as it seemeth good to thee.

12 Then were the kings ||scribes called on the thirteenth day of the first moneth, and there was written, according to all that Haman had commanded, vnto the kings Lieutenants, and to the gouernours, that *were* ouer euery prouince, and to the rulers of euery people of euery prouince, according to the writing thereof, and *to* euery people, after their language, in the name of king Ahasuerus was it written, and sealed with the kings ring.

13 And the letters were sent by posts into all the kings prouinces, to destroy, to kill, and to cause to perish all Iewes, both yong and olde, litle children and women, in one day, *euen* vpon the thirteenth *day* of the twelfth moneth (which *is* the moneth Adar) and *to take* the spoile of them for a pray.

14 The copie of the writing for a commandement to bee giuen in euery prouince, was published vnto all people, that they should bee ready against that day.

15 The postes went out, being hastened by the kings commandement, and the decree was giuen in Shushan the palace: and the king and Haman sate downe to drinke, but the citie Shushan was perplexed.

CHAP. IIII.

1 The great mourning of Mordecai and the Iewes. 4 Esther vnderstanding it, sendeth to Mordecai, who sheweth the cause, and aduiseth her to vndertake the suit. 10 Shee excusing her selfe is threatned by Mordecai. 15 She appointing a fast, vndertaketh the suit.

Hen Mordecai perceiued all that was done, Mordecai rent his clothes, and put on sackcloth with ashes, and went out into the midst of the citie, and cried with a loud and a bitter crie:

2 And came euen before the kings gate: for none *might* enter into the kings gate clothed with sackcloth.

3 And in euery prouince, whithersoeuer the kings commaundement, and his decree came, *there was* great mourning among the Iewes, and fasting, and weeping, and wailing, and †many lay in sackcloth and ashes.

4 ¶ So Esthers maides and her †chamberlaines came, and told it her: then was the Queene exceedingly grieued, and she sent raiment to clothe Mordecai, and to take away the sackcloth from him: but he receiued *it* not.

5 Then called Esther for Hatach, *one* of the kings chamberlaines, †whom he had appointed to attend vpon her, and gaue him a commaundement to Mordecai, to know what it *was*, and why it *was*.

6 So Hatach went forth to Mordecai, vnto the street of the citie, which *was* before the kings gate:

7 And Mordecai tolde him of all that had happened vnto him, and of the summe of the money that Haman had promised to pay to the Kings treasuries for the Iewes, to destroy them.

8 Also he gaue him the copie of the writing of the decree, that was giuen at Shushan to destroy them, to shewe *it* vnto Esther, and to declare *it* vnto her, and to charge her that she should goe in vnto the king, to make supplication vnto him, and to make request before him, for her people.

9 And Hatach came and told Esther the words of Mordecai.

10 ¶ Againe Esther spake vnto Hatach, and gaue him commaundement vnto Mordecai;

11 All the Kings seruants, and the people of the kings prouinces do know, that whosoeuer, whether man or woman, shall come vnto the King into the inner court, who is not called, *there is* one lawe of his to put him to death, except such to whom the King shall hold out the golden scepter, that he may liue: but I haue not beene called to come in vnto the King, these thirtie dayes.

12 And they tolde to Mordecai Esthers words.

13 Then Mordecai commanded to answere Esther; Thinke not with thy selfe

† Heb. to destroy them.
† Heb. weigh.

|| Or, oppressour.

|| Or, secretaries.

† He cloth ashes laid many

† He nuch

† He he befor

ſelfe that thou ſhalt eſcape in the kings houſe, more then all the Iewes.

14 For if thou altogether holdeſt thy peace at this time, *then* ſhall there †enlargement and deliuerance ariſe to the Iewes from another place, but thou and thy fathers houſe ſhall be deſtroyed: And who knoweth, whether thou art come to the kingdome for *ſuch* a time as this?

15 ¶ Then Eſther bade *them* returne Mordecai *this anſwere*:

16 Goe, gather together all the Iewes that are †preſent in Shuſhan, and faſt yee for me, and neither eate nor drinke three dayes, night or day: I alſo and my maidens will faſt likewiſe, and ſo will I goe in vnto the king, which *is* not according to the Law, and if I periſh, I periſh.

17 So Mordecai †went his way, and did according to all that Eſther had commanded him.

CHAP. V.

1 Eſther aduenturing on the kings fauour, obteineth the grace of the golden ſcepter, and inuiteth the king and Haman to a banquet. 6 She being incouraged by the king in her ſuit, inuiteth them to another banquet the next day. 9 Haman proud of his aduancement, repineth at the contempt of Mordecai. 14 By the counſell of Zereſh, he buildeth for him a paire of gallous.

 Ow it came to paſſe on the third day, that Eſther put on her royall *apparell*, and ſtood in the inner court of the kings houſe, ouer against the kings houſe: and the King ſate vpon his royall throne in the royall houſe, ouer against the gate of the houſe.

2 And it was ſo, when the king ſaw Eſther the Queene ſtanding in the court, *that* ſhee obtained fauour in his ſight: and the king helde out to Eſther the golden ſcepter that *was* in his hand: So Eſther drew neere, and touched the top of the ſcepter.

3 Then ſayd the King vnto her, What wilt thou, Queene Eſther? and what *is* thy request? it ſhall bee euen giuen thee to the halfe of the kingdome.

4 And Eſther anſwered, If it ſeeme good vnto the King, let the King and Haman come this day vnto the banquet that I haue prepared for him.

5 Then the King ſayd, Cauſe Haman to make haste, that he may doe as Eſther hath ſaid: So the king and Haman came to the banquet that Eſther had prepared.

6 ¶ And the king ſaid vnto Eſther at the banquet of wine, What *is* thy petition, and it ſhall be granted thee? and what is thy request? euen to the halfe of the kingdome it ſhall be performed.

7 Then anſwered Eſther, and ſaid, My petition, and my request *is*,

8 If I haue found fauour in the ſight of the king, and if it pleaſe the king to grant my petition, and † to performe my request, let the king, and Haman, come to the banquet that I ſhall prepare for them, and I wil do to morow, as the king hath ſaid.

9 ¶ Then went Haman foorth that day, ioyfull, and with a glad heart: but when Haman ſaw Mordecai in the kings gate, that hee ſtood not vp, nor mooued for him, hee was full of indignation against Mordecai.

10 Neuertheleſſe Haman refrained himſelfe, and when he came home, hee ſent and †called for his friends, and Zereſh his wife.

11 And Haman told them of the glory of his riches, and the multitude of his children, aud all the things wherein the king had promoted him, and how he had aduanced him aboue the Princes, and ſeruants of the king.

12 Haman ſaid moreouer, Yea Eſther the Queene did let no man come in with the king vnto the banquet that ſhe had prepared, but my ſelfe; and to morrow am I inuited vnto her alſo with the king.

13 Yet all this auaileth me nothing, ſo long as I ſee Mordecai the Iew ſitting at the kings gate.

14 ¶ Then ſaide Zereſh his wife, and all his friends vnto him, Let a †gallous be made of fifty cubits hie, and to morrow ſpeake thou vnto the king, that Mordecai may be hanged thereon: then goe thou in merily with the king vnto the banquet. And the thing pleaſed Haman, and hee cauſed the gallous to be made

CHAP. VI.

1 Ahaſuerus reading in the Chronicles of the good ſeruice done by Mordecai, taketh care for his reward. 4 Haman comming to ſue that Mordecai might bee hanged, vnawares giueth

re-
tion.

found

paſſed

† Heb. to doe.

Heb. cauſed to come.

† Heb. tree.

giueth counsell that hee might doe him honour, 12 complayning of his misfortune, his friends tell him of his finall destinie.

O N that night † could not the King sleepe, and hee commaunded to bring the booke of Records of the chronicles; and they were read before the king.

† Hebr. the kings sleepe fled away.

2 And it was found written, that Mordecai had told of ‖ Bigthana, and Teresh, two of the kings chamberleus, the keepers of the † doore, who sought to lay hand on the king Ahasuerus.

‖ Or, Bigthan, chap. 2. 21.
† Hebr. threshold.

3 And the king said, What honour and dignitie hath bene done to Mordecai for this? Then said the kings seruants that ministred vnto him, There is nothing done for him.

4 ¶ And the king said, Who is in the court? (now Haman was come into the outward court of the kings house, to speake vnto the king, to hang Mordecai on the gallous that hee had prepared for him.)

5 And the kings seruants said vnto him, Behold, Haman standeth in the court. And the King saide, Let him come in.

6 So Haman came in, and the king said vnto him, What shall be done vnto the man † whom the king delighteth to honour? (now Haman thought in his heart, To whom would the king delight to doe honour, more then to my selfe?)

† Hebr. in whose honour the King delighteth.

7 And Haman answered the king, For the man † whom the king delighteth to honour,

† Hebr. in whose honour the king delighteth.

8 † Let the royall apparell bee brought, † which the King vseth to weare, and the horse that the King rideth vpon, and the crowne royal which is set vpon his head:

† Hebr. let them bring the royall apparell.
† Heb. wherwith the king clotheth himselfe.

9 And let this apparell and horse bee deliuered to the hand of one of the kings most noble Princes, that they may aray the man withall, whom the king delighteth to honour, and † bring him on horsebacke through the streete of the city, and proclaime before him, Thus shal it be done to the man whom the king delighteth to honour.

† Heb. cause him to ride.

10 Then the king saide to Haman, Make haste, and take the apparell, and the horse, as thou hast said, and doe euen so to Mordecai the Iew, that sitteth at the Kings gate: † let nothing faile of all that thou hast spoken.

† Heb. suffer not a whit to fall.

11 Then tooke Haman the apparell, and the horse, & arayed Mordecai, and brought him on hors-backe through the streete of the city, and proclaimed before him: Thus shall it bee done vnto the man whom the King delighteth to honour.

12 ¶ And Mordecai came againe to the kings gate: but Haman hasted to his house, mourning, and hauing his head couered.

13 And Haman told Zeresh his wife, and all his friends, euery thing that had befallen him. Then saide his wise men, and Zeresh his wife vnto him, If Mordecai be of the seed of the Iewes, before whom thou hast begun to fall, thou shalt not preuaile against him, but shalt surely fall before him.

14 And while they were yet talking with him, came the kings chamberlens, and hasted to bring Haman vnto the banquet that Esther had prepared.

CHAP. VII.

1 Esther intertaining the King and Haman, maketh suit for her owne life, and her peoples. 5 She accuseth Haman. 7 The King in his anger vnderstanding of the gallous, which Haman had made for Mordecai, causeth him to be hanged thereon.

S O the King and Haman came † to banquet with Esther the Queene.

† Heb. drink

2 And the king said againe vnto Esther, on the second day at the banquet of wine, What is thy petition, Queene Esther, and it shalbe granted thee? and what is thy request? and it shall bee performed, euen to the halfe of the kingdome.

3 Then Esther the Queene answered, and said; If I haue found fauour in thy sight, O King, and if it please the King, let my life be giuen me at my petition, and my people at my request.

4 For we are sold, I, and my people, † to be destroyed, to be slaine, and to perish: but if we had bene sold for bondmen, and bondwomen, I had held my tongue, although the enemy could not counteruaile the kings dammage.

† Heb they s destro kil, an to per

5 ¶ Then the king Ahasuerus answered, & said vnto Esther the Queene: Who is he? and where is he, † that durst presume in his heart to do so?

† Heb heart filled w

6 And Esther said, † The aduersary and enemie, is this wicked Haman. Then

† Heb man sary.

at the
ence of.

Then Haman was afraid ||before the King and the Queene.

7 ¶ And the king arising from the banquet of wine in his wrath, *went* into the palace garden : and Haman stood vp to make request for his life to Esther the Queene : for he saw that there was euill determined against him by the King.

8 Then the king returned out of the palace garden, into the place of the banquet of wine, and Haman was fallen vpon the bed whereon Esther *was.* Then said the King, Will hee force the Queene also + before me in the house ? As the word went out of the Kings mouth, they couered Hamans face.

eb. with

9 And Harbonah one of the chamberlaines, said before the king ; Behold also the +gallowes, fiftie cubites high, which Haman had made for Mordecai, who had spoken good for the king, standeth in the house of Haman. Then the king said, Hang him thereon.

eb. tree.

10 So they hanged Haman on the gallows that he had prepared for Mordecai. Then was the Kings wrath pacified.

CHAP. VIII.

1 Mordecai is aduanced. 3 Esther maketh suite to reuerse Hamans letters. 7 Ahasuerus granteth to the Iewes to defend themselues. 15 Mordecais honour, and the Iewes ioy.

O N that day did the King Ahasuerus giue the house of Haman, the Iewes enemy, vnto Esther the Queene ; and Mordecai came before the King ; for Esther hade told what he *was* vnto her.

2 And the king tooke off his Ring which he had taken from Haman, and gaue it vnto Mordecai. And Esther set Mordecai ouer the house of Haman.

eb. and
wept and
night

3 ¶ And Esther spake yet againe before the king, and fell downe at his feet, +and besought him with teares, to put away the mischiefe of Haman the Agagite, and his deuice, that he had deuised against the Iewes.

4 Then the king helde out the golden scepter toward Esther. So Esther arose, and stood before the king,

5 And said, If it please the king, and if I haue found fauour in his sight, and the thing seeme right before the king, and I bee pleasing in his eyes, let it be written to reuerse +the letters deuised

eb. the
ice.

by Haman the sonne of Hammedatha the Agagite, ||which hee wrote to destroy the Iewes, which are in all the kings prouinces.

| Or, who
wrote.

6 For how can I +endure to see the euill that shall come vnto my people ? or how can I endure to see the destruction of my kinred ?

† Heb. be a-
ble that I
may see.

7 ¶ Then the king Ahasuerus said vnto Esther the Queene, and to Mordecai the Iewe, Behold, I haue giuen Esther the house of Haman, and him they haue hanged vpon the gallowes, because hee layde his hand vpon the Iewes.

8 Write ye also for the Iewes, as it liketh you, in the Kings name, and seale it with the Kings ring : for the writing which is written in the Kings name, and sealed with the Kings ring, *may no man reuerse.

* See Chap.
1. 19.

9 Then were the kings scribes called at that time, in the third moneth, (that is, the month Siuan) on the three and twentieth day thereof, and it was written (according to all that Mordecai commanded) vnto the Iewes, and to the Lieutenants, and the deputies and rulers of the prouinces, which are from India vnto Ethiopia, an hundred, twentie and seuen prouinces, vnto euery prouince according to the writing thereof, and vnto euery people after their language, and to the Iewes, according to their writing, and according to their language.

10 And he wrote in the king Ahasuerus name, and sealed *it* with the kings Ring, and sent letters by Postes, on horsebacke, *and* riders on mules, camels, *and* yong dromedaries :

11 Wherein the King granted the Iewes, which were in euery citie, to gather themselues together, and to stand for their life, to destroy, to slay, and to cause to perish all the power of the people and prouince that would assault them, *both* little ones, and women, and *to take* the spoile of them for a pray :

12 Vpon one day, in all the prouinces of king Ahasuerus, *namely* vpon the thirteenth day of the twelfth moneth, which *is* the moneth Adar.

13 The copy of the writing, for a commandement to bee giuen in euery prouince, was +published vnto all people, and that the Iewes should be readie against that day, to auenge themselues on their enemies.

† Heb. re-
uealed.

14 *So* the posts that rode vpon mules *and* camels went out, being hastened, and pressed on by the kings commandement, and the decree was giuen at Shushan the palace.

15 ¶ And Mordecai went out from the presence of the king, in royall apparell, of ||blew and white, and with a great crowne of gold, and with a garment of fine linnen, and purple, and the citie of Shushan reioyced, and was glad:

16 The Iewes had light and gladnesse, and ioy and honour.

17 And in euery prouince, and in euery city, whithersoeuer the kings commandement, and his decree came, the Iewes had ioy and gladnes, a feast and a good day: And many of the people of the land became Iewes; for the feare of the Iewes fell vpon them.

CHAP. IX.

1 The Iewes, (the rulers, for feare of Mordecai helping them) slay their enemies, with the ten sonnes of Haman. 12 Ahasuerus at the request of Esther, granteth another day of slaughter, and Hamans sonnes to be hanged. 20 The two daies of Purim are made festiuall.

Ow in the twelfth month (that is the moneth Adar) on the thirteenth day of the same, when the Kings commaundement and his decree drew neere to bee put in execution, in the day that the enemies of the Iewes hoped to haue power ouer them: (though it was turned to the contrary, that the Iewes had rule ouer them that hated them.)

2 The Iewes gathered themselues together in their cities, throughout all the prouinces of the king Ahasuerus, to lay hand on such as sought their hurt, and no man could withstand them: for the feare of them fell vpon all people.

3 And all the rulers of the prouinces, and the Lieutenants, and the deputies, and †officers of the king, helped the Iewes: because the feare of Mordecai fell vpon them.

4 For Mordecai *was* great in the kings house, and his fame went out, throughout all the prouinces: for this man Mordecai waxed greater and greater.

5 Thus the Iewes smote all their enemies with the stroke of the sword,

and slaughter, and destruction, and did †what they would vnto those that hated them.

6 And in Shushan the palace the Iewes slew and destroyed fiue hundred men:

7 And Parshandatha, and Dalphon, and Aspatha,

8 And Poratha, and Adalia, and Aridatha,

9 And Parmashta, and Arisai, and Aridai, and Vaiezatha,

10 The ten sonnes of Haman the sonne of Hammedatha, the enemie of the Iewes, slew they, but on the spoile laid they not their hand.

11 On that day, the number of those that were slaine in Shushan the palace, †was brought before the king.

12 ¶ And the king said vnto Esther the Queene; The Iewes haue slaine and destroied fiue hundred men in Shushan the palace, & the ten sonnes of Haman; what haue they done in the rest of the kings prouinces? now what *is* thy petition? and it shalbe granted thee: or what *is* thy request further? and it shall be done.

13 Then said Esther, If it please the king, Let it bee granted to the Iewes which *are* in Shushan, to doe to morow also, according vnto this dayes decree, and †let Hamans ten sonnes be hanged vpon the gallous.

14 And the king commanded it so to be done; and the decree was giuen at Shushan, and they hanged Hamans ten sonnes.

15 For the Iewes that *were* in Shushan, gathered themselues together on the fourteenth day also of the moneth Adar, and slewe three hundred men at Shushan: but on the pray they laid not their hand.

16 But the other Iewes that *were* in the kings prouinces, gathered themselues together, & stood for their liues, and had rest from their enemies, and slew of their foes seuenty and fiue thousand, but they laid not their handes on the pray.

17 On the thirteenth day of the moneth Adar, and on the fourteenth day †of the same, rested they, and made it a day of feasting and gladnes.

18 But the Iewes that *were* at Shushan, assembled together on the thirteenth *day* therof, and on the fourteenth thereof; and on the fifteenth *day* of the same,

Marginal notes left column:
‖ Or, violet.

† Heb. those which did the busines that belonged to the King.

Marginal notes right column:
† Heb. according to t. will.

† Heb. co

† Hebr. men han

† Heb. ir

same, they rested, and made it a day of feasting and gladnesse.

19 Therefore the Iewes of the villages, that dwelt in the vnwalled townes, made the fourteenth day of the moneth Adar, *a day* of gladnesse and feasting, and a good day, and of sending portions one to another.

20 ¶ And Mordecai wrote these things, and sent letters vnto all the Iewes, that *were* in all the prouinces of the king Ahasuerus, *both* nigh & farre,

21 To stablish *this* among them, that they should keepe the fourteenth day of the moneth Adar, and the fifteenth day of the same, yeerely:

22 As the dayes wherein the Iewes rested from their enemies, & the moneth which was turned vnto them, from sorrow to ioy, and from mourning into a good day: that they should make them daies of feasting and ioy, and of sending portions one to another, and gifts to the poore.

23 And the Iewes vndertooke to doe, as they had begun, and as Mordecai had written vnto them:

24 Because Haman the sonne of Hammedatha the Agagite, the enemie of all the Iewes, had deuised against the Iewes to destroy them, and had cast Pur (that *is*, the lot) to † consume them, and to destroy them. _{† crush.}

25 But † when *Esther* came before the king, he commanded by letters, that his wicked deuice which he deuised against the Iewes, should returne vpon his owne head, and that he and his sonnes, should be hanged on the gallous. _{† when me.}

26 Wherefore they called these dayes Purim, after the name of ‖ Pur: therefore for all the words of this letter, and of *that* which they had seene concerning this matter, and which had come vnto them, _{‖ is,}

27 The Iewes ordeined, and tooke vpon them, and vpon their seed, and vpon all such as ioyned themselues vnto them, so as it should not † faile, that they would keepe these two dayes, according to their writing, and according to their *appointed* time, euery yeere: _{† passe.}

28 And that these dayes *should be* remembred, and kept throughout euery generation, euery family, euery prouince, and euery citie, and that these dayes of Purim should not † faile from among the Iewes, nor the memoriall of them † perish from their seed. _{† Heb. passe.} _{† Hebr. be ended.}

29 Then Esther the Queene, the daughter of Abihail, and Mordecai the Iew, wrote with † all authoritie, to confirme this second letter of Purim. _{† Hebr. all strength.}

30 And hee sent the letters vnto all the Iewes, to the hundred, twentie and seuen prouinces of the kingdome of Ahasuerus, *with* wordes of peace and trueth:

31 To confirme these dayes of Purim, in their times *appointed*, according as Mordecai the Iew, and Esther the Queene had enioyned them, and as they had decreed † for themselues and for their seed, the matters of the fastings and their cry. _{† Hebr. for their soules.}

32 And the decree of Esther confirmed these matters of Purim, and it was written in the booke.

CHAP. X.

1 Ahasuerus his greatnesse. 3 Mordecais aduancement.

ANd the king Ahasuerus layde a tribute vpon the land, and vpon the Isles of the sea.

2 And all the actes of his power, and of his might, and the declaration of the greatnesse of Mordecai, whereunto the king † aduanced him, *are* they not written in the booke of the Chronicles of the kings of Media and Persia? _{† Heb. made him great.}

3 For Mordecai the Iew *was* next vnto King Ahasuerus, and great among the Iewes, and accepted of the multitude of his brethren, seeking the wealth of his people, and speaking peace to all his seed.

¶ THE

¶THE BOOKE OF Iob.

CHAP. I.

1 The holinesse, riches, and religious care of Iob for his children. 6 Satan appearing before God, by calumniation obtaineth leaue to tempt Iob. 13 Vnderstanding of the losse of his goods and children, in his mourning hee blesseth GOD.

THere was a man in the land of Vz, whose name *was* Iob, and that man was *perfect and vpright, and one that feared God, and eschewed euill.

* Chap. 2. 3.

2 And there were borne vnto him seuen sonnes, and three daughters.

3 His ‖substance also was seuen thousand sheepe, and three thousand camels, and fiue hundred yoke of oxen, and fiue hundred shee asses, and a very great ‖houshold; so that this man was the greatest of all the †men of the East.

‖ *Or, cattell.*

‖ *Or, husbandrie.*

† *Heb. sonnes of the East.*

4 And his sonnes went and feasted in *their* houses, euery one his day, and sent and called for their three sisters, to eate and to drinke with them.

5 And it was so, when the dayes of *their* feasting were gone about, that Iob sent and sanctified them, and rose vp early in the morning, and offered burnt offerings *according* to the number of them all: For Iob said, It may be that my sonnes haue sinned, and *cursed God in their hearts: Thus did Iob †continually.

* 1. King. 21. 10, 13.

† *Heb. all the dayes.*

6 ¶ Now there was a day, when the sons of God came to present themselues before the LORD, and †Satan came also †among them.

† *Heb. the aduersarie.*

† *Heb. in the midst of them.*

7 And the LORD said vnto Satan, Whence commest thou? Then Satan answered the LORD, and sayde, From going to and fro in the *earth, and from walking vp and downe in it.

* 1.

8 And the LORD sayd vnto Satan, †Hast thou considered my seruant Iob, that *there is* none like him in the earth? a perfect and an vpright man, one that feareth God, and escheweth euill?

† *He thou hear*

9 Then Satan answered ẏ LORD, and sayd, Doeth Iob feare God for nought?

10 Hast not thou made an hedge about him, and about his house, and about all that he hath on euery side? thou hast blessed the worke of his hands, and his ‖substance is increased in the land.

‖ *Or,*

11 But put foorth thine hand now, and touch all that he hath, †and he will curse thee to thy face.

† *He curs not t face*

12 And the LORD said vnto Satan, Behold, all that hee hath is in thy †power, onely vpon himselfe put not foorth thine hand. So Satan went forth from the presence of the LORD.

† *He*

13 ¶ And there was a day, when his sonnes and his daughters were eating and drinking wine in their eldest brothers house:

14 And there came a messenger vnto Iob, and said, The oxen were plowing, and the asses feeding beside them,

15 And the Sabeans fell *vpon them*, and tooke them away: yea they haue slaine the seruants with the edge of the sword, and I onely am escaped alone, to tell thee.

16 While he was yet speaking, there came also another, and said, ‖The fire of God is fallen from heauen, and hath burnt vp the sheepe, and the seruants, and consumed them, and I onely am escaped alone, to tell thee.

‖ *Or fire*

17 While he was yet speaking, there came also another, and said, The Caldeans

deans made out three bands, and † fell vpon the camels, and haue caried them away, yea, and slaine the seruants with the edge of the sword, and I onely am escaped alone, to tell thee.

18 While he was yet speaking, there came also another, & said, Thy sonnes, and thy daughters, were eating and drinking wine in their eldest brothers house.

19 And beholde, there came a great winde † from the wildernes, and smote the foure corners of the house, and it fell vpon the yong men, and they are dead, and I onely am escaped alone to tell thee.

20 Then Iob arose, and rent his ‖ mantle, and shaued his head, and fell downe vpon the ground and worshipped,

21 And said, * Naked came I out of my mothers wombe, and naked shall I returne thither : the LORD gaue, and the LORD hath taken away, blessed be the Name of the LORD.

22 In all this Iob sinned not, nor ‖ charged God foolishly.

CHAP. II.

1 Satan appearing againe before God, obtaineth further leaue to tempt Iob. 7 He smiteth him with sore boiles. 9 Iob reproueth his wife, moouing him to curse God. 11 His three friends condole with him in silence.

Gaine there was a day when the sonnes of God came to present themselues before the LORD, and Satan came also among them to present himselfe before the LORD.

2 And the LORD said vnto Satan, From whence commest thou ? And * Satan answered the LORD, and said, From going to & fro in the earth, and from walking vp and downe in it.

3 * And the LORD said vnto Satan, Hast thou considered my seruant Iob, that there is none like him in the earth; a perfect and an vpright man, one that feareth God, and escheweth euill ? and still hee holdeth fast his integritie, although thou moouedst mee against him, † to destroy him without cause.

4 And Satan answered the LORD, and said, Skinne for skinne, yea all that a man hath, wil he giue for his life.

5 But put foorth thine hand now, and touch his bone and his flesh, and he will curse thee to thy face.

6 And the LORD said vnto Satan, Behold, hee is in thine hand, ‖ but saue his life.

7 ¶ So went Satan foorth from the presence of the LORD, and smote Iob with sore biles, from the sole of his foote vnto his crowne.

8 And hee tooke him a potsheard to scrape himselfe withall; and hee sate downe among the ashes.

9 ¶ Then saide his wife vnto him, Doest thou still reteine thine integritie? Curse God, and die.

10 But he said vnto her, Thou speakest as one of the foolish women speaketh; what ? shall wee receiue good at the hand of God, and shall wee not receiue euill ? In all this did not Iob sinne with his lippes.

11 ¶ Now when Iobs three friends heard of all this euill, that was come vpon him, they came euery one from his owne place : Eliphaz the Temanite, and Bildad the Shuhite, and Zophar the Naamathite; for they had made an appointment together to come to mourne with him, and to comfort him.

12 And when they lift vp their eyes afarre off, and knew him not, they lifted vp their voice, and wept; and they rent euery one his mautle, and sprinckled dust vpon their heades toward heauen.

13 So they sate downe with him vpon the ground seuen dayes, and seuen nights, and none spake a word vnto him; for they saw that his griefe was very great.

CHAP. III.

1 Iob curseth the day, and seruices of his birth. 13 The ease of death. 20 He complaineth of life, because of his anguish.

Fter this, opened Iob his mouth, and cursed his day.

2 And Iob † spake, and said,

3 * Let the day perish, wherein I was borne, and the night in which it was said, There is a man-childe conceiued.

4 Let that day bee darkenesse, let not God regard it from aboue, neither let the light shine vpon it.

5 Let

Marginal notes (left column)
r.
ed.

.from &c.

robe.

cles. 5.
tim.

attri-
l folly
d.

ap. 1.

ap. 1.
1. & 8.

br. to
llow him

Marginal notes (right column)
‖ Or, onely.

† Hebr. answered.

* Chap. 10.
18, 19. iere.
20. 14.

Or, challenge it.
Or, let them terrifie it, as those who haue a bitter day.
Or, let it not reioyce among the dayes.

5 Let darkenes and the shadowe of death ‖ staine it, let a cloud dwell vpon it, ‖ let the blacknes of the day terrifie it.

6 As for that night, let darkenesse seaze vpon it, ‖ let it not be ioyned vnto the dayes of the yeere, let it not come into the number of the moneths.

7 Loe, let that night be solitarie, let no ioyfull voice come therein.

‖ *Or, Leuiathan.*

8 Let them curse it that curse the day, who are ready to raise vp ‖ their mourning.

† *Heb. the eye lids of the morning.*

9 Let the starres of the twilight thereof be darke, let it looke for light, but *haue* none, neither let it see † the dawning of the day:

10 Because it shut not vp the doores of my *mothers* wombe, nor hid sorrow from mine eyes.

11 Why died I not from the wombe? *why* did I *not* giue vp the ghost when I came out of the bellie?

12 Why did the knees preuent mee? or why the breasts, that I should sucke?

13 For now should I haue lien still and beene quiet, I should haue slept; then had I bene at rest,

14 With Kings and counsellers of the earth, which built desolate places for themselues,

15 Or with Princes that *had* golde, who filled their houses with siluer:

16 Or as an hidden vntimely birth, I had not bene; as infants *which* neuer saw light.

† *Heb. wearied in strength.*

17 There the wicked cease *from* troubling: and there the † wearie be at rest.

18 *There* the prisoners rest together, they heare not the voice of the oppressour.

19 The small and great are there, and the seruant *is* free from his master.

20 Wherefore is light giuen to him that is in misery, and life vnto the bitter *in* soule?

† *Heb. wait.*

21 Which † long for death, but it *commeth* not, and dig for it more then for hid treasures:

22 Which reioice exceedingly, *and* are glad when they can finde the graue?

*Chap. 19. 8

23 Why is light giuen to a man, whose way is hid, * and whom God hath hedged in?

† *Heb. before my meat.*

24 For my sighing commeth † before I eate, and my roarings are powred out like the waters.

† *Heb. I feared a feare, and it came vpon me.*

25 For † the thing which I greatly feared is come vpon me, and that which I was afraid of, is come vnto me.

26 I was not in safetie, neither had I rest, neither was I quiet: yet trouble came.

CHAP. IIII.

1 Eliphaz reprooueth Iob for want of religion. 7 He teacheth Gods iudgements to bee not for the righteous, but for the wicked. 12 His fearefull vision, to humble the excellencie of Creatures before God.

Hen Eliphaz the Temanite answered, and said,

2 *If* we assay † to commune with thee, wilt thou be grieued? But † who can withhold himselfe from speaking?

† *Hebr. a word.*

† *Heb. can refrain.*

3 Beholde, Thou hast instructed many, and thou hast strengthened the weake hands.

4 Thy words haue vpholden him that was falling, and thou hast strengthened † the feeble knees.

† *Hebr. bowing knees.*

5 But now it is come vpon thee, and thou faintest, it toucheth thee, and thou art troubled.

6 *Is* not this thy feare, thy confidence; the vprightnesse of thy wayes and thy hope?

7 Remember, I pray thee, who *euer* perished, being innocent? or where were the righteous cut off?

* Prou ose 10.

8 * Euen as I haue seene, they that plow iniquity, and sow wickednsse, reape the same.

* That his ang Esa. 3

9 By the blast of God they perish, and by the breath of his * nostrils are they consumed.

10 The roaring of the Lyon, and the voice of the fierce Lyon, and the teeth of the yong Lyons are broken.

11 The old Lyon perisheth for lacke of pray, and the stout Lyons whelpes are scattered abroad.

† *Heb. stealtl*

12 Nowe a thing was † secretly brought to me, and mine eare receiued a litle thereof.

13 In thoughts from the visions of the night, when deepe sleepe falleth on men:

† *Heb. mee.*
† *Heb. multin my bo*

14 Feare † came vpon me, and trembling, which made † all my bones to shake.

15 Then a spirit passed before my face: the haire of my flesh stood vp.

‖ *Or, 3 a still*

16 It stood still, but I could not discerne the forme thereof: an image *was* before mine eyes, ‖ *there was* silence, and I heard a voyce, *saying,*

17 Shall

17 Shall mortall man be more iust then God? shall a man bee more pure then his maker?

18 Behold, hee *put no trust in his seruants; || and his Angels hee charged with folly:

19 Howe much lesse *on* them that dwell in *houses of clay, whose foundation is in the dust, which are crushed before the moth.

20 They are †destroyed from morning to euening: they perish for euer, without any regarding *it*.

21 Doeth not their excellencie *which is* in them, goe away? they die, euen without wisedome.

CHAP. V.

1 The harme of inconsideration. 3 The ende of the wicked is misery. 6 God is to be regarded in affliction. 17 The happy ende of Gods correction.

All now, if there be any that wil answere thee, and to which of the Saints wilt thou ||turne?

2 For wrath killeth the foolish man, and || enuy slayeth the silly one.

3 I haue seene the foolish taking roote: but suddenly I cursed his habitation.

4 His children are farre from safetie, and they are crushed in the gate, neither *is there* any to deliuer *them*.

5 Whose haruest the hungry eateth vp, and taketh it euen out of the thorns, and the robber swalloweth vp their substance.

6 Although || affliction commeth not forth of the dust, neither doeth trouble spring out of the ground:

7 Yet man is borne vnto || trouble, as †the sparkes flie vpward.

8 I would seeke vnto God, and vnto God would I commit my cause:

9 *Which doth great things †& vnsearchable: marueilous things †without number.

10 Who giueth raine vpon the earth, and sendeth waters vpon the †fields:

11 *To set vp on high those that be low; that those which mourne, may be exalted to safetie.

12 *Hee disappointeth the deuices of the craftie, so that their hands ||cannot performe *their* enterprise.

13 *He taketh the wise in their *owne*

craftinesse: and the counsell of the froward is caried headlong.

14 * They ||meete with darkenesse in the day time, and grope in the noone day as in the night.

15 But he saueth the poore from the sword, from their mouth, and from the hand of the mightie.

16 *So the poore hath hope, and iniquitie stoppeth her mouth.

17 *Behold, happy *is* the man whom God correcteth: therefore despise not thou the chastening of the Almightie.

18 *For he maketh sore, and bindeth vp: he woundeth, and his hands make whole.

19 *Hee shall deliuer thee in sixe troubles, yea in seuen there shall no euill touch thee.

20 In famine he shall redeeme thee from death: and in warre from the †power of the sword.

21 Thou shalt be hidde ||from the scourge of the tongue: neither shalt thou be afraid of destruction, when it commeth.

22 At destruction and famine thou shalt laugh: neither shalt thou be afraid of the beasts of the earth.

23 *For thou *shalt be* in league with the stones of the field: and the beasts of the field shall be at peace with thee.

24 And thou shalt know that thy ||tabernacle *shall bee* in peace; and thou shalt visite thy habitation, and shalt not || sinne.

25 Thou shalt know also that thy seede shalbe ||great, and thine offspring as the grasse of the earth.

26 Thou shalt come to thy graue in a full age, like as a shocke of corne †commeth in, in his season.

27 Loe this, wee haue searched it, so it *is*; heare it, and know thou it †for thy good.

CHAP. VI.

1 Iob sheweth that his complaints are not causelesse. 8 Hee wisheth for death, wherein he is assured of comfort. 14 He reproueth his friends of vnkindnesse.

Vt Iob answered, and sayd,

2 Oh that my griefe were throughly weighed, and my calamitie †layd in the balances together.

3 For now it would be heauier then the

Marginal notes

ap. 15.
. pet.

, nor in
Angels,
hom
ut light.
Cor. 5. 1.

b. bean
pieces.

, looke.

, indig-
ion.

, iniquity.

, labour.
eb. the
nes of the
ning
e., lift
to flie.
ha. 9. 10.
. 11. 33.
eb. and
re is no
rch.
eb. till
re be no
mber.
eb. out-
ces.
sa. 113. 6.
sam. 2. 7.
eh. 4. 15.
. 33. 10.
8. 10.
, cannot
forme a
Cor. 3.

* Deut. 28.
29.
Or, runne
into.

* Psal. 107.
42.

* Pro. 3. 12.
iames 1. 12.
heb. 12. 5.
apoc. 3. 9.

* Deut. 32.
39. 1. sam.
2. 6. isa. 30.
26. hos. 6. 1.

* Psal. 91.3.

† Heb. from
the hands.
Or, when
the tongue
scourgeth.

* Hos. 2. 18.

Or, that
peace is thy
tabernacle.
Or, erre.

Or, much.

† Heb. ascen-
deth.

† Heb. for
thy selfe.

† Heb. lifted
vp.

the sand of the sea, therefore my words are || swallowed vp.

4 * For the arrowes of the Almightie are within me, the poyson whereof drinketh vp my spirit : the terrors of God doe set themselues in aray against mee.

5 Doeth the wilde asse bray † when he hath grasse ? or loweth the oxe ouer his fodder ?

6 Can that which is vnsauery, bee eaten without salt ? or is there any taste in the white of an egge ?

7 The things *that* my soule refused to touch, are as my sorrowfull meat.

8 O that I might haue my request ! and that God would graunt mee † the thing that I long for !

9 Euen that it would please God to destroy mee, that he would let loose his hand, and cut me off.

10 Then should I yet haue comfort, yea I would harden my selfe in sorrow ; let him not spare, for I haue not concealed the words of the holy One.

11 What *is* my strength, that I should hope ? and what *is* mine ende, that I should prolong my life ?

12 *Is* my strength the strength of stones ? or *is* my flesh † of brasse ?

13 *Is* not my helpe in me ? and *is* wisedome driuen quite from me ?

14 † To him that is afflicted, pitie *should be shewed* from his friend ; But he forsaketh the feare of the Almighty.

15 My brethren haue delt deceitfully as a brooke, & as the streame of brookes they passe away,

16 Which are blackish by reason of the yce, *and* wherein the snow is hid :

17 What time they waxe warme, † they vanish : † when it is hot, they are † consumed out of their place.

18 The pathes of their way are turned aside ; they goe to nothing, and perish.

19 The troupes of Tema looked, the companies of Sheba waited for them.

20 They were confounded because they had hoped ; they came thither, and were ashamed.

21 || For now ye are † nothing ; ye see *my* casting downe, and are afraid.

22 Did I say, Bring vnto mee ? or giue a reward for me of your substance ?

23 Or deliuer me from the enemies hand, or redeeme me from the hand of the mighty ?

24 Teach me, and I will hold my

tongue : and cause mee to vnderstand wherein I haue erred.

25 How forcible are right wordes ? but what doeth your arguing reproue ?

26 Do ye imagine to reproue words, and the speeches of one that is desperate, which *are* as winde ?

27 Yea, † ye ouerwhelme the fatherlesse, and you digge *a pit* for your friend.

28 Now therefore be content, looke vpon mee, for it is † euident vnto *you*, if I lie.

29 Returne, I pray you, let it not be iniquitie ; yea returne againe : my righteousnesse || *is* in it.

30 Is there iniquitie in my tongue ? cannot † my taste discerne peruerse things ?

CHAP. VII.

1 Iob excuseth his desire of death. 12 He complaineth of his owne restlesnesse, 17 and Gods watchfulnesse.

IS there not || an appointed time to man vpon earth ? *are* not his dayes also like the dayes of an hireling ?

2 As a seruant † earnestly desireth the shadow, and as an hireling looketh for *the reward* of his worke :

3 So am I made to possesse moneths of vanitie, and wearisome nights are appointed to me.

4 When I lie downe, I say, When shall I arise, and the † night be gone ? and I am full of tossings to and fro, vnto the dawning of the day.

5 My flesh is cloathed with wormes and clods of dust, my skinne is broken, and become loathsome.

6 * My dayes are swifter then a weauers shuttle, and are spent without hope.

7 O remember that my life is winde ; mine eye † shall no more || see good.

8 The eye of him that hath seene me, shall see mee no *more* : thine eyes *are* vpon me, and I || *am* not.

9 *As* the cloud is consumed and vanisheth away : so he that goeth downe to the graue, shall come vp no *more*.

10 Hee shall returne no more to his house : neither shall his place know him any more.

11 Therefore I will not refraine my mouth, I wil speake in the anguish of

Left margin notes:

|| That is, I want words to expresse my griefe.
* Psal. 38. 2.

† Hebr. at grasse.

† Hebr. my expectation.

† He. brasen.

† Hebr. to him that melteth.

† Hebr. they are cut off.
† Hebr. in the heat thereof.
† Hebr. extinguished.

|| Or, for now ye are like to them. Hebr. to it.
† Hebr. Not.

Right margin notes:

† Heb. cause vpon.

† Heb. your fi

|| That in this ter.

† Heb. palate.

|| Or, a fure.

† Heb. peth i

† Heb. euenin measu

* Iob psal. 9 and 10 and 16 isa. 40 iam. 4.
† Hebr. not re
|| To se is, to e

|| That can liu longer

of my spirit, I will complaine in the bitternesse of my soule.

12 Am I a sea, or a whale, that thou settest a watch ouer me?

13 When I say, My bed shal comfort me, my couch shall ease my complaint:

14 Then thou skarest mee with dreames, and terrifiest me through visions.

15 So that my soule chooseth strangling : *and* death rather †then my life.

16 I loath *it*, I would not liue alway : let me alone, for my dayes *are* vanitie.

17 *What is man, that thou shouldest magnifie him? and that thou shouldest set thine heart vpon him?

18 And *that* thou shouldest visite him euery morning, *and* trie him euery moment?

19 How long wilt thou not depart from me? nor let me alone till I swallow downe my spittle?

20 I haue sinned, what shall I doe vnto thee, O thou preseruer of men? why hast thou set me as a mark against thee, so that I am a burden to my selfe?

21 And why doest thou not pardon my transgression, and take away mine iniquitie? for now shall I sleepe in the dust, and thou shalt seeke me in the morning, but I shall not be.

CHAP. VIII.

1 Bildad sheweth Gods iustice, in dealing with men according to their workes. 8 He alledgeth antiquitie to proue the certaine destruction of the Hypocrite. 20 Hee applieth Gods iust dealing to Iob.

Hen answered Bildad the Shuhite, and said,

2 How long wilt thou speake these things? and *how long* shall the wordes of thy mouth *be like* a strong wind?

3 *Doth God peruert iudgement? or doth the Almightie peruert iustice?

4 If thy children haue sinned against him, and he haue cast them away †for their transgression:

5 *If thou wouldest seeke vnto God betimes, and make thy supplication to the Almightie:

6 If thou *wert* pure and vpright, surely now he would awake for thee, and make the habitation of thy righteousnes prosperous.

7 Though thy beginning was small, yet thy latter end should greatly increase.

8 *For enquire, I pray thee, of the former age, and prepare thy selfe to the search of their fathers.

9 (For *we are but of* yesterday, and know †nothing, because our dayes vpon earth *are* a shadow.)

10 Shall not they teach thee, *and* tell thee, & vtter words out of their heart?

11 Can the rush growe vp without myre? can the flag growe without water?

12 *Whilest it *is* yet in his greennesse, *and* not cut downe, it withereth before any *other* herbe.

13 So *are* the paths of all that forget God, and the *hypocrites hope shall perish:

14 Whose hope shall be cut off, and whose trust shall be †a spiders web.

15 He shall leane vpon his house, but it shall not stand: he shal hold it fast, but it shall not endure.

16 He *is* greene before the sunne, and his branch shooteth forth in his garden.

17 His roots are wrapped about the heape, *and* seeth the place of stones.

18 If he destroy him from his place, then *it* shal denie him, *saying*, I haue not seene thee.

19 Beholde, this *is* the ioy of his way, and out of the earth shall others grow.

20 Behold, God will not cast away a perfect man, neither will hee †helpe the euill doers:

21 Till he fill thy mouth *with* laughing, and thy lips *with* †reioycing.

22 They that hate thee shall be cloathed with shame, and the dwelling place of the wicked † shall come to nought.

CHAP. IX.

1 Iob acknowledging Gods iustice, sheweth there is no contending with him. 22 Mans innocencie is not to be condemned by afflictions.

Hen Iob answered, and said,

2 I know it *is* so of a trueth : but howe should *man be iust ‖ with God.

3 If he will contend with him, he cannot answere him one of a thousand.

4 He is wise in heart, and mightie in strength : who hath hardened *himselfe* against him, and hath prospered?

5 Which

Margin notes

* Deut. 4. 32.

* See chap. 7. 6. gen. 47 9. 1. chron. 29. 15. psal. 144. 4. psal. 39. 14.
† Heb. not.

* Psal. 129. 6. ier. 17. 6.

* Iob. 11. 20 and 18. 14. psal. 112. 10 prou. 10. 28
† Heb. a spiders house.

† Heb. take the vngodly by the hand.
† Heb. shouting for ioy.
† Heb. shall not be.

* Psal. 143. 2.
‖ Or, before God.

then *ves.*

. 8. 4. 4. 3. . 6.

32. 4 - 19. 7 14.

in the *their* *sion* . 22.

5 Which remoueth the mountains, and they know not: which ouerturneth them in his anger:

6 Which shaketh the earth out of her place, & the pillars thereof tremble:

7 Which commandeth the Sunne, and it riseth not: and sealeth vp the starres.

*Gen. 1. 6.
†Hebr. heights.

8 *Which alone spreadeth out the heauens, and treadeth vpon the ||waues of the Sea.

*Amos 5. 8.
iob. 38. 31, &c.
†Heb. Ash, Cesil, and Cimah.
*See Chap. 5. 9.

9 *Which maketh † Arcturus, Orion and Pleiades, and the chambers of the South.

10 *Which doeth great things past finding out, yea and wonders without number.

11 Loe, hee goeth by me, and I see him not: he passeth on also, but I perceiue him not.

*Isal. 45. 9.
iere. 18. 6.
rom. 9. 20.
†Heb. who can turne him away?
†Heb. helpers of pride, or strength.

12 *Behold, he taketh away, †who can hinder him? who will say vnto him, What doest thou?

13 If God will not withdraw his anger, the †proud helpers doe stoupe vnder him.

14 How much lesse shall I answere him, and choose out my words to reason with him?

15 Whom, though I were righteous, yet would I not answere, but I would make supplication to my Iudge.

16 If I had called, and he had answered me, yet would I not beleeue that he had hearkened vnto my voice:

17 For he breaketh me with a tempest, and multiplieth my wounds without cause.

18 Hee will not suffer me to take my breath, but filleth me with bitternesse.

19 If I speake of strength, loe, hee is strong: and if of iudgement, who shall set me a time to pleade?

20 If I iustifie my selfe, mine owne mouth shall condemne me: If I say, I am perfect, it shall also prooue me peruerse.

21 Though I were perfect, yet would I not know my soule: I would despise my life.

22 This is one thing, therefore I said it; he destroyeth the perfect and the wicked.

23 If the scourge slay suddenly, hee will laugh at the triall of the innocent.

24 The earth is giuen into the hand of the wicked: he couereth the faces of the Iudges thereof; if not, where, and who is hee?

25 Now my dayes are swifter then a Poste: they flee away, they see no good.

26 They are passed away as the †||swift ships: as the Eagle that hasteth to the pray.

†Hebr. of desire.
||Or, sh of Ebeh

27 If I say, I will not forget my complaint, I will leaue off my heauinesse, and comfort my selfe.

28 I am afraid of all my sorrowes, I know that thou wilt not holde me innocent.

29 If I be wicked, why then labour I in vaine?

30 If I wash my selfe with snow water, and make my handes neuer so cleane:

31 Yet shalt thou plunge me in the ditch, and mine owne clothes shall ||abhorre me.

||Or, m me to be horred.

32 For he is not a man as I am, that I should answere him, and we should come together in iudgement.

33 Neither is there †any ||dayes-man betwixt vs, that might lay his hand vpon vs both.

†Heb. that sho argus.
||Or, v pire.

34 Let him take his rodde away from me, & let not his feare terrifie me:

35 Then would I speake, and not feare him; †but it is not so with me.

†Heb. am not with my selfe.

CHAP. X.

1 Iob, taking libertie of complaint, expostulateth with God about his afflictions. 18 He complaineth of life, and craueth a little ease before death.

M Y soule is ||weary of my life, I will leaue my complaint vpon my selfe; I will speake in the bitternesse of my soule.

||Or, cu while I

2 I will say vnto God, Doe not condemne mee; shewe me wherefore thou contendest with me.

3 Is it good vnto thee, that thou shouldest oppresse? that thou shouldest despise †the worke of thine hands? and shine vpon the counsell of the wicked?

†Heb. labour thine h

4 Hast thou eyes of flesh? or seest thou as man seeth?

5 Are thy dayes as the dayes of man? are thy yeeres as mans dayes,

6 That thou enquirest after mine iniquitie, and searchest after my sinne?

7 †Thou knowest that I am not wicked, and there is none that can deliuer out of thine hand.

†Heb. vpon th knowle
†Heb. paines me.

8 Thine hands †haue made me and fashi-

fashioned me together round about; yet thou doest destroy me.

9 Remember, I beseech thee, that thou hast made me as the clay, and wilt thou bring me into dust againe?

139. 14, 10 *Hast thou not powred me out as milke, and cruddled me like cheese?

hedg- 11 Thou hast cloathed me with skin and flesh, and hast † fenced me with bones and sinewes.

12 Thou hast granted me life and fauour, and thy visitation hath preserued my spirit.

13 And these things hast thou hid in thine heart; I know that this *is* with thee.

14 If I sinne, then thou markest me, and thou wilt not acquite me from mine iniquitie.

15 If I be wicked, woe vnto me; and *if* I be righteous, *yet* will I not lift vp my head : I am full of confusion, therefore see thou mine affliction,

16 For it increaseth: thou huntest me as a fierce Lion: and againe thou shewest thy selfe marueilous vpon me.

is, gues. 17 Thou renuest thy ||witnesses against me, and increasest thine indignation vpon me ; Changes and warre are against me.

a. 3. 18 * Wherfore then hast thou brought me forth out of the wombe? Oht that I had giuen vp the ghost, and no eye had seene me!

19 I should haue bene as though I had not bene, I should haue bene caried from the wombe to the graue.

Chap. ʃͣ 7. 20 * Are not my dayes few? cease then, *and* let me alone that I may take comfort a litle,

21 Before I goe *whence* I shall not returne, *euen* to the land of darknes and the shadow of death,

22 A land of darknes, as darknes it selfe, *and* of the shadow of death, without any order, and *where* the light *is* as darkenes.

CHAP. XI.

1 Zophar reproueth Iob, for iustifying himselfe. 5 Gods wisdome is vnsearchable. 13 The assured blessing of repentance.

ʳ. a f lips. Hen answered Zophar the Naamathite, and said,

2 Should not the multitude of words be answered? and should †a man ful of talke be iustified?

3 Should thy ||lies make men hold their peace? and when thou mockest, shall no man make thee ashamed?

4 For thou hast said, My doctrine *is* pure, and I am cleane in thine eyes.

5 But, O that God would speake, and open his lippes against thee,

6 And that he would shew thee the secrets of wisedome, that *they are* double to that which is┐: know therefore that God exacteth of thee *lesse* then thine iniquitie *deserueth.*

7 Canst thou by searching finde out God? canst thou finde out the Almightie vnto perfection?

8 *It is* †as high as heauen, what canst thou doe? deeper then hell, what canst thou know?

9 The measure therof *is* longer then the earth, and broader then the sea.

10 If he ||cut off, and shut vp, or gather together, then †who can hinder him?

11 For, he knoweth vaine men : hee seeth wickednesse also, will he not then consider *it?*

12 For †vaine man would be wise; though man be borne *like* a wilde asses coult.

13 If thou prepare thine heart, and stretch out thine hands toward him :

14 If iniquitie be in thine hand, put it farre away, and let not wickednes dwell in thy tabernacles.

15 For then shalt thou lift vp thy face without spot, yea thou shalt be stedfast, and shalt not feare :

16 Because thou shalt forget *thy* misery, and remember *it* as waters that passe away :

17 And *thine* age †shalbe clearer then the noone day; thou shalt shine foorth, thou shalt be as the morning.

18 And thou shalt be secure because there is hope, yea thou shalt digge *about thee, and* thou shalt take thy rest in safety.

19 *Also thou shalt lye downe, and none shall make thee afraid ; yea many shall †make suite vnto thee.

20 But the eyes of the wicked shall faile, and †they shall not escape, and *their hope *shall be as* the ||giuing vp of the ghost.

CHAP. XII.

1 Iob mainteineth himselfe against his friends that reproue him. 7 He acknowledgeth the generall doctrine of Gods omnipotencie.

And

Marginal notes (right column):

|| *Or, deuises.*

† *Hebr. the heights of heauen.*

|| *Or, make a change.*
† *Hebr. who can turne him away?*

† *Hebr. emptie.*

† *Hebr. shall arise aboue the noone-day.*

* *Leuit. 26. 5.*
† *Hebr. entreat thy face.*
† *Heb. flight shall perish from them.*
* *Chap. 8. 14. and 18. 14.*
|| *Or, a puffe of breath.*

AND Iob answered, and sayd,

2 No doubt but ye *are* the people, and wisedome shall die with you.

3 But I haue †vnderstanding as well as you, †I am not inferiour to you : yea, †who knoweth not such things as these?

4 I am *as* one mocked of his neighbour, *who* calleth vpon God, and he answereth him : the iust vpright man is laughed to scorne.

5 He that is ready to slippe with *his* feet, is as a lamp despised in the thought of him that is at ease.

6 The tabernacles of robbers prosper, and they that prouoke God are secure, into whose hand God bringeth *abundantly.*

7 But aske now the beasts, and they shall teach thee; and the foules of the aire, and they shall tell thee.

8 Or speake to the earth, and it shall teach thee; and the fishes of the sea shall declare vnto thee.

9 Who knoweth not in all these, that the hand of the Lord hath wrought this?

10 In whose hand *is* the ‖soule of euery liuing thing, and the breath of †all mankinde.

11 *Doeth not the eare trie wordes? and the †mouth taste his meate?

12 With the ancient *is* wisedome, and in length of dayes, vnderstanding.

13 With ‖him *is* wisedome & strength, he hath counsell and vnderstanding.

14 *Behold, he breaketh downe, and it cannot be built againe : hee *shutteth †vp a man, and there can be no opening.

15 Behold, hee withholdeth the waters, and they drie vp : also hee sendeth them out, and they ouerturne the earth.

16 With him *is* strength & wisedome: the deceiued, and the deceiuer, *are* his.

17 He leadeth counsellers away spoiled, and maketh the Iudges fooles.

18 He looseth the bond of kings, and girdeth their loines with a girdle.

19 He leadeth Princes away spoiled, and ouerthroweth the mightie.

20 *He remooueth away †the speech of the trustie, and taketh away the vnderstanding of the aged.

21 He powreth contempt vpon princes, and ‖weakeneth the strength of the mightie.

22 Hee discoueereth deepe things out of darkenesse, and bringeth out to light the shadow of death.

23 He increaseth the nations, and destroyeth them : hee inlargeth the nations, and †straineth them *againe.*

24 He taketh away the heart of the chiefe of the people of the earth, and causeth them to wander in a wildernes *where there is* no way.

25 They grope in the darke without light, and hee maketh them to †stagger like a drunken man.

CHAP. XIII.

1 Iob reprooueth his friends of partialitie. 14 He professeth his confidence in God: 20 and entreateth to knowe his owne sinnes, and Gods purpose in afflicting him.

LOe, mine eye hath seene all *this,* mine eare hath heard and vnderstood it.

2 What yee know, *the same* doe I know also, I am not inferiour vnto you.

3 Surely I would speake to the Almighty, & I desire to reason with God.

4 But ye *are* forgers of lies, yee are all Physicians of no value.

5 O that you would altogether hold your peace, & it should be your wisedome.

6 Heare now my reasoning, and hearken to the pleadings of my lips.

7 Wil you speake wickedly for God? and talke deceitfully for him?

8 Will ye accept his person? will yee contend for God?

9 Is it good that he should search you out? or as one man mocketh another, doe ye so mocke him?

10 He will surely reprooue you, if yee doe secretly accept persons.

11 Shall not his excellencie make you afraid? and his dread fall vpon you?

12 Your remembrances *are* like vnto ashes, your bodies to bodies of clay.

13 †Hold your peace, let me alone that I may speake, and let come on me what *will.*

14 Wherefore doe I take my flesh in my teeth, and put my life in mine hand?

15 Though hee slay mee, yet will I trust in him : but I will †maintaine mine owne wayes before him.

16 Hee also *shall be* my saluation : for an hypocrite shall not come before him.

17 Heare diligently my speach, and my declaration with your eares.

18 Behold now, I haue ordered *my* cause, I know that I shall be iustified.

19 Who

† *Heb. an heart.*
† *Heb. I fall not lower then you.*
† *Heb. with whom are not such as these?*

‖ *Or, life.*

† *Heb. all flesh of man.*
* *Cha. 34. 3.*
† *Heb. palate.*

‖ *That is, with God.*

* *Isa. 22. 22.*
* *Apoc 3. 7.*
† *Heb. vpon.*

* *Cha. 32. 9.*
† *Heb. the lip of the faithfull.*

‖ *Or, looseth the girdle of the strong.*

† *Heb. deth of*

† *Heb. der.*

† *Heb. lent fr*

† *Heb. or arg*

19 Who is hee *that* will plead with me? for now if I hold my tongue, I shall giue vp the ghost.

20 Only doe not two things vnto me : then will I not hide my selfe from thee.

21 Withdrawe thine hand far from me : and let not thy dread make mee a-fraid.

22 Then call thou, and I will an-swere : or let me speake, and answere thou mee.

23 How many *are* mine iniquities and sinnes? make mee to knowe my trans-gression, and my sinne.

24 Wherefore hidest thou thy face, and holdest me for thine enemie?

25 Wilt thou breake a leafe driuen to and fro? and wilt thou pursue the drie stubble?

26 For thou writest bitter things a-gainst mee, and *makest me to possesse the iniquities of my youth.

27 Thou puttest my feete also in the stockes, and †lookest narrowly vn-to all my pathes; thou settest a print vp-on the †heeles of my feete.

28 And hee, as a rotten thing consu-meth, as a garment that is moth-eaten.

CHAP. XIIII.

1 Iob intreateth God for fauour, by the shortnes of life, and certainty of death. 7 Though life once lost be irrecouerable, yet he waiteth for his change. 16 By sinne the Creature is subiect to corruption.

MAN that is borne of a woman, is †of few dayes, and full of trouble.

2 * Hee commeth forth like a flower, and is cut downe : he fleeth also, as a shaddow and continueth not.

3 And doest thou open thine eies vpon such an one, and bringest me into iudgment with thee?

4 † Who * can bring a cleane thing out of an vncleane? not one.

5 *Seeing his daies *are* determined, the number of his moneths *are* with thee, thou hast appointed his bounds that he cannot passe.

6 Turne from him that hee may †rest, till he shall accomplish, as an hire-ling, his day.

7 For there is hope of a tree, if it be cut downe, that it will sprout againe, and that the tender branch thereof will not cease.

8 Though the roote thereof waxe old in the earth, and the stocke thereof die in the ground :

9 *Yet* through the sent of water it will bud, and bring forth boughes like a plant.

10 But man dyeth, and †wasteth a-way; yea, man giueth vp the ghost, and where is hee?

11 As the waters faile from the sea, and the floud decayeth and dryeth vp :

12 So man lyeth downe, and riseth not, till the heauens be no more, they shall not awake; nor bee raised out of their sleepe.

13 O that thou wouldest hide mee in the graue, that thou wouldest keepe me secret, vntill thy wrath bee past, that thou wouldest appoint me a set time, and remember me.

14 If a man die, shall he liue againe? All the dayes of my appointed time will I waite, till my change come.

15 Thou shalt call, and I will an-swer thee : thou wilt haue a desire to the worke of thine hands.

16 * For nowe thou numbrest my steppes, doest thou not watch ouer my sinne?

17 My transgression *is* sealed vp in a bagge, and thou sowest vp mine ini-quitie.

18 And surely the mountaine falling †commeth to nought : and the rocke is remoued out of his place.

19 The waters weare the stones, thou †washest away the things which growe *out* of the dust of the earth, and thou destroyest the hope of man.

20 Thou preuailest for euer against him, and hee passeth : thou changest his countenance, and sendest him away.

21 His sonnes come to honour, and he knoweth it not; and they are brought lowe, but he perceiueth *it* not of them.

22 But his flesh vpon him shall haue paine, and his soule within him shall mourne.

CHAP. XV.

1 Eliphaz reproueth Iob of impiety in iustify-ing himselfe. 17 He proueth by Tradition the vnquietnes of wicked men.

THen answered Eliphaz the Temanite, and said,

2 Should a wise man vtter †vaine knowledge, and fill his belly with the East winde?

3 Should

Marginal notes

l. 25. 7.

, obser-

. roots.

. short
yes?

l. 102.
. 103.
. 144.
0. 8. 9.

0. who
rie?
l. 51. 5.
ap. 7. 1.

. cease.

† Heb. is weakened, or cut off.

* Psal. 136. 2

† Heb. fa-deth.

† Heb. ouer-flowest.

† Heb. know-ledge of wind.

† Heb. thou
makest void.
‖ Or, speech.
† Heb. tea-
cheth.

3 Should hee reason with vnprofitable talke? or with speeches wherewith he can doe no good?

4 Yea † thou castest off feare, and restrainest ‖ prayer before God.

5 For thy mouth † vttereth thine iniquitie, and thou choosest the tongue of the craftie.

6 Thine owne mouth condemneth thee, and not I : yea thine owne lippes testifie against thee.

7 Art *thou* the first man *that* was borne? or wast thou made before the hilles?

* Rom. 11.
34.

8 *Hast thou heard the secret of God? and doest thou restraine wisedome to thy selfe?

9 What knowest thou that we know not? *what* vnderstandest thou, which is not in vs?

10 With vs are both the gray headed, and very aged men, much elder then thy father.

11 Are the consolations of God small with thee? is there any secret thing with thee?

12 Why doeth thine heart carie thee away? and what doe thine eyes winke at,

13 That thou turnest thy spirit against God, and lettest *such* words goe out of thy mouth?

* Chap. 14.
4. 1. king. 8.
46. 2. chron.
6. 36. psal.
14. 3. prou.
20. 9. 1. Iohn
1. 8.
* Iob. 4. 18.

14 *What *is* man, that he should be cleane? and he which is borne of a woman, that he should be righteous?

15 *Beholde, he putteth no trust in his Saints, yea, the heauens are not cleane in his sight.

16 How much more abominable and filthie is man, which drinketh iniquitie like water?

17 I will shew thee, heare me, and that which I haue seene, I wil declare,

18 Which wise men haue tolde from their fathers, and haue not hid *it*:

19 Vnto whom alone the earth was giuen, and no stranger passed among them.

20 The wicked man trauaileth with paine all *his* dayes, and the number of yeeres is hidden to the oppressor.

* Hebr. a
sound of
feares.

21 † A dreadfull sound *is* in his eares; in prosperitie the destroyer shall come vpon him.

22 He beleeueth not that he shall returne out of darkenesse, and he is waited for, of the sword.

23 He wandereth abroad for bread, *saying*, Where *is it?* he knoweth that the

day of darkenes is ready at his hand.

24 Trouble and anguish shall make him afraid; they shall preuaile against him, as a king ready to the battell.

25 For he stretcheth out his hand against God, and strengtheneth himselfe against the Almightie.

26 He runneth vpon him, *euen on his* necke, vpon the thicke bosses of his bucklers:

27 Because he couereth his face with his fatnesse, and maketh collops of fat on *his* flankes.

28 And he dwelleth in desolate cities, *and* in houses which no man inhabiteth, which are ready to become heapes.

29 He shall not be rich, neither shall his substance continue, neither shall he prolong the perfection thereof vpon the earth.

30 He shall not depart out of darkenesse, the flame shall drie vp his branches, and by the breath of his mouth shall he goe away.

31 Let not him that is deceiued, trust in vanitie: for vanitie shalbe his recompence.

32 It shall be ‖ accomplished before his time, and his branch shall not bee greene.

‖ Or, c

33 He shal shake off his vnripe grape as the Vine, and shall cast off his flowre as the Oliue.

34 For the congregation of hypocrites *shall be* desolate, and fire shall consume the tabernacles of briberie.

35 They conceiue mischiefe, * and bring forth ‖ vanitie, and their belly prepareth deceit.

* Esa
psal. 2
‖ Or, *
tie.*

CHAP. XVI.

1 Iob reproueth his friends of vnmercifulnesse.
7 He sheweth the pitifulnesse of his case. 17 He maintaineth his innocencie.

THen Iob answered, and said,

2 I haue heard many such things : ‖ *miserable comforters *are* ye all.

‖ Or, *
blesom·*
* Cha
4.

3 Shall † vaine words *haue* an end? or what emboldeneth thee, that thou answerest?

† Heb
of win

4 I also could speake as yee *doe*: if your soule were in my soules stead, I could heape vp words against you, and shake mine head at you.

5 *But* I would strengthen you with my mouth, and the mouing of my lips should

should assuage *your griefe.*

6 Though I speake, my griefe is not assuaged: and *though* I forbeare, †what am I eased?

† Heb. what goeth from me?

7 But now he hath made me weary: thou hast made desolate al my companie.

8 And thou hast filled mee with wrinckles, *which* is a witnesse *against me:* and my leannesse rising vp in me, beareth witnesse to my face.

9 He teareth *me* in his wrath, who hateth me: he gnasheth vpon me with his teeth; mine enemy sharpeneth his eyes vpon me.

10 They haue gaped vpon me with their mouth, they haue smitten me vpon the cheeke reprochfully, they haue gathered themselues together against mee.

11 God †hath deliuered me to the vngodly, and turned me ouer into the hands of the wicked.

Hebr. hath shut me vp.

12 I was at ease, but he hath broken me asunder: he hath also taken me by my necke, and shaken me to pieces, and set me vp for his marke.

13 His archers compasse me round about, he cleaueth my reines asunder, and doeth not spare; he powreth out my gall vpon the ground.

14 He breaketh me with breach vpon breach, he runneth vpon me like a giant.

15 I haue sowed sackcloth vpon my skin, and defiled my horne in the dust.

16 My face is fowle with weeping, and on mine eye-lids is the shadow of death,

17 Not for any iniustice in mine hands: also my prayer is pure.

18 O earth couer not thou my blood, and let my cry haue no place.

19 Also now, behold my witnesse *is* in heauen, and my record *is* †on high.

Hebr. in high places.

20 My friends †scorne me: *but* mine eye powreth out *teares* vnto God.

Hebr. are scorners.

21 O that one might plead for a man with God, as a man *pleadeth* for his ||neighbour

||friend.

22 When †a few yeeres are come, then I shall goe the way *whence* I shall not returne.

Heb. yeeres number.

CHAP. XVII.

1 Iob appealeth from men to God. 6 The vnmercifull dealing of men with the afflicted, may astonish, but not discourage the righteous. 11 His hope is not in life, but in death.

MY ||breath is corrupt, my dayes are extinct, the graues *are* ready for me.

|| Or, my spirit is spent.

2 *Are there* not mockers with mee? and doeth not mine eye †continue in their prouocation?

† Heb. lodge.

3 Lay downe now, put me in a suretie with thee; who *is* he *that* will strike hands with me?

4 For thou hast hid their heart from vnderstanding: therefore shalt thou not exalt *them.*

5 Hee that speaketh flattery to *his* friends, euen the eyes of his children shall faile.

6 He hath made me also a by-word of the people, and ||afore time I was as a tabret.

|| Or, before them.

7 Mine eye also is dimme by reason of sorrow, and all ||my members *are* as a shadow.

|| Or, my thoughts.

8 Vpright men shall be astonied at this, and the innocent shall stirre vp himselfe against the hypocrite.

9 The righteous also shall hold on his way, and he that hath cleane hands †shalbe stronger, and stronger.

† Hebr. shall adde stregth.

10 But as for you all, doe you returne, and come now, for I cannot find one wise man among you.

11 My dayes are past, my purposes are broken off, euen †the thoughts of my heart:

† Hebr. the possessions.

12 They change the night into day: the light is †short, because of darknes.

† Heb. neere.

13 If I waite, the graue *is* mine house: I haue made my bedde in the darknesse.

14 I haue †said to corruption, Thou *art* my father: to the worme, *Thou art* my mother, and my sister.

† Heb. cried, or called.

15 And where *is* now my hope? as for my hope, who shall see it?

16 They shall goe downe to the barres of the pit, when *our* rest together is in the dust.

CHAP. XVIII

1 Bildad reproueth Iob of presumption and impatiencie. 5 The calamities of the wicked.

THen answered Bildad the Shuhite and said,

2 How long *will it bee, ere* you make an ende of words? Marke, and afterwards we will speake.

3 Wherefore are wee counted as beasts, *and* reputed vile in your sight?

4 He

† Hebr. his soule.

4 He teareth †himselfe in his anger: shall the earth be forsaken for thee? and shall the rocke bee remooued out of his place?

5 Yea, the light of the wicked shalbe put out, and the sparke of his fire shall not shine.

‖ Or, tampe.

6 The light shalbe darke in his tabernacle, and his ‖ candle shalbe put out with him.

7 The steps of his strength shall be straitened, and his owne counsell shall cast him downe.

8 For hee is cast into a net by his owne feete, & he walketh vpon a snare.

9 The grinne shall take him by the heele, and the robber shall preuaile against him.

† Heb. hidden.

10 The snare is †laide for him in the ground, and a trap for him in the way.

† Heb. scatter him.

11 Terrours shall make him afraid on euery side, and shall †driue him to his feete.

† Heb. barres

12 His strength shalbe hunger-bitten, and destruction shall be ready at his side.

13 It shall deuoure the †strength of his skinne: euen the first borne of death shall deuoure his strength.

* Cha. 8. 14. and 11. 20. psa. 112. 10. pro. 10. 28.

14 * His confidence shalbe rooted out of his tabernacle, and it shall bring him to the king of terrours.

15 It shall dwell in his tabernacle, because it is none of his: brimstone shall be scattered vpon his habitation.

16 His rootes shall be dryed vp beneath: and aboue shall his branch be cut off.

* Pro. 2. 22.

17 * His remembrance shall perish from the earth, and hee shall haue no name in the streete.

† Heb. they shall driue him.

18 †He shall be driuen from light into darkenesse, and chased out of the world.

19 Hee shall neither haue sonne nor nephew among his people, nor any remaining in his dwellings.

‖ Or, liued with him.
† Heb. layd holde on horror.

20 They that come after him shalbe astonied at his day, as they that ‖went before, †were affrighted.

21 Surely such are the dwellings of the wicked, and this is the place of him that knoweth not God.

CHAP. XIX.

1 Iob complaining of his friends cruelty, sheweth there is miserie enough in him to feede their crueltie. 21. 28 Hee craueth pitie. 23 He beleeueth the resurrection.

Hen Iob answered, and sayd,

2 How long will yee vexe my soule, and breake me in pieces with words?

3 These tenne times haue ye reproched me: you are not ashamed that you ‖make your selues strange to me.

‖ Or, hard your selues against me.

4 And be it indeed that I haue erred, mine errour remaineth with my selfe.

5 If indeed yee will magnifie your selues against me, and plead against me my reproch:

6 Know now that God hath ouerthrowen me, and hath compassed me with his net.

7 Behold, I cry out of ‖ wrong, but I am not heard: I cry aloude, but there is no iudgement.

‖ Or, violence.

8 Hee hath fenced vp my way that I cannot passe; and hee hath set darkenesse in my pathes.

9 Hee hath stript me of my glory, and taken the crowne from my head.

10 He hath destroyed me on euery side, and I am gone: and mine hope hath he remooued like a tree.

11 He hath also kindled his wrath against me, and hee counteth me vnto him as one of his enemies.

12 His troupes come together, and raise vp their way against me, and encampe round about my tabernacle.

13 Hee hath put my brethren farre from me, and mine acquaintance are verely estranged from me.

14 My kinsefolke haue failed, and my familiar friends haue forgotten me.

15 They that dwell in mine house, and my maides count me for a stranger: I am an aliant in their sight.

16 I called my seruant, and he gaue me no answere: I intreated him with my mouth.

† Heb. belly.
‖ Or, the wicked

17 My breath is strange to my wife, though I entreated for the childrens sake of †mine owne body.

18 Yea, ‖yong children despised me; I arose, and they spake against me.

* Psal. and 55.
† Heb. men of secret.

19 * All †my inward friends abhorred me: and they whom I loued, are turned against me.

‖ Or, a

20 My bone cleaueth to my skinne, ‖ and to my flesh, and I am escaped with the skinne of my teeth.

21 Haue pity vpon me, haue pity vpon me, O ye my friends, for the hand of God hath touched me.

22 Why

22 Why doe ye persecute me as God, and are not satisfied with my flesh?

23 †Oh that my wordes were now written, oh that they were printed in a booke!

24 That they were grauen with an iron pen and lead, in the rocke for euer.

25 For I know *that* my Redeemer liueth, and *that* he shall stand at the latter *day*, vpon the earth:

26 ‖And *though* after my skin, *wormes* destroy this *body*, yet in my flesh shall I see God:

27 Whom I shal see for my selfe, and mine eyes shall beholde, and not †another, *though* my reines bee consumed †within me.

28 But ye should say, Why persecute we him? ‖seeing the root of the matter is found in me.

29 Bee ye afraid of the sword: for wrath *bringeth* the punishments of the sword, that yee may know there is a iudgement.

CHAP. XX.

Zophar sheweth the state and portion of the wicked.

Hen answered Zophar the Naamathite, and saide,

2 Therefore doe my thoughts cause mee to answere, and for *this* †I make haste.

3 I haue heard the checke of my reproach, and the spirit of my vnderstanding causeth me to answere.

4 Knowest thou *not* this of old, since man was placed vpon earth,

5 *That the triumphing of the wicked is †short, and the ioy of the hypocrite *but* for a moment?

6 Though his excellencie mount vp to the heauens, and his head reach vnto the †clouds:

7 *Yet* he shall perish for euer, like his owne doung: they which haue seene him, shall say, Where *is* he?

8 He shall flie away as a dreame, and shall not be found: yea he shalbe chased away as a vision of the night.

9 The eye also *which* saw him, shall see *him* no more; neither shall his place any more behold him.

10 ‖His children shall seeke to please the poore; and his hands shall restore their goods.

11 His bones are ful *of the sinne* of his

youth, which shall lye downe with him in the dust.

12 Though wickednes be sweet in his mouth, *though* hee hide it vnder his tongue;

13 *Though* he spare it, and forsake it not, but keepe it stil †within his mouth:

14 *Yet* his meate in his bowels is turned, it *is* the gall of Aspes within him.

15 He hath swallowed downe riches, and hee shall vomite them vp againe: God shall cast them out of his belly.

16 He shall sucke the poison of Aspes: the vipers tongue shall slay him.

17 Hee shall not see the riuers, ‖the floods, the brookes of hony and butter.

18 That which he laboured for, shall he restore, & shall not swallow *it* downe: †according to his substance shall the restitution *bee*, and hee shall not reioyce *therein*.

19 Because hee hath †oppressed, *and* hath forsaken the poore; *because* he hath violently taken away an *house which he builded not:

20 Surely he shall not †feele quietnesse in his belly, hee shall not saue of that which he desired.

21 ‖There shall none of his meat be left, therefore shall no man looke for his goods.

22 In the fulnesse of his sufficiencie, he shalbe in straites: euery hand of the ‖wicked shall come vpon him.

23 *When* he is about to fill his belly, *God* shall cast the furie of his wrath vpon him, and shall raine *it* vpon him while he is eating.

24 He shall flee from the iron weapon, and the bow of steele shall strike him through.

25 It is drawen, and commeth out of the body; *yea* the glistering sword commeth out of his gall; terrours *are* vpon him.

26 All darknesse *shalbe* hid in his secret places: a fire not blowen shall consume him; it shall goe ill with him that is left in his tabernacle.

27 The heauen shall reueale his iniquitie: and the earth shall rise vp against him.

28 The increase of his house shall depart, *and his goods* shall flow away in the day of his wrath.

29 This *is* the portion of a wicked man from God, and the heritage †appointed vnto him by God.

CHAP.

*b. who
giue?

, After
ll awake
gh this
y be de-
ed, yet
t shall I
God.
ebr. a
nger.
ebr. in
bosome.

, and
t roote
atter is
nd inme?

ebr. my
te is in

Psal. 37.
ebr. from
ere.

eb.cloud.

r, the
ore shall
presse his
ildren.

† Hebr. in
the midst of
his palate.

‖ Or, strea-
ming brooks.

† Hebr. ac-
cording to
thesubstance
of his ex-
change.
† Hebr.
crushed.
* Eccles. 5.
12.

‖ Heb.know.

‖ Or, there
shalbe none
left for his
meats.

‖ Or, trouble-
some.

† Hebr. of
his decree
from God.

CHAP. XXI.

1 Iob sheweth that euen in the iudgement of man, he hath reason to be grieued. 7 Sometimes the wicked doe so prosper, as they despise God. 16 Sometime their destruction is manifest. 22 The happy and vnhappy are alike in death. 27 The iudgement of the wicked is in another world.

BVt Iob answered, and sayd,

2 Heare diligently my speech, and let this be your consolations.

3 Suffer me that I may speake, and after that I haue spoken, mocke on.

4 As for mee, *is* my complaint to man? and if *it were so*, why should not my spirit be †troubled?

5 †Marke mee, and be astonished, and lay *your* hand vpon *your* mouth.

6 Euen when I remember, I am afraid, and trembling taketh holde on my flesh.

7 * Wherefore doe the wicked liue, become old, yea, are mightie in power?

8 Their seede is established in their sight with them, and their offspring before their eyes.

9 Their houses are †safe from feare, neither *is* the rod of God vpon them.

10 Their bull gendreth and faileth not, their cow calueth, and casteth not her calfe.

11 They send foorth their little ones like a flocke, and their children dance.

12 They take the timbrell and harpe, and reioyce at the sound of the organe.

13 They spend their daies ||in wealth, and in a moment goe downe to the graue.

14 * Therefore they say vnto God, Depart from vs : for we desire not the knowledge of thy wayes.

15 What *is* the Almightie, that wee should serue him? and what profite should we haue, if we pray vnto him?

16 Loe, their good *is* not in their hand, the counsell of the wicked is farre from me.

17 How oft is the ||candle of the wicked put out? and *how oft* commeth their destruction vpon them? *God* distributeth sorrowes in his anger.

18 They are as stubble before the winde, and as chaffe that the storme †carieth away.

19 God layeth vp his ||iniquitie for his children : he rewardeth him, and he shall know *it*.

20 His eyes shall see his destruction, and he shall drinke of the wrath of the Almightie.

21 For what pleasure *hath* he in his house after him, when the number of his moneths is cut off in the middest?

22 Shall *any* teach God knowledge? seeing he iudgeth those that are high.

23 One dieth †in his full strength, being wholly at ease and quiet.

24 His ||breasts are full of milke, and his bones are moistened with marrow.

25 And another dieth in the bitternesse of his soule, and neuer eateth with pleasure.

26 They shall lie downe alike in the dust, and the wormes shall couer them.

27 Behold, I know your thoughts, and the deuices *which* yee wrongfully imagine against me.

28 For ye say, Where *is* the house of the prince? and where *are* †the dwelling places of the wicked?

29 Haue ye not asked them that goe by the way? and doe ye not know their tokens?

30 * That the wicked is reserued to the day of destruction; they shall bee brought foorth to †the day of wrath.

31 Who shall declare his way to his face? and who shall repay him *what* he hath done?

32 Yet shall hee be brought to the †graue, & shall †remaine in the tombe.

33 The cloudes of the valley shalbe sweete vnto him, and euery man shall draw after him, as there are innumerable before him.

34 How then comfort ye me in vaine, seeing in your answeres there remaineth †falshood?

CHAP. XXII.

1 Eliphaz sheweth that mans goodnesse profiteth not God. 5 Hee accuseth Iob of diuers sinnes. 21 He exhorteth him to repentance, with promises of mercy.

THen Eliphaz the Temanite answered, and said,

2 Can a man be profitable vnto God? as ||hee that is wise may be profitable vnto himselfe.

3 *Is* it any pleasure to the Almighty, that thou art righteous? or *is* it gaine *to him*, that thou makest thy waies perfite?

4 Will

Marginal notes (left column)

† Heb. shortened.
† Heb. looke vnto me.

* Psal. 17. 10. and 73. 12. iere. 12. 1. hab. 1. 16.

† Heb. are peace from feare.

|| Or, in mirth.

Chap. 22. 17.

|| Or, lampe.

† Heb. stealeth away.
|| That is, the punishment of his iniquitie.

Marginal notes (right column)

† Heb. very perfection, o the stre of his p ction.
|| Or, mi pales.

† Heb. tent of tabernal of the v ked.

* Pro.

† Heb. day of wraths

† Heb. graues.
† Heb. in the h

† Heb. gressio

|| Or, i may be fitable, his goo cesse d thereof

4 Will hee reproue thee for feare of thee? will he enter with thee into iudgment?

5 Is not thy wickednesse great? and thine iniquities infinite?

6 For thou hast taken a pledge from thy brother for nought, and †stripped the naked of their clothing.

7 Thou hast not giuen water to the wearie to drinke, and thou hast withholden bread from the hungry.

8 But as for the †mightie man, hee had the earth, and †the honourable man dwelt in it.

9 Thou hast sent widowes away emptie, and the armes of the fatherlesse haue bene broken.

10 Therefore snares are round about thee, and sudden feare troubleth thee,

11 Or darkenes that thou canst not see, and abundance of waters couer thee.

12 Is not God in the height of heauen? and behold the †height of the starres how high they are.

13 And thou sayest, ‖How doth God know? can he iudge through the darke cloude?

14 Thicke cloudes are a couering to him that he seeth not, and hee walketh in the circuit of heauen.

15 Hast thou marked the olde way which wicked men haue troden?

16 Which were cut downe out of time, †whose foundation was ouerflowen with a flood.

17 *Which said vnto God, Depart from vs, and what can the Almightie doe ‖for them?

18 *Yet he filled their houses with good things: but the counsell of the wicked is farre from me.

19 *The righteous see it, and are glad, and the innocent laugh them to scorne.

20 Whereas our ‖substance is not cut downe, but the ‖remnant of them the fire consumeth.

21 Acquaint now thy selfe with ‖him, and be at peace: thereby good shal come vnto thee.

22 Receiue, I pray thee, the Lawe from his mouth, and lay vp his words in thine heart.

23 *If thou returne to the Almightie, thou shalt be built vp, thou shalt put away iniquitie farre from thy tabernacles.

24 Then shalt thou lay vp golde ‖as dust, and the gold of Ophir as the stones of the brookes.

25 Yea the Almightie shall bee thy ‖defence, and thou shalt haue†plenty of siluer.

26 For then shalt thou haue thy delight in the Almightie, and shalt lift vp thy face vnto God.

27 Thou shalt make thy prayer vnto him, and he shall heare thee, and thou shalt pay thy vowes.

28 Thou shalt also decree a thing, and it shal be established vnto thee: and the light shall shine vpon thy wayes.

29 When men are cast downe, then thou shalt say, There is lifting vp: and he shall saue the †humble person.

30 ‖He shall deliuer the Iland of the innocent: and it is deliuered by the purenesse of thine hands.

CHAP. XXIII.

1 Iob longeth to appeare before God, 6 in confidence of his mercie. 8 God who is inuisible, obserueth our wayes. 11 Iobs innocencie. 13 Gods decree is immutable.

Hen Iob answered, and said,

2 Euen to day is my complaint bitter: my †stroke is heauier then my groning.

3 O that I knewe where I might find him! that I might come euen to his seate!

4 I would order my cause before him, and fill my mouth with arguments.

5 I would know the words which he would answere me, and vnderstand what he would say vnto me.

6 Will he plead against me with his great power? No, but hee would put strength in me.

7 There the righteous might dispute with him; so should I be deliuered for euer from my Iudge.

8 Behold, I goe forward, but he is not there, and backward, but I cannot perceiue him:

9 On the left hand where hee doeth worke, but I cannot behold him: he hideth himselfe on the right hand, that I cannot see him.

10 But he knoweth †the way that I take: when he hath tried me, I shall come forth as gold.

11 My foot hath held his steps, his way haue I kept, and not declined.

12 Nei-

Margin notes

eb. strip the clo of the ed.

eb. the of arme ob. emi or ac ed for tenance.

eb. the t of the res.

, what.

b. a flood pouved their dation. ap. 21.

, to them ap. 21.

sal. 107.

, estate.
, their liencie.

at is, God.

ap. 8. 5.

, on the

Or, gold.
† Heb. siluer of strength.

† Heb. him that hath lowe eyes.
‖ Or, the innocent shall deliuer the Iland.

† Hebr. my hand.

† Heb. the way that is with me.

† Hebr. I haue hid, or layd vp.
‖ Or, my appointed portion.
* Psal. 115. 3.

12 Neither haue I gone backe from the commaundement of his lippes, †I haue esteemed the words of his mouth more then ‖my necessary food.

13 But hee is in one minde, and who can turne him? and what *his soule desireth, euen that he doeth.

14 For he performeth the thing that is appointed for mee: and many such things are with him.

15 Therefore am I troubled at his presence: when I consider, I am afraid of him.

16 For God maketh my heart soft, and the Almighty troubleth me:

17 Because I was not cut off before the darknes, neither hath he couered the darknes from my face.

CHAP. XXIIII.

1 Wickednesse goeth often vnpunished. 17 There is a secret iudgement for the wicked.

* Deut. 19. 14. and 27. 17.
‖ Or, feed them.

WHy, seeing Times are not hidden from the Almightie, doe they, that know him not, see his dayes?

2 Some remooue the *land-markes; they violently take away flocks, and ‖feed thereof.

3 They driue away the asse of the fatherlesse, they take the widowes oxe for a pledge.

4 They turne the needy out of the way: the poore of the earth hide themselues together.

5 Behold, as wilde asses in the desart, goe they foorth to their worke, rising betimes for a pray: the wildernes yeeldeth food for them, and for their children.

† Hebr. mingled corne, or dredge.
† Hebr. the wicked gather the vintage.

6 They reape euery one his †corne in the fielde: and †they gather the vintage of the wicked.

7 They cause the naked to lodge without clothing, that they haue no couering in the cold.

8 They are wet with the showres of the mountaines, and imbrace the rocke for want of a shelter.

9 They plucke the fatherlesse from the brest, and take a pledge of the poore.

10 They cause him to go naked without clothing: and they take away the sheafe from the hungry,

11 Which make oyle within their walles, and tread their winepresses, and suffer thirst.

12 Men groane from out of the city,

and the soule of the wounded crieth out: yet God layeth not folly to them.

13 They are of those that rebell against the light, they know not the wayes thereof, nor abide in the pathes thereof.

14 The murderer rising with the light, killeth the poore and needy, and in the night is as a thiefe.

15 The eye also of the adulterer waiteth for the twilight, saying, No eye shall see me: and †disguiseth his face.

† Hebr. teth his in secre

16 In the darke they digge through houses, which they had marked for themselues in the day time: they know not the light.

17 For the morning is to them euen as the shadow of death: if one know them, they are in the terrours of the shadow of death.

18 Hee is swift as the waters, their portion is cursed in the earth: he beholdeth not the way of the Vineyards.

19 Drought and heate †consume the snow waters: so doeth the graue those which haue sinned.

† Hebr. lently t it.

20 The wombe shall forget him, the worme shall feed sweetly on him, hee shall be no more remembred, and wickednes shalbe broken as a tree.

21 He euill intreateth the barren, that beareth not: and doeth not good to the widow.

22 He draweth also the mighty with his power: he riseth vp, ‖and no man is sure of life.

‖ Or, he steth n owne li

23 Though it be giuen him to be in safety, whereon he resteth; yet his eyes are vpon their wayes.

24 They are exalted for a litle while, but †are gone and brought low, they are †taken out of the way as al other, and cut off as the tops of the eares of corne.

† Hebr not.
† Hebr sed vp.

25 And if it be not so now, who will make mee a liar, and make my speach nothing worth?

CHAP. XXV.

Bildad sheweth that man cannot be iustified before God.

THen answered Bildad the Shuhite, and said:

2 Dominion and feare are with him, hee maketh peace in his high places.

3 Is there any number of his armies? and vpon whom doeth not his light arise?

4 *How

hap. 4.
&c. &
14. &c.

4 * How then can man bee iustified with God? or how can he be cleane that is borne of a woman?

5 Behold euen to the moone, and it shineth not, yea the starres are not pure in his sight.

6 How much lesse man, *that is a* worme: and the sonne of man *which is a* * worme?

sal. 22. 6.

CHAP. XXVI.

1 Iob reprouing the vncharitable spirit of Bildad, 5 acknowledgeth the power of God to be infinite and vnsearchable.

 VT Iob answered and sayd,

2 Howe hast thou helped *him* that is without power? *how* sauest thou the arme that *hath* no strength?

3 How hast thou counselled *him that hath* no wisedome? and *how* hast thou plentifully declared the thing, as it is?

4 To whom hast thou vttered words? and whose spirit came from thee?

5 Dead things are formed from vnder the waters, ‖ and the inhabitants thereof.

r, with
inhabi-
ts.
ro. 15. 11

6 * Hell *is* naked before him, and destruction *hath* no couering.

7 He stretcheth out the North ouer the emptie place, *and* hangeth the earth vpon nothing.

8 Hee bindeth vp the waters in his thicke clouds, and the cloud is not rent vnder them.

9 Hee holdeth backe the face of *his* throne, *and* spreadeth his cloud vpon it.

10 Hee hath compassed the waters with bounds, † vntill the day and night come to an end.

Ieb. vntill
end of
ht vntill
rknesse.

11 The pillars of heauen tremble, and are astonished at his reproofe.

12 Hee diuideth the sea with his power, and by his vnderstanding he smiteth through † the proud.

Ieb. pride.

13 By his spirit he hath garnished the heauens; his hand hath formed the crooked serpent.

14 Loe, these *are* parts of his waies, but how little a portion is heard of him? but the thunder of his power who can vnderstand?

CHAP. XXVII.

1 Iob protesteth his sincerity. 8 The Hypocrite is without hope. 11 The blessings, which the wicked haue, are turned into curses.

Ooreuer Iob † continued his parable, and sayd,

2 *As* God liueth, *who* hath taken away my iudgment, and the Almighty, who hath † vexed my soule;

† Heb. added
to take vp.

† Heb. made
my soule bit-
ter.

3 All the while my breath *is* in mee, and * the spirit of God *is* in my nostrils.

* That is,
the breath
which God
gaue him.

4 My lips shall not speake wickednesse, nor my tongue vtter deceit.

5 God forbid that I should iustifie you: till I die, I will not remoue my integritie from me.

6 My righteousnesse I hold fast, and will not let it goe: my heart shall not reproach *me* † so long as I liue.

† Heb. from
my daies.

7 Let mine enemie be as the wicked, and he that riseth vp against me, as the vnrighteous.

8 * For what *is* the hope of the hypocrite, though he hath gained, when God taketh away his soule?

* Mat. 16.
26.

9 * Will God heare his cry, when trouble commeth vpon him?

* Prou. 1.
28. Ezech.
8. 18. Iohn.
9. 31. Iam.
4. 3.

10 Will he delight himselfe in the Almightie? will hee alwayes call vpon God?

11 I will teach you ‖ by the hand of God: *that* which *is* with the Almightie, will I not conceale.

‖ Or, being in
the hand &c.

12 Behold, all ye your selues haue seene *it*, why then are yee thus altogether vaine?

13 This *is* the portion of a wicked man with God, and the heritage of oppressours *which* they shall receiue of the Almightie.

14 If his children be multiplied, *it is* for the sword: and his offspring shall not be satisfied with bread.

15 * Those that remaine of him shall bee buried in death: and his widowes shall not weepe.

* Psal. 78.
65.

16 Though he heape vp siluer as the dust, and prepare rayment as the clay:

17 He may prepare *it*, but the iust shall put it on, and the innocent shall diuide the siluer.

18 He buildeth his house as a moth, and as a booth *that* the keeper maketh.

19 The rich man shall lie downe, but he shall not be gathered: he openeth his eyes, and he *is* not:

20 * Terrours take hold on him as waters, a tempest stealeth him away in the night.

* Chap. 18.
11.

21 The East winde carieth him away,

way, and he departeth : and as a storme hurleth him out of his place.

22 For *God* shall cast vpon him, and not spare; † hee would faine flee out of his hand.

† Heb. in flee- inghe would flee.

23 Men shall clap their handes at him, and shall hisse him out of his place.

CHAP. XXVIII.

1 There is a knowledge of naturall things. 12 But wisedome is an excellent gift of God.

‖ Or, a mine

 Vrely there is ‖ a veine for the siluer, and a place for golde *where* they fine *it.*

‖ Or, dust.

2 Iron is taken out of the ‖ earth, and brasse is molten *out* of the stone.

3 Hee setteth an ende to darkenesse, and searcheth out all perfection . the stones of darkenesse and the shadow of death.

4 The floud breaketh out from the inhabitant ; euen the *waters* forgotten of the foote : they are dried vp, they are gone away from men.

5 As for the earth, out of it commeth bread : and vnder it, is turned vp as it were fire.

‖ Or, gold- oare.

6 The stones of it *are* the place of Saphires : and it hath ‖ dust of golde.

7 *There is* a path which no foule knoweth, and which the vulturs eye hath not seene.

8 The lyons whelps haue not tro- den it, nor the fierce lyon passed by it.

‖ Or, flint.

9 Hee putteth foorth his hand vpon the ‖ rocke ; hee ouerturneth the moun- taines by the rootes.

10 Hee cutteth out riuers among the rockes, and his eye seeth euery precious thing.

† Heb. from weeping.

11 He bindeth the flouds † from ouer- flowing, and the thing that is hid, brin- geth he foorth to light.

12 But where shall wisedome bee found ? and where *is* the place of vnder- standing ?

13 Man knoweth not the price there- of ; neither is it found in the land of the liuing.

* Rom. 11. 33, 34.

14 *The depth saith, It is not in me : and the sea saith, It is not with me.

† Heb. fine gold shall not be giuen for it.
* Pro. 3. 14. and 8. 11, 19. and 16. 16.

15 † It *cannot be gotten for golde, neither shall siluer be weighed *for* the price thereof.

16 It cannot be valued with the golde of Ophir, with the precious O- nix, or the Saphire.

17 The golde and the chrystall can- not equall it : and the exchange of it shall *not be for* ‖ iewels of fine golde.

‖ Or, ves of fine g
‖ Or, Ra moth.

18 No mention shalbe made of ‖ Co- rall, or of Pearles : for the price of wise- dome *is* aboue Rubies.

19 The Topaze of Ethiopia shall not equall it, neither shall it be valued with pure golde.

20 * Whence then commeth wise- dome ? and where *is* the place of vnder- standing ?

* Vers.

21 Seeing it is hid from the eyes of all liuing, and kept close from the foules of the ‖ ayre.

‖ Or, hea

22 Destruction and death say, Wee haue heard the fame thereof with our eares.

23 God vnderstandeth the way there- of, and he knoweth the place thereof.

24 For hee looketh to the endes of the earth, *and* seeth vnder the whole heauen :

25 To make the weight for the windes, and he weigheth the waters by measure.

26 When hee made a decree for the raine, and a way for the lightning of the thunder :

27 Then did he see it, ‖ and declare it, he prepared it, yea and searched it out.

‖ Or, did number

28 * And vnto man he said, Behold, the feare of the Lord, that *is* wisedome, and to depart from euill, is vnderstan- ding.

* Psal. ʸ 10. prou 7. & 9.

CHAP. XXIX.

Iob bemoaneth himselfe, of his former pros- peritie and honour.

 Oreouer Iob † continued his parable, and said,

† Heb. ac to take v

2 O that I were as *in* monethes past, as *in* the dayes when God preser- ued me.

3 When his ‖ candle shined vpon my head, and *when* by his light I walked *through* darkenesse .

‖ Or, lan

4 As I was in the dayes of my youth, when the secret of God was vp- on my tabernacle :

5 When the Almightie was yet with me, *when* my children were about me :

6 When I washed my steps with butter, and the rocke powred † me out riuers of oyle :

† Heb. u me.

7 When I went out to the gate, through the citie, *when* I prepared my seate in the street.

8 The

8 The yong men saw me, and hid themselues : and the aged arose, *and* stood vp.

9 The princes refrained talking, and laid *their* hand on their mouth.

eb. the ce of the les was

10 † The Nobles held their peace, and their tongue cleaued to the roofe of their mouth.

11 When the eare heard *mee*, then it blessed me, and when the eye saw *me*, it gaue witnesse to me :

12 Because I deliuered the poore that cried, and the fatherlesse, and *him* that had none to helpe him.

13 The blessing of him that was readie to perish, came vpon me : and I caused the widowes heart to sing for ioy.

14 I put on righteousnesse, and it clothed me : my iudgement was as a robe and a diademe.

15 I was eyes to the blind, and feet *was* I to the lame.

16 I *was* a father to the poore : and the cause which I knewe not, I searched out.

eb. the teeth or grinders
eb. I cast

17 And I brake the † iawes of the wicked, and †pluckt the spoile out of his teeth.

18 Then I said, I shall die in my nest, and I shall multiplie *my* dayes as the sand.

eb. ned.

19 My roote *was* †spread out by the waters, and the dew lay all night vpon my branch.

eb. new.
eb. chan-

20 My glory *was* † fresh in mee, and my bow was † renewed in my hand.

21 Vnto me *men* gaue eare, and waited, and kept silence at my counsell.

22 After my words they spake not againe, & my speach dropped vpon them,

23 And they waited for me as for the raine, and they opened their mouth wide *as* for the latter raine.

24 *If* I laughed on them, they beleeued it not, and the light of my countenance they cast not downe.

25 I chose out their way, and sate chiefe, and dwelt as a king in the army, as one *that* comforteth the mourners.

CHAP. XXX.

1 Iobs honour is turned into extreme contempt.
15 His prosperitie into calamitie.

eb. of ver dayes n I.

BVt nowe they † that are yonger then I, haue mee in derision, whose fathers I would haue disdained to haue set with the dogs of my flocke.

2 Yea whereto might the strength of their hands *profit* me, in whom olde age was perished ?

3 For want and famine they *were* || solitarie : flying into the wildernesse † in former time desolate and waste :

|| Or, darke as the night.
†Heb. yester-night.

4 Who cut vp mallowes by the bushes, and Iuniper rootes *for* their meate.

5 They were driuen foorth from among *men*, (they cried after them, as *after* a thiefe.)

6 To dwell in the clifts of the valleys, in † caues of the earth, and in the rockes.

† Heb. holes.

7 Among the bushes they brayed : vnder the nettles they were gathered together.

8 They *were* children of fooles, yea children of † base men : they were viler then the earth.

† Heb. men of no name.

9 * And now am I their song, yea I am their by-word.

* Psal. 35. 15. and 69. 12.

10 They abhorre me, they flee farre from me, † and spare not to spit in my face.

† Heb. and withhold not spittle from my face.

11 Because hee hath loosed my cord and afflicted me, they haue also let loose the bridle before me.

12 Vpon my right *hand* rise the youth, they push away my feete, and they raise vp against mee the wayes of their destruction.

13 They marre my path, they set forward my calamitie, they *haue* no helper.

14 They came *vpon me* as a wide breaking in *of waters* : in the desolation they rolled themselues *vpon me*.

15 Terrours are turned vpon mee : they pursue †my soule as the wind : and my welfare passeth away as a cloude.

† Heb. my principall one

16 And now my soule is powred out vpon me : the dayes of affliction haue taken hold vpon me.

17 My bones are pierced in mee in the night season : and my sinewes take no rest.

18 By the great force *of my disease*, is my garment changed : it bindeth mee about as the collar of my coat.

19 Hee hath cast mee into the myre, and I am become like dust and ashes.

20 I crie vnto thee, and thou doest not heare me : I stand vp, and thou regardest me *not*.

21 Thou art † become cruell to me : with † thy strong hand thou opposest thy selfe against me.

†Heb.turned to be cruell.
† Hebr. the strength of thy hand.

22 Thou

22 Thou liftest me vp to the wind : thou causest me to ride *vpon it*, and dissoluest my ‖ substance.

‖ *Or, wisedome.*

23 For I know *that* thou wilt bring me *to* death, and *to* the house appointed for all liuing.

24 Howbeit he will not stretch out his hand to the † graue, though they cry in his destruction.

† *Heb. heape.*

25 *Did not I weepe † for him that was in trouble? was *not* my soule grieued for the poore?

* *Rom. 12. 15. psal. 35. 13.*
† *Heb. for him that was hard of day.*

26 When I looked for good, then euill came vnto mee: and when I waited for light, there came darkenes.

27 My bowels boyled and rested not: the dayes of affliction preuented mee.

28 I went mourning without the Sunne: I stood vp, *and* I cried in the Congregation.

29 * I am a brother to dragons, and a companion to ‖ owles.

* *Psal. 102. 6.*
‖ *Or, ostriches.*

30 My skinne is blacke vpon mee, and my bones are burnt with heat.

31 My harpe also is turned to mourning, and my organe into the voyce of them that weepe.

CHAP. XXXI.

Iob maketh a solemne protestation of his integritie in seuerall dueties.

I Made a couenant with mine eyes; why then should I thinke vpon a mayd?

2 For what portion of God is there from aboue? and *what* inheritance of the Almighty from on high?

3 *Is* not destruction to the wicked? and a strange *punishment* to the workers of iniquitie?

4 * Doeth not he see my wayes, and count all my steps?

* *2. Chron. 16. 9. Iob 32. 21. pro. 5. 21. and 15. 3.*

5 If I haue walked with vanitie, or if my foot hath hasted to deceit;

6 † Let me bee weighed in an euen ballance, that God may know mine integritie.

† *Hebr. let him weigh mee in ballances of Iustice.*

7 If my step hath turned out of the way, and mine heart walked after mine eyes, and if any blot hath cleaued to my hands:

8 *Then* let mee sow, and let another eate, yea let my off-spring be rooted out.

9 If mine heart haue bene deceiued by a woman, or *if* I haue layde wait at my neighbours doore:

10 Then let my wife grind vnto another, and let others bow downe vpon her.

11 For this *is* an heinous crime, yea, it *is* an iniquitie *to bee punished by* the Iudges.

12 For *it is a* fire *that* consumeth to destruction, and would roote out all mine encrease.

13 If I did despise the cause of my man-seruant, or of my mayd-seruant, when they contended with me:

14 What then shall I do, when God riseth vp? and when hee visiteth, what shall I answere him?

15 Did not hee that made mee in the wombe, make him? and ‖ did not one fashion vs in the wombe?

‖ *Or, did he not fashion vs in one wombe?*

16 If I haue withhelde the poore from *their* desire, or haue caused the eyes of the widow to faile:

17 Or haue eaten my morsell my selfe alone, and the fatherlesse hath not eaten thereof:

18 (For from my youth hee was brought vp with me as *with* a father, and I haue guided ‖ her from my mothers wombe.)

‖ *That is, the widow.*

19 If I haue seene any perish for want of cloathing, or any poore without couering:

20 If his loynes haue not blessed me, and *if* hee were *not* warmed with the fleece of my sheepe:

21 If I haue lift vp my hand against the fatherlesse, when I saw my helpe in the gate:

22 *Then* let mine arme fall from my shoulder-blade, and mine arme be broken from the ‖ bone.

‖ *Or, the channell bone.*

23 For destruction *from* God was a terrour to mee: and by reason of his highnesse, I could not endure.

24 If I haue made golde my hope, or haue said to the fine gold, *Thou art* my confidence:

25 If I reioyced because my wealth was great, and because mine hand had † gotten much:

† *Heb. found much.*

26 If I beheld † the Sunne when it shined, or the Moone walking + *in* brightnesse:

† *Heb. the light.*
† *Heb. bright.*

27 And my heart hath bene secretly enticed, or † my mouth hath kissed my hand:

† *Hebr. hand hath kissed my mouth.*

28 This also were an iniquitie to be *punished by the* Iudge: For I should haue denied the God *that is* aboue.

29 If

29 If I reioyced at the destruction of him that hated me, or lift vp my selfe when euill found him :

† *Heb. my palate.*

30 (Neither haue I suffered † my mouth to sinne by wishing a curse to his soule.)

31 If the men of my tabernacle said not, Oh that we had of his flesh ! wee cannot be satisfied.

‖ *Or, to the way.*

32 The stranger did not lodge in the street : *but* I opened my doores ‖to the trauailer.

‖ *Or, after the manner of men.*

33 If I couered my transgressions, ‖as Adam : by hiding mine iniquitie in my bosome :

34 Did I feare a great multitude, or did the contempt of families terrifie me : that I kept silence, *and* went not out of the doore ?

‖ *Or, behold my signe is that the Almightie will answere mee.*

35 O that one would heare me ! ‖beholde, my desire *is, that* the Almightie would answere me, and that mine aduersary had written a booke.

36 Surely I would take it vpon my shoulder, *and* bind it as a crowne to me.

37 I would declare vnto him the number of my steps, as a prince would I goe neere vnto him.

† *Heb. weepe*

† *Heb. the strength thereof.*

† *Heb. caused the soule of the owners therof to expire, or breath out.*

† *Or, noy-some weedes*

38 If my land cry against me, or that the furrowes likewise thereof † complaine :

39 If I haue †eaten the fruits thereof without money, or haue †caused the owners thereof to loose their life :

40 Let thistles grow in stead of wheat, and ‖ cockle in stead of barley. The words of Iob are ended.

CHAP. XXXII.

1 Elihu is angry with Iob and his three friends. 6 Because wisedome cometh not from age, he excuseth the boldnesse of his youth. 11 He reproueth them for not satisfying of Iob. 16 His zeale to speake.

Heb. from answering.

S O these three men ceased †to answere Iob, because he *was* righteous in his owne eyes.

2 Then was kindled the wrath of Elihu, the sonne of Barachel the Buzite, of the kinred of Ram : against Iob was his wrath kindled, because he iustified †himselfe rather then God.

Heb. his rule.

3 Also against his three friends was his wrath kindled : because they had found no answere, and *yet* had condemned Iob.

Heb. expected Iob words.

4 Now Elihu had † waited till Iob

had spoken : because they *were* † elder then he.

† *Heb. elder for dayes.*

5 When Elihu saw that *there was* no answere in the mouth of these three men, then his wrath was kindled.

6 And Elihu the sonne of Barachel the Buzite answered and sayd : I *am* †yong, and yee *are* very old, wherefore I was afraid, and †durst not shew you mine opinion.

† *Heb. few of dayes.*
† *Heb. I feared.*

7 I said, Dayes should speake, and multitude of yeeres should teach wisedome.

8 *But there is a spirit in man : and the inspiration of the Almightie giueth them vnderstanding.

* Iob. 38. 36 prou. 2. 6. eccl. 2. 26. dan. 1. 17. & 2. 21.

9 Great men are not *alwayes* wise : neither doe the aged vnderstand iudgement.

10 Therfore I sayd, Hearken to me : I also will shew mine opinion.

11 Behold, I waited for your words : I gaue eare to your † reasons, whilest you searched out †what to say.

† *Heb. vnderstandings*
† *Heb. words*

12 Yea, I attended vnto you : and beholde , *there was* none of you that conuinced Iob, *or* that answered his words :

13 Lest ye should say, We haue found out wisdome : God thrusteth him down, not man.

14 Now he hath not ‖ directed his words against me : neither will I answere him with your speeches.

‖ *Or, ordered his words.*

15 They were amased , they answered no more, †they left off speaking.

16 When I had waited, (for they spake not, but stood still *and* answered no more.)

† *Heb. they remoued speeches from themselues.*

17 *I* sayd , I will answere also my part, I also will shew mine opinion.

18 For I am full of †matter, the †spirit within me constraineth me.

† *Heb. words*
† *Heb. the spirit of my belly.*

19 Behold, my belly *is* as wine, *which* †hath no vent , it is ready to burst like new bottles.

† *Heb. is not opened.*

20 I will speake, †that I may be refreshed : I will open my lippes, and answere.

† *Heb. that I may breath.*

21 Let me not, I pray you, accept any mans person : neither let me giue flattering titles vnto man.

22 For I know not to giue flattering titles : *in so doing* my maker would soone take me away.

CHAP. XXXIII.

1 Elihu offereth himselfe in stead of God, with sinceritie and meekenesse to reason with Iob.

8 He

8 He excuſeth God from giuing man an account of his wayes, by his greatneſſe. 14 God calleth man to repentance by viſions, 19 by afflictions, 23 and by his miniſtery. 31 Hee inciteth Iob to attention.

Herefore, Iob, I pray thee, heare my ſpeeches, and hearken to all my wordes.

2 Behold, now I haue opened my mouth, my tongue hath spoken †in my mouth.

† Heb. in my palate.

3 My words ſhalbe of the vprightneſſe of my heart : and my lippes ſhall vtter knowledge clearely.

4 The Spirit of God hath made me, and the breath of the Almightie hath giuen me life.

5 If thou canst, anſwere me, set *thy wordes* in order before me, ſtand vp.

* Cha. 9. 35. and 23. 20.
† Heb. according to thy mouth.
† Heb. cut out of the clay.

6 ** Behold, I am † according to thy wiſh in Gods ſtead : I also am †formed out of the clay.

7 Behold, my terrour ſhall not make thee afraid, neither ſhall my hand be heauie vpon thee.

† Heb. in mine eares.

8 Surely thou haſt spoken †in mine hearing, and I haue heard the voice of *thy* words, *ſaying,*

9 I *am* cleane without transgreſſion, I *am* innocent ; neither *is there* iniquitie in me.

10 Behold, hee findeth occaſions against mee, hee counteth mee for his enemie.

11 He putteth my feete in the ſtockes, he marketh all my pathes.

12 Behold, *in* this thou art not iust : I will anſwere thee, That God is greater then man.

† Heb. hee anſwereth not.

13 Why doeſt thou ſtriue against him? for † he giueth not account of any of his matters.

14 For God ſpeaketh once, yea twice, *yet man* perceiueth it not.

15 In a dreame, in a viſion of the night, when deepe ſleepe falleth vpon men, in ſlumbrings vpon the bed :

† Heb. hee reuealeth, or vncouereth.

16 Then hee † openeth the eares of men, and ſealeth their instruction,

17 That hee may withdraw man *from his* †purpoſe, and hide pride from man.

† Heb. worke.

18 Hee keepeth backe his ſoule from the pit, and his life †from periſhing by the ſword.

† Heb. from paſſing by the ſword.

19 Hee is chaſtened also with paine vpon his bed, and the multitude of his bones with strong *paine.*

20 ** So that his life abhorreth bread, and his ſoule †daintie meate.

* Pſal. 107. 17.
† Heb. meate of deſire.

21 His fleſh is consumed away that it cannot be ſeene ; and his bones that were not ſeene, ſticke out.

22 His ſoule draweth neere vnto the graue, and his life to the destroyers.

23 If there be a meſſenger with him, an interpreter, one among a thouſand, to ſhew vnto man his vprightneſſe :

24 Then hee is gracious vnto him, and ſayth, Deliuer him from going downe to the pit ; I haue found ‖ a ranſome.

‖ Or, an atonement.

25 His fleſh ſhall be freſher †then a childes : he ſhall returne to the dayes of his youth.

‖ Hebr. then childhood.

26 He ſhall pray vnto God, and hee will be fauourable vnto him, and hee ſhall ſee his face with ioy : for he will render vnto man his righteouſneſſe.

27 ‖ He looketh vpon men, *and* if any ſay, I haue ſinned, and peruerted that which was right, and it profited mee not :

‖ Or, he ſhall looke vpon men, andſay, I haue ſinned, &c.

28 ‖ Hee will deliuer his ſoule from going into the pit, and his life ſhall ſee the light.

‖ Or, he hath deliuered my ſoule &c. and my life.

29 Loe, all these things worketh God †oftentimes with man,

30 To bring backe his ſoule from the pit, to be enlightened with the light of the liuing.

† Heb. twice and thrice.

31 Marke well, O Iob, hearken vnto me, hold thy peace, and I wil ſpeake.

32 If thou haſt any thing to ſay, anſwere me : ſpeake, for I deſire to iustifie thee.

33 If not, hearken vnto me : holde thy peace, and I ſhall teach thee wiſedome.

CHAP. XXXIIII.

1 Elihu accuſeth Iob for charging God with iniuſtice. 10 God omnipotent cannot be vniuſt. 31 Man muſt humble himſelfe vnto God. 34 Elihu reprooueth Iob.

Vrthermore Elihu anſwered, and ſaid,

2 Heare my wordes, O yee wise men, and giue eare vnto me, ye that haue knowledge.

3 ** For the eare trieth words, as the †mouth taſteth meate.

* Chap. 12. 11.
† Heb. palate.

4 Let vs chuse to vs iudgement : let vs know among our ſelues what *is* good.

5 For

5 For Iob hath said, I am righteous : and God hath taken away my iudgement.

6 Should I lye against my right? †my wound is incurable without transgression.

7 What man *is* like Iob, *who* drinketh vp scorning like water?

8 Which goeth in company with the workers of iniquitie, and walketh with wicked men.

9 For hee hath said, It profiteth a man nothing, that he should delight himselfe with God.

10 Therefore hearken vnto me, ye †men of vnderstanding : * farre bee it from God, *that he should doe* wickednes, and from the Almighty, that *hee should commit* iniquitie.

11 * For the worke of a man shall he render vnto him, and cause euery man to finde according to *his* wayes.

12 Yea surely God will not doe wickedly, neither will the Almighty peruert iudgement.

13 Who hath giuen him a charge ouer the earth? or who hath disposed †the whole world?

14 * If he set his heart †vpon man, *if* he gather vnto himselfe his spirit and his breath;

15 * All flesh shall perish together, and man shall turne againe vnto dust.

16 If now thou *hast* vnderstanding, heare this : hearken to the voyce of my words.

17 Shall euen he that hateth right, †gouerne? and wilt thou condemne him that is most iust?

18 Is it *fit* to say to a King, *Thou art* wicked? *and* to Princes, *Ye are* vngodly?

19 * *How much lesse to him* that accepteth not the persons of Princes, nor regardeth the rich more then the poore? for they all are the woorke of his hands.

20 In a moment shall they die, and the people shalbe troubled at midnight, and passe away : and †the mighty shall be taken away without hand.

21 * For his eyes *are* vpon the wayes of man, and he seeth all his goings.

22 *There is* no darkenes, nor shadow of death, where the workers of iniquitie may hide themselues.

23 For hee will not lay vpon man more *then right;* that he should †enter into iudgement with God.

24 He shall breake in pieces mighty

men †without number, and set others in their stead.

25 Therefore hee knoweth their workes, and he ouerturneth *them* in the night, so that they are †destroyed.

26 He striketh them as wicked men, † in the open sight of others;

27 Because they turned backe †from him, and would not consider any of his wayes.

28 So that they cause the cry of the poore to come vnto him, and he heareth the cry of the afflicted.

29 When he giueth quietnesse, who then can make trouble? and when hee hideth *his* face, who then can beholde him? whether *it be done* against a nation, or against a man onely :

30 That the hypocrite raigne not, lest the people be ensnared.

31 Surely it is meete to be said vnto God, I haue borne *chastisement,* I will not offend *any more.*

32 That which I see not, teach thou me; If I haue done iniquitie, I will doe no more.

33 †Should it bee according to thy minde? he will recompense it, whether thou refuse, or whether thou chuse, and not I : therefore speake what thou knowest.

34 Let men †of vnderstanding tell mee, and let a wise man hearken vnto mee.

35 Iob hath spoken without knowledge, and his words *were* without wisdome.

36 ‖ My desire *is that* Iob may bee tried vnto the ende, because of *his* answeres for wicked men.

37 For he addeth rebellion vnto his sinne, hee clappeth *his* handes amongst vs, and multiplieth his words against God.

CHAP. XXXV.

1 Comparison is not to be made with God, because our good or euill cannot extend vnto him. 9 Many cry in their afflictions, but are not heard for want of faith.

 Lihu spake moreouer, and said,

2 Thinkest thou this to bee right, *that* thou saydest, My righteousnesse *is* more then Gods?

3 For thou saydst, What aduantage will it bee vnto thee, *and*, What profite shall

Hebr. mine row.

Hebr. men heart.
Exod. 32.
iob 8. 3.
36. 23.
al. 92. 15.
n. 9. 14.
Psal. 62.
pro. 24.
19. eze.
20. mat.
27. rom.
6. 2. cor.
10. 1. pet.
17. apoc.
12

Hebr. all of
Psal. 104.

Hebr. vpon n.

Eccles. 12.
gene. 3.

Heb. binde.

Deut. 10.
2. chro.
v. act. 10.
rom. 2.
gal. 2. 6.
ie. 6. 9.
os. 3. 25.
pet. 1. 17.

Heb. they all take away the ghty.
ro. 5. 21.
115. 3.
31. 4.
chro. 16.
iere. 16.

Hebr. goe.

† *Heb. without searching out.*

† *Hebr. crushed.*

† *Hebr. in the place of beholders.*
† *Hebr. from after him.*

† *Hebr. Should it be from with thee?*

† *Hebr. of heart.*

‖ *Or, My father, let Iob be tried.*

‖ Or, by it more then by my sinne.
† Heb. I wil returne to thee words.

shall I haue, ‖if I bee cleansed from my sinne?

4 †I wil answere thee, and thy companions with thee.

5 Looke vnto the heauens and see, and behold the clouds which are higher then thou.

6 If thou sinnest, what doest thou against him? or if thy transgressions be multiplied, what doest thou vnto him?

* Psal. 16. 2.
Rom. 11. 35
iob. 22. 3.

7 *If thou be righteous, what giuest thou him? or what receiueth hee of thine hand?

8 Thy wickednesse may hurt a man as thou art, and thy righteousnesse may profit the sonne of man.

9 By reason of the multitude of oppressions they make the oppressed to crie: they crie out by reason of the arme of the mightie.

10 But none saith, Where is God my maker, who giueth songs in the night?

11 Who teacheth vs more then the beasts of the earth, and maketh vs wiser then the foules of heauen?

12 There they crie, (but none giueth answere) because of the pride of euill men.

* Iob. 27. 9
prou. 1. 28.
isa. 1. 15. ier.
11. 11.

13 * Surely God wil not heare vanitie, neither wil the Almightie regard it.

14 Although thou sayest thou shalt not see him, yet iudgement is before him, therefore trust thou in him.

‖ That is God.
‖ That is, Iob.

15 But now because it is not so, ‖hee hath visited in his anger, yet ‖he knoweth it not in great extremitie:

16 Therefore doeth Iob open his mouth in vaine : he multiplieth words without knowledge.

CHAP. XXXVI.

1 Elihu sheweth how God is iust in his wayes.
16 How Iobs sinnes hinder Gods blessings.
24 Gods works are to be magnified.

† Heb. that there are yet words for God.

Lihu also proceeded, and said,

2 Suffer mee a little, and I will shewe thee, †that I haue yet to speake on Gods behalfe.

3 I will fetch my knowledge from afarre, and will ascribe righteousnesse to my Maker.

4 For truely my words shall not be false : he that is perfect in knowledge, is with thee.

† Heb. heart

5 Behold, God is mightie, and despiseth not any: he is mightie in strength and †wisedome.

6 He preserueth not the life of the wicked : but giueth right to the ‖poore.

‖ Or, afflicted.
* Psal. 34. 14.

7 * Hee withdraweth not his eyes from the righteous : but with kings are they on the throne, yea he doth establish them for euer, and they are exalted.

8 And if they bee bound in fetters, and be holden in cords of affliction :

9 Then hee sheweth them their worke, and their transgressions, that they haue exceeded.

10 He openeth also their eare to discipline, and commandeth that they returne from iniquitie.

* Iob 21.

11 If they obey and serue him, * they shall spend their dayes in prosperitie, and their yeeres in pleasures.

† Heb. the shall pass way by th sword.

12 But if they obey not, †they shall perish by the sword, and they shall die without knowledge.

13 But the hypocrites in heart heape vp wrath : they crie not when he bindeth them.

† Hebr. th soule diet
‖ Or, Sodo mites.
‖ Or, affli cted.

14 †They die in youth, and their life is among the ‖vncleane.

15 He deliuereth the ‖poore in his affliction, and openeth their eares in oppression.

† Heb. th rest of th table.

16 Euen so would he haue remooued thee out of the strait into a broad place, where there is no straitnesse, and †that which should be set on thy table, should be full of fatnesse.

‖ Or, iudg ment and stice sho vphold th

17 But thou hast fulfilled the iudgement of the wicked : ‖iudgement and iustice take hold on thee.

† Heb. tu thee asid

18 Because there is wrath, beware lest he take thee away with his stroke : then a great ransome cannot †deliuer thee.

19 Will he esteeme thy riches? no not gold, nor all the forces of strength.

20 Desire not the night, when people are cut off in their place.

21 Take heed, regard not iniquitie : for this hast thou chosen rather then affliction.

22 Beholde, God exalteth by his power : who teacheth like him?

23 Who hath inioyned him his way? or who can say, Thou hast wrought iniquitie?

24 Remember that thou magnifie his worke, which men behold.

25 Euery man may see it, man may behold it afarre off.

26 Behold, God is great, and we know him not, neither can the number of his yeeres be searched out.

27 For hee maketh small the drops of

of water : they powre downe raine according to the vapour thereof :

28 Which the clouds doe drop, and distill vpon man aboundantly.

29 Also can any vnderstand the spreadings of the clouds, *or* the noise of his tabernacle ?

30 Behold, he spreadeth his light vpon it, and couereth †the bottome of the sea.

31 For by them iudgeth he the people, he giueth meate in abundance.

32 With clouds he couereth the light, and commaundeth it *not to shine*, by *the cloud* that commeth betwixt.

33 The noise thereof sheweth concerning it, the cattel also concerning †the Vapour.

CHAP. XXXVII.

1 God is to be feared because of his great works.
15 His wisdome is vnsearchable in them.

AT this also my heart trembleth, and is moued out of his place.

2 †Heare attentiuely the noise of his voice, and the sound *that* goeth out of his mouth.

3 Hee directeth it vnder the whole heauen, and his †lightning vnto the †ends of the earth.

4 After it a voyce roareth : he thundreth with the voice of his excellencie, and hee will not stay them when his voice is heard.

5 God thundereth maruellously with his voice : great things doth hee, which we cannot comprehend.

6 For *he saith to the snow, Be thou *on* the earth : †likewise to the small raine, and to the great raine of his strength.

7 He sealeth vp the hand of euery man ; that all men may knowe his worke.

8 Then the beastes goe into dennes : and remaine in their places.

9 †Out of the South commeth the whirlewinde : and cold out of †North.

10 By the breath of God, frost is giuen : and the breadth of the waters is straitned.

11 Also by watring he wearieth the thicke cloud : hee scattereth †his bright cloud.

12 And it is turned round about by his counsels : that they may doe whatsoeuer hee commaundeth them vpon the face of the world in the earth.

13 He causeth it to come, whether for †correction, or for his land, or for mercy.

14 Hearken vnto this, O Iob : stand still, and consider the wondrous workes of God.

15 Doest thou knowe when God disposed them, and caused the light of his cloud to shine ?

16 Doest thou know the ballancings of the clouds, the wondrous workes of him which is perfect in knowledge ?

17 How thy garments are warme, when hee quieteth the earth by the South *wind* ?

18 Hast thou with him spread out the skie, *which* is strong, *and* as a molten looking glasse ?

19 Teach vs what we shall say vnto him ; *for* we cannot order *our speach* by reason of darknes.

20 Shall it bee told him that I speake ? if a man speake, surely he shalbe swallowed vp.

21 And nowe *men* see not the bright light which *is* in the clouds : but the wind passeth and cleanseth them.

22 †Faire weather commeth out of the North : with God *is* terrible maiestie.

23 Touching the Almighty, we cannot find him out : he *is* excellent in power, and in iudgement, and in plenty of iustice : he will not afflict.

24 Men doe therefore feare him : he respecteth not any that *are* wise of heart.

CHAP. XXXVIII.

1 God chalengeth Iob to answer. 4 God by his mighty workes, conuinceth Iob of Ignorance, 31 and of imbecillity.

Hen the LORD answered Iob out of the whirlewind, and sayd,

2 Who *is* this *that* darkneth counsell by words without knowledge ?

3 Gird vp nowe thy loines like a man ; for I will demaund of thee, and †answere thou me.

4 *Where wast thou when I layd the foundations of the earth ? declare, †if thou hast vnderstanding.

5 Who hath layd the measures thereof, if thou knowest ? or who hath stretched the line vpon it ?

6 Wherevpon are the †foundations

Margin notes (left column)

Heb. the ...ots.

Heb. that ...ich goeth

Heb. heare hearing.

Heb. light. Heb. wings the earth.

Psal. 147. & 17.
Heb. and the show- of raine, ...d to the ...uers of ...ine of his ...ength.

Heb. out of ... chamber.
Heb. scatte- ...g winds.

Heb. the ...ud of his ...ht.

Margin notes (right column)

† *Heb. a rod.*

† *Heb. gold*

† *Heb. make ...ne know.*
* Psal. 104.
5. prou. 30. 4.
† *Heb. if thou knowest vn- ...derstan- ...ding.*

† *Heb. soc- ...kets.*

† Heb. made to sinke.

ons thereof †fastened? or who layd the corner stone thereof?

7 When the morning starres sang together, and all the sonnes of God shouted for ioy.

* Psal. 104.9

8 *Or who shut vp the sea with doores, when it brake foorth as if it had issued out of the wombe?

9 When I made the cloud the garment thereof, and thicke darknesse a swadling band for it,

‖ Or, establi-shed my de-cree vpon it.

10 And ‖brake vp for it my decreed place, and set barres and doores,

11 And said, Hitherto shalt thou come, but no further: and heere shall

† Heb. the pride of thy waues.

†thy proud waues be stayed.

12 Hast thou commaunded the morning since thy daies? and caused the day-spring to know his place,

13 That it might take hold of the

† Heb. wings.

†endes of the earth, that the wicked might be shaken out of it?

14 It is turned as clay to the seale, and they stand as a garment.

15 And from the wicked their light is withholden, and the high arme shal-be broken.

16 Hast thou entred into the springs of the sea? or hast thou walked in the search of the depth?

17 Haue the gates of death bene opened vnto thee? or hast thou seene the doores of the shadow of death?

18 Hast thou perceiued the breadth of the earth? Declare if thou knowest it all.

19 Where is the way where light dwelleth? and as for darknesse, where is the place thereof?

‖ Or, at.

20 That thou shouldest take it ‖to the bound thereof, and that thou shouldest know the pathes to the house thereof.

21 Knowest thou it, because thou wast then borne? or because the number of thy daies is great?

22 Hast thou entred into the treasures of the snowe? or hast thou seene the treasures of the haile,

23 Which I haue reserued against the time of trouble, against the day of battaile and warre?

24 By what way is the light parted? which scattereth the East wind vpon the earth.

25 Who hath diuided a water course for the ouerflowing of waters? or a way for the lightning of thunder,

26 To cause it to raine on the earth, where no man is: on the wildernesse wherein there is no man?

27 To satisfie the desolate and waste ground, and to cause the bud of the tender herbe to spring forth?

28 Hath the raine a father? or who hath begotten the drops of dew?

29 Out of whose wombe came the yce? and the hoary frost of heauen, who hath gendred it?

30 The waters are hid as with a stone, and the face of the deepe †is frozen.

† Heb. is taken.

31 Canst thou bind the sweete influences of ‖Pleiades? or loose the bands of †Orion?

‖ Or, the s uen-starr Heb. Cim † Heb. Ce ‖ Or, the twelue sign † Heb. gu them.

32 Canst thou bring forth ‖Mazzaroth in his season, or canst thou †guide Arcturus with his sonnes?

33 Knowest thou the ordinances of heauen? canst thou set the dominion thereof in the earth?

34 Canst thou lift vp thy voice to the cloudes, that abundance of waters may couer thee?

35 Canst thou send lightnings, that they may goe, and say vnto thee, †Here we are?

† Heb. be hold vs.

36 *Who hath put wisedome in the inward parts? or who hath giuen vnderstanding to the heart?

* Chap. 3 8. Eccle. 26.

37 Who can number the cloudes in wisedome? or †who can stay the bottles of heauen,

† Heb. wh can caus lie downe

38 ‖When the dust †groweeh into hardnesse, and the clods cleaue fast together?

‖ Or, whe the dust i turned in myre. † Heb. is powred.

39 *Wilt thou hunt the pray for the lyon? or fill the †appetite of the young lyons,

* Psal. 1 21. † Heb. th life.

40 When they couch in their dennes, and abide in the couert to lie in waite?

41 *Who prouideth for the rauen his foode? when his young ones cry vnto God, they wander for lacke of meate.

* Psal. 1 9. Math. 26.

CHAP. XXXIX.

1 Of the wild goates and hinds. 5 Of the wild Asse. 9 The Vnicorne. 13 The Peacock, Storke and Ostrich. 19 The horse. 26 The hauke. 27 The Eagle.

Nowest *thou the time when the wild goates of the rocke bring forth? or canst thou marke when the hindes doe calue?

* Psal. 2

2 Canst thou number the moneths that they fulfill? or knowest thou the time when they bring forth?

3 They bowe themselues, they bring forth their young ones, they cast out their sorrowes.

4 Their

4 Their yong ones are in good liking, they grow vp with corne: they go forth, and returne not vnto them.

5 Who hath sent out the wild asse free? or who hath looosed the bands of the wild asse?

ebr. salt es.

6 Whose house I haue made the wildernesse, and †the barren lande his dwellings.

7 He scorneth the multitude of the citie, neither regardeth he the crying †of the driuer.

ebr. of exactor.

8 The range of the mountaines *is* his pasture, and hee searcheth after euery greene thing.

9 Will the Vnicorne be willing to serue thee? or abide by thy cribbe?

10 Canst thou binde the Vnicorne with his band in the furrow? or will he harrow the valleyes after thee?

11 Wilt thou trust him because his strength is great? or wilt thou leaue thy labour to him?

12 Wilt thou beleeue him that hee will bring home thy seed? and gather it into thy barne?

, the fea-s of the ke and -ich.

13 *Gauest thou* the goodly wings vnto the peacocks, or ‖wings and feathers vnto the Ostrich?

14 Which leaueth her egges in the earth, and warmeth them in dust,

15 And forgetteth that the foot may crush them, or that the wilde beast may breake them.

16 She is hardened against her yong ones, as though they were not hers: her labour is in vaine without feare.

17 Because God hath depriued her of wisedome, neither hath he imparted to her vnderstanding.

18 What time she lifteth vp her selfe on high, she scorneth the horse and his rider.

19 Hast thou giuen the horse strength? hast thou clothed his necke with thunder?

20 Canst thou make him afraid as a grashopper? the glory of his nostrils *is* †terrible.

ebr. rour. r, his feet ge.

21 ‖He paweth in the valley, and reioyceth in *his* strength: hee goeth on to meet †the armed men.

ebr. the our.

22 He mocketh at feare, and is not affrighted: neither turneth he backe from the sword.

23 The quiuer ratleth against him, the glittering speare and the shield.

24 He swalloweth the ground with fiercenesse and rage: neither beleeueth

he that it *is* the sound of the trumpet.

25 Hee saith among the trumpets, Ha, ha: and he smelleth the battaile a-farre off, the thunder of the captaines, and the shouting.

26 Doeth the hawke flie by thy wisedome, *and* stretch her wings toward the South?

27 Doeth the Eagle mount vp †at thy commaund? and make her nest on high?

† Hebr. by thy mouth.

28 She dwelleth and abideth on the rocke, vpon the cragge of the rocke, and the strong place.

29 From thence she seeketh the pray, *and* her eyes behold a farre off.

30 Her yong ones also suck vp blood: and *where the slaine *are*, there *is* he.

* Matt. 24. 28. luke 17. 37.

CHAP. XL.

1 Iob humbleth himselfe to God. 6 God stirreth him vp to shew his righteousnes, power, and wisedome. 15 Of the Behemoth.

Oreouer the LORD answered Iob, and said,

2 Shall hee that contendeth with the Almightie, instruct *him?* he that reproueth God, let him answere it.

3 ¶ Then Iob answered the LORD, and said,

4 Behold, I am vile, what shall I answere thee? I wil lay my hand vpon my mouth.

5 Once haue I spoken, but I will not answere: yea twise, but I will proceed no further.

6 ¶ Then answered the LORD vnto Iob out of the whirlewinde, and said:

7 *Gird vp thy loynes now like a man: I will demaund of thee, and declare thou vnto me.

* Chap. 38. 3.

8 * Wilt thou also disanul my iudgement? wilt thou condemne mee, that thou mayest be righteous?

* Psal. 50. 21. rom. 3. 4.

9 *Hast* thou an arme like God? or canst thou thunder with a voyce like him?

10 * Decke thy selfe now *with* Maiestie, and excellencie, and aray thy selfe with glory, and beautie.

* Psal. 104. 1.

11 Cast abroad the rage of thy wrath: and behold euery one that is proud, and abase him.

12 Looke on euery one that is proud, *and* bring him low: and tread downe the wicked in their place.

13 Hide

13 Hide them in the dust together, and binde their faces in secret.

14 Then will I also confesse vnto thee, that thine owne right hand can saue thee.

‖ *Or, the Elephant, as some thinke.*

15 ¶ Beholde now ‖ Behemoth which I made with thee, hee eateth grasse as an oxe.

16 Loe now, his strength *is* in his loynes, and his force *is* in the nauell of his belly.

‖ *Or, he setteth vp.*

17 ‖Hee moueth his taile like a Cedar: the sinewes of his stones are wrapt together.

18 His bones are *as* strong pieces of brasse: his bones are like barres of iron.

19 Hee *is* the chiefe of the wayes of God: he that made him, can make his sword to approach *vnto him.*

20 Surely the mountaines bring him foorth foode: where all the beasts of the field play.

21 He lieth vnder the shady trees, in the couert of the reede, and fennes.

22 The shady trees couer him *with* their shaddow: the willowes of the brooke compasse him about.

† *Heb. he oppresseth.*
‖ *Or, will any take him in his sight? or bore his nose with a ginne?*

23 Behold, †he drinketh vp a riuer, *and* hasteth not: he trusteth that he can draw vp Iordan into his mouth.

24 ‖He taketh it with his eyes: his nose pearceth through snares.

CHAP. XLI.

Of Gods great power in the Leuiathan.

‖ *That is, a whale or a whirlepoole.*

† *Heb. which thou drownest.*

Anst thou draw out ‖Leuiathan with an hooke? or his tongue with a corde †*which* thou lettest downe?

2 Canst thou put an hooke into his nose? or bore his iawe through with a thorne?

3 Will he make many supplications vnto thee? will he speake soft *words* vnto thee?

4 Will he make a couenant with thee? wilt thou take him for a seruant for euer?

5 Wilt thou play with him as with a birde? wilt thou binde him for thy maydens?

6 Shall the companions make a banquet of him? shall they part him among the merchants?

7 Canst thou fill his skinne with barbed irons? or his head with fish-speares?

8 Lay thine hand vpon him, re-

member the battell: doe no more.

9 Behold, the hope of him is in vaine: shall not one be cast downe euen at the sight of him?

10 None is so fierce that dare stirre him vp: who then is able to stand before me?

* *Psal.*
& 50. 15
1. cor. 1

11 *Who hath preuented me that I should repay *him*? *whatsoeuer* is vnder the whole heauen, is mine.

12 I will not conceale his parts, nor his power, nor his comely proportion.

‖ *Or, wi*

13 Who can discouer the face of his garment? or who can come *to him,* ‖with his double bridle?

† *Heb. pieces o shields.*

14 Who can open the doores of his face? his teeth *are* terrible round about.

15 *His* †scales *are his* pride, shut vp together *as with* a close seale.

16 One is so neere to another, that no ayre can come betweene them.

17 They are ioyned one to another, they sticke together, that they cannot be sundred.

18 By his neesings a light doth shine, and his eyes are like the eye-liddes of the morning.

19 Out of his mouth goe burning lampes, *and* sparkes of fire leape out.

20 Out of his nostrels goeth smoke, as *out* of a seething pot or caldron.

21 His breath kindleth coales, and a flame goeth out of his mouth.

22 In his necke remaineth strength, and †sorrowe is turned into ioy before him.

† *Heb. s reioyce*

23 †The flakes of his flesh are ioyned together: they are firme in themselues, they cannot be moued.

† *Heb. falling.*

24 His heart is as firme as a stone, yea as hard as a peece of the nether *mil-stone.*

25 When he rayseth vp himselfe, the mightie are afraid: by reason of breakings they purifie themselues.

26 The sword of him that layeth at him cannot hold: the speare, the dart, nor the ‖habergeon.

‖ *Or, b plate.*

27 He esteemeth iron as straw, *and* brasse as rotten wood.

28 The arrow cannot make him flee: sling-stones are turned with him into stubble.

29 Darts are counted as stubble: he laugheth at the shaking of a speare.

30 †Sharpe stones *are* vnder him: he spreadeth sharpe pointed things vpon the mire.

† *Heb. s pieces, potsher*

31 He maketh the deepe to boyle like a pot:

a pot : hee maketh the sea like a pot of oyntment.

32 Hee maketh a path to shine after him ; one would thinke the deepe to bee hoarie.

33 Vpon earth there is not his like : who is made without feare.

34 He beholdeth all high things : he is a king ouer all the children of pride.

CHAP. XLII.

1 Iob submitteth himselfe vnto God. 7 God preferring Iobs cause, maketh his friends submit themselues, & accepteth him. 10 He magnifieth & blesseth Iob. 16 Iobs age & death.

Hen Iob answered the Lord, and said,

2 I know that thou canst *doe* euery thing, and *that* ‖ no thought can bee withholden from thee.

3 * Who *is* he *that* hideth counsell without knowledge? therefore haue I vttered that I vnderstood not, things too wonderfull for me, which I knew not.

4 Heare, I beseech thee, and I will speake : I will demand of thee, and declare thou vnto me.

5 I haue heard of thee by the hearing of the eare : but now mine eye seeth thee.

6 Wherefore I abhorre *my selfe*, and repent in dust and ashes.

7 ¶ And it was so, that after the Lord had spoken these words vnto Iob, the Lord said to Eliphaz the Temanite, My wrath is kindled against thee, and against thy two friends : for ye haue not spoken of mee the thing that is right, as my seruant Iob hath.

8 Therefore take vnto you now seuen bullocks, and seuen rammes, and goe to my seruant Iob, and offer vp for your selues a burnt offring, and my ser-

uant Iob shal pray for you, for † him will I accept : lest I deale with you *after your* folly, in that ye haue not spoken of mee the thing which is right, like my seruant Iob.

9 So Eliphaz the Temanite, and Bildad the Shuhite, *and* Zophar the Naamathite went, and did according as the Lord commanded them : the Lord also accepted † Iob.

10 And the Lord turned the captiuitie of Iob, when he prayed for his friends : also the Lord † gaue Iob twice as much as he had before.

11 Then came there vnto him all his brethren, and all his sisters, and all they that had bin of his acquaintance before, and did eat bread with him in his house : and they bemoned him, and comforted him ouer all the euill that the Lord had brought vpon him : euery man also gaue him a piece of money, and euery one an eare-ring of gold.

12 So the Lord blessed the latter end of Iob, more then his beginning : for he had fourteene thousand sheepe, and sixe thousand camels, and a thousand yoke of oxen, and a thousand shee asses.

13 He had also seuen sonnes, and three daughters.

14 And he called the name of the first, Iemima, and the name of the second, Kezia, and the name of the third, Keren-happuch.

15 And in all the land were no women found so faire as the daughters of Iob : and their father gaue them inheritance among their brethren.

16 After this liued Iob an hundred and fourtie yeeres, and saw his sonnes, and his sonnes sonnes, *euen* foure generations.

17 So Iob died being old, and full of dayes.

Marginal notes:

† *Heb. his face or person.*

† *Heb. the face of Iob.*

† *Heb. added to Iob vnto the double.*

¶ THE

¶ THE BOOKE OF
Pſalmes.

PSALME I.

1 The happineſſe of the godly. 4 The vn-
happineſſe of the vngodly.

Leſſed *is the man
that walketh not
in the counſell of
the ||vngodly, nor
ſtandeth in the
way of ſinners,
nor ſitteth in the
ſeat of the ſcorne-
full.

2 But his delight *is* in the Law of
the LORD, *and in his Law doeth he
meditate day and night.

3 And he ſhalbe like a tree planted
by the riuers of water, that bringeth
foorth his fruit in his ſeaſon, his leafe
alſo ſhall not † wither, and whatſoeuer
he doeth, ſhall proſper.

4 The vngodly *are* not ſo: but *are*
*like the chaffe, which the winde dri-
ueth away.

5 Therefore the vngodly ſhall not
ſtand in the iudgement, nor ſinners in
the Congregation of the righteous.

6 For the LORD knoweth the
way of the righteous : but the way of
the vngodly ſhall periſh.

PSAL. II.

1 The kingdome of Chriſt. 10 Kings are exhorted to accept it.

Hy *do the heathen ||rage,
and the people † imagine
a vaine thing?

2 The Kings of the
earth ſet themſelues, and
the rulers take counſell together, a-
gainſt the LORD, and againſt his
Anoynted, *ſaying,*

3 Let vs breake their bandes aſunder, and caſt away their cords from vs.

4 * Hee that ſitteth in the heauens
ſhal laugh : the LORD ſhall haue them,
in deriſion.

5 Then ſhall hee ſpeake vnto them
in his wrath, and ||vexe them in his ſore
diſpleaſure.

6 Yet haue I ſet † my King † vpon
my holy hill of Sion.

7 * I will declare || the decree : the
LORD hath ſaid vnto mee, Thou *art*
my ſonne, this day haue I begotten
thee.

8 * Aske of me, and I ſhall giue *thee*
the heathen for thine inheritance, and
the vttermoſt parts of the earth for thy
poſſeſſion.

9 * Thou ſhalt breake them with a
rod of iron, thou ſhalt daſh them in pieces like a potters veſſell.

10 Bee wiſe now therefore , O yee
Kings : be inſtructed ye Iudges of the
earth.

11 Serue the LORD with feare,
and reioyce with trembling.

12 Kiſſe the Sonne leſt he be angry,
and ye periſh *from* the way, when his
wrath is kindled but a little : * Bleſſed
are all they that put their truſt in him.

PSAL. III.

The ſecuritie of Gods protection.

¶ *A Pſalme of Dauid when he fled
from Abſalom his ſonne.

LORD, how are they in-
creaſed that trouble mee?
many are they that riſe vp
againſt me.

2 Many *there bee which
ſay of my ſoule, *There is* no helpe for him
in God. Selah.

3 But

Margin notes (left column):

u 4.

wicked.

h. 1. 8.
119. 1.
17. 9.

br. fade.

al. 34. 5.
7. 13.

ts. 4.

tumul-
ſly as-
ole?
br. me-
e.

Margin notes (right column):

* Prou. 1.
26.

|| Or, trouble

† Hebr. an-
ointed.
|| Hebr. vpon
Sion, the hill
of my Holi-
neſſe.
* Acts. 13.
33. heb. 1.
5.
|| Or, for a
decree.
* Pſal. 72.
8.

* Apoc. 2.
27. and 19.
15.

* Prou. 16.
20. iſa. 30.
18. iete. 17.
7. rom. 9. 33
and 10. 11.
1. pet. 2. 6.

* 2. Sam. 15.
15.

Or, about.

3 But thou, O Lord, *art* a shield || for me; my glory, and the lifter vp of mine head.

4 I cryed vnto the Lord with my voyce, and he heard me out of his holy hill. Selah.

*Psal. 4. 9.

5 *I layd me downe and slept; I awaked, for the Lord sustained me.

*Psal. 27. 3.

6 *I will not be afraid of ten thousands of people, that haue set *themselues* against me round about.

7 Arise, O Lord, saue mee, O my God; for thou hast smitten all mine enemies *vpon* the cheeke bone: thou hast broken the teeth of the vngodly.

*Isa. 43. 11.
Hos. 13. 4.

8 *Saluation *belongeth* vnto the Lord: thy blessing *is* vpon thy people. Selah.

PSAL. IIII.

1 Dauid prayeth for audience. 2 He reproueth and exhorteth his enemies. 6 Mans happinesse is in Gods fauour.

Or, ouer-seer.

¶ To the || chiefe Musician on Neginoth, A Psalme of Dauid.

Or, bee gracious vnto me.

Eare me, when I call, O God of my righteousnesse: thou hast inlarged mee when *I was* in distresse, || haue mercy vpon me, and heare my prayer.

2 O ye sonnes of men, how long *will yee turne* my glory into shame? *how long* will yee loue vanitie, *and* seeke after leasing? Selah.

3 But know that the Lord hath set apart him that is godly, for himselfe: the Lord will heare when I call vnto him.

4 Stand in awe, and sinne not: commune with your owne heart vpon your bed, and be still. Selah.

*Psal. 50. 14. & 51. 19.

5 Offer *the sacrifices of righteousnesse, and put your trust in the Lord.

6 There be many that say, Who wil shew vs *any* good? Lord lift thou vp the light of thy countenance vpon vs.

7 Thou hast put gladnesse in my heart, more then in the time that their corne and their wine increased.

*Psal. 3. 5.

8 *I will both lay mee downe in peace, and sleepe: for thou Lord only makest me dwell in safetie.

PSAL. V.

1 Dauid prayeth, and professeth his studie in prayer. 4 God fauoureth not the wicked. 7 Dauid professing his faith, prayeth vnto God, to guide him, 10 To destroy his enemies, 11 and to preserue the godly.

¶ To the chiefe musician vpon Nehiloth, A Psalme of Dauid.

Iue eare to my words, O Lord, consider my meditation.

2 Hearken vnto the voice of my crie, my King, and my God: for vnto thee will I pray.

*Psal. 6.

3 *My voyce shalt thou heare in the morning, O Lord; in the morning will I direct *my prayer* vnto thee, and will looke *vp*.

4 For thou *art* not a God *that* hath pleasure in wickednesse: neither shall euill dwell with thee.

†Heb. fore tł eyes.

5 The foolish shall not stand †in thy sight: thou hatest al workers of iniquity

†Heb. man of and de

6 Thou shalt destroy them that speake leasing: the Lord will abhorre the †bloodie and deceitfull man.

7 But as for me, I will come *into* thy house in the multitude of thy mercy: *and* in thy feare will I worship toward †thy holy temple.

†Heb. temple holines
†Heb. which serue :
*Or, s. fastne
†Heb. mouth the mo any of
†Heb. kednes

8 Lead me O Lord, in thy righteousnesse, because of †mine enemies; make thy way straight before my face.

9 For *there is* no ||faithfulnes †in their mouth, their inward part *is* †very wickednesse: *their throat *is* an open sepulchre, they flatter with their tongue.

*Rom
*Or, m them g
*Or, fi their c sels.

10 ||Destroy thou them, O God, let them fall ||by their owne counsels: cast them out in the multitude of their transgressions, for they haue rebelled against thee.

†Heb. couere uer, o lectest

11 But let all those that put their trust in thee, reioyce: let them euer shout for ioy; because thou †defendest them: let them also that loue thy name, be ioyfull in thee.

†Heb crown

12 For thou, Lord, wilt blesse the righteous: with fauour wilt thou †compasse him as *with* a shield.

PSAL. VI.

1 Dauids complaint in his sicknesse. 8 By faith he triumpheth ouer his enemies.

¶ To the chiefe musician on Neginoth || vpon Sheminith, A Psalme of Dauid.

*Or, t the eig

*Psa.

*Lord, rebuke me not in thine anger, neither chasten me in thy hot displeasure.

2 Haue mercy vpon me, O Lord, for I *am* weake: O Lord heale mee, for my bones are vexed.

3 My

3 My ſoule is also ſore vexed : but thou, O LORD, how long?

4 Returne, O LORD, deliuer my ſoule : oh ſaue mee, for thy mercies ſake.

5 *For in death *there is* no remembrance of thee : in the graue who ſhall giue thee thankes?

6 I am weary with my groning, ||all the night make I my bed to ſwim : I water my couch with my teares.

7 Mine eie is conſumed becauſe of griefe ; it waxeth olde becauſe of all mine enemies.

8 *Depart from me, all yee workers of iniquitie ; for the LORD hath heard the voice of my weeping.

9 The LORD hath heard my ſupplication ; the LORD will receiue my prayer.

10 Let all mine enemies be aſhamed and ſore vexed : let them returne *and* be aſhamed ſuddainly.

PSAL. VII.

1 Dauid prayeth againſt the malice of his enemies, profeſſing his innocency. 10 By faith he ſeeth his defence and the deſtruction of his enemies.

¶ Shiggaion of Dauid ; which he ſang vnto the LORD concerning the ||words of Cuſh the Beniamite.

LORD, my God, in thee doe I put my truſt : ſaue me from all them that perſecute me, and deliuer me.

2 Leaſt hee teare my ſoule like a lyon, renting *it* in pieces, while *there is* †none to deliuer.

3 O LORD my God, if I haue done this ; if there be iniquitie in my hands :

4 If I haue rewarded euill vnto him that was at peace with me : (yea I haue deliuered him that without cauſe is mine enemie.)

5 Let the enemie perſecute my ſoule, and take *it*, yea let him tread downe my life vpon the earth, and lay mine honour in the duſt. Selah.

6 Ariſe, O LORD, in thine anger, lift vp thy ſelfe, becauſe of the rage of mine enemies : and awake for me to the iudgement *that* thou haſt commanded.

7 So ſhall the congregation of the people compaſſe thee about : for their ſakes therefore returne thou on high.

8 The LORD ſhal iudge the people : iudge me, O LORD, *according

to my righteouſneſſe, and according to mine integritie *that* is in me.

9 Oh let the wickedneſ of the wicked come to an end, but eſtabliſh the iuſt : *for the righteous God trieth the hearts and reines.

10 †My defence *is* of God, which ſaueth the vpright in heart.

11 ||God iudgeth the righteous, and God is angrie *with the wicked* euery-day.

12 If he turne not, he will whet his ſword ; he hath bent his bowe, and made it ready.

13 He hath alſo prepared for him the inſtruments of death ; he ordaineth his arrowes againſt the perſecutors.

14 *Behold, he trauelleth with iniquitie, and hath conceiued miſchiefe, and brought forth falſhood.

15 †He made a pit and digged it, *and is fallen into the ditch *which* he made.

16 His miſchiefe ſhall returne vpon his owne head, and his violent dealing ſhall come downe vpon his owne pate.

17 I will praiſe the LORD according to his righteouſneſſe : and will ſing *praiſe* to the name of the LORD moſt high.

PSAL. VIII.

Gods glory is magnified by his workes, and by his loue to man.

¶ To the chiefe Muſicion vpon Gittith, a Pſalme of Dauid.

LORD our Lord, how excellent *is* thy name in all the earth ! who haſt ſet thy glory aboue the heauens.

2 *Out of the mouth of babes and ſucklings haſt thou †ordained ſtrength, becauſe of thine enemies, that thou mighteſt ſtill the enemie and the auenger.

3 When I conſider thy heauens, the worke of thy fingers, the moone and the ſtarres which thou haſt ordained ;

4 *What *is* man, that thou art mindfull of him ? and the ſonne of man, that thou viſiteſt him ?

5 For thou haſt made him a little lower then the Angels ; and haſt crowned him with glory and honour.

6 Thou madeſt him to haue dominion ouer the workes of thy hands ; *thou haſt put all things vnder his feete.

7 †All ſheepe and oxen, yea and the beaſts of the field.

8 The

Marginal notes (left column):

30.
3. 11
17.
17.
68.

tery

7. 23.
1.
3. 27.

ſines.

not a
er.

18.

Marginal notes (right column):

* 1. Sam. 16.
7. 1. Chr. 28
9. pſal. 139.
1. Ierem. 11
20. and 17.
10. and 20.
12.
† Heb. my
buckler is
vpon God.
|| Or, God is
a righteous
Iudge.

* Iob. 15.
35. Eſa. 59.
4. Iam. 1.
15.

† Heb. hee
hath digged
a pit.
* Pſal. 9. 15.
and 10. 2.
prou. 5. 22.

* Mat. 21.
16.
† Heb. foun-
ded.

* Iob 7. 17.
pſal. 144. 3.
Heb. 2. 6.

* 1. Cor. 15.
27.

† Heb. flocks
and oxen, all
of them.

8 The foule of the aire, and the fish of the sea, *and whatsoeuer* passeth through the paths of the seas.

9 O Lord our Lord, how excellent *is* thy name in all the earth !

PSAL. IX.

1 Dauid prayseth God for executing of iudgement. 11 He inciteth others to prayse him. 13 Hee prayeth, that hee may haue cause to prayse him.

¶ To the chiefe musician vpon Muth-Labben. A Psalme of Dauid.

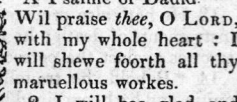

I Wil praise *thee*, O Lord, with my whole heart : I will shewe foorth all thy maruellous workes.

2 I will bee glad and reioyce in thee : I will sing prayse to thy name, O thou most High.

3 When mine enemies are turned backe, they shall fall and perish at thy presence.

4 For †thou hast maintained my right, and my cause : thou satest in the throne iudging †right.

5 Thou hast rebuked the heathen, thou hast destroyed the wicked ; thou hast put out their name for euer and euer.

6 ‖O thou enemie, destructions are come to a perpetuall end; and thou hast destroyed cities, their memoriall is perished with them.

7 But the Lord shall endure for euer : he hath *prepared his throne for iudgement.

8 And hee shall iudge the world in righteousnesse; he shall minister iudgement to the people in vprightnesse.

9 *The Lord also will bee †a refuge for the oppressed : a refuge, in times of trouble.

10 And they that know thy name will put their trust in thee : for thou Lord hast not forsaken them that seeke thee.

11 Sing *praises* to the Lord, *which* dwelleth in Sion : declare among the people his doings.

12 *When he maketh inquisition for blood, he remembreth them : he forgetteth not the crie of the ‖humble.

13 Haue mercie vpon me O Lord, consider my trouble *which I suffer* of them that hate me, thou that liftest mee vp from the gates of death :

14 That I may shew foorth all thy prayse in the gates of the daughter of

Sion : I will reioyce in thy saluation.

15 *The heathen are sunke downe in the pit *that* they made : in the net which they hid, is their own foot taken.

16 The Lord is knowen by the iudgement *which* he executeth : the wicked is snared in the worke of his owne hands. Higgaion. Selah.

17 The wicked shall be turned into hell, *and* all the nations that forget God.

18 For the needie shall not alway be forgotten : the expectation of the poore shall not perish for euer.

19 Arise, O Lord, let not man preuaile : let the heathen bee iudged in thy sight.

20 Put them in feare, O Lord : that the nations may know themselues to be but men. Selah.

PSAL. X.

1 Dauid complaineth to God of the outrage of the wicked. 12 He prayeth for remedie. 16 He professeth his confidence.

Hy standest thou afarre off, O Lord ? *why* hidest thou thy selfe in times of trouble ?

2 †The wicked in *his* pride doeth persecute the poore : *let them be taken in the deuices that they haue imagined.

3 For the wicked boasteth of his †hearts desire, ‖and blesseth the couetous, *whom* the Lord abhorreth.

4 The wicked through the pride of his countenance will not seeke *after God*: ‖God *is* not in all his *thoughts.

5 His wayes are alwayes grieuous, thy iudgements *are* farre aboue out of his sight : as for all his enemies, he puffeth at them.

6 He hath said in his heart, I shall not be moued : for *I shall* †neuer *be* in aduersitie.

7 *His mouth is full of cursing, and †deceit, and fraud : vnder his tongue *is* mischiefe and ‖vanitie.

8 He sitteth in the lurking places of the villages : in the secret places doeth he murder the innocent : his eyes †are priuily set against the poore.

9 He lieth in waite †secretly as a lyon in his denne, he lieth in wait to catch the poore : he doth catch the poore when he draweth him into his net.

10 †He croucheth, *and* humbleth himselfe, that the poore may fall ‖by his strong ones.

11 Hee

Left margin notes:

† *Hebr.* thou hast made my iudgement.
† *Hebr.* in righteousnes

‖ *Or, the destructions of the enemy are come to a perpetuall end : and their cities hast thou destroyed, &c.*
* Psal. 96. 13. and 98. 10.

* Psal. 37. 39. and 46. 1. and 91. 2.
† *Heb.* an high place.

* Gen. 9. 5

‖ *Or.* afflicted.

Right margin notes:

* Pa

† He
pria
wic
doth
cute
* Pr
and
prou
‖ Or
uete
seth
he a
the

‖ Or
thou
ther
God
* Pr

† H
gen
and
tion
* R
† H
ceit
‖ Or
qui

† H
ther

† H
secr

† H
bree
him
‖ Os
par

11 Hee hath said in his heart, God hath forgotten : *he hideth his face, hee will neuer see *it*.

12 Arise, O Lord, O God lift vp thine hand : forget not the ||humble.

13 Wherefore doeth the wicked contemne God? he hath said in his heart, Thou wilt not require *it*.

14 Thou hast seene *it*, for thou beholdest mischiefe and spite to requite *it* with thy hand : the poore †committeth himselfe vnto thee, thou art the helper of the fatherlesse.

15 Breake thou the arme of the wicked, and the euill man : seeke out his wickednes, *till* thou finde none.

16 *The Lord *is* King for euer and euer: the heathen are perished out of his land.

17 Lord, thou hast heard the desire of the humble : thou wilt ||prepare their heart, thou wilt cause thine eare to heare,

18 To iudge the fatherlesse and the oppressed, that the man of the earth may no more ||oppresse.

PSAL. XI.

1 Dauid incourageth himselfe in God, against his enemies. **4** The prouidence and iustice of God.

¶ To the chiefe Musician. A *Psalme* of Dauid.

IN the Lord put I my trust : how say yee to my soule, Flee *as* a bird to your mountaine?

2 For loe, the wicked bende their bow, they make ready their arrow vpon the string : that they may †priuily shoote at the vpright in heart.

3 If the foundations bee destroyed : what can the righteous doe?

4 *The Lord *is* in his holy Temple, the Lords Throne *is* in heauen: his eyes beholde, his eye lids trie the children of men.

5 The Lord trieth the righteous : but the wicked and him that loueth violence, his soule hateth.

6 Vpon the wicked hee shall raine snares, fire and brimstone, and ||an horrible tempest: *this shall be* the portion of their cup.

7 For the righteous Lord loueth righteousnesse : his countenance doeth behold the vpright.

PSAL. XII.

1 Dauid destitute of humane comfort, craueth helpe of God. **3** Hee comforteth himselfe with Gods iudgements on the wicked, and confidence in Gods tried promises.

¶ To the chiefe Musician ||vpon Sheminith. A Psalme of Dauid.

||Elpe Lord, for the godly man ceaseth; for the faithfull faile from among the children of men.

2 They speake vanitie euery one with his neighbour : *with* flattering lips, *and* with †a double heart do they speake.

3 The Lord shall cut off all flattering lips, *and* the tongue that speaketh †proud things.

4 Who haue said, With our tongue wil we preuaile, our lips †*are* our owne : who *is* Lord ouer vs?

5 For the oppression of the poore, for the sighing of the needy, now will I arise (saith the Lord,) I will set *him* in safetie *from him that* ||puffeth at him.

6 The wordes of the Lord are pure wordes : *as siluer tried in a fornace of earth purified seuen times.

7 Thou shalt keepe them, (O Lord,) thou shalt preserue †them, from this generation for euer.

8 The wicked walke on euery side, when the †vilest men are exalted.

PSAL. XIII.

1 Dauid complaineth of delay in helpe. **3** He prayeth for preuenting Grace. **5** Hee boasteth of Diuine mercie.

¶ To the ||chiefe Musician. *A Psalme* of Dauid.

Ow long wilt thou forget mee (O Lord) for euer? how long wilt thou hide thy face from me?

2 How long shall I take counsel in my soule, *hauing* sorrow in my heart dayly? how long shall mine enemie be exalted ouer me?

3 Consider *and* heare me, O Lord my God : lighten mine eyes, lest I sleep *the sleepe* of death.

4 Least mine enimie say, I haue preuailed against him : *and* those that trouble mee, reioyce, when I am moued.

5 But I haue trusted in thy mercy, my

Marginal notes (left column):
L. 94. 7.
ffli.
r. lea-
29. 9.
5. 13.
6. 10.
5. 10.
. 19.
sta-
errifie.
r. in esse.
k. 2.
a bur-tempest.

Marginal notes (right column):
|| *Or, vpon the eighth.*
|| *Or, saue.*
† *Hebr. an heart, and an heart.*
† *Hebr. great things.*
† *Hebr. are with vs.*
|| *Or, would ensnare him.*
* 2. Sam. 23. 31. psal. 18. 29. & 119. ver. 140. prou. 30. 5.
† *Heb. him. i. euery one of them.*
† *Hebr. the vilest of the sonnes of men are exalted.*
|| *Or, ouerseer.*

my heart ſhall reioyce in thy ſaluation.

6 I will ſing vnto the Lord, be-cauſe hee hath dealt bountifully with mee.

PSAL. XIIII.

1 Dauid deſcribeth the corruption of a naturall man. 4 He conuinceth the wicked by the light of their conſcience. 7 He glorieth in the ſaluation of God.

¶ To the chiefe muſician, *A Pſalme* of Dauid.

He *foole hath ſayd in his heart, *There is* no God: they are corrupt, they haue done abominable workes, there is none that doeth good.

* Pſal. 10. 4. and 53. 1.

2 The Lord looked downe from heauen vpon the children of men; *to ſee if there were any that did vnder-ſtand *and* ſeeke God.

* Rom. 3. 10

3 They are all gone aſide, they are *all* together become †filthy: there is none that doeth good, no not one.

† Heb. ſtinc-king.

4 Haue all the workers of iniquity no knowledge? who eate vp my people *as* they eate bread, and call not vpon the Lord.

5 †There were they in great feare; for God is in the generation of the righ-teous.

† Heb. they feared a feare.

6 You haue ſhamed the counſell of the poore; becauſe the Lord *is* his refuge.

7 †O that the ſaluation of Iſrael *were come* out of Sion! when the Lord bringeth backe the captiuitie of his peo-ple, Iacob ſhall reioyce, *and* Iſrael ſhalbe glad.

† Heb. who will giue? &c.

PSAL. XV.

Dauid deſcribeth a citizen of Sion.

¶ A Pſalme of Dauid.

Ord, *who ſhall †abide in thy tabernacle? who ſhall dwell in thy holy hill? 2 * Hee that walketh vprightly, and worketh righteouſneſſe, and ſpeaketh the trueth in his heart.

* Pſal. 24. 1. &c. † Heb. ſo-iourne. * Eſa. 33. 15.

3 Hee *that* backbiteth not with his tongue, nor doth euill to his neighbour, nor ‖taketh vp a reproach againſt his neighbour.

‖ Or, recei-ueth, or en-dureth.

4 In whoſe eies a vile perſon is contemned; but he honoureth them that feare the Lord: he that ſwea-

reth to *his owne* hurt, and changeth not.

5 *He that putteth not out his mo-ney to vſury, nor taketh reward againſt the innocent: he that doth theſe things, ſhall neuer be moued.

* Exod 24. Leuit. 36. Deu. 2 Ezech. 12. &

PSAL. XVI.

1 Dauid in diſtruſt of merites, and hatred of I-dolatry, flyeth to God for preſeruation. 5 He ſheweth the hope of his calling, of the reſur-rection, and life euerlaſting.

¶ ‖Michtam of Dauid.

Reſerue me, O God: for in thee doe I put my truſt.

2 *O my ſoule,* thou haſt ſayd vnto the Lord, Thou *art* my Lord: *my goodnes *extendeth* not to thee:

* Or, a den P of Dav

* Pſal 10. Io 2. & 3

3 *But* to the Saints, that are in the earth, and to the excellent, in whom *is* all my delight.

4 Their ſorrowes ſhalbe multipli-ed, *that* ‖haſten after another *God:* their drinke offerings of blood will I not offer, nor take vp their names into my lippes.

‖ Or, gifts ther.

5 *The Lord *is* the portion †of mine inheritance, and of my cup: thou maintaineſt my lot.

* Lam 24. D 32. V † Heb part.

6 The lines are fallen vnto mee in pleaſant places; yea, I haue a goodly heritage.

7 I will bleſſe the Lord, who hath giuen me counſell: my reines alſo inſtruct me in the night ſeaſons.

8 *I haue ſet the Lord alwaies before me: becauſe hee is at my right hand, I ſhall not be moued.

* Act 25.

9 Therefore my heart is glad, and my glory reioyceth: my fleſh alſo ſhall †reſt in hope.

† Heb confid * Act and I

10 * For thou wilt not leaue my ſoule in hell; neither wilt thou ſuffer thine holy one to ſee corruption.

11 Thou wilt ſhewe me the path of life: in thy preſence is fulneſſe of ioy, at thy right hand *there are* pleaſures for euermore.

PSAL. XVII.

1 Dauid in confidence of his integrity, craueth defence of God againſt his enemies. 10 He ſheweth their pride, craft and eagernes. 13 Hee prayeth againſt them in confidence of his hope.

¶ A prayer of Dauid.

Heare

Heb. iuſtice

Heb. with-
out lips of
deceit.

Heb. be not
moued.

Or, that
ſaueſt them
which truſt
theſe from
theſe that
riſe vp a-
gainſt thy
right hand.

Heb. that
taſte me.
Heb. my e-
nemies a-
gainſt the
ſoule.

Heb. the
Apples (i. of
euery one of
them) is as a
man that deſi
reth to rauin.
Heb. ſit-
ing.
Heb. pre-
uent his face.
Or, by thy
word.
Or, from
men by
thine hand.
Or, their
children
are full.

Eare the †right, O
Lord, attend vnto my
crie, giue eare vnto my
prayer, *that goeth* †not out
of fained lips.

2 Let my ſentence come forth from
thy preſence: let thine eyes beholde the
things that are equall.

3 Thou haſt prooued mine heart,
thou haſt viſited *me* in the night, thou
haſt tried me, *and* ſhalt find nothing: I
am purpoſed *that* my mouth ſhall not
tranſgreſſe.

4 Concerning the workes of men,
by the word of thy lips, I haue kept *me*
from the paths of the deſtroyer.

5 Hold vp my goings in thy paths,
that my footſteps †ſlip not.

6 I haue called vpon thee, for thou
wilt heare me, O God: incline thine
eare vnto me, *and* heare my ſpeach.

7 Shewe thy marueilous louing
kindneſſe, O thou ǁ that ſaueſt by thy
right hand, them which put their truſt
in thee, frō thoſe that riſe vp *againſt them.*

8 Keepe me as the apple of the eye:
hide mee vnder the ſhadowe of thy
wings,

9 From the wicked †that oppreſſe
me, *from* my †deadly enemies, *who* compaſſe me about.

10 They are incloſed in their owne
fat: with their mouth they ſpeake
proudly.

11 They haue now compaſſed vs in
our ſteps: they haue ſet their eyes bowing downe to the earth:

12 †Like as a lyon *that* is greedie of
his pray, and as it were a yong lyon
†lurking in ſecret places.

13 Ariſe, O Lord, †diſappoint him,
caſt him downe: deliuer my ſoule from
the wicked, ǁ *which is* thy ſword:

14 ǁFrom men *which are* thy hand,
O Lord, from men of the world,
which *haue* their portion in *this* life, and
whoſe belly thou filleſt with thy hid
treaſure: ǁThey are full of children, and
leaue the reſt of their ſubſtance to their
babes.

15 As for me, I will behold thy face
in righteouſneſſe: I ſhall bee ſatiſfied,
when I awake, with thy likeneſſe.

PSAL. XVIII.
Dauid praiſeth God for his manifold and
marueilous bleſſings.

¶ To the chiefe muſicion, *a pſalme* of
Dauid, the ſeruant of the Lord,
who ſpake vnto the Lord the
words of * this ſong, in the day *that*
the Lord deliuered him from the
hand of all his enemies, and from the
hand of Saul: And he ſaid,

Will loue thee, O Lord,
my ſtrength.

2 The Lord *is* my
rocke, and my fortreſſe,
and my deliuerer: my
God, †my ſtrength in whome I will
truſt, my buckler, and the horne of my
ſaluation, *and* my high tower.

3 I will call vpon the Lord, who
is worthy to be praiſed: ſo ſhall I be ſaued from mine enemies.

4 * The ſorrowes of death compaſſed me, and the floods of †vngodly men
made me afraid.

5 The ǁ ſorrowes of hell compaſſed
me about: the ſnares of death preuented me.

6 In my diſtreſſe I called vpon the
Lord, and cryed vnto my God: hee
heard my voyce out of his temple, and
my crie came before him, *euen* into his
eares.

7 Then the earth ſhooke and trembled; the foundations alſo of the hilles
mooued and were ſhaken, becauſe hee
was wroth.

8 There went vp a ſmoke †out of
his noſtrils, and fire out of his mouth
deuoured, coales were kindled by it.

9 He bowed the heauens alſo, and
came downe: and darkeneſſe *was* vnder
his feet.

10 And he rode vpon a Cherub, and
did flie: yea he did flie vpon the wings of
the wind.

11 He made darkenes his ſecret place:
his pauilion round about him, *were*
darke waters, *and* thicke cloudes of the
skies.

12 At the brightnes *that was* before him
his thicke clouds paſſed, haile *ſtones* and
coales of fire.

13 The Lord alſo thundered in
the heauens, and the higheſt gaue his
voyce; haileſtones and coales of fire.

14 Yea, he ſent out his arrowes, and
ſcattered them; and he ſhot out lightnings, and diſcomfited them.

15 Then the chanels of waters were
ſeene, and the foundations of the world
were diſcouered: at thy rebuke, O
Lord, at the blaſt of the breath of thy
noſtrils.

16 He ſent from aboue, he tooke me,
he

* 2. Sam. 22

† Heb. my
rocke.

* Pſal. 116. 3
† Heb. Be-
lial.
ǁ Or, c0ards.

† Heb. by his

he drew me out of ‖ many waters.

‖ *Or, great waters.*

17 He deliuered me from my strong enemie, and from them which hated me : for they were too strong for me.

18 They preuented me in the day of my calamitie : but the LORD was my stay.

19 He brought me forth also into a large place : he deliuered me, because he delighted in me.

20 The LORD rewarded me according to my righteousnesse, according to the cleannesse of my hands hath hee recompensed me.

21 For I haue kept the wayes of the LORD, and haue not wickedly departed from my God.

22 For all his iudgements *were* before me, and I did not put away his statutes from me.

† *Heb. with.*

23 I was also vpright † before him : and I kept my selfe from mine iniquity.

† *Heb. before his eyes.*

24 Therefore hath the LORD recompensed me according to my righteousnesse, according to the cleannesse of my hands † in his eye-sight.

25 With the mercifull thou wilt shew thy selfe mercifull, with an vpright man thou wilt shew thy selfe vpright.

26 With the pure thou wilt shewe thy selfe pure, and with the froward thou wilt ‖ shew thy selfe froward.

‖ *Or, wrestle.*

27 For thou wilt saue the afflicted people : but wilt bring downe high lookes.

28 For thou wilt light my ‖ candle : the LORD my God will enlighten my darkenesse.

‖ *Or, lampe.*

29 For by thee I haue ‖ run through a troupe? and by my God haue I leaped ouer a wall.

‖ *Or, broken.*

30 As for God, his way is perfect : * the word of the LORD is ‖ tried : he is a buckler to all those that trust in him.

* Psal. 12. 6.
&. 119. 140
prou. 30. 5.
‖ Or, refined.

31 * For who *is* God saue the LORD ? or who *is* a rocke saue our God ?

* Deut. 32.
33.
1. Sam. 2. 2.
psal. 86. 8.
Esa. 45. 5.

32 It is God that girdeth mee with strength, and maketh my way perfect.

33 Hee maketh my feete like hindes *feete*, and setteth me vpon my high places.

34 He teacheth my hands to warre, so that a bow of steele is broken by mine armes.

35 Thou hast also giuen me the shield of thy saluation : and thy right hand hath holden me vp, and thy ‖ gentlenesse hath made me great.

‖ *Or, with thy meekenesse thou hast multiplied me.*

36 Thou hast enlarged my steppes vnder me; that † my feete did not slippe.

† *Heb. ankles.*

37 I haue pursued mine enemies, and ouertaken them : neither did I turne againe till they were consumed.

38 I haue wounded them that they were not able to rise : they are fallen vnder my feete.

39 For thou hast girded mee with strength vnto the battell : thou † hast subdued vnder me, those that rose vp against me.

† *Heb.* to bow

40 Thou hast also giuen mee the neckes of mine enemies : that I might destroy them that hate me.

41 They cried, but there was none to saue *them : euen* vnto the LORD, but he answered them not.

42 Then did I beate them small as the dust before the winde : I did cast them out, as the dirt in the streetes.

43 Thou hast deliuered me from the striuings of the people, *and* thou hast made mee the head of the heathen : a people *whom* I haue not knowen, shall serue me.

44 † As soone as they heare of mee, they shall obey me : † the strangers shall ‖ submit themselues vnto me.

† Heb
the he
of the
† Heb
sonne
strang
‖ Or,
faine
dience
Heb.

45 The strangers shall fade away, and be afraid out of their close places.

46 The LORD liueth, and blessed *be* my rocke : and let the God of my saluation be exalted.

47 It is God that † auengeth mee, and ‖ subdueth the people vnder me.

† Heb.
auen
ments
me.
‖ Or,
stroye

48 He deliuereth me from mine enemies : yea thou liftest mee vp aboue those that rise vp against me; thou hast deliuered me from the † violent man.

† Heb
of vio
* Ron
‖ Or, c

49 * Therfore will I ‖ giue thankes vnto thee, (O LORD) among the heathen : and sing prayses vnto thy name.

50 Great deliuerance giueth he to his King : and sheweth mercy to his Annointed, to Dauid, and to his seede for euermore.

PSAL. XIX.

1 The creatures shew Gods glory. 7 The word his Grace. 12 Dauid prayeth for Grace.

¶ To the chiefe Musician, A Psalme of Dauid.

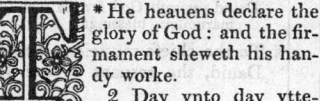 * He heauens declare the glory of God : and the firmament sheweth his handy worke.

* Gen

2 Day vnto day vttereth

reth ſpeach, and night vnto night ſheweth knowledge.

3 *There is* no ſpeach nor language, where ||their voyce is not heard.

4 || * Their line is gone out through all the earth, and their words to the end of the world : In them hath he ſet a tabernacle for the Sunne.

5 Which *is as* a bridegrome comming out of his chamber, *and* reioyceth as a ſtrong man to runne a race.

6 His going forth *is* from the end of the heauen , and his circuite vnto the ends of it : and there is nothing hidde from the heat thereof.

7 The ||Law of the LORD is perfect, ||conuerting the ſoule : the teſtimonie of the LORD is ſure, making wiſe the ſimple.

8 The Statutes of the LORD *are* right, reioycing the heart : the Commandement of the LORD *is* pure, inlightning the eyes.

9 The feare of the LORD *is* cleane, enduring for euer : the Iudgements of the LORD *are* †true, *and* righteous altogether.

10 More to bee deſired are they then gold, * yea, then much fine gold: ſweeter alſo then hony, and †the hony combe.

11 Moreouer by them is thy ſeruant warned : *and* in keeping of them *there is* great reward.

12 Who can vnderſtand *his* errours? cleanſe thou me from ſecret *faults*.

13 Keepe back thy ſeruant alſo from preſumptuous ſinnes, let them not haue dominion ouer me : then ſhall I be vpright, and I ſhalbe innocent from ||the great tranſgreſſion.

14 Let the words of my mouth, and the meditation of my heart, bee acceptable in thy ſight, O LORD †my ſtrength, and my redeemer.

PSAL. XX.

1 The Church bleſſeth the King in his exploits. 7 Her confidence in Gods ſuccour.

¶ To the chiefe Muſician. A Pſalme of Dauid.

He LORD heare thee in the day of trouble , the Name of the God of Iacob †defend thee.

2 Send †thee helpe from the Sanctuary : and †ſtrengthen thee out of Sion.

3 Remember all thy offerings, and

† accept thy burnt ſacrifice. Selah.

4 Graunt thee according to thine owne heart, and fulfill all thy counſell.

5 We will reioyce in thy ſaluation, and in the Name of our God we will ſet vp our banners: the LORD fulfill all thy petitions.

6 Now know I, that the LORD ſaueth his Anointed : he wil heare him † from his holy heauen , † with the ſauing ſtrength of his right hand.

7 Some *trust* in charets, and ſome in horſes : but wee will remember the Name of the LORD our God.

8 They are brought downe and fallen : but we are riſen, and ſtand vpright.

9 Saue LORD, let the King heare vs when we call.

PSAL. XXI.

1 A thankeſgiuing for victory. 7 Confidence of further ſucceſſe.

¶ To the chiefe Muſician. A Pſalme of Dauid.

He King ſhall ioy in thy ſtrength , O LORD : and in thy ſaluation how greatly ſhall he reioyce ?

2 Thou haſt giuen him his hearts deſire ; and haſt not withholden the requeſt of his lips. Selah.

3 For thou preuenteſt him with the bleſſings of goodneſſe : thou ſetteſt a Crowne of pure gold on his head.

4 He asked life of thee, *and* thou gaueſt *it* him, *euen* length of dayes for euer and euer.

5 His glory *is* great in thy ſaluation: honour and Maieſtie haſt thou layde vpon him.

6 For thou haſt †made him moſt bleſſed for euer : thou haſt †made him exceeding glad with thy countenance.

7 For the King truſteth in the LORD, and through the mercy of the moſt High, he ſhall not be moued.

8 Thine hand ſhall finde out all thine enemies, thy right hand ſhal finde out thoſe that hate thee.

9 Thou ſhalt make them as a fiery ouen in the time of thine anger : the LORD ſhall ſwallow them vp in his wrath, and the fire ſhall deuoure them.

10 Their fruit ſhalt thou deſtroy from the earth, and their ſeed from among the children of men.

11 For they intended euill againſt thee :

without e their e is r. with- their e heard. om. 10.

their or di- on.

do- te. reſto-

ebr. th.

ſal. 119. & 127 103. a. 8. 19. ebr. the pping of y combes.

, much.

ebr. my ke.

ebr. ſet s on an h place. ebr. thy ve. ebr. ſup- t thee.

† *Heb. turne to aſhes: or, make fat.*

† *Hebr. from the heauen of his holi- neſſe.* † *Hebr. by the ſtrength of the ſalua- tion of his right hand.*

† *Hebr. ſet him to be bleſſings.* † *Hebr. glad- ded him with ioy.*

thee : they imagined a mischieuous deuice, *which* they are not able *to performe*.

12 Therefore ‖shalt thou make them turne their † back, *when* thou shalt make ready thine *arrowes* vpon thy strings, against the face of them.

13 Be thou exalted, LORD, in thine owne strength : *so* will wee sing, aud praise thy power.

PSAL. XXII.

1 Dauid complaineth in great discouragement. 9 Hee prayeth in great distresse. 23 Hee praiseth God.

¶ To the chiefe Musician vpon ‖Aijeleth Shahar. A Psalme of Dauid.

MY God, my God, * why hast thou forsaken mee? *why* art thou so far †from helping me, *and from* the words of my roaring?

2 O my God, I crie in the day time, but thou hearest not; and in the night season, and † am not silent.

3 But thou *art* holy, *O thou* that inhabitest the praises of Israel !

4 Our fathers trusted in thee : they trusted, and thou didst deliuer them.

5 They cryed vnto thee, and were deliuered : they trusted in thee, and were not confounded.

6 But I *am* a worme, and no man ; a reproach of men, and despised of the people.

7 All they that see me, laugh me to scorne : they †shoote out the lippe, they shake the head, *saying*,

8 * † He trusted on the LORD, *that* he would deliuer him : let him deliuer him, ‖seeing he delighted in him.

9 But thou art hee that tooke mee out of the wombe ; thou ‖didst make me hope, *when I was* vpon my mothers breasts.

10 I was cast vpon thee from the wombe : thou *art* my God from my mothers belly.

11 Be not farre from me, for trouble *is* neere ; for *there is* †none to helpe.

12 Many bulles haue compassed me : strong *bulles* of Bashan haue beset me round.

13 They † gaped vpon me *with* their mouthes, *as* a rauening and a roaring Lyon.

14 I am powred out like water,

and all my bones are ‖out of ioynt : my heart is like waxe, it is melted in the middest of my bowels.

15 My strength is dried vp like a potsheard : and my tongue cleaueth to my iawes ; and thou hast brought me into the dust of death.

16 For dogges haue compassed me : the assembly of the wicked haue inclosed me : *they pierced my hands and my feete.

17 I may tell all my bones : they looke *and* stare vpon me.

18 They part my garments among them, and cast lots vpon my vesture.

19 But be not thou farre from mee, O LORD ; O my strength, hast thee to helpe me.

20 Deliuer my soule from the sword : † my darling † from the power of the dogge.

21 Saue me from the lyons mouth : for thou hast heard me from the hornes of the vnicornes.

22 *I will declare thy name vnto my brethren : in the midst of the congregation will I praise thee.

23 Yee that feare the LORD, praise him ; all yee the seede of Iacob glorifie him, and feare him all yee the seede of Israel.

24 For he hath not despised, nor abhorred the affliction of the afflicted ; neither hath he hid his face from him, but when he cried vnto him, he heard.

25 My praise *shalbe* of thee, in the great congregation : I will pay my vowes, before them that feare him.

26 The meeke shall eate and be satisfied : they shall praise the LORD that seeke him ; your heart shall liue for euer.

27 * All the ends of the world shall remember, and turne vnto the LORD : and all the kinreds of the nations shall worship before thee.

28 For the kingdome *is* the LORDS : and he *is* the gouernour among the nations.

29 All they that be fat vpon earth shall eate and worship : all they that goe downe to the dust shall bow before him, and none can keepe aliue his owne soule.

30 A seed shall serue him ; it shalbe accounted to the Lord for a generation.

31 They shall come, and shall declare his righteousnes vnto a people that shalbe borne, that he hath done *this*.

PSAL.

Marginal notes (left column)

‖ Or, thou shalt set them as a butte.
† Heb. shoulder.

‖ Or, the hind of the morning.

* Mat. 27. 46. Marc. 15. 34.
† Heb. from my saluation.

† Heb. there is no silence to me.

* Mat. 27. 39.
† Heb. open.

* Mat. 27. 43.
† Heb. hee rolled himselfe on the Lord.
‖ Or, if he delight in him.
‖ Or, keptst me in safety.

† Heb. not a helper.

† Heb. opened their mouthes against me.

Marginal notes (right column)

‖ Or, sundred.

* Mat. 35. Ma 24. Lu 33. Ioh 23. & 3

† Heb. only on
† Heb. the har

* Luc. 34. Ioh 19. 24. 2. 12.

* Psal & 72. and 86

PSAL. XXIII.

Dauids confidence in Gods grace.

¶ A Psalme of Dauid.

He Lord *is* *my shep-heard, I shall not want.

2 He maketh me to lie downe in †greene pa-stures: he leadeth mee be-side the †still waters.

3 He restoreth my soule: he leadeth me in the pathes of righteousnes, for his names sake.

4 Yea though I walke through the valley of the shadowe of death, *I will feare no euill: for thou *art* with me, thy rod and thy staffe, they comfort me.

5 Thou preparest a table before me, in the presence of mine enemies: thou †anointest my head with oyle, my cuppe runneth ouer.

6 Surely goodnes and mercie shall followe me all the daies of my life: and I will dwell in the house of the Lord †for euer.

PSAL. XXIIII.

1 Gods Lordship in the world. 3 The citizens of his spirituall kingdome. 7 An exhortation to receiue him.

¶ A Psalme of Dauid.

*He earth *is* the Lords, and the fulnesse thereof; the world, and they that dwell therein.

2 *For he hath foun-ded it vpon the seas, and established it vpon the floods.

3 *Who shall ascend into the hill of the Lord? and who shall stand in his holy place?

4 *†He that hath cleane hands, and a pure heart; who hath not lift vp his soule vnto vanitie, nor sworne deceit-fully.

5 Hee shall receiue the blessing from the Lord, and righteousnesse from the God of his saluation.

6 This *is* the generation of them that seeke him: that seeke thy face, ||O Iacob. Selah.

7 Lift vp your heads, O yee gates, and be ye lift vp ye euerlasting doores; and the King of glory shall come in.

8 Who is this king of glory? the Lord strong & mightie, the Lord mighty in battell.

9 Lift vp your heads, O ye gates, euen lift *them* vp, ye euerlasting doores;

and the king of glory shall come in.

10 Who is this king of glory? the Lord of hostes, he *is* the king of glory. Selah.

PSAL. XXV.

1 Dauids confidence in prayer. 7 Hee pray-eth for remission of sinnes, 16 and for helpe in affliction.

¶ *A Psalme* of Dauid.

Nto thee, O Lord, doe I lift vp my soule.

2 O my God, I *trust in thee, let me not be asha-med: let not mine enemies triumph ouer me.

3 *Yea let none that waite on thee, be ashamed: let them bee ashamed which transgresse without cause.

4 *Shewe mee thy wayes, O Lord: teach me thy pathes.

5 Lead me in thy trueth, and teach me: for thou *art* the God of my saluati-on, on thee doe I waite all the day.

6 *Remember, O Lord, †thy tender mercies, and thy louing kind-nesses: for they *haue beene* euer of old.

7 Remember not the sinnes of my youth, nor my transgressions: according to thy mercie remember thou me, for thy goodnesse sake, O Lord.

8 Good and vpright *is* the Lord: therefore will hee teach sinners in the way.

9 The meeke will he guide in iudge-ment: and the meeke will he teach his way.

10 All the pathes of the Lord *are* mercy and truth: vnto such as keepe his couenant, and his testimonies.

11 For thy names sake, O Lord, pardon mine iniquitie: for it *is* great.

12 What man is he that feareth the Lord? him shall he teach in the way that he shall chuse.

13 His soule †shall dwell at ease: and his seede shall inherite the earth.

14 *The secret of the Lord *is* with them that feare him: ||and he will shew them his couenant.

15 Mine eyes *are* euer towards the Lord: for hee shall †plucke my feete out of the net.

16 Turne thee vnto me, and haue mercy vpon me: for I *am* desolate and afflicted.

17 The troubles of my heart are in-larged: O bring thou me out of my di-stresses.

18 Looke

Marginal notes left column:
40.11
3. 5.
34.
9. 11.
2. 25.
pa-
often-
esse.
voa-
quiet.
3. 6.
6.
ma-
t.
to
of
1. 10.
2.
10. 12.
10.
28.
38. 6.
104. 5.
6.
15. 1.
33.
the
of
s.
Ia.

Marginal notes right column:
* Psal. 22. 5.
& 31. 2.
& 34. 9.
* Esa. 28. 16
Rom. 10. 11
* Psa. 27. 11
& 86. 11.
& 119.
* Psal. 103.
17. & 106.
1. & 107. 1.
Iere. 33. 3.
† *Heb. thy*
bowels.
† *Heb. shall*
lodge in
goodnesse.
* Pro. 3. 32.
|| *Or, and his*
couenant to
make them
know it.
† *Heb. bring*
foorth.

† *Heb. hatred of violence.*

18 Looke vpon mine affliction, aud my paine, and forgiue all my ſinnes.

19 Conſider mine enemies : for they are many, and they hate me with † cruell hatred.

20 O keepe my ſoule and deliuer me : let me not bee aſhamed, for I put my truſt in thee.

21 Let integritie and vprightneſſe preſerue me : for I wait on thee.

22 Redeeme Iſrael, O God, out of all his troubles.

PSAL. XXVI.

Dauid reſorteth vnto God, in confidence of his integritie.

¶ *A Pſalme* of Dauid.

I Vdge me, O LORD, for I haue walked in mine integritie : I haue truſted also in the LORD : *therfore* I ſhall not ſlide.

² *Pſal. 7 10*

2 *Examine me, O LORD, and proue me; try my reines and my heart.

3 For thy louing kindneſſe *is* before mine eyes : and I haue walked in thy trueth.

ᵇ *Pſal. 1. 1*

4 *I haue not ſate with vaine perſons, neither will I goe in with diſſemblers.

5 I haue hated the congregation of euill doers : and will not ſit with the wicked

6 I will waſh mine hands in innocencie : ſo will I compaſſe thine Altar, O LORD :

7 That I may publiſh with the voyce of thankeſgiuing, and tell of all thy wonderous workes.

† *Heb. of the Tabernacle of thy honor.*
‡ *Or, take not away.*
† *Heb. men of blood.*
† *Heb. filled with.*

8 LORD, I haue loued the habitation of thy houſe, and the place † where thine honour dwelleth.

9 ‖Gather not my ſoule with ſinners, nor my life with † bloody men.

10 In whoſe hands *is* miſchiefe : and their right hand is † full of bribes.

11 But as for mee, I will walke in mine integritie : redeeme me, and bee mercifull vnto me.

12 My foot ſtandeth in an euen place : in the congregations will I bleſſe the LORD.

PSAL. XXVII.

1 Dauid ſuſtaineth his faith, by the power of God, 4 By his loue to the ſeruice of God, 9 By prayer.

¶ *A Pſalme* of Dauid.

HE LORD *is* my light, and my ſaluation, whome ſhal I feare? *the LORD *is* the ſtrength of my life, of whõ ſhall I be afraid?

ᵃ *Pſal 6. micꜱ*

2 When the wicked, *euen* mine enemies and my foes † came vpon me to eat vp my fleſh, they ſtumbled and fell.

† *Heb. proach̄ gainſt*
ᵃ *Pſal*

3 *Though an hoſt ſhould encampe against me, my heart ſhall not feare : though warre ſhould riſe against me, in this will I be confident.

4 One thing haue I deſired of the LORD, that will I ſeeke after : that I may dwel in the houſe of the LORD, all the dayes of my life, to behold ‖the beautie of the LORD, and to inquire in his temple.

‖ *Or, t̄ delight̄*

5 For in the time of trouble he ſhall hide me in his pauilion : in the ſecret of his tabernacle ſhall he hide me, hee ſhall ſet me vp vpon a rocke.

6 And now ſhall mine head be lifted vp aboue mine enemies round about me : therefore will I offer in his tabernacle ſacrifices † of ioy, I will ſing, yea, I will ſing praiſes vnto the LORD.

† *Heb. ſhouti*

7 Heare, O LORD, *when* I crie with my voice : haue mercie also vpon mee, and answere me.

8 ‖*When thou ſaidſt*, Seeke ye my face, my heart ſaid vnto thee, Thy face, LORD, will I ſeeke.

‖ *Or, ṁ heart ꜱ vnto th̄ my fac̄ thy fac̄*

9 Hide not thy face farre frõ me, put not thy ſeruant away in anger : thou haſt bin my helpe, leaue me not, neither forſake me, O God of my ſaluation.

10 When my father and my mother forſake me, then the LORD † will take me vp.

† *Heb. gather*

11 *Teach me thy way, O LORD, and leade me in a † plaine path, becauſe of mine † enemies.

* *Pſal and 86 and 1̄*
† *Heb. ofplai*

12 Deliuer me not ouer vnto the will of mine enemies : for false witneſſes are riſen vp against me, and ſuch as breath out crueltie.

† *Heb. which ſerue*

13 *I had fainted*, vnleſſe I had beleeued to ſee the goodneſſe of the LORD in the land of the liuing.

14 *Wait on the LORD : be of good courage, and he ſhall ſtrengthen thine heart : wait, I ſay, on the LORD.

* *Pſa. iſa. 25 hab. 2*

PSAL. XXVIII.

1 Dauid prayeth earneſtly against his enemies. 6 He bleſſeth God. 9 Hee prayeth for the people.

¶ *A Pſalme*

¶ *A Psalme* of Dauid.

VNto thee will I cry, O LORD, my rocke, be not silent to mee : *lest if thou be silent †to me, I become like them that goe downe into the pit.

2 Heare the voyce of my supplications, when I cry vnto thee: when I lift vp my handes ||toward thy holy Oracle.

3 Draw me not away with the wicked, and with the workers of iniquitie : *which speake peace to their neighbors, but mischiefe *is* in their hearts.

4 Giue them according to their deedes, and according to the wickednes of their endeuours : giue them after the worke of their handes, render to them their desert.

5 Because they regard not the workes of the LORD, nor the operation of his hands, he shal destroy them, and not build them vp.

6 Blessed *be* the LORD, because he hath heard the voyce of my supplications.

7 The LORD *is* my strength, and my shield, my heart trusted in him and I am helped : therefore my heart greatly reioyceth, and with my song will I praise him.

8 The LORD *is* ||their strength, and hee *is* the †sauing strength of his Anointed.

9 Saue thy people, and blesse thine inheritance, ||feede them also, and lift them vp for euer.

PSAL. XXIX.

1 Dauid exhorteth Princes to giue glory to God, 3 by reason of his power, 11 and protection of his people.

¶ A Psalme of Dauid.

GIue vnto the LORD (O †ye mighty) giue vnto the LORD glory and strength.

2 Giue vnto the LORD †the glory due vnto his Name; worship the LORD ||in the beautie of holinesse.

3 The voice of the LORD *is* vpon the waters: the God of glory thundreth, the LORD *is* vpon ||many waters.

4 The voice of the LORD *is* †powerfull; the voyce of the LORD *is* †full of Maiestie.

5 The voyce of the LORD breaketh the Cedars : yea, the LORD breaketh the Cedars of Lebanon.

6 He maketh them also to skip like a calfe : Lebanon, and *Sirion like a yong Vnicorne.

7 The voyce of the LORD †diuideth the flames of fire.

8 The voyce of the LORD ||shaketh the wildernes : the LORD shaketh the wildernesse of Kadesh.

9 The voice of the LORD maketh the hindes to calue, and discouereth the forrests : and in his Temple doeth ||euery one speake of *his* glory.

10 The LORD sitteth vpon the flood : yea the LORD sitteth King for euer.

11 The LORD will giue strength vnto his people ; the LORD wil blesse his people with peace.

PSAL. XXX.

1 Dauid prayseth God for his deliuerance. 4 He exhorteth others to praise him by example of Gods dealing with him.

¶ A Psalme, *and* song *at* the dedication of the house of Dauid.

IWil extol thee, O LORD, for thou hast lifted me vp; and hast not made my foes to reioyce ouer me.

2 O LORD my God, I cried vnto thee, and thou hast healed me.

3 O LORD, thou hast brought vp my soule from the graue : thou hast kept me aliue, that I should not goe downe to the pit.

4 Sing vnto the LORD, (O yee Saints of his) and giue thanks ||at the remembrance of his holinesse.

5 For †his anger *endureth* but a moment; in *his* fauour is life : weeping may endure†for a night, but †ioy *commeth* in the morning.

6 And in my †prosperitie I said, I shall neuer be mooued.

7 LORD, by thy fauour thou hast †made my mountaine to stand strong : Thou didst hide thy face, *and* I was troubled.

8 I cried to thee, O LORD : and vnto the LORD I made supplication.

9 What profit *is there* in my blood, when I goe downe to the pit ? *Shall the dust praise thee? shall it declare thy trueth ?

10 Heare, O LORD, and haue mercie

Marginal notes (left column):
.143.
-.from
wards acle San-.
. 12. 3. 8.
his gth. r. gth of tions.
rule.
r. yee s of the y.
r. the r of me. in his usSan-y.
great 's.
r. in r. r. in stie.

Marginal notes (right column):
* Deut. 3. 9.
† Hebr. cutteth out.
|| Or, to be in paine.
|| Or, euery whit of it vttereth &c.
|| Or, to the memoriall.
† Heb. there is but a moment in his anger.
† Hebr. in the euening.
† Hebr. singing.
† Hebr. setled strength formy mountaine.
* Psal. 6. 6. and 88. 11. and 115. 17.

cie vpon me : LORD be thou my helper.

11 Thou hast turned for mee my mourning into dauncing : thou hast put off my sackecloth, and girded mee with gladnesse :

‖ That is, my tongue, or my soule.

12 To the end that ‖ my glory may sing prayse to thee, and not be silent : O LORD my God, I will giue thankes vnto thee for euer.

PSAL. XXXI.

1 Dauid shewing his confidence in God, craueth his helpe. 7 He reioyceth in his mercy. 9 He prayeth in his calamitie. 19 He prayseth God for his goodnesse.

¶ To the chiefe Musician, A Psalme of Dauid.

* Psal. 22. 5. Esa. 49. 23.

 *N thee, O LORD, doe I put my trust, let me neuer be ashamed : deliuer me in thy righteousnesse.

2 Bowe downe thine eare to me, deliuer me speedily : be thou †my strong rocke, for an house of defence to saue me.

† Heb. to me for a rocke of strength.

3 For thou *art* my rocke and my fortresse : therfore for thy names sake lead me, and guide me.

4 Pull me out of the net, that they haue layd priuily for me : for thou *art* my strength.

ᵛ Luc. 23. 46.

5 * Into thine hand I commit my spirit : thou hast redeemed mee, O LORD God of trueth.

6 I haue hated them that regard lying vanities : but I trust in the LORD.

7 I will be glad, and reioyce in thy mercie : for thou hast considered my trouble ; thou hast knowen my soule in aduersities ;

8 And hast not shut me vp into the hand of the enemie : thou hast set my feete in a large roome.

9 Haue mercy vpon me, O LORD, for I am in trouble ; mine eie is consumed with griefe, *yea* my soule and my belly.

10 For my life is spent with griefe, and my yeeres with sighing : my strength faileth, because of mine iniquitie, and my bones are consumed.

11 I was a reproch among all mine enemies, but especially among my neighbours, and a feare to mine acquaintance : they that did see me without, fled from me.

12 I am forgotten as a dead man out of minde : I am like †a broken vessell.

† Heb. ᵉ sell tha riseth.

13 For I haue heard the slaunder of many, feare was on euery side : while they tooke counsell together against me, they deuised to take away my life.

14 But I trusted in thee, O LORD : I sayd, Thou *art* my God.

15 My times *are* in thy hand : deliuer me from the hand of mine enemies, and from them that persecute me.

16 Make thy face to shine vpon thy seruant : saue me for thy mercies sake.

17 Let mee not be ashamed, O LORD, for I haue called vpon thee : let the wicked be ashamed, *and* ‖ let them be silent in the graue.

‖ Or, le them be off for t graue.

18 Let the lying lippes be put to silence : which speake †grieuous things proudly and contemptuously against the righteous.

† Heb. a thing.

19 *O how great is thy goodnesse, which thou hast layd vp for them that feare thee : *which* thou hast wrought for them that trust in thee, before the sonnes of men !

* Esa. 4. 1. Co 2. 9.

20 Thou shalt hide them in the secret of thy presence, from the pride of man : thou shalt keepe them secretly in a pauilion, from the strife of tongues.

21 Blessed *be* the LORD ; for hee hath shewed me his maruellous kindnesse, in a ‖ strong citie.

‖ Or, fe city.

22 For I sayd in my haste, I am cut off from before thine eies : Neuerthelesse thou heardest the voice of my supplications, when I cryed vnto thee.

23 O loue the LORD, all yee his Saints : *for* the LORD preserueth the faithfull, and plentifully rewardeth the proud doer.

24 * Be of good courage, and hee shall strengthen your heart : all ye that hope in the LORD.

* Psal 14.

PSAL. XXXII.

1 Blessednesse consisteth in remission of sinnes. 3 Confession of sinnes giueth ease to the conscience. 8 Gods promises bring ioy.

¶ ‖ *A Psalme* of Dauid, Maschil.

‖Or, ap of Dau giuing struct * Rom

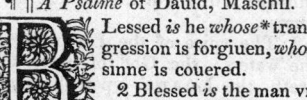 Lessed *is* he *whose** transgression is forgiuen, *whose* sinne is couered.

2 Blessed *is* the man vnto whom the LORD imputeth not iniquitie : and in whose spirit *there is* no guile.

3 When

3 When I kept silence, my bones waxed old; through my roaring all the day long.

4 For day and night thy hand was heauy vpon me : my moisture is turned into the drought of summer. Selah.

5 I acknowledged my sin vnto thee, and mine iniquitie haue I not hid : *I said, I will confesse my transgressions vnto the LORD; and thou forgauest the iniquitie of my sinne. Selah.

6 For this shall euery one that is godly pray vnto thee, †in a time when thou mayest bee found : surely in the floods of great waters, they shall not come nigh vnto him.

7 *Thou art my hiding place, thou shalt preserue mee from trouble : thou shalt compasse me about with songs of deliuerance. Selah.

8 I will instruct thee, and teach thee in the way which thou shalt goe : †I will guide thee with mine eye.

9 *Be yee not as the horse, or as the mule which haue no vnderstanding : whose mouth must be held in with bit and bridle, least they come neere vnto thee.

10 Many sorrowes shall be to the wicked : but he that trusteth in the LORD, mercy shall compasse him about.

11 Be glad in the LORD, and reioyce yee righteous : and shout for ioy all ye that are vpright in heart.

PSAL. XXXIII.

1 God is to be prayed for his goodnesse, 6 for his power, 12 and for his prouidence. 20 Confidence is to be placed in God.

Eioyce in the LORD, O yee righteous : for prayse is comely for the vpright.

2 Praise the LORD with harp : sing vnto him with the Psalterie, and an instrument of ten strings.

3 Sing vnto him a new song : play skilfully with a loud noise.

4 For the word of the LORD is right : and all his workes are done in trueth.

5 *Hee loueth righteousnesse and iudgement : the earth is ful of the ||goodnesse of the LORD.

6 *By the word of the LORD were the heauens made : and all the host of them, by the breath of his mouth.

7 He gathereth the waters of the sea together, as an heape : he layeth vp the depth in storehouses.

8 Let all the earth feare the LORD : let all the inhabitants of the world stand in awe of him.

9 For he spake, and it was done : he commanded, and it stood fast.

10 *The LORD †bringeth the counsell of the heathen to nought : he maketh the deuices of the people, of none effect.

11 *The counsaile of the LORD standeth for euer, the thoughts of his heart †to all generations.

12 *Blessed is the nation, whose God is the LORD : and the people, whom he hath chosen for his owne inheritance.

13 The LORD looketh from heauen : he beholdeth all the sonnes of men.

14 From the place of his habitation, he looketh vpon all the inhabitants of the earth.

15 He fashioneth their hearts alike : he considereth all their workes.

16 There is no king saued by the multitude of an hoste : a mightie man is not deliuered by much strength.

17 An horse is a vaine thing for safetie : neither shall he deliuer any by his great strength.

18 *Behold, the eye of the LORD is vpon them that feare him : vpon them that hope in his mercy :

19 To deliuer their soule from death, and to keepe them aliue in famine.

20 Our soule waiteth for the LORD : he is our helpe, and our shield.

21 For our heart shall reioyce in him : because we haue trusted in his holy name.

22 Let thy mercy (O LORD) be vpon vs : according as we hope in thee.

PSAL. XXXIIII.

1 Dauid prayseth God, and exhorteth other thereto by his experience. 8 They are blessed that trust in God. 11 He exhorteth to the feare of God. 15 The Priuiledges of the righteous.

¶ A Psalme of Dauid, when he changed his behauiour before || Abimelech : who droue him away & he departed.

Will blesse the LORD at all times : his prayse shall continually bee in my mouth.

2 My soule shall make her boast in the LORD : the humble shall

shall heare *thereof*, and be glad.

3 O magnifie the LORD with me, and let vs exalt his name together.

4 I sought the LORD, and hee heard me; and deliuered mee from all my feares.

Or, they flowed vnto him.

5 ‖ They looked vnto him, and were lightned : and their faces were not ashamed.

6 This poore man cried, and the LORD heard *him*; and saued him out of all his troubles.

7 The Angel of the LORD encampeth round about them that feare him, and deliuereth them.

8 O taste and see that the LORD *is* good : blessed *is* the man *that* trusteth in him.

9 O feare the LORD yee his Saints : for *there is* no want to them that feare him.

10 The young lyons doe lacke, and suffer hunger : but they that seeke the LORD, shall not want any good thing.

11 Come yee children, hearken vnto me : I will teach you the feare of the LORD.

* Pet. 3. 10.

12 * What man is hee that desireth life; *and* loueth *many* dayes, that he may see good ?

13 Keepe thy tongue from euill, and thy lippes from speaking guile.

14 Depart from euill, and doe good : seeke peace and pursue it.

* Iob. 36. 7. psal. 33. 18. 1. Pet. 3. 12.

15 * The eies of the LORD *are* vpon the righteous; and his eares *are open* vnto their crie.

16 The face of the LORD *is* against them that doe euill; to cut off the remembrance of them from the earth.

17 *The righteous* crie, and the LORD heareth; and deliuereth them out of all their troubles.

† *Heb. to the broken of heart.* † *Heb. contrite of spirit.*

18 The LORD *is* nigh † vnto them that are of a broken heart : and saueth such as be † of a contrite spirit.

19 Many *are* the afflictions of the righteous : but the LORD deliuereth him out of them all.

20 He keepeth all his bones : not one of them is broken.

‖ *Or, shalbe guilty.*

21 Euill shall slay the wicked : and they that hate the righteous ‖ shalbe desolate.

22 The LORD redeemech the soule of his seruants : and none of them that trust in him, shalbe desolate.

PSAL. XXXV.

1 Dauid prayeth for his owne safety, & his enemies confusion. 11 He complaineth of their wrongfull dealing. 22 Thereby he inciteth God against them.

¶ *A Psalme* of Dauid.

PLEAD *my cause* (O LORD) with them that striue with mee : fight against them that fight against me.

2 Take hold of shield and buckler, and stand vp for mine helpe.

3 Draw out also the speare, and stop *the way* against them that persecute me : say vnto my soule, I *am* thy saluation.

* Psal 15. &

4 * Let them be confounded and put to shame that seeke after my soule : let them be turned backe and brought to confusion, that deuise my hurt.

* Iob psal. ‖ Esa. 9 Osc. 1

5 * Let them be as chaffe before the wind : and let the Angel of the LORD chase *them*.

† *Heb. nesse slippe nesse.*

6 Let their way be † darke and slippery, and let the Angel of the LORD persecute them.

7 For without cause haue they hid for me their net *in* a pit, which without cause they haue digged for my soule.

† *He. he kn not of*

8 Let destruction come vpon him † at vnawares, and let his net that hee hath hid, catch himselfe : into that very destruction let him fall.

9 And my soule shalbe ioyfull in the LORD : it shall reioyce in his saluation.

10 All my bones shall say, LORD, who *is* like vnto thee which deliuerest the poore from him that is too strong for him, yea the poore and the needy, from him that spoileth him ?

† *Heb nesse. wron* † *Het asked*

11 † False witnesses did rise vp; † they layd to my charge things that I knew not.

† *Het uing.*

12 They rewarded mee euill for good, to the † spoiling of my soule.

‖ *Or, ed.*

13 But as for me, when they were sicke, my clothing was sack-cloth : I ‖ humbled my soule with fasting, and my prayer returned into mine owne bosome.

† *Het ked.* † *Het frien broth me.*

14 I † behaued my selfe as though *he had bene* † my friend, *or* brother : I bowed downe heauily, as one that mourneth *for his* mother.

† *Hei ting.*

15 But in mine † aduersitie they reioyced, and gathered themselues together :

ther : *yea*, the abiects gathered themselues together against me, & I knew it
not, they did teare *me*, and ceased not,

16 With hypocriticall mockers in
feasts : they gnashed vpon mee with
their teeth.

17 Lord, how long wilt thou looke
on ? rescue my soule from their destructions, †my darling from the lyons.

18 * I will giue thee thankes in the
great congregation : I will praise thee
among † much people.

19 Let not them that are mine enemies †wrongfully, reioyce ouer me : *neither* let them winke with the eye, that
hate me without a cause.

20 For they speake not peace : but
they deuise deceitfull matters against
them that are quiet in the land.

21 Yea they opened their mouth
wide against me, *and* saide, Aha, Aha,
our eye hath seene *it*.

22 *This* thou hast seene (O LORD)
keepe not silence : O Lord be not farre
from me.

23 Stirre vp thy selfe and awake to
my iudgement, *euen* vnto my cause, my
God and my Lord.

24 Iudge me O LORD my God,
according to thy righteousnesse, and let
them not reioyce ouer me.

25 Let them not say in their hearts,
† Ah, so would we haue it : let them not
say, We haue swallowed him vp.

26 Let them be ashamed and brought
to confusion together, that reioyce at
mine hurt : let them bee cloathed with
shame and dishonour, that magnifie
themselues against me.

27 Let them shoute for ioy, and bee
glad that fauour † my righteous cause :
yea let them say continually, Let the
LORD bee magnified , which hath
pleasure in the prosperity of his seruant

28 And my tongue shall speake of
thy righteousnesse, *and* of thy praise all
the day long.

PSAL. XXXVI.

1 The grieuous estate of the wicked. 5 The excellencie of Gods mercie. 10 Dauid prayeth
for fauour to Gods children.

¶ To the chiefe musician, *A Psalme* of
Dauid, the seruant of the LORD.

HE transgression of the
wicked saith within my
heart, *that there is* no feare
of God before his eyes.

2 For he flatterech him-

selfe in his owne eyes, † vntill his iniquitie be found to be hatefull.

3 The words of his mouth *are* iniquitie and deceit : he hath left off to bee
wise, *and* to doe good.

4 Hee deuiseth ‖ mischiefe vpon his
bed, he setteth himselfe in a way *that is*
not good ; he abhorreth not euill.

5 * Thy mercie (O LORD) *is* in the
heauens ; *and* thy faithfulnesse *reacheth*
vnto the cloudes.

6 Thy righteousnesse *is* like † the
great mountaines ; thy iudgements *are*
a great deepe ; O LORD, thou preseruest man and beast.

7 How †excellent *is* thy louing kindnesse, O God ! therefore the children of
men put their trust vnder the shadowe
of thy wings.

8 They shall be †abundantly satisfied with the fatnesse of thy house : and
thou shalt make them drinke of the riuer of thy pleasures.

9 For with thee *is* the fountaine of
life : in thy light shall we see light.

10 O †continue thy louing kindnesse
vnto them that know thee ; and thy
righteousnesse to the vpright in heart.

11 Let not the foot of pride come a-
gainst me, and let not the hand of the
wicked remoue me.

12 There are the workers of iniquitie fallen : they are cast downe, and shal
not be able to rise.

PSAL. XXXVII.

Dauid perswadeth to patience and confidence
in God, by the different estate of the godly
and the wicked.

¶ *A Psalme* of Dauid.

Ret *not thy selfe because
of euill doers, neither bee
thou enuious against the
workers of iniquitie.

2 For they shall soone
be cut downe like the grasse ; and wither as the greene herbe.

3 Trust in the LORD, and do good,
so shalt thou dwell in the land, and †ve-
rely thou shalt be fed.

4 Delight thy selfe also in the
LORD ; and he shall giue thee the desires of thine heart.

5 †* Commit thy way vnto the
LORD : trust also in him, and he shall
bring *it* to passe.

6 And he shall bring forth thy righteousnes as the light, and thy iudgement as the noone day

7 † Rest

Marginal notes

my
one.
40. 11
1. 1.
strong

falsly.

*ih, ah
ule.*

, my
us-

†*Heb. to find
his iniquitie
to hate.*

‖ *Or, vanitie*

* *Psal.* 57.11
and 108. 4.

† *Hebr. the
mountaines
of God.*

† *Heb. pre-
cious.*

† *Heb. wate-
red.*

† *Heb. draw
out at length*

* *Prou.* 23.
17. & 24. 1.

† *Hebr. in
trueth and
stablenesse.*

† *Heb. rolle
thy way
vpon the
Lord.*
* *Prou.* 16.3
mat. 6. 25.
1. *Pet.* 5. 7.

† *Hebr. be silent to the LORD.*

7 †Rest in the Lord, and wait patiently for him: fret not thy selfe because of him who prospereth in his way, because of the man who bringeth wicked deuices to passe.

8 Cease from anger, and forsake wrath: fret not thy selfe in any wise to doe euill.

9 For euil doers shall be cut off: but those that waite vpon the Lord, they shall inherite the earth.

10 For yet a little while, and the wicked shall not *bee* : yea, thou shalt diligently consider his place, and it *shall* not *be.*

* *Matt. 5. 5.*

11 *But the meeke shall inherite the earth : and shall delight themselues in the abundance of peace.

‖ *Or, practiseth.*

12 The wicked ‖ plotteth against the iust, and gnasheth vpon him with his teeth.

* *Psal. 2. 4.*

13 *The Lord shall laugh at him : for he seeth that his day is comming.

14 The wicked haue drawen out the sword, and haue bent their bow to cast downe the poore and needy, *and* to slay † such as be of vpright conuersation.

† *Heb. the vpright of way.*

15 Their sword shall enter into their owne heart, and their bowes shall be broken.

16 A little that a righteous man *hath, is* better then the riches of many wicked.

17 For the armes of the wicked shall be broken : but the Lord vpholdeth the righteous.

18 The Lord knoweth the dayes of the vpright : and their inheritance shall be for euer.

19 They shall not be ashamed in the euill time : and in the dayes of famine they shalbe satisfied.

20 But the wicked shall perish, and the enemies of the Lord *shall be* as † the fat of lambes : they shall consume: into smoke shall they consume away.

† *Hebr. the preciousnes of Lambes.*

21 The wicked borroweth, and payeth not againe : but the righteous sheweth mercy, and giueth.

22 For such as be blessed of him, shall inherite the earth : and they that be cursed of him, shalbe cut off.

‖ *Or, established.*

23 The steps of a *good* man are ‖ordered by the Lord : and he delighteth in his way.

24 Though hee fall, he shall not be vtterly cast downe: for the Lord vpholdeth *him* with his hand.

25 I haue bene yong, and *now* am old; yet haue I not seene the righteous forsaken, nor his seede begging bread.

26 He is †euer mercifull, and lendeth: and his seede is blessed.

† *Hebr. the da*

27 Depart from euill, and doe good; and dwell for euermore.

28 For the Lord loueth iudgement, and forsaketh not his Saints, they are preserued for euer : but the seed of the wicked shall be cut off.

29 The righteous shall inherite the land, and dwell therein for euer.

30 The mouth of the righteous speaketh wisedome ; and his tongue talketh of iudgement.

31 The Law of his God *is* in his heart : none of his ‖steps shall slide.

‖ *Or,*

32 The wicked watcheth the righteous, and seeketh to slay him.

33 The Lord will not leaue him in his hand, nor condemne him when he is iudged.

34 Wait on the Lord, and keepe his way, and he shall exalt thee to inherit the land : when the wicked are cut off, thou shalt see *it.*

35 I haue seene the wicked in great power : and spreading himselfe like ‖a greene bay tree.

‖ *Or, a tree, grow his o soyle*

36 Yet he passed away, and loe he was not : yea, I sought him, but hee could not be found.

37 Marke the perfect man, and behold the vpright : for the end of *that* man *is* peace.

38 But the transgressours shall be destroyed together : the end of the wicked shalbe cut off.

39 But the saluation of the righteous *is* of the Lord : he *is* their strength in the time of trouble.

40 And the Lord shall helpe them and deliuer them : he shall deliuer them from the wicked, and saue them because they trust in him.

PSAL. XXXVIII.

Dauid mooueth God to take compassion of his pitifull case.

¶ A Psalme of Dauid, to bring to remembrance.

 Lord, rebuke me not in thy wrath : neither chasten me in thy hot displeasure.

2 For thine arrowes sticke

ſticke faſt in me; and thy hand preſſeth me ſore.

3 *There is* no ſoundneſſe in my fleſh, becauſe of thine anger: neither *is there* any †reſt in my bones, becauſe of my ſinne.

4 For mine iniquities are gone ouer mine head: as an heauy burden, they are too heauie for me.

5 My wounds ſtinke, *and* are corrupt: becauſe of my fooliſhneſſe.

6 I am †troubled, I am bowed downe greatly; I goe mourning all the day long.

7 For my loynes are filled with a loathſome diſeaſe: and *there is* no ſoundneſſe in my fleſh.

8 I am feeble and ſore broken; I haue roared by reaſon of the diſquietneſſe of my heart.

9 Lord, all my deſire *is* before thee: and my groning is not hid from thee.

10 My heart panteth, my ſtrength faileth me: as for the light of mine eies, *not* it alſo †is gone from me.

11 My louers and my friends ſtand a *oke.* loofe from my †ſore: and ‖my kinſmen *ers.* ſtand a farre off.

12 They alſo that ſeeke after my life, lay ſnares *for me:* and they that ſeeke my hurt, ſpeake miſchieuous things, and imagine deceits all the day long.

13 But I, as a deafe man, heard not; and *I was* as a dumbe man *that* openeth not his mouth.

14 Thus I was as a man that heareth not; and in whoſe mouth *are* no reproofes.

15 For ‖in thee, O Lᴏʀᴅ, doe I *e do* hope: thou wilt ‖heare, O Lord my *or.* God.

16 For I ſaid, *heare me,* leaſt *otherwiſe* they ſhould reioyce ouer me: when my foot ſlippeth, they magnifie themſelues againſt me.

17 For I am ready †to halt, and my *or* ſorrow *is* continually before me. *s.*

18 For I will declare mine iniquitie; I will be ſory for my ſinne.

19 But mine enemies †are liuely, *and being* they are ſtrong: and they that hate mee *are* wrongfully, are multiplied.

20 They alſo that render euill for good, are mine aduerſaries: becauſe I follow the thing that good is.

21 Forſake me not, O Lᴏʀᴅ · O *or* my God, be not farre from me. *e.*

22 Make haſte †to helpe mee, O Lord my ſaluation.

PSAL. XXXIX.

1 Dauids care of his thoughts, 4 the conſideration of the breuity and vanitie of life, 7 the reuerence of Gods iudgements, 10 and prayer, are his bridles of impatiencie.

¶ To the chiefe Muſician, *euen to* * Ieduthun, A Pſalme of Dauid.

I Sayd, I will take heede to my waies, that I ſinne not with my tongue: I will keepe † my mouth with a bridle, while the wicked is before me.

2 I was dumbe with ſilence, I held my peace, *euen* from good, and my ſorrow was †ſtirred.

3 My heart was hot within mee, while I was muſing the fire burned: then ſpake I with my tongue.

4 Lᴏʀᴅ, make me to know mine end, and the meaſure of my dayes, what it *is: that* I may know ‖how fraile I am.

5 Behold, thou haſt made my dayes *as* an hand breadth, and mine age *is* as nothing before thee: verily euery man †at his beſt ſtate *is* altogether *vanitie. Selah.

6 Surely euery man walketh in †a vaine ſhew: ſurely they are diſquieted in vaine: he heapeth vp *riches,* and knoweth not who ſhall gather them.

7 And now Lord, what wait I for? my hope is in thee.

8 Deliuer me from all my tranſgreſſions: make mee not the reproch of the fooliſh.

9 I was dumbe, I opened not my mouth; becauſe thou diddeſt *it.*

10 Remooue thy ſtroke away from mee: I am conſumed by the †blowe of thine hand.

11 When thou with rebukes doeſt correct man for iniquitie, thou makeſt †his beautie to conſume away like a moth: ſurely euery man *is* vanitie. Selah.

12 Heare my prayer, O Lᴏʀᴅ, and giue eare vnto my crie, hold not thy peace at my teares: *for I am* a ſtraunger with thee, *and* a ſoiourner, as all my fathers *were.*

13 O ſpare me, that I may recouer ſtrength: before I goe hence, and be no more.

PSAL. XL.

1 The benefite of confidence in God. 6 Obedience

Marginal notes (right column)

* 1. Chron. 25. 1.

† Heb. a bridle, or mouſell for my mouth.

† Heb. troubled.

‖ Or, what time I haue here.

† Heb. ſetled.
* Pſal. 62. 9. & 144. 4.

† Hebr. image.

† Heb. conflict.

† Heb. that which is to be deſired in him, to melt away.

* Leuit. 25. 23.
1. Chron. 29. 15.
Pſal. 119. 19.
Heb. 11. 13.
1. Pet. 2. 11.

dience is the best sacrifice. 11 The sence of Dauids euils inflameth his prayer.

¶ To the chiefe Musician, *A Psalme* of Dauid.

I †Waited patiently for the LORD, and he inclined vnto me, and heard my crie.

† Heb. in waiting I waited.

2 He brought me vp also out of †an horrible pit, out of the mirie clay, and set my feete vpon a rock, *and* established my goings.

† Heb. a pit of noise.

3 And he hath put a new song in my mouth, *euen* praise vnto our God: many shall see it, and feare, and shall trust in the LORD.

4 Blessed *is* that man that maketh the LORD his truste: and respecteth not the proud, nor such as turne aside to lies.

5 Many, O LORD my God, *are* thy wonderfull workes *which* thou hast done, and thy thoughts, *which are* to vs ward: ||they cannot be reckoned vp in order vnto thee: *if* I would declare and speake *of them*, they are moe then can be numbred.

|| Or, none can order them vnto thee.

6 *Sacrifice and offering thou didst not desire, mine eares hast thou †opened: burnt offering and sinne-offering hast thou not required.

* Psal. 51. 16. Esa. 1. 11. & 66. 3. Hos. 6. 6. Heb. 10. 5. Mat. 12. 7

† Heb. digged.

7 Then sayd I, Loe, I come: in the volume of the booke it *is* written of me:

8 I delight to doe thy will, O my God: yea thy lawe *is* †within my heart.

† Heb. in the midst of my bowels.

9 I haue preached righteousnesse in the great congregation: loe, I haue not refrained my lippes, O LORD, thou knowest.

10 I haue not hid thy righteousnesse within my heart, I haue declared thy faithfulnesse and thy saluation: I haue not concealed thy louing kindnesse, and thy truth, from the great congregation.

11 With-hold not thou thy tender mercies from me, O LORD: let thy louing kindnesse, and thy trueth continually preserue me.

12 For innumerable euils haue compassed me about, mine iniquities haue taken hold vpon me, so that I am not able to looke vp: they are moe then the haires of mine head, therefore my heart †faileth me.

† Heb. forsaketh.

13 Be pleased, O LORD, to deliuer me: O LORD, make haste to helpe me.

14 *Let them be ashamed and confounded together, that seeke after my soule to destroy it: let them be driuen backward, and put to shame, that wish me euill.

* Psal. 34. 6. & 70. 3.

15 Let them be desolate, for a reward of their shame, that say vnto me, Aha, aha!

16 Let all those that seeke thee, reioyce and bee glad in thee: let such as loue thy saluation, say continually, The LORD be magnified.

17 But I *am* poore and needy, *yet* the Lord thinketh vpon me: thou *art* my helpe and my deliuerer, make no tarrying, O my God.

PSAL. XLI.

1 Gods care of the poore. 4 Dauid complaineth of his enemies trecherie. 10 He flyeth to God for succour.

¶ To the chiefe Musician. A Psalme of Dauid.

BLessed *is* he that considereth || the poore; the LORD will deliuer him †in time of trouble.

|| Or wea sick

† He day

2 The LORD will preserue him, and keepe him aliue, and he shall be blessed vpon the earth; and ||thou wilt not deliuer him vnto the will of his enemies.

|| Or thou

3 The LORD will strengthen him vpon the bed of languishing: thou wilt †make all his bed in his sicknesse.

† He

4 I sayd, LORD be mercifull vnto me, heale my soule, for I haue sinned against thee.

5 Mine enemies speake euill of me: when shall hee die, and his name perish?

6 And if hee come to see *me*, he speaketh vanity: his heart gathereth iniquitie to it selfe, *when* he goeth abroad, he telleth *it*.

7 All that hate me, whisper together against me; against me doe they deuise †my hurt.

† He to m

8 †An euill disease, *say they*, cleaueth fast vnto him; and *now* that he lyeth, he shall rise vp no more.

† He thin lial.

9 *Yea †mine owne familiar friend in whom I trusted, *which* did eate of my bread, hath †lift vp his heele against me.

* Io

† He man peac

† He nifie

10 But thou, O LORD, be mercifull vnto mee, and raise me vp that I may requite them.

11 By this I know that thou fauourest

rest me : because mine enemie doeth not triumph ouer me.

12 And as for me, thou vpholdest me in mine integritie; and settest me before thy face for euer.

13 Blessed *bee* the LORD God of Israel, from euerlasting, and to euerlasting. Amen, and Amen.

PSAL. XLII.

1 Dauids zeale to serue God in the Temple. 5 He incourageth his soule to trust in God.

¶ To the chiefe Musician, ‖ Maschil, for the sonnes of Korah.

A S the Hart † panteth after the water brookes, so panteth my soule after thee, O God.

2 My soule thirsteth for God, for the liuing God : when shall I come and appeare before God ?

3 *My teares haue bene my meate day and night; while they continually say vnto me, Where *is* thy God ?

4 When I remember these things, I powre out my soule in mee; for I had gone with the multitude, I went with them to the house of God; with the voyce of ioy and praise, with a multitude *that* kept holy day.

5 Why art thou † cast downe, O my soule, and *why* art thou disquieted in me? hope thou in God, for I shall yet ‖ praise him ‖ *for* the helpe of his countenance.

6 O my God, my soule is cast downe within me : therefore will I remember thee from the land of Iordane, and of the Hermonites, from the ‖ hill Missar.

7 Deepe calleth vnto deepe at the noyse of thy water-spouts : all thy waues, and thy billowes are gone ouer me.

8 *Yet* the LORD will command his louing kindnes in the day time, and in the night his song shalbe with me, *and* my prayer vnto the God of my life.

9 I will say vnto God, My rocke, why hast thou forgotten me ? why goe I mourning, because of the oppression of the enemy ?

10 *As* with a ‖ sword in my bones, mine enemies reproch mee : while they say dayly vnto me, Where *is* thy God?

11 Why art thou cast downe, O my soule ? and why art thou disquieted within me? hope thou in God, for I shall yet praise him, *who is* the health of my countenance, and my God.

a
ie gin-
instru-
of the
s, &c.
r.bray.

L. 80. 5.

r. bow-
one.

giue
ies.
his pre-
is sal-
n.

the
hill.

killing.

PSAL. XLIII.

1 Dauid praying to be restored to the Temple, promiseth to serue God ioyfully. 5 He encourageth his soule to trust in God.

I Vdge mee, O God, and plead my cause against an ‖ vngodly nation ; O deliuer me † from the deceitfull and vniust man.

2 For thou *art* the God of my strength, why doest thou cast me off ? why goe I mourning because of the oppression of the enemy ?

3 O send out thy light & thy trueth ; let them leade mee, let them bring mee vnto thy holy hill, and to thy Tabernacles.

4 Then will I goe vnto the Altar of God, vnto God † my exceeding ioy : yea vpon the harpe will I praise thee, O God, my God.

5 Why art thou cast downe, O my soule ? and why art thou disquieted within me? hope in God, for I shall yet praise him, *who is* the health of my * countenance, and my God.

‖ Or, vnmer-
cifull.
† Hebr. from
a man of de-
ceit, and ini-
quitie.

† Hebr. the
gladnesse of
my ioy.

* Psal. 42. 6.
aud 12.

PSAL. XLIIII.

1 The Church, in memory of former fauours, 7 complaineth of their present euils. 17 Professing her integritie, 24 She feruently prayeth for succour.

¶ To the chiefe Musician for the sonnes of Korah.

W Ee haue heard with our eares, O God, our fathers haue told vs, *what* worke thou didst in their dayes, in the times of old.

2 *How* thou didst driue out the heathen with thy hand, & plantedst them; *how* thou didst afflict the people, and cast them out.

3 For they got not the land in possession by their owne sword, neither did their owne arme saue them : but thy right hand, and thine arme, and the light of thy countenance, because thou hadst a fauour vnto them.

4 Thou art my King, O God : command deliuerances for Iacob.

5 Through thee will wee push downe our enemies : through thy Name will wee tread them vnder that rise vp against vs.

6 For I will not trust in my bow, neither shall my sword saue me.

7 But

7 But thou hast saued vs from our enemies, and hast put them to shame that hated vs.

8 In God we boast all the day long: and praise thy Name for euer. Selah.

9 But thou hast cast off and put vs to shame; and goest not forth with our armies.

10 Thou makest vs to turne backe from the enemie: and they which hate vs, spoile for themselues.

11 Thou hast giuen vs like † sheepe *appointed* for meate: and hast scattered vs among the heathen.

12 Thou sellest thy people † for nought, and doest not increase *thy wealth* by their price.

13 *Thou makest vs a reproch to our neighbours, a scorne and a derision to them that are round about vs.

14 *Thou makest vs a by-word among the heathen: a shaking of the head among the people.

15 My confusion *is* continually before me, and the shame of my face hath couered me.

16 For the voice of him that reproacheth, and blasphemeth: by reason of the enemie and auenger.

17 All this is come vpon vs; yet haue wee not forgotten thee, neither haue we dealt falsly in thy couenant.

18 Our heart is not turned backe: neither haue our ‖ steps declined from thy way,

19 Though thou hast sore broken vs in the place of dragons, and couered vs with the shadow of death.

20 If wee haue forgotten the name of our God, or stretched out our hands to a strange God:

21 Shall not God search this out? for he knoweth the secrets of the heart.

22 *Yea for thy sake are wee killed all the day long: wee are counted as sheepe for the slaughter.

23 Awake, why sleepest thou, O Lord? arise, cast *vs* not off for euer.

24 Wherefore hidest thou thy face? *and* forgettest our affliction, and our oppression?

25 For our soule is bowed downe to the dust; our belly cleaueth vnto the earth.

26 Arise † for our helpe, and redeeme vs for thy mercies sake.

PSAL. XLV.

1 The maiestie and grace of Chriſts kingdome.

10 The duetie of the Church, and the benefits thereof.

¶ To the chiefe Musician vpon Shoshannim, for the sonnes of Korah, ‖ Maschil : a song of loues.

MY heart † is inditing a good matter : I speake of the things which I haue made, touching the King: my tongue *is* the penne of a ready writer.

2 Thou art fairer then the children of men : grace is powred into thy lips : therfore God hath blessed thee for euer.

3 Gird thy sword vpon *thy* thigh, O *most* mightie : with thy glory and thy maiestie.

4 And in thy maiestie † ride prosperously, because of trueth and meekenes, *and* righteousnesse: and thy right hand shall teach thee terrible things.

5 Thine arrowes *are* sharpe in the heart of the Kings enemies; whereby the people fall vnder thee.

6 * Thy throne (O God) *is* for euer and euer: the scepter of thy kingdome *is* a right scepter.

7 Thou louest righteousnesse, and hatest wickednesse : therefore God, thy God, hath anointed thee with the oyle of gladnesse aboue thy fellowes.

8 All thy garments *smell* of myrrhe, and aloes, *and* cassia: out of the Iuorie palaces, whereby they haue made thee glad.

9 Kings daughters *were* among thy honourable women: vpon thy right hand did stand the Queene in golde of Ophir.

10 Hearken (O daughter) and consider, and incline thine eare; forget also thine owne people, and thy fathers house.

11 So shall the king greatly desire thy beautie : for he is thy Lord, and worship thou him.

12 And the daughter of Tyre *shall be* there with a gift, *euen* the rich among the people shall intreate † thy fauour.

13 The kings daughter *is* all glorious within; her clothing *is* of wrought gold.

14 She shall bee brought vnto the king in raiment of needle worke : the virgins her companions that followe her, shall be brought vnto thee.

15 With gladnesse and reioycing shall they be brought : they shall enter into the kings palace.

16 In

Side notes (left column):

† *Hebr. as sheepe of meate.*

† *Heb. without riches.*

* *Psal. 79. 4*

* *Iere. 24. 9.*

‖ *Or, goings*

* *Rom. 8. 36*

† *Heb. a help for vs.*

Side notes (right column):

‖ *Or, of instruction*
† *Hebr. leth or leth vp.*

† *Hebr. per thou ride thou*

* *Heb.*

† *Heb. face.*

16 In ſtead of thy fathers ſhall bee thy children, whom thou mayeſt make princes in all the earth.

17 I will make thy name to bee remembred in all generations : therefore ſhall the people praiſe thee for euer and euer.

PSAL. XLVI.

1 The confidence which the Church hath in God. 8 An exhortation to behold it.

¶ To the chiefe Muſician ‖ for the ſonnes of Korah , a ſong vpon Alamoth.

OD *is* our refuge and ſtrength : a very preſent helpe in trouble.

2 Therfore will not we feare , though the earth be remoued : and though the mountaines be caried into †the midſt of the ſea.

3 *Though* the waters thereof roare, *and* be troubled, *though* the mountaines ſhake with the ſwelling thereof. Selah.

4 *There is* a riuer, the ſtreames wherof ſhall make glad the citie of God: the holy place of the Tabernacles of the moſt High.

5 God *is* in the midſt of her : ſhe ſhal not be moued ; God ſhall helpe her, †*and that* right early.

6 The heathen raged , the kingdomes were mooued : he vttered his voyce, the earth melted.

7 The LORD of hoſts *is* with vs; the God of Iacob *is* †our refuge. Selah.

8 Come, behold the workes of the LORD , what deſolations hee hath made in the earth.

9 He maketh warres to ceaſe vnto the end of the earth : hee breaketh the bow, and cutteth the ſpeare in ſunder, he burneth the chariot in the fire.

10 Be ſtil, and know that I *am* God : I will bee exalted among the heathen, I will be exalted in the earth.

11 The LORD of hoſts *is* with vs; the God of Iacob *is* our refuge. Selah.

PSAL. XLVII.

The Nations are exhorted cheerefully to entertaine the Kingdome of Chriſt.

¶ To the chiefe muſician, a pſalme ‖for the ſonnes of Korah.

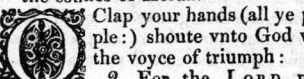 Clap your hands (all ye people:) ſhoute vnto God with the voyce of triumph :

2 For the LORD moſt

high *is* terrible; he *is* a great King ouer all the earth.

3 Hee ſhall ſubdue the people vnder vs, and the nations vnder our feet.

4 He ſhall chuſe our inheritance for vs, the excellencie of Iacob whom hee loued. Selah.

5 God is gone vp with a ſhout, the LORD with the ſound of a trumpet.

6 Sing praiſes to God, ſing praiſes : ſing praiſes vnto our King, ſing praiſes.

7 For God *is* the King of all the earth, ſing ye praiſes ‖with vnderſtanding.

8 God reigneth ouer the heathen : God ſitteth vpon the throne of his holineſſe.

9 ‖ The princes of the people are gathered together, *euen* the people of the God of Abraham : for the ſhields of the earth *belong* vnto God : hee is greatly exalted.

PSAL. XLVIII.

The Ornaments and priuiledges of the Church.

¶ A ſong, *and* Pſalme ‖for the ſonnes of Korah.

Reat *is* the LORD, and greatly to bee praiſed in the citie of our God, in the mountaine of his holineſſe.

2 Beautifull for ſituation, the ioy of the whole earth is moūt Sion, *on* the ſides of the North, the citie of the great King.

3 God is knowen in her palaces for a refuge.

4 For loe, the kings were aſſembled : they paſſed by together.

5 They ſawe *it, and* ſo they marueiled , they were troubled *and* haſted away.

6 Feare tooke holde vpon them there, *and* paine, as of a woman in trauaile.

7 Thou breakeſt the ſhips of Tarſhiſh with an Eaſt wind.

8 As we haue heard, ſo haue wee ſeene in the citie of the LORD of hoſts, in the citie of our God, God will eſtabliſh it for euer. Selah.

9 Wee haue thought of thy louing kindneſſe, O God, in the middeſt of thy Temple.

10 According to thy Name, O God, ſo *is* thy praiſe vnto the endes of the earth : thy right hand is full of righteouſneſſe.

11 Let

Marginal notes (left column):
of.

r. the of the

. when orning reth.

. an place s.

of.

Marginal notes (right column):
‖ Or, euery one *that* hath vnderſtanding.

‖ Or, the voluntarie of the people are gathered vnto *the* people of the God of A-braham.

‖ Or, of.

† *Heb. set your heart to her bulwarkes.*
‖ *Or, raise vp.*

11 Let mount Sion reioyce, let the daughters of Iudah be glad, because of thy iudgements.

12 Walke about Sion, and goe round about her : tell the towres thereof.

13 †Marke yee well her bulwarkes, ‖ consider her palaces; that yee may tell *it* to the generation following.

14 For this God *is* our God for euer, and euer; he will be our guide *euen* vnto death.

PSAL. XLIX.

1 An earnest perswasion to build the faith of Resurrection, not on worldly power, but on God. 16 Worldly prosperity is not to be admired.

¶ *To the chiefe Musician, a Psalme ‖ for the sonnes of Korah.*

‖ *Or, of.*

HEare this, all *yee* people, giue eare all yee inhabitants of the world :

2 Both low, and high, rich and poore together.

3 My mouth shall speake of wisedome : and the meditation of my heart shalbe of vnderstanding.

ᵃ *Mat. 13. 35. psal. 78. 2.*

4 *I will incline mine eare to a parable ; I will open my darke saying vpon the harpe.

5 Wherefore should I feare in the daies of euill, *when* the iniquitie of my heeles shall compasse me about ?

6 They that trust in their wealth, and boast themselues in the multitude of their riches :

7 None *of them* can by any meanes redeeme *his* brother, nor giue to God a ransome for him :

8 (For the redemption of their soule *is* precious, and it ceaseth for euer.)

9 That he should still liue for euer, *and* not see corruption.

10 For he seeth *that* wise men die, likewise the foole, and the brutish person perish, and leaue their wealth to others.

11 Their inward thought *is, that* their houses *shall continue* for euer, *and* their dwelling places † to all generations; they call *their* lands after their owne names.

† *Heb. to generation and generation.*

12 Neuerthelesse man *being* in honour abideth not : he is like the beastes *that* perish.

13 This their way *is* their follie; yet their posteritie † approue their sayings. Selah.

† *Heb. delight in their mouth.*

14 Like sheepe they are layd in the graue, death shall feede on them ; and

the vpright shall haue dominion ouer them in the morning, and their ‖ beauty shall consume ‖ in the graue, from their dwelling.

‖ *Or, sta*
‖ *Or, a graue an hal on to o one of*

15 But God will redeeme my soule †from the power of the ‖ graue; for he shall receiue me. Selah.

† *Heb. the ha the gr*

16 Be not thou afraid when one is made rich, when the glory of his house is increased.

‖ *Or, h*

17 *For when he dieth, he shall carry nothing away : his glory shall not descend after him.

* *Iob. 19.*

18 Though † whiles he liued, he blessed his soule : and men will praise thee, when thou doest well to thy selfe.

† *Heb. life.*

19 †Hee shall goe to the generation of his fathers, they shall neuer see light.

† *Heb soule goe.*

20 Man *that is* in honour and vnderstandeth not, is like the beasts *that* perish.

PSAL. L.

1 The Maiestie of God in the Church. 5 His order to gather Saints. 7 The pleasure of God is not in Ceremonies, 14 but in sinceritie of Obedience.

¶ *A Psalme ‖ of Asaph.*

‖ *Or, Asap*

THe mightie God, *euen* the LORD hath spoken, and called the earth from the rising of the sunne, vnto the going downe thereof.

2 Out of Sion the perfection of beautie, God hath shined.

3 Our God shall come, and shall not keepe silence : a fire shall deuoure before him, and it shalbe very tempestuous round about him.

4 He shall call to the heauens from aboue, and to the earth, that hee may iudge his people.

5 Gather my Saints together vnto mee : those that haue made a couenant with me, by sacrifice.

6 And the heauens shall declare his righteousnes; for God *is* iudge himselfe. Selah.

7 Heare, O my people, and I will speake, O Israel, and I will testifie against thee; I *am* God, *euen* thy God.

8 I will not reproue thee for thy sacrifices, or thy burnt offerings, *to haue bene* continually before me.

9 I will take no bullocke out of thy house, *nor* hee goates out of thy folds.

10 For euery beast of the forrest *is* mine, *and* the cattell vpon a thousand hilles.

ebr. with

ꜰod. 19.
eut. 10.

b 41. 2.
ꜱr. 10.
6.

om. 2.
ꜱ2.

ebr. thy
ꜱion was
— adul-
ꜱrs.
ꜱbr. thou
ꜱest.

ꜱbr. that
ꜱseth his

ꜱam. 12.
ꜱd 11. 1.

11 I know all the foules of the mountaines : and the wild beasts of the field *are* † mine.

12 *If I were hungry, I would not tell thee, *for the world *is* mine, and the fulnesse thereof.

13 Will I eate the flesh of bulles, or drinke the blood of goats?

14 Offer vnto God thankesgiuing, and pay thy vowes vnto the most high.

15 And call vpon mee in the day of trouble ; I will deliuer thee, and thou shalt glorifie me.

16 But vnto the wicked God saith, What hast thou to doe, to declare my Statutes, or that thou shouldest take my Couenant in thy mouth?

17 *Seeing thou hatest instruction, and castest my words behinde thee.

18 When thou sawest a thiefe, then thou consentedst with him, and † hast bene partaker with adulterers.

19 †Thou giuest thy mouth to euill, and thy tongue frameth deceit.

20 Thou sittest *and* speakest against thy brother ; thou slanderest thine owne mothers sonne.

21 These things hast thou done, and I kept silence : thou thoughtest that I was altogether such a one as thy selfe : *but* I will reproue thee, and set *them* in order before thine eyes.

22 Now consider this, ye that forget God, lest I teare *you* in pieces, and *there be* none to deliuer.

23 Who so offereth praise, glorifieth me : and to him †that ordereth *his* conuersation *aright*, will I shew the saluation of God.

PSAL. LI.

1 Dauid prayeth for remission of sinnes, where-of he maketh a deepe confession. 6 Hee prayeth for sanctification. 16 God delighteth not in sacrifice, but in sinceritie. 18 Hee prayeth for the Church.

¶ To the chiefe Musician. A Psalme of Dauid, *when Nathan the Prophet came vnto him, after hee had gone in to Bath-sheba.

Aue mercie vpon mee, O God, according to thy louing kindnesse : according vnto the multitude of thy tender mercies blot out my transgressions.

2 Wash mee throughly from mine iniquitie, and clense me from my sinne.

3 For I acknowledge my transgressions : and my sinne is euer before mee.

4 *Against thee, thee onely haue I sinned, and done this euill in thy sight : that thou mightest bee iustified when thou speakest, *and* be cleare when thou iudgest.

5 Behold, I was shapen in iniquitie : and in sinne did my mother † conceiue me.

6 Behold, thou desirest trueth in the inward parts : and in the hidden *part* thou shalt make me to know wisedome.

7 *Purge me with hyssope, and I shalbe cleane : wash me, and I shall be whiter then snow.

8 Make mee to heare ioy and gladnesse : *that* the bones *which* thou hast broken, may reioyce.

9 Hide thy face from my sinnes ; and blot out all mine iniquities.

10 Create in mee a cleane heart, O God ; and renew ‖ a right spirit within mee.

11 Cast mee not away from thy presence ; and take not thy holy Spirit from me.

12 Restore vnto me the ioy of thy saluation : and vphold mee *with thy* free Spirit.

13 *Then* will I teach transgressours thy wayes, and sinners shalbe conuerted vnto thee.

14 Deliuer mee from † blood-guiltinesse, O God, thou God of my saluation : *and* my tongue shall sing alowd of thy righteousnesse.

15 O Lord open thou my lips, and my mouth shall shew foorth thy praise.

16 For thou desirest not sacrifice : ‖ else would I giue *it* : thou delightest not in burnt offering.

17 *The sacrifices of God *are* a broken spirit : a broken and a contrite heart, O God, thou wilt not despise.

18 Doe good in thy good pleasure vnto Sion : build thou the walles of Ierusalem.

19 Then shalt thou be pleased with the sacrifices of righteousnesse, with burnt offering and whole burnt offering : then shall they offer bullockes vpon thine altar.

PSAL. LII.

1 Dauid condemning the spightfulnesse of Doeg, prophesieth his destruction. 6 The
righteous

* Rom. 3. 4.

† Hebr.
warme me.

* Leuit. 14.
6. num. 19.
18.

‖ Or, a con-
stant spirit.

† Hebr.
bloods.

‖ Or, that I
should giue
it.
᪸ Isa. 57. 15.
and 66. 2.

righteous shall reioyce at it. 8 Dauid vpon his confidence in Gods mercy, giueth thanks.

¶ To the chiefe Musician, Maschil, *A Psalme* of Dauid: * When Doeg the Edomite came and told Saul, and said vnto him, Dauid is come to the house of Ahimelech.

W Hy boastest thou thyselfe in mischiefe, O mightie man? the goodnesse of God *indureth* continually.

2 Thy tongue deuiseth mischiefes : like a sharpe rasor, working deceitfully.

3 Thou louest euill more then good ; *and* lying rather then to speake righteousnesse. Selah.

4 Thou louest all deuouring words, ‖O *thou* deceitfull tongue.

5 God shall likewise † destroy thee for euer, hee shall take thee away and plucke thee out of *thy* dwelling place, and roote thee out of the land of the liuing. Selah.

6 The righteous also shall see, and feare, and shall laugh at him.

7 Loe, this *is* the man *that* made not God his strength : but trusted in the abundance of his riches, *and* strengthened himselfe in his ‖ wickednesse.

8 But I *am* like a greene oliue tree in the house of God : I trust in the mercy of God for euer and euer.

9 I will prayse thee for euer, because thou hast done *it :* and I will wait on thy name, for it *is* good before thy Saints.

PSAL. LIII.

1 Dauid describeth the corruption of a naturall man. 4 He conuinceth the wicked by the light of their owne conscience. 6 Hee glorieth in the saluation of God.

¶ To the chiefe musician vpon Mahalath, Maschil, *A Psalme* of Dauid.

T He * foole hath sayde in his heart, *There is* no god ; Corrupt are they, and haue done abhominable iniquitie ; *there is* none that doth good.

2 God looked downe from heauen vpon the children of men, to see if there were any that did vnderstand, that did seeke God.

3 Euery one of them is gone backe, they are altogether become filthy : *there is* none *that* doth good, no not one.

4 Haue the workers of iniquitie no knowledge ? *who* eate vp my people, *as* they eate bread ; they haue not called vpon God.

5 There † were they in great feare, *where* no feare was : for God hath scattered the bones of him that incampeth *against* thee, thou hast put *them* to shame, because God hath despised them.

6 †O that the saluation of Israel *were come* out of Sion ! when God bringeth backe the captiuitie of his people, Iaakob shall reioyce, *and* Israel shall be glad.

PSAL. LIIII.

1 Dauid complaining of the Ziphims, prayeth for saluation. 4 Vpon his confidence in Gods helpe, he promiseth sacrifice.

¶ To the chiefe musician on Neginoth, Maschil, *A Psalme* of Dauid. * When the Ziphims came and sayde to Saul : doeth not Dauid hide himselfe with vs ?

S Aue me, O God, by thy name, and iudge me by thy strength.

2 Heare my prayer, O God ; giue eare to the words of my mouth.

3 For strangers are risen vp against me, and oppressors seeke after my soule ; they haue not set God before them. Selah.

4 Behold, God *is* mine helper : the Lord *is* with them that vphold my soule.

5 He shall reward euill vnto † mine enemies : cut them off in thy trueth.

6 I will freely sacrifice vnto thee ; I will praise thy name (O Lord :) for it *is* good.

7 For hee hath deliuered me out of all trouble : and mine eye hath seene *his desire* vpon mine enemies.

PSAL. LV.

1 Dauid in his prayer complaineth of his fearefull case. 9 He prayeth against his enemies, of whose wickednesse and trecherie he complaineth. 16 He comforteth himselfe in Gods preseruation of him and confusion of his enemies.

¶ To the chiefe musician on Neginoth, Maschil. *A Psalme* of Dauid.

G Iue eare to my prayer, O God : and hide not thy selfe from my supplication.

2 Attend vnto me, and heare

Marginal notes (left column)
* 1. Sam. 22. 9.

‖ Or, and the deceitfull tongue.
† Heb. beate thee downe.

‖ Or, substance.

* Psal. 14. 1. &c.
psal. 10. 4.

* Rom. 3. 16.

Marginal notes (right column)
† Heb. feared c feare.

† Heb. will giu uations

* 1. Sam 19. and 16. 1.

† Heb. t that obs me.

heare me : I mourne in my complaint, and make a noise.

3 Because of the voyce of the enemie, because of the oppression of the wicked: for they cast iniquitie vpon me, and in wrath they hate me.

4 My heart is sore pained within me: and the terrours of death are fallen vpon me.

5 Fearefulnesse and trembling are come vpon me, and horrour hath †ouerwhelmed me.

6 And I said, O that I had wings like a doue; *for then* would I flee away and be at rest.

7 Loe, *then* would I wander farre off, *and* remaine in the wildernesse. Selah.

8 I would hasten my escape from the windie storme, *and* tempest.

9 Destroy, O Lord, *and* diuide their tongues : for I haue seene violence and strife in the citie.

10 Day and night they goe about it vpon the walles thereof: mischiefe also and sorrow *are* in the midst of it.

11 Wickednesse *is* in the midst therof: deceite and guile depart not from her streets.

12 For *it was* not an enemie *that* reproached me, then I could haue borne *it*, neither *was it* hee that hated me, that did magnifie *himselfe* against me, then I would haue hid my selfe from him.

13 But *it was* thou, †a man, mine equal, my guide, and mine acquaintance.

14 †Wee tooke sweet counsell together, *and* walked vnto the house of God in companie.

15 Let death seaze vpon them, and let them goe downe quicke into ||hell: for wickednes *is* in their dwellings, *and* among them.

16 As for me, I will call vpon God: and the Lord shall saue me.

17 Euening and morning, and at noone will I pray, and crie aloud: and he shall heare my voyce.

18 He hath deliuered my soule in peace from the battell that was against me : for there were many with me.

19 God shall heare and afflict them, euen he that abideth of old, Selah : because ||they haue no changes, therefore they feare not God.

20 He hath put foorth his handes against such as be at peace with him : †he hath broken his couenant.

21 *The words* of his mouth were smoother then butter, but warre *was* in his heart: his words were softer then oyle, yet *were* they drawen swords.

22 *Cast thy ||burden vpon the Lord, and he shall sustaine thee : hee shall neuer suffer the righteous to bee moued.

23 But thou, O God, shalt bring them downe into the pit of destruction : †Bloody and deceitfull men †shall not liue out halfe their dayes, but I will trust in thee.

PSAL. LVI.

1 Dauid praying to God in confidence of his word, complaineth of his enemies. 9 Hee professeth his confidence in Gods word, and promiseth to praise him.

¶ To the chiefe musician vpon Ionath Elem Rechokim, ||Michtam of Dauid, when the *Philistines tooke him in Gath.

E mercifull vnto mee, O God, for man would swallow me vp: he fighting daily, oppresseth me.

2 †Mine enemies would dayly swallow *me* vp: for they *bee* many that fight against me, O thou most high.

3 What time I am afraide, I will trust in thee.

4 In God I will praise his worde, In God I haue put my trust, I will not feare what flesh can doe vnto me.

5 Euery day they wrest my words: all their thoughts are against mee for euill.

6 They gather themselues together; they hide themsclues, they marke my steps when they wait for my soule.

7 Shall they escape by iniquitie? in *thine* anger cast downe the people, O God.

8 Thou tellest my wanderings, put thou my teares into thy bottle: *are* they not in thy booke?

9 When I crie vnto thee, then shall mine enemies turne backe : this I know, for God *is* for me.

10 In God will I praise *his* word : in the Lord will I praise *his* word.

11 In God haue I put my trust: I will not bee afraid what man can doe vnto me.

12 Thy vowes *are* vpon me, O God: I will render praises vnto thee.

13 For thou hast deliuered my soule from death : wilt not thou *deliuer* my feet

*Psal. 37. 8
mat. 6. 25.
luk. 12. 22.
1. pet. 5. 7.
|| Or, gift.

† Heb. men of bloods and deceit.
† Hebr. shal not halfe their dayes.

|| Or, a golden psalme of Dauid.
*1. Sam. 21. 11.

†Hebr. mine obseruers.

feet from falling? that I may walke before God in the light of the liuing.

PSAL. LVII.

1 Dauid in prayer flying vnto God, complaineth of his dangerous case. 7 He incourageth himſelfe to praise God.

‖ Or, deſtroy not.
* 1. Sam. 24. 1.

¶ To the chiefe musician ‖ Al-taschith, Michtam of Dauid, *when hee fled from Saul in the caue.

BE mercifull vnto mee, O God, be merciful vnto me, for my soule trusteth in thee: yea in the shadow of thy wings will I make my refuge, vntill these calamities bee o-uerpast.

2 I will crie vnto God most high: vnto God that perfourmeth all things for mee.

‖ Or, he reproacheth him that would swallow me vp.

3 Hee shall send from heauen, and saue me ‖ from the reproch of him, that would swallow me vp; Selah. God shall send forth his mercy and his trueth.

4 My soule is among lyons, and I lie euen among them that are set on fire: euen the sonnes of men, whose teeth are speares and arrowes, and their tongue a sharpe sword.

5 Be thou exalted, O God, aboue the heauens: let thy glory be aboue all the earth.

* Psal. 7. 16. and 9. 15.

6 *They haue prepared a net for my steppes, my soule is bowed downe: they haue digged a pit before me, into the midst whereof they are fallen themselues. Selah.

* Psal. 108. 1. &c.
‖ Or, prepared.

7 *My heart is ‖fixed, O God, my heart is fixed: I will sing, and giue praise.

8 Awake vp my glory, awake psalterie and harpe; I my selfe will awake early.

9 I will praise thee, O Lord, among the people; I will sing vnto thee among the nations.

* Psal. 36. 6. & 108. 5.

10 *For thy mercy is great vnto the heauens, and thy trueth vnto the clouds.

11 Be thou exalted, O God, aboue the heauens: let thy glory be aboue all the earth.

PSAL. LVIII.

1 Dauid reprooueth wicked Iudges, 3 Describeth the nature of the wicked, 6 Deuoteth them to Gods iudgements, 10 whereat the righteous shall reioyce.

‖ Or, d● not, a ● psalme Dauid

¶ To the chiefe musician ‖ Al-taschith, Michtam of Dauid.

DOe yee indeed speake righteousnesse, O congregation? doe ye iudge vprightly, O ye sonnes of men?

2 Yea, in heart you worke wickednesse; you waigh the violence of your hands in the earth.

† Heb. the bel

3 The wicked are estranged from the wombe, they goe astray †as soone as they be borne, speaking lies.

† Heb. ding t● likene● ‖ Or, ●

4 Their poison is †like the poyson of a serpent; they are like the deafe ‖adder that stoppeth her eare:

‖ Or, b charm uer so ning.

5 Which will not hearken to the voyce of charmers, ‖charming neuer so wisely.

6 Breake their teeth, O God, in their mouth: breake out the great teeth of the young lyons, O Lord.

7 Let them melt away as waters, which runne continually: When he bendeth his bow to shoote his arrowes, let them be as cut in pieces.

8 As a snaile which melteth, let euery one of them passe away: like the vntimely birth of a woman, that they may not see the sunne.

9 Before your pots can feele the thornes, he shall take them away as with a whirlewind, †both liuing, and in his wrath.

† Heb. uing, wrath

10 The righteous shall reioyce when he seeth the vengeance: he shall wash his feete in the blood of the wicked.

11 So that a man shall say, Verily there is †a reward for the righteous: verily hee is a God that iudgeth in the earth.

† Heb. of the

PSAL. LIX.

1 Dauid prayeth to be deliuered from his enemies. 6 Hee complaineth of their cruelty. 8 Hee trusteth in God. 11 He prayeth against them. 16 He praiseth God.

‖ Or, the c● Musi● destre● a gol● psalm● Daui●
* 1. S● 11.
† Heb● on hi●

¶ To ‖the chiefe musician Al-taschith, Michtam of Dauid: *when Saul sent, and they watcht the house to kill him.

DEliuer me from mine enemies, O my God: †defend mee from them that rise vp against me.

2 Deliuer mee from the workers of iniquitie, and saue me from bloodie men.

3 For loe, they lye in wait for my soule; the mighty are gathered against me;

me; not *for* my transgression, nor *for* my sinne, O LORD.

4 They runne and prepare themselues without *my* fault: awake † to helpe me, and behold.

Hebr. to eete me.

5 Thou therefore, O LORD God of hostes, the God of Israel, awake to visite all the heathen: be not mercifull to any wicked transgressours. Selah.

6 They returne at euening: they make a noise like a dogge, and go round about the citie.

7 Behold, they belch out with their mouth: *swords *are* in their lippes; for who, *say they*, doeth heare?

Psal. 10. and 73. and 94.

8 But thou, O LORD, shalt laugh at them; thou shalt haue all the heathen in derision.

9 *Because of* his strength will I wait vpon thee: for God *is* † my defence.

Hebr. my h place.

10 The God of my mercy shall preuent me; God shall let mee see *my desire* vpon † mine enemies.

Hebr. mine eruers.

11 Slay them not, lest my people forget: scatter them by thy power; and bring them downe, O Lord our shield.

12 *For* the sinne of their mouth, *and* the words of their lips, let them euen be taken in their pride: and for cursing and lying *which* they speake.

13 Consume *them* in wrath, consume *them*, that they may not be: and let them know that God ruleth in Iacob, vnto the ends of the earth. Selah.

14 And at euening let them returne, and let them make a noise like a dogge, and goe round about the citie.

15 Let them wander vp and downe † for meate, || and grudge if they be not satisfied.

ebr. to . , if they ot satis- , then will stay ight.

16 But I will sing of thy power; yea I will sing alowd of thy mercy in the morning: for thou hast bene my defence and refuge, in the day of my trouble.

17 Vnto thee, O my strength, wil I sing: for God *is* my defence, *and* the God of my mercy.

PSAL. LX.

1 Dauid complayning to God of former iudgement, 4 now vpon better hope prayeth for deliuerance. 6 Comforting himselfe in Gods promises, he craueth that helpe whereon he trusteth.

¶ To the chiefe Musician vpon Shushan-Eduth || Michtam of Dauid, to teach. *When hee stroue with Aram Naharaim, and with Aram Zobah, *when* Ioab returned, and smote of Edom in the valley of salt, twelue thousand.

, a gol- Psalme. Sam. 8. . 1. chr.

O God, thou hast cast vs off; thou hast † scattered vs, thou hast bene displeased, O turne thy selfe to vs againe.

* Psal. 44. 10. † Hebr. broken.

2 Thou hast made the earth to tremble; thou hast broken it: heale the breaches thereof, for it shaketh.

3 Thou hast shewed thy people hard things: thou hast made vs to drinke the wine of astonishment.

4 Thou hast giuen a banner to them that feare thee: that it may be displayed because of the trueth. Selah.

5 *That thy beloued may be deliuered; saue *with* thy right hand, and heare mee.

* Psal. 108. 6. &c.

6 God hath spoken in his holinesse, I wil reioyce: I wil diuide Shechem, and mete out the valley of Succoth.

7 Gilead *is* mine, and Manasseh *is* mine; Ephraim also *is* the strength of mine head; Iudah *is* my Lawgiuer.

8 Moab *is* my wash pot, ouer Edom wil I cast out my shooe: Philistia, || triumph thou because of me.

|| Or, triumph thou ouer me. [by an ironie].

9 Who wil bring me *into* the † strong citie? who will lead me into Edom?

† Hebr. city of strength.

10 Wilt not thou, O God, *which* hadst cast vs off? and thou, *O God, which didst not goe out with our armies.

* Psal. 44. 10. and 108. 12.

11 Giue vs helpe from trouble: for vaine *is* the † helpe of man.

† Hebr. saluation.

12 Through God wee shall doe valiantly: for he *it is that* shall tread downe our enemies.

PSAL. LXI.

1 Dauid fleeth to God vpon his former experience. 4 He voweth perpetuall seruice vnto him because of his promises.

¶ To the chiefe Musician vpon Neginah. *A Psalme* of Dauid.

Heare my cry, O God, attend vnto my prayer.

2 From the end of the earth wil I cry vnto thee, when my heart is ouerwhelmed: leade me to the rocke, *that* is higher then I.

3 For thou hast bene a shelter for me, and a strong tower from the enemy.

4 I will abide in thy Tabernacle for euer: I will || trust in the couert of thy wings. Selah.

|| Or, make my refuge.

5 For

5 For thou, O God, hast heard my vowes : thou hast giuen *me* the heritage of those that feare thy name.

6 † Thou wilt prolong the kings life : *and* his yeeres †as many generations.

7 He shall abide before God for euer : O prepare mercy and trueth *which* may preserue him.

8 So will I sing praise vnto thy name for euer, that I may daily performe my vowes.

PSAL. LXII.

1 Dauid professing his confidence in God, discourageth his enemies. 5 In the same confidence he incourageth the godly. 9 No trust is to be put in worldly things. 11 Power and mercie belong to God.

¶ To the chiefe musician, to Ieduthun, A Psalme of Dauid.

 ‖Ruely my soule †waiteth vpon God : from him *commeth* my saluation.

2 He onely *is* my rocke and my saluation : *he is* my †defence, I shall not be greatly moued.

3 How long wil ye imagine mischiefe against a man ? ye shall be slaine all of you : as a bowing wall *shall ye be, and as* a tottering fence.

4 They onely consult to cast *him* downe from his excellency, they delight in lies : they blesse with their mouth, but they curse †inwardly. Selah.

5 My soule, wait thou onely vpon God : for my expectation *is* from him.

6 He onely *is* my rocke and my saluation ; *he is* my defence ; I shall not bee moued.

7 In God *is* my saluation, and my glorie : the rocke of my strength , *and* my refuge is in God.

8 Trust in him at all times ; ye people, powre out your heart before him : God *is* a refuge for vs. Selah.

9 Surely men of low degree are vanitie, *and* men of high degree *are* a lie : to be laid in the ballance, they are ‖altogether lighter then vanitie.

10 Trust not in oppression, become not vaine in robberie : if riches increase, set not your heart *vpon them.*

11 God hath spoken once ; twice haue I heard this, that ‖power *belongeth* vnto God.

12 Also vnto thee, O Lord, *belongeth* mercie : *for thou renderest to euery man according to his worke.

PSAL. LXIII.

1 Dauids thirst for God. 4 His maner of blessing God. 9 His confidence of his enemies destruction, and his owne safetie.

¶ A Psalme of Dauid, when hee was in the wildernesse of Iudah.

 God , thou *art* my God, earely will I seeke thee : my soule thirsteth for thee, my flesh longeth for thee, in a drie and †thirstie lande, †where no water is :

2 To see thy power and thy glory, so *as* I haue seen thee in the Sanctuary.

3 Because thy louing kindnes *is* better then life : my lips shal praise thee.

4 Thus will I blesse thee, while I liue : I will lift vp my handes in thy Name.

5 My soule shall be satisfied as *with* †marrow and fatnesse : and my mouth shall praise *thee* with ioyfull lips :

6 When I remember thee vpon my bed, *and* meditate on thee in the *night* watches.

7 Because thou hast bene my helpe ; therefore in the shadow of thy wings will I reioyce.

8 My soule followeth hard after thee : thy right hand vpholdeth me.

9 But those *that* seeke my soule to destroy it, shall goe into the lower parts of the earth.

10 † They shall fall by the sword : they shall be a portion for foxes.

11 But the King shal reioyce in God ; euery one that sweareth by him shall glorie : but the mouth of them that speake lies, shall be stopped.

PSAL. LXIIII.

1 Dauid prayeth for deliuerance, complaining of his enemies. 7 He promiseth himselfe to see such an euident destruction of his enemies, as the righteous shall reioyce at it.

¶ To the chiefe musician, a Psalme of Dauid.

Eare my voice, O God, in my praier ; preserue my life from feare of the enemie.

2 Hide me from the secret counsel of the wicked : from the insurrection of the workers of iniquitie :

3 * Who whet their tongue like a sword, *and* bend *their bowes to shoote* their arrowes, *euen* bitter words :

4 That

Margin notes (left column):

† *Hebr. thou shalt adde dayes to the dayes of the King.*

† *Heb. as generation and generation.*

‖ *Or, onely.*

† *Heb. is silent.*

† *Hebr. high place.*

† *Hebr. in their inward parts.*

k *Or, alike.*

‖ *Or, strength.*
* Iob 34. 11
prou. 24. 12
iere. 32. 19.
ezek. 7. 27.
mat. 16. 27.
rom. 2. 6. 2.
cor. 5. 10
eph. 6. 8.
coloss. 3. 25.
1. pet. 1. 17.
apoc. 22. 12

Margin notes (right column):

† *Heb. weary*

† *Heb. without water.*

† *Heb. fatne*

† *Hebr. the shall make him run ou like water by the hand of the swor*

* Psal. 11

4 That they may shoote in secret at the perfect : suddenly doe they shoote at him, and feare not.

speech.
b. to hide es.

5 They incourage themſelues *in* an euill ‖matter: they commune †of laying snares priuily; they say, Who shall see them ?

we are umed by which haue ghly hed.

6 They search out iniquities, ‖they accomplish †a diligent search : both the inward *thought* of euery one of them, and the heart, *is* deepe.

b. a h, sear-

7 But God shall shoote at them : *with* an arrowe, sodenly †shall they be wounded.

b. their d shal-

8 So they shall make their owne tongue to fall vpon themselues : all that see them, shall flee away.

9 And all men shall feare, and shall declare the worke of God; for they shall wisely consider of his doing.

10 The righteous shalbe glad in the LORD, and shall trust in him ; and all the vpright in heart shall glory.

PSAL. LXV.

1 Dauid prayeth God for his grace. 4 The bleſſedneſſe of Gods choſen, by reaſon of benefits.

¶ To the chiefe muſician, a Pſalme *and* ſong of Dauid.

b. is si-

Raiſe †waiteth for thee, O God, in Sion : and vnto thee shall the vowe be performed.

2 O thou that heareſt prayer, vnto thee shall all flesh come.

b. words tters of ities.

3 †Iniquities preuaile against me: as for our transgreſsions, thou shalt purge them away.

4 Bleſſed *is the man whom* thou chooseſt and causest to approach *vnto thee, that* hee may dwell in thy Courts : we shalbe ſatisfied with the goodneſſe of thy house, *euen* of thy holy temple.

5 *By* terrible things in righteouſneſſe, wilt thou anſwere vs, O God of our ſaluation : *who art* the confidence of all the ends of the earth, and of them *that are* a farre off *vpon* the sea.

6 *Which* by his strength setteth fast the mountaines ; being girded with power.

7 *Which* stilleth the noiſe of the ſeas ; the noiſe of their waues, and the tumult of the people.

8 They also that dwell in the vttermost parts are afraid at thy tokens :

thou makest the outgoings of the morning, and euening ‖to reioyce.

‖ *Or, to ſing.*

9 Thou viſitest the earth and ‖watereſt it : thou greatly inrichest it with the riuer of God *which* is full of water ; thou prepareſt them corne, when thou haſt ſo prouided for it.

‖ *Or, after thou hadſt made it to deſire raine.*

10 Thou watereſt the ridges thereof abundantly : ‖thou ſettlest the furrowes thereof : †thou makeſt it ſoft with ſhowres, thou bleſsest the ſpringing thereof.

‖ *Or, thou cauſeſt raine to deſcend into the furrowes thereof.*
† *Heb. thou diſſolueſt it.*

11 Thou crowneſt †the yeere with thy goodneſſe ; and thy paths drop fatneſſe.

† *Heb. the yeere of thy goodneſſe.*

12 They drop *vpon* the pastures of the wilderneſſe; and the little hilles †reioyce on euery ſide.

† *Heb. are girded with ioy.*

13 The pastures are cloathed with flockes ; the valleis also are couered ouer with corne; they shout for ioy, they also ſing.

PSAL. LXVI.

1 Dauid exhorteth to praiſe God, 5 To obſerue his great workes, 8 To bleſſe him for his gracious benefits. 12 He voweth for himſelfe religious ſeruice to God. 16 He declareth Gods ſpeciall goodneſſe to himſelfe.

¶ To the chiefe muſician, a ſong or Pſalme.

Ake a ioyfull noiſe vnto God, †all yee lands.

† *Heb. all the earth.*

2 Sing forth the honour of his name : make his praiſe glorious.

3 Say vnto God, How terrible *art thou in* thy workes? through the greatneſſe of thy power shall thine enemies ‖ſubmit themſelues vnto thee.

‖ *Or, yeild fained obedience. Heb. lie.*

4 All the earth shall worſhip thee ; and shall ſing vnto thee, they shall ſing *to* thy name ; Selah.

5 Come and ſee the workes of God : he is terrible *in his* doing toward the children of men.

6 He turned the ſea into dry land : they went through the flood on foote, there did we reioyce in him.

7 He ruleth by his power for euer, his eyes behold the nations : let not the rebellious exalt themſelues. Selah.

8 O bleſſe our God, yee people, and make the voice of his praiſe to be heard.

9 Which †holdeth our ſoule in life, and ſuffereth not our feete to be moued.

† *Heb. putteth.*

10 For thou, O God, hast proued vs: thou hast tried vs, as ſiluer is tryed.

11 Thou

11 Thou broughtest vs into the net; thou layedst affliction vpon our loynes.

12 Thou hast caused men to ride o-uer our heads, we went through fire, and through water: but thou brough-test vs out into a †wealthy place.

† Heb. moiſt.

13 I will goe into thy houſe, with burnt offerings: I will pay thee my vowes,

14 Which my lips haue †vttered, and my mouth hath ſpoken, when I was in trouble.

† Hebr. ope-ned.

15 I will offer vnto thee burnt ſa-crifices of †fatlings, with the incenſe of rammes: I will offer bullockes with goates. Selah.

† Hebr. mar-row.

16 Come *and* heare all ye that feare God, and I will declare what he hath done for my ſoule.

17 I cried vnto him with my mouth: and he was extolled with my tongue.

18 If I regard iniquitie in my heart: the Lord will not heare me.

19 But verily God hath heard mee; hee hath attended to the voice of my prayer.

20 Bleſſed *bee* God, which hath not turned away my prayer, nor his mercie from me.

PSAL. LXVII.

1 A prayer for the inlargement of Gods king-dome, 3 to the ioy of the people, 6 and the increaſe of Gods bleſſings.

¶ To the chiefe Muſician on Negi-noth. A Pſalme *or* ſong.

G Od be mercifull vnto vs, and bleſſe vs: *and* cauſe his face to ſhine †vpon vs. Selah.

† Hebr. with vs.

2 That thy way may bee knowen vpon earth, thy ſauing health among all nations.

3 Let the people praiſe thee, O God; let all the people praiſe thee.

4 O let the nations be glad, and ſing for ioy: for thou ſhalt iudge the people righteouſly; and †gouerne the nations vpon earth. Selah.

† Hebr. lead.

5 Let the people praiſe thee, O God, let all the people praiſe thee.

6 *Then* ſhall the earth yeeld her in-creaſe; *and* God, *euen* our owne God, ſhall bleſſe vs.

7 God ſhall bleſſe vs; and all the ends of the earth ſhall feare him.

PSAL. LXVIII.

1 A prayer at the remoouing of the Arke. 4

An exhortation to praiſe God for his mer-cies, 7 for his care of the Church, 19 for his great workes.

¶ To the chiefe Muſician. A Pſalme *or* ſong of Dauid,

L Et *God ariſe, let his ene-mies be ſcattered: let them alſo that hate him, flee †be-fore him.

* Num 36.

† Hebr his fac̄

2 As ſmoke is driuen away, *so* driue *them* away: as waxe mel-teth before the fire, *so* let the wicked pe-riſh at the preſence of God.

3 But let the righteous be glad: let them reioyce before God, yea let them †exceedingly reioyce.

† Heb̄ ioyce ✳ gladne

4 Sing vnto God, ſing praiſes to his Name: extoll *him* that rideth vpon the heauens, by his Name IAH, and reioyce before him.

5 A father of the fatherleſſe, and a iudge of the widowes, *is* God in his ho-ly habitation.

6 God ſetteth the ſolitary †in fami-lies: hee bringeth out thoſe which are bound with chaines, but the rebellious dwell in a dry land.

† Heb̄ houſe.

7 O God, when thou wenteſt forth before thy people; when thou didſt march through the wildernes, Selah.

8 The earth ſhooke, the heauens al-ſo dropped at the preſence of God: *euen* Sinai it ſelfe *was* mooued at the preſence of God, the God of Iſrael.

9 Thou, O God, didſt †ſend a plen-tifull raine, whereby thou didſt †con-firme thine inheritance, when it was weary.

†Hebr. out.
† Heb firme

10 Thy Congregation hath dwelt therein: thou, O God, haſt prepared of thy goodneſſe for the poore.

11 The Lord gaue the word: great was the †company of thoſe that pub-liſhed *it.*

† Hcb̄ mie.

12 Kings of armies †did flee apace: and ſhe that taried at home, diuided the ſpoile.

† Heb̄ flee, ◦

13 Though ye haue lien among the pots, *yet ſhall yee bee* as the wings of a doue, couered with ſiluer, and her fea-thers with yellow gold.

14 When the Almighty ſcattered Kings ‖in it, it was white as ſnow in Salmon.

‖ Or, ſhe w

15 The hil of God is *as* the hill of Ba-ſhan, an high hill *as* the hill of Baſhan.

16 Why leape ye, ye high hilles? this *is* the Hil *which* God deſireth to dwell in, yea the Lord will dwel in *it* for euer.

17 The

17 The chariots of God *are* twentie thousand, ||*euen* thousands of Angels: the Lord *is* among them *as* in Sinai, in the holy place.

18 *Thou hast ascended on high, thou hast ledde captiuitie captiue, thou hast receiued giftes †for men; yea, *for* the rebellious also, that the Lord God might dwell *among them.*

19 Blessed *be* the Lord, who daily loadeth vs *with benefits,* euen the God of our saluation. Selah.

20 Hee that *is* our God, *is* the God of saluation; and vnto GOD the Lord *belong* the issues from death.

21 But God shall wound the head of his enemies: *and* the hairy scalpe of such a one as goeth on still in his trespasses.

22 The Lord said, I will bring againe from Bashan, I will bring *my people* againe from the depthes of the sea:

23 That thy foote may be ||dipped in the blood of *thine* enemies, *and* the tongue of thy dogges in the same.

24 They haue seene thy goings, O God, *euen* the goings of my God, my King, in the Sanctuarie.

25 The singers went before, the players on instruments *followed* after; amongst *them were* the damosels playing *with* timbrels.

26 Blesse yee God, in the Congregations, *euen* the Lord, ||from the fountaine of Israel.

27 There *is* little Beniamin with their ruler, the princes of Iudah ||*and* their Councill, the princes of Zebulun, *and* the princes of Naphtali.

28 Thy God hath commanded thy strength: strengthen, O God, that *which* thou hast wrought for vs.

29 Because of thy Temple at Ierusalem, shall kings bring presents vnto thee.

30 Rebuke the ||company of spearemen, the multitude of the bulles, with the calues of the people, *till euery one* submit himselfe with pieces of siluer: ||scatter thou the people *that* delite in warre.

31 Princes shall come out of Egypt, Ethiopia shall soone stretch out her hands vnto God.

32 Sing vnto God, yee kingdomes of the earth: O sing praises *vnto* the Lord, Selah:

33 To him that rideth vpon the heauens of heauens, *which were* of olde: loe, hee doeth †send out his voice, *and that a* mightie voice.

34 Ascribe yee strength vnto God: his excellencie *is* ouer Israel, and his strength *is* in the ||cloudes.

35 O God, thou art terrible out of thy holy places: the God of Israel *is* he that giueth strength, and power vnto *his* people: blessed *be* God

PSAL. LXIX.

1 Dauid complaineth of his affliction. 13 Hee prayeth for deliuerance. 22 Hee deuoteth his enemies to destruction. 30 He praiseth God with thankesgiuing.

¶ To the chiefe musician vpon Shoshannim, *A Psalme* of Dauid.

SAue mee, O God, for the waters are come in vnto my soule.

2 I sinke in †deepe mire, where *there is* no standing: I am come into †deepe waters, where the flouds ouerflow me.

3 I am weary of my crying, my throate is dried: mine eyes faile *while* I waite for my God.

4 They that hate mee without a cause, are moe then the haires of mine head: they that would destroy me, being mine enemies wrongfully, are mightie: then I restored that which I tooke not away.

5 O God, thou knowest my foolishnesse; and my †sinnes are not hidde from thee.

6 Let not them that waite on thee, O Lord GOD of hostes, be ashamed for my sake: let not those that seeke thee, be confounded for my sake, O God of Israel.

7 Because for thy sake I haue borne reproch: shame hath couered my face.

8 I am become a stranger vnto my brethren, and an aliant vnto my mothers children.

9 *For the zeale of thine house hath eaten mee vp; *and the reproches of them that reproched thee, are fallen vpon me.

10 When I wept, and *chastened* my soule with fasting, that was to my reproch.

11 I made sackecloth also my garment: & I became a prouerbe to them.

12 They that sit in the gate, speake against mee; and *I was* the song of the †drunkards.

13 But

Marginal notes (left column): , euen y thou-s. — ph. 4. 8. — b. in the — red. — ye that of the utaine srael. — , with com-y. — , the t of the s. — he scat-th.

Marginal notes (right column): † Heb. giue. — Or, heauens. — † Heb. the myre of depth. — † Heb. depth of waters. — † Heb. guiltinesse. — * Iohn 2. 17. — * Rom. 15. 3. — † Heb. drinkers of strong drinke.

13 But as for mee, my prayer *is* vnto thee, O Lord, *in* an acceptable time: O God, in the multitude of thy mercie heare me, in the trueth of thy saluation.

14 Deliuer me out of the mire, and let me not sinke : let me bee deliuered from them that hate me, and out of the deepe waters.

15 Let not the water flood ouerflow me, neither let the deepe swallow mee vp, and let not the pit shut her mouth vpon me.

16 Heare me, O Lord, for thy louing kindnesse *is* good: turne vnto mee according to the multitude of thy tender mercies.

17 And hide not thy face from thy seruant, for I am in trouble : †heare me speedily.

† Heb. make haste to heare me.

18 Draw nigh vnto my soule, *and* redeeme it : deliuer me because of mine enemies.

19 Thou hast knowen my reproch and my shame and my dishonor: mine aduersaries are all before thee.

20 Reproch hath broken my heart, and I am full of heauines: and I looked *for some* †to take pitie, but *there was* none ; and for comforters, but I found none.

† Heb. to la- ment with me.

21 They gaue mee also gall for my meat, *and in my thirst they gaue mee vineger to drinke.

Mat. 27. 28. mar. 15. 23. iohn 19. 29.
Rom. 11. 9

22 *Let their table become a snare before them : and *that which should haue bene* for *their* welfare, *let it become* a trap.

23 Let their eyes be darkened that they see not ; and make their loines continually to shake.

24 Powre out thine indignation vpon them, and let thy wrathfull anger take hold of them.

25 Let their †habitation be desolate, *and* †let none dwell in their tents.

† Hebr. their palace.
† Hebr. let there not bee a dweller.

26 For they persecute *him* whō thou hast smitten, and they talke to the griefe of †those whom thou hast wounded.

† Hebr. thy wounded.

27 Adde ‖ iniquitie vnto their iniquitie : and let them not come into thy righteousnesse.

‖ Or, punish- ment of ini- quitie.

28 Let them bee blotted out of the booke of the liuing, and not be written with the righteous.

29 But I *am* poore, and sorowfull : let thy saluation (O God) set me vp on high.

30 I will praise the name of God with a song, and will magnifie him with thankesgiuing.

31 *This* also shall please the Lord better then an oxe *or* bullocke that hath hornes and hoofes.

32 The ‖ humble shall see this, and be glad: and your heart shall liue that seeke good.

‖ Or, m

33 For the Lord heareth the poore, and despiseth not his prisoners.

34 Let the heauen and earth praise him, the seas, and euery thing that †moueth therein.

† Hebr peth.

35 For God will saue Sion, and will build the cities of Iudah, that they may dwell there, and haue it in possession.

36 The seede also of his seruants shall inherit it : and they that loue his name shall dwell therein.

PSAL. LXX.

Dauid solliciteth God to the speedie destruction of the wicked, and preseruation of the godly.

¶ To the chiefe musician, *a psalme* of Dauid, to bring to remembrance.

Ake haste, *O God, to deliuer mee, make haste †to helpe me, O Lord.

Psal 14, &c
† Hebr my hel

2 Let them be ashamed and confounded that seeke after my soule : let them be turned backward, and put to confusion, that desire my hurt.

3 *Let them be turned backe for a reward of their shame, that say, Aha, aha.

Psal and 7

4 Let all those that seeke thee, reioyce, and be glad in thee: and let such as loue thy saluation, say continually, Let God be magnified.

5 But I *am* poore and needy, make haste vnto me, O God: Thou *art* my helpe and my deliuerer, O Lord make no tarrying.

PSAL. LXXI.

1 Danid in confidence of faith and experience of Gods fauour, prayeth both for himselfe, and against the enemies of his soule. 14 He promiseth constancie. 17 Hee prayeth for perseuerance. 19 He praiseth God, and promiseth to doe it cheerefully.

N *thee, O Lord, doe I put my trust, let me neuer be put to confusion.

Psal

2 Deliuer mee in thy righteousnesse, and cause me to escape : incline thine eare vnto me, and saue me.

3 †Bee

br. be to me a rocke bita-

3 † Bee thou my strong habitation, whereunto I may continually resort: thou hast giuen commandement to saue mee, for thou art my rocke, and my fortresse.

4 Deliuer me, O my God, out of the hand of the wicked, out of the hand of the vnrighteous, and cruel man.

5 For thou *art* my hope, O Lord God : thou *art* my trust from my youth.

6 By thee haue I bene holden vp from the wombe : thou art hee that tooke mee out of my mothers bowels, my praise *shalbe* continually of thee.

7 I am as a wonder vnto many, but thou *art* my strong refuge.

8 Let my mouth bee filled *with* thy praise, *and with* thy honour all the day.

9 Cast me not off in the time of old age ; forsake me not when my strength faileth.

10 For mine enemies speake against mee : and they that † lay waite for my soule, take counsell together,

br. i, or ue.

11 Saying, God hath forsaken him : persecute and take him, for *there is* none to deliuer *him.*

12 O God, be not farre from mee : O my God, make haste for my helpe.

13 Let them be confounded *and* consumed, that are aduersaries to my soule : let them bee couered *with* reproch and dishonour, that seeke my hurt.

14 But I wil hope continually, and will yet praise thee more and more.

15 My mouth shall shew foorth thy righteousnesse, *and* thy saluation all the day : for I know not the numbers *thereof.*

16 I will goe in the strength of the Lord God : I will make mention of thy righteousnesse, *euen* of thine onely.

17 O God, thou hast taught me from my youth : and hitherto haue I declared thy wonderous workes.

br. vnto ge, and haires. br. thine ?.

18 Now also † when I am old and gray headed, O God, forsake me not : vntill I haue shewed † thy strength vnto *this* generation, *and* thy power to euery one *that* is to come.

19 Thy righteousnes also, O God, *is* very high, who hast done great things : O God, who *is* like vnto thee ?

20 *Thou* which hast shewed mee great, and sore troubles, shalt quicken mee againe, and shalt bring mee vp againe from the depthes of the earth.

21 Thou shalt increase my great-

nesse, and comfort me on euery side.

22 I will also praise thee † with the psalterie, *euen* thy trueth, O my God : vnto thee will I sing with the harpe, O thou Holy one of Israel.

† Hebr. with the instrument of psalterie.

23 My lippes shall greatly reioyce when I sing vnto thee : and my soule, which thou hast redeemed.

24 My tongue also shall talke of thy righteousnesse all the day long : for they are confounded, for they are brought vnto shame, that seeke my hurt.

PSAL. LXXII.

1 Dauid praying for Solomon, sheweth the goodnesse and glory of his, in type, and in trueth, of Christes kingdome. 18 Hee blesseth God.

¶ *A Psalme* ‖ for Solomon.

‖ Or, of.

G Iue the King thy Iudgements, O God, and thy Righteousnesse vnto the Kings sonne.

2 Hee shall iudge thy people with righteousnesse, and thy poore with iudgement.

3 The mountaines shal bring peace to the people, and the litle hils, by righteousnesse.

4 Hee shall iudge the poore of the people, he shall saue the children of the needie, and shall breake in pieces the oppressour.

5 They shall feare thee as long as the Sunne & Moone indure, throughout all generations.

6 Hee shall come downe like raine vpon the mowen grasse : as showres *that* water the earth.

7 In his dayes shall the righteous flourish : and abundance of peace † so long as the Moone endureth.

† Hebr. till there be no moone.

8 He shall haue dominion also from sea to sea, and from the riuer, vnto the ends of the earth.

9 They that dwell in the wildernesse shall bowe before him : and his enemies shall licke the dust.

10 The kings of Tarshish and of the Isles shall bring presents : the Kings of Sheba and Seba shall offer gifts.

11 Yea, all Kings shall fall downe before him : all nations shall serue him.

12 For hee shall deliuer the needy when he crieth : the poore also, and *him* that hath no helper.

13 He shal spare the poore and needy, and

and shall saue the soules of the needy.

14 He shall redeeme their soule from deceit and violence : and precious shall their blood be in his sight.

† *Heb. one shall giue.*

15 And he shall liue, and to him † shalbe giuen of the gold of Sheba ; prayer also shalbe made for him continually, *and* daily shall he be praised.

16 There shalbe an handfull of corne in the earth vpon the top of the mountaines ; the fruit thereof shall shake like Lebanon, and *they* of the citie shall flourish like grasse of the earth.

† *Heb. shall be.*
† *Heb. shalbe as a sonne to continue his fathers name for euer.*

17 His name † shall endure for euer : † his name shalbe continued as long as the sunne : and men shalbe blessed in him ; all nations shall call him blessed.

18 Blessed *be* the Lᴏʀᴅ God, the God of Israel, who only doth wonderous things.

19 And blessed *be* his glorious name for euer, and let the whole earth be filled *with* his glory. Amen, and Amen.

20 The prayers of Dauid the sonne of Iesse, are ended.

PSAL. LXXIII.

1 The Prophet preuailing in a Temptation, 2 sheweth the occasion thereof, the prosperitie of the wicked : 13 The wound giuen thereby, diffidence. 15 The victory ouer it, knowledge of Gods purpose, in destroying of the wicked and sustaining the righteous.

‖ *Or, a Psalme for Asaph.*
‖ *Or, yet.*
† *Heb. cleane of heart.*

¶ A Psalme ‖ of Asaph.

Ruely God *is* good to Israel, *euen* to such as are † of a cleane heart.

2 But as for mee, my feete were almost gone : my steps had well-nigh slipt.

* *Iob. 21. 7. psal. 37. 1. Ierem. 12. 1*

3 * For I was enuious at the foolish, *when* I sawe the prosperity of the wicked.

4 For *there are* no bands in their death : but their strength is † firme.

† *Heb. fat.*
† *Heb. in the trouble of other men.*
† *Heb. with.*

5 They *are* not † in trouble *as other* men : neither are they plagued † like *other* men.

6 Therefore pride compasseth them about as a chaine : violence couereth them *as* a garment.

7 Their eies stand out with fatnes : † they haue more then heart could wish.

† *Heb. they passe the thoughts of the heart.*

8 They are corrupt, and speake wickedly *concerning* oppression : they speake loftily.

9 They set their mouth against the heauens ; and their tongue walketh through the earth.

10 Therefore his people returne hither : and waters of a full *cup* are wrung out to them.

11 And they say, How doth God kuow ? and is there knowledge in the most High ?

12 Behold, these *are* the vngodly : who prosper in the world, they increase *in* riches.

13 Verily I haue cleansed my heart in vaine, and washed my hands in innocencie.

14 For all the day long haue I bene plagued, and † chastened euery morning.

† *Heb. chastisewas.*

15 If I say, I will speake thus : behold, I should offend *against* the generation of thy children.

16 When I thought to know this, † it *was* too painfull for me,

† *Heb. labour mine*

17 Vntill I went into the Sanctuarie of God ; *then* vnderstood I their end.

18 Surely thou didst set them in slippery places : thou castedst them downe into destruction.

19 How are they *brought* into desolation as in a moment ? they are vtterly consumed with terrours.

20 As a dreame when one awaketh ; *so*, O Lord, when thou awakest thou shalt despise their image.

21 Thus my heart was greeued, and I was pricked in my reines.

22 So foolish was I, † and ignorant : I was *as* a beast † before thee.

† *Heb. knew* † *Heb. thee.*

23 Neuerthelesse I *am* continually with thee : thou hast holden *me* by my right hand.

24 Thou shalt guide me with thy counsell ; and afterward receiue me *to* glory.

25 Whom *haue* I in heauen *but thee* ? and *there* is none vpon earth that I desire besides thee.

26 My flesh and my heart faileth : *but* God *is* the † strength of my heart, and my portion for euer.

† *Heb*

27 For loe, they that are farre from thee, shall perish : thou hast destroyed all them that goe a whoring from thee.

28 But it is good for me, to drawe neere to God : I haue put my trust in the Lord Gᴏᴅ, that I may declare all thy workes.

PSAL. LXXIIII.

1 The Prophet complaineth of the desolation of the Sanctuarie. 10 Hee moueth God to helpe,

helpe in consideration of his power. 18 Of his reprochfull enemies, of his children, and of his Couenant.

¶ ‖ Maschil of Asaph.

O God, why hast thou cast vs off for euer ? why doeth thine anger smoke against the sheepe of thy pasture ?

2 Remember thy Congregation which thou hast purchased of olde : the ‖ rod of thine inheritance which thou hast redeemed, this mount Sion, wherein thou hast dwelt.

3 Lift vp thy feete vnto the perpetuall desolations : euen all that the enemie hath done wickedly in the Sanctuarie.

4 Thine enemies roare in the midst of thy congregations : they set vp their ensignes for signes.

5 A man was famous according as he had lifted vp axes vpon the thicke trees.

6 But now they breake downe the carued worke thereof at once, with axes and hammers.

7 † They haue cast fire into thy Sanctuary, they haue defiled by casting downe, the dwelling place of thy Name to the ground.

8 They said in their hearts, Let vs † destroy them together : they haue burnt vp all the Synagogues of God in the land.

9 We see not our signes, there is no more any prophet, neither is there among vs any that knoweth howe long.

10 O God, how long shall the aduersarie reproach ? shall the enemie blaspheme thy Name for euer ?

11 Why withdrawest thou thy hand, euen thy right hand? plucke it out of thy bosome.

12 For God is my King of old, working saluation in the midst of the earth.

13 * Thou didst † diuide the sea by thy strength : thou brakest the heads of the ‖dragons in the waters.

14 Thou brakest the heads of Leuiathan in pieces, and gauest him to bee meat to the people inhabiting the wildernesse.

15 * Thou didst cleaue the fountaine and the flood : thou driedst vp †mightie riuers.

16 The day is thine, the night also is thine : thou hast prepared the light and the sunne.

17 Thou hast set all the borders of the earth : Thou hast † made Summer and Winter.

18 Remember this, that the enemie hath reproached, O Lord, and that the foolish people haue blasphemed thy Name.

19 O deliuer not the soule of thy turtle doue vnto the multitude of the wicked forget not the Congregation of thy poore for euer.

20 Haue respect vnto the couenant : for the darke places of the earth are full of the habitations of crueltie.

21 O let not the oppressed returne ashamed : let the poore and needie praise thy name.

22 Arise, O God, plead thine owne cause : remember how the foolish man reprocheth thee daily.

23 Forget not the voyce of thine enemies : the tumult of those that rise vp against thee, †increaseth continually.

PSAL. LXXV.

1 The Prophet praiseth God. 2 Hee promiseth to iudge vprightly. 4 He rebuketh the proud by consideration of Gods prouidence. 9 He praiseth God, & promiseth to execute iustice.

¶ ‖To the chiefe musician Al-taschith, A Psalme or song of Asaph.

Vnto thee, O God, doe we giue thankes, vnto thee doe we giue thanks : for that thy name is nere, thy wonderous works declare.

2 ‖When I shall receiue the congregation, I will iudge vprightly.

3 The earth and all the inhabitants thereof are dissolued : I beare vp the pillars of it. Selah.

4 I said vnto the fooles, Deale not foolishly : and to the wicked, Lift not vp the horne.

5 Lift not vp your horne on high : speake not with a stiffe necke.

6 For promotion commeth neither from the East, nor from the West, nor from the † South.

7 But God is the iudge : he putteth downe one, and setteth vp another.

8 For in the hand of the Lord there is a cup, and the wine is red : it is full of mixture, and he powreth out of the same : but the dregges thereof all the wicked of the earth shall wring them out, and drinke them.

9 But I will declare for euer ; I will

Marginal notes (left column):

A ‖e for h to instru-

tribe.

br. they sent Sanctu-nto the

ebr. ke.

xod. 14.

ebr. ake. , whales

xo. 17. 5 n. 20. 11 n. 3. 13. eb. riuers strength.

Marginal notes (right column):

† Heb. made them.

† Heb. ascendeth.

‖ Or, to the chiefe musician (destroy not) a psalme or song for Asaph.

‖ Or, when I shall take a set time.

† Heb. desert

will sing praises to the God of Iacob.

10 All the hornes of the wicked also will I cut off; *but* the hornes of the righteous shall be exalted.

PSAL. LXXVI.

1 A declaration of Gods maiestie in the Church. 11 An exhortation to serue him reuerently.

¶ To the chiefe musician on Neginoth, a Psalme *or* song ‖of Asaph.

‖ Or, for Asaph.

I N Iudah is God knowen: his name *is* great in Israel.

2 In Salem also is his tabernacle, and his dwelling place in Sion.

3 There brake he the arrowes of the bowe, the shield, and the sword, and the battell. Selah.

4 Thou art more glorious and excellent then the mountaines of pray.

5 The stout hearted are spoiled, they haue slept their sleepe: and none of the men of might haue found their hands.

6 At thy rebuke, O God of Iacob, both the chariot and horse are cast into a dead sleepe.

7 Thou, *euen* thou art to be feared; and who may stand in thy sight when once thou art angry?

8 Thou didst cause iudgement to be heard from heauen : the earth feared and was still,

9 When God arose to iudgement, to saue all the meeke of the earth. Selah.

10 Surely the wrath of man shall praise thee : the remainder of wrath shalt thou restraine.

11 Vowe, and pay vnto the LORD your God ; let all that be round about him bring presents †vnto him that ought to be feared.

† Heb. to Feare.

12 Hee shall cut off the spirit of princes : hee *is* terrible to the kings of the earth.

PSAL. LXXVII.

1 The Psalmist sheweth what fierce combate hee had with diffidence. 10 The victory which he had by consideration of Gods great and gratious workes.

¶ To the chiefe musician, to Ieduthun, a Psalme ‖of Asaph.

‖ Or, for Asaph.

I cryed vnto God with my voice: *euen* vnto God with my voice, and he gaue eare vnto me.

2 In the day of my trouble, I sought the Lord ; †my sore ranne in the night, and ceased not : my soule refused to be comforted.

† Heb. hand.

3 I remembred God, and was troubled : I complained, and my spirit was ouerwhelmed. Selah.

4 Thou holdest mine eyes waking : I am so troubled that I cannot speake.

5 I haue considered the dayes of old, the yeeres of auncient times.

6 I call to remembrance my song in the night . I commune with mine owne heart, and my spirit made diligent search.

7 Will the Lord cast off for euer? and will hee be fauourable no more?

8 Is his mercy cleane gone for euer? doth *his* promise faile † for euermore?

† Heb. neratio genera

9 Hath God forgotten to be gracious ? hath he in anger shut vp his tender mercies? Selah.

10 And I sayd, This is my infirmitie : *but I will remember* the yeeres of the right hand of the most high.

11 I will remember the workes of the LORD : surely I will remember thy wonders of old.

12 I will meditate also of all thy worke, and talke of thy doings.

13 Thy way, O God, *is* in the Sanctuarie : who *is so* great a God, as *our* God?

14 Thou *art* the God that doest wonders ; thou hast declared thy strength among the people.

15 Thou hast with *thine* arme redeemed thy people, the sonnes of Iacob and Ioseph. Selah.

16 The waters saw thee, O God, the waters saw thee : they were afraid; the depths also were troubled.

17 † The cloudes powred out water, the skies sent out a sound ; thine arrowes also went abroad.

† Heb. clouds powred with u

18 The voice of thy thunder *was* in the heauen : the lightnings lightned the world, the earth trembled and shooke.

19 Thy way *is* in the sea, and thy path in the great waters : and thy foot-steps are not knowen.

20 * Thou leddest thy people like a flock, by the hand of Moses and Aaron.

* Exod 19.

PSAL. LXXVIII.

1 An exhortation both to learne and to preach the Law of God. 9 The story of Gods wrath against the incredulous and disobedient.

ent. 67 The Israelites being reiected, God chose Iudah, Sion, and Dauid.

¶ || Maschil of Asaph.

Giue eare, O my people, to my Lawe : incline your eares to the wordes of my mouth.

2 *I will open my mouth in a parable : I wil vtter darke sayings of old :

3 Which we haue heard, & knowen : and our fathers haue told vs.

4 We will not hide them from their children, shewing to the generation to come, the praises of the LORD : and his strength, and his wonderfull works that he hath done.

5 For he established a Testimony in Iacob, and appointed a Law in Israel, which he commauded our fathers : *that they should make them knowen to their children.

6 That the generation to come might know them, euen the children which should be borne: who should arise and declare them to their children :

7 That they might set their hope in God, and not forget the works of God: but keepe his Commandements,

8 And might not bee as their fathers, a stubborne and rebellious generation, a generation †that set not their heart aright : and whose spirit was not stedfast with God.

9 The children of Ephraim being armed, and †carying bowes, turned backe in the day of battell.

10 They kept not the couenant of God: and refused to walke in his Law :

11 And forgat his workes : and his wonders that he had shewed them.

12 Maruellous things did he, in the sight of their fathers : in the land of Egypt, in the field of Zoan.

13 *Hee diuided the Sea, and caused them to passe through: and he made the waters to stand as an heape.

14 *In the day time also he led them with a cloud : and all the night with a light of fire.

15 *Hee claue the rockes in the wildernes : and gaue them drinke as out of the great depthes.

16 Hee brought streames also out of the rocke, and caused waters to runne downe like riuers.

17 And they sinned yet more against him : by prouoking the most High in the wildernes.

18 And they tempted God in their heart : by asking meat for their lust.

19 *Yea, they spake against God : they said, Can God †furnish a table in the wildernes?

20 *Behold, he smote the rocke, that the waters gushed out, & the streames ouerflowed; can he giue bread also? can he prouide flesh for his people?

21 Therefore the LORD heard this, and was wroth, so a fire was kindled against Iacob : and anger also came vp against Israel.

22 Because they beleeued not in God : and trusted not in his saluation:

23 Though he had commanded the cloudes from aboue : and opened the doores of heauen :

24 *And had rained downe Manna vpon them to eate, and had giuen them of the corne of heauen.

25 *|| Man did eate Angels food: hee sent them meat to the full.

26 He caused an East wind to †blow in the heauen : and by his power hee brought in the South wind.

27 He rained flesh also vpon them as dust : and †feathered foules like as the sand of the sea.

28 And hee let it fall in the midst of their campe, round about their habitations.

29 So they did eate, & were well filled : for he gaue them their owne desire.

30 They were not estranged from their lust : but while their meate *was yet in their mouthes,

31 The wrath of God came vpon them, and slew the fattest of them : and †smote downe the || chosen men of Israel.

32 For all this they sinned still : and beleeued not for his wondrous works.

33 Therefore their dayes did he consume in vanitie, and their yeeres in trouble.

34 When hee slew them, then they sought him : and they returned, and inquired early after God.

35 And they remembred that God was their rocke : and the high God, their redeemer.

36 Neuerthelesse they did flatter him with their mouth : and they lyed vnto him with their tongues.

37 For their heart was not right with him : neither were they stedfast in his couenant.

38 But hee being full of compassion,
forgaue

Margin notes (left):
e for , to astru-
49. 5. 13.
t. 4. 6. 7.
r. that ed not eart.
ng
d. 14.
d. 13. d 14.
d. 17. n. 20. al. 1. . 4.

Margin notes (right):
* Num. 11. 4.
† Heb. order.
* Exod. 17. 6. num. 20. 11.
* Exod. 16. 14.
* Iohn 6. 31.
|| Or, euery one did eat the bread of the mighty.
† Hebr. to goe.
† Hebr. foule of wing.
* Num. 11. 33.
† Heb. made to bow.
|| Or, yong men.

forgaue *their* iniquity, and destroyed *them* not; yea many a time turned he his anger away, and did not stirre vp all his wrath.

39 For he remembred that they *were* but flesh; a wind that passeth away, and commeth not againe.

‖ *Or, rebell against him.*

40 How oft did they ‖prouoke him in the wildernesse : and grieue him in the desert?

41 Yea they turned backe and tempted God : and limited the holy one of Israel.

42 They remembred not his hand : *nor* the day when hee deliuered them ‖from the enemie :

‖ *Or, from affliction.*
† *Heb. set.*

43 How he had †wrought his signes in Egypt : and his wonders in the field of Zoan :

* *Exod. 7. 20.*

44 *And had turned their riuers into blood : and their flouds, that they could not drinke.

* *Exod. 8. 24. & 8. 6.*

45 *Hee sent diuers sorts of flies among them, which deuoured them : and frogges which destroyed them.

* *Exod. 10. 13.*

46 *He gaue also their increase vnto the caterpiller : and their labour vnto the locust.

* *Exod. 9. 23.*
† *Heb. killed.*
‖ *Or, great haile stones.*
† *Heb. he shut vp.*
‖ *Or, lightnings.*

47 *He †destroyed their vines with haile : and their Sycomore trees with ‖frost.

48 †He gaue vp their cattel also to the haile : and their flockes to ‖hot thunder-bolts.

49 He cast vpon them the fiercenesse of his anger, wrath and indignation, and trouble : by sending euill angels *among them.*

† *Heb. he waighed a path.*
‖ *Or, their beasts, to the murreine, Exod. 9. 3.*
* *Exod. 12. 29. & 9. 3.*

50 †He made a way to his anger, hee spared not their soule from death : but gaue ‖their life ouer to the pestilence.

51 *And smote all the first borne in Egypt : the chiefe of *their* strength in the tabernacles of Ham :

52 But made his owne people to goe forth like sheepe : and guided them in the wildernesse like a flocke.

* *Exod. 14. 27. & 15. 10.*
† *Heb. coue- red.*

53 And he led them on safely, so that they feared not : but the sea * †ouerwhelmed their enemies.

54 And he brought them to the border of his sanctuarie : *euen* to this mountaine *which* his right hand had purchased.

* *Iosu. 13. 7.*

55 *He cast out the heathen also before them, and diuided them an inheritance by line : and made the tribes of Israel to dwell in their tents.

56 Yet they tempted and prouoked

the most high God : and kept not his testimonies :

57 But turned backe, and dealt vnfaithfully like their fathers : they were turned aside like a deceitfull bowe.

58 *For they prouoked him to anger with their high places : and moued him to ielousie with their grauen images.

* *Deut 21.*

59 When God heard this, hee was wroth, and greatly abhorred Israel :

60 *So that he forsooke the tabernacle of Shiloh : the tent *which* he placed among men,

* *1. Ki 4. 10.*

61 And deliuered his strength into captiuitie : and his glory into the enemies hand.

62 He gaue his people ouer also vnto the sword : and was wroth with his inheritance.

63 The fire consumed their young men : and their maidens were not †giuen to mariage.

† *Heb. sed.*

64 Their priests fell by the sword : and their widowes made no lamentation.

65 Then the Lord awaked as one out of sleepe : *and* like a mighty man that shouteth by reason of wine.

66 And he smote his enemies in the hinder parts : he put them to a perpetuall reproch.

67 Moreouer he refused the tabernacle of Ioseph : and chose not the tribe of Ephraim.

68 But chose the tribe of Iudah : the mount Sion which he loued.

69 And he built his sanctuarie like high *palaces* : like the earth which he hath †established for euer.

† *Heb. ded.*

70 *He chose Dauid also his seruant, and tooke him from the sheepe-folds :

* *1. S 11. 2. 7. 8.*

71 *†From following the ewes great with young, hee brought him to feed Iacob his people, and Israel his inheritance.

* *2. S 2. 1. 11. 2.*
† *Heb. after.*

72 So he fed them according to the integritie of his heart : and guided them by the skilfulnesse of his hands.

PSAL. LXXIX.

1 The Psalmist complaineth of the desolation of Ierusalem. 8 Hee prayeth for deliuerance, 13 And promiseth thankefulnesse.

¶ A Psalme ‖of Asaph.

O God, the heathen are come into thine, inheritance, thy holy temple haue they defiled : they haue layd Ierusalem on heapes.

‖ *Or, f Asaph*

2 The

2 The dead bodies of thy ſeruants haue they giuen *to bee* meate vnto the foules of the heauen : the fleſh of thy Saints vnto the beaſts of the earth.

3 Their blood haue they ſhed like water round about Ieruſalem : and *there was* none to burie *them.*

4 *We are become a reproach to our neighbours : a ſcorne and deriſion to them that are round about vs.

5 *How long, LORD, wilt thou be angry, for euer? ſhall thy ielouſie burne like fire?

6 *Powre out thy wrath vpon the heathen that haue not knowen thee, and vpon the kingdomes that haue not called vpon thy name.

7 For they haue deuoured Iacob : and laid waſte his dwelling place.

8 *O remember not *against* vs ‖former iniquities, let thy tender mercies ſpeedily preuent vs : for we are brought very low.

9 Helpe vs, O God of our ſaluation, for the glory of thy Name : and deliuer vs, and purge away our ſinnes for thy Names ſake.

10 Wherfore ſhould the heathen ſay, Where *is* their God? let him be knowen among the heathen in our ſight *by* the †reuenging of the blood of thy ſeruants which is ſhed.

11 Let the ſighing of the priſoner come before thee, according to the greatneſſe of †thy power : †preſerue thou thoſe that are appointed to die.

12 And render vnto our neighbours ſeuen fold into their boſome , their reproach wherewith they haue reproched thee, O Lord.

13 So we thy people and ſheepe of thy paſture, will giue thee thankes for euer : we will ſhew forth thy praiſe †to all generations.

PSAL. LXXX.

1 The Pſalmiſt in his prayer complaineth of the miſeries of the Church. 8 Gods former fauours are turned into iudgements. 14 Hee prayeth for deliuerance.

¶ To the chiefe Muſician vpon Shoſhannim Eduth, a Pſalme ‖of Aſaph.

Iue eare, O ſhepheard of Iſrael, thou that leadeſt Ioſeph like a flocke, thou that dwelleſt *betweene* the Cherubims, ſhine forth.

2 Before Ephraim and Beniamin, and Manaſſeh, ſtirre vp thy ſtrength : and †come *and* ſaue vs.

3 Turne vs againe, O God : and cauſe thy face to ſhine, and we ſhall bee ſaued.

4 O LORD God of hoſts, how long †wilt thou bee angry againſt the prayer of thy people?

5 Thou feedeſt them with the bread of teares : and giueſt them teares to drinke in great meaſure.

6 Thou makeſt vs a ſtrife vnto our neighbours : and our enemies laugh among themſelues.

7 Turne vs againe, O God of hoſts, and cauſe thy face to ſhine, and we ſhall be ſaued.

8 Thou haſt brought a vine out of Egypt : thou haſt caſt out the heathen, and planted it.

9 Thou preparedſt *roome* before it : and didſt cauſe it to take deepe root, and it filled the land.

10 The hilles were couered with the ſhadow of it, and the boughs thereof were like †the goodly cedars.

11 She ſent out her boughs vnto the Sea : and her branches vnto the riuer.

12 Why haſt thou *then* broken downe her hedges : ſo that all they which paſſe by the way, doe plucke her?

13 The boare out of the wood doth waſte it : and the wild beaſt of the field doth deuoure it.

14 Returne, we beſeech thee, O God of hoſts : looke downe from heauen, and behold, and viſit this vine :

15 And the vineyard which thy right hand hath planted : and the branch *that* thou madeſt ſtrong for thy ſelfe.

16 It *is* burnt with fire, it *is* cut downe : they periſh at the rebuke of thy countenance.

17 Let thy hand be vpon the man of thy right hand : vpon the ſonne of man, *whom* thou madeſt ſtrong for thy ſelfe.

18 So will not wee goe backe from thee : quicken vs, and we will call vpon thy Name.

19 Turne vs againe, O LORD God of hoſts, cauſe thy face to ſhine, and wee ſhall be ſaued.

PSAL. LXXXI.

1 An exhortation to a ſolemne praiſing of God. 4 God challengeth that duetie by reaſon of his benefits. 8 God exhorting to obedience, complaineth of their diſobedience, which proueth their owne hurt.

¶ To

Marginal notes

- 44. 14
- 89. 45
- 10. 25
- 64. 9.
  the iniuries of that before
- ven-e.
- thine
- r. re-the en of
- to geneion and ation.
- for h.

† *Heb. come for ſaluation to vs.*

† *Hebr. wilt thou ſmoke?*

† *Hebr. the Cedars of God.*

¶ To the chiefe Musician vpon Gittith. *A Psalme* ||of Asaph.

|| Or, for Asaph.

Ing alowd vnto God our strength : make a ioyfull noise vnto the God of Iacob.

2 Take a Psalme, and bring hither the timbrell : the pleasant harpe with the psalterie.

3 Blow vp the trumpet in the new Moone : in the time appointed on our solemne feast day.

4 For this was a Statute for Israel : *and* a Law of the God of Iacob.

5 This he ordained in Ioseph *for a* testimonie, when he went out ||through the land of Egypt : *where* I heard a language, *that* I vnderstood not.

|| Or, against.

6 I remoued his shoulder from the burden : his handes † were deliuered from the pots.

† *Hebr. passed away.*

7 Thou calledst in trouble , and I deliuered thee, I answered thee in the secret place of thunder : I *proued thee at the waters of ||Meribah. Selah.

* Exod. 17. 6.
|| Or, strife.

8 Heare, O my people, and I will testifie vnto thee : O Israel, if thou wilt hearken vnto me :

9 There shall no strange God be in thee : neither shalt thou worship any strange God.

10 I *am* the LORD thy God, which brought thee out of the land of Egypt : open thy mouth wide, and I will fill it.

11 But my people would not hearken to my voice : and Israel would none of me.

12 *So I gaue them vp ||vnto their owne hearts lust : and they walked in in their owne counsels.

* Acts. 14. 6.
|| Or, to the hardnes of their hearts, or imagination.

13 O that my people had hearkned vnto me : *and* Israel had walked in my wayes !

14 I should soone haue subdued their enemies, and turned my hand against their aduersaries.

15 The haters of the LORD should haue ||submitted themselues vnto him : but their time should haue endured for euer.

|| Or, yeelded fained obedience. Heb. lyed.

16 Hee should haue fedde them also † with the finest of the wheat : and with honie out of the rocke, should I haue satisfied thee.

† *Hebr. with the fat of wheat.*

PSAL. LXXXII.

1 The Psalmist hauing exhorted the Iudges, 5 and reproued their negligence, 8 prayeth God to iudge.

¶ A Psalme ||of Asaph.

|| Or, Asaph.

Od standeth in the Congregation of the mightie : hee iudgeth among the gods.

2 How long will yee iudge vniustly : and accept the *persons of the wicked ? Selah.

* Deut 17.

3 † Defend the poore and fatherlesse : doe iustice to the afflicted and needie.

† Heb.

4 *Deliuer the poore and needy: rid them out of the hand of the wicked.

* Prou 11.

5 They know not, neither wil they vnderstand ; they walke on in darknes : all the foundations of the earth are † out of course.

† Heb. ued.

6 *I haue said, Ye *are* gods : and all of you *are* children of the most High :

* Ioh 34.

7 But ye shall die like men, and fall like one of the Princes.

8 Arise, O God, iudge the earth : for thou shalt inherite all nations.

PSAL. LXXXIII.

1 A complaint to God of the enemies conspiracies. 9 A prayer against them that oppresse the Church.

¶ A song *or* Psalme ||of Asaph.

|| Or, saph.

Eepe not thou silence, O God : hold not thy peace, and be not still, O God.

2 For loe, thine enemies make a tumult : and they that hate thee, haue lift vp the head.

3 They haue taken craftie counsell against thy people, and consulted against thy hidden ones.

4 They haue said, Come, and let vs cut them off from being a nation : that the name of Israel may bee no more in remembrance.

5 For they haue consulted together with one † consent : they are confederate against thee.

† Heb

6 The tabernacles of Edom, and the Ishmaelites : of Moab, and the Hagarens.

7 Gebal and Ammon, and Amalek : the Philistines, with the inhabitants of Tyre.

8 Assur also is ioyned with them : † they haue holpen the children of Lot. Selah.

† Heb haue arme childr Lot.

9 *Doe vnto them as *vnto* the Midianites : as *to* *Sisera, as *to* Iabin, at the brooke of Kison :

* Iud 22.
* Iud 15. an

10 *Which* perished at En-dor : they
                          became

became *as* dung for the earth.

11 *Make their nobles like Oreb, and like Zeeb : yea all their princes as Zebah, and as Zalmunna :

12 Who sayd, Let vs take to our selues, the houses of God in possession.

13 O my God, make them like a wheele : as the stubble before the wind.

14 As the fire burneth a wood : and as the flame setteth the mountaines on fire :

15 So persecute them with thy tempest : and make them afraid with thy storme.

16 Fill their faces with shame : that they may seeke thy name, O LORD.

17 Let them be confounded and troubled for euer : yea let them be put to shame, and perish :

18 That *men* may knowe, that thou, whose name alone *is* IEHOVAH : *art* the most High ouer all the earth.

PSAL. LXXXIIII.

1 The Prophet longing for the communion of the Sanctuarie, 4 sheweth how blessed they are that dwell vnto it. 8 Hee prayeth to be restored vnto it.

¶ To the chiefe musician vpon Gittith, a Psalme || for the sonnes of Korah.

Ow amiable *are* thy tabernacles, O LORD of hostes !

2 My soule longeth, yea euen fainteth for the courts of the LORD : my heart and my flesh cryeth out for the liuing God.

3 Yea the sparrowe hath found an house, and the swallow a nest for her selfe, where she may lay her young, *euen* thine altars, O LORD of hostes, my king and my God.

4 Blessed *are* they that dwell in thy house : they wilbe still praysing thee. Selah.

5 Blessed *is* the man whose strength *is* in thee : in whose heart *are* the wayes of them :

6 Who passing through the valley || of Baca, make it a well : the raine also † filleth the pooles.

7 They goe || from strength to strength : *euery one* of them in Zion appeareth before God.

8 O LORD God of hostes, heare my prayer : giue eare, O God of Iacob. Selah.

9 Behold, O God our shield : and looke vpon the face of thine anointed.

10 For a day in thy courts, *is* better then a thousand : †I had rather be a doore keeper in the house of my God, then to dwell in the tents of wickednesse.

11 For the LORD God *is* a sunne and shield : the LORD will giue grace and glory : no good thing will he withhold from * them that walke vprightly.

12 O LORD of hostes : blessed *is* the man that trusteth in thee.

PSAL. LXXXV.

1 The Psalmist out of the experience of former mercies prayeth for the continuance thereof. 8 He promiseth to waite thereon, out of confidence of Gods goodnesse.

¶ To the chiefe musician, a Psalme || for the sonnes of Korah.

ORD, thou hast bene || fauourable vnto thy land : thou hast brought backe the captiuity of Iacob.

2 * Thou hast forgiuen the iniquitie of thy people, thou hast couered all their sinne. Selah.

3 Thou hast taken away all thy wrath : || thou hast turned *thy selfe* from the fiercenesse of thine anger.

4 Turne vs, O God of our saluation : and cause thine anger towards vs to cease.

5 Wilt thou be angry with vs for euer ? wilt thou drawe out thine anger to all generations ?

6 Wilt thou not reuiue vs againe : that thy people may reioyce in thee ?

7 Shew vs thy mercy, O LORD ; and graunt vs thy saluation.

8 I will heare what God the LORD will speake : for hee will speake peace vnto his people, and to his Saints : but let them not turne againe to folly.

9 Surely his saluation *is* nigh them that feare him ; that glory may dwell in our land.

10 Mercy and truth are met *together:* righteousnesse and peace haue kissed *each other.*

11 Truth shall spring out of the earth : and righteousnesse shall looke downe from heauen.

12 Yea the LORD shall giue that which is good : and our land shall yeeld her increase.

13 Righte-

ng. 7.
8. 21.

of.

of mul-
trees
him
l &c.
e. coue-

from
anie to
anie.

† *Heb. I would choose rather to sit at the threshold.*

* Psal. 2. 12. & 34. 9.

|| *Or, of.*

|| *Or, well pleased.*

* Psal. 32. 1.

|| *Or, thou hast turned thine anger from waxing hot.*

13 Righteousnes shall go before him: and shall set *vs* in the way of his steps.

PSAL. LXXXVI.

1 Dauid strengtheneth his prayer by the conscience of his Religion, 5 by the goodnesse and power of God. 11 He desireth the continuance of former grace. 14 Complayning of the proud, he craueth some token of Gods goodnesse.

¶ ‖ A prayer of Dauid.

‖ *Or, a prayer, being a Psalme of Dauid.*

BOw downe thine eare, O Lord, heare me : for I *am* poore & needy.

2 Preserue my soule, for I *am* ‖ holy : O thou my God, saue thy seruant, that trusteth in thee.

‖ *Or, one whom thou fauourest.*

3 Be merciful vnto me, O Lord: for I cry vnto thee ‖ daily.

‖ *Or, all the day.*

4 Reioyce the soule of thy seruant : for vnto thee (O Lord) doe I lift vp my soule.

5 *For thou Lord *art* good, and ready to forgiue : and plenteous in mercie vnto all them that call vpon thee.

* Ioel 2. 13.

6 Giue eare O Lord, vnto my prayer : and attend to the voice of my supplications.

7 In the day of my trouble I will call vpon thee : for thou wilt answere mee.

8 Among the gods *there is* none like vnto thee (O Lord :) * neither are there any workes like vnto thy workes.

* Deut. 3. 24.

9 All nations whom thou hast made, shall come and worship before thee, O Lord : and shall glorifie thy Name.

10 For thou *art* great, and doest wonderous things : *thou *art* God alone.

11 *Teach me thy way, O Lord, I will walke in thy trueth : vnite my heart to feare thy Name.

* Deut. 6. 4. and 32. 39. isa. 37. 16. and 44. 6. mar. 12. 29. ephes. 4. 6. 1. cor. 8. 4. * Psal. 25. 3. and 119. 33.

12 I will praise thee, O Lord my God, with all my heart : and I wil glorifie thy Name for euermore.

13 For great *is* thy mercy toward me: and thou hast deliuered my soule from the lowest ‖ hell.

‖ *Or, graue.*

14 O God, the proud are risen against mee, and the assemblies of †violent men haue sought after my soule : and haue not set thee before them.

† *Hebr. terrible.*

15 *But thou, O Lord, *art* a God full of compassion, and gracious : long suffering, and plenteous in mercy and trueth.

* Deut. 34. 6. num. 14. 18. psal. 103. 8. and 139. 4. and 145. 8.

16 O turne vnto me, and haue mercie vpon me, giue thy strength vnto thy seruant : and saue the sonne of thine handmaid.

17 Shew me a token for good, that they which hate me may see *it*, and bee ashamed : because thou, Lord, hast holpen me, and comforted me.

PSAL. LXXXVII.

1 The nature and glory of the Church. 4 The increase, honour and comfort of the members thereof.

¶ A Psalme *or* song ‖ for the sonnes of Korah.

‖ *Or,*

HIs foundation is in the holy mountaines.

2 The Lord loueth the gates of Zion : more then all the dwellings of Iacob.

3 Glorious things are spoken of thee, O Citie of God. Selah.

4 I will make mention of Rahab, and Babylon, to them that know mee ; behold Philistia, and Tyre, with Ethiopia : this *man* was borne there.

5 And of Zion it shalbe said, This and that man was borne in her : and the highest himselfe shall establish her.

6 The Lord shall count when he writeth vp the people : *that* this man was borne there. Selah.

7 As wel the singers as the players on instruments *shall bee there :* all my springs *are* in thee.

PSAL. LXXXVIII.

A prayer contayning a grieuous complaint.

¶ A song *or* Psalme ‖ for the sonnes of Korah, to the chiefe Musician vpon Mahalath Leannoth, ‖ Maschil of Heman the Ezrahite.

‖ *Or,* ‖ *Or, a Psalm Heman Exraite giuing struct*

O Lord God of my saluation, I haue cried day *and* night before thee.

2 Let my prayer come before thee : incline thine eare vnto my cry.

3 For my soule is full of troubles : and my life draweth nigh vnto the graue.

4 I am counted with them that go downe into the pit : I am as a man *that hath* no strength.

5 Free among the dead, like the slaine that lie in the graue, whom thou remem-

* Or, by thy
hand.

remembrest no more : and they are cut off ||from thy hand.

6 Thou hast laid me in the lowest pit : in darkenesse, in the deepes.

7 Thy wrath lieth hard vpon me : and thou hast afflicted me with all thy waues. Selah.

8 Thou hast put away mine acquaintance farre from mee : thou hast made me an abomination vnto them : *I am* shut vp, and I cannot come forth.

9 Mine eye mourneth by reason of affliction, LORD, I haue called daily vpon thee : I haue stretched out my hands vnto thee.

10 Wilt thou shew wonders to the dead? shal the dead arise *and* praise thee? Selah.

11 Shall thy louing kindnesse be declared in the graue? *or* thy faithfulnesse in destruction?

12 Shall thy wonders be knowen in the darke? and thy righteousnesse in the land of forgetfulnesse?

13 But vnto thee haue I cried, O LORD, and in the morning shall my prayer preuent thee.

14 LORD, why castest thou off my soule? *why* hidest thou thy face from me?

15 I am afflicted and ready to die, from *my* youth vp. *while* I suffer thy terrours, I am distracted.

16 Thy fierce wrath goeth ouer me : thy terrours haue cut me off.

* Or, all the
day.

17 They came round about mee ||daily like water : they compassed mee about together.

18 Louer and friend hast thou put farre from me : *and* mine acquaintance *into* darkenesse.

PSAL. LXXXIX.

1 The Psalmist praiseth God for his couenant, 5 For his wonderfull power, 15 For the care of his Church, 19 For his fauour to the kingdome of Dauid. 38 Then complaining of contrary euents, 46 He expostulateth, prayeth, and blesseth God.

* Or, a
Pſalme for
Ethan the
Ezrahite,
to giue in-
ſtruction.

¶ || Maschil of Ethan the Ezrahite.

I Will sing of the mercies of the LORD for euer : with my mouth will I make knowen thy faithfulnesse † to all generations.

2 For I haue said, Mercie shall bee built vp for euer : thy faithfulnesse shalt thou establish in the very heauens.

3 I haue made a couenant with my

† Hebr. to
generation
and gene-
ration.

chosen : I haue * sworne vnto Dauid my seruant.

4 Thy seed will I stablish for euer : and build vp thy throne †to all generations. Selah.

5 And the heauens shall praise thy wonders, O LORD : thy faithfulnes also in the congregation of the Saints.

6 For who in the heauen can be compared vnto the LORD? *who* among the sonnes of the mightie can be likened vnto the LORD?

7 God is greatly to be feared in the assembly of the Saints : and to bee had in reuerence of all them *that are* about him.

8 O LORD God of hosts, who *is* a strong LORD like vnto thee? or to thy faithfulnesse round about thee?

9 Thou rulest the raging of the sea : when the waues thereof arise, thou stillest them.

10 Thou hast broken ||Rahab in pieces, as one that is slaine : thou hast scattered thine enemies † with thy strong arme.

11 * The heauens *are* thine, the earth also *is* thine : as for the world and the fulnes thereof, thou hast founded them.

12 The North and the South, thou hast created them : Tabor and Hermon shall reioyce in thy Name.

13 Thou *hast* † a mighty arme : strong is thy hand, *and* high is thy right hand.

14 Iustice and iudgement are the ||habitation of thy throne : mercie and trueth shall goe before thy face.

15 Blessed *is* the people that knowe the * ioyfull sound : they shall walke O LORD in the light of thy countenance.

16 In thy name shall they reioyce all the day : and in thy righteousnes shall they be exalted.

17 For thou art the glory of their strength : and in thy fauour our horne shall be exalted.

18 For the || LORD is our defence : and the holy One of Israel is our king.

19 Then thou spakest in vision to thy holy one, and saidst, I haue laid helpe vpon one that is mightie : I haue exalted one chosen out of the people.

20 * I haue found Dauid my seruant : with my holy oile haue I anointed him.

21 With whome my hand shall bee established : mine arme also shall strengthen him.

22 The enemie shall not exact vpon him :

* 2. Sam. 7.
11, &c.

† Heb. to ge-
nerationand
generation.

|| Or, Egypt.

† Heb. with
the arme of
thy strength.
* Gen. 1. 1.
psal. 24. 1.
psal. 50. 12.

† Heb. an
arme with
might.

|| Or, esta-
blishment.

* Num. 10. 6

|| Or, our
shield is of
the LORD,
and our king
is of the holy
One of
Israel.

* 1. Sam. 16
12.

him : nor the sonne of wickednesse afflict him.

23 And I will beate downe his foes before his face : and plague them that hate him.

24 But my faithfulnesse and my mercy shalbe with him : and in my name shall his horne be exalted.

25 I will set his hand also in the sea : and his right hand in the riuers.

26 He shall crie vnto mee, Thou *art* my father : my God, and the rocke of my saluation.

27 Also I will make him *my* first borne : higher then the kings of the earth.

28 My mercy will I keepe for him for euermore : and my couenant shall stand fast with him.

29 His seed also will I make *to indure* for euer : and his throne as the dayes of heauen.

30 If his children forsake my lawe, and walke not in my iudgements ;

† *Heb. pro-
fane my sta-
tutes.*

31 If they †breake my statutes, and keepe not my commandements :

32 Then will I visite their transgression with the rod, and their iniquitie with stripes.

33 Neuerthelesse, my louing kindnesse will I not vtterly take from him : nor † suffer my faithfulnesse † to faile.

† *Heb. I will
not make
voyd from
him.*
† *Heb. to lye.*

34 My couenant will I not breake : nor alter the thing that is gone out of my lippes.

35 Once haue I sworne by my holinesse ; †that I will not lye vnto Dauid.

† *Heb. if I
lie.*
* *Rom. 7.
16. Luc. 1.
33. Iohn 12
34.*

36 * His seede shall endure for euer ; and his throne as the sunne before me.

37 It shalbe established for euer as the Moone : and as a faithfull witnesse in heauen. Selah.

38 But thou hast cast off and abhorred : thou hast bene wroth with thine anointed.

39 Thou hast made voyd the couenant of thy seruant : thou hast profaned his crowne, by casting it to the ground.

40 Thou hast broken downe all his hedges : thou hast brought his strong holds to ruine.

41 All that passe by the way, spoile him : hee is a reproach to his neighbours.

42 Thou hast set vp the right hand of his aduersaries : thou hast made all his enemies to reioyce.

43 Thou hast also turned the edge

of his sword : and hast not made him to stand in the battaile.

44 Thou hast made his † glory to cease : and cast his throne downe to the ground.

† *Heb.
brightnesse.*

45 The dayes of his youth hast thou shortned : thou hast couered him with shame. Selah.

46 How long, LORD, wilt thou hide thy selfe, for euer ? shall thy wrath burne like fire ?

47 Remember how short my time is : wherefore hast thou made all men in vaine ?

48 What man *is he that* liueth, and shall not see death ? shall he deliuer his soule from the hand of the graue ? Selah.

49 Lord, where *are* thy former louing kindnesses, *which* thou *swarest vnto Dauid in thy trueth?

* *2. Sam. 7
15.*

50 Remember (Lord) the reproach of thy seruants : *how* I doe beare in my bosome *the reproache* of all the mighty people.

51 Wherewith thine enemies haue reproached, O LORD : wherewith they haue reproached the foote-steppes of thine Annointed.

52 Blessed *be* the LORD for euermore, Amen, and Amen.

PSAL. XC.

1 Moses setting foorth Gods prouidence, 3 complaineth , of humane fragility, 7 diuine chastisements, 10 and breuity of life. 12 He prayeth for the knowledge and sencible experience of Gods good prouidence.

¶ ‖ A prayer of Moses the man of God.

‖ *Or, a pra-
er, being a
psalme of
Moses.*
† *Heb. in g
neration a
generatior*

LOrd, thou hast bene our dwelling place † in all generations.

2 Before the mountaines were brought forth, or euer thou hadst formed the earth and the world : euen from euerlasting to euerlasting thou *art* God.

3 Thou turnest man to destruction : and sayest, Returne yee children of men.

4 * For a thousand yeeres in thy sight *are but* as yesterday ‖ when it is past : and *as* a watch in the night.

* *2. Pet. 3*
‖ *Or, whe
he hath p
sed them*

5 Thou carriest them away as with a flood, they are *as* a sleepe : in the morning they *are* like grasse *which* ‖ groweth vp.

‖ *Or, is ch
ged:*

6 In the morning it flourisheth, and groweth

groweth vp : in the euening it is cut downe, and withereth.

7 For we are consumed by thine anger : and by thy wrath are we troubled.

8 Thou hast set our iniquities before thee: our secret sinnes in the light of thy countenance.

9 For all our dayes are † passed away in thy wrath : we spend our yeeres ‖as a tale *that is told.*

10 † The dayes of our yeres *are* threescore yeeres and ten, and if by reason of strength they *be* fourescore yeeres, yet is their strength labour and sorrow : for it is soone cut off, and we flie away.

11 Who knoweth the power of thine anger? euen according to thy feare, *so is* thy wrath.

12 So teach vs to number our daies : that wee may † apply our hearts vnto wisedome.

13 Returne (O LORD) how long? and let it repent thee concerning thy seruants.

14 O satisfie vs early with thy mercie : that we may reioyce, and be glad all our dayes.

15 Make vs glad according to the dayes *wherein* thou hast afflicted vs : *and* the yeeres *wherein* we haue seene euil.

16 Let thy worke appeare vnto thy seruants : and thy glory vnto their children.

17 And let the beautie of the LORD our God be vpon vs, and establish thou the worke of our hands vpon vs : yea, the work of our hands establish thou it.

PSAL. XCI.

1 The state of the godly. 3 Their safety. 9 Their habitation. 11 Their seruants. 14 Their friend, with the effects of them all.

HE that dwelleth in the secret place of the most high: shall † abide vnder the shadow of the Almightie.

2 I will say of the LORD, He *is* my refuge, and my fortresse : my God, in him will I trust.

3 Surely he shall deliuer thee from the snare of the fouler: *and* from the noisome pestilence.

4 Hee shall couer thee with his feathers, and vnder his wings shalt thou trust : his trueth shall bee *thy* shield and buckler.

5 Thou shalt not bee afraid for the terrour by night : *nor* for the arrow *that* flieth by day :

6 *Nor* for the pestilence *that* walketh in darknes : *nor* for the destruction, *that* wasteth at noone-day.

7 A thousand shall fall at thy side, and ten thousand at thy right hand : *but* it shall not come nigh thee.

8 Onely with thine eyes shalt thou behold : & see the reward of the wicked.

9 Because thou hast made the LORD, which *is* my refuge, *euen* the most High, thy habitation :

10 There shall no euill befall thee : neither shall any plague come nigh thy dwelling.

11 * For hee shall giue his Angels charge ouer thee : to keepe thee in all thy wayes.

12 They shall beare thee vp in *their* hands : lest thou dash thy foot against a stone.

13 Thou shalt tread vpon the Lion, and ‖adder : the yong Lion and the dragon shalt thou trample vnder feete.

14 Because he hath set his loue vpon me, therefore will I deliuer him : I wil set him on high, because hee hath knowen my Name.

15 He shall call vpon me, and I will answere him : I *will bee* with him in trouble, I will deliuer him, and honour him.

16 With † long life wil I satisfie him : and shew him my saluation.

PSAL. XCII.

1 The Prophet exhorteth to praise God, 4 for his great workes, 6 for his iudgements on the wicked, 10 and for his goodnesse to the godly.

¶ A Psalme *or* song for the Sabbath day.

IT is a good thing to giue thanks vnto the LORD, and to sing *praises* vnto thy Name, O most High :

2 To shew foorth thy louing kindnesse in the morning : and thy faithfulnesse † euery night :

3 Vpon an instrument of tenne strings, and vpon the psalterie : vpon the ‖harpe with a solemne sound.

4 For thou, LORD, hast made me glad through thy worke : I will triumph in the workes of thy hands.

5 O LORD, how great are thy workes ! *and* thy thoughts are very deepe.

6 A brutish man knoweth not : neither doeth a foole vnderstand this.

7 When

Marginal notes:

*. turvay.

s a ation. r. as dayes yeeres, n are tie

cause e.

. lodge.

* Matt. 4. 6. luke 4. 10.

‖ Or, Aspe.

† Heb. length of dayes.

† Hebr. in the nights.

‖ Or, vpon the solemne sound with the harpe. Hebr. Higgaion.

7 When the wicked spring as the graſſe, and when all the workers of iniquitie doe flouriſh: *it is* that they ſhall be destroyed for euer.

8 ¶ But thou, LORD, art *most* high for euermore.

9 For loe, thine enemies, O LORD, for loe, thine enemies ſhall periſh: all the workers of iniquity ſhalbe ſcattred.

10 But my horne ſhalt thou exalt like *the horne* of an vnicorne: I ſhalbe anointed with freſh oyle.

11 Mine eye alſo ſhall ſee *my deſire* on mine enemies: *and* mine eares ſhall heare *my deſire* of the wicked that riſe vp against me.

*Hoſe. 14. 5   12 * The righteous ſhal flouriſh like the palme tree: hee ſhall growe like a cedar in Lebanon.

13 Thoſe that be planted in the house of the LORD, ſhall flouriſh in the courts of our God.

†Heb.greene   14 They ſhal ſtill bring forth fruit in old age: they ſhalbe fat, & †flouriſhing:

15 To ſhew that the LORD *is* vpright: hee *is* my rocke, and *there is* no vnrighteouſneſſe in him.

PSAL. XCIII.

The Maieſtie, Power, and Holineſſe of Christs Kingdome.

 He LORD reigneth, he is clothed with Maieſtie, the LORD is clothed with strength, *wherewith* hee hath girded himſelfe: the world alſo is stablished, that it cannot be moued.

†Heb. from then.   2 Thy throne is eſtabliſhed †of old: thou *art* from euerlaſting.

3 The floods haue lifted vp, O LORD, the floods haue lifted vp their voice: the floods lift vp their waues.

4 The LORD on high *is* mightier then the noiſe of many waters, *yea then* the mightie waues of the Sea.

5 Thy teſtimonies are very ſure: holineſſe becommeth thine house, O †Heb. to length of dayes.   LORD, †for euer.

PSAL. XCIIII.

1 The Prophet calling for Iustice, complaineth of tyrannie and impietie. 8 Hee teacheth Gods prouidence. 12 He ſheweth the bleſſedneſſe of affliction. 16 God is the defender of the afflicted.

†Heb. God of reuenges.   †Heb. ſhine forth.   O LORD †God, to whome vengeance belongeth: O God to whome vengeance belongeth, †ſhew thy ſelfe.

2 Lift vp thy ſelfe, thou iudge of the earth: render a reward to the proud.

3 LORD, how long ſhall the wicked? how long ſhall the wicked triumph?

4 *How long* ſhal they vtter, *and* ſpeake hard things? *and* all the workers of iniquitie boast themſelues?

5 They breake in pieces thy people, O LORD: and afflict thine heritage.

6 They ſlay the widowe and the stranger: and murder the fatherleſſe.

*Pſal. 11, 13. 20. 12.   7 * Yet they ſay, The LORD ſhall not ſee: neither ſhall the God of Iacob regard *it*.

8 Vnderſtand, yee brutiſh among the people: and *ye* fooles, when will ye be wiſe?

*Exo.   9 * He that planted the eare, ſhall he not heare? he that formed the eye, ſhall he not ſee?

10 He that chaſtiſeth the heathen, ſhall not he correct? hee that teacheth man knowledge, *ſhall not he know*?

*1. Co? 20.   11 * The LORD knoweth the thoughts of man: that they *are* vanitie.

12 Bleſſed *is* the man whome thou chaſteneſt, O LORD: and teacheſt him out of thy Law:

13 That thou mayeſt giue him reſt from the dayes of aduerſitie: vntill the pit be digged for the wicked.

14 For the LORD will not caſt off his people: neither will he forſake his inheritance.

†Hebr. be afte?   15 But iudgement ſhall returne vnto righteouſneſſe: and all the vpright in heart †ſhall follow it.

16 Who will riſe vp for mee against the euill doers? *or* who will ſtand vp for me against the workers of iniquitie?

‖Or, q?   17 Vnleſſe the LORD *had bene* my helpe: my ſoule had ‖ almoſt dwelt in ſilence.

18 When I ſaid, My foote ſlippeth: thy mercie, O LORD, held me vp.

19 In the multitude of my thoughts within me, thy comforts delight my ſoule.

20 Shal the throne of iniquitie haue fellowſhip with thee: which frameth miſchiefe by a lawe?

21 They gather themſelues together against the ſoule of the righteous: and condemne the innocent blood.

22 But the LORD is my defence: and my God *is* the rocke of my refuge.

23 And hee ſhall bring vpon them their owne iniquitie, and ſhall cut them off

off in their owne wickednesse : *yea* the Lord our God shall cut them off.

PSAL. XCV.

1 An exhortation to praise God, 3 for his greatnesse, 6 and for his goodnesse, 8 And not to tempt him,

Come, let vs sing vnto the Lord : let vs make a ioyfull noise to the rocke of our saluation.

Eb. pre-
ath his face.

2 Let vs †come before his presence with thanksgiuing : and make a ioyfull noise vnto him with psalmes.

3 For the Lord *is* a great God: and a great king aboue all Gods.

Eb. in
ose.
r, the
ghts of
hilles, are

4 †In his hand are the deepe places of the earth : ||the strength of the hilles is his also.

Eb. whose
sea is.

5 †The sea *is* his, and he made it · and his hands formed the dry land.

6 O come, let vs worship and bowe downe : let vs kneele before the Lord our maker.

7 For he *is* our God, and we *are* the people of his pasture, and the sheepe of his hand : to day if yee will heare his voyce,

Eb. 3. 7.
4. 7.
um. 14.
&c.
eb. con-
ion.
xod. 17.
nd 7.

8 * Harden not your heart, * as in the †prouocation : and as in the day of *temptation, in the wildernesse :

9 When your fathers tempted me, proued me, and sawe my worke.

10 Fortie yeeres long was I grieued with *this* generation : and sayd, It *is* a people that doe erre in their heart : and they haue not knowen my wayes

eb. if
enter
my rest.

11 Vnto whom I sware in my wrath : †that they should not enter into my rest.

PSAL. XCVI.

1 An exhortation to praise God, 4 for his greatnesse, 8 For his kingdome, 11 For his generall iudgement.

Chron.
3.

* Sing vnto the Lord a new song : sing vnto the Lord all the earth.

2 Sing vnto the Lord, blesse his name : shew forth his saluation from day to day.

3 Declare his glory among the heathen : his wonders among all people.

4 For the Lord *is* great, and greatly to be praised : hee *is* to be feared aboue all Gods.

5 For all the gods of the nations *are*

idoles : but the Lord made the heauens.

6 Honour and maiestie *are* before him : strength and beauty *are* in his sanctuary.

7 Giue vnto the Lord (O yee kinreds of the people :) giue vnto the Lord glory and strength.

8 Giue vnto the Lord the glory †*due vnto* his name : bring an offering, and come into his courts.

† *Heb. of his*
name.

9 O worship the Lord, || in the beautie of holinesse : feare before him all the earth.

|| *Or, in the*
glorious san-
ctuary.

10 * Say among the heathen, *that* the Lord reigneth : the world also shalbe established that it shall not be moued : he shall iudge the people righteously.

* Psal. 93.
1. & 97. 1.

11 Let the heauens reioyce, and let the earth be glad : let the sea roare, and the fulnesse thereof.

12 Let the field be ioyfull, and all that *is* therein : then shall all the trees of the wood reioyce

13 Before the Lord, for hee commeth, for hee commeth to iudge the earth : hee shall iudge the world with righteousnesse, and the people with his trueth.

PSAL. XCVII.

1 The Maiestie of Gods kingdome. 7 The Church reioyceth at Gods iudgements vpon Idolaters. 10 An exhortation to godlinesse and gladnesse.

He Lord raigneth, let the earth reioyce : let the †multitude of Isles bee glad thereof.

† *Heb. many,*
or, great
Isles.

2 Clouds and darkenesse *are* round about him : *righteousnesse and iudgement are the ||habitation of his throne.

* Psal. 89.
15.
|| *Or, esta-*
blishment.

3 A fire goeth before him : and burneth vp his enemies round about.

4 His lightnings inlightned the world : the earth sawe, and trembled.

5 The hilles melted like waxe at the presence of the Lord : at the presence of the Lord of the whole earth.

6 The heauens declare his righteousnesse : and all the people see his glory.

7 * Confounded be all they that serue grauen images, that boast themselues of idoles : worship him all *yee* gods.

* Exod. 20.
4. Leuit. 26
1. Deut. 5.
8. Heb. 1. 6.

8 Sion heard, and was glad, and the daughters of Iudah reioyced : because of thy iudgements, O Lord.

9 For thou, Lord, *art* high aboue all

all the earth : thou art exalted farre a-boue all gods.

* Psal. 34.
13. amos 5.
15. rom. 12.
9.

10 *Yee that loue the LORD, hate euil ; hee preserueth the soules of his Saints : hee deliuereth them out of the hand of the wicked.

11 Light is sowen for the righteous : and gladnesse for the vpright in heart.

‖ Or, to the memoriall.

12 Reioyce in the LORD, ye righ-teous : and giue thanks ‖at the remem-brance of his holinesse.

PSAL. XCVIII.

1 The Psalmist exhorteth the Iewes, 4 the Gen-tiles, 7 and all the creatures to praise God.

¶ A Psalme.

Sing vnto the LORD a New song, for hee hath done marueilous things : his right hand, and his holy arme hath gotten him the victorie.

* Isa. 52. 10.
‖ Or, reuea-led.

2 *The LORD hath made knowen his saluation : his righteousnesse hath hee ‖openly shewed in the sight of the heathen.

3 Hee hath remembred his mercie and his trueth toward the house of Is-rael : all the ends of the earth haue seene the saluation of our God.

4 Make a ioyfull noise vnto the LORD, all the earth : make a lowd noise, and reioyce, and sing praise.

5 Sing vnto the LORD with the harpe : with the harpe, and the voice of a Psalme.

6 With trumpets and sound of cor-net : make a ioyfull noise before the LORD, the King.

7 Let the sea roare, and the fulnesse thereof : the world, and they that dwell therein.

8 Let the floods clap *their* handes : let the hilles be ioyfull together

* Psal. 96. 13.

9 Before the LORD, *for he com-meth to iudge the earth : with righte-ousnesse shall hee iudge the world, and the people with equitie.

PSAL. XCIX.

1 The Prophet setting foorth the Kingdome of GOD in Zion, 5 exhorteth all, by the example of forefathers, to worship GOD at his holy Hill.

He LORD raigneth, let the people tremble : he sit-teth *betweene* the Cheru-bims, let the earth †bee mooued.

† Hebr. stag-ger.

2 The LORD *is* great in Zion : and he *is* high aboue all people.

3 Let them praise thy great and ter-rible Name : *for* it *is* holy.

4 The Kings strength also loueth iudgement, thou doest establish equitie : thou executest iudgement and righte-ousnes in Iacob.

5 Exalt yee the LORD our God, and worship at his footstoole : *for* ‖he is holy.

‖ Or, it is holy.

6 Moses and Aaron among his Priests, and Samuel among them that call vpon his Name : they called vpon the LORD, and he answered them.

7 He spake vnto them in the cloudie pillar : they kept his Testimonies, and the Ordinance *that* he gaue them.

8 Thou answeredst them, O LORD our God : thou wast a God that forga-uest them, though thou tookest venge-ance of their inuentions.

9 Exalt the LORD our God, and worship at his holy hill : for the LORD our God is holy.

PSAL. C.

1 An exhortation to praise God cheerefully, 3 for his greatnesse, 4 and for his power.

¶ A Psalme of ‖praise.

‖Or, thanks giuing.
† Hebr. a the earth.

Ake a ioyfull noise vnto the Lord, †all ye lands.

2 Serue the LORD with gladnes : come before his presence with singing.

3 Know ye that the LORD, hee *is* God, *it is* he *that* hath made vs, and ‖not we our selues : wee are his people, and the sheepe of his pasture.

‖ Or, and we are.

4 Enter into his gates with thanks-giuing, *and* into his Courts with praise : bee thankfull vnto him, *and* blesse his Name.

5 For the LORD *is* good, his mercy *is* euerlasting : and his trueth endureth †to all generations.

† Hebr. generati and gen tion.

PSAL. CI.

Dauid maketh a vow and profession of godlines.

¶ A Psalme of Dauid.

Will sing of Mercie and Iudgement : vnto thee, O LORD, wil I sing.

2 I will behaue my selfe wisely in a perfect way, O when wilt thou come vnto me ? I will walke within my house with a perfect heart.

3 I will set no †wicked thing before mine

† Heb. of Beli

mine eyes : I hate the worke of them that turne aſide, *it* ſhal not cleaue to me.

4 A froward heart ſhall depart from me, I will not knowe a wicked perſon.

5 Whoſo priuily ſlandereth his neighbour, him will I cut off : him that hath an high looke, and a proud heart, will not I ſuffer.

6 Mine eyes *ſhall be* vpon the faithfull of the land, that they may dwell with me : he that walketh ||in a perfect way, he ſhall ſerue me.

7 He that worketh deceit, ſhall not dwell within my houſe : he that telleth lies †ſhall not tarie in my ſight.

8 I will earely deſtroy all the wicked of the land : that I may cut off all wicked doers from the citie of the LORD.

¶ A prayer ||of the afflicted when he is ouerwhelmed, and powreth out his complaint before the LORD.

Eare my prayer, O LORD : and let my crie come vnto thee.

2 Hide not thy face from me in the day *when* I am in trouble, incline thine eare vnto me : in the day *when* I call, anſwere mee ſpeedily.

3 For my dayes are conſumed ||like ſmoke : and my bones are burnt as an hearth.

4 My heart is ſmitten, and withered like graſſe : ſo that I forget to eate my bread.

5 By reaſon of the voice of my groning, my bones cleaue to my ||ſkinne.

6 I am like a Pelican of the wilderneſ : I am like an owle of the deſert.

7 I watch, and am as a ſparowe alone vpon the houſe top.

8 Mine enemies reproch me all the day : *and* they that are mad againſt me, are ſworne againſt me.

9 For I haue eaten aſhes like bread : and mingled my drinke with weeping.

10 Becauſe of thine indignation and thy wrath : for thou haſt lifted me vp, and caſt me downe.

11 *My dayes *are* like a ſhadow, *that*

declineth : & I am withered like graſſe.

12 But thou, O LORD, ſhalt endure for euer : and thy remembrance vnto all generations.

13 Thou ſhalt ariſe, *and* haue mercie vpon Zion : for the time to fauour her, yea the ſet time is come.

14 For thy ſeruants take pleaſure in her ſtones : and fauour the duſt therof.

15 So the heathen ſhall feare the Name of the LORD : and all the kings of the earth thy glory.

16 When the LORD ſhall build vp Zion : he ſhall appeare in his glory.

17 He will regard the prayer of the deſtitute, and not deſpiſe their prayer.

18 This ſhall be written for the generation to come : and the people which ſhall be created, ſhall praiſe the LORD.

19 For hee hath looked downe from the height of his Sanctuarie : from heauen did the LORD beholde the earth :

20 To heare the groning of the priſoner : to looſe †thoſe that are appointed to death :

21 To declare the Name of the LORD in Zion : and his praiſe in Ieruſalem :

22 When the people are gathered together : and the kingdomes to ſerue the LORD.

23 He †weakened my ſtrength in the way : he ſhortened my dayes.

24 I ſaid, O my God, take me not away in the midſt of my dayes : thy yeres are throughout all generations.

25 *Of old haſt thou laid the foundation of the earth : and the heauens *are* the worke of thy hands.

26 They ſhall periſh, but thou ſhalt †indure, yea all of them ſhall waxe old like a garment : as a veſture ſhalt thou change them, and they ſhalbe changed.

27 But thou *art* the ſame : and thy yeeres ſhall haue no end.

28 The children of thy ſeruants ſhal continue : and their ſeed ſhall be eſtabliſhed before thee.

¶ *A Pſalme* of Dauid.

Leſſe the LORD, O my ſoule : and all that is within me, *bleſſe* his holy Name.

2 Bleſſe the LORD, O my ſoule : & forget not all his benefits.

3 Who

Marginal notes

, perfect he way.

eb. ſhall be eſtabliſhed.

, for.

(as reade) ſmoke.

fleſh.

† *Heb. the children of death.*

† *Heb. affli-cted.*

* Heb. 1. 10

† *Heb. ſtand*

* 40. 6. 1. 10.

3 Who forgiueth all thine iniquities: who healeth all thy diseases.

4 Who redeemeth thy life from destruction: who crowneth thee with louing kindnesse and tender mercies.

5 Who satisfieth thy mouth with good things: *so that* thy youth is renewed like the Eagles.

6 The LORD executeth righteousnesse: and iudgement for all that are oppressed.

7 He made knowen his wayes vnto Moses: his actes vnto the children of Israel.

8 * The LORD *is* mercifull and gracious: slow to anger, and †plenteous in mercy.

9 Hee will not alwayes chide: neither will he keepe *his anger* for euer.

10 Hee hath not dealt with vs after our sinnes: nor rewarded vs according to our iniquities.

11 For †as the heauen is high aboue the earth: *so* great is his mercy toward them that feare him.

12 As farre as the East is from the West: *so* farre hath hee remooued our transgressions from vs.

13 Like as a father pitieth *his* children: *so* the LORD pitieth them that feare him.

14 For he knoweth our frame: hee remembreth that we are dust.

15 As for man, his dayes *are* as grasse: as a flower of the field, so he flourisheth.

16 For the winde passeth ouer it, and †it is gone; and the place thereof shall know it no more.

17 But the mercy of the LORD *is* from euerlasting to euerlasting vpon them that feare him: and his righteousnesse vnto childrens children:

18 * To such as keepe his couenant: and to those that remember his commandements to doe them.

19 The LORD hath prepared his throne in the heauens: and his kingdome ruleth ouer all.

20 Blesse the LORD yee his Angels, †that excell in strength, that do his commandements: hearkening vnto the voice of his word.

21 Blesse ye the LORD all yee his hostes: ye ministers of his that doe his pleasure.

22 Blesse the LORD all his works in all places of his dominion: blesse the LORD, O my soule.

Margin left column:
* Exod. 34. 7. deut. 34. 6 nnm. 14. 18 neh. 9. 17. psal. 86. 15. ier. 32. 18.
† Heb. great of mercie.

† Heb. according to the height of the heauen.

† Heb. it is not.

* Deut. 7. 9.

† Heb. mighty in strength.

PSAL. CIIII.

1 A meditation vpon the mighty power, 7 and wonderfull prouidence of God. 31 Gods glory is eternall. 33 The Prophet voweth perpetually to praise God.

 Lesse the LORD, O my soule, O LORD my God, thou art very great: thou art clothed with honour and maiestie.

2 Who coucrest *thy selfe* with light, as *with* a garment: who stretchest out the heauens like a curtaine.

3 Who layeth the beames of his chambers in the waters, who maketh the cloudes his charet: who walketh vpon the wings of the wind.

4 * Who maketh his Angels spirits: his ministers a flaming fire.

5 † Who laid the foundations of the earth: *that* it should not be remoued for euer.

6 Thou coueredst it with the deepe as *with* a garment: the waters stood aboue the mountaines.

7 At thy rebuke they fled: at the voice of thy thunder they hasted away.

8 ‖ They go vp by the mountaines: they goe downe by the valleys vnto the place which thou hast founded for them.

9 Thou hast set a bound that they may not passe ouer: that they turne not againe to couer the earth.

10 † He sendeth the springs into the valleys: *which* †runne among the hilles.

11 They giue drinke to euery beast of the field: the wild asses †quench their thirst.

12 By them shall the foules of the heauen haue their habitation: *which* †sing among the branches.

13 He watereth the hilles from his chambers: the earth is satisfied with the fruit of thy workes.

14 He causeth the grasse to grow for the cattell, and herbe for the seruice of man: * that he may bring forth food out of the earth:

15 And wine that maketh glad the heart of man, and †oile to make *his* face to shine: and bread *which* strengtheneth mans heart.

16 The trees of the LORD are full *of sappe:* the cedars of Lebanon which he hath planted.

17 Where the birds make their nests: as for the Storke, the firre trees *are* her house.

Margin right column:
* Heb. 1. 7.

† Hebr. he hath founded the earth vpon her bases.

‖ Or, the mountaine ascend, the valleys descend.

† Hebr. wh sendeth.
† Heb. wal

† Heb. bre

† Heb. gi a voyce.

* Iosh. 9.

† Hebr. t make his face shin with oyle or more l oyle.

18 The

18 The hie hilles *are* a refuge for the wilde goates : *and* the rockes for the conies.

19 He appointed the moone for seasons ; the sunne knoweth his going downe.

20 Thou makest darkenesse, and it is night : wherein † all the beasts of the forrest doe creepe *forth*.

eb. all the sts there- loe tram- on the rest.

21 The young lyons roare after their pray : and seeke their meate from God.

22 The sunne ariseth, they gather themselues together : and lay them downe in their dennes.

23 Man goeth forth vnto his worke : and to his labour, vntill the euening.

24 O LORD, how manifold are thy workes! in wisedome hast thou made them all : the earth is full of thy riches.

25 *So is* this great and wide Sea, wherein are things creeping innumerable : both small and great beasts.

26 There goe the shippes ; *there is* that Leuiathan, *whom* thou hast † made to play therein.

eb. for- d.

sal. 145.

27 * These waite all vpon thee : that thou mayest giue them their meate in due season.

28 That thou giuest them, they gather : thou openest thine hand, they are filled with good.

29 Thou hidest thy face, they are troubled, thou takest away their breath, they die : and returne to their dust.

30 Thou sendest forth thy spirit, they are created : and thou renewest the face of the earth.

31 The glory of the LORD † shall endure for euer : the LORD shall reioyce in his workes.

eb. shalbe.

32 Hee looketh on the earth, and it trembleth ; he toucheth the hilles, and they smoke.

33 I will sing vnto the LORD as long as I liue : I will sing praise to my God, while I haue my being.

34 My meditation of him shalbe sweete : I will be glad in the LORD.

35 Let the sinners be consumed out of the earth, and let the wicked bee no more : blesse thou the LORD, O my soule. Praise yee the LORD.

PSAL CV.

1 An exhortation to praise God, and to seeke out his workes. 7 The story of Gods proui-

dence ouer Abraham, 16 Ouer Ioseph, 23 Ouer Iacob in Egypt, 26 Ouer Moses deliuering the Israelites, 37 Ouer the Israelites brought out of Egypt, fed in the wildernesse, and planted in Canaan.

O Giue * thankes vnto the LORD, call vpon his name : make knowen his deeds among the people.

*1. Chron. 16. 8. Esay. 12. 4.

2 Sing vnto him ; sing Psalmes vnto him : talke yee of all his wondrous workes.

3 Glory yee in his holy name : let the heart of them reioyce, that seeke the LORD.

4 Seeke the LORD, and his strength : seeke his face euermore.

5 Remember his maruellous workes, that hee hath done : his wonders, and the iudgements of his mouth,

6 O yee seede of Abraham his seruant : yee children of Iacob his chosen.

7 He *is* the LORD our God : his iudgements *are* in all the earth.

8 He hath remembred his couenant for euer : the word *which* he commanded to a thousand generations.

9 * Which *couenant* he made with Abraham, and his oath vnto Isaac :

* Gen. 17. 2. & 22. 16. and 26. 3. & 28. 13. & 35. 11. Luc. 1. 7, 73 Heb. 6. 17.

10 And confirmed the same vnto Iacob for a law : *and* to Israel *for* an euerlasting couenant :

11 * Saying, Vnto thee will I giue the land of Canaan : † the lot of your inheritance.

* Gen. 13. 15. & 15. 10. † Heb. the corde.

12 When they were *but* a few men in number : yea very few, & strangers in it.

13 When they went from one nation to another : from *one* kingdome to another people.

14 He suffred no man to doe them wrong : yea he reproued kings for their sakes :

15 *Saying*, Touch not mine anointed ; and doe my Prophets no harme.

16 Moreouer hee called for a famine vpon the land : he brake the whole staffe of bread.

17 Hee sent a man before them : * *euen* Ioseph, *who* was sold for a seruant.

* Gen. 37. 28.

18 * Whose feete they hurt with fetters : † he was layd in iron.

* Gen. 39. 20. † Heb. his soule came into yron.

19 Vntill the time that his word came : the word of the LORD tried him.

20 * The king sent and loosed him : *euen* the ruler of the people, and let him goe free.

* Gen. 41. 14.

21 * Hee made him lord of his house : and

* Gen. 41. 40.

† *Hebr. possession.*

and ruler of all his †substance:

22 To binde his princes at his pleasure : and teach his Senatours wisedome.

* *Gene. 46. 6.*

23 * Israel also came into Egypt : and Iacob soiourned in the land of Ham.

24 And hee increased his people greatly : and made them stronger then their enemies.

* *Exod. 1. 8.*

25 * He turned their heart to hate his people : to deale subtilly with his seruants.

* *Exod. 3. 10.*

26 * Hee sent Moses his seruant : *and* Aaron whom he had chosen.

* *Exod. 7. 9.*
† *Heb. words of his signes.*

27 * They shewed his †signes among them : and wonders in the land of Ham.

* *Exod. 10. 22.*

28 * Hee sent darknesse, and made it darke : and they rebelled not against his word.

* *Exod. 7. 20.*

29 * He turned their waters into blood : and slew their fish.

* *Exod. 8. 6.*

30 * The land brought foorth frogs in abundance : in the chambers of their kings.

* *Exod. 8. 17. and 24.*

31 * He spake, and there came diuers sorts of flies : *and* lice in all their coasts.

* *Exod. 9. 23.*
† *Hebr. he gaue their raine, haile.*

32 * † Hee gaue them haile for raine : *and* flaming fire in their laud.

33 Hee smote their Vines also, and their figge trees : and brake the trees of their coastes.

* *Exod. 10. 4.*

34 * He spake, and the locusts came : and catterpillers, and that without number,

35 And did eate vp all the herbes in their land : and deuoured the fruite of their ground.

* *Exod. 12. 29.*

36 * Hee smote also all the first borne in their land : the chiefe of all their strength.

* *Exod. 12. 29.*

37 * Hee brought them foorth also with siluer and gold : and *there was* not one feeble person among their tribes.

* *Exod. 12. 33.*

38 * Egypt was glad when they departed : for the feare of them fell vpon them.

* *Exod. 13. 21.*

39 * He spread a cloud for a couering : and fire to giue light in the night.

* *Exod. 16. 12.*

40 * *The people* asked, and he brought quailes : and satisfied them with the bread of heauen.

* *Exod. 17. 6. num. 20. 11. 1. cor. 10. 4.*

41 * He opened the rocke, and the waters gushed out : they ranne in the dry places *like* a riuer.

42 For he remembred his holy promise : *and* Abraham his seruant.

43 And he brought forth his people

with ioy : *and* his chosen with † gladnesse :

† *Heb. ging.*

44 * And gaue them the lands of the heathen : and they inherited the labour of the people :

* *Iosh. 17. de 10.*

45 That they might obserue his statutes, and keepe his Lawes. Praise ye the LORD.

PSAL. CVI.

1 The Psalmist exhorteth to praise God. 4 He prayeth for pardon of sinne, as God did with the fathers. 7 The storie of the peoples rebellion, and Gods merciè. 47 Hee concludeth with prayer, and praise.

P†Raise ye the LORD. O * giue thankes vnto the LORD, for he *is* good : for his mercie *endureth* for euer.

† *Heb. leluia*
* *Psal. 1. 118 and 13*

2 * Who can vtter the mighty acts of the LORD? *who* can shew foorth all his praise?

* *Iud. 21.*

3 Blessed *are they* that keepe iudgement : *and* he that doeth righteousnesse at all times.

4 Remember me, O LORD, with the fauour *that thou bearest vnto* thy people : O visite me with thy saluation :

5 That I may see the good of thy chosen, that I may reioyce in the gladnesse of thy nation : that I may glory with thine inheritance.

6 * Wee haue sinned with our fathers : we haue committed iniquitie, we haue done wickedly.

* *Iud. 19.*

7 Our fathers vnderstood not thy wonders in Egypt, they remembred not the multitude of thy mercies : * but prouoked *him* at the sea, *euen* at the Red-sea.

* *Exe 11, 12*

8 Neuerthelesse hee saued them for his Names sake : that hee might make his mighty power to be knowen.

9 He rebuked the Red sea also, and it was dried vp : so hee led them through the depthes, as through the wildernes.

10 And he saued them from the hand of him that hated *them* : and redeemed them from the hand of the enemie.

* *Exe 27. an 5.*

11 * And the waters couered their enemies : there was not one of them left.

* *Exe 31. & * Exe 14. &*

12 * Then beleeued they his words : they sang his praise.

† *Heb made they.*

13 * † They soone forgate his works : they waited not for his counsell :

* *Exe 2. 1. 6.*
† *Heb*

14 * But † lusted exceedingly in the wildernes : & tempted God in the desert.

† *Heb a lus*

15 * And

um. 11.
15 * And he gaue them their request : but sent leannesse into their soule.

um. 16.
16 * They enuied Moses also in the campe : *and* Aaron the Saint of the LORD.

umb. 16
leut.
5.
17 * The earth opened and swallowed vp Dathan : and couered the company of Abiram.

um. 16.
and 46.
18 * And a fire was kindled in their company : the flame burnt vp the wicked.

xo. 32. 4
19 * They made a calfe in Horeb : and worshipped the molten image.

20 Thus they changed their glory, into the similitude of an oxe that eateth grasse.

21 They forgate God their Sauiour : which had done great things in Egypt :

22 Wonderous workes in the lande of Ham : *and* terrible things by the red Sea.

xod. 33.
23 * Therefore he said that he would destroy them, had not Moses his chosen stood before him in the breach : to turne away his wrath, lest hee should destroy *them*.

ebr. a
d of de-
24 Yea, they despised † the pleasant land : they beleeued not his word :

um. 14.
25 * But murmured in their tents : *and* hearkened not vnto the voyce of the LORD.

26 Therefore he lifted vp his hande against them : to ouerthrow them in the wildernesse :

eb. to
se them
27 † To ouerthrow their seed also among the nations, and to scatter them in the lands.

um. 25.
28 * They ioyned themselues also vnto Baal-Peor : and ate the sacrifices of the dead.

29 Thus they prouoked *him* to anger with their inuentions : and the plague brake in vpon them.

um. 25.
30 * Then stood vp Phinehas, and executed iudgement : and *so* the plague was stayed.

31 And that was counted vnto him for righteousnesse : vnto all generations for euermore.

um. 20.
32 * They angred *him* also at the waters of strife : so that it went ill with Moses for their sakes :

33 Because they prouoked his spirit : so that hee spake vnaduisedly with his lippes.

eut. 7. 1.
34 * They did not destroy the nations, concerning whom the LORD commanded them :

udg. 1. 21
35 * But were mingled among the heathen, and learned their workes.

36 And they serued their idoles : which were a snare vnto them.

37 Yea they sacrificed their sonnes, and their daughters vnto deuils,

38 And shed innocent blood, *euen* the blood of their sons and of their daughters, whome they sacrificed vnto the idoles of Canaan : and the land was polluted with blood.

39 Thus were they defiled with their owne works : and went a whoring with their owne inuentions.

40 Therefore was the wrath of the LORD kindled against his people : insomuch that he abhorred his owne inheritance.

41 And he gaue them into the hand of the heathen : and they that hated them, ruled ouer them.

42 Their enemies also oppressed them : and they were brought into subiection vnder their hand.

43 * Many times did he deliuer them : but they prouoked *him* with their counsell, and were ‖ brought low for their iniquitie.

* Iudg. 2.
16.
‖ Or, impo-
uerished, or
weakened.

44 Neuertheles he regarded their affliction : when he heard their crie.

* Deu. 30. 2
45 * And hee remembred for them his couenant : and repented according to the multitude of his mercies.

46 He made them also to be pitied, of all those that caried them captiues.

47 Saue vs, O LORD our God, and gather vs from among the heathen to giue thankes vnto thy holy Name : *and* to triumph in thy praise.

48 Blessed *bee* the LORD God of Israel from euerlasting to euerlasting : and let all the people say, Amen. Praise ye the LORD.

PSAL. CVII.

1 The Psalmist exhorteth the redeemed, in praising God, to obserue his manifold prouidence 4 Ouer trauailers, 10 ouer captiues, 17 ouer sicke men, 23 ouer Sea men, 33 and in diuers varieties of life.

* Giue thankes vnto the LORD, for hee *is* good : for his mercie *endureth* for euer.

* Psa. 106. 1
& 118. 1. &
136. 1.

2 Let the redeemed of the LORD say *so* : whome he hath redeemed from the hand of the enemie :

3 And gathered them out of the lands, from the East and from the West :

† *Heb. from the sea.*

West : from the North and †from the South.

4 They wandred in the wildernes, in a solitary way : they found no citie to dwell in.

5 Hungry and thirstie : their soule fainted in them.

6 Then they cryed vnto the LORD in their trouble : *and* he deliuered them out of their distresses.

7 And hee led them forth by the right way : that they might goe to a citie of habitation.

8 Oh that *men* would praise the LORD, for his goodnesse : and for his wonderfull workes to the children of men.

9 For he satisfieth the longing soule : and filleth the hungry soule with goodnesse.

10 Such as sit in darkenesse and in the shadowe of death : being bound in affliction and yron :

11 Because they rebelled against the words of God : and contemned the counsell of the most high :

12 Therefore hee brought downe their heart with labour : they fel downe, and *there was* none to helpe.

13 Then they cryed vnto the LORD in their trouble : *and* he saued them out of their distresses.

14 Hee brought them out of darkenesse, and the shadowe of death : and brake their bands in sunder.

15 Oh that *men* would praise the LORD for his goodnesse : and for his wonderfull workes to the children of men.

16 For he hath broken the gates of brasse : and cut the barres of yron in sunder.

17 Fooles, because of their transgression, and because of their iniquities, are afflicted.

* Iob. 33. 20.

18 * Their soule abhorreth all manner of meate : and they drawe neere vnto the gates of death.

19 Then they crie vnto the LORD in their trouble : he saueth them out of their distresses.

20 Hee sent his word, and healed them : and deliuered them from their destructions.

21 Oh that *men* would praise the LORD for his goodnesse : and for his wonderfull workes, to the children of men.

22 And let them sacrifice the sacrifices of thankesgiuing : and declare his workes with †reioycing.

23 They that goe downe to the sea in shippes : that doe businesse in great waters :

24 These see the workes of the LORD : and his wonders in the deepe.

25 For he commandeth, and †raiseth the stormy winde : which lifteth vp the waues thereof.

26 They mount vp to the heauen : they goe downe againe to the depthes : their soule is melted because of trouble.

27 They reele to and fro, and stagger like a drunken man ; and †are at their wits end.

28 Then they cry vnto the LORD in their trouble : and hee bringeth them out of their distresses.

29 He maketh the storme a calme : so that the waues thereof are still.

30 Then are they glad, because they be quiet : so he bringeth them vnto their desired hauen.

31 Oh that *men* would praise the LORD for his goodnesse ; and for his wonderfull workes to the children of men :

32 Let them exalt him also in the congregation of the people, and praise him in the assembly of the Elders.

33 Hee turneth riuers into a wildernesse : and the water springs into dry ground :

34 A fruitfull land into † barrennesse ; for the wickednesse of them that dwell therein.

35 * He turneth the wildernesse into a standing water : and dry ground into water-springs.

36 And there he maketh the hungry to dwell ; that they may prepare a citie for habitation,

37 And sowe the fields, and plant vineyards ; which may yeeld fruits of increase.

38 He blesseth them also, so that they are multiplied greatly : and suffreth not their cattell to decrease.

39 Againe, they are minished and brought lowe through oppression, affliction and sorrow.

40 * Hee powreth contempt vpon princes : and causeth them to wander in the ‖ wildernesse, *where there is* no way.

41 * Yet setteth he the poore on high ‖from affliction : and maketh *him* families like a flocke.

42 * The‖

† *Heb. ging.*

† *Heb. kethkos*

† *Heb. their w dome is lowed t*

† *Heb. nesse.*

* *Isa.* 18.

* *Iob.* 21.

‖ *Or, v place.*
* 1. Sa
8. psal.
7. & 8.
‖ *Or, a*

* Iob 22.
19. and 5.
16.

42 * The righteous shall see it, and reioyce; and all iniquitie shall stop her mouth.

43 Who so is wise, and will obserue those things; euen they shall vnderstand the louing kindenesse of the LORD.

PSAL. CVIII.

1 Dauid incourageth himselfe to praise God. 5 Hee prayeth for Gods assistance according to his promise. 11 His confidence in Gods helpe.

¶ A song or Psalme of Dauid.

O God, my heart is fixed: I will sing & giue praise, euen with my glory.

2 Awake psaltery and harpe : I my selfe will awake early.

3 I will praise thee, O LORD, among the people: and I wil sing praises vnto thee among the nations.

4 For thy mercy is great aboue the heauens : and thy trueth reacheth vnto the ‖ clouds.

Or, skies.
* Psal. 60. 7.

5 * Be thou exalted, O God, aboue the heauens : and thy glory aboue all the earth :

6 That thy beloued may bee deliuered : saue with thy right hand, and answere me.

7 God hath spoken in his holinesse, I wil reioyce, I wil diuide Shechem : and mete out the valley of Succoth.

8 Gilead is mine, Manasseh is mine, Ephraim also is the strength of mine head : Iudah is my Lawgiuer.

9 Moab is my wash-pot, ouer Edom wil I cast out my shooe: ouer Philistia will I triumph.

10 Who wil bring me into the strong citie ? who will leade me into Edom ?

11 Wilt not thou, O God, who hast cast vs off? and wilt not thou, O God, goe foorth with our hostes ?

12 Giue vs helpe from trouble : for vaine is the helpe of man.

13 Through God wee shall doe valiantly: for hee it is that shall tread downe our enemies.

PSAL. CIX.

1 Dauid complayning of his slanderous enemies, vnder the person of Iudas deuoteth them. 16 He sheweth their sinne. 21 Complayning of his owne misery, hee prayeth for helpe. 29 He promiseth thankfulnesse.

¶ To the chiefe Musician, A Psalme of Dauid.

H Old not thy peace, O God of my praise.

2 For the mouth of the wicked, and the † mouth of the deceitfull † are opened against mee : they haue spoken against me with a lying tongue.

† Hebr.
mouth of de-
ceit.
† Hebr. haue
openedthem-
selues.

3 They compassed mee about also with wordes of hatred : and fought against me without a cause.

4 For my loue, they are my aduersaries : but I giue my selfe vnto prayer.

5 And they haue rewarded me euill for good : and hatred for my loue.

6 Set thou a wicked man ouer him : and let ‖ Satan stand at his right hand.

‖ Or, an ad-
uersary.

7 When he shall be iudged, let him be † condemned : and let his prayer become sinne.

† Hebr. goe
out guiltie,
or wicked.

8 * Let his dayes be few : and let another take his ‖ office.

* Act. 1. 20.
‖ Or, charge.

9 Let his children bee fatherlesse : and his wife a widow.

10 Let his children bee continually vagabonds, & begge: let them seeke their bread also out of their desolate places.

11 Let the extortioner catch all that he hath : and let the strangers spoile his labour.

12 Let there be none to extend mercy vnto him : neither let there be any to fauour his fatherlesse children.

13 Let his posteritie be cut off: and in the generation folowing let their name be blotted out.

14 Let the iniquitie of his fathers be remembred with the LORD: and let not the sinne of his mother be blotted out.

15 Let them be before the LORD continually : that he may cut off the memory of them from the earth.

16 Because that he remembred not to shew mercy, but persecuted the poore and needy man : that he might euen slay the broken in heart.

17 As he loued cursing, so let it come vnto him: as hee delighted not in blessing, so let it be farre from him.

18 As he clothed himselfe with cursing like as with his garment : so let it come into † his bowels like water, and like oyle into his bones.

† Heb. with-
in him.

19 Let it be vnto him as the garment which couereth him : and for a girdle wherewith he is girded continually.

20 Let

20 Let this be the reward of mine aduersaries from the LORD: and of them that speake euill against my soule.

21 But do thou for me, O GOD the Lord, for thy Names sake: because thy mercie *is* good: deliuer thou me.

22 For I am poore *and* needie: and my heart is wounded within me.

23 I am gone like the shadow, when it declineth: I am tossed vp and downe as the locust.

24 My knees are weake through fasting: and my flesh faileth of fatnesse.

25 I became also a reproch vnto them: *when* they looked vpon me, they shaked their heads.

26 Helpe me, O LORD my God: O saue me according to thy mercie.

27 That they may know, that this *is* thy hand: *that* thou, LORD, hast done it.

28 Let them curse, but blesse tnou: when they arise, let them be ashamed, but let thy seruant reioyce.

29 Let mine aduersaries be clothed with shame: and let them couer them selues with their owne confusion, as with a mantle.

30 I will greatly praise the LORD with my mouth: yea I will praise him among the multitude.

31 For he shal stand at the right hand of the poore: to saue *him* †from those that condemne his soule.

† *Heb. from the iudges of his soule.*

PSAL. CX.

1 The Kingdome, 4 The Priesthood, 5 The conquest, 7 And the passion of Christ.

¶ A Psalme of Dauid.

HE *LORD said vnto my Lord, Sit thou at my right hand: vntil I make thine enemies thy footestoole.

* Mätt. 22. 44. mar. 12. 36. luk. 20. 42. acts 2. 34. 1. cor. 15. 25. heb. 1. 13.

2 The LORD shall send the rod of thy strength out of Zion: rule thou in the midst of thine enemies.

3 Thy people *shalbe* willing in the day of thy power, in the beauties of holinesse ||from the wombe of the morning: thou hast the dew of thy youth.

‖ *Or, more then the wombe of the morning: thou shalt haue, &c.* * *Heb. 5. 6. and 7. 17.*

4 *The LORD hath sworne, and will not repent, thou *art* a Priest for euer: after the order of Melchizedek.

5 The Lord at thy right hand shall strike through kings in the day of his wrath.

6 He shal iudge among the heathen,

he shal fil *the places* with the dead bodies: he shall wound the heads ouer ||many countries.

‖ *Or, great.*

7 He shall drinke of the brooke in the way: therefore shall hee lift vp the head.

PSAL. CXI.

1 The Psalmist by his example inciteth others to praise God, for his glorious, 5 And gracious workes. 10 The feare of God breedeth true wisedome.

P †Raise yee the LORD. I will praise the LORD with *my* whole heart: in the assembly of the vpright, and *in* the Congregation.

† *Heb. Halleluiah.*

2 The workes of the LORD *are* great: sought out of all them that haue pleasure therein.

3 His worke *is* honourable and glorious: and his righteousnesse endureth for euer.

4 Hee hath made his wonderfull works to be remembred: the LORD *is* gracious, and full of compassion.

5 He hath giuen †meate vnto them that feare him: he will euer be mindfull of his couenant.

† *Heb. pr*

6 He hath shewed his people the power of his workes: that he may giue them the heritage of the heathen.

7 The works of his hands *are* veritie and iudgment: all his commandements are sure.

8 They †stand fast for euer and euer: *and* are done in trueth and vprightnes.

† *Heb. a stablishe*

9 He sent redemption vnto his people, hee hath commanded his couenant for euer: holy and reuerend is his Name.

10 *The feare of the LORD *is* the beginning of wisedome, ||a good vnderstanding haue all they †that doe *his commandements:* his praise endureth for euer.

* *Iob. 2 pro. 1. 7 9. 10. eccles.* ‖ *Or, go successe* † *Heb. doe the*

PSAL. CXII.

1 Godlinesse hath the promises of this life, 4 And of the life to come. 10 The prosperitie of the godly, shalbe an eye-sore to the wicked

P †Raise ye the LORD. Blessed *is* the man *that* feareth the LORD, that delighteth greatly in his Commaundements.

† *Heb. leluiah.*

2 His seed shall bee mightie vpon earth:

earth : the generation of the vpright shalbe blessed.

3 Wealth and riches *shalbe* in his house : and his righteousnesse endureth for euer.

4 Vnto the vpright there ariseth light in the darknesse : hee *is* gracious, and full of compassion, and righteous.

5 A good man sheweth fauour and lendeth : he will guide his affaires with † discretion.

Heb. iudgement.

6 Surely he shall not be moued for euer : the righteous shalbe in euerlasting remembrance.

7 He shall not be afraid of euill tidings : his heart is fixed, trusting in the LORD.

8 His heart *is* established, hee shall not be afraid, vntill he see *his desire* vpon his enemies.

2. Cor. 9. 9.

9 * He hath dispersed, he hath giuen to the poore : his righteousnesse endureth for euer ; his horne shalbe exalted with honour.

10 The wicked shall see *it*, and be grieued ; he shall gnash with his teeth, and melt away : the desire of the wicked shall perish.

PSAL. CXIII.

1 An exhortation to praise God for his excellencie, 6 for his Mercy.

Heb. Halleluiah.

†Raise yee the LORD. Praise, O yee seruants of the LORD : praise the name of the LORD.

Dan. 2. 0.

2 * Blessed *be* the name of the LORD : from this time forth and for euermore.

Mal. 1. 11.

3 * From the rising of the sunne vnto the going downe of the same : the LORDS name *is* to be praised.

4 The LORD *is* high aboue all nations : *and* his glory aboue the heauens.

5 Who *is* like vnto the LORD our God : who †dwelleth on high :

Heb. exalteth himselfe to dwell.

6 Who humbleth himselfe to behold *the things that are* in heauen, and in the earth ?

1. Sam. 2, 8. psal. 107. 41.

7 * He raiseth vp the poore out of the dust : *and* lifteth the needie out of the dung-hill :

8 That he may set *him* with princes : *euen* with the princes of his people.

Heb. to dwell in an house.

9 He maketh the barren woman †to keepe house ; to be a ioyfull mother of children : Praise yee the LORD.

PSAL. CXIII.

An exhortation by the example of the dumbe creatures, to feare God in his Church.

Exod. 13. 3.

* Hen Israel went out of Egypt, the house of Iacob from a people of strange language :

2 Iudah was his sanctuarie : *and* Israel his dominion.

Exod. 14. 21. Iosh. 3. 13.

3 * The sea sawe *it*, and fled : Iordan was driuen backe.

4 The mountaines skipped like rammes : *and* the little hilles like lambes.

5 What *ailed* thee, O thou sea, that thou fleddest ? thou Iordan, that thou wast driuen backe ?

6 Yee mountaines, *that* yee skipped like rammes : *and* yee little hilles like lambes ?

7 Tremble thou earth at the presence of the Lord : at the presence of the God of Iacob :

Exod. 17. 6. Num. 20. 11.

8 * Which turned the rocke into a standing water : the flint into a fountaine of waters.

PSAL. CXV.

1 Because God is truly glorious, 4 and Idols are vanity, 9 He exhorteth to confidence in God. 12 God is to be blessed for his blessings.

Ot vnto vs, O LORD, not vnto vs, but vnto thy name giue glory : for thy mercy, *and* for thy truthes sake.

Psal. 42. 10. & 79. 10.

2 * Wherefore should the heathen say : Where is now their God ?

Psal. 135. 6

3 * But our God *is* in the heauens : he hath done whatsoeuer he pleased.

Psal. 135. 15.

4 * Their idoles *are* siluer and gold : the worke of mens hands.

5 They *haue* mouths, but they speake not ; eies *haue* they, but they see not.

6 They *haue* eares, but they heare not : noses *haue* they, but they smell not.

7 They *haue* hands, *but* they handle not, feete *haue* they, but they walke not : neither speake they through their throat.

8 They that make them are like vnto them : *so* is euery one that trusteth in them.

9 O Israel, trust thou in the LORD : he *is* their helpe and their shield.

10 O house of Aaron, trust in the LORD : he *is* their helpe & their shield.

11 Yee

11 Ye that feare the Lord trust in the Lord : he *is* their helpe and their shield.

12 The Lord hath bene mindfull of vs, he will blesse *vs*, he will blesse the house of Israel : he will blesse the house of Aaron.

13 Hee will blesse them that feare the Lord : †*both* small and great.

† *Hebr. with.*

14 The Lord shall increase you more and more : you and your children.

15 You *are* blessed of the Lord : which made heauen and earth.

16 The heauen, *euen* the heauens *are* the Lords : but the earth hath hee giuen to the children of men.

17 The dead praise not the Lord : neither any that go downe into silence.

* *Dan. 2. 20.*

18 * But we will blesse the Lord, from this time foorth and for euermore. Praise the Lord.

PSAL. CXVI.

1 The Psalmist professeth his loue and duetie to God, for his deliuerance. 12 Hee studieth to be thankfull.

I Loue the Lord : because hee hath heard my voice, & my supplications.

2 Because hee hath inclined his eare vnto mee : therefore will I call vpon *him* †as long as I liue.

† *Hebr. in my dayes.*

* *Psal. 18. 5. 6.*
† *Hebr. found me.*

3 * The sorrowes of death compassed me, and the paines of hell †gatehold vpon me : I found trouble and sorrow.

4 Then called I vpon the Name of the Lord : O Lord, I beseech thee deliuer my soule.

5 Gracious is the Lord, and righteous : yea our God is mercifull.

6 The Lord preserueth the simple : I was brought low, and hee helped me.

7 Returne vnto thy rest, O my soule : for the Lord hath dealt bountifully with thee.

8 For thou hast deliuered my soule from death, mine eyes from teares, *and* my feete from falling.

9 I wil walke before the Lord : in the land of the liuing.

* *2. Cor. 4. 13.*

10 * I beleeued, therfore haue I spoken : I was greatly afflicted.

* *Rom. 3. 4.*

11 I said in my haste : * All men are lyers.

12 What shall I render vnto the Lord : *for* all his benefits towards mee ?

13 I will take the cup of saluation : and call vpon the Name of the Lord.

14 I will pay my vowes vnto the Lord : now in the presence of all his people.

15 Precious in ỹ sight of the Lord : *is* the death of his Saints.

16 Oh Lord, truely I *am* thy seruant, I *am* thy seruant, *and* the sonne of thy handmayde : thou hast loosed my bonds.

17 I will offer to thee the sacrifice of thankes-giuing : and will call vpon the Name of the Lord.

18 I will pay my vowes vnto the Lord : now in the presence of all his people :

19 In the Courts of the Lords house, in the middes of thee, O Ierusalem. Praise ye the Lord.

PSAL. CXVII.

An exhortation to praise God for his mercie and trueth.

* *Rom. 15 11.*

O * Praise the Lord, all ye nations : praise him all ye people.

2 For his merciful kindnesse is great toward vs : and the trueth of the Lord *endureth* for euer. Praise ye the Lord.

PSAL. CXVIII.

1 An exhortation to praise God for his mercie. 5 The Psalmist by his experience sheweth how good it is to trust in God. 19 Vnder the type of the Psalmist, the comming of Christ in his kingdome is expressed.

* *Psal. 10 1. and 10 1. & 136. 1. chron. 7.*

O * Giue thankes vnto the Lord, for hee *is* good : because his mercie *endureth* for euer.

2 Let Israel now say : that his mercy *endureth* for euer.

3 Let the house of Aaron now say : that his mercy *endureth* for euer.

4 Let them now that feare the Lord, say : that his mercy *endureth* for euer.

* *Hebr. of distres*

5 I called vpon the Lord †in distresse : the Lord answered me, *and* set *me* in a large place.

* *Heb. 1 psal. 56. 11.*
† *Hebr. me.*

6 * The Lord *is* †on my side, I will not feare : What can man doe vnto mee ?

7 The Lord taketh my part with them that helpe me : therfore shall I see

* Pſal. 146.

Hebr. cut
ſem off.

Hebr. cut
owne.

Exod. 15.
Iſa. 12. 2.

at. 21. 42
. 12. 10.
. 20. 17.
4. 11.
ct. 2. 4.
b. this
m the
RD.

at. 21. 9.

I ſee *my deſire* vpon them that hate me.

8 It *is* better to truſt in the LORD: then to put confidence in man.

9 *It *is* better to truſt in the LORD: then to put confidence in Princes.

10 All nations compaſſed me about: but in the Name of the LORD, will I † deſtroy them.

11 They compaſſed mee about, yea they compaſſed mee about: *but* in the Name of the LORD, I will deſtroy them.

12 They compaſſed mee about like Bees, they are quenched as the fire of thornes: for in the Name of the LORD I wil † deſtroy them.

13 Thou haſt thruſt ſore at mee that I might fall: but the LORD helped mee.

14 *The LORD *is* my ſtrength and ſong: and is become my ſaluation.

15 The voice of reioycing and ſaluation *is* in the tabernacles of the righteous: the Right hand of the LORD doeth valiantly.

16 The Right hand of the LORD is exalted: the Right hand of the LORD doeth valiantly.

17 I ſhall not die, but liue: and declare the workes of the LORD.

18 The LORD hath chaſtened me ſore: but he hath not giuen me ouer vnto death.

19 Open to mee the gates of righteouſneſſe: I will goe into them, *and* I will praiſe the LORD:

20 This gate of the LORD: into which the righteous ſhall enter.

21 I will praiſe thee, for thou haſt heard mee: and art become my ſaluation.

22 *The ſtone *which* the builders refuſed: is become the head *ſtone* of the corner.

23 †This is the LORDS doing: it is marueilous in our eyes.

24 This *is* the day *which* the LORD hath made; we will reioyce, and be glad in it.

25 Saue now, I beſeech thee, O LORD: O LORD, I beſeech thee, ſend now proſperitie.

26 *Bleſſed *be he* that commeth in the Name of the LORD: wee haue bleſſed you out of the houſe of the LORD.

27 God *is* the LORD, which hath ſhewed vs light, bind the ſacrifice with cords: euen vnto the horns of the Altar.

28 Thou *art* my God, and I will praiſe thee: *thou art* my God, I will exalt thee.

29 O giue thanks vnto the LORD, for he *is* good: for his mercy *endureth* for euer.

PSAL. CXIX.

This Pſalme conteineth ſundry prayers, praiſes, and profeſſions of obedience.

ALEPH.

‖ Or, perfect, or ſincere.

Leſſed *are* the ‖ vndefiled in the way: who walke in the Law of the LORD.

2 Bleſſed *are* they that keepe his teſtimonies: and *that* ſeeke him with the whole heart.

3 They alſo doe no iniquitie: they walke in his wayes.

4 Thou haſt commaunded *vs* to keepe thy precepts diligently.

5 O that my wayes were directed to keepe thy ſtatutes!

6 Then ſhall I not bee aſhamed: when I haue reſpect vnto all thy commandements.

7 I will praiſe thee with vprightneſſe of heart: when I ſhall haue learned † thy righteous iudgements.

8 I will keepe thy ſtatutes: O forſake me not vtterly.

† Hebr. iudgments of thy righteouſneſſe.

BETH.

9 WHerewithall ſhall a yong man cleanſe his way? by taking heede *thereto* according to thy word.

10 With my whole heart haue I ſought thee: O let me not wander from thy Commandements.

11 Thy word haue I hidde in mine heart: that I might not ſinne againſt thee.

12 Bleſſed *art* thou, O LORD: teach me thy ſtatutes.

13 With my lips haue I declared all the iudgements of thy mouth.

14 I haue reioyced in the way of thy teſtimonies: as *much as* in all riches.

15 I will meditate in thy precepts: and haue reſpect vnto thy wayes.

16 I will delight my ſelfe in thy ſtatutes: I will not forget thy word.

GIMEL.

17 DEale bountifully with thy ſeruant, *that* I may liue, and keepe thy word.

18 † Open

† *Heb. reueale.*

18 † Open thou mine eyes, that I may behold wonderous things out of thy Law.

* *Gen. 47. 9*
1. chro. 29.
15. pſal. 39.
12. heb. 11.
13.

19 * I am a stranger in the earth : hide not thy commandements from me.

20 My soule breaketh for the longing : *that it hath* vnto thy iudgements at all times.

21 Thou hast rebuked the proud *that are* cursed : which doe erre from thy Commandements.

22 Remooue from me reproch and contempt : for I haue kept thy testimonies.

23 Princes also did sit *and* speake against me : *but* thy seruant did meditate in thy statutes.

† *Heb. men of my counsell.*

24 Thy testimonies also *are* my delight : *and* † my counsellers.

DALETH.

25 MY soule cleaueth vnto the dust : quicken thou mee according to thy word.

26 I haue declared my wayes, and thou heardest me : * teach me thy Statutes.

* *Psal. 25. 4. and 27. 11. and 86. 11.*

27 Make me to vnderstand the way of thy precepts : so shall I talke of thy wonderous workes.

† *Heb. droppeth.*

28 My soule † melteth for heauines : strengthen thou me according vnto thy word.

29 Remoue from mee the way of lying : and grant me thy Law graciously.

30 I haue chosen the way of trueth : thy iudgements haue I laid *before me.*

31 I haue stucke vnto thy Testimonies : O LORD put me not to shame.

32 I will runne the way of thy Commandements : when thou shalt enlarge my heart.

HE.

33 TEach me, O LORD, the way of thy Statutes : and I shall keepe it *vnto* the end.

34 Giue me vnderstanding, and I shall keepe thy Law : yea I shall obserue it with *my* whole heart.

35 Make me to goe in the path of thy commandements : for therein doe I delight.

36 Incline my heart vnto thy testimonies : and not to couetousnesse.

† *Heb. make to paſſe.*

37 † Turne away mine eyes from beholding vanitie : *and* quicken thou me in thy way.

38 Stablish thy word vnto thy ser-

uant : who *is deuoted* to thy feare.

39 Turne away my reproch which I feare : for thy iudgements *are* good.

40 Behold, I haue longed after thy precepts : quicken me in thy righteousnesse.

VAV.

41 LEt thy mercies come also vnto me, O LORD : *euen* thy saluation, according to thy word.

42 ‖ So shall I haue wherewith to answere him that reprocheth me : for I trust in thy word.

‖ *Or, so sho I answere him that r proueth m in a thing.*

43 And take not the word of trueth vtterly out of my mouth : for I haue hoped in thy iudgements.

44 So shall I keepe thy Law continually : for euer and euer.

45 And I wil walke † at libertie : for I seeke thy precepts.

† *Hebr. a large.*

46 I will speake of thy testimonies also before kings, & wil not be ashamed.

47 And I will delight my selfe in thy commandements, which I haue loued.

48 My hands also will I lift vp vnto thy commandements, which I haue loued : and I will meditate in thy statutes.

ZAIN.

49 REmember the word vnto thy seruant · vpon which thou hast caused me to hope.

50 This *is* my comfort in my affliction · for thy word hath quickened me.

51 The proud haue had mee greatly in derision : *yet* haue I not declined from thy Law.

52 I remembred thy iudgements of old, O LORD : and haue comforted my selfe.

53 Horrour hath taken holde vpon me, because of the wicked that forsake thy Law.

54 Thy statutes haue bin my songs in the house of my pilgrimage.

55 I haue remembred thy name, O LORD, in the night, and haue kept thy Law.

56 This I had : because I kept thy precepts.

CHETH.

57 THou *art* my portion, O LORD, I haue said, that I would keepe thy words.

58 I intreated thy † fauour with *my* whole heart : be mercifull vnto mee according to thy word.

† *Heb.*

59 I thought on my wayes : and turned

turned my feete vnto thy Testimonies.

60 I made haste, and delayed not to keepe thy commandements.

compa- 61 The ||bands of the wicked haue robbed me : *but* I haue not forgotten thy lawe.

62 At mid-night I will rise to giue thankes vnto thee : because of thy righteous iudgements.

63 I *am* a companion of all them that feare thee : and of them that keepe thy precepts.

64 The earth, O LORD, is full of thy mercy : teach me thy statutes.

TETH.

65 THou hast dealt well with thy seruant, Oh LORD; according vnto thy word.

66 Teach me good iudgement and knowledge : for I haue beleeued thy commandements.

67 Before I was afflicted, I went astray : but now haue I kept thy word.

68 Thou *art* good, and doest good; teach me thy statutes.

69 The proud haue forged a lie against me : *but* I will keepe thy precepts with my whole heart.

70 Their heart is as fat as grease : *but* I delight in thy law.

71 It *is* good for me that I haue bene afflicted : that I might learne thy statutes.

al. 19.   72 *The law of thy mouth *is* better
ou. 8.   vnto me : then thousands of gold and siluer.

IOD.

73 THy hands haue made me and fashioned me : giue me vnderstanding, that I may learne thy commandements.

74 They that feare thee will bee glad when they see mee : because I haue hoped in thy word.

b. righ-   75 I knowe, O LORD, that thy
nesse.   iudgements *are* †right : and *that* thou in faithfulnesse hast afflicted me.

b. to   76 Let, I pray thee, thy mercifull
ort me.   kindnesse be †for my comfort; according to thy word vnto thy seruant.

77 Let thy tender mercies come vnto me, that I may liue : for thy lawe *is* my delight.

78 Let the proud be ashamed, for they dealt peruersly with me without a cause : *but* I will meditate in thy precepts.

79 Let those that feare thee turne

vnto me : and those that haue knowen thy testimonies.

80 Let my heart be sound in thy statutes; that I be not ashamed.

CAPH.

81 MY soule fainteth for thy saluation : *but* I hope in thy word.

82 Mine eyes faile for thy word : saying, When wilt thou comfort me?

83 For I am become like a bottle in the smoke : *yet* doe I not forget thy statutes.

84 How many *are* the dayes of thy seruant? when wilt thou execute iudgement on them that persecute me?

85 The proud haue digged pittes for me : which *are* not after thy law.

86 All thy commaundements *are* †faithfull : they persecute me wrongfully; helpe thou me.   † *Heb. faithfulnesse.*

87 They had almost consumed mee vpon earth : but I forsooke not thy precepts.

88 Quicken mee after thy louing kindnesse : so shall I keepe the testimonie of thy mouth.

LAMED.

89 FOr euer, O LORD, thy word is setled, in heauen.

90 Thy faithfulnesse is †vnto all generations : thou hast established the earth, and it †abideth.   † *Heb. to generation and generation.* † *Heb. standeth.*

91 They continue this day according to thine ordinances : for all *are* thy seruants.

92 Vnlesse thy lawe *had bene* my delights : I should then haue perished in mine affliction.

93 I will neuer forget thy precepts : for with them thou hast quickened me.

94 I am thine, saue me : for I haue sought thy precepts.

95 The wicked haue waited for me to destroy me : but I will consider thy testimonies.

96 I haue seene an end of all perfection : *but* thy commandement is exceeding broad.

MEM.

97 O How loue I thy Law! it is my meditation all the day.

98 Thou through thy Commandements hast made me wiser then mine enemies : for †they are euer with mee.   † *Heb. it is euer with me.*

99 I haue more vnderstanding then all

all my teachers : for thy Testimonies are my meditation.

100 I vnderstand more then the ancients : because I keepe thy precepts.

101 I haue refrained my feete from euery euill way : that I may keepe thy word.

102 I haue not departed from thy Iudgements : for thou hast taught me.

*Psal. 19. 9.
†Hebr. palat.

103 *How sweet are thy words vnto my †taste! *yea, sweeter* then hony to my mouth.

104 Through thy precepts I get vnderstanding : therefore I hate euery false way.

NVN.

‖Or, candle.

105 **T**Hy word *is* a ‖lampe vnto my feete : and a light vnto my path.

106 I haue sworne, and I will performe it : that I will keepe thy righteous iudgements.

107 I am afflicted very much : quicken mee, O Lord, according vnto thy word.

108 Accept, I beseech thee, the freewil offrings of my mouth, O LORD : and teach me thy iudgements.

109 My soule *is* continually in my hand : yet doe I not forget thy Law.

110 The wicked haue layde a snare for mee : yet I erred not from thy precepts.

111 Thy Testimonies haue I taken as an heritage for euer : for they *are* the reioycing of my heart.

† Hebr. to do.

112 I haue inclined mine heart †to performe thy Statutes, alway, *euen* vnto the end.

SAMECH.

113 **I** Hate *vaine* thoughts : but thy Law doe I loue.

114   Thou art my hiding place, and my shield : I hope in thy word.

*Matth. 7. 23.

115 *Depart from me, ye euil doers : for I will keepe the Commandements of my God.

116 Vphold mee according vnto thy word, that I may liue : and let mee not be ashamed of my hope.

117 Hold thou me vp, and I shall be safe : and I will haue respect vnto thy Statutes continually.

118 Thou hast troden downe all them that erre from thy Statutes : for their deceit *is* falshood.

† Hebr. causest to cease.

119 Thou †puttest away all the wicked of the earth *like* drosse : therefore I

loue thy Testimonies.

120 My flesh trembleth for feare of thee : and I am afraide of thy Iudgements.

AIN.

121 **I** Haue done Iudgement and iustice : leaue mee not to mine oppressours.

122 Bee suretie for thy seruant for good : let not the proud oppresse me.

123 Mine eyes faile for thy saluation : and for the word of thy righteousnesse.

124 Deale with thy seruant according vnto thy mercie : and teach me thy Statutes.

125 I *am* thy seruant, giue me vnderstanding : that I may know thy Testimonies.

126 It *is* time for thee, Lord, to worke : *for* they haue made voyde thy Law.

*Pro 11. ps 9.

127 *Therefore I loue thy Commandements : aboue gold, yea aboue fine gold.

128 Therefore I esteeme all *thy* precepts concerning all things *to be* right : *and* I hate euery false way.

PE.

129 **T**Hy Testimonies are wonderfull : therefore doeth my soule keepe them.

130 The entrance of thy wordes giueth light : it giueth vnderstanding vnto the simple.

131 I opened my mouth, and panted : for I longed for thy Commandements.

† He cord the c towa those

132 Looke thou vpon mee, and be mercifull vnto me : †as thou vsest to do vnto those that loue thy Name.

133 Order my steps in thy word : and let not any iniquitie haue dominion ouer me.

134 Deliuer me from the oppression of man : so will I keepe thy precepts.

135 Make thy face to shine vpon thy seruant : and teach me thy Statutes.

136 Riuers of waters runne downe mine eyes : because they keepe not thy Law.

TSADDI.

137 **R**Ighteous *art* thou, O Lord : and vpright *are* thy iudgements.

† He teou † He fuln *Ps ioh. † He me c

138 Thy testimonies *that* thou hast commaunded, are †righteous : and very †faithfull.

139 *My zeale hath †consumed me : because

because mine enemies haue forgotten thy words.

140 Thy word is very †pure : therefore thy seruant loueth it.

. tried ined.

141 I am small and despised : yet doe not I forget thy precepts.

142 Thy righteousnesse is an euerlasting righteousnesse: and thy law is the trueth.

found

143 Trouble and anguish haue †taken hold on me : yet thy commaundements are my delights.

144 The righteousnesse of thy Testimonies is euerlasting : giue me vnderstanding, and I shall liue.

KOPH.

145 I Cried with my whole heart : heare me, O LORD, I will keepe thy statutes.

that I keepe.

146 I cried vnto thee, saue me : ||and I shall keepe thy testimonies.

147 I preuented the dawning of the morning, and cried : I hoped in thy word.

148 Mine eyes preuent the night watches : that I might meditate in thy word.

149 Heare my voice according vnto thy louing kindnesse : O LORD quicken me according to thy iudgement.

150 They draw nigh that follow after mischiefe : they are farre from thy Law.

151 Thou art neere, O LORD : and all thy commandements are trueth.

152 Concerning thy testimonies, I haue knowen of old : that thou hast founded them for euer.

RESH.

153 C Onsider mine affliction, and deliuer me : for I doe not forget thy Law.

154 Plead my cause, and deliuer me : quicken me according to thy word.

155 Saluation is farre from the wicked : for they seeke not thy statutes.

many.

156 || Great are thy tender mercies, O LORD : quicken me according to thy iudgements.

157 Many are my persecutors, and mine enemies : yet doe I not decline from thy testimonies.

158 I beheld the transgressours, and was grieued : because they kept not thy word.

159 Consider how I loue thy precepts : quicken me, O LORD, according to thy louing kindnesse.

160 † Thy word is true from the beginning : and euery one of thy righteous iudgements endureth for euer.

† Heb. the beginning of thy word is true.

SCHIN.

161 P Rinces haue persecuted mee without a cause : but my heart standeth in awe of thy word.

162 I reioyce at thy word : as one that findeth great spoile.

163 I hate and abhorre lying : but thy Law doe I loue.

164 Seuen times a day doe I praise thee : because of thy righteous iudgements.

165 Great peace haue they which loue thy law : & †nothing shall offend them.

† Heb. they shall haue no stumbling blocke.

166 LORD, I haue hoped for thy saluation : and done thy commandements.

167 My soule hath kept thy testimonies : and I loue them exceedingly.

168 I haue kept thy precepts and thy testimonies : for all my wayes are before thee.

TAV.

169 L Et my crie come neere before thee, O LORD : giue mee vnderstanding according to thy worde.

170 Let my supplication come before thee : deliuer me according to thy word.

171 My lips shall vtter praise : when thou hast taught me thy Statutes.

172 My tongue shall speake of thy word : for all thy commandements are righteousnesse.

173 Let thine hand helpe me : for I haue chosen thy precepts.

174 I haue longed for thy saluation, O LORD : and thy Lawe is my delight.

175 Let my soule liue, and it shall praise thee : and let thy iudgments helpe me.

176 I haue gone astray like a lost sheepe, seeke thy seruant : for I doe not forget thy commandements.

PSAL. CXX.

1 Dauid prayeth against Doeg, 3 reproueth his tongue, 5 complaineth of his necessary conuersation with the wicked.

¶ A song of degrees.

I N my distresse I cried vnto the LORD : and hee heard me.

2 Deliuer my soule, O LORD, from lying lips : and from a deceitfull tongue.

3 || What

‖ Or, what
ſhall the de-
ceitfull
tongue giue
vnto thee?
or what ſhall
it profit thee?
† Heb. ad-
ded.
‖ Or, It is as
the ſharpe
arrowes of
the mighty
man with
coales of iu-
niper.
‖ Or, a man
of peace.

3 ‖ What ſhall be giuen vnto thee? or what ſhalbe †done vnto thee, thou falſe tongue?

4 ‖ Sharpe arrowes of the migh-tie : with coales of iuniper.

5 Woe is me, that I ſoiourne in Me-ſech : that I dwell in the tents of Ke-dar.

6 My ſoule hath long dwelt with him that hateth peace.

7 I am ‖ for peace : but when I ſpeake, they are for warre.

PSAL. CXXI.

1 The great ſafety of the godly, who put their truſt in Gods protection.

¶ A ſong of degrees.

‖ Or, ſhall I
lift vp mine
eies to the
hils? whence
ſhould my
helpe come?
* Pſal.
144. 7.

I ‖ Will lift vp mine eyes vn-to the hilles: from whence commeth my helpe.

2 * My helpe commeth from the LORD : which made heauen and earth.

3 He will not ſuffer thy foote to bee moued : he that keepeth thee will not ſlumber.

4 Behold, he that keepeth Iſrael; ſhall neither ſlumber nor ſleepe.

5 The LORD is thy keeper : the LORD is thy ſhade, vpon thy right hand.

6 The ſunne ſhall not ſmite thee by day; nor the moone by night.

7 The LORD ſhall preſerue thee from all euill : hee ſhall preſerue thy ſoule.

8 The LORD ſhall preſerue thy going out, and thy comming in : from this time foorth and euen for euermore.

PSAL. CXXII.

1 Dauid profeſſeth his ioy for the Church, 6 and prayeth for the peace thereof.

¶ A ſong of degrees of Dauid.

Was glad when they ſayd vnto me : Let vs goe into the houſe of the LORD.

2 Our feete ſhall ſtand within thy gates, O Ieruſalem.

3 Ieruſalem is builded as a citie, that is compact together :

4 Whither the tribes goe vp, the tribes of the LORD, vnto the teſtimo-nie of Iſrael : to giue thankes vnto the name of the LORD.

5 For there †are ſet thrones of iudg-ment : the thrones of the houſe of Da-uid.

6 Pray for the peace of Ieruſalem : they ſhall proſper that loue thee.

7 Peace be within thy walles : and proſperitie within thy palaces.

8 For my brethren and companions ſakes : I will now ſay, Peace be within thee.

9 Becauſe of the houſe of the LORD our God : I will ſeeke thy good.

† Heb.
ſit.

PSAL. CXXIII.

1 The godly profeſſe their confidence in God, 3 and pray to be deliuered from contempt.

¶ A ſong of degrees.

Nto thee lift I vp mine eyes : O thou that dwel-leſt in the heauens.

2 Beholde, as the eyes of ſeruants looke vn-to the hand of their Ma-ſters, and as the eyes of a maiden, vnto the hand of her miſtreſſe : ſo our eyes waite vpon the LORD our God, vntill that he haue mercy vpon vs.

3 Haue mercy vpon vs, O LORD, haue mercy vpon vs : for we are excee-dingly filled with contempt.

4 Our ſoule is exceedingly filled with the ſcorning of thoſe that are at eaſe : and with the contempt of the proud.

PSAL. CXXIIII.

The Church bleſſeth God, for a miraculous deli-uerance.

¶ A ſong of degrees of Dauid.

F it had not bene the LORD who was on our ſide : nowe may Iſrael ſay :

2 If it had not bene the LORD, who was on our ſide, when men roſe vp againſt vs:

3 Then they had ſwallowed vs vp quicke : when their wrath was kindled againſt vs.

4 Then the waters had ouerwhel-med vs; the ſtreame had gone ouer our ſoule.

5 Then the proud waters had gone ouer our ſoule.

6 Bleſſed be the LORD : who hath not giuen vs as a pray to their teeth.

7 Our ſoule is eſcaped as a bird out of

of the snare of the foulers; the snare is broken, and we are escaped.

8 * Our helpe *is* in the name of the LORD : who made heauen and earth.

al. 121.

PSAL. CXXV.

1 The safety of such as trust in God. 4 A prayer for the godly, and against the wicked.

¶ A song of degrees.

Hey that trust in the LORD, *shalbe* as mount Zion, *which* cannot be re-moooued, *but* abideth for euer.

2 As the mountaines *are* round a-bout Ierusalem , so the LORD *is* round about his people : from hence-foorth euen for euer.

r. wic-esse.

3 For the rod of † the wicked shall not rest vpon the lot of the righteous : lest the righteous put forth their hands vnto iniquitie.

4 Doe good, O LORD, vnto those that be good : and to them that are vp-right in their hearts.

5 As for such as turne aside vnto their crooked wayes, the LORD shall lead them foorth with the workers of iniquitie : *but* peace *shalbe* vpon Israel.

PSAL. CXXVI.

1 The Church celebrating her incredible re-turne out of captiuitie, 4 prayeth for, and prophecieth the good successe thereof.

¶ A song of degrees.

Hen the LORD † turned againe the captiuitie of Zi-on : wee were like them that dreame.

2 Then was our mouth filled with laughter , and our tongue with singing, then said they among the heathen : The LORD † hath done great things for them.

r. hath ified to ith

3 The LORD hath done great things for vs : whereof we are glad.

4 Turne againe our captiuitie, O LORD : as the streames in the South.

5 They that sow in teares : shall reape in ‖ ioy.

sing-

6 He that goeth forth and weepeth, bearing ‖ precious seed, shall doubtlesse come againe with reioycing : bringing his sheaues *with him.*

seed-t.

PSAL. CXXVII.

1 The vertue of Gods blessing. 3 Good chil-dren are his gift.

¶ A song of degrees ‖ for Solomon.

Xcept the LORD build the house, they labour in vaine that † build it: except the LORD keepe the ci-tie , the watchman wa-keth but in vaine.

2 It *is* vaine for you to rise vp early, to sit vp late , to eate the bread of sor-rowes : *for* so hee giueth his beloued sleepe.

3 Loe, children *are* an heritage of the LORD : *and* the fruit of the wombe *is his* reward.

4 As arrowes *are* in the hand of a mightie man : so *are* children of the youth.

5 Happie *is* the man that † hath his quiuer full of them, they shall not be a-shamed: but they ‖ shall speake with the enemies in the gate.

‖ Or, of So-lomon.

† Hebr. are builders of it in it.

PSAL. CXXVIII.

The sundry blessings which follow them that feare God.

¶ A song of degrees.

Lessed *is* euery one *that* feareth the LORD : that walketh in his wayes.

2 For thou shalt eat the labour of thine handes : happie *shalt* thou *bee*, and it *shall be* well with thee.

3 Thy wife *shalbe* as a fruitful Vine by the sides of thine house, thy children like Oliue plants · round about thy table.

4 Beholde that thus shall the man be blessed; that feareth the LORD.

5 The LORD shall blesse thee out of Zion : and thou shalt see the good of Ierusalem, all the dayes of thy life.

6 Yea, thou shalt see thy childrens children : *and* peace vpon Israel.

† Hebr. hath filled his qui-uer with them.

‖ Or, shall subdue, as Psal. 18. 45. or, destroy.

PSAL. CXXIX.

1 An exhortation to praise God for sauing Is-rael in their great afflictions. 5 The haters of the Church are cursed.

¶ A song of degrees.

‖ Any a time haue they af-flicted me from my youth: may Israel now say.

2 Many a time haue they afflicted me from my youth : yet they haue not preuailed a-gainst mee.

‖ Or, much.

3 The

3 The plowers plowed vpon my backe : they made long their furrowes.

4 The Lord *is* righteous : hee hath cut asunder the cordes of the wicked.

5 Let them all be confounded and turned backe, that hate Zion.

6 Let them bee as the grasse *vpon* the house tops : which withereth afore it groweth vp :

7 Wherewith the mower filleth not his hand : nor hee that bindeth sheaues, his bosome.

8 Neither doe they which goe by, say, The blessing of the Lord *be* vpon you : wee blesse you in the Name of the Lord.

PSAL. CXXX.

1 The Psalmist professeth his hope in prayer, 5 and his patience in hope. 7 Hee exhorteth Israel to hope in God.

¶ A song of degrees.

OVT of the depths haue I cryed vnto thee, O Lord.

2 Lorde, heare my voice : let thine eares be attentiue to the voice of my supplications.

3 If thou, Lord, shouldest marke iniquities : O Lord, who shal stand ?

4 But *there is* forgiuenesse with thee : that thou mayest be feared.

5 I wait for the Lord, my soule doeth waite : and in his worde doe I hope.

6 My soule *waiteth* for the Lord, more then they that watch for the morning : || I say, *more then* they that watch for the morning.

|| Or, which watch vnto the morning.

7 Let Israel hope in the Lord, for with the Lord *there is* mercy : and with him *is* plenteous redemption.

8 And hee shall redeeme Israel, from all his iniquities.

PSAL. CXXXI.

1 Dauid professing his humilitie, 3 exhorteth Israel to hope in God.

¶ A song of degrees of Dauid.

† *Heb. walke.*

LOrd, my heart is not haughtie, nor mine eyes loftie : neither doe I †exercise my selfe in great matters, or in things too † high for mee.

† *Heb. wonderfull.*

2 Surely I haue behaued and qui-

eted † my selfe as a child that is weaned of his mother : my soule is euen as a weaned childe.

3 Let Israel hope in the Lord, †from henceforth and for euer.

† *Heb. soule.*

† *Heb. now.*

PSAL. CXXXII.

1 Dauid in his prayer commendeth vnto God the religious care he had for the Arke. 8 His prayer at the remouing of the Arke, 11 with a repetition of Gods promises.

¶ A Song of degrees.

LOrd remember Dauid, *and* all his afflictions :

2 How he sware vnto the Lord, *and* vowed vnto the mightie God of Iacob.

3 Surely I will not come into the tabernacle of my house : nor goe vp into my bed.

4 I will not giue sleepe to mine eyes : *or* slumber to mine eyelids,

5 Vntill I finde out a place for the Lord : † an habitation for the mightie *God* of Iacob.

† *Heb. tation*

6 Loe, wee heard of it at Ephrata : we found it in the fields of the wood.

7 We will goe into his tabernacles : we will worship at his footstoole.

8 * Arise, O Lord, into thy rest : thou, and the Arke of thy strength.

* 2. C 6. 41. 10. 35

9 Let thy Priestes be clothed with righteousnesse : and let thy saints shout for ioy.

10 For thy seruant Dauids sake : turne not away the face of thine Anointed.

11 The Lord hath sworne *in* trueth vnto Dauid, hee will not turne from it ; * of the fruit of † thy body will I set vpon thy throne.

* 2. S 12. 1 8. 25 6. 16 9. ac † *He belly*

12 If thy children will keepe my couenant and my testimonie, that I shall teach them ; their children also shall sit vpon thy throne for euermore.

13 For the Lord hath chosen Zion : he hath desired *it* for his habitation.

14 This *is* my rest for euer : here will I dwell, for I haue desired it.

15 I will || abundantly blesse her prouision : I will satisfie her poore with bread.

|| *Or*

16 I will also clothe her priests with saluation : and her Saints shall shout aloud for ioy.

17 * There will I make the horne of Dauid to budde : I haue ordained a || lampe for mine Anointed.

* L

|| *Or*

18 His

18 His enemies will I clothe with shame : but vpon himselfe shall his crowne flourish.

PSAL. CXXXIII.

The benefite of the communion of Saints.

¶ A song of degrees of Dauid.

 Ehold how good and how pleasant *it is* : for brethren to dwell † together in vnitie.

b. euen her.

2 *It is* like the precious oyntment vpon the head, that ranne downe vpon the beard, *euen* Aarons beard : that went downe to the skirts of his garments.

3 As the dew of Hermon, *and as the dewe* that descended vpon the mountaines of Zion, for there the Lord commanded the blessing : *euen* life for euermore.

PSAL. CXXXIIII.

An exhortation to blesse God.

¶ A song of degrees.

 Eholde, blesse yee the Lord, all yee seruants of the Lord : which by night stand in the house of the Lord.

in hoſe.

2 Lift vp your hands || *in* the Sanctuary : & blesse the Lord.

3 The Lord that made heauen and earth : blesse thee out of Zion.

PSAL. CXXXV.

An exhortation to praise God for his mercy, 5 for his power, 8 for his iudgements. 15 The vanitie of Idoles. 19 An exhortation to blesse God.

Raise ye the Lord, Praise ye the Name of the Lord : prayse *him*, O ye seruants of the Lord.

2 Yee that stand in the House of the Lord : in the courts of the house of our God.

3 Praise the Lord, for the Lord *is* good : sing praises vnto his Name, for *it is* pleasant.

4 For the Lord hath chosen Iacob vnto himselfe : *and* Israel for his peculiar treasure.

5 For I know that the Lord *is* great : and *that* our Lord *is* aboue all gods.

6 Whatsoeuer the Lord pleased, *that* did he in heauen and in earth : in the Seas, and all deepe places.

7 * Hee causeth the vapours to ascend from the ends of the earth, he maketh lightnings for the raine : he bringeth the winde out of his treasuries.

8 * Who smote the first borne of Egypt : † both of man and beast.

9 *Who* sent tokens and woonders into the midst of thee, O Egypt : vpon Pharaoh, and vpon all his seruants.

10 * Who smote great nations : and slew mightie kings :

11 Sihon king of the Amorites, and Og king of Bashan : and all the kingdomes of Canaan,

12 * And gaue their land *for* an heritage : an heritage vnto Israel his people.

13 Thy Name, O Lord, *endureth* for euer : *and* thy memoriall, O Lord, † throughout all generations.

14 For the Lord will iudge his people : and he will repent himselfe concerning his seruants.

15 * The idoles of the heathen *are* siluer and golde : the worke of mens hands.

16 They *haue* mouthes, but they speake not : eyes *haue* they, but they see not :

17 They *haue* eares, but they heare not : neither is there any breath in their mouthes.

18 They that make them are like vnto them : *so is* euery one that trusteth in them.

19 Blesse the Lord, O house of Israel : blesse the Lord, O house of Aaron.

20 Blesse the Lord, O house of Leui : ye that feare the Lord, blesse the Lord.

21 Blessed *be* the Lord out of Zion ; which dwelleth at Ierusalem. Praise ye the Lord.

PSAL. CXXXVI.

An exhortation to giue thankes to God for particular mercies.

 * Giue thankes vnto the Lord, for hee *is* good : for his mercy *endureth* foreuer.

2 O giue thankes vnto the God of gods : for his mercy *endureth* for euer.

3 O giue

* Ier. 10. 13.

* Exod. 12. †Heb. from man vnto beast.

* Num. 21. 2. and 4. 25, 26, 34, 35.

* Ios. 12. 7.

† Heb. to generation and generation.

* Psal. 115. 4, 5, 6, 7, 8, 9, 10.

* Psa. 106. 1. and 107. 1. and 118. 1.

3 O giue thankes to the Lord of lords : for his mercy *endureth* for euer.

4 To him who alone doth great wonders : for his mercy *endureth* for euer.

*Gen. 1. 1.

5 *To him that by wiſedome made the heauens : for his mercy *endureth* for euer.

*Gen. 1. 6. ier. 10. 12.

6 *To him that ſtretched out the earth aboue the waters : for his mercy *endureth* for euer.

*Gen. 1. 14.

7 *To him that made great lights : for his mercy *endureth* for euer.

† Heb. for the rulings by day.

8 The ſunne † to rule by day : for his mercy *endureth* for euer.

9 The moone and ſtarres to rule by night : for his mercy *endureth* for euer.

*Exod. 12. 29.

10 *To him that ſmote Egypt in their firſt borne : for his mercy *endureth* for euer.

*Exod. 13. 17.

11 *And brought out Iſrael from among them : for his mercy *endureth* for euer.

12 With a ſtrong hand and with a ſtretched out arme : for his mercy *endureth* for euer.

*Exod. 14. 21. 22.

13 *To him which diuided the red ſea into parts : for his mercy *endureth* for euer.

14 And made Iſrael to paſſe through the midſt of it : for his mercy *endureth* for euer.

*Exod. 14. 28. †Heb.ſhaked off.

15 *But † ouerthrewe Pharaoh and his hoſte in the red ſea : for his mercy *endureth* for euer.

*Exod. 15. 22.

16 *To him which led his people through the wilderneſſe : for his mercy *endureth* for euer.

17 To him which ſmote great kings : for his mercy *endureth* for euer.

*Deut. 29. 7. pſal. 135. 10, & 11.

18 *And ſlue famous kings : for his mercy *endureth* for euer.

*Num. 21. 23.

19 *Sihon king of the Amorites : for his mercy *endureth* for euer.

*Num. 21. 33.

20 *And Og the king of Baſhan : for his mercy *endureth* for euer.

*Ioſh. 12. 7

21 *And gaue their land for an heritage : for his mercy *endureth* for euer.

22 *Euen* an heritage vnto Iſrael his ſeruant : for his mercy *endureth* for euer.

23 Who remembred vs in our lowe eſtate : for his mercy *endureth* for euer.

24 And hath redeemed vs from our enemies : for his mercy *endureth* for euer.

25 Who giueth foode to all fleſh : for his mercy *endureth* for euer.

26 O giue thankes vnto the God of heauen : for his mercy *endureth* for euer.

PSAL. CXXXVII.

The conſtancie of the Iewes in captiuity. 7 The Prophet curſeth Edom and Babel.

BY the riuers of Babylon, there wee ſate downe, yea we wept : when we remembred Zion.

2 Wee hanged our harpes vpon the willowes, in the midſt thereof.

3 For there they that carried vs away captiue, required of vs † a ſong, and they that † waſted vs, *required of vs* mirth : *ſaying*, Sing vs *one* of the ſongs of Zion.

† Heb. the words of ſong.
† Heb. laid vs on heaps.

4 How ſhall we ſing the Lords ſong : in a † ſtrange land?

† Heb. land of a ſtranger.

5 If I forget thee, O Ieruſalem : let my right hand forget *her cunning*.

6 If I doe not remember thee, let my tongue cleaue to the roofe of my mouth ; if I preferre not Ieruſalem aboue † my chiefe ioy.

† Heb. the head of my ioy.

7 Remember, O Lord, the children oi Edom, in the day of Ieruſalem ; who ſayd, † raſe it, raſe it : euen to the foundation thereof.

† Heb. make bare.

8 *O daughter of Babylon, who *art* to be † deſtroyed: happy *ſhall he be* † that rewardeth thee, as thou haſt ſerued vs.

*Obad. 12, 13.
† Heb. that is to be deſtroyed.
† Heb. that recompenſeth vnto thee thy deed which thou diddeſt to vs.

9 *Happy *ſhall he be* that taketh and daſheth thy little ones againſt † the ſtones.

*Iſa. 1
† Heb. the rocke.

PSAL. CXXXVIII.

1 Dauid praiſeth God for the truth of his word. 4 He prophecieth that the kings of the earth ſhall praiſe God. 7 He profeſſeth his confidence in God.

¶ *A Pſalme* of Dauid.

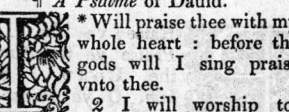

I *Will praiſe thee with my whole heart : before the gods will I ſing praiſe vnto thee.

*Pſal. 4. 6.

2 I will worſhip towards thy holy temple, and praiſe thy name, for thy louing kindneſſe and for thy trueth : for thou haſt magnified thy word aboue all thy name.

3 In the day when I cried, thou anſweredſt me: *and* ſtrengthenedſt me *with* ſtrength in my ſoule.

4 All the kings of the earth ſhall praiſe thee, O Lord : when they heare the words of thy mouth.

5 Yea they ſhall ſing in the wayes of the

the LORD: for great *is* the glory of the LORD.

6 Though the LORD be high, yet hath he respect vnto the lowly : but the proud he knoweth afarre off.

7 Though I walke in the mids of trouble, thou wilt reuiue me, thou shalt stretch foorth thine hand against the wrath of mine enemies : and thy right hand shall saue me.

8 The LORD wil perfit *that which* concerneth me : thy mercie, O LORD, *endureth* for euer: forsake not the works of thine owne hands.

PSAL. CXXXIX.

1 Dauid praiseth God for his all-seeing proui-dence, 17 And for his infinite mercies. 19 He defieth the wicked. 23 Hee prayeth for sinceritie.

¶ To the chiefe Musician, A Psalme of Dauid.

O LORD, thou hast sear-ched mee, and knowen *me.*
2 Thou knowest my downe sitting, and mine vprising : thou vnderstan-dest my thought afarre off.

3 Thou ‖compassest my path, and my lying downe, and art acquainted *with* all my wayes.

4 For *there is* not a worde in my tongue : *but* lo, O LORD, thou know-est it altogether.

5 Thou hast beset me behind, and before : and laid thine hand vpon me.

6 Such knowledge *is* too wonder-full for me : it is high, I cannot *attaine* vnto it.

7 Whither shall I goe from thy spirit ? or whither shall I flie from thy presence ?

8 *If I ascend vp into heauen, thou art there : if I make my bed in hell, behold, thou *art there.*

9 *If* I take the wings of the mor-ning : *and* dwell in the vttermost parts of the Sea :

10 Euen there shall thy hand leade me : and thy right hand shall hold me.

11 *If I say, Surely the darkenes shall couer me : euen the night shall bee light about me.

12 Yea the darkenesse †hideth not from thee, but the night shineth as the day : †the darknes and the light *are* both alike *to thee.*

13 For thou hast possessed my reines : thou hast couered me in my mothers wombe.

14 I will praise thee, for I am feare-fully *and* wonderfully made, maruei-lous *are* thy works : and *that* my soule knoweth †right well.

15 My ‖substance was not hid from thee, when I was made in secret : *and* curiously wrought in the lowest parts of the earth.

16 Thine eyes did see my substance yet being vnperfect, and in thy booke †all my members were written, ‖which in continuance were fashioned : when as yet *there was* none of them.

17 * Howe precious also are thy thoughts vnto me, O God : how great is the summe of them ?

18 *If* I should count them, they are moe in number then the sand : when I awake, I am still with thee.

19 Surely thou wilt slay the wicked, O God : depart from me therefore, ye bloody men.

20 For they speake against thee wic-kedly : *and* thine enemies take *thy name* in vaine.

21 Doe not I hate them, O LORD, that hate thee ? and am not I grieued with those that rise vp against thee ?

22 I hate them with perfect hatred : I count them mine enemies.

23 Search me, O God, and knowe my heart : trie mee, and knowe my thoughts :

24 And see if *there bee* any †wicked way in me : and leade me in the way e-uerlasting.

PSAL. CXL.

1 Dauid prayeth to be deliuered from Saul and Doeg. 8 He prayeth against them. 12 Hee comforteth himselfe by confidence in God.

¶ To the chiefe Musician, A Psalme of Dauid.

D Eliuer me, O LORD, from the euill man : pre-serue me from the† violent man.
2 Which imagine mis-chiefes in *their* heart: continually are they gathered together *for* warre.

3 *They haue sharpned their tongues like a serpent : adders poison *is* vnder their lips. Selah.

4 Keepe me, O LORD, from the hands of the wicked, preserue me from the violent man : who haue purposed to ouerthrow my goings.

5 The

Marginal notes (left column): win-ſt. · 03 9. · 26. 6. 4. 13. · darke-not. · b. as is arkenes he light

Marginal notes (right column): † Hebr. greatly. · ‖ Or, strength or body. · † Heb. all of them. · ‖ Or, what dayes they should be fashioned. · * Psal. 40. 6. · † Heb. way of paine, or griefe. · † Heb. man of violences. · * Rom. 3. 14 psal. 58. 5.

5 The proude haue hid a snare for me and cords, they haue spread a net by the way side : they haue set grinnes for me. Selah.

6 I said vnto the Lord, Thou *art* my God : heare the voyce of my supplications, O Lord.

7 O God the Lord, the strength of my saluation : thou hast couered my head in the day of battell.

8 Grant not, O Lord, the desires of the wicked : further not his wicked deuice, ||*lest* they exalt themselues. Selah.

‖ *Or, let them not be exalted.*

9 As for the head of those that compasse me about : let the mischiefe of their owne lips couer them

10 Let burning coales fall vpon them, let them be cast into the fire : into deepe pits, that they rise not vp againe.

† *Heb. a man of tongue: or, an euill speaker, a wicked man of violence be established in the earth: let him be hunted to his ouerthrow.*

11 Let not an †euill speaker bee established in the earth : euill shall hunt the violent man to ouerthrow *him*.

12 I know that the Lord will maintaine the cause of the afflicted · *and* the right of the poore.

13 Surely the righteous shall giue thankes vnto thy Name : the vpright shall dwell in thy presence.

PSAL. CXLI.

1 Dauid prayeth that his suit may bee acceptable, 3 his conscience sincere, 7 and his life safe from snares.

¶ A Psalme of Dauid.

Ord, I crie vnto thee, make haste vnto mee · giue eare vnto my voice, when I crie vnto thee

2 Let my prayer bee †set foorth before thee *as* incense : *and* the lifting vp of my hands *as* the Euening sacrifice.

† *Hebr. directed.*

3 Set a watch (O Lord) before my mouth : keepe the doore of my lips.

4 Incline not my heart to any euill thing, to practise wicked workes with men that worke iniquitie : and let mee not eate of their dainties.

‖ *Or, let the righteous smite mee kindly, and reproue me, let not their precious oile breake my head, &c.*

5 ||Let the righteous smite mee , *it shalbe* a kindnesse : and let him reprooue me, *it shalbe* an excellent oile, *which* shall not breake my head : for yet my prayer also *shalbe* in their calamities.

6 When their Iudges are ouerthrowen in stonie places , they shall heare my words, for they are sweet.

7 Our bones are scattered at the graues mouth : as when one cutteth and cleaueth *wood* vpon the earth.

8 But mine eyes *are* vnto thee , O God the Lord : in thee is my trust, †leaue not my soule destitute.

† *Heb. not my bare.*

9 Keepe mee from the snare *which* they haue laide for me, and the grinnes of the workers of iniquitie.

10 Let the wicked fall into their owne nets : whilest that I withal †escape.

† *Hebr. ouer.*

PSAL. CXLII.

Dauid sheweth that in his trouble, all his comfort was in prayer vnto God.

¶ ||Maschil of Dauid ; A prayer when he was in the caue.

‖ *Or, A Psalme Dauid uing i ction.*

Cried vnto the Lord with my voice : with my voice vnto the Lord did I make my supplication.

2 I powred out my complaint before him : I shewed before him my trouble.

3 When my spirit was ouerwhelmed within mee, then thou knewest my path : in the way wherein I walked, haue they priuily laid a snare for me.

4 ||I looked on my right hand, and beheld, but *there was* no man that would know me, refuge †failed me : †no man cared for my soule.

‖ *Or, on the hand, see.*
† *Hebr rished me.*
‖ *Hebr man so after soule.*

5 I cried vnto thee, O Lord, I said, Thou *art* my refuge, *and* my portion in the land of the liuing.

6 Attend vnto my crie, for I am brought very low, deliuer mee from my persecuters : for they are stronger then I.

7 Bring my soule out of prison, that I may praise thy Name : the righteous shall compasse me about : for thou shalt deale bountifully with me.

PSAL. CXLIII.

1 Dauid prayeth for fauour in Iudgment. 3 He complaineth of his griefes. 5 He strengthneth his faith by meditation and prayer. 7 Hee prayeth for grace, 9 for deliuerance, 10 for sanctification, 12 for destruction of his enemies.

¶ A Psalme of Dauid.

Eare my prayer , O Lord , giue eare to my supplications : in thy faithfulnesse answere me, *and* in thy righteousnes.

2 And enter not into judge-

. 34.
3. 20
. 16.

iudgement with thy ſeruant : for in *thy ſight ſhall no man liuing be iuſtified.

3 For the enemie hath perſecuted my ſoule, he hath ſmitten my life downe to the ground : hee hath made mee to dwell in darkeneſſe, as thoſe that haue bene long dead.

4 Therefore is my ſpirit ouerwhelmed within me : my heart within me is deſolate.

5 I remember the dayes of old, I meditate on all thy workes : I muſe on the worke of thy hands.

6 I ſtretch forth my hands vnto thee : my ſoule *thirſteth* after thee, as a thirſtie land, Selah.

7 Heare me ſpeedily, O Lord, my ſpirit faileth, hide not thy face from mee : ||leſt I be like vnto them that goe downe into the pit.

8 Cauſe mee to heare thy louing kindneſſe in the morning, for in thee doe I truſt, cauſe mee to knowe the way wherein I ſhould walke : for I lift vp my ſoule vnto thee.

9 Deliuer mee, O Lord, from mine enemies : †I flie vnto thee to hide me.

10 Teach me to doe thy will, for thou *art* my God, thy ſpirit *is* good : leade me into the land of vprightneſſe.

11 Quicken me, O Lord, for thy names ſake : for thy righteouſneſſe ſake bring my ſoule out of trouble.

12 And of thy mercy cut off mine enemies, and deſtroy all them that afflict my ſoule : for I *am* thy ſeruant.

PSAL. CXLIIII.

1 Dauid bleſſeth God for his mercie both to him and to man. 5 Hee prayeth that God would powerfully deliuer him from his enemies. 9 He promiſeth to praiſe God. 11 Hee prayeth for the happy ſtate of the kingdome.

¶ *A Pſalme* of Dauid.

Leſſed *be* the Lord my †ſtrength, which teacheth my hands †to warre, *and* my fingers to fight.
2 *||My goodnes and my fortreſſe, my high tower and my deliuerer, my ſhield, and *he* in whome I truſt : who ſubdueth my people vnder me.

3 *Lord, what *is* man, that thou takeſt knowledge of him? *or* the ſonne of man, that thou makeſt account of him?

*I
*me
*.

*id
*

*my
*o the
*&c.
n. 22
35.
ver-
*y

*. 17.
*5.
*6.

4 * Man is like to vanity : his dayes *are* as a ſhadow that paſſeth away.

5 Bow thy heauens, O Lord, and come downe : touch the mountaines, and they ſhall ſmoke.

6 *Caſt forth lightning, and ſcatter them : ſhoote out thine arrowes, and deſtroy them.

7 Send thine †hand from aboue, rid me, and deliuer me out of great waters : from the hand of ſtrange children,

8 Whoſe mouth ſpeaketh vanitie : and their right hand *is* a right hand of falſhood.

9 I will ſing a new ſong vnto thee, O God : vpon a pſalterie, *and* an inſtrument of ten ſtrings will I ſing praiſes vnto thee.

10 *It is he* that giueth ||ſaluation vnto kings : who deliuereth Dauid his ſeruant from the hurtfull ſword.

11 Rid me, and deliuer me from the hand of ſtrange children, whoſe mouth ſpeaketh vanitie : and their right hand *is* a right hand of falſhood.

12 That our ſonnes *may be* as plants growen vp in their youth ; *that* our daughters *may be* as corner ſtones, †poliſhed *after* the ſimilitude of a palace :

13 *That* our garners *may bee* full, affording †all maner of ſtore ; *that* our ſheepe may bring forth thouſands, and tenne thouſands in our ſtreetes.

14 That our oxen *may be* †ſtrong to labour, that *there be* no breaking in, nor going out ; that *there be* no complaining in our ſtreetes.

15 *Happy *is* that people that is in ſuch a caſe : *yea*, happy *is* that people, whoſe God is the Lord.

PSAL. CXLV.

1 Dauid praiſeth God for his fame, 8 For his goodnes, 11 For his kingdome, 14 For his prouidence, 17 For his ſauing mercie.

¶ Dauids *Pſalme* of praiſe.

Will extoll thee, my God, O King : and I will bleſſe thy name for euer and euer.
2 Euery day wil I bleſſe thee : and I will praiſe thy Name for euer and euer.

3 Great *is* the Lord, and greatly to be praiſed : †and his greatnes is vnſearchable.

4 One generation ſhall praiſe thy works to another, and ſhal declare thy mightie actes.

5 I will ſpeake of the glorious honour

* Pſal. 39. 6.
Iob 14. 2.

* Pſal. 18.
13, 14.

† Heb. hands

||Or, victory.

† Heb. cut.

† Heb. from
kind to kind.

† Heb. able
to beare bur-
dens, or loa-
den with
fleſh.

* Pſal. 33. 12
and 65. 4.

† Heb. and
of his great-
neſſe there
is no ſearch.

nour of thy maiestie : and of thy wonderous †workes.

† *Heb. things or words.*

6 And *men* shall speake of the might
of thy terrible acts : and I wil †declare
thy greatnesse.

† *Heb. declare it.*

7 They shall abundantly vtter the
memory of thy great goodnesse : and
shall sing of thy righteousnesse.

8 * The Lord *is* gracious and
full of compassion : slow to anger, and
†of great mercy.

* *Exod. 34. 6, 7. num. 14. 18. psal. 86. 5, 15. and 103. 8.*
† *Heb. great in mercie.*

9 The Lord *is* good to all : and
his tender mercies *are* ouer all his
workes.

10 All thy workes shall praise thee,
O Lord : and thy Saints shal blesse
thee.

11 They shall speake of the glory of
thy kingdome : and talke of thy power.

12 To make knowen to the sonnes
of men his mightie actes : and the glorious Maiestie of his kingdome.

13 Thy kingdome *is* †an euerlasting
kingdome : and thy dominion *endureth*
throughout all generations.

† *Hebr. a kingdome of all ages.*

14 The Lord vpholdeth all that
fall : and raiseth vp all those that bee
bowed downe.

15 The eyes of all ‖waite vpon thee :
and thou giuest them their meat in due
season.

‖ *Or, looke vnto thee.*

16 Thou openest thine hand : and
satisfiest the desire of euery liuing thing.

17 The Lord *is* righteous in all
his wayes : and ‖holy in all his works.

‖ *Or, merci-full, or boun-tifull.*

18 The Lord *is* nigh vnto all
them that call vpon him : to all that call
vpon him in trueth.

19 Hee will fulfill the desire of them
that feare him : he also will heare their
cry, and will saue them.

20 The Lord preserueth all them
that loue him : but all the wicked will
he destroy.

21 My mouth shall speake the praise
of the Lord : and let all flesh blesse
his holy Name for euer and euer.

PSAL. CXLVI.

1 The Psalmist voweth perpetuall praises to
God. 3 Hee exhorteth not to trust in man.
5 God for his power, iustice, mercy and kingdome, is onely worthy to be trusted.

† *Heb. Hal-leluiah.*

†Raise yee the Lord :
prayse the Lord, O
my soule.
2 While I liue, will
I praise the Lord : I
will sing praises vnto my

God, while I haue any being.

3 *Put not your trust in Princes :
nor in the sonne of man, in whom *there is*
no ‖helpe.

* *Psal. 8, 9.*
‖ *Or, tion.*

4 His breath goeth foorth, he returneth to his earth : in that very day his
thoughts perish.

5 Happy *is he* that *hath* the God of
Iacob for his helpe : whose hope *is* in
the Lord his God :

6 *Which* made heauen and earth, the
Sea, and all that therein is : which keepeth trueth for euer :

7 *Which* executeth iudgement for
the oppressed, *which* giueth food to the
hungry : the Lord looseth the prisoners.

8 The Lord openeth the eyes
of the blinde, the Lord raiseth them
that are bowed downe : the Lord
loueth the righteous.

9 The Lord preserueth the strangers, he relieueth the fatherlesse and widow : but the way of the wicked he turneth vpside downe.

10 * The Lord shall reigne for e-
uer, *euen* thy God, O Zion, vnto all generations : Praise ye the Lord.

* *Ex. 18.*

PSAL. CXLVII.

1 The Prophet exhorteth to praise God, for his
care of the Church : 4 his power, 6 and
his mercy : 7 To praise him for his prouidence : 12 To praise him for his blessings
vpon the kingdome : 15 for his power ouer
the Meteors : 19 and for his ordinances
in the Church.

Raise ye the Lord : for
it *is* good to sing praises vn-
to our God : for it *is* pleasant, *and* praise is comely.
2 The Lord doeth
build vp Ierusalem : he gathereth together the out-casts of Israel.

3 Hee healeth the broken in heart :
and bindeth vp their †wounds.

† *H*

4 He telleth the number of the stars :
he calleth them all by *their* names.

5 Great *is* our Lord, and of great
power : †his vnderstanding is infinite.

† *H vnd din no*

6 The Lord lifteth vp the meeke :
hee casteth the wicked downe to the
ground.

7 Sing vnto the Lord with
thanksgiuing : sing prayse vpon the
harpe vnto our God :

8 Who couereth the heauen with
cloudes, who prepareth raine for the
earth :

earth : who maketh graſſe to growe vpon the mountaines.

*b 39. 3.
* 104.
28.*

9 * He giueth to the beaſt his foode : *and* to the yong rauens which crie.

10 Hee delighteth not in the ſtrength of the horſe : he taketh not pleaſure in the legs of a man.

11 The LORD taketh pleaſure in them that feare him : in thoſe that hope in his mercie.

12 Praiſe the LORD, O Ieruſalem : praiſe thy God, O Zion.

13 For hee hath ſtrengthened the barres of thy gates : hee hath bleſſed thy children within thee.

*b. who
eth thy
er peace
b. fat
heate.*

14 † He maketh peace *in* thy borders: *and* filleth thee with the † fineſt of the wheate.

15 He ſendeth forth his commande-ment *vpon* earth · his word runneth very ſwiftly.

16 He giueth ſnow like wooll : he ſcat-tereth the hoare froſt like aſhes.

17 He caſteth forth his yce like mor-ſels : who can ſtand before his cold ?

18 He ſendeth out his word, and mel-teth them : he cauſeth his wind to blow, *and* the waters flow.

*b. his
is.*

19 He ſheweth † his word vnto Ia-cob : his ſtatutes and his iudgements vnto Iſrael.

20 He hath not dealt ſo with any na-tion : and as for *his* iudgements, they haue not knowen them. Praiſe yee the LORD.

PSAL. CXLVIII.

1 The Pſalmist exhorteth the celeſtiall, 7 The terreſtriall, 11 And the rationall creatures to praiſe God.

*b. Hal-
ah.*

† Raiſe yee the LORD. Praiſe ye the LORD from the heauens : praiſe him in the heights.

2 Praiſe yee him all his Angels : praiſe ye him all his hoſts.

3 Praiſe ye him Sunne and Moone : praiſe him all ye ſtarres of light.

4 Praiſe him ye heauens of hea-uens : and ye waters that *be* aboue the heauens.

5 Let them praiſe the Name of the LORD : for he commanded, and they were created.

6 Hee hath alſo ſtabliſhed them for euer and euer : he hath made a decree which ſhall not paſſe.

7 Praiſe the LORD from the earth :

ye dragons and all deepes.

8 Fire and haile, ſnow and vapour : ſtormie wind fulfilling his word.

9 Mountaines and all hilles ; fruit-full trees, and all cedars.

10 Beaſtes and all cattell: creeping things, and † flying foule.

*† Heb. birds
of wing.*

11 Kings of the earth, and all people : Princes, and all Iudges of the earth.

12 Both young men and maidens : olde men and children.

13 Let them praiſe the Name of the LORD, for his Name alone is †excel-lent : his glory *is* aboue the earth and heauen.

*† Heb. exal-
ted.*

14 Hee alſo exalteth the horne of his people, the praiſe of all his Saints ; euen of the children of Iſrael, a people neere vnto him. Praiſe ye the LORD.

PSAL. CXLIX.

1 The Prophet exhorteth to praiſe God for his loue to the Church, 5 and for that power, which hee hath giuen to the Church to rule the conſciences of men.

† Raiſe yee the LORD : Sing vnto the LORD a new ſong : *and* his prayſe in the Congregation of Saints.

*† Heb. Hal-
leluiah.*

2 Let Iſrael reioyce in him that made him : let the children of Zion bee ioyfull in their King.

3 Let them praiſe his Name ‖ in the dance : let them ſing praiſes vnto him with the timbrell and harpe.

*‖ Or, with
the pipe.*

4 For the LORD taketh pleaſure in his people : hee will beautifie the meeke with ſaluation.

5 Let the Saints be ioyfull in glo-ry : let them ſing aloude vpon their beddes.

6 Let the high *praiſes* of God *be* †in their mouth : and a two edged ſword in their hand :

*† Heb. in
their throat.*

7 To execute vengeance vpon the heathen : *and* puniſhments vpon the people.

8 To binde their Kings with chaines : and their Nobles with fetters of yron.

9 * To execute vpon them the iudge-ment written : This honour *haue* all his Saints. Praiſe ye the LORD.

Deut. 7. 1.

PSAL. CL.

1 An exhortation to praiſe God, 3 with all kind of inſtruments.

Praiſe

† Hallelu-
iah.

‖ Or, Cornet.

† Raise ye the Lord. Praise God in his Sanctuarie : Praise him in the firmament of his power.

2 Praise him for his mightie actes : Praise him according to his excellent greatnesse.

3 Praise him with the sound of the ‖ Trumpet : Prayse him with the Psalterie and Harpe.

4 Praise him with the timbrell and ‖ dance : praise him with stringed instruments, and Organes.

5 Praise him vpon the loud cymbals : praise him vpon the high sounding cymbals.

6 Let euery thing that hath breath, praise the Lord. Praise yee the Lord.

‖Or,

¶ THE PROVERBES.

CHAP. I.

1 The vse of the Prouerbes. 7 An exhortation to feare God and beleeue his word. 10 To auoyd the intisings of sinners. 20 Wisdome complaineth of her contempt. 24 She threatneth her contemners.

HE Prouerbes of Solomon the sonne of Dauid, King of Israel,

2 To knowe wisedome and instruction, to perceiue the words of vnderstanding,

3 To receiue the instruction of wisdome, iustice, and iudgement & † equitie.

4 To giue subtiltie to the simple, to the yong man knowledge and ‖ discretion.

5 A wise man wil heare, and wil increase learning : and a man of vnderstanding shall attaine vnto wise counsels :

6 To vnderstand a prouerbe, and ‖ the interpretation ; the wordes of the wise, and their darke sayings.

7 ¶ * The feare of the Lord is ‖ the beginning of knowledge : but fooles despise wisedome and instruction.

8 My sonne, heare the instruction of thy father, and forsake not the law of thy mother.

9 For they shall be † an ornament of grace vnto thy head, and chaines about thy necke.

† Hebr. equities.

‖ Or, aduisement.

‖ Or, an eloquchtspcach.

* Iob 28. 28. psal. 111. 10. prou. 9. 10.
‖ Or, the principall part.

† Hebr. an adding.

10 ¶ My sonne, if sinners entise thee, consent thou not.

11 If they say, Come with vs, let vs lay wait for blood, let vs lurke priuily for the innocent without cause :

12 Let vs swallow them vp aliue, as the graue, and whole, as those that goe downe into the pit :

13 Wee shall finde all precious substance, wee shall fill our houses with spoile :

14 Cast in thy lot among vs, let vs all haue one purse :

15 My sonne, walke not thou in the way with them ; refraine thy foot from their path :

16 * For their feete runne to euil, and make haste to shed blood.

17 Surely in vaine the net is spread † in the sight of any bird.

18 And they lay wait for their owne blood, they lurke priuily for their owne liues.

19 So are the waies of euery one that is greedie of gaine : which taketh away the life of the owners thereof.

20 ¶ † Wisedome crieth without, she * vttereth her voice in the streets :

21 Shee crieth in the chiefe place of concourse, in the openings of the gates : in the city she vttereth her words, saying,

22 How long, ye simple ones, will ye loue simplicitie ? and the scorners delight in their scorning, and fooles hate knowledge ?

23 Turne you at my reproofe : behold, I will powre out my spirit vnto you,

* Isa
rom.

† Hebr
the ey
euery
that h
wing.

† Hebr
dome
is, ex
wisea
* Pro

you, I will make knowen my wordes
vnto you.

s. 65. 12.
66. 4.
v. 13.
1. 8. 18

24 ¶ * Because I haue called, and
yee refused, I haue ſtretched out my
hand, and no man regarded:

25 But ye haue ſet at nought all my
counſell, & would none of my reproofe:

26 I also will laugh at your calamitie, I wil mocke when your feare commeth.

s. 27.
a. 1. 15.
1. 11.
. 12.

27 * When your feare commeth as
deſolation, and your deſtruction commeth as a whirlewinde; when diſtreſſe
and anguiſh commeth vpon you :

cah. 3. 4

28 * Then ſhall they call vpon mee,
but I will not anſwere; they ſhall ſeeke
me early, but they ſhall not finde me :

29 For that they hated knowledge,
and did not chooſe the feare of the
LORD.

30 They would none of my counſel:
they deſpiſed all my reproofe.

31 Therefore ſhall they eate of the
fruite of their owne way, and be filled
with their owne deuices.

eaſe
e ſimple.

32 For the || turning away of the ſim-
ple ſhall ſlay them, and the proſperity of
fooles ſhall deſtroy them.

33 But who ſo hearkneth vnto mee,
ſhall dwell ſafely, and ſhall be quiet
from feare of euill.

CHAP. II.

1 Wiſedome promiſeth godlineſſe to her children, 10 and ſafety from euill company,
20 and direction in good wayes.

 Y ſonne, if thou wilt re-
ceiue my words, and hide
my commaundements
with thee;

2 So that thou incline
thine eare vnto wiſe-
dome, and apply thine heart to vnderſtanding:

3 Yea if thou cryeſt after knowledge,

b. giueſt
voice.

and +lifteſt vp thy voyce for vnderſtanding :

at. 13.

4 * If thou ſeekeſt her as ſiluer, and
ſearcheſt for her, as for hid treaſures :

5 Then ſhalt thou vnderſtand the
feare of the LORD, and find the
knowledge of God.

m. 1. 5.
ng. 3. 9.

6 * For the LORD giueth wiſedome : out of his mouth commeth knowledge, and vnderſtanding.

7 He layeth vp ſound wiſedome for
the righteous : he is a buckler to them
that walke vprightly.

8 He keepeth the pathes of iudgement, and preſerueth the way of his
Saints.

9 Then ſhalt thou vnderſtand
righteouſneſſe, and iudgement, and e-
quity ; yea euery good path.

10 ¶ When wiſedome entreth into
thine heart, and knowledge is pleaſant
vnto thy ſoule ;

11 Diſcretion ſhall preſerue thee, vnderſtanding ſhall keepe thee :

12 To deliuer thee from the way of
the euill man, from the man that ſpeaketh froward things.

13 Who leaue the pathes of vprightneſſe, to walke in the wayes of darkeneſſe :

14 Who reioyce to doe euill, and delight in the frowardneſſe of the wicked.

15 Whoſe wayes are crooked, and
they froward in their pathes.

16 To deliuer thee from the ſtrange
woman, * euen from the ſtranger, which
flattereth with her words :

* Prou. 5. 3.
and 7. 5.

17 Which forſaketh the guide of her
youth, and forgetteth the couenant of
her God.

18 For her houſe inclineth vnto
death, and her pathes vnto the dead :

19 None that goe vnto her, returne
againe, neither take they hold of the
pathes of life.

20 That thou mayeſt walke in the
way of good men, and keepe the pathes
of the righteous.

21 * For the vpright ſhall dwell in
the land, and the perfect ſhall remaine
in it.

* Pſal. 37
30.

22 * But the wicked ſhall be cut off
from the earth, and the tranſgreſſours
ſhalbe || rooted out of it.

* Iob. 18.
17. pſal.
104. 35.
‖ Or, pluckt
vp.

CHAP. III.

1 An exhortation to obedience, 5 to faith, 7
to mortification, 9 to deuotion, 11 to patience. 13 The happy gaine of wiſedome. 19
The power, 21 and the benefits of wiſedome.
27 An exhortation to charitableneſſe, 30
peaceableneſſe, 31 and contentedneſſe. 33
The curſed ſtate of the wicked.

 Y ſonne, forget not my
lawe ; * but let thine heart
keepe my commaunde-
ments :

2 For length of dayes,
and +long life, and peace ſhall they adde
to thee.

* Deut. 8. 1.
& 30. 16.

† Heb. yeeres
of life.

3 Let

3 Let not mercy and trueth forsake thee : *bind them about thy necke, write them vpon the table of thine heart.

4 * So shalt thou find fauour, and || good vnderstanding in the sight of God, and man.

5 ¶ Trust in the LORD with all thine heart ; and leane not vnto thine owne vnderstanding.

6 * In all thy wayes acknowledge him, and he shall direct thy pathes.

7 ¶ * Be not wise in thine owne eyes : feare the LORD, and depart from euill.

8 It shalbe †health to thy nauill, and †marrow to thy bones.

9 * Honour the LORD with thy substance, and with the first fruits of all thine increase.

10 * So shall thy barnes be filled with plenty, and thy presses shall burst out with new wine.

11 ¶ * My sonne, despise not the chastening of the LORD : neither be weary of his correction.

12 For whom the LORD loueth, he correcteth, euen as a father the sonne, in whom he delighteth

13 ¶ Happy is the man that findeth wisedome, and †the man that getteth vnderstanding.

14 * For the merchandise of it is better then the merchandise of siluer, and the gaine thereof, then fine gold.

15 She is more precious then Rubies : and all the things thou canst desire, are not to be compared vnto her.

16 Length of dayes is in her right hand : and in her left hand, riches and honour.

17 Her wayes are wayes of plesantnesse : and all her pathes are peace.

18 She is a tree of life, to them that lay hold vpon her : and happy is euery one that retaineth her

19 The LORD by wisedome hath founded the earth ; by vnderstanding hath he || established the heauens.

20 By his knowledge the depthes are broken vp ; and the cloudes droppe downe the dew.

21 ¶ My sonne, let not them depart from thine eyes : keepe sound wisedome and discretion.

22 So shall they bee life vnto thy soule, and grace to thy necke.

23 * Then shalt thou walke in thy way safely, & thy foot shall not stumble.

24 When thou lyest downe, thou

shalt not be afraide : yea, thou shalt lye downe, and thy sleepe shalbe sweet.

25 Be not afraid of sudden feare, neither of the desolation of the wicked, when it commeth.

26 For the LORD shalbe thy confidence, and shall keepe thy foote from being taken.

27 ¶ Withhold not good from them † to whom it is due, when it is in the power of thine hand to doe it.

28 Say not vnto thy neighbour, Goe, and come againe, and to morrow I will giue, when thou hast it by thee.

29 || Deuise not euil against thy neighbour, seeing hee dwelleth securely by thee.

30 ¶ Striue not with a man without cause, if hee haue done thee no harme.

31 ¶ * Enuie thou not † the oppressour, and choose none of his wayes.

32 For the froward is abomination to the LORD : * but his secret is with the righteous.

33 ¶ * The curse of the LORD is in the house of the wicked : but he blesseth the habitation of the iust.

34 Surely he scorneth the scorners : but he giueth grace vnto the lowly.

35 The wise shall inherite glory, but shame †shalbe the promotion of fooles.

CHAP. IIII.

1 Solomon, to perswade obedience, 3 sheweth what instruction hee had of his parents, 5 to study wisdome, 14 and to shun the path of the wicked. 20 Hee exhorteth to faith, 23 and sanctification.

Eare, ye children, the instruction of a father, and attend to know vnderstanding.

2 For I giue you good doctrine : forsake you not my law.

3 For I was my fathers sonne, * tender and onely beloued in the sight of my mother.

4 * He taught me also, and said vnto me, Let thine heart reteine my wordes : keepe my commandements, and liue.

5 Get wisedome, get vnderstanding : forget it not, neither decline from the wordes of my mouth.

6 Forsake her not, and she shall preserue thee : loue her, and she shall keepe thee.

7 Wisedome is the principall thing,
therefore-

* Exod. 13. 9. deut. 6. 8.

* Psal. 111. 10.
|| Or, good successe.

* 1. Chron. 28. 9.

* Rom. 12. 16.

† Hebr. medicine.
† Hebr. watring, or moystning.
* Exod. 23. 19. and 34. 36. deut. 26. 2. &c. mala. 3. 10. &c. luke 14. 13.
* Deut. 28. 8.
* Iob 5. 17. hebr. 12. 5. apoc. 3. 19.

† Hebr. the man that draweth out vnderstanding.
* Iob 28. 15. &c. psal. 19. 10. pro 8. vers. 11. and 19. and 16. 16.

|| Or, prepared

* Psal. 37. 24. and 91. 11.

† Hebr. owners of.

|| Or, practise no

* Psal.
† Hebr. man of lence.
* Psal. 13.

* Mala.

* Iam. 1. pet.

† Hebr. alteth t fooles.

*1 Ch 29. 1.

*1 Ch 28. 9.

therefore get wisedome : and with all thy getting, get vnderstanding.

8 Exalt her, and shee shall promote thee : shee shall bring thee to honour, when thou doest imbrace her

9 * She shall giue to thine head an ornament of grace, ||a crowne of glory shall she deliuer to thee.

10 Heare, O my sonne, and receiue my sayings : and the yeeres of thy life shalbe many.

11 I haue taught thee in the way of wisedome : I haue lead thee in right pathes.

12 When thou goest, thy steps shall not be straitned, *and when thou runnest, thou shalt not stumble.

13 Take fast hold of instruction, let *her* not goe; keepe her, for she is thy life.

14 ¶ * Enter not into the path of the wicked, and goe not in the way of euill men.

15 Auoid it, passe not by it, turne from it, and passe away.

16 For they sleepe not except they haue done mischiefe : and their sleepe is taken away vnlesse they cause some to fall.

17 For they eate the bread of wickednesse, and drinke the wine of violence.

18 But the path of the iust *is* as the shining light that shineth more and more vnto the perfect day.

19 The way of the wicked *is* as darknes : they know not at what they stumble.

20 ¶ My sonne, attend to my words, incline thine eare vnto my sayings.

21 Let them not depart from thine eyes : keepe them in the midst of thine heart.

22 For they are life vnto *those* that find them, and † health to all their flesh.

23 ¶ Keepe thy heart † with all diligence : for out of it *are* the issues of life.

24 Put away from thee † a froward mouth, and peruerse lips put farre from thee.

25 Let thine eyes looke right on, and let thine eye lids looke straight before thee.

26 Ponder the path of thy feet, ||and let all thy wayes be established.

27 * Turne not to the right hande nor to the left : remoue thy foot frō euil.

CHAP. V.

1 Solomon exhorteth to the studie of wisedome.
3 He sheweth the mischiefe of whoredome and riot. 15 He exhorteth to contentednes, liberalitie, and chastitie. 22 The wicked are ouertaken with their owne sinnes.

Y sonne, attend vnto my wisedome, *and* bowe thine eare to my vnderstanding.

2 That thou mayest regard discretion, and *that* thy lips may keepe knowledge.

3 ¶ * For the lips of a strange *woman* drop *as* an hony combe, and her † mouth *is* smoother then oyle.

4 But her end is bitter as wormewood, sharpe as a two edged sword.

5 * Her feete goe downe to death : her steps take hold on hell.

6 Lest thou shouldest ponder the path of life, her wayes are moueable, *that* thou canst not know *them*.

7 Heare me now therefore, O yee children : & depart not from the words of my mouth.

8 Remoue thy way farre from her, and come not nie the doore of her house:

9 Lest thou giue thine honour vnto others, and thy yeeres vnto the cruell:

10 Lest strangers be filled with † thy wealth, and thy labors *be* in the house of a stranger,

11 And thou mourne at the last, when thy flesh and thy body are consumed,

12 And say, How haue I hated instruction, and my heart despised reproofe ?

13 And haue not obeyed the voyce of my teachers, nor inclined mine eare to them that instructed me ?

14 I was almost in all euill, in the midst of the congregation & assembly.

15 ¶ Drinke waters out of thine owne cisterne, and running waters out of thine owne well.

16 Let thy fountaines bee dispersed abroad, *and* riuers of waters in the streets.

17 Let them be onely thine owne, and not strangers with thee.

18 Let thy fountaine be blessed : and reioyce with the wife of thy youth.

19 *Let her bee as* the louing Hinde and pleasant Roe, let her breasts † satisfie thee at all times, and be thou † rauisht alwayes with her loue.

20 And why wilt thou, my sonne, be rauisht with a strange woman, and imbrace the bosome of a stranger ?

21 * For the wayes of man *are* before the eyes of the LORD, and he pondereth all his goings.

22 ¶ His

Marginal notes (left column):
hap. 1.9
, shee com- e thee a ne of .
al. 91.
ap. 1. . 1.
. me- . aboue eping.
. fro- ιesse uth ruers- lips.
ull thy shalbe ed .
t. 5. 32

Marginal notes (right column):
* Chap. 2. 16. and 6. 24.
† Heb. palate
* Chap. 7. 27.
† Hebr. thy strength.
† Heb. water thee.
† Heb. erre thou alwayes in her loue.
* Iob 31. 4. and 34. 21. chap. 15. 3. ier. 16. 17. and 32. 19.

† *Heb. sinne.*

22 ¶ His owne iniquities shall take the wicked himselfe, and he shall be holden with the coards of his †sinnes.

23 He shall die without instruction, and in the greatnesse of his folly he shal goe astray.

CHAP. VI.

1 Against suretiship, 6 Idlenesse, 12 And mischieuousnesse. 16 Seuen things hatefull to God. 20 The blessings of obedience. 25 The mischiefes of whoredome.

MY sonne, if thou bee surety for thy friend, *if* thou hast stricken thy hand with a stranger,

2 Thou art snared with the words of thy mouth, thou art taken with the wordes of thy mouth.

3 Doe this now, my sonne, and deliuer thy selfe, when thou art come into the hand of thy friend: goe, humble thy selfe, and ||make sure thy friend.

‖ *Or, so shalt thou preuaile with thy friend.*

4 Giue not sleepe to thine eyes, nor slumber to thine eyelids.

5 Deliuer thy selfe as a Roe from the hand *of the hunter,* and as a bird from the hand of the fowler.

6 ¶ Goe to the Ant, thou sluggard, consider her wayes, and be wise.

7 Which hauing no guide, ouerseer, or ruler,

8 Prouideth her meat in the Summer, *and* gathereth her food in the haruest.

* *Cha. 13. 4. and 20. 4. and 24. 33.*

9 * How long wilt thou sleepe, O sluggard? when wilt thou arise out of thy sleepe?

10 Yet a little sleepe, a little slumber, a little folding of the hands to sleepe.

11 So shall thy pouertie come as one that trauaileth, and thy want as an armed man.

12 ¶ A naughtie person, a wicked man walketh with a froward mouth.

13 He winketh with his eyes, he speaketh with his feete, hee teacheth with his fingers.

† *Heb. casteth forth.*

14 Frowardnesse *is* in his heart, he deuiseth mischiefe continually, he †soweth discord.

15 Therefore shall his calamitie come suddenly; suddenly shall hee be broken without remedie.

† *Heb. of his soule.*

16 ¶ These six things doeth the Lord hate; yea seuen are an abomination †vnto him.

17 † A proude looke, a lying tongue, and hands that shed innocent blood:

† *Hebr. haughti eyes.*

18 An heart that deuiseth wicked imaginations, *feet that be swift in running to mischiefe:

* *Rom 15.*

19 A false witnesse *that* speaketh lies; and him that soweth discord among brethren.

20 ¶ * My sonne, keepe thy fathers commandement, and forsake not the law of thy mother.

* *Cha*

21 Binde them continually vpon thine heart, *and* tie them about thy necke.

22 When thou goest, it shall leade thee; when thou sleepest, it shall keepe thee; and when thou awakest, it shall talke with thee.

23 * For the Commandement *is* a ||lampe, and the Lawe is light: and reproofes of instruction *are* the way of life:

* *Psa & 119.* ‖ *Or, c*

24 * To keepe thee from the euill woman, from the flatterie ‖ of the tongue of a strange woman.

* *Cha and 5. and 7.* ‖ *Or, strang tongu* * *Mat*

25 * Lust not after her beautie in thine heart; neither let her take thee with her eyelids.

26 For by meanes of a whorish woman, *a man is brought* to a piece of bread: and the † adulteresse will hunt for the precious life.

† *Heb woma man, mans*

27 Can a man take fire in his bosome, and his clothes not be burnt?

28 Can one goe vpon hote coales, and his feete not be burnt?

29 So he that goeth in to his neighbours wife; whosoeuer toucheth her, shall not be innocent.

30 Men doe not despise a thiefe, if he steale to satisfie his soule, when hee is hungry:

31 But *if* he be found, he shall restore seuenfold, he shall giue all the substance of his house.

32 *But* who so committeth adultery with a woman, lacketh † vnderstanding: hee that doeth it, destroyeth his owne soule.

† *Heb*

33 A wound and dishonour shall he get, and his reproch shall not be wiped away.

34 For iealousie *is* the rage of a man: therefore he will not spare in the day of vengeance.

35 † He will not regard any ransome; neither will hee rest content, though thou giuest many giftes.

† *Heb will cept of an some.*

CHAP.

CHAP. VII.

1 Solomon perſwadeth to a sincere and kind fa-
miliaritie with wisedome. 6 In an example of
his owne experience, he sheweth 10 the cunning of an whore, 22 And the desperate simplicitie of a yong wanton. 24 Hee dehorteth
from such wickednesse.

MY ſonne, keepe my words,
and lay vp my commaun-
dements with thee.

2 * Keepe my comman-
dements, and liue: and my
law as the apple of thine eye.

at. 6. 8.
10.
3. 3.

3 Bind them vpon thy fingers, write
them vpon the table of thine heart.

4 Say vnto Wisedome, Thou *art*
my sister, and call Vnderstanding *thy*
kinsewoman,

ap. 5. 3.

5 *That they may keepe thee from
the strange woman, from the stranger
which flattereth with her words.

6 ¶ For at the windowe of my
house I looked through my casement,

. the
s.

7 And behelde among the simple
ones, I discerned among †the youths,
a yong man void of vnderstanding,

8 Passing through the streete neere
her corner, and he went the way to her
house,

in the
ng of
y.

9 In the twilight †in the euening,
in the blacke and darke night :

10 And behold, there met him a woman, *with* the attire of an harlot, and
subtill of heart.

p. 9. 13

11 (* She is loud and stubburne, her
feet abide not in her house :

12 Now is shee without, now in the
streetes, and lieth in waite at euery corner.)

13 So she caught him, and kissed him,
and †with an impudent face, said vnto
him,

. shee
-thened
ce and
,

14 I *haue* †peace offerings with me :
this day haue I paid my vowes.

15 Therefore came I forth to meete
thee, diligently to seeke thy face, and I
haue found thee.

peace
gs are
me.

16 I haue deckt my bed with couerings of tapestrie, with carued workes,
with fine linnen of Egypt.

17 I haue perfumed my bed with
myrrhe, aloes, and cynamom.

18 Come, let vs take our fill of loue
vntill the morning : let vs solace our
selues with loues.

19 For the good-man *is* not at home,
he is gone a long iourney.

20 He hath taken a bag of money

†with him, *and* will come home at ǁ the
day appointed.

† Heb. in his
hand.
ǁ Or, the
New moone.

21 With much faire speech she caused
him to yeeld, with the flattering of her
lips she forced him.

22 He goeth after her †straightway,
as an oxe goeth to the slaughter, or as a
foole to the correction of the stocks,

† Heb. sud-
denly.

23 Til a dart strike through his liuer,
as a bird hasteth to the snare, and
knoweth not that it *is* for his life.

24 ¶ Hearken vnto me now therefore, O ye children, and attend to the
words of my mouth.

25 Let not thine heart decline to her
wayes, goe not astray in her paths.

26 For shee hath cast downe many
wounded : yea many strong men haue
bene slaine by her.

27 * Her house *is* the way to hell, going downe to the chambers of death.

* Chap. 2.
18. & 5. 5.

CHAP. VIII.

1 The fame, 6 and euidencie of wisedome. 10
The excellencie, 12 the nature, 15 the
power, 18 the riches, 22 and the eternitie of
wisedome. 32 Wisedome is to be desired for
the blessednesse it bringeth.

DOeth * not Wisedome crie ?
& Vnderstanding put foorth
her voice ?

2 Shee standeth in the
top of high places, by the way in the
places of the pathes.

* Cha. '. 20

3 She cryeth at the gates, at the entrie of the citie, at the comming in at the
doores.

4 Vnto you, O men, I call, and
my voice *is* to the sonnes of man.

5 O yee simple, vnderstand wisedome : and yee fooles, be yee of an vnderstanding heart.

6 Heare, for I will speake of excellent things : and the opening of my
lippes *shalbe* right things.

7 For my mouth shall speake truth,
and wickednesse *is* †an abomination to
my lippes.

† Heb. the
abomination
of my lips.

8 All the words of my mouth *are* in
righteousnes, *there is* nothing †froward
or peruerse in them.

† Heb. wrea-
thed.

9 They *are* all plaine to him that
vnderstandeth : and right to them that
find knowledge.

10 Receiue my instruction, and not
siluer : and knowledge rather then
choise gold.

* Iob 28. 15
psal. 19. 11.
chap. 3. 15.
& 16. 16.

11 *For wisedome *is* better then rubies :

|| Or, ſubtil-
tie.

bies : and all the things that may be deſired, are not to be compared to it.

12 I wiſedome dwell with || pru-
dence, and find out knowledge of witty
inuentions

. 13 The feare of the LORD *is* to
hate euill : pride and arrogancie, and the
euill way, and the froward mouth doe
I hate.

14 Counſell *is* mine, and ſound wiſedome : I *am* vnderſtanding, I *haue*
ſtrength.

15 By me kings reigne, and princes
decree iuſtice.

16 By me Princes rule, and Nobles,
euen all the Iudges of the earth.

17 I loue them that loue me, and
thoſe that ſeeke me early, ſhall find me.

* Prou. 3.
16.

18 *Riches and honour *are* with me,
yea durable riches and righteouſneſſe.

* Prou. 3.
14.

19 *My fruite *is* better then gold, yea
then fine gold, and my reuenue then
choiſe ſiluer.

|| Or, walke.

20 I ||leade in the way of righteouſ-
neſſe, in the midſt of the pathes of iudgment,

21 That I may cauſe thoſe that loue
me, to inherite ſubſtance : and I will fill
their treaſures.

22 The LORD poſſeſſed me in the
beginning of his way, before his works
of old.

23 I was ſet vp from euerlaſting,
from the beginning, or euer the earth
was.

24 When *there were* no depthes, I
was brought forth : when *there were* no
fountaines abounding with water.

25 Before the mountaines were ſetled : before the hilles, was I brought
foorth :

|| Or, open
places.
|| Or, the
chiefe part.

26 While as yet he had not made the
earth, nor the ||fields, nor the ||higheſt
part of the duſt of the world.

|| Or, a circle.

27 When hee prepared the heauens,
I was there . when he ſet ||a compaſſe
vpon the face of the depth.

28 When he eſtabliſhed the cloudes
aboue : when he ſtrengthned the fountaines of the deepe.

* Gen. 1. 10.
iob. 38. 10.
pſal. 14. 9.

29 *When he gaue to the ſea his decree, that the waters ſhould not paſſe
his commandement . when he appointed the foundations of the earth ·

30 Then I was by him, *as* one
brought vp *with him :* and I was daily
his delight, reioycing alwayes before
him :

31 Reioycing in the habitable part of

his earth, and my delights *were* with
the ſonnes of men.

32 Nowe therefore hearken vnto
me, O yee children : for bleſſed *are they*
that keepe my wayes.

* Pſa.
1, 2, 3
128. 1
11. 28

33 Heare inſtruction, and bee wiſe,
and refuſe it not.

34 Bleſſed *is* the man that heareth
me : watching daily at my gates, waiting at the poſtes of my doores.

35 For whoſo findeth mee, findeth
life, and ſhall †obtaine fauour of the
LORD

† He
foort

36 But hee that ſinneth againſt me,
wrongeth his owne ſoule : all they that
hate me, loue death.

CHAP IX.

1 The diſcipline, 4 and doctrine of wiſedome.
13 The cuſtome, 16 and error of folly.

Iſedome hath builded her
houſe : ſhe hath hewen out
her ſeuen pillars.

2 She hath killed †her
beaſtes ; ſhe hath mingled
her wine : ſhe hath alſo furniſhed her
table.

† He
killin

3 She hath ſent forth her maidens ;
ſhe cryeth vpon the higheſt places of the
citie.

4 Who ſo *is* ſimple, let him turne in
hither : as for him that wanteth vnderſtanding, ſhe ſayth to him :

5 Come, eate of my bread, and drinke
of the wine, *which* I haue mingled.

6 Forſake the fooliſh, and liue ; and
goe in the way of vnderſtanding.

7 He that reproueth a ſcorner, getteth to himſelfe ſhame : and he that rebuketh a wicked man, *getteth* himſelfe a
blot.

8 *Reproue not a ſcorner, leſt hee
hate thee : rebuke a wiſe man, and hee
will loue thee

* M
16.

9 Giue *inſtruction* to a wiſe man, and
he will be yet wiſer : teach a iuſt man,
and he will increaſe in learning.

10 *The feare of the LORD *is* the
beginning of wiſedome : and the knowledge of the holy *is* vnderſtanding.

* Io
28.
pſal
10. 6
1. 7.
* Ch
10. 2

11 *For by me thy dayes ſhall be multiplied : and the yeeres of thy life ſhalbe
increaſed.

12 If thou be wiſe, thou ſhalt be
wiſe for thy ſelfe : but *if* thou ſcorneſt,
thou alone ſhalt beare it.

13 ¶ *A fooliſh woman *is* clamo-
rous : ſhe *is* ſimple, & knoweth nothing.

* Ch
11.

14 For

14 For she ſitteth at the doore of her houſe on a ſeate, in the high places of the Citie :

15 To call paſſengers who go right on their wayes :

16 Who ſo _is_ ſimple, let him turne in hither : and as for him that wanteth vnderſtanding, ſhe ſaith to him ;

17 Stollen waters are ſweet, and bread † _eaten_ in ſecret is pleaſant.

18 But hee knoweth not that the dead _are_ there ; _and that_ her gueſts _are_ in the depths of hell.

CHAP. X.

From this Chapter to the fiue and twentieth, are sundry obseruations of morall vertues, and their contrary vices.

He Prouerbes of Solomon : * A wiſe ſonne maketh a glad father : but a fooliſh ſonne _is_ the heauineſſe of his mother.

2 * Treaſures of wickedneſſe profit nothing : but righteouſnes deliuereth from death.

3 * The LORD will not ſuffer the ſoule of the righteous to famiſh : but he caſteth away ‖ the ſubſtance of the wicked.

4 * Hee becommeth poore that dealeth _with_ a ſlacke hand : but the hand of the diligent, maketh rich.

5 Hee that gathereth in Summer, is a wiſe ſonne : _but_ hee that ſleepeth in harueſt, is a ſonne that cauſeth ſhame.

6 Bleſſings _are_ vpon the head of the iuſt : but * violence couereth the mouth of the wicked.

7 * The memorie of the iuſt _is_ bleſſed : but the name of the wicked ſhall rot.

8 The wiſe in heart wil receiue commaundements : but a † prating foole ‖ ſhall fall.

9 * He that walketh vprightly, walketh ſurely : but he that peruerteth his wayes, ſhalbe knowen.

10 * Hee that winketh with the eye, cauſeth ſorrow : but a prating foole ‖ ſhall fall.

11 * The mouth of a righteous man is a well of life : but violence couereth the mouth of the wicked.

12 * Hatred ſtirreth vp ſtrifes : but loue couereth all ſinnes.

13 In the lips of him that hath vnderſtanding, wiſedome is found : but a

rod _is_ for the backe of him that is voyd of † vnderſtanding.

14 Wiſe men lay vp knowledge : but the mouth of the fooliſh _is_ neere deſtruction.

15 * The rich mans wealth _is_ his ſtrong citie : the deſtruction of the poore _is_ their pouertie.

16 The labour of the righteous _tendeth_ to life : the fruite of the wicked to ſinne.

17 He _is in_ the way of life that keepeth inſtruction : but hee that refuſeth reproofe, ‖ erreth.

18 Hee that hideth hatred _with_ lying lippes, and he that vttereth a ſlander, is a foole.

19 In the multitude of words there wanteth not ſinne : but he that refraineth his lippes, is wiſe.

20 The tongue of the iuſt is _as_ choiſe ſiluer : the heart of the wicked is little worth.

21 The lippes of the righteous feed many : but fooles die for want † of wiſedome.

22 The bleſſing of the LORD, it maketh rich, and hee addeth no ſorrow with it.

23 * It _is_ as a ſport to a foole to doe miſchiefe : but a man of vnderſtanding _hath_ wiſedome.

24 The feare of the wicked, it ſhall come vpon him : but the deſire of the righteous ſhalbe granted.

25 As the whirlewinde paſſeth, ſo _is_ the wicked no more : but the righteous _is_ an euerlaſting foundation.

26 As vineger to the teeth, and as ſmoke to the eyes, ſo _is_ the ſluggard to them that ſend him.

27 * The feare of the LORD † prolongeth dayes : but the yeeres of the wicked ſhalbe ſhortened.

28 * The hope of the righteous _ſhall bee_ gladneſſe : but the expectation of the wicked ſhall periſh.

29 The way of the LORD _is_ ſtrength to the vpright : but deſtruction _ſhall bee_ to the workers of iniquitie.

30 * The righteous ſhall neuer bee remooued : but the wicked ſhall not inhabite the earth.

31 The mouth of the iuſt bringeth foorth wiſedome : but the froward tongue ſhalbe cut out.

32 The lips of the righteous know what is acceptable : but the mouth of the wicked ſpeaketh † frowardneſſe.

CHAP.

† _Hebr. heart._

* Chap. 18. 11.

‖ _Or, causeth to erre._

† _Hebr. of heart._

* Chap. 14. 9.

* Chap. 9. 11.
† _Hebr. addeth._

* Iob 8. 13. and 11. 20. psal. 112. 10.

* Psal. 125. 1. and 37. 22.

† _Hebr. frowardnesses._

e iuſt bleſſed.

ecies.

_p._ 15.

_p._ 11.

. 37.

the
d for
wic-
ſſe.
_p._ 12.

_ſe_ 11.

. 112.

_r. a_
of lips.
shalbe
_n._
_al._ 23. 4.

_a._ 6. 13.

shalbe
_n._
_ap._ 13.

Pet. 4. 8.
T. 13. 4.

CHAP. XI.

* Leuit. 19.
36. deut.
25. 15. cha.
16. 11. and
20. 10, 23.
† Heb. bal-
lances of de-
ceit.
† Heb. a per-
fect stone.
* Chap. 16.
18. and 15.
33. and
18. 12.
* Cha. 13. 6.

* Cha. 10. 2
ezek. 7. 19.
zeph. 1. 18.

† Heb. recti-
fie.

* Cha. 5. 22.

* Chap. 21.
18.

* Iob 6. 13.

† Heb. desti-
tute of heart.

† Heb. hee
that walketh
being a
talebearer.

* 1. King.
12. 1.

† Heb. shalbe
sore broken.
† Heb. those
that strike
hands.

A *†False ballance is abomination to the LORD: but †a iust weight is his delight.

2 *When pride commeth, then commeth shame: but with the lowly is wisedome.

3 *The integritie of the vpright shall guide them: but the peruersenesse of transgressours shall destroy them.

4 *Riches profite not in the day of wrath: but righteousnesse deliuereth from death.

5 The righteousnesse of the perfect shall †direct his way: but the wicked shall fall by his owne wickednesse.

6 *The righteousnesse of the vpright shall deliuer them: but transgressours shall be taken in their owne naughtinesse.

7 When a wicked man dieth, his expectation shall perish: and the hope of vniust men perisheth.

8 *The righteous is deliuered out of trouble, and the wicked commeth in his stead.

9 *An hypocrite with his mouth destroyeth his neighbour: but through knowledge shall the iust be deliuered.

10 When it goeth well with the righteous, the citie reioyceth: and when the wicked perish, there is shouting.

11 By the blessing of the vpright the citie is exalted; but it is ouerthrowen by the mouth of the wicked.

12 He that is †void of wisedome, despiseth his neighbour: but a man of vnderstanding holdeth his peace.

13 †A tale-bearer reuealeth secrets: but hee that is of a faithfull spirit, concealeth the matter.

14 *Where no counsell is, the people fall: but in the multitude of counsellers there is safetie.

15 Hee that is suretie for a stranger, †shall smart for it: and hee that hateth †suretiship, is sure.

16 A gracious woman retaineth honour: and strong men retaine riches.

17 The mercifull man doeth good to his owne soule: but he that is cruell, troubleth his owne flesh.

18 The wicked worketh a deceitfull worke: but to him that soweth righteousnesse, shall be a sure reward.

19 As righteousnesse tendeth to life:

so he that pursueth euill, pursueth it to his owne death.

20 They that are of a froward heart, are abomination to the LORD: but such as are vpright in their way, are his delight.

21 Though hand ioyne in hand, the wicked shall not be vnpunished: but the seede of the righteous shall be deliuered.

22 As a iewell of golde in a swines snowt; so is a faire woman which †is without discretion.

23 The desire of the righteous is onely good: but the expectation of the wicked is wrath.

24 There is that scattereth, and yet increaseth; and there is that withholdeth more then is meete, but it tendeth to pouertie.

25 *†The liberall soule shalbe made fat: and he that watereth, shall be watered also himselfe.

26 Hee that withholdeth corne, the people shall curse him: but blessing shall be vpon the head of him that selleth it.

27 *He that diligently seeketh good, procureth fauour: but hee that seeketh mischiefe, it shall come vnto him.

28 He that trusteth in his riches, shall fall: but the *righteous shall flourish as a branch.

29 Hee that troubleth his owne house, shall inherite the winde: and the foole shall be seruant to the wise of heart.

30 The fruit of the righteous is a tree of life: and hee that †winneth soules, is wise.

31 *Behold, the righteous shalbe recompensed in the earth: much more the wicked and the sinner.

† Heb.
parteth
from.

* 2. Co
† Heb.
soule o
sing.

* Psal.
and 9.
and 10.
and 57

* Psal.
and 92.
iere. 17

† Heb.
keth.

* 1. Pe
18.

CHAP. XII.

Hoso loueth instruction, loueth knowledge: but he that hateth reproofe, is brutish.

2 A good man obtaineth fauour of the LORD: but a man of wicked deuices will he condemne.

3 A man shall not bee established by wickednesse: but the *roote of the righteous shall not be mooued.

4 *A vertuous woman is a crowne to her husband: but she that maketh ashamed, is as rottennesse in his bones.

5 The thoughts of the righteous are right: but the counsels of the wicked are deceit.

* Chap
25.

* 1. Co
11. 7.

6 *The

p. 1. 18.
6 *The words of the wicked *are* to lie in waite for blood : but the mouth of the vpright shall deliuer them.

. 37. 37 11, 21.
7 *The wicked are ouerthrowen, and *are* not : but the house of the righteous shall stand.

8 A man shall be commended according to his wisedome : but hee that is †of a peruerse heart, shall be despised.

per-of

9 Hee that is despised and *hath* a seruant, *is* better then he that honoureth himselfe, and lacketh bread.

10 A righteous man regardeth the life of his beast : but the ||tender mercies of the wicked *are* cruell.

bowels.

p. 28.
11 *Hee that tilleth his land, shall bee satisfied with bread : but he that followeth vaine persons, *is* void of vnderstanding.

he esse.

12 The wicked desireth ||the net of euill men : but the roote of the righteous yeeldeth *fruit*.

. the of the d is in ans-on of

13 †*The wicked is snared by the transgression of *his* lippes : but the iust shall come out of trouble.

. 18. 7. . 13. 2.

14 *A man shall bee satisfied with good by the fruit of *his* mouth, and the recompence of a mans hands shall bee rendred vnto him.

p. 3. 7.
15 *The way of a foole *is* right in his owne eyes : but he that hearkeneth vnto counsell, *is* wise.

.in that
16 A fooles wrath is †presently knowen : but a prudent man couereth shame.

. 14. 5.
17 *He that speaketh trueth, sheweth foorth righteousnesse : but a false witnesse, deceit.

. 57. 5. 8.
18 *There is that speaketh like the pearcings of a sword : but the tongue of the wise *is* health.

19 The lippe of trueth shall bee established for euer : but a lying tongue *is* but for a moment.

20 Deceit *is* in the heart of them that imagine euill : but to the counsellours of peace, *is* ioy.

21 There shall no euill happen to the iust : but the wicked shall bee filled with mischiefe.

22 Lying lippes *are* abomination to the Lord : but they that deale truely, *are* his delight.

ap. 13. 15. 2.
23 *A prudent man concealeth knowledge : but the heart of fooles proclaimeth foolishnesse.

. 10. 4.
deceit-
24 *The hand of the diligent shall beare rule : but the ||slouthfull shall bee vnder tribute.

25 *Heauinesse in the heart of man maketh it stoope : but a good word maketh it glad.

*Chap. 15. 13.

26 The righteous *is* more ||excellent then his neighbour : but the way of the wicked seduceth them.

|| Or, abundant

27 The slouthfull *man* rosteth not that which he tooke in hunting : but the substance of a diligent man *is* precious.

28 In the way of righteousnesse *is* life, and in the path-way *thereof there is* no death.

CHAP. XIII.

A Wise sonne *heareth* his fathers instruction : but a scorner heareth not rebuke.

2 *A man shall eate good by the fruit of his mouth : but the soule of the transgressours, *shall eate* violence.

*Chap. 12. 14.

3 He that keepeth his mouth, keepeth his life : *but* hee that openeth wide his lips, *shall haue* destruction.

4 The soule of the sluggard desireth, and *hath* nothing : but the soule of the diligent shall be made fat.

5 A righteous man hateth lying : but a wicked man is loathsome, and commeth to shame.

6 *Righteousnesse keepeth *him that is* vpright in the way : but wickednesse ouerthroweth †the sinner.

*Chap. 11. 3, 5, 6. † Heb. sinne.

7 There is that maketh himselfe rich, yet *hath* nothing : there is that maketh himselfe poore, yet *hath* great riches.

8 The ransome of a mans life *are* his riches : but the poore heareth not rebuke.

9 The light of the righteous reioyceth : *but the ||lampe of the wicked shall be put out.

*Iob. 18. 6. & 21. 17. || Or, candle.

10 Onely by pride commeth contention : but with the well aduised *is* wisedome.

11 *Wealth *gotten* by vanitie shall be diminished : but he that gathereth †by labour, shall increase.

*Chap. 10. 2. & 20. 21. † Heb. with the hand.

12 Hope deferred maketh the heart sicke : but *when* the desire commeth, *it is* a tree of life.

13 Whoso despiseth the word, shall be destroyed : but he that feareth the commaundement, ||shall be rewarded.

|| Or, shall be in peace.

14 *The lawe of the wise *is* a fountaine of life, to depart from the snares of death.

*Chap. 14. 27.

15 Good

15 Good vnderstanding giueth fauour : but the way of transgressours *is* hard.

*Chap. 12.
23. & 15. 2.
†Hebr spreadeth.*

16 *Euery prudent man dealeth with knowledge : but a foole †layeth open his folly.

17 A wicked messenger falleth into mischiefe : but a faithfull ambassadour *is* health.

18 Pouerty and shame *shall be to him* that refuseth instruction : but he that regardeth reproofe, shall be honoured.

19 The desire accomplished is sweet to the soule : but it is abomination to fooles to depart from euill.

20 He that walketh with wise men, shall be wise : but a companion of fooles † shall be destroyed.

† Heb. shalbe broken.

21 Euill pursueth sinners : but to the righteous, good shall be repayd.

22 A good man leaueth an inheritance to his childrens children : and the *wealth of the sinner is layd vp for the iust.

*Iob. 27.
17.*

23 *Much food *is in* the tillage of the poore : but there is that is destroyed for want of iudgement.

*Chap. 12.
11.*

24 *He that spareth his rod, hateth his sonne : but he that loueth him, chasteneth him betimes.

*Chap. 23.
13.*

25 *The righteous eateth to the satisfying of his soule : but the belly of the wicked shall want.

*Psal. 37. 3.
& 34. 10.*

CHAP. XIIII.

EVery wise woman buildeth her house ; but the foolish plucketh it downe with her hands.

2 *He that walketh in his vprightnesse, feareth the LORD : but he that is peruerse in his wayes, despiseth him.

Iob. 12. 4.

3 In the mouth of the foolish *is* a rod of pride : but the lippes of the wise shall preserue them.

4 Where no Oxen *are*, the crib *is* cleane : but much increase *is* by the strength of the Oxe.

5 *A faithfull witnesse will not lye : but a false witnesse will vtter lyes.

*Exod. 20.
16. & 23. 1.
chap. 6. 19.
& 12. 17.*

6 A scorner seeketh wisedome, and *findeth it* not : but *knowledge is easie vnto him that vnderstandeth.

Chap. 8. 9.

7 Goe from the presence of a foolish man, when thou perceiuest not *in him* the lippes of knowledge.

8 The wisedome of the prudent *is* to vnderstand his way : but the folly of fooles *is* deceit.

9 Fooles make a mocke at *sinne : but among the righteous *there is* fauour.

*Chap
23.*

10 The heart knoweth his † owne bitternesse ; and a stranger doth not intermeddle with his ioy.

*† Heb.
bitternesse
of his s*

11 The house of the wicked shall bee ouerthrowen : but the tabernacle of the vpright shall flourish.

12 *There is a way which seemeth right vnto a man : but the end thereof *are* the wayes of death.

*Chap
23.*

13 Euen in laughter the heart is sorrowfull ; and the end of that mirth *is* heauinesse.

14 The backslider in heart shall be *filled with his owne wayes : and a good man *shall be satisfied* from himselfe.

*Chap.
31.*

15 The simple beleeueth euery word : but the prudent man looketh well to his going.

16 A wise man feareth, and departeth from euill : but the foole rageth, and is confident.

17 Hee that is soone angry, dealeth foolishly : and a man of wicked deuices is hated.

18 The simple inherite folly : but the prudent are crowned with knowledge.

19 The euill bowe before the good : and the wicked at the gates of the righteous.

20 *The poore is hated euen of his owne neighbour : but †the rich *hath* many friends.

*Chap.
7.
† Heb.
are the
uers of
rich.*

21 He that despiseth his neighbour, sinneth : *but he that hath mercy on the poore, happy *is* he.

*Psal.
9.*

22 Doe they not erre that deuise euil? but mercy and trueth *shall be* to them that deuise good.

23 In all labour there is profit : but the talke of the lippes *tendeth* onely to penury.

24 The crowne of the wise *is* their riches : *but* the foolishnesse of fooles *is* folly.

25 *A true witnesse deliuereth soules : but a deceitfull *witnesse* speaketh lyes.

Ver.

26 In the feare of the LORD *is* strong confidence : and his children shall haue a place of refuge.

27 *The feare of the LORD, *is* a fountaine of life, to depart from the snares of death.

*Chap.
14.*

28 In the multitude of people *is* the kings

kings honour : but in the want of people *is* the destruction of the prince.

Hebr. short of spirit.

29 Hee that is slow to wrath, *is* of great vnderstanding : but hee that is †hasty of spirit, exalteth folly.

30 A sound heart, *is* the life of the flesh : but enuie, the rottennesse of the bones.

Chap. 17. matt. 25.).

31 *Hee that oppresseth the poore, reprocheth his Maker : but hee that honoureth him, hath mercy on the poore.

32 The wicked is driuen away in his wickednes : but the righteous hath hope in his death.

33 Wisedome resteth in the heart of him that hath vnderstanding : but *that which is* in the midst of fooles, is made knowen.

Hebr. to ations.

34 Righteousnes exalteth a nation : but sinne *is* a reproch †to any people.

35 The Kings fauour *is* toward a wise seruant : but his wrath, is *against* him that causeth shame.

CHAP. XV.

Chap. 25,

A *Soft answere turneth away wrath : but grieuous words stirre vp anger.

2 The tongue of the wise, vseth knowledge aright : but the mouth of fooles, †powreth out *foolishnes.

Hebr. bel-eth, or bbleth. Verse 28. d chap. 23. d 13. 16. .ob 34. 21, ou. 5. 21. e. 16. 17. 1 32. 19. ər. 4. 13. Iebr. the ting of tongue. Chap. 10.

3 *The eyes of the LORD *are* in euery place, beholding the euill & the good.

4 †A wholesome tongue *is* a tree of life : but peruersnesse therein *is* a breach in the spirit.

5 *A foole despiseth his fathers instruction : but hee that regardeth reproofe, *is* prudent.

6 In the house of the righteous *is* much treasure : but in the reuenues of the wicked is trouble.

7 The lippes of the wise disperse knowledge : but the heart of the foolish, *doeth* not so

hap. 21. amos 3. isa. 1. and 66. ere. 6. 20. 7. 22.

8 *The sacrifice of the wicked *is* an abomination to the LORD : but the prayer of the vpright *is* his delight.

9 The way of the wicked *is* an abomination vnto the LORD : but he loueth him that followeth after righteousnes.

, instru-n, &c.

10 ‖Correction *is* grieuous vnto him that forsaketh the way : *and* he that hateth reproofe, shall die.

ob 26. 6.

11 *Hell and destruction *are* before the LORD : how much more then, the hearts of the children of men ?

12 A scorner loueth not one that reproueth him : neither will he goe vnto the wise.

13 *A merry heart maketh a cheerefull countenance : but by sorrow of the heart, the spirit is broken.

* Chap. 17. 22.

14 The heart of him that hath vnderstanding, seeketh knowledge : but the mouth of fooles feedeth on foolishnesse.

15 All the dayes of the afflicted *are* euill : but he that is of a merry heart, hath a continuall feast.

16 *Better *is* little with the feare of the LORD, then great treasure, and trouble therewith.

* Psal. 37 16. 1. tim. 6. 6. prou. 16. 8.

17 *Better *is* a dinner of herbes where loue is, then a stalled oxe, and hatred therewith.

* Chap 17. 1.

18 *A wrathfull man stirreth vp strife : but he that is slow to anger, appeaseth strife.

* Chap. 26. 21. and 29. 22.

19 The way of the slouthfull man *is* as an hedge of thornes : but the way of the righteous *is* made †plaine.

† Hebr. is raised vp as a causey. * Chap. 10. 1.

20 *A wise sonne maketh a glad father : but a foolish man despiseth his mother.

21 *Folly *is* ioy to him that is †destitute of wisedome : but a man of vnderstanding walketh vprightly.

* Chap. 10. 23. † Hebr. voyd of heart.

22 *Without counsell, purposes are disappointed : but in the multitude of counsellours they are established.

* See Chap. 11. ver. 14.

23 A man *hath* ioy by the answere of his mouth : and a word *spoken* †in due season, how good is it ?

† Hebr. in his season.

24 *The way of life *is* aboue to the wise, that he may depart from hell beneath.

* Phil. 3. 20. col. 3. 2.

25 *The LORD will destroy the house of the proud : but he will establish the border of the widow.

* Chap. 12. 7. and 14 11.

26 *The thoughts of the wicked *are* an abomination to the LORD : but the *wordes* of the pure, *are* †pleasant words.

* Chap. 6. 18. † Heb. words of pleasant-nesse.

27 Hee that is greedy of gaine, troubleth his owne house : but he that hateth gifts, shall liue.

28 The heart of the righteous studieth to answere : but the mouth of the wicked, powreth out euil things.

29 *The LORD *is* farre from the wicked : but hee heareth the prayer of the righteous.

* Psal. 34. 16. and 145. 18.

30 The light of the eyes reioyceth the heart : *and* a good report maketh the bones fat.

31 The

31 The eare that heareth the reproofe of life, abideth among the wise.

32 He that refuseth ‖instruction, despiseth his owne soule: but he that ‖heareth reproofe, † getteth vnderstanding.

33 The feare of the Lord is the instruction of wisedome: and *before honour is humilitie.

CHAP. XVI.

He *‖preparations of the heart in man, and the answere of the tongue, is from the Lord.

2 *All the wayes of a man are cleane in his owne eyes: but the Lord weigheth the spirits.

3 *†Commit thy workes vnto the Lord, and thy thoughts shalbe established.

4 The Lord hath made all things for himselfe: *yea, euen the wicked for the day of euill.

5 *Euery one that is proud in heart, is an abomination to the Lord: though hand ioyne in hand, he shall not be †vnpunished.

6 By mercy and trueth iniquitie is purged: and by the feare of the Lord, men depart from euill.

7 When a mans wayes please the Lord, he maketh euen his enemies to be at peace with him.

8 *Better is a little with righteousnesse, then great reuenewes without right.

9 *A mans heart deuiseth his way: but the Lord directeth his steps.

10 †A diuine sentence is in the lips of the king: his mouth transgresseth not in iudgement.

11 *A iust weight and ballance are the Lords: †all the weights of the bagge are his worke.

12 It is an abomination to kings to commit wickednesse: for the throne is established by righteousnesse.

13 Righteous lips are the delight of kings: and they loue him that speaketh right.

14 The wrath of a king is as messengers of death: but a wise man will pacifie it.

15 In the light of the kings countenance is life, and *his fauour is as a cloude of the latter raine.

16 *How much better is it to get wisedome, then gold? and to get vnderstanding, rather to be chosen then siluer?

17 The high way of the vpright is to depart from euill: hee that keepeth his way, preserueth his soule.

18 * Pride goeth before destruction: and an hautie spirit before a fall.

19 Better it is to be of an humble spirit with the lowly, then to diuide the spoile with the proud.

20 ‖He that handleth a matter wisely, shall finde good: and who so *trusteth in the Lord, happy is hee.

21 The wise in heart shall be called prudent: and the sweetnesse of the lips increaseth learning.

22 *Vnderstanding is a well-spring of life vnto him that hath it: but the instruction of fooles is folly

23 The heart of the wise †teacheth his mouth, and addeth learning to his lippes.

24 Pleasant words are as an honycombe, sweete to the soule, and health to the bones.

25 * There is a way that seemeth right vnto a man; but the end thereof are the wayes of death.

26 †Hee that laboureth, laboureth for himselfe; for his mouth †craueth it of him.

27 †An vngodly man diggeth vp euill: and in his lips there is as a burning fire.

28 *A froward man †soweth strife; & a whisperer separateth chiefe friends.

29 A violent man enticeth his neighbour, and leadeth him into the way that is not good.

30 He shutteth his eyes to deuise froward things: moouing his lips he bringeth euill to passe.

31 The hoary head is a crowne of glory, if it be found in the way of righteousnesse.

32 He that is slow to anger, is better then the mighty: and he that ruleth his spirit, then he that taketh a citie.

33 The lot is cast into the lap: but the whole disposing thereof is of the Lord.

CHAP. XVII.

Etter * is a drie morsell, and quietnesse therewith; then an house full of ‖sacrifices with strife.

2 A wise seruant shall haue rule ouer a son that causeth shame: and shall haue part of the inheritance among the brethren.

3 * The

Left margin notes:

‖ Or, correction.
‖ Or, obeyeth.
† Heb. possesseth an heart
* Cha. 18. 12

* Vers. 9. and chap. 19. 21. and 20. 24. ier. 10. 23.
‖ Or, disposings.
* Cha. 21. 2.

* Psal. 37. 5. and 55. 23. mat. 6. 25. luke 12. 22. 1. pet. 5. 4.
† Heb. rolle.
* Iob 21. 30.

* Chap. 6. 7. and 8. 13.

† Heb. helde innocent.

* Psal. 37. 16. chap. 15. 16.

* Vers. 1.

† Heb. diuination.

* Leuit. 19 36. chap 11. 1.
† Heb. all the stones

* Chap. 19. 12
* Cha. 3. 11.

Right margin notes:

* Cha. 11. and 18. 12.

‖ Or, he that vnderstandeth a matter.
* Psal. 2. 12 and 34. 9. and 125. 1. isa. 30. 18. iere. 17. 7.
* Chap. 13. 14.

* Chap. 14. 12.

† Heb. the soule of him that laboureth.
† Heb. boweth vnto him.
† Heb. a man of Belial.
* Chap. 6. 14, 19. and 15. 18 and 26. 21 and 29. 22
† Heb. sendeth foorth

* Chap. 17.
‖ Or, good cheere.

† Heb. maketh wise.

sal. 26.2.
27. 21.
17. 10.
a. 3. 3.

ap. 14.

eb. held
cent.
al. 127.
d 128.

b. a lip
cellency.
b. a lip
ing.
ap. 18.

br. a
y of
e.
ap. 10.

, procu-

a re-
re aweth
a wise
then to
e a foole
undred
.

om..12.

ess. 5.

t. 3. 9.

od. 23.7
. 23.
, 24. 24

ap. 18.

ap. 6. 1.
1. 15.
b. heart.

b. the
ard of
.

a. 10. 1.

ap. 15.
nd 12.

to a
cine.

3 * The fining pot is for siluer, and the furnace for gold : but the Lord trieth the hearts.

4 A wicked doer giueth heed to false lips : and a liar giueth eare to a naughtie tongue.

5 * Whoso mocketh the poore, reproacheth his maker : and he that is glad at calamities, shall not be † vnpunished.

6 * Childrens children are the crowne of old men : and the glory of children are their fathers.

7 † Excellent speech becommeth not a foole : much lesse doe † lying lippes a prince.

8 * A gift is as a † precious stone in the eyes of him that hath it : whithersoeuer it turneth, it prospereth.

9 * He that couereth a transgression, ‖seeketh loue ; but he that repeateth a matter, separateth very friends.

10 ‖ A reproofe entreth more into a wise man, then an hundred stripes into a foole.

11 An euill man seeketh onely rebellion ; therefore a cruell messenger shall be sent against him.

12 Let a beare robbed of her whelps meet a man, rather then a foole in his folly.

13 Whoso * rewardeth euill for good, euill shall not depart from his house.

14 The beginning of strife is as when one letteth out water : therfore leaue off contention, before it be medled with.

15 * He that iustifieth the wicked, and he that condemneth the iust : euen they both are abomination to the Lord.

16 Wherfore is there a price in the hand of a foole to get wisedome, seeing he hath no heart to it ?

17 * A friend loueth at all times, and a brother is borne for aduersitie.

18 * A man void of † vnderstanding striketh hands, and becommeth suretie in the presence of his friend.

19 He loueth transgression, that loueth strife : and he that exalteth his gate, seeketh destruction.

20 † He that hath a froward heart, findeth no good, and he that hath a peruerse tongue, falleth into mischiefe.

21 * He that begetteth a foole, doth it to his sorrow : and the father of a foole hath no ioy.

22 * A merrie heart doth good ‖like a medicine : but a broken spirit drieth the bones.

23 A wicked man taketh a gift out of the bosome, to peruert the wayes of iudgement.

24 * Wisedome is before him that hath vnderstanding : but the eyes of a foole are in the ends of the earth.

25 * A foolish sonne is a griefe to his father, & bitternes to her that bare him.

26 Also to punish the iust is not good, nor to strike princes for equitie.

27 * He that hath knowledge, spareth his words : and a man of vnderstanding is of ‖an excellent spirit.

28 * Euen a foole, when he holdeth his peace, is counted wise : and he that shutteth his lips, is esteemed a man of vnderstanding.

CHAP. XVIII.

Hrough desire a man hauing ‖separated himselfe, seeketh and intermedleth with all wisedome.

2 A foole hath no delight in vnderstanding, but that his heart may discouer it selfe.

3 When the wicked commeth, then commeth also contempt, and with ignominie, reproch.

4 * The words of a mans mouth, are as deepe waters, and the well-spring of wisedome as a flowing brooke.

5 * It is not good to accept the person of the wicked, to ouerthrowe the righteous in iudgement.

6 A fooles lips enter into contention, and his mouth calleth for strokes.

7 * A fooles mouth is his destruction, and his lips are the snare of his soule.

8 * The words of a ‖tale bearer are ‖as wounds, and they goe downe into the †innermost parts of the belly.

9 Hee also that is slouthful in his worke, is brother to him that is a great waster.

10 * The name of the Lord is a strong tower . the righteous runneth into it, and † is safe.

11 * The rich mans wealth is his strong citie : and as an high wall in his owne conceit.

12 * Before destruction the heart of man is haughtie, and before honour is humilitie.

13 He that † answereth a matter before he heareth it, it is folly and shame vnto him.

14 The spirit of a man will sustaine his infirmitie : but a wounded spirit who can beare ?

15 The

* Eccles. 2.
14. and 8. 1.

* Chap. 10.
1. & 15. 20.
and 19. 13.

* Iam. 1. 19.

‖ Or, a coole
spirit.
* Iob 13. 5.

‖ Or, he that
separateth
himselfe, see-
keth accor-
ding to his
desire, and
intermed-
leth in euery
businesse.

* Cha. 20. 5.

* Chap. 24.
23.
leuit. 19.
deut. 11. 7.
and 16. 19.

* Chap. 10.
14. and 12.
13. & 13. 3.
* Chap. 12.
18. and 26.
22.
‖ Or, whis-
perer.
‖ Or, like as
when men
are wounded
† Heb. cham-
bers.
* Psal. 18. 2.
and 27. 1. &
144. 2.
† Heb. is set
alofte.
* Chap. 10.
15.

* Chap. 11.
2. & 16. 18.
and 15. 33.

† Hebr. re-
turneth a
word.

15 The heart of the prudent getteth knowledge; and the eare of the wise seeketh knowledge.

*Chap. 17. 8.

16 *A mans gift maketh roome for him, & bringeth him before great men.

17 He that is first in his owne cause, seemeth iust; but his neighbour commeth and searcheth him.

18 The lot causeth contentions to cease, and parteth betweene the mighty.

19 A brother offended is harder to be wonne then a strong citie : and their contentions are like the barres of a castle.

*Chap. 12. 14. and 13. 2.

20 *A mans belly shall be satisfied with the fruite of his mouth ; and with the increase of his lippes shall he be filled.

21 Death and life are in the power of the tongue ; and they that loue it shall eate the fruite thereof.

*Chap. 19. 14.

22 *Who so findeth a wife, findeth a good thing, and obtaineth fauour of the LORD.

23 The poore vseth intreaties, but the rich answereth *roughly.

*Iam. 2. 3.

24 A man that hath friends must shewe himselfe friendly : *and there is a friend that sticketh closer then a brother.

*Chap. 17. 17.

CHAP. XIX.

*Chap. 28. 6.

Etter is the poore that walketh in his integrity, then he that is peruerse in his lippes, and is a foole.

2 Also, that the soule be without knowledge, it is not good; and hee that hasteth with his feete, sinneth.

3 The foolishnesse of man peruerteth his way : and his heart fretteth against the LORD.

*Chap. 14. 20.

4 *Wealth maketh many friends : but the poore is separated from his neighbour.

*Exod. 23. 1. deut. 19. 16. prou. 6. 9. and 21. 28.
†Heb. held innocent.

5 *A false witnesse shall not be †vnpunished: and he that speaketh lyes, shal not escape

6 Many will entreate the fauour of the Prince : and euery man is a friend to †him that giueth gifts.

†Heb. a man of gifts.
*Chap. 14. 20.

7 *All the brethren of the poore doe hate him, howe much more doe his friends goe farre from him ? hee pursueth them with words, yet they are wanting to him.

†Heb. an heart.

8 He that getteth †wisedome loueth his owne soule : he that keepeth vnderstanding shall find good.

9 *A false witnesse shall not be vnpunished, and hee that speaketh lyes, shall perish.

*Ver. 5.

10 Delight is not seemely for a foole : much lesse *for a seruant to haue rule ouer princes.

*Eccle. 6. prou. 22.

11 *The ||discretion of a man deferreth his anger : and it is his glory to passe ouer a transgression.

*Chap. 29.
|| Or, prudence.

12 *The kings wrath is as the roaring of a lyon : but his fauour is as dewe vpon the grasse.

*Chap. 15. and 2 2. & 28.

13 *A foolish sonne is the calamity of his father ; and the contentions of a wife are *a continuall dropping.

*Chap. 1. & 15. and 17 2 & 25. and chap. 21.
*Chap. 15.

14 House and riches, are the inheritance of fathers; and *a prudent wife is from the LORD.

*Chap. 22.

15 Slouthfulnesse casteth into a deep sleepe : and an idle soule shall *suffer hunger.

*Chap. 4. and 20 13.

16 *He that keepeth the commandement, keepeth his owne soule : but hee that despiseth his wayes, shall die.

*Luc. 1. 26.

17 *Hee that hath pity vpon the poore, lendeth vnto the LORD; and ||that which he hath giuen, will he pay him againe.

*Mat. 1 42. and 2 40. 2. cor 9. 6. and || Or, his deed.

18 *Chasten thy sonne while there is hope; and let not thy soule spare ||for his crying.

*Chap. 24. & 23.
|| Or, to h destructi or, to ca him to d

19 A man of great wrath shall suffer punishment : for if thou deliuer him, yet thou must †doe it againe.

†Heb. a

20 Heare counsell, and receiue instruction, that thou mayest be wise in thy latter end.

21 *There are many deuices in a mans heart : neuerthelesse the counsell of the LORD, that shall stand.

*Iob. 23 psal. 33. 11. prou. 1. and 9. i 46. 10

22 The desire of a man is his kindnesse : and a poore man is better then a lyar.

23 The feare of the LORD tendeth to life, and he that hath it shall abide satisfied : he shall not be visited with euill.

24 *A slouthfull man hideth his hand in his bosome, and wil not so much as bring it to his mouth againe.

*Chap. 19. & 26. and 15.

25 *Smite a scorner, and the simple †will beware ; and reproue one that hath vnderstanding, and he will vnderstand knowledge

*Chap. 11.
†Heb. u be cunni

26 He that wasteth his father, and chaseth away his mother, is a sonne that causeth shame, and bringeth reproch.

27 Cease, my sonne, to heare the instruction, that causeth to erre from the words

words of knowledge.

28 † An vngodly witnesse scorneth iudgement : and the mouth of the wicked deuoureth iniquitie.

29 Iudgements are prepared for scorners, and stripes for the backe of fooles.

CHAP. XX.

 Ine *is* a mocker, strong drinke is raging : and whosoeuer is deceiued thereby, is not wise.

2 * The feare of a king, *is as* the roaring of a Lion : *who so* prouoketh him to anger, sinneth *against* his owne soule.

3 *It is* an honour for a man to cease from strife: but euery foole will be medling.

4 * The sluggard will not plow by reason of the ‖cold ; therefore shall he begge in haruest, and haue nothing.

5 * Counsell in the heart of man is *like* deepe water : but a man of vnderstanding will draw it out.

6 Most men will proclaime euery one his owne ‖goodnes : but a faithfull man who can finde ?

7 The iust man walketh in his integritie : * his children *are* blessed after him.

8 A king that sitteth in the throne of iudgement, scattereth away all euill with his eyes.

9 * Who can say, I haue made my heart cleane, I am pure from my sinne?

10 * † Diuers weights, *and* diuers † measures, both of them *are* alike abomination to the Lord.

11 Euen a childe is knowen by his doings, whether his worke *be* pure, and whether *it be* right.

12 * The hearing eare, and the seeing eye, the Lord hath made euen both of them

13 * Loue not sleepe, lest thou come to pouertie : open thine eyes, *and* thou shalt be satisfied with bread.

14 *It is* nought, *it is* nought (saith the buyer:) but when he is gone his way, then he boasteth.

15 There is gold, and a multitude of Rubies : but the lips of knowledge *are* a precious iewell.

16 * Take his garment that is suertie *for* a stranger : and take a pledge of him for a strange woman.

17 * † Bread of deceit is sweet to a man : but afterwards his mouth shall be filled with grauell.

18 * Euery purpose is established by counsell : and with good aduice make warre.

19 * He that goeth about *as* a tale-bearer, reueileth secrets ; therefore meddle not with him that ‖flattereth with his lippes.

20 * Who so curseth his father or his mother, his ‖lampe shall be put out in obscure darkenesse.

21 An inheritance may be gotten hastily at the beginning : but the ende thereof shall not be blessed.

22 * Say not thou, I will recompence euil : *but* wait on the Lord, and he shall saue thee.

23 * Diuers waights *are* an abomination vnto the Lord : and a † false ballance *is* not good.

24 * Mans goings *are* of the Lord ; how can a man then vnderstand his owne way ?

25 *It is* a snare to the man *who* deuoureth that which is holy : and after vowes, to make inquirie.

26 * A wise king scattereth the wicked, & bringeth the wheele ouer them.

27 The spirit of man *is* the ‖candle of the Lord, searching all the inward parts of the belly.

28 * Mercy and trueth preserue the king : and his throne is vpholden by mercy.

29 * The glory of yong men *is* their strength : and the beautie of old men *is* the gray head.

30 The blewnes of a wound † cleanseth away euill : so doe stripes the inward parts of the belly.

CHAP. XXI.

 HE kings heart *is* in the hand of the Lord, *as* the riuers of water : hee turneth it whithersoeuer he will

2 * Euery way of a man *is* right in his owne eyes : but the Lord pondereth the hearts.

3 * To doe iustice and iudgement, is more acceptable to the Lord, then sacrifice.

4 * † An high looke, and a proud heart, *and* ‖the plowing of the wicked, *is* sinne.

5 The thoughts of the diligent *tend* onely to plenteousnes : but of euery one
that

Side notes (left column):

br. A esse of al.

ap. 19 nd 16.

ap. 20.

winter.

ap. 18.

bountie.

al. 112.

al. 51. 5. 4. 4. ng. 2. chro. . 1. ioh.

eut. 25. hap. 11. ad. 16. 2. br. a , and a .

ebr. an h, and phah. xod. 4. sal. 94.

nap. 19. and 12.

nap. 27.

na. 9. 17. eb. bread ying, or hood.

Side notes (right column):

* Chap. 13. 22

* Chap. 11 13.

‖ Or, entiseth.

* Exod. 21. 17. leuit. 20. 9. matt. 15. 4. ‖ Or, candle.

* Deut. 32. 35. cha. 17. 13. and 24. 29. rom. 12. 17. 1. thess. 5. 15. 1. pet. 3. 9.
* Verse 10.
† Hebr. ballances of deceit.
* Psal. 37. 23. cha. 16. 9. iere. 10. 23.

* Verse 8. psal. 101 5. &c.
‖ Or, lampe.

* Psal. 101. 1. chap. 29. 14.

* Chap. 16. 31.

† Hebr. is a purging medicine against euill.

* Chap. 16. 2.

* 1. Sam. 15. 22. isa. 1. 11. hose. 6. 6. mich. 6. 7. chap. 15. 8.
* Chap. 6. 17.
† Hebr. hautines of eyes.
‖ Or, the light of the wicked.

that is hastie, onely to want.

6 *The getting of treasures by a lying tongue, *is* a vanitie tossed to and fro of them that seeke death.

7 The robbery of the wicked shall †destroy them ; because they refuse to doe iudgement.

8 The way of man *is* froward and strange : but as for the pure; his worke *is* right.

9 *It is better to dwell in a corner of the house top ; then with a †brawling woman in †a wide house.

10 *The soule of the wicked desireth euill : his neighbour †findeth no fauour in his eyes.

11 *When the scorner is punished, the simple is made wise : and when the wise is instructed, he receiueth knowledge.

12 The righteous man wisely considereth the house of the wicked : *but God* ouerthroweth the wicked for their wickednesse.

13 *Whoso stoppeth his eares at the cry of the poore, he also shall cry himselfe, but shall not be heard.

14 *A gift in secret pacifieth anger ; and a reward in the bosome, strong wrath.

15 *It is* ioy to the iust to doe iudgement : but destruction *shalbe* to the workers of iniquitie.

16 The man that wandreth out of the way of vnderstanding, shall remaine in the congregation of the dead.

17 He that loueth ||pleasure, *shall be* a poore man : hee that loueth wine and oyle, shall not be rich.

18 *The wicked *shalbe* a ransome for the righteous ; and the transgressour for the vpright.

19 *It is better to dwell †in the wildernesse, then with a contentious and an angry woman.

20 There is treasure †to be desired, and oyle in the dwelling of the wise : but a foolish man spendeth it vp.

21 Hee that followeth after righteousnesse and mercy, findeth life, righteousnesse and honour.

22 *A wise man scaleth the citie of the mightie, and casteth downe the strength of the confidence thereof.

23 * Whoso keepeth his mouth and his tongue, keepeth his soule from troubles.

24 Proud *and* haughtie scorner, *is* his name, *who* dealeth †in proud wrath.

25 *The desire of the slouthfull kil-

leth him : for his hands refuse to labour.

26 Hee coueteth greedily all the day long : but the *righteous giueth and spareth not.

27 *The sacrifice of the wicked *is* abomination : how much more, *when he* bringeth it †with a wicked minde ?

28 * †A false witnesse shall perish : but the man that heareth, speaketh constantly.

29 A wicked man hardeneth his face : but as for the vpright, he||directeth his way.

30 *There is no wisedome, nor vnderstanding, nor counsell against the LORD.

31 *The horse is prepared against the day of battell : but *||safetie is of the LORD.

CHAP. XXII.

 *Good name is rather to be chosen then great riches, *and* ||louing fauour rather then siluer & golde.

2 *The rich and poore meet together ; the LORD *is* the maker of them all.

3 *A prudent man foreseeth the euill, and hideth himselfe : but the simple passe on, and are punished.

4 * ||By humilitie *and* the feare of the LORD, are riches, and honour, and life.

5 Thornes *and* snares *are* in the way of the froward : he that doeth keepe his soule, shalbe farre from them.

6 || Traine vp a childe †in the way he should goe : and when he is olde, hee will not depart from it.

7 The rich ruleth ouer the poore, and the borrower *is* seruant † to the lender.

8 *Hee that soweth iniquitie, shall reape vanitie : ||and the rodde of his anger shall faile.

9 * †Hee that *hath* a bountifull eye, shall bee blessed : for hee giueth of his bread to the poore.

10 *Cast out the scorner, and contention shall goe out ; yea strife, and reproch shall cease.

11 He that loueth purenesse of heart, || *for* the grace of his lips the king *shall be* his friend.

12 The eyes of the LORD preserue knowledge, and he ouerthroweth the ||words of the transgressour.

13 *The slothfull man sayth, *There is* a lyon

a lyon without, I shall be slaine in the streetes.

14 * The mouth of strange women *is* a deepe pit : he that is abhorred of the Lord shall fall therein.

15 Foolishneſſe is bound in the heart of a child : *but* * the rod of correction shal driue it farre from him.

16 Hee that oppreſseth the poore to increase his *riches, and* he that giueth to the rich, shall surely *come* to want.

17 Bow downe thine eare, and heare the words of the wise, and apply thine heart vnto my knowledge.

18 For it *is* a pleasant thing, if thou keepe them † within thee; they shall withall be fitted in thy lippes.

19 That thy trust may bee in the Lord, I haue made knowen to thee this day, ||euen to thee.

20 Haue not I written to thee excellent things in counsailes and knowledge :

21 That I might make thee knowe the certainty of the words of truth; that thou mightest answere the words of trueth ||to them that send vnto thee ?

22 Rob not the poore because he *is* poore, *neither oppreſse the afflicted in the gate.

23 * For the Lord will plead their cause, and spoile the soule of those that spoiled them.

24 Make no friendship with an angrie man : and with a furious man thou shalt not goe;

25 Lest thou learne his wayes, and get a snare to thy soule.

26 * Be not thou *one* of them that strike hands, *or* of them that are sureties for debts.

27 If thou *hast* nothing to pay, why should he take away thy bed from vnder thee ?

28 * Remoue not the ancient ||land marke, which thy fathers haue set.

29 Seest thou a man diligent in his busineſſe? hee shall stand before kings, he shall not stand before †meane men.

CHAP. XXIII.

When thou sittest to eate with a ruler, consider diligently what *is* before thee.

2 And put a knife to thy throate, if thou be a man giuen to appetite.

3 Be not desirous of his dainties :

for they *are* deceitfull meate.

4 * Labour not to bee rich : cease from thine owne wisedome.

5 † Wilt thou set thine eyes vpon that which is not ? for riches certainly make themselues wings, they fly away as an Eagle toward heauen.

6 Eate thou not the bread of *him that hath* an euill eye, neither desire thou his dainty meates.

7 For as he thinketh in his heart, so is he : Eate, and drinke, sayth he to thee, but his heart *is* not with thee.

8 The morsell *which* thou hast eaten, shalt thou vomite vp, and loose thy sweete words.

9 Speake not in the eares of a foole : for hee will despise the wisedome of thy words.

10 * Remoue not the old ||land-marke; and enter not into the fields of the fatherleſſe.

11 * For their redeemer is mighty; he shall plead their cause with thee.

12 Apply thine heart vnto instruction, and thine eares to the words of knowledge.

13 * Withhold not correction from the child : for *if* thou beatest him with the rod, he shall not die.

14 Thou shalt beate him with the rod, and shalt deliuer his soule from hell.

15 My sonne, if thine heart be wise, my heart shall reioyce, ||euen mine.

16 Yea my reines shall reioyce, when thy lippes speake right things.

17 * Let not thine heart enuy sinners, but *be thou* in the feare of the Lord all the day long.

18 * For surely there is an ||end, and thine expectation shall not be cut off.

19 Heare thou, my sonne, and be wise, and guide thine heart in the way.

20 * Be not amongst wine-bibbers; amongst riotous eaters †of flesh.

21 For the drunkard and the glutton shall come to pouerty; and drousineſſe shall cloath *a man* with ragges.

22 * Hearken vnto thy father that begate thee, and despise not thy mother when she is old.

23 Buy the trueth, and sell it not; *also* wisedome and instruction and vnderstanding.

24 * The father of the righteous shall greatly reioyce : and he that begetteth a wise *child*, shall haue ioy of him.

25 Thy father and thy mother shall be

*Chap. 2.
16. and 23.
27. and 5. 3.
and 7. 5.

*Chap. 13.
24. and 19.
18. and 23.
3. and 29.
5, 17.

Heb. in thy
belly.

Or, trust
hou also.

Or, to those
hat send
hee.

Zach. 7. 10

*Chap. 23.
1. iob. 31.
1,

*Chap. 6. 1.
nd 11. 15.

*Chap. 13.
0. deut. 19
4. & 27. 7.
Or, bound.

Heb. ob-
cure men.

* 1. Tim. 6. 9.
10.

† Heb. wilt
thou cause
thine eyes to
fly vpon ?

* Chap. 22.
28. deut. 19
14. and 27.
17.
|| Or, bound.
* Chap. 22.
21.

* Chap. 13.
24. and 19.
18. and 22.
15.

|| Or, euen I
wil reioyce.

* Chap. 24.
1. and 3. 31.
psal. 37. 1.
and 73. 3.
* Chap. 24.
14.
|| Or, reward

* Rom. 13.
13. eph. 5.
18.
† Heb. of
their flesh.

* Chap. 1. 8.

* Chap. 10.
1. & 15. 20.

be glad, and she that bare thee shall reioyce.

26 My sonne, giue me thine heart, and let thine eyes obserue my wayes.

* Chap. 22. 14.
27 * For an whore *is* a deepe ditch; and a strange woman *is* a narrow pit.

* Chap. 7. 12.
‖ *Or, as a robber.*
28 * She also lyeth in wait ‖as *for* a pray, and increaseth the transgressours among men.

* Isay. 5. 11
29 * Who *hath* woe? who *hath* sorrow? who *hath* contentions? who *hath* babbling? who *hath* wounds without cause? who *hath* rednesse of eyes?

30 They that tarry long at the wine, they that goe to seeke mixt wine.

31 Looke not thou vpon the wine when it is red, when it giueth his colour in the cup, *when* it moueth it selfe aright.

‖ *Or, a cockatrice.*
32 At the last it biteth like a serpent, and stingeth like ‖an adder.

33 Thine eyes shall behold strange women, and thine heart shall vtter peruerse things.

† *Heb. in the heart of the sea.*
34 Yea thou shalt be as he that lyeth downe †in the midst of the sea, or as he that lyeth vpon the top of a mast.

† *Heb. I knew it not.*
35 They haue striken me, *shalt thou say, and* I was not sicke: they haue beaten me, *and* † I felt it not: when shall I awake? I will seeke it yet againe.

CHAP. XXIIII.

* Chap. 23. 17. and 24. 19. psal. 37. 1. &c. and 73. 3.
* Psal. 10. 7.
BE not thou * enuious against euill men, neither desire to be with them.

2 * For their heart studieth destruction, and their lippes talke of mischiefe.

3 Through wisedome is an house builded, and by vnderstanding it is established.

4 And by knowledge shall the chambers bee filled with all precious and pleasant riches.

† *Heb. is in strength.*
† *Heb. strengthneth might.*
5 A wise man †*is* strong, yea a man of knowledge † encreaseth strength.

* Chap. 20. 18: and 11. 14. and 15. 22.
6 * For by wise counsell thou shalt make thy warre: and in multitude of counsellers *there is* safetie.

7 Wisedome *is* too high for a foole: he openeth not his mouth in the gate.

8 He that deuiseth to doe euill, shall be called a mischieuous person.

9 The thought of foolishnesse *is* sinne: and the scorner *is* an abomination to men.

† *Heb. narrow.*
10 *If* thou faint in the day of aduersitie, thy strength *is* †small:

* Psal. 82
11 * If thou forbeare to deliuer them that are drawen vnto death, and those that are ready to be slaine:

12 If thou sayest, Behold, we knew it not: doth not he that pondereth the heart, consider *it?* and he that keepeth thy soule, doth *not* he know *it?* and shall *not* hee render to euery man *according to his workes?

* Iob. 34. 11. psal. 6 12. ier. 32. 19. rom. 2 6. apoc. 2 12.
* Psal. 19 9. & 119. 103.
† *Heb. vp thy palate*
* Chap. 2 18.
13 * My sonne, eate thou honie, because it *is* good, and the honie combe, *which is* sweete †to thy taste.

14 So *shall* the knowledge of wisedome *be* vnto thy soule: when thou hast found *it,* *then there shall be a reward, and thy expectation shall not be cut off.

15 Lay not waite, (O wicked man) against the dwelling of the righteous: spoile not his resting place.

* Psal. 34 18. and 37 24. iob. 5. 19.
16 * For a iust man falleth seuen times, and riseth vp *againe:* but the wicked shall fall into mischiefe.

* Psal. 35 15. chap. 5. iob. 31. 29.
17 * Reioyce not when thine enemie falleth: and let not thine heart be glad when he stumbleth:

† *Heb. it euill in hi eyes.*
18 Lest the LORD see *it,* and †it displease him, and hee turne away his wrath from him.

* Psal. 37 chap. 23. 17.
‖ *Or, keep not compa with the u ked.*
* Chap. 1 9. iob. 21.
‖ *Or, lamp*
19 * ‖Fret not thy selfe because of euill men; neither be thou enuious at the wicked.

20 * For there shall be no reward to the euill man: the ‖candle of the wicked shall be put out.

† *Heb. changers.*
21 My sonne, feare thou the LORD, and the king: and medle not with †them that are giuen to change.

22 For their calamity shall rise suddenly, and who knoweth the ruine of them both?

23 These things also *belong* to the wise: *It is* not good to haue respect of persons in iudgement.

* Leuit. 15. chap. 5. and 28. 21. deut. 17. and 16 19. ioh. 7 24.
* Chap. 1 15. isa. 5.
24 * He that sayth vnto the wicked, Thou *art* righteous, him shall the people curse; nations shall abhorre him:

† *Heb. a blessing o good.*
25 But to them that rebuke him shall be delight, and †a good blessing shall come vpon them.

† *Heb. th answereth right wor*
26 *Euery man* shall kisse *his* lippes that †giueth a right answere.

27 Prepare thy worke without, and make it fit for thy selfe in the field; and afterwards build thine house.

28 Be not a witnesse against thy neighbour without cause: and deceiue not with thy lippes.

* Chap. 2 22.
29 * Say not, I will doe so to him as he

he hath done to mee : I will render to the man according to his worke.

30 I went by the field of the slouthfull, and by the vineyard of the man voyd of vnderstanding :

31 And loe, it was all growen ouer with thornes, and nettles had couered the face thereof, and the stone wall therof was broken downe

32 Then I saw, and †considered it well, I looked vpon it, and receiued instruction.

33 Yet a little sleepe, a little slumber, a little folding of the handes to sleepe.

34 So shall thy pouertie come, as one that traueileth, and thy want, as †an armed man.

† *Hebr. set my heart.*

* *Chap. 6. 9. &c.*

† *Hebr. a man of shield.*

CHAP. XXV.

1 Obseruations about Kings, 8 and about auoyding causes of quarrels, and sundry causes thereof.

Hese are also Prouerbes of Solomon, which the men of Hezekiah king of Iudah copied out.

2 It is the glory of God to conceale a thing : but the honour of Kings is to search out a matter.

3 The heauen for height, and the earth for depth, and the heart of Kings is †vnsearchable.

4 Take away the drosse from the siluer, and there shall come foorth a vessel for the finer.

5 * Take away the wicked from before the king, and his throne shalbe established in righteousnes.

6 † Put not forth thy selfe in the presence of the king, and stand not in the place of great men.

7 * For better it is that it be said vnto thee, Come vp hither ; then that thou shouldest be put lower in the presence of the Prince whom thine eies haue seene.

8 Goe not forth hastily to striue, lest thou know not what to doe in the ende thereof, when thy neighbour hath put thee to shame.

9 * Debate thy cause with thy neighbour himselfe ; and ||discouer not a secret to another :

10 Lest he that heareth it, put thee to shame, and thine infamie turne not away

11 A word †fitly spoken is like apples of gold in pictures of siluer.

* *Heb. there is no searching.*

* *Chap. 20. 3.*

† *Hebr. set not out thy glory.*

* *Luke 14. 10.*

* *Matth. 5. 25. and 18. 15.*

* *Or, discouer not the secret of another.*

Heb. spoken vpon his wheeles.

12 As an eare-ring of gold, and an ornament of fine gold, so is a wise reprouer vpon an obedient eare.

13 * As the cold of snow in the time of haruest, so is a faithfull messenger to them that send him : for hee refresheth the soule of his masters.

14 Who so boasteth himselfe † of a false gift, is like cloudes and winde without raine.

15 * By long forbearing is a Prince perswaded, and a soft tongue breaketh the bone.

16 Hast thou found hony ? eate so much as is sufficient for thee : lest thou be filled therewith, and vomit it.

17 || Withdraw thy foote from thy neighbours house : lest he be †weary of thee, and so hate thee.

18 A man that beareth false witnes against *his neighbour, is a maule, and a sword, and a sharpe arrow.

19 Confidence in an vnfaithfull man in time of trouble, is like a broken tooth, and a foot out of ioynt.

20 As hee that taketh away a garment in cold weather ; and as vineger vpon nitre ; so is he that singeth songs to an heauy heart.

21 * If thine enemie be hungry, giue him bread to eate : and if hee be thirstie, giue him water to drinke.

22 For thou shalt heape coales of fire vpon his head, and the LORD shall reward thee.

23 || The North winde driueth away raine : so doeth an angrie countenance a backbiting tongue.

24 * It is better to dwell in a corner of the house top, then with a brawling woman, and in a wide house.

25 As cold waters to a thirstie soule : so is good newes from a farre countrey.

26 A righteous man falling downe before the wicked, is as a troubled fountaine, aud a corrupt spring.

27 It is not good to eat much hony : so for men to search their owne glory, is not glory.

28 * Hee that hath no rule ouer his owne spirit, is like a citie that is broken downe, and without walles.

* *Chap. 13. 17.*

† *Hebr. in a gift of falshood.*

* *Chap. 15. 1. gene. 32. 4. and 16. 14. 1. sam. 25. 24.*

|| *Or, let thy foote be seldome in thy neighbours house.*
† *Hebr. full of thee.*
* *Psal. 120. 4. chap. 12. 18.*

* *Exod. 23. 4. rom. 12. 20.*

|| *Or, The Northwinde bringeth foorth raine, so doeth a backbiting tongue, an angry countenance.*
* *Chap. 21. 9. and 19. 13.*

* *Chap. 16. 32.*

CHAP. XXVI.

1 Obseruations about fooles, 13 about sluggards, 17 and about contentious busiebodies.

As

AS snow in summer, and as raine in haruest: so honour is not seemely for a foole.

2 As the bird by wandring, as the swallow by flying: so the curse causelesse shall not come.

3 * A whip for the horse, a bridle for the asse ; and a rod for the fooles backe.

4 Answere not a foole according to his folly, lest thou also be like vnto him.

5 Answere a foole according to his folly, lest hee be wise in †his owne conceit.

6 He that sendeth a message by the hand of a foole, cutteth off the feete, and drinketh ||dammage.

7 The legges of the lame † are not equall: so is a parable in the mouth of fooles.

8 || As hee that bindeth a stone in a sling; so is hee that giueth honour to a foole.

9 As a thorne goeth vp into the hand of a drunkard; so is a parable in the mouth of fooles.

10 || The great God that formed all things, both rewardeth the foole, and rewardeth transgressours.

11 * As a dogge returneth to his vomite: so a foole †returneth to his folly.

12 Seest thou a man wise in his owne conceit? there is more hope of a foole then of him.

13 * The slothfull man sayth, There is a lion in the way, a lion is in the streets.

14 As the doore turneth vpon his hinges: so doeth the slothfull vpon his bedde.

15 * The slothfull hideth his hand in his bosome, ||it grieueth him to bring it againe to his mouth.

16 The sluggard is wiser in his owne conceit, then seuen men that can render a reason.

17 He that passeth by, and ||medleth with strife belonging not to him, is like one that taketh a dog by the eares.

18 As a mad man, who casteth †firebrands, arrowes, and death:

19 So is the man that deceiueth his neighbour, & sayth, Am not I in sport?

20 * Where no wood is, there the fire goeth out: so *where there is no ||talebearer, the strife †ceaseth.

21 *As coales are to burning coales, and wood to fire; so is a contentious man to kindle strife.

22 * The words of a tale - bearer are as woundes, and they goe downe into the †innermost parts of the belly.

23 Burning lips, and a wicked heart, are like a potsheard couered with siluer drosse.

24 Hee that hateth, ||dissembleth with his lips, and layeth vp deceit within him.

25 When he †speaketh faire, beleeue him not: for there are seuen abominations in his heart.

26 || Whose hatred is couered by deceit, his wickednesse shall be shewed before the whole congregation.

27 * Whoso diggeth a pit, shall fall therein: and he that rolleth a stone, it will returne vpon him.

28 A lying tongue hateth those that are afflicted by it, and a flattering mouth worketh ruine.

CHAP. XXVII.

1 Obseruations of selfe-loue: 5 of true loue: 11 of care to auoid offences: 23 and of the housholde care.

BOast *not thy selfe of †to morrow: for thou knowest not what a day may bring foorth.

2 Let another man praise thee, and not thine owne mouth; a stranger, and not thine owne lips.

3 A stone is †heauie, and the sand weightie: but a fooles wrath is heauier then them both.

4 †Wrath is cruell, and anger is outragious: but who is able to stand before ||enuie?

5 Open rebuke is better then secret loue.

6 * Faithfull are the woundes of a friend: but the kisses of an enemy are ||deceitfull.

7 * The full soule †loatheth an honie combe: but to the hungry soule euery bitter thing is sweete.

8 As a bird that wandreth from her nest: so is a man that wandreth from his place.

9 Oyntment and perfume reioyce the heart: so doeth the sweetnesse of a mans friend †by heartie counsell.

10 Thine owne friend and thy fathers friend forsake not; neither goe in to thy brothers house in the day of thy calamitie: for *better is a neighbour that is neere, then a brother farre off.

11 * My sonne, be wise, and make my heart

Marginal notes (left column):
*Chap. 10. 13. psal. 32. 9.

† Heb. his owne eyes.

|| Or, violence.
† Heb. are lifted vp.

|| Or, as he that putteth a pretious stone in an heape of stones.

|| Or, a great man grieueth all, and hee hireth the foole, he hireth also transgressors.
* 2. Pet. 2. 22.
† Heb. iterateth his folly.

* Chap. 22. 13.

* Chap. 19. 24.
|| Or, he is weary.

|| Or, is enraged.

† Heb. flames or sparkes.

† Heb. without wood.
* Chap. 22. 10.
|| Or, whisperer.
† Heb. is silent.
* Chap. 15. 18. & 29. 22.
* Cha. 18. 8

Marginal notes (right column):
† Heb. chambers.

|| Or, is knowen.

† Heb. maketh his voice gracious.
|| Or, hatred is couered in secret.
* Eccles. 10. 5. psal. 17. 16. & 9. 18.

* Iam. 4. &c.
† Heb. to morrow day.

† Heb. heauinesse.

† Heb. wrath is crueltie and anger ouerflowing
|| Or, ielousie

* Psal. 141. 5.

|| Or, earnest or frequent.
* Iob 6. 7.
† Heb. treadeth vnder foote.

† Heb. from the counsell of the soule.

* Chap. 17. and 18. 24.
* Cha. 10. 1. and 23. 24.

heart glad, that I may answere him that reprocheth me.

12 * A prudent man foreseeth the euil, *and* hideth himselfe: *but* the simple passe on, *and* are punished.

* Chap. 22. 3

13 * Take his garment that is surety for a stranger, and take a pledge of him for a strange woman.

* Chap. 20. 16.

14 He that blesseth his friend with a loud voice, rising earely in the morning, it shall be counted a curse to him.

15 * A continuall dropping in a very rainie day, and a contentious woman, are alike.

* Chap. 19. 13.

16 Whosoeuer hideth her, hideth the wind, and the ointment of his right hand *which* bewrayeth *it selfe*

17 Iron sharpeneth iron: so a man sharpeneth the countenance of his friend.

18 Whoso keepeth the figtree, shall eate the fruit therof: so he that waiteth on his master, shall be honoured.

19 As in water face *answereth* to face: so the heart of man to man.

20 * Hell and destruction are † neuer full: so the eyes of man are neuer satisfied.

* Eccles. 1. 8
† Hebr. not.

21 * *As* the fining pot for siluer, and the furnace for gold: so *is* a man to his praise.

* Chap. 17. 3

22 Though thou shouldest bray a foole in a morter among wheate with a pestell, *yet* will not his foolishnesse depart from him.

23 Be thou diligent to knowe the state of thy flocks, *and* † looke well to thy herds.

† Hebr. set thy heart.

24 For † riches *are* not for euer: and doth the crowne *endure* † to euery generation?

† Hebr. strength.
† Hebr. to generation and generation.

25 The hay appeareth, and the tender grasse sheweth it selfe, and herbes of the mountaines are gathered.

26 The lambes *are* for thy clothing, and the goates *are* the price of thy field.

27 And thou shalt *haue* goats milke enough for thy food, for the food of thy houshold, and *for* the † maintenance for thy maidens

† Hebr. life.

CHAP XXVIII.

Generall obseruations of impietie and religious integritie.

THe * wicked flee when no man pursueth: but the righteous are bolde as a lyon.

* Leuit. 26. 36.

2 For the transgression of a land, many *are* the princes thereof: || but by a man of vnderstanding *and* knowledge *the state thereof* shall bee prolonged.

|| Or, by men of vnderstanding and wisedome shall they likewise be prolonged.

3 A poore man that oppresseth the poore, is like a sweeping raine † which leaueth no food.

† Heb. without foode.

4 They that forsake the law, praise the wicked: but such as keepe the Law, contend with them.

5 Euill men vnderstand not iudgement: but they that seeke the LORD, vnderstand all things.

6 * Better *is* the poore that walketh in his vprightnesse, then he that is peruerse *in his* wayes, though he *be* rich.

* Cha. 19. 1.

7 * Whoso keepeth the law, *is* a wise sonne: but he that † is a companion of riotous *men*, shameth his father.

* Cha. 29. 3.
|| Or, feedeth gluttons.

8 * He that by vsurie and † vniust gaine increaseth his substance, he shall gather it for him that wil pity the poore.

* Chap. 13. 22. eccles. 2 26.
† Hebr. by increase.

9 He that turneth away his eare from hearing the law, euen his prayer *shalbe* abomination.

10 * Who so causeth the righteous to goe astray in an euill way, he shall fall himselfe into his owne pit: but the vpright shall haue good things in possession.

* Chap. 26. 27.

11 The rich man *is* wise † in his owne conceit: but the poore that hath vnderstanding searcheth him out.

† Heb. in his eyes.

12 * When righteous men do reioyce, *there is* great glory: but when the wicked rise, a man is || hidden.

* Iohn 11. 10 eccles. 10. 6 and ver. 28.
|| Or, sought for.

13 * He that coucreth his sinnes, shall not prosper: but who so confesseth and forsaketh *them*, shall haue mercie.

* Psal. 32. 5. 1. ioh. 1. 9. and 10.

14 Happy *is* the man that feareth alway: * but he that hardeneth his heart, shall fall into mischiefe.

* Rom. 11 20.

15 *As* a roaring lyon and a ranging beare: so is a wicked ruler ouer the poore people.

16 The prince that wanteth vnderstanding, *is* also a great oppressour: *but* he that hateth couetousnesse, shall prolong *his* dayes.

17 * A man that doth violence to the blood of any person, shall flie to the pit, let no man stay him.

* Gen. 9. 6. exod. 21. 14

18 * Whoso walketh vprightly, shall be saued: but he that is peruerse *in his* wayes, shall fall at once.

* Chap. 10. 25.

19 * He that tilleth his land, shal haue plentie of bread; but he that followeth after vaine persons, shall haue pouerty enough.

* Chap. 12. 11.

20 A faith-

* Chap. 13.
11. and 23.
4. 1. tim. 6. 9
§ Or, vnpu-
nished.
* Chap. 18.
5. & 24. 23.
|| Or, he that
hath an euill
eye, hasteth
to be rich,
ver. 20.
* Cha. 27. 6.

† Heb. a man
destroying.

* Chap. 13.
10.

" Deut. 15.
8. cha. 22. 9.

* Chap. 29.
2. and ver.
12. of this
chapter.

† Heb. a man
of reproofes.

* Chap. 11.
10. and 28.
28. eccles.
10. 5.
|| Or, increa-
sed.
* Chap. 10.
1. and 15.
20. and 27.
11.
* Luk. 15.
13. chap. 5.
9. and 28. 7.

† Heb. a
man of ob-
lations.

* Iob 29.
16.

|| Or, set a
citie on fire.

20 A faithfull man shall abound with blessings : *but hee that maketh haste to be rich, shall not be ||innocent.

21 *To haue respect of persons, is not good : for, for a piece of bread that man will transgresse.

22 ||He that hasteth to bee rich, hath an euill eye, and considereth not that pouerty shall come vpon him.

23 *He that rebuketh a man, after-wards shall find more fauour, then he that flattereth with the tongue.

24 Who so robbeth his father or his mother, and saith, it is no transgres-sion, the same is the companion of † a de-stroyer.

25 *He that is of a proud heart, stir-reth vp strife : but he that putteth his trust in the LORD, shalbe made fat.

26 Hee that trusteth in his owne heart, is a foole : but who so walketh wisely, he shall be deliuered.

27 *He that giueth vnto the poore, shall not lacke : but he that hideth his eyes, shall haue many a curse.

28 *When the wicked rise, men hide themselues : but when they perish, the righteous increase.

CHAP. XXIX.

1 Obseruations of publike gouernement, 15 And of priuate. 22 Of anger, pride, the euery, cowardize, and corruption.

HE that being often repro-ued, hardeneth his necke, shal suddenly be destroied, and that without remedy.

2 *When the righteous are ||in authoritie, the people reioyce : but when the wicked beareth rule, the people mourne.

3 *Whoso loueth wisedome, reioy-ceth his father : *but hee that keepeth company with harlots, spendeth his substance.

4 The king by iudgement stabli-sheth the land : but †he that receiueth gifts, ouerthroweth it.

5 A man that flattereth his neigh-bour, spreadeth a net for his feet.

6 In the transgression of an euill man there is a snare : but the righteous doth sing and reioyce.

7 *The righteous considereth the cause of the poore : but the wicked regar-deth not to know it.

8 Scornefull men ||bring a citie into a snare : but wise men turne away wrath.

9 If a wise man contendeth with a foolish man, whether hee rage or laugh, there is no rest.

10 † The bloodthirstie hate the vp-right : but the iust seeke his soule.

11 A foole vttereth all his mind : but a wise man keepeth it in till after-wards.

12 If a ruler hearken to lies, all his seruants are wicked.

13 *The poore and the ||deceitful man meet together : the LORD lightneth both their eyes.

14 *The King that faithfully iudg-eth the poore, his throne shall be establi-shed for euer.

15 *The rod and reproofe giue wise-dome : but a *child left to himselfe bring-eth his mother to shame.

16 When the wicked are multiplied, transgression increaseth : *but the righ-teous shall see their fall.

17 *Correct thy sonne, and hee shall giue thee rest : yea he shall giue delight vnto thy soule.

18 Where there is no vision, the people ||perish : but he that keepeth the Law, happy is he.

19 A seruant will not be corrected by words : for though hee vnderstand, hee will not answere.

20 Seest thou a man that is hasty ||in his words ? there is more hope of a foole then of him.

21 He that delicately bringeth vp his seruant from a child, shall haue him be-come his sonne at the length.

22 *An angry man stirreth vp strife, and a furious man aboundeth in trans-gression.

23 *A mans pride shall bring him lowe : but honour shall vpholde the humble in spirit.

24 Who so is partner with a thiefe, hateth his owne soule : hee heareth cursing, and bewrayeth it not.

25 The feare of man bringeth a snare : but who so putteth his trust in the LORD, †shall be safe.

26 *Many seeke the † rulers fauour, but euery mans iudgement commeth from the LORD.

27 An vniust man is an abomination to the iust : and he that is vpright in the way, is abomination to the wicked.

CHAP. XXX.

1 Agurs confession of his faith. 7 The two points of his prayer. 10 The meanest are not

† Heb. men
of blood.

* Cha. 22.
|| Or, the v-
surer.

* Chap. 20.
28.

* See ver.
* Chap. 10.
1. and 17. 2
and 25.

* Psal. 37.
36. and 58.
11. and 91.
* Chap. 13.
24. and 22.
15. and 23.
13, 14

|| Or, is ma
naked.

|| Or, in hi
matters.

* Chap. 1
18. & 26.

* Chap. 1
33. and 1
12. iob 22.
29. luk.
11. mat.
12.

† Heb. sha
set on his
* Cha. 19.
† Hebr. t
face of a
ruler.

not to bee wronged. 11 Foure wicked generations. 15 Foure things insatiable. 17 Parents are not to bee despised. 18 Foure things hard to be knowen, 21 Foure things vntollerable. 24 Foure things exceeding wise. 29 Foure things stately. 32 Wrath is to bee preuented.

He words of Agur the sonne of Iakeh, euen the prophecy: The man spake vnto Ithiel, euen vnto Ithiel and Vcal.

2 Surely I *am* more brutish then *any* man, and *haue* not the vnderstanding of a man.

3 I neither learned wisedome, nor †haue the knowledge of the holy.

4 *Who hath ascended vp into heauen, or descended? who hath gathered the wind in his fists? who hath bound the waters in a garment? who hath established all the ends of the earth? what *is* his name, and what *is* his sonnes name, if thou canst tell?

5 *Euery word of God †*is* pure : he *is* a shield vnto them that put their trust in him.

6 *Adde thou not vnto his words, lest he reproue thee, and thou be found a lyar.

7 Two things haue I required of thee, †deny me *them* not before I die.

8 Remoue farre from mee vanity, and lyes; giue me neither pouerty, nor riches; *feede me with food †conuenient for me.

9 *Lest I be full, and †deny *thee*, and say, Who *is* the LORD? or lest I be poore, and steale, and take the name of my God *in vaine*.

10 † Accuse not a seruant vnto his master; lest he curse thee, and thou be found guilty.

11 *There is* a generation *that* curseth their father, and doth not blesse their mother.

12 *There is* a generation *that* are pure in their owne eyes, and yet is not washed from their filthinesse.

13 *There is* a generation, O howe lofty are their eyes! and their eye-lids are lifted vp.

14 *There is* a generation, whose teeth *are as* swords, and their iaw-teeth *as* kniues, to deuoure the poore from off the earth, and the needy from *among* men.

15 The horse-leach *hath* two daughters, *crying*, Giue, giue. There are three things *that* are neuer satisfied, *yea* foure things say not, †It is enough:

16 The graue; and the barren wombe; the earth *that* is not filled with water; and the fire *that* saith not, It is enough.

17 The eye *that* mocketh at *his* father, and despiseth to obey *his* mother; the rauens of ||the valley shall picke it out, and the young Eagles shall eate it.

18 There be three things *which* are too wonderfull for me; yea foure, which I know not:

19 The way of an Eagle in the ayre; the way of a serpent vpon a rocke; the the way of a ship in the †midst of the sea; and the way of a man with a maid.

20 Such *is* the way of an adulterous woman: she eateth, and wipeth her mouth, and saith, I haue done no wickednesse.

21 For three things the earth is disquieted, and for foure *which* it cannot beare :

22 *For a seruant when he reigneth, and a foole when hee is filled with meate :

23 For an odious *woman* when shee is married, and an handmayd that is heire to her mistresse.

24 There be foure things which are little vpon the earth; but they *are* †exceeding wise :

25 *The Ants *are* a people not strong, yet they prepare their meate in the summer.

26 The conies *are* but a feeble folke, yet make they their houses in the rocks

27 The locustes *haue* no king, yet goe they forth all of them †by bands.

28 The spider taketh hold with her hands, and is in kings palaces.

26 There be three things which goe well, yea foure are comely in going :

30 A lyon *which is* strongest among beastes, and turneth not away for any :

31 ||A gray-hound; an hee-goate also; and a king, against whom there is no rising vp.

32 *If thou hast done foolishly in lifting vp thy selfe, or if thou hast thought euill, *lay* thine hand vpon thy mouth.

33 Surely the churning of milke bringeth forth butter; and the wringing of the nose bringeth forth blood: so the forcing of wrath bringeth forth strife.

CHAP.

Marginal notes (left column):

Heb. know.

Iohn. 3. Iob. 38. psal. 104. isa. 40.

Psal. 12. 7. d 18. 32. 19. 8. & 9. 140. Heb. purified. Deut. 4. 2. d 12. 32. oc. 21. 19

Heb. withld not om me.

Mat. 6. 11. Heb. of my lowance. Deut. 32.

Heb. belye ee.

Heb. hurt ot with thy ngue.

Chap. 6.

Psal. 52. and 57. 5. ob. 29. 17.

Marginal notes (right column):

† Heb. wealth.

|| Or, the brooke.

† Heb. heart.

* Chap. 19. 10.

† Heb. wise made wise.

* Chap. 6. 7

† Heb. gathered together.

|| Or, horse. Heb. girt in the loynes.

* Iob. 21. 5. and 39. 37. &c. and 40. 4.

CHAP. XXXI.

1 Lemuels lesson of chastitie and temperance. 6 The afflicted are to be comforted and defended. 10 The praise and properties of a good wife.

He wordes of King Lemuel, the prophecie that his mother taught him. 2 What, my sonne! and what, the sonne of my wombe! and what, the sonne of my vowes!

3 Giue not thy strength vnto women, nor thy wayes to that which destroyeth kings

4 It *is* not for kings, O Lemuel, it is not for kings to drinke wine, nor for Princes, strong drinke †:

5 Lest they drinke, and forget the Law, and †peruert the iudgement †of any of the afflicted.

6 * Giue strong drinke vnto him that is ready to perish, and wine vnto those that be †of heauie hearts.

7 Let him drinke, and forget his pouertie, and remember his misery no more.

8 Open thy mouth for the dumbe in the cause of all such as are †appointed to destruction.

9 Open thy mouth, iudge righteously, * and plead the cause of the poore and needy.

10 ¶ * Who can finde a vertuous woman? for her price *is* farre aboue Rubies.

11 The heart of her husband doeth safely trust in her, so that he shall haue no need of spoile.

12 She will doe him good, and not euill, all the dayes of her life.

13 She seeketh wooll and flaxe, and worketh willingly with her hands.

14 She is like the merchants ships, she bringeth her food from afarre.

15 Shee riseth also while it is yet night, and giueth meate to her houshold, and a portion to her maydens.

16 She considereth a field, and †buyeth it ˙ with the fruit of her handes she planteth a Vineyard

17 She girdeth her loynes with strength, and strengtheneth her armes.

18 † She perceiueth that her merchandise *is* good, her candle goeth not out by night.

19 She layeth her handes to the spindle, and her handes hold the distaffe.

20 † She stretcheth out her hand to the poore, yea she reacheth foorth her handes to the needy

21 She is not afraid of the snow for her houshold: for all her houshold *are* cloathed with ∥scarlet.

22 She maketh herselfe couerings of tapestrie: her cloathing *is* silke and purple.

23 Her husband is known in the gates, when he sitteth among the Elders of the land.

24 She maketh fine linnen, and selleth *it*, and deliuereth girdles vnto the merchant.

25 Strength and honour *are* her cloathing; and she shall reioyce in time to come.

26 She openeth her mouth with wisedome; and in her tongue *is* the law of kindnesse.

27 She looketh well to the wayes of her housholde, and eateth not the bread of idlenesse.

28 Her children arise vp, and call her blessed; her husband *also*, and he praiseth her.

29 Many daughters ∥haue done vertuously, but thou excellest them all.

30 Fauour *is* deceitfull, and beautie *is* vaine: *but* a woman *that* feareth the Lord, she shalbe praised.

31 Giue her of the fruit of her hands, and let her owne workes praise her in the gates

Marginal notes

† Hebr. alter.
† Hebr. of all the sonnes of affliction.
* Psal. 104. 15.
† Hebr. bitter of soule.

† Hebr. the sonnes of destruction.

* Leuit. 19. 15. deut. 1. 16.
* Chap. 12. 4.

† Hebr. taketh.

† Hebr. s. tasteth.

† Hebr. s. spreadeth

∥ Or, dou garments

∥ Or, hau gotten riches.

¶ THE

¶ ECCLESIASTES,

or the Preacher.

CHAP. I.

1 The Preacher sheweth that all humane courses are vaine: 4 Because the creatures are
restlesse in their courses, 9 They bring
foorth nothing newe, and all olde things are
forgotten, 12 And because he hath found
it so in the studies of wisedome.

He wordes of the
Preacher, the son
of Dauid, King
in Ierusalem.

2 * Vanitie of
vanities, saith the
Preacher, vanitie
of vanities, all *is*
vanitie.

3 * What profite *hath* a man of all
his labour which hee taketh vnder the
Sunne?

4 *One* generation passeth away,
and *another* generation commeth : * but
the earth abideth for euer.

5 The Sunne also ariseth, and the
Sunne goeth downe, and † hasteth to
the place where he arose.

6 The winde goeth toward the
South, and turneth about vnto the
North ; it whirleth about continually,
and the winde returneth againe according to his circuits.

7 * All the riuers runne into the sea,
yet the Sea *is* not full : vnto the place
from whence the riuers come, thither
they † returne againe.

8 All things *are* full of labour, man
cannot vtter *it* : the eye is not satisfied
with seeing, nor the eare filled with
hearing.

9 * The thing that hath beene, it *is*
that which shall be : and that which is
done, is that which shall be done ; and
there is no new thing vnder the sunne.

10 Is there any thing, whereof it
may be sayd, See, this is new? it hath

beene already of olde time, which was
before vs.

11 *There is* no remembrance of former
things ; neither shall there bee any remembrance of things that are to come,
with those that shall come after.

12 ¶ I the Preacher was king ouer
Israel in Ierusalem.

13 And I gaue my heart to seeke and
search out by wisedome, concerning all
things that are done vnder heauen :
this sore trauell hath God giuen to the
sonnes of man, ‖ to be exercised therewith.

14 I haue seene all the workes that
are done vnder the Sunne, and behold,
all *is* vanitie, and vexation of spirit.

15 * That which is crooked, cannot
be made straight : and † that which is
wanting cannot be numbred.

16 I communed with mine owne
heart, saying, Loe, I am come to great
estate, and haue gotten * more wisedome
then all they that haue beene before me
in Ierusalem : yea my heart † had great
experience of wisedome & knowledge.

17 * And I gaue my heart to know
wisedome, and to know madnesse and
folly : I perceiued that this also is vexation of spirit.

18 For in much wisedome *is* much
griefe : and hee that increaseth knowledge, increaseth sorrow.

CHAP. II.

1 The vanitie of humane courses in the workes
of pleasure. 12 Though the wise be better
then the foole, yet both haue one euent. 18
The vanitie of humane labour, in leauing it
they know not to whom. 24 Nothing better
then ioy in our labour, but that is Gods gift.

Said in mine heart, Goe
to now, I wil prooue thee
with mirth, therfore enioy
pleasure : and behold, this
also *is* vanitie.

2 I said

ha. 12. 9
l. 144. 4.
l. 36. 6.
l 62. 9.

ha. 2. 22.
l 3. 9.

sal. 104.5
19. 90.

eb. pan-
.

Psal. 104.
0. iob
10.

eb. re-
ne to goe.

ha. 3. 15.

‖ Or, to af-
flict them.

* Cha. 7. 13.
† Heb. de-
fect.

* 1. King. 4.
30. and 10.
7, 23.
† Heb. had
seene much.
* Cha. 2. 12.
and 7. 23.

2 I saide of laughter, It is mad: and of mirth, What doeth it?

3 * I sought in mine heart †to giue my selfe vnto wine, (yet acquainting mine heart with wisedome) and to lay hold on folly, till I might see what *was* that good for the sonnes of men, which they should doe vnder the heauen †all the dayes of their life.

4 I made me great workes, I builded mee houses, I planted mee Vineyards.

5 I made mee gardens & orchards, and I planted trees in them of all *kinde* *of* fruits.

6 I made mee pooles of water, to water therewith the wood that bringeth foorth trees:

7 I got me seruants and maydens, and had †seruants borne in my house; also I had great possessions of great and small cattell, aboue all that were in Ierusalem before me.

8 * I gathered mee also siluer and gold, and the peculiar treasure of kings and of the prouinces: I gate mee men singers and women singers, and the delights of the sonnes of men, †as musical instruments, and that of all sorts.

9 So I was great, and increased more then all that were before mee in Ierusalem; also my wisedome remained with me.

10 And whatsoeuer mine eyes desired, I kept not from them; I withheld not my heart from any ioy : for my heart reioyced in all my labour; and this was my portion of all my labour.

11 Then I looked on all the workes that my hands had wrought, and on the labour that I had laboured to doe: and behold, all *was* *vanitie, and vexation of spirit, and *there was* no profit vnder the Sunne.

12 ¶ And I turned my selfe to behold wisedome, *and madnesse and folly: for what can the man *doe,* that commeth after the king? ||*euen* that which hath bene already done.

13 Then I saw †that wisedome excelleth folly, as farre as light excelleth darkenesse.

14 * The wise mans eyes *are* in his head, but the foole walketh in darknes: and I my selfe perceiued also that one euent happeneth to them all.

15 Then said I in my heart, As it happeneth to the foole, so it †happeneth euen to me, and why was I then more

wise? then I said in my heart, That this also *is* vanitie.

16 For *there is* no remembrance of the wise, more then of the foole for euer; seeing that which now *is,* in the dayes to come shall be forgotten; and how dieth the wise man? as the foole.

17 Therefore I hated life, because the worke that is wrought vnder the Sunne *is* grieuous vnto mee : for all *is* vanitie, and vexation of spirit.

18 ¶ Yea I hated all my labour which I had †taken vnder the Sunne: because I should leaue it vnto the man that shalbe after mee.

19 * And who knoweth whether he shall be a wise man or a foole? yet shall he haue rule ouer all my labour, wherein I haue laboured, and wherein I haue shewed my selfe wise vnder the Sunne. This *is* also vanitie.

20 Therefore I went about to cause my heart to despaire of all the labour which I tooke vnder the Sunne.

21 For there is a man whose labour *is* in wisedome and in knowledge, and in equitie : yet to a man that hath not laboured therein, shall hee †leaue it *for* his portion; This also *is* vanitie, and a great euill.

22 * For what hath man of all his labour, and of the vexation of his heart wherein hee hath laboured vnder the Sunne?

23 For all his dayes *are* *sorrowes, and his traueile, griefe; yea his heart taketh not rest in the night. This is also vanitie.

24 ¶ * *There is* nothing better for a man, *then* that he should eat and drinke, and that he ||should make his soule enioy good in his labour. This also I saw, that it *was* from the hand of God.

25 For who can eate? or who else can hasten *hereunto* more then I?

26 For *God* giueth to a man that *is* good †in his sight, wisedome, and knowledge, and ioy : but to the sinner hee giueth traueile, to gather and to heape vp that *he may giue to him that is good before God: This also *is* vanitie and vexation of spirit.

CHAP. III.

1 By the necessary change of times, vanitie is added to humane trauaile. 11 There is an excellencie in Gods workes: 16 But as for man, God shall iudge his workes there, and here he shalbe like a beast.

To

Marginal notes (left column):

* Chap. 1. 17.

† Hebr. to draw my flesh with wine.

† Hebr. the number of the dayes of their life.

†Heb. sonnes of my house.

* 1. King. 9. 28. and 10. 4.

† Hebr. musicall instrument, and instruments.

* Chap. 1. 3.

* Chap. 1. 17. and 7. 23.

‖ Or, in those things which haue bene already done.
† Hebr. That there is an excellencie in Wisedome more then in folly, &c.

* Prou. 17. 24. chap. 8. 1.

† Hebr. happeneth to me, euen to me.

Marginal notes (right column):

† Hebr. laboured.

* Psal. 49. 11. &c.

† Hebr. giue

* Chap. 1. and 3. 9.

* Iob 14. 1.

* Cha. 3. 12. 22. and 5. 17. and 8. 15.
‖ Or, delight his senses.

† Hebr. before him.

* Iob 27. 17.

*Heb. to
rare.

Heb. to be
are re from.

Or, seeke.

Chap. 1. 3.

Vers. 1.

Cha. 1. 9.

Heb. that
which is dri-
en away.

Vers. 1.

Or, that
they might
feare God,
and see, &c.

TO euery thing *there is* a sea-son, and a time to euery purpose vnder the heauen.

2 A time †to be borne, and a time to die : a time to plant, and a time to pluck vp that which is planted.

3 A time to kill, and a time to heale : a time to breake downe, and a time to build vp.

4 A time to weepe, and a time to laugh : a time to mourne, and a time to dance.

5 A time to cast away stones, and a time to gather stones *together* : a time to imbrace, and a time †to refraine from imbracing.

6 A time to ‖get, and a time to lose : a time to keepe, and a time to cast away.

7 A time to rent, and a time to sow : a time to keepe silence, and a time to speake.

8 A time to loue, and a time to hate : a time of warre, and a time of peace.

9 *What profite hath hee that worketh, in that wherein he laboureth?

10 I haue seene the trauaile which God hath giuen to the sonnes of men, to be exercised in it.

11 He hath made euery thing beautifull in his time : also hee hath set the world in their heart, so that no man can finde out the worke that God maketh from the beginning to the end.

12 I know that *there is* no good in them, but for *a* man to reioyce, and to doe good in his life.

13 And also that euery man should eate and drinke, and enioy the good of all his labour : it *is* the gift of God.

14 I know that whatsoeuer God doeth, it shalbe for euer · nothing can be put to it, nor any thing taken from it : and God doth it, that men should feare before him.

15 *That which hath beene, is now : and that which is to be, hath alreadie beene, and God requireth †that which is past.

16 ¶ And moreouer, I sawe vnder the Sunne the place of iudgement, *that* wickednesse *was* there ; and the place of righteousnesse, *that* iniquitie *was* there.

17 I said in mine heart, God shall iudge the righteous and the wicked : for *there is* *a time there, for euery purpose and for euery worke.

18 I said in my heart concerning the estate of the sonnes of men, ‖that God

might manifest them, and that they might see that they themselues are beasts.

19 *For that which befalleth the sonnes of men, befalleth beastes, euen one thing befalleth them : as the one dieth, so dieth the other ; yea they haue all one breath, so that a man hath no preheminence aboue a beast ; for all is vanitie.

20 All goe vnto one place, all are of the dust, and all turne to dust againe.

21 Who knoweth the spirit †of man that †goeth vpward ; and the spirit of the beast that goeth downeward to the earth ?

22 *Wherefore I perceiue that there is nothing better, then that a man should reioyce in his owne workes : for that is his portion ; for who shall bring him to see what shalbe after him ?

CHAP. IIII.

1 Vanitie is encreased vnto men by oppression, 4 By enuie, 5 By idlenesse, 7 By couetousnesse, 9 By solitarinesse, 13 By wilfulnesse.

SO *I returned, and considered all the oppressions that are done vnder the sunne ; & behold the teares of such as were oppressed, and they *had* no comforter : and on the †side of their oppressours *there was* power, but they *had* no comforter.

2 *Wherefore I praised the dead which are already dead, more then the liuing which are yet aliue.

3 *Yea better is he then both they, which hath not yet been, who hath not seene the euill worke that is done vnder the Sunne.

4 ¶ Againe I considered all trauaile, and †euery right worke, that †for this a man is enuied of his neighbour : this *is* also vanitie, and vexation of spirit.

5 *The foole foldeth his hands together, and eateth his owne flesh.

6 *Better is an handfull *with* quietnesse, then both the hands full *with* trauell and vexation of spirit.

7 ¶ Then I returned, and I saw vanitie vnder the Sunne.

8 There is one *alone*, and *there is* not a second ; yea, he *hath* neither childe nor brother : yet *is there* no end of all his labour, neither is his eye satisfied with riches, neither *sayth hee*, For whom doe I labour, and bereaue my soule of good ?

* Psal. 49.
21. chap.
2. 16.

† Heb. of the
sons of man.
† Heb. is as-
cending.

* Cha. 2. 24.
and 5. 17.

* Chap. 5. 7.
&c.

† Heb. hand.

* Iob 3. 17.
&c.

* Iob 3. 11,
16, 21.

† Heb. all
the rightnes
of worke.
† Heb. this is
the enuie of
a man from
his neigh-
bour.
* Prou. 6. 10
and 24. 33.
* Prou.. 15.
16. and 16.
18.

good ? this *is* also vanitie, yea it *is* a sore trauell.

9 ¶ Two *are* better then one, because they haue a good reward for their labour.

10 For if they fall, the one will lift vp his fellow, but woe to him that is alone, when he falleth : for he *hath* not another to helpe him vp.

11 Againe, if two lye together, then they haue heate ; but howe can one be warme *alone* ?

12 And if one preuaile against him, two shall withstand him ; and a threefold coard is not quickly broken.

13 ¶ Better *is* a poore and a wise child, then an old and foolish king †who will no more be admonished.

14 For out of prison hee commeth to raigne, whereas also he that is borne in his kingdome, *becommeth* poore.

15 I considered all the liuing which walke vnder the sunne, with the second child that shall stand vp in his stead.

16 *There is* no end of all the people, *euen* of all that haue beene before them : they also that come after, shall not reioyce in him : surely this also *is* vanitie, and vexation of spirit.

CHAP. V.

1 Vanities in Diuine seruice, 8 in murmuring against oppression, 9 and in Riches. 18 Ioy in riches is the gift of God.

Eepe thy foote when thou goest to the house of God, and be more ready to heare, *then to giue the sacrifice of fooles : for they consider not that they doe euill.

2 Be not rash with thy mouth, and let not thine heart be hasty to vtter any ||thing before God : for God *is* in heauen, and thou vpon earth : therefore let thy words *be few.

3 For a dreame commeth through the multitude of businesse, and a fooles voyce is *knowen* by multitude of words.

4 *When thou vowest a vow vnto God, deferre not to pay it : for he *hath* no pleasure in fooles ; *pay that which thou hast vowed.

5 Better *is* it that thou shouldest not vowe, then that thou shouldest vowe and not pay.

6 Suffer not thy mouth to cause thy flesh to sinne, neither say thou before the Angel, that it *was* an errour : wherefore should God be angrie at thy

voyce, and destroy the worke of thine hands ?

7 For in the multitude of dreames and many words, *there are* also diuers vanities : but feare thou God.

8 ¶ If thou seest the oppression of the poore, and violent peruerting of iudgement, and iustice in a prouince, maruell not †at the matter : for he that is higher then the highest, regardeth, and *there be* higher then they.

9 ¶ Moreouer the profit of the earth is for all : the king *himselfe* is serued by the field.

10 Hee that loueth siluer shall not be satisfied with siluer ; nor he that loueth abundance, with increase : this *is* also vanitie.

11 When goods increase, they are increased that eate them : and what good *is there* to the owners thereof, sauing the beholding *of them* with their eyes ?

12 The sleepe of a labouring man *is* sweete, whether he eate little or much : but the abundance of the rich will not suffer him to sleepe.

13 There is a sore euill *which* I haue seene vnder the Sun, *namely* riches kept for the owners therof to their hurt.

14 But those riches perish by euill trauell ; and he begetteth a sonne, and there is nothing in his hand.

15 *As he came forth of his mothers wombe, naked shall he returne to goe as he came, and shall take nothing of his labour, which he may carry away in his hand.

16 And this also *is* a sore euill, that in all points as he came, so shall hee goe : *and what profit *hath* he that hath laboured for the winde ?

17 All his dayes also hee eateth in darkenesse, and he hath much sorrowe, and wrath with his sicknesse.

18 ¶ *Behold that which I haue seene : †It is good and comely *for* one to eate and to drinke, and to enioy the good of all his labour that he taketh vnder the sunne, †all the dayes of his life, which God giueth him : for it is his portion.

19 Euery man also to whom God hath giuen riches and wealth, and hath giuen him power to eate thereof, and to take his portion, and to reioyce in his labour, this *is* the gift of God.

20 For he shall not much remember the dayes of his life : because God answereth *him* in the ioy of his heart.

CHAP.

† *Heb. who knoweth not to be admonished.*

* 1. Sam. 15 22. psal. 50. 8. prou. 15. 8. & 21. 27.

|| *Or, word.*

* Mat. 6. 7. prou. 10. 19

* Deut. 23. 21.

* Psal. 66. 13, 14.

† *Heb. at th will or purpose.*

* Iob. 1. 21 1. tim. 6. 7. psal. 49. 17.

* Chap. 1. 3

* Chap. 2. 24. and 3. 12. † *Heb. there which is comely, &c.* † *Heb. the number of the dayes*

|| *Or, though he giue not much, yet h remembreth &c.*

CHAP. VI.

1 The vanitie of riches without vse. 3 Of children, 6 and old age without riches. 9 The vanitie of sight and wandring desires. 11 The conclusion of vanities.

There is an euill which I haue seen vnder the Sun, and it *is* common among men:

2 A man to whom God hath giuen riches, wealth and honour, so that he wanteth nothing for his soule of all that he desireth, yet God giueth him not power to eate thereof, but a stranger eateth it : This *is* vanitie, and it *is* an euill disease.

3 ¶ If a man beget an hundred *children*, and liue many yeeres, so that the dayes of his yeeres bee many : and his soule be not filled with good, and also that he haue no buriall, I say, *that* an vntimely birth *is* better then he.

4 For he commeth in with vanitie, and departeth in darkenesse, and his name shall be couered with darkenesse.

5 Moreouer hee hath not seene the Sunne, nor knowen *any thing* : this *hath* more rest then the other.

6 ¶ Yea though he liue a thousand yeeres twice told, yet hath he seene no good : Doe not all goe to one place?

7 All the labour of man *is* for his mouth, and yet the † appetite is not filled.

8 For what *hath* the wise more then the foole? what *hath* the poore, *that* knoweth to walke before the liuing?

9 ¶ Better *is* the sight of the eyes, † then the wandering of the desire : this *is* also vanitie and vexation of spirit.

10 That which hath bene, is named already, and it is knowen that it *is* man : neither may he contend with him that is mightier then he.

11 ¶ Seeing there be many things that increase vanitie, what *is* man the better?

12 For who knoweth what *is* good for man in *this* life, † all the dayes of his vaine life, which he spendeth as *a shadow? for who can tell a man what shal be after him vnder the sunne?

CHAP. VII.

1 Remedies against vanitie, are a good name, 2 Mortification, 7 Patience, 11 Wisedome. 23 The difficultie of wisedome.

A *Good* name *is* better then precious ointment : and the day of death, then the day of ones birth.

2 ¶ It *is* better to goe to the house of mourning, then to goe to the house of feasting : for that *is* the end of all men, and the liuing will lay *it* to his heart.

3 ‖ Sorrow *is* better then laughter : for by the sadnesse of the countenance the heart is made better.

4 The heart of the wise *is* in the house of mourning : but the heart of fooles *is* in the house of mirth.

5 * It *is* better to heare the rebuke of the wise, then for a man to heare the song of fooles.

6 For as the † crackling of thornes vnder a pot, so *is* the laughter of the foole : this also *is* vanitie.

7 ¶ Surely oppression maketh a wise man mad : *and a gift destroyeth the heart.

8 Better *is* the ende of a thing then the beginning thereof : *and* the patient in spirit *is* better then the proude in spirit.

9 * Be not hastie in thy spirit to bee angry : for anger resteth in the bosome of fooles.

10 Say not thou, What is *the cause* that the former dayes were better then these? for thou doest not enquire † wisely concerning this.

11 ¶ Wisedome ‖ is good with an inheritance : and *by it* there is profite to them that see the sunne.

12 For wisedome *is* a † defence, *and* money *is* a defence : but the excellencie of knowledge *is*, that wisedome giueth life to them that haue it.

13 * Consider the worke of God : for who can make that straight, which hee hath made crooked?

14 In the day of prosperitie be ioyfull, but in the day of aduersitie consider : God also hath † set the one ouer against the other, to the end that man should find nothing after him.

15 All things haue I seene in the dayes of my vanitie : there is a iust man that perisheth in his righteousnes, and there is a wicked man that prolongeth *his life* in his wickednes.

16 Be not righteous ouer much, neither make thy selfe ouer wise : why shouldest thou † destroy thy selfe?

17 Be not ouermuch wicked, neither be

Marginal notes (left column)
† *Heb. soule.*

† *Heb. then the walking of the soule.*

† *Heb. the number of the dayes of the life of his vanitie.*
* *Psal. 144. 4.*

Marginal notes (right column)
* Prou. 22. 1. and 15. 30.

‖ *Or, anger.*

* Pro. 13. 18 & 15. 31. 32

† *Heb. sound*

* Deut. 16. 19.

* Pro. 14. 17 and 16. 32.

† *Heb. out of wisedome.*

‖ *Or, as good as an inheritance, yea, better too.*

† *Hebr. shadowe.*

* Chap. 1. 15.

† *Heb. made*

† *Heb. be desolate?*

be thou foolish : why shouldest thou die †before thy time ?

18 It *is* good that thou shouldest take holde of this, yea also from this withdraw not thine hand : for hee that feareth God, shall come foorth of them all.

19 * Wisedome strengtheneth the wise, more then ten mightie men which are in the citie.

20 * For *there is* not a iust man vpon earth, that doeth good, and sinneth not.

21 Also †take no heede vnto all words that are spoken ; lest thou heare thy seruant curse thee.

22 For often times also thine owne heart knoweth, that thou thy selfe likewise hast cursed others.

23 ¶ All this haue I prooued by wisedome : I said, I will be wise, but it *was* farre from me.

24 That which is farre off, and exceeding deepe, who can finde it out ?

25 †I applied mine heart to know, and to search, and to seeke out wisedome, and the reason *of things*, and to know the wickednes of folly, euen of foolishnesse *and* madnesse.

26 * And I finde more bitter then death, the woman whose heart is snares & nets, *and* her handes *as* bands : †who so pleaseth God, shall escape from her, but the sinner shall be taken by her.

27 Behold, this haue I found (saith the Preacher) || *counting* one by one to finde out the account :

28 Which yet my soule seeketh, but I finde not : one man among a thousand haue I found, but a woman among all those haue I not found.

29 Loe, this onely haue I found, *that God hath made man vpright : but they haue sought out many inuentions.

CHAP. VIII.

1 Kings are greatly to bee respected. 6 The Diuine prouidence is to be obserued. 12 It is better with the godly in aduersitie, then with the wicked in prosperity. 16 The worke of God is vnsearchable.

Ho *is* as the Wise man ? and who knoweth the interpretation of a thing ? * a mans wisedome maketh his face to shine, and †the boldnes of his face shalbe changed.

2 I *counsell thee*, to keepe the kings commandement, and that in regard of the oath of God.

3 Bee not hastie to goe out of his sight : stand not in an euill thing, for he doeth whatsoeuer pleaseth him.

4 Where the word of a king *is*, *there is* power : and who may say vnto him, What doest thou ?

5 Whoso keepeth the commandement, †shall feele no euill thing : and a wise mans heart discerneth both time and iudgement.

6 ¶ Because to euery purpose there is time, and iudgement ; therefore the misery of man *is* great vpon him.

7 For hee knoweth not that which shall be : for who can tell him, || when it shall be ?

8 *There is* no man that hath power *ouer the spirit to retaine the spirit; neither *hath* he power in the day of death : and *there is* no || discharge in that warre, neither shall wickednesse deliuer those that are giuen to it.

9 All this haue I seene, and applied my heart vnto euery worke that is done vnder the Sunne : *there is* a time wherein one man ruleth ouer another to his owne hurt.

10 And so I saw the wicked buried, who had come, and gone from the place of the Holy, and they were forgotten in the city, where they had so done : this *is* also vanitie.

11 Because sentence *against* an euill worke is not executed speedily ; therefore the heart of the sonnes of men is fully set in them to doe euill.

12 ¶ Though a sinner doe euill an hundred times, and his *dayes* be prolonged ; yet surely I know that * it shall be well with them that feare God, which feare before him.

13 But it shall not be well with the wicked, neither shall hee prolong *his* dayes *which are* as a shadow ; because he feareth not before God.

14 There is a vanitie which is done vpon the earth, that there be iust men vnto whom it *happeneth according to the worke of the wicked : againe, there be wicked men, to whom it happeneth according to the worke of the righteous : I said, that this also *is* vanitie.

15 * Then I commended mirth, because a man hath no better thing vnder the Sunne, then to eate and to drinke, and to be merrie : for that shall abide with him of his labour, the dayes of his life, which God giueth him vnder the Sunne.

16 ¶ When

† *Heb. not in thy time ?*

* Prou. 21. 22. and 24. 5. cha. 9. 16.

* Prou. 20. 9 1. kin. 8. 46. 1. ioh. 1. 8. † *Heb. giue not thine heart.*

† *Heb. I and mine heart compassed.*

* Prou. 22. 14.

† *He that is good before God.*

|| *Or, weighing one thing after another to finde out the reason.*

* Gen. 1. 27.

* Prou. 17. 24.

† *Heb. the strength.*

† *Heb. shall know.*

|| *Or, how it shall be ?*

* Iob 14. 5.

|| *Or, casting of weapons.*

* Psal. 37. 10, 11, 18, 19.

* Psa. 73. 13

* Cha. 3. 22

16 ¶ When I applied mine heart to know wisedome, and to see the busines that is done vpon the earth : (for also *there is that* neither day nor night seeth sleepe with his eyes.)

17 Then I behelde all the worke of God, that a man cannot finde out the worke that is done vnder the Sunne : because though a man labour to seeke *it* out, yea further though a wise man thinke to know *it*, yet shall hee not be able to finde *it*.

CHAP. IX.

1 Like things happen to good and bad. 4 There is a necessitie of death vnto men. 7 Comfort is all their portion in this life. 11 Gods prouidence ruleth ouer all. 13 Wisdome is better then strength.

Hebr. I ue, or set my heart.

FOr all this † I considered in my heart, euen to declare all this, that the righteous, and the wise, and their workes, *are* in the hand of God : no man knoweth either loue, or hatred, *by* all that *is* before them.

Mala. 3. psal. 73. & 12. 13.

2 *All things *come* alike to all : *there is* one euent to the righteous and to the wicked, to the good and to the cleane, and to the vncleane; to him that sacrificeth, and to him that sacrificeth not : as *is* the good, so *is* the sinner, *and* hee that sweareth, as he that feareth an oath.

3 This *is* an euill among all things that are done vnder the Sunne, that *there is* one euent vnto all : yea also the heart of the sonnes of men *is* full of euill, and madnesse *is* in their heart while they liue, and after that *they goe* to the dead.

4 ¶ For to him that is ioyned to all the liuing, there is hope : for a liuing dogge is better then a dead Lion.

5 For the liuing know that they shall die : but the dead know not any thing, neither *haue* they any more a reward, for the memorie of them is forgotten.

6 Also their loue, and their hatred, and their enuy is now perished; neither *haue* they any more a portion for euer in any thing that is done vnder the Sunne.

7 ¶ Goe thy way, eate thy bread with ioy, and drinke thy wine with a merry heart; for God now accepteth thy workes.

8 Let thy garments bee alwayes white; and let thy head lacke no oyntment.

9 † Liue ioyfully with the wife, whom thou louest, all the dayes of the life of thy vanitie, which he hath giuen thee vnder the Sunne, all the dayes of thy vanitie : *for that is thy portion in this life, and in thy labour which thou takest vnder the Sunne.

† Hebr. see, or enioy life.

* Chap. 2. 24. and 3. 13. and 5. 18.

10 Whatsoeuer thy hand findeth to doe, doe it with thy might : for *there is* no worke, nor deuice, nor knowledge, nor wisedome in the graue, whither thou goest.

11 ¶ I returned, and saw vnder the Sunne, That the race is not to the swift, nor the battell to the strong, neither yet bread to the wise, nor yet riches to men of vnderstanding, nor yet fauour to men of skil; but time and chance happeneth to them all.

12 *For man also knoweth not his time, as the fishes that are taken in an euil net; and as the birds that *are* caught in the snare; so are the sonnes of men snared in an euill time, when it falleth suddenly vpon them.

* Prou. 29. 6.

13 ¶ This wisedome haue I seene also vnder the Sunne, and it *seemed* great vnto me :

14 *There was* a little citie, and few men within it; and there came a great King against it, and besieged it, & built great bulwarks against it :

15 Now there was found in it a poore wise man, and hee by his wisedome deliuered the citie; yet no man remembred that same poore man.

16 *Then said I, Wisedome *is* better then strength : neuerthelesse, the poore mans wisedome *is* despised, and his words are not heard.

* Prou. 21. 22. chap. 7. 19.

17 The words of wise men *are* heard in quiet, more then the cry of him that ruleth among fooles.

18 Wisedome is better then weapons of warre : but one sinner destroyeth much good.

CHAP. X.

1 Obseruations of Wisedome and folly. 16 Of Riot, 18 Slouthfulnesse, 19 and Money. 20 Mens thoughts of Kings ought to bee reuerend.

† Hebr. flies of death.

DEad flies cause the oyntment of the Apothecarie to send foorth a stinking sauour : so doeth a little folly him that is in reputation

tation for wisedome *and* honour.

2 A wise mans heart *is* at his right *hand* : but a fooles heart at his left.

3 Yea also when hee that is a foole walketh by the way, †his wisedome faileth *him*, and hee saith to euery one *that* he is a foole.

4 If the spirit of the ruler rise vp against thee, leaue not thy place; for yeelding pacifieth great offences.

5 There is an euill *which* I haue seene vnder the Sunne, as an errour, *which* proceedeth †from the ruler.

6 Folly is set †in great dignitie; and the rich sit in lowe place.

7 I haue seene seruants *vpon horses, and princes walking as seruants vpon the earth.

8 *He that diggeth a pit, shall fall into it; and who so breaketh an hedge, a serpent shall bite him.

9 Who so remoueth stones, shall be hurt therewith : *and* hee that cleaueth wood, shalbe endangered thereby.

10 If the yron be blunt, and he doe not whet the edge, then must he put to more strength : but wisedome *is* profitable to direct.

11 Surely the serpent will bite without inchauntment, and †a babbler is no better.

12 *The words of a wise mans mouth *are* †gratious : but the lips of a foole will swallow vp himselfe.

13 The beginning of the words of his mouth *is* foolishnesse : and the end of †his talke is mischieuous madnesse.

14 *A foole also †is full of words; a man cannot tell *what shall be; and what shall bee after him who can tell him?

15 The labour of the foolish wearyeth euery one of them; because hee knoweth not how to goe to the citie.

16 ¶ *Woe to thee, O land, when thy king *is* a child, and thy princes eate in the morning.

17 Blessed *art* thou, O land, when thy king *is* the sonne of nobles, and thy princes eate in due season, for strength, and not for drunkennesse.

18 ¶ By much slouthfulnesse the building decayeth; and through idlenesse of the hands the house droppeth through.

19 ¶ A feast is made for laughter, *and wine maketh †merry : but money answereth all things.

20 ¶ *Curse not the king, no not in thy ‖thought, and curse not the rich in thy bed-chamber : for a bird of the aire shall carry the voyce, and that which hath wings shall tell the matter.

CHAP. XI.

1 Directions for charitie. 7 Death in life, 9 and the day of iudgement in the dayes of youth are to be thought on.

Ast thy bread †vpon the waters : for thou shalt find it after *many dayes.

2 Giue a portion to seuen and also to eight; for thou knowest noc what euill shall be vpon the earth.

3 If the clouds be full of raine, they emptie themselues vpon the earth : and if the tree fall toward the South, or toward the North, in the place where the tree falleth, there it shall be.

4 He that obserueth the wind, shall not sow : and hee that regardeth the clouds, shall not reape.

5 As thou knowest not what *is* the way of the spirit, nor how the bones *doe grow* in the wombe of her that is with child : euen so thou knowest not the workes of God who maketh all.

6 In the morning sowe thy seede, and in the euening withhold not thine hand : for thou knowest not whether †shall prosper, either this or that, or whether they both *shall be* alike good.

7 ¶ Truly the light *is* sweet, and a pleasant thing is it for the eyes to behold the sunne.

8 But if a man liue many yeeres, *and* reioyce in them all; yet let him remember the dayes of darkenesse, for they shall be many. All that commeth *is* vanitie.

9 ¶ Reioyce, O young man, in thy youth, and let thy heart cheere thee in the dayes of thy youth, and walke in the wayes of thine heart, and in the sight of thine eyes : but know thou, that for all these things, God will bring thee into iudgement.

10 Therefore remoue ‖sorrow from thy heart, and put away euill from thy flesh; for child-hood & youth *are* vanitie.

CHAP. XII.

1 The Creator is to be remembred in due time. 8 The Preachers care to edifie. 13 The feare of God is the chiefe Antidote of vanitie.

* Remember

† *Heb. his heart.*

† *Heb. from before.*
† *Heb. in great heights.*
* Prou. 30. 22.

* Psal. 7. 16. prou. 26. 27

† *Heb. the master of the tongue.*
* Prou. 10. 32. and 12. 13.
† *Heb. grace.*

† *Heb. his mouth.*
* Prou. 15. 2.
† *Heb. multiplieth words.*
* Chap. 3. 21. and 6. 12.

* Isa. 3. 3, 4.

* Psal. 104. 15.
† *Heb. maketh glad the life.*
* Exod. 22. 28.

‖ *Or, conscience.*

† *Heb. v. the face the wate*
* Deut. 10. Mat. 42. prou. 17.

† *Heb. s. be right.*

‖ *Or, ang*

rou. 22.6

REmember now thy Cre-
atour in the dayes of thy
youth, while the euil daies
come not, nor the yeeres
drawe nigh, when thou
shalt say, I *haue* no pleasure in them:

2 While the Sunne, or the light, or
the moone, or the starres be not darkened, nor the cloudes returne after the
raine:

3 In the day when the keepers of
the house shall tremble, and the strong
men shall bowe themselues, and the
||grinders cease, because they are fewe,
and those that looke out of the windowes be darkened:

4 And the doores shal be shut in the
streets, when the sound of the grinding
is low, and he shall rise vp at the voice
of the bird, and all the daughters of musicke shall be brought low.

5 Also *when* they shalbe afraid of that
which is high, and feares *shall bee* in the
way, and the Almond tree shall flourish, and the grashopper shall be a burden, and desire shall faile: because man
goeth to his long home, and the mourners goe about the streets:

6 Or euer the siluer corde be loosed,
or the golden bowle be broken, or the
pitcher be broken at the fountaine, or

the wheele broken at the cisterne.

7 * Then shall the dust returne to
the earth as it was: and the spirit shall
returne vnto God who gaue it.

8 ¶ *Vanitie of vanities (saith the
preacher) all is vanitie.

9 And ||moreouer because the prea-
cher was wise, he still taught the people
knowledge, yea he gaue good heed, and
sought out, *and* *set in order many prouerbes.

10 The preacher sought to finde out
†acceptable words, and that which was
written *was* vpright, *euen* wordes of
trueth.

11 The wordes of the wise *are* as
goads, and as nailes fastened *by* the masters of assemblies, *which* are giuen from
one shepheard.

12 And further, by these, my sonne, be
admonished : of making many bookes
there is no end, and much ||studie *is* a wea-
rinesse of the flesh.

13 ¶ ||Let vs heare the conclusion
of the whole matter : Feare God, and
keepe his commandements, for this *is*
the whole *duetie* of man.

14 For God *shal bring euery worke
into iudgement, with euer secret thing,
whether *it bee* good, or whether *it bee*
euill.

r, the
uders
le, be-
use they
nd litle.

* Gen. 3. 19

* Chap. 1. 2.

| Or, the
more wise
the Prea-
cher was,
&c.
‖ 1. King. 4.
32.

† Heb. words
of delight.

| Or, rea-
ding.

| Or, the end
of the mat-
ter, euen all
that hath
bene heard,
is.
*Rom. 2. 16
and 14. 10.
1. cor, 5. 10.

¶ **The Song of Solomon.**

CHAP. I.

1 The Churches loue vnto Christ. 5 Shee confesseth her deformitie, 7 And prayeth to bee
directed to his flocke. 8 Christ directeth her
to the shepheards tents. 9 And shewing his
loue to her, 11 Giueth her gracious promises. 12 The Church and Christ congratulate one another.

He song of songs,
which *is* Solo-
mons.

2 Let him
kisse mee with
the kisses of his
mouth : * for †thy
Loue *is* better
then wine.

Chap. 4.

Hebr. thy
ues.

3 Because of the sauour of thy good
ointments, thy name is *as* ointment
powred forth, therefore doe the virgins
loue thee.

4 * Draw me, we will runne after
thee : the king hath brought me into his
chambers : we will be glad and reioyce
in thee, we wil remember thy loue more
then wine : ||the vpright loue thee.

5 I *am* blacke, but comely, (O ye
daughters of Ierusalem) as the tents
of Kedar, as the curtaines of Solomon.

6 Looke not vpon me because I *am*
blacke, because the Sunne hath looked
vpon me : my mothers children were
angry with me, they made me the keeper of the vineyards, *but* mine owne
vine-

* Ioh. 6. 44.

| Or, they
loue thee
vprightly.

vineyard haue I not kept.

7 Tell me, (O thou whom my soule loueth) where thou feedest, where thou makest *thy flocke* to rest at noone : for why should I be ||as one that turneth aside by the flockes of thy companions?

‖ *Or, as one that is vai-led.*

8 ¶ If thou know not (O thou fairest among women) goe thy way forth by the footsteps of the flocke, and feede thy kiddes beside the shepheards tents.

9 I haue compared thee, O my loue, to a company of horses in Pharaohs chariots.

10 Thy cheekes are comely with rowes *of iewels*, thy necke with chaines *of golde.*

11 Wee will make thee borders of golde, with studdes of siluer.

12 ¶ While the king sitteth at his table, my spikenard sendeth foorth the smell thereof.

13 A bundle of myrrhe *is* my welbeloued vnto me ; he shall lie all night betwixt my breasts.

14 My beloued *is* vnto me, *as* a cluster of ||Camphire in the vineyards of Engedi.

‖ *Or, Cypres.*

15 Behold, thou *art* faire, ||my loue : behold, thou *art* faire, thou *hast* doues eyes.

‖ *Or, my companion.*

16 * Behold, thou *art* faire, my beloued ; yea pleasant : also our bedde *is* greene.

* *Chap. 4. 1 and 5. 12.*

17 The beames of our house are Cedar, *and* our ||rafters of firre.

‖ *Or, galleries.*

CHAP. II.

1 The mutuall loue of Christ and his Church. 8 The hope, 10 and calling of the Church. 14 Christs care of the Church. 16 The profession of the Church, her faith and hope.

Am the rose of Sharon, *and* the lillie of the valleys.

2 As the lillie among thornes, so *is* my loue among the daughters.

3 As the apple tree among the trees of the wood, so *is* my beloued among the sonnes. †I sate downe vnder his shadow with great delight, and his fruit *was* sweete to my †taste.

† *Heb. I delighted and sate downe, &c.*
† *Heb. palate*
† *Heb. house of wine.*

4 Hee brought me to the †banketing house, and his banner ouer mee, *was* loue.

5 Stay me with flagons, †comfort me with apples, for I *am* sicke of loue.

† *Heb. straw me with apples.*

6 *His left hand *is* vnder my head, and his right hand doeth imbrace me.

* *Chap. 8. 3.*

7 †*I charge you, O ye daughters of Ierusalem, by the Roes, and by the hindes of the field, that ye stirre not vp, nor awake *my* loue, till she please.

† *Heb. I ture you.*
* *Chap. 3 and 8. 4.*

8 ¶ The voice of my beloued ! behold ! hee commeth leaping vpon the mountaines, skipping vpon the hils.

9 * My beloued is like a Roe, or a yong Hart : behold, he standeth behind our wall, he looketh foorth at the windowe, †shewing himselfe through the lattesse.

* *Verse 8*
† *Heb. flo rishing.*

10 My beloued spake, and said vnto me, Rise vp, my Loue, my faire one, and come away.

11 For loe, the winter is past, the raine is ouer, *and* gone.

12 The flowers appeare on the earth, the time of the singing *of birds* is come, and the voice of the turtle is heard in our land.

13 The fig tree putteth foorth her greene figs, and the vines *with* the tender grape giue a *good* smell. Arise, my loue, my faire one, and come away.

14 ¶ O my doue ! *that art* in the clefts of the rocke, in the secret *places* of the staires : let me see thy countenance, let me heare thy voice, for sweet *is* thy voice, and thy countenance *is* comely.

15 Take vs the foxes, the litle foxes, that spoile the vines : for our vines *haue* tender grapes.

16 ¶ *My beloued *is* mine, and I *am* his : he feedeth among the lillies.

* *Chap. and 7. 10*

17 *Vntill the day breake, and the shadowes flee away : turne my beloued and be thou * like a Roe, or a yong Hart, vpon the mountaines ||of Bether.

* *Chap.*
* *Chap. 14.*
‖ *Or, of d sion.*

CHAP. III.

1 The Church her fight and victorie in temptation. 6 The Church glorieth in Christ.

Y night on my bed I sought *him* whome my soule loueth. I sought him, but I found him not.

2 I will rise now, and goe about the citie in the streets, and in the broad wayes I will seeke him whom my soule loueth : I sought him, but I found him not.

3 The watchmen that goe about the citie, found me : *to whom I said*, Saw ye him whom my soule loueth ?

4 It was but a litle that I passed from them, but I found him whome my soule loueth : I helde him, and would not let him goe, vntill I had
brought

brought him into my mothers house, and into the chamber of her that conceiued me.

5 *I charge you, O ye daughters of Ierusalem, by the Roes and by the Hindes of the field, that ye stirre not vp, nor awake my loue, till he please.

6 ¶ *Who is this that commeth out of the wildernes like pillars of smoke, perfumed with myrrhe and frankincense, with all powders of the merchant?

7 Behold his bed, which is Solomons : threescore valiant men are about it, of the valiant of Israel :

8 They all hold swords, being expert in warre : Euery man hath his sword vpon his thigh, because of feare in the night.

9 King Solomon made himselfe ||a charet of the wood of Lebanon.

10 He made the pillars thereof of siluer, the bottome thereof of gold, the couering of it, of purple; the midst thereof being paued with loue, for the daughters of Ierusalem.

11 Goe foorth, O yee daughters of Zion, and behold king Solomon with the Crowne wherewith his mother crowned him in the day of his espousals, and in the day of the gladnesse of his heart.

CHAP. IIII.

1 Christ setteth forth the graces of the Church. 8 He sheweth his loue to her. 16 The Church prayeth to be made fit for his presence.

**B**Ehold, thou art faire, my loue, behold thou art faire, thou hast doues eyes within thy lockes : thy haire is as a *flocke of goats, ||that appeare from mount Gilead.

2 Thy teeth are like a flocke of sheepe that are euen shorne, which came vp from the washing : whereof euery one beare twinnes, and none is barren among them.

3 Thy lips are like a threed of scarlet, and thy speach is comely : thy temples are like a piece of a pomegranate within thy lockes.

4 Thy necke is like the tower of Dauid builded for an armorie, whereon there hang a thousand bucklers, all shields of mightie men.

5 *Thy two breasts, are like two yong Roes, that are twinnes, which feed among the lillies.

6 *Vntill the day †breake, and the shadowes flee away, I will get mee to the mountaines of myrrhe, and to the hill of frankincense.

7 *Thou art all faire, my loue, there is no spot in thee.

8 ¶ Come with me from Lebanon (my spouse,) with me from Lebanon : looke from the top of Amana, from the top of Shenir *and Hermon, from the Lions dennes, from the mountaines of the Leopards.

9 Thou hast ||rauished my heart, my sister, my spouse; thou hast rauished my heart, with one of thine eyes, with one chaine of thy necke.

10 How faire is thy loue, my sister, *my spouse! how much better is thy loue then wine ! and the smell of thine oyntments then all spices !

11 Thy lips, O my spouse! drop as the hony combe : hony and milke are vnder thy tongue, and the smell of thy garments is like the smell of Lebanon.

12 A garden †inclosed is my sister, my spouse : a spring shut vp, a fountaine sealed.

13 Thy plants are an orchard of pomegranates, with pleasant fruits, ||Camphire, with Spikenaed,

14 Spikenard and Saffron, Calamus and Cynamom, with all trees of Frankincense, Mirrhe and Aloes, with all the chiefe spices.

15 A fountaine of gardens, a well of liuing waters, and streames from Lebanon.

16 ¶ Awake, O Northwinde, and come thou South, blow vpon my garden, that the spices thereof may flow out : let my beloued come into his garden, and eate his pleasant fruits.

CHAP. V.

1 Christ awaketh the Church with his calling. 2 The Church hauing a taste of Christes loue, is sicke of loue. 9 A description of Christ by his graces.

**I** Am come into my garden, my sister, my spouse, I haue gathered my Myrrhe with my spice, I haue eaten my honie combe with my hony, I haue drunke my wine with my milke : eate, O friends, drinke, ||yea drinke abundantly, O beloued !

2 ¶ I sleepe, but my heart waketh :

Margin notes

Chap 2. 7. and 8. 4.

Chap. 8. 5.

||r, a bed.

Chap. 1. and 5.

Chap. 6. 6. ||r, that te of, &c.

Chap. 7. 3.

*Chap. 2. 17. †Hebr. breathe.

*Ephes. 5. 27.

*Deut. 3. 9.

||Or, taken away my heart.

*Chap. 1. 2.

†Hebr. barred.

||Or, Cypres.

||Or, and be drunken with loues.

keth : *it is* the voyce of my beloued that knocketh, *saying*, Open to me, my sister, my loue, my doue, my vndefiled : for my head is filled with dewe, *and* my lockes with the drops of the night.

3 I haue put off my coate, how shall I put it on ? I haue washed my feete, how shall I defile them?

4 My beloued put in his hand by the hole *of the dore*, and my bowels were moued ||for him.

5 I rose vp to open to my beloued, and my hands dropped *with* myrrhe, and my fingers *with* †sweete smelling myrrhe, vpon the handles of the locke.

6 I opened to my beloued, but my beloued had withdrawen himselfe, *and* was gone : my soule failed when hee spake : I sought him, but I could not find him : I called him, but he gaue me no answere.

7 The watchmen that went about the citie, found me, they smote me, they wounded me, the keepers of the walles tooke away my vaile from me.

8 I charge you, O daughters of Ierusalem, if ye find my beloued, †that yee tell him, that I *am* sicke of loue.

9 ¶ What *is* thy beloued more then *another* beloued, O thou fairest among women ? what *is* thy beloued more then *another* beloued , that thou doest so charge vs ?

10 My beloued *is* white and ruddy, †the chiefest among tenne thousand.

11 His head *is* as the most fine gold, his locks *are* ||bushy, *and* blacke as a Rauen.

12 *His eyes *are* as *the eyes* of doues by the riuers of water, washed with milk, and †fitly set.

13 His cheekes *are* as a bed of spices, *as* ||sweete flowers : his lippes *like* lillies, dropping sweete smelling myrrhe.

14 His hands *are as* gold rings set with the Berill : His belly *is as* brightiuorie, ouerlayd *with* Saphires.

15 His legges *are as* pillars of marble, set vpon sockets of fine gold : his countenance *is* as Lebanon, excellent as the Cedars.

16 †His mouth is most sweete, yea he is altogether louely. This *is* my beloued, and this *is* my friend, O daughters of Ierusalem.

CHAP. VI.

1 The Church professeth her faith in Christ. 4 Christ sheweth the graces of the Church, 10 and his loue towards her.

W Hither is thy beloued gone? O thou fairest among women, whither is thy beloued turned aside ? that we may seeke him with thee.

2 My beloued is gone downe into his garden, to the beds of spices, to feede in the gardens, and to gather lillies.

3 *I *am* my beloueds, & my beloued *is* mine : he feedeth among the lillies.

4 ¶ Thou *art* beautifull , O my loue, as Tirzah, comely as Ierusalem, terrible as *an* armie with banners.

5 Turne away thine eyes from me, for they haue ||ouercome me : thy haire *is* *a flocke of goates, that appeare from Gilead.

6 Thy teeth *are* as a flocke of sheepe which goe vp from the washing, wherof euery one beareth twinnes, and there is not one barren among them.

7 As a piece of a pomegranat are thy temples within thy lockes.

8 There are threescore Queenes, and fourescore concubines, and virgins without number.

9 My doue, my vndefiled is *but* one ; she *is* the *only* one of her mother, she *is* the choice one of her that bare her : The daughters sawe her, and blessed her; *yea* the Queenes and the concubins, and they praysed her.

10 ¶ Who is she that looketh forth as the morning, faire as the moone, cleare as the sunne, *and* terrible as *an armie* with banners?

11 I went downe into the garden of nuts to see the fruits of the valley, *and* to see whether the vine flourished, *and* the pomegranats budded.

12 †Or euer I was aware, my soule ||made me like the chariots of Amminadib.

13 Returne, returne, O Shulamite : returne, returne, that we may looke vpon thee : what will yee see in the Shulamite ? as it were the company ||of two armies.

CHAP. VII.

1 A further description of the Church her graces. 10 The Church professeth her faith and desire.

H Owe beautifull are thy feete with shooes, O princes daughter ! the ioynts of thy thighs are like iewels, the worke of the hands of a cunning workman.

2 Thy

|| *Or, (as some read) in me.*

† *Heb. passing, or running about.*

† *Heb. what.*

† *Heb. a standard bearer.*

|| *Or, curled.*

* *Chap. 1. 15. & 4. 1.*

† *Heb. sitting in fulnesse, that is fitly placed, and set as a precious stone in the foile of a ring.*

|| *Or, towers of perfumes.*

† *Heb. his palate.*

* *Chap. 16. and 7. 10.*

|| *Or, they haue puft me vp.*
* *Chap. 4 1. and 2.*

† *Heb. I knew no || Or, set on the ch riot of m willing p ple.*

|| *Or of N hanaim.*

† *Heb. mix-*
ture.

2 Thy nauell *is like* a round goblet, *which* wanteth not †licour: thy belly *is like* an heape of wheate, set about with lillies.

* Chap. 4. 5

3 *Thy two breasts *are* like two yong Roes that are twinnes.

4 Thy necke *is* as a towre of yuo-ry: thine eyes *like* the fish pooles in Hesh-bon, by the gate of Bathrabbim: thy nose *is* as the towre of Lebanon, which looketh toward Damascus.

‖ *Or, crimson*

5 Thine head vpon thee *is* like ‖ Car-mel, and the haire of thine head like

† *Heb. bound*

purple, the king is †held in the galleries.

6 How faire, and how pleasant art thou, O Loue, for delights!

7 This thy stature is like to a palme tree, and thy breasts to clusters *of grapes.*

8 I said, I will goe vp to the palme tree, I will take hold of the boughes thereof: now also thy breasts shall be as clusters of the vine, and the smell of thy nose, like apples.

* *Hebr.
streightly.*
‖ *Or, of the
ancient.*
* *Chap. 2.
.6. and 6. 3*

9 And the roofe of thy mouth like the best wine, for my beloued, that goeth *downe* †sweetely, causing the lippes ‖of those that are asleepe, to speake.

10 ¶ *I *am* my beloueds, and his desire *is* towards me.

11 Come, my beloued, let vs goe forth into the field: let vs lodge in the villages.

Heb. open.

12 Let vs get vp earely to the vine-yards, let vs see if the vine flourish, *whe-ther* the tender grape †appeare, *and* the pomegranates bud forth: there will I giue thee my loues.

* Gen. 30.
4.

13 The *mandrakes giue a smell, and at our gates *are* all maner of plea-sant *fruits,* new and olde, *which* I haue laid vp for thee, O my beloued.

CHAP. VIII.

1 The loue of the Church to Christ. 6 The vehemencie of loue. 8 The calling of the Gentiles. 14 The Church prayeth for Christes comming.

* *Hebr. they
should not
despise me.*

That thou *wert* as my bro-ther that sucked the brests of my mother, *when* I should find thee without, I would kisse thee, yet †I should not be despised.

2 I would leade thee, *and* bring thee into my mothers house, *who* would in-struct me: I would cause thee to drinke of *spiced wine, of the iuice of my pome-granate.

*Prou. 9. 2.

3 *His left hand *should be* vnder my head, and his right hand should em-brace me.

*Chap. 2. 6

4 *I charge you, O daughters of Ierusalem, †that ye stirre not vp, nor awake *my* loue vntill he please.

*Chap. 3. 5.
and 2. 7.
† *Heb. why
should yee
stirre vp, or
why, &c?*
* Chap. 3. 6

5 (*Who is this that commeth vp from the wildernesse, leaning vpon her beloued?) I raised thee vp vnder the apple tree: there thy mother brought thee forth, there she brought thee forth, *that* bare thee.

6 ¶ Set mee as a seale vpon thine heart, as a seale vpon thine arme: for loue *is* strong as death, iealousie *is* †cruel as the graue: the coales thereof *are* coales of fire, *which hath* a most vehement flame.

† *Heb. hard.*

7 Many waters cannot quench loue, neither can the floods drowne it: if a man would giue all the substance of his house for loue, it would vtterly be contemned.

8 ¶ We *haue* a litle sister, and shee *hath* no breasts: what shall we doe for our sister, in the day when she shall bee spoken for?

9 If she *be* a wall, we will build vp-on her a palace of siluer: and if she *bee* a dore, we will inclose her with boards of Cedar.

10 I *am* a wall, and my breasts like towers: then was I in his eyes as one that found †fauour.

† *Heb. peace*

11 Solomon had a vineyard at Baal-hamon, hee let out the vineyard vnto keepers: euery one for the fruit thereof was to bring a thousand *pieces* of siluer.

12 My vineyard which *is* mine, *is* be-fore me: thou (O Solomon) *must haue* a thousand, and those that keepe the fruit thereof, two hundred.

13 Thou that dwellest in the gardens, the companions hearken to thy voice: cause me to heare *it.*

14 ¶ †Make haste, my beloued, and be thou like to a Roe, or to a yong Hart vpon the mountaines of spices.

† *Heb. flee
away.*

¶THE BOOKE OF THE
Prophet Isaiah.

CHAP. I.

1 Isaiah complaineth of Iudah for her rebellion. 5 He lamenteth her iudgements. 10 He vpbraideth their whole seruice. 16 He exhorteth to repentance, with promises and threatnings. 21 Bewailing their wickednesse, hee denounceth Gods iudgements. 25 Hee promiseth grace, 28 and threatneth destruction to the wicked.

HE Vision of Isaiah the sonne of Amoz, which hee sawe concerning Iudah and Ierusalem, in the dayes of Vzziah, Iotham, Ahaz, & Hezekiah kings of Iudah.

2 Heare, O *heauens, and giue eare, O earth : for the Lord hath spoken ; I haue nourished and brought vp children, and they haue rebelled against me.

3 The *oxe knoweth his owner, and the asse his masters cribbe : but Israel doeth not know, my people doeth not consider.

4 Ah sinnefull nation, a people †laden with iniquitie, a seede of euill doers, children that are corrupters : they haue forsaken the Lord, they haue prouoked the Holy one of Israel vnto anger, they are †gone away backward.

5 ¶ Why should yee be stricken any more ? yee will †reuolt more and more : the whole head is sicke, and the whole heart faint.

6 From the sole of the foote, euen vnto the head, *there is* no soundnesse in it ; but wounds, and bruises, and putrifying sores : they haue not beene closed, neither bound vp, neither mollified with ‖oyntment.

7 Your countrey *is* *desolate, your cities are burnt with fire : your land, strangers deuoure it in your presence, and *it is* desolate †as ouerthrowen by strangers.

8 And the daughter of Zion is left as a cottage in a vineyard, as a lodge in a garden of cucumbers, as a besieged citie.

9 Except the Lord of hostes had *left vnto vs a very small remnant, we should haue beene as *Sodom, *and we* should haue bene like vnto Gomorrah.

10 ¶ Heare the word of the Lord, ye rulers of Sodom, giue eare vnto the Law of our God, yee people of Gomorrah.

11 To what purpose *is* the multitude of your * sacrifices vnto me, sayth the Lord ? I am full of the burnt offerings of rammes, and the fat of fedde beasts, and I delight not in the blood of bullockes, or of lambes, or of †hee goates.

12 When ye come to †appeare before mee, who hath required this at your hand, to tread my courts ?

13 Bring no more vaine oblations, incense is an abomination vnto me : the new Moones, and Sabbaths, the calling of assemblies I cannot away with ; *it is* ‖iniquitie, euen the solemne meeting.

14 Your new Moones, and your appointed Feasts my soule hateth : they are a trouble vnto me, I am weary to beare *them*.

15 And when ye spread foorth your * handes, I will hide mine eyes from you ; yea, when yee †make many prayers I will not heare : your hands are full of *†blood.

16 ¶ Wash

---

*Deu. 32. 1.

* Iere. 8. 7.

† Heb. of heauinesse.

† Heb. alienated, or separated.
† Heb. increase reuolt.

‖ Or, oyle.

* Chap. 5. 5.
deut. 28.
51. 52.

† Heb. as the ouerthrow of strangers.

* Lam. 3. 22
rom. 9. 29.
* Gen. 19. 24.

* Prou. 15. 8
and 21. 7.
chap. 66. 3.
iere. 6. 20.
amos 5. 21.

† Heb. great hee goats.

† Heb. to be seene.

‖ Or, griefe.

* Prou. 1.
28. iere. 14
12. mic. 3. 4.
† Heb. multiply prayer.
* Cha. 59. 3.
† Heb. bloods

16 ¶ Wash yee, make you cleane, put away the euill of your doings from before mine eyes, * cease to doe euill,

* 1. Pet. 3. 11.

17 Learne to doe well, seeke iudgement, ||relieue the oppressed, iudge the fatherlesse, plead for the widow.

‖ Or, righten.

18 Come now and let vs reason together, saith the LORD : though your sinnes be as scarlet, they shall be as white as snow ; though they be red like crimsin, they shall be as wooll.

19 If yee be willing and obedient, yee shall eate the good of the land.

20 But if yee refuse and rebell, yee shalbe deuoured with the sword : for the mouth of the LORD hath spoken it.

21 ¶ Howe is the faithfull citie become an harlot ? it was full of iudgement, righteousnesse lodged in it ; but now murtherers.

22 Thy siluer is become drosse, thy wine mixt with water.

23 Thy princes are rebellious and companions of theeues : euery one loueth gifts, and followeth after rewards : they *iudge not the fatherlesse, neither doth the cause of the widowe come vnto them.

* Ier. 5. 28. Zac. 7. 10.

24 Therefore, saith the Lord, the LORD of hostes, the mighty one of Israel ; Ah, I will ease me of mine aduersaries, and auenge me of mine enemies.

25 ¶ And I will turne my hand vpon thee, and †purely purge away thy drosse, and take away all thy tinne.

† Heb. according to purenesse.

26 And I will restore thy iudges as at the first, and thy counsellers as at the beginning : afterward thou shalt be called the citie of righteousnesse, the faithfull citie.

27 Zion shall be redeemed with iudgement, and || her conuerts with righteousnesse.

‖ Or, they that returne of her.

28 ¶ And the *†destruction of the transgressours and of the sinners shall be together : and they that forsake the LORD shall be consumed.

* Iob. 31. 3. psal. 1. 6. & 5. 6. & 73. 27. & 92. 10. & 104. 35.
† Heb. breaking.

29 For they shall be ashamed of the okes which yee haue desired, and yee shalbe confounded for the gardens that yee haue chosen.

30 For yee shall be as an oke whose leafe fadeth, and as a garden that hath no water.

31 And the strong shall be as towe, ||and the maker of it as a sparke, and they shall both burne together, and none shall quench them.

‖ Or, and his worke.

CHAP. II.

1 Isaiah prophecieth the comming of Christs kingdome. 6 Wickednesse is the cause of Gods forsaking. 10 Hee exhorteth to feare, because of the powerfull effects of Gods Maiestie.

He word that Isaiah, the sonne of Amoz, sawe concerning Iudah and Ierusalem.

2 And it shall come to passe in the *last dayes, that the mountaine of the LORDS house shall be || established in the top of the mountaines, and shall be exalted aboue the hilles ; and all nations shall flow vnto it.

* Mic. 4. &c.
‖ Or, prepared.

3 And many people shall goe & say ; Come yee and let vs go vp to the mountaine of the LORD, to the house of the God of Iacob, and he will teach vs of his wayes, and we will walke in his pathes : for out of Zion shall goe forth the lawe, and the word of the LORD from Ierusalem.

4 And hee shall iudge among the nations, and shall rebuke many people : and they shall beate their swords into plow-shares, and their speares into ||pruning hookes : nation shall not lift vp sword against nation, neither shall they learne warre any more.

‖ Or, syth

5 O house of Iacob, come yee, and let vs walke in the light of the LORD.

6 ¶ Therefore thou hast forsaken thy people the house of Iacob ; because they be replenished ||from the East, and are soothsayers like the Philistines, and they ||please themselues in the children of strangers.

‖ Or, more then the East.
‖ Or, abound with the children.

7 Their land also is full of siluer and gold, neither is there any end of their treasures : their land is also full of horses ; neither is there any end of their charets.

8 Their land also is full of idoles : they worship the worke of their owne hands, that which their owne fingers haue made.

6 And the meane man boweth downe, and the great man humbleth himselfe ; therefore forgiue them not.

10 ¶ Enter into the rocke, and hide thee in the dust, for feare of the LORD, and for the glory of his Maiestie.

11 The *loftie lookes of man shalbe humbled, and the hautines of men shalbe bowed downe : and the LORD alone

* Chap. 15.

lone shalbe exalted in that day.

12 For the day of the LORD of hostes *shall bee* vpon euery one that is proud and loftie, and vpon euery one that is lifted vp, and he shalbe brought low ;

13 And vpon all the Cedars of Lebanon, that are high and lifted vp, and vpon all the okes of Bashan,

14 And vpon all the high mountaines, and vpon all the hilles that are lifted vp,

15 And vpon euery high tower, and vpon euery fenced wall,

16 And vpon all the ships of Tarshish, and vpon all †pleasant pictures.

17 And the loftinesse of man shall be bowed downe, and the hautinesse of men shalbe made low : and the LORD alone shalbe exalted in that day.

18 And ||the idoles hee shall vtterly abolish.

19 And they shall goe into the *holes of the rocks, and into the caues of the †earth for feare of the LORD, and for the glory of his Maiestie; when hee ariseth to shake terribly the earth.

20 In that day a man shall cast †his idoles of siluer, and his idoles of golde ||which they made *each one* for himselfe to worship, to the moules and to the battes :

21 To go into the clefts of the rocks, and into the tops of the ragged rockes, for feare of the LORD, and for the glorie of his Maiestie; when hee ariseth to shake terribly the earth.

22 Cease ye from man whose breath *is* in his nostrels : for wherein is hee to be accounted of ?

CHAP. III.

1 The great confusion which commeth by sinne. 9 The impudencie of the people. 12 The oppression and couetousnesse of the rulers. 16 The iudgements which shall be for the pride of the women.

Or behold, the Lord, the LORD of hostes doeth take away from Ierusalem, and from Iudah, the stay and the staffe, the whole stay of bread, and the whole stay of water,

2 The mighty man, and the man of warre; the Iudge and the Prophet, and the prudent, and the ancient,

3 The captaine of fiftie, and the †honourable man, and the counseller, and the cunning artificer, and the ||eloquent oratour.

4 And I will giue *children to bee their Princes, and babes shall rule ouer them.

5 And the people shall be oppressed, euery one by another, and euery one by his neighbour : the childe shall behaue himselfe proudly against the ancient, and the base against the honourable.

6 When a man shall take hold of his brother of the house of his father, *saying,* Thou hast clothing, be thou our ruler, and *let* this ruine *bee* vnder thy hand :

7 In that day †shall he sweare, saying, I will not be an †healer : for in my house *is* neither bread nor clothing : make me not a ruler of the people.

8 For Ierusalem is ruined, & Iudah is fallen : because their tongue and their doings *are* against the LORD, to prouoke the eyes of his glorie.

9 ¶ The shew of their countenance doeth witnesse against them, and they declare their sinne as * Sodom, they hide *it* not : woe vnto their soule, for they haue rewarded euill vnto themselues.

10 Say yee to the righteous, that *it shall be* well *with him* : for they shall eate the fruit of their doings.

11 Woe vnto the wicked, *it shall be* ill *with him* : for the reward of his handes shalbe †giuen him.

12 ¶ As for my people, children *are* their oppressours, and women rule ouer them : O my people, ||they which lead thee, cause *thee* to erre, and† destroy the way of thy paths.

13 The LORD standeth vp to plead, and standeth to iudge the people.

14 The LORD will enter into iudgement with the ancients of his people, and the Princes thereof : for ye haue ||eaten vp the Vineyard; the spoile of the poore *is* in your houses.

15 What meane yee *that* yee beat my people to pieces, and grinde the faces of the poore, saith the Lord GOD of hosts ?

16 ¶ Moreouer the LORD saith; Because the daughters of Zion are hautie, and walke with stretched forth necks, and †wanton eyes, walking and ||mincing as they goe, and making a tinkeling with their feet :

17 Therefore the Lord will smite with

Margin notes (left):
Hebr. pictures of desire.
Or, the idoles shall vtterly passe away.
Hos. 10. 8.
Luke 23. 30.
Reuel. 6. 16. and 9. 6.
Hebr. the dust.
Hebr. the idols of his siluer, &c.
Or, which they made for him.
Hebr. A muneniment in countenance.

Margin notes (right):
|| Or, skilfull of speech.
* Eccles. 10. 16.
† Hebr. lift vp the hand.
† Hebr. binder vp.
* Gen. 13. 13. and 18. 21. and 19. 5.
† Hebr. done to him.
|| Or, they which call thee blessed.
† Hebr. swallow vp.
|| Or, burnt.
† Hebr. deceiuing with their eyes.
|| Or, tripping nicely.

† *Heb. make naked.*

with a ſcab the crowne of the head of the daughters of Zion, and the LORD will †diſcouer their ſecret parts.

18 In that day the Lord will take away the brauery of their tinckling ornaments *about their feete*, and their ||caules, and their round tyres like the Moone,

|| *Or, networkes.*

|| *Or, sweetballes.*
|| *Or, spangled ornaments.*

19 The ||chaines, and the bracelets, and the ||mufflers,

20 The bonnets, and the ornaments of the legges, and the headbands, and the †tablets, and the earerings,

† *Heb. houses of the soule.*

21 The rings, and nose-iewels,

22 The changeable sutes of apparell, and the mantles, and the wimples, and the criſping pinnes,

23 The glaſſes, and the fine linnen, and the hoods, and the vailes.

24 And it ſhall come to paſſe, *that* in ſteade of ſweete ſmell, there ſhall bee ſtinke, and in ſtead of a girdle, a rent; and in ſtead of well ſet haire, baldneſſe; and in ſtead of a ſtomacher, a girding of ſackecloth ; *and* burning, in ſtead of beautie.

† *Heb. might*

25 Thy men ſhall fall by the ſword, and thy †mightie in the warre.

26 And her gates ſhall lament and mourne ; and ſhe being ||deſolate, ſhall ſit vpon the ground.

|| *Or, emptied: hebr. cleansed.*

C H A P. IIII.

In the extremitie of euils, Christes kingdome ſhall be a Sanctuarie.

Nd in that day ſeuen women ſhall take hold of one man, ſaying, We will eate our owne bread, & weare our owne apparell : onely †let vs be called by thy name, ||to take away our reproch.

† *Heb. let thy name be called vpon vs.*
|| *Or, take thou away.*
† *Heb. beauty and glory.*

2 In that day ſhall the Branch of the LORD be †beautifull and glorious, and the fruit of the earth ſhalbe excellent and comely †for them that are eſcaped of Iſrael.

† *Heb. for the escaping of Israel.*

3 And it ſhall come to paſſe, *that* hee that is left in Zion, and hee that remaineth in Ieruſalem, ſhall be called Holy, *euen* euery one that *is* written ||among the liuing in Ieruſalem,

|| *Or, to life.*

4 When the Lord ſhall haue waſhed away the filth of the daughters of Zion, and ſhall haue purged the blood of Ieruſalem from the middeſt thereof, by the ſpirit of iudgement, and by the ſpirit of burning.

5 And the LORD will create vpon euery dwelling place of mount Zion, and vpon her aſſemblies a *cloude, and ſmoke by day, and the ſhining of a flaming fire by night ; for ||vpon all the glory ſhall be †a defence.

* *Exod. 21.*
|| *Or, abo*
† *Heb. a uering.*

6 And there ſhalbe a tabernacle for a ſhadow in the day time from the heat, and for a place of refuge, and for a couert from ſtorme and from raine.

C H A P. V.

1 Vnder the Parable of a Vineyard, God excuſeth his ſeuere iudgement. 8 His iudgements vpon couetouſneſſe, 11 Vpon laſciuiouſneſſe, 13 Vpon impietie, 20 and vpon iniuſtice. 26 The executioners of Gods iudgements.

Ow will I ſing to my welbeloued, a ſong of my beloued touching his vineyard : my wellbeloued hath a *vineyard in a †very fruitfull hill.

* *Iere. 2 mat. 21. mark. 12 luke 20.*
† *Heb. t horne of sonne of*
|| *Or, ma a wall a bout it.*
† *Heb. he ed.*

2 And hee ||fenced it, and gathered out the ſtones thereof, and planted it with the choiceſt vine, and built a towre in the middeſt of it, and alſo †made a winepreſſe therein : and he looked that it ſhould bring foorth grapes, and it brought foorth wilde grapes.

3 And now, O inhabitants of Ieruſalem, and men of Iudah, Iudge, I pray you, betwixt me and my Vineyard.

4 What could haue beene done more to my Vineyard, that I haue not done in it ? wherefore when I looked that it ſhould bring foorth grapes, brought it foorth wilde grapes ?

5 And now goe to ; I will tell you what I will doe to my Vineyard, I will take away the hedge thereof, and it ſhall be eaten vp ; *and* breake downe the wall thereof, and it ſhall be †troden downe.

† *Heb. f treading*

6 And I will lay it waſte ; it ſhall not be pruned, nor digged, but there ſhall come vp briars and thornes : I will alſo command the cloudes, that they raine no raine vpon it.

7 For the Vineyard of the LORD of hoſtes *is* the houſe of Iſrael, and the men of Iudah †his pleaſant plant : and he looked for iudgement, but behold †oppreſſion ; for righteouſneſſe, but behold a crie.

† *Heb. of his pl sures.*
† *Heb. a*

8 ¶ Woe vnto them that ioyne
* houſe

Mich. 2. 2.

, this is ineeares h the RD,

eb. If not,

rou. 23. 30. , pursue n.

eb. their y are of fa- se.

sa. 2. 9. 17.

, the ho- God. Heb. God the y.

eb. that concer- g euill, It rood, &c.

rou. 3. 7. n. 12. 16 eb. be- e their ce.

house to house, that lay field to field, till *there be* no place, that they may be placed alone in the midst of the earth.

9 ‖ In mine eares *said* the LORD of hoftes, † Of a trueth many houses shall be desolate, *euen* great and faire without inhabitant.

10 Yea ten acres of vineyard shall yeeld one Bath, and the seed of an Ho-mer shall yeeld an Ephah.

11 ¶ Woe vnto them that rise vp earely in the morning, *that* they may fol-low strong * drink, that continue vntill night, *till* wine ‖ enflame them.

12 And the harpe and the viole, the tabret and pipe, and wine are in their feafts : but they regard not the worke of the LORD, neither confider the o-peration of his hands.

13 ¶ Therefore my people are gone into captiuitie, because *they haue* no knowledge : and † their honourable men *are* famished, aud their multitude dried vp with thirst.

14 Therefore hell hath enlarged her felfe, and opened her mouth without measure : and their glory, and their multitude, and their pompe, and hee that reioyceth, shall descend into it.

15 And * the meane man shall bee brought downe, and the mightie man shall be humbled, and the eyes of the loftie shall be humbled.

16 But the LORD of hosts shalbe exalted in iudgement, and ‖ God that is holy, shall bee sanctified in righteous-nesse.

17 Then shall the lambes feed after their maner, and the waste places of the fat ones shall strangers eate.

18 Woe vnto them that draw iniqui-tie with cords of vanitie, and sinne, as it were with a cart rope :

19 That say, Let him make speede, *and* hasten his worke, that we may see *it :* and let the counsell of the holy one of Israel draw nigh and come, that wee may know *it.*

20 ¶ Woe vnto them † that call euill good, and good euill, that put darkenes for light, and light for darkenesse, that put bitter for sweete, and sweete for bitter.

21 Woe *vnto them that are* * wise in their owne eyes, and prudent † in their owne sight.

22 Woe *vnto them that are* mightie to drinke wine, and men of strength to mingle strong drinke.

23 Which * iustifie the wicked for re-ward, and take away the righteousnes of the righteous from him.

24 Therfore as the † fire deuoureth the stubble, *and* the flame consumeth the chaffe, so their root shall be rottennes, and their blossome shall goe vp as dust : because they haue cast away the Lawe of the LORD of hosts, and despised the worde of the Holy One of Israel.

25 Therefore is the anger of the LORD kindled against his people, and he hath stretched foorth his hande against them, and hath smitten them : and the hilles did tremble, and their carkeises were ‖ torne in the midst of the streets : * for all this, his anger is not turned away, but his hand is stretched out still.

26 ¶ And he will lift vp an ensigne to the nations from farre, and wil hisse vnto them from the end of the earth : and behold, they shall come with speed swiftly.

27 None shalbe weary, nor stumble amongst them : none shall slumber nor sleepe, neither shall the girdle of their loynes be loosed, nor the latchet of their shooes be broken.

28 Whose arrowes *are* sharpe, and all their bowes bent, their horses hoofs shall bee counted like flint, and their wheeles like a whirlewind.

29 Their roaring *shalbe* like a lyon, they shall roare like yong lions : yea they shal roare and lay hold of the pray, and shall carie *it* away safe, and none shall deliuer *it.*

30 And in that day they shall roare against them, like the roaring of the sea : and if *one* looke vnto the land, be-hold darkenesse *and* ‖ sorrow, ‖ and the light is darkened in the heauens therof.

Pron. 17. 15.

† Hebr. the tongue of fire.

*‖ Or as doung. *Cha. 9. 11 16. 21. and 10. 4.*

‖ Or, di-stresse. ‖ Or, when it is light it shalbe darke in the de-structions thereof.

CHAP VI.

1 Isaiah in a vision of the Lord in his glory, 5 being terrified, is confirmed for his Mes-sage. 9 He sheweth the obstinacie of the people, vnto their desolation. 13 A remnant shall bee saued.

N the yeere that King Vzziah died, I * saw also the Lord sitting vpon a throne, high and lifted vp, and his ‖ traine filled the Temple.

2 Aboue it stood the Seraphims : each one *had* sixe wings, with twaine he couered

John 12. 39, 40, 41

‖ Or, the skirts there-of.

couered his face, and with twaine hee couered his feete, and with twaine hee did flie.

3 And †one cryed vnto another, and sayd; * Holy, holy, holy, *is* the LORD of hostes, †the whole earth *is* full of his glory.

4 And the posts of the †doore moued at the voyce of him that cryed, and the house was filled with smoke.

5 ¶ Then sayd I; Woe *is* me; for I am †vndone, because I *am* a man of vncleane lippes, and I dwell in the midst of a people of vncleane lippes: for mine eyes haue seene the king, the LORD of hostes.

6 Then flew one of the Seraphims vnto mee, †hauing a liue-cole in his hand, *which* hee had taken with the tongs from off the altar.

7 And †he laide *it* vpon my mouth, and sayd, Loe, this hath touched thy lippes, and thine iniquitie is taken away, and thy sinne purged.

8 Also I heard the voyce of the Lord, saying; Whom shall I send, and who will goe for * vs? Then I saide; †Heere am I, send me.

9 ¶ And he sayd, Goe and tell this people; * Heere yee ‖indeede, but vnderstand not: and see yee indeed, but perceiue not.

10 Make the heart of this people fat, and make their eares heauy, and shut their eyes: lest they see with their eyes, and heare with their eares, and vnderstand with their heart, and conuert and be healed.

11 Then sayd I; Lord, how long? And hee answered, Vntill the cities be wasted without inhabitant, and the houses without man, and the land be vtterly †desolate,

12 And the LORD haue .remoued men farre away, and *there be* x great forsaking in the midst of the land.

13 ¶ But yet in it *shalbe* a tenth, ‖and it shall returne, and shall be eaten: as a Teyle tree, and as an Oke whose ‖substance *is* in them, when they cast *their leaues: so* the holy seede *shall be* the substance thereof.

CHAP. VII.

1 Ahaz, being troubled with feare of Rezin and Pekah, is comforted by Isaiah. 10 Ahaz, hauing liberty to choose a signe, and refusing it, hath for a signe, Christ promised. 17 His iudgement is prophecied to come by Assyria.

Nd it came to passe in the dayes of * Ahaz the sonne of Iotham, the sonne of Vzziah king of Iudah, *that* Rezin the king of Syria, and Pekah, the sonne of Remaliah king of Israel, went vp towards Ierusalem to warre against it, but could not preuaile against it.

2 And it was told the house of Dauid, saying; Syria is †confederate with Ephraim: and his heart was moued, and the heart of his people as the trees of the wood are mooued with the wind.

3 Then sayd the LORD vnto Isaiah; Goe forth now to meete Ahaz, thou, & †Shear-iashub thy sonne, at the end of the * conduit of the vpper poole ‖ in the high way of the fullers field.

4 And say vnto him; Take heede and be quiet: feare not, †neither be faint hearted for the two tailes of these smoking firebrands, for the fierce anger of Rezin with Syria, and of the sonne of Remaliah.

5 Because Syria, Ephraim, and the sonne of Remaliah haue taken euill counsell against thee, saying;

6 Let vs goe vp against Iudah and ‖vexe it, and let vs make a breach therein for vs, and set a king in the midst of it, *euen* the sonne of Tabeal.

7 Thus saith the Lord GOD; It shall not stand, neither shall it come to passe.

8 For the head of Syria *is* Damascus, and the head of Damascus *is* Rezin, and within threescore and fiue yeeres, shall Ephraim be broken, †that it be not a people.

9 And the head of Ephraim *is* Samaria, and the head of Samaria *is* Remaliahs sonne: ‖if yee will not beleeue, surely yee shall not be established.

10 ¶ †Moreouer the LORD spake againe vnto Ahaz, saying;

11 Aske thee a signe of the LORD thy God; ‖aske it either in the depth, or in the height aboue.

12 But Ahaz sayd, I will not aske, neither will I tempt the LORD.

13 And he sayd; Heare yee now, O house of Dauid; *Is* it a small thing for you to wearie men, but will yee wearie my God also?

14 Therefore the Lord himselfe shal giue you a signe: *Behold, a Virgine shall conceiue and beare a Sonne, and ‖ shall

Marginal notes (left column)
† *Heb. this cried to this.*
* Reu. 4. 8.
† *Heb. his glory is the fulnesse of the whole earth.*
† *Heb. thresholds.*

† *Heb. cut off.*

† *Heb. and in his hand a liue-coale.*

† *Heb. caused it to touch.*

* Gen. 1. 26.
† *Heb. behold me.*

* Matth. 13. 14. mar. 4. 12. luc. 8. 10. ioh. 12. 40. act. 28. 26. rom. 11. 8.
‖ *Or, without ceasing, &c: Heb. heare yee in hearing, &c.*

† *Heb. desolate with desolation.*

‖ *Or, when it is returned and hath bin broused.*
‖ *Or, stocke, or stemme.*

Marginal notes (right column)
* 2. king. 16. 5.

† *Heb. leasteth on Ephraim.*

† *That is, the remnant shall returne.*
‖ *Or, causeway.*
* 2. king. 18. 17.
† *Heb. let not thy heart be tender.*

‖ *Or, waken it.*

† *Heb. a people from.*

‖ *Or, if yee will not beleeue, it is because yee are not stable.*
† *Heb. the Lord added to speake.*
‖ *Or, make thy petition deepe.*

* Matth. 1. 23. luc. 1. 31.

, thou,
Virgin,
it call.

|| shall call his name Immanuel.

15 Butter and hony shall he eat, that hee may know to refuse the euill, and choose the good.

16 For before the childe shall know to refuse the euill and choose the good; the land that thou abhorrest, shalbe forsaken of both her kings.

17 ¶ The LORD shall bring vpon thee and vpon thy people, and vpon thy fathers house, dayes that haue not come, from the day that Ephraim departed from Iudah; euen the King of Assyria.

18 And it shall come to passe in that day, that the LORD shall hisse for the flie, that is in the vttermost part of the riuers of Egypt, and for the Bee that is in the land of Assyria.

19 And they shall come, and shall rest all of them in the desolate valleys, and in the holes of the rockes, and vpon all thornes, and vpon all || bushes.

r, com-
ndable
es.
. King.
35.

20 In the same day shall the Lord shaue with a * rasor that is hired, namely by them beyond the riuer, by the king of Assyria, the head, and the haire of the feet: and it shal also consume the beard.

21 And it shall come to passe in that day, that a man shal nourish a yong cow and two sheepe.

22 And it shall come to passe, for the abundance of milke that they shall giue, he shal eate butter: for butter and hony shall euery one eate, that is left †in the land.

Hebr. in
midst of
land.

23 And it shall come to passe in that day, that euery place shalbe, where there were a thousand Vines at a thousand siluerlings, it shall euen be for briers and thornes.

24 With arrowes and with bowes shall men come thither: because all the land shall become briars and thornes.

25 And on all hilles that shalbe digged with the mattocke, there shall not come thither the feare of briars and thornes; but it shall bee for the sending foorth of oxen, and for the treading of lesser cattell.

CHAP. VIII.

Oreouer the LORD said vnto mee, Take thee a great roule, and write in it with a mans penne, concerning † Maher-shalal-hash-baz.

2 And I tooke vnto mee faithfull witnesses to record, Vriah the Priest, and Zechariah the sonne of Ieberechiah.

3 And I †went vnto the Prophetesse, and shee conceiued and bare a sonne, then said the LORD to mee, Call his name Maher-shalal-hash-baz.

4 For before the childe shall haue knowledge to cry, My father and my mother, the ||riches of Damascus, and the spoile of Samaria shalbe taken away before the king of Assyria.

5 ¶ The LORD spake also vnto me againe, saying,

6 For so much as this people refuseth the waters of Shiloah that goe softly, and reioyce in Rezin, and Remaliahs sonne:

7 Now therefore behold, the Lord bringeth vp vpon them the waters of the riuer strong and many, euen the king of Assyria, and all his glory: and he shall come vp ouer all his channels, and goe ouer all his bankes.

8 And he shall passe through Iudah, he shall ouerflow and goe ouer, he shall reach euen to the necke; and †the stretching out of his wings shall fill the breadth of thy land, O Immanuel.

9 ¶ Associate your selues, O ye people, || and yee shalbe broken in pieces; and giue eare all ye of farre countreys: gird your selues, and ye shalbe broken in pieces; gird your selues, and ye shalbe broken in pieces.

10 Take counsell together, and it shall come to nought: speake the word, and it shall not stand; for God is with vs.

11 ¶ For the LORD spake thus to me †with a strong hand, and instructed me that I should not walke in the way of this people, saying,

12 Say ye not, A confederacie to all them, to whom this people shall say, A confederacie; neither feare yee their feare, nor be afraid.

13 Sanctifie the LORD of hostes himselfe, and let him bee your feare, and let him be your dread.

14 And he shalbe for a sanctuary; but for *a stone of stumbling and for a rocke of

† Hebr. In
making
speed to the
spoile, he
hasteneth
the pray. Or,
make speed,
&c.

† Hebr. op-
proched vn-
to.

|| Or, He that
is before the
King of As-
syria shall
take away
the riches
&c.

† Hebr. The
fulnesse of
the breadth
of thy land
shall be the
stretching
out of his
wings.
|| Or, yet.

† Hebr. In
strength of
hand.

* Isa. 28. 16.
luke 2. 34.
rom. 9. 33.
1. pet. 2. 7.

of offence to both the houses of Iſrael, for a ginne, and for a snare to the inhabitants of Ieruſalem.

15 And many among them shall * stumble and fall, and be broken, and be snared, and be taken.

* Matth. 21. 44. luke 20. 18.

16 Binde vp the Teſtimonie, ſeale the Law among my disciples.

17 And I wil wait vpon the LORD that hideth his face from the house of Iacob, and I will looke for him.

* Hebr. 2. 13.

18 *Behold, I, and the children whom the LORD hath giuen me, are for signes, and for wonders in Israel : from the LORD of hostes, which dwelleth in mount Zion.

19 ¶ And when they shall ſay vnto you; Seeke vnto them that haue familiar spirits, and vnto wizards that peepe and that mutter : should not a people ſeeke vnto their God? for the liuing, to the dead?

*Heb. 2. 13.

20 *To the Law and to the Teſtimonie : if they ſpeake not according to this word, it is because there is †no light in them.

† Heb. no morning.

21 And they shall paſſe through it, hardly beſtead and hungry : and it shall come to paſſe, that when they shall be hungry, they shall fret themselues, and curſe their King, and their God, and looke vpward.

22 And they shall looke vnto the earth : and behold trouble and darkeneſſe, dimneſſe of anguish ; and they shall be driuen to darkeneſſe.

CHAP. IX.

1 What ioy shall be in the midst of afflictions, by the Kingdome and birth of Christ. 8 The iudgements vpon Israel for their pride, 13 For their hypocriſie, 18 And for their impenitencie.

N Euertheleſſe the dimneſſe shall not be such as was in her vexation ; when at the first he lightly afflicted the land of Zebulun, and the land of Naphtali, and afterward did more grieuously afflict her by the way of the Sea, beyond Iordan in Galile || of the nations.

|| Or, populous.

2 The *people that walked in darkneſſe, haue ſeene a great light : they that dwel in the land of the shadow of death, vpon them hath the light shined.

* Mat. 4. 15. ephe. 5. 14.

3 Thou hast multiplied the nation, and || not increased the ioy : they ioy before thee, according to the ioy in harueſt,

| Or, to him.

and as men reioyce when they diuide the spoile.

4 || For thou hast broken the yoke of his burden, and the ſtaffe of his shoulder, the rod of his oppreſſour, as in the day of * Midian.

| Or, wh thou bre

5 || For euery battell of the warriour is with confuſed noiſe, and garments rolled in blood ; ||but this shall be with burning and †fewell of fire.

* Iudg. cha. 10. | Or, wh the who battell o warriou was, &c | Or, an was, &c † Heb. m * Ioh. 3

6 For vnto vs a child is borne, vnto vs a *Sonne is giuen, and the gouernment shalbe vpon his shoulder : and his name shalbe called, Wonderfull, Counseller, The mightie God, The euerlasting Father, The Prince of peace.

7 Of the increase of his gouernment and peace *there shall be no end, vpon the throne of Dauid & vpon his kingdome, to order it, and to stablish it with iudgement and with iustice, from henceforth euen for euer : the *zeale of the LORD of hostes will performe this.

* Luke 32, 33.

* 2. Ki 19. 31. chap. 3

8 ¶ The Lord ſent a word into Iacob, and it hath lighted vpon Iſrael.

9 And all the people shal know, euen Ephraim and the inhabitant of Samaria, that ſay in the pride and ſtoutneſſe of heart ;

10 The brickes are fallen downe, but we will build with hewen stones : the Sycomores are cut downe, but we will change them into Cedars.

11 Therefore the LORD shall ſet vp the aduerſaries of Rezin against him, and †ioyne his enemies together.

† Heb. gle.

12 The Syrians before, and the Philistines behinde, and they shall deuoure Israel †with open mouth ; *for all this his anger is not turned away, but his hand is stretched out still.

† Heb. whole mouth. * Chap. 25. & 1

13 ¶ For the people turneth not vnto him that ſmiteth them, neither doe they ſeeke the LORD of hostes.

14 Therefore the LORD will cut off from Israel head and taile, branch and rush in one day.

15 The ancient and honourable, hee is the head : and the prophet that teacheth lies, he is the taile.

16 For the ||leaders of this people cause them to erre, and they ||that are ledde of them, are †destroyed.

| Or, th that ca them bl ſed. | Or, th that ar led bleſſe them. † Heb. lowed t

17 Therfore the Lord shall haue no ioy in their yong men, neither shal haue mercy on their fatherleſſe & widowes : for euery one is an hypocrite, and an euil doer, and euery mouth ſpeaketh ||folly : for all this his anger is not turned away,

| Or, vi

away, but his hand *is* stretched out still.

18 ¶ For wickednes burneth as the fire : it shall deuoure the briers and thornes, and shall kindle in the thickets of the forrest, and they shall mount vp *like* the lifting vp of smoke.

19 Through the wrath of the LORD of hosts is the land darkened, and the *eb. meat.* people shall be as the †fuell of the fire : no man shall spare his brother.

eb. cut. 20 And he shall †snatch on the right hand, and be hungry, and he shall eate on the left hand, and they shall not bee satisfied : they shall eate euery man the flesh of his owne arme.

21 Manasseh, Ephraim : and Ephraim, Manasseh : *and* they together *shalbe* against Iudah : for all this his anger is not turned away, but his hand *is* stretched out still.

CHAP. X.

1 The woe of tyrants. 5 Assyria, the rodde of hypocrites, for his pride shall be broken. 20 A remnant of Israel shall be saued. 24 Israel is comforted with promise of deliuerance from Assyria.

, to the
ers that
te grie-
snesse.

Woe vnto them that decree vnrighteous decrees, and ‖that write grieuousnesse *which* they haue prescribed: 2 To turne aside the needy from iudgement, and to take away the right from the poore of my people, that widdowes may be their pray, and that they may robbe the fatherles.

3 And what wil ye doe in the day of visitation, and in the desolation *which* shall come from farre? to whom wil ye flee for helpe? and where will yee leaue your glory?

ha. 5. 25
9. 12.

4 Without mee they shall bowe downe vnder the prisoners, and they shall fall vnder the slaine : *for all this his anger is not turned away, but his hand *is* stretched out still.

·, woe to
Assyri-

5 ¶ ‖O †Assyrian, the rod of mine anger, ‖and the staffe in their hand is mine indignation.

eb. As-
r ·.
, though.

6 I will send him against an hypocriticall nation, and against the people of my wrath will I giue him a charge to take the spoile, and to take the praye, and †to tread them downe like the mire of the streets.

eb. to lay
n a trea-
·.

7 Howbeit he meaneth not so, neither doth his heart thinke so, but *it is* in his heart to destroy, and cut off nations not a few.

8 *For he saith, *Are* not my princes altogether kings?

* 2. Kings 18. 24, 33. and 19. 10, &c.

9 *Is* not Calno, as Carchemish? *is* not Hamath, as Arpad? *is* not Samaria, as Damascus?

10 As my hand hath found the kingdomes of the idoles, and whose grauen images did excell them of Ierusalem and of Samaria:

11 Shall I not, as I haue done vnto Samaria and her idoles, so doe to Ierusalem and her idoles?

12 Wherefore it shall come to passe, *that* when the Lord hath performed his whole worke *vpon mount Zion, and on Ierusalem, I will †punish the fruit †of the stout heart of the king of Assyria, and the glory of his high lookes.

* 2. Kings 19. 31.
† Heb. visite vpon.
† Heb. of the greatnesseof the heart.

13 For hee saith, By the strength of my hand I haue done *it*, and by my wisedome, for I am prudent: and I haue remooued the bounds of the people, and haue robbed their treasures, and I haue put downe the inhabitants ‖like a valiant man.

‖ Or, like many people.

14 And my hand hath found as a nest the riches of the people: and as one gathereth egges that are left, haue I gathered all the earth, and there was none that moued the wing, or opened the mouth, or peeped.

15 Shall the axe boast it selfe against him that heweth therewith? *or* shal the sawe magnifie it selfe against him that shaketh it? ‖as if the rod should shake *it selfe* against them that lift it vp, *or* as if the staffe should lift vp ‖*it selfe, as if it were* no wood.

‖ Or, as if a rod should shake them that lift it vp.
‖ Or, that which is not wood.

16 Therefore shall the Lord, the Lord of hosts, send among his fat ones leannesse, and vnder his glory hee shall kindle a burning, like the burning of a fire.

17 And the light of Israel shall bee for a fire, and his Holy One for a flame : and it shall burne and deuoure his thornes and his briers in one day :

18 And shall consume the glory of his forrest, and of his fruitfull field †both soule and body : and they shall bee as when a standerd bearer fainteth.

† Heb. from the soule and euen to the flesh.

19 And the rest of the trees of his forrest shall be †few, that a child may write them.

† Heb. number.

20 ¶ And it shal come to passe in that day, *that* the remnant of Israel, and such as are escaped of the house of Iacob, shall no more againe stay vpon him that smote them : but shall stay vpon the

the LORD, the Holy One of Israel in trueth.

21 The remnant shall returne, *euen* the remnant of Iacob, vnto the mightie God.

* Cha 28. 22
rom. 9. 27.

† Heb. in or
amongst.
‖ Or, in.

* Chap. 28.
22.

‖ Or, but hee
shall lift vp
his staffe for
thee.
* Exod. 14.

* Iudg. 7. 25
cha. 9. 4.

† Hebr. shall
remoue.

† Heb. crie
shrill with
thy voice.

‖ Or, migh-
tily.

22 * For though thy people Israel be as the sand of the sea, *yet* a remnant † of them shall returne: the consumption decreed shall ouerflow ‖ with righteousnesse.

23 * For the Lord GOD of hostes shall make a consumption, euen determined in the middest of all the land.

24 ¶ Therfore thus saith the Lord GOD of hostes, O my people that dwellest in Zion, be not afraide of the Assyrian: he shall smite thee with a rod, ‖ and shall lift vp his staffe against thee, after the maner of * Egypt.

25 For yet a very litle while, and the indignation shall cease, and mine anger in their destruction.

26 And the LORD of hostes shall stirre vp a scourge for him, according to the slaughter of * Midian at the rocke Oreb: and *as* his rod *was* vpon the Sea, so shall he lift it vp after the manner of Egypt.

27 And it shall come to passe in that day, *that* his burden † shalbe taken away from off thy shoulder, and his yoke from off thy necke, and the yoke shalbe destroyed because of the anointing.

28 He is come to Aiath, hee is passed to Migron: at Michmash he hath laid vp his cariages.

29 They are gone ouer the passage: they haue taken vp their lodging at Geba, Ramah is afraid, Gebeah of Saul is fled.

30 † Lift vp thy voice, O daughter of Gallim: cause it to bee heard vnto Laish, O poore Anathoth.

31 Madmenah is remooued, the inhabitants of Gebim gather themselues to flee.

32 As yet shall hee remaine at Nob that day: he shall shake his hand *against* the mount of the daughter of Zion, the hill of Ierusalem.

33 Behold, the Lord, the LORD of hostes shall lop the bough with terrour: and the high ones of stature shal be hewen downe, and the haughtie shalbe humbled.

34 And he shall cut downe the thickets of the forrests with yron, and Lebanon shall fall ‖ by a mightie one.

CHAP. XI.

1. The peaceable kingdome of the Branch out of the root of Iesse. 10 The victorious restauration of Israel, and vocation of the Gentiles.

 Nd there shall come forth a rod out of the stemme of * Iesse, and a branch shal grow out of his rootes.

2 And the Spirit of the LORD shall rest vpon him, the spirit of wisedome and vnderstanding, the spirit of counsell and might, the spirit of knowledge, and of the feare of the LORD:

3 And shal make him of † quicke vnderstanding in the feare of the LORD, and he shall not iudge after the sight of his eyes, neither reproue after the hearing of his eares.

4 But with righteousnesse shall he iudge the poore, and ‖ reproue with equitie, for the meeke of the earth: and he shall * smite the earth with the rodde of his mouth, and with the breath of his lips shall he slay the wicked.

5 And righteousnesse shalbe the girdle of his loines, and faithfulnesse the girdle of his reines.

6 * The wolfe also shall dwell with the lambe, and the leopard shall lie downe with the kid. and the calfe and the yong lion, and the fatling together, and a litle child shall lead them.

7 And the cow and the beare shall feed, their yong ones shall lie downe together: and the lyon shall eate straw like the oxe.

8 And the sucking childe shall play on the hole of the aspe, and the weaned childe shall put his hand on the ‖ cockatrice denne.

9 They shall not hurt nor destroy in all my holy mountaine: for the earth shall bee full of the knowledge of the LORD, as the waters couer the sea.

10 ¶ And in that day there shall bee a roote of Iesse, which shall stand for an ensigne of the people; to it shall the * Gentiles seeke, and his rest shall bee † glorious.

11 And it shall come to passe in that day, *that* the Lord shall set his hande againe the second time, to recouer the remnant of his people which shalbe left, from Assyria, and from Egypt, & from Pathros, and from Cush, and from Elam, and from Shinar, and from Hamath, and from the ylands of the Sea.

12 And

* Acts
23.

† Heb. s
ot smell

‖ Or, ar

* Iohn
2. thes.

* Chap.
25.

* Rom.
12.
† Heb gl

12 And he shall set vp an ensigne for the nations, and shall assemble the outcasts of Israel, and gather together the dispersed of Iudah, from the foure †corners of the earth.

13 The enuie also of Ephraim shal depart, and the aduersaries of Iudah shalbe cut off: Ephraim shall not enuie Iudah, and Iudah shall not vexe Ephraim.

14 But they shall fly vpon the shoulders of the Philistines toward the West, they shall spoile †them of the East together : †they shall lay their hand vpon Edom and Moab, †and the children of Ammon shall obey them.

15 And the LORD shall vtterly destroy the tongue of the Egyptian sea, and with his mighty wind shall hee shake his hand ouer the riuer, and shall smite it in the seuen streames, and make *men* goe ouer †dry-shod.

16 And there shalbe an high way for the remnant of his people, which shalbe left from Assyria; like as it was to Israel in the day that hee came vp out of the land of *Egypt.

CHAP. XII.

A ioyfull thanksgiuing of the faithfull for the mercies of God.

And in that day thou shalt say, O LORD, I will praise thee : though thou wast angrie with mee, thine anger is turned away, and thou comfortedst me.

2 Behold, God *is* my saluation : I will trust, and not be afraid; for the LORD IEHOVAH *is* my *strength and *my* song, he also is become my saluation.

3 Therefore with ioy shall yee draw water out of the wels of saluation.

4 And in that day shall yee say; * Praise the LORD, ‖ call vpon his name, declare his doings among the people, make mention that his name is exalted.

5 Sing vnto the LORD, for hee hath done excellent things : this is knowen in all the earth.

6 Cry out and shout thou †inhabitant of Zion : for great *is* the holy one of Israel in the midst of thee.

CHAP. XIII.

1 God mustereth the armies of his wrath.

6 He threatneth to destroy Babylon by the Medes. 19 The desolation of Babylon.

THe burden of Babylon, which Isaiah the sonne of Amoz did see.

2 Lift yee vp a banner vpon the high mountaine, exalt the voice vnto them, shake the hand, that they may goe into the gates of the nobles.

3 I haue commanded my sanctified ones : I haue also called my mightie ones for mine anger, *euen* them that reioyce in my highnesse.

4 The noise of a multitude in the mountaines, †like as of a great people : a tumultuous noise of the kingdomes of nations gathered together : the LORD of hostes mustereth the hoste of the battell.

5 They come from a farre countrey from the end of heauen, *euen* the LORD and the weapons of his indignation, to destroy the whole land.

6 ¶ Howle yee; for the day of the LORD *is* at hand; it shall come as a destruction from the Almighty.

7 Therefore shall all hands ‖ bee faint, and euery mans heart shall melt.

8 And they shalbe afraid : pangs and sorrowes shall take hold of *them*, they shalbe in paine as a woman that trauelleth : they shalbe †amazed †one at another, their faces *shalbe* as †flames.

9 Behold, the day of the LORD commeth, cruell both with wrath and fierce anger, to lay the land desolate ; and he shall destroy the sinners thereof out of it.

10 For the starres of heauen, and the constellations thereof shall not giue their light : the sunne shalbe *darkened in his going forth, and the moone shall not cause her light to shine.

11 And I will punish the world for *their* euill, and the wicked for their iniquitie; and I will cause the arrogancie of the proud to cease, and will lay low the hautinesse of the terrible.

12 I will make a man more pretious then fine gold; euen a man then the golden wedge of Ophir.

13 Therefore I will shake the heauens, and the earth shall remoue out of her place in the wrath of the LORD of hostes, and in the day of his fierce anger.

14 And it shalbe as the chased Roe, and as a sheepe that no man taketh vp: they

---

Marginal notes (left):

,wings.

b. the ren of east.
b. Edom be the g on of hand.
b. the ren of ion obedi- e.

b. in ?s.

kod. 14.

kod. 15. al. 118.

Chron. 3. psal. 1.
• pro- ne his se.

eb. inha- esse.

Marginal notes (right):

† Heb. the likenesse of.

‖ Or, fall downe.

† Heb. won- der.
† Heb. euery man at his neighbour.
† Heb. faces of the flames.

* Ezek. 32. 7. ioel. 2. 31 and 3. 15. matth. 24. 29. mar. 13. 24. luc. 21. 25.

they shall euery man turne to his owne people, and flee euery one into his owne land.

15 Euery one that is found shall be thrust through: and euery one that is ioyned *vnto them*, shall fall by the sword.

16 Their children also shalbe *dashed to pieces before their eyes, their houses shalbe spoiled, & their wiues rauished.

* Psal. 137. 9.

17 Beholde, I will stirre vp the Medes against them, which shall not regard siluer, and as for gold, they shall not delight in it.

18 *Their* bowes also shall dash the yong men to pieces, and they shall haue no pitie on the fruit of the wombe; their eye shall not spare children.

19 ¶ And Babylon the glory of kingdomes, the beautie of the Chaldees excellencie, shall be †as when God ouerthrew *Sodom and Gomorrah.

† Hebr. As the ouerthrowing.
* Gene. 19. 25. iere. 50. 40.

20 It shall neuer be inhabited, neither shall it be dwelt in from generation to generation: neither shall the Arabian pitch tent there, neither shal the shepheards make their fold there.

21 But † wilde beastes of the desert shall lye there, and their houses shalbe full of † dolefull creatures, and ‖ owles shall dwell there, and Satyres shall daunce there.

† Heb. Ziim.
† Hebr. Ochim.
‖ Or, Ostriches.
† Hebr. daughters of the owle.

22 And the wilde † beastes of the Ilands shal cry in their ‖ desolate houses, and dragons in their pleasant palaces: and her time is neere to come, and her dayes shall not be prolonged.

† Heb. Iim.
‖ Or, palaces.

CHAP. XIIII.

1 Gods mercifull restauration of Israel. 4 Their triumphant insultation ouer Babel. 24 Gods purpose against Assyria. 29 Palestina is threatned.

FOr the LORD wil haue mercie on Iacob, and wil yet choose Israel, and set them in their owne land: and the strangers shalbe ioyned with them, and they shal cleaue to the house of Iacob.

2 And the people shall take them, and bring them to their place: and the house of Israel shall possesse them in the land of the LORD, for seruants and handmaides: and they shall take them captiues, † whose captiues they were, and they shall rule ouer their oppressours.

† Hebr. that had taken them captiues.

3 And it shall come to passe in the day that the LORD shal giue thee rest from thy sorrow, and from thy feare, and from the hard bondage wherein thou wast made to serue,

4 ¶ That thou shalt take vp this ‖ prouerbe against the king of Babylon, and say; How hath the oppressour ceased? the ‖ golden citie ceased?

‖ Or, ta- ting sp
‖ Or, e ctresse gold.

5 The LORD hath broken the staffe of the wicked, *and* the scepter of the rulers.

6 He who smote the people in wrath with † a continuall stroke; hee that ruled the nations in anger, is persecuted *and* none hindereth.

† Heb. stroke out re uing.

7 The whole earth is at rest *and* is quiet: they breake foorth into singing.

8 Yea the firre trees reioyce at thee, *and* the cedars of Lebanon, *saying*, Since thou art layd downe, no feller is come vp against vs.

9 ‖ Hell from beneath is mooued for thee to meet *thee* at thy comming: it stirreth vp the dead for thee, *euen* all the † chiefe ones of the earth; it hath raised vp from their thrones, all the kings of the nations.

‖ Or, graue
† Heb. ders, great

10 All they shall speake and say vnto thee; Art thou also become weake as we? art thou become like vnto vs?

11 Thy pompe is brought downe to the graue, *and* the noyse of thy violes: the worme is spread vnder thee, and the wormes couer thee.

12 How art thou fallen from heauen, ‖ O Lucifer, sonne of the morning? *how* art thou cut downe to the ground, which didst weaken the nations?

‖ Or, starre

13 For thou hast said in thine heart; I wil ascend into heauen, I wil exalt my throne aboue the starres of God: I wil sit also vpon the mount of the congregation, in the sides of the North.

14 I wil ascend aboue the heights of the cloudes, I wil bee like the most High.

15 Yet thou shalt be brought downe to hel, to the sides of the pit.

16 They that see thee shal narrowly looke vpon thee, *and* consider thee, *saying*; *Is* this the man that made the earth to tremble, that did shake kingdomes?

17 That made the world as a wildernesse, and destroyed the cities thereof; ‖ that opened not the house of his prisoners?

‖ Or, not lo priso loose ward

18 All the kings of the nations, *euen* all of them lie in glory, euery one in his owne house.

19 But

19 But thou art cast out of thy graue, like an abominable branch : *and* as the raiment of those that are slaine, thrust through with a sword, that goe downe to the stones of the pit, as a carkeis troden vnder feete.

20 Thou shalt not be ioyned with them in buriall, because thou hast destroyed thy land, *and* slaine thy people: * the seede of euill doers shall neuer be renowmed.

21 Prepare slaughter for his children * for the iniquitie of their fathers, that they doe not rise nor possesse the land, nor fill the face of the world with cities.

22 For I will rise vp against them, sayth the Lord of hostes, and cut off from Babylon the name, and remnant, and sonne and nephew, sayth the Lord.

23 I will also make it a possession for the Bitterne, and pooles of water : and I will sweepe it with the besome of destruction, sayth the Lord of hostes.

24 ¶ The Lord of hostes hath sworne, saying ; Surely as I haue thought, so shall it come to passe; and as I haue purposed, so shall it stand :

25 That I will breake the Assyrian in my land, and vpon my mountaines tread him vnder foote : then shall his yoke depart from off them, and his burden depart from off their shoulders.

26 This *is* the purpose, that is purposed vpon the whole earth : and this *is* the hand that is stretched out vpon all the nations.

27 For the Lord of hostes hath * purposed , and who shall disanull *it* ? and his hand *is* stretched out, and who shall turne it backe ?

28 In the yeere that king Ahaz died, was this burden.

29 ¶ Reioyce not thou whole Palestina, because the rod of him that smote thee is broken : for out of the serpents roote shall come foorth a ||cockatrice, and his fruite *shall be* a fierie flying serpent.

30 And the first borne of the poore shall feed, and the needy shall lie downe in safetie : and I will kill thy root with famine, and he shall slay thy remnant.

31 Howle, O gate, crie, O citie, thou whole Palestina art dissolued, for there shal come from the North a smoke, and ||none *shall bee* alone in his ||appointed times.

32 What shall one then answere the messengers of the nation ? * that the Lord hath founded Zion, and the poore of his people shall ||trust in it.

CHAP. XV.
The lamentable state of Moab.

He burden of Moab : because in the night Ar of Moab is laide waste *and* || brought to silence ; because in the night Kir of Moab is laide waste , *and* brought to silence :

2 Hee is gone vp to Baijth, and to Dibon, the high places, to weepe : Moab shall howle ouer Nebo, and ouer Medeba, * on all their heads *shalbe* baldnesse, *and* euery beard cut off.

3 In their streetes they shall girde themselues with sackecloth : on the toppes of their houses, and in their streetes euery one shall howle , † weeping abundantly.

4 And Heshbon shall cry, and Elealeh : their voice shalbe heard *euen* vnto Iahaz : therefore the armed souldiers of Moab shall crie out, his life shall be grieuous vnto him.

5 My heart shall cry out for Moab. ||his fugitiues *shall flee* vnto Zoar, an * heifer of three yeeres olde : for by the mounting vp of Luhith with weeping shall they goe it vp : for in the way of Horonaim, they shall raise vp a crie of † destruction.

6 For the waters of Nimrim shall be † desolate : for the hay is withered away , the grasse faileth , there is no greene thing.

7 Therefore the abundance they haue gotten, and that which they haue laide vp , shall they cary away to the ||brooke of the willowes.

8 For the cry is gone round about the borders of Moab : the howling thereof vnto Eglaim, and the howling thereof vnto Beer-Elim.

9 For the waters of Dimon shalbe full of blood : for I will bring † more vpon Dimon, lyons vpon him that escapeth of Moab, and vpon the remnant of the land.

CHAP. XVI.

1 Moab is exhorted to yeeld obedience to Christs kingdome. 6 Moab is threatned for her pride. 9 The Prophet bewaileth her. 12 The iudgement of Moab.

Send

*b 18.
*psal. 21.
and 37.
and 109

*xo. 20.5.
*t. 23. 35.

*2. Chron.
. 6. iob 9.
. prou.
. 30. dan.
32.

*Or, Adder.

*Or, he shall
*ot be alone.
*Or, assem-
*lies.

* Psal. 87. 1,
5. and 102.
17.
¶ Or, betake
themselues
vnto it.

¶ Or, cut off.

* Ier. 48. 37,
38. ezek. 7.
18.

† Heb. descending into
weeping :
or, comming
downe with
weeping.

¶ Or, to the
borders
thereof euen
to Zoar as
an heifer.
* Iere. 48.
5, 34.

† Heb. breaking

† Heb. desolations.

¶ Or, valley
of the Arabians.

† Heb. additions.

End ye the lambe to the ruler of the land from ||Sela to the wildernesse, vnto the mount of the daughter of Zion.

Or, Petra: Hebr. a rocke.

2 For it shalbe that as a wandering bird ||cast out of the nest: so the daughters of Moab shalbe at the fordes of Arnon.

Or, a nest forsaken.

3 †Take counsell, execute Iudgement, make thy shadow as the night in the middest of the nooneday, hide the outcastes, bewray not him that wandereth.

†*Heb.bring.*

4 Let mine outcasts dwel with thee, Moab, be thou a couert to them from the face of the spoiler: for the †extortioner is at an end, the spoiler ceaseth, †the oppressours are consumed out of the land.

†*Heb. wringer.*
†*Hebr. the treaders downe.*

5 And in mercy shall the throne be ||established, and hee shal *sit vpon it in trueth, in the tabernacle of Dauid, iudging and seeking iudgement, and hasting righteousnesse.

Or, prepared.
Dan. 7. 14, 27. mic. 4. 7. luke 1. 33.

6 ¶ We haue heard of the *pride of Moab (hee is very proud) *euen* of his hautines, and his pride, and his wrath: *but* his lies shall not be so.

Iere. 48. 29.

7 Therefore shall Moab *howle for Moab, euery one shal howle: for the foundations of Kir-hareseth shall yee ||mourne, surely they *are* stricken.

Iere. 48. 20.

Or, mutter.

8 For the fieldes of Heshbon languish, *and* the vine of Sibmah, the lords of the heathen haue broken downe the principall plants thereof, they are come euen vnto Iazer, they wandred *through* the wildernesse, her branches are ||stretched out, they are gone ouer the sea.

Or, plucked vp.

9 ¶ Therefore I wil bewaile with the weeping of Iazer, the Vine of Sibmah; I wil water thee with my teares, O Heshbon, and Elealeh: for ||the shouting for thy Summer fruits, and for thy haruest, is fallen.

Or, the alarme is fallen vpon, &c.

10 And *gladnesse is taken away, and ioy out of the plentifull field, and in the Vineyards there shalbe no singing, neither shal there be shouting: the treaders shall tread out no wine in their presses; I haue made their *vintage*-shouting to cease.

Iere. 48. 33.

11 Wherefore my bowels shal sound like an harpe for Moab, and mine inward parts for Kir-haresh.

12 ¶ And it shal come to passe, when it is seene that Moab is weary on the high place, that hee shall come to his Sanctuary to pray: but hee shall not preuaile.

13 This *is* the word that the LORD hath spoken concerning Moab since that time.

14 But now the LORD hath spoken, saying, Within three yeeres, as the yeeres of an hireling, and the glory of Moab shalbe contemned, with all that great multitude; and the remnant *shall be* very small and ||feeble.

Or, not many.

CHAP. XVII.

1 Syria and Israel are threatned. 6 A remnant shall forsake idolatrie. 9 The rest shalbe plagued for their impietie. 12 The woe of Israels enemies.

HE burden of Damascus: Behold, Damascus is taken away from *being* a citie, and it shalbe a ruinous heape.

2 The cities of Aroer are forsaken: they shall bee for flockes, which shall lye downe, and none shall make *them* afraid.

3 The fortresse also shall cease from Ephraim, and the kingdome from Damascus, and the remnant of Syria: they shall bee as the glorie of the children of Israel, saith the LORD of hostes.

4 And in that day it shall come to passe, *that* the glory of Iacob shall bee made thinne, and the fatnesse of his flesh shall waxe leane.

5 And it shall be as when the haruest-man gathereth the corne, and reapeth the eares with his arme; and it shalbe as he that gathereth eares in the valley of Rephaim.

6 (¶ Yet gleaning-grapes shall be left in it, as the shaking of an Oliue tree, two or three berries in the toppe of the vppermost bough: foure or fiue in the out-most fruitfull branches thereof, saith the LORD God of Israel.

7 At that day shall a man looke to his Maker, and his eyes shall haue respect to the Holy one of Israel.

8 And hee shall not looke to the altars, the worke of his handes, neither shall respect that which his fingers haue made, either the groues or the ||images.)

Or, Sunne images.

9 ¶ In that day shall his strong cities

cities be as a forsaken bough, and an vppermost branch, which they left, because of the children of Israel: and there shalbe desolation.

10 Because thou hast forgotten the God of thy saluation, and hast not beene mindfull of the rocke of thy strength: therefore shalt thou plant pleasant plants, and shalt set it with strange slips.

11 In the day shalt thou make thy plant to grow, and in the morning shalt thou make thy seede to flourish: *but* the haruest *shall be* a ||heape in the day of griefe, and of desperate sorrow.

12 ¶ Woe to the ||multitude of many people, *which* make a noise, like the noise of the seas; and to the rushing of nations, *that* make a rushing, like the rushing of ||mighty waters.

13 The nations shall rush like the rushing of many waters: but *God* shall rebuke them, and they shall flee farre off, and shalbe chased as the chaffe of the mountaines before the wind, and like a ||rolling thing before the whirlewind.

14 And behold at euening tide trouble, *and* before the morning he *is* not: this *is* the portion of them that spoile vs, and the lot of them that robbe vs.

C H A P. XVIII.

1 God in care of his people will destroy the Ethiopians. 7 An accesse thereby shall grow vnto the Church.

Oe to the land shadowing with wings, which *is* beyond the riuers of Ethiopia:

2 That sendeth ambassadours by the sea, euen in vessels of bulrushes vpon the waters, *saying*; Goe yee swift messengers to a nation ||scattered and peeled, to a people terrible from their beginning hitherto, ||a nation meted out and troden downe; ||whose land the riuers haue spoiled.

3 All yee inhabitants of the world, and dwellers on the earth, see yee, when hee lifteth vp an ensigne on the mountaines; and when he bloweth a trumpet, heare yee.

4 For so the LORD sayd vnto me; I will take my rest, and I will ||consider in my dwelling place like a cleare heate ||vpon herbes, *and* like a cloud of dew in the heate of haruest.

5 For afore the haruest when the bud is perfect, and the sowre grape is ripening in the flowre; hee shall both cut off the sprigges with pruning hookes, and take away *and* cut downe the branches.

6 They shalbe left together vnto the foules of the mountaines, and to the beasts of the earth: and the foules shall summer vpon them, and all the beastes of the earth shall winter vpon them.

7 ¶ In that time shall the present be brought vnto the LORD of hostes, of a people ||scattered and peeled, and from a people terrible from their beginning hitherto; a nation meted out and troden vnder foote, whose land the riuers haue spoiled, to the place of the name of the LORD of hostes, the mount Zion.

C H A P. XIX.

1 The confusion of Egypt. 11 The folishnesse of their Princes. 18 The calling of Egypt to the Church. 23 The couenant of Egypt, Assyria and Israel.

He burden of Egypt: Behold, the LORD rideth vpon a swift cloude, and shall come into Egypt, and the idoles of Egypt shalbe moued at his presence, and the heart of Egypt shall melt in the midst of it.

2 And I will †set the Egyptians against the Egyptians: and they shall fight euery one against his brother, and euery one against his neighbour; citie against citie, *and* kingdome against kingdome.

3 And the spirit of Egypt †shall faile in the midst thereof, and I will †destroy the counsell thereof: and they shall seeke to the idoles, and to the charmers, and to them that haue familiar spirits, and to the wizards.

4 And the Egyptians will I ||giue ouer into the hand of a cruell Lord; and a fierce king shall rule ouer them, saith the Lorde, the LORD of hostes.

5 And the waters shall faile from the sea, and the riuer shalbe wasted, and dried vp.

6 And they shall turne the riuers farre away, and the brookes of defence shall be emptied and dried vp: the reeds and flagges shall wither.

7 The

Or, remoued in the way of inheritance, and here shalbe eadly sorow.
Or, noise.

Or, many.

Or, thistledowne.

Or, outpread and polished.
Or, a nation that meeth out, and readeth downe. Heb. a nation of ine line, and reading vnder foote.
Or, whose and the riuers despise.

Or, regard my set dwelling.
Or, after raine.

|| Or, outspread and polished. &c.

† Heb. mingle.

† Heb. shall be emptied.
† Heb. swallow vp.

|| Or, shut vp.

† *Heb. and shall not be.*

7 The paper reeds by the brookes, by the mouth of the brookes, and euery thing ſowen by the brooks ſhal wither, be driuen away, † and be no *more.*

8 The fiſhers alſo ſhall mourne, and all they that caſt angle into the brookes ſhall lament, and they that ſpread nets vpon the waters ſhall languiſh.

‖ *Or, white workes.*

9 Moreouer they that worke in fine flaxe, and they that weaue ‖ net-works ſhall be confounded.

† *Heb. foundations.*
† *Heb. of liuing things.*

10 And they ſhall be broken in the † purpoſes thereof, all that make ſluces and ponds † for fiſh.

11 ¶ Surely the princes of Zoan *are* fooles, the counſell of the wiſe counſellers of Pharaoh is become brutiſh: How ſay ye vnto Pharaoh, I *am* the ſonne of the wiſe, the ſonne of ancient kings ?

12 Where *are* they ? Where *are* thy wiſe men ? and let them tell thee now, and let them know, what the LORD of hoſts hath purpoſed vpon Egypt.

13 The princes of Zoan are become fooles, the princes of Noph are deceiued, they haue alſo ſeduced Egypt, *euen* ‖ they that are the ſtay of the tribes thereof.

‖ *Or, gouernours. heb. corners.*

14 The LORD hath mingled † a peruerſe ſpirit in the midſt thereof: and they haue cauſed Egypt to erre in euery worke thereof, as a drunken man ſtaggereth in his vomit.

† *Heb. a ſpirit of peruerſities.*

15 Neither ſhall there be any worke for Egypt, which the head or taile, branch or ruſh may doe.

16 In that day ſhall Egypt bee like vnto women : and it ſhall be afraid and feare, becauſe of the ſhaking of the hand of the LORD of hoſts, which he ſhaketh ouer it.

17 And the land of Iudah ſhall bee a terrour vnto Egypt, euery one that maketh mention thereof, ſhal be afraid in himſelfe, becauſe of the counſell of the LORD of hoſts, which he hath determined againſt it.

† *Heb. the lippe.*
‖ *Or, of Hereſ: or of the Sunne.*

18 ¶ In that day ſhall fiue cities in the land of Egypt ſpeake the † language of Canaan, and ſweare to the LORD of hoſtes : one ſhalbe called the citie ‖ of deſtruction.

19 In that day ſhall there be an Altar to the LORD in the midſt of the land of Egypt, and a pillar at the border thereof to the LORD.

20 And it ſhall be for a ſigne, and for a witneſſe vnto the LORD of hoſts in the land of Egypt : for they ſhall crie vnto the LORD, becauſe of the oppreſſours, and he ſhal ſend them a Sauiour and a great One, and he ſhall deliuer them.

21 And the LORD ſhalbe knowen to Egypt, and the Egyptians ſhal know the LORD in that day, and ſhal do ſacrifice and oblation, yea they ſhall vow a vowe vnto the LORD, and performe *it.*

22 And the LORD ſhall ſmite Egypt, he ſhall ſmite and heale *it,* and they ſhall returne euen to the LORD, and he ſhalbe intreated of them, and ſhall heale them.

23 ¶ In that day ſhall there be a hie way out of Egypt to Aſſyria, and the Aſſyrian ſhall come into Egypt, and the Egyptian into Aſſyria, and the Egyptians ſhall ſerue with the Aſſyrians.

24 In that day ſhall Iſrael bee the third with Egypt, and with Aſſyria, *euen* a bleſſing in the midſt of the land :

25 Whom the LORD of hoſts ſhal bleſſe, ſaying, Bleſſed *be* Egypt my people, and Aſſyria the work of my hands, and Iſrael mine inheritance.

CHAP. XX.

A type prefiguring the ſhamefull captiuitie of Egypt and Ethiopia.

IN the yeere that Tartan came vnto Aſhdod (when Sargon the king of Aſſyria ſent him) and fought againſt Aſhdod and tooke it :

2 At the ſame time ſpake the LORD † by Iſaiah the ſonne of Amoz, ſaying, Go and looſe the ſackcloth from off thy loynes, and put off thy ſhooe from thy foot : and he did ſo, walking naked and bare foot.

† *Heb. by hand of iah.*

3 And the LORD ſaid, Like as my ſeruant Iſaiah hath walked naked and bare foote three yeeres *for* a ſigne and wonder vpon Egypt and vpon Ethiopia :

4 So ſhall the king of Aſſyria lead away the † Egyptians priſoners, and the Ethiopians captiues, yong and old, naked and bare foote, euen with their buttockes vncouered, to the † ſhame of Egypt.

† *Heb. captiuitie of Egypt.*
† *Heb. nakedneſſe.*

5 And they ſhall be afraid and aſhamed of Ethiopia their expectation, and of Egypt their glory.

6 And

‖ Or, coun-
trey.

6 And the inhabitant of this ‖ yle shall say in that day; Behold, such *is* our expectation whither we flee for helpe to be deliuered from the king of Assyria: and how shall we escape?

CHAP. XXI.

1 The Prophet, bewayling the captiuity of his people, seeth in a vision, the fall of Babylon by the Medes and Persians. 11 Edom, scorning the Prophet, is moued to repentance. 13 The set time of Arabias calamity.

He burden of the desert of the sea. As whirlewinds in the South passe thorough; *so* it commeth from the desert, from a terrible land.

† Heb. hard.

2 A †grieuous vision is declared vnto me; The treacherous dealer dealeth treacherously, and the spoiler spoileth: Goe, vp O Elam: besiege, O Media: all the sighing thereof haue I made to cease.

3 Therefore are my loynes filled with paine, pangs haue taken hold vpon me, as the pangs of a woman that trauelleth: I was bowed downe at the hearing *of it*, I was dismayed at the seeing *of it*.

‖ Or, my
minde wan-
dred.
† Heb. put.

4 ‖My heart panted, fearefulnesse affrighted me: the night of my pleasure hath he †turned into feare vnto me.

5 Prepare the table, watch in the watch-tower, eate, drinke: arise yee princes, *and* anoint the shield.

6 For thus hath the Lord sayd vnto me; Goe, set a watchman, let him declare what he seeth.

7 And he saw a charet *with* a couple of horsemen, a charet of asses, *and* a charet of camels; and hee hearkened diligently with much heede.

‖ Or, cryed
as a lyon.
* Abacuc.
2. 1.
‖ Or, euery
night.

8 And ‖he cryed; A lyon: my Lord, I stand continually vpon the *watchtower in the day time, and I am set in my ward ‖whole nights.

* Ier. 51. 8.
and 18. 2.

9 And behold, heere commeth a charet of men *with* a couple of horsemen: and he answered and sayd; *Babylon is fallen, is fallen, and all the grauen images of her Gods he hath broken vnto the ground.

† Heb. sonne.

10 O my threshing and the †corne of my floore: that which I haue heard of the Lord of hostes the God of Israel, haue I declared vnto you.

11 ¶ The burden of Dumah. Hee calleth to me out of Seir: Watchman, what of the night? Watchman, what of the night?

12 The watchman sayd; The morning commeth, and also the night: if yee will enquire, enquire yee: returne, come.

13 ¶ The burden vpon Arabia. In the forest in Arabia shall yee lodge, O yee trauelling companies of Dedanim.

14 The inhabitants of the land of Tema ‖ brought water to him that was thirsty, they preuented with their bread him that fled.

‖ Or, bring
yee.

15 For they fled from the swords, ‖from the drawen sword, and from the bent bow, and from the grieuousnesse of warre.

‖ Or, for
feare. Heb.
from the
face.

16 For thus hath the Lord sayd vnto me: Within a yeere, according to the yeeres of an hireling, and all the glory of Kedar shall faile.

17 And the residue of the number of †archers, the mighty men of the children of Kedar shalbe diminished: for the Lord God of Israel hath spoken *it*.

† Heb. bowes

CHAP. XXII.

1 The Prophet lamenteth the inuasion of Iury by the Persians. 8 He reproueth their humane wisedome and worldly ioy. 15 Hee prophesieth Shebnaes depriuation, 20 and Eliakim prefiguring the kingdome of Christ, his substitution.

He burden of the valley of vision. What ayleth thee now, that thou art wholly gone vp to the house toppes?

2 Thou that art full of stirres, a tumultuous citie, a ioyous citie: thy slaine men are not slaine with the sword, nor dead in battell.

3 All thy rulers are fled together, they are bound †by the archers: all that are found in thee are bound together, *which* haue fled from farre.

† Heb. of the
bow.

4 Therefore sayd I; *Looke away from me, †I will weepe bitterly, labour not to comfort me; because of the spoiling of the daughter of my people.

* Ier. 4. 19.
and 9. 1.
† Heb. I will
be bitter in
weeping.

5 For it *is* a day of trouble, and of treading downe, and of perplexitie by the Lord GOD of hostes in the valley of vision, breaking downe the walles, and of crying to the mountaines.

6 And

6 And Elam bare the quiuer with
charets of men *and* horsemen, and Kir
† vncouered the shield.
† *Heb. made naked.*
7 And it shall come to passe that
thy † choicest valleys shall be full of charets, and the horsemen shall set themselues in aray ‖ at the gate.
† *Heb. the choice of the valleys.*
‖ *Or, to-wards.*
8 ¶ And he discouered the couering
of Iudah, and thou diddest looke in
that day to the armour of the house of
the forrest.
9 Ye haue seene also the breaches of
the citie of Dauid, that they are many:
and ye gathered together the waters of
the lower poole.
10 And ye haue numbred the houses
of Ierusalem, and the houses haue yee
broken downe to fortifie the wall.
11 Ye made also a ditch betweene the
two walles, for the water of the olde
poole: but ye haue not looked vnto the
maker thereof, neither had respect vnto him that fashioned it long agoe.
12 And in that day did the Lord
God of hostes call to weeping and to
mourning, and to baldnesse, and to girding with sackecloth.
13 And behold ioy and gladnesse, slaying oxen and killing sheep, eating flesh,
and drinking wine; * let vs eate and
drinke, for to morrow we shall die.
* Chap. 56. 12. wisd. 2. 6. 1. cor. 15. 32.
14 And it was reuealed in mine
eares by the Lord of hostes; surely
this iniquitie shall not be purged from
you, till yee die, sayth the Lord God
of hostes.
15 ¶ Thus sayth the Lord God
of hostes, Goe, get thee vnto this treasurer, euen vnto Shebna, which *is* ouer
the house, *and say;*
16 What hast thou here? and whom
hast thou here, that thou hast hewed
thee out a sepulchre here, ‖ *as* hee that
heweth him out a sepulchre on high, *and*
that graueth an habitation for himselfe
in a rocke?
‖ *Or, O hee.*
17 Behold; ‖ the Lord will cary
thee away with a † mightie captiuitie,
and will surely couer thee.
18 He will surely violently turne and
tosse thee, *like* a ball into a † large countrey: there shalt thou die, and there the
charets of thy glory *shall be* the shame of
thy Lords house.
‖ *Or, the Lord who couered thee with an excellent couering, and clothed thee gorgeously, v. 18. shall surely, &c.*
† *Heb. the captiuitie of a man.*
† *Heb. large of spaces.*
19 And I will driue thee from thy
station, and from thy state shall he pull
thee downe.
20 ¶ And it shall come to passe in
that day, that I will call my seruant
Eliakim the sonne of Hilkiah:
21 And I will clothe him with thy
robe, and strengthen him with thy girdle, and I wil commit thy gouernment
into his hand, and he shalbe a father to
the inhabitants of Ierusalem, and to
the house of Iudah.
22 And the key of the house of Dauid will I lay vpon his shoulder: so he
shall * open and none shall shut, and he
shall shut and none shall open.
* Iob 12. [1]4. reue. 3. 7.
23 And I will fasten him *as* a naile
in a sure place, and he shalbe for a glorious throne to his fathers house.
24 And they shall hang vpon him
all the glory of his fathers house, the
offspring and the issue, all vessels of
small quantitie: from the vessels of
cups, euen to all the ‖ vessels of flagons.
‖ *Or, inst[ru]ments of violes.*
25 In that day, sayth the Lord
of hostes, shall the naile that is fastened
in the sure place, be remooued, and be
cut downe and fall: and the burden that
was vpon it shall bee cut off: for the
Lord hath spoken *it.*

CHAP. XXIII.

1 The miserable ouerthrow of Tyre. 17 Their
vnhappie returne.

The burden of Tyre. Howle
yee ships of Tarshish, for
it is laide waste, so that
there is no house, no en-
tring in: from the land of
Chittim it is reuealed to them.
2 Be † still, yee inhabitants of the
yle, thou whom the merchants of Zidon, that passe ouer the sea, haue replenished.
† *Hebr. silent.*
3 And by great waters the seede of
Sihor, the haruest of the riuer *is* her reuenew, and she is a mart of nations.
4 Be thou ashamed, O Zidon; for
the sea hath spoken, *euen* the strength of
the sea, saying; I trauell not, nor bring
foorth children, neither doe I nourish
vp yong men, *nor* bring vp virgines.
5 As at the report concerning E-
gypt, so shal they be sorely pained at the
report of Tyre.
6 Passe ye ouer to Tarshish, howle
ye inhabitants of the yle.
7 *Is* this your ioyous *citie,* whose
antiquitie is of ancient dayes? her
owne feete shall cary her † afarre off to
soiourne.
† *Heb. fro[m] afarre off.*
8 Who hath taken this counsell a-
gainst Tyre the crowning *citie,* whose
merchants

merchants are princes, whose traffiquers are the honourable of the earth?

9 The Lord of hostes hath purposed it, † to staine the pride of all glory, *and* to bring into contempt all the honorable of the earth.

10 Passe through thy land as a riuer O daughter of Tarshish : *there is* no more † strength.

11 He stretched out his hand ouer the sea, hee shooke the kingdomes : the Lord hath giuen a commandement ‖ against the merchant citie, to destroy the ‖ strong holdes thereof.

12 And he said, Thou shalt no more reioice, O thou oppressed virgin, daughter of Zidon : arise, passe ouer to Chittim, there also shalt thou haue no rest.

13 Behold, the land of the Caldeans, this people was not *till* the Assyrian founded it for them that dwel in the wildernesse : they set vp the towers thereof, they raised vp the palaces thereof, *and* he brought it to ruine.

14 Howle ye ships of Tarshish : for your strength is laid waste.

15 And it shall come to passe in that day, that Tyre shall be forgotten seuentie yeeres according to the dayes of one king : after the end of seuentie yeeres † shall Tyre sing as an harlot.

16 Take an harpe, goe about the city thou harlot, that hast beene forgotten, make sweet melody, sing many songs, that thou mayest be remembred.

17 ¶ And it shall come to passe after the ende of seuentie yeeres, that the Lord will visite Tyre, and shee shall turne to her hire, and shall commit fornication with all the kingdomes of the world vpon the face of the earth.

18 And her merchandize and her hire shall be holinesse to the Lord : it shall not be treasured nor laid vp : for her merchandize shalbe for them that dwell before the Lord, to eate sufficiently, and for † durable clothing.

CHAP. XXIIII.

1 The dolefull iudgements of God vpon the land. 13 A remnant shall ioyfully praise him. 16 God in his iudgements shall aduance his Kingdome.

**B**Ehold, the Lord maketh the earth emptie, and maketh it waste, and † turneth it vpside downe, and scattereth abroad the inhabitants thereof.

2 And it shall be as with the people, so with the ‖ * priest, as with the seruant, so with his master, as with the maid, so with her mistresse, as with the buyer, so with the seller, as with the lender, so with the borower, as with the taker of vsurie, so with the giuer of vsurie to him.

3 The land shall be vtterly emptied, and vtterly spoiled : for the Lord hath spoken this word.

4 The earth mourneth *and* fadeth away, the world languisheth and fadeth away, the † haughtie people of the earth doe languish.

5 The earth also is defiled vnder the inhabitants thereof : because they haue transgressed the lawes, changed the ordinance, broken the euerlasting couenant.

6 Therefore hath the curse deuoured the earth, and they that dwell therin are desolate : therefore the inhabitants of the earth are burned, and few men left.

7 The new wine mourneth, the vine languisheth, all the merrie hearted doe sigh.

8 The mirth * of tabrets ceaseth, the noise of them that reioyce, endeth, the ioy of the harpe ceaseth.

9 They shall not drinke wine with a song, strong drinke shall bee bitter to them that drinke it.

10 The city of confusion is broken downe : euery house is shut vp, that no man may come in.

11 There is a crying for wine in the streets, all ioy is darkened, the mirth of the land is gone.

12 In the citie is left desolation, and the gate is smitten with destruction.

13 ¶ When thus it shalbe in the midst of the land among the people : *there shall be* as the shaking of an oliue tree, *and* as the gleaning grapes when the vintage is done.

14 They shal lift vp their voice, they shal sing, for the maiesty of the Lord, they shall crie aloud from the sea.

15 Wherefore, glorifie ye the Lord in the ‖ fires, *euen* the Name of the Lord God of Israel in the yles of the Sea.

16 ¶ From the † vttermost part of the earth haue we heard songs, *euen* glory to the righteous : but I said, † My leannesse, my leannesse, woe vnto me : the treacherous dealers haue dealt treacherously,

Marginal notes (left column)
† *Heb. to pollute.*

Heb. girdle

‖ *Or, concerning a merchant man. Heb. Canaan.*

Or, strengths.

† *Heb. it shal vnto Tyre the song of a harlot.*

Heb. olde.

Heb. peruerteth the face thereof.

Marginal notes (right column)
‖ *Or, Prince.* * Hose. 4. 9.

† *Heb. the height of the people.*

* Ier. 7. 37. and 16. 9. & 25. 10. ezra 26. 13. hos. 2, 11.

‖ *Or, valleyes*

† *Heb. wing.*

† *Heb. leannesse to me or my secret to me.*

cherously, yea the treacherous dealers haue dealt very treacherously.

17 Feare, and the pit, & the snare _are_ vpon thee, O inhabitant of the earth.

18 And it shall come to passe, _that_ he who fleeth from the noise of the feare, shall fall into the *pit; and he that commeth vp out of the midst of the pit, shalbe taken in the snare : for the windowes from on high are open, and the foundations of the earth doe shake.

* Iere. 48. 44.

19 The earth is vtterly broken downe, the earth is cleane dissolued, the earth is moued exceedingly.

20 The earth shall reele to and fro, like a drunkard, and shall be remooued like a cottage, and the transgression thereof shall be heauie vpon it, and it shall fall, and not rise againe.

21 And it shall come to passe in that day, that the LORD shall †punish the hoste of the high ones _that are_ on high, and the kings of the earth vpon the earth.

† Hebr. viſite vpon.

22 And they shalbe gathered together †_as_ prisoners are gathered in the ‖pit, and shall be shut vp in the prison, and after many dayes shall they bee ‖visited.

23 Then the *Moone shall be confounded, and the Sunne ashamed, when the LORD of hosts shall reigne in mount Zion and in Ierusalem, and ‖before his ancients gloriously.

† Hebr. with the gathering of prisoners.
‖ Or, dungeon.
‖ Or, found wanting.
* Chap. 13. 10. eze. 32. 7. ioel 2. 31. and 3. 15.
‖ Or, there shalbe glory before his ancients.

CHAP. XXV.

1 The Prophet praiseth God, for his iudgements, 6 for his sauing benefits, 9 and for his victorious saluation.

 LORD, thou _art_ my God, I will exalt thee, I will praise thy Name; for thou hast done wonderfull things; _thy_ counsels of old _are_ faithfulnesse _and_ trueth.

2 For thou hast made of a citie, an heape; of a defenced city, a ruine : a palace of strangers, to be no citie, it shall neuer be built.

3 Therefore shall the strong people glorifie thee, the city of the terrible nations shall feare thee.

4 For thou hast bene a strength to the poore, a strength to the needy in his distresse, a refuge from the storme, a shadow from the heat, when the blast of the terrible ones _is_ as a storme _against_ the wall.

5 Thou shalt bring downe the noise of strangers, as the heat in a dry place; _euen_ the heat with the shadow of a cloud : the branch of the terrible ones shalbe brought low.

6 ¶ And in this mountaine shall the LORD of hostes make vnto all people a feast of fat things, a feast of wines on the lees, of fat things full of marrow, of wines on the lees well refined.

7 And he wil †destroy in this mountaine the face of the couering †cast ouer all people, and the vaile that is spread ouer all nations.

† Heb. swlow vp.
† Hebr. uered.

8 He will *swallow vp death in victorie, and the Lord GOD wil *wipe away teares from off al faces, and the rebuke of his people shall he take away from off all the earth : for the LORD hath spoken _it._

* 1. Cor. 55.
* Reuel. 17. and 2 4.

9 ¶ And it shalbe said in that day, Loe, this _is_ our God, we haue waited for him, and he will saue vs : this _is_ the LORD, we haue waited for him, we wil be glad, and reioyce in his saluation.

10 For in this mountaine shall the hand of the LORD rest, and Moab shalbe ‖troden downe vnder him, euen as straw is ‖troden downe for the doughill.

‖ Or, thr ed.
‖ Or, ed in Memenah.

11 And hee shall spread foorth his hands in the midst of them, as hee that swimmeth spreadeth foorth his _hands_ to swimme : and hee shall bring downe their pride together with the spoiles of their hands.

12 And the fortresse of the high fort of thy walles shall hee bring downe, lay low, _and_ bring to the ground, _euen_ to the dust.

CHAP. XXVI.

1 A song inciting to confidence in God, 5 for his iudgements, 12 and for his fauour to his people. 20 An exhortation to wait on God.

 N that day shall this song bee sung in the land of Iudah; Wee haue a strong citie, saluation will _God_ appoint _for_ walles and bulwarkes.

2 Open ye the gates, that the righteous nation which keepeth the †trueth may enter in.

3 Thou wilt keepe _him_ in †perfect peace, _whose_ ‖minde is stayed _on thee;_ because he trusteth in thee.

† Hebr. trueths.
† Hebr. peace, pe ‖ Or, thou or imagi tion.

4 Trust

*eb. the
ke of ages.

4 Trust ye in the L O R D for euer : for in the L O R D I E H O V A H *is* †euerlasting strength.

5 ¶ For hee bringeth downe them that dwell on high, the loftie citie he layeth it low; he layeth it low, euen to the ground, he bringeth it euen to the dust.

6 The foote shall treade it downe, *euen* the feete of the poore, *and* the steps of the needie.

7 The way of the iust *is* vprightnesse : thou most vpright, doest weigh the path of the iust.

8 Yea in the way of thy Iudgements, O L O R D, haue we waited for thee ; the desire of our soule *is* to thy Name, and to the remembrance of thee.

9 With my soule haue I desired thee in the night, yea with my spirit within me will I seeke thee early : for when thy iudgements *are* in the earth, the inhabitants of the world will learne righteousnesse.

10 Let fauour be shewed to the wicked, *yet* will hee not learne righteousnesse : in the land of vprightnesse will he deale vniustly, and will not behold the maiestie of the L O R D.

*, towards
people.*

11 L O R D, *when* thy hand is lifted vp, they will not see: *but* they shall see, and be ashamed for *their* enuie ‖at the people, yea the fire of thine enemies shall deuoure them.

, for vs.

12 ¶ L O R D, thou wilt ordaine peace for vs : for thou also hast wrought all our workes ‖in vs.

13 O L O R D our God, *other* lordes besides thee haue had dominion ouer vs : *but* by thee only will we make mention of thy Name.

14 They are dead, they shall not liue; they are deceased, they shall not rise : therefore hast thou visited and destroyed them, and made all their memory to perish.

15 Thou hast increased the nation, O L O R D, thou hast increased the nation, thou art glorified ; thou hadst remooued *it* farre *vnto* all the ends of the earth.

*Ieb. secret
eech.*

16 L O R D, in trouble haue they visited thee : they powred out a †prayer *when* thy chastening *was* vpon them.

17 Like as a woman with childe *that* draweth neere the time of her deliuerie, is in paine *and* cryeth out in her pangs; so haue wee beene in thy sight, O L O R D.

18 Wee haue beene with childe, wee haue beene in paine, we haue as it were brought foorth winde, wee haue not wrought any deliuerance in the earth, neither haue the inhabitants of the world fallen.

19 Thy dead men shall liue, *together with* my dead body shall they arise : awake and sing yee that dwell in dust : for thy dewe *is as* the dewe of herbes, and the earth shall cast out the dead.

20 ¶ Come, my people, enter thou into thy chambers, and shut thy doores about thee; hide thy selfe as it were for a little moment, vntill the indignation be ouerpast.

21 For behold, the L O R D *commeth out of his place to punish the inhabitants of the earth for their iniquitie : the earth also shall disclose her †blood, and shall no more couer her slaine.

* Mic. 1. 3.

† Heb. bloods

C H A P. XXVII.

1 The care of God ouer his vineyard. 7 His chastisements differ from iudgements. 12 The Church of Iewes and Gentiles.

N that day the L O R D with his sore and great and strong sworde shall punish Leuiathan the †piercing serpent, euen Leuiathan that crooked serpent, and hee shall slay the dragon that *is* in the Sea.

‖ Or, crossing
like a barre.

2 In that day, sing yee vnto her; A vineyard of red wine.

3 I the L O R D doe keepe it; I will water it euery moment : lest any hurt it, I will keepe it night and day.

4 Furie *is* not in mee : who would set the briars *and* thornes against me in battell ? I would ‖goe through them, I would burne them together.

‖ Or, march
against.

5 Or let him take holde of my strength, *that* he may make peace with me, *and* he shall make peace with me.

6 Hee shall cause them that come of Iacob to take roote : Israel shall blossome and budde, and fill the face of the world with fruite.

7 ¶ Hath hee smitten him, †as hee smote those that smote him ? *or is* hee slaine according to the slaughter of them that are slaine by him ?

† Heb. according to the stroke of those.

8 In measure ‖when it shooteth foorth, thou wilt debate with it : ‖hee stayeth his rough winde in the day of the East winde.

‖ Or, when thou sendest it foorth.
‖ Or, whenhe remoueth it.

9 By

9 By this therefore shall the iniquitie of Iacob be purged, and this *is* all the fruit, to take away his sinne : when he maketh all the stones of the Altar as chalke stones, that are beaten in sunder, the groues and ‖images shall not stand vp.

‖ Or, Sunne images.

10 Yet the defenced citie shall be desolate, *and* the habitation forsaken, and left like a wildernesse : there shall the calfe feede, and there shall he lie downe, and consume the branches thereof.

11 When the boughes thereof are withered, they shall be broken off : the women come *and* set them on fire : for it is a people of no vnderstanding : therefore hee that made them will not haue mercie on them, and hee that formed them, will shewe them no fauour.

12 ¶ And it shall come to passe in that day, that the LORD shall beate off from the chanell of the riuer vnto the streame of Egypt, and ye shall bee gathered one by one, O ye children of Israel.

13 And it shall come to passe in that day, that the great trumpet shall bee blowen, and they shall come which were ready to perish in the land of Assyria, and the outcasts in the land of Egypt, and shall worship the LORD in the holy mount at Ierusalem.

CHAP XXVIII.

1 The Prophet threatneth Ephraim for their pride and drunkennesse. 5 The residue shall be aduanced in the Kingdom of Christ. 7 He rebuketh their errour. 9 Their vntowardnes to learne, 14 And their securitie. 16 Christ the sure foundation is promised. 18 Their securitie shalbe tried. 23 They are incited to the consideration of Gods discreet prouidence.

Oe to the crowne of pride, to the drunkards of Ephraim, whose glorious beauty *is* a fading flowre, which are on the head of the fat valleys of them that are †ouercome with wine.

† Heb. broken.

2 Behold, the Lord *hath* a mightie and strong one, *which* as a tempest of haile *and* a destroying storme, as a flood of mightie waters ouerflowing, shall cast downe to the earth with the hand.

3 The crowne of pride, the drunkards of Ephraim shall be troden †vnder feete

† Hebr. with feete.

4 And the glorious beautie which *is* on the head of the fat valley, shall bee a fading flowre, *and* as the hastie fruite before the summer : which *when* he that looketh vpon it, seeth it, while it is yet in his hand, he †eateth it vp.

† Heb. swalloweth.

5 ¶ In that day shall the LORD of hosts be for a crowne of glory, and for a diademe of beautie vnto the residue of his people :

6 And for a spirit of iudgement to him that sitteth in iudgement, and for strength to them that turne the battell to the gate.

7 ¶ But they also haue erred through wine, and through strong drinke are out of the way : the priest and the prophet haue erred through strong drinke, they are swallowed vp of wine : they are out of the way through strong drinke, they erre in vision, they stumble *in* iudgement.

8 For all tables are full of vomite *and* filthinesse, so that there is no place *cleane.*

9 ¶ Whome shall he teach knowledge ? and whom shall he make to vnderstand †doctrine ? them that are weaned from the milke, *and* drawen from the breasts.

† Hebr. hearing.

10 For precept ‖*must be* vpon precept, precept vpon precept, line vpon line, line vpon line, here a litle, *and* there a litle.

‖ Or, hath bene.

11 For with †*stammering lips and another tongue ‖will he speake to this people.

† Heb. stammerings lippe.
‖ Or, he spoken.

12 To whom he said, This *is* the rest *wherwith* ye may cause the weary to rest, and this *is* the refreshing, yet they would not heare.

13 But the word of the LORD was vnto them, precept vpon precept, precept vpon precept, line vpon line, line vpon line, here a litle *and* there a litle : that they might goe and fall backward, and be broken, and snared, and taken.

14 ‖ Wherefore heare the worde of the LORD, yee scornefull men, that rule this people which *is* in Ierusalem.

15 Because ye haue said, Wee haue made a couenant with death, and with hell are we at agreement, when the ouerflowing scourge shall passe thorow, it shall not come vnto vs : for wee haue made lies our refuge, and vnder falsehood haue we hid our selues :

16 ¶ Therefore thus saith the Lord GOD, Beholde, I lay in Zion for a
foun-

Psal. 118.
matth.
42. acts
11. 1. pet.
6, 7, 8.
n. 9. 33.
1 10. 11.

foundation, *a stone, a tryed stone, a pretious corner stone, a sure foundation : hee that beleeueth, shall not make haste.

17 Iudgement also will I lay to the line, and righteousnesse to the plummet : and the haile shall sweepe away the refuge of lyes, and the waters shall ouerflow the hiding place.

18 ¶ And your couenant with death shalbe disanulled, and your agreement with hell shall not stand ; when the o-uerflowing scourge shall passe thorough, then yee shalbe †troden downe by it.

Heb. a
uding
one to it.

19 From the time that it goeth forth, it shall take you : for morning by morning shall it passe ouer, by day and by night, and it shalbe a vexation, onely ||to vnderstand the report.

r, when
hall make
1 to vn-
stand
trine.

20 For the bed is shorter, then that a man can stretch himselfe on it: and the couering narrower, then that he can wrap himselfe in it.

21 For the LORD shall rise vp as in mount *Perazim, he shalbe wroth as in the valley of *Gibeon, that he may doe his worke, his strange worke ; and bring to passe his act, his strange act.

. Sam. 5.
1. chro.
13.
osh. 10.
5. 1. chr.
16.

22 Now therefore be yee not mockers, lest your bands be made strong: for I haue heard from the Lord GOD of hostes a consumption euen determined vpon the whole earth.

23 ¶ Giue yee eare, and heare my voyce, hearken and heare my speach.

24 Doth the plowman plow all day to sow ? doth he open and breake the clods of his ground ?

25 When hee hath made plaine the face thereof, doth he not cast abroad the fitches, and scatter the cummin, and cast in the ||principall wheate, and the appointed barly and the || rye in their †place ?

r, the
eat in the
ncipall
ce and
ley in the
ointed
ce.
r, spelt.
Heb. bor-

26 ||For his God doth instruct him to discretion, and doth teach him.

27 For the fitches are not threshed with a threshing instrument, neither is a cart wheele turned about vpon the cummin : but the fitches are beaten out with a staffe, and the cummin with a rodde.

r, and he
deth.it in
h sort as
1 doth
ch him.

28 Bread corne is bruised ; because he will not euer be threshing it, nor breake it with the wheele of his cart, nor bruise it with his horsemen.

29 This also commeth forth from the LORD of hostes, which is wonderfull in counsell, and excellent in working.

CHAP. XXIX.

1 Gods heauy iudgement vpon Ierusalem.
7 The vnsatiablenesse of her enemies.
9 The sencelesnesse, 13 and deepe hypocrisie of the Iewes. 18 A promise of sanctification to the godly.

WOe to Ariel, to Ariel ||the citie where Dauid dwelt : adde yee yeere to yeere; let them †kill sacrifices.

|| Or, oh
Ariel that
is the lyon of
God: Or,
of the citie.
† Heb. out off
the heads.

2 Yet I will distresse Ariel, and there shalbe heauinesse and sorrow ; and it shall be vnto mee as Ariel.

3 And I will campe against thee round about, and will lay siege against thee with a mount, and I will raise forts against thee.

4 And thou shalt bee brought downe, and shalt speake out of the ground, and thy speach shall be low out of the dust, and thy voice shalbe as of one that hath a familiar spirit, out of the ground, and thy speach shall †whisper out of the dust.

† Heb. peepe
or chirpe.

5 Moreouer the multitude of thy strangers shalbe like small dust, and the multitude of the terrible ones shalbe as chaffe, that passeth away ; yea it shalbe at an instant suddenly.

6 Thou shalt bee visited of the LORD of hostes with thunder, and with earthquake, and great noise, with storme and tempest, and the flame of deuouring fire.

7 ¶ And the multitude of all the nations that fight against Ariel, euen all that fight against her and her munition, and that distresse her, shalbe as a dreame of a night vision.

8 It shall euen be as when a hungry man dreameth, and behold he eateth ; but he awaketh, and his soule is emptie : or as when a thirstie man dreameth, and behold he drinketh ; but hee awaketh, and behold he is faint, and his soule hath appetite : so shall the multitude of all the nations bee, that fight against mount Zion.

9 ¶ Stay your selues and wonder, ||cry yee out, and cry: they are drunken, but not with wine, they stagger, but not with strong drinke.

|| Or, take
your plea-
sure and
riot.

10 For the LORD hath powred out vpon you the spirit of deepe sleepe, and hath closed your eyes : the Prophets and

† *Heb. heads.*

‖ *Or, letter.*

and your †rulers, the Seers hath hee couered.

11 And the vsion of all is become vnto you, as the wordes of a ‖booke that is sealed, which men deliuer to one that is learned, saying, Reade this, I pray thee : and hee saith, I cannot, for it *is* sealed.

12 And the booke is deliuered to him that is not learned, saying, Reade this, I pray thee : and he saith, I am not learned.

* Matth. 15. 8. mar. 7. 6.

13 ¶ Wherefore the Lord said, *Forasmuch as this people draw neere mee with their mouth, and with their lips doe honour me, but haue remoued their heart farre from me, and their feare towards mee is taught by the precept of men :

† *Heb. I will adde.*

14 Therefore behold, † I will proceed to do a marueilous worke amongst this people, *euen* a marueilous worke and a wonder : *for the wisedome of their wise men shall perish, and the vnderstanding of their prudent men shall be hid.

* Ier. 49. 7. obad. ver. 8. 1. cor. 1. 19.

15 Woe vnto them that seeke deepe to hide their counsell from the LORD, and their workes are in the darke, and they say , *Who seeth vs ? and who knoweth vs ?

* Ecclus. 23. 15.

16 Surely your turning of things vpside downe shall be esteemed as the potters clay : for shall the *worke say of him that made it, He made me not ? or shall the thing framed, say of him that framed it, He had no vnderstanding ?

* Isa. 45. 19.

17 *Is* it not yet a very litle while, and Lebanon shall be turned into a fruitful field, and the fruitfull field shall be esteemed as a forrest ?

18 ¶ And in that day shall the deafe heare the words of the booke, and the eyes of the blind shall see out of obscuritie, and out of darkenesse

† *Heb. shall adde.*

19 The meeke also † shall increase *their* ioy in the LORD, and the poore among men shall reioice in the holy One of Israel.

20 For the terrible one is brought to nought , and the scorner is consumed, and all that watch for iniquitie are cut off :

21 That make a man an offendour for a word, and lay a snare for him that reproueth in the gate, and turne aside the iust for a thing of nought.

22 Therefore thus saith the LORD who redeemed Abraham , concerning

the house of Iacob : Iacob shall not now be ashamed, neither shall his face now waxe pale.

23 But when hee seeth his children the worke of mine hands in the midst of him, they shall sanctifie my Name, and sanctifie the Holy One of Iacob, and shall feare the God of Israel.

24 They also that erred in spirit †shall come to vnderstanding, and they that murmured, shall learne doctrine.

† *Hebr. know vnderstan*

CHAP. XXX.

1 The Prophet threatneth the people, for their confidence in Egypt, 8 and contempt of Gods word. 18 Gods mercies towards his Church. 27 Gods wrath, and the peoples ioy in the destruction of Assyria.

Oe to the rebellious children, sayth the LORD, that take counsell, but not of mee ; and that couer with a couering, but not of my Spirit , that they may adde sinne to sinne :

2 That walke to goe downe into Egypt, (and haue not asked at my mouth) to strengthen themselues in the strength of Pharaoh, and to trust in the shadow of Egypt.

3 Therefore shall the strength of Pharaoh be your shame, and the trust in the shadow of Egypt, *your* confusion.

4 For his princes were at Zoan, and his ambassadors came to Hanes.

5 They were all ashamed of a people *that* could not profit them, nor be an helpe nor profite, but a shame and also a reproch.

6 The burden of the beastes of the South : into the lande of trouble and anguish, from whence *come* the yong and old lyon, the viper, and fierie flying serpent, they will carie their riches vpon the shoulders of yong asses, and their treasures vpon the bunches of camels, to a people *that* shall not profite *them.*

7 For the Egyptians shall helpe in vaine, and to no purpose : Therefore haue I cried ‖concerning this : Their strength is to sit still.

‖ *Or, to*

8 ¶ Now goe, write it before them in a table, and note it in a booke, that it may bee for †the time to come for euer and euer :

† *Heb. t. latter da*

9 That this is a rebellious people, lying children , children *that* will not heare the Law of the LORD :

10 Which

10 Which say to the seers, See not; and to the prophets, Prophecie not vnto vs right things : speake vnto vs smooth things, prophecie deceits.

11 Get ye out of the way : turne aside out of the path : cause the Holy one of Israel to cease from before vs.

12 Wherefore, thus saith the Holy one of Israel : Because ye despise this word, and trust in ||oppression and peruersnesse, and stay thereon :

r, fraud.

13 Therefore this iniquitie shalbe to you as a breach ready to fall, swelling out in a high wall, whose breaking commeth suddenly at an instant.

14 And he shall breake it as the breaking of the potters †vessell, that is broken in pieces, he shall not spare ; so that there shall not be found in the bursting of it, a sheard to take fire from the hearth, or to take water *withall* out of the pit.

Iebr. the tell of ters.

15 For thus saith the Lord God, the Holy one of Israel, In returning and rest shall ye be saued, in quietnesse and in confidence shalbe your strength, and ye would not :

16 But ye said ; No, for we will flee vpon horses; therefore shall ye flee. And we will ride vpon the swift ; therefore shall they that pursue you, be swift.

17 One thousand *shall flee* at the rebuke of one : at the rebuke of fiue, shall ye flee, till ye be left as a ||beacon vpon the top of a mountaine, and as an ensigne on a hill.

r, a tree eft of nches, or ughes, or naste.

18 ¶ And therefore wil the Lord wait that he may be gracious vnto you, and therefore wil he be exalted that he may haue mercy vpon you : for the Lord is a God of Iudgment. * Blessed *are* all they that wait for him.

sal. 2. 12. d 34. 9. ju. 16. iere. 17.

19 For the people shall dwel in Zion at Ierusalem : thou shalt weepe no more : hee will be very gracious vnto thee, at the voice of thy cry ; when he shall heare it, he will answere thee.

20 And *though* the Lord giue you the bread of aduersitie, and the water of ||affliction, yet shall not thy teachers be remooued into a corner any more : but thine eyes shall see thy teachers.

r, oppres-n.

21 And thine eares shall heare a word behinde thee, saying ; This *is* the way, walke ye in it, when ye turne to the right hand, and when ye turne to the left.

22 Ye shall defile also the couering of †thy grauen images of siluer, and the

Iebr. the nuen ima-of thy sil-uer.

ornament of thy moulten images of gold : thou shalt †cast them away as a menstruous cloth, thou shalt say vnto it, Get thee hence.

†*Hebr. scatter.*

23 Then shall he giue the raine of thy seed that thou shalt sow the ground withall ; and bread of the increase of the earth, and it shalbe fat and plenteous : in that day shall thy cattell feed in large pastures.

24 The oxen likewise and the yong asses that eare the ground, shall eate ||cleane prouender which hath bene winnowed with the shouell and with the fanne.

||*Or, sauourie ; Hebr. leauened.*

25 And there shall be vpon euery high mountaine, and vpon euery †high hill, riuers *and* streames of waters, in the day of the great slaughter when the towers fall.

†*Hebr. lifted vp.*

26 Moreouer the light of the Moone shalbe as the light of the Sunne, and the light of the Sunne shall be seuenfold, as the light of seuen dayes, in the day that the Lord bindeth vp the breach of his people, and healeth the stroke of their wound.

27 ¶ Beholde, the Name of the Lord commeth from farre, burning with his anger, ||and the burden *thereof* is †heauy : his lips are full of indignation, and his tongue as a deuouring fire.

||*Or, and the grieuousnes of flame.* †*Hebr. heauinesse.*

28 And his breath as an ouerflowing streame, shall reach to the midst of the necke, to sift the nations with the sieue of vanitie : and *there shalbe* a bridle in the iawes of the people causing *them* to erre.

29 Yee shall haue a song as in the night, *when* a holy solemnitie is kept, and gladnesse of heart, as when one goeth with a pipe to come into the mountaine of the Lord, to the †mighty one of Israel.

†*Heb. rocke.*

30 And the Lord shall cause †his glorious voice to be heard, and shall shew the lighting downe of his arme, with the indignation of *his* anger, and with the flame of a deuouring fire, *with* scattering and tempest and hailestones.

†*Hebr. the glory of his voice.*

31 For through the voyce of the Lord shall the Assyrian be beaten downe, *which* smote with a rod.

32 And †in euery place where the grounded staffe shall passe, which the Lord shall †lay vpon him, it shall be with tabrets and harpes : and in battels of shaking will he fight ||with it.

†*Hebr. euery passing of the rod founded.* †*Hebr. cause to rest vpon him.* ||*Or, against them.*

33 For

† Heb. from yesterday.

33 For Tophet *is* ordained † of olde ; yea, for the king it is prepared, he hath made it deepe *and* large : the pile thereof *is* fire and much wood, the breath of the LORD, like a streame of brimstone, doeth kindle it.

CHAP. XXXI.

1 The Prophet sheweth the cursed folly, in trusting to Egypt, and forsaking of God. 6 He exhorteth to conuersion. 8 Hee sheweth the fall of Assyria.

 Oe to them that goe down to Egypt for helpe, and stay on horses, and trust in charets, because they *are* many ; and in horsemen, because they are very strong : but they looke not vnto the Holy one of Israel, neither seeke the LORD.

2 Yet he also *is* wise, and will bring euill, and wil not † call backe his words : but will arise against the house of the euill doers, and against the helpe of them that worke iniquitie

3 Now the Egyptians *are* men and not God, and their horses flesh and not spirit : when the LORD shall stretch out his hand, both he that helpeth shall fall, and hee that is holpen shall fall downe, and they all shall faile together.

4 For thus hath the LORD spoken vnto me ; Like as the lyon and the yong lyon roaring on his pray, when a multitude of shepheards is called foorth against him, he will not be afraid of their voice, nor abase himselfe for the || noyse of them : so shall the LORD of hostes come downe to fight for mount Zion, and for the hill thereof.

5 As birds flying, so wil the LORD of hostes defend Ierusalem, defending also hee will deliuer *it, and* passing ouer, he will preserue *it.*

6 ¶ Turne yee vnto him from whom the children of Israel haue deeply reuolted.

7 For in that day euery man shall * cast away his idoles of siluer, and † his idoles of gold, which your owne hands haue made vnto you for a sinne.

8 ¶ Then shall the Assyrian fall with the sword, not of a mightie man ; and the sword, not of a meane man, shal deuoure him : but hee shall flee || from the sword, and his young men shall be || discomfited.

† Heb. re-mooue.

† Or, multitude.

*.Cha. 2. 20.
† Heb. the idoles of his golde.

|| Or, for feare of the sword.
|| Or, tributarie : hebr. for melting, or tribute.

9 And hee shall passe ouer to || his strong holde for feare, and his princes shall be afraid of the ensigne, sayth the LORD, whose fire *is* in Zion, and his fornace in Ierusalem.

|| Or, his strength : hcb. rockc shall passe away for feare.

CHAP. XXXII.

1 The blessings of Christes kingdome. 9 Desolation is foreshowen. 15 Restauration is promised to succeede.

 Ehold, a King shal reigne in righteousnes, and princes shal rule in iudgement.

2 And a man shall be as an hiding place from the winde, and a couert from the tempest : as riuers of water in a drie place, as the shadow of a † great rocke in a wearie land.

3 And the eyes of them that see, shall not be dimme ; and the eares of them that heare, shall hearken.

4 The heart also of the † rash shall vnderstand knowledge, and the tongue of the stammerers shall bee readie to speake || plainely.

5 The vile person shall be no more called liberall, nor the churle sayd to be bountifull.

6 For the vile person wil speake villenie, and his heart will worke iniquitie, to practise hypocrisie, and to vtter errour against the LORD, to make emptie the soule of the hungry, and hee will cause the drinke of the thirstie to faile.

7 The instruments also of the churle *are* euill : he deuiseth wicked deuices, to destroy the poore with lying wordes, euen || when the needie speaketh right.

8 But the liberall deuiseth liberall things, and by liberall things shall hee || stand.

9 ¶ Rise vp ye women that are at ease : heare my voice, ye carelesse daughters, giue eare vnto my speech.

10 Many † dayes and yeeres shall ye be troubled, yee carelesse women : for the vintage shall faile, the gathering shall not come.

11 Tremble yee women that are at ease : be troubled, ye carelesse ones, strip ye and make ye bare, and gird *sackecloth* vpon your loynes.

12 They shall lament for the teats, for † the pleasant fieldes, for the fruitfull vine.

13 Vpon the land of my people shall come

† Heb. hea-uie.

† Heb. hastie

|| Or, elegantly.

|| Or, when he speaketh against the poore in iudgement.
|| Or, be esta-blished.

† Heb. dayes aboue a yere

† Heb. the fields of desire.

, bur-
g vpon.

come vp thornes, *and* briars, ‖ yea vpon all the houses of ioy in the ioyous citie.

14 Because the palaces ſhall be forſaken, the multitude of the citie ſhall be left, the ‖ forts and towres ſhall be for dennes for euer, a ioy of wild aſſes, a pasture of flockes ;

15 Vntill the ſpirit be powred vpon vs from on high, and the wilderneſſe be a fruitfull field, and the fruitfull field be counted for a forreſt.

16 Then * iudgement ſhall dwell in the wilderneſſe, and righteouſneſſe remaine in the fruitfull field.

17 And the worke of righteouſneſſe ſhalbe peace, and the effect of righteouſneſſe, quietneſſe and aſſurance for euer.

18 And my people ſhall dwell in a peaceable habitation, and in ſure dwellings, and in quiet reſting places :

19 When it ſhall haile, comming downe on the forreſt; ‖ and the citie ſhall be low in a low place.

20 Bleſſed *are* yee that ſow beside all waters, that ſend forth *thither* the feete of the oxe and the aſſe.

, and the
e ſhall be
rly aba-

CHAP. XXXIII.

1 Gods iudgements against the enemies of the Church. 13 The priuiledges of the godly.

Oe to thee that ſpoileſt, and thou *waſt* not ſpoiled; and dealeſt treacherouſly, and they dealt not treacherouſly with thee: when thou ſhalt ceaſe to ſpoile, thou ſhalt be ſpoiled ; *and* when thou ſhalt make an end to deale treacherouſly, they ſhall deale treacherouſly with thee.

2 O LORD, be gratious vnto vs, we haue waited for thee : be thou their arme euery morning, our ſaluation also in the time of trouble.

3 At the noiſe of the tumult the people fled : at the lifting vp of thy ſelfe the nations were ſcattered.

4 And your ſpoile ſhall be gathered *like* the gathering of the caterpiller : as the running to and fro of Locuſts ſhall he runne vpon them.

5 The LORD is exalted : for hee dwelleth on high, he hath filled Zion with iudgement and righteouſneſſe.

6 And wiſedome and knowledge ſhall be the ſtabilitie of thy times, *and* strength of † ſaluation : the feare of the LORD is his treaſure.

Heb. ſalua-
ns.

7 Behold, their ‖ valiant ones ſhall

r, meſſen-
rs.

cry without : the ambaſſadours of peace ſhall weepe bitterly.

8 The high wayes lye waſte ; the way faring man ceaſeth : he hath broken the couenant, he hath deſpiſed the cities, he regardeth no man.

9 The earth mourneth *and* languiſheth : Lebanon is aſhamed *and* ‖ hewen downe : Sharon is like a wilderneſſe, and Baſhan and Carmel ſhake off *their fruits.*

10 Now will I riſe, ſaith the LORD : now will I be exalted, now will I lift vp my ſelfe.

11 Yee ſhall conceiue chaffe, yee ſhall bring forth ſtubble : your breath *as* fire ſhall deuoure you.

12 And the people ſhalbe *as* the burnings of lyme : *as* thornes cut vp ſhall they be burnt in the fire.

13 ¶ Heare yee that are farre off, what I haue done ; and yee that are neere, acknowledge my might.

14 The ſinners in Zion are afraid, fearefulneſſe hath ſurpriſed the hypocrites : who among vs ſhall dwell with the deuouring fire ? who amongſt vs ſhall dwell with euerlaſting burnings ?

15 He that * walketh † righteouſly, and ſpeaketh † vprightly, hee that deſpiſeth the gaine of ‖ oppreſſions, that ſhaketh his hands from holding of bribes, that ſtoppeth his eares from hearing of † blood, and ſhutteth his eyes from ſeeing euill :

16 He ſhall dwell on † high : his place of defence *ſhalbe* the munitions of rocks, bread ſhalbe giuen him, his waters *ſhall be* ſure.

17 Thine eyes ſhall ſee the king in his beauty : they ſhall behold † the land that is very farre off.

18 Thine heart ſhall meditate terrour ; Where *is* the * ſcribe ? where *is* the † receiuer ? where *is* he that counted the towres ?

19 Thou ſhalt not ſee a fierce people, a people of a deeper ſpeech then thou canſt perceiue ; of a ‖ ſtammering tongue, that thou canſt not vnderſtand.

20 Looke vpon Zion, the city of our ſolemnities : thine eyes ſhall ſee Ieruſalem a quiet habitation, a tabernacle that ſhall not be taken downe, not one of the ſtakes thereof ſhall euer be remoued, neither ſhall any of the coardes thereof be broken.

21 But there the glorious LORD *will be* vnto vs a place of † broad riuers *and*

‖ Or, withe-
red away.

* Psal. 15. 2.
and 24. 3.
† Heb. in
righteouſ-
neſſes.
† Heb. vp-
rightneſſes.
‖ Or, de-
ceits.
† Heb. bloods

† Heb.
heights, or
his places.

† Heb. the
land of farre
diſtances.

* 1. Cor. 1.
20.
† Heb.
weigher.

‖ Or, ridicu-
lous.

† Heb. broad
of ſpaces or
hands.

and streames ; wherein shall goe no galley with oares , neither shall gallant ship passe thereby,

22 For the Lᴏʀᴅ *is* our Iudge, the Lᴏʀᴅ *is* our † Lawgiuer, the Lᴏʀᴅ *is* our King, he wil saue vs.

23 ‖ Thy tacklings are loosed : they could not well strengthen their mast, they could not spread the saile : then is the praye of a great spoile diuided, the lame take the praye.

24 And the inhabitant shall not say ; I am sicke : the people that dwel therein shalbe forgiuen *their* iniquitie.

CHAP. XXXIIII.

1 The iudgements wherewith God reuengeth his Church. 11 The desolation of her enemies. 16 The certaintie of the prophecie.

Ome neere ye nations to heare, and hearken ye people · let the earth heare, and † all that is therein, the world, and all things that come forth of it.

2 For the indignation of the Lᴏʀᴅ *is* vpon all nations, and *his* furie vpon all their armies : hee hath vtterly destroyed them, he hath deliuered them to the slaughter.

3 Their slaine also shalbe cast out, and their stinke shall come vp out of their carkeises, and the mountaines shalbe melted with their blood.

4 And all the hoste of heauen shalbe dissolued, and the heauens shalbe *rouled together as a scrole : and all their hoste shall fall downe as the leafe falleth off from the Vine, and as a *falling figge from the figge tree.

5 For my sword shall bee bathed in heauen · beholde, it shall come downe vpon Idumea, and vpon the people of my curse to iudgement.

6 The sword of the Lᴏʀᴅ is filled with blood, it is made fat with fatnesse, *and* with the blood of lambes and goates, with the fat of the kidneys of rammes for the Lᴏʀᴅ hath a sacrifice in Bozrah, and a great slaughter in the land of Idumea.

7 And the ‖ Vnicornes shall come downe with them, and the bullockes with the bulles, and their land shall be ‖ soaked with blood , and their dust made fat with fatnesse

8 For *it is* the day of the Lᴏʀᴅs * vengeance, *and* the yeere of recom-

pences for the controuersie of Zion.

9 And the streames thereof shalbe turned into pitch, and the dust thereof into brimstone , and the land thereof shall become burning pitch.

10 It shal not be quenched night nor day, * the smoke thereof shall goe vp for euer : from generation to generation it shall lye waste, none shal passe through it for euer and euer

11 ¶ * The ‖ cormorant and the bitterne shall possesse it, the owle also and the rauen shall dwell in it, and he shall stretch out vpon it the line of confusion, and the stones of emptinesse.

12 They shall call the nobles thereof to the kingdome, but none shall bee there, and all her Princes shall bee nothing.

13 And thornes shall come vp in her palaces, nettles and brambles in the fortresses thereof : and it shalbe an habitation of dragons, *and* a court for ‖ owles.

14 The wilde †beasts of the desert shall also meete with the *wilde beasts of the Iland and the satyre shall cry to his felow, the ‖ shrichowle also shall rest there, & finde for her selfe a place of rest.

15 There shall the great owle make her nest, and lay and hatch, and gather vnder her shadow : there shall the vultures also be gathered, euery one with her mate.

16 ¶ Seeke ye out of the booke of the Lord, and reade : no one of these shall faile, none shall want her mate : for my mouth, it hath commaunded; and his spirit, it hath gathered them.

17 And he hath cast the lot for them, and his hand hath diuided it vnto them by line : they shall possesse it for euer, from generation to generation shall they dwell therein.

CHAP XXXV.

1 The ioyfull flourishing of Christes Kingdome. 3 The weake are incouraged by the vertues and priuiledges of the Gospel.

He wildernesse and the solitarie place shall be glad for them : and the desert shall reioyce and blossome as the rose

2 It shall blossome abundantly, and reioyce euen with ioy and singing : the glory of Lebanon shal be giuen vnto it, the excellencie of Carmel and Sharon they shall see the glory of the Lᴏʀᴅ,

---

Marginal notes (left column):

† *Hebr. statute-maker.*

‖ *Or, they haue forsaken thy tacklings.*

† *Hebr. the fulnes thereof.*

* *Reuel. 6. 14.*

* *Reuel. 6. 13.*

‖ *Or, Rhinocerots.*

‖ *Or, drunken.*

* *Chap. 63. 4.*

Marginal notes (right column):

* *Reue. 2, 18. and 19. 3.*

* *Zeph. 2. 14. reuel. 18. 2.*
‖ *Or, pellicane.*

‖ *Or, ostriches. Heb. daughter of the owle*
† *Heb. 2.*
† *Heb. 1.*
‖ *Or, night monster.*

LORD, and the excellencie of our God.

3 ¶ *Strengthen yee the weake hands, and confirme the feeble knees.

4 Say to them that are of †a feare-full heart; Be strong, feare not : behold, your God will come *with* vengeance, e-*uen* God *with* a recompence, he will come and saue you.

5 Then the *eyes of the blind shall be opened, and * the eares of the deafe shalbe vnstopped.

6 Then shall the * lame man leape as an Hart, and the *tongue of the dumbe sing : for in the wildernesse shall *waters breake out, and streames in the desert.

7 And the parched ground shall be-come a poole, and the thirstie land springs of water : in the habitation of dragons, where each lay, *shalbe* ‖grasse with reeds and rushes.

8 And an high way *shalbe* there, and a way, and it shall be called the way of holinesse, the vncleane shall not passe ouer it, ‖but it shall be for those: the way-faringmen, though fooles, shall not erre *therein*.

9 No lyon shalbe there; nor any ra-uenous beast shall goe vp thereon, it shall not be found there : but the rede-med shall walke *there*.

10 And the * ransomed of the LORD shall returne and come to Zi-on with songs, and euerlasting ioy vp-on their heads : they shall obtaine ioy and gladnesse, and sorrow and sighing shall flee away.

CHAP. XXXVI.

1 Sennacherib inuadeth Iudah. 4 Rabsha-keh sent by Sennacherib, by blasphemous per-swasions solliciteth the people to reuolt. 22 His words are told to Hezekiah.

Owe *it came to passe in the fourteenth yeere of king Hezekiah, *that* Sen-nacherib king of Assyria came vp against all the de-fenced cities of Iudah, and tooke them.

2 And the king of Assyria sent Rab-shakeh, from Lachish to Ierusalem, vnto king Hezekiah, with a great ar-mie : and he stood by the conduit of the vpper poole in the high way of the fullers field.

3 Then came forth vnto him E-liakim Hilkiahs sonne, which *was*

ouer the house, and Shebna the ‖scribe, and Ioah Asaphs sonne the Recorder.

4 ¶ And Rabshakeh sayd vnto them; Say yee now to Hezekiah; Thus saith the great king, the king of Assyria; What confidence is this wherein thou trustest ?

5 I say, (sayest thou) (but *they are but* †vaine words) ‖*I haue* counsell and strength for warre : Now on whom doest thou trust, that thou rebellest a-gainst me ?

6 Loe, thou trustest in the *staffe of this broken reede, on Egypt ; whereon if a man leane, it will goe into his hand and pierce it : so *is* Pharaoh king of E-gypt to all that trust in him.

7 But if thou say to me ; We trust in the LORD our God : *Is* it not he, whose high places and whose altars Hezekiah hath taken away, and sayd to Iudah and to Ierusalem ; Yee shall worship before this altar ?

8 Now therefore giue ‖pledges, I pray thee, to my master the king of Assyria, and I will giue thee two thou-sand horses, if thou be able on thy part to set riders vpon them.

9 How then wilt thou turne away the face of one captaine of the least of my masters seruants : and put thy trust on Egypt for charets and for horsemen ?

10 And am I now come vp with-out the LORD against this land to de-stroy it ? the LORD sayd vnto me ; Goe vp against this land and destroy it.

11 ¶ Then sayd Eliakim and Sheb-na & Ioah vnto Rabshakeh ; Speake, I pray thee, vnto thy seruants in the Syrian language ; for we vnderstand *it* : and speake not to vs in the Iewes language, in the eares of the people that *are* on the wall.

12 ¶ But Rabshakeh sayd ; Hath my master sent me to thy master and to thee, to speake these words ? Hath he not *sent me* to the men that sit vpon the wall, that they may eate their owne dounge, and drinke their owne pisse with you ?

13 Then Rabshakeh stood, and cryed with a loud voice in the Iewes lan-guage, and sayd ; Heare ye the words of the great king, the king of Assyria.

14 Thus saith the king ; Let not Hezekiah deceiue you, for he shall not be able to deliuer you.

15 Neither let Hezekiah make you trust in the LORD, saying, The LORD will surely deliuer vs : this ci-tie

* 23 3

Marginal notes (left column):
ebr. 12.
eb.hastie.
Matth. 9.
and 11,
and 12.
and 20.
and 21.
ioh. 9.
Matth. 11
mar. 7.
Matth. 11
and 15.
and 21.
ioh. 5. 8,
cts 3. 2.
8. 7 and
8.
Matth. 9.
and 12.
and 15.
ioh. 7. 38.
r, a court
reedes
r, for he
lbe with
m.
hap. 51.
. Kings
13.
hron.
1.

Marginal notes (right column):
‖ Or, secreta-rie.
† Heb. a word of lips.
‖ Or, but counsell and strength are for the war.
* Eze. 29.
6, 7.
‖ Or, hosta-ges.

tie shall not be deliuered into the hand of the King of Assyria.

16 Hearken not to Hezekiah : for thus sayth the King of Assyria, ‖ Make an a-greement with mee by a present, and come out to mee : and eate yee euery one of his vine, and euery one of his figge-tree, and drinke yee euery one the wa-ters of his owne cisterne :

‖ Or, seeke my fauour by a present. Heb. make with me a blessing.

17 Vntil I come and take you away to a land like your owne land, a land of corne and wine, a land of bread and vineyards :

18 *Beware* lest Hezekiah perswade you, saying ; The Lord will deliuer vs. Hath any of the gods of the nati-ons deliuered his land out of the hand of the king of Assyria ?

19 Where *are* the gods of Hamath, and Arphad ? where *are* the gods of Sepharuaim ? and haue they deliuered Samaria out of my hand ?

20 Who *are they* amongst all the gods of these landes, that haue deliue-red their land out of my hand, that the Lord should deliuer Ierusalem out of my hand ?

21 But they held their peace, and an-swered him not a word : for the Kings commandement was, saying ; Answere him not.

22 ¶ Then came Eliakim the sonne of Hilkiah, that *was* ouer the houshold, and Shebna the Scribe, and Ioah the sonne of Asaph the Recorder, to Heze-kiah with *their* clothes rent, and tolde him the wordes of Rabshakeh.

CHAP. XXXVII.

1 Hezekiah mourning, sendeth to Isaiah to pray for them. 6 Isaiah comforteth them. 8 Sennacherib going to encounter Tirhakah, sendeth a blasphemous letter to Hezekiah. 14 Hezekiahs prayer. 21 Isaiah his pro-phecie of the pride, and destruction of Sen-nacherib, and the good of Zion. 36 An Angel slayeth the Assyrians. 37 Sennache-rib is slaine at Nineueh by his owne sonnes.

* 2. King. 19. 1, &c.

And * it came to passe when King Hezekiah heard *it*, that hee rent his clothes, and couered himselfe with sackecloth, and went into the house of the Lord.

2 And hee sent Eliakim, who *was* ouer the houshold, and Shebna the Scribe, and the Elders of the Priestes couered with sackecloth, vnto Isaiah the Prophet the sonne of Amoz.

3 And they sayd vnto him ; Thus sayth Hezekiah, This day is a day of trouble, and of rebuke, and of ‖ blasphe-mie : for the children are come to the birth, and *there is* not strength to bring foorth.

‖ Or, prou-cation.

4 It may be the Lord thy God will heare the words of Rabshakeh, whom the king of Assyria his master hath sent to reproch the liuing God, and will reproue the words which the Lord thy God hath heard : wherefore lift vp *thy* prayer for the remnant that is †left.

†Heb. four

5 So the seruants of King Hezeki-ah came to Isaiah.

6 ¶ And Isaiah sayd vnto them ; Thus shall yee say vnto your master, Thus sayth the Lord, Be not afraid of the wordes that thou hast heard, wherewith the seruants of the king of Assyria haue blasphemed me.

7 Behold, I will ‖ send a blast vp-on him, and hee shall heare a rumour, and returne to his owne land, and I will cause him to fall by the sword in his owne land.

‖ Or, put spirit into him.

8 ¶ So Rabshakeh returned and found the king of Assyria warring a-gainst Libnah : for hee had heard that he was departed from Lachish.

9 And he heard say concerning Tir-hakah king of Ethiopia, Hee is come foorth to make warre with thee : and when he heard *it*, he sent messengers to Hezekiah, saying ;

10 Thus shall ye speake to Hezekiah King of Iudah, saying, Let not thy God in whom thou trustest deceiue thee, saying, Ierusalem shall not bee giuen into the hand of the king of Assyria.

11 Behold, thou hast heard what the kings of Assyria haue done to all lands by destroying them vtterly, and shalt thou be deliuered ?

12 Haue the gods of the nations de-liuered them which my fathers haue destroyed, *as* Gozan, and Haran, and Rezeph, and the children of Eden which *were* in Telassar ?

13 Where *is* the king of Hamath, and the king of Arphad, and the king of the citie of Sepharuaim, Hena and Iuah ?

14 ¶ And Hezekiah receiued the let-ter from the hand of the messengers, and read it, and Hezekiah went vp vnto the house of the Lord, and spread it before the Lord

15 And

15 And Hezekiah prayed vnto the LORD, saying,

16 O LORD of hostes, God of Israel, that dwellest *betweene* the Cherubims, thou art the God, *euen* thou alone, of all the kingdomes of the earth, thou hast made heauen and earth.

17 Encline thine eare, O LORD, and heare, Open thine eyes, O LORD, and see, and heare all the wordes of Sennacherib, which hath sent to reproch the liuing God.

18 Of a trueth, LORD, the kings of Assyria haue laid waste all the †nations and their countreys, *eb. lands.*

19 And haue †cast their gods into the fire: for they *were* no gods, but the work of mens hands, wood and stone: therfore they haue destroyed them. *eb. giuen*

20 Now therefore, O LORD our God, saue vs from his hand, that all the kingdomes of the earth may knowe, that thou art the LORD, *euen* thou onely.

21 ¶ Then Isaiah the sonne of Amoz sent vnto Hezekiah, saying, Thus saith the LORD God of Israel, Wheras thou hast prayed to me against Sennacherib king of Assyria:

22 This *is* the worde which the LORD hath spoken concerning him: The virgin, the daughter of Zion hath despised thee, *and* laughed thee to scorne, the daughter of Ierusalem hath shaken her head at thee.

23 Whom hast thou reproched and blasphemed? and against whome hast thou exalted *thy* voice, and lifted vp thine eyes on high? *euen* against the Holy One of Israel. *Ieb. by the nd of thy uants.*

24 † By thy seruants hast thou reproched the Lord, and hast said, By the multitude of my charets am I come vp to the height of the mountaines, to the sides of Lebanon, and I wil cut downe †the tall cedars thereof, *and* the choise firre trees thereof: and I will enter into the height of his border, *and* the ||forrest of his Carmel. *Ieb. the lnesse of cedars rreof, and choise of firre es therof. r, the forst and his utifull ld. r, fenced d closed.*

25 I haue digged and drunke water, and with the sole of my feete haue I dried vp all the riuers of the ||besieged places. *ri Hast u not ard how aue made long agoe, d formed*

26 || Hast thou not heard long agoe, *how* I haue done it, *and* of ancient times, that I haue formed it? now haue I brought it to passe, that thou shouldest be to lay waste defenced cities into ruinous heapes. *of ancient nes? ould I w bring it be laide sste, and enced cis to be inous apes?*

27 Therefore their inhabitants *were* †of small power, they were dismayed and confounded: they were *as* the grasse of the field, and *as* the greene herbe, *as* the grasse on the house tops, and *as corne* blasted before it be growen vp. *† Heb. short of hand.*

28 But I know thy ||abode, and thy going out, and thy comming in, and thy rage against me. *|| Or, sitting.*

29 Because thy rage against me, and thy tumult is come vp into mine eares: therefore will I put my hooke in thy nose, and my bridle in thy lips, and I will turne thee backe by the way by which thou camest.

30 And this *shall be* a signe vnto thee, Ye shall eate this yeere such as groweth of it felfe: and the second yeere that which springeth of the same: and in the third yeere sow ye and reape, and plant vineyards, and eate the fruit thereof.

31 And the †remnant that is escaped of the house of Iudah, shal againe take roote downeward, and beare fruite vpward. *† Heb. the escaping of the house of Iudah that remaineth.*

32 For out of Ierusalem shall goe forth a remnant, and †they that escape out of mount Zion: the *zeale of the LORD of hostes shall doe this. *† Heb. the escaping. * 2. Kings 19. 11. cha. 9. 6.*

33 Therefore thus saith the LORD concerning the king of Assyria, He shall not come into this citie, nor shoot an arrow there, nor come before it with shields, nor cast a banke against it.

34 By the way that he came, by the same shall he returne, and shall not come into this citie, saith the LORD.

35 For I will *defend this citie to saue it, for mine owne sake, and for my seruant Dauids sake. ** 2. Kings 20. 6.*

36 Then the * Angel of the LORD went forth, and smote in the campe of the Assyrians a hundred and fourescore and fiue thousand: and when they arose earely in the morning, behold, they were all dead corpses. ** 2. Kings 19. 35.*

37 ¶ So Sennacherib king of Assyria departed, and went, and returned, and dwelt at Nineueh.

38 And it came to passe as hee was worshipping in the house of Nisroch his god, that Adramelech and Sharezer his sons smote him with the sword, and they escaped into the land of †Armenia: and Esarhaddon his sonne reigned in his stead. *† Heb. Ararat.*

CHAP. XXXVIII.

1 Hezekiah hauing receiued a message of death,

* 2. Kin. 21.
2. chron.
32. 24.

IN those daies was Hezekiah sicke vnto death: and Isaiah the Prophet the sonne of Amoz came vnto him, and said vnto him;

† Hebr. giue charge concerning thy house.

Thus saith the LORD, †Set thine house in order: for thou shalt die, and not liue.

2 Then Hezekiah turned his face toward the wall, and prayed vnto the LORD,

3 And said, Remember now, O LORD, I beseech thee, how I haue walked before thee in trueth, and with a perfect heart, and haue done that which is good in thy sight: and Hezekiah wept †sore.

† Hebr. with great weeping.

4 ¶ Then came the word of the LORD to Isaiah, saying,

5 Goe and say to Hezekiah, Thus saith the LORD, the God of Dauid thy father; I haue heard thy prayer, I haue seene thy teares: behold, I will adde vnto thy dayes fifteene yeeres.

6 And I will deliuer thee and this citie, out of the hand of the king of Assyria: and I will defend this citie.

7 And this *shall be* a signe vnto thee from the LORD, that the LORD will doe this thing that he hath spoken.

8 Behold, I will bring againe the shadow of the degrees which is gone downe in the †Sunne-diall of Ahaz ten degrees backward: so the Sunne returned ten degrees, by which degrees it was gone downe.

† Hebr. degrees by, or with the Sunne.

9 ¶ The writing of Hezekiah king of Iudah, when he had bene sicke, and was recouered of his sicknesse:

10 I saide in the cutting off of my dayes; I shall goe to the gates of the graue: I am depriued of the residue of my yeeres.

11 I said, I shal not see the LORD, *euen* the LORD in the land of the liuing: I shal behold man no more with the inhabitants of the world.

12 Mine age is departed, and is remoued from me as a shepheards tent: I haue cut off like a weauer my life: he will cut mee off ||with pining sicknesse: from day euen to night wilt thou make an end of me.

|| Or, From the thrum.

13 I reckoned till morning, *that* as a Lyon so will hee breake all my bones:

from day euen to night wilt thou make an end of me.

14 Like a crane or a swallow, so did I chatter; I did mourne as a doue: mine eyes faile with *looking* vpward: O LORD, I am oppressed, ||vndertake for me.

|| Or, ease me.

15 What shall I say? hee hath both spoken vnto mee, and himselfe hath done *it : I* shall goe softly, all my yeeres in the bitternesse of my soule.

16 O Lord, by these things men liue: and in all these things is the life of my spirit, so wilt thou recouer me, and make me to liue.

17 Behold, ||for peace I had great bitternesse, but †thou hast in loue to my soule *deliuered* it from the pit of corruption: for thou hast cast all my sinnes †behinde thy backe.

|| Or, on m peace cam great bitternesse.
† Hebr. th hast loued me from t pit.

18 For the graue cannot praise thee, death cannot celebrate thee: they that goe downe into the pit cannot hope for thy trueth.

19 The liuing, the liuing, hee shall praise thee, as I *doe* this day: the father to the children shall make knowen thy trueth.

20 The LORD *was ready* to saue me: therefore we will sing my songs to the stringed instruments, all the dayes of our life, in the house of the LORD.

21 For Isaiah had said, Let them take a lumpe of figges, and lay *it* for a plaister vpon the boile, and he shall recouer.

22 Hezekiah also had said, What *is* the signe, that I shall goe vp to the house of the LORD?

CHAP. XXXIX.

AT that time Merodach Baladan the sonne of Baladan king of Babylon, sent letters and a present to Hezekiah: for hee had heard that he had bene sicke, and was recouered.

* 2. Kin.
12. &c.

2 And Hezekiah was glad of them, and shewed them the house of his ||precious things, the siluer, and the golde, and the spices, and the precious oyntment, and all the house of his ||armour, and all that was found in his treasures: there

|| Or, spice
|| Or, iew heb. vesse or instru ments.

there was nothing in his house, nor in all his dominion, that Hezekiah shewed them not.

3 ¶ Then came Isaiah the Prophet vnto King Hezekiah, and sayde vnto him, What sayd these men? and from whence came they vnto thee? And Hezekiah said, They are come from a farre countrey vnto me, *euen* from Babylon.

4 Then said hee, What haue they seene in thine house? And Hezekiah answered, All that is in mine house haue they seene : there is nothing among my treasures, that I haue not shewed them.

5 Then sayde Isaiah to Hezekiah, Heare the word of the LORD of hostes.

6 Behold, the dayes come, that all that is in thine house, and that which thy fathers haue laide vp in store, vntill this day, shalbe caried to Babylon : nothing shalbe left, saith the LORD.

7 And of thy sonnes that shall issue from thee, which thou shalt beget, shall they take away; and they shall bee Eunuches in the palace of the king of Babylon.

8 Then sayde Hezekiah to Isaiah, Good *is* the word of the LORD which thou hast spoken : hee sayd moreouer, For there shalbe peace and trueth in my dayes.

CHAP XL.

1 The promulgation of the Gospel. 3 The preaching of Iohn Baptist. 9 The preaching of the Apostles. 12 The Prophet by the omnipotencie of God, 18 and his incomparablenes, 26 comforteth the people.

Omfort ye, comfort ye my people, sayth your God.

2 Speake ye †comfortably to Ierusalem, and cry vnto her, that her ‖ warrefare is accomplished, that her iniquitie is pardoned : for shee hath receiued of the LORDs hand double for all her sinnes.

3 ¶ *The voyce of him that cryeth in the wildernesse, Prepare yee the way of the LORD, make straight in the desert a high way for our God.

4 Euery valley shalbe exalted, and euery mountaine and hill shalbe made low : and the crooked shall be made ‖ straight, and the rough places ‖plaine.

5 And the glory of the LORD shall

be reuealed, and all flesh shall see *it* together : for the mouth of the LORD hath spoken *it*.

6 The voyce sayd ; Cry. And hee sayd ; What shall I cry? *All flesh *is* grasse, and all the goodlinesse thereof *is* as the flowre of the field.

7 The grasse withereth, the flowre fadeth ; because the spirit of the LORD bloweth vpon it : surely the people *is* grasse.

8 The grasse withereth, the flowre fadeth : but the * word of our God shall stand for euer.

9 ¶ ‖O Zion, that bringest good tydings, get thee vp into the high mountaine : ‖ O Ierusalem, that bringest good tidings, lift vp thy voyce with strength, lift it vp, be not afraid : say vnto the cities of Iudah ; Behold your God.

10 Behold, the Lord GOD will come ‖with strong *hand*, and his arme shall rule for him : behold , * his reward *is* with him, and ‖his worke before him.

11 He shall * feede his flocke like a shepheard : he shall gather the lambes with his arme, and carie *them* in his bosome, *and* shall gently lead those ‖that are with yoong.

12 ¶ Who hath measured the waters in the hollow of his hand? and meted out heauen with the spanne, and comprehended the dust of the earth in †a measure, and weighed the mountaines in scales, aud the hilles in a balance?

13 * Who hath directed the spirit of the LORD, or, being †his counseller, hath taught him?

14 With whom tooke he counsell, and *who* †instructed him, and taught him in the path of iudgement? and taught him knowledge, and shewed to him the way of †vnderstanding?

15 Behold, the nations *are* as a drop of a bucket, and are counted as the small dust of the balance : behold, hee taketh vp the yles as a very litle thing.

16 And Lebanon *is* not sufficient to burne, nor the beasts thereof sufficient for a burnt offring.

17 All nations before him *are* as *nothing, and they are counted to him lesse then nothing, and vanitie.

18 ¶ To whom then will ye * liken God? or what likenesse will ye compare vnto him?

19 The workeman melteth a grauen image,

*Iob. 14. 2.
psal. 112.
and 103. 15
iam. 1. 10. 1.
pet. 1. 24.

*Iohn 12.
24. 1. pet. 1.
25.
‖ Or, O thou
that tellest
good tidings
to Zion.
‖ Or, O thou
that tellest
good tidings
to Ierusalem.

‖ Or, against
the strong.
* Chap. 62.
11.
‖ Or, recompence for his
worke.
* Eze. 34.
23. Ioh. 10.
11.
‖ Or, that
giue sucke.

† Heb. a
Tierce.

* Wisd. 9.
13. rom. 11.
34. 1. cor. 2.
16.
† Heb. man
of his counsell.
† Heb. made
him vnderstand.
† Heb. vnderstandings.

*Dan. 4.
32.

*Acts.17.
20.

Heb. to the
heart.

Or, appointed time.

Mat. 3. 3.
mark. 1. 3.
luke 3. 4.
ioh. 1. 23.

Or, a
straight
place.
Or, a plaine
place.

image, and the goldsmith spreadeth it ouer with golde, and casteth siluer chaines.

† *Heb. Is poore of oblation.*

20 He that † *is* so impouerished that he hath no oblation, chooseth a tree *that* will not rot; he seeketh vnto him a cunning workeman, to prepare a grauen image *that* shall not be mooued.

21 Haue yee not knowen? haue yee not heard? hath it not beene tolde you from the beginning? haue yee not vnderstood from the foundations of the earth?

‖ *Or, him that sitteth, &c.*
* *Psa. 104. 2.*

22 ‖ *It is* he that sitteth vpon the circle of the earth, and the inhabitants thereof *are* as grashoppers; that * stretcheth out the heauens as a curtaine, and spreadeth them out as a tent to dwel in:

* *Iob 12. 21. psa. 107. 40.*

23 That bringeth the * princes to nothing; hee maketh the Iudges of the earth as vanitie.

24 Yea they shal not be planted, yea they shall not be sowen, yea their stocke shall not take roote in the earth: and he shall also blow vpon them, & they shall wither, and the whirlewinde shall take them away as stubble.

25 To whom then will ye liken me, or shal I be equall, saith the Holy One?

26 Lift vp your eyes on high, and behold who hath created these things, that bringeth out their host by number: he calleth them all by names, by the greatnesse of his might, for that hee *is* strong in power, not one faileth.

27 Why sayest thou, O Iacob, and speakest O Israel, My way is hid from the LORD, and my iudgement is passed ouer from my God?

28 ¶ Hast thou not knowen? hast thou not heard, *that* the euerlasting God, the LORD, the Creatour of the ends of the earth, fainteth not, neither

* *Psa. 147. 5.*

is wearie? * there is no searching of his vnderstanding.

29 He giueth power to the faint, and to them that haue no might, he increaseth strength.

30 Euen the youths shall faint, and be weary, and the yong men shall vtterly fall.

† *Heb. change*

31 But they that waite vpon the LORD, shall † renew *their* strength: they shall mount vp with wings as Eagles, they shal runne and not be weary, *and* they shall walke, and not faint.

CHAP. XLI.

1 God expostulateth with his people, about his

mercies to the Church, 10 about his promises, 21 and about the vanity of Idoles.

Eepe silence before me, O ylands, and let the people renew *their* strength: let them come neere, then let them speake: let vs come neere together to iudgement.

† *Heb. ri teousness*

2 Who raised vp † the righteous man from the East, called him to his foote, gaue the nations before him, and made him rule ouer kings? hee gaue *them* as the dust to his sword, *and* as driuen stuble to his bow.

† *Heb. in peace.*

3 He pursued them, *and* passed † safely; *euen* by the way, *that* hee had not gone with his feete.

4 Who hath wrought and done *it*, calling the generations from the beginning? I the LORD the * first, and with the last, I *am* he.

* *Chap. 4 10. and 4 6. and 48. 12. reu. 1 17. and 22 13.*

5 The yles saw it and feared, the ends of the earth were afraid, drew neere, and came.

6 They helped euery one his neighbour, and *euery one* sayd to his brother, † Be of good courage.

† *Heb. be strong.*

7 So the carpenter encouraged the ‖ goldsmith, *and* he that smootheth *with* the hammer ‖ him that smote the anuill, ‖ saying; It *is* ready for the sodering: and he fastened it with nayles *that* it should not be moued.

‖ *Or, four der.* ‖ *Or, the s ting.* ‖ *Or, sayi of the sode it is good.*

8 But thou Israel, *art* my seruant, Iacob whom I haue * chosen, the seede of Abraham my * friend.

* *Deut. 7. and 10. 15 and 14. 2. psal. 135. chap. 43. and 44. 1. * 2. Chron 20. 7. iam 2. 23.*

9 *Thou* whom I haue taken from the ends of the earth, and called thee from the chiefe men thereof, and sayd vnto thee; Thou art my seruant, I haue chosen thee, and not cast thee away.

10 ¶ Feare thou not, for I *am* with thee: be not dismaied, for I *am* thy God: I will strengthen thee, yea I will helpe thee, yea I will vphold thee with the right hand of my righteousnesse.

11 Behold, all they that were incensed against thee, shalbe * ashamed and confounded: they shall be as nothing, and † they that striue with thee, shall perish.

* *Exod. 2 22. chap. 60. 12. Zech. 12. † Heb. the men of th strife.*

12 Thou shalt seeke them, and shalt not find them, *euen* † them that contended with thee: † they that warre against thee shalbe as nothing, and as a thing of nought.

† *Heb. the men of th contentio † Heb. the men of th warre.*

13 For I the LORD thy God will hold thy right hand, saying vnto thee, Feare

Feare not, I will helpe thee.
14 Feare not, thou worme Iacob,
and ye ‖men of Israel : I will helpe
thee, saith the LORD, and thy Redeemer, the Holy One of Israel.
15 Behold, I will make thee a new
sharpe threshing instrument hauing
†teeth : thou shalt thresh the mountaines, and beate *them* small, and shalt
make the hilles as chaffe.
16 Thou shalt fanne them, and the
winde shall carie them away, and the
whirlewinde shall scatter them · and
thou shalt reioyce in the LORD, *and*
shalt glory in the Holy One of Israel.
17 *When* the poore and needie seeke
water and *there is* none, *and* their tongue
faileth for thirst, I the Lord will heare
them, *I* the God of Israel will not forsake them.
18 I will open *riuers in hie places,
and fountaines in the midst of the valleys : I will make the *wildernesse a
poole of water, and the dry land springs
of water.
19 I will plant in the wildernes the
Cedar, the Shittah tree, and the Myrtle, and the Oyle tree : I will set in the
desert the Firre tree, *and* the Pine and
the Boxe tree together :
20 That they may see, and knowe,
and consider, and vnderstand together,
that the hand of the LORD hath done
this, and the Holy One of Israel hath
created it.
21 †Produce your cause, saith the
LORD, bring foorth your strong *reasons*, saith the King of Iacob.
22 Let them bring *them* foorth, and
shew vs what shall happen : let them
shew the former things what they bee,
that we may †consider them, and know
the latter end of them, or declare vs
things for to come.
23 Shewe the things that are to
come hereafter, that wee may knowe
that ye are gods : yea doe good or doe
euill, that we may be dismayed, and behold *it* together.
24 Behold, ye are ‖of nothing, and
your worke ‖of nought : an abomination *is he that* chooseth you.
25 I haue raised vp *one* from the
North, and he shall come : from the rising of the Sunne shall he call vpon my
name, and he shall come *vpon* princes as
vpon morter, and as the potter treadeth clay.
26 Who hath declared from the beginning, that we may know? and before time, that we may say, *He is* righteous? yea there is none that sheweth,
yea there is none that declareth, yea
there is none that heareth your words.
27 The first *shall say* to Zion, Behold,
behold them, and I will giue to Ierusalem one that bringeth good tidings.
28 For I beheld, and *there was* no
man, euen amongst them, and *there
was* no counseller, that when I asked of
them, could †answere a word.
29 Behold, they *are* all vanitie, their
works *are* nothing : their moulten images *are* winde and confusion.

Margin notes: ‖Or, few men. — †Hebr. mouthes. — *Chap. 35. and 44. 3. — *Psal. 107. — †Heb. cause come nere. — †Heb. set our heart vpon them. — ‖Or, worse then nothing. ‖Or, worse then of a viper. — †Heb returne.

CHAP. XLII.

1 The Office of Christ, graced with meekenes and constancie. 5 Gods promise vnto him. 10 An exhortation to praise God for his Gospel. 17 He reproueth the people of incredulitie.

BEhold *my seruant whome
I vphold, mine elect *in whom*
my soule *delighteth . I
haue put my Spirit vpon
him, he shall bring forth iudgement to
the Gentiles.
2 Hee shall not crie, nor lift vp,
nor cause his voyce to bee heard in the
streete.
3 A bruised reed shall he not breake,
and the ‖smoking flaxe shall hee not
†quench : he shall bring forth iudgment
vnto trueth.
4 He shall not faile nor be †discoura-
ged, till he haue set iudgement in the
earth : and the yles shall waite for his
lawe.
5 ¶ Thus saith God the LORD,
he that created the heauens, and stretched them out, he that spread foorth the
earth and that which commeth out of
it, he that giueth breath vnto the people
vpon it, and spirit to them that walke
therein :
6 I the LORD haue called thee in
righteousnes, and wil hold thine hand,
and will keepe thee, and giue thee for a
couenant of the people, for *a light of
the Gentiles :
7 To open the blind eyes, to *bring
out the prisoners from the prison, *and*
them that sit in *darkenesse out of the
prison house.
8 I *am* the LORD; that *is* my
name, and my *glory will I not giue
to another, neither my praise to grauen
images.

Margin notes: *Mat. 12. 18. — *Mat. 3. 17. and 17. 5. eph. 1. 6. — ‖Or, dimly burning. †Hebr. quench it. — †Heb. broken. — *Chap. 49. 6. luk. 2. 32 acts. 13. 47. — *Chap. 61. 1. — *Luk. 4. 18 heb. 2. 14, 15. cha. 9. 2. — *Chap. 48. 11.

9 Behold,

9 Behold, the former things are come to paſſe, and new things doe I declare : before they ſpring forth I tell you of them.

10 Sing vnto the LORD a newe ſong, *and* his praiſe from the end of the earth : yee that goe downe to the ſea, and † all that is therin ; the yles, and the inhabitants thereof.

† *Hebr. the fulneſſe thereof.*

11 Let the wilderneſ and the cities thereof lift vp *their voyce*, the villages that Kedar doeth inhabite : let the inhabitants of the rocke ſing, let them ſhoute from the top of the mountaines.

12 Let them giue glory vnto the LORD, and declare his praiſe in the Ilands.

13 The LORD ſhall goe foorth as a mighty man, he ſhall ſtirre vp iealouſie like a man of warre : he ſhall cry, yea roare ; hee ſhall ‖ preuaile againſt his enemies.

‖ *Or, behaue himſelfe mightily*

14 I haue long time holden my peace, I haue bene ſtill *and* refrained my ſelfe : *now* wil I cry like a trauailing woman, I will deſtroy and † deuoure at once.

† *Hebr. ſwallow or ſup vp.*

15 I will make waſte mountaines and hilles, and dry vp all their herbes, and I will make the riuers Ilands, and I will dry vp the pooles.

16 And I will bring the blinde by a way *that* they knew not, I will lead them in pathes *that* they haue not knowen : I wil make darkeneſſe light before them, and crooked things † ſtraight. Theſe things will I doe vnto them, and not forſake them.

† *Hebr. into ſtraightnes.*

17 ¶ They ſhall be * turned backe, they ſhalbe greatly aſhamed, that truſt in grauen images, that ſay to the moulten images ; Ye are our gods.

* Pſal. 97. 7. chap. 1. 29. and 44. 11. and 45. 16.

18 Heare ye deafe, and looke ye blinde that ye may ſee.

19 Who *is* blinde, but my ſeruant ? or deafe, as my meſſenger *that* I ſent ? who *is* blinde as he that *is* perfit, and blinde as the LORDS ſeruant ?

20 Seeing many things, *but thou obſerueſt not : opening the eares, but he heareth not.

* Rom. 2. 2.

21 The LORD is well pleaſed for his righteouſnes ſake, he will magnifie the Law, and make ‖ *it* honourable.

‖ *Or, him.*

22 But this *is* a people robbed and ſpoiled, ‖ they *are* all of them ſnared in holes, and they are hid in priſon houſes : they are for a praye, & none deliuereth ; † for a ſpoile, and none ſaith, Reſtore.

‖ *Or, in ſnaring all the yong men of them.*
† *Hebr. a treading.*

23 Who among you will giue eare to this ? *who* will hearken, and heare † for the time to come ?

† *Hebr. the afte time.*

24 Who gaue Iacob for a ſpoile, and Iſrael to the robbers ? Did not the LORD, hee, againſt whom wee haue ſinned ? For they would not walke in his wayes, neither were they obedient vnto his Law.

25 Therefore he hath powred vpon him the furie of his anger, and the ſtrength of battell : and it hath ſet him on fire round about, yet hee knew not ; and it burned him, yet hee layed *it* not to heart.

CHAP. XLIII.

1 The Lord comforteth the Church with his promiſes. 8 Hee appealeth to the people for witneſſe of his Omnipotencie. 14 Hee foretelleth them the deſtruction of Babylon, 18 and his wonderfull deliuerance of his people. 22 He reprooueth the people as inexcuſable.

Vt now thus ſayeth the LORD that created thee, O Iacob, and hee that formed thee, O Iſrael ; Feare not : for I haue redeemed thee, I haue called *thee* by thy name, thou art mine.

2 When thou paſſeſt through the waters, I *wil be* with thee ; and through the riuers, they ſhal not ouerflow thee : when thou walkeſt through the fire, thou ſhalt not be burnt ; neither ſhall the flame kindle vpon thee.

3 For I *am* the LORD thy God, the Holy one of Iſrael, thy Sauiour : I gaue Egypt for thy ranſome, Ethiopia and Seba for thee.

4 Since thou waſt precious in my ſight, thou haſt bene honourable, and I haue loued thee : therefore will I giue men for thee, and people for thy ‖ life.

‖ *Or, p*

5 * Feare not, for I *am* with thee : I will bring thy ſeed from the Eaſt, and gather thee from the Weſt.

* Chap 1. iere. 10. an 27.

6 I wil ſay to the North, Giue vp ; and to the South, Keepe not backe : bring my ſonnes from farre, and my daughters from the ends of the earth ;

7 *Euen* euery one that is called by my Name : for I haue created him for my glory, I haue formed him, yea I haue made him.

8 ¶ Bring foorth the blinde people, that haue eyes ; and the deafe that haue eares.

9 Let

9 Let all the nations be gathered together, and let the people be assembled : * who among them can declare this, and shew vs former things? let them bring foorth their witnesses, that they may be iustified : or let them heare, and say, It is trueth.

10 Yee are my witnesses, saith the Lord, and my seruant whom I haue chosen : that ye may know and beleeue me, and vnderstand that I am he : ‖before me there was ‖no God formed, neither shall there be after me.

11 I, euen I *am the Lord, and beside me there is no Sauiour.

12 I haue declared, and haue saued, and I haue shewed, when there was no strange God among you : therefore yee are my witnesses, saith the Lord, that I am God.

13 Yea before the day was, I am hee ; and there is none that can deliuer out of my hand : I will worke, and who shall †*let it?

14 ¶ Thus sayth the Lord your Redeemer, the Holy one of Israel; For your sake I haue sent to Babylon, and haue brought downe all their †nobles, and the Caldeans, whose crie is in the shippes.

15 I am the Lord, your Holy one, the Creatour of Israel, your King.

16 Thus sayth the Lord, which *maketh a way in the sea, and *a path in the mightie waters :

17 Which bringeth foorth the charet and horse, the armie and the power : they shall lie downe together, they shall not rise : they are extinct, they are quenched as towe.

18 ¶ Remember yee not the former things, neither consider the things of olde.

19 Behold, I will doe a *new thing : now it shall spring foorth, shall yee not know it? I will euen make a way in the wildernesse, and riuers in the desert.

20 The beast of the field shall honor mee, the dragons and the ‖owles, because I giue waters in the wildernesse, and riuers in the desert, to giue drinke to my people, my chosen.

21 * This people haue I formed for my selfe, they shall shewe foorth my praise.

22 ¶ But thou hast not called vpon me, O Iacob ; but thou hast beene wearie of me, O Israel.

23 Thou hast not brought mee the ‖small cattell of thy burnt offrings, neither hast thou honoured mee with thy sacrifices. I haue not caused thee to serue with an offring, nor wearied thee with incense.

24 Thou hast bought mee no sweete cane with money, neither hast thou †filled mee with the fat of thy sacrifices : but thou hast made mee to serue with thy sins, thou hast wearied mee with thine iniquities.

25 I, euen I am hee that * blotteth out thy transgressions for mine owne sake, and will not remember thy sinnes.

26 Put mee in remembrance : let vs plead together : declare thou, that thou mayest bee iustified.

27 Thy first father hath sinned, and thy †teachers haue transgressed against mee.

28 Therefore I haue profaned the ‖princes of the Sanctuarie, and haue giuen Iacob to the curse, and Israel to reproches.

CHAP. XLIIII.

1 God comforteth the Church with his promises. 7 The vanity of Idols, 9 and folly of Idolmakers. 21 He exhorteth to prayse God for his redemption and omnipotency.

Et now heare, *O Iacob my seruant, and Israel whom I haue chosen.

2 Thus sayeth the Lord that made thee, and formed thee from the wombe, which wil helpe thee : Feare not, O Iacob, my seruant, and thou Iesurun, whom I haue chosen.

3 For I will *powre water vpon him that is thirstie, and floods vpon the dry ground : I will powre my spirit vpon thy seede, and my blessing vpon thine offspring :

4 And they shall spring vp as among the grasse, as willowes by the water courses.

5 One shall say, I am the Lords : and another shall call himselfe by the name of Iacob : and another shall subscribe with his hand vnto the Lord, and surname himselfe by the name of Israel.

6 Thus saith the Lord the king of Israel and his redeemer the Lord of hostes, *I am the first, and I am the last, and besides me there is no God.

7 And

Margin notes (left column)

Chap. 41.

cha. 41. 4.
1 44. 8.
r, nothing
med of
d.
Chap. 45.
ose. 13.

Heb. turne
acke.
ob 9. 12.
ap. 14. 17

Heb. barres

Exod. 14.
osh. 3.

. Cor. 6.
reuel.
5.

r, ostri-
es. Hebr.
ughters of
owle.

Luke 1.
75.

Margin notes (right column)

† Heb. lambs
or kids.

† Heb. made
me drunke :
or, abundant-
ly moistened.

* Ezek. 36.
22, &c.

† Heb. inter-
preters.

‖ Or, holy
princes.

* Cha. 41. 6.
Iere. 30. 10.
and 46. 27.

* Cha. 35. 7.
ioel 2. 28.
ioh. 7. 38.
acts 2. 18.

* Cha. 41. 4.
and 48. 12.
reuel. 1. 8,
17. and
22. 13.

7 And who, as I, shall call, and shall declare it, and set it in order for me, since I appointed the ancient people? and the things that are comming, and shall come? let them shew vnto them.

8 Feare yee not, neither be afraid: haue not I told thee from that time, and haue declared *it?* yee *are* euen my witnesses. Is there a God besides me? yea ** there is* no † God, I know not *any.*

* Chap. 45. 5. deut. 4. 35. 39. and 32. 39. 1. sam. 2. 2.
† Heb. rocke.

9 ¶ They that make a grauen image are all of them vanitie, and their † delectable things shall not profit, and they *are* their owne witnesses, * they see not, nor know; that they may be ashamed.

† Heb. desireable.
* Psal. 115. 4. &c.

10 Who hath formed a God, or moulten a grauen image that is profitable for nothing?

11 Behold, all his fellowes shall be * ashamed: and the workemen, they *are* of men: let them all be gathered together, let them stand *vp; yet* they shal feare, *and* they shalbe ashamed together.

* Psal. 49. 7. chap. 1. 29. and 42. 17. and 45. 16.

12 * The smith ‖ with the tonges both worketh in the coales, and fashioneth it with hammers, and worketh it with the strength of his armes: yea he is hungrie, and his strength faileth; hee drinketh no water, and is faint.

* Ier. 10. 3. wisd. 13. 11
‖ *Or, with an axe.*

13 The carpenter stretcheth out his rule: he maketh it out with the line: he fitteth it with planes, and he marketh it out with the compasse, and maketh it after the figure of a man, according to the beautie of a man; that it may remaine in the house.

14 He heweth him downe cedars, and taketh the Cypresse and the Oke, which he ‖ strengthneth for himselfe among the trees of the forrest: he planteth an Ashe, and the raine doth nourish it.

‖ *Or, taketh courage.*

15 Then shall it bee for a man to burne: for hee will take thereof and warme himselfe; yea he kindleth *it* and baketh bread; yea he maketh a God, and worshippeth it: he maketh it a grauen image, and falleth downe thereto.

16 He burneth part thereof in the fire: with part thereof he eateth flesh: he rosteth rost, and is satisfied: yea hee warmeth *himselfe,* and saith; Aha, I am warme, I haue seene the fire.

17 And the residue thereof he maketh a God, *euen* his grauen image: hee falleth downe vnto it, and worshippeth it, and prayeth vnto it, and saith; Deliuer me, for thou *art* my God.

18 They haue not knowen, nor vnderstood: for he hath † shut their eyes, that they cannot see; *and* their hearts, that they cannot vnderstand.

† *Heb. do bed.*

19 And none † considereth in his heart, neither *is there* knowledge nor vnderstanding to say; I haue burnt part of it in the fire, yea also I haue baked bread vpon the coales thereof: I haue rosted flesh and eaten *it;* and shall I make the residue thereof an abomination? shall I fall downe to † the stocke of a tree?

† *Heb. se teth to hi heart.*
† *Heb. th which co of a tree.*

20 He feedeth of ashes: a deceiued heart hath turned him aside, that he cannot deliuer his soule, nor say; *Is there* not a lie in my right hand?

21 ¶ Remember these (O Iacob and Israel) for thou *art* my seruant: I haue formed thee: thou *art* my seruant, O Israel; thou shalt not be forgotten of me.

22 I haue blotted out, as a thicke cloude, thy transgressions, and as a a cloud, thy sinnes: returne vnto me, for I haue redeemed thee.

23 Sing, O yee heauens; for the LORD hath done *it:* shout yee lower parts of the earth: breake forth into singing yee mountaines, O forrest and euery tree therein: for the LORD hath redeemed Iacob, and glorified himselfe in Israel.

24 Thus saith the LORD thy redeemer, and he that formed thee from the wombe; I *am* the LORD that maketh all things, that stretcheth forth the heauens alone, that spreadeth abroad the earth by my selfe:

25 That frustrateth the tokens of the lyers, and maketh diuiners mad, that turneth wisemen backward, and maketh their knowledge foolish:

26 That confirmeth the word of his seruant, and performeth the counsell of his messengers, that saith to Ierusalem, Thou shalt be inhabited; and to the cities of Iudah, Yee shall be built, and I will raise vp the † decayed places thereof.

† *Heb. wastes.*

27 That saith to the deepe; Be dry, and I will drie vp thy riuers.

28 That saith of Cyrus, *Hee is* my shepheard, and shall performe all my pleasure, euen saying to Ierusalem, * Thou shalt be built, and to the Temple, Thy foundation shalbe laid.

* 2. Ch 36. 22. 1. 1. ch 45. 13.

CHAP.

CHAP. XLV.

1 God calleth Cyrus for his Churches sake. 5 By his omnipotencie he challengeth obedience. 20 Hee conuinceth the idoles of vanitie, by his sauing power.

Or, strengthened.

Hus saith the LORD to his Anointed, to Cyrus whose right hande I ||haue holden, to subdue nations before him : and I will loose the loines of kings to open before him the two leaued gates, and the gates shall not be shut.

2 I will goe before thee, and make the crooked places straight, I wil break in pieces the gates of brasse, and cut in sunder the barres of yron.

3 And I will giue thee the treasures of darkenesse, & hidden riches of secret places, that thou mayest know, that I the LORD which call thee by thy name, *am* the God of Israel.

4 For Iacob my seruants sake, and Israel mine elect, I haue euen called thee by thy name : I haue surnamed thee, though thou hast not knowen me.

Deu. 4. 35.
), and 32.
), chap.
4. 9.

5 ¶ I *am* the Lord, and *there is* none els, *there is* no God besides me : I girded thee, though thou hast not knowen me :

6 That they may knowe from the rising of the Sun, and from the West, that *there is* none besides me, I am the LORD, and *there is* none else.

7 I forme the light, and create darkenesse : I make peace, and create euill : I the LORD do all these things.

8 Drop downe, ye heauens, from aboue, and let the skies powre downe righteousnesse : let the earth open, and let them bring forth saluation, and let righteousnesse spring vp together : I the LORD haue created it.

Ier. 18. 6.
m. 9. 20.

9 Woe vnto him that striueth with his maker : Let the potsheard *striue* with the potsheards of the earth : *shal the clay say to him that fashioneth it, What makest thou? or thy worke, he hath no hands?

10 Woe vnto him that saith vnto *his* father, What begettest thou? or to the woman, What hast thou brought forth?

11 Thus saith the LORD, the Holy One of Israel, and his maker, Aske me of things to come concerning my sonnes, and concerning the worke of my hands command ye me.

12 I haue made the earth, and created man vpon it : I, *euen* my handes

haue stretched out the heauens, and all their hoste haue I commanded.

13 I haue raised him vp in righteousnesse, and I will ||direct all his wayes : he shall * build my citie, and hee shall let goe my captiues, not for price nor reward, saith the LORD of hosts.

| Or, make straight.
* Chron. 36
22. ezra. 1. 1
cha. 44. 28

14 Thus saith the LORD, The labour of Egypt, and merchandise of Ethiopia, and of the Sabeans, men of stature shall come ouer vnto thee, and they shall be thine, they shall come after thee, in chaines they shall come ouer : and they shal fall downe vnto thee, they shal make supplication vnto thee, *saying*, Surely God *is* in thee, and *there is* none else, *there is* no god.

15 Verely thou *art* a God that hidest thy selfe, O God of Israel the Sauiour.

16 They shall be ashamed, and also confounded all of them : they shall goe to confusion together that are *makers of idoles.

* Chap. 44.
11.

17 *But* Israel shall bee saued in the LORD with an euerlasting saluation : ye shall not be ashamed nor confounded world without end.

18 For thus saith the LORD that created the heauens, God himselfe that formed the earth and made it, hee hath established it, he created it not in vaine, he formed it to be inhabited, I *am* the LORD, and *there is* none else.

19 I haue not spoken in * secret, in a darke place of the earth : I said not vnto the seed of Iacob, Seeke ye mee in vaine : I the LORD speake righteousnesse, I declare things that are right.

* Deut. 30.
11.

20 ¶ Assemble your selues and come : draw neere together ye that are escaped of the nations : they haue no knowledge that set vp the wood of their grauen image, and pray vnto a god *that* cannot saue.

21 Tell ye and bring *them* neere, yea let them take counsell together, who hath declared this from ancient time? *who* hath told it from that time? Haue not I the LORD? and *there is* no God else beside me, a iust God and a Sauiour, *there is* none beside me.

22 Looke vnto mee, and be ye saued all the endes of the earth : for I *am* God, and *there is* none else.

23 I haue sworne by my selfe : the word is gone out of my mouth *in* righteousnes, and shall not returne, that vnto

* Rom. 14.
11. phil. 2.
10.

‖ Or, surely
he shall say
of me, In the
Lord is all
righteousnes
and strength.
Hebr. righ-
teousnesses.

to me euery * knee shall bowe, euery
tongue shall sweare.

24 ‖ Surely, shall one say, In the
Lord haue I righteousnesse and
strength : euen to him shall men come,
and all that are incensed against him,
shalbe ashamed.

25 In the Lord shall all the seed
of Israel be iustified, and shall glory.

CHAP. XLVI.

1 The idoles of Babylon could not saue themselues. 3 God saueth his people to the end.
5 Idoles are not comparable to God for
power, 12 or present saluation.

El boweth downe, Nebo
stoupeth, their idoles were
vpon the beasts, and vpon
the cattell : your carriages
were heauie loaden, they are
a burden to the wearie beast.

2 They stoupe, they bow downe together, they could not deliuer the burden, but † themselues are gone into captiuitie.

† Hebr. their
soule.

3 ¶ Hearken vnto me, O house of
Iacob, and al the remnant of the house
of Israel, which are borne by me, from
the belly, which are caried from the
wombe.

4 And euen to your old age I am he,
and euen to hoare haires will I cary
you : I haue made, and I will beare,
euen I wil cary and wil deliuer you.

* Chap. 40.
18, 25.

5 ¶ To whom wil ye liken me, and
make me equall, and * compare me, that
we may be like?

6 They lauish gold out of the bagge,
and weigh siluer in the balance, and hire
a goldsmith, and hee maketh it a god :
they fall downe, yea they worship.

7 They beare him vpon the shoulder, they cary him and set him in his
place, and hee standeth : from his place
shall he not remooue : yea one shall cry
vnto him, yet can he not answere, nor
saue him out of his trouble.

8 Remember this, and shew your
selues men : bring it againe to minde, O
ye transgressours.

9 Remember the former things of
old, for I am God, and there is none else,
I am God, and there is none like me,

10 Declaring the end from the beginning, and from ancient times the
things that are not yet done, saying,
* My counsell shall stand, and I wil doe
all my pleasure :

* Psal. 33.
11. pro. 19.
21. and 21.
30. hebr. 6.
17.

11 Calling a rauenous bird from the

East, † the man that executeth my counsell from a farre countrey ; yea I haue
spoken it, I will also bring it to passe, I
haue purposed it, I will also doe it.

† Hebr. t
man of m
counsell.

12 ¶ Hearken vnto me, ye stout hearted, that are farre from righteousnesse.

13 I bring neere my righteousnesse :
it shall not bee farre off, and my saluation shall not tarie ; and I wil place saluation in Zion for Israel my glorie.

CHAP. XLVII.

1 Gods iudgement vpon Babylon and Cal-
dæa, 6 for their vnmercifulnesse, 7 pride,
10 and ouerboldnes, 11 shalbe vnresistable.

Ome downe and sit in the
dust : O virgin daughter
of Babylon, sit on the
ground : there is no throne,
O daughter of the Cal-
deans : for thou shalt no more be called
tender and delicate.

2 Take the milstones and grinde
meale, vncouer thy lockes : make bare
the legge: vncouer the thigh, passe ouer
the riuers.

3 Thy nakednes shalbe vncouered,
yea thy shame shalbe seene : I will take
vengeance, and I will not meet thee as a
man.

4 As for our redeemer, the Lord
of hostes is his Name, the Holy one of
Israel.

5 Sit thou silent, and get thee into
darknes, O daughter of the Caldeans : for thou shalt no more be called the
Ladie of kingdomes.

6 ¶ I was wroth with my people :
I haue polluted mine inheritance, and
giuen them into thine hand: thou didst
shew them no mercy ; vpon the ancient
hast thou very heauily layed the yoke.

7 ¶ And thou saydst, I shall bee * a
Ladie for euer : so that thou didst not lay
these things to thy heart, neither didst
remember the later end of it.

* Reue. 1
7.

8 Therefore heare now this, thou
that art giuen to pleasures, that dwellest carelesly, that sayest in thine heart,
I am, and none else besides mee, I
shall not sit as a widow, neither shall I
know the losse of children.

9 But these two * things shall come
to thee in a moment in one day ; the
losse of children, and widowhood ; they
shall come vpon thee in their perfection, for the multitude of thy sorceries,
and for the great abundance of thine inchantments.

* Chap. 8
19.

10 ¶ For

10 ¶ For thou hast trusted in thy wickednesse: thou hast said, None seeth me. Thy wisedome and thy knowledge, it hath ||peruerted thee, and thou hast said in thine heart, I *am*, and none else besides me.

11 ¶ Therefore shall euill come vpon thee, thou shalt not know † from whence it riseth : and mischiefe shall fall vpon thee, thou shalt not be able to †put it off : and desolation shall come vpon thee suddenly, *which* thou shalt not know.

12 Stand now with thine inchantments, and with the multitude of thy sorceries, wherein thou hast laboured from thy youth; if so be thou shalt be able to profite, if so be thou mayest preuaile.

13 Thou art wearied in the multitude of thy counsels : let now the †astrologers, the starre-gazers, the †monethly prognosticators stand vp, *and* saue thee from these things that shall come vpon thee.

14 Behold, they shall be as stubble : the fire shall burne them, they shall not deliuer † themselues from the power of the flame : *there shall* not *bee* a coale to warme at, *nor* fire to sit before it.

15 Thus shal they be vnto thee with whom thou hast laboured, *euen* thy merchants from thy youth, they shall wander euery one to his quarter : none shall saue thee.

CHAP. XLVIII.

1 God, to conuince the people of their foreknowen obstinacie, reuealed his prophecies. 9 He saueth them for his owne sake. 12 He exhorteth them to obedience, because of his power and prouidence. 16 Hee lamenteth their backewardnesse. 20 Hee powerfully deliuereth his out of Babylon.

Eare yee this, O house of Iacob, which are called by the name of Israel, and are come foorth out of the waters of Iudah; which sweare by the Name of the Lord, and make mention of the God of Israel, *but* not in trueth nor in righteousnes.

2 For they call themselues of the holy city, and stay themselues vpon the God of Israel, the Lord of hostes *is* his Name.

3 I haue declared the former things from the beginning : and they went foorth out of my mouth, and I shewed them, I did *them* suddenly, and they came to passe.

4 Because I knew that thou *art* †obstinate, and thy necke *is* an yron sinew, and thy brow brasse :

5 I haue euen from the beginning declared *it* to thee; before it came to passe I shewed it thee : lest thou shouldest say, Mine idole hath done them, and my grauen image, and my molten image hath commanded them.

6 Thou hast heard, see all this, and will not yee declare *it?* I haue shewed thee new things from this time, euen hidden things, and thou didst not know them.

7 They are created now, and not from the beginning, euen before the day when thou heardest them not; lest thou shouldest say, Behold, I knew them.

8 Yea thou heardest not, yea thou knewest not, yea from that time that thine eare was not opened : for I knew that thou wouldest deale very treacherously, and wast called a transgressour from the wombe.

9 ¶ For my names sake will I deferre mine anger, and for my praise will I refraine for thee, that I cut thee not off.

10 Behold, I haue refined thee, but not ||with siluer; I haue chosen thee in the fornace of affliction.

11 For mine owne sake, *euen* for mine owne sake will I doe *it*; for how should my *Name* bee polluted? and I will not giue my *glory vnto another.

12 ¶ Hearken vnto me, O Iacob, and Israel my called; I *am* hee, I *am* the *first, I also *am* the last.

13 Mine hand also hath laid the foundation of the earth, and ||my right hand hath spanned the heauens : *when* I call vnto them, they stand vp together.

14 All yee assemble your selues and heare : which among them hath declared these things? the Lord hath loued him : hee will doe his pleasure on Babylon, and his arme *shall be* on the Caldeans.

15 I, *euen* I haue spoken, yea I haue called him : I haue brought him, and he shall make his way prosperous.

16 ¶ Come ye neere vnto me; heare ye this; I haue not spoken in secret from the beginning; from the time that it was, there *am* I; and now the Lord God and his Spirit hath sent me.

17 Thus

Marginal notes

r, caused e to turne ay.

Heb. the rning reof.

Heb. exte.

Heb. viewof the uens.
Heb. that e knowe ge conning the neths.

Heb. their des.

|| *Or, for siluer.*

* Cha. 42. 8.

* Cha. 41. 4. and 44. 6. reuel. 1. 17. and 22. 13.
|| *Or, the palme of my right hand hath spread out.*

† *Heb. hard.*

17 Thus saith the LORD thy redeemer, the holy one of Israel; I *am* the LORD thy God which teacheth thee to profit, which leadeth thee by the way *that* thou shouldest goe.

18 O that thou haddest hearkened to my commandements! then had thy peace beene as a riuer, and thy righteousnesse as the waues of the sea.

19 Thy seede also had beene as the sand, and the ofspring of thy bowels like the grauell thereof : his name should not haue beene cut off, nor destroyed from before me.

20 ¶ Goe yee forth of Babylon : flee yee from the Caldeans, with a voyce of singing, declare yee, tell this, vtter it euen to the end of the earth : say yee; The LORD hath * redeemed his seruant Iacob.

21 And they thirsted not *when* he led them through the deserts; he * caused the waters to flow out of the rocke for them : he claue the rocke also, and the waters gushed out.

22 * *There is* no peace, saith the LORD, vnto the wicked.

CHAP. XLIX.

1 Christ being sent to the Iewes, complaineth of them. 5 He is sent to the Gentiles, with gracious promises. 13 Gods loue is perpetuall to his Church. 18 The ample restauration of the Church. 24 The powerfulll deliuerance out of captiuity.

Isten, O yles, vnto me, and hearken yee people from farre. The LORD hath called mee from the wombe, from the bowels of my mother hath he made mention of my name.

2 And he hath made my mouth like a sharpe sword, in the shadow of his hand hath he hid me, and made mee a polished shaft; in his quiuer hath hee hid me,

3 And sayd vnto me; Thou *art* my seruant, O Israel, in whom I will be glorified.

4 Then I said; I haue laboured in vaine, I haue spent my strength for nought, and in vaine, *yet* surely my iudgement *is* with the LORD, and ||my worke with my God.

5 ¶ And now, saith the LORD that formed me from the wombe to be his seruant, to bring Iacob againe to

him; Though Israel be ||not gathered, yet shall I be glorious in the eyes of the LORD, and my God shall bee my strength.

6 And he said, || It is a light thing that thou shouldest be my seruant to raise vp the tribes of Iacob, and to restore the || preserued of Israel : I will also giue thee for a *light to the Gentiles, that thou mayest be my saluation, vnto the end of the earth.

7 Thus saith the LORD the redeemer of Israel, *and* his holy one, ||to him whom man dispiseth, to him whom the nation abhorreth, to a seruant of rulers; Kings shall see and arise, princes also shall worship, because of the LORD, that is faithfull, *and* the holy one of Israel, and he shall choose thee.

8 Thus saith the LORD, * In an acceptable time haue I heard thee, and in a day of saluation haue I helped thee : and I will preserue thee, and giue thee for a couenant of the people, ||to establish the earth, to cause to inherite the desolate heritages :

9 That thou mayest say * to the prisoners, Goe forth ; to them that *are* in darkenesse, Shewe your selues : they shall feede in the wayes, and their pastures *shalbe* in all high places.

10 They shall not * hunger nor thirst, neither shall the heate nor sunne smite them : for he that hath mercy on them shall lead them, euen by the springs of water shall he guide them.

11 And I will make all my mountaines a way, and my high wayes shall be exalted.

12 Behold, these shall come from far : and loe, these from the North and from the West, and these from the land of Sinim.

13 ¶ Sing, O heauen, and be ioyfull, O earth, and breake forth into singing, O mountaines : for God hath comforted his people, and will haue mercy vpon his afflicted.

14 But Zion said, The LORD hath forsaken me, and my Lord hath forgotten me.

15 Can a woman forget her sucking child, † that she should not haue compassion on the sonne of her wombe? yea they may forget, yet will I not forget thee.

16 Behold, I haue grauen thee vpon the palmes of *my* hands : thy walles *are* continu-

* Exod. 19.
4. 5, 6.

* Exod. 17.
6. num. 20.
11.

* Chap. 57.
21.

|| Or, my reward.

|| Or, that
Israel ma
be gathere
to him, an
may &c.

|| Or, art th
lighter, th
that thou
shouldest
&c.
|| Or, deso
tions.
* Chap. 4
6.

|| Or, to h
that is de.
sed in sou

* 1. Cor.
2.

|| Or, ra
vp.

* Chap.
7.

* Reu. 7.

continually before mee.

17 Thy children ſhal make haſte, thy destroyers, and they that made thee waste, shall goe forth of thee.

18 ¶ *Lift vp thine eyes round about, and behold: all these gather themſelues together *and* come to thee: as I liue, saith the LORD, thou shalt surely clothe thee with them all, as with an ornament, and bind them *on thee* as a bride doeth.

19 For thy waste and thy desolate places, and the land of thy destruction shall euen now be too narrow by reason of the inhabitants, and they that swallowed thee vp, shall bee farre away.

20 The children which thou shalt haue, after thou hast lost the other, shall say againe in thine eares, The place *is* too straight for me: giue place to mee that I may dwell.

21 Then shalt thou say in thine heart, Who hath begotten me these, seeing I haue lost my children and am desolate, a captiue and remouing to and fro? and who hath brought vp these? Beholde, I was left alone, these where *had* they *beene?*

22 Thus saith the Lord GOD, Behold, I will lift vp mine hand to the Gentiles, and set vp my standerd to the people: and they shall bring thy sonnes in *their* †armes: and thy daughters shal be caried vpon *their* shoulders.

23 And kings shall be thy †nursing fathers, and their †queenes thy nurſing mothers: they shall bow downe to thee with their face toward the earth, and *licke vp the dust of thy feete, and thou shalt know that I *am* the LORD: for they shall not be ashamed that waite for me.

24 ¶ Shall the pray be taken from the mightie, or †the lawfull captiue deliuered?

25 But thus saith the LORD, Euen the †captiues of the mightie shall be taken away, and the pray of the terrible shall be deliuered: for I will contend with *him* that contendeth with thee, and I will saue thy children.

26 And I will feede them that oppresse thee, with their owne flesh, and they shall be drunken with their owne *blood, as with ‖ sweet wine: and all flesh shall know that I the LORD *am* thy Sauiour and thy Redeemer, the mightie One of Iacob.

CHAP. L.

Hus saith the LORD, Where is the bill of your mothers diuorcement, whom I haue put away? or which of my creditours *is it* to whom I haue sold you? Behold, for your iniquities haue you solde your selues, and for your transgressions is your mother put away.

2 Wherefore when I came *was there* no man? when I called, *was* there none to answere? *Is my hand shortened at all, that it cannot redeeme? or haue I no power to deliuer? Beholde, at my rebuke I *drie vp the sea: I make the *riuers a wildernes: their fish stinketh, because *there is* no water, and dieth for thirst.

3 I clothe the heauens with blackenesse, and I make sackcloth their couering.

4 The Lord GOD hath giuen me the tongue of the learned, that *I* should know how to speake a worde in season to him that *is* *wearie: I make wakeneth morning by morning, hee wakeneth mine eare to heare as the learned.

5 ¶ The Lord GOD hath opened mine eare, and I was not *rebellious, neither turned away backe.

6 *I gaue my backe to the smiters, and my cheeks to them that plucked off the haire: I hidde not my face from shame and spitting.

7 ¶ For the Lord GOD wil helpe me, therfore shall I not be confounded: therefore haue I set my face like a flint, and I know that I shall not bee ashamed.

8 *He *is* neere that iustifieth me, who will contend with me? let vs stand together: who is †mine aduersarie? let him come neere to me.

9 Behold, the Lord GOD wil helpe me, who *is he that* shall condemne mee? Loe, they all shall waxe olde as a garment: the moth shall eate them vp.

10 ¶ Who *is* among you that feareth the LORD, that obeyeth the voyce of his seruant, that walketh *in* darkenesse and hath no light? let him trust in the Name

---

Marginal notes (left column):
* Chap. 60.
4.

* Hebr. bosome.

* Heb. nourishers.
* Heb. Princesses.

* Psal. 72. 9.

* Hebr. the captiuitie of the iust.

* Heb. captiuitie.

* Reu. 14.
20. and 16.
3.
‖ Or, new vine.

Marginal notes (right column):
* Num. 11.
23. chap.
59. 1.

* Exod. 14.
21.
* Iosh. 3. 16

* Matth. 11.
28.

* Iohn 14.
31. heb. 10.
5, &c. phil.
2. 8.
* Matth. 26.
67. and 27.
26.

* Rom. 8.
32, 33.
† Heb. the master of my cause.

Name of the Lord, and stay vpon his God.

11 Behold, all ye that kindle a fire, that compasse *your selues* about with sparks : walke in the light of your fire, and in the sparkes *that* ye haue kindled. * This shall ye haue of mine hand, yee shall lie downe in sorrow.

Iohn 9. 39.

CHAP. LI.

1 An exhortation after the paterne of Abraham, to trust in Christ, 3 by reason of his comfortable promises, 4 of his righteous saluation, 7 and mans mortalitie. 9 Christ by his sanctified arme, defendeth his from the feare of man. 17 He bewaileth the afflictions of Ierusalem, 21 and promiseth deliuerance.

Earken to me, ye that follow after righteousnesse, ye that seeke the Lord : looke vnto the rocke *whence* yee are hewen, and to the hole of the pitte *whence* ye are digged.

2 Looke vnto Abraham your father, and vnto Sarah *that* bare you : for I called him alone, and blessed him, and increased him.

3 For the Lord shall comfort Zion : he wil comfort all her waste places, and he wil make her wildernes like Eden, and her desert like the garden of the Lord : ioy and gladnesse shalbe found therein, thankesgiuing, and the voice of melody.

4 ¶ Hearken vnto me, my people, and giue eare vnto me, O my nation : for a Law shall proceed from mee, and I will make my iudgement to rest for a light of the people.

5 My righteousnes *is* neere : my saluation is gone foorth, and mine armes shall iudge the people : the Iles shall wait vpon me, and on mine arme shall they trust.

6 Lift vp your eyes to the heauens, and looke vpon the earth beneath : for the heauens shall vanish away like smoke, and the earth shall waxe old like a garment, and they that dwel therein shall die in like maner : but my saluation shal be for euer, and my righteousnes shall not be abolished.

Psal. 102. 27. matth. 24. 35.

7 ¶ Hearken vnto me ye that know righteousnesse, the people * in whose heart is my Law : * Feare ye not the reproch of men, neither be yee afraid of their reuilings.

Psal. 37. 31.
Matth. 10. 27.

8 For the moth shall eate them vp like a garment, and the worme shal eate them like wooll : but my righteousnes shalbe for euer ; and my saluation from generation to generation.

9 ¶ Awake, awake, put on strength, O arme of the Lord, awake as in the ancient dayes, in the generations of old. *Art* thou not it that hath cut Rahab, *and* wounded the *dragon ?

Psal. 74. 13, 14. eze. 29. 3.
Exod. 14 21.

10 *Art* thou not it which hath * dried the sea, the waters of the great deepe, that hath made the depthes of the sea a way for the ransomed to passe ouer ?

11 Therefore the redeemed of the Lord shall * returne, and come with singing vnto Zion, and euerlasting ioy *shalbe* vpon their *head : they shall obtaine gladnesse and ioy, *and* sorrow and mourning shall flee away.

Chap. 35. 10.
Chap. 35. 10.

12 I, *euen I am* hee that comforteth you, who art thou that thou shouldest be afraid * of a man *that* shall die, and of the sonne of man *which* shall bee made *as* * grasse ?

Psal. 118 6.

13 And forgettest the Lord thy maker that hath stretched foorth the heauens, and layed the foundations of the earth ? and hast feared continually euery day, because of the furie of the oppressour, as if hee ‖were ready to destroy ? and where *is* the furie of the oppressour ?

Chap. 40. 6, 1. pet. 1, 24.

‖ Or, made himselfe ready.

14 The captiue exile hasteneth that he may be loosed, and that hee should not die in the pit, nor that his bread should faile.

15 But I *am* the Lord thy God, that *diuided the sea, whose waues roared : the Lord of hosts *is* his Name.

Iere. 31. 35.

16 And I haue put my wordes * in thy mouth, and haue couered thee in the shadow of mine hand, that I may plant the heauens, and lay the foundations of the earth, and say vnto Zion, Thou *art* my people.

Chap. 49 2, 3.

17 ¶ * Awake, awake, stand vp, O Ierusalem, which hast drunke at the hand of the Lord the cup of his furie ; thou hast drunken the dregges of the cup of trembling, *and* wrung *them* out.

Chap. 52 1.

18 *There is* none to guide her among all the sonnes *whom* shee hath brought foorth : neither *is there* any that taketh her by the hand, of all the sonnes *that* she hath brought vp.

19 * These two things † are come vnto thee ; who shall be sorie for thee ? deso-

Cha. 47.
† *Hebr. hapened.*

† *Heb. brea-king.*

desolation and † destruction, and the famine and the sword : by whom shall I comfort thee?

20 Thy sonnes haue fainted, they lie at the head of all the streetes as a wilde bull in a net; they are full of the furie of the LORD, the rebuke of thy God.

21 ¶ Therfore heare now this thou afflicted and drunken, but not with wine.

22 Thus saith thy Lord, the LORD and thy God *that* pleadeth the cause of his people, Behold, I haue taken out of thine hand the cup of trembling, *euen* the dregges of the cup of my furie : thou shalt no more drinke it againe.

23 But I will put it into the hand of them that afflict thee : which haue said to thy soule, Bow downe that wee may goe ouer : and thou hast laide thy body as the ground, and as the streete to them that went ouer.

CHAP. LII.

1 Christ perswadeth the Church to beleeue his free Redemption, 7 To receiue the Ministers thereof, 9 To ioy in the power thereof, 11 And to free themselues from bondage. 13 Christs kingdome shalbe exalted.

* *Chap. 51. 17*

AWake, *awake, put on thy strength, O Zion, put on thy beautifull garments, O Ierusalem the holy citie : for hencefoorth there shall no more come into thee the vncircumcised, and the vncleane.

2 Shake thy selfe from the dust : arise, *and* sit downe, O Ierusalem : loose thy selfe from the bandes of thy necke, O captiue daughter of Zion.

3 For thus sayth the LORD, Yee haue solde your selues for nought : and ye shall be redeemed without money.

* *Gen. 46. 6.*

4 For thus saith the Lord GOD, My people went downe aforetime into * Egypt to soiourne there, and the Assyrian oppressed them without cause.

5 Now therefore, what haue I here, sayth the LORD, that my people is taken away for nought? they that rule ouer them, make them to howle, sayth the LORD, and my Name continually euery day is * blasphemed.

* *Ezek. 36. 20, 23. rom. 2. 24.*

6 Therefore my people shall know my Name : therefore *they shall know* in that day, that I *am* he that doth speake. Behold, *it is* I.

* *Nahum. 1. 15. rom. 10. 15.*

7 ¶ * How beautifull vpon the mountaines are the feete of him that bringeth good tidings, that publisheth peace, that bringeth good tidings of good, that publisheth saluation, that sayth vnto Zion, Thy God reigneth?

8 Thy watchmen shall lift vp the voice, with the voice together shall they sing : for they shall see eye to eye when the LORD shall bring againe Zion.

9 ¶ Breake foorth into ioy, sing together, yee waste places of Ierusalem : for the LORD hath comforted his people, he hath redeemed Ierusalem.

10 The LORD hath made bare his holy arme in the eyes of all the nations, and *all the endes of the earth shall see the saluation of our God.

* *Psal. 92. 8. luke 3. 6.*

11 ¶ Depart ye, depart ye, goe ye out from thence, * touch no vncleane thing ; goe ye out of the middest of her ; be yee cleane, that beare the vessels of the LORD.

* *2. Cor. 6. 17. reuel. 18. 4.*

12 For ye shall not go out with haste, nor goe by flight : for the LORD will goe before you : and the God of Israel *will* † *be* your rereward.

† *Heb. gather you vp.* ‖ *Or, prosper.*

13 ¶ Behold, my seruant shal ‖ deale prudently, he shall be exalted and extolled, and be very high.

14 As many were astonied at thee (his * visage was so marred more then any man, and his forme more then the sonnes of men :)

* *Cha. 53. 3.*

15 So shall hee sprinckle many nations, the kings shall shut their mouthes at him : for that * which had not beene told them, shall they see, and that which they had not heard, shall they consider.

* *Rom. 15. 21.*

CHAP. LIII.

1 The Prophet complaining of incredulitie, excuseth the scandall of the crosse, 4 by the benefite of his passion, 10 and the good successe thereof.

WHo *hath beleeued our ‖ report? and to whom is the arme of the LORD reuealed?

* *Ioh. 12. 38. rom. 10. 16.* ‖ *Or, doctrine: Heb. hearing.*

2 For he shall grow vp before him as a tender plant, and as a root out of a drie ground : hee hath no forme nor comelinesse : and when wee shall see him, there is no beautie that we should desire him.

3 * He is despised and reiected of men, a man of sorrows, and acquainted with griefe : and ‖ we hid as it were our faces from him ; hee was despised, and wee esteemed him not.

* *Chap. 32. 14. mar. 9. 12.* ‖ *Or, he hid as it were his face from vs. Heb. as a hiding of faces from him or from vs.* * *Mat. 8. 18.*

4 ¶ Surely *he hath borne out griefes,

griefes, and caried our sorrowes: yet
we did esteeme him striken, smitten of
God, and afflicted.

‖ Or, tormented.
* Rom. 4. 25. 1. cor. 15. 3.
* 1. Pet. 2. 24.
† Heb. bruise.

5 But he was ‖ * wounded for our
transgressions, he was bruised for our
iniquities: the chastisement of our peace
was vpon him, and with his * † stripes we
are healed.
6 All we like sheepe haue gone
astray: we haue turned euery one to his
owne way, and the LORD hath † layd
on him the iniquitie of vs all.

† Heb. hee hath made the iniquitie of vs all to meete on him.
* Matth. 26. 63. and 27. 12. mar. 14. 61. and 15. 5.
* Actes 8. 32.

7 He was oppressed, and he was
afflicted, yet * he opened not his mouth:
he is brought as a * lambe to the slaughter, and as a sheepe before her shearers
is dumme, so he openeth not his mouth.

‖ Or, he was taken away by distresse and iudgement: but &c.
† Heb. was the stroke vpon him.
† Heb. deathes.
* 1. Pet. 2. 22. 1. ioh. 3. 5.

8 ‖ He was taken from prison, and
from iudgement: and who shall declare
his generation? for he was cut off out
of the land of the liuing, for the transgression of my people † was he stricken.
9 And he made his graue with the
wicked, and with the rich in his † death,
because he had done no violence, neither
was any * deceit in his mouth.

‖ Or, when his soule shall make an offring.

10 ¶ Yet it pleased the LORD to
bruise him, he hath put *him* to griefe:
‖ when thou shalt make his soule an offring for sinne, he shall see *his* seede, hee
shall prolong *his* daies, and the pleasure
of the LORD shall prosper in his
hand.
11 He shall see of the trauell of his
soule, *and* shalbe satisfied: by his knowledge shall my righteous seruant iustifie
many: for hee shall beare their iniquities.

* Mar. 15. 28. luc. 22. 37.
* Luc. 23. 8.

12 Therefore will I diuide him *a
portion* with the great, and he shall diuide the spoile with the strong: because
hee hath powred out his soule vnto
death: and he was * numbred with the
transgressours, and he bare the sinne of
many, and * made intercession for the
transgressours.

CHAP. LIIII.

1 The Prophet for the comfort of the Gentiles, prophesieth the amplitude of their Church. 4 Their safety, 6 their certaine deliuerance out of affliction, 11 their faire edification, 15 and their sure preseruation.

* Gal. 4. 27.

Sing * O barren thou *that*
didst not beare; breake
forth into singing, and crie
aloud thou *that* didst not
trauell with child: for
more *are* the children of the desolate then
the children of the maried wife, saith the
LORD.
2 Enlarge the place of thy tent, and
let them stretch forth the curtaines of
thine habitations: spare not, lengthen
thy cords, and strengthen thy stakes.
3 For thou shalt breake forth on the
right hand, and on the left; and thy seed
shall inherite the Gentiles, and make
the desolate cities to be inhabited.
4 Feare not: for thou shalt not be
ashamed: neither be thou confounded,
for thou shalt not be put to shame: for
thou shalt forget the shame of thy
youth, and shalt not remember the reproach of thy widowhood any more.

* Luc. 1. 32.

5 For thy maker *is* thine husband,
(the * LORD of hostes *is* his name;)
and thy redeemer the holy one of Israel, the God of the whole earth shall he
be called.
6 For the LORD hath called thee
as a woman forsaken, and grieued in
spirit, and a wife of youth, when thou
wast refused, saith thy God.
7 For a small moment haue I forsaken thee, but with great mercies will
I gather thee.
8 In a litle wrath I hid my face
from thee, for a moment; but with euerlasting kindnesse will I haue mercie on
thee, saith the LORD thy redeemer.

* Gen. 9. 11.

9 For this *is as* the waters of * Noah
vnto me: for *as* I haue sworne that the
waters of Noah should no more goe
ouer the earth; so haue I sworne that
I would not be wroth with thee, nor
rebuke thee.
10 For the mountaines shall depart,
and the hilles be remoued, but my kindnesse shall not depart from thee, neither
shall the couenant of my peace be remoued, saith the LORD, that hath mercie on thee.

* 1. Chron. 29. 2.

11 ¶ Oh thou afflicted, tossed with
tempest *and* not comforted, behold,
I will lay thy stones with * faire colours, and lay thy foundations with
Saphires.
12 And I will make thy windowes
of Agates, and thy gates of Carbun-
cles, and all thy borders of pleasant
stones.

* Ioh. 6. 45.

13 And all thy children shalbe * taught
of the LORD, and great *shalbe* the
peace of thy children.
14 In righteousnesse shalt thou be
established: thou shalt be farre from oppression, for thou shalt not feare; & from
terrour,

terrour, for it shall not come neere thee.

15 Behold, they shall surely gather together, *but* not by me: whosoeuer shal gather together against thee, shall fall for thy sake.

16 Behold, I haue created the smith that bloweth the coales in the fire, and that bringeth foorth an instrument for his worke, aud I haue created the waster to destroy.

17 ¶ No weapon that is formed against thee, shall prosper, and euery tongue *that* shall rise against thee in iudgement, thou shalt condemne. This is the heritage of the seruants of the LORD, and their righteousnesse *is* of me, saith the LORD.

CHAP. LV.

1 The Prophet, with the promises of Christ, calleth to faith, 6 and to repentance. 8 The happy successe of them that beleeue.

 *O, euery one that thirsteth, come ye to the waters, and he that hath no money : come ye, buy and eate, yea come, buy wine and milke without money, and without price.

2 Wherefore doe yee †spend money for that which is not bread ? and your labour for that which satisfieth not ? hearken diligently vnto me, and eate ye that which is good, and let your soule delight it selfe in fatnesse.

3 Incline your eare, and come vnto me: heare, and your soule shall liue, and I will make an euerlasting couenant with you, *euen* the *sure mercies of Dauid.

4 Behold, I haue giuen him for a witnesse to the people, a leader and commander to the people.

5 Behold, thou shalt call a nation *that* thou knowest not, and nations *that* knew not thee, shall runne vnto thee, because of the LORD thy God, and for the Holy One of Israel, for he hath glorified thee.

6 ¶ Seeke ye the LORD, while he may be found, call ye vpon him while he is neere.

7 Let the wicked forsake his way, & the †vnrighteous man his thoughts: and let him returne vnto the LORD, and he will haue mercie vpon him, and to our God, for hee will † abundantly pardon.

8 ¶ For my thoughts *are* not your thoughts, neither *are* your wayes my wayes, saith the LORD.

9 For *as* the heauens are higher then the earth, so are my wayes higher then your wayes, and my thoughts then your thouhts.

10 For as the raine commeth down, and the snow from heauen, and returneth not thither, but watereth the earth, and maketh it bring foorth and bud, that it may giue seed to the sower, and bread to the eater :

11 So shall my word bee that goeth forth out of my mouth : it shall not returne vnto me void, but it shall accomplish that which I please, and it shall prosper *in* the thing whereto I sent it.

12 For ye shall goe out with ioy, and bee led foorth with peace : the mountaines and the hilles shall *breake forth before you into singing, and al the trees of the field shall clap *their* hands.

13 In stead of the thorne shall come vp the Firre tree, and in stead of the brier shall come vp the Myrtle tree, and it shall be to the LORD for a name, for an euerlasting signe *that* shall not bee cut off.

CHAP. LVI.

1 The Prophet exhorteth to sanctification. 3 He promiseth it shall be generall without respect of persons. 9 He inueyeth against blinde watchmen.

Hus saith the LORD, Keepe yee ‖iudgement, and doe iustice : for my saluation *is* neere to come, and my righteousnesse to bee reuealed.

2 Blessed *is* the man *that* doeth this, and the sonne of man *that* layeth holde on it : that keepeth the Sabbath from polluting it, and keepeth his hand from doing any euill.

3 ¶ Neither let the sonne of the stranger, that hath ioyned himselfe to the LORD, speake, saying, The LORD hath vtterly separated mee from his people : neither let the Eunuch say, Behold, I *am* a drie tree.

4 For thus saith the LORD vnto the Eunuches that keep my Sabbaths, and choose the things that please mee, and take hold of my couenant :

5 Euen vnto them will I giue in mine house, and within my walles, a place and a name better then of sonnes and of daughters: I wil giue them an euer-

Margin notes (left column)
* Ioh. 7. 37.

Heb. weigh

* Acts 13. 44.

* Hebr. the man of iniquitie.

* Heb. he wil multiplie to pardon.

Margin notes (right column)
* Cha. 35. 1

‖ Or, equity.

uerlasting name, that shal not be cut off.

6 Also the sonnes of the stranger that ioyne themselues to the LORD, to serue him, and to loue the Name of the LORD, to be his seruants, euery one that keepeth the Sabbath from polluting it, and taketh hold of my Couenant :

7 Euen them will I *bring to my holy mountaine, and make them ioyfull in my house of prayer : their burnt offerings and their sacrifices *shall be* accepted vpon mine Altar: for mine house shalbe called *an house of prayer for all people.

8 The Lord GOD which gathereth the outcasts of Israel, saith, Yet will I gather *others* to him, †besides those that are gathered vnto him.

9 ¶ All ye beasts of the field, come to deuoure, *yea* all ye beasts in the forest.

10 His watchmen *are* blinde : they *are* all ignorant, they *are* all dumbe dogs, they cannot barke ; ‖ sleeping, lying downe, louing to slumber.

11 Yea they *are*† greedy dogges *which* †can neuer haue ynough, and they *are* shepheards *that* cannot vnderstand : they all looke to their owne way, euery one for his gaine, from his quarter.

12 Come ye, *say they*, I wil fetch wine, and we will fill our selues with strong drinke, and to morrow shal be as this day, *and* much more abundant.

CHAP. LVII.

1 The blessed death of the righteous. 3 God reproueth the Iewes for their whorish idolatry. 13 Hee giueth Euangelicall promises to the penitent.

HE righteous perisheth, and no man layeth it to heart ; and †*mercifull men are taken away, none considering that the righteous is taken away ‖from the euill *to come.*

2 Hee shall ‖enter *into* peace : they shall rest in their beds, each one walking ‖*in* his vprightnesse.

3 ¶ But draw neere hither, yee sonnes of the sorceresse, the seed of the adulterer, and the whore.

4 Against whom doe ye sport your selues ? against whom make ye a wide mouth, *and* draw out the tongue ? *are* ye not children of transgression, a seede of falshood ?

5 Inflaming your selues ‖with idoles *vnder euery greene tree , slaying the children in the valleys vnder the cliftes of the rockes ?

6 Among the smooth stones of the streame is thy portion ; they , they *are* thy lot : euen to them hast thou powred a drinke offering, thou hast offered a meate offering. Should I receiue comfort in these ?

7 Vpon a loftie and high mountaine hast thou set thy bed : euen thither wentest thou vp to offer sacrifice.

8 Behinde the doores also and the posts hast thou set vp thy remembrance : for thou hast discouered thy selfe *to an other* then mee, and art gone vp: thou hast enlarged thy bed, and ‖made a couenant with them : thou louedst their bed ‖where thou sawest it.

9 And ‖thou wentest to the king with oyntment , and didst increase thy perfumes , and didst send thy messengers farre off, and didst debase thy selfe euen vnto hell.

10 Thou art wearied in the greatnesse of thy way ; *yet* saydst thou not, There is no hope : thou hast found the ‖life of thine hand; therefore thou wast not grieued.

11 And of whom hast thou bene afraid or feared, that thou hast lyed, and hast not remembred me, nor layed *it* to thy heart ? haue not I held my peace euen of old, and thou fearest me not ?

12 I will declare thy righteousnes ; and thy workes, for they shall not profit thee.

13 ¶ When thou criest, let thy companies deliuer thee : but the winde shall cary them all away ; Vanitie shall take *them :* but hee that putteth his trust in me, shall possesse the land, and shall inherit my holy mountaine,

14 And shall say, *Cast yee vp, cast yee vp ; prepare the way, take vp the stumbling blocke out of the way of my people.

15 For thus saith the High and loftie One that inhabiteth eternitie, whose Name *is* Holy ; I dwell in the high and holy *place :* with him also that is of a contrite and humble spirit , to reuiue the spirit of the humble, and to reuiue the heart of the contrite ones.

16 For I will not contend for euer, neither will I be alwayes wroth : for the spirit should faile before me, and the soules *which* I haue made.

17 For the iniquitie of his couetousnesse

Marginal notes (left column):

* Chap. 2. 2.

* Matth. 21. 13. mar. 11. 17 luke 19. 46.

† Hebr. to his gathered.

‖ Or, dreaming or talking in their sleepe.
† Heb. strong of appetite.
† Heb. Know not to be satisfied.

† Hebr. men of kindnesse or godlinesse.
* Psal. 12. 2. mich. 7. 2.
‖ Or, from that which is euill.
‖ Or, goe in peace.
‖ Or, before him.

‖ Or, among the okes.

Marginal notes (right column):

* 1. Kin. 16. 4.

‖ Or, hewe it for thy selfe larger then theirs
‖ Or, thou prouidedst roome.
‖ Or, thou ſpectedſt t King.

‖ Or, liuing

* Chap. 3. and 62. 10.

nesse was I wroth, and smote him : I hid me, and was wroth, and hee went on † frowardly in the way of his heart.

18 I haue seene his wayes, and will heale him : I will leade him also, and restore comforts vnto him, and to his mourners.

19 I create the fruite of the lippes; peace, peace to him that is farre off, and to him that is neere, sayth the Lord, and I will heale him.

20 But the wicked *are* like the troubled sea, when it cannot rest, whose waters cast vp myre and dirt.

21 * *There is* no peace, sayth my God, to the wicked.

CHAP. LVIII.

1 The Prophet being sent to reproue hypocrisie, 3 expresseth a counterfeit fast, and a true. 8 He declareth what promises are due vnto godlinesse, 13 and to the keeping of the Sabbath.

RIe †aloude, spare not, lift vp thy voice like a trumpet, and shewe my people their transgression, & the house of Iacob their sins.

2 Yet they seeke mee daily, and delight to know my wayes, as a nation that did righteousnesse, and forsooke not the ordinance of their God : they aske of me the ordinances of iustice : they take delight in approching to God.

3 ¶ Wherefore haue wee fasted, *say they*, and thou seest not? *wherefore* haue wee afflicted our soule, & thou takest no knowledge ? Behold, in the day of your fast you find pleasure, and exact all your ‖ labours.

4 Behold, yee fast for strife and debate ; and to smite with the fist of wickednesse, ‖yee shall not fast as *yee doe* this day, to make your voice to be heard on high.

5 Is it * such a fast *that* I haue chosen? a * ‖day for a man to afflict his soule? *Is it* to bow down his head as a bulrush, and to spread sackecloth and ashes vnder him ? wilt thou call this a fast, and an acceptable day to the Lord ?

6 Is not this the fast that I haue chosen ? to loose the bandes of wickednesse, to vndoe † the heauie burdens, and to let the †oppressed goe free, and that ye breake euery yoke ?

7 Is it not, to * deale thy bread to the hungry, and that thou bring the poore that are ‖ cast out, to thy house? when thou seest the naked, that thou couer him, and that thou hide not thy selfe from thine owne flesh ?

8 ¶ Then shall thy light breake foorth as the morning, and thine health shall spring foorth speedily : and thy righteousnesse shall goe before thee, the glory of the Lord †shall be thy rereward.

9 Then shalt thou call, and the Lord shall answere ; thou shalt cry, and he shal say, Here I *am*: if thou take away from the midst of thee the yoke, the putting forth of the finger, and speaking vanitie :

10 And *if* thou draw out thy soule to the hungry, and satisfie the afflicted soule : then shall thy light rise in obscuritie, and thy darkenesse be as the noone day.

11 And the Lord shal guide thee continually, and satisfie thy soule in †drought, and make fat thy bones : and thou shalt be like a watered garden, and like a spring of water, whose waters †faile not.

12 And *they that shall be* of thee, * shall builde the olde waste places : thou shalt raise vp the foundations of many generations ; and thou shalt be called, the repairer of the breach, the restorer of paths to dwell in.

13 ¶ If thou turne away thy foote from the Sabbath, *from* doing thy pleasure on my Holy day, and call the Sabbath a delight, the holy of the Lord, honourable, and shalt honour him, not doing thine owne wayes, nor finding thine owne pleasure, nor speaking *thine owne* wordes :

14 Then shalt thou delight thy selfe in the Lord, and I will cause thee to * ride vpon the high places of the earth, and feede thee with the heritage of Iacob thy father ; for the mouth of the Lord hath spoken *it*.

CHAP. LIX.

1 The damnable nature of sinne. 3 The sinnes of the Iewes. 9 Calamitie is for sinne. 16 Saluation is onely of God. 20 The couenant of the Redeemer.

Eholde, the Lords hand is not * shortened, that it cannot saue: neither his eare heauie, that it cannot heare.

2 But

Marginal notes

† Hebr. turning away.

* Chap. 48. 12.

† Heb. with the throat.

‖ Or, things wherewith ye grieue others. Heb. griefes.
‖ Or, ye fast not as this day.
* Zech. 7. 5.
* Leuit. 16. 29.
† Or, to afflict his soule for a day?

† Heb. the bundles of the yoke.
† Heb. broken.
* Eze. 18. 8.

‖ Or, afflicted.

† Heb. shall gather thee vp.

† Hebr. droughts.

† Heb. lye, or deceiue.
* Cha. 61. 6.

* Deut. 32. 13.

* Num. 11. 23. chap. 50. 2.

2 But your iniquities haue separated betweene you and your God, and your sinnes ||haue hid *his* face from you, that he will not heare.

|| Or, haue made him hide.
* Chap. 1. 15.

3 For * your hands are defiled with blood, and your fingers with iniquitie, your lippes haue spoken lies, your tongue hath muttered peruersnesse.

4 None calleth for iustice, nor any pleadeth for trueth : they trust in vanity and speake lies; *they conceiue mischiefe, and bring forth iniquitie.

* Iob. 15. 35. psal. 7. 15.
|| Or, adders.

5 They hatch ||cockatrice egges, and weaue the spiders web : he that eateth of their egges dieth, and ||that which is crushed breaketh out into a viper.

|| Or, that which is sprinkled is as if there brake out a viper.
* Iob. 8. 14, 15.

6 *Their webbes shall not become garments, neither shall they couer themselues with their workes : their workes *are* workes of iniquitie, and the act of violence *is* in their hands.

* Prou. 1. 16 rom. 3. 15.

7 *Their feete runne to euill, and they make haste to shed innocent blood: their thoughts *are* thoughts of iniquity, wasting & †destruction *are* in their paths.

† Heb. breaking.
|| Or, right.

8 The way of peace they know not, and *there is* no ||iudgement in their goings : they haue made them crooked pathes ; whosoeuer goeth therein, shall not know peace.

9 ¶ Therefore is iudgement farre from vs, neither doth iustice ouertake vs : we waite for light, but behold obscuritie, for brightnesse, *but* we walke in darknesse.

10 We grope for the wall like the blind, and we grope as if we had no eies : we stumble at noone day as in the night, *we are* in desolate places as dead men.

11 We roare all like beares, and mourne sore like doues : we looke for iudgement, but *there is* none ; for saluation, *but* it is farre off from vs.

12 For our transgressions are multiplied before thee, and our sinnes testifie against vs for our transgressions *are* with vs, and as for our iniquities, we know them.

13 In transgressing and lying against the LORD, and departing away from our God, speaking oppression and reuolt, conceiuing and vttering from the heart words of falshood.

14 And iudgement is turned away backward, and iustice standeth a farre off : for truth is fallen in the streete, and equitie cannot enter.

15 Yea truth faileth, and he that departeth from euill ||maketh himselfe a pray : and the LORD saw it, and †it displeased him, that *there was* no iudgement.

|| Or, is accounted mad
† Heb. it was euill in his eyes.

16 ¶ And hee saw that *there was* no man, and wondered that *there was* no intercessour. *Therefore his arme brought saluation vnto him, and his righteousnesse, it sustained him.

* Chap. 63. 5.

17 For he put on * righteousnesse as a brestplate, and an helmet of saluation vpon his head; and he put on the garments of vengeance *for* clothing, and was clad with zeale as a cloake.

* Ephes 6. 17. 1. thes. 5. 8.

18 According to *their †deedes accordingly he will repay, furie to his aduersaries, recompence to his enemies; to the ylands he will repay recompence.

* Chap. 63. 7.
† Heb. recompenses.

19 So shall they feare the name of the LORD from the West, and his glory from the rising of the sunne : when the enemie shall come in * like a flood, the spirit of the LORD shall ||lift vp a standard against him

* Reu. 12. 15.
|| Or, put him to flight

20 ¶ And the *redeemer shall come to Zion, and vnto them that turne from transgression in Iacob, saith the LORD.

* Rom. 11. 26.

21 As for me, this *is* my couenant with them, saith the LORD; My spirit that *is* vpon thee, and my words which I haue put in thy mouth, shall not depart out of thy mouth, nor out of the mouth of the seede, nor out of the mouth of thy seedes seed, saith the LORD, from henceforth, and for euer.

CHAP. LX.

1 The glory of the Church, in the abundant accesse of the Gentiles, 15 and the great blessings after a short affliction.

Rise, ||shine, for thy light is come, and the glory of the LORD is risen vpon thee.

|| Or, be enlightened : for thy light commeth.

2 For behold, the darknesse shall couer the earth, and grosse darknesse the people : but the LORD shall arise vpon thee, and his glory shall be seene vpon thee.

3 And the * Gentiles shall come to thy light, and kings to the brightnesse of thy rising.

* Reu. 21. 24.

4 *Lift vp thine eyes round about, and see : all they gather themselues together, they come to thee : thy sonnes shall come from farre, and thy daughters shalbe nourced at *thy* side.

* Chap. 49. 18.

5 Then

5 Then thou shalt see, and flow together, and thine heart shall feare and be inlarged, because the ||abundance of the Sea shalbe conuerted vnto thee, the ||forces of the Gentiles shall come vnto thee.

Or, noise of the Sea shalbe turned toward thee.
Or, wealth

6 The multitude of camels shall couer thee, the dromedaries of Midian and Ephah : all they from Sheba shall come : they shal bring * gold and incense, and they shall shew forth the praises of the LORD.

* Chap. 61.

7 All the flockes of Kedar shall be gathered together vnto thee, the rams of Nebaioth shall minister vnto thee : they shall come vp with acceptance on mine altar, and I wil glorifie the house of my glory.

8 Who *are* these that flie as a cloude, and as the doues to their windowes ?

9 Surely the yles shall wait for me, and the ships of Tarshish first, * to bring thy sonnes from farre, their siluer and their gold with them, vnto the Name of the LORD thy God, and to the Holy One of Israel, because he hath glorified thee.

* Gen. 4. 26

10 And the sonnes of strangers shall build vp thy walles, and their kings shal minister vnto thee : for in my wrath I smote thee, but in my fauour haue I had mercie on thee.

11 Therefore thy gates * shal be open continually, they shall not bee shut day nor night, that *men* may bring vnto thee the || forces of the Gentiles, and that their kings may be brought.

* Reue. 21. 25.
* Or, wealth

12 For the nation and kingdome that will not serue thee, shall perish, yea those nations shall be vtterly wasted.

13 The glory of Lebanon shal come vnto thee, the Firre tree, the Pine tree, and the Boxe together, to beautifie the place of my Sanctuarie, and I will make the place of my feete glorious

14 The sonnes also of them that afflicted thee, shall come bending vnto thee : and all they that despised thee shal * bow themselues downe at the soles of thy feet, and they shall call thee the citie of the LORD, the Zion of the Holy One of Israel.

* Reue. 3. 9.

15 Whereas thou hast bene forsaken and hated, so that no man went thorow *thee*, I will make thee an eternall excellencie, a ioy of many generations.

16 Thou shalt also sucke the milke of the Gentiles, and shalt sucke the brest of kings, and thou shalt know that I the LORD *am* thy Sauiour and thy Redeemer, the mightie One of Iacob.

17 For brasse I will bring gold, and for yron I will bring siluer, and for wood brasse, and for stones yron : I will also make thy officers peace, and thine exactours righteousnesse.

18 Violence shall no more be heard in thy land, wasting nor destruction within thy borders, but thou shalt call thy walles saluation, and thy gates praise.

19 * The Sunne shall be no more thy light by day, neither for brightnesse shall the moone giue light vnto thee : but the LORD shall be vnto thee an euerlasting light, & thy God thy glory.

* Reue. 21, 22. & 22. 5.

20 Thy Sunne shall no more goe downe, neither shall thy moone withdraw it selfe : for the LORD shall bee thine euerlasting light, and the dayes of thy mourning shall be ended.

21 Thy people also *shall be* all righteous : they shal inherit the land for euer, the branch of my planting, the worke of my hands, that I may be glorified.

22 A litle one shall become a thousand, and a small one a strong nation : I the LORD will hasten it in his time.

CHAP. LXI.

1 The Office of Christ. 4 The forwardnesse, 7 and blessings of the faithfull.

He * Spirit of the Lord GOD *is* vpon me, because the LORD hath anointed me, to preach good tidings vnto the meeke, hee hath sent me to binde vp the broken hearted, to proclaime libertie to the captiues, and the opening of the prison to them that are bound :

* Luk. 4. 18

2 To proclaime the acceptable yere of the LORD, and the day of vengeance of our God, to comfort all that mourne :

3 To appoint vnto them that mourne in Zion, to giue vnto them beautie for ashes, the oyle of ioy for mourning, the garment of praise for the spirit of heauinesse, that they might be called trees of righteousnesse, the planting of the LORD, that he might be glorified.

4 ¶ And they shall * build the olde wastes, they shall raise vp the former desolations, and they shall repaire the waste cities, the desolations of many generations.

* Chap. 58. 12.

5 And strangers shall stand and feed

feed your flockes, and the sonnes of the alient shalbe your plowmen, and your Vine-dressers.

6 But ye shalbe named the Priests of the LORD: men shall call you the ministers of our God: *ye shall eat the riches of the Gentiles, and in their glory shall you boast your selues.

*Chap. 60. 6.

7 ¶ For your shame *you shall haue* double; and for confusion they shall reioyce in their portion: therefore in their land they shal possesse the double: euerlasting ioy shalbe vnto them

8 For I the LORD loue Iudgement, I hate robbery for burnt offering, and I will direct their worke in trueth, and I will make an euerlasting Couenant with them.

9 And their seed shalbe knowen among the Gentiles, and their offspring among the people: All that see them, shall acknowledge them, that they are the seed *which* the LORD hath blessed.

10 I will greatly reioyce in the LORD, my soule shalbe ioyfull in my God: for he hath clothed me with the garments of saluation, he hath couered me with the robe of righteousnes, as a bridegrome †decketh himselfe with ornaments, and as a bride adorneth herselfe with her iewels.

† Heb. decketh as a priest.

11 For as the earth bringeth foorth her bud, and as the garden causeth the things that are sowen in it, to spring foorth: so the Lord GOD will cause righteousnes and praise to spring forth before all the nations.

CHAP. LXII.

1 The feruent desire of the Prophet, to confirme the Church in Gods promises. 5 The office of the Ministers, (vnto which they are incited) in preaching the Gospel, 10 and preparing the people thereto.

Or Zions sake, wil I not hold my peace, and for Ierusalems sake I will not rest, vntill the righteousnesse thereof goe forth as brightnesse, and the saluation thereof as a lampe *that* burneth;

2 And the Gentiles shall see thy righteousnes, and all Kings thy glory: and thou shalt be called by a new name, which the mouth of the LORD shall name.

3 Thou shalt also be a crowne of glory in the hand of the LORD, and a royall diademe in the hand of thy God.

4 Thou shalt no more bee termed, *Forsaken; neither shall thy land any more be termed, Desolate: but thou shalt be called ‖ Hephzi-bah, and thy land, ‖Beulah: for the LORD delighteth in thee, and thy land shalbe maried.

* Ose. 1.
1. pet. 2.
‖ That is, delight is in her.
‖ That is, married.

5 ¶ For *as* a yong man marrieth a virgine, *so* shall thy sonnes marry thee: and †*as* the bridegrome reioyceth ouer the bride, *so* shall thy God reioyce ouer thee.

† Hebr. v the ioy of the bridegrom

6 I haue set watchmen vpon thy walles, O Ierusalem, which shall neuer hold their peace day nor night: ‖ye that make mention of the LORD, keepe not silence;

‖ Or, ye th are the Lor remembra cers.

7 And giue him no †rest till he establish, and till hee make Ierusalem a praise in the earth.

† Hebr. silence.

8 The LORD hath sworne by his Right hand, and by the arme of his strength, †Surely, I will no more giue thy corne to be meat for thine enemies, and the sonnes of the stranger shall not drinke thy wine, for the which thou hast laboured:

† Hebr. if giue, &c.

9 But they that haue gathered it shall eat it, and praise the LORD, and they that haue brought it together, shal drinke it in the Courts of my Holinesse.

10 ¶ *Goe through, goe through the gates: prepare you the way of the people: cast vp, cast vp the high way, gather out the stones, lift vp a standard for the people.

*Chap. 40
3. & 57. 1

11 Behold, the LORD hath proclaimed vnto the end of the world, *say ye to the daughter of Zion, Behold, thy saluation commeth; behold, his *reward *is* with him, and his ‖worke before him.

* Zach. 9.
matth. 21
5. iohn 12
15.
*Chap. 40
10.
‖ Or, reco
pence.

12 And they shall call them, The holy people: the redeemed of the LORD: and thou shalt be called, Sought out, a citie not forsaken.

CHAP. LXIII.

1 Christ sheweth who he is, 2 what his victory ouer his enemies, 7 and what his mercy toward his Church. 10 In his iust wrath hee remembreth his free Mercy. 15 The Church in their prayer, 17 and complaint, professe their Faith.

Ho *is* this that commeth from Edom, with died garments from Bozrah? this that is †glorious in his apparell,

† Hebr. decked.

parel, trauelling in the greatnesse of his strength? I that speake in righteousnesse, mightie to saue.

2 Wherefore * art thou red in thine apparell, and thy garments like him that treadeth in the winefat?

3 I haue troden the winepresse alone, and of the people *there was* none with me: for I will tread them in mine anger, and trample them in my furie, and their blood shall be sprinkled vpon my garments, and I will staine all my raiment.

4 For the * day of vengeance *is* in mine heart, and the yeere of my redeemed is come.

5 And I looked, and *there was* none to helpe; and I wondered that *there was* none to vphold: therefore mine owne * arme brought saluation vnto me, and my furie, it vpheld me.

6 And I will tread downe the people in mine anger, & make them drunke in my furie, and I will bring downe their strength to the earth.

7 ¶ I will mention the louing kindnesses of the LORD, *and* the praises of the LORD, according to all that the LORD hath bestowed on vs; and the great goodnes towards the house of Israel, which he hath bestowed on them, according to his mercies, and according to the multitude of his louing kindnesses.

8 For hee said, Surely they *are* my people, children *that* will not lie: so hee was their sauiour.

9 In all their affliction he was afflicted, and the Angel of his presence saued them: *in his loue and in his pitie hee redeemed them, and he bare them, and caried them all the dayes of olde.

10 ¶ But they * rebelled, and vexed his holy spirit: therefore hee was turned to be their enemie, *and* he fought against them.

11 Then he remembred the dayes of old, Moses *and his* people, *saying;* Where *is hee* that * brought them vp out of the Sea, with the ||shepheard of his flocke? where *is hee* that put his holy Spirit within him?

12 That led *them* by the right hand of Moses with his glorious arme, *diuiding the water before them, to make himselfe an euerlasting name?

13 That led them through the deepe as an horse in the wildernesse, *that* they should not stumble?

14 As a beast goeth downe into the valley, the Spirit of the LORD caused him to rest: so diddest thou leade thy people, to make thy selfe a glorious Name.

15 ¶ * Looke downe from heauen, and behold from the habitation of thy holinesse, and of thy glory: where *is* thy zeale and thy strength, || the sounding of thy bowels, and of thy mercies towards me? are they restrained?

16 Doubtlesse thou art our father, though Abraham be ignorant of vs, and Israel acknowledge vs not: thou, O LORD art our Father, ||our Redeemer, thy Name *is* from euerlasting.

17 ¶ O LORD, why hast thou made vs to erre from thy wayes? *and* hardened our heart from thy feare? Returne for thy seruants sake, the tribes of thine inheritance.

18 The people of thy holinesse haue possessed *it* but a little while: our aduersaries haue troden downe thy Sanctuarie.

19 Wee are *thine,* thou neuer barest rule ouer them, †they were not called by thy Name.

CHAP. LXIIII.

1 The Church prayeth for the illustration of Gods power. 5 Celebrating Gods mercy, it maketh confession of their naturall corruptions. 9 It complaineth of their affliction.

H that thou wouldest rent the heauens, that thou wouldest come downe, that the mountaines might flowe downe at thy presence,

2 As *when* † the melting fire burneth, the fire causeth the waters to boyle: to make thy Name knowen to thine aduersaries, *that* the nations may tremble at thy presence.

3 When thou diddest terrible things *which* wee looked not for, thou camest downe, the mountaines flowed downe at thy presence.

4 For since the beginning of the world * men haue not heard, nor perceiued by the eare, neither hath the eye ||seene, O God, besides thee, *what* hee hath prepared for him that waiteth for him.

5 Thou meetest him that reioyceth, and worketh righteousnesse, *those that* remember thee in thy wayes: behold, thou art wroth, for we haue sinned: in those

---

Left margin notes:

Ieu. 19.

hap. 34.

hap. 59.

Deut. 7. 8.

Exod. 15. num. 14. psal. 78. , and 9.

Exod. 14. *Or, shepards, as al. 77. 21.*

Exod. 14. iosh. . 16.

Right margin notes:

* Deut. 26. 15.

|| *Or, the multitude.*

|| *Or, our redeemer, From euerlasting is thy name,*

† *Heb. thy name was not called vpon them.*

† *Heb. the fire of meltings.*

* 1. Cor. 2. 9. psal. 31. 20. || *Or, seene a God besides thee which doeth so for him, &c.*

those is continuance, and we shall be saued.

6 But we are al as an vncleane thing, and all our righteousnesses are as filthy ragges, and we all doe * fade as a leafe, and our iniquities like the wind haue taken vs away.

† Heb. melted.

7 And there is none that calleth vpon thy name, that stirreth vp himselfe to take hold of thee : for thou hast hid thy face from vs, and hast † consumed vs because of our iniquities.

* Psal. 50. 5, 6.

8 But now, O Lord, thou *art* our father : we are the clay, and thou our potter, and we all *are* the worke of thine hand.

* Psal. 79. 8.

9 ¶ Be not * wroth very sore, O Lord, neither remember iniquitie for euer : behold, see we beseech thee, we *are* all thy people.

10 Thy holy cities *are* a wildernesse, Zion is a wildernesse, Ierusalem a desolation.

11 Our holy and our beautifull house, where our fathers praised thee, is burnt vp with fire, and all our pleasant things are layed waste :

12 Wilt thou refraine thy selfe for these things, O Lord? wilt thou hold thy peace, and afflict vs very sore?

CHAP. LXV.

1 The calling of the Gentiles. 2 The Iewes, for their incredulity, idolatry and hypocrisie, are reiected. 8 A remnant shalbe saued. 11 Iudgements on the wicked, and blessings on the godly. 17 The blessed state of the new Ierusalem.

* Rom. 10. 20.
* Rom. 9. 24, 25, 26. eph. 2. 12.

 I * Am sought *of them that* asked not *for me :* I * am found *of them* that sought me not : I said, Behold me, behold me, vnto a nation *that* was not called by my name.

2 I haue spread out my hands all the day vnto a rebellious people, which walketh in a way that *was* not good, after their owne thoughts :

3 A people that prouoketh mee to anger continually to my face, that sacrificeth in gardens, and burneth incense † vpon altars of bricke :

† Heb. vpon brickes.

4 Which remaine among the graues, and lodge in the monuments, which eate swines flesh, and ‖ broth of abominable things is in their vessels :

‖ Or, pieces.

5 Which say ; Stand by thy selfe, come not neere to me ; for I am holier then thou : these *are* a smoke in my

‖ nose, a fire that burneth all the day.

‖ *Or, ange*

6 Behold, it is written before me : I will not keepe silence, but will recompence, euen recompence into their bosome,

7 Your iniquities, and the iniquities of your fathers together, (saith the Lord) which haue burnt incense vpon the mountaines, & blasphemed mee vpon the hils : therfore will I measure their former worke into their bosome.

8 ¶ Thus saith the Lord, As the new wine is found in the cluster, and one saith, Destroy it not, for a blessing *is* in it : so wil I doe for my seruants sakes, that I may not destroy them all.

9 And I will bring forth a seede out of Iacob, and out of Iudah an inheritour of my mountaines : and mine elect shall inherit it, and my seruants shall dwell there.

10 And Sharon shall be a fold of flockes, and the valley of Achor a place for the herds to lie downe in, for my people that haue sought me.

11 ¶ But yee *are* they that forsake the Lord, that forget my holy mountaine, that prepare a table for that ‖ troope, and that furnish the drinke offring vnto that ‖ number.

‖ *Or, Gad*
‖ *Or, Me*

12 Therefore will I number you to the sword, and yee shall all bow downe to the slaughter : * because when I called, yee did not answere ; when I spake, yee did not heare, * but did euill before mine eyes, and did choose that wherein I delighted not :

* Prou. 23. ier. 7. 13.
* Chap. 4.

13 Therefore thus saith the Lord God ; Behold, my seruants shall eate, but ye shall be hungry : behold, my seruants shall drinke, but yee shall be thirstie : behold, my seruants shall reioyce, but yee shall be ashamed.

14 Behold, my seruants shall sing for ioy of heart, but yee shall cry for sorrow of heart, and shall howle for † vexation of spirit.

† Heb. b king.

15 And yee shall leaue your name for a curse vnto my chosen : for the Lord God shall slay thee, and call his seruants by another name :

16 That he who blesseth himselfe in the earth, shall blesse himselfe in the God of trueth ; and he that sweareth in the earth, shall sweare by the God of trueth ; because the former troubles are forgotten, and because they are hid from mine eyes.

17 ¶ For behold, I create * new heauens

* Chap 22. 2. p 3. 13. r 21. 1.

Heb. come vp on the eart.

uens, and a new earth: & the former shal not be remembred, nor † come into mind.

18 But bee you glad and reioyce for euer *in that* which I create : for beholde, I create Ierusalem a reioycing, and her people a ioy.

Reu. 21. 4.

19 And I wil reioyce in Ierusalem, and ioy in my people, and the *voice of weeping shall be no more heard in her, nor the voice of crying.

20 There shalbe no more thence an infant of dayes, nor an olde man, that hath not filled his dayes : for the childe shall die an hundreth yeeres olde : but the sinner being an hundreth yeres old, shalbe accursed.

21 And they shall builde houses, and inhabite *them*, and they shall plant vineyards, and eate the fruit of them.

22 They shal not build, and another inhabit : they shall not plant, and another eat : for as the daies of a tree, *are the* dayes of my people, and mine elect † shal long enioy the worke of their hands.

Heb. shall make them continue ng, or shall weare out.

23 They shall not labour in vaine, nor bring forth for trouble : for they *are* the seede of the blessed of the LORD, and their offspring with them.

Psal. 32. 5.

24 And it shal come to passe, that * before they call, I will answere, & whiles they are yet speaking, I will heare.

Isai. 11. 7.

25 The *wolfe and the lambe shall feede together , and the lyon shall eate straw like the bullocke : and dust shalbe the serpents meat. They shall not hurt nor destroy in all my holy mountaine, sayth the LORD.

CHAP. LXVI.

1 The glorious God will be serued in humble sinceritie. 5 He comforteth the humble with the maruellous generation, 10 and with the gracious benefits of the Church. 15 Gods seuere iudgements against the wicked. 19 The Gentiles shall haue an holy Church, 24 and see the damnation of the wicked.

1. Kings 8. 7. 2. cor. 6. 8. actes 7. 9. and 7. 24.

Hus sayth the LORD, *The heauen *is* my throne, and the earth *is* my footestoole : where is the house that yee builde vnto mee? and where is the place of my rest?

2 For all those things hath mine hand made, and all those things haue beene , saith the LORD : but to this *man* wil I looke, *euen* to him *that is* poore and of a contrite spirit, and trembleth at my word.

3 He that killeth an oxe *is as if* he slue

a man : he that sacrificeth a ||lambe, *as if* he cut off a dogs necke : he that offereth an oblation, *as if he offered* swines blood : he that † burneth incense, *as if* he blessed an idole : yea, they haue chosen their owne wayes, and their soule delighteth in their abominations.

4 I also will chuse their ||delusions, and will bring their feares vpon them ; * because when I called , none did answere, when I spake they did not heare: but *they did euill before mine eyes, and chose that in which I delighted not.

5 ¶ Heare the word of the LORD, ye that tremble at his word : Your brethren that hated you, that cast you out for my Names sake , sayd , *Let the LORD be glorified : but he shal appeare to your ioy, and they shalbe ashamed.

6 A voice of noyse from the city, a voice from the Temple, a voice of the LORD, that rendreth recompense to his enemies.

7 Before she trauailed, she brought foorth : before her paine came, shee was deliuered of a man childe.

8 Who hath heard such a thing? who hath seene such things? shall the earth be made to bring forth in one day, *or* shall a nation be borne at once? for as soone as Zion traueiled, shee brought foorth her children.

9 Shall I ||bring to the birth, & not cause to bring forth, saith the LORD? shall I cause to bring foorth, and shut *the wombe*, sayth thy God?

10 Reioyce ye with Ierusalem, and be glad with her, all yee that loue her: reioyce for ioy with her, all yee that mourne for her :

11 That ye may sucke and be satisfied with the breasts of her consolations : that ye may milke out, and be delighted with the ||abundance of her glory.

12 For thus sayth the LORD, Behold, I will extend peace to her like a riuer, and the glory of the Gentiles like a flowing streame : then shall ye sucke, ye shalbe *borne vpon *her* sides, and be dandled vpon her knees.

13 As one whom his mother comforteth, so wil I comfort you : and ye shall be comforted in Ierusalem.

14 And when yee see *this*, your heart shall reioyce, and your bones shall flourish like an herbe : and the hand of the LORD shall be knowen towards his seruants, and *his* indignation towards his enemies.

|| Or, kidde.

† Heb. maketh amemoriall of.

|| Or, deuices.

** Pro. 1. 24. iere. 7. 13.*

** Chap. 65. 12.*

** Cha. 5. 13.*

|| Or, beget.

|| Or, brightnesse.

** Isai 49. 22. and 60. 4.*

15 For

15 For behold, the LORD wil come with fire, and with his charets like a whirlewinde, to render his anger with furie, and his rebuke with flames of fire.

16 For by fire and by his sword, will the LORD plead with all flesh : and the slaine of the LORD shalbe many.

17 They that sanctifie themselues, and purifie themselues in the gardens, || behinde one *tree* in the midst, eating swines flesh, and the abomination, and the mouse, shall be consumed together, saith the LORD.

|| Or, one after another.

18 For I *know* their works and their thoughts : it shall come that I will gather all nations and tongues, and they shall come and see my glorie.

19 And I will set a signe among them, and I will send those that escape of them vnto the nations, to Tarshish, Pul and Lud, that draw the bow, to Tubal and Iauan, to the Iles afarre off, that haue not heard my fame, neither haue seene my glory, and they shall declare my glory among the Gentiles.

20 And they shall bring all your bre-thren for an offering vnto the LORD, out of all nations, vpon horses and in charets, and in || litters, and vpon mules, and vpon swift beasts to my holie mountaine Ierusalem, saith the LORD; as the children of Israel bring an offering in a cleane vessell, into the house of the LORD.

|| Or, coache

21 And I will also take of them for * Priestes *and* for Leuites, saith the LORD.

* Exod. 19
6. chap. 61
6. 1. pet. 2
9. reuel. 1.
* Chap. 65
17. 2. Pet.
13. reuel.
21. I.

22 For as * the new heauens, and the new earth which I wil make, shall remaine before me, saith the LORD, so shall your seed and your name remaine.

23 And it shall come to passe, that † from one new Moone to an other, and from one Sabbath to an other, shall all flesh come to worship before me, saith the LORD.

† Heb. from new Moon to his new Moone, and from Sabbath to his Sabbath.

24 And they shall goe foorth, and looke vpon the carkeises of the men that haue transgressed against me : for their * worme shall not die, neither shall their fire be quenched, and they shall be an abhorring vnto all flesh.

* Marke 9. 44.

¶ THE BOOKE OF THE
Prophet Ieremiah.

CHAP. I.

1 The time, 3 and the calling of Ieremiah : 11 His propheticall visions of an Almond rod, and a seething pot: 15 His heauy message against Iudah. 17 God incourageth him with his promise of assistance.

He wordes of Ieremiah the sonne of Hilkiah, of the Priests that *were* in Anathoth in the land of Beniamin : 2 To whom the word of the LORD came in the dayes of Iosiah the sonne of Amon king of Iudah, in the thirteenth yeere of his reigne.

3 It came also in the dayes of Iehoiakim the sonne of Iosiah king of Iudah, vnto the ende of the eleuenth yeere of Zedekiah the sonne of Iosiah king of Iudah, vnto the carrying away of Ierusalem captiue in the fift moneth.

4 Then the word of the LORD came vnto me, saying,

5 Before I * formed thee in the bellie, I knew thee ; and before thou camest forth out of the wombe, I * sanctified thee, *and* I † ordeined thee a Prophet vnto the nations.

* Isa. 49. 1, 5.
* Gal. 5. 1. 15.
† Hebr. gau

6 Then said I, Ah * Lord GOD, behold, I cannot speake, for I *am* a childe.

* Exo. 3.

7 ¶ But

* Eze. 3. 9.

* Exo. 3. 12.
deut. 31. 6,
8. iosh. 1. 5.
heb. 13. 6.

* Isai. 6 7

* Cha. 5. 14.

* Cha. 18. 7.
2. cor. 10.
4, 5.

† Heb. from
the face of
the North.
* Chap. 4. 6.
† Heb. shall
be opened.

* Cha. 5. 15.
and 6. 22.
and 10. 22.

|| Or, breake
to pieces.

* Cha. 6. 27.
and 15. 20.
Isai. 50. 7.

7 ¶ But the LORD sayd vnto me, Say not, I *am* a childe : for thou shalt goe to all that I shall send thee, and whatsoeuer I command thee, thou shalt speake.

8 * Be not afraid of their faces : for * I *am* with thee to deliuer thee, sayth the LORD.

9 Then the LORD put foorth his hand, and * touched my mouth, and the LORD said vnto me, Behold, I haue * put my words in thy mouth.

10 See, I haue this day set thee ouer the nations, and ouer the kingdomes, to * roote out, and to pull downe, and to destroy, and to throw down, to build and to plant.

11 ¶ Moreouer, the word of the LORD came vnto me, saying; Ieremiah, what seest thou? And I said, I see a rodde of an almond tree.

12 Then said the LORD vnto me, Thou hast well seene : for I will hasten my word to performe it.

13 And the worde of the LORD came vnto mee the second time, saying; What seest thou? And I said; I see a seething pot, and the face thereof *was* † towards the North.

14 Then the LORD said vnto me; Out of the * North an euill † shal breake foorth vpon all the inhabitants of the land.

15 For loe, I will * call all the families of the kingdoms of the North, saith the LORD, and they shall come, and they shall set euery one his throne at the entring of the gates of Ierusalem, and against all the walles thereof round about, & against all the cities of Iudah.

16 And I will vtter my iudgements against them touching all their wickednesse, who haue forsaken me, and haue burnt incense vnto other gods, and worshipped the workes of their owne hands.

17 ¶ Thou therefore gird vp thy loynes, and arise and speake vnto them all that I commaund thee : be not dismayed at their faces, lest I || confound thee before them.

18 For behold, I haue made thee this day * a defenced citie, and an yron pillar, and brasen walles against the whole land, against the kings of Iudah, against the princes thereof, against the Priests thereof, and against the people of the land.

19 And they shall fight against thee,

but they shall not preuaile against thee: for I *am* with thee, sayth the LORD, to deliuer thee.

CHAP. II.

1 God hauing shewed his former kindnesse, expostulateth with the Iewes, their causelesse reuolt, 9 beyond any example. 14 They are the causes of their owne calamities. 20 The sinnes of Iudah. 31 Her confidence is reiected.

Oreouer, the word of the LORD came to me, saying;

2 Goe, and crie in the eares of Ierusalem, saying; Thus sayth the LORD, I remember || thee, the kindnesse of thy * youth, the loue of thine espousals, when thou wentest after me in the wildernesse, in a land that was not sowen.

3 Israel *was* holinesse vnto the LORD, *and* the first fruites of his increase : all that deuoure him, shall offend; euill shall come vpon them, sayth the LORD.

4 Heare ye the word of the LORD, O house of Iacob, and all the families of the house of Israel.

5 ¶ Thus sayth the LORD, What iniquitie haue your fathers found in me, that they are gone farre from mee, and haue walked after vanitie, and are become vaine?

6 Neither sayd they, Where *is* the LORD that * brought vs vp out of the land of Egypt? that led vs through the wildernesse, through a land of deserts and of pittes, through a land of drought, and of the shadow of death, through a land that no man passed thorow, and where no man dwelt.

7 And I brought you into a plentifull countrey, to eate the fruit thereof, and the goodnesse thereof; but when ye entred yee * defiled my land, and made mine heritage an abomination.

8 The Priests said not, Where *is* the LORD? and they that handle the * Law knew me not : the pastours also transgressed against mee, and the Prophets prophecied by Baal, and walked after *things that* doe not profit.

9 ¶ Wherefore, I will yet pleade with you, sayth the LORD, and with your childrens children will I pleade.

10 For passe || ouer the yles of Chittim, and see; and send vnto Kedar and consider

|| Or, for thy sake.
* Eze. 16. 8.
cha. 12. 14.

* Isai. 63. 9,
11, 13. ose.
13. 4.

* Psal. 78.
58. and
106. 38.

* Rom. 2. 20

|| Or, ouer to.

consider diligently, and see if there be such a thing.

11 Hath a nation changed their Gods, which *are* *yet no Gods? but my people haue changed their glory, for *that which* doth not profit.

12 Be astonished, O yee heauens, at this, and be horribly afraid, be yee very desolate, saith the LORD.

13 For my people haue committed two euils : *they haue forsaken me, the fountaine of liuing waters, *and* hewed them out cisternes, broken cisternes that can hold no water.

14 ¶ Is Israel a seruant? is he a home-borne *slaue?* why is he †spoiled?

15 The young lyons roared vpon him *and* †yelled, and they made his land waste : his cities are burnt without inhabitant.

16 Also the children of Noph and Tahapanes haue || broken the crowne of thy head.

17 Hast thou not procured this vnto thy selfe, in that thou hast forsaken the LORD thy God, when he led thee by the way?

18 And now what hast thou to doe in the way of Egypt, to drinke the waters of Sihor? Or what hast thou to doe in the way of Assyria, to drinke the waters of the riuer?

19 Thine owne *wickednesse shall correct thee, and thy backslidings shall reproue thee : know therefore and see, that it *is* an euill thing and bitter that thou hast forsaken the LORD thy God, and that my feare *is* not in thee, saith the Lord GOD of Hostes.

20 ¶ For of old time I haue broken thy yoke, *and* burst thy bands, and thou saidst ; I will not ||transgresse : when vpon euery high *hill, and vnder euery greene tree *thou wandrest, playing the harlot.

21 Yet I had *planted thee a noble *vine, wholy a right seede : How then art thou turned into the degenerate plant of a strange vine vnto me?

22 For though thou *wash thee with nitre, and take thee much sope, *yet* thine iniquitie is marked before me, saith the Lord GOD.

23 How canst thou say, I am not polluted, I haue not gone after Baalim? see thy way in the valley, know what thou hast done : ||thou art* a swift dromedarie trauersing her wayes.

24 ||A wild asse †vsed to the wilder-

nesse, *that* snuffeth vp the wind at †her pleasure, in her occasion who can ||turne her away? all they that seeke her will not wearie themselues, in her moneth they shall find her.

25 Withhold thy foote from being vnshod, and thy throte from thirst : but thou saidst, ||There is no hope. No, for I haue loued strangers, and after them will I goe.

26 As the thiefe is ashamed, when he is found : so is the house of Israel ashamed, they, their kings, their princes, and their priests, & their prophets,

27 Saying to a stocke ; Thou *art* my father, and to a stone ; Thou hast ||brought me forth : for they haue turned †their backe vnto me, and not their face : but in the time of their *trouble, they will say ; Arise and saue vs.

28 But where *are* thy Gods that thou hast made thee? let them arise if they *can saue thee in the time of thy †trouble : for *according* to the number of thy cities, are thy Gods, O Iudah.

29 Wherefore will yee plead with me? yee all haue transgressed against me, saith the LORD.

30 In vaine haue I *smitten your children, they receiued no correction : your owne sword hath *deuoured your prophets, like a destroying lyon.

31 ¶ O generation, see yee the word of the LORD : *haue I beene a wildernesse vnto Israel? a land of darkenesse? wherefore say my people ; †We are Lords, we will come no more vnto thee?

32 Can a maide forget her ornaments, *or* a bride her attire? yet my people haue forgotten me dayes without number.

33 Why trimmest thou thy way to seeke loue? therefore hast thou also taught the wicked ones thy wayes.

34 Also in thy skirts is found the blood of the soules of the poore innocents : I haue not found it by †secret search, but vpon all these.

35 Yet thou sayest ; Because I am innocent, surely his anger shall turne from me : behold, I will plead with thee, because thou sayest, I haue not sinned.

36 Why gaddest thou about so much to change thy way? thou also shalt bee ashamed of Egypt, as thou wast ashamed of Assyria.

37 Yea thou shalt goe forth from him, and thine hands vpon thine head :

---

*Cha. 16. 20

*Chap. 17. 13. & 18. 14 psal. 36. 9.

†Heb. become a spoile.

†Heb. gaue out their voyce.

|| Or, feede on thy crown, deut. 33. 12 Isai. 8. 8.

*Isai. 3. 9. os. 5. 5.

|| Or, serue.

*Isai. 57. 5, 7.
"Ier. 3. 6.

*Matth. 21. 23. mar. 12. 1. luc. 20. 9.
*Exod. 15. 17. psal. 44, 3. and 80. 9.
Isai. 5. 2.
*Iob. 9, 30.

§ Or, O swift dromedarie.
||Or, O wild asse &c.
†Heb. taught

---

†Heb. the desire of her heart.
||Or, reuers it.

||Or, is the case desperate?

||Or, begotten me.
†Heb. the hinder part part of the necke.
*Isai. 26. 16.

*Isai. 45. 20.
†Heb. euil
*Chap. 11. 13.

*Isai. 9. 13. cha. 5.

*Matth. 2. 29. &c.

*Chap. 2.

†Heb. we haue dominion.

†Heb. digging.

head : for the LORD hath reiected thy confidences, and thou shalt not prosper in them.

CHAP. III.

1 Gods great mercy in Iudahs vile whoredome. 6 Iudah is worse then Israel. 12 The promises of the Gospel, to the penitent. 20 Israel reproued and called by God, maketh a solemne confession of their sinnes.

Heb. sayã.
Deu. 24. 4

THey †say; If a man put away his wife, and she goe from him, and become another mans, * shall hee returne vnto her againe? shall not that land be greatly polluted? but thou hast played the harlot with many louers; yet returne againe to me, saith the LORD.

2 Lift vp thine eyes vnto the high places, and see where thou hast not bene lien with : in the wayes hast thou sate for them, as the Arabian in the wildernesse, and thou hast polluted the land with thy whoredomes, and with thy wickednes.

3 Therefore the * showres haue bin withholden, and there hath bene no latter raine, and thou haddest a * whores forehead, thou refusedst to be ashamed.

4 Wilt thou not from this time cry vnto me; My father, thou *art* the guide of my youth?

5 Will he reserue *his anger* for euer? wil he keepe *it* to the end? Behold, thou hast spoken and done euill things as thou couldest.

6 ¶ The LORD said also vnto me, in the daies of Iosiah the king, Hast thou seene that which backsliding Israel hath done? she is * gone vp vpon euery high mountaine, and vnder euery greene tree, and there hath plaied the harlot.

7 And I said after she had done all these things ; Turne thou vnto me : but shee returned not, and her treacherous sister Iudah saw *it*.

8 And I saw, when for all the causes whereby backsliding Israel committed adulterie, I had put her away and giuen her a bill of diuorce : yet her treacherous sister Iudah feared not, but went and played the harlot also.

9 And it came to passe thorow the ‖lightnes of her whoredome, that shee defiled the land, and committed adultery with stones and with stockes.

10 And yet for all this her treacherous sister Iudah hath not turned vnto mee with her whole heart, but †fainedly, saith the LORD.

11 And the LORD said vnto mee, The backsliding Israel hath iustified her selfe more then treacherous Iudah.

12 ¶ Go and proclaime these words toward the North, and say, Returne thou backsliding Israel, sayeth the LORD, *and* I will not cause mine anger to fall vpon you : for I *am* * mercifull, saith the LORD, *and* I will not keepe *anger* for euer.

13 Only acknowledge thine iniquity that thou hast transgressed against the LORD thy God, and hast scattered thy wayes to the strangers vnder euery greene tree, and ye haue not obeyed my voice, saith the LORD.

14 Turne, O backesliding children, saith the LORD, for I am maried vnto you : and I will take you one of a city, and two of a family, and I wil bring you to Zion.

15 And I will giue you * Pastours according to mine heart, which shall feede you with knowledge and vnderstanding.

16 And it shall come to passe when yee bee multiplied and increased in the land; in those dayes, saith the LORD, they shal say no more ; The Arke of the Couenant of the LORD : neither shal it †come to minde, neither shall they remember it, neither shall they visit *it*, neither shall ‖*that* be done any more.

17 At that time they shall call Ierusalem the Throne of the LORD, and all the nations shalbe gathered vnto it, to the Name of the LORD, to Ierusalem : neither shall they walke any more after the ‖ imagination of their euill heart.

18 In those dayes the house of Iudah shall walke ‖ with the house of Israel, and they shall come together out of the land of the North to the land that I haue ‖giuen for an inheritance vnto your fathers.

19 But I said ; How shall I put thee among the children , and giue thee a †pleasant land, a goodly †heritage of the hostes of nations? and I said ; Thou shalt call me ; My father, and shalt not turne away †from me.

20 ¶ Surely *as* a wife treacherously departeth from her † husband : so haue you dealt treacherously with mee, O house

Deu. 24. 4

Deut. 28.
, chap. 9.

Cha. 6. 15.

Cha. 2. 20.

Or, fame.

† Hebr. in
falshood.

* Psal. 86.
15. and 103
8, 9.

* Cha. 23. 4.

† Heb. come
vp on the
heart.
‖ Or, it be
magnified.

‖ Or, stubburnnesse.

‖ Or, to.

‖ Or, caused
your fathers
to possesse.

† Heb. land
of desire.

†Hebr. from
after me.

† Hebr. friend

house of Israel, saith the LORD.

21 A voice was heard vpon the high places, weeping *and* supplications of the children of Israel : for they haue peruerted their way, *and* they haue forgotten the LORD their God.

* Ose. 14. 2.

22 * Returne ye backsliding children, *and* I wil heale your backslidings : Beholde, wee come vnto thee, for thou *art* the LORD our God.

23 Truely in vaine *is saluation hoped for* from the hilles, *and from* the multitude of mountaines : truely in the LORD our God *is* the saluation of Israel.

24 For shame hath deuoured the labour of our fathers from our youth : their flockes and their heards, their sonnes and their daughters.

25 We lie downe in our shame, and our confusion couereth vs : for we haue sinned against the LORD our God, wee and our fathers from our youth euen vnto this day, and haue not obeied the voice of the LORD our God.

CHAP. IIII.

1 God calleth Israel by his promise. 3 He exhorteth Iudah to repentance by fearefull iudgements. 19 A grieuous lamentation for the miseries of Iudah.

* Ioel 2. 12.

IF thou wilt returne, O Israel, saith the LORD, * returne vnto mee : and if thou wilt put away thine abominations out of my sight, then shalt thou not remoue.

2 And thou shalt sweare, The LORD liueth, in Trueth, in Iudgement, and in Righteousnes, and the nations shall blesse themselues in him, and in him shall they * glorie.

* 2. Cor. 10. 17.

3 ¶ For thus saith the LORD to the men of Iudah and Ierusalem, Breake vp your fallow ground, and sow not among thornes.

4 Circumcise your selues to the LORD, and take away the foreskinnes of your heart, ye men of Iudah, and inhabitants of Ierusalem, lest my furie come forth like fire, and burne that none can quench *it*, because of the euill of your doings.

5 Declare ye in Iudah, and publish in Ierusalem, and say, Blow yee the Trumpet in the land : cry, gather together, and say, Assemble your selues, and let vs goe into the defenced cities.

6 Set vp the standards toward

Zion : ||retyre, stay not ; for I wil bring euil from the * North, and a great †destruction.

* Or, strengthe
* Chap. 1
13, 14, 23.
chap. 6. 2
† Hebr.br
king.

7 The Lion is come vp from his thicket, and the destroyer of the Gentiles is on his way ; hee is gone foorth from his place to make thy land desolate, *and* thy cities shall be layed waste, without an inhabitant.

8 For this * gird you with sackcloth ; lament and howle : for the fierce anger of the LORD is not turned backe from vs.

* Chap. 6
26.

9 And it shall come to passe at that day, saith the LORD, that the heart of the King shall perish, and the heart of the Princes : and the Priests shalbe astonished, & the prophets shall wonder.

10 Then said I, Ah Lord GOD, surely thou hast greatly deceiued this people, and Ierusalem, saying, Ye shall haue peace, whereas the sword reacheth vnto the soule.

11 At that time shall it bee said to this people, and to Ierusalem ; A dry winde of the high places in the wildernes toward the daughter of my people, not to fanne, nor to cleanse,

12 *Euen* ||a full winde from those *places* shall come vnto mee : now also will I †giue sentence against them.

* Or, a f
winde th
those.
† Hebr.
ter iudg
ments.

13 Behold, hee shall come vp as cloudes, and his charets *shall bee* as a whirlewinde : his horses are swifter then Eagles : woe vnto vs, for wee are spoiled.

14 O Ierusalem, * wash thine heart from wickednesse, that thou mayest bee saued : how long shall thy vaine thoughts lodge within thee ?

* Isa. 1.

15 For a voice declareth * from Dan, and publisheth affliction from mount Ephraim.

* Chap.
16.

16 Make ye mention to the nations, behold, publish against Ierusalem, *that* watchers come from a farre countrey, and giue out their voice against the cities of Iudah.

17 As keepers of a fielde are they against her round about ; because shee hath bene rebellious against mee, saith the LORD.

18 * Thy way and thy doings haue procured these things vnto thee, this *is* thy wickednes because it is bitter, because it reacheth vnto thine heart.

* Psal.
17. isa.
1.

19 ¶ My * bowels, my bowels, I am pained at my very heart, †my heart maketh a noise in mee, I cannot hold my

* Isa. 2
chap. 9
† Hebr.
walles o
heart.

my peace, because thou hast heard, O my soule, the sound of the Trumpet, the alarme of warre.

20 Destruction vpon destruction is cried, for the whole land is spoiled : suddenly are my tents spoiled, *and* my curtaines in a moment.

21 How long shal I see the standard *and* heare the sound of the Trumpet?

22 For my people *is* foolish, they haue not knowen me, they are sottish children, and they haue none vnderstanding : they are wise to doe euill, but to doe good they haue no knowledge.

23 I beheld the earth, and loe, it *was* without forme and void : and the heauens, and they *had* no light.

24 I beheld the mountaines, and loe they trembled, and all the hilles mooued lightly.

25 I behelde, and loe, *there was* no man, and all the birdes of the heauens were fled.

26 I beheld, and loe, the fruitfull place *was* a wildernesse, and all the cities thereof were broken downe at the presence of the L O R D, *and* by his fierce anger.

ha. 5. 18.   27 For thus hath the L O R D said; The whole land shall be desolate; *yet will I not make a full ende.

28 For this shall the earth mourne, and the heauens aboue be blacke : because I haue spoken *it*, I haue purposed *it*, and will not repent, neither will I turne backe from it.

29 The whole citie shall flee, for the noise of the horsemen and bowmen, they shall goe into thickets, and climbe vp vpon the rockes : euery city shall be forsaken, and not a man dwell therein.

30 And when thou art spoiled, what wilt thou doe? though thou clothest thy selfe with crimsin, though thou deckest thee with ornaments of golde, *Heb. eyes.* though thou rentest thy †face with painting, in vaine shalt thou make thy selfe faire, thy louers will despise thee, they will seeke thy life.

31 For I haue heard a voice as of a woman in trauel, *and* the anguish as of her that bringeth foorth her first childe, the voice of the daughter of Zion, *that* bewaileth her selfe, *that* spreadeth her hands, *saying*; Woe *is* me now, for my soule is wearied because of murderers.

CHAP. V.

1 The iudgements of God vpon the Iewes, for their peruersenesse, 7 for their adulterie, 10 for their impietie, 19 for their contempt of God, 25 and for their great corruption in the Ciuill state, 30 and Ecclesiasticall.

 Vnne yee to and fro thorow the streetes of Ierusalem, and see now and knowe, and seeke in the broad places thereof, if ye can finde a man, if there be any that executeth iudgement, that seeketh the trueth, and I will pardon it.

2 And though they say, The L O R D liueth, surely they sweare falsely.

3 O L O R D, *are* not thine eyes vpon the trueth? thou hast *stricken them, but they haue not grieued; thou hast consumed them, *but* they haue refused to receiue correction : they haue made their faces harder then a rocke, they haue refused to returne.   *Isai. 9. 13. chap. 2. 30.*

4 Therefore I said, Surely these *are* poore, they are foolish : for they know not the way of the L O R D *nor* the iudgement of their God.

5 I wil get me vnto the great men, and will speake vnto them, for they haue knowen the way of the L O R D, *and* the iudgement of their God : but these haue altogether broken the yoke, *and* burst the bondes.

6 Wherfore a lyon out of the forrest shall slay them, *and* a wolfe of the ‖euenings shall spoile them, a leopard shall watch ouer their cities : euery one that goeth out thence shalbe torne in pieces, because their transgressions are many, *and* their backeslidings †are increased.   ‖ *Or, deserts.*

   † *Heb. are strong.*

7 ¶ How shall I pardon thee for this? thy children haue forsaken mee, and sworne by them *that are* no gods: when I had fed them to the full, they then committed adulterie, and assembled themselues by troupes in the harlots houses.

8 *They were as fed horses in the morning: euery one neighed after his neighbours wife: *Ezek. 22. 11.*

9 Shall I not visit for these things, sayth the L O R D, and shall not my soule bee auenged on such a nation as this?

10 ¶ Goe yee vp vpon her walles, and destroy, but make not a full ende : take away her battlements, for they *are* not the L O R D s.

11 For the house of Israel, and the house of Iudah haue dealt very treacherously against me, saith the L O R D.

12 For

12 They haue belyed the LORD, and said; *It is* not he,*neither shall euill come vpon vs, neither shal we see sword nor famine.

13 And the prophets shall become wind, and the word *is* not in them : thus shall it be done vnto them.

14 Wherfore thus saith the LORD God of Hostes; Because yee speake this word, behold, I will make my words in thy mouth, * fire, and this people wood, and it shall deuoure them.

15 Loe, I will bring a *nation vpon you from farre, O house of Israel, saith the LORD : it *is* a mighty nation, it *is* an ancient nation, a nation whose language thou knowest not, neither vnderstandest what they say.

16 Their quiuer *is* as an open sepulchre, they *are* all mighty men.

17 And they shall eate vp thine *haruest and thy bread, *which* thy sonnes and thy daughters should eate : they shall eate vp thy flockes and thine heards : they shall eate vp thy vines and thy figtrees : they shall impouerish thy fenced cities wherein thou trustedst, with the sword.

18 Neuerthelesse in those daies, saith the LORD, I *will not make a full end with you.

19 ¶ And it shall come to passe when yee shall say ; * Wherefore doth the LORD our God all these things vnto vs? then shalt thou answere them ; Like as ye haue forsaken me, & serued strange Gods in your land ; so shall yee serue strangers in a land *that is* not yours.

20 Declare this in the house of Iacob, and publish it in Iudah saying ;

21 Heare now this, O *foolish people, and without †vnderstanding, which haue eyes and see not, which haue eares and heare not.

22 Feare yee not mee, saith the LORD? will yee not tremble at my presence, which haue placed the sand for the *bound of the sea, by a perpetuall decree that it cannot passe it, and though the waues thereof tosse themselues, yet can they not preuaile, though they roare, yet can they not passe ouer it ?

23 But this people hath a reuolting and a rebellious heart : they are reuolted and gone.

24 Neither say they in their heart ; Let vs now feare the LORD our God, that giueth raine, both the *former and the later in his season : he re-

seerueth vnto vs the appointed weekes of the haruest.

25 ¶ Your iniquities haue turned away these things, & your sinnes haue withholden good things from you.

26 For among my people are found wicked men : ||they lay waite as hee that setteth snares, they set a trap, they catch men.

27 As a ||cage *is* full of birds, so are their houses full of deceit: therefore they are become great, and waxen rich.

28 They are waxen * fat, they shine: yea they ouerpasse the deedes of the wicked : they iudge not *the cause, the cause of the fatherlesse, yet they prosper: and the right of the needy doe they not iudge.

29 Shall I not visit for these things, saith the LORD? shall not my soule be auenged on such a nation as this?

30 ¶ ||A wonderfull and horrible thing is committed in the land.

31 The prophets prophecie * falsely, and the priests ||beare rule by their meanes, and my people loue *to haue it* so: and what will yee doe in the end therof?

CHAP. VI.

1 The enemies, sent against Iudah, 4 encourage themselues. 6 God setteth them on worke, because of their sinnes. 9 The prophet lamenteth the iudgements of God because of their sinnes. 18 He proclaimeth Gods wrath. 26 He calleth the people to mourne for the iudgement on their sinnes.

Yee children of Beniamin, gather your selues to flee out of the middest of Ierusalem, and blow the trumpet in Tekoa : and set vp a signe of fire in Beth-haccerem: for euill appeareth out of the North, and great destruction.

2 I haue likened the daughter of Zion to a ||comely and delicate *woman.*

3 The shepheards with their flocks shall come vnto her : they shall pitch *their* tents against her round about : they shall feede, euery one in his place.

4 Prepare yee warre against her : arise, and let vs goe vp at noone : woe vnto vs, for the day goeth away, for the shadowes of the euening are stretched out.

5 Arise, and let vs goe by night, and let vs destroy her palaces.

6 ¶ For thus hath the LORD of hostes said ; Hew yee downe trees and
||cast

* Isal. 28. 15.

* Cha. 1. 9.

* Deut. 28. 49. cha. 1. 15. and 6. 22.

* Leu. 26. 16. deut. 28. 31. 33.

* Cha. 4. 27.

* Cha. 16. 10 and 13. 22.

* Isal. 6. 9. matth. 13. 14. acts 28. 26. rom. 11. 8. Ioh. 12. 40.
† Heb. heart.

* Iob. 38. 10, 11. psal. 104. 9.

* Deut. 11. 14.

|| Or, they pry as fowlers lie in waite.

|| Or, coup

* Deut. 3 15.
* Isal. 1. zac. 7. 10.

|| Or, astonishmen a filthinesse
* Chap. 1 18. and 23 25. 26. ez. 13. 6.
|| Or, take into their hands.

|| Or, dwelling at ho

Or, powre ut the enine of shot.

Isa. 57. 20

|||cast a mount against Ierusalem : this is the citie to be visited, she *is* wholly oppression in the midst of her.

7 *As a fountaine casteth out her waters, so she casteth out her wickednesse : violence and spoile is heard in her, before me continually *is* griefe and wounds.

Heb. bee osed or disinted.

8 Be thou instructed, O Ierusalem, lest my soule †depart from thee : lest I make thee desolate, a lande not inhabited.

9 ¶ Thus saith the LORD of hosts, They shall throughly gleane the remnant of Israel as a vine : turne backe thine hand as a grape gatherer into the baskets.

Chap.7.26

10 To whome shall I speake and giue warning, that they may heare? Behold, their *eare *is* vncircumcised, and they cannot hearken : beholde, the word of the LORD is vnto them a reproch : they haue no delight in it.

11 Therefore I am full of the furie of the LORD : I am weary with holding in : I will powre it out vpon the children abroad, and vpon the assembly of yong men together : for euen the husband with the wife shall be taken, the aged with *him that is* full of dayes.

12 And their houses shall be turned vnto others, with *their* fields and wiues together : for I wil stretch out my hand vpon the inhabitants of the land, saith the LORD.

13 For from the least of them euen vnto the greatest of them, euery one is giuen to *couetousnesse, and from the prophet euen vnto the priest, euery one dealeth falsly.

* Isa. 56. 11 hap. 8. 10.

14 They haue *healed also the †hurt of the daughter of my people sleightly, saying, Peace, peace, when *there is* no peace.

Chap. 8.
. ezek.
3. 10.
Heb. bruise
r breach.

15 Were they *ashamed when they had committed abomination? nay they were not at all ashamed, neither could they blush : therefore they shall fall among them that fall : at the time that I visit them, they shall bee cast downe, saith the LORD.

* Chap. 3. 3.
nd 8. 12.

16 Thus saith the LORD, Stand ye in the wayes and see, and aske for the *old paths, where is the good way, and walke therein, and ye shall finde *rest for your soules : but they said, We will not walke *therein.*

* Isa. 8. 20.
nal. 4. 4.
uk. 16. 29.
* Mat. 11.
9.

17 Also I set watchmen ouer you, *saying,* Hearken to the sound of the trumpet : but they said, We wil not hearken.

18 ¶ Therefore heare ye nations, and know, O Congregation what *is* among them.

19 Heare, O earth, behold, I will bring euill vpon this people, *euen* the fruit of their thoughts, because they haue not hearkened vnto my wordes, nor to my law, but reiected it.

20 *To what purpose cōmeth there to me incense from Sheba? and the sweet cane from a farre countrey? your burnt offerings *are* not acceptable, nor your sacrifices sweet vnto me.

* Isa. 1. 11.
and 66. 3.
amos 5. 21.
mic. 6. 6,
&c.

21 Therefore thus saith the LORD, Behold, I will lay stumbling blockes before this people, and the fathers and the sons together shall fall vpon them : the neighbor and his friend shall perish.

22 Thus saith the LORD, Behold, a people commeth from the *North countrey, and a great nation shall bee raised from the sides of the earth.

* Chap. 1. 15
and 5. 15.
and 10. 22.

23 They shall lay hold on bowe and speare : they *are* cruell, and haue no mercie : their voice roareth like the Sea, and they ride vpon horses, set in aray as men for warre against thee, O daughter of Zion.

24 We haue heard the fame thereof, our hands waxe feeble, anguish hath taken hold of vs, *and* paine as of a woman in trauaile.

25 Goe not forth into the field, nor walke by the way : for the sword of the enemie *and* feare *is* on euery side.

26 ¶ O daughter of my people, gird *thee* with *sackcloth, and wallowe thy selfe in ashes : make thee mourning, *as* for an onely sonne, most bitter lamentation : for the spoiler shall suddenly come vpon vs.

* Chap. 4. 8.
and 25. 36.

27 I haue set thee for a towre, *and* a *fortresse among my people : that thou mayest know and trie their way.

* Chap. 1.
18. and 15.
20.

28 They are all grieuous reuolters, walking with slanders : *they are* *brasse and yron, they are all corrupters.

* Ezek. 22.
18.

29 The bellowes are burnt, the lead is consumed of the fire : the founder melteth in vaine : for the wicked are not plucked away.

30 *‖ Reprobate siluer shall men call them, because the LORD hath reiected them.

* Isa. 1. 22.
‖ Or, refuse
siluer.

CHAP. VII.

1 Ieremiah is sent to call for true repentance, to preuent the Iewes captiuitie. 8 He reiecteth their

their vaine confidence, 12 by the example of Shiloh. 17 He threatneth them for their idolatrie. 21 Hee reiecteth the sacrifices of the disobedient. 29 He exhorteth to mourne for their abominations in Tophet, 32 and the iudgements for the same.

HE word that came to Ieremiah from the LORD, saying,

2 Stand in the gate of the LORDS house, and proclaime there this word, and say, Heare the word of the LORD, all ye of Iudah, that enter in at these gates to worship the LORD.

*Chap. 26. 13. and 18. 11.

3 Thus saith the LORD of hostes the God of Israel; *Amend your wayes, and your doings, and I will cause you to dwell in this place.

4 Trust ye not in lying words, saying, The Temple of the LORD, the Temple of the LORD, the Temple of the LORD are these.

5 For if ye throughly amend your waies and your doings, if you throughly execute iudgement betweene a man and his neighbour:

6 If ye oppresse not the stranger, the fatherlesse and the widow, and shed not innocent blood in this place, neither walke after other gods to your hurt:

7 Then will I cause you to dwell in this place, in the land that I gaue to your fathers, for euer and euer.

8 ¶ Behold, ye trust in lying words, that cannot profit.

9 Will ye steale, murther, and commit adulterie, and sweare falsly, and burne incense vnto Baal, and walke after other gods, whom ye know not;

†Hebr. whereupon my Name is called.
*Isai. 56. 7.
*Matth. 21. 13. mar. 11. 17. luke 19. 46.

10 And come and stand before me in this house, †which is called by my Name, and say, We are deliuered, to do all these abominations?

11 Is *this house, which is called by my Name, become a *denne of robbers in your eies? Behold, euen I haue seen it, saith the LORD.

*1. Sam. 4. 11. psal. 78. 60. chap. 26. 6.

12 But goe yee now vnto my place which was in Shiloh, where I set my Name at the first, and see *what I did to it, for the wickednesse of my people Israel.

*Pro. 1. 24. isa. 65. 12. and 66. 4.

13 And now because ye haue done all these workes, saith the LORD, and I spake vnto you, rising vp earely, and speaking, but ye heard not; and I *called you, but ye answered not:

14 Therefore will I doe vnto this house, which is called by my Name, wherein yee trust, and vnto the place which I gaue to you, and to your fathers, as I haue done to *Shiloh.

*1. Sam. 11. psal. 78. 60. and 13. 6. chap. 26. 6.

15 And I will cast you out of my sight, as I haue cast out all your brethren, euen the whole seed of Ephraim.

16 Therefore *pray not thou for this people, neither lift vp cry nor prayer for them, neither make intercession to me, for I will not heare thee.

*Chap. 11. 14. and 14. 11. exod. 32. 10.

17 ¶ Seest thou not what they doe in the cities of Iudah, and in the streets of Ierusalem?

18 *The children gather wood, and the fathers kindle the fire, & the women knead their dough to make cakes to the ‖Queene of heauen, and to powre out drinke offerings vnto other gods, that they may prouoke me to anger.

*Chap. 44. 19.
‖Or, frame or workmanship of heauen.

19 Doe they prouoke mee to anger, saith the LORD? doe they not prouoke themselues to the confusion of their owne faces?

20 Therefore thus saith the Lord GOD, Behold, mine anger and my furie shalbe powred out vpon this place, vpon man & vpon beast, and vpon the trees of the field, and vpon the fruit of the ground, and it shall burne, and shall not be quenched.

21 ¶ Thus saith the LORD of hosts the God of Israel, *Put your burnt offrings vnto your sacrifices, & eate flesh.

*Isa. 1. chap. 6. 2 amos 5. 21

22 For I spake not vnto your fathers, nor commanded them in the day that I brought them out of the land of Egypt, †concerning burnt offerings or sacrifices.

†Hebr. concerning the matter of

23 But this thing commaunded I them, saying, Obey my voice, *and I wil be your God, and ye shalbe my people: and walke ye in all the wayes that I haue commanded you, that it may be well vnto you.

*Deut. 5.
*Exod. 5. leuit. 9 12.

24 But they hearkened not, nor inclined their eare, but walked in the counsels and in the ‖imagination of their euill heart, and †went backward, and not forward.

‖Or, stubburnnesse
†Hebr. we

25 Since the day that your fathers came forth out of the land of Egypt vnto this day, I haue euen *sent vnto you all my seruants the Prophets, daily rising vp early, and sending them.

*1. Chron. 36. 15.

26 Yet they hearkned not vnto me, nor inclined their eare, but *hardened their neck, they did worse then their fathers.

*Chap. 12.

27 There-

27 Therefore thou shalt speake all these wordes vnto them, but they will not hearken to thee : thou shalt also call vnto them, but they will not answere thee.

28 But thou shalt say vnto them ; This *is* a nation, that obeyeth not the voyce of the LORD their God, nor re-

-, instru-
n.

ceiueth ‖correction : trueth is perished, and is cut off from their mouth.

29 ¶ Cut off thine haire, *O Ierusalem,* and cast it away, and take vp a lamentation on high places, for the LORD hath reiected, and forsaken the generation of his wrath.

30 For the children of Iudah haue done euill in my sight, saith the LORD: they haue set their abominations in the house which is called by my Name, to pollute it.

Kings
10. chap.
5.

31 And they haue built the *high places of Tophet which *is* in the valley of the sonne of Hinnom, to burne their sonnes and their daughters in the fire, which I commanded *them* not, neither

‖eb. came
pon my
rt.
ha. 19. 6.

†came it into my heart.

32 ¶ Therefore behold, the dayes *come, saith the LORD, that it shall no more be called Tophet, nor the valley of the sonne of Hinnom, but the valley of slaughter : for they shall bury in Tophet, till there be no place.

hap. 34.
and. 16.
sal. 79. 2

33 And the *carkeises of this people shall be meate for the fowles of the heauen, and for the beasts of the earth, and none shall fray *them* away.

sa. 24. 7.
ap. 16. 9.
1 25. 10.
l. 33. 11.
. 26. 13.
. 2. 11.

34 Then will I cause to cease from the *cities of Iudah, and from the streets of Ierusalem, the voice of mirth and the voice of gladnesse, the voice of the bridegroome, and the voice of the bride : for the land shall be desolate.

CHAP. VIII.

1 The calamity of the Iewes, both dead and a-liue. 4 Hee vpbraideth their foolish, and shamelesse impenitencie. 13 Hee sheweth their grieuous iudgment, 18 and bewaileth their desperate estate.

AT that time, sayeth the LORD, they shall bring out the bones of the kings of Iudah, and the bones of his princes, and the bones of the Priests, and the bones of the Prophets, and the bones of the inhabitants of Ierusalem out of their graues.

2 And they shall spread them before the Sunne, and the Moone, and all the hoste of heauen whom they haue loued, and whom they haue serued, and after whom they haue walked, and whom they haue sought, and whom they haue worshipped : they shall not be gathered, nor be buried, they shall be for doung, vpon the face of the earth.

3 And death shall bee chosen rather then life, by all the residue of them that remaine of this euill family, which remaine in all the places whither I haue driuen them, saith the LORD of hosts.

4 ¶ Moreouer thou shalt say vnto them, Thus saith the LORD, Shall they fall, and not arise ? shall hee turne away, and not returne ?

5 Why *then* is this people of Ierusalem slidden backe, by a perpetual backe-sliding? they hold fast deceit, they refuse to returne.

6 I hearkened and heard, *but* they spake not aright: no man repented him of his wickednesse, saying, What haue I done ? euery one turned to his course, as the horse rusheth into the battell.

7 Yea the *Storke in the heauen knoweth her appointed times, and the turtle, and the crane, and the swallow obserue the time of their comming ; but my people know not the iudgement of the LORD.

* Isai. 1. 3.

8 How doe ye say, We *are* wise, and the Law of the LORD *is* with vs ? Loe, ‖certainly, in vaine made he it, the pen of the scribes is in vaine.

‖Or, the false
penne of the
scribes wor-
keth for fals-
hood.
* Cha. 6. 15.
‖ Or, haue
they beene
ashamed,
&c.
† Heb. the
wisedome of
what thing.

9 The *‖wise men are ashamed, they are dismayed and taken ; loe, they haue reiected the word of the LORD, and †what wisedome *is* in them ?

10 Therfore will I giue their wiues vnto others, &their fields to them that shall inherite them : for euery one from the least euen vnto the greatest is giuen to couetousnes, from the Prophet euen vnto the priest, *euery one dealeth falsly.

* Isai. 56. 11
chap. 6. 13.
* Cha. 6. 14.

11 For they haue *healed the hurt of the daughter of my people slightly, saying, *Peace, peace, when *there is* no peace.

* Eze. 13.
10.
* Chap. 3. 3.
and 6. 15.

12 Were they *ashamed when they had committed abomination ? nay, they were not at all ashamed, neither could they blush : therefore shall they fall among them that fal, in the time of their visitation they shall be cast downe, saith the LORD.

‖ Or, in ga-
thering I
will con-
sume.
* Isai. 5. 1.
* Matth. 21.
19. luke
13. 6. &c.

13 ¶ ‖I will surely consume them, saith the LORD: *there shalbe* no grapes *on the vine, nor figges on the *figtree, and the leafe shall fade, and *the things that*

I haue

I haue giuen them, shall passe away from them.

14 Why doe wee sit still? assemble your selues, and let vs enter into the defenced cities, and let vs be silent there: for the L O R D our God hath put vs to silence, and giuen vs *waters of ‖gall to drink, because we haue sinned against the L O R D.

*Cha. 9. 15.
dan. 23. 15.
‖Or, poyson.

15 We *looked for peace, but no good came: and for a time of health, and behold trouble.

*Chap. 14. 16.

16 The snorting of his horses was heard from *Dan: the whole land trembled at the sound of the neighing of his strong ones, for they are come and haue deuoured the land, and †all that is in it, the citie, and those that dwell therein.

ᵅCha. 4. 15.

†Hebr. the fulnesse therof.

17 For behold, I wil send serpents, cockatrices among you, which will not be *charmed, and they shall bite you; saith the L O R D.

*Psal. 58. 5, 6.

18 ¶ When I would comfort my selfe against sorrow, my heart is faint †in me.

†Heb. vpon.

19 Behold the voice of the crie of the daughter of my people †because of them that dwel in a farre countrey: Is not the L O R D in Zion? is not her king in her? why haue they prouoked me to anger with their grauen images, and with strange vanities?

†Heb. because of the countrey of them that are farre off.

20 The haruest is past, the summer is ended, and we are not saued.

21 For the hurt of the daughter of my people am I hurt, I am blacke: astonishment hath taken hold on me.

22 Is there no *balme in Gilead? is there no physician there? why then is not the health of the daughter of my people †recouered?

*Chap. 46. 11.

†Heb. gone vp.

CHAP. IX.

1 Ieremiah lamenteth the Iewes for their manifold sinnes, 9 and for their iudgement. 12 Disobedience is the cause of their bitter calamitie. 17 He exhorteth to mourne for their destruction, 23 and to trust, not in themselues, but in God. 25 He threatneth both Iewes and Gentiles.

†Heb. who will giue my head &c.
*Isa. 22. 4.
chap. 4. 19.

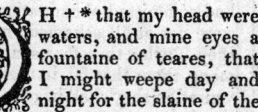O H †*that my head were waters, and mine eyes a fountaine of teares, that I might weepe day and night for the slaine of the daughter of my people.

2 Oh that I had in the wildernesse a lodging place of wayfaring men, that I might leaue my people, and goe from them: for they be all adulterers, an assembly of treacherous men.

3 And they bend their tongue like their bow for lies: but they are not valiant for the trueth vpon the earth: for they proceed from euil to euill, and they know not me, saith the L O R D.

4 *Take yee heede euery one of his ‖neighbour, and trust yee not in any brother: for euery brother will vtterly supplant, and euery neighbour will walke with slanders.

*Chap. 6. mich 5, 6.
‖Or, m

5 And they will ‖deceiue euery one his neighbour, and will not speake the trueth, they haue taught their tongue to speake lies, and weary themselues to commit iniquity.

‖Or, m

6 Thine habitation is in the middest of deceit, through deceit they refuse to know me, sayth the L O R D.

7 Therfore thus saith the L O R D of hostes; Behold, I will melt them, and trie them. for how shall I doe for the daughter of my people?

8 Their *tongue is as an arrowe shot out, it speaketh *deceit: one speaketh *peaceably to his neighbour with his mouth, but †in heart he layeth ‖his waite.

*Psal. and 28
*Psa. and 28.
†Heb. middes him.
‖Or, w for hir
*Chap. 29.

9 ¶ *Shall I not visit them for these things, saith the L O R D? shall not my soule be auenged on such a nation as this?

10 For the mountaines will I take vp a weeping and wayling, and for the ‖habitations of the wildernesse a lamentation, because they are ‖burnt vp, so that none can passe through them, neither can men heare the voyce of the cattell, †both the foule of the heauens, and the beast are fled, they are gone.

‖Or, p tures
‖Or, de
†Heb. the fou uen to

11 And I will make Ierusalem heapes, and *a denne of dragons, and I wil make the cities of Iudah †desolate, without an inhabitant.

*Cha 10, 22.
†Heb. lation.

12 ¶ Who is the wise man that may vnderstand this, and who is he to whom the mouth of the L O R D hath spoken, that hee may declare it; for what the land perisheth, and is burnt vp like a wildernesse that none passeth through?

13 And the L O R D saith; Because they haue forsaken my law, which I set before them, and haue not obeyed my voyce, neither walked therein;

14 But haue walked after the ‖imagination of their owne heart, & after Balim, which their fathers taught them:

‖Or, ė burnin

15 Therefore thus saith the L O R D of hosts, the God of Israel, Behold, I will

will feed them, *euen* this people * with wormewood, and giue them water of gall to drinke.

16 I will *scatter them also among the heathen, whome neither they nor their fathers haue knowen : and I wil send a sword after them, til I haue consumed them.

17 ¶ Thus saith the LORD of hosts, Consider yee, and call for the mourning women, that they may come, and send for cunning women, that they may come.

18 And let them make haste, and take vp a wailing for vs, that our eyes may run down with teares, and our eyelids gush out with waters.

19 For a voyce of wayling is heard out of Zion, How are we spoiled? wee are greatly confounded, because wee haue forsaken the land, because our dwellings haue cast vs out.

20 Yet heare the word of the LORD, O ye women, & let your eare receiue the word of his mouth, and teach your daughters wailing, and euery one her neighbour lamentation.

21 For death is come vp into our windowes, *and* is entred into our palaces, to cut off the children from without *and* the yong men from the streetes.

22 Speake, Thus saith the LORD, Euen the carkeises of men shall fall as dung vpon the open field, and as the handfull after the haruest man, and none shall gather *them*.

23 ¶ Thus saith the LORD, Let not the *wise man glory in his wisdom, neither let the mighty man glory in his might, let not the rich man glory in his riches.

24 But let him that glorieth, glory in this, that hee vnderstandeth and knoweth me, that I *am* the LORD which exercise louing kindnesse, iudgement and righteousnesse in the earth : for in these things I delight, saith the LORD.

† Heb. visit
vpon.

† Hebr. cut
off into cor-
ners, or ha-
uing the cor-
ners of their
haire polled.
* Chap. 25.
23.
* Rom. 2.
28, 29.

25 ¶ Behold, the dayes come, saith the LORD, that I will †punish all them which are circumcised, with the vncircumcised,

26 Egypt, and Iudah, and Edom, and the children of Ammon, and Moab, and all that are †in the * vtmost corners, that dwell in the wildernesse : for all these nations *are* vncircumcised, and all the house of Israel *are* * vncircumcised in the heart.

CHAP. X.

1 The vnequall comparison of God and idoles.
17 The Prophet exhorteth to flie from the calamitie to come. 19 Hee lamenteth the spoyle of the Tabernacle by foolish pastours.
23 He maketh an humble supplication.

HEare ye the word which the LORD speaketh vnto you, O house of Israel.

2 Thus sayeth the LORD, Learne not the way of the heathen, and be not dismayed at the signes of heauen, for the heathen are dismayed at them.

3 For the †customes of the people are vaine : for one cutteth a tree out of the forrest (the worke of the handes of the workeman) with the axe.

4 They decke it with siluer and with golde, they fasten it with nayles, and with hammers that it mooue not.

5 They *are* vpright as the palme tree, *but speake not : they must needes be *borne, because they cannot goe : be not afraid of them, for * they cannot doe euil, neither also *is it* in them to doe good.

6 Forasmuch as *there is* none *like vnto thee, O LORD, thou *art* great, and thy Name *is* great in might.

7 * Who would not feare thee, O King of nations? for ||to thee doeth *it* appertaine : forasmuch as among all the wise men of the nations, and in all their kingdomes, *there is* none like vnto thee.

8 But they are †altogether *brutish and foolish : the stocke is a doctrine of vanities.

9 Siluer spread into plates is brought from Tarshish, and gold from Vphaz, the worke of the workeman, and of the hands of the founder : blue and purple *is* their clothing : they *are* all the worke of cunning men.

10 But the LORD *is* the †true God, he *is* the liuing God, and an †euerlasting King : at his wrath the earth shal tremble, and the nations shall not be able to abide his indignation.

11 Thus shal ye say vnto them, The Gods that haue not made the heauens, & the earth, *euen* they shall perish from the earth, & from vnder these heauens.

12 Hee *hath made the earth by his power, he hath established the world by his wisedome, and hath stretched out the heauens by his discretion.

13 When he vttereth his voice, *there is* a ||mul-

† Heb. sta-
tules or ordi-
nances are
vanity.

* Psa. 115.
5.
* Isa. 46. 1,
7.
* Isa. 41. 28.

* Psal. 86.
8, 10.

* Reue. 15.
4.
|| Or, it li-
keth thee.

†Heb. in one.
or at once.
* Isa. 41. 29.
abac. 2. 18.
zec. 10. 1.

† Heb. God
of trueth.
† Heb. King
of eternity.

* Gen. 1. 6.
chap. 51. 15

‖ Or, noise.

‖ Or, for raine.

‖ Or, is more brutish, then to know.
* Chap. 51
17, 18.

a ‖multitude of waters in the heauens, and hee causeth the vapours to ascend from the ends of the earth : hee maketh lightnings ‖ with raine, and bringeth forth the wind out of his treasures.

14 Euery man is ‖ * brutish in *his* knowledge, euery founder is confounded by the grauen image : for his moulten image *is* falsehood, and *there is* no breath in them.

15 They *are* vanity, *and* the worke of errours : in the time of their visitation they shall perish.

* Chap. 51.
19.

16 * The portion of Iacob *is* not like them : for he *is* the fourmer of all things, and Israel *is* the rod of his inheritance : the Lord of hostes *is* his Name.

† Heb. in-habitresse.

17 ¶ Gather vp thy wares out of the land, O †inhabitant of the fortresse.

18 For thus saith the Lord, Behold, I will sling out the inhabitants of the land at this once, and will distresse them, that they may find *it so.*

19 ¶ Woe is mee for my hurt, my wound is grieuous : but I sayd, Truely this *is* a griefe, and I must beare it.

20 My Tabernacle is spoyled, and all my cordes are broken : my children are gone foorth of me, and they *are* not : *there is* none to stretch foorth my tent any more, and to set vp my curtaines.

21 For the Pastours are become brutish, and haue not sought the Lord : therefore they shall not prosper, and all their flockes shall be scattered.

22 Behold, the noise of the bruit is come, and a great commotion out of the * North countrey, to make the cities of Iudah desolate, *and* a *denne of dragons.

* Chap. 1.
15. and 5.
15. and 6.
22.
* Chap. 9.
11.
* Pro. 16. 1.
and 20. 44.

23 ¶ O Lord, I know that the * way of man *is* not in himselfe : it *is* not in man that walketh, to direct his steps.

* Psal. 6. 1.
and 38. 1.
cha. 30. 11.
† Hebr. di-minish me.
* Psal. 79. 6.

24 O Lord, * correct mee, but with iudgement, not in thine anger, lest thou †bring me to nothing.

25 * Powre out thy fury vpon the heathen that know thee not, and vpon the families that call not on thy Name : for they haue eaten vp Iacob, and deuoured him, and consumed him, and haue made his habitation desolate.

CHAP. XI.

1 Ieremiah proclaimeth Gods Couenant : 8
Rebuketh the Iewes disobeying thereof :
11 Prophesieth euils to come vpon them,
18 and vpon the men of Anathoth, for conspiring to kill Ieremiah.

He word that came to Ieremiah from the Lord, saying,

2 Heare yee the words of this Couenant, and speake vnto the men of Iudah, and to the inhabitants of Ierusalem.

3 And say thou vnto them, Thus saith the Lord God of Israel, * Cursed *bee* the man that obeyeth not the words of this Couenant,

* Deut. 27.
26. gal. 3.
10.

4 Which I commaunded your fathers in the day *that* I brought them foorth out of the land of Egypt, from the yron furnace, saying, * Obey my voyce, and doe them, according to all which I command you : so shall yee be my people, and I will be your God.

* Leuit. 26
3, 12.

5 That I may performe the * othe which I haue sworne vnto your fathers, to giue them a land flowing with milke and honie, as *it is* this day : then answered I, and said, †So bee it, O Lord.

* Deut. 7.
12.

† Hebr. A-men.

6 Then the Lord said vnto me, Proclaime all these wordes in the cities of Iudah, and in the streets of Ierusalem, saying, Heare ye the words of this Couenant, and doe them.

7 For I earnestly protested vnto your fathers, in the day *that* I brought them vp out of the land of Egypt, euen vnto this day, rising earely and protesting, saying, Obey my voice.

8 Yet they obeyed not, nor inclined their eare : but walked euery one in the ‖imagination of their euill heart : therefore I will bring vpon them all the words of this Couenant, which I commaunded *them* to doe ; but they did *them* not.

‖ Or, stub-burnnesse

9 And the Lord said vnto me, A conspiracie is found among the men of Iudah, and among the inhabitants of Ierusalem.

10 They are turned backe to the iniquities of their forefathers, which refused to heare my wordes : and they went after other gods to serue them : the house of Israel, and the house of Iudah haue broken my Couenant, which I made with their fathers.

11 ¶ Therefore thus sayeth the Lord, Behold, I will bring euill vpon them which they shall not be able †to escape ; and *though they shall crie vnto mee, I will not hearken vnto them.

† Hebr. to
goe forth o
* Prou. 1.
28. isa. 1.
15. cha. 14
12. eze. 8.
18. mich.
8.

12 Then shall the cities of Iudah, and

and inhabitants of Ierusalem goe, and crie vnto the gods vnto whom they offer incense; but they shall not saue them at all in the time of their †trouble.

13 For *according* to the number of thy *cities were thy gods, O Iudah, and *according* to the number of the streetes of Ierusalem haue ye set vp altars to that †shamefull thing, *euen* altars to burne incense vnto Baal.

14 Therefore *pray not thou for this people, neither lift vp a cry or prayer for them : for I will not heare them in the time that they crie vnto mee for their †trouble.

15 *†What hath my beloued to doe in mine house, *seeing* shee hath wrought lewdnesse with many ? and the holy flesh is passed from thee : ‖when thou doest euill, then thou reioycest.

16 The LORD called thy name, A greene oliue tree, faire and of goodly fruite : with the noise of a great tumult hee hath kindled fire vpon it, and the branches of it are broken.

17 For the LORD of hostes that planted thee, hath pronounced euill against thee, for the euill of the house of Israel, and of the house of Iudah, which they haue done against themselues to prouoke mee to anger in offering incense vnto Baal.

18 ¶ And the LORD hath giuen mee knowledge *of it*, and I knowe *it*, then thou shewedst me their doings.

19 But I *was* like a lambe *or* an oxe *that* is brought to the slaughter, and I knew not that they had deuised deuices against me, *saying;* Let vs destroy †the tree with the fruit thereof, and let vs cut him off from the land of the liuing, that his name may be no more remembred.

20 But, O LORD of hostes, that iudgest righteously, that * tryest the reines, and the heart; let me see thy vengeance on them, for vnto thee haue I reuealed my cause.

21 Therefore thus saith the LORD of the men of Anathoth, that seeke thy life, saying; Prophecie not in the Name of the LORD, that thou die not by our hand :

22 Therefore thus saith the LORD of hosts, Behold, I wil †punish them : the young men shall die by the sword, their sonnes and their daughters shall die by famine.

23 And there shall be no remnant of

them, for I will bring euill vpon the men of Anathoth, *euen* the yere of their visitation.

CHAP. XII.

1 Ieremiah complaining of the wickeds prosperitie, by faith seeth their ruine. 5 God admonisheth him of his brethrens treacherie against him, 7 and lamenteth his heritage. 14 Hee promiseth to the penitent, returne from captiuitie.

Ighteous *art* thou, O LORD, when I pleade with thee : ‖yet let mee talke with thee of *thy* iudgements : *Wherefore doeth the way of the wicked prosper ? *wherefore* are all they happie that deale very treacherously ?

2 Thou hast planted them, yea they haue taken root : †they grow, yea they bring foorth fruit, thou *art* neere in their mouth, and farre from their reines.

3 But thou, O LORD, *knowest me; thou hast seene me, and tried mine heart †towards thee : pull them out like sheep for the slaughter, and prepare them for the day of slaughter.

4 How long shall the land mourne, and the herbes of euery field wither, *for the wickednesse of them that dwell therein ? the beasts are consumed, and the birds, because they said; He shall not see our last end.

5 ¶ If thou hast runne with the footmen, and they haue wearied thee, then how canst thou contend with horses? and if in the land of peace, *wherein* thou trustedst, *they wearied thee,* then how wilt thou doe in the swelling of Iordan ?

6 For euen *thy brethren and the house of thy father, euen they haue dealt treacherously with thee, yea ‖they haue called a multitude after thee ; beleeue them not, though they speake †faire words vnto thee.

7 ¶ I haue forsaken mine house : I haue left mine heritage : I haue giuen †the dearely beloued of my soule into the hand of her enemies.

8 Mine heritage is vnto me as a lyon in the forrest: it‖cryeth out against me, therefore haue I hated it.

9 Mine heritage *is* vnto mee as a ‖speckled bird, the birdes round about *are* against her; come yee, assemble all the beasts of the field, ‖come to deuoure.
10 Many

Marginal notes (left column)
Heb. euill.

Cha. 2. 28.

Heb. shame

Cha. 7. 16.
& 14. 11.

Heb. euill.

Isai. 1. 11.

*Heb. what
to my be-
loued in my
house?
or, when
euill is.*

*Heb. the
like with
bread.*

*1. Sam. 16.
1. chron.
28. 9. psal.
7. 10. and
139. 12. cha.
17. 10. and
20. 12. reue.
2. 23.*

*Heb. visite
vpon.*

Marginal notes (right column)
‖ *Or, let me
reason the
case with
thee.*

* *Iob 21. 7.
psal. 37. 1.
and 73. 3.
hab. 1. 3.*

† *Heb. they
goe on.*

* *Psal. 17. 3.*

† *Heb. with
thee.*

* *Psal. 107.
34.*

° *Chap. 9. 4.*

‖ *Or, they
cryed after
thee fully.*
† *Heb. good
things.*

† *Heb. the
loue.*

‖ *Or, yelleth.
Heb. giueth
out his voice.*

‖ *Or, tallen-
ted.*
‖ *Or, cause
them to
come.*

10 Many pastors haue destroyed my vineyard; they haue troden my portion vnder foote : they haue made my † pleasant portion a desolate wildernesse.

† Heb. portion of desire.

11 They haue made it desolate, *and* being desolate it mourneth vnto me; the whole land is made desolate, because no man layeth *it* to heart.

12 The spoilers are come vpon all high places through the wildernesse: for the sword of the LORD shall deuoure from the *one* end of the land euen to the *other* end of the land: no flesh shall haue peace.

* Leuit. 26. 16. deut. 26 38. mic. 6. 15. agg. 1. 6.

13 They haue * sowen wheate, but shall reape thornes : they haue put themselues to paine, *but* shall not profit: and they shall be ashamed of your reuenues, because of the fierce anger of the LORD.

14 ¶ Thus saith the LORD against all mine euill neighbours, that touch the inheritance, which I haue caused my people Israel to inherit ; Behold, I will *plucke them out of their land, and plucke out the house of Iudah from among them.

* Deut. 30. 3. chap. 32. 37.

15 And it shall come to passe after that I haue plucked them out, I will returne, and haue compassion on them, and will bring againe euery man to his heritage, and euery man to his land.

16 And it shall come to passe, if they will diligently learne the wayes of my people to sweare by my name (The LORD liueth, as they taught my people to sweare by Baal :) then shall they be built in the middest of my people.

* Isai. 60. 12.

17 But if they will not *obey, I will vtterly plucke vp, and destroy that nation, saith the LORD.

CHAP. XIII.

1 In the Type of a linnen girdle, hidden at Euphrates, God prefigureth the destruction of his people. 12 Vnder the parable of the bottles filled with wine, he foretelleth their drunkennesse in miserie. 15 He exhorteth to preuent their future iudgements. 22 He sheweth their abominations are the cause thereof.

Hus saith the LORD vnto me; Goe and get thee a linen girdle, and put it vpon thy loynes, and put it not in water.

2 So I got a girdle, according to the word of the LORD, and put it on my loines.

3 And the word of the LORD came vnto me the second time, saying;

4 Take the girdle that thou hast got, which *is* vpon thy loines, and arise, goe to Euphrates, and hide it there in a hole of the rocke.

5 So I went and hid it by Euphrates, as the LORD commaunded mee.

6 And it came to passe after many daies, that the LORD saide vnto me; Arise, goe to Euphrates, and take the girdle from thence, which I commaunded thee to hide there.

7 Then I went to Euphrates and digged, and tooke the girdle from the place where I had hid it, and behold, the girdle was marred, it was profitable for nothing.

8 Then the word of the LORD came vnto me, saying ;

9 Thus saith the LORD; After this maner will I marre the pride of Iudah, and the great pride of Ierusalem.

10 This euill people which refuse to heare my words, which walke in the ||imagination of their heart, and walke after other Gods to serue them and to worship them, shall euen be as this girdle, which is good for nothing.

|| Or, stubburnnesse.

11 For as the girdle cleaueth to the loines of a man : so haue I caused to cleaue vnto me the whole house of Israel, and the whole house of Iudah, saith the LORD; that they might bee vnto me for a people, and for a name, and for a praise, and for a glory: but they would not heare.

12 ¶ Therefore thou shalt speake vnto them this word ; Thus saith the LORD God of Israel ; Euerie botle shalbe filled with wine : and they shall say vnto thee; Doe we not certainly know, that euery botle shall be filled with wine ?

13 Then shalt thou say vnto them; Thus saith the LORD; Behold, I will fill all the inhabitants of this land, euen the kings that sit vpon Dauids throne, and the priests and the prophets, and all the inhabitants of Ierusalem with drunkennesse.

14 And I will dash them † one against another, euen the fathers and the sonnes together, saith the LORD: I wil not pitie nor spare, nor haue mercie, †but destroy them.

† Heb. a man against his brother.

15 ¶ Heare ye and giue eare, bee not proud :

† Heb. from destroying them.

proud: for the LORD hath spoken.

16 Giue glory to the LORD your God before he cause *darknesse, and before your feet stumble vpon the darke mountaines, and while yee looke for light, he turne it into the shadowe of death, and make *it* grosse darkenesse.

* Isa. 8. 22.

17 But if ye will not heare it, my soule shall weepe in secret places for *your* pride, and *mine eye shall weepe sore, and run downe with teares, because the LORDS flocke is caried away captiue.

* Lamen. 1. 16. and 2. 18.

18 Say vnto the king, and to the queene, Humble your selues, sit downe, for your ||principalities shall come downe, *euen* the crowne of your glory.

|| Or, head-tires.

19 The cities of the South shall bee shut vp, and none shall open *them*, Iudah shall be caried away captiue all of it, it shall bee wholly caried away captiue.

20 Lift vp your eyes, and beholde them that come from the North, where is the flocke *that* was giuen thee, thy beautifull flocke?

21 What wilt thou say when he shall †punish thee (for thou hast taught them *to be* captaines *and* as chiefe ouer thee) shall not sorrowes take thee as a woman in trauaile?

† Hebr. visit vpon.

22 ¶ And if thou say in thine heart, *Wherefore come these things vpon me? for the greatnesse of thine iniquitie are thy skirts discouered, *and* thy heeles ||made bare.

* Cha. 5. 19 and 16. 10.

|| Or, shall be violently taken away.

23 Can the Ethiopian change his skinne? or the leopard his spots? *then* may ye also doe good, that are †accustomed to doe euill.

† Heb. taught.

24 Therefore will I scatter them as the stubble that passeth away by the winde of the wildernesse.

25 This *is* thy lot, the portion of thy measures from me, saith the LORD, because thou hast forgotten mee, and trusted in falshood.

26 Therefore will I discouer thy skirts vpon thy face, that thy shame may appeare.

27 I haue seene thine adulteries, and thy neighings, the lewdnesse of thy whordome, *and* thine abominations on the hils in the fields: woe vnto thee, O Ierusalem, wilt thou not bee made cleane? †when *shall it* once *be*?

† Heb. after when yet?

CHAP. XIIII.

1 The grieuous famine 7 causeth Ieremiah to
pray. 10 The Lord will not be intreated for
the people. 13 Lying prophets are no excuse
for them. 17 Ieremiah is mooued to complaine for them.

The word of the LORD that came to Ieremiah concerning the †dearth.

† Heb. the words of the dearths or restraints.

2 Iudah mourneth, and the gates thereof languish, they are blacke vnto the ground, and the crie of Ierusalem is gone vp.

3 And their nobles haue sent their litle ones to the waters, they came to the pits *and* found no water, they returned with the vessels emptie: they were ashamed and confounded, and couered their heads.

4 Because the ground is chapt, for there was no raine in the earth, the plowmen were ashamed, they couered their heads.

5 Yea the hinde also calued in the field, and forsooke *it*, because there was no grasse.

6 And the wilde asses did stand in the hie places, they snuffed vp the winde like dragons: their eyes did faile because *there was* no grasse.

7 ¶ O LORD, though our iniquities testifie against vs, doe thou *it* for thy Names sake: for our back-slidings are many, we haue sinned against thee.

8 O the hope of Israel, the Sauiour thereof in time of trouble, why shouldest thou be as a stranger in the land, and as a wayfaring man, *that* turneth aside to tarie for a night?

9 Why shouldest thou bee as a man astonied, as a mightie man *that* cannot saue? yet thou, O LORD, *art* in the midst of vs, and we are called †by thy Name, leaue vs not.

† Hebr. thy Name is called vpon vs.

10 ¶ Thus saith the LORD vnto this people, Thus haue they loued to wander, they haue not refrained their feete, therefore the LORD doeth not accept them, hee will now remember their iniquitie, and visite their sinnes.

11 Then said the LORD vnto mee, *Pray not for this people, for *their* good.

* Cha. 7. 16. and 11. 14. exod. 32. 10

12 *When they fast I will not heare their crie, and when they offer burnt offering and an oblation I wil not accept them: but I will consume them by the sword, and by the famine, and by the pestilence.

* Prou. 1. 28 isa. 1. 15. cha. 11. 11. ezek. 8. 18. mic. 3. 4.

13 ¶ Then said I Ah Lord GOD, behold, the prophets say vnto them; Ye shall not see the sword, neither shall ye

haue

850

† *Hebr peace of trueth.*

haue famine, but I will giue you † assured peace in this place.

14 Then the LORD said vnto me, The prophets prophecie lies in my Name, *I sent them not, neither haue I commanded them, neither spake vnto them: they prophecie vnto you a false vision and diuination, and a thing of nought, and the deceit of their heart.

* Chap. 23. 21. and 27. 15. and 29. 8, 9.

15 Therefore thus saith the LORD concerning the prophets that prophecie in my Name, and I sent them not, yet they say, Sword and famine shall not be in this land, By sword and famine shall those prophets be consumed.

16 And the people to whom they prophecie, shall be cast out in the streets of Ierusalem, because of the famine and the sword, and they shall haue none to burie them, them, their wiues, nor their sonnes, nor their daughters : for I will powre their wickednesse vpon them.

ᵛ Lam. 1. 16. and 2. 18. chap. 13. 17.

17 ¶ Therefore thou shalt say this word vnto them, *Let mine eies runne downe with teares night and day, and let them not cease, for the virgin daughter of my people is broken with a great breach, with a very grieuous blow.

18 If I goe forth into the field, then behold the slaine with the sword, and if I enter into the citie, then behold them that are sicke with famine, yea both the prophet and the priest ‖ goe about into a land that they know not.

‖ Or, make merchandise against a land, and menacknowledge it not, Chap. 5. 31.
* Chap. 8. 15.

19 Hast thou vtterly reiected Iudah? hath thy soule loathed Zion? why hast thou smitten vs, and *there is no healing for vs? *we looked for peace, and there is no good, and for the time of healing, and behold trouble.

20 We acknowledge, O LORD, our wickednes, and the iniquitie of our fathers · for *wee haue sinned against thee.

* Psal. 106. 6. dan. 9. 8.

21 Do not abhorre vs, for thy Names sake, doe not disgrace the Throne of thy glorie : remember, breake not thy Couenant with vs.

22 Are there any among the vanities of the Gentiles that can cause raine? or can the heauens giue showres, Art not thou he, O LORD our God? therefore we will waite vpon thee : for thou hast made all these things.

CHAP. XV.

1 The vtter reiection, and manifold iudgements of the Iewes. 10 Ieremiah complayning of their spight, receiueth a promise for himselfe, 12 and a threatning for them. 15 He praieth, 19 and receiueth a gracious promise.

Hen said the LORD vnto me, *Though *Moses and *Samuel stood before me, yet my minde could not be toward this people, cast them out of my sight, and let them goe foorth.

* Eze. 14. 14.
* Exod. 32.
* 1. Sam. 9.

2 And it shall come to passe if they say vnto thee, Whither shall wee goe foorth? then thou shalt tell them; Thus saith the LORD, *Such as are for death to death; and such as are for the sword, to the sword; and such as are for the famine, to the famine; and such as are for the captiuitie, to the captiuitie.

* Chap. 4. 11. zach. 9.

3 And I will *appoint ouer them foure † kindes, saith the LORD, the sword to slay, and the dogs to teare, and the foules of the heauen, and the beasts of the earth to deuoure and destroy.

* Leuit. 26.
† Hebr. families.

4 And † I will cause them to be *remoued into all kingdomes of the earth, because of *Manasseh the sonne of Hezekiah king of Iudah, for that which hee did in Ierusalem.

† Hebr. I giue them for a mouing.
* Deut. 28. cha.
2. Kin. 11.

5 For who shall haue pitie vpon thee, O Ierusalem? or who shall bemoane thee? or who shall goe aside to † aske how thou doest?

† Hebr. aske of thy peace.

6 Thou hast forsaken me, saith the LORD, thou art gone backward : therefore will I stretch out my hand against thee, and destroy thee, I am wearie with repenting.

7 And I will fanne them with a fanne in the gates of the land : I will bereaue them of ‖ children, I wil destroy my people, sith they returne not from their waies.

‖ Or, whosoeuer deare

8 Their widowes are increased to me aboue the sand of the seas : I haue brought vpon them ‖ against the mother of the yongmen, a spoiler at noone day : I haue caused him to fall vpon it suddenly, and terrors vpon the citie.

‖ Or, against the mother citie, a manspoiler &c. Or against mother the yongmen.
* Amos

9 *She that hath borne seuen, languisheth : she hath giuen vp the ghost : her sunne is gone down while it was yet day : shee hath bene ashamed and confounded, and the residue of them will I deliuer to the sword before their enemies, saith the LORD.

10 ¶ *Woe is mee, my mother, that that thou hast borne me a man of strife, and a man of contention to the whole earth : I haue neither lent on vsurie, nor

* Iob 3. &c. ch. 15.

nor men haue lent to me on vsurie, *yet* euery one of them doeth curse me.

11 The Lord said, Verely it shall be well with thy remnant, verely ‖I will cause the enemie to intreat thee *well* in the time of euill, and in the time of affliction.

‖ *Or, I will entreat the enemie for thee.*

12 Shall yron breake the Northren yron, and the steele?

13 Thy substance and thy treasures will I giue to the *spoile without price, and *that* for all thy sinnes, euen in all thy borders.

* Cha. 17. 3.

14 And I will make *thee* to passe with thine enemies, into a land *which* thou knowest not : for a *fire is kindled in mine anger, *which* shall burne vpon you.

* Deut. 32. 22.

15 ¶ O Lord, thou knowest, remember me, and visit me, and reuenge me of my persecutors, take mee not away in thy long suffering : know that for thy sake I haue suffered rebuke.

16 Thy wordes were found, and I did *eate them, and thy word was vnto mee, the ioy and reioycing of mine heart : for †I am called by thy Name, O Lord God of hostes.

* Eze. 3. 3. reuel. 10. 9.

† *Heb. thy Name is called vpon me.*

17 I sate not in the assembly of the mockers, nor reioyced : I sate alone because of thy hand : for thou hast filled me with indignation.

18 Why is my *paine perpetuall? and my wound incurable *which* refuseth to be healed? wilt thou be altogether vnto me as a lyar, *and as* waters that †faile?

* Chap. 30. 15.

† *Heb. be not sure?*

19 ¶ Therfore thus saith the Lord ; If thou returne, then will I bring thee againe, *and* thou shalt stand before me : and if thou take forth the precious from the vile, thou shalt be as my mouth : let them returne vnto thee, but returne not thou vnto them.

20 And I will make thee vnto this people a fenced brasen *wall, and they shall fight against thee, but they shall not *preuaile against thee : for I *am* with thee to saue thee, and to deliuer thee, sayth the Lord.

* Cha. 1. 18. and 6. 27.

* Chap. 20. 11.

21 And I will deliuer thee out of the hand of the wicked, and I will redeeme thee out of the hand of the terrible.

CHAP. XVI.

1 The Prophet, vnder the types of abstaining from marriage, from houses of mourning and feasting, foresheweth the vtter ruine of the Iewes, 10 because they were worse then their fathers. 14 Their returne from captiuitie, shall be stranger then their deliuerance out of Egypt. 16 God will doubly recompense their idolatrie.

He word of the Lord came also vnto me, saying ; 2 Thou shalt not take thee a wife, neither shalt thou haue sonnes nor daughters in this place.

3 For thus sayth the Lord concerning the sonnes and concerning the daughters that are borne in this place, and concerning their mothers that bare them, and concerning their fathers that begate them in this land :

4 They shal die of grieuous *deaths, they shall not bee *lamented, neither shall they be buried: *but* they shall be as doung vpon the face of the earth, and they shalbe consumed by the sword, and by famine, and their *carkeises shall be meate for the foules of heauen, and for the beasts of the earth.

* Cha. 15. 2.

* Chap. 25. 33.

* Chap. 7. 33 and 34. 20. psal. 39. 2.

5 For thus sayth the Lord, Enter not into the house of ‖ mourning, neither goe to lament nor bemoane them : for I haue taken away my peace from this people, sayth the Lord, *euen* louing kindnesse and mercies.

‖ *Or, mourning feast.*

6 Both the great and the small shall die in this land : they shall not be buried, neither shall men lament for them, nor cut themselues, nor make themselues balde for them.

7 Neither shall men *‖ teare *themselues* for them in mourning to comfort them for the dead, neither shall men giue them the cuppe of consolation to drinke for their father, or for their mother.

* Leuit. 19. 28. deut. 14. 1.

‖ *Or, breake bread for them, as Ezek. 24. 17.*

8 Thou shalt not also goe into the house of feasting, to sit with them to eat and to drinke.

9 For thus sayth the Lord of hostes, the God of Israel ; Behold, *I will cause to cease out of this place in your eyes, and in your dayes, the voice of mirth, and the voice of gladnesse, the voice of the bridegroome, and the voice of the bride.

* Isai. 24. 7, 8. chap. 7. 34. and 25. 10. ezek. 26. 10.

10 ¶ And it shal come to passe *when thou shalt shewe this people all these wordes, and they shall say vnto thee ; Wherefore hath the Lord pronounced all this great euill against vs? or what is our iniquitie? or what is our sinne, that we haue committed against the Lord our God?

* Cha. 5. 19. and 13. 22.

11 Then

11 Then shalt thou say vnto them; Because your fathers haue forsaken me, saith the LORD, and haue walked after other Gods, and haue serued them, and haue worshipped them, and haue forsaken mee, and haue not kept my law:

12 And yee haue done * worse then your fathers, (for behold, yee walke euerie one after the || imagination of his euill heart, that they may not hearken vnto me.)

13 * Therefore will I cast you out of this land into a land that yee knowe not, *neither* yee, nor your fathers, and there shall yee serue other Gods day and night, where I will not shewe you fauour.

14 ¶ Therefore behold, the * dayes come, saith the LORD, that it shall no more be said; The LORD liueth that brought vp the children of Israel out of the land of Egypt;

15 But, The LORD liueth, that brought vp the children of Israel from the land of the North, and from all the lands whither hee had driuen them: and I will bring them againe into their land, that I gaue vnto their fathers.

16 ¶ Behold, I will send for many fishers, saith the LORD, and they shal fish them, and after will I send for manie hunters, and they shall hunt them from euery mountaine, and from euery hill, and out of the holes of the rockes.

17 For mine * eyes *are* vpon all their waies: they are not hid from my face, neither is their iniquitie hid from mine eies.

18 And first I will recompense their iniquitie, and their sinne double, because they haue defiled my land, they haue filled mine inheritance with the carkeises of their detestable and abominable things.

19 O LORD, my strength and my fortresse, and my refuge in the day of affliction; the Gentiles shall come vnto thee from the ends of the earth, and shall say; Surely our fathers haue inherited lyes, vanitie, and *things* wherein *there is* no profit.

20 Shall a man make Gods vnto himselfe, and * they *are* no Gods?

21 Therefore behold, I will this once cause them to know: I will cause them to knowe mine hand and my might, and they shall know that my name *is* the LORD.

CHAP. XVII.

1 The captiuitie of Iudah for her sinne. 5 Trust in man is cursed, 7 in God is blessed. 9 The deceitfull heart cannot deceiue God. 12 The saluation of God. 15 The Prophet complaineth of the mockers of his prophecie. 19 He is sent to renew the couenant in hallowing the Sabbath.

He sinne of Iudah *is* written with a * pen of yron, *and* with the † point of a diamond; *it* is grauen vpon the table of their heart, and vpon the hornes of your altars:

2 Whilest their children remember their altars and their * groues by the greene trees vpon the high hilles.

3 O my mountaine, in the field * I will giue thy substance, *and* all thy treasures to the spoile, *and* thy high places for sinne, throughout all thy borders

4 And thou, † euen thy selfe shalt discontinue from thine heritage that I gaue thee, and I will cause thee to serue thine enemies in the land which thou knowest not: for yee haue kindled a fire in mine anger, *which* shall burne for euer.

5 ¶ Thus saith the LORD, Cursed *be* the man that trusteth in man, and maketh flesh his arme, and whose heart departeth from the LORD.

6 For hee shall be like the heath in the desert, and shall not see when good commeth, but shall inhabite the parched places in the wildernesse, in a salt land and not inhabited.

7 * Blessed *is* the man that trusteth in the LORD, and whose hope the LORD is.

8 For he shall be * as a tree planted by the waters, and that spreadeth out her rootes by the riuer, and shall not see when heate commeth, but her leafe shall be greene, and shall not be carefull in the yeere of || drought, neither shall cease from yeelding fruit.

9 ¶ The heart *is* deceitfull aboue all things, and desperately wicked, who can know it?

10 I the LORD * search the heart, *I* try the reines, euen to giue euery man according to his waies, *and* according to the fruit of his doings.

---

* Chap. 7. 26.

‖ *Or, stubburnnesse.*

* Deut. 4. 27. and 28. 64, 65.

* Chap. 23. 7, 8.

* Iob. 34. 21 prou. 5. 21. chap. 32. 19.

* Chap. 2. 11.

* Iob. 19. 24.
† Heb. *naile.*

* Iudg. 3. 7 Isai. 1. 29.

* Chap. 15 13.

† Heb. *in th. selfe.*

* Psal. 2. 12 and 34. 10. and 125. 1. prou. 16. 20. isa. 30. 18.
* Psal. 1. 3

‖ *Or, restraint.*

* 2. Sam. 1 7. psal. 7. 1* chap. 11. 2 and 20. 12.

11 *As* the partrich ‖ sitteth on egges, and hatcheth *them* not: *so* he that getteth riches and not by right, shall leaue them in the midst of his dayes, and at his end shall be a foole.

12 ¶ A glorious high throne from the beginning, *is* the place of our Sanctuarie.

13 O Lᴏʀᴅ, the hope of Israel, * all that forsake thee shall be ashamed, and they that depart from me shall bee written in the earth, because they haue forsaken the Lᴏʀᴅ the *fountaine of liuing waters.

14 Heale me, O Lᴏʀᴅ, and I shall be healed: saue me, and I shalbe saued: for thou *art* my praise.

15 ¶ Behold, they say vnto mee, * Where *is* the word of the Lᴏʀᴅ? let it come now.

16 As for me, I haue not hastened from being a pastour to †follow thee, *neither haue I desired the wofull day, thou knowest : that which came out of my lips, was right before thee.

17 Be not a terrour vnto me, thou *art* my hope in the day of euill.

18 *Let them bee confounded that persecute me, but let not me be confounded : let them be dismayed, but let not me be dismayed : bring vpon them the day of euill, and †* destroy them with double destruction.

19 ¶ Thus sayd the Lᴏʀᴅ vnto me, Go and stand in the gate of the children of the people, whereby the kings of Iudah come in, and by the which they goe out, and in all the gates of Ierusalem.

20 And say vnto them, Heare ye the word of the Lᴏʀᴅ, ye kings of Iudah, and all Iudah, and all the inhabitants of Ierusalem, that enter in by these gates.

21 Thus saith the Lᴏʀᴅ, * Take heed to your selues, and beare no burden on the Sabbath day, nor bring *it* in by the gates of Ierusalem.

22 Neither carie forth a burden out of your houses on the Sabbath day, neither doe ye any worke, but hallowe ye the Sabbath day, as I *commanded your fathers.

23 But they obeyed not, neither inclined their eare, but made their necke stiffe, that they might not heare nor receiue instruction.

24 And it shall come to passe, if yee diligently hearken vnto me, saith the Lᴏʀᴅ, to bring in no burden through the gates of this citie on the Sabbath day, but hallow the Sabbath day, to doe no worke therein :

25 * Then shall there enter into the gates of this citie kings and princes sitting vpon the throne of Dauid, riding in charets and on horses, they and their princes, the men of Iudah and the inhabitants of Ierusalem : and this citie shall remaine for euer.

26 And they shall come from the cities of Iudah, and from the places about Ierusalem, and from the lande of Beniamin, and from the plaine and from the mountaines, and from the South, bringing burnt offerings, and sacrifices, and meate offerings, and incense, and bringing sacrifices of praise vnto the house of the Lᴏʀᴅ.

27 But if you will not hearken vnto me to hallow the Sabbath day, and not to beare a burden, euen entring in at the gates of Ierusalem on the Sabbath day : then will I kindle a fire in the gates thereof, and it shall deuoure the palaces of Ierusalem, and it shall not be quenched.

CHAP. XVIII.

1 Vnder the type of a potter is shewed Gods absolute power in disposing of Nations. 11 Iudgements threatned to Iudah for her strange reuolt. 18 Ieremiah prayeth against his conspiratours.

THe word which came to Ieremiah from ỹ Lᴏʀᴅ saying,

2 Arise and go downe to the potters house, & there I will cause thee to heare my words.

3 Then I went downe to the potters house, and behold, hee wrought a worke on the ‖ wheeles.

4 And the vessell ‖ that he made of clay, was marred in the hand of the potter; so he †made it againe another vessell as seemed good to the potter to make *it*.

5 Then the word of the Lᴏʀᴅ came to me, saying,

6 O house of Israel, *cannot I doe with you as this potter, saith the Lᴏʀᴅ? behold, as the clay *is* in the potters hand, so *are* ye in mine hand, O house of Israel.

7 *At what* instant I shall speake concerning a nation, and concerning a kingdome, to *plucke vp and to pull downe, and to destroy *it*.

8 If

r, gathe-
young
ich shee
h not
ight
th.

sal. 73.
Isa. 1. 28

hap. 2. 3

sa. 5. 19.

Ieb. after
e.
hap. 1.
&c.

sal. 35. 4
& 40. 15.

Ieb. break
m with a
ble
ach.
ha. 11. 20

Nehe. 13.

xo. 20. 8.
& 23. 12.
& 31. 13.
& 20. 12.

Cha. 22. 8

‖ *Or, frames*
or seates.
‖ *Or, that*
he made,
was marred
as clay in the
hand of the
potter.
† *Hebr. re-*
turned and
made.
* Isa. 45. 9.
rom. 9. 10.
wisd. 15. 7.

* Chap. 1.
10.

8 If that nation against whom I haue pronounced, turne from their euill, *I will repent of the euill that I thought to doe vnto them.

*Iona. 3. 10.

9 And at what instant I shall speake concerning a nation, and concerning a kingdome to build and to plant it;

10 If it doe euill in my sight, that it obey not my voice, then I will repent of the good, wherewith I saide I would benefite them.

11 ¶ Now therefore goe to, speake to the men of Iudah, and to the inhabitants of Ierusalem, saying, Thus saith the LORD; Behold, I frame euill against you, and deuise a deuice against you: *returne ye now euery one from his euill way, and make your waies and your doings good.

*2. Kin. 17. 13. chap. 7. 3. and 25. 5. and 35. 15.
* Chap. 2. 25.

12 And they said, *There is no hope, but wee will walke after our owne deuices, and wee will euery one doe the imagination of his euil heart.

* Chap. 2. 10.

13 Therefore thus saith the LORD, *Aske ye now among the heathen, who hath heard such things? the Virgin of Israel hath done a very horrible thing.

14 Will a man leaue ‖ the *snow of Lebanon which commeth from the rocke of the fielde? or shall the colde flowing waters that come from another place, be forsaken?

‖ Or, my fields for a rocke, or for the snow of Lebanon? Shall the running waters be forsaken for the strange cold waters?
* Cha. 2. 13.
* Chap. 17. 13.
* Chap. 6. 16.

15 Because my people hath *forgotten mee, they haue burnt incense to vanitie, and they haue caused them to stumble in their waies from the *ancient paths, to walke in paths, in a way not cast vp,

*Chap. 19. 8. and 49. 13. and 50. 13.

16 To make their land *desolate and a perpetuall hissing: euery one that passeth thereby shall bee astonished, and wagge his head.

17 I will scatter them as with an East winde before the enemie: I will shew them the backe, and not the face, in the day of their calamitie.

18 ¶ Then said they, Come, and let vs deuise deuices against Ieremiah: *for the Law shall not perish from the Priest, nor counsell from the wise, nor the word from the prophet: Come and let vs smite him ‖with the tongue, and let vs not giue heede to any of his wordes.

* Mal. 2. 7.

‖ Or, for the tongue.

19 Giue heed to me, O LORD, and hearken to the voice of them that contend with me.

20 Shall euill bee recompensed for good? for they haue digged a pit for my soule: remember that I stood before thee to speake good for them, and to turne away thy wrath from them.

21 Therefore deliuer vp their children to the famine, and †*powre out their blood by the force of the sword, and let their wiues be bereaued of their children and be widowes, and let their men be put to death, let their yong men be slaine by the sword in battell.

† Heb. powre them out
* Psal. 1 10.

22 Let a crie bee heard from their houses, when thou shalt bring a troupe suddenly vpon them, for they haue digged a pit to take me, and hid snares for my feet.

23 Yet LORD thou knowest all their counsell against me †to slay mee: forgiue not their iniquitie, neither blot out their sinne from thy sight, but let them bee ouerthrowen before thee, deale thus with them in the time of thine anger.

† Hebr. death.

CHAP. XIX.

1 Vnder the type of breaking a potters vessell, is foreshewed the desolation of the Iewes for their sinnes.

 Hus saith the LORD, Goe and get a potters earthen bottell, and take of the ancients of the people, and of the ancients of the Priestes.

2 And goe forth vnto the valley of the sonne of Hinnom, which is by the entrie of the †Eastgate, and proclaime there the words that I shall tell thee:

† Hebr. Sungate

3 And say, Heare ye the word of the LORD, O kings of Iudah, and inhabitants of Ierusalem; Thus saith the LORD of hostes, the God of Israel; Behold, I will bring euill vpon this place, the which whosoeuer heareth, his eares shall *tingle.

* 1. Sam 11. 2. ki 21. 12.

4 Because they haue forsaken mee, and haue estranged this place, and haue burnt incense in it vnto other gods, whom neither they, nor their fathers haue knowen, nor the kings of Iudah, and haue filled this place with the blood of innocents.

5 They haue built also the high places of Baal, to burne their sonnes with fire for burnt offerings vnto Baal, *which I commanded not, nor spake it, neither came it into my minde.

* Chap. 31, 32.

6 Therefore behold, the daies come, saith the LORD, that this place shall no more bee called Tophet, nor the valley

valley of the sonne of Hinnom, but the valley of slaughter.

7 And I will make void the counsell of Iudah and Ierusalem in this place, and I will cause them to fall by the sword before their enemies, and by the hands of them that seek their liues: and their * carkeises will I giue to be meat for the foules of the heauen, and for the beasts of the earth:

8 And I will make this citie * desolate and an hissing: euery one that passeth thereby shalbe astonished and hisse, because of all the plagues thereof.

9 And I will cause them to eate the * flesh of their sonnes and the flesh of their daughters, and they shal eate euery one the flesh of his friend in the siege and straitnesse, wherewith their enemies, and they that seeke their liues, shall straiten them.

10 Then shalt thou breake ỹ bottle in the sight of the men that goe with thee,

11 And shalt say vnto them; Thus saith the LORD of hostes, Euen so will I breake this people and this citie as one breaketh a potters vessell that †cannot bee made whole againe, and they shall * bury them in Tophet, till there be no place else to bury.

12 Thus will I doe vnto this place, sayth the LORD, and to the inhabitants thereof, and euen make their citie as Tophet.

13 And the houses of Ierusalem, and the houses of the kings of Iudah shall bee defiled as the place of Tophet, because of all the houses vpon whose * roofes they haue burnt incense vnto all the hoste of heauen, & haue powred out drinke offrings vnto other gods.

14 Then came Ieremiah from Tophet, whither the LORD had sent him to prophecie, and hee stood in the court of the LORDS house, and said to all the people,

15 Thus saith the LORD of hostes the God of Israel, Behold, I wil bring vpon this city, and vpon all her townes all the euill that I haue pronounced against it, because they haue hardened their neckes, that they might not heare my wordes.

CHAP. XX.

Now Pashur the sonne of *Immer the Priest, who was also chiefe gouernor in the house of the LORD, heard that Ieremiah prophecied these things.

2 Then Pashur smote Ieremiah the Prophet, and put him in the stockes that were in the high gate of Beniamin, which was by the house of the LORD.

3 And it came to passe on the morrow, that Pashur brought foorth Ieremiah out of the stockes. Then sayd Ieremiah vnto him, The LORD hath not called thy name Pashur, but ǁ Magor-missabib.

4 For thus sayth the LORD, Behold, I will make thee a terrour to thy selfe, and to all thy friends, and they shall fall by the sword of their enemies, and thine eyes shall behold it, and I will giue all Iudah into the hand of the king of Babylon, and hee shall cary them captiue into Babylon, and shall slay them with the sword.

5 Moreouer, *I will deliuer all the strength of this city, and all the labours thereof, and all the precious things thereof, and all the treasures of the kings of Iudah will I giue into the hand of their enemies which shal spoile them, and take them and cary them to Babylon.

6 And thou Pashur, and all that dwell in thine house, shall goe into captiuitie, and thou shalt come to Babylon, and there thou shalt die, and shalt be buried there, thou and all thy friends to whom thou hast prophecied lies.

7 ¶ O LORD, thou hast deceiued me, and I was ǁdeceiued, thou art stronger then I, and hast preuailed : I am in derision daily, euery one mocketh me.

8 For since I spake I cryed out, I cried violence and spoyle; because the word of the LORD was made a reproch vnto me, and a derision daily?

9 Then I said; I will not make mention of him, nor speake any more in his name. But his word was in mine heart, as a *burning fire shut vp in my bones, and I was weary with forbearing, and *I could not stay.

10 ¶ For I heard the defaming of many, feare on euery side. Report, say they, and wee will report it: †all my familiars watched for my halting, saying; Peraduenture he will be enticed : and we

Marginal notes (left column)
Cha. 16. 4.
and 7. 33.

Chap. 18.
8. and 49.
ǁ. 13.

Leuit. 26.
ǁ. deu. 28.
ǁ. lam. 4.
ǁ.

Heb. be
ealed.
Cha. 7. 32.

* Chap. 32.
49.

Marginal notes (right column)
* 1. Chro.
24. 14.

ǁ That is,
feare round
about.

* 2. Kings
20. 17.

ǁ Or, enticed.

* Psal. 39. 3.

* Iob 32. 18.

† Heb. euery
man of my
peace.

we shall preuaile against him, and we shall take our reuenge on him.

11 But the LORD is with me as a mighty terrible one : *therefore my persecutours shall stumble, and they shall not preuaile, they shall be greatly ashamed, for they shall not prosper, their *euerlasting confusion shall neuer be forgotten.

12 But O LORD of hostes, that *tryest the righteous, and seest the reines and the heart, let me see thy vengeance on them : for vnto thee haue I opened my cause.

13 Sing vnto the LORD, praise yee the LORD : for hee hath deliuered the soule of the poore from the hand of euill doers.

14 ¶ Cursed be the day wherein I was borne : let not the day wherein my mother bare mee, be blessed.

15 *Cursed be the man who brought tidings to my father, saying ; A man child is borne vnto thee, making him very glad.

16 And let that man be as the cities which the LORD *ouerthrew and repented not : and let him heare the cry in the morning, and the shouting at noonetide.

17 Because he slew me not from the wombe : or that my mother might haue beene my graue, and her wombe to be alwaies great with me.

18 *Wherefore came I forth out of the wombe to see labour and sorrow, that my daies should be consumed with shame?

CHAP. XXI.

1 Zedekiah sendeth to Ieremiah to inquire the euent of Nebuchadrezzars warre. 3 Ieremiah foretelleth a hard siege and miserable captiuitie. 8 He counselleth the people to fall to the Caldeans, 11 and vpbraideth the kings house.

He word which came vnto Ieremiah from the LORD, when king Zedekiah sent vnto him Pashur the sonne of Melchiah, and Zephaniah the sonne of Maaseiah the priest, saying ;

2 Enquire, I pray thee, of the LORD for vs (for Nebuchad-rezzar king of Babylon maketh warre against vs) if so be that the LORD will deale with vs, according to all his wondrous workes, that he may goe vp from vs.

3 ¶ Then saide Ieremiah vnto them ; Thus shall yee say to Zedekiah,

4 Thus saith the LORD God of Israel ; Behold, I will turne backe the weapons of warre that are in your hands, wherewith yee fight against the king of Babylon, and against the Caldeans, which besiege you without the walles, and I will assemble them into the middest of this citie.

5 And I my selfe will fight against you with an *out stretched hand, and with a strong arme, euen in anger, and in furie, and in great wrath.

6 And I will smite the inhabitants of this citie both man and beast · they shall die of a great pestilence.

7 And afterward, saith the LORD, I will deliuer Zedekiah king of Iudah, and his seruants, and the people, and such as are left in this citie from the pestilence, from the sword, and from the famine, into the hand of Nebuchadrezzar king of Babylon, and into the hand of their enemies, and into the hand of those that seeke their life, and and he shall smite them with the edge of the sword : hee shall not spare them, neither haue pitie, nor haue mercy.

8 ¶ And vnto this people thou shalt say ; Thus saith the LORD ; Behold, I set before you the way of life, and the way of death.

9 He that *abideth in this citie, shall die by the sword, and by the famine, and by the pestilence : but he that goeth out, and falleth to the Caldeans, that besiege you, he shall liue, and his life shall be vnto him, *for a pray.

10 For I haue set my face against this citie, for euill and not for good, saith the LORD ; it shall be giuen into the hand of the king of Babylon, and he shall burne it with fire.

11 ¶ And touching the house of the king of Iudah, say ; Heare yee the word of the LORD.

12 Oh house of Dauid, thus saith the LORD, *†Execute iudgement in the morning, and deliuer him that is spoiled, out of the hand of the oppressour, lest my furie goe out like fire, and burne, that none can quench it, because of the euill of your doings.

13 Behold, I am against thee, O †inhabitant of the valley, and rocke of the plaine, saith the LORD, which say, Who

---

*Chap. 17. 18. and 15. 20.

*Chap. 23. 40.

*Chap. 11 20. and 17 10.

*Iob. 3. 3. chap. 15. 10

*Gen. 19. 25.

*Iob. 3. 20.

*Exod. 6.

*Chap. 38 2.

*Chap. 39 18. and 45. 5.

*Chap. 22 3. †Heb. iudg

†Heb. inha bitresse.

Who shall come downe against vs? or who shall enter into our habitations?

14 But I will † punish you according to the * fruit of your doings, saith the Lord: and I will kindle a fire in the forrest thereof, and it shall deuoure all things round about it.

† Heb. visite vpon.
* Pro. 1. 31.

CHAP. XXII.

1 Hee exhorteth to repentance, with promises and threats. 10 The iudgement of Shallum, 13 Of Iehoiakim, 20 and of Coniah.

Hus saith the Lord, Goe downe to the house of the king of Iudah, and speake there this word,

2 And say, Heare the word of the Lord, O king of Iudah, that sittest vpon the throne of Dauid, thou, and thy seruants, and thy people that enter in by these gates.

3 Thus saith the Lord, * Execute ye iudgement and righteousnesse, and deliuer the spoiler out of the hand of the oppressour: and doe no wrong, doe no violence to the stranger, the fatherlesse, nor the widow, neither shed innocent blood in this place.

4 For if ye doe this thing indeede, * then shall there enter in by the gates of this house, Kings sitting † vpon the throne of Dauid, riding in charets and on horses, he, and his seruants, and his people.

5 But if yee will not heare these words, I sweare by my selfe, saith the Lord, that this house shall become a desolation.

6 For thus saith the Lord vnto the kings house of Iudah, Thou *art* Gilead vnto me, *and* the head of Lebanon: *yet* surely I will make thee a wildernesse, *and* cities *which* are not inhabited.

7 And I will prepare destroyers against thee, euery one with his weapons, and they shall cut downe thy choise cedars, and cast *them* into the fire.

8 And many nations shall passe by this citie, and they shall say euery man to his neighbour, * Wherefore hath the Lord done thus vnto this great citie?

9 Then they shall answere, Because they haue forsaken the couenant of the Lord their God, and wor-

* Chap. 21. 12.

* Chap. 17. 25.
† Hebr. for Dauid vpon his throne.

* Deut. 29. 24. 1. kings 9. 8.

shipped other gods, and serued them.

10 ¶ Weepe ye not for the dead, neither bemoane him, *but* weepe sore for him that goeth away: for he shall returne no more, nor see his natiue countrey.

11 For thus saith the Lord touching Shallum, the sonne of Iosiah king of Iudah which reigned in stead of Iosiah his father, which went forth out of this place, He shall not returne thither any more.

12 But he shall die in the place whither they haue led him captiue, and shal see this land no more.

13 ¶ Woe vnto * him that buildeth his house by vnrighteousnesse, and his chambers by wrong: that vseth his neighbours seruice without wages, and giueth him not for his worke:

14 That saith, I will build mee a wide house and † large chambers, and cutteth him out ‖ windowes, and it is sieled with cedar, and painted with vermilion.

15 Shalt thou reigne because thou closest thy selfe in cedar? did not thy father eate and drinke, and doe iudgment and iustice, *and* then *it was* wel with him?

16 He iudged the cause of the poore and needy, then *it was* well *with him: was* not this to know me, saith the Lord?

17 But thine eyes and thine heart *are* not but for thy couetousnesse, and for to shed innocent blood, and for oppression, and for ‖ violence to doe *it*.

18 Therefore thus saith the Lord concerning Iehoiakim the sonne of Iosiah king of Iudah, They shall not lament for him, *saying*, Ah my brother, or ah sister: they shall not lament for him, *saying*, Ah Lord, or ah his glory.

19 He shall be buried with the buriall of an asse, drawen and cast forth beyond the gates of Ierusalem.

20 ¶ Goe vp to Lebanon, and crie, and lift vp thy voice in Bashan, and crie from the passages: for all thy louers are destroyed.

21 I spake vnto thee in thy † prosperitie, *but* thou saidest, I will not heare: this *hath bin* thy maner from thy youth, that thou obeyedst not my voice.

22 The winde shall eate vp all thy pastors, and thy louers shall goe into captiuitie, surely then shalt thou be ashamed and confounded for all thy wickednesse.

23 † O inhabitant of Lebanon, that makest

* Leuit. 19. 13. deut. 24 14, 15. habac. 2. 9.

† Hebr. through aired.
‖ Or, my windowes.

‖ Or, incursion.

† Heb. prosperities.

† Heb. inhabitresse.

makest thy nest in the Cedars, how gracious shalt thou bee when pangs come vpon thee, the paine as of a woman in trauell?

24 As I liue, saith the LORD, though Coniah the sonne of Iehoiakim king of Iudah *were* the signet vpon my right hand, yet would I plucke thee thence.

25 And I will giue thee into the hand of them that seeke thy life, and into the hand *of them* whose face thou fearest, euen into the hand of Nebuchadrezzar king of Babylon, and into the hand of the Caldeans.

26 And I will cast thee out, and thy mother that bare thee, into another countrey where ye were not borne, and there shall ye die.

27 But to the land whereunto they † desire to returne, thither shall they not returne.

† *Hebr. lift vp their minde.*

28 *Is* this man Coniah a despised broken idole? *is* hee a vessell wherein *is* no pleasure? wherefore are they cast out, he and his seed, and are cast into a land which they know not?

29 O earth, earth, earth, heare the word of the LORD:

30 Thus saith the LORD, Write ye this man childlesse, a man *that* shall not prosper in his dayes: for no man of his seed shall prosper, sitting vpon the throne of Dauid, and ruling any more in Iudah.

CHAP. XXIII.

1 Hee prophecieth a restauration of the scattered flocke. 5 Christ shall rule and saue them. 9 Against false prophets, 33 and mockers of the true prophets.

* Ezech. 34. 2.

W*Oe bee vnto the pastors that destroy and scatter the sheepe of my pasture, saith the LORD.

2 Therefore thus saith the LORD God of Israel against the pastors that feed my people; Yee haue scattered my flocke and driuen them away, and haue not visited them; behold I will visite vpon you the euill of your doings, saith the LORD.

3 And I wil gather the remnant of my flocke, out of all countreis whither I haue driuen them, and will bring them againe to their foldes, and they shalbe fruitfull and increase.

* Chap. 3. 15. ezech. 34. 11, 12.

4 And I will set vp * shepheards

ouer them which shall feed them, and they shal feare no more nor be dismaied, neither shall they bee lacking, saith the LORD.

5 ¶ Behold, *the daies come, saith the LORD, that I wil raise vnto Dauid a righteous branch, and a King shall reigne and prosper, and shall execute iudgement and iustice in the earth.

* Chap. 33. 14, 15. isa. 4. 2. and 40 11. dan. 9. 24. iohn 1. 45.

6 *In his dayes Iudah shalbe saued, and Israel shall dwell safely, and this *is* his Name whereby hee shall be called, † The LORD OVR RIGHTEOVSNES.

* Deut. 33 28.

† *Hebr. Ie houah-tsia kenu.*

7 Therefore behold, *the dayes come, saith the LORD, that they shall no more say; The LORD liueth, which brought vp the children of Israel out of the land of Egypt:

* Iere. 16. 14, 15.

8 But, The LORD liueth, which brought vp, and which led the seed of the house of Israel out of the North countrey, and from all countreis whither I had driuen them, and they shall dwell in their owne land.

9 ¶ Mine heart within me is broken because of the prophets, all my bones shake: I am like a drunken man (and like a man whom wine hath ouercome) because of the LORD, and because of the words of his Holinesse.

10 For the land is full of adulterers, for because of ||swearing the land mourneth: the pleasant places of the wildernes are dried vp, and their ||course *is* euil, and their force *is* not right.

|| *Or, cursing.*
|| *Or, violence.*

11 For both prophet and priest are prophane, yea in my house haue I found their wickednesse, saith the LORD.

12 Wherefore their way shalbe vnto them as slippery *wayes* in the darkenes: they shalbe driuen on and fall therein: for I will bring euill vpon them, *euen* the yeere of their visitation, saith the LORD.

13 And I haue seene || folly in the prophets of Samaria; they prophecied in Baal, and caused my people Israel to erre.

|| *Or, an ab surd thing Hebr. vn sauoury.*

14 I haue seene also in the prophets of Ierusalem ||an horrible thing: they commit adultery, and walke in lies: they strengthen also the hands of euill doers, that none doeth returne from his wickednesse: they are all of them vnto me as * Sodom, and the inhabitants thereof as Gomorrah.

|| *Or, filth nesse.*

* Isa. 1.

15 Therefore thus saith the LORD of

Cha. 8. 14
d 9. 15.

of hosts concerning the Prophets ; Behold, I will feede them with *wormewood, and make them drinke the water of gall : for from the Prophets of Ierusalem is ||profanenesse gone forth into all the land.

r, hypo-
sie.

16 Thus saith the Lord of hosts, Hearken not vnto the wordes of the prophets that prophecie vnto you ; they make you vaine : they speake a vision of their owne heart, and not out of the mouth of the Lord.

Cha. 6. 14.
18 8. 11.
. 13. 10.
h. 10. 2.

17 They *say still vnto them that despise me ; The Lord hath sayde, Yee shall haue peace ; and they say vnto euery one that walketh after the ||imagination of his owne heart , No euill shall come vpon you.

r, stub-
nnesse.

r, secret.

18 For who hath stood in the ||counsell of the Lord, and hath perceiued, and heard his word ? who hath marked his word, and heard it ?

Chap. 30.

19 Behold, a *whirlewinde of the Lord is gone foorth in furie, euen a grieuous whirlewinde, it shall fall grieuously vpon the head of the wicked.

Chap. 30.

20 The *anger of the Lord shall not returne, vntill hee haue executed, and til he haue performed the thoughts of his heart : in the latter dayes ye shall consider it perfectly.

Chap. 14.
and 27.

21 * I haue not sent these prophets, yet they ranne : I haue not spoken to them, yet they prophecied.

22 But if they had stood in my counsell, and had caused my people to heare my wordes, then they should haue turned them from their euil way, and from the euill of their doings.

23 Am I a God at hand, sayth the Lord, and not a God afarre off ?

Psal. 139.
&c. amos
9, 3.

24 Can any *hide himselfe in secret places that I shall not see him, saith the Lord ? doe not I fill heauen and earth, sayth the Lord ?

25 I haue heard what the prophets said, that prophecie lyes in my Name, saying ; I haue dreamed, I haue dreamed.

26 How long shall this bee in the heart of the prophets that prophecie lies ? yea they are prophets of the deceit of their owne heart ;

Iudg. 3. 7.
d 8. 33.

27 Which thinke to cause my people to *forget my Name by their dreames which they tell euery man to his neighbour, as their fathers haue forgotten my Name, for Baal.

Heb. with
som is.

28 The prophet †that hath a dreame,

let him tell a dreame ; and hee that hath my word, let him speake my word faithfully : what is the chaffe to the wheat, sayth the Lord ?

29 Is not my word like as a fire, saith the Lord ? and like a hammer that breaketh the rocke in pieces ?

30 Therefore, behold, * I am against the prophets, sayth the Lord, that steale my worde euery one from his neighbour.

* Deut. 18.
20. cha. 14.
14, 15.

31 Beholde, I am against the prophets, saith the Lord, that ||vse their tongues, and say ; He sayth.

|Or, that
smooth their
tongues.

32 Behold, I am against them that prophecie false dreames , sayeth the Lord, and doe tell them, and cause my people to erre by their lyes and by their lightnesse, yet I sent them not, nor commanded them : therefore they shall not profite this people at all, sayth the Lord.

33 ¶ And when this people , or the prophet, or a priest shall aske thee, saying ; What is the burden of the Lord ? thou shalt then say vnto them ; What burden ? I will euen forsake you, saith the Lord.

34 And as for the prophet, and the priest, and the people that shal say, The burden of the Lord, I will euen † punish that man and his house.

† Heb. visite
vpon.

35 Thus shall yee say euery one to his neighbour, and euery one to his brother, What hath the Lord answered ? and what hath the Lord spoken ?

36 And the burden of the Lord shall yee mention no more : for euery mans word shall be his burden : for yee haue peruerted the words of the liuing God, of the Lord of hostes our God.

37 Thus shalt thou say to the prophet, What hath the Lord answered thee ? and what hath the Lord spoken ?

38 But sith ye say, The burden of the Lord ; therefore thus sayeth the Lord, Because you say this word, The burden of the Lord, and I haue sent vnto you, saying ; Ye shall not say, The burden of the Lord :

39 Therefore beholde, I , euen I will vtterly forget you, and I will forsake you, and the citie that I gaue you and your fathers, and cast you out of my presence.

40 And I will bring *an euerlasting reproch

* Chap. 20.
11.

reproch vpon you, and a perpetuall shame, which shall not be forgotten.

CHAP. XXIIII.

1 Vnder the Type of good and bad figs, 4 he foreſheweth the reſtauration of them that were in captiuitie, 8 and the deſolation of Zedekiah and the reſt.

He Lord ſhewed mee, and behold, two baskets of figges were ſet before the temple of the Lord, after that Nebuchad-rezzar *king of Babylon had caried away captiue Ieconiah the sonne of Iehoiakim king of Iudah, and the princes of Iudah, with the carpenters and smiths from Ierusalem, and had brought them to Babylon.

2 One basket *had* very good figges, *euen* like the figges that are first ripe: and the other basket *had* very naughty figges, which could not be eaten, †they were so bad.

3 Then said the Lord vnto me; What seest thou Ieremiah? and I said; Figges: the good figges, very good; and the euill, very euill, that cannot be eaten, they are so euill.

4 ¶ Againe, the word of the Lord came vnto me, saying;

5 Thus saith the Lord, the God of Israel, Like these good figges, so will I acknowledge them that are caried away †captiue of Iudah, whom I haue sent out of this place into the land of the Caldeans for *their* good.

6 For I will set mine eyes vpon them for good, and I will bring them againe to this land, and I will build them, and not pull *them* downe, and I will plant them, and not plucke *them* vp.

7 And I will giue them * an heart to know me, that I *am* the Lord, and they shall be *my people, and I will be their God: for they shall returne vnto me with their whole heart.

8 ¶ And as the euill *figges which cannot be eaten, they are so euill; (Surely thus saith the Lord) so will I giue Zedekiah the king of Iudah, and his princes, and the residue of Ierusalem, that remaine in this land, and them that dwell in the land of Egypt.

9 And I will deliuer them †to *to be remoued into all the kingdomes of the earth for *their* hurt, to be a reproch and a

prouerbe, a taunt and a curse in all places whither I shall driue them.

10 And I will send the sword, the famine, and the pestilence among them, till they be consumed from off the land, that I gaue vnto them, and to their fathers.

CHAP. XXV.

1 Ieremiah reprouing the Iewes disobedience to the Prophets, 8 foretelleth the seuenty yeeres captiuitie, 12 and after that, the destruction of Babylon. 15 Vnder the Type of a cup of wine he foreſheweth the destruction of all nations. 34 The howling of the Shepheards.

He word that came to Ieremiah concerning all the people of Iudah, in the fourth yeere of Iehoiakim the sonne of Iosiah king of Iudah, that *was* the first yeere of Nebuchad-rezzar king of Babylon:

2 The which Ieremiah the prophet spake vnto all the people of Iudah, and to all the inhabitants of Ierusalem, saying;

3 From the thirteenth yere of Iosiah the sonne of Amon king of Iudah, euen vnto this day (that is the three and twentith yeere) the word of the Lord hath come vnto me, and I haue spoken vnto you, rising early and speaking, but yee haue not hearkened.

4 And the Lord hath sent vnto you all his seruants the prophets, *rising early and sending *them*, but yee haue not hearkened, nor inclined your eare to heare.

5 They sayd, *Turne yee againe now euery one from his euill way, and from the euil of your doings, and dwell in the land that the Lord hath giuen vnto you, and to your fathers for euer and euer.

6 And goe not after other Gods to serue them, and to worship them, and prouoke mee not to anger with the workes of your hands, and I will doe you no hurt.

7 Yet yee haue not hearkened vnto me, saith the Lord, that yee might prouoke me to anger with the workes of your hands, to your owne hurt.

8 ¶ Therefore thus saith the Lord of hostes; Because yee haue not heard my words:

9 Behold, I will send and take all the families of the North, saith the
Lord

* 2. Kings. 24. 2. chron. 36. 10.

† Heb. for badnesse.

† Heb. captiuitie.

* Deut. 30. 60. chap. 32 39. ezech. 11. 19. and 36. 26. 27.
* Chap. 30. 22. and 31. 33. and 32. 38..
* Chap. 29. 17.

† Heb. for remouing or vexation.
* Deut. 28. 37. chap. 15 4.

* Chap. 19.

* 2. King 17. 13. c) 18. 11. an 35. 15. lo nas 3. 8.

Lord, and Nebuchad-rezzar the king
of Babylon my seruant, and will bring
them against this land, and against the
inhabitants thereof, and against all
these nations round about, and will vtterly destroy them, and make them an
astonishment, and an hissing, and perpetuall desolations.
10 Moreouer, †I will take from
them the *voyce of myrth, and the voice
of gladnes, the voice of the bridegrome,
and the voice of the bride, the sound of
the milstones, & the light of the candle.
11 And this whole land shall be a desolation, *and* an astonishment, and these
nations shal serue the king of Babylon
seuentie yeeres.
12 ¶ And it shall come to passe *when
seuentie yeeres are accomplished, that
I will †punish the king of Babylon
and that nation, saith the Lord, for
their iniquitie, and the land of the Caldeans, and will make it perpetuall desolations.
13 And I will bring vpon that land
all my words which I haue pronounced against it, *euen* all that is written
in this booke, which Ieremiah hath
prophecied against all the nations.
14 For many nations and great
kings shall *serue themselues of them
also: and I will recompense them according to their deeds, and according to
the workes of their owne hands.
15 ¶ For thus saith the Lord God
of Israel vnto me, Take the wine *cup
of this furie at my hand, and cause all
the nations, to whom I send thee, to
drinke it.
16 And they shall drinke, and be moued, and be mad, because of the sworde
that I will send among them.
17 Then tooke I the cuppe at the
Lords hand, and made all the nations to drinke, vnto whom the Lord
had sent me:
18 *To wit* Ierusalem, and the cities
of Iudah, and the kings thereof, *and*
the princes thereof, to make them a desolation, an astonishment, an hissing,
and a curse (as *it is* this day:)
19 Pharaoh king of Egypt, and his
seruants, and his princes, and all his
people:
20 And all the mingled people, & all
the kings of the land of Vz: and all the
kings of the land of the Philistines, and
Ashkelon, and Azzah, and Ekron, and
the remnant of Ashdod:

† *Heb. I will cause to perish from them.*
* Cha. 7. 34. and 16. 9. and 25. 10. ezek. 26. 13 ose 2. 11.
* 2. Chron. 36. 22. eszr. 1. 1. chap. 29. 10. dan. 9. 2.
† *Heb. visite vpon.*
* Cha. 27. 7.
* Isa. 51. 17 psal. 75. 8. iob. 21. 20.

21 *Edom, and *Moab, and the children of *Ammon:
22 And all the kings of *Tyrus, and
all the kings of Zidon, and the kings
of the ||yles which *are* beyond the *sea:
23 *Dedan, and Tema, and Buz, and
all †that *are* in the vtmost corners:
24 And all the kings of Arabia, and
all the kings of the *mingled people
that dwell in the desert:
25 And all the kings of Zimri, and
all the kings of *Elam, and all the
kings of the Medes:
26 And all the kings of the North,
farre and neere, one with another, and
all the kingdomes of the world, which
are vpon the face of the earth, and the
king of Sheshach shall drinke after
them.
27 Therefore thou shalt say vnto
them, Thus saith the Lord of hosts,
the God of Israel, Drinke ye and bee
drunken, and spue and fall, and rise no
more, because of the sword which I wil
send among you.
28 And it shall bee, if they refuse to
take the cup at thine hand to drinke,
then shalt thou say vnto them, Thus
saith the Lord of hosts, Yee shall
certainely drinke.
29 For loe, I begin to bring euill on
the *citie, †which is called by my name,
and should yee be vtterly vnpunished?
ye shall not be vnpunished: for I will
cal for a sword vpon all the inhabitants
of the earth, saith the Lord of hosts.
30 Therefore prophecie thou against
them all these wordes, and say vnto
them, The Lord shall *roare from
an high, and vtter his voice from his
holy habitation, he shall mightily roare
vpon his habitation, hee shall giue a
shout, as they that treade the grapes,
against all the inhabitants of the earth.
31 A noise shall come euen to the ends
of the earth; for the Lord *hath* a controuersie with the nations: hee will
pleade with all flesh, he will giue them
that *are* wicked to the sword, saith the
Lord.
32 Thus saith the Lord of hosts,
Behold, euill shall goe forth from nation to nation, and a great whirlewinde
shall be raised vp from the coasts of the
earth.
33 And the slaine of the Lord shall
be at that day from one end of the earth
euen vnto the *other* ende of the earth:
they shall not be *lamented, neither gathered

* Chap. 49. 7, &c.
* Chap. 48.
* Chap. 49.
* Chap. 47.
|| *Or, region by the Sea side.*
* Chap. 49. 23.
* Chap. 49. 28.
† *Heb. cut off into corners, or hauing the corners of the haire polled, chap. 9. 26.*
* Chap. 49. 31.
* Chap. 49. 34.
* 1. Pet. 4. 17.
† *Heb. vpon which my Name is called.*
* Ioel 3. 16 amos 1. 2.
* Cha. 16. 4.

thered nor buried, they shall be doung vpon the ground.

34 ¶ * Howle yee shepheards and cry, and wallow your selues *in the ashes* ye principall of the flocke: for †the dayes of your slaughter, and of your dispersions are accomplished, and yee shall fall like †a pleasant vessell.

35 And †the shepheards shall haue no way to flee, nor the principall of the flocke to escape.

36 A voyce of the cry of the shepheards, and an howling of the principall of the flocke *shall be heard* : for the LORD hath spoiled their pasture.

37 And the peaceable habitations are cut downe because of the fierce anger of the LORD.

38 He hath forsaken his couert, as the Lyon : for their land is †desolate, because of the fiercenesse of the oppressour, and because of his fierce anger.

CHAP. XXVI.

Ieremiah by promises and threatnings, exhorteth to repentance. 8 Hee is therefore apprehended, 10 and arraigned: 11 His apologie: 16 He is quit in iudgement, by the example of Micah, 20 and of Vrijah, 24 and by the care of Ahikam.

IN the beginning of the reigne of Iehoiakim the sonne of Iosiah king of Iudah, came this word from the LORD, saying;

2 Thus saith the LORD, Stand in the Court of the LORDS house, and speake vnto all the cities of Iudah, which come to worship in the LORDS house, all the wordes that I command thee to speake vnto them : *diminish not a word;

3 If so bee they will hearken, and turne euery man from his euill way, that I may *repent me of the euill which I purpose to doe vnto them, because of the euil of their doings.

4 And thou shalt say vnto them, Thus saith the LORD; If yee will not hearken to mee to walke in my Law, which I haue set before you,

5 To hearken to the wordes of my seruants the Prophets, whom I sent vnto you, both rising vp early and sending them, (but ye haue not hearkned:)

6 Then wil I make this house like * Shiloh, and wil make this city a curse to all the nations of the earth.

7 So the priests and the prophets,

and all the people heard Ieremiah speaking these wordes in the house of the LORD.

8 ¶ Now it came to passe when Ieremiah had made an ende of speaking all that the LORD had commanded him to speake vnto all the people, that the priests and the prophets, and all the people tooke him, saying; Thou shalt surely die.

9 Why hast thou prophecied in the Name of the LORD, saying, This house shalbe like Shiloh, and this city shalbe desolate without an inhabitant? and all the people were gathered against Ieremiah in the house of the LORD.

10 ¶ When the Princes of Iudah heard these things, then they came vp from the kings house vnto the house of the LORD, and sate downe ‖ in the entrie of the new gate of the LORDS house.

11 Then spake the priests and the prophets vnto the Princes, and to all the people, saying; †This man *is* worthy to die, for he hath prophecied against this citie, as yee haue heard with your eares.

12 ¶ Then spake Ieremiah vnto all the Princes, and to all the people, saying, The LORD sent me to prophecie against this house, and against this citie, all the wordes that yee haue heard.

13 Therefore nowe * amend your wayes, and your doings, and obey the voice of the LORD your God, and the LORD will *repent him of the euill that he hath pronounced against you.

14 As for mee, behold, I *am* in your hand : doe with mee †as seemeth good and meet vnto you.

15 But know ye for certaine, That if ye put mee to death, ye shall surely bring innocent blood vpon your selues, and vpon this citie, and vpon the inhabitants thereof : for of a trueth the LORD hath sent mee vnto you, to speake all these words in your eares.

16 ¶ Then said the Princes, and all the people, vnto the priests, and to the prophets; This man *is* not worthy to die : for hee hath spoken to vs in the Name of the LORD our God.

17 Then rose vp certaine of the Elders of the land, and spake to all the assembly of the people, saying;

18 * Micah the Morashite prophecied in

Marginal notes (left column):
* Chap. 4.. 8 and 6. 26.
† *Hebr. your dayes for slaughter.*
† *Hebr. a vessell of desire.*
† *Heb. flight shall perish from the shepheards, and escaping from &c.*
† *Hebr. a desolation.*
* Acts. 20. 27.
* Chap. 18. 8.
1. Sam. 4. 12. chap. 7. 12, 14. psal. 78. 60.

Marginal notes (right column):
‖ *Or, at the doore.*
† *Hebr. the iudgement of death is for this man.*
* Chap. 7.
* Verse 19.
† *Hebr. as it is good and right in your eyes.*
* Mic. 1. and 3. 12.

in the dayes of Hezekiah king of Iudah, and spake to all the people of Iudah, saying; Thus saith the LORD of hostes, Zion shall be plowed *like* a field, and Ierusalem shall become heapes, and the mountaine of the house, the hie places of a forrest.

19 Did Hezekiah King of Iudah and all Iudah put him at all to death? did hee not feare the LORD, and besought † the LORD, and the LORD repented him of the euill which he had pronounced against them? thus might wee procure great euill against our soules.

20 And there was also a man that prophecied in the Name of the LORD, Vrijah the sonne of Shemaiah of Kiriath-iearim, who prophecied against this citie and against this land, according to all the words of Ieremiah.

21 And when Iehoiakim the king with all his mightie men, and all the princes heard his wordes, the king sought to put him to death; but when Vrijah heard *it*, he was afraid and fled, and went into Egypt.

22 And Iehoiakim the king sent men into Egypt, *namely* Elnathan the sonne of Achbor, and *certeine* men with him, into Egypt.

23 And they fet foorth Vrijah out of Egypt, and brought him vnto Iehoiakim the king, who slewe him with the sword, and cast his dead body into the graues of the † common people.

24 Neuerthelesse, the hand of Ahikam, the sonne of Shaphan, was with Ieremiah, that they should not giue him into the hand of the people, to put him to death.

CHAP. XXVII.

1 Vnder the type of bonds and yokes, hee prophecieth the subduing of the neighbour kings vnto Nebuchad-nezzar. 8 Hee exhorteth them to yeeld, and not to beleeue the false prophets. 12 The like hee doeth to Zedekiah. 19 He foretelleth the remnant of the vessels shall be caried to Babylon, and there continue vntill the day of visitation.

IN the beginning of the reigne of Iehoiakim the sonne of Iosiah King of Iudah, came this worde vnto Ieremiah from the LORD, saying,

2 Thus sayth the LORD to me,

Make thee bonds and yokes, and put them vpon thy necke.

3 And send them to the king of Edom, and to the king of Moab, and to the king of the Ammonites, and to the king of Tyrus, and to the king of Zidon, by the hand of the messengers which come to Ierusalem vnto Zedekiah king of Iudah.

4 And command them to say vnto their masters, Thus saith the LORD of hosts the God of Israel, Thus shall ye say ‖vnto your masters:

5 I haue made the earth, the man and the beast that *are* vpon the ground, by my great power, and by my outstretched arme, and * haue giuen it vnto whom it seemed meet vnto me.

6 And now haue I giuen all these landes into the hand of Nebuchadnezzar the king of Babylon * my seruant, and the beasts of the field haue I giuen him also to serue him.

7 And all nations shall serue him and his sonne, and his sonnes sonne, vntill the very time of his land come: and then many nations and great kings shall serue themselues of him.

8 And it shall come to passe, that the nation and kingdome which will not serue the same Nebuchad-nezzar the king of Babylon, and that will not put their necke vnder the yoke of the king of Babylon, that nation will I punish, sayth the LORD, with the sword, and with the famine, and with the pestilence, vntill I haue consumed them by his hand.

9 Therefore hearken not ye to your prophets, nor to your diuiners, nor to your † dreamers, nor to your inchanters, nor to your sorcerers, which speak vnto you, saying; Ye shall not serue the king of Babylon:

10 For they prophecie a lie vnto you, to remooue you farre from your land, and that I should driue you out, and ye should perish.

11 But the nations that bring their necke vnder the yoke of the king of Babylon, and serue him, those will I let remaine still in their owne land, sayth the LORD, and they shall till it, and dwell therein.

12 ¶ I spake also to Zedekiah king of Iudah according to all these wordes, saying, Bring your neckes vnder the yoke of the king of Babylon, and serue him and his people, and liue.

13 Why

Heb. the face of the LORD.

†*Heb. sons of the people.*

‖*Or, concerning their masters, saying.*

*Dan. 4. 14, 22.

*Cha. 25. 9. and 43. 10.

†*Hebr. dreames.*

13 Why will yee die, thou and thy people, by the sword, by the famine, and by the pestilence, as the LORD hath spoken against the nation that will not serue the king of Babylon?

14 Therefore hearken not vnto the words of the prophets, that speake vnto you, saying; Yee shall not serue the king of Babylon: for they prophecie * a lie vnto you.

* Chap. 14. 14. and 23. 21. and 29. 8.

15 For I haue not sent them, saith the LORD, yet they prophecie † a lye in my name, that I might driue you out, & that yee might perish, ye, and the prophets that prophecie vnto you.

† Heb. in a lie, or lying-ly.

16 Also I spake to the priests, and to all this people, saying; Thus saith the LORD, Hearken not to the words of your prophets, that prophecie vnto you, saying; Behold, the vessels of the LORDS house shall now shortly be brought againe from Babylon; for they prophecie a lie vnto you.

17 Hearken not vnto them : serue the king of Babylon, and liue : wherefore should this citie be laid waste?

18 But if they be prophets, and if the word of the LORD be with them, let them nowe make intercession to the LORD of hostes, that the vessels which are left in the house of the LORD, and in the house of the king of Iudah, and at Ierusalem, goe not to Babylon.

19 ¶ For thus saith the LORD of hostes concerning the pillars, and concerning the sea, and concerning the bases, and concerning the residue of the vessels that remaine in this citie,

20 Which Nebuchadnezzar king of Babylon tooke not, when he caried away * captiue Ieconiah the sonne of Iehoiakim king of Iudah, from Ierusalem to Babylon, and all the nobles of Iudah and Ierusalem :

* 2. Kings 24. 14, 15.

21 Yea thus saith the LORD of hostes the God of Israel, concerning the vessels that remaine in the house of the LORD, and in the house of the king of Iudah and of Ierusalem ;

22 They shall be * caried to Babylon, and there shall they be vntill the day that I * visit them, saith the LORD : then will I bring them vp, and restore them to this place.

* 2. Kings 25. 13. 2. chron. 36. 18.
* 2. Chron. 36. 22. cha. 29. 10.

CHAP. XXVIII.

1 Hananiah prophecieth falsely the returne of the vessels and of Ieconiah. 5 Ieremiah

Nd it came to passe the same yeere, in the beginning of the reigne of Zedekiah king of Iudah, in the fourth yeere, and in the fift moneth, that Hananiah the sonne of Azur the prophet, which was of Gibeon, spake vnto mee in the house of the LORD, in the presence of the priests and of all the people, saying ;

2 Thus speaketh the LORD of hostes, the God of Israel, saying ; I haue broken the yoke of the king of Babylon.

3 Within † two full yeeres will I bring againe into this place all the vessels of the LORDS house, that Nebuchadnezzar king of Babylon tooke away from this place, and caried them to Babylon.

† Heb. two yeeres of dayes.

4 And I will bring againe to this place Ieconiah the sonne of Iehoiakim king of Iudah, with all the † captiues of Iudah, that went into Babylon, saith the LORD, for I will breake the yoke of the king of Babylon.

† Heb. captiuity.

5 ¶ Then the prophet Ieremiah said vnto the prophet Hananiah in the presence of the priests, and in the presence of all the people, that stood in the house of the LORD,

6 Euen the prophet Ieremiah said ; Amen : the LORD doe so, the LORD performe the words which thou hast prophecied, to bring againe the vessels of the LORDS house, and all that is caried away captiue from Babylon into this place.

7 Neuerthelesse, heare thou now this word that I speake in thine eares, and in the eares of all the people.

8 The prophets that haue beene before mee, and before thee of old, prophecied both against many countries, and against great kingdoms, of warre, and of euill, and of pestilence.

9 The prophet which prophecieth of peace, when the word of the prophet shall come to passe, then shall the prophet be knowen, that the LORD hath truely sent him.

10 ¶ Then Hananiah the prophet tooke the * yoke from off the prophet Ieremiahs necke, and brake it.

* Chap. 27. 2.

11 And

11 And Hananiah spake in the presence of all the people, saying; Thus saith the LORD, Euen so will I breake the yoke of Nebuchadnezzer king of Babylon from the necke of all nations within the space of two full yeeres: and the Prophet Ieremiah went his way.

12 ¶ Then the word of the LORD came vnto Ieremiah the Prophet (after that Hananiah the prophet had broken the yoke from off the necke of the Prophet Ieremiah) saying,

13 Goe, and tell Hananiah, saying, Thus saith the LORD, Thou hast broken the yokes of wood, but thou shalt make for them yokes of yron.

14 For thus saith the LORD of hosts, the God of Israel, I haue put a yoke of yron vpon the neck of all these nations, that they may serue Nebuchad-nezzar king of Babylon, and they shall serue him, and I haue giuen him the beasts of the field also.

15 ¶ Then said the Prophet Ieremiah vnto Hananiah the prophet, Heare nowe Hananiah: the LORD hath not sent thee, but thou makest this people to trust in a lye.

16 Therefore thus saith the LORD, Beholde, I will cast thee from off the face of the earth: this yeere thou shalt die, because thou hast taught *†rebellion against the LORD.

17 So Hananiah the prophet died the same yeere, in the seuenth moneth.

*Deut. 13.
5. chap. 29.
32.
†Heb. re-
uolt.

CHAP. XXIX.

1 Ieremiah sendeth a letter to the captiues in Babylon, to be quiet there, 8 and not to beleeue the dreames of their prophets, 10 and that they shall returne with grace, after seuentie yeeres. 15 He foretelleth the destruction of the rest for their disobedience. 20 He sheweth the fearefull end of Ahab and Zedekiah, two lying prophets. 24 Shemaiah writeth a letter against Ieremiah. 30 Ieremiah readeth his doome.

Ow these *are* the words of the letter, that Ieremiah the prophet sent from Ierusalem vnto the residue of the elders which were caried away captiues, and to the priests, and to the prophets, and to all the people whom Nebuchad-nezzar had caried away captiue from Ierusalem to Babylon,

2 (After that *Ieconiah the king, and the queene, and the ‖eunuches, the princes of Iudah and Ierusalem, and the carpenters and the smithes were departed from Ierusalem)

3 By the hand of Elasah the sonne of Shaphan, and Gemariah the sonne of Hilkiah, whome Zedekiah king of Iudah sent vnto Babylon to Nebuchad-nezzar king of Babylon, saying,

4 Thus saith the LORD of hosts the God of Israel vnto all that are caried away captiues, whom I haue caused to be caried away from Ierusalem vnto Babylon:

5 Build ye houses and dwell *in them*, and plant gardens, and eate the fruit of them.

6 Take ye wiues, and beget sonnes and daughters, and take wiues for your sonnes, and giue your daughters to husbands, that they may beare sonnes and daughters, that ye may bee increased there, and not diminished.

7 And seeke the peace of the citie, whither I haue caused you to be caried away captiues, & pray vnto the LORD for it: for in the peace thereof shall yee haue peace.

8 ¶ For thus saith the LORD of hosts, the God of Israel, Let not your prophets and your diuiners, that *bee* in the midst of you, *deceiue you, neither hearken to your dreames which yee cause to be dreamed.

9 For they prophecie †falsly vnto you in my name: I haue not sent them, saith the LORD.

10 ¶ For thus saith the LORD, That after *seuentie yeeres be accomplished at Babylon, I will visite you, and performe my good word towards you, in causing you to returne to this place.

11 For I knowe the thoughts that I thinke towards you, saith the LORD, thoughts of peace, and not of euill, to giue you an †expected end.

12 Then shall ye *call vpon me, and ye shall goe and pray vnto mee, and I will hearken vnto you.

13 And ye shall seeke me, and finde me, when ye shall search for me with all your heart.

14 And I will be found of you, saith the LORD, and I will turne away your captiuitie, and I will gather you from all the nations, and from all the places whither I haue driuen you, saith the LORD, and I will bring you againe

*2. King.
24. 12, &c.
‖ Or, cham-
berleines.

*Chap. 14.
14. and 23.
21. and 27.
15.
†Hebr. in a
lie.

*2. Chron.
36. 22. ezra
1. 1. chap.
25. 12. and
27. 22. dan.
9. 2.

†Hebr. ende
and expecta-
tion.
*Dan. 9.

againe into the place whence I caused you to be caried away captiue.

15 ¶ Because yee haue said, The LORD hath raised vs vp prophets in Babylon :

16 *Know* that thus saith the LORD, of the king that sitteth vpon the throne of Dauid, and of all the people that dwelleth in this citie, and of your brethren that are not gone foorth with you into captiuitie.

 17 Thus saith the LORD of hosts, Beholde, I will send vpon them the *sword, the famine, and the pestilence, and will make them like *vile figges, that cannot be eaten, they are so euill.

18 And I will persecute them with the sword, with the famine, and with the pestilence, and will deliuer them to be remooued to all the kingdomes of the earth, †to be a curse and an astonishment, and an hissing, and a reproch among all the nations, whither I haue driuen them.

19 Because they haue not hearkened to my words, saith the LORD, which * I sent vnto them by my seruants the Prophets, rising vp early, and sending *them*, but ye would not heare, saith the LORD.

20 ¶ Heare yee therefore the word of the LORD, all ye of the captiuitie, whom I haue sent from Ierusalem to Babylon.

21 Thus saith the LORD of hosts the God of Israel, of Ahab the sonne of Kolaiah, and of Zedekiah the sonne of Maaseiah, which prophecie a lye vnto you in my Name, Behold, I will deliuer them into the hand of Nebuchadrezzar king of Babylon, and hee shall slay them before your eyes.

22 And of them shall bee taken vp a curse by all the captiuitie of Iudah which *are* in Babylon, saying, The LORD make thee like Zedekiah, and like Ahab, whom the king of Babylon rosted in the fire.

23 Because they haue committed villanie in Israel, and haue committed adulterie with their neighbors wiues, and haue spoken lying wordes in my Name, which I haue not commanded them, euen I know, and *am* a witnesse, saith the LORD.

24 ¶ Thus shalt thou also speake to Shemaiah the ||Nehelamite, saying;

25 Thus speaketh the LORD of hostes the God of Israel, saying, Be-

cause thou hast sent letters in thy name vnto all the people that *are* at Ierusalem, and to Zephaniah the sonne of Maaseiah the Priest, and to all the priests, saying

26 The LORD hath made thee Priest in the stead of Iehoiada the Priest, that ye should be Officers in the house of the LORD, for euery man that is *madde, and maketh himselfe a Prophet, that thou shouldest put him in prison, and in the stockes :

27 Now therefore why hast thou not reproued Ieremiah of Anathoth, which maketh himselfe a Prophet to you ?

28 For therefore he sent vnto vs in Babylon, saying, This *captiuitie is* long, build ye houses and dwell *in them*, and plant gardens, and eate the fruit of them

29 And Zephaniah the Priest read this letter in the eares of Ieremiah the Prophet.

30 ¶ Then came the word of the LORD vnto Ieremiah, saying ;

31 Send to all them of the captiuitie, saying, Thus saith the LORD, concerning Shemaiah the Nehelamite, Because that Shemaiah hath prophecied vnto you, and I sent him not, and he caused you to trust in a lye.

32 Therefore thus saith the LORD, Behold, I will punish Shemaiah the Nehelamite and his seed : he shall not haue a man to dwell among this people, neither shall hee behold the good that I will doe for my people, saith the LORD, * because he hath taught †rebellion against the LORD.

CHAP. XXX.

1 God sheweth Ieremiah the returne of the Iewes. 4 After their trouble, they shall haue deliuerance. 10 He comforteth Iacob. 18 Their returne shalbe gracious. 20 Wrath shall fall on the wicked.

He word that came to Ieremiah from the LORD, saying,

2 Thus speaketh the LORD God of Israel, saying; Write thee all the wordes that I haue spoken vnto thee, in a booke.

3 For loe, the dayes come, saith the LORD, that I will bring againe the captiuitie of my people Israel and Iudah, saith the LORD, and I wil cause them

Marginal notes

* Chap. 24. 8, 10.
* Chap. 24. 8.

† Hebr. for a curse.

* Chap. 25. 4. and 32. 3.

|| Or, dreamer.

* 2. King 11. acts. 26 24.

* Chap. 28 16.
† Hebr. reuolt.

them to returne to the land, that I gaue to their fathers, and they shall possesse it.

4 ¶ And these *are* the words that the LORD spake concerning Israel, and concerning Iudah.

5 For thus sayth the LORD, Wee haue heard a voice of trembling, ‖ of feare, and not of peace.

‖ Or, there is feare, and not peace.
† Heb. a male

6 Aske yee now and see whether †a man doeth trauaile with child? wherefore doe I see euery man with his handes on his loynes, as a woman in trauaile, and all faces are turned into palenesse?

7 * Alas, for that day *is* great, so that none *is* like it : it *is* euen the time of Iacobs trouble, but he shall be saued out of it.

* Ioel 2. 11. amos 5. 18. zeph. 1. 15.

8 For it shall come to passe in that day, saith the LORD of hostes, *that* I will breake his yoke from off thy necke, and will burst thy bondes, and strangers shall no more serue themselues of him.

9 But they shall serue the LORD their God, and *Dauid their King whom I will raise vp vnto them.

* Ezek. 34. 23. and 37. 24. hose. 3. 5.
* Isa. 41. 13. and 43. 5. and 44. 1. cha. 46. 28.

10 ¶ Therefore *feare thou not, O my seruant Iacob, saith the LORD, neither be dismayed, O Israel ; for loe, I will saue thee from afarre, and thy seede from the land of their captiuitie, and Iacob shall returne, and shall be in rest, and be quiet, and none shall make *him* afraid.

11 For I *am* with thee, sayeth the LORD, to saue thee · though I make a full end of all nations whither I haue scattered thee, yet will I not make a full ende of thee : but I will correct thee * in measure, and will not leaue thee altogether vnpunished.

* Psal. 6. 1. chap. 10. 24. and 46. 28.

12 For thus saith the LORD, Thy bruise is incurable, *and* thy wound *is* grieuous.

13 There is none to pleade thy cause, †that thou mayest bee bonnd vp : thou hast no healing medicines.

† Heb. for binding vp, or pressing.

14 All thy louers haue forgotten thee : they seeke thee not, for I haue wounded thee with the wound of an enemy, with the chastisement of a cruell one, for the multitude of thine iniquitie: *because* thy sinnes were increased.

* Chap. 13. 18.

15 Why *cryest thou for thine affliction? thy sorrow is incurable, for the multitude of thine iniquitie : *because* thy sinnes were increased, I haue done

these things vnto thee.

16 Therefore all they that deuoure thee * shalbe deuoured, and all thine aduersaries euery one of them shall goe into captiuitie : and they that spoile thee shall be a spoile, and all that pray vpon thee, will I giue for a pray.

* Exod. 23. 22. isai. 41. 11.

17 For I will restore health vnto thee, and I will heale thee of thy wounds, sayth the LORD, because they called thee an outcast, *saying*; This *is* Zion whom no man seeketh after.

18 ¶ Thus saith the LORD, Behold, I will bring againe the captiuitie of Iacobs tents, and haue mercie on his dwelling places : and the citie shall be builded vpon her owne ‖heape, and the palace shall remaine after the manner thereof.

‖ Or, little hill.

19 And out of them shall proceede thanksgiuing, and the voice of them that make merry ; and I will multiply them, and they shall not be few : I will also glorifie them, and they shall not be small.

20 Their children also shall be as aforetime, and their congregation shalbe established before me, and I will punish all that oppresse them.

21 And their nobles shall be of themselues, and their gouernour shall proceede from the middest of them, and I will cause him to draw neere, and hee shall approch vnto me : for who is this *that* engaged his heart to approch vnto me, sayth the LORD?

22 And yee shall be * my people, and I will be your God.

* Cha. 24. 7. and 31. 33. and 32. 38.

23 Behold, the *whirlewinde of the LORD goeth foorth with furie, a †continuing whirlewinde, it shall ‖fall with paine vpon the head of the wicked.

* Chap. 23. 19, 20.
† Heb. cutting.
‖ Or, remaine.

24 The fierce anger of the LORD shall not returne, vntill hee haue done *it*, and vntill he haue performed the intents of his heart in the latter dayes ye shall consider it.

CHAP. XXXI.

1 The restauration of Israel. 10 The publication thereof. 15 Rahel mourning is comforted. 18 Ephraim repenting is brought home againe. 22 Christ is promised. 27 His care ouer the Church. 31 His new couenant. 35 The stability, 38 and amplitude of the Church.

At

AT the same time, saith the LORD, wil I be the God of all the families of Israel, & they shalbe my people.

2 Thus saith the LORD; The people which were left of the sword found grace in the wildernesse, euen Israel, when I went to cause him to rest.

† Heb. from a farre.

3 The LORD hath appeared † of old vnto mee, *saying*; Yea I haue loued thee with an euerlasting loue : therefore || with louing kindnesse haue I drawen thee.

|| Or, haue I extended louing kindnesse vnto thee.

4 Againe I will build thee, and thou shalt be built, O virgine of Israel, thou shalt againe be adorned with thy *|| tabrets, and shalt goe forth in the daunces of them that make merry.

* Exod. 15. 20. iudg. 11. 34.
|| Or, timbrels.
† Heb. prophane them.

5 Thou shalt yet plant vines vpon the mountaines of Samaria, the planters shall plant, and shall † eate *them* as common things.

6 For there shall be a day, that the watchmen vpon the mount Ephraim shall cry; Arise yee, and let vs goe vp to Zion vnto the LORD our God.

7 For thus saith the LORD, Sing with gladnesse for Iacob, and shout among the chiefe of the nations : publish yee, praise yee, and say ; O LORD saue thy people the remnant of Israel.

8 Behold, I will bring them from the North countrey, and gather them from the coasts of the earth, *and* with them the blind and the lame, the woman with child, and her that trauelleth with child together, a great company shall returne thither.

|| Or, fauours.

9 They shall come with weeping, and with || supplications will I leade them : I will cause them to walke by the riuers of waters, in a straight way wherein they shall not stumble : for I am a father to Israel, and Ephraim is my *first borne.

* Exod. 4. 22.

10 ¶ Heare the word of the LORD, O yee nations, and declare *it* in the iles afarre off, and say; Hee that scattered Israel will gather him, and keepe him as a shepheard *doth* his flocke.

11 For the LORD hath redeemed Iacob, and ransomed him from the hand of him that was stronger then hee.

12 Therefore they shall come and sing in the height of Zion, and shall flow together to the goodnesse of the LORD, for wheate, and for wine, and

for oyle, and for the young of the flocke and of the herd : and their soule shall be as a *watered garden, and they shall not sorrow any more at all.

* Isai. 58. 11.

13 Then shall the virgine reioyce in the daunce, both yoong men and old together : for I will turne their mourning into ioy, and will comfort them, and make them reioyce from their sorrow.

14 And I will satiate the soule of the priests with fatnesse, and my people shall be satisfied with goodnesse, saith the LORD.

15 ¶ Thus saith the LORD; *A voyce was heard in Ramah, lamentation *and* bitter weeping : Rahel weeping for her children, refused to be comforted for her children, because they *were* not.

* Matth. 2. 18.

16 Thus saith the LORD; Refraine thy voice from weeping, and thine eyes from teares : for thy worke shall be rewarded, saith the LORD, and they shall come againe from the land of the enemie.

17 And there is hope in thine end, saith the LORD, that *thy* children shall come againe to their owne border.

18 ¶ I haue surely heard Ephraim bemoaning himselfe *thus*, Thou hast chastised me, and I was chastised, as a bullocke vnaccustomed *to the yoke:* turne thou me, and I shall be turned; thou *art* the LORD my God.

19 Surely *after that I was turned, I repented ; and after that I was instructed, I smote vpon *my* thigh : I was ashamed, yea euen confounded, because I did beare the reproch of my youth.

* Deut. 30. 2.

20 *Is* Ephraim my deare sonne ? *is* he a pleasant child? for since I spake against him, I doe earnestly remember him still : therefore my bowels † are troubled for him ; I will surely haue mercy vpon him, saith the LORD.

† Heb. soun.

21 Set thee vp way-markes; make thee high heaps : set thine heart toward the high way, *euen* the way *which* thou wentest : turne againe, O virgine of Israel, turne againe to these thy cities.

22 ¶ How long wilt thou go about, O thou backsliding daughter? for the LORD hath created a new thing in the earth : A woman shall compasse a man.

23 Thus saith the LORD of hosts the

the God of Israel, As yet they shall vse this speech in the land of Iudah, and in the cities thereof, when I shall bring againe their captiuitie, The LORD blesse thee, O habitation of iustice, and mountaine of holinesse.

24 And there shall dwell in Iudah it selfe, and in all the cities thereof together, husbandmen, and they *that* goe forth with flocks.

25 For I haue satiated the wearie soule, and I haue replenished euery sorrowfull soule.

26 Vpon this I awaked and beheld, and my sleepe was sweete vnto me.

27 ¶ Behold, the dayes come, saith the LORD, that I will sow the house of Israel, and the house of Iudah with the seed of man, and with the seed of beast.

28 And it shall come to passe, *that* like as I haue watched ouer them, to plucke vp and to breake downe, and to throw downe, and to destroy, and to afflict so will I watch ouer them, to build and to plant, saith the LORD.

29 *In those dayes they shall say no more, The fathers haue eaten a sowre grape, and the childrens teeth are set on edge.

30 But euery one shall die for his owne iniquitie, euery man that eateth the sowre grape, his teeth shall be set on edge.

31 ¶ Behold, the *dayes come, saith the LORD, that I will make a newe couenant with the house of Israel, and with the house of Iudah.

32 Not according to the couenant that I made with their fathers in the day *that* I tooke them by the hand, to bring them out of the land of Egypt, which my couenant they brake, ||although I was an husband vnto them, saith the LORD.

33 But this *shall be* the couenant, that I will make with the house of Israel, After those dayes, saith the LORD, I will put my law in their inward parts, and write it in their hearts, *and wil be their God, and they shall be my people.

34 And they shall teach no more euery man his neighbour, and euery man his brother, saying, Know the LORD: for *they shall all know mee, from the least of them vnto the greatest of them, saith the LORD; *for I will forgiue their iniquitie, and I will remember their sinne no more.

*Eze. 18. 2.

Heb. 8. 8.

Or, should haue continued a husband vnto them?

* Chap. 24. and 32. 0.

* Isa. 54. 17 oh. 6. 45.

* Chap. 33. s. mic. 7. 18 acts 10. 43.

35 ¶ Thus saith the LORD * which giueth the Sunne for a light by day, *and* the ordinances of the moone and of the starres for a light by night, which diuideth *the sea when the waues thereof roare, the LORD of hosts *is* his name.

36 *If those ordinances depart from before me, saith the LORD, then the seed of Israel also shall cease from being a nation before me for euer.

37 Thus saith the LORD, If *heauen aboue can bee measured, and the foundations of the earth searched out beneath, I will also cast off all the seed of Israel for all that they haue done, saith the LORD.

38 ¶ Behold, the dayes come, saith the LORD, that the citie shall be built to the LORD from the tower of Hananeel vnto the gate of the corner.

39 And the measuring line shall yet goe forth ouer against it, vpon the hill Gareb, and shall compasse about to Goath.

40 And the whole valley of the dead bodies, and of the ashes, and all the fields vnto the brooke of Kidron, vnto the corner of the horse gate towards the East, *shalbe* holy vnto the LORD, it shall not be plucked vp, nor throwen downe any more for euer.

* Gen. 1. 16

* Isa. 51. 15

* Isa. 54. 9. chap. 33. 20

* Chap. 33. 22.

CHAP. XXXII

1 Ieremiah being imprisoned by Zedekiah for his prophecie, 6 buyeth Hanameels field. 13 Baruch must preserue the euidences, as tokens of the peoples returne. 16 Ieremiah in his prayer complaineth to God. 26 God confirmeth the captiuitie for their sinnes, 36 and promiseth a gracious returne.

He worde that came to Ieremiah from the LORD in the tenth yeere of Zedekiah king of Iudah, which *was* the eighteenth yeere of Nebuchad-rezzar.

2 For then the king of Babylons armie besieged Ierusalem : and Ieremiah the prophet was shut vp in the court of the prison which *was* in the king of Iudahs house.

3 For Zedekiah king of Iudah had shut him vp, saying, Wherefore doest thou prophecie and say, Thus saith the LORD, *Behold, I will giue this citie into the hand of the king of Babylon, and hee shall take it ?

* Cha. 34. 2

4 And

4 And Zedekiah king of Iudah, shal not escape out of the hand of the Caldeans, but shall *surely be deliuered into the hand of the king of Babylon, and shal speake with him mouth to mouth, and his eyes shall behold his eyes.

5 And he shall lead Zedekiah to Babylon, and there shall he be vntill I visit him, saith the LORD: though ye fight with the Caldeans, yee shall not prosper.

6 ¶ And Ieremiah said; The word of the LORD came vnto me, saying;

7 Behold, Hanameel the sonne of Shallum thine vncle, shall come vnto thee, saying; Buy thee my field that is in Anathoth: for the *right of redemption is thine to buy it.

8 So Hanameel mine vncles sonne came to me in the court of the prison, according to the word of the LORD, and said vnto me; Buy my field, I pray thee, that is in Anathoth, which is in the countrey of Beniamin: for the right of inheritance is thine, and the redemption is thine, buy it for thy selfe. Then I knew that this was the word of the LORD.

9 And I bought the field of Hanameel my vncles sonne, that was in Anathoth, and weighed him the money, euen ||seuentoene shekels of siluer.

10 And I †subscribed the euidence, and sealed it, and tooke witnesses, and weighed him the money in the ballances.

11 So I tooke the euidence of the purchase, both that which was sealed according to the law and custome, and that which was open:

12 And I gaue the euidence of the purchase vnto Baruch the sonne of Neriah, the sonne of Maaseiah, in the sight of Hanameel mine vncles sonne, and in the presence of the witnesses, that subscribed the booke of the purchase, before all the Iewes that sate in the court of the prison.

13 ¶ And I charged Baruch before them, saying,

14 Thus saith the LORD of hosts the God of Israel; Take these euidences, this euidence of the purchase, both which is sealed, and this euidence which is open, and put them in an earthen vessell, that they may continue many daies.

15 For thus saith the LORD of hostes the God of Israel; Houses and fields, and Vineyards shalbe possessed againe in this land.

16 ¶ Now when I had deliuered the euidence of the purchase vnto Baruch the sonne of Neriah, I prayed vnto the LORD, saying,

17 Ah Lord GOD, beholde, thou hast made the heauen and the earth by thy great power & stretched out arme, and there is nothing ||too hard for thee.

18 Thou shewest *louing kindnesse vnto thousands, and recompensest the iniquitie of the fathers into the bosome of their children after them: the great, the mightie God, the LORD of hosts is his Name,

19 Great in counsell, and mightie in †worke, (for thine *eyes are open vpon all the wayes of the sonnes of men, to giue euery one according to his wayes, and according to the fruit of his doings)

20 Which hast set signes and wonders in the land of Egypt, euen vnto this day, and in Israel, and amongst other men, and hast made thee a Name, as at this day,

21 And hast brought foorth thy people Israel *out of the land of Egypt, with signes and with wonders, and with a strong hand, and with a stretched out arme, and with great terrour,

22 And hast giuen them this land which thou didst sweare to their fathers to giue them a land flowing with milke and honie.

23 And they came in and possessed it, but they obeied not thy voice, neither walked in thy Law, they haue done nothing of all that thou commaundedst them to doe: therefore thou hast caused all this euill to come vpon them.

24 Beholde the ||mounts, they are come vnto the citie to take it, and the citie is giuen into the hand of the Caldeans that fight against it, because of the sword, and of the famine, and of the pestilence, and what thou hast spoken is come to passe, and behold, thou seest it.

25 And thou hast said vnto mee, O Lord GOD, buy thee the field for money, and take witnesses: for the citie is giuen into the hand of the Caldeans.

26 ¶ Then came the word of the LORD vnto Ieremiah, saying,

27 Behold, I am the LORD, the *God of all flesh: Is there any thing too hard for me?

28 Therfore thus saith the LORD, Behold, I will giue this citie into the hand

---

*Chap. 34. 3.

*Leuit. 25. 24. ruth. 4. 4.

||Or, seuen shekels and ten pieces of siluer.
†Heb. wrote in the booke.

||Or, hid from thee
*Exod. 3
7. deut, 5.

†Heb. doin
*Iob 34. 21. pro. 5. 21. chap. 16. 17.

*Exod. 6.
2. sam. 7. 5
1. chro. 1
21.

||Or, engin
of shot.

*Num. 16
22.

hand of the Caldeans, and into the hand of Nebuchad-rezzar king of Babylon, and he shall take it.

29 And the Caldeans that fight against this citie, shall come and set fire on this citie, and burne it with the houses *vpon whose roofes they haue offered incense vnto Baal, and powred out drinke offerings vnto other Gods to prouoke me to anger.

Chap. 19.

30 For the children of Israel, and the children of Iudah, haue onely done euill before me from their youth: for the children of Israel haue onely prouoked mee to anger with the worke of their hands, saith the LORD.

31 For this citie hath beene to me, as † a prouocation of mine anger, and of my furie, from the day that they built it, euen vnto this day; that I should remooue it from before my face:

Heb. for y anger.

32 Because of all the euill of the children of Israel, and of the children of Iudah, which they haue done to prouoke mee to anger, they, their kings, their Princes, their Priestes, and their Prophets, and the men of Iudah, and the inhabitants of Ierusalem.

33 And they haue turned vnto mee the †*backe, and not the face, though I taught them rising vp early, and teaching them, yet they haue not hearkened to receiue instruction,

Heb. necke. Cha. 2. 27.

34 But they * set their abominations in the house (which is called by my Name) to defile it.

Chap. 23.

35 And they built the high places of Baal, which are in the valley of the sonne of Hinnom, to *cause their sonnes and their daughters to passe through the fire vnto *Molech, which I commanded them not, neither came it into my minde, that they should doe this abomination, to cause Iudah to sinne.

Cha. 7. 31. ad 19. 6.
Leuit. 18.

36 ¶ And now therefore, thus sayth the LORD the God of Israel concerning this citie, whereof ye say, It shall be deliuered into the hand of the king of Babylon, by the sword, and by the famine, and by the pestilence:

37 Behold, I wil *gather them out of all countreys, whither I haue driuen them in mine anger, and in my furie, and in great wrath, and I will bring them againe vnto this place; and I will cause them to dwell safely.

Deu. 30. 3.

38 And they shalbe *my people, and I will be their God.

39 And I will *giue them one heart,

Cha. 24. 7. ad 30. 22. ad 31. 33. Ezek. 11.

and one way, that they may feare mee †for euer, for the good of them, and of their children after them.

† Heb. all dayes.

40 And I will make an euerlasting couenant with them, that I will not turne away †from them, to doe them good, but I will put my feare in their hearts, that they shall not depart from mee.

† Heb. from after them.

41 Yea, I will reioyce oner them to doe them good, and I will plant them in this land †assuredly, with my whole heart, and with my whole soule.

† Heb. in trueth, or stabilitie.

42 For thus sayth the LORD, Like as I haue brought all this great euill vpon this people, so will I bring vpon them all the good that I haue promised them.

43 And fields shalbe bought in this land whereof ye say, It is desolate without man or beast, it is giuen into the hand of the Caldeans.

44 Men shall buy fields for money, and subscribe euidences, and seale them, and take witnesses in the land of Beniamin, and in the places about Ierusalem, and in the cities of Iudah, and in the cities of the mountaines, and in the cities of the valley, and in the cities of the South: for I will cause their captiuitie to returne, saith the LORD.

CHAP. XXXIII.

1 God promiseth to the captiuitie, a gracious returne, 9 a ioyfull state, 12 a setled gouernment, 15 Christ, the branch of righteousnesse, 17 a continuance of kingdome and Priesthood, 20 and a stabilitie of a blessed seede.

MOreouer, the word of the LORD came vnto Ieremiah the second time (while hee was yet *shut vp in the court of the prison) saying;

* Chap. 32. 23.

2 Thus saith the LORD the *maker thereof, the LORD that formed it, to establish it, the LORD is his Name.

* Isa. 37. 26.

3 Call vnto me, and I will answere thee, and shew thee great and ‖ mightie things, which thou knowest not.

‖ Or, hidden.

4 For thus sayth the LORD the God of Israel concerning the houses of this citie, and concerning the houses of the kings of Iudah, which are throwen downe by the mounts, and by the sword.

5 They come to fight with the Caldeans,

deans, but *it is* to fill them with the dead bodies of men, whome I haue slaine in mine anger, and in my fury, and for all whose wickednesse I haue hid my face from this citie.

6 Behold, I will bring it health and cure, and I will cure them, and wil reueale vnto them the abundance of peace, and trueth.

7 And I will cause the captiuitie of Iudah, and the captiuitie of Israel to returne, and will build them as at the first.

8 And I will clense them from all their iniquitie, whereby they haue sinned against mee : and I will * pardon all their iniquities whereby they haue sinned, and whereby they haue transgressed against me.

9 ¶ And it shall be to me a name of ioy, a praise and an honour before all the nations of the earth, which shall heare all the good that I doe vnto them : and they shall feare and tremble for all the goodnesse, and for all the prosperitie that I procure vnto it.

10 Thus saith the Lord; Againe there shall be heard in this place (which yee say *shalbe* desolate without man and without beast, *euen* in the cities of Iudah, and in the streetes of Ierusalem that are desolate without man and without inhabitant, & without beast.)

11 The * voyce of ioy and the voyce of gladnesse, the voyce of the bridegroome, and the voyce of the bride, the voyce of them that shall say; Praise the Lord of hostes, for the Lord *is* good, for his mercy *endureth* for euer, *and* of them that shall bring the sacrifice of praise into the house of the Lord; for I will cause to returne the captiuitie of the land, as at the first, saith the Lord.

12 Thus saith the Lord of hostes; Againe in this place which *is* desolate without man and without beast, and in all the cities thereof *shalbe* a habitation of shepheards causing their flockes to lie downe.

13 In the cities of the mountaines, in the cities of the vale, and in the cities of the South, and in the land of Beniamin, and in the places about Ierusalem, and in the cities of Iudah, shall the flockes passe againe vnder the hands of him that telleth *them*, saith the Lord.

14 Behold, the dayes come, saith the Lord, that I will performe that good thing which I haue promised vnto the house of Israel, and to the house of Iudah.

15 ¶ In those dayes; and at that time will I cause the * branch of righteousnesse to grow vp vnto Dauid, and he shall execute iudgement and righteousnesse in the land.

16 In those dayes shall Iudah be saued, and Ierusalem shall dwell safely, and this *is the name* wherewith she shall be called, † The Lord our righteousnesse.

17 ¶ For thus saith the Lord; † Dauid shall neuer * want a man to sit vpon the throne of the house of Israel.

18 Neither shall the priests the Leuites want a man before me to offer burnt offrings, and to kindle meate offrings, and to doe sacrifice continually.

19 ¶ And the word of the Lord came vnto Ieremiah, saying,

20 Thus saith the Lord; * If you can breake my couenant of the day, and my couenant of the night, and that there should not be day, and night in their season :

21 *Then* may also my couenant bee broken with Dauid my seruant, that he should not haue a sonne to reigne vpon his throne; and with the Leuites the priests my ministers.

22 As * the hoste of heauen cannot be numbred, neither the sand of the sea measured : so will I multiply the seede of Dauid my seruant, and the Leuites that minister vnto me.

23 Moreouer, the word of the Lord came to Ieremiah, saying;

24 Considerest thou not what this people haue spoken, saying; The two families, which the Lord hath chosen, he hath euen cast them off? thus they haue dispised my people, that they should be no more a nation before them.

25 Thus saith the Lord; If my couenant be not with day and night, *and* if I haue not appointed the ordinances of heauen and earth :

26 Then will I cast away the seede of Iacob and Dauid my seruant, *so that* I will not take any of his seede to be rulers ouer the seede of Abraham, Isaac and Iacob : for I will cause their captiuitie to returne, and haue mercie on them.

CHAP.

*Chap. 21. 34. mic. 7. 18.

*Chap. 7. 34. and 16. 19.

* Chap. 5. isai. 11 and 4. 2.

† Heb. *Ie-hua-tsidke-*

† Heb. th shall not cut off fr Dauid.
* 2. Sam. 16. 1. kin 2. 4.

* Chap. 36. isai. 9.

* Chap. 37.

CHAP. XXXIIII.

1 Ieremiah prophecieth the captiuitie of Zedekiah, and the Citie. 8 The Princes and the people hauing dismissed their bondseruants, contrary to the Couenant of God, reassume them. 12 Ieremiah for their disobedience, giueth them and Zedekiah, into the hands of their enemies.

2. Kings
5. 1, &c.
hap. 52.

Heb. the
ominion of
is hand.

He word which came vnto Ieremiah frō the LORD (* when Nebuchad-nezzar king of Babylon and all his armie, and all the kingdomes of the earth of his †dominion, and all the people fought against Ierusalem and against all the cities thereof) saying,

2 Thus saith the LORD, the God of Israel, Go, and speake to Zedekiah king of Iudah, and tell him, Thus saith the LORD, Behold, I will giue this citie into the hand of the king of Babylon, and he shal burne it with fire.

3 And thou shalt not escape out of his hand, but shalt surely be *taken, and deliuered into his hand, and thine eyes shall behold the eyes of the king of Babylon, and †he shall speake with thee mouth to mouth, and thou shalt goe to Babylon.

Chap. 32.

Heb. his
mouth shall
peake to thy
mouth.

4 Yet heare the word of the LORD, O Zedekiah king of Iudah : Thus saith the LORD of thee, Thou shalt not die by the sword :

5 But thou shalt die in peace, and with the burnings of thy fathers the former kings which were before thee, so shall they burne odours for thee, and they will lament thee, saying, Ah Lord; for I haue pronounced the word, saith the LORD.

6 Then Ieremiah the Prophet spake all these words vnto Zedekiah king of Iudah in Ierusalem ;

7 When the king of Babylons armie fought against Ierusalem, and against all the cities of Iudah that were left, against Lachish, and against Azekah : for these defenced cities remained of the cities of Iudah.

8 ¶ This is the word that came vnto Ieremiah from the LORD, after that the king Zedekiah had made a couenant with all the people which were at Ierusalem to proclaime *liberty vnto them,

9 That euery man should let his man seruant, and euery man his maide

* Exo. 21, 2

seruant, being an Hebrewe, or an Hebrewesse, goe free, that none should serue himselfe of them, to wit, of a Iew his brother.

10 Now when all the princes and all the people which had entred into the couenant, heard that euery one should let his man seruant, and euery one his maid seruant goe free, that none should serue themselues of them any more, then they obeyed and let them goe.

11 But afterwards they turned, and caused the seruants and the handmaids whom they had let goe free, to returne, and brought them into subiection for seruants and for handmaids.

12 ¶ Therefore the worde of the LORD came to Ieremiah, from the LORD, saying,

13 Thus saith the LORD the God of Israel, I made a couenant with your fathers in the day that I brought them forth out of the land of Egypt, out of the house of bondmen, saying,

14 At the end of *seuen yeeres, let ye go euery man his brother an Hebrew which ‖hath bene sold vnto thee : and when he hath serued thee sixe yeeres, thou shalt let him goe free from thee, but your fathers hearkened not vnto me, neither inclined their eare.

15 And ye were †now turned, and had done right in my sight, in proclaiming libertie euery man to his neighbour, and ye had made a couenant before me in the house, †which is called by my Name.

16 But yee turned and polluted my Name, and caused euery man his seruant, and euery man his handmaide, whome yee had set at libertie at their pleasure, to returne; and brought them into subiection, to bee vnto you for seruants and for handmaids.

17 Therfore thus saith the LORD, Ye haue not hearkened vnto me, in proclaiming libertie euery one to his brother, and euery man to his neighbour : behold, I proclaime a libertie for you, saith the LORD, to the sword, to the pestilence, and to the famine, and I wil make you †to be *remoued into all the kingdomes of the earth.

18 And I wil giue the men that haue transgressed my couenant, which haue not performed the wordes of the couenant which they had made before mee, when they cut the calfe in twaine, and passed betweene the parts thereof,

* Exo. 21. 2
deut. 15. 12

‖ Or, hath
sold him-
selfe.

† Heb. to day

† Heb. wher-
upon my
name is cal-
led.

† Heb. for a
remouing.
* Deut. 28.
64. chap. 29
18.

19 The

19 The princes of Iudah and the princes of Ierusalem, the eunuches, and the priests, and all the people of the land which passed betweene the parts of the calfe,

20 I will euen giue them into the hande of their enemies, and into the hand of them that seeke their life, and their *dead bodies shall bee for meate vnto the foules of the heauen, and to the beasts of the earth.

* Chap. 7. 33. and 16. 4.

21 And Zedekiah king of Iudah, and his Princes will I giue into the hand of their enemies, and into the hand of them that seeke their life, and into the hand of the king of Babylons armie, which are gone vp from you.

22 Behold, I will command, saith the LORD, and cause them to returne to this citie, and they shall fight against it, and take it, and burne it with fire, and I will make the cities of Iudah a desolation without an inhabitant.

CHAP. XXXV.

1 By the obedience of the Rechabites, 12 Ieremiah condemneth the disobedience of the Iewes. 18 God blesseth the Rechabites for their obedience.

 HE word which came vnto Ieremiah from the LORD, in the daies of Iehoiakim the sonne of Iosiah King of Iudah, saying,

2 Goe vnto the house of the Rechabites, and speake vnto them, and bring them into the house of the LORD, into one of the chambers, and giue them wine to drinke.

3 Then I tooke Iaazaniah the sonne of Ieremiah the sonne of Habaziniah and his brethren, and all his sonnes, and the whole house of the Rechabites.

4 And I brought them into the house of the LORD, into the chamber of the sonnes of Hanan, the sonne of Igdaliah a man of God, which was by the chamber of the Princes, which was aboue the chamber of Maaseiah, the sonne of Shallum, the keeper of †the doore.

† Hebr. threshold or vessell.

5 And I set before the house of the Rechabites, pottes, full of wine, and cups, and I said vnto them, Drinke ye wine.

6 But they said, We will drinke no wine: for Ionadab the sonne of Rechab our father, commanded vs, saying; Ye shall drinke no wine, neither ye, nor your sonnes for euer.

7 Neither shall ye build house, nor sow seed, nor plant Vineyard, nor haue any: but all your dayes ye shall dwell in tents, that ye may liue many dayes in the land where ye be strangers.

8 Thus haue we obeyed the voice of Ionadab the sonne of Rechab our father, in all that he hath charged vs, to drinke no wine all our dayes, we, our wiues, our sonnes, nor our daughters:

9 Nor to build houses for vs to dwel in, neither haue we Vineyard, nor field, nor seed.

10 But wee haue dwelt in tents, and haue obeyed, and done according to all that Ionadab our father commanded vs.

11 But it came to passe when Nebuchadrezzar king of Babylon came vp into the land, that we said, Come, and let vs goe to Ierusalem for feare of the armie of the Caldeans, and for feare of the armie of the Syrians: so we dwell at Ierusalem.

12 ¶ Then came the word of the LORD vnto Ieremiah, saying,

13 Thus saith the LORD of hosts, the God of Israel, Goe and tel the men of Iudah, and inhabitants of Ierusalem, Will yee not receiue instruction to hearken to my words, saith the LORD?

14 The wordes of Ionadab the sonne of Rechab, that hee commanded his sonnes, not to drinke wine, are performed; for vnto this day they drinke none, but obey their fathers commandement: notwithstanding I haue spoken vnto you, rising early, and speaking, but ye hearkened not vnto me.

15 I haue sent also vnto you all my seruants the Prophets, rising vp early and sending them, saying, *Returne ye now euery man from his euil way, and amend your doings, and goe not after other gods to serue them, and ye shall dwell in the land, which I haue giuen to you, and to your fathers: but yee haue not enclined your eare, nor hearkned vnto me.

* Chap. 11. and 5.

16 Because the sonnes of Ionadab, the sonne of Rechab, haue performed the commaundement of their father, which he commaunded them, but this people hath not hearkened vnto me;

17 Therefore thus saith the LORD God

God of hostes, the God of Israel, Behold, I will bring vpon Iudah, and vpon all the inhabitants of Ierusalem, all the euill that I haue pronounced against them : because I haue spoken vnto them, but they haue not heard, and I haue called vnto them, but they haue not answered.

18 ¶ And Ieremiah sayd vnto the house of the Rechabites, Thus sayth the LORD of hosts the God of Israel, Because ye haue obeyed the commandement of Ionadab your father, and kept all his precepts, and done according vnto all that he hath commanded you :

19 Therefore thus sayth the LORD of hostes, the God of Israel, Ionadab the son of Rechab shall not †want a man to stand before me for euer.

*Heb. there all not a in be cut *from, &c.

CHAP. XXXVI.

1 Ieremiah causeth Baruch to write his prophecie, 5 and publikely to reade it. 11 The Princes hauing intelligence thereof by Michaiah, send Iehudi to fetch the roule and reade it. 19 They will Baruch to hide himselfe and Ieremiah. 20 The king Iehoiakim being certified thereof, heareth part of it, and burneth the roule. 27 Ieremiah denounceth his iudgement. 32 Baruch writeth a newe copie.

 Nd it came to passe in the fourth yeere of Iehoiakim the sonne of Iosiah king of Iudah, *that* this word came vnto Ieremiah from the LORD, saying ;

2 Take thee a roule of a booke, and write therein all the words that I haue spoken vnto thee against Israel, and against Iudah, & against all the nations, from the day I spake vnto thee, frō the dayes of *Iosiah, euen vnto this day.

Cha. 25. 3

3 It may be that the house of Iudah will heare all the euil which I purpose to doe vnto them ; that they may returne euery man from his euill way, that I may forgiue their iniquitie, and their sinne.

4 Then Ieremiah called Baruch the sonne of Neriah, and Baruch wrote from the mouth of Ieremiah all the words of the LORD, which he had spoken vnto him, vpon a roule of a booke.

5 And Ieremiah commanded Baruch, saying, I *am* shut vp, I cannot goe into the house of the LORD.

6 Therefore goe thou and reade in the roule, which thou hast written from my mouth, the wordes of the LORD

in the eares of the people in the LORDS house vpon the fasting day : and also thou shalt reade them in the eares of all Iudah, that come out of their cities.

7 It may bee †they will present their supplication before the LORD, and will returne euery one from his euill way ; for great *is* the anger and the furie that the LORD hath pronounced against this people.

† Heb. their supplication shall fall.

8 And Baruch the sonne of Neriah did according to all that Ieremiah the Prophet commanded him, reading in the booke the wordes of the LORD, in the LORDS house.

9 And it came to passe in the fifth yeere of Iehoiakim the sonne of Iosiah king of Iudah, in the ninth moneth, *that* they proclaimed a fast before the LORD to all the people in Ierusalem, & to all the people that came from the cities of Iudah vnto Ierusalem.

10 Then read Baruch in the booke, the wordes of Ieremiah in the house of the LORD, in the chamber of Gemariah the sonne of Shaphan the scribe, in the higher court at the ‖*entry of the newe gate of the LORDS house, in the eares of all the people.

‖ Or, doore. * Chap. 26. 10.

11 ¶ When Michaiah the sonne of Gemariah the sonne of Shaphan had heard out of the booke, all the words of the LORD ;

12 Then hee went downe into the kings house into the scribes chamber, and loe, all the princes sate there, *euen* Elishama the scribe, and Delaiah the sonne of Shemaiah, and Elnathan the sonne of Achbor, and Gemariah the sonne of Shaphan, and Zedekiah the sonne of Hananiah, and all the princes.

13 Then Michaiah declared vnto them all the words that hee had heard when Baruch read the booke in the eares of the people.

14 Therefore all the princes sent Iehudi the sonne of Nethaniah, the sonne of Shelemiah, the sonne of Cushi, vnto Baruch, saying ; Take in thine hand the roule wherein thou hast read in the eares of the people, and come. So Baruch the sonne of Neriah took the roule in his hand, and came vnto them.

15 And they sayde vnto him, Sit downe now and read it in our eares. So Baruch read it in their eares.

16 Now it came to passe when they had heard all the words, they were afraid

fraid both one and other, and sayd vnto Baruch, Wee will surely tell the King of all these words.

17 And they asked Baruch, saying, Tell vs now, How diddest thou write all these words at his mouth?

18 Then Baruch answered them, Hee pronounced all these words vnto me with his mouth, and I wrote *them* with inke in the Booke.

19 Then said the Princes vnto Baruch, Go hide thee, thou and Ieremiah, and let no man know where yee *bee.*

20 ¶ And they went in to the King into the Court, bnt they layed vp the roule in the chamber of Elishama the Scribe, and told all the words in the eares of the king.

21 So the king sent Iehudi to fet the roule, and hee tooke it out of Elishama the scribes chamber, and Iehudi read it in the eares of the king, and in the eares of all the princes which stood beside the king.

22 Now the king sate in the winter house, in the ninth moneth, & there was a *fire* on the hearth burning before him.

23 And it came to passe *that* when Iehudi had read three or foure leaues, he cut it with the penknife, and cast it into the fire that *was* on the hearth, vntill all the roule was consumed in the fire that *was* on the hearth.

24 Yet they were not afraid, nor rent their garments, *neither* the king, nor any of his seruants that heard all these words.

25 Neuerthelesse Elnathan, and Delaiah & Gemariah had made intercession to the king that he would not burne the roule, but he would not heare them.

26 But the king commaunded Ierahmeel the sonne ||of Hammelech, and Seraiah the sonne of Azriel, & Shelemiah the sonne of Abdiel, to take Baruch the scribe, and Ieremiah the Prophet : but the Lord hid them.

27 ¶ Then the word of the Lord came to Ieremiah (after that the king had burnt the roule and the words which Baruch wrote at the mouth of Ieremiah) saying,

28 Take thee againe another roule, and write in it all the former words that were in the first roule, which Iehoiakim the king of Iudah hath burnt.

29 And thou shalt say to Iehoiakim king of Iudah, Thus sayth the Lord, Thou hast burnt this roule,

saying, Why hast thou written therein, saying, The king of Babylon shall certainely come and destroy this land, and shall cause to cease from thence man and beast?

30 Therefore thus saith the Lord of Iehoiakim king of Iudah ; He shall haue none to sit vpon the throne of Dauid, and his dead body shall be * cast out in the day to the heate, and in the night to the frost.

31 And I will †punish him and his seede, and his seruants for their iniquitie, and I will bring vpon them, and vpon the inhabitants of Ierusalem, and vpon the men of Iudah all the euill that I haue pronounced against them : but they hearkened not

32 ¶ Then tooke Ieremiah another roule, and gaue it to Baruch the scribe the sonne of Neriah, who wrote therein from the mouth of Ieremiah, all the words of the booke which Iehoiakim king of Iudah had burnt in the fire, and there were added besides vnto them, many †like words.

CHAP XXXVII

1 The Egyptians hauing raised the siege of the Caldeans, king Zedekiah sendeth to Ieremiah to pray for the people. 6 Ieremiah prophesieth the Caldeans certaine returne and victory. 11 He is taken for a fugitiue, beaten and put in prison. 16 He assureth Zedekiah of the captiuitie. 18 Intreating for his liberty, he obtaineth some fauour.

And king * Zedekiah the sonne of Iosiah reigned in stead of Coniah the son of Iehoiakim, who Nebuchad-rezzar king of Babylon made king in the land of Iudah.

2 But neither he, nor his seruants, nor the people of the land, did hearken vnto the words of the Lord, which he spake †by the prophet Ieremiah.

3 And Zedekiah the king sent Iehucal the sonne of Shelemiah, and Zephaniah the son of Maaseiah the priest to the prophet Ieremiah, saying, Pray now vnto the Lord our God for vs.

4 Nowe Ieremiah came in and went out among the people : for they had not put him into prison

5 Then Pharaohs armie was come forth out of Egypt : and when the Caldeans that besieged Ierusalem, heard tidings of them, they departed from Ierusalem.

6 ¶ Then

Margin notes

† *Or, of the king.*

* Chap. 22. 19.

† *Heb. vis. vpon.*

† *Heb. as they.*

* Chap. 2 24. 2. kin 24. 17. ar 2. chron. 10.

† *Heb. by the hand the prophet.*

6 ¶ Then came the word of the LORD vnto the Prophet Ieremiah, saying,

7 Thus saith the LORD, the God of Israel, Thus shall ye say to the king of Iudah, that sent you vnto me to enquire of me, Behold, Pharaohs armie which is come forth to helpe you, shall returne to Egypt into their owne land.

8 And the Caldeans shall come againe, and fight against this citie and take it, and burne it with fire.

9 Thus saith the LORD, Deceiue not your †selues, saying, The Caldeans shall surely depart from vs : for they shall not depart.

† Heb. soules

10 For though yee had smitten the whole armie of the Caldeans that fight against you, and there remained but † wounded men among them, *yet* should they rise vp euery man in his tent, and burne this citie with fire.

† Heb. thrust through.

11 ¶ And it came to passe that when the armie of the Caldeans was †broken vp from Ierusalem for feare of Pharaohs armie,

† Heb. made to ascend.

12 Then Ieremiah went forth out of Ierusalem to goe into the lande of Beniamin, ‖ to separate himselfe thence in the mids of the people.

‖ Or, to slip away from thence in the midst of the people.

13 And when he was in the gate of Beniamin, a captaine of the warde *was* there, whose name *was* Irijah, the son of Shelemiah, the sonne of Hananiah, & he tooke Ieremiah the Prophet, saying, Thou fallest away to the Caldeans

14 Then said Ieremiah, It *is* †false, I fall not away to the Caldeans : but he hearkened not to him : so Irijah tooke Ieremiah, and brought him to the princes.

† Heb. falsehood or lie.

15 Wherfore the princes were wroth with Ieremiah, and smote him, and put him in prison, in the house of Ionathan the scribe, for they had made that the prison.

16 ¶ When Ieremiah was entred into the dungeon, and into the ‖cabbins, and Ieremiah had remained there many dayes :

‖ Or, Celles.

17 Then Zedekiah the king sent and tooke him out, and the king asked him secretly in his house, and said, Is there *any* word from the LORD? and Ieremiah said, There is : for, said he, thou shalt be deliuered into the hand of the king of Babylon.

18 Moreouer Ieremiah sayd vnto king Zedekiah, What haue I offended against thee, or against thy seruants, or against this people, that yee haue put me in prison ?

19 Where *are now* your prophets, which prophecied vnto you , saying, The king of Babylon shall not come against you, nor against this land ?

20 Therefore heare now , I pray thee, O my Lord the king; †let my supplication, I pray thee, be accepted before thee, that thou cause me not to returne to the house of Ionathan the scribe, lest I die there.

† Heb. let my supplication fall.

21 Then Zedekiah the king commanded that they should commit Ieremiah into the court of the prison, and that they should giue him daily a piece of bread out of the bakers streete, vntill all the bread in the citie were spent. Thus Ieremiah remained in the court of the prison.

CHAP. XXXVIII.

1 Ieremiah by a false suggestion is put into the dungeon of Malchiah. 7 Ebed-meleech, by suite, getteth him some inlargement. 14 Vpon secret conference, he counsaileth the king by yeelding to saue his life. 24 By the kings instructions, he concealeth the conference from the Princes.

 HEN Shephatiah the sonne of Mattan, and Gedaliah the sonne of Pashur and Iucal the sonne of Shelemiah, & Pashur the sonne of Malchiah heard the words that Ieremiah had spoken vnto all the people, saying,

2 Thus saith the LORD, * He that remaineth in this citie, shall die by the sword, by the famine, and by the pestilence, but he that goeth forth to the Caldeans , shall liue : for he shall haue his life for a pray, and shall liue.

* Cha. 21. 9

3 Thus saith the LORD, This citie shall surely be giuen into the hand of the king of Babylons armie, which shall take it.

4 Therefore the princes sayd vnto the king, We beseech thee let this man be put to death : for thus he weakeneth the hands of the men of warre that remaine in this citie, and the hands of all the people, in speaking such words vnto them: for this man seeketh not the † welfare of this people, but the hurt.

† Heb. peace.

5 Then Zedekiah the king sayd, Behold, he *is* in your hand; for the king *is* not he *that* can do any thing against you.

6 Then

6 Then tooke they Ieremiah, and cast him into the dungeon of Malchiah the sonne of ‖ Hammelech that *was* in the court of the prison : and they let downe Ieremiah with cords : and in the dungeon *there was* no water, but mire : so Ieremiah sunke in the mire.

‖ Or, of the king.

7 ¶ Now when Ebed-melech the Ethiopian, one of y̆ eunuches which was in the kings house, heard that they had put Ieremiah in the dungeon (the king then sitting in the gate of Beniamin)

8 Ebed-melech went foorth out of the kings house, and spake to the king, saying,

9 My lord the king, these men haue done euill in all that they haue done to Ieremiah the Prophet, whom they haue cast into the dungeon, and †he is like to die for hunger in the place where he is, for *there is* no more bread in the city.

† Hebr. he will die.

10 Then the king commanded Ebed-melech the Ethiopian, saying, Take from hence thirtie men †with thee, and take vp Ieremiah the Prophet out of the dungeon before he die.

† Hebr. in thine hand.

11 So Ebed-melech tooke the men with him, and went into the house of the king vnder the treasurie, and tooke thence old cast cloutes, and old rotten ragges, and let them downe by cordes into the dungeon to Ieremiah.

12 And Ebed-melech the Ethiopian said vnto Ieremiah, Put now these old cast cloutes and rotten ragges vnder thine arme-holes, vnder the cordes. And Ieremiah did so.

13 So they drew vp Ieremiah with cordes, and tooke him vp out of the dungeon, and Ieremiah remained in the court of the prison.

14 ¶ Then Zedekiah the king sent, and tooke Ieremiah the Prophet vnto him into the ‖third entrie that is in the house of the Lord, and the king said vnto Ieremiah, I will aske thee a thing : hide nothing from me.

‖ Or principall.

15 Then Ieremiah said vnto Zedekiah, If I declare it vnto thee, wilt thou not surely put me to death ? and if I giue thee counsell, wilt thou not hearken vnto me ?

16 So the king sware secretly vnto Ieremiah, saying, As the Lord liueth that made vs this soule, I wil not put thee to death, neither will I giue thee into the hand of these men that seeke thy life.

17 Then said Ieremiah vnto Zede-

kiah, Thus saith the Lord the God of hostes, the God of Israel, If thou wilt assuredly goe foorth vnto the king of Babylons Princes, then thy soule shall liue, and this Citie shall not be burnt with fire, and thou shalt liue, and thine house.

18 But if thou wilt not goe foorth to the king of Babylons Princes, then shall this City be giuen into the hand of the Caldeans, and they shall burne it with fire, and thou shalt not escape out of their hand.

19 And Zedekiah the king said vnto Ieremiah, I am afraid of the Iewes that are fallen to the Caldeans, lest they deliuer mee into their hand, and they mocke me.

20 But Ieremiah said, They shall not deliuer *thee :* obey, I beseech thee, the voyce of the Lord, which I speake vnto thee : so it shall be well vnto thee, and thy soule shall liue.

21 But if thou refuse to goe foorth, this *is* the word that the Lord hath shewed me.

22 And behold, all the women that are left in the king of Iudahs house, shalbe brought forth to the king of Babylons Princes, and those *women* shall say, †Thy friends haue set thee on, and haue preuailed against thee : thy feet are sunke in the mire, *and* they are turned away backe.

† Hebr. men of thy peace.

23 So they shall bring out all thy wiues, and thy children to the Caldeans, and thou shalt not escape out of their hand, but shalt be taken by the hand of the King of Babylon : and †thou shalt cause this citie to be burnt with fire.

† Hebr. thou shalt burne, &c.

24 ¶ Then said Zedekiah vnto Ieremiah, Let no man know of these words, and thou shalt not die.

25 But if the Princes heare that I haue talked with thee, and they come vnto thee, and say vnto thee, Declare vnto vs now what thou hast said vnto the king ; hide it not from vs, and wee wil not put thee to death ; also what the king said vnto thee :

26 Then thou shalt say vnto them, I presented my supplication before the king, that he would not cause me to returne to Ionathans house to die there.

27 Then came all the Princes vnto Ieremiah, and asked him, and he told them according to all these words, that the king had commanded : so †they left off

† Hebr. the were silent from him.

off speaking with him, for the matter was not perceiued.

28 So Ieremiah abode in the court of the prison, vntill the day that Ierusalem was taken, and hee was *there* when Ierusalem was taken.

CHAP. XXXIX.

1 Ierusalem is taken. 4 Zedekiah is made blinde, and sent to Babylon. 8 The city ruinated, 9 the people captiuated. 11 Nebuchad-rezzars charge for the good vsage of Ieremiah. 15 Gods promise to Ebed-melech.

Kin. 25.
hap. 52.

IN the *ninth yeere of Zedekiah king of Iudah, in the tenth moneth, came Nebuchad rezzar king of Babylon, and all his armie against Ierusalem, and they besieged it.

2 *And* in the eleuenth yeere of Zedekiah, in the fourth moneth, the ninth day of the moneth, the citie was broken vp.

3 And all the princes of the king of Babylon came in, and sate in the middle gate, *euen* Nergal-Sharezer, Samgar-Nebo, Sarsechim, Rabsaris, Nergal-Sharezer, Rabmag, with all the residue of the princes of the king of Babylon.

4 ¶ And it came to passe, *that* when Zedekiah the king of Iudah saw them and all the men of warre, then they fled and went forth out of the citie by night, by the way of the kings garden, by the gate betwixt the two walles, and hee went out the way of the plaine.

5 But the Caldeans armie pursued after them, and ouertooke Zedekiah in the plaines of Iericho : and when they had taken him, they brought him vp to Nebuchad-nezzar king of Babylon to Riblah in the land of Hamath, where he †gaue iudgement vpon him.

br. spake
him
ements.

6 Then the king of Babylon slewe the sonnes of Zedekiah in Riblah before his eyes : also the king of Babylon slew all the nobles of Iudah.

7 Moreouer he put out Zedekiahs eyes, and bound him †with chaines, to cary him to Babylon.

eb. with
brasen
ines, or
ers.

8 ¶ And the Caldeans burnt the kings house, and the houses of the people with fire, and brake downe the wals of Ierusalem.

9 Then Nebuzaradan the ‖ captaine of the guard caried away captiue

, chiefe
rshall.
r. chiefe
e execu-
ers or
ghter

i so verse
1, &c.

into Babylon the remnant of the people that remained in the citie, and those that fell away, that fell to him, with the rest of the people that remained.

10 But Nebuzaradan the captaine of the guard left of the poore of the people which had nothing, in the land of Iudah, and gaue them vineyards and fieldes †at the same time.

† Hebr. in
that day.

11 ¶ Now Nebuchad-rezzar king of Babylon gaue charge coucerning Ieremiah †to Nebuzaradan the captaine of the guard, saying ;

† Heb. by the
hand of.

12 Take him, and †looke well to him, and doe him no harme, but doe vnto him euen as he shall say vnto thee.

† Hebr. set
thine eyes
vpon him.

13 So Nebuzaradan the captaine of the guard sent, and Nebushasban, Rabsaris, and Nergal-Sharezer, Rabmag, and all the King of Babylons Princes :

14 Euen they sent, and tooke Ieremiah out of the court of the prison, and committed him vnto Gedaliah the son of Ahikam, the sonne of Shaphan, that hee should carie him home : so hee dwelt among the people.

15 ¶ Now the word of the LORD came vnto Ieremiah, while hee was shut vp in the court of the prison, saying ;

16 Goe and speake to Ebed-melech the Ethiopian, saying, Thus sayth the LORD of hostes the God of Israel, Behold, I will bring my words vpon this citie for euill, and not for good, and they shall be *accomplished* in that day before thee.

17 But I will deliuer thee in that day, sayth the LORD, and thou shalt not be giuen into the hand of the men of whom thou *art* afraid.

18 For I wil surely deliuer thee, and thou shalt not fall by the sword, but thy life shall be for a pray vnto thee, because thou hast put thy trust in me, sayth the LORD.

CHAP XL.

1 Ieremiah being set free by Nebuzaradan, goeth to Gedaliah. 7 The dispersed Iewes repaire vnto him. 13 Iohanan reuealing Ishmaels conspiracie, is not beleeued.

THe word which came to Ieremiah fro the LORD after that Nebuzaradan the ‖captaine of the guard had let him goe from Ramath,

‖ Or, mani-
cles.

math, when hee had taken him being bound in chaines among all that were caried away captiue of Ierusalem and Iudah, which were caried away captiue vnto Babylon.

2 And the captaine of the gard took Ieremiah, and sayd vnto him, The LORD thy God hath pronounced this euill vpon this place.

3 Now the LORD hath brought *it*, and done according as he hath sayd: because yee haue sinned against the LORD, and haue not obeyed his voyce, therefore this thing is come vpon you.

4 And now behold, I loose thee this day from the chaines which *were* vpon thine hand: if it seeme good vnto thee to come with me into Babylon, come, and † I will looke well vnto thee: but if it seeme ill vnto thee to come with me into Babylon, forbeare: behold, all the land *is* before thee: whither it seemeth good and conuenient for thee to goe, thither goe.

5 Now while he was not yet gone backe, *he sayd*, Goe backe also to Gedaliah the sonne of Ahikam the sonne of Shaphan, whom the king of Babylon hath made gouernour ouer all the cities of Iudah, and dwell with him among the people: or goe wheresoeuer it seemeth conuenient vnto thee to goe. So the captaine of the gard gaue him vitailes and a reward, and let him goe.

6 Then went Ieremiah vnto Gedaliah the sonne of Ahikam to Mizpah, and dwelt with him among the people, that were left in the land.

7 ¶ Now when all the captaines of the forces which *were* in the fields, *euen* they and their men, heard that the king of Babylon had made Gedaliah the sonne of Ahikam gouernour in the land, and had committed vnto him men, and women and children, and of the poore of the land, of them that were not caried away captiue to Babylon;

8 Then they came to Gedaliah to Mizpah, euen Ishmael the sonne of Nethaniah, and Iohanan, and Ionathan the sonnes of Kareah, and Seraiah the sonne of Tanhumeth, and the sonnes of Ephai the Netophathite, and Iezaniah the sonne of a Maachathite, they and their men.

9 And Gedaliah the sonne of Ahikam the sonne of Shaphan, sware vnto them and to their men, saying, Feare

† Heb. I will set mine eye vpon thee.

not † to serue the Caldeans: dwell in the land and serue the king of Babylon, and it shalbe well with you.

10 As for me, behold, I will dwell at Mizpah to serue the Caldeans, which will come vnto vs: but yee, gather yee wine, and summer fruits, and oyle, and put them in your vessels, and dwell in your cities, that yee haue taken.

11 Likewise when all the Iewes that *were* in Moab, and among the Ammonites, and in Edom, and that *were* in all the countries, heard that the king of Babylon had left a remnant of Iudah, and that he had set ouer them Gedaliah the sonne of Ahikam the sonne of Shaphan,

12 Euen all the Iewes returned out of all places whither they were driuen, and came to the land of Iudah, to Gedaliah vnto Mizpah, and gathered wine and summer fruits, very much.

13 ¶ Moreouer Iohanan the sonne of Kareah, and all the captaines of the forces that *were* in the fields, came to Gedaliah to Mizpah,

14 And sayd vnto him, Doest thou certainly know, that Baalis the king of the Ammonites hath sent Ishmael the sonne of Nethaniah † to slay thee? But Gedaliah the sonne of Ahikam beleeued them not.

15 Then Iohanan the sonne of Kareah, spake to Gedaliah in Mizpah secretly, saying, Let me goe, I pray thee, and I will slay Ishmael the sonne of Nethaniah, and no man shall know *it*. Wherefore should he slay thee, that all the Iewes which are gathered vnto thee should be scattered, and the remnant in Iudah perish?

16 But Gedaliah the sonne of Ahikam sayd vnto Iohanan the sonne of Kareah; Thou shalt not do this thing, for thou speakest falsely of Ishmael.

† Heb. to stand before. And so verse 10.

† Heb. to strike thee in soule?

CHAP. XLI.

1 Ishmael, trecherously killing Gedaliah and others, purposeth with the residue to flie vnto the Ammonites. 11 Iohanan recouereth the captiues, and mindeth to fly into Egypt.

Ow it came to passe in the seuenth moneth, *that* Ishmael the sonne of Nethaniah the sonne of Elishamah of the seede royall, and the princes of the king, euen tenne men with him, came vnto Gedaliah the sonne of Ahikam to Mizpah, and there they

they did eate bread together in Mizpah.

2 Then arose Ishmael the sonne of Nethaniah, and the ten men that were with him, and smote Gedaliah the son of Ahikam the sonne of Shaphan with the sword, and slew him, whome the king of Babylon had made gouernour ouer the land.

3 Ishmael also slew all the Iewes that were with him, *euen* with Gedaliah at Mizpah, and the Caldeans that were found there, *and* the men of warre.

4 And it came to passe the second day after he had slaine Gedaliah, and no man knew *it*,

5 That there came certaine from Shechem, from Shiloh, and from Samaria, *euen* fourescore men, hauing their beards shauen, and their clothes rent, and hauing cut themselues, with offerings and incense in their hand, to bring *them* to the house of the LORD.

6 And Ishmael the sonne of Nethaniah went foorth from Mizpah to meete them, †weeping all along as hee went : and it came to passe as hee met them, he said vnto them, Come to Gedaliah the sonne of Ahikam.

7 And it was so when they came into the midst of the citie, that Ishmael the sonne of Nethaniah slew them, *and cast them* into the midst of the pit, he, and the men that were with him.

8 But ten men were found among them, that said vnto Ishmael, Slay vs not : for we haue treasures in the field, of wheate, and of barley, and of oyle, and of hony : so he forbare, and slewe them not among their brethren.

9 Now the pit wherein Ishmael had cast all the dead bodies of the men (whom he had slaine || because of Gedaliah) *was* it, which Asa the king had made, for feare of Baasha king of Israel, *and* Ishmael the sonne of Nethaniah filled *it* with them that were slaine.

10 Then Ishmael caried away captiue all the residue of the people, that *were* in Mizpah, *euen* the kings daughters, and al the people that remained in Mizpah, whom Nebuzaradan the captaine of the guard had committed to Gedaliah the sonne of Ahikam, and Ishmael the sonne of Nethaniah caried them away captiue, and departed to goe ouer to the Ammonites.

11 ¶ But when Iohanan the sonne of Kareah, and all the captaines of the forces that *were* with him, heard of all the euill that Ishmael the sonne of Nethaniah had done,

12 Then they tooke all the men, and went to fight with Ishmael the sonne of Nethaniah, and found him by the great waters that *are* in Gibeon.

13 Now it came to passe *that* when al the people which *were* with Ishmael, sawe Iohanan the sonne of Kareah, and all the captaines of the forces, that *were* with him, then they were glad.

14 So all the people that Ishmael had caried away captiue from Mizpah cast about and returned, and went vnto Iohanan the sonne of Kareah.

15 But Ishmael the sonne of Nethaniah escaped from Iohanan with eight men, and went to the Ammonites.

16 Then tooke Iohanan the sonne of Kareah, and all the captaines of the forces that *were* with him, all the remnant of the people whom he had recouered from Ishmael the sonne of Nethaniah, from Mizpah (after *that* he had slaine Gedaliah the sonne of Ahikam,) *euen* mighty men of warre, and the women, and the children, and the eunuches whom he had brought againe from Gibeon.

17 And they departed and dwelt in the habitation of Chimham, which *is* by Bethlehem, to goe to enter into Egypt,

18 Because of the Caldeans : for they were afraid of them, because Ishmael the sonne of Nethaniah had slaine Gedaliah the sonne of Ahikam, whom the king of Babylon made gouernour in the land.

CHAP. XLII.

1 Iohanan desireth Ieremiah to enquire of God, promising obedience to his will. 7 Ieremiah assureth him of safety in Iudea, 13 and destruction in Egypt. 19 He reproueth their hypocrisie in requiring of the Lord, that which they meant not.

Hen all the captaines of the forces, and Iohanan the sonne of Kareah, and Iezaniah the sonne of Hoshaiah, and all the people from the least euen vnto the greatest, came neere,

2 And said vnto Ieremiah the prophet, || Let, we beseech thee, our supplication be accepted before thee, and pray for vs vnto the LORD thy God, *euen* for all this remnant (for we are left *but* a few of many, as thine eies do behold vs)

3 That

*Or, neere
daliah,
b. by the
nd or by
e side of
daliah.*

|| *Or, let our
supplication
fall before
thee.*

3 That the LORD thy God may shew vs the way wherein we may walke, and the thing that we may doe.

4 Then Ieremiah the prophet sayd vnto them, I haue heard *you*; behold, I will pray vnto the LORD your God, according to your words, and it shall come to passe *that* whatsoeuer thing the LORD shall answere you, I will declare *it* vnto you: I will keepe nothing backe from you.

5 Then they sayd to Ieremiah, The LORD be a true and faithfull witnesse betweene vs, if we doe not, euen according to all things for the which the LORD thy God shall send thee to vs.

6 Whether it *be* good, or whether it *be* euill, we will obey the voice of the LORD our God, to whom we send thee, that it may be well with vs, when we obey the voice of the LORD our God.

7 ¶ And it came to passe after tenne dayes, that the word of the LORD came vnto Ieremiah.

8 Then called hee Iohanan the sonne of Kareah, and all the captaines of the forces which *were* with him, and all the people, from the least, euen to the greatest,

9 And said vnto them, Thus saith the LORD, the God of Israel, vnto whom ye sent me to present your supplication before him:

10 If ye will still abide in this land, then will I build you, and not pull *you* downe, and I will plant you, and not plucke *you* vp: for I repent mee of the euill, that I haue done vnto you.

11 Be not afraid of the king of Babylon, of whom yee are afraid : be not afraid of him, saith the LORD : for I *am* with you to saue you, and to deliuer you from his hand

12 And I will shew mercies vnto you, that he may haue mercy vpon you; and cause you to returne to your owne land.

13 ¶ But if ye say, We will not dwell in this land, neither obey the voice of the LORD your God,

14 Saying, No, but we will goe into the land of Egypt, where we shall see no warre, nor heare the sound of the Trumpet, nor haue hunger of bread, and there wil we dwell :

15 (And now therefore heare the word of the LORD, yee remnant of Iudah, Thus saith the LORD of hostes the God of Israel, If ye wholly set your faces to enter into Egypt, and goe to soiourne there:)

16 Then it shall come to passe, that the sword which yee feared, shall ouertake you there in the land of Egypt, and the famine whereof yee were afraid, †shall follow close after you in Egypt, and there ye shall die.

17 †So shall it bee with all the men that set their faces to goe into Egypt to soiourne there, they shall die by the sword, by the famine, and by the pestilence : and none of them shall remaine or escape from the euill that I will bring vpon them

18 For thus saith the LORD of hosts the God of Israel, As mine anger and my furie hath bene powred foorth vpon the inhabitants of Ierusalem · so shall my furie bee powred foorth vpon you, when yee shall enter into Egypt : and ye shall be an execration, and an astonishment, and a curse, and a reproch, and ye shall see this place no more

19 ¶ The LORD hath said concerning you, O ye remnant of Iudah, Goe ye not into Egypt : know certainly, that I haue †admonished you this day.

20 For ye ||dissembled in your hearts when ye sent me vnto the LORD your God, saying, Pray for vs vnto the LORD our God, and according vnto all that the LORD our God shall say, so declare vnto vs, and we wil doe *it*.

21 And *now* I haue this day declared *it* to you, but ye haue not obeied the voice of the LORD your God, nor any thing for the which he hath sent me vnto you.

22 Now therefore know certainly, that ye shall die by the sword, by the famine, and by the pestilence, in the place whither ye desire to go *and* to soiourne.

CHAP. XLIII.

1 Iohanan, discrediting Ieremiahs prophecie, carieth Ieremiah and others into Egypt. 8 Ieremiah prophecieth by a type the conquest of Egypt, by the Babylonians.

AND it came to passe *that* whē Ieremiah had made an end of speaking vnto all the people, al the words of the LORD their God, for which the LORD their God had sent him to them, *euen* all these words;

2 Then spake Azariah the sonne of Hoshaiah,

† *Hebr. sha- cleaue afte you.*

† *Hebr. so shall all th men be.*

† *Hebr. tes fied again you.*

‖ *Or, you haue vsed deceit a- gainst you soules.*

Hoshaiah, and Iohanan the sonne of Kareah, and all the proud men, saying vnto Ieremiah, Thou speakest falsly : the LORD our God hath not sent thee to say, Goe not into Egypt, to soiourne there.

3 But Baruch the sonne of Neriah setteth thee on against vs, for to deliuer vs into the hand of the Caldeans, that they might put vs to death , and carie vs away captiues into Babylon.

4 So Iohanan the sonne of Kareah, and all the captaines of the forces, and all the people, obeied not the voice of the LORD, to dwell in the land of Iudah.

5 But Iohanan the sonne of Kareah, and all the captaines of the forces, tooke all the remnant of Iudah, that were returned from all nations whither they had bene driuen, to dwell in the land of Iudah,

6 *Euen* men, and women, and children, and the kings daughters, and euery person that Nebuzaradan the captaine of the guard had left with Gedaliah the sonne of Ahikam, the sonne of Shaphan, and Ieremiah the Prophet, and Baruch the sonne of Neriah.

7 So they came into the land of Egypt : for they obeyed not the voyce of the LORD, thus came they euen to Tahpanhes.

8 ¶ Then came the word of the LORD vnto Ieremiah in Tahpanhes, saying ;

9 Take great stones in thine hand, and hide them in the clay in the bricke kill, which *is* at the entry of Pharaohs house in Tahpanhes, in the sight of the men of Iudah :

10 And say vnto them, Thus saieth the LORD of hosts the God of Israel ; Beholde, I will send and take Nebuchadrezzar the king of Babylon my seruant, and will set his throne vpon these stones that I haue hidde, and hee shall spread his royall pauilion ouer them.

11 And when he commeth, hee shall Chap. 15. 2 ach. 11. 2. smite the land of Egypt, *and deliuer* * such *as are* for death, to death ; and such *as are* for captiuitie to captiuitie ; and such *as are* for the sword, to the sword.

12 And I wil kindle a fire in the houses of the gods of Egypt, and hee shall burne them, and carry them away captiues, and hee shall aray himselfe with the land of Egypt, as a shepheard put-

teth on his garment ; and hee shall goe forth from thence in peace.

13 He shall breake also the †images of || Beth-shemesh that *is* in the land of Egypt, and the houses of the gods of the Egyptians shall he burne with fire.

† *Hcb. statues, or standing images.*
‡ *Or, The house of the Sunne.*

CAP. XLIIII.

1 Ieremiah expresseth the desolation of Iudah for their idolatry. 11 Hee prophesieth their destruction, who commit idolatry in Egypt. 15 The obstinacie of the Iewes. 20 Ieremiah threatneth them for the same, 29 And for a signe, prophecieth the destruction of Egypt.

He word that came to Ieremiah concerning all the Iewes which dwel in the land of Egypt, which dwell at Migdol , and at Tahpanhes, and at Noph, and in the countrey of Pathros, saying,

2 Thus saith the LORD of hosts, the God of Israel ; Ye haue seene all the euill that I haue brought vpon Ierusalem, and vpon all the cities of Iudah : and behold, this day they *are* a desolation, and no man dwelleth therein,

3 Because of their wickednes which they haue committed, to prouoke me to anger , in that they went to burne incense, *and* to serue other gods, whom they knew not, *neither* they, you, nor your fathers.

4 Howbeit I sent vnto you all my seruants the Prophets, rising early and sending *them*, saying, Oh doe not this abominable thing that I hate.

5 But they hearkened not, nor enclined their eare to turne from their wickednes, to burne no incense vnto other gods.

6 Wherefore my furie and mine anger was powred forth, and was kindled in the cities of Iudah, and in the streets of Ierusalem, and they are wasted and desolate, as at this day.

7 Therefore now thus saith the LORD the God of hostes, the God of Israel, Wherefore commit ye *this* great euill against your soules, to cut off from you man and woman, childe and suckling †out of Iudah, to leaue you none to remaine.

† *Hebr. out of the midst of Iudah.*

8 In that yee prouoke mee vnto wrath with the workes of your hands, burning incense vnto other gods in the land of Egypt whither ye bee gone to dwell, that yee might cut your selues off

off, and that ye might be a curse, and a reproch among all the nations of the earth?

† Heb. wickednesses, or, punishments &c.

9 Haue ye forgotten the †wickednes of your fathers, and the wickednesse of the kings of Iudah, and the wickednes of their wiues, and your owne wickednesse, and the wickednesse of your wiues, which they haue committed in the land of Iudah, and in the streets of Ierusalem?

† Hebr. contrite.

10 They are not †humbled euen vnto this day, neither haue they feared, nor walked in my Law, nor in my Statutes that I set before you, and before your fathers.

11 ¶ Therefore thus sayeth the LORD of hostes, the God of Israel, Behold, * I wil set my face against you for euill, and to cut off all Iudah.

* Amos 9. 4.

12 And I will take the remnant of Iudah, that haue set their faces to goe into the land of Egypt to soiourne there, and they shall all be consumed and fall in the land of Egypt: they shall euen bee consumed by the sword, and by the famine: they shall die, from the least euen vnto the greatest, by the sword and by the famine: and they shalbe an execration and an astonishment, and a curse, and a reproch.

13 For I will punish them that dwell in the land of Egypt, as I haue punished Ierusalem, by the sword, by the famine, and by the pestilence;

14 So that none of the remnant of Iudah which are gone into the land of Egypt to soiourne there, shall escape or remaine, that they should returne into the land of Iudah to the which they †haue a desire to returne to dwell there: for none shall returne but such as shall escape.

† Heb. lift vp their soule.

15 ¶ Then all the men which knew that their wiues had burnt incense vnto other Gods, and all the women that stood by, a great multitude, euen all the people that dwelt in the land of Egypt in Pathros, answered Ieremiah, saying,

16 As for the word that thou hast spoken vnto vs in the name of the LORD, we will not hearken vnto thee.

17 But we will certainly doe whatsoeuer thing goeth forth out of our owne mouth, to burne incense vnto the ‖*queene of heauen, and to powre out drinke offrings vnto her, as we haue

‖ Or, frame of heauen. * Chap. 7. 18.

done, we and our fathers, our kings and our princes in the cities of Iudah, and in the streetes of Ierusalem: for then had we plentie of † vitailes, and were well, and saw no euill.

† Heb. bread.

18 But since we left off to burne incense to the queene of heauen, and to powre out drinke offrings vnto her, we haue wanted all things, and haue beene consumed by the sword, and by the famine.

19 And *when we burnt incense to the queene of heauen, and powred out drinke offrings vnto her, did we make her cakes to worship her, and powre out drinke offrings vnto her without our ‖men?

*Chap. 7. 18.

‖ Or, husbands.

20 ¶ Then Ieremiah sayd vnto all the people, to the men and to the women, and to all the people which had giuen him that answere, saying;

21 The incense that yee burnt in the cities of Iudah, and in the streetes of Ierusalem, yee and your fathers, your kings and your princes, and the people of the land, did not the LORD remember them, and came it not into his minde?

22 So that the LORD could no longer beare, because of the euill of your doings, and because of the abominations, which yee haue committed: therefore is your land a desolation, and an astonishment, and a curse without an inhabitant, as at this day.

23 Because you haue burnt incense, and because yee haue sinned against the LORD, and haue not obeyed the voyce of the LORD, nor walked in his law, nor in his statutes, nor in his testimonies: therefore this euill is happened vnto you, as at this day.

24 Moreouer Ieremiah sayd vnto all the people, and to all the women; Heare the word of the LORD, all Iudah, that are in the land of Egypt.

25 Thus saith the LORD of hostes the God of Israel, saying; Yee and your wiues haue both spoken with your mouths, and fulfilled with your hand, saying; We will surely performe our vowes that we haue vowed, to burne incense to the queene of heauen, and to powre out drinke offrings vnto her: yee will surely accomplish your vowes, and surely performe your vowes.

26 Therefore heare yee the word of the LORD, all Iudah that dwell in the land of Egypt, Behold, I haue sworne

sworne by my great Name, saith the LORD, that my Name shal no more be named in the mouth of any man of Iudah, in all the land of Egypt, saying, The Lord GOD liueth.

27 Behold, I will watch ouer them for euill, and not for good, and all the men of Iudah that *are* in the land of Egypt shalbe consumed by the sword, & by the famin, vntil there be an end of them.

28 Yet a small number that escape the sword, shall returne out of the land of Egypt into the land of Iudah : and all the remnant of Iudah that are gone into the land of Egypt to soiourne there, shall know whose wordes shall stand, † mine or theirs.

29 ¶ And this *shalbe* a signe vnto you, saith the LORD, that I will punish you in this place, that ye may knowe that my words shal surely stand against you for euill.

30 Thus saith the LORD, Behold, I will giue Pharaoh - Hophra king of Egypt into the hand of his enemies, and into the hande of them that seeke his life, as I gaue Zedekiah king of Iudah into the hand of Nebuchadrezzar king of Babylon his enemy, and that sought his life.

CHAP. XLV.

1 Baruch being dismayed. 4 Ieremiah instructeth and comforteth him.

He word that Ieremiah the Prophet spake vnto Baruch the sonne of Neriah, when he had written these words in a booke at the mouth of Ieremiah, in the fourth yeere of Iehoiakim the sonne of Iosiah king of Iudah, saying,

2 Thus saith the LORD the God of Israel vnto thee, O Baruch,

3 Thou didst say, Woe is me now, for the LORD hath added griefe to my sorow, I fainted in my sighing, and I find no rest.

4 ¶ Thus shalt thou say vnto him, The LORD saith thus, Behold, that which I haue built will I breake downe, and that which I haue planted I will plucke vp, euen this whole land :

5 And seekest thou great things for thy selfe ? seeke *them* not : for behold, I wil bring euill vpon all flesh, saith the LORD : but thy life will I giue vnto thee *for a pray in all places whither thou goest.

CHAP. XLVI.

1 Ieremiah prophesieth the ouerthrow of Pharaohs armie at Euphrates, 13 and the conquest of Egypt, by Nebuchad - rezzar. 27 He comforteth Iacob in their chastisement.

He word of the LORD which came to Ieremiah the Prophet, against the Gentiles,

2 Against Egypt, against the armie of Pharaoh Necho king of Egypt, which was by the riuer Euphrates in Carchemish, which Nebuchad-rezzar king of Babylon smote in the fourth yeere of Iehoiakim the son of Iosiah king of Iudah.

3 Order ye the buckler and shield, and draw neere to battell.

4 Harnesse the horses, and get vp ye horsemen, and stand forth with *your* helmets, furbish the speares, *and* put on the brigandines.

5 Wherefore haue I seene them dismaid, *and* turned away backe ? and their mightie ones are † beaten downe, & are † fled apace, and looke not back : *for* feare *was* round about, saith the LORD.

6 Let not the swift flee away, nor the mightie man escape : they shal stumble and fall toward the North by the riuer Euphrates.

7 Who *is* this *that* cōmeth vp as a flood, whose waters are moued as ỹ riuers ?

8 Egypt riseth vp like a flood, and *his* waters are moued like the riuers, and he saith, I wil goe vp, *and* will couer the earth, I will destroy the citie and the inhabitants thereof.

9 Come vp ye horses, and rage yee charets, and let the mightie men come forth, the † Ethiopians and the † Libyans that handle the shield, and the Lydians that handle *and* bend the bow.

10 For this *is* the day of the Lord GOD of hostes, a day of vengeance, that he may auenge him of his aduersaries : and the sword shal deuoure, and it shall be satiate, and made drunke with their blood : for the Lord GOD of hosts hath a sacrifice in the North countrey by the riuer Euphrates.

11 Goe vp into Gilead, and take balme, O virgine, the daughter of Egypt : in vaine shalt thou vse many medicines : *for* thou shalt † not be cured.

12 The nations haue heard of thy shame, and thy crie hath filled the land : for the mightie man hath stumbled against

Marginal notes:
† *Heb. from me or from them.*

* *Chap. 39. 18.*

† *Heb. broken in pieces*
† *Heb. fled a flight.*

† *Heb. Cush.*
† *Hebr. Put.*

† *Hebr. no cure shalbe vnto thee.*

gainſt the mightie, *and* they are fallen both together.

13 ¶ The word that the LORD ſpake to Ieremiah the Prophet, how Nebuchadrezzar King of Babylon ſhould come & ſmite the land of Egypt.

14 Declare ye in Egypt, and publiſh in Migdol, and publiſh in Noph, and in Tahpanhes : ſay ye, Stand faſt, and prepare thee; for the ſword ſhal deuoure round about thee.

15 Why are thy valiant men ſwept away? they ſtood not, becauſe the LORD did driue them.

† *Hebr. multiplied the faller.*

16 † He made many to fall, yea one fell vpon another, and they ſaid, Ariſe, and let vs goe againe to our owne people, and to the land of our natiuitie, from the oppreſſing ſword.

17 They did crie there, Pharaoh king of Egypt *is but* a noiſe, he hath paſſed the time appointed.

18 As I liue, ſaith the King, whoſe Name *is* the LORD of hoſtes, Surely as Tabor *is* among the mountaines, and as Carmel by the Sea, *ſo* ſhall hee come.

† *Heb. make thee inſtruments of captiuitie.*

19 Oh thou daughter dwelling in Egypt, † furniſh thy ſelfe to goe into captiuitie : for Noph ſhalbe waſte and deſolate without an inhabitant.

20 Egypt is like a very faire heifer, *but* deſtruction commeth : it commeth out of the North.

† *Hebr. bullocks of the ſtall.*

21 Alſo her hired men *are* in the midſt of her, like † fatted bullocks, for they alſo are turned backe, *and* are fled away together; they did not ſtand, becauſe the day of their calamitie was come vpon them, *and* the time of their viſitation.

22 The voice thereof ſhall goe like a ſerpent, for they ſhall march with an armie, and come againſt her with axes, as hewers of wood.

23 They ſhall cut downe her forreſt, ſaith the LORD, though it cannot be ſearched, becauſe they are more then the graſhoppers, and *are* innumerable.

24 The daughter of Egypt ſhalbe confounded, ſhe ſhalbe deliuered into the hand of the people of the North.

‖ *Or, nouriſher.* *Heb. Amon.*

25 The LORD of hoſtes the God of Iſrael ſaith, Behold, I will puniſh the ‖ multitude of No, and Pharaoh, and Egypt, with their gods, and their kings, euen Pharaoh, and all them that truſt in him.

26 And I will deliuer them into the hand of thoſe that ſeeke their liues, and into the hand of Nebuchadrezzar king of Babylon, and into the hand of his ſeruants, and afterwards it ſhalbe inhabited, as in the dayes of old, ſaith the LORD.

27 ¶ * But feare not thou, O my ſeruant Iacob, and be not diſmaied, O Iſrael : for behold, I will ſaue thee from afarre off, and thy ſeed from the land of their captiuitie, and Iacob ſhall returne and be in reſt and at eaſe, and none ſhall make *him* afraid.

* Iſai. 41. 13. and 43. 5. and 44. 1 cha. 30. 10.

28 Feare thou not, O Iacob my ſeruant, ſaith the LORD, for I *am* with thee, for I will make a full end of all the nations whither I haue driuen thee, but I will not make * a full end of thee, but correct thee in meaſure, ‖ yet will I not leaue thee wholly vnpuniſhed.

* Chap. 30. 11. and 10. 24.
‖ *Or, not vtterly cut thee off.*

CHAP. XLVII.

The deſtruction of the Philiſtines.

He word of the LORD that came to Ieremiah the Prophet againſt the Philiſtines, before that Pharaoh ſmote † Gaza.

† *Hebr. Azzah.*

2 Thus ſaith the LORD, Behold, * waters riſe vp out of the North, and ſhall be an ouerflowing flood, and ſhall ouerflow the land, and † all that is therein, the citie, and them that dwell therein : then the men ſhall crie, and all the inhabitants of the land ſhall howle.

* Iſai. 8. 7.
† *Hebr. the fulneſſe therof.*

3 At the noiſe of the ſtamping of the hoofes of his ſtrong *horſes*, at the ruſhing of his charets, *and at* the rumbling of his wheeles, the fathers ſhall not looke backe to their children for feebleneſſe of handes.

4 Becauſe of the day that commeth to ſpoile all the Philiſtines, *and* to cut off from Tyrus and Zidon euery helper that remaineth : for the LORD will ſpoile the Philiſtines, the remnant of the † countrey of Caphtor.

† *Heb. the ile.*

5 Baldneſſe is come vpon Gaza. Aſhkelon is cut off *with* the remnant of their valley : how long wilt thou cut thy ſelfe ?

6 O thou ſword of the LORD, how long *will it be* ere thou be quiet? † put vp thy ſelfe into thy ſcabberd, reſt and be ſtill.

† *Heb. gather thy ſelfe.*

7 † How can it bee quiet, ſeeing the LORD hath giuen it a charge againſt Aſhkelon, and againſt the ſea ſhoare ? there hath he appointed it.

† *Heb. how canſt thou?*

CHAP.

CHAP. XLVIII.

1 The iudgement of Moab, 7 for their pride, 11 for their securitie, 14 for their carnall confidence, 26 & for their contempt of God and his people. 47 The restauration of Moab.

AGainst Moab thus sayth the LORD of hostes, the God of Israel, Woe vnto Nebo, for it is spoiled: Kiriathaim is confounded and taken. ‖ Misgab is confounded and dismayed.

2 *There shall bee* no more prayse of Moab : in Heshbon they haue deuised euill against it; come and let vs cut it off from *being* a nation; also thou shalt bee ‖ cut downe, O Madmen, the sword shall †pursue thee.

3 A voice of crying *shall be* from Horonaim ; Spoiling & great destruction.

4 Moab is destroyed, her little ones haue caused a crie to be heard.

5 For in the going vp of Luhith †*continuall weeping shall go vp; for in the going downe of Horonaim the enemies haue heard a crie of destruction.

6 Flee, saue your liues, and be like the ‖*heath in the wildernesse.

7 ¶ For because thou hast trusted in thy workes, and in thy treasures, thou shalt also be taken, and Chemosh shall goe foorth into captiuitie *with* his *priests and his princes together.

8 And the spoyler shall come vpon euery citie, and no citie shall escape: the valley also shal perish, & the plaine shall be destroyed, as ye LORD hath spoken.

9 Giue wings vnto Moab, that it may flee and get away : for the cities thereof shalbe desolate, without any to dwell therein.

10 Cursed *be he* that doeth the worke of the LORD ‖deceitfully, and cursed *be he* that keepeth backe his sword from blood.

11 ¶ Moab hath bene at ease from his youth, and hee hath setled on his lees, and hath not been emptied from vessell to vessell, neither hath he gone into captiuitie : therefore his taste †remained in him, and his sent is not changed.

12 Therfore behold, the dayes come, sayth the LORD, that I will send vnto him wanderers that shall cause him to wander, and shall emptie his vessels, and breake their bottles

13 And Moab shall bee ashamed of Chemosh, as the house of Israel was ashamed of Bethel their confidence.

14 ¶ How say yee, We *are* *mightie and strong men for the warre ?

15 Moab is spoiled and gone vp *out* *of* her cities, and †his chosen yong men are gone downe to the slaughter, sayth the King, whose Name *is* the LORD of hostes.

16 The calamitie of Moab is neere to come, and his affliction hasteth fast.

17 All yee that are about him bemoane him, and all yee that know his Name, say, How is the strong staffe broken, *and* the beautifull rod !

18 Thou daughter that doest inhabit Dibon, come downe from *thy* glory, and sit in thirst ; for the spoiler of Moab shall come vpon thee, *and* he shall destroy thy strong holdes.

19 O †inhabitant of Aroer, stand by the way and espie, aske him that fleeth, and her that escapeth, *and* say, What is done ?

20 Moab is confounded, for it is broken downe : *howle and cry, tell ye it in Arnon, that Moab is spoiled,

21 And iudgement is come vpon the plaine countrey, vpon Holon, and vpon Iahazah, and vpon Mephaath,

22 And vpon Dibon, and vpon Nebo, and vpon Beth-diblathaim,

23 And vpon Kiriathaim, and vpon Beth-Gamul, and vpon Beth-meon,

24 And vpon Kerioth, and vpon Bozrah, and vpon all the cities of the land of Moab farre or neere.

25 The horne of Moab is cut off, & his arme is broken, saith the LORD.

26 ¶ Make ye him drunken : for hee magnified *himselfe* against the LORD: Moab also shall wallow in his vomit, and he also shalbe in derision.

27 For was not Israel a derision vnto thee ? was hee found among theeues ? for since thou spakest of him, thou ‖skippedst for ioy.

28 O yee that dwell in Moab, leaue the cities and dwell in the rocke, and be like the doue *that* maketh her nest in the sides of the holes mouth.

29 We haue heard the *pride of Moab, (he is exceeding proud) his loftinesse and his arrogancie, and his pride, and the hautinesse of his heart.

30 I knowe his wrath, sayeth the LORD, but *it shall* not *be* so, ‖his lyes shall not so effect *it*.

31 Therefore will I howle for Moab, and I will cry out for all Moab, *mine*

Marginal notes

‖ *Or, the hie place.*

‖ *Or, bee brought to silence.*
† *Heb. goe after thee.*

† *Heb. weeping with weeping.*
* *Isal.15. 5.*

‖ *Or, a naked tree.*
* *Cha. 17. 6.*

* *Cha. 49. 5.*

‖ *Or, negligently.*

† *Heb. stood.*

* *1. Kings 12. 29.*

† *Heb. the choice of.*

† *Heb. inhabitresse.*

* *Isai. 16. 7.*

‖ *Or, mouedst thy selfe.*

* *Isai. 16. 6. &c.*

‖ *Or, those on whom hee stayeth (heb. his barres) do not right.*

mine heart shall mourne for the men of Kir-heres.

32 O vine of Sibmah, I wil weepe for thee, with the weeping of Iazer; thy plants are gone ouer the sea, they reach euen to the sea of Iazer, the spoiler is fallen vpon thy summer fruits, and vpon thy vintage.

33 And * ioy and gladnesse is taken from the plentifull field, and from the land of Moab, and I haue caused wine to faile from the winepresses, none shall tread with shouting, *their* showting *shall be* no showting.

34 From the cry of Heshbon euen vnto Elealeh, *and* euen vnto Iahaz haue they vttered their voyce, *from Zoar euen vnto Horonaim *as* an heifer of three yeeres old : for the waters also of Nimrim shall be †desolate.

35 Moreouer, I will cause to cease in Moab, saith the LORD, him that offereth in the high places, and him that burneth incense to his Gods.

36 Therefore mine heart shall sound for Moab like pipes, and mine heart shall sound like pipes for the men of Kir-heres : because the riches *that* hee hath gotten is perished.

37 For *euery head shall be bald, and euery beard †clipt : vpon all the hands *shall be* cuttings, and vpon the loines sackcloth.

38 There shall be lamentation generally vpon all the house toppes of Moab, and in the streetes thereof : for I haue broken Moab like a vessell, wherin *is* no pleasure, saith the LORD.

39 They shall howle, *saying;* How is it broken downe? how hath Moab turned the † backe with shame? so shall Moab be a derision, and a dismaying to all them about him.

40 For thus saith the LORD, Behold, hee shall fly as an eagle, and shall spread his wings vpon Maob.

41 ‖Kerioth is taken, and the strong holds are surprised, & the mighty mens hearts in Moab at that day shall be as the heart of a woman in her pangs.

42 And Moab shall be destroyed from being a people, because he hath magnified *himselfe* against the LORD

43 *Feare, and the pit, and the snare *shall be* vpon thee, O inhabitant of Moab, saith the LORD.

44 Hee that fleeth from the feare shall fall into the pit, and he that getteth vp out of the pit shall be taken in the snare : for I will bring vpon it, *euen* vpon Moab, the yeere of their visitation, saith the LORD.

45 They that fled, stood vnder the shadow of Heshbon, because of the force: but *a fire shall come forth out of Heshbon, and a flame from the middest of Sihon, and shall deuoure the corner of Moab, and the crowne of the head of the †tumultuous ones.

46 Woe be vnto thee, O Moab, the people of Chemosh perisheth : for thy sonnes are taken † captiues, and thy daughters captiues.

47 ¶ Yet will I bring againe the captiuitie of Moab in the later dayes, saith the LORD. Thus farre *is* the iudgement of Moab.

CHAP. XLIX.

1 The iudgement of the Ammonites. 6 Their restauration. 7 The iudgement of Edom, 23 of Damascus, 28 of Kedar, 30 of Hazor, 34 and of Elam. 39 The restauration of Elam.

‖Concerning the Ammonites, thus sayth the LORD; Hath Israel no sonnes? hath he no heire? Why *then* doth ‖their king inherit *God, and his people dwell in his cities?

2 Therfore behold, the dayes come, saith the LORD, that I will cause an alarme of warre to be heard in *Rabbah of the Ammonites, and it shall be a desolate heape, and her daughters shall be burnt with fire : then shall Israel be heire vnto them that were his heires, saith the LORD.

3 Howle, O Heshbon, for Ai is spoiled : cry yee daughters of Rabbah, gird yee with sackcloth : lament and runne to and fro by the hedges : for ‖their king shall goe into captiuitie : *and* his *priests and his princes together.

4 Wherfore gloriest thou in the valleys, ‖thy flowing valley, O backsliding daughter? that trusted in her treasures, *saying;* Who shall come vnto mee?

5 Behold, I will bring a feare vpon thee, saith the Lord GOD of hostes, from all those that be about thee, and yee shall be driuen out euery man right forth, and none shal gather vp him that wandereth.

6 And afterward I will bring againe the captiuitie of the children of Ammon, saith the LORD.

7 ¶ Concerning Edom thus saith the LORD

Margin notes (left column)
* Isai. 16. 10.
* Isai. 15. 5, 6.
† Heb. desolations.
* Isai. 15. 2, 3.
† Heb. diminished.
† Heb. necke.
‖ Or, the cities.
* Isai. 24. 17, 18.

Margin notes (right column)
* Num. 21. 28.
† Heb. children of nois
† Heb. in captiuitie.
‖ Or, against
‖ Or, Melcom.
* Amos 1. 13.
* Amos. 1. 14.
‖ Or, Melcom.
* Chap. 48. 7.
‖ Or, thy valley floweth away.

* Obad. ver.
3.

‖ Or, they
are turned
backe.

* Obad. ver.
5.

† Heb. their
sufficiencie.

* Obad. ver.
4.

* Obad. ver.
4.

* Chap. 50
13.

* Gen. 19.
25. chap. 50
40.

‖ Or, conuent
me in iudge-
ment.
* Iob. 21. 1.
25. chap. 50.
44, 45.

LORD of hosts; *Is wisedome no more in Teman ?: is counsell perished from the prudent? is their wisedom vanished?

8 Flee ye, ‖turne backe, dwell deepe, O inhabitants of Dedan: for I will bring the calamitie of Esau vpon him, the time that I will visite him.

9 If *grape gatherers come to thee, would they not leaue *some* gleaning grapes ? If theeues by night, they will destroy †till they haue enough.

10 But I haue made Esau bare, I haue vncouered his secret places, and he shall not be able to hide himselfe: his seed is spoiled, and his brethren and his neighbours, and he is not.

11 Leaue thy fatherlesse children, I will preserue them aliue: and let thy widowes trust in me.

12 For thus saith the LORD, Behold, they whose iudgement *was* not to drinke of the cup, haue assuredly drunken, and *art* thou he *that* shall altogether go vnpunished? thou shalt not go vnpunished, but thou shalt surely drinke *of it.*

13 For I haue sworne by my selfe, saith the LORD, that Bozrah shall become a desolation, a reproch, a waste, and a curse, and all the cities thereof shall be perpetuall wastes.

14 I haue heard a *rumor from the LORD, & an ambassadour is sent vnto the heathen, *saying,* Gather ye together & come against her, & rise vp to the battell.

15 For lo, I wil make thee smal among the heathen, *and* despised among men.

16 Thy terriblenesse hath deceiued thee, *and* the pride of thine heart, O thou that dwellest in the clefts of the rocke, that holdest the height of the hill: thogh thou shouldest make thy *nest as high as the eagle, I will bring thee downe from thence, saith the LORD

17 Also Edom shalbe a desolation: *euery one ẙ goeth by it shalbe astonished, and shall hisse at all the plagues thereof.

18 *As in the ouerthrow of Sodom and Gomorrah, and the neighbour *cities* thereof, saith the LORD: no man shall abide there, neither shall a sonne of man dwell in it.

19 Behold, he shal come vp like a lyon from the swelling of Iordane against the habitation of the strong: but I wil suddenly make him runne away from her, and who *is* a chosen man *that* I may appoynt ouer her? for who *is* like mee? and who will ‖*appoint me the time? who *is* that shepheard that

will stand before mee ?

20 Therfore heare the counsell of the LORD, that he hath taken against Edom, & his purposes that hee hath purposed against the inhabitants of Teman. surely the least of the flocke shall draw them out: surely hee shall make their habitations desolate with them.

21 The earth is moued at the noise of their fall: at the crie, the noise thereof was heard in the †red Sea

22 Behold, he shall come vp and flie as the eagle, and spread his wings ouer Bozrah. and at that day shall the heart of the mightie men of Edom, be as the heart of a woman in her pangs.

23 ¶ Concerning Damascus, Hamath is confounded, & Arpad, for they haue heard euil tidings, they are †faint hearted, *there is* sorrow ‖on the sea, it can not be quiet.

24 Damascus is waxed feeble, *and* turneth her selfe to flee, and feare hath seised on her: anguish and sorrowes haue taken her as a woman in trauell.

25 How is the citie of praise not left, the citie of my ioy ?

26 Therefore her yong men shal fall in her streets, and all the men of warre shall bee cut off in that day, saith the LORD of hosts.

27 And I will kindle a *fire in the wall of Damascus, and it shal consume the palaces of Ben-hadad.

28 ¶ Concerning Kedar, and concerning the kingdoms of Hazor, which Nebuchad-rezzar king of Babylon shall smite, Thus saith the LORD: Arise ye, goe vp to Kedar, and spoile the men of the East.

29 Their tents and their flocks shall they take away: they shal take to themselues their curtaines and all their vessels, and their camels, and they shal crie vnto them, Feare *is* on euery side.

30 ¶ *Flee, †get you farre off, dwell deepe, O ye inhabitants of Hazor, saith the LORD: for Nebuchad-rezzar king of Babylon hath taken counsel against you, and hath conceiued a purpose against you.

31 Arise, get you vp vnto the ‖wealthy nation that dwelleth without care, saith the LORD, which *haue* neither gates nor barres, *which* dwell alone.

32 And their camels shall be a bootie, and the multitude of their cattell a spoile, and I will scatter into all winds them that are in the †vtmost corners, and

† Heb. wee-
die Sea.

† Heb. mel-
ted.
‖ Or, as on
the Sea.

* Amos 1. 4.

* Verse 8.
† Heb. flit
greatly.

‖ Or, that is
at ease.

† Heb. cut off
into corners,
or that haue
the corners
of their
haire polled.

and I will bring their calamitie from all sides thereof, saith the LORD.

33 And Hazor shall be a dwelling for dragons, and a desolation for euer; there shall no man abide there, nor any sonne of man dwell in it.

34 ¶ The word of the LORD that came to Ieremiah the Prophet against Elam in the beginning of the reigne of Zedekiah king of Iudah, saying,

35 Thus saith the LORD of hosts, Behold, I will breake the bow of Elam, the chiefe of their might.

36 And vpon Elam will I bring the foure windes from the foure quarters of heauen, and will scatter them towards all those windes, and there shall be no nation, whither the outcasts of Elam shall not come.

37 For I will cause Elam to bee dismayed before their enemies, and before them that seeke their life : and I will bring euill vpon them, euen my fierce anger, saith the LORD, and I will send the sword after them, till I haue consumed them.

38 And I will set my throne in Elam, and will destroy from thence the king and the princes, saith the LORD.

39 ¶ But it shall come to passe in the *later daies, that I wil bring againe the captiuitie of Elam, saith the LORD.

*Chap. 49. 6. and 48. 47.

CHAP. L.

1. 9. 21. 35. The iudgement of Babylon. 4. 17. 33. The redemption of Israel.

He word that the LORD spake against Babylon, and against the land of the Caldeans †by Ieremiah the Prophet.

† Hebr. by the hand of Ieremiah.

2 Declare yee among the nations, and publish, and †set vp a standart, publish and conceale not : say, Babylon is taken, Bel is confounded, Merodach is broken in pieces, her idols are confounded, her Images are broken in pieces.

† Hebr. lift vp.

3 For out of the North there commeth vp a nation against her, which shall make her land desolate, and none shall dwell therein : they shall remoue, they shall depart both man and beast.

4 ¶ In those daies, and in that time, saith the LORD, the children of Israel shall come, they, and the children of Iudah together, going and weeping : they shall goe, and seeke the LORD their God.

5 They shall aske the way to Zion with their faces thitherward, saying, Come, and let vs ioyne our selues to the LORD, in a perpetuall Couenant that shall not be forgotten.

6 My people hath bene lost sheepe : their shepheards haue caused them to goe astray, they haue turned them away on the mountaines : they haue gone from mountaine to hill, they haue forgotten their †resting place.

† Hebr. place to lye downe in.

7 All that found them haue deuoured them, and their aduersaries said, We offend not, because they haue sinned against the LORD, the habitation of iustice, euen the LORD, the hope of their fathers.

8 *Remoue out of the midst of Babylon, and goe foorth out of the land of the Caldeans, and be as the hee goats before the flocks.

*Isai. 48. 20. chap. 51. 6. reue. 18. 4.

9 ¶ For loe, I will raise and cause to come vp against Babylon, an assembly of great nations from the North countrey, and they shall set themselues in aray against her, from thence shee shalbe taken : their arrowes shalbe as of a mightie ||expert man : none shall returne in vaine.

|| Or, destroyer.

10 And Caldea shall bee a spoile : all that spoile her shall be satisfied, saith the LORD.

11 Because ye were glad, because yee reioyced, O ye destroyers of mine heritage, because ye are growen †fat, as the heifer at grasse, and bellow as bulles :

† Heb. bigge or corpulent.

12 Your mother shalbe sore confounded, she that bare you shalbe ashamed : beholde, the hindermost of the nations shalbe a wildernes, a dry land, & a desert.

13 Because of the wrath of the LORD, it shall not be inhabited, but it shalbe wholly desolate : *euery one that goeth by Babylon shall be astonished, and hisse at all her plagues.

*Chap. 49. 17.

14 Put your selues in aray against Babylon round about : all ye that bend the bow, shoot at her; spare no arrows : for she hath sinned against the LORD,

15 Shout against her round about : shee hath giuen her hand : her foundations are fallen, her walls are throwen downe : for it is the vengeance of the LORD : take vengeance vpon her; as she hath done, doe vnto her.

16 Cut off the sower from Babylon, and him that handleth the ||sickle in the time of haruest : for feare of the oppressing sword, they shall turne euery one to his people, and they shall flee euery one

|| Or, sythe.

one to his owne lande.

17 ¶ Israel *is* a scattered sheepe, the lyons haue driuen *him* away : first the king of Assyria hath deuoured him, and last this Nebuchad-rezzar king of Babylon hath broken his bones.

18 Therefore thus saith the Lord of hostes the God of Israel; Behold, I will punish the king of Babylon and his land, as I haue punished the king of Assyria.

19 And I will bring Israel againe to his habitation, and he shal feed on Carmel and Bashan, and his soule shall be satisfied vpon mount Ephraim and Gilead.

20 In those dayes, and in that time, sayth the Lord, the iniquitie of Israel shall be sought for, and *there shall be* none; and the sinnes of Iudah, and they shall not be found : for I will pardon them whom I reserue.

21 ¶ Goe vp against the land ||of Merathaim, *euen* against it, and against the inhabitants || of Pekod : waste and vtterly destroy after them, sayeth the Lord, and doe according to all that I haue commanded thee.

22 A sound of battell *is* in the land, and of great destruction.

23 How is the hammer of the whole earth cut asunder and broken ? how is Babylon become a desolation among the nations ?

24 I haue laide a snare for thee, and thou art also taken, O Babylon, and thou wast not aware : thou art found and also caught, because thou hast striuen against the Lord.

25 The Lord hath opened his armorie, and hath brought foorth the weapons of his indignation : for this *is* the worke of the Lord God of hosts, in the land of the Caldeans.

26 Come against her † from the vtmost border, open her store-houses : ||cast her vp as heapes, and destroy her vtterly : let nothing of her be left.

27 Slay all her bullocks : let them goe downe to the slaughter : woe vnto them, for their day is come, the time of their visitation.

28 The voice of them that flee & escape out of the land of Babylon to declare in Zion the vengeance of the Lord our God, the vengeance of his Temple.

29 Call together the archers against Babylon : all yee that bend the bow, campe against it round about; let none

thereof escape : recompense her according to her worke ; according to all that shee hath done vnto her : for shee hath bene proud against the Lord, against the Holy one of Israel.

30 Therefore shall her yong men fall in the streets, & all her men of war shall be cut off in that day, saith the Lord.

31 Behold, I *am* against thee, O thou most †proud, sayth the Lord God of hostes : for thy day is come, the time *that* I will visit thee.

32 And the most †proude shall stumble and fall, and none shal raise him vp : and I will kindle a fire in his cities, and it shall deuoure all round about him.

33 ¶ Thus saith the Lord of hosts; The children of Israel and the children of Iudah *were* oppressed together, and all that tooke them captiues, held them fast, they refused to let them goe.

34 Their Redeemer *is* strong, the Lord of hosts *is* his Name, he shall throughly pleade their cause, that hee may giue rest to the land, and disquiet the inhabitants of Babylon.

35 ¶ A sword *is* vpon the Caldeans, saith the Lord, and vpon the inhabitants of Babylon, and vpon her princes, and vpon her wise men.

36 A sword *is* vpon the ||lyers, and they shall dote : a sword *is* vpon her mighty men, and they shalbe dismayed.

37 A sword *is* vpon their horses, and vpon their charets, and vpon all the mingled people that *are* in the middest of her, and they shall become *as* women: a sword *is* vpon her treasures, and they shall be robbed.

38 A drought *is* vpon her waters, and they shalbe dried vp : for it *is* the land of grauen images, and they are madde vpon their idoles.

39 Therefore the wilde beasts of the desert with the wilde beastes of the Ilands shall dwel *there*, and the owles shall dwell therein : & it shalbe no more inhabited for euer : neither shall it bee dwelt in fro generation to generation.

40 * As God ouerthrew Sodom and Gomorrah, and the neighbour *cities* thereof, sayth the Lord : *so* shall no man abide there, neither shal any sonne of man dwell therein.

41 Behold, a people shall come from the North, and a great nation, and many kings shall bee raised vp from the coasts of the earth.

42 They shall holde the bow and the

Marginal notes:

|| Or, of the rebels.

|| Or, visitation.

† Heb. from the end.

|| Or, tread her.

† Heb. pride.

† Heb. pride.

|| Or, chiefe stayes. Heb. barres.

* Gen. 19. 25. chap. 49. 18.

the lance : they are cruell and will not shewe mercy : their voice shall roare like the sea, and they shall ride vpon horses, *euery one* put in aray like a man to the battell, against thee, O daughter of Babylon.

43 The king of Babylon hath heard the report of them, and his hands waxed feeble ; anguish tooke hold of him, *and* pangs as of a woman in trauell.

*Chap. 49. 19.

44 Behold, he shall come vp *like a lyon from the swelling of Iordan, vnto the habitation of the strong : but I will make them suddenly runne away from her ; and who is a chosen man *that* I may appoint ouer her? for who is like me, and *who will ||appoint me the time? and who *is* that shepheard that will stand before me?

* Iob. 41. 1. chap. 49. 19.
|| Or, conuent me to plead.

45 Therefore heare yee the counsell of the Lord that hee hath taken against Babylon, and his purposes that he hath purposed against the land of the Caldeans : surely the least of the flocke shall drawe them out : surely he shall make *their* habitation desolate with them.

46 At the noise of the taking of Babylon the earth is moued, and the cry is heard among the nations.

CHAP. LI.

1 The seuere iudgement of God against Babylon, in reuenge of Israel. 59 Ieremiah deliuereth the booke of this prophecie to Sheraiah, to be cast into Euphrates, in token of the perpetuall sinking of Babylon.

† Heb. heart.

Hus saith the Lord; Behold, I will raise vp against Babylon, and against them that dwell in the †middest of them that rise vp against me, a destroying wind ;

2 And will send vnto Babylon fanners, that shall fanne her, and shall emptie her land : for in the day of trouble they shall be against her round about.

3 Against *him that* bendeth let the archer bend his bow, and against *him that* lifteth himselfe vp in his brigandine ; and spare yee not her young men, destroy yee vtterly all her hoste.

4 Thus shall the slaine fall in the land of the Caldeans, and they that are thrust through in her streetes.

5 For Israel hath not beene forsaken, nor Iudah of his God, of the Lord of hostes; though their land was filled with sinne against the holy one of Israel.

6 *Flee out of the middest of Babylon, and deliuer euery man his soule : bee not cut off in her iniquitie : for this is the time of the Lords vengeance : he will render vnto her a recompence.

*Chap. 50. 8. reu. 18. 4

7 Babylon *hath beene* a golden cup in the Lords hand, that made all the earth drunken : the nations haue drunken of her wine, therefore the nations are mad.

8 Babylon is suddenly *fallen and destroyed : howle for her, take balme for her paine, if so be she may be healed.

*Isa. 21. 9 reu. 14. 8. and 18. 2.

9 We would haue healed Babylon, but she is not healed : forsake her, and let vs goe euery one into his owne countrey : for her iudgement reacheth vnto heauen , and is lifted vp euen to the skies.

10 The Lord hath brought forth our righteousnesse : come and let vs declare in Zion the worke of the Lord our God.

11 Make †bright the arrowes : gather the shields : the Lord hath raised vp the spirit of the kings of the Medes : for his deuice is against Babylon, to destroy it ; because it *is* the vengeance of the Lord, the vengeance of his temple.

† Heb. pur

12 Set vp the standart vpon the walles of Babylon, make the watch strong : set vp the watchman : prepare †the ambushes : for the Lord hath both deuised and done that, which hee spake against the inhabitants of Babylon.

† Heb. lye in waite.

13 O thou that dwellest vpon many waters, abundant in treasures ; thine end is come, *and* the measure of thy couetousnesse.

14 *The Lord of hostes hath sworne †by himselfe, *saying*, Surely I will fill thee with men , as with caterpillers ; and they shall †lift vp a shoute against thee.

*Amos. 6
† Heb. by soule.
† Heb. vtt

15 * Hee hath made the earth by his power, he hath established the world by his wisedome , and hath stretched out the heauen by his vnderstanding.

*Gen. 6. 6. chap. 12. &c.

16 When he vttereth *his* voyce, *there is* a ||multitude of waters in the heauens, and he causeth the vapours to ascend from the ends of the earth , he maketh lightnings with raine , and bringeth forth the wind out of his treasures.

|| Or, nois

17 *Euery

* Chap. 10. 14.
|| *Or, is more brutish then to know.*

17 * Euery man is ||brutish by *his* knowledge : euery founder is confounded by the grauen image : for his moulten image *is* falsehood, and *there is* no breath in them.

18 They *are* vanitie, the worke of errours : in the time of their visitation they shall perish.

19 The portion of Iacob *is* not like them, for he *is* the former of all things, and * *Israel is* the rod of his inheritance: the Lord of hostes *is* his Name.

* Chap. 10. 16.

20 Thou *art* my battel-axe *and* weapons of warre : for ||with thee will I breake in pieces the nations , and with thee will I destroy kingdomes ;

|| *Or, in thee, or by thee.*

21 And with thee will I breake in pieces the horse and his rider, and with thee will I breake in pieces the charet, and his rider ;

22 With thee also will I breake in pieces man and woman, and with thee will I breake in pieces old and yong, and with thee will I breake in pieces the yong man and the maide.

23 I will also breake in pieces with thee, the shepheard and his flocke, and with thee will I breake in pieces the husbandman, and his yoke of oxen, and with thee will I breake in pieces Captaines and rulers.

24 And I will render vnto Babylon, and to all the inhabitants of Caldea, all their euil that they haue done in Zion in your sight, saith the Lord.

25 Behold, I *am* against thee, O destroying mountaine, saith the Lord, which destroiest all the earth, and I wil stretch out mine hand vpon thee, and roule thee downe from the rockes, and will make thee a burnt mountaine.

26 And they shall not take of thee a stone for a corner, nor a stone for foundations, but thou shalt be † desolate for euer, saith the Lord.

† Hebr. euerlasting desolations.

27 Set ye vp a standart in the land, blow the trumpet among the nations : prepare the nations against her : call together against her the kingdomes of Ararat, Minni, & Ashchenaz : appoint a captaine against her : cause her horses to come vp as the rough caterpillers.

28 Prepare against her the nations with the kings of the Medes, the captaines thereof, and all the rulers thereof, and all the land of his dominion.

29 And the land shall tremble and sorrow : for euery purpose of the Lord shalbe performed against Babylon, to make the land of Babylon a desolation without an inhabitant.

30 The mightie men of Babylon haue forborne to fight : they haue remained in their holdes : their might hath failed, they became as women : they haue burnt their dwelling places : her barres are broken.

31 One poste shall runne to meet another, and one messenger to meete another, to shew the king of Babylon that his citie is taken at *one* end,

32 And that the passages are stopped, and the reedes they haue burnt with fire , and the men of warre are afrighted.

33 For thus saith the Lord of hostes, the God of Israel ; The daughter of Babylon *is* like a threshing floore; ||*it is* time to thresh her : yet a little while, and the time of her haruest shall come.

|| *Or, in the time that he thresheth her.*

34 Nebuchadrezzar the king of Babylon hath deuoured me, he hath crushed me ; he hath made me an emptie vessell : hee hath swallowed mee vp like a dragon ; he hath filled his bellie with my delicates, he hath cast me out.

35 † The violence done to me and to my ||flesh, *be* vpon Babylon, shall the †inhabitant of Zion say ; and my blood vpon the inhabitants of Caldea, shall Ierusalem say.

† Hebr. my violence.
|| Or, remainder.
† Hebr. inhabitresse.

36 Therefore thus saith the Lord, Behold, I wil plead thy cause, and take vengeance for thee , and I will drie vp her sea, and make her springs drie.

37 And Babylon shal become heaps, a dwelling place for dragons , an astonishment, and an hissing without an inhabitant.

38 They shall roare together like lions ; they shall ||yell as lions whelps.

|| *Or, shake themselues.*

39 In their heat I will make their feasts, and I will make them drunken, that they may reioyce, and sleepe a perpetuall sleepe, and not wake, saith the Lord.

40 I will bring them downe like lambes to the slaughter, like rammes with hee goates.

41 How is Sheshach taken ? and how is the praise of the whole earth surprised ? how is Babylon become an astonishment among the nations ?

42 The sea is come vp vpon Babylon : she is couered with the multitude of the waues thereof.

43 Her cities are a desolation, a dry land and a wildernes, a land wherein no

no man dwelleth, neither doeth any sonne of man passe thereby.

44 And I will punish Bel in Babylon, and I will bring forth out of his mouth that which he hath swallowed vp, and the nations shall not flow together any more vnto him, yea, the wall of Babylon shall fall.

45 My people, goe ye out of the midst of her, and deliuer ye euery man his soule frō the fierce anger of the Lord,

46 And lest your heart faint, and ye feare for the rumour that shall be heard in the land: a rumour shall both come one yeere, and after that in *another* yeere *shall come* a rumour, and violence in the land, ruler against ruler.

47 Therefore behold, the dayes come, that I will †doe iudgment vpon the grauen images of Babylon, and her whole land shall bee confounded, and all her slaine shall fall in the midst of her.

† *Heb. visit vpon.*

48 Then the heauen and the earth, and all that *is* therein, shall sing for Babylon: for the spoilers shall come vnto her from the North, saith the Lord.

49 ‖ As Babylon *hath caused* the slaine of Israel to fall: so at Babylon shall fall the slaine of all ‖ the earth.

‖ *Or, both Babylon is to fall, O ye slaine of Israel, & with Babylon, &c.*
‖ *Or, the countrey.*

50 Ye that haue escaped the sword, go away, stand not still: remember the Lord afarre off: and let Ierusalem come into your mind.

51 We are confounded, because wee haue heard reproch, shame hath couered our faces: for strangers are come into the Sanctuaries of the Lords house.

52 Wherfore behold, the dayes come, saith the Lord, that I will do iudgment vpon her grauen images, and through all her land the wounded shall grone.

53 Though Babylon should mount vp to heauen, and though shee should fortifie the height of her strength, *yet* from me shall spoilers come vnto her, saith the Lord.

54 A sound of a crie *commeth* from Babylon, and great destruction from the land of the Caldeans.

55 Because the Lord hath spoiled Babylon, and destroyed out of her the great voyce when her waues doe roare like great waters, a noise of their voice is vttered.

56 Because the spoiler is come vpon her, *euen* vpon Babylon, and her migh-

tie men are taken, euery one of their bowes is broken, for the Lord God of recompenses shall surely requite.

57 And I will make drunke her princes and her wise men, her captaines and her rulers, and her mightie men: and they shall sleepe a perpetuall sleepe, and not wake, saith the king, whose Name *is* the Lord of hosts.

58 Thus saith the Lord of hosts, The ‖ broad walles of Babylon shalbe vtterly ‖ broken, and her high gates shal be burnt with fire, and the people shall labour in vaine, and the folke in the fire, and they shall be weary.

‖ *Or, the walles of broad Babylon.*
‖ *Or, made naked.*

59 ¶ The word which Ieremiah the prophet commanded Seraiah the sonne of Neriah, the sonne of Maaseiah, when he went ‖ with Zedekiah the king of Iudah into Babylon, in the fourth yeere of his reigne, and this Seraiah was a ‖ quiet prince.

‖ *Or, on the behalfe of.*
‖ *Or, prince of Menucha or chiefe chamberlaine.*

60 So Ieremiah wrote in a booke all the euill that should come vpon Babylon: *euen* all these wordes that are written against Babylon.

61 And Ieremiah said to Seraiah, When thou commest to Babylon, and shalt see, and shalt read all these words,

62 Then shalt thou say, O Lord, thou hast spoken against this place, to cut it off, that none shall remaine in it, neither man nor beast, but that it shalbe †desolate for euer.

† *Heb. desolations.*

63 And it shall bee when thou hast made an end of reading this booke, *that* thou shalt binde a stone to it, and cast it into the midst of Euphrates.

64 And thou shalt say, Thus shall Babylon sinke, and shall not rise from the euill that I will bring vpon her: and they shall be wearie. Thus farre *are* the words of Ieremiah.

CHAP. LII.

1 Zedekiah rebelleth. 4 Ierusalem is besieged and taken. 8 Zedekiahs sonnes killed, and his owne eyes put out. 12 Nebuzaradan burneth and spoileth the citie. 24 Hee carieth away the captiues. 32 Euil-merodach aduanceth Iehoiakim.

Edekiah *was* * one and twentie yeere olde when he †began to reigne, and he reigned eleuen yeeres in Ierusalem, and his mothers name *was* Hamutal the daughter of Ieremiah of Libnah.

* 2. Kings 24. 18.
† *Heb. reigned.*

2 And

2 And hee did that *which was* euill in the eyes of the LORD, according to all that Iehoiakim had done.

3 For through the anger of the LORD it came to passe in Ierusalem and Iudah, till hee had cast them out from his presence, that Zedekiah rebelled against the king of Babylon.

2. Kings 25. 1. chap. 39. 1.

4 ¶ And it came to passe in the *ninth yere of his reigne, in the tenth moneth, in the tenth *day* of the moneth, *that* Nebuchad-rezzar king of Babylon came, hee, and all his armie against Ierusalem, and pitched against it, and built fortes against it round about.

5 So the citie was besieged vnto the eleuenth yeere of king Zedekiah.

6 And in the fourth moneth, in the ninth *day* of the moneth, the famine was sore in the citie, so that there was no bread for the people of the land.

7 Then the city was broken vp, and all the men of warre fled, and went foorth out of the citie by night, by the way of the gate between the two wals, which *was* by the kings garden (now the Caldeans *were* by the city round about) and they went by the way of the plaine.

8 ¶ But the armie of the Caldeans pursued after the king, and ouertooke Zedekiah in the plaines of Iericho, & all his armie was scattered from him.

9 Then they tooke the king, and caried him vp vnto the king of Babylon to Riblah in the land of Hamath : where he gaue iudgement vpon him.

10 And the king of Babylon slew the sonnes of Zedekiah before his eyes : he slewe also all the princes of Iudah in Riblah.

† *Heb. blinded.*

11 Then he †put out the eyes of Zedekiah, and the king of Babylon bound him ‖in chaines, and caried him to Babylon, and put him in †prison till the day of his death.

‖ *Or, fetters.*
† *Heb. house of the wards.*

12 ¶ Now in the fifth moneth, in the tenth *day* of the moneth (which *was* the nineteenth yeere of Nebuchad-rezzar king of Babylon) came Nebuzaradan ‖captaine of the guard, which †serued the king of Babylon, into Ierusalem;

‖ *Or, chiefe Marshall. Heb. chiefe of the executioners or slaughtermen. And so vers. 14. &c.*
† *Heb. stood before.*

13 And burnt the house of the LORD, and the kings house, and all the houses of Ierusalem, and all the houses of the great men burnt he with fire.

14 And all the armie of the Caldeans that *were* with the captaine of the guard, brake downe all the walles of Ierusalem round about.

15 Then Nebuzaradan the captaine of the guard, caried away captiue *certaine* of the poore of the people, and the residue of the people that remained in the citie, and those that fell away, that fell to the king of Babylon, and the rest of the multitude.

16 But Nebuzaradan the captaine of the guard, left *certaine* of the poore of the land for Vine-dressers and for husbandmen.

17 Also the * pillars of brasse that *were* in the house of the LORD, and the bases, and the brasen sea that *was* in the house of the LORD, the Caldeans brake, and caried all the brasse of them to Babylon.

* *Chap. 27. 19.*

18 The cauldrons also, and the ‖shouels, and the snuffers, and the ‖bolles, and the spoones, and all the vessels of brasse wherewith they ministred, tooke they away.

‖ *Or, instruments to remooue the ashes.*
‖ *Or, basons.*

19 And the basons, and the ‖firepans, and the bolles, and the cauldrons, and the candlestickes, and the spoones, and the cuppes; that which *was* of golde, *in* golde, and that which *was* of siluer, *in* siluer, tooke the captaine of the guard away :

‖ *Or, censers.*

20 The two pillars, one Sea, and twelue brasen bulles, that *were* vnder the bases, which king Solomon had made in the house of the LORD : † the brasse of all these vessels was without weight.

† *Heb. their brasse.*

21 And concerning the *pillars, the height of one pillar *was* eighteene cubites, and a †fillet of twelue cubites did compasse it, and the thickenesse thereof *was* foure fingers : *it was* hollow.

* *1. King. 7. 15. 2. kíng. 25. 17. 2. chro. 3. 15.*
† *Heb. threed*

22 And a chapiter of brasse *was* vpon it, and the height of one chapiter *was* fiue cubites, with networke and pomegranates vpon the chapiters round about, all of brasse: the second pillar also and the pomegranates *were* like vnto these.

23 And there were ninetie and sixe pomegranates on a side, *and* all the pomegranates vpon the networke *were* an hundreth round about.

24 ¶ And the captaine of the guard tooke Seraiah the chiefe Priest, and Zephaniah the second Priest, and the three keepers of the †doore.

† *Heb. threshold.*

25 Hee tooke also out of the citie an Eunuch, which had the charge of the men of warre, and seuen men of them that

† *Heb. saw the face of the king.*

‖ *Or, scribe of the captaine of the hoste.*

that † were neere the kings person which were found in the citie, and the ‖principall Scribe of the host, who mustered the people of the land, and threescore men of the people of the land, that were found in the middest of the citie.

26 So Nebuzar-adan the captaine of the guard tooke them, and brought them to the king of Babylon to Riblah.

27 And the king of Babylon smote them, and put them to death in Riblah, in the land of Hamath : thus Iudah was caried away captiue out of his owne land.

28 This *is* the people whom Nebuchad rezzar caried away captiue in the seuenth yeere, three thousand Iewes and three and twentie.

29 In the eighteenth yeere of Nebuchad-rezzar hee caried away captiue from Ierusalem eight hundreth, thirtie and two † persons.

† *Heb. soules.*

30 In the three and twentith yeere of Nebuchad-rezzar, Nebuzar-adan

the captaine of the guard, caried away captiue of the Iewes seuen hundreth fortie and fiue persons : all the persons *were* foure thousand and sixe hundreth.

31 ¶ And it came to passe in the seuen and thirtieth yeere of the captiuitie of Iehoiakin king of Iudah, in the twelfth moneth, in the fiue and twentieth *day* of the moneth, *that* Euil-merodach king of Babylon, in the *first* yeere of his reigne, lifted vp the head of Iehoiakin king of Iudah, and brought him forth out of prison,

32 And spake † kindly vnto him, and set his throne aboue the throne of the kings that *were* with him in Babylon,

† *Heb. good things with him.*

33 And changed his prison garments : and hee did continually eate bread before him all the dayes of his life.

34 And for his diet, there was a continuall diet giuen him of the king of Babylon, † euery day a portion vntill the day of his death, all the dayes of his life.

† *Heb. the matter of the day in his day.*

¶ The Lamentations of Ieremiah.

CHAP. I.

1 The miserable estate of Ierusalem by reason of her sinne, 12 Shee complaineth of her griefe, 18 and confesseth Gods iudgement to be righteous.

Ow doeth the citie sit solitarie *that was* full of people? how is she become as a widow? She *that was* great among the nations, and princesse among the prouinces, *how* is she become tributarie?

* *Ier.* 13. 17.

* *Iob.* 7. 3.

2 Shee * weepeth sore in the * night, and her teares *are* on her cheekes : among all her louers she *hath* none to comfort her, all her friends haue dealt treacherously with her, they are become her enemies.

† *Heb. for the greatnesse of seruitude.*

3 Iudah is gone into captiuitie, because of affliction, and † because of great seruitude : she dwelleth among the heathen, she findeth no rest : all her persecu-

tors ouertooke her betweene the straits.

4 The wayes of Zion do mourne, because none come to the solemne feasts : all her gates are desolate : her priests sigh : her virgins are afflicted, and she *is* in bitternesse.

5 Her aduersaries * are the chiefe, her enemies prosper : for the LORD hath afflicted her ; for the multitude of her transgressions, her * children are gone into captiuitie before the enemie.

* *Deut.* 28. 13.

* *Ier.* 52. 28.

6 And from the daughter of Zion all her beautie is departed : her princes are become like Harts *that* find no pasture, & they are gone without strength before the pursuer.

7 Ierusalem remembred in the dayes of her affliction, and of her miseries, all her ‖ pleasant things that she had in the dayes of old, when her people fell into the hand of the enemie, and none did helpe her, the aduersaries saw her, *and* did mocke at her Sabbaths.

‖ *Or, desireable.*

8 Ierusalem hath grieuously sinned, there-

therefore she †is remoued : all that honoured her, despise her, because they
haue seene her nakednesse : yea, shee
sigheth and turneth backward.

9 Her filthines *is* in her skirts, she remembreth not her last end, therfore she
came downe wonderfully : shee *had* no
comforter : O Lord, behold my affliction : for ỹ enemie hath magnified *himselfe*.

10 The aduersarie hath spread out
his hand vpon all her ‖pleasant things :
for she hath seene *that* the heathen entred
into her Sanctuarie, whom thou didst
command *that* *they should not enter
into thy congregation.

11 All her people sigh, they seek bread,
they haue giuen their pleasant things
for meate to ‖relieue the soule : see, O
Lord, & consider : for I am become vile.

12 ¶ ‖*Is it* nothing to you, all ye that
†passe by ? behold and see, if there be any
sorow like vnto my sorowe, which is
done vnto me, wherewith the Lord
hath afflicted *me*, in the day of his fierce
anger.

13 From aboue hath he sent fire into
my bones, and it preuaileth against
them : he hath spread a net for my feete,
he hath turned me backe : he hath made
me desolate, *and* faint all the day.

14 The yoke of my transgressions is
bound by his hand : they are wreathed,
and come vp vpon my necke : he hath
made my strength to fall, the Lord
hath deliuered me into *their* hands, *from
whom* I am not able to rise vp.

15 The Lord hath troden vnder foot
all my mightie men in the midst of me :
he hath called an assembly against mee,
to crush my yong men. The Lord hath
troden ‖the virgine, the daughter of
Iudah, *as* in a wine presse.

16 For these things I weepe, *mine
eye, mine eye runneth downe with water, because the comforter that should
†relieue my soule is farre from me : my
children are desolate, because the enemy
preuailed.

17 Zion spreadeth forth her hands,
and there is none to comfort her : the
Lord hath commanded concerning
Iacob, that his aduersaries *should bee*
round about him : Ierusalem is as a
menstruous woman among them.

18 ¶ The Lord is *righteous, for
I haue rebelled against his †comman-
dement : heare, I pray you, all people,
and behold my sorow : my virgins and
my yong men are gone into captiuitie.

19 I called for my louers, *but* they deceiued me : my priests and mine elders
gaue vp the ghost in the citie, while they
sought their meat to relieue their soules

20 Behold, O Lord : for I *am* in distresse : my *bowels are troubled : mine
heart is turned within mee, for I haue
grieuously rebelled : abroad the sword
bereaueth, at home *there is* as death.

21 They haue heard that I sigh, *there
is* none to comfort me : all mine enemies
haue heard of my trouble, they are glad
that thou hast done it : thou wilt bring
the day *that* thou hast ‖called, and they
shall be like vnto me.

22 Let all their wickednes come before thee : and doe vnto them, as thou
hast done vnto me for all my transgressions : for my sighes *are* many, and my
heart *is* faint.

CHAP. II.

1 Ieremiah lamenteth the misery of Ierusalem.
20 He complaineth thereof to God.

Ow hath the Lord couered
the daughter of Zion with
a cloud, in his anger, *and* cast
downe from heauen vnto
the earth the beautie of Israel, and remembred not his footstoole
in the day of his anger ?

2 The Lord hath swallowed vp all
the habitations of Iacob, and hath not
pitied : he hath throwen downe in his
wrath the strong holds of the daughter
of Iudah : he hath †brought *them* down
to the ground : hee hath polluted the
kingdome and the princes thereof.

3 He hath cut off in his fierce anger
all the horne of Israel : he hath drawen
backe his right hand from before the e-
nemy, and he burned against Iacob like
a flaming fire *which* deuoureth round a-
bout.

4 He hath bent his bow like an enemy : he stood with his right hand as an
aduersary, and slew all that were †plea-
sant to the eye, in the tabernacle of the
daughter of Zion : he powred out his
furie like fire.

5 The Lord was as an enemie : he
hath swallowed vp Israel, hee hath
swallowed vp all her palaces : he hath
destroyed his strong holds, and hath
increased in the daughter of Iudah
mourning and lamentation.

6 And he hath violently *taken away
his ‖tabernacle, as *if it were of* a garden,
hee hath destroyed his places of the
assem-

† *Heb. is be-
come a re-
mouing or
wandering.*

‖ *Or, desire-
able.*

* *Deu. 23.3*

‖ *Or, to make
the soule to
come againe.*
‖ *Or, it is no-
thing.*
† *Heb. passe
by the way.*

‖ *Or, the
winepresse
of the vir-
gine, &c.*
* *Ier. 13.17
and 14.17.
chap. 2.18.*
† *Heb. bring
backe.*

* *Dan. 9.7.*
† *Heb. mouth*

* *Isa. 16.11.
iere. 48.36.*

‖ *Or, pro-
claimed.*

† *Heb. made
to couch.*

† *Heb. all the
desireable of
the eye.*

* *Psal. 80.
13. and 89.
41. and isa.
5. 5.*
‖ *Or, hedge.*

† *Heb. shut vp.*

† *Hebr. swallowing vp.*

* *Psal. 74. 9.*

‖ *Or, faint.*

* *Iere. 2. 8. and 5. 31. and 14. 14. and 23. 16.*

† *Hebr. by the way.*

assembly : the LORD hath caused the solemne feasts and Sabbaths to be forgotten in Zion, and hath despised in the indignation of his anger the King and the Priest.

7 The Lord hath cast off his Altar : hee hath abhorred his Sanctuarie : he hath †giuen vp into the hand of the enemie the walles of her palaces : they haue made a noise in the house of the LORD, as in the day of a solemne Feast.

8 The LORD hath purposed to destroy the wall of the daughter of Zion : he hath stretched out a line : he hath not withdrawen his hand from † destroying : therefore hee made the rampart and the wall to lament : they languished together.

9 Her gates are sunke into the ground : he hath destroyed and broken her barres : her King and her Princes *are* among the Gentiles : the Law *is* no *more*, her *prophets also finde no vision from the LORD.

10 The Elders of the daughter of Zion sit vpon the ground *and* keepe silence : they haue cast vp dust vpon their heads : they haue girded themselues with sackcloth : the virgins of Ierusalem hang downe their heades to the ground.

11 Mine eyes doe faile with teares : my bowels are troubled : my liuer is powred vpon the earth, for the destruction of the daughter of my people, because the children and the sucklings ‖swoone in the streets of the citie.

12 They say to their mothers, Where *is* corne and wine ? when they swooned as the wounded in the streets of the citie, when their soule was powred out into their mothers bosome.

13 What thing shall I take to witnesse for thee ? what thing shall I liken to thee, O daughter of Ierusalem ? what shall I equal to thee, that I may comfort thee, O Virgin daughter of Zion ? for thy breach *is* great like the sea : who can heale thee ?

14 Thy *Prophets haue seene vaine and foolish things for thee, and they haue not discouered thine iniquitie, to turne away thy captiuitie : but haue seene for thee false burdens, and causes of banishment.

15 All that passe †by, clap their hands at thee : they hisse and wagge their head at the daughter of Ierusalem, *saying, Is*

this the citie that men call *the perfection of beauty, the ioy of the whole earth ?

16 All thine enemies haue opened their mouth against thee : they hisse and gnash the teeth : they say, We haue swallowed *her* vp : certainly this *is* the day that we looked for : we haue found, we haue seene *it.*

17 The LORD hath done that which he had *deuised : he hath fulfilled his word that he had commanded in the dayes of old : hee hath throwen downe and hath not pitied : and he hath caused thine enemie to reioyce ouer thee, hee hath set vp the horne of thine aduersaries.

18 Their heart cried vnto the Lord, *O wall of the daughter of Zion, let teares runne downe like a riuer, day and night : giue thy selfe no rest, let not the apple of thine eyes cease.

19 Arise, cry out in the night : in the beginning of the watches powre out thine heart like water before the face of the Lord : lift vp thy handes toward him, for the life of thy yong children, that faint for hunger in the top of euery streete.

20 ¶ Behold, O LORD, and consider to whom thou hast done this : shal the women eat their fruit, *and* children of a ‖spanne long ? shall the priest and the prophet be slaine in the Sanctuary of the Lord ?

21 The yong and the old lye on the ground in the streets : my virgins and my yong men are fallen by the sword : thou hast slaine *them* in the day of thy anger : thou hast killed, and not pitied.

22 Thou hast called as in a solemne day my terrours round about, so that in the day of the LORDS anger, none escaped nor remained : those that I haue swadled and brought vp, hath mine enemy consumed.

* *Psal. 48. 2.*

* *Leuit. 26. 16. deut. 28. 15.*

* *Iere. 14. 17. chap. 1. 16.*

‖ *Or, swadled with their hands.*

CHAP. III.

1 The faithfull bewaile their calamities. 22 By the mercies of God they nourish their hope. 37 They acknowledge Gods iustice. 55 They pray for deliuerance, 64 and vengeance on their enemies.

 *Am* the man *that* hath seene affliction by the rod of his wrath.

2 He hath led me and brought *mee into* darkenesse, but not into light.

3 Surely against me is he turned, he turneth

turneth his hand *against me* all the day.

4 My flesh and my skinne hath he made old, he hath broken my bones.

5 He hath builded against me, and compassed *me* with gall and trauel.

6 He hath set me in darke places, as they that be dead of old.

7 He hath hedged me about, that I cannot get out : hee hath made my chaine heauie.

8 Also when I cry and shout, he shutteth out my prayer.

9 Hee hath inclosed my wayes with hewen stone : he hath made my pathes crooked.

10 He *was* vnto me *as* a Beare lying in waite, *and as* a Lion in secret places.

11 Hee hath turned aside my wayes, and pulled me in pieces : hee hath made me desolate.

12 He hath bent his bow, and set me as a marke for the arrow.

13 Hee hath caused the †arrowes of his quiuer to enter into my reines.

14 I was a *derision to all my people, *and* their song all the day.

15 Hee hath filled me with †bitternesse, hee hath made me drunken with wormewood.

16 He hath also broken my teeth with grauell stones, hee hath ‖couered me with ashes.

17 And thou hast remoued my soule farre off from peace : I forgate †prosperitie.

18 And I said, My strength and my hope is perished from the LORD :

19 ‖Remembring mine affliction and my miserie, the wormewood & the gall.

20 My soule hath *them* still in remembrance, and is †humbled in me.

21 This I †recall to my mind, therefore haue I hope.

22 ¶ *It is of* the LORDS mercies that wee are not consumed, because his compassions faile not.

23 *They are* newe euery morning : great *is* thy faithfulnesse.

24 The LORD *is* my *portion, sayth my soule, therefore will I hope in him.

25 The LORD *is* good vnto them that waite for him, to the soule *that* seeketh him.

26 *It is* good that *a man* should both hope and quietly wait for the saluation of the LORD.

27 *It is* good for a man that he beare the yoke in his youth.

28 Hee sitteth alone and keepeth silence, because hee hath borne *it* vpon him.

29 He putteth his mouth in the dust, if so be there may be hope.

30 Hee giueth his cheeke to him that smiteth him, hee is filled full with reproch.

31 For the Lord will not cast off for euer.

32 But though hee cause griefe, yet will hee haue compassion according to the multitude of his mercies.

33 For he doth not afflict †willingly, nor grieue the children of men.

34 To crush vnder his feete all the prisoners of the earth,

35 To turne aside the right of a man before the face of the ‖most high,

36 To subuert a man in his cause, the Lord ‖approoueth not.

37 ¶ Who *is* hee *that* sayth, and it commeth to passe, *when* the Lord commandeth *it* not ?

38 Out of the mouth of the most hie proceedeth not *euill and good ?

39 Wherefore doeth a liuing man ‖complaine, a man for the punishment of his sinnes ?

40 Let vs search and try our waies, and turne againe to the LORD.

41 Let vs lift vp our heart with our hands vnto God in the heauens.

42 We haue transgressed, and haue rebelled, thou hast not pardoned.

43 Thou hast couered with anger, and persecuted vs: thou hast slaine, thou hast not pitied.

44 Thou hast couered thy selfe with a cloud, that our prayer should not passe through.

45 Thou hast made vs as the *off-scouring and refuse in the middest of the people.

46 All our enemies haue opened their mouthes against vs.

47 *Feare and a snare is come vpon vs, desolation and destruction.

48 Mine eye runneth downe with riuers of water, for the destruction of the daughter of my people.

49 Mine eye trickleth downe and ceaseth not, without any intermission :

50 Till the LORD looke downe, and behold from heauen.

51 Mine eye affecteth †mine heart, ‖because of all the daughters of my city.

52 Mine enemies chased me sore like a bird, without cause.

53 They

Marginal notes (left column):

† Heb. *sons.*

* Iere. 20.7.

† Heb. *bitternesses.*

‖ Or, *rolled me in the ashes.*

† Heb. *good.*

‖ Or, *remember.*

† Heb. *bowed*

† Heb. *make to returne to my heart.*

* Psal. 16.5. and 73. 26. and 119. 57. Iere. 10. 16.

Marginal notes (right column):

† Heb. *from his heart.*

‖ Or, *a superiour.*

‖ Or, *seeth not.*
* Psal. 33. 9.

* Amos 3. 6

‖ Or, *murmure.*

* 1. Cor. 4. 13.

* Isai. 24.17.

† Heb. *my soule.*
‖ Or, *more then all.*

53 They haue cut off my life in the dungeon, and cast a stone vpon me.

54 Waters flowed ouer mine head, *then* I sayd, I am cut off.

55 ¶ I called vpon thy name, O LORD, out of the low dungeon.

56 Thou hast heard my voice, hide not thine eare at my breathing, at my crie.

57 Thou drewest neere in the day that I called vpon thee : thou saidst, Feare not.

58 O Lord, thou hast pleaded the causes of my soule, thou hast redeemed my life.

59 O LORD, thou hast seene my wrong, iudge thou my cause.

60 Thou hast seene all their vengeance; *and* all their imaginations against me.

61 Thou hast heard their reproch, O LORD, *and* all their imaginations against me :

62 The lippes of those that rose vp against me, and their deuice against me all the day.

63 Behold, their sitting downe and their rising vp, I *am* their musicke.

64 ¶ Render vnto them a recompense, O LORD, according to the worke of their hands.

65 Giue them ||sorrow of heart, thy curse vnto them.

66 Persecute and destroy *them* in anger, from vnder the *heauens of the LORD.

Or, obstinacie of heart.

* Psal. 8. 4.

CHAP. IIII.

1 Zion bewaileth her pitifull estate. 13 She confesseth her sinnes. 21 Edom is threatned. 22 Zion is comforted.

Ow is the gold become dimme! *how* is the most fine gold changed! the stones of the sanctuarie are powred out in the top of euery streete.

2 The precious sonnes of Zion, comparable to fine gold, how are they esteemed as earthen pitchers, the worke of the hands of the potter!

3 Euen the ||sea-monsters draw out the breast, they giue sucke to their young ones : the daughter of my people *is become* cruell, like the ostriches in the wildernesse.

4 The tongue of the sucking child cleaueth to the roofe of his mouth for thirst : the young children aske bread,

Or, sea calues.

and no man breaketh *it* vnto them.

5 They that did feede delicately, are desolate in the streetes : they that were brought vp in scarlet, embrace dounghilles.

6 For the ||punishment of the iniquitie of the daughter of my people, is greater then the punishment of the sinne of Sodom, that was *ouerthrowen as in a moment, and no hands stayed on her.

Or, iniquitie.

* Gen. 19. 25.

7 Her Nazarites were purer then snow, they were whiter then milke, they were more ruddie in body then rubies, their polishing *was* of Saphir.

8 Their visage is † blacker then a cole : they are not knowen in the streets : their skinne cleaueth to their bones : it is withered, it is become like a sticke.

† *Heb. darker then blacknesse.*

9 They that bee slaine with the sword, are better then they that be slain with hunger : for these † pine away, stricken through for *want* of the fruits of the field.

† *Heb. flow out.*

10 The hands of the pitifull women haue *sodden their owne children, they were their meate in the destruction of the daughter of my people.

* 2. Kings 6. 29. deut. 28. 57.

11 The LORD hath accomplished his furie, he hath powred out his fierce anger, and hath kindled a fire in Zion, and it hath deuoured the foundations thereof.

12 The kings of the earth, and all the inhabitants of the world would not haue beleeued, that the aduersarie and the enemie should haue entred into the gates of Ierusalem.

13 ¶ *For the sinnes of her prophets, *and* the iniquities of her priests, that haue shed the blood of the iust in the middest of her :

* Ier. 5. 31. and 23. 21.

14 They haue wandred *as* blind men in the streetes, they haue polluted themselues with blood, ||so that men could not touch their garments.

Or, in that they could not but touch.

15 They cryed vnto them; Depart yee, ||*it is* vncleane, depart, depart, touch not, when they fled away and wandred : they said among the heathen, They shall no more soiourne *there.*

Or, yee polluted.

16 The ||anger of the LORD hath diuided them, he will no more regard them : they respected not the persons of the priests, they fauoured not the elders.

Or, face.

17 As for vs, our eyes as yet failed for our vaine helpe : in our watching we haue watched for a nation *that* could not saue vs.

18 They

18 They hunt our steps that we cannot goe in our streets: our end is neere, our dayes are fulfilled, for our ende is come.

19 Our persecutours are swifter then the eagles of the heauen : they pursued vs vpon the mountaines, they laide waite for vs in the wildernesse.

20 The *breath of our nostrels, the anointed of the Lord was taken in their pits, of whom we said, Vnder his shadowe we shall liue among the heathen.

21 ¶ Reioyce and be glad, O daughter of Edom, that dwellest in the lande of Vz, the cup also shall passe through vnto thee : thou shalt be drunken, and shalt make thy selfe naked.

22 ¶ The ||punishment of thine iniquitie is accomplished, O daughter of Zion, he will no more carie thee away into captiuitie : hee will visit thine iniquitie, O daughter of Edom, hee will ||discouer thy sinnes.

CHAP. V.

A pitifull complaint of Zion, in prayer vnto God.

Remember, O Lord, what is come vpon vs : consider and beholde our reproch.

2 Our inheritance is turned to strangers, our houses to aliants.

3 We are orphanes and fatherlesse, our mothers are as widowes.

4 We haue drunken our water for money, our wood †is sold vnto vs.

5 †Our neckes are vnder persecution : we labour and haue no rest.

6 We haue giuen the hand to the Egyptians, and to the Assyrians, to be satisfied with bread.

7 *Our fathers haue sinned and are not, and wee haue borne their iniquities.

8 Seruants haue ruled ouer vs : there is none that doeth deliuer vs out of their hand.

9 We gate our bread with the perill of our liues, because of the sword of the wildernesse.

10 Our *skinne was blacke like an ouen, because of the ||terrible famine.

11 They rauished the women in Zion, and the maides in the cities of Iudah.

12 Princes are hanged vp by their hand : the faces of Elders were not honoured.

13 They tooke the young men to grinde, and the children fell vnder the wood.

14 The Elders haue ceased from the gate, the young men from their musicke.

15 The ioy of our heart is ceased, our daunce is turned into mourning.

16 The crowne is fallen from our head : Woe vnto vs, that wee haue sinned.

17 For this our heart is faint, for these things our eyes are dimme.

18 Because of the mountaine of Zion, which is desolate, the foxes walke vpon it.

19 Thou, O Lord, * remainest for euer : thy throne from generation to generation.

20 Wherefore doest thou forget vs for euer, and forsake vs †so long time?

21 *Turne thou vs vnto thee, O Lord, and we shall be turned : renew our dayes as of old.

22 ||But thou hast vtterly reiected vs : thou art very wroth against vs.

¶ THE

*Gen. 2. 7.

| Or, thine iniquitie.

† Or, carie thee captiue for thy sinnes

† Heb. commeth for price.
† Heb. on our necks are we persecuted.

*Ier. 31. 29 ezek. 16. 2.

*Psal. 11. 38
† Or, terrors or stormes.

† Hebr. the crowne of our head is fallen.

*Psal. 9. 8. and 29. 10. and 102. 13. & 145. 13.

† Heb. for length of dayes.
*Ier. 31. 18

| Or, for wilt thou vtterly reiect vs?

¶ THE BOOKE OF THE
Prophet Ezekiel.

CHAP. I.

1 The time of Ezekiels prophecie at Chebar. 4 His vision of foure Cherubims, 15 Of the foure wheeles, 26 and of the glory of God.

Ow it came to passe in the thirtieth yeere, in the fourth *moneth*, in the fifth *day* of the moneth, (as I was among † the captiues by the riuer of Chebar) *that* the heauens were opened, and I saw visions of God.

† *Hebr. captiuitie.*

2 In the fifth *day* of the moneth, (which *was* the fifth yeere of king Iehoiakins captiuitie,)

3 The word of the LORD came expresly vnto † Ezekiel the Priest, the sonne of Buzi, in the land of the Caldeans, by the riuer Chebar, and the hand of the Lord was there vpon him.

† *Hebr. Iehezkel.*

4 ¶ And I looked, and behold, a whirlewinde came out of the North, a great cloude, and a fire † infoulding it selfe, and a brightnesse *was* about it, and out of the midst thereof as the colour of amber, out of the midst of the fire.

† *Heb. catching it selfe.*

5 Also out of the midst thereof *came* the likenesse of foure liuing creatures, and this *was* their appearance : they had the likenesse of a man.

6 And euery one had foure faces, and euery one had foure wings.

7 And their feet *were* † straight feet, and the sole of their feet *was* like the sole of a calues foot, and they sparkled like the colour of burnished brasse.

† *Heb. a straight foot.*

8 And they had the handes of a man vnder their wings on their foure sides, and they foure *had* their faces and their wings.

9 Their wings were ioyned one to another, they turned not when they went : they went euery one straight forward.

10 As for the likenesse of their faces, they foure *had* the face of a man, and the face of a lyon on the right side, and they foure *had* the face of an oxe on the left side : they foure also *had* the face of an eagle.

11 Thus *were* their faces : and their wings were ‖ stretched vpward, two *wings* of euery one were ioyned one to an other, and two couered their bodies.

‖ *Or, diuided aboue.*

12 And they went euery one straight forward : whither the spirit was to goe, they went : *and* they turned not when they went.

13 As for the likenesse of the liuing creatures, their appearance *was* like burning coles of fire, *and* like the appearance of lamps : it went vp and downe among the liuing creatures, and the fire was bright, and out of the fire went foorth lightning.

14 And the liuing creatures ranne, and returned as the appearance of a flash of lightning.

15 ¶ Now as I behelde the liuing creatures : behold one wheele vpon the earth by the liuing creatures, with his foure faces.

16 The appearance of the wheeles, and their worke *was* like vnto the colour of a Berill : and they foure *had* one likenesse, and their appearance and their worke *was* as it were a wheele in the middle of a wheele.

17 When they went, they went vpon their foure sides : *and* they returned not when they went.

18 As for their rings, they were so high, that they were dreadful, and their ‖ rings were full of eyes round about them foure.

‖ *Or, strakes*

19 And when the liuing creatures went,

went, the wheeles went by them : and when the liuing creatures were lift vp from the earth, the wheels were lift vp.

20 Whitherſoeuer the spirit *was* to goe, they went, thither *was their* spirit to goe, and the wheeles were lifted vp *Or, of life.* ouer against them : for the spirit ||of the liuing creature *was* in the wheeles.

21 When those went, *these* went, and *Or, of life.* when those stood, *these* stood; and when those were lifted vp from the earth, the wheeles *were* lifted vp ouer against them : for the spirit ||of the liuing creature *was* in the wheeles.

22 And the likenesse of the firmament vpon the heads of the liuing creature *was* as the colour of the terrible chryſtall, stretched foorth ouer their heads aboue.

23 And vnder the firmament *were* their wings straight, the one toward the other, euery one had two which couered on this side, & euery one had two, which couered on that side their bodies.

24 And when they went, I heard the noise of their wings, like the noise of great waters, as the voice of the Almightie, the voice of speech, as the noise of an hoste : when they stood, they let downe their wings.

25 And there was a voice from the firmament, that *was* ouer their heads, when they stood, *and* had let downe their wings.

26 ¶ And aboue the firmament that *was* ouer their heads, *was* the likenesse of a Throne, as the appearance of a Saphyre stone, and vpon the likenesse of the Throne *was* the likenesse as the appearance of a man aboue vpon it.

27 And I saw as the colour of amber, as the appearance of fire round about within it : from the appearance of his loynes euen vpward, and from the appearance of his loynes euen downeward, I saw as it were the appearance of fire, & it *had* brightnesse round about.

28 As the appearance of the bow that is in the cloude in the day of raine, so *was* the appearance of the brightnesse round about. This *was* the appearance of the likenesse of the glory of the LORD: and when I saw it, I fell vpon my face, and I heard a voice of one that spake.

CHAP. II.

1 Ezekiels commission : 6 His instruction.
9 The roule of his heauie prophecie.

Nd he said vnto me, Son of man, stand vpon thy feete, and I will speake vnto thee.

2 And the spirit entred into me, when hee spake vnto me, and set me vpon my feete, that I heard him that spake vnto me :

3 And hee said vnto me, Sonne of man, I send thee to the children of Israel, to a rebellious †nation that hath †*Heb. natiōs.* rebelled against mee : they and their fathers haue transgressed against mee, euen vnto this very day.

4 For they *are* †impudent children †*Heb. hard of face.* and stiffe hearted : I doe send thee vnto them, and thou shalt say vnto them, Thus sayth the Lord GOD.

5 And they, whether they wil heare or whether they will forbeare, (for they are a rebellious house) yet shall know that there hath bene a Prophet among them.

6 ¶ And thou sonne of man, be not afraid of them, neither be afraid of their wordes, though || bryars and thornes |*Or, rebels.* *be* with thee, and thou doest dwell among scorpions : be not afraid of their words, nor be dismayed at their lookes, though they *be* a rebellious house.

7 And thou shalt speake my words vnto them, whether they will heare or whether they will forbeare, for they *are* most †rebellious. †*Heb. rebellion.*

8 But thou, sonne of man, heare what I say vnto thee; Be not thou rebellious like that rebellious house : open thy mouth and * eate that I giue *Reu. 10. 9.* thee.

9 ¶ And when I looked, behold, an hand *was* sent vnto mee, and loe, a roule of a booke *was* therein.

10 And he spread it before me, and it was written within and without, and there was written therein lamentations, and mourning, and woe.

CHAP. III.

1 Ezekiel eateth the roule. 4 God encourageth him. 15 God sheweth him the rule of prophecie. 22 God shutteth and openeth the Prophets mouth.

Oreouer he said vnto me, Sonne of man, eate that thou findest : eate this roule, and goe, speake vnto the house of Israel.

2 So I opened my mouth, and hee caused me to eate that roule.

3 And

3 And he said vnto mee; Sonne of man, cause thy belly to eate, and fill thy bowels with this roule that I giue thee. Then did I *eate it, and it was in my mouth as honie for sweetnesse.

4 ¶ And he said vnto me, Sonne of man, goe, get thee vnto the house of Israel, and speake with my words vnto them.

5 For thou art not sent to a people of a †strange speach, and of an hard language, but to the house of Israel.

6 Not to many people of a strange speach and of an †hard language, whose words thou canst not vnderstand : ||surely had I sent thee to them, they would haue hearkened vnto thee :

7 But the house of Israel will not hearken vnto thee; for they will not hearken vnto me : for all the house of Israel are †impudent and hard hearted.

8 Behold, I haue made thy face strong against their faces, and thy forehead strong against their foreheads.

9 As an adamant harder then flint haue I made thy forehead : *feare them not, neither be dismayed at their lookes, though they be a rebellious house.

10 Moreouer he said vnto me, Sonne of man, all my words that I shall speake vnto thee, receiue in thine heart, and heare with thine eares.

11 And goe, get thee to them of the captiuity, vnto thy people, and speake vnto them and tell them, Thus saith the Lord God, whether they will heare, or whether they will forbeare.

12 Then the spirit tooke me vp, and I heard behind me a voyce of a great rushing, saying; Blessed be the glory of the Lord from his place.

13 I heard also the noise of the wings of the liuing creatures that † touched one another, and the noise of the wheeles ouer against them, and a noise of a great rushing.

14 So the spirit lifted me vp, and tooke me away, and I went in †bitternesse, in the †heate of my spirit, but the hand of the Lord was strong vpon mee.

15 ¶ Then I came to them of the captiuity at Tel-abib, that dwelt by the riuer of Chebar, and I sate where they sate, and remained there astonished among them seuen daies.

16 And it came to passe at the end of seuen dayes, that the word of the Lord came vnto me, saying;

17 *Sonne of man, I haue made thee a watchman vnto the house of Israel : therefore heare the word at my mouth, & giue them warning from me.

18 When I say vnto the wicked; Thou shalt surely die, and thou giuest him not warning, nor speakest to warne the wicked from his wicked way to saue his life; the same wicked man shall die in his iniquitie : but his blood will I require at thine hand.

19 Yet if thou warne the wicked, and he turne not from his wickednesse, nor from his wicked way, he shall die in his iniquity, but thou hast deliuered thy soule.

20 Againe, when a *righteous man doth turne from his † righteousnesse and commit iniquity, and I lay a stumbling blocke before him, he shall die : because thou hast not giuen him warning, he shall die in his sinne, and his righteousnesse which he hath done shal not be remembred : but his blood will I require at thine hand.

21 Neuerthelesse if thou warne the righteous man, that the righteous sinne not, and he doth not sinne; he shall surely liue, because he is warned : also thou hast deliuered thy soule.

22 ¶ And the hand of the Lord was there vpon me, and he said vnto me; Arise, goe forth into the plaine, and I will there talke with thee.

23 Then I arose and went forth into the plaine, and behold, the glory of the Lord stood there as the glory which I *saw by the riuer of Chebar, and I fell on my face.

24 Then the spirit entred into me, and set me vpon my feet, and spake with me, and said vnto me, Goe shut thy selfe within thine house.

25 But thou, O sonne of man, behold, they shall put bands vpon thee, and shall bind thee with them, and thou shalt not goe out among them.

26 And I will make thy tongue cleaue to the roofe of thy mouth, that thou shalt be dumme and shalt not be to them ||a reprouer : for they are a rebellious house.

27 But when I speake with thee, I will open thy mouth, and thou shalt say vnto them; Thus saith the Lord God, He that heareth, let him heare, and he that forbeareth, let him forbeare : for they are a rebellious house.

CHAP.

---

*Reu. 10. 9.

† Heb. deepe of lippes and heauie of tongue, and so ver. 6.
† Heb. deepe of lip, and heauie language.
| Or, if I had sent thee &c. would they not haue hearkened vnto thee?
† Heb. stiffe of forhead and hard of heart.

*Ier. i. 6.

† Heb. kissed.

† Heb. bitter.
† Heb. hot anger.

*Chap. 33.

*Chap. 18 24.
† Heb. righteousnesse

*Chap. 1.

| A man reprouing.

CHAP. IIII.

1 Vnder the type of a siege, is shewed the time from the defection of Ieroboam to the captiuitie. 9 By the prouision of the siege, is shewed the hardnesse of the famine.

Hou also sonne of man, take thee a tile, and lay it before thee, and pourtray vpon it the citie, *euen* Ierusalem,

2 And lay siege against it, and build a fort against it, and cast a mount against it : set the campe also against it, and set ‖ *battering* rammes against it round about:

Or, chiefe raders.

3 Moreouer take thou vnto thee an ‖ yron panne, and set it for a wall of yron betweene thee and the city, and set thy face against it, and it shalbe besieged, and thou shalt lay siege against it : this *shalbe* a signe to the house of Israel.

Or, a flat plate, or slice.

4 Lie thou also vpon thy left side, and lay the iniquitie of the house of Israel vpon it : *according* to the number of the dayes that thou shalt lie vpon it, thou shalt beare their iniquitie.

5 For I haue layed vpon thee the yeeres of their iniquitie, according to the number of the dayes, three hundreth and ninetie daies. * So shalt thou beare the iniquitie of the house of Israel.

* Num. 14. 34.

6 And when thou hast accomplished them, lie againe on thy right side, and thou shalt beare the iniquitie of the house of Iudah fourtie dayes : I haue appointed thee † each day for a yeere.

† Hebr. a day for a yeere, a day for a yeere.

7 Therefore thou shalt set thy face toward the siege of Ierusalem, and thine arme *shalbe* vncouered, and thou shalt prophecie against it.

8 And behold, I wil lay bands vpon thee, and thou shalt not turne thee † from one side to an other, till thou hast ended the dayes of thy siege.

† Hebr. from thy side to thy side.

9 ¶ Take thou also vnto thee wheat, and barley, and beanes, and lentils, and millet, and ‖ fitches, and put them in one vessell, and make thee bread thereof *according* to the number of the dayes that thou shalt lie vpon thy side; three hundreth and ninetie dayes shalt thou eate thereof.

‖ Or, spelt.

10 And thy meate which thou shalt eat, *shalbe* by weight twentie shekels a day : from time to time shalt thou eat it.

11 Thou shalt drinke also water by measure, the sixt part of an hin : from time to time shalt thou drinke.

12 And thou shalt eate it *as* barley cakes, & thou shalt bake it with doung that commeth out of man in their sight.

13 And the LORD said; Euen thus shall the children of Israel eat their defiled bread among the Gentiles, whither I will driue them.

14 Then said I, Ah Lord GOD, behold, my soule hath not bene polluted : for from my youth vp euen til now, haue I not eaten of that which dieth of it selfe, or is torne in pieces, neither came there abominable flesh into my mouth.

15 Then he said vnto me, Loe, I haue giuen thee cowes doung for mans doung and thou shalt prepare thy bread therewith.

16 Moreouer he said vnto me, Sonne of man, behold, I wil breake the * staffe of bread in Ierusalem, and they shall eat bread by weight, and with care, and they shal drinke water by measure, and with astonishment:

* Leuit. 26. 26. chap. 5. 16. and 13. 13.

17 That they may want bread and water, & be astonied one with an other, and consume away for their iniquitie.

CHAP. V.

1 Vnder the type of haire, 5 is shewed the iudgement of Ierusalem for their rebellion, 12 by famine, sword and dispersion.

ANd thou sonne of man, take thee a sharpe knife, take thee a barbours rasor, and cause *it* to passe vpon thine head and vpon thy beard : then take the ballances to weigh, and diuide the *haire*.

2 Thou shalt burne with fire a third part in the midst of the city, when the dayes of the siege are fulfilled, and thou shalt take a third part, and smite about it with a knife, and a third part thou shalt scatter in the winde, and I will draw out a sword after them.

3 Thou shalt also take thereof a few in number, and bind them in thy † skirts.

† Hebr. wings.

4 Then take of them againe, and cast them into the midst of the fire, and burne them in the fire : *for* thereof shall a fire come foorth into all the house of Israel.

5 ¶ Thus saith the Lord GOD; This *is* Ierusalem : I haue set it in the midst of the nations and countreys *that are* round about her.

6 And she hath changed my iudgements into wickednesse more then the nations

nations, and my statutes more then the countreyes that *are* round about her : for they haue refused my iudgements and my statutes, they haue not walked in them.

7 Therefore thus saith the Lord God, Because yee multiplied more then the nations that *are* round about you, *and* haue not walked in my Statutes, neither haue kept my iudgments, neither haue done according to the iudgements of the nations that *are* round about you :

8 Therefore thus saith the Lord God, Behold, I, euen I *am* against thee, and will execute iudgements in the midst of thee in the sight of the nations.

9 And I will doe in thee that which I haue not done, and whereunto I will not doe any more the like, because of all thine abominations.

* Leuit. 26. 29. deut. 28. 53. 2. kin. 6. 29. lamen. 4. 10. baruch. 2. 3.

10 Therefore the fathers shall * eate the sonnes in the midst of thee, and the sonnes shall eate their fathers, and I will execute iudgements in thee, and the whole remnant of thee will I scatter into all the windes.

11 Wherefore, as I liue, saith the Lord God, Surely because thou hast defiled my Sanctuary with all thy detestable things, and with all thine abominations, therefore will I also diminish *thee*, neither shall mine * eye spare, neither will I haue any pitie.

* Chap. 7. 4, 14.

12 ¶ A third part of thee shall die with the pestilence, and with famine shall they be consumed in the middest of thee : and a third part shall fall by the sword round about thee : and I will scatter a third part into all the windes, and I wil draw out a sword after them.

13 Thus shall mine anger be accomplished, and I will cause my fury to rest vpon them, and I will be comforted : and they shal know that I the Lord haue spoken *it* in my zeale, when I haue accomplished my fury in them.

14 Moreouer I will make thee waste, and a reproch among the nations that *are* round about thee, in the sight of all that passe by.

* Deut. 28. 37.

15 So it shall bee a * reproch and a taunt, an instruction and an astonishment vnto the nations that *are* round about thee, when I shall execute iudgments in thee in anger and in furie, and in furious rebukes : I the Lord haue spoken *it*.

16 When I shall send vpon them the euill arrowes of famine, which shall be for *their* destruction, *and* which I will send to destroy you : and I wil increase the famine vpon you, and will breake your * staffe of bread.

* Leuit. 26. chap. 4. 1 and 14. 13 * Leuit. 2 22.

17 So will I send vpon you famine, and * euill beasts, and they shall bereaue thee, and pestilence and blood shal passe through thee, and I will bring the sword vpon thee : I the Lord haue spoken *it*.

CHAP. VI.

1 The iudgement of Israel for their idolatrie. 8 A remnant shall be blessed. 11 The faithfull are exhorted to lament their calamities.

ND the worde of the Lord came vnto mee, saying,

2 Sonne of man, set thy face towardes the * mountaines of Israel, and prophecie against them,

* Cha. 36

3 And say, Ye mountaines of Israel, Heare the word of the Lord God, Thus saith the Lord God to the mountaines and to the hilles, to the riuers and to the valleys, Behold, I, *euen* I will bring a sword vpon you, and I will destroy your high places.

4 And your altars shalbe desolate, and your ‖images shall be broken : and I will cast downe your slaine men before your idoles.

‖ Or, sun images, o so vers. 6

5 And I will † lay the dead carkeises of the children of Israel before their idoles, and I will scatter your bones round about your altars.

† Heb. gi

6 In all your dwelling places the cities shall be laid waste, and the high places shalbe desolate, that your altars may be laid waste and made desolate, and your idols may be broken and cease, and your images may bee cut downe, and your workes may be abolished.

7 And the slaine shall fall in the midst of you, and ye shall knowe that I *am* the Lord.

8 ¶ Yet will I leaue a remnant, that he may leaue *some*, that shall escape the sword among the nations, when ye shalbe scattered through the countreys.

9 And they that escape of you shall remember me among the nations, whither they shalbe caried captiues, because I am broken with their whorish heart which hath departed from me, and with their eyes which goe a whoring after their idoles : and they shall loathe them-

themselues for the euils which they haue committed in all their abominations.

10 And they shall know that I *am* the Lord, *and that* I haue not said in vaine, that I would doe this euill vnto them.

Chap. 21.

11 ¶ Thus sayth the Lord God; Smite * with thine hand, and stampe with thy foot, and say, Alas, for all the euill abominations of the house of Israel: for they shall fall by the sword, by the famine, and by the pestilence.

12 He that is farre off shall die of the pestilence, and he that is neere shall fall by the sword, and hee that remaineth and is besieged, shall die by the famine: thus will I accomplish my furie vpon them.

13 Then shal ye know that I *am* the Lord, when their slaine men shalbe among their idoles round about their altars, vpon euery high hill in all the tops of the mountaines, and vnder euery greene tree, and vnder euery thicke oke, the place where they did offer sweet sauour to all their idoles.

Or, desolate from the wildernesse.

14 So will I stretch out my hand vpon them, and make the land desolate, yea more ||desolate then the wildernesse towards Diblath, in all their habitations, and they shall know that I *am* the Lord.

CHAP. VII.

1 The final desolation of Israel. 16 The mournfull repentance of them that escape. 20 The enemies defile the Sanctuarie, because of the Israelites abominations. 23 Vnder the type of a chaine, is shewed their miserable captiuitie.

Oreouer the word of the Lord came vnto mee, saying;

2 Also thou sonne of man, thus saith the Lord God vnto the land of Israel, An end, the ende is come vpon the foure corners of the land.

3 Now *is* the ende *come* vpon thee, and I will send mine anger vpon thee, and will iudge thee according to thy wayes, and will † recompense vpon thee all thine abominations.

† Heb. giue.

4 And mine eye shal not spare thee, neither will I haue pitie : but I will recompense thy wayes vpon thee, and thine abominations shalbe in the midst of thee, and yee shall know that I *am* the Lord.

5 Thus sayth the Lord God, An euill, an onely euill, behold, is come.

6 An end is come, the end is come, it † watcheth for thee, behold, it is come.

† Heb. awaketh against thee.

7 The morning is come vnto thee, O thou that dwellest in the land : the time is come, the day of trouble *is* neere, and not the ||sounding againe of the mountaines.

|| Or, eccho.

8 Now will I shortly powre out my furie vpon thee, and accomplish mine anger vpon thee: and I wil iudge thee according to thy wayes, and will recompense thee for all thine abominations.

9 And mine eye shall not spare, neither will I haue pitie : I will recompense † thee according to thy wayes, and thine abominations that are in the middest of thee, and yee shall know that I *am* the Lord that smiteth.

† Heb. vpon thee.

10 Behold the day, behold, it is come, the morning is gone foorth, the rodde hath blossomed, pride hath budded.

11 Violence is risen vp into a rod of wickednesse : none of them *shall remaine*, nor of ||their multitude, nor of any of theirs, neither shall there be wailing for them.

|| Or, their tumultuous persons. Hebr. tumult.

12 The time is come, the day draweth neere, let not the buyer reioyce, nor the seller mourne : for wrath is vpon all the multitude thereof.

13 For the seller shall not returne to that which is solde, † although they were yet aliue : for the vision *is* touching the whole multitude thereof which shal not returne : neither shall any strengthen himselfe in ||the iniquity of his life.

† Heb. thogh their life were yet among the liuing.
|| Or, whose life is in his iniquitie. Hebr. his iniquitie.

14 They haue blowen the trumpet, euen to make all ready, but none goeth to the battell : for my wrath *is* vpon all the multitude thereof.

15 The sword *is* without, and the pestilence and the famine within : he that *is* in the field shall die with the sword, and hee that *is* in the city, famine and pestilence shall deuoure him.

16 ¶ But they that escape of them, shall escape, and shall be on the mountaines like doues of the valleys, all of them mourning, euery one for his iniquitie.

17 All *hands shall be feeble, and all knees † shalbe weake *as* water.

• Isai. 13. 7. iere. 6. 24.
† Heb. goe into water.

18 They shall also *girde *themselues* with sackcloth, and horrour shall couer them, and shame *shall be* vpon all faces, and baldnesse vpon all their heads.

• Isa. 15. 2, 3. iere. 48. 37.

19 They

19 They shall cast their siluer in the
streets, and their golde shalbe †remoo-
ued: their *siluer and their golde shall
not be able to deliuer them in the day of
the wrath of the LORD: they shall
not satisfie their soules, neither fill their
bowels: ||because it is the stumbling
blocke of their iniquitie.
20 ¶ As for the beautie of his ornament, he set it in maiestie: but they made
the images of their abominations, *and*
of their detestable things therein: there-
fore haue I ||set it farre from them.
21 And I will giue it into the hands
of the strangers for a pray, and to the
wicked of the earth for a spoile, and they
shall pollute it.
22 My face will I turne also from
them, and they shall pollute my secret
place: for the ||robbers shall enter into
it and defile it.
23 ¶ Make a chaine: for the land is
full of bloody crimes, the citie is full of
violence.
24 Wherfore I will bring the worst
of the heathen, and they shall possesse
their houses: I will also make the
pompe of the strong to cease, and ||their
holy places shall be defiled.
25 †Destruction commeth, and they
shall seeke peace, and *there shall be* none.
26 Mischiefe shall come vpon mischiefe, and rumour shall be vpon rumour, then shall they seeke a vision of
the prophet: but the law shall perish
from the priest, and counsell from the
ancients.
27 The king shall mourne, and the
prince shall be clothed with desolation,
and the hands of the people of the land
shall be troubled: I will doe vnto
them after their way, and †according to
their deserts will I iudge them, and
they shall know that I *am* the LORD.

† Heb. *for a separation or vncleannesse.*
* Prou. 11. 4. zeph. 1. 18. ecclus. 5. 8.
|| Or, *because their iniquitie is their stumbling blocke.*
|| Or, *made it vnto them an vncleane thing.*
|| Or, *burglers.*
|| Or, *they shall inherit their holy places.*
† Heb. *cutting off.*
† Heb. *with their iudgements.*

CHAP. VIII.

1 Ezekiel in a vision of God, at Ierusalem, 5 is shewed the image of Ielousie. 7 The chambers of Imagery. 13 The mourners for Tammuz, 15 the worshippers towards the Sunne. 18 Gods wrath for their idolatry.

AND it came to passe in the
sixt yeere, in the sixt *moneth*,
in the fift *day* of the month,
as I sate in mine house,
and the elders of Iudah
sate before me; that the hand of the
Lord GOD fell there vpon me.
2 Then I beheld, and loe, a likenesse as the appearance of fire: from the
appearance of his loines euen downeward, fire: and from his loines euen
vpward, as the appearance of brightnesse, as the colour of amber.
3 And he *put forth the forme of an
hand, and tooke me by a locke of mine
head, and the spirit lift me vp betweene
the earth and the heauen, and brought
me in the visions of God to Ierusalem,
to the doore of the inner gate, that looketh toward the North, where *was* the
seate of the image of ielousie, which prouoketh to ielousie.
4 And behold, the glory of the God
of Israel *was* there according to the vision that I *saw in the plaine.
5 ¶ Then said he vnto me, Sonne
of man, lift vp thine eyes now the way
towards the North: so I lift vp mine
eyes the way toward the North, and
behold, Northward at the gate of the
altar, this image of ielousie in the entry.
6 He said furthermore vnto me,
Sonne of man, seest thou what they
doe? *euen* the great abominations that
the house of Israel committeth heere,
that I should goe farre off from my
sanctuarie? but turne thee yet againe,
and thou shalt see greater abominations.
7 ¶ And hee brought me to the
doore of the court, and when I looked,
behold a hole in the wall.
8 Then said he vnto me, Sonne of
man, digge now in the wall: and when
I had digged in the wall, behold a
doore.
9 And he said vnto me, Goe in, and
behold the wicked abominations that
they doe heere.
10 So I went in and saw, and behold euery forme of creeping things,
and abominable beasts, and all the idols
of the house of Israel purtrayed vpon
the wall round about.
11 And there stood before them seuentie men of the ancients of the house of
Israel, and in the middest of them stood
Iaazaniah the sonne of Shaphan,
with euery man his censer in his hand,
and a thicke cloud of incense went vp.
12 Then said he vnto me, Sonne of
man, hast thou seene what the ancients
of the house of Israel doe in the darke,
euery man in the chambers of his imagery? for they say, *The LORD seeth
vs not, the LORD hath forsaken the
earth.

* Dan. 5
* Chap. 23.
* Chap

13 ¶ Hee said also vnto me, Turne thee yet againe, *and* thou shalt see greater abominations that they doe.

14 Then he brought me to the doore of the gate of the LORDS house which *was* towards the North, and behold, there sate women weeping for Tammuz.

15 ¶ Then said hee vnto me, Hast thou seene *this*, O sonne of man? Turne thee yet againe, *and* thou shalt see greater abominations then these.

16 And he brought me into the inner court of the LORDS house, and behold at the doore of the Temple of the LORD, betweene the porch and the altar, *were* about fiue and twentie men, with their backes toward the temple of the LORD, and their faces towards the East, and they worshipped the sunne towards the East.

17 ¶ Then he said vnto me, Hast thou seene *this*, O sonne of man? ‖Is it a light thing to the house of Iudah, that they commit the abominations, which they commit heere? for they haue filled the land with violence, and haue returned to prouoke me to anger : and loe, they put the branch to their nose.

18 Therefore will I also deale in furie : mine *eye shall not spare, neither will I haue pitie : and though they *crie in mine eares with a loud voyce, *yet* will I not heare them.

CHAP. IX.

1 A vision whereby is shewed the preseruation of some, 5 and the destruction of the rest. 8 God cannot be intreated for them.

Ee cryed also in mine eares, with a loude voyce, saying ; Cause them that haue charge ouer the citie, to draw neere, euen euery man *with* his destroying weapon in his hand.

2 And behold, sixe men came from the way of the higher gate, †which lyeth toward the North, and euery man a †slaughter weapon in his hand : and one man among them was clothed with linnen, with a writers inkehorne †by his side, and they went in and stood beside the brasen altar.

3 And the glory of the God of Israel was gone vp from the Cherub whereupon hee was, to the threshold of the house, and he called to the man clothed

with linnen, which *had* the writers inkehorne by his side.

4 And the LORD sayd vnto him, Goe through the middest of the citie, through the middest of Ierusalem, and set +*a marke vpon the foreheads of the men that sigh, and that cry for all the abominations, that bee done in the middest thereof.

5 ¶ And to the *others* he said in †mine hearing, Goe ye after him through the citie, and smite : let not your eye spare, neither haue ye pitie.

6 Slay †vtterly olde *and* yong ; both maides, and litle children, and women : but come not neere any man vpon whom *is* the marke, and begin at my sanctuary : then they began at the ancient men which *were* before the house.

7 And hee sayd vnto them, Defile the house, and fill the courts with the slaine, goe ye forth : and they went forth and slew in the citie.

8 ¶ And it came to passe while they were slaying them, and I was left, that I fell vpon my face, and cryed and said, Ah, Lord GOD, wilt thou destroy all the residue of Israel, in thy powring out of thy fury vpon Ierusalem ?

9 Then sayd he vnto me ; The iniquity of the house of Israel and Iudah *is* exceeding great, and the land is †full of blood, and the citie full of ‖peruersenesse : for they say ; *The LORD hath forsaken the earth, and the LORD seeth not.

10 And as for me also, mine *eye shal not spare, neither will I haue pitie, *but* I will recompence their way vpon their head.

11 And behold, the man clothed with linnen, which *had* the inkehorne by his side, †reported the matter, saying ; I haue done as thou hast commanded me.

CHAP. X.

1 The vision of the coales of fire, to bee scattered ouer the citie. 8 The vision of the Cherubims.

Hen I looked, and beholde, in the *firmament that *was* aboue the head of the Cherubims, there appeared ouer them as *it were* a Saphir stone, as the appearance of the likenesse of a throne.

2 And hee spake vnto the man clothed with linnen, and sayd, Goe in betweene the wheeles, *euen* vnder the Cherub,

---

Marginal notes (left column):

r, is there y thing hter then commit ?

Chap. 5. and 7. 4.
Pro. 1. 28.
. 15.
. 11. 11.
ch. 7. 4.

Heb. which turned.

Heb. a weapon of his eaking in nces.

Heb. vpon loines.

Marginal notes (right column):

† Heb. *marke a marke.*
* Exod. 12. 7.
reuel. 7. 3.

† Heb. *mine eares.*

† Hebr. *to destruction.*

† Heb. *filled with.*
‖ Or, *wresting of ludgement.*
* Cha. 8. 12.

* Cha. 5. 11. and 7. 4. & 8. 18.

† Heb. *returned the word.*

* Cha. 1. 22.

† *Heb. the hollow of thine hand.*

rub, and †fill thine hand with coales of fire from betweene the Cherubims, and scatter them ouer the city. And he went in my sight.

3 Now the Cherubims stood on the right side of the house, when the man went in, and the cloud filled the inner court.

† *Hebr. was lifted vp.*

4 Then the glory of the LORD †went vp from the Cherub, *and stood* ouer the threshold of the house, and the house was filled with the cloud, and the court was full of the brightnesse of the LORDS glory.

* *Chap. 1. 24.*

5 And the *sound of the Cherubims wings was heard euen to the vtter court, as the voice of the Almighty God when he speaketh.

6 And it came to passe *that* when he had commanded the man clothed with linnen, saying ; Take fire from betweene the wheeles, from betweene the Cherubims ; then he went in and stood beside the wheeles.

† *Hebr. sent foorth.*

7 And one Cherub †stretched forth his hand from betweene the Cherubims vnto the fire that *was* betweene the Cherubims : and tooke *thereof,* and put it into the handes of him that was clothed with linnen, who tooke it, and went out.

8 ¶ And there appeared in the Cherubims, the forme of a mans hand vnder their wings.

9 And when I looked, behold the foure wheeles by the Cherubims, one wheele by one Cherub, and an other wheele by an other Cherub : and the appearance of the wheeles *was* as the

* *Chap. 1. 16.*

colour of a *Berill stone.

10 And as for their appearances, they foure *had* one likenes, as if a wheele had bene in the midst of a wheele.

11 When they went, they went vpon their foure sides ; they turned not as they went, but to the place whither the head looked, they followed it ; they turned not as they went.

† *Hebr. flesh.*

12 And their whole †body, and their backes, and their handes, and their wings, and the wheeles, *were* ful of eyes round about, *euen* the wheeles that they foure *had.*

‖ *Or, they were called in my hearing, wheele, or Galgal.*

13 As for the wheeles, ‖it was cried vnto them in my hearing, O wheele.

14 And euery one *had* foure faces : the first face *was* the face of a Cherub, and the second face *was* the face of a man, and the third the face of a lion, and

the fourth the face of an eagle.

15 And the Cherubims were lifted vp, this *is* the liuing creature that I saw by the riuer of Chebar.

16 And when the Cherubims went, the wheeles went by them : and when the Cherubims lift vp their wings, to mount vp from the earth, the same wheels also turned not frō beside them.

17 When they stood, *these* stood, and when they were lifted vp, *these* lift vp themselues *also* : for the spirit of the ‖liuing creature *was* in them.

‖ *Or, of life.*

18 Then the glory of the LORD departed from off the threshold of the house, and stood ouer the Cherubims.

19 And the Cherubims lift vp their wings, and mounted vp from the earth in my sight : when they went out, the wheeles also *were* besides them, and euery one stood at the doore of the East gate of the LORDS house, and the glorie of the God of Israel *was* ouer them aboue.

20 This *is* the liuing creature that I saw vnder the God of Israel, by the riuer of Chebar, and I knew that they *were* the Cherubims.

21 Euery one had foure faces a piece, and euery one foure wings, and the likenesse of the handes of a man *was* vnder their wings.

22 And the likenesse of their faces *was* the same faces which I saw by the riuer of Chebar, their appearances and themselues : they went euery one straight forward.

CHAP. XI.

1 The presumption of the Princes. 4 Their sinne and iudgement. 13 Ezekiel complaining, God sheweth him his purpose in sauing a remnant, 21 and punishing the wicked. 22 The Glory of God leaueth the Citie. 24 Ezekiel is returned to the captiuitie.

Oreouer the Spirit lift me vp, and brought me vnto the East gate of the LORDS house, which looketh Eastward : and behold at the doore of the gate fiue and twenty men ; among whom I saw Iaazaniah the sonne of Azur, and Pelatiah the sonne of Benaiah, Princes of the people.

2 Then said he vnto me ; Sonne of man, these *are* the men that deuise mischiefe, & giue wicked counsel in this city.

3 Which say, It ‖*is* not *neere, let vs build

‖ *Or, it is not for vs to build house neere.*
* 2. Pet. 3.

build houses: this *citie is* the caldron, and we be the flesh.

4 ¶ Therefore prophecie against them, prophecie, O ſonne of man.

5 And the Spirit of the LORD fell vpon me, and said vnto me, Speake, thus ſaith the LORD; Thus haue ye said, O house of Israel : for I know the things that come into your minde, euery one *of them.*

6 Ye haue multiplyed your slaine in this citie, and yee haue filled the streetes thereof with the slaine.

7 Therefore thus sayth the Lord GOD; Your slaine whom ye haue laid in the middest of it, they *are* the flesh, and this *citie is* the cauldron : but I wil bring you foorth out of the middest of it.

8 Ye haue feared the sword, and I will bring a sword vpon you, saith the Lord GOD.

9 And I will bring you out of the middest thereof, and deliuer you into the hands of strangers, and will execute iudgements among you.

10 Yee shall fall by the sword, I will iudge you in the border of Israel, and ye shall know that I *am* the LORD.

11 This *citie* shall not be your cauldron, neither shall ye be the flesh in the middest thereof, *but* I will iudge you in the border of Israel.

12 And ye shall know that I *am* the LORD: for ||yee haue not walked in my statutes, neither executed my iudgements, but haue done after the maners of the heathen that *are* round about you.

13 ¶ And it came to passe, when I prophecied, that Pelatiah the sonne of Benaiah died : then fell I downe vpon my face, and cried with a loud voice, and said; Ah Lord GOD, wilt thou make a full end of the remnant of Israel ?

14 Againe the word of the LORD came vnto me, saying;

15 Sonne of man, thy brethren, *euen* thy brethren, the men of thy kinred, and all the house of Israel wholly *are they,* vnto whom the inhabitants of Ierusalem haue sayd ; Get yee farre from the LORD : vnto vs is this land giuen in possession.

16 Therefore say, Thus sayth the Lord GOD; Although I haue cast them farre off among the heathen, and although I haue scattered them among the countreys, yet will I be to them as a little Sanctuarie in the countreys where they shall come.

Or, which haue not walked.

17 Therefore say, Thus saith the Lord GOD; I will euen gather you from the people, and assemble you out of the countreys where ye haue beene scattered, and I will giue you the land of Israel.

18 And they shall come thither, and they shall take away all the detestable things thereof, and all the abominations thereof from thence.

19 And *I will giue them one heart, and I wil put a new spirit within you: and I will take the stonie heart out of their flesh, and will giue them an heart of flesh,

* Ier. 31. 39. cha. 36. 26.

20 That they may walke in my statutes, and keepe mine ordinances, and doe them : and they shall be my people, and I will be their God.

21 But *as for them* whose heart walketh after the heart of their detestable things, and their abominations, I wil recompense their way vpon their owne heads, saith the Lord GOD.

22 ¶ Then did the Cherubims lift vp their wings, and the wheeles besides them, and the glory of the God of Israel *was* ouer them aboue.

23 And the glory of the LORD went vp from the middest of the citie, and stood vpon the mountaine, which *is* on the East side of the citie.

24 ¶ Afterwards the spirit tooke me vp, and brought me in vision by the spirit of God into Caldea to them of the captiuity : so the vision that I had seene, went vp from me.

25 Then I spake vnto them of the captiuity, all the things that the LORD had shewed me.

CHAP. XII.

1 The type of Ezekiels remouing. 8 It shewed the captiuitie of Zedekiah. 17 Ezekiels trembling sheweth the Iewes desolation. 21 The Iewes presumptuous prouerbe is reproued. 26 The speedinesse of the Vision.

 He word of the LORD also came vnto me, saying; 2 Sonne of man, thou dwellest in the middest of a rebellious house, which haue eyes to see, and see not : they haue eares to heare, and heare not : for they *are* a rebellious house.

3 Therefore thou ſonne of man, prepare thee ||stuffe for remoouing, and remooue by day in their sight, and thou shalt

Or, instruments.

shalt remoue from thy place to another place in their sight; it may be they will consider , though they *bee* a rebellious house.

4 Then shalt thou bring foorth thy stuffe by day in their sight, as stuffe for remoouing : and thou shalt goe foorth at euen in their sight, † as they that goe foorth iuto captiuitie.

† *Heb. as the goings foorth of captiuity.*
† *Hebr. digge for thee.*

5 † Digge thou through the wall in their sight, and cary out thereby.

6 In their sight shalt thou beare it vpon *thy* shoulders, *and* cary *it* foorth in the twy light : thou shalt couer thy face, that thou see not the ground : for I haue set thee for a signe vnto the house of Israel.

7 And I did so as I was commanded : I brought forth my stuffe by day, as stuffe for captiuity, and in the euen I †digged through the wall with mine hand, I brought *it* foorth in the twy light, *and* I bare *it* vpon *my* shoulder in their sight.

† *Heb. digged for me.*

8 ¶ And in the morning came the word of the LORD vnto me, saying,

9 Sonne of man, hath not the house of Israel, the rebellious house, sayd vnto thee , What doest thou ?

10 Say thou vnto them; Thus saith the Lord GOD; This burden *concerneth* the Prince in Ierusalem, and all the house of Israel that *are* among them.

11 Say, I *am* your signe: like as I haue done, so shall it be done vnto them: †they shall remoue *and* goe into captiuitie.

† *Heb. by removing goe into captiuitie.*

12 And the Prince that *is* among them, shall beare vpon his shoulder in the twylight, and shall goe forth : they shall digge through the wall to cary out thereby : he shall couer his face, that he see not the ground with *his* eyes.

13 My *net also will I spread vpon him, and he shall be taken in my snare, and I wil bring him to Babylon to the land of the Caldeans, yet shall hee not see it, though he shall die there.

* *Chap. 17. 20.*

14 And I will scatter toward euery winde all that are about him to helpe him, and all his bands, and I wil draw out the sword after them.

15 And they shall know that I *am* the LORD, when I shal scatter them among the nations, and disperse them in the countreys.

16 But I will leaue † a few men of them from the sword, from the famine,

† *Heb. men of number.*

and from the pestilence, that they may declare all their abominations among the heathen whither they come , and they shall know that I *am* the LORD.

17 ¶ Moreouer , the worde of the LORD came to me, saying;

18 Sonne of man , eate thy bread with quaking , and drinke thy water with trembling and with carefulnesse,

19 And say vnto the people of the land ; Thus sayth the Lord GOD, of the inhabitants of Ierusalem, and of the land of Israel ; They shall eat their bread with carefulnes, and drinke their water with astonishment, that her land may be desolate from †all that is therein, because of the violence of them that dwell therein.

† *Heb. the fulnesse thereof.*

20 And the cities that are inhabited, shall be laid waste, and the land shall be desolate, and yee shall know that I *am* the LORD.

21 ¶ And the word of the LORD came vnto me, saying ;

22 Sonne of man, what *is* that prouerbe, that ye haue in the land of Israel, saying ; The dayes are prolonged, and euery vision faileth ?

23 Tell them therefore, Thus sayth the Lord GOD ; I will make this prouerbe to cease, and they shall no more vse it as a prouerbe in Israel : but say vnto them, The dayes are at hand, and the effect of euery vision.

24 For there shall bee no more any vaine vision , nor flattering diuination, within the house of Israel.

25 For I *am* the LORD : I will speake, & the word that I shall speake, shall come to passe : it shall be no more prolonged : for in your dayes, O rebellious house , will I say the word, and will performe it, sayth the Lord GOD.

26 ¶ Againe the word of the LORD came to me, saying ;

27 Sonne of man, behold, *they of* the house of Israel say ; The vision that he seeth *is* * for many dayes *to come*, and he prophecieth of the times that are far off.

*2. Pet. 3. ♦

28 Therefore say vnto them, Thus saith the Lord GOD, There shal none of my words be prolonged any more, but the worde which I haue spoken, shall be done, sayth the Lord GOD.

CHAP. XIII.

And

A ND the worde of the LORD came vnto mee, saying;

2 Sonne of man, prophecie against the Prophets of Israel that prophecie, and say thou vnto them that † prophecie out of their owne * hearts, Heare ye the word of the LORD.

3 Thus saith the Lord GOD; Woe vnto the foolish prophets, that † follow their owne spirit, ‖ and haue seene nothing.

4 O Israel, thy prophets *are* like the foxes in the deserts.

5 Yee haue not gone vp into the ‖ gaps, neither † made vp the hedge for the house of Israel, to stand in the battell in the day of the LORD.

6 They haue seene vanity, and lying diuination, saying; The LORD saith, and the LORD hath not sent them : and they haue made *others* to hope, that they would confirme the word.

7 Haue ye not seene a vaine vision, and haue ye not spoken a lying diuination, whereas yee say, The LORD sayth *it*, albeit I haue not spoken ?

8 Therefore thus saith the Lord GOD; Because ye haue spoken vanity and seene lyes, therefore behold, I *am* against you, saith the Lord GOD.

9 And mine hand shall be vpon the Prophets that see vanitie, and that diuine lyes : they shall not bee in the ‖ assembly of my people, neither shall they be written in the writing of the house of Israel, neither shall they enter into the land of Israel, and ye shall know that I *am* the Lord GOD.

10 ¶ Because, euen because they haue seduced my people, saying; * Peace, and *there was* no peace : and one built vp a ‖ wall, and loe, others dawbed it with vntempered morter,

11 Say vnto them which dawbe *it* with vntempered *morter*, that it shall fall : there shall bee an ouerflowing showre, and yee, O great haile stones, shal fall, and a stormie wind shal rent *it*.

12 Loe, when the wall is fallen, shall it not bee sayde vnto you; Where *is* the dawbing wherwith ye haue dawbed *it?*

13 Therefore thus sayth the Lord GOD; I will euen rent *it* with a stormie wind in my fury: and there shall be an ouerflowing showre in mine anger, and great hailestones in *my* fury, to consume *it*.

14 So wil I breake downe the wall that ye haue dawbed with vntempered *morter*, & bring it downe to the ground, so that the foundation thereof shall be discouered, and it shall fall, and ye shall be consumed in the middest thereof: and ye shall know that I *am* the LORD.

15 Thus will I accomplish my wrath vpon the wall, and vpon them that haue dawbed it with vntempered *morter*, and will say vnto you; The wall *is* no *more*, neither they that dawbed it:

16 *To wit*, the Prophets of Israel which prophecie concerning Ierusalem, and which see visions of peace for her, and *there is* no peace, sayth the Lord GOD.

17 ¶ Likewise thou sonne of man, set thy face against the daughters of thy people; which prophecie out of their owne heart, and prophecie thou against them,

18 And say, Thus saith the Lord GOD; Woe to the *women* that sow pillowes to all ‖ arme holes, and make kerchiefes vpon the head of euery stature to hunt soules : Will ye hunt the soules of my people, and will yee saue the soules aliue *that come* vnto you?

19 And will yee pollute me among my people for handfuls of barley, and for pieces of bread, to slay the soules that should not die, and to saue the soules aliue that should not liue, by your lying to my people that heare *your* lyes?

20 Wherefore thus sayth the Lord GOD, Behold, I *am* against your pillowes, wherewith yee there hunt the soules to make ‖ *them* flie, and I will teare them from your armes, and will let the soules goe, *euen* the soules that ye hunt to make them flie.

21 Your kerchiefes also will I teare, and deliuer my people out of your hand, and they shalbe no more in your hand to be hunted, and yee shall know that I *am* the LORD.

22 Because with lyes yee haue made the heart of the righteous sad whom I haue not made sad; and strengthened the hands of the wicked, that hee should not returne from his wicked way ‖ by promising him life :

23 Therefore yee shall see no more vanitie, nor diuine diuinations, for I will deliuer my people out of your hand, and ye shall knowe that I *am* the LORD.

CHAP.

† Heb. them that are prophets out of their owne hearts.

* Ier. 23. 16.

† Heb. walke after.

‖ Or, and things which they haue not seene.

‖ Or, breaches.

† Heb. hedged the hedge.

‖ Or, secret or counsell.

* Ier. 6. 14.

‖ Or, a sleight wall.

‖ Or, elbowes.

‖ Or, into gardens.

‖ Or, that I should saue his life. Hebr. by quickning him.

CHAP. XIIII.

1 God answereth idolaters according to their owne heart. 6 They are exhorted to repent, for feare of iudgements, by meanes of seduced prophets. 12 Gods irreuocable sentence of famine, 15 of noisome beasts, 17 of the sword, 19 and of pestilence. 22 A remnant shalbe reserued for example of others.

Hen came certaine of the Elders of Israel vnto me, and sate before me.

2 And the word of the LORD came vnto me, saying,

3 Sonne of man, these men haue set vp their idoles in their heart, and put the stumbling blocke of their iniquitie before their face: should I be enquired of at all by them?

4 Therefore speake vnto them, and say vnto them, Thus saith the Lord GOD; Euery man of the house of Israel that setteth vp his idoles in his heart, and putteth the stumbling blocke of his iniquitie before his face, and commeth to the Prophet, I the LORD will answere him that commeth, according to the multitude of his idoles,

5 That I may take the house of Israel in their owne heart, because they are all estranged from mee through their idoles.

6 ¶ Therefore say vnto the house of Israel, Thus saith the Lord GOD, Repent, and turne || your selues from your idoles, and turne away your faces from all your abominations.

margin: || Or, others.

7 For euery one of the house of Israel, or of the stranger that soiourneth in Israel, which separateth himselfe from me, and setteth vp his idols in his heart, and putteth the stumbling blocke of his iniquitie before his face, and commeth to a prophet to enquire of him concerning me, I the LORD will answere him by my selfe.

8 And I wil set my face against that man, and will make him a *signe and a prouerbe, and I will cut him off from the midst of my people, and yee shall know that I am the LORD.

*margin: * Deut. 28. 37. chap. 5. 15.*

9 And if the prophet bee deceiued when hee hath spoken a thing, I the LORD *haue deceiued that prophet, and I will stretch out my hand vpon him, and will destroy him from the midst of my people Israel.

*margin: * 1. Kings. 22. 23.*

10 And they shall beare the punishment of their iniquitie : the punishment of the prophet shall bee euen as the punishment of him that seeketh vnto him:

11 That the house of Israel may goe no more astray from me, neither be polluted any more with all their transgressions; but that they may be my people, and I may bee their God, sayeth the Lord GOD.

12 ¶ The word of the LORD came againe to me, saying,

13 Sonne of man, when the land sinneth against mee by trespassing grieuously, then will I stretch out mine hand vpon it, and will breake the *staffe of the bread thereof, and will send famine vpon it, and will cut off man and beast from it.

*margin: * Leuit. 26. 26. chap. 4. 16. and 5. 26.*

14 * Though these three men, Noah, Daniel and Iob were in it, they should deliuer but their owne soules by their righteousnes, saith the Lord GOD.

*margin: * Iere. 15. 1.*

15 ¶ If I cause noisome beastes to passe through the land, and they ||spoile it, so that it bee desolate, that no man may passe through because of the beasts:

margin: || Or, bereaue.

16 Though these three men were † in it, as I liue, saith the Lord GOD, they shall deliuer neither sonnes nor daughters: they onely shalbe deliuered, but the land shalbe desolate.

margin: † Hebr. in the midst of it.

17 ¶ Or if I bring a sword vpon that land, and say, Sword, goe through the lande, so that I cut off man and beast from it :

18 Though these three men were in it, as I liue, saith the Lord GOD, they shall deliuer neither sonnes nor daughter, but they onely shall bee deliuered themselues.

19 ¶ Or if I send a pestilence into that land, and powre out my fury vpon it in blood, to cut off from it man and beast :

20 Though Noah, Daniel and Iob were in it, as I liue, saith the Lord God, they shal deliuer neither son nor daughter : they shall but deliuer their owne soules by their righteousnes.

21 For thus saith the Lord GOD, ||How much more when I send my foure sore iudgements vpon Ierusalem ; the sword, and the famine, and the noisome beast, and the pestilence, to cut off from it man and beast ?

margin: || Or, also when.

22 ¶ Yet behold, therein shalbe left a remnant that shalbe brought foorth, both sonnes and daughters : behold, they shall come foorth vnto you, and ye shall see their way and their doings : and

and ye shalbe comforted concerning the euill that I haue brought vpon Ierusalem, *euen* concerning all that I haue brought vpon it.

23 And they shall comfort you when yee see their wayes and their doings: and ye shal know that I haue not done without cause, all that I haue done in it, saith the Lord God.

CHAP. XV.

1 By the vnfitnesse of the Vine branch for any worke, 16 is shewed the reiection of Ierusalē.

Nd the word of ỹ Lord came vnto me, saying; 2 Sonne of man, What is the Vine tree more then any tree, or *then* a branch which is among the trees of the forrest?

3 Shall wood bee taken thereof to doe any worke? or, will men take a pin of it, to hang any vessell thereon?

† *Heb. will it prosper?*

4 Behold, it is cast into the fire for fewell: the fire deuoureth both the ends of it, and the middest of it is burnt. †Is it meete for *any* worke?

† *Heb. made fit.*

5 Behold, when it was whole it was †meete for no worke: how much lesse shall it be meete yet for any worke, when the fire hath deuoured it, and it is burned?

6 ¶ Therefore thus saith the Lord God; As the Vine tree among the trees of the forrest, which I haue giuen to the fire for fewell, so will I giue the inhabitants of Ierusalem.

7 And I will set my face against them, they shall goe out from *one* fire, and *another* fire shall deuoure them, and ye shall know that I *am* the Lord, when I set my face against them.

† *Heb. tres-passed a tres-passe.*

8 And I will make the land deso-late, because they haue †committed a trespasse, saith the Lord God.

CHAP. XVI.

1 Vnder the similitude of a wretched infant, is shewed the naturall state of Ierusalem. 6 Gods extraordinarie loue towards her. 15 Her monstrous whoredome. 35 Her grie-uous Iudgement. 44 Her sinne, matching her mother, and exceeding her sisters, So-dome and Samaria, calleth for Iudgements. 60 Mercy is promised her in the end.

Gaine the worde of the Lord came vnto me, say-ing; 2 Son of man, cause Ie-rusalem to know her abominations,

3 And say, Thus saith the Lord God vnto Ierusalem; Thy †birth and thy natiuitie *is* of the land of Ca-naan, thy father *was* an Amorite, and thy mother an Hittite.

† *Heb. out-ting out, or habitation.*

4 And as for thy natiuity in the day thou wast borne, thy nauell was not cut, neither wast thou washed in water to ‖supple thee: thou wast not salted at all, nor swadled at all.

‖ *Or, when I looked vpon thee.*

5 None eye pitied thee to doe any of these vnto thee, to haue compassion vp-on thee, but thou wast cast out in the o-pen field, to the lothing of thy person, in the day that thou wast borne.

6 ¶ And when I passed by thee, and saw thee ‖polluted in thine owne blood, I said vnto thee *when thou wast* in thy blood, Liue: yea I said vnto thee *when thou wast* in thy blood, Liue.

‖ *Or, troden vnder foot.*

7 I haue †caused thee to multiply as the bud of the field, and thou hast in-creased and waxen great, and thou art come to †excellent ornaments: *thy* breasts are fashioned, and thine haire is growen, whereas thou *wast* naked and bare.

† *Heb. made thee a mil-lion.*

† *Heb. orna-mento fornaments.*

8 Now when I passed by thee, and looked vpon thee, behold, thy time *was* the time of loue, and I spread my skirt ouer thee, and couered thy nakednesse: yea, I sware vnto thee, and entred into a couenant with thee, sayth the Lord God, and thou becamest mine.

9 Then washed I thee with water: yea, I throughly washed away thy †blood from thee, and I anointed thee with oyle.

† *Heb. bloods.*

10 I clothed thee also with broidred worke, & shod thee with badgers skin, and I girded thee about with fine linen, and I couered thee with silke.

11 I decked thee also with orna-ments, and I put bracelets vpon thine hands, and a chaine on thy necke.

12 And I put a iewell on thy fore-head, and eare-rings in thine eares, and a beautifull crowne vpon thine head.

13 Thus wast thou decked with gold and siluer, and thy raiment *was* of fine linen & silke, and broidered worke, thou didst eate fine floure and honie and oyle, and thou wast exceeding beautiful, and thou didst prosper into a kingdome.

14 And thy renowme went foorth among the heathen for thy beautie: for it *was* perfect through my comelinesse which I had put vpon thee, sayth the Lord God.

15 ¶ But

15 ¶ But thou diddest trust in thine owne beauty, and playedst the harlot, because of thy renowne, and powredst out thy fornications on euery one that passed by; his it was.

16 And of thy garments thou diddest take, and deckedst thy high places with diuers colours, and playedst the harlot thereupon : *the like* things shall not come, neither shall it be *so.*

17 Thou hast also taken thy faire iewels of my gold and of my siluer, which I had giuen thee, and madest to thy selfe images † of men, and diddest commit whoredome with them,

† Heb. of a male.

18 And tookest thy broidered garments and coueredst them : and thou hast set mine oyle and mine incense before them.

19 My meate also which I gaue thee, fine flowre, and oyle, and honie *wherewith* I fed thee, thou hast euen set it before them for a † sweete sauour : and *thus* it was, saith the Lord God.

† Heb. a sauour of rest.

20 Moreouer thou hast taken thy sonnes and thy daughters, whom thou hast borne vnto me, and these hast thou sacrificed vnto them † to be deuoured : *is this* of thy whoredomes a small matter,

† Heb. to deuoure.

21 That thou hast slaine my children, and deliuered them to cause them to passe through *the fire* for them?

22 And in all thine abominations and thy whooredomes, thou hast not remembred the dayes of thy youth, when thou wast naked and bare, *and* wast polluted in thy blood.

23 And it came to passe after all thy wickednesse (woe, woe vnto thee, saith the Lord God.)

24 *That* thou hast also built vnto thee an ‖ eminent place, and hast made thee an high place in euery streete.

‖ Or, brothell house.

25 Thou hast built thy high place at euery head of the way, and hast made thy beauty to be abhorred, and hast opened thy feete to euery one that passed by, and multiplied thy whooredomes.

26 Thou hast also committed fornication with the Egyptians thy neighbours great of flesh, & hast increased thy whooredomes, to prouoke me to anger.

27 Behold therefore, I haue stretched out my hand ouer thee, and haue diminished thine ordinarie *foode,* and deliuered thee vnto the will of them that hate thee, the ‖ daughters of the Philistines, which are ashamed of thy lewd way.

‖ Or, cities.

28 Thou hast played the whoore also with the Assyrians, because thou wast vnsatiable : yea thou hast played the harlot with them, and yet couldest not be satisfied.

29 Thou hast moreouer multiplied thy fornication in the land of Canaan vnto Caldea, and yet thou wast not satisfied heerewith.

30 How weake is thine heart, saith the Lord God, seeing thou doest all these things, the work of an imperious whorish woman?

31 In ‖ that thou buildest thine eminent place in the head of euery way, and makest thine high place in euery streete, and hast not beene as an harlot, in that thou scornest hire :

‖ Or, in thy daughters is thine &c.

32 *But as* a wife that committeth adulterie, *which* taketh strangers in steede of her husband.

33 They giue gifts to all whores, but thou giuest thy gifts to all thy louers, and † hyrest them, that they may come vnto thee on euery side for thy whoredome.

† Heb. bribest.

34 And the contrary is in thee from *other* women in thy whoredomes, whereas none followeth thee to commit whoredomes : and in that thou giuest a reward, and no reward is giuen vnto thee : therefore thou art contrary.

35 ¶ Wherefore, O harlot, heare the word of the Lord.

36 Thus saith the Lord God, Because thy filthinesse was powred out, and thy nakednesse discouered through thy whoredomes with thy louers, and with all the idols of thy abominations, and by the blood of thy children, which thou diddest giue vnto them,

37 Behold therefore, I will gather all thy louers, with whom thou hast taken pleasure, and all them that thou hast loued, with all them that thou hast hated : I will euen gather them round about against thee, and will discouer thy nakednesse vnto them, that they may see all thy nakednesse.

38 And I will iudge thee, † as women that breake wedlocke and shead blood are iudged, and I will giue thee blood in fury and iealousie.

† Heb. with iudgements of.

39 And I will also giue thee into their hand, and they shal throw downe thine eminent place, and shall breake downe thy high places : they shall strip thee also of thy clothes, and shall take thy

*Heb.instru-
nents of
hine orna-
ment.*

thy †faire iewels, and leaue thee naked and bare.

40 They shall also bring vp a companie against thee, and they shall stone thee with stones, and thrust thee thorough with their swords.

*2. Kings.
25. 9. ier. 52
3.*

41 And they shall *burne thine houses with fire, and execute iudgements vpon thee in the sight of many women: and I wil cause thee to cease from playing the harlot, and thou also shalt giue no hire any more.

42 So will I make my fury towards thee to rest, and my iealousie shall depart from thee, and I will be quiet, and will be no more angry.

43 Because thou hast not remembred the dayes of thy youth, but hast fretted mee in all these things; behold therefore, I also will recompence thy way vpon *thine* head, saith the Lord God: and thou shalt not commit this lewdnesse, aboue all thine abominations.

44 ¶ Behold, euery one that vseth prouerbs, shall vse *this* prouerbe against thee, saying, As *is* the mother, *so is* her daughter.

45 Thou *art* thy mothers daughter, that lotheth her husband and her children, and thou *art* the sister of thy sisters which lothed their husbands, and their children : your mother *was* an Hittite, and your father an Amorite.

*Heb. lesser
hen thou.*

46 And thine elder sister *is* Samaria, she and her daughters, that dwell at thy left hand : and thy †younger sister that dwelleth at thy right hand, *is* Sodom and her daughters.

*Or, that
was lothed
as a small
hing.*

47 Yet hast thou not walked after their wayes, nor done after their abominations: but as *if* ‖ *that were* a very litle *thing*, thou wast corrupted more then they in all thy wayes.

48 As I liue, saith the Lord God, Sodom thy sister hath not done, she nor her daughters, as thou hast done, thou and thy daughters.

49 Behold, this was the iniquitie of thy sister Sodom ; Pride, fulnesse of bread, and aboundance of idlenesse was in her and in her daughters, neither did she strengthen the hand of the poore and needy.

*Gen. 19.
24.*

50 And they were hautie, and committed abomination before me : *therefore I tooke them away, as I saw *good*.

51 Neither hath Samaria committed halfe of thy sinnes, but thou hast multiplied thine abominations more then they, and hast iustified thy sisters in all thine abominations, which thou hast done.

52 Thou also which hast iudged thy sisters, beare thine owne shame for thy sinnes, that thou hast committed more abominable then they : they are more righteous then thou : yea be thou confounded also, and beare thy shame, in that thou hast iustified thy sisters.

53 When I shall bring againe their captiuitie, the captiuitie of Sodom and her daughters, and the captiuitie of Samaria and her daughters, then *will I bring againe* the captiuity of thy captiues in the midst of them ;

54 That thou mayest beare thine owne shame, and mayest be confounded in all that thou hast done, in that thou art a comfort vnto them.

55 When thy sisters, Sodom and her daughters shal returne to their former estate, and Samaria and her daughters shall returne to their former estate, then thou and thy daughters shall returne to your former estate.

56 For thy sister Sodom was not †mentioned by thy mouth in the day of thy †pride ;

*† Heb. for a
report or
hearing.
† Heb. prides
or excellen-
cies.*

57 Before thy wickednesse was discouered, as at the time of thy reproch of the daughters of † Syria, and all *that are* round about her, the daughters of the Philistines which ‖ despise thee round about.

*‡ Heb. A-
ram.
‖ Or spoile.*

58 Thou hast †borne thy lewdnesse, and thine abominations, saith the Lord.

*† Heb. borne
them.*

59 For thus saith the Lord God ; I will euen deale with thee as thou hast done, which hast despised the oath in breaking the couenant.

60 ¶ Neuerthelesse I will remember my couenant with thee in the dayes of thy youth, and I will establish vnto thee an euerlasting couenant.

61 Then thou shalt remember thy wayes and be ashamed, when thou shalt receiue thy sisters, thine elder and thy younger, and I will giue them vnto thee for *daughters, but not by thy couenant.

Gal. 4. 26.

62 And I will establish my couenant with thee, and thou shalt know that I *am* the Lord :

63 That thou mayest remember, and bee confounded, and neuer open thy mouth

mouth any more : because of thy shame, when I am pacified toward thee, for all that thou hast done, sayeth the Lord God.

CHAP. XVII.

1 Vnder the parable of two Eagles and a Vine, 11 is shewed Gods iudgement vpon Ierusalem for reuolting from Babylon to Egypt. 22 God promiseth to plant the Cedar of the Gospel.

AND the word of the Lord came vnto mee, saying,

2 Sonne of man, put foorth a riddle, and speake a parable vnto the house of Israel,

3 And say, Thus saith the Lord God, A great eagle with great wings, long wing'd, full of feathers, which had †diuers colours, came vnto Lebanon, and tooke the highest branch of the Cedar.

† *Hebr. em-broydering.*

4 Hee cropt off the top of his yong twigs, and caried it into a land of traffique; he set it in a city of merchants.

5 Hee tooke also of the seed of the land, and †planted it in a fruitfull field, he placed it by great waters, *and* set it *as* a willow tree.

† *Hebr. put it in a field of seed.*

6 And it grew, and became a spreading Vine of low stature, whose branches turned toward him, and the roots thereof were vnder him : so it became a Vine, and brought forth branches, and shot foorth sprigges.

7 There was also an other great eagle, with great wings and many feathers, and behold, this Vine did bend her rootes towards him, and shot forth her branches toward him, that hee might water it by the furrowes of her plantation.

8 It was planted in a good †soile by great waters, that it might bring forth branches, and that it might beare fruit, that it might be a goodly Vine.

† *Hebr. field.*

9 Say thou, Thus saith the Lord God; Shall it prosper ? shall he not pull vp the rootes thereof, and cut off the fruit thereof, that it wither ? it shall wither in all the leaues of her spring, euen without great power, or many people to plucke it vp by the rootes thereof.

10 Yea behold, being planted, shall it prosper ? shall it not vtterly wither, when the East wind toucheth it ? it shal wither in the furrowes where it grew.

11 ¶ Moreouer the word of the Lord came vnto me, saying,

12 Say now to the rebellious house, Know ye not what these things *meane?* tell them, behold, the king of Babylon is come to Ierusalem, and hath taken the King thereof, and the Princes thereof, and ledde them with him to Babylon,

13 And hath taken of the kings seed, and made a couenant with him, and hath †taken an oath of him : he hath also taken the mighty of the land,

† *Hebr. brought him to an oath.*

14 That the kingdome might bee base, that it might not lift it selfe vp, †*but* that by keeping of his Couenant it might stand.

† *Hebr. to keepe his couenant to stand to it.*

15 But he rebelled against him in sending his ambassadours into Egypt, that they might giue him horses and much people: shall he prosper? shall he escape that doeth such things ? or shall hee breake the Couenant, and bee deliuered ?

16 As I liue, saith the Lord God, surely in the place *where* the king *dwelleth* that made him king, whose oath he despised, and whose couenant he brake, *euen* with him, in the midst of Babylon he shall die.

17 Neither shall Pharaoh with *his* mightie armie and great companie make for him in the warre by casting vp mounts, and building forts, to cut off many persons.

18 Seeing hee despised the oath by breaking the couenant (when loe, he had giuen his hand) and hath done all these things, he shall not escape.

19 Therefore thus saith the Lord God, As I liue, surely mine oath that he hath despised, and my Couenant that he hath broken, euen it will I recompense vpon his owne head.

20 And I will *spread my net vpon him, & he shalbe taken in my snare, and I will bring him to Babylon, and will plead with him there for his trespasse, that he hath trespassed against me.

* *Chap. 12. 13. and 32. 3.*

21 And all his fugitiues, with all his bands, shall fall by the sword, and they that remaine shalbe scattered towards all windes: and ye shall know that I the Lord haue spoken *it.*

22 ¶ Thus saith the Lord God, I wil also take of the highest branch of the high Cedar, and will set *it*, I will croppe off from the top of his yong twigges a tender one, and will plant *it* vpon

vpon an high mountaine and eminent.

23 In the mountaine of the height of Israel will I plant it : and it shall bring foorth boughes, and beare fruite, and be a goodly Cedar, and vnder it shall dwell all foule of euery wing : in the shadow of the branches thereof shal they dwell.

24 And all the trees of the field shall know that I the Lord haue brought downe the high tree, haue exalted the low tree, haue dried vp the greene tree, and haue made the drie tree to flourish: I the Lord haue spoken, and haue done it.

CHAP. XVIII.

1 God reprooueth the vniust parable of sowre grapes. 5 He sheweth how he dealeth with a iust father : 10 with a wicked sonne of a iust father : 14 with a iust sonne of a wicked father : 19 with a wicked man repenting : 24 with a iust man reuolting. 25 Hee defendeth his iustice, 31 and exhorteth to repentance.

A Nd the word of ẙ Lord came vnto me againe, saying ;

2 What meane ye that yee vse this prouerbe concerning the land of Israel, saying, The *fathers haue eaten sowre grapes, and the childrens teeth are set on edge?

3 As I liue, saith the Lord God, yee shall not haue *occasion* any more to vse this prouerbe in Israel.

4 Behold, all soules are mine, as the soule of the father, so also the soule of the sonne is mine : the soule that sinneth, it shall die.

5 ¶ But if a man be iust, and do that which is †lawfull and right :

6 And hath not eaten vpon the mountaines, neither hath lift vp his eyes to the idoles of the house of Israel, neither hath * defiled his neighbours wife, neither hath come neere to * a menstruous woman,

7 And hath not * oppressed any, *but* hath restored to the debtour his *pledge, hath spoiled none by violence, hath *giuen his bread to the hungrie, and hath couered the naked with a garment,

8 He *that* hath not giuen foorth vpon * vsurie, neither hath taken any increase, that hath withdrawen his hand from iniquitie, hath executed true iudgment betweene man and man,

9 Hath walked in my Statutes, and

hath kept my Iudgements to deale truely ; hee *is* iust, hee shall surely liue, saith the Lord God.

10 ¶ If hee beget a sonne that is a ‖robber, a shedder of blood, and ‖that doth the like to any one of these things,

11 And that doeth not any of those *duties*, bnt euen hath eaten vpon the mountaines, and defiled his neighbours wife,

12 Hath oppressed the poore and needie, hath spoiled by violence, hath not restored the pledge, and hath lift vp his eyes to the idoles, hath committed abomination,

13 Hath giuen foorth vpon vsurie, and hath taken encrease : shall he then liue? hee shall not liue : hee hath done all these abominations, hee shall surely die, his †blood shalbe vpon him.

14 ¶ Now loe, *if* hee beget a sonne that seeth all his fathers sinnes which he hath done, and considereth, and doth not such like,

15 *That* hath not eaten vpon the mountaines, neither hath lift vp his eyes to the idoles of the house of Israel, hath not defiled his neighbours wife,

16 Neither hath oppressed any, †hath not withholden the pledge, neither hath spoiled by violence, *but* hath giuen his bread to the hungry, and hath couered the naked with a garment,

17 *That* hath taken off his hand from the poore, *that* hath not receiued vsurie nor increase, hath executed my Iudgements, hath walked in my Statutes, he shall not die for the iniquitie of his father, he shall surely liue.

18 As for his father, because hee cruelly oppressed, spoiled his brother by violence, and did that which *is* not good among his people, loe, euen he shall die in his iniquitie.

19 ¶ Yet say yee, * Why? doeth not the sonne beare the iniquitie of the father? when the sonne hath done that which is lawfull and right, *and* hath kept all my Statutes, and hath done them, he shall surely liue.

20 The soule that sinneth, it shal die: the sonne shall not beare the iniquitie of the father, neither shal the father beare the iniquitie of the sonne ; the righteousnesse of the righteous shall bee vpon him, and the wickednesse of the wicked shalbe vpon him.

21 But if the wicked will turne from all

* Iee. 31. 29.

• Heb. iudgment and ustice.

* Leuit. 18.
20.
* Leuit. 18.
19. and
20. 18.
* Exod. 22.
21. leuit. 19.
13. and 25.
14.
* Deut. 24.
12. exod.
22. 20.
* Deu. 15. 7.
sal. 58: 7.
nat. 25. 35.
* Exod. 22.
25. leuit. 25.
36, 37. deu.
23. 19. psal.
15. 5.

‖ Or, breaker vp of an house.
‖ Or, that doeth to his brother, besides any of these.

† Heb. bloods

† Heb. hath not pledged the pledge or taken to pledge.

* Deut. 24.
16. 2. kings
14. 6. 2.
chron. 25. 4.
iere. 31. 29.

all his sinnes that he hath committed and keepe all my statutes, and doe that which is lawful and right, he shall surely liue, he shall not die.

22 All his transgressions that he hath committed, they shall not be mentioned vnto him : in his righteousnesse, that he hath done, he shall liue.

*Chap. 33. 11.

23 * Haue I any pleasure at all that the wicked should die, saith the Lord GOD? *And* not that he should returne from his wayes, and liue ?

24 ¶ But when the righteous turneth away fro his righteousnes, & committeth iniquitie, *and* doth according to all the abominations that the wicked man doth, shall he liue ? all his righteousnesse that he hath done, shall not be mentioned : in his trespasse that he hath trespassed, and in his sinne that he hath sinned, in them shall he die.

*Chap. 33. 20.

25 ¶ Yet yee say ; * The way of the Lord is not equall. Heare now, O house of Israel ; Is not my way equall? are not your wayes vnequall ?

26 When a righteous man turneth away from his righteousnesse, & committeth iniquitie, and dieth in them ; for his iniquitie that he hath done, shall he die.

27 Againe, when the wicked man turneth away from his wickednesse that he hath committed, and doth that which is lawfull and right, he shall saue his soule aliue.

28 Because he considereth and turneth away from all his transgressions that he hath committed, he shall surely liue, he shall not die.

29 Yet saith the house of Israel ; The way of the Lord is not equall. O house of Israel, are not my wayes e-quall ? are not your wayes vnequall ?

*Matth. 3. 2.
‖ *Or*, others.

30 Therefore I will iudge you, O house of Israel, euery one according to his wayes, saith the Lord GOD ; *repent, and turne ‖ your selues from all your transgressions : so iniquitie shall not be your ruine.

*Ier. 32. 39 chap. 11. 19. and 36. 26.

31 ¶ Cast away from you all your transgressions, wherby yee haue transgressed, and make you a * new heart and a new spirit : for why will yee die, O house of Israel ?

*Chap. 33. 11. 2. pet. 3. 9.
‖ *Or*, others.

32 For * I haue no pleasure in ỹ death of him that dieth, saith the Lord GOD : wherefore turne ‖ your selues, & liue ye.

CHAP. XIX.

1 A lamentation for the Princes of Israel, vnder the parable of Lyons whelpes taken in a pit, 10 and for Ierusalem, vnder the parable of a wasted vine.

M Oreouer, take thou vp a lamentation for the princes of Israel,

2 And say, What *is* thy mother ? a lyonesse : shee lay downe among lions, she nourished her whelpes among yong lions.

3 And shee brought vp one of her whelps : it became a yong lion, & it learned to catch the pray, it deuoured men.

4 The nations also heard of him, hee was taken in their pit, and they brought him with chaines vnto the land of *Egypt.

*2. Kings 23. 33. ier. 22. 11.

5 Now when she saw that shee had waited, *and* her hope was lost, then she tooke another of her whelps, *and* made him a yong lion.

6 And he went vp and downe among the lions, he became a yong lion, and learned to catch the pray, *and* deuoured men.

7 And he knew there ‖ desolate palaces, and he laied waste their cities, and the land was desolate, and the fulnesse thereof by the noise of his roaring.

‖ *Or, their widowes.*

8 Then the nations set against him on euery side from the prouinces, and spread their net ouer him : he was taken in their pit.

9 And they put him in ward ‖ in chaines, and brought him to the king of Babylon, they brought him into holds, that his voyce should no more be heard vpon the mountaines of Israel.

‖ *Or, in hookes.*

10 ¶ Thy mother *is* like a vine ‖ in thy blood, planted by the waters, she was fruitfull and full of branches by reason of many waters,

‖ *Or, in thy quietnesse or in thy likenesse.*

11 And she had strong rods for the scepters of them that beare rule, and her stature was exalted among the thicke branches, & she appeared in her height with the multitude of her branches.

12 But she was plucked vp in fury : she was cast downe to the ground, and the *East wind dryed vp her fruite : her strong rods were broken and withered, the fire consumed them.

*Os. 13. 15.

13 And now she *is* planted in the wildernesse, in a dry and thirsty ground.

14 And fire is gone out of a rod of her branches, *which* hath deuoured her fruite, so that she hath no strong rod *to be* a scepter to rule : this *is* a lamentation, and shall be for a lamentation.

CHAP.

CHAP. XX.

1 God refuseth to be consulted by the Elders of Israel. 5 He sheweth the story of their rebellions in Egypt, 10 in the wildernes, 27 and in the land. 33 He promiseth to gather them by the Gospel. 45 Vnder the name of a forest he sheweth the destruction of Ierusalem.

Nd it came to passe in the seuenth yeere, in the fift *moneth*, the tenth *day* of the moneth, *that* certaine of the elders of Israel came to enquire of the Lord, and sate before me.

2 Then came the word of the Lord vnto me, saying,

3 Sonne of man, speake vnto the elders of Israel, and say vnto them, Thus saith the Lord God, Are you come to enquire of me? As I liue, saith the Lord God, I will not be enquired of by you.

4 Wilt thou ‖ *iudge them, sonne of man, wilt thou iudge *them*? cause them to know the abominations of their fathers :

5 ¶ And say vnto them, Thus saith the Lord God, In the day when I chose Israel, and ‖lifted vp mine hand vnto the seed of the house of Iacob, and made my selfe *knowen vnto them in the land of Egypt, when I lifted vp mine hand vnto them, saying, I *am* the Lord your God,

6 In the day *that* I lifted vp mine hand vnto them to bring them foorth of the land of Egypt, into a lande that I had espied for them, flowing with milke and hony, *which* is the glory of all lands:

7 Then said I vnto them, Cast ye away euery man the abominations of his eyes, and defile not your selues with the idoles of Egypt : I *am* the Lord your God.

8 But they rebelled against me, and would not hearken vnto mee : they did not euery man cast away the abominations of their eyes, neither did they forsake the idoles of Egypt : then I said, I will powre out my furie vpon them, to accomplish my anger against them in the middest of the land of Egypt.

9 But I wrought for my names sake that it should not be polluted before the heathen, among whom they *were*, in whose sight I made my selfe knowen vnto them, in bringing them foorth out of the land of Egypt.

10 ¶ Wherefore I *caused them to goe foorth out of the land of Egypt, and brought them into the wildernesse.

11 And I gaue them my statutes, and †shewed them my iudgements, *which if a man doe, he shall euen liue in them.

12 Moreouer also, I gaue them my *Sabbaths, to be a signe betweene mee and them, that they might know that I *am* the Lord that sanctifie them.

13 But the house of Israel rebelled against me in the wildernesse : they walked not in my statutes, and they despised my iudgements, which if a man doe, hee shall euen liue in them, and my sabbaths they greatly * polluted : then I said I would powre out my furie vpon them in the *wildernesse, to consume them :

14 But I wrought for my names sake, that it should not bee polluted before the heathen, in whose sight I brought them out.

15 Yet also I lifted vp my hand vnto them in the wildernesse, that I would not bring them into the land which I had giuen *them*, flowing with milke and hony, *which* is the glory of all lands,

16 Because they despised my iudgements, and walked not in my statutes, but polluted my Sabbaths : for their heart went after their idoles.

17 Neuerthelesse, mine eye spared them from destroying them, neither did I make an end of the in the wildernes.

18 But I said vnto their children in the wildernesse ; Walke ye not in the statutes of your fathers, neither obserue their iudgements, nor defile your selues with their idoles.

19 I *am* the Lord your God : walke in my statutes, and keepe my iudgements, and doe them :

20 And hallow my Sabbaths, and they shall be a signe betweene mee and you, that yee may know that I *am* the Lord your God.

21 Notwithstanding the children rebelled against me : they walked not in my statutes, neither kept my iudgements to doe them, which if a man doe, hee shall euen liue in them ; they polluted my Sabbaths : then I said I would powre out my furie vpon them, to accomplish my anger against them in the wildernesse.

22 Neuerthelesse I withdrew mine hand and wrought for my names sake, that it should not be polluted in the sight

‖ Or, plead for them.
* Chap. 22. 2. and 23. 36.

‖ Or, sware, and so verse 6, &c.
* Exod. 31. 9. and 4. 31.

* Exod. 13. 18.

† Heb. made them to know.
* Leuit. 18. 5.
rom. 10. 5.
gal. 3. 12.
* Exod. 20. 8. and 31. 13, &c. and 35. 2. deut. 5. 12.

* Exod. 16. 26.
* Numb. 14. 29. and 26. 65.

sight of the heathen, in whose sight I brought them foorth.

23 I lifted vp mine hand vnto them also in the wildernesse, that I would scatter them among the heathen, and disperse them through the countreys;

24 Because they had not executed my iudgements, but had despised my Statutes, and had polluted my Sabbaths, and their eyes were after their fathers idoles.

25 Wherefore I gaue them also statutes that were not good, and iudgements whereby they should not liue.

26 And I polluted them in their owne gifts, in that they caused to passe *through *the fire* all that openeth the wombe, that I might make them desolate, to the end, that they might know that I *am* the L O R D.

*Chap. 16. 21.

27 ¶ Therfore sonne of man, speake vnto the house of Israel, and say vnto them, Thus saith the Lord G O D, Yet in this your fathers haue blasphemed me, in that they haue †committed a trespasse against me.

†Heb. trespassed a trespasse.

28 *For* when I had brought them into the land, for the which I lifted vp mine hand to giue it to them, then they saw euery high hill, and all the thicke trees, and they offered there their sacrifices, and there they presented the prouocation of their offering: there also they made their sweet sauour, and powred out there their drinke offerings.

29 Then ||I said vnto them, What is the high place whereunto ye goe? and the name thereof is called Bamah vnto this day.

||Or, *I told them what the hie place was,* or *Bamah.*

30 Wherefore say vnto the house of Israel, Thus saith the Lord G O D, Are ye polluted after the maner of your fathers? and commit ye whoredome after their abominations?

31 For when yee offer your gifts, when yee make your sonnes to passe through the fire, ye pollute your selues with all your idoles euen vnto this day: and shall I be inquired of by you, O house of Israel? As I liue, saith the Lord G O D, I will not be inquired of by you.

32 And that which cometh into your minde, shall not be at all, that ye say, We wil be as the heathen, as the families of the countreys, to serue wood and stone.

33 ¶ As I liue, sayeth the Lord G O D, surely with a mighty hand, and with a stretched out arme, and with fu-

rie powred out, will I rule ouer you.

34 And I will bring you out from the people, and will gather you out of the countreys wherein ye are scattered, with a mighty hand, & with a stretched out arme, and with fury powred out.

35 And I wil bring you into the wildernes of the people, and there will I plead with you face to face.

36 Like as I pleaded with your fathers in the wildernes of the land of Egypt, so wil I plead with you, saith the Lord G O D.

37 And I will cause you to passe vnder the rod, and I will bring you into the ||bond of the Couenant.

||Or, *a deliuering.*

38 And I will purge out from among you the rebels, and them that transgresse against mee: I will bring them foorth out of the countrey where they soiourne, and they shall not enter into the land of Israel, and yee shall know that I *am* the L O R D.

39 As for you, O house of Israel, thus saith the Lord G O D, Goe yee, serue ye euery one his idoles, and hereafter *also*, if ye wil not hearken vnto me: but pollute ye my holy Name no more with your gifts, and with your idoles.

40 For in mine holy mountaine, in the mountaine of the height of Israel, saith the Lord G O D, there shall all the house of Israel, all of them in the land serue me: there will I accept them, and there wil I require your offerings, and the ||first fruits of your oblations, with all your holy things.

||Or, *chief.*

41 I will accept you with your †sweet sauour, when I bring you out from the people, and gather you out of the countreys wherein yee haue bene scattered, and I wil be sanctified in you before the heathen.

†Hebr. *sauour of rest.*

42 And ye shall know that I *am* the L O R D, when I shall bring you into the land of Israel, into the countrey for the which I lifted vp mine hand, to giue it to your fathers.

43 And there shall yee remember your wayes, & all your doings, wherein ye haue bene defiled, and ye shal lothe your selues in your owne sight, for all your euils that ye haue committed.

44 And ye shal know that I *am* the L O R D, when I haue wrought with you for my Names sake, not according to your wicked wayes, nor according to your corrupt doings, O yee house of Israel, saith the Lord G O D.

45 ¶ More-

45 ¶ Moreouer, the worde of the LORD came vnto me, saying,

46 Sonne of man, set thy face toward the South, and drop *thy word* toward the South, and prophesie against the forrest of the South field.

47 And say to the forest of ẙ South, Heare the word of the Lord GOD; Behold, I will kindle a fire in thee, and it shall deuoure euery greene tree in thee, and euery dry tree: the flaming flame shal not be quenched, and all faces from the South to the North shalbe burnt therein.

48 And all flesh shall see that I the LORD haue kindled it: it shall not be quenched.

49 Then said I, Ah Lord GOD, they say of me, Doeth he not speake parables?

CHAP. XXI.

1 Ezekiel prophecieth against Ierusalem, with a signe of sighing. 8 The sharpe and bright sword, 18 against Ierusalem, 25 against the kingdome, 28 and against the Ammonites.

ANd the word of ẙ LORD came vnto me, saying,

2 Sonne of man, set thy face toward Ierusalem, and drop *thy word* toward the holy places, and prophecie against the land of Israel,

3 And say to ẙ land of Israel, Thus saith the LORD, Behold, I *am* against thee, and will draw forth my sword out of his sheath, and will cut off from thee the righteous and the wicked.

4 Seeing then that I will cut off from thee the righteous and the wicked, therefore shall my sword goe forth out of his sheath against all flesh from the South to the North:

5 That all flesh may know, that I the LORD haue drawen foorth my sword out of his sheath: it shall not returne any more.

6 Sigh therefore thou sonne of man with the breaking of *thy* loynes, and with bitternesse sigh before their eyes.

7 And it shall be, when they say vnto thee; Wherefore sighest thou? that thou shalt answere, For the tidings, because it commeth: and euery heart shall melt, and all hands shalbe feeble, and euery spirit shal faint, and all knees †shal be weake *as* water: behold, it commeth, and shalbe brought to passe, sayth the Lord GOD.

† *Heb. shall goe into water.*

8 ¶ Againe, the word of the LORD came vnto me, saying,

9 Sonne of man, prophecie and say, Thus sayth the LORD, Say, A sword, a sword is sharpened, and also fourbished.

10 It is sharpened to make a sore slaughter; it is fourbished, that it may glitter: should we then make mirth? ‖It contemneth the rod of my sonne, *as* euery tree.

‖ *Or, it is the rod of my sonne, it despiseth euery tree.*

11 And he hath giuen it to be fourbished, that it may be handled: this sword is sharpened, and it is fourbished to giue it into the hand of the slayer.

12 Cry and howle, sonne of man, for it shalbe vpon my people, it *shalbe* vpon all the princes of Israel: ‖terrours, by reason of the sword, shall be vpon my people: * smite therefore vpon *thy* thigh.

‖ *Or, they are thrust downe to the sword with my people.*
* Iere. 31. 19.

13 ‖Because it is a tryall, and what if *the sword* contemne euen the rodde? it shall be no *more*, sayth the Lord GOD.

‖ *Or, when the triall hath beene, what then? shall they not also belong to the despising rod?*

14 Thou therefore sonne of man, prophecie and smite thine †hands together, and let the sword bee doubled the third time, the sword of the slaine, it *is* the sword of the great men, that are slaine, which entreth into their priuie chambers.

† *Heb. hand to hand.*

15 I haue set the ‖point of the sword against all their gates, that *their* heart may faint, and their ruines be multiplied. Ah, it is made bright, it is ‖wrapt vp for the slaughter.

‖ *Or, glittering, or feare.*
‖ *Or, sharpened.*

16 Goe thee one way or other, either on the right hand, †or on the left, whithersoeuer thy face is set.

† *Heb. set thy selfe, take the left hand.*

17 I will also smite mine hands together, and I wil cause my furie to rest: I the LORD haue sayd *it*.

18 ¶ The word of the LORD came vnto me againe, saying,

19 Also thou sonne of man, appoint thee two wayes, that the sword of the king of Babylon may come: both twaine shall come forth out of one land: and choose thou a place, choose it at the head of the way to the citie.

20 Appoint a way, that the sword may come to Rabbath of the Ammonites, and to Iudah in Ierusalem the defenced.

21 For the king of Babylon stood at the †parting of the way, at the head of the two wayes, to vse diuination: he made his ‖arrowes bright, he consulted with †images, he looked in the liuer.

† *Heb. mother of the way.*
‖ *Or, kniues.*
† *Heb. Teraphim.*

22 At his right hand was the diuination

nation for Ierusalem to appoint ‖ captaines, to open the mouth in the slaughter, to lift vp the voice with shouting, to
appoint *battering-rammes* against the
gates, to cast a mount *and* to build a fort.

23 And it shall be vnto them as a
false diuination in their sight, ‖ to them
that haue sworne oathes : but he will
call to remembrance the iniquitie, that
they may be taken.

24 Therefore thus saith the Lord
God, Because yee haue made your
iniquitie to be remembred, in that your
transgressions are discouered, so that in
all your doings your sinnes doe appeare: because, *I say*, that yee are come to
remembrance, yee shall be taken with
the hand.

25 ¶ And thou prophane wicked
prince of Israel, whose day is come,
when iniquitie *shall haue* an end,

26 Thus saith the Lord God, Remoue the diademe, and take off the
crowne: this *shall* not *be* the same : exalt
him that is low, and abase him that is
high.

27 † I will ouerturne, ouerturne,
ouerturne it, and it shall be no more, vntill he come, whose right it is, and I will
giue it him.

28 ¶ And thou sonne of man, prophecie, and say, Thus saith the Lord
God concerning the Ammonites,
and concerning their reproch : Euen say
thou ; The sword, the sword *is* drawen,
for the slaughter it *is* furbished, to consume because of the glittering :

29 Whiles they see vanitie vnto thee,
whiles they diuine a lie vnto thee, to
bring thee vpon the necks of them that
are slaine, of the wicked whose day is
come, when their iniquitie *shall haue* an
end.

30 ‖ Shall I cause it to returne into
his sheath? I will iudge thee in the
place where thou wast created, in the
land of thy natiuitie.

31 And I will powre out mine indignation vpon thee, I will blow a-
gainst thee in the fire of my wrath, and
deliuer thee into the hand of ‖ brutish
men *and* skilfull to destroy.

32 Thou shalt be for fuell to the fire :
thy blood shall be in the middest of the
land, thou shalt be no *more* remembred:
for I the Lord haue spoken *it*.

CHAP. XXII.

1 A Catalogue of sinnes in Ierusalem. 13 God
will burne them as drosse in his furnace. 23
The generall corruption of Prophets,
Priests, Princes, and people.

Moreouer the word of the
Lord came vnto me,
saying ;

2 Now thou sonne of
man, *wilt thou † iudge,
wilt thou iudge the † bloodie citie? yea
thou † shalt shew her all her abominations.

3 Then say thou, Thus saith the
Lord God; The citie sheadeth blood
in the middest of it, that her time may
come, and maketh idoles against herselfe to defile herselfe.

4 Thou art become guilty in thy
blood that thou hast *shed, and hast defiled thy selfe in thine idoles, which thou
hast made, and thou hast caused thy
daies to draw neere, and art come euen
vnto thy yeeres ; therfore haue I made
thee a reproch vnto the heathen, and a
mocking to all countries.

5 Those that be neere, and those
that be farre from thee, shall mocke thee
which art † infamous, *and* much vexed.

6 Behold the princes of Israel, euerie one were in thee to their † power to
shead blood.

7 In thee haue they set light by father and mother : in the middest of thee
haue they dealt by ‖ oppression with the
stranger : in thee haue they vexed the
fatherlesse and the widow.

8 Thou hast despised mine holy
things, & hast prophaned my sabbaths:

9 In thee are † men that carie tales
to shead blood : and in thee they eate
vpon the mountaines : in the middest of
thee they commit lewdnesse.

10 In thee haue they * discouered
their fathers nakednesse : in thee haue
they humbled her that was *set apart
for pollution.

11 And ‖ one hath committed *abomination with his neighbours *wife,
and ‖ an other hath ‖ lewdly defiled his
*daughter in law, and an other in thee
hath humbled his sister, his fathers
daughter.

12 In thee haue they taken gifts to
shead blood : thou hast taken vsury and
increase, and thou hast greedily gained
of thy neighbours by extortion, and hast
forgotten me, saith the Lord God.

13 ¶ Behold therefore, I haue *smitten mine hand at thy dishonest gaine
which thou hast made, and at thy blood
which

Marginal notes

‖ *Or,* batte-
ring *rams.*
† *Heb.* rams.

‖ *Or, for the
oathes made
vnto them.*

† *Heb. per-
uerted, per-
uerted, per-
uerted will
I make it.*

‖ *Or, cause to
it to returne.*

‖ *Or, bur-
ning.*

* Chap. 20
41. and 23.
36.
† *Or, plead
for.*
† *Heb. citi*
of bloods.
† *Heb. ma*
her know.

* 2. Kings
21. 16.

† *Heb.* poll*
ted of name
much in
vexation.*
† *Heb. arm*

‖ *Or, decei*

† *Heb. men*
of slaunders

* Leuit. 18
8. and 20.
11.
* Leuit. 18
19.

‖ *Or, euery*
one.
* Leuit. 18
20.
* Ier. 5. 8.
‖ *Or, euery*
one.
‖ *Or, by*
lewdnesse.
* Leuit. 18
9.

* Chap. 21
22.

which hath bene in the midst of thee.

14 Can thine heart indure, *or* can thine hands be strong in the dayes that I shall deale with thee? I the Lord haue spoken *it*, and will doe *it*.

15 And I will scatter thee among the heathen, and disperse thee in the countreys, and will consume thy filthinesse out of thee.

16 And thou ||shalt take thine inheritance in thy selfe in the sight of the heathen, and thou shalt know that I *am* the Lord.

Or, shalt beprophaned

17 And the word of the Lord came vnto me, saying,

18 Sonne of man, the house of Israel is to me become drosse: all they *are* brasse, and tinne, and yron, and lead in the midst of the furnace: they are *euen* the †drosse of siluer.

†*Heb. drosses.*

19 Therefore thus saith the Lord God, Because ye are all become drosse, behold therefore I will gather you into the midst of Ierusalem.

20 †*As* they gather siluer, and brasse, and yron, and lead, and tinne into the midst of the furnace, to blow the fire vpon it, to melt *it* : so will I gather *you* in mine anger, and in my fury, and I will leaue *you there*, and melt you.

†*Heb. according to the gathering.*

21 Yea, I will gather you, and blow vpon you in the fire of my wrath, and ye shalbe melted in the midst thereof.

22 As siluer is melted in the midst of the furnace, so shall ye be melted in the middest thereof, and ye shall know that I the Lord haue powred out my furie vpon you.

23 ¶ And the word of the Lord came vnto me, saying,

24 Son of man, say vnto her, Thou art the land that is not cleansed, nor rained vpon in the day of indignation.

25 *There is* a conspiracie of her prophets in the middest thereof like a roaring lyon, rauening the praye: they *haue deuoured soules : they haue taken the treasure and precious things: they haue made her many widowes in the midst thereof.

*Matth. 23. 4.

26 Her priests haue † violated my law, and haue prophaned mine holy things : they haue put no difference betweene the holy and prophane, neither haue they shewed *difference* between the vncleane and the cleane, and haue hid their eyes from my Sabbaths, and I am prophaned among them.

†*Heb. offered violence to.*

27 Her *princes in the midst thereof

*Mic. 3. 11 Zeph. 3. 3.

are like wolues rauening the praye, to shed blood, *and* to destroy soules, to get dishonest gaine.

28 And her prophets haue dawbed them with vntempered *morter*, seeing vanity, and diuining lies vnto them, saying, Thus saith the Lord God, when the Lord hath not spoken.

29 The people of the land haue vsed ||oppression, and exercised robbery, and haue vexed the poore and needie : yea, they haue oppressed the stranger †wrongfully.

*Or, deceit.

†*Heb. without right.*

30 And I sought for a man among them, that should make vp the hedge, and stand in the gap before me for the land, that I should not destroy it : but I found none.

31 Therefore haue I powred out mine indignation vpon them, I haue consumed them with the fire of my wrath : their owne way haue I recompensed vpon their heads, saith the Lord God.

CHAP. XXIII.

1 The whoredomes of Aholah & Aholibah. 22 Aholibah is to be plagued by her louers. 36 The Prophet reproueth the adulteries of them both, 45 and sheweth their iudgements.

He word of the Lord came againe vnto me, saying,

2 Sonne of man, there were two women, the daughters of one mother.

3 And they committed whordomes in Egypt, they committed whordomes in their youth: there were their brests pressed, and there they bruised the teats of their virginitie.

4 And the names of them *were* Aholah the elder, and Aholibah her sister : and they were mine, & they bare sonnes and daughters : thus *were* their names: Samaria *is* Aholah, and Ierusalem Aholibah

5 And Aholah played the harlot, when she was mine, & she doted on her louers, on the Assyrians *her* neighbors,

6 Which were clothed with blew, captaines and rulers, all of them desireable yong men, horsemen riding vpon horses.

7 Thus † she committed her whordomes with them, with all them that were the †chosen men of Assyria, and with all on whom she doted, with all their idoles she defiled her selfe.

†*Heb. bestowed her whoredomes vpon them.*
†*Heb. the choise of the children of Asshur.*

8 Nei-

8 Neither left she her whoredomes *brought* from Egypt : for in her youth they lay with her, and they bruised the breasts of her virginitie, and powred their whoredome vpon her.

9 Wherefore I haue deliuered her into the hand of her louers, into the hand of the * Assyrians, vpon whom she doted.

* 2. Kings 17. 18.

10 These discouered her nakednes, they tooke her sonnes and her daughters, and slew her with the sword : and she became †famous among women, for they had executed iudgement vpon her.

† Heb. a name.

11 And when her sister Aholibah saw *this*, she †was more corrupt in her inordinate loue then she, and in her whoredoms†more then her sister in *her* whoredomes.

† Heb. she corrupted her inordinate loue more then &c.
† Heb. more then the whoredomes of her sister.
* 2. Kings. 16. 7.

12 She doted vpon the * Assyrians *her* neighbours, captaines and rulers clothed most gorgeously, horsemen riding vpon horses, all of them desireable young men.

13 Then I saw that she was defiled, that they *tooke* both one way ;

14 And that she increased her whoredomes : for when shee saw men pourtrayed vpon the wall, the images of the Caldeans pourtrayed with vermilion,

15 Girded with girdles vpon their loynes, exceeding in dyed attire vpon their heads, all of them princes to looke to, after the maner of the Babylonians of Caldea, the land of their natiuitie :

16 And †assoone as shee saw them with her eyes, she doted vpon them, and sent messengers vnto them into Caldea.

† Hebr. at the sight of her eyes.

17 And the † Babylonians came to her into the bed of loue, and they defiled her with their whoredome, and shee was polluted with them, and her mind was †alienated from them.

† Hebr. children of Babel.
† Hebr. loosed or disioynted.

18 So shee discouered her whoredomes, and discouered her nakednesse; then my mind was alienated from her, like as my minde was alienated from her sister

19 Yet shee multiplied her whoredomes, in calling to remembrance the dayes of her youth, wherein she had played the harlot in the land of Egypt.

20 For she doted vpon their paramours, whose flesh *is as* the flesh of asses, and whose issue *is like* the issue of horses.

21 Thus thou calledst to remembrance the lewdnesse of thy youth, in bruising thy teates by the Egyptians, for the paps of thy youth.

22 ¶ Therefore, O Aholibah, thus saith the Lord GOD, Behold, I will raise vp thy louers against thee, from whom thy minde is alienated, and I will bring them against thee on euery side,

23 The Babylonians, and all the Caldeans, Pekod, and Shoah, and Koa, all the Assyrians with them, all of them desireable young men, captaines and rulers, great lords and renowmed, all of them riding vpon horses.

24 Aud they shall come against thee with charets, wagons and wheeles, and with an assemblie of people *which* shall set against thee buckler, and shield, and helmet round about : and I will set iudgement before them, and they shal iudge thee according to their iudgements.

25 And I will set my ielousie against thee, and they shall deale fnriously with thee: they shall take away thy nose and thine eares, and thy remnant shall fall by the sword: they shall take thy sonnes and thy daughters, and thy residue shal be deuoured by the fire.

26 They shall also strippe thee out of thy clothes, and take away thy †faire iewels.

† Hebr. instruments of thy decking

27 Thus will I make thy lewdnesse to cease from thee, and thy whoredome *brought* from the land of Egypt: so that thou shalt not lift vp thine eyes vnto them, nor remember Egypt any more.

28 For thus saith the Lord GOD; Beholde, I will deliuer thee into the hand *of them* whom thou hatest; into the hand *of them* from whom thy mind is alienated.

29 And they shall deale with thee hatefully, and shall take away all thy labour, and shall leaue thee naked and bare, and the nakednesse of thy whoredomes shall bee discouered, both thy lewdnesse and thy whoredomes.

30 I wil doe these things vnto thee, because thou hast gone a whoring after the heathen, *and* because thou art polluted with their idoles.

31 Thou hast walked in the way of thy sister, therefore will I giue her cup into thine hand.

32 Thus sayth the Lord GOD, Thou

Thou shalt drinke of thy sisters cuppe deepe and large : thou shalt be laughed to scorne and had in derision ; it containeth much.

33 Thou shalt be filled with drunkennesse and sorrow , with the cup of astonishment and desolation, with the cup of thy sister Samaria.

34 Thou shalt euen drinke it and sucke it out, and thou shalt breake the sheards thereof, and plucke off thine owne breasts : for I haue spoken it, saith the Lord God.

35 Therefore thus sayth the Lord God, Because thou hast forgotten me, and cast me behinde thy backe, therfore beare thou also thy lewdnesse, and thy whoredomes.

36 ¶ The Lord said moreouer vnto mee ; Sonne of man, wilt thou * ||iudge Aholah and Aholibah? yea declare vnto them their abominations ;

* Cha. 20. 4. and 22. 2.
|| Or, plead for.

37 That they haue committed adulterie, and blood is in their handes, and with their idoles haue they committed adulterie, and haue also caused their sonnes, whom they bare vnto me, to passe for them through the fire to deuoure them.

38 Moreouer this they haue done vnto me : they haue defiled my Sanctuarie in the same day, and haue profaned my Sabbaths.

39 For when they had slaine their children to their idoles, then they came the same day into my Sanctuarie to profane it, and loe, *thus haue they done in the middest of mine house.

* 2. Kings 21. 4.

40 And furthermore that yee haue sent for men †to come from farre, vnto whom a messenger was sent, and loe they came ; for whom thou didst wash thy selfe, paintedst thy eyes, and deckedst thy selfe with ornaments,

† Heb. comming.

41 And satest vpon a †stately bedde, and a table prepared before it, *whereupon thou hast set mine incense and mine oile.

† Heb. honourable.
* Prou. 7. 17

42 And a voice of a multitude being at ease was with her, and with the men of the †common sort were brought ||Sabeans from the wildernesse, which put bracelets vpon their hands, and beautifull crownes vpon their heads.

† Heb. of the multitude of men.
|| Or, drunkards.

43 Then said I vnto her that was olde iu adulteries ; Will they now commit ||whoredomes with her, and shee with them ?

|| Her whordomes.

44 Yet they went in vnto her, as they goe in vnto a woman that playeth the harlot : so went they in vnto Aholah & vnto Aholibah the lewd women.

45 ¶ And the righteous men, they shall *iudge them after the manner of adulteresses, and after the manner of women that shed blood ; because they are adulteresses , and blood is in their handes.

* Chap. 16. 38.

46 For thus sayth the Lord God, I will bring vp a company vpon them, and will giue them †to be remoued and spoiled.

† Heb. for a remoouing and spoyle.

47 And the companie shall stone them with stones , and ||dispatch them with their swords : they shall slay their sonnes and their daughters, and burne vp their houses with fire.

|| Or, single them out.

48 Thus will I cause lewdnesse to cease out of the land , that all women may be taught not to doe after your lewdnesse.

49 And they shall recompense your lewdnesse vpon you, and ye shall beare the sinnes of your idoles, and yee shall know that I am the Lord God.

CHAP. XXIIII.

1 Vnder the parable of a boiling pot, 6 is shewed the irreuocable destruction of Ierusalem. 15 By the signe of Ezekiel not mourning for the death of his wife, 19 is shewed the calamity of the Iewes to be beyond all sorow.

Gaine in the ninth yeere, in the tenth moneth, in the tenth day of the moneth, the word of the Lord came vnto me, saying ;

2 Sonne of man , Write thee the name of the day, euen of this same day : the king of Babylon set himselfe against Ierusalem this same day.

3 And vtter a parable vnto the rebellious house, and say vnto them, Thus sayth the Lord God, Set on a pot, set it on, and also powre water into it.

4 Gather the pieces thereof into it, euen euery good piece, the thigh, and the shoulder ; fill it with the choice bones.

5 Take the choice of the flocke, and ||burne also the bones vnder it, and make it boyle well, and let him seethe the bones of it therein.

|| Or, heape.

6 ¶ Wherefore thus sayth the Lord God, Woe to the bloodie citie, to the pot whose scumme is therein, and whose scumme

scumme is not gone out of it; bring it out
piece by piece, let no lot fall vpon it.

7 For her blood is in the middest of
her: she set it vpon the toppe of a rocke,
she powred it vpon the ground to couer
it with dust:

8 That it might cause furie to come
vp to take vengeance: I haue set her
blood vpon the top of a rocke, that it
should not be couered.

9 Therefore thus saith the Lord
God; * Woe to the bloody citie, I will
euen make the pile for fire, great.

*Nah. 3. 1.
Abac. 2.
12.

10 Heape on wood, kindle the fire,
consume the flesh, and spice it well, and
let the bones be burnt.

11 Then set it empty vpon the coales
thereof, that the brasse of it may be hot
and may burne, and that the filthinesse
of it may be molten in it, that the scum of
it may be consumed.

12 She hath wearied *herselfe* with
lies, and her great scumme went not
forth out of her: her scumme *shall be* in
the fire.

13 In thy filthinesse *is* lewdnesse, because I haue purged thee, and thou
wast not purged, thou shalt not be purged from thy filthinesse any more, till I
haue caused my fury to rest vpon thee.

14 I the Lord haue spoken *it*, it
shall come to passe, and I will doe *it*,
I will not goe backe, neither will I
spare, neither will I repent, according
to thy wayes and according to thy doings, shall they iudge thee, saith the
Lord God.

15 ¶ Also the word of the Lord
came vnto me, saying;

16 Sonne of man, behold, I take a-
way from thee the desire of thine eyes
with a stroke: yet neither shalt thou
mourne, nor weepe, neither shall thy
teares †runne downe.

†Heb. goe.
†Heb. be si-
lent.

17 †Forbeare to crie, make no mourning for the dead, bind the tire of thine
head vpon thee, and put on thy shooes
vpon thy feete, and couer not thy †lips,
and eate not the bread of men.

†Heb. vpper
lip. And so
vers. 22

18 So I spake vnto the people in the
morning, and at euen my wife died, and
I did in the morning as I was commanded.

19 ¶ And the people said vnto me;
Wilt thou not tell vs what these things
are to vs, that thou doest *so*?

20 Then I answered them, The
word of the Lord came vnto me,
saying,

21 Speake vnto the house of Israel;
Thus saith the Lord God; Behold,
I will prophane my sanctuarie, the excellencie of your strength, the desire of
your eyes, and †that which your soule
pitieth; and your sonnes and your
daughters, whom yee haue left, shall
fall by the sword.

†Heb. the
pitie of you
soule.

22 And yee shall doe as I haue
done: yee shall not couer your lips, nor
eate the bread of men.

23 And your tires *shall be* vpon your
heads, and your shooes vpon your feet:
yee shall not mourne nor weepe, but yee
shall pine away for your iniquities, and
mourne one towards an other.

24 Thus Ezekiel is vnto you a
signe: according to all that he hath done,
shall yee doe: and when this commeth,
yee shall know that I *am* the Lord
God.

25 Also thou sonne of man, *shall it
not be* in the day when I take from
them their strength, the ioy of their glorie, the desire of their eyes, and †that
whereupon they set their minds, their
sonnes and their daughters;

†Heb. the
lifting vp o
the soule.

26 That he that escapeth in that day,
shall come vnto thee, to cause *thee* to
heare it with *thine* eares?

27 In that day shall thy mouth be
opened to him which is escaped, and
thou shalt speake & be no more dumbe,
and thou shalt be a signe vnto them, and
they shall know that I *am* the Lord.

CHAP. XXV.

1 Gods vengeance, for their insolencie against
the Iewes, vpon the Ammonites. 8 Vpon
Moab and Seir. 12 Vpon Edom, 15 and
vpon the Philistines.

He word of the Lord
came againe vnto me, say-
ing;

2 Sonne of man, *set
thy face against the Am-
monites, and prophecie against them,

*Ier. 49.
1. &c.

3 And say vnto the Ammonites,
Heare the word of the Lord God,
Thus saith the Lord God; Because
thou saidst, Aha, against my sanctuarie, when it was prophaned, and a-
gainst the land of Israel, when it was
desolate, & against the house of Iudah,
when they went into captiuitie;

4 Behold therefore, I will deliuer
thee to the †men of the East for a possession, and they shall set their palaces
in thee, and make their dwellings in
thee:

†Heb. chil
dren.

thee : they shall eate thy fruit, and they shall drinke thy milke.

5 And I will make Rabbah a stable for camels, and the Ammonites a couching place for flocks: and ye shal know that I *am* the LORD.

6 For thus saith the Lord GOD, Because thou hast clapped thine † hands and stamped with the † feete, and reioyced in † heart with all thy despite against the land of Israel :

7 Behold therefore, I will stretch out mine hand vpon thee, and will deliuer thee for a ||spoile to the heathen, and I will cut thee off from the people, and I wil cause thee to perish out of the countreys : I will destroy thee, and thou shalt know that I *am* the LORD.

8 ¶ Thus saith the Lord GOD, * Because that Moab and Seir doe say, Behold, the house of Iudah *is* like vnto all the heathen :

9 Therefore beholde, I will open † the side of Moab from the cities, from his cities *which are* on his frontiers, the glory of the countrey Beth-ieshimoth, Baal-meon and Kiriathaim,

10 Vnto the men of the East || with the Ammonites, and will giue them in possession, that the Ammonites may not be remembred among the nations.

11 And I will execute iudgments vpon Moab, and they shall know that I *am* the LORD.

12 ¶ Thus saith the Lord GOD, Because that Edom hath dealt against the house of Iudah † by taking vengeance, and hath greatly offended, and reuenged himselfe vpon them :

13 Therefore thus saith the Lord GOD, I will also stretch out mine hand vpon Edom, and will cut off man and beast from it, and I will make it desolate from Teman, and || they of Dedan shall fall by the sword.

14 And I will lay my vengeance vpon Edom by the hand of my people Israel, and they shall doe in Edom according to mine anger, and according to my furie, and they shall know my vengeance, saith the Lord GOD.

15 ¶ Thus saith the Lord GOD, Because the Philistines haue dealt by reuenge, and haue taken vengeance with a despiteful heart, to destroy *it* || for the old hatred :

16 Therefore thus saith the Lord GOD, Behold, I will stretch out mine hand vpon the Philistines, and I will

cut off the Cherethims, and destroy the remnant of the || Sea coast.

17 And I wil execute great † vengeance vpon them with furious rebukes, and they shall knowe that I *am* the LORD, when I shall lay my vengeance vpon them.

CHAP. XXVI.

1 Tyrus, for insulting against Ierusalem, is threatned. 7 The power of Nebuchadrezzar against her. 15 The mourning and astonishment of the sea, at her fall.

Nd it came to passe in the eleuenth yeere, in the first *day* of the moneth, *that* the word of the LORD came vnto me, saying,

2 Sonne of man, because that Tyrus hath said against Ierusalem, Aha, she is broken *that was* the gates of the people, she is turned vnto me, I shalbe replenished *now* she is laid waste :

3 Therefore thus saith the Lord GOD, Behold, I *am* against thee, O Tyrus, and will cause many nations to come vp against thee, as the sea causeth his waues to come vp.

4 And they shall destroy the walles of Tyrus, and breake downe her towres : I will also scrape her dust from her, and make her like the top of a rocke.

5 It shall be a place for the spreading of nets in the middest of the sea : for I haue spoken *it*, saith the Lord GOD, and it shall become a spoile to the ñations.

6 And her daughters which *are* in the field shall be slaine by the sword, and they shall know that I *am* the LORD.

7 ¶ For thus saith the Lord GOD ; Behold, I will bring vpon Tyrus, Nebuchadrezzar king of Babylon, a king of kings, from the North, with horses, and with charets, and with horsemen, and companies, and much people.

8 Hee shall slay with the sword thy daughters in the field, and he shal make a fort against thee, and ||cast a mount against thee, and lift vp the buckler against thee.

9 Hee shall set engines of warre against thy walles, and with his axes he shall breake downe thy towres.

10 By reason of the abundance of his horses, their dust shall couer thee : thy walles shall shake at the noise of the

---

Marginal notes (left column):

† Heb. hand.
† Heb. foote.
† Heb. soule.

|| Or, meate.

* Ier. 48. 1, &c.

† Heb. shoulder of Moab

|| Or, against the children of Ammon.

† Heb. by reuenging reuengement.

|| Or, they shall fall by the sword vnto Dedan.

|| Or, with perpetuall hatred.

Marginal notes (right column):

|| Or, hauen of the Sea.
† Heb. vengeances.

|| Or, powre out the engine of shot.

the horsemen, and of the wheeles, and of the charets, when he shall enter into thy gates, †as men enter into a citie wherein is made a breach.

† Hebr. according to the entrings of a city broken vp.

11 With the hoofes of his horses shall he tread downe all thy streets : he shall slay thy people by the sword, and thy strong garisons shall goe downe to the ground.

12 And they shall make a spoile of thy riches, and make a pray of thy merchandise, and they shall breake downe thy walles, and destroy † thy pleasant houses, and they shall lay thy stones, and thy timber, and thy dust in the midst of the water.

† Heb. houses of thy desire.

13 * And I wil cause the noise of thy songs to cease, and the sound of thy harpes shalbe no more heard.

* Isa. 24. 8. iere. 7. 34. and 16. 9.

14 And I will make thee like the top of a rocke : they shall bee a place to spread nets vpon : thou shalt bee built no more : for I the LORD haue spoken it, saith the Lord GOD.

15 ¶ Thus saith the Lord GOD to Tyrus; Shall not the Iles shake at the sound of thy fall, when the wounded crie, when the slaughter is made in the midst of thee ?

16 Then all the Princes of the sea shall come downe from their thrones, and lay away their robes, and put off their broidred garments . they shall cloth themselues with † trembling, they shall sit vpon the ground, aud shall tremble at euery moment, and be astonished at thee.

† Hebr. tremblings.

17 And they shall take vp a * lamentation for thee, and say to thee, How art thou destroyed that wast inhabited of †Sea-faring men, the renowned citie, which wast strong in the sea, she and her inhabitants, which cause their terrour to be on all that haunt it ?

* Reuel. 18. 9.

† Hebr. of the seas.

18 Now shall the Iles tremble in the day of thy fall, yea the Iles that are in the sea, shall bee troubled at thy departure.

19 For thus saith the Lord GOD; When I shal make thee a desolate citie, like the cities that are not inhabited, when I shall bring vp the deepe vpon thee, and great waters shall couer thee ;

20 When I shall bring thee downe, with them that descend into the pit, with the people of old time, and shall set thee in the low parts of the earth, in places desolate of olde, with them that goe downe to the pit, that thou bee not

inhabited, and I shall set glorie in the land of the liuing :

21 I will make thee a †terrour, and thou shalt bee no more : though thou be sought for, yet shalt thou neuer bee found againe, saith the Lord GOD.

† Hebr. terrours.

CHAP. XXVII.

1 The rich supply of Tyrus. 26 The great and vnrecouerable fall thereof.

 He word of the LORD came againe vnto mee, saying,

2 Now thou sonne of man; take vp a lamentation for Tyrus;

3 And say vnto Tyrus, O thou that art situate at the entrie of the sea, which art a merchant of the people for many Iles, Thus saith the Lord GOD; O Tyrus, thou hast said, I am †of perfit beautie.

† Hebr. perfit of beautie.

4 Thy borders are in the †midst of the seas, thy builders haue perfected thy beautie.

† Hebr. heart.

5 They haue † made all thy shippe bords of firre trees of Senir : they haue taken Cedars from Lebanon, to make mastes for thee.

† Hebr. buil

6 Of the okes of Bashan haue they made thine ‖ oares : the † companie of the Ashurites haue made thy benches of Yuorie, brought out of the Iles of Chittim.

‖ Or, they haue made hatches of Yuorie wel troden.
† Heb. the daughter.

7 Fine linnen with broidred worke from Egypt, was that which thou spreddest forth to be thy saile, ‖ blew and purple from the Iles of Elishah was that which couered thee.

‖ Or, purple and scarlet.

8 The inhabitants of Zidon and Aruad were thy mariners : thy wise men, O Tyrus, that were in thee, were thy pilots.

9 The ancients of Gebal, and the wise men thereof were in thee thy ‖calkers, all the ships of the sea with their mariners were in thee, to occupie thy merchandise.

‖ Or, stoppers of chinks. Heb strengthners.

10 They of Persia, and of Lud, and of Phut were in thine army, thy men of warre : they hanged the shield and helmetin thee : they set forth thy comelines.

11 The men of Aruad with thine armie were vpon thy wals round about, and the Gammadims were in thy towres : they hanged their shields vpon thy wals round about : they haue made thy beautie perfect.

12 Tar-

12 Tarshish *was* thy merchant by reason of the multitude of all *kinde of* riches : with siluer, yron, tinne, and lead they traded in thy faires.

13 Iauan, Tubal and Meshech, they *were* thy merchants : they traded the persons of men, and vessels of brasse in thy ‖ market.

Or, mer-sandise.

14 They of the house of Togarmah traded in thy faires with horses, and horsemen, and mules.

15 The men of Dedan *were* thy merchants, many Iles *were* the merchandise of thine hand : they brought thee for a present, hornes of Iuorie, and Ebenie.

16 Syria *was* thy merchant by reason of the multitude of the † wares of thy making : they occupied in thy faires with Emeraulds, purple, and broidered worke, and fine linen, and Corall, and ‖ Agate.

Hebr. orkes.

Or, Chrys-prase.

17 Iudah and the land of Israel they *were* thy merchants : they traded in thy market wheate of Minnith, and Pannag, and honie, and oyle, & ‖ balme.

Or, rosin.

18 Damascus *was* thy merchant in the multitude of the *wares* of thy making, for the multitude of all riches : in the wine of Helbon, and white wooll.

19 Dan also and Iauan ‖ going to and fro, occupied in thy faires : bright yron, Cassia and Calamus were in thy market.

Or, Meu-ull.

20 Dedan *was* thy merchant in † precious clothes for charets.

Hebr. othes of reedome.

21 Arabia and all the princes of Kedar, † they occupied with thee in lambes and rammes and goats : in these *were* they thy merchants.

Heb. they ere the erchants † thy hand.

22 The merchants of Shebah and Raamah, they were thy merchants : they occupied in thy faires with chiefe of all spices, and with all precious stones and golde.

23 Haran, and Canneh, and Eden, the merchants of Shebah, Asshur *and* Chilmad *were* thy merchants.

24 These *were* thy merchants in all ‖ sorts *of things*, in blewe † clothes and broidered worke, and in chests of rich apparell, bound with cordes and made of Cedar among thy merchandise.

Or, excel-ent things. Heb. fol-ings.

25 The ships of Tarshish did sing of thee in thy market, and thou wast replenished, and made very glorious in the middest of the seas.

26 ¶ Thy rowers haue brought thee into great waters . the East winde hath broken thee in the † middest of the Seas.

† *Heb. heart.*

27 Thy * riches and thy faires, thy merchandise, thy mariners, and thy pilots, thy calkers, and the occupiers of thy merchandise, and all thy men of warre that *are* in thee, ‖ and in all thy company, which *is* in the midst of thee, shall fall into the‖ middest of the seas, in the day of thy ruine.

* *Reu. 18. 9, &c.*

‖ *Or, euen withall.*

‖ *Or, heart.*

28 The ‖ suburbs shall shake at the sound of the crie of thy pilots.

‖ *Or, waues.*

29 And all that handle the oare ; the mariners, *and* all the pilots of the Sea, shal come downe from their ships, they shall stand vpon the land ;

30 And shall cause their voice to be heard against thee, and shall crie bitterly, and shall cast vp dust vpon their heads, they shall wallow themselues in the ashes.

31 And they shall make themselues vtterly balde for thee, and girde them with sackecloth, and they shall weepe for thee with bitternesse of heart *and* bitter wailing.

32 And in their wailing, they shall take vp a lamentation for thee, and lament ouer thee, *saying*; What *citie is* like Tyrus, like the destroyed in the middest of the sea ?

33 When thy wares went foorth out of the seas, thou filledst many people, thou didst enrich the kings of the earth, with the multitude of thy riches, and of thy merchandise.

34 In the time *when* thou shalt be broken by the seas in the depths of the waters, thy merchandise and all thy companie in the middest of thee shal fall.

35 All the inhabitants of the Iles shall bee astonished at thee, and their kings shall be sore afraid, they shall be troubled in *their* countenance.

36 The merchants among the people shall hisse at thee, thou shalt bee a † terrour, and † neuer *shalt be* any more.

† *Heb. ter-rours.*

† *Heb. shalt not be for euer.*

C H A P. XXVIII.

1 Gods iudgement vpon the prince of Tyrus, for his sacrilegious pride. 11 A lamentation, of his great glory corrupted by sinne. 20 The iudgement of Zidon. 24 The restauration of Israel.

 He word of the LORD came againe vnto me, saying,

2 Sonne of man, say vnto the prince of Tyrus, Thus

Thus saith the Lord God; Because thine heart is lifted vp, and thou hast said, I *am* a God, I sit *in* the seate of God in the †middest of the seas; *yet thou *art* a man and not God, though thou set thine heart as the heart of God.

† Heb. heart.
* Isai. 31. 13.

3 Behold, thou *art* wiser then Daniel: there is no secret that they can hide from thee.

4 With thy wisedome and with thine vnderstanding thou hast gotten thee riches, and hast gotten gold and siluer into thy treasures.

5 †By thy great wisedome, *and* by thy traffique hast thou increased thy riches, and thine heart is lifted vp because of thy riches.

† Heb. by the greatnesse of thy wisedome.

6 Therefore thus saith the Lord God; Because thou hast set thine heart as the heart of God;

7 Behold therefore, I will bring strangers vpon thee, the terrible of the nations: and they shall draw their swords against the beautie of thy wisedome, & they shall defile thy brightnesse.

8 They shall bring thee downe to the pit, and thou shalt die the deaths of them, that are slaine in the middest of the seas.

9 Wilt thou yet say before him that slayeth thee, I *am* God? but thou *shalt be* a man, and no God in the hand of him that ‖slayeth thee.

‖ Or, woundeth.

10 Thou shalt die the deaths of the vncircumcised, by the hand of strangers: for I haue spoken *it*, saith the Lord God.

11 ¶ Moreouer the word of the Lord came vnto me, saying;

12 Sonne of man, take vp a lamentation vpon the king of Tyrus, and say vnto him, Thus saith the Lord God; Thou sealest vp the summe, full of wisedome and perfect in beautie.

13 Thou hast beene in Eden the garden of God; euery precious stone *was* thy couering, the ‖Sardius, Topaze, and the Diamond, the ‖Beril, the Onyx, and the Iasper, the Saphir, the ‖Emeraude, and the Carbuncle and gold: the workmanship of thy tabrets and of thy pipes was prepared in thee, in the day that thou wast created.

‖ Or, ruby.
‖ Or, chrysolite.
‖ Or, Chrysoprase.

14 Thou art the annointed Cherub that couereth: and I haue set thee *so*; thou wast vpon the holy mountaine of God; thou hast walked vp and downe in the middest of the stones of fire.

15 Thou *wast* perfect in thy wayes from the day that thou wast created, till iniquitie was found in thee.

16 By the multitude of thy merchandise they haue filled the middest of thee with violence, and thou hast sinned: therefore I will cast thee as prophane out of the mountaine of God: and I wil destroy thee, O couering Cherub, from the middest of the stones of fire.

17 Thine heart was lifted vp because of thy beautie, thou hast corrupted thy wisedome by reason of thy brightnesse: I will cast thee to the ground: I will lay thee before kings, that they may behold thee.

18 Thou hast defiled thy sanctuaries by the multitude of thine iniquities, by the iniquitie of thy traffique: therefore will I bring forth a fire from the middest of thee, it shall deuoure thee: and I will bring thee to ashes vpon the earth in the sight of all them that behold thee.

19 All they that know thee among the people, shall be astonished at thee: thou shalt be a †terrour, and neuer *shalt* thou *be* any more.

† Heb. terrours.

20 ¶ Againe the word of the Lord came vnto me, saying;

21 Sonne of man, set thy face against Zidon, and prophecie against it,

22 And say, Thus saith the Lord God; Behold, I *am* against thee, O Zidon, and I will be glorified in the middest of thee: and they shall know that I *am* the Lord, when I shall haue executed iudgements in her, and shall be sanctified in her.

23 For I will send into her, pestilence, and blood into her streetes, and the wounded shall be iudged in the middest of her by the sword vpon her on euery side, and they shall know that I *am* the Lord.

24 ¶ And there shall be no more a pricking briar vnto the house of Israel, nor *any* grieuing thorne of all that *are* round about them that despised them, and they shal know that I *am* the Lord God.

25 Thus saith the Lord God; When I shall haue gathered the house of Israel fro the people among whom they are scattered, and shall be sanctified in them in the sight of the heathen, then shall they dwell in their land, that I haue giuen to my seruant Iacob.

26 And they shal dwell ‖safely therein, and shall build houses, and plant vineyards:

‖ Or, with confidence.

vineyards yea, they shall dwell with confidence when I haue executed iudgments vpon all those that ||despise them round about them, and they shal know that I am the Lord their GOD.

CHAP. XXIX.

1 The iudgement of Pharaoh, for his treachery to Israel. 8 The desolation of Egypt. 13 The restauration thereof, after fourtie yeeres. 17 Egypt the reward of Nebuchad-rezzar. 21 Israel shall be restored.

IN the tenth yeere, in the tenth *moneth*, in the twelft *day* of the moneth, the word of the LORD came vnto me, saying,

2 Sonne of man, set thy face against Pharaoh king of Egypt, and prophecie against him, and against all Egypt.

3 Speake and say, Thus saith the Lord GOD, Behold, I *am* against thee, Pharaoh king of Egypt, the great *dragon that lieth in the middest of his riuers, which hath saide, My riuer *is* mine owne, and I haue made *it* for my selfe.

4 But I will put hookes in thy chawes, and I will cause the fish of thy riuers to sticke vnto thy scales, and I will bring thee vp out of the middest of thy riuers, and all the fish of thy riuers shall sticke vnto thy scales.

5 And I will leaue thee *throwen* into the wildernes, thee and all the fish of thy riuers thou shalt fall vpon the †open fields, thou shalt not be brought together, nor gathered : I haue giuen thee for meat to the beastes of the field, and to the foules of the heauen.

6 And all the inhabitants of Egypt shall know that I *am* the LORD, because they haue bene a*staffe of reede to the house of Israel.

7 When they tooke hold of thee by thy hand, thou didst breake, and rent all their shoulder · and when they leaned vpon thee, thou brakest, and madest all their loynes to be at a stand.

8 ¶ Therefore thus saith the Lord GOD, Behold, I will bring a sword vpon thee, and cut off man and beast out of thee.

9 And the land of Egypt shalbe desolate and waste, and they shall knowe that I *am* the LORD : because he hath saide, The riuer *is* mine, and I haue made *it*.

10 Beholde therefore, I *am* against thee, and against thy riuers, and I wil make the land of Egypt †vtterly waste and desolate, from the towre of †Syene euen vnto the border of Ethiopia.

11 No foot of man shal passe through it, nor foote of beast shall passe through it, neither shall it bee inhabited fourtie yeeres.

12 And I will make the land of Egypt desolate in the midst of the countreys that are desolate, and her cities among the cities that are layed waste, shall be desolate fourtie yeeres : and I will scatter the Egyptians among the nations, and wil disperse them through the countreys.

13 ¶ Yet thus saith the Lord GOD, At the *end of fourtie yeeres will I gather the Egyptians from the people whither they were scattered.

14 And I will bring againe the captiuitie of Egypt, and will cause them to returne into the land of Pathros, into the land of their ||habitation, and they shall be there a †base kingdome.

15 It shall be the basest of the kingdomes, neither shall it exalt it selfe any more aboue the nations: for I will diminish them, that they shall no more rule ouer the nations.

16 And it shall be no more the confidence of the house of Israel, which bringeth *their* iniquity to remembrance, when they shall looke after them : but they shall know that I *am* the Lord GOD.

17 ¶ And it came to passe in the seuen and twentieth yeere, in the first *moneth*, in the first *day* of the moneth, the worde of the LORD came vnto me, saying,

18 Sonne of man, Nebuchad-rezzar king of Babylon caused his armie to serue a great seruice against Tyrus : euery head was made balde, and euery shoulder was peeled: yet had he no wages, nor his armie for Tyrus, for the seruice that he had serued against it.

19 Therefore thus saith the Lord GOD, Behold, I will giue the land of Egypt vnto Nebuchad-rezzar king of Babylon, and he shall take her multitude, and †take her spoile, and take her praye, and it shall be the wages for his armie.

20 I haue giuen him the land of Egypt ||for his labour wherewith he serued against it, because they wrought for me, saith the Lord GOD.

21 ¶ In

Margin notes

||Or, spoile.

Psal. 74. 8, 14. isa. 2. 1. & 51.

Heb. face of the field.

* 2. Kings 8. 21. isa. 36. 6.

† Heb. wastes of waste.
† Heb. Seueneh.

* Isai. 19. 23. ier. 46. 26.

||Or, birth.
† Heb. low.

† Heb. spoile her spoile and prayher pray.

||Or, for his hire.

21 ¶ In that day will I cause the horne of the house of Israel to budde forth, and I will giue thee the opening of the mouth in the midst of them, and they shal know that I *am* the LORD.

CHAP. XXX.

1 The desolation of Egypt, and her helpers. 20 The arme of Babylon shalbe strengthened to breake the arme of Egypt.

THE word of the LORD came againe vnto me, saying,
2 Sonne of man, prophecie and say, Thus saith the Lord GOD, Howle ye, woe worth the day.
3 For the day *is* neere, euen the day of the LORD *is* neere, a cloudie day; it shalbe the time of the heathen.
4 And the sword shall come vpon Egypt, and great ||paine shalbe in Ethiopia, when the slaine shall fall in Egypt, and they shall take away her multitude, and her foundations shalbe broken downe.
5 Ethiopia, and †Libya, and Lydia, and all the mingled people, and Chub, and the †men of the land that is in league, shal fal with them by the sword.
6 Thus saith the LORD, They also that vphold Egypt shall fall, and the pride of her power shall come downe: from the towre of Syene shall they fall in it by the sword, saith the Lord GOD.
7 And they shall bee desolate in the midst of the countries that are desolate, and her cities shalbe in the midst of the cities that are wasted.
8 And they shall know that I *am* the LORD, when I haue set a fire in Egypt, and *when* all her helpers shall be †destroied.
9 In that day shall messengers goe foorth from me in shippes, to make the carelesse Ethiopians afraid, and great paine shall come vpon them, as in the day of Egypt: for loe, it commeth.
10 Thus saith the Lord GOD, I will also make the multitude of Egypt to cease by the hand of Nebuchad-rezzar, king of Babylon.
11 He and his people with him, the terrible of the nations shall be brought to destroy the land: and they shall draw their swords against Egypt, and fill the land with the slaine.

|| Or, feare.
† Heb. Phut.
† Hebr. children.
† Hebr. broken.

12 And I wil make the riuers †drie, and sell the land into the hand of the wicked, and I wil make the land wast, and †all that is therein, by the hand of strangers: I the LORD haue spoken *it*.
13 Thus saith the Lord GOD, I will also *destroy the idoles, and I will cause *their* images to cease out of Noph: and there shalbe no more a Prince of the land of Egypt, and I will put a feare in the land of Egypt.
14 And I wil make Pathros desolate, and wil set fire in ||Zoan, and will execute iudgements in No.
15 And I wil powre my furie vpon ||Sin, the strength of Egypt, and I wil cut off the multitude of No.
16 And I will set fire in Egypt, Sin shall haue great paine, and No shall be rent asunder, and Noph shall haue distresses daily.
17 The yong men of ||Auen and of ||Phibeseth, shall fall by the sword: and these *cities* shall goe into captiuitie.
18 At Tehaphnehes also the day shalbe ||darkened when I shall breake there the yokes of Egypt: & the pompe of her strength shall cease in her: as for her, a cloud shall couer her, and her daughters shall goe into captiuitie.
19 Thus will I execute iudgements in Egypt, and they shall know that I *am* the LORD.
20 ¶ And it came to passe in the eleuenth yeere, in the first *moneth*, in the seuenth *day* of the moneth, *that* the word of the LORD came vnto me, saying,
21 Sonne of man, I haue broken the arme of Pharaoh king of Egypt, and loe, it shall not be bound vp to be healed, to put a rouler to binde it, to make it strong to hold the sword.
22 Therefore thus saith the Lord GOD, Behold, I *am* against Pharaoh king of Egypt, and will breake his armes, the strong, and that which was broken; and I wil cause the sword to fall out of his hand.
23 And I wil scatter the Egyptians among the nations, and wil disperse them through the countries.
24 And I wil strengthen the armes of the king of Babylon, and put my sword in his hand: but I will breake Pharaohs armes, and he shall grone before him, with the groanings of a deadly wounded man.
25 But I wil strengthen the armes of

† Hebr. drought.
† Hebr. the fulnesse thereof.
* Zach. 13. 2.
|| Or, Tanis.
|| Or, Pelusium.
|| Or, Heliopolis.
|| Or, Pubastum.
|| Or, restrained.

of the king of Babylon, and the armes of Pharaoh shall fall downe, and they shall knowe that I *am* the LORD, when I shall put my sword into the hand of the king of Babylon, & he shall stretch it out vpon the land of Egypt.

26 And I wil scatter the Egyptians among the nations, and disperse them among the countreys, and they shall know that I *am* the LORD.

CHAP. XXXI.

1 A relation vnto Pharaoh, 3 of the glory of Assyria, 10 and the fall thereof, for pride. 18 The like destruction of Egypt.

Nd it came to passe in the eleuenth yeere, in the third *moneth*, in the first *day* of the moneth, *that* the word of the LORD came vnto mee, saying;

2 Sonne of man, speake vnto Pharaoh king of Egypt, and to his multitude, Whom art thou like in thy greatnesse?

3 ¶ Behold, the Assyrian *was* a Cedar in Lebanon †with faire branches, and with a shadowing shrowd, and of an hie stature, and his top was among the thicke boughes.

4 The waters ‖made him great, the deepe ‖set him vp on high with her riuers running round about his plants, and sent out her †little riuers vnto all the trees of the field.

5 Therefore his height was exalted aboue all the trees of the field, and his boughes were multiplied, and his branches became long because of the multitude of waters, ‖when he shot foorth.

6 All the *foules of heauen made their nests in his boughes, and vnder his branches did all the beastes of the field bring foorth their yong, and vnder his shadow dwelt all great nations.

7 Thus was hee faire in his greatnesse, in the length of his branches : for his roote was by great waters.

8 The Cedars in the *garden of God could not hide him : the Firre trees were not like his boughes, and the chesnut trees were not like his branches : not any tree in the garden of God, was like vnto him in his beautie.

9 I haue made him faire by the multitude of his branches : so that all the trees of Eden, that *were* in the garden of God, enuied him.

10 ¶ Therefore thus saith the Lord

GOD, Because thou hast lifted vp thy selfe in height, and hee hath shot vp his top among the thicke boughes, and his heart is lifted vp in his height ;

11 I haue therefore deliuered him into the hand of the mightie one of the heathen : hee shall surely †deale with him, I haue driuen him out for his wickednesse.

12 And strangers, the terrible of the nations haue cut him off, and haue left him : vpon the mountaines and in all the valleys his branches are fallen, and his boughes are broken by all the riuers of the land, and all the people of the earth are gone downe from his shadow, and haue left him.

13 Vpon his ruine shal all the foules of the heauen remaine, & all the beasts of the field shalbe vpon his branches,

14 To the ende that none of all the trees by the waters exalt themselues for their height, neither shoot vp their top among the thicke boughes, neither ‖their trees stand vp in their height, all that drinke water : for they are all deliuered vnto death, to the nether parts of the earth, in the middest of the children of men, with them that go downe to the pit.

15 Thus saith the Lord GOD, In the day when hee went downe to the graue, I caused a mourning, I couered the deepe for him, and I restrained the floods therof, and the great waters were stayed ; and I caused Lebanon ‖to mourne for him, and all the trees of the field fainted for him.

16 I made the nations to shake at the sound of his fall, when I cast him downe to hell with them that descend into the pit : and all the trees of Eden, the choice and best of Lebanon, all that drinke water, shall be comforted in the nether parts of the earth.

17 They also went downe into hell with him vnto them that be slaine with the sword, and *they that were* his arme, *that* dwelt vnder his shadow in the middest of the heathen.

18 ¶ To whom art thou thus like in glory & in greatnesse among the trees of Eden? yet shalt thou be brought downe with the trees of Eden vnto the nether parts of the earth : thou shalt lie in the middest of the vncircumcised, with them that be slaine by the sword : this *is* Pharaoh and all his multitude, saith the Lord GOD.

CHAP.

Side notes:

† *Heb. faire of branches.*

‖ *Or, nourished.*
‖ *Or, brought him vp.*
† *Heb. continuis.*

‖ *Or, when it sent them foorth.*
* *Dan. 4.*

* *Gen. 2.*

† *Heb. in doing hee shall doe vnto him.*

‖ *Or, stand vpon themselues for their height.*

† *Hebr. to be blacke.*

CHAP. XXXII.

1 A lamentation for the fearefull fall of Egypt. 11 The sword of Babylon shall destroy it. 17 It shall be brought downe to hell, among all the vncircumcised Nations.

AND it came to passe in the twelfth yeere, in the twelft moneth, in the first *day* of the moneth, *that* the word of the LORD came vnto me, saying;

2 Sonne of man, take vp a lamentation for Pharaoh king of Egypt, and say vnto him; Thou art like a young lyon of the nations, & thou *art* as ‖ a whale in the seas: and thou camest forth with thy riuers, and troubledst the waters with thy feet, and fouledst their riuers.

‖ *Or, dragon.*

3 Thus saith the Lord GOD; I will therefore * spread out my net ouer thee, with a company of many people, and they shall bring thee vp in my net.

* Chap. 12. 13. and 17. 20.

4 Then will I leaue thee vpon the land, I will cast thee forth vpon the open field, and will cause all the foules of the heauen to remaine vpon thee, and I will fill the beasts of the whole earth with thee.

5 And I will lay thy flesh vpon the mountaines, and fill the valleis with thy height.

6 I will also water with thy blood ‖ the land wherein thou swimmest, *euen* to the mountaines, and the riuers shall be full of thee.

‖ *Or, the land of thy swimming.*

7 And when I shall ‖ * put thee out, I wil couer the heauen, and make the starres thereof darke: I will couer the sunne with a cloud, and the moone shall not giue her light.

‖ *Or, extinguish.* * Isai. 13. 10. ioel. 2. 31. and 3. 15. matth. 24. 29.

8 All the † bright lights of heauen will I make † darke ouer thee, and set darkenesse vpon thy land, saith the Lord GOD.

† *Heb. lights of the light in heauen.* † *Heb. them darke.*

9 I wil also † vex the hearts of many people, when I shall bring thy destruction among the nations, into the countries which thou hast not knowen.

† *Heb, prouoke to anger, or griefe.*

10 Yea I will make many people amazed at thee, and their kings shall be horribly afraide for thee, when I shall brandish my sword before them, and they shall tremble at *euery* moment; euerie man for his owne life, in the day of thy fall.

11 ¶ For thus saith the Lord GOD, The sword of the king of Babylon shal come vpon thee.

12 By the swords of the mighty will I cause thy multitude to fall, the terrible of the nations all of them: and they shall spoile the pompe of Egypt, and all the multitude therof shall be destroyed.

13 I will destroy also all the beasts thereof from besides the great waters, neither shall the foote of man trouble them any more, nor the hoofes of beasts trouble them.

14 Then will I make their waters deepe, and cause their riuers to runne like oyle, saith the Lord GOD.

15 When I shall make the land of Egypt desolate, and the countrey shall be † destitute of that wherof it was full; when I shall smite all them that dwell therein, then shal they know that I *am* the LORD.

† *Heb. desolate from the fulnesse therof.*

16 This *is* the lamentation wherewith they shall lament her: the daughters of the nations shall lament her: they shall lament for her, *euen* for Egypt and for al her multitude, saith the Lord GOD.

17 ¶ It came to passe also in the twelfth yeere, in the fifteenth *day* of the moneth, *that* the word of the LORD came vnto me, saying;

18 Sonne of man, waile for the multitude of Egypt, & cast them downe, *euen* her, and the daughters of the famous nations, vnto the nether parts of the earth, with them that goe downe into the pit.

19 Whom doest thou passe in beautie? goe downe, and be thou layed with the vncircumcised.

20 They shall fall in the middest of them that are slaine by the sword: she is deliuered ‖ to the sword; draw her and all her multitudes.

‖ *Or, the sword is layd.*

21 The strong among the mighty shall speake to him out of the middest of hell with them that helpe him: they are gone downe, they lie vncircumcised, slaine by the sword.

22 Ashur *is* there, and all her companie: his graues *are* about him: al of them slaine, fallen by the sword.

23 Whose graues are set in the sides of the pit, and her company is round about her graue: all of them slaine, fallen by the sword, which caused ‖ terrour in the land of the liuing.

‖ *Or, dismaying.*

24 There *is* Elam and all her multitude round about her graue, all of them slaine, fallen by the sword, which are gone downe vncircumcised into the

the nether parts of the earth, which caused their terrour in the lande of the liuing, yet haue they borne their shame with them that goe downe to the pit.

25 They haue set her a bed in the midst of the slaine with all her multitudes : her graues *are* round about him, all of them vncircumcised, slaine by the sword : though their terrour was caused in the land of the liuing, yet haue they borne their shame with them that goe downe to the pit : he is put in the midst of them that be slaine.

26 There *is* Meshech, Tubal, and all her multitude : her graues *are* round about him : all of them vncircumcised, slaine by the sword, though they caused their terrour in the land of the liuing.

27 And they shall not lie with the mightie, *that are* fallen of the vncircumcised, which are gone downe to hell † with their weapons of warre : and they haue laid their swords vnder their heads, but their iniquities shalbe vpon their bones, though *they were* the terrour of the mightie in the land of the liuing.

Hebr. with weapons of their warre.

28 Yea thou shalt be broken in the midst of the vncircumcised, and shalt lie with them that are slaine with ẙ sword.

29 There *is* Edom, her kings and all her princes, which with their might are † laid by them that were slaine by the sword : they shall lie with the vncircumcised, and with them that go downe to the pit.

Heb. giuen or put.

30 There *be* the princes of the North all of them, and all the Zidonians : which are gone downe with the slaine, with their terrour they are ashamed of their might, and they lie vncircumcised with them that be slaine by the sword, and beare their shame with them that goe downe to the pit.

31 Pharaoh shall see them, and shall bee comforted ouer all his multitude, *euen* Pharaoh and all his armie slaine by the sword, saith the Lord God.

32 For I haue caused my terrour in the land of the liuing : and he shall bee laid in the midst of the vncircumcised with them that are slaine with the sword, *euen* Pharaoh and all his multitude, saith the Lord God.

CHAP. XXXIII.

1 According to the duetie of a watchman, in warning the people, 7 Ezekiel is admonished of his duetie. 20 God sheweth the iustice of his wayes towards the penitent, and towards reuolters. 17 Hee maintaineth his Iustice. 21 Vpon the newes of the taking of Ierusalem, he prophecieth the desolation of the land. 30 Gods iudgment vpon the mockers of the Prophets.

Gaine the worde of the Lord came vnto mee, saying,

2 Sonne of man, speake to the children of thy people, and say vnto them, † When I bring the sword vpon a land, if the people of the land take a man of their coasts, and set him for their watchman,

† Heb. a land when I bring a sword vpon her.

3 If when he seeth the sword come vpon the land, hee blow the trumpet, and warne the people,

4 Then † whosoeuer heareth the sound of the trumpet, and taketh not warning, if the sword come, and take him away, his blood shall be vpon his owne head.

† Heb. hee that hearing heareth.

5 Hee heard the sound of the trumpet, and tooke not warning, his blood shall be vpon him : but he that taketh warning, shall deliuer his soule.

6 But if the watchman see the sword come, and blow not the trumpet, and the people be not warned : if the sword come and take any person from among them, he is taken away in his iniquitie : but his blood will I require at the watchmans hand.

7 ¶ *So thou, O sonne of man, I haue set thee a watchman vnto the house of Israel : therefore thou shalt heare the worde at my mouth, and warne them from me.

* Chap. 3. 17, &c.

8 When I say vnto the wicked, O wicked man, thou shalt surely die, if thou doest not speake to warne the wicked from his way, that wicked man shall die in his iniquitie : but his blood will I require at thine hand.

9 Neuerthelesse if thou warne the wicked of his way to turne from it : if he do not turne from his way, he shal die in his iniquitie : but thou hast deliuered thy soule.

10 Therefore, O thou sonne of man, speake vnto the house of Israel, Thus ye speake, saying, If our transgressions and our sinnes *be* vpon vs, & we pine away in them, how should we then liue?

11 Say vnto them, *As I liue, saith the Lord God, I haue no pleasure in the death of the wicked, but that the wicked turne from his way & liue : turne ye,

* 2. Sam. 14 14. chap. 18 32.

* Chap. 18.
31.

ye, turne ye from your euill wayes, for *why wil ye die, O house of Israel?

12 Therefore thou sonne of man, say vnto the children of thy people, The *righteousnes of the righteous shal not deliuer him in the day of his transgression : as for the wickednes of the wicked, he shall not fall thereby in the day that hee turneth from his wickednes, neither shall the righteous bee able to liue *for his righteousnes* in the day that he sinneth.

* Chap. 18.
24.

13 When I shal say to the righteous, that he shall surely liue; if he trust to his owne righteousnes and commit iniquitie, all his righteousnesses shall not be remembred; but for his iniquitie that he hath committed, he shall die for it.

14 Againe, when I say vnto the wicked, Thou shalt surely die, if hee turne from his sinne, and do that which is †lawfull and right;

† Heb. iudgement and iustice.

15 *If* the wicked restore the pledge, giue againe that he had robbed, walke in the Statutes of life without committing iniquitie, hee shall surely liue, hee shall not die.

16 None of his sinnes that hee hath committed, shall be mentioned vnto him : he hath done that which is lawfull and right; he shall surely liue.

17 ¶ Yet the children of thy people say, The way of the Lord is not equall : but as for them, their way is not equall.

18 When the righteous turneth from his righteousnes, and committeth iniquitie, he shall euen die thereby.

19 But if the wicked turne from his wickednes, and doe that which is lawfull and right, he shall liue thereby.

* Chap. 18.
25.

20 ¶ Yet yee say, *The way of the Lord is not equall, O yee house of Israel; I will iudge you euery one after his wayes.

21 ¶ And it came to passe in the twelfth yeere of our captiuitie, in the tenth *moneth,* in the fifth *day* of the moneth, *that* one that had escaped out of Ierusalem, came vnto mee, saying,

* 2. Kings.
25.

*The city is smitten.

22 Now the hand of the Lord was vpon mee in the euening, afore hee that was escaped came, and had opened my mouth vntill hee came to mee in the morning, and my mouth was opened,

* Chap. 24.
27.

and I was no more *dumbe.

23 Then the word of the Lord came vnto me, saying,

24 Sonne of man, they that inhabite those wastes of the land of Israel, speake, saying, Abraham was one, and he inherited the land : but we *are* many, the land is giuen vs for inheritance.

25 Wherefore say vnto them, Thus saith the Lord God, Ye eate with the blood, and lift vp your eyes toward your idoles, and shed blood; and shal ye possesse the land?

26 Yee stand vpon your sword; yee worke abomination, and ye defile euery one his neighbours wife, and shall ye possesse the land?

27 Say thou thus vnto them, Thus saith the Lord God, As I liue, surely they that are in the wastes, shall fall by the sword, and him that is in the open field will I giue to the beasts †to be deuoured : and they that *be* in the forts and in the caues, shall die of the pestilence.

† Hebr. to deuoure him.

28 For I will lay the land †most desolate, and the *pompe of her strength shall cease : and the mountaines of Israel shall bee desolate, that none shall passe through.

† Hebr. desolation and desolation.
* Chap. 7.
24. and 24.
21. and 39.
6, 7.

29 Then shall they know that I *am* the Lord, when I haue layed the land most desolate, because of all their abominations which they haue committed.

30 ¶ Also thou sonne of man, the children of thy people still are talking against thee by the walles, and in the doores of the houses, and speake one to another, euery one to his brother, saying, Come, I pray you, and heare what is the word that commeth foorth from the Lord.

31 And they come vnto thee †as the people commeth, and they ‖sit before thee *as* my people, and they heare thy words, but they will not doe them : for with their mouth †they shew much loue, *but* their heart goeth after their couetousnesse.

† Hebr. according to the comming of the people.
‖ Or, my people sit before thee.
† Hebr. the, make loues or iestes.

32 And loe, thou *art* vnto them as †a very louely song of one that hath a pleasant voyce, and can play well on an instrument : for they heare thy wordes, but they doe them not.

† Hebr. a song of loues

33 And when this commeth to passe, (loe it will come) then shall they know that a Prophet hath bene among them.

CHAP. XXXIIII.

1 A reproofe of the shepheards. 7 Gods iudgement against them. 11 His prouidence for his flocke. 20 The kingdome of Christ.

And

Iere. 23. 1.

Nd the word of ẙ Lord came vnto me, saying;

2 Sonne of man, prophecie against the *shepheards of Israel, prophecie and say vnto them, Thus saith the Lord God vnto the shepheards, Woe *be* to the shepheards of Israel that doe feede themselues : should not the shepheards feede the flockes ?

3 Yee eate the fat, and ye clothe you with the wooll, yee kill them that are fed : *but* ye feede not the flocke.

4 The diseased haue ye not strengthened, neither haue yee healed that which was sicke, neither haue ye bound vp that which was broken, neither haue yee brought againe that which was driuen away, neither haue yee sought that which was lost; but with *force and with crueltie haue yee ruled them.

1. Pet. 5. 3.

Or, without a shepheard: and verse 8.

5 And they were scattered ||because *there is* no shepheard: and they became meate to all the beasts of the field, when they were scattered.

6 My sheepe wandered through all the mountaines, and vpon euery high hill : yea my flocke was scattered vpon all the face of the earth, and none did search or seeke *after them.*

7 ¶ Therefore, yee shepheards, heare the word of the Lord.

8 As I liue, saith the Lord God, surely because my flocke became a pray, and my flocke became meate to euery beast of the field, because *there was* no shepheard, neither did my shepheards search for my flocke, but the shepheards fed themselues, and fed not my flocke:

9 Therefore, O yee shepheards, heare the word of the Lord.

10 Thus saith the Lord God, Behold, I *am* against the shepheards, and I will require my flocke at their hand, and cause them to cease from feeding the flocke, neither shall the shepheards feede themselues any more : for I will deliuer my flock from their mouth, that they may not be meat for them.

11 ¶ For thus saith the Lord God, Behold, I, *euen* I will both search my sheepe, and seeke them out.

Heb. according to the ſecking.

12 †As a shepheard seeketh out his flocke in the day that hee is among his sheepe that are scattered : so wil I seeke out my sheep, and will deliuer them out of all places, where they haue bene scattered in the cloudie and darke day.

13 And I will bring them out from the people, and gather them from the countreys, and will bring them to their owne land, and feede them vpon the mountaines of Israel by the riuers, and in all the inhabited places of the countrey,

14 I will feede them in a good pasture, and vpon the high mountaines of Israel shall their folde be : there shall they lie in a good folde, and *in* a fat pasture shall they feede vpon the mountaines of Israel.

15 I will feed my flocke, and I will cause them to lie downe, saith the Lord God.

16 I will seeke that which was lost, and bring againe that which was driuen away, and will bind vp that which was broken, and will strengthen that which was sicke : but I will destroy the fat and the strong, I will feed them with iudgement.

17 And as for you, O my flocke, thus saith the Lord God, Behold, I iudge betweene †cattell and cattell, betweene the rammes and the †hee goates.

† Heb. small cattell of lambes and kids.
† Heb. great hee goats.

18 Seemeth it a small thing vnto you, to haue eaten vp the good pasture, but ye must tread downe with your feet the residue of your pastures ? and to haue drunke of the deepe waters, but yee must fonle the residue with your feete ?

19 And as for my flocke, they eate that which yee haue troden with your feete : and they drinke that which yee haue fouled with your feete.

20 ¶ Therefore thus saith the Lord God vnto them, Behold, I, *euen* I will iudge betweene the fat cattell, and betweene the leane cattell.

21 Because yee haue thrust with side and with shoulder, and pusht all the diseased with your hornes, till yee haue scattered them abroad :

22 Therefore will I saue my flocke, and they shall no more be a pray, and I will iudge betweene cattell and cattell.

23 And I will set vp one *shepheard ouer them, and hee shall feede them, *euen* my seruant Dauid; he shall feede them, and hee shall be their shepheard.

* Isai 40. 11.
Ioh. 10. 11.

24 And I the Lord will be their God, and my seruant Dauid a prince among them, I the Lord haue spoken *it.*

25 And|

25 And I will make with them a couenant of peace, and will cause the euill beasts to cease out of the land : and they shall dwell safely in the wildernesse, and sleepe in the woods.

26 And I will make them and the places round about my hill, a blessing ; and I will cause the showre to come downe in his season : there shall bee showres of blessing.

27 And the tree of the field shal yeeld her fruite, and the earth shall yeeld her increase, and they shall be safe in their land, and shall know that I *am* the LORD, when I haue broken the bands of their yoke, and deliuered them out of the hand of those that serued themselues of them.

28 And they shall no more be a pray to the heathen, neither shall the beasts of the land deuoure them; but they shall dwell safely, and none shall make *them* afraide.

29 And I will raise vp for them a *plant ||of renowne, and they shall be no more †consumed with hunger in the land, neither beare the shame of the heathen any more.

30 Thus shall they know that I the LORD their God *am* with them, and that they, *euen* the house of Israel, *are* my people, saith the Lord GOD.

31 And yee my *flocke of my pasture, *are* men, *and* I *am* your God, saith the Lord GOD.

CHAP. XXXV.

The iudgment of Mount Seir, for their hatred of Israel.

Oreouer the word of the LORD came vnto mee, saying;

2 Sonne of man, set thy face against mount Seir, and prophecie against it,

3 And say vnto it, Thus saith the Lord GOD; Behold, O mount Seir, I *am* against thee, and I will stretch out mine hand against thee, and I will make thee †most desolate.

4 I will lay thy cities waste, and thou shalt be desolate, and thou shalt know that I *am* the LORD.

5 Because thou hast had a ||perpetuall hatred, and hast †shed the *blood* of the children of Israel by the †force of the sword in the time of their calamitie, in the time that *their* iniquitie *had* an end;

6 Therefore, as I liue, saith the Lord GOD, I will prepare thee vnto blood, and blood shall pursue thee : sith thou hast not hated blood, euen blood shall pursue thee.

7 Thus will I make mount Seir †most desolate, and cut off from it him that passeth out, & him that returneth.

8 And I will fill his mountaines with his slaine men : in thy hilles, and in thy valleis, and in all thy riuers shall they fall that are slaine with the sword.

9 I will make thee perpetuall desolations, & thy cities shall not returne, and ye shal know that I *am* the LORD

10 Because thou hast said; These two nations, and these two countries shall be mine, and we will *possesse it, ||whereas the LORD was there :

11 Therefore, as I liue, saith the Lord GOD, I will euen doe according to thine anger, and according to thine enuie, which thou hast vsed out of thy hatred against them : and I will make my selfe knowen amongst them, when I haue iudged thee.

12 And thou shalt know, that I am the LORD, *and that* I haue heard all thy blasphemies which thou hast spoken against the mountaines of Israel, saying; They are layed desolate, they are giuen vs †to consume.

13 Thus with your mouth yee haue †boasted against me, & haue multiplied your words against me : I haue heard *them*.

14 Thus saith the Lord GOD; When the whole earth reioyceth, I will make thee desolate.

15 As thou didst reioyce at the inheritance of the house of Israel, because it was desolate, so will I doe vnto thee : thou shalt be desolate, O mount Seir, and all Idumea, *euen* all of it, and they shall know that I *am* the LORD.

CHAP. XXXVI.

1 The land of Israel is comforted, both by destruction of the heathen, who spitefully vsed it, 8 and by the blessings of God promised vnto it. 16 Israel was reiected for their sinne, 21 and shall be restored without their desert. 25 The blessings of Christs kingdome.

Lso thou sonne of man, prophecie vnto the mountaines of Israel, and say; Ye mountaines of Israel, Heare the word of the LORD.

2 Thus saith the Lord GOD,
*Because

*Isai. 11. 1.
ier. 23. 5.
|| Or, for renowne.
† Heb. taken away.

*Ioh. 10.
11.

† Heb. desolation and desolation.

* Psal. 83.
4, 13.
|| Or, though the Lord was there.

† Heb. to deuoure.
† Heb. magnified.

† Heb. desolation and desolation.

|| Or, hatred of old.
† Heb. powred out the children.
† Heb. hands.

Chap. 62.

*Heb. be-
auſe for be-
auſe.*

*Or, ye are
ade to
ome vp on
e lip of the
ngue.*

*Or, bot-
omes or
ales.*

* Becauſe the enemy had ſaid againſt you, Aha, euen the ancient high places are ours in poſſeſſion:

3 Therfore prophecie and ſay, Thus ſaith the Lord GOD, †Becauſe they haue made you deſolate, and ſwallowed you vp on euery ſide, that ye might be a poſſeſſion vnto the reſidue of the heathen, and ‖ye are taken vp in the lips of talkers, and *are* an infamy of the people:

4 Therefore ye mountaines of Iſrael, heare the word of the Lord GOD, Thus ſaith the Lord GOD to the mountaines and to the hilles, to the ‖riuers and to the valleys, to the deſolate waſtes, and to the cities that are forſaken, which became a pray and deriſion to the reſidue of the heathen that *are* round about:

5 Therefore thus ſaith the Lord GOD, Surely in the fire of my ielouſie haue I ſpoken againſt the reſidue of the heathen, and againſt al Idumea, which haue appointed my land into their poſſeſſion, with the ioy of all *their* heart, with deſpitefull minds to caſt it out for a praye.

6 Prophecie therefore concerning the land of Iſrael, and ſay vnto the mountaines and to the hilles, to the riuers and to the valleys, Thus ſaith the Lord GOD, Behold, I haue ſpoken in my ielouſie and in my furie, becauſe ye haue borne the ſhame of the heathen,

7 Therefore thus ſaith the Lord GOD, I haue lifted vp mine hand, Surely the heathen that *are* about you, they ſhall beare their ſhame.

8 ¶ But ye, O mountaines of Iſrael, ye ſhall ſhoot forth your branches, and yeeld your fruit to my people of Iſrael, for they are at hand to come.

9 For behold, I *am* for you, and I will turne vnto you, and ye ſhall be tilled and ſowen.

10 And I will multiplie men vpon you, all the houſe of Iſrael, *euen* all of it, and the cities ſhall be inhabited, and the waſtes ſhall be builded.

11 And I will multiply vpon you man and beaſt, and they ſhall increaſe and bring fruite, and I will ſettle you after your olde eſtates: and will doe better vnto you, then at your beginnings, and ye ſhall know that I *am* the LORD.

12 Yea I will cauſe men to walke vpon you, *euen* my people Iſrael, and they ſhall poſſeſſe thee, and thou ſhalt

be their inheritance, and thou ſhalt no more henceforth bereaue them *of men.*

13 Thus ſaith the Lord GOD, Becauſe they ſay vnto you, Thou *land* deuoureſt vp men, and haſt bereaued thy nations,

14 Therefore thou ſhalt deuoure men no more, neither ‖bereaue thy nations any more, ſaith the Lord GOD.

15 Neither will I cauſe men to heare in thee the ſhame of the heathen any more, neither ſhalt thou beare the reproch of the people any more, neither ſhalt thou cauſe the nations to fall any more, ſaith the Lord GOD.

16 ¶ Moreouer the worde of the LORD came vnto me, ſaying,

17 Sonne of man, when the houſe of Iſrael dwelt in their own land, they defiled it by their owne way, and by their doings: their way was before me as the vncleanneſſe of a remooued woman.

18 Wherefore I powred my furie vpon them for the blood that they had ſhed vpon the land, and for their idoles *wherewith* they had polluted it.

19 And I ſcattered them among the heathen, and they were diſperſed through the countreys: according to their way and according to their doings I iudged them.

20 And when they entred vnto the heathen whither they went, they *prophaned my holy Name, when they ſaid to them, Theſe *are* the people of the LORD, and are gone forth out of his land.

21 ¶ But I had pitie for mine holy Name, which the houſe of Iſrael had prophaned among the heathen, whither they went.

22 Therefore ſay vnto the houſe of Iſrael, Thus ſaith the Lord GOD, I doe not *this* for your ſakes, O houſe of Iſrael, but for mine holy Names ſake, which ye haue prophaned among the heathen, whither ye went.

23 And I will ſanctifie my great Name which was prophaned among the heathen, which ye haue prophaned in the midſt of them, and the heathen ſhall know, that I *am* the LORD, ſaith the Lord GOD, when I ſhall be ſanctified in you before ‖their eyes.

24 For I will take you from among the heathen, and gather you out of all countreys, and will bring you into your owne land.

25 Then

‖ *Or, cauſe
to fall.*

* Iſa. 52. 5.
rom. 2. 24.

‖ *Or, your.*

25 ¶ Then will I sprinckle cleane water vpon you, and ye shalbe cleane: from all your filthinesse, and from all your idoles wil I cleanse you.

*Iere. 32. 39. chap. 11. 19.

26 A *new heart also will I giue you, and a new spirit will I put within you, and I will take away the stonie heart out of your flesh, and I will giue you an heart of flesh.

*Chap. 11. 19.

27 And I wil put my *Spirit within you, and cause you to walke in my Statutes, and ye shall keepe my iudgements, and doe them.

28 And ye shall dwel in the land that I gaue to your fathers, and ye shall be my people, and I wil be your God.

29 I wil also saue you from all your vncleannesses, and I will call for the corne, and will increase it, and lay no famine vpon you.

30 And I will multiply the fruit of the tree, and the increase of the field, that yee shall receiue no more reproch of famine among the heathen.

31 Then shall yee remember your owne euil waies, and your doings that were not good, and shall lothe your selues in your owne sight for your iniquities, and for your abominations.

32 Not for your sakes doe I this, saith the Lord GOD, be it knowen vnto you: be ashamed and confounded for your owne wayes, O house of Israel.

33 Thus saith the Lord GOD, In the day that I shall haue cleansed you from all your iniquities, I will also cause you to dwell in the cities, and the wastes shalbe builded.

34 And the desolate land shalbe tilled, whereas it lay desolate in the sight of all that passed by.

*Chap. 28. 13.

35 And they shall say, This land that was desolate, is become like the garden of *Eden, and the waste and desolate and ruined cities, are become fenced, and are inhabited.

36 Then shall the heathen that are left round about you, shall know that I the LORD build the ruined places, and plant that that was desolate : I *the LORD haue spoken it, and I wil doe it.

*Chap. 17. 24. and 22. 14. and 37. 14.

37 Thus saith the Lord GOD, I wil yet for this bee enquired of by the house of Israel, to doe it for them : I will increase them with men like a flocke.

†Hebr. flocke of holy things.

38 As the †holy flocke, as the flocke of Ierusalem in her solemne feastes, so shal the waste cities be filled with flocks of men, and they shall know that I am the LORD.

CHAP. XXXVII.

1 By the resurrection of dry bones, 11 the dead hope of Israel is reuiued, 15 by the vniting of two stickes, 18 is shewed the incorporation of Israel into Iudah. 20 The promises of Christs kingdome.

He hand of the LORD was vpon mee, and caried mee out in the Spirit of the LORD, and set mee downe in the middest of the valley which was full of bones,

2 And caused mee to passe by them round about, and beholde, there were very many in the open ‖valley, and loe, they were very drie.

‖Or, champian.

3 And hee said vnto mee, Sonne of man, can these bones liue ? and I answered, O Lord GOD, thou knowest.

4 Againe he said vnto me, Prophecie vpon these bones, and say vnto them ; O yee drie bones, heare the word of the LORD.

5 Thus saith the Lord GOD vnto these bones, Behold, I wil cause breath to enter into you, and ye shall liue.

6 And I wil lay sinewes vpon you, and wil bring vp flesh vpon you, and couer you with skinne, and put breath in you, and ye shall liue, and ye shall know that I am the LORD.

7 So I prophecied as I was commanded : and as I prophecied, there was a noise, and beholde a shaking, and the bones came together, bone to his bone.

8 And when I beheld, loe, the sinews and the flesh came vp vpon them, and the skin couered them aboue ; but there was no breath in them.

9 Then said he vnto mee, Prophecie vnto the ‖winde, prophecie sonne of man, and say to the winde, Thus saith the Lord GOD ; Come from the foure windes, O breath, and breathe vpon these slaine, that they may liue.

‖Or, breath.

10 So I prophecied as he commanded mee, and the breath came into them, and they liued, and stood vp vpon their feet, an exceeding great armie.

11 ¶ Then he said vnto me, Sonne of man, these bones are the whole house of Israel : behold, they say ; Our bones are

are dried, and our hope is lost, wee are cut off for our parts.

12 Therefore prophecie and say vnto them, Thus saith the Lord G O D, Behold, O my people, I wil open your graues, and cause you to come vp out of your graues, and bring you into the land of Israel.

13 And ye shall know that I *am* the L O R D, when I haue opened your graues, O my people, and brought you vp out of your graues,

14 And shall put my spirit in you, and yee shall liue, and I shall place you in your owne land : then shall ye know that I the L O R D haue spoken *it*, and perfourmed *it*, saith the L O R D.

15 ¶ The word of the L O R D came againe vnto me, saying ;

16 Moreouer thou sonne of man, take thee one sticke, and write vpon it, For Iudah and for the children of Israel his companions : then take another sticke, and write vpon it ; For Ioseph the sticke of Ephraim, and for all the house of Israel his companions.

17 And ioyne them one to another into one sticke, and they shall become one in thine hand.

18 ¶ And when the children of thy people shall speake vnto thee, saying ; Wilt thou not shew vs what thou *meanest* by these ?

19 Say vnto them, Thus saith the Lord G O D, Behold, I will take the sticke of Ioseph which *is* in the hand of Ephraim, and the tribes of Israel his fellowes, and will put them with him, *euen* with the sticke of Iudah, and make them one sticke, and they shall be one in mine hand.

20 ¶ And the stickes whereon thou writest, shalbe in thine hand before their eyes.

21 And say vnto them, Thus saith the Lord G O D, Behold, I will take the children of Israel from among the heathen whither they be gone, and will gather them on euery side, and bring them into their owne land.

22 And I will make them one nation in the land vpon the mountaines of Israel, and *one King shall be king to them all : and they shalbe no more two nations, neither shall they bee diuided into two kingdomes any more at all.

23 Neither shall they defile themselues any more with their idoles, nor with their detestable things, nor with

Iohn 10. 3.

any of their transgressions : but I will saue them out of all their dwelling places, wherein they haue sinned, and will cleanse them : so shall they be my people, and I will be their God.

24 And *Dauid my seruant *shall be* King ouer them, and they all shall haue one shepheard : they shall also walke in my iudgements, and obserue my statutes, and doe them.

25 And they shall dwell in the land that I haue giuen vnto Iacob my seruant, wherin your fathers haue dwelt, and they shall dwell therein, *euen* they and their children, and their childrens children for euer, and my seruant Dauid *shalbe* their prince for euer.

26 Moreouer I will make a *couenant of peace with them, it shall be an euerlasting couenant wich them, and I will place them and multiply them, and will set my *Sanctuary in the middest of them for euermore.

27 My Tabernacle also shalbe with them : yea, I will be *their God, and they shalbe my people.

28 And the heathen shal know that I the L O R D doe sanctifie Israel, when my Sanctuarie shalbe in the middest of them for euermore.

C H A P. XXXVIII.

1 The armie, 8 and malice of Gog. 14 Gods iudgement against him.

A Nd the word of ỹ L O R D came vnto me, saying ;

2 Sonne of man, set thy face against *Gog, the land of Magog the ‖chiefe prince of Meshech and Tubal, and prophecie against him,

3 And say, Thus saith the Lord G O D ; Behold, I *am* against thee, O Gog, the chiefe prince of Meshech and Tubal.

4 And I will turne thee backe, and put *hookes into thy chawes, and I will bring thee foorth, and all thine armie, horses and horsemen, all of them clothed with all sorts *of armour*, *euen* a great company with bucklers & shields, all of them handling swordes.

5 Persia, Ethiopia and ‖Libya with them ; all of them with shield & helmet :

6 Gomer and all his bandes, the house of Togarmah of the North quarters, and all his bands, *and* many people with thee.

7 Be

* Isai 40. 11.
iere. 23. 5.
and 30. 9.
cha. 34. 23.

* Psal. 89. 4.
cha. 34. 25.

* 2. Cor. 6.
16.

* Chap. 11.
20. and
14. 11.

* Reu. 20. 8.
‖ Or, prince
of the chiefe.

* Cha. 39. 2.

‖ Or. Phut.

7 Be thou prepared, and prepare for thy selfe, thou and all thy company, that are assembled vnto thee, and be thou a guard vnto them.

8 ¶ After many daies thou shalt be visited: in the latter yeeres thou shalt come into the land, that is brought backe from the sword, *and* is gathered out of many people against the mountaines of Israel, which haue beene alwayes waste: but it is brought forth out of the nations, and they shall dwell safely all of them.

9 Thou shalt ascend and come like a storme, thou shalt be like a cloud to couer the land, thou and all thy bands, and many people with thee.

10 Thus saith the Lord GOD; It shall also come to passe, *that* at the same time shall things come into thy minde, and thou shalt ‖ thinke an euill thought.

‖ *Or, conceiue a mischieuous purpose.*

11 And thou shalt say; I will goe vp to the land of vnwalled villages; I will goe to them that are at rest, that dwell ‖ safely all of them dwelling without walles, and *hauing* neither barres nor gates;

‖ *Or, confidently.*

12 † To take a spoile, and to take a praye, to turne thine hand vpon the desolate places that are *now* inhabited, and vpon the people that are gathered out of the nations which haue gotten cattel and goods, that dwell in the † middest of the land.

† *Heb. to spoile the spoile, and to praye the praye.*

† *Heb. nauell.*

13 Sheba, and Dedan, and the marchants of Tarshish, with all the young lyons thereof, shall say vnto thee, Art thou come to take a spoile? hast thou gathered thy company to take a praye? to carie away siluer and gold, to take away cattell and goods, to take a great spoile?

14 ¶ Therefore, sonne of man, prophecie and say vnto Gog, Thus saith the Lord GOD; In that day when my people of Israel dwelleth safely, shalt thou not know it?

15 And thou shalt come from thy place out of the North parts, thou and many people with thee, all of them riding vpon horses, a great company, and a mighty armie.

16 And thou shalt come vp against my people of Israel, as a cloud to couer the land; it shall be in the latter dayes, and I will bring thee against my land, that the heathen may know me, when I shall be sanctified in thee, O Gog, before their eyes.

17 Thus saith the Lord GOD; Art thou hee, of whom I haue spoken in old time † by my seruants the prophets of Israel, which prophecied in those dayes *many* yeeres, that I would bring thee against them?

† *Heb. by the hands.*

18 And it shall come to passe at the same time, when Gog shal come against the land of Israel, saith the Lord GOD, *that* my furie shall come vp in my face.

19 For in my iealousie, *and* in the fire of my wrath haue I spoken: surely in that day, there shall be a great shaking in the land of Israel.

20 So that the fishes of the sea, and the foules of the heauen, and the beasts of the field, and all creeping things that creepe vpon the earth, and all the men that are vpon the face of the earth, shall shake at my presence, and the mountaines shall be throwen downe, and the ‖ steepe places shall fall, and euery wall shall fall to the ground.

‖ *Or, towre Or staires.*

21 And I will call for a sword against him throughout all my mountaines, saith the Lord GOD: euery mans sword shalbe against his brother.

22 And I will plead against him with pestilence and with blood, and I will raine vpon him and vpon his bands, and vpon the many people that *are* with him, an ouerflowing raine, and great hailestones, fire, and brimstone.

23 Thus will I *magnifie my selfe, and sanctifie my selfe, and I will be knowen in the eyes of many nations, and they shall know that I *am* the LORD.

* *Chap. 36 33. and 37. 28.*

CHAP. XXXIX.

1 Gods iudement vpon Gog. 8 Israels victory. 11 Gogs buriall in Hamon-Gog. 17 The feast of the Foules. 23 Israel hauing beene plagued for their sinnes, shall be gathered againe with eternall fauour.

 Herefore thou sonne of man, prophecie against Gog, and say, Thus saith the Lord GOD; Behold, I *am* against thee O Gog, the chiefe prince of Meshech & Tubal.

2 And I will turne thee backe, and ‖ leaue but the sixt part of thee, and will cause thee to come vp from the † North parts, and will bring thee vpon the mountaines of Israel:

‖ *Or, strike thee with size plagu Or, drawe thee backe with an h of six teen as chap. 3 4.*

† *Heb. the sides of th North.*

3 And I will smite thy bow out of thy

thy left hand, and will cause thine arrowes to fall out of thy right hand.

4 Thou shalt fall vpon the mountaines of Israel, thou & all thy bands, and the people that *is* with thee : I will giue thee vnto the rauenous birds of euery †sort, and to the beasts of the field †to be deuoured.

5 Thou shalt fall vpon †the open field, for I haue spoken *it*, saith the Lord God.

6 And I will send a fire on Magog, and among them that dwell ||carelesly in the yles, and they shall know that I *am* the Lord.

7 So will I make my holy Name knowen in the midst of my people Israel, and I will not let *them* pollute my holy Name any more, and the heathen shall know that I *am* the Lord, the holy One in Israel.

8 ¶ Behold, it is come, and it is done, saith the Lord God, this *is* the day whereof I haue spoken.

9 And they that dwell in the cities of Israel, shall goe forth, and shall set on fire, and burne the weapons, both the shields and the bucklers, the bowes and the arrowes, and the ||handstaues and the speares, and they shall ||burne them with fire seuen yeeres.

10 So that they shall take no wood out of the field, neither cut downe *any* out of the forrests : for they shall burne the weapons with fire, and they shall spoile those that spoiled them, and rob those that robbed them, saith the Lord God.

11 ¶ And it shal come to passe at that day, *that* I will giue vnto Gog a place there of graues in Israel, the valley of the passengers on the East of the Sea : and it shall stop the ||*noses* of the passengers, and there shall they burie Gog, and all his multitude, and they shal call *it*, the valley of ||Hamon-gog.

12 And seuen moneths shall the house of Israel bee burying of them, that they may cleanse the land.

13 Yea all the people of the land shall burie *them*, and it shall be to them a renowne the day that I shall be glorified, saith the Lord God.

14 And they shall seuer out †men of continual emploiment, passing through the land, to burie with the passengers those that remaine vpon the face of the earth to clense it: after the end of seuen moneths shall they search.

15 And the passengers *that* passe through the lande, when *any* seeth a mans bone, then shall he †set vp a signe by it, till the buriers haue buried it in the valley of Hamon-gog.

16 And also the name of the citie *shall be* ||Hamonah : thus shal they clense the land.

17 ¶ And thou sonne of man, Thus saith the Lord God, Speake †vnto euery feathered foule, and to euery beast of the field, Assemble your selues, and come, gather your selues on euery side to my ||sacrifice that I doe sacrifice for you, *euen* a great sacrifice vpon the mountaines of Israel, that ye may eat flesh and drinke blood.

18 Ye shall eate the flesh of the mightie, and drinke the blood of the princes of the earth, of rammes, of lambes and of †goats, of bullocks, all of them fatlings of Bashan.

19 And yee shall eate fat till yee be full, and drinke blood till yee be drunken, of my sacrifice which I haue sacrificed for you.

20 Thus yee shall be filled at my table with horses and charets, with mightie men, and with all men of warre, saith the Lord God.

21 And I will set my glory among the heathen, and all the heathen shal see my iudgement that I haue executed, and my hande that I haue laid vpon them.

22 So the house of Israel shall know that I *am* the Lord their God from that day and forward.

23 ¶ And the heathen shall knowe that the house of Israel went into captiuitie for their iniquitie : because they trespassed against me, therefore hid I my face from them, and gaue them into the hand of their enemies : so fell they all by the sword.

24 According to their vncleannesse, and according to their transgressions haue I done vnto them, and hid my face from them.

25 Therefore thus saith the Lord God, Now will I bring againe the captiuitie of Iacob, and haue mercie vpon the whole house of Israel, and will be ielous for my holy Name :

26 After that they haue borne their shame, and all their trespasses, wherby they haue trespassed against me, when they dwelt safely in their lande, and none made *them* afraid.

27 When

Marginal notes (left column):

Heb. wing.
Heb. to deuure.
Hebr. the ..ce of the ..eld.

Or, confi-..ntly.

Or, iaue-..as.
Or, make a ..re of them.

Or, ..outhes.

That is, ..e multi-..de of Gog.

Heb. men ..f continu-..nce.

Marginal notes (right column):

† Heb. build

‡ That is, the multitude.

‡ Heb. to the foule of eue-ry wing.

‡ Or, slaugh-ter.

† Heb. great goats.

27 When I haue brought them a-gaine from the people, and gathered them out of their enemies lands, and *am sanctified in them in the sight of many nations;

28 Then shall they know that I *am* the Lord their God, †which caused them to be led into captiuitie among the heathen: but I haue gathered them vnto their owne land, and haue left none of them any more there.

29 Neither will I hide my face any more from them: for I haue * powred out my Spirit vpon the house of Israel, saith the Lord God.

CHAP. XL.

1 The time, maner and end of the vision. 6 The description of the East gate, 20 of the North gate, 24 of the South gate; 32 of the East gate, 35 and of the North gate. 39 Eight Tables. 44 The chambers. 48 The porch of the house.

N the fiue and twentieth yeere of our captiuitie, in the beginning of the yere, in the tenth *day* of the moneth, in the fourteenth yeere after that the citie was smitten, in the selfe same day, the hand of the Lord was vpon mee, and brought me thither.

2 In the visions of God brought he me into the land of Israel, and set mee vpon a very high mountaine, ‖ by which *was* as the frame of a citie on the South.

3 And he brought mee thither, and behold, *there was* a man, whose appearance *was* like the appearance of brasse, with a line of flaxe in his hand, & a measuring reed; and he stood in the gate.

4 And the man saide vnto mee; Sonne of man, behold with thine eyes, and heare with thine eares, & set thine heart vpon all that I shall shew thee: for to the intent that I might shew *them* vnto thee, art thou brought hither: declare all that thou seest, to the house of Israel.

5 And behold a wall on the outside of the house round about: and in the mans hand a measuring reed of sixe cubites *long*, by the cubite, and an hand breadth: so hee measured the breadth of the building, one reed, and the height one reed.

6 ¶ Then came hee vnto the gate †which looketh toward the East, and went vp the staires thereof, and measured the threshold of the gate, *which was* one reed broad, and the other threshold of the *gate, which was* one reed broad.

7 And *euery* little chamber *was* one reed long, and one reed broad, and betweene the litle chambers *were* fiue cubites, & the threshold of the gate within *was* one reed.

8 He measured also the porch of the gate within, one reed.

9 Then measured hee the porch of the gate, eight cubites, and the postes thereof two cubits, and the porch of the gate *was* inward.

10 And the litle chambers of the gate Eastward, *were* three on this side, and three on that side, they three *were* of one measure, and the postes had one measure on this side, and on that side.

11 And hee measured the breadth of the entrie of the gate, ten cubits, *and* the length of the gate, thirteene cubits.

12 The † space also before the litle chambers *was* one cubite *on this side*, and the space *was* one cubite on that side, and the litle chambers *were* sixe cubites on this side, and sixe cubits on that side.

13 Hee measured then the gate from the roofe of the one litle chamber to the roofe of another: the breadth *was* fiue and twentie cubits, doore against doore.

14 He made also postes of threescore cubites, euen vnto the poste of the court round about the gate.

15 And from the face of the gate of the entrance, vnto the face of the porch of the inner gate, *were* fiftie cubits.

16 And *there were* †narrow windows to the litle chambers, and to their posts within the gate round about, and likewise to the ‖ arches: and windowes *were* round about ‖ inward: and vpon ech post *were* palme-trees.

17 Then brought he me into the outward court, and loe *there were* chambers, and a pauement, made for the court round about: thirtie chambers *were* vpon the pauement.

18 And the pauement by the side of the gates ouer against the length of the gates, *was* the lower pauement.

19 Then hee measured the breadth from the forefront of the lower gate, vnto the forefront of the inner court ‖ without, an hundred cubits Eastward and Northward.

20 ¶ And the gate of the outward court,

* Chap. 36. 23.

† Hebr. by my causing of them &c.

* Ioel 2. 28. acts. 2. 17.

‖ Or, vpon which.

‖ Heb. wh face was way towa the East.

† Hebr. li mit, or bound.

† Heb. clos

‖ Or, galle ries, or po ches.
‖ Or, with in.

‖ Or, from without.

Heb. whose
ice was.

court, †that looked toward the North,
he measured the length thereof, and the
breadth thereof.

Or, galle-
ies or por-
hes.

21 And the little chambers thereof
were three on this side, and three on that
side, and the postes thereof, and the ‖arches thereof were after the measure of
the first gate : the length thereof *was* fiftie cubites, and the breadth fiue and
twentie cubites.

22 And their windowes, and their
arches, and their palme trees, *were* after
the measure of the gate that looketh towards the East, and they went vp vnto it by seuen steps, and the arches thereof *were* before them.

23 And the gate of the inner court
was ouer against the gate toward the
North and toward the East, and hee
measured from gate to gate an hundreth cubites.

24 ¶ After that hee brought me toward the South, and behold a gate toward the South, and he measured the
postes thereof, and the arches thereof
according to these measures.

25 And *there were* windowes in it,
and in the arches thereof round about,
like those windowes, the length *was* fiftie cubites, and the breadth fiue and
twentie cubites.

26 And *there were* seuen steps to goe
vp to it, and the arches thereof *were* before them, and it had palme trees, one
on this side, and another on that side
vpon the postes thereof.

27 And *there was* a gate in the inner
court toward the South, and he measured from gate to gate toward the
South an hundred cubites.

28 And hee brought me to the inner
court by the South gate, and he measured the South gate according to these
measures,

29 And the little chambers thereof,
and the postes thereof, and the arches
thereof according to these measures,
and *there were* windowes in it, and in the
arches thereof round about : *it was* fiftie
cubites long, and fiue and twentie cubites broad.

30 And the arches round about *were*
fiue and twenty cubits long, and fiue cubites †broad.

† Hebr.
breadth.

31 And the arches thereof *were* toward the vtter court, and palme trees
were vpon the postes thereof, and the
going vp to it *had* eight steps.

32 ¶ And hee brought me into the

inner court toward the East, and hee
measured the gate according to these
measures.

33 And the little chambers thereof,
and the postes thereof, and the arches
thereof *were* according to these measures, and *there were* windowes therein,
and in the arches thereof round about,
it was fiftie cubites long, and fiue and
twentie cubits broad.

34 And the arches thereof *were* toward the outward court, and palme
trees *were* vpon the postes thereof on
this side, and on that side, and the going
vp to it *had* eight steps.

35 ¶ And hee brought me to the
North gate, and measured *it* according
to these measures.

36 The little chambers thereof, the
postes thereof, and the arches thereof
and the windowes to it round about :
the length *was* fiftie cubites, and the
breadth fiue and twentie cubites.

37 And the postes thereof *were* toward the vtter court, and palme trees
were vpon the posts thereof on this side,
and on that side, and the going vp to it
had eight steps.

38 And the chambers, and the entries thereof *were* by the postes of the
gates, where they washed the burnt offering.

39 ¶ And in the porch of the gate *were*
two tables on this side, and two tables
on that side, to slay thereon the burnt offering, and the sinne offering, and the
trespasse offering.

40 And at the side without, ‖as one
goeth vp to the entry of the North gate,
were two tables, and on the other side,
which *was* at the porch of the gate, *were*
two tables.

‖ Or, at the
steppe.

41 Foure tables *were* on this side, and
foure tables on that side, by the side of
the gate ; eight tables, whereupon they
slew *their sacrifices.*

42 And the foure tables *were* of hewen
stone for the burnt offering, of a cubite
and an halfe long, and a cubite & a halfe
broad, and one cubit high : whereupon
also they laide the instruments wherewith they slewe the burnt offering and
the sacrifice.

43 And within *were* ‖hooks, an hand
broad, fastened round about, and vpon
the tables *was* the flesh of the offering.

‖ Or, andirons or the
two harthstones.

44 ¶ And without the inner gate
were the chambers of the singers in the
inner court, which *was* at the side of the
North

North gate : and their prospect *was* toward the South, one at the side of the East gate, hauing the prospect toward the North.

45 And hee said vnto me ; This chamber whose prospect *is* toward the South, *is* for the priests, the keepers of the ||charge of the house.

| Or, ward:
or, ordi-
nance, and
so ver. 46.

46 And the chamber whose prospect *is* toward the North, *is* for the priests the keepers of the charge of the altar : these *are* the sonnes of Zadok among the sonnes of Leui, which come neere to the Lᴏʀᴅ to minister vnto him.

47 So he measured the court, an hundreth cubites long, and an hundreth cubites broad foure square, and the altar *that was* before the house.

48 ¶ And he brought me to the porch of the house, and measured *each* post of the porch, fiue cubites on this side, and fiue cubites on that side : and the bredth of the gate *was* three cubites on this side, and three cubites on that side.

49 The length of the porch *was* twentie cubites, and the bredth eleuen cubites, and *he brought me* by the steps, whereby they went vp to it, and *there were* pillars by the posts, one on this side, and another on that side.

CHAP. XLI.

The measures, parts, chambers and ornaments of the Temple.

Fterward he brought me to the Temple, and measured the posts, six cubites broad on the one side, and six cubites broad on the other side, *which was* the bredth of the Tabernacle.

| Or, en-
trance.

2 And the bredth of the ||doore *was* tenne cubites, and the sides of the doore *were* fiue cubites on the one side, and fiue cubites on the other side, and he measured the length thereof fortie cubites, and the bredth twentie cubites.

3 Then went he inward, and measured the post of the doore two cubites, and the doore six cubites, and the bredth of the doore seuen cubites.

4 So he measured the length therof twentie cubites, and the bredth twentie cubites before the temple, and he said vnto me ; This *is* the most holy place.

5 After he measured the wall of the house sixe cubites, and the bredth of euerie side-chamber foure cubites round a-bout the house on euery side.

6 And the side-chambers *were* †three, one ouer an other, and ||thirtie in order, and they entred into the wall which *was* of the house for the side chambers round about, that they might † haue hold, but they had not hold in the wall of the house.

† Heb. side-
chamber o-
uer side-
chamber.
|| Or, three
and thirty
times, or 500
† Heb. be
holden.

7 And †there was an enlarging and a winding about still vpward to the side-chambers, for the winding about of the house went still vpward round about the house : therefore the bredth of the house *was still* vpward, and so increased *from* the lowest *chamber* to the highest by the middest.

† Heb. it was
made broa-
der and wid
round.

8 I saw also the height of the house round about ; the foundations of the side-chambers *were* a full reede of sixe great cubites.

9 The thicknesse of the wall which *was* for the side chamber without, *was* fiue cubites, and that which was left, *was* the place of the side-chambers that *were* within.

10 And betweene the chambers *was* the widenesse of twentie cubites round about the house on euery side.

11 And the doores of the side-chambers *were* toward the place that was left, one doore toward the North, and an other doore toward the South, and the bredth of the place that was left, *was* fiue cubites round about.

12 Now the building that *was* before the seperate place, at the end toward the West, *was* seuenty cubites broad, and the wall of the building *was* fiue cubites thicke round about, and the length thereof ninety cubites.

13 So he measured the house, an hundreth cubites long, and the separate place and the building with the walles thereof, an hundreth cubites long.

14 Also the bredth of the face of the house, and of the separate place toward the East, an hundreth cubites.

15 And he measured the length of the building ouer against the separate place which *was* behind it, and the ||galleries thereof on the one side, and on the other side an hundreth cubites with the inner temple, and the porches of the court.

| Or, seue-
rall walkes
Or, walkes
with pillars.

16 The doore-posts and the narrow windows, and the galleries round about on their three stories, ouer against the doore †sieled with wood round about, ||and from the ground vp to the windows, & the windows *were* couered

† Heb. sielin
of wood.
| Or, and
the ground
vnto the
windowes.

17 To

17 To that aboue the doore, euen vnto the inner house and without, and by all the wall round about within and without by †measure.

† *Heb. measures.*

18 And it was made with Cherubims and Palme trees, so that a Palme tree *was* betweene a Cherub and a Cherub, and *euery* Cherub had two faces.

19 So that the face of a man *was* toward the Palme-tree on the one side, and the face of a yong lyon toward the Palme-tree on the other side : it was made through all the house round about.

20 From the ground vnto aboue the doore *were* Cherubims and Palme-trees made, & on the wall of the temple.

† *Heb. poste.*

21 The †postes of the Temple were squared, *and* the face of the Sanctuary, the appearance *of the one* as the appearance *of the other.*

22 The altar of wood *was* three cubits high, and the length thereof two cubits; and the corners thereof and the length thereof and the walles thereof *were* of wood : and hee said vnto me; This *is* the Table that *is* before the LORD.

23 And the Temple and the Sanctuarie had two doores.

24 And the doores *had* two leaues a piece, two turning leaues, two leaues for the one doore, and two leaues for the other doore.

25 And there were made on them, on the doores of the Temple, Cherubims and Palme-trees, like as were made vpon the walles, and *there were* thicke planckes vpon the face of the porch without.

26 And *there were* narrow windowes and Palme-trees on the one side and on the other side, on the sides of the porch, and vpon the side chambers of the house, and thicke plankes.

CHAP. XLII.

1 The chambers for the Priests. 13 The vse thereof. 19 The measures of the outward court.

Hen he brought me foorth into the vtter court, the way toward the North, and hee brought mee into the chamber, that *was* ouer against the separate place, & which *was* before the building toward the North.

2 Before the length of an hundreth cubites *was* the North doore, and the breadth *was* fiftie cubits.

3 Ouer against the twentie *cubites* which *were* for the inner court, and ouer against the pauement which *was* for the vtter court, *was* gallerie against gallery in three *stories.*

4 And before the chambers *was* a walke of ten cubites breadth inward, a way of one cubite, and their doores toward the North.

5 Now the vpper-chambers *were* shorter : for the galleries ||were higher then these, ||then the lower, and then the middlemost of the building.

‖ *Or, did eate of these.*
‖ *Or, and the building consisted of the lower and the middlemost.*

6 For they *were* in three *stories*, but *had* not pillars as the pillars of the courts : therefore *the building* was straitned more then the lowest, and the middlemost from the ground.

7 And the wall that *was* without ouer against the chambers towards the vtter court on the forepart of the chambers, the length thereof *was* fiftie cubites.

8 For the length of the chambers that *were* in the vtter court *was* fiftie cubites : and loe, before the Temple *were* an hundreth cubites.

9 And ||from vnder these chambers ||*was* the entrie on the East side, ||as one goeth into them from the vtter court.

‖ *Or, from the place.*
‖ *Or, he, that brought me.*
‖ *Or, as hee came.*

10 The chambers *were* in the thicknes of the wall of the court toward the East, ouer against the separate place, and ouer against the building.

11 And the way before them *was* like the appearance of the chambers, which *were* toward the North, as long as they *and* as broad as they, and all their goings out were both according to their fashions, and according to their doores.

12 And according to the doores of the chambers that *were* toward the South, *was* a doore in the head of the way, *euen* the way directly before ŷ wall toward the East, as one entreth into them.

13 ¶ Then sayd hee vnto mee, The North chambers, *and* the South chambers, which *are* before the separate place, they *be* holy chambers, where ŷ Priests that approach vnto the LORD shall eate the most holy things : there shall they lay the most holy things, and the meat offering, & the sinne offering, and the trespasse offring, for the place *is* holy.

14 When the Priests enter therein, then shall they not goe out of the holy place into the vtter court, but there they shall lay their garments, wherein they minister : for they *are* holy, and shall

shall put on other garments, and shall approch to those things which *are* for the people.

15 Now when hee had made an end of measuring the inner house, hee brought mee foorth toward the gate, whose prospect is toward the East, and measured it round about.

† *Heb. wind.*

16 He measured the East †side with the measuring reede, fiue hundreth reedes, with the measuring reed round about.

17 Hee measured the North side fiue hundreth reedes, with a measuring reed round about.

18 Hee measured the South side fiue hundreth reedes, with the measuring reede.

19 ¶ Hee turned about to the West side, *and* measured fiue hundreth reedes with the measuring reed.

20 He measured it by the foure sides: it *had* a wall round about fiue hundreth *reedes* long, and fiue hundreth broad, to make a separation betweene the Sanctuary *and* the prophane place.

CHAP. XLIII.

1 The returning of the glory of God into the Temple. 7 The sinne of Israel hindered Gods presence. 10 The Prophet exhorteth them to repentance, and obseruation of the Law of the house. 13 The measures, 18 and the ordinances of the Altar.

* Chap. 1. 24.

* Chap. 1. 4. and 8. 4.

‖ *Or, when I came to prophecie that the citie should be destroyed. See chap. 9. 2, 5.*

Fterward he brought me to the gate, *euen* the gate that looketh toward the East.

2 And behold, the glory of the God of Israel came from the way of the East: and his voice *was* like a noise of many *waters, and the earth shined with his glory.

3 And *it was* * according to the appearance of the vision which I saw, *euen* according to the vision that I saw, ‖when I came to destroy the citie: and the visions *were* like the vision that I saw by the riuer Chebar: *and* I fell vpon my face.

4 And the glorie of the LORD came into the house by the way of the gate, whose prospect *is* toward the East.

5 So the Spirit tooke me vp, and brought mee into the inner court, and behold, the glory of the LORD filled the house.

6 And I heard *him* speaking vnto me out of the house, & the man stood by me.

7 ¶ And he said vnto me, Sonne of man, the place of my throne, and the place of the soles of my feete, where I will dwell in the midst of the children of Israel for euer, and my holy Name, shall the house of Israel no more defile, neither they, nor their kings, by their whoredome, nor by the carkeises of their kings in their high places.

8 In their setting of their threshold by my thresholds, and their post by my postes, ‖and the wall betweene me and them, they haue euen defiled my holy Name by their abominations that they haue committed : wherefore I haue consumed them in mine anger.

‖ *Or, for there was but a wall betweene m. and them.*

9 Now let them put away their whoredome, and the carkeises of their kings farre from me, and I wil dwell in the middest of them for euer.

10 ¶ Thou sonne of man, shew the house to the house of Israel, that they may be ashamed of their iniquities, and let them measure the ‖patterne.

‖ *Or, summe or number.*

11 And if they be ashamed of all that they haue done; shew them the forme of the house, and the fashion thereof, and the goings out thereof, and the commings in thereof, and all the formes thereof, and all the ordinances thereof, and all the formes thereof, and all the lawes thereof : & write it in their sight, that they may keepe the whole forme thereof, and all the Ordinances therof, and doe them.

12 This is the law of the house ; Vpon the top of the mountaine, the whole limit thereof round about *shall be* most holy : behold, this *is* the law of the house.

13 ¶ And these *are* the measures of the Altar after the cubites; the cubite *is* a cubite and an hand breadth, euen the † bottom *shalbe* a cubite, and the breadth a cubite, and the border thereof by the † edge therof round about *shalbe* a spanne, and this *shalbe* the higher place of the Altar.

† *Hebr. bosome.*

† *Hebr. lippe*

14 And from the bottom *vpon* the ground, euen to the lower settle, *shalbe* two cubits, and the breadth one cubite, and from the lesser settle euen to the greater settle *shalbe* foure cubites, and the breadth *one* cubite.

15 So the † Altar *shalbe* foure cubites, and from the † altar and vpward *shalbe* foure hornes.

† *Heb. Mareel, that is, the Mountaine of Go*
† *Hebr. Ariel, that is, the Lyon of God.*

16 And the altar *shalbe* twelue *cubites* long, twelue broad, square in the foure squares thereof.

17 And

17 And the settle *shall bee* fourteene *cubites* long, and fourteene broad in the foure squares thereof, and the border about it *shalbe* halfe a cubite, and the bottome thereof *shall be* a cubite about, and his staires shall looke toward the East.

18 ¶ And he said vnto me, Sonne of man, thus saith the Lord GOD, These *are* the ordinances of the Altar in the day when they shall make it to offer burnt offrings thereon, and to sprinkle blood thereon.

19 And thou shalt giue to the Priests the Leuites that be of the seede of Zadok, which approch vnto me, to minister vnto me, saith the Lord GOD, a yong bullocke for a sinne offering.

20 And thou shalt take of the blood thereof, and put *it* on the foure hornes of it, and on the foure corners of the settle, and vpon the border round about : thus shalt thou cleanse and purge it.

21 Thou shalt take the bullocke also of the sinne offering, and he shall burne it in the appointed place of the house without the Sanctuary.

22 And on the second day thou shalt offer a kidde of the goats without blemish for a sinne offering, and they shall cleanse the Altar, as they did cleanse it with the bullocke.

23 When thou hast made an ende of cleansing it, thou shalt offer a yong bullocke without blemish, and a ramme out of the flocke, without blemish.

24 And thou shalt offer them before the LORD, and the Priests shall cast salt vpon them, and they shall offer them vp for a burnt offering vnto the LORD.

25 Seuen dayes shalt thou prepare euery day a goate for a sinne offering : they shall also prepare a yong bullocke, and a ramme out of the flocke, without blemish.

† *Heb. fill their hands.*

26 Seuen dayes shal they purge the Altar and purifie it, and they shall † consecrate themselues.

‖ *Or, thanke-offrings.*

27 And when these dayes are expired, it shall be *that* vpon the eight day and so forward, the Priests shall make your burnt offerings vpon the Altar, and your ‖ peace offerings ; and I will accept you, saith the Lord GOD.

CHAP. XLIIII.

1 The East gate assigned onely to the Prince. 4 The Priestes reproued for polluting of the Sanctuary. 9 Idolaters vncapable of the Priests office. 15 The sonnes of Zadok are accepted therto. 17 Ordinances for the Priests.

THen he brought me backe the way of the gate of the outward Sanctuarie which looketh toward the East, and it *was* shut.

2 Then said the LORD vnto me, This gate shall be shut, it shall not be opened, and no man shall enter in by it ; because the LORD the God of Israel hath entred in by it, therefore it shall be shut.

3 *It is* for the Prince ; the Prince, hee shall sit in it to eate bread before the LORD : hee shall enter by the way of the porch of that gate, and shall goe out by the way of the same.

4 ¶ Then brought he me the way of the North gate before the house, and I looked, and behold, the glory of the LORD filled the house of the LORD, and I fell vpon my face.

5 And the LORD said vnto me ; Sonne of man, † marke well, and behold with thine eyes, and heare with thine eares, all that I say vnto thee, concerning all the ordinances of the house of ehe LORD, and all the lawes thereof, and marke well the entring in of the house, with euery going foorth of the Sanctuary.

† *Heb. set thine heart.*

6 And thou shalt say to the rebellious, *euen* to the house of Israel, Thus sayth the Lord GOD ; O yee house of Israel, let it suffice you, of all your abominations ;

7 In that ye haue brought into my Sanctuarie † strangers vncircumcised in heart, and vncircumcised in flesh, to be in my Sanctuarie to pollute it, *euen* my House, when ye offer my bread, the fat and the blood, and they haue broken my Couenant, because of all your abominations.

† *Heb. children of a stranger.*

8 And yee haue not kept the charge of mine holy things : but ye haue set keepers of my ‖ charge in my Sanctuarie for your selues.

‖ *Or, ward, or ordinance. And so verse 14. and 16.*

9 ¶ Thus sayth the Lord GOD, No stranger vncircumcised in heart, nor vncircumcised in flesh, shall enter into my Sanctuarie, of any stranger that *is* among the children of Israel.

10 And the Leuites that are gone away farre from me, when Israel went astray, which went astray away from me after their idoles, they shall euen beare their iniquitie.

11 Yet

11 Yet they shall be ministers in my Sanctuary, *hauing* charge at the gates of the house, and ministring to the house: they shall slay the burnt offring, and the sacrifice for the people, and they shall stand before them to minister vnto them:

† Heb. were for a stumbling blocke of iniquitie vnto &c.

12 Because they ministred vnto them before their idoles, and † caused the house of Israel to fall into iniquitie; therefore haue I lift vp mine hand against them, saith the Lord God, and they shall beare their iniquitie.

13 And they shall not come neere vnto me to doe the office of a priest vnto me, nor to come neere to any of my holy things, in the most holy place: but they shall beare their shame, and their abominations which they haue committed.

14 But I will make them keepers of the charge of the house for all the seruice thereof, and for all that shalbe done therein.

15 ¶ But the priests the Leuites, the sonnes of Zadok, that kept the charge of my sanctuarie, when the children of Israel went astray from me, they shall come neere to me to minister vnto me, and they shall stand before me to offer vnto me the fat and the blood, saith the Lord God.

16 They shall enter into my sanctuarie, and they shall come neere to my table to minister vnto mee, and they shall keepe my charge.

17 ¶ And it shall come to passe *that* when they enter in at the gates of the inner court, they shall be clothed with linnen garments, and no wooll shall come vpon them, whiles they minister in the gates of the inner court and within.

18 They shall haue linnen bonets vpon their heads, and shall haue linnen breeches vpon their loynes: they shall not girde *themselues* with any thing ‖ that causeth sweat.

‖ Or, in sweating places. Heb. in, or with sweat.

19 And when they goe forth into the vtter court, *euen* into the vtter court to the people, they shall put off their garments wherein they ministred, and lay them in the holy chambers, and they shall put on other garments, and they shall not sanctifie the people with their garments.

20 Neither shall they shaue their heads, nor suffer their lockes to grow long, they shall only polle their heads.

21 Neither shall any priest drinke wine, when they enter into the inner court.

22 Neither shall they take for their wiues a *widow, or her that is †put away: but they shall take maidens of the seede of the house of Israel, or a widow †that had a priest before.

* Leuit. 21. 13.
† Heb. thrust foorth.
† Heb. from a priest.

23 And they shall teach my people *the difference* betweene the holy and prophane, and cause men to discerne betweene the vncleane and the cleane.

24 And in controuersie they shall stand in iudgement, and they shall iudge it according to my iudgements: and they shall keepe my lawes and my statutes in all mine assemblies, and they shall halow my Sabbaths.

25 And they shall come at no *dead person to defile themselues: but for father or for mother, or for sonne or for daughter, for brother or for sister, that hath had no husband, they may defile themselues.

* Leuit. 21. 1, 11.

26 And after he is cleansed, they shal reckon vnto him seuen dayes.

27 And in the day that he goeth into the sanctuarie, vnto the inner court to minister in the sanctuarie, he shall offer his sinne offring, saith the Lord God.

28 And it shall be vnto them for an inheritance; I *am their inheritance: and yee shall giue them no possession in Israel; I *am* their possession.

* Numb. 18 20. deut. 10 9. and 18. 1, 2. iosh. 14, 33.

29 They shal eate the meate offring, and the sinne offring, and the trespasse offring, and euery ‖dedicate thing in Israel shall be theirs.

‖ Or, deuoted.

30 And the ‖*first of all the first fruits of all things, and euery oblation of all of euery sort of your oblations shall be the priests: yee shall also giue vnto the priest the first of your dough, that he may cause the blessing to rest in thine house.

‖ Or, chiefe * Exod. 13 2. and 22. 29. and ver 30. numb. 13. and 18. 12.

31 The priests shall not eate of any thing that is *dead of it selfe or torne, whether it be foule or beast.

* Exod. 22 31. leuit. 2 8.

CHAP. XLV.

1 The portion of land for the Sanctuarie, 6 for the citie, 7 and for the Prince. 9 Ordinances for the Prince.

OREOUER, †when yee shall diuide by lot the land for inheritance, yee shall offer an oblation vnto the Lord, †an holy portion of the land: the length *shall be* the length of fiue

† Heb. wh yee cause t land to fal

† Heb. hol nesse.

fiue and twentie thousand *reedes*, and the bredth *shalbe* ten thousand: this *shall be* holy in all the borders thereof round about.

2 Of this there shal be for the Sanctuarie fiue hundreth *in length*, with fiue hundreth *in bredth*, square round about, and fiftie cubites round about, for the ||suburbs thereof.

|| Or, void places.

3 And of this measure shalt thou measure the length of fiue and twentie thousand, and the bredth of ten thousand : and in it shall be the Sanctuarie *and* the most holy place.

4 The holy portion of the land shal bee for the priests the ministers of the Sanctuarie, which shall come neere to minister vnto the LORD, and it shall be a place for *their* houses, and an holy place for the Sanctuarie.

5 And the fiue and twenty thousand of length, and the tenne thousand of breadth, shall also the Leuites the ministers of the house haue for themselues, for a possession for twentie chambers.

6 ¶ And ye shall appoint the possession of the citie fiue thousand broad, and fiue and twentie thousand long ouer against the oblation of the holy portion : it shall be for the whole house of Israel.

7 ¶ And *a portion shalbe* for the prince on the one side, and on the other side of the oblation of the holy *portion*, and of the possession of the citie, before the oblation of the holy *portion*, and before the possession of the citie from the West side Westward, and from the East side Eastward, and the length *shalbe* ouer against one of the portions from the West border vnto the East border.

8 In the land shall be his possession in Israel, and my princes shall no more oppresse my people, and *the rest* of the land shall they giue to the house of Israel according to their tribes.

9 ¶ Thus saith the Lord GOD, Let it suffice you, O princes of Israel : remoue violence and spoile, and execute iudgement and iustice, take away your † exactions from my people, saith the Lord GOD.

† Heb. expulsions.

* Leuit. 19. 3, 35, 36.

10 Ye shall haue iust *ballances, and a iust Ephah, and a iust Bath.

11 The Ephah and the Bath shal be of one measure, that the Bath may containe the tenth part of an Homer, and the Ephah the tenth part of an Ho-

mer : the measure thereof shall be after the Homer.

12 And the *shekell *shall be* twentie Gerahs : twenty shekels, fiue and twentie shekels, fifteene shekels shall be your Maneh.

* Exod. 30. 13. leuit. 27 25. numb. 3 47.

13 This *is* the oblation that ye shal offer, the sixt part of an Ephah of an Homer of wheat, & ye shal giue the sixt part of an Ephah of an Homer of barley.

14 Concerning the ordinance of oile, the Bath of oyle, *ye shall offer* the tenth part of a Bath out of the Cor, *which is* an Homer of ten Baths, for ten Baths *are* an Homer.

15 And one ||lambe out of the flocke, out of two hundred, out of the fat pastures of Israel for a meate offering, and for a burnt offering, and for ||peace offerings to make reconciliation for them, saith the Lord GOD.

|| Or. kidde.

|| Or, thanke offrings.

16 All the people of the land †shall *giue* this oblation ||for the prince in Israel.

† Heb. shall be for. || Or, with.

17 And it shall be the princes part *to giue* burnt offerings, and meat offrings, and drinke offerings, in the feasts, and in the new moones, and in the Sabbaths, in all solemnities of the house of Israel : he shall prepare the sinne offering, and the meate offering, and the burnt offering, and the ||peace offrings, to make reconciliation for the house of Israel.

|| Or, thanke offrings.

18 Thus saith the Lord GOD, In the first *moneth*, in the first *day* of the moneth, thou shalt take a yong bullock without blemish, and clense the Sanctuarie.

19 And the priest shall take of the blood of the sinne offering, and put it vpon the postes of the house, and vpon the foure corners of the settle of the Altar, and vpon the postes of the gate of the inner court.

20 And so thou shalt doe the seuenth *day* of the moneth, for euery one that erreth; and for him that is simple : so shall ye reconcile the house.

21 In the first *moneth*, in the fourteenth day of the moneth, ye shall haue the passeouer a feast of seuen dayes, vnleauened bread shall be eaten.

22 And vpon that day shall the prince prepare for himselfe, and for all the people of the land, a bullocke for a sinne offering.

23 And seuen dayes of the feast he shall prepare a burnt offering to the LORD,

LORD, seuen bullockes, and seuen rammes without blemish dayly the seuen dayes, and a kidde of the goats daily for a sinne offering.

24 And hee shall prepare a meat offering of an Ephah for a bullocke, and an Ephah for a ramme, and an Hin of oyle for an Ephah.

25 In the seuenth *moneth*, in the fifteenth day of the moneth shall he doe the like in the *feast of the seuen dayes, according to the sinne offring, according to the burnt offering, & according to the meat offering, and according to the oile.

*Num. 29. 12.

CHAP. XLVI.

1 Ordinances for the Prince, in his worship, 9 and for the people. 16 An order for the Princes inheritance. 19 The courts for boyling and baking.

Hus saith the Lord GOD, The gate of the inner court, that looketh toward the East, shalbe shut the sixe working dayes: but on the Sabbath it shall be opened, and in the day of the New moone it shalbe opened.

2 And the Prince shall enter by the way of the porch of that gate without, and shall stand by the post of the gate, and the Priests shall prepare his burnt offering, and his peace offerings, and he shall worship at the threshold of the gate : then he shall goe foorth, but the gate shall not be shut vntil the euening.

3 Likewise the people of the land shall worship at the doore of this gate before the LORD, in the Sabbaths, and in the New moones.

4 And the burnt offering that the Prince shall offer vnto the LORD in the Sabbath day, *shall be* sixe lambes without blemish, and a ramme without blemish.

5 And the meat offring *shalbe* an Ephah for a ramme, and the meate offering for the lambes † as he shalbe able to giue, and an Hin of oile to an Ephah.

† Hebr. the gift of his hand.

6 And in the day of the New moone *it shall be* a yong bullocke without blemish, and sixe lambes, and a ramme : they shalbe without blemish.

7 And hee shall prepare a meat offering, an Ephah for a bullocke, and an Ephah for a ramme, and for the lambs, according as his hand shall attaine vnto, and an Hin of oile to an Ephah.

8 And when the Prince shall enter, he shall goe in by the way of the porch of that gate, and he shall goe foorth by the way thereof.

9 ¶ But when the people of the land shall come before the LORD, in the solemne feasts, he that entreth in by the way of the North gate to worship, shall goe out by the way of the South gate : and he that entreth by the way of the South gate, shall goe forth by the way of the North gate : he shall not returne by the way of the gate whereby he came in, but shall goe foorth against it.

10 And the Prince in the midst of them when they goe in, shal goe in, and when they goe foorth, shall goe forth.

11 And in the feasts, and in the solemnities, the meat offering shalbe an Ephah to a bullocke, and an Ephah to a ramme, and to the lambes, as he is able to giue, and an Hin of oile to an Ephah.

12 Now when the Prince shall prepare a voluntary burnt offering or peace offerings, voluntarily vnto the LORD, one shall then open him the gate that looketh toward the East, and he shall prepare his burnt offering, and his peace offerings, as hee did on the Sabbath day, then he shall goe foorth, and after his going foorth, one shall shut the gate.

13 Thou shalt daily prepare a burnt offering vnto the LORD, of a lambe of † the first yeere, without blemish thou shalt prepare it † euery morning.

† Hebr. of his yeere.
† Hebr. morning by morning.

14 And thou shalt prepare a meat offering for it euery morning; the sixt part of an Ephah, and the third part of an Hin of oyle, to temper with the fine flowre ; a meat offering continually, by a perpetual ordinance vnto the LORD.

15 Thus shall they prepare the lambe, and the meat offering, and the oyle, euery morning, for a continuall burnt offering.

16 ¶ Thus saith the Lord GOD, If the prince giue a gift vnto any of his sonnes, the inheritance thereof shall be his sonnes, *it shall be* their possession by inheritance :

17 But if hee giue a gift of his inheritance to one of his seruants, then it shalbe his to the yeere of libertie : after, it shall returne to the Prince, but his inheritance shalbe his sonnes for them.

18 Moreouer, the Prince shall not take of the peoples inheritance by oppression,

pression, to thrust them out of their possession : *but* hee shall giue his sonnes inheritance out of his owne possession, that my people be not scattered euery man from his possession.

19 ¶ After, he brought me through the entry, which *was* at the side of the gate, into the holy chambers of the Priests which looked toward ẙ North : and behold, there *was* a place on the two sides Westward.

20 Then said hee vnto me, This *is* the place where the Priests shall boyle the trespasse offring, and the sinne offering, where they shall bake the meate offering : that they beare *them* not out into the vtter court, to sanctifie the people.

21 Then hee brought me foorth into the vtter court, and caused me to passe by the foure corners of the court, and behold, †in euery corner of the court *there was* a court.

> †*Heb.a court in a corner of a court, and a court in a corner of a court.*
> ‖*Or, made with chimneys.*
> †*Heb. cornered.*

22 In the foure corners of the court *there were* courts ‖ioyned of fourtie *cubits* long, and thirtie broad : these †foure corners *were* of one measure.

23 And *there was* a new *building* round about in them, round about them foure; and it was made with boyling places vnder the rowes round about.

24 Then said he vnto me, These *are* the places of them that boyle, where the ministers of the house shall boyle the sacrifice of the people.

CHAP. XLVII.

1 The vision of the holy waters. 6 The vertue of them. 13 The borders of the land. 22 The diuision of it by lot.

Fterward hee brought me againe vnto the doore of the house, and behold, waters issued out from vnder the threshold of the house Eastward : for the forefront of the house *stood* toward the East, and the waters came downe from vnder from the right side of the house, at the South side of the Altar.

2 Then brought hee me out of the way of the gate Northward, and ledde me about the way without vnto the vtter gate by the way that looketh Eastward, and behold, there ranne out waters on the right side.

3 And when the man that had the line in his hand, went forth Eastward, he measured a thousand cubites, and he brought me through the waters : †the waters *were* to the ancles.

> †*Heb. waters of the ancles.*

4 Againe he measured a thousand, and brought me through the waters ; the waters *were* to the knees : againe he measured a thousand, and brought mee through ; the waters *were* to the loynes.

5 Afterward hee measured a thousand, *and it was* a riuer, that I could not passe ouer : for the waters were risen, †waters to swimme in, a riuer that could not be passed ouer.

> †*Heb. waters of swimming.*

6 ¶ And hee said vnto me, Sonne of man, hast thou seene *this* ? Then hee brought me, and caused me to returne to the brinke of the riuer.

7 Now when I had returned, behold, at the †banke of the riuer *were* very many * trees on the one side and on the other.

> †*Heb. lip.*
> * Reu. 22. 2.

8 Then said he vnto me, These waters issue out toward the East country, and go downe into the ‖desert, and goe into the sea : which being brought foorth into the sea, the waters shalbe healed.

> ‖*Or, plaine.*

9 And it shall come to passe, that euery thing that liueth, which mooueth, whithersoeuer the † riuers shall come, shall liue, and there shall be a very great multitude of fish, because these waters shall come thither : for they shall be healed, and euery thing shall liue whither the riuer commeth.

> †*Heb. two riuers.*

10 And it shall come to passe *that* the fishers shall stand vpon it, from Engedi euen vnto En-eglaim ; they shall be a place to spread foorth nets, their fish shall bee according to their kindes, as the fish of the great Sea, exceeding many.

11 But the myrie places thereof, and the marishes thereof, ‖shall not be healed, they shall be giuen to salt.

> ‖*Or, and that which shall not be healed.*

12 And by the riuer vpon the banke thereof on this side, and on that side, †shall grow all trees for meat, whose leafe shal not fade, neither shal the fruit thereof be consumed : it shall bring forth ‖new fruit, according to his moneths, because their waters they issued out of the Sanctuarie, and the fruite thereof shall be for meate, and the leafe thereof ‖for * medicine.

> †*Heb. shall come vp.*
> ‖*Or, principall.*
> ‖*Or, for bruises and sores.*
> * Reu. 22. 2.

13 ¶ Thus sayth the Lord God, This *shall be* the border, whereby yee shall inherite the land, according to the twelue tribes of Israel : Ioseph *shall haue* two portions.

14 And

ℓ Or, swore.
ª Gen. 12.
7. and 17.
8. and 26.
3. and 28.
13.

14 And yee shall inherite it, one as well as an other : concerning the which I ‖*lifted vp mine hand to giue it vnto your fathers, and this land shal fall vnto you for inheritance.

15 And this *shall be* the border of the land toward the North side from the great Sea, the way of Hethlon, as men goe to Zedad :

16 Hamath, Berothah, Sibraim, which *is* betweene the border of Damascus, and the border of Hamath : ‖Hazar Hatticon, which *is* by the coast of Hauran.

‖ Or, the middle village.

17 And the border from the Sea shall be Hazar-enan, the border of Damascus, and the North northward, and the border of Hamath : and *this is* the North side.

18 And the East side yee shall measure from Hauran, and †from Damascus, and from Gilead, and from the land of Israel *by* Iordan, from the border vnto the East sea : & *this is* the East side.

† Heb. from betweene.

19 And the South side Southward from Tamar, euen to the waters of ‖strife *in* Kadesh, the ‖riuer, to the great Sea ; and *this is* the South side ‖Southward.

ℓ Or, Meribah.
‖ Or, valley.
‖ Or, toward Teman.

20 The West side also *shall be* the great Sea from the border, till a man come ouer against Hamath : this *is* the West side.

21 So shall yee diuide this land vnto you according to the Tribes of Israel.

22 ¶ And it shall come to passe, *that* yee shall diuide it by lot for an inheritance vnto you, and to the strangers that soiourne among you, which shall beget children among you, and they shall be vnto you as borne in the countrey among the children of Israel ; they shall haue inheritance with you among the Tribes of Israel.

23 And it shall come to passe *that* in what Tribe the stranger soiourneth, there shall yee giue *him* his inheritance, saith the Lord God.

CHAP. XLVIII.

1. 23 The portions of the twelue Tribes, 8 of the Sanctuarie, 15 of the citie and Suburbs, 21 and of the Prince. 30 The dimensions and gates of the citie.

Ow these *are* the names of the Tribes, from the North end to the coast of the way of Hathlon, as one goeth to Hamath, Hazar-

enan, the border of Damascus Northward, to ў coast of Hamath (for these are his sides East & West) *a portion* for Dan.

2 And by the border of Dan, from the East side vnto the West, *a portion* for Asher.

3 And by the border of Asher, from the East side euen vnto the West side, *a portion* for Naphtali.

4 And by the border of Naphtali, from the East side vnto the West side, *a portion* for Manasseh.

5 And by the border of Manasseh, from the East side vnto the West side, *a portion* for Ephraim.

6 And by the border of Ephraim, from the East side euen vnto the West side, *a portion* for Reuben.

7 And by the border of Reuben, from the East side vnto the West side, *a portion* for Iudah.

8 ¶ And by the border of Iudah, from the East side vnto the West side, shall be the offring which they shall offer of fiue and twentie thousand *reedes in* bredth, and *in* length as one of the other parts, from the East side vnto the West side, and the Sanctuarie shall be in the midst of it.

9 The oblation that yee shall offer vnto the Lord, *shall be* of fiue and twentie thousand in length, and of ten thousand in bredth.

10 And for them, *euen* for the priests shall be this holy oblation, toward the North, fiue and twentie thousand *in length*, and toward the West ten thousand in bredth, and toward the East ten thousand in bredth, and toward the South fiue and twentie thousand in length, & the sanctuarie of the Lord shall be in the midst thereof.

11 *It shall be* ‖for the Priests that are sanctified, of the sonnes of Zadok, which haue kept ‖my charge, which went not astray when the children of Israel went astray, as the Leuites went astray.

‖ Or, the sanctified portion shall be for the priests.
‖ Or, ward or, ordinance.

12 And *this* oblation of the land that is offred, shalbe vnto them a thing most holy by the border of the Leuites.

13 And ouer against the border of the Priests, the Leuites *shall haue* fiue and twentie thousand in length, and tenne thousand in bredth : all the length *shalbe* fiue and twentie thousand, and the bredth tenne thousand.

14 And they shall not sell of it, neither exchange, nor alienate the first fruits

fruits of the land : for it *is* holy vnto the LORD.

15 ¶ And the fiue thousand that are left in the breadth ouer against the fiue and twentie thousand, shall bee a prophane place for the citie, for dwelling, and for suburbs, and the citie shall be in the midst thereof.

16 And these *shall bee* the measures thereof, the North side foure thousand and fiue hundred, and the South side foure thousand and fiue hundred, and on the East side foure thousand, and fiue hundred, and the West side foure thousand and fiue hundred.

17 And the suburbs of the city shall be toward the North two hundred and fiftie, and toward the South two hundred and fifty, and toward the East two hundred and fiftie, and toward the West two hundred and fiftie.

18 And the residue in length ouer against the oblation of the holy portion, *shalbe* ten thousand Eastward, and ten thousand Westward : and it shall be ouer against the oblation of the holy portion, and the increase thereof shall bee for food vnto them that serue the citie.

19 And they that serue the citie, shall serue it out of all the tribes of Israel.

20 All the oblation *shall bee* fiue and twentie thousand, by fiue and twentie thousand : ye shall offer the holy oblation foure square, with the possession of the citie.

21 ¶ And the residue *shall bee* for the prince on the one side, and on the other of the holy oblation, and of the possession of the citie ouer against the fiue and twentie thousand, of the oblation toward the East border, and Westward ouer against the fiue and twentie thousand toward the West border, ouer against the portions for the prince, and it shall be the holy oblation, and the Sanctuarie of the house *shall be* in the middest thereof.

22 Moreouer, from the possession of the Leuites, and from the possession of the citie, *being* in the midst of that which is the princes, betweene the border of Iudah, and the border of Beniamin, shall bee for the prince.

23 As for the rest of the tribes, from the East side vnto the West side, Beniamin *shall haue* †a portion :

24 And by the border of Beniamin, from the East side vnto the West side, Simeon *shall haue a portion :*

25 And by the border of Simeon, from the East side vnto the West side, Issachar *a portion :*

26 And by the border of Issachar, from the East side vnto the West side, Zebulun *a portion :*

27 And by the border of Zebulun from the East side vnto the West side, Gad *a portion :*

28 And by the border of Gad, at the South side Southward, the border shall be euen from Tamar, *vnto* the waters of ‖ strife *in* Kadesh, *and* to the riuer toward the great Sea.

29 This *is* the land which ye shal diuide by lot vnto the tribes of Israel for inheritance, and these *are* their portions, saith the Lord GOD.

30 ¶ And these *are* the goings out of the citie, on the North side foure thousand and fiue hundred measures.

31 And the gates of the citie *shall bee* after the names of the tribes of Israel, three gates Northward, one gate of Reuben, one gate of Iudah, one gate of Leui.

32 And at the East side foure thousand and fiue hundred : and three gates; and one gate of Ioseph, one gate of Beniamin, one gate of Dan.

33 And at the South side foure thousand and fiue hundred measures, and three gates : one gate of Simeon, one gate of Issachar, one gate of Zebulun.

34 At the West side foure thousand and fiue hundred, *with* their three gates : one gate of Gad, one gate of Asher, one gate of Naphtali.

35 *It was* round about eighteene thousand *measures*, and the name of the citie from that day *shall be*, †The LORD *is* there.

Marginal notes:

† *Heb. one portion.*

‖ *Or, Meribah Kadesh.*

† *Heb. Iehouah Shammah.*

¶ THE

¶ THE BOOKE OF
Daniel.

CHAP. I.

1 Iehoiakims captiuitie. 3 Ashpenaz taketh Daniel, Hananiah, Mishael and Azariah. 8 They refusing the Kings portion, doe prosper with pulse and water. 17 Their excellencie in wisdome.

IN the thirde yere of the reigne of *Iehoiakim King of Iudah, came Nebuchadnezzar King of Babylon, vnto Ierusalem, and besieged it.

2 And the Lord gaue Iehoiakim king of Iudah into his hand, with part of the vessels of the house of God, which he caried into the land of Shinar to the house of his god, and he brought the vessels into the treasure house of his god.

3 ¶ And the king spake vnto Ashpenaz the master of his Eunuches, that he shonld bring *certaine* of the children of Israel, and of the kings seed, and of the Princes :

4 Children in whom *was* no blemish, but well fauoured, and skilfull in all wisedome, and cunning in knowledge, and vnderstanding science, and such as *had* abilitie in them to stand in the Kings palace, and whom they might teach the learning, and the tongue of the Caldeans.

5 And the King appointed them a daily prouision of the kings meat, and of †the wine which he dranke : so nourishing them three yeeres, that at the ende thereof they might stand before the king.

6 Now among these were of the children of Iudah, Daniel, Hananiah, Mishael, and Azariah :

7 Vnto whom the Prince of the Eunuches gaue names : for he gaue vn-

to Daniel *the name* of Belteshazzar ; and to Hananiah, of Shadrach ; and to Mishael, of Meshach ; and to Azariah of Abednego.

8 ¶ But Daniel purposed in his heart, that he would not defile himselfe with the portion of the kings meat, nor with the wine which he dranke : therefore hee requested of the Prince of the Eunuches, that hee might not defile himselfe.

9 Now God had brought Daniel into fauour and tender loue with the Prince of the Eunuches,

10 And the Prince of the Eunuches said vnto Daniel, I feare my lord the king, who hath appointed your meat, and your drinke : for why should he see your faces †worse liking then the children which *are* of your ||sort ? then shall yee make mee indanger my head to the King.

11 Then said Daniel to ||Melzar, whom the Prince of the Eunuches had set ouer Daniel, Hananiah, Mishael, and Azariah,

12 Proue thy seruants, I beseech thee, ten dayes, and let them giue †pulse †to eat, and water to drinke.

13 Then let our countenances be looked vpon before thee, and the countenance of the children that eat of the portion of the Kings meate : and as thou seest, deale with thy seruants.

14 So hee consented to them in this matter, and proued them ten dayes.

15 Aud at the end of ten dayes, their countenances appeared fairer, and fatter in flesh, then all the children, which did eate the portion of the kings meat.

16 Thus Melzar tooke away the portion of their meat, and the wine that they should drink: and gaue them pulse.

17 ¶ As for these foure children, God gaue them knowledge, and skil in all learning and wisedome, ||and Daniel

---

Marginal notes (left column):

* 2. Kings. 24. 2. 2. chro. 36. 6.

† Hebr. the wine of his drinke.

Marginal notes (right column):

† Hebr. sadder.
|| Or, terme or continuance.

|| Or, the steward.

† Hebr. of pulse.
† Hebr. that wee may eat &c.

|| Or, hee made Daniel vnderstand.

niel had vnderstanding in all visions and dreames.

18 Now at the end of the dayes that the King had said he should bring them in, then the Prince of the Eunuches brought them in before Nebuchadnezzar.

19 And the King communed with them : and among them all was found none like Daniel, Hananiah, Mishael, and Azariah : therefore stood they before the King.

20 And in all matters of † wisedome *and* vnderstanding that the king enquired of them, hee found them ten times better then all the Magicians *and* Astrologers that *were* in all his Realme.

† Heb. wiselome of vnterstanding.

21 And Daniel continued euen vnto the first yeere of king Cyrus.

CHAP. II.

1 Nebuchad-nezzar forgetting his dreame, requireth it of the Caldeans, by promises and threatnings. 10 They acknowledging their inabilitie, are iudged to die. 14 Daniel obtaining some respite, findeth the dreame. 19 He blesseth God. 24 He staying the Decree, is brought to the King. 31 The dreame. 36 The interpretatio. 46 Daniels aduancement.

AND in the second yeere of the reigne of Nebuchadnezzar, Nebuchad-nezzar dreamed dreames, wherewith his spirit was troubled, and his sleepe brake from him.

2 Then the King commanded to call the Magicians, and the Astrologers, and the Sorcerers, and the Caldeans, for to shew the King his dreames : so they came and stood before the king.

3 And the King said vnto them, I haue dreamed a dreame, and my spirit was troubled to know the dreame.

* Dan. 3. 9.

4 Then spake the Caldeans to the King in Syriacke ; *O king, liue for euer : tell thy seruants the dreame, and we will shew the interpretation.

5 The King answered, and said to the Caldeans, The thing is gone from mee : if ye will not make knowen vnto me the dreame, with the interpretation thereof, yee shall be * † cut in pieces, and your houses shalbe made a dunghill.

* Dan. 3. 29.
† Cald. made pieces.

6 But if yee shewe the dreame, and the interpretation thereof, yee shall receiue of me giftes and ‖ rewards, and great honour : therefore shewe me the dreame, and the interpretation thereof.

‖ Or, Fee, Dan. 5. 17.

7 They answered againe, and said, Let the King tell his seruants the dreame, and we will shew the interpretation of it.

8 The King answered, and said, I know of certeinty that ye would † gaine the time, because ye see the thing is gone from me.

† Cald. buy.

9 But if yee will not make knowen vnto me the dreame, *there is but* one decree for you : for ye haue prepared lying, and corrupt words to speake before me, till the time be changed : therefore tell me the dreame, and I shall know that yee can shewe mee the interpretation thereof.

10 ¶ The Caldeans answered before the King, and said, There is not a man vpon the earth that can shew the kings matter : therefore there is no King, lord, nor ruler, that asked such things at any Magician, or Astrologer, or Caldean.

11 And *it is* a rare thing that the king requireth, and there is none other that can shew it before the King, except the gods, whose dwelling is not with flesh.

12 For this cause the King was angry and very furious, and commanded to destroy all the wise men of Babylon.

13 And the decree went foorth that the wise men should be slaine, and they sought Daniel and his fellowes to be slaine.

14 ¶ Then Daniel † answered with counsell and wisedome to Arioch the ‖ captaine of the Kings guard, which was gone foorth to slay the wise men of Babylon.

† Cald. returned.
‖ Or, chiefe marshall. Cald. chiefe of the executioners or slaughtermen.

15 Hee answered and said to Arioch the Kings captaine, Why is the decree so hastie from the King? Then Arioch made the thing knowen to Daniel.

16 Then Daniel went in and desired of the King, that hee would giue him time, and that he would shew the king the interpretation.

17 Then Daniel went to his house, and made the thing knowen to Hananiah, Mishael, and Azariah his companions :

18 That they would desire mercies † of the God of heauen concerning this secret, that Daniel and his fellowes ‖ should not perish with the rest of the Wise men of Babylon.

† Cald. from before God.
‖ Or, that they should not destroy Daniel, &c.

19 ¶ Then was the secret reueuled vnto Daniel in a night vision : then Daniel blessed the God of heauen.

20 Daniel

* Psal. 113.
2. and 115.
18.

20 Daniel answered and said; *Blessed be the name of God for euer and euer : for wisedome and might are his :

21 And he changeth the times and the seasons : he remoueth Kings, and setteth vp Kings : he giueth wisedome vnto the wise, and knowledge to them that know vnderstanding.

22 He reuealeth the deepe and secret things : hee knoweth what is in the darknes, & the light dwelleth with him.

23 I thanke thee and praise thee, O thou God of my fathers, who hast giuen me wisedome and might, and hast made knowen vnto me now what we desired of thee : for thou hast now made knowen vnto vs the kings matter.

24 ¶ Therefore Daniel went in vnto Arioch whom the king had ordained to destroy the wise men of Babylon : he went and said thus vnto him, Destroy not the wise men of Babylon : bring me in before the king, and I will shew vnto the king the interpretation.

25 Then Arioch brought in Daniel before the king in haste, & said thus vnto him, †I haue found a man of the †captiues of Iudah, that will make knowen vnto the king the interpretation.

† Cald. that
I haue found.
† Cald.
children of
the captiui-
tie of Iudah.

26 The King answered and said to Daniel whose name was Belteshazzar, Art thou able to make knowen vnto me the dreame which I haue seene, and the interpretation thereof?

27 Daniel answered in the presence of the King, and said, The secret which the King hath demanded, cannot the wise men, the astrologians, the magicians, ỹ southsaiers shew vnto the king:

28 But there is a God in heauen that reuealeth secrets, and †maketh knowen to the king Nebuchad-nezzar, what shalbe in the latter dayes. Thy dreame, and the visions of thy head vpon thy bed, are these.

† Cald.
hath made
knowen.

29 As for thee, O King, thy thoughts †came into thy minde vpon thy bed, what should come to passe hereafter : and he that reuealeth secrets, maketh knowen to thee, what shall come to passe.

† Cald. came
vp.

30 But as for me, this secret is not reuealed to me, for any wisdome that I haue more then any liuing, but for their sakes that shall make knowen the interpretation to the King, and that thou mightest know the thoughts of thy heart.

31 ¶ Thou, O King, †sawest, and behold a great image : this great image whose brightnesse was excelleut, stood before thee, and the forme thereof was terrible.

† Cald. was
seeing.

32 This images head was of fine gold, his breast and his armes of siluer, his belly and his ‖thighes of brasse :

‖ Or, sides.

33 His legs of yron, his feete part of yron, and part of clay.

34 Thou sawest till that a stone was cut out ‖without hands, which smote the image vpon his feete that were of yron and clay, and brake them to pieces.

‖ Or, which
was not in
hands. As
verse 45.

35 Then was the yron, the clay, the brasse, the siluer, and the golde broken to pieces together, and became like the chaffe of the summer threshing floores, and the wind caried them away, that no place was found for them : & the stone that smote the image became a great mountaine, and filled the whole earth.

36 ¶ This is the dreame, and we will tell the interpretation thereof before the King.

37 Thou, O King, art a king of Kings : for the God of heauen hath giuen thee a kingdome, power, and strength, and glory.

38 And wheresoeuer the children of men dwel, the beasts of the field, and the foules of the heauen hath he giuen into thine hand, and hath made thee ruler ouer them all : thou art this head of gold.

39 And after thee shall arise an other kingdome inferiour to thee, and another third kingdome of brasse, which shall beare rule ouer all the earth.

40 And the fourth kingdome shall be strong as yron : forasmuch as yron breaketh in pieces and subdueth all things ; and as yron that breaketh all these, shall it breake in pieces and bruise.

41 And whereas thou sawest the feete and toes, part of potters clay, and part of yron : the kingdome shalbe diuided, but there shalbe in it of the strength of the yron, forasmuch as thou sawest the yron mixt with myrie clay.

42 And as the toes of the feete were part of yron, and part of clay ; so the kingdome shall be partly strong, and partly ‖broken.

‖ Or, brittle

43 And whereas thou sawest yron mixt with myrie clay, they shall mingle themselues with the seede of men : but they shall not cleaue †one to an other, euen as yron is not mixed with clay.

† Cald. this
with this.

44 And in †the daies of these Kings shall

† Cald. thei
dayes.

* Chap. 4. 3,
34. and 6.
27. and 7.
14, 27.
mich. 4. 7.
luke 1. 33.
† Cald. king-
dome there-
of.

‖ Or, which
was not in
hand.

† Cald. after
this.

shall the God of heauen set vp a king-dome, *which shall neuer be destroyed: and the † Kingdome shall not be left to other people, *but* it shall breake in pieces, and consume all these kingdomes, and it shall stand for euer.

45 Forasmuch as thou sawest that the stone was cut out of the mountaine ‖without hands, and that it brake in pieces the yron, the brasse, the clay, the siluer, and the gold: the great God hath made knowen to the King what shall come to passe † hereafter, & the dreame *is* certaine, and the interpretation there-of sure.

46 ¶ Then the King Nebuchad-nezzar fell vpon his face, and worship-ped Daniel, and commanded that they should offer an oblation, and sweet o-dours vnto him.

47 The King answered vnto Da-niel and said, Of a trueth *it is*, that your God is a God of gods, and a Lord of Kings, and a reuealer of secrets, seeing thou couldest reueale this secret.

48 Then the King made Daniel a great man, and gaue him many great gifts, & made him ruler ouer the whole prouince of Babylon, and *chiefe of the gouernours ouer all the wise men of Babylon.

49 Then Daniel requested of the King, and he set Shadrach, Meshach, and Abednego ouer the affaires of the prouince of Babylon: but Daniel *sate* in the gate of the King.

CHAP. III.

1 Nebuchad-nezzar dedicateth a golden image in Dura. 8 Shadrach, Meshach and Abed-nego are accused for not worshipping the image. 13 They being threatned, make a good confession. 19 God deliuereth them out of the furnace. 26 Nebuchad-nezzar seeing the miracle, blesseth God.

Ebuchad nezzar the king made an image of gold, whose height *was* three-score cubits, *and ŷ* breadth thereof six cubites: he set it vp in the plaine of Dura, in the pro-uince of Babylon.

2 Then Nebuchad-nezzar the king sent to gather together the Princes, the Gouernours, and the Captaines, the Iudges, the Treasurers, the Counsel-lers, the Sherifes, and all the rulers of the Prouinces, to come to the dedica-tion of the image which Nebuchad-nez-

zar the King had set vp.

3 Then the Princes, the Gouer-nours and Captaines, the Iudges, the Treasurers, the Counsellers, the She-rifes, and all the rulers of the Prouin-ces were gathered together vnto the dedicatio of the image, that Nebuchad-nezzar the King had set vp, and they stood before the image that Nebuchad-nezzar had set vp.

4 Then an herauld cryed † aloud, To you †it is commaunded, O people, nations, and languages,

5 *That* at what time yee heare the sound of the cornet, flute, harpe, sack-but, psalterie, ‖dulcimer, and all kinds of musicke, yee fall downe, and worship the golden image that Nebuchad-nez-zar the King hath set vp:

6 And who so falleth not down and worshippeth, shall the same houre bee cast into the middest of a burning fierie furnace.

7 Therefore at that time, when all the people heard the sound of the cor-net, flute, harpe, sackbut, psalterie, and all kindes of musicke, all the people, the nations, and the languages fell downe *and* worshipped the golden image, that Nebuchad-nezzar the King had set vp.

8 ¶ Wherefore at that time certaine Caldeans came neere, and accused the Iewes.

9 They spake and sayd to the King Nebuchad-nezzar, O King, liue for euer.

10 Thou, O King, hast made a de-cree, that euery man that shal heare the sound of the cornet, flute, harpe, sackbut, psalterie, and dulcimer, and all kinds of musicke, shall fall downe and worship the golden image:

11 And who so falleth not downe & worshippeth, *that* he should be cast in-to the midst of a burning fierie furnace.

12 There are certain Iewes whom thou hast set ouer the affaires of the prouince of Babylon, Shadrach, Me-shach, and Abednego: these men, O King, †haue not regarded thee; they serue not thy gods, nor worship the gol-den image, which thou hast set vp.

13 ¶ Then Nebuchad-nezzar in his rage and furie commaunded to bring Shadrach, Meshach, and Abednego: then they brought these men before the King.

14 Nebuchad-nezzar spake and said vnto them, Is it ‖true, O Shadrach, Me-

† Cald. with
might.
† Cald. they
command.

‖Or, singing.
Cald. Sym-
phonie.

† Cald. haue
set no regard
vpon thee.

‖ Or, of pur-
pose: as Exo-
dus 21. 13.

Meshach and Abednego? doe not yee serue my gods, nor worship the golden image which I haue set vp?

15 Now if ye be ready that at what time yee heare the sound of the cornet, flute, harpe, sackbut, psalterie, and dulcimer, and all kindes of musicke, ye fall downe, and worship the image which I haue made, *well:* but if yee worship not, ye shall be cast the same houre into the midst of a fierie furnace, and who is that God that shall deliuer you out of my handes?

16 Shadrach, Meshach, and Abednego answered and said to the king; O Nebuchad-nezzar, we are not carefull to answere thee in this matter.

17 If it be *so,* our God whom wee serue, is able to deliuer vs from the burning fierie furnace, and he will deliuer vs out of thine hand, O king.

18 But if not, bee it knowen vnto thee, O king, that we will not serue thy gods, nor worship thy golden image, which thou hast set vp.

19 ¶ Then was Nebuchad-nezzar †full of furie, and the forme of his visage was changed against Shadrach, Meshach and Abednego: *therefore* he spake and commanded, that they should heat the furnace one seuen times more then it was wont to be heat. †*Cal. filled.*

20 And hee commaunded the most †mighty men that were in his armie, to binde Shadrach, Meshach and Abednego, *and* to cast them into the burning fierie furnace. †*Cald. mightie of strength.*

21 Then these men were bound in their ‖coates, their hosen, and their ‖hats, and their *other* garments, and were cast into the midst of the burning fierie furnace. ‖*Or, mantle.* ‖*Or, turbant.*

22 Therefore because the Kings †commandement was vrgent, and the furnace exceeding hot, the ‖flame of the fire slew those men that tooke vp Shadrach, Meshach and Abednego. †*Cald. word.* ‖*Or, sparke.*

23 And these three men, Shadrach, Meshach, and Abednego, fell downe bound into the midst of the burning fierie furnace.

24 Then Nebuchad-nezzar the king was astonied, and rose vp in haste, *and* spake and said vnto his ‖counsellers, Did not wee cast three men bound into the midst of the fire? They answered and said vnto the king; True, O king. ‖*Or, gouernours.*

25 He answered and said, Loe, I see foure men loose, walking in the midst of the fire, and †they haue no hurt, and the forme of the fourth is like the sonne of God. †*Cal. there. is no hurt in them.*

26 ¶ Then Nebuchad-nezzar came neere to the †mouth of the burning fierie furnace, *and* spake and said, Shadrach, Meshach and Abednego, ye seruants of the most High God, come forth, and come *hither.* Then Shadrach, Meshach, and Abednego came forth of the midst of the fire. †*Cald. doore.*

27 And the princes, gouernours, and captaines, and the kings counsellers, being gathered together, saw these men, vpon whose bodies the fire had no power, nor was an haire of their head singed, neither were their coats changed, nor the smell of fire had passed on them.

28 *Then* Nebuchad-nezzar spake and said; Blessed *bee* the God of Shadrach, Meshach, and Abednego, who hath sent his Angel, and deliuered his seruants that trusted in him, and haue changed the Kings word, and yeelded their bodies, that they might not serue nor worship any God, except their owne God.

29 Therefore †I make a decree, That euery people, nation, and language, which speake †any thing amisse against the God of Shadrach, Meshach, and Abednego, shall be *∗†cut in pieces, and their houses shall be made a dunghill, because there is no other God, that can deliuer after this sort. †*Cald. a decree is mad by me.* †*Cald. errour.* ∗*Chap. 2. 5* †*Cald. made pieces.*

30 Then the King † promoted Shadrach, Meshach, and Abednego in the prouince of Babylon. †*Cald. mad to prosper.*

CHAP. IIII.

1 Nebuchad-nezzar confesseth Gods Kingdome, 4 maketh relation of his dreames, which the Magitians could not interpret. 8 Daniel heareth the dreame. 19 Hee interpreteth it. 28 The storie of the euent.

Ebuchad-nezzar the king, vnto all people, nations, and languages that dwell in all the earth, Peace be multiplied vnto you.

2 †I thought it good to shew the signes, and wonders, that the high God hath wrought toward me. †*Cald. it was seemely before me.*

3 How great *are* his signes? and how mighty *are* his wonders? his kingdome *is* ∗an euerlasting kingdome, and his dominion *is* fro generation to generation. ∗*Chap. 2. 34.*

4 ¶ I

4 ¶ I Nebuchadnezzar was at rest in mine house, and flourishing in my palace.

5 I saw a dreame which made me afraid, and the thoughts vpon my bed, and the visions of my head troubled me.

6 Therefore made I a decree, to bring in all the wise men of Babylon before mee, that they might make knowen vnto me the interpretation of the dreame.

7 Then came in the Magicians, the Astrologers, the Caldeans, and the Southsayers : and I tolde the dreame before them ; but they did not make knowen vnto mee the interpretation thereof.

8 ¶ But at the last Daniel came in before me, (whose name *was* Belteshazzar, according to the name of my God, and in whom *is* the spirit of the holy Gods) & before him I told the dreame, *saying,*

*Cha. 1. 48.

9 O Belteshazzar, * master of the Magicians, because I know that the spirit of the holy Gods is in thee, and no secret troubleth thee, tell me the visions of my dreame that I haue seene, and the interpretation thereof.

† Cald. I was seeing.

10 Thus *were* the visions of mine head in my bed : †I saw, and behold, a tree in the middest of the earth, and the height thereof *was* great.

11 The tree grew, and was strong, and the height thereof reached vnto heauen, and the sight thereof to the end of all the earth.

12 The leaues thereof *were* faire, and the fruite thereof much, and in it *was* meate for all : the beasts of the field had shadow vnder it, and the foules of the heauen dwelt in the boughes thereof, and all flesh was fed of it.

† Cald. with might.

13 I sawe in the visions of my head vpon my bed, & behold, a watcher and an holy one came downe from heauen.

14 He cryed †aloude, and said thus; Hew downe the tree, and cut off his branches; shake off his leaues, and scatter his fruite ; let the beasts get away from vnder it, and the foules from his branches.

15 Neuerthelesse leaue the stumpe of his rootes in the earth, euen with a band of yron and brasse, in the tender grasse of the field, and let it be wet with the dew of heauen, and let his portion *be* with the beastes in the grasse of the earth.

16 Let his heart bee changed from mans, and let a beasts heart be giuen vnto him, and let seuen times passe o-uer him.

17 This matter *is* by the decree of the watchers, and the demaund by the word of the Holy ones : to the intent that the liuing may know, that the most High ruleth in the kingdome of men, and giueth it to whomsoeuer hee will, and setteth vp ouer it the basest of men.

18 This dreame, I king Nebuchadnezzar haue seene : Now thou, O Belteshazzar, declare the interpretation thereof, forasmuch as all the Wise men of my kingdome are not able to make knowen vnto mee the interpretation : but thou art able, for the spirit of the holy Gods *is* in thee.

19 ¶ Then Daniel (whose name *was* Belteshazzar) was astonied for one houre, and his thoughts troubled him : The King spake, and said, Belteshazzar, let not the dreame, or the interpretation thereof trouble thee. Belteshazzar answered; and said; My lord, the dreame *be* to them that hate thee, and the interpretation thereof to thine enemies.

20 The tree that thou sawest, which grew, and was strong, whose height reached vnto the heauen, and the sight thereof to all the earth .

21 Whose leaues *were* faire, and the fruit thereof much, and in it *was* meate for all, vnder which the beasts of the field dwelt, and vpon whose branches the foules of the heauen had their habitation :

22 It is thou, O King, that art growen and become strong : for thy greatnesse is growen and reacheth vnto heauen, and thy dominion to the end of the earth.

23 And whereas the King saw a watcher, and an holy one comming downe from heauen, and saying, Hew the tree downe, and destroy it, yet leaue the stumpe of the rootes thereof in the earth, euen with a band of yron and brasse in the tender grasse of the field, and let it be wet with the dewe of heauen, and let his portion be with the beasts of the field, till seuen times passe ouer him :

24 This *is* the interpretation, O king, & this *is* the decree of the most Hie, which is come vpon my lord the king :

25 That

* Chap. 5.
20. &c.

25 That they shall *driue thee from men, and thy dwelling shall be with the beasts of the field, and they shall make thee to eate grasse as oxen, and they shall wet thee with the dew of heauen, and seuen times shall passe ouer thee, till thou know that the most high ruleth in the kingdome of men, and giueth it to whomsoeuer he will.

26 And whereas they commanded to leaue the stumpe of the tree rootes ; thy kingdome shall be sure vnto thee, after that thou shalt haue knowen that the heauens doe rule.

27 Wherefore, O King, let my counsell be acceptable vnto thee, and breake off thy sinnes by righteousnesse, and thine iniquities by shewing mercy to the poore; if it may be ||a lengthening of thy tranquillitie.

| Or, an healing of thine errour.

28 ¶ All this came vpon the King Nebuchad-nezzar

| Or, vpon.

29 At the end of twelue moneths he walked ||in the palace of the kingdome of Babylon.

30 The King spake, and said, Is not this great Babylon, that I haue built for the house of the kingdome, by the might of my power, and for the honour of my maiestie?

31 While the word *was* in the Kings mouth, there fell a voice from heauen, *saying*, O King Nebuchad-nezzar, to thee it is spoken ; The kingdome is departed from thee.

32 And they shall driue thee from men, and thy dwelling *shall be* with the beasts of the field ; they shall make thee to eate grasse as oxen, and seuen times shall passe ouer thee, vntill thou know that the most high ruleth in the kingdome of men, and giueth it to whomsoeuer he will.

33 The same houre was the thing fulfilled vpon Nebuchad-nezzar, and he was driuen from men, and did eate grasse as oxen, and his body was wet with the dew of heauen, till his haires were growen like Egles *feathers*, and his nailes like birds *clawes*.

34 And at the end of the dayes, I Nebuchad-nezzar lift vp mine eyes vnto heauen, and mine vnderstanding returned vnto me, and I blessed the most high, and I praised, and honoured him that liueth for euer, whose dominion *is* *an euerlasting dominion, and his kingdome *is* from generation to generation.

* Chap. 7
14. mic. 4. 7
luc. 1. 33.

35 And all the inhabitants of the earth are reputed as nothing : and hee doth according to his will in the armie of heauen, and *among* the inhabitants of the earth : and none can stay his hand, or *say vnto him, What doest thou?

* Iob. 9. 12.
isai. 45. 9.

36 At the same time my reason returned vnto me, and for the glory of my kingdome, mine honour, and brightnes returned vnto me, and my counsellers, and my Lords sought vnto me, and I was established in my kingdome, and excellent Maiestie was added vnto me.

37 Now I Nebuchad-nezzar praise, and extoll and honour the King of heauen, all whose workes *are* truth, and his waies iudgement, and those that walke in pride he is able to abase.

CHAP. V.

1 Belshazzars impious feast.   5 A hand writing, vnknowen to the Magitians, troubleth the king.   10 At the commendation of the Queene, Daniel is brought.   17 He reprouing the king of pride and idolatry,   25 readeth and interpreteth the writing.   30 The Monarchie is translated to the Medes.

BElshazzar the King made a great feast to a thousand of his Lords, and dranke wine before the thousand.

2 Belshazzar, whiles he tasted the wine, commaunded to bring the golden and siluer vessels, which his father Nebuchad-nezzar had †taken out of the temple which *was* in Ierusalem, that the king and his princes, his wiues, and his concubines might drinke therein.

† Cald.
brought foorth.

3 Then they brought the golden vessels that were taken out of the temple of the house of God, which *was* at Ierusalem, and the king and his princes, his wiues, and his concubines dranke in them.

4 They drunke wine, and praised the gods of gold and of siluer, of brasse, of yron, of wood, and of stone.

5 ¶ In the same houre came forth fingers of a mans hand, and wrote ouer against the candlesticke vpon the plaister of the wall of the Kings palace, and the king saw the part of the hand that wrote.

6 Then the kings † countenance †was changed, and his thoughts troubled him, so that the ||ioints of his loines were

† Cald.
brightnesse.
† Cald. changed it.
| Or, girdles
Cald. bindings or
knots.

were loosed, and his knees smote one against another.

7 The king cried †aloud to bring in the Astrologers, the Caldeans, and the soothsayers: *and* the king spake and said to the wise men of Babylon, Whosoeuer shall reade this writing, and shewe me the interpretation thereof, shall bee clothed with ‖scarlet, and *haue* a chaine of gold about his necke, and shall be the third ruler in the kingdome.

8 Then came in all the kings wise men, but they could not reade the writing, nor make knowen to the king the interpretation thereof.

9 Then was King Belshazzar greatly troubled, and his †countenance was changed in him, and his lordes were astonied.

10 ¶ *Now* the queene, by reason of the wordes of the king and his lords, came into the banquet house, *and* the queene spake and said, O king, liue for euer: let not thy thoughts trouble thee, nor let thy countenance be changed.

11 *There is a man in thy kingdom, in whome *is* the spirit of the holy gods, and in the dayes of thy ‖father light and vnderstanding and wisedome like the wisedome of the gods, was found in him: whom the king Nebuchad-nezzar‖ thy father, the king, *I say,* thy father made *master of the magicians, astrologers, Caldeans, *and* soothsayers,

12 Forasmuch as an excellent spirit and knowledge and vnderstanding, ‖interpreting of dreames, and shewing of hard sentences, & ‖dissoluing of †doubts were found in the same Daniel, whom the king named Belteshazzar: now let Daniel be called, and he will shewe the interpretation.

13 Then was Daniel brought in before the king, *and* the king spake and said vnto Daniel, *Art* thou that Daniel, which *art* of the children of the captiuity of Iudah, whom the king my ‖father brought out of Iewrie?

14 I haue euen heard of thee, that the spirit of the gods *is* in thee, and *that* light, and vnderstanding, and excellent wisedome is found in thee.

15 And now the wise men, the astrologers haue bene brought in before me, that they should reade this writing, and make knowen vnto me the interpretation thereof: but they could not shewe the interpretation of the thing.

16 And I haue heard of thee, that

thou canst †make interpretations, and dissolue doubts: now if thou canst read the writing, and make knowen to mee the interpretation thereof, thou shalt be clothed with scarlet, & *haue* a chaine of gold about thy necke, and shalt bee the third ruler in the kingdome.

17 ¶ Then Daniel answered and said before the king, Let thy gifts be to thy selfe, and giue thy ‖rewards to an other, yet I will reade the writing vnto the king, and make knowen to him the interpretation.

18 O thou king, the most high God gaue Nebuchad-nezzar thy father a kingdome, and maiestie, and glory, and honour.

19 And for the maiestie that hee gaue him, all people, nations, and languages trembled and feared before him: whom he would, he slew, & whom he would, he kept aliue, and whom he would hee set vp, and whom he would hee put downe.

20 But when his heart was lifted vp, and his minde hardened ‖in pride: hee was †deposed from his kingly throne, and they tooke his glory from him.

21 And hee was *driuen from the sonnes of men, and ‖his heart was made like the beasts, and his dwelling was with the wilde asses: they fed him with grasse like oxen, and his body was wet with the dew of heauen, till hee knew that the most high God ruled in the kingdome of men, and that hee appointeth ouer it whomsoeuer he will.

22 And thou his sonne, O Belshazzar, hast not humbled thine heart, though thou knewest all this:

23 But hast lifted vp thy selfe against the Lord of heauen, and they haue brought the vessels of his house before thee, and thou and thy lords, thy wiues and thy concubines haue drunke wine in them, and thou hast praised the gods of siluer, and golde, of brasse, yron, wood and stone, which see not, nor heare, nor knowe: and the God in whose hande thy breath *is,* and whose are all thy wayes, hast thou not glorified.

24 Then was the part of the hand sent from him, and this writing was written.

25 ¶ And this *is* the writing that was written, *MENE, MENE, TEKEL VPHARSIN.*

26 This

Marginal notes:

† *Calde. with might.*

‖ *Or, purple.*

† *Calde. brightnesses.*

*Cha. 2. 48

‖ *Or, grandfather.*

‖ *Or, grandfather.* *Cha. 4. 6.

‖ *Or, of an interpreter, &c.* ‖ *Or, of a dissoluer.* † *Calde. knots.*

‖ *Or, grandfather.*

† *Calde. interprete.*

‖ *Or, fee, as chap. 2. 6.*

‖ *Or, to deale proudly.* † *Cal. made to come downe.* *Cha. 4. 22 ‖ Or, hee made his heart equall, &c.*

26 This *is* the interpretation of the thing, *MENE*, God hath numbred thy kingdome, and finished it.

27 *TEKEL*, thou art weighed in the balances, and art found wanting.

28 *PERES*, thy kingdome is diuided, and giuen to the Medes and Persians.

29 Then commanded Belshazzar, and they clothed Daniel with scarlet, and *put* a chaine of gold about his necke, and made a Proclamation concerning him, that he should be the third ruler in the kingdome.

30 ¶ In that night was Belshazzar the king of the Caldeans slaine.

† *Cald. he as the Sonne of, &c.*
‖ *Or, now.*

31 And Darius the Median tooke the kingdome, † being ‖ about threescore and two yeere old.

CHAP. VI.

1 Daniel is made chiefe of the Præsidents. 4 They conspiring against him, obtaine an idolatrous decree. 10 Daniel accused of the breach thereof, is cast into the Lions denne. 18 Daniel is saued. 24 His aduersaries deuoured, 25 and God magnified by a decree.

I T pleased Darius to set ouer the kingdome an hundred and twenty Princes, which should be ouer the whole kingdome.

2 And ouer these, three Presidents, (of whom Daniel *was* first) that the Princes might giue accompts vnto them, and the King should haue no damage.

3 Then this Daniel was preferred aboue the Presidents, and Princes, because an excellent spirit *was* in him, and the king thought to set him ouer the whole realme.

4 ¶ Then the Presidents and Princes sought to finde occasion against Daniel concerning the kingdome, but they could finde none occasion, nor fault : forasmuch as he *was* faithfull, neither was there any errour or fault found in him.

5 Then said these men, We shall not finde any occasion against this Daniel, except wee finde it against him concerning the Law of his God.

‖ *Or, came tumultuously.*

6 Then these Presidents and Princes ‖ assembled together to the king, and said thus vnto him, King Darius, liue for euer.

7 All the Presidents of the kingdome, the gouernours, and the Princes, the counsellers and the captaines haue consulted together to establish a royall statute, and to make a firme ‖ decree, that whosoeuer shall aske a petition of any God or man for thirty dayes, saue of thee, O King, hee shall be cast into the denne of Lions.

‖ *Or, interdict.*

8 Now, O king, establish the decree, and signe the writing, that it be not changed, according to the * law of the Medes & Persians, which † altereth not.

* *Esth. 2. 1. and 8. 8.*
† *Cald. passeth not.*

9 Wherefore King Darius signed the writing and the decree.

10 ¶ Now when Daniel knew that the writing was signed, hee went into his house, and his windowes being open in his chamber * toward Ierusalem, hee kneeled vpon his knees * three times a day, and prayed, and gaue thankes before his God, as hee did afore time.

* *1. King. 8. 48.*
* *Psal. 55. 18.*

11 Then these men assembled, and found Daniel praying, and making supplication before his God.

12 Then they came neere, and spake before the king concerning the kings decree ; Hast thou not signed a decree, that euery man that shall aske a petition of any God or man, within thirty dayes, saue of thee, O king, shalbe cast into the denne of Lions ? The king answered and said, The thing *is* true, according to the law of the Medes and Persians, which altereth not.

13 Then answered they and said before the king ; That Daniel which *is* of the captiuity of the children of Iudah, regardeth not thee, O king, nor the decree that thou hast signed, but maketh his petition three times a day.

14 Then the king, when hee heard these wordes, was sore displeased with himselfe, and set his heart on Daniel to deliuer him : and he laboured till the going downe of the sunne, to deliuer him.

15 Then these men assembled vnto the king, and said vnto the king, Know O king, that the law of the Medes and Persians *is*, that no decree nor statute which the king establisheth, may bee changed.

16 Then the king commanded, and they brought Daniel, and cast *him* into the denne of Lions : now the king spake and saide vnto Daniel ; Thy God, whom thou seruest continually, he will deliuer thee.

17 And a stone was brought and laid vpon the mouth of the denne, and the King

King sealed it with his owne signet, and with the signet of his lords; that the purpose might not be changed concerning Daniel.

18 ¶ Then the king went to his palace, and passed the night fasting : neither were ‖ instruments of musicke brought before him, and his sleepe went from him.

19 Then the king arose very early in the morning, and went in haste vnto the den of Lyons.

20 And when he came to the den, he cryed with a lamentable voice vnto Daniel, and the king spake and said to Daniel; O Daniel, seruant of the liuing God, Is thy God whom thou seruest continually, able to deliuer thee from the Lyons?

21 Then said Daniel vnto the king, O king, liue for euer.

22 My God hath sent his Angel, and hath shut the lyons mouthes that they haue not hurt me : forasmuch as before him, innocencie was found in me; and also before thee, O king, haue I done no hurt.

23 Then was the king exceeding glad for him, and commanded that they should take Daniel vp out of the denne: so Daniel was taken vp out of the den, and no maner of hurt was found vpon him, because he beleeued in his God.

24 ¶ And the king commanded, and they brought those men which had accused Daniel, and they cast them into the den of Lyons, them, their children, and their wiues : and the Lyons had the mastery of them, and brake all their bones in pieces or euer they came at the bottome of the den.

25 ¶ Then king Darius wrote vnto all people, nations, and languages that dwell in all the earth; Peace be multiplied vnto you.

26 I make a decree, That in euery dominion of my kingdome, men tremble and feare before the God of Daniel: for he is the liuing God, and stedfast for euer, and his kingdome *that, which shal not be *destroyed, and his dominion shall be euen vnto the end.

27 He deliuereth and rescueth, and he worketh signes and wonders in heauen and in earth : who hath deliuered Daniel from the †power of the lyons.

28 So this Daniel prospered in the reigne of Darius, and in the reigne of *Cyrus the Persian.

CHAP. VII.

1 Daniels vision of foure beastes. 9 Of Gods kingdome. 15 The interpretation thereof.

N the first yeere of Belshazzar king of Babylon, Daniel † had a dreame, and visions of his head vpon his bed: then he wrote the dreame, and tolde the summe of the ‖ matters.

2 Daniel spake, and said, I saw in my vision by night, & behold, the foure windes of the heauen stroue vpon the great Sea.

3 And foure great beastes came vp from the sea, diuers one from another.

4 The first was like a Lyon, and had Eagles wings : I beheld till the wings thereof were pluckt, ‖ and it was lifted vp from the earth, and made stand vpon the feete as a man, and a mans heart was giuen to it.

5 And behold, another beast, a second, like to a Beare, and ‖ it raised vp it selfe on one side, and it had three ribbes in the mouth of it betweene the teeth of it, and they said thus vnto it, Arise, deuoure much flesh.

6 After this I beheld, and loe, another like a Leopard, which had vpon the backe of it foure wings of a foule, the beast had also foure heads, and dominion was giuen to it.

7 After this I saw in the night visions, and behold, a fourth beast, dreadfull and terrible, and strong exceedingly; and it had great yron teeth: it deuoured and brake in pieces, and stamped the residue with the feete of it, and it was diuers from all the beasts that were before it, and it had ten hornes.

8 I considered the hornes, and behold, there came vp among them another little horne, before whom there were three of the first hornes pluckt vp by the roots : and behold, in this horne were eyes like the eyes of man, and a mouth speaking great things.

9 ¶ I beheld till the thrones were cast downe, and the Ancient of dayes did sit, whose garment was white as snow, and the haire of his head like the pure wooll : his throne was like the fierie flame, and his wheeles as burning fire.

10 A fierie streame issued, and came foorth from before him : *thousand thousands ministred vnto him, and ten thousand times ten thousand stood before

---

Margin notes (left column):

‖ Or, table.

* Cha. 2. 44.
and 4. 3.
and 7. 14,
27. luke
1. 33.

† Heb. hand.

* Cha. 1. 22.

Margin notes (right column):

† Cald. saw.

‖ Or, words.

‖ Or, wherewith.

‖ Or, it raised vp one dominion.

* Reu. 5. 11.

* Reu. 22.
12.

fore him : the iudgement was set, and the *bookes were opened.

11 I beheld then, because of the voice of the great words which the horne spake : I beheld euen till the beast was slaine, and his body destroyed, and giuen to the burning flame.

12 As concerning the rest of the beasts, they had their dominion taken away : yet †their liues were prolonged for a season and time.

† Cald. a prolonging in life was giuen them.

13 I saw in the night visions, and behold, *one* like the sonne of man, came with the clouds of heauen, and came to the Ancient of daies, and they brought him neere before him.

14 And there was giuen him dominion and glory, and a kingdome, that all people, nations, and languages should serue him : his dominion *is* *an euerlasting dominion, which shall not passe away ; and his kingdome *that*, which shall not be destroyed.

* Chap. 2. 44. mic. 4. 7. luc. 1. 33.

15 ¶ I Daniel was grieued in my spirit in the midst of *my* †body, and the visions of my head troubled me.

† Cald. sheath.

16 I came neere vnto one of them that stood by, and asked him the truth of all this : so he told mee, and made me know the interpretation of the things.

17 These great beasts, which are foure, *are* foure Kings, *which* shall arise out of the earth.

18 But the Saints of the †most high shall take the kingdome, & possesse the kingdome for euer, euen for euer & euer.

† Cald. high ones, i. things or, places.

19 Then I would know the truth of the fourth beast, which was diuerse †from al the others, exceeding dreadful, whose teeth were of yron, and his nailes of brasse, *which* deuoured, brake in pieces, and stamped the residue with his feete,

† Cald. from all those.

20 And of the ten hornes that *were* in his head, and of the other, which came vp, and before whom three fell, euen of that horne that *had* eyes, and a mouth that spake very great things, whose looke *was* more stout then his fellowes.

21 I beheld, and the same horne made warre with the Saints, and preuailed against them ;

22 Vntill the Ancient of daies came, and iudgment was giuen to the Saints of the most high : and the time came that the Saints possessed the kingdome.

23 Thus he said, The fourth kingdome shall be the fourth kingdome vpon earth, which shall be diuerse from all kingdomes, & shall deuoure the whole earth, and shall tread it downe, and breake it in pieces.

24 And the tenne hornes out of this kingdome *are* tenne Kings *that* shall arise : and an other shall rise after them, and he shall be diuerse from the first, and he shall subdue three Kings.

25 And he shall speake great words against the most high, and shall weare out the Saints of the most high, and thinke to change times, and lawes : and they shall be giuen into his hand, vntill a time and times, & the diuiding of time.

26 But the iudgement shall sit, and they shall take away his dominion, to consume, and to destroy *it* vnto the end.

27 And the *kingdome and dominion, and the greatnesse of the kingdome vnder the whole heauen, shall be giuen to the people of the Saints of the most high, whose kingdome is an euerlasting kingdome, and all ‖dominions shall serue and obey him.

* Luc. 1. 3

‖ Or, rulers

28 Hitherto *is* the end of the matter. As for me Daniel, my cogitations much troubled me, and my countenance changed in me : but I kept the matter in my heart.

CHAP. VIII.

1 Daniels vision, of the Ram, and he Goate. 13 The 2300. daies of sacrifice. 15 Gabriel comforteth Daniel, and interpreteth the vision.

IN the third yeere of the reigne of King Belshazzar, a vision appeared vnto mee, *euen* vnto me Daniel, after that which appeared vnto me at the first.

2 And I saw in a vision (and it came to passe when I saw, that I *was* at Shushan *in* the palace, which *is* in the prouince of Elam) and I saw in a vision, and I was by the riuer of Vlai.

3 Then I lifted vp mine eyes, and saw, and behold, there stood before the riuer, a ramme which *had* two hornes, and the two hornes *were* high : but one *was* higher then † the other, and the higher came vp last.

† Heb. the second.

4 I saw the ramme pushing Westward, & Northward, and Southward : so that no beasts might stand before him, neither *was* there any that could deliuer out of his hand, but he did according to his will, and became great.

5 And as I was considering, behold, an he goat came frõ the west on the face of the whole earth, & ‖touched not the ground :

‖ Or, none touched hi in the eart

† *Hebr. a horne of sight.*

ground : and the goate *had* †a notable horne betweene his eyes.

6 And he came to the ramme that had two hornes, which I had seene standing before the riuer, and ranne vnto him in the furie of his power.

7 And I saw him come close vnto the ramme, and he was mooued with choler against him, and smote the ramme, and brake his two hornes, and there was no power in the ramme to stand before him, but he cast him downe to the ground, and stamped vpon him, and there was none that could deliuer the ramme out of his hand.

8 Therefore the hee goate waxed very great, and when he was strong, the great horne was broken : and for it came vp foure notable ones, * toward the foure windes of heauen.

* *Cha. 11. 4*

9 And out of one of them came forth a litle horne, which waxed exceeding great, toward the South, and toward the East, and toward the *pleasant *land*.

* *Psal. 48.2 ezek. 20. 6.*
‖ *Or, against the hoste.*

10 And it waxed great euen ‖ to the hoste of heauen, and it cast downe *some* of the hoste, and of the starres to the ground, and stamped vpon them.

‖ *Or, against*
‖ *Or, from him.*

11 Yea he magnified *himselfe* euen ‖ to the prince of the hoste, and ‖ by him the dayly *sacrifice* was taken away, and the place of his Sanctuary was cast down.

‖ *Or, the host was giuen ouer for the transgression against the daily sacrifice.*

12 And ‖ an hoste was giuen *him* against the daily *sacrifice* by reason of transgression, and it cast downe the trueth to the ground, and it practised, and prospered.

‖ *The numberer of secrets, or, the wonderfull numberer. Heb. Palmoni.*
‖ *Or, making desolate.*
† *Heb. euening morning.*
† *Heb. iustified.*

13 ¶ Then I heard one Saint speaking, and another Saint saide vnto ‖ that certaine *Saint* which spake, How long *shall bee* the vision concerning the daily *sacrifice*, and the transgression ‖ of desolation, to giue both the Sanctuary, and the hoste to be troden vnder foot?

14 And he said vnto me, Vnto two thousand and three hundred †dayes : then shall the Sanctuary be †clensed.

15 ¶ And it came to passe, when I, *euen* I Daniel had seene the vision, and sought for the meaning, then beholde, there stood before me as the appearance of a man.

16 And I heard a mans voyce betweene *the bankes of* Vlai, which called and said, * Gabriel, make this man to vnderstand the vision.

* *Cha. 9. 21.*

17 So he came neere where I stood : and when he came, I was afraid, and fell vpon my face : but he said vnto mee,

Vnderstand, O sonne of man : for at the time of the end *shalbe* the vision.

18 Now as he was speaking with me, I was in a deepe sleepe on my face toward the ground : but he touched me, and †set me vpright.

† *Heb. made me stand vp on my standing.*

19 And he said, Behold, I wil make thee know what shall be in the last end of the indignation : for at the time appointed the end *shalbe*.

20 The ramme which thou sawest hauing two hornes, *are* the kings of Media, and Persia.

21 And the rough goat *is* the king of Grecia, and the great horne that *is* betweene his eyes, is the first king.

22 Now that being broken, whereas foure stood vp for it, foure kingdomes shall stand vp out of the nation, but not in his power.

23 And in the latter time of their kingdome, when the transgressours †are come to the full, a king of fierce countenance, and vnderstanding darke sentences, shall stand vp.

† *Heb. are accomplished.*

24 And his power shall be mighty, but not by his owne power : and hee shall destroy wonderfully, and shall prosper, and practise, and shall destroy the mightie, and the †holy people.

† *Heb. people of the holy ones.*

25 And through his policie also hee shall cause craft to prosper in his hand, and hee shall magnifie *himselfe* in his heart, and by ‖ peace shal destroy many : he shall also stand vp against the prince of princes, but he shalbe * broken without hand.

‖ *Or, prosperitie.*
* *2. Mac. 6. 9*

26 And the vision of the euening, and the morning, which was tolde, is true : wherfore shut thou vp the vision, for it *shalbe* for many dayes.

27 And I Daniel fainted and was sicke *certaine* dayes : afterward I rose vp and did the kings businesse, and I was astonished at the vision, but none vnderstood it.

CHAP. IX.

1 Daniel considering the time of the captiuitie, 3 maketh confession of sinnes, 16 and prayeth for the restauration of Ierusalem. 20 Gabriel informeth him of the seuentie weekes.

N the first yeere of Darius the sonne of Ahasuerus, of the seede of the Medes, ‖ which was made King ouer the realme of the Caldeans,

‖ *Or, in which he, &c.*

2 In

2 In the first yeere of his reigne, I Daniel vnderstood by bookes the number of the yeeres, whereof the word of the LORD came to * Ieremiah the Prophet, that he would accomplish seuentie yeeres in the desolations of Ierusalem.

3 ¶ And I set my face vnto the Lord God to seeke by prayer, and supplications, with fasting, and sackcloth, and ashes.

4 And I prayed vnto the LORD my God, and made my confession, and said, O * Lord, the great and dreadfull God, keeping the couenant, and mercy to them that loue him, and to them that keepe his Commandements:

5 *We haue sinned, and haue committed iniquitie, and haue done wickedly, and haue rebelled, euen by departing from thy precepts, and from thy iudgements.

6 Neither haue we hearkened vnto thy seruants the Prophets, which spake in thy Name to our kings, our princes, and our fathers, and to all the people of the land.

7 O Lord, righteousnes ||belongeth vnto thee, but vnto vs confusion of faces, as at this day : to the men of Iudah, and to the inhabitants of Ierusalem, and vnto all Israel that are neere, and that are farre off, through all the countreys whither thou hast driuen them, because of their trespasse, that they haue trespassed against thee.

8 O Lord, *to vs belongeth confusion of face, to our kings, to our princes, and to our fathers; because we haue sinned against thee.

9 To the Lord our God belong mercies and forgiuenesses, though we haue rebelled against him.

10 Neither haue we obeyed the voice of the LORD our God, to walke in his Lawes which he set before vs, by his seruants the Prophets.

11 Yea, all Israel haue transgressed thy Law, euen by departing, that they might not obey thy voice, therefore the curse is powred vpon vs, and the othe that is written in the *Law of Moses the seruant of God, because we haue sinned against him.

12 And he hath confirmed his words which he spake against vs, and against our Iudges that iudged vs, by bringing vpon vs a great euill : for vnder the whole heauen hath not bene done, as

hath bene done vpon Ierusalem.

13 As *it is written in the Law of Moses, all this euill is come vpon vs : yet †made we not our prayer before the LORD our God, that we might turne from our iniquities, and vnderstand thy trueth.

14 Therefore hath the LORD watched vpon the euil, and brought it vpon vs : for the LORD our God is righteous in all his workes, which he doeth : for we obeyed not his voice.

15 And now O Lord our God, that hast *brought thy people forth out of the land of Egypt with a mighty hand, and hast †gotten thee renowne, as at this day, wee haue sinned, wee haue done wickedly.

16 ¶ O Lord, according to all thy righteousnes, I beseech thee, let thine anger and thy furie bee turned away from thy citie Ierusalem, thy holy Mountaine : because for our sinnes, and for the iniquities of our fathers, Ierusalem and thy people are become a reproch to all that are about vs.

17 Now therefore, O our God, heare the prayer of thy seruant, and his supplications, and cause thy face to shine vpon thy Sanctuary that is desolate, for the Lords sake.

18 O my God, encline thine eare and heare : open thine eyes, and behold our desolations, & the city, †which is called by thy name: for we do not †present our supplications before thee for our righteousnesses, but for thy great mercies.

19 O Lord heare, O Lord forgiue, O Lord hearken and doe : deferre not for thine owne sake, O my God : for thy citie, & thy people are called by thy Name.

20 ¶ And whiles I was speaking, and praying, and confessing my sinne, and the sinne of my people Israel, and presenting my supplication before the LORD my God, for the holy Mountaine of my God :

21 Yea whiles I was speaking in praier, euen the man *Gabriel, whom I had seene in the vision at the beginning, being caused to flie†swiftly, touched me about the time of the euening oblation.

22 And he informed mee, and talked with mee, and said; O Daniel, I am now come foorth †to giue thee skill and vnderstanding.

23 At the beginning of thy supplications the †commandement came forth, and I am come to shew thee : for thou art

* Iere. 25. 12. and 29. 10.

* Nehe. 1. 5. deut. 7. 9.

* Bar. 1. 17.

‖ Or, thou hast, &c.

* Bar. 1. 15.

* Leuit. 26. 14. &c. deu. 28. 15. &c. and 29. 20. &c. and 30. 17, 18. and 31. 17. &c. and 32. 19. &c.

* Leuit. 26. 14. deu. 28. 15. lament. 2. 17.
† Hebr. intreated the face.

* Exod. 14. 28.

† Heb. made thee a name.

† Heb. wherupon thy Name is called.
† Heb. cause to fall.

* Dan. 8. 16.

† Hebr. with wearinesse or flight.

† Hebr. to make thee skilfull of vnderstanding.

† Heb. word.

† *Heb.* a man *of desires.*

art †greatly beloued : therefore vnderstand the matter, & consider the vision.

24 Seuentie weekes are determined vpon thy people, and vpon thy holy citie, ||to finish the transgression, and to ||make an ende of sinnes, and to make reconciliation for iniquitie, and to bring in euerlasting righteousnes, and to seale vp the vision and † prophecie, and to anoynt the most Holy.

25 Know therefore and vnderstand, *that* from the going foorth of the commandement to restore and to build Ierusalem, vnto the Messiah the Prince, *shall be* seuen weekes; and threescore and two weekes, the street †shall be built againe, and the || wall, euen † in troublous times.

26 And after threescore and two weekes, shall Messiah be cut off, ||but not for himselfe, and the people of the Prince that shall come, shall destroy the citie, and the Sanctuarie, and the ende thereof *shall be* with a flood, and vnto the ende of the warre ||desolations are determined.

27 And hee shall confirme the couenant with many for one weeke : and in the midst of the weeke he shall cause the sacrifice and the oblation to cease, and ||for the ouerspreading of *abominations hee shall make *it* desolate, euen vntill the consummation, & that determined, shalbe powred vpon the desolate.

CHAP. X.

1 Daniel hauing humbled himselfe, seeth a vision. 10 Being troubled with feare, hee is comforted by the Angel.

IN the third yere of Cyrus King of Persia, a thing was reuealed vnto Daniel (whose name was called Belteshazzar) and the thing *was* true, but the time appointed *was* †long, and he vnderstood the thing, and had vnderstanding of the vision.

2 In those dayes, I Daniel was mourning three † full weekes.

3 I ate no †pleasant bread, neither came flesh, nor wine in my mouth, neither did I anoynt my selfe at all, till three whole weekes were fulfilled.

4 And in the foure and twentieth day of the first moneth, as I was by the side of the great riuer, *which is* *Hiddekel:

5 Then I lift vp mine eyes and looked, and behold, †a certaine man clothed in linen, whose loynes were *girded with fine gold of Vphaz.

6 His body also *was* like the Berill, and his face as the appearance of lightning, and his eyes as lampes of fire, and his armes, and his feete like in colour to polished brasse, and the voice of his words like the voice of a multitude.

7 And I Daniel alone saw the vision : for the men that were with mee saw not the vision : but a great quaking fell vpon them, so that they fled to hide themselues.

8 Therefore I was left alone, and saw this great vision, and there remained no strength in me : for my ||*comelinesse was turned in me into corruption, and I retained no strength.

9 Yet heard I the voice of his words : and when I heard the voice of his wordes, then was I in a deepe sleepe on my face, and my face toward the ground.

10 ¶ And behold, an hand touched me, which †set me vpon my knees, and *vpon* the palmes of my hands.

11 And hee said vnto me, O Daniel, †a man greatly beloued, vnderstand the wordes that I speake vnto thee, and †stand vpright : for vnto thee am I now sent ; and when he had spoken this word vnto me, I stood trembling.

12 Then sayd hee vnto me ; Feare not, Daniel : for from the first day that thou diddest set thine heart to vnderstand, and to chasten thy selfe before thy God, thy wordes were heard, and I am come for thy words.

13 But the prince of the kingdome of Persia withstood mee one and twentie dayes : but loe, Michael ||one of the chiefe Princes came to helpe mee, and I remained there with the Kings of Persia.

14 Now I am come to make thee vnderstand what shall befall thy people, in the latter dayes : for yet the vision *is* for *many* dayes.

15 And when hee had spoken such words vnto me, I set my face toward the ground, and I became dumbe.

16 And behold, *one* like the similitude of the sonnes of men touched my lippes : then I opened my mouth, and spake, and sayd vnto him that stoode before me ; O my Lord, by the vision my sorrowes are turned vpon me, and I haue retained no strength.

17 For how can ||the seruant of this my Lord, talke with this my Lord ? for

|| *Or, to restraine.* || *Or, to seale vp.*

- *Heb.* prophet.

|| *Heb.* shall returne and be built. || *Or, breach or ditch.* † *Hebr.* in strait of times. || *Or,* shall haue nothing.

|| *Or, it shall be cut off by desolations.*

|| *Or, with the abominable armies.* *Mat. 24. 15. marke 13. 14. luke 21. 20.

† *Hcb.* great.

† *Heb.* weekes of dayes. † *Heb.* bread of desires.

*Gen. 2. 14.

† *Heb.* one man. *Reu. 1. 13, 14, 15.

† *Or, vigor.* *Dan. 7. 28.

† *Heb.* mooued.

† *Heb.* a man *of desires.* † *Heb.* stand vpon thy standing.

|| *Or, the first.*

|| *Or, this seruant of my Lord.*

as|

as for me, straightway there remained no strength in mee, neither is there breath left in me.

18 Then there came againe and touched me *one* like the appearance of a man, and he strengthned me,

19 And said; O man greatly beloued, feare not : peace *be* vnto thee, be strong, yea be strong ; and when he had spoken vnto me, I was strengthened, and said; Let my Lord speake: for thou hast strengthened me.

20 Then said hee, Knowest thou wherefore I come vnto thee ? and now will I returne to fight with the prince of Persia : and when I am gone forth, loe, the prince of Grecia shall come.

21 But I will shew thee that which is noted in the Scripture of trueth : and there is none that †holdeth with me in these things, but Michael your prince.

† Heb. strengtheneth himselfe.

CHAP. XI.

1 *The ouerthrow of Persia by the king of Grecia.* 5 *Leagues and conflicts, betweene the kings of the South and of the North.* 30 *The inuasion and tyrannie of the Romanes.*

ALso I, in the first yeere of Darius the Mede, *euen* I stood to confirme and to strengthen him.

2 And now will I shew thee the trueth. Behold, there shall stand vp yet three Kings in Persia, & the fourth shalbe farre richer then they all : and by his strength through his riches he shall stirre vp all against the realme of Grecia.

3 And a mighty King shal stand vp, that shall rule with great dominion, and doe according to his will.

4 And when he shall stand vp, his kingdome shall be broken, and shall be diuided toward the foure winds of heauen ; and not to his posteritie, nor according to his dominion which he ruled : for his kingdome shall be pluckt vp, euen for others besides those.

5 ¶ And the King of the South shall be strong, and *one* of his princes, and he shall be strong aboue him, and haue dominion : his dominion *shall be* a great dominion.

6 And in the end of yeeres they shall †ioyne themselues together : for the Kings daughter of the South shall come to the King of the North to make †an agreement, but she shall not retaine the power of the arme, neither shall he

† Heb. shall associate themselues.

† Heb. rights.

stand, nor his arme : but she shall be giuen vp, and they that brought her, and ||he that begate her, and he that strengthened her in these times.

7 But out of a branch of her rootes shall one stand vp in his estate, which shall come with an armie, and shall enter into the fortresse of the King of the North, and shall deale against them, and shall preuaile :

8 And shall also carie captiues into Egypt their gods with their princes, *and* with their †precious vessels of siluer and of gold, and he shall continue *moe* yeeres then the King of the North.

9 So the King of the South shall come into *his* kingdome, and shall returne into his owne land.

10 But his sonnes || shall be stirred vp, and shall assemble a multitude of great forces · and *one* shall certainly come and ouerflow and passe through : then shall he returne, and be stirred vp euen to his fortresse.

11 And the King of the South shall be moued with choler, and shall come forth and fight with him, *euen* with the King of the North : and hee shall set forth a great multitude, but the multitude shall be giuen into his hand.

12 *And* when he hath taken away the multitude, his heart shall be lifted vp : and he shall cast downe *many* tenne thousands : but he shall not be strengthened *by it.*

13 For the King of the North shall returne, and shall set forth a multitude greater then the former, and shall certainly † come (after certaine yeeres) with a great armie & with much riches.

14 And in those times there shall many stand vp against the King of the South : also †the robbers of thy people shall exalt themselues to establish the vision, but they shall fall.

15 So the King of the North shall come, and cast vp a mount, and take †the most fenced cities, and the armes of the South shall not withstand, neither †his chosen people, neither *shall there be* any strength to withstand.

16 But he that commeth against him, shall doe according to his owne will, and none shall stand before him : and he shall stand in the ||glorious land, which by his hand shall be consumed.

17 He shall also set his face to enter with the strength of his whole kingdome and ||vpright ones with him : thus shall

Or, whom she brought forth.

† *Heb. vessels of their desire.*

Or, shall warre.

† *Heb. at the end of times of yeeres.*

† *Heb. the children of robbers.*

† *Heb. the citie of munitions.*

† *Heb. the people of his choices.*

|| *Or, goodly land. Heb. The land of ornament.*

|| *Or, much vprightnes Or equall conditions.*

*Heb. to cor-
rupt.*

shall he doe, and he shall giue him the daughter of women †corrupting her : but she shall not stand *on his side*, neither be for him.

18 After this shall he turne his face vnto the yles, and shall take many, but a prince †for his own behalfe shall cause †the reproch offred by him to cease without his owne reproch : he shall cause *it* to turne vpon him.

*Heb. for
him.
Heb. his
reproch.*

19 Then he shall turne his face towards the fort of his owne lande : but he shall stumble and fall, and not bee found.

20 Then shall stand vp in his estate †a raiser of taxes *in* the glory of the kingdome, but within few dayes he shall be destroyed, neither in †anger, nor in battell.

*Heb. one
that causeth
an exactour
to passe ouer.
* Heb. an-
gers.*

21 And in his estate shall stand vp a vile person, to whom they shal not giue the honour of the kingdome : but hee shall come in peaceably, and obtaine the kingdome by flatteries.

22 And with the armes of a flood shall they bee ouerflowen from before him, and shall be broken : yea also the prince of the couenant.

23 And after the league *made* with him he shall worke deceitfully, for hee shall come vp, and shall become strong with a small people.

*‖ Or, into the
peaceable or
fat, &c.*

24 He shall enter ‖peaceably euen vpon the fattest places of the prouince, and he shall doe that which his fathers haue not done, nor his fathers fathers, he shall scatter among them the praye and spoile, and riches : yea and he shall †forecast his deuices against the strong holdes, euen for a time.

*†Heb. thinke
thoughts.*

25 And he shall stirre vp his power, and his courage against the king of the South with a great army, and the king of the South shall bee stirred vp to battell with a very great and mightie armie : but he shall not stand : for they shall forecast deuices against him.

26 Yea they that feede of the portion of his meate, shall destroy him, and his armie shall ouerflow : and many shall fall downe slaine.

*†Heb. their
hearts.*

27 And both these kings †hearts *shall be* to doe mischiefe, and they shall speake lies at one table : but it shall not prosper : for yet the end *shall bee* at the time appointed.

28 Then shall hee returne into his land with great riches, and his heart *shall be* against the holy couenant : and

he shall doe *exploits*, and returne to his owne land.

29 At the time appointed he shall returne, and come toward the South : but it shall not be as the former, or as the latter.

30 ¶ For the ships of Chittim shall come against him : therefore he shall be grieued and returne, and haue indignation against the holy Couenant : so shal he doe, he shall euen returne, and haue intelligence with them that forsake the holy Couenant.

31 And armes shal stand on his part, and they shall pollute the Sanctuarie of strength, and shall take away the daily *sacrifice*, and they shal place the abomination that ‖maketh desolate.

*‖ Or, astoni-
sheth.*

*‖ Or, cause
to dissemble.*

32 And such as doe wickedly against the couenant, shall hee ‖corrupt by flatteries : but the people that do know their God, shall be strong and doe *exploits*.

33 And they that vnderstand among the people shall instruct many : yet they shall fall by the sword, and by flame, by captiuitie, and by spoile *many* dayes.

34 Now when they shall fall, they shalbe holpen with a litle help : but many shall cleaue to them with flatteries.

35 And *some* of them of vnderstanding shall fall, to trie ‖them, and to purge, and to make them white, euen to the time of the end : because *it is* yet for a time appointed.

‖ Or, by them

36 And the king shall doe according to his will, and he shall exalt himselfe, and magnifie himselfe aboue euery god, and shall speake maruelous things against the God of gods, & shall prosper till the indignation be accomplished : for that that is determined, shall be done.

37 Neither shall hee regard the god of his fathers, nor the desire of women, nor regard any god : for he shall magnifie himselfe aboue all.

38 But in his estate shall he honour the god of ‖forces : and a God whome his fathers knew not, shall hee honour with gold, and siluer, and with precious stones, and †pleasant things.

*‖ Or, mu-
nitions. Heb.
Mauzzim,
or, as for
the almighty
God in his
seate he shall
honour, yea
he shall ho-
nour a God,
&c.
† Heb. things
desired.
† Heb. for-
tresses of mu-
nitions.
†Heb. a price*

39 Thus shall hee doe in the †most strong holds with a strange god, whom he shall acknowledge *and* increase with glory : and he shall cause them to rule ouer many, and shall diuide the land for †gaine.

40 And at the time of the end shall the king of the South push at him, and the king of the North shal come against him

him like a whirlewind with charets, and with horsemen, and with many ships, and he shall enter into the countreys, and shall ouerflow and passe ouer.

Or, goodly land. Hebr. land of delight, or ornament.

41 He shall enter also into the ||glorious land, and many *countreys* shall be ouerthrowen : but these shall escape out of his hand, *euen* Edom, and Moab, and the chiefe of the children of Ammon.

†*Hebr. send foorth.*

42 He shall †stretch foorth his hand also vpon the countreys, and the land of Egypt shall not escape.

43 But he shall haue power ouer the treasures of gold and of siluer, and ouer all the precious things of Egypt : and the Libyans and the Ethiopians *shalbe* at his steps.

44 But tidings out of the East, and out of the North shall trouble him : therefore he shall goe foorth with great fury to destroy, and vtterly to make away many.

Or, goodly. Hebr. mountaine of delight of holinesse.

45 And hee shall plant the tabernacles of his palace betweene the seas in the ||glorious holy mountaine, yet he shall come to his end, and none shall helpe him.

CHAP. XII.

1 Michael shall deliuer Israel from their troubles. 5 Daniel is informed of the times.

Nd at that time shall Michael stand vp, the great Prince which standeth for the children of thy people, and there shalbe a time of trouble, such as neuer was since there was a nation, euen to that same time : and at that time thy people shalbe deliuered, euery one that shalbe found written in the booke.

Matt. 25, 45. ioh. 5. 29.

2 And many of them that sleepe in the dust of the earth shall awake, *some to euerlasting life, and some to shame *and* euerlasting contempt.

Or, teachers.
Matth. 13. 43.

3 And they that be ||wise shall *shine as the brightnesse of the firmament,

and they that turne many to righteousnesse, as the starres for euer and euer.

4 But thou, O Daniel, shut vp the wordes, and seale the booke euen to the time of the ende : many shall runne to and fro, and knowledge shall bee increased.

5 ¶ Then I Daniel looked, and behold, there stood other two, the one on this side of the banke of the riuer, and the other on that side of the †banke of the riuer.

†*Hebr. lip*

6 And *one* said to the man clothed in *linnen, which *was* ||vpon the waters of the riuer; How long *shall it bee* to the end of these wonders ?

*Dan. 10.
Or, from aboue.

7 And I heard the man clothed in linnen, which *was* vpon the waters of the riuer, when he *held vp his right hand, and his left hand vnto heauen, and sware by him that liueth for euer, that *it shalbe* for a time, times, and ||an halfe : and when hee shall haue accomplished to scatter the power of the holy people, all these things shall bee finished.

Reuel. 5.

Or, part

8 And I heard, but I vnderstood not : then said I, O my Lord, what *shalbe* the end of these things ?

9 And he said, Goe thy way, Daniel : for the wordes are closed vp and sealed till the time of the end.

10 Many shalbe purified, and made white and tried : but the wicked shall doe wickedly : and none of the wicked shall vnderstand, but the wise shall vnderstand.

11 And from the time that the dayly *sacrifice* shalbe taken away, and †the abomination ||that maketh desolate set vp, *there shalbe* a thousand two hundred and ninetie dayes.

†*Hebr. to vp the abomination &c.*
Or, astonisheth.

12 Blessed is he that waiteth, and commeth to the thousand, three hundred and fiue and thirtie dayes.

13 But goe thou thy way till the end *be*: ||for thou shalt rest, and stand in the lot at the end of the dayes.

Or, and thou, &c.

¶ HOSEA.

¶HOSEA.

CHAP. I.

1 Hosea to shew Gods iudgement for spirituall whoredome, taketh Gomer, 4 and hath by her Iezreel, 6 Lo-ruhamah, 8 and Lo-ammi. 10 The restauration of Iudah and Israel.

HE word of the LORD that came vnto Hosea, the sonne of Beeri, in the dayes of Vzziah, Iotham, Ahaz, and Hezekiah kings of Iudah, and in the dayes of Ieroboam the sonne of Ioash king of Israel.

2 The beginning of the word of the LORD by Hosea : and the LORD sayd to Hosea, Goe, take vnto thee a wife of whoredomes, and children of whoredomes : for the land hath committed great whoredome, *departing* from the LORD.

3 So he went and tooke Gomer the daughter of Diblaim, which conceiued and bare him a sonne.

4 And the LORD said vnto him, Call his name Iezreel; for yet a little *while,* and I will †auenge the blood of Iezreel vpon the house of Iehu, and will cause to cease the kingdome of the house of Israel.

Heb. visit.

5 And it shall come to passe at that day, that I will breake the bow of Israel in the valley of Iezreel.

6 ¶ And shee conceiued againe and bare a daughter, and *God* sayd vnto him, Call her name ‖Lo-ruhamah : for †I will no more haue mercy vpon the house of Israel : ‖ but I will vtterly take them away.

That is, not auing ob-ained mer-ie.
Heb. I will ot adde any ore to.
Or, that I hould alto-ether par-on them.

7 But I will haue mercy vpon the house of Iudah, and will saue them by the LORD their God, and will not saue them by bow, nor by sword, nor by battell, by horses nor by horsemen.

8 ¶ Now when shee had weaned Lo-ruhamah, she couceiued and bare a sonne.

9 Then sayde *God,* Call his name ‖Lo-ammi : for yee *are* not my people, and I will not be your *God.*

‖ *That is, not my people.*

10 ¶ Yet the number of the children of Israel shall be as the sand of the sea, which cannot bee measured nor numbred, *and it shall come to passe, that* ‖in the place where it was said vnto them, Yee *are* not my people, there it shall be said vnto them, *Ye are* the sonnes of the liuing God.

* Rom. 9. 25, 26.
‖ *Or, in stead of that.*

11 Then shall the children of Iudah and the children of Israel be *gathered together, and appoint themselues one head, and they shall come vp out of the land : for great *shalbe* the day of Iezreel.

* Iere. 3. 18. ezek. 34. 37

CHAP. II.

1 The idolatrie of the people. 6 Gods iudgements against them. 14 His promises of reconciliation with them.

AY ye vnto your brethren, ‖Ammi, & to your sisters, ‖Ruhamah :

2 Plead with your mother, plead : for *she is not my wife, neither *am* I her husband : let her therefore put away her whordomes out of her sight, and her adulteries from betweene *her breasts ;

‖ *That is, my people.*
‖ *That is, ha-uing obtai-ned mercy.*
* Isai. 50. 1.

3 Lest I strip her naked, and set her as in the day that shee was *borne, and make her as a wildernesse, and set her like a drie land, and slay her with thirst.

* Eze. 16. 25

* Eze. 16. 4.

4 And I will not haue mercy vpon her children, for they *be* the children of whoredomes.

5 For their mother hath played the harlot : shee that conceiued them hath done shamefully : for shee sayd, I will goe after my louers, that giue *me* my bread and my water, my wooll and my flaxe, mine oyle, and my †drinke.

† *Heb. drinks*

6 ¶ Therefore behold, I wil hedge vp thy way with thornes, and †make a wall,

† *Heb. wall a wall.*

wall, that she shall not find her pathes.

7 And she shall follow after her louers, but she shall not ouertake them, and she shall seeke them, but shall not find *them* : then shall she say, I will goe and returne to my first husband, for then *was* it better with me then now.

8 For she did not know that I gaue her corne, and † wine, and oyle, and multiplied her siluer and gold, ||which they prepared for Baal.

9 Therefore will I returne, and take away my Corne in the time thereof, and my wine in the season thereof, and wil ||recouer my wooll and my flaxe *giuen* to couer her nakednesse.

10 And now will I discouer her †lewdnesse in the sight of her louers, and none shall deliuer her out of mine hand.

11 I will also cause all her mirth to cease, her feast daies, her new moones, and her Sabbaths, and all her solemne feasts.

12 And I will †destroy her vines and her figge trees, whereof she hath said; These *are* my rewards that my louers haue giuen me : and I will make them a forrest, and the beasts of the field shall eate them.

13 And I will visite vpon her the daies of Baalim, wherein she burnt incense to them, and she decked her selfe with her eare-rings, and her Iewels, and she went after her louers, and forgate me, saith the Lord.

14 ¶ Therefore behold, I will allure her, and bring her into the wildernesse, and speake ||comfortably vnto her.

15 And I wil giue her, her vineyards from thence, and the valley of Achor for a doore of hope, and she shall sing there, as in the dayes of her youth, and as in the day when she came vp out of the land of Egypt.

16 And it shall be at that day, saith the Lord, *that* thou shalt call mee †Ishi; and shalt call mee no more †Baali.

17 For I will take away the names of Baalim out of her mouth, & they shal no more be remembred by their name.

18 And in that day will I make a *couenant for them with the beasts of the field, and with the foules of heauen, and with the creeping things of the ground ; and I will breake the bow and the sword, and the battell out of the earth, and will make them to lie downe safely.

19 And I will betroth thee vnto me for euer; yea, I will betroth thee vnto me in righteousnesse, and in iudgement, and in louing kindnesse, and in mercies.

20 I will euen betroth thee vnto me in faithfulnesse, and thou shalt know the Lord.

21 And it shall come to passe in that day, I will heare, saith the Lord, I will heare the heauens, and they shall heare the earth,

22 And the earth shall heare the corne, and the wine, and the oyle, and they shall heare Iezreel.

23 And I will sow her vnto me in the earth, and I will haue mercy vpon her that had not obtained mercy, and I *will say *to them* which were not my people; Thou *art* my people, and they shall say, *Thou art* my God.

CHAP. III.

1 By the expiation of an adulteresse, 4 is shewed the desolation of Israel before their restauration.

Hen said the Lord vnto me, Goe yet, loue a woman (beloued of *her* friend, yet an adulteresse) according to the loue of the Lord toward the children of Israel, who looke to other gods, and loue flagons †of wine.

2 So I bought her to me for fifteene *pieces* of siluer, and for an homer of barley and an †halfe *homer* of barley.

3 And I said vnto her, Thou shalt *abide for me many dayes, thou shalt not play the harlot, & thou shalt not be for *an other* man, so *will* I also *be* for thee.

4 For the children of Israel shall abide many dayes without a King, and without a Prince, and without a sacrifice, and without †an image, and without an Ephod, and *without* Teraphim.

5 Afterward shall the children of Israel returne, and seeke the Lord their God, and *Dauid their King, and shall feare the Lord, and his goodnesse in the *latter dayes.

CHAP. IIII.

1 Gods iudgements against the sinnes of the people, 6 and of the priests, 12 and against their idolatrie. 15 Iudah is exhorted to take warning by Israels calamitie.

Heare

Marginal notes (left column)

† *Heb. new wine.*
|| *Or, wherewith they made Baal.*

|| *Or, take away.*

† *Heb. folly or villanie.*

† *Heb. make desolate.*

| *Or, friendly. Heb. to her heart.*

† *That is, my husband.*
† *That is, my Lord.*

* *Iob. 5. 23.*

Marginal notes (right column)

* Rom. 9. 26. 1. pet. 2. 10.

† *Heb. of grapes.*

† *Heb. lethech.*

* *Deut. 21. 3.*

† *Heb. a standing or statue.*

* Ier. 30. 9. ezech. 34. 23.
* Isai. 2. 1.

* Mica. 6. 2.

† Hebr.
bloods.

† Heb. cut off

† Heb. cut off

† Heb. lift
vp their
soule to their
iniquitie.
* Isa. 24. 2.
† Heb. visite
vpon.
† Heb. cause
to returne.

‖ Or, shall I
not? &c.

HEare the worde of the LORD, yee children of Israel : for the LORD hath a * controuersie with the inhabitants of the land, because *there is* no trueth, nor mercie, nor knowledge of God in the land.

2 By swearing, and lying, and killing, and stealing, and committing adulterie, they breake out, and blood toucheth † blood.

3 Therefore shall the land mourne, and euery one that dwelleth therein shall languish, with the beastes of the field, and with the foules of heauen, yea the fishes of the Sea also shall be taken away.

4 Yet let no man striue, nor reproue another : for this people *are* as they that striue with the priest.

5 Therefore shalt thou fall in the day, and the prophet also shall fall with thee in the night, and I will † destroy thy mother.

6 ¶ My people are † destroyed for lacke of knowledge : because thou hast reiected knowledge, I will also reiect thee, that thou shalt be no priest to me : seeing thou hast forgotten the lawe of thy God, I wil also forget thy children.

7 As they were increased, so they sinned against me : *therfore* wil I change their glory into shame.

8 They eate vp the sinne of my people, and they † set their heart on their iniquitie.

9 And there shall be like people, like * priest : and I will † punish them for their wayes, and † reward them their doings.

10 For they shall eate, and not haue enough : they shall commit whordome, and shall not increase, because they haue left off to take heed to the LORD.

11 Whoredome, and wine, and newe wine take away the heart.

12 ¶ My people aske counsel at their stocks, and their staffe declareth vnto them : for the spirit of whordomes hath caused *them* to erre, and they haue gone a whoring from vnder their God.

13 They sacrifice vpon the tops of the mountaines, and burne incense vpon the hilles vnder okes and poplars, and elmes, because the shadowe thereof *is* good : therefore your daughters shall commit whoredome, and your spouses shall commit adulterie.

14 I ‖ will not punish your daughters when they commit whordome, nor your spouses when they commit adulterie : for themselues are separated with whores, and they sacrifice with harlots : therfore the people *that* doth not vnderstand, ‖ shall fall.

15 ¶ Though thou Israel play the harlot, *yet* let not Iudah offend, and come not ye vnto Gilgal, neither goe ye vp to * Beth-auen, nor sweare, The LORD liueth :

16 For Israel slideth backe, as a backe sliding heifer : now the LORD will feede them as a lambe in a large place.

17 Ephraim *is* ioyned to idoles : let him alone.

18 Their drinke † is sowre : they haue committed whordome continually : her † rulers *with* shame doe loue, Giue ye.

19 The wind hath bound her vp in her wings, and they shall be ashamed because of their sacrifices.

‖ Or, be punished.

* 1. King. 12. 29.

† Hebr. is gone.

† Hebr. shields.

CHAP. V.

1 Gods iudgements against the Priests, the people, and the princes of Israel for their manifold sinnes, 15 vntill they repent.

HEare yee this, O priests, and hearken, ye house of Israel, and giue yee eare, O house of the king : for iudgement *is* toward you, because yee haue beene a snare on Mizpah, and a net spread vpon Tabor.

2 And the reuolters are profound to make slaughter, ‖ though I haue bene † a rebuker of them all.

3 I know Ephraim, and Israel is not hid from me : for now, O Ephraim, thou committest whordome, *and* Israel is defiled.

4 † They will not frame their ‖ doings to turne vnto their God : for the spirit of whoredomes *is* in the midst of them, and they haue not knowen the LORD.

5 And the pride of Israel doth testifie to his face : therefore shall Israel and Ephraim fall in their iniquity : Iudah also shall fall with them.

6 They shall goe with their flocks, and with their heards to seeke the LORD : but they shall not finde *him*, he hath withdrawen himselfe from them.

7 They haue dealt treacherously against the LORD : for they haue begotten strange children, now shall a moneth

‖ Or, and, &c.
† Heb. a correction.

† Heb. they will not giue.
‖ Or, their doings will not suffer them.

moneth deuoure them with their portions.

8 Blow yee the cornet in Gibeah, *and* the trumpet in Ramah : cry alowd at Beth-auen : after thee, O Beniamin.

9 Ephraim shall be desolate in the day of rebuke : among the tribes of Israel haue I made knowen that which shall surely be.

10 The Princes of Iudah were like them that remooue the bound : *therefore* I will powre out my wrath vpon them like water.

11 Ephraim is oppressed, *and* broken in iudgement : because he willingly walked after the commandement.

12 Therefore *wil I be* vnto Ephraim as a moth : and to the house of Iudah as ||rottennesse.

|| *Or, a worme.*

13 When Ephraim saw his sicknesse, and Iudah *saw* his wound : then went Ephraim to the Assyrian, and sent ||to king Iareb; yet could he not heale you, nor cure you of your wound.

|| *Or, to the king of Iareb. Or, to the king that should plead.*

14 For I *will bee* vnto Ephraim as a Lion, and as a yong Lion to the house of Iudah : I, *euen* I wil teare and goe away : I will take away, and none shall rescue *him.*

15 ¶ I will goe *and* returne to my place, †till they acknowledge their offence, and seeke my face : in their affliction they will seeke me early.

† *Heb. till they be guiltie.*

CHAP. VI.

1 An exhortation to repentance. 4 A complaint of their vntowardnesse, and iniquitie.

Ome, and let vs returne vnto the LORD : for hee hath torne, and hee will heale vs : he hath smitten, and he will binde vs vp.

2 *After two daies will he reuiue vs, in the third day he will raise vs vp, and we shall liue in his sight.

* *1. Cor. 15. 4.*

3 Then shal we know, if we follow on to know the LORD : his going forth is prepared, as the morning; & he shall come vnto vs, as the raine; as the latter *and* former raine vnto the earth.

4 ¶ O Ephraim, what shall I doe vnto thee? O Iudah, what shall I do vnto thee? for your ||goodnesse *is* as a morning cloud, and as the early dew it goeth away.

|| *Or, mercy, or kindnesse.*

5 Therefore haue I shewed *them* by the Prophets : I haue slaine them by the wordes of my mouth, ||and thy

|| *Or, that thy iudgements might be, &c.*

iudgements *are as* the light *that* goeth foorth.

6 For I desired * mercie, and not sacrifice; and the knowledge of God, more then burnt offerings.

* *Matth. 9. 13. and 10. 7. eccles. 4. 17. 1. sam. 15. 22.*

7 But they || like men haue transgressed the Couenant : there haue they dealt treacherously against me.

|| *Or, like Adam.*

8 Gilead *is* a city of them that worke iniquitie; *and is* ||polluted with blood.

|| *Or, cunning for blood.*

9 And as troupes of robbers waite for a man, *so* the company of priestes murther in the way †by consent : for they commit ||lewdnesse.

† *Hebr. with one shoulder. Or, to Sichem.*

|| *Or, enormitie.*

10 I haue seene an horrible thing in the house of Israel : there *is* the whoredome of Ephraim, Israel is defiled.

11 Also O Iudah, hee hath set an haruest for thee, when I returned the captiuitie of my people.

CHAP. VII.

1 A reproofe of manifold sinnes. 11 Gods wrath against them for their hypocrisie.

Hen I would haue healed Israel, then the iniquitie of Ephraim was discouered, and the †wickednesse of Samaria : for they commit falsehood : and the thiefe commeth in, *and* the troupe of robbers †spoileth without.

† *Hebr. euils.*

† *Hebr. strippeth.*

2 And they †consider not in their hearts *that* I remember al their wickednesse : now their owne doings haue beset them about, they are before my face.

† *Hebr. say not to.*

3 They make the king glad with their wickednesse, and the princes with their lies.

4 They *are* al adulterers, as an ouen heated by the baker : ||who ceaseth ||from raising after he hath kneaded the dough, vntill it be leauened.

|| *Or, the raiser will cease.* || *Or, from waking.*

5 In the day of our King, the princes haue made *him* sicke ||with bottels of wine, he stretched out his hand with scorners.

|| *Or, with heat through wine.*

6 For they haue ||made ready their heart like an ouen, whiles they lie in wait : their baker sleepeth all the night, in the morning it burneth as a flaming fire.

|| *Or, applied.*

7 They are all hot as an ouen, and haue deuoured their Iudges; all their Kings are fallen, there is none among them that calleth vnto me.

8 Ephraim, he hath mixed himselfe among the people, Ephraim is a cake not turned.

9 Stran-

9 Strangers haue deuoured his strength, and hee knoweth *it* not : yea, gray haires are †here and there vpon him, yet he knoweth not.

10 And the *pride of Israel testifieth to his face, and they doe not returne to the Lord their God, nor seeke him for all this.

11 ¶ Ephraim also is like a silly doue, without heart : they call to Egypt ; they goe to Assyria.

12 When they shall goe, I wil spread my net vpon them, I will bring them downe as the foules of the heauen : I will chastise them as their congregation hath heard.

13 Woe vnto them, for they haue fled from me : †destruction vnto them, because they haue transgressed against me, though I haue redeemed them, yet they haue spoken lies against me.

14 And they haue not cryed vnto me with their heart, when they howled vpon their beds : they assemble themselues for corne and wine, *and* they rebell against me.

15 Though I ‖haue bound, *and* strengthened their armes, yet doe they imagine mischiefe against me.

16 They returne, *but* not to the most High : they are like a deceitfull bow : their princes shall fall by the sword, for the *rage of their tongue : this *shall be* their derision in the land of Egypt.

CHAP. VIII.

1. 12 Destruction is threatned for their impietie, 5 and idolatrie.

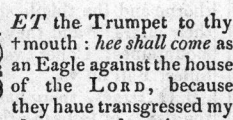ET the Trumpet to thy †mouth : *hee shall come* as an Eagle against the house of the Lord, because they haue transgressed my Lawe.

2 Israel shall crie vnto me, My God, we know thee.

3 Israel hath cast off the thing that is good : the enemie shall pursue him.

4 They haue set vp Kings, but not by me : they haue made Princes, and I knew *it* not : of their siluer and their golde haue they made them idoles, that they may be cut off.

5 ¶ Thy calfe, O Samaria, hath cast thee off : mine anger is kindled against them : how long will it bee ere they attaine to innocencie ?

6 For from Israel *was* it also, the workeman made it, therefore it is not God : but the calfe of Samaria shall be broken in pieces.

7 For they haue sowen the winde, and they shall reape the whirlewinde : it hath no ‖stalke : the budde shall yeeld no meale : if so be it yeeld, the strangers shall swallow it vp.

8 Israel is swallowed vp, now shal they be among the Gentiles, as a vessell wherein *is* no pleasure.

9 For they are gone vp to Assyria, a wilde Asse alone by himselfe ; Ephraim hath hired †louers.

10 Yea, though they haue hired among the nations, now will I gather them, and they shall ‖sorrow a little for the burden of the King of princes.

11 Because Ephraim hath made many altars to sinne, altars shall be vnto him to sinne.

12 I haue written to him the great things of my Law, *but* they were counted as a strange thing.

13 They sacrifice flesh ‖for the sacrifices of mine offerings, and eate *it* ; *but* the Lord accepteth them not : now will he remember their iniquitie, and visite their sinnes : they shal returne to Egypt.

14 For Israel hath forgotten his maker, and buildeth temples ; and Iudah hath multiplied fenced cities : but I will send a fire vpon his cities, and it shall deuoure the palaces thereof.

CHAP. IX.

The distresse and captiuitie of Israel, for their sinnes and idolatrie.

Eioyce not, O Israel, for ioy as *other* people : for thou hast gone a whoring from thy God, thou hast loued a * reward ‖vpon euery corne floore.

2 The floore and the ‖winepresse shall not feede them, and the new wine shall faile in her.

3 They shal not dwel in ỹ Lords land : but Ephraim shall returne to Egypt, and they shall eat vncleane things in Assyria.

4 They shall not offer wine *offrings* to the Lord : neither shall they be pleasing vnto him : *their sacrifices shalbe* vnto them as the bread of mourners : all that eate thereof shall be polluted : for their bread for their soule shall not come into the house of the Lord.

5 What

Margin notes:

† *Heb. sprinkled.*
* *Cha. 5. 5.*
† *Heb. spoile.*
‖ *Or, chastened.*
* *Psal. 73. 9.*
† *Heb. the roofe of thy mouth.*
‖ *Or, standing corne.*
† *Heb. loues.*
‖ *Or, begin.*
‖ *Or, in the sacrifices of mine offerings, they &c.*
* *Iere. 44. 17.*
‖ *Or, in, &c.*
‖ *Or, winefat.*

5 What will yee doe in the solemne day, and in the day of the feast of the LORD?

6 For loe they are gone, because of † destruction : Egypt shall gather them vp, Memphis shall burie them : ‖ the pleasant places for their siluer, netles shal possesse them : thornes shall be in their Tabernacles.

7 The dayes of visitation are come, the dayes of recompence are come, Israel shall know it ; the Prophet is a foole, † the spirituall man is madde, for the multitude of thine iniquitie and the great hatred.

8 The watchman of Ephraim was with my God : but the Prophet is a snare of a fouler in all his wayes, and hatred ‖ in the house of his God.

9 They haue deeply corrupted themselues as in the dayes of * Gibeah : therefore he will remember their iniquitie, he will visite their sinnes.

10 I found Israel like grapes in the wildernesse : I saw your fathers as the first ripe in the fig tree at her first time: but they went to * Baalpeor, and separated themselues vnto that shame, and their abominations were according as they loued.

11 As for Ephraim, their glory shall flee away like a bird from the birth and from the wombe, and from the conception.

12 Though they bring vp their children, yet wil I bereaue them that there shall not be a man left : yea, woe also to them when I depart from them.

13 Ephraim, as I saw Tyrus, is planted in a pleasant place : but Ephraim shall bring foorth his children to the murderer.

14 Giue them, O LORD : what wilt thou giue ? giue them a † miscarying wombe, and drie breasts.

15 All their wickednesse * is in Gilgal : for there I hated them : for the wickednesse of their doings I will driue them out of mine house, I will loue them no more : all their princes are reuolters.

16 Ephraim is smitten, their roote is dried vp, they shall beare no fruite : yea though they bring foorth, yet wil I slay euen † the beloued fruite of their wombe.

17 My God will cast them away, because they did not hearken vnto him : and they shalbe wanderers among the nations.

CHAP. X.
Israel is reproued and threatned for their impietie and idolatry.

ISrael is ‖ an empty vine, he bringeth forth fruite vnto himselfe : according to the multitude of his fruite, he hath increased the altars, according to the goodnesse of his land, they haue made goodly † images.

2 ‖ Their heart is diuided : now shall they be found faultie : hee shall † breake downe their altars : he shall spoile their images.

3 For now they shall say, We haue no King, because we feared not the LORD, What then should a King doe to vs ?

4 They haue spoken words, swearing falsely in making a couenant : thus iudgement springeth vp as hemlocke in the furrowes of the field.

5 The inhabitants of Samaria shall feare, because of the calues of Bethauen : for the people thereof shall mourne ouer it, and the ‖ priests thereof that reioyced on it, for the glory thereof, because it is departed from it.

6 It shall be also caried vnto Assyria for a present to * King Iareb : Ephraim shall receiue shame, and Israel shall be ashamed of his owne counsell.

7 As for Samaria, her King is cut off as the fome vpon † the water.

8 The high places also of Auen, the sinne of Israel, shall be destroyed : the thorne and the thistle shall come vp on their altars ; * and they shall say to the mountaines, Couer vs ; and to the hilles, Fall on vs.

9 O Israel, thou hast sinned from the dayes of Gibeah : there they stood : the battell in Gibeah against the children of iniquitie did not ouertake them.

10 It is in my desire that I should chastise them, and the people shall be gathered against them, ‖ when they shall bind themselues in their two furrowes.

11 And Ephraim is as an heifer that is taught and loueth to tread out the corne, but I passed ouer vpon † her faire necke : I will make Ephraim to ride : Iudah shall plow, and Iacob shall breake his clods.

12 Sow to your selues in righteousnesse, reape in mercie : * breake vp your fallow

---

Marginal notes (left column):

† Heb. spoile.

‖ Or, their siluer shall be desired, the nettle &c: Heb. the desire.

† Heb. man of the spirit.

‖ Or, against

* Iudg. 19. 18.

* Num. 25. 3.

† Heb. that casteth the fruite.
* Chap. 12. 11.

† Heb. the desires.

Marginal notes (right column):

‖ Or, a v emptyin fruite to it giueth

† Heb. s tues, or standing mages.
‖ Or, he diuided their hea
† Heb. he head.

‖ Chemarims.

* Chap. 13.

† Heb. th face of th water.

* Isai. 2 luc. 23. 3 reu. 6. 16 and 9. 6.

‖ Or, whe I shall bi them for their two transgres ons, or in their two bitations.
† Heb. the beautie o her necke

* Ier. 4. 4

fallow ground : for *it is* time to seeke the LORD, till he come and raine righteousnesse vpon you.

13 Ye haue plowed wickednesse, yee haue reaped iniquitie, ye haue eaten the fruite of lies : because thou didst trust in thy way, in the multitude of thy mightie men.

14 Therefore shall a tumult arise among thy people, and all thy fortresses shall bee spoiled, as Shalman spoiled *Beth-arbel in the day of battell : the mother was dashed in pieces vpon her children.

2. King. 18
9.

15 So shall Bethel doe vnto you, because of †your great wickednesse : in a morning shall the king of Israel be vtterly cut off.

Hebr. the
uill of your
uill.

CHAP. XI.

1 The ingratitude of Israel vnto God for his benefits. 5 His iudgement. 8 Gods mercy toward them.

Mat. 2. 15

Hen Israel *was* a childe, then I loued him, and *called my sonne out of Egypt.

2 *As* they called them, so they went from them : they sacrificed vnto Baalim, and burnt incense to grauen images.

3 I taught Ephraim also to goe, taking them by their armes : but they knew not that I healed them.

4 I drew them with cords of a man, with bands of loue, and I was to them as they that †take off the yoke on their iawes, and I laid meat vnto them.

Heb. lift
vp.

5 ¶ He shall not returne into the land of Egypt; but the Assyrian shall be his king, because they refused to returne

6 And the sword shall abide on his cities, and shall consume his branches, and deuoure *them*, because of their own counsels.

7 And my people are bent to backesliding from mee : though they called them to the most High, †none at all would exalt *him*.

Hebr. toge-
her they ex-
alted not.

8 How shall I giue thee vp, Ephraim? *how* shall I deliuer thee, Israel? how shall I make thee as *Admah? *how* shall I set thee as Zeboim? mine heart is turned within mee, my repentings are kindled together.

* Gene. 19.
22. amos 4.
1.

9 I will not execute the fiercenes of mine anger, I will not returne to destroy Ephraim, for I *am* God, and not man, the Holy One in the midst of thee,

and I will not enter into the citie.

10 They shal walke after the LORD : he shall roare like a lyon : when he shall roare, then the children shall tremble from the West.

11 They shall tremble as a bird out of Egypt, and as a doue out of the land of Assyria : and I will place them in their houses, saith the LORD.

12 Ephraim compasseth mee about with lies, and the house of Israel with deceit : but Iudah yet ruleth with God, and is faithfull ||with the Saints.

|| Or, with
the most holy

CHAP. XII.

1 A reproofe of Ephraim, Iudah, and Iacob. 3 By former fauours he exhorteth to repentance. 7 Ephraims sinnes prouoke God.

Phraim feedeth on winde, and followeth after the East winde : hee daily increaseth lies and desolation, and they doe make a couenant with the Assyrians, and oyle is caried into Egypt.

2 The LORD hath also a controuersie with Iudah, and will †punish Iacob according to his wayes, according to his doings will he recompense him.

† Heb. visit
vpon.

3 ¶ Hee tooke his brother *by the heele in the wombe, and by his strength he †*had power with God.

* Gene. 25.
26.
† Heb. was a
prince, or be-
haued him-
selfe princely
* Gen. 32.
24.

4 Yea, he had power ouer the Angel and preuailed : hee wept and made supplication vnto him : he found him in *Bethel, and there he spake with vs.

* Gen. 35.
9, 10.

5 Euen the LORD God of hosts, the LORD *is* his *memoriall.

* Exo. 3. 15

6 Therefore turne thou to thy God : keepe mercie and iudgement, and wait on thy God continually.

7 ¶ *He is* ||a merchant, che balances of deceit *are* in his hand : hee loueth to ||oppresse.

|| Or, Canaan

|| Or, deceiue

8 And Ephraim said, Yet I am become rich, I haue found mee out substance : ||*in* all my labours they shall finde none iniquitie in mee, †that *were* sinne.

|| Or, all my
labours suf-
fice me not:
hee shall
haue punish-
ment of ini-
quitie in
whom is
sinne.
† Heb. which

9 And I *that am* the LORD thy God from the lande of Egypt, will yet make thee to dwell in tabernacles, as in the dayes of the solemne feast.

10 I haue also spoken by the prophets, and I haue multiplied visions, and vsed similitudes, †by the ministerie of the prophets.

† Heb. by the
hand.

11 *Is*

11 *Is there* iniquitie in Gilead ? surely they are vanitie, they sacrifice bullocks in *Gilgal, yea their altars *are* as heapes in the furrowes of the fields.

12 And Iacob *fled into the countrey of Syria, and Israel serued for *a wife, and for a wife he kept *sheepe.*

13 And *by a Prophet the LORD brought Israel out of Egypt, and by a Prophet was he preserued.

14 Ephraim prouoked him to anger, †most bitterly : therefore shall he leaue his †blood vpon him, and his reproch shall his Lord returne vnto him.

CHAP. XIII.

1 Ephraims glory, by reason of idolatry, vanisheth. 5 Gods anger for their vnkindnes. 9 A promise of Gods mercie. 15 A iudgement for rebellion.

WHen Ephraim spake, trembling, he exalted himselfe in Israel, but, when he offended in Baal, he died.

2 And now †they sinne more and more, and haue made them molten images of their siluer, *and* idoles according to their owne vnderstanding, all of it the worke of the craftesmen : they say of them, Let the ||men that sacrifice, kisse the calues.

3 Therefore they shalbe as the morning cloud, and as the early dew it passeth away, as the chaffe that is driuen with a whirlewinde out of the floore, and as the smoke out of the chimney.

4 Yet I am the LORD thy God *from the land of Egypt, and thou shalt know no God, but me : for *there is* no sauiour beside me.

5 ¶ I did know thee in the wildernesse, in the land of †great drought.

6 According to their pasture, so were they filled : they were filled, and their heart was exalted : therefore haue they forgotten me.

7 Therefore I will bee vnto them as a Lion, as a Leopard by the way will I obserue *them.*

8 I will meet them as a beare that is bereaued *of her whelpes,* and will rent the kall of their heart, and there will I deuoure them like a Lion : †the wilde beast shall teare them.

9 ¶ O Israel, thou hast destroied thy selfe, but in me †*is* thine helpe.

10 I will be thy King : where *is any other* that may saue thee in all thy cities?

and thy Iudges of whom thou saidst, Giue me a King and Princes ?

11 I gaue thee a *king in mine anger, and tooke *him* away in my wrath.

12 The iniquitie of Ephraim is bound vp : his sinne is hid.

13 The sorrowes of a traueiling woman shall come vpon him, he *is* an vnwise sonne, for he should not stay †long in the place of the breaking foorth of children.

14 I will ransome them from the †power of the graue : I will redeeme them from death : *O death, I will be thy plagues, O graue, I will be thy destruction ; repentance shall be hid from mine eyes.

15 ¶ Though he be fruitfull among *his* brethren, * an Eastwinde shall come, the winde of the LORD shall come vp from the wildernesse, and his spring shall become drie, and his fountaine shalbe dried vp : he shall spoile the treasure of all †pleasant vessels.

16 Samaria shall become desolate, for she hath rebelled against her God : they shall fall by the sword : their infants shalbe dashed in pieces, and their women with childe shalbe ript vp.

CHAP. XIIII.

1 An exhortation to repentance. 4 A promise of Gods blessing.

**O** Israel, returne vnto the LORD thy God ; for thou hast fallen by thine iniquitie.

2 Take with you words, and turne to the LORD, say vnto him, Take away all iniquitie, and || receiue *vs* graciously : so will wee render the *calues of our lips.

3 Asshur shall not saue vs, we will not ride vpon horses, neither will wee say any more to the work of our hands, *Yee are* our gods: for in thee the fatherlesse findeth mercie.

4 ¶ I will heale their backsliding, I will loue them freely : for mine anger is turned away from him.

5 I wil be as the dew vnto Israel : hee shall ||grow as the lillie, and †cast foorth his rootes as Lebanon.

6 His branches shall †spread, and his beautie shalbe as the oliue tree, and his smell as Lebanon.

7 They that dwell vnder his shadow shall returne : they shall reuiue *as* the corne, & ||grow as the vine, the ||sent there-

---

*Chap. 4. 15. and 9. 15.
*Gen. 28. 5.
*Gene. 29. 20, 28.
*Exod. 12. 50, 51. and 13. 3.

†Hebr. with bitternesses.
†Hebr. bloods.

†Hebr. they adde to sinne.

||Or, the sacrificers of men.

*Isa. 43. 11. chap. 12. 10.

†Hebr. droughts.

†Hebr. the beast of the field.

†Hebr. in thy helpe.

*1. Sam. 8. and 15. 23. and 10. 1.

†Hebr. time.

†Hebr. hand.
*1. Cor. 55.

*Eze. 19. 12.

†Hebr. sels of desire.

||Or, giue good.
*Hebr. 15,

||Or, giue good.

10r, grow.
†Heb. strike.

†Hebr. goe.

||Or, blossome.
||Or, memoriall.

thereof *shalbe* as the wine of Lebanon,

8 Ephraim *shall say*, What haue I to doe any more with idoles? I haue heard *him*, and obserued him: I *am* like a greene firre tree, from me *is* thy fruite found.

9 Who *is* wise, and hee shall vnderstand these things? prudent, and hee shall know them? for the wayes of the LORD *are* right, and the iust shall walke in them: but the transgressours shall fall therein.

¶IOEL.

CHAP. I.

1 Ioel, declaring sundry iudgements of God, exhorteth to obserue them, 8 and to mourne. 14 He prescribeth a fast, for complaint.

HE word of the LORD that came to Ioel the sonne of Pethuel.

2 Heare this, yee oldemen, and glue eare, all yee inhabitants of the lande: Hath this been in your dayes, or euen in the dayes of your fathers?

3 Tell ye your children of it, and let your children *tell* their children, and their children another generation.

4 † That which the palmer worme hath left, hath the locust eaten; and that which the locust hath left, hath the canker-worme eaten; and that which the canker-worme hath left, hath the caterpillar eaten.

5 Awake ye drunkards, and weepe, and howle all yee drinkers of wine, because of the new wine, for it is cut off from your mouth.

6 For a nation is come vp vpon my lande, strong, and without number, whose teeth *are* the teeth of a lyon, and he *hath* the cheeke-teeth of a great lyon.

7 He hath laide my vine waste: and †barked my figge-tree: hee hath made it cleane bare, and cast *it* away, the branches thereof are made white.

8 ¶ Lament like a virgine girded with sackecloth for the husband of her youth.

9 The meate offring and the drinke offering is cut off from the house of the LORD, the Priestes the LORDS ministers mourne.

10 The field is wasted, the lande mourneth; for the corne is wasted: the new wine is ‖dried vp, the oyle languisheth.

11 Be yee ashamed, O yee husbandmen: howle, O yee vine-dressers, for the wheate and for the barley; because the haruest of the field is perished.

12 The vine is dried vp, and the figgetree languisheth, the pomegranate tree, the palme tree also and the apple tree, *euen* all the trees of the field are withered: because ioy is withered away from the sonnes of men.

13 Gird your selues, and lament, yee Priests: howle, ye ministers of the Altar: come, lie all night in sackecloth, ye ministers of my God: for the meat offering and the drinke offering is withholden from the house of your God.

14 ¶ * Sanctifie yee a fast: call a ‖solemne assembly: gather the Elders, *and* all the inhabitants of the land *into* the house of the LORD your God, and cry vnto the LORD:

15 Alas for the day: for * the day of the LORD *is* at hand, and as a destruction from the Almightie shall it come.

16 Is not the meate cut off before your eyes, *yea* ioy and gladnesse from the house of our God?

17 The †seede is rotten vnder their clods: the garners are laide desolate: the barnes are broken downe, for the corne is withered.

18 How doe the beastes grone? the heards of cattell are perplexed, because they haue no pasture, yea the flockes of sheepe are made desolate.

Heb. the esidue of he palmer-vorme.

† *Heb. laid my figgetree for a barking.*

‖ *Or, ashamed.*

* Cha. 2. 15.
‖ *Or, day of restraint.*

* Isai. 13. 6.

† *Heb.grains*

Or, habitations.

19 O Lord, to thee will I crie: for the fire hath deuoured the ‖pastures of the wildernesse, and the flame hath burnt all the trees of the field.

20 The beasts of the field crie also vnto thee : for the riuers of waters are dried vp, and the fire hath deuoured the pastures of the wildernesse.

CHAP. II.

1 He sheweth vnto Zion the terriblenesse of Gods iudgement. 12 He exhorteth to repentance, 15 Prescribeth a fast, 18 Promiseth a blessing thereon. 21 He comforteth Zion with present, 28 and future blessings.

Or, cornet.

BLow yee the ‖trumpet in Zion, & sound an alarme in my holy mountaine : let all the inhabitants of the land tremble: for the day of the Lord cōmeth, for *it is* nie at hand;

2 A day of darkenesse and of gloominesse, a day of clouds and of thicke darkenesse, as the morning spread vpon the mountaines : a great people and a strong, there hath not beene euer the like, neither shall be any more after it, euen to the yeres †of many generations.

† *Heb. of generation and generation.*

3 A fire deuoureth before them, and behind them a flame burneth : the land *is* as the garden of Eden before them, and behind them a desolate wildernes, yea and nothing shall escape them.

4 The appearance of them *is* as the appearance of horses; and as horse men, so shall they runne.

5 Like the noise of charets on the tops of mountaines shall they leape, like the noise of a flame of fire that deuoureth the stubble, as a strong people, set in battell aray.

6 Before their face the people shall be much pained : all faces shall gather †blacknesse.

† *Heb pot.*

7 They shall runne like mighty men, they shall clime the wall like men of warre, *and* they shall march euery one on his wayes, and they shall not breake their rankes.

8 Neither shall one thrust another, they shall walke euery one in his path : and when they fall vpon the ‖sword, they shall not be wounded.

‖ *Or, dart.*

9 They shall runne to and fro in the citie : they shall runne vpon the wall : they shall clime vp vpon the houses : they shall enter in at the windowes, like a theefe.

* *Isai. 13. 10. ezech. 32. 2.*

10 The *earth shall quake before

them, the heauens shall tremble, the Sun & the Moone shall be darke, & the starres shall withdrawe their shining.

11 And the Lord shall vtter his voyce before his armie, for his campe is very great : for *he is* strong that executeth his word : for the * day of the Lord *is* great and very terrible, and who can abide it?

* *Ier. 39. 5. am. 5. 18. zeph. 1. 15.*

12 ¶ Therefore also now, saith the Lord, *turne yee euen to me with all your heart, and with fasting, and with weeping, and with mourning.

* *Ier. 4. 1.*

13 And rent your heart and not your garments; and turne vnto the Lord your God : for he is *gracions and mercifull, slow to anger, and of great kindnesse, and repenteth him of the euill.

* *Exod. 34 6. psal. 86. 35. ion. 4. 2*

14 * Who knoweth *if* he will returne and repent, and leaue a blessing behind him, *euen* a meate offring and a drinke offring vnto the Lord your God?

* *Ion. 3. 9.*

15 ¶ Blow the trumpet in Zion, *sanctifie a fast, call a solemne assembly.

* *Chap. 1. 14.*

16 Gather the people : sanctifie the congregation : assemble the elders : gather the children, and those that sucke the breasts : let the bridegroome goe forth of his chamber, and the bride out of her closet.

17 Let the priests, the ministers of the Lord, weepe betweene the porch and the altar, & let them say; Spare thy people O Lord, and giue not thine heritage to reproch; that the heathen should ‖rule ouer them : * Wherefore should they say among the people, Where *is* their God?

‖ *Or, vse a byword against the* * *Psal. 42. 11. and 79. 10. and 115 2.*

18 ¶ Then will the Lord be iealous for his land, and pitie his people.

19 Yea the Lord will answere and say vnto his people; Behold, I will send you corne and wine, and oyle, and yee shall be satisfied therewith : and I will no more make you a reproch among the heathen.

20 But I will remoue farre off from you the northren *armie*, & will driue him into a land barren and desolate, with his face toward the East sea, and his hinder part towards the vtmost Sea, and his stinke shall come vp, and his ill sauour shall come vp, because †he hath done great things.

† *Heb. hee hath magnified to d*

21 ¶ Feare not, O land, be glad and reioyce : for the Lord will doe great things.

22 Be not afraid, yee beasts of the field: for the pastures of the wildernesse doe

doe spring, for the tree beareth her fruit, the fig tree and the vine doe yeeld their strength.

23 Be glad then, ye children of Zion, and reioyce in the LORD your God: for he hath giuen you the ‖former raine †moderately, and he * will cause to come downe for you the raine, the former raine, & the latter raine in the first *month.*

24 And the floores shall bee full of wheate, and the fats shall ouerflowe with wine and oyle.

25 And I will restore to you the yeeres that the locust hath eaten, the canker worme, and the caterpiller, and the palmer worme, my great armie which I sent among you.

26 And ye shall eate in plentie, and be satisfied, aud praise the Name of the LORD your God, that hath dealt wonderously with you : and my people shall neuer be ashamed.

27 And ye shal know that I *am* in the midst of Israel, and that I *am* the LORD your God, and none else : and my people shall neuer be ashamed.

28 ¶ And it shall come to passe afterward, *that* I will *powre out my Spirit vpon all flesh, and your sonnes and your daughters shall prophecie, your old men shall dreame dreames, your yong men shall see visions.

29 And also vpon the seruants, and vpon the handmaids in those dayes will I powre out my Spirit.

30 And I will shew wonders in the heauens, and in the earth, blood and fire, and pillars of smoke.

31 *The Sunne shall be turned into darkenesse, and the Moone into blood, before the great and the terrible day of the LORD come.

32 And it shall come to passe *that* *whosoeuer shall call on the Name of the LORD, shall bee deliuered : for in mount Zion and in Ierusalem shalbe deliuerance, as the LORD hath said, and in the remnant, whom the LORD shall call.

CHAP. III.

1 Gods iudgements against the enemies of his people. 9 God will be knowen in his iudgement. 18 His blessing vpon the Church.

Or behold, in those dayes and in that time, when I shall bring againe the captiuitie of Iudah and Ierusalem,

2 I wil also gather all nations, and will bring them downe into the valley of Iehoshaphat, and wil plead with them there for my people, and for my heritage Israel, whom they haue scattered among the nations, and parted my land.

3 And they haue cast lots for my people, and haue giuen a boy for a harlot, and solde a girle for wine, that they might drinke.

4 Yea and what haue ye to do with me, O Tyre and Zidon, and all the coasts of Palestine ? will ye render mee a recompence ? and if ye recompense me, swiftly *and* speedily will I returne your recompense vpon your owne head.

5 Because yee haue taken my siluer and my gold, and haue caried into your temples my goodly †pleasant things.

6 The children also of Iudah and the children of Ierusalem haue ye sold vnto †the Grecians, that yee might remoue them farre from their border.

7 Behold, I will raise them out of the place whither yee haue sold them, and wil returne your recompense vpon your owne head.

8 And I will sell your sonnes and your daughters into the hande of the children of Iudah, and they shall sell them to the Sabeans, to a people farre off, for the LORD hath spoken *it.*

9 ¶ Proclaime ye this among the gentiles : †prepare warre, wake vp the mightie men, let all the men of warre draw neere, let them come vp.

10 * Beate your plowe shares into swords, and your ‖pruning hookes into speares, let the weake say, I am strong.

11 Assemble your selues, and come all ye heathen, and gather your selues together round about : thither ‖cause thy mightie ones to come downe, O LORD.

12 Let the heathen be wakened, and come vp to the valley of Iehoshaphat: for there will I sit to iudge all the heathen round about.

13 * Put ye in the sickle, for the haruest is ripe, come, get you downe, for the presse is full, the fats ouerflowe, for the wickednesse is great.

14 Multitudes, multitudes in the valley of ‖decision : for ŷ day of the LORD *is* neere in the valley of decision.

15 The *Sunne and the Moone shall be darkened, and the starres shall withdraw their shining.

16 The

Marginal notes (left column):

‖ *Or, a teacher of righteousnesse.*
† *Heb. according to righteousnesse.*
* *Leuit. 26. deut. 14.*

* Isa. 44. 8. acts 2. 17.

* Cha. 3. 15

* Rom. 10. 13.

Marginal notes (right column):

† *Heb. desireable.*

† *Heb. the sonnes of the Grecians.*

† *Heb. sanctifie.*

* *Isa. 2. 4.*
‖ *Or, sythes.*

‖ *Or, the Lord shall bring downe.*

* *Reue. 14. 15.*

‖ *Or, concision, or threshing.*
* *Cha. 2. 31.*

* Iere. 25.
30. amos 1.
2.

† Hebr. place
of repaire, or
harbour.

† Hebr. ho-
linesse.
* Reuel. 21.
27.
* Amos 9.
13.

16 The LORD also shal * roare out of Zion, and vtter his voice from Ierusalem, and the heauens and the earth shall shake, but the LORD *will be* the † hope of his people, and the strength of the children of Israel.

17 So shall ye know that I *am* the LORD your God, dwelling in Zion, my holy Mountaine : then shall Ierusalem be † holy, and there shall no * strangers passe through her any more.

18 ¶ And it shall come to passe in that day, *that* the mountaines shal * drop downe new wine, and the hils shall flow with milke, and all the riuers of Iudah shall † flow with waters, and a fountaine shall come forth of the house of the LORD, and shall water the valley of Shittim.

19 Egypt shall be a desolation, and Edom shall be a desolate wildernes, for the violence *against* the children of Iudah, because they haue shed innocent blood in their land.

20 But Iudah shall ‖ dwell for euer, and Ierusalem from generation to generation.

21 For I wil cleanse their blood, *that* I haue not cleansed, ‖ for the LORD dwelleth in Zion.

† Hebr goe

‖ Or, abide

‖ Or, Euen
the Lord
that dwel-
leth in Zio

¶ AMOS.

CHAP. I.

1 Amos sheweth Gods iudgement vpon Syria, 6 vpon the Philistines, 9 vpon Tyrus, 11 vpon Edom, 13 vpon Ammon.

HE wordes of Amos, who was among the heardmen of Tekoa, which hee sawe concerning Israel, in the daies of Vzziah King of Iudah, and in the dayes of Ieroboam the sonne of Ioash king of Israel, two yere before the * earthquake.

* Zech. 14.
5.

* Iere. 25.
30. ioel 3.
18.

‖ Or, he for
foure.
‖ Or, conuert
it, or let it
be quiet.
And so ver.
6. &c.

2 And he said, The LORD will * roare from Zion, and vtter his voice from Ierusalem : and the habitations of the shepheards shall mourne, and the top of Carmel shall wither.

3 Thus saith the LORD ; For three transgressions of Damascus, and ‖ for foure I wil not ‖ turne away *the punishment* thereof, because they haue threshed Gilead, with threshing instruments of yron.

4 But I will send a fire into the house of Hazael, which shall deuoure the palaces of Benhadad.

5 I wil breake also the barre of Damascus, and cut off the inhabitant from the ‖ plaine of Auen : and him that holdeth the scepter from the ‖ house of Eden, and the people of Syria shall goe into captiuitie, vnto Kir, saith the LORD.

6 ¶ Thus saith the LORD, For three transgressions of * Gaza, and for foure I will not turne away *the punishment* thereof : because they ‖ caried away captiue the whole captiuitie, to deliuer *them* vp to Edom.

7 But I wil send a fire on the wall of Gaza, which shall deuoure the palaces thereof.

8 And I wil cut off the inhabitant from Ashdod, and him that holdeth the scepter from Ashkelon, and I wil turne mine hand against Ekron; and the remnant of the Philistines shall perish, saith the Lord GOD.

9 ¶ Thus saith the LORD, For three transgressions of Tyrus, and for foure I wil not turne away *the punishment* thereof, because they deliuered vp the whole captiuitie to Edom, and remembred not † the brotherly couenant.

10 But I wil send a fire on the wall of Tyrus, which shall deuoure the palaces thereof.

11 ¶ Thus saith the LORD, For three transgressions of Edom, and for foure,

‖ Or, Bikath-Auen.
‖ Or, Beth-Eden.

* 2. Chro.
28. 18.

‖ Or, caried
them away
with an en-
tire captiui-
tie.

† Hebr. the
couenant of
brethren.

foure, I will not turne away *the punishment* thereof, because he did pursue his brother with the sword, and did † cast off all pitie, and his anger did teare perpetually, and kept his wrath for euer.

Heb. corrupted his compassions.

12 But I will send a fire vpon Teman, which shall deuoure the palaces of Bozrah.

13 ¶ Thus sayth the LORD, For three transgressions of the children of Ammon, and for foure, I wil not turne away *the punishment* thereof; because they haue ‖ ript vp the women with childe of Gilead, that they might enlarge their border.

Or, diuided the mountaines.

14 But I will kindle a fire in the wall of Rabbah, and it shall deuoure the palaces thereof, with showting in the day of battell, with a tempest in the day of the whirlewinde.

15 And their king shall goe into captiuitie, hee, and his princes together, sayth the LORD.

CHAP. II.

1 Gods wrath against Moab, 4 vpon Iudah, 6 and vpon Israel. 9 God complaineth of their vnthankefulnesse.

Hus sayth the LORD, For three transgressions of Moab, and for foure, I wil not turne away *the punishment* thereof, because hee *burnt the bones of the King of Edom into lime.

2. Kings. 3. 27.

2 But I will send a fire vpon Moab, and it shall deuoure the palaces of Kerioth, and Moab shall die with tumult, with shouting, *and* with the sound of the trumpet:

3 And I will cut off the iudge from the middest thereof, and wil slay all the princes thereof with him, sayeth the LORD.

4 ¶ Thus sayth the LORD, For three transgressions of Iudah, and for foure, I will not turne away *the punishment* thereof; because they haue despised the Law of the LORD, and haue not kept his Commandements, and their lies caused them to erre, after the which their fathers haue walked.

5 But I will send a fire vpon Iudah, and it shall deuoure the palaces of Ierusalem.

6 ¶ Thus sayth the LORD, For three transgressions of Israel, and for foure, I will not turne away *the punish-*

ment thereof; because * they solde the righteous for siluer, and the poore for a paire of shooes:

Chap. 8. 8.

7 That pant after the dust of the earth on the head of the poore, and turne aside the way of the meeke; and a man and his father will goe in vnto the *same* ‖ maid, to profane my holy Name.

Or, young woman.

8 And they lay themselues downe vpon clothes laide to pledge, by euery Altar, and they drinke the wine of ‖ the condemned *in* the house of their God.

Or, such as haue fined or mulcted.

9 ¶ Yet destroyed I the *Amorite before them, whose height *was* like the height of the Cedars, and hee was strong as the okes, yet I destroyed his fruite from aboue, and his rootes from beneath.

Num. 21. 24. deut. 2. 31. iosh. 24. 8.

10 Also I brought you vp from the land of *Egypt, and ledde you fourtie yeeres through the wildernesse, to possesse the land of the Amorite.

Exod. 12. 51.

11 And I raised vp of your sonnes for Prophets, and of your young men for Nazarites. *Is it* not euen thus, O ye children of Israel, saith the LORD?

12 But ye gaue the Nazarites wine to drinke, and commaunded the Prophets, * saying, Prophecie not.

Cha. 7. 12.

13 Behold, ‖ I am pressed vnder you, as a cart is pressed that is ful of sheaues.

Or, I will presse your place as a cart full of sheaues presseth.

14 Therefore the flight shall perish from the swift, and the strong shall not strengthen his force, neither shall the mightie deliuer † himselfe:

Heb. his soule or life.

15 Neither shall hee stand that handleth the bow, and hee that is swift of foote, shall not deliuer *himselfe*, neither shall hee that rideth the horse, deliuer himselfe.

16 And hee that is † couragious among the mighty, shall flee away naked in that day, saith the LORD.

Heb. strong of his heart.

CHAP. III.

1 The necessitie of Gods iudgement against Israel. 9 The publication of it, with the causes thereof.

Eare this word that the LORD hath spoken against you, O children of Israel, against the whole family, which I brought vp from the land of Egypt, saying;

2 You onely haue I knowen of all the families of the earth: therefore I will † punish you for all your iniquities.

Heb. visit vpon.

3 Can two walke together, except they be agreed?

4 Will

† *Heb. giue foorth his voyce.*

4 Will a lyon roare in the forrest, when he *hath* no pray? will a young lyon †cry out of his den, if he haue taken nothing?

5 Can a bird fall in a snare vpon the earth, where no ginne *is* for him? shall one take vp a snare from the earth, and haue taken nothing at all?

‖ *Or, not runne together.*
‖ *Or, and shall not the L. doe somewhat?*

6 Shall a trumpet be blowen in the citie, and the people ‖not be afraid? shall there be euill in a citie, ‖and the Lᴏʀᴅ hath not done *it?*

7 Surely the Lord Gᴏᴅ will doe nothing, but he reuealeth his secret vnto his seruants the Prophets.

8 The lyon hath roared, Who will not feare? the Lord Gᴏᴅ hath spoken, Who can but prophecie?

9 ¶ Publish in the palaces at Ashdod, and in the palaces in the land of Egypt, and say; Assemble your selues vpon the mountaines of Samaria: and behold the great tumults in the midst thereof, and the ‖oppressed in the midst thereof.

‖ *Or, oppressions.*

10 For they know not to doe right, saith the Lᴏʀᴅ; who store vp violence, and ‖robberie in their palaces.

‖ *Or, spoile.*

11 Therefore thus saith the Lord Gᴏᴅ An aduersarie *there shall be* euen round about the land: and he shal bring downe thy strength from thee, and thy palaces shall be spoiled.

† *Heb. deliuereth.*

12 Thus saith the Lᴏʀᴅ, As the shepheard †taketh out of the mouth of the lyon two legges or a piece of an eare; so shall the children of Israel be taken out that dwell in Samaria, in the corner of a bed, and in ‖Damascus *in* a couch.

‖ *Or, on the beds feete.*

13 Heare yee and testifie in the house of Iacob, saith the Lord Gᴏᴅ, the God of hostes;

‖ *Or, punish Israel for.*

14 That in the day that I shall ‖visite the transgressions of Israel vpon him, I will also visite the altars of Bethel, and the hornes of the altar shall be cut off, and fall to the ground.

15 And I will smite the winter house with the summer house; and the houses of yuorie shall perish, and the great houses shall haue an end, saith the Lᴏʀᴅ.

CHAP. IIII.

1 He reproueth Israel, for oppression. 4 for idolatry, 6 and for their incorrigiblenesse.

 Eare this word yea kine of Bashan, that *are* in the mountaine of Samaria, which oppresse the poore, which crush the needy, which say to their masters; Bring, and let vs drinke.

2 The Lord Gᴏᴅ hath sworne by his holinesse, that loe, the dayes shall come vpon you, that he will take you away with hookes, and your posteritie with fish-hookes.

3 And yee shall goe out at the breaches, euery *Cow* at that *which is* before her, and ‖yee shall cast them into the palace, saith the Lᴏʀᴅ.

‖ *Or, yee shall cast way the things of t palace.*

4 ¶ Come to Bethel and transgresse, at Gilgal multiplie transgression; and bring your sacrifices euery morning, *and* your tithes after †three *yeeres.*

† *Heb. thr yeeres of dayes.*
† *Heb. off by burnin*
† *Heb. so s loue.*

5 And †offer a sacrifice of thanksgiuing with leauen, and proclaime and publish the free offrings; for † this liketh you, O yee children of Israel, saith the Lord Gᴏᴅ.

6 ¶ And I also haue giuen you cleannesse of teeth in all your cities, and want of bread in all your places: yet haue yee not returned vnto me, saith the Lᴏʀᴅ.

7 And also I haue withholden the raine from you, when *there were* yet three moneths to the haruest, and I caused it to raine vpon one citie, and caused it not to raine vpon an other city: one piece was rained vpon, & the piece wherupon it rained not, withered.

8 So two *or* three cities wandered vnto one citie, to drinke water; but they were not satisfied: yet haue yee not returned vnto me, saith the Lᴏʀᴅ.

9 I haue smitten you with blasting and mildew; ‖when your gardens and your vineyards, and your fig trees, and your oliue trees increased, the palmer worme deuoured *them:* yet haue yee not returned vnto me, saith the Lᴏʀᴅ.

‖ *Or, the multitude yourgard &c: did the palme worme &*

10 I haue sent among you the pestilence, ‖after the maner of Egypt: your yongmen haue I slain with the sword, and †haue taken away your horses, & I haue made the stinke of your campes to come vp vnto your nostrils, yet haue ye not returned vnto me, saith the Lᴏʀᴅ.

‖ *Or, in th way.*
† *Heb. wi the captiu tie of you horses.*

11 I haue ouerthrowen *some* of you, as God ouerthrew *Sodome & Gomorrah, and yee were as a firebrand pluckt out of the burning: yet haue yee not returned vnto me, saith the Lᴏʀᴅ.

* *Gen. 19 24.*

12 Therefore

12 Therefore thus will I doe vnto thee, O Israel : *and* because I will doe this vnto thee, prepare to meete thy God, O Israel.

13 For loe, he that formeth the mountaines, and createth the ||wind, and declareth vnto man, what *is* his thought, that maketh the morning darkenesse, and treadeth vpon the high places of the earth : the LORD, the God of hostes *is* his Name.

Or, spirit.

CHAP. V.

1 A Lamentation for Israel. 4 An exhortation to repentance. 21 God reiecteth their hypocriticall seruice.

Eare ye this word which I take vp against you, *euen* a lamentation, O house of Israel.

2 The virgin of Israel is fallen, she shall no more rise: she is forsaken vpon her land, there *is* none to raise her vp.

3 For thus saith the Lord GOD, The citie that went out *by* a thousand, shall leaue an hundred, and that which went foorth *by* an hundred, shall leaue ten to the house of Israel.

4 ¶ For thus saith the LORD vnto the house of Israel, Seeke ye mee, and ye shall liue.

5 But seeke not *Bethel, nor enter into Gilgal and passe not to Beer-sheba : for Gilgal shall surely goe into captiuitie, and Bethel shal come to nought.

*Ier. 4. 4.

6 Seeke the LORD, and ye shall liue, lest hee breake out like fire in the house of Ioseph and deuoure *it*, and *there be* none to quench *it* in Bethel.

7 Ye who turne iudgment to wormwood, and leaue off righteousnesse in the earth :

8 *Seeke him* that maketh the *seuen starres and Orion, and turneth the shadow of death into the morning, and maketh the day darke with night : that *calleth for the waters of the Sea, and powreth them out vpon the face of the earth : the LORD *is* his Name.

*Iob. 9. 9. and 38. 31.

*Chap. 9. 6.

9 That strengtheneth the †spoiled against the strong : so that the spoiled shall come against the fortresse.

†Heb. spoile.

10 They hate him that rebuketh in the gate : and they abhorre him that speaketh vprightly.

11 Forasmuch therfore as your treading *is* vpon the poore, and ye take from him burdens of wheate, *ye haue built

*Zeph. 1. 13.

houses of hewen stone, but ye shall not dwell in them : yee haue planted †pleasant vineyards, but ye shall not drinke wine of them.

†Heb. vineyards of desire.

12 For I know your manifold transgressions, and your mighty sinnes : they afflict the iust, they take ||a bribe, and they turne aside the poore in the gate *from their right*.

|Or, a ransome.

13 Therefore the prudent shall keepe silence in that time, for it *is* an euill time.

14 Seeke good and not euill, that ye may liue : and so the LORD, the God of hosts shall be with you, as yee haue spoken.

15 *Hate the euill, and loue the good, and establish iudgement in the gate : it may be that the LORD God of hostes will bee gracious vnto the remnant of Ioseph.

*Psal. 74. 15. & 79. 10. rom. 12. 9.

16 Therefore the LORD, the God of hostes, the Lord saith thus : Wailing *shall be* in all streets, and they shall say in all the high wayes, Alas, Alas : and they shall call the husbandman to mourning, and such as are skilful of lamentation, to wailing.

17 And in all vineyards *shall be* wailing : *for* I will passe through thee, saith the LORD.

18 *Woe vnto you that desire the day of the LORD : to what ende is it for you ? the day of the LORD *is* darknes and not light.

*Isai. 5. 19. ier. 30. 7. ioel 2. 2. zeph. 1. 15.

19 As if a man did flee from a lyon, and a beare met him, or went into the house, and leaned his hand on the wall, and a serpent bit him.

20 Shall not the day of the LORD *be* darkenes, and not light ? euen very darke, and no brightnesse in it ?

21 ¶ *I hate, I despise your feast dayes, and I will not ||smell in your solemne assemblies.

*Isa. 1. 11. ier. 6. 20. |Or, smell your holy dayes.

22 Though ye offer me burnt offerings, and your meat offerings, I will not accept *them* : neither will I regard the ||peace offerings of your fat beasts.

|Or, thanke offerings.

23 Take thou away from mee the noise of thy songs : for I will not heare the melodie of thy violes.

24 But let iudgement †run downe as waters, and righteousnesse as a mightie streame.

†Heb. roule.

25 *Haue yee offered vnto mee sacrifices and offerings in the wildernesse fourtie yeeres, O house of Israel ?

*Acts 7. 42

26 But yee haue borne the ||tabernacle of your Moloch, and Chiun your images,

|Or, Siccuth your king.

images, the starre of your god, which ye made to your selues.

27 Therefore wil I cause you to go into captiuitie beyond Damascus, saith the LORD, whose Name *is* the God of hostes.

CHAP. VI.

1 The wantonnes of Israel, 7 shalbe plagued with desolation, 12 and their incorrigiblenes.

*Luke 6.
24.
‖ Or, are secure.

*Exod. 19.
5.
‖ Or, first
fruits.

Oe to *them that ‖are at ease in Zion, and trust in the mountaine of Samaria, which are named *‖chiefe of the nations, to whom the house of Israel came.

2 Passe ye vnto Calneh, and see, and from thence go ye to Hemath the great: then goe downe to Gath of the Philistines: bee they better then these kingdomes? or their border greater then your border?

*Exek. 12.
27.
*Chap. 5.
18.
‖ Or, habitation.
‖ Or, abound
with superfluities.

3 Ye that *put farre away the *euil day, and cause the ‖ seat of violence to come neere:

4 That lie vpon beds of Yuorie, and ‖ stretch themselues vpon their couches, and eate the lambes out of the flocke, and the calues out of the midst of the stall:

‖ Or, quauer.

5 That ‖chaunt to the sound of the Viole, *and* inuent to themselues instruments of musicke, like Dauid:

‖ Or, in
bowles of
wine.

6 That drinke ‖ wine in bowles, and anoint themselues with the chiefe ointments: but they are not grieued for the †affliction of Ioseph.

† Hebr.
breach.

7 ¶ Therefore now shall they goe captiue, with the first that goe captiue, and the banquet of them that stretched themselues, shalbe remoued.

*Iere. 52.
14.

8 *The Lord GOD hath sworne by himselfe, saith the LORD the God of hostes, I abhorre the excellencie of Iacob, and hate his palaces: therefore wil I deliuer vp the citie, with †all that is therein.

† Hebr. the
fulnesthereof.

9 And it shall come to passe, if there remaine tenne men in one house, *that* they shall die.

10 And a mans vncle shall take him vp, and he that burneth him, to bring out the bones out of the house, and shall say vnto him that is by the sides of the house; *Is* there yet any with thee? and hee shall say, No. Then shall he say,

*Chap. 5.
13.
‖ Or, they
will not, or
haue not.

*Holde thy tongue: for ‖ wee may not make mention of the Name of the LORD.

11 For beholde, the LORD commandeth, and hee will smite the great house with ‖ breaches, and the little house with clefts.

‖ Or, drop
pings.

12 ¶ Shall horses runne vpon the rocke? wil one plow *there* with oxen? for ye haue turned iudgement into gall, and the fruite of righteousnesse into hemlocke.

13 Yee which reioyce in a thing of nought, which say, Haue we not taken to vs hornes by our owne strength?

14 But beholde, I wil raise vp against you a nation, O house of Israel, saith the LORD, the God of hostes, and they shall afflict you from the entring in of Hemath, vnto the ‖riuer of the wildernesse.

‖ Or, valle

CHAP. VII.

1 The iudgements of the grashoppers, 4 and of the fire, are diuerted hy the prayer of Amos. 7 By the wall of a plumb-line, is signified the reiection of Israel. 10 Amaziah complaineth of Amos. 14 Amos sheweth his calling, 16 and Amaziahs iudgement.

‖ Or, gree
wormes.

Hus hath the Lord GOD shewed vnto me, and behold, he formed ‖ grassehoppers in the beginning of the shooting vp of the latter grouth: and loe, *it was* the latter grouth after the kings mowings.

2 And it came to passe, *that* when they had made an ende of eating the grasse of the land, then I said; O Lord GOD, forgiue, I beseech thee, ‖by whom shal Iacob arise? for he *is* small.

‖ Or, who
of (or for
Iacob sha
stand?

3 The LORD repented for this. It shall not be, saith the LORD.

4 ¶ Thus hath the Lord GOD shewed vnto me; and behold, the Lord GOD called to contend by fire, and it deuoured the great deepe, and did eate vp a part.

5 Then said I, O Lord GOD, cease, I beseech thee, by whom shal Iacob arise? for he *is* small.

6 The LORD repented for this. This also shall not bee, saith the Lord GOD.

7 ¶ Thus hee shewed mee, and behold, the Lord stood vpon a wall *made by* a plumbline, with a plumbline in his hand.

8 And the LORD said vnto mee, Amos, what seest thou? And I sayd, A plumb-line. Then sayd the Lord, Behold,

Behold, I will set a plumb-line in the midst of my people Israel, I will not againe passe by them any more.

9 And the high places of Isaac shall be desolate, and the Sanctuaries of Israel shalbe laide waste : and I will rise against the house of Ieroboam with the sword.

10 ¶ Then Amaziah the Priest of Beth-el sent to Ieroboam king of Israel, saying ; Amos hath conspired against thee in the midst of the house of Israel : the land is not able to beare all his words.

11 For thus Amos saith, Ieroboam shall die by the sword, and Israel shall surely be led away captiue, out of their owne land.

12 Also Amaziah said vnto Amos, O thou Seer, goe, flee thee away into the land of Iudah, and there eate bread, and prophecie there.

13 But prophecie not againe any more at Beth-el : for it ‖*is* the Kings ‖Chappell, and it *is* the †Kings Court.

14 ¶ Then answered Amos, and sayde to Amaziah ; I *was* no Prophet, neither *was* I a Prophets sonne, but I *was* an heardman, and a gatherer of ‖Sycomore fruit.

15 And the LORD tooke me †as I followed the flocke, and the LORD said vnto me, Goe, prophecie vnto my people Israel.

16 ¶ Now therefore heare thou the worde of the LORD ; Thou sayest, Prophecie not against Israel, and *drop not *thy word* against the house of Isaac.

17 Therfore thus sayth the LORD ; Thy wife shall be an harlot in the city, and thy sonnes and thy daughters shall fall by the sword, and thy land shall be diuided by line : and thou shalt die in a polluted land, and Israel shall surely goe into captiuitie foorth of his land.

CHAP. VIII.

1 By a basket of Summer fruite, is shewed the propinquitie of Israels end. 4 Oppression is reproued. 11 A famine of the word threatned.

Hus hath the Lord GOD shewed vnto me, and beholde, a basket of Summer fruit.

2 And he said, Amos, what seest thou ? And I sayde, A basket of Summer fruite. Then said the LORD vnto mee, The ende is come vpon my people of Israel ; I will not

againe passe by them any more.

3 And the songs of the Temples †shalbe howlings in that day, sayth the Lord GOD : *there shall be* many dead bodies in euery place, they shall cast *them* foorth †with silence.

4 ¶ Heare this, O ye that swallow vp the needy, euen to make the poore of the land to faile,

5 Saying, When will the ‖newe Moone be gone, that we may sell corne? and the Sabbath, that wee may †set forth wheat, making the Ephah small, and the shekel great, and †falsifying the balances by deceit ?

6 That wee may buy the poore for *siluer, & the needie for a paire of shoes ; yea, and sell the refuse of the wheate ?

7 The LORD hath sworne by the excellencie of Iacob, Surely I will neuer forget any of their workes.

8 Shall not the land tremble for this, and euery one mourne that dwelleth therein ? and it shall rise vp wholly as a flood ; and it shall be cast out and drowned, as by the flood of Egypt.

9 And it shall come to passe in that day, saith the Lord GOD, that I will cause the Sunne to go downe at noone, and I will darken the earth in the cleare day.

10 And I will turne your feasts into mourning, and all your songs into lamentation, and I will bring vp sackcloth vpon all loynes, and baldnesse vpon euery head : and I will make it as the mourning of an onely *sonne*, and the end thereof as a bitter day.

11 ¶ Behold, the daies come, saith the Lord GOD, that I will send a famine in the land, not a famine of bread, nor a thirst for water, but of hearing the words of the LORD.

12 And they shall wander from Sea to Sea, and from the North euen to the East they shall runne to and fro, to seeke the worde of the LORD, and shall not finde *it*.

13 In that day shall the faire virgines and young men faint for thirst.

14 They that sweare by the sinne of Samaria, and say, Thy God, O Dan, liueth, and the manner of Beer-sheba liueth, euen they shall fall, and neuer rise vp againe.

CHAP. IX.

1 The certeintie of the desolation. 11 The restoring of the Tabernacle of Dauid.

I saw

Margin notes

Or, Sanctuarie.
Heb. house of the kingdome.

Or, wilde figges.
Heb. from behind.

Eze. 21. 2.

† *Heb. shall howle.*

† *Heb. be silent.*

‖ *Or, moneth.*

† *Heb. open.*

† *Heb. peruerting the balances of deceit.*

* *Chap. 2. 6.*

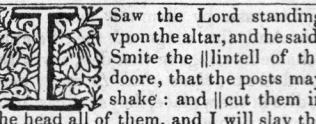

‖ Or, chapiter, or knop.

‖ Or, wound them.

I Saw the Lord standing vpon the altar, and he said, Smite the ‖lintell of the doore, that the posts may shake : and ‖cut them in the head all of them, and I will slay the last of them with the sword : hee that fleeth of them, shall not flee away, and he that escapeth of them, shall not be deliuered.

* Psal. 139. 8. &c :

2 * Though they digge into hell, thence shall mine hand take them : though they clime vp to heauen, thence will I bring them downe.

3 And though they hide themselues in the top of Carmel, I will search and take them out thence, and though they be hid from my sight in the bottome of the Sea, thence will I commaund the serpent, and he shall bite them.

4 And though they goe into captiuitie before their enemies, thence will I commaund the sword, and it shall slay them : and * I will set mine eyes vpon them for euill, and not for good.

* Ier. 44. 11.

5 And the Lord God of hostes is he that toucheth the land, and it shall melt, and all that dwelleth therein shall mourne, and it shall rise vp wholly like a flood, and shall be drowned as by the flood of Egypt.

‖ Or, spheares heb. ascensions.
* Psal. 104. 3.
‖ Or, bundell.
* Chap. 5. 8.

6 It is he that buildeth his ‖*stories in the heauen, and hath founded his ‖troupe in the earth, he that *calleth for the waters of the Sea, and powreth them out vpon the face of the earth : the Lord is his name.

7 Are yee not as children of the Ethiopians vnto me, O children of Israel, saith the Lord? haue not I brought vp Israel out of the land of Egypt? and the *Philistines from Caph-

* Ier. 47. 4.

tor, and the Syrians from Kir?

8 Behold, the eyes of the Lord God are vpon the sinfull kingdome, and I will destroy it from off the face of the earth; sauing that I will not vtterly destroy the house of Iacob, saith the Lord.

9 For loe, I will commaund, and I will †sift the house of Israel among all nations, like as corne is sifted in a sieue, yet shall not the least †graine fall vpon the earth.

† Heb. cause to moue.
† Heb. stone.

10 All the sinners of my people shall die by the sword, which say : The euill shall not ouertake nor preuent vs.

11 ¶ In that day will I raise vp the *tabernacle of Dauid, that is fallen, and †close vp the breaches thereof, and I will raise vp his ruines, and I will build it as in the dayes of old ;

* Acts 15. 16.
† Heb. hedge, or wall.

12 That they may possesse the remnant of Edom, and of all the heathen ; †which are called by my name, saith the Lord that doth this.

† Heb. vpon whom my name is called.

13 Behold, the daies come, saith the Lord, that the plowman shall ouertake the reaper, & the treader of grapes him that †soweth seede, and the mountaines shall drop ‖*sweete wine, and all the hils shall melt.

† Heb. draweth forth.
‖ Or, new wine.
* Ioel. 3. 18.

14 And I will bring againe the captiuitie of my people of Israel : and they shall build the waste cities, and inhabit them ; and they shall plant vineyards, and drinke the wine thereof : they shall also make gardens, and eate the fruite of them

15 And I will plant them vpon their land, and they shall no more be pulled vp out of their land, which I haue giuen them, saith the Lord thy God.

¶ OBADIAH.

1 The destruction of Edom, 3 for their pride, 10 and for their wrong vnto Iacob. 17 The saluation and victory of Iacob.

* Ier. 49. 14.

He vision of Obadiah : Thus saith the Lord God, concerning Edom ; *Wee haue heard a rumour from the Lord, and an am-

bassador is sent among the heathen : Arise yee, and let vs rise vp against her in battell.

2 Behold, I haue made thee small among the heathen : thou art greatly despised.

3 ¶ The pride of thine heart hath deceiued thee : thou that dwellest in the clefts of the rocke, Whose habitation is high,

high, that saith in his heart; Who shall bring me downe to the ground?

4 *Though thou exalt thy selfe as the eagle, and though thou set thy nest among the starres, thence will I bring thee downe, saith the LORD.

5 If *theeues came to thee, if robbers by night (how art thou cut off?) would they not haue stollen til they had enough? if the grape gatherers came to thee, would they not leaue ||some grapes?

6 How are the things of Esau searched out? how are his hid things sought vp?

7 All the men of thy confederacie haue brought thee euen to the border: †the men that were at peace with thee, haue deceiued thee, and preuailed against thee: †they that eate thy bread haue laide a wound vnder thee: there is none vnderstanding ||in him.

8 *Shal I not in that day, saith the LORD, euen destroy the wise men out of Edom, and vnderstanding out of the mount of Esau?

9 And thy mightie men, O Teman, shall be dismayed, to the end that euery one of the mount of Esau may be cut off by slaughter.

10 ¶ For thy *violence against thy brother Iacob shame shall couer thee, and thou shalt be cut off for euer.

11 In the day that thou stoodest on the other side, in the day that the strangers ||caried away captiue his forces, and forreiners entred into his gates, and cast lots vpon Ierusalem, euen thou wast as one of them.

12 But ||thou shouldest not haue looked on the day of thy brother in the day that hee became a stranger, neither shouldest thou haue reioyced ouer the children of Iudah in the day of their destruction: neither shouldest thou haue †spoken proudly in the day of distresse.

13 Thou shouldest not haue entred into the gate of my people in the day of

their calamitie: yea, thou shouldest not haue looked on their affliction in the day of their calamitie, nor haue laid hands on their ||substance in the day of their calamitie.

14 Neither shouldest thou haue stood in the crosse way to cut off those of his that did escape, neither shouldest thou haue ||deliuered vp those of his that did remaine in the day of distresse.

15 For the day of the LORD is neere vpon all the heathen: *as thou hast done, it shall bee done vnto thee, thy reward shall returne vpon thine owne head.

16 For as ye haue drunke vpon my holy mountaine, so shall all the heathen drinke continually: yea, they shall drinke, and they shall ||swallow downe, and they shall bee as though they had not bene.

17 ¶ But vpon mount Zion shall be ||deliuerance, and there ||shall be holinesse, and the house of Iacob shall possesse their possessions.

18 And the house of Iacob shall bee a fire, and the house of Ioseph a flame, and the house of Esau for stubble, and they shall kindle in them and deuoure them, and there shall not be any remaining of the house of Esau, for the LORD hath spoken it.

19 And they of the South shall possesse the mount of Esau, and they of the plaine, the Philistines: and they shall possesse the fields of Ephraim, and the fields of Samaria, and Beniamin shall possesse Gilead.

20 And the captiuitie of this hoste of the children of Israel shall possesse that of the Canaanites euen vnto Zarephath, and the captiuitie of Ierusalem ||which is in Sepharad, shall possesse the cities of the South.

21 And *Sauiours shall come vp on mount Zion to iudge the mount of Esau, and the *kingdome shall be the LORDS.

¶IONAH.

Margin notes (left column):

* Ier. 49. 16.

* Ier. 49. 9.

Or, gleanings.

Hebr. the men of thy peace.
Heb. the men of thy bread.
Or, of it.
* Isa. 49. 14.
* Ier. 49. 7.

* Gen. 27. 1. ezek. 35. amos 1. 1.

Or, caried way his substance.

Or, doe not behold, &c.

Heb. magnified thy mouth.

Margin notes (right column):

|| Or, forces.

|| Or, shut vp

* Ezek. 35. 15.

|| Or, sup vp.

|| Or, they that escape.
|| Or, it shall be holy.

|| Or, shall possesse that which is in Sepharad.
* 1. Tim. 4. 16. iames 5 20.
* Luke 1. 33

¶IONAH.

CHAP. I.

1 Ionah sent to Nineueh, fleeth to Tarshish.
4 He is bewrayed by a tempest, 11 throwen
into the sea, 17 and swallowed by a fish.

Ow the word of
the LORD came
vnto ‖ Ionah the
sonne of Amittai,
saying,

2 Arise, goe
to Nineueh that
* great citie, and
cry against it: for
their wickednes is come vp before me.

3 But Ionah rose vp to flee vnto
Tarshish, from the presence of the
LORD, and went downe to Ioppa,
and he found a ship going to Tarshish:
so he payed the fare thereof, and went
downe into it, to goe with them vnto Tarshish from the presence of the
LORD.

4 ¶ But the LORD †sent out a
great winde into the sea, and there was
a mightie tempest in the sea, so that the
ship †was like to be broken.

5 Then the Mariners were afraid,
and cried euery man vnto his god, and
cast foorth the wares that were in the
ship, into the sea, to lighten it of them:
but Ionah was gone downe into the
sides of the ship, and hee lay, and was
fast asleepe.

6 So the shipmaster came to him,
and said vnto him; What meanest thou,
O sleeper? Arise, call vpon thy God, if
so be that God wil thinke vpon vs, that
we perish not.

7 And they said euery one to his fellow; Come, and let vs cast lots, that we
may know for whose cause this euil is
vpon vs. So they cast lots, and the lot
fell vpon Ionah.

8 Then said they vnto him, Tel vs,
we pray thee, for whose cause this euill
is vpon vs: What is thine occupation?
and whence commest thou? What is thy
countrey? and of what people art thou?

9 And hee said vnto them, I am an
Hebrew, and I feare the LORD the
God of heauen, which hath made the
sea, and the dry land.

10 Then were the men †exceedingly
afraid, and saide vnto him; Why hast
thou done this? (for the men knew that
he fled from the presence of the LORD,
because he had told them.)

11 ¶ Then said they vnto him, What
shall we doe vnto thee, that the sea †may
be calme vnto vs? (for the sea ‖ wrought
and was tempestuous.)

12 And he said vnto them, Take me
vp, and cast mee foorth into the sea; so
shall the sea be calme vnto you: for I
know that for my sake this great tempest is vpon you.

13 Neuerthelesse the men †rowed
hard to bring it to the land, but they
could not: for the sea wrought, and was
tempestuous against them.

14 Wherefore they cried vnto the
LORD, and said, We beseech thee, O
LORD, We beseech thee, let vs not perish for this mans life, and lay not vpon
vs, innocent blood: for thou, O LORD,
hast done as it pleased thee.

15 So they tooke vp Ionah, and cast
him foorth into the sea, and the sea †cea-
sed from her raging.

16 Then the men feared the LORD
exceedingly, and †offered a sacrifice vnto the LORD, and made vowes.

17 ¶ Now the LORD had prepa-
red a great fish to swallow vp *Ionah,
and Ionah was in the †belly of the fish
three dayes, and three nights.

CHAP. II.

1 The prayer of Ionah. 10 Hee is deliuered
from the fish.

Hen Ionah prayed vnto
the LORD his God, out
of the fishes belly,

2 And said, I *cried ‖ by
reason of mine affliction
vnto the LORD, and hee heard mee;
out of the belly of ‖ hell cried I, and thou
heardest my voyce.

3 For thou hadst cast mee into the
deepe,

‖ Called,
Matth. 12.
39. Ionas.

* Gene. 10.
11, 12. cha.
3. 3.

† Heb. cast
foorth.

† Hebr.
thought to
be broken.

† Hebr. with
great feare.

† Hebr. may
be silent
from vs.
‖ Or grew
more and
more tem-
pestuous.
Heb. wentt.

† Hebr. dig-
ged.

†Hebr.stood.

† Hebr. sa-
crificed a sa-
crifice, and
vowed
vowes.
* Matt. 12.
40. and 16.
4. luke 11.
30.
† Hebr.
bowels.

* Psal. 120.
1.
‖ Or, out of
mine affli-
ction.
‖ Or, the
graue.

Heb. heart.

deepe, in the †middest of the Seas, and the floods compassed me about : all thy billowes & thy waues passed ouer me.

4 Then I said, I am cast out of thy sight ; yet I will looke againe toward thy holy Temple.

Psal. 69. 2.

5 The *waters compassed mee about euen to the soule ; the depth closed mee round about ; the weedes were wrapt about my head.

Heb. cuttings off.

6 I went downe to the †bottomes of the mountaines : the earth with her barres *was* about me for euer : yet hast

Or, the pit.

thou brought vp my life from ‖corruption, O Lord my God.

7 When my soule fainted within mee, I remembred the Lord, and my prayer came in vnto thee, into thine holy Temple.

8 They that obserue lying vanities, forsake their owne mercy.

*Psal. 50.
8. 23. and
6. 7. hos.
4. 2. heb.
8. 5.*

9 But I wil sacrifice vnto thee with the voice of *thanksgiuing, I will pay that that I haue vowed : *saluation is of the Lord.

Psal. 3. 9.

10 ¶ And the Lord spake vnto the fish, and it vomited out Ionah vpon the drie land.

CHAP. III.

1 Ionah sent againe, preacheth to the Nineuites.
5 Vpon their repentance, 10 God repenteth.

Nd the word of ỹ Lord came vnto Ionah the second time, saying ;

2 Arise, goe vnto Nineueh that great citie, and preach vnto it the preaching that I bid thee.

3 So Ionah arose and went vnto Nineueh, according to the word of the Lord : now Nineueh was an †exceeding great citie of three dayes iourney.

*Heb. of
od.*

4 And Ionah began to enter into the citie a dayes iourney, and hee cryed, and said ; Yet fourtie dayes, and Niniueh shalbe ouerthrowen.

*Matth. 12.
k. luke
k. 32.*

5 ¶ So the people of Nineueh *beleeued God, and proclaimed a fast, and put on sackecloth from the greatest of them euen to the least of them.

6 For word came vnto the King of Nineueh, and he arose from his throne, and he laid his robe from him and couered *him* with sackcloth, & sate in ashes.

Heb. said.

*Heb. great
nen.*

7 And he caused it to be proclaimed and †published through Nineueh (by the decree of the King and his †nobles) saying ; Let neither man nor beast,

herd nor flocke taste any thing; let them not feede, nor drinke water.

8 But let man and beast be couered with sackecloth, and cry mightily vnto God : yea, let them turne euery one from his euill way, and from the violence that *is* in their hands.

9 *Who can tell *if* God will turne and repent, and turne away from his fierce anger, that we perish not?

Ioel 2. 14.

10 ¶ And God saw their workes, that they turned from their euill way, and God repented of the euill that hee had sayd, that he would doe vnto them, and he did *it* not.

CHAP. IIII.

1 Ionah repining at Gods mercy, 4 is reprooued by the type of a Gourd.

Vt it displeased Ionah exceedingly, and he was very angry.

2 And he prayed vnto the Lord, and sayd, I pray thee, *O Lord, *was* not this my saying, when I was yet in my countrey? Therefore I fledde before vnto Tarshish : for I knew that thou *art* a *gracious God, and mercifull, slow to anger, and of great kindnesse, and repentest thee of the euill.

Chap. 1. 8.

*Exo. 34. 6.
psal. 86. 5.
ioel 2. 13.*

3 Therefore now, O Lord, Take, I beseech thee, my life from me; for it *is* better for me to die then to liue.

4 ¶ Then said the Lord, ‖ Doest thou well to be angry?

*Or, art
thou greatly angry?*

5 So Ionah went out of the citie, and sate on the East side of the city, and there made him a boothe, and sate vnder it in the shadow, till hee might see what would become of the citie.

6 And the Lord God prepared a ‖gourd, and made it to come vp ouer Ionah, that it might be a shadow ouer his head, to deliuer him from his griefe. So Ionah was †exceeding glad of the gourd.

*Or, palme-
crist. Heb.
Kikaion.*

*Heb. reioyced with
great ioy.*

7 But God prepared a worme when the morning rose the next day, and it smote the gourd that it withered.

8 And it came to passe when the Sunne did arise, that God prepared a ‖vehement East wind ; and the Sunne beat vpon the head of Ionah, that hee fainted, and wished in himselfe to die, and said, It *is* better for me to die, then to liue.

Or, silent.

9 And God said to Ionah, ‖ Doest thou well to be angry for the gourd? and

*Or, art
thou greatly
angry?*

| Or, I am greatly angry. |

| Or, spared. |

† Heb. was the ſonne of the night.

and he said, ||I doe well to be angry, e-uen vnto death.

10 Then said the LORD, Thou hast || had pitie on the gourde, for the which thou hast not laboured, neither madest it grow, which †came vp in a night, and perished in a night :

11 And should not I spare Nineueh that great citie, wherein are more then sixscore thousand persons, that cannot discerne betweene their right hand and their left hand, and *also* much cattell ?

¶ M I C A H.

CHAP. I.

1 Micah sheweth the wrath of God a-gainst Iacob, for idolatry. 10 Hee ex-horteth to mourning.

He word of the LORD that came to Micah the Morasthite in the dayes of Iotham, Ahaz, *and* Hezekiah Kings of Iu-dah, which hee saw con-cerning Samaria and Ierusalem.

† Heb. heare yee people all of them.
* Deut. 32.
1. isai. 1. 2.
† Heb. the fulnesse therof.
* Isai. 26. 21 psal. 115. 3.
* Deut. 32. 13. and 33. 29.
* Psal. 97. 5.

2 † Heare *all ye people, hearken O earth ; and †all that therein is, and let the Lord GOD be witnesse against you, the Lord from his holy temple.

3 For behold, *the LORD com-meth forth out of his *place, and will come downe and tread vpon the *high places of the earth.

† Heb. a des-cent.

4 And * the mountaines shall be molten vnder him, and the valleis shall be cleft : as waxe before the fire, *and* as the waters that are powred downe †a steepe place.

5 For the transgression of Iacob *is* all this, and for the sinnes of the house of Israel : What *is* the transgression of Iacob ? *Is* it not Samaria ? and what *are* the high places of Iudah ? *are* they not Ierusalem ?

6 Therfore I will make Samaria *as* an heape of the field, *and as* plantings of a vineyard ; and I will powre downe the stones therof into the valley, and I will discouer the foundations thereof.

7 And all the grauen images there-of shall be beaten to pieces, and all the hires thereof shall be burnt with the fire, and all the idoles therof will I lay desolate : for she gathered it of the hire of an harlot, and they shall returne to the hire of an harlot.

8 Therfore I wil waile and houle,

I will goe stript and naked : I will make a wailing like the dragons, and mourning as the †owles.

9 For ||her wound *is* incurable, for it is come vnto Iudah : he is come vnto the gate of my people, *euen* to Ierusalem.

10 ¶ *Declare yee *it* not at Gath, weepe yee not at all : In the house of ||Aphrah *rowle thy selfe in the dust.

11 Passe yee away thou † inhabitant of ||Saphir, hauing thy *shame naked ; the inhabitant of ||Zaanan came not forth in the mourning of ||Beth-ezel, he shall receiue of you his standing.

12 For the inhabitant of Maroth ||waited carefully for good, but euill came downe from the LORD vnto the gate of Ierusalem.

13 O thou inhabitant of Lachish, bind the charet to the swift beast : she *is* the beginning of the sinne to the daugh-ter of Zion : for the transgressions of Israel were found in thee.

14 Therfore shalt thou giue presents || to Moresheth-Gath : the houses of || Achzib *shalbe* a lie to ẙ kings of Israel.

15 Yet wil I bring an heire vnto thee, O inhabitant of Mareshah : ||he shall come vnto Adullam, the glory of Israel

16 Make thee *bald, and polle thee for thy delicate children, enlarge thy bald-nesse as the Eagle, for they are gone in-to captiuitie from thee.

† Heb. daughters of the owle.
|| Or, she is grieuously sicke of her wounds.
* 2. Sam. 1. 20.

|| That is, dust.
† Ier. 6. 26.
† Heb. inha-bitresse.
|| Or, thou that dwelleſt fairely.
* Isai. 47. 30.
|| Or, the countrey of flockes.
|| Or, a place neere.
|| Or, was grieued.

|| Or, for.
|| That is, a lie.

|| Or, the glory of Is-rael shall come &c.
* Isai. 22. 12

CHAP. II.

1 Against oppression. 4 A lamentation. 7 A reproofe of iniustice and idolatrie. 12 A pro-mise of restoring Iacob.

Oe to them that deuise iniquitie, and worke euill vpon their beds : when the morning is light, they practise it, because it is in the power of their hand.

*Isa. 5. 8.

‖ Or, de-
fraude.

† Heb. with
a lamentati-
on of lamen-
tations.
‖ Or, in stead
of restoring.

* Deut. 32.
8, 9.

‖ Or, prophe-
cie not, as
they prophe-
cie.
† Heb. drop,
&c.
* Isa. 30. 10.
‖ Or, shorte-
ned.

† Hebr. vp-
right.
† Heb. ye-
sterday.
† Heb. ouer
against a
garment.
‖ Or, wiues.

‖ Or, walke
with the
winde, and
lie falsly.

2 And they couet *fields and take *them* by violence: and houses, and take *them* away: so they ‖oppresse a man and his house, euen a man and his heritage.

3 Therefore thus saith the Lord, Behold, against this familie doe I deuise an euill, from which ye shall not remoue your necks, neither shall ye goe haughtily: for this time *is* euill.

4 ¶ In that day shall one take vp a parable against you, and lament with a †dolefull lamentation, *and* say, We be vtterly spoiled: hee hath changed the portion of my people: how hath he remoued it from me? ‖turning away hee hath diuided our fields.

5 Therefore thou shalt haue none that shall *cast a cord by lot in the Congregation of the Lord.

6 ‖†*Prophecie ye not, *say they, to them that* prophecie: they shall not prophecie to them, *that* they shall not take shame.

7 ¶ O thou that art named the house of Iacob, is the Spirit of the Lord ‖straitned? *are* these his dongs? doe not my words do good to him that walketh †vprightly?

8 †Euen of late, my people is risen vp as an enemie: ye pull off the robe †with the garment, frō them that passe by securely, as men auerse from warre.

9 The ‖women of my people haue ye cast out from their pleasant houses, from their children haue ye taken away my glory for euer

10 Arise ye and depart, for this *is* not *your* rest: because it is polluted, it shall destroy *you* euen with a sore destruction.

11 If a man ‖walking in the spirit and falshood, doe lie, *saying*, I will prophecie vnto thee of wine and of strong drinke, he shall euen bee the prophet of this people.

12 ¶ I will surely assemble, O Iacob, all of thee: I will surely gather the remnant of Israel, I will put them together as the sheepe of Bozrah, as the flocke in the midst of their fold: they shall make great noise by reason of *the multitude of* men.

13 The breaker is come vp before them: they haue broken vp and haue passed through the gate, and are gone out by it, and their king shal passe before them, & the Lord on the head of them.

CHAP. III.

And I said, Heare, I pray you, O heads of Iacob, and ye princes of the house of Israel: *is it* not for you to know iudgement?

2 Who hate the good and loue the euill, who plucke off their skinne from off them, and their flesh from off their bones.

3 Who also eate the flesh of my people, and flay their skinne from off them, and they breake their bones, and chop them in pieces, as for the pot, and as flesh within the cauldron.

4 Then shall they cry vnto the Lord, but he will not heare them: he will euen hide his face from them at that time, as they haue behaued themselues ill in their doings.

5 ¶ Thus saith the Lord concerning the Prophets that make my people erre, that *bite with their teeth and crie; Peace: and he that putteth not into their mouths, they euen prepare warre against him:

6 Therefore night *shall be* vnto you, †that yee shall not haue a vision, and it shall be darke vnto you, †that yee shall not diuine, and the Sunne shall goe downe ouer the Prophets, and the day shall be darke ouer them.

7 Then shall the seers be ashamed, and the diuiners confounded: yea, they shall all couer their †lips, for *there is* no answere of God.

8 ¶ But truely I am full of power by the spirit of the Lord, and of iudgment and of might, to declare vnto Iacob his transgression, and to Israel his sinne.

9 Heare this, I pray you, yee heads of the house of Iacob, and princes of the house of Israel, that abhorre iudgement and peruert all equitie.

10 They build vp Zion with *†blood, and Ierusalem with iniquitie.

11 The heads thereof iudge for reward, and the priests thereof teach for hyre, and the Prophets thereof diuine for money: yet will they leane vpon the Lord, †and say; Is not the Lord among vs? none euill can come vpon vs.

12 Therefore shall Zion for your sake be *plowed *as* a field, and Ierusalem shal become heapes, and the mountaine of the house, as the high places of the forrest.

CHAP.

* Chap. 2. 11

† Hebr. from
a vision.
† Heb. from
diuining.

† Heb. vpper
lippe.

* Ezek: 22.
27. zeph. 3.
3.
† Heb.
bloods.

† Heb. say-
ing.

* Ier. 26. 18

CHAP. IIII.

1 The Glory, 3 Peace, 8 Kingdome, 11 and Victorie of the Church.

* Isai. 2. 2.
&c.

 Vt *in the last dayes it shal come to passe, *that* the mountaine of the house of the Lord shall be established in the top of the mountaines, and it shalbe exalted aboue the hilles, and people shall flow vnto it.

2 And many nations shall come, and say; Come, and let vs goe vp to the mountaine of the Lord, and to the house of the God of Iacob, and he will teach vs of his wayes, and wee will walke in his pathes : for the Law shall goe foorth of Zion, and the word of the Lord from Ierusalem.

3 ¶ And he shall iudge among many people, and rebuke strong nations afarre off, and they shall beate their swords into * plowshares, and their speares into ‖ pruning hookes : nation shall not lift vp a sword against nation, neither shall they learne warre any more.

* Isa. 2. 4.
ioel 3. 10.
‖ Or, sythes.

4 But they shall sit euery man vnder his Vine, and vnder his figgetree, and none shal make *them* afraid : for the mouth of the Lord of hostes hath spoken *it*.

5 For all people will walke euery one in the name of his god, and we will walke in the Name of the Lord our God for euer and euer.

6 In that day, saith the Lord, will I assemble her that halteth, and I will gather her that is driuen out, and her that I haue afflicted.

7 And I will make her that * halted, a remnant ; and her that was cast farre off, a strong nation ; and the Lord *shall reigne ouer them, in Mount Zion from hencefoorth, euen for euer.

* Zeph. 3.
19.

8 ¶ And thou, O towre of the flock, the strong hold of the daughter of Zion, vnto thee shall it come, euen the first dominion, the kingdome shall come to the daughter of Ierusalem.

* Dan. 7. 14.
luke 1. 33.

9 Now why doest thou cry out alowd? *is there* no king in thee? is thy counseller perished? for pangs haue taken thee, as a woman in trauell.

10 Bee in paine and labour to bring forth, O daughter of Zion, like a woman in trauell : for now shalt thou goe foorth out of the citie, and thou shalt dwel in the field, and thou shalt go euen to Babylon : there shalt thou be deliuered : there the Lord shall redeeme thee from the hand of thine enemies.

11 ¶ Now also many nations are gathered against thee, that say, Let her be defiled, & let our eye looke vpon Zion.

12 But they know not the thoughts of the Lord, neither vnderstand they his counsell : for hee shall gather them as the sheaues into the floore.

13 Arise and thresh, O daughter of Zion : for I will make thine horne yron, & I will make thy hooues brasse, and thou shalt beat in pieces many people : and I will consecrate their gaine vnto the Lord, and their substance vnto the Lord of the whole earth.

CHAP. V.

1 The birth of Christ. 4 His Kingdome. 8 His conquest.

Ow gather thy selfe in troupes, O daughter of troupes : he hath laid siege against vs : they shal smite the Iudge of Israel with a rod vpon the cheeke.

2 But thou *Beth-leem Ephratah, *though* thou bee little among the thousands of Iudah, *yet* out of thee shall he come foorth vnto mee, *that is* to be ruler in Israel : whose goings foorth *haue bene* from of old, †from euerlasting.

* Matth. 2
6. ioh. 7. 4

† Hebr. the
dayes of
eternitie.

3 Therefore will hee giue them vp, vntill the time that shee which trauaileth, hath brought forth : then the remnant of his brethren shall returne vnto the children of Israel.

4 ¶ And he shall stand and ‖feed in the strength of the Lord, in the Maiestie of the Name of the Lord his God, and they shall abide : for now shall he be great vnto the ends of the earth.

‖ Or, rule.

5 And this *man* shall bee the peace when the Assyrian shall come into our land : and when hee shall tread in our palaces, then shall we raise against him seuen Shepheards, and eight †principall men.

† Heb. pri
ces of men

6 And they shall †waste the land of Assyria with the sword, and the land of Nimrod ‖ in the entrances thereof : thus shall hee deliuer *vs* from the Assyrian, when he commeth into our land, and when hee treadeth within our borders.

† Hebr. ea
vp.

‖ Or, with
her owne ▪
ked sword

7 And

7 And the remnant of Iacob shall be in the midst of many people, as a dew from the Lord, as the showres vpon the grasse that tarieth not for man, nor waiteth for the sonnes of men

8 ¶ And the remnant of Iacob shal be among the Gentiles in the middest of many people, as a Lyon among the beasts of the forrest, as a yong Lyon among the flockes of ||sheepe : who if he goe through, both treadeth downe, and teareth in pieces, and none can deliuer.

9 Thine hand shall be lift vp vpon thine aduersaries, aud all thine enemies shalbe cut off.

10 And it shall come to passe in that day, sayth the Lord, that I will cut off thy horses out of the midst of thee, and I will destroy thy charets.

11 And I will cut off the cities of thy land, and throw downe all thy strong holdes.

12 And I will cut off witchcrafts out of thine hand, and thou shalt haue no more Southsayers.

13 Thy grauen images also will I cut off, and thy ||standing images out of the midst of thee : & thou shalt no more worship the worke of thine hands.

14 And I will plucke vp thy groues out of the middest of thee : so will I destroy thy ||cities.

15 And I will execute vengeance in anger, and furie vpon the heathen, *such* as they haue not heard.

CHAP. VI.

1 Gods controuersie for vnkindnesse, 6 for ignorance, 10 for iniustice, 16 and for idolatry.

HEare yee now what the Lord saith, Arise, contend thou || before the *mountaines , and let the hilles heare thy voice

2 Heare yee , O mountaines , the Lords controuersie, and ye strong foundations of the earth : for the Lord hath a controuersie with his people, and he will pleade with Israel.

3 O my people , what haue I done vnto thee , and wherein haue I wearied thee ? testifie against me.

4 For I brought thee vp out of the land of *Egypt, and redeemed thee out of the house of seruants, and I sent before thee Moses, Aaron and Miriam.

5 O my people , remember now what *Balak king of Moab consulted,

and what Balaam the sonne of Beor answered him from *Shittim vnto Gilgal, that yee may know the righteousnesse of the Lord.

6 ¶ Wherewith shall I come before the Lord, *and* bow my selfe before the high God ? shall I come before him with burnt offerings, with calues †of a yeere olde ?

7 Will the Lord be pleased with thousands of rammes , *or* with tenne thousands of riuers of oyle ? shall I giue my first borne *for* my transgression, the fruit of my † body *for* the sinne of my soule ?

8 Hee hath *shewed thee, O man, what *is* good ; and what doeth the Lord require of thee, but to do iustly, and to loue mercy, and to †walke humbly with thy God ?

9 The Lords voice cryeth vnto the citie, and ||the *man* of wisedome shall see thy Name : heare ye the rodde, and who hath appointed it.

10 ¶ ||*Are* there yet the treasures of wickednesse in the house of the wicked, and the †scant measure that is abominable.

11 ||Shall I count *them* pure with the wicked balances, and with the bag of deceitfull weights ?

12 For the rich men thereof are full of violence, and the inhabitants thereof haue spoken lies, and their tongue *is* deceitfull in their mouth.

13 Therefore also will I make thee sicke in smiting thee, in making *thee* desolate, because of thy sinnes.

14 Thou shalt eate, but not be satisfied, and thy casting downe *shall be* in the midst of thee, and thou shalt take holde, but shalt not deliuer : & that which thou deliuerest, will I giue vp to the sword.

15 Thou shalt *sow , but thou shalt not reape : thou shalt tread the oliues, but thou shalt not anoint thee with oile ; & sweet wine, but shalt not drinke wine.

16 ¶ For ||the statutes of *Omri are kept, and all the workes of the house of *Ahab, and ye walke in their counsels, that I should make thee a ||desolation, and the inhabitants thereof an hissing : therefore yee shall beare the reproch of my people.

CHAP. VII.

1 The Church complaining of her small number, 3 and the generall corruption, 5 putteth her confidence, not in man but in God. 8 Shee

Marginal notes:

|| Or, goats

|| Or, statues.

|| Or, enemies.

|| Or, with
* Isai 1. 2.

* Exod. 12. 51. and 14. 30.

* Num. 22. 5. and 23. 7.

* Num. 25.
* Iosh. 5.

† Heb. sonnes of a yeere.

† Heb. belly.

* Deut. 10. 12.

† Heb. humble thy selfe to walke.

|| Or, thy name shall see that which is.

¶ Or, is there yet vnto euery man an house of the wicked? &c.
† Heb. measure of leannesse.
|| Or, shall I be pure with, &c.

* Deut. 28. 38. hagg. 1. 6.

|| Or, he doth much keepe the &c.
* 1. Kin. 16.
* 1. Kin. 16. 30, &c.
|| Or, astonishment.

8 She triumpheh ouer her enemies. 14 God comforteth her by promises, 16 by confusion of the enemies, 18 and by his mercies.

Oe is mee, for I am as when they haue gathered the † summer fruits, as the grape gleanings of the vintage : *there is* no cluster to eate : my soule desired the first ripe fruit.

† *Heb. the gatherings of summer.*

2 The * ‖ good man is perished out of the earth, and *there is* none vpright among men : they all lie in waite for blood : they hunt euery man his brother with a net.

* *Psal. 12.*
3. *isai. 57. 1.*
‖ *Or, godly, or mercifull.*

3 ¶ That they may doe euill with both hands earnestly, the prince asketh, and the iudge *asketh* for a reward : and the great man, he vttereth his † mischieuous desire : so they wrap it vp.

† *Heb. the mischiefe of the soule.*

4 The best of them *is* as a brier : the most vpright *is sharper* then a thorne hedge : the day of thy watchmen, *and* thy visitation commeth ; now shall be their perplexitie.

5 ¶ Trust yee not in a friend, put ye not confidence in a guide : keepe the doores of thy mouth from her that lyeth in thy bosome.

6 For * the sonne dishonoureth the father : the daughter riseth vp against her mother : the daughter in law against her mother in law ; a mans enemies *are* the men of his owne house.

* *Matth. 10.*
21, 35, 36.
luc. 24. 16.

7 Therefore I will looke vnto you the LORD : I will waite for the God of my saluation : my God will heare me.

8 ¶ Reioyce not against mee, O mine enemie : When I fall, I shall arise ; when I sit in darknes, the LORD *shall be* a light vnto me.

9 I will beare the indignation of the LORD, because I haue sinned against him, vntill he plead my cause, and execute iudgement for me : he will bring me forth to the light, *and* I shall behold his righteousnesse.

10 Then ‖ she that is mine enemie shall see *it*, and shame shall couer her * which said vnto mee ; Where is the LORD thy God ? mine eyes shall behold her : now shall † she bee troden downe, as the myre of the streets.

‖ *Or, and thou wilt s her that is mine enem and couer her with shame.*
* *Psal. 79.*
10. *and 115*
2. *ioel. 2.*
† *Heb. she shall be for a treading downe.*
* *Amos 9.*
11. *&c :*
‖ *Or, euen to.*

11 *In* the day that thy * walles are to be built, *in* that day shall the decree bee farre remoued.

12 *In* that day also he shal come euen to thee from Assyria, and ‖ *from* the fortified cities, and *from* the fortresse euen to the riuer, and from Sea to Sea, and *from* mountaine to mountaine ;

13 ‖ Notwithstanding the land shall be desolate because of them that dwell therein, for the fruite of their doings.

‖ *Or, after that it hat beene.*

14 ¶ ‖ Feede thy people with thy rod, the flocke of thine heritage, which dwell solitarily *in* the wood, in the midst of Carmel : let them feede in Bashan and Gilead, as in the dayes of old.

‖ *Or, rule.*

15 According to the dayes of thy comming out of the land of Egypt will I shew vnto him meruailous things.

16 ¶ The nations shall see, and be confounded at all their might : they shall lay their hand vpon *their* mouth : their eares shall be deafe.

17 They shall licke the * dust like a serpent, they shall moue out of their holes like ‖ wormes of the earth : they shall be afraid of the LORD our God, and shall feare because of thee.

* *Psal. 72*
9.
‖ *Or, creeping thing*

18 Who *is* a God like vnto thee, that * pardoneth iniquitie, and passeth by the transgression of the remnant of his heritage ? hee retaineth not his anger for euer, because he delighteth *in* mercy.

* *Exod. 3*
6, 7.

19 He wil turne againe, he will haue compassion vpon vs : he will subdue our iniquities, and thou wilt cast all their sinnes into the depths of the Sea.

20 Thou wilt performe the trueth to Iacob, *and* the mercy to Abraham, which thou hast sworne vnto our fathers from the dayes of old.

¶ N A H V M

¶ NAHVM.

CHAP. I.

The Maiestie of God, in goodnesse to his people, and seueritie against his enemies.

He burden of Nineueh. The book of the vision of Nahum the Elkoshite.

2 ‖ God *is* *ielous, and the LORD reuengeth : the LORD reuengeth, and *is* †furious, the LORD wil take vengeance on his aduersaries, and he reserueth *wrath* for his enemies.

3 The LORD *is* * slow to anger, and great in power, and will not at all acquit *the wicked* : the LORD *hath* his way in the whirlewind , and in the storme, and the clouds *are* the dust of his feete.

4 He rebuketh the sea, and maketh it drie, and drieth vp all the riuers : Bashan languisheth, and Carmel, and the floure of Lebanon languisheth.

5 The mountaines quake at him, and the hilles melt, and the earth is burnt at his presence, yea the world and all that dwell therein.

6 Who can stand before his indignation? and who can †abide in the fiercenesse of his anger? his furie is powred out like fire, and the rocks are throwen downe by him.

7 The LORD is good, a ‖strong hold in the day of trouble, & he knoweth them that trust in him.

8 But with an ouer-running flood he will make an vtter ende of the place thereof, and darkenesse shall pursue his enemies.

9 What doe ye imagine against the LORD? he will make an vtter ende : affliction shall not rise vp the second time.

10 For while they be folden together *as* thornes, and while they are drunken *as* drunkards, they shall be deuoured as stubble fully drie.

11 There is one come out of thee, that imagineth euill against the LORD : †a wicked counseller.

12 Thus saith the LORD, ‖Though they *be* quiet, and likewise many, yet thus shall they be †cut downe, when he shall passe through : though I haue afflicted thee, I will afflict thee no more.

13 For now will I breake his yoke from off thee, and will burst thy bonds in sunder.

14 And the LORD hath giuen a commandement concerning thee, *that* no more of thy name be sowen : out of the house of thy gods will I cut off the grauen image, and the molten image, I wil make thy graue, for thou art vile.

15 Behold vpon the * mountaines the feete of him that bringeth good tidings, that publisheth peace. O Iudah †keepe thy solemne feasts, performe thy vowes : for the †wicked shall no more passe through thee, he is vtterly cut off.

CHAP. II.

The fearefull and victorious armies of God, against Nineueh.

‖E that dasheth in pieces is come vp before thy face : keep the munition, watch the way : make *thy* loines strong : fortifie *thy* power mightily.

2 * For the LORD hath turned away the ‖excellencie of Iacob, as the excellencie of Israel : for the emptiers haue emptied them out, and marred their vine branches.

3 The shield of his mightie men is made red, the valiant men are ‖in scarlet : the charets *shall bee* with †flaming torches in the day of his preparation, and the firre trees shall bee terribly shaken.

4 The charets shall rage in the streets, they shall iustle one against another in the broad wayes : †they shall seeme like torches, they shall runne like the lightnings.

5 He

Marginal notes (left column):

‖ *Or, the Lord is a ielous God, and reuenger, &c.*

* Exo. 20. 5

* *Heb. that hath fury.*

* Exo. 34. 7

Heb. stand vp.

Or, strength

Marginal notes (right column):

† *Hebr. a counseller of Belial.*

‖ *Or, if they would haue bin at peace, so should they haue beene many, and so should they haue bene shorne, & he should haue passed away.*

† *Heb. shorne*

* Isa. 52. 7 rom. 10. 15.

† *Heb. feast.*

† *Heb. Belial.*

‖ *Or, the disperser or hammer.*

* Isa. 10. 12.

‖ *Or, the pride of Iacob and the pride of Israel.*

‖ *Or, died scarlet.*

† *Heb. fierie torches.*

† *Heb. their show.*

† Or, gallants

† Hebr. coue-
ring or coue-
rer.

‖ Or, molten.

‖ Or, That
which was e-
stablished,
or, there was
astandmade.
‖ Or, discoue-
red.
‖ Or, from
the dayes
that she hath
bene.
‖ Or, cause
them to turn.

‖ Or, And
their infinite
store, &c.
† Heb. vessels
of desire..

* Isai. 13.
7, 8.

5 Hee shall recount his †worthies: they shall stumble in their walke : they shall make haste to the wal thereof, and the †defence shall bee prepared.

6 The gates of the riuers shall bee opened, and the palace shall bee ‖dissolued.

7 And ‖Huzzab shall be ‖led away captiue, she shall be brought vp, and her maids shall leade her as with the voyce of doues, tabring vpon their breasts.

8 But Nineueh is ‖of olde like a poole of water : yet they shall flee away. Stand, stand shall they cry : but none shal ‖looke backe.

9 Take ye the spoyle of siluer, take the spoile of golde : ‖for there is none end of the store, and glory out of all the †pleasant furniture.

10 Shee is emptie, and voide, and waste, and the *heart melteth, and the knees smite together, and much paine is in all loynes, and the faces of them all gather blacknesse.

11 Where is the dwelling of the Lions, and the feeding place of the yong Lions? where the Lion, euen the olde Lion walked, and the Lions whelpe, and none made them afraid.

12 The Lion did teare in pieces enough for his whelpes, and strangled for his Lionesses, and filled his holes with pray, and his dens with rauine.

13 Behold, I am against thee, saith the LORD of hosts, and I will burne her charets in the smoke, and the sword shall deuoure thy yong Lions, and I wil cut off thy pray from the earth, and the voice of thy messengers shall no more be heard.

CHAP. III.

The miserable ruine of Nineueh.

† Heb. Citie
of bloods.
* Eze. 24. 9.
hab. 2. 10.

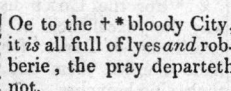

Oe to the † *bloody City, it is all full of lyes and robberie, the pray departeth not.

2 The noise of a whip, and the noise of the rattling of the wheeles, and of the praunsing horses, and of the iumping charets.

3 The horseman lifteth vp both the †bright sword, & the glittering speare, and there is a multitude of slaine, and a great number of carkeises : and there is none ende of their corpses. they stumble vpon their corpses,

† Heb. the
flame of
the sword
and the
lightning of
the speare.

4 Because of the multitude of the whoredomes of the wel-fauoured harlot, the mistresse of witchcrafts, that selleth nations through her whoredomes, and families through her witchcrafts.

5 Behold, *I am against thee, saith the LORD of hostes, and I will discouer thy skirtes vpon thy face, and I will shew the nations thy nakednesse, and the kingdomes thy shame.

Esa. 47. 3.
ezek. 16.
37.

6 And I will cast abominable filth vpon thee, and make thee vile, and will set thee as a gazing stocke.

7 And it shall come to passe, that all they that looke vpon thee, shall flee from thee, and say ; Nineueh is layde waste, who will bemoane her? whence shall I seeke comforters for thee?

8 Art thou better then ‖populous No, that was scituate among the riuers that had the waters round about it, whose rampart was the sea, and her wall was from the sea?

‖ Or, nouri
shing.
Hebr. No
Amon.

9 Ethiopia and Egypt were her strength, and it was infinit, Put and Lubim were †thy helpers.

† Heb. in the
helpe.

10 Yet was she caried away, she went into captiuitie : her yong children also were dashed in pieces at the top of all the streetes : and they cast lots for her honourable men, and all her great men were bound in chaines.

11 Thou also shalt be *drunken : thou shalt bee hid, thou also shalt seeke strength because of the enemie.

* Iere. 25.
17.

12 All thy strong holds shall be like fig trees with the first ripe figs : if they bee shaken, they shall euen fall into the mouth of the eater.

13 Beholde, thy people in the midst of thee are women : the gates of thy land shall be set wide open vnto thine enemies, the fire shall deuoure thy barres.

14 Draw thee waters for the siege : fortifie thy strong holdes, goe into clay, and tread the morter : make strong the bricke-kill.

15 There shall the fire deuoure thee : the sword shall cut thee off : it shall eate thee vp like the cankerworme : make thy selfe many as the cankerworme, make thy selfe many as the locusts

16 Thou hast multiplied thy merchants aboue the starres of heauen; the cankerworme ‖spoileth & flieth away.

‖ Or, sprea
deth him-
selfe.

17 The crowned are as the locusts, and thy captains as the great grashoppers which campe in the hedges in the cold

∥ Or, valiant
mes.

cold day : *but* when the Sunne ariseth, they flee away, and their place is not knowen where they *are*.

18 Thy shepheards slumber, O king of Assyria: thy ∥nobles shall dwell *in the dust :* thy people is scattered vpon the mountaines, & no man gathereth *them.*

19 There is no †healing of thy bruise: thy wound is grieuous : all that heare the bruit of thee, shall clap the hands o-uer thee ; for vpon whom hath not thy wickednesse passed continually ?

† Heb. wrin-
kling.

¶ HABAKKVK.

CHAP. I.

1 Vnto Habakkuk complaining of the iniquitie of the land, 5 is shewed the fearefull ven-geance by the Caldeans. 12 Hee complai-neth, that vengeance should be executed by them who are farre worse.

He burden which Habakkuk ÿ Pro-phet did see.

2 O Lord, howe long shall I crie, and thou wilt not heare! *euen* cry out vnto thee *of* violence, and thou wilt not saue ?

3 Why doest thou shew me iniquity, & cause me to behold grieuance? for spoi-ling and violence *are* before me : & there are *that* raise vp strife and contention.

4 Therefore the Lawe is slacked, and iudgement doeth neuer goe foorth : for the *wicked doeth compasse about the righteous : therfore ∥wrong iudge-ment proceedeth.

5 ¶ Behold ye *among the heathen, and regard, and wonder marueilously : for I wil worke a worke in your daies, *which* yee will not beleeue, though it be tolde *you.*

6 For loe, I raise vp the Caldeans, that bitter and hastie nation, which shall march through the †breadth of the land, to possesse the dwelling places *that are* not theirs.

7 They are terrible and dreadfull : ∥their iudgement and their dignity shal proceed of themselues.

8 Their horses also are swifter then the leopards, and are more †fierce then the *euening wolues : & their horsemen shall spread themselues, and their horse-men shall come from farre, they shall flie as the Eagle *that* hasteth to eate.

* Iob 21. 7.
iere. 12. 1.
∥Or,wrested.

* Actes 13.
41.

† Hebr.
breadths.

∥ Or, from
them shall
proceed the
iudgement
of these, and
the captiuity
of these.
† Heb.sharp.
* Zeph. 3. 3.

9 They shall come all for violence: †their faces shall sup vp *as* the East winde, and they shall gather the capti-uitie as the sand.

10 And they shal scoffe at the Kings, and the Princes *shall bee* a scorne vnto them : they shall deride euery strong holde, for they shall heape dust & take it.

11 Then shall *his* minde change, and he shall passe ouer, and offend, *imputing* this his power vnto his God.

12 ¶ *Art* thou not from euerlasting, O Lord my God, mine Holy one ? we shall not die: O Lord, thou hast ordained them for iudgement, and O †mightie God, thou hast † established them for correction.

13 *Thou art* of purer eyes then to be-holde euill, and canst not looke on ∥ini-quitie : wherefore lookest thou vpon them that deale treacherously, *and* hol-dest thy tongue when the wicked de-uoureth the man that is more righte-ous then hee ?

14 And makest men as the fishes of the Sea, as the ∥creeping things, that *haue* no ruler ouer them.

15 They take vp all of them with the angle : they catch them in their net, and gather them in their ∥dragge ; therefore they reioyce and are glad.

16 Therefore they sacrifice vnto their net, and burne incense vnto their drag: because by them their portion *is* fat, and their meat ∥plenteous.

17 Shall they therefore emptie their net, and not spare continually to slay the nations ?

† Heb. the
suppingvpof
their faces,
&c. Or, their
faces shall
looke toward
the East :
Heb. the op-
position of
their faces
toward the
East.

† Heb. rocke.
† Heb. foun-
ded.

∥ Or, grie-
uance.

∥ Or, moo-
uing.

∥ Or, flue-net

∥Or, daintie:
Heb. fat.

CHAP. II.

1 Vnto Habakkuk, waiting for an answere, is shewed that he must waite by faith. 5 The iudgement vpon the Caldean for vnsatiable-nesse, 9 for couetousnesse, 12 for crueltie, 15 for drunkennesse, 18 and for idolatrie.

I will

I Will * stand vpon my
watch, & set mee vpon the
†towre, and will watch to
see what he will say ‖ vnto
me, and what I shall an-
swere ‖ when I am reproued.
2 And the LORD answered me
and said, Write the vision, and make it
plaine vpon tables, that he may runne
that readeth it.
3 For the vision is yet for an appointed time, but at the the end it shall speak,
and not lie: though it tary, wait for it, because it will *surely come, it wil not tary.
4 Behold, his soule *which* is lifted
vp, is not vpright in him; but the *iust
shall liue by his faith.
5 ¶ ‖ Yea also, because he transgresseth by wine, he is a proud man, neither
keepeth at home, who enlargeth his desire as hell, and is as death, and cannot
be satisfied, but gathereth vnto him all
nations, & heapeth vnto him all people:
6 Shal not all these take vp a parable against him, and a tanting prouerbe
against him, and say; ‖ Woe to him that
increaseth *that which* is not his: how
long? and to him that ladeth himselfe
with thicke clay.
7 Shall they not rise vp suddenly
that shall bite thee? and awake, that
shall vexe thee? and thou shalt be for
booties vnto them?
8 Because thou hast spoiled many
nations, all the remnant of the people
shal spoile thee: because of mens † blood,
and for the violence of the land, of the citie, and of all that dwell therein.
9 ¶ Woe to him that * ‖ coueteth an
euill couetousnesse to his house, that he
may set his nest on high, that hee may
be deliuered from the † power of euill.
10 Thou hast consulted shame to thy
house, by cutting off many people, and
hast sinned *against* thy soule.
11 For the stone shall crie out of the
wall, and the ‖ beame out of the timber
‖ shall answere it.
12 ¶ Woe to him that buildeth a
towne with * † blood, and stablisheth a
citie by iniquitie.
13 Behold, *is* it not of the LORD of
hostes, that the people shall labour in
the very fire, and the people shal wearie
themselues for ‖ very vanitie?
14 For the earth shall be filled ‖ with
the * knowledge of the glory of the
LORD, as the waters couer the Sea.
15 ¶ Woe vnto him that giueth his
neighbour drinke: that puttest thy bot-
tell to *him*, and makest *him* drunken also; that thou mayest looke on their nakednesse.
16 Thou art filled ‖ with shame for
glory: * drinke thou also, and let thy
foreskin bee vncouered: the cup of the
LORDS right hand shall be turned
vnto thee, and shamefull spewing *shalbe*
on thy glory.
17 For the violence of Lebanon
shall couer thee: and the spoile of beasts,
which made them afraide, because of
mens blood, and for the violence of the
land, of the city, & of al that dwel therin.
18 ¶ What profiteth the grauen
image, that the maker thereof hath grauen it; the molten image, and a * teacher
of lies, that † the maker of his worke,
trusteth therin, to make dumbe idoles.
19 Woe vnto him that saith to the
wood, Awake: to the dumbe stone,
Arise, it shall teach: behold, it is layed
ouer with gold and siluer, and *there is* no
breath at all in the middest of it.
20 But * the LORD *is* in his holy
temple: † let all the earth keepe silence
before him.

* Isai. 21. 8.
† *Heb. fenced place.*
‖ *Or, in me.*
‖ *Or, when I am argued with. Heb. vpon my reproofe or arguing.*
* Hebr. 10. 37.
* Iohn 3. 36. rom. 1. 7. gal. 3. 11. heb. 10. 38.
‖ *Or, how much more.*
‖ *Or, hoe, he.*
† *Heb. bloods.*
* Ier. 22. 13.
‖ *Or, gaineth an euill gaine.*
† *Heb. palme of the hand.*
‖ *Or, piece, or, fastening.*
‖ *Or, witnesse against it.*
* Ezech. 24. 9. nahum. 3. 1.
† *Heb. bloods.*
‖ *Or, in vaine.*
‖ *Or, by knowing the glory of the Lord.*
* Isai. 11. 9.
‖ *Or, more with shame then with glory.*
* Ier. 25. 2[...]
* Ier. 10. 8[...] 14. zec. 10. 2.
† *Heb. The facioner o[f] his facion.*
* Psal. 11.
† *Heb. be s[i]lent all the earth befo[re] him.*

CHAP. III.

1 Habakkuk in his prayer, trembleth at Gods
Maiestie. 17 The confidence of his faith.

A Prayer of Habakkuk the
prophet ‖ vpon Sigionoth.
2 O LORD, I haue
heard † thy speach, *and* was
afraide: O LORD, ‖ re-
uiue thy worke in the midst of the
yeeres, in the midst of the yeeres make
knowen; in wrath remember mercy.
3 God came from ‖ Teman, and the
holy on from mount Paran Selah.
His glory couered the heauens and the
earth was full of his praise.
4 And *his* brightnesse was as the
light: he *had* ‖ hornes *comming* out of his
hand, and there was the hiding of his
power:
5 Before him went the pestilence,
and ‖ burning coales went forth at his
feete.
6 He stood and measured the earth:
hee beheld and droue asunder the nations, and the euerlasting mountaines
were scattered, the perpetuall hilles did
bowe: his wayes *are* euerlasting.
7 I saw the tents of ‖ Cushan ‖ in
affliction: *and* the curtaines of the land
of Midian did tremble.

‖ *Or, according to variable songs or tunes called in hebrew, Shigianoth.*
† *Heb. thy report or th[y] hearing.*
‖ *Or, preserue aliue.*
‖ *Or, the South.*
‖ *Or, bright beames out of his side.*
‖ *Or, burning diseases.*
‖ *Or, Ethi[o]pia.*
‖ *Or, vnde[r] affliction o[r] vanitie.*

8 Was

8 Was the Lord displeased against the riuers? *was* thine anger against the riuers? *was* thy wrath against the Sea, that thou didst ride vpon thine horses, *and* ||thy charets of saluation?

9 Thy bow was made quite naked *according* to the oathes of the tribes, *euen thy* word. Selah. ||Thou didst cleaue the earth with riuers.

10 The mountaines sawe thee, *and* they trembled: the ouerflowing of the water passed by: the deepe vttered his voyce, *and* lift vp his hands on high.

11 The Sunne *and* Moone * stood still in *their* habitation: ||at the light of thine * arrowes they went, *and* at the shining of thy glittering speare.

12 Thou didst march through the land in indignation, thou didst thresh the heathen in anger.

13 Thou wentest forth for the saluation of thy people, *euen* for saluation with thine Anointed, thou woundedst the head out of the house of the wicked, †by discouering the foundation vnto the necke. Selah.

14 Thou didst strike through with his staues the head of his villages: they †came out as a whirle-winde to scatter me: their reioycing *was* as to deuoure the poore secretly.

15 Thou didst walke through the Sea with thine horses, *through* the ||heape of great waters.

16 When I heard, my belly trembled: my lips quiuered at the voice: rottennesse entred into my bones, and I trembled in my selfe, that I might rest in the day of trouble: when hee commeth vp vnto the people, he wil ||inuade them with his troupes.

17 ¶ Although the fig tree shall not blossome, neither *shall* fruite *bee* in the vines: the labour of the Oliue shall †faile, and the fields shal yeeld no meat, the flocke shall be cut off from the folde, and there *shalbe* no heard in the stalles:

18 Yet I will reioyce in the Lord: I will ioy in the God of my saluation.

19 The Lord God *is* my strength, and he will make my feet like *hindes feet*, and he will make me to walke vpon mine high places. To the chiefe singer on my †stringed instruments.

Margin notes (left):
|| *Or, thy charets were saluation.*
|| *Or, thou tidst cleaue the riuers of the earth.*
* Iosh. 10. 12.
|| *Or, thine arrowes swalced in the light, &c.*
* Iosh. 10. 1
Heb. making naked.

Margin notes (right):
† *Heb. were tempestuous.*
|| *Or, mud.*
|| *Or, cut them in pieces.*
† *Heb. lie.*
* 2. Sam. 22. 34. psal. 18. 34.
† *Heb. Neginoth.*

¶ ZEPHANIAH.

CHAP. I·

Gods seuere iudgement against Iudah for diuers sinnes.

He worde of the Lord which came vnto Zephaniah the son of Cushi, the son of Gedaliah, the sonne of Amariah, the sonne of Hizkiah, in the dayes of Iosiah, the sonne of Amon king of Iudah.

2 I †will vtterly consume all things from off †the land, saith the Lord.

3 I will consume man and beast: I will consume the foules of the heauen and the fishes of the sea, and the ||stumbling blocks with the wicked, and I will cut off man from off the land, saith the Lord.

4 I will also stretch out mine hand vpon Iudah, and vpon all the inhabitants of Ierusalem, and I will cut off the remnant of Baal from this place, *and* the name of the Chemarims with the priests:

5 And them that worship the hoste of heauen vpon the house tops, & them that worship, *and* that sweare ||by the Lord, *and* that sweare by Malcham:

6 And them that are turned backe from the Lord, & those that haue not sought ӯ Lord, nor enquired for him.

7 Hold thy peace at the presence of the Lord God: for the day of the Lord is at hand: for the Lord hath prepared a sacrifice: he hath †bid his ghests.

8 And it shall come to passe in the day of the Lords Sacrifice, that I will †punish the princes, and the kings children, and al such as are clothed with strange apparell.

9 In the same day also wil I punish all

Margin notes (left):
|| *Heb. by taking away I will make an end.*
* *Heb. the face of the land.*
|| *Or, Idoles.*

Margin notes (right):
|| *Or, to the Lord.*
† *Heb. sanctified or prepared.*
† *Heb. visite vpon.*

all those that leape on the threshold,
which fill their masters houses with
violence and deceit.
10 And it shall come to passe in that
day, saith the LORD, *that there shall be*
the noise of a cry from the fish gate, and
an howling from the second, and a
great crashing from the hils.
11 Howle yee inhabitants of Maktesh,
for all the merchant people are cut
downe: all they that beare siluer are
cut off.
12 And it shall come to passe at that
time, *that* I wil search Ierusalem with
candles, and punish the men that are
†setled on their lees, that say in their
heart, The LORD will not doe good,
neither will he doe euill.

† *Hebr. curded, or thickned.*

13 Therefore their goods shall become
a booty, and their houses a desolation:
they shall also build houses, but
*not inhabite *them*, and they shall plant
Vineyards, but not drinke the wine
thereof.

* Deu. 28. 36, 39. amos 5. 11.

14 The great day of the LORD *is*
neere, it is neere, and hasteth greatly,
euen the voice of the day of the LORD:
the mighty man shall cry there bitterly.
15 That day *is* a day of *wrath, a day
of trouble and distresse, a day of wastenesse
and desolation, a day of darknesse
and gloominesse, a day of cloudes and
thicke darkenesse;

* Iere. 30. 7. ioel 2. 11. amos 5. 18.

16 A day of the trumpet and alarme
against the fenced cities, and against the
high towres.
17 And I will bring distresse vpon
men, that they shall walke like blinde
men, because they haue sinned against
the LORD, and their blood shall bee
powred out as dust, and their flesh as
the doung.
18 *Neither their siluer nor their
golde shall be able to deliuer them in the
day of the LORDS wrath; but the
whole land shall bee *deuoured by the
fire of his iealousie: for hee shall make
euen a speedy riddance of all them that
dwell in the land.

* Prou. 11. 4. ezek. 7. 19.
* Zeph. 3. 8.

CHAP. II.

1 An exhortation to repentance. 4 The iudgement of the Philistines, 8 Of Moab and Ammon, 12 Of Ethiopia and Assyria.

GAther your selues together,
yea gather together,
O nation ||not desired.
2 Before the decree
bring foorth, *before* the day
passe as the chaffe, before the fierce anger
of the LORD come vpon you, before
the day of the LORDS anger
come vpon you.

|| *Or, not desirous.*

3 Seeke ye the LORD all ye meeke
of the earth, which haue wrought his
iudgement, seeke righteousnesse, seeke
meeknesse: it may be, ye shall be hid in
the day of the LORDS anger.
4 ¶ For Gaza shall bee forsaken,
and Ashkelon a desolation: they shall
driue out Ashdod at the noone day, and
Ekron shall be rooted vp.
5 Woe vnto the inhabitants of the
sea coast: the nation of the Cherethites,
the word of the LORD *is* against you:
O Canaan, the land of the Philistines,
I will euen destroy thee, that there shal
be no inhabitant.
6 And the sea coast shall bee dwellings
and cottages for shepheards, and
foldes for flockes.
7 And the coast shall bee for the
remnant of the house of Iudah, they
shall feede thereupon, in the houses of
Ashkelon shall they lie downe in the euening:
||for the LORD their God
shall visite them, and turne away their
captiuitie.

|| *Or, when, &c.*

8 ¶ I haue heard the reproach of
Moab, and the reuilings of the children
of Ammon, whereby they haue reproched
my people, and magnified *themselues*
against their border.
9 Therefore, as I liue, saith the
LORD of hostes the God of Israel,
surely Moab shalbe as Sodom, and the
children of Ammon as Gomorrah,
euen the breeding of netles, and salt pits,
and a perpetuall desolation, the residue
of my people shall spoile them, and
the remnant of my people shall possesse
them.
10 This shall they haue for their
pride, because they *haue* reproched and
magnified *themselues* against the people
of the LORD of hostes.
11 The LORD *will be* terrible vnto
them: for he will †famish all the gods of
the earth, and men shall worship him,
euery one from his place, *euen* all the
Iles of the heathen.

† *Heb. make leane.*

12 ¶ Ye Ethiopians also, ye shalbe
slaine by my sword.
13 And he wil stretch out his hand
against the North, and destroy Assyria,
and wil make Nineueh a desolation,
and dry like a wildernes.
14 And flocks shall lie downe in the
midst

*r, Pellican
Isai 34. 11,
c.

*r, knops,
chapters.

*r, when
hath vn-
uered.

Isai 47. 8.

*r, glut-
sous. Heb.
w.

*r, instru-
on.

Ezek. 22.
mic. 3.

Ier. 23. 11.
se. 9, 7.

Ezek. 22.

Heb. mor-
ng by mor-
ng.

*r, corners.

midst of her, all the beasts of the nations : both the || Cormorant, and the Bitterne, shall *lodge in the || vpper lintels of it : *their* voice shal sing in the windowes, desolation *shall be* in the thresholds : ||for he shall vncouer the Cedar worke.

15 This is the reioycing citie that dwelt carelessely, that said in her heart, *I *am*, and there is none beside me: how is shee become a desolation, a place for beasts to lie downe in ! euery one that passeth by her, shall hisse *and* wagge his hand.

CHAP. III.

1 A sharpe reproofe of Ierusalem for diuers sinnes. 8 An exhortation to wait for the restauration of Israel : 14 and to reioyce for their saluation by God.

WOe to her that is ||filthie and polluted, to the oppressing citie.

2 She obeyed not the voice: she receiued not||correction : she trusted not in the Lord : she drew not neere to her God.

3 Her princes within her are roaring *lyons ; her Iudges *are* euening wolues, they gnaw not the bones till the morrow.

4 Her *prophets are light *and* treacherous persons : her priests haue polluted the Sanctuarie, they haue done *violence to the Law.

5 The iust Lord *is* in the middest thereof : he will not doe iniquitie : †euery morning doeth hee bring his iudgement to light, he faileth not : but the vniust knoweth no shame.

6 I haue cut off the nations : their || towres are desolate, I made their streetes waste, that none passeth by : their cities are destroied, so that there is no man, that there is none inhabitant.

7 I said, Surely thou wilt feare mee : thou wilt receiue instruction : so their dwelling should not bee cut off, howsoeuer I punished them : but they rose early, & corrupted all their doings.

8 ¶ Therefore waite ye vpon mee, sayth the Lord, vntill the day that I rise vp to the pray : for my determination *is* to gather the nations, that I may assemble the kingdomes to powre vpon them mine indignation, *euen* all my fierce anger : for all the earth shalbe

deuoured with the fire of my *iealousie.

9 For then will I turne to the people a pure †language, that they may all call vpon the Name of the Lord, to serue him with one †consent.

10 From beyond the riuers of Ethiopia, my suppliants, *euen* the daughter of my dispersed shal bring mine offring.

11 In that day shalt thou not be ashamed for all thy doings, wherein thou hast transgressed against me : for then I will take away out of the midst of thee them that reioyce in thy pride, and thou shalt no more be haughty †because of mine holy mountaine.

12 I will also leaue in the middest of thee an afflicted and poore people : and they shall trust in the Name of the Lord.

13 The remnant of Israel shall not doe iniquitie, nor speake lies : neither shall a deceitful tongue be found in their mouth : for they shall feede, and lie downe, and none shall make *them* afraid.

14 ¶ Sing, O *daughter of Zion : shout, O Israel : be glad and reioyce with all the heart, O daughter of Ierusalem.

15 The Lord hath taken away thy iudgements, he hath cast out thine enemy : the King of Israel, *euen* the Lord *is* in the middest of thee : thou shalt not see euill any more.

16 In that day it shall be said to Ierusalem, Feare thou not : *and* to Zion, Let not thine hands be ||slacke.

17 The Lord thy God in the midst of thee *is* mightie : hee will saue, he will reioyce ouer thee with ioy : †hee will rest in his loue, hee will ioy ouer thee with singing.

18 I will gather them that are sorrowfull for the solemne assembly, who are of thee, *to whom* the †reproch of it *was* a burden.

19 Behold, at that time I will vndoe all that afflict thee, and I will saue her that *halteth, and gather her that was driuen out, and †I will get them praise and fame in euery land, †where they haue beene put to shame.

20 At that time will I bring you *againe* euen in the time that I gather you : for I will make you a name and a praise among all people of the earth, when I turne backe your captiuitie before your eyes, saith the Lord.

* Chap. 1. 18.

† Heb. lip.

† Heb. shoulder.

† Heb. in my holy.

* Isai 12. 6. and 54. 1.

|| Or, faint.

† Heb. he will be silent.

† Heb. the burden vpon it was reproch.

* Mic. 4. 7.
† Heb. I will set them for a praise.
† Hebr. of their shame.

¶HAG-

¶HAGGAI.

CHAP. I.

1 Haggai reproueth the people for neglecting the building of the house. 7 Hee inciteth them to the building. 12 He promiseth Gods assistance to them being forward.

I N the second yeere of Darius the king, in the sixtmoneth, in the first day of the moneth came the worde of the LORD †by Haggai the Prophet vnto Zerubbabel the sonne of Shealtiel, ||gouernour of Iudah, and to Iosuah the sonne of Iosedech the high priest, saying;

† *Heb. by the hand of Haggai.*

‖ *Or, captaine.*

2 Thus speaketh the LORD of hostes, saying; This people say, The time is not come, the time that the LORDS house should be built.

3 Then came the word of the LORD by Haggai the prophet, saying;

4 *Is it* time for you, O yee, to dwell in your sieled houses, and this house lie waste?

5 Nowe therefore thus saith the LORD of hostes, † Consider your wayes.

† *Heb. set your heart on your wayes.*
* Deut. 28. 38. mic. 6. 14, 15.

6 Yee haue *sowen much and bring in litle : ye eate, but ye haue not inough : yee drinke, but yee are not filled with drinke : yee cloth you, but there is none warme : and hee that earneth wages, earneth wages *to put it* into a bag †with holes

† *Heb. pierced through.*

7 ¶ Thus saith the LORD of hostes, Consider your wayes.

8 Goe vp to the mountaine, and bring wood, and build the house; and I will take pleasure in it, and I will be glorified, saith the LORD

9 Ye looked for much, and loe *it came* to litle : and when yee brought it home, I did ‖blow vpon it : Why, saith the LORD of hostes? because of mine house that is waste, and yee runne euery man vnto his owne house.

‖ *Or, blow it away.*

10 Therefore the heauen ouer you is stayed from dew, and the earth *is staied *from* her fruite.

* Deut. 23.

11 And I called for a drought vpon the land and vpon the mountaines, and vpon the corne, and vpon the new wine, and vpon the oyle, and vpon that which the ground bringeth forth, & vpon men, and vpon cattell, and vpon all the labour of the hands.

12 ¶ Then Zerubbabel the sonne of Shealtiel, and Iosuah the sonne of Iosedech the high priest, with all the remnant of the people obeyed the voyce of the LORD their God, and the words of Haggai the Prophet (as the LORD their God had sent him) and the people did feare before the LORD.

13 Then spake Haggai the LORDS messenger in the LORDS message vnto the people, saying; I *am* with you, saith the LORD.

14 And the LORD stirred vp the spirit of Zerubbabel the sonne of Shealtiel gouernour of Iudah, and the spirit of Iosuah the sonne of Iosedech the high priest, and the spirit of all the remnant of the people, and they came and did worke in the house of the LORD of hostes their God :

15 In the foure and twentieth day of the sixt moneth, in the second yeere of Darius the King.

CHAP. II.

1 He incourageth the people to the worke, by promise of greater glory to the second Temple, then was in the first. 10 In the type, of holy things and vncleane, hee sheweth their sinnes hindred the worke. 20 Gods promise to Zerubbabel.

I N the seuenth moneth, in the one and twentith *day* of the moneth, came the word of the LORD †by the Prophet Haggai, saying;

† *Heb. by hand of.*

2 Speake now to Zerubbabel the sonne of Shealtiel, gouernour of Iudah, and to Iosuah the sonne of Iosedech

dech the high priest, and to the residue of the people, saying,

3 Who is left among you that sawe this house in her first glory? and how do ye see it now? *Is it* not in your eyes in comparison of it, as nothing?

4 Yet now be strong, O Zerubbabel, saith the LORD, and bee strong, O Ioshua, sonne of Iosedech the high Priest, and be strong all ye people of the land, saith the LORD, and worke : (for I *am* with you, saith the LORD of hosts,)

5 *According to* the word that I couenanted with you, when ye came out of Egypt, so my Spirit remaineth among you, Feare ye not.

6 For thus saith the LORD of hosts, *Yet once, it *is* a litle while, and I will shake the heauens, and the earth, and the sea, and the drie land.

7 And I will shake all nations, and the desire of all nations shall come, and I will fill this house with glory, saith the LORD of hosts.

8 The siluer *is* mine, and the gold *is* mine, saith the LORD of hosts.

9 The glory of this latter house shal be greater then of the former, saith the LORD of hostes : and in this place will I giue peace, saith the LORD of hostes.

10 ¶ In the foure and twentieth *day* of the ninth *moneth*, in the second yeere of Darius, came y word of the LORD by Haggai the Prophet, saying,

11 Thus saith the LORD of hosts, Aske now the priests *concerning* the law, saying,

12 If one beare holy flesh in the skirt of his garment, and with his skirt doe touch bread or pottage, or wine, or oile, or any meate, shall it be holy? and the priests answered and said, No.

13 Then said Haggai, If one that is vncleane by a dead body, touch any of these, shal it be vncleane? and the priests answered and said, It shalbe vncleane.

14 Then answered Haggai, and said,

So *is* this people, and so *is* this nation before me, saith the LORD, and so *is* euery worke of their hands, and that which they offer there, is vncleane.

15 And now I pray you consider from this day and vpward, from before a stone was laid vpon a stone in the Temple of the LORD.

16 Since those *dayes* were, when one came to an heape of twentie *measures*, there were but ten : when one came to the presse-fatte for to draw out fiftie *vessels* out of the presse, there were but twentie.

17 I smote you *with blasting, and with mildew, and with haile in all the labours of your hands : yet yee *turned* not to me, saith the LORD.

18 Consider now from this day, and vpward from the foure and twentieth day of the ninth *moneth, euen* from the day that the foundatiō of the LORDS Temple was laid, consider it.

19 *Is* the seed yet in the barne? yea, as yet the vine and the fig tree, & the pomegranate, and the Oliue tree hath not brought foorth : from this day will I blesse *you*.

20 ¶ And againe the worde of the LORD came vnto Haggai in the foure and twentieth *day* of the moneth, saying,

21 Speake to Zerubbabel gouernor of Iudah, saying, I wil shake the heauens and the earth.

22 And I will ouerthrow the throne of kingdomes, and I will destroy the strength of the kingdomes of the heathen, and I will ouerthrow the charets, and those that ride in them, and the horses and their riders shall come downe, euery one by the sword of his brother.

23 In that day, saith the LORD of hosts, will I take thee, O Zerubbabel, my seruant, the son of Shealtiel, saith the LORD, and will make thee as a signet : for I haue chosen thee, saith the LORD of hosts.

eb. 12.

* Amos 4. 9

¶ Z E-

¶ ZECHARIAH.

CHAP. I.

1 Zechariah exhorteth to repentance. 7 The vision of the horses. 12 At the prayer of the Angel, comfortable promises are made to Ierusalem. 18 The vision of the foure hornes, and the foure Carpenters.

N the eight moneth, in the seconde yeere of Darius, came the word of the LORD vnto Zechariah, the sonne of Barachiah, the sonne of Iddo the Prophet, saying,

2 The LORD hath bene †sore displeased with your fathers.

† Hebr. with displeasure.

3 Therefore say thou vnto them, Thus saith the LORD of hostes; *Turne ye vnto me, saith the LORD of hostes, and I will turne vnto you, saith the LORD of hostes.

* Mal. 3. 7.

4 *Be ye not as your fathers, vnto whom the former Prophets haue cried, saying, Thus saith the LORD of hostes, Turne ye now from your euill wayes, and from your euil doings: but they did not heare, nor hearken vnto me, saith the LORD.

* Isa. 31. 6. iere. 3. 12. and 18. 11. eze. 18. 30. hose. 14. 1.

5 Your fathers, where *are* they? and the Prophets, doe they liue for euer?

6 But my words and my statutes, which I commanded my seruants the Prophets, did they not ‖take holde of your fathers? and they returned and saide; *Like as the LORD of hostes thought to doe vnto vs, according to our wayes, and according to our doings, so hath he dealt with vs.

‖ Or, ouertake.

* Lam. 1. 18.

7 ¶ Vpon the foure and twentieth day of the eleuenth moneth, which is the moneth Sebat, in the second yere of Darius, came the word of the LORD vnto Zechariah, the sonne of Barachiah, the sonne of Iddo the Prophet, saying;

8 I saw by night, and behold a man riding vpon a red horse, and he stood among the mirtle trees that *were* in the bottome, and behinde him *were there* red horses, ‖speckled and white.

‖ Or, bay.

9 Then said I, O my Lord, what *are* these? And the Angel that talked with me, said vnto me, I wil shew thee what these be.

10 And the man that stood among the myrtle trees answered, and said, These *are* they, whom the LORD hath sent to walke to and fro through the earth.

11 And they answered the Angel of the LORD that stood among the mirtle trees, and said, Wee haue walked to and fro through the earth: and behold, all the earth sitteth still, and is at rest.

12 ¶ Then the Angel of the LORD answered, and said, O LORD of hosts, how long wilt thou not haue mercie on Ierusalem, and on the cities of Iudah, against which thou hast had indignation these threescore and ten yeeres?

13 And the LORD answered the Angel that talked with me, with good words, *and* comfortable words.

14 So the Angel that communed with me, said vnto me; Cry thou, saying; Thus saith the LORD of hosts, I am *iealous for Ierusalem, and for Zion, with a great iealousie.

* Chap. 8

15 And I am very sore displeased with the heathen that are at ease: for I was but a little displeased, and they helped forward the affliction.

16 Therefore thus saith the LORD, I am returned to Ierusalem with mercies: my house shall bee built in it, saith the LORD of hostes, and a line shalbe stretched forth vpon Ierusalem.

17 Cry yet, saying, Thus saith the LORD of hostes, My cities through †prosperitie shall yet be spread abroad, and the LORD shall yet comfort Zion, and shall yet choose Ierusalem.

† Hebr. g

18 ¶ Then lift I vp mine eyes, and saw, and behold foure hornes.

19 And I said vnto the Angel that talked with me; What *be* these? and he answered mee, These *are* the hornes which

which haue scattered Iudah, Israel, and Ierusalem.

20 And the LORD shewed mee foure carpenters.

21 Then said I, What come these to doe? And hee spake, saying, These *are* the hornes which haue scattered Iudah, so that no man did lift vp his head: but these are come to fray them, to cast out the hornes of the Gentiles, which lift vp their horne ouer the land of Iudah to scatter it.

CHAP. II.

1 God in the care of Ierusalem sendeth to measure it. 6 The redemption of Zion. 10 The promise of Gods presence.

 Lift vp mine eyes againe, and looked, and behold, a man with a measuring line in his hand.

2 Then said I, Whither goest thou? And hee said vnto me, To measure Ierusalem, to see what *is* the breadth thereof, and what *is* the length thereof.

3 And behold, the Angel that talked with me, went foorth, and another Angel went out to meete him:

4 And said vnto him, Run, speake to this young man, saying; Ierusalem shall be inhabited as townes without walles, for the multitude of men and cattell therein.

5 For I, saith the LORD, will be vnto her a wall of fire round about, and will be the glory in the midst of her.

6 ¶ Ho, ho, *come foorth*, and flee from the land of the North, saith the LORD: for I haue spread you abroad as the foure windes of the heauen, sayth the LORD.

7 Deliuer thy selfe, O Zion, that dwellest *with* the daughter of Babylon.

8 For thus sayth the LORD of hostes, After the glory hath he sent me vnto the nations which spoiled you: for he that * toucheth you, toucheth the apple of his eye.

9 For behold, I will shake mine hand vpon them, and they shall bee a spoile to their seruants: and yee shall know that the LORD of hostes hath sent me.

10 ¶ * Sing and reioyce, O daughter of Zion: for loe, I come, and I * will dwell in the middest of thee, sayth the LORD.

11 And many nations shalbe ioyned

to the LORD in that day, and shall be my people: and I will dwel in the middest of thee, and thou shalt know that the LORD of hostes hath sent me vnto thee.

12 And the LORD shall inherite Iudah his portion in the holy land, and shall choose Ierusalem againe.

13 Be silent, O all flesh, before the LORD: for he is raised vp out of † his holy habitation.

CHAP. III.

1 Vnder the type of Ioshua, the restauration of the Church. 18 Christ the Branch is promised.

Nd he shewed me Ioshua the high Priest, standing before the Angel of the LORD, and ‖ Satan standing at his right hand † to resist him.

2 And the LORD said vnto Satan; * The LORD rebuke thee, O Satan, euen the LORD that hath chosen Ierusalem rebuke thee. *Is* not this a brand pluckt out of the fire?

3 Now Ioshua was clothed with filthie garments, and stood before the Angel.

4 And he answered, and spake vnto those that stood before him, saying, Take away the filthie garments from him. And vnto him he said, Behold, I haue caused thine iniquity to passe from thee, and I wil clothe thee with change of raiment.

5 And I said, Let them set a faire mitre vpon his head. So they set a faire mitre vpon his head, and clothed him with garments, and the Angel of the LORD stood by.

6 And the Angel of the LORD protested vnto Ioshua, saying;

7 Thus sayth the LORD of hosts, If thou wilt walke in my wayes, and if thou wilt keepe my ‖ charge, then thou shalt also iudge my House, and shalt also keepe my Courts, and I will giue thee † places to walke among these that stand by.

8 Heare now, O Ioshua the high Priest, thou and thy fellowes that sit before thee: for they *are* † men wondred at: for behold, I will bring foorth my seruant the * BRANCH.

9 For behold the stone that I haue layd before Ioshua: vpon one stone *shall be* seuen eyes, behold, I will engraue the grauing thereof, saith the LORD of

---

Marginal notes (left column):

Deut. 32.
9. psal.
7. 8.

Isai 12. 6.
and 54. 1.
Leuit. 26.
2. ezek.
7. 27. 2.
or. 6. 18.

Marginal notes (right column):

† Heb. the habitation of his holines.

‖ That is, an aduersarie.

† Heb. to be his aduersarie.

* Iude 9.

‖ Or, ordinance.

† Heb. walks.

† Heb. men of wonder.

* Isai 11. 1.
iere. 23. 5.
and 33. 15.
chap. 6. 12.
luke 1. 78.

of hostes, and I will remoue the iniquitie of that land in one day.

10 In that day, saith the LORD of hostes, shal ye call euery man his neighbour vnder the vine and vnder the figge tree.

CHAP. IIII.

1 By the golden Candlesticke is foreshewed the good successe of Zerubbabels foundation. 11 By the two Oliue trees the two anointed ones.

Nd the Angell that talked with me, came againe and waked me, as a man that is wakened out of his sleepe:

Heb. with her bowle.

Or, seuen seuerall pipes to the lampes &c.

2 And said vnto mee, What seest thou? and I said, I haue looked, and behold a candlesticke all of gold, †with a bowle vpon the top of it, and his seuen lampes thereon, and || seuen pipes to the seuen lampes, which were vpon the top thereof.

3 And two Oliue trees by it, one vpon the right side of the bowle, and the other vpon the left side thereof.

4 So I answered and spake to the Angell that talked with mee, saying: What are these, my Lord?

5 Then the Angel that talked with me, answered and said vnto me; Knowest thou not what these be? and I said; No, my Lord.

6 Then hee answered and spake vnto mee, saying; This is the word of the LORD vnto Zerubbabel, saying; Not by ||might, nor by power, but by my spirit, saith the LORD of hostes.

Or, armie.

7 Who art thou, O great mountaine? before Zerubbabel thou shalt become a plaine, and he shall bring forth the head stone thereof with shoutings, crying; Grace, grace vnto it.

8 Moreouer the word of the LORD came vnto me, saying;

9 The hands of Zerubbabel haue layed the foundation of this house: his hands shall also finish it, and thou shalt know that the LORD of hostes hath sent me vnto you.

10 For who hath despised the day of small things? || for they shall reioyce and shall see the †plummet in the hand of Zerubbabel with those seuen: * they are the eyes of the LORD, which run to and fro through the whole earth.

Or, sith the seueneyes of the Lord shall reioyce.
†*Heb. stone of tinne.*
Chap. 3. 9.

11 ¶ Then answered I, and said vn-

to him; What are these two oliue trees vpon the right side of the candlesticke, and vpon the left side thereof?

12 And I answered againe and said vnto him, What be these two oliue branches, which †through the two golden pipes || emptie †the golden oyle out of themselues?

†*Heb. by hand.*
Or, emptie out of themselues oyl into the gold.
†*Heb. the gold.*

13 And hee answered mee and said; Knowest thou not what these be? and I said, No, my Lord.

14 Then said he; These are the two †annointed ones, that stand by the Lord of the whole earth.

†*Heb.sons of oyle.*

CHAP. V.

1 By the flying rowle, is shewed the curse of Theeues and Swearers. 5 By a woman pressed in an Ephah, the finall damnation of Babylon.

Hen I turned, and lift vp mine eyes, and looked, and behold, a flying roule.

2 And hee said vnto mee, What seest thou? and I answered, I see a flying roule; the length thereof is twentie cubites, and the breadth thereof tenne cubites.

3 Then said hee vnto mee; This is the curse, that goeth forth ouer the face of the whole earth : for ||euery one that stealeth shall be cut off as on this side, according to it; and euery one that sweareth shall be cut off as on that side, according to it.

Or, euery one of this people that stealeth, is held himselfe guiltlesse as it doth.

4 I will bring it forth, saith the LORD of hostes, and it shall enter into the house of the theefe, and into the house of him that sweareth falsely by my name: and it shall remaine in the midst of his house, and shall consume it, with the timber thereof, and the stones thereof.

5 ¶ Then the Angell that talked with me, went forth and said vnto me, Lift vp now thine eyes, and see what is this that goeth forth.

6 And I said, What is it? and hee said, This is an Ephah that goeth forth. Hee said moreouer, This is their resemblance through all the earth.

7 And behold, there was lift vp a ||talent of lead: and this is a woman that sitteth in the midst of the Ephah.

Or, weighty piece.

8 And he said, This is wickednesse, and he cast it into the midst of the Ephah, and he cast the weight of lead vpon the mouth thereof.

9 Then

9 Then lift I vp mine eyes, and looked, & behold, there came out two women, and the winde *was* in their wings (for they had wings like the wings of a storke) and they lift vp the Ephah betweene the earth and the heauen.

10 Then saide I to the Angel that talked with me, Whither do these beare the Ephah?

11 And he said vnto mee, To build it an house in the land of Shinar, and it shall be established, and set there vpon her owne base.

CHAP. VI.

1 The vision of the foure charets. 9 By the Crownes of Ioshua, is shewed the Temple and Kingdome of Christ the Branch.

Nd I turned, and lift vp mine eyes, and looked, and beholde, there came foure charets out from betweene two mountaines, and the mountaines *were* mountaines of brasse.

2 In the first charet *were* red horses, and in the second charet, blacke horses.

3 And in the third charet white horses, and in the fourth charet grisled *and* ||bay horses.

|| *Or, strong.*

4 Then I answered, and said vnto the Angel that talked with mee, What *are* these, my LORD?

5 And the Angel answered and said vnto me, These *are* the foure ||spirits of the heauens, which go forth from standing before the Lord of all the earth.

|| *Or, winds.*

6 The blacke horses which are therin, goe forth into the North countrey, and the white goe forth after them, and the grisled goe forth toward the South countrey.

7 And the baye went foorth, and sought to goe, that they might walke to and fro through the earth: and he said, Get ye hence, walke to and fro through the earth. So they walked to and fro through the earth.

8 Then cried he vpon me, and spake vnto me, saying, Behold, these that goe toward the North countrey, haue quieted my spirit, in the North countrey.

9 ¶ And the word of the LORD came vnto me, saying,

10 Take of *them of* the captiuitie, *euen* of Heldai, of Tobijah, and of Iedaiah, which are come from Babylon, and come thou the same day, and go into the house of Iosiah the son of Zephaniah.

11 Then take siluer, and golde, and make crownes, and set *them* vpon the head of Ioshua the sonne of Iosedech, the high priest.

12 And speake vnto him, saying, Thus speaketh the LORD of hostes, saying, Behold, the man whose name *is* the *BRANCH, and he shall ||growe vp out of his place, and he shal build the Temple of the LORD:

*Chap. 3. 4
|| Or, branch
vp from vn-
der him.

13 Euen he shall build the temple of the LORD, and he shal beare the glory, and shall sit and rule vpon his throne, and he shall be a priest vpon his throne, and the counsell of peace shall bee betweene them both.

14 And the crownes shall bee to Helem, and to Tobijah, and to Iedaiah, and to Hen the sonne of Zephaniah for a memoriall, in the Temple of the LORD.

15 And they that are farre off, shall come and build in the Temple of the LORD, and ye shall knowe that the LORD of hosts hath sent me vnto you. And *this* shall come to passe, if ye will diligently obey the voyce of the LORD your God.

CHAP. VII.

1 The captiues enquire of fasting. 4 Zechariah reproueth their fasting. 8 Sinne the cause of their captiuitie.

Nd it came to passe in the fourth yeere of King Darius, that the word of the LORD came vnto Zechariah in the fourth *day* of the ninth moneth, *euen* in Chisleu.

2 When they had sent vnto the house of God, Sherezer and Regem-melech, and their men † to pray before the LORD,

† Heb. to in-
treat the
face of the
Lord.

3 *And* to speake vnto the priestes, which *were* in the house of the LORD of hosts, and to the prophets, saying, Should I weepe in the fift moneth, separating my selfe, as I haue done these so many yeeres?

4 ¶ Then came the word of the LORD of hosts vnto me, saying,

5 Speake vnto all the people of the land, and to the priests, saying, When ye *fasted and mourned in the fift and seuenth *moneth*, euen those seuenty yeeres; did ye at all fast vnto me, *euen* to me?

*Isa. 58. 5.

6 And when ye did eat, and when ye did drinke, ||did not ye eat *for your selues*, and drinke *for your selues*?

|| Or, be not
ye they that
&c.

7 ||Should

*Or, are not these the wordes.
†Hebr. by the hand of, &c.

†Heb. iudge iudgement of trueth.

*Exod. 22. 21. isa. 1. 23. iere. 5. 28.

†Hebr. they gaue a back-slidingshoulder.
†Hebr. made heauie.

†Hebr. by the hand of &c.

*Pro. 1. 28. isa. 1. 15. iere. 11. 11. and 14. 2.

†Heb. land of desire.

*Cha. 1. 14.

7 ‖Should yee not heare the wordes, which the LORD hath cried †by the former Prophets, when Ierusalem was inhabited, and in prosperitie, and the cities thereof round about her, when men inhabited the South of the plaine?

8 ¶ And the word of the LORD came vnto Zechariah, saying;

9 Thus speaketh the LORD of hostes, saying, † Execute true iudgement, and shew mercie and compassions euery man to his brother.

10 And oppresse not the *widow, nor the fatherlesse, the stranger, nor the poore, and let none of you imagine euill against his brother in your heart.

11 But they refused to hearken, and †pulled away the shoulder, and †stopped their eares, that they should not heare.

12 Yea, they made their hearts as an adamant stone, lest they should heare the Law, and the wordes which the LORD of hostes hath sent in his spirit †by the former Prophets: therefore came a great wrath from the LORD of hostes.

13 Therefore it is come to passe, that as he cried, and they would not heare, so *they cried, and I would not heare, saith the LORD of hostes.

14 But I scattered them with a whirlewinde among all the nations, whom they knew not: thus the land was desolate after them, that no man passed through, nor returned: for they layed the †pleasant land desolate.

CHAP. VIII.

1 The restauration of Ierusalem. 9 They are incouraged to the building by Gods fauour to them. 16 Good workes are required of them. 18 Ioy and inlargement are promised.

Gaine the word of the LORD of hostes came to me, saying;

2 Thus sayeth the LORD of hostes, I was iealous for Zion, with great iealousie; and I was *iealous for her with great furie.

3 Thus saith the LORD, I am returned vnto Zion, and will dwell in the midst of Ierusalem, and Ierusalem shall be called a Citie of trueth, and the Mountaine of the LORD of hostes, the holy Mountaine.

4 Thus saith the LORD of hostes;

†Hebr. for multitude of dayes.

‖Or, hard or difficult.

†Hebr. the countrey of the going downe of the Sunne.

‖Or, the hire of man became nothing. &c. Haggai. 1. 6.

†Hebr. of peace.

There shall yet old men, and old women, dwell in the streets of Ierusalem, and euery man with his staffe in his hand †for very age.

5 And the streets of the citie shall be full of boyes and girles playing in the streets thereof.

6 Thus saith the LORD of hosts, If it bee maruelous in the eyes of the remnant of this people in these dayes, should it also bee ‖maruelous in my eyes, saith the LORD of hostes?

7 Thus saith the LORD of hosts, Beholde, I will saue my people from the East countrey, and from the †West countrey.

8 And I will bring them, and they shall dwell in the midst of Ierusalem, and they shalbe my people, and I will bee their God, in Trueth and in Righteousnesse.

9 ¶ Thus saith the LORD of hostes, Let your handes be strong, ye that heare in these dayes, these wordes by the mouth of the Prophets, which were in the day that the foundation of the house of the LORD of hosts was laied, that the Temple might be built.

10 For before these daies there was no ‖*hire for man, nor any hire for beast, neither was there any peace to him that went out, or came in, because of the affliction: for I set all men, euery one against his neighbour.

11 But now I will not bee vnto the residue of this people, as in the former daies, saith the LORD of hostes.

12 For the seed shalbe †prosperous: the Vine shall giue her fruit, and the ground shall giue her increase, and the heauens shall giue their dew, and I will cause the remnant of this people to possesse all these things.

13 And it shall come to passe, that as yee were a curse among the heathen, O house of Iudah, and house of Israel; so will I saue you, and ye shalbe a blessing: feare not, but let your handes bee strong.

14 For thus saith the LORD of hostes, As I thought to punish you, when your fathers prouoked mee to wrath, saith the LORD of hostes, and I repented not:

15 So againe haue I thought in these dayes to doe well vnto Ierusalem, and to the house of Iudah: feare ye not.

16 ¶ These are the things that yee shall

* Ephes. 4. 25.
† Heb. iudge trueth, and the iudgement of peace.

† Hebr. solemne, or set times.

* Isa. 2. 2. mic. 4. 12.
‖ Or, continually. Hebr. going.
† Hebr. to intreat the face.

* Isa. 2. 2. mic. 4. 12.

* Ezek. 28. 3. &c.

shall doe; * Speake yee euery man the truth to his neighbor: † execute the iudgment of trueth and peace in your gates.

17 And let none of you imagine euill in your hearts against his neighbour, and loue no false oath: for all these are things that I hate, saith the LORD.

18 ¶ And the word of the LORD of hostes came vnto me, saying,

19 Thus saith the LORD of hosts; The fast of the fourth moneth, and the fast of the fift, and the fast of the seuenth, and the fast of the tenth shall be to the house of Iudah ioy and gladnesse, and cheerefull † feasts: therefore loue the trueth and peace.

20 Thus saith the LORD of hosts, It shall yet come to passe, that there shall come people, and the inhabitants of many cities.

21 And the inhabitants of one citie shall goe to another, saying, * Let vs goe ‖speedily to † pray before the LORD, and to seeke the LORD of hostes: I will goe also.

22 Yea many people and strong nations shall come to seeke the LORD of hostes in Ierusalem, and to pray before the LORD.

23 Thus saith the LORD of hosts, In those daies it shall come to passe, that ten men shall take holde out of all languages of the nations, euen shall take hold of the skirt of him that is a Iew, saying, Wee will goe with you: for we haue heard that God is with you.

CHAP. IX.

1 God defendeth his Church. 9 Zion is exhorted to reioyce for the comming of Christ, and his peaceable Kingdome. 12 Gods promises of Victory and Defence.

He burden of the word of the LORD in the land of Hadrach, and Damascus shall bee the rest thereof: when the eyes of man, as of all the tribes of Israel shalbe toward the LORD.

2 And Hamath also shall border thereby; Tyrus and Zidon, though it be very *wise.

3 And Tyrus did builde her selfe a strong hold, and heaped vp siluer as the dust, and fine golde as the myre of the streets.

4 Behold, the Lord wil cast her out, and he will smite her power in the sea,

and she shalbe deuoured with fire.

5 Ashkelon shall see it, and feare, Gaza also shall see it and be very sorrowfull, and Ekron: for her expectation shalbe ashamed, and the king shall perish from Gaza, and Ashkelon shal not be inhabited.

6 And a bastard shall dwell in Ashdod, and I will cut off the pride of the Philistines.

7 And I wil take away his †blood out of his mouth, and his abominations from betweene his teeth: but he that remaineth, euen hee shalbe for our God, and he shall be as a gouernour in Iudah; and Ekron as a Iebusite.

8 And I will encampe about mine house because of the armie, because of him that passeth by, and because of him that returneth: and no oppressour shall passe through them any more: for now haue I seene with mine eyes.

9 ¶ *Reioyce greatly, O daughter of Zion; shout O daughter of Ierusalem: beholde, thy King commeth vnto thee: hee is iust, and ‖hauing saluation, lowly, and riding vpon an asse, and vpon a colt, the foale of an asse.

10 And I wil cut off the charet from Ephraim, and the horse from Ierusalem: and the battell bow shalbe cut off, and he shall speake peace vnto the heathen, and his dominion shalbe *from sea euen to sea, and from the Riuer, euen to the ends of the earth.

11 As for thee also, ‖by the blood of thy Couenant, I haue sent foorth thy *prisoners out of the pit, wherein is no water.

12 ¶ Turne ye to the strong hold, ye prisoners of hope, euen to day doe I declare that I will render double vnto thee

13 When I haue bent Iudah for me, filled the bow with Ephraim, and raised vp thy sonnes O Zion, against thy sonnes, O Greece, and made thee as the sword of a mightie man.

14 And the LORD shalbe seene ouer them, and his arrow shall goe forth as the lightning: and the Lord GOD shall blow the trumpet, and shall goe with whirlewinds of the South.

15 The LORD of hostes shall defend them, and they shall deuoure, and ‖subdue with sling stones, and they shal drinke and make a noise, as through wine, and they ‖ shall bee filled like bowles, and as the corners of the Altar.

16 And

† Hebr. bloods.

* Isa. 62. 11. matth. 21. 5. ioh. 12. 15.
‖ Or, sauing himselfe.

* Psal. 72. 8.

‖ Or, whose Couenant is by blood.
* Isa. 61. 1.

‖ Or, subdue the stones of the sling.
‖ Or, shall fill both the bowles, &c.

16 And the LORD their God shall saue them in that day as the flock of his people, for *they shall be as* the stones of a crowne lifted vp as an ensigne vpon his land.

17 For how great *is* his goodnesse, and how great *is* his beautie? corne shal make the yong men ||cheerefull , and new wine the maides.

CHAP. X.

1 God is to be sought vnto, and not idoles. 5 As he visited his flocke for sinne, so he will saue and restore them.

Ske yee of the LORD raine in the time of the latter raine, *so* the LORD shal make ||bright clouds, and giue them showres of raine, to euery one grasse in the field.

2 For the **†idoles haue spoken vanitie, and the diuiners haue seene a lye, and haue told false dreames; they comfort in vaine : therefore they went their way as a flocke, they ||were troubled because there *was* no shepheard.

3 Mine anger was kindled against the shepheards, and I †punished the goats : for the LORD of hostes hath visited his flocke the house of Iudah, and hath made them as his goodly horse in the battell.

4 Out of him *came forth* the corner, out of him the naile, out of him the battell bow, out of him euery oppressour together.

5 ¶ And they shall bee as mightie men which tread downe *their enemies* in the myre of the streets in the battell, and they shall fight because the LORD *is* with them, and the ||riders on horses shall be confounded.

6 And I will strengthen the house of Iudah, and I will saue the house of Ioseph, and I will bring them againe to place them, for I haue mercie vpon them : and they shall be as though I had not cast them off : for I *am* the LORD their God, & will heare them.

7 And *they of* Ephraim shall be like a mightie man, and their heart shall reioyce as through wine : yea, their children shall see *it*, and be glad, their heart shall reioyce in the LORD.

8 I will hisse for them and gather them, for I haue redeemed them : and they shall increase as they haue increased.

9 And I will sow them among the people, and they shall remember me in farre countries, and they shall liue with their children, and turne againe.

10 I will bring them againe also out of the land of Egypt, and gather them out of Assyria, and I will bring them into the land of Gilead and Lebanon, and *place* shall not be found for them.

11 And he shall passe through the sea with affliction, & shall smite the waues in the Sea, and all the deepes of the riuer shall dry vp : and the pride of Assyria shall be brought downe, and the scepter of Egypt shall depart away.

12 And I will strengthen them in the LORD, and they shall walke vp and downe in his name, saith the LORD.

CHAP. XI.

1 The destruction of Ierusalem. 3 The elect being cared for, the rest are reiected. 10 The staues of beauty and bands broken by the reiection of Christ. 15 The Type and curse of a foolish Shepheard.

Pen thy doores, O Lebanon, that the fire may deuoure thy cedars.

2 Howle firre tree, for the cedar is fallen; because all the ||mighty are spoiled; howle O yee okes of Bashan, for the ||forrest of the vintage is come downe.

3 ¶ *There is* a voyce of the howling of the shepheards; for their glory is spoiled : a voyce of the roaring of young lyons; for the pride of Iordan is spoiled.

4 Thus saith the LORD my God; Feede the flocke of the slaughter;

5 Whose possessours slay them, and hold themselues not guiltie : and they that sell thē say, Blessed *be* the LORD; for I am rich : and their owne shepheards pitie them not.

6 For I will no more pitie the inhabitants of the land, saith the LORD : but loe, I will †deliuer the men euery one into his neighbours hand, and into the hand of his King, and they shall smite the land, and out of their hand I will not deliuer *them*.

7 And I will feede the flocke of slaughter, *euen* you, O ||poore of the flock . and I tooke vnto me two staues; the one I called Beautie, and the other I called || Bandes , and I fed the flocke.

8 Three

Margin notes (left column):

‖ Or, *grow, or speake.*

‖ Or, *lightnings.*

* Ier. 10. 8. abac. 2. 18.
† Heb. *teraphims.*

‖ Or, *answered that &c.*

† Heb. *visited vpon.*

‖ Or, *they shall make the riders on horses ashamed.*

Margin notes (right column):

‖ Or, *gallants.*
‖ Or, *the defenced for rest.*

† Heb. *made to be found*

‖ Or, *verily the poore*

‖ Or, *binder*

† *Hebr. was straitened for them.*

8 Three shepheards also I cut off in one moneth, and my soule †loathed them, and their soule also abhorred mee.

* Ier. 15. 2.

9 Then said I, I *will not feede you: that that dieth, let it die: and that that is to be cut off, let it be cut off, and let the rest eate, euery one the flesh of †another.

† *Hebr. of his fellow or neighbour.*

10 ¶ And I tooke my staffe, *euen* Beautie, and cut it asunder, that I might breake my couenant which I had made with all the people.

11 And it was broken in that day: and so ‖the poore of the flocke that waited vpon me, knew that it *was* the word of the Lord.

‖ *Or, the poore of the flocke, &c. certainly knewe.*
† *Hebr. if it be good in your eyes.*

12 And I said vnto them, †If yee thinke good, giue *me* my price: and if not, forbeare: so they *weighed for my price thirtie *pieces* of siluer.

* Matth. 26. 15.

13 And the Lord said vnto mee, Cast it vnto the *potter: a goodly price, that I was prised at of them. And I tooke the thirtie *pieces* of siluer, and cast them to the potter in the house of the Lord.

* Matth. 27. 9.

14 Then I cut asunder mine other staffe, *euen* ‖Bands, that I might breake the brotherhood betweene Iudah and Israel.

‖ *Or, binders.*

15 ¶ And the Lord said vnto me, Take vnto thee yet the instruments of a foolish shepheard.

16 For loe, I wil raise vp a shepherd in the land, *which* shall not visit those that bee ‖cut off, neither shall seeke the yong one, nor heale that that is broken, nor ‖feed that that standeth still: but he shal eate the flesh of the fat, and teare their clawes in pieces.

‖ *Or, hidden.*
‖ *Or, beare.*

17 *Woe to the idoll shepheard that leaueth the flocke: the sword *shall be* vpon his arme, and vpon his right eye: his arme shall be cleane dryed vp, and his right eye shall be vtterly darkened.

* Iere. 23. 1. ezek. 34. 2. iohn 10. 12.

CHAP. XII.

1 *Ierusalem a cup of trembling to her selfe,* 3 *and a burdensome stone to her aduersaries.* 6 *The victorious restoring of Iudah.* 9 *The repentance of Ierusalem.*

HE burden of the word of the Lord for Israel, saith the Lord, which stretcheth foorth the Heauens, and laith the foundation of the earth, and formeth the spirit of man within him.

2 Behold, I will make Ierusalem a cup of ‖trembling vnto all the people round about, ‖when they shall be in the siege both against Iudah *and* against Ierusalem.

‖ *Or, slumber or poison.*
‖ *Or, and also against Iudah shall he be which shall be in siege against Ierusalem.*

3 ¶ And in that day will I make Ierusalem a burdensome stone for all people : all that burden themselues with it, shall be cut in pieces; though all the people of the earth bee gathered together against it.

4 In that day, saith the Lord, I will smite euery horse with astonishment, and his rider with madnesse, and I will open mine eyes vpon the house of Iudah, and will smite euery horse of the people with blindnesse.

5 And the gouernours of Iudah shall say in their heart, ‖The inhabitants of Ierusalem *shall be* my strength in the Lord of hostes their God.

‖ *Or, there is strength to me and to the inhabitants, &c.*

6 ¶ In that day will I make the gouernours of Iudah like a harth of fire among the wood, and like a torch of fire in a sheafe; and they shall deuoure all the people round about, on the right hand and on the left: and Ierusalem shall bee inhabited againe in her owne place, *euen* in Ierusalem.

7 The Lord also shall saue the tents of Iudah first, that the glory of the house of Dauid, and the glory of the inhabitants of Ierusalem do not magnifie *themselues* against Iudah.

8 In that day shall the Lord defend the inhabitants of Ierusalem, and he that is ‖feeble among them at that day shall be as Dauid; and the house of Dauid *shall be* as God, as the Angel of the Lord before them.

‖ *Or, abiect. Hebr. fallen.*

9 ¶ And it shall come to passe in that day, *that* I will seeke to destroy all the nations that come against Ierusalem.

10 And I wil powre vpon the house of Dauid, and vpon the inhabitants of Ierusalem the spirit of grace and of supplications, and they shall *looke vpon me whom they haue pearced, and they shal mourne for him, as one mourneth for *his* onely *sonne,* and shall be in bitternesse for him, as one that is in bitternesse for *his* first borne.

* Ioh. 19. 34, 37. reuel. 1. 7.

11 In that day shall there bee a great mourning in Ierusalem, as the *mourning of *Hadadrimmon in the valley of Megiddon.

* Acts 2. 37.
* 2. Chron. 35. 22.
† *Heb. families, families.*

12 And the land shal mourne, †euery familie

familie apart, the familie of the house of Dauid apart, and their wiues apart, the familie of the house of Nathan apart, and their wiues apart:

13 The familie of the house of Leui apart, and their wiues apart: the familie of Shimei apart, and their wiues apart:

14 All the families that remaine, euery family apart, & their wiues apart.

CHAP. XIII.

1 The fountaine of purgation for Ierusalem, 2 from idolatrie, and false prophecie. 7 The death of Christ, and the triall of a third part.

N that day there shalbe a fountaine opened to the house of Dauid, and to the inhabitants of Ierusalem, for sinne, and for †vncleannesse.

† Heb. seperation for vncleannesse.

* Ezek. 30. 13.

2 ¶ And it shal come to passe in that day, saith the LORD of hostes, that I will *cut off the names of the idoles out of the land: and they shal no more be remembred: and also I wil cause the prophets, and the vncleane spirit to passe out of the land.

3 And it shal come to passe that when any shall yet prophecie, then his father and his mother that begate him, shall say vnto him, Thou shalt not liue: for thou speakest lies in the Name of the LORD: and his father and his mother, that begate him, shall thrust him through when he prophecieth.

4 And it shall come to passe in that day, that the prophets shalbe ashamed euery one of his vision, when hee hath prophecied: neither shall they weare a †rough garment †to deceiue.

† Hebr. a garment of haire.
† Hebr. to lie.

5 But he shal say, I am no prophet, I am an husbandman: for man taught me to keepe cattell from my youth.

6 And one shal say vnto him, What are these wounds in thine hands? Then hee shall answere: Those with which I was wounded in the house of my friends.

7 ¶ Awake, O sword, against my shepheard, and against the man that is my fellow, saith the LORD of hostes: * smite the Shepheard, and the sheepe shalbe scattered; and I wil turne mine hand vpon the litle ones.

*ᶜMatt. 26. 31. mar. 14. 27.

8 And it shall come to passe, that in all the land, saith the LORD, two parts therein shall be cut off, and die,

but the third shall be left therein.

9 And I will bring the thirde part through the fire, and wil *refine them as siluer is refined, & will try them as gold is tried: they shall call on my Name, and I wil heare them: I wil say, It is my people: and they shall say, The LORD is my God.

* 1. Pet. 1. 6, 7.

CHAP. XIIII.

1 The destroyers of Ierusalem, destroied. 4 The comming of Christ, and the graces of his kingdome. 12 The plague of Ierusalems enemies. 16 The remnant shal turne to the Lord, 20 And their spoiles shalbe holy.

Eholde, the day of the LORD commeth, and thy spoile shall be diuided in the midst of thee.

2 For I wil gather all nations against Ierusalem to battell, and the citie shall be taken, & the houses rifeled, and the women rauished, and halfe of the citie shall goe forth into captiuitie, and the residue of the people shal not be cut off from the citie.

3 Then shall the LORD goe forth and fight against those nations, as when he fought in the day of battel.

4 ¶ And his feet shall stand in that day vpon the mount of Oliues, which is before Ierusalem on the East, and the mount of Oliues shall cleaue in the midst thereof toward the East, and toward the West, and there shall bee a very great valley, and halfe of the Mountaine shall remoue toward the North, and halfe of it toward the South.

5 And ye shal flee to the valley of ‖the mountaines: ‖for the valley of the mountaines shal reach vnto Azal: yea, ye shall flee like as yee fled from before the *earthquake in the dayes of Vzziah king of Iudah: and the LORD my God shall come, and all the Saints with thee.

‖ Or, my mountaines.
‖ Or, when he shal touch the valley of the mountaines to the place he separated.
* Amos 1. 1.

6 And it shall come to passe in that day, that the light shall not be †cleare, nor †darke.

† Hebr. precious.
† Hebr. thickenesse.

7 But ‖it shall be *one day, which shalbe knowen to the LORD, not day nor night: but it shal come to passe that at *euening time it shalbe light.

‖ Or, the day shalbe one.
* Reuel. 20. 25.
* Isa. 60. 26. reu. 21. 23.

8 And it shal be *in that day, that liuing *waters shall goe out from Ierusalem: halfe of them toward the ‖former Sea, and halfe of them toward the hinder Sea: in Summer and in winter shall it be.

* Eze. 47. 1. ioel 3. 18. reue. 22. 1.
‖ Or, Easterne.

9 And

9 And the LORD shall be King ouer all the earth : in that day shal there be one LORD, and his Name one.

10 All the land shall be ||turned as a plaine from Geba to Rimmon, South of Ierusalem : and it shall be lifted vp and ||inhabited in her place : from Beniamins gate vnto the place of the first gate, vnto the corner gate, and *from* the towre of Hananiel vnto the Kings winepresses.

|| Or, compassed.

|| Or, shall abide.

11 And men shall dwell in it, and there shalbe no more vtter destruction : but Ierusalem ||shalbe safely inhabited.

|| Or, shall abide.

12 ¶ And this shall be the plague, wherewith the LORD will smite all the people, that haue fought against Ierusalem : their flesh shall consume away, while they stand vpon their feete, and their eyes shall consume away in their holes, and their tongue shall consume away in their mouth

13 And it shall come to passe in that day, *that* a great tumult from the LORD shalbe among them, and they shall lay holde euery one on the hand of his neighbour, and his hand shall rise vp against the hand of his neighbour.

14 And ||Iudah also shall fight ||at Ierusalem ; and the wealth of all the heathen round about shall be gathered together, golde and siluer, and apparell, in great abundance.

|| Or, thou also O Iudah shalt.

|| Or, against.

15 And so shall be the plague of the horse, of the mule, of the camell, and of the asse, and of all the beasts that shall be in these tents, as this plague

16 ¶ And it shall come to passe that euery one that is left of all the nations which came against Ierusalem, shall euen goe vp from yeere to yeere to worship the King the LORD of hostes, and to keepe the feast of Tabernacles.

17 And it shall be, *that* who so will not come vp of *all* the families of the earth vnto Ierusalem, to worship the King the LORD of hostes, euen vpon them shall be no raine.

18 And if the family of Egypt goe not vp, and come not, that †haue no *raine:* there shall bee the plague wherewith the LORD will smite the heathen that come not vp to keepe the feast of Tabernacles.

† Heb. vpon whom there is not.

19 This shall be the ||punishment of Egypt, and the punishment of all nations that come not vp to keepe the feast of Tabernacles.

|| Or, sinne.

20 ¶ In that day shall there be vpon the ||bels of the horses, HOLINES VNTO THE LORD, and the pots in the LORDS house shall bee like the bowles before the Altar.

|| Or, bridles.

21 Yea, euery pot in Ierusalem and in Iudah shall bee Holinesse vnto the LORD of hostes, and all they that sacrifice, shall come and take of them, and seethe therein : and in that day there shall be no more the *Canaanite in the house of the LORD of hostes.

* Isai 35. 8. ioel 3. 17. reu. 21. 27. and 22. 15.

¶ MALACHI.

CHAP. I.

1 Malachi complaineth of Israels vnkindnesse. 6 Of their irreligiousnes, 12 and profanenesse.

THe burden of the word of ẏ LORD to Israel by †Malachi.

† Heb. by the hand of Malachi.

2 I haue loued you, sayth the LORD: yet yee say, Wherein hast thou loued vs? *was* not Esau Iacobs brother, sayth the LORD? yet I *loued Iacob,

* Rom. 9. 13.

3 And I hated Esau, and layde his mountaines, and his heritage waste, for the dragons of the wildernesse.

4 Whereas Edom sayth, Wee are impouerished, but we will returne and build the desolate places; Thus sayth the LORD of hostes, They shal build, but I will throw downe; and they shal call them, The border of wickednesse, & the people against whom the LORD hath indignation for euer.

5 And your eyes shall see, and yee shall say; The LORD will be magnified ||from the border of Israel.

|| Or, vpon. Heb. from vpon.

6 ¶ A sonne honoureth *his* father, and

and a seruant his Master. If then I *be* a father, where *is* mine honour? and if I *be* a Master, where *is* my feare, saith the Lord of hostes, vnto you O priests, that despise my name? and yee say, Wherein haue we despised thy name?

‖ Or, bring vnto &c.

7 ‖Yee offer polluted bread vpon mine altar; and yee say, Wherein haue we polluted thee? In that yee say, The table of the Lord is contemptible.

† Heb. to sacrifice.

8 And if hee offer the blind †for sacrifice, *is it* not euill? and if yee offer the lame and sicke, *is it* not euill? offer it now vnto thy gouernour : will he be pleased with thee, or accept thy person, saith the Lord of hostes?

† Heb. the face of God.
† Heb. from your hand.

9 And now I pray you, beseech †God, that hee will be gracious vnto vs : this hath beene †by your meanes : will he regard your persons, saith the Lord of hostes?

10 Who is there euen among you that would shut the doores *for nought?* neither doe yee kindle *fire* on mine altar for nought. I *haue* no pleasure in you, saith the Lord of hostes, neither will I accept an *offring at your hand.

* Isai. 1. 11. ier. 6. 20. amos. 5. 21.

11 For from the rising of the Sunne, euen vnto the going downe of the same my name *shall be* great among the Gentiles, and in euery place incense *shall be* offered vnto my name, and a pure offring : for my name *shall be* great among the heathen, saith the Lord of hostes.

12 ¶ But yee haue prophaned it, in that yee say; The table of the Lord is polluted, and the fruite thereof, *euen* his meate, is contemptible.

‖ Or, whereas you might haue blowen it away.

13 Yee said also; Behold what a wearinesse *is it*, and ‖yee haue snuffed at it, saith the Lord of hostes, and yee brought that which was torne, and the lame, and the sicke: thus yee brought an offring : should I accept this of your hand, saith the Lord?

† Heb. in whose flocke is.

14 But cursed *be* the deceiuer, †which hath in his flocke a male, and voweth and sacrificeth vnto the Lord a corrupt thing : for I *am* a great King, saith the Lord of hostes, and my name *is* dreadfull among the heathen.

CHAP. II.

1 He sharpely reproueth the Priests for neglecting their couenant. 11 and the people for idolatrie, 14 for adulterie, 17 and for infidelitie.

 Nd now, O yee Priests, this commaundement *is* for you.

2 If ye will not heare, and if yee will not lay *it* to heart, to giue glory vnto my name, saith the Lord of hostes; I will euen send a *curse vpon you, and will curse your blessings : yea, I haue cursed them already, because yee doe not lay *it* to heart.

* Leuit. 26. 14. deut. 28. 15.

3 Behold, I will ‖corrupt your seed, and †spread doung vpon your faces, *euen* the doung of your solemne feasts, and ‖one shall take you away with it.

‖Or, reproue
† Heb. scatter.
‖ Or, it shall take you away to it.

4 And yee shall know that I haue sent this commaundement vnto you, that my couenant might be with Leui, saith the Lord of hostes.

5 My couenant was with him of life and peace, and I gaue them to him, *for* the feare, wherewith he feared mee, and was afraid before my name.

6 The law of truth was in his mouth, and iniquitie was not found in his lips : he walked with me in peace and equitie, and did turne many away from iniquitie.

7 For the priests lips should keepe knowledge, and they should seeke the law at his mouth : for he *is* the messenger of the Lord of hostes.

8 But yee are departed out of the way : ye haue caused many to ‖stumble at the law : ye haue corrupted the couenant of Leui, saith the Lord of hostes.

‖ Or, fall in the law.

9 Therefore haue I also made you contemptible and base before al the people, according as yee haue not kept my wayes, but ‖haue bin partiall in ỹ law.

‖ Or, lifted vp the face against. Hel accepted faces.

10 *Haue* we not all one father? hath not one God created vs? Why doe we deale treacherously euery man against his brother, by prophaning the couenant of our fathers?

* Eph. 4. 6.

11 ¶ Iudah hath dealt treacherously, and an abomination is committed in Israel and in Ierusalem : for Iudah hath prophaned the holinesse of the Lord which ‖he loued, and hath maried the daughter of a strange God.

‖ Or, ought to loue.

12 The Lord will cut off the man that doth this : the ‖Master and the scholler out of the tabernacles of Iacob, and him that offereth an offring vnto the Lord of hostes.

‖ Or, him that waketh and him he answereth.

13 And this haue yee done againe, couering the Altar of the Lord with teares,

teares, with weeping and with crying out, in so much that hee regardeth not the offering any more, or receiueth it with good will at your hand.

14 ¶ Yet ye say, Wherefore? Because the LORD hath bene witnes betweene thee and the wife of thy youth, against whome thou hast dealt treacherously: yet *is* she thy companion, and the wife of thy couenant.

Or, excel-lencie.
† Heb. a seed of God.

15 And did not he make one? yet *had* he the ||residue of the spirit: and where-fore one? that hee might seeke †a godly seed: therefore take heed to your spirit, and let none deale || treacherously a-gainst the wife of his youth

Or, on-faithfully.

Or, if hee hate her, put her away.
† Heb. to put away

16 For the LORD the God of Is-rael saith, that ||he hateth †putting a-way: for one couereth violence with his garment, saith the LORD of hosts, therfore take heed to your spirit, that ye deale not treacherously.

17 ¶ Ye haue wearied the LORD with your words: yet ye say, Wherein haue we wearied him? when ye say, E-uery one that doeth euill, *is* good in the sight of the LORD, and he delighteth in them, or where *is* the God of iudge-ment?

CHAP. III.

1 Of the Messenger, Maiesty, & Grace of Christ. 7 Of the rebellion, 8 sacriledge, 13 and in-fidelitie of the people. 16 The promise of blessing to them that feare God.

Matt. 11. 10. mar. 1. 2 luk. 1. 76. & 7. 27.

BEholde, I *will send my messenger, and he shal pre-pare the way before mee: and the LORD whom ye seeke, shall suddenly come to his Temple: euen ỹ messenger of the Couenant, whom we delight in: behold, he shall come, saith the LORD of hosts.

2 But who may abide the day of his comming? and who shall stand when he appeareth? for he *is* like a refi-ners fire, and like fullers sope.

3 And he shall as *as* a refiner and pu-rifier of siluer: and he shall purifie the sonnes of Leui, and purge them as gold & siluer, that they may offer vnto the LORD an offring in righteousnes.

4 Then shall the offerings of Iu-dah and Ierusalem bee pleasant vnto the LORD, as in the dayes of old, and as in ||former yeeres.

Or, ancient.

5 And I will come neere to you to iudgement, and I will bee a swift wit-nesse against the sorcerers, and against

the adulterers, and against false swea-rers, and against those that ||oppresse the hireling in *his* wages, the widowe, and the fatherlesse, and that turne aside the stranger *from his right*, and feare not me, saith the LORD of hosts.

Or, defraud

6 For I *am* the LORD, I change not: therefore ye sonnes of Iacob are not consumed.

7 ¶ Euen from the dayes of your fathers yee are gone away from mine ordinances, and haue not kept *them*: *re-turne vnto me, and I will returne vnto you, saith the LORD of hosts: But ye said, Wherein shall we returne?

*Zech. 1. 3.

8 ¶ Wil a man rob God? yet ye haue robbed me. But ye say, Wherein haue we robbed thee? In tithes & offerings.

9 Ye are cursed with a curse: for ye haue robbed me, *euen* this whole nation.

10 Bring ye all the tithes into the store-house, that there may be meate in mine house, & proue me now herewith, saith the LORD of hostes, if I will not open you the *windowes of hea-uen, and †powre you out a blessing, that *there shall* not *be* roome enough *to receiue it.*

*Gen. 7. 11
† Heb. emp-tie out.

11 And I wil rebuke the deuourer for your sakes: and he shal not †destroy the fruits of your ground, neither shal your vine cast her fruit before the time in the field, saith the LORD of hosts.

† Heb. cor-rupt.

12 And all nations shall call you bles-sed: for ye shall be a delightsome land, saith the LORD of hosts.

13 ¶ Your words haue bin *stout a-gainst me, saith the LORD, yet ye say, What haue we spoken so much against thee?

*Iob 21. 14

14 Ye haue said, It *is* vaine to serue God: and what profit *is it*, that we haue kept his †ordinance, and that wee haue walked †mournfully before the LORD of hosts?

† Heb. his obseruation.
† Hebr. in blacke.

15 And now we call the proud happy: yea, they that worke wickednes †are set vp, yea they that *tempt God, are euen deliuered.

† Heb. are built.
Psal. 95. 9.

16 ¶ Then they that feared the LORD, spake often one to another, and the LORD hearkened and heard *it*, & a booke of remembrance was writ-ten before him, for them that feared the LORD, & that thought vpon his name.

17 And they shall be mine, saith the LORD of hosts, in that day when I make vp my ||iewels, and I wil spare them as a man spareth his owne sonne that serueth him.

Or, speciall treasure.

18 Then

18 Then shall yee returne and discerne betweene the righteous and the wicked, betweene him that serueth God, and him that serueth him not.

CHAP. IIII.

1 Gods iudgement on the wicked, 2 and his blessing on the good. 4 Hee exhorteth to the studie of the Law, 5 and telleth of Eliiahs comming, and Office.

Or beholde, the day commeth, that shall burne as an ouen, and all the proud, yea and all that doe wickedly shalbe stubble: and the day that commeth, shal burne them vp, saith the LORD of hostes, that it shall leaue them neither roote nor branch.

2 ¶ But vnto you that feare my Name, shall the *Sunne of righteousnesse arise with healing in his wings, and shall goe foorth and grow vp as calues of the staule.

3 And yee shall treade downe the wicked: for they shall bee ashes vnder the soles of your feet, in the day that I shall doe this, saith the LORD of hosts.

4 ¶ Remember yee the * Law of Moses my seruant, which I commanded vnto him in Horeb for all Israel, with the Statutes and iudgements.

5 ¶ Beholde, I will send you * Eliiah the Prophet, before the comming of the great and dreadfull day of the LORD.

6 And hee shall turne the heart of the fathers to the children, and the heart of the children to their fathers, lest I come and smite the earth with a curse.

* Luke 1. 3.

* Exod. 20. 3.

* Matth. 11, 14. luke 1. 17. mark. 9. 11.

✠ The end of the Prophets.

APO-

APOCRYPHA.

¶ I. ESDRAS.

CHAP. I.

1 Iosias his charge to the Priests and Leuites. 7 A great Passeouer is kept. 32 His death is much lamented : 34 His Successours. 53 The Temple, Citie, and people are destroyed. 56 The rest are caried vnto Babylon.

* 2. King. 23.
22. 2. chro.
35. 1.

Nd Iosias helde the *Feast of the Passeouer in Ierusalem vnto his Lord, and offered the Passeouer the fourteenth day of the first moneth:

2 Hauing set the Priests according to their daily courses, being arayed in long garments, in the Temple of the Lord.

3 And hee spake vnto the Leuites the holy ministers of Israel, that they should hallow themselues vnto the Lord, to set the holy Arke of the Lord, in the house that king Solomon the sonne of Dauid had built :

4 And said, Ye shall no more beare the Arke vpon your shoulders : now therefore serue the Lord your God, and minister vnto his people Israel, and prepare you after your families and kinreds.

5 According as Dauid the king of Israel prescribed, & according to the magnificence of Solomon his sonne : & standing in the Temple according to the seuerall dignitie of the families of you the Leuites, who minister in the presence of your brethren the children of Israel.

6 Offer the Passeouer in order, and make ready the sacrifices for your brethren, and keepe the Passeouer according to the commaundement of the Lord, which was giuen vnto Moyses.

7 And vnto the people that was found there, Iosias gaue thirtie thousand lambes, and kids, and three thousand calues : these things were giuen of the kings allowance, according as hee promised to the people, to the Priestes, and to the Leuites.

8 And Helkias, Zacharias, and ‖Sielus the gouernours of the Temple, gaue to the Priests for the Passeouer, two thousand and sixe hundred sheepe, and three hundreth calues.

9 And Iechonias, and Samaias, and Nathanael his brother, and Assabias, and Ochiel, and Ioram captaines ouer thousands, gaue to the Leuites for the Passeouer fiue thousand sheepe, and ‖seuen hundreth calues.

10 And when these things were done, the Priests and Leuites hauing the vnleauened bread, stood in very comely order according to the kinreds,

11 And according to the seuerall dignities of the fathers, before the people, to offer to the Lord, as it is written in the booke of Moyses : †And thus did they in the morning.

12 And they rosted the Passeouer with fire, as appertaineth : as for the sacrifices, they sodde them in brasse pots, and pannes ‖with a good sauour.

13 And set them before all the people, and afterward they prepared for themselues, and for the Priests their brethren the sonnes of Aaron.

14 For the Priests offered the fat vntill night : and the Leuites prepared for themselues, and the Priests their brethren the sonnes of Aaron.

15 The holy Singers also, the sonnes of Asaph, were in their order, according to

‖ Or, Iehiel.

‖ Fiue hundred calues, 2. chro. 35. 9.

†2. Chron. 35. 12. And so of the bullockes.

‖ With good speed, or willingly, 2. chron. 35. 13.

*30

* 2. Chron.
35. 15.
of Dauid
and Asaph.
* 2. Chro.
35. 15. the
kings seer.

to the appointment of *Dauid, to wit, Asaph, Zacharias, and Ieduthun, who was *of the kings retinue.

16 Moreouer the porters were at e-uery gate : it was not lawfull for any to goe from his ordinary seruice : for their brethren the Leuites prepared for them.

17 Thus were the things that be-longed to the sacrifices of the Lord ac-complished in that day, that they might hold the Passeouer,

18 And offer sacrifices vpon the altar of the Lord, according to the comman-dement of king Iosias.

19 So the children of Israel which were present, held the Passeouer at that time, and the feast of sweet bread seuen dayes.

20 And such a Passeouer was not kept in Israel since the time of the Pro-phet Samuel.

21 Yea all the kings of Israel held not such a Passeouer as Iosias, and the Priests and the Leuites, & the Iewes held with all Israel that were found dwelling at Ierusalem.

22 In the eighteenth yeere of the reigne of Iosias was this Passeouer kept.

23 And the workes of Iosias were vpright before his Lord with an heart full of godlinesse.

24 As for the things that came to passe in his time, they were written in former times, concerning those that sin-ned, and ||did wickedly against the Lord aboue all people and kingdomes, and how they grieued him ||exceedingly, so that the words of the Lord rose vp a-gainst Israel.

|| Or, were vngodly.

||Or, sensibly.

* 2. Chron. 35. 20.

25 *Now after all these acts of Io-sias, it came to passe that Pharao the king of Egypt came to raise warre at Carchamis vpon Euphrates · and Io-sias went out against him.

26 But the king of Egypt sent to him saying, What haue I to doe with thee, O king of Iudea?

27 I am not sent out from the Lord God against thee : for my warre is vp-on Euphrates, and now the Lord is with mee, yea the Lord is with mee hasting me forward : Depart from me and be not against the Lord.

28 Howbeit Iosias did not turne backe his chariot from him, but vnder-tooke to fight with him, not regarding the words of the Prophet Ieremie,

spoken by the mouth of the Lord :

29 But ioyned battell with him in the plaine of Magiddo, and the princes came against king Iosias.

30 Then said the king vnto his ser-uants, carry me away out of the battell for I am very weake : and immediate-ly his seruants tooke him away out of the battell.

31 Then gate he vp vpon his second chariot, and being brought backe to Ie-rusalem, dyed, and was buried in his fa-thers sepulchre.

32 And in all Iury they mourned for Iosias, yea Ieremie the Prophet lamented for Iosias, and the cheefe men with the women made lamentati-on for him vnto this day : and this was giuen out for an ordinance to be done continually in all the nation of Israel.

33 These things are written in the booke of the stories of the kings of Iu-dah, and euery one of the acts that Io-sias did, and his glory, and his vnder-standing in the law of the Lord, and the things that he had done before, and the things now recited, are reported in the bookes of the Kings of Israel and Iudea.

34 *And the people tooke Ioachaz the sonne of Iosias, and made him king in stead of Iosias his father, when hee was twentie and three yeeres old.

* 2. King. 23. 30. 2. chron. 36.

35 And he reigned in Iudea and in Ierusalem three moneths : and then the King of Egypt deposed him from reigning in Ierusalem.

36 And he set a taxe vpon the land of an hundreth talents of siluer, and one talent of gold.

37 The king of Egypt also made king Ioacim his brother king of Iu-dea and Ierusalem.

38 And hee bound Ioacim and the nobles : but Zaraces his brother he apprehended, and brought him out of Egypt.

39 Fiue and twentie yeere old was Ioacim †when he was made king in the land of Iudea and Ierusalem, and he did euill before the Lord.

† 2. Chro. 36. 45. Ie-hoiakim, or Eliakim.

40 Wherefore against him Nabu-chodonosor the King of Babylon came vp, and bound him with a chaine of brasse, and carried him vnto Babylon.

41 Nabuchodonosor also tooke of the holy vessels of the Lord, and carri-ed them away, and set them in his owne temple at Babylon.

42 But

42 But those things that are recorded of him, and of his vncleannes, and impietie, are written in the Chronicles of the kings.

43 And Ioacim his sonne reigned in his stead: he was made king being eighteene yeeres old,

44 And reigned but three moneths and ten dayes in Ierusalem, and did euill before the Lord.

45 So after a yere Nabuchodonosor sent, and caused him to be brought into Babylon with ẏ holy vessels of ẏ Lord,

46 And made Zedechias king of Iudea and Ierusalem, when he was one and twentie yeeres old, and he reigned eleuen yeeres:

47 And he did euill also in the sight of the Lord, & cared not for the words that were spoken vnto him, by the Prophet Ieremie from the mouth of the Lord.

48 And after that king Nabuchodonosor had made him to sweare by the Name of the Lord, he forswore himselfe, and rebelled, and hardening his necke, and his heart, hee transgressed the lawes of the Lord God of Israel.

49 The gouernours also of the people and of the priests did many things against the lawes, and passed al the pollutions of all nations, and defiled the Temple of the Lord which was sanctified in Ierusalem.

50 Neuerthelesse, the God of their fathers sent by his messenger to call them backe, because he spared them and his tabernacle also:

51 But they had his messengers in derision, and looke when the Lorde spake vnto them, they made a sport of his prophets,

52 So farre foorth that he being wroth with his people for their great vngodlinesse, commanded the kings of the Caldees to come vp against them.

53 Who slew their yong men with the sword, yea euen within the compasse of their holy Temple, & spared neither yong man nor maid, old man nor child among them, for hee deliuered all into their hands.

54 And they tooke all the holy vessels of the Lord, both great and small, with the vessels of the Ark of God, and the kings treasures, and caried them away into Babylon.

55 As for the house of the Lord they burnt it, brake downe the walles of Ie-

rusalem, set fire vpon her towres.

56 And as for her glorious things, they neuer ceased til they had consumed and brought them all to nought, and the people that were not slaine with the sword, he caried vnto Babylon:

57 Who became seruants to him and his children, till the Persians reigned, to fulfill the *word of the Lord spoken by the mouth of Ieremie:

58 Vntill the land had enioyed her Sabbaths, the whole time of her desolation shal she ||rest, vntill the full terme of seuentie yeeres.

*Ier. 25. 11 and 29. 10.

|| Or, Keepe Sabbath.

CHAP. II.

1 Cyrus is moued by God to build the Temple, 5 And giueth leaue to the Iewes to returne & contribute to it. 11 He deliuereth againe the vessels which had bin taken thence. 25 Artaxerxes forbiddeth the Iewes to build any more.

IN the first yeere of Cyrus king of the Persians, that the worde of the Lorde might bee accomplished, that hee had promised by the mouth of Ieremie:

*2. Chron. 36. 22. ezra 1. 1, &c.

2 The Lord raised vp the spirit of Cyrus the king of the Persians, and he made proclamation thorow al his kingdome, and also by writing,

3 Saying, Thus saith Cyrus king of the Persians, The Lord of Israel the most high Lord, hath made me king of the whole world,

4 And commanded me to build him an house at Ierusalem in Iurie.

5 If therefore there bee any of you that are of his people, let the Lord, euen his Lord be with him, and let him goe vp to Ierusalem that is in Iudea, and build the house of the Lord of Israel: for ||he is the Lord that dwelleth in Ierusalem.

|| Or, this.

6 Whosoeuer then dwell in the places about, let them helpe him, those I say that are his neighbours, with gold and with siluer,

7 With gifts, with horses, and with cattell, and other things, which haue bene set forth by vowe, for the Temple of the Lord at Ierusalem.

8 ¶ Then the chiefe of the families of Iudea, and of the tribes of Beniamin stood vp: the priests also and the Leuites, and all they whose minde the Lord had moued to goe vp, and to build an house for the Lord at Ierusalem,

9 And they that dwelt round about them,

† *Hebr. substance, Ezr. 1. 6.*

them, and helped them in all things with siluer and gold, with † horses and cattell, and with very free gifts of a great number whose mindes were stirred vp thereto.

10 King Cyrus also brought foorth the holy vessels which Nabuchodonosor had caried away from Ierusalem, and had set vp in his temple of idoles.

11 Now when Cyrus king of the Persians had brought them foorth, hee deliuered them to Mithridates his treasurer:

12 And by him they were deliuered to † Sanabassar ỹ gouernour of Iudea.

† *Shash-bazar. Greek. the first part of the word is corruptly ioyned to the word going before, Ezra 1. 8.*
† *Hebr. kniues, Ezra 1. 9.*
† *Ezra. 1. 10. but foure hundred and ten.*
† *Ezra. 1. 11. but fiue thousand foure hundred.*

13 And this was the number of them, a thousand golden cuppes, and a thousand of siluer, † censers of siluer twentie nine, vials of gold thirtie, and of siluer † two thousand foure hundred and ten, and a thousand other vessels.

14 So all the vessels of gold, and of siluer which were caried away, were † fiue thousand, foure hundred, threescore and nine.

15 These were brought back by Sanabassar, together with them of the captiuity, from Babylon to Ierusalem.

* *Ezra 4. 6.*

16 *But in the time of Artaxerxes king of the Persians, Belemus, and Mithridates, and Tabellius, and † Rathumus, and Beeltethmus, and † Semellius the Secretarie, with others that were in commission with them, dwelling in Samaria and other places, wrote vnto him against them that dwelt in Iudea and Ierusalem, these letters following.

† *Bahumus and the name which followeth, is but an epithete to the former, Ezra 4. 9.*
† *Shimshai, Ezra 4. 8.*

17 To King Artaxerxes our lord, Thy seruants Rathumus the story writer, and Semellius the scribe, and the rest of their counsell, and the Iudges that are in Coelosyria and Phenice.

18 Be it now knowen to the lord the king, that the Iewes that are come vp from you to vs, being come into Ierusalem (that rebellious and wicked citie,) doe build the market places, and repaire the walles of it, and doe lay the foundation of the Temple.

19 Now if this citie, and the walles thereof be made vp againe, they will not onely refuse to giue tribute, but also rebell against kings.

20 And forasmuch as the things pertaining to the Temple, are now in hand, we thinke it meete not to neglect such a matter,

21 But to speake vnto our lord the king, to the intent that if it be thy pleasure, it may be sought out in the bookes of thy fathers:

22 And thou shalt finde in the Chronicles, what is written concerning these things, and shalt vnderstand that that citie was rebellious, troubling both kings and cities:

23 And that the Iewes were rebellious, and raised alwayes warres therin, for the which cause euen this citie was made desolate.

24 Wherefore now wee doe declare vnto thee, (O lord the king) that if this citie bee built againe, and the walles thereof set vp anew, thou shalt from hencefoorth haue no passage into Coelosyria and Phenice.

25 Then the King wrote backe againe to Rathumus the storie-writer, to Beeltethmus, to Semellius the scribe, and to the rest that were in commission, and dwellers in Samaria and Syria, and Phenice, after this maner.

26 I haue read the Epistle which ye haue sent vnto mee : therefore I commanded to make diligent search, and it hath bene found, that that city was from the beginning practising against Kings.

27 And the men therein were giuen to rebellion, and warre, and that mightie Kings and fierce were in Ierusalem, who reigned and exacted tributes in Coelosyria and Phenice.

28 Now therefore I haue commanded to hinder those men from building the citie, and heed to be taken that there be no more done in it,

29 And that those wicked workers proceed no further to the annoyance of Kings.

30 Then king Artaxerxes his letters being read, Rathumus and Semellius the scribe, and the rest that were in commission with them, remoouing in hast towards Ierusalem with a troupe of horsemen, and a ‖ multitude of people in battell aray, began to hinder the builders, and the building of the Temple in Ierusalem ceased vntill the second yeere of the reigne of Darius King of the Persians.

‖ *Or, a great number of souldiers.*

CHAP. III.

4 Three striue to excell each other in wise speaches.   9 They referre themselues to the iudgement of the King.   18 The first declareth the strength of Wine.

Now

Ow when Darius reigned, hee made a great feast vnto all his Subiects and vnto all his houshold, and vnto all the princes of Media and Persia,

2 And to all the gouernours and captaines, and lieutenants that were vnder him, from India vnto Ethiopia, of an hundreth twenty and seuen prouinces.

3 And when they had eaten and drunken, and being satisfied were gone home, then Darius the king went into his bed-chamber, and slept, and soone after awaked.

4 Then three yong men that were of the guard, that kept the kings body, spake one to another:

5 Let euery one of vs speake a sentence : hee that shall ouercome, & whose sentence shall seeme wiser then the others, vnto him shall the king Darius giue great gifts, and great things in token of victory :

6 As to be clothed in purple, to drink in golde, and to sleepe vpon golde, and a chariot with bridles of golde, and an head-tyre of fine linen, and a chaine about his necke :

7 And hee shall sit next to Darius, because of his wisedome, and shalbe called, Darius his cousin.

8 And then euery one wrote his sentence, sealed it, and laide it vnder king Darius his pillow,

9 And sayd, that when the king is risen, some will giue him the writings, and of whose side the king, and the three princes of Persia shall iudge, that his sentence is the wisest, to him shall the victory be giuen as was appointed.

10 The first wrote: Wine is the strongest.

11 The second wrote : The King is strongest.

12 The third wrote; Women are strongest, but aboue all things trueth beareth away the victory.

13 ¶ Now when the king was risen vp, they tooke their writings, and deliuered them vnto him, and so hee read them.

14 And sending foorth, hee called all the Princes of Persia and Media, and the gouernours, and the captaines, and the lieutenants, and the chiefe officers,

15 And sate him downe in the ||royall seate of Iudgement, and the writings

|| Or, counsell.

were read before them :

16 And he said, Call the young men, and they shall declare their owne sentences : so they were called, and came in.

17 And hee said vnto them, Declare vnto vs your minde, concerning the writings. Then began the first, who had spoken of the strength of wine ;

18 And he said thus : O ye men, how exceeding strong is wine ! it causeth all men to erre that drinke it :

19 It maketh the minde of the king, and of the fatherlesse childe to be all one; of the bondman and of the freeman, of the poore man and of the rich :

20 It turneth also euery thought into iollitie and mirth, so that a man remembreth neither sorow nor debt :

21 And it maketh euery heart rich, so that a man remembreth neither king nor gouernour; and it maketh to speake all things by talents :

22 And when they are in their cups, they forget their loue both to friends and brethren, and a litle after draw out swords :

23 But when they are from the wine, they remember not what they haue done.

24 O ye men, is not wine the strongest, that enforceth to doe thus ? And when hee had so spoken, hee helde his peace.

CHAP. IIII.

1 The second declareth the power of a King. 14 The third, the force of women : 33 and of Trueth. 41 The third is iudged to be wisest, 47 and obtaineth Letters of the King to build Ierusalem. 58 He praiseth God, and sheweth his brethren what he had done.

Hen the second that had spoken of the strength of the King, began to say ;

2 O yee men, doe not men excel in strength, that ||beare rule ouer Sea and land, and all things in them ?

|| Or, haue the command.

3 But yet the King is more mighty : for hee is lord of all these things, and hath dominion ouer them, and whatsoeuer he commandeth them, they doe :

4 If hee bid them make warre the one against the other, they doe it : if hee send them out against the enemies, they goe, and breake downe mountaines, walles and towres.

5 They slay and are slaine, and transgresse not the Kings commandement :

ment: if they get the victory, they bring all to the King, as well the spoile as all things else.

6 Likewise for those that are no souldiers, and haue not to doe with warres, but vse husbandrie; when they haue reaped againe, that which they had sowen, they bring it to the King, and compell one another to pay tribute vnto the King.

7 And yet he is but one man; if hee commaund to kill, they kill, if he command to spare, they spare.

8 If he command to smite, they smite; if he command to make desolate, they make desolate; if hee command to build, they build:

9 If he command to cut downe, they cut downe; if he command to plant, they plant.

10 So all his people and his armies obey him; furthermore he lieth downe, he eateth and drinketh, & taketh his rest.

11 And these keepe (watch) round about him, neither ||may any one depart, and doe his owne businesse, neither disobey they him in any thing.

‖ *Or, can.*

12 O yee men, how should not the King be mightiest, when in such sort he is obeyed? and he held his tongue.

13 ¶ Then the third, who had spoken of women, and of the truth (this was Zorobabel) beganne to speake.

14 O yee men, it is not the great King, nor the multitude of men, neither is it wine that †excelleth; who is it then that ruleth them, or hath the lordship ouer them, are they not women?

† *Heb. is of force.*

15 Women haue borne the King and all the people, that beare rule by sea and land.

16 Euen of the came they: & they nourished them vp that planted the vineyards from whence the wine commeth.

17 These also make garments for men; these bring glory vnto men, and without women cannot men be.

18 Yea and if men haue gathered together gold and siluer, or any other goodly thing, doe they not loue a woman, which is comely in fauour and beautie?

19 And letting all those things goe, doe they not gape, and euen with open mouth fixe their eyes fast on her; and haue not all men more desire vnto her, then vnto siluer or gold, or any goodly thing whatsoeuer?

20 A man leaueth his owne father

that brought him vp, and his owne countrie, and cleaueth vnto his wife.

21 He stickes not to spend his life with his wife, and remembreth neither father, nor mother, nor countrey.

22 By this also you must know, that women haue dominion ouer you: doe yee not labour and toyle, and giue and bring all to the woman?

23 Yea a man taketh his sword, and goeth his way to rob, and to steale, to saile vpon the sea, and vpon riuers,.

24 And looketh vpon a lyon, and goeth in the darknesse, and when he hath stolen, spoiled and robbed, he bringeth it to his loue.

25 Wherefore a man loueth his wife better then father and mother.

26 Yea many there be that haue ||run out of their wits for women, and become seruants for their sakes:

‖ *Or, growen desperate.*

27 Many also haue perished, haue erred, and sinned for women.

28 And now doe yee not belieue me? is not the King great in his power? doe not all regions feare to touch him?

29 Yet did I see him and Apame the Kings concubine, the daughter of the admirable Bartacus, sitting at the right hand of the King,

Ioseph.antiq. lib. 11. cap. 4. Rabsaces Themasius.

30. And taking the crowne from the Kings head, and setting it vpon her owne head; she also strooke the King with her left hand.

31 And yet ||for all this, the King gaped and gazed vpon her with open mouth: if she laughed vpon him, hee laughed also: but if she tooke any displeasure at him, the King was faine to flatter, that she might ||be reconciled to him againe.

‖ *Or, heere at.*

‖ *Or, be friends with him.*

32 O ye men, how can it be but women should be strong, seeing they doe thus?

33 Then the king & the princes looked one vpon another: so he began to speake of the trueth.

34 O ye men, are not women strong? great is the earth, high is the heauen, swift is the Sunne in his course, for he compasseth the heauens round about, and fetcheth his course againe to his owne place in one day.

35 Is he not great that maketh these things? therefore great is the truth, and stronger then all things.

36 All the earth ||calleth vpon the truth, & the heauen blesseth it, all works shake and tremble at it, and with it is no vnrighteous thing.

‖ *Or, praiseth the truth. Athanas.*

37 Wine

37 Wine is wicked, the king is wicked, women are wicked, all the children of men are wicked, and such are all their wicked workes, and there is no trueth in them. In their vnrighteousnes also they shall perish.

38 As for the trueth it endureth, and is alwayes strong, it lieueth and conquereth for euermore.

39 With her there is no accepting of persons, or rewards, but she doeth the things that are iust, and refraineth from all vniust and wicked things, and all men doe well like of her workes.

40 Neither in her iudgement is any vnrighteousnesse, & she is the strength, kingdome, power and maiestie of all ages. Blessed be the God of trueth.

41 And with that he held his peace, and al the people then shouted and said, Great is trueth, and mightie aboue all things.

42 Then saide the king vnto him, Aske what thou wilt, more then is appointed in the writing, and we wil giue it thee, because thou art found wisest, and thou shalt sit next me, and shalt bee called my cousin.

43 Then said hee vnto the king, Remember thy vow which thou hast vowed to build Ierusalem in the day when thou camest to the kingdome,

44 And to send away all the vessels that were taken away out of Ierusalem, which Cyrus set apart, when hee vowed to destroy Babylon, and to send them againe thither.

45 Thou also hast vowed to build vp the Temple, which the Edomites burnt when Iudea was made desolate by the Chaldees.

46 And now, O lord the king, this is that which I require, and which I desire of thee, and this is the princely liberalitie proceeding from thy selfe : I desire therefore that thou make good the vow, the performance wherof with thine owne mouth thou hast vowed to the king of heauen.

47 Then Darius the king stood vp and kissed him, and wrote letters for him vnto all the treasurers and lieutenants, and captaines and gouernours that they should safely conuey on their way, both him, and all those that go vp with him to build Ierusalem.

48 Hee wrote letters also vnto the lieutenants that were in Coelosyria and Phenice, and vnto them in Libanus, that they should bring Cedar wood from Libanus vnto Ierusalem, and that they should build the city with him

49 Moreouer he wrote for all the Iewes that went out of his realme vp into Iurie, concerning their freedome, that no officer, no ruler, no lieutenant, nor ‖treasurer, should forcibly enter into their dores,   ‖ *Or, steward.*

50 And that all the countrey which they hold, should be free without tribute, & that the Edomites should giue ouer the villages of the Iewes which then they held,

51 Yea that there should be yereely giuen twentie talents to ỹ building of the Temple, vntill ỹ time that it were built,

52 And other tenne talents yeerely, to maintaine the burnt offerings vpon the Altar euery day (as they had a commandement to offer seuenteene)

53 And that all they that went from Babylon to build the citie, should haue free liberty as well they as their posteritie, and all the priests that went away.

54 He wrote also concerning the charges, and the priests vestments wherein they minister :

55 And likewise for the charges of the Leuites, to be giuen them, vntill the day that the house were finished, and Ierusalem builded vp.

56 And he commanded to giue to all that kept the city, ‖pensions and wages.   ‖ *Or, portions of land.*

57 He sent away also all the vessels fro Babylon that Cyrus had set apart, and all that Cyrus had giuen in commandement, the same charged hee also to be done, and sent vnto Ierusalem.

58 Now when this yong man was gone forth, he lifted vp his face to heauen toward Ierusalem, and praised the king of heauen.

59 And said, From thee commeth victory, from thee commeth wisedom, and thine is the glory, & I am thy seruant.

60 Blessed art thou who hast giuen me wisedom : for to thee I giue thanks, O Lord of our fathers.

61 And so he tooke the letters, and went out, and came vnto Babylon, and told it all his brethren.

62 And they praised the God of their fathers: because he had giuen them freedome and libertie

63 To goe vp, and to build Ierusalem, and the Temple which is called by his Name, and they feasted with instruments of musick, & gladnes seuen dayes.

CHAP.

CHAP. V.

4 The names and number of the Iewes that returned home. 50 The Altar is set vp in his place. 57 The foundation of the Temple is layd. 73 The worke is hindred for a time.

AFter this were the principall men of the families chosen according to their tribes, to go vp with their wiues, and sonnes, and daughters, with their men-seruants and maid-seruants, and their cattel.

2 And Darius sent with them a thousand horsmen, til they had brought them backe to Ierusalem safely, and with musicall [instruments,] tabrets and flutes.

3 And all their brethren played, and hee made them goe vp together with them.

4 And these are the names of the men which went vp, according to their families, amongst their tribes, after their seuerall heads.

5 The Priestes the sonnes of Phinees, the sonne of Aaron : Iesus the sonne of Iosedec, the sonne of Saraias, and ||Ioachim the sonne of Zorobabel, the sonne of Salathiel of the house of Dauid, out of the kindred of Phares, of the tribe of Iuda.

6 [a]Who spake wise sentences before Darius the king of Persia, in the second yeere of his reigne, in the moneth Nisan, which is the first moneth.

7 And these are they of Iewrie that came vp from the captiuitie, where they dwelt as strangers, whom Nabuchodonosor the king of Babylon had carried away vnto Babylon.

8 And they returned vnto Ierusalem, and to the other parts of Iurie euery man to his owne city, who came with Zorobabel, with Iesus, Nehemias, and [b]Zacharias, and Reesaias, Enenius, Mardocheus, Beelsarus, [c]Aspharasus, [d]Reelius, Roimus, and Baana their guides.

9 The number of them of the nation, and their gouernours : sonnes of [e]Phoros two thousand an hundred seuentie and two : the sonnes of [f]Saphat [g]foure hundred seuentie and two ;

10 The sonnes of Ares seuen hundred fiftie and six :

11 The sonnes of Phaath Moab, two thousand eight hundred & twelue :

12 The sonnes of Elam, a thousand two hundred fifty and foure : the sonnes of [h]Zathui, nine hundred fourtie and fiue : the sonnes of [i]Corbe seuen hundred and fiue : the sonnes of Bani, sixe hundred fourtie and eight :

13 The sonnes of Bebai, sixe hundred twentie and three : the sonnes of [k]Sadas, three thousand two hundred twentie and two :

14 The sonnes of Adonican, sixe hundred sixtie and seuen : the sonnes of [l]Bagoi, two thousand sixtie and sixe : the sonnes of Adin, foure hundred fiftie and foure :

15 The sonnes of [m]Aterezias, ninetie and two : the sonnes of Ceilan and Azetas, threescore and seuen : the sonnes of Azuran, foure hundred thirtie & two.

16 The sonnes of Ananias, an hundred and one : the sonnes of Arom thirtie two, and the sonnes of [n]Bassa, three hundred twentie and three : the sonnes of Azephurith, an hundred and two :

17 The sonnes of Meterus, three thousand and fiue : the sonnes of [o]Bethlomon, an hundred twentie and three.

18 They of Netophah fiftie and fiue : they of Anathoth, an hundred fiftie and eight : they of [p]Bethsamos, fourtie and two :

19 They of [q]Kiriathiarius, twentie and fiue : they of Caphira and Beroth, seuen hundred fourtie and three : they of Pyra, seuen hundred :

20 They of Chadias and Ammidioi, foure hundred twenty and two : they of [r]Cyrama, and [s]Gabdes, sixe hundred twentie and one :

21 They of [t]Macalon, an hundred twentie and two : they of [u]Betolius fiftie and two : the sonnes of [x]Nephis, an hundred fiftie and sixe.

22 The sonnes of [y]Calamolalus, and Onus, seuen hundred twentie and fiue : the sonnes of Ierechus, two hundred fourtie and fiue :

23 The sonnes of [z]Annaas, three thousand three hundred and thirtie :

24 The Priests, the sonnes of [a]Ieddu, the sonne of Iesus, among the sonnes of Sanasib, nine hundred seuentie and two : the sonnes of [b]Meruth, a thousand fiftie and two :

25 The sonnes of [c]Phassaron, a thousand fourtie and seuen : the sonnes of [d]Carme [e]a thousand and seuenteene.

26 The Leuites : the sonnes of Iessue, and Cadmiel, and Banuas, and Sudias, seuentie and foure.

27 The

Left margin notes

|| Ioachim and Zorobabel. This place is corrupt: For Ioachim was the sonne of Iosedech, Neh. 12. 10. and not Zorobabel, who was of the tribe of Iuda.
[a] Zorobabel.

[b] Saraiah.
[c] Or Mispar.
[d] Or Reelaiah.
[e] Parosh, Ezra 2. 3.
Nehem. 7. 9. where for breuity looke for the true numbers of the particulars following : for here they vary much, & the names much more.
[f] Shephatia.
[g] Or, three hundred seuentie two.

Right margin notes

[h] Zattu.
[i] Zacchai.

[k] Asgad.

[l] Bigui.

[m] Alerhezekia.

[n] Besai.

[o] Bethlehem.

[p] Asmaueth

[q] Kiriashia rim.

[r] Rama.
[s] Gabah.
[t] Michmas.
[u] Bethel.
[x] Maghbis.

[y] Lodhadid.

[z] Senaah.

[a] Iedaiah.

[b] Immar.
[c] Pashur.
[a] Harim.
[e] Or, 777. according to some copies
[†] Thus it is read, Ezra 2. 40. the sonnes of Ieshua, and Cadmeel, of the sonnes of Hodouiah.

27 The holy singers: the sonnes of Asaph an hundred twentie and eight.

28 The porters: the sonnes of [a]Salum, the sonnes of [b]Iatal, the sonnes of Talmon, the sonnes of [c]Dacobi, the sonnes of [d]Teta, the sonnes of [e]Sami, in all an hundred thirty and nine.

29 The seruants of the Temple: the sonnes of [f]Esau, the sonnes of [g]Asipha, the sonnes of Tabaoth, the sonnes of [h]Ceras: the sonnes of [i]Sud, the sonnes of [k]Phaleas, the sonnes of Labana, the sonnes of [l]Graba:

30 The sonnes of [m]Acua, the sonnes of Vta, the sonnes of [n]Cetab, the sons of Agaba, the sonnes of [o]Subai, the sonnes of Anan, the sonnes of [p]Cathua, the sonnes of [q]Geddur:

31 The sonnes of [r]Airus, the sonnes of [s]Daisan, the sonnes of [t]Noeba, the sonnes of Chaseba, the sonnes of [u]Gazera, the sonnes of [x]Azia, the sonnes of [y]Phinees, the sonnes of Azara, the sonnes of [z]Bastai, the sonnes of [a]Asana the sonnes of [b]Meani, the sonnes of [c]Naphisi, the sonnes of [d]Acub, the sons of [e]Asipha, the sonnes of [f]Assur, the sonnes of Pharacim, the sons of [g]Basaloth.

32 The sonnes of [h]Meeda: the sons of Coutha, the sonnes of [i]Charea, the sonnes of [k]Chareus, the sonnes of [l]Aserer, the sonnes of [m]Thomoi, the sonnes of [n]Nasith, the sons of Atipha.

33 The sons of the seruants of Solomon: the sonnes of [o]Azaphion, the sonnes of [p]Pharira, the sonnes of [q]Ioeli, the sonnes of [r]Lozon, the sonnes of [s]Isdael, the sonnes of [t]Sapheth:

34 The sonnes of [u]Hagia, the sons of [x]Phacareth, the sonnes of Sabie, the sonnes of Sarothie, the sonnes of Masias, the sonnes of Gar, the sons of Addus, the sonnes of Suba, the sonnes of Apherra, the sonnes of Barodis, the sonnes of Sabat, the sonnes of Allom.

35 All the ministers of the Temple, and the sonnes of the seruants of Solomon, were three hundred seuenty & two.

36 These came vp from Thermeleth, and Thelersas, Charaathalar leading them and Aalar.

37 Neither could they shewe their families, nor their stock, how they were of Israel: the sonnes of [y]Ladan, the sonnes of [z]Ban, the sonnes of [a]Necodan, sixe hundred fiftie and two.

38 And of the Priests that vsurped the office of the Priesthood, and were not found, the sonnes of [b]Obdia: the sonnes of [c]Accoz, the sonnes of [d]Addus, who married Augia one of the daughters of Berzelus, and was named after his name.

39 And when the description of the kinred of these men was sought in the Register, and was not found, they were remooued from executing the office of the Priesthood.

40 For vnto them said || Nehemias, and Atharias, that they should not be partakers of the holy things, till there arose vp an high Priest, clothed with † Doctrine and Trueth.

41 So of Israel from them of twelue yeeres olde and vpward, they were all in number fourtie thousand, besides men seruants and women seruants, two thousand three hundred and sixtie.

42 Their ||men seruants and handmaids were seuen thousand three hundred fourtie and seuen: the singing men and singing women, two hundred fortie and fiue.

43 Foure hundred thirtie and fiue camels, seuen thousand thirtie and sixe horses, two hundred fourtie and fiue mules, *fiue thousand fiue hundred twentie & fiue ||beasts vsed to the yoke.

44 And certaine of the chiefe of their families, when they came to the Temple of God that is in Ierusalem, vowed to set vp the house againe in his owne place according to their abilitie:

45 And to giue into the holy treasurie of the workes, a thousand pounds of golde, fiue thousand of siluer, and an hundred priestly vestments.

46 And so dwelt the Priests, and the Leuites, and the people in Ierusalem, and in the countrey: the Singers also, and the Porters, and all Israel in their villages.

47 But when the seuenth moneth was at hand, and when the children of Israel were euery man in his owne place, they came all together with one consent into the open place of the ||first gate, which is towards the East.

48 Then stood vp Iesus the sonne of Iosedec, and his brethren the Priests, and Zorobabel the sonne of Salathiel, and his brethren, and made ready the Altar of the God of Israel,

49 To offer burnt sacrifices vpon it, according as it is expresly commanded in the booke of Moses the man of God.

50 And there were gathered vnto them

[a] Shallum. [b] Ater. [c] Akkub. [d] Hatita. [e] Shobai. [f] Zich. [g] Hasupha. [h] Keros. [i] Siaha. [k] Padon. [l] Agabah. [m] Akkub. [n] Hagab. [o] Shamlai. [p] Giddes. [q] Gahar. [r] Reaiah. [s] Rezin. [t] Necodah. [u] Gazam. [x] Huzza. [y] Paseah. [z] Besai. [a] Asnah. [b] Neumin. [c] Nephusin. [d] Bakbuk. [e] Hacupa. [f] Harhur. [g] Bazluth. [h] Mehida. [i] Harsha. [k] Barcos. [l] Sisera. [m] Thamai. [n] Neziah. [o] Sophereth. [p] Peruda. [q] Iaalah. [r] Darcon. [s] Giddel. [t] Shephatiah [u] Hatti. [x] Phoceroth Hazzebaim, Ezra 2. 25.

[y] Delaiah. [z] Tobiah. [a] Necodah.

[b] Hobaiah. [c] Cos. [d] Barzelai.

|| Nehemias, who also is Atharias, two of one. Nehe. 8. 9. and 10. 2. chap. 2. 63. † Heb. Vrim and Thummim.

|| See Nehe. 7. 66.

* Ezra 2. 67. || Asses.

|| Or, before the East gate.

them out of the other nations of the land, and they erected the Altar vpon his owne place, because all the nations of the land were at enmitie with them, and oppressed them, and they offered sacrifices according to the time, and burnt offerings to the Lord both morning, and euening.

51 Also they held the feast of Tabernacles, as it is commanded in the law, and *offered* sacrifices daily as was meet:

‖ *Or, daily sacrifice.*

52 And after, that the ‖ continuall oblations, and the sacrifice of the Sabbaths, and of the new Moones, and of all holy feasts.

† *Grek. hallowed.*

53 And all they that † had made any vow to God, beganne to offer sacrifices to God from the first day of the seuenth moneth, although the Temple of the Lord was not yet built.

54 And they gaue vnto the Masons and Carpenters, money, meate and drinke with cheerefulnesse.

55 Vnto them of Sidon also and Tyre, they gaue carres that they should bring Cedar trees from Libanus, which should bee brought by flotes to the hauen of Ioppe, according as it was commanded them by Cyrus King of the Persians.

56 And in the second yeere and second moneth, after his comming to the Temple of God at Ierusalem, beganne Zorobabel the sonne of Salathiel, and Iesus the sonne of Iosedec, and their brethren and the priests, and the Leuites, and all they that were come vnto Ierusalem out of the captiuity:

57 And they layd the foundation of the house of God, in the first day of the second moneth, in the second yeere after they were come to Iury & Ierusalem.

‖ *See Ezra 3. 9.*

58 ‖ And appointed the Lenites from twenty yeeres old, ouer the workes of the Lord. Then stood vp Iesus and his sonnes, and brethren, and Cadmiel his brother, & the sonnes of Madiabun, with the sonnes of Ioda the sonne of Eliadun, with their sonnes and brethren, all Leuites, with one accord ‖ setters forward of the businesse, labouring to aduance the workes in the house of God. So the workmen built the temple of the Lord.

‖ *Or, ouerseers or encouragers of them that wrought in the house of the Lord.*

59 And the Priests stood arayed in their vestiments with musicall instruments, and trumpets, and the Leuites the sonnes of Asaph had Cymbals,

60 Singing songs of thanksgiuing, and praising the Lord ‖ according as Dauid the king of Israel had ordained.

‖ *Or, after the maner of Dauid king of Israel.*

61 And they sung *with* loud voices songs to the praise of the Lord : because his mercy and glory is for euer in all Israel.

62 And all the people sounded trumpets, and shouted with a loud voyce, singing songs of thankesgiuing vnto the Lord for the rearing vp of the house of the Lord.

63 * Also of the Priests and Leuites, and of the chiefe of their families the ancients who had seene the former house, came to the building of this with weeping and great crying.

* Ezra 3. 12 13.

64 But many with trumpets and ioy shouted with loud voyce.

65 Insomuch that the trumpets might not be ‖ heard for the weeping of the people : yet the multitude sounded marueilously, so that it was heard a farre off.

‖ *Or, discerned.*

66 Wherefore when the enemies of the Tribe of Iuda and Beniamin heard it, they came to know what that noise of trumpets should meane.

67 And they perceiued, that they that were of the captiuity did build the temple vnto the Lord God of Israel.

68 So they went to Zorobabel and Iesus, and to the chiefe of the families, and said vnto them, We will build together with you.

69 For we likewise, as you, doe obey your Lord, and doe sacrifice vntó him from the dayes of ‖ Asbazareth the king of the Assyrians who brought vs hither

‖ *Asar-haddon, chap. 4. 2.*

70 Then Zorobabel and Iesus, and the chiefe of the families of Israel said vnto them, It is not for vs and you to build together an house vnto the Lord our God.

71 We our selues alone will build vnto the Lord of Israel, according as Cyrus the King of the Persians hath commanded vs.

72 But the heathen of the land lying heauy vpon the inhabitants of Iudea, and holding them straite, hindred their building :

73 And by their secret plots, and popular perswasions, and commotions, they hindred the finishing of the building, all the time that king Cyrus liued, so they were hindered from building for the space of ‖ two yeeres, vntill the reigne of Darius.

‖ *Vntill the second yeere of Darius.* Ezra 4. 5, 6, 7.

CHAP.

C H A P. VI.

1 The Prophets stirre vp the people to build the Temple. 8 Darius is solicited to hinder it. 27 But he doth further it by all meanes, 32 and threatneth those that shall hinder it.

Ow in the second yeere of the reigne of Darius, Aggeus, and Zacharias the sonne of ‖ Addo, the prophets prophesied vnto the Iewes, in Iurie and Ierusalem in the Name of the Lord God of Israel ‖ which was vpon them.

Or, Iddo.

Or, which was called on them.

2 Then stood vp Zorobabel the sonne of Salathiel, and Iesus the son of Iosedec, and beganne to build the house of the Lord at Ierusalem, the prophets of the Lord being with them, *and* helping them.

3 * At the same time came vnto them ‖ Sisinnes the gouernor of Syria, and Phenice, with ‖ Sathrabuzanes, and his companions, and said vnto them,

* Ezra. 5. 3.

Or, Tatnai

Or, Sheher-boznai.

7 By whose appointment doe you build this house, and this roofe, and performe all the other things? and who are the workemen that performe these things?

5 Neuerthelesse the Elders of the Iewes obtained fauour : because the Lord had visited the captiuitie.

6 And they were not hindred from building vntil such time as signification was giuen vnto Darius concerning them, and an answere receiued.

7 The copie of the letters which Sisinnes gouernour of Syria, and Phenice, and Sathrabuzanes with their companions rulers in Syria and Phenice, wrote and sent vnto Darius, To king Darius, greeting.

8 Let all things bee knowen vnto our lord the King, that being come into the countrey of Iudea, and entred into the citie of Ierusalem, we found in the citie of Ierusalem the ancients of the Iewes that were of the captiuitie ;

9 Building an house vnto the Lord, great, *and* newe, of hewen and costly stones, and the timber already laid vpon the walles.

10 And those workes are done with great speede, and the worke goeth on prosperously in their handes, and with all glory and diligence is it made.

11 Then asked wee these Elders, saying, By whose commaundement builde you this house, and lay the foundations of these workes?

12 Therefore to the intent that wee might giue knowledge vnto thee by writing, we demanded of them who were the chiefe doers, and we required of them the names in writing of their principall men.

13 So they gaue vs this answere : We are the seruants of the Lord which made heauen and earth.

14 And as for this house, it was builded many yeeres agoe, by a king of Israel great and strong, and was finished.

15 But when our fathers prouoked God vnto wrath, and sinned against the Lord of Israel which is in heauen, hee gaue them ouer into the power of Nabuchodonosor king of Babylon of the Chaldees :

16 Who pulled downe the house and burnt it, and caried away the people captiues vnto Babylon.

17 But in the first yeere that King Cyrus reigned ouer the country of Babylon, Cyrus the king wrote to build vp this house.

18 And the holy vessels of gold and of siluer, that Nabuchodonosor had caried away out of the house at Ierusalem, and had set them in his owne temple, those Cyrus the king brought forth againe out of the temple at Babylon, and they were deliuered to ‖ Zorobabel and to Sanabassarus the ruler,

Or, Zorobabel, which is also Sanabassar the ruler, so as Zorobabel seemeth to be added to the text, Ezra 1. 8.

19 With commaundement that hee should carrie away the same vessels, and put them in the Temple at Ierusalem, and that the Temple of ỹ Lord should be built in his place.

20 Then came the same Sanabassarus being come hither, laid the foundations of the house of the Lord at Ierusalem, and from that time to this, being still a building, it is not yet fully ended.

21 Now therefore if it seeme good vnto the king, let search be made among the ‖ records of King Cyrus,

22 And if it be found, that the building of the house of the Lord at Ierusalem hath bene done with the consent of King Cyrus, and if our lord the king be so minded, let him signifie vnto vs thereof.

Or, roules.

23 Then commanded king Darius to seeke among the records at Babylon : and so at Ecbatana the palace which is in the countrey of Media, there

Or, place.

there was found a ‖ roule wherein these things were recorded.

24 In the first yeere of the reigne of Cyrus, king Cyrus commaunded that the house of the Lord at Ierusalem should bee built againe where they doe sacrifice with continuall fire.

25 Whose height shalbe sixtie cubits, and the breadth sixtie cubits, with three rowes of hewen stones, and one row of new wood of that countrey, and the expenses thereof to bee giuen out of the house of king Cyrus.

26 And that the holy vessels of the house of the Lord, both of gold and siluer that Nabuchodonosor tooke out of the house at Ierusalem, and brought to Babylon, should be restored to the house at Ierusalem, and bee set in the place where they were before.

27 And also he commanded that Sisinnes the gouernour of Syria and Phenice, and Sathrabuzanes, and their companions, and those which were appointed rulers in Syria, and Phenice should be carefull not to meddle with the place, but suffer Zorobabel the seruant of the Lord, and gouernour of Iudea, and the Elders of the Iewes, to build the house of the Lord in that place.

28 I haue commanded also to haue it built vp whole againe, and that they looke diligently to helpe those that be of the captiuitie of the Iewes, till the house of the Lord be finished.

29 And out of the tribute of Coelosyria, and Phenice, a portion carefully to be giuen these men, for the sacrifices of the Lord *that is*, to Zorobabel the gouernour, for bullocks, and rammes, and lambes;

30 And also corne, salt, wine and oile, and that continually euery yeere without further question, according as the Priests that be in Ierusalem shall signifie, to be daily spent:

‖ Drinke offerings.

31 That ‖ offrings may be made to the most high God, for the king and for his children, and that they may pray for their liues.

32 And he commanded, that whosoeuer should transgresse, yea, or make light of any thing afore spoken or written, out of his owne house should a tree be taken, and he thereon be hanged, and all his goods seized for the king.

33 The Lord therfore whose Name is there called vpon, vtterly destroy eue-

ry king and nation, that stretcheth out his hand to hinder or endammage that house of the Lord in Ierusalem.

34 I Darius the king haue ordeined, that according vnto these things it be done with diligence.

CHAP. VII.

1 Sisinnes and others, helpe forward the building. 5 The Temple is finished, and dedicated. 10 The Passeouer is kept.

Hen * Sisinnes the gouernour of Coelosyria, and Phenice, and Sathrabuzanes, with their companions, following the commandements of king Darius,

* Ezra 6. 13.

2 Did very carefully ouersee the holy workes, assisting the ancients of the Iewes, & gouernours of the Temple.

3 And so the holy workes prospered, when Aggeus, and Zacharias the Prophets prophecied.

4 And they finished these things, by the commandement of the Lord God of Israel, and with ‖ the consent of Cyrus, Darius, and Artaxerxes, kings of Persia.

‖ Or, the decree.

5 And thus was the holy house finished, in the † three and twentieth day of the moneth Adar, in the sixt yeere of Darius king of the Persians.

† Hebr. the third day, Ezra 6. 15.

6 And the children of Israel : the Priests, and the Leuites, and other that were of the captiuitie, that were added vnto them, did according to the things written in the booke of Moses.

7 And to the dedication of the Temple of the Lord, they offered an hundred bullockes, two hundred rammes, foure hundred lambes;

8 And twelue goats for the sinne of all Israel, according to the number of ‖ the chiefe of the tribes of Israel.

‖ Or, tribes.

9 The Priests also and the Leuites, stood arayed in their vestments according to their † kinreds, in the seruices of the Lord God of Israel, according to the booke of Moses : and the porters at euery gate.

† Hebr. diuisions, Esdr. 6. 18.

10 And the children of Israel ‖ that were of the captiuitie, held the Passeouer the fourteenth day of the first moueth, after that the Priests and the Leuites were sanctified.

‖ Or, with those that, &c.

11 They that were of the captiuitie were not all sanctified together : but the Leuites were all sanctified together,

12 And

12 And so they offered the Passeouer for all them of the captiuitie, and for their brethren the Priestes, and for themselues.

13 And the children of Israel that came out of the captiuitie, did eate, euen all they that had separated themselues from the abominations of the people of the land, and sought the Lord.

14 And they kept the feast of vnleauened bread seuen dayes, making merry before the Lord,

Or, mind. 15 For that he had turned the ||counsell of the King of Assyria towards them to strengthen their hands in the workes of the Lord God of Israel.

CHAP. VIII.

1 Esdras bringeth the Kings Commission to build. 8 The copy of it. 28 He declareth the names and number of those that came with him: 61 And his iourney. 71 Hee lamenteth the sinnes of his people, 96 And sweareth the Priestes to put away their strange wiues.

Azarias. AND after these things, when Artaxerxes the king of the Persians reigned, came Esdras the sonne of Saraias, the sonne of ||Ezerias, the sonne of Helchiah, the sonne of Salum,

Azarias. Meraioth. 2 The sonne of Sadduc, the sonne of Achitob, the sonne of Amarias, the sonne of ||Ozias, the sonne of ||Memeroth, the sonne of Zaraias, the sonne of ||Sauias, the sonne of Boccas, the sonne of Abisum, the sonne of Phinees, the sonne of Eleasar, the sonne of Aaron the †chiefe Priest.

Vzzi. Some copies want these three names.

Heb. was first, Ezra 1. 3 This Esdras went vp from Babylon, as a Scribe being very ready in the Law of Moyses, that was giuen by the God of Israel,

4 And the king did him honour: for he found grace in his sight in all his requests.

5 There went vp with him also certaine of the children of Israel, of the Priests, of the Leuites, of the holy Singers, Porters, and ||Ministers of the Temple, vnto Ierusalem,

Nethinims.

See Ezra 1. 7, 8, 9. 6 In †the seuenth yere of the reigne of king Artaxerxes, in the fifth moneth, (this was the kings seuenth yeere) for they went from Babylon in the first day of the first moneth, and came to Ierusalem, according to the ||prosperous

Or, successe

iourney which the Lord gaue them.

7 For Esdras had very great skill, so that he omitted nothing of the Law and Commaundements of the Lord, but taught all Israel the Ordinances and Iudgements.

8 Now the copy of the ||Commission which was written from Artaxerxes the King, and came to Esdras the priest and reader of the Law of the Lord, is this that followeth. | *Or, decree.*

9 King Artaxerxes vnto Esdras the Priest and reader of the Law of the Lord, sendeth greeting.

10 Hauing determined to deale graciously, I haue giuen order, that such of the nation of the Iewes, and of the Priests and Leuites being within our Realme, as are willing and desirous, should goe with thee vnto Ierusalem.

11 As many therefore as haue a minde thereunto, let them depart with thee, as it hath seemed good both to me, & my seuen friends the counsellors,

12 That they may looke vnto the affaires of Iudea and Ierusalem, agreeably to that which is in the Law of the Lord.

13 And cary the gifts vnto the Lord of Israel to Ierusalem, which I and my friends haue vowed, and all the golde and siluer that in the countrey of Babylon can be ||found, to the Lord in Ierusalem, | *Or, got.*

14 With that also which is giuen of the people, for the Temple of the Lord their God at Ierusalem: and that siluer and golde may be collected for bullocks, rammes and lambes, and things thereunto appertaining,

15 To the end that they may offer sacrifices vnto the Lord, vpon the Altar of the Lord their God, which is in Ierusalem.

16 And whatsoeuer thou and thy brethren will doe ||with the siluer and golde, that doe according to the will of thy God. | *With the rest of, Ezra 7. 18.*

17 And the holy vessels of the Lord which are giuen thee, for the vse of the Temple of thy God which is in Ierusalem, thou shalt set before thy God in Ierusalem.

18 And whatsoeuer thing else thou shalt remember for the vse of the Temple of thy God, thou shalt giue it out of the kings treasury.

19 And I, king Artaxerxes, haue also commaunded the keepers of the trea-

treasures in Syria and Phenice, that whatsoeuer Esdras the priest, and the reader of the law of the most high God shall send for, they should giue it him with speed,

20 To the summe of an hundred talents of siluer: likewise also of wheat euen to an hundred ||cores, and an hundred pieces of wine, and other things in abundance.

21 Let all things be performed after the law of God diligently vnto the most high God, that wrath come not vpon the kingdome of the King and his sonnes.

22 I command you also that yee require no taxe, nor any other imposition of any of the Priests or Leuites, or holy singers, or porters, or ministers of the temple, or of any that haue doings in this temple, and that no man haue authority to impose any thing vpon them.

23 And thou, Esdras, according to the wisedome of God, ordaine iudges, and iustices, that they may iudge in all Syria and Phenice, †all those that know the law of thy God, and those that know it not thou shalt teach.

24 And *whosoeuer shal transgresse the law of thy God, and of the king, shall be punished diligently, whether it be by death or other punishment, by penalty of money, or by imprisonment.

25 ¶ Then said Esdras the Scribe, Blessed be the onely Lord God of my fathers, who hath put these things into the heart of the king, to glorifie his house that is in Ierusalem;

26 And hath honoured mee in the sight of the king and his counsellers, and all his friends and Nobles.

27 Therefore was I encouraged, by the helpe of the Lord my God, and gathered together men of Israel to goe vp with me:

28 And these are the chiefe according to their families and seuerall dignities, that went vp with me from Babylon in the reigne of king Artaxerxes.

29 Of the sonnes of Phinees, Gerson: of the sonnes of Ithamar, ||Gamael: of the sonnes of Dauid; ||Lettus *the sonne of Sechenias:

30 Of the sonnes of Pharez, Zacharias, and with him were counted, an hundred and fifty men:

31 Of the sonnes of Pahath, Moab; Eliaonias, the sonne of ||Zaraias, and

with him two hundred men:

32 Of the sonnes of ||Zathoe, Sechenias, the sonne of Iezelus, and with him three hundred men; Of the sonnes of Adin, Obeth the sonne of Ionathan, and with him †two hundred and fifty men.

33 Of the sonnes of Elam, Iosias sonne of || Gotholias, and with him seuenty men:

34 Of the sonnes of Saphatias, ||Zaraias sonne of Michael, and with him ||threescore and ten men:

35 Of the sonnes of Ioab, ||Abadias sonne of ||Iezelus, and with him two hundred and ||twelue men:

36 Of the sonnes of Banid, ||Assalimoth sonne of Iosaphias, and with him an hundred and threescore men:

37 Of the sonnes of Babi, Zacharias sonne of Bebai, and with him twentie and eight men:

38 Of the sonnes of || Astath, Iohannes *sonne of* ||Acatan, and with him an hundred and ten men:

39 Of the sonnes of Adonicam the last, and these are the names of them, Eliphalet, Ieuel, and ||Samaias and with them ||seuenty men:

40 Of the sonnes of †Bago, Vthi, the sonne of Istalcurus, and with him seuenty men:

41 And these I gathered together to the riuer, called, ||Theras, where we pitched our tents three dayes, and then I suruayed them

42 But when I had found there, none of the priests and Leuites,

43 Then sent I vnto Eleazar and ||Iduel, and ||Masman,

44 And Alnathan, and Mamaias, and ||Ioribas, and Nathan, Eunatan, Zacharias, and Mosollamon principal men and learned.

45 And I bad them that they should goe vnto Saddeus the captaine, who was in the place of the treasury:

46 And commanded them that they should speake vnto Daddeus, and to ||his brethren, and to the treasurers in that place, to send vs such men as might execute the Priests office in the house of the Lord.

47 And by the mighty hand of our Lord they brought vnto vs skilful men of the sonnes of ||Moli, the sonne of Leui, the sonne of Israel, ||Asebebia and his sonnes and his brethren, who were eighteene.

48 And

|| Or, measures or salt, Ezra 7. 22.

† Heb. of those that know Ezra 7. 25.
* Ezra 7. 26.

|| Or, Daniel.
|| Or, Chattus.
* Ezra 8. 3. of the sons of Secheniah, of the sonnes of Parosh.
|| Zerachaiah.

|| Or, of the sonnes of Shecheniah, the sonne of Iahaziel.
† Heb. fifty men.

|| Or, Athaliah.

|| Or, Zebadiah.
|| Or, foure score men.
|| Or, Obadiah.
|| Or, Iehiel.
|| Or, eighteene men.
|| Or, of the sonnes of Shelomith the sonne of Iosiphiah.

|| Or, Azgad.
|| Or, Catan.

|| Or, Shemaia.
|| Or, sixty men.
|| Or, to the riuer called Ahaue. E. 8. 11.

|| Or, he numbred the people and the priests but found none of the sonnes of Leui.

|| Or, Ariel.
|| Or, Shemaiah.
|| Or, Iarib.
|| Or, these mens names with their generation are rightly distinguished Ezra 8. 16.
|| Or, Iddo.
|| Or, of
|| Or, Casiphia.
|| Or, the Nethinim at the place of Casiphia.
|| Or, Macli.
|| Sherebiah Ezra 8. 18.
|| Or, also Hashabia and with him Ieshaiah of the sonnes of Merari with his brethren, Ezra 8. 19.

48 And Asebia, and Annuus, and Osaias his brother of the sonnes of Channuneus, and their sonnes were twentie men.

49 And of the seruants of the Temple whom Dauid had ordeined, and the principall men, for the seruice of the Leuites (to wit) the seruants of the Temple, two hundred and twentie, the catalogue of whose names were shewed.

50 And there I ||vowed a fast vnto the yong men before our Lord, to desire of him a prosperous iourney, both for vs, and them that were with vs: for our children and for the †cattell:

|| Proclaimed.

* Heb. substance.

51 For I was ashamed to aske the king footmen, & horsemen, and conduct for safegard against our aduersaries:

52 For wee had said vnto the king, that the power of the Lord our God, should be with them that seeke him, to support them in all wayes.

53 And againe wee besought our Lord, as touching these things, & found him fauourable vnto vs.

54 Then I separated twelue of the chiefe of the priests, ||Esebrias, & Assanias, and ten men of their brethren with them.

|| Serenias and Hassibias.

55 And I weighed them the golde, and the siluer, and the holy vessels of the house of our Lord, which the king and his counsell, and the princes, and all Israel had giuen.

56 And when I had weighed it, I deliuered vnto them sixe hundred and fiftie talents of siluer, and siluer vessels of an hundred talents, and an hundred talents of gold,

57 And twentie golden vessels, and †twelue vessels of brasse, euen of fine brasse, glittering like gold.

* Heb. two vessels, Ezr. 8. 27.

58 And I said vnto them, Both you are holy vnto the Lord, and the vessels are holy, and the golde, and the siluer is a vowe vnto the Lord, the Lord of our fathers.

59 Watch ye, and keepe them till yee deliuer them to the chiefe of the priestes and Leuites, and to the principall men of the families of Israel in Ierusalem into the chambers of the house of our God.

60 So the priests and the Leuites who had receiued the siluer & the golde, and the vessels, brought them vnto Ierusalem into the Temple of the Lord.

61 And from the riuer Theras wee departed the twelft day of the first moneth, and came to Ierusalem by the mightie hand of our Lord, which was with vs: and from the beginning of our ||iourney, the Lord deliuered vs from euery enemy, and so wee came to Ierusalem.

|| Dangers in the way.

62 And when wee had bene there three dayes, the golde and siluer that was weighed, was deliuered in the house of our Lord on the fourth day vnto ||Marmoth the priest, the sonne of Iri.

|| Or, vnto Merimoth the sonne of Vriah the Priest.

63 And with him was Eleazar the sonne of Phinees, and with them were Iosabad the sonne of Iesu, and ||Moeth the sonne of Sabban, Leuites: all was deliuered them by number and weight.

|| Noadiah the sonne of Binnui.

64 And all the weight of them was written vp the same houre.

65 Moreouer they that were come out of the captiuitie offered sacrifice vnto the Lord God of Israel, euen twelue bullocks for all Israel, fourescore and sixteene rammes,

66 †Threescore and twelue lambes, goates for a peace offering, twelue, all of them a sacrifice to the Lord.

† Heb. 77. lambes, 12. hee goats for a sinne offering, Ezra 8. 31.

67 And they deliuered the kings commandements vnto the kings stewards, and to the gouernours of Coelosyria, and Phenice, and they honoured the people, and the Temple of God.

68 Now when these things were done, the rulers came vnto me, and said:

69 The nation of Israel, the princes, the priests, and Leuites haue not put away from them the strange people of the land: nor the pollutions of the Gentiles, to wit, of the Chanaanites, Hittites, Pheresites, Iebusites, and the Moabites, Egyptians, and Edomites.

* Ezra 9. 2.

70 For both they, and their sonnes, haue maried with their daughters, and the holy seed is mixed with the strange people of the land, and from the beginning of this matter, the rulers and the great men haue bene partakers of this iniquitie.

71 And assoone as I had heard these things, I rent my clothes, and the holy garment, and pulled off the haire from off my head, and beard, and sate me downe sad, and very heauy.

72 So all they that were then mooued at the word of the Lord God of Israel, assembled vnto me, whilest I mour-

mourned for the iniquitie : but I sate still full of heauinesse, vntill the euening sacrifice.

73 Then rising vp from the fast with my clothes and the holy garment rent, and bowing my knees, and stretching foorth my hands vnto the Lord :

74 I said, O Lord, I am confounded, and ashamed before thy face ;

† Greeke. haue aboun-ded

75 For our sinnes † are multiplied aboue our heads, and our ignorances haue reached vp vnto heauen.

76 For euer since the time of our fathers wee *haue bene* and are in great sinne, euen vnto this day :

77 And for our sinnes and our fathers, we with our brethren, and our kings, and our priests, were giuen vp vnto the Kings of the earth, to the sword, and to captiuitie, and for a pray with shame, vnto this day.

78 And now in some measure hath mercy bene shewed vnto vs, from thee, O Lord, that there should be left vs a roote, and a name, in the place of thy Sanctuary.

† Hebr. life, Ezr. 9. 8.

79 And to discouer vnto vs a light in the house of the Lord our God, and to giue vs †foode in the time of our seruitude.

80 Yea, when we were in bondage, we were not forsaken of our Lord ; but he made vs gracious before the Kings of Persia, so that they gaue vs food ;

81 Yea, and honoured the Temple of our Lord, and raised vp the desolate Sion, that they haue giuen vs a sure abiding in Iurie, and Ierusalem.

82 And now, O Lord, what shall wee say hauing these things ? for wee haue transgressed thy Commaundements, which thou gauest by the hand of thy seruants the Prophets, saying,

83 That the land which ye enter into to possesse as an heritage, is a land polluted with the pollutions of the strangers of the land, and they haue filled it with their vncleannesse.

84 Therefore now shal ye not ioyne your daughters vnto their sonnes, neither shall ye take their daughters vnto your sonnes.

85 Moreouer you shall neuer seeke to haue peace with them, that yee may be strong, and eate the good things of the land, and that ye may leaue the inheritance of the land vnto your children for euermore.

86 And all that is befallen, is done

vnto vs for our wicked workes, and great sinnes : for thou, O Lord, didst make our sinnes light :

87 And didst giue vnto vs such a roote : but we haue turned backe againe to transgresse thy Law, and to mingle our selues with the vncleannesse of the nations of the land.

‖ Or, be n angry, &

88 ‖ Mightest not thou be angry with vs to destroy vs, till thou hadst left vs neither root, seed, nor name ?

89 O Lord of Israel, thou art true : for we are left a root this day.

90 Behold, now are we before thee in our iniquities, for wee cannot stand any longer by reason of these things before thee.

91 And as Esdras in his praier made his confession, weeping, and lying flat vpon the ground before the Temple, there gathered vnto him from Ierusalem, a very great multitude of men, and women, & children : for there was great weeping among the multitude.

92 Then Iechonias the sonne of Ieelus, one of the sonnes of Israel called out and saide, O Esdras, wee haue sinned against the Lord God, wee haue maried strange women of the nations of the land; & now is all Israel ‖aloft.

‖ Or, exal ted, Deut. 28. 13. & Baruch.

93 Let vs make an oath to the Lord, that wee will put away all our wiues, which we haue taken of the heathen, with their children,

94 Like as thou hast decreed, and as many as doe obey the Law of the Lord.

95 Arise, and put in execution : for to thee doeth this matter appertaine, and wee will bee with thee : doe valiantly.

96 So Esdras arose, and tooke an oath of the chiefe of the Priestes, and Leuites of all † Israel, to do after these things, and *so* they sware.

† Hebr. of all Isr Ezr. 10.

CHAP. IX.

3 Esdras assembleth all the people. 10 They promise to put away the strange wiues. 20 The names and number of them that did so. 40 The Law of Moses is read and declared before all the people. 49 They weepe, and are put in mind of the Feast day.

 Hen Esdras rising from the court of the Temple, went to the chamber of Ioanan the sonne of Eliasib,

2 And

2 And remained there, and did eate no meate nor drinke water, mourning for the great iniquities of the multitude.

3 And there was a proclamation in all Iury and Ierusalem, to all them that were of the captiuitie, that they should be gathered together at Ierusalem:

4 And that whosoeuer met not there within two or three dayes according as the Elders that bare rule, appointed, their cattell should be seized to the vse of the Temple, and himselfe ||cast out from them that were of the captiuitie.

|| Vtterly destroyed, Iosh. 10. 8.

5 And in three dayes were all they of the tribe of Iuda and Beniamin gathered together at Ierusalem the twentieth day of the ninth moneth.

6 And all the multitude sate trembling in the broad court of the Temple, because of the present foule weather.

7 So Esdras arose vp, and said vnto them, Ye haue transgressed the law in marrying strange wiues, thereby to increase the sinnes of Israel.

8 And now by confessing giue glory vnto the Lord God of our fathers,

9 And doe his will, and separate your selues from the heathen of the land, and from the strange women.

10 Then cryed the whole multitude, and sayd with a loude voice; Like as thou hast spoken, so will we doe.

11 But forasmuch as the people are many, and it is foule weather, so that wee cannot stand without, and this is not a worke of a day or two, seeing our sinne in these things is spread farre:

12 Therefore let the rulers of the multitude ||stay, and let all them of our habitations that haue strange wiues, come at the time appointed,

|| Or, stand.

13 And with them the Rulers and Iudges of euery place, till we turne away the wrath of the Lord from vs, for this matter.

14 Then Ionathan the sonne of Azael, and Ezechias the sonne of Theocanus, accordingly tooke this matter vpon them: and Mosollam, and Leuis, and Sabbatheus helped them.

15 And they that were of the capt iutie, did according to all these things.

16 And Esdras the Priest chose vnto him the principal men of their families, all by name: and in the first day of the tenth moneth, they sate together to examine the matter.

17 So their cause that helde strange wiues, was brought to an ende in the first day of the first moneth.

18 And of the Priests that were come together, and had strange wiues, there were found:

19 Of the sonnes of Iesus the sonne of Iosedec, and his brethren, ||Matthelas, and Eleazar, and ||Ioribus, and ||Ioadanus.

20 And they gaue their hands to put away their wiues, & to offer †rammes, to make reconcilement for their ||errors.

21 And of the sonnes of Emmer, Ananias, and Zabdeus, and [a]Eanes, and [b]Sameius, and [c]Hierel, and [d]Azarias.

22 And of the sonnes of [e]Phaisur, Ellionas, Massias, Ismael, and Nathanael, and [f]Ocidelus, and [g]Talsas.

23 And of the Leuites: Iosabad, and Semis, and [h]Colius who was called [i]Calitas, and [k]Patheus, and Iudas, and Ionas.

24 Of the holy Singers: [l]Eleazurus, Bacchurus.

25 Of the Porters: Sallumus, and [m]Tolbanes.

26 Of them of Israel, of the sonnes of [n]Phoros, [o]Hiermas, and [p]Eddias, and Melchias, and [q]Maelus, and Eleazar, and [r]Asibias, and Baanias.

27 Of the sonnes of Ela, Matthanias, Zacharias, and [s]Hierielus, and Hieremoth, and [t]Aedias.

28 And of the sonnes of [u]Zamoth, [x]Eliadas, [y]Elisimus, [z]Othonias, Iarimoth, and [a]Sabatus, and [b]Sardeus.

29 Of the sonnes of Bebai, Iohannes, and Ananias, and [c]Iosabad, and [d]Amatheis.

30 Of the sonnes of [e]Many, [f]Olamus, [g]Mamuchus, [h]Iedeus, Iasubus, [i]Iasael, and Hieremoth.

31 †And of the sonnes of Addi, Naathus, and Moosias, Lacunus, and Naidus, and Mathanias, and Sesthel, Balunus, and Manasseas.

32 And of the sonnes of Annas, Elionas, and Aseas, and Milchias, and Sabbeus, and Simon Chosameus.

33 Aud of the sonnes of Asom, [k]Altaneus, and [l]Matthias, and [m]Bannaia, Eliphalat, and Manasses, and Semei.

34 And of the sonnes of Maani, Ieremias, Momdis, Omaerus, Iuel, Mabdai, and Pelias, and Anos, Carabasion, and Enasibus, & Mamnitanaimus, Eliasis, Bannus, Eliali, Samis, Selenias, Nathanias: And of the sons of

|| Maasias. || Iarib. || Gedaliah.
† Hebr. a ramme. || Or, purification.
[a] Harim. [b] Maasiah. [c] Iehiel. [d] Vzziah. [e] Pashur. [f] Iosabad. [g] Elasah. [h] Kelaiah. [i] Kelitah. [k] Pethahiah. [l] Eliashib. [m] Telem. [n] Parosh. [o] Ramiah. [p] Iesaiah. [q] Miamin. [r] Malchuah. [s] Iehiel. [t] Abdi. [u] Zattu. [x] Elioenai. [y] Eliashib. [z] Mattaniah. [a] Sabad. [b] Aziza. [c] Zabbai. [d] Athlai. [e] Bani. [f] Meshullam [g] Malluch. [h] Adaiah. [i] Sheal.
† Of the names in vers. 31, 32, 34, 35, See Ezr. 10. 30, 31. 34, &c.
[k] Mattenai. [l] Mattithiah [m] Zabad.

of Ozora, Sesis, Esril, Azailus, Samatus, Zambis, Iosiphus,

35 And of the sonnes of Ethma, Mazitias, Zabadaias, Edes, Iuel, Banaias.

36 All these had taken strange wiues, and they put them away with their children.

37 And the priests, and Leuites, and they that were of Israel dwelt in Ierusalem, and in the countrey, in the first day of y seuenth month: so the children of Israel were in their ||habitations.

||Or, villages.
* Nehe. 8. 1.

38 * And the whole multitude came together with one accord, into the broad place of the holy porch toward the East.

39 And they spake vnto Esdras the priest and reader, that he would bring the law of Moses, that was giuen of the Lord God of Israel.

40 So Esdras the chiefe priest, brought the law vnto the whole multitude from man to woman, and to all the priests, to heare the law in the first day of the seuenth moneth.

41 And hee read in the broad court before the holy porch from morning vnto midday, before both men and women; and all the multitude gaue heed vnto the law.

42 And Esdras the priest, and reader of the law stood vp, vpon a pulpit of wood which was made *for that purpose.*

||Or, Hilkiah.
||Or, Maasiah.
||Or, Pedaiah.
||Or, Hashum.
|| See Nehom. 8. 4.

43 And there stood vp by him Matathias, Sammus, Ananias, Azarias, Vrias, ||Ezecias, ||Balasamus, vpon the right hand.

44 And vpon his left hand stood ||Phaldaius, Misael, Melchias, ||Lothasubus and ||Nabarias.

45 Then tooke Esdras the booke of the law before the multitude: for he sate †honourably in the first place in the sight of them all.

† Heb. aboue them all.

46 And when hee opened the law, they stood all streight vp. So Esdras blessed the Lord God most high, the God of hostes Almighty.

47 And all the people answered Amen, and lifting vp their hands they fell to the ground, & worshipped the Lord.

48 Also Iesus, Anus, Sarabias, Adinus, Iacubus, Sabateus, ||Auteas, Maianeas, and Calitas, Azarias, and Ioazabdus, and Ananias, Biatas, the Leuites taught the law of the Lord, making them withall to vnderstand it.

||Or, Hodiah.

49 ||Then spake Attharates vnto Esdras the chiefe priest, and reader, and to the Leuites that taught the multitude, euen to all, saying,

50 This day is holy vnto y Lord; for they all wept when they heard the law.

51 Goe then and eate the fat, and drinke the sweet, and send part to ||them that haue nothing.

52 For this day is holy vnto the Lord, and be not sorrowfull; for the Lord will bring you to honour.

||Then Nehemiah and Ezra the priest and Scribe, and the Leuites that instructed the people, said vnto all the people, Nehem. 8.
||Or, the poore.

53 So the Leuites published all things to the people, saying: This day is holy to the Lord, be not sorrowfull.

54 Then went they their way, euery one to eate and drinke, & make mery, and to giue part to them that had nothing, and to make great cheere,

55 Because they vnderstood the words wherein they were instructed, and for y which they had bin assembled.

¶ II. ESDRAS.

CHAP. II.

1 Esdras is commanded to reproue the people. 24 God threatneth to cast them off, 35 and to giue their houses to a people of more grace then they.

* Ezra 7. 1.

 He second booke of the Prophet * Esdras the sonne of Saraias, the sonne of Azarias, the sonne of Helchias, the sonne of ||Sadamias, the

||Or, Shallum.

sonne of Sadoc, the sonne of Achitob,

2 The sonne of Achias, the sonne of Phinees, the sonne of Heli, the sonne of Amarias, the sonne of Aziei, the sonne of Marimoth, the sonne of Arna, the sonne of Ozias, the sonne of Borith, the sonne of Abisei, the sonne of Phinees, the sonne of Eleazar,

3 The sonne of Aaron, of the Tribe of Leui, which was captiue in the land of the Medes, in the reigne of Artaxerxes king of the Persians.

4 * And

* Isa. 58. 1.

4 *And the word of the Lord came vnto me, saying,

5 Goe thy way, and shew my people their sinfull deeds, and their children their wickednes which they haue done against me, that they may tell their childrens children,

6 Because the sinnes of their fathers are increased in them : for they haue forgotten me, & haue offered vnto strange gods.

7 Am not I euen hee that brought them out of the land of Egypt, from the house of bondage ? but they haue prouoked me vnto wrath, and despised my counsels.

8 Pull thou off then the haire of thy head, and cast all euill vpon them, for they haue not beene obedient vnto my law, but it is a rebellious people.

9 How long shall I forbeare them vnto whō I haue done so much good ?

* Exod. 14. 28.

10 *Many kings haue I destroyed for their sakes, Pharao with his seruants, and all his power haue I smitten downe.

* Num. 21. 24. iosh. 8. 12.

11 All the nations haue I destroyed before them, *& in the East I haue scattered the people of two prouinces, euen of Tyrus and Sidon, and haue slaine all their enemies.

12 Speake thou therefore vnto them saying, Thus saith the Lord,

* Eod. 14. 29.
‖ Or, street.
* Exo. 3. 10. and 4. 14.
* Exod. 13. 21.

13 *I led you through the Sea, and in the beginning gaue you a large and safe ‖passage, *I gaue you Moyses for a leader, and Aaron for a priest,

14 *I gaue you light in a pillar of fire, and great wonders haue I done among you, yet haue you forgotten me, saith the Lord.

* Exod. 16. 13. psal. 104 40.

15 Thus saith the Almightie Lord, The quailes *were as a token for you, I gaue you tents for your safegard, neuerthelesse you murmured there,

16 And triumphed not in my name for the destruction of your enemies, but euer to this day doe ye yet murmure.

17 Where are the benefits that I haue done for you ? when you were hungry and thirstie in the wildernesse, *did you not crie vnto me ?

* Num. 14. 3.

18 Saying, Why hast thou brought vs into this wildernesse to kill vs ? It had bin better for vs to haue serued the Egyptians, then to die in this wildernesse.

* Wisd. 16. 20.

19 Then had I pity vpon your mournings, and gaue you Manna to eat, *so ye did eate Angels bread.

* Numb. 20 11. wisd. 11 4.
‖ Or, abundantly.

20 *When ye were thirstie, did I not cleaue the rocke, and waters flowed out ‖to your fill ? for the heate I couered you with the leaues of the trees.

21 I diuided amongst you a fruitfull land, I cast out the Canaanites, the Pherezites, and the Philistines before you : *what shall I yet doe more for you, saith the Lord ?

* Isa. 5. 4. & exod. 15. 23

22 Thus saith the Almighty Lord, when you were in the wildernes in the riuer of the ‖Amorites, being athirst, and blaspheming my Name,

‖ Or, at the bitter waters, or waters of Marah.

23 I gaue you not fire for your blasphemies, but cast a tree in the water, and made the riuer sweet.

24 What shall I doe vnto thee, O Iacob ? thou *Iuda wouldest not obey me : I will turne me to other nations, and vnto those will I giue my Name, that they may keepe my Statutes.

* Exo. 32. 8.

25 Seeing yee haue forsaken mee, I will forsake you also : when yee desire me to be gracious vnto you, I shall haue no mercy vpon you.

26 *Whensoeuer you shall call vpon me, I will not heare you : for yee haue defiled your hands with blood, and your feete are swift to commit manslaughter.

* Isa. 1. 15.

27 Yee haue not as it were forsaken me, but your owne selues, saith the Lord.

28 Thus saith the Almighty Lord, Haue I not prayed you as a father his sonnes, as a mother her daughters, and a nurse her young babes,

29 That yee would be my people, ‖and I shoud be your God, that ye would be my children, and I should be your father ?

‖ Or, as I am your God

30 *I gathered you together, as a henne gathereth her chickens vnder her wings : but now, what shall I doe vnto you ? I will cast you out from my face.

* Mat. 23. 37.

31 *When you offer vnto me, I will turne my face from you : for your solemne feast dayes, your newe Moone, and your circumcisions haue I forsaken.

* Isa. 1. 13.

32 I sent vnto you my seruants the Prophets, whom yee haue taken and slaine, and torne their bodies in pieces, whose blood I will require of your hands, saith the Lord.

33 Thus saith the Almighty Lord, Your house is desolate, I will cast you out,

out, as the wind doth stubble.

34 And your children shall not bee fruitful : for they haue despised my Commandement, and done the thing that is euill before me.

35 Your houses wil I giue to a people that shall come, which not hauing heard of mee, yet shall beleeue mee, to whom I haue shewed no signes, yet they shall doe that I haue commaunded them.

36 They haue seene no Prophets, yet they shall call their sinnes to remembrance, and acknowledge them.

37 I take to witnesse the grace of the people to come, whose little ones reioyce in gladnesse : and though they haue not seene me with bodily eyes, yet in spirit they beleeue the thing that I say.

38 And now brother, behold what glory : and see the people that commeth from the East.

39 Vnto whom I will giue for leaders, Abraham, Isaac, and Iacob, Oseas, Amos, and Micheas, Ioel, Abdias, and Ionas,

40 Nahum, and Abacuc, Sophonias, Aggeus, Zacharie, and Malachie, which is called also an * Angel of the Lord.

* Mala. 3. 1.

CHAP. II.

1 God complaineth of his people : 10 Yet Esdras is willed to comfort them. 34 Because they refused, the Gentiles are called. 43 Esdras seeth the Sonne of God, and those that are crowned by him.

Hus saith the Lord, I brought this people out of bondage, and I gaue them my Commaundements by my seruants the prophets, whom they would not heare, but despised my counsailes.

2 The mother that bare them, saith vnto them, Goe your way ye children, for I am a widow, and forsaken.

3 I brought you vp with gladnesse, but with sorrow and heauinesse haue I lost you : for yee haue sinned before the Lord your God, and done that thing that is euil before him.

4 But what shall I now doe vnto you? I am a widow and forsaken : goe your way, O my children, and aske mercy of the Lord.

5 As for mee, O father, I call vpon thee for a witnesse ouer the mother of

these children, which would not keepe my Couenant,

6 That thou bring them to confusion, and their mother to a spoile, that there may be no off spring of them.

7 Let them bee scattered abroad among the heathen, let their names bee put out of the earth : for they haue despised my ‖ Couenant.

‖ Sacrament or oath.

8 Woe be vnto thee Assur, thou that hidest the vnrighteous in thee, O thou wicked people, remember * what I did vnto Sodome and Gomorrhe.

* Gene. 19 24.

9 Whose land lieth in clods of pitch and heapes of ashes : euen so also wil I doe vnto them that heare me not, saith the Almightie Lord.

10 Thus saith the Lord vnto Esdras, Tell my people that I will giue them the kingdome of Hierusalem, which I would haue giuen vnto Israel.

11 Their glory also wil I take vnto mee, and giue these the euerlasting Tabernacles, which I had prepared for them.

12 They shall haue the tree of Life for an oyntment of sweet sauour, they shall nether labour, nor be weary.

13 Goe and yee shall receiue : pray for few dayes vnto you, that they may be shortned : the kingdome is already prepared for you : Watch.

14 Take heauen and earth to witnesse; for I haue broken the euill in pieces, and created the good; for I liue, saith the Lord.

15 Mother, embrace thy children, and ‖ bring them vp with gladnesse, make their feet as fast as a pillar : for I haue chosen thee, saith the Lord.

‖ Or, bring them vp with gladnesse as a doue : make their feet fast. For, &c.

16 And those that be dead wil I raise vp againe from their places, and bring them out of the graues : for I haue knowen ‖ my Name in Israel.

‖ Or, thy name, O Israel.

17 Feare not thou mother of the children : for I haue chosen thee, saith the Lord.

18 For thy helpe I will send my seruants Esay and Ieremie, after whose counsaile I haue sanctified and prepared for thee twelue trees, laden with diuers fruits;

19 And as many fountaines flowing with milke and hony : and seuen mightie mountaines, whereupon there grow roses and lillies, whereby I will fill thy children with ioy.

20 Doe right to the widow, iudge for

for the fatherlesse, giue to the poore, defend the orphane, clothe the naked,

21 Heale the broken and the weake, laugh not a lame man to scorne, defend the maimed, and let the blind man come into the sight of my clearenesse.

22 Keepe the olde and yong within thy walles.

23 * Wheresoeuer thou findest the dead, †take them and bury them, and I will giue thee the first place in my resurrection.

* Tob. 17. 18.
† Signing bury them.

24 Abide still, O my people, and take thy rest, for thy quietnesse shall come.

25 Nourish thy children, O thou good nouroe, stablish their feete.

26 As for the seruants whom I haue giuen thee, there shall not one of them perish; for I will require them from among thy number.

27 Be not weary, for when the day of trouble and heauinesse commeth, others shal weepe and be sorrowfull, but thou shalt be merry, and haue abundance.

28 The heathen shall enuie thee, but they shall be able to doe nothing against thee, sayth the Lord.

29 My hands shal couer thee, so that thy children shall not see hell.

30 Be ioyfull, O thou mother, with thy children, for I will deliuer thee, sayth the Lord.

31 Remember thy children that sleep, for I shall bring them out of the sides of the earth, and shew mercy vnto them: for I am mercifull, sayth the Lord Almightie.

32 Embrace thy children vntill I come and ‖shew mercy vnto them: for my welles runne ouer, and my grace shall not faile.

‖ Or, preach.

33 I Esdras receiued a charge of the Lord vpon the mount Oreb, that I should goe vnto Israel; but when I came vnto them, they set me at nought, and despised the commandement of the Lord.

34 And therefore I say vnto you, O yee heathen, that heare and vnderstand, Looke for your shepheard, hee shall giue you euerlasting rest; for he is nigh at hand, that shall come in the end of the world.

35 Be ready to the reward of the kingdome, for the euerlasting light shal shine vpon you for euermore.

36 Flee the shadow of this world, receiue the ioyfulnesse of your glory: I testifie my Sauiour openly.

37 O receiue the gift that is giuen you, and be glad, giuing thankes vnto him that hath called you to the heauenly kingdome.

38 Arise vp and stand, behold the number of those that be sealed ‖in the feast of the Lord:

‖ Or, for.

39 Which are departed from the shadow of the world, and haue receiued glorious garments of the Lord.

40 Take thy number, O Sion, and †shut vp those of thine that are clothed in white, which haue fulfilled the Law of the Lord.

† Lat. conclude.

41 The number of thy children whom thou longedst for, is fulfilled: beseech the power of the Lord, that thy people which haue been called from the beginning, may be hallowed.

42 *I Esdras saw vpon the mount Sion a great people, whom I could not number, and they all praised the Lord with songs.

* Reu. 7. 9.

43 And in the middest of them there was a young man of a high stature, taller then all the rest, and vpon euery one of their heads he set crownes, and was more exalted, which I marueiled at greatly.

44 So I asked the Angel, and said, ‖Sir, what are these?

‖ Or, Lord.

45 Hee answered, and said vnto me, These be they that haue put off the mortall clothing, and put on the immortall, and haue confessed the Name of God: now are they crowned, and receiue palmes.

46 Then sayd I vnto the Angel, What yong person is it that crowneth them, and giueth them palmes in their handes?

47 So hee answered, and said vnto me, It is the sonne of God, whom they haue confessed in the world. Then began I greatly to commend them, that stood so stiffely for the Name of the Lord.

48 Then the Angel sayd vnto me, Goe thy way, and tell my people what maner of things, and how great wonders of the Lord thy God thou hast seene.

CHAP. III.

1 Esdras is troubled, 13 and acknowledgeth the sinnes of the people: 28 yet complaineth that the heathen were lords ouer them, being more wicked then they.

In

N the thirtieth yeere after the ruine of the citie, I was in Babylon, and lay troubled vpon my bed, and my thoughts came vp ouer my heart.

2 For I saw the desolation of Sion, and the wealth of them that dwelt at Babylon.

3 And my spirit was sore moued, so that I began to speake words full of feare to the most High, and said,

4 O Lord, who bearest rule, thou spakest at the beginning, when thou didst plant the earth (and that thy selfe alone) and commandedst the people,

*Gen. 2. 7.   5 *And gauest a body vnto Adam without soule, which was the workemanship of thine hands, & didst breathe into him the breath of life, and he was made liuing before thee.

6 And thou leddest him into paradise, which thy right hand had planted, before euer the earth came forward.

7 And vnto him thou gauest commandement to loue thy way, which he transgressed, and immediatly thou appointedst death in him, and in his generations, of whom came nations, tribes, people, and kinreds out of number.

*Gen. 6. 12.   8 *And euery people walked after their owne will, and did wonderfull things before thee, and despised thy commandements.

*Gen. 7. 10   9 *And againe in processe of time thou broughtest the flood vpon those that dwelt in the world, and destroyedst them.

10 And it came to passe in euery of them, that as death was to Adam, so was the flood to these.

*1. Pet. 3. 20.   11 Neuerthelesse one of them thou leftest, namely *Noah with his household, of whom came all righteous men.

12 And it happened, that when they that dwelt vpo the earth began to multiply, and had gotten them many children, and were a great people, they beganne againe to be more vngodly then the first.

*Gen. 12. 1   13 Now when they liued so wickedly before thee, *thou diddest choose thee a man from among them, whose name *Gen. 17. 5   was *Abraham.

14 Him thou louedst, and vnto him onely thou shewedst thy will:

15 And madest an euerlasting couenant with him, promising him that thou wouldest neuer forsake his seede.

16 *And vnto him, thou gauest Isahac, and *vnto Isahac also thou gauest Iacob and Esau. As for Iacob thou *didst choose him to thee, and put by Esau: and so Iacob became a great multitude.

17 And it came to passe, that when thou leddest his seede out of Egypt, *thou broughtest them vp to the mount Sina.

18 And bowing the heauens, thou didst set fast the earth, mouedst the whole world, and madest the depth to tremble, and troubledst the men of that age.

19 And thy glory went through foure gates, of fire, and of earthquake, and of wind, and of cold, that thou mightest giue the law vnto the seed of Iacob, ||and diligence vnto the generation of Israel.

20 And yet tookest thou not away from them a wicked heart, that thy law might bring forth fruite in them.

21 For the first Adam bearing a wicked heart transgressed, and was ouercome; and so be all they that are borne of him.

22 Thus infirmity was made permanent; and the law (also) in the heart of the people with the malignity of the roote, so that the good departed away, and the euill abode still.

23 So the times passed away, and the yeeres were brought to an end: *then diddest thou raise thee vp a seruant, called Dauid,

24 * Whom thou commandedst to build a citie vnto thy name, and to offer incense and oblations vnto thee therein.

25 When this was done many yeeres, then they that inhabited the citie forsooke thee,

26 And in all things did euen as Adam, and all his generations had done, for they also had a wicked heart.

27 And so thou gauest the citie ouer into the hands of thine enemies.

28 Are their deeds then any better that inhabite Babylon, that they should therefore haue the dominion ouer Sion?

29 For when I came thither, and had seene impieties without number, then my soule saw many euill doers in this thirtieth yeere, so that my heart failed me.

30 For I haue seene how thou sufferest

*Gen. 21. 2, 3.
* Gen. 25. 25, 26.

* Mal. 1. 2,

* Rom. 9.
13. exod.
19. 1. deut.
4. 10.

|| And to all the generation of Israel that they should keepe it with diligence.

* 1. Sam. 16. 13.

* 2. Sam. 5 1. and 7. 5. 13.

rest them sinning, and hast spared wicked doers : and hast destroyed thy people, and hast preserued thine enemies, and hast not signified it.

31 ‖I doe not remember how this way may be left : Are they then of Babylon better then they of Sion?

Or, I conceiue.

32 Or is there any other people that knoweth thee besides Israel? or what generation hath so beleeued thy Couenants as Iacob?

33 And yet their reward appeareth not, and their labour hath no fruite : for I haue gone here and there through the heathen, and I see that they ‖flowe in wealth, and think not vpon thy commandements.

Or, abound

34 Weigh thou therfore our wickednesse now in the ballance, and theirs also that dwell in the world : and so shall thy Name no where be found , but in Israel.

35 Or when was it that they which dwell vpon the earth, haue not sinned in thy sight? or what people hath so kept thy commandements?

36 Thou shalt find that Israel by name hath kept thy precepts : but not the heathen.

CHAP. IIII.

1 The Angel declareth the ignorance of Esdras in Gods iudgments, 13 and aduiseth him not to meddle with things aboue his reach. 23 Neuerthelesse Esdras asketh diuers questions, and receiueth answeres to them.

Nd the Angel that was sent vnto me, whose name was Vriel , gaue mee an answere,

2 And said, Thy heart hath gone too farre in this world, and thinkest thou to comprehend the way of the most High?

3 Then said I , Yea my Lord : and he answered me and said, I am sent to shew thee three wayes, and to set forth three similitudes before thee.

4 Whereof if thou canst declare me one, I will shew thee also the way that thou desirest to see, & I shall shew thee from whence the wicked heart cometh.

5 And I said, Tel on my Lord. Then said he vnto me, Goe thy way, weigh me the weight of the fire, or measure me the blast of the wind, or call me againe the day that is past.

6 Then answered I and said, What man is able to doe that, that thou shouldest aske such things of mee?

7 And he said vnto me, If I should aske thee how great dwellings are in the midst of ẙ sea, or how many springs are in the beginning of the deepe , or how many springs are aboue the firmament, or which are the outgoings of Paradise :

8 Peraduenture thou wouldest say vnto me, I neuer went downe into the deepe, nor as yet into hell, neither did I euer climbe vp into heauen.

9 Neuerthelesse, now haue I asked thee but onely of the fire and winde, and of the day where through thou hast passed, and of things frō which thou canst not be separated, and yet canst thou giue me uo answeere of them.

10 He said moreouer vnto me, Thine owne things, and such as are growen vp with thee, canst thou not know.

11 How should thy vessel then bee able to comprehend the way of the highest, and the world being now outwardly corrupted, to vnderstand the ‖corruption that is euident in my sight?

‖ Or, incorruption.

12 Then said I vnto him , It were better that we were not at all, then that we should liue still in wickednesse, and to suffer, and not to know wherefore.

13 He answered me and said, I went into a forest into a plaine, and the *trees tooke counsell.

* Iudg. 9. 8. 2. chron. 25 18.

14 And said, Come, let vs goe and make warre against the Sea , that it may depart away before vs, and that we may make vs more woods.

15 The floods of the Sea also in like maner tooke counsell, and said, Come, let vs goe vp and subdue the woods of the plaine, that there also we may make vs another countrey.

16 The thought of the wood was in vaine, for the fire came and consumed it.

17 The thought of the floods of the Sea came likewise to nought, for the sand stood vp and stopped them.

18 If thou wert iudge now betwixt these two, whom wouldest thou begin to iustifie, or whom wouldest thou condemne?

19 I answered and said, Verily it is a foolish thought that they both haue deuised : for the ‖ground is giuen vnto the wood, and the sea also hath his place to beare his ‖floods.

‖ Or, the land.

‖ Or, waues.

20 Then answered he me and said, Thou hast giuen a right iudgment, but why iudgest thou not thy selfe also?

21 For

‖ *The land.*

* Isay 55.
9, 9 iohn 3.
31. 1. cor. 2.
13.

21 For like as ‖the ground is giuen vnto the wood, & the sea to his floods: euen so *they that dwell vpon the earth may vnderstand nothing, but that which is vpon the earth: and hee that dwelleth aboue the heauens, may onely vnderstand the things that are aboue the height of the heauens.

22 Then answered I, and said, I beseech thee, O Lord, let me haue vnderstanding.

23 For it was not my minde to be curious of the high things, but of such as passe by vs dayly, namely wherefore Israel is giuen vp as a reproch to the heathen, and for what cause the people whom thou hast loued, is giuen ouer vnto vngodly nations, and why the Lawe of our forefathers is brought to nought, and the written Couenants come to ‖none effect.

‖ *Or, no where.*

24 And wee passe away out of the world as grassehoppers, and our life is astonishment and feare, and we are not worthy to obtaine mercie.

25 What will he then doe vnto his Name, whereby we are called? of these things haue I asked.

26 Then answered he me, and said, The more thou searchest, the more thou shalt marueile, for the world hasteth fast to passe away,

27 And cannot comprehend the things that are promised to the righteous in time to come: for this world is ful of vnrighteousnesse and infirmities.

28 But as concerning the things whereof thou askest me, I wil tell thee; for the euil is sowen, but the destruction thereof is not yet come.

29 If therefore that which is sowen, be not turned vpside downe; and if the place where the euil is sowen passe not away, then cannot it come that is sowen with good.

30 For the graine of euill seed hath bene sowen in the heart of Adam from the beginning, and how much vngodlinesse hath it brought vp vnto this time? and how much shall it yet bring foorth vntill the ‖time of threshing come.

‖ *Or, floore.*

31 Ponder now by thy selfe, how great fruit of wickednesse the graine of euil seed hath brought forth.

32 And when the eares shall bee cut downe, which are without number, how great a floore shall they fill?

33 Then I answered and said, How and when shall these things come to passe? wherefore are our yeeres few and euill?

34 And he answered me, saying, Do not thou hasten aboue the most Highest: for thy haste is in vaine to be aboue him, for thou hast much exceeded.

35 Did not the soules also of the righteous aske question of these things in their chambers, saying, How long shall I hope on this fashion? when commeth the fruit of the floore of our reward?

36 And vnto these things ‖Vriel the Archangel gaue them answere, and said, Euen when the number of seedes is filled in you: for he hath weighed the world in the ballance.

‖ *Ieremiel.*

37 By measure hath hee measured the times, and by number hath he numbred the times; and he doeth not mooue nor stirre them, vntill the said measure be fulfilled.

38 Then answered I, and said, O Lord that bearest rule, euen we all are full of impietie.

39 And for our sakes peraduenture it is that the floores of the righteous are not filled, because of the sinnes of them that dwell vpon the earth.

40 So he answered me, and said, Go thy way to a wman with childe, and aske of her, when she hath fulfilled her nine moneths, if her wombe may keepe the birth any longer within her?

41 Then said I, No Lord, that can she not. And he said vnto mee, In the graue, the chambers of soules are like the wombe of a woman:

42 For like as a woman that trauaileth, maketh haste to escape the necessitie of the trauaile: euen so doe these places haste to deliuer those things that are committed vnto them.

43 From the beginning looke what thou desirest to see, it shalbe shewed thee.

44 Then answered I, and said, If I haue found fauour in thy sight, and if it be possible, and if I be meet therefore,

45 Shew me then whether there be more to come then is past, or more past then is to come.

46 What is past I know; but what is for to come I know not.

47 And he said vnto me, Stand vp vpon the right side, and I shal expound the similitude vnto you.

48 So I stood and saw, and behold an hot burning ouen passed by before mee: and it happened that when the flame

flame was gone by, I looked, and behold, the smoke remained still.

49 After this there passed by before me a watrie cloude, and sent downe much raine with a storme, and when the stormie raine was past, the drops remained still.

50 Then said he vnto me, Consider with thy selfe : as the raine is more then the drops, and as the fire is greater then the smoke : but the drops and the smoke remaine behind : so the ||quantitie which is past, did more exceede.

51 Then I prayed, and sayd, May I liue, thinkest thou, vntill that time? ||or what shall happen in those dayes?

52 He answered me, and sayd, As for the tokens whereof thou askest me, I may tell thee of them in part ; but as touching thy life, I am not sent to shew thee, for I doe not know it.

CHAP. V.

1 The signes of the times to come. 23 He asketh why God choosing but one people, did cast them off. 30 Hee is taught, that Gods Iudgements are vnsearchable : 46 and that God doeth not all at once.

NEuertheles as concerning the tokens, beholde, the dayes shall come that they which dwell vpon earth, ||shall bee taken in a great number, and the way of trueth shall be hidden, and the land shall be barren of faith.

2 But *iniquitie shalbe increased aboue that which now thou seest, or that thou hast heard long agoe.

3 And the land ||that thou seest now to haue roote, shalt thou see wasted suddenly.

4 But if the most high graunt thee to liue, thou shalt see after the third trumpet, that the Sunne shall suddenly shine againe in the night, and the Moone thrice in the day.

5 And blood shal drop out of wood, and the stone shall giue his voice, and the people shalbe troubled.

6 And enen he shal rule whom they looke not for that dwel vpon the earth, and the foules shall take their flight away together.

7 And the Sodomitish sea shall cast out fish, and make a noyse in the night, which many haue not knowen : but they shall all heare the voice thereof.

8 There shall be a confusion also in many places, and the fire shalbe oft ||sent out againe, and the wilde beasts shall change their places, and menstruous women shall bring foorth monsters.

9 And salt waters shall be found in the sweete, and all friends shall destroy one another : then shall wit hide it selfe, and vnderstanding withdraw it selfe into his secret chamber,

10 And shall be sought of many, and yet not be found : then shall vnrighteousnesse and incontinencie be multiplyed vpon earth.

11 One land also shall aske another, and say, Is righteousnes that maketh a man righteous, gone through thee? And it shall say, No.

12 At the same time shall men hope, but nothing obtaine : they shall labour, but their wayes shall not ||prosper.

13 To shew thee such tokens I haue leaue : and if thou wilt pray againe, and weepe as now, and fast seuen dayes, thou shalt heare yet greater things.

14 Then I awaked, & an extreme fearefulnesse went through all my body, and my minde was troubled, so that it fainted.

15 So the Angel that was come to talke with me, helde me, comforted me, and set me vp vpon my feete.

16 And in the second night it came to passe, that Salathiel the captaine of the people came vnto mee, saying, Where hast thou beene? and why is thy countenance so heauie?

17 Knowest thou not that Israel is committed vnto thee, in the land of their captiuitie?

18 Vp then, and eate bread, and forsake vs not as the shepheard that leaueth his flocke in the handes of cruell wolues.

19 Then sayd I vnto him, Goe thy waies from me, and come not nigh me : And he heard what I said, and went from me.

20 And so I fasted seuen dayes, monrning and weeping, like as Vriel the Angel commanded me.

21 And after seuen dayes, so it was that the thoughts of my heart were very grieuous vnto me againe.

22 And my soule recouered the spirit of vnderstanding, and I began to talke with the most high againe,

23 And said, O Lord, that bearest rule of euery wood of the earth, and of all

Margin notes

Or, measure.

Or, who shalbe manuscript?

Shalbe found with great wealth

Mat. 24. 12

Or, that hou treadest vpon and seest.

Or, slaked.

Or, be reiected.

all the trees thereof, thou hast chosen thee one onely vine.

24 And of all lands of the whole world thou hast chosen thee one pit : and of all the flowers thereof, one Lillie.

25 And of all the depths of the Sea, thou hast filled thee one riuer : and of all builded cities, thou hast hallowed Sion vnto thy selfe.

26 And of all the foules that are created, thou hast named thee one Doue : and of all the cattell that are made, thou hast prouided thee one sheepe.

27 And among all the multitudes of peoples, thou hast gotten thee one people : and vnto this people whom thou louedst, thou gauest a law that is approued of all.

‖ Or, ouer.   28 And now O Lord, why hast thou giuen this one people ouer vnto many? and ‖ vpon the one roote hast thou prepared others, and why hast thou scattered thy onely one people among many?

29 And they which did gainesay thy promises, and beleeued not thy couenants, haue trodden them downe.

30 If thou didst so much hate thy people, yet shouldest thou punish them with thine owne hands.

31 Now when I had spoken these words, the Angell that came to me the night afore, was sent vnto me,

32 And said vnto me, Heare me, and I will instruct thee, hearken to the thing that I say, & I shal tell thee more.

33 And I said, Speake on, my Lord : then said he vnto me, thou art sore troubled in minde for Israels sake : louest thou that people better then hee that made them?

34 And I said, No Lord, but of very griefe haue I spoken : For my reines paine me euery houre, while I labour to comprehend the way of the most High, and to seeke out part of his iudgement.

35 And he said vnto me, Thou canst not : and I said, wherfore Lord? wherunto was I borne then? or why was not my mothers wombe then my graue, that I might not haue seene the trauell of Iacob, and the wearisome toyle of the stocke of Israel?

36 And he said vnto me, Number me the things that are not yet come, gather me together the droppes that are scattered abroad, make mee the flowres greene againe that are withered.

37 Open me the places that are closed, and bring me forth the winds that in them are shut vp, shew me the image of a voyce : and then I will declare to thee the thing that thou labourest to knowe.

38 And I said, O Lord, that bearest rule, who may know these things, but hee that hath not his dwelling with men?

39 As for me, I am vnwise : how may I then speake of these things whereof thou askest me?

40 Then said he vnto me, Like as thou canst doe none of these things that I haue spoken of, euen so canst thou not find out my iudgement, or in the end the loue that I haue promised vnto my people.

41 And I said, behold, O Lord, yet art thou nigh vnto them that be reserued till the end; and what shall they doe that haue beene before me, or we (that be now) or they that shall come after vs?

42 And he said vnto me, I wil liken my iudgement vnto a ring : like as there is no slacknesse of the last, euen so there is no swiftnesse of the first.

43 So I answered and said, Couldst thou not make those that haue beene made, and be now, and that are for to come, at once, that thou mightest shewe thy iudgement the sooner?

44 Then answered he me, and said, The creature may not hast aboue the maker, neither may the world hold them at once that shalbe created therin.

45 And I said, As thou hast said vnto thy seruant, that thou which giuest life to all, hast giuen life at once to the creature that thou hast created, and the creature bare it : euen so it might now also beare them that now be present at once.

46 And he said vnto me, Aske the wombe of a woman, & say vnto her, If thou bringest forth children, why doest thou it not together, but one after another? pray her therefore to bring forth tenne children at once.

47 And I said, She cannot : but must doe it by distance of time.

48 Then said he vnto me, Euen so haue I giuen the wombe of the earth to those that be sowen in it, in their times.

49 For like as a young child may not bring forth the things that belong to the aged, euen so haue I disposed the world which I created.

50 And

50 And I asked and said, Seeing thou hast now giuen me the way, I will *proceed to* speak before thee : for our mother of whom thou hast told me that she is yong, draweth now nigh vnto age.

51 He answered me and said, Aske a woman that beareth children, and shee shall tell thee.

52 Say vnto her, Wherefore are not they whome thou hast now brought forth, like those that were before, but lesse of stature ?

53 And she shall answere thee, They that be borne in the strength of youth, are of one fashion, and they that are borne in the time of age (when the wombe faileth) are otherwise.

54 Consider thou therfore also, how that yee are lesse of stature then those that were before you.

55 And so are they that come after you lesse then ye, as the creatures which now begin to be old, and haue passed ouer the strength of youth.

56 Then saide I, Lord, I beseech thee, if I haue found fauor in thy sight, shew thy seruant by whom thou visitest thy creature.

CHAP. VI.

1 Gods purpose is eternall. 8 The next world shall follow this immediatly. 13 What shall fall out at the last. 31 Hee is promised more knowledge, 38 and reckoneth vp the workes of the creation, 57 and complaineth that they haue no part in the world for whome it was made.

Or, circle of the earth.

Nd he said vnto me, in the beginning when ỹ ‖earth was made, before the borders of the world stood, or euer the windes blew,

2 Before it thundred and lightned, or euer the foundations of Paradise were laide,

3 Before the faire flowers were seene, or euer the moueable powers were established, before ỹ innumerable multitude of Angels were gathered together,

4 Or euer the heights of the aire were lifted vp, before the measures of the firmament were named, or euer the chimnies in Sion were hot,

5 And ere the present yeeres were sought out, and or euer the inuentions of them that now sinne were turned, before they were sealed that haue gathered faith for a treasure :

6 Then did I consider these things, and they all were made through mee alone, and through none other : by mee also they shall be ended, & by none other.

7 Then answered I and said, What shall bee the parting asunder of the times ? or when shall be the ende of the first, and the beginning of it that followeth ?

8 And he said vnto me, From Abraham vnto Isaac, when Iacob and Esau were borne of him, *Iacobs hand held ‖first the heele of Esau.

9 For Esau is the end of the world, and Iacob is the beginning of it that followeth.

10 The hand of man is betwixt the heele and the hand : other question, Esdras, aske thou not.

11 ¶ I answered then and said, O Lord that bearest rule, if I haue found fauour in thy sight,

12 I beseech thee, shew thy seruant the end of thy tokens, whereof thou shewedst me part the last night.

13 So he answered and said vnto me, Stand vp vpon thy feete, and heare a mightie sounding voyce.

14 And it shall be as it were a great ‖motion, but the place where thou standest, shall not be moued.

15 And therefore when it speaketh be not afraid : for the word is of the end, and the foundation of the earth is vnderstood.

16 And why ? because the speech of these things trembleth and is mooued : for it knoweth that the ende of these things must be changed.

17 And it happened that when I had heard it, I stood vp vpon my feet, and hearkened, & behold, there was a voice that spake, and the sound of it was like the sound of many waters.

18 And it said, Behold, the dayes come, that I will begin to draw nigh, and to visit them that dwell vpon the earth,

19 And will begin to make inquisition of them, what they be that haue hurt vniustly with their vnrighteousnesse, and when the affliction of Sion shalbe fulfilled.

20 And when the world that shal begin to vanish away shall bee ‖finished : then will I shew these tokens, the books shalbe opened before the firmament, and they shall see all together.

21 And the children of a yeere olde shall speake with their voyces, the women

*Gen. 25.
26.
‖Or, from the beginning.

‖Or, earthquake.

‖Or, sealed.

men with childe shall bring foorth vntimely children, of three or foure moneths old : and they shall liue, and bee raised vp.

22 And suddenly shal the sowen places appeare vnsowen, the full storehouses shall suddenly be found empty.

23 And the trumpet shall giue a sound, which when euery man heareth they shalbe suddenly afraid.

24 At that time shall friendes fight one against another like enemies, and the earth shall stand in feare with those that dwell therein, the springs of the fountaines shall stand still, and in three houres they shall not runne.

25 Whosoeuer remaineth from all these that I haue told thee, shall escape, and see my saluation, and the ende of your world.

26 And the men that are receiued, shall see it, who haue not tasted death from their birth : and the heart of the inhabitants shalbe changed, and turned into another meaning.

27 For euil shalbe put out, and deceit shalbe quenched.

28 As for faith, it shall flourish, corruption shalbe ouercome, & the trueth which hath bene so long without fruit, shalbe declared.

29 And when hee talked with mee, behold, I looked by little and little vpon him before whom I stood.

30 And these words said he vnto me, I am come to shew thee the time of the night to come.

31 If thou wilt pray yet more, & fast seuen daies againe, I shal tel thee greater things ‖by day, then I haue heard.

‖ See cap. 13. vers. 52.

32 For thy voice is heard before the most High : for the mighty hath seene thy righteous dealing, he hath seene also thy chastitie, which thou hast had euer since thy youth.

33 And therefore hath he sent mee to shew thee al these things, and to say vnto thee, Be of good comfort, & feare not.

34 And hasten not with the times that are past, to thinke vaine things, that thou mayest not hasten from the latter times.

35 And it came to passe after this, that I wept againe, and fasted seuen dayes in like maner, that I might fulfill the three weekes which he told me.

36 And in the eight night was my heart vexed within mee againe, and I began to speake before the most High.

37 For my spirit was greatly set on fire, and my soule was in distresse.

38 And I said, O Lord, thou spakest from the beginning of the creation, euen the first day, & saidest thus, *Let heauen and earth bee made : and thy word was a perfect worke.

* Gen. 1. 1.

39 And then was the spirit, and darkenesse, and silence were on euery side ; the sound of mans voice was not yet formed.

40 Then commandedst thou a faire light to come foorth of thy treasures, that thy worke might appeare.

41 Vpon the second day thou madest the spirit of the firmament, and commandedst it to part asunder, and to make a diuision betwixt the waters, that the one part might goe vp, and the other remaine beneath.

42 Vpon the thirde day thou didst commaund that the waters should bee gathered in the seuenth part of the earth : sixe parts hast thou dried vp and kept them, to the intent that of these some being planted of God and tilled, might serue thee.

43 For as soone as thy word went foorth, the worke was made.

44 For immediatly there was great and innumerable fruit, and many and diuers pleasures for the taste, & flowers of vnchangeable colour, and odours of wonderfull smell : and this was done the third day.

45 *Vpon the fourth day thou commandedst that the Sunne should shine, and the Moone giue her light, and the starres should be in order,

* Gen. 1. 14.

46 And gauest them a charge to do *seruice vnto man, that was to be made.

Gen. 1. 15. deut. 4. 19.

47 Vpon the fift day, thou saydst vnto the seuenth part, * where the waters were gathered, that it should bring foorth liuing creatures, foules and fishes : and so it came to passe.

Gene. 1. 20.

48 For the dumbe water, and without life, brought foorth liuing things at the commandement of God, that al people might praise thy wondrous works.

49 Then didst thou ordeine two liuing creatures, the one thou calledst ‖Enoch, and the other Leuiathan,

‖ Behemoth.

50 And didst separate the one from the other : for the seuenth part (namely where the water was gathered together) might not hold them both.

51 Vnto Enoch thou gauest one part which was dried vp the third day, that he

he should dwel in the same part, where-in are a thousand hilles.

52 But vnto Leuiathan thou gauest the seuenth part, namely the moist, and hast kept him to be deuoured of whom thou wilt, and when.

53 Vpon the sixt day thou gauest commaundement vnto the earth, that before thee it should bring foorth beasts, cattell, and creeping things:

54 And after these, Adam also whom thou madest lord of all thy creatures, of him come wee all, and the people also whom thou hast chosen.

55 All this haue I spoken before thee, O Lord, because thou madest the world for our sakes.

56 As for the other people which also come of Adam, thou hast said that they are nothing, but be like vnto spittle, and hast likened the abundance of them vnto a drop that falleth from a vessell.

57 And now, O Lord, behold, these heathen, which haue euer been reputed as nothing, haue begun to be lordes o-uer vs, and to deuoure vs:

58 But wee thy people (whom thou hast called thy first borne, thy onely begotten, and thy feruent louer) are giuen into their hands.

59 If the world now be made for our sakes, why doe we not possesse an inheritance with the world? how long shall this endure?

CHAP. VII.

4 The way is narrow. 12 When it was made narrow. 28 All shall die and rise againe. 33 Christ shall sit in iudgement. 46 God hath not made Paradise in vaine, 62 & is merciful.

ND when I had made an ende of speaking these words, there was sent vn-to mee the Angel which had beene sent vnto mee the nights afore.

2 And he said vnto me, Vp Esdras, and heare the wordes that I am come to tell thee.

3 And I said, Speake on, my God. Then said he vnto me, The Sea is set in a wide place, that it might be deepe and great.

4 But put the case the entrance were narrow, and like a riuer,

5 Who then could goe into the Sea to looke vpon it, and to rule it? If hee

went not through the narrow, how could he come into the broad?

6 There is also another thing. A city is builded, and set vpon a broad field, and is full of all good things.

7 The entrance thereof is narrow, and is set in a ‖ dangerous place to fall, like as if there were a fire on the right hand, and on the left a deepe water.   ‖ Or, steepe place.

8 And one only path between them both, euen betweene the fire and the water, so small that there could but one man goe there at once.

9 If this city now were giuen vn-to a man for an inheritance, if he neuer shall passe the danger set before it, how shall he receiue this inheritance?

10 And I said, It is so, Lord. Then said he vnto me, Euen so also is Israels portion:

11 Because for their sakes I made the world: and when Adam transgressed my Statutes, then was decreed that now is done.

12 Then were the entrances of this world made narrow, full of sorrow and trauaile: they are but few and euill, full of perils, and very painefull.

13 For the entrances of the ‖ elder world were wide and sure, and brought immortall fruit.   ‖ Or, greater

14 If then they that liue, labour not to enter these strait and vaine things, they can neuer receiue those that are laide vp for them.

15 Now therefore why disquietest thou thy selfe, seeing thou art but a cor-ruptible man? and why art thou moo-ued, whereas thou art but mortall?

16 Why hast thou not considered in thy minde this thing that is to come, ra-ther then that which is present?

17 Then answered I, and sayd, O Lord, that bearest rule, thou hast ordai-ned in thy *Law, that the righteous should inherite these things, but that the vngodly should perish: * Deut. 8. 1.

18 Neuerthelesse, the righteous shal suffer strait things, and hope for wide: for they that haue done wickedly, haue suffered the strait things, and yet shall not see the wide.

19 And he said vnto me, There is no iudge aboue God, and none that hath vnderstanding aboue the highest.

20 For there be many that perish in this life, because they despise the Lawe of God that is set before them.

21 For God hath giuen strait com-mande-

mandement to such as came, what they should doe to liue, euen as they came, and what they should obserue to auoid punishment.

22 Neuerthelesse they were not obedient vnto him, but spake against him, and imagined vaine things:

23 And deceiued themselues by their wicked deeds, and sayd of the most Hie, that he is not, and knew not his waies.

24 But his Law haue they despised, and denied his couenants; in his statutes haue they not beene faithfull, and haue not performed his workes.

25 And therfore Esdras, for the emptie, are emptie things, and for the ful, are the full things.

26 Behold, the time shall come, that these tokens which I haue told thee, shall come to passe, and the bride shall appeare, and she comming forth shall be seene, that now is withdrawen from the earth.

27 And whosoeuer is deliuered from the foresaid euils, shall see my wonders.

28 For my sonne Iesus shall be reuealed with those that be with him, and they that remaine shall reioyce within foure hundred yeeres.

29 After these yeeres shall my sonne Christ die, and all men that haue life.

30 And the world shall be turned into the old silence seuen dayes, like as in the || former iudgements : so that no man shall remaine.

| Or, first beginning.

31 And after seuen dayes, the world that yet awaketh not shall be raised vp, and that shall die, that is corrupt.

32 And the earth shall restore those that are asleepe in her, and so shall the dust those that dwell in silence, and the secret places shall deliuer those soules that were committed vnto them.

33 And the most high shall appeare vpon the seate of iudgement, and miserie shall passe away, and the long suffering shall haue an end.

34 But iudgement onely shall remaine, trueth shall stand, and faith shall waxe strong.

35 And the worke shall follow, and the reward shall be shewed, and the good deeds shall be of force, and wicked deeds shall beare no rule.

* Gen. 18. 13.
* Exod. 32. 11.

36 Then said I, * Abraham prayed first for the Sodomites, and *Moses for the fathers that sinned in the wildernesse.

37 And Iesus after him for Israel in the time of || Achan,

| Or, Achar

38 And Samuel; and Dauid for the destruction : and * Solomon for them that should come to the sanctuary.

* 2. Sam. 1 17. 2. chro 6. 14.

39 And *Helias for those that receiued raine, & for the dead that hee might liue.

* 1. King. 21. and 18. 42. 45.

40 And * Ezechias for the people in the time of Sennacherib : and many for many.

* 2. King. 19. 15.

41 Euen so now seeing corruption is growen vp, and wickednesse increased, and the righteous haue prayed for the vngodly : wherefore shall it not be so now also?

42 He answered me and said, This present life is not the end where much glory doth abide; therefore haue they prayed for the weake.

43 But the day of doome shall be the end of this time, and the beginning of the immortality for to come, wherein corruption is past.

44 Intemperancie is at an end, infidelity is cut off, righteousnesse is growen, and trueth is sprung vp.

45 Then shall no man be able to saue him that is destroyed, nor to oppresse him that hath gotten the victory.

46 I answered then and said, This is my first and last saying; that it had beene better not to haue giuen the earth vnto Adam : or else when it was giuen him, to haue restrained him from sinning.

47 For what profit is it for men now in this present time to liue in heauinesse, and after death to looke for punishment?

48 O thou Adam, what hast thou done? for though it was * thou that sinned, thou art not fallen alone, but we all that come of thee.

* Rom. 5 18.

49 For what profit is it vnto vs, if there be promised vs an immortall time, wheras we haue done the works that bring death?

50 And that their is promised vs an euerlasting hope, whereas our selues being most wicked are made vaine?

51 And that there are layd vp for vs dwellings of health and safety, whereas we haue liued wickedly?

52 And that the glory of the most high is kept to defend them which haue led ||a wary life, whereas we haue walked in the most wicked wayes of all?

| Or, a ch life.

53 And that there should be shewed

a

a paradise whose fruite endureth for e-uer, wherein is ||securitie and medicine, sith we shall not enter into it?

Or, fulnes.

54 For we haue walked in vnpleasant places.

55 And that the faces of them which haue vsed abstinence, shall shine aboue the starres, whereas our faces shall bee blacker then darkenesse?

56 For while we liued and committed iniquitie, we considered not that we should begin to suffer for it after death.

57 Then answered he and saide, This is the ||condition of the battell, which man that is borne vpon the earth shall fight,

Or, intent.

58 That if he be ouercome, he shall suffer as thou hast said, but if he get the victorie, he shall receiue the thing that I say

59 For this is the life whereof Moses spake vnto the people while hee liued, saying, *Choose thee life that thou mayest liue.

Deut. 30. 19.

60 Neuerthelesse they beleeued not him, nor yet the prophets after him, no nor me which haue spoken vnto them,

61 That there should not be such heauinesse in their destruction, as shall bee ioy ouer them that are perswaded to saluation.

62 I answered then and saide, I know, Lord, that the most Hie is called mercifull, in that he hath mercy vpon them, which are not yet come into the world,

63 And vpon those also that turne to his Law,

64 And that *he is patient, and long suffereth those that haue sinned, as his creatures,

Rom. 2. 4.

65 And that he is bountifull, for hee is ready to giue where it needeth,

66 And that is of great mercie, for he multiplieth more and more mercies to them that are present, and that are past, & also to them which are to come.

67 For if he shall not multiplie his mercies, the world would not continue with them that inherit therein.

68 And he pardoneth : for if hee did not so of his goodnesse, that they which haue committed iniquities might be eased of them, the ten thousand part of men should not remaine liuing.

69 And being Iudge, if he should not forgiue them that are ||cured with his word, and put out the multitude of ||contentions,

Or, created.
Or, contempts.

70 There should bee very fewe left peraduenture in an innumerable multitude.

CHAP. VIII.

1 Many created, but few saued. 6 Hee asketh why God destroyeth his owne worke, 26 and prayeth God to looke vpon the people which onely serue him. 41 God answereth that all seed commeth not to God, 52 and that glory is prepared for him and such like.

Nd he answered me, saying, The most High hath made this world for many, but the world to come for fewe.

2 I will tell thee a similitude, Esdras, As when thou askest the earth, it shall say vnto thee, that it giueth much mold wherof earthen vessels are made, but litle dust that golde commeth of : euen so is y course of this present world.

3 *There be many created, but few shall be saued.

Mat. 20. 16.

4 So answered I and said, Swallow then downe O my soule, vnderstanding, and deuoure wisedome.

5 For thou hast agreed to giue eare, and art willing to prophesie for thou hast no longer space then onely to liue.

6 O Lord, if thou suffer not thy seruant that we may pray before thee, and thou ||giue vs seed vnto our heart, and culture to our vnderstanding, that there may come fruit of it, howe shall each man liue that is corrupt, who beareth the place of a man?

Or, to giue vs.

7 For thou art alone, and we all one workemanship of thine hands, like as thou hast said.

8 For when the body is fashioned now in the mothers wombe, and thou giuest it members, ||thy creature is preserued in fire & water, and nine months doeth thy workemanship endure thy creature which is created in her.

Or, how is the body fashioned.

9 But that which keepeth, and is kept, shall both be preserued : and when the time commeth, the wombe preserued, deliuereth vp the things that grew in it.

10 For thou hast commanded out of the parts of the body, that is to say, out of the breasts milke to be giuen, which is the fruit of the breasts,

11 That the thing which is fashioned, may bee nourished for a time, till thou disposest it to thy mercy

12 Thou broughtest it vp with thy righ-

* Iob 10. 8.
psal. 139.
14. &c.

righteousnesse, and nourturedst it in thy Law, and reformedst it with thy iudgement.

13 And thou shalt mortifie it as thy creature, and quicken it as thy worke.

14 If therefore thou shalt destroy him which with so great *labour was fashioned, it is an easie thing to be ordeined by thy Commaundement, that the thing which was made might be preserued.

15 Now therefore, Lord, I will speake (touchiug man in generall, thou knowest best) but touching thy people, for whose sake I am sory,

16 And for thine inheritance, for whose cause I mourne, and for Israel, for whom I am heauy, and for Iacob, for whose sake I am troubled:

17 Therefore will I begin to pray before thee, for my selfe, and for them: for I see the falles of vs that dwell in the land.

18 But I haue heard the swiftnesse of the Iudge which is to come.

19 Therefore heare my voyce, and vnderstand my wordes, and I shall speake before thee : this is the beginning of the words of Esdras, before he was taken vp : and I said ;

20 O Lord, Thou that dwellest in euerlastingnes, which beholdest from aboue, things in the heauen, & in the aire,

21 Whose Throne is inestimable, whose glory may not be comprehended, before whom the hosts of Angels stand with trembling,

22 (Whose seruice is conuersant in wind and fire,) whose word is true, and sayings constant, whose Commaundement is strong, and ordinance fearefull,

23 Whose looke drieth vp the depths, and indignation maketh the mountaines to melt away, which the trueth witnesseth :

24 O heare the prayer of thy seruant, and giue eare to the petition of thy creature.

25 For while I liue, I will speake, and so long as I haue vnderstanding, I will answere.

26 O looke not vpon the sinnes of thy people : but on them which serue thee in trueth.

27 Regard not the wicked inuentions of the heathen : but the desire of those that keepe thy Testimonies in afflictions.

28 Thinke not vpon those that

haue walked fainedly before thee : but remember them, which according to thy will haue knowen thy feare.

29 Let it not bee thy will to destroy them, which haue liued like beasts : but to looke vpon them that haue clearely taught thy Law.

30 Take thou no indignation at them which are deemed worse then beasts : but loue them that alway put their trust in thy righteousnesse, and glory.

31 For we and our fathers ||doe languish of such diseases; but because of vs sinners, thou shalt be called mercifull.   ‖ *Are sick*

32 For if thou ||hast a desire to haue mercy vpon vs, thou shalt bee called mercifull, to vs namely, that haue no workes of righteousnesse.   ‖ *Be willin*

33 For the iust which haue many good workes layed vp with thee, shall out of their owne deedes receiue reward.

34 For what is man that thou shouldest take displeasure at him ? or what is a corruptible generation, that thou shouldest be so bitter toward it ?

35 *For in trueth there is no man among them that be borne, but he hath dealt wickedly, and among the faithfull, there is none which hath not done amisse.   * 1. King. 46. and 2. chro. 6. 3

36 For in this, O Lord, thy righteousnesse, and thy goodnesse shalbe declared, if thou be mercifull vnto them which haue not the ||confidence of good workes.   ‖ *Or, substance.*

37 Then answered he mee, and said, Some things hast thou spoken aright, and according vnto thy words it shalbe.

38 For indeed I will not thinke on the disposition of them which haue sinned before death, before iudgement, before destruction.

39 But *I will reioyce ouer the disposition of the righteous, and I wil remember also their pilgrimage, and the saluation, and the reward that they shall haue.   * Gen. 4.

40 Like as I haue spoken now, so shall it come to passe.

41 For as the husbandmau soweth much seed vpon the ground, and planteth many trees, and yet the thing that is sowen good in his season, commeth not vp, neither doeth all that is planted take root : euen so is it of them that are sowen in the world, they shall not all be saued.

42 I answered then, and said, If I haue found grace, let me speake.

43 Like as the husbandmans seede perisheth, if it come not vp, and receiue not the raine in due season, or if there come too much raine and corrupt it :

44 Euen so perisheth man also which is formed with thy hands, and is called thine owne image, because thou art like vnto him, for whose sake thou hast made all things, and likened him vnto the husbandmans seede.

45 Be not wroth with vs, but spare thy people, and haue mercy vpon thine owne inheritance : for thou art mercifull vnto thy creature.

46 Then answered he me, and said, Things present are for the present; and things to come, for such as be to come.

47 For thou commest farre short, that thou shouldest be able to loue my creature more then I : but I haue oft times drawen nigh vnto thee, and vnto it, but neuer to the vnrighteous.

48 In this also thou art marueilous before the most high ;

49 In that thou hast humbled thy selfe as it becommeth thee, and hast not iudged thy selfe worthy to be much glorified among the righteous.

50 For many great miseries shall be done to them, that in the latter time shal dwell in the world, because they haue walked in great pride.

51 But vnderstand thou for thy selfe, and seeke out the glory for such as be like thee.

52 For vnto you is Paradise opened, the tree of life is planted, the time to come is prepared, plenteousnesse is made ready, a citie is builded, and rest is allowed, yea perfect goodnesse and wisedome.

53 The root of euil is sealed vp from you, weakenesse and the moth is hidde from you, and corruption is fled into *Or, graue.* ||hell to be forgotten.

54 Sorrows are passed, & in the end is shewed the treasure of immortalitie.

55 And therefore aske thou no more questions concerning the multitude of them that perish.

56 For when they had taken liberty, they despised the most High, thought scorne of his Lawe, and forsooke his wayes.

57 Moreouer, they haue troden downe his righteous,

Psal. 14. 1. nd 53. 1. 58 And *said in their heart, that there

is no God, yea and that knowing they must die.

59 For as the things aforesaid shall receiue you, so thirst and paine are prepared for them ; for it was not his will that men should come to nought.

60 But they which be created, haue defiled the Name of him that made them, and were vnthankefull vnto him which prepared life for them.

61 And therefore is my iudgement now at hand.

62 These things haue I not shewed vnto all men, but vnto thee, and a fewe like thee. Then answered I, and said,

63 Behold, O Lord, now hast thou shewed me the multitude of the wonders which thou wilt begin to doe in the last times : but at what time, thou hast not shewed me.

CHAP. IX.

7 Who shall be saued, and who not. 19 All the world is now corrupted : 22 Yet God doeth saue a few. 33 Hee complaineth that those perish which keepe Gods Law : 38 and seeth a woman lamenting in a field.

Ee answered me then, and sayde, Measure thou the time diligently in it selfe : and when thou seest part of the signes past, which I haue tolde thee before,

2 Then shalt thou vnderstand, that it is the very same time, wherein the highest will begin to visite the time which he made.

3 Therefore when there shall bee seene *earthquakes and vprores of the *Mat. 24. 7 people in the world :

4 Then shalt thou wel vnderstand, that the most high spake of those things from the dayes that were before thee, euen from the beginning.

5 For like as all that is made in the world hath a beginning, and an ende, and the end is manifest :

6 Euen so the times also of the highest, haue plaine beginnings in wonders and powerfull workes, and endings in effects and signes.

7 And euery one that shalbe saued, and shalbe able to escape by his works, and by faith, whereby ye haue beleeued,

8 Shall be preserued from the sayd perils, and shall see my saluation, in my land, and within my borders : for I haue sanctified them for me, from the beginning.

9 Then

‖ Or, they shall mar-uell.

9 Then shall they ‖be in pitifull case which now haue abused my wayes: and they that haue cast them away des-spitefully, shall dwell in torments.

10 For such, as in their life haue re-ceiued benefits, & haue not knowen me:

11 And they that haue loathed my law, while they had yet liberty, and when as yet place of repentance was open vnto them, vnderstood not, but despised it:

12 The same must know it after death by paine.

13 And therefore be thou not curi-ous, how the vngodly shalbe punished and when: but enquire how the righ-teous shall be saued, whose the world is, and for whom the world is created.

14 Then answered I, and said,

15 I haue said before, and now doe speake, and will speake it also heereaf-ter: that there be many moe of them which perish, then of them which shall be saued,

16 Like as a waue is greater then a droppe.

17 And he answered me, saying: like as the field is, so is also the seed: as the flowres be, such are the colours also: such as the workeman is, such also is the worke: and as the husbandman is himselfe, so is his husbandry also: for it was the time of the world.

‖ And now because the time of the world was come, when I was pre-paring the world &c.

18 ‖And now when I prepared the world, which was not yet made, euen for them to dwell in that now liue, no man spake against me.

‖ But when the world was made, both now and then, the maners of euery one created were corrupted by a neuer fai-ling haruest, and a law vnsearch-able.

19 For then euery one obeyed, ‖but now the maners of them which are cre-ated in this world that is made, are cor-rupted by a perpetuall seed, & by a law which is vnsearchable, rid themselues.

20 So I considered the world, and behold there was perill, because of the deuices that were come into it.

21 And I saw and spared it greatly, and haue kept me a ‖grape of the cluster, and a plant of a great people.

‖ Or, graine.

22 Let the multitude perish then, which was borne in vaine, and let my ‖grape be kept and my plant: for with great labour haue I made it perfect.

‖ Or, graine.

23 Neuerthelesse if thou wilt cease yet seuen dayes moe (but thou shalt not fast in them.)

24 But goe into a field of flowres, where no house is builded, and eate on-ly the flowres of the field, Tast no flesh, drinke no wine, but eate flowres onely.

25 And pray vnto the Highest conti-nually, then wil I come and talke with thee.

26 So I went my way into the field which is called Ardath, like as he com-manded me, and there I sate amongst the flowres, and did eate of the herbes of the field, and the meate of the same sa-tisfied me.

27 After seuen dayes I sate vpon the grasse, and my heart was vexed within me, like as before.

28 And I opened my mouth, and beganne to talke before the most High and said,

29 O Lord, thou that shewest thy selfe vnto vs, thou wast *shewed vnto our fathers in the wildernesse, in a place where no man ‖treadeth, in a barren place when they came out of Egypt.

* Exod. 19. and 24.
3. deut. 4. 12.
‖ Or, com-meth.

30 And thou spakest, saying, Heare me, O Israel, and marke my words, thou seed of Iacob.

31 For behold I sow my law in you, and it shall bring fruite in you, and yee shall be honoured in it for euer.

32 But our fathers which receiued the law, kept it not, and obserued not thy ordinances, and though the fruite of thy law did not perish, neither could it, for it was thine:

33 Yet they that receiued it, perished, because they kept not the thing that was sowen in them.

34 And loe, it is a custome when the ground hath receiued seed, or the Sea a ship, or any vessel, meate or drinke, that, that being perished wherein it was sowen, or cast into,

35 That thing also which was sowen or cast therein, or receiued, doth perish, and remaineth not with vs: but with vs it hath not happened so.

36 For we that haue receiued the law perish by sinne, and our heart also which receiued it.

37 Notwithstanding the law peri-sheth not, but remaineth in his force.

38 And when I spake these things in my heart, I looked backe with mine eyes, & vpon the right side I saw a wo-man, and behold, she mourned, & wept with a loud voyce, and was much grie-ued in heart, and her clothes were rent, and she had ashes vpon her head.

39 Then let I my thoughts goe that I was in, and turned me vnto her,

40 And said vnto her, Wherefore weepest thou? why art thou so grieued in thy minde?

41 And

41 And she said vnto me, Sir, let me alone, that I may bewaile my selfe, and adde vnto my sorow, for I am sore vexed in my minde, and brought very low.

42 And I said vnto her, What aileth thee? Tell me.

43 She said vnto me, I thy seruant haue bene barren, and had no childe, though I had an husband thirty yeres.

44 And those thirtie yeeres I did nothing else day and night, and euery houre, but make my prayer to ẙ highest.

45 After thirtie yeeres, God heard me thine handmaid, looked vpon my misery, considered my trouble, and gaue me a sonne : and I was very glad of him, so was my husband also, and all my neighbours, and we gaue great honour vnto the Almightie.

46 And I nourished him with great trauaile.

47 So when he grew vp, and came to the time that he should haue a wife, I made a feast.

CHAP. X.

1 Hee comforteth the woman in the field. 17 She vanisheth away, and a citie appeareth in her place. 40 The Angel declareth these visions in the field.

ANd it so came to passe, that when my sonne was entred into his wedding chamber, he fell downe and died.

2 Then we all ouerthrew the lights, and all my ||neighbours rose vp to comfort me, so I tooke my rest vnto the second day at night.

|| Or countrey men citizens.

3 And it came to passe when they had all left off to comfort me, to the end I might be quiet : then rose I vp by night and fled, and came hither into this field, as thou seest.

4 And I doe now purpose not to returne into the citie, but here to stay, and neither to eate nor drinke, but continually to mourne, & to fast vntil I die.

5 Then left I the || meditations wherein I was, and spake to her in anger, saying,

|| Or, speeches.

6 Thou foolish woman aboue all other, seest thou not our mourning, and what happeneth vnto vs?

7 How that Sion our mother is full of all heauinesse, and much humbled, mourning very sore?

8 And now seeing we all mourne, and are sad, for we are all in heauinesse,

art thou grieued for one sonne?

9 For aske the earth, and she shall tell thee, that it is she, which ought to mourne, for the fall of so many that grow vpon her.

10 For out of her came all at the first, and out of her shal all others come: and behold they walke almost all into destruction, and a multitude of them is vtterly ||rooted out.

|| Or, abolished.

11 Who then should make more mourning, then she that hath lost so great a multitude, and not thou which art sory but for one?

12 But if thou sayest vnto me, My lamentation is not like the earths, because I haue lost the fruit of my womb, which I brought foorth with paines, and bare with sorrowes.

13 ||But the earth *not so:* for the multitude present in it, according to the course of the earth, is gone, as it came.

|| But the earth after the maner of the earth: whereinto the present multitude is gone againe, as it came out.

14 Then say I vnto thee, Like as thou hast brought foorth with labour : euen so the earth also hath giuen her fruit, namely man, euer sithence the beginning, vnto him that made her.

15 Now therefore keepe thy sorrow to thy selfe, and beare with a good courage that which hath befallen thee.

16 For if thou shalt acknowledge the determination of God to be iust, thou shalt both receiue thy sonne in time, and shalt be commended amongst women.

17 Goe thy way then into the citie, to thine husband.

18 And she said vnto me, That will I not doe : I will not goe into the city, but here will I die.

19 So I proceeded to speake further vnto her, and said,

20 Doe not so, but bee counselled by me . for how many are the aduersities of Sion? Bee comforted in regard of the sorow of Ierusalem.

21 For thou seest that our Sanctuary is laid waste, our Altar broken downe, our Temple destroyed.

22 Our Psaltery is laid on ẙ ground, our song is put to silence, our reioycing is at an end, the light of our candlesticke is put out, the Arke of our Couenant is spoiled, our holy things are defiled, and the Name that is called vpon vs, is almost prophaned: our children are put to shame, our priests are burnt, our Leuites are gone into captiuitie, our virgines are defiled, and our wiues rauished, our righteous men caried away, our

our litle ones destroyed, our yong men are brought in bondage, and our strong men are become weake.

23 And which is the greatest of all, the seale of Sion hath now lost her honour : for she is deliuered into the hands of them that hate vs.

24 And therefore shake off thy great heauinesse, and put away the multitude of sorrowes, that the mighty may be mercifull vnto thee againe, and the highest shal giue thee rest, and ease from thy labour.

25 And it came to passe while I was talking with her, behold her face vpon a sudden shined exceedingly, & her countenance glistered, so that I was afraid of her, and mused what it might be.

26 And behold suddenly, she made a great cry very fearful : so that the earth shooke at the noise of the woman.

27 And I looked, and beholde, the woman appeared vnto me no more, but there was a city builded, and a large place shewed it selfe from the foundations : then was I afraid, and cried with a lowd voice, and said,

^{* Chap. 4. 1.}   28 Where is *Vriel the Angel, who came vnto mee at the first? for hee hath

^{‡ Or, into the multitude in a traunce.} caused me to fall into many ‖traunces, and mine end is turned into corruption, and my prayer to rebuke.

29 And as I was speaking these wordes, behold, he came vnto me, and looked vpon me.

30 And loe, I lay as one that had bene dead, & mine vnderstanding was taken from me, and he tooke me by the right hand, and comforted mee, and set me vpon my feet, and said vnto me,

31 What aileth thee? and why art thou so disquieted, and why is thine vnderstanding troubled, & the thoughts of thine heart?

32 And I said, because thou hast forsaken me, and yet I did according to thy

^{* Chap. 5. 20.} *words, and I went into the field, and loe I haue seene, and yet see, that I am not able to expresse.

33 And hee said vnto me, Stand vp manfully, and I wil aduise thee.

34 Then said I, Speake on, my lord in me, onely forsake me not, lest I die frustrate of my hope.

35 For I haue seene, that I knew not, and heare that I do not know.

36 Or, is my sense deceiued, or my soule in a dreame?

37 Now therfore, I beseech thee, that

thou wilt shew thy seruant of this ‖visiō. ^{‡ Or, traunce.}

38 He answered me then, & said, Heare me, and I shall enforme thee, and tell thee wherefore thou art afraid : for the highest will reueile many secret things vnto thee.

39 Hee hath seene that thy ‖way is ^{‡Or,purpos} right : for that thou sorrowest continually for thy people, and makest great lamentation for Sion.

40 This therefore is the meaning of the vision which thou lately sawest.

41 Thou sawest a woman mourning, and thou beganst to comfort her:

42 But now seest thou the likenesse of the woman no more, but there appeared vnto thee a city builded.

43 And whereas she told thee of the death of her sonne, this is the ‖solution. ^{‡ Or, Inte pretation.}

44 This woman whom thou sawest, is Sion : and whereas she said vnto thee (euen she whom thou seest as a city builded.)

45 Whereas I say, she said vnto thee, that she hath bene thirty yeres barren : those are the thirty yeeres wherein there was no offering made in her.

46 But after thirtie yeeres, Solomon builded the city, & offered offrings : and then bare the barren a sonne.

47 And whereas she told thee that shee nourished him with labour : that was the dwelling in Hierusalem.

48 But whereas she said vnto thee, That my sonne comming into his marriage chamber, happened to haue a fall, and died, this was the destruction that came to Hierusalem.

49 And behold, thou sawest her likenesse, and because she mourned for her sonne, thou beganst to comfort her, and of these things which haue chaunced, these are to be opened vnto thee.

50 For now the most High seeth, that thou art grieued vnfainedly, & sufferest from thy whole heart for her, so hath he shewed thee the brightnes of her glory, and the comelinesse of her beautie.

51 And therfore I bad thee remaine in ỹ field, where no house was builded.

52 For I knew that the Highest would shew this vnto thee.

53 Therefore I commanded thee to goe into the field, where no foundation of any building was.

54 For in the place wherein the Highest beginneth to shew his city, ther can no mans building be able to stand.

55 And therfore feare not, let not thy heart

heart be afrighted, but goe thy way in, and see the beautie and greatnesse of the building, as much as thine eyes be able to see :

56 And then shalt thou heare as much as thine eares may comprehend.

57 For thou art blessed aboue many other, and art ||called with the highest, and so are but few.

58 But to morrow at night thou shalt remaine here.

59 And so shall the highest shew thee visions of the ||high things, which the most high will do vnto them, that dwel vpon earth in the last dayes. So I slept that night and another, like as he commanded me.

C H A P. XI.

1 Hee seeth in his dreame an Eagle comming out of the Sea : 37 And a Lion out of a wood talking to the Eagle.

THen saw I a dreame, and beholde, there came vp from the Sea an Eagle, which had twelue feathered wings, & three heads.

2 And I saw, and behold, she spred her wings ouer all the earth, and all the windes of the ayre blewe on her, and were gathered together.

3 And I beheld, and out of her feathers there grewe other contrary feathers, and they became little feathers, and small.

4 But her heads were at rest: the head in the middest was greater then the other, yet rested † it with the residue.

5 Moreouer I beheld, and loe, the Eagle flew with her feathers, and reigned vpon earth, and ouer them that dwelt therein.

6 And I saw that all things vnder heauen were subiect vnto her, and no man spake against her, no not one creature vpon earth.

7 And I beheld, and loe, the Eagle rose vpon her talents, and spake to her feathers, saying,

8 Watch not all at once, sleepe euery one in his own place, & watch by course.

9 But let the heads be preserued for the last.

10 And I beheld, and loe, the voice went not out of her heads, but from the middest of her body.

11 And I numbred her contrary feathers, and behold, there were eight of them.

12 And I looked, and behold, on the right side there arose one feather, and reigned ouer all the earth.

13 And so it was, that when it reigned, the ende of it came, and the place thereof appeared no more : so the next following stood vp and reigned, and had a great time.

14 And it happened, that when it reigned, the end of it came also, like as the first, so that it appeared no more.

15 Then came there a voice vnto it, and sayd,

16 Heare, thou that hast borne rule ouer the earth so long : this I say vnto thee, before thou beginnest to appeare no more.

17 There shall none after thee attaine vnto thy time, neither vnto the halfe thereof.

18 Then arose the third, and reigned as the other before : and appeared no more also.

19 So went it with all the residue one after another, as that euery one reigned, and then appeared no more.

20 Then I beheld, & loe, in processe of time, the feathers that folowed, stood vp vpon the right side, that they might rule also, and some of them ruled, but within a while they appeared no more :

21 For some of them were set vp, but ruled not.

22 After this I looked, and behold, the twelue feathers appeared no more, nor the two little feathers :

23 And there was no more vpon the Eagles body, but three heads that rested, and sixe little wings.

24 Then saw I also that two little feathers diuided themselues from the sixe, and remained vnder the head, that was vpon the right side : for the foure continued in their place.

25 And I beheld, & loe, the feathers that were vnder the wing, thought to set vp themselues, and to haue the rule.

26 And I beheld, & loe, there was one set vp, but shortly it appeared no more.

27 And the second was sooner away then the first.

28 And I beheld, and loe, the two that remained, thought also in themselues to reigne.

29 And when they so thought, behold, there awaked one of the heads that were at rest, namely it that was in the middest, for that was greater then the two other heads.

30 And

30 And then I saw, that the two other heads were ioyned with it.

31 And behold, the head was turned with them that were with it, and did eate vp the two feathers vnder the wing that would haue reigned.

32 But this head put the whole earth in feare, and bare rule in it ouer all those that dwelt vpon the earth, with much oppression, and it had the gouernance of the world more then all the wings that had beene.

33 And after this I beheld, and loe the head that was in the midst, suddenly appeared no more, like as the wings.

34 But there remained the two heads, which also in like sort ruled vpon the earth, and ouer those that dwelt therein.

35 And I beheld, and loe, the head vpon the right side, deuoured it, that was vpon the left side.

36 Then I heard a voyce, which said vnto me, Looke before thee, and consider the thing that thou seest.

37 And I beheld, and loe, as it were a roaring Lyon, chased out of the wood : and I saw that hee sent out a mans voyce vnto the Eagle, and said,

38 Heare thou, I will talke with thee, and the highest shall say vnto thee,

39 Art not thou it that remainest of the foure beasts, whom I made to raigne in my world, that the end of their times might come through them ?

40 And the fourth came and ouercame all the beasts that were past, and had power ouer the world with great fearefulnesse, and ouer the whole compasse of the earth with much wicked oppression, and so long time dwelt he vpon the earth with deceit.

41 For the earth hast thou not iudged with trueth.

42 For thou hast afflicted the meeke, thou hast hurt the peaceable, thou hast loued lyers, and destroyed the dwellings of them that brought forth fruite, and hast cast downe the walles of such, as did thee no harme.

43 Therefore is thy wrongfull dealing come vp vnto the Highest, and thy pride vnto the Mighty.

44 The Highest also hath looked vpon the proud times, and behold, they are ended, and his abominations are fulfilled.

45 And therefore appeare no more thou Eagle, nor thy horrible wings, nor thy wicked feathers, nor thy malitious heads, nor thy hurtfull clawes, nor all thy vaine body :

46 That all the earth may be refreshed, and may returne, being deliuered from thy violence, and that she may hope for the iudgement, and mercy of him that made her.

CHAP. XII.

3 The Eagle which hee saw, is destroyed. 10 The vision is interpreted. 37 He is bid to write his visions, 39 and to fast, that he may see more. 46 He doth comfort those, that were grieued for his absence.

And it came to passe whiles the Lyon spake these words vnto the Eagle, I saw :

2 And behold, the head that remained, and the foure wings appeared no more, and the two went vnto it, and set themselues vp to raigne, and their kingdome was small and full of vprore.

3 And I saw, and behold, they appeared no more, and the whole body of the Eagle was burnt, so that the earth was in great feare : then awaked I out of the trouble and traunce of my minde, and from great feare, and said vnto my spirit,

4 Loe, this hast thou done vnto me, in that thou searchest out the wayes of the Highest.

5 Loe, yet am I weary in my mind, and very weake in my spirit : and litle strength is there in me ; for the great feare, wherewith I was affrighted this night.

6 Therefore wil I now beseech the Highest, that hee will comfort me vnto the end.

7 And I said, Lord, that bearest rule, If I haue found grace before thy sight, and if I am iustified with thee, before many others, and if my prayer indeed be come vp before thy face,

8 Comfort me then, and shew me thy seruant the interpretation, and plaine difference of this fearefull vision, that thou maist perfectly comfort my soule.

9 For thou hast iudged me worthy, to shew me the last times.

10 And he said vnto me, This is the interpretation of the vision.

11 The Eagle whom thou sawest come vp from the sea, is the kingdome which

* Daniel
7. 7.

which was seene, in the *vision of thy brother Daniel.

12 But it was not expounded vnto him, therefore now I declare it vnto thee.

13 Behold, the dayes will come, that there shall rise vp a kingdome vpon earth, and it shall be feared aboue all the kingdomes that were before it.

14 In the same shall twelue kings reigne, one after another.

15 Whereof the second shall begin to reigne, and shall haue more time then any of the twelue.

16 And this doe the twelue wings signifie which thou sawest.

17 As for the voice which thou heardest speake, and that thou sawest not to goe out from the heads, but from the mids of the body thereof, this is the interpretation:

18 That after the time of that kingdome, there shall arise great striuings, and it shall stand in perill of falling: neuerthelesse it shall not then fall, but shal be restored againe to his beginning.

19 And whereas thou sawest the eight small vnder feathers sticking to her wings, this is the interpretation:

20 That in him there shal arise eight kings, whose time shall bee but small, and their yeeres swift.

21 And two of them shall perish: the middle time approching, foure shall bee kept vntill their end begin to approch: but two shall be kept vnto the end.

22 And whereas thou sawest three heads resting, this is the interpretation

23 In his last dayes shall the most High raise vp three kingdomes, and renew many things therein, and they shal haue the dominion of the earth,

24 And of those that dwell therein with much oppression, aboue all those that were before them: therefore are they called the heads of the Eagle.

25 For these are they that shal accomplish his wickednesse, and that shall finish his last end.

26 And whereas thou sawest that the great head appeared no more, it signifieth that one of them shall die vpon his bed, and yet with paine.

27 For the two that remaine, shall be slaine with the sword.

28 For the sword of the one shall deuoure the other: but at the last shall he fall through the sword himselfe.

29 And whereas thou sawest two feathers vnder the wings passing ouer the head, that is on the right side:

30 It signifieth that these are they whom the Highest hath kept vnto their end: this is the small kingdom and full of trouble, as thou sawest.

31 And the Lyon whom thou sawest rising vp out of the wood, and roaring, and speaking to the Eagle, and rebuking her for her vnrighteousnesse, with all the words which thou hast heard,

32 This is the Anointed which the Highest hath kept for them, and for their wickednesse vnto the end: he shall reprooue them, and shall vpbraid them with their crueltie.

33 For hee shall set them before him aliue in iudgement, and shall rebuke them and correct them.

34 For the rest of my people shall he deliuer with mercie, those that haue bin preserued vpon my borders, and he shal make them ioyfull vntill the comming of the day of iudgement, whereof I haue spoken vnto thee from the beginning.

35 This is the dreame that thou sawest, and these are the interpretations.

36 Thou onely hast bene meete to know this secret of the Highest.

37 Therefore write all these things that thou hast seene, in a booke, and hide them.

38 And teach them to the wise of the people, whose hearts thou knowest may comprehend, & keepe these seerets.

39 But wait thou here thy selfe yet seuen dayes moe, that it may be shewed thee whatsoeuer it pleaseth the Highest to declare vnto thee: And with that he went his way.

40 And it came to passe when all the people saw that the seuen dayes were past, and I not come againe into the citie, they gathered them all together, from the least vnto the greatest, and came vnto me, and said,

41 What haue we offended thee? and what euill haue we done against thee, that thou forsakest vs, and sittest here in this place?

42 For of all the ||prophets thou only art left vs, as a cluster of the vintage, and as a candle in a darke place, and as a hauen or ship preserued from the tempest:

|| Or, people.

43 Are not the euils which are come to vs, sufficient?

44 If thou shalt forsake vs, how much

much better had it bene for vs, if we also had bene burnt in the midst of Sion.

45 For we are not better then they that died there. And they wept with a loud voice : then answered I them, and said,

46 Be of good comfort, O Israel, and be not heauy thou house of Iacob.

47 For the Highest hath you in remembrance, and the mighty hath not forgotten you in temptation.

48 As for mee, I haue not forsaken you, neither am I departed from you : but am come into this place, to pray for the desolation of Sion, and that I might seeke mercy for the low estate of your Sanctuary.

49 And now goe your way home euery man, and after these dayes will I come vnto you.

50 So the people went their way into the city, like as I commanded them:

51 But I remained still in the field seuen dayes, as the Angel commanded me, and did eate onely in those dayes, of the flowers of the fielde, and had my meat of the herbes.

CHAP. XIII.

1 Hee seeth in his dreame a man comming out of the sea. 25 The declaration of his dreame. 54 He is praised, and promised to see more.

[‖] *A certaine man as the winde. Iunius.*

[‖] *Clouds.*

ANd it came to passe after seuen dayes, I dreamed a dreame by night.

2 And ‖loe, there arose a winde from the sea that it mooued all the waues thereof.

3 And I beheld, and loe, that man waxed strong with the ‖thousands of heauen : and when he turned his countenance to looke, all the things trembled that were seene vnder him.

4 And whensoeuer the voyce went out of his mouth, all they burnt, that heard his voyce, like as the earth faileth when it feeleth the fire.

5 And after this I beheld, and loe, there was gathered together a multitude of men out of number, from the foure windes of the heauen, to subdue the man that came out of the sea.

6 But I beheld, and loe, hee had graued himselfe a great mountaine, and flew vp vpon it.

7 But I would haue seene the region, or place, whereout the hill was grauen, and I could not.

8 And after this I beheld, and loe,

all they which were gathered together to subdue him, were sore afraid, and yet durst fight.

9 And loe, as hee saw the violence of the multitude that came, hee neither lift vp his hand, nor held sword, nor any instrument of warre.

10 But onely I saw that he sent out of his mouth, as it had bene a blast of fire, and out of his lippes a flaming breath, and out of his tongue he cast out sparkes and tempests,

11 And they were all mixt together ; the blast of fire, the flaming breath, and the great tempest, and fel with violence vpon the multitude, which was prepared to fight, and burnt them vp euery one, so that vpon a sudden, of an innumerable multitude, nothing was to be perceiued, but onely dust and smell of smoke : whē I saw this, I was afraid.

12 Afterward saw I the same man come downe from the mountaine, and call vnto him an other peaceable multitude.

13 And there came much people vnto him, whereof some were glad, some were sory, some of them were bound, and other some brought of ‖them that were offred : then was I sicke through great feare, and I awaked and said,

[‖] *Iunius. Of the things that were offred.*

14 Thou hast shewed thy seruant wonders from the beginning, and hast counted me worthy that thou shouldest receiue my prayer :

15 Shew mee now yet the interpretation of this dreame.

16 For as I conceiue in mine vnderstanding, woe vnto them that shall be left in those dayes; and much more woe vnto them that are not left behinde.

17 For they that were not left, were in heauinesse.

18 Now vnderstand I the things that are layde vp in the latter dayes, which shall happen vnto them, and to those that are left behinde.

19 Therefore are they come into great perils, and many necessities, like as these dreames declare.

20 Yet is it easier for him that is in danger, to come into ‖these things, then to passe away as a cloud out of the world, and not to see the things that happen in the last dayes. And he answered vnto me, and said,

[‖] *Or, this day.*

21 The interpretation of the vision shal I shew thee, and I wil open vnto thee, the thing that thou hast required.

22 Where-

22 Wheras thou hast spoken of them that are left behinde, this is the interpretation.

23 He that shall endure the perill in that time, hath kept himselfe: they that be fallen into danger, are such as haue workes, and faith towards the Almightie.

24 Know this therefore, that they which be left behinde, are more blessed then they that be dead.

25 This is the meaning of the vision: Whereas thou sawest a man comming vp from the middest of the Sea:

26 The same is hee whom God the highest hath kept a great season, which by his owne selfe shall deliuer his creature: and hee shall order them that are left behinde.

27 And whereas thou sawest, that out of his mouth there came as a blast of winde, and fire, and storme:

28 And that he helde neither sword, nor any instrument of warre, but that the rushing in of him destroyed the whole multitude that came to subdue him, this is the interpretation.

29 Behold, the dayes come, when the most high wil begin to deliuer them that are vpon the earth.

30 And he shall come to the astonishment of them that dwell on the earth.

31 And one shall vndertake to fight against another, one city against another, one place against another, *one people against another, and one realme against another.

32 And the time shalbe, when these things shall come to passe, and the signes shall happen which I shewed thee before, and then shall my sonne be declared, whom thou sawest as a man ascending.

33 And when all the people heare his voice, euery man shall in their owne land, leaue the battaile they haue one against another.

34 And an innumerable multitude shalbe gathered together, as thou sawest them willing to come, and to ouercome him by fighting.

35 But hee shall stand vpon the top of the mount Sion.

36 And Sion shall come and shall be shewed to all men, being prepared and builded, like as thou sawest the hill grauen without hands.

37 And this my sonne shall rebuke the wicked inuentions of those nations,

*Mat. 24. 7.

which for their wicked life are fallen into the tempest,

38 And shall lay before them their euill thoughts, and the torments wherwith they shall begin to be tormented, which are like vnto a flame: and hee shall destroy them without labour, by the law which is like vnto fire.

39 And whereas thou sawest that hee gathered another peaceable multitude vnto him;

40 Those are the ten tribes, which were caried away prisoners out of their owne land, in the time of Osea the king, whom *Salmanasar the king of Assyria ledde away captiue, and hee caried them ouer the waters, and so came they into another land.

41 But they tooke this counsaile amongst themselues, that they would leaue the multitude of the heathen, and goe foorth into a further countrey, where neuer mankind dwelt,

42 That they might there keepe their statutes, which they neuer kept in their owne land.

43 And they entred into Euphrates by the narrow passages of the Riuer.

44 For the most high then shewed *signes for them, and held still the flood, till they were passed ouer.

45 For through that countrey there was a great way to goe; namely, of a yeere and a halfe: and the same region is called ‖ Arsareth.

46 Then dwelt they there vntill the latter time; and now when they shall begin to come,

47 The highest shall stay the springs of the streame againe, that they may go through: therefore sawest thou the multitude with peace.

48 But those that be left behinde of thy people, are they that are found within my borders.

49 Now when hee destroyeth the multitude of the nations that are gathered together, he shal defend his people that remaine.

50 And then shall hee shewe them great wonders.

51 Then said I, O Lord, that bearest rule, shew me this: Wherefore haue I seene the man comming vp from the midst of the Sea?

52 And he said vnto me, Like as thou canst neither seeke out, nor know the things that are in the deepe of the sea: euen so can no man vpon earth see my sonne,

* 2. Kings 17. 3.

* Exod. 14. 21. Iosh. 3. 15, 16.

‖ Or, Ararath.

sonne, or those that be with him, but in the day time.

53 This is the interpretation of the dreame which thou sawest, and whereby thou onely art here lightened.

54 For thou hast forsaken thine owne way, and applied thy diligence vnto my law, and sought it.

55 Thy life hast thou ordered in wisdome, and hast called vnderstanding thy mother.

56 And therefore haue I shewed thee the treasures of the Highest: After other three dayes, I will speake other things vnto thee, and declare vnto thee mightie and wonderous things.

57 Then went I forth into the field giuing praise and thanks greatly vnto the most High, because of his wonders which he did in time,

58 And because hee gouerneth the same, and such things as fall in their seasons, and there I sate three dayes.

CHAP. XIIII.

1 A voice out of a bush calleth Esdras, 10 and telleth him that the world waxeth old. 22 He desireth, because the Law was burnt, to write all againe, 24 and is bid to get swift writers. 39 Hee and they are filled with vnderstanding: 45 but hee is charged not to publish all that is written.

Nd it came to passe, vpon the third day I sate vnder an oke, and behold, there came a voyce out of a bush ouer against me, and said, Esdras, Esdras.

2 And I said, Here am I Lord, and I stood vp vpon my feet.

3 Then said he vnto me, * In the bush I did manifestly reueale my selfe vnto Moses, and talked with him, when my people serued in Egypt.

4 And I sent him, and led my people out of Egypt, and brought him vp to the mount of Sinai, where I held him by me, a long season,

5 And told him many wonderous things, and shewed him the secrets of the times, and the end, and commanded him, saying,

6 These wordes shalt thou declare, and these shalt thou hide.

7 And now I say vnto thee,

8 That thou lay vp in thy heart the signes that I haue shewed, and the dreames that thou hast seene, and the

*Exod. 3. 2, 6.

interpretations which thou hast heard:

9 For thou shalt be taken away from all, and from henceforth thou shalt remaine with my sonne, and with such as be like thee, vntill the times be ended.

10 For the world hath lost his youth, and the times begin to waxe old.

11 For the world is diuided into twelue parts, and the ten parts of it are gone already, and halfe of a tenth part.

12 And there remaineth that which is after the halfe of the tenth part.

13 Now therefore set thine house in order, and reproue thy people, comfort such of them as be in trouble, and now renounce corruption.

14 Let go frō thee mortall thoughts, cast away the burdens of man, put off now the weake nature,

15 And set aside the thoughts that are most heauy vnto thee, and haste thee to flie from these times.

16 For *yet greater euils then those which thou hast seene happen, shall bee done hereafter.

17 For looke how much the world shall be weaker through age : so much the more shall euils increase vpon them that dwell therein.

18 For the trueth is fled farre away, and leasing is hard at hand : For now hasteth the vision to come, which thou hast seene.

19 Then answered I before thee, and said,

20 Behold, Lord, I will go as thou hast commanded me, and reproue the people which are present, but they that shall be borne afterward, who shall admonish them ? thus the world is set in darkenes, and they that dwell therein, are without light.

21 For thy law is burnt, therefore no man knoweth the things that are done of thee, or the works that shal begin.

22 But if I haue found grace before thee, send the holy Ghost into me, and I shall write all that hath bene done in the world, since the beginning, which were written in thy Lawe, that men may find thy path, and that they which will liue in the latter dayes, may liue.

23 And he answered me, saying, Goe thy way, gather the people together, and say vnto them, that they seeke thee not for fourtie dayes.

24 But looke thou prepare thee many ‖boxe trees, and take with thee Sarea, Dabria, Selemia, ‖Ecanus and Asiel,

* Mat. 24.

‖ Or, boxe tables to write on, See ver. 44.
‖ Or, Banus.

Asiel, these fiue which are ready to write swiftly.

25 And come hither, and I shall light a candle of vnderstanding in thine heart, which shall not be put out, till the things be performed which thou shalt beginne to write.

26 And when thou hast done, some things shalt thou publish, and some things shalt thou shew secretly to the wise: to morrowe this houre shalt thou beginne to write.

27 Then went I foorth as he commanded, and gathered all the people together, and said,

28 Heare these words, O Israel.

* Gene. 47. 4.

29 * Our fathers at the beginning were strangers in Egypt, from whence they were deliuered:

* Act. 7 53.

30 * And receiued the law of life which they kept not, which ye also haue transgressed after them.

31 Then was the land, euen the land of Sion, parted among you by lot, but your fathers, and yee your selues haue done vnrighteousnesse, and haue not kept the wayes which the Highest commanded you.

32 And for as much as he is a righteous iudge, hee tooke from you in time, the thing that he had giuen you.

33 And now are you heere, and your brethren amongst you.

34 Therefore if so be that you will subdue your owne vnderstanding, and reforme your hearts, yee shall be kept aliue, and after death yee shall obtaine mercy.

35 For after death, shall the iudgement come, when we shall liue againe: and then shall the names of the righteous be manifest, and the workes of the vngodly shall be declared.

36 Let no man therefore come vnto me now, nor seeke after me these fourty dayes.

37 So I tooke the fiue men as hee commanded me, and we went into the field, and remained there.

* Ezek. 3. 2.

38 And the next day behold a voyce called mee saying, Esdras, * open thy mouth and drinke that I giue thee to drinke.

39 Then opened I my mouth, and behold, he reached me a full cup, which was full as it were with water, but the colour of it was like fire.

40 And I tooke it, and dranke: and when I had drunke of it, my heart vt-

tered vnderstanding: and wisedome grew in my brest, for my spirit strengthened my memory.

41 And my mouth was opened and shut no more.

42 The highest gaue vnderstanding vnto the fiue men, and they wrote the wonderfull visions of the night, that were told, which they knew not: And they sate fourty dayes, and they wrote in the day, and at night they ate bread.

43 As for me I spake in the day, and held not my tongue by night:

‖ Or, 904

44 In fourty dayes they wrote ‖ two hundred and foure bookes.

45 And it came to passe when the fourty dayes were fulfilled, that the Highest spake, saying, The first that thou hast written, publish openly, that the worthy and vnworthy may read it.

46 But keepe the seuenty last, that thou mayest deliuer them onely to such as be wise, among the people.

‖ Or, the light of knowledge.

47 For in them is the spring of vnderstanding, the fountains of wisedome, and the ‖ streame of knowledge.

48 And I did so.

CHAP. XV.

1 This prophecie is certaine. 5 God will take vengeance vpon the wicked, 12 Vpon Egypt, 28 An horrible vision. 43 Babylon and Asia are threatned.

Ehold, speake thou in the eares of my people the words of prophesie, which I will put in thy mouth, saith the Lord.

2 And cause them to be written in paper: for they are faithfull and true.

3 Feare not the imaginations against thee, let not the incredulity of them trouble thee, that speake against thee.

4 For all the vnfaithfull shall die in their vnfaithfulnesse.

5 Behold, saith the Lord, I will bring plagues vpon the world; the sword, famine, death, and destruction.

6 For wickednesse hath exceedingly polluted the whole earth, and their hurtfull workes are fulfilled.

7 Therefore saith the Lord,

8 I will hold my tongue no more as touching their wickednesse, which they prophanely commit, neither wil I suffer them in those things, in which they wickedly exercise themselues: behold, the * innocent & righteous blood cryeth

* Reuel. 6. 10. and 19. 2.

cryeth vnto me, and the soules of the iust complaine continually.

9 And therefore saith the Lord, I wil surely auenge them, and receiue vnto me, all the innocent blood from among them.

10 Beholde, my people is ledde as a flocke to the slaughter: I wil not suffer them now to dwel in the land of Egypt.

11 But I will bring them with a mighty hand, and a stretched out arme, and smite Egypt with plagues as before, and wil destroy al the land thereof.

12 Egypt shal mourne, and the foundation of it shall bee smitten with the plague and punishment, that God shall bring vpon it.

13 They that till the ground shall mourne: for their seedes shall faile, through the blasting, and haile, and with a fearefull constellation.

14 Woe to the world, and them that dwell therein.

15 For the sword and their destruction draweth nigh, and one people shall stand vp to fight against another, and swords in their hands.

16 For there shalbe sedition among men, and inuading one another, they shal not regard their kings, nor princes, and the course of their actions shall stand in their power.

17 A man shall desire to goe into a citie, and shall not be able.

18 For because of their pride, the cities shalbe troubled, the houses shalbe destroyed, and men shalbe afraid.

19 A man shall haue no pitie vpon his neighbour, but shall destroy their houses with the sword, and spoile their goods, because of the lacke of bread, and for great tribulation.

20 Behold, saith God, I will call together all the Kings of the earth to reuerence me, which are from the rising of the Sunne, from the South, from the East, and Libanus: to turne themselues one against another, and repay the things that they haue done to them.

21 Like as they doe yet this day vnto my chosen, so will I doe also and recompense in their bosome, Thus saith the Lord God;

22 My right hand shall not spare the sinners, and my sword shal not cease ouer them, that shed innocent blood vpon earth.

23 The fire is gone foorth from his wrath, and hath consumed the foundations of the earth, and the sinners like the straw that is kindled.

24 Wo to them that sinne and keepe not my comandements, saith the Lord.

25 I will not spare them: goe your way ye children from the power, defile not my Sanctuary:

26 For the Lord knoweth all them that sinne against him, and therefore deliuereth he them vnto death and destruction.

27 For now are the plagues come vpon the whole earth, and ye shall remaine in them, for God shal not deliuer you, because ye haue sinned against him.

28 Behold an horrible vision, and the appearance thereof from the East.

29 Where the nations of the dragons of Arabia shall come out with many charets, and the multitude of them shalbe caried as the winde vpon earth, that all they which heare them, may feare and tremble.

30 Also the Carmanians raging in wrath, shall go forth as the wilde bores of the wood, and with great power shall they come, and ioyne battell with them, and shall waste a portion of the land of the Assyrians.

31 And then shall the dragons haue the vpper hand, remembring their nature, and if they shall turne themselues, conspiring together in great power to persecute them,

32 Then these shalbe troubled, and keepe silence through their power, and shall flee.

33 And from the land of the Assyrians, shall the enemy besiege them, and consume some of them, and in their host shall be feare, and dread and strife ‖ among their kings.   ‖ *Or, against*

34 Behold clouds from the East, and from the North, vnto the South, and they are very horrible to looke vpon; full of wrath and storme.

35 They shall smite one vpon another, & they shall smite downe a great multitude of starres vpon the earth, euen their owne starre; and blood shalbe from the sword vnto the belly.

36 And doung of men vnto the camels ‖ hough.   ‖ *Or, Pasterne, or litter.*

37 And there shalbe great fearefulnesse and trembling vpon earth: and they that see the wrath, shall be afraid, and trembling shall come vpon them.

38 And then shall there come great stormes, from the South, and from the North,

North, & another part from the West.

39 And strong winds shal arise from the East, and shall open it, and the cloud which hee raised vp in wrath, and the starre stirred to cause feare toward the East and West winde, shalbe destroyed.

40 The great and mightie cloudes shall be lifted vp full of wrath, and the starre, that they may make all the earth afraid, and them that dwel therein, and they shall powre out ouer euery high and eminent place, an horrible starre.

41 Fire and haile, and fleeing swords, and many waters, that all fields may be full, and all riuers with the abundance of great waters.

42 And they shal breake downe the cities, and walls, mountaines and hils, trees of the wood, and grasse of the medowes, and their corne.

43 And they shal goe stedfastly vnto *Or,destroy.* Babylon, and ||make her afraid.

44 They shall come to her, and besiege her, the starre and all wrath shall they powre out vpon her, then shall the dust and smoke goe vp vnto the heauen: and all they that be about her, shall bewaile her.

45 And they that remaine vnder her, shall doe seruice vnto them that haue put her in feare.

46 And thou Asia that art ||parta- *Or, like vn-to Babylon.* ker of the hope of Babylon, and art the glory of her person:

47 Woe be vnto thee thou wretch, because thou hast made thy selfe like vnto her, and hast deckt thy daughters in whoredome, that they might please and glory in thy louers, which haue alway desired to commit whordome with thee.

48 Thou hast followed her, that is hated in all her works and inuentions: therefore sayth God,

49 I will send plagues vpon thee: widowhood, pouertie, famine, sword, and pestilence, to waste thy houses with destruction and death.

50 And the glory of thy power shall be dried vp as floure, when the heate shall arise that is sent ouer thee.

51 Thou shalt bee weakened as a poore woman with stripes, and as one chastised with woundes, so that the mightie and louers shall not be able to receiue thee.

52 Would I with iealousie haue so proceeded against thee, saith the Lord,

53 If thou haddest not alway slaine my chosen, exalting the stroke of thine hands, & saying ouer their †dead, when thou wast drunken,   *† Lat. death.*

54 Set foorth the beauty of thy countenance.

55 The reward of thy whoredome shall be in thy bosome, therefore shalt thou receiue recompense.

56 Like as thou hast done vnto my chosen, sayth the Lord; euen so shall God doe vnto thee, and shall deliuer thee into mischiefe.

57 Thy children shall die of hunger, and thou shalt fall through the sword: thy cities shalbe broken downe, and all thine shall perish with the sword in the field.

58 They that be in the mountaines shall die of hunger, and eate their owne flesh, and drinke their owne blood, for very hunger of bread, & thirst of water.

59 Thou, as vnhappy, shalt come through the Sea, and receiue plagues againe.

60 And in the passage, they shall rush on the idle citie, and shall destroy some portion of thy land, and consume part of thy glory, and shall returne to Babylon that was destroyed.

61 And thou shalt be cast downe by them, as stubble, and they shall be vnto thee as fire,

62 And shall consume thee and thy cities, thy land and thy mountaines, all thy woods and thy fruitfull trees shall they burne vp with fire.

63 Thy children shall they cary away captiue, and looke what thou hast, they shall spoile it, and ||marre the beauty of thy face.   *||Or,blemish.*

CHAP. XVI.

1 Babylon and other places are threatned with plagues that cannot be auoided: 23 and with desolation. 40 The seruants of the Lorde must looke for troubles: 51 and not hide their sinnes, 74 but leaue them, and they shall be deliuered.

W Oe be vnto thee, Babylon and Asia, woe be vnto thee Egypt and Syria.

2 Gird vp your selues with clothes of sacke and haire, bewaile your children, and be sory, for your destruction is at hand.

3 A sword is sent vpon you, and who may turne it backe?

4 A fire is sent among you, and who may quench it?

5 Plagues are sent vnto you, and what

what is he that may driue them away?

6 May any man driue away a hungry Lion in the wood? or may any one quench the fire in stubble, when it hath begun to burne?

7 May one turne againe the arrow that is shot of a strong archer?

8 The mightie Lord sendeth the plagues, and who is hee that can driue them away?

9 A fire shall goe foorth from his wrath: & who is he that may quench it?

10 He shall cast lightnings, and who shall not feare? he shall thunder, and who shall not be afraid?

11 The Lord shall threaten, and who shall not be vtterly beaten to powder at his presence?

12 The earth quaketh and the foundations thereof, the sea ariseth vp with waues from the deepe, and the waues of it are troubled, and the fishes thereof also before the Lord, and before the glorie of his power.

13 For strong is his right hand that bendeth the bow, his arrowes that hee shooteth are sharpe, and shall not misse when they begin to bee shot into the ends of the world.

14 Behold, the plagues are sent, and shall not returne againe, vntill they come vpon the earth.

15 The fire is kindled, and shall not be put out, till it consume the foundation of the earth.

16 Like as an arrow which is shot of a mightie archer returneth not backward: euen so the plagues that shall be sent vpon earth, shall not returne againe.

17 Woe is me, woe is me, who will deliuer me in those dayes?

18 The beginning of sorrowes, and great mournings, the beginning of famine, and great death: the beginning of warres, and the powers shall stand in feare, the beginning of euils, what shall I doe when these euils shal come?

19 Behold, famine, and plague, tribulation and anguish, are sent as scourges for amendment.

20 But for all these things they shall not turne from their wickednes, nor be alway mindfull of the scourges.

21 Behold, victuals shall be so good cheape vpon earth, that they shal think themselues to be in good case, and euen then shall || euils growe vpon earth, sword, famine, and great confusion.

|| Or, plagues

22 For many of them that dwell vpon earth, shall perish of famine, and the other that escape the hunger, shall the sword destroy.

23 And the dead shall be cast out as doung, and there shalbe no man to comfort them, for the earth shall be wasted, and the cities shall be cast downe.

24 There shall be no man left to till the earth, and to sow it.

25 The trees shall giue fruite, and who shall gather them?

26 The grapes shall ripe, and who shall treade them? for all places shall be desolate of men.

27 So that one man shall desire to see another, and to heare his voyce.

28 For of a citie there shalbe ten left, and two of the field which shall hide themselues in the thicke groues, and in the clefts of rockes.

29 As in an orchard of oliues, vpon euery tree there are left three or foure oliues:

30 Or, when as a vineyard is gathered, there are left some clusters of them that diligently seek through y vineyard:

31 Euen so in those dayes there shalbe three or foure left by them that search their houses with the sword.

32 And the earth shall be laid waste, and the fields therof shal waxe old, and her wayes and all her paths shall grow full of thornes, because no man shall trauaile therethrough.

33 The virgins shall mourne hauing no bridegromes, ŷ women shal mourne hauing no husbands, their daughters shall mourne hauing no helpers.

34 In the warres shall their bridegromes bee destroyed, and their husbands shall perish of famine.

35 Heare now these things, and vnderstand them, ye seruants of the Lord.

36 Behold the word of the Lord, receiue it, beleeue not the gods of whom the Lord spake.

37 Behold, the plagues draw nigh, and are not slacke.

38 As when a woman with childe in the ninth month bringeth forth her son, within two or three houres of her birth great paines compasse her wombe, which paines, when the child commeth forth, they slacke not a moment,

39 Euen so shall not the plagues bee slacke to come vpon the earth, and the world shall mourne, and sorrowes shal come vpon it on euery side.

40 O my

40 O my people , Heare my word : make you ready to the battell , and in those euils , be euen as pilgrimes vpon the earth.

41 He that selleth let him be as hee that fleeth away : and he that buyeth, as one that will loose.

42 He that occupieth merchandize, as he that had no profit by it : and he that buildeth , as hee that shall not dwell therein.

43 He that soweth, as if he should not reape : so also he that planteth the vineyard, as he that shal not gather the grapes.

44 They that marry, as they that shall get no children : and they that marrie not, as the widowers.

45 And therefore they that labour, labour in vaine.

46 For strangers shall reape their fruits , and spoile their goods , ouerthrowe their houses ; and take their children captiues, for in captiuity and famine shall they get children.

47 And they that occupy their merchandize with robbery, the more they decke their citties, their houses, their possessions and their owne persons :

48 The more will I be angry with them for their sinne, saith the Lord.

49 Like as an whore enuieth a right honest and vertuous woman :

50 So shall righteousnesse hate iniquity, when she decketh her selfe, and shall accuse her , to her face, when he commeth that shall defend him that diligently searcheth out euery sinne vpon earth.

51 And therfore be yee not like therunto, nor to the workes thereof.

52 For yet a little iniquitie shall be taken away out of the earth, and righteousnesse shall reigne among you.

53 Let not the sinner say that he hath not sinned : for God shall burne coales of fire vpon his head, which saith before the Lord God and his glory, I haue not sinned.

* Luke 16. 15.

54 Behold, the Lord knoweth all the workes of men , *their imaginations, their thoughts, and their hearts :

* Gene. 1. 1.

55 Which spake but the word, let the earth be made, *and it was made : let the heauen be made, and it was created.

* Psal. 146. 4.

56 In his word were the starres made, and he knoweth the *number of them.

57 He searcheth the deepe, and the treasures thereof, he hath measured the Sea, and what it containeth.

58 He hath shut the Sea in the midst of the waters , and with his word hath he hanged the earth vpon the waters.

59 He spreadeth out the heauens like a vault, vpon the waters hath he founded it.

60 In the desert hath hee made springs of water , and pooles vpon the tops of the mountaines , that the floods might powre downe from the high rockes to water the earth.

61 He made man, and put his heart in the midst of the body, and gaue him breath, life, and vnderstanding.

62 Yea and the spirit of Almighty God, which made all things, and searcheth out all hidden things in the secrets of the earth.

63 Surely he knoweth your inuentions , and what you thinke in your hearts, euen them that sinne, and would hide their sinne.

64 Therefore hath the Lord exactly searched out all your workes, and he will put you all to shame.

65 And when your sinnes are brought foorth yee shalbe ashamed before men, and your owne sinnes shall be your accusers in that day.

66 What will yee doe ? or how will yee hide your sinnes before God and his Angels ?

67 Behold , God himselfe is the iudge, feare him : leaue off from your sinnes, and forget your iniquities to medle no more with them for euer, so shall God lead you forth , and deliuer you from all trouble.

68 For behold , the burning wrath of a great multitude is kindled ouer you, and they shall take away certaine of you, and feede you ‖being idle with things offered vnto idoles.

‖ Or, being vnable to resist.

69 And they that consent vnto them shall be had in derision, and in reproch, and troden vnder foote.

70 For there shall be in euery place, and in the next cities a great insurrection vpon those that feare the Lord.

71 They shall be like mad men, sparing none, but still spoiling and destroying those that feare the Lord.

72 For they shal waste and take away their goods, and cast them out of their houses.

73 Then shall they be knowen who are

are my chosen, and they shall be tried, as the gold in the fire:

74 Heare, O yee my beloued, saith the Lord : behold, the dayes of trouble are at hand, but I will deliuer you from the same.

75 Be yee not afraid, neither doubt, for God is your guide,

76 And the guide of them who keepe my commaundements, and precepts, saith the Lord God : Let not your

sinnes weigh you downe, and let not your iniquities lift vp themselues.

77 Woe bee vnto them that are bound with their sinnes, and couered with their iniquities : like as a field is couered ouer with bushes, and the path thereof couered with thornes, that no man may trauell through.

78 It is ‖left vndressed, and is cast into the fire, to bee consumed there-with

‖ *Or, shut out.*

¶ TOBIT.

‖ Or, acts

HE Booke of the ‖wordes of Tobit, sonne of Tobiel, the son of Ananiel, the sonne of Aduel, the sonne of Gabael, of the seed of Asael, of the Tribe of Nephthali,

2 Who in the time of Enemessar king of the Assyrians, was led captiue out of *Thisbe which is at the right hand of that citie, which is called ‖pro-perly Nephthali in Galile aboue Aser.

* 2. King. 17. 3.
‖ Or, Kedes of Nephthali in Galile, Iudg. 4 6.

3 I Tobit haue walked all the dayes of my life in the way of trueth, and iustice, and I did many almes deeds to my brethren, and my nation, who came with me to Nineue, into the land of the Assyrians.

4 And when I was in mine owne countrey, in the land of Israel, being but yong, all the tribe of Nephthali my father, fell from the house of Ierusa-lem, which was chosen out of all the tribes of Israel, that all the tribes should sacrifice *there* where the Temple of the habitation of the most High was consecrated, and built for all ages.

5 Now all the tribes which toge-

ther reuolted, and the house of my fa-ther Nephthali sacrificed vnto the *heifer Baal

* 1. King. 12. 30. Or, to the power of Baal, or the god Baal.

6 But I alone went often to Ieru-salem at the Feasts, as it was ordeined vnto al the people of Israel by an euer-lasting decree, * hauing the first fruits, and tenths of encrease, with that which was first shorne, and them gaue I at the Altar to the Priestes the children of Aaron.

* Exod. 22. 29. deu. 12. 6.

7 The first tenth part of al increase, I gaue to the sonnes of ‖Aaron, who ministred at Ierusalem : another tenth part I sold away, and went, and spent it euery yeere at Ierusalem.

‖ Or, Leui

8 And the third, I gaue vnto them to whom it was meet, as Debora my fathers mother had commanded mee, because I was left an orphane by my father.

9 Furthermore when I was come to the age of a man, I married Anna of mine *owne kinred, and of her I be-gate Tobias

* Num. 36. 7.

10 And when we were caried away captiues to Nineue, all my brethren, and those that were of my kinred, did eate of the * bread of the Gentiles.

* Gene. 43. 32.

11 But I kept †my selfe from eating;

† Greek. my soule.

12 Because I remembred God with all my heart

13 And the most High gaue me grace, and fauour before Enemessar, so that I was his †purueyour.

† Greek. byer.

14 And I went into Media, and left in trust with Gabael, the brother of Ga-brias ‖at Rages a citie of Media, ten ta-lents of siluer

‖ Or, in the land or coun-trey of Me-dia.

15 Now

Gr. the
payes of
whom were
nsetled.

15 Now when Enemessar was dead, Sennacherib his sonne reigned in his stead, †whose estate was troubled, that I could not goe into Media.

16 And in the time of Enemessar, I gaue many almes to my brethren, and gaue my bread to the hungry,

Or, behind
e walles.

17 And my clothes to the naked: and if I saw any of my nation dead, or cast ‖about the walles of Nineue, I buried him.

2. Kin. 19.
, 36. isal.
. 36, 37.
clus. 48.
, 22, 1.
acc. 7. 41.
mac. 8.

18 And if the king Sennacherib had slaine any, when hee was come, *and fledde from Iudea, I buried them priuily, (for in his wrath hee killed many) but the bodies were not found, when they were sought for of the king.

19 And when one of the Nineuites went, and complained of me to the king that I buried them, and hid my selfe: vnderstanding that I was sought for to be put to death, I withdrew my selfe for feare.

20 Then all my goods were forcibly taken away, neither was there any thing left me, besides my wife Anna, and my sonne Tobias.

. King.
37. 2.
r. 32. 21.
Or, Esar-
addon.

21 And there passed not fiue and fiftie dayes before two of his sonnes *killed him, and they fled into the mountaines of Ararath, and ‖Sarchedonus his sonne reigned in his stead, who appointed ouer his fathers accounts, and ouer all his affaires, Achiacharus my brother Anaels sonne.

', Esar-
addon.

22 And Achiacharus entreating for me, I returned to Nineue: now Achiacharus was Cup-bearer, and keeper of the Signet, and Steward, and ouerseer of the accounts: and ‖Sarchedonus appointed him next vnto him: and hee was my brothers sonne.

CHAP. II.

1 Tobit leaueth his meate to bury the dead, 10 and becommeth blinde. 11 His wife taketh in worke to get her liuing. 14 Her husband and she fall out about a kidde.

 Ow when I was come home againe, and my wife Anna was restored vnto me, with my sonne Tobias, in the feast of Pentecost, which is the holy Feast of the seuen weekes, there was a good dinner prepared me, in the which I sate down to eate.

2 And when I saw abundance of meate, I sayd to my sonne, Goe and bring what poore man soeuer thou shalt finde out of our brethren, who is mindfull of the Lord, and loe, I tarie for thee.

3 But he came againe and said, Father, one of our nation is strangled, and is cast out in the market place.

4 Then before I had tasted of any meate, I start vp and tooke him vp into a roume, vntill the going downe of the Sunne.

5 Then I returned and washed my selfe, and ate my meate in heauinesse,

6 Remembring that prophesie *of Amos, as hee said; Your feasts shall be turned into mourning, and all your mirth into lamentation.

* Amos 8.
10.

7 Therefore I wept: and after the going downe of the Sunne, I went and made a graue, and buried him.

8 But my neighbours mocked me, and said, This man is not yet afraide to be put to death for this matter, *who fledde away, and yet loe, he burieth the dead againe.

* Cha. 1. 19.

9 The same night also I returned from the buriall, and slept by the wall of my court yard, being polluted, and my face was vncouered:

10 And I knewe not that there were ‖Sparrowes in the wall, and mine eyes being open, the Sparrowes muted warme doung into mine eyes, and a ‖whitenesse came in mine eyes, and I went to the Physicians, but they helped me not: moreouer Achiacharus did nourish mee, vntill I went into Elymais.

‖ Or, Swallowes.

‖ Or, white filmes.

11 And my wife Anna ‖did take womens workes to doe.

12 And when shee had sent ‖them home to the owners, they payd her wages, and gaue her also besides a kid.

‖ Or, was hired to spinne in the womens rooms.
‖ Or, her worke.

13 And when it was in mine house, and beganne to crie, I said vnto her, From whence is this kidde? is it not stollen? render it to the owners, *for it is not lawfull to eate any thing that is stollen.

* Deu. 22. 1.

14 *But shee replyed vpon me, It was giuen for a gift more then the wages: Howbeit I did not beleeue her, but bade her render it to the owners: and I was abashed at her. But she replyed vpon me, Where are thine almes, and thy righteous deedes? ‖behold, thou and all thy workes are knowen.

* Iob 2. 9.

‖ Or, loe all things are knowen to thee.

CHAP.

CHAP. III.

1 Tobit grieued with his wiues taunts, prayeth.
11 Sara reproched by her fathers maides,
prayeth also. 17 An Angel is sent to helpe
them both.

 Hen I being grieued, did
weepe, and in my sorrowe
prayed, saying,

2 O Lord, thou art iust
and all thy workes, and
all thy wayes are mercie and trueth,
and thou iudgest truely & iustly for euer.

3 Remember me, and looke on me,
punish me not for my sinnes and ignorances, and *the sinnes of* my fathers, who
haue sinned before thee.

4 For they obeyed not thy commandements, wherefore thou hast deliuered
vs *for a spoile, and vnto captiuitie, and
vnto death, and for a prouerbe of reproch to all the nations among whom
we are dispersed.

*Deut. 28.
15, 37.*

5 And now thy iudgments are many and true: Deale with me according
to my sinnes, and my fathers: because
we haue not kept thy commandements,
neither haue walked in trueth before
thee.

6 Now therefore deale with me as
seemeth best vnto thee, and command
my spirit to be taken from me, that I
may be ||dissolued, and become earth:
for it is profitable for me to die, rather
then to liue, because I haue heard false
reproches, and haue much sorow: command therfore that I may now be deliuered out of this distresse, and goe into
the euerlasting place: turne not thy face
away from me.

*|| Or, dismis-
sed, or deli-
uered.*

7 It came to passe the same day,
that in Ecbatane a citie of Media, Sara the daughter of Raguel, was also reproched by her fathers maides.

8 Because that she had bin maried
to seuen husbands, whom Asmodeus
the euill spirit had killed, before they had
lien with her. Doest thou not knowe,
said they, that thou hast strangled thine
husbands? thou hast had already seuen
husbands, neither wast thou named after any of them.

9 Wherefore doest thou beate vs for
them? If they be dead, goe thy wayes
after them, let vs neuer see of thee either
sonne or daughter.

10 When she heard these things, she
was very sorowful, so that she thought
to haue strangled her selfe, and she said,

I am the onely daughter of my father,
and if I doe this, it shall bee a reproch
vnto him, and I shall bring his old age
with sorow vnto the graue.

11 Then she prayed toward the window, & said, Blessed art thou, O Lord
my God, and thine holy and glorious
Name is blessed, and honourable for e-
uer, let al thy works praise thee for euer.

12 And now, O Lord, I set mine
eyes and my face toward thee,

13 And say, take me out of the earth,
that I may heare no more the reproch.

14 Thou knowest, Lord, that I am
pure from all sinne with man,

15 And that I neuer polluted my
name, nor the name of my father in the
land of my captiuitie: I am the onely
daughter of my father, neither hath he
any child to bee his heire, neither any
||neere kinseman, nor any sonne of his
aliue, to whome I may keepe my selfe
for a wife: my seuen husbands are already dead, and why should I liue? but
if it please not thee that I should die,
command some regard to be had of me,
and pitie taken of me, that I heare no
more reproch.

i Or, brot

16 So the prayers of them both were
heard before the Maiesty of the great
God.

17 And Raphael was sent to heale
them both, that is, to scale away the
whitenesse of Tobits eyes, and to giue
Sara the daughter of Raguel, for a
wife to Tobias the sonne of Tobit, and
to bind Asmodeus the euill spirit, because she belongeth to Tobias by right
of inheritance. The selfe same time came
Tobit home, and entred into his house,
and Sara, the daughter of Raguel
came downe from her vpper chamber.

CHAP. IIII.

3 Tobit giueth instructions to his sonne Tobias, 20 and telleth him of money left with
Gabael in Media.

 N that day Tobit remem-
bred the money, which he
had committed to Gabael
in Rages of Media,

2 And said with him-
selfe, I haue wished for death, wherefore doe I not call for my sonne Tobias, that I may signifie to him *of the
money* before I die.

3 And when he had called him, he
said; My sonne, when I am dead, bury
me, and despise not thy mother, *but
honour

*Exod. 5
12. ecclus
27.*

honour her all the dayes of thy life, and doe that which shall please her, and greiue her not.

4 Remember, my sonne, that shee saw many dangers for thee, *when thou wast* in her wombe, and when shee is dead, bury her by me in one graue.

5 My sonne, be mindfull of the Lord our God all thy dayes, and let not thy will be set to sinne, or to transgresse his Commandements : doe vprightly all thy life long, and follow not the wayes of vnrighteousnesse.

6 For if thou deale truely, thy doings shall prosperously succeed to thee, and to all them that liue iustly.

7 *Giue almes of thy substance, and when thou giuest almes, let not thine eye be enuious, neither turne thy face from any poore, and the face of God shall not be turned away from thee.

8 If thou hast abundance, * giue almes accordingly : if thou haue but a litle, be not afraid to giue according to that litle.

9 For thou layest vp a good treasure for thy selfe against the day of necessitie.

10 *Because that almes doth deliuer from death, and suffereth not to come into darknesse.

11 For almes is a good gift vnto all that giue it, in the sight of the most High.

12 Beware of all *whoredome, my sonne, and chiefly take a wife of the seed of thy fathers, and take not a strange woman to wife, which is not of thy fathers tribe : for we are the children of the Prophets, Noe, Abraham, Isaak, and Iacob : remember, my sonne, that our fathers from the beginning, euen that they all maried wiues of their owne kinred, and were blessed in their children, and their seede shall inherite the land.

13 Now therefore my sonne, loue thy brethren, and despise not in thy heart thy brethren, the sonnes and daughters of thy people, in not taking a wife of them : for in pride is destruction and much trouble, and in lewdnesse is decay, and great want : for lewdnesse is the mother of famine.

14 Let not the *wages of any man, which hath wrought for thee, tary with thee, but giue him it out of hand : for if thou serue God he will also repay thee : be circumspect, my sonne, in all things thou doest, and be wise in all thy conuersation.

15 *Doe that to no man which thou hatest : drinke not wine to make thee drunken ; neither let drunkennesse goe with thee in thy iourney.

16 *Giue of thy bread to the hungry, and of thy garments to them that are naked, *and according to thine abundance giue almes, and let not thine eye be enuious, when thou giuest almes.

17 Powre out thy bread on the buriall of the iust, but giue nothing to the wicked.

18 Aske counsell of all that are wise, and despise not any counsell that is profitable.

19 Blesse the Lord thy God alway, and desire of him that thy wayes may be directed, and that all thy pathes, and counsels may prosper : for euery nation hath not counsell, but the Lord himselfe giueth all good things, and hee humbleth whom he will, as he will ; now therefore my sonne, remember my commandements, neither let them be put out of thy minde.

20 And now I signifie this to thee, that I committed tenne talents to Gabael the sonne of Gabrias at Rages in Media.

21 And feare not my sonne, that we are made poore, for thou hast much wealth, if thou feare God, and depart from all sinne, and doe that which is pleasing in his sight.

CHAP. V.

4 Yong Tobias seeketh a guide into Media. 6 The Angel will goe with him, 12 and saith he is his kinsman. 16 Tobias and the Angel depart together. 17 But his mother is grieued for her sonnes departing.

Obias then answered and said, Father, I will doe all things, which thou hast commanded me.

2 But how can I receiue the money, seeing, I know him not?

3 Then he gaue him the handwriting, and said vnto him, Seeke thee a man which may goe with thee whiles I yet liue, and I will giue him wages, and goe, and receiue the money.

4 Therefore when he went to seeke a man, he found Raphael that was an Angell.

5 But he knew not ; and he said vnto him, Canst thou goe with me to Rages? & knowest thou those places well?

6 To

rou. 3. 9.
le. 4. 1.
14. 13.
e 14. 13.

Ecclu. 35.

Ecclu. 29.

, Thess. 4.

Leuit. 19.
. deut.
. 14. 15.

* Matth. 7.
12. luc. 6.
31.

* Luc. 14.
13.

* Matth. 6. 1

6 To whom the Angel said, I will goe with thee, and I know the way well : for I haue lodged with our brother Gabael.

7 Then Tobias said vnto him, Tary for me till I tell my father.

8 Then he said vnto him, Goe and tary not; so he went in, and said to his father; Behold, I haue found one, which wil goe with me. Then he said, Call him vnto me, that I may know of what tribe he is, and whether hee be a trustie man to goe with thee.

9 So he called him, and he came in, and they saluted one another.

10 Then Tobit said vnto him, Brother, shew me of what tribe and family thou art.

11 To whom hee said, Doest thou seeke for a tribe or family, or an hired man to goe with thy sonne? Then Tobit said vnto him, I would know, brother, thy kinred, and name.

12 Then he said, I am Azarias, the sonne of Ananias the great, and of thy brethren.

13 Then Tobit said, Thou art welcome brother, be not now angry with mee, because I haue enquired to know thy tribe, and thy family, for thou art my brother, of an honest & good stocke: for I know Ananias, and Ionathas sonnes of that great Samaias : as we went together to Ierusalem to worship, and offered the first borne, and the tenths of the fruits, and they were not seduced with the errour of our brethren: my brother, thou art of a good stocke.

14 But tell me, what wages shall I giue thee? *wilt thou* a drachme a day? and things necessary as to my owne sonne?

15 Yea moreouer, if ye returne safe, I will adde some thing to the wages.

16 So they were well pleased. Then said he to Tobias; Prepare thy selfe for the iourney, and God send you a good iourney. And when his sonne had prepared all things for the iourney, his father said; Goe thou with this man, and God which dwelleth in heauen prosper your iourney, & the Angel of God keepe you company. So they went foorth both, and the yong mans dogge with them.

17 But Anna his mother wept, and said to Tobit, Why hast thou sent away our sonne? is hee not the staffe of our hand, in going in and out before vs?

18 Be not greedy (to adde) money to money : but let it bee ||as refuse in respect of our childe.

19 ||For that which the Lord hath giuen vs to liue with, doeth suffice vs.

20 Then said Tobit to her, Take no care my sister, he shal returne in safety, and thine eyes shall see him.

21 For the good Angel will keepe him company, and his iourney shall be prosperous, and he shall returne safe.

22 Then she made an end of weeping.

Marginal notes:
||Let not money be added, but be the off scoring of our sonne.
||Or, so long as God hath granted vs to liue, this is sufficient.

CHAP. VI.

4 The Angel biddeth Tobias to take the liuer, heart and gall out of a fish, 10 And to marry Sara the daughter of Raguel; 16 And teacheth how to driue the wicked spirit away.

Nd as they went on their iourney, they came in the euening to the riuer Tigris, & they lodged there.

2 And when the yong man went downe to wash himselfe, a fish leaped out of the riuer, and would haue deuoured him.

3 Then the Angel said vnto him, Take the fish; and the yong man layd hold of the fish, and ||drew it to land.

Marginal note: ||Cast it on the la...

4 To whom the Angel said, Open the fish, and take the heart, and the liuer and the gall, and put them vp safely.

5 So the yong man did as the Angel commaunded him, and when they had rosted the fish, they did eate it : then they both went on their way, till they drew neere to Ecbatane.

6 Then the yong man saide to the Angel; Brother Azarias, to what vse is the heart, and the liuer, and the gall of the fish?

7 And he said vnto him, Touching the heart and the liuer, if a deuil, or an euil spirit trouble any, we must make a smoke thereof before the man or the woman, and the party shalbe no more vexed.

8 As for the gall *it is good* to anoint a man that hath whitenesse in his eyes, and he shalbe healed.

9 And when they were come neere to Rages;

10 The Angel said to the yong man, Brother, to day wee shall lodge with Raguel, who is thy cousin; hee also hath one onely daughter, named Sara, I wil speake for her, that she may be giuen thee for a wife.

11 For

‖ Or, inheri-
tance.
* Num. 27.
8. & 36. 8.

11 For to thee doth the ‖ *right of her appertaine, seeing thou onely art of her kinred.

12 And the maide is faire and wise, now therefore heare me, & I wil speake to her father, and when wee returne from Rages, we will celebrate the mariage : for I know that Raguel cannot marry her to another according to the Law of Moses, but he shalbe guiltie of death, because the right of inheritance doeth rather appertaine to thee, then to any other.

13 Then the yong man answered the Angel, I haue heard, brother Azarias, that this maide hath beene giuen to seuen men, who all died in the marriage chamber :

14 And now I am the onely sonne of my father, and I am afraid, lest if I goe in vnto her, I die, as the other before ; for a wicked spirit loueth her, which hurteth no body, but those which come vnto her ; wherefore I also feare, lest I die, and bring my fathers and my mothers life (because of me) to the graue with sorrow, for they haue no other sonne to bury them.

15 Then the Angel said vnto him, Doest thou not remember the precepts, which thy father gaue thee, that thou shouldest marrie a wife of thine owne kinred? wherefore heare me, O my brother, for she shall be giuen thee to wife, and make thou no reckoning of the euil spirit, for this same night shall shee be giuen thee in mariage.

‖ Or, imbers.

16 And when thou shalt come into the mariage chamber, thou shalt take the ‖ashes of perfume, and shalt lay vpon them, some of the heart, and liuer of the fish, and shalt make a smoke with it.

17 And the deuill shall smell it, and flee away, and neuer come againe any more : but when thou shalt come to her, rise vp both of you, and pray to God, which is mercifnll, who will haue pity on you, and saue you : feare not, for shee is appointed vnto thee from the beginning ; and thou shalt preserue her, and shee shall goe with thee. Moreouer I suppose that shee shall beare thee children. Now when Tobias had heard these things, he loued her, and his heart was ‖effectually ioyned to her.

‖ Or, vehe-
mently.

CHAP. VII.

11 Raguel telleth Tobias what had happened to his daughter : 12 and giueth her in marriage

vnto him. 17 She is conueyed to her chamber, and weepeth. 18 Her mother cõforteth her.

 Nd when they were come to Ecbatane, they came to the house of Raguel ; and Sara met them : and after that they had saluted one another, shee brought them into the house.

2 Then sayd Raguel to Edna his wife, How like is this yong man to Tobit my cousin?

3 And Raguel asked them, From whence are you, brethren? To whom they said, We are of the sonnes of Nephthali, which are captiues in Nineue.

4 Then hee said to them, Doe yee know Tobit our kinseman? And they said, We know him. Then said hee, Is he in good health?

5 And they said, Hee is both aliue, and in good health : And Tobias sayd, He is my father.

6 Then Raguel leaped vp, and kissed him, and wept,

7 And blessed him, and said vnto him, Thou art the sonne of an honest and good man : but when he had heard that Tobit was blinde, he was sorowfull, and wept.

8 And likewise Edna his wife, and Sara his daughter wept. Moreouer, they entertained them cheerefully, and after that they had killed a ‖ramme of the flocke, they set store of meat on the table. Then said Tobias to Raphael, Brother Azarias, speak of those things, of which thou diddest talke in the way, and let this businesse be dispatched.

‖ A sucking
ramme or
lambe. Iu-
nius.

9 So he communicated the matter with Raguel, and Raguel said to Tobias, Eate and drink, and make merry :

10 For it is meet that thou shouldest marry my daughter : neuerthelesse I will declare vnto thee the trueth.

11 I haue giuen my daughter in mariage to seuen men, who died that night they came in vnto her : neuerthelesse for the present be merry : But Tobias said, I will eate nothing here, till we agree and sweare one to another.

12 Raguel said, Then take her from henceefoorth according to the ‖manner, for thou art her cousin, and she is thine, and the mercifull God giue you good successe in all things.

‖ Or, Law.

13 Then he called his daughter Sara, and she came to her father, and hee tooke her by the hand, and gaue her to be

be wife to Tobias, saying, Behold, take her after *the Law of Moses, and leade her away to thy father : And he blessed them,

* Num. 36. 6

14 And called Edna his wife, & tooke paper, and did write an instrument *of conenants*, and sealed it.

15 Then they began to eate.

16 After Raguel called his wife Edna, and said vnto her, Sister, prepare another chamber, & bring her in thither.

17 Which when she had done as hee had bidden her, she brought her thither, and she wept, & she ||receiued the teares of her daughter, and said vnto her,

‖ Or, licked.

18 Be of good comfort, my daughter, the Lord of heauen and earth giue thee ioy for this thy sorow : be of good comfort, my daughter.

CHAP. VIII.

3 Tobias driueth the wicked spirit away, as hee was taught. 4 He and his wife rise vp to pray. 10 Raguel thought he was dead : 15 But finding him aliue, praiseth God, 12 and maketh a wedding feast.

ANd when they had supped, they brought Tobias in vnto her.

2 And as he went, he remembred the wordes of Raphael, and tooke the ||ashes of the perfumes, and put the heart, and the liuer of the fish thereupon, and made a smoke *therewith.*

‖ Or, imbers

3 The which smell, when the euill spirit had smelled, hee fled into the outmost parts of Egypt, and the Angel bound him.

4 And after that they were both shut in together, Tobias rose out of the bed and said, Sister, arise, and let vs pray, that God would haue pitie on vs.

5 Then began Tobias to say, Blessed art thou, O God of our fathers, and blessed is thy holy and glorious Name for euer, let the heauens blesse thee, and all thy creatures.

6 Thou madest Adam, and gauest him *Eue his wife for an helper & stay: of them came mankind : thou hast said, It is not good that man should bee alone, let vs make vnto him an aide like to himselfe.

* Gen. 2. 7, 18, 22.

7 And now, O Lord, I take not this my sister for lust, but vprightly: therefore mercifully ordeine, that wee may become aged together.

8 And she said with him, Amen.

9 So they slept both that night, and Raguel arose, and went & made a graue

10 Saying, *I feare* lest he be dead.

11 But when Raguel was come into his house,

12 He said vnto his wife Edna, Send one of the maids, and let her see, whether he be aliue: if *he be* not, that we may bury him, and no man know it.

13 So the maid opened the doore and went in, and found them both asleepe,

14 And came forth, and told them, that he was aliue.

15 Then Raguel praised God, and said, O God, thou art worthy to be praised with all pure and holy praise : therefore let thy Saints praise thee with all thy creatures, and let all thine Angels and thine elect praise thee for euer.

16 Thou art to be praised, for thou hast made mee ioyfull, and that is not come to me, which I suspected : but thou hast dealt with vs according to thy great mercie.

17 Thou art to be praised, because thou hast had mercie of two, that were the onely begotten children of their fathers, grant them mercy, O Lord, and finish their life in health, with ioy and mercie.

18 Then Raguel bade his seruants to fill the graue.

19 And hee kept the wedding feast fourteene dayes.

20 For before the dayes of the mariage were finished, Raguel had said vnto him by an othe, that he should not depart, till the fourteene dayes of the mariage were expired,

21 And then he should take the halfe of his goods, and goe in safetie to his father, and should haue the rest when I and my wife be dead.

CHAP. IX.

1 Tobias sendeth the Angel vnto Gabael for the money. 6 The Angel bringeth it, and Gabael to the wedding.

THen Tobias called Raphael, and said vnto him, 2 Brother Azarias, Take with thee a seruant, and two camels, and go to Rages of Media to Gabael, & bring me the money, & bring him to the wedding.

3 For Raguel hath sworne that I shall not depart.

4 But my father counteth the dayes, and if I tarie long, he will be very sorie.

5 So

5 So Raphael went out and lodged with Gabael, and gaue him the handwriting, who brought forth bags, which were sealed vp, and gaue them to him.

6 And earely in the morning they went forth both together, and came to the wedding, and ||Tobias blessed his wife.

|| Or, Gabael blessed Tobias and his wife. Iunius.

CHAP. X.

1 Tobit and his wife long for their sonne. 7 She will not be comforted by her husband. 10 Raguel sendeth Tobias and his wife away, with halfe their goods, 12 and blesseth them.

Owe Tobit his father counted euery day, and when the dayes of the iourney were expired, and they came not:

2 Then Tobit said, Are they detained? or is Gabael dead? and there is no man to giue him the money?

3 Therefore he was very sory.

4 Then his wife said to him, My sonne is dead, seeing hee stayeth long, and she beganne to bewaile him, and said,

5 *Now I care for nothing*, my sonne, *since I haue let thee goe*, the light of mine eyes.

6 To whom Tobit said, Hold thy peace, take no care; for he is safe.

7 But she said, Hold thy peace, and deceiue me not: my sonne is dead, and she went out euery day into the way which they went, and did eate no meat on the day time, and ceased not whole nights, to bewaile her sonne Tobias, vntill the foureteene dayes of the wedding were expired, which Raguel had sworne, that he should spend there: Then Tobias said to Raguel, Let me goe, for my father, and my mother look no more to see me.

8 But his father in law said vnto him, Tary with me, and I will send to thy father, and they shall declare vnto him, how things goe with thee.

9 But Tobias said, No: but let me goe to my father.

10 Then Raguel arose and gaue him Sara his wife, and halfe his goods, seruants, & cattell, and money.

11 And hee blessed them, and sent them away, saying, The God of heauen giue you a prosperous iourney, my children.

12 And he said to his daughter, Honour thy father and thy mother in law, which are now thy parents, that I may heare good report of thee: and hee kissed her. Edna also said to Tobias, The Lord of heauen restore thee, my deare brother, and grant that I may see thy children of my daughter Sara before I die, that I may reioyce before the Lord: behold, I commit my daughter vnto thee ||of speciall trust, wherefore doe not entreate her euill.

|| Or, to be safely kept.

CHAP. XI.

6 Tobits mother spieth her sonne comming. 10 His father meeteth him at the doore, and recouereth his sight. 14 Hee praiseth God, 17 And welcommeth his daughter in Lawe.

Fter these things Tobias went his way, praising God that he had giuen him a prosperous iourney, and blessed Raguel, and Edna his wife, and went on his way till they drew neere vnto Nineue.

2 Then Raphael said to Tobias, Thou knowest brother, how thou didst leaue thy father.

3 Let vs haste before thy wife, and prepare the house.

4 And take in thine hand the gall of the fish: so they went their way, and the dog went after them.

5 Now Anna sate looking about towards the way for her sonne.

6 And when she espied him comming, she said to his father, Behold, thy sonne commeth, and the man that went with him.

7 Then said Raphael, I know, Tobias, that thy father will open his eyes.

8 Therefore annoint thou his eies with the gall, and being pricked therewith he shall rub, and the whitenesse shall fall away, and he shall see thee.

9 Then Anna ran forth, and fell vpon the necke of her sonne, and said vnto him, seeing I haue seene thee my sonne, from henceforth, I am content to die, and they wept both.

10 Tobit also went forth toward the doore, and stumbled: but his sonne ran vnto him,

11 And tooke hold of his father, and he strake of the gall on his fathers eyes, saying, Be of good hope, my father.

12 And

12 And when his eyes beganne to smart, he rubbed them.

13 And the whitenesse pilled away from the corners of his eyes, and when he saw his sonne, he fell vpon his necke.

14 And he wept, and said, Blessed art thou, O God, and blessed is thy Name for euer, and blessed are all thine holy Angels:

15 For thou hast scourged, and hast taken pitie on me : for behold, I see my sonne Tobias. And his sonne went in reioycing, and told his father the great things that had happened to him in Media.

16 Then Tobit went out to meete his daughter in law at the gate of Niniue, reioycing and praysing God : and they which saw him goe, marueiled because he had receiued his sight.

17 But Tobit gaue thankes before them : because God had mercy on him. And when hee came neere to Sara his daughter in Law, hee blessed her, saying, Thou art welcome daughter : God be blessed which hath brought thee vnto vs, and blessed be thy father and thy mother ; And there was ioy amongst all his brethren which were at Nineue.

‖ *Iunius,who is also called Nasbas.* 18 And Achiacharus, ‖and Nasbas his brothers sonne came.

19 And Tobias wedding was kept seuen dayes with great ioy

CHAP. XII.

5 Tobit offereth halfe to the Angel for his paines; 6 But he calleth them both aside, and exhorteth them, 15 and telleth them that he was an Angel, 21 and was seene no more.

Hen Tobit called his son Tobias, and said vnto him, My sonne, see that the man haue his wages, which went with thee, and thou must giue him more.

2 And Tobias said vnto him, O father, it is no harme to me to giue him halfe of those things which I haue brought.

3 For he hath brought me againe to thee in safety, and made whole my wife, and brought mee the money, and likewise healed thee.

4 Then the old man said : It is due vnto him.

5 So he called the Angell, and he said vnto him, Take halfe of all that yee haue brought, and goe away in safety.

6 Then he tooke them both apart, and sayd vnto them, Blesse God, praise him, and magnifie him, and praise him for the things which he hath done vnto you in the sight of all that liue. It is good to praise God and exalt his name, & ‖honorably to shew forth the works of God, therfore be not slacke to praise him.

‖ *Or, with honour.*

7 It is good to keepe close the secret of a King, but it is honorable to reueale the works of God : do that which is good, and no euill shall touch you.

8 Praier is good with fasting, and almes and righteousnesse : a little with righteousnes is better then much with vnrighteousnesse : it is better to giue almes then to lay vp gold.

9 For almes doth deliuer from death, and shall purge away all sinne. Those that exercise almes, and righteousnesse, shall be filled with life.

10 But they that sinne are enemies to their owne life.

11 Surely I will keepe close nothing from you. For I said, it was good to keepe close the secret of a King, but that it was honorable to reueale the works of God.

12 Now therefore, when thou didst pray, and Sara thy daughter in Law, I did bring the remembrance of your prayers before the holy one, and when thou didst bury the dead, I was with thee likewise.

13 And when thou didst not delay to rise vp, and leaue thy dinner †to go and couer the dead, thy good deede was not hidde from me : but I was with thee.

† *Greek, to and bury.*

14 And now God hath sent mee to heale thee, & Sara thy daughter in law.

15 I am Raphael one of the seuen holy Angels, which present the prayers of the Saints, and which go in and out before the glory of the Holy one

16 Then they were both troubled, and fel vpon their faces : for they feared.

17 But he said vnto them, feare not, for it shall go well with you, praise God therefore.

18 For not of any fauour of mine, but by the will of our God I came, wherefore praise him for euer.

19 *All these daies I did appeare vnto you, but I did neither eat nor drinke, but you did see a vision.

* Gen. 18 19. 3. Iudg. 13. 16.

20 Now therefore giue God thanks : for I go vp to him ỹ sent me, but write all things which are done, in a booke.

21 And when they rose, they saw him no more.

22 Then

22 Then they confessed the great and wonderfull workes of God, and how the Angel of the Lord had appeared vnto them.

CHAP. XIII.

The thankesgiuing vnto God, which Tobit wrote.

Hen Tobit wrote a prayer of reioycing, and said, Blessed be God that liueth for euer, and blessed be his kingdome:

* Deut. 32. 39. 1. sam. 2. 6. wisd. 16. 13.

2 * For he doeth scourge, and hath mercy : hee leadeth downe to hell, and bringeth vp againe : neither is there any that can auoid his hand.

3 Confesse him before the Gentiles, ye children of Israel : for he hath scattered vs among them.

4 There declare his greatnesse, and extoll him before all the liuing, for he is our Lord, and he is the God our father for euer :

5 And he wil scourge vs for our iniquities, and will haue mercy againe, and will gather vs out of all nations, among whom he hath scattered vs.

6 If you turne to him with your whole heart, and with your whole minde, and deale vprightly before him, then will hee turne vnto you, and will not hide his face from you : Therefore see what he will doe with you, and confesse him with your whole mouth, and praise the Lord of might, and extoll the euerlasting King: in the land of my captiuitie doe I praise him, and declare his might and maiesty to a sinnefull nation: O yee sinners turne, and doe iustice before him : who can tell if he will accept you, and haue mercy on you ?

7 I wil extoll my God, and my soule shal praise the King of heauen, and shal reioyce in his greatnesse.

8 Let all men speake, and let all praise him for his righteousnesse.

|| Or, he will lay a scourge vpon the workes of thy children.

9 O Ierusalem the holy Citie, || he will scourge thee for thy childrens workes, and will haue mercy againe on the sonnes of the righteous.

10 Giue praise to the Lord, for hee is good : and praise the euerlasting King, that his Tabernacle may bee builded

| Or, to make.

in thee againe with ioy : and || let him make ioyfull there in thee, those that are captiues, and loue in thee for euer those that are miserable.

11 Many nations shall come from farre to the Name of the Lord God, with gifts in their hands, euen giftes to the King of heauen : all generations shall praise thee with great ioy.

12 Cursed are all they which hate thee, and blessed shall all be, which loue thee for euer.

13 Reioyce & be glad for the children of the iust : for they shall be gathered together, & shall blesse the Lord of the iust.

14 O blessed are they which loue thee, for they shall reioyce in thy || peace : blessed are they which haue been sorowfull for all thy scourges, for they shal reioyce for thee, when they haue seene all thy glory, and shalbe glad for euer.

| Or, prosperitie.

15 Let my soule blesse God the great King.

16 For Ierusalem shall be built vp with Saphires, and Emerauds, and precious stone : thy walles and towres, and battlements with pure golde.

17 And the streets of Ierusalem shal be paued with Berill, and Carbuncle, and stones of Ophir.

18 And all her streets shall say, Halleluiah, and they shall praise him, saying, Blessed be God which hath extolled it for euer.

CHAP. XIIII.

3 Tobit giueth instructions to his sonne, 8 Specially to leaue Nineue. 11 Hee and his wife die, and are buried. 12 Tobias remoueth to Ecbatane, 14 and there died, after hee had heard of the destruction of Nineue.

O Tobit made an ende of praising God.

2 And he was eight and fifty yeeres olde when hee lost his sight, which was restored to him after eight yeeres, and he gaue almes, and he || increased in the feare of the Lord God, and praised him.

| Or, did more and more feare.

3 And when he was very aged, hee called his sonne, and the sixe sons of his sonne, and said to him, My sonne, take thy children; for behold, I am aged, and am ready to depart out of this life.

4 Goe into Media, my sonne, for I surely beleeue those things which Ionas the Prophet spake of Nineue, that it shall be ouerthrowen, and that for a time peace shal rather be in Media, and that our brethren shall lie scattered in the earth from that good land, and Ierusalem shall be desolate, and the house of God in it shalbe burned, and shall be desolate for a time :

5 * And

* Ezra 3. 6.
and 6. 14.

5 * And that againe God will haue mercie on them, and bring them againe into the land where they shall build a Temple, but not like to the first, vntill the time of that age be fulfilled, and afterward they shall returne from all places of their captiuitie, and build vp Ierusalem gloriously, and the house of God shall be built in it ||for euer, with a glorious building, as the prophets haue spoken thereof.

|| For euer
is not in the
Rom. copie.

6 And all nations shall turne, and feare the Lord God truely, and shall burie their idoles.

7 So shall all nations praise the Lord, and his people shal confesse God, and the Lord shall exalt his people, and all those which loue the Lord God in trueth and iustice, shall reioyce, shewing mercie to our brethren.

8 And now, my sonne, depart out of Nineue, because that those things which the Prophet Ionas spake, shall surely come to passe.

9 But keepe thou the Law and the Commandements, and shew thy selfe mercifull and iust, that it may goe well with thee.

10 And burie me decently, and thy mother with me, but tarie no longer at Nineue. Remember, my sonne, how Aman handled Achiacharus ỹ brought him vp, how out of light he brought him into darkenes, and how he rewarded him againe : yet Ahiacharus was ||saued, but the other had his reward, for hee went downe into darkenesse. ||Manasses gaue almes, and escaped the snares of death ||which they had set for him : but Aman fell into the snare and perished.

|| Or, preserued.
|| Junius reaeth Nitsban.
|| Rom. which he had set.

11 Wherefore now, my sonne, consider what almes doeth, and how righteousnesse doth deliuer. When he had said these things, he gaue vp the ghost in the bed, being an hundred, and eight and fiftie yeeres old, and ||he buried him honourably.

|| Or, they.

12 And when Anna his mother was dead, he buried her with his father: but Tobias departed with his wife and children to Ecbatane, to Raguel his father in law:

13 Where hee became old with honour, and hee buried his father and mother in lawe honourably, and hee ||inherited their substance, and his father Tobits.

|| Or, possessed.

14 And he died at Ecbatane in Media, being an hundred and seuen and twentie yeeres old.

15 But before he died, he heard of the destruction of Nineue, which was taken by Nabuchodonosor & Assuerus: and before his death hee reioyced ouer Nineue.

¶ IVDETH.

IN the twelfth yeere of ỹ reigne of Nabuchodonosor, who reigned in Nineue the great citie, (in the dayes of Arphaxad, which reigned ouer the Medes in Ecbatane,

2 And built in Ecbatane walles round abont of stones hewen, three cubites broad, and six cubites long, and made the height of the wall seuenty cubites, and the breadth thereof fiftie cubites :

3 And set the towers thereof vpon the gates of it, an hundred cubites *high*, and the breadth thereof in the foundation threescore cubites.

4 And he made the gates thereof, euen gates that were raised to the height of seuentie cubites, & the breadth of them was fourtie cubites, for the going foorth of his mightie armies, and for the setting in aray of his footmen.)

5 Euen in those dayes, king Nabuchodo-

chodonosor made warre with king Arphaxad in the great plaine, which is the plaine in the borders of Ragau.

6 And there came vnto him, all they that dwelt in the hill countrey, and all that dwelt by Euphrates, and Tigris, and Hydaspes, and the plaine of Arioch the king of the Elimeans, and very many nations of the sonnes of Chelod, assembled themselues to the battell.

7 Then Nabuchodonosor king of the Assyrians, sent vnto all that dwelt in Persia, and to all that dwelt Westward, and to those that dwelt in Cilicia, and Damascus and Libanus, and Antilibanus, and to all that dwelt vpon the Sea coast,

8 And to those amongst the nations that were of Carmel, and Galaad, and the higher Galile, and the great plaine of Esdrelon,

9 And to all that were in Samaria, and the cities thereof : and beyond Iordan vnto Ierusalem, and Betane, and Chellus, and Kades, and the riuer of Egypt, and Taphnes, and Ramesse, and all the land of Gesem,

10 Vntill you come beyond Tanis, and Memphis, and to all the inhabitants of Egypt, vntill you come to the borders of Ethiopia.

11 But all the inhabitants of the land made light of the commandement of Nabuchodonosor king of the Assyrians, neither went they with him to the battell : for they were not afraid of him : yea he was before them as one man, and they sent away his Ambassadours from them without effect, and with disgrace.

12 Therefore Nabuchodonosor was very angry with all this countrey, and sware by his throne and kingdome, that hee would surely be auenged vpon all those coasts of Cilicia, and Damascus, and Syria, and that he would slay with the sword all the inhabitants of the land of Moab, and the children of Ammon, and all Iudea, and all that were in Egypt, till you come to the borders of the two Seas.

13 Then he marched in battell aray with his power against king Arphaxad in the seuenteenth yeere, and he preuailed in his battell : for he ouerthrew all the power of Arphaxad, and all his horsemen and all his chariots,

14 And became Lord of his cities,

and came vnto Ecbatane, and took towers, and spoiled the streetes thereof, and turned the beauty thereof into shame.

15 Hee tooke also Arphaxad in the mountaines of Ragau, and smote him through with his dartes, and destroyed him vtterly that day.

16 So he returned afterward to Nineue, both he and all his company of sundry nations : being a very great multitude of men of warre, and there he tooke his ease and banketted, both he and his armie an hundred and twenty dayes.

CHAP. II.

4 Olofernes is appointed generall, 11 and charged to spare none, that will not yeeld. 15 His armie and prouision, 23 the places which he wonne and wasted, as he went.

Nd in the eighteenth yeere, the two and twentieth day of the first month, there was talke in the house of Nabuchodonosor king of the Assyrians, that he should as he said auenge himselfe on all the earth.

2 So he called vnto him all his officers, and all his nobles, and communicated with them his secret counsell, * and concluded the afflicting of the whole earth out of his owne mouth.

3 Then they decreed to destroy all flesh that did not obey the commaundement of his mouth.

4 And when he had ended his counsell, Nabuchodonosor king of the Assyrians called Olofernes the chiefe captaine of his army, which was †next vnto him, and said vnto him,

5 Thus saith the great king, the Lord of the whole earth : behold, thou shalt goe forth from my presence, and take with thee men that trust in their owne strength, of footemen an hundred and twenty thousand, and the number of horses with their riders twelue thousand.

6 And thou shalt goe against all the West countrey, because they disobeyed my commandement.

7 And thou shalt declare vnto them that they prepare for me ‖ earth and water : for I will goe forth in my wrath against them, and will couer the whole face of the earth with the feete of mine armie, and I will giue them for a spoile vnto them.

8 So

* 1. Sam. 20 7. and 25. 17.

† Gre. second man.

‖ Or, after the maner of the kings of Persia, to whom earth and water was wont to be giuen to acknowledge that they were Lords of land and sea. Herodotus.

8 So that their slaine shall fill their vallies, and brookes, and the riuer shall be filled with their dead, til it ouerflow.

9 And I will lead them captiues to the vtmost parts of all the earth.

10 Thou therefore shalt goe foorth, and take before hand for me all their coasts, and if they will yeeld themselues vnto thee, thou shalt reserue them for me till the day of their punishment.

11 But concerning them that rebell, let not thine eye spare them : but put them to the slaughter, and spoile them wheresoeuer thou goest.

12 For as I liue, and by the power of my kingdome, whatsoeuer I haue spoken, that will I doe by mine hand.

13 And take thou heede that thou transgresse none of the Commaundements of thy Lord, but accomplish them fully, as I haue commaunded thee, and deferre not to doe them.

14 Then Olofernes went foorth from the presence of his Lord, and called all the gouernours and Captaines, and the officers of the army of Assur.

15 And he mustered the chosen men for the battell, as his Lord had commaunded him, vnto an hundred and twenty thousand, & twelue thousand archers on Horsebacke.

16 And he ranged them as a great army is ordered for the warre.

17 And he tooke Camels, and Asses for their cariages a very great number, and sheepe, and Oxen, & Goates without number, for their prouision,

18 And plenty of vittaile for euery man of the army, and very much gold, and siluer, out of the Kings house.

19 Then he went foorth and all his power to go before King Nabuchodonosor in the voyage, and to couer al the face of the earth Westward with their charets, and horsemen, and their chosen footmen.

20 A great multitude also of sundry countries came with them, like locusts, and like the sand of the earth : for the multitude was without number.

21 And they went foorth of Nineue, three dayes iourney toward the plaine of Bectileth, and pitched from Bectileth neere the mountaine, which is at the left hand of the vpper Cilicia.

22 Then he tooke all his armie, his footmen, and horsemen and chariots, and went from thence into the hill countrey,

23 And destroyed Phud, and Lud : and spoiled all the children of Rasses, and the children of Ismael, which were toward the wildernesse at the South of the land of the Chellians.

24 Then he went ouer Euphrates, and went through Mesopotamia, and destroyed all the high cities that were vpon the riuer Arbonai, till you come to the sea.

25 And hee tooke the borders of Cilicia, and killed all that resisted him, and came to the borders of Iapheth, which were toward the South, ouer against Arabia.

26 He compassed also all the children of Madian, and burnt vp their tabernacles, and spoiled their sheepcoats.

27 Then hee went downe into the plaine of Damascus in the time of wheat-haruest, and burnt vp all their fieldes, and destroyed their flockes, and heards, also he spoiled their cities, and vtterly wasted their countreys, and smote all their yong men with the edge of the sword.

28 Therefore the feare and dread of him, fell vpon all the inhabitants of the sea coastes, which were in Sidon and Tyrus, and them that dwelt in Sur, and Ocina, and all that dwelt in Iemnaan, and they that dwelt in Azotus, and Aschalon feared him greatly.

CHAP. III.

1 They of the Sea-coasts entreat for peace. 7 Olofernes is receiued there : 8 Yet he destroyeth their gods, that they might worship onely Nabuchodonosor. 9 He commeth neere to Iudea.

 O they sent Embassadours vnto him, to treat of peace, saying,

2 Behold, we the seruants of Nabuchodonosor the great king lie before thee ; vse vs as shall be good in thy sight.

3 Behold, our houses, and all our places, and all our fieldes of wheat, and flockes, and heards, and all the lodges of our tents, lie before thy face : vse them as it pleaseth thee.

4 Behold, euen our cities and the inhabitants thereof are thy seruants, come and deale with them, as seemeth good vnto thee.

5 So the men came to Holofernes, & declared vnto him after this maner.

6 Then came hee downe toward the

the Sea coast, both hee and his armie, and set garisons in the high cities, and tooke out of them chosen men for aide.

7 So they and all the countrey round about, receiued them with garlands, with dances, and with timbrels.

8 Yet hee did cast downe their frontiers, and cut downe their groues: for hee had decreed to destroy all the gods of the land, that all nations should worship Nabuchodonosor onely, and that all tongues and tribes should call vpon him as God.

9 Also he came ouer against ||Esdraelon neere vnto ||Iudea, ouer against the †great strait of Iudea.

10 And hee pitched betweene Geba, and Scythopolis, and there he taried a whole moneth, that he might gather together all the cariages of his armie.

Marginal notes left:
‖ Or, Esdrelom.
‖ Or, Dotæa, Dothan. Iunius. Genes. 37. 17.
† Gr. great saw.

CHAP. IIII.

4 The Iewes are afraid of Holofernes, 5 and fortifie the hilles. 6 They of Bethulia take charge of the passages. 9 All Israel fall to fasting and prayer.

Ow the children of Israel that dwelt in Iudea, heard all that Holofernes the chiefe captaine of Nabuchodonosor king of the Assyrians had done to the nations, and after what manner hee had spoiled all their Temples, and brought them to nought.

2 Therefore they were exceedingly afraid of him, and were troubled for Ierusalem, and for the Temple of the Lord their God.

3 For they were newly returned from the captiuitie, and all the people ||of Iudea were lately gathered together: and the vessels, and the Altar, and the house, were sanctified after the profanation.

4 Therefore they sent into all the coasts of Samaria, and the villages, and to Bethoron, and Belmen, and Iericho, and to Choba, and Esora, and to the valley of Salem.

5 And possessed themselues beforehand of all the tops of the high mountaines, and fortified the villages that were in them, and laid vp victuals for the prouision of warre: for their fieldes were of late reaped.

6 Also Ioacim the hie Priest which was in those daies in Ierusalem, wrote

Marginal note left:
‖ Or, out of Iudea.

to them that dwelt in Bethulia, and Betomestham which is ouer against ||Esdraelon toward the ||open countrey neere to Dothaim,

7 Charging them to keepe the passages of the hill countrey: for by them there was an entrance into Iudea, and it was easie to stoppe them that would come vp, because the passage was strait ||for two men at the most.

8 And the children of Israel did as Ioacim the hie Priest had commanded them, with the ||ancients of all the people of Israel, which dwelt at Ierusalē.

9 Then euery man of Israel cryed to God with great feruencie, and with great vehemency did they humble their soules:

10 Both they and their wiues, and their children, and their cattell, and euery stranger and hireling, and their seruants bought with money, put sackecloth vpon their loynes.

11 Thus euery man and woman, and the little children, & the inhabitants of Ierusalem fell before the temple, and cast ashes vpon their heads, and spread out their sackcloth before the face of the Lord : also they put sackecloth about the Altar,

12 And cryed to the God of Israel all with one consent earnestly, that hee would not giue their children for a pray, and their wiues for a spoile, and the cities of their inheritance to destruction, and the Sanctuary to profanation and reproch, & for the nations to reioyce at.

13 So God heard their prayers, and looked vpon their afflictions : for the people fasted many dayes in all Iudea, and Ierusalem, before the Sanctuary of the Lord Almighty.

14 And Ioacim the high Priest, and all the Priestes that stood before the Lord, and they which ministred vnto the Lord, had their loines girt with sackecloth, and offered the daily burnt offerings, with the vowes and free gifts of the people,

15 And had ashes on their miters, and cried vnto the Lord with all their power, that he would looke vpon all the house of Israel graciously.

Marginal notes right:
‖ Or, Esdrelom.
‖ Or, plaine.
‖ Or, two against all.
‖ Or, gouernours.

CHAP. V.

5 Achior telleth Holofernes what the Iewes are, 8 and what their God had done for them : 21 and aduiseth not to meddle with them. 22 All that heard him, were offended at him. Then

Hen was it declared to Holofernes the chief captaine of the armie of Assur that the children of Israel had prepared for warre, and had shut vp the passages of the hill † *Gre. all the toppe.* countrey, and had fortified † all the tops of the high hilles, and had laide impediments in the champion countreys.

2 Wherewith he was very angry, and called all the princes of Moab, and the captaines of Ammon, and all the gouernours of the Sea coast.

3 And he said vnto them, Tell mee now, ye sonnes of Canaan, who this people is that dwelleth in the hill countrey? and what are the cities that they inhabite? and what is the multitude of their armie? and wherein is their power and strength, and what king is set ouer them, or captaine of their armie?

4 And why haue they determined not to come and meet me, more then all the inhabitants of the West?

* *Chap. 11. 7, 9.* 5 * Then said Achior, the captaine of all the sonnes of Ammon: Let my lord now heare a word from the mouth of thy seruant, and I will declare vnto thee the trueth, concerning this people which dwelleth neere thee, and inhabiteth the hill countreys: and there shall no lie come out of the mouth of thy seruant.

6 This people are descended of the Caldeans,

* *Gen. 11. 31.* 7 * And they soiourned heretofore in Mesopotamia, because they would not follow the gods of their fathers, which were in the land of Caldea.

‖ *Or, went out of.* 8 For they ‖ left the way of their ancestours, and worshipped the God of heauen, the God whom they knew: so they cast them out from the face of their gods, and they fled into Mesopotamia, and soiourned there many dayes.

* *Gen. 12. 1* 9 Then * their God commaunded them to depart from the place where they soiourned, and to goe into the land of Chanaan, where they dwelt, and were increased with gold and siluer, and with very much cattell.

10 But when a famine couered all the land of Chanaan, they went downe into Egypt, and soiourned there, while they were nourished, and became there a great multitude, so that one could not number their nation.

11 Therefore the king of Egypt rose vp against them, and dealt subtilly with them, and brought them low, with labouring in bricke, & made them slaues.

12 Then they cried vnto their God, and he smote all the land of Egypt with incurable plagues, so the * Egyptians cast them out of their sight.   * *Exod. 1. 8.* * *Exod. 12. 31, 33.*

13 And * God dried the red Sea before them: * *Exod. 14.*

14 And * brought them to mount † Sina, and Cades Barne, and cast forth all that dwelt in the wildernesse.   * *Exod. 19.1* † *Greek. into the way of the wildernes of Sina.*

15 So they dwelt in the land of the Amorites, and they destroyed by their strength all them of Esebon, and passing ouer Iordan they possessed all the hill countrey.

16 * And they cast forth before them, the Chanaanite, the Pheresite, the Iebusite, and the Sychemite, and all the Gergesites, and they dwelt in that countrey many dayes.   * *Iosh. 12. 8*

17 And whilest they sinned not before their God, they prospered, because the God that hateth iniquitie, was with them.

18 But * when they departed from the way which he appointed them, they were destroyed in many battels very sore, * and were led captiues into a land that was not theirs, and the Temple of their God was cast to the ground, and their cities were taken by the enemies.   * *Iudg. 2. 14 and 3. 8.* * *2. Kings 25. 1, 11.*

19 But * nowe are they returned to their God, and are come vp from the places, where they were scattered, and haue possessed Ierusalem, where their Sanctuary is, and ‖ are seated in the hill countrey, for it was desolate.   * *Ezra 1. 1, 3.* ‖ *Or, haue their dwellings.*

20 Now therefore, my lord and gouernour, if there be any errour in this people, & they sinne against their God, let vs consider that this shal be their ruine, and let vs goe vp, and we shal ouercome them.

21 But if there be no iniquitie in their nation, let my lord now passe by, lest their Lord defend them, and their God be for them, and wee become a reproch before all the world.

22 And when Achior had finished these sayings, all the people standing round about the tent, murmured, and the chiefe men of Holofernes, and all that dwelt by the Sea side, and in Moab, spake that he should kill him.

23 For, *say they,* we will not be afraid of the face of the children of Israel, for loe, it is a people that haue no strength, nor

†*Greagainst a mighty armie.*

nor power †for a strong battell.

24 Now therefore, Lord Holofernes, we will goe vp, and they shall be a pray, to be deuoured of all thine armie.

CHAP. VI.

3 Holofernes despiseth God. 7 He threatneth Achior and sendeth him away. 14 The Bethulians receiue and heare him. 18 They fall to prayer, and comfort Achior.

Nd when the tumult of men that were about the councell was ceased, Holofernes the chiefe captaine of the armie of Assur, said vnto Achior and all the Moabites, before all the company of other nations,

2 And who art thou Achior and the hirelings of Ephraim, that thou hast prophesied amongst vs as to day, and hast said, that we should not make warre with the people of Israel, because their God will defend them? and who is God but Nabuchodonosor?

3 He will send his power, and will destroy them from the face of the earth, and their God shall not deliuer them: but we his seruants will destroy them as one man, for they are not able to sustaine the power of our horses.

4 For with them we will tread them vnder foote, and their mountains shall be drunken with their blood, and their fields shall be fiilled with their dead bodies, and their footesteps shall not be able to stand before vs, for they shal vtterly perish; saith king Nabuchodonosor Lord of all the earth; for hee said, none of my words shall be in vaine.

5 And thou Achior, an hireling of Ammon, which hast spoken these words in the day of thine iniquity, shalt see my face no more, from this day vntill I take vengeance of this nation that came out of Egypt.

6 And then shall the sword of mine armie, and the multitude of them that serue me, passe through thy sides, and thou shalt fal among their slaine, when I returne.

7 Now therefore my seruants shall bring thee backe into the hill countrey, and shall set thee in one of the cities of the passages.

8 And thou shalt not perish till thou be destroyed with them.

9 And if thou perswade thy selfe in thy minde, that they shall not be taken, let not thy countenance fall : I haue spoken it, and none of my words shall be in vaine.

10 Then Holofernes commanded his seruants that waited in his tent, to take Achior and bring him to Bethulia, and deliuer him into the hands of the children of Israel.

11 So his seruants tooke him, and brought him out of the campe into the plaine, and they went from the midst of the plaine into the hill countrey, and came vnto the fountaines that were vnder Bethulia.

12 And when the men of the citie saw them, they tooke vp their weapons, and went out of the citie to the toppe of the hill, and euery man that vsed a sling from comming vp by casting of stones against them.

13 Neuerthelesse hauing gotten priuily vnder the hill, they bound Achior and cast him downe, and left him at the foote of the hill, and returned to their Lord.

14 But the Israelites descended from their citie, and came vnto him, and loosed him, and brought him into Bethulia, and presented him to the gouernours of the citie,

15 Which were in those dayes Ozias the sonne of Micha of the tribe of Simeon, and Chabris the sonne of Gothoniel, and Charmis the sonne of Melchiel.

16 And they called together all the ancients of the citie, and all their youth ranne together, and their women to the assembly, and they set Achior in the midst of all their people. Then Ozias asked him of that which was done.

17 And he answered and declared vnto them the words of the counsell of Holofernes, and all the words that he had spoken in the midst of the princes of Assur, and whatsoeuer Holofernes had spoken proudly against the house of Israel.

18 Then the people fell downe, and worshipped God, and cryed vnto God, saying,

19 O Lord God of heauen, behold their pride, and pity the low estate of our nation, and looke vpon the face of those that are sanctified vnto thee this day.

20 Then they comforted Achior and praised him greatly.

21 And Ozias tooke him out of the assembly vnto his house, and made a feast

feast to the Elders, & they called on the God of Israel all that night for helpe.

CHAP. VII.

1 Holofernes besiegeth Bethulia, 7 and stoppeth the water from them. 22 They faint and murmure against the gouernours, 30 Who promise to yeeld within fiue dayes.

He next day Holofernes commanded all his army, and all his people which were come to take his part, that they should remooue their campe against Bethulia, to take aforehand the ascents of the hill countrey, and to make warre against the children of Israel.

2 Then their strong men remoued their campes in that day, and the armie of the men of warre was, an hundred and seuenty thousand footmen, and twelue thousand horsemen, beside the baggage, & other men that were afoot amongst them, a very great multitude.

3 And they camped in the valley neere vnto Bethulia, by the fountaine, and they spred themselues in breadth ouer ||Dothaim, euen to Belmaim, and in length from Bethulia vnto †Cyamon which is ouer against Esdraelon.

|| From Dothaim. Iunius.
† Greek beane field.

4 Now the children of Israel, when they saw the multitude of them, were greatly troubled, and said euery one to his neighbour : Now will these men licke vp the face of the earth; for neither the high mountaines, nor the valleys, nor the hils, are able to beare their waight.

5 Then euery man tooke vp his weapons of warre, and when they had kindled fires vpon their towers, they remained and watched all that night.

6 But in the second day Holofernes brought foorth all his horsemen, in the sight of the children of Israel which were in Bethulia,

7 And viewed the passages vp to the city, and came to the fountaine of their waters, and tooke them, and set garrisons of men of warre ouer them, and he himselfe remooued towards his people.

8 Then came vnto him all the chiefe of the children of Esau, and al the gouernours of the people of Moab, and the captaines of the sea coast, and said,

9 Let our lord now heare a word, that there be not an ouerthrow in thine armie.

10 For this people of the children of Israel do not trust in their speares, but in the height of the mountaines wherein they dwell, because it is not easie to come vp to the tops of their mountaines.

11 Now therefore my lord, fight not against them in battell aray, and there shall not so much as one man of thy people perish

12 Remaine in thy campe, and keepe all the men of thine army, and let thy seruants get into their hands the fountaine of water which issueth foorth of the foot of the mountaine.

13 For all the inhabitants of Bethulia haue their water thence : so shall thirst kil them, & they shall giue vp their citie, and we and our people shal goe vp to the tops of the mountaines that are neere, and will campe vpon them, to watch that none goe out of the city.

14 So they and their wiues, and their children shalbe consumed with famine, and before the sword come against them, they shall be ouerthrowen in the streets where they dwel.

15 Thus shalt thou render them an euil reward : because they rebelled and met not thy person peaceably.

16 And these words pleased Holofernes, and al his seruants, and he appointed to doe as they had spoken.

17 So the campe of the children of Ammon departed, and with them fiue thousand of the Assyrians, and they pitched in the valley, and tooke the waters, and the fountaines of the waters of the children of Israel.

18 Then the children of Esau went vp, with the children of Ammon, and camped in the hil countrey ouer against Dotha-em : and they sent some of them toward the South, & toward the East ouer against Ekrebel, which is neere vnto Chusi, that is vpon the brooke Mochmur, and the rest of the army of the Assyrians camped in the plaine, and couered the face of the whole land, and their tents and cariages were pitched to a very great multitude.

19 Then the children of Israel cried vnto the Lord their God, because their heart failed, for all their enemies had compassed them round about, & there was no way to escape out from among them.

20 Thus all the company of Assur remained about them, both their footmen, charets and horsemen, foure and thirtie

Or, pits.

thirtie dayes, so that all their vessels of water failed all the inhabitants of Bethulia.

21 And the ‖cisternes were emptied, and they had not water to drinke their fill, for one day; for they gaue them drinke by measure.

22 Therefore their young children were out of heart, and their women and yong men fainted for thirst, and fell downe in the streetes of the city, and by the passages of the gates, and there was no longer any strength in them.

23 Then all the people assembled to Ozias, and to the chiefe of the city, both young men, and women, and children, and cryed with a loude voice, and saide before all the Elders;

Exo. 5. 21.

24 God *be Iudge betweene vs and you: for you haue done vs great iniury in that you haue not required peace of the children of Assur.

25 For now we haue no helper: but God hath sold vs into their hands, that wee should be throwne downe before them with thirst, and great destruction.

26 Now therefore call them vnto you, and deliuer the whole citie for a spoile to the people of Olofernes, and to all his armie.

27 For it is better for vs to be made a spoile vnto them, then to die for thirst: for wee will be his seruants, that our soules may liue, and not see the death of our infants before our eyes, nor our wiues nor our children to die.

28 We take to witnesse against you, the heauen and the earth, and our God, and Lord of our fathers, which punisheth vs according to our sinnes, and the sinnes of our fathers, that ‖hee doe not according as we haue said this day.

‖ Or, lest he doe: meaning, Olofernes.

29 Then there was great weeping with one consent in the middest of the assembly, and they cryed vnto the Lord God with a loude voice.

30 Then said Ozias to them, Brethren, be of good courage, let vs yet endure fiue dayes, in the which space the Lord our God may turne his mercy toward vs, for he will nòt forsake vs vtterly.

31 And if these dayes passe, and there come no helpe vnto vs, I wil doe according to your word.

32 And he dispersed the people euery one to their owne charge, and they went vnto the walles and towres of their citie, and sent the women and children into their houses, and they were very low brought in the city.

CHAP. VIII.

1 The state and behauiour of Iudeth a widow. 12 She blameth the gouernors for their promise to yeeld: 17 and aduiseth them to trust in God. 28 They excuse their promise. 32 She promiseth to doe something for them.

Ow at that time Iudeth heard thereof, which was the daughter of Merari the sonne of Ox, the sonne of Ioseph, the sonne of Oziel, the sonne of Elcia, the sonne of Ananias, the sonne of Gedeon, the sonne of Raphaim, the son of Acitho, the sonne of Eliu, the sonne of Eliab, the sonne of Nathanael, the sonne of ‖ Samael, the sonne of Salasadai, the son of Israel.

‖ Or, Samaliel.

2 And Manasses was her husband of her tribe and kinred, who died in the barley haruest.

3 For as hee stood ouerseeing them that bound sheaues in the field, the heat came vpon his head, and hee fell on his bed, and died in the city of Bethulia, and they buried him with his fathers, in the field betweene Dothaim and Balamo.

4 So Iudeth was a widow in her house three yeeres, and foure moneths.

5 And she made her a tent vpon the top of her house, and put on sackecloth on her loynes, and ware her widowes apparell.

6 And she fasted all the dayes of her widowhood, saue the eues of the Sabbath, and the Sabbaths, and the eues of the newe Moones, and the newe Moones, and the Feasts, and solemne dayes of the house of Israel.

7 Shee was also of a goodly countenance, and very beautifull to behold: and her husband Manasses had left her golde and siluer, and men seruants and maide seruants, and cattell, and lands, ‖and she remained vpon them.

‖ Or, and she kept them.

8 And there was none that gaue her an ill worde; for shee feared God greatly.

9 Now when shee heard the euill wordes of the people against the gouernor, that they fainted for lacke of water (for Iudeth had heard all the wordes that Ozias had spoken vnto them, and that he had *sworne to deliuer the citie vnto the Assyrians after fiue dayes)

*Cha. 7. 26.

10 Then shee sent her waiting woman that had the gouernment of all things

things that she had, to call Ozias, and Chabris, and Charmis, the ancients of the citie.

11 And they came vnto her, and she said vnto them, Heare me now, O yee gouernours of the inhabitants of Bethulia : for your wordes that you haue spoken before the people this day are not right, touching this othe which ye made, and pronounced betweene God and you, and haue promised to deliuer the citie to our enemies, vnlesse within these daies the Lord turne to helpe you.

12 And now who are you, that haue tempted God this day, & stand in stead of God amongst the children of men ?

13 And now trie the Lord Almighty, but you shall neuer know any thing.

14 For you cannot find the depth of the heart of man, neither can ye perceiue the things that he thinketh : then how can you search out God, that hath made all these things, and knowe his minde, or comprehend his purpose ? Nay my brethren, prouoke not the Lord our God to anger.

15 For if he will not helpe vs within these few dayes, he hath power to defend vs when he will, euen euery day, or to destroy vs before our enemies.

|| Or, ingage.
* Numb. 23
19.

16 Doe not ||binde the counsels of the Lord our God, for * God is not as man, that he may be threatned, neither is he as the sonne of man that he should bee wauering.

17 Therefore let vs waite for saluation of him, and call vpon him to helpe vs, and he will heare our voyce if it please him.

18 For there arose none in our age, neither is there any now in these daies, neither tribe, nor familie, nor ||people, nor city among vs, which worship gods made with hands, as hath bene aforetime.

|| Or, towne.

19 For the which cause our fathers * were giuen to the sword, & for a spoile, and had a great fall before our enemies.

* Iudg. 2. 11
and 4. 1.
and 6. 1.

20 But we know none other god : therefore we trust that he will not despise vs, nor any of our nation.

21 For if we be taken so, all Iudea shall lie waste, and our Sanctuarie shal be spoiled, and he will require the prophanation thereof, at our mouth.

|| Or, feare.

22 And the ||slaughter of our brethren, and the captiuitie of the countrey, and the desolation of our inheritance, will he turne vpon our heads among the Gentiles, wheresoeuer we shall bee in bondage, and we shall be an offence and a reproch to all them that possesse vs.

23 For our seruitude shall not be directed to fauour : but the Lord our God shall turne it to dishonour.

24 Now therefore, O brethren, let vs shew an example to our brethren, because their hearts depend vpon vs, and the Sanctuary, and the house, and the Altar rest vpon vs.

25 Moreouer, let vs giue thankes to the Lord our God, which trieth vs, euen as he did our fathers.

26 Remember what things he did to * Abraham, and how he tried Isaac, and what happened to * Iacob in Mesopotamia of Syria, when he kept the sheepe of Laban his mothers brother. * Gen. 22. 1
* Gen. 28. 7

27 For, hee hath not tried vs in the fire as he did them, for the examination of their hearts, neither hath hee taken vengeance on vs : but the Lord doeth scourge them that come neere vnto him to admonish them.

28 Then said Ozias to her, All that thou hast spoken, hast thou spoken with a good heart, and there is none that may gainesay thy words.

29 For this is not the first day wherin thy wisedome is manifested, but from the beginning of thy dayes all thy people haue knowen thy vnderstanding, because the disposition of thine heart is good.

30 But the people were very thirsty, and compelled vs to doe vnto them as we haue spoken, and to bring an othe vpon our selues, which wee will not breake.

31 Therefore now pray thou for vs, because thou art a godly woman , and the Lord will send vs raine to fill our cisternes, and we shall faint no more.

32 Then said Iudeth vnto them, Heare me, and I wil doe a thing, which shall goe throughout all generations, to the children of our nation.

33 You shall stand this night in the gate, and I will goe foorth with my waiting woman : and within the dayes that you haue promised to deliuer the citie to our enemies, the Lord will visit Israel by mine hand.

34 But inquire not you of mine act : for I will not declare it vnto you, til the things be finished that I doe.

35 Then said Ozias and the princes vnto her, Goe in peace, and the Lord God

God be before thee, to take vengeance on our enemies.

36 So they returned from the tent, and went to their wards.

CHAP. IX.

1 Iudeth humbleth herselfe, 2 and prayeth God to prosper her purpose against the enemies of his sanctuarie.

Hen Iudeth fell vpon her face, and put ashes vpon her head, and vncouered the sackcloth wherewith she was clothed, and about the time, that the incense of that euening was offered in Ierusalem, in the house of the Lord, Iudeth cryed with a loud voyce, and said,

* Gen. 34. 2, 23.

2 O Lord God of my father *Simeon, to whom thou gauest a sword to take vengeance of the strangers, who loosened the girdle of a maide to defile her, and discoured the thigh to her shame, and polluted her virginity to her reproch, (for thou saidst it shall not be so, and yet they did so.)

3 Wherefore thou gauest their rulers to be slaine, so that they died their bed in blood, being deceiued, and smotest the seruants with their Lords, and the Lords vpon their thrones:

4 And hast giuen their wiues for a pray, and their daughters to bee captiues, and all their spoiles to be diuided amongst thy deere children: which were mooued with thy zeale, and abhorred the pollution of their blood, and called vpon thee for aide: O God, O my God, heare me also a widow.

5 For thou hast wrought not onely those things, but also the things which fell out before, and which ensewed after, thou hast thought vpon the things which are now, and which are to come.

6 Yea what things thou didst determine were redy at hand, and said, loe we are heere; for all thy wayes are prepared, and thy iudgements are in thy foreknowledge.

7 For behold, the Assyrians are multiplyed in their power : they are exalted with horse and man : they glory in the strength of their footemen : they trust in shield and speare, and bow, and sling, and know not that thou art the Lord that breakest the battels : the Lord is thy name.

8 Throw downe their strength in thy power, and bring downe their force in thy wrath; for they haue purposed to defile thy Sanctuary, and to pollute the Tabernacle, where thy glorious name resteth, and to cast downe with sword the horne of thy altar.

9 Behold their pride, and send thy wrath vpon their heads : giue into mine hand which am a widow, the power that I haue conceiued.

10 *Smite by the deceit of my lips the seruant with the prince, and the prince with the seruant : breake downe their statelinesse by the hand of a woman.

* Iudg. 4. 21. & 5. 26.

11 *For thy power standeth not in multitude, nor thy might in strong men, for thou art a God of the afflicted, an helper of the oppressed, an vpholder of the weake, a protector of the forelorne, a sauiour of them that are without hope.

* Iudg. 7. 2. 2. chro. 14. 11. and 16. 8. & 20. 6.

12 I pray thee, I pray thee, O God of my father, and God of the inheritance of Israel, Lord of the heauens, and earth, creator of the waters, king of euery creature : heare thou my prayer :

13 And make my speech and deceit to be their wound & stripe, who haue purposed cruell things against thy couenant, and thy hallowed house, and against the top of Sion, and against the house of the possession of thy children.

14 And make euery nation and tribe to acknowledge that thou art the God of all power and might, and that there is none other that protecteth the people of Israel but thou.

CHAP. X.

3 Iudeth doth set forth herselfe. 10 She and her maide goe forth into the campe. 17 The watch take and conduct her to Olofernes.

Ow after that she had ceased to cry vnto the God of Israel, and had made an end of all these words,

2 She rose where she had fallen downe, and called her maide, and went downe into the house, in the which she abode in the Sabbath dayes and in her feast dayes,

3 And pulled off the sackcloth which she had on, and put off the garments of her widowhood, and washed her body all ouer with water, and annointed herselfe with precious ointment, and braided the haire of her head, and put on †a tire vpon it, and put on her garments of gladnesse, wherewith she was clad during the life of Manasses her husband.

† Gre. miter.

4 And she tooke sandals vpon her feete,

feete, and put about her, her bracelets and her chaines, and her rings, and her earerings, and all her ornaments, and decked her selfe brauely to allure the eyes of all men that should see her.

5 Then she gaue her mayd a bottle of wine, and a cruse of oyle, and filled a bagge with parched corne, and lumpes of figs, and with fine bread, so she ‖folded all these things together, and layd them vpon her.

‖ Wrapped, or packed.

6 Thus they went forth to the gate of the citie of Bethulia, and found standing there Ozias, and the ancients of the city Chabris, and Charmis.

7 And when they saw her, that her countenance was altered, and her apparel was changed, they wondered at her beautie very greatly, and said vnto her,

8 The God, the God of our fathers giue thee fauour, and accomplish thine enterprises to the glory of the children of Israel, and to the exaltation of Ierusalem : then they worshipped God.

9 And she said vnto them, Command the gates of the city to be opened vnto me, that I may goe forth to accomplish the things, whereof you haue spoken with me ; so they commanded the yong men to open vnto her, as shee had spoken.

10 And when they had done so, Iudeth went out, she and her mayd with her, and the men of the citie looked after her, vntill shee was gone downe the mountaine, and till she had passed the valley, and could see her no more.

11 Thus they went straight foorth in the valley : and the first watch of the Assyrians met her ;

12 And tooke her, and asked her, Of what people art thou ? and whence cōmest thou ? and whither goest thou ? And she said, I am a woman of the Hebrewes, and am fled from them : for they shalbe giuen you to be consumed :

13 And I am comming before Olofernes the chiefe captaine of your army, to declare words of trueth, and I will shew him a way, whereby he shall goe, and winne all the hil countrey, without loosing the body or life of any one of his men.

14 Now when the men heard her wordes, and beheld her countenance, they wondered greatly at her beautie, and said vnto her ;

15 Thou hast saued thy life, in that thou hast hasted to come downe to the presence of our lord : now therfore come to his tent, and some of vs shall conduct thee, vntill they haue deliuered thee to his hands.

16 And when thou standest before him, bee not afraid in thine heart : but shew vnto him according to thy word, and he will intreat thee well.

17 Then they chose out of them an hundred men, to ‖accompany her and her mayd, and they brought her to the tent of Olofernes.

‖ Or, and they prepared a charict for her.

18 Then was there a concourse throughout all the campe : for her comming was noised among the tents, and they came about her, as she stood without the tent of Olofernes, till they told him of her.

19 And they wondered at her beautie, and admired the children of Israel because of her, and euery one said to his neighbour ; Who would despise this people, that haue among them such women, surely it is not good that one man of them be left, who being let goe, might deceiue the whole earth.

20 And they that lay neere Olofernes, went out, and all his seruants, and they brought her into the tent.

21 Now Olofernes rested vpon his bed vnder a canopie which was wouen with purple, and gold, and emeraudes, and precious stones.

22 So they shewed him of her, and he came out before his tent, with siluer lampes going before him.

23 And when Iudeth was come before him and his seruants, they all marueiled at the beautie of her countenance ; and she fel downe vpon her face, and did reuerence vnto him ; and his seruants tooke her vp.

CHAP. XI.

3 Olofernes asketh Iudeth the cause of her comming. 6 She telleth him how, and when hee may preuaile. 20 Hee is much pleased with her wisedome and beautie.

 Hen said Olofernes vnto her, Woman, bee of good comfort, feare not in thine heart : for I neuer hurt any, that was willing to serue Nabuchodonosor the king of all the earth.

2 Now therefore if thy people that dwelleth in the mountaines, had not set light by me, I would not haue lifted vp my

my speare against them : but they haue done these things to themselues.

3 But now tell me wherefore thou art fled from them, and art come vnto vs : for thou art come for safeguard, be of good comfort , thou shalt liue this night, and hereafter.

4 For none shall hurt thee, but intreat thee well, as they doe the seruants of king Nabuchodonosor my lord.

5 Then Iudeth said vnto him, Receiue the words of thy seruant, and suffer thine handmaid to speake in thy presence, and I will declare no lie to my lord this night.

6 And if thou wilt follow the words of thine handmaid, God will bring the thing perfectly to passe by thee, and my lord shall not faile of his purposes,

7 As Nabuchodonosor king of all the earth liueth, and as his power liueth, who hath sent thee for the vpholding of euery liuing thing : for not only men shall serue him by thee, but also the beasts of the field, and the cattell, and the foules of the aire shall liue by thy power, vnder Nabuchodonosor and all his house.

8 For wee haue heard of thy wisedome, and thy policies, and it is reported in all the earth, that thou onely art ‖ excellent in all the kingdome , and mightie in knowledge, and wonderfull in feates of warre. *‖ Or, in fauour.*

9 Now as concerning the matter which Achior did speake in thy counsell, we haue heard his words ; for the men of Bethulia ‖ saued him, and hee declared vnto them all that hee had spoken vnto thee. *‖ Or, gate him.*

10 Therefore, O lord and gouernor, reiect not his word, but lay it vp in thine heart, for it is true, for our nation shall not be punished, neither can the sword preuaile against them, except they sinne against their God.

11 And now, that my lord be not defeated , and frustrate of his purpose, euen death is now fallen vpon them, and their sinne hath ouertaken them, wherewith they will prouoke their God to anger, whensoeuer they shall doe that which is not fit to be done.

12 For their victuals faile them, and all their water is scant , and they haue determined to lay hands vpon their cattell, and purposed to consume all those things, that God hath forbidden them to eate by his Lawes,

13 And are resolued to spend the first fruits of the corne, & the tenths of wine and oyle, which they had sanctified, and reserued for the Priests that serue in Ierusalem, before the face of our God, the which things it is not lawfull for any of the people so much as to touch with their hands.

14 For they haue sent some to Ierusalem, because they also that dwel there haue done the like, to bring them a license from the Senate.

15 Now when they shall bring them word, they will forthwith doe it, and they shall be giuen thee to be destroyed the same day.

16 Wherefore I thine handmaide knowing all this, am fledde from their presence, & God hath sent me to worke things with thee, whereat all the earth shalbe astonished, and whosoeuer shall heare it.

17 For thy seruant is religious, and serueth the God of heauen day & night: now therefore, my lord, I will remaine with thee, and thy seruant will goe out by night into the valley, and I will pray vnto God, and he wil tel me when they haue committed their sinnes.

18 And I will come, and shew it vnto thee : then thou shalt goe forth with all thine army, and there shall be none of them that shall resist thee.

19 And I will leade thee through the midst of Iudea, vntill thou come before Ierusalem, and I will set thy throne in the midst thereof, and thou shalt driue them as sheep that haue no shepheard, and a dogge shall not so much as ‖ open his mouth at thee : for ‖ these things were tolde mee , according to my foreknowledge, and they were declared vnto me, and I am sent to tell thee. *‖ Or, barke. ‖ Or, these things haue I spoken.*

20 Then her wordes pleased Olofernes , and all his seruants, and they marueiled at her wisedome, and said,

21 There is not such a woman from one end of the earth to the other, both for beautie of face , and wisedome of wordes.

22 Likewise Olofernes said vnto her, God hath done well to send thee before the people, that strength might be in our hands, and destruction vpon them that lightly regard my lord :

23 And now thou art both beautifull in thy countenance, and wittie in thy wordes ; surely if thou doe as thou hast spoken, thy God shall be my God, and

and thou shalt dwel in the house of king Nabuchodonosor, and shalt be renowmed through the whole earth.

CHAP. XII.

2 Iudeth will not eate of Olofernes meate. 7 She taried three dayes in the campe, and euerie night went forth to pray. 13 Bagoas doth moue her to be merry with Olofernes, 20 who for ioy of her companie drunke much.

Hen hee commaunded to bring her in, where his plate was set, and bad that they should prepare for her of his owne meats, and that she should drinke of his owne wine.

* Gen. 43. 32. dan. 1. 8 tob. 1. 11.

2 And Iudeth said, * I will not eat thereof, lest there bee an offence : but prouision be made for mee of the things that I haue brought.

3 Then Olofernes said vnto her, If thy prouision should faile, howe should we giue thee the like? for there be none with vs of thy nation.

4 Then said Iudeth vnto him, As thy soule liueth, my lord, thine handemaid shall not spend those things that I haue, before the Lord worke by mine hand, the things y̆ he hath determined.

5 Then the seruants of Olofernes brought her into the tent, and shee slept til midnight, and she arose when it was towards the morning watch,

6 And sent to Olofernes, saying, Let my lord now command, that thine handmaid may goe forth vnto prayer.

7 Then Olofernes commaunded his guard that they should not stay her : thus she abode in the camp three dayes, and went out in the night into the valley of Bethulia, and washed her selfe in a fountaine of water by the campe.

8 And when she came out, shee besought the Lord God of Israel to direct her way, to the raising vp of the children of her people.

9 So she came in cleane, and remained in the tent, vntill shee did eate her meat at euening.

10 And in the fourth day Olofernes made a feast to his owne seruants only, and called none of the officers to the banquet.

11 Then said he to Bagoas the Eunuch, who had charge ouer all that he had : Goe now, and perswade this Ebrewe woman which is with thee, that she come vnto vs, and eate and drinke with vs.

12 For loe, it will be a shame for our person, if we shall let such a woman go, not hauing had her company : for if we draw her not vnto vs, she will laugh vs to scorne.

13 Then went Bagoas from the presence of Olofernes, and came to her, and he said, Let not this faire damosell feare to come to my lord, and to bee honoured in his presence, and drink wine, and be merry with vs, and be made this day as one of the daughters of the Assyrians, which serue in the house of Nabuchodonosor.

14 Then said Iudeth vnto him, Who am I now, that I should gainesay my lord? surely whatsoeuer pleaseth him, I will doe speedily, and it shall bee my ioy vnto the day of my death.

15 So she arose, and decked her selfe with her apparell, and all her womans attire, and her maid went and laid soft skinnes on the ground for her, ouer against Olofernes, which she had receiued of Bagoas for her daily vse, that she might sit, and eate vpon them.

16 Now when Iudeth came in, and sate downe, Olofernes his heart was rauished with her, and his minde was moued, and he desired greatly her company, for hee waited a time to deceiue her, from the day that he had seene her.

17 Then said Olofernes vnto her, Drinke now, and be merry with vs.

18 So Iudeth saide, I will drinke now my lord, because my life is magnified in me this day, more then all the dayes since I was borne.

19 Then she tooke and ate and dranke before him what her maide had prepared.

20 And Olofernes tooke great delight in her, & dranke much more wine, then he had drunke at any time in one day, since he was borne.

CHAP. XIII.

2 Iudeth is left alone with Olofernes in his tent. 4 She prayeth God to giue her strength 8 She cut off his head while hee slept : 10 And returned with it to Bethulia : 17 They saw it, and commend her.

Ow when the euening was come, his seruants made haste to depart, and Bagoas shut his tent without, and dismissed the waiters

waiters from the presence of his lord, and they went to their beds : for they were all weary, because the feast had bene long.

2 And Iudeth was left alone in the tent, and Olofernes lying along vpon his bed, for hee was filled with *wine.

Ecclesl. 20. 25.

3 Now Iudeth had commanded her maide to stand without her bedchamber, and to waite for her comming forth as she did daily : for she said, she would goe forth to her prayers, and she spake to Bagoas, according to the same purpose.

4 So all went forth, and none was left in the bedchamber, neither little, nor great. Then Iudeth standing by his bed, said in her heart : O Lord God of all power, looke at this present vpon the workes of mine hands for the exaltation of Ierusalem.

5 For now is the time to helpe thine inheritance, and to execute mine enterprises, to the destruction of the enemies, which are risen against vs.

6 Then she came to the pillar of the bed, which was at Olofernes head, and tooke downe his fauchin from thence,

7 And approched to his bed, and tooke hold of the haire of his head, and said, Strengthen mee, O Lord God of Israel, this day.

8 And she smote twise vpon his necke with all her might, and she tooke away his head from him,

9 And tumbled his body downe from the bed, and pulled downe the canopy from the pillars, and anon after she went forth, and gaue Olofernes his head to her maide.

10 And she put it in her bag of meate, so they twaine went together according to their custome vnto prayer, and when they passed the campe, they compassed the valley, and went vp the mountaine of Bethulia, and came to the gates thereof.

11 Then said Iudeth a farre off to the watchmen at the gate, Open, open now the gate : God, euen our God is with vs, to shew his power yet in Ierusalem, and his forces against the enemie, as he hath euen done this day.

12 Now when the men of her citie heard her voyce, they made haste to goe downe to the gate of their citie, and they called the Elders of the citie.

13 And then they ranne altogether both small and great, for it was strange vnto them that she was come : so they opened the gate, and receiued them, and made a fire for a light, and stood round about them.

14 Then she said to them with a loud voyce, Praise, praise God, praise God, (I say) for hee hath not taken away his mercy from the house of Israel, but hath destroyed our enemies by mine hands this night.

15 So she tooke the head out of the bag, and shewed it, and said vnto them, Behold the head of Olofernes the chiefe captaine of the armie of Assur, and behold the canopy wherein he did lie in his drunkennesse, and the Lord hath smitten him by the hand of a woman.

16 As the Lord liueth, who hath kept me in my way that I went, my countenance hath deceiued him to his destruction, and yet hath hee not committed sinne with mee, to defile and shame mee.

17 Then all the people were wonderfully astonished, and bowed themselues, and worshipped God, and said with one accord : Blessed be thou, O our God, which hast this day brought to nought the enemies of thy people.

18 Then said Ozias vnto her, O daughter, blessed art thou of the most high God, aboue all the women vpon the earth, and blessed be the Lord God, which hath created the heauens, and the earth, which hath directed thee to the cutting off of the head of the chiefe of our enemies.

19 For this thy confidence shall not depart from the heart of men, which remember the power of God for euer.

20 And God turne these things to thee for a perpetuall praise, to visite thee in good things, because thou hast not spared thy life for ỹ affliction of our nation, but hast reuenged our ruine, walking a straight way before our God : and all the people said, So be it, so be it.

CHAP. XIIII.

8 Achior heareth Iudeth shewe what she had done, and is circumcised, 11 the head of Olofernes is hanged vp, 15 hee is found dead, and much lamented.

 Hen saide Iudeth vnto them, Heare me now, my brethren, & take this *head, and hang it vpon the highest place of your walles.

* 2. Mac. 15. 35.

2 And

2 And so soone as the morning shall appeare, and the Sunne shal come forth vpon the earth, take you euery one his weapons, and goe forth euery valiant man out of the city, & set you a captaine ouer them, as though you would goe downe into the field toward the watch of the Assyrians, but goe not downe.

3 Then they shal take their armour, and shal goe into their campe, and raise vp the captaines of the armie of Assur, and they shall runne to the tent of Olofernes, but shall not finde him, then feare shall fall vpon them, and they shall flee before your face.

4 So you, and all that inhabite the coast of Israel, shall pursue them, and ouerthrow them as they goe.

5 But before you doe these things, call me Achior the Ammonite, that hee may see and know him that despised the house of Israel, and that sent him to vs as it were to his death.

6 Then they called Achior out of the house of Ozias, and when hee was come, and saw the head of Olofernes in a mans hand, in the assembly of the people, he fell downe on his face, and his spirit failed.

7 But when they had recouered him, hee fell at Iudeths feete, and reuerenced her, and said : Blessed art thou in all the tabernacle of Iuda, and in all nations, which hearing thy name shall be astonished.

8 Now therefore tell mee all the things that thou hast done in these dayes : Then Iudeth declared vnto him in the midst of the people, all that shee had done from the day that shee went foorth, vntill that houre she spake vnto them.

9 And when shee had left off speaking, the people shouted with a lowd voice, & made a ioyful noise in their citie.

10 And when Achior had seene all that the God of Israel had done, hee beleeued in God greatly, and circumcised the foreskinne of his flesh, and was ioyned vnto the house of Israel vnto this day.

11 And assoone as the morning arose, they hanged the head of Olofernes vpon the wall, and euery man took his weapons, and they went foorth by bandes vnto the ‖straits of the mountaine.   ‖ Or, ascents.

12 But when the Assyrians sawe them, they sent to their leaders, which came to their Captaines, and tribunes, and to euery one of their rulers.

13 So they came to Olofernes tent, and said to him that had the charge of all his things, Waken now our lord : for the slaues haue beene bold to come downe against vs to battell, that they may be vtterly destroyed.

14 Then went in Bagoas, and knocked at the doore of the tent : for he thought that he had slept with Iudeth.

15 But because none answered, he opened it, and went into the bedchamber, and found him cast vpon the floore dead, & his head was taken from him.

16 ‖Therefore he cried with a lowd voice, with weeping, and sighing, and a mighty cry, and rent his garments.   ‖ Then.

17 After, hee went into the tent, where Iudeth lodged, and when hee found her not, he leaped out to the people, and cried ;

18 These slaues haue dealt treacherously, one woman of the Hebrewes hath brought shame vpon the house of king Nabuchodonosor : for behold, Olofernes lieth vpon the ground without a head.

19 When the captaines of the Assyrians armie heard these words, they rent their couts, and their minds were wonderfully troubled, and there was a cry, and a very great noise throughout the campe.

CHAP. XV.

1 The Assyrians are chased and slaine. 8 The high Priest commeth to see Iudeth. 11 The stuffe of Olofernes is giuen to Iudeth. 13 The women crowne her with a garland.

And when they that were in the tents heard, they were astonished at the thing that was done.

2 And feare and trembling fell vpon them, so that there was no man that durst abide in the sight of his neighbour, but rushing out altogether, they fled into euery way of the plaine, and of the hill countrey.

3 They also that had camped in the mountaines, round about Bethulia, fled away. Then the children of Israel euery one that was a warriour among them, rushed out vpon them.

4 Then sent Ozias to Bethomasthem, and to Bebai, and Chobai, and Cola, and to all the coasts of Israel, such as should tell the things that were done,

done, and that all should rush forth vpon their enemies to destroy them.

5 Now when the children of Israel heard it, they all fell vpon them with one consent, and slewe them vnto Choba : likewise also they that came from Ierusalem, and from all the hill country, for men had told them what things were done in the campe of their enemies, and they that were in Galaad and in Galile ||chased them with a great slaughter, vntill they were past Damascus, and the borders thereof.

‖ Or, ouer-
came.

6 And the residue that dwelt at Bethulia, fell vpon the campe of Assur, and spoiled them, & were greatly enriched.

7 And the children of Israel that returned from the slaughter, had that which remained, and the villages, and the cities that were in the mountaines, and in the plaine, gate many spoiles : for the multitude was very great.

8 Then Ioacim the high Priest, and the Ancients of the children of Israel that dwelt in Ierusalem, came to behold the good things that God had shewed to Israel, and to see Iudeth, and to salute her.

9 And when they came vnto her, they blessed her with one accord, and said vnto her, Thou art the exaltation of Ierusalem : thou art the great glory of Israel : thou art the great reioycing of our nation.

10 Thou hast done all these things by thine hand : thou hast done much good to Israel, and God is pleased therewith : blessed bee thou of the Almightie Lord for euermore : and all the people said, So be it.

11 And the people spoiled the campe, the space of thirty dayes, and they gaue vnto Iudeth Olofernes his tent, and all his plate, and beds, and vessels, and all his stuffe : and she tooke it, and laide it on her mule, and made ready her carts, and laid them thereon.

12 Then all the women of Israel ran together to see her, and blessed her, and made a dance among them for her : and shee tooke branches in her hand, & gaue also to the women that were with her.

13 And they put a garland of oliue vpon her, and her maid that was with her, and shee went before the people in the dance, leading all the women : and all the men of Israel followed in their armor with garlands, and with songs in their mouthes.

CHAP. XVI.

Hen Iudeth began to sing this thankesgiuing in all Israel, and all the people sang after her ||this song of praise.

‖ Or, this
praising.

2 And Iudeth said, Begin vnto my God with timbrels, sing vnto my Lord with cymbals : tune vnto him a ||newe Psalme : exalt him, & cal vpon his name.

‖ Or, Psalme
and praise.

3 For God breaketh the battels : for amongst the campes in the midst of the people hee hath deliuered me out of the hands of them that persecuted me.

4 Assur came out of the mountaines from the North, he came with ten thousands of his army, the *multitude wherof stopped the torrents, and their horsemen haue couered the hilles.

* Chap. 2.
11, 15.

5 He bragged that he would burne vp my borders, and kill my young men with the sword, and dash the sucking children against the ground, and make mine infants as a pray, and my virgins as a spoile.

6 But the Almighty Lord hath disappointed them by the hand of a woman.

7 For the mighty one did not fall by the yong men, neither did the sonnes of the Titans smite him, nor high gyants set vpon him : but Iudeth the daughter of Merari weakned him with the beautie of her countenance.

8 For she put off the garment of her widowhood, for the exaltation of those that were oppressed in Israel, and anointed her face with oyntment, & bound her haire in a †tyre, and tooke a linnen garment to dcceiue him.

† Gr. or mi-
ter.

9 Her sandals rauished his eyes, her beautie tooke his minde prisoner, and the fauchin passed through his necke.

10 The Persians quaked at her boldnesse, and the Medes were ||daunted at her hardinesse.

‖ Or, con-
founded.

11 Then my afflicted shouted for ioy, and my weake ones cryed aloude ; but ||they were astonished : these lifted vp their voices, but they were ouerthrowen.

‖ The Assy-
rians.

12 The sonnes of the damosels haue pierced them through, and wounded them as fugitiues children : they perished by the battell of the Lord.

13 I

‖ Or, a song of praise.

13 I will sing vnto the Lord a ‖new song, O Lord thou art great and glorious, wonderfull in strength & inuincible.

14 Let all creatures serue thee: for thou spakest, and they were made, thou didst send forth thy spirit, and it created them, and there is none that can resist thy voyce.

15 For the mountaines shall be mooued from their foundations with the waters, the rockes shall melt as waxe at thy presence : yet thou art mercifull to them that feare thee.

16 For all sacrifice is too little for a sweete sauour vnto thee, and all the fat is not sufficient, for thy burnt offering : but he that feareth the Lord is great at all times.

17 Woe to the nations that rise vp against my kinred : the Lord almighty will take vengeance of them in the day of iudgement in putting fire & wormes in their flesh, and they shall feele them and weepe for euer.

18 Now assoone as they entred into Ierusalem, they worshipped the Lord, and assoone as the people were purified, they offered their burnt offerings, and their free offerings, and their gifts.

19 Iudeth also dedicated all the stuffe of Olofernes, which the people had giuen her, and gaue the canopy which she had taken out of his bed chamber, for a gift vnto the Lord.

20 So the people continued feasting in Ierusalem before the Sanctuarie, for the space of three moneths, and Iudeth remained with them.

21 After this time, euery one returned to his owne inheritance, and Iudeth went to Bethulia, and remained in her owne possession, and was in her time honourable in all the countrey.

22 And many desired her, but none knew her all the dayes of her life, after that Manasses her husband was dead, and was gathered to his people.

23 But she encreased more and more in honour, and waxed olde in her husbands house, being an hundred and fiue yeeres olde, and made her maide free, so shee died in Bethulia : and they buried her in the ‖caue of her husband Manasses.

‖ Or, sepulchre.

24 And the house of Israel lamented her * seauen dayes, and before shee dyed, she did distribute her goods to all them that are neerest of kinred to Manasses her husband : and to them that were the neerest of her kinred.

* Gen. 50. 10.

25 And there was none that made the children of Israel any more afraide, in the dayes of Iudeth, nor a long time after her death.

¶ The rest of the Chapters of the Booke of Esther, which are found neither in the Hebrew, nor in the Calde.

Part of the tenth Chapter after the Greeke.

5 Mardocheus remembreth and expoundeth his dreame, of the riuer and the two dragons.

THen Mardocheus saide, God hath done these things.

5 For I remember a dreame, which I sawe concerning these matters and nothing thereof hath failed.

6 A little fountaine became a riuer, and there was light, & the Sunne, and much water : this riuer is Esther, whō the King married and made Queene.

7 And the two Dragons are I, and Aman.

8 And the nations were those that were assembled, to destroy the name of the Iewes.

9 And my nation is this Israel, which cryed to God and were saued : for the Lord hath saued his people, and the Lord hath deliuered vs from all those euils, and God hath wrought signes, and great wonders, which haue not bin done among the Gentiles.

10 There-

10 Therefore hath hee made two lots, one for the people of God, and another for all the Gentiles.

11 And these two lots came at the houre, and time, and day of iudgement before God amongst all nations.

12 So God remembred his people, and iustified his inheritance.

13 Therefore those dayes shall be vnto them in the moneth Adar, the foureteenth and fifteenth day of the same moneth, with an assembly, and ioy, and with gladnesse, before God, according to the generations for euer among his people.

CHAP. XI.

2 The stocke and qualitie of Mardocheus. 6 He dreameth of two dragons comming forth to fight, 10 and of a little fountaine, which became a great water.

 N the fourth yeere of the raigne of Ptolomeus, and Cleopatra, Dositheus, who said hee was a priest and Leuite, and Ptolomeus his sonne brought this Epistle of Phurim, which they said was the same, and that Lysimachus the sonne of Ptolomeus, that was in Ierusalem, had interpreted it.

2 In the second yeere of the raigne of Artaxerxes the great : in the first day of the moneth Nisan, Mardocheus the sonne of Iairus, the sonne of Semei, the sonne of Cisai of the tribe of Beniamin, had a dreame.

3 Who was a Iew and dwelt in the citie of Susa, a great man, being a seruitour in the kings court.

4 He was also one of the captiues, which Nabuchodonosor the king of Babylon caried from Ierusalem, with Iechonias king of Iudea ; and this was his dreame.

5 Behold a noise of a tumult with thunder, and earthquakes, and vproare in the land.

6 And behold, two great dragons came forth ready to fight, and their crie was great.

7 And at their cry all nations were prepared to battel, that they might fight against the righteous people.

8 And loe a day of darknesse and obscurity : tribulation, and anguish, affliction, and great vproare vpon the earth.

9 And the whole righteous nation was troubled, fearing their owne euils, and were ready to perish.

10 Then they cryed vnto God, and vpon their cry, as it were from a little fountaine, was made a great flood, euen much water.

11 The light and the Sunne rose vp, and the lowly were exalted, and deuoured the glorious.

12 Now when Mardocheus, who had seene this dreame, and what God had determined to doe, was awake : he bare this dreame in minde, and vntill night by all meanes was desirous to know it.

CHAP. XII.

2 The conspiracie of the two Eunuchs is discouered by Mardocheus, 5 for which he is entertained by the king and rewarded.

 Nd Mardocheus tooke his rest in the court with Gabatha, and Thara, the two Eunuches of the king, and keepers of the palace.

2 * And he heard their deuices, and searched out their purposes, and learned that they were about to lay hands vpon Artaxerxes the king, and so he certified the king of them. * Ester 2. 21. and 6. 2.

3 Then the king examined the two Eunuches, and after that they had confessed it, they were strangled.

4 And the king made a record of these things, and Mardocheus also wrote thereof.

5 So the king commaunded Mardocheus to serue in the court, and for this he rewarded him.

6 Howbeit Aman the sonne of Amadathus the Agagite, who was in great honour with the king, sought to molest Mardocheus and his people, because of the two Eunuches of the king.

CHAP. XIII.

1 The copie of the kings letters to destroy the Iewes. 8 The prayer of Mardocheus for them.

 He copy of the letters was this. The great king Artaxerxes, writeth these things to the princes, and gouernours that are vnder him from India vnto Ethiopia, in an hundred and seuen and twentie prouinces. Ios. antiq. lib. 11. cap. 6

2 After that I became Lord ouer many nations, and had dominion ouer the

the whole world, not lifted vp with presumption of my authoritie, but carying my selfe alway with equitie and mildenesse, I purposed to settle my subiects continually in a quiet life, and making my kingdome ‖peaceable, and open for passage to the vtmost coastes, to renue peace which is desired of all men.

‖ Or, milde.

3 Now when I asked my counsellers how this might bee brought to passe, Aman that excelled in wisedome among vs, and was approoued for his constant good will, and stedfast fidelitie, and had the honour of the second place in the kingdome,

4 Declared vnto vs, that in all nations throughout the world, there was scattered a certaine malitious people, that had Lawes contrary to all nations, and continually despised the commandements of Kings, so as the vniting of our kingdomes honourably intended by vs, cannot ‖goe forward.

‖ Or, be setled.

5 Seeing then we vnderstand that this people alone is continually in opposition vnto all men, differing in the strange maner of their Lawes, and euill affected to our state, working all the mischiefe they can, that our kingdome may not be firmely stablished :

6 Therefore haue we commanded that al they that are signified in writing vnto you by Aman (who is ordained ouer the affaires, and is ‖next vnto vs) shall all with their wiues and children bee vtterly destroyed, by the sword of their enemies, without all mercie and pitie, the fourteenth day of the twelfth moneth Adar of this present yeere :

‖ Or, second from vs.

7 That they, who of old, and now also are malitious, may in one day with violence goe into the graue, and so euer hereafter, cause our affaires to be well settled, and without trouble.

8 Then Mardocheus thought vpon all the works of the Lord, and made his prayer vnto him,

9 Saying, O Lord, Lord, the king Almightie : for the whole world is in thy power; and if thou hast appointed to saue Israel, there is no man that can gainesay thee.

10 For thou hast made heauen and earth, and all the wonderous things vnder the heauen.

11 Thou art Lord of all things, and there is no man that can resist thee, which art the Lord.

12 Thou knowest all things, and

thou knowest Lord, that it was neither in contempt nor pride, nor for any desire of glory, that I did not bow downe to proud Aman.

13 For I could haue bene content with good will for the saluation of Israel, to kisse the soles of his feet.

14 But I did this, that I might not preferre the glory of man aboue the glory of God : neither will I worship any but thee, O God, neither wil I doe it in pride.

15 And now, O Lord God, and King, spare thy people : for their eyes are vpon vs, to bring vs to nought, yea they desire to destroy the inheritance that hath beene thine from the beginning.

16 Despise not the portion which thou hast deliuered out of Egypt for thine owne selfe :

17 Heare my prayer, and be mercifull vnto thine inheritance : turne our sorrow into ioy, that wee may liue, O Lord, and praise thy Name : and ‖destroy not the mouthes of them that praise thee, O Lord.

‖ Or, shut or stop not

18 All Israel in like maner cried most †earnestly vnto the Lord, because their death was before their eyes.

† Greeke mightily.

CHAP. XIIII.

1 The prayer of Queene Esther, for herselfe, and her people.

OVeene Esther also being in feare of death, resorted vnto the Lord,

2 And layd away her glorious apparel, and put on the garments of anguish, & mourning : and in stead of pretious oyntments, she couered her head with ashes, & doung, and she humbled her body greatly, and all the places of her ioy she filled with her torne haire.

3 And shee prayed vnto the Lord God of Israel, saying, O my Lord, thou onely art our king : helpe me desolate woman, which haue no helper but thee :

4 *For my danger is in mine hand.

* 1. Sam. 21. iob 13 14. psa. 1 109.

5 From my youth vp I haue heard in the tribe of my family, that thou, O Lord, tookest Israel from among all people, and our fathers from all their predecessours, for a perpetuall inheritance, and thou hast performed whatsoeuer thou didst promise them.

6 And

6 And now we haue sinned before thee : therefore hast thou giuen vs into the hands of our enemies,

7 Because wee worshipped their gods : O Lord, thou art righteous.

8 Neuertheles it satisfieth them not, that we are in bitter captiuitie, but they haue striken hands with their idols,

9 That they will abolish the thing, that thou with thy mouth hast ordained, and destroy thine inheritance, and stop the mouth of them that praise thee, and quench the glory of thy house, and of thine Altar,

10 And open the mouthes of the heathen to set foorth the praises of the † Idoles, and to magnifie a fleshly king for euer.

11 O Lord, giue not thy scepter vnto them that † be nothing, and let them not laugh at our fall, but turne their deuice vpon themselues, and make him an example that hath begunne this against vs.

12 Remember, O Lord, make thy selfe knowen in time of our affliction, and giue mee boldnesse, O King of the ‖nations, and Lord of all power.

13 Giue me eloquent speech in my mouth before the lyon : turne his heart to hate him that fighteth against vs, that there may be an end of him, and of all that are like minded to him :

14 But deliuer vs with thine hand, and helpe me that am desolate, & which haue no other helper but thee.

15 Thou knowest all things, O Lord, thou knowest that I hate the glory of the vnrighteous, and abhorre the bed of the vncircumcised, and of † all the heathen.

16 Thou knowest my necessitie : for I abhorre the signe of my † high estate, which is vpon mine head, in the dayes wherein I shewe my selfe, and that I abhorre it as a menstruous ragge, and that I weare it not when I am † priuate by my selfe.

17 And that thine handmaid hath not eaten at Amans table, and that I haue not greatly esteemed the Kings feast, nor drunke the wine of the drinke offerings :

18 Neither had thine handmaid any ioy, since the day † that I was brought hither to this present, but in thee, O Lord God of Abraham.

19 O thou mightie God aboue all, heare the voice of the forlorne, and deliuer vs out of the handes of the mischieuous, and deliuer me out of my feare.

CHAP. XV.

6 Esther commeth into the Kings presence. 7 Hee looketh angerly, and she fainteth. 8 The king doth take her vp, and comfort her.

Nd vpon the third day when shee had ended her prayer, she laide away her mourning garments, and put on her glorious apparell.

2 And being gloriously adorned, after she had called vpon God, who is the beholder, and Sauiour of all things, she tooke two maids with her.

3 And vpon the one shee leaned as carying her selfe ‖daintily.

4 And the other followed bearing vp her traine.

5 And she was ‖ruddy through the perfection of her beautie, and her countenance was cheerefull, and very ‖amiable : but her heart was in anguish for feare.

6 Then hauing passed through all the doores, shee stood before the King, who sate vpon his royall throne, and was clothed with all his robes of maiestie, all glittering with golde and precious stones, and he was very dreadfull.

7 Then lifting vp his countenance that shone with maiestie, he looked very fiercely vpon her : and the Queene fell downe and was pale, and fainted, and bowed her selfe vpon the head of the maide that went ‖before her.

8 Then God changed the spirit of the king into mildnesse, who in a † feare leaped from his throne, and tooke her in his armes till she came to her selfe againe, and comforted her with louing words, and sayd vnto her,

9 Esther, what is the matter ? I am thy brother, be of good cheere.

10 Thou shalt not die, though our cōmandement be ‖generall : come neere.

11 And so he held vp his golden scepter, and laid it vpon her necke,

12 And embraced her, & said, Speake vnto me.

13 Then said shee vnto him, I saw thee, my lord, as an Angel of God, and my heart was troubled for feare of thy maiestie.

14 For wonderfull art thou, lord, and thy countenance is full of grace.

15 And

r. vaine ings.

Gr. be not

Or, gods.

Gr. euery ranger.

Gr. pride.

Gr. quiet, priuate.

Gr. of my hange.

‖ Or, delicately.

‖ Or, rose coloured.

‖ Or, as amiable or smiling.

‖ Or, with her, or by her.
† Gr. in an agonie.

‖ Or, as well thine as mine.

Or, she fell in a swoone.

15 And as she was speaking, ‖she fell downe for faintnesse.

16 Theu the king was troubled, and all his seruants comforted her.

CHAP. XVI.

1 The Letter of Artaxerxes, 10 wherein hee taxeth Aman, 17 and reuoketh the decree procured by Aman to destroy the Iewes, 22 and commandeth the day of their deliuerance to be kept holy.

Ioseph. Ant. lib. 11 c. 6.

He great king Artaxerxes vnto the princes and gouernours of an hundreth and seuen and twenty prouinces, from India vnto Ethiopia, and vnto all ‖our faithfull Subiects, greeting.

‖ Or, well affected to our State.

2 Many, the more often they are honoured with the great bountie of their †gracious princes, the more proud they are waxen,

† Gr. their benefactors.

3 And endeauour to hurt not our Subiects onely, but not being able to beare abundance, doe take in hand to practise also against those that doe them good:

4 And take not only thankfulnesse away from among men, but also lifted vp with the glorious words of ‖lewde persons ‖that were neuer good, they thinke to escape the iustice of God, that seeth all things, and hateth euill.

‖ Or, needie.

‖ Or, that neuer tasted prosperitie.

5 Often times also faire speech of ‖those that are put in trust to manage their friends affaires, hath caused many that are in authority to be partakers of innocent blood, and hath enwrapped them in remedilesse calamities:

‖ Or, of our friends put in trust to manage the affaires.

6 Beguiling with the falshood and deceit of their lewd disposition, the innocencie and goodnesse of princes.

7 Now yee may see this as we haue declared, not so much by ancient histories, as yee may, if ye search what hath beene wickedly done of late through the pestilent behauiour of them that are vnworthily placed in authoritie.

8 And we must take care for the time to come, that our kingdome may bee quiet and peaceable for all men,

9 Both by changing our purposes, and alwayes iudging things that are euident, with more equall proceeding.

10 For Aman a Macedonian the son of Amadatha, being indeed a stranger from the Persian blood, and far distant from our goodnesse, and as a stranger receiued of vs:

11 Had so farre forth obtained the fauour that wee shew toward euery nation, as that he was called our father, and was continually honoured of all men, as the next person vnto the king.

12 But he not bearing his great dignitie, went about to depriue vs of our kingdome and life:

13 Hauing by manifold and cunning deceits sought of vs the destruction as well of Mardocheus, who saued our life, and continually procured our good, as also of blamelesse Esther partaker of our kingdome, with their whole nation.

14 For by these meanes he thought, finding vs destitute of friends, to haue translated the kingdome of the Persians to the Macedonians.

15 But wee finde that the Iewes, whom this wicked wretch hath deliuered to vtter destruction, are no euill doers, but liue by most iust lawes:

16 And that they be children of the most high and most mighty liuing God, who hath ‖ordered the kingdome both vnto vs, and to our progenitors in the most excellent maner.

‖ Or, prospered.

17 Wherefore ye shall doe well not to put in execution the Letters sent vnto you by Aman the sonne of Amadatha.

18 For hee that was the worker of these things, is hanged at the gates of Susa with all his family : God, who ruleth all things, speedily rendring vengeance to him according to his deserts.

19 Therefore ye shall publish the copy of this Letter in all places, that the Iewes may freely liue after their owne lawes

20 And ye shall aide them, that euen the same day, being the thirteenth day of the twelfth moneth Adar, they may be auenged on them, who in the time of their affliction shall set vpon them.

21 For Almightie God hath turned to ioy vnto them the day, wherein the chosen people should haue perished.

22 You shall therefore among your solemne feasts keepe it an high day with all feasting,

23 That both now and hereafter there may be safetie to vs, and the well affected Persians : but to those which doe conspire against vs, a memoriall of destruction.

24 There-

24 Therefore euery citie and countrey whatsoeuer, which shall not doe according to these things, shall bee destroyed without mercy, with fire and sword, and shall be made not onely vnpassable for men, but also most hatefull to wilde beasts and foules for euer.

¶ The Wisedome of Solomon.

CHAP. I.

2 To whom God sheweth himselfe, 4 and Wisedome herselfe. 6 An euill speaker can not lie hid. 12 We procure our owne destruction: 13 for God created not death.

Oue * righteousnesse, yee that be iudges of the earth : thinke of the Lord with a good (heart) and in simplicitie of heart seeke him.

1. King. 3.
. esay. 56. 1
3. 4.

2 For hee will be found of them that tempt him not : and sheweth himselfe vnto such as doe not *distrust him.

Deut. 4.
9. 2. chro.

3 For froward thoughts separate from God : and his power when it is tryed, ||reprooueth the vnwise.

Or, maketh
manifest.

4 For into a malitious soule wisedome shall not enter : nor dwell in the body that is subiect vnto sinne.

5 *For the holy spirit of discipline will flie deceit, & remoue from thoughts that are without vnderstanding : and will not ||abide when vnrighteousnesse commeth in.

Iere. 4. 22.

Or, is re-
nuked, or
heweth it
elfe.
Gal. 5. 22.

6 For wisedome is a *louing spirit : and will not acquite a blasphemour of his ||words : for God is witnesse of his reines, and a true beholder of his heart, and a hearer of his tongue.

Or, lippes.

7 For the spirit of the Lord filleth the world : and that which ||containeth all things hath knowledge of the voice.

Or, vphol-
deth.

8 Therefore he that speaketh vnrighteous things, cannot be hid : neither shal vengeance, when it punisheth. passe by him.

9 For inquisition shall be made into the counsels of the vngodly : and the sound of his words, shall come vnto the Lord, for the ||manifestation of his wicked deedes.

Or, repro-
uing.

10 For the eare of iealousie heareth al things : and the noise of murmurings is not hid.

11 Therefore beware of murmuring, which is vnprofitable, and refraine your tongue from backbiting : for there is no word so secret that shall goe for nought : and the mouth that ||belieth, slayeth the soule.

Or, slande-
reth.

12 Seeke not death in the errour of your life : and pull not vpon your selues *destruction, with the workes of your hands.

Deut. 4.
23.

13 For God made not death : neither hath he pleasure in the destruction of the liuing.

14 For he created all things, that they might haue their being : and the generations of the world were healthfull : and there is no poyson of destruction in them : nor the kingdome of death vpon the earth.

15 For righteousnesse is immortall.

16 But vngodly men with their workes, and words called it to them : for when they thought to haue it their friend, they consumed to nought, and made a couenant with it, because they are worthy to take part with it.

CHAP. II.

1 The wicked thinke this life short, 5 and of no other after this. 6 Therefore they will take their pleasure in this, 10 and conspire against the iust. 21 What that is which doth blind them.

Or the *vngodly* said, reasoning with themselues, but not aright : *Our life is short and tedious, *and in the death of a man there is no remedie : neither was there any man knowen to haue returned from the graue.

Iob. 7. 1.
Math. 22.
23. 1. cor. 15
32.

2 For wee are borne at all aduenture : & we shalbe heereafter as though we had neuer bene : for the breath in our nostrils is as smoke, and a little sparke in the mouing of our heart.

3 Which

3 Which being extinguished, our body shall be turned into ashes, and our spirit shall vanish as the ||soft aire :

4 And our name shalbe forgotten in time, and no man shall haue our works in remembrance, and our life shall passe away as the trace of a cloud : and shall be dispersed as a mist that is driuen away with the beames of the Sunne, and ||ouercome with the heat thereof.

5 * For our time is a very shadow that passeth away : and after our end there is no returning : for ||it is fast sealed, so that no man commeth againe.

6 Come on therefore, let vs enioy the good things * that are present : and let vs ||speedily vse the * creatures like as in youth.

7 Let vs fill our selues with costly wine, and ointments : and let no flower of the Spring passe by vs.

8 Let vs crowne our selues with Rose buds, before they be withered.

9 Let none of vs goe without his part of our || voluptuousnesse : let vs leaue tokens of our ioyfulnesse in euery place : for this is our portion, and our lot is this.

10 Let vs oppresse the poore righteous man, let vs not spare the widow, nor reuerence the ancient gray haires of the aged.

11 Let our strength bee the Lawe of iustice : for that which is feeble is found to be nothing worth.

12 Therefore let vs lye in wait for the righteous : because he is not for our turne, and he is cleane contrary to our doings : he vpbraideth vs with our offending the Law, and obiecteth to our infamy the transgressings of our education.

13 Hee professeth to haue the knowledge of God : and hee calleth himselfe the childe of the Lord.

14 Hee was made to * reproue our thoughts.

15 Hee is grieuous vnto vs euen to beholde : * for his life is not like other mens, his waies are of another fashion.

16 We are esteemed of him as ||counterfeits : he abstaineth from our wayes as from filthinesse : he pronounceth the end of the iust to be blessed, and maketh his boast that God is his father.

17 Let vs see if his wordes be true : and let vs proue what shall happen in the end of him.

18 For if the iust man be the * sonne of God, he will helpe him, and deliuer him from the hand of his enemies.

19 Let vs * examine him with despitefulnesse and torrture, that we may know his meekenesse, and prooue his patience.

20 Let vs condemne him with a shamefull death : for by his owne saying, he shall be respected.

21 Such things they did imagine, and were deceiued : for their owne wickednesse hath blinded them.

22 As for the mysteries of God, they knew them not : neither hoped they for the wages of righteousnesse : nor †discerned a reward for blamelesse soules.

23 For God created man to bee immortall, and made him to be an * image of his owne eternitie.

24 * Neuerthelesse through enuie of the deuill came death into the world : and they that doe holde of his side doe finde it.

CHAP. III.

1 The godly are happie in their death, 5 and in their troubles ; 10 The wicked are not, nor their children : 5 But they that are pure, are happie, though they haue no children : 16 For the adulterer and his seed shall perish.

Vt * the soules of the righteous are in the hand of God, and there shall no torment touch them.

2 * In the sight of the vnwise they seemed to die: and their departure is taken for misery,

3 And their going from vs to be vtter destruction : but they are in peace.

4 For though they bee punished in the sight of men : yet is their * hope full of immortalitie.

5 And hauing bene a little chastised, they shalbe greatly ||rewarded : for God * proued them, and found them ||worthy for himselfe.

6 As gold in the furnace hath hee tried them, and receiued them as a burnt offering.

7 And in the time of their * visitation, they shall shine and runne to and fro, like sparkes among the stubble.

8 They * shall iudge the nations, and haue dominion ouer the people, and their Lord shall raigne for euer.

9 They that put their trust in him, shall vnderstand the trueth : ||and such as be faithfull in loue, shall abide with him : for grace & mercy is to his saints, and

---

Marginal notes (left column):

|| Or, moist.

|| Or, oppressed.
* 1. Chr. 29. 15.

|| Or, he.

* Isa. 22. 13. and 56. 12.
|| Or, earnestly.
* 1. Cor. 15. 32.

|| Or, iolitie.

* Iohn 7. 7. ephes. 5. 13, 14.

* Isai. 53. 3.

|| Or, false coine.

* Psal. 22. 8. 9. matth. 27. 43.

Marginal notes (right column):

* Iere. 11. 19.

† Greeke, preferred or esteemed the reward.

* Gen. 1. 26. 27. and 5. 1. eccle. 17. 3.
* Gen. 3. 12.

* Deut. 33. 3.

* Chap. 5. 4.

* Rom. 8. 24. 1. cor. 5. 1. 1. pet. 1. 13.
|| Or, benefited.
* Exod. 16. 4. deut. 8. 2.
|| Or, meet.

* Matth. 13. 43.

* Matt. 19. 28. 1. cor. 6. 2.

|| Or, and such as be faithfull shall remaine with him in loue

and he hath care for his elect.

10 But the *vngodly shalbe punished according to their owne imaginations, which haue neglected the righteous, and forsaken the Lord.

11 For who so despiseth wisedome, and nurture, he is miserable, and their hope is vaine, their labours vnfruitfull, and their works vnprofitable.

12 Their wiues are ‖ foolish, and their children wicked.

13 Their of-spring is cursed : wherefore blessed is the barren that is vndefiled, which hath not knowen the sinfull bed : she *shall haue fruit in the visitation of soules.

14 And *blessed is* the Eunuch which with his hands hath wrought no iniquitie : nor imagined wicked things against God : for vnto him shall be giuen the *†speciall gift of faith, and an inheritance in the Temple of the Lord more acceptable to his minde.

15 For glorious is the fruit of good labours : and the root of wisedom shall neuer fall away.

16 As for the children of adulterers, they shall not ‖come to their perfection, and the seed of an vnrighteous bed shal be rooted out.

17 For though they liue long, yet shall they bee nothing regarded : and their last age shall be without honour.

18 Or if they die quickly, they haue no hope, neither comfort in the day of ‖triall.

19 For horrible is the end of the vnrighteous generation.

CHAP. IIII.

1 The chaste man shall be crowned. 3 Bastard slips shall not thriue. 6 They shall witnesse against their parents. 7 The iust die yong, and are happie. 19 The miserable ende of the wicked.

BEtter it is to haue no children, and to haue vertue : for the memoriall thereof is immortal : because it is ‖knowen with God and with men.

2 When it is present, men take example at it, and when it is gone they desire it : it weareth a crown, and triumpheth for euer, hauing gotten the victorie, striuing for vndefiled rewards.

3 But the multiplying brood of the vngodly shall not thriue, nor take deepe rooting from bastard slips, nor lay any fast foundation.

4 For though they flourish in branches for a time : *yet standing not fast, they shall be shaken with the winde : and through the force of windes they shall be rooted out.

5 The vnperfect branches shall bee broken off, their fruit vnprofitable, not ripe to eate : yea meet for nothing.

6 For children begotten of vnlawfull †beds, are witnesses of wickednes against their parents in their triall.

7 But though the righteous be preuented with death : yet shal he be in rest.

8 For honourable age is not that which standeth in length of time, nor that is measured by number of yeeres.

9 But wisedome is the gray haire vnto men, & an vnspotted life is old age.

10 *He pleased God, and was beloued of him : so that liuing amongst sinners, he was translated.

11 Yea, speedily was he taken away, lest that wickednes should alter his vnderstanding, or deceit beguile his soule.

12 For the bewitching of naughtines doth obscure things that are honest : and the wandring of concupiscence, doth †vndermine the simple mind.

13 He being made ‖perfect in a short time, fulfilled a long time.

14 For his soule pleased the Lord : therefore hasted he *to take him away,* from among the wicked.

15 This the people saw, and vnderstood it not : neither laid they vp this in their mindes, That his grace and mercie is with his Saints, and that he hath respect vnto his chosen.

16 Thus the righteous that is dead, shall condemne the vngodly, which are liuing, and youth that is soone perfected, the many yeeres and old age of the vnrighteous.

17 For they shall see the end of the wise, & shall not vnderstand what God in his counsell hath decreed of him, and to what end the Lord hath set him in safetie.

18 They shal see him and despise him, but God shall laugh them to scorne, and they shal hereafter be a vile carkeis, and a reproch among the dead for euermore.

19 For he shall rend them, and cast them downe headlong, that they shalbe speechles : and he shal shake them from the foundation : aud they shall bee vtterly laid waste, and be in sorow : and their memoriall shall perish.

20 And ‖when they cast vp the accounts

Marginal notes

Mat. 25.

Or, light, vnchaste.

Esai. 56. 5.

Esai. 56. 5.
Gre. the losen, or amongst the people.

Or, be partakers of holy things.

Or, hearing

Or, approued.

*Mat. 7. 19.

†Gre. sleeps.

*Gen. 5. 24 heb. 11. 5.

†Gre. peruert.
‖Or, sanctified or consummated.

‖Or, to the casting vp of the account.

counts of their ſinnes, they ſhall come with feare: and their owne iniquities ſhall conuince them to their face.

CHAP. V.

1 The wicked ſhal wonder at the godly, 4 and confeſſe their errour, 5 and the vanitie of their liues. 15 God will reward the Iuſt, 17 and warre againſt the wicked.

Hen ſhal the righteous man ſtand in great boldneſſe, before the face of ſuch as haue afflicted him, and made no account of his labours.

2 When they ſee it, they ſhalbe troubled with terrible feare, & ſhall be amazed at the ſtrangeneſſe of his ſaluation, ſo farre beyond all that they looked for.

3 And they repenting, and groning for anguiſh of ſpirit, ſhall ſay within themſelues, This was he whom wee ‖ *Or, parable* had ſometimes in deriſion, and a ‖prouerbe of reproch.

Chap. 3. 2 4 * We fooles accounted his life madnes, and his end to be without honour.

5 How is hee numbred among the children of God, and his lot is among the Saints?

6 Therefore haue wee erred from the way of trueth, and the light of righteouſneſſe hath not ſhined vnto vs, and the Sunne of righteouſneſſe roſe not vpon vs.

‖ *Or, filled our ſelues, or ſurfeited.* 7 We ‖wearied our ſelues in the way of wickedneſſe, and deſtruction : yea, we haue gone through deſerts, where there lay no way: but as for the way of the Lord, we haue not knowen it.

8 What hath pride profited vs? or what good hath riches with our vaunting brought vs?

1. Chron. 29. 15. and 2. 5. 9 All thoſe things are *paſſed away like a ſhadow, and as a Poſte that haſted by.

10 And as a ſhip that paſſeth ouer the waues of the water, which when it is gone by, the trace thereof cannot bee found: neither the path way of the keele in the waues.

Pro. 30. 19 ‖ Or, flyeth. 11 *Or as when a bird ‖hath flowen thorow the aire, there is no token of her way to be found, but the light aire being beaten with the ſtroke of her wings, and parted with the violent noiſe and motion of them, is paſſed thorow, and therin afterwards no ſigne where ſhe went, is to be found.

12 Or like as when an arrow is ſhot at a marke, it parteth the aire, which immediatly commeth together againe : ſo that a man cannot know where it went thorow :

13 Euen ſo we in like maner, aſſoone as we were borne, began to draw to our end, and had no ſigne of vertue to ſhew : but were conſumed in our owne wickedneſſe.

14 * For the hope of the vngodly is like †duſt that is blowen away with ẏ wind, like a thinne froth that is driuen away with ẏ ſtorme : like as the ‖ſmoke which is *diſperſed here and there with a tempeſt, and paſſeth away as the remembrance of a gueſt that tarieth but a day.

Iob 8. 9. †Gre. thiſtle downe. ‖ Or, chaffe. Pſal. 2. 4. & 103. 14. pro. 10. 25. and 11. 7. Iam. 1. 10, 11.

15 But ẏ righteous liue for euermore, their reward alſo is with the Lord, and the care of them is with the moſt High.

16 Therfore ſhall they receiue a glorious ‖kingdome, & a beautiful crowne from the Lords hande : for with his right hand ſhall he couer them, and with his arme ſhall he protect them.

‖ Or, palace vnleſſe the word be taken vnproperly, as 2. Mac. 2. 17.

17 He ſhall take to him his ielouſie for cōplete armour, & make the creature his weapon for the reuenge of his enemies.

18 He ſhal put on * righteouſneſſe as a breſtplate, and true iudgement in ſtead of an helmet.

Eſa. 59. 17

19 He ſhall take ‖holineſſe for an inuincible ſhield.

‖ Or, equity

20 His ſeuere wrath ſhall he ſharpen for a ſword, and the world ſhall fight with him againſt the vnwiſe.

21 Then ſhal the right-aiming thunder bolts goe abroad, and from the cloudes, as from a well-drawen bow, ſhall they flie to the marke.

22 And haileſtones full of wrath ſhal be caſt as out of a ſtonebow, and the water of the Sea ſhall rage againſt them, & the floods ſhall cruelly drowne them.

23 Yea a mightie wind ſhall ſtand vp againſt them, & like a ſtorme ſhall blow them away : thus iniquity ſhal lay waſt the whole earth, and ill dealing ſhall ouerthrow the thrones of the mightie.

CHAP. VI.

1 Kings muſt giue eare. 3 They haue their power from God, 5 Who will not ſpare them. 12 Wiſedome is ſoone found. 21 Princes muſt ſeeke for it : 24 For a wiſe Prince is the ſtay of his people.

Eare therefore, O ye kings, and vnderſtand, learne yee that be iudges of the ends of the earth.

2 Giue eare you that rule the people, and

and glory in the multitude of nations.

* Rom. 13.
1, 2.

3 For *power is giuen you of the Lord, & soueraigntie from the Highest, who shall try your workes, and search out your counsels.

4 Because being Ministers of his kingdome, you haue not iudged aright, nor kept the law, nor walked after the counsell of God,

5 Horribly and speedily shall he come vpon you: for a sharpe iudgement shall be to them that be in high places.

6 For mercy will soone pardon the meanest: but mightymen shall be mightily tormented.

* 2. Chro.
9. 17. deut.
10. 17. iob.
34. 19.
ecclesi. 35.
12. 16. act.
10. 24. rom.
2. 11. gal. 2.
5. ephe. 6. 9
col. 3. 25.
. pet. 1. 17.

7 For he which is Lord ouer all, shall feare no *mans person: neither shall he stand in awe of any mans greatnesse: for he hath made the small and great, and careth for all alike.

8 But a sore triall shall come vpon the mighty.

9 Vnto you therefore, *O kings*, doe I speake, that yee may learne wisedome, and not fall away.

10 For they that keepe holinesse holily, shall be ||iudged holy: and they that haue learned such things, shall find ||what to answere.

|| Or, iusti-
fied.

|| Or, a de-
fence.

11 Wherefore set your affection vpon my words, desire them, and yee shall be instructed.

12 Wisedome is glorious and neuer fadeth away: yea she is easily seene of them that loue her, and found of such as seeke her.

13 She preuenteth them that desire her, in making herselfe first knowen vnto them.

14 Whoso seeketh her earely, shall haue no great trauaile: for he shall find her sitting at his doores.

15 To thinke therefore vpon her is perfection of wisedome: and who so watcheth for her, shall quickly be without care.

16 For she goeth about seeking such as are worthy of her, sheweth herselfe fauourably vnto them in the wayes, and meeteth them in euery thought.

||Or, nurture

17 For the very true beginning of her, is the desire of ||discipline, and the care of discipline is loue:

18 And loue is the keeping of her lawes; and the giuing heed vnto her lawes, is the assurance of incorruption.

19 And incorruption maketh vs neere vnto God.

20 Therefore the desire of wisedome

bringeth to a kingdome.

21 If your delight be then in thrones and scepters, O ye kings of the people, honour wisedome that yee may raigne for euermore.

22 As for wisedome what she is; and how she came vp, I will tell you, and will not hide mysteries from you: but will seeke her out from the beginning of her natiuity, & bring the knowledge of her into light, and will not passe ouer the trueth.

23 Neither will I goe with consuming enuy: for such a man shall haue no fellowship with wisedome.

24 But the multitnde of the wise is the welfare of the world: and a wise king is the vpholding of the people.

25 Receiue therefore instruction thorough my words, and it shall doe you good.

CHAP. VII.

1 All men haue their beginning and end alike.
6 He preferred wisedome before all things
   else. 8 God gaue him all the knowledge,
   which he had. 22 The praise of wisedome.

My selfe also am a mortall man, like to all, and the offspring of him that was first made of the earth,

2 And in my mothers wombe was fashioned to be flesh in the time of tenne moneths *being compacted in blood, of the seed of man, and the pleasure that came with sleepe.

* Iob. 10.
12.

3 And when I was borne, I drew in the common aire, and fell vpon the earth which is of like nature, and the first voice which I vttered, was crying as all others doe.

4 I was nursed in swadling clothes, and that with cares.

5 For there is no king that had any other beginning of birth.

6 *For all men haue one entrance vnto life, and the like going out.

* Iob. 1. 21.
1. Timo. 6, 7

7 Wherefore I prayed, and vnderstanding was giuen mee: I called *vpon God*, and the spirit of wisedome came to me.

8 I preferred her before scepters, and thrones, and esteemed riches nothing in comparison of her.

9 Neither compared I vnto her any †precious stone, because all gold in respect of her is as a little sand, and siluer shalbe counted as clay before her.

† Gre. stone
of inestima-
ble price.

10 I loued her aboue health and beautie,

beautie, and chose to haue her in stead of light : for the light that commeth from her neuer goeth out.

* 1. King. 3. 13. matt. 6. 33.

11 All *good things together came to me with her, and innumerable riches in her hands.

12 And I reioyced in *them* all, because wisedome goeth before them : and I knew not that shee was the mother of them.

† *Greeke, without guile.*
† *Gr. without enuie.*

13 I learned †diligently, and doe communicate *her* †liberally : I doe not hide her riches.

14 For shee is a treasure vnto men that neuer faileth : which they that vse, ||become the friends of God : being commended for the gifts that come from learning.

|| *Or, enter friendship with God.*

15 God hath ||granted me to speake as I would, and to conceiue as is meet for the things ||that are giuen mee : because it is hee that leadeth vnto wisedome, and directeth the wise.

|| *Or, God grant.*
|| *Or, are to be spoken of.*

16 For in his hand are both we and our wordes : all wisedome also and knowledge of workemanship.

17 For hee hath giuen mee certaine knowledge of the things that are, namely to know how the world was made, & the operation of the elements :

18 The beginning, ending, and midst of the times : the alterations of the turning *of the Sunne*, and the change of seasons :

19 The circuits of yeres, and the positions of starres :

20 The natures of liuing creatures, and the furies of wilde beasts : the violence of windes, and the reasonings of men : the diuersities of plants, and the vertues of rootes ·

21 And all such things as are either secret or manifest : them I know.

22 For wisedome which is the worker of all things, taught mee : for in her is an vnderstanding spirit, holy, †one onely, manifold, subtile, liuely, cleare, vndefiled, plaine, not subiect to hurt, louing the thing that is good, quicke, which cãnot be letted, ready to do good:

† *Greeke, onely begotten.*

23 Kinde to man, stedfast, sure, free from care, hauing all power, ouerseeing all things, and going through all vnderstanding, pure, and most subtile spirits.

24 For wisedome is more moouing then any motion : she passeth and goeth through all things by reason of her purenesse.

25 For she is the ||breath of the power of God, and a pure ||influence flowing from the glory of the Almighty : therefore can no vndefiled thing fall into her.

|| *Or, vapour.*
|| *Or, streame.*

26 For shee is the *brightnesse of the euerlasting light : the vnspotted mirrour of the power of God, and the Image of his goodnesse.

*Hebr. 1. 3.

27 And being but one she can doe all things : and remayning in her selfe, she ||maketh all things new : and in all ages entring into holy soules, she maketh them friends of God, & Prophets.

|| *Or, createth.*

28 For God loueth none but him, that dwelleth with wisedome.

29 For she is more beautiful then the Sunne, and aboue all the order of starres, being compared with the light, she is found before it.

30 For after this commeth night : but vice shall not preuaile against wisedome.

CHAP. VIII.

2 He is in loue with wisedome : 4 For he that hath it, hath euery good thing. 21 It cannot be had, but from God.

Isdome reacheth from one ende to another mightily : and ||sweetly doeth she order all things.

|| *Or, profitably.*

2 I loued her and sought *her* out, from my youth I desired ||to make her my spouse, and I was a louer of her beautie.

|| *Or, to marry her to my selfe.*

3 In that she is conuersant with God, she magnifieth her nobilitie : yea, the Lord of all things himselfe loued her.

4 For she is ||priuy to the mysteries of the knowledge of God, and a ||louer of his workes.

|| *Or, teacher.*
|| *Or, chuser.*

5 If riches be a possession to be desired in this life : what is richer then wisedome that worketh all things ?

6 And if *prudence worke ; who of all that are, is a more cunning workeman then she ?

*Exod. 31. 40.

7 And if a man loue righteousnesse, her labours are vertues : for she teacheth temperance and prudence : iustice and fortitude, which are such things as men can haue nothing more profitable in their life.

8 If a man desire much experience : she knoweth things of old, and coniectureth *aright* what is to come : shee knoweth the subtilties of speaches, and can expound darke sentences : she

she foreseeth signes and wonders, and the euents of seasons and times.

9 Therefore I purposed to take her to me to liue with mee, knowing that shee †would be a counsellour of good things, and a comfort in cares & griefe.

† Gr. will.

10 For her sake I shall haue estimation among the multitude, and honour with the Elders, though I be yong.

11 I shall be found of a quicke conceit in iudgement, and shall be admired in the sight of great men.

12 * When I hold my tongue they shal bide my leisure, and when I speake they shall giue good eare vnto me : if I talke much, they shall lay their handes vpon their mouth.

* Iob 29. 8, 9, 10, 11.

13 Moreouer, by the meanes of her, I shall obtaine immortalitie, and leaue behind me an euerlasting memoriall to them that come after me.

14 I shall ‖ set the people in order, and the nations shalbe subiect vnto me.

‖Or,gouerne.

15 Horrible tyrants shall be afraide when they doe but heare of me, I shall be ‖found good among the multitude, and valiant in warre.

‖Or,appeare.

16 ‖ After I am come into mine house, I will repose my selfe with her : for her conuersation hath no bitternes, and to liue with her, hath no sorrow, but mirth and ioy.

‖ Or, being entred into mine house.

17 Now when I considered these things in my selfe, and * pondered them in mine heart, how that to be allyed vnto wisedome, is immortalitie,

* Prou. 7. 3.

18 And great pleasure it is to haue her friendship, and in the workes of her hands are infinite riches, and in the exercise of conference with her, prudence : and in talking with her a ‖good report : I went about seeking how to ‖ take her to me.

‖ Or, fame.
‖ Or, marry her.

19 For I was a wittie child, and had a good spirit

20 Yea rather being good, I came into a body vndefiled.

21 Neuerthelesse when I perceiued that I could not otherwise obtaine her, except God gaue her me (and that was a point of wisdome also to know whose gift she was) I ‖prayed vnto the Lord, and besought him, and with my whole heart I said:

‖ Or, went.

CHAP. IX.

1 A prayer vnto God for his wisedome, 6 without which the best man is nothing worth, 13 neither can he tell how to please God.

O God of my fathers, and Lord of mercy, who hast made all things with thy word,

2 And ordained man through thy wisedome, that he should haue * dominion ouer the creatures, which thou hast made,

* Gen. 1. 28.

3 And order the world according to equitie and righteousnesse, and execute iudgement with an vpright heart :

4 Giue * me wisedome that sitteth by thy Throne, and reiect me not from among thy children :

* 1. Kin. 3. 5.

5 For I *thy seruant and sonne of thine handmaide , am a feeble person, and of a short time, and too young for the vnderstanding of iudgement and lawes.

* Psal. 116. 16.

6 For though a man be neuer so perfect among the children of men, yet if thy wisedome be not with him, hee shall be nothing regarded.

7 Thou hast chosen me to be a king of thy people, and a Iudge of thy sons and daughters :

* 1. Chron. 28. 5. 2. chro. 1. 9.

8 Thou hast commaunded me to build a Temple vpon thy holy mount, and an Altar in the city wherein thou dwellest, a resemblance of the holy Tabernacle which thou hast prepared from the beginning:

9 And * wisedome was with thee : which knoweth thy workes, and was present when thou madest the world, and knew what was acceptable in thy sight , and right in thy Commaundements.

* Pro. 8. 22. ioh. 1. 2, 3, 10.

10 O send her out of thy holy heauens, and from the Throne of thy glory, that being present shee may labour with mee, that I may know what is pleasing vnto thee.

11 For she knoweth and vnderstandeth all things, and shee shall leade me soberly in my doings, and preserue me ‖in her power.

12 So shall my workes be acceptable, and then shall I iudge thy people righteously, and be worthy to sit in my fathers seate.

‖ Or, by her power or glory.

13 For what man is hee that can know the counsell of God ? or who can thinke what the will of the Lord is ?

* Isai 40. 13. rom. 11. 34. 1. cor. 2. 16.

14 For the thoughts of mortall men are ‖miserable, and our deuices are but vncertaine.

‖ Or, fearefull.

15 For the corruptible body presseth downe the soule, and the earthy tabernacle

nacle weigheth downe the minde that museth vpon many things.

16 And hardly doe we geſſe aright at things that are vpon earth, and with labour doe wee find the things that are †before vs : but the things that are in heauen, who hath searched out?

† Gre. at hand.

17 And thy counsell who hath knowen, except thou giue wisedome, and send thy holy spirit from aboue?

18 For so the wayes of them which liued on the earth were reformed, and men were taught the things that are pleasing vnto thee, and were saued through wisedome.

CHAP. X.

1 What wisedome did for Adam, 4 Noe, 5 Abraham, 6 Lot, and against the fiue cities, 10 for Iacob, 13 Ioseph, 16 Moses, 17 and the Israelites.

He preserued the first formed father of the world that was created alone, and brought him out of his fall,

* Gen. 2. 20.

2 And *gaue him power to rule all things.

* Gen. 4. 8.

3 *But when the vnrighteous went away from her in his anger, he perished also in the fury wherwith he murdered his brother.

* Gen. 7. 21

4 For whose cause the *earth being drowned with the flood, Wiſedome againe preserued it, & directed the course of the righteous, in a piece of wood, of small value.

* Gen. 11. 9

5 Moreouer, *the nations in their wicked conspiracie being confounded, she found out the righteous, and preserued him blamelesse vnto God, and kept him strong ||against his tender compassion towards his sonne.

‖ Or, in.

* Gen. 22. 10. gen. 19. 16.

6 *When the vngodly perished, shee deliuered the righteous man, who fled from the fire which fell downe vpon the †fiue cities.

† Gre. Pentapolis.

7 Of whose wickednesse euen to this day the waste land that smoketh, is a testimonie, and plants bearing fruite that neuer come to ripenesse: and a standing pillar of salt is a monument of an vnbeleeuing soule.

8 For regarding not wisedome, they gate not only this hurt, that they knew not the things which were good : but also left behind them to the world a memoriall of their foolishnes : so that in the things wherein they offended, they could not so much as be hid.

9 But Wisedome deliuered from paine those that attended vpon her.

10 When the righteous fled from his brothers wrath, she guided him in right paths : shewed him the kingdome of God : and gaue him knowledge of holy things, made him rich in his trauailes, and multiplied the fruit of his labours.

11 In the couetousnesse of such as oppressed him, she stood by him, and made him rich.

12 She defended him from his enemies, and kept him safe from those that lay in wait, and in a sore conflict she gaue him the victory, that he might knowe that godlinesse is stronger then all.

13 *When the righteous was solde, she forsooke him not, but deliuered him from sinne : she went downe with him into the pit,

* Gen. 37. 38. & 39. 7. acts 7. 10.

14 And left him not in bonds till she brought him the scepter of the kingdome and ||power against those that oppressed him : as for them that had accused him, she shewed them to be liers, and gaue them perpetuall glory.

‖ Or, the power of them that ruled ouer him.

15 *She deliuered the ||righteous people, and blamelesse seed from the nation that oppressed them.

* Exo. 1. 10 and 12. 42. ‖ Or, holy.

16 She entred into the soule of the seruant of the Lord, and *withstood dreadfull kings in wonders and signes,

* Exod. 5. 1

17 Rendred to the righteous a reward of their labours, guided them in a marueilous way, and was vnto them for a couer by day, and a light ||of starres in the night season :

‖ Or, flame.

18 *Brought them through the red sea, and led them thorow much water.

* Exod. 14. 21, 22. psal. 78. 13.

19 But she drowned their enemies, and cast them vp out of the bottome of the deepe.

20 Therefore the righteous spoiled the vngodly, & *praised thy holy Name, O Lord, and magnified with one accord thine hand that fought for them.

* Exo. 15.

21 For wisedome opened the mouth of the dumbe, and made the tongues of them that cannot speake, eloquent.

CHAP. XI.

5 The Egyptians were punished, and the Israelites reserued in the same thing. 15 They were plagued by the same things, wherein they sinned. 20 God could haue destroyed them otherwise, 23 but he is mercifull to all.

She

He prospered their works in the hand of the holy Prophet.

2 * They went thorough the wildernesse that was not inhabited, and pitched tents in places where there lay no way.

* Exod.
16. 1. exod.
17. 10, 11.

3 They stood against their enemies, and were auenged of their aduersaries.

4 When they were thirsty they called vpon thee, and water was giuen them out of the flinty rocke, and their thirst was quenched out of the hard stone.

5 For by what things their enemies were punished, by the same they in their neede were benefited.

6 For in stead of a fountaine of a perpetuall running riuer, troubled with foule blood,

7 For a manifest reproofe of that commandement, whereby the infants were slaine, thou gauest vnto them abundance of water by a meanes which they hoped not for,

8 Declaring by that thirst then, *how thou hadst punished their aduersaries.

* Exod. 7.
20.

9 For when they were tryed, albeit but in mercy chastised, they knew how the vngodly were iudged in wrath and tormented thirsting in another maner then the Iust.

10 For these thou didst admonish, and trie as a father: but the other as a seuere king thou didst condemne and punish.

11 Whether they were absent, or present, they were vexed alike.

12 For a double griefe came vpon them, and a groaning for the remembrance of things past.

13 For when they heard by their owne punishments the other to be benefited, they ||had some feeling of the Lord.

Or, percei-
ued.

14 For whom they reiected with scorne when hee was long before throwen out at the casting forth of the infants, him in the end, when they saw what came to passe, they admired.

15 But for the foolish deuises of their wickednesse, wherewith being deceiued, they worshipped serpents voyd of reason, and vile beasts: thou didst send a multitude of vnreasonable beasts vpon them for vengeance,

16 That they might knowe that wherewithall a man sinneth, by the same also shall he be punished.

17 For thy Almighty hand that made the world of matter without forme, wanted not meanes to send among them a multitude of Beares, or fierce Lyons,

18 Or vnknowen wild beasts full of rage newly created, breathing out either a fiery vapour, or filthy sents of scattered smoake, or shooting horrible sparkles out of their eyes:

19 Whereof not onely the harme might dispatch them at once: but also the terrible sight vtterly destroy them.

20 Yea and without these might they haue fallen downe with one blast, being persecuted of vengeance, and scattered abroad thorough the breath of thy power, but thou hast ordered all things in measure, and number, and weight.

21 For thou canst shew thy great strength at all times when thou wilt, and who may withstand the power of thine arme?

22 For the whole world before thee is as a litle ||graine of the ballance, yea as a drop of the morning dew that falleth downe vpon the earth.

|| Or, little
waight.

23 But thou hast mercy vpon all: for thou canst doe all things, and winkest at the sinnes of men: because they should amend.

24 For thou louest all the things that are, and abhorrest nothing which thou hast made: for neuer wouldest thou haue made any thing, if thou hadst hated it.

25 And how could any thing haue endured if it had not beene thy will? or beene preserued, if not called by thee?

26 But thou sparest all: for they are thine, O Lord, thou louer of soules.

CHAP. XII.

2 God did not destroy those of Canaan all at once. 12 If he had done so, who could controll him? 19 but by sparing them hee taught vs, 27 they were punished with their Gods.

For thine vncorruptible spirit is in all things.

2 Therefore chastnest thou them by little, and little, that offend, and warnest them by putting them in remembrance, wherin they haue offended, that leauing their wickednesse they may beleeue on thee O Lord.

3 For it was thy will to destroy by the

the handes of our fathers, both those ||old inhabitants of thy holy land,

Or, ancient.

4 Whom thou hatedst for doing most odious workes of || witchcrafts, and wicked sacrifices ;

Or, sorce-ries.

5 And also those mercilesse murderers of children, & deuourers of mans flesh, and the feasts of blood ;

6 With their Priests out of the midst of their idolatrous crew, and the parents that killed with their owne hands, soules destitute of helpe :

7 That the land which thou esteemedst aboue all other, might receiue a worthy ||colonie of Gods children.

Or, new in-habitance.

8 Neuerthelesse, euen those thou sparedst as men, and didst send *waspes forerunners of thine hoste, to destroy them by little and little.

Exod. 33. 2. deut. 2. 22.

9 Not that thou wast vnable to bring the vngodly vnder the hand of the righteous in battell, or to destroy them at once with cruel beastes, or with one rough word :

10 But executing thy iudgements vpon them by little and little, thou gauest them place of repentance, not being ignorant that they were a naughtie generation, and that their malice, was bred in them, and that their cogitation would neuer be changed.

11 For it was a *cursed seed, from the beginning, neither didst thou for feare of any man giue them pardon for those things wherein they sinned.

Gen. 9. 25.

12 For who shall say, *What hast thou done? or who shall withstand thy iudgement, or who shall accuse thee for the nations that perish whom thou hast made? or who shall come to ||stand against thee, to be ||reuenged for the vnrighteous men ?

Rom. 9. 20.

Or, in thy presence.
Or, a re-uenger.

13 For neither is there any God but thou, that *careth for all, to whom thou mightest shew that thy iudgement is not vnright.

1. Pet. 5. 7

14 Neither shall king or tyrant bee able to set his face against thee, for any whom thou hast punished.

15 For so much then as thou art righteous thy selfe, thou orderest all things righteously : *thinking it not agreeable with thy power to condemne him ỹ hath not deserued to be punished.

Iob 10. 2.

16 For thy power is the beginning of righteousnesse, and because thou art the Lord of all, it maketh thee to be gracious vnto all.

17 For when men will not beleeue,

that thou art of a || full power, thou shewest thy strength, and among them that know it, thou makest their boldnesse manifest.

Or, per

18 But thou, mastering thy power, iudgest with equitie, and orderest vs with great fauour : for thou mayest vse power when thou wilt.

19 But by such workes hast thou taught thy people, that the iust man should be mercifull, and hast made thy children to be of a good hope, that thou giuest repentance for sinnes.

20 For if thou didst punish the enemies of thy children, and the condemned to death with such deliberation, giuing them time and place, wherby they might be deliuered from their malice.

21 With how great circumspection diddest thou iudge thine owne sonnes, vnto whose fathers thou hast sworne, and made couenants of good promises?

23 Therefore whereas thou doest chasten vs, thou scourgest our enemies a thousand times more, to the intent that when wee iudge, wee should carefully thinke of thy goodnesse, and when we our selues are iudged, wee should looke for mercy.

23 Wherefore, whereas men haue liued dissolutely and vnrighteously, thou hast tormented them with their owne ||abominations.

Or, ab-nable io
Chap 13. rom 23.

24 *For they went astray very farre in the wayes of errour, & held them for gods (which euen amongst the beasts of their enemies were despised) being deceiued as children of no vnderstanding.

25 Therefore vnto them, as to children without the vse of reason, thou didst send a iudgement to mocke them.

26 But they that would not bee refourmed by that correction wherein he dallied with them, shall feele a iudgement worthy of God.

27 For looke, for what things they grudged when they were punished, (that is) for them whom they thought to be gods, [now] being punished in them; when they saw it, they acknowledged him to be the true God, whome before they denyed to know : and therefore came extreme damnation vpon them.

CHAP. XIII.

1 They were not excused that worshipped any of Gods workes : 10 But most wretched are they that worship the works of mens hands.

Surely|

SVrely vaine are all men by nature, who are ignorant of God, and could not out of the good things that are seene, know him that is : neither by considering the workes, did they acknowledge the worke-master ;

Rom. 1. 9.
eut. 4. 19.
nd 17. 3.

2 * But deemed either fire, or wind, or the swift aire, or the circle of the stars, or the violent water, or the lights of heauen to be the gods which gouerne the world :

3 With whose beautie, if they being delighted, tooke them to be gods : let them know how much better the Lord of them is; for the first Author of beautie hath created them.

4 But if they were astonished at their power and vertue, let them vnderstand by them, how much mightier he is that made them.

5 For by the greatnesse and beautie of the creatures, proportionably the Maker of them is seene.

6 But yet for this they are the lesse to bee blamed : for they peraduenture erre seeking God, and desirous to finde him.

Rom. 1. 21
Or, seeke.

7 For being * conuersant in his workes, they ||search *him* diligently, and beleeue their sight : because the things are beautifull that are seene.

8 Howbeit, neither are they to bee pardoned.

9 For if they were able to know so much, that they could aime at the world; how did they not sooner finde out the Lord thereof ?

10 But miserable are they, and in dead things is their hope, who called them gods which are the workes of mens hands, golde and siluer, to shewe arte in, and resemblances of beasts, or a stone good for nothing, the worke of an ancient hand.

Isai 44. 13.
Or, timber-
ight.

11 * Now a ||carpenter that felleth timber, after hee hath sawen downe a tree meet for the purpose, and taken off all the barke skilfully round about, and hath wrought it handsomely, & made a vessell thereof fit for the seruice of mans life :

Or, chips.

12 And after spending the ||refuse of his worke to dresse his meat, hath filled himselfe :

13 And taking the very refuse among those which serued to no vse (being a crooked piece of wood, and ful of knots)

hath carued it diligently when hee had nothing else to doe, and formed it by the skill of his vnderstanding, and fashioned it to the image of a man :

14 Or made it like some vile beast, laying it ouer with vermilion , and with paint, colouring it red, and couering euery spot therein :

15 And when he had made a conuenient roume for it, set it in a wall, and made it fast with yron :

16 For he prouided for it, that it might not fall : knowing that it was vnable to helpe it selfe, (for it is an image and hath neede of helpe :)

17 Then maketh hee prayer for his goods, for his wife and children, and is not ashamed to speake to that which hath no life.

18 For health, hee calleth vpon that which is weake : for life, prayeth to that which is dead : for aide, humbly beseecheth †that which hath least meanes to helpe : and for a good iourney, hee asketh of that which cannot set a foot forward :

† Gr. that
hath no ex-
perience
at all.

19 And for gaining and getting, and for good successe of his hands, asketh abilitie to doe, of him that is most vnable to doe any thing.

CHAP. XIIII.

1 Though men doe not pray to their shippes, 5 Yet are they saued rather by them then by their Idoles. 8 Idoles are accursed, and so are the makers of them. 14 The beginning of Idolatrie, 23 And the effects thereof. 30 God wil punish them that sweare falsely by their Idoles.

AGaine, one preparing himselfe to saile, and about to passe through the raging waues, calleth vpon a piece of wood more rotten then the ||vessell that carieth him.

|| Or, ship.

2 For verely desire of gaine deuised ||that, and the workeman built it by his skill :

|| Or, vessell
or ship.

3 But thy prouidence, O Father, gouerneth it : for thou hast * made a way in the Sea, and a safe path in the waues :

* Exod. 14.
22.

4 Shewing that thou canst saue from all danger : yea though a man went to Sea without arte.

5 Neuerthelesse thou wouldest not that the works of thy wisedome should be idle, and therefore doe men commit their

their liues to a small piece of wood, and passing the rough sea in a weake vessell, are saued.

*Gen. 6. 4. and 7. 10.

6 * For in the old time also when the proud gyants perished, the hope of the world gouerned by thy hand, escaped in a weake vessell, and left to all ages a seed of generation.

7 For blessed is the wood, whereby righteousnesse commeth.

* Psal. 115. 8. baruc. 6. 3

8 But that which is made with hands, is cursed, aswell *it, as hee that made it : he, because he made it, and it, because being corruptible it was called God.

* Psal. 5. 5.

9 *For the vngodly and his vngod-lines are both alike hatefull vnto God.

10 For that which is made, shall bee punished together with him that made it.

‖ Or, to or by.

11 Therfore euen vpon ‖the idoles of the Gentiles shall there be a visitation: because in the creature of God they are become an abomination and *†stumb-ling blocks to the soules of men, and a ‖snare to the feet of the vnwise.

* Ier. 10. 8. abac. 2. 18. † Gre. scan-dales. ‖ Or, trap.

12 For the deuising of idoles was the beginning of spiritual fornication, and the inuention of them the corruption of life.

13 For neither were they from the beginning, neither shall they be for euer.

14 For by the vaine glory of men they entred into the world, and therefore shall they come shortly to an end.

15 For a father afflicted with vn-timely mourning, when he hath made an image of his childe soone taken a-way, now honoured him as a god, which was then a dead man, and deli-uered to those that were vnder him, ce-remonies and sacrifices.

‖ Gre. in time

16 Thus †in process of time an vn-godly custome growen strong, was kept as a law, and grauen images were worshipped by the commandements of ‖kings,

‖ Or, tyrants ‖ Or, in sight

17 Whom men could not honour ‖in presence, because they dwelt farre off, they tooke the counterfeit of his visage from farre, and made an expresse image of a king whom they honoured, to the end that by this their forwardnes, they might flatter him that was absent, as if he were present.

18 Also the singular diligence of the artificer did helpe to set forward the ig-norant to more superstition.

19 For he peraduenture willing to please one in authoritie, forced all his

skill to make the resemblance †of the best fashion.

† Gre. to th better.

20 And so the multitude allured by the grace of the worke, tooke him now for a god, which a litle before was but honoured as a man.

21 And this was an occasion to de-ceiue the world : for men seruing either calamitie or tyrannie, did ascribe vnto stones, and stockes, the incommunica-ble ‖Name.

‖ Of God.

22 Moreouer this was not enough for them, that they erred in the know-ledge of God, but whereas they liued in the great warre of ignorance, those so great plagues called they peace.

23 For whilest they *slew their chil-dren in sacrifices, or vsed secret cereme-nies, or made reuellings of strange rites

* Deut. 18 10. ier. 7. and 19. 4.

24 They kept neither liues nor ma-riages any longer vndefiled : but either one slew another traiterously, or grie-ued him by adulterie :

25 So that there reigned in all men ‖without exception, blood, manslaugh-ter, theft, and dissimulation, corrupti-on, vnfaithfulnesse, tumults, periurie,

‖ Or, conj sedly.

26 Disquieting of good men, forget-fulnesse of good turnes, defiling of soules, changing of ‖kinde, disorder in mariages, adulterie, and shameles vn-cleannesse.

‖ Or, sexe

27 For the worshipping of idoles †not to be named, is the beginning, the cause, and the end of all euill.

† Gre. nam lesse.

28 For either they are mad when they be merry, or prophesie lies, or liue vniustly, or else lightly forsweare them-selues.

29 For insomuch as their trust is in idoles which haue no life, though they sweare falsly, yet they looke not to bee hurt.

30 Howbeit for both causes shal they be iustly puuished : both because they thought not well of God, ‖giuing heed vnto idols, and also vniustly swore in de-ceit, despising holinesse.

‖ Or, deue ted.

31 For it is not the power of them by whom they sweare : but it is the iust vengeance of sinners, that punisheth alwaies the offence of the vngodly.

CHAP. XV.

1 We doe acknowledge the true God. 7 The follie of Idole-makers, 14 and of the ene-mies of Gods people : 15 because besides the idoles of the Gentiles, 18 they worshipped vile beasts.

But

Vt thou O God, art gracious and true: long suffering, and in mercy ordering all things.

2 For if we sinne we are thine, knowing thy power: but we will not sinne, knowing that we are counted thine.

3 For to know thee is perfect righteousnesse: yea to know thy power is the roote of immortality.

4 For neither did the mischieuous inuention of men deceiue vs: nor an image spotted with diuers colours, the painters fruitlesse labour.

Or, turneth
a reproch to
the foolish.

5 The sight wherof ||entiseth fooles to lust after it, and so they desire the forme of a dead image that hath no breath.

6 Both they that make them, they that desire them, and they that worship them, are louers of euill things, and are worthy to haue such things to trust vpon.

* Rom. 9. 11

7 For the *potter tempering soft earth fashioneth, euery vessell with much labour for our seruice: yea of the same clay hee maketh both the vessels that serue for cleane vses: and likewise also all such as serue to the contrary: but what is the vse of either sort, the potter himselfe is the iudge.

8 And employing his labours lewdly, he maketh a vaine God of the same clay, euen he which a little before was made of earth himselfe, and within a little while after returneth to the same out of the which he was taken: when

* Luke 12.
20.

his *life which was lent him shall be demanded.

9 Notwithstanding his care is, not that hee shall haue much labour, nor

Or, be sicke
or die.

that ||his life is short: but striueth to excel goldsmiths, and siluersmiths, and endeuoureth to doe like the workers in brasse, and counteth it his glory to make counterfeit things.

10 His heart is ashes, his hope is more vile then earth, and his life of lesse value then clay:

11 Forasmuch as hee knew not his maker, and him that inspired into him an actiue soule, and breathed in a liuing spirit.

† Gre. life.

12 But they counted our life a pastime, & our †time here a market for gaine: for, say they, we must be getting euery way, though it be by euil meanes.

|| Or, so.

13 ||For this man that of earthly matter maketh brickle vessels, and grauen images, knoweth himselfe to offend aboue all others.

14 And all the enemies of thy people, that hold them in subiection are most foolish and are more miserable then very babes.

15 For they counted all the idoles of the heathen to be gods: which neither haue the vse of eyes to see, nor noses to draw ||breath, nor eares to heare, nor fingers of hands to handle, and as for their feete they are slow to goe.

|| Or, ayre.

16 For man made them, and he that borrowed his owne spirit fashioned them, but no man can make a god like vnto himselfe.

17 For being mortall he worketh a dead thing with wicked hands: for hee himselfe is better then the things which he worshippeth: whereas he liued once, but they neuer.

18 Yea they worshipped those beasts also that are most hatefull: for being compared together, some are worse then others.

19 Neither are they beautifull, so much, as to bee desired in respect of beasts, but they went without the praise of God and his blessing.

CHAP. XVI.

2 God gaue strange meate to his people, to stirre vp their appetite, and vile beasts to their enemies to take it from them. 5 Hee stung with his serpents, 12 but soone healed them by his word onely. 17 The creatures altred their nature to pleasure Gods people, and to offend their enemies.

Herefore by the like were they punished worthily, and by the multitude of beasts *tormented.

* Num. 21.
6. chap. 11.
15, 16.

2 In stead of which punishment, dealing graciously with thine owne people thou preparedst for them meate of a strange taste: euen *quailes to stirre vp their appetite:

* Num. 11.
31.

3 To the end that they desiring food might for the ougly sight of the beasts sent among them, loath euen that which they must needs desire: but these suffering penury for a short space, might be made partakers of a strange taste.

4 For it was requisite, that vpon them excercising tyranny should come penury which they could not auoyde: but to these it should onely be shewed how their enemies were tormented.

5 For

‖ Or, thy people.
* Num. 21. 6. 1. cor. 10. 9.

5 For when the horrible fierceneſſe of beasts came vpon ‖ these, and they periſhed with the *stings of crooked serpents, thy wrath endured not for euer.

* Num. 21. 9.

6 But they were troubled for a smal season that they might be admonished, hauing a * signe of saluation, to put them in remembrance of the commandement of thy Law.

7 For hee that turned himselfe towards it, was not saued by the thing that he saw : but by thee that art the sauiour of all.

8 And in this thou madest thine enemies confesse, that it is thou who deliuerest from all euill :

* Exod. 8. 24. and 10. 4. reuel. 9. 7.

9 For * them the bitings of grassehoppers and flies killed, neither was there found any remedy for their life : for they were worthy to bee punished by such.

10 But thy sonnes, not the very teeth of venemous dragons ouercame : for thy mercy was *euer* by them, and healed them.

† Hebr. stung.

11 For they were † pricked, that they should remember thy words, and were quickly saued, that not falling into deep forgetfulnesse, they might be ‖ continually mindefull of thy goodnesse.

‖ Or, neuer drawen from.

12 For it was neither herbe, nor mollifying plaister that restored them to health : but thy word, O Lord, which healeth all things.

* Psal. 105. deut. 32. 39. 1. sam. 2. 6.

13 For thou hast power of life and death : thou * leadest to the gates of hell, and bringest vp againe.

14 A man indeed killeth through his malice : but the spirit when it is gone foorth returneth not ; neither the soule receiued vp, commeth againe.

15 But it is not possible to escape thine hand.

* Exod. 9. 23.

16 * For the vngodly that denied to know thee, were scourged by the strength of thine arme : with strange raines, hailes, and showers were they persecuted, that they could not auoyd, and through fire were they consumed.

17 For, which is most to be wondered at, the fire had more force in the water that quencheth all things : for the

* Iud. 5. 20.

* world fighteth for the righteous.

18 For sometimes the flame was mitigated, that it might not burne vp the beasts that were sent against the vngodly : but themselues might see and perceiue that they were persecuted with the iudgement of God.

19 And at another time it burneth euen in the midst of water, aboue the power of fire, that it might destroy the fruits of an vniust land.

* Exod. 16. 14. num. 11. 7. psal. 78. 25. ioh. 6. 31.

20 * In stead whereof thou feddest thine owne people, with Angels food, and didst send them from heauen bread prepared without their labour, able to content euery mans delight, and agreeing to euery taste.

* Iudg. 6. 4
‖ Or, Manna.
‖ Or, was tempered.

21 * For thy ‖ sustenance declared thy sweetnesse vnto thy children, and seruing to the appetite of the cater ‖ tempered it selfe to euery mans liking.

* Chap. 19. 20.

22 * But snow and yce endured the fire and melted not, that they might know that fire burning in the haile, and sparkling in the raine, did destroy the fruits of the enemies.

23 But this againe did euen forget his owne strength, that the righteous might be nourished.

24 For the creature that serueth thee who art the maker, encreaseth his strength against the vnrighteous for their punishment, and abateth his strength for the benefit of such as put their trust in thee.

‖ Or, thing

25 Therefore euen then was it altered into all ‖ fashions, and was obedient to thy grace that nourisheth all things, according to the desire ‖ of them that had need :

‖ Or, of the that praye

26 That thy children, O Lord, whom thou louest, might know that * it is not the growing of fruits that nourisheth man : but that it is thy word which preserueth them that put their trust in thee.

* Deut. 8. matth. 4.

27 For that which was not destroied of the fire, being warmed with a litle Sunne beame, soone melted away,

28 That it might bee knowen, that wee must preuent the Sunne, to giue thee thanks, and at the day-spring pray vnto thee.

29 For the hope of the vnfaithfull, shal melt away as the Winters hoarefrost, and shall runne away as vnprofitable water.

CHAP. XVII.

1 Why the Egyptians were punished with darkenesse. 4 The terrours of that darknes. 12 The terrours of an ill conscience.

 Or great are thy Iudgements, and cannot be expressed : therefore ‖ vnnourtured soules haue erred.

‖ Or, sou that will be reforn

2 For

2 For when vnrighteous men thought to oppresse the holy nation: they being shut vp ||in their houses, the prisoners of darkenesse, and fettered with the bondes of a long night, lay [there] ||exiled from the eternall prouidence.

3 For while they supposed to lie hid in their secret sinnes, they were scattered ||vnder a darke vaile of forgetfulnesse, being horribly astonished, and troubled with (strange) || apparitions.

4 For neither might the corner that helde them keepe them from feare: but noises (as of waters) falling downe, sounded about them, and sadde visions appeared vnto them with heauie countenances.

5 No power of the fire might giue them light: neither could the bright flames of the starres endure to lighten that horrible night.

6 Onely there appeared vnto them a fire kindled of it selfe, very dreadfull: for being much terrified, they thought the things which they saw to be worse then the sight they saw not.

7 *As for the illusions of arte Magicke, they were put downe, and their vaunting in wisedome was reprooued with disgrace.

8 For they that promised to driue away terrours, and troubles from a sicke soule, were sicke themselues of feare worthy to be laughed at.

9 For though no terrible thing did feare them: yet being skared with beasts that passed by, and hissing of serpents,

10 They died for feare, ||denying that they saw the ayre, which could of no side be auoided.

11 For wickednesse condemned by her owne witnesse, is very timorous, and being pressed with conscience, alwayes forecasteth grieuous things.

12 For feare is nothing else, but a betraying of the succours which reason offereth.

13 And the expectation from within being lesse, counteth the ignorance more then the cause which bringeth the torment.

14 But they sleeping the same sleepe that night ||which was indeed intolerable, and which came vpon them out of the bottomes of ineuitable hell:

15 Were partly vexed with monstrous apparitions, and partly fainted,

their heart failing them: for a suddaine feare and not looked for, came vpon them.

16 So then, whosoeuer there fell downe, was straitly kept, shut vp in a prison without yron barres.

17 For whether hee were husbandman, or shepheard, or a labourer in the ||field, he was ouertaken, and endured that necessitie, which could not be auoided: for they were all bound with one chaine of darkenesse.

18 Whether it were a whistling winde, or a melodious noise of birdes among the spreading branches, or a pleasing fall of water running violently:

19 Or a ||terrible sound of stones cast downe, or a running that could not be seene of skipping beasts, or a roaring voice of most sauage wilde beasts, or a rebounding Eccho from the hollow mountaines: these things made them to swoone for feare.

20 For the whole world shined with cleare light, and none were hindered in their labour.

21 Ouer them onely was spread an heauie night, an image of that darkenesse which should afterwards receiue them: but yet were they vnto themselues more grieuous then the darkenesse.

CHAP. XVIII.

4 Why Egypt was punished with darkenesse, 5 and with the death of their children, 18 They themselues saw the cause thereof. 20 God also plagued his owne people. 11 By what meanes that plague was stayed.

EuertheIesse, thy Saints had a very great *light, whose voice they hearing and not seeing their shape, because they also had not suffered the same things, they counted them happy.

2 But for that they did not hurt them *now*, of whom they had beene wronged before, they thanked them, and besought them pardon, for that they had beene enemies.

3 *In stead whereof thou gauest them a burning pillar of fire, both to be a guide of the vnknowen iourney, and an harmelesse Sunne to entertaine them honourably.

4 For they were worthy to be depriued of light, and imprisoned in darkenesse, who had kept thy sonnes shut vp,

by

r, vnder ir roofes.

r, fugi-es.

r, in.

r, sights.

Exo. 7. 12. d 8. 7, 19.

r, refusing looke vpon.

Or, wherein sey could be nothing.

|| Or, desert.

||Or, hideous.

* Exod. 10. 23.

* Exo. 13. 21 and 14. 24. psal. 78. 14. & 105. 29.

by whom the ‖vncorrupt light of the law was to be giuen vnto the world.

Or, incorruptible.

Exod. 14. 24, 25.

5 *And when they had determined to slay the babes of the Saints, one child being cast forth, and saued : to reproue them, thou tookest away the multitude of their children, and destroyedst them altogether in a mightie water.

Exod. 11. 4.

6 *Of that night were our fathers certified afore, that assuredly knowing vnto what oathes they had giuen credence, they might afterwards bee of good cheere.

7 So of thy people was accepted both the saluation of the righteous, and destruction of the enemies.

8 For wherewith thou didst punish our aduersaries, by the same thou didst glorifie vs whom thou hadst called.

Exod. 12.

9 *For the righteous children of good men did sacrifice secretly, and with one consent made a ‖holy lawe, that the Saints should bee alike partakers of the same good and euill, the fathers now singing out the songs of praise.

‖ *Or, a couenant of God, or league, see psal. 50. 5.*

10 But on the other side there sounded an ill-according crie of the enemies, and a lamentable noise was caried abroad for children that were bewailed.

Exo. 11. 5 and 12. 29.

11 *The master and the seruaunt were punished after one maner, and like as the king, so suffered the common person.

12 So they altogether had innumerable dead with one kind of death, neither were the liuing sufficient to burie them : for in one moment the noblest offspring of them was destroyed.

13 For whereas they would not beleeue any thing by reason of the enchantments, vpon the destruction of the first borne, they acknowledged this people to be the sonnes of God.

14 For while all things were in quiet silence, and that night was in the midst of her swift course,

15 Thine almighty word leapt downe from heauen, out of thy royall throne, as a fierce man of warre into the midst of a land of destruction,

16 And brought thine vnfained commandement as a sharpe sword, and standing vp filled all things with death, and it touched the heauen, but it stood vpon the earth.

‖ *Or, imaginations.*

17 Then suddenly ‖visions of horrible dreames troubled them sore, and terrours came vpon them vnlooked for.

18 And one throwen here, another there halfe dead, shewed the cause of his death.

19 For the dreames that troubled them, did foreshew this, lest they should perish, and not know why they were afflicted.

20 Yea, the tasting of death touched the righteous also, and there was a destruction of the *multitude in the wildernes : but the wrath endured not long.

Num. 16. 46.

21 For then the blamelesse man made haste, and stood foorth to defend them, and bringing the shield of his proper ministerie, euen prayer and the propitiation of incense, set himselfe against the wrath, and so brought the calamity to an end, declaring that hee was thy seruant.

22 So hee ouercame the destroyer, not with strength of body, nor force of armes, but with a word subdued he him that punished, alleaging the oathes and couenants made with the fathers.

23 For when the dead were now fallen downe by heaps one vpon another, standing betweene, he staied the wrath, and ‖parted the way to the liuing.

‖ *Or, cut*

24 *For in the long garment was the whole world, & in the foure rowes of the stones was the glory of the fathers grauen, and thy maiestie vpon the diademe of his head.

Exo. 28. and 11. 10

25 Vnto these the destroyer gaue place, and was afraid of them : for it was enough that they onely tasted of the wrath.

CHAP. XIX.

1 Why God shewed no mercie to the Egyptians. 5 And how wonderfully hee dealt with his people. 14. The Egyptians were worse then the Sodomites. 18 The wonderfull agreement of the creatures to serue Gods people.

A S for the vngodly, wrath came vpon them without mercie vnto the end : for he knew before what they would doe ;

2 Howe that hauing giuen them leaue to depart, and sent them hastily away, they would repent and pursue them.

3 For whilest they were yet mourning, and making lamentation at the graues of the dead, they added another foolish

foolish deuice, and pursued them as fugitiues, whom they had ||entreated to be gone.

|| Or, cast out by entreaty.

4 For the destiny, whereof they were worthy, drew them vnto this end, and made them forget the things that had already happened, that they might fulfill the punishment which was wanting to their torments,

5 And that thy people might passe a wonderfull way : but they might find a strange death.

6 For the whole creature in his proper kind was fashioned againe anew, seruing the peculiar commandements that were giuen vnto them, that thy children might be kept without hurt.

7 *As namely*, a cloud shadowing the campe, and where water stood before drie land appeared, and out of the red Sea a way without impediment, and out of the violent streame a greene field :

8 Where-thorough all the people went that were defended with thy hand, seeing thy marueilous strange wonders.

9 For they went at large like horses, and leaped like lambes, praising thee O Lord, who hadst deliuered them.

10 For they were yet mindefull of the things that were done while they soiourned in the strange land, how the ground brought forth ||flies in stead of cattell, and how the riuer cast vp a multitude of frogs in stead of fishes.

|| Or, lice.

11 But afterwards they saw a new generation of foules, when being led with their appetite they asked delicate meates.

12 For quailes came vp vnto them from the Sea, for their ||contentment.

|| Or, comfort.

13 And punishments came vpon the sinners not without former signes by the force of thunders : for they suffered iustly, according to their owne wickednesse, insomuch as they vsed a more hard and hatefull behauiour towards strangers :

14 For the *Sodomits* did not receiue those whom they knew not when they came : but these brought friends into bondage, that had well deserued of them.

15 And not onely so : but peraduenture some respect shall be had of those, because they vsed strangers not friendly.

16 But these very grieuously afflicted them, whom they had receiued with feastings, and were already made partakers of the same lawes with them.

17 Therefore euen with blindnesse were these stricken, as those were at the doores of the righteous man : when being compassed about with horrible great darkenesse, euery one sought the passage of his owne doores.

18 For the elements were changed †in themselues by a kind of harmonie, like as in a Psaltery notes change the name of the tune, and yet are alwayes sounds, which may well be perceiued by the sight of the things that haue beene done.

† Gre. by themselues.

19 For earthly things were turned into watry, and the things that before swamme in the water, now went vpon the ground.

20 The fire had power in the water, forgetting his owne vertue : and the water forgat his owne quenching nature.

21 On the other side, the flames wasted not the flesh of the corruptible liuing things, though they walked therin, neither melted they the ycie kind of heauenly meate, that was of nature apt to melt.

22 For in all things, O Lord, thou didst magnifie thy people, and glorifie them, neither didst thou lightly regard them : but didst assist them in euery time and place.

¶ THE

¶ THE WISDOME OF

Iesus the sonne of Sirach,

Or Ecclesiasticus.

✠ A Prologue made by an vncertaine Authour.

Some referre this Pro-logue to A-thanasius, because it is found in his Synopsis.

‖ Or, colle-cted.

THis Iesus was the sonne of Sirach, and grand-childe to Iesus of the same name with him; This man therefore liued in the latter times, after the people had bene led away captiue, and called home againe, and almost after all the Prophets. Now his grandfather Iesus (as he himselfe witnesseth) was a man of great diligence and wisedome among the Hebrewes, who did not onely gather the graue and short Sentences of wise men, that had bene before him, but himselfe also vttered some of his owne, full of much vnderstanding and wisedome. When as therefore the first Iesus died, leauing this booke almost ‖ perfected, Sirach his sonne receiuing it after him, left it to his owne sonne Iesus, who hauing gotten it into his hands, compiled it all orderly into one Volume, and called it Wisdome, Intituling it, both by his owne name, his fathers name, and his grandfathers, alluring the hearer by the very name of Wisedome, to haue a greater loue to the studie of this Booke. It conteineth therefore wise Sayings, darke Sentences, and Parables, and certaine particular ancient godly stories of men that pleased God: Also his Prayer and Song. Moreouer, what benefits God had vouchsafed his people, and what plagues he had heaped vpon their enemies. This Iesus did imitate Solomon, and was no lesse famous for Wisedome, and learning, both being indeed a man of great learning, and so reputed also.

¶ *The Prologue of the Wisdome of Jesus the sonne of Sirach.*

‖ Or, of an other nation.

† Greeke, prophecies. ‖ Or, excel-lencie.

‖ Or, helpe of learning.

WHereas many and great things haue bene deliuered vnto vs by the Law and the Prophets, and by others that haue followed their steps, for the which things Israel ought to be commended for learning and Wisedome, and whereof not onely the Readers must needs become skilful themselues, but also they that desire to learne, be able to profit them which are ‖ without, both by speaking and writing: My grandfather Iesus, when he had much giuen himselfe to the reading of the Law, and the Prophets, and other Bookes of our fathers, and had gotten therein good iudgement, was drawen on also himselfe, to write something pertayning to learning and Wisedome, to the intent that those which are desirous to learne, and are addicted to these things, might profit much more in liuing according to the Law Wherefore, let me intreat you to reade it with fauour and attention, and to pardon Vs, wherein wee may seeme to come short of some words which we haue laboured to interprete. For the same things vttered in Hebrew, and translated into an other tongue, haue not the same force in them: and not onely these things, but the Law it selfe, and the † Prophets, and the rest of the Bookes, haue no small ‖ difference, when they are spoken in their owne language. For in the eight and thirtieth yeere comming into Egypt, when Euergetes was King, and continuing there some time, I found a ‖ Booke of no small learning, therefore I thought it most necessary for mee, to bestow some diligence and trauaile to interprete it: Vsing great watchfulnesse, and skill in that space, to bring the Booke to an end, and set it foorth for them also, which in a strange countrey are willing to learne, being prepared before in maners to liue after the Law

CHAP.

CHAP. I.

1 All wisedome is from God. 10 He giueth it to them that loue him. 12 The feare of God is full of many blessings. 28 To feare God without hypocrisie.

ALL * wisedome *commeth* from the Lord, and is with him for euer.

2 Who can number the sand of the sea, and the drops of raine, and the dayes of eternity?

3 Who can finde out the height of heauen, and the breadth of the earth, and the deepe, and wisedome?

4 Wisedome hath beene created before all things, and the vnderstanding of prudence from euerlasting.

5 The word of God most high, is the fountaine of wisdome, & her wayes are euerlasting commandements.

6 *To whom hath the root of wisdome beene reuealed? or who hath knowen her wise counsels?

7 [Vnto whom hath the knowledge of wisedome beene made manifest? and who hath vnderstood her great experience?]

8 There is one wise and greatly to bee feared; the Lord sitting vpon his Throne.

9 He created her, and saw her, and numbred her, and powred her out vpon all his workes.

10 Shee [is] with all flesh according to his gift, and hee hath giuen her to them that loue him.

11 The feare of the Lord is honour, and glory, and gladnesse, and a crowne of reioycing.

12 *The feare of the Lord maketh a merrie heart, and giueth ioy and gladnesse, and a long life.

13 Who so feareth the Lord, it shall goe well with him at the last, & he ||shall finde fauour in the day of his death.

14 To feare the Lord, is the beginning of wisedome: and it was created with the faithfull in the wombe.

15 Shee hath built an euerlasting foundation with men, and she shal continue *with their seede.

16 To feare the Lord, is fulnesse of wisedome, and filleth men with her fruits.

17 Shee filleth all their house with things desireable, and the garners with her increase.

18 The feare of the Lord is a crowne of wisedome, making peace and perfect health to flourish, both which are the gifts of God: and it enlargeth their reioycing that loue him.

19 Wisedome raineth downe skill and knowledge of vnderstanding, and exalteth them to honour that holde her fast.

20 The root of wisedome is to feare the Lord, and the branches thereof are long life.

21 The feare of the Lord driueth away sinnes: and where it is present, it turneth away wrath.

22 A furious man cannot ||be iustified, for the sway of his fury shalbe his destruction.

23 A patient man will beare for a time, and afterward ioy shall spring vp vnto him.

24 He wil hide his words for a time, and the lippes of many shall declare his wisedome.

25 The parables of knowledge are in the treasures of wisedome: but godlines is an abomination to a sinner.

26 If thou desire wisedome, keepe the commaundements, and the Lord shall giue her vnto thee.

27 For the feare of the Lord is wisdome, and instruction: and faith and meekenesse are his delight.

28 || Distrust not the feare of the Lord when thou art poore: and come not vnto him with a double heart.

29 Be not an hypocrite in the sight of men, and take good heede what thou speakest.

30 Exalt not thy selfe, lest thou fall, and bring dishonor vpon thy soule, and so God discouer thy secrets, and cast thee downe in the midst of the congregation, because thou camest not in trueth, to the feare of the Lord: but thy heart is full of deceit.

CHAP. II.

1 Gods seruants must looke for trouble, 7 and be patient, and trust in him. 12 For woe to them that doe not so. 15 But they that feare the Lord, will doe so.

MY sonne, if *thou come to serue the Lorde, prepare thy soule for temptation.

2 Set thy heart aright, and

Margin notes

* 1. Kings 3. 9.

* Rom. 11. 34.

* Prou. 1. 7. psal. 110. 10

|| Or, shalbe blessed.

* 2. Chron. 20. 21.

|| Or, escape punishment.

|| Or, be not disobedient to.

* Mat. 4. 11. 2. tim. 3. 12. 1. pet. 4. 12.

| Or, haste not.

and constantly endure, and ||make not haste in time of trouble.

3 Cleaue vnto him, and depart not away, that thou mayest be increased at thy last end.

4 Whatsoeuer is brought vpon thee, take cheerefully, and bee patient when thou art changed to a lowe estate.

* Wisd. 3. 6 pro. 17. 3.

5 * For gold is tried in the fire, and acceptable men in the furnace of aduersitie.

6 Beleeue in him, and he will helpe thee, order thy way aright, and trust in him.

7 Ye that feare the Lord, waite for his mercie, and goe not aside, lest ye fall.

8 Yee that feare the Lord, beleeue him, and your reward shall not faile.

9 Ye that feare the Lord, hope for good, and for euerlasting ioy and mercy.

10 Looke at the generations of old, and see, did euer any trust in the Lord, and was confounded? or did any abide in his feare, & was forsaken? or whom did hee euer despise, that called vpon him?

* Psal. 37. 25

11 For the * Lord is full of compassion, and mercie, long suffering, and very pitifull, and forgiueth sinnes, and saueth in time of affliction.

12 Woe be to fearefull hearts, and faint hands, and the sinner that goeth two wayes.

13 Woe vnto him that is faint hearted, for he beleeueth not, therefore shall he not be defended.

14 Woe vnto you that haue lost patience: and what will ye doe when the Lord shall visite you?

* Ioh. 14. 20

15 They * that feare the Lord, will not disobey his word, and they that loue him, will keepe his wayes.

16 They that feare the Lord, will seeke that which is well pleasing vnto him, and they that loue him, shall bee filled with the Law.

17 They that feare the Lord, will prepare their hearts, and humble their soules in his sight:

18 *Saying*, We will fal into the hands of the Lord, and not into the hands of men: for as his maiestie is, so is his mercie.

CHAP. III.

3 Children must honour, and helpe both their parents. 21 We may not desire to knowe all things. 26 The incorrigible must needes perish. 30 Almes are rewarded.

 Eare mee your father, O children, and doe thereafter, that ye may be safe.

* Exo. 20. deut. 5. 10.

2 For the Lord hath giuen *the father honour ouer the children, and hath confirmed the ||authoritie of the mother ouer the sonnes.

| Or, iudgement.

3 Who so honoureth his father, maketh an atonement for his sinnes.

4 And he that honoureth his mother, is as one that layeth vp treasure.

5 Who so honoureth his father, shal haue ioy of *his owne* children, and when he maketh his prayer, hee shall bee heard.

6 He that honoureth his father, shal haue a long life, and he that is obedient vnto the Lord, shall bee a comfort to his mother.

7 He that feareth the Lord, will honour his father, and will doe seruice vnto his parents, as to his masters.

8 * Honour thy father and mother, both in word and deed, that a blessing may come vpon thee from them.

* Exod. 20. 12. deut. 5. 10.

9 For the *blessing of the father establisheth the houses of children, but the curse of the mother rooteth out foundations.

* Gene. 27. 27. deu. 33. 1.

10 Glory not in the dishonour of thy father, for thy fathers dishonour is no glory vnto thee.

11 For the glory of a man, is from the honour of his father, and a mother in dishonour, is a reproch to the children.

12 My sonne, helpe thy father in his age, and grieue him not as long as hee liueth.

13 And if his vnderstanding faile, haue patience with him, and despise him not, when thou art ||in thy ful strength.

| Or, in all thine habilitie.

14 For the relieuing of thy father shall not be forgotten: and in stead of sinnes it shall be added to build thee vp.

15 In the day of thine affliction it shall be remembred, thy sinnes also shal melt away, as the yce in ŷ faire warme weather.

16 He that forsaketh his father, is as a blasphemer, and he that angreth his mother, is cursed of God.

17 My sonne, goe on with thy businesse in meekenesse, so shalt thou be beloued of him that is approued.

18 *The greater thou art, the more humble thy selfe, and thou shalt find fauour before the Lord.

* Phil. 2. 3

19 Many are in high place and of renowne:

* Psal. 25.
9, 14.

nowne : but *mysteries are reueiled vnto the meeke.

20 For the power of the Lord is great, and hee is honoured of the lowly.

* Prou. 25.
27. rom. 12.
3.

21 * Seeke not out the things that are too hard for thee, neither search the things that are aboue thy strength.

22 But what is commaunded thee, thinke thereupon with reuerence, for it is not needfull for thee, to see *with thine eyes*, the things that are in secret.

23 Be not curious in vnnecessarie matters : for moe things are shewed vnto thee, then men vnderstand.

24 For many are deceiued by their owne vaine opinion, and an euill suspition hath ouerthrowen their iudgement.

25 Without eyes thou shalt want light : professe not the knowledge therfore that thou hast not.

26 A stubborne heart shall fare euill at the last, and he that loueth danger shall perish therein.

27 An obstinate heart shall be laden with sorrowes, and the wicked man shall heape sinne vpon sinne.

‖ Or, the
proud man is
not healed
by his pu-
nishment.

28 ‖ In the punishment of the proud there is no remedie : for the plant of wickednesse hath taken roote in him.

29 The heart of the prudent will vnderstand a parable, and an attentiue eare is the desire of a wise man.

* Psal. 40. 2.
dan. 4. 24.
matth. 5. 7.

30 * Water will quench a flaming fire, and almes maketh an attonement for sinnes.

31 And hee that requiteth good turnes, is mindfull of that which may come heereafter : and when he falleth he shall find a stay.

CHAP. III.

1 We may not despise the poore or fatherlesse, 11 but seeke for Wisedome, 20 and not be ashamed of some things, nor gainsay the trueth, 30 nor be as lyons in our houses.

MY sonne, defraude not the poore of his liuing, and make not the needy eies to waite long.

2 Make not an hungry soule sorrowfull, neither prouoke a man in his distresse.

3 Adde not more trouble to an heart that is vexed, and deferre not to giue to him that is in neede.

4 Reiect not the supplication of the afflicted, neither turne away thy face from a poore man.

5 Turne not away thine eye from ‖ the needy, and giue him none occasion to curse thee :

‖ Or, him that
asketh.

6 For if he curse thee in the bitternesse of his soule, his prayer shall be heard of him that made him.

7 Get thy selfe the loue of the congregation, and bow thy head to a great man.

8 Let it not grieue thee to bowe downe thine eare to the poore, and giue him a friendly answere with meekenesse.

9 Deliuer him that suffreth wrong, from the hand of the oppressour, and be not faint hearted when thou sittest in iudgement.

10 Be as a father vnto the fatherlesse, and in stead of a husband vnto their mother, so shalt thou be as the sonne of the most high, and he shall loue thee more then thy mother doeth.

11 Wisedome exalteth her children, and layeth hold of them that seeke her.

12 He that loueth her, loueth life, and they that seeke to her early, shall be filled with ioy.

13 He that holdeth her fast shall inherit glory, and wheresoeuer she entreth, the Lord will blesse.

14 They that serue her shall minister ‖ to the Holy one, and them that loue her, the Lord doth loue.

‖ Or, in the
sanctuary.

15 Who so giueth eare vnto her, shall iudge the nations, and he that attendeth vnto her, shall dwell securely.

16 If a man commit himselfe vnto her, he shall inherite her, and his generation shall hold her in possession.

17 For at the first she will walke with him by crooked wayes, and bring feare and dread vpon him, and torment him with her discipline, vntill she may trust his soule, and try him by her Lawes.

18 Then wil she returne the straight way vnto him, and comfort him, and shew him her secrets.

19 But if he goe wrong, she will forsake him, and giue him ouer to his owne ruine.

20 Obserue the opportunitie, and beware of euill, and be not ashamed when it concerneth thy soule.

21 For *there* is a shame that bringeth sinne, and there is a shame which is glorie and grace.

22 Accept

22 Accept no person against thy soule, and let not the reuerence of any man cause thee to fall:

† *Greeke, in time of sa- uing.*

23 And refraine not to speake, †*when* there is *occasion to doe good,* and hide not thy wisedome in her beautie

24 For by speach wisedome shall be knowen, and learning by the word of the tongue

25 In no wise speake against the trueth, but be abashed of the errour of thine ignorance.

‖ *Or, and striue not a- gainst the streame.*

26 Bee not ashamed to confesse thy sinnes, ‖and force not the course of the riuer.

27 Make not thy selfe an vnderling to a foolish man, neither accept the person of the mighty.

28 Striue for the trueth vnto death, and the Lord shall fight for thee.

29 Be not hastie in thy tongue, and in thy deeds slacke and remisse.

30 Bee not as a Lion in thy house, nor franticke among thy seruants.

‖ *Or, giue.*

31 Let not thine hand bee stretched out to receiue, and shut when thou shouldest ‖repay.

CHAP. V.

1 Wee must not presume of our wealth and strength, 6 Nor of the mercie of God to sinne. 9 We must not be double tongued, 12 Nor answere without knowledge.

* Luke 12. 15.

SEt not thy heart vpon thy goods, and say not, *I haue ynough for my life.

2 Folow not thine owne minde, and thy strength, to walke in the wayes of thy heart:

3 And say not, Who shall controll mee for my workes? for the Lord will surely reuenge thy pride.

4 Say not, I haue sinned, and what harme hath happened vnto mee? for the Lord is long-suffering, he wil in no wise let thee goe.

5 Concerning propitiation, bee not without feare to adde sinne vnto sinne.

* Ecclus. 21. 1.

6 And say not, His *mercy is great, hee will be pacified for the multitude of my sinnes: for mercy and wrath come from him, and his indignation resteth vpon sinners.

* Chap. 16. 13.

7 *Make no tarying to turne to the Lord, and put not off from day to day: for suddenly shal the wrath of the Lord come foorth, and in thy securitie thou shalt be destroyed, and perish in the day of vengeance.

8 *Set not thy heart vpon goods vniustly gotten: for they shall not profit thee in the day of calamitie

* Pro. 10. 2. and 11. 4. ezek. 7. 19.

9 Winnow not with euery winde, and goe not into euery way: for so doth the sinner that hath a double tongue.

10 Be stedfast in thy vnderstanding, and let thy word be the same.

11 *Be swift to heare, and let thy life be sincere, & with patience giue answere.

* Iam. 1. 19

12 If thou hast vnderstanding, answer thy neighbour, if not, lay thy hand vpon thy mouth.

13 Honour and shame is in talke; and the tongue of man is his fall

14 Be not called a whisperer, and lye not in wait with thy tongue : for a foule shame is vpon the thiefe, and an euill condemnation vpon the double tongue.

15 Be not ignorant of any thing, in a great matter or a small.

CHAP. VI.

2 Doe not extoll thy owne conceit, 7 But make choise of a friend. 18 Seeke wisedome betimes: 20 It is grieuous to some, 28 yet the fruits thereof are pleasant. 35 Be ready to heare wise men.

**I**N stead of a friend, become not an enemie ; for [thereby] thou shalt inherite an ill name, shame, and reproch: euen so shall a sinner that hath a double tongue.

2 Extoll not thy selfe in the counsell of thine owne heart, that thy soule bee not torne in pieces as a bull [straying alone.]

3 Thou shalt eat vp thy leaues, and loose thy fruit, and leaue thy selfe as a dry tree.

4 A wicked soule shall destroy him that hath it, and shall make him to be laughed to scorne of his enemies.

† *Greeke, a sweet throat*

5 †Sweet language will multiply friends : and a faire speaking tongue will increase kinde greetings.

6 Be in peace with many : neuerthelesse haue but one counseller of a thousand.

‖ *Or, get him in the time of trouble.*

7 If thou wouldst get a friend, ‖proue him first, and be not hasty to credit him.

8 For some man is a friend for his owne occasion, and will not abide in the day of thy trouble.

9 And there is a friend, who being turned to enmitie, and strife, will discouer thy reproch.

10 Againe

* Cha. 37. 5.

10 *Againe some friend is a companion at the table, and will not continue in the day of thy affliction.

11 But in thy prosperitie hee will be as thy selfe, and will be bould ouer thy seruants.

12 If thou be brought low, he will be against thee, and will hide himselfe from thy face.

13 Separate thy selfe from thine enemies, and take heed of thy friends.

14 A faithfull friend is a strong defence : and hee that hath found such an one, hath found a treasure.

15 Nothing doeth counteruaile a faithful friend, and his excellencie is vnualuable.

16 A faithfull friend is the medicine of life, and they that feare the Lord shal finde him.

17 Who so feareth the Lord shall direct his friendship aright, for as he is, so shall his neighbour be also.

18 My sonne, gather instruction from thy youth vp : so shalt thou finde wisedome till thine old age.

19 Come vnto her as one that ploweth, and soweth, and wait for her good fruits, for thou shalt not toile much in labouring about her, but thou shalt eat of her fruits right soone.

20 She is very vnpleasant to the vnlearned : he that is without ||vnderstanding, will not remaine with her. *||Or, heart.*

21 She wil lye vpon him as a *mightie stone of triall, and hee will cast her from him ere it be long. *Zech. 12. 4*

22 For wisedome is according to her name, and she is not manifest vnto many.

23 Giue eare, my sonne, receiue my aduice, and refuse not my counsell,

24 And put thy feet into her fetters, and thy necke into her ||chaine. *||Or, coller.*

25 Bow *downe thy shoulder, and beare her, and be not grieued with her bonds. *Mat. 11. 29.*

26 Come vnto her with thy whole heart, and keepe her wayes with all thy power.

27 Search and seeke, and shee shall bee made knowen vnto thee, and when thou hast got hold of her, let her not goe.

28 For at the last thou shalt finde her rest, and that shalbe turned to thy ioy.

29 Then shall her fetters be a strong defence for thee, and her chaines a robe of glory

30 For there is a golden ornament vpon her, and her bandes are ||purple lace. *Or, a ribband of bleu silke, Numb. 15. 38.*

31 Thou shalt put her on as a robe of honour : and shalt put her about thee as a crowne of ioy.

32 My sonne, if thou wilt, thou shalt bee taught : and if thou wilt apply thy minde, thou shalt be prudent.

33 If thou loue to heare, thou shalt receiue vnderstanding : and if thou bow thine eare, thou shalt be wise.

34 Stand in the multitude of the *elders, and cleaue vnto him that is wise. *Ecclus. 8.9*

35 Be willing to heare euery godly discourse, and let not the parables of vnderstanding escape thee.

36 And if thou seest a man of vnderstanding, get thee betimes vnto him, and let thy foote weare the steps of his doore.

37 Let thy minde be vpon the ordinances of the Lord, & *meditate continually in his commandements : he shal establish thine heart, and giue thee wisedome at thine owne desire. *Psal. 1. 2.*

CHAP. VII.

1 Wee are exhorted from sinne, 4 from ambition, 8 presumption, 10 and fainting in prayer : 12 from lying and backebiting, 18 and how to esteeme a friend : 19 A good wife : 20 a seruant : 22 our cattell : 23 our children and parents : 31 The Lord and his Priests : 32 the poore and those that mourne.

Oe no euill, so shall no harme come vnto thee.

2 Depart from the vniust, and iniquitie shall turne away from thee.

3 My sonne, sow not vpon the furrowes of vnrighteousnesse, and thou shalt not reape them seuen solde.

4 Seeke not of the Lord preheminence, neither of the King the seate of honour.

5 *Iustifie not thy selfe before the Lord, and boast not of thy wisedome before the king. *Psal. 142. 2. eccles. 7. 17. Iob 9. 20. luke 18. 11.*

6 Seeke not to be iudge, being not able to take away iniquitie, lest at any time thou feare the person of the mightie, and lay a stumbling blocke in the way of thy vprightnesse.

7 Offend not against the multitude of a city, and then thou shalt not cast thy selfe downe among the people.

8 Bind not one sinne vpon another, for

for in one thou shalt not be vnpunished.

9 Say not, God wil looke vpon the multitude of my oblations, and when I offer to the most High God, he will accept it.

10 Be not faint hearted when thou makest thy prayer, and neglect not to giue almes.

11 Laugh no man to scorne in the bitternesse of his soule : for there is one which humbleth and exalteth.

† *Gre. plough not.*

12 †Deuise not a lie against thy brother : neither doe the like to thy friend.

13 Vse not to make any maner of lie: for the custome thereof is not good.

* *Mat. 6.5, 7*
‖ *Or; vaine repetition.*

14 Vse not many words in a multitude of Elders, *and *make not* ‖*much babling* when thou prayest.

15 Hate not laborious worke, neither husbandrie, which the most High hath †ordeined.

† *Gre. created.*

16 Number not thy selfe among the multitude of sinners, but remember that wrath will not tary long.

17 Humble thy soule greatly : for the vengeance of the vngodly is fire and wormes.

18 Change not a friend for any good by no meanes: neither a faithfull brother for the gold of Ophir.

19 Forgoe not a wise and good woman : for her grace is aboue gold.

* *Leuit. 19. 15.*

20 * Whereas thy seruant worketh truely, entreate him not euill, nor the hireling that bestoweth himselfe wholly for thee.

21 Let thy soule loue a good seruant, and defraud him not of liberty.

* *Deu. 25. 4*

22 *Hast thou cattell? haue an eye to them, and if they be for thy profit, keepe them with thee.

23 Hast thou children? instruct them, and bow downe their necke from their youth.

24 Hast thou daughters? haue care of their body, and shewe not thy selfe cheerefull toward them.

25 Marrie thy daughter, and so shalt thou haue performed a weightie matter : but giue her to a man of vnderstanding.

26 Hast thou a wife after thy minde? forsake her not, but giue not thy selfe ouer to a ‖light woman.

‖ *Or, hatefull*

27 Honour thy father with thy whole heart, and forget not the sorrowes of thy mother.

28 Remember that thou wast begot of them, and how canst thou recom-

pense them the things that they haue done for thee?

29 Feare the Lord with all thy soule, and reuerence his priests.

30 Loue him that made thee with all thy strength, and forsake not his ministers.

31 Feare the Lord, and honour the priest : and giue him his portion, as it is commanded thee, the first fruits, and the trespasse offering, & the gift of the shoulders, and the sacrifice of sanctification, and the first fruits of the holy things.

32 * And stretch thine hand vnto the poore, that thy ‖*blessing* may be perfected

* *Deut. 15. 10.*
‖ *Or, thy liberality.*

33 A gift hath grace in the sight of euery man liuing, and for the dead deteine it not.

34 Faile not to bee with them that weepe, and mourne with them that mourne.

35 Be not slow to visit the sicke : for that shall make thee to be beloued.

36 Whatsoeuer thou takest in hand, remember the end, and thou shalt neuer doe amisse.

CHAP. VIII.

1 Whom we may not striue with, 8 nor despise, 10 nor prouoke, 15 nor haue to doe with.

Striue not with a mighty man, lest thou fall into his hands.

2 Bee not at variance with a rich man, lest he ouerweigh thee: for gold *hath destroyed many, and peruerted the hearts of kings.

* *Mat. 5. 25. chap. 31. 6*
‖ *Or, of an euill tongue.*

3 Striue not with a man that is ‖full of tongue, and heape not wood vpon his fire.

4 Iest not with a rude man, lest thy ancestours be disgraced.

5 Reproch not a man that turneth from sinne, but remember that we are all worthy *of punishment.

6 *Dishonour not a man in his old age : for euen some of vs waxe old.

* *Gal. 6. 2. 1. cor. 2. 6. * Leuit. 19. 32.*

7 Reioice not ouer thy greatest enemie being dead, but remember that we die all.

8 *Despise not the discourse* of the wise, but acquaint thy selfe with their prouerbs ; for of them thou shalt learne instruction, & how to serue great men with ease.

9 Misse not the discourse of the Elders : for they also learned of their fathers, and of them thou shalt learne vnderstanding, and to giue answere as need requireth.

10 Kindle

10 Kindle not the coales of a sinner, lest thou be burnt with the flame of his fire.

11 Rise not vp (in anger) at the presence of an iniurious person, least he lie in waite to ||entrap thee in thy words.

Or, for thy mouth.

12 Lend not vnto him that is mightier then thy selfe; for if thou lendest him, count it but lost.

13 Be not surety aboue thy power : for if thou be surety, take care to pay it.

14 Goe not to law with a iudge, for they will iudge for him according to his ||honour.

Or, opinion.
* Gene. 4. 8.

15 *Trauaile not by the way with a bold fellow, least he become grieuous vnto thee : for he will doe according to his owne will, and thou shalt perish with him through his folly.

* Prou. 22. 24.

16 *Striue not with an angry man, and goe not with him into a solitary place : for blood is as nothing in his sight, and where there is no helpe, he will ouerthrow thee.

17 Consult not with a foole ; for he cannot keepe counsell.

18 Doe no secret thing before a stranger, for thou knowest not what he will bring forth.

19 Open not thine heart to euery man, least he requite thee with a shrewd turne.

CHAP. IX.

1 We are aduised how to vse our wiues. 3 What women to auoide. 10 And not to change an old friend. 13 Not to be familiar with men in authority, 14 But to knowe our neighbours, 15 And to conuerse with wise men.

BE not iealous ouer the wife of thy bosome, and teach her not an euil lesson against thy selfe.

2 Giue not thy soule vnto a woman, to set her foot vpon thy substance.

3 Meete not with an harlot, least thou fall into her snares.

4 Vse not much the companie of a woman that ||is a singer, least thou be taken with her attempts.

Or, playeth vpon instruments.

5 Gaze not on a maide, that thou fall not by those things, that are pretious in her.

6 Giue not thy soule vnto harlots, that thou loose not thine inheritance.

7 Looke not round about thee, in the streets of the citie, neither wander thou in the solitary places thereof.

8 *Turne away thine eye from a beautifull woman, and looke not vpon anothers beautie : for many haue beene deceiued by the beautie of a woman, for heerewith loue is kindled as a fire.

* Gen. 34. 22. 2. sam. 11. 2. iudg. 10. 17.

9 Sit not at all with another mans wife, nor sit downe with her in thine armes, and spend not thy money with her at the wine, least thine heart incline vnto her, and so thorough *thy desire* thou fall into destruction.

10 Forsake not an old friend, for the new is not comparable to him : a new friend is as new wine : when it is old, thou shalt drinke it with pleasure.

11 Enuy not the glory of a sinner : for thou knowest not what shall be his end.

12 Delight not in the thing that the vngodly haue pleasure in, but remember they shall not goe vnpunished vnto their graue.

13 Keepe thee farre from the man that hath power to kill, so shalt thou not doubt the feare of death : and if thou come vnto him, make no fault, least he take away thy life presently : remember that thou goest in the midst of snares, and that thou walkest vpon the battlements of the citie.

14 As neere as thou canst, ghesse at thy neighbour, and consult with the wise.

15 Let thy talke be with the wise, and all thy communication in the law of the most High.

16 And let iust men eate and drinke with thee, and let thy glorying be in the feare of the Lord.

17 For the hand of the artificer, the worke shall be commended : and the wise ruler of the people, for his speech.

18 A man of an ill tongue is dangerous in his citie, and he that is rash in his talke shall be hated.

CHAP. X.

1 The commodities of a wise ruler. 4 God setteth him vp. 7 The inconueniences of pride, iniustice, and couetousnesse. 14 What God hath done to the proud. 19 Who shall be honored, 29 And who not.

A Wise iudge will instruct his people, & the gouernement of a prudent man is well ordered.

2 *As the iudge of the people is himselfe, so are his officers, and what maner of man the ruler of the

* Prou. 29. 12.

the citie is, such are all they that dwell therein.

3 An vnwise king destroyeth his people, but through the prudence of them which are in authoritie, the citie shalbe inhabited.

4 The power of the earth is in the hand of the Lord, and in due time hee will set ouer it one that is profitable.

5 In the hand of God is the prosperitie of man : and vpon the ||person of the scribe shall he lay his honour.

6 Beare not hatred to thy neighbour for *euery wrong, and do nothing at all by iniurious practises.

7 Pride is hatefull before God, and man : and by both doeth one commit iniquitie.

8 Because of vnrighteous dealings, iniuries, and riches got by deceit, the kingdome is translated from one people to another.

9 Why is earth and ashes proude? There is not a more wicked thing, then a couetous man : for such an one setteth his owne soule to sale, because while he liueth, he casteth away his bowels.

10 The Phisition cutteth off a long disease, and he that is to day a King, to morrow shall die.

11 For when a man is dead, hee shall inherite creeping things, beastes and wormes.

12 The beginning of pride is, when one departeth from God, and his heart is turned away from his maker.

13 For pride is the beginning of sinne, and hee that hath it, shall powre out abomination : and therefore the Lord brought vpon them strange calamities, and ouerthrew them vtterly.

14 The Lord hath cast downe the thrones of proud Princes, and set vp the meeke in their stead.

15 The Lord hath plucked vp the rootes of the proud nations : and planted the lowly in their place.

16 The Lord ouerthrew countreys of the heathen : and destroyed them to the foundations of the earth.

17 He tooke some of them away, and destroyed them, and hath made their memoriall to cease from the earth.

18 Pride was not made for men, nor furious anger for them that are borne of a woman.

19 They that feare the Lord are a sure seed, and they that loue him, an honourable plant : they that regard not the Law, are a dishonourable seed, they that transgresse the commandements, are a ||deceiuable seed.

20 Among brethren he that is chiefe is honourable, so are they that feare the Lord in his eyes.

21 The feare of the Lord goeth before ||the obtayning of authoritie : but roughnesse and pride, is the loosing thereof.

22 Whether hee bee rich, noble, or poore, their glorie is the feare of the Lord.

23 It is not meet to despise the poore man that hath vnderstanding, neither is it conuenient to magnifie a sinnefull man.

24 Great men, and Iudges, and Potentates shall bee honoured, yet is there none of them greater then he that feareth the Lord.

25 Vnto the seruant that is wise, shall they that are free doe seruice : and hee that hath knowledge, *will not grudge when he is reformed.

26 Be not otherwise in doing thy busines, and boast not thy selfe in the time of thy distresse.

27 Better is he that laboureth and aboundeth in all things, then hee that boasteth himselfe, and wanteth *bread.

28 My sonne, glorifie thy soule in meekenesse, and giue it honour according to the dignitie thereof.

29 Who wil iustifie him that sinneth against his owne soule? and who will honour him that dishonoureth his owne life?

30 The poore man is honoured for his skill, and the rich man is honoured for his riches.

31 Hee that is honoured in pouertie, how much more in riches? And he that is dishonourable in riches, how much more in pouertie?

CHAP. XI.

4 Wee may not vaunt or set foorth our selues, 8 Nor answere rashly, 10 Nor meddle with many matters. 14 Wealth and all things else, are from God. 14 Bragge not of thy wealth, 29 Nor bring euery man into thy house.

Isedome lifteth vp the head ||of him that is of low degree, and *maketh him to sit among great men.

2 Commend not a man for

Margin notes (left column)
||Or, face.

*Leuit. 19. 17.

Margin notes (right column)
||Or, vnstable generation.

||Or, princpalitie.

*Pro. 17. 2. Sam. 12 13.

*Pro. 12.

||Or, of the lowly.
*Gen. 40. 40. dan. 6.

for his beautie, neither abhorre a man for his outward appearance

3 The Bee is little among such as flie, but her fruite is the chiefe of sweete things.

* Act. 12. 21

4 *Boast not of thy cloathing and raiment, and exalt not thy selfe in the day of honour : for the workes of the Lord are wonderfull, and his workes among men are hidden.

†Gr.tyrants.

5 Many †kings haue sit downe vpon the ground, and one that was neuer thought of, hath worne the crowne.

* 1. Kin. 15. 28. hest. 6. 10.

6 *Many mightie men haue beene greatly disgraced : and the honourable deliuered into other mens hands.

* Deut. 12. 24.

7 *Blame not before thou hast examined the trueth : vnderstand first, and then rebuke.

* Pro. 8. 13.

8 *Answere not, before thou hast heard the cause : neither interrupt men in the midst of their talke.

‖ Or, in the iudgement of sinners.

9 Striue not in a matter that concerneth thee not : and sit not ‖in iudgement with sinners.

10 My sonne, meddle not with many matters : for if thou meddle much, thou shalt not be innocent : and if thou follow after, thou shalt not obtaine, neither shalt thou ‖escape by flying.

‖ Or, escape hurt.
* Mat. 19. 12. 1. tim. 6. 9. prou. 10. 13.

11 *There is one that laboureth and taketh paines, and maketh haste, and is so much the more behinde.

* Iob 1. 12. ezek. 28. 4.

12 Againe, there is another that is slow, and hath neede of helpe, wanting abilitie, and full of pouertie, *yet the eye of the Lord looked vpon him for good, and set him vp from his low estate,

13 And lifted vp his head from miserie, so that many that saw it, marueiled at him.

14 Prosperitie and aduersitie, life and death, pouerty and riches, come of the Lord.

15 Wisedome, knowledge, and vnderstanding of the Lawe, are of the Lord : loue, & the way of good workes, are from him.

16 Errour and darkenesse had their beginning together with sinners : and euill shall waxe old with them that glory therein.

17 The gift of the Lord remaineth with the godly, and his fauour bringeth prosperitie for euer.

18 There is that waxeth rich by his warinesse, and pinching, and this is the portion of his reward :

* Luke 12. 19.

19 Whereas he sayth, *I haue found rest, and now will eate continually of my goods, and yet hee knoweth not what time shall ‖come vpon him, and that hee must leaue those things to others, and die.

‖ Or, passe.

20 Be *stedfast in thy couenant, and be conuersant therein, and waxe olde in thy worke

* Matt. 10. 22.

21 Marueile not at the workes of sinners, but trust in the Lord, and abide in thy labour : for it is an easie thing in the sight of the Lord, on the sudden to make a poore man rich.

22 The blessing of the Lord is ‖in the reward of the godly, and suddenly he maketh his blessing to flourish.

‖ Or, for a reward.

23 Say not, *What profit is there of my seruice? and what good things shal I haue hereafter?

* Mal. 3. 14.

24 Againe, say not, I haue enough, and possesse many things; and what euill can come to me hereafter?

25 In the day of prosperitie, there is a forgetfulnesse of affliction : and in the day of affliction, there is no remembrance of prosperitie.

26 For it is an easie thing vnto the Lord in the day of death, to reward a man according to his wayes.

27 The affliction of an houre, maketh a man forget pleasure : and in his end, his deeds shalbe discouered.

28 Iudge none blessed before his death : for a man shall bee knowen in his children.

29 Bring not euery man into thine house, for the deceitfull man hath many traines.

30 Like as a Partrich taken [and kept] in a cage, so is the heart of the proud; aud like as a spie, watcheth hee for thy fall.

31 For hee lieth in wait, and turneth good into euill, and in things worthy praise, will lay blame vpon thee.

32 Of a sparke of fire, a heape of coales is kindled : and a sinnefull man layeth waite for blood.

33 Take heed of a mischieuous man, (for hee worketh wickednesse) lest hee bring vpon thee a perpetuall blot.

34 Receiue a stranger into thine house, and hee will disturbe thee, and turne thee out of thine owne.

CHAP. XII.

2 Be not liberall to the vngodly. 10 Trust not thine enemie, nor the wicked.

When|

When thou wilt doe good, know to whō thou doest it, so shalt thou be thanked for thy benefites.

2 Do good to the godly man, and thou shalt find a recompence, and if not from him, yet from the most High.

3 There can no good come to him that is alwayes occupied in euill: nor to him that giueth no almes.

4 Giue to the godly man, and helpe not a sinner.

5 Doe well vnto him that is lowly, but giue not to the vngodly: hold backe thy bread, and giue it not vnto him, lest he ouermaster thee thereby. For [else] thou shalt receiue twice as much euill, for all the good thou shalt haue done vnto him.

6 For the most High hateth sinners, and will repay vengeance vnto the vngodly, and keepeth them against the mightie day of their punishment.

7 Giue vnto the good, and helpe not the sinner.

8 A friend cannot be knowen in prosperitie, and an enemy cannot be hidden in aduersitie.

9 In the prosperitie of a man, enemies will be grieued, but in his aduersitie, euen a friend will depart.

10 Neuer trust thine enemie: for like as ||yron rusteth, so is his wickednesse. | Or, brasse.

11 Though he humble himselfe, and goe crouching, yet take good heed, and beware of him, and thou shalt bee vnto him, as if thou hadst wiped a looking glasse, and thou shalt knowe that his rust hath not beene altogether wiped away.

12 Set him not by thee, lest when he hath ouerthrowen thee, he stand vp in thy place, neither let him sit at thy right hand, lest he seeke to take thy seat, and thou at the last remember my wordes, and be pricked therewith.

13 Who will pitie a charmer that is bitten with a serpent, or any such as come nigh wilde beasts?

14 So one that goeth to a sinner, and is ||defiled with him in his sinnes, who will pitie? | Or, mingled.

15 For a while hee will abide with thee, but if thou begin to fall, he wil not tarie.

16 An enemie speaketh sweetly with *his lippes, but in his heart he imagineth how to throw thee into a pit: hee | Ier. 41. 6. will weepe with his eyes, but if he find opportunitie, hee will not be satisfied with blood.

17 If aduersitie come vpon thee, thou shalt find him there first, & though he pretend to helpe thee, yet shal he||vndermine thee. | Or, supplant.

18 He will shake his head and clap his handes, and whisper much, and change his countenance.

CHAP. XIII.

1 Keepe not companie with the proude, or a mightier then thy selfe. 15 Like will to like. 21 The difference betweene the rich and the poore. 25 A mans heart will change his countenance.

He that toucheth pitch, shal be defiled therewith, and *hee that hath fellowship with a proude man, shall be like vnto him. | * Deu. 7. 2

2 Burthen not thy selfe aboue thy power, while thou liuest, and haue no fellowship with one that is mightier, and richer then thy selfe. For how agree the kettle and the earthen pot together? †for if the one be smitten against the other, it shall be broken. | † Gre. this shal smite against it, and be broken.

3 The rich man hath done wrong, and yet he threatneth withall: the poore is wronged, and he must intreat also.

4 If thou be for his profit, he will vse thee: but if thou haue nothing, he will forsake thee.

5 If thou haue any thing, he will liue with thee, yea he will make thee bare, and will not be sorie for it.

6 If he haue need of thee, hee will deceiue thee, and smile vpon thee, and put thee in hope, he will speake thee faire, and say, What wantest thou?

7 And hee will shame thee by his meates, vntill he haue drawen thee drie twice or thrice, and at the last hee will laugh thee to scorne: afterward when he seeth thee, he will forsake thee, and shake his head at thee.

8 Beware that thou bee not deceiued, and brought downe ||in thy iolitie. | Or, by thy simplicitie

9 If thou be inuited of a mighty man, withdraw thy selfe, and so much the more will he inuite thee.

10 Presse thou not vpon him, lest thou be put backe, stand not farre off, lest thou be forgotten.

11 ||Affect not to be made equall vnto him in talke, ||and beleeue not his many words: for with much communication will | | Or, forbeare not. | Or, but.

will he tempt thee, and smiling vpon thee will get out thy secrets.

12 But cruelly he will lay vp thy words, and will not spare to doe thee hurt, and to put thee in prison.

13 Obserue and take good heed, for thou walkest in peril of thy ouerthrowing : when thou hearest these things, awake in thy sleepe.

14 Loue the Lord all thy life, and call vpon him for thy saluation.

15 Euery beast loueth his like, and euery man loueth his neighbour.

16 All flesh consorteth according to kind, and a man will cleaue to his like :

17 What fellowship hath the wolfe with the lambe? so the sinner with the godly.

18 What agreement is there betweene the Hyena and a dogge? and what peace betweene the rich and the poore?

19 As the wilde asse is the lyons pray in the wildernesse : so the rich eate vp the poore.

20 As the proud hate humilitie : so doth the rich abhorre the poore.

21 A rich man beginning to fall, is held vp of his friends : but a poore man being downe, is thrust also away by his friends.

22 When a rich man is fallen, he hath many helpers : he speaketh things not to be spoken, and yet men iustifie him : the poore man slipt, and yet they rebuked him too : he spake wisely, and could haue no place.

23 When a rich man speaketh, euery man holdeth his tongue, and looke what hee sayeth, they extoll it to the clouds : but if the poore man speake, they say, What fellow is this? and if he stumble, they will helpe to ouerthrowe him.

24 Riches are good vnto him that hath no sinne, and pouerty is euill in the mouth of the vngodly.

25 The heart of a man changeth his countenance, whether it be for good or euill : and a merry heart maketh a cheerefull countenance.

26 A cheerefull countenance is a token of a heart that is in prosperity, and the finding out of parables, is a wearisome labour of the minde.

CHAP. XIIII.

1 A good conscience maketh men happie.
5 The niggard doth good to none. 13 But

doe thou good.   10 Men are happy that draw neere to wisedome.

BLessed is the man that *hath not slipt with his mouth, and is not pricked with the || multitude of sinnes.

2 Blessed is hee whose conscience hath not condemned him, and who is not fallen from his hope in the Lord.

3 Riches are not comely for a niggard : and what should an enuious man doe with money?

4 He that gathereth by defrauding his owne soule, gathereth for others, that shall spend his goods riotously.

5 Hee that is euill to himselfe, to whom will he be good? he shall not take pleasure in his goods.

6 There is none worse then he that enuieth himselfe ; and this is a recompence of his wickednesse.

7 And if he doth good, he doth it vnwillingly, and at the last he will declare his wickednesse.

8 The enuious man hath a wicked eye, he turneth away his face and despiseth men.

9 A *couetous mans eye is not satisfied with his portion, and the iniquity of the wicked dryeth vp his soule.

10 A wicked eye enuieth [his] bread, and he is a niggard at his table.

11 My sonne, according to thy habilitie doe good to thy selfe, and giue the Lord his due offering.

12 Remember that death will not be long in comming, and that the couenant of the graue is not shewed vnto thee.

13 *Doe good vnto thy friend before thou die, and according to thy abilitie, stretch out thy hand and giue to him.

14 Defraud not thy selfe of || the good day, and let not the part of a good desire ouerpasse thee.

15 Shalt thou not leaue thy trauailes vnto another? and thy labours to be diuided by lot?

16 Giue, and take, and sanctifie thy soule, for there is no seeking of dainties in the graue.

17 *All flesh waxeth old as a garment : for the couenant from the beginning is ; thou shalt die the death.

18 As of the greene leaues on a thicke tree, some fall, and some grow ; so is the generation of flesh and blood, one commeth

*Chap. 19. 16. and 25.
s. iam. 3. 2.

|| Or, sorrow.

* Prou. 17. 20.

* Tobit. 4. 7.
luc. 14. 13.

|| Or, the feast day.

* Isai. 40. 5.
iam. 1. 10.
1. pet. 1. 24.

meth to an end, and another is borne.

19 Euery worke rotteth and consumeth away, and the worker therof shal goe withall.

20 *Blessed is the man that doeth meditate good things in wisdome, and that reasoneth of holy things by his vnderstanding.

* Psal. 1. 2.

21 He that considereth her wayes in his heart, shall also haue vnderstanding in her secrets.

22 Goe after her as one that traceth, and lie in wait in her wayes.

23 Hee that prieth in at her windowes, shal also hearken at her doores.

24 Hee that doeth lodge neere her house, shall also fasten a ||pin in her walles.

|| Or, stake.

25 He shall pitch his tent nigh vnto her, and shall lodge in a lodging where good things are.

26 He shal set his children vnder her shelter, and shall lodge vnder her branches.

27 By her he shall be couered from heat, and in her glory shall he dwell.

CHAP. XV.

2 Wisedome embraceth those that feare God. 7 The wicked shall not get her. 11 We may not charge God with our faults: 14 For he made, and left vs to our selues.

E that feareth the Lord will doe good, and he that hath the knowledge of the Law shal obtaine her.

2 And as a mother shall she meet him, and receiue him as a wife maried of a virgin.

3 With the bread of vnderstanding shall she feed him, and giue him the water of wisedome to drinke.

4 Hee shall be stayed vpon her, and shall not be moued, and shall rely vpon her, and shall not be confounded.

5 Shee shall exalt him aboue his neighbours, and in the midst of the congregation shall she open his mouth.

6 He shall finde ioy, and a crowne of gladnesse, and she shall cause him to inherit an euerlasting name.

7 But foolish men shall not attaine vnto her, and sinners shall not see her.

8 For she is farre from pride, and men that are liers cannot remember her.

9 ||Praise is not seemly in the mouth of a sinner, for ||it was not sent him of the Lord :

|| Or, a parable.
|| Or, he was not sent of, &c.

10 For ||praise shalbe vttered in wisdome, and the Lord wil prosper it.

|| Or, rather a parable.

11 Say not thou, It is through the Lord, that I fell away, for thou oughtest not to doe the things that he hateth.

12 Say not thou, He hath caused mee to erre, for hee hath no need of the sinfull man.

13 The Lord hateth all abomination, and they that feare God loue it not.

14 Hee himselfe made man from the *beginning, and left him in the hand of his counsell,

* Gene. 1. 20.

15 If thou wilt, to keepe the Commandements, and to performe acceptable faithfulnesse.

16 He hath set fire and water before thee : stretch forth thy hand vnto whether thou wilt.

17 *Before man is life and death, and whether him liketh shalbe giuen him.

* Iere. 21.

18 For the wisedome of the Lord is great, and he is mighty in power, and beholdeth all things,

19 And *his eyes are vpon them that feare him, & hee knoweth euery worke of man.

* Psal. 33. 16.

20 Hee hath commanded no man to do wickedly, neither hath he giuen any man license to sinne.

CHAP. XVI.

1 It is better to haue none then many lewd children. 6 The wicked are not spared for their number. 12 Both the wrath and the mercy of the Lord are great. 17 The wicked cannot be hid. 20 Gods workes are vnsearchable.

Esire not a multitude of vnprofitable children, neither delight in vngodly sonnes.

2 Though they multiply, reioyce not in them, except the feare of the Lord be with them.

3 Trust not thou in their life, neither respect their múltitude : for one that is iust, is better then a thousand, and better it is to die without children, then to haue them that are vngodly.

4 For by one that hath vnderstanding, shall the city be replenished, but the ||kindred of the wicked, shall speedily become desolate.

|| Or, tribe.

5 Many such things haue I seene with mine eyes, and mine eare hath heard greater things then these.

6 *In the congregation of the vngodly, shall a fire be kindled, and in a rebellious nation, wrath ||is set on fire.

* Chap. 21. 10.
|| Or, hath bene.

7 He

Gen. 6. 4.

* Gen. 19.
4.

Num. 14.
6. and 16.
0. and 20.

Chap. 5. 6.

7 *Hee was not pacified towards the olde giants, who fell away in the strength of their foolishnesse.

8 *Neither spared he the place where Lot soiourned, but abhorred them for their pride.

9 Hee pitied not the people of perdition, who were taken away in their sinnes.

10 *Nor the sixe hundreth thousand footmen, who were gathered together in the hardnesse of their hearts.

11 And if there be one stiffe-necked among the people, it is marueile, if he escape vnpunished; for *mercy and wrath are with him, hee is mighty to forgiue, and to powre out displeasure.

12 As his mercy is great, so is his correction also : he iudgeth a man according to his workes.

13 The sinner shall not escape with his spoiles, and the patience of the godly shall not be frustrate.

14 Make way for euery worke of mercy : for euery man shall finde according to his workes.

15 The Lord hardened Pharaoh, that hee should not know him, that his powerfull workes might be knowen to the world.

16 His mercy is manifest to euery creature, and hee hath separated his light from the darkenesse with an ‖Adamant.

Or, strong
partition.

17 Say not thou, I will hide my selfe from the Lord : shall any remember me from aboue? I shall not be remembred among so many people : for what is my soule among such an infinite number of creatures?

1. King. 8.
*. 2. chron.
18. 2. pet.
10.

18 *Behold, the heauen, and the heauen of heauens, the deepe and the earth, and all that therein is, shall be mooued when he shall visit.

19 The mountaines also, and foundations of the earth shall bee shaken with trembling, when the Lord looketh vpon them.

20 No heart can thinke vpon these things worthily : and who is able to conceiue his wayes?

21 It is a tempest, which no man can see : for the most part of his workes are hidde.

22 Who can declare the workes of his iustice? or who can endure them? for his Couenant is afarre off, and the triall of all things is in the ende.

23 He that wanteth vnderstanding,

will thinke vpon vaine things : and a foolish man erring, imagineth follies.

24 My sonne, hearken vnto mee, and learne knowledge, and marke my words with thy heart.

25 I will shewe foorth doctrine in weight, and declare his knowledge exactly

26 The works of the Lord are done in iudgement from the beginning : and from the time he made them, hee disposed the parts thereof.

27 Hee garnished his workes for euer, and in his hand are the ‖chiefe of them vnto all generations : they neither labour, nor are weary, nor cease from their workes.

‖ Or, beginnings.

28 None of them hindreth another, and they shall neuer disobey his word.

29 After this, the Lord looked vpon the earth, and filled it with his blessings.

30 With all maner of liuing things hath hee couered the face thereof, and they shall returne into it againe.

CHAP. XVII.

1 How God created and furnished man. 14 Auoid all sinne : 19 For God seeth all things. 25 Turne to him while thou liuest.

 He Lord *created man of the earth, and turned him into it againe.

2 *He gaue them few dayes, and a short time, and power also ouer the things therein.

* Gen. 1. 27
and 5. 2.
wisd. 2. 23.
and 7. 1, 6.
1. cor. 11. 7.
col. 3. 10.
* Gen. 1. 26.
1. cor. 11. 7.

3 He endued them with strength by themselues, and made them according to his image,

4 And put the feare ‖of man vpon all flesh, and gaue him dominion ouer beasts and foules.

‖ Or, of him.

5 [They receiued the vse of the fiue operations of the Lord, and in the sixt place he imparted them vnderstanding, and in the seuenth, speech, an interpreter of the cogitations thereof.]

6 Counsell, and a tongue, and eyes, eares, and a heart, gaue he them to vnderstand.

7 Withall, hee filled them with the knowledge of vnderstanding, & shewed them good and euill.

8 Hee set his eye vpon their hearts, that he might shew them the greatnesse of his workes.

9 He gaue them to glory in his maruelous actes for euer, that they might declare his works with vnderstanding.

10 And

10 And the elect shall praise his holy Name.

11 Beside this he gaue them knowledge, and the law of life for an heritage.

12 He made an euerlasting couenant with them, and shewed them his iudgements.

13 Their eyes saw the maiestie of his glory, and their eares heard his glorious voyce.

14 And he said vnto them, Beware of all vnrighteousnes, and he *gaue euery man commandement concerning his neighbour,

15 Their wayes are euer before him, and shall not be hid from his eyes.

16 Euery man from his youth is giuen to euill, neither could they make to themselues fleshie hearts for stonie.

17 For in the diuision of the nations of the whole earth, he set a *ruler ouer euery people, but *Israel is the Lords portion.

18 Whom being his first borne, hee nourisheth with discipline, and giuing him the light of his loue, doth not forsake him.

19 Therefore all their workes are as the Sunne before him, and his eyes are continually vpon their wayes.

20 None of their vnrighteous deeds are hid from him, but all their sinnes are before the Lord:

21 But the Lord being gracious, and knowing his workemanship, neither left nor forsooke them, but spared them.

22 The *almes of a man is as a signet with him, and he will keep the good deedes of man, as the apple of the eye, and giue repentance to his sonnes and daughters.

23 *Afterward he will rise vp and reward them, and render their recompense vpon their heads.

24 *But vnto them that repent, he granted them returne, and comforted those that faile in patience.

25 *Returne vnto the Lord, and forsake thy sinnes, make thy prayer before his face, and ||offend lesse.

26 Turne againe to the most High, and turne away from iniquitie: for he will leade thee out of darkenesse into the ||light of health, and hate thou abomination vehemently.

27 *Who shall praise the most High in the graue, in stead of them which liue and giue thanks?

28 Thankesgiuing perisheth from the dead, as from one that is not: the liuing and sound in heart, shall praise the Lord.

29 How great is the louing kindnes of the Lord our God, and his compassion vnto such as turne vnto him in holinesse?

30 For all things cannot bee in men, because ỹ sonne of man is not immortal.

31 *What is brighter then the Sun? yet the light thereof faileth: and flesh and blood wil imagine euill.

32 Hee vieweth the power of the height of heauen, and all men are but earth and ashes.

CHAP. XVIII.

4 Gods workes are to be wondred at. 9 Mans life is short. 11 God is mercifull. 15 Doe not blemish thy good deeds with ill wordes. 22 Deferre not to bee iustified. 30 Followe not thy lustes.

 Ee that liueth for euer, *created all things in generall.

2 The Lord onely is righteous, and there is none other but he.

3 Who gouerneth the world with the palme of his hand, and all things obey his will, for he is the king of all, by his power *diuiding holy things among them from prophane.

4 To whom hath he giuen power to declare his workes? *and who shall finde out his noble actes?

5 Who shall number the strength of his maiestie? and who shall also tel out his mercies?

6 As for the wonderous workes of the Lord, there may nothing bee taken from them, neither may any thing bee put vnto them, neither can the ground of them be found out.

7 When a man hath done, then he beginneth, and when hee leaueth off, then he shall be doubtfull.

8 What is man, and whereto serueth he? what is his good, & what is his euil?

9 *The number of a mans dayes at the most are an hundred yeeres.

10 As a drop of water vnto the Sea, and a grauell stone in comparison of the sand, so are a *thousand yeeres to the dayes of eternitie.

11 Therfore is God patient with them, & powreth forth his mercy vpon them.

12 He saw and perceiued their end to be euill, therefore he multiplied his compassion.

13 The

Marginal notes (left column)

* Exod. 20. 16. &. 22. 23.

* Deu. 32. 8. rom. 13. 1.
* Deu. 4. 20 and 10. 15.

* Cha. 29. 13

* Mat. 25. 35.

* Acts 3. 19

* Iere. 3. 12

||Or, lessen thy offence.

|| Or, illumination.

* Psal. 6. 6. isa. 38. 19.

Marginal notes (right column)

* Iob 25. 4, 5.

* Gen. 1.

* Leuit. 1 6.

* Psal. 10

*Psal. 90.

* 2. Pet. 3.

13 The mercy of man is toward his neighbour, but the mercy of the Lord is vpon all flesh : he reprooueth and nurtureth, and teacheth, & bringeth againe as a shepheard his flocke.

14 He hath mercy on them that receiue discipline, and that diligently seeke after his iudgements.

*Chap. 41. 23.

15 * My sonne, blemish not thy good deeds, neither vse vncomfortable words when thou giuest any thing.

16 Shall not the deaw asswage the heate? so is a word better then a gift.

17 Loe is not a word better then a gift? but both are with a gracious man.

18 A foole will vpbraide churlishly, and a gift of the enuious consumeth the eyes.

19 Learne before thou speake, and vse phisicke, or euer thou be sicke.

*1. Cor. 11. 28. 31.

20 Before iudgement *examine thy selfe, and in the day of visitation thou shalt find mercy.

21 Humble thy selfe before thou be sicke, and in the time of sinnes shew repentance.

22 Let nothing hinder thee to pay thy vowe in due time, and deferre not vntill death to be iustified.

23 Before thou prayest, prepare thy selfe, and be not as one that tempteth the Lord.

*Chap. 7. 17, 36.

24 * Thinke vpon the wrath that shall be at the end; and the time of vengeance when he shall turne away his face.

25 When thou hast enough remember the time of hunger, and when thou art rich thinke vpon pouerty and need.

26 From the morning vntill the euening the time is changed, and all things are soone done before the Lord.

*Prou. 28. 14.

27 *A wise man will feare in euery thing, and in the day of sinning he will beware of offence : but a foole will not obserue time.

28 Euery man of vnderstanding knoweth wisedome, and wil giue praise vnto him that found her.

29 They that were of vnderstanding in sayings, became also wise themselues, and powred forth exquisite parables.

*Rom. 6. 6. and 13. 14.

30 *Goe not after thy lustes, but refraine thy selfe from thine appetites.

31 If thou giuest thy soule the desires that please her, she will make thee a laughing stocke to thine enemies, that maligne thee.

32 Take not pleasure in much good

cheere, neither be tyed to the expence thereof.

33 Be not made a begger by banquetting vpon borrowing, when thou hast nothing in thy purse, for thou shalt lie in waite for thy owne life : and be talked on.

CHAP. XIX.

2 Wine and women seduce wise men. 7 Say not all thou hearest. 17 Reproue thy friend without anger. 22 There is no wisedome in wickednesse.

A Labouring man that is giuen to drunkennesse shal not be rich, and hee that contemneth small things shall fall by little & little.

2 Wine and women will make men of vnderstanding to fall away, and he that cleaueth to harlots will become impudent.

3 Mothes and wormes shall haue him to heritage, and a bold man shall be taken away.

*Iosh. 22. 11.

4 * He that is hasty to giue credit is light minded, and he that sinneth shall offend against his owne soule.

5 Who so taketh pleasure in wickednesse shall be condemned, but he that resisteth pleasures, crowneth his life.

6 He that can rule his tongue shall liue without strife, and he that hateth babbling, shall haue lesse euill.

7 Rehearse not vnto another that which is told vnto thee, and thou shalt fare neuer the worse.

‖Or, of friend or foe.

8 Whether it be ‖to friend or foe, talk not of other mens liues, and if thou canst without offence reueale them not.

‖Or, shewe his hatred.

9 For he heard and obserued thee, and when time commeth he will ‖hate thee.

10 If thou hast heard a word, let it die with thee, and be bold it will not burst thee.

11 A foole trauaileth with a word, as a woman in labour of a child.

‖Or, heart.

12 As an arrowe that sticketh in a mans thigh, so is a word within a fooles ‖belly.

*Leuit. 19. 17. matth. 18. 15.

13 *Admonish a friend, it may be he hath not done it, and if he haue [done it] that he doe it no more.

‖Or, reproue.

14 ‖ Admonish thy friend, it may be he hath not said it, and if he haue, that he speake it not againe.

15 Admonish a friend : for many times it is a slander, & beleeue not euery tale.

16 There

‖ *Or, wil-*
lingly.

16 There is one that slippeth in his speach, but not ‖from his heart, and who is he that hath not offended with his * tongue?

* Iam. 3. 2.

‖*Or, reproue.*

17 ‖Admonish thy neighbour before thou threaten him, and not being angry giue place to the Law of the most high.

18 The feare of the Lord is the first step ‖to be accepted [of him,] and wise-dome obtaineth his loue.

‖ *Or, of re-*
ceiuing him.

19 The knowledge of the Commandements of the Lord, is the doctrine of life, and they that do things that please him, shall receiue the fruit of the tree of immortalitie.

20 The feare of the Lord is all wisedome, and in all wisedome is the performance of the Law, and the knowledge of his omnipotencie.

21 If a seruant say to his master, I will not doe as it pleaseth thee, though afterward hee doe it, hee angereth him that nourisheth him.

22 The knowledge of wickednes is not wisedome, neither at any time the counsell of sinners, prudence.

23 There is a wickednesse, and the same is abomination, and there is a foole wanting in wisedome.

24 He that hath smal vnderstanding and feareth God, is better then one that hath much wisedome, and transgresseth the Law of the most High.

25 There is an exquisite subtilty, and the same is vniust, and there is one that turneth aside to make iudgement appeare: and there is a wise man that ‖iustifieth in iudgement.

‖ *Or, iudg-*
eth.

26 There is a wicked man that hangeth downe his head ‖sadly; but inwardly he is full of deceit,

‖ *Or, in*
blacke.

27 Casting downe his countenance, and making as if he heard not: where he is not knowen, he will do thee a mischiefe before thou be aware.

28 And if for want of power hee be hindered from sinning, yet when he findeth opportunitie he wil doe euil.

29 A man may bee knowen by his looke, and one that hath vnderstanding, by his countenance, when thou meetest him.

30 A mans attire, and excessiue laughter, and gate, shew what he is.

CHAP. XX.

1 Of silence and speaking. 10 Of gifts, and gaine. 18 Of slipping by the tongue. 24 Of lying. 27 Of diuers aduertisements.

 Here is a reproofe that is not ‖comely: againe some man holdeth his tongue, and he is wise.

‖ *Or, seaso-*
nable.

2 It is much better to reproue, then to be angry secretly, and he that confesseth his fault, shall be preserued from hurt.

3 How good is it when thou art reproued, to shew repentance? for so shalt thou escape wilfull sinne.

4 As is the lust of an * Eunuch to defloure a virgine; so is he that executeth iudgement with violence.

* Chap. 30.
20.

5 There is one that keepeth silence and is found wise: and another by much babling becommeth hatefull.

6 Some man holdeth his tongue, because hee hath not to answere, and some keepeth silence, * knowing his time.

* Eccle. 3.7

7 A wise man wil hold his * tongue till he see opportunitie: but a babler and a foole will regard no time.

* Cha. 32. 4

8 He that vseth many words shalbe abhorred; and hee that taketh to himselfe authoritie therein, shalbe hated.

9 There is a sinner that hath good success in euill things; and there is a gaine that turneth to losse.

10 There is a gift that shall not profit thee; and there is a gift whose recompence is double.

11 There is an abasement because of glory; and there is that lifteth vp his head from a low estate.

12 There is that buyeth much for a little, and repayeth it seuen fold.

13 *A wise man by his words maketh himselfe beloued: but the ‖graces of fooles shalbe ‖powred out.

* Chap. 6. 5
‖ *Or, plea-*
santconceits
‖ *Lost, or*
spilt.

14 The gift of a foole shall doe thee no good when thou hast it; neither yet of the enuious for his necessitie: for hee †looketh to receiue many things for one.

† *Gr. for, hi*
eyes are ma-
ny for one t
receiue.

15 Hee giueth little and vpbraideth much; hee openeth his mouth like a crier; to day he lendeth, and to morrow will he ask it againe: such an one is to be hated of God and man.

16 The foole saith, I haue no friends, I haue no thanke for all my good deeds and they that eate my bread speake euill of me.

17 How oft, and of how many shall he be laughed to scorne? for hee knoweth not aright what it is to haue; and it is all one vnto him, as if he had it not.

18 To

18 To slip vpon a pauement, is better then to slip with the tongue : so, the fall of the wicked shall come speedily.

19 ‖ An vnseasonable tale will alwayes be in the mouth of the vnwise.

20 A wise sentence shall be reiected when it commeth out of a fools mouth: for he will not speake it in due season.

21 There is that is hindred from sinning through want : and when hee taketh rest, he †shall not be troubled.

22 There is that destroyeth his owne soule through bashfulnesse, and by accepting of persons ouerthroweth himselfe

23 There is that for bashfulnes promiseth to his friend, and maketh him his enemy for nothing.

24 *A lie is a foule blot in a man, yet it is continually in the mouth of the vntaught.

25 A thiefe is better then a man that is accustomed to lie : but they both shall haue destruction to heritage

26 The disposition of a liar is ‖dishonourable, and his shame is euer with him.

27 A wise man shall promote himselfe *to honour* with his words : and hee that hath vnderstanding, will please great men.

28 *He that tilleth his land, shall increase his heape : and he that pleaseth great men, shal get pardon for iniquity.

29 *Presents and gifts blind the eyes of the wise, and ‖stoppe vp his mouth that he cannot reprooue.

30 Wisedome that is hidde, and treasure that is hoarded vp, what profit is in them both ?

31 Better is he that hideth his folly, then a man that hideth his wisedome.

32 Necessary patience in seeking the Lord, is better then he that leadeth his life without a guide.

CHAP. XXI.

2 Flee from sinne as from a serpent. 4 His oppression will vndoe the rich. 9 The ende of the vniust shall be naught. 12 The differences betweene the foole and the wise.

Y sonne, hast thou sinned? doe so no more, but *aske pardon for thy former sinnes.

2 Flee from sinne as from the face of a Serpent : for if thou commest too neere it, it will bite thee : the teeth thereof, are as the teeth of a lyon, slaying the soules of men.

3 All iniquitie is as a two edged sword, the wounds whereof cannot be healed.

4 To terrifie and doe wrong, will waste riches : thus the house of proude men shalbe made desolate.

5 A *prayer out of a poore mans mouth reacheth to the eares of God, and his iudgement commeth speedily.

6 He that hateth to be reprooued, is in the way of sinners : but hee that feareth the Lord, will †repent from his heart.

7 An eloquent man is knowen farre and neere, but a man of vnderstanding knoweth when he slippeth.

8 He that buildeth his house with other mens money, is like one that gathereth himselfe stones for the tombe of his buriall.

9 *The congregation of the wicked is like tow wrapped together : and the end of them is a flame of fire to destroy them.

10 The way of sinners is made plaine with stones, but at the end thereof is the pit of hell.

11 Hee that keepeth the Law of the Lord, getteth the vnderstanding thereof : and the perfection of the feare of the Lord, is wisedome.

12 *He that is not ‖wise, will not be taught : but there is a ‖wisedome which multiplieth bitternesse.

13 The knowledge of a wise man shall abound like a flood : and his counsell is like a pure fountaine of life.

14 *The inner parts of a foole, are like a broken vessell, and he will holde no knowledge as long as he liueth.

15 If a skilfull man heare a wise word, hee will commend it, and *adde vnto it : but assoone as one of no vnderstanding heareth it, it displeaseth him, and he casteth it behinde his backe.

16 The talking of a foole is like a burden in the way : but grace shall be found in the lips of the wise.

17 They inquire at the mouth of the wise man in the congregation, and they shall ponder his words in their heart.

18 As is a house that is destroyed, so is wisedome to a foole : and the knowledge of the vnwise, is as talke ‖without sense.

19 Doctrine vnto fooles, is as fetters on the feete, and like manacles on the right hand.

20 *A

Margin notes:
r, an vnpleasant low.

r. shall be pried.

ha. 25. 2.

r, ignoie.

rou. 12. and 28.

xo. 23. 8. . 16. 19. ., as a zzle in mouth.

sal. 41. 4. 15. 21.

* Exod. 3. 9. and 22. 23

† Gr. be conuerted.

* Chap. 16. 16.

* Eccles. 1. 18. ‖ Or, wittie. ‖ Or, subtilie.

* Cha. 33. 5.

* Pro. 9. 9.

‖ Or, not to be enquired after.

* Chap. 19.
27, 28.

20 * A foole lifteth vp his voyce with laughter, but a wise man doeth scarce smile a litle.

21 Learning is vnto a wise man, as an ornament of gold, and like a bracelet vpon his right arme.

22 A foolish mans foote is soone in his [neighbours] house : but a man of experience is ashamed of him.

23 A foole will peepe in at the doore into the house, but he that is well nurtured, will stand without.

24 It is the rudenesse of a man to hearken at the doore : but a wise man will be grieued with the disgrace.

25 The lips of talkers will bee telling such things as pertaine not vnto them : but the words of such as haue vnderstanding, are weighed in the ballance.

26 The heart of fooles is in their mouth, but the mouth of the wise is in their heart.

27 When the vngodly curseth Satan, he curseth his owne soule.

* Chap. 28.
13.

28 * A whisperer defileth his owne soule , and is hated wheresoeuer hee dwelleth.

C H A P. XXII.

1 Of the slouthfull man, 3 and a foolish daughter. 11 Weepe rather for fooles, then for the dead. 13 Meddle not with them. 16 The wise mans heart will not shrinke. 20 What will lose a friend.

Slouthful man is compared to a filthy stone, and euery one will hisse him out to his disgrace.

2 A slouthfull man is compared to the filth of a dunghill : euery man that takes it vp, will shake his hand.

3 An euill nurtured sonne is the dishonour of his father that begate him : and a [foolish] daughter is borne to his losse.

* Prou. 13.
22.
‖ Or, shalbe
the heire of
her husband

4 * A wise daughter shall bring an ‖inheritance to her husband : but shee that liueth dishonestly, is her fathers heauinesse.

5 Shee that is bold , dishonoureth both her father and her husband, but they both shall despise her.

6 A tale out of season [is as] musick in mourning : but stripes and correction of wisedome are neuer out of time.

7 Who so teacheth a foole, is as one that gleweth a potsheard together, and

as hee that waketh one from a sound sleepe.

8 Hee that telleth a tale to a foole, speaketh to one in a slumber : when hee hath told his tale, he will say, What is the matter ?

9 If children liue honestly, and haue ‖wherewithall, they shall couer the basenesse of their parents.

‖ Or, an as

10 But children being haughtie through disdaine, and want of nurture, doe staine the nobilitie of their kinred.

11 * Weepe for the dead, for hee hath lost the light : and weepe for the foole, for he wanteth vnderstanding : make litle weeping for the dead, for hee is at rest : but the life of the foole is worse then death.

* Chap. 38
16.

12 Seuen dayes doe men mourne for him that is dead; but for a foole, and an vngodly man, all the dayes of his life.

13 Talke not much with a foole, and goe not to him that hath no vnderstanding, *beware of him lest thou haue trouble, and thou shalt neuer be defiled ‖with his fooleries : depart from him, and thou shalt find rest, and neuer bee ‖disquieted with madnesse.

* Cha. 12.
‖ Or, when
he shakes
his filth.
‖ Or, weare

14 What is heauier then lead ? and what is the name thereof, but a foole ?

15 * Sand , and salt , and a masse of yron is easier to beare then a man without vnderstanding.

* Pro. 27.

16 As timber girt and bound together in a building, cannot be loosed with shaking : so the heart that is stablished by aduised counsel, shal feare at no time.

17 A heart setled vpon a thought of vnderstanding, is as a faire plaistering ‖on the wall of a gallerie.

‖ Or, of a
polished w

18 Pales set on an high place will neuer stand against the wind: so a feareful heart in the imagination of a foole, can not stand against any feare.

19 He that pricketh the eye, wil make teares to fall : and he that pricketh the heart, maketh it to shewe her knowledge.

20 Who so casteth a stone at the birds, frayeth them away, and he that vpbraideth his friend, breaketh friendship.

21 Though thou drewest a sword at thy friend , yet despaire not , for there way be a returning (to fauour.)

22 If thou hast opened thy mouth against thy friend, feare not, for there may be a reconciliation : except for vpbraiding, or pride, or disclosing of secrets,

or

or a treacherous wound, for, for these things euery friend will depart.

23 Be faithfull to thy neighbour in his pouertie, that thou mayest reioyce in his prosperitie : abide stedfast vnto him in the time of his trouble, that thou mayest bee heire with him in his heritage : for a meane estate is not alwayes to be contemned, nor the rich that is foolish, to be had in admiration.

24 As the vapour and smoke of a furnace goeth before the fire : so reuiling before blood.

25 I will not be ashamed to defend a friend : neither will I hide my selfe from him.

26 And if any euill happen vnto me by him, euery one that heareth it will beware of him.

Psal. 141.

27 * Who shall set a watch before my mouth, and a seale of wisedome vpon my lippes, that I fall not suddenly by them, & that my tongue destroy me not?

CHAP. XXIII.

1 A prayer for grace to flee sinne. 9 We may not vse swearing : 14 But remember our parents. 16 Of three sorts of sinne. 23 The adultresse wife sinneth many waies.

Lord, father and gouernour of all my whole life, leaue me not to their counsels, and let me not fall by them.

2 Who will set scourges ouer my thoughts, and the discipline of wisedome ouer mine heart? that they spare me not for mine ignorances and it passe not by my sinnes :

3 Least mine ignorances increase, and my sinnes abound to my destruction, and I fall before mine aduersaries, and mine enemie reioyce ouer mee, whose hope is farre from thy mercy.

4 O Lord, father and God of my life, giue me not a proud looke, but turne away from thy seruants alwaies a ||haughty minde :

Or, a giant like.

5 Turne away from mee vaine hopes, and concupiscence, and thou shalt hold him vp that is desirous alwaies to serue thee.

6 Let not the greedinesse of the belly, nor lust of the flesh take hold of me, and giue not ouer me thy seruant into an impudent minde.

7 Heare, O yee children, the discipline of the mouth : He that keepeth it,

shall neuer be taken in his lippes.

8 The sinner shall be left in his foolishnesse : both the euill speaker and the proud shall fall thereby.

9 * Accustome not thy mouth to swearing : neither vse thy selfe to the naming of the holy one.

* Exod. 20. 7. chap. 27. 15. math. 5. 33.

10 For as a seruant that is continually beaten, shall not be without a blew marke : so hee that sweareth and nameth God continually, shal not be faultlesse.

11 A man that vseth much swearing shall be filled with iniquity, and the plague shall neuer depart from his house : If he shall offend, his sinne shall be vpon him : and if he acknowledge not his sinne, hee maketh a double offence, and if he sweare in vaine, he shall not be †innocent, but his house shall be full of calamities.

† Gre. iustified.

12 There is a word that is clothed about with death : God graunt that it be not found in the heritage of Iacob, for all such things shall be farre from the godly, and they shall not wallow in their sinnes.

13 Vse not thy mouth to vntemperate swearing, for therein is the word of sinne.

14 Remember thy father and thy mother, when thou sittest among great men. Be not forgetfull before them, and so thou by thy custome become a foole, and wish that thou hadst not beene borne, and curse the day of thy natiuitie.

15 * The man that is accustomed to opprobrious words, will neuer be reformed all the daies of his life.

* 2. Sam. 16. 17.

16 Two sorts of men multiply sinne, and the third will bring wrath : a hot minde is as a burning fire, it will neuer be quenched till it be consumed : a fornicatour in the body of his flesh, will neuer cease till he hath kindled a fire.

17 * All bread is sweete to a whoremonger, he will not leaue off till he die.

* Prou. 9. 17.

18 A man that breaketh wedlocke, saying thus in his heart, * Who seeth me? I am compassed about with darknesse : the walles couer me ; & no body seeth me, what neede I to feare? The most high wil not remember my sinnes :

* Isai. 29. 15. iob. 24. 15.

19 Such a man only feareth the eies of men, and knoweth not that the eies of the Lord are tenne thousand times brighter then the Sunne, beholding all the waies of men, and considering the most secret parts.

20 He

20 He knew all things ere euer they were created, so also after they were perfited, he looked vpon them all :

* Leuit. 20. 10. deut. 22. 22.

21 * This man shall bee punished in the streets of the citie, and where he suspecteth not, he shall be taken.

22 Thus shall it goe also with the wife, that leaueth her husband, and bringeth in an heire by ||another :

|| Or, a stranger.
* Exod. 20. 14.

23 For * first she hath disobeyed the Law of the most High : and secondly, she hath trespassed against her owne husband, and thirdly, she hath played the whore in adultery, and brought children by another man.

|| Or, visitation.

24 Shee shall be brought out into the congregation, and ||inquisition shalbe made of her children.

* Wisd. 4. 3.

25 Her * children shall not take root, and her branches shall bring foorth no fruit.

26 She shall leaue her memorie to be cursed, and her reproch shall not be blotted out.

27 And they that remaine, shall know that there is nothing better then the feare of the Lord, and that there is nothing sweeter then to take heed vnto the Commandement of the Lord.

28 It is great glory to follow the Lord, & to be receiued of him is long life.

CHAP. XXIIII.

2 Wisedome doeth praise herselfe, shew her beginning, 4 Her dwelling, 13 Her glory, 17 Her fruit, 26 Her increase, and perfection.

The praise of wisedome.

WIsedome shall praise her selfe, and shall glory in the midst of her people.

2 In the Congregation of the most high, shall she open her mouth, and triumph before his power.

3 I came out of the mouth of the most High, and couered the earth as a ||cloud.

|| Or, a miste.
* Iob. 22. 14.

4 *I dwelt in high places, and my throne is in a cloudy pillar.

5 I alone compassed the circuit of heauen, and walked in the bottome of the deepe.

6 In the waues of the sea, and in all the earth, and in euery people, and nation, I got a possession.

7 With all these I sought rest : and in whose inheritance shall I abide ?

8 So the creatour of all things gaue mee a commandement, and hee that made me, caused my tabernacle to rest:

and said, Let thy dwelling be in Iacob, and thine inheritance in Israel.

9 Hee * created mee from the beginning before the world, and I shall neuer faile.

* Pro. 8. 23.

10 In the *holy Tabernacle I serued before him : and so was I established in Sion.

* Exod. 31. 3.

11 *Likewise in the ||beloued citie he gaue mee rest, and in Ierusalem was my power.

* Psal. 132. 8.
|| Or, holy.

12 And I tooke roote in an honourable people, euen in the portion of the Lords inheritance.

13 I was exalted like a Cedar in Libanus, and as a Cypresse tree vpon the mountaines of Hermon.

14 I was exalted like a palme tree in ||Engaddi, and as a rose-plant in Iericho, as a faire oliue tree in a pleasant fielde, and grew vp as a planetree ||by the water.

|| Or, Cades.
|| Or, in the water.

15 I gaue a sweete smell like cinamon, and aspalathus, and I yeelded a pleasant odour like the best mirrhe, as Galbanum and Onix, and sweet Storax, and as the fume of franckincense in the * Tabernacle.

* Exod. 30 34.

16 As the Turpentine tree, I stretched out my branches, and my branches are the branches of honour and grace.

17 As the Vine brought I foorth pleasant sauour, and my flowers are the fruit of honour and riches.

* Ioh. 15.)

18 I am the mother of faire loue, and feare, and knowledge, and holy hope, I therefore being eternall, am giuen to all my children which are ||named of him.

|| Or, choser

19 Come vnto me all ye that are desirous of mee, and fill your selues with my fruits.

20 For my memorial is sweeter then hony, and mine inheritance then the hony combe.

* Psal. 19. 10, 11.

21 They that eate mee shall yet be hungry, and they that drinke me shall yet be thirstie.

22 He that obeyeth me, shall neuer be confounded, and they that worke by me, shall not doe amisse.

23 All these things are the booke of the Couenant of the most high God, euen a *Law which Moses commanded for an heritage vnto the Congregations of Iacob.

* Exod. 20 1. and 24. 1 deut. 4. 1. and 29. 2.

24 Faint not to bee strong in the Lord; that he may confirme you, cleaue vnto him : for the Lord Almightie is God

God alone, and besides him there is no other Sauiour.

25 He filleth all things with his wisdome, as * Physon, and as Tigris in the time of the new fruits.

26 He maketh the vnderstanding to abound like Euphrates, and as * Iorden in the time of the haruest.

27 He maketh the doctrine of knowledge appeare as the light, and as Geon in the time of vintage.

28 The first man knew her not perfectly: no more shall the last finde her out.

29 For her thoughts are more then the Sea, and her counsels profounder then the great deepe.

30 I also came out as a ||brooke from a riuer, and as a conduit into a garden.

31 I said, I will water my best garden, and will water abundantly my garden bedde : and loe, my brooke became a riuer, and my riuer became a sea.

32 I will yet make doctrine to shine as the morning, and will send forth her light afarre off.

33 I will yet powre out doctrine as prophecie, and leaue it to all ages for euer.

34 *Behold that I haue not laboured for my selfe onely, but for all them that seeke wisedome.

CHAP. XXV.

1 What things are beautifull, and what hatefull. 6 What is the crowne of age. 7 What things make men happy. 13 Nothing worse then a wicked woman.

IN three things I ||was beautified, and stoode vp beautiful, both before God and men : the * vnitie of brethren, the loue of neighbours, a man and a wife that agree together.

2 Three sorts of men my soule hateth, and I am greatly offended at their life : a poore man that is proud, a rich man that is a lyar, and an olde adulterer that doteth.

3 If thou hast gathered nothing in thy youth, how canst thou finde any thing in thine age ?

4 Oh how comely a thing is iudgement for gray haires, and for ancient men to know counsell ?

5 Oh how comely is the wisedome of olde men, and vnderstanding and counsell to men of honour ?

6 Much experience is the crowne of olde men, and the feare of God is their glory.

7 There be nine things which I haue iudged in mine heart to be happy, and the tenth I will vtter with my tongue : a man that hath ioy of his children, and he that liueth to see the fall of his enemie.

8 Well is him that dwelleth with a wife of vnderstanding, and that hath not *slipped with his tongue, and that hath not serued a man more vnworthy then himselfe.

9 Well is him that hath found ||prudence, and he that speaketh in the eares of him that will heare.

10 Oh how great is he that findeth wisedome ! yet is there none aboue him that feareth the Lord.

11 But the loue of the Lord passeth all things for illumination : he that holdeth it, ||whereto shall he be likened ?

12 The feare of the Lord is the beginning of his loue : and faith is the beginning of cleauing vnto him.

13 [Giue mee] any plague, but the plague of the heart : and any wickednesse, but the wickednesse of a woman.

14 And any affliction, but the affliction from them that hate me : and any reuenge, but the reuenge of enemies.

15 There is no head aboue the head of a serpent, and there is no wrath aboue the wrath of an enemie.

16 *I had rather dwell with a lyon and a dragon, then to keepe house with a wicked woman.

17 The wickednesse of a woman changeth her face, and darkeneth her countenance like ||sackecloth.

18 Her husband shall sit among his neighbours : and when hee heareth it, shall sigh bitterly.

19 All wickednesse is but little to the wickednesse of a woman : let the portion of a sinner fall vpon her.

20 As the climbing vp a sandie way is to the feete of the aged, so is a wife ||full of words to a quiet man.

21 *Stumble not at the beautie of a woman, and desire her not for pleasure.

22 A woman, if shee maintaine her husband, is full of anger, impudencie, and much reproch.

23 A wicked woman abateth the courage, maketh a heauie countenance, and a wounded heart : a woman that will not comfort her husband in distresse,

---

*Gen. 2. 11.

*Iosh. 3. 15.

|| Or, draine or ditch.

*Chap. 33. 16.

|| Or, gloried.

*Gen. 13. 2, 5. rom. 12. 10.

*Cha. 14. 1. and 19. 16. iam. 3. 2.

||Or, a friend

|Or, to whom.

*Pro. 21. 19

|| Or, like a Beare.

|| Or, scolding.
*2. Sam. 11.
42. 2.
2. chap.

stresse maketh weake hands, and feeble knees.

* Gen. 3. 6.
1. tim. 2. 14

24 Of * the woman came the beginning of sinne, & through her wee all die

25 Giue the water no passage: neither a wicked woman libertie to gad abroad.

26 If she goe not as thou wouldest haue her, cut her off from thy flesh, and giue her a bill of diuorce, and let her goe.

CHAP. XXVI.

1 A good wife, 4 and a good conscience doe glad men. 6 A wicked wife is a fearefull thing. 13 Of good and bad wiues. 28 Of three things that are grieuous. 20 Merchants and hucksters are not without sinne.

Lessed is the man that hath a vertuous wife, for the number of his dayes shall be double.

2 A vertuous woman reioyceth her husband, and he shall fulfill the yeeres of his life in peace.

3 A good wife is a good portion, which shall be giuen in the portion of them that feare the Lord.

4 Whether a man be rich or poore, if he haue a good heart towards the Lord, he shall at all times reioyce with a cheerefull countenance.

5 There bee three things that mine heart feareth: and for the fourth I was sore afraid: † the slander of a citie, the gathering together of an vnruly multitude, and a false accusation: all these are worse then death.

† Gr. an euill report.

6 But a griefe of heart and sorrow, is a woman that is ielous ouer another woman, and a scourge of the tongue which communicateth withall.

7 An euill wife is a ||yoke shaken to and fro: he that hath hold of her, is as though he held a scorpion.

|| Or, a yoke of oxen.

8 A drunken woman and a gadder abroad, causeth great anger, and shee will not couer her owne shame.

9 The whordome of a woman may be knowen in her haughtie lookes, and eye lids.

10 * If thy daughter be shamelesse, keepe her in straitly: lest she abuse her selfe through ouermuch libertie.

* Chap. 44. 11.

11 Watch ouer an impudent eye: and marueile not, if shee trespasse against thee.

12 Shee will open her mouth as a thirstie traueiler, when he hath found a fountaine: and drinke of euery water

neere her: by euery ||hedge will she sit downe, and open her quiuer against euery arrow.

|| Or, stake.

13 The grace of a wife delighteth her husband, and her discretion will fat his bones.

14 A silent and louing woman is a gift of the Lord, and there is nothing so much worth, as a mind well instructed.

15 A shamefast and faithfull woman is a double grace, and her continent mind cannot be valued.

16 As the Sunne when it ariseth in the † high heauen: so is the beautie of a good wife in the ||ordering of her house.

† Gre. in the highest places of the Lord.
|| Or, ornament.

17 As the cleare light is vpon the holy candlesticke: so is the beautie of the face ||in ripe age.

|| Or, in constant age.

18 As the golden pillars are vpon the sockets of siluer: so are the ||faire feete with a constant ||heart.

|| Or, comely.
|| Or, brest.

19 My sonne, keepe the flowre of thine age sound: and giue not thy strength to strangers.

20 When thou hast gotten a fruitfull possession through all the field: sowe it with thine owne seede, trusting in the goodnesse of thy stocke.

21 So thy race which thou leauest shalbe magnified, hauing the confidence of their good descent.

22 An harlot shall bee accounted as ||spittle: but a maried woman is a towre against death to her husband.

|| Or, a swine.

23 A wicked woman is giuen as a portion to a wicked man: but a godly woman is giuen to him that feareth the Lord.

24 A dishonest woman contemneth shame, but an honest woman will reuerence her husband.

25 A shamelesse woman shalbe counted as a dog: but she that is shamefast will feare the Lord.

26 A woman that honoureth her husband, shall bee iudged wise of all: but she that dishonoureth him in her pride, shall be counted vngodly of all.

27 A loude crying woman, and a scolde, shall be sought out to driue away the enemies.

28 There be two things that grieue my heart: and the third maketh me angry: a man of warre that suffereth pouerty, and men of vnderstanding that are not set by: and one that returneth from righteousnesse to sinne: the Lord prepareth such a one for the sword.

29 A merchant shall hardly keepe him-

himselfe from doing wrong : and an huckster shall not be freed from sinne.

CHAP. XXVII.

1 Of sinnes in selling and buying. 7 Our speach will tell what is in vs. 16 A friend is lost by discouering his secrets. 25 Hee that diggeth a pit shall fall into it.

M *Any haue sinned for ‖ a smal matter : & he that seeketh for abundance will turne his eies away.

2 *As a naile sticketh fast betweene the ioynings of the stones: so doth sinne sticke close betweene buying and selling.

3 Vnlesse a man hold himselfe diligently in the feare of the Lord, his house shall soone be ouerthrowen.

4 As when one sifteth with a sieue, the refuse remaineth, so the filth of man in his ‖ talke.

5 The furnace prooueth the potters vessell : so the *triall of man is in his reasoning.

6 *The fruite declareth if the tree haue beene dressed : so is the vtterance of a conceit in the heart of man.

7 Praise no man before thou hearest him speake, for this is the triall of men.

8 If thou followest righteousnesse, thou shalt obtaine her, and put her on, as a glorious long robe.

9 The birds will resort vnto their like, so will truth returne vnto them that practise in her.

10 As the Lyon lieth in waite for the pray : so sinne for them that worke iniquity.

11 The discourse of a godly man is alwaies with wisedome : but a foole changeth as the Moone.

12 If thou be among the vndiscreet, obserue the time : but be continually among men of vnderstanding.

13 The discourse of fooles is irksome, and their sport is in the wantonnesse of sinne.

14 The talke of him that sweareth much, maketh the haire stand vpright : and their braules make one stop his eares.

15 The strife of the proud is bloodshedding, and their reuilings are grieuous to the eare.

16 Who so discouereth secrets, looseth his credit : and shall neuer find friend to his minde.

17 Loue thy friend, and be faithfull vnto him : but if thou bewrayest his secrets, follow no more after him.

18 For as a man hath destroyed his enemie : so hast thou lost the loue of thy neighbour.

19 As one that letteth a bird goe out of his hand, so hast thou let thy neighbour goe, and shalt not get him againe.

20 Follow after him no more, for he is too far off, he is as a roe escaped out of the snare.

21 As for a wound it may be bound vp, and after reuiling there may be reconcilement : but he that bewrayeth secrets is without hope.

22 He *that winketh with the eies worketh euil, and he that knoweth him will depart from him.

23 When thou art present he will speake sweetly, and will admire thy words : but at the last he will ‖ writhe his mouth, and slander thy sayings.

24 I haue hated many things, but nothing like him, for the Lord will hate him.

25 Who so casteth a stone on high, casteth it on his owne head, and a deceitfull stroke shall make wounds.

26 Who so diggeth a *pit shall fall therein : and he that setteth a trap shall be taken therein.

27 He that worketh mischiefe, it shall fall vpon him, and he shall not know whence it commeth.

28 Mockery and reproach are from the proud : but *vengeance as a Lyon shall lie in waite for them.

29 They that reioyce at the fall of the righteous shalbe taken in the snare, and anguish shall consume them before they die.

30 Malice and wrath, euen these are abhominations, and the sinfull man shall haue them both.

CHAP XXVIII.

1 Against reuenge. 8 Quarrelling, 10 Anger, 15 And backbiting.

H E that reuengeth shall find vengeance from the Lord, and he will surely keepe his sinnes (in remembrance.)

2 Forgiue thy neighbour the hurt that he hath done vnto thee, so shall thy sinnes also be forgiuen when thou prayest.

3 One man beareth hatred against another,

Marginal notes

* Prou. 28. 21.
‖ Or, a thing indifferent.
* Prou. 23. 4. 1. tim. 6. 3.
‖ Or, thought
* Prou. 27. 21.
* Matth. 7. 7.
* Prou. 10. 10.
‖ Or, alter his speach.
* Psal. 7. 15. prou. 26. 27. ecclesi. 8. 10.
* Deut. 32. 35. rom. 12. 19.

another, and doeth he seeke pardon from the Lord?

4 Hee sheweth no mercy to a man, which is like himselfe: and doeth hee aske forgiuenesse of his owne sinnes?

5 If he that is but flesh nourish hatred, who will intreat for pardon of his sinnes?

6 Remember thy end, and let enimitie cease, [remember] corruption and death, and abide in the Commandements.

7 Remember the Commaundements, & beare no malice to thy neighbour: [remember] the Couenant of the highest, and winke at ignorance.

*Chap. 8. 1. 8 *Abstaine from strife, and thou shalt diminish thy sinnes: for a furious man will kindle strife.

9 A sinfull man disquieteth friends, and maketh debate among them that be at peace.

*Prou. 26. 21. 10 *As the matter of the fire is, so it burneth: and as a mans strength is, so is his wrath, and according to his riches his anger riseth, and the stronger they are which contend, the more they will be inflamed.

11 An hastie contention kindleth a fire, and an hasty fighting sheddeth blood.

12 If thou blow the sparke, it shall burne: if thou spit vpon it, it shall bee quenched, and both these come out of thy mouth.

*Chap. 21 28. 13 *Curse the whisperer, and double tongued: for such haue destroyed many that were at peace.

14 A backbiting tongue hath disquieted many, and driuen them from nation to nation, strong cities hath it pulled down, and ouerthrowen the houses of great men.

‖Or, third. 15 A ‖backbiting tongue hath cast out vertuous women, and depriued them of their labours.

16 Who so hearkeneth vnto it, shall neuer finde rest, and neuer dwel quietly.

17 The stroke of the whip maketh markes in the flesh, but the stroke of the tongue breaketh the bones.

18 Many haue fallen by the edge of the sword: but not so many as haue fallen by the tongue.

19 Well is hee that is defended from it, and hath not passed through the venime thereof: who hath not drawen the yoke thereof, nor hath bene bound in her bands.

20 For the yoke thereof is a yoke of yron, and the bands thereof are bandes of brasse.

21 The death therof is an euil death, the graue were better then it.

22 It shall not haue rule ouer them that feare God, neither shall they be burnt with the flame thereof.

23 Such as forsake the Lord shall fall into it, and it shall burne in them, and not be quenched, it shalbe sent vpon them as a Lion, and deuoure them as a Leopard.

24 Looke that thou hedge thy possession about with thornes, and binde vp thy siluer and gold:

25 And weigh thy words in a ballance, and make a doore and barre for thy mouth.

26 Beware thou slide not by it, lest thou fall before him that lieth in wait.

CHAP. XXIX.

2 Wee must shew mercy and lend: 4 but the borower must not defraud the lender. 9 Giue almes. 14 A good man will not vndoe his suretie. 18 To be suretie and vndertake for others is dangerous. 22 It is better to liue at home, then to soiourne.

Ee that is mercifull, will lende vnto his neighbour, and hee that strengthneth his hande, keepeth the Commandements.

*Deut. 15 8. matth. 42. luke 6. 35. 2 Lend to thy neighbour in time of his *need, and pay thou thy neighbour againe in due season.

3 Keepe thy word & deale faithfully with him, and thou shalt alwaies finde the thing that is necessary for thee.

4 Many when a thing was lent them, reckoned it to be found, and put them to trouble that helped them.

5 Till he hath receiued, he will kisse a mans hand: and for his neighbours money he will speake submissely: but when he should repay, he will prolong the time, and returne words of griefe, and complaine of the time.

‖Or, if he able. 6 If he preuaile, he shall hardly receiue the halfe, and he will count as if he had found it: if not; he hath depriued him of his money, and he hath gotten him an enemy without cause: he payeth him with cursings, and raylings: and for honour he will pay him disgrace.

7 Many

7 Many therefore haue refused to lend for other mens ill dealing, fearing to be defrauded.

8 Yet haue thou patience with a man in poore estate, and delay not to shew him mercy.

9 Helpe the poore for the commandements sake, and turne him not away because of his pouertie.

10 Lose thy money for thy brother and thy friend, and let it not rust vnder a stone to be lost.

11 *Lay vp thy treasure according to the commandements of the most high, and it shall bring thee more profite then golde.

12 *Shut vp almes in thy storehouses : and it shall deliuer thee from all affliction.

13 It shal fight for thee against thine enemies, better then a mightie shield and strong speare.

14 An honest man is suretie for his neighbour : but hee that is impudent, will ||forsake him.

15 Forget not the friendship of thy suretie : for hee hath giuen his life for thee.

16 A sinner will ouerthrow the good estate of his suretie :

17 And he that is of an vnthankfull minde, will leaue him in [danger] that deliuered him.

18 Suretiship hath vndone many of good estate, and shaked them as a waue of the Sea : mightie men hath it driuen from their houses, so that they wandred among strange nations.

19 A wicked man transgressing the commandements of the Lord, shall fall into suretiship : and hee that vndertaketh and followeth other mens businesse for gaine, shall fall into suits.

20 Helpe thy neighbour according to thy power, and beware that thou thy selfe fall not into the same.

21 The *chiefe thing for life is water and bread, and clothing, and an house to couer shame.

22 Better is the life of a poore man in a meane cottage, then delicate fare in another mans house.

23 Be it little or much, holde thee contented, that thou heare not the reproch of thy house.

24 For it is a miserable life to goe from house to house : for where thou art a stranger, thou darest not open thy mouth.

25 Thou shalt entertaine and feast, and haue no thankes : moreouer, thou shalt heare bitter words.

26 Come thou stranger, and furnish a table, and feede me of that thou hast ready.

27 Giue place thou stranger to an honourable man, my brother commeth to be lodged, and I haue neede of mine house.

28 These things are grieuous to a man of vnderstanding : the vpbraiding of house-roome, and reproching of the lender.

CHAP. XXX.

1 It is good to correct our children, 7 and not to cocker them. 14 Health is better then wealth. 22 Health and life are shortened by griefe.

Ee *that loueth his sonne, causeth him oft to feele the rodde, that hee may haue ioy of him in the end.

2 He that chastiseth his sonne, shall haue ||ioy in him, and shall reioyce of him among his ||acquaintance.

3 *He that teacheth his sonne, grieueth the enemie : and before his friends he shall reioyce of him.

4 Though his father die, yet he is as though hee were not dead : for hee hath left one behinde him that is like himselfe.

5 While he liued, he *saw and reioyced in him : and when he died hee was not sorrowfull.

6 He left behinde him an auenger against his enemies, and one that shall requite kindnesse to his friends.

7 He that maketh too much of his sonne, shall binde vp his wounds, and his bowels wil be troubled at euery cry.

8 An horse not broken becommeth headstrong : and a childe left to himselfe will be wilfull.

9 Cocker thy childe, and hee shall make thee ||afraid : play with him, and he will bring thee to heauinesse.

10 Laugh not with him, lest thou haue sorrow with him, and lest thou gnash thy teeth in the end.

11 *Giue him no liberty in his youth, and winke not at his follies.

12 Bow downe his necke while hee is young, and beate him on the sides while he is a childe, lest hee waxe stubborne, and be disobedient vnto thee, and so bring sorrow to thine heart.

13 Cha-

Margin notes (left column)

*Dan. 4. 24
matt. 6. 20.
uke 11. 41.
and 12. 33.
.cts 10. 4.
. tim. 6.
8, 19.
*Iob 4 8,
, 10.

Or, faile.

Chap. 39.
3.

Margin notes (right column)

Of children.
*Prou. 13.
24. and 23.
13.

||Or, good by him.
||Or, kinsefolke.

*Deut. 6. 7.

*Psal. 128.

||Or, astonished.

*Cha. 7. 23.

13 Chastise thy sonne, and hold him to labour, lest his lewd behauiour be an offence vnto thee

Of health.

14 Better is the poore being sound and strong of constitution, then a rich man that is afflicted in his body.

15 Health and good state of body are aboue all gold, and a strong body aboue infinite wealth.

16 There is no riches aboue a sound body, and no ioy aboue the ioy of the heart.

17 Death is better then a bitter life, or continuall sickenesse.

18 Delicates powred vpon a mouth shut vp, are as messes of meat set vpon a graue.

19 What good doth the offering vnto an idole? for neither can it eat nor smell: so is he that is ‖persecuted of the Lord.

‖ Or, affli-cted.

20 Hee seeth with his eyes and gro-neth, as an Eunuch that embraceth a virgine, and sigheth.

* Pro. 12. 25. & 15. 13. and 17. 22.

21 * Giue not ouer thy mind to hea-uinesse, and afflict not thy selfe in thine owne counsell.

22 The gladnesse of the heart is the life of man, and the ‖ioyfulnes of a man prolongeth his dayes.

‖ Or, exul-tation.

23 Loue thine owne soule, and com-fort thy heart, remoue sorrow far from thee : for sorrow hath killed many, and there is no profit therein

24 Enuie and wrath shorten the life, and carefulnesse bringeth age before the time.

‖ Or, a noble.

25 ‖A cherefull and good heart will haue a care of his meat and diet.

CHAP. XXXI.

1 Of the desire of riches. 12 Of moderation and excesse in eating, or drinking wine.

* 1. Tim. 6. 9, 10.

Atching for *riches, consu-meth the flesh, and the care therof driueth away sleepe.

2 Watching care will not let a man slumber, as a sore disease breaketh sleepe.

3 The rich hath great labour in gathering riches together, and when he resteth, he is filled with his delicates.

4 The poore laboureth in his poore estate, and when he leaueth off, hee is still needie.

5 He that loueth gold shall not bee iustified, and he that followeth corrupti-on, shall haue enough thereof.

* Chap. 8. 2

6 *Gold hath bin the ruine of many, and their destruction was present.

7 It is a stumbling block vnto them that sacrifice vnto it, and euery foole shall be taken therewith.

8 *Blessed is the rich that is found without blemish, and hath not gone af-ter gold :

* Luke 6. 24.

9 Who is he? and we will call him blessed: for wonderfull things hath hee done among his people.

10 Who hath bene tried thereby, and found perfit? then let him glory. Who might offend and hath not offended, or done euill, and hath not done it?

11 His goods shall be established, and the congregatiō shall declare his almes.

12 If thou sit at a bountifull table, *bee not greedy vpon it, and †say not, There is much meate on it.

* Psa. 111. pro. 23. 1.
†Gr.open not thy throat vpon it.

13 Remember that a wicked eye is an euill thing : and what is created more wicked then an eye? therefore it wee-peth ‖vpon euery occasion.

‖ Or, before euery thing that is pre-sented.

14 Stretch not thine hand whither-soeuer it looketh, and thrust it not with him into the dish.

15 Iudge of thy neighbour by thy selfe : and be discreet in euery point.

16 Eate as it becommeth a man those things which are set before thee: and de-uoure not, lest thou be hated.

17 Leaue off first for maners sake, and be not vnsatiable, lest thou offend.

18 *When thou sittest among many, reach not thine hand out first of all.

* Chap. 37. 29.

19 A very litle is sufficient for a man well nurtured, ‖and he fetcheth not his wind short vpon his bed.

‖ Or, & lieth not puffing and blowing

20 Sound sleepe commeth of mode-rate eating : he riseth early, and his wits are with him, but the paine of wat-ching and choller, and pangs of the bel-lie are with an vnsatiable man.

21 And if thou hast bin forced to eate, arise, goe forth, vomit, and thou shalt haue rest.

22 My sonne, heare me, and despise me not, and at the last thou shalt finde as I told thee : in all thy workes bee quicke, so shall there no sickenesse come vnto thee.

23 *Who so is liberall of his meat, men shall speake well of him, and the report of his good housekeeping will be beleeued.

* Prou. 22 9.

24 But against him that is a. nig-gard of his meate, the whole citie shall murmure ; and the testimonies of his niggardnesse shall not be doubted of.

25 Shew not thy * valiantnesse in wine,

* Isal. 5. 1 Iudet. 13.

wine, for wine hath destroyed many.

26 The furnace prooueth the edge by dipping : so doth wine the hearts of the proud by drunkennesse.

27 Wine is as good as life to a man if it be drunke moderatly : what life is then to a man that is without wine? for it was made to make men glad.

28 Wine measurably drunke, and in season, bringeth gladnesse of the heart and cheerefulnesse of the minde.

29 But wine drunken with excesse, maketh bitternesse of the minde, with brawling and quarreling.

30 Drunkennesse increaseth the rage of a foole till he offend, it diminisheth strength, and maketh wounds.

31 Rebuke not thy neighbour at the wine, and despise him not in his mirth: giue him no despitefull words, and presse not vpon him with vrging him (to drinke.)

CHAP. XXXII.

1 Of his duty that is cheefe or master in a feast. 14 Of the feare of God. 18 Of counsell. 20 Of a ragged and a smooth way. 23 Trust not to any but to thy selfe and to God.

IF thou be made the master (of the feast) lift not thy selfe vp, but bee among them as one of the rest, take diligent care for them, and so sit downe.

2 And when thou hast done all thy office, take thy place that thou mayest be merry with them, and receiue a crowne for thy well ordering of the feast.

3 Speake thou that art the elder, for it becometh thee, but with sound iudgement, and hinder not musicke.

4 Powre not out words where *there is a musitian, and shew not forth wisedome out of time.

5 A consort of musicke in a banket of wine, is as a signet of Carbuncle set in gold.

6 As a signet of an Emeraud set in a worke of gold, so is the melodie of musicke with pleasant wine.

7 Speake yong man, if there be need of thee : and yet scarsely when thou art twise asked :

8 Let thy speach be short, comprehending much in few words, be as one that knoweth, and yet holdeth his tongue.

9 *If thou be among great men,

make not thy selfe equall with them, and when ancient men are in place, vse not many words.

10 Before the thunder goeth lightening : and before a shamefast man shall goe fauour.

11 Rise vp betimes, and be not the last : but get thee home without delay.

12 There take thy pastime, & do what thou wilt: but sinne not by proud speach

13 And for these things blesse him that made thee, and hath replenished thee with his good things.

14 Who so feareth the Lord, will receiue his discipline, and they that seeke him early, shall find fauour.

15 He that seeketh the law, shall be filled therewith : but the hypocrite will be offended thereat.

16 They that feare the Lord shall find iudgement, and shall kindle iustice as a light.

17 A sinfull man will not be reproued, but findeth an excuse according to his will.

18 A man of counsell will be considerate, but a strange and proud man is not daunted with feare, euen when of himselfe he hath done without counsell.

19 Doe nothing without aduice, and when thou hast once done, repent not.

20 Goe not in a way wherein thou maiest fall, and stumble not among the stones.

21 Be not confident in a plaine way.

22 And beware of thine owne children.

23 *In euery good worke trust thy owne soule : for this is the keeping of the commandements.

24 He that beleeueth in the Lord, taketh heed to the commandement, and he that trusted in him, ||shall fare neuer the worse.

CHAP. XXXIII.

1 The safety of him that feareth the Lord. 2 The wise and the foolish. 7 Times and seasons are of God. 10 Men are in his hands, as clay in the hands of the potter. 18 Cheefely regard thy selfe. 24 Of seruants.

THere shall no euill happen vnto him that feareth the Lord, but in temptation euen againe he wil deliuer him.

2 A wise man hateth not the Law, but he that is an hypocrite therein, is as a ship in a storme.

*Eccle. 3. 7. chap. 20. 7.

* Iob. 33. 6.

* Rom. 14. 5.

||Or, shall not be hurt.

3 A

3 A man of vnderstanding trusteth in the Law, and the Law is faithfull vnto him, ||as an oracle.

4 Prepare what to say, and so thou shalt be heard, and binde vp instruction, and then make answere.

5 The † heart of the * foolish is like a cartwheele : and his thoughts are like a rolling axeltree.

6 A stallion horse is as a mocking friend, hee neigheth vnder euery one that sitteth vpon him

7 Why doth one day excell another? when as all the light of euery day in the yeere is of the Sunne.

8 By the knowledge of the Lord they were distinguished : and he altered seasons and feasts.

9 Some of them hath hee made high dayes, and hallowed *them*, and some of them hath hee ||made ordinary dayes.

10 And all men are from the ground, and * Adam was created of earth.

11 In much knowledge the Lord hath diuided them, and made their wayes diuers.

12 Some of them hath hee blessed, and exalted, and some of them hath hee sanctified, and set neere himselfe : but some of them hath hee cursed, and brought low, and turned out of their ||places.

13 * As the clay is in the potters hand to fashion it at his pleasure : so man is in the hand of him that made him, to render to them as liketh him best.

14 Good is set against euill, and life against death : so is the godly against the sinner, and the sinner against the godly.

15 So looke vpon all the workes of the most High, and there are two and two, one against another.

16 I awaked vp last of all, as one that ||gathereth after the grape-gathe-rers : by the blessing of the Lord I pro-fited, and filled my wine-presse, like a gatherer of grapes.

17 * Consider that I laboured not for my selfe onely, but for all them that seeke learning;

18 Heare me, O ye great men of the people, and hearken with your eares ye rulers of the Congregation :

19 Giue not thy sonne, and wife, thy brother and friend power ouer thee while thou liuest, and giue not thy goods to another, lest it repent thee :

and thou intreat for the same againe.

20 As long as thou liuest and hast breath in thee, ||giue not thy selfe ouer to any.

21 For better it is that thy children should seeke to thee, then that thou shouldst ||stand to their courtesie.

22 In all thy workes keepe to thy selfe the preheminence, leaue not a staine in thine honour.

23 At the time when thou shalt end thy dayes, and finish thy life, distribute thine inheritance.

24 Fodder, a wand, and burdens, *are* for the asse : and bread, correction, and worke for a seruant.

25 If thou set thy seruant to la-bour, thou shalt finde rest : but if thou let him goe idle, he shall seeke libertie.

26 A yoke and a collar doe bow the necke : so are tortures and torments for an euill seruant.

27 Sende him to labour that hee be not idle : for idlenesse teacheth much euill.

28 Set him to worke, as is fit for him; if he be not obedient, put on more heauy fetters.

29 But be not excessiue toward any, and without discretion doe nothing.

30 * If thou haue a seruant, let him bee vnto thee as thy selfe, because thou hast bought him † with a price.

31 If thou haue a seruant, in-treate him as a brother : for thou hast neede of him, as of thine owne soule : if thou intreate him euill, and he runne from thee, which way wilt thou goe to seeke him?

CHAP. XXXIIII.

1 Of dreames. 13 The praise and blessing of them that feare the Lord. 18 The offering of the ancient, and praier of the poore innocent.

 HE hopes of a man voyd of vnderstanding are vaine, and false : and dreames lift vp fooles.

2 Who so ||regardeth dreames, is like him that catcheth at a shadow, and follow-eth after the winde.

3 The vision of dreames is the re-semblance of one thing to another, euen as the * likenesse of a face to a face.

4 * Of an vncleane thing, what can be cleansed? and from that thing which is false, what trueth can come?

5 Diui-

Side notes (left column):

‖ *Or, as the asking of Vrim.*

† *Greeke, bowels.*
* *Chap. 21. 16.*

‖ *Or, ordai-ned for the number of dayes.*
* *Gen. 1. 27. and 2. 7.*

‖ *Or, stan-dings.*
* *Esay 45. 9. rom. 9. 20, 21.*

‖ *Or, glea-neth.*

* *Chap. 24. 39.*

Side notes (right column):

‖ *Or, sell not.*

‖ *Or, looke to their hands.*

Of seruants.

* *Chap. 7. 20.*
† *Greeke, in blood.*

Of dreames.

‖ *Or, hath his minde vpon.*

* *Prou. 27 19.*
* *Iob 14. 4*

5 Diuinations, and soothsayings, and dreames are vaine : and the heart fancieth as a womans heart in trauell.

6 If they be not sent from the most high in thy visitation, ||set not thy heart vpon them.

Or, regard them not.

7 For dreames haue deceiued many, and they haue failed that put their trust in them.

8 The Law shall be found perfect without lies : and wisedome is perfection to a faithfull mouth.

9 A man that hath trauailed knoweth many things : and hee that hath much experience, wil declare wisedome.

10 He that hath no experience, knoweth little : but he that hath trauailed, is full of prudence.

11 When I trauailed, I saw many things : and I vnderstand more, then I can expresse.

12 I was oft times in danger of death, yet I was deliuered because of these things.

13 The spirit of those that feare the Lord shall liue, for their hope is in him that saueth them.

14 Who so feareth the Lord, shall not feare nor be afraid, for hee is his hope.

15 Blessed is the soule of him that feareth the Lord : to whom doeth hee looke ? and who is his strength ?

Psal. 33. 18. and 61. 1, 2.

16 For *the eyes of the Lord are vpon them that loue him, he is their mightie protection, and strong stay, a defence from heat, and a couer from the Sunne at noone, a preseruation from stumbling, and a helpe from falling.

17 He raiseth vp the soule, and lighteneth the eyes : hee giueth health, life, and blessing.

Prou. 21. 27.

18 *Hee that sacrificeth of a thing wrongfully gotten, his offering is ridiculous, and the ||giftes of vniust men are not accepted.

Or, the mockeries.

Pro. 15. 8.

19 *The most high is not pleased with the offerings of the wicked, neither is he pacified for sinne by the multitude of sacrifices.

20 Who so bringeth an offering of the goods of the poore, doeth as one that killeth the sonne before his fathers eyes.

21 The bread of the needie, is their life : he that defraudeth him thereof, is a man of blood.

22 Hee that taketh away his neighbours liuing, slayeth him : and hee that

*defraudeth the labourer of his hire, is a bloodshedder.

Deut. 24. 14, 15. cha. 7. 20.

23 When one buildeth, and another pulleth downe, what profite haue they then but labour ?

24 When one prayeth, and another curseth, whose voice will the Lorde heare ?

25 *He that washeth himselfe after the touching of a dead body, if he touch it againe, what auaileth his washing ?

Num. 19. 11, 12.

26 So is it with a man that fasteth for his sinnes, and goeth againe and doeth the same : who will heare his prayer, or what doeth his humbling profit him ?

CHAP. XXXV.

1 Sacrifices pleasing God. 14 The prayer of the fatherlesse, of the widow, and of the humble in spirit. 20 Acceptable mercy.

Ee *that keepeth the law, bringeth offerings enow : he that taketh heed to the commandement, offereth a peace offering.

1. Sam. 15. 22. iere. 7. 3, 5, 6, 7.

2 He that requiteth a good turne, offereth fine floure : and he that giueth almes, sacrificeth praise.

3 To depart from wickednesse is a thing pleasing to the Lord : and to forsake vnrighteousnesse, is a propitiation.

4 *Thou shalt not appeare emptie before the Lord :

Exod. 23. 15. deut. 16. 16.

5 For all these things [are to bee done] because of the commandement.

6 The offering of the righteous maketh the Altar fat, and the sweete sauour thereof *is* before the most high.

7 The sacrifice of a iust man is acceptable, and the memoriall thereof shall neuer be forgotten.

8 Giue the Lord his honour with a good eye, and diminish not the first fruits of thine hands.

9 *In all thy gifts shew a cheerefull countenance, and ||dedicate thy tithes with gladnesse.

2. Cor. 9. 7. *Or, set apart.*

10 *Giue vnto the most high, according as hee hath enriched thee, and as thou hast gotten, giue with a cheerefull eye.

Tob. 4. 8.

11 For the Lord recompenseth, and will giue thee seuen times as much.

12 ||Doe not thinke to corrupt with gifts, *for such he will not receiue : and trust not to vnrighteous sacrifices, for the

Or, diminish nothing of thy offerings. *Leuit. 22. 21, 22. deu. 16. 21.*

* Deut. 10.
17. 2. chr. 19
7. Iob 34. 19
wisd. 6. 7.
acts 10. 34.
rom. 2. 11.
gal. 2. 6.
eph. 6. 9.
colos. 3. 25.
1. pet. 1. 17.

the Lord is iudge, and with him is *no respect of persons.

13 Hee will not accept any person against a poore man : but will heare the prayer of the oppressed.

14 He will not despise the supplication of the fatherlesse : nor the widowe when she powreth out her complaint

15 Doeth not the teares run downe the widowes cheeks ? and is not her crie against him that causeth them to fall ?

16 He that serueth the Lord, shall be accepted with fauour, and his prayer shall reach vnto the cloudes

17 The prayer of the humble pierceth the clouds : and till it come nigh he will not be comforted : and will not depart till the most High shall beholde to iudge righteously, and execute iudgement.

18 For the Lord will not be slacke, neither will the mightie be patient towards them, till he hath smitten in sunder the loines of the vnmercifull, and repaid vengeance to the heathen : till he haue taken away the multitude of the ||proud, and broken the scepter of the vnrighteous :

|| Or, cruell oppressours.

19 Till he haue rendred to euery man according to his deeds, and to the works of men according to their deuises, till he haue iudged the cause of his people· and made them to reioyce in his mercie,

20 Mercie is †seasonable in the time of affliction, as cloudes of raine in the time of drought.

† Gre. faire.

CHAP. XXXVI.

1 A prayer for the Church against the enemies thereof. 18 A good heart and a froward. 21 Of a good wife.

Aue mercie vpon vs , O Lord God of all, and behold vs :

2 And send thy feare vpon all the nations that seeke not after thee.

3 *Lift vp thy hand ||against the strange nations, and let them see thy power.

* Ier. 10. 25
|| Or, vpon.

4 As thou wast sanctified in vs before them : so be thou magnified among them before vs

5 And let them know thee, as we haue knowen thee, that there is no God, but onely thou, O God.

6 Shew new signes, and make other strange wonders : glorifie thy hand and thy right arme, that they may set forth thy wonderous workes,

7 Raise vp indignation, and powre out wrath : take away the aduersarie and destroy the enemie.

8 Make the time short, remember the †couenant, and let them declare thy wonderfull works.

† Gre. othe

9 Let him that escapeth, be consumed by the rage of the fire, and let them perish that oppresse the people

10 Smite in sunder the heads of the rulers of the heathen, that say, There is none other but we.

11 Gather all the tribes of Iacob together, and inherit thou them, as from the beginning

12 O Lord haue mercie vpon the people, that is called by thy name, and vpon Israel, * whom thou hast named thy first borne.

* Exo. 4.

13 O bee mercifull vnto Ierusalem thy holy citie, the place of thy rest.

14 Fill Sion with ||thine vnspeakable oracles, and thy people with thy glory.

|| Or, that may mag fie thine racles.

15 Giue testimonie vnto those that thou hast possessed from the beginning, and raise vp ||prophets that haue bin in thy name.

|| Or, prop cies.

16 Reward them that wait for thee, and let thy prophets be found faithfull.

17 O Lord heare the prayer of thy ||seruants, according to the *blessing of Aaron ouer thy people, that all they which dwel vpon the earth, may know that thou art the Lord, the eternall God.

|| Or, suppliants.
* Num. 6
25.

18 The belly deuoureth all meates, yet is one meat better then another.

19 *As the palate tasteth diuers kinds of venison : so doth an heart of vnderstanding false speeches

* Iob 34.

20 A froward heart causeth heauinesse : but a man of experience will recompense him.

21 A woman will receiue euery man, yet is one daughter better then another

22 The beautie of a woman cheareth the countenance, and a man loueth nothing better.

23 If there be kindnesse, meekenes, and comfort in her tongue, then is not her husband like ||other men.

|| Or, con mon.

24 He that getteth a wife, beginneth || a possession, a helpe like vnto himselfe, and a pillar of rest.

|| Or, to thriue.

25 Where no hedge is, there the possession is spoiled : and he that hath no wife will wander vp and downe mourning.

26 Who

26 Who will trust a thiefe well appointed, that skippeth from citie to citie? so [who will beleeue] a man that hath no house? and lodgeth wheresoeuer the night taketh him?

CHAP. XXXVII.

1 How to know friends and counsellers. 12 The descretion and wisedome of a godly man blesseth him. 27 Learne to refraine thine appetite.

Very friend saieth, I am his friend also : but there is a friend which is onely a friend in name.

2 Is it not a griefe vnto death, when a companion and friend is turned to an enemie?

3 O wicked imagination, whence camest thou in to couer the earth with deceit?

4 There is a companion, which reioyceth in the prosperity of a friend : but in the time of trouble will be against him.

5 There is a companion which helpeth his friend for the belly, and taketh vp the buckler ||against the enemie.

‖ *Or, in presence of the enemie.*

6 Forget not thy friend in thy minde, and be not vnmindfull of him in thy riches.

7 Euery counseller extolleth counsell; but there is some that counselleth for himselfe.

8 Beware of a counseller, and know before ||what neede he hath (for he will counsell for himselfe) lest hee cast the lot vpon thee :

‖ *Or, what vse there is of him.*

9 And say vnto thee, Thy way is good : and afterward he stand on the other side, to see what shall befall thee.

10 Consult not with one that suspecteth thee : and hide thy counsell from such as enuie thee.

11 Neither consult with a woman touching her of whom she is iealous; neither with a coward in matters of warre, nor with a merchant concerning exchange; nor with a buyer of selling; nor with an enuious man of thankfulnesse; nor with an vnmercifull man touching kindnesse; nor with the slouthfull for any worke; nor with an hireling for a yeere, of finishing worke; nor with an idle seruant of much businesse : Hearken not vnto these in any matter of counsell.

12 But be continually with a godly man, whom thou knowest to keepe the commandements of the Lord, whose minde is according to thy minde, and will sorrow with thee, if thou shalt miscarry.

13 And let the counsell of thine owne heart stand : for there is no man more faithfull vnto thee then it.

14 For a mans minde is sometime wont to tell him more then seuen watchmen, that sit aboue in an high towre.

15 And aboue all this pray to the most high, that he will direct thy way in trueth.

16 Let reason goe before euery enterprise, & counsell before euery action.

17 The countenance is a signe of changing of the heart.

18 Foure maner of things appeare : good and euill, life and death : but the tongue ruleth ouer them continually.

19 There is one that is wise and teacheth many, and yet is vnprofitable to himselfe.

20 There is one that sheweth wisedome in words, and is hated : he shall be destitute of all ||foode.

‖ *Or, wisedome.*

21 For grace is not giuen him from the Lord : because he is depriued of all wisedome.

22 Another is wise to himselfe : and the fruits of vnderstanding are commendable in his mouth.

23 A wise man instructeth his people, and the fruits of his vnderstanding faile not.

24 A wise man shall be filled with blessing, and all they that see him, shall count him happy.

25 The daies of the life of man may be numbred : but the daies of Israel are innumerable.

26 A wise man shall inherite ||glory among his people, and his name shalbe perpetuall.

‖ *Or, credit.*

27 My sonne prooue thy soule in thy life, and see what is euill for it, and giue not that vnto it.

28 For all things are not profitable for all men, neither hath euery soule pleasure in euery thing.

29 Be not vnsatiable in any dainty thing : nor too greedy vpon meates.

30 For ||excesse of meates, bringeth sicknesse, and surfetting will turne into choler.

‖ *Or, varietie of meates.*

31 By surfetting haue many perished, but hee that taketh heed, prolongeth his life.

CHAP.

CHAP. XXXVIII.

1 Honour due to the Phisitian, and why 16 How to weepe and mourne for the dead. 24 The wisedome of the learned man, and of the Labourer and Artificer: with the vse of them both

 Onour a Phisitian with the honour due vnto him, for the vses which you may haue of him: for the Lord hath created him.

2 For of the most High commeth healing, and he shall receiue ‖honour of the King.

‖ *Or, a gift.*

3 The skill of the Phisitian shall lift vp his head: and in the sight of great men he shalbe in admiration.

4 The Lord hath created medicines out of the earth; and he that is wise will not abhorre them.

5 Was not the water made sweet with wood, that the *vertue thereof might be knowen?

* Exod. 15. 25.

6 And he hath giuen men skill, that hee might be honoured in his marueilous workes.

7 With such doeth he heale [men,] and taketh away their paines.

8 Of such doeth the Apothecarie make a confection, and of his workes there is no end, and from him is peace ouer all the earth.

9 My sonne, in thy sickenesse be not negligent: but *pray vnto the Lord, and he will make thee whole.

* Esay. 38. 2.

10 Leaue off from sinne, and order thy hands aright, and cleanse thy heart from all wickednesse.

11 Giue a sweet sauour, and a memoriall of fine flowre: and make a fat offering, as ‖not being.

‖ *Or, as a dead man.*

12 Then giue place to the phisitian, for the Lord hath created him: let him not go from thee, for thou hast need of him.

13 There is a time when in their hands there is good successe.

14 For they shall also pray vnto the Lord, that hee would prosper that, which they giue, for ease and ‖remedy to prolong life.

‖ *Or, euring.*

15 He that sinneth before his maker, let him fal into the hand of the Phisitian.

16 My sonne, let teares fall downe ouer the dead, and begin to lament, as if thou hadst suffered great harme thy selfe: and then couer his body according to the custome, & neglect not his buriall.

17 Weepe bitterly, and make great moane, and vse lamentation, as hee is worthy, and that a day or two, lest thou be euill spoken of: and then comfort thy selfe for thy heauinesse.

18 For of heauinesse commeth death, and the heauinesse of the *heart, breaketh strength.

* Prou. 15. 13. and 17. 22.

19 In affliction also sorrow remaineth: and the life of the poore, is the curse of the heart.

20 Take no heauines to heart: driue it away, and remember the last end.

21 Forget it not, for there is no turning againe: thou shalt not doe him good, but hurt thy selfe

22 Remember ‖my iudgement: for thine also shall be so; yesterday for me, and to day for thee.

‖ *Or, the sentence vpon him.*

23 When the dead is at *rest, let his remembrance rest, & be comforted for him, when his spirit is departed from him.

* 2. Sam. 12. 20.

24 The wisedome of a learned man cometh by opportunitie of leasure: & he that hath litle busines shal become wise.

25 How can he get wisdome that holdeth the plough, and that glorieth in the goad; that driueth oxen, and is occupied in their labours, and whose talke is †of bullocks?

† *Greeke, of the breed of bullocks.*

26 He giueth his minde to make furrowes: and is diligent to giue the kine fodder.

27 So euery carpenter, and workemaster, that laboureth night and day: and they that cut and graue seales, and are diligent to make great variety, and giue themselues to counterfait imagerie, and watch to finish a worke.

28 The smith also sitting by the anuill, & considering the iron worke; the vapour of the fire wasteth his flesh, and he fighteth with the heat of the furnace: the noise of the hammer & the anuill is euer in his eares, and his eies looke still vpon the patterne of the thing that he maketh, he setteth his mind to finish his worke, & watcheth to polish it perfitly.

29 So doeth the potter sitting at his worke, and turning the wheele about with his feet, who is alway carefully set at his worke: and maketh all his worke by number

30 He fashioneth the clay with his arme, and ‖boweth downe his strength before his feet: he applieth himselfe to lead it ouer; and he is diligent to make cleane the furnace.

‖ *Or, tempereth it with his feet.*

31 All these trust to their hands: and euery one is wise in his worke.

32 With-

32 Without these cannot a citie be inhabited : and they shall not dwell where they will, nor goe vp and downe.

33 They shall not be sought for in publike counsaile, nor sit high in the congregation : they shal not sit on the Iudges seate, nor vnderstand the sentence of iudgement : they cannot declare iustice, and iudgement, and they shall not be found where parables are spoken.

34 But they will maintaine the state of the world, and [all] their desire is in the worke of their craft.

CHAP. XXXIX.

1 A description of him that is truely wise. 12 An exhortation to praise God for his workes, which are good to the good, and euill to them that are euill.

BVT hee that giueth his minde to the Law of the most high, and is occupied in the meditation thereof, wil seeke out the wisdome of all the ancient, and be occupied in prophecies.

2 Hee will keepe the sayings of the renowned men : and where subtile parables are, he will be there also.

3 Hee will seeke out the secrets of graue sentences, and be conuersant in darke parables.

4 He shall serue among great men, and appeare before princes : he will trauaile through strange countreys, for hee hath tried the good, and the euill among men.

5 Hee will giue his heart to resort early to the Lord that made him, and will pray before the most high, and will open his mouth in prayer, and make supplication for his sinnes.

6 When the great Lord will, he shall bee filled with the spirit of vnderstanding : he shal powre out wise sentences, and giue thankes vnto the Lord in his prayer.

7 Hee shall direct his counsell and knowledge, and in his secrets shall hee meditate.

8 Hee shall shew foorth that which he hath learned, and shall glory in the Law of the couenant of the Lord.

9 Many shall commend his vnderstanding, and so long as the world endureth, it shall not be blotted out, his memoriall shall not depart away, and his name shall liue from generation to generation.

10 * Nations shall shewe foorth his wisedome, and the congregation shall declare his praise.

11 If hee die, he shall leaue a greater name then a thousand : and if he liue, he shall ||increase it.

12 Yet I haue more to say which I haue thought vpon, for I am filled as the Moone at the full.

13 Hearken vnto me, ye holy children, and budde foorth as a rose growing by the ||brooke of the field :

14 And giue yee a sweete sauour as frankincense, and flourish as a lilly, send foorth a smell, and sing a song of praise, blesse the Lord in all his workes.

15 Magnifie his Name, and shewe foorth his praise with the songs of your lips, and with harpes, and in praising him you shall say after this maner :

16 * Al the works of the Lord are exceeding good, & whatsoeuer hee commandeth, shalbe _accomplished_ in due season.

17 And none may say, What is this ? wherefore is that ? for at time conuenient they shall all be sought out : at his commaundement the waters stood as an heape, & at the wordes of his mouth the receptacles of waters.

18 At his commandement is done whatsoeuer pleaseth him, and none can hinder when he will saue.

19 The workes of all flesh are before him, & nothing can be hid from his eyes.

20 He seeth from euerlasting to euerlasting, and there is nothing wonderfull before him.

21 A man neede not to say, What is this ? wherefore is that ? for hee hath made all things for their vses.

22 His blessing couered the dry land as a riuer, and watered it as a flood.

23 As hee hath turned the waters into saltnesse : so shall the heathen inherite his wrath.

24 * As his wayes are plaine vnto the holy, so are they stumbling blockes vnto the wicked.

25 For the good, are good things created from the beginning : so euill things for sinners.

26 The principall things for the whole vse of mans life, are water, fire, yron, and salt, floure of wheate, honie, milke, and the blood of the grape, and oyle, and clothing

27 All these things are for good to the godly : so to the sinners they are turned into euill.

28 There

* Chap. 44. 15.

‖ Or, gaine vnto it.

‖ Or, riuers of water.

* Gen. 1. 31. mark. 7. 37.

* Ose 14. 10.

28 There be spirits that are created for vengeance, which in their furie lay on sore strokes, in the time of destruction they powre out their force, and appease the wrath of him that made them.

29 Fire, and haile, and famine, and death : all these were created for vengeance :

‖ Or, vipers.

30 Teeth of wild beasts, and scorpions, ‖serpents, & the sword, punishing the wicked to destruction.

31 They shall reioice in his commandement, and they shall bee ready vpon earth when neede is, and when their time is come, they shall not transgresse his word.

32 Therefore from the beginning I was resolued, and thought vpon these things, and haue left them in writing.

33 All the workes of the Lord are good : and he will giue euery needefull thing in due season.

34 So that a man cannot say, This is worse then that : for in time they shall all be well approued.

35 And therefore praise ye the Lord with the whole heart and mouth, and blesse the Name of the Lord.

CHAP. XL.

1 Many miseries in a mans life. 12 The reward of vnrighteousnesse, and the fruit of true dealing. 17 A vertuous wife, & an honest friend reioyce the heart, but the feare of the Lord is aboue all. 28 A beggers life is hatefull.

* Eccles. 1.3

Reat *trauaile is created for euery man, and an heauy yoke is vpon the sons of Adam, from the day that they goe out of their mothers wombe, till the day that they returne to the mother of all things.

2 Their imagination of things to come, & the day of death [trouble] their thoughts, and [cause] feare of heart :

3 From him that sitteth on a throne of glory, vnto him that is humbled in earth and ashes.

‖ Or, to the porter.

4 From him that weareth purple, and a crown, ‖vnto him that is clothed with a linnen frocke.

5 Wrath, and enuie, trouble and vnquietnesse, feare of death, and anger, and strife, and in the time of rest vpon his bed, his night sleepe doe change his knowledge,

6 A litle or nothing is his rest, and afterward he is in his sleepe, as in a day

of keeping watch, troubled in the vision of his heart, as if he were escaped out of a battell :

7 When all is safe, he awaketh, and marueileth that the feare was nothing.

8 [Such things happen] vnto all flesh, both man and beast, and that is seuen fold more vpon sinners.

* Chap. 39. 29, 30.

9 *Death and bloodshed, strife and sword, calamities, famine, tribulation, and the scourge :

10 These things are created for the wicked, and for their sakes came the *flood.

* Gen. 7. 1

11 *All things that are of the earth shal turne to the earth againe: and that which is of the *waters doeth returne into the Sea.

* Gen. 3. 19 chap. 41. 10

* Eccles 1.

12 All †briberie and iniustice shall be blotted out : but true dealing shall endure for euer.

† Gre. bribe

13 The goods of the vniust shall bee dried vp like a riuer, and shall vanish with noise, like a great thunder in raine.

14 While he openeth his hand he shal reioyce : so shall transgressours come to nought.

15 The children of the vngodly shall not bring forth many branches: but are as vncleane roots vpon a hard rocke.

* Iob. 8. 11 and 16. 12. gen. 41. 2.

16 *The weed growing vpon euery water, and banke of a riuer, shall bee pulled vp before all grasse.

‖ Or, a garden that is blessed.

17 Bountifulnes is as a most ‖fruitfull garden, and mercifulnesse endureth for euer.

* Phil. 4. 11 1. tim. 6. 6

18 To *labour & to be content with that a man hath, is a sweet life : but hee that findeth a treasure, is aboue them both.

19 Children and the building of a citie continue a mans name : but a blamelesse wife is counted aboue them both.

20 Wine & musicke reioyce the heart: but the loue of wisedome is aboue them both.

21 The pipe and the psalterie make sweet melodie : but a pleasant tongue is aboue them both.

22 Thine eye desireth fauour and beautie : but more then both, corne while it is greene.

23 A friend and companion neuer meet amisse : but aboue both is a wife with her husband.

24 Brethren and helpe are against time of trouble : but almes shall deliuer more then them both.

25 Golde and siluer make the foote stand

* Isai. 4. 15.
|| Or, a garden that is blessed.

stand sure : but counsell is esteemed aboue them both.

26 Riches and strength lift vp the heart : but the feare of the Lord is aboue them both : there is no want in the feare of the Lord, and it needeth not to seeke helpe.

27 * The feare of the Lord is a || fruitfull garden, and couereth him aboue all glory.

28 My sonne, lead not a beggers life : for better it is to die then to beg.

29 The life of him that dependeth on another mans table, is not to be counted for a life : for he polluteth himselfe with other mens meate, but a wise man well nurtured will beware thereof.

30 Begging is sweet in the mouth of the shamelesse : but in his belly there shall burne a fire.

CHAP. XLI.

1 The remembrance of Death. 3 Death is not to be feared. 5 The vngodly shall be accursed. 11 Of an euill and a good name. 14 Wisedome is to be vttered. 16 Of what things we should be ashamed.

|| Or, to whom euery thing is troublesome.

Death, how bitter is the remembrance of thee to a man that liueth at rest in his possessions, vnto the man that hath nothing to vexe him, and that hath prosperity in all things : yea vnto him that is yet able to receiue meate ?

2 O death, acceptable is thy sentence vnto the needy, and vnto him whose strength faileth, that is now in the last age, and is || vexed with all things, and to him that despaireth and hath lost patience.

3 Feare not the sentence of death, remember them that haue beene before thee, and that come after, for this is the sentence of the Lord ouer all flesh.

4 And why art thou against the pleasure of the most High ? there is no inquisition in the graue, whether thou haue liued ten, or a hundred, or a thousand yeeres.

5 The children of sinners, are abhominable children : and they that are conuersant in the dwelling of the vngodly.

6 The inheritance of sinners children shal perish, and their posterity shal haue a perpetuall reproch.

7 The children will complaine of an vngodly father, because they shall be reproched for his sake.

8 Woe be vnto you vngodly men which haue forsaken the law of the most high God : for if you encrease, it shall be to your destruction.

9 And if you be borne, you shall be borne to a curse : and if you die, a curse shall be your portion.

10 * All that are of the earth shall turne to earth againe : so the vngodly shall goe from a curse to destruction.

* Chap. 40. 11.

11 The mourning of men is about their bodies : but an ill name of sinners shall be blotted out.

12 Haue regard to thy name : for that shall continue with thee aboue a thousand great treasures of gold.

13 A good life hath but few daies : but a good name endureth for euer.

14 My children, keepe discipline in peace : for wisedome that is hid, and a treasure that is not seene, what profit is in them both ?

15 A man that hideth his foolishnesse is better then a man that hideth his wisedome.

16 Therefore be shamefast according to my word : for it is not good to retaine all shamefastnesse, neither is it altogether approoued in euery thing.

17 Be ashamed of whoredome before father and mother, and of a lie before a prince and a mighty man :

18 Of an offence before a iudge and ruler, of iniquitie before a congregation and people, of vniust dealing before thy partner and friend :

19 And of theft in regard of the place where thou soiournest, and in regard of the trueth of God and his couenant, and to leane with thine elbow vpon the meate, and of scorning to giue and take :

20 And of silence before them that salute thee, and to look vpon an harlot :

21 And to turne away thy face from thy kinsman, or to take away a portion or a gift, or to gaze vpon another mans wife,

22 Or to bee ouerbusie with his maide, and come not neere her bed, or of vpbraiding speaches before friends ; and after thou hast giuen, vpbraide not :

23 Or of iterating and speaking againe that which thou hast heard, and of reuealing of secrets.

24 So

24 So shalt thou be truely shame-fast, and finde fauour before all men.

CHAP. XLII.

1 Whereof we should not be ashamed. 9 Be carefull of thy daughter. 12 Beware of a wo-man. 15 The workes and greatnes of God.

 F these things be not thou ashamed, and accept no person to sinne thereby.

2 Of the Law of the most High, and his Coue-nant, and of iudgement to iustifie the vngodly :

|| *Or, of thy partners speech.*
|| *Or, compa-nions.*
|| *Or, of the giuing.*
|| *Or, with-out profit.*

3 Of ||reckoning with thy part-ners, and ||traueilers : or of the ||gift of the heritage of friends :

4 Of exactnesse of ballance, and waights : or of getting much or little :

5 And of merchants ||indifferent sel-ling, of much correction of children, and to make the side of an euill seruant to bleed.

6 Sure keeping is good where an euill wife is, and shut vp where many hands are.

7 Deliuer all things in number and waight, and put al in writing that thou ||giuest out, or receiuest in.

1 *Or, dealest for.*
|| *Or, rebuke.*

8 Be not ashamed to ||informe the vnwise and foolish, and the extreeme aged ||that contendeth with those that are yong, thus shalt thou bee truely learned and approued of all men liuing.

1 *Or, that is accused of fornication.*

9 The father waketh for the daugh-ter when no man knoweth, and the care for her taketh away sleepe ; when shee is yong lest shee passe away the flowre of her age, and being married, lest she should be hated :

10 In her virginitie lest she should be defiled, and gotten with childe in her fa-thers house ; and hauing an husband, lest she should misbehaue herselfe : and when shee is married, lest shee should be barren.

11 Keepe a sure watch ouer a shame-lesse daughter, lest shee make thee a laughing stocke to thine enemies, and a by-word in the citie, and a reproch a-mong the people, and make thee asha-med before the multitude.

* *Chap. 25. 23.*

12 Behold not euery bodies *beauty, and sit not in the midst of women.

* *Gene. 3. 6.*
1 *Or, wic-kednesse.*

13 For from garments commeth a moth, and *from women wickednesse.

14 Better is the ||churlishnesse of a man, then a courteous woman, a wo-man *I say*, which bringeth shame and reproch.

15 I will now remember the works of the Lord, and declare the things that I haue seene : in the words of the Lord are his workes.

16 The Sunne that giueth light, looketh vpon all things : and the worke thereof is full of the glory of the Lord.

17 The Lord hath not giuen power to the Saints to declare all his maruei-lous workes, which the Almightie Lord firmely setled, that whatsoeuer is, might be established for his glory.

|| *Or, the highest.*

18 He seeketh out the deepe and the heart, and considereth their crafty de-uices : for ||the Lord knoweth all that may be knowen, and he beholdeth the signes of the world.

19 Hee declareth the things that are past, and for to come, and reueileth the steps of hidden things.

* *Iob 41.*
esay 21. 1

20 No *thought escapeth him, nei-ther any word is hidden from him.

21 Hee hath garnished the excellent workes of his wisedome, and hee is from euerlasting to euerlasting, vnto him may nothing be added, neither can he be diminished, and he hath no need of any counseller.

22 O how desireable are all his workes : and that a man may see euen to a sparke.

23 All these things liue and remaine for euer, for all vses, and they are all obedient.

24 All things are double one against another : and hee hath made nothing vnperfit.

25 One thing establisheth the good of another : and who shalbe filled with beholding his glory ?

CHAP. XLIII.

1 The workes of God in heauen, and in earth, and in the sea, are exceeding glorious and wonderfull. 29 Yet God himselfe in his power and wisedome is aboue all.

 He pride of the height, the cleare firmament, the beautie of heauen, with his glorious shew ;

2 The Sunne when it appeareth, declaring at his rising, a marueilous ||instrument, the worke of the most High.

|| *Or, vesse*

3 At noone it parcheth the country, and who can abide the burning heate thereof ?

4 A man blowing a furnace is in
works of heat, but the Sunne burneth
the mountaines three times more; breathing out fiery vapours, and sending
foorth bright beames, it dimmeth the
eyes.
5 Great is the Lord that made it,
and at his commandement †it runneth
hastily.
6 *He made the Moone also to serue
in her season, for a declaration of times,
and a signe of the world.
7 *From the Moone is the signe of
Feasts, a light that decreaseth in her
perfection.
8 The moneth is called after her
name, encreasing wonderfully in her
changing, being an instrument of the
armies aboue, shining in the firmament
of heauen,
9 The beautie of heauen, the glory
of the starres, an ornament giuing light
in the highest places of the Lord.
10 At the commandement of the holy One, they will stand in their order,
and neuer faint in their watches.
11 *Looke vpon the rainebow, and
praise him that made it, very beautifull
it is in the brightnesse thereof.
12 *It compasseth the heauen about
with a glorious circle, and the hands of
the most high haue bended it.
13 By his commandement hee maketh the snow to fall apace, and sendeth
swiftly the lightnings of his iudgment.
14 Through this the treasures are
opened, and clouds flie forth as foules.
15 By his great power hee maketh
the cloudes firme, and the hailestones
are broken small.
16 At his sight the mountaines are
shaken, and at his will the South wind
bloweth.
17 The noise of the thunder maketh
the earth to ||tremble: so doth the Nor-
thren storme, and the whirlewinde: as
birds flying he scattereth the snow, and
the falling downe thereof, is as the lighting of grashoppers.
18 The eye marueileth at the beauty
of the whitenesse thereof, and the heart
is astonished at the raining of it.
19 The hoare frost also as salt hee
powreth on the earth, and being con-
gealed, ||it lieth on the toppe of sharpe
stakes.
20 When the colde North-winde
bloweth, and the water is congealed
into yce, it abideth vpon euery gathering together of water, and clotheth
the water as with a brestplate.
21 It deuoureth the mountaines,
and burneth the wildernesse, and consumeth the grasse as fire.
22 A present remedy of all is a miste
comming speedily: a dew comming ||after
heate, refresheth.
23 By his counsell he appeaseth the
deepe, and planteth Ilands therein.
24 They that saile on the Sea, tell
of the danger thereof, and when wee
heare it with our eares, wee marueile
thereat.
25 For therein be strange and wonderous workes, variety of all kindes
of beasts, and whales created.
26 By him the ende of them hath
prosperous successe, and by his word all
things consist.
27 We may speake much, & yet come
short: wherefore in summe, he is all.
28 How shall wee be able to magnifie him? for hee is great aboue all his
workes.
29 *The Lord is terrible and very
great, and marueilous is his power.
30 When you glorifie the Lord exalt
him as much as you can: for euen yet
wil he farre exceed, and when you exalt
him, put foorth all your strength, and
be not weary: for you can neuer goe
farre enough.
31 *Who hath seene him, that hee
might tell vs? and who can magnifie
him as he is?
32 There are yet hid greater things
then these be, for wee haue seene but a
few of his workes:
33 For the Lord hath made all things,
and to the godly hath hee giuen wisedome.

† Gr. hee stayed his course.
* Gen. 1. 16.
* Exo. 12. 2.
* Gen. 9. 13.
* Esa. 40. 12.
|| Or, to grone as a woman in her trauaile.
|| Or, it is as the point of sharp stakes.
|| Or, vpon the heat.
* Psal. 107. 23.
* Psal. 96. 42
* Psal. 106. 2 ioh. 1. 18.

CHAP. XLIIII.

1 The praise of certaine holy men: 16 Of Enoch, 17 Noah, 19 Abraham, 22 Isaac, 23 and Iacob.

LEt vs now praise famous
men, and our Fathers
that begat vs.
2 The Lorde hath
wrought great glory by
them, through his great power from
the beginning.
3 Such as did beare rule in their
kingdomes, men renowmed for their
power, giuing counsell by their vnderstanding, and declaring prophecies:
4 Leaders of the people by their
coun-

The praise of the fathers.

counsels, and by their knowledge of learning meet for the people, wise and eloquent in their instructions.

5 Such as found out musical tunes, and reiected ||verses in writing.

|| Or, ditties.

6 Rich men furnished with abilitie, liuing peaceably in their habitations.

7 All these were honoured in their generations, and were the glory of their times.

8 There be of them, that haue left a name behind them, that their praises might be reported.

9 And some there be, which haue no memorial, * who are perished as though they had neuer bene, and are become as though they had neuer bene borne, and their children after them.

* Gen. 7. 22

10 But these were mercifull men, whose righteousnesse hath not beene forgotten.

11 With their seed shall continually remaine a good inheritance, and their children are within the couenant.

12 Their seed stands fast, and their children ||for their sakes.

|| Or, after them.

13 Their seed shall remaine for euer, and their glory shall not be blotted out.

14 Their bodies are buried in peace, but their name liueth for euermore.

15 *The people will tell of their wisdome, and the congregation will shew forth their praise.

* Chap. 39. 10.

16 *Enoch pleased the Lord, and was translated, being an example of repentance, to all generations.

* Gen. 5. 24 heb. 11. 5.

17 *Noah was found perfect and righteous, in the time of wrath, he was taken in exchange (for the world) therefore was he left as a remnant vnto the earth, when the flood came.

* Gen. 6. 9. and 7. 1. heb. 11. 7.

18 An *euerlasting Couenant was made with him, that all flesh should perish no more by the flood.

* Gen. 9. 11.

19 Abraham was a *great father of many people : in glory was there none like vnto him :

* Gen. 12. 3 and 15. 5. and 17. 4.

20 Who kept the Law of the most High, and was in couenant with him, hee established the Couenant in *his flesh, and when he was proued, he was found faithfull.

* Gen. 21. 4.

21 Therefore he assured him by an *othe, that he would blesse the nations in his seed, and that he would multiply him, as the dust of the earth, and exalt his seed as the starres, and cause them to inherit from Sea to Sea, & from the riuer vnto the vtmost part of the land.

* Gen. 22. 16, 17, 18. gal. 3. 8.

22 With * Isaac did he establish likewise [for Abraham his fathers sake] the blessing of all men and the couenant,

* Gen. 27. 28. and 28. 14.

23 And made it rest vpon the head of Iacob. Hee acknowledged him in his blessing, and gaue him an heritage, and diuided his portions, among the twelue tribes did he part them.

CHAP. XLV.

1 The praise of Moses, 6 Of Aaron, 23 and of Phinees.

ANd he brought out of him a mercifull man, which found fauour in the sight of all flesh, euen * Moses beloued of God and men, whose memoriall is blessed :

* Exo. 11. 3

2 He made him like to the glorious Saints, and magnified him, so that his enemies stood in feare of him.

3 By his words he caused the wonders to cease, and he made him *glorious in the sight of kings, and gaue him a commaundement for his people, and shewed him part of his glory.

* Exod. 6. 7, 8, 9. chap.

4 *He sanctified him *in* his faithfulnesse, and meekenesse, and chose him out of all men.

* Num. 12. 3

5 He made him to heare his voyce, and brought him into the darke cloud, and *gaue him commandements before his face, euen the law of life and knowledge, that hee might teach Iacob his Couenants, and Israel his iudgments.

* Exo. 17. 4

6 He *exalted Aaron an holy man like vnto him, euen his brother, of the tribe of Leui.

* Exo. 4. 28

7 An euerlasting couenant he made with him, and gaue him the priesthood among the people, he †beautified him with comely ornaments, and clothed him with a robe of glory.

† Gr. he blessed.

8 Hee put vpon him perfect glory : and strengthened him with †rich garments, with breeches, with a long robe, and the Ephod :

† Greeke, vessels or instruments.

9 And he compassed him with pomegranates, and with many golden bels round about, that as he went, there might be a *sound, and a noise made that might be heard in the Temple, for a memoriall to the children of his people.

* Exod. 28. 35.

10 With an holy garment, with gold and blew silke, and purple the worke of the embroiderer ; with a brestplate of iudgement, and with Vrim &. Thummim.

11 With twisted scarlet, the worke of the

the cunning workeman, with precious stones grauen like seales, and set in gold, the worke of the Ieweller, with a writing engraued for a memoriall, after the number of the tribes of Israel.

12 He set a crowne of gold vpon the miter, wherein was engraued holinesse an ornament of honour, a costly worke, the desires of the eies goodly & beautiful.

13 Before him there were none such, neither did euer any stranger put them on, but onely his children, and his childrens children perpetually

14 Their sacrifices shall be wholy consumed euery day twise continually.

15 Moises consecrated him, and annointed him with holy oile, this was appointed vnto him by an euerlasting couenant, and to his seed so long as the heauens should remaine, that they should minister vnto him, and execute the office of the priesthood, and blesse the people in his name.

16 He chose him out of all men liuing to offer sacrifices to the Lord, incense and a sweet sauour, for a memoriall, to make reconciliation for his people.

^{Deut. 17
0. and 21.} 17 *He gaue vnto him his commandements, and authority in the statutes of iudgements, that he should teach Iacob the testimonies, and informe Israel in his lawes.

^{Num. 16.
2.} 18 *Strangers conspired together against him, and maligned him in the wildernesse, euen the men that were of Dathans, and Abirons side, and the congregation of Core with fury and wrath.

19 This the Lord saw and it displeased him, and in his wrathfull indignation, were they consumed: he did wonders vpon them, to consume them with the fiery flame.

^{Num. 17.
4.} 20 *But he made Aaron more honourable, and gaue him an heritage, and diuided vnto him the first fruits of the encrease, especially he prepared bread in abundance:

21 For they eate of the sacrifices of the Lord, which he gaue vnto him and his seed:

^{Deut. 12.
12. and 18.
0.} 22 *Howbeit in the land of the people he had no inheritance, neither had he any portion among the people, for the Lord himselfe is his portion and inheritance.

^{Num. 25.
2, 13. 1.
mac. 2. 54.} 23 *The third in glory is Phinees the sonne of Eleazar, because he had zeale in the feare of the Lord, and stood vp with

good courage of heart, when the people were turned backe, and made reconciliation for Israel.

24 Therfore was there a couenant of peace made with him, that he should be the cheefe of the sanctuary, and of his people, and that he, and his posteritie should haue the dignitie of the Priesthood for euer.

25 According to the couenant made with Dauid sonne of Iesse, of the tribe of Iuda, that the inheritance of the king should be to his posterity alone: so the inheritance of Aaron should also be vnto his seed.

26 God giue you wisedome in your heart to iudge his people in righteousnesse, that their good things be not abolished, and that their glory may endure for euer.

CHAP. XLVI.

1 The praise of Ioshua, 9 Of Caleb, 13 Of Samuel.

Esus the sonne of Naue was valiant in the wars, and was the successor of Moses in prophesies, who according to his name was made great for the sauing of the elect of God, and taking vengeance of the enemies that rose vp against them, that he might set Israel in their inheritance. ^{*Num. 27.
18. deut. 34
9. iosh. 1. 2.
and 12. 7.}

2 *How great glory gat he when he did lift vp his hands, and stretched out his sword against the cities? ^{* Iosh. 10.
12, 13, 14.}

3 Who before him so stood to it? for the Lord himselfe brought his enemies vnto him.

4 Did not the Sunne goe backe by his meanes? and was not one day as long as two?

5 He called vpon the most high Lord, when the enemies pressed vpon him on euery side, & the great Lord heard him.

6 And with hailestones of mighty power he made the battell to fall violently vpon the nations, and in the descent (of Bethoron) hee destroyed them that resisted, that the nations might know all their strength, because hee fought in the sight of the Lord, and he followed the mightie one.

7 In the time of Moses also, he did a worke of mercie, hee and Caleb the sonne of Iephunne, in that they withstood the Congregation, and withheld the people from sinne, and appeased the wicked murmuring.

8 And

* Num. 26.
65. deu. 35.
36.

8 * And of sixe hundred thousand people on foot, they two were preserued to bring them into the heritage, euen vnto the land that floweth with milk & hony.

9 The Lord gaue strength also vnto Caleb, which remained with him vnto his old age, so that he entred vpon the high places of the land, and his seed obtained it for an heritage.

10 That all the children of Israel might see that it is good to follow the Lord.

11 And concerning the Iudges, euery one by name, whose heart went not a whoring, nor departed from the Lord, let their memory be blessed.

* Chap. 49.
12.

12 Let their bones * flourish out of their place, and let the name of them that were honoured, be continued vpon their children.

* 1. Sam. 1.
10. and 16.
19.

13 * Samuel the Prophet of the Lord, beloued of his Lord, established a kingdom, & anointed princes ouer his people.

14 By the Law of the Lord hee iudged the Congregation, and the Lord had respect vnto Iacob.

15 By his faithfulnes he was found a true Prophet, and by his word he was knowen to be faithfull in vision.

* 1. Sam 7.
9.

16 He called vpon the mighty Lord, when his enemies pressed vpon him on euery side, when he offered the * sucking lambe.

17 And the Lord thundered from heauen, and with a great noise made his voice to be heard.

18 And he destroyed the rulers of the Tyrians, and all the princes of the Philistines.

* 1. Sam. 12.
3.

19 And before his long sleepe hee made * protestations in the sight of the Lord, and his anoynted, I haue not taken any mans goods, so much as a shoe, and no man did accuse him.

* 1. Sam. 28.
18, 19.

20 And after his death hee * prophesied, and shewed the King his end, and lift vp his voyce from the earth in prophesie, to blot out the wickednesse of the people.

CHAP. XLVII.

1 The praise of Nathan, 2 Of Dauid, 12 Of Solomon his glory, and infirmities. 23 Of his end and punishment.

* 2. Sam. 12.
1.

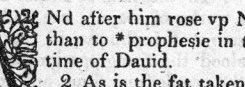

Nd after him rose vp Nathan to * prophesie in the time of Dauid.

2 As is the fat taken away from the peace of-

fering, so was Dauid chosen out of the children of Israel.

1 Or, he
smote Li
* 1. Sam
34.

3 Hee ||played with Lions as with kids, and with * beares as with lambs.

* 1. Sam
49, 50, 5.

4 * Slew he not a gyant when hee was yet but yong ? and did he not take away reproch from the people, when he lifted vp his hand with the stone in the sling, and beat downe the boasting of Goliah ?

5 For he called vpon the most high Lord, and he gaue him strength in his right hand to slay that mighty warriour, and set vp the horne of his people :

* 1. Sam
7.

6 So the people honoured him with * ten thousands, and praised him in the blessings of the Lord, in that hee gaue him a crowne of glory.

* 2. Sam
7.
|| Or, con
temned.

7 For hee destroyed the enemies on euery side, and * brought to nought the Philistines his ||aduersaries, and brake their horne in sunder vnto this day.

8 In all his workes hee praised the holy one most High, with words of glory, with his whole heart he sung songs, and loued him that made him.

* 1. Chr
4.

9 He set singers also before the * Altar, that by their voyces they might make sweet melody, and daily sing praises in their songs.

|| Or, per
fectly.

10 He beautified their feasts, and set in order the solemne times, ||vntill the ende, that they might praise his holy Name, and that the Temple might sound from morning.

* 1. Sam
13.
|| Or, of (
kingdom

11 The Lord tooke away his sinnes, and exalted his * horne for euer: he gaue him a couenant of kings, and a throne ||of glory in Israel.

12 After him rose vp a wise sonne, and for his sake he dwelt at large.

* 1. Kin
21, 24.

13 * Salomon reigned in a peaceable time, and was honoured; for God made all quiet round about him, that hee might build an house in his Name, and prepare his Sanctuary for euer

* 1. Kin
29, 30.

14 * How wise wast thou in thy youth, & as a flood filled with vnderstanding.

15 Thy soule couered the whole earth, and thou filledst it with dark parables.

16 Thy name went farre vnto the Ilands, and for thy peace thou wast beloued.

* 1. Kin
31, 32.

17 The countreys marueiled at thee for thy * Songs, and Prouerbs, and Parables, and interpretations.

* 1. Kin.
27.

18 By the Name of the Lord God, which is called the Lord God of Israel, thou didst * gather gold as tinne, and

and didst multiply siluer as lead.

19 *Thou didst bow thy loines vnto women, and ||by thy body thou wast brought into subiection.

20 Thou dist staine thy honour, and pollute thy seed, so that thou broughtest wrath vpon thy children, and wast grieued for thy folly.

21 *So the kingdome was diuided, and out of Ephraim ruled a rebellious kingdome.

22 *But the Lord will neuer leaue off his mercy, neither shall any of his workes perish, neither will hee abolish the posterity of his elect, and the seed of him that loueth him he will not take away : wherefore he gaue a remnant vnto Iacob, and out of him a roote vnto Dauid.

23 Thus rested Solomon with his fathers, and of his seede he left behinde him Roboam, euen the foolishnesse of the people, and one that had no vnderstanding ; who *turned away the people through his counsell : there was also Ieroboam the sonne of Nabat, who *caused Israel to sinne, and shewed Ephraim the way of sinne :

24 And their sinnes were multiplied exceedingly, that they were driuen out of the land.

25 For they sought out all wickednes, till the vengeance came vpon them.

CHAP. XLVIII.

1 The praise of Elias, 12 of Elizeus, 17 and of Ezekias.

Hen stood vp *Elias the Prophet as fire, and his word burnt like a lampe.

2 He brought a sore famine vpon them, and by his zeale he diminished their number.

3 By the word of the Lord he ||shut vp the heauen, *and also three times brought downe fire.

4 O Elias, how wast thou honoured in thy wondrous deedes ! and who may glory like vnto thee !

5 *Who didst raise vp a dead man from death, & his soule from the ||place of the dead by the word of the most Hie.

6 *Who broughtest kings to destruction, and honourable men from their ||bedde.

7 Who heardest the rebuke of the Lord in Sinai, *and in Horeb the iudgment of vengeance.

8 *Who anointed kings to take re-

uenge, & Prophets to succeed after him:

9 *Who wast taken vp in a whirlewinde of fire, and in a charet of fierie horses :

10 Who wast ||ordained *for reproofes in their times, to pacifie the wrath of the Lordes iudgement before it brake foorth into fury, and to turne the heart of the father vnto the sonne, and to ||restore the tribes of Iacob.

11 Blessed are they that saw thee, and ||slept in loue, for we shal surely liue.

12 *Elias it was, who was couered with a whirlewinde : and Elizeus was filled with his spirit : whilest he liued he was *not mooued [with the presence] of any prince, neither could any bring him into subiection.

13 ||No word could ouercome him, * & after his death his body prophecied.

14 He did wonders in his life, and at his death were his works marueilous.

15 For all this the people repented not, neither departed they from their sinnes, *till they were spoiled and caried out of their land, and were scattered through all the earth : yet there remained a small people, and a ruler in the house of Dauid :

16 Of whom, some did that which was pleasing to God, and some multiplied sinnes.

17 *Ezekias fortified his citie, and brought in water into the midst thereof : he digged the hard rocke with yron, and made welles for waters.

18 In his time *Sennacherib came vp, and sent Rabsaces, and lift vp his hand against Sion, & boasted proudly.

19 Then trembled their hearts and handes, and they were in paine as women in trauell.

20 But they called vpon the Lord which is mercifull, and stretched out their hands towards him, and immediatly the holy One heard them out of heauen, and deliuered them by the ||ministery of Esay.

21 *He smote the hoste of the Assyrians, and his Angel destroyed them.

22 For Ezekias had done the thing that pleased the Lord, and was strong in the wayes of Dauid his father, as Esay the Prophet, who was great and faithfull in his vision, had commaunded him.

23 *In his time the Sunne went backeward, and hee lengthened the kings life.

24 He

*1. King. 1. 1. *Or, in.

*1. Kin 12. 5, 16, 17.

*2. Sam. 7. 6.

1. Kin. 12. 0, 11, 13, 4.

1. Kin. 12. 9, 30.

1. King. 7. 1.

Or, made heauen to holde vp. *1. Kin. 18. 38. 2. king. . 10, 12.

*1. Kin. 17. 21, 22. Or, graue.

*2. Kings 4. 16. Or, seate.

*1. Kings 19. 15.

*1. Kin. 19. 16.

*2. King. 2. 11.

|| Or, written of. *Mal. 4. 3.

|| Or, establish.

|| Or, were adorned with loue. *2. King. 2. 11, 15.

|| Or, Nothing. *2. King. 13. 21.

*2. Kin. 18. 11, 12.

*2. King. 18. 2.

*2. King. 18. 13.

1 Or, hand.

*2. Kin. 19. 35. isa. 37. 18. 1. mac. 7. 41. 2. mac. 8. 19.

*2. King. 20. 10. isa. 38. 8.

24 Hee sawe by an excellent spirit what should come to passe at the last, and hee comforted them that mourned in Sion.

25 He shewed what should come to passe for euer, and secret things or euer they came.

CHAP. XLIX.

1 The praise of Iosias, 4 Of Dauid and Ezekias, 6 Of Ieremie, 8 Of Ezechiel, 11 Zorobabel, 12 Iesus the sonne of Iosedec. 13 Of Nehemiah, Enoch, Seth, Sem, and Adam.

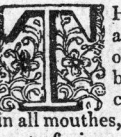

He remembrance of * Iosias is like the composition of the perfume ẏ is made by the arte of the Apothecarie : it is sweete as hony in all mouthes, and as musicke at a banquet of wine.

2 He ||behaued himselfe vprightly in the conuersion of the people, and tooke away the abominations of iniquitie.

3 * He directed his heart vnto the Lord, and in the time of the vngodly he established the worship of God.

4 All, except Dauid and Ezechias, and Iosias, were defectiue : for they forsooke the Law of the most High, (euen) the kings of Iudah failed :

5 Therefore he gaue their ||power vnto others, & their glory to a strange nation.

6 *They burnt the chosen citie of the Sanctuarie, and made the streets desolate ||according to the prophecie of Ieremias :

7 For they *entreated him euil, who neuerthelesse was a prophet *sanctified in his mothers wombe, that he might root out and afflict & destroy, and that he might build vp also and plant.

8 * It was Ezechiel who sawe the glorious vision, which was shewed him vpon the chariot of the Cherubims

9 For he *made mention of the enemies vnder [the figure of] the raine, and ||directed them that went right.

10 * And of the twelue prophets let the memorial be blessed, and let their bones flourish againe out of their place : for they comforted Iacob, and deliuered them by assured hope.

11 *How shall we magnifie Zorobabel ? euen he was as a signet on the right hand.

12 *So was Iesus the sonne of Iosedec : who in their time builded the house, and set vp an holy Temple to the Lord, which was prepared for euerlasting glory.

13 *And among the elect was Neemias whose renowme is great, who raised vp for vs, the walles that were fallen, and set vp the gates & the barres, and raised vp our ruines againe.

14 But vpon the earth was no man created like Enoch, for he was taken from the earth.

15 Neither was there a man borne like vnto * Ioseph, a gouernour of his brethren, a stay of the people, whose bones were regarded of the Lord.

16 *Sem and Seth were in great honour among men, and so was Adam aboue euery liuing thing in the creation.

CHAP. L.

1 Of Simon the sonne of Onias. 22 How the people were taught to praise God, and pray. 27 The conclusion.

Imon * the high priest the sonne of Onias, who in his life repaired the house againe, and in his dayes fortified the Temple :

2 And by him was built from the foundation the double height, the high fortresse of the wall about the Temple.

3 In his dayes the * cisterne to receiue water being in compasse as the sea, was couered with plates of brasse.

4 He tooke care of the Temple that it should not fall, and fortified the citie against besieging.

5 How was he honoured in the midst of the people, in his comming out of the + Sanctuarie ?

6 He was as the morning starre in the midst of a cloud : and as the moone at the full.

7 As the Sunne shining vpon the Temple of the most High, and as the rainebow giuing light in the bright cloudes.

8 And as the flowre of roses in the spring of the yeere, as lillies by the riuers of waters, and as the branches of the frankincense tree in the time of summer.

9 As fire and incense in the censer, and as a vessell of beaten gold set with all maner of precious stones,

10 And as a faire oliue tree budding forth fruit, and as a Cypresse tree which groweth vp to the cloudes.

11 When he put on the robe of honour, and was clothed with the perfection

* 2. King. 22
1. and 23. 2.
2. chr. 3. 34.

|| Or, prospered.

* 2. Kin. 23.
4.

|| Or, horne.

* 2. King.
25. 9.
|| Or, by the hand of Ieremie.
* Ier. 36. 6.
* Ier. 1. 5.

* Eze. 1. 3,
15.

* Eze. 13. 11
and 36. 11.
16. & 46. 12
hag. 2. 24.
ezr. 3. 2.
|| Or, did good.
* Ezek. 13.
13. & 38. 22

* Zach. 3. 1.
ezr. 3. 2.
hag. 1. 12.
and 2. 3.
* Nehe. 7. 1.

* Gen. 5.
heb. 11. 5

* Gen. 41.
44. and
6. & 45.

* Gen. 5.
and 11. 1

* 2. Mac.

* 1. King
23.

+ Gr. the house of vaile.

tion of glory, when he went vp to the holy altar, he made the garment of holinesse honourable.

12 When he tooke the portions out of the priests hands, hee himselfe stood by the hearth of the altar, compassed with his brethren round about, as a yong cedar in Libanus, and as palme trees compassed they him round about.

13 So were all the sonnes of Aaron in their glory, and the oblations of the Lord in their hands, before all the congregation of Israel.

14 And finishing the seruice at the altar, that he might adorne the offring of the most high Almighty,

15 He stretched out his hand to the cup, and powred of the blood of the grape, he powred out at the foote of the altar, a sweet smelling sauour vnto the most high King of all.

16 Then shouted the sonnes of Aaron, and sounded ||the siluer trumpets, and made a great noise to be heard, for a remembrance before the most High.

Or, trumpets beaten forth with e hammer.

17 Then all the people together hasted, and fell downe to the earth vpon their faces to worship their Lord God almighty the most High.

18 The singers also sang praises with their voices, with great variety of sounds was there made sweete melodie.

19 And the people besought the Lord the most High by prayer before him that is mercifull, till the solemnity of the Lord was ended, and they had finished his seruice.

20 Then he went downe, and lifted vp his hands ouer the whole congregation of the children of Israel, to giue the blessing of the Lord with his lips, and to reioyce in his name.

21 And they bowed themselues downe to worship the second time, that they might receiue a blessing from the most High.

22 Now therefore blesse yee the God of all, which onely doth wonderous things euery where, which exalteth our daies from the wombe, and dealeth with vs according to his mercy.

23 He grant vs ioyfulnesse of heart, and that peace may be in our daies in Israel for euer.

24 That hee would confirme his mercy with vs, and deliuer vs at his time.

25 **There be two maner of nations** which my heart abhorreth, and the third is no nation.

26 They that sit vpon the mountaine of Samaria, and they that dwell amongst the Philistines, and that foolish people that dwell in Sichem.

27 Iesus the sonne of Sirach of Hierusalem hath written in this booke, the instruction of vnderstanding and knowledge, who out of his heart powred forth wisedome.

28 Blessed is he that shall be exercised in these things, and hee that layeth them vp in his heart, shall become wise.

29 For if he doe them, hee shall be strong to all things, for the light of the Lord leadeth him, who giueth wisedome to the godly : blessed be the Lord for euer. Amen. Amen.

CHAP. LI.

¶ A Prayer of Iesus the sonne of Sirach.

I Will thanke thee, O Lord and king, and praise thee O God my Sauiour, I doe giue praise vnto thy name:

2 For thou art my defeuder, and helper, and hast preserued my body from destruction, and from the snare of the slanderous tongue, and from the lippes that forge lies, and hast beene my helper against mine aduersaries.

3 And hast deliuered me according to the multitude of thy mercies, and greatnesse of thy name, from the † teeth of them that were ready to deuoure me, and out of the hands of such as sought after my life, and from the manifold afflictions which I had :

† Gre. the gnashing of the teeth.

4 From the choking of fire on euery side, and from the mids of the fire, which I kindled not :

5 From the depth of the belly of hel, from an vncleane tongue, and from lying words.

6 By an accusation to the king from an vnrighteous tongue, my soule drew neere euen vnto death, my life was neere to the hell beneath :

7 They compassed me on euery side, and there was no man to helpe me: I looked for the succour of men, but there was none :

8 Then thought I vpon thy mercy, O Lord, and vpon thy acts of old, how thou deliuerest such as waite for thee,

thee, and sauest them out of the hands of the enemies :

9 Then lifted I vp my supplication from the earth, and prayed for deliuerance from death.

10 I called vpon the Lord the father of my Lord, that he would not leaue me in the dayes of my trouble, & in the time of the proud when there was no helpe.

11 I will praise thy Name continually, and will sing praise with thankesgiuing, and so my prayer was heard :

12 For thou sauedst me from destruction, and deliuerest mee from the euill time : therefore will I giue thankes and praise thee, and blesse thy Name, O Lord.

‖ Or, went astray.

13 When I was yet yong, or euer I ‖went abroad, I desired wisedome openly in my prayer.

14 I prayed for her before the Temple, & will seeke her out euen to the end :

15 Euen from the flowre till the grape was ripe, hath my heart delighted in her, my foot went the right way, from my youth vp sought I after her.

16 I bowed downe mine eare a litle and receiued her, & gate much learning.

17 I profited therein, [therefore] will I ascribe the glory vnto him that giueth me wisedome :

18 For I purposed to doe after her, and earnestly I followed that which is good, so shall I not be confounded :

19 My soule hath wrestled with her, and in my doings I was exact, I stretched foorth my hands to the heauen aboue, & bewailed my ignorances of her.

20 ‖I directed my soule vnto her, and I found her in purenesse, I haue had my heart ioyned with her from the beginning, therefore shall I not bee forsaken.

‖ Or, I & understa ding.

21 My ‖heart was troubled in seeking her : therefore haue I gotten a good possession.

‖ Or, bou

22 The Lord hath giuen mee a tongue for my reward, and I wil praise him therewith.

23 Draw neere vnto me you vnlearned, and dwell in the house of learning.

24 Wherefore are you slow, and what say you of these things, seeing your soules are very thirstie ?

25 *I opened my mouth, and said, buy her for your selues without money.

*Esay 5.

26 Put your necke vnder the yoke, and let your soule receiue instruction, she is hard at hand to finde.

27 *Behold with your eies, how that I haue had but little labour, and haue gotten vnto me much rest.

* Chap. 18.

28 Get learning with a great summe of money, and get much gold by her.

29 Let your soule reioyce in his mercy, and be not ashamed of his praise.

30 Worke your worke betimes, & in his time he will giue you your reward.

¶ BARVCH.

CHAP. I.

1 Baruch wrote a booke in Babylon. 5 The Iewes there wept at the reading of it. 7 They sende money and the booke, to the brethren at Hierusalem.

Nd these are the wordes of the booke, which Baruch the sonne of Nerias, the sonne of Maasias, the sonne of Sedecias, the sonne of Asadias, the son of Chelcias, wrote in Babylon,

2 In the fift yere, and in the seuenth day of the moneth, what time as the Caldeans tooke Ierusalem, and burnt it with fire.

3 And Baruch did reade the words of this booke, in the hearing of Iechonias, the sonne of ‖Ioachim king of Iuda, and in the eares of all the people, that came to [heare] the booke.

‖ Or, Ioac

4 And in the hearing of the nobles, and of the kings sonnes, and in the hearing of the Elders, and of all the people from the lowest vnto the highest, euen of all them that dwelt at Babylon, by the riuer Sud.

5 Whereupon they wept, fasted, ‖and

|| and prayed before the Lord.

6 They made also a collection of money, according to euery mans power.

|| Or, and vowed vowes.

7 And they sent it to Ierusalem vnto || Ioachim the hie Priest the sonne of Chelcias, sonne of Salom, and to the Priestes, and to all the people which were found with him at Ierusalem,

|| Or, Ioacim.

8 At the same time, when he receiued the vessels of the house of the Lord that were caried out of the Temple, to returne them into the land of Iuda the tenth day of the moneth Siuan, [namely] siluer vessels, which Sedecias the sonne of Iosias king of Iuda had made,

9 After that Nabuchodonosor king of Babylon had caried away Iechonias, and the Princes, and the || captiues, and the mightie men, and the people of the land from Ierusalem, and brought them vnto Babylon:

|| Or, prisoners.

10 And they said, Behold, we haue sent you money, to buy you burnt offerings, and sinne offerings, and incense, and prepare yee † Manna, and offer vpon the Altar of the Lord our God,

† Gr. corruptly for Mincha, a meat offering.

11 And pray for the life of Nabuchodonosor king of Babylon, and for the life of Balthasar his sonne, that their dayes may be vpon earth as the dayes of heauen.

12 And the Lord wil giue vs strength, and lighten our eyes, and we shall liue vnder the shadow of Nabuchodonosor king of Babylon, and vnder the shadow of Balthasar his sonne, and wee shall serue them many dayes, and finde fauour in their sight.

13 Pray for vs also vnto the Lord our God, (for wee haue sinned against the Lord our God, and vnto this day the fury of the Lord, and his wrath is not turned from vs)

14 And yee shall reade this booke, which we haue sent vnto you, to make confession in the house of the Lord, vpon the feasts and solemne dayes.

15 And yee shall say, * To the Lord our God belongeth righteousnesse, but vnto vs the confusion of faces, as it is come to passe this day vnto them of Iuda, & to the inhabitants of Ierusalem,

* Chap. 2. 6.

16 And to our kings, and to our princes, and to our Priests, and to our Prophets, and to our fathers.

17 For wee haue * sinned before the Lord,

* Dan. 9. 5.

18 And disobeyed him, aud haue not hearkened vnto the voice of the Lord our God, to walke in the commaundements that he gaue vs openly:

19 Since the day that the Lorde brought our forefathers out of the land of Egypt, vnto this present day, wee haue beene disobedient vnto the Lord our God, and we haue beene negligent in not hearing his voice.

20 * Wherefore the euils cleaued vnto vs, and the curse which the Lord appointed by Moses his seruant, at the time that he brought our fathers out of the land of Egypt, to giue vs a land that floweth with milke and honie, like as it is to see this day.

* Deut. 28. 15.

21 Neuerthelesse we haue not hearkened vnto the voice of the Lord our God, according vnto all the wordes of the Prophets, whom he sent vnto vs.

22 But euery man followed the imagination of his owne wicked heart, to serue strange gods, and to doe euill in the sight of the Lord our God.

CHAP. II.

The prayer and confession which the Iewes at Babylon made, and sent in that booke vnto the brethren in Ierusalem.

Herefore the Lord hath made good his worde, which hee pronounced against vs, and against our Iudges that iudged Israel, and against our kings, and against our princes, and against the men of Israel and Iuda,

2 To bring vpon vs great plagues, such as neuer happened vnder the whole heauen, as it came to passe in Ierusalem, according to the things that were written in the Law of Moses,

3 That a man should * eat the flesh of his owne sonne, and the flesh of his owne daughter.

* Deut. 28. 53.

4 Moreouer, he hath deliuered them to be in subiection to all the kingdomes that are round about vs, to be as a reproch and desolation among all the people round about, where the Lord hath scattered them.

5 Thus wee † were cast downe and not exalted, because wee haue sinned against the Lord our God, and haue not beene obedient vnto his voice.

† Gr. were beneath and not aboue.

6 * To the Lord our God appertaineth righteousnesse : but vnto vs and to our fathers open shame, as appeareth this day.

* Cha. 1. 15

7 For

7 For all these plagues are come vpon vs, which the Lord hath pronounced against vs,

8 Yet haue we not prayed before the Lord, ŷ we might turne euery one from the imaginations of his wicked heart.

9 Wherefore the Lord watched ouer vs for euill, and the Lord hath brought it vpon vs : for the Lord is righteous in all his works, which he hath commanded vs.

10 Yet we haue not hearkened vnto his voice, to walk in the cōmandements of the Lord, that he hath set before vs.

Dan. 9. 15 11 *And now O Lord God of Israel, that hast brought thy people out of the land of Egypt with a mighty hand, and high arme, and with signes & with wonders, & with great power, and hast gotten thy selfe a name, as appeareth this day :

12 O Lord our God, we haue sinned, we haue done vngodly, wee haue dealt vnrighteously in all thine ordinances.

13 Let thy wrath turne from vs : for we are but a few left among the heathen, where thou hast scattered vs.

14 Heare our prayers, O Lord, and our petitions, and deliuer vs for thine owne sake, and giue vs fauour in the sight of them which haue led vs away :

† *Gr. thy name is called vpon Israel.* 15 That all the earth may know that thou art ŷ Lord our God, because Israel & his posteritie is † called by thy name.

* *Deut. 26. 15. esa. 63. 15.* 16 O Lord *looke downe from thy holy house, & consider vs : bow downe thine eare, O Lord, to heare vs.

* *Psal. 6. 5. and 115. 17 esa. 38. 18, 19.* 17 *Open thine eyes and behold : for the dead that are in the graues, whose † soules are taken from their bodies, wil giue vnto the Lord neither praise nor righteousnesse.

† *Gr. spirit or life.* 18 But ŷ soule that is greatly vexed, which goeth stouping & feeble, and the eyes that faile, and the hungry soule wil giue thee praise & righteousnes O Lord.

* *Dan. 9. 20.* 19 *Therfore wee doe not make our humble supplication before thee, O Lord our God, for the righteousnes of our fathers, and of our kings.

20 For thou hast sent out thy wrath & indignation vpon vs, as thou hast spoken by thy seruants ŷ prophets, saying,

* *Ier. 27. 7, 8* 21 *Thus saith the Lord, bow down your shoulders to serue the king of Babylon : so shall ye remaine in the lande that I gaue vnto your fathers.

22 But if ye will not heare the voice of the Lord to serue ŷ king of Babylon,

23 I will cause to cease out of the cities of Iuda, and from without Ierusalem the voice of mirth, and the voice of ioy : the voice of the bridegrome, and the voice of the bride, and the whole land shall be desolate of inhabitants.

24 But we would not hearken vnto thy voyce, to serue the king of Babylon : therefore hast thou made good the wordes that thou spakest by thy seruants the prophets, namely that the bones of our kings, and the bones of our fathers should be taken out of their places.

25 And loe, they are cast out to the heat of the day, and to the frost of the night, and they died in great miseries, by famine, by sword, and by pestilence.

26 And the house which is called by thy name (hast thou laid waste) as it is to be seene this day, for the wickednesse of the house of Israel, and the house of Iuda.

27 O Lord our God, thou hast dealt with vs after all thy goodnesse, and according to all that great mercie of thine.

28 As thou spakest by thy seruant Moses in the day when thou didst command him to write thy Law, before the children of Israel, saying,

* *Leuit 14. deu 15.* 29 *If ye will not heare my voyce, surely † this very great multitude shalbe turned into a smal [number] among the nations, where I will scatter them.

† *Gr. th great swarme*

30 For I knew that they would not heare me : because it is a stiffenecked people : but in the land of their captiuities, they shall ||remember themselues,

‖ *Or, co to them selues.*

31 And shall know that I am the Lord their God : For I giue them an heart, and eares to heare.

32 And they shal praise me in the land of their captiuitie, and thinke vpon my name,

33 And returne from their stiffe † neck, and from their wicked deeds : for they shal remember the way of their fathers which sinned before the Lord.

† *Gr. be*

34 And I will bring them againe into the land which I promised with an oath vnto their fathers, Abraham, Isaac, and Iacob, and they shall bee lords of it, and I will increase them, and they shall not be diminished.

35 And I will make an euerlasting couenant with them, to be their God, and they shall be my people : and I will no more driue my people of Israel out of the land that I haue giuen them.

CHAP.

CHAP. III.

3 The rest of their prayer & confession contained in that book, which Baruch writ and sent to Hierusalem. 30 Wisdome was shewed first to Iacob, and was seene vpon the earth.

O Lord almighty, God of Israel, the soule in anguish, the troubled spirit crieth vnto thee.

2 Heare O Lord, and haue mercy: for thou art mercifull, and haue pitty vpon vs, because we haue sinned before thee.

3 For thou endurest for euer, and we perish vtterly.

4 O Lord almighty, thou God of Israel, heare now the prayers of the dead Israelites, and of their children, which haue sinned before thee, and not hearkened vnto the voice of thee their God: for the which cause these plagues cleaue vnto vs.

5 Remember not the iniquities of our forefathers: but thinke vpon thy power and thy name, now at this time.

6 For thou art the Lord our God, and thee, O Lord, will we praise.

7 And for this cause thou hast put thy feare in our hearts, to the intent that we should call vpon thy name, and praise thee in our captiuity: for *we haue called to minde all the iniquity of our forefathers that sinned before thee.

8 Behold, we are yet this day in our captiuity, where thou hast scattered vs, for a reproch and a curse, and to be subiect to payments, according to all the iniquities of our fathers which departed from the Lord our God.

9 Heare, Israel, the commandements of life, giue eare to vnderstand wisedome.

10 How happeneth it, Israel, that thou art in thine enemies land, that thou art waxen old in a strange countrey, that thou art defiled with the dead?

11 That thou art counted with them that goe downe into the graue?

12 Thou hast forsaken the fountaine of wisedome.

13 For if thou hadst walked in the way of God, thou shouldest haue dwelled in peace for euer.

14 Learne where is wisedome, where is strength, where is vnderstanding, that thou mayest know also where is length of daies, and life, where is the light of the eyes and peace.

* Deut. 30. 1.

15 Who hath found out her *place? or who hath come into her treasures?

16 Where are the princes of the heathen become, and such as ruled the beasts vpon the earth.

17 They that had their pastime with the foules of the aire, and they that hoorded vp siluer and gold wherein men trust, and made no end of their getting?

18 For they that wrought in siluer, and were so carefull, and whose workes are vnsearchable,

19 They are vanished, and gone downe to the graue, and others are come vp in their steads.

20 Young men haue seene light, and dwelt vpon the earth: but the way of knowledge haue they not knowen,

21 Nor vnderstood the pathes thereof, nor laid hold of it: their children were farre off from that way.

22 It hath not beene heard of in Chanaan: neither hath it beene seene in Theman.

23 The Agarenes that seek wisdome vpon earth, the marchants of Merran, and of Theman, the ‖authors of fables, and searchers out of vnderstanding: none of these haue knowen the way of wisedome, or remember her pathes.

24 O Israel, how great is the house of God? and how large is the place of his possession?

25 Great, and hath none end: high, and vnmeasurable.

26 There were the gyants, famous from the beginning, that were of so great stature, and so expert in warre.

27 Those did not the Lord chuse, neither gaue he the way of knowledge vnto them.

28 But they were destroyed, because they had no wisedome, and perished through their owne foolishnesse.

29 Who hath gone vp into heauen and taken her, and brought her downe from the clouds?

30 Who hath gone ouer the Sea, and found her, & wil bring her for pure gold?

31 No man knoweth her way, nor thinketh of her path.

32 But he that knoweth all things, knoweth her, and hath found her out with his vnderstanding: he that prepared the earth for euermore, hath filled it with fourefooted beasts.

33 He that sendeth forth light, and it goeth: calleth it againe, and it obeyeth him with feare.

* Iob. 28. 12. 20.

‖ Or, expounders.

34 The

34 The starres shined in their watches, and reioyced : when he calleth them, they say, Here we be, and so with cheerefulnesse they shewed light vnto him that made them.

35 This is our God, and there shall none other be accounted of in comparison of him.

36 He hath found out all the way of knowledge, and hath giuen it vnto Iacob his seruant, & to Israel his beloued.

*Pro. 8. 31. iohn 1. 14.

37 *Afterward did he shew himselfe vpon earth, and conuersed with men.

CHAP. IIII.

1 The booke of Commandements, is that Wisdome which was commended in the former chapter. 25 The Iewes are mooued to patience, and to hope for the deliuerance.

His is the Booke of the commandements of God : and the Law that endureth for euer : all they that keepe it shall come to life: but such as leaue it, shall die.

2 Turne thee, O Iacob, & take heed of it : walke † in the presence of the light therof, that thou mayest be illuminated.

† Greeke, to the shining, before the light thereof.

3 Giue not thine honour to another, nor the things that are profitable vnto thee, to a strange nation.

4 O Israel, happie are wee : for things that are pleasing to God, are made knowen vnto vs.

5 Be of good cheare, my people, the memoriall of Israel.

6 Ye were sold to the nations, not for [your] destruction : but because you moued God to wrath, ye were deliuered vnto the enemies.

*1. Cor. 10. 20.

7 For yee prouoked him that made you, by *sacrificing vnto deuils, and not to God.

8 Ye haue forgotten the euerlasting God, that brought you vp, and ye haue grieued Ierusalem that noursed you.

9 For when shee saw the wrath of God coming vpon you, she said ; Hearken, O ye that dwell about Sion : God hath brought vpō me great mourning.

10 For I saw the captiuitie of my sonnes and daughters, which the euerlasting brought vpon them.

11 With ioy did I nourish them: but sent them away with weeping and mourning.

12 Let no man reioyce ouer me a widow, and forsaken of many, who for the sinnes of my children, am left desolate:

because they departed from the Law of God.

13 They knew not his statutes, nor walked in the waies of his Commandements, nor trode in the pathes ||of discipline in his righteousnesse.

|| Or, of his discipline righteousnes.

14 Let them that dwell about Sion come, and remember ye the captiuity of my sonnes and daughters, which the euerlasting hath brought vpon them.

15 For he hath brought a nation vpon them from far : a shamelesse nation, and of a strange language, who neither reuerenced old man nor pitied childe.

16 These haue caried away the deare beloued children of the widow, and left her that was alone, desolate without daughters.

17 But what can I helpe you .

18 For he that brought these plagues vpon you, will deliuer you from the hands of your enemies.

19 Goe your way, O my children, goe your way : for I am left desolate.

20 I haue put off the clothing of ||peace, and put vpon me the sackcloth of my prayer. I will cry vnto the euerlasting ||*in my dayes.

|| Or, prosperitie.

|| Or, in the time of my affliction. * Psa. 116 and 137. 7

21 Be of good cheare, O my children, cry vnto the Lord : & he shal deliuer you from the power & hand of the enemies.

22 For my hope is in the Euerlasting that hee will saue you, and ioy is come vnto me from the Holy one, because of the mercy which shall soone come vnto you from the euerlasting our Sauiour.

23 For I sent you out with mourning and weeping : but God will giue you to mee againe, with ioy and gladnesse for euer.

24 Like as now the neighbours of Sion haue seene your captiuity: so shall they see shortly your saluation from our God, which shall come vpon you with great glory, and brightnesse of the euerlasting.

25 My children, suffer patiently the wrath that is come vpon you from God : for thine enemy hath persecuted thee : but shortly thou shalt see his destruction, & shalt tread vpon his necke.

26 My ||delicate ones haue gone rough wayes, and were taken away as a flocke caught of the enemies.

|| Or, my dearelings

27 Be of good comfort, O my children, and cry vnto God : for you shall be remembred of him that brought these things vpon you.

28 For as it was your minde to goe astray

astray from God : so being returned seeke him ten times more.

29 For he that hath brought these plagues vpon you, shall bring you euerlasting ioy againe with your saluation.

30 Take a good heart, O Ierusalem : for hee that gaue thee that name, will comfort thee.

31 Miserable are they that afflicted thee, and reioyced at thy fall.

32 Miserable are the cities which thy children serued: miserable is she that receiued thy sonnes.

33 For as shee reioyced at thy ruine, and was glad of thy fall : so shall she be grieued for her owne desolation.

34 For I will take away the reioycing of her great multitude, and her pride shalbe turned into mourning.

35 For fire shal come vpon her frō the euerlasting, long to endure : and she shal be inhabited of deuils for a great time.

36 O Ierusalem, looke about thee toward the East, and behold the ioy that commeth vnto thee from God.

37 Loe, thy sonnes come whom thou sentest away : they come gathered together from the East to the West, by the word of the holy One, reioycing in the glory of God

CHAP. V.

1 Ierusalem is moued to reioyce, 5 and to behold their returne out of captiuity with glory.

Vt off, O Ierusalem, the garment of thy mourning and affliction, and put on the comelinesse of the glory that commeth from God for euer.

2 Cast about thee a double garment of the righteousnesse which commeth from God, and set a diademe on thine head of the glory of the euerlasting.

3 For God wil shew thy brightnesse vnto euery countrey vnder heauen.

4 For thy name shall bee called of God for euer, The peace of righteousnesse, and the glory of Gods worship.

5 Arise, O Ierusalem, and stand on high, and looke about toward the East, and behold thy children gathered from the West vnto the East by the word of the holy One, reioycing in the remembrance of God.

6 For they departed from thee on foote, and were ledde away of their enemies : but God bringeth them vnto thee exalted with glory, as children of the kingdome.

7 For God hath appointed that euery high hill, and banks of long continuance should be cast downe, and valleys filled vp, to make euen the ground, that Israel may goe safely in the glory of God.

8 Moreouer, euen the woods, & euery sweet smelling tree, shall ouershadow Israel by the commandement of God.

9 For God shall leade Israel with ioy, in the light of his glory, with the mercy and righteousnes that commeth from him.

¶ *The Epistle of Ieremie.*

CHAP. VI.

1 The cause of the captiuity is their sinne. 3 The place whereto they were caried, is Babylon: the vanitie of whose idols and idolatry are set foorth at large in this Chapter.

 Copy of an Epistle which Ieremie sent vnto them which were to be led captiues into Babylon, by the king of the Babylonians, to certifie them as it was commanded him of God

2 Because of ŷ sinnes which ye haue committed before God, ye shall be led away captiues vnto Babylon by Nabuchodonosor king of the Babylonians.

3 So when ye be come vnto Babylon, ye shal remaine there many yeeres, and for a long season, namely seuen generations : and after that I will bring you away peaceably from thence.

4 * Now shal ye see in Babylon gods of siluer, and of gold, and of wood, borne vpon shoulders, which cause the nations to feare.

5 Beware therefore that yee in no wise be like to strangers, neither be yee afraid of them, when yee see the multitude before them, and behinde them, worshipping them.

6 But say yee in your hearts, O Lord, we must worship thee.

7 For mine Angel is with you, and I my selfe caring for your soules.

8 As for their tongue, it is polished by the workeman, and they themselues are guilded and laid ouer with siluer, yet are they but false and cannot speake.

9 And taking golde, as it were for a virgine that loues to go gay, they make crownes for the heads of their gods.

10 Sometimes also the Priests conuey from their gods golde and siluer, and bestow it vpon themselues.

11 Yea

* Esai. 44. 8, 9, 10. and 46. 5, 7. psal. 115. 4. wis. 13. 10.

11 Yea they will giue thereof to the ‖common harlots, and decke them as men with garments [being] gods of siluer, and gods of gold, and wood.

Or, which prostitute themselues openly.

12 Yet cannot these gods saue themselues from rust and moths, though they be couered with purple raiment.

13 They wipe their faces because of the dust of the Temple, when there is much vpon them.

14 And he that cannot put to death one that offendeth him, holdeth a scepter as though hee were a iudge of the countrey.

15 Hee hath also in his right hand a dagger, and an axe : but cannot deliuer himselfe from warre and theeues.

16 Whereby they are knowen not to bee gods, therefore feare them not.

17 For like as a vessell that a man v-seth, is nothing worth when it is broken : euen so it is with their gods : when they be set vp in the Temple, their eyes be full of dust, thorow the feet of them that come in.

Or, courts.

18 And as the ‖doores are made sure on euery side, vpon him that offendeth the king, as being committed to suffer death : euen so the priests make fast their temples, with doores, with lockes and barres, lest their gods bee spoiled with robbers.

19 They light them candles, yea, more then for themselues, whereof they cannot see one.

20 They are as one of the beames of the temple, yet they say, their hearts are †gnawed vpon by things creeping out of the earth, & when they eate them and their clothes, they feele it not.

†*Gr. licked.*

21 Their faces are blacked, thorow the smoke that comes out of the temple.

22 Vpon their bodies and heads, sit battes, swallowes, and birds, and the cats also.

23 By this you may know that they are no gods : therefore feare them not.

24 Notwithstanding the gold that is about them, to make them beautifull, except they wipe off the rust they will not shine : for neither when they were molten did they feele it.

Or, any price.
Esa. 46. 7.

25 The things wherein there is no breath, are bought for ‖a most hie price.

26 *They are borne vpon shoulders, hauing no feete, whereby they declare vnto men that they be nothing worth.

27 They also that serue them, are a-shamed : for if they fall to the ground at any time, they cannot rise vp againe of themselues : neither if one set them vp-right can they moue of themselues : neither if they be bowed downe, can they make themselues streight : but they set ‖gifts before them as vnto dead men.

Or, offring

28 As for the things that are sacrificed vnto them, their priests sell and ‖abuse : in like maner their wiues lay vp part thereof in salt : but vnto the poore and impotent, they giue nothing of it.

Or, spend

29 Menstruous women, and women in childbed * eate their sacrifices : by these things ye may know that they are no gods : feare them not.

*Leu. 12.

30 For how can they be called gods ? because women set meate before the gods of siluer, gold, and wood.

31 And the priests sit in their temples, hauing their clothes rent, and their heads and beards shauen, and nothing vpon their heads.

32 They roare and crie before their gods : as men doe at the feast when one is dead.

33 The priestes also take off their garments, and clothe their wiues and children.

34 Whether it be euill that one doth vnto them, or good : they are not able to recompense it : they can neither set vp a king, nor put him downe.

35 In like maner, they can neither giue riches nor money : though a man make a vowe vnto them, and keepe it not, they will not require it.

36 They can saue no man from death, neither deliuer the weake from the mightie.

37 They cannot restore a blind man to his sight, nor helpe any man in his distresse.

38 They can shew no mercie to the widow : nor doe good to the fatherlesse.

39 Their gods of wood, and which are ouerlaid with gold, and siluer, are like the stones that be hewen out of the mountaine : they that worship them shall be confounded.

40 How should a man then thinke and say that they are gods ? when euen the Chaldeans thēselues dishonor them.

41 Who if they shall see one dumbe that cannot speake, they ‖bring him and intreate Bel that he may speake, as though he were able to vnderstand.

Or, bid h call vpon Bel.

42 Yet they cannot vnderstand this themselues, and leaue them : for they haue no ‖knowledge.

Or, sence

43 The

43 The women also with cordes about them, sitting in the wayes, burne branne for perfume: but if any of them drawen by some that passeth by, lie with him, she reproacheth her fellow that she was not thought as worthy as her selfe, nor her cord broken.

44 Whatsoeuer is done among them is false: how may it then be thought or said that they are gods?

45 They are made of carpenters, and goldsmiths, they can be nothing else, then the workman will haue them to be.

46 And they themselues that made them, can neuer continue long, how should then the things that are made of them, be gods?

47 For they left lies and reproaches to them that come after.

48 For when there commeth any warre or plague vpon them, the priests consult with themselues, where they may be hidden with them.

49 How then cannot men perceiue, that they be no gods, which can neither saue themselues from warre nor from plague?

50 *For seeing they be but of wood, and ouerlaide with siluer and gold: it shall be knowen heereafter that they are false.

* Psal. 115. 4. wisdom. 13. 10.

51 And it shall manifestly appeare to all nations and kings, that they are no gods: but the workes of mens hands, and that there is no worke of God in them

52 Who then may not know that they are no gods?

53 For neither can they set vp a king in the land, nor giue raine vnto men

54 Neither can they iudge their owne cause, nor redresse a wrong being vnable: for they are as crowes between heauen and earth.

55 Whereupon when fire falleth vpon the house of gods of wood, or layd ouer with gold or siluer, their priests will fly away, & escape: but they themselues shall be burnt asunder like beames.

56 Moreouer they cannot withstand any king or enemies: how can it then be thought or said that they be gods?

57 Neither are those gods of wood, and layd ouer with siluer or gold able to escape either from theeues or robbers.

58 Whose gold, and siluer, and garments wherwith they are clothed, they that are strong doe take, and goe away withall: neither are they able to helpe themselues.

59 Therefore it is better to be a king that sheweth his power, or else a profitable vessell in an house, which the owner shall haue vse of, then such false gods: or to be a doore in an house to keepe such things safe as be therein, then such false gods: or a pillar of wood in a palace, then such false gods.

60 For Sunne, Moone, and starres, being bright and sent to doe their offices, are obedient.

61 In like maner the lightning when it breaketh forth is easie to bee seene, and after the same maner ||the wind bloweth in euery country.

|| Or, the same wind.

62 And when God commandeth the clouds to goe ouer the whole world: they doe as they are bidden:

63 And the fire sent from aboue to consume hilles and woods, doth as it is commanded: but these are like vnto them neither in shew, nor power.

64 Wherefore it is neither to be supposed nor said, that they are gods, seeing they are able, neither to iudge causes, nor to doe good vnto men.

65 Knowing therefore that they are no gods, feare them not.

66 For they can neither curse nor blesse kings.

67 Neither can they shew signes in the heauens among the heathen: nor shine as the Sunne, nor giue light as the Moone.

68 The beasts are better then they: for they can get vnder a couert, and helpe themselues.

69 It is then by no meanes manifest vnto vs that they are gods: therefore feare them not

70 For as a scarcrow in a garden of Cucumbers keepeth nothing: so are their gods of wood, and laid ouer with siluer and gold.

71 And likewise their gods of wood, and laid ouer with siluer and gold, are like to a white thorne in an orchard that euery bird sitteth vpon: as also to a dead body, that is cast into the darke.

72 And you shall know them to be no gods, by the ||bright purple that rotteth vpon them: and they themselues afterward shall be eaten, and shall be a reproach in the country.

|| Or, purple and brightnesse.

73 Better therefore is the iust man that hath none idoles: for he shall be farre from reproach.

¶ The

¶ The Song of the three holy children,

which followeth in the third Chapter of Daniel after

this place, [And they walked in the midst of the fire, praising God, and blessing the Lord.] That which followeth is not in the Hebrew; to wit, [Then Azarias stood vp] vnto these wordes, [And Nabuchodonosor.]

1 Azarias his praier and confession in the flame, 24 wherewith the Chaldeans about the ouen were consumed, but the three children within it were not hurt. 28 The Song of the three children in the ouen.

THEN Azarias stood vp & prayed on this manner, and opening his mouth in the midst of the fire, said,

2 Blessed art thou, O Lord God of our fathers: thy Name is worthy to be praised, and glorified for euermore.

3 For thou art righteous in all the things that thou hast done to vs : yea, true are all thy workes : thy wayes are right, and *all thy iudgements trueth.

4 In all the things that thou hast brought vpon vs, and vpon the holy citie of our fathers, euen Ierusalem, thou hast executed true iudgement : for according to trueth and iudgement, didst thou bring all these things vpon vs, because of our sinnes.

5 For wee haue sinned and committed iniquitie, departing from thee.

6 In all things haue we trespassed, and not obeyed thy Commandements, nor kept them, neither done as thou hast commanded vs, that it might goe well with vs.

7 Wherefore all that thou hast brought vpon vs, and euery thing that thou hast done to vs, thou hast done in true iudgement.

8 And thou didst deliuer vs into the hands of lawlesse enemies, most hatefull forsakers [of God] and to an vniust King, and the most wicked in all the world.

9 And now wee can not open our

*Psal. 25. 10.

mouthes, we are become a shame, and reproch to thy seruants, and to them that worship thee.

10 Yet deliuer vs not vp wholly for thy Names sake, neither disanull thou thy Couenant :

11 And cause not thy mercy to depart from vs : for thy beloued Abrahams sake : for thy seruant Isaacs sake, and for thy holy Israels sake.

12 To whom thou hast spoken and promised, That thou wouldest multiply their seed as the starres of heauen, and as the sand that lyeth vpon the sea shore.

13 For we, O Lord, are become lesse then any nation, and bee kept vnder this day in all the world, because of our sinnes.

14 Neither is there at this time, Prince, or Prophet, or leader, or burnt offering, or sacrifice, or oblation, or incense, or place to sacrifice before thee, and to finde mercie.

15 Neuerthelesse in a contrite heart, and an humble spirit, let vs be accepted.

16 Like as in the burnt offering of rammes and bullockes, and like as in ten thousands of fat lambes : so let our sacrifice bee in thy sight this day, and [grant] that wee may wholy goe after thee : for they shall not bee confounded that put their trust in thee.

17 And now wee follow thee, with all our heart, wee feare thee, and seeke thy face.

18 Put vs not to shame : but deale with vs after thy louing kindenesse, and according to the multitude of thy mercies.

19 Deliuer vs also according to thy marueilous workes, and giue glory to thy Name, O Lord, and let all them that doe thy seruants hurt be ashamed.

20 And let them be ‖confounded in all

‖ Or, by thy power and might.

all their power and might, and let their strength be broken.

21 And let them know that thou art Lord, the onely God, and glorious ouer the whole world.

22 And the kings seruants that put them in, ceased not to make the ouen hote with ||rosin, pitch, towe, and small wood.

|| Or, Naptha, which is a certaine kind of fat and chalkie clay, Plin. lib. 2. c. 105.

23 So that the flame streamed forth aboue the fornace, fourtie and nine cubites :

24 And it passed through, and burnt those Caldeans it found about the fornace.

25 But the Angel of the Lord came downe into the ouen, together with Azarias and his fellowes, and smote the flame of the fire out of the ouen :

26 And made the mids of the fornace, as it had bene a ||moist whistling wind, so that the fire touched them not at all, neither hurt nor troubled them.

|| Or, coole.

27 Then the three, as out of one mouth, praised, glorified, and blessed God in the fornace, saying ;

28 Blessed art thou, O Lord God of our fathers : and to be praised and exalted aboue all for euer.

29 And blessed is thy glorious and holy Name : and to be praised and exalted aboue all for euer.

30 Blessed art thou in the Temple of thine holy glory: and to be praised and glorified aboue all for euer.

31 Blessed art thou that beholdest the depths, and sittest vpon the Cherubims, and to be praised and exalted aboue all for euer.

32 Blessed art thou on the glorious Throne of thy kingdome : and to bee praised and glorified aboue all for euer.

33 Blessed art thou in the firmament of heauen : and aboue all to be praised and glorified for euer.

34 O all yee workes of the Lorde, blesse ye the Lord : praise and exalt him ||aboue all for euer.

|| Or, highly exalt : and so in the rest.
* Psal. 148. 4

35 **O ye heauens, blesse ye the Lord: praise and exalt him aboue all for euer.

36 O yee Angels of the Lord, blesse ye the Lord : praise and exalt him aboue all for euer.

37 O all ye waters that be aboue the heauen, blesse yee the Lord : praise and exalt him aboue all for euer.

38 O all yee powers of the Lord, blesse ye the Lord : praise and exalt him aboue all for euer.

39 O yee Sunne and Moone, blesse ye the Lord : praise and exalt him aboue all for euer.

40 O ye starres of heauen, blesse ye the Lord : praise and exalt him aboue all for euer.

41 O euery showre and dew, blesse ye the Lord : praise and exalt him aboue all for euer.

42 O all ye windes, blesse yee the Lord : praise and exalt him aboue all for euer.

43 O yee fire and heate, blesse ye the Lord : praise and exalt him aboue all for euer.

44 O yee Winter and Summer, blesse ye the Lord : praise and exalt him aboue all for euer.

45 O ye dewes and stormes of snow, blesse ye the Lord : praise and exalt him aboue all for euer.

46 O ye nights and dayes, blesse ye the Lord : praise and exalt him aboue all for euer.

47 O ye light and darkenesse, blesse ye the Lord : praise and exalt him aboue all for euer.

48 O yee yce and colde, blesse ye the Lord : praise and exalt him aboue all for euer.

49 O ye frost and snow, blesse ye the Lord : praise and exalt him aboue all for euer.

50 O ye lightnings and clouds, blesse ye the Lord : praise and exalt him aboue all for euer.

51 O let the earth blesse the Lord : praise and exalt him aboue all for euer.

52 O ye mountaines and little hils, blesse ye the Lord : praise and exalt him aboue all for euer.

53 O all ye things that grow on the earth, blesse ye the Lord : praise and exalt him aboue all for euer.

54 O yee fountaines, blesse yee the Lord : praise and exalt him aboue all for euer.

55 O ye seas and riuers, blesse ye the Lord : praise and exalt him aboue all for euer.

56 O ye whales and all that mooue in the waters, blesse ye the Lord : praise and exalt him aboue all for euer.

57 O all ye foules of the †aire, blesse ye the Lord : praise and exalt him aboue all for euer.

† Gr. heauen.

58 O all ye beasts and cattell, blesse ye the Lord : praise and exalt him aboue all for euer.

59 O ye

59 O ye children of men, blesse yee the Lord: praise and exalt him aboue all for euer.

60 O Israel blesse ye the Lord: praise and exalt him aboue all for euer.

61 O ye priests of the Lord, blesse ye the Lord: praise and exalt him aboue all for euer.

62 O ye seruants of the Lord, blesse ye the Lord: praise and exalt him aboue all for euer.

63 O ye spirits and soules of the righteous, blesse ye the Lord, praise and exalt him aboue all for euer.

‖ Or, Saints

64 O ye ‖holy and humble men of heart, blesse ye the Lord: praise and ex-alt him aboue all for euer.

65 O Ananias, Azarias, and Misael, blesse ye the Lord, praise and exalt him aboue all for euer: for hee hath deliuered vs from ‖hell, and saued vs from the hand of death, and deliuered vs out of the mids of the furnace, [and] burning flame: euen out of the mids of the fire hath he deliuered vs.

‖ Or, graue

66 O giue thanks vnto the Lord, because he is gracious: for his mercie endureth for euer.

67 O all ye that worship the Lord, blesse the God of gods, praise him, and giue him thankes: for his mercie endureth for euer.

¶ The historie of Susanna, set apart from

the beginning of Daniel, because it is not in He-

brew, as neither the narration of † Bel and the Dragon.

† Gr, Bel *Dragon.*

16 Two Iudges hide themselues in the garden of Susanna to haue their pleasure of her: 28 which when they could not obteine, they accuse and cause her to be condemned for adulterie, 46 but Daniel examineth the matter againe, and findeth the two iudges false.

Here dwelt a man in Babylon, called Ioacim.

2 And hee tooke a wife, whose name was Susanna, the daughter of Chelcias, a very faire woman, and one that feared the Lord.

3 Her parents also were righteous, and taught their daughter according to the Law of Moses.

4 Now Ioacim was a great rich man, and had a faire garden ioyning vnto his house, and to him resorted the Iewes: because he was more honourable then all others.

5 The same yeere were appointed two of the Ancients of the people to be iudges, such as the Lord spake of, that wickednesse came from Babylon from ancient iudges, who seemed to gouerne the people.

6 These kept much at Ioacims house: and all that had any suits in lawe, came vnto them.

7 Now when the people departed away at noone, Susanna went into her husbands garden to walke.

8 And the two Elders saw her going in euery day and walking: so that their lust was inflamed toward her.

9 And they peruerted their owne mind, and turned away their eyes, that they might not looke vnto heauen, nor remember iust iudgements.

10 And albeit they both were wounded with her loue: yet durst not one shew another his griefe.

11 For they were ashamed to declare their lust, that they desired to haue to doe with her.

12 Yet they watched diligently from day to day to see her.

13 And the one said to the other, Let vs now goe home: for it is dinner time.

14 So when they were gone out, they parted the one from the other, and turning backe againe they came to the same place, and after that they had asked one another the cause, they acknowledged their lust: then appointed they a time both together, when they might find her alone.

15 And it fell out as they watched a fit time, she went in †as before, with two maids onely, and she was desirous to

† Gr. as ye sterday an the day be fore.

to wash her selfe in the garden : for it was hot.

16 And there was no body there saue the two Elders, that had hid them-selues, and watched her.

17 Then she said to her maids, Bring me oile and washing bals, and shut the garden doores, that I may wash me.

18 And they did as she bad them, and shut the garden doores, and went out themselues at ||priuie doores to fetch the things that she had commaunded them : but they saw not the Elders, be-cause they were hid.

Or, side oores.

19 Now when the maids were gone forth, the two Elders rose vp, and ran vnto her, saying,

20 Behold, the garden doores are shut, that no man can see vs, and we are in loue with thee : therefore consent vn-to vs, and lie with vs.

21 If thou wilt not, we will beare witnesse against thee, that a young man was with thee : and therefore thou didst send away thy maides from thee.

22 Then Susanna sighed and said, I am straited on euery side : for if I doe this thing, it is death vnto me : and if I doe it not, I cannot escape your hands.

23 It is better for me to fall into your hands, and not doe it : then to sinne in the sight of the Lord.

24 With that Susanna cried with a loud voice : and the two Elders cried out against her.

25 Then ranne the one, and opened the garden doore.

26 So when the seruants of the house heard the crie in the garden, they rushed in at a priuie doore to see what was done vnto her.

27 But when the Elders had decla-red their matter, the seruants were greatly ashamed : for there was neuer such a report made of Susanna.

28 And it came to passe the next day, when the people were assembled to her husband Ioacim, the two Elders came also full of mischieuous imagination a-gainst Susanna to put her to death,

29 And said before the people, Send for Susanna, the daughter of Chelcias, Ioacims wife. And so they sent.

30 So she came with her father and mother, her children and all her kinred.

31 Now Susanna was a very deli-cate woman and beauteous to behold.

32 And these wicked men comman-ded to vncouer her face (for she was co-

uered) that they might be filled with her beautie.

33 Therefore her friends, and all that saw her, wept.

34 Then the two Elders stood vp in the mids of the people, and laid their hands vpon her head.

35 And she weeping looked vp to-wards heauen : for her heart trusted in the Lord.

36 And the Elders said, As we wal-ked in the garden alone, this woman came in, with two maides, and shut the garden doores, & sent the maides away.

37 Then a young man who there was hid, came vnto her & lay with her.

38 Then we that stood in a corner of the garden, seeing this wickednesse, ran vnto them.

39 And when we saw them toge-ther, the man we could not hold : for he was stronger then we, and opened the doore, and leaped out.

40 But hauing taken this woman, we asked who the young man was : but she would not tell vs : these things doe we testifie.

41 Then the assembly beleeued them, as those that were the Elders and Iudges of the people : so they condem-ned her to death.

42 Then Susanna cried out with a loud voice and said : O euerlasting God that knowest the secrets, and knowest all things before they be :

43 Thou knowest that they haue borne false witnesse against me, and be-hold I must die : whereas I neuer did such things, as these men haue malici-ously inuented against me.

44 And the Lord heard her voice.

45 Therefore when she was led to be put to death : the Lord raised vp the holy spirit of a young youth, whose name was Daniel,

46 Who cried with a loud voice : I am cleare frō the blood of this woman.

47 Then all the people turned them towards him, & said : what meane these words that thou hast spoken ?

48 So he standing in the mids of them, said, Are ye such fooles ye sonnes of Israel, that without examination or knowledge of the truth, ye haue con-demned a daughter of Israel ?

49 Returne againe to the place of iudgement : for they haue borne false witnesse against her

50 Wherefore all the people turned againe

againe in hast, and the Elders said vnto him, Come sit downe among vs, and shew it vs, seeing God hath giuen thee the honour of an Elder.

51 Then said Daniel vnto them, Put these two aside one farre from another, and I will examine them.

52 So when they were put asunder one from another, hee called one of them, and said vnto him, O thou that art waxen old in wickednesse : now thy sinnes which thou hast committed aforetime, are come [to light.]

53 For thou hast pronounced false iudgement, and hast condemned the innocent, and hast let the guiltie goe free, albeit the Lord saith, * The innocent and righteous shalt thou not slay.

*Exod. 23. 7.

54 Now then if thou hast seene her : tell mee, Vnder what tree sawest thou them companying together ? who answered, Vnder a †masticke tree.

† Gr. lentiske tree.

55 And Daniel said, Very wel; Thou hast lied against thine owne head : for euen now the Angel of God hath receiued the sentence of God, to cut thee in two.

56 So hee put him aside, and commanded to bring the other, & said vnto him, O thou seed of Chanaan, and not of Iuda, beauty hath deceiued thee, and lust hath peruerted thine heart.

57 Thus haue yee dealt with the daughters of Israel, and they for feare companied with you : but the daughter of Iuda would not abide your wickednesse.

58 Now therefore tell mee, Vnder what tree didst thou take them companying together ? who answered, Vnder a ∥holme tree.

∥ Or, ki of oake.

59 Then said Daniel vnto him, Well : thou hast also lied against thine owne head : for the Angel of God waiteth with the sword to cut thee in two, that he may destroy you.

60 With that all the assembly cried out with a lowd voice, and praised God who saueth them that trust in him.

61 And they arose against the two Elders, (for Daniel had conuicted them of false witnesse by their owne mouth)

62 And according to the Law of Moses, they did vnto them in such sort as they *malitiously intended to doe to their neighbour : And they put them to death. Thus the innocent blood was saued the same day.

*Deut. 19. prou 19. 5.

63 Therefore Chelcias and his wife praised God for their daughter Susanna, with Ioacim her husband, and all the kinred : because there was no dishonestie found in her.

64 From that day foorth was Daniel had in great reputation in the sight of the people.

¶ The history of the destruction of †Bel and the Dragon, cut off from the end of Daniel.

† Gr. B Dragon.

19 The fraud of Bels Priests, is discouered by Daniel, 27 and the Dragon slaine, which was worshipped. 33 Daniel is preserued in the Lions denne. 42 The King doeth acknowledge the God of Daniel, and casteth his enemies into the same denne.

∥ Or, liued with the King.

ANd King Astyages was gathered to his fathers, and Cyrus of Persia receiued his kingdome.

2 And Daniel ∥ conuersed with the king, and was honored aboue all his friends.

3 Now the Babylonians had an Idol called Bel, and there were spent vpon him euery day twelue great measures of fine flowre, and fourtie sheepe, and six vessels of wine.

4 And the king worshipped it, and went daily to adore it : but Daniel worshipped his owne God. And the king said vnto him, Why doest not thou worship Bel ?

5 Who answered and said, Because I may not worship idols made with hands, but the liuing God, who hath created the heauen, and the earth, and hath soueraigntie ouer all flesh.

6 Then saide the King vnto him, Thinkest thou not that Bel is a liuing god ? seest thou not how much he eateth

eateth and drinketh euery day?

7 Then Daniel smiled, and said, O king, be not deceiued : for this is but clay within, and brasse without, and did ne-uer * eate or drinke any thing.

* Ecclus. 30. 9.

8 So the king was wroth, and cal-led for his Priests, and said vnto them, If yee tell me not who this is that de-uoureth these expenses, ye shall die.

9 But if ye can certifie me that Bel deuoureth them, then Daniel shall die : for hee hath spoken blasphemie against Bel. And Daniel sayd vnto the king, Let it be according to thy word.

10 (Now the Priests of Bel were threescore and tenne, beside their wiues and children) and the king went with Daniel into the temple of Bel.

11 So Bels Priests said, Loe, wee goe out : but thou, O king, set on the meate, and make ready the wine, and shut the doore fast, and seale it with thine owne signet :

12 And to morrow, when thou com-mest in, if thou findest not that Bel hath eaten vp all, wee will suffer death ; or else Daniel, that speaketh falsely a-gainst vs.

13 And they little regarded it : for vnder the table they had made a priuie entrance, whereby they entred in con-tinually, and consumed those things.

14 So when they were gone forth, the king set meates before Bel. Now Daniel had commanded his seruants to bring ashes, and those they strewed throughout all the temple, in the pre-sence of the king alone : then went they out and shut the doore, & sealed it with the kings signet, and so departed.

15 Now in the night came the Priests with their wiues and children (as they were woont to doe) and did eate and drinke vp all.

16 In the morning betime the king arose, and Daniel with him.

17 And the king said, Daniel, are the seales whole? And he said, Yea, O king, they be whole.

18 And assoone as he had opened the doore, the king looked vpon the table, and cried with a loude voice, Great art thou, O Bel, and with thee is no deceit at all.

19 Then laughed Daniel, and helde the king that he should not goe in, and sayd, Behold now the pauement, and marke well whose footsteps are these.

20 And the king said, I see the foot-

steps of men, women and children : and then the king was angry,

21 And tooke the Priests, with their wiues and children, who shewed him the priuy doores, where they came in, and consumed such things as were vp-on the table.

22 Therefore the king slewe them, and deliuered Bel into Daniels power, who destroyed him and his temple.

23 ‖ And in that same place there was a great Dragon, which they of Babylon worshipped.

‖ Some adde this title : Of the Dragon.

24 And the king said vnto Daniel, Wilt thou also say that this is of brasse? loe, he liueth, he eateth and drinketh, thou canst not say, that he is no liuing God : therefore worship him.

25 Then said Daniel vnto the king, I will worship the Lord my God : for he is the liuing God.

26 But giue me leaue, O king, and I shall slay this dragon without sword or staffe. The king sayde, I giue thee leaue.

27 Then Daniel tooke pitch, fat, and haire, and did seethe them toge-ther, and made lumpes thereof : this hee put in the Dragons mouth, and so the Dragon burst in sunder : and Da-niel said, ‖ Loe, these are the gods you worship.

‖ Or, Behold what you worship.

28 When they of Babylon heard that, they tooke great indignation, and conspired against the king, saying, The king is become a Iew, and he hath de-stroyed Bel, he hath slaine the Dragon, and put the Priests to death.

29 So they came to the king, and said, Deliuer vs Daniel, or else we will destroy thee and thine house.

30 Now when the king sawe that they pressed him sore, being constrained, he * deliuered Daniel vnto them :

* Dan. C. 16.

31 Who cast him into the lions den, where he was sixe dayes.

32 And in the den there were seuen lyons, and they had giuen them euery day ‖ two carkeises, and two sheepe: which then were not giuen to them, to the intent they might deuoure Da-niel.

‖ Or, two slaues.

33 Now there was in Iury a Pro-phet called Habacuc, who had ‖ made pottage, & had broken bread in a boule, and was going into the field, for to bring it to the reapers.

‖ Or, sodde.

34 But the Angel of the Lord said vnto Habacuc, Goe carrie the dinner that

that thou hast into Babylon vnto Daniel, who is in the lions denne.

35 And Habacuc said, Lord, I neuer saw Babylon : neither do I know where the denne is.

* Ezek. 8. 3.

36 Then the Angel of the Lord tooke him by the crown, and *bare him by the haire of his head, and through the vehemencie of his spirit, set him in Babylon ouer the den.

* 1. King. 17. 4.

37 And Habacuc cryed, saying, O Daniel, Daniel, * take the dinner which God hath sent thee.

38 And Daniel saide, Thou hast remembred mee, O GOD : neither hast thou forsaken them that seeke

thee, and loue thee.

39 So Daniel arose and did eate : and the Angel of the Lord set Habacuc in his owne place againe immediatly.

40 Vpon the seuenth day the king went to bewaile Daniel : and when he came to the den, he looked in, and behold, Daniel was sitting.

41 Then cried the king with a loud voyce, saying, Great art thou, O Lord God of Daniel, and there is none other besides thee.

42 *And he drew him out : and cast those that were the cause of his destruction into the den : and they were deuoured in a moment before his face.

* Ier. 37.

¶ The prayer of Manasses King of Iuda, when he was holden captiue in Babylon.

 Lord, Almightie God of our Fathers, Abraham, Isaac, and Iacob, and of their righteous seed : who hast made heauen and earth, with all the ornament thereof : who hast bound the Sea by the word of thy Commandement : who hast shut vp the deepe, and sealed it by thy terrible and glorious Name, whome all men feare, and tremble before thy power : for the Maiestie of thy glory cannot bee borne, and thine angry threatning towards sinners is importable : but thy mercifull promise is vnmeasurable and vnsearchable : for thou art the most High Lord, of great compassion, long suffering, very mercifull, and repentest of the euils of men. Thou, O Lord, according to thy great goodnesse hast promised repentance, and forgiuenesse to them that haue sinned against thee : and of thine infinite mercies hast appointed repentance vnto sinners that they may be saued. Thou therefore, O Lord, that art the God of the iust, hast not appointed repentance to the iust, as to Abraham, and Isaac, and Iacob, which haue not sinned against thee : but thou hast appointed repentance vnto me that am a sinner : for I haue sinned aboue the number of the sands of the Sea. My transgressions, O Lord, are multiplied : my transgressions are multiplied, and I am not worthy to behold and see the height of heauen, for the multitude of mine iniquitie. I am bowed downe with many yron bands, that I cannot lift vp mine head, ‖neither haue any release : For I haue prouoked thy wrath, and done euill before thee, I did not thy will, neither kept I thy Commandements : I haue set vp abominations, and haue multiplied offences. Now therefore I bow the knee of mine heart, beseeching thee of grace : I haue sinned, O Lord, I haue sinned, and I acknowledge mine iniquities : wherefore I humbly beseech thee, forgiue me, O Lord, forgiue me, and destroy me not with mine iniquities. Be not angry with me for euer, by reseruing euill for me, neither condemne mee into the lower parts of the earth. For thou art the God, euen the God of them that repent : and in me thou wilt shew all thy goodnesse : for thou wilt saue me that am vnworthy, according to thy great mercie. Therefore I will praise thee for euer all the dayes of my life : for all the powers of the heauens doe praise thee, and thine is the glory for euer and euer, Amen.

‖ Or, neither take my breath.

¶ The

¶ The firſt booke of the Maccabees.

CHAP. I.

14 Antiochus gaue leaue to set vp the fashions of the Gentiles in Hierusalem, 22 And spoiled it, & the temple in it, 57 And set vp therin the abomination of desolation, 63 And slew those that did circumcise their children.

Or, Chettiim.

Nd it happened, after that Alexander sonne of Philip, the Macedonian, who came out of the land of ‖Chettiim , had smitten Darius king of the Persians and Medes, that hee reigned in his stead, the first ouer Greece,

2 And made many wars, and wan many strong holds, and slew the kings of the earth,

3 And went through to the ends of the earth, and tooke spoiles of many nations, insomuch, that the earth was quiet before him, whereupon ‖he was exalted, and his heart was lifted vp.

4 And he gathered a mighty strong hoste, and ruled ouer countries, and nations and ‖kings, who became tributaries vnto him.

5 And after these things he fell sicke, and perceiued †that he should die.

6 Wherefore he called his seruants, such as were honourable, and had bin brought vp with him from his youth, and parted kis kingdome among them, while he was yet aliue:

7 So Alexander reigned twelue yeeres, and (then) died.

8 And his seruants bare rule euery one in his place.

9 And after his death they all put crownes [vpon themselues] so did their sonnes after them, many yeeres, and e- uils were multiplied in the earth.

10 And there came out of them a wicked roote, Antiochus [surnamed] Epiphanes, sonne of Antiochus the king, who had beene an hostage at Rome, and he reigned in the hundreth and thir-

(margin left:)
Or, his heart was exalted and lifted vp.

Or, kingmes which came &c.

Gre. that s dieth.

ty and seuenth yeere of the kingdome of the Greekes.

11 In those daies went there out of Israel wicked men , who perswaded many, saying; Let vs goe, and make a couenant with the heathen , that are round about vs : for since we departed from them, †we haue had much sorrow.

12 So this deuise pleased them well.

13 Then certaine of the people were so forward heerein, that they went to the king, who gaue them licence to doe after the ordinances of the heathen.

14 Whereupon ‖they built a place of exercise at Ierusalem, according to the customes of the heathen,

15 And made themselues, vncircumcised, and forsooke the holy couenant, and ioyned themselues to the heathen, and were sold to doe mischiefe.

16 Now when the kingdome was established , before Antiochus , hee thought to reigne ouer Egypt, that he might haue ỹ dominion of two realms :

17 Wherefore he entred into Egypt with a great multitude, with chariots, and elephants, and horsemen , and a great nauie.

18 And made warre against Ptolomee king of Egypt, but Ptolomee was afraide of him, and fled : and many were wounded to death.

19 Thus they got the strong cities in the land of Egypt, and hee tooke the spoiles thereof.

20 And after that Antiochus had smitten Egypt, he returned againe in the hundreth fortie and third yeere, and went vp against Israel and Ierusalem with a great multitude.

21 And entred proudly into the sanctuarie, and tooke away the golden altar, and the candlesticke of light, and all the vessels thereof,

22 And the table of the shewbread, and the powring vessels, and the vials, and the censers of gold, & the vaile, and the crownes, & the golden ornaments that were before the temple, ‖all which he pulled off.

(margin right:)
† Gre. many euils haue found vs.

‖ Or, set vp an open schoole at Ierusalem.

‖ Or, he pilled all things.

23 He

† Gr. desire-able.

23 Hee tooke also the siluer and the gold, and the †pretious vessels : also he tooke the hidden treasures which hee found :

24 And when hee had taken all away, he went into his owne land, hauing made a great massacre, and spoken very proudly.

25 Therfore there was great mourning in Israel, in euery place where they were ;

26 So that the Princes and Elders mourned, the virgines and yong men were made feeble, and the beautie of women was changed.

27 Euery bridegrome tooke vp lamentation, and she that sate in the marriage chamber, was in heauinesse.

28 The land also was moued for the inhabitants thereof, and all the house of Iacob was couered with confusion.

29 And after two yeeres fully expired, the king sent his chiefe collectour of tribute vnto the cities of Iuda, who came vnto Ierusalem with a great multitude,

30 And spake peaceable wordes vnto them, but [all was] deceit : for when they had giuen him credence, he fell suddenly vpon the citie, and smote it very sore, & destroyed much people of Israel.

31 And when hee had taken the spoiles of the citie, hee set it on fire, and pulled downe the houses, and walles thereof on euery side.

32 But the women & children tooke they captiue, and possessed the cattell.

33 Then builded they the citie of Dauid with a great and strong wall, [and] with mightie towers, and made it a strong hold for them,

34 And they put therein a sinfull nation, wicked men, and fortified [themselues] therein.

35 They stored it also with armour and victuals, and when they had gathered together the spoiles of Ierusalem, they layd them vp there, and so they became a sore snare.

36 For it was a place to lie in wait against the Sanctuary, and an euill aduersary to Israel.

37 Thus they shed innocent blood on euery side of the Sanctuary, and defiled it.

38 In so much that the inhabitants of Ierusalem fledde because of them, whereupon [the citie] was made an habitation of strangers, & became strange to those that were borne in her, and her owne children left her :

39 Her Sanctuary was laid waste like a wildernesse, her feasts were turned into mourning, her Sabbaths into reproch, her honour into contempt.

40 As had bene her glory, so was her dishonour encreased, and her excellencie was turned into mourning.

41 Moreouer king Antiochus wrote to his whole kingdome, that all should be one people,

42 And euery one should leaue his lawes : so all the heathen agreed, according to the commandement of the king.

43 Yea many also of the Israelites consented to his religion, and sacrificed vnto idols, and prophaned the Sabbath.

44 For the king had sent letters by messengers vnto Ierusalem, and the cities of Iuda, that they should follow ‖ the strange lawes of the land,

‖ Or, the lawes an rites of th strangers the land.

45 And forbid burnt offerings, and sacrifice, and drinke offerings in the temple; and that they should prophane the Sabbaths, and festiuall dayes :

46 And pollute the Sanctuarie and holy people :

47 Set vp altars, and groues, and chappels of idols, and sacrifice swines flesh, and vncleane beasts :

48 That they should also leaue their children vncircumcised, and make their soules abominable with all maner of vncleannesse, and prophanation :

49 To the end they might forget the Law, and change all the ordinances.

50 And whosoeuer would not doe according to the commandement of the king [he said] he should die.

51 In the selfe same maner wrote he to his whole kingdome, and appointed ouerseers ouer all the people, commanding the cities of Iuda to sacrifice, citie by citie.

52 Then many of the people were gathered vnto them, to wit, euery one that forsooke the Lawe, and so they committed euils in the land :

53 ‖ And droue the Israelites into secret places, euen wheresoeuer they could flie for succour.

‖ Or, and they mad Israel hi themselue in holes, euery pla of succour

54 Now the fifteenth day of the moneth Casleu, in the hundreth fourtie and fift yeere, they set vp the abomination of desolation vpon the Altar, and builded idole altars throughout the cities of Iuda, on euery side :

55 And

55 Aud burnt incense at the doores of their houses, and in the streetes.

56 And when they had rent in pieces the bookes of the Lawe which they found, they burnt them with fire.

57 And wheresoeuer was found with any, the booke of the Testament, or if any consented to the Lawe, † the kings commandement was, that they should put him to death.

Or. the ngs commandement t him to uth.

58 Thus did they by their authority, vnto the Israelites euery moneth, to as many as were found in the cities.

59 Now the fiue and twentieth day of the moneth, they did sacrifice vpon the idole altar, which was vpon the Altar of God.

60 At which time, according to the commandement, they put to death certaine women † that had caused their children to be circumcised.

Or. that d circumed their ildren.

61 And they hanged the infants about their neckes, and rifled their houses, and slewe them that had circumcised them.

62 Howbeit, many in Israel were fully resolued and confirmed in themselues, not to eate any vncleane thing.

63 Wherfore they chose rather to die, that they might not be defiled with meats, and that they might not profane the holy Couenant : So then they died.

64 And there was very great wrath vpon Israel.

CHAP. II.

6 Mattathias lamenteth the case of Ierusalem. 24 He slayeth a Iewe that did sacrifice to Idoles in his presence, and the Kings messenger also. 34 He and his are assailed vpon the Sabbath, and make no resistance. 50 Hee dieth, and instructeth his sons: 66 and maketh their brother Iudas Maccabeus generall.

 N those daies ‖ arose Mattathias the son of Iohn, the sonne of Simeon, a Priest of the sonnes of Ioærib, from Ierusalem, and dwelt in Modin.

r. Matthias the n of Iohn, c. arose om Ierusalem, or out Ierusalem.

2 And he had fiue sonnes, Ioannan ‖ called ‖ Caddis :

3 Simon, called Thassi :

4 Iudas, who was called Maccabeus :

Or, who as called : ad so afterst. Caddis.

5 Eleazar, called ‖ Auaran, and Ionathan, whose surname was Apphus.

Or, Auan, or A-ron.

6 And when hee saw the blasphemies that were committed in Iuda and Ierusalem,

7 He said, Woe is me, wherfore was I borne to see this misery of my people, and of the holy citie, and to dwell there, when it was deliuered into the hand of the enemie, and the Sanctuary into the hand of strangers ?

8 Her Temple is become as a man without glory.

9 Her glorious vessels are caried away into captiuitie, her infants are slaine in the streets, her yong men with the sword of the enemie.

10 What nation hath not had a part in her kingdome, and gotten of her spoiles ?

11 All her ornaments are taken away, of a free-woman shee is become a bondslaue.

12 And behold, our ‖ Sanctuarie, euen our beautie, aud our glory is laid waste, & the Gentiles haue profaned it.

‖ *Or, holy thing.*

13 To what ende therefore shall we liue any longer ?

14 Then Mattathias and his sons rent their clothes, and put on sackcloth, and mourned very sore.

15 In the meane while the kings officers, such as compelled the people to reuolt, came into the city Modin to make them sacrifice.

16 And when many of Israel came vnto them, Mattathias also and his sonnes came together.

17 Then answered the kings officers, and said to Mattathias on this wise ; Thou art a ruler, and an honourable and great man in this citie, and strengthened with sons and brethren :

18 Now therefore come thou first and fulfill the kings commandement, like as all the heathen haue done ; yea and the men of Iuda also, and such as remaine at Ierusalem : so shalt thou and thine house be in the number of the kings friends, and thou and thy children shall be honoured with siluer, and golde, and many rewards.

19 Then Mattathias answered, and spake with a loude voice, Though all the nations that are vnder the kings dominion obey him, and fall away euery one from the religion of their fathers, and giue consent to his commandements :

20 Yet will I, and my sonnes, and my brethren walke in the couenant of our fathers.

21 God forbid that we should forsake the Law, and the ordinances :

22 We

22 We will not hearken to the kings words, to goe from our religion, either on the right hand, or the left.

23 Now when he had left speaking these words, there came one of the Iewes in the sight of all, to sacrifice on the altar, which was at Modin, according to the kings commandement.

24 Which thing when Mattathias saw, he was inflamed with zeale, and his reines trembled, neither could hee forbeare to shew his anger according to iudgement: wherefore he ranne, and slew him vpon the altar.

25 Also the kings commissioner who compelled men to sacrifice, he killed at that time, & the altar he pulled downe.

26 Thus dealt he zealously for the Law of God, like as *Phineas did vnto Zambri the sonne of Salom.

27 And Mattathias cried throughout the citie with a loud voyce, saying, Whosoeuer is zealous of the law, and maintaineth the couenant, let him follow me.

28 So he and his sonnes fled into the mountaines, and left all that euer they had in the citie.

29 Then many that sought after iustice and iudgement, went downe into the wildernesse to †dwell there.

30 Both they and their children, and their wiues, and their cattell, †because afflictions increased sore vpon them.

31 Now when it was told the kings seruants, and the hoste that was at Ierusalem, in the citie of Dauid, that certaine men, who had broken the kings commandement, were gone downe into the secret places in the wildernesse.

32 They pursued after them, a great number, and hauing ouertaken them, they camped against them, and made war against them on the Sabbath day.

33 And they said vnto them, Let that which you haue done hitherto, suffice: Come foorth, and doe according to the commandement of the king, and you shall liue.

34 But they said, We will not come forth, neither will we do the kings commandement to profane the Sabbath day.

35 So then †they gaue them the battell with all speed.

36 Howbeit they answered them not, neither cast they a stone at them, nor stopped the places where they lay hid,

37 But said, Let vs die all in our †innocencie: heauen and earth shall testifie for vs, that you put vs to death wrongfully.

38 So they rose vp against them in battell on the Sabbath, and they slew them with their wiues & children, and their cattell, to the number of a thousand †people.

39 Now when Mattathias and his friends vnderstood hereof, they mourned for them right sore.

40 And one of them said to another: If we all do as our brethren haue done, and fight not for our liues, and lawes against the heathen, they wil now quickly root vs out of the earth.

41 At that time therfore they decreed, saying, Whosoeuer shall come to make battell with vs on the Sabbath day, we will fight against him, neither will wee die all, as our brethren that were murdered in the secret places.

42 Then came there vnto him a company of Assideans, who were mightie men of Israel, euen all such as were voluntarily deuoted vnto the Lawe.

43 Also all they that fled for persecution ioyned themselues vnto them, and were a stay vnto them.

44 So they ioyned their forces, and smote sinfull men in their anger, and wicked men in their wrath: but the rest fled to the heathen for succour.

45 Then Mattathias & his friends went round about, and pulled downe the altars.

46 And what children soeuer they found within the coast of Israel vncircumcised, those they circumcised ‖ valiantly.

47 They pursued also after ŷ proud men, & the work prospered in their hand.

48 So they recouered the Law out of the hand of the Gentiles, and out of the hande of Kings, neither †suffered they the sinner to triumph.

49 Now when the time drew neere, that Mattathias should die, he said vnto his sonnes, Now hath pride & rebuke gotten strength, and the time of destruction, and the wrath of indignation:

50 Now therefore, my sonnes, be ye zealous for the Law, & giue your liues for the couenant of your fathers.

51 Call to remembrance what actes our fathers did in their †time, so shall ye receiue great honour, & an euerlasting name.

52 *Was

Marginal notes

* Num. 25. 9.

† Gr. sit, abide.

† Gr. euils were multiplied vpon them.

† Gr. the Iewes.

† Gr. simplicitie.

† Gr. soul of men.

‖ Or, by ƒ

† Gr. ga they the horne to sinner.

† Gr. ge rations.

* Gene. 22.
9, 10. rom.
4. 3.

* Gene. 41.
40.

* Num. 25.
13. ecclus.
45. 23, 24.

* Iosh. 1. 2.

* Num. 14.
5, 7. iosh.
14. 13.

* 2. Sam. 2.
4.

* 2. Kin. 2.
11.

* Dan. 3. 16.
17. 18, and
26.
* Dan. 6. 22.

52 * Was not Abraham found faithfull intentation, and it was imputed vnto him for righteousnesse?

53 * Ioseph in the time of his distresse kept the commaundement, and was made Lord of Egypt.

54 * Phineas our father in being zealous and feruent, obtained the couenant of an euerlasting priesthood.

55 * Iesus for fulfilling the word, was made a iudge in Israel.

56 * Caleb for bearing witnesse, before the congregation, receiued the heritage of the land.

57 * Dauid for being mercifull, possessed the throne of an euerlasting kingdome.

58 * Elias for being zealous and feruent for the law, was taken vp into heauen.

59 * Ananias, Azarias, and Misael, by beleeuing were saued out of the flame

60 * Daniel for his innocencie was deliuered from the mouth of Lyons.

61 And thus consider ye throughout all ages, that none that put their trust in him shall be ouercome.

62 Feare not then the words of a sinfull man : for his glory shall bee dung and wormes.

63 To day he shall be lifted vp, and to morrow hee shall not be found, because he is * returned into his dust, and his thought is come to nothing.

* Psal. 146.
4.

64 Wherefore you my sonnes be valiant, and shew your selues men in the behalfe of the law, for by it shall you obtaine glory.

65 And behold, I know that your brother Simon is a man of counsell, giue eare vnto him alway : he shall be a father vnto you.

66 As for Iudas Maccabeus hee hath bin mighty and strong, euen from his youth vp, let him be your captaine, and || fight the battaile of the people.

|| Or fight yee the battaile of the people.

67 Take also vnto you, all those that obserue the law, and auenge ye the wrong of your people.

68 Recompence fully the heathen, and take heed to the commandements of the law.

69 So he blessed them, and was gathered to his fathers.

70 And he died in the hundreth fortie, and sixth yeere, and his sonnes buried him in the Sepulchre of his fathers, at Modin, and all Israel made great lamentation for him.

CHAP. III.

1 The valour and fame of Iudas Maccabeus. 10 He ouerthroweth the forces of Samaria and Syria. 27 Antiochus sendeth a great power against him. 44 He and his fall to fasting and prayer, 58 and are encouraged.

 Hen his sonne Iudas, called Maccabeus, rose vp in his stead.

2 And all his brethren helped him, and so did all they that held with his father, and they fought with cheerefulnesse, the battaile of Israel.

3 So he gate his people great honor, and put on a brestplate as a giant, and girt his warlike harnesse about him, and he made battels, protecting the host with his sword.

4 In his acts he was like a lyon, and like a lyons whelp roaring for his pray.

5 For hee pursued the wicked, and sought them out, and burnt vp those that vexed his people.

6 Wherefore the wicked shrunke for feare of him, and all the workers of iniquity were troubled, because saluation prospered in his hand.

7 He grieued also many kings, and made Iacob glad with his acts, and his memoriall is blessed for euer.

8 Moreouer he went through the citties of Iuda, destroying the vngodly out of them, and turning away wrath from Israel.

9 So that he was renowned vnto the vtmost part of the earth, & he † receiued vnto him such as were ready to perish.

† Gre. gathered together.

10 Then Apollonius gathered the Gentiles together, and a great host out of Samaria to fight against Israel.

11 Which thing when Iudas perceiued he went forth to meete him, and so he smote him, and slew him, many also fell downe slaine, but the rest fled.

12 Wherefore Iudas tooke their spoiles, and Apollonius sword also, and therewith he fought, all his life long.

13 Now when Seron a prince of the armie of Syria, heard say that Iudas had gathered vnto him a multitude and company of the faithfull, to goe out with him to warre.

14 He said, I will get me a name and honour in the kingdome, for I will goe fight with Iudas, and them that are with him, who despise the kings commandement.

15 So

15 So he made him ready to goe vp, and there went with him a mighty host of the vngodly to helpe him, and to be auenged of the children of Israel.

16 And when hee came neere to the going vp of Bethoron, Iudas went forth to meet him with a smal company.

17 Who when they saw the host comming to meet them, said vnto Iudas; How shall wee be able, being so few to fight against so great a multitude, and so strong, seeing wee are ready to faint with fasting all this day?

18 Vnto whom Iudas answered: *It is no hard matter for many to bee shut vp in the hands of a few; and with the God of heauen it is all one, to deliuer with a great multitude, or a small company:

19 For the victory of battell standeth not in the multitude of an hoste, but strength commeth from heauen.

‖ Or, vnto vs.
† Greek. in multitude of pride, or enuie, and iniquitie.

20 They come ‖against vs †in much pride and iniquitie to destroy vs, and our wiues & children, and to spoile vs:

21 But wee fight for our liues, and our Lawes.

22 Wherefore the Lord himselfe will ouerthrow them before our face: and as for you, be ye not afraid of them.

23 Now as soone as hee had left off speaking, he lept suddenly vpon them, and so Seron and his host was ouerthrowen before him.

† Gr. in the going downe.

24 And they pursued them †from the going downe of Bethoron., vnto the plaine, where were slaine about eight hundred men of them; and the residue fledde into the land of the Philistines.

25 Then began the feare of Iudas and his brethren, & an exceeding great dread to fall vpon the nations round about them:

26 In so much, as his fame came vnto the king, and all nations talked of the battels of Iudas.

27 Now when King Antiochus heard these things, he was full of indignation: wherefore hee sent and gathered together all the forces of his realme [euen] a very strong armie.

28 He opened also his treasure, and gaue his souldiers pay for a yeere, commanding them to be ready, †whensoeuer he should need them.

† Gr. or at euery need.
† Gr. that the collectors of tribute in the countrey were few.

29 Neuerthelesse, when he saw that the money of his treasures failed, and †that the tributes in the countrey were

small, because of the dissention, and plague which he had brought vpon the land, ‖ in taking away the Lawes which had bene of old time,

‖ Or, for th taking aw of the Law
† Gr. that should not haue.

30 Hee feared †that he should not be able to beare the charges any longer, nor to haue such gifts to giue so liberally, as he did before: for hee had abounded aboue the Kings that were before him.

31 Wherefore, being greatly perplexed in his minde, hee determined to goe into Persia, there to take the tributes of the countreys, and to gather much money.

32 So hee left Lysias a noble man, and one of the blood royall, to ouersee the affaires of the King, from the riuer Euphrates, vnto the borders of Egypt:

33 And to bring vp his sonne Antiochus, vntill he came againe.

34 Moreouer he deliuered vnto him the halfe of his forces, and the Elephants, and gaue him charge of all things that he would haue done, as also concerning them that dwelt in Iuda and Ierusalem.

35 To wit, that he should send an armie against them, to destroy and root out the strength of Israel, and the remnant of Ierusalem, and to take away their memoriall from that place:

36 And that he should place strangers in all their quarters, and diuide their land by lot.

37 So the king tooke the halfe of the forces that remained, and departed from Antioch †his royall city, the hundreth fourtie and seuenth yeere, and hauing passed the riuer Euphrates, hee went through the high countreys.

† Gr. a cit of his king dome.

38 Then Lysias chose Ptoleme, the son of Dorymenes and Nicanor, & Gorgias, mighty men of the kings friends:

39 And with them hee sent fourtie thousand footmen, and seuen thousand horsemen to goe into the land of Iuda, and to destroy it as the king cōmanded.

40 So they went forth with all their power, and came and pitched by Emmaus in the plaine countrey.

41 And the merchants of the countrey, hearing the fame of them, tooke siluer, & gold very much, with ‖seruants, and came into the campe to buy the children of Israel for slaues; A power also of Syria, and of the land ‖of the Philistines, ioyned themselues vnto them.

‖ Or, fette

‖ Or, of stra gers.

42 Now

42 Now when Iudas and his brethren saw that miseries were multiplied, & that the forces did encampe themselues in their borders, (for they knewe how the king had giuen commaundement to destroy the people, and vtterly abolish them.)

43 They said one to another, Let vs restore the decayed estate of our people, and let vs fight for our people and the Sanctuarie.

44 Then was the Congregation gathered together, that they might be ready for battell, and that they might pray, and aske mercy and compassion.

45 Now Ierusalem lay voide as a wildernesse, there was none of her children that went in or out : the Sanctuarie also was troden downe, and aliens kept the strong holde : the heathen had their habitation in that place, and ioy was taken from Iacob, and the pipe with the harpe ceased.

46 Wherefore the Israelites assembled themselues together, and came to ‖ Maspha ouer-against Ierusalem ; for in Maspha was the place where they prayed aforetime in Israel.

Or, Mitz-pa.

47 Then they fasted that day, and put on sackecloth, and cast ashes vpon their heads, and rent their clothes :

48 And laide open the booke of the Law, ‖wherein ỹ heathen had sought to paint the likenesse of their images.

Or, for the which the heathen had made diligent search that they might paint therein the likenesse of their idols.
Num. 6. 2.

49 They brought also the Priestes garments, and the first fruits, and the tithes, and the *Nazarites they stirred vp, who had accomplished their dayes.

50 Then cried they with a loud voice toward heauen, saying, What shall we doe with these, and whither shall wee cary them away ?

51 For thy Sanctuarie is troden downe and profaned, and thy Priestes are in heauinesse, and brought low.

52 And loe, the heathen are assembled together against vs, to destroy vs : what things they imagine against vs, thou knowest.

53 How shall wee be able to stand against them, except thou (O God) be our helpe ?

54 Then sounded they with trumpets, and cryed with a loude voice.

55 And after this, Iudas ordained captaines ouer the people, euen captaines ouer thousands, and ouer hundreds, and ouer fifties, and ouer tennes.

*Deu. 20. 5.

56 But as for such as *were building houses, or had betrothed wiues, or were planting vineyards, or *were fearefull, those hee commanded that they should returne, euery man to his owne house, according to the Law.

*Iudg. 7. 3.

57 So the campe remooued, and pitched vpon the South side of Emmaus.

58 And Iudas sayde, Arme your selues, and be valiant men, and see that ye be in readinesse against the morning, that yee may fight with these nations, that are assembled together against vs, to destroy vs and our Sanctuarie.

59 For it is better for vs to die in battell, then to behold the calamities of our people, and our Sanctuarie.

60 Neuerthelesse, as the will [of God] is in heauen, so let him doe.

CHAP. IIII.

6 Iudas defeateth the plot 14 and forces of Gorgias, 23 and spoileth their tents, 34 and ouerthroweth Lysias. 45 He pulleth downe the Altar which the heathen had prophaned, and setteth vp a newe, 60 and maketh a wall about Sion.

THen tooke Gorgias fiue thousand footmen, and a thousand of the best horsemen, and remooued out of the campe by night,

2 To the end he might rush in vpon the camp of the Iewes, and smite them suddenly. And the men of the fortresse were his guides.

3 Now when Iudas heard thereof, hee himselfe remooued, and the valiant men with him, that hee might smite the Kings armie which was at Emmaus,

4 While as yet the forces were dispersed from the campe.

5 In the meane season came Gorgias by night into the campe of Iudas : and when hee found no man there, hee sought them in the mountaines : for said hee, these fellowes flee from vs.

6 But assoone as it was day, Iudas shewed himselfe in the plaine with three thousand men, who neuerthelesse had neither ‖armour, nor swordes to their mindes.

‖Or, targets.

7 And they sawe the campe of the heathen, that it was strong, and well harnessed, and compassed round about with horsemen ; and these were expert of warre.

8 Then said Iudas to the men that were

were with him : feare ye not their multitude, neither be ye afraid of their assault

9 Remember how our fathers were
deliuered in the red Sea, when Pharao
pursued them with an armie.

10 Now therfore let vs crie vnto heauen, if peraduenture the Lord wil haue
mercie vpon vs, and remember the couenant of our fathers, and destroy this
hoste before our face this day.

11 That so all the heathen may know
that there is one, who deliuereth and
saueth Israel.

12 Then the strangers lift vp their
eyes, & saw them comming ouer against
them.

13 Wherefore they went out of the
campe to battell, but they that were
with Iudas sounded their trumpets.

14 So they ioyned battell, and the
heathen being discomfited, fled into the
plaine.

15 Howbeit all the hindmost of them
were slaine with the sword : for they
pursued them vnto Gazera, and vnto
the plaines of Idumea, and Azotus,
and Iamnia, so that there were slaine
of them, vpon a three thousand men.

16 This done, Iudas returned a-
gaine with his hoste frō pursuing them,

17 And said to the people, Bee not
greedie of the spoiles, in as much as
there is a battell before vs,

18 And Gorgias and his hoste are
here by vs in the mountaine, but stand
ye now against your enemies, and ouercome them, & after this you may boldly
take the spoiles.

19 As Iudas was yet speaking these
words, there appeared a part of them
looking out of the mountaine.

20 Who when they perceiued that
the Iewes had put their hoste to flight,
and were burning the tents : (for the
smoke that was seene declared what
was done)

21 When therefore they perceiued
these things, they were sore afraid, and
seeing also the hoste of Iudas in the
plaine ready to fight :

22 They fled euery one into the land
of strangers.

23 Then Iudas returned to spoile
the tents, where they got much golde,
and siluer, and blew silke, and purple of
the sea, and great riches.

24 After this, they went home, and
sung a song of thankesgiuing, & praised
the Lord in heauen : because it is good,

because his mercie endureth for euer.

25 Thus Israel had a great deliuerance that day.

26 Now all the strangers that had
escaped, came and told Lysias what
had happened.

27 Who when hee heard thereof,
was confounded, and discouraged, because neither such things as he would,
were done vnto Israel, nor such things
as the king commanded him were come
to passe.

28 The next yeere therefore following, Lysias gathered together threescore thousand choice men of foote, and
fiue thousand horsemen, that he might
subdue them.

29 So they came into Idumea, and
pitched their tents at Bethsura, and Iudas met with them ten thousand men.

30 And when he saw that mighty
armie, he prayed, and said, Blessed art
thou, O sauiour of Israel, *who diddest quaile the violence of the mighty
man by the hand of thy seruant Dauid,
and gauest, the host of ||strangers into
the hands of *Ionathan the sonne of
Saul, and his armour bearer.

31 Shut vp this armie in the hand of
thy people Israel, and let them be confounded in their power and horsemen.

32 Make them to be of no courage,
and cause the boldnesse of their strength
to †fall away, & let them quake at their
destruction.

33 Cast them downe with the sword
of them that loue thee, and let all those
that know thy name, praise thee with
thanksgiuing.

34 So they ioyned battaile, and there
were slaine of the host of Lysias about
fiue thousand men, euen before them
were they slaine.

35 Now when Lysias saw his armie put to flight, and the manlinesse of
Iudas souldiers, and how they were
ready, either to liue or die valiantly, he
went into Antiochia, and gathered together a company of strangers, and hauing made his armie greater then it
was, he purposed to come againe into
Iudea.

36 Then saide Iudas and his brethren, behold our enemies are discomfi-
ted : let vs goe vp to cleanse, and ||dedi-
cate the Sanctuarie.

37 Vpon this all the host assembled
themselues together, and went vp into
mount Sion.

38 And

* 1. Sam.)
50, 51.

‖ Or, Phili-
stines.
* 1. Sam.)
13, 14.

† Gr. melt.

‖ Or, repai

38 And when they saw the sanctuarie desolate, and the altar prophaned, and the gates burnt vp, and shrubs growing in the courts, as in a forrest; or in one of the mountaines, yea and the priests chambers pulled downe,

39 They rent their clothes, and made great lamentation, and cast ashes vpon their heads,

40 And fell downe flat to the ground vpon their faces, and blew an alarme with the trumpets, and cried towards heauen.

41 Then Iudas appointed certaine men to fight against those that were in the fortresse, vntill he had clensed the Sanctuarie.

42 So he chose priests of blamelesse conuersation, such as had pleasure in the law.

43 Who cleansed the Sanctuarie, and bare out the defiled stones into an vncleane place.

44 And when as they consulted what to doe with the altar of burnt offrings which was prophaned,

45 They thought it best to pull it downe, lest it should be a reproch to them, because the heathen had defiled it; wherefore they pulled it downe,

46 And laide vp the stones in the mountaine of the temple in a conuenient place, vntill there should come a Prophet, to shew what should be done with them.

* Exod. 20 5. deut. 27 , & iosh. 8.

47 Then they tooke whole stones * according to the law, and built a new altar, according to the former:

48 And made vp the Sanctuarie, and the things that were within the temple, and hallowed the courts.

49 They made also new holy vessels, and into the temple they brought the candlesticke, and the altar of burnt offerings, and of incense, and the table.

50 And vpon the altar they burnt incense, and the lamps that were vpon the candlesticke they lighted, that they might giue light in the temple.

Or, spread abroad the hangings, or hanged vp the vailes.

51 Furthermore they set the loaues vpon the table, and ||spread out the veiles, and finished all the workes which they had begunne to make.

52 Now on the fiue and twentieth day of the ninth moneth, (which is called the moneth Casleu) in the hundreth fourty and eight yeere they rose vp betimes in the morning,

53 And offered sacrifice according to the law vpon the new altar of burnt offerings, which they had made.

54 Looke at what time, and what day the heathen had prophaned it, euen in that was it dedicated with songs, and cittherns, and harpes, & cimbals.

55 Then all the people fell vpon their faces, worshipping and praising the God of heauen, who had giuen them good successe.

56 And so they kept the dedication of the altar eight dayes, and offered burnt offerings with gladnesse, and sacrificed the sacrifice of ||deliuerance and praise.

|| Or, peace offerings.

57 They deckt also the forefront of the temple with crownes of gold; and with shields, and the gates, and the chambers they ||renewed and ||hanged doores vpon them.

|| Or, dedicated.
|| Or, made doores for them.

58 Thus was there very great gladnesse among the people, for that the reproch of the heathen was put away.

59 Moreouer Iudas and his brethren with the whole congregation of Israel ordained that the daies of the dedication of the altar, should be kept in their season from yeere to yeere by the space of eight dayes, from the fiue and twentieth day of the moneth Casleu, with mirth and gladnesse.

60 At that time also they builded vp the mount Sion with high walles, and strong towres round about, lest the Gentiles should come & tread it downe, as they had done before.

61 And they set there a garison to keepe it: and fortified Bethsura to preserue it, that the people might haue a defence against Idumea.

CHAP. V.

3 Iudas smiteth the children of Dan, Bean, and Ammon. 17 Simon is sent into Galile. 15 The exploits of Iudas in Galaad. 51 He destroyeth Ephron, for denying him to passe through it. 56 Diuerse, that in Iudas absence would fight with their enemies, are slaine.

Ow when the nations round about heard that the Altar was built, & the Sanctuarie renewed as before, it displeased them very much.

2 Wherfore they thought to destroy the generation of Iacob that was among them, and thereupon they began to slay and destroy the people.

3 Then

‖ Or, Ara-
bathene, or
Arabattan,
or Arabet-
tine.

‖ Or, malice.

‖ Or, Haran,
Gene. 36.
27. & num.
33. 3, 32.

3 Then Iudas fought against the children of Esau in Idumea at ‖ Arabattine, because they besieged Israel: and hee gaue them a great ouerthrow, and abated their courage, and tooke their spoiles.

4 Also he remembred the ‖iniurie of the children of ‖ Bean, who had bene a snare and an offence vnto the people, in that they lay in waite for them in the wayes.

5 Hee shut them vp therefore in the towres, and incamped against them, and destroyed them vtterly, and burnt the towers of that place with fire, and all that were therein.

6 Afterward he passed ouer to the children of Ammon, where he found a mighty power, and much people, with Timotheus their captaine.

7 So he fought many battels with them, till at length they were discomfited before him ; and he smote them.

8 And when hee had taken Iazar, with the townes belonging thereto, he returned into Iudea.

9 Then the heathen that were at Galead, assembled themselues together against the Israelites that were in their quarters to destroy them but they fled to the fortresse of Dathema ;

10 And sent letters vnto Iudas and his brethren . The heathen that are round about vs, are assembled together against vs to destroy vs ;

11 And they are preparing to come and take the fortresse whereunto wee are fled, Timotheus being captaine of their host.

12 Come now therefore and deliuer vs from their handes, for many of vs are slaine.

13 Yea all our brethren that were in the places of Tobie, are put to death, their wiues and their children ; Also they haue caried away captiues, and borne away their stuffe, and they haue destroied there about a thousand men.

14 While these letters were yet reading, behold there came other messengers from Galilee with their clothes rent, who reported on this wise,

15 And said : They of Ptolemais, and of Tyrus, and Sidon, and all Galilee of the Gentiles are assembled together against vs to consume vs.

16 Now when Iudas and the people heard these wordes, there assembled a great congregation together, to consult what they should doe for their brethren, that were in trouble and assaulted of them.

17 Then said Iudas vnto Simon his brother, Choose thee out men, and goe, and deliuer thy brethren that are in Galilee, for I and Ionathan my brother, will goe into the countrey of Galaad.

18 So hee left Ioseph the sonne of Zacharias, and Azarias captaines of the people, with the remnant of the hoste in Iudea to keepe it,

19 Vnto whom he gaue commandement, saying, Take yee the charge of this people, and see that you make not warre against the heathen, vntill the time that we come againe.

20 Now vnto Simon were giuen three thousand men to goe into Galilee, and vnto Iudas eight thousand men for the countrey of Galaad.

21 Then went Simon into Galilee, where hee fought many battels with the heathen, so that the heathen were discomfited by him.

22 And hee pursued them vnto the gate of Ptolemais ; And there were slaine of the heathen about three thousand men, whose spoiles he tooke.

23 And ‖those that were in Galilee and in Arbattis, with their wiues and their children , and all that they had, tooke he away [with him] and brought them into Iudea, with great ioy.

24 Iudas Maccabeus also and his brother Ionathan, went ouer Iordan, and trauailed three dayes iourney in the wildernesse,

25 Where they met with the Nabathites, who came vnto them in peaceable maner, and told them euery thing that had happened to their brethren in the land of Galaad.

26 And how that many of them were shut vp in ‖ Bosora, and Bosor, in Alema, ‖Casphor, Maked & Carnaim (all these cities are strong and great.)

27 And that they were shut vp in the rest of the cities of the countrey of Galaad, and that against to morrow ‖they had appointed to bring their host against the forts, and to take them, and to destroy them all in one day.

28 Hereupon Iudas and his host turned suddenly by the way of the wildernesse vnto ‖ Bosorra, and when he had wonne the citie, hee slew all the males with the edge of the sword, and tooke

‖ Or, captiue
Iewes.

‖ Or, Bosor-
ra.
‖ Or, Chas-
cor

‖ Or, the
heathen.

‖ Or, Bosor.

tooke all their spoiles, and burnt the citie with fire.

29 From whence hee remooued by night, and went till he came to the fortresse.

30 And betimes in the morning they †looked vp, & behold, there was an innumerable people bearing ladders, and other engines of warre, to take the fortresse : for ‖they assaulted them.

† Gr. lift vp their eyes.

‖ The heathen assaulted the Iewes.

31 When Iudas therefore saw that the battaile was begun, and that the cry of the citie went vp to heauen, with trumpets, and a great sound,

32 He said vnto his hoste, Fight this day for your brethren.

33 So he went foorth behinde them in three companies, who sounded their trumpets, and cryed with prayer.

34 Then the hoste of Timotheus knowing that it was Maccabeus, fled from him : wherefore hee smote them with a great slaughter : so that there were killed of them that day about eight thousand men.

35 This done, Iudas turned aside to Maspha, and after he had assaulted it, hee tooke it, and slewe all the males therein, and receiued the spoiles therof, and burnt it with fire.

36 From thence went he, and tooke Casphon, Maged, Bosor, and the other cities of the countrey of Galaad.

37 After these things, gathered Timotheus another hoste, and encamped against Raphon beyond the brooke.

38 So Iudas sent [men] to espie the hoste, who brought him word, saying ; All the heathen that be round about vs, are assembled vnto them, euen a very great hoste.

39 Hee hath also hired the Arabians to helpe them, and they haue pitched their tents beyond the brooke, readie to come and fight against thee : vpon this Iudas went to meet them.

40 Then Timotheus said vnto the captaines of his hoste, When Iudas and his hoste come neere the brooke, if he passe ouer first vnto vs, we shall not be able to withstand him, for hee will mightily preuaile against vs.

41 But if he be afraid, and campe beyond the riuer, we shall goe ouer vnto him, and preuaile against him.

42 Now when Iudas came neere the brooke, he caused the Scribes of the people to remaine by the brooke : vnto whom hee gaue commandement, say-

ing, Suffer no man to remaine in the campe, but let all come to the battell.

43 So he went first ouer vnto them, and all the people after him : then all the heathen being discomfited before him, cast away their weapons, and fled vnto the Temple that was at Carnaim.

44 But ‖they tooke the citie, and burnt the Temple, with all that were therein. Thus was Carnaim subdued, neither could they stand any longer before Iudas.

‖ Iudas and his company.

45 Then Iudas gathered together all the Israelites that were in the countrey of Galaad from the least vnto the greatest, euen their wiues and their children, and their stuffe, a very great hoste, to the ende they might come into the land of Iudea.

46 Now when they came vnto Ephron (this was a great city in the way as they should goe, very well fortified) they could not turne from it, either on the right hand or the left, but must needs passe through the midst of it.

47 Then they of the city shut them out, and stopped vp the gates with stones.

48 Whereupon Iudas sent vnto them in peaceable maner, saying ; Let vs passe through your land to goe into our owne countrey, and none shall doe you any hurt, we will onely passe thorow on foote : howbeit they would not open vnto him.

49 Wherefore Iudas commaunded a proclamation to be made throughout the hoste, that euery man should pitch his tent in the place where he was.

50 So the souldiers pitched, and assaulted the city all that day, and all that night, till at the length the city was deliuered into his hands :

51 Who then slew all the males with the edge of the sword, and rased the city, and tooke the spoiles therof, and passed through the city ouer them that were slaine.

52 After this went they ouer Iordan, into the great plaine before Bethsan.

53 And Iudas gathered together those that ‖came behind, and ‖exhorted the people all the way through, till they came into the land of Iudea.

‖ Or, went hindmost, Num. 10. 25
‖ Or, comforted, or encouraged.

54 So they went vp to mount Sion with ioy and gladnesse, where they offered ‖burnt offerings, because not one of them were slaine, vntill they had returned in peace.

‖ Peace offerings, Ioseph. Antiq. 12. 12.

55 Now

55 Now what time as Iudas and Ionathan were in the land of Galaad, and Simon his brother in Galilee before Ptolemais,

56 Ioseph the sonne of Zacharias, and Azarias, captaines of the garisons, heard of the valiant actes and warlike deeds which they had done.

57 Wherefore they said, Let vs also get vs a name, and goe fight against the heathen that are round about vs.

58 So when they had giuen charge vnto the garison that was with them, they went towards Iamnia.

59 Then came Gorgias and his ⟨† Gr. to meet them in battell.⟩ men out of the citie †to fight against them.

60 And so it was, that Ioseph and Azarias were put to flight, and pursued vnto the borders of Iudea, and there were slaine that day of the people of Israel about two thousand men.

61 Thus was there a great ouerthrow among the children of Israel, because they were not obedient vnto Iudas, and his brethren, but thought to doe some valiant act.

62 Moreouer these men came not of the seed of those, by whose hand deliuerance was giuen vnto Israel.

63 Howbeit the man Iudas and his brethren were greatly renowned in the sight of all Israel, and of all the heathen wheresoeuer their name was heard of,

64 Insomuch as the people assembled vnto them with ioyfull acclamations.

65 Afterward went Iudas foorth with his brethren, and fought against the children of Esau in the land toward the South, where he smote Hebron, ⟨† Gr. daughters.⟩ and the † townes thereof, and pulled downe the fortresse of it, and burnt the townes thereof round about.

66 From thence he remoued to goe ⟨† Gr. strangers.⟩ into the land of the † Philistines, and passed through Samaria.

67 At that time certaine priests desirous to shew their valour, were slaine in battell, for that they went out to fight vnaduisedly.

68 So Iudas turned to Azotus in the land of the Philistines, and when he had pulled downe their altars, and burnt their carued images with fire, and spoiled their cities, he returned into the land of Iudea.

CHAP. VI.

8 Antiochus dieth, 12 and confesseth that he is plagued for the wrong done to Ierusalem. 20 Iudas besiegeth those in the towre at Hierusalem. 28 They procure Antiochus the yonger to come into Iudea. 51 He besiegeth Sion, 60 and maketh peace with Israel: 62 yet ouerthroweth the wall of Sion.

Bout that time king Antiochus trauailing through the high countreys, heard say that Elimais in the countrey of Persia, was a citie greatly renowned for riches, siluer, and gold,

2 And that there was in it a very rich temple, wherein were ‖couerings ⟨‖ Or, shiel⟩ of gold, and brestplates, and ‖shields ⟨‖ Or, arme⟩ which Alexander sonne of Philippe the Macedonian King, who reigned first among the Grecians, had left there.

3 Wherefore he came and sought to take the citie, and to spoile it, but he was not able, because they of the citie hauing had warning thereof,

4 Rose vp against him in battell: So he fled and departed thence with great heauinesse, and returned to Babylon.

5 Moreouer there came one, who brought in tidings into Persia, that the armies which went against the land of Iudea, were put to flight:

6 And that Lysias who went forth first with a great power, was driuen away of the Iewes, and that they were made strong by the armour, and power, and store of spoiles, which they had gotten of the armies, whom they had destroyed.

7 Also that they had pulled downe the abomination which hee had set vp vpon the altar in Ierusalem, and that they had compassed about the Sanctuarie with high wals as before, and his citie Bethsura.

8 Now when the king heard these words, he was astonished, and sore moued, whereupon hee laide him downe vpon his bedde, and fell sicke for griefe, because it had not befallen him, as hee looked for.

9 And there hee continued many dayes : for his griefe was euer more and more, and he made account that he should die.

10 Where-

10 Wherefore he called for all his friends, and said vnto them, The sleepe is gone from mine eyes, and my heart faileth for very care.

11 And I thought with my selfe: Into what tribulation am I come, and how great a flood [of miserie] is it wherein now I am? for I was bountifull, and beloued in my power.

12 But now I remember the euils that I did at Ierusalem, and that I tooke all the vessels of gold and siluer that were therein, and sent to destroy the inhabitants of Iudea without a cause.

13 I perceiue therefore that for this cause these troubles are come vpon me, and behold I perish through great griefe in a strange land.

14 Then called he for Philip one of his friends whom he made ruler ouer all his realme:

15 And gaue him the crowne and his robe, and his signet, to the end ‖hee should bring vp his sonne Antiochus, and nourish him vp for the kingdome.

‖ Or, hee should take his sonne Antiochus to him.

16 So king Antiochus died there in the hundreth forty and ninth yeere.

17 Now when Lysias knew that the king was dead, he set vp Antiochus his sonne (whom he had brought vp being yong) to reigne in his stead, and his name he called Eupator.

18 About this time they that were in the towre shut vp the Israelites round about the Sanctuarie, and sought alwayes their hurt, and the strengthening of the heathen.

19 Wherefore Iudas purposing to destroy them, called all the people together to besiege them.

20 So they came together, and besieged them in the hundred and fiftith yeere, and he made mounts for shot against them, and [other] engines:

21 Howbeit certaine of them that were besieged got forth, vnto whom some vngodly men of Israel ioyned themselues.

22 And they went vnto the king and said, How long will it be ere thou execute iudgement, and auenge our brethren?

23 We haue beene willing to serue thy father, and to doe as he would haue vs, and to obey his commandements.

24 For which cause they of our nation besiege the towre, and are alienated from vs: Moreouer as many of vs as they could light on, they slew, and spoiled our inheritance.

25 Neither haue they stretched out their hand against vs only, but also against all their borders.

26 And behold this day are they besieging the towre at Ierusalem to take it: the Sanctuary also, and Bethsura haue they fortified.

27 Wherefore if thou doest not preuent them quickly, they wil doe greater things then these, neither shalt thou be able to rule them.

28 Now when the king heard this, he was angry, and gathered together all his friends, and the captaines of his armie, and those that had charge of the horse.

29 There came also vnto him from other kingdomes, and from Isles of the Sea bands of hired souldiers.

30 So that the number of his armie was an hundred thousand foote men, and twentie thousand horsemen, and two and thirty Elephants exercised in battell.

31 These went through Idumea, and pitched against Bethsura which they assaulted many daies, making engines of warre: but they [of Bethsura] came out, and burnt them with fire, and fought valiantly.

32 Vpon this Iudas remoued from the towre, and pitched in Bathzacharias, ouer against the kings campe.

33 Then the king rising very early marched fiercely with his host toward Bathzacharias, where his armies made them ready to battell, and sounded the trumpets.

34 And to the end they might prouoke the elephants to fight, they shewed them the blood of grapes & mulberies.

35 Moreouer, they diuided the beasts among the armies, and for euery elephant they appointed a thousand men, armed with coats of male, and with helmets of brasse on their heads, and besides this, for euery beast were ordained fiue hundred horsemen of the best.

36 These were ready at euery occasion: wheresoeuer the beast was, and whithersoeuer ỹ beast went, they went also, neither departed they from him.

37 And vpon the beastes were there strong towres of wood, which couered euery one of them, and were girt fast vnto them with deuices: there were also vpon euery one

two

two and thirtie strong men that fought vpon them, besides the Indian that ruled him.

38 As for the remnant of the horsemen they set them on this side, and that side, at the two parts of the host ‖ giuing them signes what to do, and being harnessed all ouer amidst the rankes.

‖ Or, stirring them vp, and being compassed with the rankes, or defended with the valleys.

39 Now when the Sunne shone vpon the shields of golde, and brasse, the mountaines glistered therewith, and shined like lampes of fire.

40 So part of the kings armie being spred vpon the high mountaines, and part on the valleyes below, they marched on safely, and in order.

41 Wherefore all that heard the noise of their multitude, and the marching of the company, and the ratling of the harnesse, were moued : for the army was very great and mighty.

42 Then Iudas and his host drew neere, and entred into battell, and there were slaine of the kings army, sixe hundred men.

43 ¶ Eleazar also (syrnamed) Sauaran, perceiuing that one of the beasts, armed with royall harnesse, was higher then all the rest, and supposing that the king was vpon him,

44 Put himselfe in ieopardie, to the end hee might deliuer his people, and get him a perpetuall name :

45 Wherefore hee ranne vpon him courageously through the midst of the battell, slaying on the right hand, and on the left, ‖ so that they were diuided from him on both sides.

‖ Or, so that he cut them in pieces.

46 Which done, he crept vnder the Elephant, and thrust him vnder and slew him : whereupon the Elephant fell downe vpon him, and there he died.

47 How be it [the rest of the Iewes] seeing the strength of the king, and the violence of his forces, turned away from them.

48 ¶ Then the kings armie went vp to Ierusalem to meet them, and the king pitched his tents ‖ against Iudea, and against mount Sion.

‖ Or, in Iudea.

49 But with them that were in Bethsura hee made ‖ peace : for they came out of the citie, because they had no victuals there, to endure the siege, it being a yeere of rest to the land.

‖ Adde out of Iosephus, and yeelded themselues.

50 So the King tooke Bethsura, and set a garison there to keepe it.

51 As for the Sanctuarie hee besieged it many dayes : ‖ and set there artillerie with engins, and instruments to cast fire and stones, and pieces to cast darts, and slings.

‖ Or, made there mounts for shot.

52 Whereupon ‖ they also made engins, against their engins, and helde them battell a long season.

‖ Or, the Iewes.

53 Yet at the last their vessels being without victuals, (for that it was the seuenth yeere, and they in Iudea that were deliuered from the Gentiles, had eaten vp the residue of the store)

54 There were but a few left in the Sanctuary, because the famine did so preuaile against them, that they were faine to disperse themselues, euery man to his owne place.

55 At that time Lysias heard say, that Philip (whom Antiochus the King whiles hee liued had appointed to bring vp his sonne Antiochus, that he might be king)

56 Was returned out of Persia, and Media, and the Kings host also that went with him, and that hee sought to take vnto him the ruling of the affaires.

57 Wherefore hee went in all haste, and said to the King, and the captaines of the host, and the company, Wee decay dayly, and our victuals are but small, and the place wee lay siege vnto is strong : and the affaires of the kingdome lie vpon vs.

58 Now therefore let vs †be friends with these men, and make peace with them, and with all their nation.

† Gr. giue hands.

59 And couenant with them, that they shall liue after their Lawes, as they did before : for they are therefore displeased, & haue done all these things because wee abolished their Lawes.

60 So the King and the Princes were content : wherefore hee sent vnto them to make peace, and they accepted thereof.

61 Also the King and the Princes made an oath vnto them : whereupon they went out of the strong hold.

62 Then the King entred into mount Sion, but when hee saw the strength of the place, hee brake his oath that hee had made, and gaue commandement to pull downe the wall round about.

63 Afterward departed hee in all haste, and returned vnto Antiochia, where hee found Philip to bee master of the citie ; So he fought against him, and tooke the citie by force.

CHAP.

CHAP. VII.

1 Antiochus is slaine, and Demetrius reigneth
in his stead. 5 Alcimus would be hie Priest,
and complaineth of Iudas to the king. 16 He
slayeth threescore Asideans. 43 Nicanor is
slaine, and the kings forces are defeated by
Iudas. 49 The day of this victorie is kept
holy euery yeere.

‖ Tripolis:
Ioseph. Ant.
ib. 10, 12.
* Gr. house
of the king-
lome of his
father.

N the hundreth and one
and fiftieth yeere, Deme-
trius the sonne of Seleu-
cus departed from Rome,
and came vp with a fewe
men vnto a ‖citie of the Sea coast, and
reigned there.

2 And as he entred into the †palace
of his ancestors, so it was, that his forces had taken Antiochus and Lysias to
bring them vnto him.

3 Wherefore when he knew it, hee
said; Let me not see their faces.

4 So his hoste slewe them. Now
when Demetrius was set vpon the
throne of his kingdome,

5 There came vnto him all the wic-
ked and vngodly men of Israel, hauing
Alcimus (who was desirous to be high
Priest) for their captaine.

6 And they accused the people to the
king, saying; Iudas and his brethren
haue slaine all thy friends, and driuen
vs out of our owne land.

7 Now therefore send some man
whom thou trustest, and let him goe
and see what hauocke he hath made a-
mongst vs, and in the kings land, and
let him punish them with all them that
aide them.

8 Then the king chose Bacchides a
friend of the king, who ruled beyond
the flood, and was a great man in the
kingdome, and faithfull to the king.

9 And him hee sent with that wicked Alcimus, whom hee made high
Priest, and commanded that he should
take vengeance of the children of Israel.

10 So they departed, and came with
a great power into the land of Iudea,
where they sent messengers to Iudas
and his brethren with peaceable words
deceitfully.

11 But they gaue no heede to their
words, for they sawe that they were
come with a great power.

‖ Or, officers,
gouernours,
chiefe men,
or men in au-
thoritie.

12 Then did there assemble vnto Alcimus and Bacchides, a company of
‖Scribes, to require iustice.

13 Now the Assideans were the first
among the children of Israel, that
sought peace of them:

14 For, said they, one that is a Priest
of the scede of Aaron, is come with this
armie, and he will doe vs no wrong.

15 So he spake vnto them peaceably,
and sware vnto them, saying; We will
procure the harme neither of you nor
your friends.

16 Whereupon they beleeued him:
howbeit hee tooke of them threescore
men, and slewe them in one day, according to the words which he wrote:

17 *The flesh of thy Saints [haue
they cast out] and their blood haue they
shed round about Ierusalem, and there
was none to bury them.

* Psal. 79.
2, 3.

18 Wherefore the feare and dread of
them fell vpon all the people, who said,
There is neither trueth, nor †righteous-
nesse in them; for they haue broken the
couenant and othe that they made.

† Gr. iudge-
ment.

19 After this remooued Bacchides
from Ierusalem, and pitched his tents
in Bezeth, where he sent and tooke many of the men that had forsaken him,
and certaine of the people also, and
when he had slaine them, [he cast them]
into the great pit.

20 Then committed he the countrey
to Alcimus, and left with him a power
to aide him : so Bacchides went vnto
the king.

21 But Alcimus ‖contended for the
high Priesthood.

‖ Or, labou-
red to de-
fend his high
Priesthood.

22 And vnto him resorted all such
as troubled the people, who after they
had gotten the land of Iuda into their
power, did much hurt in Israel.

23 Now when Iudas saw all the
mischiefe that Alcimus and his company had done among the Israelites, euen
aboue the heathen,

24 He went out into all the coast of
Iudea round about, and tooke vengeance of them that had ‖reuolted from
him, so that they durst no more ‖goe
foorth into the countrey.

‖ Or, fledde
from him to
the enemie.
‖ Or, inuade
the countrey.

25 On the other side, when Alcimus
saw that Iudas and his company ‖had
gotten the vpper hand, and knew that
he was not able to †abide their force, he
went againe to the king, and said all the
worst of them that he could.

‖ Or, were
growen very
strong.
† Gr. to a-
bide them.

26 Then the king sent Nicanor one
of his honourable princes, a man that
bare deadly hate vnto Israel, with commandement to destroy the people.

27 So

† *Gr. peaceable.*

27 So Nicanor came to Ierusalem with a great force : and sent vnto Iudas and his brethren deceitfully with †friendly words, saying,

† *Gr. see your faces.*

28 Let there be no battell betweene me and you, I will come with a fewe men, that I may †see you in peace.

29 He came therefore to Iudas, and they saluted one another peaceably. Howbeit the enemies were prepared to take away Iudas by violence.

30 Which thing after it was knowen to Iudas (to wit) that he came vnto him with deceit, he was sore afraid of him, and would see his face no more.

† *Gr. meet Iudas in battell.*
‖ *Or, Carphasalama.*

31 Nicanor also when he saw that his counsell was discouered, went out to †fight against Iudas besides ‖Caphar-salama.

32 Where there were slaine of Nicanors side, about fiue thousand men, and [the rest] fled into the citie of Dauid.

33 After this went Nicanor vp to mount Sion, and there came out of the Sanctuarie certaine of the priestes, and certaine of the elders of the people to salute him peaceably, and to shewe him the burnt sacrifice that was offred for the king.

† *Gr. defiled them.*

34 But he mocked them, and laughed at them, and †abused them shamefully, and spake proudly,

35 And swore in his wrath, saying, vnlesse Iudas and his hoste be now deliuered into my hands, if euer I come againe †in safetie, I will burne vp this house : and with that he went out in a great rage.

† *Gr. in peace*

36 Then the priests entred in, and stood before the altar, and the Temple, weeping, and saying,

37 Thou O Lord didst choose this house, to be called by thy Name, and to be a house of prayer and petition for thy people.

38 Be auenged of this man and his hoste, and let them fall by the sword : Remember their blasphemies, and suffer them not to continue any longer.

39 So Nicanor went out of Ierusalem, & pitched his tents in Bethoron, where an hoste out of Syria met him.

40 But Iudas pitched in Adasa with three thousand men, and there he prayed, saying,

ª 2. Kings 19. 35. esai. 37. 36. ecclus. 48. 22. 2. mac. 8. 19

41 *O Lord, when they that were sent from the king of the Assyrians blasphemed, thine Angel went out, and smote a hundred, fourescore, and fiue

thousand of them.

42 Euen so destroy thou this host before vs this day, that the rest may know that he hath spoken blasphemously against thy Sanctuary, and iudge thou him according to his wickednesse.

43 So the thirteenth day of the moneth Adar, the hostes ioyned battell, but Nicanors host was discomfited, & he himselfe was first slaine in the battell.

44 Now when Nicanors host saw that he was slaine, they cast away their weapons, and fled.

‖ *Or, the Iewes.*

45 Then ‖they pursued after them a dayes iourney from Adasa, vnto Gasera, sounding an alarme after them with their trumpets.

46 Whereupon they came forth out of all the townes of Iudea round about, and closed them in, so that they turning backe vpon them that pursued them, were all slaine with the sword, and not one of them was left.

47 Afterwards they tooke ẙ spoiles, and the pray, and smote off Nicanors head, & his right hand, which he stretched out so proudly, and brought them away, and hanged them vp, towards Ierusalem.

48 For this cause the people reioyced greatly, and they kept that day, a day of great gladnesse.

49 Moreouer they ordeined to keepe yeerely this day, being the thirteenth of Adar.

50 Thus the land of Iuda was in rest a litle while.

CHAP. VIII.

1 Iudas is informed of the power and policie of the Romanes, 20 and maketh a league with them. 24 The articles of that league.

Ow Iudas had heard of the fame of the Romanes, that they were mighty and valiant men, and such as would louingly accept all that ioyned themselues vnto them, and make a league of amitie with all that came vnto them,

‖ *Or, Frmen.*

2 And that they were men of great valour : It was told him also of their warres and noble acts which they had done amongst the ‖Galatians, and how they had conquered them, and brought them vnder tribute.

3 And what they had done in ẙ countrey of Spaine, for the winning of the mines of the siluer & gold which is there

4 And

4 And that by their policie and patience, they had conquered ‖ all that place (though it were very farre from them) and the kings also that came against them from the vttermost part of the earth, till they had discomfited them, & giuen them a great ouerthrow, so that the rest did giue them tribute euery yere.

⸗ Or, euery place.

5 Besides this, how they had discomfited in battell Philip, and Perseus king of the ‖Citims, with others that lift vp themselues against them, and had ouercome them.

⸗ Or, Macedonians.

6 How also Antiochus the great king of Asia that came against them in battaile, hauing an hundred and twentie Elephants with horsemen and chariots, and a very great armie, was discomfited by them.

7 And how they tooke him aliue, and couenanted that hee and such as reigned after him, should pay a great tribute, and giue hostages, and that which was agreed vpon,

8 And the country of India, and Media, and Lidia, and of the goodliest countries: which they tooke of him, and gaue to king Eumenes.

9 Moreouer how the Grecians had determined to come and destroy them.

10 And that they hauing knowledge thereof sent against them a certaine captaine, and fighting with them slew many of them, and caried away captiues, their wiues, and their children, and spoiled them, and tooke possession of their lands, and pulled downe their strong holds, and brought them to be their seruants vnto this day.

11 [It was told him besides] how they destroyed and brought vnder their dominion, all other kingdomes and isles that at any time resisted them.

12 But with their friends, and such as relied vpon them they kept amitie: and that they had conquered kingdomes both farre and nigh, insomuch as all that heard of their name were afraid of them.

13 Also that whom they would helpe to a kingdome, those raigne, and whom againe they would, they displace: finally that they were greatly exalted.

14 Yet for all this, none of them wore a crowne, or was clothed in purple to be magnified thereby.

15 Moreouer how they had made for themselues a senate house, wherin three hundred and twentie men sate in coun-

sell daily, consulting alway for the people, to the end they might be wel ordered

16 And that they committed their gouernment to one man euery yeere, who ruled ouer all their countrie, and that all were obedient to that one, and that there was neither enuy, nor emulation amongst them.

17 In consideration of these things Iudas chose Eupolemus the sonne of Iohn, the sonne of Accas, and Iason the sonne of Eleazar, and sent them to Rome to make a league of amitie and confederacie with them,

18 [And to intreate them] that they would take the yoke from them, for they saw that the kingdome of the Grecians did oppresse Israel with seruitude

19 They went therefore to Rome (which was a very great iourney) and came into the Senate, where they spake and said,

20 Iudas Maccabeus with his brethren, and the people of the Iewes, haue sent vs vnto you, to make a confederacie, and peace with you, and that we might be registred, your confederats and friends.

21 So that matter pleased the Romanes well.

22 And this is the copie of the Epistle which (the Senate) wrote backe againe, in tables of brasse: and sent to Ierusalem, that there they might haue by them a memorial of peace & confederacy.

23 Good successe be to the Romans and to the people of the Iewes, by Sea, and by land for euer: the sword also and enemie, be farre from them.

24 If there come first any warre vpon the Romans or any of their confederats throughout all their dominion,

25 The people of the Iewes shall helpe them, as the time shall be appointed, with all their heart.

26 Neither shal they giue any thing, vnto them that make war vpon them, or aide them with victuals, weapons, money, or ships, as it hath seemed good vnto the Romans, but they shall keepe their couenant without taking any thing therefore.

27 In the same maner also, if warre come first vpon the nation of the Iewes, the Romans shall helpe them with all their heart, according as the time shall be appointed them.

28 Neither shal victuals be giuen to thē that take part against thē, or weapons,

or

or money, or ships, as it hath seemed good to the Romanes; but they shall keepe their couenants, and that without deceit.

29 According to these articles did the Romanes make a couenant with the people of the Iewes.

30 Howbeit, if hereafter the one partie or the other, shall thinke meete to adde or diminish any thing, they may doe it at their pleasures, and whatsoeuer they shall adde or take away, shalbe ratified.

31 And as touching the euils that Demetrius doeth to the Iewes, wee haue written vnto him, saying, Wherefore hast thou made thy yoke heauie vpon our friends, and confederats the Iewes?

32 If therefore they complaine any more against thee: wee will doe them iustice, and fight with thee by sea and by land.

CHAP. IX.

1 Alcimus and Bacchides come againe with new forces into Iudea. 7 The armie of Iudas flee from him, 17 and he is slaine. 30 Ionathan is in his place, 40 and reuengeth his brother Iohns quarrell. 55 Alcimus is plagued, and dieth. 70 Bacchides maketh peace with Ionathan.

† *Gr. he added or proceeded to send.*

‖ *Or, the right wing.*

Vrthermore, when Demetrius heard that Nicanor and his hoste were slaine in battell, †hee sent Bacchides and Alcimus into the land of Iudea the second time, and with them the ‖chiefe strength of his hoste.

‡ *Or, Galilea.*

2 Who went forth by the way that leadeth to ‖Galgala, and pitched their tents before Masaloth, which is in Arbela, and after they had wonne it, they slew much people.

3 Also the first moneth of the hundred fiftie and second yeere, they encamped before Ierusalem.

‡ *Or, Berretho. Ios.*

4 From whence they remoued and went to ‖Berea, with twentie thousand footmen, and two thousand horsemen.

5 Now Iudas had pitched his tents at Eleasa, and three thousand chosen men with him.

6 Who seeing the multitude of the other army to be so great, were sore afraide, whereupon many conueyed themselues out of the hoste, insomuch

as there abode of them no moe but eight hundred men.

7 When Iudas therefore saw that his hoste slipt away, and that the battell pressed vpon him, he was sore troubled in mind, and much distressed, for that he had no time to gather them together.

8 Neuerthelesse vnto them that remained, he said; Let vs arise and goe vp against our enemies, if peraduenture we may be able to fight with them.

9 But they dehorted him, saying, Wee shall neuer be able : ‖Let vs now rather saue onr liues, and hereafter we will returne with our brethren, and fight against them : for we are but few.

‖ *We follo here the mane cop*

10 Then Iudas said, God forbid that I should doe this thing, and flee away from them : If our time be come, let vs die manfully for our brethren, and †let vs not staine our honour.

11 With that the hoste [of Bacchides] remoued out of their tents, and stood ouer against ‖them, their horsemen being diuided into two troupes, and their slingers and archers going before the hoste, and they that marched in the foreward were all mighty men.

† *Gr. let v notleauea iust cause behinde v why our glory sho be spoken gainst.*

‖ *Or the Iewes.*

12 As for Bacchides, hee was in the right wing, so the hoste drew neere on the two parts, and sounded their trumpets.

13 They also of Iudas side, euen they sounded their trumpets also, so that the earth shooke at the noise of the armies, and the battell continued from morning till night.

14 Now when Iudas perceiued that Bacchides and the strength of his armie were on the right side, he tooke with him all the hardy men,

15 Who discomfited the right wing, and pursued them vnto the mount Azotus.

16 But when they of the left wing, saw that they of the right wing were discomfited, they followed vpon Iudas and those that were with him hard at the heeles from behinde :

17 Whereupon there was a sore battell, insomuch as many were slaine on both parts.

18 Iudas also was killed, and the remnant fled.

19 Then Ionathan and Simon tooke Iudas their brother, and buried him in the sepulchre of his fathers in Modin.

20 Moreouer they bewailed him, and

and all Israel made great lamentation for him, and mourned many dayes, saying;

21 How is the valiant man fallen, that deliuered Israel?

22 As for the other things concerning Iudas and his warres, and the noble actes which he did, and his greatnesse, they are not written : for they were very many.

23 ¶ Now after the death of Iudas, the wicked began to put foorth their heads in all the coasts of Israel, and there rose vp all such as wrought iniquitie.

24 In those dayes also was there a very great famine, by reason whereof the countrey reuolted, and went with ‖ them.

25 Then Bacchides chose the wicked men, and made them lordes of the countrey.

26 And they made enquirie & search for Iudas friends, and brought them vnto Bacchides, who tooke vengeance of them, and † vsed them despitefully.

27 So was there a great affliction in Israel, the like whereof was not since the time that a Prophet was not seene amongst them.

28 For this cause all Iudas friends came together, & said vnto Ionathan,

29 Since thy brother Iudas died, we haue no man like him to goe foorth against our enemies, and Bacchides, and against them of our nation that are aduersaries to vs.

30 Now therefore wee haue chosen thee this day to be our prince, and captaine in his stead, that thou mayest fight our battels.

31 Vpon this, Ionathan tooke the gouernance vpon him at that time, and rose vp in stead of his brother Iudas.

32 But when Bacchides gat knowledge thereof, he sought for to slay him.

33 Then Ionathan and Simon his brother, and all that were with him, perceiuing that, fled into the wildernes of Thecoe, and pitched their tents by the water of the poole Asphar.

34 ‖ Which when Bacchides vnderstood, he came neere to Iordan with all his hoste vpon the Sabbath day.

35 Now Ionathan had sent his brother [‖ Iohn] a captaine of the people, to pray his friendes the Nabbathites † that they might leaue with them their cariage, which was much.

36 But the children of Iambri came out of Medaba, and tooke Iohn and all that hee had, and went their way with it.

37 After this came word to Ionathan and Simon his brother, that the children of Iambri made a great mariage, and were bringing the bride from ‖ Nadabatha with a great traine, as being the daughter of one of the great princes of Canaan.

38 Therfore they remembred Iohn their brother, and went vp and hidde themselues vnder the couert of the mountaine.

39 Where they lift vp their eyes, and looked, & behold, there was much adoe and great cariage : and the bridegrome came foorth, and his friends & brethren to meet them with ‖ drums and ‖ instruments of musicke, and many weapons.

40 Then Ionathan and they that were with him, rose vp against them from the place where they lay in ambush, and made a slaughter of them in such sort, as many fell downe dead, and the remnant fledde into the mountaine, and they tooke all their spoiles.

41 Thus was the mariage turned into mourning, and the noise of their melody into lamentation.

42 So when they had auenged fully the blood of their brother, they turned againe to the marish of Iordan.

43 Now when Bacchides heard hereof, hee came on the Sabbath day vnto the banks of Iordan with a great power.

44 Then Ionathan sayde to his company, Let vs goe vp now and fight for our liues, for it standeth not with vs to day, as in time past :

45 For behold, the battell is before vs and behinde vs, and the water of Iordan on this side and that side, the marish likewise and wood, neither is there place for vs to turne aside.

46 Wherefore cry ye now vnto heauen, that ye may be deliuered from the hand of your enemies.

47 With that they ioyned battel, and Ionathan stretched foorth his hand to smite Bacchides, but hee turned backe from him.

48 Then Ionathan and they that were with him, leapt into Iordan, and swamme ouer vnto the farther banke : howbeit the other passed not ouer Iordan vnto them.

49 So

Margin notes:

‖ Bacchides and his company.

† Gr. mocked them.

‖ Or, Which when Bacchides vnderstood, on the Sabbath day he came neere.

‖ Ios. Antiq. lib. 13. c. 1.

† Gr. that he might leaue with them their cariage or stuffe.

‖ Or, Medaba.

‖ Or, timbrels

‖ Or, musicians.

† Two thousand men. Ioseph. ant. lib. 13. cap. 1
‖ Or, built.

49 So there were slaine of Bacchides side that day about a †thousand men

50 Afterward returned [Bacchides] to Ierusalem, and ‖repaired the strong cities in Iudea : the fort in Iericho, and Emmaus, and Bethoron, and Bethel, and Thamnatha, Pharathoni, and ‖Taphon (these did he strengthen with high wals, with gates, & with barres.)

‖ Ioseph. Techoa.

51 And in them he set a garison, that they might worke malice vpon Israel.

52 He fortified also †the citie Bethsura, and Gazara, and the towre, and put forces in them, and prouision of victuals.

† Gr. the citie in Bethsura.

53 Besides, he tooke the chiefe mens sonnes in the country for hostages, and put them into the towre at Ierusalem to be kept.

54 Moreouer, in the hundred, fiftie and third yere, in the second moneth, Alcimus commanded that the wall of the inner court of the Sanctuarie should be pulled downe, he pulled downe also the workes of the prophets.

55 And as he began to pull downe, euen at that time was Alcimus plagued, and his enterprises hindered : for his mouth was stopped, and he was taken with a palsie, so that hee could no more speake any thing, nor giue order concerning his house.

56 So Alcimus died at that time with great torment.

57 Now when Bacchides saw that Alcimus was dead, he returned to the king, whereupon the land of Iudea was in rest two yeere.

58 Then all the vngodly men held a counsell, saying, Behold, Ionathan and his companie are at ease, and dwell without care : now therefore wee will bring Bacchides hither, who shall take them all in one night.

59 So they went, and consulted with him.

60 Then remoued he, and came with a great hoste, and sent letters priuily to his adherents in Iudea, that they should take Ionathan, and those that were with him : Howbeit they could not, because their counsell was knowen vnto them.

61 Wherefore they tooke of the men of the countrey that were authours of that mischiefe, about fiftie persons, and slew them.

62 Afterward Ionathan and Simon, and they that were with him, got them away to Bethbasi, which is in the wildernesse, and they repaired the decayes thereof, and made it strong.

63 Which thing when Bacchides knew, he gathered together all his host, and sent word ‖to them that were of Iudea.

‖ Or, to suː of the couː trey as weː his friends takc his paː

64 Then went he and laid siege against Bethbasi, & they fought against it a long season, and made engines of warre.

65 But Ionathan left his brother Simon in the citie, and went forth himselfe into the countrey, and with a certaine number went he forth.

66 And he smote ‖Odonarkes and his brethren, and the children of Phasiron in their tent.

‖ Or, Odomarra.

67 And when he began to smite them, and came vp with his forces, Simon and his company went out of the citie, and burnt vp the engines of warre.

68 And fought against Bacchides, who was discomfited by them, and they afflicted him sore. For his counsell and trauaile was in vaine.

69 Wherefore he was very wroth at the wicked men that gaue him counsell to come into the countrey, insomuch as he slew many of them, and purposed to returne into his owne countrey.

70 Whereof when Ionathan had knowledge, he sent ambassadours vnto him, to the end he should make peace with him, & deliuer them the prisoners.

71 Which thing hee accepted, and did according to his demaunds, and sware vnto him that hee would neuer doe him harme all the dayes of his life.

72 When therefore hee had restored vnto him the prisoners that he had taken aforetime out of the land of Iudea, he returned and went his way into his owne land, neither †came he any more into their borders.

† Gr. adde he to come any more.

73 Thus the sword ceased from Israel : but Ionathan dwelt at Machmas, and began to †gouerne the people, and he destroyed the vngodly men out of Israel.

† Gr. iudg

CHAP. X.

In

‖ Ios. the sonne of Antiochus Epiphanes.

 N the hundreth & sixtieth yere, Alexander the ‖sonne of Antiochus surnamed Epiphanes, went vp and tooke Ptolemais : for the people had receiued him, by meanes whereof he reigned there.

2 Now when king Demetrius heard thereof, he gathered together an exceeding great host, and went foorth against him to fight.

3 Moreouer Demetrius sent letters vnto Ionathan with louing wordes, so as he magnified him.

4 For, said hee, Let vs first make peace with him before he ioyne with Alexander against vs.

5 Else he wil remember all the euils that we haue done against him, and against his brethren and his people.

6 Wherefore he gaue him authority to gather together an host, and to prouide weapons that hee might aide him in battell : he commaunded also that the hostages that were in the towre, should be deliuered him.

7 Then came Ionathan to Ierusalem, and read the letters in the audience of all the people, and of them that were in the towre.

8 Who were sore afraid when they heard that the king had giuen him authoritie to gather together an host.

9 Whereupon they of the towre deliuered their hostages vnto Ionathan, & he deliuered them vnto their parents.

10 This done, Ionathan setled himselfe in Ierusalem, and began to build and repaire the citie.

11 And he commaunded the workemen to build the wals, and the mount Sion round about with square stones, for fortification, and they did so.

12 Then the strangers that were in the fortresses which Bacchides had built, fled away :

13 Insomuch as euery man left his place, and went into his owne country.

14 Onely at Bethsura certaine of those that had forsaken the law, and the commaundements remained still : for it was their place of refuge.

15 Now when king Alexander had heard what promises Demetrius had sent vnto Ionathan : when also it was told him of the battels and noble acts which he & his brethren had done, and of the paines that they had indured,

16 He said, Shal we find such another man ? Now thereforee we will make him our friend, and confederate.

17 Vpon this he wrote a letter and sent it vnto him according to these words, saying :

18 King Alexander to his brother Ionathan, sendeth greeting :

19 We haue heard of thee, that thou art a man of great power, and meete to be our friend.

20 Wherefore now this day we ordaine thee to bee the high priest of thy nation, and to be called the kings friend, (and therewithall he sent him a purple robe and a crowne of gold) [and require thee] to take our part, and keepe friendship with vs.

21 So in the seuenth moneth of the hundreth and sixtieth yere, at the feast of the Tabernacles, Ionathan put on the holy robe, and gathered together forces, and prouided much armour.

22 Wherof when Demetrius heard, he was very sory, and said,

23 What haue we done that Alexander hath preuented vs, in making amity with the Iewes to strengthen himself ?

24 I also will write vnto them words of encouragement [and promise them] dignities and gifts, that I may haue their ayde.

25 He sent vnto him therefore, to this effect : King Demetrius vnto the people of the Iewes, sendeth greeting :

26 Whereas you haue kept couenants with vs, & continued in our friendship, not ioyning your selues with our enemies, we haue heard hereof, & are glad :

27 Wherefore now continue yee still to be faithful vnto vs, and we will well recompence you for the things you doe in our behalfe,

28 And will grant you many immunities, and giue you rewards.

29 And now I doe free you, and for your sake I release all the Iewes from tributes, and from the customes of salt, and from crowne taxes,

30 And frō that which appertaineth vnto me to receiue for the third part of the seed, and the halfe of the fruit of the trees, I release it from this day forth, so that they shall not be taken of the land of Iudea, nor of the three gouernments which are added thereunto out of the country of Samaria and Galile, from this day forth for euermore.

31 Let Ierusalem also bee holy and free, with the borders thereof,
both

both from tenths and tributes.

32 And as for the towre which is at Ierusalem, I yeeld vp my authoritie ouer it, and giue it to the high Priest, that he may set in it such men as he shall choose to keepe it.

33 Moreouer I freely set at libertie euery one of the Iewes that were carried captiues out of the land of Iudea, into any part of my kingdome, and I will that all my officers remit the tributes, euen of their cattell.

34 Furthermore, I will that all the Feasts and Sabbaths, & New moones and solemne dayes, and the three dayes before the Feast, and the three dayes after the Feast, shall be all dayes of immunitie and freedom for all the Iewes in my realme.

35 Also no man shall haue authoritie to meddle with them, or to molest any of them in any matter.

36 [I will further] that there be enrolled amongst the kings forces about thirtie thousand men of the Iewes, vnto whom pay shall be giuen as belongeth to all the kings forces.

37 And of them some shalbe placed in the kings strong holds, of whom also some shall be set ouer the affaires of the kingdome, which are of trust : and I will that their ouerseers and gouernours be of themselues, and that they † liue after their owne lawes, euen as the King hath commanded in the land of Iudea.

† Gr. walke.

38 And concerning the three gouernments that are added to Iudea from the countrey of Samaria, let them be ioyned with Iudea, that they may be reckoned to be vnder one, nor bound to obey other authoritie then ỹ high priests

39 As for Ptolemais and the land pertaining thereto, I giue it as a free gift to the Sanctuary at Ierusalem, for the necessary expences ‖ of the Sanctuary.

‖ Or, of the holy things.

40 Moreouer, I giue euery yeere fifteene thousand shekels of siluer, out of the Kings accompts from the places appertaining.

41 And all the ouerplus which the officers payed not in as in former time, from henceforth shalbe giuen towards the workes of the Temple.

42 And besides this, the fiue thousand shekels of siluer, which they tooke from the vses of the Temple out of the accompts yeere by yeere, euen those

things shall be released, because they appertaine to the Priests that minister.

43 And whosoeuer they be that flee vnto the Temple at Ierusalem, or be within the liberties thereof, being indebted vnto the King, or for any other matter, let them be at libertie, and all that they haue in my realme.

44 For the building also and repairing of the workes of the Sanctuary, expences shalbe giuen of the Kings accompts.

45 Yea, and for the building of the walles of Ierusalem, and the fortifying thereof round about, expences shall bee giuen out of the Kings accompts, as also for building of the walles in Iudea.

46 Now when Ionathan and the people heard these words, they gaue no credite vnto them, nor receiued them, because they remembred the great euill that he had done in Israel; for hee had afflicted them very sore.

47 But with Alexander they were well pleased, because hee was the first that entreated of ‖ peace with them, and they were confederate with him alwayes.

‖ True.

48 Then gathered king Alexander great forces, and camped ouer against Demetrius.

49 And after the two Kings had ioyned battell, Demetrius hoste fled : but Alexander followed after him, and preuailed against them.

50 And he continued the battell very sore vntill the Sunne went downe, and that day was Demetrius slaine.

51 Afterward Alexander sent Embassadors to Ptoleme king of Egypt, with a message to this effect;

52 Forsomuch as I am come againe to my realme, and am set in the throne of my progenitors, and haue gotten the dominion, and ouerthrowen Demetrius, and recouered our countrey,

53 (For after I had ioyned battell with him, both he, and his hoste was discomfited by vs, so that we sit in the throne of his kingdome)

54 Now therefore let vs make a league of amitie together, and giue me now thy daughter to wife : & I will be thy son in law, and will giue both thee and her, gifts according to thy dignity.

55 Then Ptoleme the king gaue answere, saying, Happy be the day wherein thou diddest returne into the land of thy

thy fathers, and satest in the throne of their kingdome.

56 And now will I doe to thee, as thou hast written : meet me therefore at Ptolemais, that wee may see one another, for I will marry my daughter to thee according to thy desire.

57 So Ptolome went out of Egypt with his daughter Cleopatra, and they came vnto Ptolemais in the hundred threescore and second yeere.

58 Where king Alexander meeting him, gaue vnto him his daughter Cleopatra, and celebrated her marriage at Ptolemais with great glory, as the maner of kings is.

59 Now king Alexander had written vnto Ionathan, that hee should come and meete him.

60 Who thereupon went honourably to Ptolemais, where he met the two kings, and gaue them and their friends siluer and golde, and many presents, and found fauour in their sight.

61 At that time certaine pestilent fellowes of Israel, men of a wicked life, assembled themselues against him, to accuse him : but the king would not heare them.

62 Yea more then that, the king commanded to take off his garments, and clothe him in purple : and they did so.

63 Also he made him sit by himselfe, and said vnto his princes, Goe with him into the midst of the city, and make proclamation, that no man complaine against him of any matter, and that no man troble him for any maner of cause.

64 Now when his accusers sawe that he was honoured according to the proclamation, and clothed in purple, they fled all away.

65 So the king honoured him, and wrote him amongst his chiefe friends, and made him a duke, and ||partaker of his dominion.

|| Or, gouernour of a prouince.

66 Afterward Ionathan returned to Ierusalem with peace and gladnes.

67 Furthermore, in the hundreth threescore and fifth yeere, came Demetrius sonne of Demetrius, out of Crete into the land of his fathers.

68 Whereof when king Alexander heard tell, he was right sory, and returned into Antioch.

69 Then Demetrius made Apollonius the gouernour of Coelosyria his general, who gathered together a great hoste, and camped in Iamnia, and sent

vnto Ionathan the high Priest, saying,

70 Thou alone liftest vp thy selfe against vs, and I am laughed to scorne for thy sake, and reproched, and why doest thou vaunt thy power against vs in the mountaines?

71 Now therefore if thou trustest in thine owne strength, come downe to vs into the plaine field, and there let vs trie the matter together, for with me is the power of the cities.

72 Aske and learne who I am, and the rest that take our part, and they shal tel thee that thy foot is not able to stand before our face; for thy fathers haue bene twice put to flight in their owne land.

73 Wherefore now thou shalt not be able to abide the horsemen and so great a power in the plaine, where is neither stone nor flint, nor place to flee vnto.

74 So when Ionathan heard these words of Apollonius, he was moued in his mind, & choosing ten thousand men, he went out of Ierusalē, where Simon his brother met him for to helpe him.

75 And hee pitched his tents against Ioppe : but they of Ioppe shut him out of the citie, because Apollonius had a garison there.

76 Then Ionathan laid siege vnto it : whereupon they of the city let him in for feare : & so Ionathan wan Ioppe.

77 Wherof when Apollonius heard, he tooke three thousand horsemen with a great hoste of footmen, and went to Azotus ||as one that iourneyed, & therewithal ||drew him forth into the plaine, because he had a great number of horsemen, in whom he put his trust.

|| Or, as thogh he would passe thorow it.
|| Or, led his company.

78 Then Ionathan followed after him to Azotus, where the armies ioyned battell.

79 Now Apollonius had left a thousand horsemen in ambush.

80 And Ionathan knew that there was an ambushment behinde him ; for they had compassed in his host, and cast darts at the people, from morning till euening.

81 But the people stood still, as Ionathan had commanded them : and so the ||enemies horses were tired.

82 Then brought Simon forth his hoste, and set them against the footmen, (for the horsemen were spent) who were discomfited by him, and fled.

|| Ios. Antiq. lib. 13. c. 8.

83 The horsemen also being scattered in the field, fled to Azotus, and went into Bethdagō their idols temple for safety.

84 But

84 But Ionathan set fire on Azotus, and the cities round about it, and tooke their spoiles, and the temple of Dagon, with them that were fled into it, he burnt with fire.

85 Thus there were burnt and slaine with the sword, well nigh eight thousand men.

86 And from thence Ionathan remoued his hoste, and camped against Ascalon, where the men of the city came forth, and met him with great pompe.

87 After this, returned Ionathan and his hoste vnto Ierusalem, hauing many spoiles.

88 Now when king Alexander heard these things, he honoured Ionathan yet more,

89 And sent him a buckle of golde, as the vse is to be giuen to such as are of the kings blood: he gaue him also Accaron with the borders thereof in possession.

CHAP. XI.

12 Ptolomeus taketh away his daughter from Alexander, and entreth vpon his kingdome. 17 Alexander is slaine, and Ptolemeus dieth within three dayes. 20 Ionathan besiegeth the towre at Ierusalem. 26 The Iewes and he are much honoured by Demetrius, 48 Who is rescued by the Iewes from his owne subiects in Antioch. 57 Antiochus the yonger honoureth Ionathan. 61 His exploits in diuers places

Nd the king of Egypt gathered together a great host like the sand that lieth vpon the Sea shore, and many ships, and went about through deceit to get Alexanders kingdome, and ioyne it to his owne.

2 Whereupon he tooke his iourney into Syria in peaceable maner, so as they of the cities opened vnto him, and met him: for king Alexander had commanded them so to doe, because he was his father in law.

3 Now as Ptolomee entred into the cities, he set in euery one of them a garison of souldiers to keepe it.

4 And when he came neere to Azotus, they shewed him the temple of Dagon that was burnt, and Azotus, and the suburbs thereof that were destroyed, and the bodies that were cast abroad, and them that he had burnt in the battell, for they had made heapes of them by the way where he should passe.

5 Also they told the king whatsoe-

uer Ionathan had done, to the intent he might blame him: but the king helde his peace.

6 Then Ionathan met the king with great pompe at Ioppa, where they saluted one another, and † lodged.

7 Afterward Ionathan when he had gone with the king to the riuer called Eleutherus, returned againe to Ierusalem.

8 King Ptolomee therefore hauing gotten the dominion of the cities by the sea, vnto Seleucia vpon the sea coast, imagined wicked counsels against Alexander.

9 Whereupon he sent embassadours vnto king Demetrius, saying, Come, let vs make a league betwixt vs, and I will giue thee my daughter whome Alexander hath, and thou shalt reigne in thy fathers kingdome:

10 For I repent ỹ I gaue my daughter vnto him, for he sought to slay me.

11 Thus did he slander him, because he was desirous of his kingdome.

12 Wherefore he tooke his daughter from him, and gaue her to Demetrius, and forsooke Alexander, so that their hatred was openly knowen.

13 Then Ptolomee entred into Antioch, where he set two crownes vpõ his head, the crowne of Asia, and of Egypt.

14 In the meane season was king Alexander in Cilicia, because those ỹ dwelt in those parts, had reuolted from him.

15 But when Alexander heard of this, hee came to warre against him, whereupon king Ptolomee brought forth his hoste, and met him with a mightie power, and put him to flight.

16 So Alexander fled into Arabia, there to be defended, but king Ptolomee was exalted.

17 For Zabdiel the Arabian tooke off Alexanders head, and sent it vnto Ptolomee.

18 King Ptolomee also died the third day after, † & they that were in the strong holds, were slaine one of another.

19 By this meanes Demetrius reigned in the hundreth, threescore and seuenth yeere.

20 At the same time Ionathan gathered together them that were in Iudea, to take the towre that was in Ierusalem, and he made many engines of warre against it.

21 Then certaine vngodly persons who hated their owne people, went vnto

Margin notes:
† Gr. slept.

† Gr. and those that were in the holds were slaine of those that were in the holds.

to the king, and told him that Ionathan besieged the towre.

22 Whereof when he heard, he was angry, and immediately remouing, he can to Ptolemais, and wrote vnto Ionathan, that he should not lay siege to the towre, but come and speake with him at Ptolemais in great haste.

23 Neuerthelesse Ionathan when he heard this, commanded to besiege it [still] and he chose certaine of the Elders of Israel, and the priests, and put himselfe in perill,

24 And tooke siluer and gold, and rayment, and diuers presents besides, and went to Ptolemais, vnto the king, where he found fauour in his sight.

25 And though certaine vngodly men of the people, had made complaints against him,

26 Yet the king entreated him as his predecessors had done before, & promoted him in the sight of all his friends,

27 And confirmed him in the high priesthood, and in all the honours that hee had before, and gaue him preeminence among his chiefe friends.

28 Then Ionathan desired the king, that hee would make Iudea free from tribute, as also the three gouernments with the countrey of Samaria, & he promised him three hundred talents

29 So the king consented and wrote letters vnto Ionathan, of all these things after this maner.

30 King Demetrius vnto his brother Ionathan, and vnto the nation of the Iewes, sendeth greeting.

31 We send you heere a copie of the letter, which we did write vnto our cousin Lasthenes, concerning you, that you might see it.

32 King Demetrius vnto his father Lasthenes, sendeth greeting:

33 We are determined to doe good to the people of the Iewes, who are our friends, and keepe couenants with vs, because of their good will towards vs.

‖ Iosep. antiq. lib. 13. cap. 8.

34 ‖ Wherefore we haue ratified vnto them the borders of Iudea, with the three gouernments of Apherema, and Lidda, and Ramathem, that are added vnto Iudea, from the countrie of Samaria, and all things appertaining vnto them, for all such, as doe sacrifice in Ierusalem, in stead of the paiments, which the king receiued of them yeerely aforetime out of the fruits of the earth, and of trees.

35 And as for other things that belong vnto vs of the tithes and customes pertaining vnto vs, as also the salt pits, and the crowne taxes, which are due vnto vs, we discharge them of them all for their reliefe.

36 And nothing heereof shall be reuoked from this time foorth for euer.

37 Now therefore see that thou make a copie of these things, and let it be deliuered vnto Ionathan, and set vpon the holy mount in a conspicuous place.

38 After this, when king Demetrius saw that the land was quiet before him, and that no resistance was made against him, he sent away all his forces euery one to his owne place, except certaine bands of strangers, whom he had gathered from the iles of the heathen, wherefore all the forces of his fathers hated him.

39 Moreouer there was one Tryphon, that had beene of Alexanders part afore, who seeing that all the hoste murmured against Demetrius, went to Simalcue the Arabian, that brought vp Antiochus ỹ yong sonne of Alexander,

40 And lay sore vpon him, to deliuer him [this young Antiochus] that he might raigne in his fathers stead: he told him therefore all that Demetrius had done, and how his men of warre were at enmitie with him, and there he remained a long season.

41 In the meane time Ionathan sent vnto king Demetrius, that hee would cast those of the towre out of Ierusalem, and those also in the fortresses. For they fought against Israel.

42 So Demetrius sent vnto Ionathan, saying, I will not onely doe this for thee, and thy people, but I will greatly honour thee and thy nation, if opportunitie serue.

43 Now therefore thou shalt do wel if thou send me men to helpe me; for all my forces are gone from me.

44 Vpon this Ionathan sent him three thousand strong men vnto Antioch, and when they came to ỹ king, the king was very glad of their comming.

45 Howbeit, they that were of the citie, gathered themselues together into the midst of the citie, to the number of an hundreth and twentie thousand men, and would haue slaine the king.

46 Wherefore the king fled into the court, but they of the citie kept the passages of the citie, and began to fight.

47 Then

47 Then the king called to the Iewes for helpe, who came vnto him all at once, and dispersing themselues through the city, slew that day in the citie to the number of an hundred thousand.

48 Also they set fire on the citie, and gat many spoiles that day, and deliuered the king.

49 So when they of the city saw, that the Iewes had got the city as they would, their courage was abated, wherefore they made supplication to the king, and cried, saying:

50 ‖ Graunt vs peace, and let the Iewes cease from assaulting vs and the citie.

‖ Or, bee friends with vs.

51 With that they cast away their weapons, and made peace, and the Iewes were honoured in the sight of the king, and in the sight of all that were in his realme, and they returned to Ierusalem hauing great spoiles.

52 So king Demetrius sate on the throne of his kingdome, and the land was quiet before him.

53 Neuerthelesse hee dissembled in all that euer hee spake, and estranged himselfe from Ionathan, neither rewarded he him, according to the benefits which hee had receiued of him, but troubled him very sore.

54 After this returned Tryphon, and with him the yong childe Antiochus, who reigned and was crowned.

55 Then there gathered vnto him all the men of warre whom Demetrius had put away, and they fought against Demetrius, who turned his backe and fled.

† Gr. beasts.

56 Moreouer Triphon tooke the † Elephants, and wonne Antioch.

57 At that time yong Antiochus wrote vnto Ionathan, saying; I confirme thee in the high Priesthood, and appoint thee ruler ouer the foure gouernments, and to be one of the kings friends.

† Gr. and seruice.

58 Vpon this he sent him golden vessels † to be serued in, and gaue him leaue to drinke in gold, and to bee clothed in purple, and to weare a golden buckle.

‖ Or, went beyond the riuer, and passed through the cities : Or, went and passed beyond the riuer, and through the cities, Gr.

59 His brother Simon also he made captaine from the place called the ladder of Tyrus, vnto the borders of Egypt.

60 Then Ionathan ‖ went foorth and passed through the cities beyond the water, and all the forces of Syria,

gathered themselues vnto him for to helpe him : and when he came to Ascalon, they of the city met him honorably.

61 From whence he went to Gaza, but they of Gaza shut him out ; wherefore hee layd siege vnto it, and burned ‖ the suburbs thereof with fire, and spoiled them.

‖ Or, the places ther about.

62 Afterward when they of Gaza made supplication vnto Ionathan, † he made peace with them, and tooke the sonnes of the chiefe men for hostages, and sent them to Ierusalem, and passed through the countrey vnto Damascus.

† Gr. he ga them the right hand

63 Now when Ionathan heard that Demetrius Princes were come to Cades which is in Galilee, with a great power, purposing to ‖ remoue him out of the countrey,

‖ Or, to remooue him from the a faires of t kingdome.

64 Hee went to meet them, and left Simon his brother in the countrey.

65 Then Simon encamped against Bethsura, and fought against it a long season, and shut it vp :

66 But they desired to haue peace with him, which he granted them, and then put them out from thence, and tooke the city, and set a garrison in it.

67 As for Ionathan and his hoste, they pitched at the water of Gennesar, from whence betimes in the morning they gate them to the plaine of Nasor.

68 And behold, the hoste of strangers met them in the plaine, who hauing layed men in ambush for him in the mountaines, came themselues ouer against him.

69 So when they that lay in ambush rose out of their places, and ioyned battel, al that were of Ionathans side fled.

70 In so much as there was not one of them left, except Mattathias the sonne of Absolon, and Iudas the sonne of Calphi the captaines of the hoste.

71 Then Ionathan rent his clothes, and cast earth vpon his head, and prayed.

72 Afterwards turning againe to battell, he put them to flight, and so they ranne away.

73 Now when his owne men that were fled saw this, they turned againe vnto him, and with him pursued them to Cades, euen vnto their owne tents, and there they camped.

74 So there were slaine of the heathen that day, about three thousand men, but Ionathan returned to Ierusalem.

CHAP.

CHAP. XII.

1 Ionathan reneweth his league with the Romanes and Lacedemonians. 28 The forces of Demetrius thinking to surprise Ionathan, flee away for feare. 35 Ionathan fortifieth the castles in Iudea, 48 and is shut vp by the fraud of Tryphon in Ptolemais.

Owe when Ionathan saw that the time serued him, he chose certaine men and sent them to Rome, for to confirme and renew the friendship that they had with them.

2 He sent letters also to the Lacedemonians, and to other places, for the same purpose.

3 So they went vnto Rome, and entred into the Senate, and said, Ionathan the high Priest, and the people of the Iewes sent vs vnto you, to the end you should renew the friendship which you had with them, and league, as in former time.

4 Vpon this the Romanes gaue them letters vnto the gouernours of euery place, that they should bring them into the land of Iudea peaceably.

5 And this is the copy of the letters which Ionathan wrote to the Lacedemonians :

6 Ionathan the hie Priest, and the Elders of the nation, and the Priestes and the other people of the Iewes, vnto the Lacedemonians their brethren, send greeting.

7 There were letters sent in times past vnto Onias the high Priest from ||Darius, who reigned then among you, to signifie that you are our brethren, as the copy here vnder-written doeth specifie.

8 At which time Onias intreated the Embassador that was sent, honourably, and receiued the letters, wherein declaration was made of the ||league and friendship.

9 Therefore we also, albeit we need none of these things, for that wee haue the holy bookes of Scripture in our hands to comfort vs,

10 Haue neuerthelesse attempted to send vnto you, for the renewing of brotherhood and friendship, lest we should become strangers vnto you altogether : for there is a long time passed since you sent vnto vs.

11 We therefore at all times without ceasing, both in our Feasts, and other conuenient dayes, doe remember you in the sacrifices which we offer, and in our prayers, as reason is, and as it becommeth vs to thinke vpon our brethren :

12 And wee are right glad of your honour.

13 As for our selues, wee haue had great troubles and warres on euery side, forsomuch as the kings that are round about vs haue fought against vs.

14 Howbeit wee would not be troublesome vnto you, nor to others of our confederates & friends in these warres :

15 For wee haue helpe from heauen that succoureth vs, so as we are deliuered from our enemies, and our enemies are brought vnder foote.

16 For this cause we chose Numenius the son of Antiochus, and Antipater the sonne of Iason, and sent them vnto the Romanes, to renew the amitie that we had with them, and the former league.

17 We commanded them also to goe vnto you, and to salute you, and to deliuer you our letters, concerning the renewing of our brotherhood.

18 Wherefore now ye shall doe well to giue vs an answere thereto.

19 And this is the copy of the letters which ||Omiares sent :

20 Areus king of the Lacedemonians, to Onias the hie Priest, greeting.

21 It is found in writing, that the Lacedemonians and Iewes are brethren, and that they are of the stocke of Abraham :

22 Now therefore, since this is come to our knowledge, you shall doe well to write vnto vs of your †prosperitie.

23 We doe write backe againe to you, that your cattell and goods are ours, and ours are yours. We doe command therefore [our Embassadours] to make report vnto you on this wise.

24 Now when Ionathan heard that Demetrius princes were come to fight against him with a greater hoste then afore,

25 Hee remooued from Ierusalem, and met them in the land of Amathis : for he gaue them no respite ||to enter his countrey.

26 He sent spies also vnto their tents, who came againe, and tolde him, that they were appointed to come vpon them in the night season.

27 Wherefore so soone as the Sunne was downe, Ionathan commaunded his men to watch, and to be in armes, that

Marginal notes

|| Areus : looke Ioseph. Ant. lib. 13. cap. 8.

|| Or, kinred, Ios. Ant.

|| Read out of Ios. which Areus sent to Onias.

† Gr. peace.

|| Or, to set foote in his countrey: or, to inuade his countrey.

that all the night long they might bee ready to fight: Also he sent foorth sentinels round about the hoste.

28 But when the aduersaries heard that Ionathan and his men were ready for battell, they feared, and trembled in their hearts, and ‖ they kindled fires in their campe.

‖ Ioseph. lib. ant. 13. 9. they went away.

29 Howbeit Ionathan and his company knew it not till the morning : for they saw the lights burning.

30 Then Ionathan pursued after them, but ouertooke them not : for they were gone ouer the riuer Eleutherus.

31 Wherefore Ionathan turned to the Arabians, who were called † Zabadeans, and smote them, and tooke their spoiles.

† Ios. gr. Nabatheans, or Zabatheans.

32 And remouing thence, he came to Damascus, and so passed through all the countrey.

33 Simon also went foorth, and passed through the countrey vnto Ascalon, and the holds there adioyning, from whence he turned aside to Ioppe, and wanne it.

34 For he had heard that they would deliuer the hold vnto them that tooke Demetrius part, wherefore he set a garison there to keepe it.

35 After this came Ionathan home againe, and calling the Elders of the people together, hee consulted with them about building steong holdes in Iudea,

36 And making the walles of Ierusalem higher, and raising a great mount betweene the towre and the city, for to separate it from the city, that so it might be alone, that men might neither sell nor buy in it.

37 Vpon this they came together, to build vp the citie ‖ forasmuch as [part of] the wall toward the brooke on the East side was fallen down, & they repaired that which was called Caphenatha.

‖ Or, according to the Romane reading, and he came neere to the wall of the brooke toward the East.

38 Simon also set vp Adida, in Sephela, and made it strong with gates and barres.

39 Now Tryphon went about to get the kingdome of Asia, and to kill Antiochus the king, that hee might set the crowne vpon his owne head.

40 Howbeit, he was afraid that Ionathan would not suffer him, and that he would fight against him, wherefore he sought a way, howe to take Ionathan, that he might kill him. So he remoued, and came to Bethsan.

41 Then Ionathan went out to meet him with fourtie thousand men, chosen for the battell, and came to Bethsan.

42 Now when Tryphon saw that Ionathan came with so great a force, hee durst not stretch his hande against him,

43 But receiued him honourably, and comended him vnto all his friends, and gaue him gifts, and commaunded his men of warre to be as obedient vnto him, as to himselfe.

44 Vnto Ionathan also hee said, Why hast thou put all this people to so great trouble, seeing there is no warre betwixt vs ?

45 Therefore send them now home againe, and chuse a few men to waite on thee, and come thou with me to Ptolemais, for I will giue it thee and the rest of the strong holds and forces, and all that haue any charge : as for me, I will returne and depart : for this is the cause of my comming.

46 So Ionathan beleeuing him, did as he bade him, and sent away his host, who went into the land of Iudea.

47 And with himselfe hee retained but three thousand men, of whome he † sent two thousand into Galile, and one thousand went with him.

† Gr. left two thousand in Galile.

48 Now assoone as Ionathan entred into Ptolemais, they of Ptolemais shut the gates, and tooke him, and all them that came with him, they slewe with the sword.

49 Then sent Tryphon an hoste of footmen, and horsemen into Galile, and into the great plaine, to destroy all Ionathans company.

50 But when they knew that Ionathan and they that were with him were taken and slaine, they encouraged one another, and went close together, prepared to fight.

51 They therfore that followed vpon them, perceiuing ỹ they were ready to fight for their liues, turned back againe.

52 Whereupon they all came into the land of Iudea peaceably, and there they bewailed Ionathan & them that were with him, & they were sore afraid, wherfore all Israel made great lamentation.

53 Then all the heathen that were round about them, sought to destroy them. For, said they, they haue no captaine, nor any to helpe them. Now therfore let vs make war vpon them, & take away their memorial frō amongst men.

CHAP.

CHAP. XIII.

8 Simon is made captaine in his brother Ionathans roume. 19 Tryphon getteth two of
Ionathans sonnes into his hands, and slayeth
their father. 27 The tombe of Ionathan.
36 Simon is fauoured by Demetrius, 46 and
winneth Gaza, and the towre at Hierusalem.

Ow when Simon heard
that Tryphon had gathe-
red together a great hoste
to inuade the land of Iu-
dea, and destroy it,

2 And saw that the people was in
great trembling and feare, he went vp
to Ierusalem, and gathered the people
together,

3 And gaue them exhortation, saying : Yee your selues know, what great
things I and my brethren, and my fathers house haue done for the lawes,
and the Sanctuarie, the battels also,
and troubles which we haue seene,

4 By reason whereof all my brethren are slaine for Israels sake, and I
am left alone.

5 Now therefore be it farre from
me, that I should spare mine owne life
in any time of trouble : for I am no better then my brethren.

6 Doubtlesse I will auenge my nation and the Sanctuarie, & our wiues,
and our children : for all the heathen are
gathered to destroy vs, of very malice.

7 Now as soone as the people
heard these words, their spirit reuiued.

8 And they answered with a loud
voice, saying, Thou shalt bee our leader
in stead of Iudas and Ionathan thy
brother.

9 Fight thou our battels, & what soeuer thou commandest vs, that will we
doe.

10 So then he gathered together all
the men of warre, and made hast to finish the walles of Ierusalem, and he
fortified it round about.

11 Also he sent Ionathan, the sonne
of Absolom, & with him a great power
to Ioppe, who casting out them that
were therein, remained there in it.

12 So Tryphon remoued from Ptolemais, with a great power to inuade
the land of Iudea, and Ionathan was
with him in warde.

13 But Simon pitched his tents at
Adida, ouer against the plaine.

14 Now when Tryphon knew that
Simon, was risen vp in stead of his bro-

ther Ionathan, and meant to ioyne
battell with him, he sent messengers vnto him, saying,

15 Whereas we haue Ionathan thy
brother in hold, it is for money that he
is owing vnto the kings treasure, ||con-
cerning the businesse that was committed vnto him.

16 Wherefore, now send an hundred
talents of siluer, and two of his sonnes
for hostages, that when he is at liberty
he may not reuolt from vs, and we will
let him goe.

17 Heereupon Simon, albeit he perceiued that they spake deceiptfully vnto
him, yet sent he the money, and the children, lest peraduenture he should procure to himselfe great hatred of the
people :

18 Who might haue said, Because I
sent him not the money, and the children, therefore is [Ionathan] dead.

19 So he sent them the children, and
the hundred talents : Howbeit [Try-
phon] dissembled, neither would he let
Ionathan goe.

20 And after this came Tryphon to
inuade the land, and destroy it, going
round about by the way that leadeth
vnto Adora, but Simon and his host
marched against him in euery place
wheresoeuer he went.

21 Now they that were in the towre,
sent messengers vnto Tryphon, to the
end that he should hasten his comming
vnto them by the wildernesse, and send
them victuals.

22 Wherefore Tryphon made readie all his horsemen to come that night,
but there fell a very great snow, by reason whereof he came not : So he departed & came into the countrey of Galaad.

23 And when he came neere to Bas-
cama, he slew Ionathan, who was buried there.

24 Afterward Tryphon returned,
and went into his owne land.

25 Then sent Simon and tooke the
bones of Ionathan his brother, and
buried them in Modin the citie of his
fathers.

26 And all Israel made great lamentation for him, and bewailed him
many daies.

27 Simon also built a monument
vpon the Sepulchre of his father and
his brethren, and raised it aloft to the
sight, with hewen stone behind and before.

28 Moreouer

|| Or, for the
affaires, or
officers that
he had, for
the necessary
vses which
he had.

28 Moreouer hee set vp seuen pyramides one against another, for his father and his mother, and his foure brethren.

29 And in these he made cunning deuices, about the which he set great pillars, and vpon the pillars he made all their armour for a perpetuall memory, and by the armour, ships carued, that they might be seene of all that saile on the sea.

30 This is the Sepulchre which he made at Modin, and it standeth yet vnto this day.

31 Now Tryphon dealt deceitfully with the yong king Antiochus, and slew him,

32 And he raigned in his stead, and crowned himselfe king of Asia, and brought a great calamitie vpō the land.

33 Then Simon built vp the strong holds in Iudea, and fensed them about with high towres, and great walles and gates and barres, and layd vp victuals † therein.

† Gr. in the strong holds.

34 Moreouer Simon chose men, and sent to king Demetrius, to the end he should giue the land an immunitie, because †all that Tryphon did, was to spoyle.

† Gr. All Tryphons doings were robberies.

35 Vnto whom king Demetrius answered and wrote after this maner.

36 King Demetrius vnto Simon the high Priest, and friend of kings, as also vnto the Elders and nation of the Iewes, sendeth greeting.

37 The golden crowne, and the scarlet robe which ye sent vnto vs, we haue receiued, and wee are ready to make a stedfast peace with you, yea and to write vnto our officers to confirme the immunities which we haue granted.

38 And whatsoeuer couenants we haue made with you, shall stand, and the strong holdes which yee haue builded shalbe your owne.

39 As for any ouersight or fault committed vnto this day, we forgiue it, and the crowne taxe also which yee owe vs, if there were any other tribute paide in Ierusalem, it shall no more be paide.

40 And looke who are meet among you to be in our court, let them be inrolled, and let there be peace betwixt vs.

41 Thus the yoke of the heathen was taken away from Israel, in the hundred and seuentieth yeere.

42 Then the people of Israel began to write in their instruments, and contracts, in the first yeere of Simon the high Priest, the gouernour, and leader of the Iewes.

43 In those dayes Simon camped against Gaza, and besieged it round about; he made also an engine of warre, and set it by the city, and battered a certaine towre, and tooke it.

44 And they that were in the Engine leapt into the citie, whereupon there was a great vproare in the citie:

45 Insomuch as the people of the citie rent their clothes, and climed vpon the walles, with their wiues and children, and cried with a lowd voice, beseeching Simon †to grant them peace.

† Gr. to giue them his right hand.

46 And they said, Deale not with vs according to our wickednesse, but according to thy mercy.

47 So Simon was appeased towards them, and fought no more against them, but put them out of the citie, and cleansed the houses wherein the idols were: and so entred into it, with songs, and thankesgiuing.

48 Yea, he put all vncleannesse out of it, and placed such men there, as would keepe the Law, and made it stronger then it was before, and built therein a dwelling place for himselfe.

49 They also of the towre in Ierusalem were kept so strait, that they could neither come foorth, nor goe into the countrey, nor buy, nor sell, wherefore they were in great distresse for want of victuals, and a great number of them perished through famine.

50 Then cried they to Simon, beseeching him ‖to bee at one with them, which thing hee graunted them, and when he had put them out from thence, he cleansed the towre from pollutions:

‖ Or, to make peace with them.

51 And entred into it the three and twentieth day of the second moneth, in the hundred seuentie and one yere, with thankesgiuing, and branches of palme trees, and with harpes, and cymbals, and with viols and hymnes, and songs: because there was destroyed a great enemy out of Israel.

52 Hee ordained also that that day should be kept euery yeere with gladnes. Moreouer, the hill of the Temple that was by the towre he made stronger then it was, and there hee dwelt himselfe with his company.

53 And when Simon sawe that Iohn his sonne was a valiant man, he made

made him captaine of all the hostes and
dwelt in Gazara.

CHAP. XIIII.

3 Demetrius is taken by the King of Persia. 4
The good deedes of Simon to his countrey.
18 The Lacedemonians and Romans renew
their league with him. 26 A memoriall of his
actes is set vp in Sion.

Ow in the hundred three-
score and twelfth yeere,
king Demetrius gathered
his forces together, and
went into Media, to get
him helpe to fight against Tryphon.

2 But when Arsaces the king of
Persia & Media, heard that Demetrius
was entred within his borders, he sent
one of his princes to take him aliue.

3 Who went and smote the hoste of
Demetrius, and tooke him and brought
him to Arsaces, by whom hee was put
in warde.

4 As for the land of Iudea, that
was quiet all the dayes of Simon : for
he sought the good of his nation, in such
wise, as that euermore his authoritie
and honour pleased them well.

5 And as he was honourable (in all
his acts) so in this, that he tooke Ioppe
for an hauen, and made an entrance to
the yles of the Sea,

6 And enlarged the boundes of his
nation, and recouered the countrey,

7 And gathered together a great
number of captiues, and had the dominion of Gazara and Bethsura, and the
towre, out of the which he tooke all vncleannesse, neither was there any that
resisted him.

8 Then did they till their ground in
peace, and the earth gaue her increase,
and the trees of the field their fruit.

9 The ancient men sate all in the
streetes, communing together of ||good
things, and the young men put on glorious and warrelike apparell.

10 He prouided victuals for the cities,
and set in them all maner of munition,
so that his honourable name was renowmed vnto the end of the world.

11 He made peace in the land, and Israel reioyced with great ioy :

12 For *euery man sate vnder his
vine, and his figgetree, and there was
none to fray them :

13 Neither was there any left in
the lande to fight against them : yea,
the Kings themselues were ouer-

|| Or, the
wealth of
the land.

* 1. Kings
4. 25.

throwen in those dayes.

14 Moreouer hee strengthened all
those of his people that were brought
low : the Law he searched out, and euery contemner of the Law, and wicked
person, he tooke away.

15 He beautified the Sanctuary, and
multiplied the vessels of the Temple.

16 Now when it was heard at
Rome, & as far as Sparta, that Ionathan was dead, they were very sorie.

17 But assoone as they heard that
his brother Simon was made high
Priest in his stead, and ruled the countrey, and the cities therein,

18 They wrote vnto him in tables of
brasse, to renew the friendship & league
which they had made with Iudas and
Ionathan his brethren :

19 Which writings were read before
the Congregation at Ierusalem.

20 And this is the copy of the letters
that the Lacedemonians sent : The rulers of the Lacedemonians, with the
city, vnto Simon the high Priest, and
the Elders and Priestes, and residue of
the people of the Iewes, our brethren,
send greeting.

21 The Embassadors that were sent
vnto our people, certified vs of your
glory and honour, wherefore we were
glad of their comming,

22 And did register the things that
they spake, in the counsell of the people,
in this maner : Numenius sonne of Antiochus, and Antipater sonne of Iason,
the Iewes Embassadours, came vnto
vs, to renew the friendship they had
with vs.

23 And it pleased the people to entertaine the men honourably, and to put
the copy of their embassage in publike
records, to the end the people of the Lacedemonians might haue a memoriall
therof : furthermore we haue written a
copy thereof vnto Simon the hie Priest.

24 After this, Simon sent Numenius to Rome, with a great shield of
golde of a thousand pound weight, to
confirme the league with them.

25 Whereof when the people heard,
they said, What thankes shall wee giue
to Simon and his sonnes ?

26 For hee and his brethren, and the
house of his father, haue established Israel, and chased away in fight their enemies from them, and confirmed their
libertie.

27 So then they wrote [it] in tables
of

of brasse, which they set vpon pillars in mount Sion, and this is the copie of the writing. The eighteenth day of the moneth Elul, in the hundred threescore and twelft yeere, being the third yeere of Simon the hie priest,

‖ Or, Ierusalem, peraduenture by corruption and transposition of letters, or as some thinke, the common hall where they met to consult of matters of estate.

28 At ‖Saramel in the great congregation of the priests and people, and rulers of the nation, & elders of the countrey, were these things notified vnto vs.

29 Forsomuch as often times there haue bin warres in the countrey, wherin for the maintenance of their Sanctuarie, and the law, Simon the sonne of Mattathias of the posteritie of Iarib, together with his brethren, put themselues in ieopardie, and resisting the enemies of their nation, did their nation great honour.

30 (For after that Ionathan hauing gathered his nation together, and bene their hie priest, was added to his people,

31 Their enemies purposed to inuade their countrey that they might destroy it, and lay hands on the Sanctuary.

32 At which time Simon rose vp, and fought for his nation, and spent much of his own substance, & armed ‖the valiant men of his nation, & gaue them wages,

‖ Or, the men of warre.

33 And fortified the cities of Iudea, together with Bethsura that lieth vpon the borders of Iudea, where the ‖armour of the enemies had bin before, but he set a garison of Iewes there.

‖ Or, weapons.

34 Moreouer, hee fortified Ioppe which lieth vpon the Sea, and ‖Gazara that bordereth vpon Azotus, where the enemies had dwelt before : but hee placed Iewes there, and furnished them with all things conuenient for the reparation thereof.)

‖ Or, Gaza.

35 The people therefore seeing the acts of Simon, and vnto what glory he thought to bring his nation, made him their gouernor and chiefe priest, because he had done all these things, and for the iustice and faith which hee kept to his nation, and for that hee sought by all meanes to exalt his people.

36 For in his time things prospered in his hands, so that the heathen were taken out of their countrey, and they also that were in the citie of Dauid in Ierusalem, who had made themselues a towre, out of which they issued, and polluted all about the Sanctuarie, and did much hurt ‖in the holy place.

‖ Or, vnto religion.

37 But he placed Iewes therein, and fortified it for the safetie of the coun-

trey, and the city, and raised vp the wals of Ierusalem.

38 King Demetrius also confirmed him in the high priesthood, according to those things,

39 And made him one of his friends, and honoured him with great honour.

40 For he had heard say, that the Romanes had called the Iewes their friends, and confederates, and brethren, and that they had entertained the Embassadours of Simon honourably.

41 Also that the Iewes & priests were wel pleased that Simon should be their gouernour, and high priest for euer vntil there should arise a faithfull prophet.

42 Moreouer, that he should be their captaine, and should take charge of the Sanctuarie, to set them ouer their workes, and ouer the countrey, and ouer the armour, and ouer the fortresses, that (I say) he should take charge of the Sanctuarie.

43 Besides this, that he should be obeyed of euery man, and that all the writings in the countrey should be made in his name, and that he should be clothed in purple, and weare gold.

44 Also that it should be lawfull for none of the people or priests, to breake any of these things, or to gainesay his words, or to gather an assembly in the countrey without him, or to bee clothed in purple, or weare a buckle of gold.

45 And whosoeuer should do otherwise, or breake any of these things, he should be punished.

46 Thus it liked all y̆ people to deale with Simon, & to do as hath bene said.

47 Then Simon accepted hereof, and was well pleased to be high Priest, and captaine, and gouernour of the Iewes, & priests, & to defend them all.

48 So they commanded that this writing should be put in tables of brasse, and that they should be set vp within the compasse of the Sanctuary in a conspicuous place.

49 Also y̆ the copies therof should be laid vp in the treasurie, to the ende that Simon & his sonnes might haue them.

CHAP. XV.

4 Antiochus desireth leaue to passe through Iudea, & granteth great honours to Simon and the Iewes. 16 The Romanes write to diuerse kings & nations to fauour the Iewes. 27 Antiochus quarrelleth with Simon, 38 and sendeth some to annoy Iudea.

More-

Oreouer Antiochus sonne of Demetrius the king, sent letters from the isles of the Sea, vnto Simon the priest, and prince of the Iewes, and to all the people.

2 The contents whereof were these : King Antiochus, to Simon the high Priest, and prince of his nation, and to the people of the Iewes, greeting,

3 For as much as certaine pestilent men, haue vsurped the kingdome of our fathers, and my purpose is to chalenge it againe, that I may restore it to the old estate, and to that end haue gathered a multitude of forraine souldiers together, and prepared shippes of warre,

4 My meaning also being to goe through the countrey, that I may be a-uenged of them that haue destroyed it, and made many cities in the kingdome desolate :

5 Now therefore I confirme vnto thee, all the oblations which the kings before me granted thee, and whatsoeuer gifts besides they granted.

6 I giue thee leaue also to coine money for thy countrey with thine owne stampe.

7 And as concerning Ierusalem, and the Sanctuarie, let them be free, and al the armour that thou hast made, and fortresses that thou hast built, and keepest in thy hands, let them remaine vnto thee.

8 And if any thing bee, or shall be owing to the king, let it be forgiuen thee, from this time forth for euermore.

9 Furthermore, when we haue obtained our kingdome, ye will honour thee, and thy nation, and thy temple with great honour, so that your honour shall bee knowen throughout the world.

10 In the hundred threescore and fourteenth yeere, went Antiochus into the land of his fathers, at which time all the forces came together vnto him, so that few were left with Tryphon.

11 Wherefore being pursued by king Antiochus, he fled vnto Dora, which lieth by the Sea side.

12 For he saw, that troubles came vpon him all at once, and that his forces had forsaken him.

13 Then camped Antiochus against Dora, hauing with him, an hundred and twentie thousand men of warre, and eight thousand horsemen.

14 And when he had compassed the citie round about, and ioyned ships close to the towne on the Sea side, hee vexed the citie by land, and by Sea, neither suffered he any to goe out or in.

15 In the meane season came Numenius, & his company from Rome hauing letters to the kings and countries, wherein were written these things.

16 Lucius, Consul of the Romanes, vnto king Ptolomee greeting.

17 The Iewes Embassadors our friends and confederates, came vnto vs to renew the old friendship and league, being sent from Simon the high Priest, and from the people of the Iewes.

18 And they brought a shield of gold, of a thousand pound :

19 We thought it good therefore, to write vnto the kings and countries, that they should doe them no harme, nor fight against them, their cities, or countries, nor yet aide their enemies against them.

20 It seemed also good to vs, to receiue the shield of them.

21 If therefore there be any pestilent fellowes, that haue fled from their countrie vnto you, deliuer them vnto Simon the high priest, that hee may punish them according to their owne lawe.

22 The same thing wrote hee likewise vnto Demetrius the king, and Attalus, to ||Ariarathes, and Arsaces, || *Or, Arathes.*

23 And to all the countries, and to ||Sampsames, & the Lacedemonians, || *Or, Sampsaces.* and to Delus, and Myndus, and Sycion, and Caria, and Samos, and Pamphylia, and Lycia, and Halicarnassus, and Rhodus, and ||Phaseilis, and Cos, || *Or, Basilis.* and Sidee, and Aradus, and Gortina, and Cnidus, and Cyprus, and Cyrene.

24 And the copy heereof they wrote, to Simon the high Priest.

25 So Antiochus the king camped against Dora, the second day, †assaul- † *Grc. bringing his forces to it.* ting it continually, and making engins, by which meanes he shut vp Tryphon, that he could neither goe out nor in.

26 At that time Simon sent him two thousand chosen men to aide him : siluer also, and gold, and much armour.

27 Neuerthelesse, he would not receiue them, but brake all the couenants which he had made with him afore, and became strange vnto him.

28 Further-

28 Furthermore hee sent vnto him Athenobius, one of his friends to commune with him and say : you withhold Ioppe and Gazara with the towre that is in Ierusalem, which are cities of my realme.

29 The borders thereof yee haue wasted and done great hurt in the land, and got the dominion of many places within my kingdome.

30 Now therefore deliuer the cities which ye haue taken, and the tributes of the places whereof yee haue gotten dominion ||without the borders of Iudea.

|| Or, except the borders, &c.

31 Or else giue me for them fiue hundred talents of siluer, and for the harme that you haue done, and the tributes of the cities other fiue hundred talents : if not, we wil come and ||fight against you.

|| Or, subdue you in fight.

32 So Athenobius the kings friend came to Ierusalem, and when hee saw the glory of Simon, and the cupboard of gold, and siluer plate, and his great attendance, he was astonished and told him the kings message.

33 Then answered Simon, and said vnto him, We haue neither taken other mens land, nor holden that which apperteineth to others, but the inheritance of our fathers, which our enemies had wrongfully in possession a certaine time.

34 Wherefore we hauing opportunitie, hold the inheritance of our fathers.

35 And whereas thou demaundest Ioppe and Gazara; albeit they did great harme vnto the people in our countrey, yet will we giue an hundred talents for them. Hereunto Athenobius answered him not a word,

36 But returned in a rage to the king, and made report vnto him of these speaches, and of the glory of Simon, and of all that hee had seene : whereupon the king was exceeding wroth.

37 In the meane time fled Tryphon by ship vnto Orthosias.

38 Then the king made Cendebeus captaine of the sea coast, and gaue him an hoste of footmen and horsemen,

39 And commanded him to remoue his hoste toward Iudea : also hee commanded him to build vp Cedron, and to fortifie the gates, & to warre against the people, but as for the king [himselfe] he pursued Tryphon.

40 So Cendebeus came to Iamnia, and began to prouoke the people, and to inuade Iudea, and to take the people prisoners, and slay them.

41 And when hee had built vp Cedron, he set horsemen there, and an host [of footmen] to the end that issuing out, they might make outroades vpon the wayes of Iudea, as the king had commanded him.

CHAP. XVI.

3 Iudas and Iohn preuaile against the forces sent by Antiochus. 11 The captaine of Hierico inuiteth Simon and two of his sonnes into his castle, and there treacherously murdereth them. 19 Iohn is sought for, 22 and escapeth, and killeth those that sought for him.

THen came vp Iohn from Gazara, and told Simon his father, what Cendebeus had done.

2 Wherefore Simon called his two eldest sonnes, Iudas and Iohn, and said vnto them, I and my brethren, and my fathers house haue euer from our youth vnto this day fought against the enemies of Israel, and things haue prospered so well in our hands, that wee haue deliuered Israel oftentimes.

3 But now I am old, and yee [by Gods mercy] are of a sufficient age : Be ye in stead of mee, and my brother, and goe and fight for our nation, and the helpe from heauen be with you.

4 So hee chose out of the countrey twentie thousand men of warre with horsemen, who went out against Cendebeus, and rested that night at Modin.

5 And when as they rose in the morning, and went into the plaine, behold, a mighty great hoste both of footmen, and horsemen, came against them : Howbeit there was a water brooke betwixt them.

6 So hee and his people pitched ouer against them, and when hee saw that the people were afraid to goe ouer the water brooke, hee went first ouer himselfe, and then the men seeing him, passed through after him.

7 [That done] he diuided his men, and set the horsemen in the midst of the footemen : for the enemies horsemen were very many.

8 Then sounded they with the holy Trumpets : whereupon Cendebeus and his hoste were put to flight, so that many of them were slaine, and the remnant gat them to the strong hold.

9 At

9 At that time was Iudas Iohns brother wounded : But Iohn still followed after them, vntill he came to Cedron which [Cendebeus] had built.

10 ‖ So they fled euen vnto the towres in the fields of Azotus, wherefore hee burnt it with fire : So that there were slaine of them about two thousand men. Afterward hee returned into the land of Iudea in peace.

11 Moreouer, in the plaine of Iericho was Ptolomeus the sonne of Abubus made captaine, and hee had abundance of siluer and golde.

12 For he was the hie Priests sonne in lawe.

13 Wherefore his heart being lifted vp, hee thought to get the countrey to himselfe, and thereupon consulted deceitfully against Simon and his sons, to destroy them.

14 Now Simon was visiting the cities that were in the countrey, and taking care for the good ordering of them, at which time hee came downe himselfe to Iericho with his sons, Mattathias and Iudas, in the hundreth threescore and seuenth yeere, in the eleuenth moneth called Sabat.

15 Where the sonne of Abubus receiuing them deceitfully into a little holde called Docus, which he had built, made them a great banquet : howbeit he had hidde men there.

16 So when Simon and his sonnes

margin: 1 Or, which when he had set fire, they fled vnto the towres in the fields of Azotus, and there were slaine, &c.

had drunke largely, Ptolome and his men rose vp, and tooke their weapons, and came vpon Simon into the banketting place, and slewe him and his two sonnes, and certaine of his seruants.

17 In which doing, he committed a great treachery, and recompensed euill for good.

18 Then Ptolome wrote these things, and sent to the king, that he should send him an hoste to aide him, and he would deliuer him the countrey and cities.

19 He sent others also to Gazara to kill Iohn, & vnto the †tribunes he sent letters to come vnto him, that he might giue them siluer, and golde, & rewards.

20 And others he sent to take Ierusalem, and the mountaine of the temple.

21 Now one had runne afore to Gazara, and tolde Iohn that his father and brethren were slaine, and [quoth he] Ptolome hath sent to slay thee also.

22 Hereof when he heard, hee was sore astonished : So he laide hands on them that were come to destroy him, and slew them, for hee knew that they sought to make him away.

23 As concerning the rest of the actes of Iohn, and his wars & worthy deeds which hee did, and the building of the walles which he made, and his doings,

24 Behold, these are written in the Chronicles of his Priesthood, from the time he was made high Priest after his father.

margin: † Gr. captaines of thousands.

¶ The second booke of the Maccabees.

CHAP. I.

1 A letter of the Iewes from Ierusalem to them of Egypt, to thanke God for the death of Antiochus. 19 Of the fire that was hidde in the pit. 24 The prayer of Nehemias.

He brethren the Iewes that bee at Ierusalem, and in the lande of Iudea, wish vnto the brethren the Iewes that are throughout Egypt, health and peace.

2 God be gracious vnto you, and remember his Couenant that hee made with Abraham, Isaac, and Iacob, his faithfull seruants :

3 And giue you all an heart to serue him, and to doe his will, with a good courage, and a willing minde :

4 And open your hearts in his law and commandements, & send you peace :

5 And heare your prayers, and be at one with you, and neuer forsake you in time of trouble.

6 And now wee be here praying for you.

7 What time as Demetrius reigned, in the hundred threescore and ninth yeere, wee the Iewes wrote vnto you, in the extremitie of trouble, that came vpon vs in those yeeres, from the time that Iason and his company reuolted from the holy land, and kingdome,

8 And burnt the porch, and shed innocent blood. Then we prayed vnto the Lord, and were heard : we offered also sacrifices, and fine flowre, and lighted the lampes, and set forth the loaues.

9 And now see that ye keepe the feast

of

* Leuit. 23.
34.

of * Tabernacles in the moneth Casleu.

10 In the hundreth, fourescore, and eight yeere, the people that were at Ierusalem, and in Iudea, and the counsel, and Iudas, sent greeting and health vnto Aristobulus, king Ptolomeus master, who was of the stock of the anointed priests, and to the Iewes that were in Egypt.

11 Insomuch as God hath deliuered vs from great perils, wee thanke him highly, as hauing bin in battell against a king.

12 For he cast them out that fought within the holy citie.

13 For when the leader was come into Persia, and the armie with him that seemed inuincible, they were slaine in the temple of Nanea, by the deceit of Naneas priests.

14 For Antiochus, as though hee would marrie her, came into the place, and his friends that were with him, to receiue money in name of a dowrie.

15 Which when the priests of Nanea had set forth, and he was entred with a small company into the compasse of the temple, they shut the temple assoone as Antiochus was come in.

16 And opening a priuie doore of the roofe, they threw stones like thunderbolts, and stroke downe the captaine, hewed them in pieces, smote off their heads, and cast them to those that were without.

17 Blessed be our God in all things, who hath deliuered vp the vngodly.

18 Therefore whereas we are nowe purposed to keep the purification of the Temple vpon the fiue & twentieth day of the moneth * Casleu, we thought it necessary to certifie you thereof, that ye also might keepe it, as the [feast] of the tabernacles, and of the fire [which was giuen vs] when Neemias offered sacrifice, after that he had builded the Temple, and the Altar.

19 For when our fathers were led into Persia, the Priests that were then deuout, took the fire of the Altar priuily, & hid it in a hollow place of a pit without water, where they kept it sure, so that the place was vnknowen to all men.

20 Now after many yeeres, when it pleased God, Neemias being sent from the king of Persia, did send of the posteritie of those Priests that had hid it, to the fire : but when they tolde vs they found no fire, but thicke water,

* Leuit. 23.
numb. 29.

21 Then cōmanded he them to draw it vp, and to bring it : and when the sacrifices were laid on, Neemias cōmanded the Priests to sprinkle y̆ wood, and the things laid therupon with y̆ water.

22 When this was done, and the time came that the Sun shone which afore was hid in the cloude, there was a great fire kindled, so that euery man marueiled.

23 And the Priests made a prayer whilest the sacrifice was consuming, [I say] both the Priests, and all the rest, Ionathan beginning, and the rest answering thereunto, as Neemias did.

24 And the prayer was after this maner, O Lord, Lord God, Creatour of all things, who art fearefull, and strong, and righteous, and mercifull, and the onely, and gracious king,

25 The onely giuer of all things, the onely iust, almightie & euerlasting, thou that deliuerest Israel from al trouble, & didst choose the fathers, & sanctifie them :

26 Receiue the sacrifice for thy whole people Israel, and preserue thine owne portion, and sanctifie it.

27 Gather those together that are scattered frō vs, deliuer them that serue among the heathen, looke vpon them that are despised & abhorred, and let the heathen know that thou art our God.

28 Punish them that oppresse vs, and with pride doe vs wrong.

29 Plant thy people againe in thy holy place, as Moises hath spoken.

30 And the Priests sung psalmes of thankesgiuing.

31 Now when the sacrifice was consumed, Neemias commanded the water that was left, to bee powred on the great stones.

32 When this was done, there was kindled a flame : but it was consumed by the light that shined from the Altar.

33 So when this matter was knowen, it was told the king of Persia, that in the place, where the Priests that were led away, had hid the fire, there appeared water, and that || Neemias had purified the sacrifices therewith.

34 Then the king inclosing the place, made it holy after he had tried y̆ matter.

35 And the king tooke many gifts, and bestowed thereof, on those whom he would gratifie.

36 And Neemias called this thing Naphthar, which is as much to say as a cleansing : but many men call it Nephi.

‖ Or, Neemias his company.

CHAP.

CHAP. II.

1 What Ieremie the Prophet did. 5 How he hid the Tabernacle, the Arke, and the Altar. 13 What Neemias, and Iudas wrote. 20 What Iason wrote in fiue bookes, 25 And how those were abridged by the author of this booke.

 T is also found in the records, that Ieremie the Prophet , commaunded them that were caried away, to take of the fire as it hath beene signified,

2 And how that the Prophet hauing giuen them the law, charged them not to forget the commaundements of the Lord, and that they should not erre in their minds, when they see images of siluer, and gold, with their ornaments.

3 And with other such speeches exhorted he them, that the law should not depart from their hearts.

4 It was also contained in the same writing, that the Prophet being warned of God, commanded the Tabernacle, and the Arke to goe with him, as he went forth into the mountaine, where Moises climed vp, and sawe the heritage of God.

5 And when Ieremie came thither, he found an hollow caue wherin he laid the Tabernacle, and the Arke, and the altar of incense, & so stopped the doore.

6 And some of those that followed him, came to marke the way, but they could not find it.

7 Which when Ieremie perceiued, hee blamed them, saying, As for that place, it shall be vnknowen vntill the time that God gather his people againe together, and receiue them vnto mercy.

8 Then shall the Lord shew them these things, and the glory of the Lord shall appeare, and the cloud also as it was shewed vnder Moises, and as when Solomon desired that the place might be honourably sanctified.

9 It was also declared that he being wise, offered the sacrifice of dedication, and of the finishing of the Temple.

10 And as when Moises prayed vnto the Lord, the fire came down from heauen, and consumed the sacrifices : euen so prayed Solomon also, and the fire came downe from heauen, and consumed the burnt offerings.

11 And Moises said, because the sinne offering was not to be eaten, it was consumed.

12 So Solomon kept those eight dayes.

13 The same things also were reported in the writings, and commentaries of Neemias, and how he founding a librarie, gathered together the acts of the Kings, and the Prophets, and of Dauid, and the Epistles of the Kings concerning the holy gifts.

14 In like maner also, Iudas gathered together all those things that were lost, by reason of the warre we had, and they remaine with vs.

15 Wherefore if yee haue neede thereof, send some to fetch them vnto you.

16 Whereas we then are about to celebrate the purification, we haue written vnto you, and yee shall doe well if yee keepe the same dayes.

17 † We hope also that the God, that deliuered all his people, and gaue them all an heritage, and the kingdome, and the priesthood, and the Sanctuarie,

18 As he promised in the lawe, will shortly haue mercy vpon vs, and gather vs together out of euery land vnder heauen into the holy place : for he hath deliuered vs out of great troubles, and hath purified the place.

19 Now as concerning Iudas Maccabeus, and his brethren, and the purification of the great Temple, and the dedication of the altar,

20 And the warres against Antiochus Epiphanes, & Eupator his sonne,

21 And the manifest signes that came from heauen, vnto those that behaued themselues manfully to their honour for Iudaisme : so that being but a few, they ouercame the whole country, and chased barbarous multitudes,

22 And recouered againe the Temple renowned all the world ouer, and freed the citie, and vpheld the lawes, which were going downe, the Lord being gracious vnto them with al fauour :

23 All these things (I say) being declared by Iason of Cyrene in fiue books, we will assay to abridge in one volume.

24 For considering the infinite number, and the difficulty, which they find that desire to looke into the narrations of the story, for the variety of ỹ matter,

25 We haue beene carefull, that they that will read might haue delight, and that they that are desirous to commit to memorie, might haue ease, and that all,

† Gre. now God it is that saued all his people, and rendred the heritage, and the kingdome, and the priesthood, and the Sanctuarie, as he promised in the lawe. For we hope in God that he will shortly, &c.

all, into whose hands it comes might haue profit.

26 Therefore to vs that haue taken vpon vs this painefull labour of abridging, it was not easie, but a matter of sweat, and watching.

27 Euen as it is no ease vnto him, that prepareth a banquet, and seeketh the benefit of others: yet ||for the pleasuring of many we will vndertake gladly this great paines:

|| Or, to deserue well of many.

28 Leauing to the authour the exact handling of euery particular, and labouring to follow the rules of an abridgement.

29 For as the master builder of a new house, must care for the whole building : but hee that vndertaketh to set it out, and paint it, must seeke out fit things for the adorning thereof : euen so I thinke it is with vs.

30 To stand vpon euery point, and goe ouer things at large, and to be curious in particulars, belongeth to the first authour of the storie.

31 But to vse breuitie, and auoyde much labouring of the worke, is to bee granted to him that will make an abridgement.

32 Here then will we begin the story: onely adding thus much to that which hath bene said, That it is a foolish thing to make a long prologue, and to be short in the story it selfe.

CHAP. III.

1 Of the honour done to the Temple by the Kings of the Gentiles. 4 Simon vttereth what treasures are in the Temple. 7 Heliodorus is sent to take them away. 24 He is stricken of God, and healed at the praier of Onias.

Ow when the holy Citie was inhabited with all peace, and the Lawes were kept very well, because of the godlinesse of Onias the high Priest, and his hatred of wickednesse,

2 It came to passe that euen the Kings themselues did honour the place, and magnifie the Temple with their best gifts ;

3 Insomuch that Seleucus king of Asia, of his owne reuenues, bare all the costes belonging to the seruice of the sacrifices.

4 But one Simon of the tribe of Beniamin, who was made gouernour of the Temple, fell out with the high Priest about disorder in the citie.

5 And when he could not ouercome Onias, he gate him to Apollonius the sonne of Thraseas, who then was gouernour of Coelosyria, and Phenice,

6 And told him that the treasurie in Ierusalem was full of infinite summes of money, so that the multitude of their riches which did not pertaine to the account of the sacrifices, was innumerable, and that it was possible to bring all into the kings hand.

7 Now when Apollonius came to the king, and had shewed him of the money, whereof he was told, the king chose out Heliodorus his treasurer, and sent him with a commaundement, to bring him the foresaid money.

8 So foorthwith Heliodorus tooke his iourney vnder a colour of visiting the cities of Coelosyria, and Phenice, but indeed to fulfill the kings purpose.

9 And when he was come to Ierusalem, & had bene courteously receiued of the high Priest of the citie, hee told him what intelligence was giuen of the money, & declared wherefore hee came, and asked if these things were so in deed.

10 Then the high Priest tolde him that there was such money layde vp for the reliefe of widowes, and fatherlesse children,

11 And that some of it belonged to Hircanus, sonne of Tobias, a man of great dignitie, and not as that wicked Simon had misinformed : the summe whereof in all was foure hundred talents of siluer, and two hundred of gold,

12 And that it was altogether impossible that such wrong should be done vnto them, that had committed it to the holinesse of the place, and to the maiestie and inuiolable sanctitie of the Temple, honoured ouer all the world.

13 But Heliodorus because of the kings commandement giuen him, said, That in any wise it must be brought into the kings treasury.

14 So at the day which hee appointed, hee entred in to order this matter, wherefore, there was no small agonie throughout the whole citie.

15 But the Priests prostrating themselues before the Altar in their Priests Vestments, called vnto heauen vpon him that made a Lawe concerning things giuen to bee kept, that they should safely bee preserued for such as had committed them to be kept.

16 Then

16 Then whoso had looked the hie Priest in the face, it would haue wounded his heart : for his countenance, and the changing of his colour, declared the inward agonie of his minde :

17 For the man was so compassed with feare, and horror of the body, that it was manifest to them that looked vpon him, what sorrow hee had now in his heart.

18 Others ran flocking out of their houses ||to the generall Supplication, because the place was like to come into contempt.

||*Or, to make generall supplication.*

19 And the women girt with sackecloth vnder their breasts, abounded in the streetes ; and the virgins that were kept in, ran some to the gates, and some to the walles, and others looked out of the windowes :

20 And all holding their handes towards heauen, made supplication.

21 Then it would haue pitied a man to see the falling downe of the multitude of all sorts, and the †feare of the hie Priest, being in such an agony.

†*Gr. expectation.*

22 They then called vpon the Almightie Lord, to keepe the things committed of trust, safe and sure, for those that had committed them.

23 Neuerthelesse Heliodorus executed that which was decreed.

24 Now as hee was there present himselfe with his guard about the treasurie, the ||Lord of spirits, & the Prince of all power caused a great apparition, so that all that presumed to come in with him, were astonished at the power of God, and fainted, and were sore afraid.

||*Or, Lord of our fathers.*

25 For there appeared vnto them a horse, with a terrible rider vpon him, and adorned with a very faire couering, and he ranne fiercely, and smote at Heliodorus with his forefeet, and it seemed that hee that sate vpon the horse, had complete harnesse of golde.

26 Moreouer two other yong men appeared before him, notable in strength, excellent in beautie, and comely in apparell, who stood by him on either side, and scourged him continually, and gaue him many sore stripes.

27 And Heliodorus fell suddenly vnto the ground, and was compassed with great darkenesse : but they that were with him, tooke him vp, and put him into a litter.

28 Thus him that lately came with a great traine, and with all his guard into the said treasury, they caried out, being vnable to helpe himselfe with his weapons : and manifestly they acknowledged the power of God.

29 For hee by the hand of God was cast downe, and lay speechlesse without all hope of life.

30 But they praised the Lord that had miraculously honoured his owne place : for the Temple which a little afore was full of feare and trouble, when the Almightie Lord appeared, was filled with ioy and gladnesse.

31 Then straightwayes certaine of Heliodorus friends, prayed Onias that hee would call vpon the most High to graunt him his life, who lay ready to giue vp the ghost.

32 So the high Priest suspecting lest the king should misconceiue that some treachery had beene done to Heliodorus by the Iewes, offered a sacrifice for the health of the man.

33 Now as the high Priest was making an atonement, the same yong men, in the same clothing, appeared and stood beside Heliodorus, saying, Giue Onias the high Priest great thankes, insomuch as for his sake the Lord hath granted thee life.

34 And seeing that thou hast beene scourged from heauen, declare vnto all men the mightie power of God : and when they had spoken these wordes, they appeared no more.

35 So Heliodorus after he had offered sacrifice vnto the Lord, and made great vowes vnto him that had saued his life, and saluted Onias, returned with his hoste to the king.

36 Then testified hee to all men, the workes of the great God, which he had seene with his eyes.

37 And when the king asked Heliodorus, who might be a fit man to be sent yet once againe to Ierusalem, he said,

38 If thou hast any enemy or traitor, send him thither, and thou shalt receiue him well scourged, if he escape with his life : for in that place, no doubt, there is an especiall power of God.

39 For hee that dwelleth in heauen hath his eye on that place, and defendeth it, and hee beateth and destroyeth them that come to hurt it.

40 And the things concerning Heliodorus, and the keeping of the treasurie, fell out on this sort.

CHAP.

CHAP. IIII.

1 Simon slandereth Onias. 7 Iason by corrupting the king, obteineth the office of the hie Priest. 24 Menelaus getteth the same from Iason by the like corruption. 34 Andronicus traiterously murdereth Onias. 36 The King being informed thereof, causeth Andronicus to be put to death. 39 The wickednes of Lysimachus, by the instigation of Menelaus.

His Simon now (of whō wee spake afore) hauing bin a bewrayer of the money, and of his countrey, slandered Onias, as if he had terrified Heliodorus, and bene the worker of these euils.

2 Thus was hee bold to call him a traitour, that had deserued well of the citie, and tendred his owne nation, and was so zealous of the lawes.

3 But when their hatred went so farre, that by one of Simons faction murthers were committed,

4 Onias seeing the danger of this contention, and that Appollonius, as being the gouernour of Coelosyria and Phenice, did rage, and increase Simons malice,

5 He went to the king, not to be an accuser of his countrey men, but seeking the good of all, both publike, & priuate.

6 For he saw that it was impossible, that the state should continue quiet, and Simon leaue his folly, vnlesse the king did looke thereunto.

7 But after the death of Seleucus, when Antiochus called Epiphanes, tooke the kingdom, Iason the brother of Onias, laboured vnder hand to bee hie Priest,

8 Promising vnto the king by intercession, three hundred and threescore talents of siluer, and of another reuenew, eightie talents:

9 Besides this, he promised to assigne an hundred and fiftie more, if he might haue licence to set him vp a place for exercise, and for the training vp of youth in the fashions of the heathen, and to write them of Ierusalem [by the name of] Antiochians.

10 Which when the king had granted, and hee had gotten into his hand the rule, he foorthwith brought his owne nation to the Greekish fashion.

11 And the royal priuiledges granted of speciall fauour to the Iewes, by the meanes of Iohn the father of Eupolemus, who went Embassador to Rome, for amitie and aid, he tooke away, and putting down the gouernments which were according to the law, he brought vp new customes against the law.

12 For he built gladly a place of exercise vnder the towre it selfe, and brought the chiefe yong men vnder his subiection, and made them weare a hat.

13 Now such was the height of Greek fashions, and increase of heathenish maners, through the exceeding profanenes of Iason that vngodly wretch, and no high priest:

14 That the priests had no courage to serue any more at the altar, but despising the Temple, and neglecting the sacrifices, hastened to be partakers of the vnlawfull allowance in the place of exercise, after the game of ‖ Discus called them forth. ‖ *Or, the Discus which was a stone with an hole in the midst.*

15 Not setting by the honours of their fathers, but liking the glory of the Grecians best of all.

16 By reason whereof sore calamity came vpon them : for they had them to be their enemies and auengers, whose custome they followed so earnestly, and vnto whom they desired to be like in all things.

17 For it is not a light thing to doe wickedly against the lawes of God, but the time following shall declare these things.

18 Now when the game that was vsed euery fift yere was kept at Tyrus, the king being present,

19 This vngracious Iason sent † speciall messengers from Ierusalem, who were Antiochians, to carie three hundred drachmes of siluer to the sacrifice of Hercules, which euen the bearers therof thought fit not to bestow vpon the sacrifice, because it was not conuenient, but to be reserued for other charges. † *Gr. who were religious embassadours.*

20 This money then in regard of the sender, was appointed to Hercules sacrifice, but because of the bearers thereof, it was imployed to the making of gallies.

21 Now when Apollonius the sonne of Manastheus was sent vnto Egypt, for the ‖ coronation of king Ptolomeus Philometor, Antiochus vnderstanding him not to bee well affected to his affaires, prouided for his owne safetie : whereupon he came to Ioppe, & from thence to Ierusalem. ‖ *Or, inthronizing.*

22 Where he was honourably receiued

ued of Iason, and of the citie, and was brought in with torchlight, and with great shoutings : and so afterward went with his hoste vnto Phenice.

23 Three yeere afterward, Iason sent Menelaus the foresaid Simons brother, to beare the money vnto the king, and to put him in minde of certaine necessary matters.

24 But he being brought to the presence of the king, when he had magnified him, for the glorious appearance of his power, got the priesthood to himselfe, offering more then Iason by three hundred talents of siluer.

25 So he came with the kings Mandate, bringing nothing worthy the high priesthood, but hauing the fury of a cruell Tyrant, and the rage of a sauage beast.

26 Then Iason, who had vndermined his owne brother, being vndermined by another, was cōpelled to flee into the countrey of the Ammonites.

27 So Menelaus got the principalitie : but as for the money that he had promised vnto the king, hee tooke no good order for it, albeit Sostratus the ruler of the castle required it.

28 For vnto him appertained the gathering of the customes. Wherefore they were both called before the king.

29 Now Menelaus left his brother Lysimachus in his stead in the priesthood, and Sostratus left Crates, who was gouernour of the Cyprians.

30 While those things were in doing, they of Tharsus and Mallos made insurrection, because they were giuen to the kings concubine called Antiochis.

31 Then came the king in all haste to appease matters, leauing Andronicus a man in authority, for his deputy.

32 Now Menelaus supposing that he had gotten a conuenient time, stole certaine vessels of gold, out of the temple, and gaue some of them to Andronicus, and some he sold into Tyrus, and the cities round about.

33 Which when Onias knew of a suretie, he reproued him, and withdrew himselfe into a Sanctuarie at Daphne, that lieth by Antiochia.

34 Wherefore Menelaus, taking Andronicus apart, prayed him to get Onias into his hands, who being perswaded thereunto, and comming to Onias in deceit, gaue him his right hand with othes, and though hee were sus-

pected (by him) yet perswaded he him to come forth of the Sanctuarie : whom forthwith he shut vp without regard of Iustice.

35 For the which cause not onely the Iewes, but many also of other nations tooke great indignation, and were much grieued for the vniust murder of the man.

36 And when the king was come againe from the places about Cilicia, the Iewes that were in the citie, and certaine of the Greekes, that abhorred the fact also, complained because Onias was slaine without cause.

37 Therefore Antiochus was heartily sorry, and mooued to pity, and wept, because of the sober and modest behauiour of him that was dead.

38 And being kindled with anger, forthwith he tooke away Andronicus his purple, and rent off his clothes, and leading him through the whole city vnto that very place, where he had committed impietie against Onias, there slew he the cursed murtherer. Thus the Lord rewarded him his punishment, as he had deserued.

39 Now when many sacriledges had beene committed in the citie by Lysimachus, with the consent of Menelaus, and the bruit therof was spread abroad, the multitude gathered themselues together against Lysimachus, many vessels of gold being already caried away.

40 Whereupon the common people rising, and being filled with rage, Lysimachus armed about three thousand men, and beganne first to offer violence on ‖ Auranus, being the leader, a man farre gone in yeeres, & no lesse in folly. ‖ Or, Tyrannus.

41 They then seeing the attempt of Lysimachus, some of them caught stones, some clubs, others taking handfuls of dust, that was next at hand, cast them all together vpon Lysimachus, and those that set vpon them.

42 Thus many of them they wounded, & some they stroke to the ground, and all [of them] they forced to flee : but as for the Churchrobber himselfe, him they killed besides the treasury.

43 Of these matters therefore there was an accusation laide against Menelaus.

44 Now when the king came to Tyrus, three men that were sent from the Senate, pleaded the cause before him :

45 But

45 But Menelaus being now con-uicted, promised Ptolomee the sonne of Dorymenes, to giue him much money, if hee would pacifie the King towards him.

46 Whereupon Ptolomee taking the king aside into a certaine gallerie, as it were to take the aire, brought him to be of another minde;

47 Insomuch that hee discharged Menelaus from the accusations, who notwithstanding was cause of all the mischiefe : and those poore men, who if they had told their cause, yea, before the Scythians, should haue bene iudged innocent, them he condemned to death.

48 Thus they that followed the matter for the citie, and for the people, and for the holy vessels, did soone suffer vniust punishment.

49 Wherefore euen they of Tyrus mooued with hatred of that wicked deed, caused them to bee honourably buried.

50 And so through the couetousnesse of them that were in power, Menelaus remained still in authority, increasing in malice, and being a great traitour to the citizens.

CHAP. V.

2 Of the signes and tokens seene in Ierusalem. 6 Of the end and wickednesse of Iason. 11 The pursuit of Antiochus against the Iewes. 15 The spoiling of the Temple. 27 Maccabeus fleeth into the wildernes.

ABout the same time Antiochus prepared his second voyage into Egypt:

2 And then it happened, that through all the citie, for the space almost of fourtie dayes, there were seene horsemen running in the aire, in cloth of golde, and armed with lances, like a band of souldiers,

3 And troupes of horsemen in aray, incountring, and running one against another with shaking of shieldes, and multitude of ||pikes, and drawing of swords, and casting of darts, and glittering of golden ornaments, and harnesse of all sorts.

Or, staues.

4 Wherefore euery man praied that that apparition might turne to good.

5 Now when there was gone forth a false rumour, as though Antiochus had bene dead, Iason tooke at the least a thousand men, and suddenly made an assault vpon the citie, and they that

were vpon the walles, being put backe, and the citie at length taken, Menelaus fled into the castle :

6 But Iason slew his owne citizens without mercy, (not considering that to get the day of them of his owne nation, would be a most vnhappy day for him : but thinking *they had bene his enemies*, and not his countrey men whom he conquered.)

7 Howbeit, for all this hee obtained not the principalitie, but at the last receiued shame for the reward of his treason, and fled againe into the countrey of the Ammonites.

8 In the end therefore hee had an vnhappy returne, being accused before Aretas the king of the Arabians, fleeing from city to city, pursued of all men, hated as a forsaker of the Lawes, and being had in abomination, as an open ||enemie of his countrey, and countreymen, he was cast out into Egypt.

Or, executioner.

9 Thus hee that had driuen many out of their countrey, perished in a strange land, retiring to the Lacedemonians, and thinking there to finde succour by reason of his kindred.

10 And hee that had cast out many vnburied, had none to mourne for him, nor any solemne funerals at all, nor sepulchre with his fathers.

11 Now when this that was done came to the kings eare, he thought that Iudea had reuolted, whereupon remouing out of Egypt in a furious minde, he tooke the citie by force of armes,

12 And commaunded his men of warre not to spare such as they met, and to slay such as went vp vpon the houses.

13 Thus there was killing of yong and old, making away of men, women and children, slaying of virgins and infants.

14 And there were destroyed within the space of three whole daies, fourescore thousand, whereof fourty thousand were slaine in the conflict; and no fewer sold, then slaine.

15 Yet was he not content with this, but presumed to goe into the most holy Temple of all the world : Menelaus that traitour to the Lawes, and to his owne countrey, being his guide.

16 And taking the holy vessels with polluted handes, and with prophane handes, pulling downe the things that were dedicated by other kings, to the augmen-

augmentation and glory and honour of the place, he gaue them away.

17 And so haughtie was Antiochus in minde, that hee considered not that the Lord was angry for a while for the sinnes of them that dwelt in the citie, and therefore his eye was not vpon the place.

18 For had they not beene formerly wrapped in many sinnes, this man as soone as hee had come, had foorthwith beene scourged, and put backe from his presumption, as Heliodorus was, whom Seleucus the king sent to view the treasurie.

19 Neuerthelesse God did not choose the people for the places sake, but the place for the peoples sake.

20 And therefore the place it selfe that was partaker with them of the aduersities that happened to the nation, did afterward communicate in the benefits sent from the Lord: and as it was forsaken in the wrath of the Almighty, so againe the great Lord being reconciled, it was set vp with all glory.

21 So when Antiochus had caried out of the Temple, a thousand and eight hundred talents, hee departed in all haste into Antiochia, weening in his pride to make the land nauigable, and the Sea passable by foot: such was the haughtinesse of his minde.

22 And he left gouernours to vexe the nation: at Ierusalem Philip, for his countrey a Phrygian, and for manners more barbarous then hee that set him there:

23 And at Garizim, Andronicus; and besides, Menelaus, who worse then all the rest, bare an heauie hand ouer the citizens, hauing a malicious minde against his countreymen the Iewes.

24 He sent also that detestable ringleader Apollonius, with an armie of two and twentie thousand, commaunding him to slay all those that were in their best age, and to sell the women and the yonger sort:

25 Who comming to Ierusalem, and pretending peace, did forbeare till the holy day of the Sabbath, when taking the Iewes keeping holy day, hee commanded his men to arme themselues.

26 And so hee slewe all them that were gone to the celebrating of the Sabbath, and running through the city with weapons, slewe great multitudes.

27 But Iudas Maccabeus, † with nine others, or thereabout, withdrew himselfe into the wildernesse, and liued in the mountaines after the maner of beasts, with his company, who fed on herbes continually, lest they should be partakers of the pollution.

† Gr. who was the tenth.

CHAP. VI.

1 The Iewes are compelled to leaue the Law of God. 4 The Temple is defiled. 8 Crueltie vpon the people and the women. 12 An exhortation to beare affliction, by the example of the valiant courage of Eleazarus, cruelly tortured.

OT long after this, the king sent an olde man of ‖ Athens, to compell the Iewes to depart from the lawes of their fathers, and not to liue after the Lawes of God:

‖ Antioch: the Latine interpreters.

2 And to pollute also the Temple in Ierusalem, and to call it the Temple of Iupiter Olympius: and that in Garizim, of Iupiter the defender of strangers, as they ‖ did desire that dwelt in the place.

‖ Out of Ios. lib. 12. c. 7. or, as they were.

3 The comming in of this mischiefe was sore and grieuous to the people:

4 For the Temple was filled with riot and reuelling, by the Gentiles, who dallied with harlots, and had to doe with women within the circuit of the holy places, and besides that, brought in things that were not lawfull.

5 The Altar also was filled with profane things, which the Law forbiddeth.

6 Neither was it lawfull for a man to keepe Sabbath dayes, or ancient Feasts, or to professe himselfe at all to be a Iewe.

7 And in the day of the kings birth, euery moneth they were brought by bitter constraint to eate of the sacrifices; and when the Feast of Bacchus was kept, the Iewes were compelled to goe in procession to Bacchus, carying Iuie.

8 Moreouer there went out a decree to the neighbour cities of the † heathen, by the suggestion of Ptolomee, against the Iewes, that they should obserue the same fashions, and be partakers of their sacrifices.

† Gr. Grecians.

9 And whoso would not conforme themselues to the maners of the Gentiles, should be put to death: then might a man hane seene the present misery.

10 For there were two women brought

brought, who had circumcised their children, whom when they had openly led round about the citie, the babes hanging at their breasts, they cast them downe headlong from the wall.

11 And others that had run together into caues neere by, to keepe the Sabbath day secretly, being discouered to Philip, were all burnt together, because they made a conscience to helpe themselues, for the honour of the most sacred day.

12 Now I beseech those that reade this booke, that they be not discouraged for these calamities, but that they iudge those punishments not to be for destruction, but for a chastening of our nation.

13 For it is a token of his great goodnesse, when wicked doers are not suffered any long time, but forthwith punished.

14 For not as with other nations whom the Lord patiently forbeareth to punish, till they be come to the fulnesse of their sinnes, so dealeth he with vs,

15 Lest that being come to the height of sinne, afterwards hee should take vengeance of vs.

16 And therfore he neuer withdraweth his mercie from vs : and though he punish with aduersitie, yet doeth he neuer forsake his people.

17 But let this that we haue spoken be for a warning vnto vs : And nowe will wee come to the declaring of the matter in few words.

18 Eleazar one of the principall Scribes, an aged man, and of a well fauoured countenance, was constrained to open his mouth, and to eate swines flesh.

19 But he chusing rather to die gloriously, then to liue stained with such an abomination, spit it forth, and came of his owne accord to the torment,

20 As it behoued them to come, that are resolute to stand out against such things, as are not lawfull for loue of life to be tasted.

21 But they that had the charge of that wicked feast, for the olde acquaintance they had with the man, taking him aside, besought him to bring flesh of his owne prouision, such as was lawfull for him to vse, and make as if he did eate of the flesh, taken from the sacrifice commanded by the king,

22 That in so doing hee might bee deliuered from death, and for the olde friendship with them, find fauour.

23 But he began to consider discreetly, and as became his age, and the excellencie of his ancient yeeres, and the honour of his gray head, whereunto hee was come, and his most honest education from a child, or rather the holy lawe made, and giuen by God : therefore hee answered accordingly, and willed them straightwaies to send him to the graue.

24 For it becommeth not our age, said he, in any wise to dissemble, whereby many yong persons might thinke, that Eleazar being fourescore yeres old and ten, were now gone to a strange religion,

25 And so they through mine hypocrisie, and desire to liue a litle time, and a moment longer, should bee deceiued by me, and I get a staine to mine olde age, and make it abominable.

26 For though for the present time I should be deliuered from the punishment of men : yet should I not escape the hand of the Almightie, neither aliue nor dead.

27 Wherefore now manfully changing this life, I will shew my selfe such an one, as mine age requireth,

28 And leaue a notable example to such as bee yong, to die willingly, and couragiously, for the honourable and holy lawes : and when he had said these words, immediatly he went to the torment,

29 They that led him, changing the good will they bare him a litle before, into hatred, because the foresaid speaches proceeded as they thought, from a ‖desperate minde.

‖ *Or, madnes or pride.*

30 But when hee was readie to die with stripes, he groned, and said, It is manifest vnto the Lord, that hath the holy knowledge, that wheras I might haue bin deliuered from death, I [now] endure sore paines in body, by being beaten : but in soule am well content to suffer these things, because I feare him.

31 And thus this man died, leauing his death for an example of a noble courage, and a memoriall of vertue not only vnto yong men, but vnto all his nation.

CHAP. VII.

The constancie and cruell death of seuen brethren and their mother in one day, because they would not eate swines flesh at the kings commandement.

It

T came to passe also that seuen brethren with their mother were taken, and compelled by the king against the lawe to taste swines flesh, and were tormented with scourges, and whips:

2 But one of them that spake first said thus: What wouldest thou aske, or learne of vs? we are ready to die, rather then to transgresse the lawes of our fathers.

3 Then the king being in a rage, commanded pannes, and caldrons to be made whot.

4 Which forthwith being heated, he commanded to cut out the tongue of him that spake first, and to cut off the vtmost parts of his body, the rest of his brethren, and his mother looking on.

5 Now when he was thus maimed in all his members, he commanded him being yet aliue, to be brought to the fire, and to be fried in the panne: and as the vapour of the panne was for a good space dispersed, they exhorted one another, with the mother, to die manfully, saying thus:

6 The Lord God looketh vpon vs, and in trueth hath comfort in vs, as * Moises in his song, which witnessed to their faces declared, saying, And he shall be comforted in his seruants.

7 So when the first was dead, after this maner, they brought the second to make him a mocking stocke: and when they had pulled off the skin of his head with the haire, they asked him, Wilt thou eate before thou bee punished throughout euery member of thy body?

8 But hee answered in his owne language, and said, No. Wherefore hee also receiued the next torment in order, as the former did.

9 And when hee was at the last gaspe, hee said, Thou like a fury takest vs out of this present life, but the king of the world shall raise vs vp, who haue died for his lawes, vnto euerlasting life.

10 After him was the third made a mocking stocke, and when he was required, he put out his tongue, and that right soone, holding forth his hands manfully,

11 And said couragiously, These I had from heauen, and for his lawes I despise them, and from him I hope to receiue them againe.

12 Insomuch that the king, and

they that were with him marueiled at the yong mans courage, for that he nothing regarded the paines.

13 Now when this man was dead also, they tormented and mangled the fourth in like maner.

14 So when he was ready to die, he said thus, It is good, being put to death by men, to looke for hope from God to be raised vp againe by him: as for thee thou shalt haue no resurrection to life.

15 Afterward they brought the fift also, and mangled him.

16 Then looked hee vnto the king and said, Thou hast power ouer men, thou art corruptible, thou doest what thou wilt, yet thinke not that our nation is forsaken of God.

17 But abide a while, and behold his great power, how he will torment thee, and thy seed.

18 After him also they brought the sixt, who being ready to die, said, Be not deceiued without cause: for we suffer these things for our selues, hauing sinned against our God. Therefore marueilous things are done (vnto vs.)

19 But thinke not thou that takest in hand to striue against God, that thou shalt escape vnpunished.

20 But the mother was marueilous aboue all, and worthy of honorable memorie: for when shee sawe her seuen sonnes slaine within the space of one day, she bare it with a good courage, because of the hope that she had in ỹ Lord

21 Yea she exhorted euery one of them in her owne language, filled with couragious spirits, and stirring vp her womanish thoughts, with a manly stomacke, she said vnto them,

22 I cannot tell how you came into my wombe: for I neither gaue you breath, nor life, neither was it I that formed the mēbers of euery one of you.

23 But doubtlesse the Creator of the world, who formed the generation of man, and found out the beginning of all things, wil also of his owne mercy giue you breath, and life againe, as you now regard not your owne selues for his Lawes sake.

24 Now Antiochus thinking himselfe despised, and suspecting it to be a reprochfull speach, whiles the yongest was yet aliue, did not onely exhort him by wordes, but also assured him with oathes, that he would make him both a rich, and a happy man, if hee would
turne

Deut. 32.
3.

turne from the Lawes of his fathers, and that also he would take him for his friend, and trust him with affaires.

25 But when the yong man would in no case hearken vnto him, the king called his mother, and exhorted her, that she would counsell the yong man to saue his life.

26 And when hee had exhorted her with many words, she promised him that she would counsell her sonne.

27 But shee bowing her selfe towards him, laughing the cruell tyrant to scorne, spake in her countrey language on this maner; O my sonne, haue pitie vpon mee that bare thee nine moneths in my wombe, and gaue thee sucke three yeeres, and nourished thee, and brought thee vp vnto this age, and endured the troubles of education.

28 I beseech thee, my sonne, looke vpon the heauen, and the earth, and all that is therein, and consider that God made them of things that were not, and so was mankinde made likewise;

29 Feare not this tormentour, but being worthy of thy brethren, take thy death, that I may receiue thee againe in mercy, with thy brethren.

30 Whiles she was yet speaking these words, the yong man said, Whom wait ye for? I will not obey the kings commandement: but I will obey the commandement of the Law that was giuen vnto our fathers, by Moses.

31 And thou that hast bene the authour of all mischiefe against the Hebrewes, shalt not escape the handes of God.

32 For wee suffer because of our sinnes.

33 And though the liuing Lord bee angrie with vs a little while for our chastening and correction, yet shall hee be at one againe, with his seruants.

34 But thou, O godlesse man, and of all other most wicked, be not lifted vp without a cause, nor puffed vp with vncertaine hopes, lifting vp thy hand against the seruants of God:

35 For thou hast not yet escaped the iudgement of Almightie God, who seeth all things.

36 For our brethren who now haue suffered a short paine, are dead vnder Gods Couenant of euerlasting life: but thou through the iudgement of God, shalt receiue iust punishment for thy pride.

37 But I, as my brethren, offer vp my body, and life for the Lawes of our fathers, beseeching God that he would speedily bee mercifull vnto our nation, and that thou by torments & plagues mayest confesse, that he alone is God;

38 And that in me, and my brethren, the wrath of the Almighty, which is iustly brought vpon all our nation, may cease.

39 Then the King being in a rage, handled him worse then all the rest, and took it grieuously that he was mocked.

40 So this man died vndefiled, and put his whole trust in the Lord.

41 Last of all after the sonnes, the mother died.

42 Let this be ynough now to haue spoken cōcerning the idolatrous feasts, and the extreme tortures.

CHAP. VIII.

1 Iudas gathereth an hoste. 9 Nicanor is sent against him: who presumeth to make much money of his prisoners. 16 Iudas encourageth his men, and putteth Nicanor to flight, 28 and diuideth the spoiles. 30 Other enemies are also defeated, 35 And Nicanor fleeth with griefe to Antioch.

THen Iudas Maccabeus and they that were with him, went priuily into the townes, and called their kinsefolkes together, and tooke vnto them all such as continued in the Iewes religion, and assembled about six thousand men.

2 And they called vpon the Lord, that hee would looke vpon the people that was troden downe of all, and also pitie the Temple, prophaned of vngodly men,

3 And that he would haue compassion vpon the city sore defaced and ready to be made euen with the ground, and heare the blood that cried vnto him,

4 And remember the wicked slaughter of harmelesse infants, and the blasphemies committed against his Name, and that hee would shew his hatred against the wicked.

5 Now when Maccabeus had his company about him, hee could not be withstood by the heathen: for the wrath of the Lord was turned into mercy.

6 Therefore he came at vnawares, and burnt vp townes and cities, and got into his hands the most commodious

ous places, and ouercame & put to flight no small number of his enemies.

7 But specially tooke he aduantage of the night, for such priuie attempts, insomuch that the bruite of his manlinesse was spread euery where.

8 So when Philip sawe that this man encreased by little and little, & that things prospered with him still more and more, hee wrote vnto Ptolemeus, the gouernour of Coelosyria & Phenice, to yeeld more aide to the kings affaires.

9 Then forthwith choosing Nicanor the son of Patroclus, one of his speciall friends, he sent him with no fewer then twentie thousand of all nations vnder him, to root out the whole generation of the Iewes; and with him he ioyned also Gorgias a captaine, who in matters of warre had great experience.

10 So Nicanor vndertooke to make so much money of the captiue Iewes, as should defray the tribute of two thousand talents, which the king was to pay to the Romanes.

11 Wherefore immediatly he sent to the cities vpon the sea coast, proclaiming a sale of the captiue Iewes, and promising that they should haue fourescore and ten bodies for one talent, not expecting the vengeance that was to follow vpon him from the Almighty God.

12 Now when word was brought vnto Iudas of Nicanors coming, and he had imparted vnto those that were with him, that the army was at hand,

13 They that were fearefull, and distrusted the iustice of God, fled, and conueyed themselues away.

14 Others sold all that they had left, and withall besought the Lord to deliuer them, being solde by the wicked Nicanor before they met together:

15 And if not for their owne sakes, yet for ỹ couenants he had made with their fathers, and for his holy and glorious Names sake, by which they were called

16 So Maccabeus called his men together vnto the number of sixe thousand, and exhorted them not to be stricken with terrour of the enemie, nor to feare the great multitude of the heathen who came wrongfully against them, but to fight manfully,

17 And to set before their eyes, the iniury that they had vniustly done to the holy place, and the cruell handling of the city, whereof they made a mockery, and also the taking away of the gouernment of their forefathers:

18 For they, said he, trust in their weapons and boldnesse, but our confidence is in the Almightie God, who at a becke can cast downe both them that come against vs, and also all the world.

19 Moreouer, hee recounted vnto them what helps their forefathers had found, and how they were deliuered, when vnder Sennacherib an hundred fourescore and fiue thousand perished.

20 And he told them of ỹ battel that they had in Babylon with the Galatians, how they came but eight thousand in all to ỹ busines, with foure thousand Macedonians, and that the Macedonians being perplexed, the eight thousand destroyed an hundred and twenty thousand, because of the helpe that they had from heauen, & so receiued a great booty.

21 Thus when hee had made them bold with these words, and ready to die for the Lawes, and the countrey, he diuided his army into foure parts:

22 And ioyned with himselfe his owne brethren, leaders of each band, to wit, Simon, and Ioseph, & Ionathan, giuing each one fifteene hundred men.

23 Also (hee appointed) Eleazar to reade the holy booke: and when he had giuen them this watchword, The help of God; himselfe leading the first band, he ioyned battell with Nicanor:

24 And by the helpe of the Almightie, they slew aboue nine thousand of their enemies, and wounded and maimed the most part of Nicanors hoste, and so put all to flight:

25 And tooke their money that came to buy them, and pursued them farre: but lacking time, they returned.

26 For it was the day before the Sabbath, and therefore they would no longer pursue them.

27 So when they had gathered their ||armour together, and spoiled their enemies, they occupied themselues about the Sabbath, yeelding exceeding praise, & thanks to the Lord, who had preserued them vnto ỹ day, which was the beginning of mercy, distilling vpon them.

28 And after the Sabbath, when they had giuen part of the spoiles to the ||maimed, and the widdowes, and Orphanes, the residue they diuided among themselues, and their seruants.

29 When this was done, and they had made a common supplication, they besought the mercifull Lord to be reconciled with his seruants for euer.

30 Moreouer,

That is, the enemies armour.

Or, lamed, with tortures.

‖ Or, lamed.

30 Moreouer of those that were with Timotheus & Bacchides, who fought against them, they slewe aboue twentie thousand, and very easily got high and strong holds, & diuided amongst them selues many spoiles more, and made the ‖maimed, orphanes, widowes, yea, & the aged also, equal in spoiles w̄ themselues

31 And when they had gathered their armour together, they laid them vp all carefully in couenient places, and the remnant of the spoiles they brought to Ierusalem.

32 They slew also Philarches that wicked persō who was w̄ Timotheus, & had annoied the Iewes many waies.

33 Furthermore at such time as they kept the feast for the victorie in their coū-try, they burnt Calisthenes that had set fire vpon the holy gates, who was fled into a litle house, and so he receiued a re-ward meet for his wickednesse.

34 As for that most vngracious Ni-canor, who had brought a thousand merchants to buy the Iewes,

35 He was through the helpe of the Lord brought downe by them, of whō he made least account, & putting off his glorious apparell, and discharging his company, he came like a fugitiue seruant through the mid land vnto Antioch, ha-uing very great dishonour for that his hoste was destroyed.

36 Thus he that tooke vpon him to make good to the Romanes, their tri-bute by meanes of the captiues in Ieru-salem, told abroad, that the Iewes had God to fight for them, and therfore they could not be hurt, because they followed the lawes that he gaue them.

CHAP. IX.

1 Antiochus is chased from Persepolis. 5 Hee is striken with a sore disease, 14 and promiseth to become a Iew. 28 He dieth miserably.

‖ Or, disor-derly.

 Bout that time came An-tiochus with ‖dishonor out of the countrey of Persia.

2 For he had entred the citie called Persepolis, and went about to rob the Temple, and to hold the citie, whereupon the multitude running to defend thēselues with their weapons, put them to flight, & so it hap-pened y Antiochus being put to flight of the inhabitants, returned with shame.

3 Now when he came to Ecbatana, newes was brought him what had happened vnto Nicanor & Timotheus.

4 Then swelling with anger, hee thought to auenge vpon the Iewes the disgrace done vnto him by those that made him flie. Therfore commanded he his chariot man to driue without cea-sing, and to dispatch the iourney, the iudgement of God now following him. For he had spoken proudly in this sort, y he would come to Ierusalem, & make it a common burying place of y Iewes.

5 But the Lord almightie, the God of Israel smote him with an incurable and inuisible plague: for assoone as hee had spoken these words, a paine of the bowels that was remediles, came vpon him, & sore torments of the inner parts.

6 And that most iustly : for hee had tormented other mens bowels with many and strange torments.

7 Howbeit hee nothing at all ceased from his bragging, but still was filled with pride, breathing out fire in his rage against the Iewes, and commanding to haste the iourney : but it came to passe that he fel downe frō his chariot, caried violently, so that hauing a sore fal, al the mēbers of his body were much pained.

8 And thus hee that a little afore thought he might command the waues of the sea (so proud was hee beyond the condition of man) and weigh the high mountaines in a ballance, was now cast on the ground, and carried in an horselitter, shewing foorth vnto all, the manifest power of God.

9 So that the wormes rose vp out of the body of this wicked man, and whiles hee liued in sorrow and paine, his flesh fell away, and the filthinesse of his smell was noysome to all his army.

10 And the man that thought a little afore he could reach to the starres of heauen, no man could endure to carry for his intollerable stinke.

11 Here therefore being plagued, hee began to leaue off his great pride, and to come to the knowledge [of himselfe] by the scourge of God, his paine encrea-sing euery moment.

12 And when hee himselfe could not abide his owne smell, hee saide these wordes : It is meete to bee subiect vnto God, and that a man that is mortall, should not proudly thinke of himselfe, as if he were God.

13 This wicked person vowed also vn-to the Lord, (who now no more would haue mercy vpon him) saying thus :

14 That the holy citie (to the which hee was going in haste to lay it euen with

with the ground, & to make it a common burying place) he would set at liberty.

15 And as touching the Iewes, whom hee had iudged not worthy so much as to be buried, but to be cast out with their children to be deuoured of the foules, and wild beasts, he would make them al equals to ȳ citizens of ‖ Athens.

Or, Antioch.

16 And the holy Temple, which before he had spoiled, hee would garnish with goodly gifts, and restore all the holy vessels with many more, and out of his owne reuenew defray the charges belonging to the sacrifices:

17 Yea, and that also hee would become a Iew himselfe, and goe through all the world that was inhabited, and declare the power of God.

18 But for all this his paines would not cease: for the iust iudgement of God was come vpō him: therfore despairing of his health, he wrote vnto the Iewes the letter vnderwritten, containing the forme of a supplicatiō, after this maner.

19 Antiochus king and gouernour, to the good Iewes his Citizens, wisheth much ioy, health, and prosperity.

20 If ye, and your children fare well, and your affaires be to your contentment, I giue very great thankes to God, hauing my hope in heauen.

21 As for mee I was weake, or else I would haue remembred kindly your honour, and good will. Returning out of Persia, and being taken with a grieuous disease, I thought it necessary to care for the common safety of all:

22 Not distrusting mine health, but hauing great hope to escape this sicknes

23 But considering that euen my father, at what time he led an armie into the hie countries, appointed a successor,

24 To the end, that if any thing fell out contrary to expectation, or if any tidings were brought that were grieuous, they of the land knowing to whom ‖ the state was left, might not be troubled.

Or, common affaires.

25 Againe considering, how that the princes that are borderers, and neighbors vnto my kingdome, waite for opportunities, and expect what shalbe the euent, I haue appointed my sonne Antiochus king, whom I often cōmitted, and cōmended vnto many of you, when I went vp into the high prouinces, to whom I haue written as followeth.

26 Therefore I pray, and request you to remember the benefits that I

haue done vnto you generally, and in speciall, and that euery man will be still faithfull to me, and my sonne.

27 For I am perswaded that hee ‖ vnderstanding my minde, will fauourably & graciously yeeld to your desires.

‖ Or, following.

28 Thus the murtherer, and blasphemer hauing suffered most grieuously, as he entreated other men, so died he a miserable death in a strange countrey in the mountaines.

29 And Philip that was brought vp with him, caried away his body, who also fearing the son of Antiochus, went into Egypt to Ptolomeus Philometor.

CHAP. X.

1 Iudas recouereth the Citie, and purifieth the Temple. 14 Gorgias vexeth the Iewes. 16 Iudas winneth their holds. 29 Timotheus and his men are discomfited. 35 Gazara is taken, and Timotheus slaine.

NOw Maccabeus, and his company, the Lord guiding them, recouered the Temple, and the citie.

2 But the altars, which the heathen had built in the open street, & also the Chappels they pulled downe.

3 And hauing cleansed the Temple, they made another Altar, and striking stones, they tooke fire out of them, and offered a sacrifice after two yeeres, & set forth incense, & lights, and Shewbread.

4 When that was done, they fell flat downe, and besought the Lord that they might come no more into such troubles: but if they sinned any more against him, that he himselfe would chasten them with mercie, and that they might not bee deliuered vnto the blasphemous, and barbarous nations.

5 Now vpon the same day that the strangers prophaned the Temple, on the very same day it was cleansed againe, euen the fiue and twentieth day of the same moneth, which is Casleu.

6 And they kept eight dayes with gladnes as in the feast of the Tabernacles, remembring that not long afore they had helde the feast of the Tabernacles, when as they wandered in the mountaines, and dennes, like beasts.

7 Therefore they bare branches, and faire boughes and palmes also, and sang Psalmes vnto him, that had giuen them good successe in clensing his place.

8 They ordeined also by a common statute, and decree, That euery yeere those

those dayes should be kept of the whole nation of the Iewes.

9 And this was the ende of Antiochus called Epiphanes.

10 Now will wee declare the acts of Antiochus Eupator, who was the sonne of this wicked man, gathering briefly the calamities of the warres.

11 So when he was come to y̆ crowne, he set one Lysias ouer the affaires of his Realme, and [appointed him] chiefe gouernour of Coelosyria and Phenice.

12 For Ptolomeus that was called Macron, chosing rather to doe iustice vnto the Iewes, for the wrong that had bene done vnto them, endeuoured to continue peace with them.

13 Whereupon being accused of [the kings] friends, before Eupator, & called traitor at euery word, because he had left Cyprus that Philometor had cōmitted vnto him, & departed to Antiochus Epiphanes; ||and seeing that hee was in no honorable place, he was so discouraged, that he poysoned himselfe and died.

|| *Or, and not bearing his authoritie as it becommeth a noble man.*

14 But when Gorgias was gouernour of the ||holds, hee hired souldiers, and nourished warre continually with the Iewes :

|| *Or, strong places.*

15 And therewithall the Idumeans hauing gotten into their handes the most commodious holdes, kept the Iewes occupied, and receiuing those that were banished from Ierusalem, they went about to nourish warre.

16 Then they that were wich Maccabeus made supplication, & besought God, that he would be their helper, and so they ranne with violence vpon the strong holds of the Idumeans,

17 And assaulting them strongly, they wanne the holds, and kept off all that fought vpon the wall, and slew all that fell into their hands, and killed no fewer then twentie thousand.

18 And because certaine (who were no lesse then nine thousand) were fled together into two very strong castles, hauing all maner of things conuenient to sustaine the siege,

19 Maccabeus left Simon, & Ioseph, and Zaccheus also, and them that were with him, who were enow to besiege them, and departed himselfe vnto those places, which more needed his helpe.

|| *Or, Simon.*

20 Now ||they that were with Simon, being led with couetousnes, were perswaded for money (through certaine of those that were in the castle) and

tooke seuentie thousand drachmes, and let some of them escape.

21 But when it was told Maccabeus what was done, hee called the gouernours of the people together, and accused those men, that they had sold their brethren for money, & set their enemies free to fight against them.

22 So he slew those that were found traitors, and immediately tooke the two castles.

23 And hauing good successe with his weapons in all things hee tooke in hand, hee slew in the two holdes, more then twentie thousand.

24 Now Timotheus whom the Iewes had ouercome before, when he had gathered a great multitude of forraine forces, and horses out of Asia not a few, came as though hee would take Iewrie by force of armes.

25 But when hee drew neere, ||they that were with Maccabeus, turned themselues to pray vnto God, and sprinckled earth vpon their heads, and girded their loynes with sackcloth,

|| *Or, Maccabeus, they that were with him.*

26 And fell downe at the foot of the Altar, and besought him to be mercifull to them, and to be an *enemie to their enemies, and an aduersarie to their aduersaries, as the Law declareth.

Deut.

27 So after the prayer, they tooke their weapons, & went on further from the city : and when they drew neere to their enemies, they kept by themselues.

28 Now the Sunne being newly risen, they ioyned both together; the one part hauing, together with their vertue, their refuge also vnto the Lord, for a ||pledge of their successe and victorie: the other side making their rage leader of their battell.

|| *Or, warrant, or stie.*

29 But when the battaile waxed strong, there appeared vnto the enemies from heauen, fiue comely men vpon horses, with bridles of golde, and two of them ledde the Iewes,

30 And tooke Maccabeus betwixt them, and couered him on euery side with their weapons, and kept him safe, but shot arrowes & lightenings against the enemies : so that being confounded with blindnesse, and full of trouble, they were killed.

31 And there were slaine [of footemen] twentie thousand and fiue hundred, and sixe hundred horsemen.

32 As for Timotheus himselfe, hee fled into a very strong holde, called Gazara,

zara, where Chereas was gouernour.

33 But they that were with Maccabeus, laid siege against the fortresse couragiously foure dayes.

34 And they y were within, trusting to the strength of the place, blasphemed exceedingly, & vttered wicked words.

35 Neuerthelesse, vpon the fifth day early, twentie yong men of Maccabeus company, inflamed with anger because of the blasphemies, assaulted the wall manly, and with a fierce courage killed all that they met withall.

36 Others likewise ascending after them, whiles they were busied with them that were within, burnt the towres, and kindling fires, burnt the blasphemers aliue, and others broke open the gates, and hauing receiued in the rest of the army, tooke the city,

37 And killed Timotheus that was hidde in a certaine pit, and Chereas his brother, with Apollophanes.

38 When this was done, they praised the Lord with Psalmes and thankesgiuing, who had done so great things for Israel, and giuen them the victory.

CHAP. XI.

3 Lysias thinking to get Ierusalem, 8 Is put to flight. 16 The letters of Lysias to the Iewes: 22 Of the king vnto Lysias: 27 and to the Iewes: 34 Of the Romanes to the Iewes.

.tutour.

NOt long after this, Lysias the kings †protectour & cousin, who also managed the affaires, tooke sore displeasure for the things that were done.

2 And when he had gathered about fourescore thousand, with all the horsemen, he came against the Iewes, thinking to make the citie an habitation of the ‖Gentiles,

, Greci-

3 And to make a gaine of the Temple, as of the other Chappels of the heathen, and to set the high Priesthood to sale euery yeere:

4 Not at all considering the power of God, but puffed vp with his ten thousand footmen, and his thousand horsemen, and his fourescore Elephants.

5 So he came to Iudea, & drew neere to Bethsura, which was a strong town, but distant from Ierusalem about fiue furlongs, and he laid sore siege vnto it.

*acca-
s and his
pany.*

6 Now when ‖they that were with Maccabeus heard that he besieged the holdes, they and all the people with lamentation and teares besought the Lord, that he would send a good Angel to deliuer Israel.

7 Then Maccabeus himselfe first of all tooke weapons, exhorting the other, that they would ieopard themselues together with him, to helpe their brethren : so they went forth together with a willing minde.

8 And as they were at Ierusalem, there appeared before them on horsebacke, one in white clothing, shaking his armour of gold.

9 Then they praised the mercifull God altogether, and tooke heart, insomuch that they were ready not onely to fight with men, but with most cruell beasts, & to pierce through wals of yron.

10 Thus they marched forward in their armour, hauing an helper from heauen : for the Lord was mercifull vnto them.

11 And giuing a charge vpō their enemies like lions, they slew eleuen thousand footmen, & sixteene hundred horsemen, and put all the other to flight.

12 Many of them also being wounded, escaped naked, and Lysias himselfe fled away shamefully, and so escaped.

13 Who as hee was a man of vnderstanding, casting with himselfe what losse he had had, and considering that the Hebrewes could not be ouercome, because the Almighty God helped them, he sent vnto them,

14 And perswaded them to agree to all reasonable conditions, & [promised] that hee would perswade the king, that he must needs be a friend vnto them.

15 Then Maccabeus consented to all that Lysias desired, being carefull of the common good ; and whatsoeuer Maccabeus wrote vnto Lysias concerning the Iewes, the king granted it.

16 For there were letters written vnto the Iewes from Lysias, to this effect : Lysias vnto the people of the Iewes, sendeth greeting.

17 Iohn and Absalon, who were sent from you, deliuered me the petition subscribed, and made request for the performance of the contents thereof.

18 Therefore what things soeuer were meet to be reported to the king, I haue declared them, and he hath granted as much as might be.

19 If then you wil keepe your selues loyall to the state, hereafter also will I endeuour to be a meanes of your good.

20 But of the particulars I haue giuen

Or, Dioscoros.

uen order, both to these, & the other that came from me, to commune with you.

21 Fare ye wel. The hundred & eight and fortie yeere, the foure and twentie day of the moneth Dioscorinthius.

22 Now the kings letter conteined these words, King Antiochus vnto his brother Lysias sendeth greeting.

23 Since our father is translated vnto ỹ gods, our will is, that they that are in our realme liue quietly, that euery one may attend vpon his own affaires.

24 Wee vnderstand also that the Iewes would not consent to our father for to bee brought vnto the custome of the Gentiles, but had rather keepe their owne manner of liuing : for the which cause they require of vs that we should suffer thē to liue after their own lawes.

25 Wherefore our mind is, that this nation shall be in rest, and we haue determined to restore them their Temple, that they may liue according to the customes of their forefathers.

Or, giue them assurance.

26 Thou shalt doe well therefore to send vnto them, and ||grant them peace, that whē they are certified of our mind, they may be of good comfort, & euer goe cheerefully about their owne affaires.

27 And the letter of ỹ king vnto the nation of the Iewes was after this maner : king Antiochus sendeth greeting vnto the counsel, & the rest of the Iewes

28 If ye fare well, we haue our desire, we are also in good health.

29 Menelaus declared vnto vs, that your desire was to returne home, and to follow your owne businesse.

30 Wherefore they that will depart shall haue safe conduct, till the thirtieth day of Xanthicus with securitie.

31 And the Iewes shal vse their owne kind of meats, and lawes, as before, and none of them any maner of wayes shal be molested for things ignorantly done.

32 I haue sent also Menelaus, that he may comfort you.

Or, Aprill.

33 Fare ye wel. In the hundred, forty and eight yeere, and the fifteenth day of the moneth ||Xanthicus.

34 The Romanes also sent vnto them a letter containing these wordes : Quintus Memmius, & Titus Manlius *Or, consuls* ||embassadours of ỹ Romanes, send greeting vnto the people of the Iewes.

35 Whatsoeuer Lysias the kings cousin hath granted, therewith we also are well pleased.

36 But touching such things as hee

iudged to be referred to the king : after you haue aduised therof, send one forthwith, that we may declare as it is conuenient for you : for we are now going to Antioch.

37 Therefore send some with speed, that we may know what is your mind.

38 Farewell, this hundred and eight and fortie yeere, the fifteenth day of the moneth Xanthicus.

CHAP. XII.

1 The Kings lieutenants vexe the Iewes. 3 They of Ioppe drowne two hundred Iewes. 6 Iudas is auenged vpon them. 11 Hee maketh peace with the Arabians, 16 and taketh Caspis. 22 Timotheus armies ouerthrowen.

WHen these Couenants were made, Lysias went vnto the king, and the Iewes were about their husbandrie.

2 But of the gouernours of seueral places, Timotheus, and Apollonius the sonne of Genneus, also Hieronymus, and Demophon, and besides them Nicanor y gouernor of Cyprus would not suffer them to be quiet, and liue in peace.

3 The men of Ioppe also did such an vngodly deed : they prayed the Iewes that dwelt among them, to goe with their wiues, and children into the boats which they had prepared, as though they had meant them no hurt.

4 Who accepted of it according to the common decree of the citie, as being desirous to liue in peace, and suspecting nothing : but when they were gone forth into the deepe, they drowned no lesse then two hundred of them.

5 When Iudas heard of this crueltie done vnto his countrey men, he commanded those that were with him [to make them ready.]

6 And calling vpon God the righteous iudge, he came against those murtherers of his brethren, & burnt the hauen by night, and set the boats on fire, and those that fled thither, he slew.

Or, with purpose returne

7 And when the towne was shut vp, he went backward, ||as if he would returne to root out all them of the citie of Ioppe.

8 But when he heard that y Iamnites were minded to doe in like maner vnto the Iewes ỹ dwelt among them,

9 He came vpon the Iamnites also by night, and set fire on the hauen, & the nauy, so that the light of the fire was seene at Ierusalem, two hundred and fortie furlongs off.   10 Now

10 Now when they were gone from thence nine furlongs in their iourney toward Timotheus, no fewer then fiue thousand men on foote, & fiue hundred horse men of the Arabians, set vpon him.

11 Whereupon there was a very sore battell; but Iudas side by the helpe of God got the victory, so that the Nomades of Arabia being ouercome, besought Iudas for peace, promising both to giue him cattell, and to pleasure him otherwise.

12 Then Iudas thinking indeede that they would be profitable in many things, granted them peace, wherupon they shooke hands, and so they ‖departed to their tents.

Or, went om place place, with eir fami- es and cat- ll.

13 Hee went also about to make a bridge to a certaine strong citie, which was fenced about with walles, and inhabited by people of diuers countries, and the name of it was Caspis.

14 But they that were within it put such trust in the strength of the walles, and prouision of victuals, that they behaued themselues rudely towards them that were with Iudas, railing, and blaspheming, and vttering such words, as were not to be spoken.

15 Wherefore Iudas with his company, calling vpon the great Lord of the world (who without any rammes, or engines of warre did cast downe Iericho in the time of Iosua) gaue a fierce assault against the walles,

16 And tooke the citie by the will of God, and made vnspeakeable slaughters, insomuch that a lake two furlongs broad, neere adioining thereunto, being filled ful, was seen running with blood.

17 Then departed they from thence seuen hundred and fifty furlongs, and came to Characa vnto the Iewes that are called Tubieni.

18 But as for Timotheus they found him not in the places, for before hee had dispatched any thing, he departed from thence, hauing left a very strong garrison in a certaine hold:

19 Howbeit, Dositheus, and Sosipater, who were of Maccabeus captaines, went forth, and slew those that Timotheus had left in the fortresse, aboue tenne thousand men.

Dositheus, ıd Sosipa- r.

20 And Maccabeus ranged his armie by bands, & set ‖them ouer the bands, and went against Timotheus, who had about him & hundred and twentie

thousand men of foote, and two thousand, and fiue hundred horsemen.

21 Nowe when Timotheus had knowledge of Iudas comming, he sent the women and children, and the other baggage vnto a fortresse called Carnion (for the towne was hard to besiege and vneasie to come vnto, by reason of the straitnesse of all the places.)

22 But when Iudas his first band came in sight, the enemies (being smitten with feare, and terrour through the appearing of him that seeth all things) fled amaine, one running this way, another that way, so as that they were often hurt of their owne men, and wounded with ẙ points of their owne swords

23 Iudas also was very earnest in pursuing them, killing those wicked wretches, of whom he slew about thirtie thousand men.

24 Moreouer, Timotheus himselfe fell into the hands of Dositheus, & Sosipater, whom he besought with much craft to let him goe with his life, because hee had many of the Iewes parents, and the brethren of some of them, who, if they put him to death, should not be regarded.

25 So when hee had assured them with many words, that hee would restore them without hurt according to the agreement, they let him goe for the sauing of their brethren.

26 Then Maccabeus marched forth to Carnion, & to the Temple of ‖Atargatis, and there he slew fiue and twenty thousand persons.

‖ *i. Venus.*

27 And after he had put to flight, and destroyed them, Iudas remooued the hoste towards Ephron, a strong citie, wherin Lysias abode, and a great multitude of diuers nations, and the strong yong men kept the wals, and defended them mightily : wherin also was great prouision of engines, and darts.

28 But when Iudas and his company had called vpon Almighty God (who with his power breaketh the strength of his enemies) they wanne the citie, and slew twentie and fiue thousand of them that were within.

29 From thence they departed to Scythopolis, which lieth sixe hundreth furlongs from Ierusalem.

30 But when the Iewes that dwelt there had testified that the Scythopolitans dealt louingly with them, and entreated them kindely in the time of their aduersitie :   13 They

31 They gaue them thankes, desiring them to be friendly stil vnto them, and so they came to Ierusalem, the feast of the weekes approching.

32 And after the feast called Pentecost, they went foorth against Gorgias the gouernour of Idumea,

33 Who came out w̄ three thousand men of foot, & foure hundred horsemen.

34 And it happened that in their fighting together, a few of the Iewes were slaine.

35 At which time Dositheus one of Bacenors company, who was on horsbacke, and a strong man, was still vpon Gorgias, and taking hold of his coate, drew him by force, and when he would haue taken that cursed man aliue, a horseman of Thracia comming vpon him, smote off his ||shoulder, so that Gorgias fled vnto Marisa.

36 Now when they that were with Gorgias had fought long & were wearie, Iudas called vpon the Lord that he would shew himselfe to be their helper, and leader of the battell.

37 And with that he beganne in his owne language, & sung Psalmes with a lowd voyce, & rushing vnawares vpon Gorgias men, he put them to flight.

38 So Iudas gathered his host, and came into the city of Odollam. And when the seuenth day came, they purified themselues (as the custome was) and kept the Sabbath in the same place.

39 And vpon the day following ||as the vse had bene, Iudas and his company came to take vp the bodies of them that were slaine, and to bury them with their kinsmen, in their fathers graues.

40 Now vnder the coats of euery one that was slaine, they found things consecrated to the idoles of the Iamnites, which is forbidden the Iewes by *the Law. Then euery man saw that this was ȳ cause wherefore they were slaine.

41 All men therefore praising the Lord the righteous Iudge, who had opened the things that were hid,

42 Betooke themselues vnto praier, and besought him that the sinne committed, might wholy bee put out of remembrance. Besides, that noble Iudas exhorted the people to keep themselues from sinne, forsomuch as they saw before their eyes the things that came to passe, for the sinne of those ȳ were slaine.

43 And when he had made a gathering throughout the company, to the

sum of two thousand drachmes of siluer, hee sent it to Ierusalem to offer a sinne offering, doing therein very well, and honestly, in that he was mindfull of the resurrection.

44 (For if he had not hoped that they that were slaine should haue risen againe, it had bin superfluous and vaine, to pray for the dead.)

45 And also in that he perceiued that there was great fauour layed vp for those that died godly. (It was an holy, and good thought) wherupon he made a reconciliation for the dead, that they might be deliuered from sinne.

CHAP. XIII.

1 Eupator inuadeth Iudea. 15 Iudas by night slayeth many. 18 Eupators purpose is defeated. 23 He maketh peace with Iudas.

IN the hundreth forty and ninth yere it was told Iudas that Antiochus Eupator was coming with a great power into Iudea;

2 And with him Lysias his protector, and ruler of his affaires, hauing either of them a Grecian power of footemen, an hundred and ten thousand, and horsmen fiue thousand, & three hundred, and Elephants two & twenty, and three hundred charets armed w̄ hooks.

3 Menelaus also ioyned himself with them, and with great dissimulation encouraged Antiochus, not for the safegard of the countrey, but because hee thought to haue bin made gouernour.

4 But the King of kings mooued Antiochus minde against this wicked wretch, and Lysias enformed the king, that this man was the cause of all mischiefe, so that the king commanded to bring him vnto Berea, and to put him to death, as the maner is in that place.

5 Now there was in that place a towre of fifty cubites high full of ashes, and it had a round instrumēt which on euery side hanged down into the ashes.

6 And whosoeuer was condemned of sacriledge, or had committed any other grieuous crime, there did all men thrust him vnto death.

7 Such a death it happened that wicked man to die, not hauing so much as buriall in the earth, & that most iustly.

8 For inasmuch as he had committed many sinnes about the altar whose fire and ashes were holy, hee receiued his death in ashes.

9 Now

Put by his armie: wounded him in the shoulder: or stroke him in the shoulder.

Or, at such time, &c.

Deut. 26. ver. 7.

9 Now ẙ king came with a barbarous & hautie mind, to do far worse to ẙ Iewes then had beene done in his fathers time.

10 Which things when Iudas perceiued, hee commanded the multitude to call vpon the Lord night & day, that if euer at any other time, he would now also helpe them, being at the point to be put from their Law, from their country, and from the holy Temple :

11 And that hee would not suffer the people, that ||had euen now been but a little refreshed, to be in subiection to the blasphemous nations.

Or, had ad a litle espite.

12 So when they had all done this together, and besought the mercifull Lord with weeping, and fasting, and lying flat vpon the ground three daies long, Iudas hauing exhorted them, commanded they should be in a readinesse.

13 And Iudas being apart with the Elders, determined before the kings host should enter into Iudea and get the city, to goe foorth and try the matter [in fight] by the helpe of the Lord.

14 So when he had committed [all] to the ||Creator of the world, & exhorted his souldiers to fight manfully, euen vnto death, for the Lawes, the Temple, the çity, the country, and the common-wealth, he camped by Modin.

Or, Lord

15 And hauing giuen the watchword to them that were about him, Victory is of God ; with the most valiant and choice yong men, he went in into the kings tent by night, & slewe in the campe about foure thousand men, and the chiefest of the Elephants, with all that were vpon him.

16 And at last they filled the campe with feare and tumult, and departed with good successe.

17 This was done in the breake of the day, because the protection of the Lord did helpe him.

18 Now when the king had taken a taste of the manlinesse of the Iewes, hee went about to take the holds by policie,

19 And marched towards Bethsura, which was a strōg hold of ẙ Iews, but he was put to flight, failed, & lost of his men.

20 For Iudas had conueyed vnto them ẙ were in it, such things as were necessary.

21 But Rhodocus who was in ẙ Iewes hoste, disclosed the secrets to the enemies, therefore he was sought out, & when they had gotten him, they put him in prison.

22 The king treated with them in Bethsura the second time, gaue his hand, tooke theirs, departed, fought with Iudas, was ouercome :

23 Heard that Philip who was left ouer the affaires in Antioch ||was desperately bent, confounded, intreated the Iewes, submitted himselfe, and sware to all equal conditions, agreed with them, and offred sacrifice, honoured the Temple, and dealt kindly with the place,

Or, rebelled.

24 And accepted well of Maccabeus, made him principall gouernor from Ptolemais vnto the Gerrhenians,

25 Came to Ptolemais, the people there were grieued for the couenants : for they stormed because they would make their couenants voide.

26 Lysias went vp to the iudgement seat, said as much as could be in defence of the cause, perswaded, pacified, made them well affected, returned to Antioch. Thus it went touching the kings comming and departing.

CHAP. XIIII.

6 Alcimus accuseth Iudas. 18 Nicanor maketh peace with Iudas. 39 He seeketh to take Rhasis, 46 who to escape his hands, killeth himselfe.

Fter three yeres was Iudas enformed that Demetrius the sonne of Seleucus hauing entred by the hauen of Tripolis with a great power and nauie,

2 Had taken the countrey, and killed Antiochus, and Lysias his protectour.

3 Now one Alcimus who had beene hie Priest, and had defiled himselfe wilfully in the times of their mingling (with the Gentiles) seeing that by no meanes hee could saue himselfe, nor haue any more accesse to the holy Altar,

4 Came to king Demetrius in the hundreth and one and fiftieth yeere, presenting vnto him a crowne of golde, and a palme, and also of the boughes which were ||vsed solemnly in the Temple : and so that day he helde his peace.

Or, thought to be of the Temple.

5 Howbeit hauing gotten opportunity to further his foolish enterprise, [and] being called into counsel by Demetrius, & asked how the Iewes stood affected, and what they intēded, he answered therunto ;

6 Those of the Iewes that bee called Asideans (whose captaine is Iudas Maccabeus) nourish warre, and are seditious, and will not let the realme be in peace.

7 Therfore I being depriued of mine ancestors honor (I meane the hie Priesthood) am now come hither.

8 First verily for the vnfained care I haue of things pertaining to the king, and secondly, euen for that I intend the good
of

of mine owne countrey men : for all our nation is in no small misery, through the vnaduised dealing of them aforesaid.

9 Wherefore, O king, seeing thou knowest all these things, bee carefull for the countrey, and our nation, which is pressed on euery side, according to the clemency that thou readily shewest vnto all.

10 For as long as Iudas liueth, it is not possible that the state should be quiet.

11 This was no sooner spoken of him, but others of the kings friends being malitiously set against Iudas, did more incense Demetrius.

12 And foorthwith calling Nicanor, who had bene master of the Elephants, and making him gouernour ouer Iudea, he sent him forth,

13 Cōmanding him to slay Iudas, & to scatter them that were ẇ him, & to make Alcimus high priest of the great Temple.

14 Then the heathen that had fled out of Iudea from Iudas, came to Nicanor by flocks, thinking the harme and calamities of the Iewes, to be their well-fare.

15 Now when the Iewes heard of Nicanors comming, and that the heathen ‖ were vp against them, they cast earth vpon their heads, and made supplication to him that had stablished his people for euer, and who alwayes helpeth his portion with manifestation of his presence.

‖ Or, were ioyned to them.

16 So at the commandement of the captaine, they remooued straightwayes from thence, and came neere vnto them, at the towne of Dessaro.

17 Now Simon, Iudas brother, had ioyned battell with Nicanor, but was somewhat discomfited, through the suddaine silence of his enemies.

18 Neuerthelesse Nicanor hearing of the manlinesse of them that were with Iudas, and the courageousnes that they had to fight for their countrey, durst not try the matter by the sword.

19 Wherefore he sent Posidonius, and Theodotus, & Mattathias to make peace.

20 So when they had taken long aduisement thereupon, and the captaine had made ẏ multitude acquainted therewith, and it appeared that they were all of one minde, they consented to the couenants,

21 And appointed a day to meet in together by themselues, & when the day came, and stooles were set for either of them,

22 Iudas placed armed men ready in conuenient places, lest some treachery should bee suddenly practised by the enemies; so they made a peaceable cōference.

23 Now Nicanor abode in Ierusalem, and did no hurt, but sent away the people that came flocking vnto him.

24 And hee would not willingly haue Iudas out of his sight : for hee loued the man from his heart.

25 He praied him also to take a wife, and to beget children: so he maried, was quiet, and ‖ tooke part of this life.

‖ Or, liued together wit him.

26 But Alcimus perceiuing the loue that was betwixt them, and considering the couenants that were made, came to Demetrius, and tolde him that Nicanor was not well affected towards the state, for that he had ordained Iudas, a traitor to his realme, to be the kings successour.

27 Then the king being in a rage, and prouoked with the accusations of the most wicked man, wrote to Nicanor, signifying that he was much displeased with the couenants, and commaunding him that hee should send Maccabeus prisoner in all haste vnto Antioch.

28 When this came to Nicanors hearing, he was much cōfounded in himselfe, and tooke it grieuously, that hee should make voyd the articles which were agreed vpon, the man being in no fault.

29 But because there was no dealing against the king, hee watched his time to accomplish this thing by pollicie.

30 Notwithstāding when Maccabeus saw that Nicanor began to bee churlish vnto him, and that he entreated him more roughly then he was wont, perceiuing y such sowre behauiour came not of good, hee gathered together not a few of his men, and withdrew himselfe frō Nicanor.

31 But the other knowing that he was notably preuented by Iudas policie, came into the great and holy Temple, and commanded the Priestes that were offering their vsual sacrifices, to deliuer him ẏ man.

32 And whē they sware that they could not tel where ẏ man was, whō he sought,

33 Hee stretched out his right hand toward the Temple, & made an oath in this maner : If you wil not deliuer me Iudas as a † prisoner, I will lay this Temple of God euen with the ground, and I will breake downe the Altar, and erect a notable temple vnto Bacchus.

† Greeke bound.

34 After these words he departed; then the Priests lift vp their handes towards heauen, & besought him ẏ was euer a defēder of their nation, saying in this maner :

35 Thou, O Lord of all things, who hast neede of nothing, wast pleased that the Temple of thine habitation should be among vs.

                             36 There-

36 Therefore now, O holy Lord of all holinesse, keepe this house euer vndefiled, which lately was cleansed, and stop euery vnrighteous mouth.

37 Now was there accused vnto Nicanor, one Razis, one of the Elders of Ierusalem, a louer of his countrey men, and a man of very good report, who for his kindnesse was called a father of ẙ Iewes.

38 For in the former times, when they mingled not themselues with the Gentiles, he had bin accused of Iudaisme, and did boldly ieopard his body and life with al vehemency for the religion of ẙ Iewes.

39 So Nicanor willing to declare the hate that he bare vnto the Iewes, sent aboue fiue hūdred men of war to take him.

40 For he thought by taking him to do [the Iewes] much hurt.

41 Now when the multitude would haue taken the towre, and violently broken into the vtter doore, and bade that fire should be brought to burne it, he being ready to be taken on euery side, fell vpon his sword,

42 Chusing rather to die manfully, then to come into the hands of the wicked to be abused otherwise then beseemed his noble birth.

43 But missing his stroke through haste, the multitude also rushing within the doores, he ran boldly vp to the wall, and cast himselfe downe manfully among the thickest of them.

44 But they quickly giuing backe, and a space being made, he fell downe into the midst of the void place.

45 Neuerthelesse while there was yet breath within him, being inflamed with anger, he rose vp, and though his blood gushed out like spouts of water, and his wounds were grieuous, yet hee ranne through the midst of the throng, and standing vpon a steepe rocke,

46 When as his blood was now quite gone, hee pluckt out his bowels, & taking them in both his hands, hee cast them vpon the throng, and calling vpon the Lord of life and spirit to restore him those againe, he thus died.

CHAP. XV.

Vt Nicanor hearing that Iudas and his company were in the strong places about Samaria, resolued without any danger to set vpon them on ẙ sabbath day.

2 Neuertheles, the Iewes that were compelled to go with him, said, O destroy not so cruelly and barbarously, but giue honour to that day, which he that seeth all things, hath honoured with holinesse aboue [other dayes.]

3 Then this most vngracious wretch demanded, if there were a mightie one in heauen that had commanded the Sabbath day to be kept.

4 And when they said, There is in heauen a liuing Lord, and mightie, who commanded the seuenth day to be kept,

5 Then said the other, And I also am mightie vpon earth, & I cōmand to take armes, and to do the kings busines: yet he obteined not to haue his wicked wil done.

6 So Nicanor in exceeding pride and haughtinesse, determined to set vp a publike moument of his victorie ouer Iudas, and them that were with him.

7 But Maccabeus had euer sure confidence that the Lord would helpe him.

8 Wherfore he exhorted his people not to feare the comming of the heathen against them, but to remember the helpe which in former times they had receiued from heauen, and now to expect the victory, and aid which should come vnto them from the Almightie.

9 And so comforting them out of the law, and the prophets, and withall putting them in mind of the battels that they won afore, he made them more cheerefull.

10 And when he had stirred vp their minds, he gaue them their charge, shewing them therewithall the falshood of the heathen, and the breach of othes.

11 Thus he armed euery one of them not so much with defence of shields and speares, as with comfortable and good words : and besides that, he tolde them a dreame worthy to be beleeued, as if it had bin so indeed, which did not a litle reioyce them.

12 And this was his vision : that Onias, who had bin high Priest, a vertuous, and a good man, reuerend in conuersation, gentle in condition, well spoken also, and exercised from a child in all points of vertue, holding vp his hands, prayed for the whole bodie of the Iewes.

13 This done, in like maner there appeared a man with gray haires, & exceeding glorious, who was of a wonderfull and excellent maiestie.

14 Then Onias answered, saying, This is a louer of the brethren, who prayeth much for the people, and for the holy citie,

citie, (to wit) Ieremias ỹ prophet of God.

15 Whereupon Ieremias, holding forth his right hand, gaue to Iudas a sword of gold, and in giuing it spake thus:

16 Take this holy sword a gift from God, with the which thou shalt wound the aduersaries.

17 Thus being well comforted by the words of Iudas, which were very good, and able to stirre them vp to valour, and to encourage the hearts of the yong men, they determined not to pitch campe, but couragiously to set vpon them, and manfully to trie the matter by conflict, because the citie, and the Sanctuarie, and the Temple were in danger.

18 For the care that they tooke for their wiues, and their children, their brethren, and kinsfolkes, was in least account with them : but the greatest, and principall feare, was for the holy Temple.

19 Also they that were in the citie, tooke not the least care, being troubled for the conflict abroad.

20 And now when as all looked what should bee ỹ triall, & the enemies were already come neere, and the armie was set in aray, and the beasts conueniently placed, and the horsemen set in wings :

21 Maccabeus seeing the comming of the multitude, and the diuers preparations of armour, and the fiercenesse of the beasts, stretched out his hands towards heauen, and called vpon the Lord, that worketh wonders, knowing that victorie commeth not by armes, but euen as it seemeth good to him, he giueth it to such as are worthy :

22 Therefore in his prayer he said after this maner : O Lord, thou diddest send thine Angel in the time of Ezekias king of Iudea, and diddest slay in the host of Sennacherib, an hundred, fourescore, and fiue thousand.

23 Wherfore now also O Lord of heauen, send a good Angel before vs, for a feare, and dread vnto them.

24 And through the might of thine arme, let those bee stricken with terror, that come against thy holy people to blaspheme. And he ended thus.

25 Then Nicanor, and they that were with him came forward with trumpets, and songs.

26 But Iudas, and his company encountred the enemies with inuocation, and prayer.

27 So that fighting with their hands,

and praying vnto God with their hearts, they slew no lesse then thirty and fiue thousand men : for through the appearance of God, they were greatly cheered.

28 Now when the battell was done, returning againe with ioy, they knew that Nicanor lay dead in his harnesse.

29 Then they made a great shout, and a noise, praising the Almighty in their owne language :

30 And Iudas, who was euer the chiefe defender of the citizens both in body, and minde, and who continued his loue towards his countrymen all his life, commanded to strike off Nicanors head, and his hand, with his shoulder, & bring them to Ierusalem.

31 So when he was there, and had called them of his nation together, and set the priests before the altar, he sent for them that were of the Towre :

32 And shewed them vile Nicanors head, and the hand of that blasphemer, which with proud brags he had stretched out against the holy Temple of the Almightie.

33 And when he had cut out the tongue of that vngodly Nicanor, he commanded that they should giue it by pieces vnto the foules, and hang vp the reward of his madnesse before the Temple.

34 So euery man praised towards the heauen the glorious Lord, saying Blessed be hee that hath kept his owne place vndefiled.

35 He hanged also Nicanors head vpon the Towre, an euident, and manifest signe vnto all, of the helpe of the Lord.

36 And they ordained all with a common decree, in no case to let that day passe without solemnitie : but to celebrate the thirteenth day of the twelfth moneth, which in the Syrian tongue is called Adar, the day before Mardocheus day.

37 Thus went it with Nicanor, and from that time forth, the Hebrewes had the citie in their power : and heere will I make an end.

38 And if I haue done well, and as is fitting the story, it is that which I desired: but if slenderly, and meanly, it is that which I could attaine vnto.

39 For as it is hurtfull to drinke wine, or water alone ; & as wine mingled with water is pleasant, and delighteth the tast: euen so speech finely framed, delighteth the eares of them that read the storie. And heere shall be an end.

The end of Apocrypha.

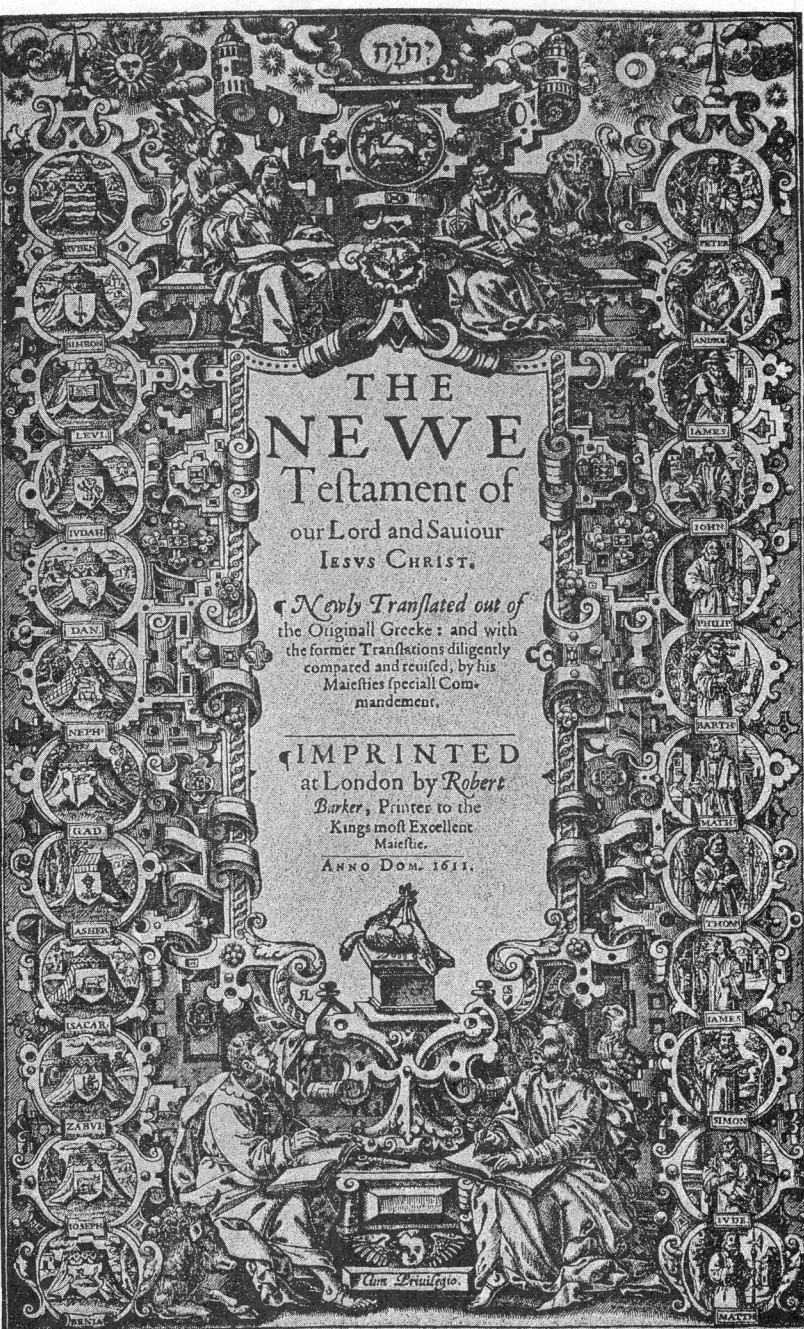

יהוה

THE
NEWE
Testament of
our Lord and Saviour
Iesvs Christ.

¶ Newly Translated out of
the Originall Greeke : and with
the former Translations diligently
compared and reuised, by his
Maiesties speciall Com-
mandement.

¶ IMPRINTED
at London by Robert
Barker, Printer to the
Kings most Excellent
Maiestie.
Anno Dom. 1611.

Cum Priuilegio.

RVBEN
SIMEON
LEVI
IVDAH
DAN
NEPH
GAD
ASHER
ISACAR
ZABVL
IOSEPH
BENI.

PETER
ANDR.
IAMES
IOHN
PHILIP
BARTH.
MATH.
THOM.
IAMES
SIMON
IVDE
MATH.

THE
GOSPEL ACCORDING
to S. Matthew.

CHAP. I.

1 The genealogie of Christ from Abraham to
Ioseph. 18 Hee was conceiued by the holy
Ghost, and borne of the Virgin Mary when
she was espoused to Ioseph. 19 The Angel
satisfieth the misdeeming thoughts of Ioseph,
and interpreteth the names of Christ.

Luke 3.
3.

Gen. 21. 3.

* Gene. 25.
6.
* Gen. 29.
5.
* Gen. 38.
7.
* 1. Chro. 2.
ruth. 4.
8.

* 1. Sam. 16.
and 17.
2.
* 2. Sam. 12.
24.
* 1. Chro. 3.
0.

* 2. King.
20. 21. 1.
chro. 3. 13.

THE booke of the *genera-tion of Iesus Christ, the sonne of Dauid, the sonne of Abraham.
2 * Abraham begate Isaac, and * Isaac begate Iacob, and * Iacob begate Iudas and his brethren.

3 And * Iudas begate Phares and Zara of Thamar, and * Phares begate Esrom, and Esrom begate Aram.

4 And Aram begate Aminadab, and Aminadab begate Naasson, and Naasson begate Salmon.

5 And Salmon begat Boos of Rachab, and Boos begate Obed of Ruth, and Obed begate Iesse.

6 And * Iesse begate Dauid the King, & * Dauid the King begat Solomon of her *that had bin* the wife of Vrias.

7 And * Solomon begat Roboam, and Roboam begate Abia, and Abia begate Asa.

8 And Asa begate Iosaphat, and Iosaphat begate Ioram, and Ioram begate Ozias.

9 And Ozias begat Ioatham, and Ioatham begate Achas, and Achas begate Ezekias.

10 And * Ezekias begate Manasses,

and Manasses begate Amon, and Amon begate Iosias.

11 And ‖ Iosias begate Iechonias and his brethren, about the time they were caried away to Babylon.

12 And after they were brought to Babylon, * Iechonias begat Salathiel, and Salathiel begate Zorobabel.

13 And Zorobabel begat Abiud, and Abiud begate Eliakim, and Eliakim begate Azor.

14 And Azor begate Sadoc, & Sadoc begat Achim, and Achim begat Eliud.

15 And Eliud begate Eleazar, and Eleazar begate Matthan, and Matthan begate Iacob.

16 And Iacob begate Ioseph the husband of Mary, of whom was borne Iesus, who is called Christ.

17 So all the generations from Abraham to Dauid, are fourteene generations : and from Dauid vntill the carying away into Babylon, are fourteene generations : and from the carying away into Babylon vnto Christ, are fourteene generations.

18 ¶ Now the *birth of Iesus Christ was on this wise : When as his mother Mary was espoused to Ioseph (before they came together) shee was found with childe of the holy Ghost.

19 Then Ioseph her husband being a iust man, and not willing to make her a publique example, was minded to put her away priuily.

20 But while hee thought on these things, behold, the Angel of the Lord appeared vnto him in a dreame, saying, Ioseph thou sonne of Dauid, feare not to take vnto thee Mary thy wife ; for that which is conceiued in her, is of the holy Ghost.

‖ Some read,
Iosias begate
Iakim, and
Iakim begat
Iechonias.

* 1. Chro. 3.
16, 17.

* Luke 1.
27.

21 And

21 And she shall bring forth a sonne, *and thou shalt call his Name Iesus: for hee shall saue his people from their sinnes.

*Luke 1. 31.

22 (Now all this was done, that it might be fulfilled which was spoken of the Lord by the Prophet, saying,

23 *Behold, a Virgin shall be with childe, and shall bring foorth a sonne, and ||they shall call his name Emmanuel, which being interpreted, is, God with vs.)

*Esai. 7. 14.

|| Or, his name shall be called.

24 Then Ioseph, being raised from sleepe, did as the Angel of the Lord had bidden him, & tooke vnto him his wife:

25 And knewe her not, till shee had brought forth her first borne sonne, and he called his name Iesus.

CHAP. II.

1 The Wise men out of the East, are directed to Christ by a Starre. 11 They worship him, and offer their presents. 14 Ioseph fleeth into Egypt, with Iesus and his mother. 16 Herod slayeth the children: 20 Himselfe dyeth. 23 Christ is brought backe againe into Galilee to Nazareth.

*Luk. 2. 6.

Ow when *Iesus was borne in Bethlehem of Iudea, in the dayes of Herod the king, behold, there came Wise men from the East to Hierusalem,

2 Saying, Where is he that is borne King of the Iewes? for we haue seene his Starre in the East, and are come to worship him.

3 When Herod the king had heard *these things*, he was troubled, and all Hierusalem with him.

4 And when he had gathered all the chiefe Priests and Scribes of the people together, hee demanded of them where Christ should be borne.

5 And they said vnto him, In Bethlehem of Iudea: For thus it is written by the Prophet;

6 *And thou Bethlehem *in* the land of Iuda, art not the least among the Princes of Iuda: for out of thee shall come a Gouernour, that shall ||rule my people Israel.

*Mic. 5. 2. iohn 7. 41.

|| Or, feede.

7 Then Herod, when he had priuily called the Wise men, enquired of them diligently what time the Starre appeared:

8 And he sent them to Bethlehem, and said, Goe, and search diligently for the yong child, and when ye haue found him, bring me word againe, that I may come and worship him also.

9 When they had heard the King, they departed, and loe, the Starre which they saw in the East, went before them, till it came and stood ouer where the young childe was.

10 When they saw the Starre, they reioyced with exceeding great ioy.

11 ¶ And when they were come into the house, they saw the yong child with Mary his mother, and fell downe, and worshipped him: and when they had opened their treasures, they ||presented vnto him gifts, gold, and frankincense, and myrrhe.

|| Or, offere

12 And being warned of God in a dreame, that they should not returne to Herode, they departed into their owne countrey another way.

13 And when they were departed, behold, the Angel of the Lord appeareth to Ioseph in a dreame, saying, Arise and take the young childe, and his mother, and flee into Egypt, and bee thou there vntill I bring thee word: for Herode will seeke the young childe, to destroy him.

14 When he arose, he tooke the yong childe and his mother by night, and departed into Egypt:

15 And was there vntill the death of Herode, that it might be fulfilled which was spoken of the Lord by the Prophet, saying, *Out of Egypt haue I called my sonne.

*Ose. 11. 1

16 ¶ Then Herode, when hee saw that hee was mocked of the Wise men, was exceeding wroth, and sent foorth, and slewe all the children that were in Bethlehem, and in all the coasts thereof, from two yeeres olde and vnder, according to the time, which he had diligently enquired of the Wise men.

17 Then was fulfilled that which was spoken by *Ieremie the Prophet, saying,

*Ier. 31. 1.

18 In Rama was there a voice heard, lamentation, and weeping, and great mourning, Rachel weeping *for* her children, and would not be comforted, because they are not.

19 ¶ But when Herode was dead, behold, an Angel of the Lord appeareth in a dreame to Ioseph in Egypt,

20 Saying, Arise, and take the yong childe and his mother, and goe into the land of Israel: for they are dead which sought the yong childes life.

21 And

21 And he arose, and tooke the yong childe and his mother, and came into the land of Israel.

22 But when he heard that Archelaus did reigne in Iudea in the roome of his father Herod, hee was afraid to goe thither : notwithstanding, beeing warned of God in a dreame, he turned aside into the parts of Galilee :

23 And hee came and dwelt in a city called Nazareth, that it might be fulfilled which was spoken by the Prophets, He shalbe called a Nazarene.

CHAP. III.

1 Iohn preacheth : his office : life, and Baptisme. 7 He reprehendeth the Pharises, 13 and baptizeth Christ in Iordane.

Marke 1. luke 3. 2.

IN those daies came *Iohn the Baptist, preaching in the wildernesse of Iudea,

2 And saying, Repent yee : for the kingdome of heauen is at hand.

Esay 40. marke 1.

3 For this is he that was spoken of by the Prophet Esaias, saying, *The voyce of one crying in the wildernes, Prepare ye the way of the Lord, make his paths straight.

4 And the same Iohn had his raiment of camels haire, and a leatherne girdle about his loynes, and his meate was locusts and wilde hony.

5 Then went out to him Hierusalem, and all Iudea, and all the region round about Iordane,

6 And were baptized of him in Iordane, confessing their sinnes.

7 ¶ But when he saw many of the Pharisees and Sadducees come to his Baptisme, he said vnto them, *O generation of vipers, who hath warned you to flee from the wrath to come ?

Cha. 12.

8 Bring forth therefore fruits ||meet for repentance.

Or, answeable to a-mendment of life.

9 And thinke not to say within your selues, *Wee haue Abraham to *our* father : For I say vnto you, that God is able of these stones to raise vp children vnto Abraham.

Iohn 18.

10 And now also the axe is layd vnto the root of the trees : *Therefore euery tree which bringeth not foorth good fruite, is hewen downe, and cast into the fire.

Chap. 7.

11 I indeed baptize you with water vnto repentance : but he that commeth after mee, is mightier then I, whose shooes I am not worthy to beare, hee

Mark 1. 8. ohn 1. 26. ke 3. 16.

shall baptize you with the holy Ghost, and with fire.

12 Whose fanne is in his hand, and he will throughly purge his floore, and gather his wheat into the garner : but wil burne vp the chaffe with vnquenchable fire.

13 ¶ *Then commeth Iesus from Galilee to Iordane, vnto Iohn, to be baptized of him :

Mark. 1. 9. luke 3. 21.

14 But Iohn forbade him, saying, I haue need to bee baptized of thee, and commest thou to me ?

15 And Iesus answering, said vnto him, Suffer it to be so now : for thus it becommeth vs to fulfill all righteousnesse. Then he suffered him.

16 And Iesus, when hee was baptized, went vp straightway out of the water : and loe, the heauens were opened vnto him, and he saw the Spirit of God descending like a doue, and lighting vpon him.

17 And loe, a voice from heauen, saying, This is my beloued Sonne, in whom I am well pleased.

CHAP. IIII.

1 Christ fasteth, and is tempted. 11 The Angels minister vnto him. 13 Hee dwelleth in Capernaum, 17 beginneth to preach, 18 calleth Peter, and Andrew, 21 Iames, and Iohn : 23 and healeth all the diseased.

THen was *Iesus led vp of the Spirit into the wildernesse, to bee tempted of the deuill.

Marke 1. 12. luke 4. 1.

2 And when hee had fasted forty dayes and forty nights, hee was afterward an hungred.

3 And when the tempter came to him, hee said, If thou be the sonne of God, command that these stones bee made bread.

4 But he answered, and said, It is written, *Man shall not liue by bread alone, but by euery word that proceedeth out of the mouth of God.

Deut. 8. 3.

5 Then the deuill taketh him into the holy Citie, and setteth him on a pinacle of the Temple,

6 And saith vnto him, If thou bee the Sonne of God, cast thy selfe downe: For it is written, *He shall giue his Angels charge concerning thee, & in their handes they shall beare thee vp, lest at any time thou dash thy foote against a stone.

Psal. 91. 11.

7 Iesus

7 Iesus said vnto him, It is written againe, * Thou shalt not tempt the Lord thy God.

*Deu. 6. 16

8 Againe the Deuill taketh him vp into an exceeding high mountaine, and sheweth him all the kingdomes of the world, and the glory of them :

9 And saith vnto him, All these things will I giue thee, if thou wilt fall downe and worship me.

10 Then saith Iesus vnto him, Get thee hence, Satan : for it is written, *Thou shalt worship the Lord thy God, and him onely shalt thou serue.

*Deu. 6. 13 and 10. 20.

11 Then the deuill leaueth him, and behold, Angels came and ministred vnto him.

12 ¶ * Now when Iesus had heard that Iohn was ‖ cast into prison, he departed into Galilee.

*Mar. 1. 14. luke 4. 14. iohn 4. 43. ‖ Or, deliue-red vp.

13 And leauing Nazareth, he came and dwelt in Capernaum, which is vpon the Sea coast, in the borders of Zabulon and Nephthali :

14 That it might be fulfilled which was spoken by Esaias the Prophet, saying,

15 *The land of Zabulon, and the land of Nephthali, by the way of the Sea beyond Iordane, Galilee of the Gentiles :

*Esai. 9. 1.

16 The people which sate in darkenesse, saw great light : and to them which sate in the region and shadow of death, light is sprung vp.

17 ¶ *From that time Iesus began to preach, and to say, Repent, for the kingdome of heauen is at hand.

*Mar. 1. 14

18 ¶ *And Iesus walking by the sea of Galilee, saw two brethren, Simon, called Peter, and Andrew his brother, casting a net into the Sea (for they were fishers)

*Mar. 1. 16.

19 And he saith vnto them, Follow mee : and I will make you fishers of men.

20 And they straightway left their nets, and followed him.

21 And going on from thence, hee sawe other two brethren, Iames the sonne of Zebedee, and Iohn his brother, in a ship with Zebedee their father, mending their nets : and he called them.

22 And they immediatly left the shippe and their father, and followed him.

23 ¶ And Iesus went about all Galilee, teaching in their Synagogues, and preaching the Gospel of the kingdome, and healing all maner of sickenesse, and all maner of disease among the people.

24 And his fame went thorowout all Syria : and they brought vnto him all sicke people that were taken with diuerse diseases and torments, and those which were possessed with deuils, and those which were lunaticke, and those that had the palsie, and he healed them.

25 And there followed him great great multitudes of people, from Galilee, and from Decapolis, and from Hierusalem, and from Iudea, and from beyond Iordane.

CHAP. V.

Christ beginneth his Sermon in the Mount : 3 declaring who are blessed, 13 who are the salt of the earth, 14 the light of the world, the citie on an hill, 15 the candle : 17 that he came to fulfill the Law : 21 what it is to kill, 27 to commit adulterie, 33 to sweare : 38 Exhorteth to suffer wrong, 44 to loue euen our enemies, 38 and to labour after perfectnesse.

Nd seeing the multitudes, he went vp into a mountaine : and when he was set, his disciples came vnto him.

2 And he opened his mouth, and taught them, saying,

3 *Blessed are the poore in spirit : for theirs is the kingdome of heauen.

*Luk. 6.

4 Blessed are they that mourne : for they shall be comforted.

5 *Blessed are the meeke : for they shall inherit the earth.

*Psa. 37.

6 Blessed are they which doe hunger and thirst after righteousnesse : *for they shall be filled.

*Esa. 65

7 Blessed are the mercifull : for they shall obtaine mercie.

8 *Blessed are the pure in heart : for they shall see God.

*Psal. 24.

9 Blessed are the peacemakers : for they shall bee called the children of God.

10 *Blessed are they which are persecuted for righteousnesse sake : for theirs is the kingdome of heauen.

*1. Pet. 3

11 Blessed are ye, when men shall reuile you, and persecute you, and shal say all manner of *euill against you †falsly for my sake.

*1. Pet. 14. † Gr. lyin

12 Reioyce,

12 Reioyce, and be exceeding glad : for great is your reward in heauen : For so persecuted they the Prophets which were before you.

Marke 9.
. luke. 14

13 ¶ Yee are the salt of the earth : *But if the salt haue lost his sauour, wherewith shall it bee salted ? It is thenceforth good for nothing, but to be cast out, and to be troden vnder foote of men.

14 Yee are the light of the world. A citie that is set on an hill, cannot be hid.

The word
the origi-
all, signifi-
th a mea-
sre contai-
ng about a
nt lesse
en a pecke.
Marke 4.
. luke 8.
8. and 11.

1. Pet. 2.
.

15 Neither doe men ||light a candle, and put it vnder a *bushell : but on a candlesticke, and it giueth light vnto all that are in the house.

16 Let your light so shine before men, * that they may see your good workes, and glorifie your father which is in heauen.

17 ¶ Thinke not that I am come to destroy the lawe or the Prophets. I am not come to destroy, but to fulfill.

Luke 16.
.

18 For verily I say vnto you, *Till heauen and earth passe, one iote or one title, shall in no wise passe from the law, till all be fulfilled.

Iames 2.
.

19 *Whosoeuer therfore shall breake one of these least commaundements, and shall teach men so, he shall be called the least in the kingdome of heauen : but whosoeuer shall doe, and teach *them*, the same shall be called great in the king-dome of heauen.

20 For I say vnto you, That except your righteousnesse shall exceede the righteousnesse of the Scribes and Pha-risees, yee shall in no case enter into the kingdome of heauen.

21 ¶ Yee haue heard, that it was saide || by them of old time, *Thou shalt not kill : and, Whosoeuer shall kill, shalbe in danger of the iudgement.

Or, to them
Exod. 20.
3. deut. 5.
7.

22 But I say vnto you, that who-soeuer is angry with his brother with-out a cause, shall be in danger of the Iudgement : and whosoeuer shall say to his brother, Racha, shal be in danger of the counsell : but whosoeuer shall say, *Thou* foole, shalbe in danger of hell fire.

23 Therefore if thou bring thy gift to the altar, and there remembrest that thy brother hath ought against thee :

24 Leaue there thy gift before the altar, and goe thy way, first be reconci-led to thy brother, and then come and offer thy gift.

* Luke 12.
58.

25 *Agree with thine aduersarie quickly, whiles thou art in the way with him : least at any time the aduer-sarie deliuer thee to the iudge, and the iudge deliuer thee to the officer, and thou be cast into prison.

26 Verily I say vnto thee, thou shalt by no meanes come out thence, till thou hast payd the vttermost far-thing.

27 ¶ Yee haue heard that it was said by them of old time, * Thou shalt not commit adulterie.

* Exod. 20.
14.

28 But I say vnto you, That who-soeuer looketh on a woman to lust after her, hath committed adulterie with her already in his heart.

29 *And if thy right eie ||offend thee, plucke it out, and cast it from thee. For it is profitable for thee that one of thy members should perish, and not that thy whole body should be cast into hell.

* Chap. 18.
8. marke 9.
47.
|| Or, doe
cause thee to
offend.

30 And if thy right hand offend thee, cut it off, and cast it from thee. For it is profitable for thee that one of thy mem-bers should perish, and not that thy whole body should be cast into hell.

31 It hath beene said, *Whosoeuer shall put away his wife, let him giue her a writing of diuorcement.

* Deut. 24.
1. luke 16.
18. 1. cor.
7. 10.

32 But I say vnto you, that whoso-euer shall put away his wife, sauing for the cause of fornication, causeth her to commit adultery : and whosoeuer shall marie her that is diuorced, committeth adulterie.

33 ¶ Againe, yee haue heard that it hath beene said by them of old time, * Thou shalt not forsweare thy selfe, but shalt performe vnto the Lord thine othes.

* Exod. 20.
7. leuit. 19.
12. deut. 5.
11.

34 But I say vnto you, Sweare not at all, neither by heauen, for it is Gods throne :

35 Nor by the earth, for it is his foot-stoole : neither by Hierusalem, for it is the citie of the great king.

36 Neither shalt thou sweare by thy head, because thou canst not make one haire white or blacke.

37 *But let your communication bee Yea, yea : Nay, nay : For whatsoeuer is more then these, commeth of euill.

* Iam. 5. 12.

38 ¶ Yee haue heard that it hath beene said, *An eie for an eie, and a tooth for a tooth.

* Exod. 21.
24. leuit. 24
20. deut. 19
21.

39 But I say vnto you, *that yee re-sist not euill : but whosoeuer shall smite thee on thy right cheeke, turne to him the other also.

* Luke 6.
29. rom. 12.
17. 1. cor. 6.
7.

40 And

40 And if any man will sue thee at the law, and take away thy coate, let him haue thy cloake also.

41 And whosoeuer shall compell thee to goe a mile, goe with him twaine.

* Deut. 15. 8.

42 Giue to him that asketh thee : and * from him that would borrow of thee, turne not thou away.

* Leuit. 19. 18.

43 ¶ Yee haue heard, that it hath beene said, * Thou shalt loue thy neighbour, and hate thine enemie :

* Luke 6. 27.

44 But I say vnto you, * Loue your enemies, blesse them that curse you, doe good to them that hate you,

* Luke 23. 34. acts 7. 60.

and * pray for them which despitefully vse you, and persecute you :

45 That yee may be the children of your father which is in heauen : for he maketh his sunne to rise on the euill and on the good, and sendeth raine on the iust, and on the vniust.

* Luke 6. 32.

46 * For if yee loue them which loue you, what reward haue yee ? Doe not euen the Publicanes the same ?

47 And if yee salute your brethren only, what do you more *then others?* Doe not euen the Publicanes so ?

48 Be yee therefore perfect, euen as your father, which is in heauen, is perfect.

CHAP. VI.

1 Christ continueth his Sermon in the Mount, speaking of almes, 5 prayer, 14 forgiuing our brethren, 16 fasting, 19 where our treasure is to be layed vp, 24 of seruing God, and Mammon, 25 Exhorteth not to bee carefull for worldly things : 33 but to seeke Gods kingdome.

‖ Or, with.

Ake heed that yee doe not your almes before men, to bee seene of them : otherwise yee haue no reward ‖ of your father which is in heauen.

* Rom. 12. 8
‖ Or, cause not a trumpet to be sounded.

2 Therefore, * when thou doest thine almes, ‖ doe not sound a trumpet before thee, as the hypocrites doe, in the Synagogues, and in the streetes, that they may haue glory of men. Verily, I say vnto you, they haue their reward.

3 But when thou doest almes, let not thy left hand know, what thy right doeth :

4 That thine almes may be in secret : And thy father which seeth in secret, himselfe shall reward thee openly.

5 ¶ And when thou prayest, thou shalt not be as the hypocrites are : for

they loue to pray standing in the Synagogues, and in the corners of the streets, that they may be seene of men. Verily I say vnto you, they haue their reward.

6 But thou when thou prayest, enter into thy closet, and when thou hast shut thy doore, pray to thy father which is in secret, and thy father which seeth in secret, shall reward thee openly.

7 But when yee pray, vse not vaine * repetitions, as the heathen doe. For they thinke that they shall be heard for their much speaking.

* Ecclus. 16.

8 Be not yee therefore like vnto them : For your father knoweth what things yee haue neede of, before yee aske him.

9 After this maner therefore pray yee : * Our father which art in heauen, hallowed be thy name.

* Luke 11

10 Thy kingdome come. Thy will be done, in earth, as it is in heauen.

11 Giue vs this day our daily bread.

12 And forgiue vs our debts, as we forgiue our debters.

13 And lead vs not into temptation, but deliuer vs from euill : For thine is the kingdome, and the power, and the glory, for euer, Amen.

14 * For, if yee forgiue men their trespasses, your heauenly father will also forgiue you.

* Marke 25.

15 But, if yee forgiue not men their trespasses, neither will your father forgiue your trespasses.

16 ¶ Moreouer, when yee fast, be not as the Hypocrites, of a sad countenance : for they disfigure their faces, that they may appeare vnto men to fast : Verily I say vnto you, they haue their reward.

17 But thou, when thou fastest, anoint thine head, and wash thy face :

18 That thou appeare not vnto men to fast, but vnto thy father which is in secret : and thy father which seeth in secret, shall reward thee openly.

19 ¶ Lay not vp for your selues treasures vpon earth, where moth and rust doth corrupt, and where theeues breake thorow, and steale.

20 * But lay vp for your selues treasures in heauen, where neither moth nor rust doth corrupt, & where theeues doe not breake thorow, nor steale.

* Luke 1 33. 1. tim 19.

21 For where your treasure is, there will your heart be also.

22 * The light of the body is the eye :

* Luke 1 34.

If

If therefore thine eye be single, thy whole body ſhalbe full of light.

23 But if thine eye be euill, thy whole body ſhall be full of darkneſſe. If therfore the light that is in thee be darkeneſſe, how great is that darkeneſſe?

24 ¶ *No man can ſerue two maſters : for either he will hate the one and loue the other, or elſe hee will holde to the one, and deſpiſe the other. Ye cannot ſerue God and Mammon.

25 Therfore I ſay vnto you, *Take no thought for your life, what yee ſhall eate, or what ye ſhall drinke, nor yet for your body, what yee ſhall put on : Is not the life more then meate? and the body then raiment?

26 Behold the foules of the aire : for they ſow not, neither do they reape, nor gather into barnes, yet your heauenly father feedeth them. Are yee not much better then they?

27 Which of you by taking thought, can adde one cubite vnto his ſtature?

28 And why take ye thought for raiment? Conſider the lillies of the field, how they grow : they toile not, neither doe they ſpinne.

29 And yet I ſay vnto you, that euen Solomon in all his glory, was not arayed like one of theſe.

30 Wherefore, if God ſo clothe the graſſe of the field, which to day is, and to morrow is caſt into the ouen : ſhall he not much more clothe you, O yee of little faith?

31 Therefore take no thought, ſaying, What ſhall we eate? or, what ſhall we drinke? or wherewithall ſhall wee be clothed?

32 (For after all theſe things doe the Gentiles ſeeke :) for your heauenly father knoweth that ye haue neede of all theſe things.

33 But ſeeke ye firſt the kingdome of God, and his righteouſneſſe, and all theſe things ſhalbe added vnto you.

34 Take therefore no thought for the morrow : for the morrow ſhall take thought for the things of it ſelfe : ſufficient vnto the day is the euill thereof.

CHAP. VII.

1 Chriſt ending his Sermon in the Mount, reprooueth raſh iudgement, 6 Forbiddeth to caſt holy things to dogges, 7 Exhorteth to prayer, 13 To enter in at the ſtrait gate, 15 To beware of falſe prophets, 21 Not to be hearers, but doers of the word : 24 like

houſes builded on a rocke, 26 And not on the ſand.

Vdge *not, that ye be not iudged.

2 For with what iudgment ye iudge, yee ſhall be iudged : *and with what meaſure ye mete, it ſhall be meaſured to you againe.

3 *And why beholdeſt thou the mote that is in thy brothers eye, but conſidereſt not the beame that is in thine owne eye?

4 Or how wilt thou ſay to thy brother, Let mee pull out the mote out of thine eye, and beholde, a beame is in thine owne eye?

5 Thou hypocrite, firſt caſt out the beame out of thine owne eye : and then ſhalt thou ſee clearely to caſt out the mote out of thy brothers eye.

6 ¶ Giue not that which is holy vnto the dogs, neither caſt ye your pearles before ſwine : leſt they trample them vnder their feete, and turne againe and rent you.

7 ¶ *Aske, and it ſhalbe giuen you : ſeeke, and ye ſhall finde : knocke, and it ſhalbe opened vnto you.

8 For euery one that aſketh, receiueth : and he that ſeeketh, findeth : and to him that knocketh, it ſhalbe opened.

9 Or what man is there of you, whom if his ſonne aſke bread, will hee giue him a ſtone?

10 Or if he aſke a fiſh, will hee giue him a ſerpent?

11 If ye then being euill, know how to giue good giftes vnto your children, how much more ſhall your Father which is in heauen, giue good things to them that aſke him?

12 Therefore all things *whatſoeuer ye would that men ſhould doe to you, doe ye euen ſo to them : for this is the Law and the Prophets.

13 ¶ *Enter ye in at the ſtrait gate, for wide is the gate, and broad is the way that leadeth to deſtruction, and many there be which goe in thereat :

14 ‖Becauſe ſtrait is the gate, and narrow is the way which leadeth vnto life, and few there be that finde it.

15 ¶ Beware of falſe prophets which come to you in ſheepes clothing, but inwardly they are rauening wolues.

16 Yee ſhall knowe them by their fruits : *Doe men gather grapes of thornes, or figges of thiſtles?

17 Euen

Margin notes (left column)
uke 16.

uke 12.
psal. 55.
1. pet.

Margin notes (right column)
* Luk. 6. 37.
rom. 2. 1.

* Mar. 4. 24.
luke 6. 38.

* Luk. 6. 41.

* Chap. 21.
22. marke
11. 24. luke
11. 9. iohn
16. 24. iam.
1. 6.

* Luk. 6. 31.

* Luk. 13.
24.

‖ Or, how.

* Luk. 6. 43.

17 Euen so, euery good tree bringeth forth good fruit : but a corrupt tree bringeth forth euill fruit.

18 A good tree cannot bring forth euil fruit, neither can a corrupt tree bring forth good fruit.

* Cha. 3. 10

19 * Euery tree that bringeth not forth good fruit, is hewen downe, and cast into the fire.

20 Wherefore by their fruits ye shall know them.

* Rom. 2. 13
iam. 1. 22.

21 ¶ Not euery one that saith vnto me, * Lord, Lord, shall enter into the kingdome of heauen : but he that doth the will of my father which is in heauen.

22 Many will say to me in that day, Lord, Lord, haue we not prophecied in thy name? and in thy name haue cast out deuils? and in thy name done many wonderfull works?

* Luk. 13. 27
* Psal. 6. 8.

23 And then wil I professe vnto them, * I neuer knew you : * Depart from me, ye that worke iniquity.

* Luk. 6. 47.

24 ¶ Therefore, * whosoeuer heareth these sayings of mine, and doeth them, I wil liken him vnto a wise man, which built his house vpon a rocke :

25 And the raine descended, and the floods came, and the windes blew, and beat vpon that house : and it fell not, for it was founded vpon a rocke.

26 And euery one that heareth these sayings of mine, and doeth them not, shall bee likened vnto a foolish man, which built his house vpon the sand :

27 And the raine came, and the floods came, and the windes blew, and beat vpon that house, and it fell, and great was the fall of it.

* Mar. 1. 22
luke 4. 32.

28 And it came to passe, when Iesus had ended these sayings, * the people were astonished at his doctrine.

29 For he taught them as one hauing authoritie, and not as the Scribes.

CHAP. VIII.

2 Christ clenseth the leper, 5 healeth the Centurions seruant, 14 Peters mother in lawe, 16 and many other diseased : 18 Sheweth how he is to be followed : 23 stilleth the tempest on the Sea, 28 driueth the deuils out of two men possessed, 31 and suffereth them to goe into the swine.

* Mar. 1. 40.
luke 5. 12.

W Hen he was come downe from the Mountaine, great multitudes folowed him.

2 * And behold, there came a leper, and worshipped him, saying, Lord, If thou wilt, thou canst make me cleane.

3 And Iesus put forth his hand, and touched him, saying, I will, bee thou cleane. And immediatly his leprosie was cleansed.

4 And Iesus saith vnto him, See thou tell no man, but go thy way, shew thy selfe to the priest, and offer the gift that * Moses commanded, for a testimonie vnto them.

* Leui.

5 ¶ * And when Iesus was entred into Capernaum, there came vnto him a Centurion, beseeching him,

* Luke

6 And saying, Lord, my seruant lieth at home sicke of the palsie, grieuously tormented.

7 And Iesus saith vnto him, I will come, and heale him.

8 The Centurion answered, and said, Lord, I am not worthy that thou shouldest come vnder my roofe : but speake the word onely, and my seruant shalbe healed.

9 For I am a man vnder authority, hauing souldiers vnder me : and I say to this man, Goe, and he goeth : and to another, Come, and he commeth : and to my seruant, Doe this, and he doth it.

10 When Iesus heard it, he marueiled, and said to them that followed, Verely, I say vnto you, I haue not found so great faith, no not in Israel.

11 And I say vnto you, that many shall come from the East and West, and shal sit downe with Abraham, and Isaac, & Iacob, in the kingdome of heauen:

12 But the children of the kingdome shall be cast out into outer darkenesse : there shalbe weeping and gnashing of teeth.

13 And Iesus said vnto the Centurion, Go thy way, and as thou hast beleeued, so be it done vnto thee. And his seruant was healed in the self same houre.

* Mar.
luke 4.

14 ¶ * And when Iesus was come into Peters house, hee saw his wiues mother laid, and sicke of a feuer :

15 And he touched her hand, and the feuer left her : and she arose, and ministred vnto them.

* Mar.
luke 4.

16 ¶ * When the Euen was come, they brought vnto him many that were possessed with deuils : and hee cast out the spirits with his worde, and healed all that were sicke,

* Esai.
1. pet. 2.

17 That it might be fulfilled which which was spoken by Esaias the Prophet, saying, * Himselfe tooke our infirmities,

mities, and bare our sicknesses.

18 ¶ Now when Iesus saw great multitudes about him, hee gaue commaundement to depart vnto the other side.

Luke 9.

19 * And a certaine Scribe came, and said vnto him, Master, I will follow thee whithersoeuer thou goest.

20 And Iesus saith vnto him, The Foxes haue holes, and the birds of the ayre haue nests : but the sonne of man hath not where to lay his head.

21 And another of his Disciples said vnto him, Lord, suffer me first to goe, and bury my father.

22 But Iesus said vnto him, Follow me, & let the dead, bury their dead.

23 ¶ And when he was entred into a ship, his Disciples followed him.

Marke. 4.
. luke 8.
.

24 * And behold, there arose a great tempest in the Sea, insomuch that the ship was couered with the waues : but he was asleepe.

25 And his Disciples came to him, and awoke, saying, Lord, saue vs : we perish.

26 And he saith vnto them, Why are yee fearefull, O yee of litle faith? Then hee arose, and rebuked the winds and the Sea, and there was a great calme.

27 But the men marueiled, saying, What maner of man is this, that euen the winds and the Sea obey him ?

Marke 5.
luk. 8.
5.

28 ¶ * And when hee was come to the other side, into the countrey of the Gergesenes, there met him two possessed with deuils, comming out of the tombes, exceeding fierce, so that no man might passe by that way.

29 And behold, they cryed out, saying, What haue we to doe with thee, Iesus thou sonne of God ? Art thou come hither to torment vs befor y time?

30 And there was a good way off from them, an heard of many swine, feeding.

31 So the deuils besought him, saying, If thou cast vs out, suffer vs to goe away into the herd of swine.

32 And he said vnto them, Goe. And when they were come out, they went into the herd of swine : and behold, the whole herd of swine ranne violently downe a steepe place into the Sea, and perished in the waters.

33 And they that kept them, fled, and went their waies into the citie, and told euery thing, and what was befallen to the possessed of the deuils.

34 And behold, the whole citie came out to meete Iesus : and when they saw him, they besought him that hee would depart out of their coasts.

CHAP. IX.

2 Christ curing one sicke of the palsey, 9 calleth Matthew from the receite of custome, 10 eateth with Publicanes, and sinners, 14 defendeth his Disciples for not fasting, 20 cureth the bloody issue, 23 raiseth from death Iairus daughter, 27 giueth sight to two blind men, 32 healeth a dumbe man possessed of a deuil, 36 and hath compassion of the multitude.

Nd hee entred into a ship, and passed ouer, and came into his owne citie.

2 * And behold, they brought to him a man sicke of the palsie, lying on a bed : and Iesus seeing their faith, said vnto the sicke of the palsie, Sonne, be of good cheere, thy sinnes be forgiuen thee.

* Marke 2. 3
luke 5. 18.

3 And behold, certaine of the Scribes said within themselues, This man blasphemeth.

4 And Iesus knowing their thoughts, said, Wherefore thinke yee euill in your hearts ?

5 For whether is easier to say, Thy sinnes be forgiuen thee : or to say, Arise, and walke ?

6 But that yee may know that the sonne of man hath power on earth to forgiue sinnes, (Then saith hee to the sicke of the palsie) Arise, take vp thy bed, and goe vnto thine house.

7 And he arose, and departed to his house.

8 But when the multitudes saw it, they marueiled, & glorified God, which had giuen such power vnto men.

9 ¶ * And as Iesus passed forth from thence, he saw a man named Matthew, sitting at the receite of custome : and he saith vnto him, Follow me. And he arose and followed him.

* Marke 2.
14. luke 5.
27.

10 ¶ And it came to passe, as Iesus sate at meate in the house, behold, many publicanes and sinners, came and sate downe with him and his Disciples.

11 And when the Pharisees saw *it*, they said vnto his disciples, Why eateth your master with publicanes & sinners.

12 But when Iesus heard *that*, hee said vnto them, They that be whole neede not a Physicion, but they that are sicke.

13 But

* Ose. 6. 6.
chap. 12. 7.

* 1. Tim. 1.
25.

* Mar. 2. 18.
luke 5. 33.

‖ Or, raw, or
vnwrought
cloth.

* Mar. 5. 22.
luke 8. 41.

‖ Or, this
same.

13 But goe ye and learne what that meaneth, *I will haue mercy and not sacrifice : for I am not come to call the righteous, *but sinners to repentance.

14 ¶ Then came to him the disciples of Iohn, saying, *Why doe we and the Pharisees fast oft, but thy disciples fast not?

15 And Iesus saide vnto them, Can the children of the bride-chamber mourne, as long as the bridegrome is with them? But the dayes will come when the bridegrome shall bee taken from them, and then shall they fast.

16 No man putteth a piece of ‖new cloth vnto an olde garment : for that which is put in to fill it vp, taketh from the garment, & the rent is made worse.

17 Neither doe men put new wine into old bottels : else the bottels breake, and the wine runneth out, and the bottels perish : but they put new wine into new bottels, and both are preserued.

18 ¶ *While hee spake these things vnto them, beholde, there came a certaine ruler and worshipped him, saying, My daughter is euen now dead : but come, and lay thy hand vpon her, and she shall liue.

19 And Iesus arose, and followed him, and so did his disciples.

20 (¶ And behold, a woman which was diseased with an issue of blood twelue yeeres, came behinde him, and touched the hemme of his garment.

21 For she said within her selfe, If I may but touch his garment, I shall be whole.

22 But Iesus turned him about, and when he saw her, he said, Daughter, bee of good comfort, thy faith hath made thee whole. And the woman was made whole from that houre.)

23 And when Iesus came into the rulers house, and saw the minstrels and the people making a noise,

24 He said vnto them, Giue place, for the mayd is not dead, but sleepeth. And they laughed him to scorne.

25 But when the people were put foorth, he went in, and tooke her by the hand : and the mayd arose.

26 And ‖the fame hereof went abroad into all that land.

27 ¶ And when Iesus departed thence, two blinde men followed him, crying, and saying, Thou sonne of Dauid, haue mercy on vs.

28 And when he was come into the house, the blinde men came to him : and Iesus saith vnto them, Beleeue ye that I am able to doe this? They said vnto him, Yea, Lord.

29 Then touched he their eyes, saying, According to your faith, bee it vnto you.

30 And their eyes were opened : and Iesus straitly charged them, saying, See that no man know it.

31 But they, when they were departed, spread abroad his fame in all that countrey.

32 ¶ *As they went out, beholde, they brought to him a dumbe man possessed with a deuill.

33 And when the deuill was cast out, the dumbe spake, and the multitudes marueiled, saying, It was neuer so seene in Israel.

34 But the Pharisees said, *He casteth out the deuils through the prince of the deuils.

35 *And Iesus went about all the cities and villages, teaching in their Synagogues, and preaching the Gospel of the kingdome, and healing euery sickenesse, and euery disease among the people.

36 ¶ *But when he saw the multitudes, he was moued with compassion on them, because they ‖fainted, and were scattered abroad, *as sheepe hauing no shepheard.

37 Then saith he vnto his disciples, *The haruest truely is plenteous, but the labourers are few.

38 Pray ye therefore the Lord of the haruest, that hee will send foorth labourers into his haruest.

CHAP. X.

1 Christ sendeth out his twelue Apostles, enabling them with power to doe miracles, 5 giueth them their charge, teacheth them, 16 comforteth them against persecutions : 40 and promiseth a blessing to those that receiue them.

Nd *when hee had called vnto him his twelue disciples, he gaue them power ‖against vncleane spirits, to cast them out, and to heale all maner of sickenesse, and all maner of disease.

2 Now the names of the twelue Apostles are these : The first, Simon, who is called Peter, and Andrew his brother,

* Luke
14.

* Chap.
24. mar.
3. 22. lu.
11. 15.

* Mar.
luke 13.

* Mar.

‖ Or, we
tyred an
lay dow.
* Num.
17.

* Luke
2.

* Mar.
luke 9.

‖ Or, ou

brother, Iames the sonne of Zebedee, and Iohn his brother:

3 Philip, and Bartholomew, Thomas, and Matthew the Publicane, Iames the sonne of Alpheus, and Lebbeus, whose surname was Thaddeus:

4 Simon the Canaanite, and Iudas Iscariot, who also betrayed him.

5 These twelue Iesus sent foorth, and commanded them, saying, Goe not into the way of the Gentiles, and into *any* city of the Samaritans enter ye not:

6 * But goe rather to the lost sheepe of the house of Israel.

7 And as yee goe, preach, saying, * The kingdome of heauen is at hand:

8 Heale the sicke, cleanse the lepers, raise the dead, cast out deuils: freely ye haue receiued, freely giue.

9 * ‖ Prouide neither gold, nor siluer, nor brasse in your purses:

10 Nor scrippe for your iourney, neither two coats, neither shooes, nor yet staues: (* for the workeman is worthy of his meat.)

11 * And into whatsoeuer city or towne ye shall enter, inquire who in it is worthy, and there abide till yee goe thence.

12 And when ye come into an house, salute it.

13 And if the house be worthy, let your peace come vpon it: but if it be not worthy, let your peace returne to you.

14 * And whosoeuer shall not receiue you, nor heare your words: when yee depart out of that house, or city, * shake off the dust of your feete.

15 Verely I say vnto you, it shall be more tolerable for the land of Sodom and Gomorrha in the day of iudgment, then for that citie.

16 ¶ * Behold, I send you foorth as sheepe in the middest of wolues: be yee therefore wise as serpents, and ‖ harmelesse as doues.

17 But beware of men: for they will deliuer you vp to the Councils, and they will scourge you in their Synagogues,

18 And yee shall be brought before Gouernours and Kings for my sake, for a testimonie against them, and the Gentiles.

19 * But when they deliuer you vp, take no thought, how or what ye shall speake, for it shall bee giuen you in that same houre what ye shall speake.

20 For it is not yee that speake, but the Spirit of your Father, which speaketh in you.

21 * And the brother shall deliuer vp the brother to death, and the father the childe: and the children shall rise vp against their parents, and cause them to be put to death.

22 And yee shall be hated of all men for my Names sake: * but he that endureth to the end, shalbe saued.

23 But when they persecute you in this citie, flee ye into another: for verely I say vnto you, ye shall not ‖ haue gone ouer the cities of Israel, till the Sonne of man be come.

24 * The disciple is not aboue his master, nor the seruant aboue his lord.

25 It is enough for the disciple that he be as his master, and the seruant as his Lord: If they haue called the Master of the house Beelzebub, how much more shall they call them of his household?

26 Feare them not therefore: * for there is nothing couered, that shall not be reueiled; and hidde, that shall not be knowen.

27 What I tell you in darkenesse, *that* speake yee in light: and what yee heare in the eare, that preach yee vpon the house tops.

28 * And feare not them which kill the body, but are not able to kill the soule: but rather feare him which is able to destroy both soule and body in hell.

29 Are not two Sparrowes solde for a ‖ farthing? And one of them shall not fall on the ground without your Father.

30 * But the very haires of your head are all numbred.

31 Feare yee not therefore, ye are of more value then many Sparrowes.

32 * Whosoeuer therefore shall confesse mee before men, him will I confesse also before my Father which is in heauen.

33 * But whosoeuer shall deny me before men, him will I also deny before my Father which is in heauen.

34 * Thinke not that I am come to send peace on earth: I came not to send peace, but a sword.

35 For I am come to set a man at variance * against his father, & the daughter against her mother, and the daughter in law against her mother in law.

36 And

Margin notes (left column):
cts 13.
uke 10. 9
Mark. 6. 8.
e 9. 3.
22. 35.
r, get.
Tim. 5.
luke
7.
uk. 10. 8.
Mar. 6. 11.
Acts 13.
uk. 10. 3.
r, simple.
Marke 13.
, luke
, 11.

Margin notes (right column):
* Luke 21. 16.
* Mark. 13. 13.
‖ Or, end or finish.
* Luk. 6. 40. iohn 13. 16.
* Mar. 4. 22. luke 8. 17. and 12. 2.
* Luk. 12. 4.
‖ It is in valuehalfepeny farthing, in the originall: as being the tenth part of the Romane peny.
* 2. Sam. 14. 11. actes 27. 34.
* Luk. 12. 8.
* Mar. 8. 38. luke 9. 26. 2. tim. 2. 12.
* Luke 12. 51.
* Mic. 7. 6.

36 And a mans foes *shalbe* they of his owne houshold.

37 *He that loueth father or mother more then me, is not worthy of me : and he that loueth sonne or daughter more then me, is not worthy of me.

38 *And he that taketh not his crosse, and followeth after me, is not worthy of me.

39 *He that findeth his life, shall lose it : and he that loseth his life for my sake, shall find it.

40 ¶ *He that receiueth you, receiueth me : and he that receiueth mee, receiueth him that sent me.

41 He that receiueth a Prophet in the name of a Prophet, shall receiue a Prophets reward : and he that receiueth a righteous man, in the name of a righteous man, shal receiue a righteous mans reward.

42 *And whosoeuer shall giue to drinke vnto one of these litle ones, a cup of cold water onely, in the name of a disciple, verily I say vnto you, hee shall in no wise lose his reward.

CHAP. XI.

2 Iohn sendeth his disciples to Christ. 7 Christs testimonie concerning Iohn. 18 The opinion of the people, both concerning Iohn, and Christ. 20 Christ vpbraideth the vnthankfulnesse, and vnrepentance of Chorazin, Bethsaida, and Capernaum : 25 and praising his fathers wisedome in reueiling the Gospel to the simple, 28 hee calleth to him all such as feele the burden of their sinnes.

And it came to passe, when Iesus had made an end of commaunding his twelue Disciples, hee departed thence to teach and to preach in their cities.

2 *Now when Iohn had heard in the prison the workes of Christ, he sent two of his disciples,

3 And said vnto him, Art thou hee that should come? Or doe wee looke for another?

4 Iesus answered and saide vnto them, Go and shew Iohn againe those things which ye doe heare and see :

5 *The blind recciue their sight, and the lame walke, the lepers are cleansed, and the deafe heare, the dead are raised vp, and *the poore haue the Gospel preached to them.

6 And blessed is he, whosoeuer shal not be offended in me.

7 ¶ And as they departed, Iesus began to say vnto the multitudes concerning Iohn, What went ye out into the wildernesse to see ? a reede shaken with the winde ?

8 But what went ye out for to see ? A man clothed in soft raiment? Behold, they that weare soft cloathing, are in kings houses.

9 But what went ye out for to see ? A Prophet ? yea, I say vnto you, and more then a Prophet.

10 For this is he of whom it is written, *Behold, I send my messenger before thy face, which shall prepare thy way before thee.

11 Verely I say vnto you, Among them that are borne of women, there hath not risen a greater then Iohn the Baptist : notwithstanding, hee that is least in the kingdome of heauen, is greater then he.

12 *And from the dayes of Iohn the Baptist, vntill now, the kingdome of heauen ||suffereth violence, and the violent take it by force.

13 For all the Prophets, and the Law prophecied vntill Iohn.

14 And if ye wil receiue *it*, this is *Elias which was for to come.

15 Hee that hath eares to heare, let him heare.

16 ¶ *But whereunto shall I liken this generation? It is like vnto children, sitting in the markets, and calling vnto their fellowes,

17 And saying, We haue piped vnto you, and ye haue not danced : wee haue mourned vnto you, and ye haue not lamented.

18 For Iohn came neither eating nor drinking, and they say, He hath a deuill.

19 The sonne of man came eating and drinking, and they say, Behold a man gluttonous, and a wine bibber, a friend of publicanes and sinners : but wisedom is iustified of her children.

20 ¶ *Then began he to vpbraid the cities wherein most of his mighty workes were done, because they repented not.

21 Woe vnto thee Chorazin, woe vnto thee Bethsaida : for if the mightie workes which were done in you, had bene done in Tyre and Sidon, they would haue repented long agoe in sackcloth and ashes.

22 But I say vnto you, It shall bee more tolerable for Tyre and Sidon at the day of iudgement, then for you.

23 And

Marginal notes (left column)

* Luke 14. 26.

* Chap. 16. 24. luke. 9. 23. mar. 8. 34.

* Iohn 12. 25.

* Luk. 10. 16. ioh. 13. 20.

* Mar. 9. 41

* Luk. 7. 18

* Esai. 35. 6

* Esai. 61. 1

Marginal notes (right column)

* Mala. 3

* Luk. 16.

|| Or, is gotten by force and they that thrust men.

* Mala. 4

* Luk. 7.

* Luk. 10. 13.

23 And thou Capernaum, which art exalted vnto heauen, shalt be brought downe to hell : For if the mighty works which haue beene done in thee, had bin done in Sodome, it would haue remained vntill this day.

24 But I say vnto you, that it shall be more tolerable for the land of Sodom, in ỹ day of iudgment, then for thee.

Luke 10.

25 ¶ *At that time Iesus answered, and said, I thanke thee, O Father, Lord of heauen and earth, because thou hast hid these things frō the wise & prudent, & hast reueiled them vnto babes.

26 Euen so, Father, for so it seemed good in thy sight.

Iohn 3. 35

27 *All things are deliuered vnto me of my father : and no man knoweth the sonne but the father: *neither knoweth any man the father, saue the sonne, and hee to whomsoeuer the sonne will reueile him.

Iohn 6.

28 ¶ Come vnto me all yee that labour, and are heauy laden, and I will giue you rest.

29 Take my yoke vpon you, and learne of me, for I am meeke and lowly in heart : *and yee shall find rest vnto your soules.

Iere. 6. 16

30 *For my yoke is easie, and my burden is light.

1. Iohn 5.

CHAP. XII.

1 Christ reprooueth the blindnesse of the Pharisees concerning the breach of the Sabbath, 3 by Scriptures, 9 by reason, 13 and by a miracle. 22 He healeth the man possessed that was blind, and dumbe. 31 Blasphemie against the holy Ghost shall neuer be forgiuen. 36 Account shalbe made of idle words. 38 He rebuketh the vnfaithfull, who seeke after a signe : 49 and sheweth who is his brothe, sister, and mother.

*Marke 2.
2, luke 6. 1.
eut. 23. 25*

AT that time, *Iesus went on the Sabbath day thorow the corne, & his Disciples were an hungred, and beganne to pluck the eares of corne, and to eate.

2 But when the Pharises saw it, they said vnto him, Behold, thy Disciples doe that which is not lawfull to doe vpon the Sabbath day.

1. Sam. 21.

3 But he said vnto them, Haue yee not read *what Dauid did when hee was an hungred, and they that were with him,

4 How he entred into the house of God, and did eate the shew bread, which

was not lawfull for him to eate, neither for them which were with him , *but only for the Priests ?

5 Or haue yee not read in the *law, how that on the Sabbath dayes the Priests in the Temple profane the Sabbath, and are blamelesse ?

6 But I say vnto you, that in this place is *one* greater then the Temple.

7 But if yee had knowen what this meaneth, *I will haue mercy, and not sacrifice, yee would not haue condemned the guiltlesse.

8 For the sonne of man is Lord euen of the Sabbath day.

9 *And when hee was departed thence, he went into their Synagogue.

10 ¶ And behold, there was a man which had his hand withered, and they asked him, saying, Is it lawfull to heale on the Sabbath dayes ? that they might accuse him.

11 And hee said vnto them , What man shal there be among you, that shall haue one sheepe : and if it fall into a pit on the Sabbath day, will hee not lay hold on it, and lift it out ?

12 How much then is a man better then a sheepe ? Wherefore it is lawfull to doe well on the Sabbath dayes.

13 Then saith he to the man, Stretch forth thine hand : and hee stretched it forth, and it was restored whole, like as the other.

14 ¶ Then the Pharises went out, and ‖held a counsell against him, how they might destroy him.

15 But when Iesus knew it, hee withdrew himselfe from thence : and great multitudes followed him, and he healed them all,

16 And charged them that they should not make him knowen :

17 That it might be fulfilled which was spoken by Esaias the Prophet, saying,

18 *Behold , my seruant whom I haue chosen, my beloued in whom my soule is well pleased : I will put my spirit vpon him, and he shall shew iudgement to the Gentiles.

19 He shall not striue, nor cry, neither shall any man heare his voice in the streets.

20 A bruised reed shal he not breake, and smoking flaxe shall he not quench, till he send forth iudgment vnto victory.

21 And in his name shall the Gentiles trust.

22 ¶ *Then

Exod. 29. 33. leuit. 8. 31. and 24. 9.
Num. 28. 9.

Osee 6. 7. chap. 9. 13.

Marke 3. 1. luke 6. 6.

‖ *Or, tooke counsell.*

Esai. 42. 1.

* Luke 11. 14.

22 ¶ * Then was brought vnto him one possessed with a deuill, blinde, and dumbe : and hee healed him, insomuch that the blinde and dumbe both spake and saw.

23 And all the people were amazed, and said, Is this the sonne of Dauid ?

* Cha. 9. 34

24 * But when the Pharisees heard it, they said, This *fellow* doeth not cast out deuils, but by Beelzebub the prince of the deuils.

25 And Iesus knew their thoughts, and said vnto them, Euery kingdome diuided against it selfe, is brought to desolation : and euery citie or house diuided against it selfe, shall not stand.

26 And if Satan cast out Satan, he is diuided against himselfe ; how shall then his kingdome stand ?

27 And if I by Beelzebub cast out deuils, by whom doe your children cast them out ? Therefore they shall be your Iudges.

28 But if I cast out deuils by the Spirit of God, then the kingdome of God is come vnto you.

29 Or else, how can one enter into a strong mans house, & spoile his goods, except hee first binde the strong man, and then he will spoile his house.

30 He that is not with me, is against me : and hee that gathereth not with me, scattereth abroad.

* Mar. 3. 28. luke 12. 10. 1. iohn 5. 16.

31 ¶ Wherefore I say vnto you, * All maner of sinne and blasphemie shall be forgiuen vnto men : but the blasphemie against the *holy* Ghost, shall not bee forgiuen vnto men.

32 And whosoeuer speaketh a word against the sonne of man, it shall be forgiuen him : but whosoeuer speaketh against the holy Ghost, it shall not be forgiuen him, neither in this world, neither in the world to come.

33 Either make the tree good, and his fruit good : Or else make the tree corrupt, and his fruit corrupt : For the tree is knowen by his fruit.

34 O generation of vipers, how can ye, being euil, speake good things ? * For

* Luke 6. 45.

out of the abundance of the heart the mouth speaketh.

35 A good man out of the good treasure of the heart, bringeth foorth good things : and an euill man out of the euill treasure, bringeth foorth euill things.

36 But I say vnto you, That euery idle word that men shall speake, they

shall giue accompt thereof in the day of Iudgement.

37 For by thy wordes thou shalt bee iustified, and by thy words thou shalt be condemned.

* Chap. 1. luke 29. 1. co 1. 22.

38 ¶ * Then certaine of the Scribes, and of the Pharisees, answered, saying, Master, we would see a signe from thee.

39 But hee answered, and said to them, An euill and adulterous generation seeketh after a signe, and there shall no signe be giuen to it, but the signe of the Prophet Ionas.

* Iona.

40 * For as Ionas was three dayes and three nights in the whales belly : so shal the sonne of man be three daies and three nights in the heart of the earth.

41 The men of Nineue shall rise in iudgement with this generation, and shall condemne it, * because they repented at the preaching of Ionas, and behold, a greater then Ionas is here.

* Iona.

* 1. Kin 1.

42 * The Queene of the South shall rise vp in the iudgement with this generation, and shall condemne it : for she came from the vttermost parts of the earth to heare the wisedome of Solomon, and behold, a greater then Solomon is here.

* Luke 24.

43 * When the vncleane spirit is gone out of a man, hee walketh thorow dry places, seeking rest, and findeth none.

44 Then he saith, I will returne into my house from whence I came out ; And when he is come, he findeth it emptie, swept, and garnished.

* Heb. and 10. 2. pet. 2

45 Then goeth he, and taketh with himselfe seuen other spirits more wicked then himselfe, and they enter in and dwell there : * And the last state of that man is worse then the first. Euen so shal it be also vnto this wicked generation.

* Mar 31. luk 20.

46 ¶ While he yet talked to the people, * behold, his mother and his brethren stood without, desiring to speake with him.

47 Then one saide vnto him, Behold, thy mother and thy brethren stand without, desiring to speake with thee.

48 But he answered, and said vnto him that told him, Who is my mother? And who are my brethren ?

49 And hee stretched forth his hand toward his disciples, and said, Behold, my mother and my brethren.

50 For whosoeuer shall doe the will of my Father which is in heauen, the same is my brother, and sister, and mother.

CHAP.

C H A P. XIII.

3 The parable of the Sower, and the seed: 18 the exposition of it. 24 The parable of the tares, 31 of the mustard seed, 33 of the leuen, 44 of the hidden treasure, 45 of the pearle, 47 of the drawnet cast into the Sea, 53 And how Christ is contemned of his own countrymen.

Mark. 4. 1. He same day went Iesus out of the house, *and sate by the sea side.

2 And great multitudes were gathered together vnto him, so that hee went into a ship, and sate, and the whole multitude stood on the shore.

3 And hee spake many things vnto **Luke 8. 5.** them in parables, saying, *Behold, a sower went foorth to sow.

4 And when he sowed, some seedes fell by the wayes side, and the foules came, and deuoured them vp.

5 Some fell vpon stony places, where they had not much earth : and foorthwith they sprung vp, because they had no deepenesse of earth.

6 And when the Sunne was vp, they were scorched : and because they had not root, they withered away.

7 And some fell among thorns : and the thornes sprung vp, & choked them.

8 But other fell into good ground, and brought foorth fruit, some an hundred folde, some sixtie folde, some thirty folde.

9 Who hath eares to heare, let him heare.

10 And the disciples came, and sayd vnto him, Why speakest thou vnto them in parables?

11 He answered, and said vnto them, Because it is giuen vnto you to know the mysteries of the kingdome of heauen, but to them it is not giuen.

Chap. 25. 12 *For whosoeuer hath, to him shall **8.** be giuen, and he shall haue more abundance : but whosoeuer hath not, from him shall be taken away, euen that hee hath.

13 Therefore speake I to them in parables : because they seeing, see not : and hearing, they heare not, neither doe they vnderstand.

14 And in them is fulfilled the prophecie of Esaias, which saith, *By hea-
Esai 6. 9.
mark. 4. 12. ring ye shall heare, and shall not vnder-
ke 8. 10. stand : and seeing yee shall see, and shall
oh. 12. 40. not perceiue.
cts 28. 26.
om. 11. 8. 15 For this peoples heart is waxed

grosse, and their eares are dull of hearing, and their eyes they haue closed, lest at any time they should see with their eyes, and heare with their eares, and should vnderstand with their heart, and should be conuerted, and I should heale them.

16 But blessed are your eyes, for they see : and your eares, for they heare.

17 For verely I say vnto you, *that *** Luke 10.** many Prophets, and righteous men **24.** haue desired to see those things which yee see, and haue not seene them : and to heare those things which ye heare, and haue not heard them.

18 ¶ Heare ye therefore the parable of the sower.

19 When any one heareth the word of the kingdome, and vnderstandeth it not, then commeth the wicked one, and catcheth away that which was sowen in his heart : this is hee which receiued seede by the way side.

20 But he that receiued the seed into stony places, the same is he that heareth the word, & anon with ioy receiueth it :

21 Yet hath hee not root in himselfe, but dureth for a while : for when tribulation or persecution ariseth because of the word, by and by he is offended.

22 He also that receiued seed among the thorns, is he that heareth the word, and the care of this world, and the deceitfulnesse of riches choke the word, and he becommeth vnfruitfull.

23 But he that receiued seed into the good ground, is hee that heareth the word, and vnderstandeth it, which also beareth fruit, and bringeth foorth, some an hundred fold, some sixtie, some thirty.

24 ¶ Another parable put he forth vnto them, saying ; The kingdome of heauen is likened vnto a man which sowed good seed in his field :

25 But while men slept, his enemy came & sowed tares among the wheat, and went his way.

26 But when the blade was sprung vp, and brought foorth fruit, then appeared the tares also.

27 So the seruants of the housholder came, and said vnto him, Sir, didst not thou sow good seede in thy field ? from whence then hath it tares ?

28 He said vnto them, An enemy hath done this. The seruants said vnto him, Wilt thou then that we goe and gather them vp ?

29 But he said, Nay : lest while yee gather

gather vp the tares, ye root vp also the wheat with them.

30 Let both grow together vntil the haruest : and in the time of haruest, I will say to the reapers, Gather ye together first the tares, and binde them in bundels to burne them : but gather the wheat into my barne.

31 ¶ Another parable put he foorth vnto them, saying, * The kingdome of heauen is like to a graine of mustard seed, which a man tooke, and sowed in his field.

32 Which indeed is the least of al seeds : but when it is growen, it is the greatest among herbes, and becommeth a tree : so that the birds of the aire come and lodge in the branches thereof.

33 ¶ *Another parable spake he vnto them, The kingdome of heauen is like vnto leauen, which a woman tooke, and hid in three †measures of meale, till the whole was leauened.

34 * All these things spake Iesus vnto the multitude in parables, and without a parable spake hee not vnto them :

35 That it might bee fulfilled which was spoken by the Prophet, saying, * I will open my mouth in parables, I wil vtter things which haue bin kept secret from the foundation of the world.

36 Then Iesus sent the multitude away, and went into the house : and his disciples came vnto him, saying, Declare vnto vs the parable of the tares of the field.

37 He answered, and said vnto them, Hee that soweth the good seed, is the sonne of man.

38 The field is the world. The good seed, are the children of the kingdome : but the tares are the children of the wicked one.

39 The enemie that sowed them, is the deuill. * The haruest, is the ende of the world. And the reapers are the Angels.

40 As therefore the tares are gathered and burnt in the fire : so shall it be in the end of this world.

41 The Sonne of man shall send forth his Angels, and they shall gather out of his kingdome all ‖things that offend, and them which doe iniquitie :

42 And shall cast them into a furnace of fire : there shall be wayling and gnashing of teeth.

43 * Then shall the righteous shine foorth as the Sunne, in the kingdome

of their father. Who hath eares to heare, let him heare.

44 ¶ Againe, the kingdome of heauen is like vnto treasure hid in a field : the which when a man hath found, hee hideth, and for ioy thereof goeth and selleth all that hee hath, and buyeth that field.

45 ¶ Againe, the kingdome of heauen is like vnto a marchant man, seeking goodly pearles :

46 Who when hee had found one pearle of great price, he went and solde all that he had, and bought it.

47 ¶ Againe, the kingdome of heauen is like vnto a net that was cast into the sea, and gathered of euery kind,

48 Which, when it was full, they drew to shore, and sate downe, and gathered the good into vessels, but cast the bad away.

49 So shall it be at the ende of the world : the Angels shal come forth, and seuer the wicked from among the iust,

50 And shal cast them into the furnace of fire : there shall be wailing, and gnashing of teeth.

51 Iesus saith vnto them, Haue ye vnderstood all these things ? They say vnto him, Yea, Lord.

52 Then said he vnto them, Therefore euery Scribe which is instructed vnto the kingdome of heauen, is like vnto a man that is an housholder, which bringeth foorth out of his treasure things new and old.

53 ¶ And it came to passe, that when Iesus had finished these parables, hee departed thence.

54 *And when hee was come into his owne countrey, he taught them in their Synagogue, insomuch that they were astonished, and said, Whence hath this man this wisedome, and these mighty works ?

55 *Is not this the Carpenters sonne ? Is not his mother called Marie ? and his brethren, Iames, and Ioses, and Simon, and Iudas ?

56 And his sisters, are they not all with vs ? whence then hath this man all these things ?

57 And they were offended in him. But Iesus said vnto them, * A Prophet is not without honour, saue in his owne countrey, and in his owne house.

58 And hee did not many mighty workes there, because of their vnbeliefe.

CHAP.

* Mar. 4. 30
luke 13. 19

* Luke 13.
20.

† The worde
in the Greek
is a measure
conteining
about a peck
and an halfe,
wanting little
more then
a pinte.
* Marke 4.
33.
* Psal. 78. 2.

* Ioel. 3. 13.
reue. 14. 15

‖ Or, scandales.

* Dan. 12. 3

* Marke
luke. 4. 1

* Ioh. 6.

* Mar. 6.
luke 4. 24
iohn 4. 4

CHAP. XIIII.

1 Herods opinion of Christ. 3 Wherefore Iohn Baptist was beheaded. 13 Iesus departeth into a desert place: 15 Where hee feedeth fiue thousand men with fiue loaues, and two fishes: 22 he walketh on the Sea to his Disciples: 34 and landing at Gennezaret, healeth the sicke by the touch of the hemme of his garment.

Marke 6.
4. luke 9. 7

AT that time * Herod the Tetrarch heard of the fame of Iesus,

2 And said vnto his seruants, This is Iohn the Baptist, hee is risen from the dead, and therfore mighty workes ||doe shew foorth themselues in him.

Or, are
rought by
im.
Luke 3.
9.

3 ¶ *For Herode had layd hold on Iohn, and bound him, and put him in prison for Herodias sake, his brother Philips wife.

Leuit. 18.
6. and 20.
4.

4 For Iohn said vnto him, *It is not lawfull for thee to haue her.

5 And when he would haue put him to death, hee feared the multitude, * because they counted him as a Prophet.

Chap. 21.
6.

6 But when Herods birth day was kept, the daughter of Herodias daunced before them, and pleased Herode.

7 Whereupon he promised with an oath, to giue her whatsoeuer she would aske.

8 And she, being before instructed of her mother, said, Giue me heere Iohn Baptists head in a charger.

9 And the king was sorie : neuerthelesse for the othes sake, and them which sate with him at meate, he commanded it to be giuen her :

10 And he sent, and beheaded Iohn in the prison.

11 And his head was brought in a charger, and giuen to the Damsell : and she brought it to her mother.

12 And his Disciples came, and took vp the body, and buried it, and went and told Iesus.

* Marke 6.
32. luke 9.
40.

13 ¶ *When Iesus heard of it, he departed thence by ship, into a desert place apart : and when the people had heard thereof, they followed him on foote, out of the cities.

14 And Iesus went forth, and saw a great multitude, and was mooued with compassion toward them, and he healed their sicke.

* Iohn 6. 5.
marke 6.
35.

15 ¶ *And when it was euening, his Disciples came to him, saying, This is a desert place, and the time is now past; send the multitude away, that they may goe into the villages, and buy themselues victuals.

16 But Iesus said vnto them, They neede not depart; giue yee them to eate.

17 And they say vnto him, We haue heere but fiue loaues, and two fishes.

18 He said, Bring them hither to me.

19 And hee commanded the multitude to sit downe on the grasse, & tooke the fiue loaues, and the two fishes, and looking vp to heauen, hee blessed, and brake, and gaue the loaues to his Disciples, and the Disciples to the multitude.

20 And they did all eat, & were filled: and they tooke vp of the fragments that remained twelue baskets full.

21 And they that had eaten, were about fiue thousand men, beside women and children.

22 ¶ And straightway Iesus constrained his Disciples to get into a ship, and to goe before him vnto the other side, while he sent the multitudes away.

* Marke 6.
46.

23 * And when he had sent the multitudes away, he went vp into a mountaine apart to pray : * and when the euening was come, he was there alone :

* Iohn 6.
16.

24 But the ship was now in the midst of the Sea, tossed with waues : for the wind was contrary.

25 And in the fourth watch of the night, Iesus went vnto them, walking on the Sea.

26 And when the Disciples saw him walking on the Sea, they were troubled, saying, It is a spirit : and they cried out for feare.

27 But straightway Iesus spake vnto them, saying, Be of good cheere: it is I, be not afraid.

28 And Peter answered him, and said, Lord, if it be thou, bid me come vnto thee on the water.

29 And he said, Come. And when Peter was come downe out of the ship, he walked on the water, to go to Iesus.

* Or, strong.

30 But when he saw the wind ||boysterous, he was afraid : and beginning to sinke, he cried, saying, Lord saue me.

31 And immediately Iesus stretched foorth his hand, and caught him, and said vnto him, O thou of little faith, wherefore didst thou doubt ?

32 And when they were come into the ship, the wind ceased.

33 Then they that were in the ship, came and worshipped him, saying, Of a trueth

* Marke 6.
53.

34 ¶ *And when they were gone o-
uer, they came into ỹ land of Genesaret.

35 And when the men of that place
had knowledge of him, they sent out into all that countrey round about, and
brought vnto him al that were diseased,

36 And besought him, that they
might onely touch the hemme of his
garment; and as many as touched,
were made perfectly whole.

CHAP. XV.

3 Christ reprooueth the Scribes, and Pharisees,
for transgressing Gods Commaundements
through their owne traditions: 11 teacheth
how that which goeth into the mouth, doeth
not defile a man. 21 He healeth the daughter of the woman of Canaan, 30 and other
great multitudes: 32 and with seuen loaues
and a few little fishes feedeth foure thousand
men, beside women and children.

* Mark. 7. 1.

THEN *came to Iesus
Scribes and Pharisees,
which were of Hierusa-
lem, saying,
2 Why do thy disciples
transgresse the tradition of the Elders?
for they wash not their handes when
they eat bread.

3 But hee answered, and said vnto
them, Why doe you also transgresse the
Commaundement of God by your tradition?

4 For God commaunded, saying,
* Exod. 20.
12. deut. 5.
16.
* Honour thy father and mother: And
* Exod. 21.
17. leui. 20.
9. pro. 20.
20.
* Mar. 7. 11,
12.
*hee that curseth father or mother, let
him die the death.

5 But yee say, Whosoeuer shall say
to his father or his mother, *It is a gift
by whatsoeuer thou mightest bee profited by me,

6 And honour not his father or his
mother, *hee shall be free.* Thus haue yee
made the Commaundement of God of
none effect by your tradition.

7 Yee hypocrites, well did Esaias
prophecie of you, saying,

* Esa. 29.
14.
8 *This people draweth nigh vnto
mee with their mouth, and honoureth
mee with their lips: but their heart is
farre from me.

9 But in vaine they do worship me,
teaching for doctrines, the commandements of men.

* Marke 7.
14.
10 ¶ *And he called the multitude, and
said vnto them, Heare and vnderstand.

11 Not that which goeth into the
mouth defileth a man: but that which

commeth out of the mouth, this defileth
a man.

12 Then came his disciples, and said
vnto him, Knowest thou that the Pharisees were offended after they heard
this saying?

* Ioh. 15. 2
13 But he answered, and said, *Euery
plant which my heauenly father hath
not planted, shalbe rooted vp.

* Luke 6.
39.
14 Let them alone: *they be blinde
leaders of the blinde. And if the blinde
lead the blinde, both shall fall into the
ditch.

* Mar. 7. 17
15 *Then answered Peter, and said
vnto him, Declare vnto vs this parable.

16 And Iesus said, Are yee also yet
without vnderstanding?

17 Doe not yee yet vnderstand, that
whatsoeuer entreth in at the mouth,
goeth into the belly, and is cast out into
the draught?

18 But those things which proceed
out of the mouth, come forth from the
heart, and they defile the man.

* Gen. 6. 5.
and 8. 21.
19 *For out of the heart proceed euill
thoughts, murders, adulteries, fornications, thefts, false witnes, blasphemies.

20 These are the things which defile a man: But to eate with vnwashen
hands, defileth not a man.

* Marke 7.
24.
21 ¶ *Then Iesus went thence, and
departed into the coastes of Tyre and
Sidon.

22 And behold, a woman of Canaan came out of the same coasts, & cried
vnto him, saying, Haue mercy on me, O
Lord, thou sonne of Dauid, my daughter is grieuously vexed with a deuill.

23 But he answered her not a word.
And his disciples came, and besought
him, saying, Send her away, for she cryeth after vs.

* Chap. 10
6.
24 But he answered, and said, *I am
not sent, but vnto the lost sheepe of the
house of Israel.

25 Then came she, and worshipped
him, saying, Lord, helpe me.

26 But he answered, and said, It is
not meete to take the childrens bread,
and to cast it to dogs.

27 And she said, Trueth Lord: yet
the dogs eat of the crummes which fall
from their masters table.

28 Then Iesus answered, and said
vnto her, O woman, great is thy faith:
be it vnto thee euen as thou wilt. And
her daughter was made whole from
that very houre.

29 *And

* Marke 7.
*1.

* Esay 35. 5.

* Mark. 8. 1.

29 *And Iesus departed frō thence, and came nigh vnto the sea of Galile, and went vp into a mountaine, and sate downe there.

30 *And great multitudes came vnto him, hauing with them those that were lame, blinde, dumbe, maimed, and many others, and cast them downe at Iesus feet, and he healed them :

31 Insomuch that the multitude wondred, when they saw the dumbe to speake, the maimed to be whole, the lame to walke, and the blind to see : and they glorified the God of Israel.

32 ¶ *Then Iesus called his disciples vnto him, and said, I haue compassion on the multitude, because they continue with me now three dayes, and haue nothing to eate : and I will not send them away fasting, lest they faint in the way.

33 And his disciples say vnto him, Whence should we haue so much bread in the wildernesse, as to fill so great a multitude ?

34 And Iesus saith vnto them, How many loaues haue yee ? And they said, Seuen, and a few little fishes.

35 And hee commaunded the multitude to sit downe on the ground.

36 And he tooke the seuen loaues and the fishes, and gaue thankes, and brake them, and gaue to his disciples, and the disciples to the multitude.

37 And they did all eate, and were filled : and they tooke vp of the broken meate that was left, seuen baskets full.

38 And they that did eat, were foure thousand men, beside women and children.

39 And he sent away the multitude, and tooke ship, and came into the coasts of Magdala.

CHAP. XVI.

1 The Pharises require a signe. 6 Iesus warneth his disciples of the leauen of the Pharises and Sadduces. 13 The peoples opinion of Christ, 16 and Peters confession of him. 21 Iesus foresheweth his death, 23 Reproouing Peter for disswading him from it: 24 And admonisheth those that will follow him, to beare the Crosse.

* Mar. 8. 11.
Luke 12. 54.

He *Pharises also, with the Sadduces, came, and tempting, desired him that hee would shew them a signe from heauen.

2 He answered, and said vnto them, When it is euening, yee say, It will bee faire weather : for the skie is red.

3 And in the morning, It will be foule weather to day : for the skie is red and lowring. O ye hypocrites, yee can discerne the face of the skie, but can ye not discerne the signes of the times ?

4 A wicked and adulterous generation seeketh after a signe, and there shall no signe be giuen vnto it, but the signe of the Prophet Ionas. And hee left them, and departed.

5 And when his disciples were come to the other side, they had forgotten to take bread.

6 ¶ Then Iesus said vnto them, Take heed and beware of the leauen of the Pharises, and of the Sadduces.

7 And they reasoned among themselues, saying, It is because we haue taken no bread.

8 Which when Iesus perceiued, he said vnto them, O ye of little faith, why reason ye among your selues, because ye haue brought no bread ?

9 *Doe ye not yet vnderstand, neither remember the fiue loaues of the fiue thousand, and how many baskets ye tooke vp ?

10 *Neither the seuen loaues of the foure thousand, and how many baskets ye tooke vp ?

11 How is it that ye doe not vnderstand, that I spake it not to you concerning bread, that ye should beware of the leauen of the Pharises, and of the Sadduces ?

12 Then vnderstood they how that he bade them not beware of the leauen of bread : but of the doctrine of the Pharisees, and of the Sadduces.

13 ¶ When Iesus came into the coasts of Cesarea Philippi, he asked his disciples, saying, *Whom doe men say, that I, the sonne of man, am ?

14 And they said, Some say that thou art Iohn the Baptist, some Elias, and others Ieremias, or one of ȳ Prophets.

15 He saith vnto them, But whom say ye that I am ?

16 And Simon Peter answered, and said, *Thou art Christ the sonne of the liuing God.

17 And Iesus answered, and said vnto him, Blessed art thou Simon Bar Iona : for flesh and blood hath not reueiled it vnto thee, but my Father which is in heauen.

18 And

* Chap. 14.
17.

* Chap. 15.
34.

* Mar. 8. 27.
luke 9. 18.

* Ioh. 6. 69.

18 And I say also vnto thee, that *thou art Peter, and vpon this rocke I will build my Church : and the gates of hell shall not preuaile against it.

19 * And I will giue vnto thee the keyes of the kingdome of heauen : and whatsoeuer thou shalt bind on earth, shall be bound in heauen : whatsoeuer thou shalt loose on earth, shall be loosed in heauen.

20 Then charged hee his disciples that they should tel no man that he was Iesus the Christ.

21 ¶ From that time foorth began Iesus to shew vnto his disciples, how that he must goe vnto Hierusalem, and suffer many things of the Elders and chiefe Priests & Scribes, and be killed, and be raised againe the third day.

22 Then Peter tooke him, and began to rebuke him, saying, Be it farre from thee Lord : This shal not be vnto thee.

23 But he turned, and said vnto Peter, Get thee behind mee, Satan, thou art an offence vnto me : for thou sauourest not the things that *be* of God, but those that *be* of men.

24 ¶ * Then said Iesus vnto his disciples, If any man will come after me, let him denie himselfe, and take vp his crosse, and follow me.

25 For whosoeuer will saue his life, shall lose it : and whosoeuer will lose his his life for my sake, shall finde it.

26 For what is a man profited, if hee shal gaine the whole world, and lose his owne soule ? Or what shall a man giue in exchange for his soule ?

27 For the sonne of man shall come in the glory of his father, with his Angels : * and then he shall reward euery man according to his works.

28 Verely I say vnto you, * There be some standing here, which shall not taste of death, till they see the Sonne of man comming in his Kingdome.

CHAP. XVII.

1 The transfiguration of Christ. 14 He healeth the lunatike, 22 foretelleth his owne passion, 24 and payeth tribute.

Nd *after six dayes, Iesus taketh Peter, Iames, and Iohn his brother, and bringeth them vp into an high mountaine apart,

2 And was transfigured before them,

and his face did shine as the Sunne, and his raiment was white as the light.

3 And behold, there appeared vnto them Moses, and Elias, talking with him.

4 Then answered Peter, and saide vnto Iesus, Lord, it is good for vs to be here : If thou wilt, let vs make here three tabernacles : one for thee, and one for Moses, and one for Elias.

5 * While he yet spake, behold, a bright cloud ouershadowed them : and behold a voyce out of the cloude, which saide, This is my beloued sonne, in whom I am well pleased : heare ye him.

6 And when the disciples heard it, they fell on their face, and were sore a-fraid.

7 And Iesus came and touched them, and said, Arise, and be not afraid.

8 And when they had lift vp their eyes, they saw no man, saue Iesus only.

9 And as they came downe from the mountaine, Iesus charged them, saying, Tell the vision to no man, vntil the sonne of man bee risen againe from the dead.

10 And his disciples asked him, saying, * Why then say the Scribes that Elias must first come ?

11 And Iesus answered, and said vnto them, Elias truely shall first come, and restore all things :

12 But I say vnto you, that Elias is come already, and they knew him not, but haue done vnto him whatsoeuer they listed : Likewise shall also the Son of man suffer of them.

13 Then the Disciples vnderstood that he spake vnto them of Iohn the Baptist.

14 ¶ * And when they were come to the multitude, there came to him a certaine man, kneeling downe to him, and saying,

15 Lord, haue mercie on my sonne, for he is lunatike, and sore vexed : for oft times he falleth into the fire, and oft into the water.

16 And I brought him to thy disciples, and they could not cure him.

17 Then Iesus answered, and said, O faithlesse and peruerse generation, how long shall I bee with you ? howe long shal I suffer you? bring him hither to me.

18 And Iesus rebuked the deuill, and hee departed out of him : and the childe was cured from that very houre.

19 Then

* Ioh. 1. 42.

* Ioh. 20. 23.

* Chap. 10. 38. mar. 8. 34.

* Psa. 62. 12 rom. 2. 6.

* Mar. 9. 1. luke 9. 27.

* Mark. 9. 2. luke 9. 28.

* 2. Pet. 1. 17.

* Chap. 11. 14. mark. 9. 11.

* Mar. 9. 17. luke 9. 38.

19 Then came the Disciples to Iesus apart, and said, Why could not we cast him out?

20 And Iesus said vnto them, Because of your vnbeliefe : for verily I say vnto you, *If yee haue faith as a graine of mustard seed, yee shall say vnto this mountaine ; Remoue hence to yonder place : and it shall remoue, and nothing shall be vnpossible vnto you.

* Luke 17. 6.

21 Howbeit, this kind goeth not out, but by prayer and fasting.

22 ¶ *And while they abode in Galilee, Iesus said vnto them, The sonne of man shall be betraied into the hands of men :

* Mat. 20. 17. mar. 9. 31. luke 9. 44.

23 And they shall kill him, and the third day he shall be raised againe : And they were exceeding sorie.

24 ¶ And when they were come to Capernaum, they that receiued ‖tribute money, came to Peter, and said, Doeth not your master pay tribute?

‖ Called in the originall Didrachma, being in value fifteene pence.

25 Hee saith, Yes. And when hee was come into the house, Iesus preuented him, saying, What thinkest thou, Simon? of whom doe the kings of the earth take custome or tribute? of their owne children, or of strangers?

26 Peter saith vnto him, Of strangers. Iesus saith vnto him, Then are the children free.

27 Notwithstanding, least we should offend them, goe thou to the Sea, and cast an hooke, and take vp the fish that first commeth vp : and when thou hast opened his mouth, thou shalt find ‖a piece of money : that take, and giue vnto them for me, and thee.

‖ Or, a stater. It is halfe an ounce of siluer, in value two shillings sixe pence, after fiue shillings the ounce.

CHAP. XVIII.

1 Christ warneth his Disciples to be humble and harmelesse : 7 To auoide offences, and not to despise the little ones : 15 Teacheth howe we are to deale with our brethren, when they offend vs : 21 And how oft to forgiue them : 23 Which hee setteth forth by a parable of the King, that tooke account of his seruants, 32 And punished him, who shewed no mercie to his fellowe.

* Marke 9. 33. luke 9. 46.

**A**T the same time came the Disciples vnto Iesus, saying, Who is the greatest in the Kingdome of heauen?

2 And Iesus called a little child

vnto him, and set him in the midst of them,

3 And said, Verily I say vnto you, *Except yee be conuerted, and become as little children, yee shall not enter into the kingdome of heauen.

* Chap. 19. 14. 1. cor. 14. 20.

4 Whosoeuer therefore shall humble himselfe as this little childe, the same is greatest in the Kingdome of heauen.

5 And who so shall receiue one such little child in my name, receiueth me.

6 *But who so shall offend one of these little ones which beleeue in me, it were better for him that a milstone were hanged about his necke, and that hee were drowned in the depth of the Sea.

* Marke 9. 42. luke 17. 1, 2.

7 ¶ Woe vnto the world because of offences : for it must needs be that offences come : but wo to that man by whom the offence commeth.

8 *Wherefore if thy hand or thy foote offend thee, cut them off, and cast them from thee : it is better for thee to enter into life halt or maimed, rather then hauing two hands or two feete, to be cast into euerlasting fire.

* Chap. 5. 30. mar. 9. 45.

9 And if thine eie offend thee, plucke it out, and cast it from thee : it is better for thee to enter into life with one eie, rather then hauing two eies, to be cast into hell fire.

10 Take heed that yee despise not one of these little ones : for I say vnto you, that in heauen their Angels do alwaies behold the face of my father which is in heauen.

11 *For the sonne of man is come to saue that which was lost.

* Luke 19. 10.

12 *How thinke yee? if a man haue an hundred sheepe, and one of them be gone astray, doth he not leaue the ninetie and nine, and goeth into the mountaines, and seeketh that which is gone astray?

* Luke 15. 4.

13 And if so be that he find it, Verily I say vnto you, hee reioyceth more of that sheepe, then of the ninetie and nine which went not astray.

14 Euen so, it is not the will of your father which is in heauen, that one of these little ones should perish.

15 ¶ Moreouer, *if thy brother shall trespasse against thee, goe and tell him his fault betweene thee and him alone : if he shall heare thee, thou hast gained thy brother.

* Leuit. 19. 17. luke 17. 3.

16 But if he will not heare thee, then take

* Deut. 19.
15. iohn 8.
17. 2. cor.
13. 1. hebr.
10. 28.

* 1. Cor. 5.
9. 2. thes. 3.
14.
* Iohn 20.
23. 1. cor.
5. 4.

* Luke 17.
4.

‖ A talent
is 750. oun-
ces of siluer,
which after
fiue shillings
the ounce, is
187.li. 10.s.

‖ Or, be-
sought him.

‖ The Ro-
mane penie
is the eighth
part of an
ounce, which
after 8. shil-
lings the
ounce is 7.d.
ob.

take with thee one or two more, that in * the mouth of two or three witnesses, euery word may be established.

17 And if hee shall neglect to heare them, tell it vnto the Church : But if he neglect to heare the Church, let him be vnto thee as an * heathen man, and a Publicane.

18 Verily I say vnto you, * Whatsoeuer ye shall binde on earth, shall bee bound in heauen : and whatsoeuer yee shall loose on earth, shall be loosed in heauen.

19 Againe I say vnto you, that if two of you shall agree on earth as touching any thing that they shall aske, it shall bee done for them of my father which is in heauen.

20 For where two or three are gathered together in my Name, there am I in the midst of them.

21 ¶ Then came Peter to him, and said, Lord, how oft shall my brother sinne against mee, and I forgiue him ? * till seuen times ?

22 Iesus saith vnto him, I say not vnto thee, Vntill seuen times : but, Vntill seuentie times seuen.

23 ¶ Therefore is the kingdome of heauen likened vnto a certaine king, which would take accompt of his seruants.

24 And when hee had begun to reckon, one was brought vnto him which ought him ten thousand ‖ talents.

25 But forasmuch as hee had not to pay, his lord commanded him to bee sold, and his wife, and children, and all that he had, and payment to be made.

26 The seruant therfore fell downe, and ‖ worshipped him, saying, Lord, haue patience with mee, and I will pay thee all.

27 Then the Lord of that seruant was moued with compassion, and loosed him, and forgaue him the debt.

28 But the same seruant went out, and found one of his fellow-seruants, which ought him an hundred ‖ pence : and hee layd handes on him, and tooke him by the throte, saying, Pay mee that thou owest.

29 And his fellow seruant fell downe at his feete, and besought him, saying, Haue patience with me, and I will pay thee all.

30 And he would not : but went and cast him into prison, till hee should pay the debt.

31 So when his fellow-seruants saw what was done, they were very sorie, and came, and told vnto their lord all that was done.

32 Then his lord, after that hee had called him, said vnto him, O thou wicked seruant , I forgaue thee all that debt because thou desiredst me :

33 Shouldest not thou also haue had compassion on thy fellow-seruant, euen as I had pitie on thee ?

34 And his lord was wroth, and deliuered him to the tormentors, till hee should pay all that was due vnto him.

35 So likewise shall my heauenly Father doe also vnto you, if yee from your hearts forgiue not euery one his brother their trespasses.

CHAP. XIX.

2 Christ healeth the sicke : 3 answereth the Pharisees concerning diuorcement : 10 sheweth when mariage is necessary : 13 receiueth litle children : 16 instructeth the yong man how to attaine eternall life, 20 and how to be perfect : 23 telleth his disciples how hard it is for a rich man to enter into the kingdom of God, 27 and promiseth reward to those that forsake any thing, to follow him.

ANd it came to passe, * that when Iesus had finished these sayings, he departed from Galilee, and came into the coastes of Iudea, beyond Iordane :

2 And great multitudes followed him, and he healed them there.

3 ¶ The Pharisees also came vnto him, tempting him, and saying vnto him, Is it lawfull for a man to put away his wife for euery cause ?

4 And hee answered, and said vnto them, Haue ye not read, * that he which made them at the beginning, made them male and female ?

5 And said, * For this cause shall a man leaue father and mother, and shall cleaue to his wife : and * they twaine shalbe one flesh.

6 Wherefore they are no more twaine, but one flesh. What therefore God hath ioyned together, let not man put asunder.

7 They say vnto him, * Why did Moses then command to giue a writing of diuorcement, and to put her away ?

8 Hee saith vnto them, Moses, because of the hardnesse of your hearts, suffered

* Mar. 10.
1.

* Gen. 1. 27.

* Gen. 2. 24.
ephe. 5. 31.
* 1. Cor. 6.
16.

* Deut. 24.
1.

suffered you to put away your wiues : but from the beginning it was not so.

9 *And I say vnto you, Whosoeuer shall put away his wife, except it be for fornication, and shall marry another, committeth adultery : and whoso marrieth her which is put away, doth commit adultery.

10 ¶ His disciples say vnto him, If the case of the man be so with his wife, it is not good to marrie.

11 But hee said vnto them, All men cannot receiue this saying, saue they to whom it is giuen.

12 For there are some Eunuches, which were so borne from their mothers wombe : and there are some Eunuches, which were made Eunuches of men : and there be Eunuches, which haue made themselues Eunuches for the kingdome of heauens sake. He that is able to receiue *it*, let him receiue *it*.

13 ¶ *Then were there brought vnto him little children, that he should put his hands on them, and pray : and the disciples rebuked them.

14 But Iesus said, Suffer little children, and forbid them not to come vnto me : for of such is ẙ kingdome of heauen.

15 And he laide his hands on them, and departed thence.

16 ¶ *And behold, one came and said vnto him, Good master, what good thing shall I do, that I may haue eternall life ?

17 And he said vnto him, Why callest thou me good ? there is none good but one, *that is* God : but if thou wilt enter into life, keepe the commandements.

18 He saith vnto him, Which ? Iesus said, *Thou shalt do no murder, Thou shalt not commit adultery, Thou shalt not steale, Thou shalt not beare false witnesse,

19 Honour thy father and thy mother : and, Thou shalt loue thy neighbour as thy selfe.

20 The young man saith vnto him, All these things haue I kept from my youth vp : what lacke I yet ?

21 Iesus said vnto him, If thou wilt be perfect, goe and sell that thou hast, and giue to the poore, and thou shalt haue treasure in heauen : and come and follow me.

22 But when the young man heard that saying, he went away sorrowfull : for he had great possessions.

23 ¶ Then said Iesus vnto his dis-

ciples, Verely I say vnto you, that a rich man shall hardly enter into the kingdome of heauen.

24 And againe I say vnto you, It is easier for a camel to goe thorow the eye of a needle, then for a rich man to enter into the kingdome of God.

25 When his disciples heard it, they were exceedingly amazed, saying, Who then can be saued ?

26 But Iesus beheld them, and said vnto them, With men this is vnpossible, but with God al things are possible.

27 ¶ *Then answered Peter, and said vnto him, Behold, we haue forsaken all, and followed thee, what shall we haue therefore ?

28 And Iesus said vnto them, Verily I say vnto you, that ye which haue followed me, in the regeneration when the Sonne of man shal sit in the throne of his glory, *ye also shal sit vpon twelue thrones, iudging the twelue tribes of Israel.

29 And euery one that hath forsaken houses, or brethren, or sisters, or father, or mother, or wife, or children, or lands, for my Names sake, shall receiue an hundred fold, and shall inherite euerlasting life.

30 *But many that are first, shall be last, and the last shall be first.

CHAP. XX.

1 Christ by the similitude of the labourers in the vineyard, sheweth that God is debter vnto no man : 17 Foretelleth his passion : 20 By answering the mother of Zebedeus children, teacheth his disciples to be lowly : 30 and giueth two blinde men their sight.

Or the kingdome of heauen is like vnto a man that is an housholder, which went out early in the morning to hire labourers into his vineyard.

2 And when hee had agreed with the labourers for a ‖peny a day, he sent them into his vineyard.

3 And he went out about the third houre, and saw others standing idle in the market place,

4 And said vnto them, Go ye also into the vineyard, & whatsoeuer is right, I wil giue you. And they went their way.

5 Againe he went out about the sixth and ninth houre, and did likewise.

6 And about the eleuenth houre, he went out, and found others standing idle,

*Cha. 5. 32.
mar. 10. 11.
luke 16. 18.
1. cor. 7. 11.

*Mark. 10.
13. luke 18.
15.

*Marke 10.
17. luke
18. 18.

*Exod. 20.
13.

*Mark. 10.
28. luke
18. 28.

*Luke 22.
30.

*Chap. 20.
16. mark.
10. 31. luk.
13. 30.

‖ The Romane peny is the eight part of an ounce, which after fiue shillings the ounce, is seuen pence halfepeny.

idle, and saith vnto them, Why stand ye here all the day idle?

7 They say vnto him, Because no man hath hired vs. He saith vnto them, Go ye also into the vineyard : and whatsoeuer is right, that shall ye receiue.

8 So when euen was come, the lord of the vineyard saith vnto his Steward, Call the labourers, and giue them their hire, beginning from the last, vnto the first.

9 And when they came that *were hired* about the eleuenth houre, they receiued euery man a penie.

10 But when the first came, they supposed that they should haue receiued more, and they likewise receiued euery man a penie.

11 And when they had receiued it, they murmured against the good man of the house,

‖ *Or, haue continued one houre onely.*

12 Saying, These last ‖haue wrought *but* one houre, and thou hast made them equall vnto vs, which haue borne the burden, and heat of the day.

13 But he answered one of them and said, Friend, I do thee no wrong : didst not thou agree with me for a penie?

14 Take that thine is, and goe thy way, I will giue vnto this last, euen as vnto thee.

15 Is it not lawfull for mee to doe what I wil with mine owne? Is thine eye euill, because I am good?

* Chap. 19. 30.

16 * So the last shall be first, and the first last : for many bee called, but fewe chosen.

* Mar. 10. 32. luke 18. 31.

17 ¶ * And Iesus going vp to Hierusalem, tooke the twelue disciples apart in the way, and said vnto them,

18 Behold, we goe vp to Hierusalem, and the Sonne of man shall be betraied vnto the chiefe Priests, and vnto the Scribes, and they shall condemne him to death,

* Ioh. 18. 32

19 * And shal deliuer him to the Gentiles to mocke, and to scourge, and to crucifie him : and the third day he shall rise againe.

* Mar. 10. 35:

20 ¶ * Then came to him the mother of Zebedees children, with her sonnes, worshipping him, and desiring a certaine thing of him.

21 And he said vnto her, What wilt thou? She saith vnto him, Grant, that these my two sonnes may sit, the one on thy right hand, and the other on the left in thy kingdome.

22 But Iesus answered, and said,

Ye know not what ye aske. Are ye able to drinke of the cup that I shall drinke of, and to be baptized with the baptisme that I am baptized with? They say vnto him, We are able.

23 And he saith vnto them, Yee shall drinke indeed of my cup, and be baptized with the baptisme that I am baptized with : but to sit on my right hand, and on my left, is not mine to giue, but *it shall be giuen* to them for whom it is prepared of my father.

24 And when the ten heard it, they were moued with indignation against the two brethren.

* Luk. 22. 25.

25 But Iesus called them vnto him, and said, * Ye know that the princes of the Gentiles exercise dominion ouer them, and they that are great, exercise authoritie vpon them.

26 But it shall not be so among you: But whosoeuer will bee great among you, let him be your minister.

27 And whosoeuer will be chiefe among you, let him be your seruant.

* Phil. 2. 7

28 Euen as the * Sonne of man came not to be ministred vnto, but to minister, and to giue his life a ransome for many.

* Mar. 10. 46. luke 18. 35.

29 * And as they departed from Hiericho, a great multitude followed him.

30 ¶ And behold, two blind men sitting by the way side, when they heard that Iesus passed by, cried out, saying, Haue mercie on vs, O Lord, thou sonne of Dauid.

31 And the multitude rebuked them, because they should holde their peace: but they cried the more, saying, Haue mercie on vs, O Lord, thou sonne of Dauid.

32 And Iesus stood still, and called them, and saide, What will yee that I shall doe vnto you?

33 They say vnto him, Lord, that our eyes may be opened.

34 So Iesus had compassion on them, and touched their eyes : and immediatly their eyes receiued sight, and they followed him.

CHAP. XXI.

1 Christ rideth into Hierusalem vpon an asse, 12 driueth the buyers and sellers out of the Temple, 17 curseth the fig-tree, 23 putteth to silence the Priests and Elders, 28 and rebuketh them by the similitude of the two sonnes, 35 and by the husbandmen, who slew such as were sent vnto them.

And

* Marke 11.
1. luke 19.
29.

**A**Nd when they drewe nigh vnto Hierusalem, and were come to Bethphage, vnto the mount of Oliues, then sent Iesus two Disciples,

2 Saying vnto them, Goe into the village ouer against you, and straightway yee shall find an Asse tied, and a colt with her : loose them, and bring them vnto me.

3 And if any man say ought vnto you, yee shall say, The Lord hath need of them, and straightway hee will send them.

4 All this was done, that it might be fulfilled which was spoken by the Prophet, saying,

* Esai. 62.
11. zach. 9.
9. iohn 12.
15.

5 *Tell yee the daughter of Sion, Behold, thy king commeth vnto thee, meeke, and sitting vpon an Asse, and a colt, the foale of an Asse.

* Marke 11.
2.

6 * And the Disciples went, and did as Iesus commanded them,

7 And brought the Asse, and the colt, and put on them their clothes, and they set him thereon.

8 And a very great multitude spread their garments in the way, others cut downe branches from the trees, and strawed them in the way.

9 And the multitudes that went before, and that followed, cried, saying, Hosanna to the sonne of Dauid : Blessed is he that commeth in the Name of the Lord, Hosanna in the highest.

* Marke 11.
15. luke 19.
45. iohn 2.
13.

10 *And when hee was come into Hierusalem, all the citie was mooued, saying, Who is this ?

11 And the multitude said, This is Iesus the Prophet of Nazareth of Galilee.

12 ¶ And Iesus went into the temple of God, and cast out all them that sold and bought in the Temple, and ouerthrew the tables of the money changers, and the seats of them that solde doues,

13 And said vnto them, It is written, *My house shall be called the house of prayer, * butyee haue made it a denne of theeues.

* Esai. 56. 7.
* Iere. 7. 11.
mar. 11. 17.
luke 19. 46.

14 And the blind and the lame came to him in the Temple, & he healed them.

15 And when the chiefe Priests and Scribes saw the wonderfull things that he did, & the children crying in the temple, & saying, Hosanna to the sonne of Dauid, they were sore displeased,

16 And said vnto him, Hearest thou what these say ? And Iesus saith vnto them, Yea, haue yee neuer read, *Out of the mouth of babes and sucklings thou hast perfected praise ?

* Psal. 8. 2.

17 ¶ And he left them, and went out of the citie into Bethany, and he lodged there.

18 Now in the morning, as hee returned into the citie, he hungred.

19 * And when he saw a figge tree in the way, hee came to it, and found nothing thereon but leaues only, and said vnto it, Let no fruite growe on thee hence forward for euer. And presently the figge tree withered away.

* Marke 11.
13.

20 And when the Disciples saw it, they marueiled, saying, How soone is the figge tree withered away ?

21 Iesus answered, and said vnto them, Verily I say vnto you, if yee haue faith, and doubt not, yee shall not onely doe this *which is done* to the figge tree, but also, if ye shall say vnto this mountaine, Be thou remoued, and be thou cast into the Sea, it shall be done.

22 And all things whatsoeuer yee shall aske in prayer, beleeuing, ye shall receiue.

23 ¶ *And when he was come into the temple, the chiefe Priests and the Elders of the people came vnto him as he was teaching, and said, By what authoritie doest thou these things ? and who gaue thee this authoritie ?

* Marke 11.
27. luke 20.
1.

24 And Iesus answered, and said vnto them, I also will aske you one thing, which if ye tell me, I in like wise will tell you by what authoritie I doe these things.

25 The baptisme of Iohn, whence was it ? from heauen, or of men ? and they reasoned with themselues saying, If we shall say, From heauen, hee will say vnto vs, Why did ye not then beleeue him ?

26 But if we shall say, Of men, we feare the people, *for all hold Iohn as a Prophet.

* Chap. 14.
5.

27 And they answered Iesus, and said, We cannot tell. And he said vnto them, Neither tell I you by what authoritie I doe these things.

28 ¶ But what thinke you ? A certaine man had two sonnes, and he came to the first, and said, Sonne, goe worke to day in my vineyard.

29 He answered, & said, I will not : but afterward he repented, and went.

30 And

30 And hee came to the second, and said likewise : and hee answered, and said, I *goe* sir, and went not.

31 Whether of them twaine did the will of his father ? They say vnto him, The first. Iesus saith vnto them, Verely I say vnto you, that the Publicanes and the harlots go into the kingdome of God before you.

* Chap. 3. 1.

32 For *Iohn came vnto you in the way of righteousnesse, and ye beleeued him not : but the Publicanes and the harlots beleeued him. And ye when ye had seene it, repented not afterward, that ye might beleeue him.

* Esa. 5 1. iere. 2. 21. mark. 12. 1. luke 20. 9.

33 ¶ Heare another parable. There was a certaine house-holder, *which planted a Vineyard, and hedged it round about, and digged a wine-presse in it, and built a tower, and let it out to husbandmen, and went into a farre countrey.

34 And when the time of the fruite drew neere, he sent his seruants to the husbandmen, that they might receiue the fruits of it.

35 And the husbandmen tooke his seruants, and beat one, and killed another, and stoned another.

36 Againe hee sent other seruants, moe then the first, and they did vnto them likewise.

37 But last of all, he sent vnto them his sonne, saying, They will reuerence my sonne.

* Chap. 26. 3. iohn. 11. 53.

38 But when the husbandmen saw the sonne, they said among themselues, *This is the heire, come, let vs kill him, and let vs sease on his inheritance.

39 And they caught him, and cast him out of the Vineyard, and slew him.

40 When the Lord therefore of the Vineyard commeth, what will he doe vnto those husbandmen ?

41 They say vnto him, He will miserably destroy those wicked men, and will let out his Vineyard vnto other husbandmen, which shall render him the fruits in their seasons.

* Psal. 118. 22. acts. 4. 11.

42 Iesus saith vnto them, *Did ye neuer reade in the Scriptures, The stone which the builders reiected, the same is become the head of the corner? This is the Lords doing, and it is marueilous in our eyes.

43 Therefore say I vnto you, the kingdome of God shall be taken from you, and giuen to a nation bringing forth the fruits thereof.

44 And *whosoeuer shall fall on this stone, shalbe broken : but on whom soeuer it shall fall, it will grinde him to powder.

* Rom. 9. 33. 1. pet. 2 7. esa. 8. 14.

45 And when the chiefe Priests and Pharisees had heard his parables, they perceiued that he spake of them.

46 But when they sought to lay hands on him, they feared the multitude, because they tooke him for a Prophet.

CHAP. XXII.

1 The parable of the marriage of the Kings sonne. 9 The vocation of the Gentiles. 12 The punishment of him that wanted the wedding garment. 15 Tribute ought to be payed to Cæsar. 23 Christ confuteth the Sadducees for the Resurrection : 34 answereth the Lawyer, which is the first and great Commandement : 41 and poseth the Pharisees about the Messias.

And Iesus answered, *and spake vnto them againe by parables, and said,

* Luke 14. 16. reuel. 19. 9.

2 The Kingdome of heauen is like vnto a certaine King, which made a marriage for his sonne,

3 And sent forth his seruants to call them that were bidden to the wedding, and they would not come.

4 Againe, hee sent foorth other seruants, saying, Tell them which are bidden, Beholde, I haue prepared my dinner; my oxen, and my fatlings are killed, and all things are ready : come vnto the marriage.

5 But they made light of it, and went their wayes, one to his farme, another to his merchandize :

6 And the remnant tooke his seruants, and intreated them spitefully, and slew them.

7 But when the king heard *thereof,* he was wroth, and hee sent foorth his armies, and destroyed those murderers, and burnt vp their citie.

8 Then saith hee to his seruants, The wedding is ready, but they which were bidden, were not worthy.

9 Goe yee therefore into the high wayes, and as many as yee shall finde, bid to the marriage.

10 So those seruants went out into the high wayes, and gathered together all as many as they found, both bad and good, and the wedding was furnished with ghests.

11 ¶ And

11 ¶ And when the King came in to see the guests, hee sawe there a man, which had not on a wedding garment,

12 And hee sayth vnto him, Friend, how camest thou in hither, not hauing a wedding garment? And hee was speechlesse.

13 Then said the king to the seruants, Binde him hand and foot, and take him away, and cast him into outer darkenesse, there shall be weeping and gnashing of teeth.

14 *For many are called, but few are chosen.

15 ¶ *Then went the Pharises, and tooke counsell, how they might intangle him in his talke.

16 And they sent out vnto him their disciples, with the Herodians, saying, Master, wee know that thou art true, and teachest the way of God in trueth, neither carest thou for any man; for thou regardest not the person of men.

17 Tell vs therefore, what thinkest thou? Is it lawfull to giue tribute vnto Cesar, or not?

18 But Iesus perceiued their wickednesse, and said, Why tempt ye me, ye hypocrites?

19 Shew me the tribute money. And they brought vnto him a ‖peny.

20 And he sayth vnto them, Whose is this image and ‖superscription?

21 They say vnto him, Cesars. Then sayth he vnto them, *Render therefore vnto Cesar, the things which are Cesars: and vnto God, the things that are Gods.

22 When they had heard *these wordes*, they marueiled, and left him, and went their way.

23 ¶ *The same day came to him the Sadduces, *which say that there is no resurrection, and asked him,

24 Saying, Master, *Moses said, If a man die, hauing no children, his brother shall marrie his wife, and raise vp seed vnto his brother.

25 Now there were with vs seuen brethren, and the first when he had maried a wife, deceased, and hauing no issue, left his wife vnto his brother.

26 Likewise the second also, and the third, vnto the seuenth.

27 And last of al the woman died also.

28 Therefore, in the resurrection, whose wife shall she be of the seuen? for they all had her.

29 Iesus answered, and said vnto them, Yee doe erre, not knowing the Scriptures, nor the power of God.

30 For in the resurrection they neither marry, nor are giuen in marriage, but are as the Angels of God in heauen.

31 But as touching the resurrection of the dead, haue ye not read that which was spoken vnto you by God, saying,

32 *I am the God of Abraham, and the God of Isaac, and the God of Iacob? God is not the God of the dead, but of the liuing.

33 And when the multitude heard this, they were astonished at his doctrine.

34 ¶ *But when the Pharises had heard that he had put the Sadduces to silence, they were gathered together.

35 Then one of them, which was a Lawyer, asked *him* a question, tempting him, and saying,

36 Master, which is the great Commandement in the Law?

37 Iesus sayd vnto him, *Thou shalt loue the Lord thy God with all thy heart, and with all thy soule, and with all thy minde.

38 This is the first and great Commandement.

39 And the second is like vnto it, *Thou shalt loue thy neighbour as thy selfe.

40 On these two Commandements hang all the Law and the Prophets.

41 ¶ *While the Pharises were gathered together, Iesus asked them,

42 Saying, What thinke yee of Christ? whose sonne is hee? They say vnto him, The sonne of Dauid.

43 He saith vnto them, How then doth Dauid in spirit call him Lord, saying,

44 The Lord said vnto my Lord, *Sit thou on my right hand, till I make thine enemies thy footstoole?

45 If Dauid then call him Lord, how is he his sonne?

46 And no man was able to answere him a word, neither durst any man (from that day foorth) aske him any moe questions.

CHAP. XXIII.

1 Christ admonisheth the people to follow the good doctrine, not the euill examples of the Scribes and Pharises. 5 His disciples must beware of their ambition. 13 Hee denounceth eight woes against their hypocrisie and blindnesse: 34 and prophecieth of the destruction of Hierusalem.

Then

Marginal notes

* Chap. 20. 16.

* Marke 12. 13. luke 20. 20.

‖ In value seuen pence halfepeny, chap. 20. 2.
‖ Or, inscription.
* Rom. 13. 7.

* Marke 12. 18. luke 20. 27.
* Acts 23. 8.
* Deu. 25. 5.

* Exod. 3. 6.

* Marke 12. 28.

* Deut. 6. 5. luke 10. 27.

* Leuit. 19. 18.

* Marke 12. 35. luke 20. 41.

* Psal. 110. 1.

Hen spake Iesus to the multitude, and to his disciples,

2 Saying, The Scribes and the Pharises sit in Moses seate :

3 All therefore whatsoeuer they bid you obserue, that obserue and doe, but doe not ye after their workes : for they say, and doe not.

4 *For they binde heauie burdens, and grieuous to be borne, and lay them on mens shoulders, but *they themselues* will not mooue them with *one* of their fingers.

5 But all their workes they doe, for to be seene of men : *they make broad their phylacteries, and enlarge the borders of their garments,

6 *And loue the vppermost roomes at feasts, and the chiefe seats in the Synagogues,

7 And greetings in the markets, and to be called of men, Rabbi, Rabbi.

8 *But be not ye called Rabbi : for one is your Master, *euen* Christ, and all ye are brethren.

9 And call no man your father vpon the earth : *for one is your father which is in heauen.

10 Neither be ye called masters : for one is your Master, *euen* Christ.

11 But hee that is greatest among you, shall be your seruant.

12 *And whosoeuer shall exalt himselfe, shall be abased : and he that shall humble himselfe, shall be exalted.

13 ¶ But *woe vnto you, Scribes and Pharisees, hypocrites; for yee shut vp the kingdome of heauen against men: For yee neither goe in your selues, neither suffer ye them that are entring, to goe in.

14 *Woe vnto you Scribes and Pharisees, hypocrites; for yee deuoure widowes houses, and for a pretence make long prayer ; therefore ye shall receiue the greater damnation.

15 Woe vnto you Scribes and Pharises, hypocrites; for yee compasse Sea and land to make one Proselyte, and when hee is made, yee make him two fold more the childe of hell then your selues.

16 Woe vnto you, yee blind guides, which say, Whosoeuer shall sweare by the Temple, it is nothing : but whosoeuer shal sweare by the gold of the Temple, he is a debter.

17 Ye fooles and blind : for whether is greater, the gold, or the Temple that sanctifieth the gold ?

18 And whosoeuer shall sweare by the Altar, it is nothing : but whosoeuer sweareth by the gift that is vpon it, he is ||guiltie.

19 Ye fooles and blind : for whether is greater, the gift, or the Altar that sanctifieth the gift ?

20 Who so therefore shall sweare by the Altar, sweareth by it, and by all things thereon.

21 And who so shall sweare by the Temple, sweareth by it , and by him that dwelleth therein.

22 And he that shall sweare by heauen, sweareth by the throne of God, and by him that sitteth thereon.

23 Woe vnto you Scribes and Pharisees, hypocrites; *for yee pay tithe of mint, and annise , and cummine , and haue omitted the weightier matters of the Law, iudgement, mercie and faith: these ought ye to haue done, and not to leaue the other vndone.

24 Ye blind guides, which straine at a gnat, and swallow a camel.

25 Woe vnto you Scribes and Pharisees, hypocrites; *for yee make cleane the outside of the cup, and of the platter, but within they are full of extortion and excesse.

26 Thou blind Pharisee, cleanse first that which is within the cup and platter, that the outside of them may bee cleane also.

27 Woe vnto you Scribes and Pharisees, hypocrites, for yee are like vnto whited sepulchres , which indeed appeare beautifull outward, but are within full of dead mens bones, and of all vncleannesse.

28 Euen so, yee also outwardly appeare righteous vnto men, but within ye are full of hypocrisie and iniquitie.

29 Woe vnto you Scribes and Pharisees, hypocrites, because ye build the tombes of the Prophets, and garnish the sepulchres of the righteous,

30 And say, If wee had beene in the dayes of our fathers, wee would not haue bene partakers with them in the blood of the Prophets.

31 Wherefore ye bee witnesses vnto your selues, that yee are the children of them which killed the Prophets.

32 Fil ye vp then the measure of your fathers.

33 Yee

* Luk. 11. 46

* Num. 15. 38. deut. 22 12.

* Mark. 12. 38. luke 11 43.

* Iames 3. 1

* Mala. 1. 6.

* Luk. 14. 11 and 18. 14.

* Luk. 11. 52.

* Mar. 12. 40. luk. 20. 47.

|| Or, a debter, or bou

* Luk. 11.

* Luk. 11.

33 Yee serpents, yee generation of vipers, How can yee escape the damnation of hell?

34 ¶ Wherefore behold, I send vnto you Prophets, and wisemen, and Scribes, and some of them yee shall kill and crucifie, and some of them shall yee scourge in your synagogues, and persecute them from citie to citie:

35 That vpon you may come all the righteous blood shed vpon the earth, *from the blood of righteous Abel, vnto the blood of Zacharias, sonne of Barachias, whom yee slew betweene the temple and the altar.

36 Verily I say vnto you, All these things shal come vpon this generation.

37 *O Hierusalem, Hierusalem, thou that killest the Prophets, *and stonest them which are sent vnto thee, how often would *I haue gathered thy children together, euen as a hen gathereth her chickens vnder her wings, and yee would not?

38 Behold, your house is left vnto you desolate.

39 For I say vnto you, yee shall not see me henceforth, till ye shall say, Blessed is he that commeth in the Name of the Lord.

CHAP. XXIIII.

1 Christ foretelleth the destruction of the temple: 3 what, and how great calamities shall be before it: 29 the signes of his comming to iudgement. 36 And because that day and houre is vnknowen, 42 we ought to watch like good seruants expecting euery moment our masters comming.

And *Iesus went out, and departed from the temple, and his Disciples came to him, for to shew him the buildings of the temple.

2 And Iesus said vnto them, See yee not all these things? Verily I say vnto you, *there shall not be left heere one stone vpon another, that shall not be throwen downe.

3 ¶ And as he sate vpon the mount of Oliues, the Disciples came vnto him priuately, saying, Tell vs, when shall these things be? and what shall be the signe of thy comming, and of the end of the world?

4 And Iesus answered, and said vnto them, Take heed that no man deceiue you.

5 For many shall come in my name,

saying, I am Christ: and shall deceiue many.

6 And yee shall heare of warres, and rumors of warres: See that yee be not troubled: for all these things must come to passe, but the end is not yet.

7 For nation shall rise against nation, and kingdome against kingdome, and there shall be famines, and pestilences, and earthquakes in diuers places.

8 All these are the beginning of sorrowes.

9 *Then shall they deliuer you vp to be afflicted, and shall kill you: and yee shall bee hated of all nations for my names sake.

10 And then shall many be offended, and shall betray one another, and shall hate one another.

11 And many false Prophets shall rise, and shall deceiue many.

12 And because iniquitie shal abound, the loue of many shall waxe cold.

13 But he that shall endure vnto the end, the same shall be saued.

14 And this Gospell of the kingdome shall be preached in all the world, for a witnesse vnto al nations, and then shall the end come.

15 *When yee therefore shall see the abomination of desolation, spoken of by *Daniel the Prophet, stand in the holy place, (who so readeth, let him vnderstand.)

16 Then let them which be in Iudea, flee into the mountaines.

17 Let him which is on the house top, not come downe, to take any thing out of his house:

18 Neither let him which is in the field, returne backe to take his clothes.

19 And woe vnto them that are with child, and to them that giue sucke in those dayes.

20 But pray yee that your flight bee not in the winter, neither on the Sabbath day:

21 For then shall be great tribulation, such as was not since the beginning of the world to this time, no, nor euer shall be.

22 And except those dayes should be shortned, there should no flesh be saued: but for the elects sake, those dayes shall be shortned.

23 *Then if any man shall say vnto you, Loe, heere is Christ, or there: beleeue it not.

24 For there shall arise false Christs, and

Marginal notes (left column):

Gen. 4. 8.

Luke 13. 4.
2. Chro. 4. 21.
4. Esd. 1. 0.

Mar. 13. 1.
Luke 21. 5.

Luke 19. 4.

Marginal notes (right column):

* Chap. 10. 17. luke 21. 12. iohn 16. 2.

* Mar. 13. 14.

* Dan. 9. 27.

* Mar. 13. 21. luke 17. 23.

and false prophets, and shal shew great signes and wonders : insomuch that (if it were possible,) they shall deceiue the very elect.

25 Behold, I haue told you before.

26 Wherefore, if they shall say vnto you, Behold, he is in the desert, goe not foorth : Behold, he is in the secret chambers, beleeue it not.

27 For as the lightening commeth out of the East, and shineth euen vnto the West : so shall also the comming of the Sonne of man be.

*Luke 17. 37.

28 *For whersoeuer the carkeise is, there will the Eagles bee gathered together.

*Marke 13. 24. luke 21. 25. esay 13. 10. ioel 2. 31. ezek. 32. 7.

29 ¶ Immediatly after the tribulation of those dayes, *shall the Sunne be darkned, and the Moone shall not giue her light, and the starres shall fall from heauen, and the powers of the heauens shall be shaken.

30 And then shall appeare the signe of the Sonne of man in heauen : and then shall all the Tribes of the earth mourne, *and they shall see the Sonne of man comming in the clouds of heauen, with power and great glory.

*Reuel. 1. 7.

*1. Cor. 15. 52. 1. thes. 4. 16. ‖ Or, with a Trumpet and a great voice.

31 *And hee shall send his Angels with ‖a great sound of a trumpet, and they shall gather together his Elect from the foure windes, from one end of heauen to the other.

32 Now learne a parable of the figtree : when his branch is yet tender, and putteth foorth leaues, yee know that Summer is nigh :

33 So likewise yee, when ye shall see all these things, know that it is neere, *euen* at the doores.

34 Verely I say vnto you, this generation shall not passe, till all these things be fulfilled.

*Mark. 13. 31.

35 *Heauen and earth shall passe away, but my wordes shall not passe away.

36 ¶ But of that day and houre knoweth no man, no, not the Angels of heauen, but my Father onely.

37 But as the dayes of Noe were, so shall also the comming of the Sonne of man be.

*Gene. 7. luke 17. 26.

38 *For as in the dayes that were before the Flood, they were eating, and drinking, marrying, and giuing in mariage, vntill the day that Noe entred into the Arke,

39 And knew not vntill the Flood came, and tooke them all away : so shall also the comming of the Sonne of man be.

40 *Then shall two be in the field, the one shalbe taken, and the other left.

*Luke 17. 36.

41 Two women shall be grinding at the mill : the one shall be taken, and the other left.

42 ¶ *Watch therfore, for ye know not what houre your Lord doth come.

*Mark. 13. 35.

43 *But know this, that if the good man of the house had knowen in what watch the thiefe would come, he would haue watched, and would not haue suffered his house to be broken vp.

*Luke 12. 39. 1. thes. 5. 2. reue. 16. 15.

44 Therefore bee yee also ready : for in such an houre as you thinke not, the sonne of man commeth.

45 *Who then is a faithfull and wise seruant, whom his Lord hath made ruler ouer his houshold, to giue them meat in due season ?

*Luke 12. 42.

46 Blessed is that seruant, whome his Lord when he commeth, shall finde so doing.

47 Verely I say vnto you, that hee shal make him ruler ouer all his goods.

48 But and if that euill seruant shal say in his heart, My Lord delayeth his comming,

49 And shall begin to smite his fellow seruants, and to eate and drinke with the drunken :

50 The Lord of that seruant shall come in a day when hee looketh not for him, and in an houre that hee is not ware of :

51 And shall cut him ‖asunder, and appoint him his portion with the hypocrites : there shall be weeping and gnashing of teeth.

‖ Or, cut off.

CHAP. XXV.

1 The parable of the tenne Virgins, 14 and of the talents. 31 Also the description of the last Iudgement.

Hen shall the kingdome of heauen be likened vnto ten Virgins, which tooke their lamps, & went forth to meet the bridegrome.

2 And fiue of them were wise, and fiue were foolish.

3 They that were foolish tooke their lampes, and tooke no oyle with them :

4 But the wise tooke oyle in their vessels with their lampes.

5 While the bridegrome taried, they all slumbred and slept.

6 And

6 And at midnight there was a cry made, Behold, the bridegrome commeth, goe ye out to meet him.

7 Then all those virgins arose, and trimmed their lampes.

8 And the foolish said vnto the wise, Give vs of your oyle, for our lampes are ||gone out.

9 But the wise answered, saying, *Not so*, lest there be not ynough for vs and you, but goe ye rather to them that sell, and buy for your selues.

10 And while they went to buy, the bridegrome came, and they that were ready, went in with him to the marriage, and the doore was shut.

11 Afterward came also the other virgines, saying, Lord, Lord, open to vs.

12 But he answered, and said, Verely I say vnto you, I know you not.

13 * Watch therefore, for ye know neither the day, nor the houre, wherein the Sonne of man commeth.

14 ¶ *For the kingdome of heauen is* as a man trauailing into a farre countrey, who called his owne seruants, and deliuered vnto them his goods:

15 And vnto one he gaue fiue ||talents, to another two, and to another one, to euery man according to his seuerall ability, & straightway tooke his iourney.

16 Then hee that had receiued the fiue talents, went and traded with the same, and made *them* other fiue talents.

17 And likewise he that had receiued two, he also gained other two.

18 But hee that had receiued one, went and digged in the earth, and hid his lordes money.

19 After a long time, the lord of those seruants commeth, and reckoneth with them.

20 And so hee that had receiued fiue talents, came and brought other fiue talents, saying, Lord, thou deliueredst vnto me fiue talents, behold, I haue gained besides them, fiue talents moe.

21 His lord said vnto him, Well done, thou good and faithfull seruant, thou hast been faithfull ouer a few things, I wil make thee ruler ouer many things : enter thou into the ioy of thy lord.

22 He also that had receiued two talents, came and said, Lord, thou deliueredst vnto me two talents : behold, I haue gained two other talents besides them.

23 His lord said vnto him, Well done, good and faithfull seruant, thou hast

beene faithfull ouer a few things, I wil make thee ruler ouer many things : enter thou into the ioy of thy lord.

24 Then he which had receiued the one talent, came & said, Lord, I knew thee that thou art an hard man, reaping where thou hast not sowen, & gathering where thou hast not strawed :

25 And I was afraid, and went and hidde thy talent in the earth : loe, there thou hast that is thine.

26 His lord answered, and said vnto him, Thou wicked and slouthfull seruant, thou knewest that I reape where I sowed not, and gather where I haue not strawed :

27 Thou oughtest therefore to haue put my money to the exchangers, and then at my comming I should haue receiued mine owne with vsurie.

28 Take therefore the talent from him, and giue it vnto him which hath ten talents.

29 *For vnto euery one that hath shall be giuen, and he shall haue abundance : but from him that hath not, shal be taken away, euen that which he hath.

30 And cast yee the vnprofitable seruant into outer darkenesse, there shall be weeping and gnashing of teeth.

31 ¶ When the Sonne of man shall come in his glory, and all the holy Angels with him, then shall hee sit vpon the throne of his glory :

32 And before him shall be gathered all nations, and he shall separate them one from another, as a shepheard diuideth his sheepe from the goats.

33 And he shall set the sheepe on his right hand, but the goats on the left.

34 Then shall the King say vnto them on his right hand, Come ye blessed of my Father, inherit the kingdome prepared for you from the foundation of the world.

35 *For I was an hungred, and yee gaue me meate : I was thirstie, and ye gaue me drinke : I was a stranger, and ye tooke me in :

36 Naked, and ye clothed me : I was sicke, and yee visited me : I was in prison, and ye came vnto me.

37 Then shal the righteous answere him, saying, Lord, when saw we thee an hungred, and fedde thee ? or thirstie, and gaue thee drinke ?

38 When saw wee thee a stranger, and tooke thee in ? or naked, and clothed thee ?

39 Or

Or, going out,

" Chap. 24.
2. marke
3. 33.

" Luke 19.
2.

A talent is
87. pound
0. shillings,
hap. 18. 24.

* Chap. 13.
12. marke
4. 25. luke
8. 18.

" Esai 58. 7.
ezec. 18. 7.

39 Or when saw we thee sicke, or in prison, and came vnto thee?

40 And the King shall answere, and say vnto them, Verely I say vnto you, in as much as ye haue done it vnto one of the least of these my brethren, ye haue done it vnto me.

41 Then shall he say also vnto them on the left hand, * Depart from me, ye cursed, into euerlasting fire, prepared for the deuill and his angels.

42 For I was an hungred, and yee gaue me no meat: I was thirstie, and ye gaue me no drinke:

43 I was a stranger, and yee tooke me not in: naked, and ye clothed mee not: sicke, and in prison, and yee visited me not.

44 Then shall they also answere him, saying, Lord, when saw we thee an hungred, or athirst, or a stranger, or naked, or sicke, or in prison, and did not minister vnto thee?

45 Then shall he answere them, saying, Verely, I say vnto you, in as much as ye did it not to one of the least of these, ye did it not to me.

46 And * these shall goe away into euerlasting punishment: but the righteous into life eternall.

CHAP. XXVI.

1 The rulers conspire against Christ. 6 The woman anointeth his feet. 14 Iudas selleth him. 17 Christ eateth the Passeouer: 26 instituteth his holy Supper: 36 prayeth in the garden: 47 and being betrayed with a kisse, 57 is caried to Caiaphas, 69 and denied of Peter.

And it came to passe, when Iesus had finished al these sayings, hee said vnto his disciples,

2 * Ye know that after two dayes is the feast of the Passeouer, and the Sonne of man is betrayed to be crucified.

3 * Then assembled together the chiefe Priests, and the Scribes, and the Elders of the people, vnto the palace of the high Priest, who was called Caiaphas,

4 And consulted that they might take Iesus by subtiltie, and kill him.

5 But they said, Not on the feast day, lest there bee an vproare among the people.

6 ¶ * Now when Iesus was in Bethanie, in the house of Simon the leper,

7 There came vnto him a woman, hauing an alabaster boxe of very precious ointment, and powred it on his head, as he sate at meat.

8 But when his disciples saw it, they had indignation, saying, To what purpose is this waste?

9 For this ointment might haue bin sold for much, and giuen to the poore.

10 When Iesus vnderstood it, he said vnto them, Why trouble ye the woman? for she hath wrought a good worke vpon me.

11 * For ye haue the poore alwayes with you, but me ye haue not alwayes.

12 For in that she hath powred this ointment on my body, shee did it for my buriall.

13 Verely I say vnto you, Wheresoeuer this Gospel shall be preached in the whole world, there shall also this, that this woman hath done, be told for a memoriall of her.

14 ¶ * Then one of the twelue, called Iudas Iscariot, went vnto the chiefe Priests,

15 And said vnto them, What will ye giue me, and I will deliuer him vnto you? and they couenanted with him for thirtie pieces of siluer.

16 And from that time he sought opportunitie to betray him.

17 ¶ * Now the first day of the feast of vnleauened bread, the disciples came to Iesus, saying vnto him, Where wilt thou that we prepare for thee to eat the Passeouer?

18 And he said, Goe into the citie to such a man, and say vnto him, The Master saith, My time is at hand, I will keepe the Passeouer at thy house with my disciples.

19 And the disciples did, as Iesus had appointed them, and they made ready the Passeouer.

20 * Now when the euen was come, he sate downe with the twelue.

21 And as they did eate, he said, Verely I say vnto you, that one of you shal betray me.

22 And they were exceeding sorowfull, and began euery one of them to say vnto him, Lord, Is it I?

23 And he answered and said, * Hee that dippeth his hand with mee in the dish, the same shall betray me.

24 The sonne of man goeth as it is written of him: but woe vnto that man by whom the sonne of man is betrayed:

It

Marginal references (left column):

* Psal. 6. 8. chap. 7. 23.

* Dan. 12. 2 iohn 5. 29.

* Mar. 14. 1 luke 22. 1. iohn 13. 1.

* Ioh. 11. 47

* Mar. 14. 3 iohn 11. 1.

Marginal references (right column):

* Deu. 15.

* Marke 1 10. luke 22. 3.

* Mar. 14. 12. luke 22. 7.

* Mark. 18. luke 14. ioh. 1 21.

* Psal. 41.

It had bin good for that man, if hee had not bene borne.

25 Then Iudas, which betrayed him, answered, and said, Master, Is it I? He said vnto him, Thou hast said.

26 ¶ And as they were eating, * Ieſus took bread, and ||bleſſed it, and brake it, and gaue it to the Disciples, and said, Take, eate, this is my body.

27 And he tooke the cup, and gaue thankes, and gaue it to them, saying, Drinke ye all of it:

28 For this is my blood of the new Testament, which is shed for many for the remission of sinnes.

29 But I say vnto you, I will not drinke henceforth of this fruite of the vine, vntill that day when I drinke it new with you in my fathers kingdom.

30 And when they had sung an ||hymne, they went out into the mount of Oliues.

31 Then saith Iesus vnto them, * All ye shall be offended because of me this night, For it is written, * I will smite the Shepheard, and the sheepe of the flocke shall be scattered abroad.

32 But after I am risen againe, * I will goe before you into Galilee.

33 Peter answered, and said vnto him, Though all men shall be offended because of thee, yet will I neuer be offended.

34 Iesus said vnto him, * Verily I say vnto thee, that this might before the cocke crow, thou shalt denie me thrise.

35 Peter said vnto him, Though I should die with thee, yet will I not denie thee. Likewise also said all the Disciples.

36 ¶ * Then commeth Iesus with them vnto a place called Gethsemane, and saith vnto the Disciples, Sit yee heere, while I goe and pray yonder.

37 And hee tooke with him Peter, and the two sonnes of Zebedee, and beganne to be sorrowful, and very heauie.

38 Then saith he vnto them, My soule is exceeding sorrowfull, euen vnto death : tary ye heere, & watch with me.

39 And he went a little further, and fell on his face, and prayed, saying, O my father, if it be possible, let this cup passe from me : neuerthelesse, not as I will, but as thou wilt.

40 And he commeth vnto the Disciples, and findeth them asleepe, and saith vnto Peter, What, could ye not watch with me one houre?

41 Watch and pray, that yee enter not into temptation : The spirit indeed is willing, but the flesh *is* weake.

42 He went away again the second time, and prayed, saying, O my father, if this cup may not passe away from me, except I drinke it, thy will be done.

43 And he came and found them asleepe againe : For their eies were heauie.

44 And he left them, and went away againe, and prayed the third time, saying the same words.

45 Then commeth he to his Disciples, and saith vnto them, Sleepe on now, and take your rest, behold, the houre is at hand, and the sonne of man is betrayed into the hands of sinners.

46 Rise, let vs be going : behold, he is at hand that doeth betray me.

47 ¶ And * while he yet spake, loe, Iudas one of the twelue came, and with him a great multitude with swords and staues from the chiefe Priests and Elders of the people.

48 Now he that betrayed him, gaue them a signe, saying, Whomsoeuer I shall kisse, that same is he, hold him fast.

49 And forthwith hee came to Iesus, and said, Haile master, and kissed him.

50 And Iesus said vnto him, Friend, Wherefore art thou come? Then came they, and laid handes on Iesus, and tooke him.

51 And behold, one of them which were with Iesus, stretched out his hand, and drew his sword, and stroke a seruant of the high Priests, and smote off his eare.

52 Then said Iesus vnto him, Put vp againe thy sword into his place : * for all they that take the sword, shall perish with the sword.

53 Thinkest thou that I cannot now pray to my father, and he shall presently giue me more then twelue legions of Angels?

54 But how then shall the Scriptures be fulfilled, * that thus it must be?

55 In that same houre said Iesus to the multitudes, Are ye come out as against a thiefe with swords and staues for to take mee? I sate daily with you teaching in the Temple, and ye laide no hold on me.

56 But all this was done, that the * Scriptures of the Prophets might be fulfilled. Then all the Disciples forsooke him, and fled:

57 ¶ * And

* 1. Cor. 11
24.
|| Many
Greeke co-
pies haue,
gaue thanks.

|| Or, psalme.

* Marke 14.
27. iohn.
16. 32.

* Zach. 13.
7.

* Mar. 14.
28. and 16.
7.

* Iohn 13.
38.

* Marke 14
32. luke 22.
39.

* Mar. 14.
43. luke 22.
47. iohn 18
3.

* Gen. 9. 6.
reuel. 13.
10.

* Esai. 53.
10.

* Lamen. 4.
20.

* Mark. 14.
53. luke
22. 54. iohn
18. 13.

57 ¶ *And they that had laid hold on Iesus, led him away to Caiaphas the high Priest, where the Scribes and the Elders were assembled.

58 But Peter followed him afarre off, vnto the high Priests palace, and went in, and sate with the seruants to see the end.

59 Now the chiefe Priests and Elders, and all the councell, sought false witnesse against Iesus to put him to death,

60 But found none: yea, though many false witnesses came, yet found they none. At the last came two false witnesses,

* Iohn 2.
19.

61 And said, This *fellow* said, *I am able to destroy the Temple of God, and to build it in three dayes.

62 And the high Priest arose, and said vnto him, Answerest thou nothing? what is it, which these witnesse against thee?

63 But Iesus held his peace. And the high Priest answered, and said vnto him, I adiure thee by the liuing God, that thou tell vs, whether thou bee the Christ the Sonne of God.

64 Iesus saith vnto him, Thou hast saide: Neuerthelesse I say vnto you, *Hereafter shall yee see the Sonne of man sitting on the right hand of power, and comming in the clouds of heauen.

* Chap. 16.
27. 1. thess.
4. 16. rom.
14. 10.

65 Then the high Priest rent his clothes, saying, He hath spoken blasphemie: what further need haue wee of witnesses? Behold, now ye haue heard his blasphemie.

66 What thinke ye? They answered and said, He is guiltie of death.

* Esay. 50.
6.
‖ Or, rods.

67 *Then did they spit in his face, and buffeted him, and others smote him with ‖the palmes of their hands,

68 Saying, Prophecie vnto vs, thou Christ, who is he that smote thee?

* Mark. 14.
66. luke 22.
55. iohn 18.
25.

69 ¶ *Now Peter sate without in the palace: and a damosell came vnto him, saying, Thou also wast with Iesus of Galilee.

70 But hee denied before them all, saying, I know not what thou saiest.

71 And when he was gone out into the porch, another maide saw him, and saide vnto them that were there, This fellow was also with Iesus of Nazareth.

72 And againe hee denied with an oath, I doe not know the man.

73 And after a while came vnto him they that stood by, and saide to Peter, Surely thou also art one of them, for thy speech bewrayeth thee.

74 Then beganne hee to curse and to sweare, *saying*, I know not the man. And immediatly the cocke crew.

75 And Peter remembred the words of Iesus, which said vnto him, Before the cocke crow, thou shalt denie mee thrice. And hee went out, and wept bitterly.

CHAP. XXVII.

1 Christ is deliuered bound to Pilate. 3 Iudas hangeth himselfe. 19 Pilate admonished of his wife, 24 washeth his hands: 26 and looseth Barabbas. 29 Christ is crowned with thornes, 34 crucified, 40 reuiled, 50 dieth, and is buried: 66 his Sepulchre is sealed, and watched.

W Hen the morning was come, *all the chiefe Priests and Elders of the people, tooke counsell against Iesus to put him to death.

* Mark. 15.
1. luke 22.
66. ioh 18.
28.

2 And when they had bound him, they led him away, and deliuered him to Pontius Pilate the gouernour.

3 ¶ Then Iudas, which had betraied him, when he saw that hee was condemned, repented himselfe, and brought againe the thirtie pieces of siluer to the chiefe Priests and Elders,

4 Saying, I haue sinned, in that I haue betraied the innocent blood. And they said, What is that to vs? see thou to that.

* Act. 1. 18.

5 And hee cast downe the pieces of siluer in the Temple, *and departed, and went and hanged himselfe.

6 And the chiefe Priests tooke the siluer pieces, and said, It is not lawfull for to put them into the treasurie, because it is the price of blood.

7 And they tooke counsell, and bought with them the potters field, to burie strangers in.

* Acts 1.
19.

8 Wherefore that field was called, *The field of blood vnto this day.

* Zach. 11.
12.
‖ Or, whom
they bought
of the children of Israel.

9 (Then was fulfilled that which was spoken by Ieremie the Prophet, saying, *And they tooke the thirtie pieces of siluer, the price of him that was valued, ‖whom they of the children of Israel did value:

10 And gaue them for the potters field, as the Lord appointed me.)

11 And Iesus stood before the gouernour, and the gouernour asked him, saying; Art thou the King of the Iewes?

Iewes? And Iesus sayd vnto him, Thou sayest.

12 And when hee was accused of the chiefe Priests and Elders, he answered nothing.

13 Then saith Pilate vnto him, Hearest thou not how many things they witnesse against thee?

14 And he answered him to neuer a word : insomuch that the Gouernour marueiled greatly.

15 *Now at *that* feast the Gouernor was woont to release vnto the people a prisoner, whom they would.

16 And they had then a notable prisoner, called Barabbas.

17 Therefore when they were gathered together, Pilate said vnto them, Whom will ye that I release vnto you? Barabbas, or Iesus, which is called Christ?

18 For hee knew that for enuie they had deliuered him.

19 ¶ When he was set downe on the Iudgement seate, his wife sent vnto him, saying, Haue thou nothing to doe with that iust man : for I haue suffered many things this day in a dreame, because of him.

20 *But the chiefe Priestes and Elders perswaded the multitude that they should aske Barabbas, & destroy Iesus.

21 The Gouernour answered, and said vnto them, Whether of the twaine will ye that I release vnto you? They said, Barabbas.

22 Pilate said vnto them, What shall I doe then with Iesus, which is called Christ? They all sayde vnto him, Let him be crucified.

23 And the Gouernour said, Why, what euil hath he done? But they cried out ȳ more, saying, Let him be crucified.

24 ¶ When Pilate saw that he could preuaile nothing, but that rather a tumult was made, hee tooke water, and washed his hands before the multitude, saying, I am innocent of the blood of this iust person : see yee to it.

25 Then answered all the people, and said, His blood *be* on vs, and on our children.

26 ¶ Then released hee Barabbas vnto them, and when he had scourged Iesus, he deliuered him to be crucified.

27 *Then the souldiers of the Gouernour tooke Iesus into the ‖ common hall, and gathered vnto him the whole band *of souldiers*.

28 And they stripped him, and put on him a scarlet robe.

29 ¶ And when they had platted a crowne of thornes, they put it vpon his head, and a reed in his right hand : and they bowed the knee before him, and mocked him, saying, Haile king of the Iewes.

30 And they spit vpon him, and tooke the reed, and smote him on the head.

31 And after that they had mocked him, they tooke the robe off from him, and put his owne raiment on him, and led him away to crucifie him.

32 *And as they came out, they found a man of Cyrene, Simon by name : him they compelled to beare his Crosse.

33 *And when they were come vnto a place called Golgotha, that is to say, a place of a skull,

34 ¶ They gaue him vineger to drinke, mingled with gall : and when hee had tasted thereof, hee would not drinke.

35 And they crucified him, and parted his garments, casting lots : that it might be fulfilled which was spoken by the Prophet, *They parted my garments among them, and vpon my vesture did they cast lots.

36 And sitting downe, they watched him there :

37 And set vp ouer his head, his accusation writtten, *THIS IS IESVS THE KING OF THE IEWES*.

38 Then were there two theeues crucified with him : one on the right hand, and another on the left.

39 ¶ And they that passed by, reuiled him, wagging their heads,

40 And saying, Thou that destroyest the Temple, & buildest it in three dayes, saue thy selfe : If thou be the Sonne of God, come downe from the Crosse.

41 Likewise also the chiefe Priests mocking him, with the Scribes and Elders, said,

42 He saued others, himselfe he cannot saue : If he be the King of Israel, let him now come downe from the Crosse, and we will beleeue him.

43 *He trusted in God, let him deliuer him now if hee will haue him : for he said, I am the Sonne of God.

44 The thieues also which were crucified with him, cast ȳ same in his teeth.

45 Now from the sixth houre there was darkenesse ouer all the land vnto the ninth houre.

46 And

* Luke 23. 17.

* Iohn 18. 40. actes 3. 14.

* Ioh. 19. 1.

‖ Or, *gouernours house*.

* Marke 15. 21. luke 23. 26.

* Iohn 19. 17.

* Psal. 22. 18.

* Psal. 22. 8. wisd. 2. 15, 16.

*Psal. 22. 1.

46 And about the ninth houre, Iesus cried with a loud voyce, saying, *Eli, Eli, Lamasabachthani*, that is to say, * My God, my God, why hast thou forsaken mee?

47 Some of them that stood there, when they heard that, said, This man calleth for Elias.

*Psa. 69. 22

48 And straightway one of them ran, and tooke a spunge, * and filled it with vineger, and put it on a reede, and gaue him to drinke.

49 The rest said, Let bee, let vs see whether Elias will come to saue him.

50 ¶ Iesus, when hee had cried againe with a loud voice, yeelded vp the ghost.

51 And behold, the vaile of the Temple was rent in twaine, from the top to the bottome, and the earth did quake, and the rocks rent.

52 And the graues were opened, and many bodies of Saints which slept, arose,

53 And came out of the graues after his resurrection, and went into the holy citie, and appeared vnto many.

54 Now when the Centurion, and they that were with him, watching Iesus, saw the earthquake, & those things that were done, they feared greatly, saying, Truely this was the Son of God.

55 And many women were there (beholding afarre off) which followed Iesus from Galilee, ministring vnto him.

56 Among which was Mary Magdalene, & Mary the mother of Iames and Ioses, and the mother of Zebedees children.

*Mar. 15. 42. luk. 23. 50. ioh. 19. 38.

57 * When the Euen was come, there came a rich man of Arimathea, named Ioseph, who also himselfe was Iesus disciple:

58 He went to Pilate, and begged the body of Iesus : then Pilate commanded the body to be deliuered.

59 And when Ioseph had taken the body, hee wrapped it in a cleane linnen cloth,

60 And laide it in his owne newe tombe, which he had hewen out in the rocke : and he rolled a great stone to the doore of the sepulchre, and departed.

61 And there was Mary Magdalene, and the other Mary, sitting ouer against the sepulchre.

62 ¶ Now the next day that followed the day of the preparation, the chiefe Priests and Pharisees came together vnto Pilate,

63 Saying, Sir, we remember that that deceiuer said, while he was yet aliue, After three daies I wil rise againe.

64 Command therfore that the sepulchre be made sure, vntill the third day, lest his disciples come by night, & steale him away, and say vnto the people, He is risen from the dead : so the last errour shalbe worse then the first.

65 Pilate said vnto them, Yee haue a watch, goe your way, make it as sure as you can.

66 So they went, and made the sepulchre sure, sealing the stone, and setting a watch.

CHAP. XXVIII.

1 Christs resurrection is declared by an Angel, to the women. 9 He himselfe appeareth vnto them. 11 The high Priests giue the souldiers money to say that he was stollen out of his sepulchre. 16 Christ appeareth to his disciples, 12 and sendeth them to baptize and teach all Nations.

*Mar. 16. 1 iohn 20. 1.

IN the * ende of the Sabbath, as it began to dawne towards the first day of the weeke, came Mary Magdalene, and the other Mary, to see the sepulchre.

2 And behold, there ‖ was a great earthquake, for the Angel of the Lord descended from heauen, and came and rolled backe the stone from the doore, and sate vpon it.

‖ Or, had bin

3 His countenance was like lightning, and his raiment white as snowe.

4 And for feare of him, the keepers did shake, and became as dead men.

5 And the Angel answered, and said vnto the women, Feare not ye : for I know that ye seeke Iesus, which was crucified.

6 He is not here : for he is risen, as hee said: Come, see the place where the Lord lay.

7 And goe quickly, and tell his disciples that he is risen from the dead. And behold, hee goeth before you into Galilee, there shall ye see him : loe, I haue told you.

8 And they departed quickly from the sepulchre, with feare and great ioy, and did run to bring his disciples word.

9 ¶ And as they went to tell his disciples, behold, Iesus met them, saying, All haile. And they came, and held him

by

by the feet, and worshipped him.

10 Then said Iesus vnto them, Be not afraid : Goe tell my brethren that they goe into Galilee, and there shall they see me.

11 ¶ Now when they were going, behold, some of the watch came into the citie, and shewed vnto the chiefe Priests all the things that were done.

12 And when they were assembled with the Elders, and had taken counsell, they gaue large money vnto the souldiers,

13 Saying, Say ye, His disciples came by night, and stole him away while we slept.

14 And if this come to the gouernours eares, wee will perswade him, and secure you.

15 So they tooke the money, and did as they were taught. And this saying is commonly reported among the Iewes vntill this day.

16 ¶ Then the eleuen disciples went away into Galilee, into a mountaine where Iesus had appointed them.

17 And when they saw him, they worshipped him : but some doubted.

18 And Iesus came, and spake vnto them, saying, All power is giuen vnto me in heauen and in earth.

19 ¶ *Goe ye therefore, and teach all nations, baptizing them in the Name of the Father, and of the Sonne, and of the holy Ghost:

20 Teaching them to obserue all things, whatsoeuer I haue commanded you : and loe, I am with you alway, euen vnto the end of the world. Amen.

*Mark. 16. 15.

¶ The Goſpel according to S.Marke.

CHAP. I.

1 *The office of Iohn the Baptist. 9 Iesus is baptized, 12 tempted, 14 he preacheth : 16 calleth Peter, Andrew, Iames and Iohn : 23 healeth one that had a deuill, 29 Peters mother in law, 32 many diseased persons, 41 and cleanseth the Leper.

He beginning of the Gospel of Iesus Christ, the Sonne of God,

2 As it is written in the Prophets, *Behold, I send my messenger before thy face, which shall prepare thy way before thee.

*Mala. 3. 1.

3 *The voice of one crying in the wildernesse, Prepare ye the way of the Lord, make his paths straight.

*Esa. 40. 3. luke 3. 4. iohn 1. 23.

4 *Iohn did baptize in the wildernesse, and preach the baptisme of repentance, ||for the remission of sinnes.

*Matt. 3. 1.
|| Or, vnto.

5 *And there went out vnto him all the land of Iudea, and they of Ierusalem, and were all baptized of him in the riuer of Iordane, cōfessing their sinnes.

*Matt. 3. 5.

6 And Iohn was *clothed with camels haire, and with a girdle of a skin about his loines : and he did eat locusts and wilde honie,

*Matt. 3. 1.

7 And preached, saying, There commeth one mightier then I after me, the latchet of whose shooes I am not worthy to stoupe downe, and vnloose.

8 I indeed haue baptized you with water : but hee shall baptize you with the holy Ghost.

9 *And it came to passe in those daies, that Iesus came from Nazareth of Galilee, and was baptized of Iohn in Iordane.

*Matth. 3. 13.

10 And straightway comming vp out of the water, hee saw the heauens ||opened, and the Spirit like a doue descending vpon him.

|| Or, clouen, or rent.

11 And there came a voice from heauen, saying, Thou art my beloued Sonne, in whom I am well pleased.

12 *And immediately the Spirit drieth him into the wildernesse.

*Matt. 4. 1.

13 And he was there in the wildernesse fourtie daies tempted of Satan, and was with the wildbeasts, and the Angels ministred vnto him.

14 Now after that Iohn was put in

* Matth. 4.
12.
in prison, *Iesus came into Galilee, preaching the Gospell of the kingdome of God,

15 And saying, The time is fulfilled, and the kingdome of God is at hand: repent ye, and beleeue the Gospell.

* Matth. 4.
18.
16 *Now as he walked by the Sea of Galilee, he saw Simon, and Andrew his brother, casting a net into the Sea (for they were fishers.)

17 And Iesus said vnto them, Come ye after me; and I will make you to become fishers of men.

18 And straightway they forsooke their nets, and followed him.

19 And when hee had gone a little further thence, hee saw Iames the sonne of Zebedee, and Iohn his brother, who also were in the ship mending their nets.

20 And straightway he called them: and they left their father Zebedee in the ship with the hired seruants, and went after him.

* Matth. 4.
13.
21 * And they went into Capernaum, and straightway on the Sabbath day he entred into the Synagogue, and taught.

* Matth. 7.
28.
22 *And they were astonished at his doctrine : for hee taught them as one that had authority, and not as the Scribes.

* Luke 4.
33.
23 *And there was in their Synagogue a man with an vncleane spirit, and he cried out,

24 Saying, Let vs alone, what haue we to doe with thee, thou Iesus of Nazareth? Art thou come to destroy vs? I know thee who thou art, the holy One of God.

25 And Iesus rebuked him, saying, Hold thy peace, and come out of him.

26 And when the vncleane spirit had torne him, and cried with a lowd voice, he came out of him.

27 And they were all amased, insomuch that they questioned among themselues, saying, What thing is this? What new doctrine is this? For with authoritie commandeth he euen the vncleane spirits, and they doe obey him.

28 And immediatly his fame spread abroad throughout al the region round about Galilee.

* Matth. 8.
14.
29 *And forthwith, when they were come out of the Synagogue, they entered into the house of Simon, and Andrew, with Iames and Iohn.

30 But Simons wiues mother lay sicke of a feuer : and anone they tell him of her.

31 And he came and tooke her by the hand, and lift her vp, and immediately the feuer left her, and she ministred vnto them.

32 And at euen, when the Sunne did set, they brought vnto him all that were diseased, and them that were possessed with diuels :

33 And all the citie was gathered together at the doore.

34 And he healed many that were sicke of diuers diseases, and cast out many deuils, and suffered not the deuils ||to speake, because they knew him.

|| Or, to say
that they
knew him.
35 And in the morning, rising vp a great while before day, hee went out, and departed into a solitarie place, and there prayed.

36 And Simon, and they that were with him, followed after him :

37 And when they had found him, they said vnto him, All men seek for thee.

38 And he said vnto them, Let vs goe into ẏ next townes, that I may preach there also : for therefore came I foorth.

39 And he preached in their Synagogues throughout all Galilee, and cast out deuils.

40 *And there came a leper to him, beseeching him, and kneeling downe to him, and saying vnto him, If thou wilt, thou canst make me cleane.

* Matth. 8.
41 And Iesus mooued with compassion, put foorth his hand, and touched him, and saith vnto him, I will, be thou cleane.

42 And assoone as he had spoken, immediately the leprosie departed from him, and he was cleansed.

43 And he straitly charged him, and forthwith sent him away,

44 And saith vnto him, See thou say nothing to any man : but goe thy way, shew thy selfe to the Priest, and offer for thy clensing those things which Moses commanded, for a testimony vnto them.

45 *But he went out, and beganne to publish it much, and to blase abroad the matter : insomuch that Iesus could no more openly enter into the citie, but was without in desert places : and they came to him from euery quarter.

* Luke 5.
15.

CHAP. II.

1 Christ healeth one sicke of the palsie, 14 calleth Matthew from the receit of Custome,
15 eateth

15 eateth with Publicanes, and sinners,
18 excuseth his disciples for not fasting,
23 and for plucking the eares of corne on
the Sabbath day.

*Matt. 9. 1.

Nd againe *hee entred into Capernaum after some dayes, and it was noysed that he was in the house.

2 And straightway many were gathered together, insomuch that there was no roome to receiue *them,* no not so much as about the doore: and he preached the word vnto them.

3 And they come vnto him, bringing one sicke of the palsie, which was borne of foure.

4 And when they could not come nigh vnto him for preasse, they vncouered the roofe where he was : and when they had broken it vp, they let downe the bed wherin the sick of the palsie lay.

5 When Iesus saw their faith, hee said vnto the sicke of the palsie, Sonne, thy sinnes be forgiuen thee.

6 But there were certaine of the Scribes sitting there, and reasoning in their hearts,

*Iob 14. 4.
esay 43. 25.

7 Why doeth this man thus speake blasphemies? *Who can forgiue sinnes but God onely ?

8 And immediatly, when Iesus perceiued in his Spirit, that they so reasoned within themselues, he said vnto them, Why reason ye these things in your hearts?

9 Whether is it easier to say to the sicke of the palsie, Thy sinnes be forgiuen thee : or to say, Arise, and take vp thy bed and walke?

10 But that yee may know that the Sonne of man hath power on earth to forgiue sinnes, (Hee saith to the sicke of the palsie,)

11 I say vnto thee, Arise, & take vp thy bed, & goe thy way into thine house.

12 And immediatly he arose, tooke vp the bed, and went foorth before them all, insomuch that they were all amazed, and glorified God, saying, Wee neuer saw it on this fashion.

13 And he went foorth againe by the sea side, and all the multitude resorted vnto him, and he taught them.

*Matt. 9. 9.
‖ Or, at the
place where
the Custome
was recei-
ued.

14 *And as he passed by, he saw Leui the son of Alpheus sitting ‖at the receit of Custome, and said vnto him, Follow me. And he arose, and followed him.

15 And it came to passe, that as Iesus sate at meate in his house, many Publicanes and sinners sate also together with Iesus and his disciples : for there were many, & they followed him.

16 And when the Scribes and Pharisees saw him eate with Publicanes and sinners, they said vnto his disciples, How is it that hee eateth and drinketh with Publicanes and sinners ?

17 When Iesus heard it, he saith vnto them, They that are whole, haue no need of the Physition, but they that are sicke : I came not to call the righteous, but sinners to repentance.

*Matth. 9.
14 luke 5.
32.

18 *And the disciples of Iohn, and of the Pharisees vsed to fast ; and they come, and say vnto him, Why doe the disciples of Iohn, and of the Pharisees fast, but thy disciples fast not ?

19 And Iesus said vnto them, Can the children of the bride-chamber fast, while the Bridegrome is with them ? As long as they haue the Bridegrome with them, they cannot fast.

20 But the dayes will come, when the Bridegrome shall bee taken away from them, and then shall they fast in those dayes.

‖ Or, raw, or
vnwrought.

21 No man also soweth a piece of ‖new cloth on an old garment : else the new piece that filled it vp, taketh away from the old, & the rent is made worse.

22 And no man putteth new wine into old bottles, else the new wine doeth burst the bottles, and the wine is spilled, and the bottles will bee marred : But new wine must bee put into new bottles.

*Matt. 12.
1.

23 *And it came to passe, that he went thorow the corne fields on the Sabbath day, & his disciples began as they went, to plucke the eares of corne.

24 And the Pharisees saide vnto him, Behold, why do they on the Sabbath day that which is not lawfull?

25 And he said vnto them, Haue ye neuer read what Dauid did, when hee had need, and was an hungred, he, and they that were with him ?

26 How hee went into the house of God in the dayes of Abiathar the high Priest, and did eate the Shew-bread, which is not lawfull to eate, but for the Priests, and gaue also to them which were with him ?

27 And hee said vnto them, The Sabbath was made for man, and not man for the Sabbath:

28 Therefore the Sonne of man is Lord also of the Sabbath.

CHAP.

CHAP. III.

1 Christ healeth the withered hand, 10 and many other infirmities: 11 Rebuketh the vncleane spirits: 13 Chooseth his twelue Apostles: 22 Conuinceth the blasphemie of casting out deuils by Beelzebub: 31 and sheweth who are his brother, sister and mother.

* Mat. 12. 9

 ND *he entred againe into the Synagogue, and there was a man there which had a withered hand:

2 And they watched him, whether hee would heale him on the Sabbath day, that they might accuse him.

3 And he saith vnto the man which had the withered hand, Stand forth.

4 And hee saith vnto them, Is it lawfull to doe good on the Sabbath dayes, or to doe euill? to saue life, or to kill? but they held their peace.

5 And when he had looked round about on them with anger, being grieued for the ‖hardnesse of their hearts, He saith vnto the man, Stretch foorth thine hand. And he stretched it out: and his hand was restored whole as the other.

‖ Or, blindnesse.

6 And the Pharisees went forth, and straightway tooke counsel with the Herodians against him, how they might destroy him.

7 But Iesus withdrew himselfe with his disciples to the Sea: and a great multitude from Galilee followed him, and from Iudea,

8 And from Hierusalem, and from Idumea, and from beyond Iordane, and they about Tyre & Sydon, a great multitude, when they had heard what great things he did, came vnto him.

9 And he spake to his disciples that a small ship should wait on him, because of the multitude, lest they should throng him.

10 For he had healed many, insomuch that they ‖preassed vpon him, for to touch him, as many as had plagues.

‖ Or, rushed

11 And vncleane spirits, when they saw him, fell downe before him, and cried, saying, Thou art the Sonne of God.

12 And he straitly charged them, that they should not make him knowen.

* Matt. 10. 1

13 * And he goeth vp into a mountaine, and calleth vnto him whom he would: and they came vnto him.

14 And he ordeined twelue, that they should be with him, and that hee might send them foorth to preach:

15 And to haue power to heale sicknesses, and to cast out deuils.

16 And Simon he surnamed Peter.

17 And Iames the sonne of Zebedee, and Iohn the brother of Iames (and he surnamed them Boanerges, which is, The sonnes of thunder.)

18 And Andrew, and Philip, and Bartholomew, and Matthew, and Thomas, and Iames the sonne of Alpheus, and Thaddeus, and Simon the Canaanite,

19 And Iudas Iscariot, which also betrayed him: and they went ‖into an house.

‖ Or, home.

20 And the multitude commeth together againe, so that they could not so much as eate bread.

21 And when his ‖friends heard of it, they went out to lay hold on him, for they said, He is beside himselfe.

‖ Or, kinsemen.

22 ¶ And the Scribes which came downe from Hierusalem, said, *He hath Beelzebub, and by the prince of the deuils, casteth he out deuils.

* Mat. 9. 34

23 And he called them vnto him, and said vnto them in parables, Howe can Satan cast out Satan?

24 And if a kingdome be diuided against it selfe, that kingdome cannot stand.

25 And if a house be diuided against it selfe, that house cannot stand.

26 And if Satan rise vp against himselfe, and be diuided, hee cannot stand, but hath an end.

27 No man can enter into a strong mans house, and spoile his goods, except he will first bind the strong man, and then he will spoile his house.

28 *Verely I say vnto you, All sinnes shalbe forgiuen vnto the sonnes of men, and blasphemies, wherewith soeuer they shall blaspheme:

* Matt. 12. 31.

29 But he that shal blaspheme against the holy Ghost, hath neuer forgiuenesse, but is in danger of eternall damnation.

30 Because they said, He hath an vncleane spirit.

31 ¶ *There came then his brethren, and his mother, and standing without, sent vnto him, calling him.

* Mat. 12. 46.

32 And the multitude sate about him, and they said vnto him, Behold, thy mother and thy brethren without seeke for thee.

33 And he answered them, saying, Who is my mother, or my brethren?

34 And

34 And he looked round about on them which sate about him, and saide, Behold my mother and my brethren.

35¶ For whosoeuer shall doe the will of God, the same is my brother, and my sister, and mother.

CHAP. IIII.

1 The parable of the sower, 14 and the meaning thereof. 21 We must communicate the light of our knowledge to others. 26 The parable of the seede growing secretly, 30 and of the Mustard seede. 35 Christ stilleth the tempest on the Sea.

*Matth. 13. 1.

A Nd * he beganne againe to teach by the Sea side : and there was gathered vnto him a great multitude, so that he entred into a ship, and sate in the Sea : and the whole multitude was by the Sea on the land.

2 And he taught them many things by parables, and said vnto them in his doctrine,

3 Hearken, Behold, there went out a sower to sow :

4 And it came to passe as he sowed, some fell by the way side, and the foules of the aire came, & deuoured it vp.

5 And some fell on stonie ground, where it had not much earth : and immediately it sprang vp, because it had no depth of earth.

6 But when the Sunne was vp, it was scorched, and because it had no roote, it withered away.

7 And some fell among thornes, and the thornes grew vp, and choked it, and it yeelded no fruite.

8 And other fell on good ground, and did yeeld fruite that sprang vp, and increased, and brought foorth some thirtie, & some sixtie, & some an hundred.

9 And he said vnto them, He that hath eares to heare, let him heare.

10 And when hee was alone, they that were about him, with the twelue, asked of him the parable.

11 And he said vnto them, Vnto you it is giuen to know the mystery of the kingdome of God : but vnto them that are without, all these things are done in parables :

*Matth. 13. 14.

12 * That seeing they may see, and not perceiue, and hearing they may heare, and not vnderstand, lest at any time they should be conuerted, and their sinnes should be forgiuen them.

13 And he said vnto them, Know ye not this parable? And how then will you know all parables?

14 ¶ The Sower soweth the word.

15 And these are they by the way side, where the word is sowen, but when they haue heard, Satan commeth immediately, and taketh away the word that was sowen in their hearts.

16 And these are they likewise which are sowen on stonie ground, who when they haue heard the word, immediately receiue it with gladnesse :

17 And haue no roote in themselues, and so endure but for a time : afterward when affliction or persecution ariseth for the words sake, immediately they are offended.

18 And these are they which are sowen among thornes : such as heare the word,

*1. Tim. 6. 17.

19 And the cares of this world, * and the deceitfulnesse of riches, and the lusts of other things entring in, choke the word, and it becommeth vnfruitfull.

20 And these are they which are sowen on good ground, such as heare the word, and receiue it, & bring foorth fruit, some thirty fold, some sixtie, and some an hundred.

*Matth. 5. 15. ‖ The word in the originall, signifieth a lesse measure as Mat. 5. 15. *Matth. 10. 26.

21 ¶ * And he said vnto them, Is a candle brought to be put vnder a ‖bushell, or vnder a bed? & not to be set on a candlesticke?

22 * For there is nothing hid, which shall not be manifested : neither was any thing kept secret, but that it should come abroad.

23 If any man haue eares to heare, let him heare.

*Matth. 7. 2.

24 And he said vnto them, Take heed what you heare : * With what measure ye mete, it shalbe measured to you : And vnto you that heare, shal more be giuen.

*Matth. 13. 12.

25 * For he that hath, to him shall be giuen : and he that hath not, from him shall be taken, euen that which he hath.

26 ¶ And he said, So is the kingdome of God, as if a man should cast seede into the ground,

27 And should sleepe, and rise night and day, and the seed should spring, and grow vp, he knoweth not how.

28 For the earth bringeth foorth fruite of herselfe, first the blade, then the eare, after that the full corne in the eare.

‖Or, ripe.

29 But when the fruite is ‖brought foorth, immediately he putteth in the sickle, because the haruest is come.

*Matth. 13. 31.

30 ¶ And he said, *Wherunto shal we liken the kingdome of God? Or with what

what comparison shall we compare it?

31 It is like a graine of mustard seed: which when it is sowen in the earth, is lesse then all the seedes that be in the earth.

32 But when it is sowen, it groweth vp, and becommeth greater then all herbes, & shooteth out great branches, so that the fowles of the aire may lodge vnder the shadow of it.

33 *And with many such parables spake hee the word vnto them, as they were able to heare it.

34 But without a parable spake he not vnto them, and when they were a-lone, hee expounded all things to his disciples.

35 *And the same day, when the E-uen was come, he saith vnto them, Let vs passe ouer vnto the other side.

36 And when they had sent away the multitude, they tooke him, euen as he was in the ship, and there were also with him other litle ships.

37 And there arose a great storme of wind, and the waues beat into the ship, so that it was now full.

38 And he was in the hinder part of the ship asleepe on a pillow : and they a-wake him, and say vnto him, Master, carest thou not, that we perish?

39 And hee arose, and rebuked the winde, and said vnto the sea, Peace, be still : and the winde ceased, and there was a great calme.

40 And he said vnto them, Why are ye so fearefull? How is it that you haue no faith?

41 And they feared exceedingly, and saide one to another, What maner of man is this, that euen the winde and the sea obey him?

CHAP. V.

1 Christ deliuering the possessed of the Legion of deuils, 13 They enter into the swine, 25 Hee healeth the woman of the bloody issue, 35 and raiseth from death Iairus his daughter.

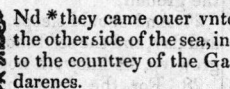

Nd *they came ouer vnto the other side of the sea, in-to the countrey of the Ga-darenes.

2 And when hee was come out of the ship, immediatly there met him out of the tombes, a man with an vncleane spirit,

3 Who had his dwelling among the tombs, and no man could binde him, no not with chaines :

4 Because that hee had bene often bound with fetters and chaines, and the chaines had bene plucked asunder by him, and the fetters broken ip pie-ces : neither could any man tame him.

5 And alwayes night and day, hee was in the mountaines, and in the tombes, crying, and cutting himselfe with stones.

6 But when hee saw Iesus afarre off, he came and worshipped him,

7 And cried with a lowd voice, and said, What haue I to doe with thee, Ie-sus, thou Sonne of the most high God? I adiure thee by God, that thou tor-ment me not.

8 (For he said vnto him, Come out of the man, thou vncleane spirit.)

9 And he asked him, What is thy name? And hee answered, saying, My name is Legion : for we are many.

10 And hee besought him much, that he would not send them away out of the countrey.

11 Now there was there nigh vnto the mountaines a great herd of swine, feeding.

12 And all the deuils besought him, saying, Send vs into the swine, that we may enter into them.

13 And forthwith Iesus gaue them leaue. And the vncleane spirits went out, and entred into the swine, and the herd ranne violently downe a steepe place into the sea (they were about two thousand) and were choked in the sea.

14 And they that fed the swine fled, and tolde it in the citie, and in the coun-trey. And they went out to see what it was that was done.

15 And they come to Iesus, and see him that was possessed with the deuill, and had the Legion, sitting, and clo-thed, and in his right minde : and they were afraid.

16 And they that saw it, tolde them how it befell to him that was possessed with the deuill, and also concerning the swine.

17 And they began to pray him to de-part out of their coasts.

18 And when hee was come into the ship, he that had bene possessed with the deuill prayed him that hee might bee with him.

19 Howbeit Iesus suffered him not, but saith vnto him, Goe home to thy friends, and tel them how great things the Lord hath done for thee, and hath
had

* Matth. 13. 34.

* Matth. 8. 23.

* Matth. 8. 28.

had compassion on thee.

20 And hee departed, and began to publish in Decapolis, how great things Iesus had done for him : and all men did marueile.

21 And when Iesus was passed ouer againe by ship vnto the other side, much people gathered vnto him, and he was nigh vnto the Sea.

^{* Mat. 9. 18.} 22 *And behold, there commeth one of the Rulers of the Synagogue, Iairus by name, and when he saw him, he fell at his feete,

23 And besought him greatly, saying, My litle daughter lieth at the point of death, *I pray thee* come and lay thy hands on her, that shee may be healed, and she shall liue.

24 And Iesus went with him, and much people followed him, and thronged him.

25 And a certaine woman which had an issue of blood twelue yeeres,

26 And had suffered many things of many Physicians, and had spent all that she had, and was nothing bettered, but rather grew worse,

27 When shee had heard of Iesus, came in the prease behinde, and touched his garment.

28 For she said, If I may touch but his clothes, I shalbe whole.

29 And straightway the fountaine of her blood was dried vp : and she felt in her body that she was healed of that plague.

30 And Iesus immediatly knowing in himselfe that vertue had gone out of him, turned him about in the preasse, and said, Who touched my clothes?

31 And his disciples said vnto him, Thou seest the multitude thronging thee, and sayest thou, Who touched me?

32 And he looked round about to see her that had done this thing.

33 But the woman fearing and trembling, knowing what was done in her, came and fell downe before him, and tolde him all the trueth.

34 And he said vnto her, Daughter, thy faith hath made thee whole, goe in peace, and be whole of thy plague.

35 While hee yet spake, there came from the Ruler of the Synagogues *house*, certaine which said, Thy daughter is dead, why troublest thou the Master any further?

36 Assoone as Iesus heard the word that was spoken, he saith vnto the Ru-

ler of the Synagogue, Be not afraid, onely beleeue.

37 And he suffered no man to follow him, saue Peter, & Iames, and Iohn the brother of Iames.

38 And hee commeth to the house of the Ruler of the Synagogue, and seeth the tumult, and them that wept and wailed greatly.

39 And when he was come in, hee saith vnto them , Why make yee this adoe, and weepe? the damosell is not dead, but sleepeth.

40 And they laughed him to scorne : but when he had put them all out, hee taketh the father and the mother of the damosell , and them that were with him, and entreth in where the damosell was lying.

41 And he tooke the damosell by the hand, and said vnto her, *Talitha cumi*, which is, being interpreted, Damosell (I say vnto thee) Arise.

42 And straightway the damosell arose, and walked, for shee was of the age of twelue yeeres : and they were astonished with a great astonishment.

43 And hee charged them straitly, that no man should know it : and commanded that some thing should be giuen her to eate.

CHAP. VI.

1 Christ is contemned of his countreymen. 7 He giueth the twelue power ouer vncleane spirits. 14 Diuers opinions of Christ. 18 Iohn Baptist is beheaded, 29 and buried. 30 The Apostles returne from preaching. 34 The miracle of fiue loaues and two fishes. 45 Christ walketh on the Sea : 53 And healeth all that touch him.

A^{* Mat. 13. 54.}Nd *hee went out from thence, and came into his owne countrey, and his disciples follow him.

2 And when the Sabbath day was come, he began to teach in the Synagogue : and many hearing him, were astonished, saying, From whence hath this man these things? And what wisedome is this which is giuen vnto him, that euen such mightie workes are wrought by his hands?

3 Is not this the carpenter, the sonne of Mary, the brother of Iames and Ioses, and of Iuda, and Simon? And are not his sisters heere with vs? And they were offended at him.

4 But Iesus sayde vnto them,
*A Pro-

* Iohn 4. 44

* A Prophet is not without honour, but in his owne countrey, and among his owne kinne, and in his owne house.

5 And he could there doe no mightie worke, saue that he laid his hands vpon a few sicke folke, and healed them.

6 And he marueiled because of their vnbeliefe. *And he went round about the villages, teaching.

* Mat. 9. 35 luke 13. 22.

* Mat. 10. 1.

7 ¶ *And he calleth vnto him the twelue, and began to send them foorth, by two and two, and gaue them power ouer vncleane spirits.

8 And commanded them that they should take nothing for their iourney, saue a staffe onely: no scrip, no bread, no ||money in their purse:

|| The word signifieth a piece of brasse money, in value lesse then a farthing, mat. 10. 9. but here it is taken in generall formony.

9 But be shod with sandales: and not put on two coats.

10 And he said vnto them, In what place soeuer yee enter into an house, there abide til ye depart from that place.

* Mat. 10. 14
* Act. 13. 51

11 *And whosoeuer shall not receiue you, nor heare you, when yee depart thence, *shake off the dust vnder your feet, for a testimonie against them: Verely I say vnto you, it shalbe more tolerable for Sodom and Gomorrha in the day of iudgement, then for that citie.

12 And they went out, and preached that men should repent.

* Iam. 5. 14.

13 And they cast out many deuils, *and anointed with oyle many, that were sicke, and healed them.

* Mat. 14. 1

14 *And king Herod heard of him (for his name was spread abroad:) and hee said that Iohn the Baptist was risen from the dead, and therefore mightie workes doe shew foorth themselues in him.

15 Others said, That it is Elias. And others said, That it is a Prophet, or as one of the Prophets.

* Luk. 3. 19

16 *But when Herod heard thereof, he said, It is Iohn, whome I beheaded, he is risen from the dead.

17 For Herod himselfe had sent forth and laid hold vpon Iohn, and bound him in prison for Herodias sake, his brother Philips wife, for hee had maried her.

* Leuit. 18. 16.

18 For Iohn had said vnto Herod, *It is not lawfull for thee to haue thy brothers wife.

|| Or, an inward grudge

19 Therfore Herodias had ||a quarrel against him, & would haue killed him, but she could not.

20 For Herod feared Iohn, knowing that he was a iust man, and an holy,

and ||obserued him: and when he heard him, hee did many things, and heard him gladly.

|| Or, kept him or saue him.

21 And when a conuenient day was come, that Herod on his birth day made a supper to his lords, high captaines, and chiefe estates of Galilee:

22 And when the daughter of the said Herodias came in, and danced, and pleased Herod, and them that sate with him, the king said vnto the damosell, Aske of me whatsoeuer thou wilt, and I will giue it thee.

23 And he sware vnto her, Whatsoeuer thou shalt aske of me, I will giue it thee, vnto the halfe of my kingdome.

24 And she went forth, and said vnto her mother, What shall I aske? And she said, The head of Iohn ẙ Baptist.

25 And she came in straightway with haste, vnto the king, and asked, saying, I will that thou giue me by and by in a charger, the head of Iohn the Baptist.

26 And the king was exceeding sory, yet for his othes sake, and for their sakes which sate with him, hee would not reiect her.

27 And immediately the king sent ||an executioner, and commaunded his head to be brought, and he went, and beheaded him in the prison,

|| Or, one of his guard.

28 And brought his head in a charger, and gaue it to the damosell, and the damosell gaue it to her mother.

29 And when his disciples heard of it, they came and tooke vp his corpse, and laid it in a tombe.

30 *And the Apostles gathered themselues together vnto Iesus, and tolde him all things, both what they had done, and what they had taught.

* Luk. 9. 1

31 And he said vnto them, Come yee your selues apart into a desert place, and rest a while. For there were many comming and going, and they had no leisure so much as to eate.

32 *And they departed into a desert place by ship priuately.

* Mat. 14. 13.

33 And the people saw them departing, and many knew him, and ranne afoote thither out of all cities, and outwent them, and came together vnto him.

34 *And Iesus when he came out, saw much people, and was moued with compassion toward them, because they were as sheepe not hauing a shepherd: and hee beganne to teach them many things.

* Mat. 6. 3

35 *And

Matth. 14.
6.

35. * And when the day was now far spent, his Disciples came vnto him, and said, This is a desert place, and now the time is farre passed.

36 Send them away, that they may goe into the countrey round about, and into the villages, and buy themselues bread : for they haue nothing to eate.

37 He answered and said vnto them, Giue yee them to eate. And they say vnto him, Shall we goe and buy two hundred ||penniworth of bread, and giue them to eate?

The Rom.
enie is
euen pence
alfe penie
s Mat. 18.
8

38 He saith vnto them, How many loaues haue yee? goe, and see. And when they knew, they say, Fiue, and two fishes.

39 And he commanded them to make all sit downe by companies vpon the greene grasse.

40 And they sate downe in rankes by hundreds, and by fifties.

41 And when he had taken the fiue loaues, and the two fishes, he looked vp to heauen, and blessed, and brake the loaues, and gaue them to his disciples to set before them; and the two fishes diuided he among them all.

42 And they did all eate, and were filled.

43 And they tooke vp twelue baskets full of the fragments, and of the fishes.

44 And they that did eate of the loaues, were about fiue thousand men.

45 And straightway he constrained his disciples to get into the ship, and to goe to the other side before ||vnto Bethsaida, while he sent away the people.

Or, ouer a-
ainst Beth-
aida.

46 And when hee had sent them away, he departed into a mountaine to pray.

* Matth. 14
3.

47 * And when Euen was come, the ship was in the midst of the Sea, and he alone on the land.

48 And he saw them toiling in rowing (for the wind was contrary vnto them :) and about the fourth watch of the night, he commeth vnto them, walking vpon the Sea, and would haue passed by them.

49 But when they saw him walking vpon the Sea, they supposed it had bene a spirit, and cried out.

50 (For they all saw him, and were troubled) and immediately hee talked with them, and saith vnto them, Be of good cheere, It is I, be not afraid.

51 And hee went vp vnto them into the ship, and the wind ceased : and they were sore amazed in themselues beyond measure, and wondered.

52 For they considered not the miracle of the loaues, for their heart was hardened.

53 * And when they had passed ouer, they came into the land of Genesareth, and drew to the shore.

* Matth. 14.
34.

54 And when they were come out of the ship, straightway they knew him,

55 And ran through that whole region round about, and beganne to carrie about in beds, those that were sicke, where they heard he was.

56 And whithersoeuer he entred, into villages, or cities, or countrie, they laide the sicke in the streetes, & besought him that they might touch if it were but the border of his garment : and as many as touched ||him, were made whole.

|| Or, it.

CHAP. VII.

1 The Pharises find fault at the disciples for eating with vnwashen hands. 8 They breake the commandement of God, by the traditions of men. 4 Meate defileth not the man. 24 Hee healeth the Syrophenician womans daughter of an vncleane spirit, 31 and one that was deafe, and stammered in his speach.

* Matth. 15
1.

H*Hen came together vnto him the Pharises, and certain of the Scribes, which came from Hierusalem.

2 And when they saw some of his disciples eate bread with ||defiled (that is to say, with vnwashen) hands, they found fault.

|| Or, com-
mon.

3 For the Pharises and all the Iewes, except they wash their hands ||oft, eate not, holding the tradition of the elders.

4 And when they come from the market, except they wash, they eate not. And many other things there be, which they haue receiued to hold, as the washing of cups and ||pots, brasen vessels, and of ||tables.

|| Or, dili-
gently, in the
Originall,
with the fist:
Theophilact,
vp to the el-
bowe.

|| Or, beds.

|| Sextarius,
is about a
pinte and an
halfe.

5 Then the Pharises and Scribes asked him, Why walke not thy disciples according to the tradition of the Elders, but eate bread with vnwashen hands?

6 He answered and said vnto them, Well hath Esaias prophesied of you Hypocrites, as it is written, *This people honoureth mee with their lips, but their heart is farre from me.

Esai. 29.
13. mat. 15.
8.

7 Howbeit in vaine doe they worship

ship me, teaching for doctrines, the commandements of men.

8 For laying aside the Commandement of God, yee hold the tradition of men, as the washing of pots, and cups: and many other such like things ye doe.

9 And he said vnto them, Full well ye ||reiect the Commandement of God, that ye may keepe your owne tradition.

Or, frustrate.

10 For Moses said, Honour thy father & thy mother: and who so curseth father or mother, let him die the death.

11 But ye say, If a man shall say to his father or mother, It is *Corban, that is to say, a gift, by whatsoeuer thou mightest be profited by me: *he shalbe free.*

* Matth. 15. 5.

12 And ye suffer him no more to doe ought for his father, or his mother:

13 Making the word of God of none effect through your tradition, which ye haue deliuered: And many such like things doe ye.

14 ¶ *And when he had called all the people vnto him, hee said vnto them, Hearken vnto me euery one of you, and vnderstand.

* Matt. 15. 10.

15 There is nothing from without a man that entring into him, can defile him: but the things which come out of of him, those are they that defile the man.

16 If any man haue eares to heare, let him heare.

17 And when hee was entred into the house from the people, his disciples asked him concerning the parable.

18 And he saith vnto them, Are ye so without vnderstanding also? Doe yee not perceiue that whatsoeuer thing from without entreth into the man, it cannot defile him,

19 Because it entreth not into his heart, but into the belly, and goeth out into the draught, purging all meats?

20 And he said, That which commeth out of the man, that defileth the man.

21 *For from within, out of the heart of men, proceed euill thoughts, adulteries, fornications, murders,

* Gen. 6. 5. and 8. 21.

22 *Thefts, couetousnesse, wickednesse, deceit, lasciuiousnesse, an euill eye, blasphemie, pride, foolishnesse:

* Matth. 15. 19.

23 All these euill things come from within, and defile the man.

24 ¶ *And from thence he arose, and went into the borders of Tyre and Sidon, and entred into an house, and would haue no man know it, but hee could not be hid.

* Matt. 15. 21.

25 For a certaine woman, whose yong daughter had an vncleane spirit, heard of him, and came and fell at his feete.

26 (The woman was a ||Greeke, a Syrophenician by nation:) and she besought him that he would cast forth the deuill out of her daughter.

||*Or, Gentile.*

27 But Iesus said vnto her, Let the children first be filled: for it is not meet to take the childrens bread, and to cast it vnto the dogges.

28 And she answered and said vnto him, Yes Lord, yet the dogges vnder the table eat of the childrens crummes.

29 And hee said vnto her, For this saying, goe thy way, the deuill is gone out of thy daughter.

30 And when shee was come to her house, she found the deuill gone out, and her daughter laied vpon the bed.

31 ¶ And againe departing from the coastes of Tyre and Sidon, he came vnto the sea of Galilee, thorow the midst of the coasts of Decapolis.

32 And they bring vnto him one that was deafe, and had an impediment in his speech: and they beseech him to put his hand vpon him.

33 And he tooke him aside from the multitude, and put his fingers into his eares, and he spit, and touched his tongue,

34 And looking vp to heauen, hee sighed, and saith vnto him, Ephphatha, that is, Be opened.

35 And straightway his eares were opened, and the string of his tongue was loosed, and he spake plaine.

36 And hee charged them that they should tell no man: but the more hee charged them, so much the more a great deale they published it,

37 And were beyond measure astonished, saying, Hee hath done all things well: hee maketh both the deafe to heare, and the dumbe to speake.

CHAP. VIII.

1 Christ feedeth the people miraculously: 10 refuseth to giue a signe to the Pharisees: 14 admonisheth his disciples to beware of the leuen of the Pharisees, and of the leuen of Herode: 22 giueth a blinde man his sight: 27 acknowledgeth that hee is the Christ, who should suffer and rise againe: 34 and exhorteth to patience in persecution for the profession of the Gospel.

In

Mat. 15.
2.

 N those dayes * the multitude being very great, and hauing nothing to eat, Iesus called his disciples vnto him, & saith vnto them,

2 I haue compassion on the multitude, because they haue now bene with me three daies, and haue nothing to eat:

3 And if I send them away fasting to their owne houses, they will faint by the way : for diuers of them came from farre.

4 And his disciples answered him, From whence can a man satisfie these men with bread here in the wildernes ?

5 And hee asked them, How many loaues haue ye ? And they said, Seuen.

6 And he commanded the people to sit downe on the ground : and he tooke the seuen loaues, and gaue thanks, and brake, and gaue to his disciples to set before them : and they did set them before the people.

7 And they had a few small fishes : and he blessed, and commaunded to set them also before them.

8 So they did eate, and were filled : and they tooke vp, of the broken meate that was left, seuen baskets.

9 And they that had eaten were about foure thousand, and he sent them away.

10 ¶ And straightway he entred into a ship with his disciples, and came into the parts of Dalmanutha.

* Mat. 16. 1

11 *And the Pharisees came foorth, and began to question with him, seeking of him a signe from heauen, tempting him.

12 And he sighed deepely in his spirit, and saith, Why doeth this generation seeke after a signe ? Verely I say vnto you, There shall no signe be giuen vnto this generation.

13 And he left them, & entring into the ship againe, departed to the other side.

* Mat. 16. 5.

14 ¶ *Now the disciples had forgotten to take bread, neither had they in the ship with them more then one loafe.

15 And hee charged them, saying, Take heed, beware of the leauen of the Pharisees, and of the leauen of Herode.

16 And they reasoned among themselues, saying, It is, *because we haue no bread.

* Mat. 16. 7.

17 And when Iesus knew it, he saith vnto them, Why reason ye, because yee haue no bread ? Perceiue ye not yet, neither vnderstand ? Haue yee your heart yet hardened ?

18 Hauing eyes, see ye not ? and hauing eares heare ye not ? And doe ye not remember ?

19 When I brake the fiue loaues among fiue thousand, how many baskets full of fragments tooke yee vp ? They say vnto him, Twelue.

20 And when the seuen among foure thousand : how many baskets full of fragments tooke ye vp ? And they said, Seuen.

21 And he said vnto them, How is it that ye doe not vnderstand ?

22 ¶ And he commeth to Bethsaida, and they bring a blind man vnto him, and besought him to touch him :

23 And he tooke the blind man by the hand, and led him out of the towne, and when he had spit on his eyes, & put his hands vpon him, he asked him, if hee saw ought.

24 And he looked vp, and saide, I see men as trees, walking.

25 After that hee put his handes againe vpon his eies, and made him look vp : and he was restored, and saw euery man clearely.

26 And hee sent him away to his house, saying, Neither goe into the towne, nor tell it to any in the towne.

* Mat. 16.
13.

27 ¶ *Iesus went out, and his disciples, into the townes of Cesarea Philippi : and by the way he asked his disciples, saying vnto them, Whom doe men say that I am ?

28 And they answered, Iohn the Baptist : but some say, Elias : & others, one of the Prophets.

29 And hee saith vnto them, But whom say yee that I am ? And Peter answereth and saith vnto him, Thou art the Christ.

30 And he charged them that they should tell no man of him.

31 And hee beganne to teach them, that the Sonne of man must suffer many things, and be reiected of the Elders, and of the chiefe Priests, & Scribes, and be killed, & after three dayes rise againe.

32 And he spake that saying openly. And Peter tooke him, and beganne to rebuke him.

33 But when he had turned about, & looked on his disciples, he rebuked Peter, saying, Get thee behind me, Satan : for thou sauourest not the things that be of God, but the things that be of men

34 ¶ And

* Matt. 10.
38.

34 ¶ And when he had called the people vnto him, with his disciples also, he said vnto them , *Whosoeuer will come after me, let him denie himselfe, and take vp his crosse and follow mee.

35 For whosoeuer will saue his life shall lose it, but whosoeuer shall lose his life for my sake and the Gospels , the same shall saue it.

36 For what shall it profit a man, if he shall gaine the whole world, and lose his owne soule ?

37 Or what shall a man giue in exchange for his soule ?

* Mat. 10.
33.

38 *Whosoeuer therefore shall be ashamed of me, and of my words, in this adulterous and sinfull generation, of him also shall the Sonne of man bee ashamed, when he commeth in the glory of his Father, with the holy Angels.

CHAP. IX.

2 Iesus is transfigured. 11 Hee instructeth his disciples, concerning the comming of Elias: 14 casteth forth a dumbe, and deafe spirit: 30 foretelleth his death and resurrection : 33 exhorteth his disciples to humilitie: 38 bidding them, not to prohibite such as be not against thē, nor to giue offence to any of the faithfull.

* Mat. 16.
28.

Nd hee said vnto them, *Verely I say vnto you, that there be some of them that stand here, which shal not taste of death, till they haue seene the kingdome of God come with power.

Mat. 17. 1.

2 ¶ *And after six dayes, Iesus taketh with him Peter, and Iames, and Iohn, and leadeth them vp into an high mountaine apart by themselues : and he was transfigured before them.

3 And his raiment became shining, exceeding white as snow : so as no Fuller on earth can white them.

4 And there appeared vnto them Elias with Moses : and they were talking with Iesus.

5 And Peter answered, and saide to Iesus, Master, it is good for vs to bee here, and let vs make three Tabernacles; one for thee, and one for Moses, and one for Elias.

6 For he wist not what to say, for they were sore afraid.

7 And there was a cloud that ouershadowed them : and a voyce came out of the cloud, saying, This is my beloued Sonne : heare him.

8 And suddenly when they had looked round about, they saw no man any more, saue Iesus only with themselues.

9 And as they came downe from the mountaine, he charged them that they should tell no man, what things they had seene, till the Sonne of man were risen from the dead.

10 And they kept that saying with themselues, questioning one with another, what the rising from the dead should meane.

11 ¶ And they asked him, saying, Why say the Scribes that Elias must first come ?

12 And he answered, and told them, Elias verely commeth first, and restoreth al things, and *how it is written of the Sonne of man, that he must suffer many things, and be set at nought.

* Esai. 53. 2

13 But I say vnto you, that Elias is indeed come, and they haue done vnto him whatsoeuer they listed, as it is written of him.

14 ¶ *And when he came to his disciples, he saw a great multitude about them, and the Scribes questioning with them.

* Mat. 17.
14.

15 And straightway all the people, when they beheld him, were greatly amazed, & running to him, saluted him.

16 And he asked the Scribes, What question ye ||with them ?

|| Or, amon,
your selues

17 And one of the multitude answered, and said, Master, I haue broughe vnto thee my son, which hath a dumbe spirit :

18 And wheresoeuer he taketh him, he ||teareth him, & he fometh, and gnasheth with his teeth, and pineth away : and I spake to thy disciples, that they should cast him out, and they could not.

|| Or, dashe
him.

19 He answereth him , and saith, O faithlesse generation, how long shall I be with you, how long shall I suffer you ? Bring him vnto me.

20 And they brought him vnto him : and when he saw him, straightway the spirit tare him, and he fel on the ground, and wallowed, foming.

21 And he asked his father, Howe long is it agoe since this came vnto him? And he said, Of a child.

22 And oft times it hath cast him into the fire, and into the waters to destroy him : but if thou canst doe any thing, haue compassion on vs, and helpe vs.

23 Iesus said vnto him, If thou canst beleeue, all things are possible to him that beleeueth.

24 And

24 And straightway the father of the child cried out and said with teares, Lord, I beleeue, helpe thou mine vnbeliefe.

25 When Iesus saw that the people came running together, he rebuked the foule spirit, saying vnto him, Thou dumbe and deafe spirit, I charge thee come out of him, and enter no more into him.

26 And the *spirit* cried, and rent him sore, and came out of him, and he was as one dead, insomuch that many said, He is dead.

27 But Iesus tooke him by the hand, and lifted him vp, and he arose.

28 And when he was come into the house, his disciples asked him priuately, Why could not we cast him out?

29 And hee said vnto them, This kind can come forth by nothing, but by prayer, and fasting.

Mat. 17.

30 ¶ *And they departed thence, and passed through Galilee, and he would not ŷ any man should know it.

31 For he taught his disciples, and said vnto them, The sonne of man is deliuered into the hands of men, and they shall kill him, and after that he is killed, he shall rise the third day.

32 But they vnderstood not that saying, and were afraid to aske him.

Mat. 18. 1.

33 ¶ *And he came to Capernaum; and being in the house, he asked them, What was it that yee disputed among your selues by the way?

34 But they held their peace : For by the way they had disputed among themselues, who *should be* the greatest.

35 And he sate downe, and called the twelue, and saith vnto them, If any man desire to be first, the same shall be last of all, and seruant of all.

36 And he tooke a child, and set him in the midst of them : & when he had taken him in his armes, he said vnto them,

37 Whosoeuer shall receiue one of such children in my Name, receiueth me : and whosoeuer shall receiue me, receiueth not me, but him that sent me.

Luke 9.
9.

38 ¶ *And Iohn answered him, saying, Master, we saw one casting out deuils in thy Name, and he followeth not vs, and we forbade him, because he followeth not vs.

1. Cor. 12.

39 But Iesus said, Forbid him not, *for there is no man, which shall doe a miracle in my Name, that can lightly speake euill of me.

40 For he that is not against vs, is on our part.

41 *For whosoeuer shall giue you a cup of water to drinke in my Name, because yee belong to Christ : Verily I say vnto you, he shall not lose his reward.

Mat. 10. 42.

42 *And whosoeuer shall offend one of these litle ones that beleeue in me, it is better for him, that a milstone were hanged about his necke, and he were cast into the Sea.

Mat. 18. 6.

43 *And if thy hand ||offend thee, cut it off : It is better for thee to enter into life maimed, then hauing two hands, to goe into hell, into the fire that neuer shall be quenched :

Mat. 5. 29 and 18. 8.
I Or, cause thee to offend.

44 *Where their worme dieth not, and the fire is not quenched.

Esai. 66. 24.

45 And if thy foote offend thee, cut it off : it is better for thee to enter halt into life, then hauing two feete, to be cast into hell, into the fire that neuer shall be quenched :

46 Where their worme dieth not, and the fire is not quenched.

47 And if thine eye ||offend thee, pluck it out : it is better for thee to enter into the kingdome of God with one eye, then hauing two eyes, to be cast into hel fire :

I Or, cause thee to offend.

48 Where their worme dieth not, and the fire is not quenched.

49 For euery one shall be salted with fire, *and euery sacrifice shall be salted with salt.

Leuit. 2. 13.

50 *Salt is good : but if the salt haue lost his saltnesse, wherewith will you season it ? Haue salt in your selues, and haue peace one with another.

Mat. 5. 13.

CHAP. X.

2 Christ disputeth with the Pharisees, touching diuorcement : 13 blesseth the children that are brought vnto him : 17 resolueth a rich man how he may inherite life euerlasting : 23 telleth his disciples of the danger of riches : 28 promiseth rewards to them that forsake any thing for the Gospell : 32 Foretelleth his death, & resurrection : 35 Biddeth the two ambitious suiters to thinke rather of suffring with him : 46 And restoreth to Bartimeus his sight.

*Nd he rose from thence, & commeth into the coasts of Iudea by the farther side of Iordan : and the people resort vnto him againe, and as he was wont, he taught them againe.

Mat. 19. 1.

2 ¶ And the Pharises came to him, and asked him, Is it lawfull for a man to

to put away his wife? tempting him.

3 And he answered, and saide vnto them, What did Moses command you?

4 And they said, Moses suffered to write a bill of diuorcement, and to put her away.

5 And Iesus answered, and said vnto them, For the hardnesse of your heart, he wrote you this precept.

6 But from the beginning of the creation, God made them male, and female.

7 For this cause shall a man leaue his father and mother, and cleaue to his wife,

8 And they twaine shalbe one flesh : so then they are no more twaine, but one flesh.

9 What therefore God hath ioyned together, let not man put asunder.

10 And in the house his disciples asked him againe of the same matter.

* Matth. 5. 32. and 19. 9.

11 And he saith vnto them, * Whosoeuer shall put away his wife, and marry another, committeth adultery against her.

12 And if a woman shall put away her husband, and bee married to another, she committeth adulterie.

* Matth. 19. 13.

13 ¶ * And they brought yong children to him, that he should touch them, and his disciples rebuked those that brought them.

14 But when Iesus saw it, hee was much displeased, and said vnto them, Suffer the little children to come vnto mee, and forbid them not : for of such is the kingdome of God.

15 Verily I say vnto you, Whosoeuer shall not receiue the kingdome of God as a little childe, he shall not enter therein.

16 And hee tooke them vp in his armes, put his handes vpon them, and blessed them.

* Matth. 19. 16.

17 ¶ * And when he was gone forth into the way, there came one running, and kneeled to him, and asked him, Good master, what shall I doe that I may inherit eternall life?

18 And Iesus said vnto him, Why callest thou me good? There is no man good, but one, that is God.

19 Thou knowest the Commandements, Doe not commit adulterie, Doe not kill, Doe not steale, Doe not beare false witnesse, Defraud not, Honour thy father, and mother.

20 And hee answered, and saide vnto him, Master, all these haue I obserued from my youth.

21 Then Iesus beholding him, loued him, and said vnto him, One thing thou lackest ; Goe thy way, sell whatsoeuer thou hast, and giue to the poore, and thou shalt haue treasure in heauen, and come, take vp the crosse & folow me.

22 And hee was sad at that saying, and went away grieued : for hee had great possessions.

23 ¶ And Iesus looked round about, and saith vnto his disciples, How hardly shall they that haue riches enter into the kingdome of God?

24 And the disciples were astonished at his words. But Iesus answereth againe, and saith vnto them, Children, how hard is it for them that trust in riches, to enter into the kingdom of God?

25 It is easier for a camel to goe thorow the eye of a needle, then for a rich man to enter into the kingdom of God.

26 And they were astonished out of measure, saying among themselues, Who then can be saued?

27 And Iesus looking vpon them, saith, With men it is impossible, but not with God : for with God all things are possible.

* Mat 27.

28 ¶ * Then Peter began to say vnto him, Loe, we haue left all, and haue followed thee.

29 And Iesus answered, and said, Verily I say vnto you, There is no man that hath left house, or brethren, or sisters, or father, or mother, or wife, or children, or lands, for my sake, and the Gospels,

30 But hee shall receiue an hundred fold now in this time, houses, and brethren, and sisters, and mothers, and children, and lands, with persecutions ; and in the world to come eternall life:

* Mat 30.

31 * But many that are first, shall be last : and the last, first.

* Mat 17.

32 ¶ * And they were in the way going vp to Hierusalem : and Iesus went before them, and they were amazed, and as they followed, they were afraid: and he tooke againe the twelue, and began to tell them what things should happen vnto him,

33 Saying, Behold, we go vp to Hierusalem, and the Sonne of man shall be deliuered vnto the chiefe Priests, and vnto the Scribes : and they shall condemne him to death, and shall deliuer him to the Gentiles.

34 And

34 And they shall mocke him, and shall scourge him, and shall spit vpon him, and shall kil him, and the third day he shall rise againe.

* Matth. 20. 20.

35 ¶ *And Iames, and Iohn the sonnes of Zebedee come vnto him, saying, Master, we would ẏ thou shouldest do for vs whatsoeuer we shall desire.

36 And hee saide vnto them, What would ye that I should doe for you?

37 They said vnto him, Grant vnto vs that wee may sit, one on thy right hand, and the other on thy left hand, in thy glory.

38 But Iesus said vnto them, Yee know not what ye aske : Can ye drinke of the cup that I drinke of? and be baptized with the baptisme that I am baptized with?

39 And they said vnto him, Wee can. And Iesus said vnto them, Ye shall indeed drinke of the cup that I drinke of: and with the baptisme that I am baptized withall, shall ye be baptized :

40 But to sit on my right hand and on my left hand, is not mine to giue, but it shall be giuen to them for whom it is prepared.

41 And when the ten heard it, they beganne to bee much displeased with Iames and Iohn.

* Luke 22. 25.
‖ Or, thinke good.

42 But Iesus called them to him, and saith vnto them, *Yee know that they which ‖are accompted to rule ouer the Gentiles, exercise Lordship ouer them : and their great ones exercise authoritie vpon them.

43 But so shall it not be among you : but whosoeuer will bee great among you, shall be your minister :

44 And whosoeuer of you will bee the chiefest, shalbe seruant of all.

45 For euen the Sonne of man came not to bee ministred vnto, but to minister, and to giue his life a ransome for many.

* Matth. 20. 29.

46 ¶ *And they came to Iericho : and as he went out of Iericho with his disciples, and a great number of people; blinde Bartimeus, the son of Timeus, sate by the high wayes side, begging.

47 And when he heard that it was Iesus of Nazareth, he began to cry out, and say, Iesus thou Sonne of Dauid, haue mercie on me.

48 And many charged him, that he should hold his peace : But he cried the more a great dealc, Thou Sonne of Dauid, haue mercy on me.

49 And Iesus stood still, and commanded him to bee called : and they call the blinde man, saying vnto him, Be of good comfort, rise, he calleth thee.

50 And hee casting away his garment, rose, and came to Iesus.

51 And Iesus answered, and said vnto him, What wilt thou that I should doe vnto thee? The blinde man said vnto him, Lord, that I might receiue my sight.

52 And Iesus saide vnto him, Goe thy way, thy faith hath ‖made thee whole : And immediately hee receiued his sight, & followed Iesus in the way.

‖ Or, saued thee.

CHAP. XI.

1 Christ rideth with triumph into Hierusalem : 12 curseth the fruitlesse leafie tree : 15 purgeth the Temple : 20 exhorteth his disciples to stedfastnesse of faith, and to forgiue their enemies : 27 and defendeth the lawfulnes of his actions, by the witnesse of Iohn, who was a man sent of God.

*ND when they came nigh to Hierusalem, vnto Bethphage, and Bethanie, at the mount of Oliues, hee sendeth foorth two of his disciples,

* Matth. 21. 1.

2 And saith vnto them, Goe your way into the village ouer against you, and assoone as ye bee entred into it, yee shall finde a colt tied, whereon neuer man sate, loose him, and bring him.

3 And if any man say vnto you, Why doe yee this? Say yee, that the Lord hath need of him : and straightway he will send him hither.

4 And they went their way, and found the colt tied by the doore without, in a place where two wayes met : and they loose him.

5 And certaine of them that stood there, said vnto them, What doe ye loosing the colt?

6 And they said vnto them euen as Iesus had commanded : and they let them goe.

7 And they brought the colt to Iesus, and cast their garments on him, and he sate vpon him.

8 And many spread their garments in the way : and others cut downe branches of the trees, and strawed them in the way.

9 And they that went before, and they that followed, cryed, saying, Hosanna, blessed is hee that commeth in the

10 Blessed be the kingdome of our father Dauid, that commeth in the Name of the Lord, *Hosanna* in the highest.

11 And Iesus entred into Hierusalem, and into the Temple, and when hee had looked round about vpon all things, & now the euentide was come, he went out vnto Bethanie with the twelue.

12 ¶ And on the morow when they were come from Bethanie, hee was hungry.

13 *And seeing a figtree a farre off, hauing leaues, hee came, if haply hee might find any thing thereon, & when he came to it, hee found nothing but leaues : for the time of figs was not *yet*.

14 And Iesus answered, and said vnto it, No man eate fruite of thee hereafter for euer. And his disciples heard *it*.

15 ¶ *And they come to Hierusalem, and Iesus went into the Temple, and beganne to cast out them that sold and bought in the Temple, and ouerthrew the tables of the money changers, and the seats of them that sold doues,

16 And would not suffer that any man should carie any vessell thorow the Temple.

17 And he taught, saying vnto them, Is it not written, My house shalbe called of all nations the house of prayer ? but ye haue made it a den of theeues.

18 And the Scribes and chiefe Priests heard *it*, and sought how they might destroy him : for they feared him, because all the people was astonished at his doctrine.

19 And when Euen was come, Hee went out of the citie.

20 ¶ *And in the morning, as they passed by, they saw the fig tree dried vp from the roots.

21 And Peter calling to remembrance saith vnto him, Master, behold, the fig tree which thou cursedst, is withered away.

22 And Iesus answering, saith vnto them, ||Haue faith in God.

23 For verely I say vnto you, that whosoeuer shall say vnto this mountaine, Bee thou remoued, and bee thou cast into the sea, and shall not doubt in his heart, but shall beleeue that those things which hee saith, shall come to passe : he shal haue whatsoeuer he saith.

24 Therfore I say vnto you, *What things soeuer ye desire when ye pray, be-

*Matt. 21. 19.

*Matt. 21. 12.

*Matt. 21. 19.

¶ *Or, haue the faith of God.*

*Matt. 7. 7.

leeue that ye receiue *them*, and ye shall haue *them*.

25 And when ye stand, praying, *forgiue, if ye haue ought against any : that your Father also which is in heauen, may forgiue you your trespasses.

26 But if you doe not forgiue, neither will your Father which is in heauen, forgiue your trespasses.

27 ¶ And they come againe to Hierusalem, * and as he was walking in the Temple, there come to him the chiefe Priests, and the Scribes, & the Elders,

28 And say vnto him, By what authoritie doest thou these things ? and who gaue thee this authority to doe these things?

29 And Iesus answered, and saide vnto them, I will also aske of you one ||question, and answere me, and I will tell you by what authoritie I doe these things.

30 The baptisme of Iohn, was it from heauen, or of men ? Answere me.

31 And they reasoned with themselues, saying, If we shall say, From heauen, he will say, Why then did ye not beleeue him ?

32 But if we shall say, Of men, they feared the people : for all men counted Iohn, that he was a Prophet indeed.

33 And they answered and said vnto Iesus, We cannot tell. And Iesus answering, saith vnto them, Neither do I tell you by what authority I doe these things.

* Mat. 6.

* Matt. 2. 23.

‖ Or, thing

CHAP. XII.

1 In a parable of the vineyard let out to vnthankfull husbandmen, Christ foretelleth the reprobation of the Iewes, and the calling of the Gentiles : 13 Hee auoideth the snare of the Pharisees and Herodians about paying tribute to Cesar : 18 conuinceth the errour of the Sadducees, who denied the resurrection : 28 resolueth the Scribe who questioned of the first commandement : 35 refuteth the opinion that the Scribes held of Christ : 38 Bidding the people to beware of their ambition, and hypocrisie : 41 and commendeth the poore widow for her two mites, aboue all.

Nd *hee began to speake vnto them by parables. A certaine man planted a vineyard, and set an hedge about it, and digged *a place for the wine fat, and built a towre, and let it out to husbandmen, and went into a farre countrey.

* Mat. 2

2 And

2 And at the season, he sent to the husbandmen a seruant, that he might receiue from the husbandmen of the fruite of the vineyard.

3 And they caught him, and beat him, and sent him away emptie.

4 And againe, hee sent vnto them another seruant; and at him they cast stones, and wounded him in the head, and sent him away shamefully handled.

5 And againe, he sent another, and him they killed : and many others, beating some, and killing some.

6 Hauing yet therefore one sonne his welbeloued, he sent him also last vnto them, saying, They will reuerence my sonne.

7 But those husbandmen said amongst themselues, This is the heire, come, let vs kill him, and the inheritance shall be ours.

8 And they tooke him, and killed him, and cast him out of the vineyard.

9 What shall therefore the Lord of the vineyard doe? He will come and destroy the husbandmen, and will giue the vineyard vnto others.

Psal. 118.
.
10 * And haue ye not read this Scripture? The stone which the builders reiected, is become the head of the corner:

11 This was the Lords doing, and it is maruellous in our eies.

12 And they sought to lay hold on him, but feared the people, for they knew that he had spoken the parable against them : and they left him, and went their way.

Matth. 22
5.
13 ¶ * And they send vnto him certaine of the Pharises, and of the Herodians, to catch him in his words.

14 And when they were come, they say vnto him, Master, we know that thou art true, and carest for no man : for thou regardest not the person of men, but teachest the way of God in truth. Is it lawfull to giue tribute to Cesar, or not?

15 Shall we giue, or shall we not giue? But he knowing their hypocrisie, said vnto them, Why tempt yee mee? Bring me a ||penny that I may see it.

|| Valewing four money euen pence alſe penie, s Mat. 18. 8.
16 And they brought it : and he saith vnto them, Whose is this image and superscription? And they said vnto him, Cesars.

17 And Iesus answering, said vnto them, Render to Cesar the things that are Cesars : and to God the things that are Gods. And they maruailed at him.

18 ¶ *Then come vnto him the Sadducees, which say there is no resurrection, and they asked him, saying,

* Matth. 22.
23.

19 Master, Moses wrote vnto vs, If a mans brother die, and leaue his wife behind him, and leaue no children, that his brother should take his wife, and raise vp seed vnto his brother.

20 Now there were seuen brethren : and the first tooke a wife, and dying left no seede.

21 And the second tooke her, and died, neither left he any seed, and the third likewise.

22 And the seuen had her, and left no seede : last of all the woman died also.

23 In the resurrection therefore, when they shall rise, whose wife shall she be of them? for the seuen had her to wife.

24 And Iesus answering, said vnto them, Doe ye not therefore erre, because yee know not the scriptures, neither the power of God?

25 For when they shall rise from the dead, they neither marry, nor are giuen in marriage : but are as the Angels which are in heauen.

26 And as touching the dead, that they rise : haue ye not read in the booke of Moses, how in the bush God spake vnto him, saying, I am the God of Abraham, and the God of Isahac, and the God of Iacob?

27 Hee is not the God of the dead, but the God of the liuing : yee therefore doe greatly erre.

28 ¶ *And one of the Scribes came, and hauing heard them reasoning together, and perceiuing that he had answered them well, asked him which is the first commandement of all.

* Matth. 22.
35.

29 And Iesus answered him, The first of al the commandements is, Heare, O Israel, the Lord our God is one Lord:

30 And thou shalt loue the Lord thy God with all thy heart, and with all thy soule, and with all thy minde, and with all thy strength : This is the first commandement.

31 And the second is like, namely this, Thou shalt loue thy neighbour as thy selfe : there is none other commandement greater then these.

32 And the Scribe said vnto him, Well master, thou hast said the truth : for there is one God, and there is none other but he.

33 And

33 And to loue him with all the heart, and with all the vnderstanding, and with all the soule, and with all the strength, and to loue his neighbour as himselfe, is more then all whole burnt offerings and sacrifices.

34 And when Iesus saw that he answered discreetly, hee saide vnto him, Thou art not far from the kingdome of God. And no man after that durst aske him any question.

*Matth. 22. 41.

35 ¶ *And Iesus answered, and said, while hee taught in the Temple, How say the Scribes that Christ is the sonne of Dauid?

36 For Dauid himselfe said by the holy Ghost, The Lord said to my Lord, Sit thou on my right hand, til I make thine enemies thy footstoole.

37 Dauid therefore himselfe calleth him Lord, and whence is hee then his sonne? And the common people heard him gladly.

*Matth. 23. 5.

38 ¶ And he said vnto them in his doctrine, *Beware of the Scribes, which loue to goe in long clothing, and loue salutations in the market places,

39 And the chiefe seates in the Synagogues, and the vppermost roomes at feasts:

*Matth. 23. 14.

40 *Which deuoure widowes houses, and for a pretence make long prayers: These shall receiue greater damnation.

*Luke 21. 1.

41 ¶ *And Iesus sate ouer against the treasurie, and behold how the people cast ‖money into the treasurie: and many that were rich, cast in much.

‖ A piece of brasse money, See Matth. 10. 9.
‖ It is the seuenth part of one piece of that brasse money.

42 And there came a certaine poore widow, and she threw in two ‖mites, which make a farthing.

43 And he called vnto him his disciples, and saith vnto them, Verily I say vnto you, that this poore widow hath cast more in, then all they which haue cast into the treasurie.

44 For all they did cast in of their abboundance: but she of her want, did cast in all that she had, euen all her liuing.

CHAP. XIII.

*Matth. 1.

ANd *as he went out of the Temple, one of his disciples saith vnto him, Master, see what maner of stones, and what buildings are here.

2 And Iesus answering, said vnto him, Seest thou these great buildings? there shall not be left one stone vpon another, that shal not be throwen downe.

3 And as he sate vpon the mount of Oliues, ouer against the Temple, Peter, and Iames, and Iohn, and Andrew asked him priuately,

*Matth. 3.

4 *Tell vs, when shall these things be? And what shalbe the signe when all these things shalbe fulfilled?

5 And Iesus answering them, began to say, Take heed lest any man deceiue you.

6 For many shal come in my Name, saying, I am Christ: and shall deceiue many.

7 And when yee shall heare of warres, and rumors of warres, be yee not troubled: For such things must needs be, but the end shall not be yet.

8 For nation shall rise against nation, and kingdome against kingdome: and there shalbe earthquakes in diuers places, and there shall be famines, and troubles: these are the beginnings of ‖sorrowes.

‖ The wo in the or ginall, in porteth, paines of woman i trauaile.

9 ¶ But take heed to your selues: for they shall deliuer you vp to councels, and in the Synagogues ye shall be beaten, and ye shalbe brought before rulers and kings for my sake, for a testimony against them.

10 And the Gospel must first be published among all nations.

*Matth. 19.

11 *But when they shall lead you, and deliuer you vp, take no thought before hand what ye shall speake, neither doe yee premeditate: but whatsoeuer shall bee giuen you in that houre, that speake yee: for it is not yee that speake, but the holy Ghost.

12 Now the brother shall betray the brother to death, and the father the sonne: and children shall rise vp against their parents, and shall cause them to be put to death.

13 And yee shall bee hated of all men for my Names sake: but hee that shall endure vnto the ende, the same shall be saued.

14 ¶ *But

Matt. 24.

14 ¶ * But when ye shall see the abomination of desolation spoken of by Daniel the Prophet, standing where it ought not (let him that readeth vnderstand) then let them that be in Iudea, flee to the mountaines:

15 And let him that is on the house top, not goe downe into the house, neither enter therin, to take any thing out of his house.

16 And let him that is in the field, not turne backe againe for to take vp his garment.

17 But woe to them that are with child, and to them that giue suck in those dayes.

18 And pray ye that your flight bee not in the winter.

19 For in those dayes shall be affliction, such as was not from the beginning of the creation which God created, vnto this time, neither shall be.

20 And except that the Lord had shortened those dayes, no flesh should be saued: but for the elects sake whome he hath chosen, he hath shortned the daies.

Matt. 24.

21 * And then, if any man shall say to you, Loe, here is Christ, or loe, hee is there: beleeue him not.

22 For false Christs and false prophets shall rise, and shall shewe signes and wonders, to seduce, if it were possible, euen the elect.

23 But take ye heed: behold, I haue foretold you all things.

Matt. 24.

24 ¶ * But in those dayes, after that tribulation, the Sunne shalbe darkned, and the Moone shall not giue her light.

25 And the Starres of heauen shall fall, and the powers that are in heauen shall be shaken.

26 And then shal they see the Sonne of man comming in the cloudes, with great power and glory.

27 And then shal he send his Angels, and shall gather together his elect from the foure winds, from the vttermost part of the earth, to the vttermost part of heauen.

28 Now learne a parable of the fig tree. When her branch is yet tender, and putteth forth leaues, ye know that summer is neere:

29 So ye in like maner, when ye shal see these things come to passe, knowe that it is nigh, euen at the doores.

30 Verely I say vnto you, that this generation shall not passe, till all these things be done.

31 Heauen and earth shal passe away: but my words shall not passe away.

32 ¶ But of that day and that houre knoweth no man, no not the Angels which are in heauen, neither the Son, but the Father.

33 * Take ye heed, watch and pray: for ye know not when the time is.   *Mat. 24. 42

34 For the Sonne of man is as a man taking a farre iourney, who left his house, and gaue authority to his seruants, and to euery man his worke, and commanded the porter to watch:

35 Watch ye therefore (for ye knowe not when the master of the house commeth, at Euen, or at midnight, or at the cocke crowing, or in the morning.)

36 Lest comming suddenly, he finde you sleeping.

37 And what I say vnto you, I say vnto all, Watch.

CHAP. XIIII.

1 A conspiracie against Christ. 3 Precious ointment is powred on his head by a woman. 10 Iudas selleth his master for money. 12 Christ himselfe foretelleth how he shall be betrayed of one of his disciples: 22 after the Passeouer prepared, & eaten, instituteth his Supper: 26 declareth aforehand the flight of all his disciples, and Peters deniall. 43 Iudas betrayeth him with a kisse. 46 Hee is apprehended in the garden, 53 Falsly accused, and impiously condemned of the Iewes counsell: 65 shamefully abused by them: 66 and thrise denied of Peter.

Fter * two dayes was the feast of the Passeouer, and of vnleauened bread: and the chiefe Priests, and the Scribes sought how they might take him by craft, and put him to death.   *Mat. 26. 2

2 But they said, Not on the feast day, lest there be an vprore of the people.

3 ¶ * And being in Bethanie, in the house of Simon the leper, as he sate at meat, there came a woman, hauing an Alabaster boxe of oyntment of ||spikenard very precious, and shee brake the boxe, and powred it on his head.   *Mat. 26. 6

   || Or, pure nard: or liquid nard.

4 And there were some that had indignation within themselues, and said, Why was this waste of the oyntment made?

5 For it might haue bene solde for more then three hundred ||pence, and haue bene giuen to the poore: and they murmured against her. || See Matt. 18. 28.

6 And

6 And Iesus said, Let her alone, why trouble you her? Shee hath wrought a good worke on me.

7 For ye haue the poore with you alwayes, and whensoeuer ye will yee may doe them good: but me ye haue not alwayes.

8 She hath done what she could: she is come aforehand to anoint my body to the burying.

9 Verely I say vnto you, Wheresoeuer this Gospel shalbe preached thorowout the whole world, this also that she hath done, shall be spoken of for a memoriall of her.

*Mat. 26. 14.

10 ¶ *And Iudas Iscariot, one of the twelue, went vnto the chiefe Priests, to betray him vnto them.

11 And when they heard it, they were glad, and promised to giue him money. And he sought how he might conueniently betray him.

*Mat. 26. 17. ‖ Or, sacrificed.

12 ¶ *And the first day of vnleauened bread, when they ‖ killed the Passeouer, his disciples said vnto him, Where wilt thou that we goe, and prepare, that thou mayest eate the Passeouer?

13 And he sendeth forth two of his disciples, and saith vnto them, Goe yee into the citie, and there shall meet you a man bearing a pitcher of water: follow him.

14 And wheresoeuer he shall goe in, say yee to the good man of the house, The Master saith, Where is the guest chamber, where I shall eate the Passeouer with my disciples?

15 And he will shew you a large vpper roome furnished, and prepared: there make ready for vs.

16 And his disciples went forth, and came into the citie, and found as hee had said vnto them: and they made readie the Passeouer.

17 And in the euening hee commeth with the twelue.

*Mat. 26. 20.

18 *And as they sate, and did eat, Iesus said, Verily I say vnto you, one of you which eateth with me, shall betray mee.

19 And they began to be sorowfull, and to say vnto him, one by one, Is it I? And another said, Is it I?

20 And he answered, and saide vnto them, It is one of the twelue, that dippeth with me in the dish.

21 The sonne of man indeed goeth, as it is written of him: but woe to that man by whom the Sonne of man is betrayed: Good were it for that man, if he had neuer bene borne.

*Mat. 2 26.

22 ¶ *And as they did eate, Iesus tooke bread, and blessed, and brake it, and gaue to them, and said, Take, eate: this is my body.

23 And he tooke the cup, and when he had giuen thanks, he gaue it to them: and they all dranke of it.

24 And he said vnto them, This is my blood of the new Testament, which is shed for many.

25 Verely I say vnto you, I will drinke no more of the fruit of the Vine, vntill that day that I drinke it new in the kingdome of God.

26 ¶ And when they had sung an ‖hymne, they went out into the mount of Oliues.

‖ Or, psa

*Mat. 2 31.

27 *And Iesus saith vnto them, All ye shall be offended because of mee this night: for it is written, I will smite the shepheard, and the sheepe shall be scattered.

28 But after that I am risen, I will goe before you into Galilee.

*Mat. 2 33.

29 *But Peter said vnto him, Although al shalbe offended, yet wil not I.

30 And Iesus saith vnto him, Verily I say vnto thee, that this day, euen in this night before the cocke crow twise, thou shalt denie me thrise.

31 But he spake the more vehemently, If I should die with thee, I will not denie thee in any wise. Likewise also said they all.

*Matth. 36.

32 *And they came to a place which was named Gethsemani, and hee saith to his disciples, Sit yee here, while I shall pray.

33 And hee taketh with him Peter, and Iames, and Iohn, and began to be sore amazed, and to be very heauy,

34 And saith vnto them, My soule is exceeding sorowful vnto death: tarie ye here, and watch.

35 And he went forward a litle, and fell on the ground, and prayed, that if it were possible, the houre might passe from him.

36 And he said, Abba, father, all things are possible vnto thee, take away this cup from me: Neuerthelesse, not that I will, but what thou wilt.

37 And hee commeth, and findeth them sleeping, and saith vnto Peter, Simon, sleepest thou? Couldest not thou watch one houre?

38 Watch ye and pray, lest yee enter
into

into temptation : The spirit truly is ready, but the flesh is weake.

39 And againe he went away, and prayed, and spake the same words.

40 And when he returned, he found them asleepe againe, (for their eies were heauie) neither wist they what to answere him.

41 And he commeth the third time, and saith vnto them, Sleepe on now, and take your rest : it is enough, the houre is come, behold, the Son of man is betrayed into the hands of sinners.

42 Rise vp, let vs goe, Loe, he that betrayeth me, is at hand.

_{Mat. 26. 7.}

43 ¶ *And immediately, while hee yet spake, commeth Iudas, one of the twelue, and with him a great multitude with swords, and staues, from the chiefe Priests, and the Scribes, & the Elders.

44 And he that betrayed him, had giuen them a token, saying, Whomsoeuer I shall kisse, that same is he ; take him, and lead him away safely.

45 And assoone as he was come, he goeth straightway to him, and sayeth, Master, Master, and kissed him.

46 ¶ And they layed their hands on him, and tooke him.

47 And one of them that stood by, drew a sword, and smote a seruant of the high Priest, and cut off his eare.

48 And Iesus answered, & said vnto thē, Are ye come out as against a theefe, with swords, & with staues to take me ?

49 I was daily with you in the Temple, teaching, and yee tooke me not ; but the Scriptures must be fulfilled.

50 And they all forsooke him, & fled.

51 And there followed him a certaine yong man, hauing a linnen cloth cast about his naked body, and the yong men laid hold on him.

52 And he left the linnen cloth, and fled from them naked.

*Mat. 26. 57.

53 ¶ *And they led Iesus away to the high Priest, and with him were assembled all the chiefe Priests, and the Elders, and the Scribes.

54 And Peter followed him a farre off, euen into the pallace of the high Priest : and he sate with the seruants, and warmed himselfe at the fire.

*Mat. 26. 59.

55 *And the chiefe Priests, and all the counsell sought for witnesse against Iesus, to put him to death, & found none.

56 For many bare false witnesse against him, but their witnesse agreed not together.

57 And there arose certaine, and bare false witnesse against him, saying,

58 We heard him say, I will destroy this Temple that is made with hands, and within three dayes I will build another made without hands.

59 But neither so did their witnesse agree together.

60 And the high Priest stood vp in the mids, and asked Iesus, saying, Answerest thou nothing ? What is it which these witnesse against thee ?

61 But he held his peace, and answered nothing. Againe, the high Priest asked him, and said vnto him, Art thou the Christ, the sonne of the Blessed ?

62 And Iesus said, I am : *and yee shall see the sonne of man sitting on the right hand of power, and comming in the clouds of heauen.

*Mat. 24. 30.

63 Then the high Priest rent his clothes, and saith, What neede we any further witnesses ?

64 Yee haue heard the blasphemy : what thinke yee ? And they all condemned him to be guilty of death.

65 And some beganne to spit on him, and to couer his face, and to buffet him, and to say vnto him, Prophecie : And the seruants did stricke him with the palmes of their hands.

66 ¶ *And as Peter was beneath in the palace, there commeth one of the maides of the high Priest.

*Mat. 26. 69.

67 And when she saw Peter warning himselfe, she looked vpon him, and said, And thou also wast with Iesus of Nazareth.

68 But hee denied, saying, I know not, neither vnderstand I what thou sayest. And he went out into the porch, and the cocke crew.

69 And a maide saw him againe, and beganne to say to them that stood by, This is one of them.

70 And he denied it againe. And a little after, they that stood by said againe to Peter, Surely thou art one of them : for thou art a Galilean, and thy speach agreeth thereto.

71 But he beganne to curse and to sweare, *saying*, I know not this man of whom yee speake.

72 *And the second time the cocke crew : and Peter called to minde the word that Iesus said vnto him, Before the cocke crow twise, thou shalt denie me thrise. And when he thought thereon, ‖he wept.

*Mat. 26. 75.

‖ *Or, he wept abundantly, or he began to wept.*

CHAP.

CHAP. XV.

1 Ieſus brought bound, and accuſed before Pilate. 15 Vpon the clamour of the common people, the murderer Barabbas is looſed, and Ieſus deliuered vp to be crucified : 17 hee is crowned with thornes, 19 ſpit on, and mocked : 21 fainteth in bearing his croſſe : 27 hangeth betweene two theeues, 29 ſuffreth the triumphing reproches of the Iewes : 39 but confeſſed by the Centurion, to bee the Sonne of God : 43 and is honourably buried by Ioſeph.

* Matth. 27. 1.

ANd * ſtraightway in the morning the chiefe Prieſts helde a conſultation with the Elders and Scribes, and the whole Councell, and bound Ieſus, and caried him away, and deliuered him to Pilate.

2 And Pilate asked him, Art thou the King of the Iewes ? And hee anſwering, ſaid vnto him, Thou ſayeſt it.

3 And the chiefe Prieſts accuſed him of many things : but hee anſwered nothing.

* Matth. 27. 13.

4 * And Pilate asked him againe, ſaying, Answereſt thou nothing ? behold how many things they witneſſe againſt thee.

5 But Ieſus yet anſwered nothing, ſo that Pilate marueiled.

6 Now at that Feaſt he releaſed vnto them one priſoner, whomſoeuer they deſired.

7 And there was one named Barabbas, which lay bound with them that had made inſurrection with him, who had committed murder in the inſurrection.

8 And the multitude crying alowd, began to deſire him to doe as he had euer done vnto them.

9 But Pilate anſwered them, ſaying, Will ye that I releaſe vnto you the King of the Iewes ?

10 (For hee knew that the chiefe Prieſts had deliuered him for enuie.)

11 But the chiefe Prieſts mooued the people, that hee ſhould rather releaſe Barabbas vnto them.

12 And Pilate anſwered, and ſaid againe vnto them, What will yee then that I ſhall do vnto him whom ye call the King of the Iewes ?

13 And they cried out againe, Crucifie him.

14 Then Pilate ſaide vnto them,

Why, what euill hath hee done ? And they cried out the more exceedingly, Crucifie him.

15 ¶ And ſo Pilate, willing to content the people, released Barabbas vnto them, and deliuered Ieſus, when he had ſcourged him, to be crucified.

16 And the ſouldiers led him away into the hall, called Pretorium, and they call together the whole band.

17 And they clothed him with purple, and platted a crowne of thornes, and put it about his head,

18 And beganne to ſalute him, Haile King of the Iewes.

19 And they ſmote him on the head with a reed, and did ſpit vpon him, and bowing their knees, worſhipped him.

20 And when they had mocked him, they tooke off the purple from him, and put his owne clothes on him, and led him out to crucifie him.

21 * And they compell one Simon a Cyrenian, who paſſed by, comming out of the country, the father of Alexander and Rufus, to beare his Croſſe.

* Matth. 32.

22 And they bring him vnto the place Golgotha, which is, being interpreted, the place of a ſkull.

23 And they gaue him to drinke, wine mingled with myrrhe : but he receiued it not.

24 And when they had crucified him, they parted his garments, caſting lots vpon them, what euery man ſhould take.

25 And it was the third houre, and they crucified him.

26 And the ſuperſcription of his accuſation was written ouer, THE KING OF THE IEWES.

27 And with him they crucifie two theeues, the one on his right hand, and the other on his left.

28 And the Scripture was fulfilled, which ſayeth, * And hee was numbred with the tranſgreſſours.

* Eſay 53. 12.

29 And they that paſſed by, railed on him, wagging their heads, and ſaying, Ah thou that deſtroyeſt the Temple, and buildeſt it in three dayes,

30 Saue thy ſelfe, and come downe from the Croſſe.

31 Likewiſe alſo the chiefe Prieſts mocking, ſaid among themſelues with the Scribes, He ſaued others, himſelfe he cannot ſaue.

32 Let Chriſt the King of Iſrael deſcend now from the Croſſe, that we may

may see and beleeue : And they that were crucified with him, reuiled him.

33 And when the sixth houre was come, there was darkenesse ouer the whole land, vntill the ninth houre.

34 And at the ninth houre, Iesus cryed with a loude voice, saying, * Eloi, Eloi, lamasabachthani? which is, being interpreted, My God, my God, why hast thou forsaken me?

35 And some of them that stood by, when they heard it, said, Behold, he calleth Elias.

36 And one ranne, and filled a spunge full of vineger, and put it on a reed, and gaue him to drinke, saying, Let alone, let vs see whether Elias will come to take him downe.

37 And Iesus cryed with a loude voice, and gaue vp the ghost.

38 And the vaile of the Temple was rent in twaine, from the top to the bottome.

39 ¶ And when the Centurion which stood ouer against him, saw that hee so cryed out, and gaue vp the ghost, hee said, Truely this man was the Sonne of God.

40 There were also women looking on afarre off, among whom was Mary Magdalene, and Mary the mother of Iames the lesse, and of Ioses, and Salome :

41 Who also when hee was in Galile, * followed him, and ministred vnto him, and many other women which came vp with him vnto Hierusalem.

42 ¶ * And now when the euen was come, (because it was the Preparation, that is, the day before the Sabbath)

43 Ioseph of Arimathea, an honourable counseller, which also waited for the kingdome of God, came, and went in boldly vnto Pilate, and craued the body of Iesus.

44 And Pilate marueiled if he were already dead, and calling vnto him the Centurion, hee asked him whether hee had beene any while dead.

45 And when he knew it of the Centurion, he gaue the body to Ioseph.

46 And hee bought fine linnen, and tooke him downe, and wrapped him in the linnen, and laide him in a sepulchre, which was hewen out of a rocke, and rolled a stone vnto the doore of the sepulchre.

47 And Mary Magdalene, and

Mary the mother of Ioses behelde where he was laide.

CHAP. XVI.

1 An Angel declareth the resurrection of Christ to three women. 9 Christ himselfe appeareth to Mary Magdalene : 12 to two going into the countrey : 14 then, to the Apostles, 15 whom he sendeth foorth to preach the Gospel : 19 and ascendeth into heauen.

Nd when the Sabbath was past, Mary Magdalene, and Mary the mother of Iames, and Salome, had bought sweete spices, that they might come and anoint him.

2 * And very early in the morning, the first day of the week they came vnto the sepulchre, at the rising of the sunne :

3 And they said among themselues, Who shall roll vs away the stone from the doore of the sepulchre?

4 (And when they looked, they saw that the stone was rolled away) for it was very great.

5 * And entring into the sepulchre, they sawe a young man sitting on the right side, clothed in a long white garment, and they were affrighted.

6 And hee sayth vnto them, Be not affrighted; ye seeke Iesus of Nazareth, which was crucified : he is risen, hee is not here : behold the place where they laide him.

7 But goe your way, tell his disciples, and Peter, that hee goeth before you into Galile, there shall ye see him, * as he said vnto you.

8 And they went out quickely, and fledde from the sepulchre, for they trembled, and were amazed, neither sayd they any thing to any man, for they were afraid.

9 ¶ Now when *Iesus* was risen early, the first day of the weeke, * he appeared first to Mary Magdalene, * out of whom he had cast seuen deuils.

10 And she went and told them that had beene with him, as they mourned and wept.

11 And they, when they had heard that he was aliue, and had beene seene of her, beleeued not.

12 ¶ After that, he appeared in another forme * vnto two of them, as they walked, and went into the countrey.

13 And they went and tolde it vnto the residue, neither beleeued they them.

14 ¶ * Af-

* Mat. 27. 46.

* Luke 8. 3.

* Mat. 27. 57.

* Luk. 24. 1 ioh. 20. 1.

* Iohn 20. 11.

* Mat. 26. 32.

* Iohn 20. 14. * Luke 8. 2.

* Luke 24. 13.

* Luk. 24.
36. iohn 20
19.
|| Or, toge-
ther.

* Mat. 28.
19.

* Ioh. 12. 48

* Act. 16. 18

14 ¶ *Afterward he appeared vnto the eleuen, as they sate ||at meat, and vpbraided them with their vnbeliefe, and hardnesse of heart, because they beleeued not them, which had seene him after he was risen.

15 *And he said vnto them, Goe yee into all the world, and preach the Gospel to euery creature.

16 He that beleeueth and is baptized, shalbe saued, *but he that beleeueth not, shall be damned.

17 And these signes shal follow them that beleeue, *In my Name shall they cast out deuils, *they shall speake with new tongues,

18 *They shall take vp serpents, and if they drinke any deadly thing, it shall not hurt them, *they shall lay hands on the sicke, and they shall recouer.

19 ¶ So then after the Lord had spoken vnto them, he was receiued vp into heauen, *and sate on the right hand of God.

20 And they went foorth, and preached euery where, the Lord working with them, *and confirming the worde with signes following. Amen.

* Acts

* Act.

* Act.

* Luk.
51.

* Heb

¶ The Goſpel according to S.Luke.

CHAP. I.

1 The Preface of Luke to his whole Gospel. 5 The conception of Iohn the Baptist, 26 and of Christ. 39 The prophecie of Elizabeth, and of Mary, concerning Christ. 57 The natiuitie & circumcision of Iohn. 67 The prophesie of Zachary both of Christ, 76 and of Iohn.

Orasmuch as many haue taken in hande to set foorth in order a declaration of those things which are most surely beleeued among vs,

2 Euen as they deliuered them vnto vs, which from the beginning were eye-witnesses, & ministers of the word:

3 It seemed good to me also, hauing had perfect vnderstanding of things from the very first, to write vnto thee in order, most excellent Theophilus,

4 That thou mightest know the certainetie of those things wherein thou hast bene instructed.

5 ¶ THere was in the dayes of Herode the king of Iudea, a certaine Priest, named Zacharias, of the course of Abia, and his wife was of the daughters of Aaron, and her name was Elizabeth.

6 And they were both righteous before God, walking in all the Commandements and ordinances of the Lord, blamelesse.

7 And they had no childe, because that Elizabeth was barren, and they both were now well striken in yeeres.

8 And it came to passe, that while he executed the Priests office before God in the order of his course,

9 According to the custome of the Priests office, his lot was to burne incense when he went into the Temple of the Lord.

10 *And the whole multitude of the people were praying without, at the time of incense.

11 And there appeared vnto him an Angel of the Lord, standing on the right side of the Altar of incense.

12 And when Zacharias sawe him, hee was troubled, and feare fell vpon him.

13 But the Angel said vnto him, Feare not, Zacharias, for thy prayer is heard, and thy wife Elizabeth shall beare thee a sonne, and thou shalt call his name Iohn.

14 And thou shalt haue ioy and gladnesse, and many shall reioyce at his birth:

15 For he shall be great in the sight of the Lord, and shal drinke neither wine, nor strong drinke, and he shall bee filled with the holy Ghost, euen from his mothers wombe.

16 *And many of the children of Israel shall hee turne to the Lord their God.

* Exo
leuit.

* Mal

17 And

Or, by.

17 And hee shall goe before him in the spirit and power of Elias, to turne the hearts of the fathers to the children, and the disobedient || to the wisedome of the iust, to make ready a people prepared for the Lord.

18 And Zacharias said vnto the Angel, Whereby shall I know this? For I am an old man, and my wife well striken in yeeres.

19 And the Angel answering, said vnto him, I am Gabriel that stand in the presence of God, and am sent to speake vnto thee, and to shew thee these glad tidings.

20 And behold, thou shalt be dumbe, and not able to speake, vntill the day that these things shall bee performed, because thou beleeuest not my words, which shall bee fulfilled in their season.

21 And the people waited for Zacharias, and maruelled that hee taried so long in the temple.

22 And when he came out, he could not speake vnto them: and they perceiued that he had seene a vision in the temple: for he beckened vnto them, and remained speechlesse.

23 And it came to passe, that as soone as the dayes of his ministration were accomplished, he departed to his owne house.

24 And after those dayes his wife Elizabeth conceiued, and hid her selfe fiue moneths, saying,

25 Thus hath the Lord dealt with me in the dayes wherein he looked on me, to take away my reproch among men.

26 And in the sixt moneth, the Angel Gabriel was sent from God, vnto a citie of Galilee, named Nazareth,

27 To a virgine espoused to a man whose name was Ioseph, of the house of Dauid, and the virgins name was Marie.

Or, gracisly accept-, or much uced, see rse 30.

28 And the Angel came in vnto her, and said, Haile thou that art || highly fauoured, the Lord is with thee: Blessed art thou among women.

29 And when she saw him, she was troubled at his saying, and cast in her minde what maner of salutation this should be.

30 And the Angel said vnto her, Feare not, Marie, for thou hast found fauour with God.

Esai. 7. 14 at. 1. 21.

31 * And behold, thou shalt conceiue in thy wombe, and bring forth a sonne, and shalt call his name Iesus.

32 He shall be great, and shall be called the sonne of the Highest, and the Lord God shall giue vnto him the throne of his father Dauid.

* Dan. 7. 14. mich. 4. 7.

33 * And hee shall reigne ouer the house of Iacob for euer, and of his kingdome there shall be no end.

34 Then said Marie vnto the Angel, How shall this be, seeing I know not a man?

35 And the Angel answered and said vnto her, The holy Ghost shall come vpon thee, and the power of the Highest shall ouershadow thee. Therefore also that holy thing which shall bee borne of thee, shall bee called the sonne of God.

36 And behold, thy cousin Elizabeth, she hath also conceiued a sonne in her old age, and this is the sixt moneth with her, who was called barren.

37 For with God no thing shall be vnpossible.

38 And Marie said, Behold the handmaide of the Lord, be it vnto me according to thy word: and the Angel departed from her.

39 And Marie arose in those dayes, and went into the hill countrey with haste, into a citie of Iuda,

40 And entred into the house of Zacharias, and saluted Elizabeth.

41 And it came to passe that when Elizabeth heard the salutation of Marie, the babe leaped in her wombe, and Elizabeth was filled with the holy Ghost.

42 And she spake out with a loud voyce, and saide, Blessed art thou among women, and blessed is the fruite of thy wombe.

43 And whence is this to me, that the mother of my Lord should come to mee?

44 For loe, assoone as the voice of thy salutation sounded in mine eares, the babe leaped in my wombe for ioy.

45 And blessed is she || that beleeued, for there shalbe a performance of those things, which were told her from the Lord.

|| Or, which beleeued, that there.

46 And Marie said, My soule doth magnifie the Lord.

47 And my spirit hath reioyced in God my sauiour.

48 For hee hath regarded the low estate of his handmaiden: for behold, from

from hencefoorth all generations shall call me blessed.

49 For he that is mighty hath done to mee great things, and holy is his Name.

50 And his mercy is on them that feare him, from generation to generation.

*Esay 51. 9.
*Psal. 33. 10.

51 * Hee hath shewed strength with his arme, * he hath scattered the proud, in the imagination of their hearts.

*1. Sam. 2. 8.

52 * He hath put downe the mighty from their seates, and exalted them of low degree.

*Psal. 34. 10.

53 * Hee hath filled the hungry with good things, and the rich hee hath sent emptie away.

*Iere. 31. 3. 20.
*Psal. 132. 10. gen. 17. 19.

54 Hee hath holpen his seruant Israel, * in remembrance of his mercy,

55 * As he spake to our fathers, to Abraham, and to his seed for euer.

56 And Mary abode with her about three moneths, and returned to her owne house.

57 Now Elizabeths full time came, that shee should be deliuered, and shee brought foorth a sonne.

58 And her neighbours and her cousins heard how the Lord had shewed great mercy vpon her, and they reioyced with her.

59 And it came to passe that on the eight day they came to circumcise the childe, and they called him Zacharias, after the name of his father.

60 And his mother answered, and said, Not so, but he shalbe called Iohn.

61 And they said vnto her, There is none of thy kinred that is called by this name.

62 And they made signes to his father, how he would haue him called.

63 And he asked for a writing table, and wrote, saying, His name is Iohn: and they marueiled all.

64 And his mouth was opened immediatly, and his tongue *loosed*, and hee spake, and praised God.

|| Or, things.

65 And feare came on all that dwelt round about them, and all these ||sayings were noised abroad thorowout all the hill countrey of Iudea.

66 And all they that had heard them, layde them vp in their hearts, saying, What maner of childe shal this be? And the hand of the Lord was with him.

67 And his father Zacharias was filled with the holy Ghost, and prophesied, saying,

68 Blessed bee the Lord God of Israel, for hee hath visited and redeemed his people,

*Psal. 1 18.

69 * And hath raised vp an horne of saluation for vs, in the house of his seruant Dauid,

*Iere. 23 and 30. 9.

70 * As he spake by the mouth of his holy Prophets, which haue bene since the world began:

71 That wee should be saued from our enemies, and from the hand of all that hate vs,

72 To performe the mercy promised to our fathers, and to remember his holy Couenant,

*Gene. 2 16.

73 * The oath which he sware to our father Abraham,

74 That hee would grant vnto vs, that wee beeing deliuered out of the hands of our enemies, might serue him without feare,

75 In holinesse and righteousnesse before him, all the dayes of our life.

76 And thou childe shalt bee called the Prophet of the Highest: for thou shalt goe before the face of the Lord to prepare his wayes,

|| Or, for.

77 To giue knowledge of saluation vnto his people, ||by the remission of their sinnes,

|| Or, bow of the mer
|| Or, Sun rising, or branch, Z
3. 8. esay
1. malach
2. numb.
17.

78 Through the ||tender mercy of our God, whereby the ||day-spring from on high hath visited vs,

79 To giue light to them that sit in darknes, and in the shadow of death, to guide our feet into the way of peace.

80 And the childe grew, and waxed strong in spirit, and was in the deserts, till the day of his shewing vnto Israel.

CHAP. II.

1 Augustus taxeth all the Romane Empire: 6 The natiuitie of Christ: 3 one Angel relateth it to the shepherds: 13 many sing praises to God for it. 21 Christ is circumcised. 22 Mary purified: 28 Simeon and Anna prophecie of Christ: 40 who increaseth in wisdome, 46 questioneth in the Temple with the doctours, 51 and is obedient to his parents.

AND it came to passe in those dayes, that there went out a decree from Cesar Augustus, that all the world should be ||taxed.

|| Or, inre led.

2 (And this taxing was first made whē Cyrenius was gouernor of Syria)

3 And all went to bee taxed, euery one into his owne citie.

4 And Ioseph also wēt vp frō Galilee,
out

Iohn 7. 42.

out of the citie of Nazareth, into Iudea, vnto the *citie of Dauid, which is called Bethlehem, (because he was of the house and linage of Dauid,)

5 To be taxed with Mary his espoused wife, being great with child.

6 And so it was, that while they were there, the dayes were accomplished that she should be deliuered.

7 And she brought foorth her first borne sonne, and wrapped him in swadling clothes, and laid him in a manger, because there was no roome for them in the Inne.

8 And there were in the same countrey shepheards abiding in ÿ field, keeping ‖watch ouer their flocke by night.

*Or, the
ight wat-
ies.*

9 And loe, the Angel of the Lord came vpon them, and the glory of the Lord shone round about them, and they were sore afraid.

10 And the Angel said vnto them, Feare not : For behold, I bring you good tidings of great ioy, which shall be to all people.

11 For vnto you is borne this day, in the citie of Dauid, a Sauiour, which is Christ the Lord.

12 And this shall be a signe vnto you; yee shall find the babe wrapped in swatling clothes lying in a manger.

13 And suddenly there was with the Angel a multitude of the heauenly hoste praising God, and saying,

14 Glory to God in the highest, and on earth peace, good wil towards men.

15 And it came to passe, as the Angels were gone away from them into heauen, the shepheards said one to another, Let vs now goe euen vnto Bethlehem, and see this thing which is come to passe, which the Lord hath made knowen vnto vs.

16 And they came with haste, and found Mary and Ioseph, and the babe lying in a manger.

17 And when they had seene it, they made knowen abroad the saying, which was told them, concerning this child.

18 And all they that heard it, wondered at those things, which were tolde them by the shepheards.

19 But Mary kept all these things, and pondered them in her heart.

20 And the shepheards returned, glorifying & praising God for all the things that they had heard and seene, as it was told vnto them.

* Gen. 17.
2.

21 *And when eight dayes were ac-

complished for the circumcising of the childe, his name was called *Iesus, which was so named of the Angel before he was conceiued in the wombe.

* Mat. 1.
21.

22 And when the dayes of her purification according to the law of Moses, were accomplished, they brought him to Hierusalem, to present him to the Lord,

23 (As it is written in the law of the Lord, *Euery male that openeth the wombe, shalbe called holy to the Lord)

* Exod. 13.
2. numb. 18
16.

24 And to offer a sacrifice according to *that which is said in the Law of the Lord, a paire of turtle doues, or two yong pigeons.

* Leuit. 12.
2; 6.

25 And behold, there was a man in Hierusalem, whose name was Simeon, and the same man was iust and deuout, waiting for the consolation of Israel : and the holy Ghost was vpon him.

26 And it was reuealed vnto him by the holy Ghost, that he should not see death, before he had seene the Lords Christ.

27 And hee came by the spirit into the Temple : and when the parents brought in the child Iesus, to doe for him after the custome of the Lawe,

28 Then tooke hee him vp in his armes, and blessed God, and said,

29 Lord now lettest thou thy seruant depart in peace, according to thy word.

30 For mine eyes haue seene thy saluation.

31 Which thou hast prepared before the face of all people.

32 A light to lighten the Gentiles, and the glory of thy people Israel.

33 And Ioseph and his mother marueiled at those things which were spoken of him.

34 And Simeon blessed them, and said vnto Marie his mother, Behold, this child is set for the *fall and rising againe of many in Israel : and for a signe which shall be spoken against,

* Esai. 8. 14.
rom. 9. 32.

35 (Yea a sword shall pearce thorow thy owne soule also) that the thoughts of many hearts may be reuealed.

36 And there was one Anna a Prophetesse, the daughter of Phanuel, of the tribe of Aser; she was of a great age, and had liued with an husband seuen yeeres from her virginitie.

37 And she was a widow of about fourescore and foure yeeres, which departed

Or, Israel.

parted not from the Temple, but serued God with fastings and prayers night and day.

38 And she comming in that instant, gaue thankes likewise vnto the Lord, and spake of him to al them that looked for redemption in ‖Hierusalem.

39 And when they had performed all things according to the Lawe of the Lord, they returned into Galilee, to their owne citie Nazareth.

40 And the child grew, and waxed strong in spirit filled with wisedome, and the grace of God was vpon him.

* Deu. 16. 1.

41 Now his parents went to Hierusalem *euery yeere, at the feast of the Passeouer.

42 And when he was twelue yeeres old, they went vp to Hierusalem, after the custome of the feast.

43 And when they had fulfilled the dayes, as they returned, the childe Iesus taried behind in Hierusalem, and Ioseph and his mother knew not of it.

44 But they supposing him to haue bene in the company, went a daies iourney, and they sought him among their kinsefolke and acquaintance.

45 And when they found him not, they turned backe againe to Hierusalem, seeking him.

46 And it came to passe, that after three daies they found him in the Temple, sitting in the midst of the Doctours, both hearing them, and asking them questions.

47 And all that heard him were astonished at his vnderstanding, and answeres.

48 And when they sawe him, they were amazed: and his mother said vnto him, Sonne, why hast thou thus dealt with vs? Behold, thy father and I haue sought thee sorrowing.

49 And he said vnto them, How is it that ye sought me? Wist yee not that I must bee about my fathers businesse?

50 And they vnderstood not the saying which he spake vnto them.

51 And he went downe with them, and came to Nazareth, and was subiect vnto them: But his mother kept all these sayings in her heart.

‖ *Or, age.*

52 And Iesus increased in wisedom and ‖stature, and in fauour with God and man.

CHAP. III.

1 The preaching and baptisme of Iohn: 15 His testimonie of Christ. 20 Herode imprisoneth Iohn. 21 Christ baptized, receiueth testimony from heauen. 23 The age, and genealogie of Christ, from Ioseph vpwards.

 Ow in the fifteenth yeere of the reigne of Tiberius Cesar, Pontius Pilate being Gouernour of Iudea, & Herode being Tetrarch of Galilee, and his brother Philip Tetrarch of Iturea, and of the region of Trachonitis, and Lysanias the Tetrarch of Abilene,

2 Annas and Caiaphas being the high Priests, the word of God came vnto Iohn the sonne of Zacharias, in the wildernesse.

* Mat.

3 *And he came into all the countrey about Iordane, preaching the baptisme of repentance, for the remissiō of sinnes,

* Esai.

4 As it is written in the book of the words of Esaias the Prophet, saying, *The voyce of one crying in the wildernesse, Prepare ye the way of the Lord, make his paths straight.

5 Euery valley shall be filled, and euery mountaine and hill shalbe brought low, and the crooked shall bee made straight, and the rough wayes shall be made smooth.

6 And all flesh shal see the saluation of God.

7 Then said hee to the multitude that came forth to bee baptized of him, *O generation of vipers, who hath warned you to flee from the wrath to come?

* Mat.

8 Bring forth therfore fruits ‖worthy of repentance, and begin not to say within your selues, We haue Abraham to our father: For I say vnto you, that God is able of these stones to raise vp children vnto Abraham.

‖ *Or, me for.*

9 And now also the axe is laid vnto the root of the trees: Euery tree therefore which bringeth not foorth good fruit, is hewen downe, and cast into the fire.

10 And the people asked him, saying, What shall we doe then?

11 He answereth, and saith vnto them, * He that hath two coats, let him impart to him that hath none, and he that hath meat, let him doe likewise.

* Iam.
1. ioh.

12 Then came also Publicanes to be baptized, and said vnto him, Master, what shall we doe?

13 And he said vnto them, Exact no more then that which is appointed you.

14 And

14 And the ſouldiers likewiſe demanded of him, ſaying, And what ſhall put no infeare. we doe? And he ſaid vnto them, ‖Doe violence to no man, neither accuſe any allow- falſely, & be content with your ‖wages.

15 And as the people were ‖in expectation, and all men ‖muſed in their in ſus- hearts of Iohn, whether he were the reaſo- or deba- Chriſt or not:

16 Iohn anſwered, ſaying vnto at. 3. 11 them all, *I indeede baptize you with water, but one mightier then I commeth, the latchet of whoſe ſhooes I am not worthy to vnlooſe, he ſhall baptize you with the holy Ghoſt, and with fire.

17 Whoſe fanne is in his hand, and he will thorowly purge his floore, and will gather the wheat into his garner, but the chaffe he will burne with fire vnquencheable.

18 And many other things in his exhortation preached he vnto the people.

19 *But Herode the Tetrarch being at. 14. reprooued by him for Herodias his brother Philips wife, and for all the euils which Herode had done,

20 Added yet this aboue all, that he ſhut vp Iohn in priſon.

21 Now when all the people were at. 3. baptized, *and it came to paſſe that Ieſus alſo being baptized, and praying, the heauen was opened:

22 And the holy Ghoſt deſcended in a bodily ſhape like a Doue vpon him, and a voice came from heauen, which ſaid, Thou art my beloued ſonne, in thee I am well pleaſed.

23 And Ieſus himſelfe began to be about thirty yeeres of age, being (as was ſuppoſed) the ſonne of Ioſeph, which was *the ſonne* of Heli,

24 Which was *the ſonne* of Matthat, which was *the ſonne* of Leui, which was *the ſonne* of Melchi, which was *the ſonne* of Ianna, which was *the ſonne* of Ioſeph,

25 Which was *the ſonne* of Matthathias, which was *the ſonne* of Amos, which was *the ſonne* of Naum, which was *the ſonne* of Eſli, which was *the ſonne* of Nagge,

26 Which was *the ſonne* of Maath, which was *the ſonne* of Matthathias, which was *the ſonne* of Semei, which was *the ſonne* of Ioſeph, which was *the ſonne* of Iuda,

27 Which was *the ſonne* of Ioanna, which was *the ſonne* of Rheſa, which was *the ſonne* of Zorobabel, which was *the ſonne* of Salathiel, which was *the ſonne* of Neri,

28 Which was *the ſonne* of Melchi, which was *the ſonne* of Addi, which was *the ſonne* of Coſam, which was *the ſonne* of Elmodam, which was *the ſonne* of Er,

29 Which was *the ſonne* of Ioſe, which was *the ſonne* of Eliezer, which was *the ſonne* of Iorim, which was *the ſonne* of Matthat, which was *the ſonne* of Leui,

30 Which was *the ſonne* of Simeon, which was *the ſonne* of Iuda, which was *the ſonne* of Ioſeph, which was *the ſonne* of Ionan, which was *the ſonne* of Eliakim,

31 Which was *the ſonne* of Melea, which was *the ſonne* of Menam, which was *the ſonne* of Mattatha, which was *the ſonne* of Nathan, which was *the ſonne* of Dauid,

32 Which was *the ſonne* of Ieſſe, which was *the ſonne* of Obed, which was *the ſonne* of Booz, which was *the ſonne* of Salmon, which was *the ſonne* of Naaſſon,

33 Which was *the ſonne* of Aminadab, which was *the ſonne* of Aram, which was *the ſonne* of Eſrom, which was *the ſonne* of Phares, which was *the ſonne* of Iuda,

34 Which was *the ſonne* of Iacob, which was *the ſonne* of Iſaac, which was *the ſonne* of Abraham, which was *the ſonne* of Thara, which was *the ſonne* of Nachor,

35 Which was *the ſonne* of Saruch, which was *the ſonne* of Ragau, which was *the ſonne* of Phaleg, which was *the ſonne* of Heber, which was *the ſonne* of Sala,

36 Which was *the ſonne* of Cainan, which was *the ſonne* of Arphaxad, which was *the ſonne* of Sem, which was *the ſonne* of Noe, which was *the ſonne* of Lamech,

37 Which was *the ſonne* of Mathuſala, which was *the ſonne* of Enoch, which was *the ſonne* of Iared, which was *the ſonne* of Maleleel, which was *the ſonne* of Cainan,

38 Which was *the ſonne* of Enos, which was *the ſonne* of Seth, which was *the ſonne* of Adam, which was *the ſonne* of God.

CHAP. IIII.

1 The temptation and faſting of Chriſt: 13 He
ouercom-

overcommeth the deuill : 14 Beginneth to preach : 16 The people of Nazareth admire his gratious words : 33 he cureth one possessed of a deuill, 38 Peters mother in law, 40 and diuers other sicke persons. 41 The deuils acknowledge Christ, and are reproued for it : 43 he preacheth through the cities.

*Matth. 4. 1.

ANd *Iesus being full of the holy Ghost, returned from Iordane, and was led by the spirit into the wildernesse,

2 Being fourtie dayes tempted of the deuil, and in those dayes he did eat nothing : and when they were ended, he afterward hungred.

3 And the deuil saide vnto him, If thou be the Sonne of God, command this stone that it be made bread.

4 And Iesus answered him, saying, It is written, that man shall not liue by bread alone, but by euery word of God.

5 And the deuil taking him vp into an high mountaine, shewed vnto him all the kingdomes of the world in a moment of time.

6 And the deuil said vnto him, All this power will I giue thee, and the glory of them ; for that is deliuered vnto me, & to whomsoeuer I will, I giue it.

|Or, fall downe before me.

7 If thou therefore wilt ||worship me, all shalbe thine.

8 And Iesus answered and said vnto him, Get thee behinde me, Satan : for it is written, Thou shalt worship the Lord thy God; and him onely shalt thou serue.

9 And hee brought him to Hierusalem, and set him on a pinacle of the Temple, and said vnto him, If thou be the Sonne of God, cast thy selfe downe from hence.

10 For it is written, He shall giue his Angels charge ouer thee, to keepe thee.

11 And in their handes they shall beare thee vp, lest at any time thou dash thy foot against a stone.

12 And Iesus answering, said vnto him, It is said, Thou shalt not tempt the Lord thy God.

13 And when the deuill had ended all the temptation, hee departed from him for a season.

14 ¶ And Iesus returned in the power of the Spirit into Galilee, and there went out a fame of him through all the region round about.

15 And hee taught in their Syna-

gogues, being glorified of all.

16 ¶ And hee came to *Nazareth, where he had bene brought vp, and as his custome was, he went into the Synagogue on the Sabbath day, and stood vp for to reade.

*Matt 54.

17 And there was deliuered vnto him the booke of the Prophet Esaias, and when he had opened the Booke, he found the place where it was written,

18 *The Spirit of the Lord is vpon mee, because hee hath anointed mee, to preach the Gospel to the poore, he hath sent mee to heale the broken hearted, to preach deliuerance to the captiues, and recouering of sight to the blinde, to set at libertie them that are bruised,

*Esay

19 To preach the acceptable yeere of the Lord.

20 And he closed the booke, and hee gaue it againe to the minister, and sate downe : and the eyes of all them that were in the Synagogue were fastened on him.

21 And hee began to say vnto them, This day is this Scripture fulfilled in your eares.

22 And all bare him witnesse, and wondered at the gracious wordes, which proceeded out of his mouth. And they said, Is not this Iosephs sonne ?

23 And hee said vnto them, Yee will surely say vnto me this prouerbe, Physition, heale thy selfe : Whatsoeuer wee haue heard done in Capernaum, doe also here in thy countrey.

24 And hee said, Verely I say vnto you, no *Prophet is accepted in his owne countrey.

*Mat 57.

25 But I tell you of a trueth, *many widowes were in Israel in the dayes of Elias, when the heauen was shut vp three yeres and sixe moneths : when great famine was throughout all the land :

*1. K 17. 9.

26 But vnto none of them was Elias sent, saue vnto Sarepta *a citie* of Sidon, vnto a woman that was a widow.

27 *And many lepers were in Israel in the time of Elizeus the Prophet: and none of them was cleansed, sauing Naaman the Syrian.

*2. K 14.

28 And all they in the Synagogue, when they heard these things, were filled with wrath,

29 And rose vp, and thrust him out of the citie, & led him vnto the ||brow of the hill (whereon their city was built) that they might cast him downe headlong.

|Or, e

30 But

30 But he passing thorow the mids of them, went his way :

31 And came downe to Capernaum, a citie of Galile, and taught them on the Sabbath dayes.

32 And they were astonished at his doctrine : * for his worde was with power.

Mat. 7. 29.

33 ¶ * And in the Synagogue there was a man which had a spirit of an vncleane deuill, and cryed out with a loud voice,

Mar. 1. 23.

34 Saying, ‖ Let vs alone, what haue wee to doe with thee, thou Iesus of Nazareth ? art thou come to destroy vs ? I know thee who thou art, the Holy One of God.

Or, away.

35 And Iesus rebuked him, saying, Holde thy peace, and come out of him. And when the deuill had throwen him in the middes, hee came out of him, and hurt him not.

36 And they were all amazed, and spake among themselues, saying, What a word is this ? for with authoritie and power hee commaundeth the vncleane spirits, and they come out.

37 And the fame of him went out into euery place of the countrey round about.

38 ¶ * And he arose out of the Synagogue, and entred into Simons house : and Simons wiues mother was taken with a great feuer, and they besought him for her.

Mat. 8. 14.

39 And he stood ouer her, and rebuked the feuer, & it left her. And immediatly she arose, & ministred vnto them.

40 ¶ Now when the Sunne was setting, all they that had any sicke with diuers diseases, brought them vnto him : and hee laid his handes on euery one of them, and healed them.

41 * And deuils also came out of many, crying out, and saying, Thou art Christ the Sonne of God. And hee rebuking them, suffered them not ‖ to speake : for they knewe that hee was Christ.

Mar. 1. 34.

‖ Or, to say that they knew him to be Christ.

42 And when it was day, he departed, and went into a desert place : and the people sought him, and came vnto him, and stayed him, that he should not depart from them.

43 And hee said vnto them, I must preach the kingdome of God to other cities also : for therefore am I sent.

44 And hee preached in the Synagogues of Galile.

CHAP. V.

1 Christ teacheth the people out of Peters ship. 4 In a miraculous taking of fishes, sheweth how he wil make him and his partners fishers of men : 12 Cleanseth the leper : 16 Prayeth in the wildernesse : 18 Healeth one sicke of the palsie : 27 Calleth Matthew the Publicane : 29 Eateth with sinners, as being the Physician of soules : 34 Foretelleth the fastings and afflictions of the Apostles after his ascension : 35 And likeneth faint hearted and weake disciples, to olde bottels and worne garments.

Nd * it came to passe, that as the people preassed vpon him to heare the word of God, hee stood by the lake of Genesareth,

* Mat. 4. 18.

2 And sawe two ships standing by the lake : but the fishermen were gone out of them, and were washing their nets.

3 And he entred into one of the ships, which was Simons, and prayed him, that he would thrust out a little from the land : and he sate downe, and taught the people out of the ship.

4 Now when he had left speaking, he said vnto Simon, Lanch out into the deepe, and let downe your nets for a draught.

5 And Simon answering, said vnto him, Master, wee haue toiled all the night, and haue taken nothing : neuerthelesse at thy word I will let downe the net.

6 And when they had this done, they inclosed a great multitude of fishes, and their net brake :

7 And they beckened vnto their partners, which were in the other ship, that they should come and helpe them. And they came, & filled both the ships, so that they began to sinke.

8 When Simon Peter saw it, he fell downe at Iesus knees, saying, Depart from me, for I am a sinfull man, O Lord.

9 For he was astonished, and al that were with him, at the draught of the fishes which they had taken.

10 And so was also Iames, and Iohn the sonnes of Zebedee, which were partners with Simon. And Iesus said vnto Simon, Feare not, from henceforth thou shalt catch men.

11 And when they had brought their ships

* Mat. 8. 2.

ships to land, they forsooke all, and followed him.

12 ¶ *And it came to passe, when he was in a certaine citie, behold a man full of leprosie : who seeing Iesus, fell on his face, & besought him, saying, Lord, if thou wilt, thou canst make me cleane.

13 And he put forth his hand, and touched him, saying, I wil : be thou cleane. And immediatly the leprosie departed from him.

14 And hee charged him to tell no man : but, Goe, and shewe thy selfe to the Priest, and offer for thy clensing, according as Moses commanded, for a testimonie vnto them.

15 But so much the more went there a fame abroad of him, and great multitudes came together to heare, and to be healed by him of their infirmities.

16 ¶ And he withdrew himselfe into the wildernesse, and prayed.

17 And it came to passe on a certaine day, as hee was teaching, that there were Pharisees and Doctours of the Law sitting by, which were come out of euery towne of Galilee, and Iudea, and Hierusalem : and the power of the Lord was *present* to heale them.

* Mat. 9. 2.

18 ¶ *And behold, men brought in a bed a man which was taken with a palsie : and they sought meanes to bring him in, and to lay him before him.

19 And when they could not find by what way they might bring him in, because of the multitude, they went vpon the house top, & let him downe through the tiling with his couch, into the midst before Iesus.

20 And when he saw their faith, hee said vnto him, Man, thy sinnes are forgiuen thee.

21 And the Scribes and the Pharisees began to reason, saying, Who is this which speaketh blasphemies? Who can forgiue sinnes, but God alone?

22 But when Iesus perceiued their thoughts, he answering, saide vnto them, What reason ye in your hearts?

23 Whether is easier to say, Thy sinnes be forgiuen thee : or to say, Rise vp and walke?

24 But that ye may know that the Sonne of man hath power vpon earth to forgiue sinnes (he said vnto the sicke of the palsie,) I say vnto thee, Arise, and take vp thy couch, and go into thine house.

25 And immediatly he rose vp before them, and tooke vp that whereon hee lay, and departed to his owne house, glorifying God.

26 And they were all amazed, and they glorified God, and were filled with feare, saying, Wee haue seene strange things to day.

27 ¶ *And after these things hee went foorth, and sawe a Publicane, named Leui, sitting at the receit of custome : and hee said vnto him, Follow me.

* Mat. 9.

28 And he left all, rose vp, and followed him.

29 And Leui made him a great feast in his owne house : and there was a great company of Publicanes, and of others that sate downe with them.

30 But their Scribes and Pharisees murmured against his disciples, saying, Why doe ye eate and drinke with Publicanes and sinners?

31 And Iesus answering, said vnto them, They that are whole need not a physician : but they that are sicke.

32 I came not to call the righteous, but sinners to repentance.

33 ¶ And they said vnto him, *Why doe the disciples of Iohn fast often, and make prayers, and likewise the disciples of the Pharisees : but thine eat and drinke?

* Mat. 9.

34 And he said vnto them, Can yee make the children of the Bride-chamber fast, while the Bridegrome is with them?

35 But the dayes will come, when the Bridegrome shall bee taken away from them, and then shall they fast in those dayes.

36 ¶ And he spake also a parable vnto them, No man putteth a piece of a newe garment vpon an olde : if otherwise, then both the newe maketh a rent, and the piece that was *taken* out of the new, agreeth not with the olde.

37 And no man putteth new wine into old bottles : else the new wine will burst the bottles, and be spilled, and the bottles shall perish.

38 But newe wine must be put into newe bottles, and both are preserued.

39 No man also hauing drunke olde wine, straightway desireth new : for he saith, The old is better.

CHAP.

CHAP. VI.

1 Christ reproueth the Pharises blindnesse about the obseruation of the Sabbath, by Scripture, reason, and miracle: 13 Chooseth twelue Apostles: 17 Healeth the diseased: 20 Preacheth to his disciples before the people of blessings, and curses: 27 How we must loue our enemies: 46 And ioyne the obedience of good workes, to the hearing of the word: least in the euill day of temptation, we fall like an house built vpon the face of the earth, without any foundation.

Marke 12.

*Nd it came to passe on the second Sabbath after the first, that he went thorow the corne fields : and his disciples plucked the eares of corne, and did eate, rubbing them in their hands.

2 And certaine of the Pharisees said vnto them, Why doe yee that which is not lawfull to doe on the Sabbath dayes?

3 And Iesus answering them, said, Haue yee not read so much as this what Dauid did, when himselfe was an hungred, and they which were with him:

4 How he went into the house of God, and did take and eate the Shew bread, and gaue also to them that were with him, which it is not lawful to eate but for the Priests alone?

5 And he said vnto them, That the sonne of man is Lord also of the Sabbath.

* Mat. 12.

6 * And it came to passe also on another Sabbath, that he entred into the Synagogue, and taught : and there was a man whose right hand was withered.

7 And the Scribes and Pharisees watched him, whether he would heale on the Sabbath day : that they might find an accusation against him.

8 But he knew their thoughts, and said to the man which had the withered hand, Rise vp, and stand foorth in the mids. And he arose, and stood foorth.

9 Then said Iesus vnto them, I will aske you one thing, Is it lawfull on the Sabbath dayes to doe good, or to doe euill? to saue life, or to destroy it?

10 And looking round about vpon them all, he said vnto the man, Stretch foorth thy hand. And he did so : and his hand was restored whole as the other.

11 And they were filled with madnesse, and communed one with another what they might doe to Iesus.

12 And it came to passe in those dayes, that hee went out into a mountaine to pray, and continued all night in prayer to God.

13 ¶ And when it was day, he called vnto him his disciples : *and of them he chose twelue; whom also hee named Apostles :

* Mat. 10. 1

14 Simon, (whom he also named Peter,) and Andrew his brother : Iames and Iohn, Philip and Bartholomew,

15 Matthew and Thomas, Iames the sonne of Alpheus, and Simon, called Zelotes.

16 And Iudas *the brother of Iames, and Iudas Iscariot, which also was the traitour.

* Iude. 1.

17 ¶ And hee came downe with them, and stood in the plaine, and the company of his disciples, and a great multitude of people, out of all Iudea and Hierusalem, and from the Sea coast of Tyre and Sidon, which came to heare him, and to be healed of their diseases,

18 And they that were vexed with vncleane spirits : and they were healed.

19 And the whole multitude sought to touch him : for there went vertue out of him, and healed them all.

20 ¶ And hee lifted vp his eyes on his disciples, and said, *Blessed be yee poore : for yours is the kingdome of God.

* Mat. 5. 3.

21 Blessed are yee that hunger now : for yee shall be filled. Blessed are yee that weepe now, for yee shall laugh.

22 Blessed are yee when men shall hate you, and when they shall separate you *from their company*, and shal reproach you, and cast out your name as euill, for the Sonne of mans sake.

23 Reioice yee in that day, and leape for ioy : for behold, your reward is great in heauen for in the like maner did their fathers vnto the Prophets.

24 *But woe vnto you that are rich : for yee haue receiued your consolation.

* Amos. 6. 1

25 *Woe vnto you that are full : for yee shall hunger. Woe vnto you that laugh now : for yee shall mourne and weepe.

* Esai. 65. 13.

26 Woe vnto you when all men shall speake well of you : for so did their fathers to the false Prophets.

27 ¶ * But

*Matth. 5. 44.
*Matth. 5. 39.
* 1. Cor. 6. 7.
*Matth. 7. 12. tob. 4. 16.
*Matth. 5. 46.
*Matth. 5. 42.
*Matt. 7. 1.
*Matth. 15. 14.
*Matth. 10. 24.
‖ Or, ſhalbe perfected as his maſter.
*Matth. 7. 3.

27 ¶ *But I say vnto you which heare, Loue your enemies, doe good to them which hate you,

28 Blesse them that curse you, & pray for them which despitefully vse you.

29 * And vnto him that smiteth thee on the *one* cheeke, offer also the other: *and him that taketh away thy cloake, forbid not to take thy coat also.

30 Giue to euery man that asketh of thee, and of him that taketh away thy goods, aske them not againe.

31 * And as yee would that men should doe to you, doe yee also to them likewise.

32 * For if yee loue them which loue you, what thanke haue ye? for sinners also loue those that loue them.

33 And if ye doe good to them which doe good to you, What thanke haue ye? for sinners also doe euen the same.

34 * And if ye lend to them of whom ye hope to receiue, What thanke haue ye? for sinners also lend to sinners, to receiue as much againe.

35 But loue yee your enemies, and doe good, and lend, hoping for nothing againe : and your reward shall be great, and ye shalbe the children of the Highest : for hee is kinde vnto the vnthankfull, and to the euill.

36 Be ye therefore mercifull, as your Father also is mercifull.

37 *Iudge not, and ye shall not bee iudged : condemne not, and ye shall not be condemned : forgiue, and ye shall be forgiuen.

38 Giue, and it shall bee giuen vnto you, good measure, preassed downe, and shaken together, and running o-uer, shall men giue into your bosome : for with the same measure that ye mete withall, it shall bee measured to you againe.

39 And hee spake a parable vnto them, * Can the blinde leade the blinde? Shall they not both fall into the ditch ?

40 *The disciple is not aboue his master : but euery one ‖ that is perfect shalbe as his master.

41 * And why beholdest thou the mote that is in thy brothers eye, but perceiuest not the beame that is in thine owne eye ?

42 Either how canst thou say to thy brother, Brother, let mee pull out the mote that is in thine eye : when thou thy selfe beholdest not the beame that is in thine owne eye ? Thou hypo-

crite, cast out first the beame out of thine owne eye, and then shalt thou see clear-ly to pul out the mote that is in thy bro-thers eye.

* Matth. 16.

43 * For a good tree bringeth not foorth corrupt fruit : neither doeth a corrupt tree bring foorth good fruit.

44 For euery tree is knowen by his owne fruit : for of thornes men doe not gather figs, nor of a bramble bush ga-ther they grapes.

45 A good man out of the good trea-sure of his heart, bringeth foorth that which is good : and an euill man out of the euill treasure of his heart, bringeth foorth that which is euill : For of the abundance of the heart, his mouth speaketh.

* Matth. 21.

46 ¶ * And why call ye mee Lord, Lord, and doe not the things which I say ?

47 Whosoeuer commeth to me, and heareth my sayings, and doeth them, I will shew you to whom he is like.

48 He is like a man which built an house, and digged deepe, and layd the foundation on a rocke. And when the flood arose, the streame beat vehement-ly vpon that house, and could not shake it : for it was founded vpon a rocke.

49 But he that heareth, and doeth not, is like a man that without a foun-dation built an house vpon the earth : against which the streame did beate ve-hemently, and immediatly it fell, and the ruine of that house was great.

CHAP. VII.

1 Christ findeth a greater faith in the Centuri-on a Gentile, then in any of the Iewes: 10 Healeth his seruant being absent: 11 Rai-seth from death the widowes sonne at Naim: 10 Answereth Iohns messengers with the declaration of his miracles: 24 Testifieth to the people what opinion hee held of Iohn: 30 Inueigheth against the Iewes, who with neither the maners of Iohn, nor of Iesus could be wonne: 36 and sheweth by occasi-on of Marie Magdalene, how he is a friend to sinners, not to maintaine them in sinnes, but to forgiue them their sinnes, vpon their faith and repentance.

* Matth 5.

Ow when hee had ended all his sayings in the audi-ence of the people, *hee en-tred into Capernaum.

2 And a certaine Cen-turions seruant, who was deare vnto him, was sicke and ready to die.

3 And

3 And when he heard of Iesus, he sent vnto him the Elders of the Iewes, beseeching him that he would come and heale his seruant.

4 And when they came to Iesus, they besought him instantly, saying, that hee was worthy for whome hee should doe this.

5 For he loueth our nation, and hee hath built vs a Synagogue.

6 Then Iesus went with them. And when he was now not farre from the house, the Centurion sent friends to him, saying vnto him, Lord, trouble not thy selfe : for I am not worthy that thou shouldest enter vnder my roofe.

7 Wherefore neither thought I my selfe worthy to come vnto thee : but say in a worde, and my seruant shall bee healed.

8 For I also am a man set vnder authoritie, hauing vnder mee souldiers : and I say vnto one, Goe, and he goeth : and to another, Come, and hee commeth : and to my seruant, Doe this, and he doeth it.

9 When Iesus heard these things, hee marueiled at him, and turned him about, and saide vnto the people that followed him, I say vnto you, I haue not found so great faith, no, not in Israel.

10 And they that were sent, returning to the house, found the seruant whole that had bene sicke.

11 ¶ And it came to passe the day after, that he went into a citie called Naim : and many of his disciples went with him, and much people.

12 Now when he came nigh to the gate of the citie, behold, there was a dead man caried out, the onely sonne of his mother, and shee was a widow : and much people of the citie was with her.

13 And when the Lord saw her, he had compassion on her, and saide vnto her, Weepe not.

14 And hee came and touched the ‖beere (and they that bare him, stood still.) And he said, Yong man, I say vnto thee, Arise.

15 And he that was dead, sate vp, and began to speake : and he deliuered him to his mother.

16 And there came a feare on all, and they glorified God, saying, that a great Prophet is risen vp among vs, and that God hath visited his people.

Or, coffin.

17 And this rumour of him went foorth throughout all Iudea, and throughout all the region round about.

18 * And the disciples of Iohn shewed him of all these things.

19 ¶ And Iohn calling vnto him two of his disciples, sent them to Iesus, saying, Art thou hee that should come, or looke we for another ?

20 When the men were come vnto him, they said, Iohn Baptist hath sent vs vnto thee, saying, Art thou hee that should come, or looke we for another ?

21 And in that same houre hee cured many of their infirmities and plagues, and of euill spirits, and vnto many that were blind, he gaue sight.

22 Then Iesus answering, said vnto them, Go your way, and tell Iohn what things ye haue seene and heard, how that the blind see, the lame walke, the lepers are clensed, the deafe heare, the dead are raised, to the poore the Gospel is preached.

23 And blessed is he whosoeuer shall not be offended in me.

24 ¶ And when the messengers of Iohn were departed, hee beganne to speake vnto ỹ people concerning Iohn : What went ye out into the wildernesse for to see ? A reede shaken with the winde ?

25 But what went ye out for to see ? A man clothed in soft raiment ? Behold, they which are gorgeously apparelled, and liue delicately, are in kings courts.

26 But what went ye out for to see ? A Prophet ? Yea, I say vnto you, and much more then a Prophet.

27 This is he of whome it is written, Behold, I send my messenger before thy face, which shall prepare thy way before thee.

28 For I say vnto you, among those that are borne of women, there is not a greater Prophet then Iohn the Baptist : but he that is least in the kingdome of God, is greater then he.

29 And all the people that heard *him*, and the Publicanes, iustified God, being baptized with the baptisme of Iohn.

30 But the Pharisees and Lawyers ‖reiected the counsell of God ‖against themselues, being not baptized of him.

31 ¶ And the Lord said, * Whereunto

* Mat. 11. 2.

‖ Or, frustrated.
‖ Or, within themselues.

* Mat. 11. 16

to then shall I liken the men of this generation? and to what are they like?

32 They are like vnto children sitting in the market place, & calling one to another, and saying, We haue piped vnto you, and ye haue not danced : wee haue mourned to you, and yee haue not wept.

33 For Iohn the Baptist came, neither eating bread, nor drinking wine, and ye say, He hath a deuill.

34 The sonne of man is come, eating, and drinking, and ye say, Behold a gluttonous man, and a wine bibber, a friend of Publicanes and sinners.

35 But wisedome is iustified of all her children.

*Mar. 14. 3

36 ¶ *And one of the Pharisees desired him that he would eat with him. And he went into the Pharisees house, and sate downe to meat.

37 And behold, a woman in the citie which was a sinner, when shee knew that Iesus sate at meat in the Pharisees house, brought an Alabaster boxe of ointment,

38 And stood at his feet behind him, weeping, and began to wash his feete with teares, and did wipe them with the haires of her head, and kissed his feet, and anointed them with the oyntment.

39 Now when the Pharisee which had bidden him, saw it, he spake within himselfe, saying, This man, if he were a Prophet, would haue knowen who, and what maner of woman this is that toucheth him : for she is a sinner.

40 And Iesus answering, said vnto him, Simon, I haue somewhat to say vnto thee. And he saith, Master, say on.

¶ See Mat. 18. 29.

41 There was a certaine creditour, which had two debtors : the one ought fiue hundred ||pence, and the other fiftie.

42 And when they had nothing to pay, he frankly forgaue them both. Tell me therefore, which of them will loue him most?

43 Simon answered, and saide, I suppose, that hee to whome he forgaue most. And he said vnto him, Thou hast rightly iudged.

44 And hee turned to the woman, and said vnto Simon, Seest thou this woman? I entred into thine house, thou gauest me no water for my feete : but shee hath washed my feete with teares, and wiped them with the haires of her head.

45 Thou gauest me no kisse : but this woman, since the time I came in, hath not ceased to kisse my feet.

46 Mine head with oile thou didst not anoint : but this woman hath anointed my feet with oyntment.

47 Wherefore, I say vnto thee, her sinnes, which are many, are forgiuen, for she loued much : but to whom litle is forgiuen, the same loueth litle.

48 And he said vnto her, Thy sinnes are forgiuen.

49 And they that sate at meat with him, began to say within themselues, Who is this that forgiueth sinnes also?

50 And he said to the woman, Thy faith hath saued thee, goe in peace.

CHAP. VIII.

3 Women minister vnto Christ of their substance 4 Christ after he had preached from place to place, attended with his Apostles, propoundeth the parable of the sower, 16 and of the candle : 21 declareth who are his mother, and brethren : 22 rebuketh the winds : 26 casteth the Legion of deuils out of the man, into the heard of swine : 37 is reiected of the Gadarenes : 43 healeth the woman of her bloodie issue, 49 and raiseth frō death Iairus daughter

Nd it came to passe afterward, ẙ he went throughout euery citie and village preaching, and shewing the glad tidings of the kingdome of God : and the twelue were with him,

2 And certaine women which had bene healed of euill spirits and infirmities, Mary called Magdalene *out of whom went seuen deuils,   *Mar. 16

3 And Ioanna the wife of Chuza, Herods steward, and Susanna, and many others which ministred vnto him of their substance.

4 ¶ *And when much people were gathered together, and were come to him out of euery citie, he spake by a parable :   *Mat. 13

5 A Sower went out to sowe his seed : and as he sowed, some fell by the wayes side, and it was troden downe, and the foules of the aire deuoured it.

6 And some fell vpon a rocke, and assoone as it was sprung vp, it withered away, because it lacked moisture.

7 And some fell among thornes, and the thornes sprang vp with it, and choked it.

8 And other fell on good ground, and

and sprang vp, and bare fruite an hundred fold. And when hee saide these things, he cryed, He that hath eares to heare, let him heare.

9 And his disciples asked him, saying, What might this parable be?

10 And he said, Vnto you it is giuen to know the mysteries of the kingdome of God : but to others in parables, that seeing, they might not see, and hearing, they might not vnderstand.

Mat. 13. 11 * Now the parable is this : The seed is the word of God.

12 Those by the way side, are they that heare : then commeth the deuil, and taketh away the word out of their hearts, least they should beleeue, and be saued.

13 They on the rocke, are they which when they heare, receiue the word with ioy; and these haue no roote, which for a while beleeue, and in time of temptation fall away.

14 And that which fell among thornes, are they, which when they haue heard, goe forth, and are choked with cares and riches, and pleasures of *this* life, and bring no fruite to perfection.

15 But that on the good ground, are they, which in an honest and good heart hauing heard the word, keepe it, and bring foorth fruite with patience.

Mat. 5. 15. 16 ¶ * No man when he hath lighted a candle, couereth it with a vessell, or putteth it vnder a bed : but setteth it on a candlesticke, that they which enter in, may see the light.

Mat. 10. 17 * For nothing is secret, that shall not be made manifest : neither any thing hid, that shall not be knowen, and come abroad.

18 Take heede therefore how yee Mat. 13. heare : * for whosoeuer hath, to him shall bee giuen; and whosoeuer hath not, from him shall be taken, euen that Or, thinketh that he hath. which he ‖ seemeth to haue.

Mat. 12. 19 ¶ * Then came to him his mother and his brethren, and could not come at him for the prease.

20 And it was told him *by certaine* which saide, Thy mother and thy brethren stand without, desiring to see thee.

21 And hee answered and said vnto them, My mother and my brethren are these which heare the word of God, and doe it.

Mat. 8. 23. 22 ¶ * Now it came to passe on a certaine day, that he went into a ship, with his disciples : and hee said vnto them, Let vs goe ouer vnto the other side of the lake, and they lanched foorth.

23 But as they sailed, he fell asleepe, and there came downe a storme of wind on the lake, and they were filled *with water*, and were in ieopardie.

24 And they came to him, and awoke him, saying, Master, master, we perish. Then he rose, and rebuked the wind, and the raging of the water : and they ceased, and there was a calme.

25 And he saide vnto them, Where is your faith? And they being afraide wondred, saying one to another, What maner of man is this? For he commandeth euen the winds and water, and they obey him.

26 ¶ * And they arriued at the countrey of the Gadarenes, which is ouer against Galilee. * Mat. 8. 28.

27 And when he went forth to land, there met him out of the citie a certaine man which had deuils long time, and ware no clothes, neither abode in *any* house, but in the tombes.

28 When he saw Iesus, he cried out, and fell downe before him, and with a loud voyce said, What haue I to doe with thee, Iesus, thou sonne of God most high? I beseech thee torment me not.

29 (For he had commanded the vncleane spirit to come out of the man : For oftentimes it had caught him, and he was kept bound with chaines, and in fetters : and he brake the bands, and was driuen of the deuil into the wildernesse.)

30 And Iesus asked him, saying, What is thy name? And he said, Legion : because many deuils were entred into him.

31 And they besought him, that he would not command them to goe out into the deepe.

32 And there was there an herd of many swine feeding on the mountaine : and they besought him that he would suffer them to enter into them : and he suffered them.

33 Then went the deuils out of the man, and entred into the swine : and the herd ran violently downe a steepe place into the lake, and were choked.

34 When they that fed them saw what was done, they fled, and went, and

and tolde it in the citie, and in the countrey.

35 Then they went out to see what was done, and came to Iesus, and found the man, out of whom the deuils were departed, sitting at the feete of Iesus, clothed, and in his right minde: and they were afraid.

36 They also which saw it, told them by what meanes he that was possessed of the deuils, was healed.

37 ¶ Then the whole multitude of the countrey of the Gadarenes round about, besought him to depart from them, for they were taken with great feare: and he went vp into the ship, and returned back againe.

38 Now the man, out of whom the deuils were departed, besought him that he might be with him: but Iesus sent him away, saying,

39 Returne to thine owne house, and shew how great things God hath done vnto thee. And he went his way, and published throughout the whole citie how great things Iesus had done vnto him.

40 And it came to passe, that when Iesus was returned, the people gladly receiued him: for they were all waiting for him.

* Matth. 9. 18.

41 ¶ *And behold, there came a man named Iairus, and hee was a ruler of the Synagogue, and hee fell downe at Iesus feete, and besought him that hee would come into his house:

42 For hee had one onely daughter about twelue yeeres of age, and she lay a dying. (But as hee went the people thronged him.

43 ¶ And a woman hauing an issue of blood twelue yeres, which had spent all her liuing vpon Phisitions, neither could be healed of any,

44 Came behinde him, and touched the border of his garment: and immediatly her issue of blood stanched.

45 And Iesus saide, Who touched mee? When all denied, Peter and they that were with him, said, Master, the multitude throng thee, and preasse thee, and sayest thou, Who touched me?

46 And Iesus saide, Some body hath touched mee: for I perceiue that vertue is gone out of me.

47 And when the woman saw that she was not hid, shee came trembling, and falling downe before him, shee declared vnto him before all the people, for what cause shee had touched him, and how she was healed immediatly.

48 And he said vnto her, Daughter, be of good comfort, thy faith hath made thee whole, goe in peace.)

49 ¶ While hee yet spake, there commeth one from the ruler of the Synagogues house, saying to him, Thy daughter is dead, trouble not the Master.

50 But when Iesus heard it, he answered him, saying, Feare not, beleeue onely, and she shalbe made whole.

51 And when hee came into the house, hee suffered no man to goe in, saue Peter, and Iames, and Iohn, and the father and the mother of the mayden.

52 And all wept, and bewailed her: but he said, Weepe not, she is not dead, but sleepeth.

53 And they laughed him to scorne, knowing that she was dead.

54 And hee put them all out, and tooke her by the hand, and called, saying, Mayd, arise.

55 And her spirit came againe, and shee arose straightway: and hee commanded to giue her meat.

56 And her parents were astonished: but hee charged them that they should tell no man what was done.

CHAP. IX.

1 Christ sendeth his Apostles to worke miracles, and to preach. 7 Herod desired to see Christ. Christ feedeth fiue thousand: 38 inquireth what opinion the world had of him: foretelleth his passion: 23 proposeth to all, the paterne of his patience. 28 The transfiguration. 37 Hee healeth the lunaticke: 43 Againe forewarneth his disciples of his Passion: 46 commendeth humilitie: 51 biddeth them to shew mildnesse towards all, without desire of reuenge. 57 Diuers would follow him, but vpon conditions.

* Matth. 1.

Hen *he called his twelue disciples together, and gaue them power and authority ouer all deuils, and to cure diseases.

2 And hee sent them to preach the Kingdome of God, and to heale the sicke.

3 And he said vnto them, Take nothing for your iourney, neither staues, nor scrip, neither bread, neither money, neither haue two coates apeece.

4 And

4 And whatsoeuer house yee enter into, there abide, and thence depart.

5 And whosoeuer will not receiue you, when ye goe out of that city, shake off the very dust from your feete, for a testimonie against them.

6 And they departed, and went through the townes, preaching the Gospel, and healing euery where.

Mat. 14. 1. 7 ¶ * Now Herode the Tetrarch heard of all that was done by him : and hee was perplexed, because that it was said of some, that Iohn was risen from the dead :

8 And of some, that Elias had appeared : and of others, that one of the olde Prophets was risen againe.

9 And Herode said, Iohn haue I beheaded : but who is this of whom I heare such things? And hee desired to see him.

Mat. 14. 10 ¶ And the Apostles when they were returned, tolde him all that they had done. *And hee tooke them, and went aside priuately into a desert place, belonging to the citie called Bethsaida.

11 And the people when they knew it, followed him, and he receiued them, and spake vnto them of the kingdome of God, and healed them that had need of healing.

Mat. 14. 12 *And when the day beganne to weare away, then came the twelue, and said vnto him, Send the multitude away, that they may go into the townes and countrey round about, and lodge, and get victuals : for we are here in a desert place.

13 But he said vnto them, Giue yee them to eate. And they said, Wee haue no more but fiue loaues and two fishes, except we should goe and buy meate for all this people.

14 For they were about fiue thousand men. And he said to his disciples, Make them sit downe by fifties in a company.

15 And they did so, and made them all sit downe.

16 Then he tooke the fiue loaues and the two fishes, and looking vp to heauen, hee blessed them, and brake, and gaue to the disciples to set before the multitude.

17 And they did eate, and were all filled. And there was taken vp of fragments that remained to them, twelue baskets.

18 ¶ *And it came to passe, as he was alone praying, his disciples were with him : and he asked them, saying, Whom say the people that I am?

19 They answering, said, Iohn the Baptist : but some say, Elias : and others say, that one of the old Prophets is risen againe.

20 He said vnto them, But whom say yee that I am? Peter answering, said, The Christ of God.

21 And he straitly charged them, and commanded them to tell no man that thing,

22 Saying, *The Sonne of man must suffer many things, and be reiected of the Elders, and chiefe Priests, and Scribes, and be slaine, and be raised the third day.

23 ¶ *And he said to them all, If any man will come after me, let him denie himselfe, and take vp his crosse daily, and follow me.

24 For whosoeuer will saue his life, shall lose it : but whosoeuer will lose his life for my sake, the same shall saue it.

25 *For what is a man aduantaged, if hee gaine the whole world, and lose himselfe, or be cast away?

26 *For whosoeuer shall bee ashamed of me, and of my wordes, of him shall the Sonne of man be ashamed, when he shall come in his owne glory, and in his Fathers, and of the holy Angels.

27 *But I tell you of a trueth, there be some standing here, which shall not taste of death, till they see the kingdome of God.

28 ¶ *And it came to passe, about an eight dayes after these ‖sayings, hee tooke Peter, and Iohn, and Iames, and went vp into a mountaine to pray :

29 And as hee prayed, the fashion of his countenance was altered, and his raiment was white and glistering.

30 And behold, there talked with him two men, which were Moses and Elias,

31 Who appeared in glory, and spake of his decease, which he should accomplish at Hierusalem.

32 But Peter, and they that were with him, were heauie with sleepe : and when they were awake, they saw his glory, and the two men that stood with him.

33 And

* Mat. 16. 13.

* Mat. 17. 22.

* Mat. 10. 38.

* Mat. 16. 26. marke 8. 36.

* Matt. 10. 33.

* Matt. 16. 20.

* Mat. 17. 1. ‖ Or, things.

33 And it came to passe, as they departed from him, Peter said vnto Iesus, Master, it is good for vs to be here, and let vs make three tabernacles, one for thee, and one for Moses, and one for Elias : not knowing what he said.

34 While he thus spake, there came a cloud, and ouershadowed them, & they feared, as they entred into the cloude.

35 And there came a voice out of the cloud, saying, This is my beloued Son, heare him.

36 And when the voyce was past, Iesus was found alone, and they kept it close, & told no man in those dayes any of those things which they had seene.

*Mat. 17. 14 37 ¶ *And it came to passe, that on the next day, when they were come downe from the hill, much people met him.

38 And behold, a man of the companie cried out, saying, Master, I beseech thee looke vpon my sonne, for he is mine onely child.

39 And loe, a spirit taketh him, and hee suddenly crieth out, and it teareth him that he fometh againe, and bruising him, hardly departeth from him.

40 And I besought thy disciples to cast him out, and they could not.

41 And Iesus answering, said, O faithlesse, and peruerse generation, how long shal I be with you, and suffer you? bring thy sonne hither.

42 And as he was yet a comming, the deuill threw him downe, and tare him : and Iesus rebuked the vncleane spirit, and healed the child, and deliuered him againe to his father.

43 ¶ And they were al amazed at the mightie power of God : But while they wondred euery one at all things which Iesus did, he said vnto his disciples,

*Matth. 17. 22. 44 *Let these sayings sinke downe into your eares : for the Sonne of man shall bee deliuered into the handes of men.

45 But they vnderstood not this saying, and it was hid from them, that they perceiued it not : and they feared to aske him of that saying.

*Mat. 18. 1 mark. 9. 34. 46 ¶ *Then there arose a reasoning among them, which of them should be greatest.

47 And Iesus perceiuing ẏ thought of their heart, tooke a child, and set him by him,

48 And said vnto them, Whosoeuer shall receiue this child in my Name, re-

ceiueth me : and whosoeuer shal receiue me, receiueth him that sent me : For hee that is least among you all, the same shalbe great.

49 ¶ *And Iohn answered, and said, Master, we saw one casting out deuils in thy Name, and we forbade him, because he followeth not with vs. *Mar. 9

50 And Iesus said vnto him, Forbid him not : for he that is not against vs, is for vs.

51 ¶ And it came to passe, when the time was come that he should bee receiued vp, he stedfastly set his face to goe to Hierusalem,

52 And sent messengers before his face, and they went and entred into a village of the Samaritanes to make ready for him.

53 And they did not receiue him, because his face was as though he would goe to Hierusalem.

54 And when his disciples, Iames and Iohn sawe this, they said, Lord, wilt thou that wee command fire to come downe from heauen, and consume them, euen as *Elias did ? *2. King 10.

55 But he turned, and rebuked them, and said, Ye know not what maner spirit ye are of.

56 For the Sonne of man is not come to destroy mens liues, but to saue them. And they went to another village.

57 ¶ *And it came to passe that as they went in the way, a certaine man said vnto him, Lord, I wil follow thee whithersoeuer thou goest. *Mat. 8

58 And Iesus said vnto him, Foxes haue holes, and birds of the aire haue nests, but the Sonne of man hath not where to lay his head.

59 *And he said vnto another, Follow me : But he said, Lord, suffer mee first to goe and bury my father. *Mat. 8

60 Iesus said vnto him, Let the dead bury their dead : but go thou and preach the kingdome of God.

61 And another also said, Lord, I will follow thee : but let me first goe bid them farewel, which are at home at my house.

62 And Iesus said vnto him, No man hauing put his hand to the plough, and looking backe, is fit for the kingdome of God.

CHAP. X.

1 Christ sendeth out at once, seuenty disciples to worke miracles, and to preach : 17 Admoni-

Admonisheth them to be humble, and wherin to reioyce: 21 Thanketh his father for his grace: 23 Magnifieth the happy estate of his Church: 25 Teacheth the Lawyer, how to attaine eternall life, and to take euery one for his neighbour, that needeth his mercy: 41 Reprehendeth Martha, and commendeth Mary her ſister.

Mat. 10. 1.

A Fter *these things, the Lord appointed other seuenty also, and sent them two and two before his face, into euery citie and place, whither hee himselfe would come.

2 Therefore said hee vnto them,

Mat. 9. 37. *The haruest truly is great, but the labourers are few; pray ye therefore the Lord of the haruest, that he would send foorth labourers into his haruest.

Mat. 10. 3 Go your wayes : *Behold, I send you forth as lambes among wolues.

4 Cary neither purse nor scrip, nor shoes, and salute no man by the way.

Mat. 10. 5 * And into whatsoeuer house yee enter, first say, Peace bee to this house.

6 And if the sonne of peace be there, your peace shall rest vpon it : if not, it shall turne to you againe.

7 And in the same house remaine, eating and drinking such things as they giue : For the labourer is worthy of his hire. Goe not from house to house.

8 And into whatsoeuer citie yee enter, and they receiue you, eate such things as are set before you :

9 And heale the sicke that are therein, and say vnto them, The kingdome of God is come nigh vnto you.

10 But into whatsoeuer citie yee enter, and they receiue you not, goe your waies out into the streetes of the same, and say,

11 Euen the very dust of your citie which cleaueth on vs, we doe wipe off against you : notwithstanding, be yee sure of this, that the kingdome of God is come nigh vnto you.

12 But I say vnto you, That it shall be more tolerable in that day for Sodome, then for that citie.

Mat. 11. 13 *Woe vnto thee Chorazin, wo vnto thee Bethsaida : For if the mighty workes had beene done in Tyre and Sidon, which haue beene done in you, they had a great while agoe repented, sitting in sackcloth and ashes.

14 But it shall be more tolerable for Tyre and Sidon at the iudgment, then for you.

15 And thou Capernaum, which art exalted to heauen, shalt be thrust downe to hell.

16 * Hee that heareth you, heareth me : and he that despiseth you, despiseth me : and he that despiseth me, despiseth him that sent me. 　*Mat. 10. 40.*

17 ¶ And the seuenty returned againe with ioy, saying, Lord, euen the deuils are subiect vnto vs through thy name.

18 And he said vnto them, I beheld Satan as lightning fall from heauen.

19 Behold, I giue vnto you power to tread on serpents and scorpions, and ouer all the power of the enemie : and nothing shall by any meanes hurt you.

20 Notwithstanding in this reioyce not, that the spirits are subiect vnto you : but rather reioyce, because your names are written in heauen.

21 ¶ In that houre Iesus reioyced in spirit, and said, I thanke thee, O father, Lord of heauen and earth, that thou hast hid these things from the wise and prudent, and hast reuealed them vnto babes : euen so father, for so it seemed good in thy sight.

22 ‖All things are deliuered to me of my father : and no man knoweth who the sonne is, but the father : and who the father is, but the sonne, and he to whom the sonne will reueale him.　‖ *Many ancient copies adde these words, And turning to his Disciples he said.*

23 ¶ And he turned him vnto his disciples, and said priuately, * Blessed are the eyes which see the things that yee see.　*Mat. 13. 16.*

24 For I tell you, that many Prophets, and kings haue desired to see those things which yee see, and haue not seene them : & to heare those things which yee heare, and haue not heard them.

25 ¶ And behold, a certaine Lawyer stood vp, and tempted him, saying, *Master, what shall I doe to inherite eternall life? He said vnto him,　*Mat. 22. 35.*

26 What is written in the law? how readest thou?

27 And he answering, said, Thou shalt loue the Lord thy God with all thy heart, and with all thy soule, and with all thy strength, and with all thy minde, and thy neighbour as thy selfe.

28 And

28 And he said vnto him, Thou hast answered right : this do, and thou shalt liue.

29 But he willing to iustifie himselfe, said vnto Iesus, And who is my neighbour ?

30 And Iesus answering, said, A certaine man went downe from Hierusalem to Iericho, and fel among theeues, which stripped him of his raiment, and wounded him, and departed, leauing him halfe dead.

31 And by chaunce there came downe a certaine Priest that way, and when he saw him, he passed by on the other side.

32 And likewise a Leuite, when hee was at the place, came and looked on him, and passed by on the other side.

33 But a certaine Samaritane as he iourneyed, came where he was ; and when hee saw him, hee had compassion on him,

34 And went to him, and bound vp his wounds, powring in oile and wine, and set him on his owne beast, and brought him to an Inne, and tooke care of him.

See Matt. 20. 2. 35 And on the morrow when he departed, hee tooke out two ||pence, and gaue them to the hoste, and saide vnto him, Take care of him, and whatsoeuer thou spendest more, when I come againe I will repay thee.

36 Which now of these three, thinkest thou, was neighbour vnto him that fell among the theeues ?

37 And he said, He that shewed mercie on him. Then said Iesus vnto him, Goe, and doe thou likewise.

38 ¶ Now it came to passe, as they went, that he entred into a certaine village : and a certaine woman named Martha, receiued him into her house.

39 And shee had a sister called Mary, which also sate at Iesus feet, and heard his word :

40 But Martha was cumbred about much seruing, and came to him, and said, Lord, doest thou not care that my sister hath left mee to serue alone ? Bid her therefore that she helpe me.

41 And Iesus answered, and saide vnto her, Martha, Martha, thou art carefull, and troubled about many things :

42 But one thing is needefull, and Mary hath chosen that good part, which shall not bee taken away from her.

CHAP. XI.

1 Christ teacheth to pray, and that instantly : 11 assuring that God so will giue vs good things. 14 He casting out a dumbe deuil, rebuketh the blasphemous Pharisees : 28 and sheweth who are blessed : 29 preacheth to the people, 37 and reprehendeth the outward shew of holinesse in the Pharisees, Scribes and Lawyers.

Nd it came to passe, that as he was praying in a certaine place, when hee ceased , one of his disciples said vnto him, Lord, teach vs to pray, as Iohn also taught his disciples.

2 And hee said vnto them, When ye pray, say, *Our Father which art in heauen, Halowed be thy Name, Thy kingdome come, Thy will be done as in heauen, so in earth.   * Matth. 9.

3 Giue vs ||day by day our dayly bread. || *Or, for day.*

4 And forgiue vs our sinnes : for we also forgiue euery one that is indebted to vs. And lead vs not into temptation, but deliuer vs from euill.

5 And he said vnto them, Which of you shall haue a friend, and shall goe vnto him at midnight, and say vnto him, Friend, lend me three loaues.

6 For a friend of mine ||in his iourney is come to me, and I haue nothing to set before him, || *Or, out his way.*

7 And he from within shal answere and say, Trouble mee not, the doore is now shut, and my children are with me in bed : I cannot rise and giue thee.

8 I say vnto you, Though he will not rise, and giue him, because he is his friend : yet because of his importunitie, hee will rise and giue him as many as he needeth.

9 *And I say vnto you, Aske, and it shalbe giuen you : seeke, and ye shal find : knocke, and it shalbe opened vnto you.   * Matth. 7.

10 For euery one that asketh, receiueth : and he that seeketh, findeth : and to him that knocketh, it shalbe opened.

11 *If a sonne shall aske bread of any of you that is a father, will hee giue him a stone? Or if he aske a fish, will he for a fish giue him a serpent ?   * Matth. 9.

12 Or if he shall aske an egge, will he offer him a scorpion ?

13 If ye then, being euill, know how to giue good gifts vnto your children : how much more shall your heauenly Father

Father giue the holy Spirit to them that aske him?

14 ¶ And he was casting out a deuil, and it was dumbe. And it came to passe, when the deuill was gone out, the dumbe spake : and the people wondred.

15 But some of them said, * Hee casteth out deuils through Beelzebub the chiefe of the deuils.

Mat. 9. 34. and 12. 24.

16 And other tempting him, sought of him a signe from heauen.

17 But he knowing their thoughts, said vnto them, Euery kingdome diuided against it selfe, is brought to desolation: and a house *diuided* against a house, falleth.

18 If Satan also be diuided against himselfe, how shall his kingdom stand? Because yee say that I cast out deuils through Beelzebub.

19 And if I by Beelzebub cast out deuils, by whom doe your sonnes cast them out? therefore shall they be your iudges.

20 But if I with the finger of God cast out deuils, no doubt the kingdome of God is come vpon you.

21 When a strong man armed keepeth his palace, his goods are in peace:

22 But when a stronger then he shal come vpon him, and ouercome him, hee taketh from him all his armour wherein he trusted, and diuideth his spoiles.

23 He that is not with me, is against me : and hee that gathereth not with me, scattereth.

24 * When the vncleane spirit is gone out of a man, he walketh through drie places, seeking rest : and finding none, he sayth, I will returne vnto my house whence I came out.

Mat. 12. 3.

25 And when hee commeth, hee findeth it swept and garnished.

26 Then goeth he, and taketh to him seuen other spirits more wicked then himselfe, and they enter in, and dwell there, and the last state of that man is worse then the first.

27 ¶ And it came to passe as hee spake these things, a certaine woman of the company lift vp her voice, and said vnto him, Blessed is the wombe that bare thee, and the pappes which thou hast sucked.

28 But hee said, Yea, rather blessed are they that heare the word of God, and keepe it.

29 ¶ * And when the people were gathered thicke together, hee began to

Matt. 12. 38.

say, This is an euill generation, they seeke a signe, and there shall no signe be giuen it, but the signe of Ionas the Prophet :

30 For as Ionas was a signe vnto the Nineuites, so shall also the Sonne of man be to this generation.

31 The Queene of the South shall rise vp in the iudgement with the men of this generation, & condemne them : for shee came from the vtmost parts of the earth, to heare the wisedome of Solomon : and behold, a greater then Solomon is here.

32 The men of Nineue shall rise vp in the iudgement with this generation, and shall condemne it: for they repented at the preaching of Ionas, and behold, a greater then Ionas is here.

33 * No man when he hath lighted a candle, putteth it in a secret place, neither vnder a ||bushell, but on a candlesticke, that they which come in may see the light.

Mat. 5. 15.
|| See Matt. 5. 15.

34 * The light of the body is the eye: therefore when thine eye is single, thy whole body also is full of light : but when thine eye is euill, thy body also is full of darkenesse.

Mat. 6. 22.

35 Take heede therefore, that the light which is in thee, be not darknesse.

36 If thy whole body therefore be full of light, hauing no part darke, the whole shalbe full of light, as when the bright shining of a candle doeth giue thee light.

37 ¶ And as he spake, a certaine Pharise besought him to dine with him : and he went in, and sate downe to meate.

38 And when the Pharise saw it, he marueiled that he had not first washed before dinner.

39 * And the Lord said vnto him, Now doe ye Pharises make cleane the outside of the cup and the platter : but your inward part is full of rauening and wickednesse.

Mat. 23. 25.

40 Yee fooles, did not he that made that which is without, make that which is within also?

41 But rather giue almes of such things ||as you haue : and behold, all things are cleane vnto you.

|| Or, as you are able.

42 But woe vnto you Pharises : for ye tythe Mint and Rue, and all maner of herbes, and passe ouer iudgement, and the loue of God : these ought yee to haue done, and not to leaue the other vndone.

43 * Woe

* Mat. 23. 6.

43 * Woe vnto you Pharisees: for ye loue the vppermost seats in the Synagogues, and greetings in the markets.

44 Woe vnto you Scribes and Pharisees, hypocrites: for ye are as graues which appeare not, and the men that walk ouer them, are not aware of them.

45 ¶ Then answered one of the Lawyers, and said vnto him, Master, thus saying, thou reprochest vs also.

* Mat. 23. 4

46 * And he said, Woe vnto you also ye lawyers: for ye lade men with burdens grieuous to be borne, and ye your selues touch not the burdens with one of your fingers.

* Matth. 23. 29.

47 * Woe vnto you . for ye build the sepulchres of the Prophets, and your fathers killed them.

48 Truely ye beare witnesse that ye allowe the deeds of your fathers: for they indeed killed them, and yee build their sepulchres.

49 Therefore also said the wisedome of God, I wil send them Prophets and Apostles, and some of them they shal slay and persecute:

50 That the blood of all the Prophets, which was shed from the foundation of the world, may be required of this generation,

* Gen. 4. 8.

51 * From the blood of Abel vnto the blood of Zacharias, which perished betweene the Altar and the Temple: Verely I say vnto you, it shall be required of this generation.

* Matth. 23 13.

52 * Woe vnto you Lawyers: for ye haue taken away the key of knowledge: ye entred not in your selues, and

‖ Or, forbade

them that were entring in, ye ‖hindred.

53 And as he said these things vnto them, the Scribes and the Pharisees began to vrge him vehemently, and to prouoke him to speake of many things:

54 Laying wait for him, and seeking to catch something out of his mouth, that they might accuse him.

CHAP. XII.

1 Christ preacheth to his disciples to auoid hypocrisie, and fearefulnesse in publishing his doctrine: 13 Warneth the people to beware of couetousnes, by the parable of the rich man who set vp greater barnes. 22 We must not be ouer carefull of earthly things, 31 but seeke the kingdome of God, 33 giue almes, 36 bee ready at a knocke to open to our Lord whensoeuer he commeth. 41 Christs ministers are to see to their charge, 49 and looke for persecution. 54 The people must take this time

of grace, 58 because it is a fearefull thing to die without reconciliation.

IN * the meane time, when there were gathered together an innumerable multitude of people, insomuch that they trode one vpon another, he began to say vnto his disciples first of all, Beware yee of the leauen of the Pharisees, which is hypocrisie.

* Mat. 16. 6

2 * For there is nothing couered, that shall not be reuealed, neither hid, that shall not be knowen.

* Matth. 10 26.

3 Therefore, whatsoeuer yee haue spoken in darkenesse, shall bee heard in the light: and that which yee haue spoken in the eare, in closets, shal be proclaimed vpon the house tops.

4 * And I say vnto you my friends, Be not afraid of them that kill the body, and after that, haue no more that they can doe.

* Matth. 10 28.

5 But I will forewarne you whom you shall feare: Feare him, which after he hath killed, hath power to cast into hell, yea, I say vnto you, Feare him.

6 Are not fiue sparrowes solde for two ‖farthings, and not one of them is forgotten before God?

‖ See Matt. 10. 29.

7 But euen the very haires of your head are all numbred: Feare not therefore, ye are of more value then many sparrowes.

8 * Also I say vnto you, Whosoeuer shall confesse me before men, him shall the Sonne of man also confesse before the Angels of God.

* Matth. 1 32. 2. tim. 2 12.

9 But he that denieth me before men, shalbe denied before the Angels of God.

10 And whosoeuer shall speake a word against the Sonne of man, it shall be forgiuen him: but vnto him that blasphemeth against the holy Ghost, it shal not be forgiuen.

11 * And when they bring you vnto the Synagogues, and vnto Magistrates, & powers, take yee no thought how or what thing ye shall answere, or what ye shall say:

* Matth. 10 19.

12 For the holy Ghost shal teach you in the same houre, what ye ought to say.

13 ¶ And one of the company saide vnto him, Master, speake to my brother, that he diuide the inheritance with me.

14 And he said vnto him, Man, who made mee a iudge, or a diuider ouer you?

15 And he said vnto them, Take heed and

and beware of couetousnes : for a mans life consisteth not in the abundance of the things which he possesseth.

16 And he spake a parable vnto them, saying, The ground of a certaine rich man brought foorth plentifully.

17 And he thought within himselfe, saying, What shall I doe, because I haue no roome where to bestow my fruits ?

18 And he said, This will I doe, I will pull downe my barnes, and build greater, and there will I bestow all my fruits, and my goods.

19 And I will say to my soule, Soule, thou hast much goods layd vp for many yeeres, take thine ease, eate, drinke, and be merry.

20 But God said vnto him, Thou foole, this night † thy soule shal be required of thee : then whose shal those things be which thou hast prouided ?

† Gre. doe they require thy soule.

21 So is he that laieth vp treasure for himselfe, and is not rich towards God.

22 ¶ And he said vnto his disciples, Therefore I say vnto you, *Take no thought for your life what yee shall eate, neither for the body what yee shall put on.

* Mat. 6. 25.

23 The life is more then meate, and the body is more then raiment.

24 Consider the rauens, for they neither sow nor reape, which neither haue storehouse nor barne, and God feedeth them : How much more are yee better then the foules ?

25 And which of you with taking thought can adde to his stature one cubite ?

26 If yee then bee not able to doe that thing which is least, why take yee thought for the rest ?

27 Consider the Lillies how they growe, they toile not ; they spinne not : and yet I say vnto you, that Solomon in all his glory, was not arayed like one of these.

28 If then God so clothe the grasse, which is to day in the field, and to morrow is cast into the ouen : how much more *will he clothe* you, O ye of litle faith?

29 And seeke not yee what yee shall eate, or what ye shall drinke, ||neither be ye of doubtfull minde.

|| Or, liue not in carefull suspence.

30 For all these things doe the nations of the world seeke after : and your father knoweth that yee haue neede of these things.

31 ¶ But rather seeke yee the kingdome of God, and all these things shall be added vnto you.

32 Feare not, litle flocke, for it is your fathers good pleasure to giue you the kingdome.

33 Sell that yee haue, and giue almes : *prouide your selues bagges which waxe not old, a treasure in the heauens that faileth not, where no theefe approcheth, neither moth corrupteth.

*Mat. 6. 20.

34 For where your treasure is, there will your heart be also.

35 *Let your loines be girded about, and your lights burning,

* 1. Pet. 1. 13.

36 And ye your selues like vnto men that waite for their Lord, when he will returne from the wedding, that when he commeth and knocketh, they may open vnto him immediately.

37 Blessed are those seruants, whom the Lord when he commeth, shall find watching : Verily, I say vnto you, That he shall girde himselfe, and make them to sit downe to meate, and will come foorth and serue them.

38 And if he shall come in the second watch, or come in the third watch, and find them so, blessed are those seruants.

39 *And this know, that if the good man of the house had knowen what houre the theefe would come, he would haue watched, and not haue suffred his house to be broken thorow.

* Mat. 24. 43.

40 Be yee therefore ready also : for the sonne of man commeth at an houre when yee thinke not.

41 ¶ Then Peter said vnto him, Lord, speakest thou this parable vnto vs, or euen to all ?

42 And the Lord said, Who then is that faithfull and wise steward, whom his Lord shall make ruler ouer his houshold, to giue them their portion of meate in due season ?

43 Blessed is that seruant, whom his Lord when he commeth, shall find so doing.

44 Of a trueth, I say vnto you, that hee will make him ruler ouer all that he hath.

45 But and if that seruant say in his heart, My Lord delayeth his comming; and shall beginne to beat the men seruants, and maidens, and to eate and drinke, and to be drunken :

46 The Lord of that seruant will
come

come in a day when hee looketh not for him, and at an houre when hee is not ware, and will ‖cut him in sunder, and will appoint him his portion with the vnbeleeuers.

‖ Or, cut him off.

47 And that seruant which knew his Lords will, and prepared not *himselfe*, neither did according to his will, shalbe beaten with many stripes.

48 But hee that knew not, and did commit things worthy of stripes, shall bee beaten with few stripes. For vnto whomsoeuer much is giuen, of him shall bee much required: and to whom men haue committed much, of him they will aske the more.

49 ¶ I am come to send fire on the earth, and what will I, if it be already kindled?

50 But I haue a baptisme to be baptized with, and how am I ‖straitned till it be accomplished?

‖ Or, pained.

51 *Suppose yee that I am come to giue peace on earth? I tell you, Nay, but rather diuision.

* Matt. 10. 34.

52 For from henceforth there shalbe fiue in one house diuided, three against two, and two against three.

53 The father shall bee diuided against the sonne, and the sonne against the father: the mother against the daughter, and the daughter against the mother: the mother in lawe against her daughter in lawe, and the daughter in law against her mother in lawe.

54 ¶ And he said also to the people, *When ye see a cloud rise out of the West, straightway yee say, There commeth a showre, and so it is.

* Matt. 16. 2.

55 And when ye see the Southwind blow, ye say, There will be heat, and it commeth to passe.

56 Ye hypocrites, ye can discerne the face of the skie, and of the earth: but how is it that yee doe not discerne this time?

57 Yea, and why euen of your selues iudge ye not what is right?

58 ¶ *When thou goest with thine aduersary to the magistrate, as thou art in the way, giue diligence that thou mayest be deliuered from him, lest hee hale thee to the Iudge, and the Iudge deliuer thee to the officer, and the officer cast thee into prison.

* Matth. 5. 25.

59 I tell thee, Thou shalt not depart thence, till thou hast payd the very last ‖mite.

‖ See Mar. 12. 42.

CHAP. XIII.

1 Christ preacheth repentance vpon the punishment of the Galileans, and others. 6 The fruitlesse figge tree may not stand. 11 Hee healeth the crooked woman: 18 sheweth the powerfull working of the word in the hearts of his chosen, by the parable of the graine of mustard seed, and of leuen: 24 exhorteth to enter in at the straite gate, 31 and reproueth Herode, and Hierusalem.

 Here were present at that season, some that told him of the Galileans, whose blood Pilate had mingled with their sacrifices.

2 And Iesus answering, said vnto them, Suppose ye that these Galileans were sinners aboue all the Galileans, because they suffered such things?

3 I tell you, Nay: but except yee repent, ye shall all likewise perish.

4 Or those eighteene, vpon whom the towre in Siloe fell, and slew them, thinke ye that they were ‖sinners aboue all men that dwelt in Hierusalem?

‖ Or, debters.

5 I tell you, Nay; but except yee repent, ye shall all likewise perish.

6 ¶ Hee spake also this parable, A certaine man had a figtree planted in his Vineyard, and he came and sought fruit thereon, and found none.

7 Then said hee vnto the dresser of his Vineyard, Beholde, these three yeeres I come seeking fruit on this figtree, and finde none: cut it downe, why cumbreth it the ground?

8 And he answering, said vnto him, Lord, let it alone this yeere also, till I shall digge about it, and doung it:

9 And if it beare fruit, *Well*: and if not, then after that, thou shalt cut it downe.

10 And he was teaching in one of the Synagogues on the Sabbath.

11 ¶ And beholde, there was a woman which had a spirit of infirmitie eighteene yeeres, and was bowed together, and could in no wise lift vp her selfe.

12 And when Iesus saw her, he called her to him, and said vnto her, Woman, thou art loosed frō thy infirmitie.

13 And hee layd his handes on her, and immediatly she was made straight, and glorified God.

14 And the ruler of the Synagogue answered with indignation, because that Iesus had healed on the Sabbath day,

day, and said vnto the people, There are sixe dayes in which men ought to worke : in them therefore come and be healed, and not on the Sabbath day.

15 The Lord then answered him, and said, Thou hypocrite, doeth not each one of you on the Sabbath loose his oxe or his asse from the stall, and leade him away to watering?

16 And ought not this woman being a daughter of Abraham, whom Satan hath bound, loe these eighteene yeeres, be loosed from this bond on the Sabbath day?

17 And when hee had said these things, all his aduersaries were ashamed : & all the people reioyced for all the glorious things that were done by him.

* Mat. 13. 31.
18 ¶ * Then said he, Vnto what is the kingdome of God like? and whereunto shall I resemble it?

19 It is like a graine of mustard seed, which a man tooke, and cast into his garden, and it grew, and waxed a great tree : and the foules of the aire lodged in the branches of it.

20 And againe hee said, Whereunto shall I liken the kingdome of God?

‡ See Mat. 13. 33.
21 It is like leauen, which a woman tooke and hidde in three ||measures of meale, till the whole was leauened.

* Mat. 9. 35.
22 * And he went thorow the cities and villages, teaching and iourneying towards Hierusalem.

23 Then said one vnto him, Lord, are there few that be saued? And he said vnto them,

* Mat. 7. 13.
24 ¶ * Striue to enter in at the strait gate : for many, I say vnto you, will seeke to enter in, and shall not be able.

25 When once the master of the house is risen vp, & hath shut to the doore, and ye begin to stand without, & to knocke at the doore, saying, Lord, Lord, open vnto vs, and he shal answere, & say vnto you, I know you not whence you are :

26 Then shall ye begin to say, Wee haue eaten and drunke in thy presence, and thou hast taught in our streets.

* Mat. 7. 23.
27 * But he shall say, I tell you, I know you not whence you are ; depart from me all ye workers of iniquitie.

28 There shall be weeping and gnashing of teeth, when yee shall see Abraham, and Isaac, and Iacob, and all the Prophets in the kingdome of God, and you *your selues* thrust out.

29 And they shall come from the East, and from the West, and from the North, and from the South, and shall sit downe in the kingdome of God.

* Mat. 19. 30.
30 * And behold, there are last, which shall be first; and there are first, which shall be last.

31 ¶ The same day there came certaine of the Pharises, saying vnto him, Get thee out, and depart hence; for Herode will kill thee.

32 And he said vnto them, Go ye and tell that Foxe, behold, I cast out deuils, and I doe cures to day and to morrow, and the third day I shall be perfected.

33 Neuerthelesse, I must walke to day and to morrow, and the day following : for it cannot be that a Prophet perish out of Hierusalem.

* Mat. 23. 37.
34 * O Hierusalem, Hierusalem, which killest the Prophets, and stonest them that are sent vnto thee; how often would I haue gathered thy children together, as a henne doeth gather her brood vnder her wings, & ye would not?

35 Behold, your house is left vnto you desolate. And verely I say vnto you, ye shall not see me, vntill the time come when yee shall say, Blessed is hee that commeth in the Name of the Lord.

CHAP. XIIII.

2 Christ healeth the dropsie on the Sabbath: 7 teacheth humilitie: 12 to feast the poore: 15 Vnder the parable of the great supper, sheweth how worldly minded men, who contemne the word of God, shalbe shut out of heauen. 25 Those who wil be his disciples, to beare their crosse must make their accounts aforehand, lest with shame they reuolt from him afterward, 34 and become altogether vnprofitable, like salt that hath lost his sauour.

ANd it came to passe, as he went into the house of one of the chief Pharises to eat bread on ẏ Sabbath day, that they watched him.

2 And behold, there was a certaine man before him, which had the dropsie.

3 And Iesus answering, spake vnto the Lawyers and Pharises, saying, Is it lawfull to heale on the Sabbath day?

4 And they held their peace. And he tooke him, and healed him, & let him go,

5 And answered them, saying, Which of you shall haue an asse or an oxe fallen into a pit, and will not straightway pull him out on the Sabbath day?

6 And they could not answere him againe to these things.

7 ¶ And he put foorth a parable to those

those which were bidden, when he marked howe they chose out the chiefe roumes, saying vnto them,

8 When thou art bidden of any man to a wedding, sit not downe in the highest roume : lest a more honourable man then thou be bidden of him,

9 And hee that bade thee and him, come, and say to thee, Giue this man place : and thou begin with shame to take the lowest roume.

10 * But when thou art bidden, goe and sit downe in the lowest roume, that when he that bade thee commeth, hee may say vnto thee, Friend, goe vp higher : then shalt thou haue worship in the presence of them that sit at meate with thee.

11 *For whosoeuer exalteth himselfe, shalbe abased : and hee that humbleth himselfe, shalbe exalted.

12 ¶ Then said hee also to him that bade him, When thou makest a dinner or a supper, call not thy friends, nor thy brethren, neither thy kinsemen, nor thy rich neighbours, lest they also bid thee againe, and a recompence be made thee.

13 But when thou makest a feast, call *the poore, the maimed, the lame, the blinde,

14 And thou shalt be blessed, for they cannot recompense thee : for thou shalt be recompensed at the resurrection of the iust.

15 ¶ And when one of them that sate at meate with him, heard these things, he said vnto him, *Blessed is hee that shall eate bread in the kingdom of God.

16 *Then said hee vnto him, A certaine man made a great supper, and bade many :

17 And sent his seruant at supper time, to say to them that were bidden, Come, for all things are now ready.

18 And they all with one consent began to make excuse : The first said vnto him, I haue bought a piece of ground, and I must needs goe and see it : I pray thee haue me excused.

19 And another said, I haue bought fiue yoke of oxen, and I goe to prooue them : I pray thee haue me excused.

20 And another said, I haue maried a wife : and therefore I cannot come.

21 So that seruant came, and shewed his lord these things. Then the master of the house being angry sayde to his seruant, Goe out quickely into the streetes and lanes of the city, and bring

in hither the poore, and the maimed, and the halt, and the blinde.

22 And the seruant said, Lord, it is done as thou hast commanded, and yet there is roume.

23 And the Lord said vnto the seruant, Goe out into the high wayes and hedges, and compell them to come in, that my house may be filled.

24 For I say vnto you, that none of those men which were bidden, shall taste of my supper.

25 ¶ And there went great multitudes with him : and hee turned, and said vnto them,

26 *If any man come to me, and hate not his father, and mother, and wife, and children, and brethren, and sisters, yea and his owne life also, hee cannot be my disciple.

27 And whosoeuer doeth not beare his crosse, and come after me, cannot be my disciple.

28 For which of you intending to build a towre, sitteth not downe first, and counteth the cost, whether he haue sufficient to finish it ?

29 Lest haply after hee hath laide the foundation, and is not able to finish it, all that behold it, begin to mock him,

30 Saying, This man beganne to build, and was not able to finish.

31 Or what king going to make war against another king, sitteth not downe first, and consulteth whether he be able with ten thousand, to meete him that commeth against him with twentie thousand ?

32 Or else, while the other is yet a great way off, hee sendeth an ambassage, and desireth conditions of peace.

33 So likewise, whosoeuer he be of you, that forsaketh not all that he hath, he cannot be my disciple.

34 ¶ * Salt is good : but if the salt haue lost his sauour, wherewith shall it be seasoned ?

35 It is neither fit for the land, nor yet for the dunghill : but men cast it out. He that hath eares to heare, let him heare.

CHAP. XV.

1 The parable of the lost sheep : 8 Of the piece of siluer : 11 Of the prodigall sonne.

Hen drew neere vnto him all the Publicanes and sinners, for to heare him.

2 And the Pharises and Scribes murmured, saying,

Margin notes (left column):
* Prou. 25. 5
* Mat. 23. 12.
* Tob. 4. 7.
* Reu. 19. 9.
* Mat. 22. 2.

Margin notes (right column):
* Matth. 10. 37.
* Mat. 5.

murmured, saying, This man receiueth sinners, and eateth with them.

3 ¶ And he spake this parable vnto them, saying,

4 * What man of you hauing an hundred sheepe, if he loose one of them, doth not leaue the ninety and nine in the wildernesse, and goe after that which is lost, vntill he find it?

5 And when he hath found it, hee layeth it on his shoulders, reioycing.

6 And when he commeth home, he calleth together his friends, and neighbours, saying vnto them, Reioyce with me, for I haue found my sheepe which was lost.

7 I say vnto you, that likewise ioy shall be in heauen ouer one sinner that repenteth, more then ouer ninety and nine iust persons, which need no repentance.

8 ¶ Either what woman hauing ten ||pieces of siluer, if she lose one piece, doth not light a candle, and sweepe the house, and seeke diligently till shee find it?

9 And when she hath found it, she calleth her friends and her neighbours together, saying, Reioyce with me, for I haue found ỹ piece which I had lost.

10 Likewise I say vnto you, there is ioy in the presence of the Angels of God, ouer one sinner that repenteth.

11 ¶ And hee said, A certaine man had two sonnes:

12 And the yonger of them said to his father, Father, giue me the portion of goods that falleth to me. And he diuided vnto them his liuing.

13 And not many dayes after, the yonger sonne gathered al together, and tooke his iourney into a farre countrey, and there wasted his substance with riotous liuing.

14 And when he had spent all, there arose a mighty famine in that land, and he beganne to be in want.

15 And he went and ioyned himselfe to a citizen of that countrey, and he sent him into his fields to feed swine.

16 And he would faine haue filled his belly with the huskes that the swine did eate: & no man gaue vnto him.

17 And when he came to himselfe, he said, How many hired seruants of my fathers haue bread inough and to spare, and I perish with hunger?

18 I will arise and goe to my father, and will say vnto him, Father, I

haue sinned against heauen and before thee.

19 And am no more worthy to be called thy sonne: make me as one of thy hired seruants.

20 And he arose and came to his father. But when he was yet a great way off, his father saw him, and had compassion, and ranne, and fell on his necke, and kissed him.

21 And the sonne said vnto him, Father, I haue sinned against heauen, and in thy sight, and am no more worthy to be called thy sonne.

22 But the father saide to his seruants, Bring foorth the best robe, and put it on him, and put a ring on his hand, and shooes on his feete.

23 And bring hither the fatted calfe, and kill it, and let vs eate and be merrie.

24 For this my sonne was dead, and is aliue againe: hee was lost, & is found. And they began to be merie.

25 Now his elder sonne was in the field, and as he came and drew nigh to the house, he heard musicke & dauncing,

26 And he called one of the seruants, and asked what these things meant.

27 And he said vnto him, Thy brother is come, and thy father hath killed the fatted calfe, because he hath receiued him safe and sound.

28 And he was angry, and would not goe in: therefore came his father out, and intreated him.

29 And he answering said to his father, Loe, these many yeeres doe I serue thee, neither transgressed I at any time thy commandement, and yet thou neuer gauest mee a kid, that I might make merry with my friends:

30 But as soone as this thy sonne was come, which hath deuoured thy liuing with harlots, thou hast killed for him the fatted calfe.

31 And he said vnto him, Sonne, thou art euer with me, and all that I haue is thine.

32 It was meete that we should make merry, and be glad: for this thy brother was dead, and is aliue againe: and was lost, and is found.

CHAP. XVI.

1 The parable of the vniust steward. 14 Christ reprooueth the hypocrisie of the couetous Pharisees. 19 The rich glutton, and Lazarus the begger.

And

* Matth. 18.
2.

Drachma
heere transated a piece
of siluer, is
he eight
art of an
ounce, which
ommeth to
euen pence
alfe penie,
and is equall
o the Ro-
nane penie,
Mat. 18. 28

Nd hee said also vnto his disciples, There was a certaine rich man which had a Steward, and the same was accused vnto him that he had wasted his goods.

2 And hee called him, and said vnto him, How is it that I heare this of thee? Giue an accompt of thy stewardship : for thou mayest bee no longer Steward.

3 Then the Steward said within himselfe, What shall I doe, for my lord taketh away from mee the Stewardship? I cannot digge, to begge I am ashamed.

4 I am resolued what to doe, that when I am put out of the stewardship, they may receiue me into their houses.

5 So hee called euery one of his lords detters vnto him, and said vnto the first, How much owest thou vnto my lord?

6 And hee said, An hundred ‖measures of oyle. And hee saide vnto him, Take thy bill, and sit downe quickly, and write fiftie.

The word Batus in the originall conteineth nine gallons 3. quarts.

7 Then said hee to another, And how much owest thou? And hee said, An hundred ‖measures of wheat. And hee saide vnto him, Take thy bill and write fourescore.

The word here interpreted a measure, in the originall conteineth about foureteene bushels and a pottle.

8 And the lord commended the vniust Steward, because he had done wisely : for the children of this world are in their generation wiser then the children of light.

9 And I say vnto you, Make to your selues friends of the ‖Mammon of vnrighteousnesse, that when ye faile, they may receiue you into euerlasting habitations.

‖ Or, riches.

10 Hee that is faithfull in that which is least, is faithfull also in much : and he that is vniust in the least, is vniust also in much.

11 If therefore yee haue not bene faithfull in the vnrighteous ‖Mammon, who will commit to your trust the true riches?

‖ Or, riches.

12 And if ye haue not bene faithful in that which is another mans, who shall giue you that which is your owne?

* Matth. 6. 24.

13 ¶ *No seruant can serue two masters, for either he will hate the one, and loue the other : or else he will hold to the one, and despise the other : yee cannot serue God and Mammon.

14 And the Pharisees also who were couetous, heard all these things: and they derided him.

15 And he said vnto them, Ye are they which iustifie your selues before men, but God knoweth your hearts: for that which is highly esteemed amongst men, is abomination in the sight of God.

16 * The law and the Prophets were vntill Iohn : since that time the kingdome of God is preached, and euery man preasseth into it.

* Matth. 11. 12.

17 *And it is easier for heauen and earth to passe, then one title of the law to faile.

* Matth. 5. 18.

18 * Whosoeuer putteth away his wife, & marrieth another, committeth adultery : and whosoeuer marrieth her that is put away from her husband, committeth adultery.

* Matth. 5. 32.

19 ¶ There was a certaine rich man, which was clothed in purple and fine linnen, and fared sumptuously euery day.

20 And there was a certaine begger named Lazarus, which was layde at his gate full of sores,

21 And desiring to bee fed with the crummes which fel from the rich mans table : moreouer the dogges came and licked his sores.

22 And it came to passe that the begger died, and was caried by the Angels into Abrahams bosome : the rich man also died, and was buried.

23 And in hell he lift vp his eyes being in torments, and seeth Abraham afarre off, and Lazarus in his bosome:

24 And he cried, and said, Father Abraham, haue mercy on mee, and send Lazarus, that he may dip the tip of his finger in water, and coole my tongue, for I am tormented in this flame.

25 But Abraham saide, Sonne, remember that thou in thy life-time receiuedst thy good things, and likewise Lazarus euill things, but now he is comforted, and thou art tormented.

26 And besides all this, betweene vs and you there is a great gulfe fixed, so that they which would passe from hence to you, cannot, neither can they passe to vs, that would come from thence.

27 Then he said, I pray thee therefore father, that thou wouldest send him to my fathers house:

28 For I haue fiue brethren, that he may testifie vnto them, lest they also come into this place of torment.

29 Abraham

29 Abraham saith vnto him, They haue Moses and the Prophets, let them heare them.

30 And hee said, Nay, father Abraham : but if one went vnto them from the dead, they will repent.

31 And hee said vnto him, If they heare not Moses and the Prophets, neither will they be perswaded, though one rose from the dead.

CHAP. XVII.

1 Christ teacheth to auoid occasions of offence. 3 One to forgiue another. 6 The power of faith. 7 How we are bound to God, and not he to vs. 11 Hee healeth ten lepers. 22 Of the kingdome of God, and the comming of the Sonne of man.

*Mat. 18.7.

Hen said he vnto the disciples, *It is impossible but that offences will come, but wo vnto him through whom they come.

2 It were better for him that a milstone were hanged about his necke, and he cast into the Sea, then that he should offend one of these little ones.

*Mat. 18. 21.

3 ¶ Take heed to your selues : *If thy brother trespasse against thee, rebuke him, and if he repent, forgiue him.

4 And if hee trespasse against thee seuen times in a day, and seuen times in a day turne againe to thee, saying, I repent, thou shalt forgiue him.

5 And the Apostles said vnto the Lord, Increase our faith.

*Mat. 17. 20.

6 *And the Lord said, If yee had faith as a graine of mustard seede, yee might say vnto this Sycamine tree, Be thou plucked vp by the root, and be thou planted in the sea, & it should obey you.

7 But which of you hauing a seruant plowing, or feeding cattell, will say vnto him by & by when he is come from the field, Goe and sit downe to meate?

8 And will not rather say vnto him, Make ready wherewith I may suppe, and gird thy selfe, and serue me, till I haue eaten and drunken : and afterward thou shalt eate and drinke.

9 Doeth he thanke that seruant, because hee did the things that were commanded him? I trow not.

10 So likewise ye, when ye shal haue done all those things which are commanded you, say, Wee are vnprofitable seruants : wee haue done that which was our duety to doe.

11 ¶ And it came to passe, as he went to Hierusalem, that hee passed thorow the mids of Samaria and Galile.

12 And as he entred into a certaine village, there met him tenne men that were lepers, which stood afarre off.

13 And they lifted vp their voices, and said, Iesus master haue mercy on vs.

14 And when he saw them, hee said vnto them, *Goe shew your selues vnto the Priests. And it came to passe, that as they went, they were cleansed.   *Leu. 14. 2.

15 And one of them when hee sawe that he was healed, turned backe, and with a loud voice glorified God,

16 And fell downe on his face at his feet, giuing him thanks : and he was a Samaritane.

17 And Iesus answering, said, Were there not ten cleansed, but where are the nine?

18 There are not found that returned to giue glory to God, saue this stranger.

19 And he said vnto him, Arise, go thy way, thy faith hath made thee whole.

20 ¶ And when hee was demanded of the Pharises, when the kingdome of God should come, hee answered them, and said, The kingdome of God commeth not with ||obseruation.   ‖ Or, with outward shew.

21 Neither shall they say, Loe here, or loe there : for behold, the kingdome of God is ||within you.   ‖ Or, among you.

22 And hee said vnto the disciples, The dayes will come, when ye shall desire to see one of the dayes of the Sonne of man, and ye shall not see it.

23 *And they shall say to you, See here, or see there : Goe not after them, nor follow them.   *Mat. 24. 23.

24 For as the lightning that lighteneth out of the one part vnder heauen, shineth vnto the other part vnder heauen : so shall also the Sonne of man be in his day.

25 But first must hee suffer many things, & be reiected of this generation.

26 *And as it was in the dayes of Noe : so shal it be also in the dayes of the Sonne of man.   *Gen. 7.

27 They did eate, they dranke, they married wiues, they were giuen in mariage, vntill the day that Noe entred into the arke : and the flood came, and destroyed them all.

28 *Likewise also as it was in the dayes of Lot, they did eat, they dranke, they bought, they sold, they planted, they builded :   *Gen. 19.

29 But

29 But the same day that Lot went out of Sodome, it rained fire and brimstone from heauen, & destroyed them all:

30 Euen thus ſhall it bee in the day when the Sonne of man is reuealed.

31 In that day he which ſhall be vpon the house top, and his stuffe in the house, let him not come downe to take it away : and he that is in the field, let him likewise not returne backe.

32 * Remember Lots wife.

33 * Whosoeuer ſhall seeke to saue his life, ſhall lose it, and whosoeuer ſhall lose his life, ſhall preserue it.

34 * I tell you, in that night there ſhall be two men in one bed; the one ſhal be taken, the other ſhall be left.

35 Two women ſhall bee grinding together; the one ſhall be taken, and the other left.

36 ‖ Two men ſhall be in the field; the one ſhall be taken, and the other left.

37 And they answered, and said vnto him, * Where, Lord? And he said vnto them, Wheresoeuer the body is, thither will the Eagles be gathered together.

*Gen. 19. 26.
* Mat. 16. 25
* Mat. 24. 40
‖ This 36. verse is wanting in most of the Greek copies.
* Mat. 24. 28

CHAP. XVIII.

3 Of the importunate widow. 9 Of the Pharisee and the Publicane. 15 Children brought to Christ. 18 A ruler that would folow Christ but is hindred by his riches. 28 The reward of them, that leaue all for his sake. 31 Hee foresheweth his death, 35 and restoreth a blinde man to his sight.

ANd he spake a parable vnto them, *to this ende*, that men ought * alwayes to pray, and not to faint,

2 Saying, There was in a city a Iudge, which feared not God neither regarded man.

3 And there was a widowe in that citie, and she came vnto him, saying, Auenge me of mine aduersarie :

4 And hee would not for a while. But afterward he said within himselfe, Though I feare not God, nor regard man,

5 Yet because this widow troubleth me, I will auenge her, lest by her continuall comming, she wearie me.

6 And the Lord said, Heare what the vniust iudge saith.

7 And ſhall not God auenge his owne elect, which crie day and night vnto him, thogh he beare long with them?

8 I tell you that he wil auenge them

*1. Thes. 5. 17.

speedily. Neuerthelesse, when the Son of man commeth, ſhall hee find faith on the earth?

9 And he spake this parable vnto certaine which trusted in themselues ‖ that they were righteous, & despised other:

10 Two men went vp into the Temple to pray, the one a Pharisee, and the other a Publicane.

11 The Pharisee stood and prayed thus with himselfe, God, I thank thee, that I am not as other men are, extortioners, vniust, adulterers, or euen as this Publicane.

12 I fast twise in the weeke, I giue tithes of all that I possesse.

13 And the Publicane standing afarre off, would not lift vp so much as his eyes vnto heauen : but smote vpon his breast, saying, God me mercifull to mee a sinner.

14 I tell you, this man went downe to his house iustified rather then the other : * For euery one that exalteth himselfe, ſhall be abased : and hee that humbleth himselfe, ſhall be exalted.

15 And they brought vnto him also infants, that he would touch them : but when his disciples saw it, they rebuked them.

16 But Iesus called them vnto him, and said, Suffer litle children to come vnto me, and forbid them not : for of such is the kingdome of God.

17 Verely I say vnto you, Whosoeuer ſhall not receiue the kingdome of God as a litle child, ſhal in no wise enter therein.

18 And a certaine ruler asked him, saying, Good master, what ſhall I doe to inherit eternall life?

19 * And Iesus said vnto him, Why callest thou mee good? None is good saue one, *that is* God.

20 Thou knowest the commaundements, Doe not commit adulterie, Doe not kill, Doe not steale, Doe not beare false witnesse, Honour thy father and thy mother.

21 And he said, All these haue I kept from my youth vp.

22 Now when Iesus heard these things, hee said vnto him, Yet lackest thou one thing : Sell all that thou hast, and distribute vnto the poore, and thou shalt haue treasure in heauen, and come, follow me.

23 And when he heard this, he was very sorowfull, for he was very rich.

24 And

‖ Or, as being righteou
* Matth. 12.
* Matth. 16.

24 And when Iesus saw that hee was very sorrowfull, he said, How hardly shal they that haue riches, enter into the kingdome of God?

25 For it is easier for a camel to goe thorow a needles eye, then for a rich man to enter into the kingdom of God.

26 And they that heard it, said, Who then can be saued?

27 And he said, The things which are vnpossible with men, are possible with God.

Mat. 19. 7.

28 * Then Peter said, Loe, we haue left all, and followed thee.

29 And he said vnto them, Verily, I say vnto you, there is no man that hath left house, or parents, or brethren, or wife, or children, for the kingdome of Gods sake,

30 Who shall not receiue manifold more in this present time, and in the world to come life euerlasting.

* Mat. 20. 7.

31 ¶ * Then hee tooke vnto him the twelue, and said vnto them, Behold, we goe vp to Hierusalem, and al things that are written by the Prophets concerning the sonne of man, shall be accomplished.

32 For he shall be deliuered vnto the Gentiles, and shall be mocked, and spitefully intreated, and spitted on:

33 And they shall scourge him, and put him to death, and the third day he shall rise againe.

34 And they vnderstood none of these things: and this saying was hid from them, neither knew they the things which were spoken.

* Mat. 20. 29.

35 ¶ * And it came to passe, that as he was come nigh vnto Iericho, a certaine blinde man sate by the way side, begging,

36 And hearing the multitude passe by, he asked what it meant.

37 And they tolde him that Iesus of Nazareth passeth by.

38 And he cried, saying, Iesus thou sonne of Dauid, haue mercie on me.

39 And they which went before, rebuked him, that hee should holde his peace: but hee cried so much the more, Thou Sonne of Dauid, haue mercie on mee.

40 And Iesus stood and commanded him to be brought vnto him: and when he was come neere, he asked him,

41 Saying, What wilt thou that I shall doe vnto thee? And he said, Lord, that I may receiue my sight.

42 And Iesus said vnto him, Receiue thy sight, thy faith hath saued thee.

43 And immediately he receiued his sight, and followed him, glorifying God: and all the people when they saw it, gaue praise vnto God.

CHAP. XIX.

1 Of Zacheus a Publicane. 11 The ten pieces of money. 28 Christ rideth into Hierusalem with triumph: 41 weepeth ouer it: 45 driueth the buiers and sellers out of the Temple: 47 teaching dayly in it. The rulers would haue destroyed him, but for feare of the people.

ANd *Iesus* entred, and passed thorow Iericho.

2 And behold, there was a man named Zacheus, which was the cheefe among the Publicanes, and he was rich.

3 And he sought to see Iesus who he was, and could not for the prease, because he was litle of stature.

4 And he ranne before, and climed vp into a sycomore tree to see him, for he was to passe that way.

5 And when Iesus came to the place, he looked vp and saw him, and said vnto him, Zacheus, make haste, & come downe, for to day I must abide at thy house.

6 And he made haste, and came downe, and receiued him ioyfully.

7 And when they saw it, they all murmured, saying, That he was gone to be guest with a man that is a sinner.

8 And Zacheus stood, and said vnto the Lord, Behold, Lord, the halfe of my goods I giue to the poore, & if I haue taken any thing from any man by false accusation, I restore him foure fold.

9 And Iesus said vnto him, This day is saluation come to this house, forsomuch as he also is the sonne of Abraham.

* Matt. 18. 11.

10 * For the sonne of man is come to seeke, and to saue that which was lost.

11 And as they heard these things, he added, and spake a parable, because he was nigh to Hierusalem, and because they thought that the kingdome of God should immediately appeare.

* Matt. 25. 14.

12 * He said therefore, A certaine noble man went into a farre countrey, to receiue for himselfe a kingdome, and to returne.

13 And hee called his ten seruants, and

‖ *Mina here translated a pound, is twelue ounces and an halfe, which according to fiue shillings the ounce, is 3. pounds two shillings sixe pence.*

and deliuered them ten ‖pounds, and said vnto them, Occupy till I come

14 But his citizens hated him, and sent a message after him, saying, We wil not haue this man to reigne ouer vs.

15 And it came to passe, that when he was returned, hauing receiued the kingdome, then hee commaunded these seruants to be called vnto him, to whom he had giuen the money, that hee might know how much euery man had gained by trading.

16 Then came the first, saying, Lord, thy pound hath gained ten pounds.

17 And he said vnto him, Well, thou good seruant : because thou hast bene faithfull in a very little, haue thou authoritie ouer ten cities.

18 And the second came, saying, Lord, thy pound hath gained fiue pounds.

19 And hee said likewise to him, Bee thou also ouer fiue cities.

20 And another came, saying, Lord, behold, here is thy pound which I haue kept layd vp in a napkin :

21 For I feared thee, because thou art an austere man : thou takest vp that thou layedst not downe, and reapest that thou didst not sow.

22 And hee saith vnto him, Out of thine owne mouth will I iudge thee, thou wicked seruant : Thou knewest that I was an austere man, taking vp that I layde not downe, and reaping that I did not sow.

23 Wherefore then gauest not thou my money into the bancke, that at my comming I might haue required mine owne with vsury ?

24 And he said vnto them that stood by, Take from him the pound, and giue it to him that hath ten pounds.

25 And they said vnto him, Lord, he hath ten pounds.

* Matth. 13. 12.

26 For I say vnto you, * That vnto euery one which hath, shalbe giuen, and from him that hath not, euen that hee hath shalbe taken away from him

27 But those mine enemies which would not that I should reigne ouer them, bring hither, and slay them before mee.

28 ¶ And when he had thus spoken, he went before, ascending vp to Hierusalem.

* Matth. 21. 1.

29 *And it came to passe when he was come nigh to Bethphage and Bethanie, at the mount called the mount of Oliues, he sent two of his disciples,

30 Saying, Goe ye into the village ouer against you, in the which at your entring ye shall find a Colt tied, whereon yet neuer man sate : loose him, and bring him hither.

31 And if any man aske you, Why do ye loose him? Thus shall ye say vnto him, Because the Lord hath neede of him.

32 And they that were sent, went their way, and found euen as hee had said vnto them.

33 And as they were loosing the colt, the owners thereof said vnto them, Why loose ye the Colt ?

34 And they said, The Lord hath need of him.

35 And they brought him to Iesus : and they cast their garments vpon the Colt, and they set Iesus thereon.

36 And as he went, they spread their clothes in the way.

37 And when he was come nigh euen now at the descent of the mount of Oliues, the whole multitude of the disciples began to reioyce and praise God with a loud voice, for all the mighty workes that they had seene,

38 Saying, Blessed bee the King that commeth in the Name of the Lord, peace in heauen, and glory in the Highest.

39 And some of the Pharisees from among the multitude saide vnto him, Master, rebuke thy disciples.

40 And he answered, and said vnto them, I tell you, that if these should holde their peace, the stones would immediatly cry out.

41 ¶ And when he was come neere, he beheld the city and wept ouer it,

42 Saying, If thou hadst knowen, euen thou, at least in this thy day, the things which belong vnto thy peace ! but now they are hid from thine eyes.

43 For the dayes shall come vpon thee, that thine enemies shall cast a trench about thee, and compasse thee round, and keepe thee in on euery side,

44 And shall lay thee euen with the ground, and thy children within thee : and they shall not leaue in thee one stone vpon another, because thou knewest not the time of thy visitation.

* Matth. 12.

45 *And he went into the Temple, and began to cast out them that solde therein, and them that bought,

46 Saying vnto them, It is written

ten, My house is the house of prayer : but ye haue made it a denne of theeues.

47 And he taught daily in the Temple. But the chiefe Priestes and the Scribes, and the chiefe of the people sought to destroy him,

48 And could not finde what they might doe : for all the people were ‖very attentiue to heare him.

*r, han-
ł on him.*

CHAP. XX.

1 Christ auoucheth his authoritie by a question of Iohns Baptisme. 9 The parable of the Vineyard. 19 Of giuing tribute to Cesar. 27 He coniunceth the Sadduces that denied the resurrection. 41 How Christ is the sonne of Dauid. 45 Hee warneth his disciples to beware of the Scribes.

Matt. 21.

Nd *it came to passe, that on one of those dayes, as he taught the people in the Temple, and preached the Gospel, the chiefe Priests and the Scribes came vpon him, with the Elders,

2 And spake vnto him, saying, Tell vs, by what authoritie doest thou these things? or who is hee that gaue thee this authoritie?

3 And hee answered, and said vnto them, I will also aske you one thing, and answere me.

4 The Baptisme of Iohn, was it from heauen, or of men?

5 And they reasoned with themselues, saying, If wee shall say, From heauen, he will say, Why then beleeued yee him not?

6 But and if we say, Of men, all the people will stone vs : for they be perswaded that Iohn was a Prophet.

7 And they answered, that they could not tell whence *it was*.

8 And Iesus said vnto them, Neither tell I you by what authoritie I doe these things.

*Mat. 21.
3.

9 Then began hee to speake to the people this parable : *A certaine man planted a vineyard, and let it foorth to husbandmen, and went into a farre countrey for a long time.

10 And at the season, hee sent a seruant to the husbandmen, that they should giue him of the fruit of the vineyard, but the husbandmen beat him, and sent him away emptie.

11 And againe hee sent another seruant, and they beat him also, and en-

treated him shamefully, and sent him away emptie.

12 And againe he sent the third, and they wounded him also, & cast him out.

13 Then said the lord of the vineyard, What shall I doe? I will send my beloued sonne : it may be they will reuerence him when they see him.

14 But when the husbandmen saw him, they reasoned among themselues, saying, This is ẏ heire, come, let vs kill him, that the inheritance may be ours.

15 So they cast him out of the vineyard, and killed him. What therefore shall the lord of the vineyard doe vnto them?

16 Hee shall come and destroy these husbandmen, and shall giue the vineyard to others. And when they heard it, they said, God forbid,

17 And hee beheld them, and said, What is this then that is written, *The stone which the builders reiected, the same is become the head of the corner?

*Psal. 118.
22.*

18 Whosoeuer shall fall vpon that stone, shalbe broken : but on whomsoeuer it shall fall, it will grinde him to powder.

19 ¶ And the chiefe Priests and the Scribes the same houre sought to lay hands on him, and they feared the people : for they perceiued that he had spoken this parable against them.

20 And they watched him, and sent foorth spies, which should faine themselues iust men, that they might take holde of his words, that so they might deliuer him vnto the power and authoritie of the gouernour.

21 And they asked him, saying, *Master, we know that thou sayest and teachest rightly, neither acceptest thou the person *of any*, but teachest the way of God ‖truely.

*Mat. 22.
16.

‖ Or, of a
trueth.*

22 Is it lawfull for vs to giue tribute vnto Cesar, or no?

23 But he perceiued their craftines, and said vnto them, Why tempt ye me?

24 Shew me a ‖peny : whose image and superscription hath it? They answered, and said, Cesars.

‖ See Matt.
18. 28.

25 And he said vnto them, Render therefore vnto Cesar the things which be Cesars, and vnto God the things which be Gods.

26 And they could not take holde of his wordes before the people, and they marueiled at his answere, and helde their peace.

27 ¶ *Then

* Mat. 22.
23.

27 ¶ *Then came to him certaine of the Sadduces (which denie that there is any resurrection) and they asked him,

28 Saying, Master, Moses wrote vnto vs, If any mans brother die, hauing a wife, and hee die without children, that his brother should take his wife, and raise vp seede vnto his brother.

29 There were therefore seuen brethren, and the first tooke a wife, and died without children.

30 And the second tooke her to wife, and he died childlesse.

31 And the third tooke her, and in like maner the seuen also. And they left no children, and died.

32 Last of all the woman died also.

33 Therefore in the resurrection, whose wife of them is she? for seuen had her to wife.

34 And Iesus answering, said vnto them, The children of this world, marrie, and are giuen in marriage:

35 But they which shall be accompted worthy to obtaine that world, and the resurrection from the dead, neither marrie, nor are giuen in marriage.

36 Neither can they die any more; for they are equall vnto the Angels, and are the children of God, being the children of the resurrection.

* Exod. 3. 6.

37 Now that the dead are raised, *euen Moses shewed at the bush, when he calleth the Lord, the God of Abraham, and the God of Isahac, and the God of Iacob.

38 For he is not a God of the dead, but of the liuing; for all liue vnto him.

39 ¶ Then certaine of the Scribes answering, said, Master, Thou hast well said.

40 And after that, they durst not aske him any question at all.

* Mat. 22.
42.

41 And he said vnto them, * How say they that Christ is Dauids sonne?

42 And Dauid himselfe saith in the booke of Psalmes, The Lord said to my Lord, Sit thou on my right hand,

43 Till I make thine enemies thy footestoole.

44 Dauid therefore calleth him, Lord, how is he then his sonne?

45 ¶ Then in the audience of all the people, he said vnto his disciples,

* Mat. 23.5.

46 *Beware of the Scribes, which desire to walke in long robes, and loue greetings in the markets, and the highest seates in the Synagogues, and the chiefe roumes at feasts:

47 Which deuoure widowes houses, and for a shew make long prayers: the same shall receiue greater damnation.

CHAP. XXI.

1 Christ commendeth the poore widow. 5 Hee foretelleth the destruction of the Temple, and of the citie Hierusalem : 25 The signes also which shall be before the last day. 34 He exhorteth them to be watchfull.

AND he looked vp, *and saw the rich men casting their giftes into the treasurie.

* Marke
41.

2 And hee saw also a certaine poore widow, casting in thither two ‖mites.

‖ See Ma
12. 42.

3 And he said, Of a truth, I say vnto you, that this poore widow hath cast in more then they all.

4 For all these haue of their abundance cast in vnto the offerings of God, but shee of her penurie hath cast in all the liuing that she had.

* Mat. 2

5 ¶ *And as some spake of the Temple, how it was adorned with goodly stones, and gifts, he said,

6 As for these things which yee behold, the dayes will come, in the which there shal not be left one stone vpon another, that shal not be throwen downe.

7 And they asked him, saying, Master, but when shall these things be? and what signe wil there be, when these things shall come to passe?

8 And he said, Take heede that yee be not deceiued : for many shall come in my Name, saying, I am Christ, and the time draweth neere : goe yee not therefore after them.

9 But when ye shall heare of wars, and commotions, be not terrified : for these things must first come to passe, but the end is not by and by.

* Matt.
7.

10 *Then said he vnto them, Nation shall rise against nation, and kingdome against kingdome:

11 And great earthquakes shall be in diuers places, and famines, and pestilences : and fearefull sights and great signes shall there be from heauen.

12 But before all these, they shall lay their hands on you, and persecute you, deliuering you vp to the Synagogues, and into prisons, being brought before Kings and rulers for my Names sake.

13 And

13 And it shall turne to you for a te-stimony.

Matth. 10. 14 *Settle it therfore in your hearts, not to meditate before what ye shall an-swere.

15 For I will giue you a mouth and wisedome, which all your aduersaries shall not be able to gainsay, nor resist.

16 And yee shall be betrayed both by parents and brethren, and kinsefolkes and friends, and some of you shall they cause to be put to death.

17 And ye shalbe hated of all men for my Names sake.

Matth. 10. 18 *But there shall not a haire of your head perish.

19 In your patience possesse ye your soules.

Matth. 24. 20 *And when yee shall see Hierusa-lem compassed with armies, then know that the desolation thereof is nigh.

21 Then let them which are in Iu-dea, flee to the mountaines, and let them which are in the midst of it, depart out, and let not them that are in the coun-treys, enter thereinto.

22 For these be the dayes of venge-ance, that all things which are written may be fulfilled.

23 But woe vnto them that are with childe, and to them that giue sucke in those dayes, for there shalbe great di-stresse in the land, and wrath vpon this people.

24 And they shall fall by the edge of the sword, and shall bee led away cap-tiue into all nations, and Hierusalem shall be troden downe of the Gentiles, vntill the times of the Gentiles bee ful-filled.

Matth. 24. 9. 25 ¶ *And there shalbe signes in the Sunne, and in the Moone, and in the Starres, and vpon the earth distresse of nations, with perplexity, the Sea and the waues roaring,

26 Mens hearts failing them for feare, and for looking after those things which are comming on the earth ; For the powers of heauen shall be shaken.

27 And then shall they see the sonne of man comming in a cloud with power and great glory.

28 And when these things begin to come to passe, then looke vp, and lift vp your heads, for your redemption draw-eth nigh.

29 And he spake to them a parable, Behold the figge tree, and all the trees,

30 When they now shoot foorth, yee see and know of your owne selues, that summer is now nigh at hand.

31 So likewise yee, when yee see these things come to passe, know ye that the kingdome of God is nigh at hand.

32 Verily I say vnto you, this ge-neration shall not passe away, till all be fulfilled.

33 Heauen and earth shall passe a-way, but my words shall not passe a-way.

34 ¶ And take heed to your selues, least at any time your hearts be ouer-charged with surfetting, and drunken-nesse, and cares of this life, and so that day come vpon you vnawares.

35 For as a snare shall it come on all them that dwell on the face of the whole earth.

36 Watch ye therefore, and pray al-wayes, that ye may be accompted wor-thy to escape all these things that shall come to passe, and to stand before the sonne of man.

37 And in the day time he was tea-ching in the Temple, and at night hee went out, and abode in the mount that is called the mount of Oliues.

38 And all the people came earely in the morning to him in the Temple, for to heare him.

CHAP. XXII.

1 The Iewes conspire against Christ. 3 Satan prepareth Iudas to betray him. 7 The A-postles prepare the Passeouer. 19 Christ instituteth his holy supper, 21 couertly fore-telleth of the traitour, 24 dehorteth the rest of his Apostles from ambition, 31 assu-reth Peter his faith should not faile: 34 and yet he should denie him thrise. 39 He pray-eth in the mount, and sweateth blood, 47 is betrayed with a kisse: 50 hee healeth Malchuseare, 54 he is thrise denied of Peter, 63 shamefully abused, 66 and confesseth himselfe to be the sonne of God.

 *Ow ẙ feast of vnleuened bread drew nigh which is called the Passeouer. * Matth. 26. 2.

2 And the chiefe Priests and Scribes sought how they might kill him; for they feared the people.

3 ¶ *Then entred Satan into Iu-das surnamed Iscariot, being of the number of the twelue. * Matth. 26. 14.

4 And he went his way, and com-muned with the chiefe Priests and cap-taines,

taines, how he might betray him vnto them.

5 And they were glad, and couenanted to giue him money.

‖ Or, without tumult.

6 And he promised, and sought opportunitie to betray him vnto them ‖in the absence of the multitude.

* Matth. 26. 17.

7 ¶ *Then came the day of vnleauened bread, when the Passeouer must be killed.

8 And he sent Peter and Iohn, saying, Goe and prepare vs the Passeouer, that we may eate.

9 And they said vnto him, Where wilt thou that we prepare?

10 And he said vnto them, Behold, when ye are entred into the citie, there shall a man meet you, bearing a pitcher of water, follow him into the house where he entreth in.

11 And yee shall say vnto the goodman of the house, The Master saith vnto thee, Where is the ghest-chamber where I shall eate the Passeouer with my disciples?

12 And he shall shew you a large vpper roume furnished, there make ready.

13 And they went, and found as hee had said vnto them, and they made readie the Passeouer.

* Matth. 26. 20.

14 *And when the houre was come, he sate downe, and the twelue Apostles with him.

‖ Or, I haue heartily desired.

15 And he said vnto them, ‖With desire I haue desired to eate this Passeouer with you before I suffer.

16 For I say vnto you, I will not any more eate thereof, vntill it be fulfilled in the kingdome of God.

17 And hee tooke the cup, and gaue thanks, and said, Take this, and diuide it among your selues.

18 For I say vnto you, I will not drinke of the fruit of the Vine, vntill the kingdome of God shall come.

* Matt. 26. 26.

19 ¶ *And hee tooke bread, and gaue thankes, and brake *it*, and gaue vnto them, saying, This is my body which is giuen for you, this doe in remembrance of me.

20 Likewise also the cup after supper, saying, This cup is the New Testament in my blood, which is shed for you.

* Matth. 26. 21.

21 ¶ *But beholde, the hand of him that betrayeth mee, is with mee on the table.

22 And truely the Sonne of man goeth as it was determined, but woe vnto that man by whom he is betraied.

23 And they began to enquire among themselues, which of them it was that should doe this thing.

24 ¶ And there was also a strife among them, which of them should bee accompted the greatest.

* Matth. 25.

25 *And hee saide vnto them, The Kings of the Gentiles exercise lordship ouer them, & they that exercise authoritie vpon them, are called benefactors.

26 But ye shall not be so; but he that is greatest among you, let him be as the yonger, and he that is chiefe, as he that doeth serue.

27 For whether is greater, hee that sitteth at meat, or hee that serueth? Is not he that sitteth at meat? But I am among you as he that serueth.

28 Ye are they which haue continued with me in my temptations.

29 And I appoint vnto you a kingdome, as my Father hath appointed vnto me,

* Matth. 26.

30 That yee may eate and drinke at my table in my kingdome, *and sit on thrones iudging the twelue Tribes of Israel.

* 1. Pet. 5

31 ¶ And the Lord said, Simon, Simon, beholde, *Satan hath desired *to haue* you, that he may sift you as wheat:

32 But I haue prayed for thee, that thy faith faile not; and when thou art conuerted, strengthen thy brethren.

33 And hee said vnto him, Lord, I am ready to goe with thee both into prison, and to death.

* Matth. 34.

34 *And hee said, I tell thee Peter, the cocke shall not crow this day, before that thou shalt thrise denie that thou knowest me.

* Matth. 9.

35 *And he said vnto them, When I sent you without purse, and scrip, and shooes, lacked ye any thing? And they said, Nothing.

36 Then saide hee vnto·them, But now he that hath a purse, let him take it, and likewise his scrip : and hee that hath no sword, let him sel his garment, and buy one.

* Esay. 5 12.

37 For I say vnto you, that this that is written, must yet be accomplished in me, *And he was reckoned among the transgressors : For the things concerning me haue an end.

38 And they said, Lord, behold, here are two swords. And hee saide vnto them, It is ynough.

* Matth. 36.

39 ¶ *And he came out, and went, as hee

hee was wont, to the mount of Oliues, and his disciples also followed him.

Mat. 26.

40 *And when he was at the place, he said vnto them, Pray, that yee enter not into temptation.

41 And he was withdrawen from them about a stones cast, and kneeled downe, and prayed,

42 Saying, Father, if thou be willing, remooue this cup from me : neuerthelesse, not my will, but thine be done.

43 And there appeared an Angel vnto him from heauen, strengthening him.

44 And being in an agonie, he prayed more earnestly, and his sweat was as it were great drops of blood falling downe to the ground.

45 And when he rose vp from prayer, and was come to his disciples, hee found them sleeping for sorrow,

46 And said vnto them, Why sleepe yee ? Rise, and pray, lest yee enter into temptation.

Mat. 26.

47 ¶ And while he yet spake, *behold, a multitude, and hee that was called Iudas, one of the twelue, went before them, and drewe neere vnto Iesus, to kisse him.

48 But Iesus said vnto him, Iudas, betrayest thou the sonne of man with a kisse ?

49 When they which were about him, saw what would follow, they said vnto him, Lord, shall wee smite with the sword ?

50 ¶ And one of them smote the seruant of the high Priest, and cut off his right eare.

51 And Iesus answered, and said, Suffer ye thus farre. And he touched his eare, and healed him.

52 Then Iesus said vnto the chiefe Priests, and captaines of the Temple, and the Elders which were come to him, Be ye come out as against a thiefe, with swords and staues ?

53 When I was daily with you in the Temple , yee stretched foorth no hands against mee : but this is your houre, and the power of darkenesse.

Mat. 26.

54 ¶ *Then tooke they him, and led him, and brought him into the high Priests house, and Peter followed afarre off.

Mat. 26.

55 *And when they had kindled a fire in the middes of the hall, and were set downe together, Peter sate downe among them.

56 But a certaine maide beheld him as he sate by the fire, and earnestly looked vpon him, and said, This man was also with him.

57 And he denied him, saying, Woman, I know him not.

58 And after a little while another saw him, & said, Thou art also of them. And Peter said, Man, I am not.

59 And about the space of one houre after, another confidently affirmed, saying, Of a trueth this fellow also was with him ; for he is a Galilean.

60 And Peter said, Man, I know not what thou sayest. And immediatly while he yet spake, the cocke crew.

61 And the Lord turned, and looked vpon Peter ; and Peter remembred the word of the Lord, how he had said vnto him, Before the cocke crow, thou shalt deny me thrise.

62 And Peter went out, and wept bitterly.

63 ¶ And the men that helde Iesus, mocked him, and smote him.

64 And when they had blindfolded him, they stroke him on the face, and asked him, saying, Prophesie, who is it that smote thee ?

65 And many other things blasphemously spake they against him.

66 ¶ *And assoone as it was day, the Elders of the people, & the chiefe Priests and the Scribes came together, and led him into their Councell, saying, *Mat. 27. 1.

67 Art thou the Christ ? Tell vs. And hee said vnto them, If I tell you, you will not beleeue.

68 And if I also aske you, you will not answere me, nor let me goe.

69 Hereafter shal the sonne of man sit on the right hand of the power of God.

70 Then said they all, Art thou then the Sonne of God ? And hee said vnto them, *Ye say that I am. *Mark. 14. 62.

71 And they said, What need we any further witnesse ? For wee our selues haue heard of his owne mouth.

CHAP. XXIII.

1 Iesus is accused before Pilate, and sent to Herode. 8 Herode mocketh him. 12 Herode and Pilate are made friends. 13 Barabbas is desired of the people, and is loosed by Pilate, and Iesus is giuen to be crucified. 27 He telleth the women that lament him , the destruction of Hierusalem : 34 Prayeth for his enemies. 39 Two euill doers are crucified with him. 46 His death. 50 His buriall.

And|

Nd the whole multitude of them arose, and led him vnto Pilate.

2 And they began to accusehim, saying, We found this fellow peruerting the nation, and forbidding to giue tribute to Cesar, saying, that he himselfe is Christ a king.

[*] Matth. 27 11.

3 *And Pilate asked him, saying, Art thou the king of the Iewes? And he answered him, & said, Thou sayest it.

4 Then saide Pilate to the chiefe Priests, and to the people, I finde no fault in this man.

5 And they were the more fierce, saying, He stirreth vp the people, teaching thorowout all Iurie, beginning from Galilee to this place.

6 When Pilate heard of Galilee, he asked whether the man were a Galilean.

7 And assoone as he knew that hee belonged vnto Herods iurisdiction, hee sent him to Herode, who himselfe also was at Hierusalem at that time.

8 ¶ And when Herode saw Iesus, he was exceeding glad, for hee was desirous to see him of a long season, because he had heard many things of him, and hee hoped to haue seene some miracle done by him.

9 Then he questioned with him in many words, but he answered him nothing.

10 And the chiefe Priests and Scribes stood, and vehemently accused him.

11 And Herod with his men of warre set him at naught, and mocked him, and arayed him in a gorgeous robe, and sent him againe to Pilate.

12 ¶ And the same day Pilate and Herod were made friends together; for before, they were at enmitie betweene themselues.

[*] Matth. 27 23.

13 ¶ *And Pilate, when hee had called together the chiefe Priests, and the rulers, and the people,

14 Said vnto them, Ye haue brought this man vnto me, as one that peruerteth the people, and behold, I hauing examined him before you, haue found no fault in this man, touching those things whereof ye accuse him.

15 No, nor yet Herod: for I sent you to him, and loe, nothing worthy of death is done vnto him.

16 I will therefore chastise him, and release him.

17 For of necessitie hee must release one vnto them at the Feast.

18 And they cried out all at once, saying, Away with this man, and release vnto vs Barabbas,

19 Who for a certaine sedition made in the citie, and for murder, was cast in prison.

20 Pilate therefore willing to release Iesus, spake againe to them:

21 But they cried, saying, Crucifie him, crucifie him.

22 And hee said vnto them the third time, Why, what euill hath he done? I haue found no cause of death in him, I will therefore chastise him, & let him goe.

23 And they were instant with loud voyces, requiring that he might be crucified: and the voyces of them, and of the chiefe Priests preuailed.

24 And Pilate ||gaue sentence that it should be as they required.

^{||} Or, asse ted.

25 And he released vnto them, him that for sedition and murder was cast into prison, whom they had desired, but he deliuered Iesus to their will.

26 * And as they led him away, they laid hold vpon one Simon a Cyrenian, comming out of the countrey, and on him they laid the crosse, that hee might beare it after Iesus.

[*] Matth. 32.

27 ¶ And there followed him a great company of people, and of women, which also bewailed & lamented him.

28 But Iesus turning vnto them, said, Daughters of Hierusalem, weepe not for me, but weepe for your selues, and for your children.

29 For beholde, the dayes are comming, in the which they shall say, Blessed are the barren, and the wombs that neuer bare, and the paps which neuer gaue sucke.

30 * Then shall they begin to say to the mountaines, Fall on vs, and to the hils, Couer vs.

[*] Isa. 2. hos. 10. 8 reuel. 6.

31 *For if they doe these things in a green tree, what shalbe done in the drie?

[*] 1. Pet. 17.

32 * And there were also two other malefactors led with him, to bee put to death.

[*] Matth. 38.

33 And when they were come to the place which is called ||Caluarie, there they crucified him, and the malefactors, one on the right hand, and the other on the left.

^{||} Or, the place of a skull.

34 ¶ Then said Iesus, Father, forgiue them, for they know not what they doe: And they parted his raiment, and cast lots.

35 And

35 And the people stood beholding, & the rulers also with them derided him, saying, Hee saued others, let him saue himselfe, if he be Christ, ẙ chosen of God.

36 And the souldiers also mocked him, comming to him, and offering him vineger,

37 And saying, If thou be the king of the Iewes, saue thy selfe.

38 And a superscription also was written ouer him in letters of Greeke, and Latin, & Hebrew, *THIS IS THE KING OF THE IEWES*.

39 ¶ And one of ẙ malefactors, which were hanged, railed on him, saying, If thou be Christ, saue thy selfe and vs.

40 But the other answering, rebuked him, saying, Doest not thou feare God, seeing thou art in the same condemnation ?

41 And we indeed iustly ; for we receiue the due reward of our deeds, but this man hath done nothing amisse.

42 And he said vnto Iesus, Lord, remember me when thou commest into thy kingdome.

43 And Iesus said vnto him, Verily, I say vnto thee, to day shalt thou be with me in Paradise.

44 And it was about the sixt houre, and there was a darkenesse ouer all the ||earth, vntill the ninth houre.

| Or, land.

45 And the Sunne was darkened, and the vaile of the temple was rent in the mids.

46 ¶ And when Iesus had cried with a loud voice, he said, * Father, into thy hands I commend my spirit : And hauing said thus, he gaue vp the ghost.

* Psal. 31. 6.

47 Now when the Centurion saw what was done, he glorified God, saying, Certainly this was a righteous man.

48 And all the people that came together to that sight, beholding the things which were done, smote their breasts, and returned.

49 And all his acquaintance, and the women that followed him from Galilee, stood a farre off, beholding these things.

50 ¶ * And behold, there was a man named Ioseph, a counseller, and hee was a good man, and a iust.

* Mat. 27. 57.

51 (The same had not consented to the counsell and deede of them) he was of Arimathea, a city of the Iewes (who also himselfe waited for the kingdome of God.)

52 This man went vnto Pilate, and begged the body of Iesus.

53 And he tooke it downe, and wrapped it in linnen, and layd it in a Sepulchre that was hewen in stone, wherein neuer man before was layd.

54 And that day was the Preparation, and the Sabbath drew on.

55 And the women also which came with him from Galilee, followed after, and beheld the Sepulchre, and how his body was layd.

56 And they returned, and prepared spices and ointments, and rested the Sabbath day, according to the commandement.

CHAP. XXIIII.

1 Christs Resurrection is declared by two Angels, to the women that come to the Sepulchre. 9 These report it to others. 13 Christ himselfe appeareth to the two disciples that went to Emmaus : 36 Afterwards he appeareth to the Apostles, and reproueth their vnbeleefe : 47 Giueth them a charge : 49 Promiseth the holy Ghost : 51 And so ascendeth into heauen.

Ow *vpon the first day of the weeke, very earely in the morning, they came vnto the Sepulchre, bringing the spices which they had prepared, and certaine others with them.

* Mat. 28. 1.

2 And they found the stone rolled away from the Sepulchre.

3 And they entred in, and found not the body of the Lord Iesus.

4 And it came to passe, as they were much perplexed thereabout, behold, two men stood by them in shining garments.

5 And as they were afraid, and bowed downe their faces to the earth, they said vnto them, Why seek ye ||the liuing among the dead ?

|Or, him that liueth.

6 He is not heere, but is risen · *Remember how he spake vnto you when he was yet in Galilee,

* Mat. 17 23.

7 Saying, The Sonne of man must be deliuered into the hands of sinfull men, and be crucified, and the third day rise againe.

8 And they remembred his words,

9 And returned from the Sepulchre, and told all these things vnto the eleuen, and to all the rest.

10 It was Marie Magdalene, & Ioanna, & Mary *the mother* of Iames, and other

other women that were with them, which tolde these things vnto the Apostles.

11 And their words seemed to them as idle tales, and they beleeued them not.

* Iohn 20. 6.

12 *Then arose Peter, and ranne vnto the Sepulchre, and stowping downe, hee behelde the linnen clothes layd by themselues, and departed, wondering in himselfe at that which was come to passe.

* Marke 16. 12.

13 ¶ *And behold, two of them went that same day to a village called Emaus, which was from Hierusalem about threescore furlongs.

14 And they talked together of all these things which had happened.

15 And it came to passe, that while they communed together, and reasoned, Iesus himselfe drew neere, and went with them.

16 But their eyes were holden, that they should not know him.

17 And he said vnto them, What maner of communications are these that yee haue one to another as yee walke, and are sad?

18 And the one of them, whose name was Cleophas, answering, saide vnto him, Art thou onely a stranger in Hierusalem, and hast not knowen the things which are come to passe there in these dayes?

19 And hee saide vnto them, What things? And they said vnto him, Concerning Iesus of Nazareth, which was a Prophet, mighty in deede and word before God, and all the people.

20 And how the chiefe Priests and our rulers deliuered him to be condemned to death, and haue crucified him.

21 But wee trusted that it had bene hee, which should haue redeemed Israel: and beside all this, to day is the third day since these things were done.

22 Yea, and certaine women also of our company made vs astonished, which were early at the Sepulchre:

23 And when they found not his bodie, they came, saying, that they had also seene a vision of Angels, which saide that he was aliue.

24 And certaine of them which were with vs, went to the Sepulchre, and found it euen so as the women had said, but him they saw not.

25 Then hee saide vnto them, O fooles, and slow of heart to beleeue all that the Prophets haue spoken:

26 Ought not Christ to haue suffered these things, and to enter into his glorie?

27 And beginning at Moses, and all the Prophets, hee expounded vnto them in all the Scriptures, the things concerning himselfe.

28 And they drew nigh vnto the village, whither they went, and hee made as though hee would haue gone further.

29 But they constrained him, saying, Abide with vs, for it is towards euening, and the day is farre spent: And he went in, to tarrie with them.

30 And it came to passe, as hee sate at meate with them, hee tooke bread, and blessed it, and brake, and gaue to them.

31 And their eyes were opened, and they knew him, and he ‖vanished out of their sight.

‖ Or, ceased to be seene of them.

32 And they said one vnto another, Did not our heart burne within vs, while hee talked with vs by the way, and while hee opened to vs the Scriptures?

33 And they rose vp the same houre, and returned to Hierusalem, and found the eleuen gathered together, and them that were with them,

34 Saying, The Lord is risen indeed, and hath appeared to Simon.

35 And they told what things were done in the way, & how he was knowen of them in breaking of bread.

36 ¶ *And as they thus spake, Iesus himselfe stood in the midst of them, and sayeth vnto them, Peace bee vnto you.

* Marke 16. 14.

37 But they were terrified, and afrighted, and supposed that they had seene a spirit.

38 And he said vnto them, Why are yee troubled, and why doe thoughts arise in your hearts?

39 Beholde my hands and my feete, that it is I my selfe: handle me, and see, for a spirit hath not flesh and bones, as ye see me haue.

40 And when hee had thus spoken, hee shewed them his handes and his feete.

41 And while they yet beleeued not for ioy, and wondered, hee saide vnto them, Haue ye here any meat?

42 And they gaue him a piece of a broyled fish, and of an hony combe.

43 And

43 And he tooke it, and did eate before them.

44 And hee said vnto them, These are the words which I spake vnto you, while I was yet with you, ẏ all things must be fulfilled, which were written in the Law of Moses, & in the Prophets, and in the Psalmes concerning me.

45 Then opened he their vnderstanding, that they might vnderstand the Scriptures,

46 And said vnto them, Thus it is written, & thus it behoued Christ to suffer, & to rise from the dead the third day:

47 And that repentance and remission of sinnes should be preached in his Name, among all nations, beginning at Hierusalem.

48 And yee are witnesses of these things.

49 ¶ *And behold, I send the promise of my Father vpon you : but tarie ye in the citie of Hierusalem, vntill ye be indued with power from on high.

*Iohn 15. 26. actes 1. 4.

50 ¶ And he led them out as farre as to Bethanie, and hee lift vp his hands, and blessed them.

51 *And it came to passe, while hee blessed them, hee was parted from them, and caried vp into heauen.

*Mar. 16. 19. actes 1. 9.

52 And they worshipped him, and returned to Hierusalem, with great ioy:

53 And were continually in the Temple, praising and blessing God. Amen.

¶ The Goſpel according to S. Iohn.

CHAP. I.

1 The Diuinitie, Humanitie, and Office of Iesus Christ. 15 The testimonie of Iohn. 39 The calling of Andrew, Peter, &c.

IN the beginning was the Word, & the Word was with God, and the Word was God.

2 *The same was in the beginning with God.

*Gen. 1. 1.

3 *All things were made by him, and without him was not any thing made that was made.

*Col. 1. 16.

4 In him was life, and the life was the light of men.

5 And the light shineth in darknesse, and the darknesse comprehended it not.

6 ¶ *There was a man sent from God, whose name was Iohn.

*Mat. 3. 1.

7 The same came for a witnesse, to beare witnesse of the light, that all men through him might beleeue.

8 Hee was not that light, but was sent to beare witnesse of that light.

9 That was the true light, which lighteth euery man that commeth into the world.

10 Hee was in the world, and *the world was made by him, and the world knew him not.

*Heb. 11. 3.

11 Hee came vnto his owne, and his owne receiued him not.

12 But as many as receiued him, to them gaue hee ‖power to become the sonnes of God, euen to them that beleeue on his Name :

‖ Or, the right or priuiledge.

13 Which were borne, not of blood, nor of the will of the flesh, nor of the will of man, but of God.

14 *And the Word was made flesh, and dwelt among vs (& we beheld his glory, the glory as of the onely begotten of the Father) full of grace and trueth.

*Mat. 1. 16.

15 ¶ Iohn bare witnesse of him, and cried, saying, This was he of whom I spake, He that commeth after me, is preferred before me, for he was before me.

16 And of his *fulnesse haue all wee receiued, and grace for grace.

*Col. 1. 19.

17 For the Law was giuen by Moses, but grace and trueth came by Iesus Christ.

18 *No man hath seene God at any time : the onely begotten Sonne, which is in the bosome of the Father, he hath declared him.

*1. Iohn 4. 12. 1. tim. 6. 16.

19 ¶ And this is the record of Iohn, when the Iewes sent Priests and Leuites from Hierusalem, to aske him, Who art thou ?

20 And he confessed, and denied not: but confessed, I am not the Christ.

21 And

‖ Or, a Pro-
phet.

21 And they asked him, What then? Art thou Elias? And he saith, I am not. Art thou ‖that Prophet? And hee answered, No.

22 Then said they vnto him, Who art thou, that we may giue an answere to them that sent vs? What sayest thou of thy selfe?

* Mat. 3. 3.

23 *He said, I am the voice of one crying in the wildernesse : Make straight the way of the Lord, as said the Prophet Esaias.

24 And they which were sent, were of the Pharises.

25 And they asked him, and said vnto him, Why baptizest thou then, if thou be not that Christ, nor Elias, neither that Prophet?

26 Iohn answered them, saying, I baptize with water, but there standeth one among you, whom ye know not,

* Mat. 3. 11.
acts 19. 4.

27 *He it is, who comming after me, is preferred before me, whose shoes latchet I am not worthy to vnloose.

28 These things were done in Bethabara beyond Iordane, where Iohn was baptizing.

‖ Or, beareth.

29 ¶ The next day, Iohn seeth Iesus comming vnto him, and saith, Behold the Lambe of God, which ‖taketh away the sinne of the world.

30 This is he of whom I said, After me commeth a man, which is preferred before me : for he was before me.

31 And I knew him not : but that he should be made manifest to Israel, therfore am I come baptizing with water.

* Mat. 3. 16.

32 *And Iohn bare record saying, I saw the Spirit descending from heauen, like a Doue, and it abode vpon him.

33 And I knew him not : but he that sent me to baptize with water, the same said vnto me, Vpon whom thou shalt see the Spirit descending, & remaining on him, the same is he which baptizeth with the holy Ghost.

34 And I saw, and bare record, that this is the sonne of God.

35 ¶ Againe the next day after, Iohn stood, and two of his disciples.

36 And looking vpon Iesus as he walked, he saith, Behold the Lambe of God.

37 And the two disciples heard him speake, and they followed Iesus.

38 Then Iesus turned, and saw them following, and saith vnto them, What seeke ye? They said vnto him, Rabbi, (which is to say being interpre-

‖ Or, abidest.

ted, Master) where ‖dwellest thou?

39 He saith vnto them, Come and see. They came and saw where he dwelt, and abode with him that day : for it was ‖about the tenth houre.

‖ That was
two houres
before night.

40 One of the two which heard Iohn speake, and followed him, was Andrew, Simon Peters brother.

41 He first findeth his owne brother Simon, and saith vnto him, We haue found the Messias, which is, being interpreted, ‖the Christ.

‖ Or, the a-
nointed.

42 And he brought him to Iesus. And when Iesus beheld him, he said, Thou art Simon the sonne of Iona, thou shalt be called Cephas, which is by interpretation, ‖a stone.

‖ Or, Peter.

43 ¶ The day following, Iesus would goe foorth into Galilee, & findeth Philip, & saith vnto him, Follow me.

44 Now Philip was of Bethsaida, the citie of Andrew and Peter.

45 Philip findeth Nathaneel, and saith vnto him, We haue found him of whom *Moses in the Law, and the *Prophets did write, Iesus of Nazareth the sonne of Ioseph.

* Gen. 49.
10. Ieuit. 18
16.
* Esai. 4. 2.

46 And Nathaneel said vnto him, Can there any good thing come out of Nazareth? Philip saith vnto him, Come and see.

47 Iesus saw Nathaneel comming to him, and saith of him, Behold an Israelite indeed in whom is no guile.

48 Nathaneel sayeth vnto him, Whence knowest thou me? Iesus answered, and said vnto him, Before that Philip called thee, when thou wast vnder the figge tree, I saw thee.

49 Nathaneel answered, and saith vnto him, Rabbi, thou art the Sonne of God, thou art the king of Israel.

50 Iesus answered, and said vnto him, Because I said vnto thee, I saw thee vnder the figge tree, beleeuest thou? thou shalt see greater things then these.

51 And hee saith vnto him, Verily, verily I say vnto you, heereafter yee shall see heauen open, and the Angels of God ascending, and descending vpon the sonne of man.

CHAP. II.

1 Christ turneth water into wine, 12 Departeth into Capernaum, to Ierusalem, 14 Where hee purgeth the temple of buyers and sellers. 19 He foretelleth his death and resurrection. 23 Many beleeued because of his miracles, but he would not trust himselfe with them.

And

Nd the third day there was a mariage in Cana of Galilee, and the mother of Iesus was there.

2 And both Iesus was called, and his disciples, to the mariage.

3 And when they wanted wine, the mother of Iesus saith vnto him, They haue no wine.

4 Iesus saith vnto her, Woman, what haue I to doe with thee? mine houre is not yet come.

5 His mother saith vnto ẙ seruants, Whatsoeuer he saith vnto you, doe it.

6 And there were set there sixe water pots of stone, after the maner of the purifying of the Iewes, conteining two or three firkins apeece.

7 Iesus saith vnto them, Fill the water pots with water. And they filled them vp to the brimme.

8 And hee saith vnto them, Drawe out now, and beare vnto the gouernor of the feast. And they bare it.

9 When the ruler of the feast had tasted the water that was made wine, and knew not whence it was, (but the seruants which drew the water knew) the gouernor of the feast called the bridegrome,

10 And saith vnto him, Euery man at the beginning doth set foorth good wine, and when men haue well drunke, then that which is worse: but thou hast kept the good wine vntill now.

11 This beginning of miracles did Iesus in Cana of Galilee, and manifested forth his glory, and his disciples beleeued on him.

12 ¶ After this hee went downe to Capernaum, hee and his mother, and his brethren, and his disciples, and they continued there not many dayes.

13 ¶ And the Iewes Passeouer was at hand, & Iesus went vp to Hierusalem

14 And found in the Temple those that sold oxen, and sheepe, and doues, and the changers of money, sitting.

15 And when he had made a scourge of small cordes, he droue them all out of the Temple, and the sheepe & the oxen, and powred out the changers money, and ouerthrew the tables,

16 And said vnto them that sold doues Take these things hence, make not my fathers house an house of merchandize.

17 And his disciples remembred that it was written, * The zeale of thine house hath eaten me vp.

* Psal. 69. 9.

18 ¶ Then answered the Iewes, and said vnto him, What signe shewest thou vnto vs, seeing that thou doest these things?

19 Iesus answered, and said vnto them, * Destroy this temple, and in three dayes I will raise it vp.

* Mat. 26. 61.

20 Then said the Iewes, Fourty and six yeres was this Temple in building, and wilt thou reare it vp in three dayes?

21 But he spake of the temple of his body.

22 When therefore hee was risen from the dead, his disciples remembred that hee had said this vnto them: and they beleeued the Scripture, and the word which Iesus had said.

23 ¶ Now when hee was in Hierusalem at the Passeouer, in the feast day, many beleeued in his Name, when they saw the miracles which he did.

24 But Iesus did not commit himselfe vnto them, because he knew al men,

25 And needed not that any should testifie of man: for hee knew what was in man.

CHAP. III.

1 Christ teacheth Nicodemus the necessitie of regeneration. 14 Of faith in his death. 16 The great loue of God towards the world. 18 Condemnation for vnbeliefe. 23 The baptisme, witnes & doctrine of Iohn concerning Christ.

Here was a man of the Pharisees, named Nicodemus, a ruler of ẙ Iewes:

2 The same came to Iesus by night, and said vnto him, Rabbi, wee know that thou art a teacher come from God: for no man can doe these miracles that thou doest, except God be with him.

3 Iesus answered, and said vnto him, Verily, verily I say vnto thee, except a man be borne ‖ againe, he cannot see the kingdome of God.

‖ Or, from aboue.

4 Nicodemus saith vnto him, How can a man be borne when he is old? can he enter the second time into his mothers wombe, and be borne?

5 Iesus answered, Verily, verily I say vnto thee, except a man be borne of water and of the spirit, he cannot enter into the kingdome of God.

6 That which is borne of the flesh, is flesh, and that which is borne of the spirit, is spirit.

7 Marueile not that I saide vnto thee, Ye must be borne ‖ againe.

‖ Or, from aboue.

8 The

8 The winde bloweth where it liſteth, and thou heareſt the sound thereof, but canst not tel whence it commeth, and whither it goeth : So is euery one that is borne of the Spirit.

9 Nicodemus answered, and said vnto him, How can these things be?

10 Iesus answered, and saide vnto him, Art thou a master of Israel, and knowest not these things?

11 Verely, verely I say vnto thee, We speake that we doe know, and testifie that wee haue seene; and yee receiue not our witnesse.

12 If I haue tolde you earthly things, and ye beleeue not : how shall ye beleeue if I tell you of heauenly things?

13 And no man hath ascended vp to heauen, but hee that came downe from heauen, *euen* the Sonne of man which is in heauen.

*Num. 21. 9.

14 ¶ *And as Moses lifted vp the serpent in the wildernesse : euen so must the Sonne of man be lifted vp :

15 That whosoeuer beleeueth in him, should not perish, but haue eternall life.

*1. Iohn 4. 9.

16 ¶ *For God so loued ẙ world, that he gaue his only begotten Sonne : that whosoeuer beleeueth in him, should not perish, but haue euerlasting life.

*Chap. 12. 47.

17 *For God sent not his Sonne into the world to condemne the world : but that the world through him might be saued.

18 ¶ He that beleeueth on him, is not condemned : but hee that beleeueth not, is condemned already, because hee hath not beleeued in the Name of the onely begotten Sonne of God.

*Cha. 1. 4.

19 And this is the condemnation, *that light is come into the world, and men loued darknesse rather then light, because their deedes were euill.

20 For euery one that doeth euill, hateth the light, neither commeth to the light, lest his deeds should be ||reproued.

|| Or, discouered.

21 But hee that doeth trueth, commeth to the light, that his deeds may be made manifest, that they are wrought in God.

22 ¶ After these things, came Iesus and his disciples into the land of Iudea, and there hee taried with them, *and baptized.

*Chap. 4. 2.

23 ¶ And Iohn also was baptizing in Aenon, neere to Salim, because there was much water there : and they came, and were baptized.

24 For Iohn was not yet cast into prison.

25 ¶ Then there arose a question betweene some of Iohns disciples and the Iewes, about purifying.

26 And they came vnto Iohn, and said vnto him, Rabbi, he that was with thee beyond Iordane, *to whom thou barest witnesse, behold, the same baptizeth, and all men come to him.

*Chap. 1. 7, 34.

27 Iohn answered, and said, *A man can ||receiue nothing, except it be giuen him from heauen.

*Heb. 5. 4.
|| Or, take vnto himselfe.

28 Ye your selues beare me witnesse, that I said, *I am not the Christ, but that I am sent before him.

*Chap. 1. 20.

29 He that hath the bride, is the bridegrome : but the friend of the bridegrome, which standeth and heareth him, reioyceth greatly because of the bridegromes voice : This my ioy therefore is fulfilled.

30 Hee must increase, but I must decrease.

31 Hee that commeth from aboue, is aboue all : hee that is of the earth, is earthly, and speaketh of the earth : hee that cōmeth from heauen is aboue all :

32 And what hee hath seene and heard, that he testifieth, and no man receiueth his testimony :

33 He that hath receiued his testimonie, *hath set to his seale, that God is true.

*Rom. 3. 4

34 For he whom God hath sent, speaketh the words of God : For God giueth not the Spirit by measure *vnto him*.

35 *The Father loueth the Sonne, and hath giuen al things into his hand.

*Matth. 11 27.

36 *He that beleeueth on the Sonne, hath euerlasting life : and he that beleeueth not the Sonne, shall not see life : but the wrath of God abideth on him.

*Habac. 2. 4. 1. iohn 5. 10.

CHAP. IIII.

1 Christ talketh with a woman of Samaria, and reueileth himselfe vnto her. 27 His disciples marueile. 31 He declareth to them his zeale to Gods glory. 39 Many Samaritanes beleeue on him. 43 He departeth into Galile, and healeth the Rulers sonne that lay sicke at Capernaum.

Hen therefore the Lord knew how the Pharisees had heard that Iesus made and baptized moe disciples then Iohn,

2 (Though Iesus himselfe baptized not, but his disciples :)

3 He

3 He left Iudea, and departed againe into Galile.

4 And hee must needs goe thorow Samaria.

5 Then commeth he to a city of Samaria, which is called Sychar, neere to the parcell of ground *that Iacob gaue to his sonne Ioseph.

˒Gen. 33.
19. and 48.
22. iosh.
24. 23.

6 Now Iacobs Well was there. Iesus therefore being wearied with his iourney, sate thus on the Well: and it was about the sixth houre.

7 There commeth a woman of Samaria to draw water: Iesus sayth vnto her, Giue me to drinke.

8 For his disciples were gone away vnto the city to buy meate.

9 Then saith the woman of Samaria vnto him, How is it that thou, being a Iewe, askest drinke of me, which am a woman of Samaria? For the Iewes haue no dealings with the Samaritanes.

10 Iesus answered, and said vnto her, If thou knewest the gift of God, and who it is that sayth to thee, Giue me to drinke; thou wouldest haue asked of him, and hee would haue giuen thee liuing water.

11 The woman saith vnto him, Sir, thou hast nothing to drawe with, and the Well is deepe: from whence then hast thou that liuing water?

12 Art thou greater then our father Iacob, which gaue vs the Well, and dranke thereof himselfe, and his children, and his cattell?

13 Iesus answered, and said vnto her, Whosoeuer drinketh of this water, shall thirst againe:

14 But whosoeuer drinketh of the water that I shal giue him, shall neuer thirst: but the water that I shall giue him, shalbe in him a well of water springing vp into euerlasting life.

15 The woman saith vnto him, Sir, giue me this water, that I thirst not, neither come hither to draw.

16 Iesus saith vnto her, Goe, call thy husband, and come hither.

17 The woman answered, and said, I haue no husband. Iesus said vnto her, Thou hast well said, I haue no husband:

18 For thou hast had fiue husbands, and he whom thou now hast, is not thy husband: In that saidest thou truely.

19 The woman saith vnto him, Sir, I perceiue that thou art a Prophet.

20 Our fathers worshipped in this mountaine, and ye say, that *in Hierusalem is the place where men ought to worship.

*Deu. 12. 5.

21 Iesus saith vnto her, Woman, beleeue me, the houre commeth when ye shall neither in this mountaine, nor yet at Hierusalem, worship the Father.

22 Ye worship ye know not what: we know what we worship: for saluation is of the Iewes.

23 But the houre commeth, and now is, when the true worshippers shall worship the Father in spirit, and in trueth: for the Father seeketh such to worship him.

24 *God is a Spirit, and they that worship him, must worship him in spirit, and in trueth.

*2. Cor. 3.
17.

25 The woman saith vnto him, I know that Messias commeth, which is called Christ: when he is come, hee will tell vs all things.

26 Iesus saith vnto her, I that speake vnto thee, am hee.

27 ¶ And vpon this came his disciples, and marueiled that he talked with the woman: yet no man said, What seekest thou, or, Why talkest thou with her?

28 The woman then left her waterpot, and went her way into the city, and sayth to the men,

29 Come, see a man, which tolde me all things that euer I did: Is not this the Christ?

30 Then they went out of the citie, and came vnto him.

31 ¶ In the meane while his disciples prayed him, saying, Master, eate.

32 But hee said vnto them, I haue meate to eate that ye know not of.

33 Therefore said the disciples one to another, Hath any man brought him ought to eate?

34 Iesus saith vnto them, My meat is, to doe the will of him that sent mee, and to finish his worke.

35 Say not ye, There are yet foure moneths, and then commeth haruest? Behold, I say vnto you, Lift vp your eyes, and looke on the fields: *for they are white already to haruest.

*Mat. 9. 37.

36 And hee that reapeth receiueth wages, and gathereth fruite vnto life eternall: that both he that soweth, and he that reapeth, may reioyce together.

37 And herein is that saying true: One soweth, and another reapeth.

38 I sent

38 I sent you to reape that, whereon ye bestowed no labour : other men laboured, and yee are entred into their labours.

39 ¶ And many of the Samaritanes of that citie beleeued on him, for the saying of the woman, which testified, Hee told me all that euer I did.

40 So when the Samaritanes were come vnto him, they besought him that he would tarie with them, and he abode there two dayes.

41 And many moe beleeued, because of his owne word :

42 And said vnto the woman, Now we beleeue, not because of thy saying, for we haue heard him our selues, and know that this is indeed the Christ, the Sauiour of the world.

* Matth. 13 57.

43 ¶ *Now after two dayes he departed thence, and went into Galilee :

44 For Iesus himselfe testified, that a Prophet hath no honour in his owne countrey.

45 Then when hee was come into Galilee, the Galileans receiued him, hauing seene all the things that hee did at Hierusalem at the Feast   for they also went vnto the Feast.

* Chap. 2. 1

46 So Iesus came againe into Cana of Galilee, *where hee made the water wine.   And there was a certaine ‖noble man, whose sonne was sicke at Capernaum.

‖ Or, Courtier, or ruler.

47 When he heard that Iesus was come out of Iudea into Galilee, hee went vnto him, and besought him that he would come downe, and heale his sonne : for he was at the point of death.

48 Then said Iesus vnto him, Except ye see signes and wonders, yee will not beleeue.

49 The noble man saith vnto him, Syr, come downe ere my child die.

50 Iesus saith vnto him, Go thy way, thy sonne liueth. And the man beleeued the word that Iesus had spoken vnto him, and he went his way.

51 And as he was now going down, his seruants met him, and told him, saying, Thy sonne liueth.

52 Then inquired hee of them the houre when he began to amend : and they said vnto him, Yesterday at the seuenth houre the feuer left him.

53 So the father knewe that it was at the same houre, in the which Iesus said vnto him, Thy sonne liueth, and himselfe beleeued, and his whole house.

54 This is againe the second miracle that Iesus did, when hee was come out of Iudea into Galilee.

CHAP. V.

1 Iesus on the Sabbath day cureth him that was diseased eight & thirtie yeeres. 10 The Iewes therefore cauill, and persecute him for it. 17 He answereth for himselfe, and reprooueth them, shewing by the testimonie of his Father, 32 of Iohn, 36 of his workes, 39 and of the Scriptures, who he is.

A Fter *this there was a feast of the Iewes, and Iesus went vp to Hierusalem.

* Leuit. 23, 2. deut. 16.

2 Now there is at Hierusalem by the sheepe ‖market, a poole, which is called in the Hebrew tongue Bethesda, hauing fiue porches.

‖ Or, gate.

3 In these lay a great multitude of impotent folke, of blind, halt, withered, waiting for the mouing of the water.

4 For an Angel went downe at a certaine season into the poole, and troubled the water : whosoeuer then first after the troubling of the water stepped in, was made whole of whatsoeuer disease he had.

5 And a certaine man was there, which had an infirmitie thirtie and eight yeeres.

6 When Iesus saw him lie, & knew that hee had beene now a long time in that case, he sayth vnto him, Wilt thou be made whole ?

7 The impotent man answered him, Sir, I haue no man when the water is troubled, to put mee into the poole : but while I am comming, another steppeth downe before me.

8 Iesus sayth vnto him, Rise, take vp thy bed, and walke.

9 And immediatly the man was made whole, and tooke vp his bed, and walked : And on the same day was the Sabbath.

10 ¶ The Iewes therefore said vnto him that was cured, It is the Sabbath day, *it is not lawfull for thee to cary thy bed.

* Ier. 17. 22

11 He answered them, He that made me whole, the same said vnto me, Take vp thy bed, and walke.

12 Then asked they him, What man is that which said vnto thee, Take vp thy bed, and walke ?

13 And he that was healed, wist not who it was : for Iesus had conueyed himselfe

‖ Or, from the multitude that was.

himselfe away, ‖a multitude being in that place.

14 Afterward Iesus findeth him in the Temple, & said vnto him, Behold, thou art made whole: sinne no more, lest a worse thing come vnto thee.

15 The man departed, and tolde the Iewes that it was Iesus which had made him whole.

16 And therefore did the Iewes persecute Iesus, and sought to slay him, because he had done these things on the Sabbath day.

17 ¶ But Iesus answered them, My Father worketh hitherto, & I worke.

18 Therefore the Iewes sought the more to kill him, not onely because hee had broken the Sabbath, but said also, that God was his father, making himselfe equall with God.

19 Then answered Iesus, and saide vnto them, Verily, verily I say vnto you, The sonne can doe nothing of himselfe, but what he seeth the Father doe: for what things soeuer he doeth, these also doth the sonne likewise.

20 For the father loueth the sonne, and sheweth him all things that himselfe doth : & he will shew him greater works then these, that ye may marueile.

21 For as the Father raiseth vp the dead, and quickeneth them : euen so the Sonne quickeneth whom he will.

22 For the Father iudgeth no man : but hath committed all iudgement vnto the Sonne:

23 That all men should honour the Son, euen as they honour the Father. He that honoureth not ẙ Sonne, honoreth not y Father which hath sent him.

24 Verily, verily I say vnto you, Hee that heareth my word, & beleeueth on him that sent mee, hath euerlasting life, and shall not come into condemnation : but is passed from death vnto life.

25 Verily, verily I say vnto you, The houre is comming, & now is, when the dead shall heare the voice of the Sonne of God : and they that heare, shall liue.

26 For as the Father hath life in himselfe : so hath he giuen to the Sonne to haue life in himselfe :

27 And hath giuen him authority to execute iudgement also, because he is the Sonne of man.

28 Marueile not at this : for the houre is comming, in the which all that are in the graues shall heare his voice,

29 And shall come foorth, * they that

haue done good, vnto the resurrection of life, and they that haue done euill, vnto the resurrection of damnation.

30 I can of mine owne selfe doe nothing : as I heare, I iudge : and my iudgement is iust, because I seeke not mine owne will, but the will of the Father, which hath sent me.

31 * If I beare witnesse of my selfe, my witnesse is not true.

32 ¶ * There is another that beareth witnesse of me, & I know that the witnesse which he witnesseth of me, is true.

33 Ye sent vnto Iohn, * and he bare witnesse vnto the trueth.

34 But I receiue not testimonie from man : but these things I say, that ye might be saued.

35 He was a burning and a shining light : and ye were willing for a season to reioyce in his light.

36 ¶ But I haue greater witnesse then that of Iohn : for the workes which the Father hath giuen me to finish, the same workes that I doe, beare witnesse of mee, that the Father hath sent me.

37 And the Father himselfe which hath sent me, * hath borne witnesse of me. Ye haue neither heard his voyce at any time, * nor. seene his shape.

38 And ye haue not his word abiding in you : for whom he hath sent, him ye beleeue not.

39 ¶ Search the Scriptures, for in them ye thinke ye haue eternall life, and they are they which testifie of me.

40 And ye will not come to me, that ye might haue life.

41 I receiue not honour from men.

42 But I know you, that ye haue not the loue of God in you.

43 I am come in my Fathers name, and ye receiue me not : if another shall come in his owne Name, him ye will receiue.

44 *How can ye beleeue, which receiue honour one of another, & seeke not the honour that commeth from God onely ?

45 Doe not thinke that I will accuse you to the Father : there is one that accuseth you, euen Moses, in whom ye trust ?

46 For had ye beleeued Moses, ye would haue beleeued me : *for he wrote of me.

47 But if ye beleeue not his writings, how shall ye beleeue my words ?
CHAP.

* Matth. 25. 46.

* Chap. 8. 14.

* Matth. 3. 17.

* Chap. 1. 7

* Matth. 3. 17. and 17. 5.
* Deut. 4. 12.

* Chap. 12. 43.

* Gen. 3. 15. deut. 18. 15

CHAP. VI.

1 Christ feedeth fiue thousand men with fiue loaues and two fishes. 15 Thereupon the people would haue made him King. 16 But withdrawing himselfe, he walked on the sea to his disciples : 26 Reprooueth the people flocking after him, and all the fleshly hearers of his word : 32 Declareth himselfe to be the Bread of life to beleeuers. 66 Many disciples depart from him. 68 Peter confesseth him. 70 Iudas is a deuil.

Fter these things Iesus went ouer the sea of Galilee, which is the sea of Tiberias :

2 And a great multitude followed him, because they saw his miracles which hee did on them that were diseased.

3 And Iesus went vp into a mountaine, and there hee sate with his disciples.

4 * And the Passeouer, a feast of the Iewes, was nigh.

5 ¶ * When Iesus then lift vp his eyes, and saw a great company come vnto him, he saith vnto Philip, Whence shall we buy bread, that these may eate?

6 (And this he said to proue him : for he himselfe knew what he would doe)

7 Philip answered him, Two hundred peny-worth of bread is not sufficient for them, that euery one of them may take a litle.

8 One of his disciples, Andrew, Simon Peters brother, saith vnto him,

9 There is a lad here, which hath fiue barley loaues, and two small fishes : but what are they among so many?

10 And Iesus said, Make the men sit downe. Now there was much grasse in the place. So the men sate downe, in number about fiue thousand.

11 And Iesus tooke the loaues, and when he had giuen thankes, hee distributed to the disciples, and the disciples to them that were set downe, and likewise of the fishes, as much as they would.

12 When they were filled, he said vnto his disciples, Gather vp the fragments that remaine, that nothing be lost.

13 Therefore they gathered them together, and filled twelue baskets with the fragments of the fiue barley loaues, which remained ouer and aboue, vnto them that had eaten.

*Leuit. 23.
5. deut. 16.
1.
* Matt. 14.
15.

14 Then, those men, when they had seene the miracle that Iesus did, said, This is of a trueth that Prophet that should come into the world.

15 ¶ When Iesus therefore perceiued that they would come and take him by force, to make him a King, hee departed againe into a mountaine, himselfe alone.

16 * And when euen was now come, his disciples went downe vnto the sea,

17 And entred into a ship, and went ouer the sea towards Capernaum : and it was now darke, and Iesus was not come to them.

18 And the sea arose, by reason of a great winde that blew.

19 So when they had rowed about fiue and twentie, or thirtie furlongs, they see Iesus walking on the sea, and drawing nigh vnto the ship : and they were afraid.

20 But he saith vnto them, It is I, be not afraid.

21 Then they willingly receiued him into the ship, and immediatly the ship was at the land whither they went.

22 ¶ The day following, when the people which stood on the other side of the sea, saw that there was none other boat there, saue that one whereinto his disciples were entred, and that Iesus went not with his disciples into the boat, but that his disciples were gone away alone :

23 Howbeit there came other boats from Tiberias, nigh vnto the place where they did eate bread, after that the Lord had giuen thankes :

24 When the people therefore saw that Iesus was not there, neither his disciples, they also tooke shipping, and came to Capernaum, seeking for Iesus.

25 And when they had found him on the other side of the sea, they saide vnto him, Rabbi, when camest thou hither?

26 Iesus answered them, and said, Verely, verely I say vnto you, Ye seeke me, not because ye saw the miracles, but because yee did eate of the loaues, and were filled.

27 ||Labour not for the meat which perisheth, but for that meat which endureth vnto euerlasting life, which the Sonne of man shall giue vnto you : *for him hath God the Father sealed.

28 Then said they vnto him, What shall

* Matth. 14.
23.

|| Or, worke
not.

* Matth. 3.
17.

shall we doe, that we might worke the workes of God?

29 Iesus answered, and said vnto them, *This is the worke of God, that ye beleeue on him whom he hath sent.

*1. Ioh. 3. 23.

30 They said therefore vnto him, What signe shewest thou then, that we may see, and beleeue thee? What doest thou worke?

31 *Our fathers did eate Manna in the desert, as it is written, *He gaue them bread from heauen to eate.

* Exod. 16. 15. numb. 11. 7.
* Psal. 78. 25.

32 Then Iesus said vnto them, Verely, verely I say vnto you, Moses gaue you not that bread from heauen, but my Father giueth you the true bread from heauen.

33 For the bread of God is hee which commeth downe from heauen, and giueth life vnto the world.

34 Then said they vnto him, Lord, euermore giue vs this bread.

35 And Iesus said vnto them, I am the bread of life : hee that commeth to me, shall neuer hunger : and he that beleeueth on me, shall neuer thirst.

36 But I said vnto you, that ye also haue seene me, and beleeue not.

37 All that the Father giueth mee, shall come to mee ; and him that commeth to me, I will in no wise cast out.

38 For I came downe from heauen, not to doe mine owne will, but the will of him that sent me.

39 And this is the Fathers wil which hath sent me, that of all which he hath giuen mee, I should lose nothing, but should raise it vp againe at the last day.

40 And this is the will of him that sent me, that euery one which seeth the Sonne, and beleeueth on him, may haue euerlasting life : and I will raise him vp at the last day.

41 The Iewes then murmured at him, because hee said, I am the bread which came downe from heauen.

42 And they said, *Is not this Iesus the sonne of Ioseph, whose father and mother we know? How is it then that hee sayth, I came downe from heauen?

* Mat. 13. 55.

43 Iesus therefore answered, and said vnto them, Murmure not among your selues.

44 No man can come to me, except the Father which hath sent me, draw him : and I will raise him vp at the last day.

* Esai 54. 13. Iere. 31. 34.

45 *It is written in the Prophets, And they shall be all taught of God. Euery man therefore that hath heard, and hath learned of the Father, commeth vnto me,

46 Not that any man hath seene the Father ; *saue hee which is of God, hee hath seene the Father.

* Mat. 11. 27.

47 Verely, verely I say vnto you, Hee that beleeueth on me, hath euerlasting life.

48 I am that bread of life.

49 Your fathers did eate Manna in the wildernesse, and are dead.

50 This is the bread which commeth downe from heauen, that a man may eate thereof, and not die.

51 I am the liuing bread, which came downe from heauen. If any man eate of this bread, he shall liue for euer : and the bread that I will giue, is my flesh, which I will giue for the life of the world.

52 The Iewes therefore stroue amongst themselues, saying, How can this man giue vs his flesh to eate?

53 Then Iesus sayd vnto them, Verely, verely I say vnto you, Except yee eate the flesh of the sonne of man, and drinke his blood, yee haue no life in you.

54 Whoso eateth my flesh, and drinketh my blood, hath eternall life, and I will raise him vp at the last day.

55 For my flesh is meate indeed, and my blood is drinke indeed.

56 He that eateth my flesh, and drinketh my blood, dwelleth in me, and I in him.

57 As the liuing Father hath sent me, and I liue by the Father : so, he that eateth me, euen he shall liue by me.

58 This is that bread which came downe from heauen : not as your fathers did eate Manna, and are dead : he that eateth of this bread, shall liue for euer.

59 These things said hee in the Synagogue, as he taught in Capernaum.

60 Many therefore of his disciples, when they had heard *this*, said, This is an hard saying, who can heare it?

61 When Iesus knew in himselfe, that his disciples murmured at it, hee said vnto them, Doeth this offend you?

62 *What and if yee shall see the sonne of man ascend vp where hee was before?

* Cha. 3. 13.

63 It is the Spirit that quickeneth, the flesh profiteth nothing : the wordes that

that I speake vnto you, they are Spirit, and they are life.

64 But there are some of you that beleeue not. For Iesus knew from the beginning, who they were that beleeued not, and who should betray him.

65 And he said, Therefore said I vnto you, that no man can come vnto me, except it were giuen vnto him of my Father.

66 ¶ From that time many of his disciples went backe, and walked no more with him.

67 Then said Iesus vnto the twelue, Will ye also goe away ?

68 Then Simon Peter answered him, Lord, to whom shall we goe ? Thou hast the words of eternall life.

*Matth. 16 16.

69 * And we beleeue and are sure that thou art that Christ, the Sonne of the liuing God.

70 Iesus answered them, Haue not I chosen you twelue, and one of you is a deuill ?

71 He spake of Iudas Iscariot the sonne of Simon : for hee it was that should betray him, being one of the twelue.

CHAP. VII.

Iesus reprooueth the ambition and boldnesse of his kinsemen : 10 goeth vp from Galilee to the feast of Tabernacles, 14 teacheth in the Temple. 40 Diuers opinions of him among the people. 45 The Pharisees are angry that their officers tooke him not, & chide with Nicodemus for taking his part.

Fter these things, Iesus walked in Galilee : for hee would not walk in Iurie, because the Iewes sought to kill him.

*Leuit. 23.

2 * Now the Iewes feast of Tabernacles was at hand.

3 His brethren therefore saide vnto him, Depart hence, and go into Iudea, that thy Disciples also may see the works that thou doest.

4 For there is no man that doth any thing in secret, and hee himselfe seeketh to be knowen openly : If thou doe these things, shew thy selfe to ÿ world.

5 For neither did his brethren beleeue in him.

6 Then Iesus said vnto them, My time is not yet come : but your time is alway ready.

7 The world cannot hate you, but me it hateth, because I testifie of it, that the workes thereof are euill.

8 Goe ye vp vnto this feast : I goe not vp yet vnto this feast, * for my time is not yet full come.

*Cha. 8. 30

9 When he had said these words vnto them, he abode still in Galilee.

10 ¶ But when his brethren were gone vp, then went he also vp vnto the feast, not openly, but as it were in secret.

11 Then the Iewes sought him at the feast, and said, Where is he ?

12 And there was much murmuring among the people, concerning him : For some said, Hee is a good man : Others said, Nay, but he deceiueth the people.

13 Howbeit, no man spake openly of him, for feare of the Iewes.

14 ¶ Now about the middest of the feast, Iesus went vp into the Temple, and taught.

15 And the Iewes maruelled, saying, How knoweth this man ||letters, hauing neuer learned ?

|| Or, learning.

16 Iesus answered them, My doctrine is not mine, but his that sent me.

17 If any man will doe his will, he shall know of the doctrine, whether it be of God, or whether I speake of my selfe.

18 He that speaketh of himselfe, seeketh his owne glory: but he that seeketh his glory that sent him, the same is true, and no vnrighteousnesse is in him.

19 * Did not Moses giue you the Law, and yet none of you keepeth the Law ? * Why goe ye about to kill me ?

*Exo. 24. 3
*Cha. 5. 18

20 The people answered, and sayd, Thou hast a deuill : Who goeth about to kill thee ?

21 Iesus answered, and saide vnto them, I haue done one worke, and yee all maruelle.

22 * Moses therefore gaue vnto you Circumcision (not because it is of Moses, * but of the fathers) and yee on the Sabbath day circumcise a man.

*Leui. 12.
*Gen. 17. 1

23 If a man on the Sabbath day receiue circumcision, || that the Lawe of Moses should not be broken ; are ye angry at me, because I haue made a man euery whit whole on the Sabbath day ?

|| Or, without breakin the Law of Moses.

24 * Iudge not according to the appearance, but iudge righteous iudgement.

*Deu. 1. 1

25 Then said some of them of Hierusalem, Is not this hee, whome they seeke to kill ?

26 But loe, he speaketh boldly, and they say nothing vnto him : Doe the rulers

rulers know indeede that this is the very Christ?

27 Howbeit wee know this man whence he is : but when Christ commeth, no man knoweth whence he is.

28 Then cried Iesus in the Temple as he taught, saying, Ye both know me, and ye know whence I am, and I am not come of my selfe, but he that sent me, is true, whom ye know not.

29 But I know him, for I am from him, and he hath sent me.

30 Then they sought to take him : but no man laid hands on him, because his houre was not yet come.

31 And many of the people beleeued on him, & said, When Christ commeth, will hee doe moe miracles then these which this man hath done?

32 ¶ The Pharisees heard that the people murmured such things concerning him : And the Pharisees and the chiefe Priests sent officers to take him.

33 Then said Iesus vnto them, Yet a litle while am I with you, and then I goe vnto him that sent me.

34 *Ye shall seeke me, and shall not find me : and where I am, thither yee cannot come.

35 Then saide the Iewes among themselues, Whither will hee goe, that we shall not find him? will he goe vnto the dispersed among the || Gentiles, and teach the Gentiles?

36 What maner of saying is this that he said, Ye shall seeke me, and shall not find me? and where I am, thither ye cannot come?

37 *In the last day, that great day of the feast, Iesus stood, and cried, saying, If any man thirst, let him come vnto me, and drinke.

38 *He that beleeueth on me, as the Scripture hath saide, out of his belly shall flow riuers of liuing water.

39 *(But this spake he of the Spirit which they that beleeue on him, should receiue. For the holy Ghost was not yet *giuen*, because that Iesus was not yet glorified.)

40 ¶ Many of the people therefore, when they heard this saying, saide, Of a trueth this is the Prophet.

41 Others said, This is the Christ. But some said, Shall Christ come out of Galilee?

42 *Hath not the Scripture saide, that Christ commeth of the seede of Dauid, and out of the towne of Beth-

lehem, where Dauid was?

43 So there was a diuision among the people because of him.

44 And some of them would haue taken him, but no man layed hands on him.

45 ¶ Then came the officers to the chiefe Priests and Pharises, and they said vnto them, Why haue ye not brought him?

46 The officers answered, Neuer man spake like this man.

47 Then answered them the Pharisees, Are ye also deceiued?

48 Haue any of the rulers, or of the Pharises beleeued on him?

49 But this people who knoweth not the Law, are cursed.

50 Nicodemus saith vnto them, (* He that came to Iesus by night, being one of them,)

51 *Doth our Law iudge any man before it heare him, & know what he doth?

52 They answered, and said vnto him, Art thou also of Galilee? Search, and looke : for out of Galilee ariseth no Prophet.

53 And euery man went vnto his owne house.

CHAP. VIII.

1 Christ deliuereth the woman taken in adultery. 12 He preacheth himselfe the light of the world, and iustifieth his Doctrine : 33 Answereth the Iewes that boasted of Abraham, 59 And conueigheth himselfe from their crueltie.

Esus went vnto ỹ Mount of Oliues :

2 And earely in the morning hee came againe into the Temple, and all the people came vnto him, and he sate downe, and taught them.

3 And the Scribes and Pharisees brought vnto him a woman taken in adultery, and when they had set her in the mids,

4 They say vnto him, Master, this woman was taken in adultery, in the very act.

5 *Now Moses in the Law commanded vs, that such should be stoned : but what sayest thou?

6 This they said, tempting him, that they might haue to accuse him. But Iesus stouped downe, and with his finger wrote on the ground as though he heard them not.

7 So

---

*Chap. 13. 33.

‖ Or, Greeks.

* Leuit. 23. 36.

* Deut. 18. 15.

* Ioel. 2. 28. esai. 44. 3.

* Mat. 2. 5.

*Chap. 3. 2.

* Deut. 17. 10. and 19. 15.

* Leuit. 20. 10.

‖ Deut. 17.
7.

7 So when they continued asking him, hee lift vp himselfe, and saide vnto them, *Hee that is without sinne among you, let him first cast a stone at her.

8 And againe, hee stouped downe, and wrote on the ground.

9 And they which heard it, being conuicted by their owne conscience, went out one by one, beginning at the eldest, euen vnto the last : and Iesus was left alone, and the woman standing in the midst.

10 When Iesus had lift vp himselfe, and saw none but the woman, hee said vnto her, Woman, where are those thine accusers? Hath no man condemned thee?

11 She saide, No man, Lord. And Iesus saide vnto her, Neither doe I condemne thee : Goe, and sinne no more.

‖ Chap. 1.
5. and 9. 5.

12 ¶ Then spake Iesus againe vnto them, saying, *I am the light of the world : he that followeth mee, shall not walke in darkenesse, but shall haue the light of life.

13 The Pharisees therefore said vnto him, Thou bearest record of thy selfe, thy record is not true.

‖ Chap. 5.
31.

14 Iesus answered, and said vnto them, *Though I beare record of my selfe, yet my record is true : for I know whence I came, and whither I goe : but ye cannot tell whence I come, and whither I goe.

15 Yee iudge after the flesh, I iudge no man.

16 And yet if I iudge, my iudgement is true : for I am not alone, but I and the Father that sent me.

‖ Deut. 17.
6. matt. 18.
16.

17 *It is also written in your Law, that the testimonie of two men is true.

18 I am one that beare witnesse of my selfe, and the Father that sent mee, beareth witnesse of me.

19 Then said they vnto him, Where is thy Father? Iesus answered, Ye neither know me, nor my Father : if ye had knowen mee, yee should haue knowen my Father also.

20 These words spake Iesus in the treasury, as hee taught in the Temple; and no man layd hands on him, for his houre was not yet come.

21 Then saide Iesus againe vnto them, I goe my way, and ye shall seeke me, & shall die in your sinnes: Whither I goe, ye cannot come.

22 Then said the Iewes, Will hee kill himselfe? because he saith, Whither I goe, ye cannot come.

23 And hee said vnto them, Yee are from beneath, I am from aboue : Yee are of this world, I am not of this world.

24 I said therefore vnto you, that ye shall die in your sinnes. For if yee beleeue not that I am hee, yee shall die in your sinnes.

25 Then said they vnto him, Who art thou? And Iesus saith vnto them, Euen the same that I saide vnto you from the beginning.

26 I haue many things to say, and to iudge of you : But hee that sent mee is true, and I speake to the world, those things which I haue heard of him.

27 They vnderstood not that hee spake to them of the Father.

28 Then saide Iesus vnto them, When yee haue lift vp the Sonne of man, then shall ye know that I am he, and that I doe nothing of my selfe : but as my Father hath taught mee, I speake these things.

29 And he that sent me, is with me : the Father hath not left mee alone : for I doe alwayes those things that please him.

30 As hee spake those words, many beleeued on him.

31 Then said Iesus to those Iewes which beleeued on him, If ye continue in my word, then are yee my disciples indeed.

32 And ye shall know the Trueth, and the Trueth shall make you free.

33 ¶ They answered him, We be Abraham seed, and were neuer in bondage to any man : how sayest thou, Yee shall be made free?

34 Iesus answered them, Verily, verily I say vnto you, *Whosoeuer committeth sinne, is the seruant of sinne.

* Rom. 6.
20. 2. pet.
2. 19.

35 And the seruant abideth not in the house for euer : but the Sonne abideth euer.

36 If the Sonne therfore shall make you free, ye shall be free indeed.

37 I know that yee are Abrahams seed, but ye seeke to kill mee, because my word hath no place in you.

38 I speake that which I haue seene with my Father : and ye do that which ye haue seene with your father.

39 They

39 They answered, and said vnto him, Abraham is our father. Iesus sayth vnto them, If yee were Abrahams children, ye would doe the workes of Abraham.

40 But now yee seeke to kill me, a man that hath tolde you the trueth, which I haue heard of God : this did not Abraham.

41 Ye doe the deeds of your father. Then said they to him, We be not borne of fornication, wee haue one Father, euen God.

42 Iesus said vnto them, If God were your Father, yee would loue me, for I proceeded foorth, and came from God : neither came I of my selfe, but he sent me.

43 Why doe yee not vnderstand my speech? euen because yee cannot heare my word.

*1. Ioh. 3. 8. 44 *Ye are of your father the deuill, and the lusts of your father ye will doe: hee was a murtherer from the beginning, and abode not in the trueth, because there is no truth in him. When hee speaketh a lie, he speaketh of his owne: for he is a liar, and the father of it.

45 And because I tell you the truth, ye beleeue me not.

46 Which of you conuinceth mee of sinne? And if I say the trueth, why doe ye not beleeue me?

*1. Ioh. 4. 6. 47 *He that is of God, heareth Gods words : ye therefore heare them not, because ye are not of God.

48 Then answered the Iewes, and said vnto him, Say wee not well that thou art a Samaritane, & hast a deuill?

49 Iesus answered, I haue not a deuill : but I honour my Father, and ye doe dishonour me.

50 And I seeke not mine owne glory, there is one that seeketh & iudgeth.

51 Verely, verely I say vnto you, If a man keepe my saying, hee shall neuer see death.

52 Then said the Iewes vnto him, Now we know that thou hast a deuill. Abraham is dead, and the Prophets : and thou sayest, If a man keepe my saying, he shall neuer taste of death.

53 Art thou greater then our father Abraham, which is dead? and the Prophets are dead : whom makest thou thy selfe?

54 Iesus answered, If I honour my selfe, my honour is nothing : it is my Father that honoureth me, of whom

ye say, that he is your God:

55 Yet ye haue not knowen him, but I know him : and if I should say, I know him not, I shalbe a lyar like vnto you : but I know him, and keepe his saying.

56 Your father Abraham reioyced to see my day : and he saw it, & was glad.

57 Then said the Iewes vnto him, Thou art not yet fiftie yeeres olde, and hast thou seene Abraham?

58 Iesus said vnto them, Verely, verely I say vnto you, Before Abraham was, I am.

59 Then tooke they vp stones to cast at him : but Iesus hidde himselfe, and went out of the Temple, going thorow the midst of them, and so passed by.

CHAP. IX.

1 The man that was borne blinde restored to sight. 8 Hee is brought to the Pharises. 13 They are offended at it, and excommunicate him: 35 But hee is receiued of Iesus, and confesseth him. 39 Who they are whome Christ enlighteneth.

 Nd as Iesus passed by, he saw a man which was blinde from his birth.

2 And his disciples asked him, saying, Master, who did sinne, this man, or his parents, that he was borne blinde?

3 Iesus answered, Neither hath this man sinned, nor his parents : but that the workes of God should be made manifest in him.

4 I must worke the workes of him that sent me, while it is day : the night commeth when no man can worke.

5 As long as I am in the world, *I am the light of the world.   * Chap. 1. 9.

6 When he had thus spoken, he spat on the ground, and made clay of the spettle, and he ||anointed the eyes of the blinde man with the clay,   ‖ Or, spread the clay vpon the eyes of the blinde man.

7 And said vnto him, Goe wash in the poole of Siloam (which is by interpretation, Sent.) He went his way therfore, and washed, and came seeing.

8 ¶ The neighbours therefore, and they which before had seene him, that he was blinde, said, Is not this he that sate and begged?

9 Some said, This is hee : others said, Hee is like him : but hee sayd, I am hee.

10 Therefore said they vnto him, How were thine eyes opened?

11 He

11 He answered and said, A man that is called Iesus, made clay, and anointed mine eyes, and said vnto me, Goe to the poole of Siloam, and wash : and I went and washed, and I receiued sight.

12 Then said they vnto him, Where is he? He said, I know not.

13 ¶ They brought to the Pharisees him that aforetime was blind.

14 And it was the Sabbath day when Iesus made the clay, and opened his eyes.

15 Then againe the Pharisees also asked him how he had receiued his sight. He said vnto them, Hee put clay vpon mine eyes, and I washed, and doe see.

16 Therefore said some of the Pharisees, This man is not of God, because hee keepeth not the Sabbath day. Others said, How can a man that is a sinner, doe such miracles? and there was a diuision among them.

17 They say vnto the blind man againe, What sayest thou of him, that he hath opened thine eyes? He said, Hee is a Prophet.

18 But the Iewes did not beleeue concerning him, that hee had bin blind, and receiued his sight, vntill they called the parents of him that had receiued his sight.

19 And they asked them, saying, Is this your sonne, who ye say was borne blind? how then doth he now see?

20 His parents answered them, and said, We know that this is our sonne, and that he was borne blind:

21 But by what meanes he now seeth, we know not, or who hath opened his eyes we know not : hee is of age, aske him, he shall speake for himselfe.

22 These words spake his parents, because they feared the Iewes : for the Iewes had agreed already, that if any man did confesse that he was Christ, he should be put out of the Synagogue.

23 Therefore said his parents, He is of age, aske him.

24 Then againe called they the man that was blind, and said vnto him, Giue God the praise, we know that this man is a sinner.

25 He answered, and said, Whether he be a sinner or no, I know not : One thing I know, that whereas I was blind, now I see.

26 Then saide they to him againe, What did he to thee? How opened hee thine eyes?

27 He answered them, I haue told you already, and ye did not heare: wherfore would you heare it againe? Will ye also be his disciples?

28 Then they reuiled him, and said, Thou art his disciple, but we are Moses disciples.

29 Wee know that God spake vnto Moses : as for this fellow, we knowe not from whence he is.

30 The man answered, and said vnto them, Why herein is a marueilous thing, that ye know not from whence he is, and yet he hath opened mine eyes.

31 Now we know that God heareth not sinners : but if any man bee a worshipper of God, and doth his will, him he heareth.

32 Since the world began was it not heard that any man opened the eyes of one that was borne blinde :

33 If this man were not of God, he could doe nothing.

34 They answered, and saide vnto him, Thou wast altogether borne in sinnes, and doest thou teach vs? And they ‖cast him out.

‖ *Or, excommunicated him.*

35 Iesus heard that they had cast him out; and when hee had found him, he said vnto him, Doest thou beleeue on the Sonne of God?

36 He answered and said, Who is he, Lord, that I might beleeue on him?

37 And Iesus said vnto him, Thou hast both seene him, and it is he that talketh with thee.

38 And he said, Lord, I beleeue : and he worshipped him.

39 ¶ And Iesus said, For iudgment I am come into this world, that they which see not, might see, and that they which see, might be made blind.

40 And some of the Pharisees which were with him, heard these words, and saide vnto him, Are wee blinde also?

41 Iesus saide vnto them, If yee were blind, ye should haue no sinne : but now ye say, We see, therfore your sinne remaineth.

CHAP. X.

1 Christ is the doore and the good Shepheard. 19 Diuers opinions of him. 24 He proueth by his workes, that he is Christ the Sonne of God, 39 Escapeth the Iewes, 40 and went againe beyond Iordane, where many beleeued on him.

Verily|

Erily, verily I say vnto you, He that entreth not by ẙ doore into the sheepe-fold, but climeth vp some other way, the same is a theefe, and a robber.

2 But hee that entreth in by the doore, is the shepherd of the sheepe.

3 To him the porter openeth, and the sheepe heare his voyce, and he calleth his owne sheepe by name, and leadeth them out.

4 And when he putteth foorth his owne sheepe, he goeth before them, and the sheepe follow him : for they know his voyce.

5 And a stranger will they not follow, but will flee from him, for they know not the voyce of strangers.

6 This parable spake Iesus vnto them : but they vnderstood not what things they were which he spake vnto them.

7 Then said Iesus vnto them againe, Verily, verily I say vnto you, I am the doore of the sheepe.

8 All that euer came before me, are theeues and robbers : but the sheepe did not heare them.

9 I am the doore ; by me if any man enter in, he shall be saued, and shall goe in and out, and find pasture.

10 The theefe commeth not, but for to steale and to kill, and to destroy : I am come that they might haue life, and that they might haue it more abundantly.

11 * I am the good shepheard : the good shepheard giueth his life for the sheepe.

12 But hee that is an hireling and not the shepheard, whose owne the sheepe are not, seeth the woolfe comming, and leaueth the sheep, and fleeth : and the woolfe catcheth them, and scattereth the sheepe.

13 The hireling fleeth, because he is an hireling, & careth not for the sheepe.

14 I am the good shepheard, and know my sheepe, and am knowen of mine.

15 As the father knoweth me, euen so know I the father : & I lay downe my life for the sheepe.

16 And other sheepe I haue, which are not of this fold : them also I must bring, and they shall heare my voyce ; *and there shall be one fold, and one shepheard.

17 Therefore doth my father loue me, *because I lay downe my life that I might take it againe.

18 No man taketh it from me, but I lay it downe of my selfe : I haue power to lay it downe, and I haue power to take it againe. *This commandement haue I receiued of my father.

19 ¶ There was a diuision therefore againe among the Iewes for these sayings.

20 And many of them said, He hath a deuill, and is mad, why heare ye him?

21 Others said, These are not the words of him that hath a deuill. Can a deuill open the eyes of the blind?

22 ¶ And it was at Hierusalem the *feast of the dedication, & it was winter.

23 And Iesus walked in the temple in Solomons porch.

24 Then came the Iewes round about him, and said vnto him, How long doest thou ‖make vs to doubt? If thou be the Christ, tell vs plainely.

25 Iesus answered them, I told you, and ye beleeued not : the workes that I doe in my Fathers name, they beare witnesse of me.

26 But ye beleeue not, because ye are not of my sheepe, as I said vnto you.

27 My sheepe heare my voyce, and I know them, and they follow me.

28 And I giue vnto them eternall life, and they shall neuer perish, neither shall any man plucke them out of my hand.

29 My father which gaue them me, is greater then all : and no man is able to plucke them out of my fathers hand.

30 I and my father are one.

31 Then the Iewes tooke vp stones againe to stone him.

32 Iesus answered them, Many good workes haue I shewed you from my Father : for which of those workes doe ye stone me?

33 The Iewes answered him, saying, For a good worke we stone thee not, but for blasphemy, and because that thou, being a man, makest thy selfe God.

34 Iesus answered them, *Is it not written in your law, I said, ye are gods?

35 If hee called them gods, vnto whom the word of God came, and the Scripture cannot be broken :

36 Say ye of him, whom the father hath sanctified and sent into the world, Thou

* Esai. 40.
1. ezech.
34. 23.

* Esai. 37.
22.

* Esay. 53.
7, 8.

* Acts 2. 24.

* 1. Macc. 4.
59.

‖ Or, hold vs
in suspence.

* Psal. 82. 6.

Thou blasphemest; because I said, I am the Sonne of God?

37 If I doe not the workes of my Father, beleeue me not.

38 But if I doe, though yee beleeue not me, beleeue the workes : that ye may know and beleeue that the Father is in me, and I in him.

39 Therefore they sought againe to take him : but hee escaped out of their hand,

40 And went away againe beyond Iordane, into the place where Iohn at first baptized : and there he abode.

41 And many resorted vnto him, and said, Iohn did no miracle : but all things that Iohn spake of this man, were true.

42 And many beleeued on him there.

CHAP. XI.

1 Christ raiseth Lazarus, foure dayes buried. 45 Many Iewes beleeue. 47 The high Priests and Pharisees gather a counsel against Christ. 49 Caiaphas prophecieth. 54 Iesus hid himselfe. 55 At the Passeouer they enquire after him, and lay wait for him.

Ow a certaine man was sicke, named Lazarus of Bethanie, the towne of Mary, and her sister Martha.

* Matt. 26. 7.

2 (*It was that Mary which anoynted the Lord with oyntment, and wiped his feete with her haire, whose brother Lazarus was sicke.)

3 Therefore his sister sent vnto him, saying, Lord, behold, hee whom thou louest, is sicke.

4 When Iesus heard that, hee said, This sickenesse is not vnto death, but for the glory of God, that the Sonne of God might be glorified thereby.

5 Now Iesus loued Martha, and her sister, and Lazarus.

6 When he had heard therefore that he was sicke, he abode two dayes still in the same place where he was.

7 Then after that, saith hee to his disciples, Let vs go into Iudea againe.

8 His disciples say vnto him, Master, the Iewes of late sought to stone thee, and goest thou thither againe?

9 Iesus answered, Are there not twelue houres in the day? If any man walke in the day, he stumbleth not, because he seeth the light of this world.

10 But if a man walke in the night,

hee stumbleth, because there is no light in him.

11 These things said hee, and after that, hee saith vnto them, Our friend Lazarus sleepeth, but I goe, that I may awake him out of sleepe.

12 Then said his disciples, Lord, if he sleepe, he shall doe well.

13 Howbeit Iesus spake of his death : but they thought that hee had spoken of taking of rest in sleepe.

14 Then saide Iesus vnto them plainly, Lazarus is dead :

15 And I am glad for your sakes, that I was not there (to the intent yee may beleeue :) Neuerthelesse, let vs goe vnto him.

16 Then said Thomas, which is called Didymus, vnto his fellow disciples, Let vs also goe, that we may die with him.

17 Then when Iesus came, hee found that hee had lien in the graue foure dayes already.

18 (Now Bethanie was nigh vnto Hierusalem, || about fifteene furlongs off :)

|| That is about two mile.

19 And many of the Iewes came to Martha, and Mary, to comfort them concerning their brother.

20 Then Martha, as soone as shee heard that Iesus was comming, went and met him : but Mary sate still in the house.

21 Then saide Martha vnto Iesus, Lord, if thou hadst bene here, my brother had not died.

22 But I know, that euen now, whatsoeuer thou wilt aske of God, God will giue it thee.

23 Iesus saith vnto her, Thy brother shall rise againe.

24 Martha sayeth vnto him, *I know that he shall rise againe in the resurrection at the last day.

| Luke 14. 14. chap. 29.

25 Iesus said vnto her, I am the resurrection, and the *life : hee that beleeueth in me, though he were dead, yet shall he liue.

* Chap. 35.

26 And whosoeuer liueth, and beleeueth in mee, shall neuer die. Beleeuest thou this?

27 She saith vnto him, Yea Lord, I beleeue that thou art the Christ the Sonne of God, which should come into the world.

28 And when shee had so said, shee went her way, and called Mary her sister secretly, saying, The Master is

is come, and calleth for thee.

29 Assoone as she heard that, she arose quickely, and came vnto him.

30 Now Iesus was not yet come into the towne, but was in that place where Martha met him.

31 The Iewes then which were with her in the house, and comforted her, when they saw Mary that she rose vp hastily, and went out, followed her, saying, Shee goeth vnto the graue, to weepe there.

32 Then when Mary was come where Iesus was, and saw him, shee fell downe at his feete, saying vnto him, Lord, if thou hadst beene here, my brother had not dyed.

33 When Iesus therefore sawe her weeping, and the Iewes also weeping which came with her, hee groned in the Spirit, and † was troubled,

† Gr. Hee troubled himselfe.

34 And said, Where haue ye laid him? They say vnto him, Lord, come, & see.

35 Iesus wept.

36 Then said the Iewes, Behold, how he loued him.

37 And some of them said, Could not this man, * which opened the eyes of the blinde, haue caused that euen this man should not haue died?

* Chap. 9. 6.

38 Iesus therefore againe groning in himselfe, commeth to the graue. It was a caue, and a stone lay vpon it.

39 Iesus said, Take yee away the stone. Martha, the sister of him that was dead, sayth vnto him, Lord, by this time he stinketh : for he hath beene dead foure dayes.

40 Iesus saith vnto her, Said I not vnto thee, that if thou wouldst beleeue, thou shouldest see the glory of God?

41 Then they tooke away the stone from the place where the dead was laid. And Iesus lift vp his eyes, and said, Father, I thanke thee, that thou hast heard me.

42 And I knewe that thou hearest me alwayes : but because of the people which stand by, I said it, that they may beleeue that thou hast sent me.

43 And when hee thus had spoken, he cryed with a loude voice, Lazarus, come foorth.

44 And he that was dead, came forth, bound hand & foot with graue-clothes: and his face was bound about with a napkin. Iesus saith vnto them, Loose him, and let him goe.

45 Then many of the Iewes which came to Mary, and had seene the things which Iesus did, beleeued on him.

46 But some of them went their wayes to the Pharises, and tolde them what things Iesus had done.

47 ¶ Then gathered ỹ chiefe Priests and the Pharises a councell, and said, What doe wee? for this man doeth many miracles.

48 If we let him thus alone, all men will beleeue on him, and the Romanes shall come, and take away both our place and nation.

49 And one of them named Caiaphas, being the high Priest that same yeere, said vnto them, Ye know nothing at all,

50 * Nor consider that it is expedient for vs, that one man should die for the people, and that the whole nation perish not.

* Chap. 18. 14.

51 And this spake he not of himselfe: but being high Priest that yeere, he prophecied that Iesus should die for that nation :

52 And not for that nation only, but that also hee should gather together in one, the children of God that were scattered abroad.

53 Then from that day foorth, they tooke counsell together for to put him to death.

54 Iesus therefore walked no more openly among the Iewes : but went thence vnto a countrey neere to the wildernesse, into a city called Ephraim, and there continued with his disciples.

55 ¶ And the Iewes Passeouer was nigh at hand, and many went out of the countrey vp to Hierusalem before the Passeouer to purifie themselues.

56 Then sought they for Iesus, and spake among themselues, as they stood in the Temple, What thinke ye, that he will not come to the feast?

57 Now both the chiefe Priests and the Pharises had giuen a commandement, that if any man knew where hee were, he should shew it, that they might take him.

CHAP. XII.

1 Iesus excuseth Mary anointing his feet. 9 The people flocke to see Lazarus. 10 The high Priests consult to kill him. 12 Christ rideth into Ierusalem. 20 Greekes desire to see Iesus. 23 He foretelleth his death. 37 The Iewes are generally blinded : 42 yet many chiefe rulers beleeue, but do not confesse him : 44 therfore Iesus calleth earnestly for confession of faith.

Then

Hen Iesus, sixe dayes before the Passouer, came to Bethanie, where Lazarus was, which had bene dead, whom hee raised from the dead.

2 There they made him a supper, and Martha serued : but Lazarus was one of them ẏ sate at the table with him.

3 Then tooke Mary a pound of ointment, of Spikenard, very costly, and anointed the feet of Iesus, & wiped his feet with her haire : and the house was filled with the odour of the ointment.

4 Then saith one of his disciples, Iudas Iscariot, Simons sonne, which should betray him,

5 Why was not this ointment sold for three hundred pence, and giuen to the poore ?

* Cha. 13. 29　6 *This he said, not that he cared for the poore : but because hee was a thiefe, and had the bag, and bare what was put therein.

7 Then said Iesus, Let her alone, against the day of my burying hath she kept this.

8 For the poore alwayes yee haue with you : but me ye haue not alwayes.

9 Much people of the Iewes therefore knew that he was there : and they came, not for Iesus sake onely, but that they might see Lazarus also, whom he had raised from the dead.

10 ¶ But the chiefe Priests consulted, ẏ they might put Lazarus also to death,

11 Because that by reason of him many of the Iewes went away and beleeued on Iesus.

* Cha. 21. 8.　12 ¶ *On the next day, much people that were come to the feast, when they heard that Iesus was comming to Hierusalem,

13 Tooke branches of Palme trees, and went foorth to meet him, and cried, Hosanna, blessed is the king of Israel that cōmeth in the Name of the Lord.

14 And Iesus, when he had found a yong asse, sate thereon, as it is written,

' Zach. 9. 9.　15 *Feare not, daughter of Sion, behold, thy King commeth, sitting on an asses colt.

16 These things vnderstood not his disciples at the first : but when Iesus was glorified, then remēbred they that these things were written of him, and that they had done these things vnto him.

17 The people therefore that was with him, when he called Lazarus out

of his graue, and raised him from the dead, bare record.

18 For this cause the people also met him, for that they heard that hee had done this miracle.

19 The Pharisees therefore saide among themselues, Perceiue ye how yee preuaile nothing? Behold, the world is gone after him.

20 ¶ And there were certaine Greeks among them, that came vp to worship at the feast:

21 The same came therefore to Philip which was of Bethsaida of Galilee, and desired him, saying, Sir, we would see Iesus.

22 Philip commeth and telleth Andrew : and againe Andrew and Philip told Iesus.

23 ¶ And Iesus answered them, saying, The houre is come, that the Sonne of man should be glorified.

24 Verely, verely, I say vnto you, Except a corne of wheat fall into the ground, and die, it abideth alone : but if it die, it bringeth forth much fruit.

25 *He that loueth his life, shall lose it : and hee that hateth his life in this world, shall keepe it vnto life eternall.　* Matth. 10. 39.

26 If any man serue me, let him follow me, and where I am, there shall also my seruant be: If any man serue me, him will my father honour.

27 Now is my soule troubled, and what shall I say? Father, saue me from this houre, but for this cause came I vnto this houre.

28 Father, glorifie thy Name. Then came there a voice from heauen, saying, I haue both glorified it, and wil glorifie it againe.

29 The people therefore that stood by, and heard it, said, that it thundered: others said, An Angel spake to him.

30 Iesus answered, and said, This voice came not because of mee, but for your sakes.

31 Now is the iudgement of this world : now shall the prince of this world be cast out.

32 And I, if I be lifted vp from the earth, will draw all men vnto me.

33 (This hee said, signifying what death he should die)

34 The people answered him, *We haue heard out of the Law, that Christ abideth for euer : and how sayest thou, The Sonne of man must bee lift vp? Who is this Sonne of man ?　* Psal. 110.

35 Then

35 Then Iesus said vnto them, Yet a little while is the light with you : walke while ye haue the light, lest darkdesse come vpon you : For he that walketh in darkenesse, knoweth not whither he goeth.

36 While ye haue light, beleeue in the light, that ye may bee the children of light. These things spake Iesus, and departed, and did hide himselfe from them.

37 ¶ But though he had done so many miracles before them, yet they beleeued not on him :

38 That the saying of Esaias the Prophet might be fulfilled, which hee spake, *Lord, who hath beleeued our report? and to whom hath the arme of the Lord beene reuealed?

*Esai. 53. 1. rom. 10. 16.

39 Therefore they could not beleeue, because that Esaias said againe,

40 *He hath blinded their eyes, and hardned their heart, that they should not see with their eyes, nor vnderstand with their heart, and be conuerted, and I should heale them.

*Mat. 13. 14.

41 These things said Esaias, when he saw his glory, and spake of him.

42 ¶ Neuerthelesse, among the chiefe rulers also, many beleeued on him; but because of the Pharisees they did not confesse him, lest they should be put out of the Synagogue.

43 *For they loued the praise of men, more then the praise of God.

*Chap. 5. 44.

44 ¶ Iesus cried, and said, He that beleeueth on me, beleeueth not on me, but on him that sent me.

45 And he that seeth me, seeth him that sent me.

46 *I am come a light into the world, that whosoeuer beleeueth on me, should not abide in darkenesse.

*Chap. 3. 19.

47 *And if any man heare my words, and beleeue not, I iudge him not; For I came not to iudge the world, but to saue the world.

*Chap. 3. 17.

48 He that reiecteth me, and receiueth not my words, hath one that iudgeth him : *ẙ word that I haue spoken, the same shall iudge him in the last day.

*Marke 16 16.

49 For I haue not spoken of my selfe ; but the Father which sent me, gaue me a commaundement what I should say, and what I should speake.

50 And I know that his commandement is life euerlasting : whatsoeuer I speake therefore, euen as the Father said vnto me, so I speake.

CHAP. XIII.

1 Iesus washeth the disciples feete : exhorteth them to humilitie and charitie. 18 He foretelleth, and discouereth to Iohn by a token that Iudas should betray him : 31 Commandeth them to loue one another, 36 And forewarneth Peter of his deniall.

Ow *before the feast of the Passeouer, when Iesus knew that his houre was come, that he should depart out of this world vnto the Father, hauing loued his owne which were in the world, he loued them vnto the end.

*Mat. 26. 2.

2 And supper being ended (the deuill hauing now put into the heart of Iudas Iscariot Simons sonne to betray him.)

3 Iesus knowing that the Father had giuen all things into his hands, and that he was come from God, and went to God :

4 He riseth from supper, and layed aside his garments, and tooke a towell, and girded himselfe.

5 After that, he powreth water into a bason, and beganne to wash the disciples feete, and to wipe them with the towell wherewith he was girded.

6 Then commeth he to Simon Peter : and Peter saith vnto him, Lord, doest thou wash my feete ?

7 Iesus answered, and said vnto him, What I doe, thou knowest not now : but thou shalt know heereafter.

8 Peter saith vnto him, Thou shalt neuer wash my feete. Iesus answered him, If I wash thee not, thou hast no part with me.

9 Simon Peter saith vnto him, Lord, not my feete only, but also my hands, and my head.

10 Iesus saith to him, He that is washed, needeth not, saue to wash his feet, but is cleane euery whit : and ye are cleane, but not all.

11 For he knew who should betray him, therefore said he, Ye are not all cleane.

12 So after he had washed their feet, and had taken his garments, and was set downe againe, he said vnto them, Know ye what I haue done to you ?

13 Ye call me Master and Lord, and ye say well : for so I am.

14 If I then your Lord and Master haue washed your feete, yee also ought

ought to wash one anothers feete.

15 For I haue giuen you an example, that yee should doe, as I haue done to you.

16 *Verily, verily I say vnto you, the seruant is not greater then his lord, neither he that is sent, greater then hee that sent him.

17 If yee know these things, happy are ye if ye doe them.

18 ¶ I speake not of you all, I know whom I haue chosen : but that the Scripture may be fulfilled, *He that eateth bread with mee, hath lift vp his heele against me.

19 ‖Now I tell you before it come, that when it is come to passe, yee may beleeue that I am he.

20 *Verily, verily I say vnto you, he that receiueth whomsoeuer I send, receiueth me : and he that receiueth me, receiueth him that sent me.

21 *When Iesus had thus sayd, hee was troubled in spirit, and testified, and said, Verily, verily I say vnto you, that one of you shall betray me.

22 Then the disciples looked one on another, doubting of whom hee spake.

23 Now there was leaning on Iesus bosome one of his disciples, whom Iesus loued.

24 Simon Peter therefore beckened to him, that he should aske who it should be of whom he spake.

25 Hee then lying on Iesus breast, saith vnto him, Lord, who is it ?

26 Iesus answered, Hee it is to whom I shall giue a ‖soppe, when I haue dipped it. And when he had dipped the sop, he gaue it to Iudas Iscariot the sonne of Simon.

27 And after the soppe, Satan entred into him, Then said Iesus vnto him, That thou doest, doe quickly.

28 Now no man at the table knew, for what intent he spake this vnto him.

29 For some of them thought, because Iudas had the bagge, that Iesus had sayd vnto him, Buy those things that wee haue need of against the feast : or that he should giue some thing to the poore.

30 He then hauing receiued the sop, went immediatly out : and it was night.

31 ¶ Therefore when hee was gone out, Iesus sayd, Now is the Sonne of man glorified : and God is glorified in him.

32 If God be glorified in him, God shall also glorifie him in himselfe, and shall straightway glorifie him.

33 Litle children, yet a litle while I am with you. Ye shall seeke mee, *and as I said vnto the Iewes, whither I go, ye cannot come : so now I say to you.

34 *A new commandement I giue vnto you, That yee loue one another, as I haue loued you, that yee also loue one another.

35 By this shall all men know that ye are my disciples, if yee haue loue one to another.

36 ¶ Simon Peter sayd vnto him, Lord, whither goest thou ? Iesus answered him, Whither I goe, thou canst not follow me now : but thou shalt follow me afterwards.

37 Peter said vnto him, Lord, why can not I follow thee now ? I will *lay downe my life for thy sake.

38 Iesus answered him, Wilt thou lay downe thy life for my sake ? Verily, verily I say vnto thee, the Cocke shall not crow, til thou hast denied me thrise.

CHAP. XIIII.

1 Christ comforteth his Disciples with the hope of heauen : 6 professeth himselfe the Way, the Trueth, and the Life, and one with the Father : 13 Assureth their praiers in his Name to be effectuall : 15 Requesteth loue and obedience, 16 promiseth the holy Ghost the comforter, 27 and leaueth his peace with them.

Et not your heart be troubled : yee beleeue in God, beleeue also in me.

2 In my Fathers house are many mansions ; if it were not so, I would haue told you : I goe to prepare a place for you.

3 And if I goe and prepare a place for you, I will come againe, and receiue you vnto my selfe, that where I am, there ye may be also.

4 And whither I goe yee know, and the way ye know.

5 Thomas saith vnto him, Lord, we know not whither thou goest : and how can we know the way ?

6 Iesus saith vnto him, I am the Way, the Trueth, and the Life : no man commeth vnto the Father but by mee.

7 If ye had knowen me, ye should haue knowen my Father also : and from henceforth ye know him, and haue seene him.

8 Philip sayth vnto him, Lord, shew

*Matth. 10. 24. chap. 15. 20.

*Psal. 41. 10.

‖Or, from henceforth.

*Matth. 10. 40.

*Matth. 26. 21.

‖Or, morsell.

*Chap. 7 34.

*Chap. 1 17. leui. 18. 1. Ioh 4. 21.

*Matt. 2 33.

shew vs the Father, and it sufficeth vs.

9 Iesus saith vnto him, Haue I bin so long time with you, and yet hast thou not knowen me, Philip? he that hath seene me, hath seene the father, and how sayest thou then, Shew vs the father?

10 Beleeuest thou not that I am in the father, and the father in mee? The words that I speake vnto you, I speak not of my selfe: but the Father that dwelleth in me, he doth the works.

11 Beleeue me that I am in the Father, and the Father in mee: or else beleeue me for the very workes sake.

12 Verely, verely I say vnto you, he that beleeueth on me, the works that I doe, shall hee doe also, and greater workes then these shall he doe, because I goe vnto my Father.

13 *And whatsoeuer ye shall aske in my Name, that will I doe, that the Father may be glorified in the Sonne.

14 If ye shall aske any thing in my Name, I will doe it.

15 ¶ If ye loue me, keepe my commandements.

16 And I will pray the Father, and hee shall giue you another Comforter, that he may abide with you for euer,

17 *Euen* the Spirit of trueth, whom the world cannot receiue, because it seeth him not, neither knoweth him: but ye know him, for hee dwelleth with you, and shall be in you.

18 I wil not leaue you ||comfortlesse, I will come to you.

19 Yet a litle while, and the world seeth me no more: but ye see me, because I liue, ye shall liue also.

20 At that day ye shall know, that I am in my Father, and you in me, and I in you.

21 He that hath my commandements, and keepeth them, hee it is that loueth me: and he that loueth me shall be loued of my Father, and I will loue him, and will manifest my selfe to him.

22 Iudas saith vnto him, not Iscariot, Lord, how is it that thou wilt manifest thy selfe vnto vs, and not vnto the world?

23 Iesus answered, and saide vnto him, If a man loue mee, he will keepe my wordes: and my Father will loue him, and wee will come vnto him, and make our abode with him.

24 He that loueth mee not, keepeth not my sayings, and the word which you heare, is not mine, but the Fa-

Mat. 7. 7.

‖ Or, orphanes.

thers which sent mee.

25 These things haue I spoken vnto you, being yet present with you.

26 But the Comforter, *which is* the holy Ghost, whom the Father wil send in my name, he shal teach you al things, & bring al things to your remembrance, whatsoeuer I haue said vnto you.

27 Peace I leaue with you, my peace I giue vnto you, not as the world giueth, giue I vnto you: let not your heart bee troubled, neither let it bee afraid.

28 Ye haue heard how I saide vnto you, I goe away, and come againe vnto you. If ye loued mee, yee would reioyce, because I said, I go vnto the Father: for my Father is greater then I.

29 And now I haue told you before it come to passe, that when it is come to passe, ye might beleeue.

30 Heereafter I will not talke much with you: for the prince of this world commeth, and hath nothing in me.

31 But that the world may know that I loue the Father: and as the Father gaue me commandement, euen so I doe: Arise, let vs goe hence.

CHAP. XV.

1 The Consolation and mutuall loue betweene Christ and his members, vnder the parable of the vine. 18 A comfort in the hatred and persecution of the world. 26 The office of the holy Ghost, and of the Apostles.

I Am the true vine, and my Father is ȳ husbandman.

2 *Euery branch in me that beareth not fruit, hee taketh away: and euery branch that beareth fruit, he purgeth it, that it may bring foorth more fruit.

3 *Now ye are cleane through the word which I haue spoken vnto you.

4 Abide in me, and in you: As the branch cannot beare fruit of it selfe, except it abide in the vine: no more can ye, except ye abide in me.

5 I am the vine, ye are the branches: He that abideth in me, and I in him, the same bringeth forth much fruit: for ||without me ye can doe nothing.

6 If a man abide not in me, he is cast forth as a branch, and is withered, and men gather them, and cast them into the fire, and they are burned.

7 If ye abide in me, and my words abide in you, ye shall aske what ye will, and it shall be done vnto you.

*Mat. 15. 13.

*Iohn. 13. 10.

‖ Or, seuered from me.

8 Here-

8 Herein is my Father glorified, that ye beare much fruit, so shall ye bee my Disciples.

9 As the Father hath loued me, so haue I loued you : continue ye in my loue.

10 If ye keepe my Commandements, ye shal abide in my loue, euen as I haue kept my Fathers Commandements, and abide in his loue.

11 These things haue I spoken vnto you, that my ioy might remaine in you, and that your ioy might be full.

12 *This is my Commaundement, that ye loue one another, as I haue loued you.

*Chap. 13. 34. 1. thes. 4. 9. 1. iohn 3. 11.

13 Greater loue hath no man then this, that a man lay downe his life for his friends.

14 Ye are my friends, if ye do whatsoeuer I command you.

15 Henceforth I call you not seruants, for the seruant knoweth not what his lord doth, but I haue called you friends: for all things that I haue heard of my Father, I haue made knowen vnto you.

16 Ye haue not chosen me, but I haue chosen you, and *ordeined you, that you should goe and bring foorth fruit, and that your fruite should remaine : that whatsoeuer ye shall aske of the Father in my Name, he may giue it you.

*Mat. 28. 19

17 These things I commaund you, that ye loue one another.

18 If the world hate you, yee know that it hated me before it hated you.

19 If ye were of the world, the world would loue his owne : But because yee are not of the world, but I haue chosen you out of the world, therfore the world hateth you.

20 *Remember the word that I said vnto you, The seruant is not greater then the Lord : if they haue persecuted me, they will also persecute you . if they haue kept my saying, they will keepe yours also.

*Chap. 13. 16. mat. 10. 24.

21 But all these things will they doe vnto you for my Names sake, because they know not him that sent me.

22 If I had not come, and spoken vnto them, they had not had sinne : but now they haue no ||cloke for their sinne.

|Or, excuse.

23 He that hateth me, hateth my Father also.

24 If I had not done among the the works which none other man did, they had not had sinne : but now haue they both seene, & hated both me & my father.

25 But this commeth to passe, that the word might be fulfilled that is written in their law, *They hated me without a cause.

*Psa. 35. 19.

26 *But when the Comforter is come, whom I wil send vnto you from the Father, euen the Spirit of trueth, which proceedeth from the Father, hee shall testifie of me.

*Chap. 14. 26. luke 24 49.

27 And ye also shall beare witnesse, because ye haue bene with me from the beginning.

CHAP. XVI

1 Christ comforteth his Disciples against tribulation by the promise of the holy Ghost, and by his Resurrection and Ascension: 23 Assureth their prayers made in his Name to be acceptable to his Father. 33 Peace in Christ, and in the world affliction.

 Hese things haue I spoken vnto you, that yee should not be offended.

2 They shall put you out of the Synagogues : yea, the time commeth, that whosoeuer killeth you, will thinke that hee doeth God seruice.

3 And these things will they doe vnto you, because they haue not knowen the Father, nor me.

4 But these things haue I told you, that when the time shall come, ye may remember that I told you of them. And these things I said not vnto you at the beginning, because I was with you.

5 But now I goe my way to him that sent mee, and none of you asketh me, Whither goest thou ?

6 But because I haue saide these things vnto you, sorow hath filled your heart.

7 Neuerthelesse, I tell you the trueth, it is expedient for you that I goe away : for if I goe not away, the Comforter will not come vnto you : but if I depart, I will send him vnto you.

8 And when he is come, he will ||reproue the world of sinne, and of righteousnesse, and of iudgement.

|Or, conuince

9 Of sinne, because they beleeue not on me.

10 Of righteousnesse, because I goe to my Father, and ye see me no more.

11 Of iudgement, because the prince of this world is iudged.

12 I haue yet many things to say vnto you, but ye cannot beare them now:

13 How-

13 Howbeit, when hee the ſpirit of trueth is come, he wil guide you into all trueth : For he ſhall not ſpeake of himſelfe : but whatſoeuer he ſhall heare, that ſhall he ſpeake, and he will ſhew you things to come.

14 He ſhall glorifie me, for he ſhall receiue of mine, and ſhall ſhew it vnto you.

15 All things that the Father hath, are mine : therefore ſaid I that he ſhall take of mine, and ſhal ſhew it vnto you.

16 A litle while, and ye ſhall not ſee me : and againe a litle while, & ye ſhall ſee me : becauſe I goe to the Father.

17 Then ſaide ſome of his diſciples among themſelues, What is this that he ſaith vnto vs, A litle while, and ye ſhal not ſee me: and againe, a litle while, and ye ſhall ſee me : and, becauſe I goe to the Father ?

18 They ſaid therefore, What is this that he ſaith, A litle while ? we cannot tell what he ſaith.

19 Now Ieſus knew that they were deſirous to aſke him, & ſaid vnto them, Doe ye enquire among your ſelues of that I ſaide, A litle while, and ye ſhall not ſee mee : and againe; A little while and ye ſhall ſee me ?

20 Verily, verily I ſay vnto you, that ye ſhall weepe and lament, but the world ſhall reioyce : And ye ſhall be ſorrowfull, but your ſorrow ſhall be turned into ioy.

21 A woman, when ſhe is in trauaile, hath ſorrow, becauſe her houre is come : but aſſoone as ſhe is deliuered of the child, ſhe remembreth no more the anguiſh, for ioy that a man is borne into the world.

22 And ye now therefore haue ſorrow : but I will ſee you againe, and your heart ſhall reioyce, and your ioy no man taketh from you.

Mat. 7. 7. 23 And in that day ye ſhall aſke me nothing : *Verily, verily I ſay vnto you, Whatſoeuer yee ſhall aſke the Father in my Name, he will giue it you.

24 Hitherto haue ye aſked nothing in my Name : aſke, and ye ſhall receiue, that your ioy may be full.

Or, para-les. 25 Theſe things haue I ſpoken vnto you in ‖prouerbs : the time commeth when I ſhall no more ſpeake vnto you *Or, para-les.* in ‖prouerbes, but I ſhall ſhew you plainly of the Father.

26 At that day ye ſhall aſke in my Name : and I ſay not vnto you that I will pray the Father for you :

27 For the Father himſelfe loueth you, becauſe ye haue loued me, and haue beleeued that I came out from God.

28 I came foorth from the Father, and am come into the world : againe, I leaue the world, and goe to the Father.

29 His diſciples ſaid vnto him, Loe, now ſpeakeſt thou plainly, and ſpeakeſt no ‖prouerbe. *Or, para-ble.*

30 Now are we ſure that thou knoweſt al things, and needeſt not that any man ſhould aſke thee : By this we beleeue that thou cameſt foorth from God.

31 Ieſus anſwered them, Doe yee now beleeue ?

32 *Behold, the houre commeth, **Mat. 26. 31.** yea is now come, that ye ſhall be ſcattered, euery man to his ‖owne, and ſhall *Or, his owne home.* leaue me alone : and yet I am not alone, becauſe the Father is with me.

33 Theſe things I haue ſpoken vnto you, that in me ye might haue peace, in the world ye ſhall haue tribulation : but be of good cheare, I haue ouercome the world.

CHAP. XVII.

1 Chriſt prayeth to his Father to glorifie him, 6 To preſerue his Apoſtles 11 In vnitie, 17 And trueth, 20 To glorifie them, and all other beleeuers with him in heauen.

Heſe words ſpake Ieſus, and lift vp his eyes to heauen, and ſaid, Father, the houre is come, glorifie thy Sonne, that thy Sonne also may glorifie thee.

2 *As thou haſt giuen him power **Mat. 28. 18.** ouer all fleſh, that he ſhould giue eternall life to as many as thou haſt giuen him.

3 And this is life eternall, that they might know thee the onely true God, and Ieſus Chriſt whom thou haſt ſent.

4 I haue glorified thee on the earth : I haue finiſhed the worke which thou gaueſt me to doe.

5 And now O Father, glorifie thou me, with thine owne ſelfe, with the glory which I had with thee before the world was.

6 I haue manifeſted thy Name vnto the men which thou gaueſt me out of the world : thine they were; and thou gaueſt them me; and they haue kept thy word.

7 Now

7 Now they haue knowen that all things whatsoeuer thou hast giuen me, are of thee.

8 For I haue giuen vnto them the words which thou gauest me, and they haue receiued them, * and haue knowen surely that I came out from thee, and they haue beleeued that thou didst send me.

*Chap. 16. 27.

9 I pray for them, I pray not for the world : but for them which thou hast giuen me, for they are thine.

10 And all mine are thine, and thine are mine : and I am glorified in them.

11 And now I am no more in the world, but these are in the world, and I come to thee. Holy Father, keep through thine owne Name, those whom thou hast giuen mee, that they may bee one, as we are.

12 While I was with them in the world, I kept them in thy Name : those that thou gauest me, I haue kept, and none of them is lost, but the sonne of perdition : *that the Scripture might be fulfilled.

*Psal. 109. 7.

13 And now come I to thee, and these things I speake in the world, that they might haue my ioy fulfilled in themselues.

14 I haue giuen them thy word, and the world hath hated them, because they are not of the world, euen as I am not of the world.

15 I pray not that thou shouldest take them out of the world, but that thou shouldest keepe them from the euill.

16 They are not of the world, euen as I am not of the world.

17 Sanctifie them through thy trueth : thy word is trueth.

18 As thou hast sent mee into the world : euen so haue I also sent them into the world.

19 And for their sakes I sanctifie my selfe, that they also might be ||sanctified through the trueth.

|| Or, truely sanctified.

20 Neither pray I for these alone; but for them also which shall beleeue on me through their word :

21 That they all may be one, as thou Father art in mee, and I in thee, that they also may bee one in vs : that the world may beleeue that thou hast sent mee.

22 And the glory which thou gauest me, I haue giuen them : that they may be one, euen as we are one :

23 I in them, and thou in mee, that they may bee made perfect in one, and that the world may know that thou hast sent me, and hast loued them, as thou hast loued me.

24 *Father, I will that they also whom thou hast giuen me, be with me where I am, that they may behold my glory which thou hast giuen mee : for thou louedst mee before the foundation of the world.

* Chap. 12 26.

25 O righteous Father, the world hath not knowen thee, but I haue knowen thee, and these haue knowen that thou hast sent me.

26 And I haue declared vnto them thy Name, and will declare it : that the loue wherewith thou hast loued mee, may be in them, and I in them.

CHAP. XVIII.

1 Iudas betrayeth Iesus. 6 The Officers fall to the ground. 10 Peter smiteth off Malchus eare. 12 Iesus is taken, and led vnto Annas and Caiaphas. 15 Peters deniall. 19 Iesus examined before Caiaphas. 28 His arraignment before Pilate. 36 His Kingdome. 40 The Iewes aske Barabbas to be let loose.

When Iesus had spoken these wordes, *hee went foorth with his disciples o-uer the Brooke Cedron, where was a garden, into the which hee entred and his disciples.

* Matth. 2 36.

2 And Iudas also which betrayed him, knew the place : for Iesus oft times resorted thither with his disciples.

3 *Iudas then hauing receiued a band of men, and officers from the chiefe Priests and Pharisees, commeth thither with lanternes and torches, and weapons.

* Matth. 2 47.

4 Iesus therefore knowing all things that should come vpon him, went foorth, and sayde vnto them, Whom seeke ye?

5 They answered him, Iesus of Nazareth. Iesus saith vnto them, I am hee. And Iudas also which betrai-ed him, stood with them.

6 Assoone then as he had said vnto them, I am he, they went backeward, and fell to the ground.

7 Then asked hee them againe, Whom seeke ye? And they said, Iesus of Nazareth.

8 Iesus answered, I haue tolde you that I am he : If therefore ye seeke me, let these goe their way :

9 That

Chap. 17.
.

9 That the saying might be fulfilled which he spake, *Of them which thou gauest me, haue I lost none.

10 Then Simon Peter hauing a sword, drewe it, and smote the high Priests seruant, & cut off his right eare: The seruants name was Malchus.

11 Then said Iesus vnto Peter, Put vp thy sword into the sheath : the cup which my father hath giuen me, shall I not drinke it?

12 Then the band and the captaine, and officers of the Iewes, tooke Iesus, and bound him,

13 And led him away to Annas first, (for he was father in law to Caiaphas) which was the high Priest that same yeere.||

And An-
s sent
rist
nd vnto
iaphas
e high
riest, ver.

Chap. 11.

Mat. 26.

14 *Now Caiaphas was he which gaue counsell to the Iewes, that it was expedient that one man should die for the people.

15 ¶ *And Simon Peter followed Iesus, and so did another disciple : that disciple was knowen vnto the high Priest, and went in with Iesus into the palace of the high Priest.

16 But Peter stood at the doore without. Then went out that other disciple, which was knowen vnto the high Priest, and spake vnto her that kept the doore, and brought in Peter.

17 Then saith the damosell that kept the doore vnto Peter, Art not thou also one of this mans disciples ? He sayth, I am not.

18 And the seruants and officers stood there, who had made a fire of coales, (for it was colde) and they warmed themselues : and Peter stood with them, and warmed himselfe.

19 ¶ The high Priest then asked Iesus of his disciples, and of his doctrine.

20 Iesus answered him, I spake openly to the world, I euer taught in the Synagogue, and in the Temple, whither the Iewes alwayes resort, and in secret haue I said nothing:

21 Why askest thou me ? Aske them which heard me, what I haue said vnto them : behold, they know what I said.

22 And when hee had thus spoken, one of the officers which stood by, stroke Iesus ||with the palme of his hand, saying, Answerest thou the hie priest so?

r, with
od.

23 Iesus answered him, If I haue spoken euill, beare witnesse of the euill : but if well, why smitest thou me?

Mat. 26.

24 *Now Annas had sent him bound vnto Caiaphas the high Priest.

25 And Simon Peter stood and warmed himselfe : *They said therefore vnto him, Art not thou also one of his disciples ? Hee denied it, and said, I am not.

*Mat. 26.
69.

26 One of the seruants of the high Priests (being his kinsman whose eare Peter cut off) saith, Did not I see thee in the garden with him ?

27 Peter then denied againe, and immediatly the cocke crew.

28 ¶ *Then led they Iesus from Caiaphas vnto || the hall of Iudgement : And it was earely, *and they themselues went not into the Iudgement hall, lest they should be defiled : but that they might eat the Passeouer.

*Mat. 27. 2.
|| Or, Pilats
house.
* Acts 10.
28.

29 Pilate then went out vnto them, and said, What accusation bring you against this man ?

30 They answered, & said vnto him, If he were not a malefactor, we would not haue deliuered him vp vnto thee.

31 Then saide Pilate vnto them, Take ye him, and iudge him according to your law. The Iewes therefore said vnto him, It is not lawfull for vs to put any man to death :

32 *That the saying of Iesus might be fulfilled, which hee spake, signifying what death he should die.

*Mat. 20.
19.

33 *Then Pilate entred into the Iudgement hall againe, and called Iesus, and saide vnto him, Art thou the King of the Iewes ?

*Mat. 27.
11.

34 Iesus answered him, Sayest thou this thing of thy selfe ? or did others tell it thee of me ?

35 Pilate answered, Am I a Iew ? Thine owne nation, and the chiefe Priests haue deliuered thee vnto mee : What hast thou done ?

36 Iesus answered, My kingdome is not of this world : if my kingdome were of this world, then would my seruants fight, that I should not be deliuered to the Iewes : but now is my kingdome not from hence.

37 Pilate therefore saide vnto him, Art thou a King then ? Iesus answered, Thou saiest that I am a King. To this end was I borne, and for this cause came I into the world, that I should beare witnesse vnto the trueth : euery one that is of the trueth heareth my voice.

38 Pilate saith vnto him, What is trueth ? And when hee had said this, he

he went out againe vnto the Iewes, and saith vnto them, I find in him no fault at all.

* Matth. 27 15.

39 * But yee haue a custome that I should release vnto you one at the Passeouer: will ye therefore that I release vnto you the king of the Iewes?

* Act. 3. 14.

40 * Then cried they all againe, saying, Not this man, but Barabbas. Now Barabbas was a robber.

CHAP. XIX.

1 Christ is scourged, crowned with thornes, and beaten. 4 Pilate is desirous to release him, but being ouercome with the outrage of the Iewes, he deliuered him to bee crucified. 23 They cast lots for his garments. 26 He commendeth his mother to Iohn. 28 Hee dieth. 31 His side is pierced. 38 He is buried by Ioseph and Nicodemus.

* Matth. 27. 26.

Hen * Pilate therfore tooke Iesus, and scourged him. 2 And the souldiers platted a crowne of thornes, and put it on his head, and they put on him a purple robe,

3 And said, Haile king of the Iewes: and they smote him with their hands.

4 Pilate therefore went foorth againe, and saith vnto them, Behold, I bring him foorth to you, that yee may know that I find no fault in him.

5 Then came Iesus forth, wearing the crowne of thornes, and the purple robe: and *Pilate* saith vnto them, Behold the man.

6 When the chiefe Priests therefore and officers saw him, they cried out, saying, Crucifie him, crucifie him. Pilate saith vnto them, Take ye him, and crucifie him: for I find no fault in him.

7 The Iewes answered him, We haue a law, and by our law he ought to die, because hee made himselfe the Son of God.

8 ¶ When Pilate therefore heard that saying, he was the more afraid,

9 And went againe into the iudgement hall, & saith vnto Iesus, Whence art thou? But Iesus gaue him no answere.

10 Then saith Pilate vnto him, Speakest thou not vnto me? Knowest thou not, that I haue power to crucifie thee, and haue power to release thee?

11 Iesus answered, Thou couldest haue no power at all against me, except it were giuen thee from aboue: therfore

he that deliuered me vnto thee, hath the greater sinne.

12 And from thenceforth Pilate sought to release him: but the Iewes cried out, saying, If thou let this man goe, thou art not Cesars friend: whosoeuer maketh himselfe a king, speaketh against Cesar.

13 ¶ When Pilate therefore heard that saying, he brought Iesus foorth, and sate downe in the iudgement seate, in a place that is called the pauement, but in the Hebrew, Gabbatha.

14 And it was the preparation of the Passeouer, and about the sixt houre: and he saith vnto the Iewes, Beholde your King.

15 But they cried out, Away with him, away with him, crucifie him. Pilate saith vnto them, Shall I crucifie your King? The chiefe Priests answered, Wee haue no king but Cesar.

* Matth. 2 31.

16 * Then deliuered he him therfore vnto them to be crucified: and they took Iesus, and led him away.

17 And he bearing his crosse, went foorth into a place called the place of a skull, which is called in the Hebrewe, Golgotha:

18 Where they crucified him, and two other with him, on either side one, and Iesus in the middest.

19 ¶ And Pilate wrote a title, and put it on the crosse. And the writing was, *IESVS OF NAZARETH, THE KING OF THE IEWES.*

20 This title then read many of the Iewes: for the place where Iesus was crucified, was nigh to the citie, and it was written in Hebrewe, and Greeke, and Latine.

21 Then said the chiefe Priests of the Iewes to Pilate, Write not, The king of the Iewes: but that he said, I am King of the Iewes.

22 Pilate answered, What I haue written, I haue written.

* Matth. 35.

23 ¶ * Then the souldiers, when they had crucified Iesus, tooke his garments, (and made foure parts, to euery souldier a part) and also his coat: Now the coate was without seame, ‖wouen from the top thorowout.

‖ Or, wrought.

24 They said therefore among themselues, Let not vs rent it, but cast lots for it, whose it shall bee: * that the Scripture might bee fulfilled, which saith, They parted my raiment among them, and for my vesture they did cast lots.

* Psal. 22

lots. These things therefore the soul-diers did.

25 ¶ Now there stood by the crosse of Iesus, his mother, and his mothers sister, Mary *the wife* of ||Cleophas, and Mary Magdalene.

I Or, Clopas.

26 When Iesus therefore saw his mother, and the disciple standing by, whom he loued, he saith vnto his mother, Woman, behold thy sonne.

27 Then saith he to the disciple, Be-hold thy mother. And from that houre that disciple tooke her vnto his owne home.

28 ¶ After this, Iesus knowing that all things were now accomplish-ed, *that the Scripture might be fulfil-led, saith, I thirst.

* Psal. 69. 22.

29 Now there was set a vessell, full of vineger : And they filled a spunge with vineger, and put it vpon hyssope, and put it to his mouth.

30 When Iesus therefore had recei-ued the vineger, he said, It is finished, and he bowed his head, and gaue vp the ghost.

31 The Iewes therefore, because it was the preparation, that the bodies should not remaine vpon the Crosse on the Sabbath day (for that Sabbath day was an high day) besought Pilate that their legs might be broken, and that they might be taken away.

32 Then came the souldiers, and brake the legs of the first, and of the o-ther, which was crucified with him.

33 But when they came to Iesus, and saw that he was dead already, they brake not his legs.

34 But one of the souldiers with a speare pierced his side, and forthwith came there out blood and water.

35 And he that saw it, bare record, and his record is true, and he knoweth that hee saith true, that yee might be-leeue.

36 For these things were done, *that the Scripture should be fulfilled, *A bone of him shall not be broken.

* Num. 9. 12. exod. 12 46.
* Psa. 34. 21

37 *And againe another Scripture saith, They shall looke on him whom they piersed.

* Zach. 12. 10.

38 ¶ *And after this, Ioseph of A-rimathea (being a disciple of Iesus, but secretly for feare of the Iewes) be-sought Pilate that he might take away the body of Iesus, and Pilate gaue him leaue : he came therefore, and tooke the body of Iesus.

* Mat. 27. 57.

39 And there came also Nicodemus, which at the first came to Iesus by night, and brought a mixture of myrrhe and aloes, about an hundred pound *weight.*

40 Then tooke they the body of Ie-sus, & wound it in linnen clothes, with the spices, as the maner of the Iewes is to burie :

41 Now in the place where he was crucified, there was a garden, and in the garden a new Sepulchre, wherein was neuer man yet layd.

42 There laid they Iesus there-fore, because of the Iewes preparation day, for the Sepulchre was nigh at hand.

CHAP. XX.

1 Mary commeth to the Sepulchre. 3 So doe Peter and Iohn ignorant of the Resurrection. 11 Iesus appeareth to Mary Magdalene, 19 And to his Disciples. 24 The incredulitie, and confession of Thomas. 30 The Scripture is sufficient to saluation.

*He first day of the weeke, commeth Mary Magda-lene earely when it was yet darke, vnto the Sepul-chre, and seeth the stone taken away from the Sepulchre.

* Mat. 28. 1. mark. 16. 1.

2 Then she runneth and commeth to Simon Peter, and to the *other dis-ciple whom Iesus loued, and saith vn-to them, They haue taken away the Lord out of the Sepulchre, and we know not where they haue laid him.

* Chap. 13. 23. and 21. 20.

3 Peter therefore went forth, and that other disciple, and came to the Se-pulchre.

4 So they ranne both together, and the other disciple did outrun Peter, and came first to the Sepulchre.

5 And he stouping downe and loo-king in, saw the linnen clothes lying, yet went he not in.

6 Then commeth Simon Peter following him, and went into the Se-pulchre, and seeth the linnen clothes lie,

7 And the napkin that was about his head, not lying with the linnen clo-thes, but wrapped together in a place by it selfe.

8 Then went in also that other dis-ciple which came first to the Sepulchre, and he saw, and beleeued.

9 For as yet they knew not the Scripture, that hee must rise againe from the dead.

10 Then

10 Then the disciples went away againe vnto their owne home.

11 ¶ But Mary stood without at the sepulchre, weeping : & as shee wept, she stouped downe, and looked into the Sepulchre,

12 And seeth two Angels in white, sitting, the one at the head, and the other at the feete, where the body of Iesus had layen :

13 And they say vnto her, Woman, why weepest thou ? Shee saith vnto them, Because they haue taken away my Lord, and I know not where they haue laied him.

14 And when she had thus said, she turned herselfe backe, and saw Iesus standing, and knew not that it was Iesus.

15 Iesus saith vnto her, Woman, why weepest thou? whom seekest thou? She supposing him to be the gardiner, saith vnto him, Sir, if thou haue borne him hence, tell me where thou hast laied him, and I will take him away.

16 Iesus saith vnto her, Mary. She turned herselfe, and saith vnto him, Rabboni, which is to ṣay, Master.

17 Iesus saith vnto her, Touch me not : for I am not yet ascended to my Father : but goe to my brethren, and say vnto them, I ascend vnto my Father, and your Father, and to my God, and your God.

18 Mary Magdalene came and told the disciples that shee had seene the Lord, and that hee had spoken these things vnto her.

* Marke 16.
14.

19 ¶ * Then the same day at euening, being the first day of the weeke, when the doores were shut, where the disciples were assembled for feare of the Iewes, came Iesus, and stood in the midst, and saith vnto them, Peace bee vnto you.

20 And when hee had so saide, hee shewed vnto them his hands and his side. Then were the disciples glad, when they saw the Lord.

21 Then said Iesus to them againe, Peace be vnto you : As my Father hath sent me, euen so send I you.

22 And when he had said this, hee breathed on them, and saith vnto them, Receiue ye the holy Ghost.

* Matth. 18.
18.

23 * Whose soeuer sinnes yee remit, they are remitted vnto them, and whose soeuer sinnes yee retaine, they are retained.

24 ¶ But Thomas one of the twelue, called Didymus, was not with them when Iesus came.

25 The other disciples therefore said vnto him, We haue seene the Lord. But he said vnto them, Except I shall see in his hands the print of the nailes, and put my finger into the print of the nailes, and thrust my hand into his side, I will not beleeue.

26 ¶ And after eight dayes, againe his disciples were within, and Thomas with them : *Then* came Iesus, the doores being shut, and stood in the midst, and said, Peace be vnto you.

27 Then saith he to Thomas, Reach hither thy finger, and beholde my hands, and reach hither thy hand, and thrust it into my side, and bee not faithlesse, but beleeuing.

28 And Thomas answered, and said vnto him, My Lord, and my God.

29 Iesus saith vnto him, Thomas, because thou hast seene mee, thou hast beleeued: blessed are they that haue not seene, and yet haue beleeued.

* Chap. 2?
25.

30 ¶ * And many other signes truely did Iesus in the presence of his disciples, which are not written in this booke :

31 But these are written, that yee might beleeue that Iesus is the Christ the Sonne of God, and that beleeuing ye might haue life through his Name.

CHAP. XXI.

1 Christ appearing againe to his disciples was knowen of them by the great draught of fishes. 12 Hee dineth with them : 15 earnestly commandeth Peter to feed his Lambes and sheepe : 18 Foretelleth him of his death : 22 Rebuketh his curiositie touching Iohn. 25 The conclusion.

A Fter these things Iesus shewed himselfe againe to the disciples at the sea of Tiberias, and on this wise shewed he himselfe.

2 There were together Simon Peter, and Thomas called Didymus, and Nathaneel of Cana in Galilee, and the sonnes of Zebedee, and two other of his disciples.

3 Simon Peter saith vnto them, I goe a fishing. They say vnto him, Wee also goe with thee. They went foorth and entred into a ship immediatly, and that night they caught nothing.

4 But when the morning was now

now come, Ieſus ſtood on the ſhore: but the diſciples knewe not that it was Ieſus.

5 Then Ieſus ſaith vnto them, *Or, Sirs.* ‖Children, haue ye any meat? They anſwered him, No.

6 And he ſaid vnto them, Caſt the net on the right ſide of the ſhip, and yee ſhall finde. They caſt therfore, and now they were not able to draw it, for the multitude of fiſhes.

7 Therefore that Diſciple whome Ieſus loued, ſaith vnto Peter, It is the Lord. Now when Simon Peter heard that it was the Lord, he girt his fiſhers coate vnto him, (for hee was naked) & did caſt himſelfe into the ſea.

8 And the other diſciples came in a litle ſhip (for they were not farre from land, but as it were two hundred cubites) dragging the net with fiſhes.

9 Aſſoone then as they were come to land, they ſaw a fire of coales there, and fiſh laid thereon, and bread.

10 Ieſus ſaith vnto them, Bring of the fiſh, which ye haue now caught.

11 Simon Peter went vp, & drewe the net to land full of great fiſhes, an hundred and fiftie and three: and for all there were ſo many, yet was not the net broken.

12 Ieſus ſaith vnto them, Come, and dine. And none of the diſciples durſt aſke him, Who art thou? knowing that it was the Lord.

13 Ieſus then commeth, and taketh bread, and giueth them, and fiſh likewiſe.

14 This is nowe the third time that Ieſus ſhewed himſelfe to his diſciples, after that hee was riſen from the dead.

15 ¶ So when they had dined, Ieſus ſaith to Simon Peter, Simon, ſonne of Ionas, loueſt thou mee more then theſe? He ſaith vnto him, Yea, Lord, thou knoweſt that I loue thee. He ſaith vnto him, Feed my lambes.

16 He ſaith to him againe the ſecond time, Simon ſonne of Ionas, loueſt thou me? He ſaith vnto him, Yea Lord, thou knoweſt that I loue thee. He ſaith vnto him, Feed my ſheepe.

17 He ſaid vnto him the third time, Simon ſonne of Ionas, loueſt thou mee? Peter was grieued, becauſe hee ſaide vnto him the third time, Loueſt thou me? And he ſaid vnto him, Lord, thou knoweſt all things, thou knoweſt that I loue thee. Ieſus ſayth vnto him, Feed my ſheepe.

18 Verily, verily I ſay vnto thee, whē thou waſt yong, thou girdedſt thy ſelfe, and walkedſt whither thou wouldeſt: but when thou ſhalt be old, thou ſhalt ſtretch forth thy hands, and another ſhall gird thee, and carie thee whither thou wouldeſt not.

19 This ſpake hee, ſignifying by what death he ſhould glorifie God. And when he had ſpoken this, he ſayth vnto him, Follow me.

20 Then Peter turning about, ſeeth the Diſciple *whom Ieſus loued, following, which alſo leaned on his breaſt at ſupper, and ſaid, Lord, which is hee that betraieth thee? * Iohn. 13.
23 & 20. 2.

21 Peter ſeeing him, ſaith to Ieſus, Lord, and what ſhall this man *doe*?

22 Ieſus ſaith vnto him, If I will that he tary till I come, what is that to thee? Follow thou me.

23 Then went this ſaying abroad among the brethren, that that Diſciple ſhould not die: yet Ieſus ſayd not vnto him, He ſhall not die: but, If I will that he tary till I come, what is that to thee?

24 This is the Diſciple which teſtifieth of theſe things, and wrote theſe things, and we know that his teſtimonie is true.

25 * And there are alſo many other things which Ieſus did, the which if they ſhould be written euery one, I ſuppoſe that euen the world it ſelfe could not conteine the bookes that ſhould be written, Amen. * Chap. 20.
30.

¶ THE

¶ THE ACTES OF
the Apoſtles.

CHAP. I.

1 Christ preparing his Apostles to the beholding of his ascension, gathereth them together into the mount Oliuet, commandeth them to expect in Hierusalem the sending downe of the holy Ghost, promiseth after fewe dayes to send it : by vertue whereof they should be witnesses vnto him euen to the vtmost parts of the earth. 9 After his ascension they are warned by two Angels to depart, and to set their mindes vpon his second comming. 12 They accordingly returne, and giuing themselues to prayer, chuse Matthias Apostle inthe place of Iudas.

He former treatise haue I made, O Theophilus, of al that Iesus began both to doe and teach,

2 Vntill the day in which hee was taken vp, after that he through the holy Ghost had giuen commaundements vnto the Apostles, whom he had chosen.

3 To whom also he shewed himselfe aliue after his passion, by many infallible proofes, being seene of them fourty dayes, and speaking of the things perteining to the kingdome of God :

‖ Or, eating together with them.

4 And ‖ being assembled together with them, commanded them that they should not depart from Hierusalem, but wait for the promise of the Father, *which, saith he,* ye haue heard of me.

* Luke 24. 49.
* Matth. 3. 11.

5 *For Iohn truely baptized with water, but ye shall be baptized with the holy Ghost, not many dayes hence.

6 When they therefore were come together, they asked of him, saying, Lord, wilt thou at this time restore againe the kingdome to Israel ?

7 And he said vnto them, It is not for you to knowe the times or the sea-

sons, which the Father hath put in his owne power.

8 *But ye shall receiue ‖power after that the holy Ghost is come vpon you, and ye shall be witnesses vnto me, both in Hierusalem, and in all Iudea, and in Samaria, and vnto the vttermost part of the earth.

* Chap. 2
‖ Or, the power of holy Ghost comming vpon you.

9 *And when hee had spoken these things, while they beheld, hee was taken vp, and a cloud receiued him out of their sight.

* Luke 24.
51.

10 And while they looked stedfastly toward heauen, as he went vp, behold, two men stood by them in white apparell,

11 Which also said, Yee men of Galililee, why stand yee gazing vp into heauen ? This same Iesus, which is taken vp from you into heauen, shall so come, in like maner as yee haue seene him goe into heauen.

12 Then returned they vnto Hierusalem, from the mount called Oliuet, which is from Hierusalem a Sabbath dayes iourney.

13 And when they were come in, they went vp into an vpper roome, where abode both Peter & Iames, & Iohn, and Andrew, Philip, and Thomas, Bartholomew, and Matthew, Iames *the sonne* of Alpheus, and Simon Zelotes, and Iudas *the brother* of Iames.

14 These all continued with one accord in prayer and supplication, with the women, and Mary the mother of Iesus, and with his brethren.

15 ¶ And in those dayes Peter stood vp in the mids of the disciples, and said, (The number of names together were about an hundred and twentie)

16 Men and brethren, This Scripture must needs haue beene fulfilled, *which the holy Ghost by the mouth of Dauid spake before concerning Iudas, which was guide to them ỹ took Iesus.

* Psal. 4

17 For

17 For hee was numbred with vs, and had obtained part of this ministerie.

* Mat. 27. 7.

18 * Now this man purchased a field with the reward of iniquity, and falling headlong, he burst asunder in the mids, and all his bowels gushed out.

19 And it was knowen vnto all the dwellers at Hierusalem, insomuch as that field is called in their proper tongue, Aceldama, that is to say, The field of blood.

* Psal. 69. 26.

20 * For it is written in the booke of Psalmes, Let his habitation be desolate, and let no man dwell therein:

* Psal. 109. 7.
‖ Or, office: or, charge.

* And his ‖ Bishopricke let another take.

21 Wherefore of these men which haue companied with vs all the time that the Lord Iesus went in and out among vs,

22 Beginning from the baptisme of Iohn, vnto that same day that he was taken vp from vs, must one be ordained to be a witnesse with vs of his resurrection.

23 And they appointed two, Ioseph called Barsabas, who was surnamed Iustus, and Matthias.

24 And they prayed, and said, Thou Lord, which knowest the hearts of all men, shew whether of these two thou hast chosen,

25 That hee may take part of this ministerie and Apostleship, from which Iudas by transgression fell, that hee might goe to his owne place.

26 And they gaue foorth their lots, and the lot fell vpon Matthias, and hee was numbred with the eleuen Apostles.

CHAP. II.

1 The Apostles filled with the holy Ghost, and speaking diuers languages, are admired by some, and derided by others. 14 Whom Peter disprouing, and shewing that the Apostles spake by the power of the holy Ghost, that Iesus was risen from the dead, ascended into heauen, had powred downe the same holy Ghost, and was the Messias, a man knowen to them to be approued of God by his miracles, wonders, and signes, and not crucified without his determinate counsell, and foreknowledge: 37 He baptizeth a great number that were conuerted. 41 Who afterwards deuoutly, and charitably conuerse together: the Apostles working many miracles, and God daily increasing his Church.

And when the day of Pentecost was fully come, they were all with one accord in one place.

2 And suddenly there came a sound from heauen as of a rushing mighty wind, and it filled all the house where they were sitting.

3 And there appeared vnto them clouen tongues, like as of fire, and it sate vpon each of them.

4 And they were all filled with the holy Ghost, and began to speake with other tongues, as the spirit gaue them vtterance.

5 And there were dwelling at Hierusalem Iewes, deuout men, out of euery nation vnder heauen.

† Gre. when this voice was made.
‖ Or, troubled in mind.

6 Now † when this was noised abroad, the multitude came together, and were ‖ confounded, because that euery man heard them speake in his owne language.

7 And they were all amazed, and marueiled, saying one to another, Behold, are not all these which speake, Galileans?

8 And how heare we euery man in our owne tongue, wherein we were borne?

9 Parthians, and Medes, and Elamites, and the dwellers in Mesopotamia, and in Iudea, and Cappadocia, in Pontus, and Asia,

10 Phrygia, and Pamphylia, in Egypt, and in the parts of Libya, about Cyrene, & strangers of Rome, Iewes and Proselites,

11 Cretes, and Arabians, we doe heare them speake in our tongues the wonderfull workes of God.

12 And they were all amazed, and were in doubt, saying one to another, What meaneth this?

13 Others mocking said, These men are full of new wine.

14 ¶ But Peter standing vp with the eleuen, lift vp his voyce, and said vnto them, Ye men of Iudea, & all ye that dwell at Hierusalem, be this knowen vnto you, and hearken to my words:

15 For these are not drunken, as ye suppose, seeing it is but the third houre of the day.

* Ioel. 2. 28. esai. 44. 3.

16 * But this is that which was spoken by the Prophet Ioel,

17 And it shall come to passe in the last dayes (saith God) I will powre out of my Spirit vpon all flesh: and
your

your sonnes and your daughters shall prophesie, and your yong men shall see visions, and your old men shall dreame dreames:

18 And on my seruants, and on my handmaidens, I will powre out in those daies of my Spirit, and they shall prophesie:

19 And I wil shew wonders in heauen aboue, and signes in the earth beneath: blood, and fire, and vapour of smoke.

*Ioel 2. 31.

20 * The Sunne shall be turned into darkenesse, and the Moone into blood, before that great and notable day of the Lord come.

*Rom. 10. 13.

21 * And it shall come to passe, that whosoeuer shall call on the Name of the Lord, shalbe saued.

22 Yee men of Israel, heare these words, Iesus of Nazareth, a man approued of God among you, by miracles, wonders, and signes, which God did by him in the midst of you, as yee your selues also know:

23 Him, being deliuered by the determinate counsell and foreknowledge of God, yee haue taken, and by wicked hands, haue crucified, and slaine:

24 Whom God hath raised vp, hauing loosed the paines of death: because it was not possible that hee should be holden of it.

*Psal. 16. 9.

25 For Dauid speaketh concerning him, * I foresaw the Lord alwayes before my face, for he is on my right hand, that I should not be moued:

26 Therefore did my heart reioyce, and my tongue was glad: Moreouer also, my flesh shall rest in hope,

27 Because thou wilt not leaue my soule in hell, neither wilt thou suffer thine Holy one to see corruption.

28 Thou hast made knowen to mee the wayes of life, thou shalt make mee full of ioy with thy countenance.

‖ Or, I may.

*1. King. 2. 10.

29 Men and brethren, ‖let me freely speake vnto you * of the Patriarch Dauid, that he is both dead & buried, and his sepulchre is with vs vnto this day:

*Psal. 132. 11.

30 Therefore being a Prophet, *and knowing that God had sworne with an oath to him, that of the fruit of his loines, according to the flesh, hee would raise vp Christ, to sit on his throne:

*Psal. 16. 11.

31 He seeing this before, spake of the resurrection of Christ, *that his soule was not left in hell, neither his flesh did see corruption.

32 This Iesus hath God raised vp, whereof we all are witnesses.

33 Therefore being by the right hand of God exalted, and hauing receiued of the Father the promise of the holy Ghost, he hath shed forth this, which ye now see and heare.

34 For Dauid is not ascended into the heauens, but he saith himselfe, *The Lord said vnto my Lord, Sit thou on my right hand,

*Psal. 1 1.

35 Vntill I make thy foes thy footstoole.

36 Therefore let all the house of Israel know assuredly, that God hath made that same Iesus, whom ye haue crucified, both Lord and Christ.

37 ¶ Now when they heard this, they were pricked in their heart, and said vnto Peter, and to the rest of the Apostles, Men and brethren, What shall we doe?

38 Then Peter said vnto them, Repent, and be baptized euery one of you in the Name of Iesus Christ, for the remission of sinnes, and ye shal receiue the gift of the holy Ghost.

39 For the promise is vnto you, and to your children, and to all that are afarre off, euen as many as the Lord our God shall call.

40 And with many other words did hee testifie and exhort, saying, Saue your selues from this vntoward generation.

41 ¶ Then they that gladly receiued his word, were baptized: and the same day there were added vnto them about three thousand soules.

42 And they continued stedfastly in the Apostles doctrine and fellowship, and in breaking of bread, and in praiers.

43 And feare came vpon euery soule: and many wonders and signes were done by the Apostles.

44 And all that beleeued were together, and had all things common,

45 And solde their possessions and goods, and parted them to all men, as euery man had need.

46 And they continuing daily with one accord in the Temple, and breaking bread ‖from house to house, did eat their meat with gladnesse and singlenesse of heart,

‖ Or, at home.

47 Praising God, and hauing fauour with all the people. And the Lord added to the Church dayly such as should be saued.

CHAP.

CHAP. III.

Peter preaching to the people that came to see a lame man restored to his feete, 12 professeth the cure not to haue beene wrought by his, or Iohns owne power, or holinesse, but by God, and his sonne Iesus, and through faith in his Name: 13 Withall reprehending them for crucifying Iesus. 17 Which because they did it through ignorance, and that thereby were fulfilled Gods determinate counsell, and the Scriptures: 19 He exhorteth them by repentance and faith to seeke remission of their sinnes, and saluation in the same Iesus.

Owe Peter and Iohn went vp together into the Temple at the houre of prayer, *beeing* the ninth houre.

2 And a certaine man lame from his mothers womb was caried, whom they laide daily at the gate of the Temple which is called Beautifull, to aske almes of them that entred into the Temple.

3 Who seeing Peter & Iohn about to go into the Temple, asked an almes.

4 And Peter fastening his eyes vpon him, with Iohn, said, Looke on vs.

5 And he gaue heede vnto them, expecting to receiue something of them.

6 Then Peter said, Siluer and gold haue I none, but such as I haue, giue I thee: In the Name of Iesus Christ of Nazareth, rise vp and walke.

7 And hee tooke him by the right hand, & lift him vp: aud immediately his feete and ancle bones receiued strength.

8 And hee leaping vp, stood, and walked, and entred with them into the Temple, walking, and leaping, and praising God.

9 And all the people saw him walking, and praising God.

10 And they knew that it was hee which sate for almes at the beautifull gate of the Temple: and they were filled with wonder and amazement at that which had happened vnto him.

11 And as the lame man which was healed, helde Peter and Iohn, all the people ranne together vnto them in the porch, that is called Solomons, greatly wondring.

12 ¶ And when Peter sawe it, hee answered vnto the people, Yee men of Israel, why marueile ye at this? or why looke yee so earnestly on vs, as though by our owne power or holinesse we had made this man to walke?

13 The God of Abraham, and of Isaac, and of Iacob, the God of our fathers hath glorified his sonne Iesus, whom ye deliuered vp, and denied him in the presence of Pilate, when hee was determined to let him goe.

14 *But ye denied the Holy one, and the Iust, and desired a murderer to be granted vnto you, | *Matt. 27. 20.

15 And killed ‖ the Prince of life, whom God hath raised from the dead, whereof we are witnesses. | ‖ Or, author.

16 And his Name through faith in his Name hath made this man strong, whom ye see and know: yea, the faith which is by him, hath giuen him this perfect soundnesse in the presence of you all.

17 And now brethren, I wote that through ignorance yee did it, as did also your rulers.

18 But those things which God before had shewed by the mouth of all his Prophets, that Christ should suffer, hee hath so fulfilled.

19 ¶ Repent yee therefore, and bee conuerted, that your sins may be blotted out, when the times of refreshing shal come from the presence of the Lord.

20 And hee shall send Iesus Christ, which before was preached vnto you.

21 Whom the heauen must receiue, vntill the times of restitution of all things, which God hath spoken by the mouth of all his holy Prophets since the world began.

22 *For Moses truely said vnto the fathers, A Prophet shall the Lord your God raise vp vnto you of your brethren, like vnto me; him shall yee heare in all things whatsoeuer he shal say vnto you. | *Deut. 18. 15. chap. 7. 37.

23 And it shall come to passe, that euery soule which will not heare that Prophet, shalbe destroyed from among the people.

24 Yea and all the Prophets from Samuel, and those that follow after, as many as haue spoken, haue likewise foretold of these dayes.

25 Yee are the children of the Prophets, and of the couenant which God made with our fathers, *saying vnto Abraham, And in thy seed shall all the kinreds of the earth be blessed. | *Gen. 12. 3.

26 Vnto you first, God hauing raised vp his Sonne Iesus, sent him to blesse you, in turning away euery one of you from his iniquities.

CHAP.

CHAP. IIII.

1 The rulers of the Iewes offended with Peters Sermon, 4 (though thousands of the people were conuerted that heard the word) imprison him, and Iohn. 5 After, vpon examination Peter boldly auouching the lame man to be healed by the Name of Iesus, and that by the same Iesus onely we must bee eternally saued, 13 They command him and Iohn to preach no more in that Name, adding also threatning, 23 Whereupon the Church fleeeth to prayer. 31 And God by mouing the place where they were assembled, testified that he heard their prayer: confirming the Church with the gift of the holy Ghost, and with mutuall loue and charitie.

|| Or, ruler.

And as they spake vnto the people, the Priests and the ||captaine of the Temple, and the Sadduces came vpon them,

2 Being grieued that they taught the people, and preached through Iesus the resurrection from the dead.

3 And they laid hands on them, and put them in hold vnto the next day : for it was now euentide.

4 Howbeit, many of them which heard the word, beleeued, and the number of the men was about fiue thousand.

5 ¶ And it came to passe on the morow, that their rulers, and Elders, and Scribes,

6 And Annas the high Priest, and Caiphas, and Iohn, and Alexander, and as many as were of the kinred of the high Priest, were gathered together at Hierusalem.

7 And when they had set them in the middest, they asked, By what power, or by what name haue ye done this?

8 Then Peter filled with the holy Ghost, said vnto them, Ye rulers of the people, and Elders of Israel,

9 If we this day be examined of the good deed done to the impotent man, by what meanes he is made whole,

10 Be it knowen vnto you all, and to all the people of Israel, that by the Name of Iesus Christ of Nazareth, whom ye crucified, whome God raised from the dead, euen by him, doeth this man stand here before you, whole.

*Psal. 118. 22. mat. 21. 42.

11 *This is the stone which was set at nought of you builders, which is become the head of the corner.

12 Neither is there saluation in any other : for there is none other name vnder heauen giuen among men whereby we must be saued.

13 ¶ Now when they sawe the boldnesse of Peter and Iohn, and perceiued that they were vnlearned and ignorant men, they marueiled, and they tooke knowledge of them, that they had bene with Iesus.

14 And beholding the man which was healed, standing with them, they could say nothing against it.

15 But when they had commanded them to go aside out of the Council, they conferred among themselues,

16 Saying, What shall we do to these men ? for that indeed a notable miracle hath bene done by them, is manifest to all them that dwell in Hierusalem, and we cannot denie it.

17 But that it spread no farther among the people, let vs straitly threaten them, that they speake henceforth to no man in this Name.

18 And they called them, and commanded them, not to speake at all, nor teach in the Name of Iesus.

19 But Peter and Iohn answered, and said vnto them, Whether it be right in the sight of God, to hearken vnto you more then vnto God, iudge ye.

20 For wee cannot but speake the things which we haue seene and heard.

21 So when they had further threatned them, they let them goe, finding nothing how they might punish them, because of the people : for all men glorified God for that which was done.

22 For the man was aboue fourtie yeeres olde, on whome this miracle of healing was shewed.

23 ¶ And being let goe, they went to their owne company, and reported all that the chiefe Priests and Elders had said vnto them.

24 And when they heard that, they lift vp their voyce to God with one accord, & said, Lord, thou art God which hast made heauen and earth, and the sea, and all that in them is,

* Psal. 2. 1

25 * Who by the mouth of thy seruant Dauid hast saide, Why did the heathen rage, and the people imagine vaine things ?

26 The Kings of the earth stood vp, and the rulers were gathered together against the Lord, & against his Christ.

27 For of a trueth against thy holy child Iesus, whom thou hast anointed, both

both Herod, and Pontius Pilate, with the Gentiles, and the people of Israel were gathered together,

28 For to doe whatsoeuer thy hand and thy counsell determined before to be done.

29 And now Lord, behold their threatnings, and graunt vnto thy seruants, that with all boldnesse they may speake thy word,

30 By stretching foorth thine hand to heale : and that signes and wonders may be done by the Name of thy holy child Iesus.

31 ¶ And when they had prayed, the place was shaken where they were assembled together, and they were all filled with the holy Ghost, and they spake the word of God with boldnesse.

32 And the multitude of them that beleeued, were of one heart, and of one soule : Neither said any of them, that ought of the things which he possessed, was his owne, but they had all things common.

33 And with great power gaue the Apostles witnesse of the resurrection of the Lord Iesus, and great grace was vpon them all.

34 Neither was there any among them that lacked : For as many as were possessors of lands, or houses, sold them, and brought the prices of the things that were solde,

35 And laide them downe at the Apostles feete And distribution was made vnto euery man according as hee had neede.

36 And Ioses, who by the Apostles was surnamed Barnabas (which is, being interpreted, The sonne of consolation) a Leuite, and of the Countrey of Cyprus,

37 Hauing land, sold it, and brought the money, & laid it at the Apostles feet.

CHAP. V.

After that Ananias and Sapphira his wife for their hypocrisie at Peters rebuke had fallen downe dead, 12 and that the rest of the Apostles had wrought many miracles, 14 to the increase of the faith : 17 The Apostles are againe imprisoned, 19 But deliuered by an Angel bidding them to preach openly to all : 21 When, after their teaching accordingly in the temple, 29 and before the Councill, 33 they are in danger to be killed, through the aduise of Gamaliel, a great councellour among the Iewes, they be kept aliue,

40 and are but beaten : for which they glorifie God, and cease no day from preaching.

Vt a certaine man named Ananias, with Sapphira his wife, solde a possession,

2 And kept backe *part* of the price, his wife also being priuy *to it*, and brought a certaine part, and layd it at the Apostles feete.

3 But Peter said, Ananias, Why hath Satan filled thine heart ||to lie to the holy Ghost, and to keepe backe *part* of the price of the land ? ⫽*Or, to deceiue.*

4 Whiles it remained, was it not thine owne ? and after it was sold, was it not in thine owne power ? why hast thou conceiued this thing in thine heart ? thou hast not lied vnto men, but vnto God.

5 And Ananias hearing these words, fell downe, and gaue vp the ghost : and great feare came on all them that heard these things.

6 And the yong men arose, wound him vp, and caried him out, and buried him.

7 And it was about the space of three houres after, when his wife, not knowing what was done, came in.

8 And Peter answered vnto her, Tell me whether ye sold the land for.so much. And she saide, Yea, for so much.

9 Then Peter saide vnto her, How is it that ye haue agreed together, to tempt the Spirit of the Lord ? behold, the feete of them which haue buried thy husband, are at the doore, and shall cary thee out.

10 Then fell she downe straightway at his feete, and yeelded vp the ghost : And the yong men came in, and found her dead, and carying her forth, buried her by her husband.

11 And great feare came vpon all the Church, and vpon as many as heard these things.

12 ¶ And by the hands of the Apostles, were many signes and wonders wrought among the people. (And they were all with one accord in Solomons porch.

13 And of the rest durst no man ioyne himselfe to them : But the people magnified them.

14 And beleeuers were the more added to the Lord, multitudes both of men and women.)

15 Insomuch ŷ they brought foorth the sicke ||into the streetes, and layed them ⫽*Or, in euery streete.*

them on beds and couches, that at the least the shadow of Peter passing by, might ouershadow some of them.

16 There came also a multitude *out* of the cities round about vnto Hierusalem, bringing sicke folkes, and them which were vexed with vncleane spirits : and they were healed euery one.

17 ¶ Then the high Priest rose vp, and al they that were with him, (which is the sect of the Sadduces) and were filled with ||indignation,

‖ Or, enuie.

18 And laid their hands on the Apostles, & put them in the common prison.

19 But the Angel of the Lord by night opened the prison doores, and brought them foorth, and said,

20 Goe, stand and speake in the Temple to the people all the words of this life.

21 And when they heard that, they entred into the Temple early in the morning, & taught : but the high Priest came, and they that were with him, and called the Councill together, and all the Senate of the children of Israel, and sent to the prison to haue them brought.

22 But when the officers came, and found them not in the prison, they returned, and told,

23 Saying, The prison truely found we shut with all safety, and the keepers standing without before the doores, but when we had opened, we found no man within.

24 Now when the high Priest, and the captaine of the Temple, and the chiefe Priests heard these things, they doubted of them wherunto this would grow.

25 Then came one, and told them, saying, Behold, the men whom ye put in prison, are standing in the Temple, and teaching the people.

26 Then went the captaine with the officers, and brought them without violence : (For they feared the people, lest they should haue bene stoned.)

27 And when they had brought them, they set them before the Councill, and the high Priest asked them,

28 Saying, *Did not wee straitly command you, that you should not teach in this Name ? And behold, yee haue filled Hierusalem with your doctrine, and intend to bring this mans blood vpon vs.

* Chap. 4. 18.

29 ¶ Then Peter, and the other Apostles answered, and saide, Wee

ought to obey God rather then men.

30 The God of our fathers raised vp Iesus, whom yee slew and hanged on a tree.

31 Him hath God exalted with his right hand *to bee* a Prince and a Sauiour, for to giue repentance to Israel, and forgiuenesse of sinnes.

32 And we are his witnesses of these things, and so is also the holy Ghost, whom God hath giuen to them that obey him.

33 ¶ When they heard that, they were cut to the heart, and tooke counsell to slay them.

34 Then stood there vp one in the Councill, a Pharisee, named Gamaliel, a doctour of Law, had in reputation among all the people, and commanded to put the Apostles forth a litle space,

35 And said vnto them, Yee men of Israel, take heed to your selues, what ye intend to doe as touching these men.

36 For before these dayes rose vp Theudas, boasting himselfe to be some body, to whom a number of men, about foure hundred, ioyned themselues: who was slaine, and all, as many as ||obeied him, were scattered, & brought to nought.

‖ Or, beleeued.

37 After this man rose vp Iudas of Galilee, in the dayes of the taxing, and drew away much people after him : hee also perished, and all, euen as many as obeyed him, were dispersed.

38 And now I say vnto you, refraine from these men, and let them alone : for if this counsell or this worke be of men, it will come to nought.

39 But if it be of God, ye cannot ouerthrow it, lest haply yee be found euen to fight against God.

40 And to him they agreed : and when they had called the Apostles, and beaten them, they commanded that they should not speake in the Name of Iesus, and let them goe.

41 ¶ And they departed from the presence of the Councill, reioycing that they were counted worthy to suffer shame for his Name.

42 And dayly in the Temple, and in euery house, they ceased not to teach and preach Iesus Christ.

CHAP. VI.

1 The Apostles desirous to haue the poore regarded for their bodily sustenance, as also carefull

carefull themselues to dispense the word of God, the foode of the soule : 3 Appoint the office of Deaconship to seuen chosen men. 5 Of whom, Steuen a man full of faith, & of the holy Ghost, is one. 12 Who is taken of those, whom he confounded in disputing, 13 and after falsely accused of blasphemie against the law and the temple.

Nd in those dayes when the number of the Disciples was multiplied, there arose a murmuring of the Grecians against the Hebrewes, because their widowes were neglected in the daily ministration.

2 Then the twelue called the multitude of the disciples vnto them, and said, It is not reason that we should leaue the word of God, and serue tables.

3 Wherefore brethren, looke ye out among you seuen men of honest report, full of the holy Ghost, and wisedome, whom we may appoint ouer this businesse.

4 But we will giue our selues continually to prayer, and to the ministerie of the word.

5 ¶ And the saying pleased the whole multitude : and they chose Steuen, a man full of faith and of the holy Ghost, and Philip, and Prochorus, and Nicanor, and Timon, and Permenas, and Nicolas a proselyte of Antioch.

6 Whom they set before the Apostles : and when they had praied, they layd their hands on them.

7 And the word of God encreased, and the number of the Disciples multiplied in Hierusalem greatly, and a great company of the Priests were obedient to the faith.

8 And Steuen full of faith and power, did great wonders and miracles among the people.

9 ¶ Then there arose certaine of the Synagogue, which is called *the Synagogue* of the Libertines, and Cyrenians, and Alexandrians, and of them of Cilicia, and of Asia, disputing with Steuen.

10 And they were not able to resist the wisedome and the spirit by which he spake.

11 Then they suborned men which said, We haue heard him speake blasphemous words against Moses, and against God.

12 And they stirred vp the people, and the Elders, and the Scribes, and

came vpon him, and caught him, and brought him to the Councell,

13 And set vp false witnesses, which said , This man ceaseth not to speake blasphemous words against this holy place, and the Law.

14 For we haue heard him say, that this Iesus of Nazareth shall destroy this place, & shall change the ‖ Customes which Moses deliuered vs.   ‖ Or, rites.

15 And all that sate in the Councell, looking stedfastly on him, saw his face as it had bene the face of an Angel.

CHAP. VII.

1 Steuen permitted to answere to the accusation of blasphemie, 2 Sheweth that Abraham worshipped God rightly, and how God chose the Fathers 20 before Moses was borne, and before the Tabernacle and Temple were built: 37 that Moses himselfe witnessed of Christ: 44 and that all outward Ceremonies were ordeined according to the heauenly paterne, to last but for a time : 51 reprehending their rebellion, and murthering of Christ, the Iust One, whome the Prophets foretold should come into the world. 54 Whereupon they stone him to death, who commendeth his soule to Iesus, and humbly prayeth for them.

Hen said the high Priest, Are these things so ?

2 And hee said, Men, brethren, and fathers, hearken : The God of glory appeared vnto our father Abraham, when he was in Mesopotamia, before he dwelt in Charran,

3 And said vnto him, * Get thee out of thy countrey, and from thy kinred, and come into the land which I shall shew thee.   * Gen. 12. 1

4 Then came he out of the land of the Chaldeans, and dwelt in Charran : and from thence, when his father was dead, he remoued him into this lande wherein ye now dwell.

5 And he gaue him none inheritance in it, no not *so much as* to set his foote on : yet he promised that he would giue it to him for a possession, and to his seed after him, when as yet he had no child

6 And God spake on this wise, that his seede should soiourne in a strange land, and that they should bring them into bondage , and intreate them euill foure hundreth yeeres.

7 And the nation to whom they shal bee in bondage , will I iudge , saide God :

God : And after that shall they come forth, and serue me in this place.

Gen. 17. 9

8 *And he gaue him the couenant of Circumcision : *and so *Abraham* begate Isaac, and circumcised him the eight day : *and Isaac *begate* Iacob, *and Iacob *begate* the twelue Patriarchs.

Gen. 21. 3

Gene. 25. 26.

Gen. 29. 31.

Gen. 37. 28.

9 *And the Patriarchs moued with enuie, sold Ioseph into Egypt : but God was with him,

10 And deliuered him out of all his afflictions, *and gaue him fauour and wisedome in the sight of Pharao king of Egypt : and he made him gouernour ouer Egypt and all his house.

Gen. 41. 37.

11 Now there came a dearth ouer all the land of Egypt, and Chanaan, and great affliction, and our fathers found no sustenance.

12 *But when Iacob heard that there was corne in Egypt, he sent out our fathers first.

Gen. 42. 1

13 *And at the second *time* Ioseph was made knowen to his brethren, and Iosephs kinred was made knowen vnto Pharao.

Gen. 45. 4

14 Then sent Ioseph, and called his father Iacob to him, and all his kinred, threescore and fifteene soules.

15 *So Iacob went downe into Egypt, *and died, he and our fathers,

Gen. 46. 5

Gen. 49. 33.

16 And were caried ouer into Sichem, and laid in the sepulchre that Abraham bought for a summe of money of the sonnes of Emor *the father* of Sichem.

17 But when the time of the promise drew nigh, which God had sworne to Abraham, the people grew and multiplied in Egypt,

18 Till another king arose, which knew not Ioseph.

19 The same dealt subtilly with our kinred, and euill intreated our fathers, so that they cast out their yong children, to the end they might not liue.

20 *In which time Moses was borne, and *was ||exceeding faire, and nourished vp in his fathers house three moneths :

Exo. 2. 2.

Heb. 11. 23.

|| Or, faire to God.

21 And when he was cast out, Pharaohs daughter tooke him vp, and nourished him for her owne sonne.

22 And Moses was learned in all the wisedome of the Egyptians, and was mightie in words and in deeds.

23 And when he was full forty yeres old, it came into his heart to visit his brethren the children of Israel.

24 *And seeing one of them suffer

Exod. 2. 11.

wrong, he defended him, and auenged him that was oppressed, and smote the Egyptian :

25 For he supposed his brethren would haue vnderstood, how that God by his hand would deliuer them, but they vnderstood not.

26 *And the next day he shewed himselfe vnto them as they stroue, and would haue set them at one againe, saying, Sirs, ye are brethren, Why doe yee wrong one to another ?

Exo. 2. 13

27 But hee that did his neighbour wrong, thrust him away, saying, Who made thee a ruler and a Iudge ouer vs?

28 Wilt thou kill me, as thou diddest the Egyptian yesterday ?

29 Then fled Moses at this saying, and was a stranger in the land of Madian, where he begate two sonnes.

30 *And when fourtie yeeres were expired, there appeared to him in the wildernes of mount Sina, an Angel of the Lord in a flame of fire in a bush.

Exod. 3.

31 When Moses saw it, he wondred at the sight : and as he drew neere to behold it, the voyce of the Lord came vnto him,

32 *Saying*, I am the God of thy fathers, the God of Abraham, and the God of Isaac, and the God of Iacob. Then Moses trembled, and durst not behold.

33 Then said the Lord to him, Put off thy shooes from thy feet : for the place where thou standest, is holy ground.

34 I haue seene, I haue seene the affliction of my people which is in Egypt, and I haue heard their groning, & am come downe to deliuer them : And now come, I will send thee into Egypt.

35 This Moses whom they refused, saying, Who made thee a ruler and a Iudge? the same did God send to bee a ruler and a deliuerer, by the handes of the Angel which appeared to him in the bush.

36 *He brought them out, after that he had shewed wonders and signes in the land of Egypt, and in the red Sea, *and in the wildernesse fortie yeeres.

Exod. 7. 9

Exo. 16.

37 ¶ This is that Moses which said vnto the children of Israel, *A Prophet shall the Lord your God raise vp vnto you of your brethren, ||like vnto mee : him shall ye heare.

Deut. 18. 15.

|| Or, as my selfe.

38 *This is he that was in y̎ Church in the wildernesse with the Angel, which spake to him in the mount Sina, and

Exo. 19.

and with our fathers : who receiued the liuely oracles, to giue vnto vs.

39 To whom our fathers would not obey, but thrust *him* from them, and in their hearts turned backe againe into Egypt,

*Exod. 32.
1.

40 *Saying vnto Aaron, Make vs gods to goe before vs. For as for this Moses, which brought vs out of the land of Egypt, we wote not what is become of him.

41 And they made a calfe in those dayes, and offered sacrifice vnto the idole, and reioyced in the workes of their owne hands.

42 Then God turned, and gaue them vp to worship the hoste of heauen,

*Amos 5.
25.

*as it is written in the booke of the Prophets, O ye house of Israel, haue ye offered to me slaine beasts, and sacrifices, by the space of fourty yeeres in the wildernesse?

43 Yea, ye tooke vp the Tabernacle of Moloch, and the starre of your God Remphan, figures which ye made, to worship them : and I will carie you away beyond Babylon.

44 Our fathers had the Tabernacle of witnesse in the wildernesse, as hee had appointed, speaking vnto Moses,

*Exod. 25.
40.

*that he should make it according to the fashion that he had seene.

45 Which also our fathers that came after, brought in with Iesus into the possession of the Gentiles, whom God draue out before the face of our fathers, vnto the dayes of Dauid,

46 Who found fauour before God, and desired to find a Tabernacle for the God of Iacob.

*1. Chro.
17. 12.

47 *But Solomon built him an house.

*Chap. 17.
24.

48 *Howbeit the most high dwelleth not in temples made with hands, as saith the Prophet,

49 Heauen is my throne, and earth is my footestoole : What house will ye build me, saith the Lord? Or what is the place of my rest?

50 Hath not my hand made all these things?

51 ¶ Ye stifnecked and vncircumcised in heart, and eares, ye doe alwayes resist the holy Ghost? as your fathers did, *so* doe ye.

52 Which of the Prophets haue not your fathers persecuted? And they haue slaine them which shewed before of the comming of the Iust one, of

whom ye haue bene now the betrayers and murderers :

53 Who haue receiued the Lawe by the disposition of Angels, and haue not kept it.

54 ¶ When they heard these things, they were cut to the heart, and they gnashed on him with their teeth.

55 But hee being full of the holy Ghost, looked vp stedfastly into heauen, and saw the glory of God, and Iesus standing on the right hand of God,

56 And said, Behold, I see the heauens opened, and the Sonne of man standing on the right hand of God.

57 Then they cried out with a loud voice, and stopped their eares, and ran vpon him with one accord,

58 And cast him out of the citie, and stoned him : and the witnesses layd downe their clothes at a yong mans feete, whose name was Saul.

59 And they stoned Steuen, calling *vpon God,* and saying, Lord Iesus receiue my spirit.

60 And he kneeled downe, and cried with a loud voice, Lord lay not this sinne to their charge. And when he had said this, he fell asleepe.

CHAP. VIII.

By occasion of the persecution in Hierusalem, the Church being planted in Samaria, 5 By Philip the Deacon who preached, did miracles, and baptized many, among the rest Simon the sorcerer a great seducer of the people : 14 Peter and Iohn come to confirme, and inlarge the Church : where by prayer, and imposition of hands giuing the holy Ghost, 18 When Simon would haue bought the like power of them, 20 Peter sharpely reprouing his hypocrisie, and couetousnesse, and exhorting him to repentance: together with Iohn preaching the word of the Lord, returne to Hierusalem. 26 But the Angel sendeth Philip to teach, & baptize the Ethiopian Eunuch.

 Nd Saul was consenting vnto his death. And at that time there was a great persecution against the Church which was at Hierusalem, and they were all scattered abroad through out the regions of Iudea, and Samaria, except the Apostles.

2 And deuout men carried Steuen *to his buriall,* and made great lamentation ouer him.

3 As for Saul, he made hauocke of the

the Church, entring into euery house, and hailing men and women, committed them to prison.

4 Therefore they that were scattered abroad, went euery where preaching the word.

5 Then Philip went downe to the citie of Samaria, and preached Christ vnto them.

6 And the people with one accord gaue heed vnto those things which Philip spake, hearing and seeing the miracles which he did.

7 For vncleane spirits, crying with lowd voyce, came out of many that were possessed with them : and many taken with palsies, and that were lame, were healed.

8 And there was great ioy in that citie.

9 But there was a certaine man called Simon, which before time in the same citie vsed sorcery, and bewitched the people of Samaria, giuing out that himselfe was some great one.

10 To whom they all gaue heed from the least to the greatest, saying, This man is the great power of God.

11 And to him they had regard, because that of long time he had bewitched them with sorceries.

12 But when they beleeued Philip preaching the things concerning the kingdome of God, and the Name of Iesus Christ, they were baptized, both men and women.

13 Then Simon himselfe beleeued also : and when hee was baptized, hee continued with Philip, and wondered, beholding the miracles and signes which were done.

14 Now when the Apostles which were at Hierusalem, heard that Samaria had receiued the word of God, they sent vnto them Peter and Iohn.

15 Who when they were come downe, praied for them that they might receiue the holy Ghost.

16 (For as yet hee was fallen vpon none of them : onely they were baptized in the Name of the Lord Iesus.)

17 Then layde they their hands on them, and they receiued the holy Ghost.

18 And when Simon saw that through laying on of the Apostles hands, the holy Ghost was giuen, hee offered them money,

19 Saying, Giue me also this power, that on whomsoeuer I lay handes,

hee may receiue the holy Ghost.

20 But Peter said vnto him, Thy money perish with thee, because thou hast thought that the gift of God may be purchased with money.

21 Thou hast neither part nor lot in this matter, for thy heart is not right in the sight of God.

22 Repent therefore of this thy wickednesse, and pray God, if perhaps the thought of thine heart may be forgiuen thee.

23 For I perceiue that thou art in the gall of bitternesse, and in the bond of iniquitie.

24 Then answered Simon, and said, Pray ye to the Lord for mee, that none of these things which ye haue spoken, come vpon me.

25 And they, when they had testified and preached the word of the Lord, returned to Hierusalem, and preached the Gospel in many villages of the Samaritanes.

26 And the Angel of the Lord spake vnto Philip, saying, Arise, and goe toward the South, vnto the way that goeth downe from Hierusalem vnto Gaza, which is desert.

27 And hee arose, and went : and behold, a man of Ethiopia, an Eunuch of great authority vnder Candace queene of the Ethiopians, who had the charge of all her treasure, and had come to Hierusalem for to worship,

28 Was returning, and sitting in his charet, read Esaias the Prophet.

29 Then the Spirit saide vnto Philip, Goe neere, and ioyne thy selfe to this charet.

30 And Philip ran thither to him, and heard him reade the Prophet Esaias, and said, Vnderstandest thou what thou readest ?

31 And hee said, How can I, except some man should guide me? And he desired Philip, that hee would come vp, and sit with him.

32 The place of the Scripture, which hee read, was this, *Hee was led as a sheepe to the slaughter, & like a Lambe dumbe before the shearer, so opened he not his mouth :   * Esay. 53. 7.

33 In his humiliation, his Iudgement was taken away : and who shall declare his generation? For his life is taken from the earth.

34 And the Eunuch answered Philip, and said, I pray thee, of whom speaketh

keth the Prophet this? of himſelfe, or of some other man?

35 Then Philip opened his mouth, and began at the same Scripture, and preached vnto him Iesus.

36 And as they went on their way, they came vnto a certaine water : and the Eunuch said, See, here is water, what doeth hinder me to be baptized?

37 And Philip said, If thou beleeuest with all thine heart, thou mayest. And he answered, and said, I beleeue that Iesus Christ is the Sonne of God.

38 And he commanded the charet to stand still : and they went downe both into the water, both Philip, and the Eunuch, and he baptized him.

39 And when they were come vp out of the water, the Spirit of the Lord caught away Philip, that the Eunuch saw him no more : and hee went on his way reioycing.

40 But Philip was found at Azotus : and passing thorow he preached in all the cities, till he came to Cesarea.

CHAP. IX.

1 Saul going towards Damascus, 4 is strikẽ downe to the earth, 10 is called to the Apostleship, 18 and is baptized by Ananias. 20 He preacheth Christ boldly. 23 The Iewes lay wait to kil him: 29 So doe the Grecians, but hee escapeth both. 31 The Church hauing rest, Peter healeth Æneas of the palsie, 36 and restoreth Tabitha to life.

Nd Saul yet breathing out threatnings & slaughter against the disciples of the Lord, went vnto the high Priest,

2 And desired of him letters to Damascus, to the Synagogues, that if hee found any of this way, whether they were men or women, hee might bring them bound vnto Hierusalem.

3 And as he iourneyed he came neere Damascus, and suddenly there shined round about him a light from heauen.

4 And he fel to the earth, and heard a voice saying vnto him, Saul, Saul, why persecutest thou me?

5 And he said, Who art thou Lord? And the Lord said, I am Iesus whom thou persecutest : It is hard for thee to kicke against the prickes.

6 And he trembling and astonished, said, Lord, what wilt thou haue mee to doe? And the Lord said vnto him, Arise, and goe into the citie, and it shall

be told thee what thou must doe.

7 And the men which iourneyed with him, stood speechlesse, hearing a voice, but seeing no man.

8 And Saul arose from the earth, and when his eyes were opened, he saw no man : but they led him by the hand, and brought him into Damascus.

9 And he was three dayes without sight, and neither did eate, nor drinke.

10 ¶ And there was a certaine disciple at Damascus, named Ananias, and to him said the Lord in a vision, Ananias. And he said, Behold, I *am here*, Lord.

11 And the Lord said vnto him, Arise, and goe into the street, which is called Straight, and inquire in the house of Iudas, for one called Saul of Tarsus : for behold, he prayeth,

12 And hath seene in a vision a man named Ananias, comming in, and putting his hand on him, that he might receiue his sight.

13 Then Ananias answered, Lord, I haue heard by many of this man, how much euill hee hath done to thy Saints at Hierusalem :

14 And here he hath authoritie from the chiefe Priests, to binde all that call on thy Name.

15 But the Lord said vnto him, Goe thy way : for hee is a chosen vessell vnto me, to beare my Name before the Gentiles, and Kings, and the children of Israel.

16 For I will shew him how great things hee must suffer for my Names sake.

17 And Ananias went his way, and entred into the house, and putting his hands on him, said, Brother Saul, the Lord (euen Iesus that appeared vnto thee in the way as thou camest) hath sent me, that thou mightest receiue thy sight, and be filled with the holy Ghost.

18 And immediatly there fell from his eyes as it had bene scales, and he receiued sight forthwith, and arose, and was baptized.

19 And when hee had receiued meat, he was strengthened. Then was Saul certaine dayes with the disciples which were at Damascus.

20 And straightway hee preached Christ in the Synagogues, that hee is the Sonne of God.

21 But all that heard him, were amazed, and said, Is not this he that destroyed

stroyed them which called on this Name in Hierusalem, and came hither for that intent that he might bring them bound vnto the chiefe Priests?

22 But Saul increased the more in strength, and confounded the Iewes which dwelt at Damascus, proouing that this is very Christ.

23 ¶ And after that many dayes were fulfilled, the Iewes tooke counsel to kill him.

* 2. Cor. 11 32.

24 * But their laying awaite was knowen of Saul: and they watched the gates day and night to kill him.

25 Then the disciples tooke him by night, and let him downe by the wall in a basket.

26 And when Saul was come to Hierusalem, he assayed to ioyne himselfe to the disciples, but they were all afraid of him, and beleeued not that he was a disciple.

27 But Barnabas tooke him, and brought him to the Apostles, and declared vnto them how hee had seene the Lord in the way, and that hee had spoken to him, and how hee had preached boldly at Damascus in the Name of Iesus.

28 And he was with them comming in, and going out at Hierusalem.

29 And he spake boldly in the Name of the Lord Iesus, and disputed against the Grecians: but they went about to slay him.

30 Which when the brethren knewe, they brought him downe to Cesarea, and sent him foorth to Tarsus.

31 Then had the Churches rest thorowout all Iudea, and Galilee, and Samaria, and were edified, and walking in the feare of the Lord, and in the comfort of the holy Ghost, were multiplied.

32 ¶ And it came to passe, as Peter passed thorowout all quarters, he came downe also to the Saints, which dwelt at Lydda.

33 And there he found a certaine man named Aeneas, which had kept his bed eight yeeres, and was sicke of the palsie.

34 And Peter said vnto him, Aeneas, Iesus Christ maketh thee whole: arise, and make thy bed. And he arose immediately.

35 And all that dwelt at Lydda, and Saron, saw him, and turned to the Lord.

36 ¶ Now there was at Ioppa a certain disciple, named Tabitha, which by interpretation is called Dorcas: This woman was full of good works, and almes deeds, which she did.

37 And it came to passe in those dayes that she was sicke, and died: whome when they had washed, they laid her in an vpper chamber.

38 And forasmuch as Lydda was nigh to Ioppa, and the disciples had heard that Peter was there, they sent vnto him two men, desiring him that he would not ||delay to come to them. || Or, be grie ued.

39 Then Peter arose and went with them: when he was come, they brought him into the vpper chamber: And all the widowes stood by him weeping, and shewing the coats and garments which Dorcas made, while shee was with them.

40 But Peter put them all forth, and kneeled downe, and prayed, and turning him to the body, said, Tabitha, arise. And she opened her eyes, and when she saw Peter, she sate vp.

41 And he gaue her his hand, and lift her vp: and when hee had called the Saints & widowes, presented her aliue.

42 And it was knowen thorowout all Ioppa, and many beleeued in the Lord.

43 And it came to passe, that he taried many dayes in Ioppa, with one Simon a Tanner.

CHAP. X.

1 Cornelius a deuout man, 5 being commaunded by an Angel, sendeth for Peter: 11 Who by a vision, 15. 20 is taught not to despise the Gentiles. 34 As he preacheth Christ to Cornelius and his companie, 44 The holy Ghost falleth on them, 48 and they are baptized.

 Here was a certaine man in Cesarea, called Cornelius, a Centurion of ŷ band called the Italian band,

2 A deuout man, and one that feared God with all his house, which gaue much almes to the people, and prayed to God alway.

3 He saw in a vision euidently, about the ninth houre of the day, an Angel of God comming in to him, and saying vnto him, Cornelius.

4 And when he looked on him, hee was afraid, and said, What is it, Lord? And he said vnto him, Thy praiers and thine almes are come vp for a memorial before God.

5 And

5 And now send men to Ioppa, and call for one Simon, whose sirname is Peter.

6 Hee lodgeth with one Simon a Tanner, whose house is by the Sea side; he shall tell thee what thou oughtest to doe.

7 And when the Angel which spake vnto Cornelius, was departed, he called two of his houshold seruants, and a deuout souldier of them that waited on him continually.

8 And when he had declared all these things vnto them, he sent them to Ioppa.

9 ¶ On the morrow as they went on their iourney, and drew nigh vnto the citie, Peter went vp vpon the house to pray, about the sixth houre.

10 And he became very hungry, and would haue eaten : But while they made ready, he fell into a traunce,

11 And saw heauen opened, and a certaine vessell descending vnto him, as it had beene a great sheete, knit at the foure corners, and let downe to the earth :

12 Wherein were all maner of foure footed beasts of the earth, and wilde beasts, and creeping things, and foules of the ayre.

13 And there came a voyce to him, Rise, Peter : kill, and eate.

14 But Peter said, Not so, Lord ; for I haue neuer eaten any thing that is common or vncleane.

15 And the voice spake vnto him againe the second time, What God hath cleansed, that call not thou common.

16 This was done thrise : & the vessel was receiued vp againe into heauen.

17 Now while Peter doubted in himselfe what this vision which he had seene, should meane : behold, the men which were sent from Cornelius, had made inquirie for Simons house, and stood before the gate,

18 And called, and asked whether Simon, which was sirnamed Peter, were lodged there.

19 ¶ While Peter thought on the vision, the spirit said vnto him, Behold, three men seeke thee.

20 Arise therefore, and get thee downe, and goe with them, doubting nothing : for I haue sent them.

21 Then Peter went downe to the men, which were sent vnto him from Cornelius, and said, Behold, I am hee,

whom ye seeke : what is the cause wherefore ye are come ?

22 And they saide, Cornelius the Centurion, a iust man, and one that feareth God, and of good report among all the nation of the Iewes, was warned from God by an holy Angel, to send for thee into his house, and to heare words of thee.

23 Then called he them in, and lodged them : And on the morrowe Peter went away with them, and certaine brethren from Ioppa accōpanied him.

24 And the morrow after they entred into Cesarea : and Cornelius waited for them, and had called together his kinsmen and neere friends.

25 And as Peter was comming in, Cornelius met him, and fell downe at his feete, and worshipped him.

26 But Peter tooke him vp, saying, Stand vp, I my selfe also am a man.

27 And as he talked with him, hee went in, and found many that were come together.

28 And he said vnto them, Ye know how that it is an vnlawfull thing for a man that is a Iewe, to keepe company or come vnto one of another nation : but God hath shewed me, that I should not call any man common or vncleane.

29 Therfore came I vnto you without gainesaying, as soone as I was sent for. I aske therefore, for what intent ye haue sent for me.

30 And Cornelius said, Foure daies agoe I was fasting vntill this houre, and at the ninth houre I prayed in my house, and behold, a man stood before me in bright clothing,

31 And said, Cornelius, thy prayer is heard, and thine almes are had in remembrance in the sight of God.

32 Send therfore to Ioppa, and call hither Simon, whose sirname is Peter; he is lodged in the house of one Simon a Tanner, by the Sea side, who when he cōmeth, shall speake vnto thee.

33 Immediately therefore I sent to thee, and thou hast well done, that thou art come. Now therefore are we all heere present before God, to heare all things that are cōmanded thee of God.

34 ¶ Then Peter opened his mouth, and said, *Of a trueth I perceiue ỹ God is no respecter of persons:

35 But in euery nation, he that feareth him, and worketh righteousnesse, is accepted with him.

36 The

* Deut. 10. 17. rom. 2. 11. 1. pet. 1. 17.

36 The word which God sent vnto the children of Israel, preaching peace by Iesus Christ (he is Lord of all.)

37 That word (I say) you knowe which was published thorowout all Iudea, and began from Galilee, after the baptisme which Iohn preached :

38 How God anointed Iesus of Nazareth with the holy Ghost, and with power, who went about doing good, and healing all that were oppressed of the deuill : for God was with him.

39 And we are witnesses of all things which hee did both in the land of the Iewes, and in Hierusalem, whom they slew and hanged on a tree.

40 Him God raised vp the third day, and shewed him openly,

41 Not to all the people, but vnto witnesses, chosen before of God, euen to vs who did eate and drinke with him after he rose from the dead.

42 And he commanded vs to preach vnto the people, and to testifie that it is he which was ordeined of God to be the Iudge of quicke and dead.

*Ier. 31. 34. mich. 7. 18.

43 *To him giue all the Prophets witnesse, that through his Name whosoeuer beleeueth in him, shall receiue remission of sinnes.

44 ¶ While Peter yet spake these words, the holy Ghost fell on all them which heard the word.

45 And they of the circumcision which beleeued, were astonished, as many as came with Peter, because that on the Gentiles also was powred out the gift of the holy Ghost.

46 For they heard them speake with tongues, and magnifie God. Then answered Peter,

47 Can any man forbid water, that these should not bee baptized, which haue receiued the holy Ghost, as well as wee?

48 And hee commanded them to be baptized in the Name of the Lord. Then prayed they him to tarie certaine dayes.

CHAP. XI.

1 Peter, being accused for going in to the Gentiles, 5 maketh his defence, 18 which is accepted. 19 The Gospel being spread into Phenice and Cyprus, and Antioch, Barnabas is sent to confirme them. 26 The disciples there are first called Christians. 27 They send reliefe to the brethren in Iudea in time of famine.

Nd the Apostles, and brethren that were in Iudea, heard that the Gentiles had also receiued the word of God.

2 And when Peter was come vp to Hierusalem, they that were of the circumcision contended with him,

3 Saying, Thou wentest in to men vncircumcised, & didst eate with them.

4 But Peter rehearsed the matter from the beginning, and expounded it by order vnto them, saying,

5 I was in the citie of Ioppa praying, and in a trance I saw a vision, a certaine vessell descend, as it had beene a great sheete, let downe from heauen by foure corners, and it came euen to me.

6 Vpon the which when I had fastened mine eyes, I considered, and saw foure footed beasts of the earth, and wild beasts, and creeping things, and foules of the aire.

7 And I heard a voyce, saying vnto me, Arise Peter, slay, and eate.

8 But I said, Not so, Lord : for nothing common or vncleane hath at any time entred into my mouth.

9 But the voyce answered me againe from heauen, What God hath cleansed, that call not thou common.

10 And this was done three times : and all were drawen vp againe into heauen.

11 And behold, immediately there were three men already come vnto the house where I was, sent from Cesarea vnto me.

12 And the spirit bad me goe with them, nothing doubting : Moreouer, these sixe brethren accompanied me, and we entred into the mans house :

13 And he shewed vs how hee had seene an Angell in his house, which stood and said vnto him, Send men to Ioppa, and call for Simon, whose sirname is Peter :

14 Who shall tell thee words, wherby thou, and all thy house shal be saued.

15 And as I began to speake, the holy Ghost fell on them, *as on vs at the beginning.   *Chap. 2. 4.

16 Then remembred I the word of the Lord, how that he said, *Iohn indeede baptized with water : but ye shall be baptized with the holy Ghost.   *Iohn 1. 26.

17 Forasmuch then as God gaue them the like gift as hee did vnto vs, who beleeued on the Lord Iesus Christ :

Christ : what was I that I could withstand God ?

18 When they heard these things,
they held their peace, and glorified God,
saying, Then hath God also to the Gentiles granted repentance vnto life.

* Chap. 8. 1.

19 ¶ * Now they which were scattered abroad vpon the persecution that
arose about Steuen, trauailed as farre
as Phenice, and Cyprus, and Antioch,
preaching the word to none, but vnto
the Iewes onely.

20 And some of them were men of
Cyprus, and Cyrene, which when they
were come to Antioch, spake vnto the
Grecians, preaching the Lord Iesus.

21 And the hand of the Lord was
with them : and a great number beleeued, and turned vnto the Lord.

22 ¶ Then tidings of these things
came vnto the eares of the Church,
which was in Hierusalem : and they
sent foorth Barnabas, that hee should
goe as farre as Antioch.

23 Who when hee came, and had
seene the grace of God, was glad, and
exhorted them all, that with purpose
of heart they would cleaue vnto the
Lord.

24 For he was a good man, and full
of the holy Ghost, and of faith : and
much people was added vnto the
Lord.

25 Then departed Barnabas to
Tarsus, for to seeke Saul.

26 And when he had found him, he
brought him vnto Antioch. And it came
to passe, that a whole yeere they assem-

‖ Or, in the Church.

bled themselues ‖ with the Church, and
taught much people, and the disciples
were called Christians first in Antioch.

27 ¶ And in these dayes, came Prophets from Hierusalem vnto Antioch.

28 And there stood vp one of them,
named Agabus, and signified by the
spirit, that there should be great dearth
throughout all the world : which came
to passe in the dayes of Claudius Cesar.

29 Then the disciples, euery man
according to his abilitie, determined to
send reliefe vnto the brethren which
dwelt in Iudea.

30 Which also they did, and sent it to
the Elders by the hands of Barnabas
and Saul.

CHAP. XII.

1 King Herode persecuteth the Christians, killeth Iames, and imprisoneth Peter ; whome
an Angel deliuereth vpon the prayers of the
Church. 20 In his pride taking to himselfe
the honour due to God, he is stricken by an
Angel, and dieth miserably. 24 After his
death, the word of God prospereth.

‖ Or, began.

Ow about that time, He-
rode the King ‖ stretched
foorth his hands, to vexe
certaine of the Church.
2 And he killed Iames
the brother of Iohn with the sword.

3 And because he saw it pleased the
Iewes, hee proceeded further, to take
Peter also. (Then were the dayes of
vnleauened bread.)

4 And when hee had apprehended
him, hee put him in prison, and deliuered him to foure quaternions of souldiers to keepe him, intending after
Easter to bring him forth to the people.

‖ Or, instant
and earnest
prayer was
made.

5 Peter therefore was kept in prison, but prayer was made ‖ without
ceasing of the Church vnto God for
him.

6 And when Herode would haue
brought him foorth, the same night Peter was sleeping betweene two Souldiers, bound with two chaines, and
the Keepers before the doore kept the
prison.

7 And beholde, the Angel of the
Lord came vpon him, and a light shined in the prison : and hee smote Peter
on the side, and raised him vp, saying,
Arise vp quickely. And his chaines fell
off from his hands.

8 And the Angel said vnto him,
Girde thy selfe, and binde on thy sandales : And so he did. And he sayth vnto him, Cast thy garment about thee,
and follow me.

9 And hee went out, and followed
him, and wist not that it was true
which was done by the Angel : but
thought he saw a vision.

10 When they were past the first and
the second ward, they came vnto the
yron gate that leadeth vnto the citie,
which opened to them of his owne accord : and they went out and passed on
thorow one streete, and foorthwith the
Angel departed from him.

11 And when Peter was come to
himselfe, hee said, Now I know of a
suretie, that the Lord hath sent his Angel, and hath deliuered mee out of the
hand of Herode, and from all the expectation of the people of the Iewes.

12 And

12 And when he had considered the thing, he came to the house of Mary the mother of Iohn whose sirname was Marke, where many were gathered together praying.

13 And as Peter knocked at the doore of the gate, a damosell came ‖to hearken, named Rhoda.

‖ *Or, to aske who was there.*

14 And when she knew Peters voice, she opened not the gate for gladnes, but ran in, and told how Peter stood before the gate.

15 And they said vnto her, Thou art mad. But she constantly affirmed that it was euen so. Then said they, It it his Angel.

16 But Peter continued knocking: and when they had opened *the doore*, and saw him, they were astonished.

17 But he beckening vnto them with the hand, to hold their peace, declared vnto them how the Lord had brought him out of the prison : And he said, Goe shew these things vnto Iames, and to the brethren. And he departed, and went into another place.

18 Now assoone as it was day, there was no smal stirre among the souldiers, what was become of Peter.

19 And when Herode had sought for him, and found him not, hee examined the keepers, and commanded that they should be put to death. And hee went downe from Iudea to Cesarea, & there abode.

20 ¶ And Herode ‖was highly displeased with them of Tyre and Sidon : but they came with one accord to him, and hauing made Blastus †the kings chamberlaine their friend, desired peace, because their countrey was nourished by the kings countrey.

‖ *Or, bare an hostile mind intending warre.*

† *Gr. that was ouer the kings bedchamber.*

21 And vpon a set day Herod arayed in royall apparell, sate vpon his throne, and made an Oration vnto them.

22 And the people gaue a shout, *saying*, It is the voice of a God, and not of a man.

23 And immediatly the Angel of the Lord smote him, because hee gaue not God the glory, and hee was eaten of wormes, and gaue vp the ghost.

24 ¶ But the word of God grewe, and multiplied.

25 And Barnabas and Saul returned from Hierusalem, when they had fulfilled their ‖ministerie, and tooke with them Iohn, whose syrname was Marke.

‖ *Or, charge, chap. 11. 29, 30.*

CHAP. XIII.

1 Paul and Barnabas are chosen to goe to the Gentiles. 7 Of Sergius Paulus, and Elymas the sorcerer. 14 Paul preacheth at Antioch, that Iesus is Christ. 42 The Gentiles beleeue : 45 but the Iewes gainesay and blaspheme : 46 whereupon they turne to the Gentiles. 48 As many as were ordained to life, beleeued.

Owe there were in the Church that was at Antioch, certaine Prophets and teachers : as Barnabas, and Simeon that was called Niger, and Lucius of Cyrene, and Manaen, which had bene ‖brought vp with Herod the Tetrarch, and Saul.

‖ *Or, Herods foster brother.*

2 As they ministred to the Lord, and fasted, the holy Ghost said, Separate me Barnabas and Saul, for the worke whereunto I haue called them.

3 And when they had fasted and prayed, and laid their handes on them, they sent them away.

4 ¶ So they being sent forth by the holy Ghost, departed vnto Seleucia, and from thence they sailed to Cyprus.

5 And when they were at Salamis, they preached the word of God in the Synagogues of the Iewes : and they had also Iohn to their Minister.

6 And when they had gone thorow the Ile vnto Paphos, they found a certaine sorcerer, a false prophet, a Iewe, whose name was Bariesus :

7 Which was with the deputie of the countrey Sergius Paulus, a prudent man : who called for Barnabas and Saul, and desired to heare the word of God.

8 But Elymas the sorcerer (for so is his name by interpretation) withstood them, seeking to turne away the deputy from the faith.

9 Then Saul (who also is *called* Paul) filled with the holy Ghost, set his eyes on him,

10 And said, O full of all subtilty and all mischiefe, thou child of the deuil, thou enemie of all righteousnesse, wilt thou not cease to peruert the right wayes of the Lord ?

11 And now behold, the hand of the Lord is vpon thee, & thou shalt be blind, not seeing the Sunne for a season. And immediatly there fell on him a mist and a darkenes, and he went about, seeking some to lead him by the hand.

12 Then

12 Then the Deputie when he ſawe what was done, beleeued, being aſtoniſhed at the doctrine of the Lord.

13 Now when Paul and his company looſed from Paphos, they came to Perga in Pamphylia : and Iohn departing from them, returned to Hieruſalem.

14 ¶ But when they departed from Perga, they came to Antioch in Piſidia, and went into the ſynagogue on the Sabbath day, and ſate downe.

15 And after the reading of the Law and the Prophets, the rulers of the ſynagogue ſent vnto them, ſaying, Ye men and brethren, if ye haue any word of exhortation for the people, ſay on.

16 Then Paul ſtood vp, and beckning with his hand, ſaid, Men of Iſrael, and ye that feare God, giue audience.

17 The God of this people of Iſrael choſe our fathers, and exalted the people *when they dwelt as ſtrangers in the land of Egypt, *and with an high arme brought he them out of it.

18 *And about the time of fourtie yeeres †ſuffered he their maners in the wilderneſſe.

19 And when he had deſtroyed ſeuen nations in the land of Chanaan, *he diuided their land to them by lot:

20 And after that *he gaue vnto them iudges, about the ſpace of foure hundred and fifty yeeres vntill Samuel the Prophet.

21 And afterward they deſired a King, *and God gaue vnto them Saul the ſonne of Cis, a man of the tribe of Beniamin, by the ſpace of fourty yeres.

22 And when he had remoued him, *hee raiſed vp vnto them Dauid to be their king, to whom alſo he gaue teſtimonie, and ſaid, *I haue found Dauid the ſonne of Ieſſe, a man after mine own heart, which ſhal fulfill all my wil.

23 *Of this mans ſeed hath God, according to his promiſe, raiſed vnto Iſrael a Sauiour, Ieſus:

24 *When Iohn had firſt preached before his comming, the baptiſme of repentance to all the people of Iſrael.

25 And as Iohn fulfilled his courſe, he ſaid, *Whom thinke ye that I am? I am not he. But behold, there commeth one after me, whoſe ſhooes of his feete I am not worthy to looſe.

26 Men and brethren, children of the ſtocke of Abraham, and whoſoeuer among you feareth God, to you is the word of this ſaluation ſent.

27 For they that dwell at Hieruſalem, & their rulers, becauſe they knew him not, nor yet the voices of the Prophets which are read euery Sabbath day, they haue fulfilled them in condemning him.

28 *And though they found no cauſe of death in him, yet deſired they Pilate that he ſhould be ſlaine.

29 And when they had fulfilled all that was written of him, they tooke him downe from the tree, and layd him in a Sepulchre.

30 *But God raiſed him frō the dead:

31 And he was ſeene many dayes of them which came vp with him from Galilee to Hieruſalem, who are his witneſſes vnto the people.

32 And we declare vnto you glad tidings, how that the promiſe which was made vnto the fathers,

33 God hath fulfilled the ſame vnto vs their children, in that he hath raiſed vp Ieſus againe, as it is alſo written in the *ſecond Pſalme : Thou art my Sonne, this day haue I begotten thee.

34 And as concerning that he raiſed him vp from the dead, now no more to returne to corruption, he ſaid on this wiſe, *I will giue you the ſure †mercies of Dauid.

35 Wherfore he ſaith alſo in another Pſalme, *Thou ſhalt not ſuffer thine holy one to ſee corruption.

36 For Dauid after he had ſerued his ‖owne generation by the will of God, *fell on ſleepe, and was laide vnto his fathers, and ſaw corruption :

37 But hee whom God raiſed againe, ſaw no corruption.

38 ¶ Be it knowen vnto you therefore, men and brethren, that through this man is preached vnto you the forgiueneſſe of ſinnes.

39 And by him all ȳ beleeue, are iuſtified from all things, from which ye could not be iuſtified by the Law of Moſes.

40 Beware therefore, leaſt that come vpon you which is ſpoken of *in the Prophets,

41 Behold, yee deſpiſers, and wonder, and periſh : for I worke a worke in your dayes, a worke which you ſhall in no wiſe beleeue, though a man declare it vnto you.

42 And when the Iewes were gone out of the Synagogue, the Gentiles beſought that theſe words might be

* Exod. 1. 1.
* Exod. 13. 14.

* Exod. 13. 16.
‡ Grīgreoποφόenσιs, perhaps, for ετροφοφόρησεν, as a nurſe beareth or feedeth her childe, Deut. 1. 31. 2. macc 7. 27. according to the Sept. and ſo Chryſoſt.
* Ioſh. 14. 1
* Iudg. 3. 9.

* 1. Sam. 8. 5.

* 1. Sam. 16. 13.

* Pſal. 89. 21.

* Eſai. 11. 1.

* Mat. 3. 1.

* Iohn 1. 20

* Mat. 27. 22.

* Mat. 28. 6

* Pſal. 2. 7. heb. 1. 5.

* Eſai. 55. 3. † Gre. τὰ ὅσια, holy or iuſt things, which word the Sept. both in the place of Eſai 55. 3. and in many others, vſe for that which is inthe Hebrew, Mercies.
* Pſal. 16. 11.
‖ Or, after he had in his owne age ſerued the will of God.
* 1. Kings 2. 10.

* Habac. 1. 5

1 Or, in the weeke betweene, or in the Sabbath betweene.

be preached to them ‖ the next Sabbath.

43 Now when the Congregation was broken vp, many of the Iewes, and religious Proselytes followed Paul and Barnabas, who speaking to them, perswaded them to continue in the grace of God.

44 ¶ And the next Sabbath day came almost the whole citie together to heare the word of God.

45 But when the Iewes saw the multitudes, they were filled with enuie, and spake against those things which were spoken by Paul, contradicting, and blaspheming.

46 Then Paul and Barnabas waxed bold, and said, It was necessary that the word of God should first haue bene spoken to you: but seeing yee put it from you, and iudge your selues vnworthy of euerlasting life, loe, we turne to the Gentiles.

* Esay 49. 6.

47 For so hath the Lord cōmanded vs, saying, * I haue set thee to bee a light of the Gentiles, that thou shouldest be for saluation vnto the ends of the earth.

48 And when the Gentiles heard this, they were glad, and glorified the word of the Lord : and as many as were ordeined to eternall life, beleeued.

49 And the word of the Lord was published throughout all the region.

50 But the Iewes stirred vp the deuout and honourable women, and the chiefe men of the citie, and raised persecution against Paul and Barnabas, and expelled them out of their coasts.

* Matth. 10. 14.

51 *But they shooke off the dust of their feete against them, and came vnto Iconium.

52 And the disciples were filled with ioy, and with the holy Ghost.

CHAP. XIIII.

1 Paul and Barnabas are persecuted from Iconium. 7 At Lystra Paul healeth a creeple, wherupon they are reputed as gods. 19 Paul is stoned. 21 They passe through diuers Churches, confirming the disciples in faith and patience. 26 Returning to Antioch, they report what God had done with them.

Nd it came to passe in Iconium, that they went both together into the synagogue of the Iewes, and so spake, that a great multitude both of the Iewes, and also of the Greekes, beleeued.

2 But the vnbeleeuing Iewes stirred vp the Gentiles, and made their mindes euill affected against the brethren.

3 Long time therefore abode they speaking boldly in the Lord, which gaue testimonie vnto the word of his grace, and granted signes and wonders to be done by their hands.

4 But the multitude of the city was diuided : and part held with the Iewes, and part with the Apostles.

5 And when there was an assault made both of the Gentiles, and also of the Iewes, with their rulers, to vse them despitefully, and to stone them,

6 They were ware of it, and fled vnto Lystra and Derbe, cities of Lycaonia, and vnto the region that lyeth round about.

7 And there they preached the Gospell.

8 ¶ And there sate a certaine man at Lystra, impotent in his feete, being a creeple from his mothers wombe, who neuer had walked.

9 The same heard Paul speake : who stedfastly beholding him, and perceiuing that he had faith to be healed,

10 Said with a lowd voice, Stand vpright on thy feete ; And he leaped and walked.

11 And when the people saw what Paul had done, they lift vp their voyces, saying in the speech of Lycaonia, The gods are come downe to vs in the likenesse of men.

12 And they called Barnabas Iupiter, and Paul Mercurius, because hee was the chiefe speaker.

13 Then the priest of Iupiter, which was before their city, brought oxen, and garlands vnto the gates, and would haue done sacrifice with the people.

14 Which when the Apostles, Barnabas and Paul heard of, they rent their clothes, and ranne in among the people, crying out,

15 And saying, Sirs, Why doe yee these things? Wee also are men of like passions with you, and preach vnto you, that ye should turne from these vanities, vnto the liuing God, *which made heauen and earth, and the sea, and all things that are therein.

* Gen. 1. 1. psal. 146. 6. reuel. 14. 7.

16 *Who in times past, suffred all nations to walke in their owne wayes.

* Psal. 81. 13.

17 Neuerthelesse, he left not himselfe without witnesse, in that he did good, and gaue vs raine from heauen, and fruit-

fruitful ſeaſons, filling our hearts with food and gladneſſe.

18 And with theſe ſayings ſcarſe reſtrained they the people, that they had not done ſacrifice vnto them.

19 ¶ And there came thither certaine Iewes from Antioch and Iconium, who perſwaded the people, *and hauing ſtoned Paul, drew him out of the citie, ſuppoſing he had beene dead.

*2. Cor. 11. 25.

20 Howbeit, as the diſciples ſtood round about him, he roſe vp, and came into the citie, and the next day he departed with Barnabas to Derbe.

21 And when they had preached the Goſpel to that city, and had taught many, they returned againe to Lyſtra, and to Iconium, and Antioch,

22 Confirming the ſoules of the diſciples, and exhorting them to continue in the faith, aud that we muſt through much tribulation enter into the kingdome of God.

23 And when they had ordeined them Elders in euery Church, and had prayed with faſting, they commended them to the Lord, on whom they beleeued.

24 And after they had paſſed throughout Piſidia, they came to Pamphylia.

25 And when they had preached the word in Perga, they went downe into Attalia,

26 And thence ſailed to Antioch, from whence they had been recommended to the grace of God, for the worke which they fulfilled.

27 And when they were come, and had gathered the Church together, they rehearſed all that God had done with them, and how he had opened the doore of faith vnto the Gentiles.

28 And there they abode long time with the diſciples.

CHAP. XV.

Great diſſention ariſeth touching Circumciſion. 6 The Apoſtles conſult about it, 22 and ſend their determination by letters to the Churches. 36 Paul and Barnabas thinking to viſit the brethren together, fall at ſtrife, and depart aſunder.

*Galat. 5. 1.

ANd certaine men which came downe from Iudea, taught the brethren, _and ſaid,_*Except ye be circumciſed after the manner of Moſes, ye cannot be ſaued.

2 When therefore Paul and Barnabas had no ſmall diſſention and diſpu-

tation with them, they determined that Paul and Barnabas, and certeine other of them, ſhould goe vp to Hieruſalem vnto the Apoſtles and Elders about this queſtion.

3 And being brought on their way by the Church, they paſſed thorow Phenice and Samaria, declaring the conuerſion of the Gentiles: and they cauſed great ioy vnto all the brethren.

4 And when they were come to Hieruſalem, they were receiued of the Church, and of the Apoſtles, and Elders, and they declared all things that God had done with them.

5 But there roſe vp certaine of the ſect of the Phariſees which beleeued, ſaying, that it was needfull to circumciſe them, and to cōmand them to keepe the Law of Moſes.

6 ¶ And the Apoſtles & Elders came together for to conſider of this matter.

7 And when there had bene much diſputing, Peter roſe vp, and ſaid vnto them, * Men and brethren, ye know how that a good while agoe, God made choiſe among vs, that the Gentiles by my mouth ſhould heare the worde of the Goſpel, and beleeue.

*Chap. 10. 20. and 11. 13.

8 And God which knoweth the hearts, bare them witnes, giuing them the holy Ghoſt, euen as he did vnto vs,

9 *And put no difference between vs & them, purifying their hearts by faith.

*Chap. 10. 43. 1. cor. 1. 2.

10 Now therfore why tempt ye God, *to put a yoke vpon the necke of the diſciples, which neither our fathers nor we were able to beare?

*Mat. 23. 4.

11 But we beleeue that through the grace of the Lord Ieſus Chriſt, we ſhal be ſaued euen as they.

12 ¶ Then all the multitude kept ſilence, and gaue audience to Barnabas and Paul, declaring what miracles and wonders God had wrought among the Gentiles by them.

13 ¶ And after they had helde their peace, Iames anſwered, ſaying, Men and brethren, hearken vnto me.

14 Simeon hath declared how God at the firſt did viſite the Gentiles to take out of them a people for his Name.

15 And to this agree the words of the Prophets, as it is written,

16 * After this I will returne, and wil build againe the Tabernacle of Dauid, which is fallen downe: and I will build againe the ruines thereof, and I will ſet it vp:

*Amos 9. 11

17 That

17 That the residue of men might seeke after the Lord, and all the Gentiles, vpon whom my Name is called, sayth the Lord, who doeth all these things.

18 Knowen vnto God are all his workes frō the beginning of the world.

19 Wherefore my sentence is, that we trouble not them, which from among the Gentiles are turned to God:

20 But that wee write vnto them, that they abstaine from pollutions of Idoles, and from fornication, and from things strangled, and from blood.

21 For Moses of olde time hath in euery citie them that preach him, being read in the Synagogues euery Sabbath day.

22 Then pleased it the Apostles and Elders with the whole Church, to send chosen men of their owne company to Antioch, with Paul and Barnabas: *namely*, Iudas surnamed Barsabas, & Silas, chiefe men among the brethren,

23 And wrote letters by them after this maner, The Apostles and Elders, and brethren, send greeting vnto the brethren, which are of the Gentiles in Antioch, and Syria, and Cilicia.

24 Forasmuch as we haue heard, that certaine which went out from vs, haue troubled you with words, subuerting your soules, saying, Ye must be circumcised, and keepe the Law, to whom we gaue no such commandement:

25 It seemed good vnto vs, being assembled with one accord, to send chosen men vnto you, with our beloued Barnabas and Paul,

26 Men that haue hazarded their liues for the Name of our Lord Iesus Christ.

27 Wee haue sent therefore Iudas and Silas, who shall also tell you the same things by mouth.

28 For it seemed good to the holy Ghost, and to vs, to lay vpon you no greater burden then these necessarie things;

29 That ye abstaine from meates offered to idoles, and from blood, & from things strangled, and from fornication: from which if ye keepe your selues, yee shall doe well. Fare ye well.

30 So when they were dismissed, they came to Antioch: and when they had gathered the multitude together, they deliuered the Epistle.

31 Which when they had read, they reioyced for the ||consolation.

|| Or, exhortation.

32 And Iudas and Silas, being Prophets also themselues, exhorted the brethren with many words, and confirmed them:

33 And after they had taried there a space, they were let goe in peace from the breehren vnto the Apostles.

34 Notwithstanding it pleased Silas to abide there still.

35 Paul also and Barnabas continued in Antioch, teaching and preaching the word of the Lord, with many others also.

36 ¶ And some dayes after, Paul said vnto Barnabas, Let vs go againe and visit our brethren, in euery city where we haue preached the word of the Lord, *and see* how they doe.

37 And Barnabas determined to take with them Iohn, whose surname was Marke.

38 But Paul thought not good to take him with them; who departed from them from Pamphylia, and went not with them to the worke.

39 And the contention was so sharpe betweene them, that they departed asunder one from the other: & so Barnabas tooke Marke, & sailed vnto Cyprus.

40 And Paul chose Silas, and departed, being recommended by the brethren vnto the grace of God.

41 And he went thorow Syria and Cilicia, confirming the Churches.

CHAP. XVI.

1 Paul hauing circumcised Timothy, 7 and being called by the Spirit from one countrey to another, 14 conuerteth Lydia, 16 casteth out a spirit of diuination. 19 For which cause he and Silas are whipped and imprisoned. 26 The prison doores are opened. 31 The Iayler is conuerted, 37 and they are deliuered.

Hen came he to Derbe, and Lystra: and behold, a certaine disciple was there, *named Timotheus, the son of a certaine woman which was a Iewesse, and beleeued: but his father was a Greeke:

*Rom. 16. 21.

2 Which was well reported of by the brethren that were at Lystra and Iconium.

3 Him would Paul haue to go forth with him, and tooke, and circumcised him, because of the Iewes which were in those quarters: for they knew all, that his father was a Greeke.

4 And

4 And as they went through the cities, they deliuered them the decrees for to keepe, * that were ordeined of the Apostles and Elders, which were at Hierusalem.

* Chap. 15. 28.

5 And so were the Churches established in the faith, and increased in number dayly.

6 Now when they had gone thorowout Phrygia, and the region of Galatia, and were forbidden of the holy Ghost to preach the word in Asia,

7 After they were come to Mysia, they assayed to goe into Bithynia : but the Spirit suffered them not.

8 And they passing by Mysia, came downe to Troas.

9 And a vision appeared to Paul in the night : There stood a man of Macedonia, and prayed him, saying, Come ouer into Macedonia, and helpe vs.

10 And after he had seene the vision, immediatly we endeuoured to goe into Macedonia, assuredly gathering, that the Lord had called vs for to preach the Gospel vnto them.

11 Therfore loosing from Troas, we came with a straight course to Samothracia, and the next day to Neapolis :

12 And from thence to Philippi, which is ‖ the chiefe citie of that part of Macedonia, and a Colonie : and we were in that citie abiding certaine dayes.

‖ Or, the first.

13 And on the Sabboth we went out of the citie by a riuer side, where prayer was wont to be made, & we sate downe, and spake vnto the women which resorted thither.

14 ¶ And a certaine woman named Lydia, a seller of purple, of the citie of Thyatira, which worshipped God, heard vs : whose heart the Lord opened, that she attended vnto the things which were spoken of Paul.

15 And when she was baptized, and her houshold, she besought vs, saying, If ye haue iudged me to bee faithfull to the Lord, come into my house, and abide there. And she constrained vs.

16 ¶ And it came to passe, as we went to prayer, a certaine Damosell possessed with a spirit of ‖ diuination, met vs : which brought her masters much gaine by soothsaying.

‖ Or, of Python.

17 The same followed Paul and vs, and cried, saying, These men are the seruants of the most hie God, which shew vnto vs the way of saluation.

18 And this did she many dayes : but Paul being grieued, turned and said to the spirit, I command thee in the Name of Iesus Christ, to come out of her. And he came out the same houre.

19 ¶ And when her Masters saw that the hope of their gaines was gone, they caught Paul and Silas, and drew them into the ‖ market place, vnto the rulers,

‖ Or, court.

20 And brought them to the Magistrates, saying, These men being Iewes, do exceedingly trouble our city,

21 And teach customes which are not lawfull for vs to receiue, neither to obserue, being Romanes.

22 And the multitude rose vp together against them, and the Magistrates rent off their clothes, * and commanded to beate them.

* 2. Cor. 11 25. 1. thes. 2. 2.

23 And when they had layed many stripes vpon them, they cast them into prison, charging the Iaylour to keepe them safely.

24 Who hauing receiued such a charge, thrust them into the inner prison, & made their feet fast in the stockes.

25 ¶ And at midnight, Paul and Silas prayed, and sang praises vnto God : and the prisoners heard them.

26 And suddenly there was a great earthquake, so that the foundations of the prison were shaken : and immediatly all the doores were opened, and euery ones bands were loosed.

27 And the keeper of the prison awaking out of his sleepe, and seeing the prison doores open, he drew out his sword, and would haue killed himselfe, supposing that the prisoners had beene fled.

28 But Paul cried with a loud voice, saying, Doe thy selfe no harme, for we are all heere.

29 Then hee called for a light, and sprang in, and came trembling, and fell downe before Paul and Silas,

30 And brought them out, and said, Sirs, what must I doe to be saued ?

31 And they saide, Beleeue on the Lord Iesus Christ, and thou shalt be saued, and thy house.

32 And they spake vnto him the word of the Lord, and to all that were in his house.

33 And hee tooke them the same houre of the night, and washed their stripes, and was baptized, hee and all his, straightway.

34 And when he had brought them into

into his house, hee set meat before them, and reioyced, beleeuing in God with all his house.

35 And when it was day, the Magistrates sent the Sergeants, saying, Let those men goe.

36 And the keeper of the prison told this saying to Paul, The Magistrates haue sent to let you goe : Now therefore depart, and goe in peace.

37 But Paul said vnto them, They haue beaten vs openly vncondemned, being Romanes, and haue cast vs into prison, and now doe they thrust vs out priuily? Nay verily, but let them come themselues, and fetch vs out.

38 And the Sergeants tolde these words vnto the Magistrates : and they feared when they heard that they were Romanes.

39 And they came and besought them, and brought them out, and desired them to depart out of the citie.

*Chap. 16. 14.

40 And they went out of the prison, *and entred into *the house* of Lydia, and when they had seene the brethren, they comforted them, and departed.

CHAP. XVII.

1 Paul preacheth at Thessalonica, 4 where some beleeue, and others persecute him. 10 Hee is sent to Berea, and preacheth there. 13 Being persecuted at Thessalonica, 15 hee commeth to Athens, and disputeth, and preacheth the liuing God to them vnknowen, 34 whereby many are conuerted vnto Christ.

Ow when they had passed thorow Amphipolis, and Apollonia, they came to Thessalonica, where was a synagogue of the Iewes.

2 And Paul, as his maner was, went in vnto them, and three Sabbath dayes reasoned with them out of the Scriptures,

3 Opening and alleadging, that Christ must needs haue suffered and risen againe from the dead : and that this Iesus whom I preach vnto you, is Christ.

4 And some of them beleeued, and consorted with Paul and Silas : and of the deuout Greekes a great multitude, and of the chiefe women not a few.

5 ¶ But the Iewes which beleeued not, mooued with enuie, tooke vnto them certaine lewd fellowes of the baser sort, and gathered a company, and

set all the citie on an vprore, and assaulted the house of Iason, and sought to bring them out to the people.

6 And when they found them not, they drew Iason, and certaine brethren vnto the rulers of the citie, crying, These that haue turned the world vpside downe, are come hither also,

7 Whom Iason hath receiued : and these all doe contrary to the decrees of Cesar, saying, that there is another King, *one* Iesus.

8 And they troubled the people, and the rulers of the citie, when they heard these things.

9 And when they had taken securitie of Iason, and of the other, they let them goe.

10 ¶ And the brethren immediatly sent away Paul and Silas by night vnto Berea : who comming thither, went into the Synagogue of the Iewes.

11 These were more noble then those in Thessalonica, in that they receiued the word with all readinesse of minde, and searched the Scriptures dayly, whether those things were so.

12 Therefore many of them beleeued : also of honourable women which were Greekes, and of men not a few.

13 But when the Iewes of Thessalonica had knowledge that the word of God was preached of Paul at Berea, they came thither also, and stirred vp the people.

14 And then immediatly the brethren sent away Paul, to goe as it were to the sea : but Silas and Timotheus abode there still.

15 And they that conducted Paul, brought him vnto Athens, and receiuing a commaundement vnto Silas and Timotheus, for to come to him with all speed, they departed.

16 ¶ Now while Paul waited for them at Athens, his spirit was stirred in him, when hee saw the city ‖wholy giuen to idolatrie.

‖Or, full of idoles.

17 Therefore disputed he in the Synagogue with the Iewes, and with the deuout persons, and in the market dayly with them that met with him.

18 Then certaine Philosophers of the Epicureans and of the Stoikes, encountred him : and some said, What will this ‖babbler say? Other some, He seemeth to be a setter foorth of strange gods : because hee preached vnto them Iesus, and the resurrection.

‖Or, base fellow.

19 And

19 And they tooke him, and brought him vnto ‖ Areopagus, saying, May we know what this new doctrine, whereof thou speakest, is?

‖ Or, Mars-hill : It was the highest court in Athens.

20 For thou bringest certaine strange things to our eares : we would know therefore what these things meane.

21 (For all the Athenians and strangers which were there, spent their time in nothing else, but either to tell or to heare some new thing.)

22 ¶ Then Paul stood in the mids of ‖ Mars-hill, and said, Yee men of Athens, I perceiue that in all things yee are too superstitious.

‖ Or, court of the Areopagites.

23 For as I passed by, and beheld your ‖ deuotions, I found an Altar with this inscription, *TO THE VNKNOWEN GOD.* Whom therefore yee ignorantly worship, him declare I vnto you.

‖ Or, gods that you worship, 2. Thess. 2. 4.

24 * God that made the world, and all things therein, seeing that hee is Lord of heauen and earth, dwelleth not in Temples made with hands :

* Cha. 7. 48.

25 Neither is worshipped with mens hands * as though he needed any thing, seeing hee giueth to all, life and breath, and all things,

* Psal. 50. 8.

26 And hath made of one blood all nations of men, for to dwell on all the face of the earth, and hath determined the times before appointed, and the bounds of their habitation :

27 That they should seeke the Lord, if haply they might feele after him and finde him, though he be not farre from euery one of vs.

28 For in him we liue, and mooue, and haue our being, as certaine also of your owne Poets haue said, For we are also his offspring.

29 Forasmuch then as wee are the offspring of God, * wee ought not to thinke that the Godhead is like vnto golde, or siluer, or stone grauen by arte, and mans deuice.

* Esai 40. 18

30 And the times of this ignorance God winked at, but now commandeth all men euery where to repent :

31 Because hee hath appointed a day in the which he will iudge the world in righteousnesse, by that man whom hee hath ordeined, whereof he ‖ hath giuen assurance vnto all men, in that he hath raised him from the dead.

‖ Or, offered faith.

32 ¶ And when they heard of the resurrection of the dead, some mocked : and others said, Wee will heare thee againe of this matter.

33 So Paul departed from among them.

34 Howbeit, certaine men claue vnto him, and beleeued : among the which was Dionysius the Areopagite, and a woman named Damaris, and others with them.

CHAP. XVIII.

3 Paul laboureth with his hands, and preacheth at Corinth to the Gentiles. 9 The Lord encourageth him in a vision. 12 Hee is accused before Gallio the deputie, but is dismissed. 18 Afterwards passing from citie to citie, he strengtheneth the disciples. 24 Apollos, being more perfectly instructed by Aquila and Priscilla, 28 preacheth Christ with great efficacie.

Fter these things, Paul departed from Athens, and came to Corinth,

2 And found a certaine Iewe named * Aquila, borne in Pontus, lately come from Italy, with his wife Priscilla, (because that Claudius had commanded all Iewes to depart from Rome) and came vnto them.

* Rom. 16. 3

3 And because hee was of the same craft, he abode with them, and wrought (for by their occupation they were tentmakers.)

4 And hee reasoned in the Synagogue euery Sabbath, and perswaded the Iewes, and the Greekes.

5 And when Silas and Timotheus were come from Macedonia, Paul was pressed in spirit, and testified to the Iewes, that Iesus was Christ.

6 And when they opposed themselues, and blasphemed, * he shooke his raiment, and said vnto them, Your blood be vpon your owne heads, I am cleane : from henceforth I will goe vnto the Gentiles.

* Mat. 10. 14.

7 ¶ And hee departed thence, and entred into a certaine mans house, named Iustus, one that worshipped God, whose house ioyned hard to the Synagogue.

8 * And Crispus, the chiefe ruler of the Synagogue, beleeued on the Lord, with all his house : and many of the Corinthians, hearing, beleeued, and were baptized.

* 1. Cor. 1. 14.

9 Then spake the Lord to Paul in the night by a vision, Be not afraid, but speake, and holde not thy peace:

10 For

10 For I am with thee, and no man shal set on thee, to hurt thee : for I haue much people in this city.

† Gr. sate there.

11 And hee † continued there a yeere and sixe monethes, teaching the word of God among them.

12 ¶ And when Gallio was the Deputie of Achaia, the Iewes made insurrection with one accord against Paul, and brought him to the iudgement seat,

13 Saying, This fellow perswadeth men to worship God contrary to the Law.

14 And when Paul was now about to open his mouth, Gallio said vnto the Iewes, If it were a matter of wrong, or wicked lewdnesse, O yee Iewes, reason would that I should beare with you.

15 But if it be a question of words, and names, and of your law, looke ye to it : for I wil be no iudge of such matters.

16 And he draue them from the iudgment seate.

17 Then all the Greekes tooke Sosthenes the chiefe ruler of the Synagogue, and beat him before the Iudgement seat : and Gallio cared for none of those things.

18 ¶ And Paul after this taried there yet a good while, and then tooke his leaue of the brethren, and sailed thence into Syria, and with him Priscilla and Aquila: hauing shorne his head in Cenchrea : for he had a vow.

19 And he came to Ephesus, and left them there : but he himselfe entred into the Synagogue, and reasoned with the Iewes.

20 When they desired him to tary longer time with them, hee consented not :

21 But bade them farewell, saying, I must by all meanes keepe this feast that commeth, in Hierusalem ; but I will returne againe vnto you, *if God will : and he sailed from Ephesus.

* 1. Cor. 4. 19. iam. 4. 15.

22 And when he had landed at Cesarea, and gone vp, and saluted the Church, he went downe to Antioch.

23 And after he had spent some time there, hee departed, and went ouer all the countrey of Galatia and Phrygia in order, strengthening all the disciples.

24 ¶ *And a certaine Iew, named Apollos, borne at Alexandria, an eloquent man, and mightie in the Scriptures, came to Ephesus.

* 1. Cor. 1. 12.

25 This man was instructed in the way of the Lord, and being feruent in the spirit, he spake and taught diligently the things of the Lord, knowing onely the baptisme of Iohn.

26 And he began to speake boldly in the Synagogue : whom when Aquila and Priscilla had heard, they tooke him vnto them, and expounded vnto him the way of God more perfectly.

27 And when hee was disposed to passe into Achaia, the brethren wrote, exhorting the disciples to receiue him : who, when he was come, helped them much which had beleeued throgh grace.

28 For hee mightily conuinced the Iewes, and that publikely, shewing by the scriptures, that Iesus was Christ.

CHAP. XIX

6 The holy Ghost is giuen by Pauls hands. 9 The Iewes blaspheme his doctrine, which is confirmed by miracles. 13 The Iewish exorcists 16 are beaten by the deuill. 19 Coniuring books are burnt. 24 Demetrius, for loue of gaine, raiseth an vprore against Paul, 35 which is appeased by the Towne-clerke.

Nd it came to passe, that while Apollos was at Corinth, Paul hauing passed thorow the vpper coasts, came to Ephesus, and finding certaine disciples,

2 He said vnto them, Haue ye receiued the holy Ghost since yee beleeued? And they saide vnto him, Wee haue not so much as heard whether there be any holy Ghost.

3 And he said vnto them, Vnto what then were ye baptized? And they saide, Vnto Iohns Baptisme.

4 *Then saide Paul, Iohn verely baptized with the baptisme of repentance, saying vnto the people, that they should beleeue on him which should come after him, that is, on Christ Iesus.

* Mat. 3. 11.

5 When they heard this, they were baptized in the Name of the Lord Iesus.

6 And when Paul had laide his hands vpon them, the holy Ghost came on them, and they spake with tongues, and prophecied.

7 And all ŷ men were about twelue.

8 And hee went into the Synagogue, and spake boldly for the space of three moneths, disputing and perswading the things concerning the Kingdome of God.

9 But

9 But when diuers were hardened, and beleeued not, but spake euill of that way before the multitude, he departed from them, and separated the disciples, disputing daily in the schoole of one Tyrannus.

10 And this continued by the space of two yeeres, so that all they which dwelt in Asia, heard the word of the Lord Iesus, both Iewes and Greeks.

11 And God wrought speciall miracles by the hands of Paul:

12 So that from his body were brought vnto the sicke handkerchiefs or aprons, and the diseases departed from them, and the euill spirits went out of them.

13 ¶ Then certaine of the vagabond Iewes, exorcistes, tooke vpon them to call ouer them which had euill spirits, the Name of the Lord Iesus, saying, We adiure you by Iesus whom Paul preacheth.

14 And there were seuen sonnes of one Sceua a Iewe, and chiefe of the Priests, which did so.

15 And the euill spirit answered, and said, Iesus I knowe, and Paul I know, but who are ye?

16 And the man in whom the euill spirit was, leapt on them, and ouercame them, and preuailed against them, so that they fled out of that house naked and wounded.

17 And this was knowen to all the Iewes and Greekes also dwelling at Ephesus, and feare fell on them all, and the Name of the Lord Iesus was magnified.

18 And many that beleeued came, and confessed, and shewed their deedes.

19 Many also of them which vsed curious arts, brought their bookes together and burned them before all men: and they counted the price of them, and found it fifty thousand pieces of siluer.

20 So mightily grew the word of God, and preuailed.

21 ¶ After these things were ended, Paul purposed in the spirit, when hee had passed thorow Macedonia and Achaia, to go to Hierusalem, saying, After I haue bin there, I must also see Rome.

22 So hee sent into Macedonia two of them that ministred vnto him, Timotheus and Erastus, but he himselfe stayed in Asia for a season.

23 And the same time there arose no small stirre about that way.

24 For a certaine man named Demetrius, a siluer smith, which made siluer shrines for Diana, brought no small gaine vnto the craftsmen:

25 Whom he called together, with the workemen of like occupation, and said, Sirs, ye know that by this craft we haue our wealth.

26 Moreouer, ye see & heare, that not alone at Ephesus, but almost throughout all Asia, this Paul hath perswaded and turned away much people, saying, that they bee no gods, which are made with hands.

27 So that not only this our craft is in danger to be set at nought: but also that the Temple of the great goddesse Diana should be despised, and her magnificence should be destroyed, whom all Asia, and the world worshippeth.

28 And when they heard these sayings, they were ful of wrath, & cried out, saying, Great is Diana of ỹ Ephesians.

29 And the whole citie was filled with confusion, and hauing caught Gaius and Aristarchus men of Macedonia Pauls companions in trauaile, they rushed with one accord into the Theatre.

30 And when Paul would haue entred in vnto the people, the disciples suffered him not.

31 And certaine of the chiefe of Asia, which were his friends, sent vnto him, desiring him that he would not aduenture himselfe into the Theatre.

32 Some therefore cried one thing, and some another: for the assembly was confused, and the more part knew not wherefore they were come together.

33 And they drew Alexander out of the multitude, the Iewes putting him forward. And Alexander beckened with the hand, and would haue made his defence vnto the people.

34 But when they knew that he was a Iewe, all with one voyce about the space of two houres cried out, Great is Diana of the Ephesians.

35 And when the towne clarke had appeased the people, he said, Ye men of Ephesus, what man is there ỹ knoweth not how that the citie of the Ephesians is †a worshipper of the great goddesse Diana, and of the *image* which fell downe from Iupiter?

36 Seeing then that these things cannot be spoken against, ye ought to be quiet, and to doe nothing rashly.

37 For

† Gre. the temple keeper.

37 For ye haue brought hither these men, which are neither robbers of Churches, nor yet blasphemers of your goddesse:

38 Wherefore if Demetrius, and the craftesmen which are with him, haue a matter against any man, ‖ the law is open, and there are deputies, let them implead one another.

‖ Or, the Court dayes are kept.

39 But if yee enquire any thing concerning other matters, it shalbe determined in a ‖ lawfull assembly.

‖ Or, ordinary.

40 For we are in danger to be called in question for this dayes vprore, there being no cause whereby we may giue an accompt of this concourse.

41 And when hee had thus spoken, he dismissed the assembly.

CHAP. XX.

1 Paul goeth to Macedonia. 7 He celebrateth the Lords Supper, and preacheth. 9 Eutychus hauing fallen downe dead, 10 is raised to life. 17 At Miletum he calleth the Elders together, telleth them what shall befall to himselfe, 28 committeth Gods flocke to them, 29 warneth them of false teachers, 32 commendeth them to God, 36 prayeth with them, and goeth his way.

Nd after the vprore was ceased, Paul called vnto him the disciples, and imbraced them, & departed, for to go into Macedonia.

2 And when he had gone ouer those parts, and had giuen them much exhortation, he came into Greece,

3 And there abode three moneths: and when the Iewes layed waite for him, as hee was about to saile into Syria, hee purposed to returne thorow Macedonia.

4 And there accompanied him into Asia, Sopater of Berea: and of the Thessalonians, Aristarchus, and Secundus, and Gaius of Derbe, and Timotheus: and of Asia Tychicus and Trophimus.

5 These going before, taried for vs at Troas:

6 And wee sailed away from Philippi, after the dayes of vnleauened bread, and came vnto them to Troas in fiue dayes, where we abode seuen daies.

7 And vpon the first day of the weeke, when the disciples came together *to breake bread, Paul preached vnto them, ready to depart on the mor-

* Chap. 2. 46.

row, and continued his speach vntill midnight.

8 And there were many lights in the vpper chamber where they were gathered together.

9 And there sate in a window a certaine yong man named Eutychus, being fallen into a deepe sleepe, and as Paul was long preaching, hee sunke downe with sleepe, and fel downe from the third loft, and was taken vp dead.

10 And Paul went downe, and fell on him, and embracing him, saide, Trouble not your selues, for his life is in him.

11 When hee therefore was come vp againe, & had broken bread, and eaten, and talked a long while, euen till breake of day, so he departed.

12 And they brought the yong man aliue, and were not a little comforted.

13 ¶ And wee went before to ship, and sailed vnto Assos, there intending to take in Paul: for so had hee appointed, minding himselfe to goe afoote.

14 And when he met with vs at Assos, wee tooke him in, and came to Mitylene.

15 And wee sailed thence, and came the next day ouer against Chios, and the next day we arriued at Samos, and taried at Trogyllium: and the next day we came to Miletus.

16 For Paul had determined to saile by Ephesus, because he would not spend the time in Asia: for he hasted, if it were possible for him, to be at Hierusalem the day of Pentecost.

17 ¶ And from Miletus hee sent to Ephesus, and called the Elders of the Church.

18 And when they were come to him, he said vnto them, Ye know from the first day that I came into Asia, after what maner I haue bene with you at all seasons,

19 Seruing the Lord with all humilitie of minde, and with many teares, and temptations, which befell me by the lying in wait of the Iewes:

20 And how I kept backe nothing that was profitable vnto you, but haue shewed you, and haue taught you publikely, and from house to house,

21 Testifying both to the Iewes and also to the Greekes, repentance toward God, and faith toward our Lord Iesus Christ.

22 And now behold, I goe bound in

Or, waite for me.

in the spirit vnto Hierusalem, not knowing the things that shal befall me there:

23 Saue that the holy Ghost witnesseth in euery city, saying that bonds and afflictions || abide me.

24 But none of these things mooue me, neither count I my life deare vnto my self, so that I might finish my course with ioy, & the ministery which I haue receiued of the Lord Iesus, to testifie the Gospel of the grace of God.

25 And now behold, I know that ye all, among whom I haue gone preaching the kingdom of God, shall see my face no more.

26 Wherefore I take you co record this day, that I am pure from the blood of all men. ‖

27 For I haue not shunned to declare vnto you all the counsell of God.

28 ¶ Take heed therefore vnto your selues, & to all the flocke, ouer the which the holy Ghost hath made you ouerseers, to feed the Church of God, which he hath purchased with his own blood.

29 For I know this, that after my departing shall grieuous wolues enter in among you, not sparing the flocke.

30 Also of your owne selues shal men arise, speaking peruerse things, to draw away disciples after them.

31 Therefore watch, and remember that by the space of three yeeres, I ceased not to warne euery one night and day with teares.

32 And now brethren, I commend you to God, and to the word of his grace, which is able to build you vp, and to giue you an inheritance among all them which are sanctified.

33 I haue coueted no mans siluer, or golde, or apparell.

1. Cor. 4. 12. 1. thess. 2. 9. 2. thes. 3. 8.

34 Yea, you your selues know, *that these handes haue ministred vnto my necessities, and to them that were with me.

35 I haue shewed you all things, how that so labouring, yee ought to support the weake, and to remember the words of the Lord Iesus, how he said, It is more blessed to giue, then to receiue.

36 ¶ And when he had thus spoken, he kneeled downe, & prayed with them all.

37 And they all wept sore, and fell on Pauls necke, and kissed him,

38 Sorrowing most of all for the words which he spake, that they should see his face no more. And they accompanied him vnto the ship.

CHAP. XXI.

Paul will not by any meanes be disswaded from going to Ierusalem. 9 Philips daughters Prophetesses. 17 Paul commeth to Ierusalem: 27 where he is apprehended, & in great danger, 31 but by the chiefe captaine is rescued, and permitted to speake to the people.

Nd it came to passe, that after wee were gotten frō them, and had lanched, wee came with a straight course vnto Choos, and the day following vnto Rhodes, and from thence vnto Patara.

2 And finding a ship sailing ouer vnto Phenicea, wee went abroad, and set foorth.

3 Now when wee had discouered Cyprus, we left it on the left hand, and sailed into Syria, and landed at Tyre: for there the shippe was to vnlade her burden.

4 And finding disciples, wee taried there seuen dayes : who said to Paul through the Spirit, that hee should not goe vp to Hierusalem.

5 And when we had accomplished those dayes, we departed, and went our way, and they all brought vs on our way, with wiues and children, till wee were out of the citie : and wee kneeled downe on the shore, and prayed.

6 And when we had taken our leaue one of another, we tooke ship, and they returned home againe.

7 And when wee had finished our course from Tyre, wee came to Ptolemais, and saluted the brethren, and abode with them one day.

8 And the next day we that were of Pauls company, departed, and came vnto Cesarea, and wee entred into the house of Philip the Euangelist (* which was one of the seuen) & abode with him.

*Chap. 6. 5.

9 And ỹ same man had foure daughters, virgins, which did prophesie.

10 And as wee taried there many dayes, there came downe from Iudea a certaine Prophet, named Agabus.

11 And when he was come vnto vs, he tooke Pauls girdle, and bound his owne hands and feete, and said, Thus sayth the holy Ghost, So shall the Iewes at Hierusalem binde the man that oweth this girdle, and shall deliuer him into the hands of the Gentiles.

12 And when we heard these things, both we and they of that place, besought
him

him not to goe vp to Hierusalem.

13 Then Paul answered, What meane ye to weepe and to breake mine heart? for I am ready, not to bee bound onely, but also to die at Hierusalem for the Name of the Lord Iesus.

14 And when he would not bee perswaded, we ceased, saying, The will of the Lord be done.

15 And after those dayes we tooke vp our cariages, & went vp to Hierusalem.

16 There went with vs also certaine of the disciples of Cesarea, and brought with them one Mnason of Cyprus, an old disciple, with who we should lodge.

17 And when we were come to Hierusalem, the brethren receiued vs gladly

18 And the day following Paul went in with vs vnto Iames, and all the Elders were present.

19 And when hee had saluted them, hee declared particularly what things God had wrought among the Gentiles by his ministerie.

20 And when they heard it, they glorified the Lord, & said vnto him, Thou seest, brother, how many thousands of Iewes there are which beleeue, and they are all zealous of the Law.

21 And they are informed of thee, that thou teachest all the Iewes which are among the Gentiles, to forsake Moses, saying, that they ought not to circumcise their children, neither to walke after the customes.

22 What is it therefore? the multitude must needs come together: for they will heare that thou art come.

23 Doe therefore this that we say to thee: Wee haue foure men which haue a vow on them,

24 Them take, and purifie thy selfe with them, & bee at charges with them, that they may *shaue their heads: and all may know that those things wherof they were informed concerning thee, are nothing, but that thou thy selfe also walkest orderly, and keepest the Law.

25 As touching the Gentiles which beleeue, *wee haue written and concluded, that they obserue no such thing, saue onely that they keepe themselues from things offered to idoles, and from blood, and from strangled, and from fornication.

26 Then Paul tooke the men, and the next day purifying himselfe with them, entred into the Temple, * to signifie the accomplishment of the dayes

* Num. 6. 18. chap. 18. 18.

* Chap. 15. 20.

* Num. 6. 13

of purification, vntill that an offering should be offered for euery one of them:

27 And when the seuen dayes were almost ended, the Iewes which were of Asia, when they saw him in the Temple, stirred vp all the people, and laide hands on him,

28 Crying out, Men of Israel, helpe: this is ẙ man that teacheth al men euery where against the people, and the law, and this place: and farther brought Greeks also into the Temple, and hath polluted this holy place.

29 (For they had seene before with him in the citie, Trophimus an Ephesian, whome they supposed that Paul had brought into the Temple.)

30 And all the citie was moued, and the people ran together: and they tooke Paul, and drew him out of the Temple: and forthwith the doores were shut.

31 And as they went about to kil him, tidings came vnto the chiefe captaine of the band, that all Hierusalem was in an vprore.

32 Who immediatly tooke souldiers, and Centurions, and ran downe vnto them: and when they saw the chiefe captaine and the souldiers, they left beating of Paul.

33 Then the chiefe captain came neere, and tooke him, & commanded him to be bound with two chaines, and demanded who he was, and what hee had done.

34 And some cried one thing, some another, among the multitude: and when he could not know the certaintie for the tumult, he commanded him to be caried into the castle.

35 And when he came vpon ẙ staires, so it was that he was borne of the souldiers, for the violence of the people.

36 For the multitude of the people followed after, crying, Away with him.

37 And as Paul was to bee led into the castle, hee saide vnto the chiefe captaine, May I speake vnto thee? Who saide, Canst thou speake Greeke?

38 *Art not thou that Egyptian which before these daies madest an vprore, and leddest out into the wildernesse foure thousand men that were murtherers?

39 But Paul said, I am a man which am a Iew of Tarsus, a citie in Cilicia, a citizen of no meane citie: & I beseech thee suffer me to speake vnto the people.

40 And when he had giuen him licence, Paul stood on the staires, and beckened with the hand vnto the people:

* Chap. 5. 36.

ple : and when there was made a great silence, he spake vnto them in the Hebrew tongue, saying.

CHAP. XXII.

1 Paul declareth at large, how he was conuerted to the faith, 17 and called to his Apostleship. 22 At the very mentioning of the Gentiles, the people exclaime on him. 24 He should haue bene scourged, 25 but clayming the priuilege of a Romane, he escapeth.

MEn, brethren, and fathers, heare ye my defence which I make now vnto you.

2 (And when they heard that hee spake in the Hebrew tongue to them, they kept the more silence : and he saith,)

3 *I am verely a man which am a Iew, borne in Tarsus *a citie* in Cilicia, yet brought vp in this citie at the feete of Gamaliel, and taught according to the perfect maner of the law of the fathers, and was zealous towards God, as ye all are this day.

4 *And I persecuted this way vnto the death, binding and deliuering into prisons both men and women,

5 As also the high Priest doth beare me witnesse, and all the estate of the elders : from whom also I receiued letters vnto the brethren, and went to Damascus, to bring them which were there, bound vnto Hierusalem, for to be punished.

6 And it came to passe, that as I made my iourney, & was come nigh vnto Damascus about noone, suddenly there shone from heauen a great light round about me.

7 And I fell vnto the ground, and heard a voice saying vnto mee, Saul, Saul, why persecutest thou me?

8 And I answered, Who art thou, Lord? And he said vnto me, I am Iesus of Nazareth who thou persecutest.

9 And they that were with me saw indeede the light, and were afraid; but they heard not the voice of him that spake to me.

10 And I saide, What shall I doe, Lord? And the Lord said vnto me, Arise, and goe into Damascus, and there it shall be told thee of all things which are appointed for thee to doe.

11 And when I could not see for the glory of that light, being led by the hand of them that were with me, I came into Damascus.

* Chap. 21. 39.

* Chap. 8. 3

12 And one Ananias, a deuout man according to the law, hauing a good report of al the Iewes which dwelt *there*,

13 Came vnto me, and stood, & said vnto me, Brother Saul, receiue thy sight. And the same houre I looked vp vpon him.

14 And he said, The God of our fathers hath chosen thee, ẏ thou shouldest know his will, & see that Iust one, and shouldest heare the voice of his mouth.

15 For thou shalt be his witnes vnto al men, of what thou hast seene & heard.

16 And now, why tariest thou? Arise, and be baptized, and wash away thy sinnes, calling on the name of the Lord.

17 And it came to passe, that when I was come againe to Hierusalem, euen while I prayed in the temple, I was in a trance,

18 And saw him saying vnto mee, Make haste, and get thee quickly out of Hierusalem : for they will not receiue thy testimony concerning me.

19 And I said, Lord, they know that I imprisoned, and beat in euery synagogue them that beleeued on thee.

20 *And when ẏ blood of thy martyr Steuen was shed, I also was standing by, and consenting vnto his death, and kept the raiment of them that slew him.

21 And he said vnto me, Depart : for I will send thee farre hence, vnto the Gentiles.

22 And they gaue him audience vnto this word, and then lift vp their voices, and said, Away with such a fellow from the earth : for it is not fit that he should liue.

23 And as they cried out, and cast off their clothes, & threw dust into the aire,

24 The chiefe captaine commanded him to be brought into the castle, and bade that hee should be examined by scourging : that he might know wherfore they cried so against him.

25 And as they bound him with thongs, Paul said vnto the Centurion that stood by, Is it lawfull for you to scourge a man that is a Romane, and vncondemned?

26 When the Centurion heard that, hee went and told the chiefe captaine, saying, Take heede what thou doest, for this man is a Romane.

27 Then the chiefe captaine came; and said vnto him, Tell me, art thou a Romane? He said, Yea.

28 And the chiefe captaine answered, With

* Chap. 7. 58.

Or, tortured him.

With a great summe obteined I this freedome. And Paul said, But I was free borne.

29 Then straightway they departed from him which should haue ‖ examined him : and the chiefe captaine also was afraid after he knew that he was a Romane, & because he had bound him.

30 On the morrow, because he would haue knowen the certaintie wherefore he was accused of the Iewes, he loosed him from his bands, and commanded the chiefe Priests and all their Councill to appeare, and brought Paul downe, and set him before them.

CHAP. XXIII.

1 As Paul pleadeth his cause, 2 Ananias commandeth them to smite him. 7 Dissension among his accusers. 11 God encourageth him. 14 The Iewes laying waite for Paul, 20 is declared vnto the chiefe captaine. 27 He sendeth him to Felix the gouernour.

Nd Paul earnestly beholding the council, said, Men and brethren, I haue liued in all good conscience before God vntill this day.

2 And the high Priest Ananias commanded them that stood by him, to smite him on the mouth.

3 Then saith Paul vnto him, God shall smite thee, thou whited wall : for sittest thou to iudge mee after the Law, and commandest mee to be smitten contrary to the Law?

4 And they that stood by, said, Reuilest thou Gods high Priest?

Exod. 22. 27.

5 Then said Paul, I wist not, brethren, that hee was the high Prist : For it is written, *Thou shalt not speake euill of the ruler of thy people.

6 But when Paul perceiued that the one part were Sadducees, and the other Pharisees, hee cryed out in the Councill, Men and brethren, *I am a Pharisee, the sonne of a Pharisee : *of the hope and resurrection of the dead, I am called in question.

*Phil. 3. 5.
*Chap. 24. 21.

7 And when hee had so said, there arose a dissension betweene the Pharisees and the Sadducees : and the multitude was diuided.

*Matt. 22. 23.

8 *For the Sadducees say that there is no resurrection, neither Angel, nor spirit : but the Pharisees confesse both.

9 And there arose a great cry : and the Scribes that were of the Pharisees part arose, and stroue, saying, Wee finde

no euill in this man : but if a spirit or an Angel hath spoken to him, let vs not fight against God.

10 And when there arose a great dissension, the chiefe captaine fearing lest Paul should haue bene pulled in pieces of them, commanded the souldiers to goe downe, and to take him by force from among them, and to bring him into the castle.

11 And the night folowing, the Lord stood by him, and saide, Bee of good cheere, Paul : for as thou hast testified of mee in Hierusalem, so must thou beare witnesse also at Rome.

12 And when it was day, certaine of the Iewes banded together, and bound themselues vnder ‖ a curse, saying, that they would neither eate nor drinke till they had killed Paul.

Or, with an oath of execration.

13 And they were more then fourtie which had made this conspiracie.

14 And they came to the chiefe Priests and Elders, and said, Wee haue bound our selues vnder a great curse, that wee will eate nothing vntill wee haue slaine Paul.

15 Now therefore ye with the Councill, signifie to the chiefe captaine that he bring him downe vnto you to morrow, as though yee would enquire something more perfectly concerning him : and we, or euer he come neere, are ready to kill him.

16 And when Pauls sisters sonne heard of their laying in wait, hee went and entred into the castle, & told Paul.

17 Then Paul called one of the Centurions vnto him, and said, Bring this yong man vnto the chiefe captaine : for he hath a certaine thing to tell him.

18 So he took him, and brought him to the chiefe captaine, and said, Paul the prisoner called me vnto him, and praied mee to bring this yong man vnto thee, who hath something to say vnto thee.

19 Then the chiefe captaine tooke him by the hand, and went with him aside priuately, and asked him, What is that thou hast to tell me?

20 And he said, The Iewes haue agreed to desire thee, that thou wouldest bring downe Paul to morrow into the Council, as though they would enquire somewhat of him more perfectly.

21 But do not thou yeeld vnto them : for there lie in wait for him of them moe then fourtie men, which haue bound themselues with an othe, that they will

neither

neither eate nor drinke, till they haue killed him : and now are they ready, looking for a promiſe from thee.

22 So the chiefe captaine then let the yong man depart, and charged him, See thou tell no man, that thou haſt ſhewed theſe things to me.

23 And he called vnto him two Centurions, ſaying, Make ready two hundred ſouldiers to goe to Ceſarea, and horſemen threeſcore and ten, and ſpearemen two hundred, at the third houre of the night.

24 And prouide them beaſts, that they may ſet Paul on, and bring him ſafe vnto Felix the gouernour.

25 And hee wrote a letter after this manner:

26 Claudius Lyſias, vnto the moſt excellent Gouernour Felix, ſendeth greeting.

27 This man was taken of the Iewes and ſhould haue beene killed of them : Then came I with an armie, and reſcued him, hauing vnderſtood that he was a Romane.

28 And when I would haue knowen the cauſe wherefore they accuſed him, I brought him foorth into their Council.

29 Whom I perceiued to be accuſed of queſtions of their lawe, but to haue nothing laide to his charge worthy of death or of bonds.

30 And when it was tolde me, how that the Iewes laid waite for the man, I ſent ſtraightway to thee, and gaue commandement to his accuſers alſo, to ſay before thee what they had againſt him. Farewell.

31 Then the ſouldiers, as it was commaunded them, tooke Paul, and brought him by night to Antipatris.

32 On the morow, they left the horſemen to goe with him, and returned to the caſtle.

33 Who when they came to Ceſarea, and deliuered the Epiſtle to the gouernour, preſented Paul alſo before him.

34 And when the gouernour had read *the letter*, he asked of what prouince he was. And when he vnderſtood that he was of Cilicia :

35 I will heare thee, ſaid hee, when thine accuſers are alſo come. And hee commanded him to be kept in Herods iudgement hall.

CHAP. XXIIII.

1 Paul being accuſed by Tertullus the Oratour,

10 anſwereth for his life and doctrine. 24 He preacheth Christ to the gouernour and his wife. 26 The gouernour hopeth for a bribe, but in vaine. 27 At last, going out of his office, hee leaueth Paul in priſon.

And after fiue dayes, Ananias the hie Prieſt deſcended with the Elders, and with a certaine Oratour named Tertullus, who enformed the gouernour against Paul.

2 And when he was called foorth, Tertullus began to accuſe him, ſaying, Seeing that by thee we enioy great quietneſſe, and that very worthy deeds are done vnto this natiõ by thy prouidence:

3 Wee accept it alwayes, and in all places, moſt noble Felix, with all thankfulneſſe.

4 Notwithſtanding, that I be not farther tedious vnto thee, I pray thee, that thou wouldeſt heare vs of thy clemencie a few words.

5 For we haue found this man a peſtilent fellow, and a moouer of ſedition among all the Iewes throughout the world, and a ringleader of the ſect of the Nazarenes.

6 Who alſo hath gone about to profane the Temple : whom we tooke, and would haue iudged according to our lawe.

7 But the chiefe captaine Lyſias came vpon vs, and with great violence tooke him away out of our hands :

8 Commanding his accuſers to come vnto thee, by examining of whom thy ſelfe mayeſt take knowledge of all theſe things, whereof we accuſe him.

9 And the Iewes alſo aſſented, ſaying that theſe things were ſo.

10 Then Paul, after that the gouernour had beckened vnto him to ſpeake, anſwered, Foraſmuch as I know that thou haſt been of many yeeres a Iudge vnto this nation, I do the more cheerefully anſwere for my ſelfe :

11 Becauſe that thou mayeſt vnderſtand, that there are yet but twelue dayes, ſince I went vp to Hieruſalem for to worſhip.

12 And they neither found me in the Temple diſputing with any man, neither raiſing vp the people, neither in the Synagogues, nor in the citie :

13 Neither can they proue the things whereof they now accuſe me.

14 But this I confeſſe vnto thee, that after the way which they call hereſie,

heresie, so worship I the God of my fathers, beleeuing all things which are written in the Law and the Prophets,

15 And haue hope towards God, which they themselues also allow, that there shall be a resurrection of the dead, both of the iust and vniust.

16 And herein doe I exercise my selfe to haue alwayes a conscience void of offence toward God, and toward men.

17 Now after many yeeres, I came to bring almes to my nation, & offrings:

* Chap. 21. 27.

18 * Wherupon certaine Iewes from Asia found me purified in the Temple, neither with multitude, nor with tumult.

19 Who ought to haue beene here before thee, and obiect, if they had ought against me.

20 Or else let these same here say, if they haue found any euill doing in mee, while I stood before the Councill,

* Chap. 23. 6.

21 Except it be for this one voice, that I cried standing among them, * Touching the resurrection of the dead I am called in question by you this day.

22 And when Felix heard these things, hauing more perfect knowledge of that way, he deferred them and said, When Lysias the chiefe captaine shall come downe, I will know the vttermost of your matter.

23 And he commanded a Centurion to keepe Paul, and to let him haue libertie, and that he should forbid none of his acquaintance to minister, or come vnto him.

24 And after certaine dayes, when Felix came with his wife Drusilla, which was a Iew, he sent for Paul, and heard him cōcerning the faith in Christ.

25 And as he reasoned of righteousnesse, temperance, and iudgement to come, Felix trembled and answered, Go thy way for this time, when I haue a conuenient season, I will call for thee.

26 He hoped also that money should haue bene giuen him of Paul, that hee might loose him: wherefore hee sent for him the oftner, and comuned with him.

27 But after two yeeres, Portius Festus came into Felix roome: and Felix willing to shew the Iewes a pleasure, left Paul bound.

CHAP. XXV.

2 The Iewes accuse Paul before Festus. 8 He answereth for himselfe, 11 and appealeth vnto Cesar. 14 Afterwards, Festus openeth his matter to king Agryppa, 23 and he is brought forth. 25 Festus cleareth him to haue done nothing worthy of death.

N Owe when Festus was come into the prouince, after three dayes he ascended frō Cesarea to Hierusalem.

2 Then the high Priest, and the chiefe of the Iewes informed him against Paul, and besought him,

3 And desired fauour against him, that he would send for him to Hierusalem, laying wait in the way to kill him.

4 But Festus answered, that Paul should be kept at Cesarea, and that hee himselfe would depart shortly *thither*.

5 Let them therefore, said he, which among you are able, go downe with *me*, and accuse this man, if there be any wickednesse in him.

6 And when hee had taried among them ||more then ten dayes, he went downe vnto Cesarea, and the next day sitting in the iudgement seat, commanded Paul to be brought.

|| Or, as some copies reade no more then the eight or ten dayes.

7 And when hee was come, the Iewes which came downe from Hierusalem, stood round about, and laide many and grieuous complaints against Paul, which they could not proue,

8 While hee answered for himselfe, Neither against the law of the Iewes, neither against the Temple, nor yet against Cesar, haue I offended any thing at all.

9 But Festus willing to doe the Iewes a pleasure, answered Paul, and said, Wilt thou goe vp to Hierusalem, and there be iudged of these things before me?

10 Then said Paul, I stand at Cesars iudgement seat, where I ought to bee iudged: to the Iewes haue I done no wrong, as thou very well knowest.

11 For if I be an offender, or haue committed any thing worthy of death, I refuse not to die: but if there be none of these things whereof these accuse me, no man may deliuer me vnto them. I appeale vnto Cesar.

12 Then Festus when he had conferred with the Councill, answered, Hast thou appealed vnto Cesar? vnto Cesar shalt thou goe.

13 And after certaine dayes, king Agrippa and Bernice, came vnto Cesarea, to salute Festus.

14 And when they had beene there many dayes, Festus declared Pauls cause

cause vnto the king, saying, There is a certaine man left in bonds by Felix:

15 About whom when I was at Hierusalem, the chiefe Priests and the Elders of the Iewes enformed me, desiring to haue iudgement against him.

16 To whom I answered, It is not the maner of the Romanes to deliuer any man to die, before that he which is accused, haue the accusers face to face, and haue licence to answere for himselfe concerning the crime laid against him.

17 Therefore when they were come hither, without any delay, on the morrow I sate on the iudgement seate, and comanded the man to be brought forth.

18 Against whom when the accusers stood vp, they brought none accusation of such things as I supposed:

19 But had certaine questions against him of their owne superstition, and of one Iesus, which was dead, whom Paul affirmed to be aliue.

20 And because ‖I doubted of such maner of questions, I asked him whether he would goe to Hierusalem, and there be iudged of these matters.

‖ Or, I was doubtfull how to inquire heereof.

21 But when Paul had appealed to bee reserued vnto the ‖hearing of Augustus, I commanded him to be kept, till I might send him to Cesar.

‖ Or, iudgement.

22 Then Agrippa said vnto Festus, I would also heare the man my selfe. To morrow, said he, thou shalt heare him.

23 And on the morrow when Agrippa was come and Bernice, with great pompe, and was entred into the place of hearing, with the chiefe captaines, and principall men of the citie; at Festus commaundement Paul was brought foorth.

24 And Festus said, King Agrippa, and all men which are heere present with vs, ye see this man, about whom all the multitude of the Iewes haue dealt with me, both at Hierusalem, and also heere, crying that he ought not to liue any longer.

25 But when I found that he had committed nothing worthy of death, and that he himselfe hath appealed to Augustus, I haue determined to send him.

26 Of whom I haue no certaine thing to write vnto my Lord: Wherefore I haue brought him foorth before you, and specially before thee, O king Agrippa, that after examination had,

I might haue somewhat to write.

27 For it seemeth to me vnreasonable, to send a prisoner, and not withall to signifie the crimes laid against him.

CHAP. XXVI.

2 Paul, in the presence of Agrippa, declareth his life from his childhood, 12 and how miraculously he was conuerted, and called to his Apostleship. 24 Festus chargeth him to be mad, whereunto he answereth modestly. 28 Agrippa is almost perswaded to be a christian. 31 The whole company pronounce him innocent.

THen Agrippa said vnto Paul, Thou art permitted to speake for thy selfe. Then Paul stretched foorth the hand, and answered for himselfe,

2 I thinke my selfe happy, king Agrippa, because I shall answere for my selfe this day before thee touching all the things whereof I am accused of the Iewes:

3 Especially, because I know thee to be expert in all customes and questions which are among the Iewes: wherefore I beseech thee to heare mee patiently.

4 My maner of life from my youth, which was at the first among mine owne nation at Hierusalem, know all the Iewes,

5 Which knew me from the beginning, (if they would testifie) that after the most straitest sect of our religion, I liued a Pharisee.

6 And now I stand, and am iudged for the hope of the promise made of God vnto our fathers:

7 Vnto which promise our twelue tribes instantly seruing God day and night, hope to come: For which hopes sake, King Agrippa, I am accused of the Iewes.

8 Why should it be thought a thing incredible with you, that God should raise the dead?

9 I verily thought with my selfe, that I ought to doe many things contrary to the name of Iesus of Nazareth:

10 *Which thing I also did in Hierusalem, and many of the Saints did I shut vp in prison, hauing receiued authoritie from the chiefe Priests, and when they were put to death, I gaue my voyce against them.

* Chap. 8. 3.

11 And

11 And I punished them oft in euery Synagogue, and compelled them to blaspheme, and being exceedingly mad against them, I persecuted them euen vnto strange cities.

* Chap. 9. 2.

12 *Whereupon, as I went to Damascus, with authoritie and commission from the chiefe Priests:

13 At midday, O king, I saw in the way a light from heauen, aboue the brightnes of the Sunne, shining round about mee, and them which iourneyed with me.

14 And when wee were all fallen to the earth, I heard a voice speaking vnto me, and saying in the Hebrew tongue, Saul, Saul, why persecutest thou me? It is hard for thee to kicke against the prickes.

15 And I said, Who art thou, Lord? And hee said, I am Iesus whom thou persecutest.

16 But rise, and stand vpon thy feete, for I haue appeared vnto thee for this purpose, to make thee a minister and a witnesse, both of these things which thou hast seene, & of those things in the which I will appeare vnto thee,

17 Deliuering thee from the people, and from the Gentiles, vnto whom now I send thee,

18 To open their eyes, and to turne them from darknesse to light, and from the power of Satan vnto God, that they may receiue forgiuenesse of sinnes, and inheritance among them which are sanctified by faith that is in me.

19 Whereupon, O king Agrippa, I was not disobedient vnto the heauenly vision:

20 But shewed first vnto them of Damascus, and at Hierusalem, and thorowout all the coasts of Iudea, and then to the Gentiles, that they should repent and turne to God, and do works meete for repentance.

21 For these causes the Iewes caught mee in the Temple, and went about to kill me.

22 Hauing therefore obteined helpe of God, I continue vnto this day, witnessing both to small and great, saying none other things then those which the Prophets and Moses did say should come:

23 That Christ should suffer, and that hee should be the first that should rise from the dead, & should shew light vnto the people, and to the Gentiles.

24 And as hee thus spake for himselfe, Festus saide with a lowd voyce, Paul, thou art beside thy selfe, much learning doeth make thee mad.

25 But he said, I am not mad, most noble Festus, but speake foorth the words of trueth and sobernesse.

26 For the King knoweth of these things, before whom also I speake freely: for I am perswaded, that none of these things are hidden from him, for this thing was not done in a corner.

27 King Agrippa, beleeuest thou the Prophets? I know that thou beleeuest.

28 Then Agrippa saide vnto Paul, Almost thou perswadest mee to bee a Christian.

29 And Paul said, I would to God, that not onely thou, but also all that heare mee this day, were both almost, and altogether such as I am, except these bonds.

30 And when hee had thus spoken, the king rose vp, and the gouernour, and Bernice, & they that sate with them.

31 And when they were gone aside, they talked betweene themselues, saying, This man doeth nothing worthy of death, or of bonds.

32 Then said Agrippa vnto Festus, This man might haue bene set at libertie, if he had not appealed vnto Cesar.

CHAP. XXVII.

1 Paul shipping toward Rome, 10 foretelleth of the danger of the voyage, 11 but is not beleeued. 14 They are tossed to and fro with tempest, 41 and suffer shipwracke, 22 34. 44 yet all come safe to land.

Nd when it was determined, that wee should saile into Italy, they deliuered Paul, & certaine other prisoners, vnto one named Iulius, a centurion of Augustus band.

2 And entring into a ship of Adramyttium, wee lanched, meaning to saile by the coasts of Asia, one Aristarchus a Macedonian, of Thessalonica, beeing with vs.

3 And the next day wee touched at Sidon: And Iulius courteously entreated Paul, and gaue him libertie to goe vnto his friends to refresh himselfe.

4 And when we had lanched from thence, we sailed vnder Cyprus, because the winds were contrary.

5 And when we had sailed ouer the
sea

sea of Cilicia and Pamphylia, wee came to Myra a citie of Lysia.

6 And there the Centurion found a ship of Alexandria sailing into Italy, and he put vs therein.

7 And when wee had sailed slowly many dayes, and scarse were come ouer against Gnidus, the wind not suffering vs, wee sailed vnder ||Creete, ouer against Salmone,

||Or, Candy.

8 And hardly passing it, came vnto a place which is called the Faire hauens, nigh whereunto was the citie of Lasea.

9 Now when much time was spent, and when sailing was now dangerous, because the Fast was now alreadie past, Paul admonished them,

10 And said vnto them, Sirs, I perceiue that this voyage will be with ||hurt and much damage, not onely of the lading & ship, but also of our liues.

||Or, iniurie.

11 Neuerthelesse, the Centurion beleeued the master and the owner of the shippe, more then those things which were spoken by Paul.

12 And because the hauen was not commodious to winter in, the more part aduised to depart thence also, if by any meanes they might attaine to Phenice, and there to winter; which is an hauen of Creete, and lieth toward the Southwest, and Northwest.

13 And when the South wind blew softly, supposing that they had obtained their purpose, loosing thence, they sailed close by Creete.

14 But not long after, there ||arose against it a tempestuous winde, called Euroclydon.

||Or, beat.

15 And when the ship was caught, and could not beare vp into the winde, we let her driue.

16 And running vnder a certaine yland, which is called Clauda, wee had much worke to come by the boate:

17 Which when they had taken vp, they vsed helpes, vnder-girding the ship; and fearing lest they should fall into the quicke-sands, strake saile, and so were driuen.

18 And being exceedingly tossed with a tempest the next day, they lightened the ship:

19 And the third day we cast out with our owne handes the tackling of the shippe.

20 And when neither Sunne nor starres in many dayes appeared, and

no small tempest lay on vs; all hope that wee should be saued, was then taken away.

21 But after long abstinence, Paul stood foorth in the middes of them, and said, Sirs, yee should haue hearkened vnto mee, and not haue loosed from Creete, and to haue gained this harme and losse.

22 And now I exhort you to be of good cheere : for there shall be no losse of any mans life among you, but of the shippe.

23 For there stood by me this night the Angel of God, whose I am, and whom I serue,

24 Saying, Feare not Paul, thou must be brought before Cesar, and loe, God hath giuen thee all them that saile with thee.

25 Wherefore, sirs, be of good cheere: for I beleeue God, that it shall be euen as it was tolde me.

26 Howbeit, we must be cast vpon a certaine Iland.

27 But when the fourteenth night was come, as wee were driuen vp and downe in Adria about midnight, the shipmen deemed that they drew neere to some countrey :

28 And sounded, and found it twentie fathoms: and when they had gone a little further, they sounded againe, and found it fifteene fathoms.

29 Then fearing lest we should haue fallen vpon rockes, they cast foure ancres out of the sterne , and wished for the day.

30 And as the shipmen were about to flee out of the ship, when they had let downe the boat into the sea, vnder colour as though they would haue cast ancres out of the fore-ship,

31 Paul said to the Centurion, and to the souldiers, Except these abide in the ship, ye cannot be saued.

32 Then the souldiers cut off the ropes of the boat, and let her fall off.

33 And while the day was comming on, Paul besought them all to take meat, saying, This day is the fourteenth day that ye haue taried, and continued fasting, hauing taken nothing.

34 Wherefore, I pray you to take some meat, for this is for your health : for there shall not an haire fall from the head of any of you.

35 And when hee had thus spoken, hee tooke bread, and gaue thankes to
God

God in presence of them all, and when he had broken it, he began to eate.

36 Then were they all of good cheere, and they also tooke some meat.

37 And we were in all, in the ship, two hundred, threescore and sixteene soules.

38 And when they had eaten enough, they lightened the ship, and cast out the wheat into the sea.

39 And when it was day, they knew not the land: but they discouered a certaine creek, with a shore, into the which they were minded, if it were possible, to thrust in the ship.

Or, cut the ankers, they left them in the sea, &c.

40 And when they had ‖ taken vp the ankers, they committed *themselues* vnto the sea, & loosed the rudder bands, and hoised vp the maine saile to the winde, and made toward shore.

41 And falling into a place where two seas met, they ranne the shippe a ground, and the forepart stucke fast, and remained vnmoueable, but the hinder part was broken with the violence of the waues.

42 And the souldiers counsel was to kil the prisoners, lest any of them should swimme out, and escape.

43 But the Centurion, willing to saue Paul, kept them from their purpose, and commanded that they which could swimme, should cast themselues first into the sea, and get to land:

44 And the rest, some on boords, and some on broken pieces of the ship: and so it came to passe that they escaped all safe to land.

CHAP. XXVIII.

1 Paul, after his shipwracke is kindly entertained of the Barbarians. 5 The viper on his hand hurteth him not. 8 He healeth many diseases in the Iland. 11 They depart towards Rome. 17 Hee declareth to the Iewes the cause of his comming. 14 After his preaching some were perswaded, and some beleeued not. 30 Yet he preacheth there two yeeres.

And when they were escaped, then they knew that the Iland was called Melita.

2 And the barbarous people shewed vs no little kindnesse: for they kindled a fire, and receiued vs euery one because of the present raine, and because of the cold.

3 And when Paul had gathered a bundle of stickes, and layde them on the fire, there came a Viper out of the heat, and fastened on his hand.

4 And when the Barbarians saw the venomous beast hang on his hand, they saide among themselues, No doubt this man is a murtherer, whom though hee hath escaped the Sea, yet Vengeance suffereth not to liue.

5 And hee shooke off the beast into the fire, and felt no harme.

6 Howbeit, they looked when hee should haue swollen, or fallen downe dead suddenly: but after they had looked a great while, and saw no harme come to him, they changed their minds, and said that he was a God.

7 In the same quarters were possessions of the chiefe man of the Iland, whose name was Publius, who receiued vs, and lodged vs three dayes courteously.

8 And it came to passe that the father of Publius lay sicke of a feuer, and of a bloody-flixe, to whom Paul entred in, and prayed, and layed his hands on him, and healed him.

9 So when this was done, others also which had diseases in the Iland, came, and were healed:

10 Who also honoured vs with many honours, and when wee departed, they laded vs with such things as were necessary.

11 And after three moneths wee departed in a ship of Alexandria, which had wintered in the Ile, whose signe was Castor and Pollux.

12 And landing at Syracuse wee taried there three dayes.

13 And from thence wee fet a compasse, and came to Rhegium, and after one day the South winde blew, and we came the next day to Puteoli:

14 Where wee found brethren, and were desired to tary with them seuen dayes: and so we went toward Rome.

15 And from thence, when the brethren heard of vs, they came to meet vs as farre as Appii forum, and the three Tauernes: whom when Paul saw, he thanked God, and tooke courage.

16 And when we came to Rome, the Centurion deliuered the prisoners to the Captaine of the guard: but Paul was suffered to dwell by himselfe, with a souldier that kept him.

17 And it came to passe, that after three dayes, Paul called the chiefe of the Iewes together. And when they were come

come together, he said vnto them, Men and brethren, though I haue committed nothing against the people, or customes of our fathers, yet was I deliuered prisoner from Hierusalem into the hands of the Romanes.

18 Who when they had examined me, would haue let me goe, because there was no cause of death in me.

19 But when the Iewes spake against it, I was constrained to appeale vnto Cesar, not that I had ought to accuse my nation of.

20 For this cause therefore haue I called for you, to see you, and to speake with you : because that for the hope of Israel I am bound with this chaine.

21 And they saide vnto him, Wee neither receiued letters out of Iudea concerning thee, neither any of the brethren that came, shewed or spake any harme of thee.

22 But we desire to heare of thee what thou thinkest : for as concerning this sect, we know that euery where it is spoken against.

23 And when they had appointed him a day, there came many to him into his lodging, to whom he expounded and testified the kingdome of God, perswading them concerning Iesus, both out of the law of Moses, and out of the Prophets, from morning till euening.

24 And some beleeued the things which were spoken, and some beleeued not.

25 And when they agreed not among themselues, they departed, after that Paul had spoken one word, Well spake the holy Ghost by Esaias the Prophet, vnto our fathers,

26 Saying, * Goe vnto this people, and say, Hearing ye shall heare, and shall not vnderstand, and seeing ye shall see, and not perceiue.

27 For the heart of this people is waxed grosse, and their eares are dull of hearing, and their eyes haue they closed, lest they should see with their eyes, and heare with their eares, and vnderstand with their heart, and should bee conuerted, and I should heale them.

28 Be it knowen therfore vnto you, that the saluation of God is sent vnto the Gentiles, and that they wil heare it.

29 And when hee had saide these words, the Iewes departed, and had great reasoning among themselues.

30 And Paul dwelt two whole yeeres in his owne hired house, and receiued all that came in vnto him,

31 Preaching the kingdome of God, and teaching those things which concerne the Lord Iesus Christ, with all confidence, no man forbidding him.

*Esai. 6. 9.
mat. 13. 14.
mar. 4. 12.
luke 8. 4.
ioh. 12. 40.
rom. 11. 8.

¶ *The end of the Acts of the Apostles.*

¶ THE

THE
EPISTLE OF PAVL THE
Apostle to the Romanes.

CHAP. I.

1 Paul commendeth his calling to the Romanes, 9 and his desire to come to them. 16 What his Gospel is, and the righteousnesse which it sheweth. 18 God is angry with all maner of sin. 21 What were the sinnes of the Gentiles.

AVL a seruant of Iesus Christ, called *to bee* an Apostle, * separated vnto the Gospel of God,

2 (Which he had promised afore by his Prophets in the holy Scriptures,)

3 Concerning his Sonne Iesus Christ our Lord, which was made of the seed of Dauid according to the flesh,

4 And †declared to be the Sonne of God, with power, according to the Spirit of holinesse, by the resurrection from the dead.

5 By whom we haue receiued grace and Apostleship ‖ for obedience to the faith among all nations for his Name,

6 Among whom are ye also the called of Iesus Christ.

7 To all that be in Rome, beloued of God, *called to be* Saints: Grace to you and peace from God our Father, and the Lord Iesus Christ.

8 First I thanke my God through Iesus Christ for you all, that your faith is spoken of throughout the whole world.

9 For God is my witnesse, whom I serue ‖ with my spirit in the Gospel of his Sonne, that without ceasing I make mention of you, alwayes in my prayers,

10 Making request, (if by any meanes now at length I might haue a prosperous iourney by the will of God) to come vnto you.

11 For I long to see you, that I may impart vnto you some spirituall gift, to the end you may be established,

12 That is, that I may be comforted together ‖ with you, by the mutuall faith both of you and me.

13 Now I would not haue you ignorant, brethren, that oftentimes I purposed to come vnto you, (but was let hitherto) that I might haue some fruit ‖ among you also, euen as among other Gentiles.

14 I am debter both to the Greeks, and to the Barbarians, both to the wise, and to the vnwise.

15 So, as much as in mee is, I am ready to preach the Gospel to you that are at Rome also.

16 For I am not ashamed of the Gospel of Christ : for it is the power of God vnto saluation, to euery one that beleeueth, to the Iew first, and also to the Greeke.

17 For therein is the righteousnesse of God reueiled from faith to faith : as it is written, * The iust shall liue by faith.

18 For the wrath of God is reueiled from heauen against all vngodlinesse, and vnrighteousnesse of men, who hold the trueth in vnrighteousnesse.

19 Because that which may bee knowen of God, is manifest in ‖ them, for God hath shewed it vnto them.

20 For the inuisible things of him from the Creation of the world, are clearely seene, being vnderstood by the things that are made, *euen* his eternall Power and Godhead, ‖ so that they are without excuse :

21 Because that when they knew God, they glorified him not as God, neither were thankefull, but became vaine in

* Acts. 13. 1.

† Gr. determined.

‖ Or, to the obedience of faith.

‖ Or, in my spirit.

‖ Or, in you.

‖ Or, in you.

* Abac. 2. 4.

‖ Or, to them.

‖ Or, that they may be.

in their imaginations, and their foolish heart was darkened:

22 Professing themſelues to be wise, they became fooles:

23 And changed the glory of the vncorruptible *God, into an image made like to corruptible man, and to birdes, and foure footed beasts, and creeping things:

24 Wherefore God also gaue them vp to vncleannesse, through the lusts of their owne hearts, to dishonour their owne bodies betweene themselues:

25 Who changed the trueth of God into a lye, and worshipped and serued the creature more then the Creatour, who is blessed for euer. Amen.

26 For this cause God gaue them vp vnto vile affections: for euen their women did change the naturall vse into that which is against nature:

27 And likewise also the men, leauing the naturall vse of the woman, burned in their lust one towards another, men with men working that which is vnseemely, and receiuing in themselues that recompense of their errour which was meet.

28 And euen as they did not like to ‖retaine God in *their* knowledge, God gaue them ouer to ‖a reprobate minde, to doe those things which are not conuenient:

29 Being filled with all vnrighteousnes, fornication, wickednesse, couetousnes, maliciousnes, full of enuie, murther, debate, deceit, malignitie, whisperers,

30 Backbiters, haters of God, despitefull, proude, boasters, inuenters of euill things, disobedient to parents;

31 Without vnderstanding, couenant breakers, without ‖naturall affection, implacable, vnmercifull;

32 Who knowing the iudgement of God, (that they which commit such things, are worthy of death) not onely do the same, but ‖haue pleasure in them that doe them.

CHAP. II.

1 They that sinne, though they condemne it in others, cannot excuse themselues, 6 and much lesse escape the iudgement of God, 9 whether they be Iewes or Gentiles. 14 The Gentiles cannot escape, 17 nor yet the Iewes, 25 whom their Circumcision shall not profit, if they keepe not the Law.

Herefore, thou art inexcusable, O man, whosoeuer thou art that iudgest: for wherein thou iudgest another, thou condemnest thy selfe, for thou that iudgest doest the same things.

2 But wee are sure that the iudgement of God is according to trueth, against them which commit such things.

3 And thinkest thou this, O man, that iudgest them which doe such things, and doest the same, that thou shalt escape the iudgement of God?

4 Or despisest thou the riches of his goodnesse, and forbearance, and long suffering, not knowing that the goodnes of God leadeth thee to repentance?

5 But after thy hardnesse, and impenitent heart, *treasurest vp vnto thy selfe wrath, against the day of wrath, and reuelation of the righteous iudgement of God:

6 *Who will render to euery man according to his deedes:

7 To them, who by patient continuance in well doing, seeke for glorie, and honour, and immortalitie, eternall life:

8 But vnto them that are contentious, & doe not obey the trueth, but obey vnrighteousnes, indignation, & wrath,

9 Tribulation, and anguish vpon euery soule of man that doeth euill, of the Iew first, and also of the †Gentile.

10 But glory, honour, and peace, to euery man that worketh good, to the Iew first, and also to the †Gentile.

11 For there is no respect of persons with God.

12 For as many as haue sinned without Law, shall also perish without Law: and as many as haue sinned in the Law, shalbe iudged by the Law.

13 (For not the hearers of the Law are iust before God, but the doers of the Law shalbe iustified;

14 For when the Gentiles which haue not the Law, doe by nature the things contained in the Law: these hauing not the Law, are a Law vnto themselues,

15 Which shew the worke of the Law written in their hearts, their ‖conscience also bearing witnesse, and their thoughts ‖the meane while accusing, or else excusing one another:

16 In the day when God shall iudge the secrets of men by Iesus Christ, according to my Gospel.

17 Be-

Marginal notes (left column):

* Psal. 106. 20.

‖ Or, to acknowledge.
‖ Or, a minde voyde of iudgement.

‖ Or, vnsociable.

‖ Or, consent with them.

Marginal notes (right column):

* Iames 5 3.

* Psal. 62. 12. matth. 16. 27. reuel. 22. 12.

† Gr. Greeke

† Gr. Greeke

‖ Or, the conscience witnessing with them.
‖ Or, betweene themselues.

17 Behold, thou art called a Iew, and restest in the Law, and makest thy boast of God:

|| Or, triest the things that differ.

18 And knowest *his* will, and ||approuest the things that are more excellent, being instructed out of the Law,

19 And art confident that thou thy selfe art a guide of the blinde, a light of them *which are* in darkenesse:

20 An instructour of the foolish, a teacher of babes: which hast the forme of knowledge and of the trueth in the Law:

21 Thou therefore which teachest another, teachest thou not thy selfe? thou that preachest a man should not steale, doest thou steale?

22 Thou that sayest a man should not commit adulterie, doest thou commit adulterie? thou that abhorrest idols, doest thou commit sacriledge?

23 Thou that makest thy boast of the Law, through breaking the Law dishonourest thou God?

24 For the Name of God is blasphemed among the Gentiles, through you, as it is *written:

* Esay 52. 5. ezech. 36. 20, 23.

25 For Circumcision verily profiteth if thou keepe the Law: but if thou be a breaker of the Law, thy Circumcision is made vncircumcision.

26 Therefore, if the vncircumcision keepe the righteousnesse of the Law, shall not his vncircumcision be counted for Circumcision?

27 And shall not vncircumcision which is by nature, if it fulfill the Law, iudge thee, who by the letter, and Circumcision, doest transgresse the Law?

28 For hee is not a Iew, which is one outwardly, neither is that Circumcision, which is outward in the flesh:

29 But he is a Iew which is one inwardly, and Circumcision is, that of the heart, in the spirit, and not in the letter, whose praise is not of men, but of God.

CHAP. III.

1 The Iewes prerogatiue: 3 which they haue not lost: 9 Howbeit the Law conuinceth them also of sinne: 20 Therefore no flesh is iustified by the Law, 28 but all, without difference, by faith onely: 31 And yet the Law is not abolished.

WHat aduantage then hath the Iew? or what profit is there of Circumcision?

2 Much euery way: chiefly, because that vnto them were committed the Oracles of God.

3 For what if some did not beleeue? shall their vnbeliefe make the faith of God without effect?

4 God forbid: yea, let God be true, but euery man a lier, as it is written, *That thou mightest be iustified in thy sayings, and mightest ouercome when thou art iudged.

* Psal. 51. 4.

5 But if our vnrighteousnesse commend the righteousnesse of God, what shall we say? is God vnrighteous who taketh vengeance? (I speake as a man)

6 God forbid: for then how shall God iudge the world?

7 For if the trueth of God hath more abounded through my lye vnto his glory? why yet am I also iudged as a sinner?

8 And not *rather* as wee be slanderously reported, and as some affirme that we say, Let vs doe euill, that good may come: whose damnation is iust.

9 What then? are wee better *then they?* No in no wise: for we haue before † proued both Iewes, and Gentiles, that they are all vnder sinne,

† Gr. charged.

10 As it is written, There is none righteous, no not one:

11 There is none that vnderstandeth, there is none that seeketh after God.

12 They are all gone out of the way, they are together become vnprofitable, there is none that doeth good, no not one.

13 Their throat is an open sepulchre, with their tongues they haue vsed deceit, the poyson of Aspes is vnder their lippes:

14 Whose mouth is full of cursing and bitternesse:

15 Their feet are swift to shed blood.

16 Destruction & misery are in their wayes:

17 And the way of peace haue they not knowen.

18 There is no feare of God before their eyes.

19 Now we know that what things soeuer the Law saith, it saith to them who are vnder the Law: that euery mouth may bee stopped, and all the world may become ||guilty before God.

|| Or, subiect to the iudgement of God.

20 Therefore by the deedes of the Law, there shall no flesh be iustified in his sight: for by the Law *is* the knowledge of sinne.

21 But

21 But nowe the righteousnesse of God without the Lawe is manifested, being witnessed by the Lawe and the Prophets.

22 Euen the righteousnesse of God, which is by faith of Iesus Christ vnto all, and vpon all them that beleeue : for there is no difference :

23 For all haue sinned , and come short of the glory of God,

24 Being iustified freely by his grace, through the redemption that is in Iesus Christ :

‖ Or, fore-ordeined.

25 Whom God hath ‖ set forth to bee a propitiation , through faith in his blood, to declare his righteousnesse for the ‖ remission of sinnes, that are past, through the forbearance of God.

‖ Or, passing ouer.

26 To declare, I say, at this time his righteousnesse : that hee might bee iust, and the iustifier of him which beleeueth in Iesus.

27 Where is boasting then ? It is excluded. By what Law ? Of workes ? Nay : but by the Law of faith.

28 Therefore wee conclude, that a man is iustified by faith, without the deeds of the Law.

29 Is he the God of the Iewes only ? Is he not also of the Gentiles ? Yes, of the Gentiles also :

30 Seeing it is one God which shal iustifie the circumcision by faith, and vncircumcision through faith.

31 Doe we then make void the lawe through faith ? God forbid : yea, we establish the Law.

CHAP. IIII.

1 Abrahams faith was imputed to him for righteousnesse, 10 before hee was circumcised. 13 By faith only he and his seed receiued the promise. 16 Abraham is the father of all that beleeue. 24 Our faith also shall be imputed to vs for righteousnes.

WHat shall we say then, that Abraham our father, as perteining to the flesh, hath found ?

2 For if Abraham were iustified by workes, hee hath *whereof* to glory, but not before God.

3 For what saith the Scripture ? Abraham beleeued God, and it was counted vnto him for righteousnes.

4 Now to him that worketh, is the reward not reckoned of grace, but of debt.

5 But to him that worketh not, but beleeueth on him that iustifieth the vngodly ; his faith is counted for righteousnesse.

6 Euen as Dauid also describeth the blessednesse of the man, vnto whom God imputeth righteousnesse without works :

7 *Saying*, Blessed are they whose iniquities are forgiuen, and whose sinnes are couered.

8 Blessed is the man to whome the Lord will not impute sinne.

9 *Commeth* this blessednes then vpon the circumcision *onely*, or vpon the vncircumcision also ? for wee say that faith was reckoned to Abraham for righteousnesse.

10 How was it then reckoned ? when he was in circumcision, or in vncircumcision ? not in circumcision, but in vncircumcision.

11 And hee receiued the signe of circumcision, a seale of the righteousnesse of the faith, which *hee had yet* being vncircumcised : that he might be the father of all them that beleeue, though they be not circumcised ; that righteousnesse might be imputed vnto them also :

12 And the father of circumcision, to them who are not of the circumcision onely, but also walke in the steppes of that faith of our father Abraham, *which he had* being yet vncircumcised.

13 For the promise that he should be the heire of the world, *was* not to Abraham, or to his seed through the Lawe, but through the righteousnesse of faith.

14 For if they which are of the law be heires, faith is made voide, and the promise made of none effect.

15 Because the law worketh wrath : for where no Lawe is, *there* is no transgression.

16 Therefore *it is* of faith, that it might bee by grace; to the ende the promise might be sure to all the seede, not to that onely which is of the Law, but to that also which is of the faith of Abraham, who is the father of vs all,

17 (As it is written, *I haue made thee a father of many nations) ‖ before him whom he beleeued, *euen* God who quickeneth the dead, and calleth those things which bee not, as though they were,

* Gen. 17. 5
 ‖ Or, like vnto him.

18 Who against hope , beleeued in hope, that hee might become the father of many nations : according to that which

* Gen. 15. 5.

which was spoken, *So shall thy seede bee.

19 And being not weake in faith, hee considered not his owne body now dead, when hee was about an hundred yere old, neither yet the deadnes of Saraes wombe.

20 Hee staggered not at the promise of God through vnbeliefe : but was strong in faith, giuing glory to God :

21 And being fully perswaded, that what he had promised, he was able also to performe.

22 And therefore it was imputed to him for righteousnesse.

23 Now it was not written for his sake alone, that it was imputed to him :

24 But for vs also, to whome it shall bee imputed, if wee beleeue on him that raised vp Iesus our Lord from the dead,

25 Who was deliuered for our offences, and was raised againe for our iustification.

CHAP. V.

1 Being iustified by faith, wee haue peace with God, 2 and ioy in our hope, 8 that sith we were reconciled by his blood, when wee were enemies, 10 wee shall much more be saued being reconciled. 12 As sinne and death came by Adam, 17 so much more righteousnesse and life by Iesus Christ. 20 Where sinne abounded, grace did superabound.

Herefore being iustified by faith, wee haue peace with God, through our Lord Iesus Christ.

2 By whom also wee haue accesse by faith, into this grace wherein wee stand, and reioyce in hope of the glory of God.

3 And not onely so, but we glory in tribulations also, knowing that tribulation worketh patience :

4 And patience, experience : and experience, hope :

5 And hope maketh not ashamed, because the loue of God is shed abroad in our hearts, by the holy Ghost, which is giuen vnto vs.

‖ Or, according to the time.

6 For when wee were yet without strength, ‖in due time, Christ died for the vngodly.

7 For scarcely for a righteous man will one die : yet peraduenture for a good man, some would euen dare to dye.

8 But God commendeth his loue towards vs, in that, while we were yet sinners, Christ died for vs.

9 Much more then being now iustified by his blood, we shalbe saued from wrath through him.

10 For if when wee were enemies, we were reconciled to God, by the death of his sonne : much more being reconciled, we shalbe saued by his life.

11 And not onely so, but wee also ioy in God, through our Lorde Iesus Christ, by whom we haue now receiued the atonement.

12 Wherefore, as by one man sinne entred into the world, and death by sin : and so death passed vpon all men, ‖for that all haue sinned.

‖ Or, in whom

13 For vntill the Law sinne was in the world : but sin is not imputed when there is no Law.

14 Neuertheles, death reigned from Adam to Moses, euen ouer them that had not sinned after the similitude of Adams transgression, who is the figure of him that was to come :

15 But not as the offence, so also is the free gift : for if through the offence of one, many bee dead : much more the grace of God, and the gift by grace, which is by one man Iesus Christ, hath abounded vnto many.

16 And not as it was by one that sinned, so is the gift : for the iudgement was by one to condemnation : but the free gift is of many offences vnto iustification.

17 For if ‖by one mans offence, death raigned by one, much more they which receiue abundance of grace and of the gift of righteousnes, shall reigne in life by one, Iesus Christ.

‖ Or, by one offence.

18 Therfore as ‖by the offence of one, iudgment came vpon all men to condemnation : euen so by the ‖righteousnes of one, the free gift came vpon all men vnto iustification of life.

‖ Or, by one offence.
‖ Or, by one righteousnes

19 For as by one mans disobedience many were made sinners : so by the obedience of one, shall many bee made righteous.

20 Moreouer, the Lawe entred, that the offence might abound : but where sinne abounded, grace did much more abound.

21 That as sinne hath reigned vnto death ; euen so might grace reigne thorow righteousnes vnto eternall life, by Iesus Christ our Lord.

CHAP.

CHAP. VI.

1 Wee may not liue in sinne, 2 for wee are dead vnto it, 3 as appeareth by our baptisme. 12 Let not sinne raigne any more, 18 because wee haue yeelded our selues to the seruice of righteousnesse, 23 and for that death is the wages of sinne.

Hat shall we say then? shall wee continue in sinne : that grace may abound ?

2 God forbid : how shall wee that are dead to sinne, liue any longer therein ?

3 Know ye not, that so many of vs as ||were baptized into Iesus Christ, were baptized into his death ?

‖Or, are.

4 Therefore wee are buryed with him by baptisme into death , that like as Christ was raised vp from the dead by the glorie of the Father : euen so wee also should walke in newnesse of life.

5 For if we haue bene planted together in the likenesse of his death : wee shalbe also in the likenesse of his resurrection :

6 Knowing this, that our old man is crucified with him, that the bodie of sinne might bee destroyed, that hencefoorth we should not serue sinne.

7 For he that is dead, is †freed from sinne.

†Gr. iustified

8 Now if we be dead with Christ, we beleeue that we shal also liue with him:

9 Knowing that Christ being raysed from the dead, dieth no more, death hath no more dominion ouer him.

10 For in that he dyed, he dyed vnto sinne once : but in that hee liueth, hee liueth vnto God.

11 Likewise reckon yee also your selues to be dead indeed vnto sinne : but aliue vnto God, through Iesus Christ our Lord.

12 Let not sinne reigne therfore in your mortall body, that ye should obey it in the lusts thereof.

13 Neither yeeld yee your members as †instruments of vnrighteousnes vnto sinne : but yeelde your selues vnto God, as those that are aliue from the dead, and your members as instruments of righteousnesse vnto God.

†Gr. armes, or weapons.

14 For sinne shall not haue dominion ouer you, for yee are not vnder the Law, but vnder Grace.

15 What then? shal we sinne, because wee are not vnder the Law, but vnder Grace? God forbid.

16 Know ye not, that to whom yee yeeld your selues seruants to obey, his seruants ye are to whom ye obey : whether of sinne vnto death, or of obedience vnto righteousnesse ?

17 But God bee thanked, that yee were the seruants of sinne : but ye haue obeyed from the heart that fourme of doctrine, †which was deliuered you.

†Gr. whereto ye were deliuered.

18 Being then made free from sinne, yee became the seruants of righteousnesse.

19 I speake after the maner of men, because of the infirmitie of your flesh : for as yee haue yeelded your members seruants to vncleannesse and to iniquitie, vnto iniquitie : euen so now yeelde your members seruants to righteousnesse, vnto holinesse.

20 For when yee were the seruants of sinne ye were free †from righteousnesse.

†Gr. to righteousnesse.

21 What fruit had yee then in those things, whereof ye are now ashamed? for the end of those things is death.

22 But now being made free from sinne, and become seruants to God, yee haue your fruit vnto holinesse, and the end euerlasting life.

23 For the wages of sinne is death : but the gift of God is eternall life, through Iesus Christ our Lord.

CHAP. VII.

1 No law hath power ouer a man, longer then hee liueth. 4 But wee are dead to the law. 7 Yet is not the law sinne, 12 but holy, iust, good, 16 as I acknowledge, who am grieued because I cannot keepe it.

Now ye not, brethren (for I speake to them that knowe the Lawe) how that the Lawe hath dominion ouer a man, as long as he liueth ?

2 For the woman which hath an husbaud, is bound by the law to her husband, so long as he liueth : but if the husband be dead, she is loosed from the law of the husband.

3 So then if while her husband liueth, shee be married to another man, shee shalbe called an adulteresse : but if her husband be dead, shee is free from that law, so that she is no adulteresse, though she be married to another man.

4 Where-

4 Wherefore my brethren, yee also are become dead to the law by the body of Christ, that ye should be married to another, euen to him who is raised from the dead, that wee should bring forth fruit vnto God,

5 For when wee were in the flesh, the †motions of sinnes which were by the law, did worke in our members, to bring foorth fruit vnto death.

†Gr.passions

6 But now wee are deliuered from the law, ||that being dead wherein we were held, that we should serue in newnesse of spirit, and not in the oldnesse of the letter.

‖ Or, being dead to that.

7 What shall wee say then? is the law sinne? God forbid. Nay, I had not knowen sinne, but by the lawe: for I had not knowen ||lust, except the Law had said, Thou shalt not couet.

‖ Or. concupiscence.

8 But sinne taking occasion by the commaundement, wrought in me all maner of concupiscence. For without the Law sinne *was* dead.

9 For I was aliue without the Law once, but when the commandement came, sinne reuiued, and I died.

10 And the commandement which was *ordained* to life, I found to be vnto death.

11 For sinne taking occasion by the commandement, deceiued me, and by it slew me.

12 Wherefore the Law is holy, and the Commandement holy, and iust, and good.

13 Was that then which is good, made death vnto me? God forbid. But sinne, that it might appeare sinne, working death in mee by that which is good: that sinne by the Commaundement might become exceeding sinfull.

14 For wee know that the Law is spirituall: but I am carnall, sold vnder sinne.

† Gr. know.

15 For that which I do, I †allow not: for what I would, that do I not, but what I hate, that doe I.

16 If then I doe that which I would not, I consent vnto the Law, that it is good.

17 Now then, it is no more I that doe it: but sinne that dwelleth in me.

18 For I know, that in me (that is, in my flesh) dwelleth no good thing. For to will is present with me: but *how* to performe that which is good, I find not.

19 For the good that I would, I do

not: but the euill which I would not, that I doe.

20 Now if I doe that I would not, it is no more I that do it, but sinne that dwelleth in me.

21 I find then a Law, that when I would do good, euil is present with me.

22 For I delight in the Lawe of God, after the inward man.

23 But I see another Lawe in my members, warring against the Lawe of my minde, and bringing me into captiuity to the Law of sinne, which is in my members.

24 O wretched man that I am! who shall deliuer me from ||the body of this death?

‖ Or, this body of death.

25 I thanke God through Iesus Christ our Lord. So then, with the mind I my self serue the Law of God: but with the flesh, the law of sinne.

CHAP. VIII.

1 They that are in Christ, and liue according to the Spirit, are free from condemnation. 5. 13 What harme commeth of the flesh, 6. 14 and what good of the Spirit: 17 and what of being Gods childe, 19 whose glorious deliuerance all things long for, 29 was before hand decreed from God. 38 What can seuer vs from his loue?

Here is therefore now no condemnation to them which are in Christ Iesus, who walke not after the flesh, but after the spirit.

2 For the law of the spirit of life, in Christ Iesus, hath made me free from the law of sinne and death.

3 For what the law could not doe, in that it was weake through the flesh, God sending his owne Sonne, in the likenesse of sinnefull flesh, and ||for sinne condemned sinne in the flesh:

‖Or, by a sacrifice for sin.

4 That the righteousnesse of the law might be fulfilled in vs, who walke not after the flesh, but after the spirit.

5 For they that are after the flesh, doe minde the things of the flesh: but they that are after the spirit, the things of the spirit.

6 For to †be carnally minded, is death: but †to be spiritually minded, is life and peace:

† Gr. the minding of the flesh.
† Gr. the minding of the spirit.

7 Because † the carnall minde is enmitie against God: for it is not subiect to the law of God, neither indeed can be.

† Gr. the minding of the spirit.
† Gr. the minding of the flesh.

8 So then they that are in the flesh, cannot please God.

9 But

9 But ye are not in the flesh, but in the spirit, if so be that the spirit of God dwell in you. Now if any man haue not the spirit of Christ, he is none of his.

10 And if Christ be in you, the body is dead because of sinne : but the spirit is life, because of righteousnesse.

11 But if the spirit of him that raised vp Iesus from the dead, dwell in you : he that raised vp Christ from the dead, shall also quicken your mortall bodies, ‖ by his spirit that dwelleth in you.

‖ Or, because of his spirit.

12 Therfore brethren, we are detters, not to the flesh, to liue after the flesh.

13 For if ye liue after the flesh, ye shall die : but if ye through the spirit doe mortifie the deeds of the body, ye shall liue.

14 For as many as are led by the spirit of God, they are the sonnes of God.

15 For ye haue not receiued the spirit of bondage againe to feare : but ye haue receiued the spirit of adoption, whereby we cry, Abba, father.

16 The spirit it selfe beareth witnes with our spirit, that we are the children of God.

17 And if children, then heires, heires of God, and ioynt heires with Christ : if so be that we suffer with *him*, that wee may be also glorified together.

18 For I reckon, that the sufferings of this present time, are not worthy to be compared with the glory which shall be reuealed in vs.

19 For the earnest expectation of the creature, waiteth for the manifestation of the sonnes of God.

20 For the creature was made subiect to vanitie, not willingly, but by reason of him who hath subiected the same in hope :

21 Because the creature it selfe also shall bee deliuered from the bondage of corruption, into the glorious libertie of the children of God.

22 For wee know that ‖ the whole creation groaneth, and trauaileth in paine together vntill now.

‖ Or, euery creature.

23 And not only *they*, but our selues also which haue the first fruites of the spirit, euen we our selues groane within our selues, waiting for the adoption, *to wit*, the *redemption of our body.

* Luke 21. 28.

24 For wee are saued by hope : but hope that is seene, is not hope : for what a man seeth, why doth he yet hope for?

25 But if wee hope for that wee see not, then doe wee with patience waite for it.

26 Likewise the spirit also helpeth our infirmities : for we know not what wee should pray for as wee ought : but the spirit it selfe maketh intercession for vs with groanings, which cannot bee vttered.

27 And he that searcheth the hearts, knoweth what is the minde of the spirit, ‖ because he maketh intercession for the Saints, according to *the will of* God.

‖ Or, that

28 And wee know that all things worke together for good, to them that loue God, to them who are the called according to *his* purpose.

29 For whom he did foreknow, he also did predestinate to be conformed to the image of his sonne, that hee might bee the first borne amongst many brethren.

30 Moreouer, whom he did predestinate, them he also called : and whom he called, them he also iustified : and whom he iustified, them he also glorified.

31 What shall wee then say to these things? If God be for vs, who can bee against vs?

32 He that spared not his owne son, but deliuered him vp for vs all : how shall hee not with him also freely giue vs all things?

33 Who shall lay any thing to the charge of Gods elect? It is God that iustifieth :

34 Who is he that condemneth? It is Christ that died, yea rather that is risen againe, who is euen at the right hand of God, who also maketh intercession for vs.

35 Who shall separate vs from the loue of Christ? *shall* tribulation, or distresse, or persecution, or famine, or nakednesse, or perill, or sword?

36 (As it is written, *for thy sake we are killed all the day long, wee are accounted as sheepe for the slaughter.)

* Psal. 44. 22.

37 Nay in all these things wee are more then conquerours, through him that loued vs.

38 For I am perswaded, that neither death, nor life, nor angels, nor principalities, nor powers, nor things present, nor things to come,

39 Nor height, nor depth, nor any other creature, shalbe able to separate vs from the loue of God, which is in Christ Iesus our Lord.

CHAP. IX.

1 Paul is sory for the Iewes. 7 All the seed of Abraham

Abraham were not the children of the promise. 18 God hath mercy vpon whom hee will. 21 The potter may doe with his clay what he list. 25 The calling of the Gentiles, and reiecting of the Iewes were foretold. 32 The cause why so few Iewes embraced the righteousnesse of faith.

I Say the trueth in Christ, I lie not, my conscience also bearing mee witnesse in the holy Ghost,

2 That I haue great heauinesse, and continuall sorrow in my heart.

3 For I could wish that my selfe were ||accursed from Christ, for my brethren my kinsemen according to the flesh :

|| Or, separated.

4 Who are Israelites : to whom perteineth the adoption, and the glory, and the ||couenants, and the giuing of the Law, and the seruice of God, and the promises :

|| Or, testaments.

5 Whose are the fathers, and of whom as concerning the flesh Christ came, who is ouer all, God blessed for euer, Amen.

6 Not as though the word of God hath taken none effect. For they are not all Israel which are of Israel :

7 Neither because they are the seed of Abraham are they all children : but *in Isaac shall thy seed be called.

* Gen. 21. 12.

8 That is, They which are the children of the flesh, these are not the children of God : but the children of the promise are counted for the seed.

9 For this is the word of promise, *At this time will I come, and Sara shall haue a sonne.

* Gen. 18. 10.

10 And not onely this, but when Rebecca also had conceiued by one, euen by our father Isaac,

11 (For the children being not yet borne, neither hauing done any good or euil, that the purpose of God according to election might stand, not of workes, but of him that calleth.)

12 It was said vnto her, The *||elder shall serue the ||yonger.

* Gene. 25. 23.
||. Or, greater.
|| Or, lesser.
* Mala. 1. 2.

13 As it is written, *Iacob haue I loued, but Esau haue I hated.

14 What shall we say then ? Is there vnrighteousnes with God ? God forbid.

15 For hee saith to Moses, *I will haue mercy on whom I wil haue mercie, and I will haue compassion on whom I will haue compassion.

* Exod. 33. 19.

16 So then it is not of him that willeth, nor of him that runneth, but of God that sheweth mercy.

17 For the Scripture saith vnto Pharaoh, *Euen for this same purpose haue I raised thee vp, that I might shew my power in thee, and that my Name might bee declared throughout all the earth.

* Exod 9. 16.

18 Therefore hath hee mercie on whom hee will haue mercy, and whom he will, he hardeneth.

19 Thou wilt say then vnto mee ; Why doeth he yet find fault ? For who hath resisted his will ?

20 Nay but O man, who art thou that ||repliest against God ? Shall the thing formed say to him that formed it, *Why hast thou made me thus ?

|| Or, answerest againe, or disputest with God ?
* Esay 45. 9.
* Iere. 18. 6. wisd. 15. 7.

21 Hath not the *potter power ouer the clay, of the same lumpe, to make one vessell vnto honour, and another vnto dishonour ?

22 What if God, willing to shew his wrath, & to make his power knowen, indured with much long suffering the vessels of wrath ||fitted to destruction :

| Or, made vp.

23 And that he might make knowen the riches of his glory on the vessels of mercy, which hee had afore prepared vnto glorie ?

24 Euen vs whom hee hath called, not of the Iewes onely, but also of the Gentiles.

25 As he saith also in Osee, *I will call them my people, which were not my people : and her, beloued, which was not beloued.

* Ose. 2. 23. 1. pet. 2. 10.

26 *And it shall come to passe, that in the place where it was saide vnto them, Ye are not my people, there shall they bee called the children of the liuing God.

* Ose. 1. 10.

27 Esaias also crieth concerning Israel, *Though the number of the children of Israel be as the sand of the sea, a remnant shalbe saued.

* Esay 10. 22, 23.

28 For he will finish the ||worke, and cut it short in righteousnesse : because a short ||worke will the Lord make vpon the earth.

|| Or, the account.

29 And as Esaias said before, *Except the Lord of Sabboth had left vs a seed, we had bene as Sodoma, and bene made like vnto Gomorrha.

* Esay 1. 9.

30 What shall wee say then ? That the Gentiles which followed not after righteousnesse, haue attained to righteousnesse, euen the righteousnesse which is of faith :

31 But

31 But Israel which followed after the Law of righteousnesse, hath not attained to the Law of righteousnes.

32 Wherefore? because *they sought it*, not by faith, but as it were by the workes of the Law: for they stumbled at that stumbling stone,

*Esay 8. 14 and 28. 16. 1. pet. 2. 6.

33 As it is written, *Beholde, I lay in Sion a stumbling stone, and rocke of offence: and whosoeuer beleeueth on him, shall not be ||ashamed.

|| Or, confounded.

CHAP. X.

5 The Scripture sheweth the difference betwixt the righteousnes of the Law, and this of faith, 11 and that all both Iew and Gentile that beleeue, shal not be cōfounded, 18 and that the Gentiles shall receiue the word and beleeue. 19 Israel was not ignorant of these things.

BRethren, my hearts desire and prayer to God for Israel is, that they might be saued.

2 For I beare them record, that they haue a zeale of God, but not according to knowledge.

3 For they being ignorant of Gods righteousnesse, and going about to establish their owne righteousnesse, haue not submitted themselues vnto the righteousnesse of God.

4 For Christ is the end of the Law for righteousnes to euery one that beleeueth.

*Leu. 18. 5 ezek. 20. 11 gal. 3. 12.

5 For Moses describeth the righteousnesse which is of the Law, that *the man which doeth those things shall liue by them.

6 But the righteousnesse which is of faith, speaketh on this wise: *Say not in thine heart, Who shall ascend into heauen? That is to bring Christ down from aboue.

*Deut. 30. 12.

7 Or, Who shall descend into the deepe? That is to bring vp Christ againe from the dead.

*Deut. 30. 14.

8 But what saith it? *The word is nigh thee, *euen* in thy mouth, and in thy heart, that is the word of faith which we preach,

9 That if thou shalt confesse with thy mouth the Lord Iesus, and shalt beleeue in thine heart, that God hath raised him from the dead, thou shalt be saued.

10 For with the heart man beleeueth vnto righteousnesse, and with the mouth confession is made vnto saluation.

11 For the Scripture saith, *Whosoeuer beleeueth on him, shall not bee ashamed.

*Esa. 28. 16

12 For there is no difference betweene the Iew and the Greeke: for the same Lord ouer all, is rich vnto all, that call vpon him.

13 *For whosoeuer shall call vpon the Name of the Lord, shall be saued.

*Ioel 2. 32. acts 2. 21.

14 How then shall they call on him in whom they haue not beleeued? and how shal they beleeue in him, of whom they haue not heard? and how shall they heare without a Preacher?

15 And how shall they preach, except they be sent? as it is written: *How beautifull are the feete of them that preach the *Gospel of peace, and bring glad tidings of good things!

*Esa. 52. 7. naum. 1. 15

16 But they haue not all obeyed the Gospel. For Esaias saith, *Lord, who hath beleeued our ||†report?

*Esa. 53. 1. iohn 12. 38 || Or, preaching. † Gr. the hearing of vs.

17 So then, faith *commeth* by hearing, and hearing by the word of God.

18 But I say, haue they not heard? yes verely, *their sound went into all the earth, and their words vnto the ends of the world.

*Psal. 19. 4.

19 But I say, Did not Israel know? First Moses saith, *I will prouoke you to iealousie by them that are no people, & by a foolish nation I will anger you.

*Deut. 32. 21.

20 But Esaias is very bold, and saith, *I was found of them that sought me not: I was made manifest vnto them, that asked not after me.

*Esa. 65. 1.

21 But to Israel he sayth, *All day long I haue stretched foorth my hands vnto a disobedient and gainesaying people.

*Esa. 65. 2.

CHAP. XI.

1 God hath not cast off all Israel. 7 Some were elected, though the rest were hardened. 16 There is hope of their conuersion. 18 The Gentiles may not insult vpon them: 26 For there is a promise of their saluation. 33 Gods iudgements are vnsearchable.

I Say then, Hath God cast away his people? God forbidde. For I also am an Israelite of the seede of Abraham, of the tribe of Beniamin.

2 God hath not cast away his people which hee foreknew. Wote yee not what the Scripture saieth of Elias? how hee maketh intercession to God against Israel, saying,

3 *Lord,

*1. Reg. 19. 14.

3 *Lord, they haue killed thy Prophets, and digged downe thine Altars, and I am left alone, and they seeke my life.

*1. Reg. 19. 18.

4 But what saieth the answere of God vnto him? *I haue reserued to my selfe seuen thousand men, who haue not bowed the knee to *the image of* Baal.

5 Euen so then at this present time also there is a remnant according to the election of grace.

6 And if by grace, then is it no more of workes : otherwise grace is no more grace. But if it bee of workes, then is it no more grace, otherwise worke is no more worke.

7 What then? Israel hath not obtained that which he seeketh for, but the election hath obtained it, and the rest were ‖blinded,

‖ Or, hardened.
* Esa. 29. 10
‖ Or, remorse
* Esa. 6. 9.

8 According as it is written, *God hath giuen them the spirit of ‖slumber: *eyes that they should not see, and eares that they should not heare vnto this day.

* Psa. 69. 22

9 And Dauid sayth; *Let their table be made a snare, and a trap, and a stumbling blocke, and a recompense vnto them.

* Psa. 69. 23

10 *Let their eyes be darkened, that they may not see, and bow downe their backe alway.

11 I say then; Haue they stumbled that they should fall? God forbid, But *rather* through their fall, saluation *is come* vnto the Gentiles, for to prouoke them to ielousie.

‖ Or, decay, or losse.

12 Now if the fall of them be the riches of the world, and the ‖diminishing of them, the riches of the Gentiles: how much more their fulnesse?

13 For I speake to you Gentiles, in as much as I am the Apostle of the Gentiles, I magnifie mine office :

14 If by any means I may prouoke to emulation them which are my flesh, and might saue some of them.

15 For if the casting away of them be the reconciling of the world : what shal the receiuing *of them* be, but life from the dead?

16 For if the first fruite bee holy, the lumpe is also *holy :* and if the root be holy, so *are* the branches.

17 And if some of the branches bee broken off, and thou being a wilde oliue tree wert graffed in ‖amongst them, and with them partakest of the roote and fatnesse of the Oliue tree :

‖ Or, for them.

18 Boast not against the branches : but if thou boast, thou bearest not the root, but the root thee.

19 Thou wilt say then, The branches were broken off, that I might bee graffed in.

20 Well : because of vnbeliefe they were broken off, and thou standest by fayth. Be not high minded, but feare.

21 For if God spared not the natural branches, *take heede* least hee also spare not thee.

22 Beholde therefore the goodnesse and seueritie of God : on them which fell, seueritie ; but towards thee, goodnesse, if thou continue in his goodnesse: otherwise thou also shalt be cut off.

23 And they also, if they bide not still in vnbeliefe, shall be graffed in : for God is able to graffe them in againe.

24 For if thou wert cut out of the Oliue tree which is wilde by nature, and wert graffed contrary to nature into a good Oliue tree : how much more shall these which be the natural *branches*, bee graffed into their owne Oliue tree?

25 For I would not, brethren, that ye should bee ignorant of this mysterie (least yee should bee wise in your owne conceits) that ‖blindnesse in part is happened to Israel, vntill the fulnes of the Gentiles be come in.

‖ Or, hardnesse.

26 And so all Israel shall be saued, as it is written, *There shall come out of Sion the Deliuerer, and shall turne away vngodlinesse from Iacob.

* Esa. 59. 20

27 For this is my couenant vnto them, when I shall take away their sinnes.

28 As concerning the Gospel, they are enemies for your sake : but as touching the election, they are beloued for the fathers *sakes*.

29 For the gifts and calling of God are without repentance.

30 For as yee in times past haue not ‖beleeued God, yet haue now obtained mercy through their vnbeliefe :

‖ Or, obeyed

31 Euen so haue these also now not ‖beleeued, that through your mercy they also may obtaine mercy.

‖ Or, obeyed

32 For God hath ‖concluded them all in vnbeliefe, that he might haue mercy vpon all.

‖ Or, shut them all vp together.

33 O the depth of the riches both of the wisedome and knowledge of God! how vnsearchable are his iudgements, and his wayes past finding out!

34 *For who hath knowen the mind of

* Esa. 40. 1
wisd. 9. 13.
1. cor. 2. 16.

of the Lord, or who hath bene his counseller?

35 Or who hath first giuen to him, and it shall bee recompensed vnto him againe?

36 For of him, and through him, and to him are all things : to whom be glory for euer. Amen.

CHAP. XII.

1 Gods mercies must mooue vs to please God. 3 No man must thinke too well of himselfe, 6 But attend, euerie one, on that calling, wherein he is placed. 9 Loue, and many other dueties are required of vs. 19 Reuenge is specially forbidden.

I Beseech you therefore brethren, by the mercies of God, that yee present your bodies a liuing sacrifice, holy, acceptable vnto God, *which is* your reasonable seruice.

2 And bee not conformed to this world : but be ye transformed by the renuing of your minde, that ye may proue what is that good, that acceptable and perfect will of God.

3 For I say, through the grace giuen vnto mee, to euery man that is among you, not to thinke of himselfe more highly then hee ought to thinke, but to thinke † soberly, according as God hath dealt to euery man the measure of faith.

4 For as we haue many members in one body, and all members haue not the same office :

5 So we being many are one bodie in Christ, and euery one members one of another.

6 Hauing then gifts, differing according to the grace that is giuen to vs, whether prophecie, *let vs prophecie* according to the proportion of faith.

7 Or ministery, *let vs wait*, on our ministring : or hee that teacheth, on teaching :

8 Or he that exhorteth, on exhortation : he that ‖giueth, *let him doe it* ‖with simplicitie : hee that ruleth, with diligence : hee that sheweth mercy, with cheerefulnesse.

9 Let loue bee without dissimulation : abhorre that which is euill, cleaue to that which is good.

10 Bee kindly affectioned one to another ‖with brotherly loue, in honour preferring one another.

11 Not slouthfull in busines : feruent in spirit, seruing the Lord.

12 Reioycing in hope, patient in tribulation, continuing instant in prayer.

13 Distributing to the necessitie of Saints ; giuen to hospitalitie.

14 Blesse them which persecute you, blesse, and curse not.

15 Reioyce with them that doe reioice, and weepe with them that weepe.

16 Be of the same mind one towards another. Minde not high things, but ‖condescend to men of low estate. Bee not wise in your owne conceits.

17 Recompence to no man euill for euill. Prouide things honest in the sight of all men.

18 If it be possible, as much as lyeth in you, liue peaceably with all men.

19 Dearely beloued, auenge not your selues, but rather giue place vnto wrath : for it is written, *Vengeance is mine, I will repay, saith the Lord.

20 *Therefore if thine enemie hunger, feed him : if he thirst, giue him drink. For in so doing thou shalt heape coales of fire on his head.

21 Be not ouercome of euill, but ouercome euill with good.

CHAP. XIII.

1 Subiection, and many other dueties wee owe to the Magistrates. 8 Loue is the fulfilling of the Law. 11 Gluttonie and drunkennes, and the workes of darkenesse, are out of season in the time of the Gospel.

L Et euery ſoule bee subiect vnto the higher powers : For there is no power but of God. The powers that be, are ‖ordeined of God.

2 Whosoeuer therefore resisteth the power, resisteth the ordinance of God : and they that resist, shall receiue to themselues damnation.

3 For rulers are not a terrour to good works, but to the euill. Wilt thou then not bee afraide of the power ? doe that which is good, and thou shalt haue praise of the same.

4 For hee is the minister of God to thee for good : but if thou do that which is euill, be afraid : for he beareth not the sword in vaine : for he is the minister of God, a reuenger *to execute* wrath vpon him that doeth euill.

5 Wherfore ye must needs be subiect, not onely for wrath, but also for conscience sake.

6 For, for this cause pay you tribute also :

† Gr. to sobrietie.

‖ Or, imparteth.
‖ Or, liberally.

‖ Or, in the loue of the brethren.

‖ Or, be contented with meane things.

* Deut. 32. 35.

* Pro. 25. 21

‖ Or, ordered.

also : for they are Gods ministers, attending continually vpon this very thing.

7 Render therfore to all their dues, tribute to whom tribute *is due*, custome to whome custome, feare to whome feare, honour to whom honour.

8 Owe no man any thing, but to loue one another : for hee that loueth another hath fulfilled the Law.

9 For this, Thou shalt not commit adulterie, Thou shalt not kill, Thou shalt not steale, Thou shalt not beare false witnesse, Thou shalt not couet : and if there be any other commandement, it is briefly comprehended in this saying, namely, Thou shalt loue thy neighbour as thy selfe.

10 Loue worketh no ill to his neighbour, therefore loue is the fulfilling of the Law.

11 And that, knowing the time, that now it is high time to awake out of sleepe : for now is our saluation neerer then when we beleeued.

12 The night is farre spent, the day is at hand : let vs therefore cast off the workes of darkenesse, and let vs put on the armour of light.

‖ *Or, decently.*

13 Let vs walke ‖honestly as in the day, not in rioting and drunkennesse, not in chambring and wantonnes, not in strife and enuying.

14 But put yee on the Lord Iesus Christ, and make not prouision for the flesh, to *fulfill* the lusts *thereof.*

CHAP. XIIII.

3 Men may not contemne nor condemne one the other for things indifferent: 13 But take heed that they giue no offence in them : 15 For that the Apostle prooueth vnlawfull by many reasons.

‖ *Or, not to iudge his doubtfull thoughts.*

Im that is weake in the faith receiue you, but not to ‖doubtfull disputations.

2 For one beleeueth that he may eat all things: another who is weake, eateth herbes.

3 Let not him that eateth, despise him that eateth not : and let not him which eateth not, iudge him that eateth. For God hath receiued him.

4 Who art thou that iudgest another mans seruant ? to his owne master he standeth or falleth ; Yea he shall bee holden vp : for God is able to make him stand.

5 One man esteemeth one day aboue another : another esteemeth euery day *alike.* Let euery man bee ‖fully perswaded in his owne minde.

‖ *Or, fully assured.*

6 He that ‖regardeth a day, regardeth it vnto the Lord ; and hee that regardeth not the day, to the Lord hee doeth not regard it. He that eateth, eateth to the Lord, for hee giueth God thankes : and hee that eateth not, to the Lord hee eateth not, and giueth God thankes.

‖ *Or, obserueth.*

7 For none of vs liueth to himselfe, and no man dieth to himselfe.

8 For whether we liue, we liue vnto the Lord : and whether wee die, we die vnto the Lord : whether wee liue therefore or die, we are the Lords.

9 For to this ende Christ both died, and rose, and reuiued, that hee might be Lord both of the dead and liuing.

10 But why doest *thou iudge thy brother? or why dost thou set at nought thy brother ? wee shall all stand before the Iudgement seat of Christ.

* 2. Cor. 5. 10.

11 For it is written, *As I liue, saith the Lord, euery knee shall bow to mee, and euery tongue shall confesse to God.

* Esay 45. 23.

12 So then euery one of vs shall giue accompt of himselfe to God.

13 Let vs not therefore iudge one another any more : but iudge this rather, that no man put a stumbling blocke, or an occasion to fall in his brothers way.

14 I know, and am perswaded by the Lord Iesus, that there is nothing †vncleane of it selfe : but to him that esteemeth any thing to bee †vncleane, to him it is vncleane.

† *Gr. common.*
† *Gr. common.*

15 But if thy brother be grieued with *thy* meate : now walkest thou not †charitably. Destroy not him with thy meat, for whom Christ died.

† *Gr. according to charitie. 1. Co 8. 11.*

16 Let not then your good be euill spoken of.

17 For the kingdome of God is not meat and drinke ; but righteousnes, and peace, and ioy in the holy Ghost.

18 For hee that in these things serueth Christ, is acceptable to God, and approued of men.

19 Let vs therefore follow after the things which make for peace, and things wherewith one may edifie another.

20 For meat, destroy not the worke of God : all *things indeed are pure ; but it is euill for that man who eateth with offence.

* Tit. 1. ‖

21 It is good neither to eate *flesh, nor to drinke wine, nor *any thing* whereby

* 1. Cor. 13.

by thy brother stumbleth , or is offended, or is made weake.

22 Hast thou faith? haue it to thy selfe before God. Happie is he that condemneth not himselfe in that *thing which* hee alloweth.

‖ Or, discerneth, & putteth a difference betweene meats

23 And hee that ‖ doubteth, is damned if hee eate , because *hee eateth* not of faith : For whatsoeuer is not of faith, is sinne.

CHAP. XV.

1 The strong must beare with the weake. 2 We may not please our selues, 3 for Christ did not so, 7 but receiue one the other, as Christ did vs all, 8 both Iewes 9 and Gentiles. 15 Paul excuseth his writing, 28 and promiseth to see them, 30 and requesteth their prayers.

 Ee then that are strong, ought to beare the infirmities of the weake, and not to please our selues.

2 Let euery one of vs please his neighbour for *his* good to edification.

* Psal. 69. 9.

3 For euen Christ pleased not himselfe, but as it is written, * The reproches of them that reproched thee, fell on mee.

4 For whatsoeuer things were written aforetime, were written for our learning, that we through patience and comfort of the Scriptures might haue hope.

* 1. Cor. 1. 10.

‖ Or, after the example of.

5 * Now the God of patience and consolation graunt you to be like minded one towards another, ‖ according to Christ Iesus :

6 That ye may with one mind and one mouth glorifie God, euen the Father of our Lord Iesus Christ.

7 Wherfore receiue yee one another, as Christ also receiued vs, to the glory of God.

8 Now I say, that Iesus Christ was a Minister of the circumcision for the trueth of God, to confirme the promises *made* vnto the fathers :

* Psal. 18. 50

9 And that the Gentiles might glorifie God for his mercie, as it is written, * For this cause I will confesse to thee among the Gentiles, and sing vnto thy Name.

* Deut. 32. 43.

10 And againe he saith, * Reioyce yee Gentiles with his people.

* Psal. 117. 1

11 And againe, * Praise the Lord all ye Gentiles, and laud him all ye people.

* Es. 11. 10.

12 And againe Esaias saith, * There

shal be a roote of Iesse, and he that shal rise to raigne ouer the Gentiles, in him shall the Gentiles trust.

13 Nowe the God of hope fill you with all ioy and peace in beleeuing, that yee may abound in hope through the power of the holy Ghost.

14 And I my selfe also am perswaded of you, my brethren, that ye also are full of goodnesse, filled with all knowledge, able also to admonish one another.

15 Neuerthelesse, brethren, I haue written the more boldly vnto you, in some sort, as putting you in mind, because of the grace that is giuen to mee of God,

16 That I should be the minister of Iesus Christ to the Gentiles, ministring the Gospel of God, that the ‖ offering vp of the Gentiles might be acceptable, being sanctified by the holy Ghost.

‖ Or, sacrificing.

17 I haue therfore whereof I may glory through Iesus Christ , in those things which pertaine to God.

18 For I will not dare to speake of any of those things, which Christ hath not wrought by me, to make the Gentiles obedient, by word and deede,

19 Through mighty signes and wonders, by the power of the Spirit of God, so that from Hierusalem and round about vnto Illyricum , I haue fully preached the Gospel of Christ.

20 Yea, so haue I striued to preach the Gospel, not where Christ was named, lest I should build vpon another mans foundation :

21 But as it is written, * To whom hee was not spoken of, they shall see : and they that haue not heard, shall vnderstand.

* Esa. 52. 15

22 For which cause also I haue been ‖ much hindered from comming to you.

‖ Or, many wayes, or oftentimes.

23 But now hauing no more place in these parts, and hauing a great desire these many yeeres to come vnto you :

24 Whensoeuer I take my iourney into Spaine, I will come to you : for I trust to see you in my iourney, and to be brought on my way thitherward by you, if first I be somewhat filled with † your *company.*

† Gr. with you. Ver. 32.

25 But now I goe vnto Hierusalem, to minister vnto the Saints.

26 For it hath pleased them of Macedonia and Achaia, to make a certaine contribution for the poore Saints which are at Hierusalem.

27 It hath pleased them *verely,* and their

their detters they are. For if the Gentiles haue bene made partakers of their spirituall things, their duetie is also to minister vnto them in carnall things.

28 When therefore I haue performed this, and hane sealed to them this fruit, I will come by you into Spaine.

29 And I am sure that when I come vnto you, I shall come in the fulnes of the blessing of ẙ Gospel of Christ.

30 Now I beseech you, brethren, for the Lord Iesus Christs sake, and for the loue of the Spirit, that ye striue together with me, in your praiers to God for me,

31 That I may bee deliuered from them that ‖ do not beleeue in Iudea, and that my seruice which I haue for Hierusalem, may bee accepted of the Saints:

‖ Or, are disobedient.

32 That I may come vnto you with ioy by the will of God, and may with you be refreshed.

33 Now the God of peace bee with you all. Amen.

CHAP. XVI.

3 Paul willeth the brethren to greete many, 17 and aduiseth them to take heede of those which cause dissention and offences, 21 and after sundry salutations endeth with praise and thankes to God.

 Commend vnto you Phebe our sister, which is a seruant of the Church which is at Cenchrea:

2 That ye receiue her in the Lord as becommeth Saints, and that ye assist her in whatsoeuer businesse she hath need of you: for she hath beene a succourer of many, and of my selfe also.

3 Greete Priscilla and Aquila, my helpers in Christ Iesus:

4 (Who haue for my life laid downe their owne neckes : vnto whome not onely I giue thankes, but also all the Churches of the Gentiles.)

5 Likewise *greet* the Church that is in their house. Salute my welbeloued Epenetus, who is the first fruits of Achaia vnto Christ.

6 Greete Marie, who bestowed much labour on vs.

7 Salute Andronicus and Iunia my kinsmen, and my fellow prisoners, who are of note among the Apostles, who also were in Christ before me.

8 Greet Amplias my beloued in the Lord.

9 Salute Vrbane our helper in Christ, and Stachys my beloued.

10 Salute Appelles approoued in Christ. Salute them which are of Aristobulus ‖ houshold.

‖ Or, friends

11 Salute Herodion my kinsman. Greet them that be of the ‖ houshold of Narcissus, which are in the Lord.

‖ Or, friend

12 Salute Tryphena and Tryphosa, who labour in the Lord. Salute the beloued Persis, which laboured much in the Lord.

13 Salute Rufus chosen in the Lord, and his mother and mine.

14 Salute Asyncritus, Phlegon, Hermas, Patrobas, Hermes, and the brethren which are with them.

15 Salute Philologus & Iulia, Nereus, and his sister, and Olympas, and all the Saints which are with them.

16 Salute one another with an holy kisse. The Churches of Christ salute you.

17 Now I beseech you, brethren, marke them which cause diuisions and offences, contrary to the doctrine which ye haue learned, and auoide them.

18 For they that are such, serue not our Lord Iesus Christ, but their owne belly, and by good wordes and faire speeches deceiue the hearts of the simple.

19 For your obedience is come abroad vnto all men. I am glad therefore on your behalfe : but yet I would haue you wise vnto that which is good, and ‖ simple concerning euill.

‖ Or, harmelesse.

20 And the God of peace shal ‖ bruise Satan vnder your feete shortly. The grace of our Lord Iesus Christ be with you. Amen.

‖ Or, tread

21 Timotheus my worke-fellow, and Lucius, and Iason, and Sosipater my kinsemen salute you.

22 I Tertius who wrote this Epistle, salute you in the Lord.

23 Gaius mine hoste, and of the whole Church, saluteth you. Erastus the Chamberlaine of the citie saluteth you, and Quartus a brother.

24 The grace of our Lord Iesus Christ be with you all. Amen.

25 Now to him that is of power to stablish you according to my Gospel, and the preaching of Iesus Christ, according to the reuelation of the the mysterie,

sterie, which was kept secret since the world began:

26 But now is made manifest, and by the Scriptures of the Prophets according to the commandement of the euerlasting God, made known to all nations for the obedience of faith,

27 To God, onely wise, bee glorie through Iesus Christ, for euer. Amen.

¶ Written to the Romanes from Corinthus, *and sent* by Phebe seruant of the Church at Cenchrea.

¶ THE FIRST EPISTLE

of Paul the Apoſtle to the

Corinthians.

CHAP. I.

After his salutation, and thankesgiuing, 10 he exhorteth them to vnitie, and 12 reproueth their dissentions. 18 God destroyeth the wisedome of the wise, 21 by the foolishnesse of preaching, and 26 calleth not the wise, mighty, and noble, but 27 28 the foolish, weake, and men of no accompt.

Aul called *to be* an Apostle of Iesus Christ, through the will of God, and Sosthenes *our* brother,

2 Vnto the Church of God which is at Corinth, to them that * are sanctified in Christ Iesus, called *to be* Saints, * with all that in euery place call vpon the Name of Iesus Christ our Lord, both theirs and ours.

3 Grace be vnto you, and peace from God our Father, and *from* the Lord Iesus Christ.

4 I thanke my God alwayes on your behalfe, for the grace of God which is giuen you by Iesus Christ,

5 That in euery thing yee are enriched by him, in all vtterance, and in all knowledge:

6 Euen as the Testimony of Christ was confirmed in you.

7 So that yee come behinde in no gift; wayting for the † comming of our Lord Iesus Christ,

8 Who shall also confirme you vnto

the end, that yee may be blamelesse in the day of our Lord Iesus Christ.

9 * God is faithfull by whom ye were called vnto the felowship of his Sonne Iesus Christ our Lord.

10 Now I beseech you brethren by the Name of our Lord Iesus Christ, that yee all speake the same thing, and that there be no † diuisions among you: but that ye be perfectly ioyned together in the same minde, and in the same iudgement.

11 For it hath bene declared vnto me of you, my brethren, by them which are of the house of Cloe, that there are contentions among you.

12 Now this I say, that euery one of you saith, I am of Paul, and I of * Apollo, and I of Cephas, and I of Christ.

13 Is Christ diuided? was Paul crucified for you? or were yee baptized in the name of Paul?

14 I thanke God that I baptized none of you, but * Crispus and Gaius:

15 Lest any should say, that I had baptized in mine owne name.

16 And I baptized also the household of Stephanas: besides, I know not whether I baptized any other.

17 For Christ sent me not to baptize, but to preach the Gospel: * not with wisedome of ‖ words, lest the Crosse of Christ should be made of none effect.

18 For the preaching of the Crosse is to them that perish, foolishnesse: but vnto vs which are saued, it is the * power of God.

19 For

Left margin notes:
* Acts. 15. 9.
* Rom. 1. 7.

† *Gr. Reuelation.*

Right margin notes:
* 1. Thess. 5. 24.

† *Greeke, schismes.*

* Acts. 18. 24.

* Acts. 18. 8.

* 2. Pet. 1. 16.
‖ *Or, speech.*

* Rom. 1. 16.

19 For it is written, I will destroy the wiſedome of the wise, and wil bring to nothing the *vnderstanding of the prudent.

*Esa. 29. 14

20 *Where is the wise ? where is the Scribe ? where is the disputer of this world? Hath not God made foolish the wiſedome of this world ?

*Esa. 33. 18

21 *For after that, in the wisdom of God, the world by wiſedome knew not God, it pleased God by the foolishneſſe of preaching, to saue them that beleeue.

*Rom. 1. 20

22 For the *Iewes require a signe, and the Greekes seeke after wiſedome.

*Matt. 12. 38.

23 But wee preach Christ crucified, vnto the Iewes a stumbling block, and vnto the Greekes, foolishneſſe:

24 But vnto them which are called, both Iewes and Greekes, Christ, the power of God, & the wiſedome of God.

25 Because the foolishneſſe of God is wiser then men : and the weakeneſſe of God is stronger then men.

26 For ye see your calling, brethren, how that not many wise men after the flesh, not many mighty, not many noble *are called.*

27 But God hath chosen the foolish things of the world, to confound the wise : and God hath chosen the weake things of the world, to confound the things which are mighty.

28 And base things of the world, and things which are despised, hath God chosen, *yea* and things which are not, to bring to nought things that are,

29 That no flesh should glory in his presence.

30 But of him are ye in Christ Ieſus, who of God is made vnto vs wiſedome, and righteouſneſſe, and sanctification, and redemption:

*Iere. 9. 23.

31 That according as it is written, *He that glorieth, let him glory in the Lord.

CHAP. II.

Hee declareth that his preaching, 1 though it bring not excellency of speech, or of 4 humane wiſedome : yet consisteth in the 4. 5 power of God : and so farre excelleth 6 the wiſedome of this world, and 9 humane sense, as that 14 the naturall man cannot vnderstand it.

*Wis. 1. 17.

ND I, brethren, when I came to you, *came not with excellencie of speech, or of wiſedome, declaring vnto you the testimony of God.

2 For I determined not to know any thing amõg you, saue Ieſus Christ, and him crucified.

3 And I was with you in weakeneſſe, and in feare, and in much trembling.

4 And my speech, and my preaching *was not with ||entiſing words of mans wiſedome, but in demonstration of the Spirit, and of power:

*2. Pet. 1. 10.
||Or, perswasible.
† Gr. be.

5 That your faith should not stand in the wiſdome of men, but in the power of God.

6 Howbeit wee speake wiſedome among them that are perfect : yet not the wiſedome of this worlde, nor of the Princes of this worlde, that come to nought:

7 But wee speake the wiſedome of God in a mysterie, *euen* the hidden *wiſedome* which God ordeined before the world, vnto our glory.

8 Which none of the princes of this world knewe . for had they knowen it, they would not haue crucified the Lord of glory.

9 But as it is written, *Eye hath not seene, nor eare heard, neither haue entred into the heart of man, the things which God hath prepared for them that loue him.

*Esa. 64. 4.

10 But God hath reueiled *them* vnto vs by his Spirit . for the Spirit searcheth all things, yea, the deepe things of God.

11 For what man knoweth the things of a man, saue the spirit of man which is in him? Euen so the things of God knoweth no man, but the Spirit of God.

12 Now wee haue receiued, not the spirit of the world, but the Spirit which is of God, that wee might know the things that are freely giuen to vs of God.

13 *Which things also we speake, not in the words which mans wiſedome teacheth, but which the holy Ghost teacheth, comparing spirituall things with spirituall.

*2. Pet. 1. 16

14 But the naturall man receiueth not the things of the Spirit of God, for they are foolishneſſe vnto him : neither can he know *them,* because they are spiritually discerned.

*Pro. 27. 19
||Or, discerneth.

15 *But he that is spirituall, ||iudgeth all things, yet he himselfe is ||iudged of no man.

||Or, discerned.
*Rom. 11 34. esa. 40. 13.

16 *For who hath knowen the mind of

† *Gr. shall.*

of the Lord that he † may instruct him? But we haue the mind of Christ.

CHAP. III.

2 Milke is fit for children. 3 Strife and diuision, arguments of a fleshly minde. 7 Hee that planteth, and hee that watereth, is nothing. 9 The ministers are Gods fellowe workemen. 11 Christ the only foundation. 16 Men the temples of God, which 17 must bee kept holy. 19 The wisedome of this world is foolishnesse with God.

Nd I, brethren, could not speake vnto you as vnto spirituall, but as vnto carnall, *euen* as vnto babes in Christ.

2 I haue fed you with milke, and not with meate : for hitherto yee were not able *to beare it*, neither yet now are ye able.

‖*Or, factions*
† *Gr. according to man.*

3 For ye are yet carnall : for whereas there is among you enuying, and strife, and ‖diuisions, are ye not carnall, and walke † as men ?

4 For while one saieth, I am of Paul, and another, *I am* of Apollo, are ye not carnall ?

5 Who then is Paul ? and who is Apollo ? but ministers by whom ye beleeued, euen as the Lord gaue to euery man.

6 I haue planted, Apollo watered : but God gaue the encrease.

7 So then, neither is he that planteth any thing, neither hee that watereth : but God that giueth the increase.

* *Psal. 63. 13* gal. 6. 5.

8 Now hee that planteth, and hee that watereth, are one : * and euery man shal receiue his own reward according to his owne labour.

‖ *Or, tillage.*

9 For wee are labourers together with God, ye are Gods ‖husbandry, yee are Gods building.

10 According to the grace of God which is giuen vnto mee, as a wise master builder I haue laid the foundation, and another buildeth thereon. But let euery man take heede how hee buildeth thereupon.

11 For other foundation can no man lay, then that is laide, which is Iesus Christ.

12 Now if any man build vpon this foundation, gold, siluer, precious stones, wood, hay, stubble :

13 Euery mans worke shall be made manifest. For the day shall declare it, be-

cause it † shall bee reuealed by fire, and the fire shall trie euery mans worke of what sort it is.

† *Gr. is reuealed.*

14 If any mans worke abide which he hath built thereupon, he shal receiue a reward.

15 If any mans worke shall bee burnt, he shall suffer losse : but he himselfe shall be saued : yet so, as by fire.

16 * Knowe yee not that yee are the Temple of God, and that the Spirit of God dwelleth in you ?

* 1. Cor. 6. 19.

17 If any man ‖defile the Temple of God, him shall God destroy : for the Temple of God is holy, which *Temple* ye are.

‖*Or, destroy.*

18 Let no man deceiue himselfe : If any man among you seemeth to bee wise in this world, let him become a foole, that he may be wise.

19 For the wisedome of this world is foolishnesse with God : for it is written, * Hee taketh the wise in their owne craftinesse.

* Iob. 5. 13.

20 And againe, * The Lord knoweth the thoughts of the wise, that they are vaine.

* Psal. 94. 11.

21 Therefore let no man glory in men, for all things are yours.

22 Whether Paul, or Apollo, or Cephas, or the world, or life, or death, or things present, or things to come, all are yours.

23 And yee are Christs, and Christ *is* Gods.

CHAP. IIII.

1 In what account the Ministers ought to bee had. 7 We haue nothing which wee haue not receiued. 9 The Apostles spectacles to the world, Angels and men, 13 The filth and off-scouring of the worlde : 15 Yet our fathers in Christ, 16 Whome wee ought to followe.

Et a man so account of vs, as of the ministers of Christ, and stewards of the mysteries of God.

2 Moreouer, it is required in stewards, that a man be found faithfull.

3 But with mee it is a very small thing that I should bee iudged of you, or of mans † iudgement : yea, I iudge not mine owne selfe.

† *Gr. day.*

4 For I know nothing by my selfe, yet am I not hereby iustified : but hee that iudgeth me is the Lord.

5 * Therefore iudge nothing before the

* Matt. 7. 1.
rom. 2. 1.

the time, vntill the Lord come, who both will bring to light the hidden things of darkenesse, and will make manifest the counsels of the hearts: and then shall euery man haue prayse of God.

6 And these things, brethren, I haue in a figure transferred to my selfe, and to Apollo, for your sakes : that ye might learne in vs not to thinke *of men,* aboue that which is written, that no one of you bee puffed vp for one against another.

† *Gr. distinguisheth thee?*

7 For who †maketh thee to differ *from another?* And what hast thou that thou didst not receiue ? Now if thou didst receiue it, why doest thou glory as if thou hadst not receiued it ?

8 Now ye are full, now ye are rich, ye haue reigned as kings without vs, and I would to God ye did reigne, that we also might reigne with you.

9 For I thinke that God hath set forth vs the Apostles last, as it were approued to death. For wee are made a

†*Gr. theater.* †spectacle vnto the world, and to Angels, and to men.

10 We *are* fooles for Christs sake, but ye *are* wise in Christ. We *are* weake, but ye *are* strong : yee are honourable, but we are despised.

11 Euen vnto this present houre we both hunger and thirst, and are naked, and are buffeted, and haue no certaine dwelling place,

* Act. 20. 34
1 thess. 2. 9.
2 thess. 3. 8.

12 *And labour, working with our owne hands : being reuiled, wee blesse: being persecuted, we suffer it :

* Mat. 5. 44

13 *Being defamed, we intreate : we are made as the filth of the world, and *are* the off-scouring of all things vnto this day.

14 I write not these things to shame you, but as my beloued sonnes I warne you.

15 For though you haue ten thousand instructors in Christ, yet *haue yee* not many fathers : For in Christ Iesus I haue begotten you through the Gospel.

16 Wherefore I beseech you, be yee followers of me.

17 For this cause haue I sent vnto you Timotheus, who is my beloued sonne, and faithfull in the Lord, who shal bring you into remembrance of my wayes which be in Christ, as I teach euery where in euery Church.

18 Nowe some are puffed vp as

though I would not come to you.

19 *But I wil come to you shortly, if the Lord will, and will knowe, not the speach of them which are puffed vp, but the power.

* Acts 19.
21. iam 4.
15.

20 For the kingdome of God is not in word, but in power.

21 What will ye ? Shall I come vnto you with a rod, or in loue, and in the spirit of meekenesse ?

CHAP. V.

1 The incestuous person   6 is cause rather of shame vnto them, then of reioycing. 7 The olde leauen is to be purged out. 10 Heinous offenders are to be shamed & auoided.

IT is reported commonly, *that there is* fornication among you, and such fornication, as is not so much as named amongst the Gentiles, that one should haue his fathers wife.

2 And yee are puffed vp, and haue not rather mourned, that he that hath done this deed, might bee taken away from among you.

3 *For I verily as absent in body, but present in spirit, haue ||iudged alreadie, as though I were present, concerning him that hath so done this deed,

* Col. 2. 5.
|| *Or, determined.*

4 In the Name of our Lord Iesus Christ, when yee are gathered together, and my spirit, with the power of our Lord Iesus Christ,

5 *To deliuer such *a one* vnto Satan for the destruction of the flesh, that the spirit may be saued in the day of the Lord Iesus.

* 1. Tim. 1
20.

6 Your glorying is not good : *know ye not that a little leauen leaueneth the whole lumpe ?

* Gal. 5. 9.

7 Purge out therefore the olde leauen, that ye may be a new lumpe, as ye are vnleauened. For *euen* Christ our Passeouer ||is sacrificed for vs.

|| *Or, is slain*

8 Therefore let vs keepe || the Feast, not with old leauen, neither with the leauen of malice and wickednesse : but with the vnleauened bread of sinceritie and trueth.

|| *Or, holiday.*

9 I wrote vnto you in an Epistle, not to company with fornicators.

10 Yet not altogether with the fornicatours of this world, or with the couetous, or extortioners, or with idolaters; for then must yee needs goe out of the world.

11 But now I haue written vnto you,

you, not to keepe company, if any man that is called a brother bee a fornicator, or couetous, or an idolater, or a railer, or a drunkard, or an extortioner : with such a one, no, not to eate.

12 For what haue I to doe to iudge them also that are without? doe not ye iudge them that are within?

13 But them that are without, God iudgeth. Therefore put away from among your selues that wicked person.

CHAP. VI.

1 The Corinthians must not vexe their brethren, in going to law with them : 6 Especially vnder Infidels. 9 The vnrighteous shall not inherite the kingdome of God. 15 Our bodies are the members of Christ, 19 And Temples of the holy Ghost. 16. 17 They must not therefore be defiled.

 Are any of you, hauing a matter against another, goe to law before the vniust, and not before the Saints?

2 Do ye not know that the Saints shall iudge the world? And if the world shalbe iudged by you, are ye vnworthy to iudge the smallest matters?

3 Know ye not that we shall iudge Angels? How much more things that perteine to this life?

4 If then yee haue iudgements of things perteining to this life, set them to iudge who are least esteemed in the Church.

5 I speake to your shame. Is it so, that there is not a wise man amongst you? no not one that shall bee able to iudge betweene his brethren?

6 But brother goeth to law with brother, & that before the vnbeleeuers?

7 Now therefore, there is vtterly a fault among you, because yee goe to law one with another : Why doe ye not rather take wrong? Why doe yee not rather suffer your selues to be defrauded?

8 Nay, you do wrong and defraud, and that your brethren.

9 Know yee not that the vnrighteous shall not inherite the kingdome of God? Be not deceiued : neither fornicatours, nor idolaters, nor adulterers, nor effeminate, nor abusers of themselues with mankinde,

10 Nor theeues, nor couetous, nor drunkards, nor reuilers, nor extortioners, shall inherit the kingdom of God.

11 And such were some of you : but

ye are washed, but ye are sanctified, but ye are iustified in the Name of the Lord Iesus, and by the Spirit of our God.

12 All things are lawfull vnto mee, but all things are not ||expedient : all things are lawfull for mee, but I will not bee brought vnder the power of any. ‖ Or, profitable.

13 Meats for the belly, and the belly for meates : but God shall destroy both it and them. Now the body is not for fornication, but for the Lord : and the Lord for the body.

14 And God hath both raised vp the Lord, and will also raise vp vs by his owne power.

15 Know yee not that your bodies are the members of Christ? Shall I then take the members of Christ, and make them the members of an harlot? God forbid.

16 What, know ye not that he which is ioyned to an harlot, is one body? for two (saith he) shalbe one flesh.

17 But hee that is ioyned vnto the Lord, is one spirit.

18 Flee fornication : Euery sinne that a man doeth, is without the body : but he that committeth fornication, sinneth against his owne body.

19 What, know ye not that your body is the Temple of the holy Ghost which is in you, which yee haue of God, and ye are not your owne?

20 For yee are bought with a price : therefore glorifie God in your body, and in your spirit, which are Gods.

CHAP. VII.

2 He treateth of mariage, 4 shewing it to be a remedy against fornication : 10 And that the bond thereof ought not lightly to be dissolued. 18. 20 Euery man must be content with his vocation. 25 Virginitie wherefore to be imbraced. 35 And for what respects we may either marry, or abstaine from marying.

 Ow cōcerning the things wherof ye wrote vnto me, It is good for a man not to touch a woman.

2 Neuerthelesse, to auoid fornication, let euery man haue his owne wife, and let euery woman haue her owne husband.

3 Let the husband render vnto the wife due beneuolence : and likewise also the wife vnto the husband.

4 The wife hath not power of her owne body, but the husband : and likewise

wise also the husband hath not power of his owne body, but the wife.

5 Defraud you not one the other, except *it bee* with consent for a time, that yee may giue your selues to fasting and prayer, and come together againe, that Satan tempt you not for your incontinencie.

6 But I speake this by permission, and not of commandement.

7 For I would that all men were euen as I my selfe : but euery man hath his proper gift of God, one after this maner, and another after that.

8 I say therefore to the vnmaried and widowes, It is good for them if they abide euen as I.

9 But if they cannot conteine, let them marry : for it is better to marrie then to burne.

10 And vnto the married, I command, *yet* not I, but the Lord, Let not the wife depart from her husband ·

11 But and if shee depart, let her remaine vnmaried, or be reconciled to her husband : and let not the husband put away his wife.

12 But to the rest speake I, not the Lord, If any brother hath a wife that beleeueth not, and shee bee pleased to dwell with him, let him not put her away.

13 And the woman which hath an husband that beleeueth not, and if hee be pleased to dwell with her, let her not leaue him.

14 For the vnbeleeuing husband is sanctified by the wife, and the vnbeleeuing wife is sanctified by the husband ; else were your children vncleane, but now are they holy.

15 But if the vnbeleeuing depart, let him depart. A brother or a sister is not vnder bondage in such *cases :* but God †*Gr. in peace* hath called vs † to peace.

16 For what knowest thou, O wife, whether thou shalt saue thy husband ? or how knowest thou, O man, whether thou shalt saue thy wife ?

17 But as God hath distributed to euery man, as the Lord hath called euery one, so let him walke, and so ordeine I in all Churches.

18 Is any man called being circumcised ? let him not become vncircumcised : Is any called in vncircumcision ? let him not be circumcised.

19 Circumcision is nothing, and vncircumcision is nothing, but the keeping of the Commandements of God.

20 Let euery man abide in the same calling wherein he was called.

21 Art thou called *being* a seruant ? care not for it : but if thou maist be made free, vse it rather.

22 For he that is called in the Lord, *being* a seruant, is the Lords †free man : likewise also hee that is called *being* free, is Christs seruant. †*Gr. made free.*

23 Ye are bought with a price, be not ye the seruants of men.

24 Brethren, let euery man wherin he is called, therein abide with God.

25 Nowe concerning virgins, I haue no commaundement of the Lord : yet I giue my iudgement as one that hath obtained mercy of the Lord to be faithfull.

26 I suppose therefore that this is good for the present ||distresse, *I say*, that it is good for a man so to be. ||*Or, necessitie.*

27 Art thou bound vnto a wife ? seeke not to bee loosed. Art thou loosed from a wife ? seeke not a wife.

28 But and if thou marry, thou hast not sinned, and if a virgin marry, shee hath not sinned : neuerthelesse, such shall haue trouble in the flesh : but I spare you.

29 But this I say, brethren, the time is short. It remaineth, that both they that haue wiues, be as though they had none :

30 And they that weepe, as though they wept not : and they that reioyce, as though they reioyced not : and they that buy, as though they possessed not :

31 And they that vse this world, as not abusing it : for the fashion of this world passeth away

32 But I would haue you without carefulnesse. He that is vnmarried, careth for the things that belongeth to the Lord, how he may please the Lord :

33 But hee that is maried, careth for the things that are of the world, how he may please his wife.

34 There is difference also between a wife and a virgin : the vnmaried woman careth for the things of the Lord, that shee may be holy, both in body and in spirit : but she that is married, careth for the things of the worlde, how shee may please her husband.

35 And this I speake for your owne profite, not that I may cast a snare vpon you, but for that which is comely, and that you may attend vpon

on the Lord without distraction.

36 But if any man thinke that he be-haueth himselfe vncomely toward his virgin, if she passe the floure of *her* age, and neede so require, let him doe what hee will, hee sinneth not: let them marry.

37 Neuerthelesse, hee that standeth stedfast in his heart, hauing no necessi-tie, but hath power ouer his owne will, and hath so decreed in his heart that he will keepe his virgin, doeth well.

38 So then he that giueth her in ma-riage, doeth wel: but he that giueth her not in mariage, doeth better.

39 The wife is bound by the Lawe as long as her husband liueth: but if her husband bee dead, shee is at liberty to bee maried to whom shee will, onely in the Lord.

40 But shee is happier if shee so bide, after my iudgment: and I thinke also that I haue the Spirit of God.

CHAP. VIII.

1 To abstaine from meates offered to Idoles: 8. 9 We must not abuse our Christian liber-tie, to the offence of our brethren: 11 but must bridle our knowledge with Charitie.

Ow as touching things offered vnto idoles, wee know that wee all haue knowledge. Knowledge puffeth vp: but Cha-ritie edifieth.

2 And if any man thinke that hee knoweth any thing, hee knoweth no-thing yet as he ought to know.

3 But if any man loue God, the same is knowen of him.

4 As concerning therefore the ea-ting of those things that are offered in sacrifice vnto idoles, wee know that an idole is nothing in the world, and that there is none other God but one.

5 For though there bee that are cal-led gods, whether in heauen or in earth (as there be gods many, and lords ma-ny:)

6 But to vs there is but one God, the Father, of whom are all things, ‖*Or, for him,* Rom. 11. 36. and we ‖in him, and one Lord Iesus Christ, by whom are all things, and we by him.

7 Howbeit there is not in euerie man that knowledge: for some with conscience of the idole vnto this houre, eate it as a thing offred vnto an idole,

and their conscience being weake, is de-filed.

8 But meate commendeth vs not to God: for neither if we eate, ‖are we ‖*Or, haue we the more.* ‖*Or, haue we the lesse.* the better: neither if wee eate not, ‖are we the worse.

9 But take heed lest by any meanes, this ‖libertie of yours become a stum-bling blocke to them that are weake. ‖*Or, power.*

10 For if any man see thee which hast knowledge, sit at meat in the idols tem-ple: shall not the conscience of him which is weake, be †emboldened to eat †*Gr. edified.* those things which are offered to idols?

11 And through thy knowledge shal the weake brother perish, for whome Christ died?

12 But when ye sinne so against the brethren, and wound their weake con-science, ye sinne against Christ.

13 Wherefore if meate make my bro-ther to offend, I will eat no flesh while the world standeth, lest I make my bro-ther to offend.

CHAP. IX.

1 He sheweth his libertie, 7 and that the mi-nister ought to liue by the Gospel: 15 yet that himselfe hath of his owne accord abstai-ned, 18 to be either chargeable vnto them: 22 or offensiue vnto any, in matters indiffer-ent. 24 Our life is like vnto a race.

M I not an Apostle? am I not free? haue I not seene Iesus Christ our Lord? Are not you my worke in the Lord?

2 If I bee not an Apostle vnto o-thers, yet doubtlesse I am to you: for the seale of mine Apostleship are yee in the Lord.

3 Mine answere to them that doe examine me, is this:

4 Haue wee not power to eate and to drinke?

5 Haue we not power to lead about a sister a ‖wife aswel as other Apostles, ‖*Or, woman.* and as the brethren of the Lord, and Cephas?

6 Or I onely and Barnabas, haue not we power to forbeare working?

7 Who goeth a warfare any time at his owne charges? who planteth a vineyard, and eateth not of the fruite thereof? or who feedeth a flocke, and eateth not of the milke of the flocke?

8 Say I these things as a man? or saith not the Law the same also?

9 For

* Deut. 25.
4.

9 For it is written in the Law of Moyses, * Thou shalt not muzzell the mouth of the oxe that treadeth out the corne : doth God take care for oxen ?

10 Or saith hee it altogether for our sakes ? for our sakes, no doubt, *this* is written : that hee that ploweth, should plow in hope : and that hee that thresheth in hope, should bee partaker of his hope.

* Rom. 15.
27.

11 * If we haue sowen vnto you spirituall things, is it a great thing if wee shall reape your carnall things ?

12 If others bee partakers of this power ouer you, *are* not we rather ? Neuerthelesse, we haue not vsed this power : but suffer all things, lest wee should hinder the Gospel of Christ.

* Deut. 18.
1.
‖ Or, feed.

13 * Do ye not know that they which minister about holy things, ‖liue of the things of the Temple ? and they which wait at the altar, are partakers with the altar ?

14 Euen so hath the Lord ordeined, that they which preach the Gospel, should liue of the Gospel.

15 But I haue vsed none of these things. Neither haue I written these things, that it should bee so done vnto me : for it were better for me to die, then that any man should make my glorying voyd.

16 For though I preach the Gospel, I haue nothing to glorie of : for necessitie is laid vpon mee, yea, woe is vnto me, if I preach not the Gospel.

17 For if I doe this thing willingly, I haue a reward : but if against my will, a dispensation *of the Gospel* is committed vnto me.

18 What is my reward then ? verily that when I preach the Gospel, I may make the Gospel of Christ without charge, that I abuse not my power in the Gospel.

19 For though I bee free from all men, yet haue I made my selfe seruant vnto all, that I might gaine the more.

20 And vnto the Iewes, I became as a Iew, that I might gaine the Iewes : to them that are vnder the Law, as vnder the Law, that I might gaine them that are vnder the Law :

21 To them that are without Law, as without Law (being not without Law to God, but vnder the Law to Christ,) that I might gaine them that are without Law.

22 To the weake became I as weake, that I might gaine the weake : I am made all things to all men, that I might by all meanes saue some.

23 And this I doe for the Gospels sake, that I might be partaker thereof with *you.*

24 Know yee not that they which runne in a race, runne all, but one receiueth the price ? So runne, that yee may obteine.

25 And euery man that striueth for the masterie, is temperate in all things : Now they *doe it* to obtaine a corruptible crowne, but we an incorruptible.

26 I therefore so runne, not as vncertainely : so fight I, not as one that beateth the ayre :

27 But I keepe vnder my body, and bring it into subiection : lest that by any meanes when I haue preached to others, I my selfe should be a castaway.

CHAP. X.

1 The Sacraments of the Iewes, 6 are types of ours, 7 and their punishments, 11 examples for vs. 14 We must flie from idolatrie. 21 We must not make the Lords Table the table of deuils : 24 And in things indifferent, we must haue regard of our brethren.

OREOUER brethren, I would not that yee should be ignorant, how that all our fathers were vnder the cloud, and all passed thorow the Sea :

2 And were all baptized vnto Moyses in the cloud, and in the sea :

3 And did all eat the same spirituall meat :

4 And did all drinke the same spirituall drinke : (for they dranke of that spirituall Rocke that ‖followed them : and that Rocke was Christ)

‖ Or, went with them.

5 But with many of them God was not well pleased : for they were ouerthrowen in the wildernesse.

6 Now these things were †our examples, to the intent wee should not lust after euil things, as they also lusted.

† Gr. our figures.

7 Neither be ye idolaters, as *were* some of them, as it is written, * The people sate downe to eate and drinke, and rose vp to play.

* Exod. 32
6. psal. 106
14.

8 Neither let vs commit fornication, as some of them committed, and *fell in one day three and twentie thousand.

* Num. 25
9.

9 Neither let vs tempt Christ, as some

* Num. 21. 6.
some of them also tempted, * and were destroyed of serpents.

10 Neither murmure ye, as some of them also murmured, and were * destroyed of the destroyer.

11 Now all these things happened vnto them for ||ensamples : and they are written for our admonition , vpon whom the ends of the world are come.

12 Wherefore, let him that thinketh he standeth, take heed lest he fall.

13 There hath no temptation taken you, but such as is ||common to man : but God is faithfull, who wil not suffer you to bee tempted aboue that you are able : but will with the temptation also make a way to escape, that ye may bee able to beare it.

14 Wherefore my dearely beloued, flee from idolatrie.

15 I speake as to wise men : iudge ye what I say.

16 The cup of blessing which wee blesse, is it not the communion of the blood of Christ? The bread which we breake, is it not the communion of the body of Christ?

17 For we being many are one bread, and one body : for we are all partakers of that one bread.

18 Behold Israel after the flesh : are not they which eat of the sacrifices, partakers of the Altar?

19 What say I then? that the idole is any thing? or that which is offered in sacrifice to idols is any thing?

20 But *I say* that the things which the Gentiles * sacrifice, they sacrifice to deuils, and not to God : and I would not that yee should haue fellowship with deuils.

21 Yee cannot drinke the cup of the Lord, and the cup of deuils : ye cannot be partakers of the Lords Table, and of the table of deuils.

22 Doe we prouoke the Lord to iealousie? are we stronger then he?

23 All things are lawfull for me, but all things are not expedient : All things are lawfull for mee, but all things edifie not.

24 Let no man seeke his owne : but euery man anothers wealth.

25 Whatsoeuer is solde in the shambles, that eate, asking no question for conscience sake.

26 For * the earth is the Lords, and the fulnesse thereof.

27 If any of them that beleeue not,

* Num. 14. 37.

‖ Or, Types.

‖ Or, moderate.

* Deut. 32. 17. psal. 106. 37.

* Deut. 10. 14. psal. 24. 1.

bid you *to a feast*, and yee be disposed to goe, whatsoeuer is set before you, eate, asking no question for conscience sake.

28 But if any man say vnto you, This is offered in sacrifice vnto idoles, eate not for his sake that shewed it, and for conscience sake. * The earth is the Lords, and the fulnesse thereof.

29 Conscience I say, not thine owne, but of the others : for why is my libertie iudged of another mans conscience?

30 For, if I by ||grace be a partaker, why am I euill spoken of, for that for which I giue thankes?

31 Whether therfore ye eat or drinke, or whatsoeuer ye doe, doe all to the glory of God.

32 Giue none offence, neither to the Iewes, nor to the † Gentiles, nor to the Church of God :

33 Euen as I please all men in all things, not seeking mine owne profit, but the profit of many, that they may be saued.

Deut. 10. 14. psal. 24. 1.

‖Or, thankesgiuing.

† Gr. Greeks

CHAP. XI.

1 He reprooueth them, because in holy assemblies, 4 their men prayed with their heads couered, and 6 women with their heads vncouered, 17 and because generally their meetings were not for the better but for the worse, as 21 namely in profaning with their owne feasts the Lords Supper. 25 Lastly, he calleth them to the first institution thereof.

BE yee followers of mee, euen as I also am of Christ.

2 Now I prayse you, brethren, that you remember me in all things, and keepe the ||ordinances, as I deliuered them to you.

3 But I would haue you knowe, that the head of euery man is Christ : and the head of the woman is the man, and the head of Christ is God.

4 Euery man praying or prophecying, hauing his head couered, dishonoureth his head.

5 But euery woman that prayeth or prophesieth with her head vncouered, dishonoureth her head : for that is euen all one as if she were shauen.

6 For if the woman be not couered, let her also bee shorne : but if it bee a shame for a woman to be shorne or shauen, let her be couered.

7 For a man in deede ought not to couer his head, forasmuch as hee is the image

‖ Or, traditions.

image and glory of God : but the woman is the glory of the man.

8 For the man is not of the woman : but the woman of the man.

9 Neither was the man created for the woman : but the woman for the man.

10 For this cause ought the woman to haue power ‖on her head, because of the Angels.

‖ *That is, a couering, in signe that she is vnder the power of her husband*

11 Neuerthelesse, neither is the man without the woman, neither the woman without the man in the Lord.

12 For as the woman is of the man : euen so is the man also by the woman ; but all things of God.

13 Iudge in your selues, is it comely that a woman pray vnto God vncouered ?

14 Doeth not euen nature it selfe teach you, that if a man haue long haire, it is a shame vnto him ?

15 But if a woman haue long haire, it is a glory to her : for her haire is giuen her for a ‖couering.

‖ *Or, vaile.*

16 But if any man seeme to be contentious, we haue no such custome, neither the Churches of God.

17 Now in this that I declare *vnto you*, I praise you not, that you come together not for the better, but for the worse.

18 For first of all when yee come together in the Church, I heare that there be ‖diuisions among you, and I partly beleeue it.

‖ *Or, schismes.*

19 For there must bee also ‖heresies among you, that they which are approued may be made manifest among you.

‖ *Or, sects.*

20 When yee come together therefore into one place, *this is* ‖not to eate the Lords Supper.

‖ *Or, ye cannot eate.*

21 For in eating, euery one taketh before *other*, his owne supper : and one is hungry, and an other is drunken.

22 What, haue ye not houses to eate and to drinke in ? Or despise yee the Church of God, and shame ‖them that haue not ? What shall I say to you ? shall I praise you in this ? I prayse you not.

‖ *Or, them that are poore.*

23 For I haue receiued of the Lord that which also I deliuered vnto you, that the Lord Iesus, the same night in which he was betrayed, tooke bread :

24 *When he had giuen thanks, he brake it, and sayd, Take, eate, this is my body, which is broken for you : this doe ‖in remembrance of mee.

* *Mat. 26. 16 mar. 14. 22. luk. 22. 19.*

‖ *Or, for a remembrance.*

25 After the same manner also *hee* tooke the cup when he had supped, saying, This cup is the new Testament in my blood : this do ye, as oft as ye drinke it, in remembrance of me.

26 For as often as ye eate this bread, and drinke this cup, ‖yee doe shew the Lords death till he come.

‖ *Or, shew yee.*

27 Wherefore, whosoeuer shall eate this bread, and drinke this cup of the Lord vnworthily, shall be guilty of the body and blood of the Lord.

28 But let a man examine himselfe, and so let him eate of that bread, and drinke of that cup.

29 For hee that eateth and drinketh vnworthily, eateth and drinketh ‖damnation to himselfe, not discerning the Lords body.

‖ *Or, iudgement.*

30 For this cause many are weake and sickly among you, and many sleepe.

31 For if we would iudge our selues, we should not be iudged.

32 But when we are iudged, we are chastened of the Lord, that wee should not be condemned with the world.

33 Wherefore my brethren, when ye come together to eate, tary one for another.

34 And if any man hunger, let him eate at home, that ye come not together vnto ‖condemnation. And the rest wil I set in order, when I come.

‖ *Or, iudgement.*

CHAP. XII.

1 Spirituall gifts 4 are diuers, 7 yet all to profit withall. 8 And to that ende, are diuersly bestowed : 12 That by the like proportion, as the members of a naturall body, tend all to the 16 mutuall decency, 22 seruice, and 26 succour of the same body ; 27 so wee should doe one for another, to make vp the mysticall body of Christ.

NOw concerning spirituall *giftes*, brethren, I would not haue you ignorant.

2 Yee know that yee were Gentiles, caryed away vnto these dumbe idoles, euen as ye were led.

3 Wherefore I giue you to vnderstand, that no man speaking by the spirit of God, calleth Iesus ‖accursed : and that no man can say that Iesus is the Lord, but by the holy Ghost.

‖ *Or, Anathema.*

4 Nowe there are diuersities of gifts, but the same spirit.

5 And there are differences of administrations, but the same Lord.

6 And

6 And there are diuersities of operations, but it is the same God, which worketh all in all.

7 But the manifestation of the spirit, is giuen to euery man to profit withall.

8 For to one is giuen by the spirit, the word of wisedome, to another the word of knowledge, by the same spirit.

9 To another faith, by the same spirit : to another the gifts of healing, by the same spirit :

10 To another the working of miracles, to another prophecie, to another discerning of spirits, to another *diuers* kindes of tongues, to another the interpretation of tongues.

11 But all these worketh that one and the selfe same spirit, diuiding to euery man seuerally as he will.

12 For as the body is one, and hath many members, and all the membrs of that one body, being many, are one bodie : so also *is* Christ.

13 For by one spirit are we all baptized into one bodie, whether *wee bee* †Iewes or †Gentiles, whether *wee bee* bond or free : and haue beene all made to drinke into one spirit.

†*Gr. Greeks.*

14 For the body is not one member, but many.

15 If the foot shall say, Because I am not the hand, I am not of the body : is it therefore not of the body ?

16 And if the eare shall say, Because I am not the eye, I am not of the body : is it therefore not of the body ?

17 If the whole body were an eye, where were the hearing ? If the whole were hearing, where were the smelling ?

18 But now hath God set the members, euery one of them in the body, as it hath pleased him.

19 And if they were all one member, where were the body ?

20 But now are they many members, yet but one body.

21 And the eye cannot say vnto the hand, I haue no need of thee : nor againe, the head to the feete, I haue no neede of you.

22 Nay, much more those members of the bodie, which seeme to bee more feeble, are necessary.

23 And those *members* of the bodie, which wee thinke to bee lesse honourable, vpon these we ‖bestow more abundant honour, and our vncomely parts

‖ *Or, put on.*

haue more abundant comelinesse.

24 For our comely *parts* haue no need : but God hath tempered the bodie together, hauing giuen more abundant honour to that part which lacked :

25 That there should be no ‖schisme in the body : but that the members should haue the same care one for another.

‖ *Or, diui-sion.*

26 And whether one member suffer, all the members suffer with it : or one member be honoured, all the members reioyce with it.

27 Now yee are the body of Christ, and members in particular.

28 And God hath set some in the Church, first Apostles, secondarily Prophets, thirdly Teachers, after that miracles, then gifts of healings, helpes in gouernmēts, ‖diuersities of tongues.

‖ *Or, kinds.*

29 Are all Apostles? are all Prophets? are all Teachers? are all ‖workers of miracles?

‖ *Or, powers.*

30 Haue all the gifts of healing? doe all speake with tongues? doe all interpret?

31 But couet earnestly the best gifts : And yet shew I vnto you a more excellent way.

CHAP. XIII.

1 All giftes, 2. 3 how excellent soeuer, are nothing worth without charitie. 4 The praises therof, and 13 prelation before hope & faith.

Hough I speake with the tongues of men & of Angels, and haue not charity, I am become as sounding brasse or a tinkling cymbal.

2 And though I haue the gift of prophesie, and vnderstand all mysteries and all knowledge : and though I haue all faith, so that I could remooue mountaines, and haue no charitie, I am nothing.

3 And though I bestowe all my goods to feede the poore, and though I giue my body to bee burned, and haue not charitie, it profiteth me nothing.

4 Charitie suffereth long, and is kinde : charitie enuieth not : charitie ‖vaunteth not it selfe, is not puffed vp,

‖ *Or, is not rash.*

5 Doeth not behaue it selfe vnseemly, seeketh not her owne, is not easily prouoked, thinketh no euill,

6 Reioyceth not in iniquitie, but reioyceth ‖in the trueth :

‖ *Or, with the trueth.*

7 Beareth all things, beleeueth all things, hopeth all things, endureth all things.

8 Cha-

8 Charitie neuer faileth : but whether there be prophesies, *they* shall faile; whether there bee tongues, *they* shall cease; whether there bee knowledge, *it* shall vanish away.

9 For we know in part, and we prophesie in part.

10 But when that which is perfect is come, then that which is in part, shalbe done away.

11 When I was a childe, I spake as a childe, I vnderstood as a childe, I ‖thought as a childe: but when I became a man, I put away childish things.

‖ *Or, reasoned.*

12 For now we see through a glasse, †darkely : but then face to face : now I know in part, but then shall I know euen as also I am knowen.

† *Gr. in a riddle.*

13 And now abideth faith, hope, charitie, these three, but the greatest of these is charitie.

CHAP. XIIII.

1 Prophecie is commended, 2. 3. 4 and preferred before speaking with tongues, 6 by a comparison drawen from musicall instruments. 12 Both must bee referred to edification, 22 as to their true and proper end. 26 The true vse of each is taught, 27 and the abuse taxed. 34 Women are forbidden to speake in the Church.

Ollow after charitie, and desire spirituall giftes, but rather that yee may prophesie.

2 For he that speaketh in an *vnknowen* tongue, speaketh not vnto men, but vnto God : for no man †vnderstandeth him : howbeit in the spirit he speaketh mysteries.

† *Gr. heareth*

3 But he that prophesieth, speaketh vnto men to edification, and exhortation, and comfort.

4 He that speaketh in an *vnknowen* tongue, edifieth himselfe : but hee that prophesieth, edifieth the Church.

5 I would that yee all spake with tongues, but rather that ye prophesied: for greater is hee that prophesieth, then hee that speaketh with tongues, except hee interprete, that the Church may receiue edifying.

6 Now brethren, if I come vnto you speaking with tongues, what shall I profit you, except I shall speake to you either by reuelation, or by knowledge, or by prophesying, or by doctrine?

7 And euen things without life giuing sound, whether pipe or harpe, except they giue a distinction in the ‖sounds, how shall it be knowen what is piped or harped?

‖ *Or, tunes.*

8 For if the trumpet giue an vncertaine sound, who shall prepare himselfe to the battell?

9 So likewise you, except ye vtter by the tongue words †easie to be vnderstood, how shall it be knowen what is spoken? for ye shall speake into the aire.

† *Gr. signifi-cant.*

10 There are, it may bee, so many kindes of voices in the world, and none *of them* are without signification.

11 Therefore if I know not the meaning of the voyce, I shall bee vnto him that speaketh, a Barbarian, and he that speaketh shall be a Barbarian vnto mee.

12 Euen so ye, forasmuch as yee are zealous †of spirituall *gifts*, seeke that yee may excell to the edifying of the Church.

† *Gr. of spirits.*

13 Wherefore let him that speaketh in an *vnknowen* tongue, pray that he may interprete.

14 For if I pray in an *vnknowen* tongue, my spirit prayeth, but my vnderstanding is vnfruitfull.

15 What is it then? I will pray with the spirit, and wil pray with vnderstanding also : I will sing with the spirit, and I will sing with the vnderstanding also.

16 Else, when thou shalt blesse with the spirit, how shall hee that occupieth the roome of the vnlearned, say Amen at thy giuing of thankes, seeing he vnderstandeth not what thou sayest?

17 For thou verily giuest thankes well : but the other is not edified.

18 I thanke my God, I speake with tongues more then you all.

19 Yet in the Church I had rather speake fiue words with my vnderstanding, that *by my voyce* I might teach others also, then ten thousand words in an *vnknowen* tongue.

20 Brethren, bee not children in vnderstanding : how be it, in malice be yee children, but in vnderstanding be †men.

† *Gr. perfect or of a ripe age.* Esa. 28. 11.

21 In the Law it is *written, With *men of* other tongues, and other lippes will I speake vnto this people : and yet for all that will they not heare me, saith the Lord.

22 Wherfore tongues are for a signe, not to them that beleeue, but to them that beleeue not : But prophesying *serueth*

ueth not for them that beleeue not, but for them which beleeue.

23 If therefore the whole Church be come together into some place, and all speake with tongues, & there come in those that are vnlearned, or vnbeleeuers, will they not say that ye are mad?

24 But if all prophesie, and there come in one that beleeueth not, or one vnlearned : he is conuinced of all, he is iudged of all.

25 And thus are the secrets of his heart made manifest, and so falling downe on his face, hee will worship God, and report that God is in you of a trueth.

26 How is it then brethren? when ye come together, euery one of you hath a Psalme, hath a doctrine, hath a tongue, hath a reuelatiō, hath an interpretatiō: Let all things be done vnto edifying.

27 If any man speake in *an vnknowen* tongue, let it be by two, or at the most by three, and that by course, and let one interprete.

28 But if there be no interpreter, let him keepe silence in the Church, and let him speake to himselfe, and to God.

29 Let the Prophets speake two or three, and let the other iudge.

30 If *any thing* be reueiled to another that sitteth by, let the first hold his peace.

31 For yee may all prophesie one by one, that all may learne, and all may be comforted.

32 And the spirits of the Prophets are subiect to the Prophets.

† *Gr. tumult, or vnquietnesse.*

33 For God is not *the authour* of † confusion, but of peace, as in all Churches of the Saints.

34 Let your women keepe silence in the Churches, for it is not permitted vnto them to speake; but *they are commanded* to bee vnder obedience : as also

* Gen. 3. 16.

saith the *Law.

35 And if they will learne any thing, let them aske their husbands at home : for it is a shame for women to speake in the Church.

36 What? came the word of God out from you? or came it vnto you onely?

37 If any man thinke himselfe to be a Prophet, or spirituall, let him acknowledge, that the things that I write vnto you, are the commandements of the Lord.

38 But if any man bee ignorant, let him be ignorant.

39 Wherefore brethren, couet to pro-

phesie, and forbid not to speake with tongues.

40 Let all things be done decently, and in order.

CHAP. XV.

3 By Christés resurrection, 12 he proueth the necessitie of our resurrection, against all such as deny the resurrection of the body. 21 The fruit, 35 and maner thereof, 51 And of the changing of them, that shall bee found aliue at the last day.

Oreouer brethren, I declare vnto you the Gospel which I preached vnto you, which also you haue receiued, and wherein yee stand.

2 By which also yee are saued, if yee ||keepe in memorie †what I preached vnto you, vnlesse yee haue beleeued in vaine.

|| *Or, hold fast.*
† *Gr. by what speech.*

3 For I deliuered vnto you first of all, that which I also receiued, how that Christ died for our sinnes according to the Scriptures :

4 And that he was buried, and that he rose againe the third day according to the Scriptures.

5 And that he was seene of Cephas, then of the twelue.

5 And that hee was seene of aboue fiue hundred brethren at once : of whom the greater part remaine vnto this present, but some are fallen asleepe.

7 After that, he was seen of Iames, then of all the Apostles.

8 And last of all he was seene of me also, as of †one borne out of due time.

|| *Or, an abortiue.*

9 For I am the least of the Apostles, that am not meet to be called an Apostle because I persecuted ÿ Church of God.

10 But by the grace of God I am what I am : and his grace which was *bestowed* vpō me, was not in vaine : But I laboured more abundantly then they all, yet not I, but the grace of God which was with me :

11 Therefore, whether it were I or they, so we preach, aud so ye beleeued.

12 Now if Christ be preached that he rose from the dead, how say some among you, that there is no resurrection of the dead?

13 But if there be no resurrection of the dead, then is Christ not risen.

14 And if Christ be not risen, then is our preaching vaine, and your faith is also vaine:

15 Yea,

15 Yea, and we are found false witnesses of God, because we haue testified of God, that he raised vp Christ : whom hee raised not vp, if so bee that the dead rise not.

16 For if the dead rise not, then is not Christ raised.

17 And if Christ be not raised, your faith is vaine, ye are yet in your sinnes.

18 Then they also which are fallen asleepe in Christ, are perished.

19 If in this life only we haue hope in Christ, wee are of all men most miserable.

20 But now is Christ risen from the dead, *and* become the first fruits of them that slept.

21 For since by man *came* death, by man *came* also the resurrection of the dead.

22 For as in Adam all die, euen so in Christ shall all be made aliue.

23 But euery man in his owne order. Christ the first fruits, afterward they that are Christs, at his comming.

24 Then *commeth* the end, when he shall haue deliuered vp the kingdome to God euen the Father, when he shall haue put downe all rule, and all authority and power.

25 For he must reigne, till hee hath put all enemies vnder his feete.

26 The last enemie *that* shall be destroyed, *is* death.

27 For he hath put all things vnder his feete; but when hee saith all things are put vnder him, it is manifest that he is excepted which did put all things vnder him.

28 And when all things shall bee subdued vnto him, then shal the Sonne also himselfe bee subiect vnto him that put all things vnder him, that God may be all in all.

29 Else what shal they do, which are baptized for the dead, if the dead rise not at all, why are they then baptized for the dead?

30 And why stand we in ieopardy euery houre?

31 I protest by ||your reioycing which I haue in Christ Iesus our Lord, I die dayly.

32 If ||after the maner of men I haue fought with beasts at Ephesus, what aduantageth it me, if the dead rise not? let vs eate and drinke, for to morrowe wee die.

33 Bee not deceiued : euill commu-

‖ Some reade, *our*.

‖ *Or, to speak after the maner of men.*

nications corrupt good manners.

34 Awake to righteousnesse, and sinne not : for some haue not the knowledge of God, I speake this to your shame.

35 But some man will say, How are the dead raysed vp? and with what body doe they come?

36 Thou foole, that which thou sowest, is not quickened except it die.

37 And that which thou sowest, thou sowest not that body that shall be, but bare graine, it may chance of wheate, or of some other *graine*.

38 But God giueth it a body as it hath pleased him, and to euery seed his owne body.

39 All flesh is not the same flesh, but there is one *kind of* flesh of men, another flesh of beasts, another of fishes, and another of birds.

40 There are also celestiall bodies, and bodies terrestriall : But the glorie of the celestiall is one, and the glorie of the terrestriall is another.

41 There is one glory of the sunne, another of the moone, and another glorie of the starres : for *one* starre differeth from *another* starre in glorie.

42 So also is the resurrection of the dead, it is sowen in corruption, it is raised in incorruption.

43 It is sowen in dishonour, it is raysed in glorie : it is sowen in weakenesse, it is raysed in power :

44 It is sowen a naturall body, it is raised a spirituall bodie. There is a naturall bodie, and there is a spirituall bodie.

45 And so it is written : The first man Adam was made a liuing soule, the last Adam was made a quickening spirit.

46 Howbeit that was not first which is spirituall : but that *which is* naturall, and afterward that *which is* spirituall.

47 The first man *is* of the earth, earthy : The second man *is* the Lord from heauen.

48 As is the earthy, such are they that are earthy, and as is the heauenly, such *are* they also that are heauenly.

49 And as we haue borne the image of the earthy, wee shall also beare the image of the heauenly.

50 Now this I say, brethren, that flesh & blood cannot inherite the kingdome of God : neither doth corruption inherite incorruption.

51 Be-

51 Behold, I shew you a mysterie: we shall not all sleepe, but wee shall all be changed,

52 In a moment, in the twinckling of an eye, at the last trumpe, (for the trumpet shall sound, and the dead shall be raised incorruptible, and we shall be changed.)

53 For this corruptible must put on incorruption, and this mortall must put on immortalitie.

54 So when this corruptible shall haue put on incorruption, & this mortall shall haue put on immortality, then shall be brought to passe the saying that is written, *Death is swallowed vp in victorie.

Ose. 13. 14

55 O death, where is thy sting? O ||graue, where is thy victorie?

‖ Or, hell.

56 The sting of death is sinne, and the strength of sinne is the law.

57 But thankes bee to God, which giueth vs the victorie, through our Lord Iesus Christ.

58 Therefore my beloued brethren, be yee stedfast, vnmoueable, alwayes abounding in the worke of the Lord, forasmuch as you know that your labour is not in vaine in the Lord.

CHAP. XVI.

1 Hee exhorteth them to relieue the want of the brethren at Ierusalem. 10 Commendeth Timothy, 13 And after friendly admonitions, 16 Shutteth vp his Epistle with diuers salutations.

Ow concerning the collection for the Saints, as I haue giuen order to the Churches of Galatia, euen so doe ye.

2 Vpon the first *day* of the weeke, let euery one of you lay by him in store, as *God* hath prospered him, that there be no gatherings when I come.

3 And when I come, whomsoeuer you shall approue by *your* letters, them wil I send to bring your †liberality vnto Ierusalem.

† Gr. gift.

4 And if it be meet that I goe also, they shall goe with me.

5 Now I wil come vnto you, when I shall passe through Macedonia: for I doe passe through Macedonia.

6 And it may bee that I will abide, yea, and winter with you, that yee may bring me on my iourny, whithersoeuer I goe.

7 For I will not see you now by the way, but I trust to tarry a while with you, if the Lord permit.

8 But I will tarry at Ephesus vntill Pentecost.

9 For a great doore and effectuall is opened vnto mee, and there are many aduersaries.

10 Now if Timotheus come, see that he may be with you without feare: for hee worketh the worke of the Lord, as I also doe.

11 Let no man therefore despise him: but conduct him forth in peace, that hee may come vnto me: for I looke for him with the brethren.

12 As touching *our* brother Apollos, I greatly desired him to come vnto you with y brethren, but his wil was not at all to come at this time: but he wil come when hee shall haue conuenient time.

13 Watch yee, stand fast in the faith, quit you like men: be strong.

14 Let all your things be done with charitie.

15 I beseech you, brethren, (ye know the house of Stephanas, that it is the first fruits of Achaia, and that they haue addicted themselues to the ministery of the Saints,)

16 That ye submit your selues vnto such, and to euery one that helpeth with vs and laboureth.

17 I am glad of the comming of Stephanas, and Fortunatus, and Achaicus: for that which was lacking on your part, they haue supplied.

18 For they haue refreshed my spirit and yours: therefore acknowledge yee them that are such.

19 The Churches of Asia salute you: Aquila and Priscilla salute you much in the Lord, with the Church that is in their house.

20 All the brethren greet you: greet ye one another with an holy kisse.

21 The salutation of me Paul, with mine owne hand.

22 If any man loue not the Lord Iesus Christ, let him bee Anathema Maranatha.

23 The grace of our Lord Iesus Christ be with you.

24 My loue be with you all in Christ Iesus, Amen.

¶ The first Epistle to the Corinthians was written from Philippi by Stephanas, and Fortunatus, and Achaicus, and Timotheus.

THE

¶ THE SECOND EPISTLE
of Paul the Apostle to the
Corinthians.

CHAP. I.

3 The Apostle incourageth them against troubles, by the comforts and deliuerances which God had giuen him, as in all his afflictions, 8 so particularly in his late danger in Asia. 12 And calling both his owne conscience, and theirs to witnesse, of his sincere maner of preaching the immutable trueth of the Gospel, 15 Hee excuseth his not comming to them, as proceeding not of lightnesse, but of his lenitie towards them.

Aul an Apostle of Iesus Christ by the will of God, and Timothie *our* brother, vnto the Church of God, which is at Corinth, with all the Saints, which are in all Achaia:

2 Grace *bee* to you and peace, from God our Father, and *from* the Lord Iesus Christ.

3 Blessed be God, euen the Father of our Lord Iesus Christ, the Father of mercies, and the God of all comfort,

4 Who comforteth vs in all our tribulation, that we may be able to comfort them which are in any trouble, by the comfort, wherewith we our selues are comforted of God.

5 For as the sufferings of Christ abound in vs, so our consolation also aboundeth by Christ.

6 And whether we be afflicted, *it is* for your consolation and saluation, which is ‖effectuall in the enduring of the same sufferings, which wee also suffer : or whether we be comforted, *it is* for your consolation, and saluation.

‖ *Or, is wrought.*

7 And our hope of you is stedfast, knowing, that as you are partakers of the sufferings, so *shall yee be* also of the consolatiou.

8 For we would not, brethren, haue you ignorant of our trouble which came to vs in Asia, that we were pressed out of measure, aboue strength, in so much that we dispaired euen of life.

9 But we had the ‖sentence of death in our selues, that we should not trust in our selues, but in God which raiseth the dead.

‖ *Or, answere.*

10 Who deliuered vs from so great a death, and doeth deliuer : in whom we trust that he will yet deliuer *vs* :

11 You also helping together by prayer for vs, that for the gift *bestowed* vpon vs by the meanes of many persons, thankes may bee giuen by many on our behalfe.

12 For our reioycing is this, the testimony of our conscience, that in simplicitie and godly sinceritie, not with fleshly wisedome, but by the grace of God, wee haue had our conuersation in the world, and more aboundantly to youwards.

13 For we write none other things vnto you, then what you reade or acknowledge, and I trust you shall acknowledge euen to the end.

14 As also you haue acknowledged vs in part, that we are your reioycing, euen as ye also are ours, in the day of the Lord Iesus.

15 And in this confidence I was minded to come vnto you before, that you might haue a second ‖benefit :

‖ *Or, grace.*

16 And to passe by you into Macedonia, and to come againe out of Macedonia vnto you, and of you to bee brought on my way toward Iudea.

17 When I therefore was thus minded, did I vse lightnesse ? or the things that I purpose, doe I purpose according to the flesh, that with mee there should be yea yea, and nay nay ?

18 But *as* God is true, our ‖word toward you, was not yea and nay.

‖ *Or, preaching.*

19 For

19 For the Sonne of God Iesus Christ, who was preached among you by vs, *euen* by me, and Syluanus and Timotheus, was not Yea, and Nay, but in him, was yea.

20 For all the promises of God in him are Yea, and in him Amen, vnto the glory of God by vs.

21 Now hee which stablisheth vs with you, in Christ, and hath anoynted vs, *is* God,

22 Who hath also sealed vs, and giuen the earnest of the Spirit in our hearts.

23 Moreouer, I call God for a record vpõ my soule, that to spare you I came not as yet vnto Corinth.

24 Not for that we haue dominion ouer your faith, but are helpers of your ioy : for by faith ye stand.

CHAP. II.

1 Hauing shewed the reason why he came not to them, 6 Hee requireth them to forgiue and to comfort that excommunicated person, 10 Euen as himselfe also vpon his true repentance had forgiuen him, 12 declaring withall why hee departed from Troas to Macedonia, 14 and the happy successe which God gaue to his preaching in all places.

 Vt I determined this with my selfe, that I would not come againe to you in heauinesse.

2 For if I make you sorie, who is hee then that maketh mee glad, but the same which is made sorie by me.

3 And I wrote this same vnto you, least when I came, I should haue sorrow from them of whome I ought to reioyce, hauing confidence in you all, that my ioy is *the ioy* of you all.

4 For out of much affliction and anguish of heart, I wrote vnto you with many teares, not that you should bee grieued, but that yee might knowe the loue which I haue more abundantly vnto you.

5 But if any haue caused griefe, hee hath not grieued mee, but in part : that I may not ouercharge you all.

Or, censure 6 Sufficient to such a man is this ||punishment, which *was inflicted* of many.

7 So that contrariwise, yee ought rather to forgiue him, and comfort him, lest perhaps, such a one should be swallowed vp with ouermuch sorrow.

8 Wherefore I beseech you, that you would confirme *your* loue towards him.

9 For to this end also did I write, that I might know the proofe of you, whether ye be obedient in all things.

10 To whom yee forgiue any thing, I *forgiue* also : *for* if I forgaue any thing, to whom I forgaue it, for your sakes forgaue I it, in ||the person of Christ, *Or, in the sight.*

11 Lest Satan should get an aduantage of vs : for wee are not ignorant of his deuices.

12 Furthermore when I came to Troas, to *preach* Christs Gospel, and a doore was opened vnto mee of the Lord,

13 I had no rest in my spirit, because I found not Titus my brother, but taking my leaue of them, I went from thence into Macedonia.

14 Now thankes bee vnto God, which alwayes causeth vs to triumph in Christ, and maketh manifest the sauour of his knowledge by vs in euery place.

15 For wee are vnto God, a sweet sauour of Christ, in them that are saued, and in them that perish.

16 To the one *wee are* the sauour of death vnto death; and to the other, the sauour of life vnto life : and who is sufficient for these things ?

17 For wee are not as many which ||corrupt the word of God : but as of sinceritie, but as of God, in the sight of God speake we in Christ. *Or, deale deceitfully with.*

CHAP. III.

1 Lest their false teachers should charge him with vaineglory, hee sheweth the faith and graces of the Corinthians, to bee a sufficient commendation of his ministerie. 6 Whereupon entring a comparison betweene the ministers of the Law & of the Gospel, 12 he proueth that his ministerie is so far the more excellent, as the Gospel of life and libertie is more glorious then the law of condemnation.

 Oe wee begin againe to commend our selues ? or need wee, as some *others*, Epistles of commendation to you, or *letters* of commendation from you ?

2 Ye are our Epistle written in our hearts, knowen and read of all men.

3 *Forasmuch as* yet are manifestly declared *to be* the Epistle of Christ ministred by vs, written not with inke, but with

with the spirit of the liuing God, not in tables of stone, but in fleshy tables of the heart.

4 And such trust haue wee through Christ to Godward:

5 Not that wee are sufficient of our selues to thinke any thing as of our selues: but our sufficiencie *is* of God:

6 Who also hath made vs able ministers of the New Testament, not of the letter, but of the spirit: for the letter killeth, but the spirit ||giueth life.

| Or, quick-neth.

7 But if the ministration of death written, and ingrauen in stones, was glorious, so that the children of Israel could not stedfastly beholde the face of Moses, for the glory of his countenance, which *glorie* was to be done away:

8 How shall not the ministration of the spirit, be rather glorious?

9 For if the ministration of condemnation bee glory, much more doth the ministration of righteousnesse exceed in glorie.

10 For euen that which was made glorious, had no glorie in this respect by reason of the glorie that excelleth.

11 For if that which is done away, was glorious, much more that which remaineth is glorious.

12 Seeing then that wee haue such hope, we vse great ||plainnesse of speech.

| Or, boldnes.

13 And not as Moses, which put a vaile ouer his face, that the children of Israel could not stedfastly looke to the end of that which is abolished;

14 But their mindes were blinded: for vntill this day remaineth the same vaile vntaken away, in the reading of the old testament: which vaile is done away in Christ.

15 But euen vnto this day, when Moses is read, the vaile is vpon their heart.

16 Neuerthelesse, when it shall turne to the Lord, the vaile shall be taken away.

17 Now the Lord is that spirit, and where the Spirit of the Lord *is*, there *is* libertie.

18 But we all, with open face beholding as in a glasse the glory of the Lord, are changed into the same image, from glorie to glorie, euen as ||by the spirit of the Lord.

| Or, of the Lord the spirit.

CHAP. IIII.

1 He declareth how hee hath vsed all synceritie

and faithfull diligence in preaching the Gospel, 7 and how the troubles and persecutions which he dayly indured for the same, did redound to the praise of Gods power, 12 to the benefit of the Church, 16 and to the Apostles owne eternall glory.

Therefore, seeing we haue this ministery, as we haue receiued mercie wee faint not:

2 But haue renounced the hidden things of †dishonesty, not walking in craftines, nor handling the word of God deceitfully, but by manifestation of the trueth, commending our selues to euery mans conscience, in the sight of God.

† Gr. shame.

3 But if our Gospel be hid, it is hid to them that are lost:

4 In whom the God of this world hath blinded the minds of them which beleeue not, lest the light of the glorious Gospel of Christ, who is the image of God, should shine vnto them.

5 For we preach not our selues, but Christ Iesus the Lord, and our selues your seruants for Iesus sake.

6 For God who commaunded the light to shine out of darkenes, hath shined in our hearts, *to giue* the light of the knowledge of the glory of God, in the face of Iesus Christ.

7 But we haue this treasure in earthen vessels, that the excellencie of the power may be of God, and not of vs.

8 Wee are troubled on euery side, yet not distressed; we are perplexed, but ||not in despaire,

9 Persecuted, but not forsaken; cast downe, but not destroyed.

|| Or, not altogether without help or meanes.

10 Alwayes bearing about in the body, the dying of the Lord Iesus, that the life also of Iesus might bce made manifest in our body.

11 For we which liue, are alway deliuered vnto death for Iesus sake, that the life also of Iesus might bee made manifest in our mortall flesh.

12 So then death worketh in vs, but life in you.

13 We hauing the same spirit of faith, according as it is written, *I beleeued, and therefore haue I spoken: wee also beleeue, and therefore speake.

Ps. 116. 10

14 Knowing that hee which raised vp the Lord Iesus, shall raise vp vs also by Iesus, and shall present vs with you.

15 For all things are for your sakes, that

that the abundāt grace might, through the thanksgiuing of many, redound to the glory of God.

16 For which cause we faint not, but though our outward man perish, yet the inward man is renewed day by day.

17 For our light affliction, which is but for a momēt, worketh for vs a farre more exceeding *and* eternall waight of glory,

18 While we looke not at the things which are seene, but at ỹ things which are not seene : for the things which are seene, are temporall, but the things which are not seene, are eternall.

CHAP. V.

1 That in his assured hope of immortall glorie, 9 and in expectance of it, and of the generall iudgement, hee laboureth to keepe a good conscience, 12 not that he may herein boast of himselfe, 14 but as one that hauing receiued life from Christ, indeuoureth to liue as a new creature to Christ onely, 18 and by his ministery of reconciliation to reconcile others also in Christ to God.

Or we know, that if our earthly house of this Tabernacle were dissolued, wee haue a building of God, an house not made with hand, eternall in the heauens.

2 For in this we grone earnestly, desiring to be clothed vpō with our house, which is from heauen.

3 If so be that being clothed we shal not be found naked.

4 For, we that are in this tabernacle, doe grone, being burdened, not for that wee would bee vnclothed, but clothed vpon, that mortalitie might bee swallowed vp of life.

5 Now he ỹ hath wrought vs for the selfe same thing, *is* God, who also hath giuen vnto vs the earnest of the spirit.

6 Therefore we are alwayes confident, knowing that whilest wee are at home in the body, wee are absent from the Lord.

7 (For we walke by faith, not by sight.)

8 We are confident, I say, and willing rather to be absent from the body, and to be present with the Lord.

9 Wherefore we ‖labour, that whether present or absent, we may be accepted of him.

‖ Or, indeuour.

10 For we must all appeare before the iudgement seat of Christ, that euery one may receiue the things done in his body, according to that hee hath done, whether it be good or bad.

11 Knowing therefore the terrour of the Lord, we perswade men ; but we are made manifest vnto God, & I trust also, are made manifest in your consciences.

12 For we commend not our selues againe vnto you, but giue you occasion to glory on our behalfe, that you may haue somewhat *to answere* them, which glory †in appearance, and not in heart.

† Gr. in the face.

13 For whether wee bee besides our selues, it is to God : or whether we bee sober, *it is* for your cause.

14 For the loue of Christ constreineth vs, because wee thus iudge : that if one died for all, then were all dead :

15 And that he died for all, that they which liue, should not hencefoorth liue vnto themselues, but vnto him which died for them, and rose againe.

16 Wherefore hencefoorth know we no man, after the flesh : yea, though we haue knowen Christ after the flesh, yet now hencefoorth knowe wee him no more.

17 Therfore if any man *be* in Christ, ‖*hee is* a new creature : *old things are past away, behold, al things are become new.

‖ Or, let him be.
* Esa. 43. 19 reuel. 21. 5.

18 And all things are of God, who hath reconciled vs to himselfe by Iesus Christ, and hath giuen to vs the ministery of reconciliation,

19 To wit, that God was in Christ, reconciling the world vnto himselfe, not imputing their trespasses vnto them, and hath †committed vnto vs the word of reconciliation.

† Gr. put in vs.

20 Now then we are Ambassadors for Christ, as though God did beseech you by vs; we pray you in Christs stead, that be ye reconciled to God.

21 For he hath made him to be sinne for vs, who knewe no sinne, that wee might bee made the righteousnesse of God in him.

CHAP. VI.

That hee hath approued himselfe a faithfull minister of Christ, both by his exhortations, 3 and by integritie of life, 4 and by patient enduring all kinds of affliction and disgraces for the Gospel. 10 Of which hee speaketh the more boldly amongst them, because his heart

heart is open to them, 13 And he expecteth the like affection from them againe, 14 Exhorting to flee the societie and pollutions of Idolaters, as being themselues Temples of the liuing God.

Ee then, as workers together *with him*, beseech you also, that ye receiue not the grace of God in vaine.

Esa. 49. 8.

2 (For he saith, *I haue heard thee in a time accepted, and in the day of saluation haue I succoured thee: beholde, now is the accepted time, behold, now is the day of saluation)

3 Giuing no offence in any thing, that the ministery be not blamed:

† Gr. commending.

4 But in all things ‖approuing our selues, as the Ministers of God, in much patience, in afflictions, in necessities, in distresses,

‖ Or, in tossings to and fro,

5 In stripes, in imprisonments, in ‖tumults, in labours, in watchings, in fastings,

6 By purenesse, by knowledge, by long suffering, by kindnesse, by the holy Ghost, by loue vnfained,

7 By the worde of trueth, by the power of God, by the armour of righteousnesse, on the right hand, and on the left,

8 By honour and dishonour, by euil report and good report, as deceiuers and yet true:

9 As vnknowen, & yet wel knowen: as dying, and behold, we liue: as chastened, and not killed:

10 As sorrowfull, yet alway reioycing: as poore, yet making many rich: as hauing nothing, and yet possessing all things.

11 O yee Corinthians, our mouth is open vnto you, our heart is enlarged.

12 Yee are not straitened in vs, but yee are straitned in your owne bowels.

13 Nowe for a recompense in the same, (I speake as vnto *my* children) be ye also inlarged.

14 Be ye not vnequally yoked together with vnbeleeuers : for what fellowship hath righteousnesse with vnrighteousnesse? and what communion hath light with darknesse?

15 And what concord hath Christ with Belial? or what part hath he that beleeueth, with an infidel?

16 And what agreement hath the Temple of God with idoles? for ye are the Temple of the liuing God, as God

hath saide, *I will dwell in them, and walke in *them*, and I will be their God, and they shall be my people.

• Leuit. 26. 12.

17 *Wherefore come out from among them, and bee yee separate, saieth the Lord, and touch not the vncleane thing, and I will receiue you,

• Esa. 52. 11

18 *And will bee a Father vnto you, and ye shall bee my sonnes and daughters, saith the Lord Almightie.

• Iere. 31. 1

CHAP. VII.

1 Hee proceedeth in exhorting them to puritie of life, 2 and to beare him like affection as hee doeth to them. 3 Whereof, lest hee might seeme to doubt, hee declareth what comfort he tooke in his afflictions, by the report which Titus gaue of their godly sorrow, which his former Epistle had wrought in them, 13 and of their louing kindnes and obedience towards Titus, answerable to his former boastings of them.

Auing therefore these promises (dearely beloued) let vs cleanse our selues from all filthines of the flesh and spirit, perfecting holinesse in the feare of God.

2 Receiue vs, we haue wronged no man, wee haue corrupted no man, wee haue defrauded no man.

3 I speake not this to condemne *you* : for I haue said before, that you are in our hearts to die and liue with *you*.

4 Great is my boldnesse of speach toward you, great is my glorying of you, I am filled with comfort, I am exceeding ioyfull in all our tribulation.

5 For when wee were come into Macedonia, our flesh had no rest, but we were troubled on euery side; without *were* fightings, within *were* feares.

6 Neuerthelesse, God that comforteth those that are cast downe, comforted vs by the comming of Titus.

7 And not by his comming onely, but by the consolation wherewith hee was comforted in you, when he told vs your earnest desire, your mourning, your feruent minde toward me, so that I reioyced the more.

8 For though I made you sory with a letter, I doe not repent, though I did repent : For I perceiue that the same Epistle hath made you sory, thogh it were but for a season.

9 Now I reioyce, not that ye were made sorie, but that ye sorrowed to repentance : for ye were made sorie ‖after a godly

‖ Or, according to God.

godly maner, that ye might receiue damage by vs in nothing.

10 For godly sorrow worketh repentance to saluation not to be repented of, but the sorrow of the world worketh death.

11 For behold this selfe same thing that yee sorrowed after a godly sort, what carefulnesse it wrought in you, yea, *what* clearing of your selues, yea, *what* indignation, yea *what* feare, yea *what* vehement desire, yea *what* zeale, yea *what* reuenge; In all things yee haue approued your selues to be cleare in this matter.

12 Wherefore though I wrote vnto you, *I did it* not for his cause that had done the wrong, nor for his cause that suffered wrong, but that our care for you in the sight of God might appeare vnto you.

13 Therefore we were comforted in your comfort, yea and exceedingly the more ioyed wee for the ioy of Titus, because his spirit was refreshed by you all.

14 For if I haue boasted any thing to him of you, I am not ashamed; but as we spake all things to you in trueth, euen so our boasting which I made before Titus, is found a trueth.

15 And his † inward affection is more abundant toward you, whilest he remembreth the obedience of you all, how with feare and trembling you receiued him.

16 I reioyce therefore that I haue confidence in you in all things.

† Gr. bowels.

CHAP. VIII.

1 He stirreth them vp to a liberall contribution for the poore Saints at Ierusalem, by the example of the Macedonians, 7 by commendation of their former forwardnesse, 9 by the example of Chrift, 14 and by the spirituall profit that shall redound to themselues thereby: 16 Commending to them the integritie and willingnesse of Titus, and those other brethren, who vpon his request, exhortation and commendation, were purposely come to them for this businesse.

Oreouer, brethren, wee do you to wit of the grace of God bestowed on the Churches of Macedonia, 2 How that in a great trial of affliction, the abundance of their ioy, and their deepe pouertie, abounded vnto the riches of their liberalitie.

3 For to *their* power (I beare record)

yea, and beyond their power *they were* willing of themselues:

4 Praying vs with much entreatie, that we would receiue the gift, and take vpon vs the fellowship of the ministring to the Saints.

5 And this *they did*, not as we hoped, but first gaue their owne selues to the Lord, and vnto vs, by the will of God.

6 In so much that wee desired Titus, that as he had begun, so hee would also finish in you, the same grace also.

7 Therefore (as ye abound in euery thing, in faith, and vtterance, & knowledge, and in all diligence, and in your loue to vs) *see* that yee abound in this grace also.

8 I speake not by commandement, but by occasion of the forwardnesse of others, and to prooue the sinceritie of your loue.

9 For yee know the grace of our Lord Iesus Christ, that though he was rich, yet for your sakes he became poore, that yee through his pouertie might be rich.

10 And herein I giue my aduice, for this is expedient for you, who haue begun before, not onely to doe, but also to be †forward a yeere agoe.

11 Now therefore performe the doing of it, that as *there was* a readinesse to will, so there may be a performance also out of that which you haue.

12 For if there bee first a willing minde, it is accepted according to that a man hath, and not according to that he hath not.

13 For *I meane* not that other men bee eased, and you burthened:

14 But by an equalitie : that now at this time your abundance may be *a supply* for their want, that their abundance also may be *a supply* for your want, that there may be equalitie,

15 As it is written, *Hee that had *gathered* much, had nothing ouer, and hee that had *gathered* little, had no lacke.

16 But thankes bee to God which put the same earnest care into the heart of Titus for you.

17 For indeed he accepted the exhortation, but being more forward, of his owne accord he went vnto you.

18 And wee haue sent with him the brother, whose praise is in the Gospel, throughout all the Churches.

19 And not that onely, but who was also chosen of the Churches to trauaile with

† Gr. willing.

* Exod. 16. 18.

‖ *Or, gift.*

with vs with this ‖grace which is administred by vs to the glorie of the same Lord, and *declaration* of your readie minde.

20 Auoyding this, that no man should blame vs in this aboundance which is administred by vs.

21 Prouiding for honest things, not onely in the sight of the Lord, but in the sight of men.

22 And we haue sent with them our brother, whom wee haue often times proued diligent in many things, but now much more diligent, vpon the great confidence which ‖I haue in you.

‖ *Or, hee hath.*

23 Whether *any doe enquire* of Titus; he is my partner and fellow helper concerning you : or our brethren *bee enquired of, they are* the messengers of the Churches, *and* the glorie of Christ.

24 Wherefore shew ye to them, and before the Churches, the proofe of your loue, & of our boasting on your behalfe.

CHAP. IX.

1 Hee yeeldeth the reason why, though hee knewe their forwardnesse, yet hee sent Titus and his brethren before hand. 6 And hee proceedeth in stirring them vp to a bountifull almes, as being but a kind of sowing of seed, 10 which shall returne a great increase to them, 13 and occasion a great sacrifice of thanksgiuings vnto God.

Or as touching the ministring to the Saints, it is superfluous for mee to write to you.

2 For I know the forwardnesse of your mind, for which I boast of you to them of Macedonia, that Achaia was ready a yeere agoe, and your zeale hath prouoked very many.

3 Yet haue I sent the brethren, least our boasting of you should bee in vaine in this behalfe, that as I saide, yee may be readie.

4 Lest happily if they of Macedonia come with mee, & find you vnprepared, wee (that wee say not, you) should bee ashamed in this same confident boasting.

5 Therefore I thought it necessary to exhort the brethren, that they would go before vnto you, and make vp before hand your †bountie, ‖whereof yee had notice before, that the same might bee readie, as a matter of bountie, not of couetousnesse.

† *Gr. blessing* ‖ *Or, which hath bene so much spoken of before.*

6 But this *I say*, Hee which soweth sparingly, shall reape sparingly : and he which soweth bountifully, shall reape bountifully.

7 Euerie man according as he purposeth in his heart, *so let him giue* ; not grudgingly, or of necessitie: for * God loueth a cheerefull giuer.

* Pro. 11. 2. rom. 12. 8. ecclu. 35. 9.

8 And God is able to make all grace abound towards you, that ye alwayes hauing all sufficiencie in all things, may abound to euery good worke.

9 (As it is written : * Hee hath dispersed abroad : Hee hath giuen to the poore : his righteousnesse remaineth for euer.

* Psa. 112.

10 Now he that *ministreth seede to the sower, both minister bread for your foode, and multiply your seede sowen, and encrease the fruites of your righteousnesse)

* Esa. 55. 1

11 Being enriched in euery thing to al bountifulnes, which causeth through vs thankesgiuing to God.

12 For the administration of this seruice, not onely supplieth the want of the Saints, but is abundant also by many thanksgiuings vnto God,

13 Whiles by the experiment of this ministration, they glorifie God for your professed subiection vnto the Gospel of Christ, and for your liberall distribution vnto them, and vnto all men :

14 And by their prayer for you, which long after you for the exceeding grace of God in you.

15 Thanks be vnto God for his vnspeakeable gift.

CHAP. X.

Against the false Apostles, who disgraced the weakenesse of his person and bodily presence, he setteth out the spirituall might and authoritie, with which hee is armed against all aduersary powers, 7 assuring them that at his comming hee will bee found as mightie in word, as hee is now in writing beeing absent, 12 And withall taxing them for reaching out themselues beyond their compasse, and vanting themselues into other mens labors.

Ow I Paul my selfe beseech you, by the meekenes and gentlenesse of Christ, who ‖in presence am base among you, but being absent, am bold toward you :

‖ *Or, in outward appearance.*

2 But I beseech you, that I may not bee bold when I am present, with that confidence wherewith I thinke to be

Or, reckon.

be bold against some, which ||thinke of vs as if wee walked according to the flesh.

3 For though we walke in the flesh, we doe not warre after the flesh:

Or, to God.

4 (For the weapons of our warfare are not carnal, but mighty ||through God to the pulling downe of strong holds.)

Or, reasonings.

5 Casting down ||imaginations, and euery high thing that exalteth it selfe against the knowledge of God, and bringing into captiuitie euery thought to the obedience of Christ:

6 And hauing in a readinesse to reuenge all disobedience, when your obedience is fulfilled.

7 Doe ye looke on things after the outward appearance? if any man trust to himselfe, that he is Christs, let him of himselfe thinke this againe, that as he is Christs, euen so are we Christs.

8 For though I should boast somewhat more of our authority (which the Lord hath giuen vs for edification, and not for your destruction) I should not be ashamed:

9 That I may not seeme as if I would terrifie you by letters.

10 For his letters (say they) are waighty and powerfull, but *his* bodily presence is weake, and his speach contemptible.

11 Let such a one thinke this: that such as we are in word by letters, when we are absent, such *will we be also* in deede when we are present.

12 For we dare not make our selues of the number, or compare our selues with some that commend themselues: but they measuring themselues by themselues, and comparing themselues amongst themselues, ||are not wise.

Or, understand it not.

Or, line.

13 But we will not boast of things without our measure, but according to the measure of the ||rule, which God hath distributed to vs, a measure to reach euen vnto you.

14 For we stretch not our selues beyond our measure as though wee reached not vnto you, for wee are come as farre as to you also, in *preaching* the Gospel of Christ.

15 Not boasting of things without our measure, *that is*, of other mens labours, but hauing hope, when your faith is increased, that wee shall bee ||enlarged by you, according to our rule abundantly.

Or, magnified in you.

16 To preach the Gospel in the regions beyond you, and not to boast in another mans ||line of things made ready to our hand.

Or, rule.

17 *But he that glorieth, let him glory in the Lord.

Iere. 9. 24, 1. cor. 1. 31

18 For, not he that commendeth himselfe is approued, but whom the Lord commendeth.

CHAP. XI.

1 Out of his ieloufie ouer the Corinthians, who seemed to make more account of the false apostles, then of him, he entreth into a forced commendation of himselfe, 5 of his equalitie with the chiefe Apostles, 7 of his preaching the Gospel to them freely, and without any their charge, 13 shewing that hee was not inferiour to those deceitfull workers, in any legall prerogatiue, 13 and in the seruice of Christ, and in all kind of sufferings for his ministery, farre superiour.

W Ould to God you could beare with mee a little in my folly, & in deede ||beare with me.

Or, you do beare with me.

2 For I am iealous ouer you with godly iealousie, for I haue espoused you to one husband, that I may present you as a chaste virgin to Christ.

3 But I feare lest by any meanes, as the Serpent beguiled Eue through his subtilty, so your mindes should bee corrupted from the simplicitie that is in Christ.

4 For if he that commeth preacheth another Iesus whome wee haue not preached, or if yee receiue another spirit, which ye haue not receiued, or another Gospel, which ye haue not accepted, yee might well beare *with him*.

5 For, I suppose, I was not a whit behinde the very chiefest Apostles.

6 But though I be rude in speach, yet not in knowledge; but we haue bene throughly made manifest among you in all things.

7 Haue I committed an offence in abasing my selfe, that you might be exalted, because I haue preached to you the Gospel of God freely?

8 I robbed other Churches, taking wages of them to doe you seruice.

9 And when I was present with you, and wanted, I was chargeable to no man: For that which was lacking to mee, the brethren which came from Macedonia supplied, and in all things I haue

*43

I haue kept my selfe from being burthensome to you, and so will I keepe
my selfe.

10 As the trueth of Christ is in mee,
no man shall †stop mee of this boasting
in the regions of Achaia.

† Gr. this boasting shal not be stop-ped in me.

11 Wherefore? because I loue you
not? God knoweth.

12 But what I doe, that I wil doe,
that I may cut off occasion from them
which desire occasion, that wherein
they glory, they may bee found euen
as we.

13 For such are false Apostles, deceitfull workers, transforming themselues
into the Apostles of Christ.

14 And no marueile, for Sathan
himselfe is transformed into an Angel
of light.

15 Therefore it is no great thing if
his ministers also bee transformed as
the ministers of righteousnesse, whose
end shall be according to their workes.

16 I say againe, Let no man thinke
mee a foole; if otherwise, yet as a foole
||receiue me, that I may boast my selfe
a little.

|| Or, suffer.

17 That which I speake, I speake
it not after the Lord, but as it were foolishly in this confidence of boasting.

18 Seeing that many glory after the
flesh, I will glory also.

19 For ye suffer fooles gladly, seeing
ye your selues are wise.

20 For ye suffer if a man bring you
into bondage, if a man deuoure you, if a
man take of you, if a man exalt himselfe,
if a man smite you on the face.

21 I speake as concerning reproch,
as though we had bene weake: howbeit, wherein soeuer any is bold, I speake
foolishly, I am bold also.

22 Are they Hebrewes? so am I: are
they Israelites? so am I: are they the
seed of Abraham? so am I:

23 Are they ministers of Christ? I
speake as a foole, I am more: in labors
more abundant: in stripes aboue measure: in prisons more frequent: in
deaths oft.

24 Of the Iewes fiue times receiued I *forty stripes saue one.

* Deut. 25. 3.

25 Thrice was I beaten with rods,
once was I stoned: thrice I suffered
shipwracke: a night and a day I haue
bene in the deepe.

26 In iourneying often, in perils of
waters, in perils of robbers, in perils
by my owne countreymen, in perils by

the heathen, in perils in the citie, in perils in the wildernesse, in perils in the
sea, in perils among false brethren, *

27 In wearinesse and painfulnesse,
in watchings often, in hunger & thirst,
in fastings often, in cold and nakednes.

28 Besides those things that are
without, that which commeth vpon me
dayly, the care of all the Churches.

29 Who is weake, and I am not
weake? who is offended, and I burne
not?

30 If I must needes glory, I will
glory of the things which concerne
mine infirmities.

31 The God and Father of our Lord
Iesus Christ, which is blessed for euermore, knoweth that I lie not.

32 In Damascus the gouernour
vnder Aretas the King, kept the citie
with a garison, desirous to apprehend
mee.

33 And through a window in a basket was I let downe, by the wall, and
escaped his hands.

CHAP. XII.

1 For commending of his Apostleship, though
he might glory of his wonderfull reuelations,
9 Yet hee rather chuseth to glory of his infirmities, 11 blaming them for forcing him
to this vaine boasting. 14 Hee promiseth to
come to them againe: but yet altogether in
the affection of a father, 10 although hee
feareth he shall to his griefe finde many offenders, and publike disorders there.

T is not expedient for me,
doubtlesse, to glory, I wil
come to visions and reue-
lations of the Lord.

2 I knewe a man in
Christ aboue fourteene yeeres agoe,
whether in the body, I cannot tell, or
whether out of the body, I cannot tell,
God knoweth: such a one, caught vp
to the third heauen.

3 And I knew such a man (whether in the body, or out of the body, I
cannot tell, God knoweth.)

4 How that he was caught vp into
Paradise, and heard vnspeakeable
wordes, which it is not ||lawfull for a
man to vtter.

||Or, possib-

5 Of such a one will I glory, yet of
my selfe I will not glory, but in mine
infirmities.

6 For though I would desire to
glory, I shall not be a foole: for I will
say the trueth. But now I forbeare,
lest

lest any man should thinke of me aboue *that* which hee seeth me *to bee*, or *that* hee heareth of me:

7 And least I should bee exalted aboue measure through the abundance of the reuelations, there was giuen to me a * thorne in the flesh, the messenger of Sathan to buffet me, lest I should be exalted aboue measure.

* See Ezek. 28. 24.

8 For this thing I besought the Lord thrice, that it might depart from mee.

9 And he said vnto me, My grace is sufficient for thee: for my strength is made perfect in weaknes. Most gladly therefore will I rather glory in my infirmities, that the power of Christ may rest vpon me.

10 Therefore I take pleasure in infirmities, in reproches, in necessities, in persecutions, in distresses for Christes sake: for when I am weake, then am I strong.

11 I am become a foole in glorying, ye haue compelled me. For I ought to haue beene commended of you: for in nothing am I behinde the very chiefest Apostles, though I be nothing.

12 Truely the signes of an Apostle were wrought among you in all patience, in signes and wonders, and mightie deeds.

13 For what is it wherein yee were inferior to other Churches, except *it bee* that I my selfe was not burthensome to you? forgiue me this wrong.

14 Behold, the third time I am readie to come to you, and I will not bee burthensome to you: for I seeke not yours, but you: for the children ought not to lay vp for the parents, but the parents for the children.

15 And I wil very gladly spend and bee spent for †you, though the more abundantly I loue you, the lesse I bee loued.

† Gr. your soules.

16 But be it so: I did not burthen you: neuerthelesse beeing craftie, I caught you with guile.

17 Did I make a gaine of you by any of them, whom I sent vnto you?

18 I desired Titus, and with him I sent a brother: did Titus make a gaine of you? Walked wee not in the same spirit? *walked wee* not in the same steps?

19 Againe, thinke you that we excuse our selues vnto you? wee speake before God in Christ: but *wee doe* all things,

dearely beloued, for your edifying.

20 For I feare lest when I come, I shall not find you such as I would, and that I shall bee found vnto you such as ye would not, lest there bee debates, enuyings, wraths, strifes, backebitings, whisperings, swellings, tumults,

21 And least when I come againe, my God will humble mee among you, and that I shall bewaile many which haue sinned alreadie, and haue not repented of the vncleannesse, and fornication, and lasciuiousnesse which they haue committed.

CHAP. XIII.

1 He threatneth seueritie, and the power of his Apostleship against obstinate sinners. 5 And aduising them to a triall of their faith, 7 and to a reformation of their sinnes before his comming, 11 He concludeth his Epistle with a generall exhortation and a prayer.

 His is the third time I am comming to you: in the mouth of two or three witnesses shal euery word be established.

2 I told you before, and foretell you as if I were present the second time, and being absent, now I write to them which heretofore haue sinned, and to all other, that if I come againe I will not spare:

3 Since ye seeke a proofe of Christ, speaking in me, which to you-ward is not weake, but is mightie in you.

4 For though hee was crucified through weaknesse, yet he liueth by the power of God: for wee also are weake ||in him, but wee shall liue with him by the power of God toward you. || *Or, with him.*

5 Examine your selues, whether ye be in the faith: proue your owne selues. Know yee not your owne selues, how that Iesus Christ is in you, except ye be reprobates?

6 But I trust that yee shall knowe that we are not reprobates.

7 Now I pray to God, that ye doe no euill, not that we should appeare approued, but that ye should doe ẏ which is honest, though we be as reprobates.

8 For wee can doe nothing against the trueth, but for the trueth.

9 For wee are glad when wee are weake, and ye are strong: and this also we wish, euen your perfection.

10 Therefore I write these things being absent, lest being present I should

vse

vse sharpnesse, according to the power which the Lord hath giuen me to edification, and not to destruction.

11 Finally, brethren, farewell: Bee perfect, bee of good comfort, bee of one minde, liue in peace, and the God of loue and peace shalbe with you.

12 Greet one another with an holy kisse.

13 All the Saints salute you.

14 The grace of the Lord Iesus Christ, and the loue of God, and the communion of the holy Ghost, be with you all. Amen.

The second Epistle to the Corinthians, was written from Philippos *a citie* of Macedonia, by Titus and Lucas.

¶THE EPISTLE OF
Paul to the Galatians.

CHAP. I.

6 He wondereth that they haue so soone left him, and the Gospel, 8 And accurseth those that preach any other Gospel then hee did. 11 He learned the Gospel not of men, but of God: 14 And sheweth what he was before his calling, 17 and what he did presently after it.

Aul an Apostle, not of men, neither by man, but by Iesus Christ, and God the Father, who raised him frō the dead,

2 And all the brethren which are with mee, vnto the Churches of Galatia:

3 Grace bee to you and peace, from God the Father, and from our Lord Iesus Christ,

4 Who gaue himselfe for our sinnes, that he might deliuer vs from this present euill world, according to the will of God, and our Father,

5 To whom *bee* glorie for euer and euer, Amen.

6 I marueile, that you are so soone remoued from him, that called you into the grace of Christ, vnto an other Gospel:

7 Which is not another; but there bee some that trouble you, and would peruert the Gospel of Christ.

8 But though we, or an Angel from heauen, preach *anyother Gospel* vnto you, then that which wee haue preached vn-to you, let him be accursed.

9 As we said before, so say I now againe, If any man preach any other Gospel vnto you, then that yee haue receiued, let him be accursed.

10 For doe I now perswade men, or God? or doe I seeke to please men? For if I yet pleased men, I should not bee the seruant of Christ.

11 But I certifie you, brethren, that the Gospel which was preached of me, is not after man.

12 For I neither receiued it of man, neither was I taught *it*, but by the reuelation of Iesus Christ.

13 For yee haue heard of my conuersation in time past, in the Iewes Religion, *how* that beyond measure I persecuted the Church of God, and wasted it:

14 And profited in the Iewes Religion, aboue many my †equals in mine owne nation, being more exceedingly zealous of the traditions of my fathers.   † *Gr. equal in yeeres.*

15 But when it pleased God, who separated me from my mothers wombe, and called *me* by his grace,

16 To reueale his sonne in mee, that I might preach him among the heathen, immediately I conferred not with flesh and blood:

17 Neither went I vp to Ierusalem, to them which *were* Apostles before me, but I went into Arabia, and returned againe vnto Damascus.

18 Then after three yeeres, I ‖went vp to Ierusalem to see Peter, and abode with him fifteene dayes.   ‖ *Or, returned.*

19 But other of the Apostles saw I none,

none, saue Iames the Lords brother.

20 Now the things which I write vnto you, behold, before God I lye not.

21 Afterwards I came into the regions of Syria and Cilicia,

22 And was vnknowen by face vnto the Churches of Iudea, which were in Christ.

23 But they had heard onely, that he which persecuted vs in times past, now preacheth the faith, which once hee destroyed.

24 And they glorified God in me.

CHAP. II.

1 He sheweth when he went vp againe to Hierusalem, and for what purpose: 3 And that Titus was not circumcised: 11 And that he resisted Peter, and told him the reason, 14 why hee and other being Iewes, doe beleeue in Christ to bee Iustified by faith, and not by workes: 20 And that they liue not in sinne, who are so iustified.

‖ Or, seuerally.

Hen fourteene yeeres after, I went vp againe to Ierusalem with Barnabas, and tooke Titus with me also.

2 And I went vp by reuelation, and communicated vnto them that Gospel, which I preach among the Gentiles, but ‖priuately to them which were of reputation, lest by any meanes I should runne, or had runne in vaine.

3 But neither Titus, who was with me, being a Greeke, was compelled to be circumcised:

4 And that because of false brethren vnawares brought in, who came in priuily to spie out our libertie, which wee haue in Christ Iesus, that they might bring vs into bondage.

5 To whom wee gaue place by subiection, no not for an houre, that the trueth of the Gospel might continue with you.

6 But of these, who seemed to bee somewhat, (whatsoeuer they were, it maketh no matter to mee, God accepteth no mans person,) for they who seemed *to be somewhat*, in conference added nothing to me.

7 But contrariwise, when they saw that the Gospel of the vncircumcision was committed vnto me, as the Gospel of the circumcision was vnto Peter:

8 (For he that wrought effectually in Peter to the Apostleship of the circumcision, the same was mightie in me towards the Gentiles.)

9 And when Iames, Cephas and Iohn, who seemed to bee pillars, perceiued the grace that was giuen vnto me, they gaue to me and Barnabas the right hands of fellowship, that wee *should goe* vnto the heathen, and they vnto the circumcision.

10 Onely *they would* that wee should remember the poore, the same which I also was forward to doe.

11 But when Peter was come to Antioch, I withstood him to the face, because he was to be blamed.

12 For before that certaine came from Iames, he did eate with the Gentiles: but when they were come, hee withdrew, and separated himselfe, fearing them *which were* of the Circumcisiõ.

13 And the other Iewes dissembled likewise with him, insomuch that Barnabas also was caried away with their dissimulation.

14 But when I saw that they walked not vprightly according to the truth of the Gospel, I said vnto Peter before them al, If thou, being a Iew, liuest after the maner of Gentiles, and not as doe the Iewes, why compellest thou the Gentiles to liue as do the Iewes?

15 We *who are* Iewes by nature, and not sinners of the Gentiles,

16 Knowing that a man is not iustified by the works of the Law, but by the faith of Iesus Christ, euen we haue beleeued in Iesus Christ, that we might be iustified by the faith of Christ, and not by the workes of the Law: for by the workes of the Law shall no flesh be iustified.

17 But if while we seeke to be iustified by Christ, wee our selues also are found sinners, is therefore Christ the minister of sinne? God forbid.

18 For if I build againe the things which I destroyed, I make my selfe a transgressour.

19 For I through ỹ Law, am dead to the Law, that I might liue vnto God.

20 I am crucified with Christ. Neuertheles, I liue, yet not I, but Christ liueth in me, and the life which I now liue in the flesh, I liue by the faith of the sonne of God, who loued mee, and gaue himselfe for me.

21 I doe not frustrate the grace of God: for if righteousnes *come* by the Lawe, then Christ is dead in vaine.

CHAP.

CHAP. III.

1 He asketh what moued them to leaue the faith, and hang vpon the Law? 6 They that beleeue are iustified, 9 & blessed with Abraham. 10 And this he sheweth by many reasons.

 Foolish Galatians, who hath bewitched you, that you should not obey the trueth, before whose eyes Iesus Christ hath been euidently set forth, crucified among you?

2 This onely would I learne of you, receiued ye the spirit, by the works of the Law, or by the hearing of faith?

3 Are ye so foolish? hauing begun in the Spirit, are ye now made perfect by the flesh?

4 Haue ye suffered ‖ so many things in vaine? if it be yet in vaine.

‖ Or, so great

5 He therfore that ministreth to you the Spirit, and worketh miracles among you, doeth he it by the workes of the Law, or by the hearing of faith?

6 Euen as Abraham beleeued God, and it was ‖ accounted to him for righteousnesse.

‖ Or, imputed.

7 Knowe yee therefore, that they which are of faith, the same are the children of Abraham.

8 And the Scripture foreseeing that God would iustifie the heathen through faith, preached before the Gospel vnto Abraham, *saying*, *In thee shall all nations be blessed.

* Gen. 12. 3

9 So then, they which bee of faith, are blessed with faithfull Abraham.

10 For as many as are of the works of the lawe, are vnder the curse : for it is written, *Cursed is euery one that continueth not in all things which are written in the booke of the Law to doe them.

* Deu. 27. 26.

11 But that no man is iustified by the Lawe in the sight of God, it is euident: for, *The iust shall liue by faith.

* Abac. 2. 4. rom. 1. 17.

12 And the Law is not of faith : but *the man that doeth them, shall liue in them.

* Leui. 18. 5

13 Christ hath redeemed vs from the curse of the Law, being made a curse for vs : for it is written, *Cursed is euery one that hangeth on tree :

* Deut. 21. 23.

14 That the blessing of Abraham might come on the Gentiles, through Iesus Christ : that wee might receiue the promise of the Spirit through faith.

15 Brethren, I speake after the maner of men : though it be but a mans ‖comment.

‖ Or, testament.

uenant, yet if it bee confirmed, no man disanulleth, or addeth thereto.

16 Now to Abraham and his seede were the promises made. He saith not, And to seeds, as of many, but as of one, And to thy seed, which is Christ.

17 And this I say, that the Couenant that was confirmed before of God in Christ, the Lawe which was foure hundred and thirtie yeres after, cannot disanul, that it should make the promise of none effect.

18 For if the inheritance bee of the Law, it is no more of promise : but God gaue it to Abraham by promise.

19 Wherefore then *serueth* the Law? it was added because of transgressions, till the seed should come, to whome the promise was made, *and it was* ordeyned by Angels in the hand of a Mediatour.

20 Now a mediatour is not *a Mediatour* of one, but God is one.

21 Is the Lawe then against the promises of God? God forbid : for if there had beene a Lawe giuen which could haue giuen life, verily righteousnesse should haue bene by the Law.

22 But the Scripture hath concluded all vnder sinne, that the promise by faith of Iesus Christ might be giuen to them that beleeue.

23 But before faith came, wee were kept vnder the Law, shut vp vnto the faith, which should afterwards bee reuealed.

24 Wherefore the Law was our Schoolemaster *to bring vs* vnto Christ, that we might be iustified by Faith.

25 But after that Faith is come, we are no longer vnder a Schoolemaster.

26 For ye are all the children of God by faith in Christ Iesus.

27 For as many of you as haue bene baptized into Christ, haue put on Christ.

28 There is neither Iewe, nor Greeke, there is neither bond nor free, there is neither male nor female : for ye are all one in Christ Iesus.

29 And if *yee be* Christs, then are ye Abrahams seed, and heires according to the promise.

CHAP. IIII.

1 We were vnder the Law till Christ came, as the heire is vnder his gardian till he be of age. 5 But Christ freed vs from the Law : 7 therefore we are seruants no longer to it. 14 He remembreth their good will to him, and his
to

to them, 22 and sheweth that wee are the sonnes of Abraham by the free woman.

Ow I say, that the heire, as long as hee is a child, differeth nothing from a seruant, though hee bee Lord of all,

2 But is vnder tutors and gouernours vntill the time appointed of the father.

3 Euen so we, when wee were children, were in bondage vnder the ‖ Elements of the world:

‖ *Or, rudiments.*

4 But when the fulnes of the time was come, God sent foorth his Sonne made of a woman, made vnder the Law,

5 To redeeme them that were vnder the Law, that we might receiue the adoption of sonnes.

6 And because yee are sonnes, God hath sent foorth the spirit of his Sonne into your hearts, crying Abba, Father.

7 Wherefore thou art no more a seruant, but a sonne; and if a sonne, then an heire of God through Christ.

8 Howbeit, then when ye knew not God, yee did seruice vnto them which by nature are no Gods.

9 But now after that yee haue knowen God, or rather are knowen of God, how turne ye ‖againe to the weak and beggerly ‖ Elements, whereunto ye desire againe to be in bondage?

‖ *Or, backe.*
‖ *Or, rudiments.*

10 Yee obserue dayes, and moneths, and times, and yeeres.

11 I am afraide of you, lest I haue bestowed vpon you labour in vaine.

12 Brethren, I beseech you, be as I *am;* for I *am* as ye are, ye haue not iniured me at all.

13 Ye know how through infirmitie of the flesh, I preached the Gospel vnto you at the first.

14 And my temptation which was in my flesh ye despised not, nor reiected, but receiued mee as an Angel of God, *euen* as Christ Iesus.

15 ‖ Where is then the blessednes you spake of? for I beare you record, that if it had bin possible, ye would haue plucked out your own eyes, and haue giuen them to me.

‖ *Or, what was then?*

16 Am I therefore become your enemie, because I tell you the trueth?

17 They zelously affect you, but not well: yea, they would exclude ‖you, that you might affect them.

‖ *Or, vs.*

18 But it is good to bee zealously af-fected alwayes in a good thing, and not onely when I am present with you.

19 My litle children, of whom I trauaile in birth againe, vntill Christ bee formed in you:

20 I desire to bee present with you now, and to change my voyce, for I ‖stand in doubt of you.

‖ *Or, I am perplexed for you.*

21 Tell me, ye that desire to be vnder the Law, doe ye not heare the Law?

22 For it is written, that Abraham had two sonnes, the one by a bond-maid, the other by a free woman.

23 But he who was of the bondwoman, was borne after the flesh: but hee of the freewoman, *was* by promise.

24 Which things are an Allegorie; for these are the two ‖Couenants; the one from the mount Sinai, which gendereth to bondage, which is Agar.

‖ *Or, testaments.*

25 For this, Agar is mount Sinai in Arabia, and ‖answereth to Ierusalem, which now is, and is in bondage with her children.

‖ *Or, is in the same ranke with.*

26 But Ierusalem which is aboue is free, which is the mother of vs all.

27 For it is written, *Reioyce thou barren that bearest not, breake foorth and cry thou that trauailest not; for the desolate hath many moe children then she which hath an husband.

* *Esay 54. 1*

28 Now wee, brethren, as Isaac was, are the children of promise.

29 But as then hee that was borne after the flesh, persecuted him that was *borne* after the Spirit, euen so it is now.

30 Neuerthelesse, what saith the Scripture? *Cast out the bondwoman and her sonne: for the son of the bond-woman shall not bee heire with the son of the freewoman.

* *Gen. 21 10.*

31 So then, brethren, we are not children of the bondwoman, but of the free.

CHAP. V.

1 Hee mooueth them to stand in their libertie, 3 and not to obserue circumcision: 13 but rather loue, which is the summe of the Law. 19 He reckoneth vp the workes of the flesh, 22 and the fruits of the spirit, 25 and exhorteth to walke in the spirit.

Tand fast therefore in the libertie wherewith Christ hath made vs free, and bee not intangled againe with the yoke of bondage.

2 Beholde, I Paul say vnto you, that if ye be circumcised, Christ shal profite you nothing.

3 For

3 For I testifie againe to euery man that is circumcised, that he is a debtor to doe the whole Law.

4 Christ is become of no effect vnto you, whosoeuer of you are iustified by the Law : ye are fallen from grace.

5 For we through the spirit waite for the hope of righteousnesse by faith.

6 For in Iesus Christ, neither circumcision auaileth any thing, nor vncircumcision, but faith which worketh by loue.

Or, who did driue you backe?

7 Ye did run well ; ||who did hinder you, that ye should not obey the trueth?

8 This perswasion commeth not of him that calleth you.

9 A little leauen leaueneth the whole lumpe.

10 I haue confidence in you through the Lord, that you will be none otherwise minded ; but he that troubleth you, shall beare *his* iudgement, whosoeuer hee be.

11 And I, brethren, if I yet preach circumcision, why doe I yet suffer persecution? then is the offence of the crosse ceased.

12 I would they were euen cut off which trouble you.

13 For brethren, ye haue beene called vnto liberty, onely *vse* not libertie for an occasion to the flesh, but by loue serue one another.

* Leu. 19. 18 mat. 22. 39.

14 For all the Law is fulfilled in one word, *euen* in this: * Thou shalt loue thy neighbour as thy selfe.

15 But if yee bite and deuoure one another, take heed ye be not consumed one of another.

|| Or, fulfill not.

16 This I say then, Walke in the spirit, and ||ye shall not fulfill the lust of the flesh.

17 For the flesh lusteth against the Spirit, and the spirit against the flesh : and these are contrary the one to the other : so that yee cannot doe the things that yee would.

18 But if yee be lead of the spirit, yee are not vnder the Law.

19 Nowe the workes of the flesh are manifest, which are *these*, adulterie, fornication, vncleannesse, lasciuiousnesse,

20 Idolatrie, witchcraft, hatred, variance, emulations, wrath, strife, seditions, heresies,

21 Enuyings, murthers, drunkennesse, reuellings, and such like : of the which I tell you before, as I haue also tolde you in time past, that they which do such things shall not inherite the kingdome of God.

22 But the fruit of the spirit is loue, ioy, peace, longsuffering, gentlenesse, goodnesse, faith,

23 Meekenesse, temperance : against such there is no law.

24 And they that are Christs, haue crucified the flesh with the ||affections and lustes.

Or, passions

25 If we liue in the Spirit, let vs also walke in the Spirit.

26 Let vs not be desirous of vaine glory, prouoking one another, enuying one another.

CHAP. VI.

1 He moueth them to deale mildly with a brother that hath slipped, 2 and to beare one anothers burden. 6 To bee liberall to their teachers, 9 and not wearie of well doing. 12 He sheweth what they intend that preach circumcision. 14 He glorieth in nothing, saue in the Crosse of Christ.

Rethren, ||if a man bee ouertaken in a fault : yee which are spirituall, restore such a one in the spirit of meekenesse, considering thy selfe least thou also be tempted.

Or, although.

2 Beare ye one anothers burthens, and so fulfill the Law of Christ.

3 For if a man thinke himselfe to be some thing, when he is nothing, hee deceiueth himselfe.

4 But let euery man prooue his owne worke, and then shall he haue reioycing in him selfe alone, and not in an other.

5 For euery man shall beare his owne burthen.

6 Let him that is taught in the word, communicate vnto him that teacheth, in all good things.

7 Be not deceiued, God is not mocked : for whatsoeuer a man soweth, that shall he also reape.

8 For hee that soweth to his flesh, shall of the flesh reape corruption : but he that soweth to the spirit, shall of the spirit reape life euerlasting.

9 And let vs not bee weary in well doing : for in due season we shall reape, if we faint not.

10 As we haue therefore opportunitie, let vs doe good vnto all men, especially vnto them who are of the houshold of faith.

11 Yee

11 Ye see how large a letter I haue written vnto you with mine owne hand.

12 As many as desire to make a faire shew in the flesh, they constraine you to be Circumcised: onely least they should suffer persecution for the Crosse of Christ.

13 For neither they themselues who are circumcised, keepe the Law, but desire to haue you circumcised, that they may glory in your flesh.

14 But God forbid that I should glory, saue in the Crosse of our Lord Iesus Christ, || by whom the world is ‖ *Or, whereby.*

crucified vnto me, & I vnto the world.

15 For in Christ Iesus neither circumcision auaileth any thing nor vncircumcision, but a new creature.

16 And as many as walke according to this rule, peace be on them, and mercie, and vpon the Israel of God.

17 From henceforth let no man trouble mee, for I beare in my body the markes of the Lord Iesus.

18 Brethren, the grace of our Lord Iesus Christ *be* with your spirit. Amen.

¶ Vnto the Galatians, written from Rome.

¶ THE EPISTLE OF PAVL
the Apoſtle to the Epheſians.

CHAP. I.

1 *After the salutation,* 3 *and thankesgiuing for the Ephesians,* 4 *he treateth of our Election,* 6 *and Adoption by grace,* 11 *which is the true and proper fountaine of mans saluation.* 13 *And because the height of this mysterie cannot easily be atteined vnto,* 16 *he praieth that they may come* 18 *to the full knowledge, and* 20 *possession thereof in Christ.*

PAul an Apostle of Iesus Christ by the will of God, to the Sainсts which are at Ephesus, and to the faithfull in Christ Iesus.

2 Grace *be* to you, and peace from God our Father, and *from* the Lord Iesus Christ.

3 Blessed be the God and Father of our Lord Iesus Christ, who hath blessed vs with all spirituall blessings in heauenly || places in Christ: ‖ *Or, things.*

4 According as he hath chosen vs in him, before the foundation of the world, that wee should bee holy, and without blame before him in loue:

5 Hauing predestinated vs vnto the adoption of children by Iesus Christ to himselfe, according to the good pleasure of his will:

6 To the praise of the glorie of his grace, wherein he hath made vs accepted in the beloued:

7 In whom wee haue redemption through his blood, the forgiuenesse of sinnes, according to the riches of his grace,

8 Wherein hee hath abounded toward vs in all wisedome and prudence:

9 Hauing made knowen vnto vs the mysterie of his will, according to his good pleasure, which he had purposed in himselfe,

10 That in the dispensation of the fulnesse of times, he might gather together in one all things in Christ, both which are in †heauen, and which are on earth, euen in him: † *Gr. the heauens.*

11 In whom also we haue obteined an inheritance, being predestinated according to the purpose of him who worketh all things after the counsell of his owne will:

12 That we should be to the praise of his glorie, who first ||trusted in Christ. ‖ *Or, hoped.*

13 In whom ye also *trusted* after that ye heard the word of trueth, the Gospel of your saluation: in whom also after that yee beleeued, yee were sealed with that holy Spirit of promise,

14 Which

14 Which is the earnest of our inheritance, vntill the redemption of the purchased possession, vnto the praise of his glorie.

15 Wherefore I also, after I heard of your faith in the Lord Iesus, and loue vnto all the Saints,

16 Cease not to giue thankes for you, making mention of you in my prayers,

17 That the God of our Lord Iesus Christ the Father of glorie, may giue vnto you the Spirit of wisedome and *reuelation ‖ in the knowledge of him :

‖ *Or, for the acknowledgment.*

18 The eyes of your vnderstanding being inlightned : that yee may know what is the hope of his calling, and what the riches of the glorie of his inheritance in the Saints :

19 And what is the exceeding greatnesse of his power to vs-ward who beleeue, according to the working †of his mightie power :

† *Gr. of the might of his power.*

20 Which he wrought in Christ when he raised him from the dead, and set him at his owne right hand in the heauenly *places*,

21 Farre aboue all principalitie, and power, and might, and dominion, and euery name that is named, not onely in this world, but also in that which is to come :

22 And hath put all things vnder his feete, and gaue him to be the head ouer all things to the Church,

23 Which is his body, the fulnesse of him that filleth all in all.

CHAP. II.

1 By comparing what we were by 3 nature, with what we are 5 by grace : 10 He declareth, that wee are made for good workes; and 13 beeing brought neere by Christ, should not liue as 11 Gentiles, and 12 forreiners in time past, but as 19 citizens with the Saints, and the family of God.

Nd you *hath hee quickned* who were dead in trespasses, and sinnes,

2 Wherein in time past ye walked according to the course of this world, according to the prince of the power of the aire, the spirit that now worketh in the children of disobedience,

3 Among whom also we all had our conuersation in times past, in the lusts of our flesh, fulfilling †the desires of the flesh, and of the minde, and were by

‡ *Gr. the wills.*

nature the children of wrath, euen as others :

4 But God who is rich in mercie, for his great loue wherewith hee loued vs,

5 Euen when wee were dead in sinnes, hath quickned vs together with Christ, (by grace ye are saued)

6 And hath raised *vs* vp together, and made *vs* sit together in heauenly places in Christ Iesus :

7 That in the ages to come, hee might shew the exceeding riches of his grace, in *his* kindenesse towards vs, through Christ Iesus.

8 For by grace are ye saued, through faith, and that not of your selues : *it is* the gift of God :

9 Not of workes, lest any man should boast.

10 For wee are his workemanship, created in Christ Iesus vnto good workes, which God hath before ‖ ordeined, that we should walke in them.

‖ *Or, prepared.*

11 Wherefore remember that ye *being* in time passed Gentiles in the flesh, who are called vncircumcision by that which is called the Circumcision in the flesh made by hands,

12 That at that time yee were without Christ, being aliens from the common wealth of Israel, and strangers from the couenants of promise, hauing no hope, & without God in the world.

13 But now in Christ Iesus, ye who sometimes were far off, are made nigh by the blood of Christ.

14 For hee is our peace, who hath made both one, and hath broken downe the middle wall of partition betweene vs :

15 Hauing abolished in his flesh the enmitie, *euen* the Lawe of Commandements *conteined* in Ordinances, for to make in himselfe, of twaine, one newe man, so making peace.

16 And that he might reconcile both vnto God in one body by the crosse, hauing slaine the enmitie ‖ thereby,

‖ *Or, in himselfe.*

17 And came, and preached peace to you, *which were* afarre off, and to them that were nigh,

18 For through him wee both haue an accesse by one Spirit vnto the Father.

19 Now therefore yee are no more strangers and forreiners ; but fellow citizens with the Saints, and of the houshold of God,

20 And

20 And are built vpon the foundation of the Apostles and Prophets, Iesus Christ himselfe being the chiefe corner stone,

21 In whom all the building fitly framed together, groweth vnto an holy Temple in the Lord:

22 In whom you also are builded together for an habitation of God thorow the Spirit.

CHAP. III.

5 The hidden mysterie, 6 that the Gentiles should be saued, 3 was made knowen to Paul by reuelation: 8 And to him was that grace giuen, that 9 he should preach it. 13 He desireth them not to faint for his tribulation, 14 and praieth, 19 that they may perceiue the great loue of Christ toward them.

 Or this cause I Paul, the prisoner of Iesus Christ for you Gentiles,

2 If ye haue heard of the dispensation of the grace of God, which is giuen me to youward:

3 How that by reuelation hee made knowen vnto me the mysterie, (as I wrote ‖ afore in few words,

‖ Or, a little before.

4 Whereby when ye reade, ye may vnderstand my knowledge in the mysterie of Christ.)

5 Which in other ages was not made knowen vnto the sonnes of men, as it is now reueiled vnto his holy Apostles and Prophets by the Spirit,

6 That the Gentiles should be fellow heires, and of the same body, and partakers of his promise in Christ, by the Gospel:

7 Whereof I was made a Minister, according to the gift of the grace of God giuen vnto mee, by the effectuall working of his power.

8 Vnto mee, who am lesse then the least of all Saints, is this grace giuen, that I should preach among the Gentiles the vnsearchable riches of Christ,

9 And to make all men see, what is the fellowship of the mysterie, which from the beginning of the world, hath bene hid in God, who created all things by Iesus Christ:

10 To the intent that now vnto the principalities and powers in heauenly places, might be knowen by the church, the manifold wisedome of God,

11 According to the eternall purpose which he purposed in Christ Iesus our Lord:

12 In whom we haue boldnesse and accesse, with confidence, by the faith of him.

13 Wherefore I desire that yee faint not at my tribulations for you, which is your glory.

14 For this cause I bow my knees vnto the Father of our Lord Iesus Christ,

15 Of whom the whole family in heauen and earth is named,

16 That he would grant you according to the riches of his glory, to bee strengthened with might, by his Spirit in the inner man,

17 That Christ may dwell in your hearts by faith, that yee being rooted and grounded in loue,

18 May be able to comprehend with all Saints, what is the breadth, and length, and depth, and height:

19 And to know the loue of Christ, which passeth knowledge, that yee might bee filled with all the fulnesse of God.

20 Now vnto him that is able to do exceeding abundantly aboue all that wee aske or thinke, according to the power that worketh in vs,

21 Vnto him be glory in the Church by Christ Iesus, throughout all ages, world without end. Amen.

CHAP. IIII.

1 He exhorteth to vnitie, 7 and declareth that God therefore giueth diuers 11 gifts vnto men, that his Church might be 13 edified, and 16 growen vp in Christ. 18 He calleth them from the impuritie of the Gentiles. 24 To put on the new man. 25 To cast of lying, and 29 corrupt communication.

 Therefore the prisoner ‖ of the Lord, beseech you that yee walke worthy of the vocation wherewith ye are called,

‖ Or, in the Lord.

2 With all lowlinesse and meekenesse, with long suffering, forbearing one another in loue.

3 Endeuouring to keepe the vnitie of the Spirit in the bond of peace.

4 *There is* one body, and one spirit, euen as yee are called in one hope of your calling.

5 One Lord, one Faith, one Baptisme,

6 One

6 One God and Father of all, who is aboue all, & through all, & in you all.

7 But vnto euery one of vs is giuen grace, according to the measure of the gift of Christ.

8 Wherefore he saith : * When he ascended vp on high, he led || captiuitie captiue, and gaue gifts vnto men.

* Psal. 68.
18.
‖ Or, a multitude of captiues.

9 (Now that he ascended, what is it but that hee also descended first into the lower parts of the earth ?

10 He that descended, is the same also that ascended vp far aboue all heauens, that he might || fill all things.)

‖ Or, fulfill.
* 1. Cor. 12.
28.

11 * And he gaue some, Apostles: and some, Prophets : and some, Euangelists : and some, Pastors, and teachers :

12 For the perfecting of the Saints, for the worke of the ministerie, for the edifying of the body of Christ :

13 Till we all come || in the vnitie of the faith, and of the knowledge of the Sonne of God, vnto a perfect man, vnto the measure of the || stature of the fulnesse of Christ :

‖ Or, into the vnitie.

‖ Or, age.

14 That we henceforth be no more children, tossed to and fro, and caried about with euery winde of doctrine, by the sleight of men, and cunning craftinesse, whereby they lye in waite to deceiue :

15 But || speaking the trueth in loue, may grow vp into him in all things which is the head, euen Christ :

‖ Or, being sincere.

* Col. 2. 19.

16 * From whom the whole body fitly ioyned together, and compacted by that which euery ioynt supplyeth, according to the effectuall working in the measure of euery part, maketh increase of the body, vnto the edifying of it selfe in loue.

17 This I say therefore and testifie in the Lord, that yee henceforth walke not as other Gentiles walke in the vanitie of their minde,

18 Hauing the vnderstanding darkened, being alienated from the life of God, through the ignorance that is in them, because of the * || blindnesse of their heart :

* Rom. 1. 21
‖ Or, hardnesse.

19 Who being past feeling, haue giuen themselues ouer vnto lasciuiousnesse, to worke all vncleannesse with greedinesse.

20 But ye haue not so learned Christ:

21 If so be that ye haue heard him, and haue bene taught by him, as the trueth is in Iesus,

22 That yee put off concerning the former conuersation , the olde man, which is corrupt according to the deceitfull lusts :

23 And bee renewed in the spirit of your minde :

24 And that yee put on that new man, which after God is created in righteousnesse, and || true holinesse.

‖ Or, holines of trueth.

25 Wherefore putting away lying, speake euery man truth with his neighbour : for we are members one of another.

26 Be ye angry and sinne not, let not the Sunne go down vpon your wrath :

27 Neither giue place to the deuill.

28 Let him that stole, steale no more: but rather let him labour, working with his handes the thing which is good, that he may haue || to giue to him that needeth.

‖ Or, to distribute.

29 Let no corrupt communication proceede out of your mouth, but that which is good || to the vse of edifying, that it may minister grace vnto the hearers.

‖ Or, to edifie profitably.

30 And grieue not the holy Sririt of God, whereby yee are sealed vnto the day of redemption.

31 Let all bitternes, and wrath, and anger, and clamour, and euill speaking, be put away from you, with all malice,

32 * And bee ye kinde one to another. tender hearted, forgiuing one another, euen as God for Christs sake hath forgiuen you.

* 2. Cor. 2.
10.

CHAP. V.

2 After generall exhortations, to loue, 3 to flie fornication, 4 and all vncleannesse, 7 not to conuerse with the wicked, 15 to walke warily, and to be 18 filled with the spirit, 22 he descendeth to the particular dueties, how wiues ought to obey their husbands, 25 and husbands ought to loue their wiues, 32 euen as Christ doth his Church.

BE ye therefore followers of God, as deare children.

2 And walke in loue, as Christ also hath loued vs, and hath giuen himselfe for vs, an offering and a sacrifice to God for a sweet smelling sauour ;

3 But fornication and all vncleannesse, or couetousnesse, let it not be once named amongst you, as becommeth Saints :

4 Neither filthinesse, nor foolish talking,

talking, nor iesting, which are not conuenient : but rather giuing of thankes.

5 For this ye know, that no whoremonger, nor vncleane person, nor couetous man who is an idolater, hath any inheritance in the kingdome of Christ, and of God.

6 Let no man deceiue you with vaine words : for because of these things commeth the wrath of God vpon the children of ‖disobedience.

‖ Or, vnbeliefe.

7 Bee not yee therefore partakers with them.

8 For yee were sometimes darkenesse, but now *are yee* light in the Lord: walke as children of light,

9 (For the fruite of the spirit is in all goodnesse and righteousnesse & trueth.)

10 Proouing what is acceptable vnto the Lord :

11 And haue no fellowship with the vnfruitfull workes of darkenesse, but rather reproue them.

12 For it is a shame euen to speake of those things which are done of them in secret.

13 But all things that are ‖reprooued, are made manifest by the light : for whatsoeuer doth make manifest, is light.

‖ Or, discouered.

14 Wherfore hee saith : * Awake thou that sleepest, and arise from the dead, and Christ shall giue thee light.

* Esai. 60. 1.

15 * See then that yee walke circumspectly, not as fooles, but as wise,

* Col. 4. 5.

16 Redeming the time, because the dayes are euill.

17 Wherefore be ye not vnwise, but vnderstanding what the will of the Lord is.

18 And bee not drunke with wine, wherein is excesse : but bee filled with the Spirit :

19 Speaking to your selues, in Psalmes, and Hymnes, and Spirituall songs, singing and making melodie in your heart to the Lord,

20 Giuing thankes alwayes for all things vnto God, and the Father, in the Name of our Lord Iesus Christ,

21 Submitting your selues one to another in the feare of God.

22 Wiues, submit your selues vnto your own husbands, as vnto the Lord.

23 For the husband is the head of the wife, euen as Christ is the head of the Church : and he is the sauiour of the body.

24 Therefore as the Church is sub-

iect vnto Christ, so let the wiues *bee* to their owne husbands in euery thing.

25 Husbands, loue your wiues, euen as Christ also loued the Church, and gaue himselfe for it :

26 That he might sanctifie & cleanse *it* with the washing of water, by the word,

27 That hee might present it to himselfe a glorious Church, not hauing spot or wrinckle, or any such thing : but that it should bee holy and without blemish.

28 So ought men to loue their wiues, as their owne bodies : hee that loueth his wife, loueth himselfe.

29 For no man euer yet hated his owne flesh : but nourisheth and cherisheth it, euen as the Lord the Church:

30 For we are members of his body, of his flesh, and of his bones.

31 For this cause shall a man leaue his father and mother, and shall be ioyned vnto his wife, and they two shalbe one flesh.

32 This is a great mysterie : but I speake concerning Christ and the Church.

33 Neuerthelesse, let euery one of you in particular, so loue his wife euen as himselfe, and the wife *see* that she reuerence her husband.

CHAP. VI.

1 The duetie of children towards their parents, 5 Of seruants towards their masters. 10 Our life is a warfare, 12 Not onely against flesh and blood, but also spiritual enemies. 13 The complete armor of a Christian, 18 and how it ought to be vsed. 21 Tychicus is cõmended.

 Hildren, obey your parents in the Lord : for this is right.

2 Honour thy father and mother, (which is the first commandement with promise,)

3 That it may bee well with thee, and thou maiest liue long on the earth.

4 And *yee* fathers, prouoke not your children to wrath : but bring them vp in the nourture and admonition of the Lord.

5 Seruants, bee obedient to them that are your masters according to the flesh, with feàre and trembling, in singlenesse of your heart, as vnto Christ:

6 Not with eye seruice as men pleasers, but as the seruants of Christ, doing the will of God from the heart:

7 With

7 With good will doing seruice, as to the Lord, and not to men,

8 Knowing that whatsoeuer good thing any man doeth, the same shall he receiue of the Lord, whether he be bond or free.

9 And ye masters, do the same things vnto them, || forbearing threatning: knowing that ||your master also is in heauen, neither is there respect of persons with him.

|| Or, moderating.
|| Some reade, both your, and their master.

10 Finally, my brethren, be strong in the Lord, & in the power of his might.

11 Put on the whole armour of God, that ye may be able to stand against the wiles of the deuill.

12 For wee wrestle not against flesh and blood, but against principalities, against powers, against the rulers of the darkes of this world, against ||spirituall wickednes in ||high places.

|| Or, wicked spirits.
|| Or, heauenly.

13 Wherfore take vnto you the whole armour of God, that yee may be able to withstand in the euill day, and ||hauing done all, to stand.

|| Or, hauing ouercome all.

14 Stand therefore, hauing your loynes girt about with trueth, and hauing on the breast-plate of righteousnesse:

15 And your feete shod with the preparation of the Gospel of peace.

16 Aboue all, taking the shielde of Faith, wherewith yee shall bee able to quench all the fierie dartes of the wicked.

17 And take the helmet of saluation, and the sword of the Spirit, which is the word of God:

18 Praying alwayes with all prayer and supplication in the spirit, and watching thereunto with all perseuerance, and supplication for all Saints,

19 And for mee, that vtterance may be giuen vnto me, that I may open my mouth boldly, to make knowen the mysterie of the Gospel:

20 For which I am an ambassador ||in bonds, that ||therein I may speake boldly, as I ought to speake.

|| Or, in a chaine.
|| Or, thereof.

21 But that yee also may know my affaires, *and* how I doe, Tychicus a beloued brother, and faithfull minister in the Lord, shall make knowen to you all things.

22 Whom I haue sent vnto you for the same purpose, that yee might know our affaires, and that he might comfort your hearts.

23 Peace *be* to the brethren, and loue, with faith from God the Father, and the Lord Iesus Christ.

24 Grace be with all them that loue our Lord Iesus Christ ||in sinceritie.

|| Or, with incorruption.

¶ Written from Rome vnto the Ephesians by Tychicus.

¶ THE

¶THE EPISTLE OF PAVL

the Apostle to the Philippians.

CHAP. I.

3 He testifieth his thankefulnesse to God, and his loue toward them, for the fruits of their faith and fellowship, in his sufferings, 9 dayly praying to him for their increase in grace: 12 Hee sheweth what good the faith of Christ had receiued by his troubles at Rome, 21 and how ready he is to glorifie Christ either by his life or death, 27 exhorting them to vnitie, 28 and to fortitude in persecution.

Aul and Timotheus the seruants of Iesus Christ, to all the Saints in Christ Iesus, which are at Philippi, with the Bishops and Deacons :

2 Grace *be* vnto you, and peace, from God our Father, and *from* the Lord Iesus Christ.

3 I thanke my God vpon euery ||remembrance of you,

4 Alwayes in euery prayer of mine for you all making request, with ioy

5 For your felowship in the Gospel from the first day vntill now ;

6 Being confident of this very thing, that he which hath begun a good work in you, ||will performe it vntil the day of Iesus Christ :

7 Euen as it is meete for mee to thinke this of you all, because I ||haue you in my heart, in as much as both in my bonds, and in the defence and confirmation of the Gospel, ye all are ||partakers of my grace.

8 For God is my record, how greatly I long after you all, in the bowels of Iesus Christ.

9 And this I pray, that your loue may abound yet more & more in knowledge, and in all ||iudgment.

10 That ye may ||approue things that ||are excellent, that ye may be sincere, and without offence till the day of Christ.

11 Being filled with the fruites of righteousnesse, which *are* by Iesus Christ vnto the glory and praise of God.

12 But I would yee should vnderstand brethren, that the things which happened vnto mee, haue fallen out rather vnto the furtherance of the Gospel.

13 So that my bonds ||in Christ, are manifest in all the ||palace, and in ||all other *places*.

14 And many of the brethren in the Lord, waxing confident, by my bonds, are much more bold to speake the word without feare.

15 Some in deed preach Christ, euen of enuie and strife, and some also of good will.

16 The one preach Christ of contention, not syncerely, supposing to adde affliction to my bonds :

17 But the other of loue, knowing that I am set for the defence of the Gospel.

18 What then ? Notwithstanding euery way, whether in pretence, or in trueth : Christ is preached, and I therein doe reioyce, yea, and will reioyce.

19 For I know that this shall turne to my saluation through your prayer, and the supplie of the spirit of Iesus Christ,

20 According to my earnest expectation, and my hope, that in nothing I shalbe ashamed : but that with all boldnes, as alwayes, *so* now also Christ shal be magnified in my body, whether it be by life or by death.

21 For to me to liue is Christ, and to die is gaine.

22 But if I liue in the flesh, this is the fruit of my labour : yet what I shal chuse, I wote not.

23 For I am in a strait betwixt two, hauing a desire to depart, & to bee with Christ, which is farre better.

24 Neuer-

Margin notes left column:

|| *Or, mention.*

|| *Or, will finish it.*

|| *Or, you haue me in your heart.*

|| *Or, partakers with me of grace.*

|| *Or, sence.*

¶ *Or, trie.*

Margin notes right column:

|| *Or, differ.*

|| *Or, for Christ.*

|| *Or, Cæsars Court.*

|| *Or, to all others.*

24 Neuertheles, to abide in the flesh, *is* more needfull for you.

25 And hauing this confidence, I know that I shall abide and continue with you all, for your furtherance and ioy of faith,

26 That your reioycing may bee more abundant in Iesus Christ for me, by my comming to you againe.

27 Onely let your conuersation bee as it becommeth the Gospel of Christ, that whether I come and see you, or else be absent, I may heare of your affaires, that yee stand fast in one spirit, with one minde, striuing together for the faith of the Gospel,

28 And in nothing terrified by your aduersaries, which is to them an euident token of perdition : but to you of saluation, and that of God.

29 For vnto you it is giuen in the behalfe of Christ, not onely to beleeue on him, but also to suffer for his sake,

30 Hauing the same conflict which ye saw in me, and now heare *to be* in me.

CHAP. II.

He exhorteth them to vnitie, and to all humblenesse of minde, by the example of Christs humilitie and exaltation : 12 To a carefull proceeding in the way of saluation, that they bee as lights to the wicked world, 16 and comforts to him their Apostle, who is now ready to bee offered vp to God. 19 He hopeth to send Timothie to them, whom hee greatly commendeth, 25 as Epaphroditus also, whom he presently sendeth to them.

IF *there bee* therefore any consolation in Christ, if any comfort of loue, if any fellowship of the Spirit, if any bowels, & mercies;

2 Fulfill ye my ioy, that yee be like minded, hauing the same loue, being of one accord, of one minde.

3 Let nothing bee *done* through strife, or vaine glory, but in lowlinesse of minde let each esteeme other better then themselues.

4 Looke not euery man on his owne things, but euery man also on the things of others.

5 Let this minde bee in you, which was also in Christ Iesus:

6 Who being in the forme of God, thought it not robbery to bee equall with God:

7 But made himselfe of no reputation, and tooke vpon him the forme of

a seruant, and was made in the ‖likenesse of men. ‖ *Or, habite.*

8 And being found in fashion as a man, he humbled himselfe, and became obedient vnto death, euen the death of the Crosse.

9 Wherefore God also hath highly exalted him, and giuen him a Name which is aboue euery name .

10 That at the Name of Iesus euery knee should bow, of *things* in heauen, and *things* in earth, and *things* vnder the earth :

11 And that euery tongue should confesse, that Iesus Christ is Lord, to the glory of God the Father.

12 Wherefore, my beloued, as yee haue alwayes obeyed, not as in my presence onely, but now much more in my absence ; worke out your owne saluation with feare, and trembling.

13 For it is God which worketh in you, both to will, and to doe, of *his* good pleasure.

14 Doe all things without murmurings, and disputings :

15 That yee may bee blamelesse and ‖harmelesse, the sonnes of God, without rebuke, in the middes of a crooked and peruerse nation, among whom ‖ye shine as lights in the world : ‖ *Or, syncere.* ‖ *Or, shine ye*

16 Holding foorth the word of life, that I may reioyce in the day of Christ, that I haue not runne in vaine, neither laboured in vaine.

17 Yea, and if I bee † offered vpon the sacrifice and seruice of your faith, I ioy, and reioyce with you all. † *Gr. powred foorth.*

18 For the same cause also doe ye ioy, and reioyce with me.

19 ‖But I trust in the Lord Iesus, to send Timotheus shortly vnto you, that I also may bee of good comfort, when I know your state. ‖ *Or, moreouer.*

20 For I haue no man ‖like minded, who will naturally care for your state. ‖ *Or, so deare vnto mee.*

21 For all seeke their owne, not the things which are Iesus Christs.

22 But ye know the proofe of him, That as a sonne with the father, hee hath serued with me, in the Gospel.

23 Him therefore I hope to send presently, so soone as I shall see how it wil goe with me.

24 But I trust in the Lord, that I also my selfe shall come shortly.

25 Yet I supposed it necessary, to send to you Epaphroditus my brother and companion in labour, and fellow souldiour,

souldiour, but your messenger, and hee that ministred to my wants.

26 For hee longed after you all, and was full of heauinesse, because that yee had heard that he had bene sicke.

27 For indeed he was sicke nigh vnto death, but God had mercy on him : and not on him onely, but on mee also, lest I should haue sorow vpon sorow.

28 I sent him therefore the more carefully, that when ye see him againe, ye may reioyce, and that I may bee the lesse sorrowfull.

Or, honor uch. 29 Receiue him therfor in the Lord with all gladnesse, and ‖ hold such in reputation :

30 Because for the worke of Christ he was nigh vnto death, not regarding his life, to supply your lacke of seruice toward me.

C H A P. III.

1 Hee warneth them to beware of the false teachers of the Circumcision, 4 shewing that himself hath greater cause then they, to trust in the righteousnesse of the Law : 7 which notwithstanding hee counteth as doung and losse, to gaine Christ and his righteousnesse, 12 therein acknowledging his owne imperfection. 15 Hee exhorteth them to be thus minded, 17 and to imitate him, 18 and to decline the waies of carnall Christians.

Inally, my brethren, reioyce in the Lorde. To write the same things to you, to me indeed is not grieuous : but for you it is safe.

2 Beware of dogs, beware of euill workers : beware of the concision.

3 For we are the circumcision, which worship God in the spirit, and reioyce in Christ Iesus, and haue no confidence in the flesh.

4 Though I might also haue confidence in the flesh. If any other man thinketh that hee hath whereof hee might trust in the flesh, I more :

5 Circumcised the eight day, of the stocke of Israel, of the tribe of Beniamin, an Hebrew of the Hebrewes, as touching the Law, a Pharise :

6 Concerning zeale, persecuting the Church : touching the righteousnesse which is in the Law, blamelesse.

7 But what things were gaine to me, those I counted losse for Christ.

8 Yea doubtlesse, and I count all things but losse, for the excellencie of the knowledge of Christ Iesus my Lord : for whom I haue suffered the losse of all things, and doe count them but doung, that I may win Christ,

9 And be found in him, not hauing mine owne righteousnesse, which is of the Law, but that which is through the faith of Christ, the righteousnesse which is of God by faith :

10 That I may know him, and the power of his resurrection, and the fellowship of his sufferings, being made conformable vnto his death,

11 If by any meanes I might attaine vnto the resurrection of the dead.

12 Not as though I had already attained, either were already perfect : but I follow after, if that I may apprehend that for which also I am apprehended of Christ Iesus.

13 Brethren, I count not my selfe to haue apprehended : but this one thing *I doe,* forgetting those things which are behinde, and reaching forth vnto those things which are before,

14 I presse toward the marke, for the price of the high calling of God in Christ Iesus.

15 Let vs therefore, as many as bee perfect, bee thus minded : and if in any thing ye be otherwise minded, God shal reueale euen this vnto you.

16 Neuerthelesse, whereto wee haue alreadie attained, let vs walke by the same rule, let vs minde the same thing.

17 Brethren, be followers together of me, and marke them which walke so, as ye haue vs for an ensample.

18 (For many walke, of whome I haue told you often, and now tell you euen weeping, *that they are* the enemies of the crosse of Christ :

19 Whose end *is* destruction, whose God *is* their belly, and whose glorie is in their shame, who minde earthly things.)

20 For our conuersation is in heauen, from whence also we looke for the Sauiour, the Lord Iesus Christ :

21 Who shall change our vile bodie, that it may bee fashioned like vnto his glorious body, according to the working whereby he is able euen to subdue all things vnto himselfe.

C H A P. IIII.

1 From particular admonitions 4 hee proceedeth to generall exhortations, 10 shewing how hee reioyced at their liberalitie towards

wards him lying in prison, not so much for the supply of his owne wants, as for the grace of God in them. 19 And so he concludeth with prayer and salutations.

THerefore, my brethren, dearely beloued and longed for, my ioy and crowne, so stand fast in the Lord, my dearely beloued.

2 I beseech Euodias, and beseech Syntiche, that they be of the same mind in the Lord.

3 And I entreat thee also, true yoke-fellow, helpe those women which laboured with me in the Gospel, with Clement also, and with other my fellow labourers, whose names are in the booke of life.

4 Reioyce in the Lord alway : and againe I say, Reioyce.

5 Let your moderation be knowen vnto all men. The Lord is at hand.

6 Bee carefull for nothing : but in euery thing by prayer and supplication with thankesgiuing, let your request be made knowen vnto God.

7 And the peace of God which passeth all vnderstanding, shall keepe your hearts & minds through Christ Iesus.

8 Finally, brethren, whatsoeuer things *are* true, whatsoeuer things *are* ‖honest, whatsoeuer things *are* iust, whatsoeuer things *are* pure, whatsoeuer things *are* louely, whatsoeuer things *are* of good report : if there bee any vertue, and if there bee any praise, thinke on these things :

‖ Or, venerable.

9 Those things which ye haue both learned and receiued, and heard, and seene in mee, doe : and the God of peace shall be with you.

10 But I reioyced in the Lorde greatly, that now at the last your care of me ‖hath flourished againe, wherein yee were also carefull, but ye lacked opportunitie.

‖ Or, is reuiued.

11 Not that I speake in respect of want : for I haue learned in whatsoeuer state I am, therewith to bee content.

12 I know both how to bee abased, and I knowe how to abound : euerie where, and in all things I am instructed, both to bee full, and to bee hungrie, both to abound, and to suffer need.

13 I can do all things through Christ, which strengtheneth me.

14 Notwithstanding, yee haue well done, that ye did communicate with my affliction.

15 Now ye Philippians know also, that in the beginning of the Gospel, when I departed from Macedonia, no Church communicated with mee, as concerning giuing and receiuing, but ye onely.

16 For euen in Thessalonica, ye sent once, and againe vnto my necessitie.

17 Not because I desire a gift : but I desire fruit that may abound to your account.

18 But ‖I haue all, and abound. I am full, hauing receiued of Epaphroditus the things *which were sent* from you, an odour of a sweet smell, a sacrifice acceptable, well pleasing to God.

‖ Or, I haue receiued a

19 But my God shall supply all your need, according to his riches in glory, by Christ Iesus.

20 Now vnto God and our Father *be* glory for euer and euer. Amen.

21 Salute euery Saint in Christ Iesus : the brethren which are with me, greet you.

22 All the Saints salute you, chiefly they that are of Cesars houshold.

23 The grace of our Lord Iesus Christ *be* with you all. Amen.

¶ It was written to the Philippians from Rome, by Epaphroditus.

¶ THE

¶THE EPISTLE OF PAVL
the Apoſtle to the Coloſſians.

CHAP. I.

1 After salutation hee thanketh God for their faith, 7 confirmeth the doctrine of Epaphras, 9 Praieth further for their increase in grace, 14 describeth the true Christ, 21 encourageth them to receiue Iesus Christ, and commendeth his owne ministery.

Aul an Apostle of Iesus Christ, by ẙ will of God, and Timotheus our brother,

2 To the saints and faithfull brethren in Christ, which are at Colosse, grace be vnto you, and peace from God our Father, and the Lord Iesus Christ.

3 We giue thanks to God, and the Father of our Lord Iesus Christ, praying alwayes for you,

4 Since we heard of your faith in Christ Iesus, and of the loue which yee haue to all the Saints,

5 For the hope which is layd vp for you in heauen, whereof ye heard before in the word of the trueth of the Gospel,

6 Which is come vnto you as *it is* in all the world, and bringeth foorth fruit, as it doth also in you, since the day yee heard *of it*, and knew the grace of God in trueth,

7 As yee also learned of Epaphras our deare felow seruant, who is for you a faithfull Minister of Christ:

8 Who also declared vnto vs your loue in the spirit.

9 For this cause wee also, since the day we heard it, doe not cease to pray for you, and to desire that ye might be filled with the knowledge of his will, in all wisedome and spirituall vnderstanding:

10 That ye might walke worthy of the Lord vnto all pleasing, being fruit-full in euery good worke, & increasing in the knowledge of God:

11 Strengthened with all might according to his glorious power, vnto all patience and long suffering with ioyfulnesse:

12 Giuing thanks vnto the Father, which hath made vs meete to be partakers of the inheritance of the Saints in light:

13 Who hath deliuered vs from the power of darkenesse, and hath translated *vs* into the kingdome of †his deare Sonne,

14 In whom we haue redemption through his blood, *euen* the forgiuenesse of sinnes:

15 Who is the image of the inuisible God, the first borne of euery creature.

16 For by him were all things created that are in heauen, and that are in earth, visible and inuisible, whether *they be* thrones, or dominions, or principalities, or powers: all things were created by him, and for him.

17 *And he is before all things, and by him all things consist.

18 And hee is the head of the body, the Church: who is the beginning, the first borne from the dead, that ‖in all things he might haue the preeminence:

19 For it pleased *the Father* that in him should all fulnesse dwell,

20 And (‖hauing made peace through the blood of his crosse) by him to reconcile all things vnto himself, by him, *I say*, whether they bee things in earth, or things in heauen.

21 And you that were sometimes alienated, and enemies ‖in your minde by wicked workes, yet now hath hee reconciled,

22 In the body of his flesh through death, to present you holy & vnblameable, and vnreprooueable in his sight,

23 If ye continue in the faith grounded and setled, and be not moued away from

† *Gr. the Sonne of his loue.*

* 1. Cor. 8. 6 Ioh. 1. 3.

‖ *Or, among all.*

‖ *Or, making peace.*

‖ *Or, by your mind in wicked works.*

from the hope of the Gospel, which yee haue heard, *and* which was preached to euery creature which is vnder heauen, whereof I Paul am made a Minister.

24 Who now reioyce in my sufferings for you, and fill vp that which is behind of the afflictions of Christ in my flesh, for his bodies sake, which is the Church,

25 Whereof I am made a Minister, according to the dispensation of God, ‖ Or, *fully to preach the word of God, Rom.* 1. 19. which is giuen to mee for you, ‖to fulfill the word of God :

26 *Euen* the mystery which hath been hid from ages, and from generations, but now is made manifest to his saints,

27 To whom God would make knowen what is the riches of the glory of this mysterie among the Gentiles, ‖ Or, a-mongst you. which is Christ ‖in you, the hope of glory :

28 Whom we preach, warning euery man, and teaching euery man in all wisedome, that we may present euery man perfect in Christ Iesus.

29 Whereunto I also labour, striuing according to his working, which worketh in me mightily.

CHAP. II.

1 Hee still exhorteth them to bee constant in Christ, 8 To beware of Philosophie, and vaine traditions, 18 worshipping of Angels, 20 and Legall Ceremonies, which are ended in Christ.

‖ Or, *feare or care.*

 Or I would that ye knew what great ‖ conflict I haue for you, and for them at Laodicea, and for as many as haue not seene my face in the flesh :

2 That their hearts might be comforted, being knit together in loue, and vnto all riches of the full assurance of vnderstanding, to the acknowledgement of the mysterie of God, and of the Father, and of Christ,

‖ Or, *where-in.* 3 ‖In whom are hid all the treasures of wisedome, and knowledge.

4 And this I say, lest any man should beguile you with entising words.

5 For though I bee absent in the flesh, yet am I with you in the spirit, ioying and beholding your order, and the stedfastnesse of your faith in Christ.

6 As yee haue therefore receiued Christ Iesus the Lord, *so* walke yee in him :

7 Rooted and built vp in him, and stablished in the faith, as yee haue bene taught, abounding therein with thanksgiuing.

8 Beware lest any man spoile you through Philosophie and vaine deceit, after the tradition of men, after the ‖rudiments of the world, and not after Christ : ‖ Or, *elements.*

9 For in him dwelleth all the fulnesse of the Godhead bodily.

10 And ye are complete in him, which is the head of all principalitie, & power.

11 In whom also ye are circumcised with the Circumcision made without handes, in putting off the body of the sinnes of the flesh, by the Circumcision of Christ :

12 Buried with him in Baptisme, wherein also you are risen with *him* through the faith of the operation of God, who hath raised him from the dead.

13 And you being dead in your sinnes, and the vncircumcision of your flesh, hath hee quickened together with him, hauing forgiuen you all trespasses,

14 Blotting out the handwriting of ordinances, that was against vs, which was contrary to vs, and tooke it out of the way, nayling it to his Crosse :

15 And hauing spoyled principalities and powers, he made a shew of them openly, triumphing ouer them ‖in it. ‖ Or, *in his selfe.*

16 Let no man therefore iudge you in ‖meat, or in drinke, or in ‖respect of an ‖ Or, *for eating and drinking.* Holy day, or of the New moone, or of ‖ Or, *in part* the Sabbath *dayes :*

17 Which are a shadow of things to come, but the body *is* of Christ.

18 Let no man ‖beguile you of your reward, †in a voluntary humilitie, and ‖ Or, *iudge against you* worshipping of Angels, intruding into † Gr. *being* those things which hee hath not seene, *a voluntary* vainely puft vp by his fleshly minde : *in humilit*

19 And not holding the head, from which all the body by ioynts and bands hauing nourishment ministred, and knit together, increaseth with the increase of God.

20 Wherefore if yee bee dead with Christ frō the ‖rudiments of the world : ‖ Or, *elements.* why, as though liuing in the world, are ye subiect to ordinances ?

21 (Touch not, taste not, handle not :

22 Which all are to perish with the vsing) after the commandements and doctrines of men :

23 Which things haue in deed a shew of

‖ Or, punishing, or not sparing.

of wisedome in will-worship and humilitie, and ‖ neglecting of the body, not in any honour to the satisfying of the flesh.

CHAP. III.

1 Hee sheweth where wee should seeke Christ. 5 Hee exhorteth to mortification, 10 to put off the olde man, and to put on Christ, 12 exhorting to charitie, humilitie, and other seuerall dueties.

 F yee then bee risen with Christ, seeke those things which are aboue, where Christ sitteth on the right hand of God:

‖ Or, minde.

2 Set your ‖ affection on things aboue, not on things on the earth.

3 For yee are dead, and your life is hid with Christ in God.

4 When Christ, who is our life, shall appeare, then shall yee also appeare with him in glorie.

5 Mortifie therefore your members which are vpon the earth : fornication, vncleannesse, inordinate affection, euill concupiscence, and couetousnesse, which is idolatrie :

6 For which things sake, the wrath of God commeth on the children of disobedience,

7 In the which yee also walked sometime, when ye liued in them.

8 But now you also put off all these, anger, wrath, malice, blasphemie, filthy communication out of your mouth.

9 Lie not one to another, seeing that yee haue put off the old man with his deedes :

10 And haue put on the new man, which is renued in knowledge, after the image of him that created him,

11 Where there is neither Greeke, nor Iew, circumcision, nor vncircumcision, Barbarian, Scythian, bond, nor free : but Christ is all, and in all.

12 Put on therefore (as the elect of God, holy and beloued) bowels of mercies, kindnesse, humblenesse of minde, meekenesse, long suffering,

‖ Or, complaint.

13 Forbearing one another, and forgiuing one another, if any man haue a ‖ quarrell against any : euen as Christ forgaue you, so also *doe* yee.

14 And aboue all these things *put on* charitie, which is the bond of perfectnesse.

15 And let the peace of God rule in your hearts, to the which also yee are called in one body : and be yee thankefull.

16 Let the word of Christ dwell in you richly in all wisdome, teaching and admonishing one another in Psalmes, and Hymnes, and Spirituall songs, singing with grace in your hearts to the Lord.

17 And whatsoeuer yee doe in word or deed, *doe* all in the Name of the Lord Iesus, giuing thankes to God and the Father, by him.

18 Wiues, submit your selues vnto your owne husbands, as it is fit in the Lord.

19 Husbands, loue your wiues, and be not bitter against them.

20 Children, obey your parents in all things, for this is well pleasing vnto the Lord.

21 Fathers, prouoke not your children *to anger*, lest they be discouraged.

22 Seruants, obey in all things your masters according to the flesh : not with eye seruice as men pleasers, but in singlenesse of heart, fearing God :

23 And whatsoeuer yee doe, doe it heartily, as to the Lord, and not vnto men :

24 Knowing, that of the Lord yee shall receiue the reward of the inheritance : for ye serue the Lord Christ.

25 But he that doeth wrong, shall receiue for the wrong which hee hath done : and there is no respect of persons.

CHAP. IIII.

1 Hee exhorteth them to bee feruent in prayer, 5 to walke wisely toward them that are not yet come to the true knowledge of Christ. 10 Hee saluteth them, and wisheth them all prosperitie.

 Asters, giue vnto your seruants that which is iust and equall, knowing that yee also haue a Master in heauen.

2 Continue in prayer, and watch in the same with thankesgiuing :

3 Withall, praying also for vs, that God would open vnto vs a doore of vtterance, to speake the mystery of Christ, for which I am also in bonds :

4 That I may make it manifest, as I ought to speake.

5 Walke in wisdome toward them that are without, redeeming the time.

6 Let your speech bee alway with grace,

grace, seasoned with salt, that you may know how yee ought to answere euery man.

7 All my state shall Tychicus declare vnto you, *who is* a beloued brother, and a faithfull minister, and fellow seruant in the Lord:

8 Whom I haue sent vnto you for the same purpose, that hee might know your estate, and comfort your hearts.

9 With Onesimus a faithfull and beloued brother, who is one of you. They shall make knowen vnto you all things which *are* done here.

10 Aristarchus my fellow prisoner saluteth you, and Marcus sisters sonne to Barnabas, (touching whome yee receiued commandements; if he come vnto you, receiue him:)

11 And Iesus, which is called Iustus, who are of the circumcision. These onely are my fellow workers vnto the kingdome of God, which haue beene a comfort vnto me.

12 Epaphras, who is one of you, a seruant of Christ, saluteth you, alwaies ‖ *Or, striuing* ‖labouring feruently for you in praiers,

that ye may stand perfect, and ‖complete ‖ *Or, filled.* in all the will of God.

13 For I beare him record, that hee hath a great zeale for you, and them *that are* in Laodicea, and them in Hierapolis.

14 Luke the beloued physician, and Demas greet you.

15 Salute the brethren which are in Laodicea, and Nymphas, & the church which is in his house.

16 And when this Epistle is read amongst you, cause that it be read also in the church of the Laodiceans: and that ye likewise reade the Epistle from Laodicea,

17 And say to Archippus, Take heede to the ministerie, which thou hast receiued in the Lord, that thou fulfill it.

18 The salutation by the hand of me Paul. Remember my bonds. Grace be with you. Amen.

¶ Written from Rome to the Colossians, by Tychicus and Onesimus.

¶THE FIRST EPISTLE OF
Paul the Apoſtle to the Theſſalonians.

CHAP. I.

1 The Thessalonians are giuen to vnderstand both how mindfull of them S. Paul was at all times in thanks-giuing, & prayer: 5 and also how well he was perswaded of the truth, and sinceritie of their faith, & conuersion to God.

Aul and Siluanus, and Timotheus, vnto the Church of the Thessalonians, *which is* in God the Father, and in the Lord Iesus Christ: grace *be* vnto you, and peace from God our Father, and the Lord Iesus Christ.

2 We giue thankes to God alwaies for you all, making mention of you in our prayers,

3 Remembring without ceasing your worke of faith, and labour of loue, and patience of hope in our Lord Iesus Christ, in the sight of God and our Father:

4 Knowing, brethren ‖beloued, ‖ *Or, beloued of God youreiectio* your election of God.

5 For our Gospel came not vnto you in word onely: but also in power, and in the holy Ghost, and in much assurance, as yee know what maner of men we were among you for your sake.

6 And yee became followers of vs, and of the Lord, hauing receiued the word in much affliction, with ioy of the holy Ghost:

7 So that ye were ensamples to all that beleeue in Macedonia and Achaia.

8 For

8 For from you sounded out the Word of the Lord, not onely in Macedonia & Achaia, but also in euery place your faith to Godward is spred abroad, so that we need not to speak any thing.

9 For they themselues shew of vs, what maner of entring in we had vnto you, and how yee turned to God from idols, to serue the liuing, and true God,

10 And to waite for his sonne from heauen, whom he raised from the dead, *euen* Iesus which deliuered vs from the wrath to come.

CHAP. II.

In what manner the Gospel was brought and preached to the Thessalonians, and in what sort also they receiued it. 18 A reason is rendred both why Saint Paul was so long absent from them, and also why hee was so desirous to see them.

Or your selues, brethren, knowe our entrance in vnto you, that it was not in vaine.

2 But euen after that wee had suffered before, and were shamefully entreated, as ye know, at Philippi, wee were bold in our God, to speake vnto you the Gospel of God with much contention.

3 For our exhortation was not of deceite, nor of vncleannesse, nor in guile:

4 But as we were allowed of God to bee put in trust with the Gospel, euen so wee speake, not as pleasing men, but God, which trieth our hearts.

5 For neither at any time vsed wee flattering wordes, as yee knowe, nor a cloke of couetousnesse, God *is* witnesse:

6 Nor of men sought we glorie, neither of you, nor yet of others, when we might haue beene ||burdensome, as the Apostles of Christ.

‖ Or, vsed authority.

7 But wee were gentle among you, euen as a nurse cherisheth her children:

8 So being affectionately desirous of you, we were willing to haue imparted vnto you, not the Gospel of God onely, but also our owne soules, because ye were deare vnto vs.

9 For yee remember, brethren, our labour and trauaile: for labouring night and day, because wee would not bee chargeable vnto any of you, wee preached vnto you the Gospel of God.

10 Yee *are* witnesses, and God *also*, how holily, and iustly, and vnblameably wee behaued our selues among you that beleeue.

11 As you know, how wee exhorted and comforted, and charged euery one of you, (as a father doeth his children,)

12 That ye would walke worthy of God, who hath called you vnto his kingdome and glory.

13 For this cause also thanke wee God without ceasing, because when yee receiued the word of God, which yee heard of vs, yee receiued it not as the word of men, but (as it is in trueth) the word of God, which effectually worketh also in you that beleeue.

14 For yee, brethren, became followers of the Churches of God, which in Iudea are in Christ Iesus: for ye also haue suffered like things of your owne countreymen, euen as they haue of the Iewes:

15 Who both killed the Lord Iesus, and their owne Prophets, and haue ||persecuted vs: and they please not God, and are contrary to all men:

‖ Or, chased vs out.

16 Forbidding vs to speake to the Gentiles, that they might bee saued, to fill vp their sinnes alway: for the wrath is come vpon them to the vttermost.

17 But wee, brethren, beeing taken from you for a short time, in presence, not in heart, endeuored the more abundantly to see your face with great desire.

18 Wherefore we would haue come vnto you (euen I Paul) once & againe: but Satan hindered vs.

19 For what is our hope, or ioy, or crowne of ||reioycing? Are not euen ye in the presence of our Lord Iesus Christ at his comming?

‖ Or, glorying

20 For, ye are our glory and ioy.

CHAP. III.

1 S. Paul testifieth his great loue to the Thessalonians, partly by sending Timothie vnto them to strengthen and comfort them: partly by reioycing in their weldoing: 10 and partly by praying for them, and desiring a safe comming vnto them.

Herefore when wee could no longer forbeare, wee thought it good to bee left at Athens alone:

2 And sent Timotheus our brother and minister of God, and our fellow labourer in the Gospel of Christ,

Christ, to establish you, and to comfort you concerning your faith

3 That no man should be mooued by these afflictions : for your selues know that we are appointed therunto.

4 For verily when wee were with you, we told you before, that we should suffer tribulation, euen as it came to passe and ye know.

5 For this cause when I could no longer forbeare, I sent to know your faith, lest by some meanes the tempter haue tempted you, and our labor be in vaine.

6 But now when Timotheus came from you vnto vs, and brought vs good tidings of your faith and charitie, and that ye haue good remembrance of vs alwayes, desiring greatly to see vs, as we also *to see* you :

7 Therefore brethren, wee were comforted ouer you in all our affliction and distresse, by your faith :

* Rom. 7. 9.

8 For now we *liue, if ye stand fast in the Lord.

9 For what thankes can we render to God againe for you, for all the ioy wherewith wee ioy for your sakes before our God,

10 Night & day praying exceedingly that we might see your face, and might perfect that which is lacking in your faith ?

‖ Or, guide.

11 Now God himselfe and our Father, and our Lord Iesus Christ ‖ direct our way vnto you.

12 And the Lorde make you to increase, & abound in loue one towards another, and towards all men, euen as we *doe* towards you :

13 To the end hee may stablish your hearts vnblameable in holinesse before God euen our Father, at the comming of our Lord Iesus Christ with all his Saints.

CHAP. IIII.

Hee exhorteth them to goe on forward in all manner of godlinesse, 6 to liue holily and iustly, 9 to loue one another, 11 and quietly to followe their owne businesse : 13 and last of all to sorrow moderately for the dead. 17 And vnto this last exhortation is annexed a briefe description of the resurrection, and second comming of Christ to iudgement.

‖ Or, request
¶ Or, beseech

Vrthermore then we ‖beseech you, brethren, and‖exhort you by the Lord Iesus, that as yee haue receiued of vs, how ye ought to walke, and to please God, so yee would abound more and more.

2 For yee know what commandements wee gaue you, by the Lord Iesus.

3 For this is the will of God, *euen* your sanctification, that yee should absteine from fornication :

4 That euery one of you should know how to possesse his vessell in sanctification and honour :

5 Not in the lust of concupiscence, euen as the Gentiles which know not God :

6 That *no man* goe beyond and ‖defraud his brother‖in *any* matter, because that the Lord is the auenger of all such: as we also haue forewarned you, and testified :

‖Or, oppresse, or, ouer-reach.
‖ Or, in the matter.

7 For God hath not called vs vnto vncleannesse, but vnto holinesse.

8 He therefore that ‖despiseth, despiseth not man, but God, who hath also giuen vnto vs his holy Spirit.

‖ Or, reieteth.

9 But as touching brotherly loue, ye need not that I write vnto you · for yee your selues are taught of God to loue one an other

10 And in deed ye doe it towards all the brethren, which are in all Macedonia : but we beseech you, brethren, that ye increase more and more

11 And that ye studie to be quiet, and to doe your owne businesse, and to worke with your owne hands, (as wee commanded you :)

12 That ye may walke honestly toward them that are without, and that ye may haue lacke of ‖nothing.

‖ Or, of no man.

13 But I would not haue you to be ignorant, brethren, concerning them which are asleepe, that ye sorrow not, euen as others which haue no hope.

14 For if we beleeue that Iesus died, and rose againe : euen so them also which sleepe in Iesus, will God bring with him

15 For this we say vnto you by the word of the Lord, That we which are aliue and remaine vnto the comming of the Lord, shall not preuent them which are asleepe.

16 For the Lord himselfe shall descend from heauen with a shout, with the voyce of the Archangel, and with the trumpe of God : and the dead in Christ shall rise first.

17 Then we which are aliue, and remaine, shalbe caught vp together with them

them in the clouds, to meet the Lord in the aire : and so shall wee euer bee with the Lord.

Or, exhort.   18 Wherefore, ||comfort one an other with these words.

CHAP. V.

1 Hee proceedeth in the former description of Christs comming to iudgement, 16 and giueth diuers precepts, 23 and so concludeth the Epistle.

Vt of the times and the seasons, brethren, yee haue no need that I write vnto you.

2 For your selues knowe perfectly that the day of the Lord so commeth as a thiefe in the night.

3 For when they shal say, Peace and safety : then sudden destructiō commeth vpon them, as trauaile vpon a woman with childe, and they shall not escape.

4 But ye, brethren, are not in darkenesse, that that day should ouertake you as a thiefe.

5 Yee are all the children of light, and the children of the day : we are not of the night, nor of darkenesse.

6 Therefore let vs not sleepe, as *doe* others : but let vs watch and be sober.

7 For they that sleepe, sleepe in the night, and they that bee drunken, are drunken in the night.

8 But let vs who are of the day, bee sober, putting on the brestplate of faith and loue, and for an helmet, the hope of saluation.

9 For God hath not appointed vs to wrath : but to obtaine saluation by our Lord Iesus Christ,

10 Who died for vs, that whether we wake or sleepe, we should liue together with him.

Or, exhort.   11 Wherefore, ||comfort your selues together, and edifie one another, euen as also ye doe.

12 And we beseech you, brethren, to know them which labour among you, and are ouer you in the Lord, and admonish you :

13 And to esteeme them very highly in loue for their workes sake, and be at peace among your selues.

14 Now we ||exhort you, brethren, warne them that are ||vnruly, comfort the feeble minded, support the weake, be patient toward all men.   *Or, beseech | Or, disorderly.*

15 See that none render euill for euill vnto any man : but euer follow that which is good, both among your selues and to all men.

16 Reioyce euermore :

17 Pray without ceasing :

18 In euery thing giue thankes : for this is the will of God in Christ Iesus concerning you.

19 Quench not the spirit :

20 Despise not prophecyings :

21 Proue all things : hold fast that which is good.

22 Abstaine from all appearance of euill.

23 And the very God of peace sanctifie you wholly : and *I pray God* your whole spirit, and soule, and body be preserued blamelesse vnto the comming of our Lord Iesus Christ.

24 Faithfull is hee that calleth you, who also will doe it.

25 Brethren, pray for vs.

26 Greete all the brethren with an holy kisse.

27 I ||charge you by the Lord, that this Epistle bee read vnto all the holy brethren.   *Or, adiure.*

28 The grace of our Lord Iesus Christ *be* with you, Amen.

¶ The first Epistle vnto the Thessalonians, was written from Athens.

¶ THE

¶ THE SECOND EPISTLE
of Paul the Apoſtle to the
Thessalonians.

CHAP. I.

1 S. Paul certifieth them of the good opinion which hee had of their faith, loue, and patience: 11 And therewithall vseth diuers reasons for the comforting of them in persecution, whereof the chiefest is taken from the righteous iudgement of God.

Aul and Siluanus, and Timotheus vnto the Church of the Thessaloniãs, in God our Father, and the Lord Iesus Christ:

2 Grace vnto you, and peace from God our Father, and the Lorde Iesus Christ.

3 Wee are bound to thanke God alwayes for you, brethren, as it is meete, because that your faith groweth exceedingly, and the charitie of euery one of you al towards each other aboundeth:

4 So that wee our selues glorie in you in the Churches of God, for your patience and faith in all your persecutions and tribulations that yee endure.

5 *Which is* a manifest token of the righteous iudgement of God, that yee may bee counted worthy of the kingdome of God, for which yee also suffer;

6 Seeing it is a righteous thing with God to recompence tribulation to them that trouble you :

7 And to you who are troubled, rest with vs, when the Lord Iesus shalbe reuealed from heauen, †with his mightie Angels,

8 In flaming fire, ‖ taking vengeance on them that know not God, and that obey not the Gospel of our Lorde Iesus Christ,

9 Who shalbe punished with euerlasting destruction from the presence of the Lord, and from the glory of his power :

12 When hee shall come to bee glorified in his Saints, and to bee admired in all them that beleeue (because our testimony among you was beleeued) in that day.

11 Wherefore also we pray alwayes for you, that our God would ‖ count you worthy of this calling, and fulfill all the good pleasure of *his* goodnesse, and the worke of faith with power :

12 That the Name of our Lord Iesus Christ may bee glorified in you, and ye in him, according to the grace of our God, and the Lord Iesus Christ.

CHAP. II.

1 Hee willeth them to continue stedfast in the trueth receiued, 3 Sheweth that there shall bee a departure from the faith, 9 and a discouery of Antichrist, before the day of the Lord come. 15 And thereupon repeateth his former exhortation, & prayeth for them.

Ow wee beseech you, brethren, by the comming of our Lord Iesus Christ, and by our gathering together vnto him,

2 That yee bee not soone shaken in minde, or bee troubled, neither by spirit, nor by word, nor by letter, as from vs, as that the day of Christ is at hand,

3 Let no man deceiue you by any meanes, for *that day shall not come*, except there come a falling away first, and that man of sinne bee reuealed, the sonne of perdition,

4 Who opposeth and exalteth himselfe aboue all that is called God, or that is worshipped : so that he as God, sitteth in the Temple of God, shewing himselfe that he is God.

5 Remember yee not, that when I was yet with you, I tolde you these things ?

6 And

† Gr. the angels of his power.
‖ Or, yeelding.

‖ Or, vouchsafe.

‖ *Or, holdeth.*

6 And now yee know what ‖withholdeth, that hee might be reuealed in his time.

7 For the mysterie of iniquitie doth alreadie worke : onely he who now letteth, *will let*, vntill he be taken out of the way.

8 And then shall that wicked bee reuealed, whome the Lord shall consume with the spirit of his mouth, and shall destroy with the brightnesse of his comming :

9 *Euen him* whose comming is after the working of Satan, with all power and signes, and lying wonders,

10 And with all deceiueablenesse of vnrighteousnesse, in them that perish : because they receiued not the loue of the trueth, that they might be saued.

11 And for this cause God shall send them strong delusion, that they should beleeue a lye :

12 That they all might bee damned who beleeued not the trueth, but had pleasure in vnrighteousnes.

13 But we are bound to giue thanks alway to God for you, brethren, beloued of the Lord, because God hath from the beginning chosen you to saluation, through sanctification of the spirit, and beleefe of the trueth,

14 Whereunto he called you by our Gospel, to the obteining of the glorie of the Lord Iesus Christ.

15 Therefore, brethren, stand fast, and hold the traditions which yee haue beene taught, whether by word or our Epistle.

16 Now our Lorde Iesus Christ himselfe, and God euen our Father, which hath loued vs, and hath giuen vs euerlasting consolation, and good hope through grace,

17 Comfort your hearts, and stablish you in euery good word and worke.

CHAP. III.

He craueth their prayers for himselfe, 3 testifieth what confidence hee hath in them, 5 maketh request to God in their behalfe, 6 giueth them diuers precepts, especially to shun idlenesse, and ill company, 16 And last of all concludeth with prayer and salutation.

† *Gr. may runne.*

Inally, brethren, pray for vs, that the word of the Lord †may haue *free* course, and be glorified, euen as *it is* with you :

2 And that we may

† *Gr. absurd.*

bee deliuered from †vnreasonable and wicked men : for all men haue not faith.

3 But the Lord is faithfull, who shall stablish you, and keepe you from euill.

4 And wee haue confidence in the Lord touching you, that yee both doe, and will doe the things which we command you.

5 And the Lord direct your hearts into the loue of God, and into ‖the patient waiting for Christ.

‖ *Or, the patience of Christ.*

6 Now we command you, brethren, in the Name of our Lord Iesus Christ, that ye withdraw your selues from euery brother that walketh disorderly, and not after the tradition which hee receiued of vs.

7 For your selues know how yee ought to follow vs : for wee behaued not our selues disorderly among you,

8 Neither did wee eate any mans bread for nought : but wrought with labour and trauaile night and day, that wee might not bee chargeable to any of you.

9 Not because we haue not power, but to make our selues an ensample vnto you to follow vs.

10 For euen when wee were with you, this wee commanded you, that if any would not worke, neither should he eate.

11 For we heare that there are some which walke among you disorderly, working not at all, but are busi-bodies.

12 Now them that are such, we command, and exhort by our Lord Iesus Christ, that with quietnesse they worke, and eat their owne bread.

13 But ye, brethren, ‖be not wearie in well doing.

‖ *Or, faint not.*

14 And if any man obey not our word, by this Epistle ‖note that man, and haue no company with him, that he may be ashamed.

‖ *Or, signifie that man by an Epistle.*

15 Yet count him not as an enemie, but admonish him as a brother.

16 Now the Lord of peace himselfe, giue you peace alwayes, by all meanes. The Lord be with you all.

17 The salutation of Paul, with mine owne hand, which is the token in euery Epistle : so I write.

18 The grace of our Lord Iesus Christ *be* with you all, Amen.

¶ The second *Epistle* to the Thessalonians was written from Athens.
¶ THE

¶ THE FIRST EPISTLE
of Paul the Apoſtle to Timothie.

CHAP. I.

1 Timothie is put in mind of the charge which was giuen vnto him by Paul at his going to Macedonia. 5 Of the right vse and end of the Law. 11 of Saint Pauls calling to be an Apostle, 20 and of Hymeneus & Alexander.

Aul an Apostle of Ie-
sus Christ by the com-
maundement of God
our Sauiour, & Lord
Iesus Christ *which is*
our hope,

2 Vnto Timothie *my* own sonne in the Faith : Grace, mer-cie, *and* peace from God our Father, and Iesus Christ our Lord.

3 As I besought thee to abide still at Ephesus when I went into Mace-donia, that thou mightest charge some that they teach no other doctrine,

4 Neither giue heed to fables, and endlesse genealogies, which minister questions, rather then edifying which is in faith : so doe.

5 Now the end of the commande-ment is charity, out of a pure heart, and of a good conscience, and of faith vn-fained.

‖ *Or, not ai-ming at.*

6 From which some ‖ hauing swar-ued, haue turned aside vnto vaine iang-ling,

7 Desiring to bee teachers of the Law, vnderstāding neither what they say, nor whereof they affirme.

8 But we know that the Law is good, if a man vse it lawfully.

9 Knowing this, that the Law is not made for a righteous man, but for the lawlesse and disobedient, for the vngodly, and for sinners, for vnholy, and profane, for murderers of fathers, and murderers of mothers, for man-slayers,

10 For whoremongers, for them that defile themselues with mankinde, for men-stealers, for liars, for periured persons, and if there be any other thing

that is contrary to sound doctrine,

11 According to the glorious Gospel of the blessed God, which was commit-ted to my trust.

12 And I thanke Christ Iesus our Lord, who hath enabled mee : for that he counted me faithfull, putting me in-to the Ministerie,

13 Who was before a blasphemer, and a persecuter, and iniurious. But I obtained mercie, because I did it ig-norantly, in vnbeliefe.

14 And the grace of our Lord was exceeding abundant, with faith, & loue, which is in Christ Iesus.

15 This is a faithfull saying, and worthy of all acceptation, that Christ Iesus came into the world to saue sin-ners, of whom I am chiefe.

16 Howbeit, for this cause I obtai-ned mercy, that in me first, Iesus Christ might shew foorth all long suffering, for a paterne to them which should hereafter beleeue on him to life euerla-sting.

17 Now vnto ỹ king eternal, immor-tall, inuisible, the onely wise God, be ho-nour and glory for euer & euer. Amen.

18 This charge I commit vnto thee, sonne Timothie, according to the pro-phesies which went before on thee, that thou by them mightest warre a good warfare,

19 Holding faith, and a good consci-ence, which some hauing put away, con-cerning faith, haue made shipwracke.

20 Of whom is Hymeneus and Alex-ander, whome I haue deliuered vnto Satan, that they may learne not to blaspheme.

CHAP. II.

1 That it is meete to pray and giue thanks for all men, and the reason why. 9 How women should be attired. 12 They are not permit-ted to teach. 15 They shalbe saued, notwith-standing the testimonies of Gods wrath, in childbirth, if they continue in faith.

I ‖ ex-

‖ Or, desire.

‖Exhort therefore, that first of all, supplications, prayers, intercessions, and giuing of thanks be made for all men:

‖ Or, eminent place.

2 For Kings, and for all that are in ‖authoritie, that we may leade a quiet and peaceable life in all godlinesse and honestie.

3 For this is good and acceptable in the sight of God our Sauiour,

4 Who will haue all men to bee saued, and to come vnto the knowledge of the trueth.

5 For *there is* one God, and one Mediatour betweene God and men, the man Christ Iesus,

‖ Or, a testimony.

6 Who gaue himselfe a ransome for all, ‖to be testified in due time.

7 Whereunto I am ordained a preacher, and an Apostle (I speake the trueth in Christ, and lie not) a teacher of the Gentiles in faith and veritie.

8 I will therefore that men pray euery where, lifting vp holy handes without wrath, and doubting.

9 In like maner also, that women adorne themselues in modest apparell, with shamefastnesse and sobrietie, not with ‖broided haire, or gold, or pearles, or costly aray,

‖ Or, plaited.

10 But (which becommeth women professing godlines) with good works.

11 Let the woman learne in silence with all subiection :

12 But I suffer not a woman to teach, nor to vsurpe authoritie ouer the man, but to be in silence.

13 For Adam was first formed, then Eue :

14 And Adam was not deceiued, but the woman being deceiued was in the transgression :

15 Notwithstanding she shall be saued in child-bearing, if they continue in faith and charitie, and holinesse, with sobrietie.

CHAP. III.

How Bishops, and Deacons, and their wiues should be qualified, 14 and to what end S. Paul wrote to Timothie of these things. 15 Of the Church, and the blessed trueth therein taught and professed.

His is a true saying : If a man desire the office of a Bishop, he desireth a good worke.

2 A Bishop then must be blamelesse, the husband of one wife, vigilant, sober, ‖of good behauiour, giuen to hospitalitie, apt to teach ,

‖ Or, modest.

3 Not ‖giuen to wine, no striker, not greedy of filthy lucre, but patient, not a brawler, not couetous ;

‖ Or, not ready to quarell and offer wrong, as one in wine.

4 One that ruleth well his owne house, hauing his children in subiection with all grauitie.

5 (For if a man know not how to rule his owne house, how shall he take care of the Church of God ?)

6 Not a ‖nouice, lest being lifted vp with pride, hee fall into the condemnation of the deuill.

‖ Or, one newly come to the faith.

7 Moreouer, hee must haue a good report of them which are without, lest he fall into reproch, and the snare of the deuill.

8 Likewise must the Deacons bee graue, not double tongued, not giuen to much wine, not greedy of filthy lucre,

9 Holding the mysterie of the faith in a pure conscience.

10 And let these also first be proued ; then let them vse the office of a Deacon, being *found* blamelesse.

11 Euen so must their wiues be graue ; not slanderers, sober, faithfull in all things.

12 Let the Deacons be the husbands of one wife, ruling their children, and their owne houses well.

13 For they that ‖haue vsed the office of a Deacon well, purchase to themselues a good degree, and great boldnesse in the faith, *which is* in Christ Iesus.

‖ Or, ministred.

14 These things write I vnto thee, hoping to come vnto thee shortly.

15 But if I tary long, that thou mayest know how thou oughtest to behaue thy selfe in the House of God, which is the Church of the liuing God, the pillar and ‖ground of the trueth.

‖ Or, stay.

16 And without controuersie, great is the mysterie of godlinesse · God was manifest in the flesh, iustified in the Spirit, seene of Angels, preached vnto the Gentiles, beleeued on in the world, receiued vp into glory.

CHAP. IIII.

He foretelleth that in the latter times there shall be a departure from the faith. 6 And to the end that Timothie might not faile in doing his duetie, he furnisheth him with diuers precepts belonging thereto.

Now

Ow the Spirit speaketh expresly, that in the latter times some shall depart from the faith, giuing heed to seducing spirits, and doctrines of deuils:

2 Speaking lies in hypocrisie, hauing their conscience seared with a hote iron,

3 Forbidding to marry, *and commanding* to absteine from meates, which God hath created to bee receiued with thankesgiuing of them which beleeue, and know the trueth.

4 For euery creature of God *is* good, and nothing to be refused, if it be receiued with thankesgiuing:

5 For it is sanctified by the word of God, and prayer.

6 If thou put the brethren in remembrance of these things, thou shalt be a good minister of Iesus Christ, nourished vp in the wordes of faith, and of good doctrine, whereunto thou hast attained.

7 But refuse prophane and olde wiues fables, and exercise thy selfe *rather* vnto godlinesse.

‖ *Or, for a little time.*

8 For bodily exercise profiteth ‖litle, but godlinesse is profitable vnto all things, hauing promise of the life that now is, and of that which is to come.

9 This *is* a faithful saying, and worthy of all acceptation:

10 For therfore we both labour, and suffer reproch, because we trust in the liuing God, who is the Sauiour of all men, specially of those that beleeue.

11 These things command & teach.

12 Let no man despise thy youth, but be thou an example of the beleeuers, in word, in conuersation, in charitie, in spirit, in faith, in puritie.

13 Till I come, giue attendance to reading, to exhortation, to doctrine.

14 Neglect not the gift that is in thee, which was giuen thee by prophesie, with the laying on of the hands of the Presbyterie.

15 Meditate vpon these things, giue thy selfe wholly to them, that thy profiting may appeare ‖to all.

‖ *Or, in all things.*

16 Take heed vnto thy selfe, and vnto the doctrine: continue in them: for in doing this, thou shalt both saue thy selfe, and them that heare thee.

CHAP. V.

1 Rules to be obserued in reprouing.   3 *Of*

widowes. 17 Of Elders. 23 A precept for Timothies health. 24 Some mens sinnes goe before vnto iudgement, and some mens doe follow after.

Ebuke not an Elder, but intreate him as a father, and the yonger men as brethren:

2 The elder women as mothers, the yonger as sisters with all puritie.

3 Honour widowes that are widowes indeed.

4 But if any widow haue children or nephewes, let them learne first to shew ‖pietie at home, and to requite their parents: for that is good and acceptable before God.

‖ *Or, kindenesse.*

5 Now she that is a widow in deed, and desolate, trusteth in God, and continueth in supplications and prayers night and day.

6 But she that liueth ‖in pleasure, is dead while she liueth.

‖ *Or, delicately.*

7 And these things giue in charge, that they may be blamelesse.

8 But if any prouide not for his owne, & specially for those of his owne ‖house, hee hath denied the faith, and is worse then an infidel.

‖ *Or, kindred*

9 Let not a widow bee ‖taken into the number, vnder threescore yeeres old, hauing bene the wife of one man,

‖ *Or, chosen.*

10 Well reported of for good works, if shee haue brought vp children, if she haue lodged strangers, if she haue washed the Saints feet, if shee haue releeued the afflicted, if shee haue diligently followed euery good worke.

11 But the yonger widowes refuse: for when they haue begunne to waxe wanton against Christ, they will marry,

12 Hauing damnation, because they haue cast off their first faith.

13 And withall they learne *to bee* idle, wandering about from house to house; and not onely idle, but tatlers also, and busibodies, speaking things which they ought not.

14 I will therefore that the yonger women marry, beare children, guid the house, giue none occasion to the aduersary †to speake reprochfully.

† *Gr. for their railing.*

15 For some are already turned aside after Satan.

16 If any man or woman that beleeueth haue widowes, let them relieue them, and let not the Church be charged,

ged, that it may relieue them that are widowes indeed.

17 Let the Elders that rule well, be counted worthy of double honour, especially they who labour in the word and doctrine.

* Deut. 25. 4.

18 For the Scripture saith, *Thou shalt not mousell the oxe that treadeth out the corne : and, *The labourer is worthy of his reward.

* Matth. 10. 10.

19 Against an Elder receiue not an accusation, but ‖before two or three witnesses.

‖ Or, vnder.

20 Them that sinne rebuke before all, that others also may feare.

21 I charge thee before God, and the Lord Iesus Christ, and the elect Angels, that thou obserue these things ‖without preferring one before another, doing nothing by partialitie.

‖ Or, without preiudice.

22 Lay hands suddenly on no man, neither bee partaker of other mens sinnes. Keepe thy selfe pure.

23 Drinke no longer water, but vse a little wine for thy stomackes sake, and thine often infirmities.

24 Some mens sinnes are open before hand, going before to iudgement : and some *men* they follow after.

25 Likewise also the good works *of some* are manifest before hand, and they that are otherwise, cannot be hid.

CHAP. VI.

1 Of the duetie of seruants. 3 Not to haue fellowship with newfangled teachers. 6 Godlinesse is great gaine, 10 and loue of money the roote of all euill. 11 What Timothie is to flie, and what to follow, 17 and whereof to admonish the rich. 20 To keepe the puritie of true doctrine, and to auoyd prophane ianglings.

Et as many seruants as are vnder the yoke, count their owne masters worthy of all honour, that the Name of God, and his doctrine be not blasphemed.

2 And they that haue beleeuing masters, let them not despise *them* because they are brethren : but rather doe *them* seruice, because they are ‖faithfull and beloued, partakers of the benefite : These things teach and exhort.

‖ Or, beleeuing.

3 If any man teach otherwise, and consent not to wholesome words, *euen* the wordes of our Lord Iesus Christ, and to the doctrine which is according to godlinesse :

4 Hee is ‖proud, knowing nothing, but ‖doting about questions, and strifes of wordes, whereof commeth enuie, strife, railings, euill surmisings,

‖ Or, a foole. ‖ Or, sicke.

5 ‖Peruerse disputings of men of corrupt mindes, and destitute of the trueth, supposing that gaine is godlinesse : From such withdraw thy selfe.

‖ Or, gallings one of another.

6 But godlinesse with contentment is great gaine.

7 For we brought nothing into this world, *and* it is certaine we can cary nothing out.

8 And hauing food and raiment let vs be therewith content.

9 But they that wil be rich, fall into temptation and a snare, and into many foolish & hurtfull lusts, which drowne men in destruction and perdition.

10 For the loue of money is the root of all euill, which while some coueted after, they haue ‖erred from the faith, and pierced themselues through with many sorrowes.

‖ Or, bene seduced.

11 But thon, O man of God, flie these things ; and follow after righteousnesse, godlinesse, faith, loue, patience, meekenesse.

12 Fight the good fight of faith, lay hold on eternall life, whereunto thou art also called, and hast professed a good profession before many witnesses.

13 I giue thee charge in the sight of God, who quickneth all things, and *before* Christ Iesus, who before Pontius Pilate witnessed a good ‖Confession,

‖ Or, profession.

14 That thou keepe this commandement without spot, vnrebukeable, vntill the appearing of our Lord Iesus Christ.

15 Which in his times he shall shew, who is the blessed, and onely Potentate, the King of kings, and Lord of lords :

16 Who onely hath immortalitie, dwelling in the light, which no man can approch vnto, whom no man hath seene, nor can see : to whom *be* honour and power euerlasting. Amen.

17 Charge them that are rich in this world, that they bee not high minded, nor trust in †vncertaine riches, but in the liuing God, who giueth vs richly all things to enioy,

† Gr. vncertaintie of riches.

18 That they doe good, that they be rich in good works, ready to distribute, ‖willing to communicate,

‖ Or, sociable.

19 Laying vp in store for themselues a good foundation against the time to come,

come, that they may lay holde on eternall life.

20 O Timothie, keepe that which is committed to thy trust, auoyding prophane *and* vaine bablings, and oppositions of science, fasly so called :

21 Which some professing, haue erred concerning the faith. Grace *be* with thee. Amen.

¶ The first to Timothie was written from Laodicea, which is the chiefest citie of Phrygia Pacaciana.

¶ THE SECOND EPISTLE
of Paul the Apostle to Timothie.

CHAP. I.

Pauls loue to Timothie, and the vnfained faith which was in Timothie himselfe, his mother, and grandmother. 6 Hee is exhorted to stirre vp the gift of God which was in him, 8 to be stedfast and patient in persecution, 13 and to persist in the fourme and trueth of that doctrine which hee had learned of him. 15 Phygellus and Hermogenes, and such like are noted, and Onesiphorus is highly commended.

Aul an Apostle of Iesus Christ by the will of God, according to the promise of life, which is in Christ Iesus,

2 To Timothie *my* dearely beloued sonne : grace, mercie, *and* peace from God the Father, and Christ Iesus our Lord.

3 I thanke God, whom I serue from *my* forefathers with pure conscience, that without ceasing I haue remembrance of thee in my prayers night and day,

4 Greatly desiring to see thee, being mindfull of thy teares, that I may bee filled with ioy,

5 When I call to remembrance the vnfained faith that is in thee, which dwelt first in thy grandmother Lois, and thy mother Eunice : and I am perswaded that in thee also.

6 Wherefore I put thee in remembrance, that thou stirre vp the gift of God which is in thee, by the putting on of my hands.

7 For God hath not giuen vs the spirit of feare, but of power, of loue, and of a sound minde.

8 Bee not thou therefore ashamed of the testimony of our Lord, nor of me his prisoner, but bee thou partaker of the afflictions of the Gospel according to the power of God,

9 Who hath saued vs, and called vs with an holy calling, not according to our workes, but according to his owne purpose and grace, which was giuen vs in Christ Iesus, before the world began,

10 But is now made manifest by the appearing of our Sauiour Iesus Christ, who hath abolished death, and hath brought life and immortalitie to light, through the Gospel :

11 Whereunto I am appointed a Preacher, and an Apostle, and a teacher of the Gentiles.

12 For the which cause I also suffer these things ; neuerthelesse, I am not ashamed : for I know whom I haue ‖ beleeued, and I am perswaded that he is able to keepe that which I haue committed vnto him against that day. ‖ *Or, trusted*

13 Holde fast the fourme of sound words, which thou hast heard of mee, in faith and loue, which is in Christ Iesus.

14 That good thing which was committed vnto thee, keepe, by the holy Ghost which dwelleth in vs.

15 This thou knowest, that all they which are in Asia be turned away from me, of whom are Phygellus and Hermogenes.

16 The

16 The Lord giue mercie vnto the house of Onesiphorus, for hee oft refreshed mee, and was not ashamed of my chaine.

17 But when he was in Rome, hee sought mee out very diligently, and found *me*.

18 The Lord grant vnto him, that he may finde mercie of the Lord in that day : And in how many things hee ministred vnto mee at Ephesus, thou knowest very well.

CHAP. II.

1 He is exhorted againe to constancie and perseuerance, and to doe the duetie of a faithfull seruant of the Lord in diuiding the word aright, and staying prophane and vaine bablings. 17 Of Hymeneus and Philetus. 19 The foundation of the Lord is sure. 22 Hee is taught whereof to beware, and what to follow after, and in what sort the seruant of the Lord ought to behaue himselfe.

Or, by.

Hou therefore, my sonne, be strong in the grace that is in Christ Iesus.

2 And the things that thou hast heard of mee ||among many witnesses, the same commit thou to faithfull men, who shall be able to teach others also.

3 Thou therefore indure hardnesse, as a good souldier of Iesus Christ.

4 No man that warreth, intangleth himselfe with the affaires of *this* life, that hee may please him who hath chosen him to be a souldier.

5 And if a man also striue for masteries, *yet* is hee not crowned except hee striue lawfully.

Or, the husbandman labouring first, must be partaker of the fruites.

6 || The husbandman that laboureth, must bee first partaker of the fruites.

7 Consider what I say, and the Lord giue thee vnderstanding in all things.

8 Remember that Iesus Christ of the seede of Dauid, was raised from the dead, according to my Gospel :

9 Wherein I suffer trouble as an euill doer, *euen* vnto bonds : but the word of God is not bound.

10 Therefore I indure all things for the elects sakes, that they may also obtaine the saluation which is in Christ Iesus, with eternall glory.

11 *It is* a faithfull saying : for if we bee dead *with him*, wee shall also liue *with him*.

12 If we suffer, we shall also reigne *with him :* if wee denie him, hee also will denie vs.

13 If we beleeue not, *yet* he abideth faithfull, he cannot denie himselfe.

14 Of these things put *them* in remembrance, charging *them* before the Lord, that they striue not about words to no profite, *but* to the subuerting of the hearers.

15 Studie to shewe thy selfe approued vnto God, a workman that needeth not to be ashamed, rightly diuiding the word of trueth.

16 But shun profane and vaine bablings, for they will increase vnto more vngodlinesse.

17 And their word will eate as doth a ||canker : of whom is Hymeneus and Philetus.

|| Or, gangrene.

18 Who concerning the trueth haue erred, saying that the resurrection is past alreadie, and ouerthrow the faith of some.

19 Neuerthelesse the foundation of God standeth ||sure, hauing the seale, the Lord knoweth them that are his. And, let euery one that nameth the Name of Christ, depart from iniquitie.

|| Or, steady.

20 But in a great house, there are not onely vessels of gold, and of siluer, but also of wood, & of earth : and some to honour, and some to dishonour.

21 If a man therefore purge himselfe from these, he shal be a vessell vnto honour, sanctified, and meete for the Masters vse, and prepared vnto euery good worke.

22 Flie also youthfull lusts : but follow righteousnesse, faith, charitie, peace with them that call on the Lord out of a pure heart.

23 But foolish and vnlearned questions auoid, knowing that they doe gender strifes.

24 And the seruant of the Lord must not striue : but bee gentle vnto all men, apt to teach, ||patient,

|| Or, forbearing.

25 In meekenesse instructing those that oppose themselues, if God peraduenture will giue them repentance to the acknowledging of the trueth.

26 And that they may †recouer themselues out of the snare of the deuill, who are †taken captiue by him at his will.

† Gr. awake.

† Gr. taken aliue.

CHAP. III.

1 Hee aduertiseth him of the times to come, 6 describeth the enemies of the trueth, 10 pro-

propoundeth vnto him his owne example, 16 and commendeth the holy Scriptures.

His know also, that in the last dayes perillous times shall come.

2 For men shall bee louers of their owne selues, couetous, boasters, proude, blasphemers, disobedient to parents, vnthankfull, vnholy,

3 Without naturall affection, trucebreakers, ||false accusers, incontinent, fierce, despisers of those that are good,

|| *Or, makebates.*

4 Traitours, heady, high minded, louers of pleasures more then louers of God,

5 Hauing a forme of godlinesse, but denying the power thereof : from such turne away.

6 For of this sort are they which creep into houses, and leade captiue silly women laden with sinnes, led away with diuers lusts,

7 Euer learning, and neuer able to come to the knowledge of the trueth.

8 Now as Iannes and Iambres withstood Moses, so do these also resist the trueth : men of corrupt mindes, ||reprobate concerning the faith.

|| *Or, of no iudgement.*

9 But they shal proceede no further: for their folly shall be manifest vnto all *men*, as theirs also was.

10 But ||thou hast fully knowen my doctrine, maner of life, purpose, faith, long suffering, charitie, patience,

|| *Or, thou hast been a diligent follower of.*

11 Persecutions, afflictions which came vnto me at Antioch, at Iconium, at Lystra, what persecutions I indured : but out of them all the Lord deliuered me.

12 Yea, and all that will liue godly in Christ Iesus, shall suffer persecution.

13 But euill men and seducers shall waxe worse and worse, deceiuing, and being deceiued.

14 But continue thou in the things which thou hast learned, and hast been assured of, knowing of whome thou hast learned *them*.

15 And that from a childe thou hast knowen the holy Scriptures, which are able to make thee wise vnto saluation through faith which is in Christ Iesus.

16 All Scripture *is* giuen by inspiration of God, & *is* profitable for doctrine, for reproofe, for correction, for instrution in righteousnesse,

17 That the man of God may be perfect, ||throughly furnished vnto all good workes.

|| *Or, perfected.*

CHAP. IIII.

1 Hee exhorteth him to doe his duety with all care and diligence, 6 certifieth him of the neerenesse of his death, 9 willeth him to come speedily vnto him, and to bring Marcus with him, and certaine other things which he wrote for, 14 warneth him to beware of Alexander the smith, 16 informeth him what had befallen him at this first answering, 19 and soone after hee concludeth.

 Charge *thee* therefore before God, and the Lord Iesus Christ, who shall iudge the quicke and the dead at his appearing, and his kingdome :

2 Preach the word, be instant in season, out of season, reprooue, rebuke, exhort with all long suffering & doctrine.

3 For the time wil come when they will not endure sound doctrine, but after their owne lusts shall they heape to themselues teachers, hauing itching eares :

4 And they shall turne away their eares from the trueth, and shall be turned vnto fables.

5 But watch thou in all things, indure afflictions, doe the worke of an Euangelist, ||make full proofe of thy ministery.

|| *Or, fulfil*

6 For I am now readie to bee offered, and the time of my departure is at hand.

7 I haue fought a good fight, I haue finished my course, I haue kept the faith.

8 Hencefoorth there is layde vp for me a crowne of righteousnesse, which the Lord the righteous iudge shall giue me at that day : and not to me only, but vnto them also that loue his appearing.

9 Doe thy diligence to come shortly vnto me :

10 For Demas hath forsaken me, hauing loued this present world, and is departed vnto Thessalonica : Crescens to Galatia, Titus vnto Dalmatia.

11 Onely Luke is with me. Take Marke and bring him with thee : for he is profitable to me for the ministerie.

12 And Tychicus haue I sent to Ephesus.

13 The cloke that I left at Troas with

withı Carpus, when thou commest, bring *with thee*, but especially the parchments.

14 Alexander the Coppersmith did mee much euill, the Lord reward him according to his works.

15 Of whom bee thou ware also, for he hath greatly withstood ||our words.

|| Or, our ʒreachings.

16 At my first answere no man stood with mee, but all men forsooke mee : *I pray God* that it may not bee laid to their charge.

17 Notwithstanding the Lord stood with me, and strengthened me, that by me the preaching might be fully knowen, and that all the Gentiles might heare : and I was deliuered out of the mouth of the Lyon.

18 And the Lord shall deliuer mee from euery euill worke, and will pre-serue me vnto his heauenly kingdome; to whom *bee* glory for euer, and euer. Amen.

19 Salute Prisca and Aquila, and the houshold of Onesiphorus.

20 Erastus abode at Corinth : but Trophimus haue I left at Miletum sicke.

21 Doe thy diligence to come before winter. Eubulus greeteth thee, and Pudens, and Linus, and Claudia, and all the brethren.

22 The Lord Iesus Christ *bee* with thy spirit. Grace *be* with you. Amen.

¶ The second Epistle vnto Timotheus, ordeined the first Bishop of the Church of the Ephesians, was written from Rome, when Paul was brought before Nero the second time.

¶ THE EPISTLE OF
Paul to Titus.

CHAP. I.

1 For what end Titus was left in Crete. 6 How they that are to bee chosen ministers, ought to bee qualified. 11 The mouthes of euill teachers to bee stopped : 12 and what manner of men they bee.

Aul a seruant of God, and an Apostle of Iesus Christ, according to the Faith of Gods Elect, and the acknowledging of the trueth which is after godlinesse,

|| Or, for.

2 ||In hope of eternall life, which God that cannot lie, promised before the world began :

3 But hath in due times manifested his word through preaching, which is committed vnto mee according to the commandement of God our Sauiour :

4 To Titus mine owne Sonne after the common faith, Grace, mercie, and peace from God the Father, and the Lord Iesus Christ our Sauiour.

5 For this cause left I thee in Crete, that thou shouldest set in order the things that ||are wanting, and ordaine Elders in euery citie, as I had appointed thee.

|| Or, left vndone.

6 If any be blamelesse, the husband of one wife, hauing faithfull children, not accused of riot, or vnruly.

7 For a Bishop must be blamcles, as the steward of God : not selfewilled, not soone angry, not *giuen to wine, no striker, not giuen to filthie lucre,

* 1. Tim. 3. 6.

8 But a louer of hospitality, a louer of ||good men, sober, iust, holy, temperate,

|| Or, good things.

9 Holding fast the faithfull word, ||as hee hath beene taught, that he may bee able by sound doctrine, both to exhort and to conuince the gainsayers.

|| Or, in teaching.

10 For there are many vnruly and vaine talkers and deceiuers, specially they of the circumcision :

11 Whose mouthes must be stopped, who subuert whole houses, teaching things which they ought not, for filthie lucres sake.

12 One

12 One of themselues, *euen* a Prophet of their owne, said : The Cretians are alway lyers, euill beasts, slow bellies.

13 This witnesse is true : wherefore rebuke them sharpely that they may be sound in the faith ;

14 Not giuing heede to Iewish fables, and commandements of men that turne from the trueth.

15 Vnto the pure all things are pure, but vnto them that are defiled, and vnbeleeuing, is nothing pure : but euen their mind and conscience is defiled.

16 They professe that they know God; but in workes they deny him, being abominable, and disobedient, and ‖ *Or, voide of iudgment.* vnto euery good worke ‖reprobate.

CHAP. II.

1 Directions giuen vnto Titus both for his doctrine and life. 9 Of the duetie of seruants, and in generall of all Christians.

Vt speake thou the things which become sound doctrine :

‖ *Or, vigilant* 2 That the aged men be ‖sober, graue, temperate, sound in faith, in charitie, in patience.

‖ *Or, holy women.* 3 The aged women likewise that *they be* in behauiour as becommeth ‖holinesse, not ‖false accusers, not giuen to much wine, teachers of good things,

‖ *Or, makebates.*

‖ *Or, wise.* 4 That they may teach the young women to bee ‖sober, to loue their husbands, to loue their children,

5 *To be* discreet, chaste, keepers at home, good, obedient to their own husbands, that the word of God bee not blasphemed.

6 Yong men likewise exhort, to bee ‖sober minded.

‖ *Or, discreet*

7 In all things shewing thy selfe a patterne of good workes : in doctrine *shewing* vncorruptnesse, grauity, sinceritie,

8 Sound speech that cannot be condemned, that hee that is of the contrarie part, may bee ashamed, hauing no euill thing to say of you.

9 *Exhort* seruants to be obedient vnto their own masters, and to please *them* well in all things, not ‖answering againe :

‖ *Or, gainesaying.*

10 Not purloyning, but shewing all good fidelitie, that they may adorne the doctrine of God our Sauiour in all things.

‖ *Or, that bringeth saluation to all men, hath appeared.*

11 For the grace of God ‖that brin-

geth saluatiō, hath appeared to all men,

12 Teaching vs that denying vngodlinesse and worldly lusts we should liue soberly, righteously and godly in this present world,

13 Looking for that blessed hope, and the glorious appearing of the great God, and our Sauiour Iesus Christ,

14 Who gaue himselfe for vs, that he might redeeme vs from all iniquitie, and purifie vnto himselfe a peculiar people, zealous of good workes.

15 These things speake and exhort, and rebuke with all authoritie. Let no man despise thee.

CHAP. III.

1 Titus is yet further directed by Paul, both concerning the things he should teach, and not teach. 10 He is willed also to reiect obstinate Heretikes : 12 which done, hee appointeth him both time and place, wherein hee should come vnto him, & so concludeth.

Vt them in minde to bee subiect to Principalities & Powers, to obey magistrates, to be ready to euery good worke,

2 To speake euill of no man, to bee no brawlers, *but* gentle, shewing all meekenesse vnto all men.

3 For we our selues also were sometimes foolish, disobedient, deceiued, seruing diuers lusts and pleasures, liuing in malice and enuy, hatefull, *and* hating one another.

4 But after that the kindnesse and ‖loue of God our Sauiour toward man appeared,

‖ *Or, pitie*

5 Not by workes of righteousnesse which wee haue done, but according to his mercy he saued vs, by the washing of regeneration, and renewing of the holy Ghost,

6 Which hee shed on vs †abundantly, through Iesus Christ our Sauiour :

† *Gr. richly.*

7 That being iustified by his grace, we should bee made heires according to the hope of eternall life.

8 *This is* a faithfull saying, and these things I will that thou affirme constantly, that they which haue beleeued in God, might be carefull to maintaine good works : these things are good and profitable vnto men.

9 But auoyd foolish questions, and genealogies, and contentions, and striuings about the lawe ; for they are vnprofitable and vaine.

10 A

10 A man that is an heretike, after the first and second admonition, reiect:

11 Knowing that hee that is such, is subuerted, and sinneth, being condemned of himselfe.

12 When I shall send Artemas vnto thee, or Tychicus, be diligent to come vnto mee to Nicopolis : for I haue determined there to winter.

13 Bring Zenas the Lawyer, and Apollos, on their iourney diligently,

that nothing be wanting vnto them.

14 And let ours also learne to ‖maintaine good workes for necessarie vses, that they be not vnfruitfull.

‖Or, profeſſe honest trades.

15 All that are with mee salute thee. Greete them that loue vs in the faith. Grace be with you all. Amen.

¶ It was written to Titus ordeined the first Bishop of the Church of the Cretians, from Nicopolis of Macedonia.

¶ THE EPISTLE OF
Paul to Philemon.

4 Hee reioyceth to heare of the faith and loue of Philemon, 9 Whom he desireth to forgiue his seruant Onesimus, and louingly to receiue him againe.

Aul a prisoner of Iesus Christ, & Timothie our brother vnto Philemon our dearely beloued, and fellow labourer,

2 And to our beloued Apphia, and Archippus our fellow Souldier, and to the Church in thy house.

3 Grace to you, and peace from God our Father, and the Lord Iesus Christ.

4 I thanke my God, making mention of thee alwayes in my prayers,

5 Hearing of thy loue, and faith, which thou hast toward the Lord Iesus, and toward all Saints :

6 That the communication of thy faith may become effectuall by the acknowledging of euery good thing, which is in you in Christ Iesus.

7 For wee haue great ioy and consolation in thy loue, because the bowels of the Saints are refreshed by thee, brother.

8 Wherefore, though I might bee much bolde in Christ to enioyne thee that which is conuenient ;

9 Yet for loues sake I rather beseech thee, being such a one as Paul the aged, and now also a prisoner of Iesus Christ.

10 I beseech thee for my sonne Onesimus, whome I haue begotten in my bonds,

11 Which in time past was to thee vnprofitable : but now profitable to thee and to me :

12 Whom I haue sent againe : thou therfore receiue him, that is mine owne bowels.

13 Whome I would haue reteined with mee, that in thy stead hee might haue ministred vnto me in the bonds of the Gospel.

14 But without thy minde would I doe nothing, that thy benefite should not bee as it were of necessitie, but willingly.

15 For perhaps hee therefore departed for a season, that thou shouldest receiue him for euer :

16 Not now as a seruant, but aboue a seruant, a brother beloued, specially to mee, but how much more vnto thee, both in the flesh, and in the Lord ?

17 If thou count mee therefore a partner, receiue him as my selfe.

18 If hee hath wronged thee, or oweth *thee ought*, put that on mine account.

19 I Paul haue written it with mine own hand, I will repay it : albeit I doe not say to thee how thou owest vnto me,

me, euen thine owne selfe besides:

20 Yea, brother, let mee haue ioy of thee in the Lord : refresh my bowles in the Lord.

21 Hauing confidence in thy obedience, I wrote vnto thee, knowing that thou wilt also doe more then I say.

22 But withall prepare mee also a lodging : for I trust that through your prayers I shall be giuen vnto you.

23 There salute thee Epaphras, my fellow prisoner in Christ Iesus :

24 Marcus, Aristarchus, Demas, Lucas, my fellow labourers.

25 The grace of our Lord Iesus Christ *be* with your spirit. Amen.

¶ Written from Rome to Philemon, by Onesimus a seruant.

¶THE EPISTLE OF PAVL
the Apoftle to the Hebrewes.

CHAP. I.

1 Christ in these last times comming to vs from the Father, 4 is preferred aboue the Angels, both in Person and Office.

Od who at sundry times, and in diuers manners, spake in time past vnto the Fathers by the Prophets, 2 Hath in these lastdayes spoken vnto vs by *his* Sonne, whom he hath appointed heire of all things, by whom also he made the worlds,

" Wis. 7. 26.

3 * Who being the brightnesse of his glory, and the expresse image of his person, and vpholding all things by the word of his power, when hee had by himselfe purged our sinnes, sate down on ŷ right hand of the Maiestie on high,

4 Being made so much better then the Angels, as hee hath by inheritance obtained a more excellent Name then they.

5 For vnto which of the Angels said he at any time, Thou art my sonne, this day haue I begotten thee? And again, I will be to him a Father, and he shall be to me a Sonne.

6 And againe, when he bringeth in the first begotten into the world, hee saith, And let all the Angels of God worship him.

7 And of the Angels he saith : Who maketh his Angels spirits, and his ministers a flame of fire.

8 But vnto the Sonne, *he saith,* Thy throne, O God, *is* for euer and euer : a scepter of †righteousnesse *is* the scepter of thy kingdome.

† *Gr. rightnesse, or straightnes.*

9 Thou hast loued righteousnesse, and hated iniquitie, therefore God, *euen* thy God hath anointed thee with the oyle of gladnesse aboue thy fellowes.

10 And, *thou Lord in the beginning hast layed the foundation of the earth: and the heauens are the works of thine hands.

* Psa. 102. 2 esa. 34. 4.

11 They shall perish, but thou remainest : and they all shal waxe old as doth a garment.

12 And as a vesture shalt thou fold them vp, and they shall be changed, but thou art the same, and thy yeeres shall not faile?

13 But to which of the Angels said hee at any time, *Sit on my right hand, vntill I make thine enemies thy footstoole?

* Psal. 110. 1. matt. 22. 44.

14 Are they not all ministring spirits, sent foorth to minister for them, who shall be heires of saluation?

CHAP. II.

1 Wee ought to bee obedient to Christ Iesus, 5 and that because he vouchsafed to take our nature vpon him, 14 as it was necessarie.

Herefore we ought to giue the more earnest heede to the things which we haue heard, lest at any time we should †let them slip.

† *Gr. run ou as leaking vessels.*

2 For

2 For if the word spoken by Angels was stedfast, and euery transgression and disobedience receiued a iust recompense of reward :

3 How shall we escape, if we neglect so great saluation, which at the first began to be spoken by the Lord, *and* was confirmed vnto vs by them that heard *him*,

4 God also bearing them witnesse, both with signes & wonders, and with diuers miracles, ||and gifts of the holy Ghost, according to his owne will ?

5 For vnto the Angels hath he not put in subiection the world to come, whereof we speake.

6 But one in a certaine place testified, saying : * What is man, that thou art mindfull of him : or the Sonne of man that thou visitest him ?

7 Thou madest him a ||little lower then the Angels, thou crownedst him with glory and honor, and didst set him ouer the workes of thy hands.

8 Thou hast put all things in subiection vnder his feete. For in that he put all in subiection vnder him, hee left nothing that is not put vnder him. But now wee see not yet all things put vnder him.

9 But wee see Iesus, who was made a little lower then the Angels, ||for the suffering of death, crowned with glory and honour, that hee by the grace of God should taste death for euery man.

10 For it became him, for whom are all things, and by whom are all things, in bringing many sonnes vnto glory, to make the Captaine of their saluation perfect through sufferings.

11 For both hee that sanctifieth, and they who are sanctified, are all of one : for which cause he is not ashamed to cal them brethren,

12 Saying, I will declare thy Name vnto my brethren, in the midst of the Church will I sing praise vnto thee.

13 And againe, * I will put my trust in him : and againe, * Behold, I, and the children which God hath giuen me.

14 Forasmuch then as the children are partakers of flesh and blood, he also himselfe likewise took part of the same, that through death hee might destroy him that had the power of death, that is, the deuill :

15 And deliuer them, who through feare of death were all their life time subiect to bondage.

16 For verely he † tooke not on him *the nature of* Angels: but he tooke on *him* the seed of Abraham.

17 Wherfore in all things it behooued him to bee made like vnto his brethren, that he might be a mercifull and faithfull high Priest, in things pertaining to God, to make reconciliation for the sinnes of the people.

18 For in that he himselfe hath suffered, being tempted, he is able to succour them that are tempted.

CHAP III.

1 Christ is more worthy then Moses, 7 therefore if we beleeue not in him, we shalbe more worthy punishmēt then hard hearted Israel.

Herfore holy brethrē, partakers of the heauenly calling, consider the Apostle and high Priest of our profession Christ Iesus,

2 Who was faithfull to him that † appointed him, as also Moses was faithfull in all his house.

3 For this *man* was counted worthy of more glory then Moses, in as much as he who hath builded the house, hath more honour then the house.

4 For euery house is builded by some man, but hee that built all things is God.

5 And Moses verely was faithfull in all his house as a seruant, for a testimonie of those things which were to be spoken after.

6 But Christ as a Sonne ouer his owne house, whose house are wee, if we hold fast the confidence, and the reioycing of the hope firme vnto the end.

7 Wherfore as the holy Ghost saith, * To day if ye will heare his voyce,

8 Harden not your hearts, as in the prouocation, in the day of temptation in the wildernesse :

9 When your fathers tempted me, prooued me, and saw my works fourty yeeres.

10 Wherefore I was grieued with that generation, and sayd, They doe alway erre in their hearts, and they haue not knowen my wayes.

11 So I sware in my wrath : † they shall not enter into my rest.

12 Take heed, brethren, lest there be in any of you an euill heart of vnbeleefe, in departing from the liuing God.

13 But

‖ Or, distributions.

* Psal. 8. 4.

‖ Or, a little while inferiour to.

‖ Or, by.

* Psal. 18. 2.
* Esay 8. 18.

† Gr. hee taketh not hold of Angels, but of the seede of Abraham he taketh hold.

† Gr. made, 1. Sam. 12. 6

Psal. 95. 7.

† Gr. if they shall enter.

13 But exhort one another dayly, while it is called To day, least any of you be hardned through the deceitfulnesse of sinne.

14 For wee are made partakers of Christ, if we hold the beginning of our confidence stedfast vnto the end.

15 Whilest it is sayd, To day if yee will heare his voice, harden not your hearts, as in the prouocation.

16 For some when they had heard, did prouoke : howbeit not all that came out of Egypt by Moses.

17 But with whom was he grieued fourty yeeres ? *was it* not with them that had sinned, whose carcases fell in the wildernesse ?

18 And to whom sware he that they should not enter into his rest, but to them that beleeued not ?

19 So we see that they could not enter in, because of vnbeleefe.

CHAP. IIII.

1 The rest of Christians is attained by faith. 12 The power of Gods word. 14 By our High Priest Iesus the sonne of God, subiect to infirmities, but not sinne, 16 wee must and may go boldly to the throne of grace.

Et vs therefore feare, lest a promise being left *vs*, of entring into his rest, any of you should seeme to come short of it.

2 For vnto vs was the Gospel preached, as well as vnto thē : but †the word preached did not profit them, ‖not being mixed with faith in them that heard *it*.

† *Gr. the word of hearing.*
‖ *Or, because they were not vnited by faith to.*

3 For we which haue beleeued do enter into rest, as hee said, As I haue sworne in my wrath, if they shall enter into my rest, although the works were finished from the foundation of the world.

4 For he spake in a certaine place of the seuenth day on this wise : And God did rest the seuenth day from all his works.

5 And in this place againe : If they shall enter into my rest.

6 Seeing therfore it remaineth that some must enter therein, and they to whom ‖it was first preached, entred not in because of vnbeleefe :

‖ *Or, the Gospel was first preached.*

7 Againe, hee limiteth a certaine day, saying in Dauid, To day, after so long a time ; as it is saide, To day if ye will heare his voyce, harden not your hearts.

8 For if ‖Iesus had giuen them rest, then would he not afterward haue spoken of another day.

‖ *That is, Iosuah.*

9 There remaineth therefore a ‖rest to the people of God.

‖ *Or, keepin of a Sabbath*

10 For he that is entred into his rest, hee also hath ceased from his owne works, as God *did* from his.

11 Let vs labour therefore to enter into that rest, lest any man fall after the same example of ‖vnbeleefe.

‖ *Or, disobe dience.*

12 For the word of God is quicke and powerfull, and sharper then any two edged sword, pearcing euen to the diuiding asunder of soule and spirit, and of the ioynts and marrowe, and is a discerner of the thoughts and intents of the heart.

13 Neither is there any creature that is not manifest in his sight : but all things *are* naked, and opened vnto the eyes of him with whome wee haue to doe.

14 Seeing then that wee haue a great high Priest, that is passed into the heauens, Iesus the Sonne of God, let vs hold fast *our* profession.

15 For wee haue not an high Priest which cannot bee touched with the feeling of our infirmities : but was in all points tempted like as we are, *yet* without sinne.

16 Let vs therefore come boldly vnto the throne of grace, that wee may obtaine mercy, and finde grace to helpe in time of need.

CHAP. V.

1 The authoritie and honour of our Sauiours Priesthood. 11 Negligence in the knowledge thereof is reproued.

Or euery high Priest taken from among men, is ordeined for men in things *pertaining* to God, that hee may offer both giftes & sacrifices for sins.

2 Who ‖can haue compassion on the ignorant, and on them that are out of the way, for that he himselfe also is compassed with infirmitie.

‖ *Or, can rea sonably beare with.*

3 And by reason heereof hee ought as for the people, so also for himselfe, to offer for sinnes.

4 And no man taketh this honour vnto himselfe, but hee that is called of God, as *was* Aaron.

5 So also, Christ glorified not himselfe, to bee made an High Priest : but hee

hee that saide vnto him, Thou art my Sonne, to day haue I begotten thee.

6 As he saith also in another place, Thou *art* a Priest for euer after the order of Melchisedec.

7 Who in the dayes of his flesh, when hee had offered vp prayers and supplications, with strong crying and teares, vnto him that was able to saue him from death, and was heard, ||in that he feared.

|| Or, for his pietie.

8 Though hee were a Sonne, yet learned hee obedience, by the things which he suffered:

9 And being made perfect, he became the authour of eternall saluation vnto all them that obey him,

10 Called of God an high Priest after the order of Melchisedec:

11 Of whom we haue many things to say, and hard to be vttered, seeing ye are dull of hearing.

12 For when for the time yee ought to bee teachers, yee haue neede that one teach you againe which be the first principles of the Oracles of God, and are become such as haue need of milke, and not of strong meat.

13 For euery one that vseth milke, is †vnskilful in the word of righteousnes: for he is a babe.

† Gr. hath no experience.

14 But strong meate belongeth to them that are ||of full age, *euen* those who by reason ||of vse haue their senses exercised to discerne both good and euil.

|| Or, perfect.
|| Or, of an habite, or perfection.

CHAP. VI.

1 Hee exhorteth not to fall backe from the faith, 11 But to bee stedfast, 12 diligent, and patient to waite vpon God, 13 because God is most sure in his promise.

|| Or, the word of the beginning of Christ.

Hereforeleauing the||principles of the doctrine of Christ, let vs goe on vnto perfection, not laying againe the foundation of repentance from dead workes, and of faith towards God,

2 Of the doctrine of Baptismes, and of laying on of hands, and of resurrection of the dead, and of eternall iudgement.

3 And this will we doe, if God permit.

4 For it is impossible for those who were once inlightned, and haue tasted of the heauenly gift, and were made partakers of the holy Ghost,

5 And haue tasted the good word of God, and the powers of the world to come;

6 If they shall fall away, to renue them againe vnto repentance : seeing they crucifie to themselues the Sonne of God afresh, and put him to an open shame.

7 For the earth which drinketh in the raine that commeth oft vpon it, and bringeth forth herbes meet for them ||by whome it is dressed, receiueth blessing from God.

|| Or, for.

8 But that which beareth thornes and briers, is reiected, and is nigh vnto cursing, whose end is to be burned.

9 But beloued, wee are perswaded better things of you, and things that accompany saluation, though we thus speake.

10 For God is not vnrighteous, to forget your worke and labour of loue, which yee haue shewed toward his Name, in that yee haue ministred to the Saints, and doe minister.

11 And wee desire, that euery one of you doe shewe the same diligence, to the full assurance of hope vnto the ende :

12 That yee be not slothfull, but followers of them, who through faith and patience inherite the promises.

13 For when God made promise to Abraham, because hee could sweare by no greater, he sware by himselfe,

14 Saying, Surely, blessing I will blesse thee, and multiplying I wil multiply thee.

15 And so after he had patiently indured, he obtained the promise.

16 For men verily sweare by the greater, and an oath for confirmation is to them an end of all strife.

17 Wherein God willing more abundantly to shewe vnto the heyres of promise the immutabilitie of his counsell, †confirmed *it* by an oath :

† Gr.interposed himselfe by an oath.

18 That by two immutable things, in which it was impossible for God to lye, wee might haue a strong consolation, who haue fled for refuge to lay hold vpon the hope set before vs.

19 Which *hope* we haue as an anker of the soule both sure and stedfast, and which entreth into that within the vaile,

20 Whither the forerunner is for vs entrrd; *euen* Iesus, made an high Priest for euer after the order of Melchisedec.

CHAP.

CHAP. VII.

1 Christ Iesus is a Priest after the order of Melchisedec, 11 And so, farre more excellent then the Priests of Aarons order.

OR this Melchisedec king of Salem, Priest of the most high God, who met Abraham returning from the slaughter of the Kings, and blessed him :

2 To whom also Abraham gaue a tenth part of all : first being by interpretation king of righteousnesse, and after that also king of Salem, which is, king of peace.

3 † Without father, without mother, †without descent, hauing neither beginning of dayes nor end of life : but made like vnto the Sonne of God, abideth a Priest continually.

† Gr. without pedigree.

4 Now consider how great this man was, vnto whō euen the patriarch Abraham gaue the tenth of the spoiles.

5 And verily they that are of the sonnes of Leui, who receiue the office of the Priesthood, haue a commandement to take Tithes of the people according to the Law, that is of their brethren, though they come out of the loines of Abraham :

6 But he whose ‖descent is not counted from them, receiued tithes of Abraham, and blessed him that had the promises.

‖ Or, pedigree.

7 And without all contradiction, the lesse is blessed of the better.

8 And here men that die receiue tithes : but there hee *receiueth them*, of whom it is witnessed that he liueth.

9 And as I may so say, Leui also who receiueth tithes, payed tithes in Abraham.

10 For hee was yet in the loynes of his Father when Melchisedec met him.

11 If therefore perfection were by the Leuiticall Priesthood (for vnder it the people receiued the Law) what further neede was there, that another Priest should rise after the order of Melchisedec, and not bee called after the order of Aaron ?

12 For the Priesthood being chaunged, there is made of necessitie a change also of the Law.

13 For hee of whom these things are spoken, pertaineth to another tribe, of which no man gaue attendance at the Altar.

14 For it is euident that our Lorde sprang out of Iuda, of which tribe Moses spake nothing cōcerning Priesthood.

15 And it is yet farre more euident : for that after the similitude of Melchisedec there ariseth another Priest,

16 Who is made not after the Law of a carnall commandement, but after the power of an endles life.

17 For hee testifieth ; Thou art a Priest for euer, after the order of Melchisedec.

18 For there is verily a disanulling of the commandement going before, for the weakenesse and vnprofitablenesse thereof.

19 For the Law made nothing perfect, ‖but the bringing in of a better hope *did* : by the which wee draw nigh vnto God.

‖ Or, but it was the bringing in.

20 And in as much as not without an othe *he was made Priest*,

21 (For those *Priests* were made ‖without an oath : but this with an oath, by him ȳ said vnto him, * The Lord sware and wil not repent, thou art a Priest for euer after the order of Melchisedec)

‖ Or, without swearing of an othe.
* Psa. 110.

22 By so much was Iesus made a suertie of a better Testament.

23 And they truely were many Priests, because they were not suffered to continue by reason of death.

24 But this man because hee continueth euer, hath an ‖vnchangeable Priesthood.

‖ Or, which passeth not from one to another.

25 Wherefore he is able also to saue them ‖to the vttermost, that come vnto God by him, seeing hee euer liueth to make intercession for them.

‖ Or, euermore.

26 For such an high Priest became vs, *who is* holy, harmelesse, vndefiled, separate from sinners, and made higher then the heauens.

27 Who needeth not daily, as those high Priests, to offer vp sacrifice, first for his owne sins and then for the peoples : for this he did once, when he offered vp himselfe.

28 For the Law maketh men high Priests which haue infirmitie, but the word of the othe which was since the Law, *maketh* the Sonne, who is †consecrated for euermore.

† Gr. perfected.

CHAP. VIII.

1 By the eternall Priesthood of Christ, the Leuiticall Priesthood of Aaron is abolished. 7 And the temporall Couenant with the Fathers, by the eternal Couenant of the Gospel.
Now

Ow of the things which we haue spoken, *this is the* summe : wee haue such an high Priest, who is set on the right hand of the throne of the Maiestie in the heauens:

2 A minister ||of the Sanctuary, and of the true Tabernacle, which the Lord pitched, and not man.

3 For euery high Priest is ordeined to offer gifts and sacrifices : wherefore it is of necessitie that this man haue somewhat also to offer.

4 For if he were on earth, he should not bee a Priest, seeing that ||there are Priests that offer gifts according to the Law :

5 Who serue vnto the example and shadow of heauenly things, as Moses was admonished of God when he was about to make the Tabernacle. For see (saith he) that thou make all things according to the paterne shewed to thee in the mount.

6 But now hath he obtained a more excellent ministerie, by how much also he is the Mediatour of a better ||Couenant, which was established vpon better promises.

7 For if that first *Couenant* had bene faultles, then should no place haue bene sought for the second.

8 For finding fault with them, hee saith, Behold, the dayes come (saith the Lord) when I will make a new couenant with the house of Israel, and the house of Iudah.

9 Not according to the Couenant that I made with their fathers, in the day when I tooke them by the hand to lead them out of the land of Egypt, because they continued not in my Couenant, and I regarded them not, saith the Lord.

10 For this is the Couenant that I will make with the house of Israel after those dayes, saith the Lord : *I will +put my Lawes into their minde, and write them ||in their hearts : and I will be to them a God, and they shalbe to me a people.

11 And they shall not teach euery man his neighbour, and euery man his brother, saying, Know the Lord : For all shall know me, from the least to the greatest.

12 For I will be mercifull to their vnrighteousnes, and their sins & their iniquities will I remember no more.

13 In that he saith, A new *Couenant,* he hath made the first olde. Now that which decayeth and waxeth old, is readie to vanish away.

CHAP. IX.

1 The description of the rites and bloody sacrifices of the Law, 11 farre inferiour to the dignitie and perfection of the blood and sacrifice of Christ.

Hen verily the first *Couenant* had also ||ordinances of diuine Seruice, and a worldly Sanctuary.

2 For there was a Tabernacle made, the first, wherein was the Candlesticke, and the Table, and the Shewbread, which is called ||the Sanctuarie.

3 And after the second vaile, the Tabernacle which is called ŷ Holiest of all:

4 Which had the golden Censor, and the Arke of the Couenant ouerlayed round about with gold, wherein was the Golden pot that had Manna, and Aarons rod that budded, and the Tables of the Couenant.

5 And ouer it the Cherubims of glory shadowing the Mercyseat; of which we cannot now speake particularly.

6 Now when these things were thus ordained, the Priestes went alwayes into the first Tabernacle, accomplishing the seruice of God.

7 But into the second *went* the high Priest alone once euery yeere, not without blood, which he offered for himselfe, and for the errors of the people.

8 The holy Ghost this signifying, that the way into the Holiest of all, was not yet made manifest, while as the first Tabernacle was yet standing :

9 Which *was* a figure for the time then present, in which were offred both gifts and sacrifices, that could not make him that did the seruice perfect, as pertayning to the conscience,

10 *Which stood* onely in meates and drinkes, and diuers washings, and ||carnall ordinances imposed on them vntill the time of reformation.

11 But Christ being come an high Priest of good things to come, by a greater and more perfect Tabernacle, not made with hands, that is to say, not of this building :

12 Neither by the blood of Goats and Calues : but by his owne blood hee entred in once into the Holy place, hauing

Margin notes
|| *Or, of holy things.*

|| *Or, they are Priests.*

|| *Or, Testament.*

* Ier. 31. 33.
† *Gr. giue.*
|| *Or, vpon.*

|| *Or, ceremonies.*

‖ *Or, holy.*

|| *Or, rites, or ceremonies.*

uing obtained eternall redemption *for vs.*

13 For if the blood of Bulls, and of goats, and the ashes of an heifer sprinkling the vncleane, sanctifieth to the purifying of the flesh:

14 How much more shall the blood of Christ, who through the eternal Spirit, offered himselfe without ||spot to God, purge your conscience from dead workes, to serue the liuing God?

Or, fault.

15 And for this cause hee is the Mediatour of the New Testament, that by meanes of death, for the redemption of the transgressions *that were* vnder the first Testament, they which are called, might receiue the promise of eternall inheritance.

16 For where a Testament is, there must also of necessitie ||bee the death of the Testatour.

Or, bee brought in.

17 For a Testament is of force after men are dead : otherwise it is of no strength at all whilest the Testatour liueth.

18 Whereupon, neither the first *Testament* was ||dedicated without blood.

Or, purified.

19 For when Moses had spoken euery precept to all the people according to the Law, he tooke the blood of Calues and of Goates, with water and ||scarlet wooll, and hysope, and sprinckled both the booke and all the people,

Or, purple.

20 Saying, This is the blood of the Testament which God hath enioyned vnto you.

21 Moreouer, hee sprinkled with blood both the Tabernacle, and all the vessels of the Ministery.

22 And almost all things are by the Law purged with blood : and without shedding of blood is no remission.

23 It was therefore necessary that the patterns of things in the heauens should bee purified with these, but the heauenly things themselues with better sacrifices then these.

24 For Christ is not entred into the Holy places made with handes, which are the figures of the true, but into heauen it selfe, now to appeare in the presence of God for vs.

25 Nor yet that he should offer himselfe often, as the high Priest entreth into the Holy place, euery yeere with blood of others:

26 For then must hee often haue suffered since the foundation of the world: but now once in the end of the world,

hath he appeared to put away sinne by the sacrifice of himselfe.

27 And as it is appointed vnto men once to die, but after this the Iudgement:

28 So Christ was once offered to beare the sinnes of many, & vnto them that looke for him shall hee appeare the second time without sinne, vnto saluation.

CHAP. X.

1 The weakenesse of the Law sacrifices. 10 The sacrifice of Christs body once offered, 14 for euer, hath taken away sinnes. 19 An exhortation to hold fast the faith, with patience and thanksgiuing.

Or the Law hauing a shadow of good things to come, and not the very Image of the things, can neuer with those sacrifices which they offered yeere by yeere continually, make the commers thereunto perfect :

2 For then would they not haue ceased to be offered, because that the worshippers once purged, should haue had no more conscience of sinnes?

3 But in those sacrifices *there is* a remembrance againe *made* of sinnes euery yeere.

4 For it is not possible that the blood of Bulles and of Goats, should take away sinnes.

5 Wherefore when hee commeth into the world, he saith, Sacrifice and offering thou wouldest not, but a body hast thou ||prepared mee :

Or, thou hast fitted me.

6 In burnt offerings, and sacrifices for sinne thou hast had no pleasure :

7 Then said I, Loe, I come. (In the volume of the booke it is written of me) to doe thy will, O God.

8 Aboue when hee said, Sacrifice, and offering, and burnt offerings, and offering for sinne thou wouldest not, neither hadst pleasure therein, which are offered by the Law :

9 Then said he, Loe, I come to doe thy will (O God :) He taketh away the first, that he may establish the second.

10 By the which will wee are sanctified, through the offering of the body of Iesus Christ once for all.

11 And euery Priest standeth dayly ministring and offering oftentimes the same sacrifices which can neuer take away sinnes.

12 But

12 But this man after he had offered one sacrifice for sinnes for euer, sate downe on the right hand of God,

13 From henceforth expecting till his enemies be made his footstoole.

14 For by one offering hee hath perfected for euer them that are sanctified.

15 Whereof the holy Ghost also is a witnesse to vs : for after that he had said before,

16 This is the Couenant that I wil make with them after those dayes, saith the Lord : I will *put my Lawes into their hearts, and in their mindes will I write them :

*Iere. 31. 33.

17 And their sinnes and iniquities will I remember no more.

18 Now, where remission of these is, there is no more offering for sinne.

19 Hauing therefore, brethren, ‖boldnesse to enter into the Holiest by the blood of Iesus,

‖ Or, libertie.

20 By a new and liuing way which hee hath ‖consecrated for vs, through the vaile, that is to say, His flesh :

‖ Or, new made.

21 And *hauing* an high Priest ouer the house of God :

22 Let vs drawe neere with a true heart in full assurance of faith, hauing our hearts sprinkled from an euill conscience, and our bodies washed with pure water.

23 Let vs hold fast the profession of our faith without wauering (for he is faithfull that promised)

24 And let vs consider one another to prouoke vnto loue, and to good workes :

25 Not forsaking the assembling of our selues together, as the manner of some is : but exhorting one another, and so much the more, as ye see the day approching.

26 For if we sinne wilfully after that we haue receiued the knowledge of the trueth, there remaineth no more sacrifice for sinnes,

27 But a certaine fearefull looking for of iudgement, and fiery indignation, which shall deuoure the aduersaries.

28 Hee that despised Moses Lawe, died without mercy, vnder two or three witnesses.

29 Of how much sorer punishment *suppose ye*, shall hee be thought worthy, who hath troden vnder foote ỹ Sonne of God, and hath counted the blood of the couenant wherwith he was sanctified, an vnholy thing, and hath done de-

spite vnto the spirit of grace ?

30 For we know him that hath said, *Vengeance belongeth vnto me, I wil recompence, saith the Lord : and again, The Lord shall iudge his people.

*Deut. 32. 35. Rom. 12. 19.

31 It is a fearefull thing to fall into the hands of the liuing God.

32 But call to remembrance the former dayes, in which after yee were illuminated, ye indured a great fight of afflictions :

33 Partly whilest ye were made a gazing stocke both by reproches & afflictions, and partly whilest ye became companions of them that were so vsed.

34 For yee had compassion of me in my bonds, and tooke ioyfully the spoyling of your goods, knowing in your selues that yee haue in heauen a better and an induring substance.

35 Cast not away therfore your confidence which hath great recompense of reward.

36 For ye haue need of patience, that shall after ye haue done the will of God ye might receiue the promise.

37 For yet a litle while, and he that shall come will come, and will not tary.

38 Now the iust shall liue by faith : but if any man drawe backe, my soule shall haue no pleasure in him.

39 But wee are not of them who draw backe vnto perdition : but of them that beleeue, to the sauing of the soule.

CHAP. XI.

1 What faith is. 6 Without faith we cannot please God. 7 The worthy fruits thereof in the Fathers of old time.

Ow faith is the ‖substance of things hoped for, the euidence of things not seen.

‖ Or, ground, or confidence

2 For by it the Elders obtained a good report.

3 Through faith we vnderstand that the worlds were framed by the word of God, so that things which are seene were not made of things which doe appeare.

4 By faith Abel offered vnto God a more excellent sacrifice then Kain, by which he obtained witnes that he was righteous, God testifying of his gifts : and by it he being dead, ‖yet speaketh.

‖ Or, is yet spoken of.

5 By faith Enoch was translated, that he should not see death, and was not found, because God had translated him : For before his translation he had this testimonie, that he pleased God.

6 But

6 But without faith it is impossible to please him: for hee that commeth to God, must beleeue that he is, and that he is a rewarder of them that diligently seeke him.

7 By faith Noah being warned of God of things not seene as yet, ||moued with feare, prepared an Arke to the sauing of his house, by the which he condemned the world, and became heire of the righteousnesse which is by faith.

|| Or, being wary.

8 By faith Abraham when he was called to goe out into a place which hee should after receiue for an inheritance, obeyed, and he went out, not knowing whither he went.

9 By faith hee soiourned in the land of promise, as in a strange countrey, dwelling in tabernacles with Isaac and Iacob, the heires with him of the same promise.

10 For hee looked for a citie which hath foundations, whose builder and maker is God.

11 Through faith also Sara her selfe receiued strength to conceiue seede, and was deliuered of a child when she was past age, because she iudged him faithful who had promised.

12 Therfore sprang there euen of one, and him as good as dead, *so many* as the starres of the skie in multitude, and as the sand which is by the sea shore innumerable.

13 These all died †in faith, not hauing receiued the promises, but hauing seene them a farre off, and were perswaded of *them*, and embraced *them*, and confessed that they were strangers and pilgrims on the earth.

† Gr. according to faith.

14 For they that say such things, declare plainly that they seeke a countrey.

15 And truly if they had been mindfull of that *countrey*, from whence they came out, they might haue had opportunitie to haue returned:

16 But now they desire a better countrey, that is, an heauenly: wherefore God is not ashamed to bee called their God: for he hath prepared for thē a city.

17 By faith Abraham when he was tried, offered vp Isaac: and he that had receiued the promises, offered vp his onely begotten sonne,

18 ||Of whom it was said, That, in Isaac shall thy seed be called:

|| Or, To.

19 Accounting that God was able to raise *him* vp, euen from the dead: from whence also he receiued him in a figure.

20 By faith Isaac blessed Iacob and Esau concerning things to come.

21 By faith Iacob when hee was a dying, blessed both the sonnes of Ioseph, and worshipped *leaning* vpon the top of his staffe.

22 By faith, Ioseph when hee died, ||made mention of the departing of the children of Israel: and gaue commandement concerning his bones.

|| Or, remembred.

23 By faith, Moses when hee was borne was hid three moneths of his parents, because they saw he was a proper childe, and they not afraid of the Kings commandement.

24 By faith Moses when hee was come to yeeres, refused to bee called the sonne of Pharaohs daughter,

25 Chusing rather to suffer affliction with the people of God, then to enioy the pleasures of sinne for a season:

26 Esteeming the reproch ||of Christ greater riches then the treasures in Egypt: for he had respect vnto the recompense of the reward.

|| Or, for Christ.

27 By faith hee forsooke Egypt, not fearing the wrath of the king: for he indured, as seeing him who is inuisible.

28 Through faith he kept the Passeouer, and the sprinkling of blood, lest he that destroyed the first borne, should touch them.

29 By faith they passed through the red sea, as by drie land: which the Egyptians assaying to do, were drowned.

30 By faith the walles of Iericho fell downe, after they were compassed about seuen dayes.

31 By faith the harlot Rahab perished not with them ||that beleeued not, when shee had receiued the spies with peace.

|| Or, that were disobedient.

32 And what shall I more say? for the time would faile mee to tell of Gideon, and of Barak, and of Sampson, and of Iephthah, of Dauid also and Samuel, and of the Prophets:

33 Who through faith subdued kingdomes, wrought righteousnesse, obteined promises, stopped the mouthes of Lions,

34 Quenched the violence of fire, escaped the edge of the sword, out of weakenesse were made strong, waxed valiant in fight, turned to flight the armies of the aliens.

35 Women receiued their dead raised to life againe: and others were *tortured, not accepting deliuerance, that they

* 2. Macc. 7. 7.

they might obtaine a better resurrection.

36 And others had triall of cruell mockings and scourgings, yea moreouer, of bonds and imprisonment.

37 They were stoned, they were sawen asunder, were tempted, were slaine with the sword : they wandered about in sheepskinnes, and goat skins, being destitute, afflicted, tormented.

38 Of whome the world was not worthy : they wandered in deserts, and in mountains, and in dennes and caues of the earth.

39 And these all hauing obtained a good report through faith, receiued not the promise :

40 God hauing ‖prouided some better thing for vs, that they without vs, should not be made perfect.

Or, fore-ene.

CHAP. XII.

1 An exhortation to constant faith, patience, and godlinesse. 22 A commendation of the New Testament aboue the old.

Wherefore, seeing wee also are compassed about with so great a cloude of witnesses, let vs lay aside euery weight, & the sinne which doth so easily beset vs, and let vs runne with patience vnto the race that is set before vs.

2 Looking vnto Iesus the ‖Authour and finisher of *our* faith, who for the ioy that was set before him, endured the crosse, despising the shame, and is set down at the right hand of the throne of God.

Or, begin-r.

3 For consider him that indured such contradiction of sinners against himselfe, lest ye be wearied and faint in your mindes.

4 Yee haue not yet resisted vnto blood, striuing against sinne.

5 And ye haue forgotten the exhortation which speaketh vnto you as vnto children, My sonne, despise not thou the chastening of the Lord, nor faint when thou art rebuked of him.

6 For whome the Lord loueth hee chasteneth, and scourgeth euery sonne whom he receiueth.

7 If yee endure chastening, God dealeth with you as with sonnes : for what sonne is he whom the father chasteneth not ?

8 But if ye be without chastisement, whereof all are partakers, then are ye bastards, and not sonnes.

9 Furthermore, wee haue had fathers of our flesh, which corrected vs, and we gaue them reuerence : shall we not much rather bee in subiection vnto the Father of Spirits, and liue ?

10 For they verily for a fewe dayes chastened vs after their owne pleasure, but hee for our profit, that we might bee partakers of his holinesse.

11 Now no chastening for the present seemeth to be ioyous, but grieuous : neuerthelesse, afterward it yeeldeth the peaceable fruite of righteousnesse, vnto them which are exercised thereby.

12 Wherefore lift vp the handes which hang downe , and the feeble knees.

13 And make ‖straight paths for your feete, lest that which is lame bee turned out of the way, but let it rather bee healed.

‖ *Or, euen.*

14 Followe peace with all men, and holinesse, without which no man shall see the Lord :

15 Looking diligently, lest any man ‖faile of the grace of God, lest any roote of bitternesse springing vp, trouble *you*, and thereby many be defiled :

‖ *Or, fal from*

16 Lest there bee any fornicatour, or profane person, as Esau, who for one morsell of meat sold his birthright.

17 For yee know how that afterward when hee would haue inherited the blessing, he was reiected : for hee found no ‖place of repentance, though he sought it carefully with teares.

‖ *Or, way to change his minde.*

18 For yee are not come vnto the mount that might be touched, and that burned with fire, nor vnto blacknesse, and darknes, and tempest,

19 And the sound of a trumpet, and the voyce of wordes, which *voyce* they that heard, entreated that the word should not bee spoken to them any more.

20 For they could not indure that which was commaunded : And if so much as a beast touch the Mountaine, it shall be stoned, or thrust thorow with a dart.

21 And so terrible was the sight, that Moses sayde, I exceedingly feare, and quake.

22 But ye are come vnto mount Sion, and vnto the citie of the liuing God the heauenly Ierusalem, and to an innumerable company of Angels :

23 To

23 To the generall assembly, and Church of the first borne which are ||written in heauen, and to God the Iudge of all, and to the spirits of iust men made perfect:

‖ Or, inrouled.

24 And to Iesus the mediatour of the new ||Couenant, and to the blood of sprinckling, that speaketh better things then that of Abel.

‖ Or, Testament.

25 See that yee refuse not him that speaketh : for if they escaped not who refused him that spake on earth, much more shall not we *escape* if wee turne away from him that *speaketh* from heauen.

26 Whose voice then shooke the earth, but now he hath promised, saying, Yet once more I shake not the earth onely, but also heauen.

27 And this *word* Yet once more, signifieth the remouing of those things that ||are shaken, as of things that are made, that those things which cannot be shaken may remaine.

‖ Or, may be shaken.

28 Wherefore wee receiuing a kingdome which cannot bee moued, ||let vs haue grace, whereby wee may serue God acceptably, with reuerence and godly feare.

‖ Or, let vs hold fast.

29 For our God is a consuming fire.

CHAP. XIII.

1 Diuers admonitions, as to Charitie, 4 To honest life, 5 To auoide couetousnes, 7 To regarde Gods preachers, 9 To take heed of strange doctrines, 10 To confesse Christ, 16 To giue almes, 17 To obey gouernors, 18 To pray for the Apostle. 20 The Conclusion.

Et brotherly loue continue.

2 Bee not forgetfull to entertaine strangers, for thereby some haue entertayned Angels vnawares.

3 Remember them that are in bonds, as bound with them, *and* them which suffer aduersitie, as being your selues also in the body.

4 Mariage *is* honorable in all, and the bed vndefiled : but whoremongers, and adulterers God will iudge.

5 Let your conuersation bee without couetousnesse : and be content with such things as yee haue. For hee hath said, *I will neuer leaue thee, nor forsake thee.

* Ios. 1. 5.

6 So that wee may boldly say, The Lord is my helper, and I will not feare what man shall doe vnto me.

7 Remember them which ||haue the rule ouer you, who haue spoken vnto you the word of God, whose faith follow, considering the end of their conuersation.

‖ Or, are your guides

8 Iesus Christ the same yesterday, and to day, and for euer.

9 Be not caried about with diuers and strange doctrines : for it is a good thing that the heart be established with grace, not with meates, which haue not profited them that haue beene occupied therein.

10 Wee haue an altar whereof they haue no right to eate, which serue the Tabernacle.

11 For the bodies of those beasts, whose blood is brought into the Sanctuary by the high Priest for sinne, are burnt without the campe.

12 Wherefore Iesus also, that hee might sanctifie the people with his own blood, suffered without the gate.

13 Let vs goe foorth therefore vnto him without the campe, bearing his reproch.

14 *For here haue we no continuing citie, but we seeke one to come.

* Mich. 2.

15 By him therefore let vs offer the sacrifice of praise to God continually, that is, the fruit of *our* lippes, †giuing thankes to his Name.

† Gr. confessing to.

16 But to doe good, and to communicate forget not, for with such sacrifices God is well pleased.

17 Obey them that ||haue the rule ouer you, and submit your selues : for they watch for your soules, as they that must giue account, that they may doe it with ioy, and not with griefe : for that is vnprofitable for you.

‖ Or, guide

18 Pray for vs : for we trust wee haue a good conscience in all things, willing to liue honestly.

19 But I beseech you the rather to doe this, that I may be restored to you the sooner.

20 Now the God of peace, that brought againe from the dead our Lord Iesus, that great shepheard of the sheepe, through the blood of the euerlasting ||Couenant,

‖ Or, Testament.

21 Make you perfect in euery good worke to doe his will, ||working in you that which is well pleasing in his sight, through Iesus Christ, to whom be glorie for euer and euer. Amen.

‖ Or, doing

22 And I beseech you brethren, suffer

fer the word of exhortation, for I haue written a letter vnto you in few words.

23 Know yee, that our brother Timothie is ſet at libertie, with whom if he come shortly, I will see you.

24 Salute all them that haue the rule ouer you, and al the Saints. They of Italy salute you.

25 Grace be with you all. Amen.

¶ Written to the Hebrewes, from Italy, by Timothie.

¶THE GENERALL
Epiſtle of Iames.

CHAP. I.

Wee are to reioyce vnder the Crosse, 5 To aske patience of God, 13 And in our trials not to impute our weakenesse, or sinnes vnto him, 19 but rather to hearken to the word, to meditate in it, and to doe thereafter. 26 Otherwise men may seeme, but neuer be truely religious.

Ames a seruant of God, and of the Lord Iesus Christ, to the twelue Tribes which are scattered abroad, greeting.

2 My brethren, count it all ioy when ye fall into diuers temptations,

3 Knowing *this*, that the trying of your faith worketh patience,

4 But let patience haue *her* perfect worke, that ye may be perfect, and entier, wanting nothing.

5 If any of you lacke wisedome, let him aske of God, that giueth to all men liberally, and vpbraideth not : and it shalbe giuen him.

6 But let him aske in faith, nothing wauering : for he that wauereth is like a waue of the sea, driuen with the wind, and tossed.

7 For let not that man thinke that he shall receiue any thing of the Lord.

8 A double minded man *is* vnstable in all his wayes.

‖ Or, glory. 9 Let the brother of low degree, ‖reioyce in that he is exalted :

10 But the rich, in that hee is made low : because as the floure of the grasse he shall passe away.

11 For the Sunne is no sooner risen with a burning heate, but it withereth the grasse ; and the flowre thereof falleth, and the grace of the fashion of it perisheth : so also shall the rich man fade away in his wayes.

12 Blessed is the man that endureth temptation : for when hee is tried, hee shall receiue the crowne of life, which the Lord hath promised to them that loue him.

13 Let no man say when he is tempted, I am tempted of God : for God cannot be tempted with ‖euill, neither tempteth he any man. *‖ Or, euils.*

14 But euery man is tempted, when hee is drawen away of his owne lust, and entised.

15 Then when lust hath conceiued, it bringeth forth sinne : and sinne, when it is finished, bringeth forth death.

16 Doe not erre, my beloued brethren.

17 Euery good gift, and euery perfect gift is from aboue, & commeth downe from the Father of lights, with whom is no variablenesse, neither shadow of turning.

18 Of his owne will begate hee vs, with the word of Trueth, that wee should bee a kinde of first fruites of his creatures.

19 Wherefore my beloued brethren, let euery man bee swift to heare, slow to speake, slow to wrath.

20 For the wrath of man worketh not the righteousnesse of God.

21 Wherefore lay apart all filthinesse, and superfluitie of naughtinesse, & receiue with meeknesse the engrafted word, which is able to saue your soules.

22 But be ye doers of the word, and not

not hearers onely, deceiuing your owne selues.

23 For if any be a hearer of the word and not a doer, he is like vnto a man beholding his naturall face in a glasse :

24 For hee beholdeth himselfe, and goeth his way, and straightway forgetteth what maner of man he was.

25 But who so looketh into the perfect Law of libertie, and continueth *therein*, he being not a forgetfull hearer, but a doer of the worke, this man shall be blessed in his ||deed.

|| *Or, doing.*

26 If any man among you seeme to be religious, & bridleth not his tongue, but deceiueth his owne heart, this mans religion is vaine.

27 Pure religion and vndefiled before God and the Father, is this, to visit the fatherlesse and widowes in their affliction, *and* to keepe himselfe vnspotted from the world.

CHAP. II.

It is not agreeable to Christian profession to regard the rich, and to despise the poore brethren : 13 rather wee are to be louing, and mercifull : 14 And not to boast of faith where no deedes are, 17 which is but a dead faith, 19 the faith of deuils, 21 not of Abraham, 25 and Rahab.

Y brethren, haue not the faith of our Lord Iesus Christ *the Lord* of glorie, with respect of persons.

2 For if there come vnto your †assembly a man with a gold ring, in goodly apparel, and there come in also a poore man, in vile raiment :

† *Gr. Syna-gogue.*

3 And yee haue respect to him that weareth the gay clothing, and say vnto him, Sit thou here ||in a good place : and say to the poore, Stand thou there, or sit here vnder my footstoole :

|| *Or, well, or seemely.*

4 Are yee not then partiall in your selues, and are become iudges of euill thoughts ?

5 Hearken, my beloued brethren, Hath not God chosen the poore of this world, rich in faith, and heires of || the kingdome, which hee hath promised to them that loue him ?

|| *Or, that.*

6 But yee haue despised the poore. Doe not rich men oppresse you, and draw you before the Iudgement seats ?

7 Doe not they blaspheme that worthy Name, by the which ye are called ?

8 If ye fulfil the royall Law, accor-

ding to the Scripture, Thou shalt loue thy neighbour as thy selfe, ye doe well.

9 But if ye haue respect to persons, ye commit sinne, *and* are conuinced of the Law, as transgressours.

10 For whosoeuer shall keepe the whole Law, & yet offend in one point, he is guilty of all.

11 For he †that said, Doe not commit adultery ; sayd also, Do not kill. Now if thou commit no adultery, yet if thou kill, thou art become a transgressour of the Law.

† *Or, that Law which said.*

12 So speake ye, and so doe, as they that shall bee iudged by the Law of libertie.

13 For he *shall haue* iudgement without mercie, that hath shewed no mercy, & mercie ||reioyceth against iudgement.

|| *Or, gloriet*

14 What doth it profit, my brethren, though a man say hee hath faith, and haue not workes ? can faith saue him ?

15 If a brother or sister be naked, and destitute of dayly foode,

16 And one of you say vnto them, Depart in peace, be you warmed & filled : notwithstanding ye giue them not those things which are needfull to the body : what doth it profit ?

17 Euen so faith, if it hath not works, is dead being †alone.

† *Gr. by it selfe.*

18 Yea, a man may say, Thou hast faith, and I haue workes : shew mee thy faith ||without thy workes, and I will shew thee my faith by my workes.

|| *Some copies reade, by thy workes.*

19 Thou beleeuest that there is one God, thou doest well : the deuils also beleeue, and tremble.

20 But wilt thou knowe, O vaine man, that faith without workes is dead ?

21 Was not Abraham our father iustified by works, when hee had offered Isaac his sonne vpon the altar ?

22 ||Seest thou how faith wrought with his works, and by works was faith made perfect ?

|| *Or, thou seest.*

23 And the Scripture was fullfiled which saith, *Abraham beleeued God, and it was imputed vnto him for righteousnes : and he was called the friend of God.

* Gen. 15. rom. 4. 3. gal. 3. 6.

24 Ye see then, how that by workes a man is iustified, and not by faith only.

25 Likewise also, was not Rahab the harlot iustified by works, when she had recciued the messengers, and had sent them out another way ?

26 For as the body without the ||spirit is

|| *Or, breath*

rit is dead, so faith without workes is dead also.

CHAP. III.

1 We are not rashly or arrogantly to reproue others : 5 but rather to bridle the tongue, a little member, but a powerfull instrument of much good, and great harme. 13 They who be truely wise, be milde, and peaceable, without enuying, and strife.

MY brethren, bee not many masters, knowing that we shall receiue the greater ||condemnation.

|| Or, iudgement.

2 For in many things we offend all. If any man offend not in word, the same is a perfect man, and a-ble also to bridle the whole body.

3 Behold, we put bittes in the hor-ses mouthes, that they may obey vs, and we turne about their whole body.

4 Behold also the ships, which though they be so great, and are driuen of fierce windes, yet are they turned a-bout with a very small helme, whither-soeuer the gouernour listeth.

5 Euen so the tongue is a little mem-ber, and boasteth great things : behold, how great ||a matter a litle fire kindleth.

|| Or, wood.

6 And the tongue is a fire, a world of iniquitie : so is the tongue amongst our members, that it defileth the whole body, and setteth on fire the course of nature, and it is set on fire of hell.

7 For euery †kind of beasts, and of birds, and of serpents, and things in the sea, is tamed, and hath been tamed of †mankind.

† Gr. nature.

† Gr. nature of man.

8 But the tongue can no man tame, *it is* an vnruly euill, ful of deadly poyson.

9 Therewith blesse wee God, euen the Father : and therewith curse wee men, which are made after the simili-tude of God.

10 Out of the same mouth proceedeth blessing and cursing : my brethren, these things ought not so to be.

11 Doeth a fountaine send foorth at the same ||place sweet water and bitter?

|| Or, hole.

12 Can ẙ figtree, my brethren, beare o-liue berries? either a vine, figs ? so *can* no fountaine both yeeld salt water & fresh.

13 Who is a wise man and indued with knowledge amongst you ? let him shew out of a good conuersation his workes with meekenes of wisedome.

14 But if ye haue bitter enuying and strife in your hearts, glory not, and lie not against the trueth.

15 This wisedome descendeth not from aboue, but *is* earthly, ||sensuall, deuilish.

|| Or, natural

16 For where enuying and strife is, there is † confusion, and euery euill worke.

† Gr. tumult or vnquietnesse.

17 But the wisedome that is from aboue, is first pure, then peaceable, gentle, and easie to be intreated, full of mercy, and good fruits, ||without par-tialitie, and without hypocrisie.

|| Or, without wrangling.

18 And the fruit of righteousnesse is sowen in peace, of them that make peace.

CHAP. IIII.

1 Wee are to striue against couetousnesse, 4 intemperance, 5 pride, 11 detraction, and rash iudgement of others : 13 and not to bee confident in the good successe of worldly businesse, but mindfull euer of the vncer-taintie of this life, to commit our selues, and all our affaires to Gods prouidence.

FRom whence come warres and ||fightings among you ? come they not hence, euen of your ||lusts, that warre in your members ?

|| Or, braw-lings.

|| Or, plea-sures.

2 Ye lust, and haue not : yee kill, and desire to haue, and cannot obtaine : yee fight and warre, yet yee haue not, be-cause ye aske not.

3 Ye aske and receiue not, because ye aske amisse, that yee may consume it vpon your ||lusts.

|| Or, plea-sures.

4 Ye adulterers, and adulteresses, know yee not that the friendship of the world is enmity with God ? whosoeuer therefore will be a friend of the world, is the enemy of God.

5 Doe ye thinke that the Scripture saith in vaine, the spirit that dwelleth in vs lusteth ||to enuy ?

|| Or, enui-ously.

6 But he giueth more grace, where-fore he saith, *God resisteth the proude, but giueth grace vnto the humble.

* Pro. 3. 34.
1. pet. 5. 5.

7 Submit your selues therefore to God : resist the deuill, and hee will flee from you.

8 Draw nigh to God, and hee will draw nigh to you : cleanse your hands ye sinners, and purifie your hearts yee double minded.

9 Bee afflicted, and mourne, and weepe : let your laughter be turned to mourning, and your ioy to heauinesse.

10 Humble your selues in the sight of the Lord, and he shall lift you vp.

11 Speake

11 Speake not euill one of another (brethren:) he that speaketh euill of his brother, and iudgeth his brother, speaketh euill of the Law, and iudgeth the Law: but if thou iudge the Law, thou art not a doer of the Law, but a iudge.

12 There is one Lawgiuer, who is able to saue, and to destroy: who art thou that iudgest another?

13 Goe to now ye that say, To day or to morrow wee will goe into such a city and continue there a yere, and buy, and sell, and get gaine:

14 Whereas yee know not what *shalbe on the morow: *for what is your life? ‖ It is euen a vapour that appeareth for a litle time, and then vanisheth away.

* Pro. 27. 1.
‖ Or, for it is.

15 For that yee ought to say, if the Lord will, we shall liue, and doe this, or that.

16 But now yee reioyce in your boastings: all such reioycing is euill.

17 Therefore to him that knoweth to doe good, and doth it not, to him it is sinne.

CHAP. V.

1 Wicked rich men are to feare Gods vengeance. 7 We ought to be patient in afflictions, after the example of the Prophets, and Iob: 12 to forbeare swearing, 13 to pray in aduersitie, to sing in prosperitie: 16 to acknowledge mutually our seuerall faults, to pray one for another, 19 and to reduce a straying brother to the trueth.

Oe to now, yee rich men, weepe and howle for your miseries that shall come vpon you.

2 Your riches are corrupted, and your garments motheaten:

3 Your gold and siluer is cankered, and the rust of them shall bee a witnesse against you, and shall eate your flesh as it were fire: ye haue heaped treasure together for the last dayes.

4 Beholde, the hire of the labourers which haue reaped downe your fieldes, which is of you kept backe by fraud, cryeth: and the cryes of them which haue reaped, are entred into the eares of the Lord of Sabaoth.

5 Yee haue liued in pleasure on the earth, and bene wanton: ye haue nourished your hearts, as in a day of slaughter:

6 Yee haue condemned, *and* killed

the iust, *and* he doth not resist you.

7 ‖ Be patient therefore, brethren, vnto the comming of the Lord: behold, the husbandman waiteth for the precious fruit of the earth, and hath long patience for it, vntill hee receiue the early and latter raine.

‖ Or, be long patient, or suffer with longpatience

8 Be yee also patient; stablish your hearts: for the comming of the Lorde draweth nigh.

9 ‖ Grudge not one against another, brethren, lest ye be condemned: behold, the Iudge standeth before the doore.

‖ Or, groane or grieue not.

10 Take, my brethren, the Prophets, who haue spoken in the Name of the Lord, for an example of suffering affliction, and of patience.

11 Beholde, wee count them happie which endure. Ye haue heard of the patience of Iob, and haue seene the end of the Lord: that the Lord is very pitifull and of tender mercie.

12 But aboue all things, my brethren, sweare not, neither by heauen, neither by the earth, neither by any other othe: but let your yea, be yea, and your nay, nay: lest yee fall into condemnation.

13 Is any among you afflicted? let him pray. Is any merry? let him sing Psalmes.

14 Is any sicke among you? let him call for the Elders of the Church, and let them pray ouer him, anointing him with oyle in the Name of the Lord:

15 And the prayer of Faith shall saue the sicke, and the Lord shall raise him vp: and if hee haue committed sinnes, they shall be forgiuen him.

16 Confesse your faults one to another, and pray one for another, that yee may bee healed: the effectuall feruent prayer of a righteous man auaileth much.

17 Elias was a man subiect to like passions as we are, and he prayed ‖ earnestly that it might not raine: and it rained not on the earth by the space of three yeeres and sixe monethes.

‖ Or, in his prayer.

18 And hee prayed againe, and the heauen gaue raine, and the earth brought foorth her fruit.

19 Brethren, if any of you doe erre from the trueth, and one conuert him,

20 Let him know, that hee which conuerteth the sinner from the errour of his way, shall saue a soule from death, and shall hide a multitude of sinnes.

THE

¶THE FIRST EPISTLE
generall of Peter.

CHAP. I.

Hee blesseth God for his manifolde spirituall graces: 10 shewing that the saluation in Christ is no newes, but a thing prophesied of olde: 13 And exhorteth them accordingly to a godly conuersation, forasmuch as they are now borne anew by the word of God.

Eter an Apostle of Iesus Christ, to the strangers scattred thorowout Pontus, Galatia, Cappadocia, Asia, and Bithynia,

2 Elect, according to the foreknowledge of God the Father, through sanctification of the Spirit vnto obedience, and sprinkling of the blood of Iesus Christ : Grace vnto you and peace be multiplied.

3 Blessed be the God and Father of our Lord Iesus Christ, which according to his †abundant mercy, hath begotten vs againe vnto a liuely hope, by the resurrection of Iesus Christ from the dead,

4 To an inheritance incorruptible, and vndefiled, and that fadeth not away, reserued in heauen ||for you,

5 Who are kept by the power of God through faith vnto saluation, ready to be reuealed in the last time.

6 Wherin ye greatly reioyce, though now for a season (if neede bee) yee are in heauinesse through manifolde temptations :

7 That the triall of your faith, being much more precious then of golde that perisheth, though it bee tryed with fire, might be found vnto praise, and honor, and glory, at the appearing of Iesus Christ :

8 Whom hauing not seene, yee loue, in whom though now ye see *him* not, yet beleeuing, ye reioyce with ioy vnspeakeable, and full of glory,

9 Receiuing the ende of your faith, euen the saluation of your soules :

10 Of which saluation the Prophets haue inquired, and searched diligently, who prophesied of the grace *that should come* vnto you,

11 Searching what, or what maner of time the Spirit of Christ which was in them did signifie, when it testified beforehand the suffrings of Christ, and the glory that should follow.

12 Vnto whome it was reuealed, that not vnto themselues, but vnto vs, they did minister the things which are now reported vnto you, by them that haue preached the Gospel vnto you, with the holy Ghost sent downe from heauen, which things the Angels desire to looke into.

13 Wherefore gird vp the loynes of your minde, bee sober, and hope †to the end, for the grace that is to bee brought vnto you at the reuelation of Iesus Christ :

14 As obedient children, not fashioning your selues according to the former lusts, in your ignorance :

15 But as hee which hath called you is holy, so be ye holy in all maner of conuersation ;

16 Because it is written, *Be ye holy, for I am holy.

17 And if ye call on the Father, who without respect of persons iudgeth according to euery mans worke, passe the time of your soiourning here in feare :

18 For as much as ye know that yee were not redeemed with corruptible things, as siluer and golde, from your vaine conuersation *receiued* by tradition from your fathers ;

19 But with the precious blood of Christ, as of a Lambe without blemish and without spot,

20 Who verily was foreordeined before the foundation of the world, but was manifest in these last times for you :

21 Who by him do beleeue in God that raised

† Gr. much.

|| Or, for vs.

† Gr. perfectly.

* Leuit. 11. 44. and 19. 2. and 20. 7.

raiſed him vp from the dead, and gaue him glorie, that your faith and hope might be in God.

22 Seeing yee haue purified your ſoules in obeying the truth through the Spirit, vnto vnfained loue of the brethren : ſee that ye loue one another with a pure heart feruently,

23 Being borne againe, not of corruptible ſeed, but of incorruptible, by the word of God which liueth and abideth for euer.

Or, for that   24 ‖ For all fleſh *is* as graſſe, and all the glory of man as the flowre of graſſe: the graſſe withereth, and the flowre thereof falleth away.

25 But the word of the Lord endureth for euer : & this is the word which by the Goſpel is preached vnto you.

CHAP. II.

He dehorteth them from the breach of charitie; 4 ſhewing that Chriſt is the foudation wherupon they are built. 11 He beſeecheth them also to abſtaine from fleſhly luſtes, 13 To bee obedient to magiſtrates, 18 and teacheth ſeruants how to obey their maſters, 20 patiently ſuffering for well doing after the example of Chriſt.

Herefore laying aſide all malice, and all guile, and hypocriſies, and enuies, and euill ſpeakings,

2 As new borne babes deſire the ſincere milke of the word, that ye may grow thereby,

3 If ſo bee yee haue taſted that the Lord is gracious.

4 To whom comming *as* vnto a liuing Stone, diſallowed in deed of men, but choſen of God, and precious,

Or, be ye built.   5 Ye alſo as liuely ſtones, ‖ are built vp a ſpirituall houſe, an holy Prieſthood to offer vp ſpirituall ſacrifice, acceptable to God by Ieſus Chriſt.

Eſa. 28. 16 pſa. 118. 22 mat. 21. 42 actes 4. 12.   6 Wherefore it is contained in the Scripture, *Beholde, I lay in Sion a chiefe corner ſtone, elect, precious, and he that beleeueth on him, ſhall not be confounded.

Or, he is an honour.   7 Vnto you therfore which beleeue hee is ‖ precious ; but vnto them which be diſobedient, the ſtone which the builders diſallowed, the ſame is made the head of the corner,

Eſa. 8. 14.   8 *And a Stone of ſtumbling, and a Rocke of offence, *euen to them* which ſtumble at the word, being diſobedient, whereunto alſo they were appointed.

9 But yee are a choſen generation, a royall Prieſthood, an holy nation, a ‖ peculiar people, that yee ſhould ſhewe forth the ‖ praiſes of him, who hath called you out of darknes into his marueilous light :

Or, a purchaſed people.   ‖ *Or, vertues*

10 Which in time paſt were not a people, but are now the people of God : *which had not obteined mercie, but now haue obteined mercy.

Oſe. 2. 23.

11 Dearely beloued, I beſeech you as ſtrangers and pilgrimes, abſtaine from fleſhly luſts, which warre againſt the ſoule,

12 Hauing your conuerſation honeſt among the Gentiles, that ‖ whereas they ſpeake againſt you as euill doers, they may by *your* good works which they ſhall behold, glorifie God in the day of viſitation.

‖ *Or, wherin.*

13 Submit your ſelues to euery ordinance of man for the Lordes ſake, whether it be to the King, as ſupreme,

14 Or vnto gouernours, as vnto them that are ſent by him, for the puniſhment of euill doers, and for the praiſe of them that doe well.

15 For ſo is the will of God, that with well doing yee may put to ſilence the ignorance of fooliſh men.

16 As free, and not † vſing your libertie for a cloake of maliciouſneſſe, but as the ſeruants of God.

† *Gr. hauing*

17 ‖ Honour all men. Loue the brotherhood. Feare God. Honour the King.

‖ *Or, eſteeme.*

18 Seruants, be ſubiect to your maſters with al feare, not only to the good and gentle, but alſo to the froward.

19 For this is thanke-worthie, if a man for conſcience toward God endure griefe, ſuffering wrongfully.

20 For what glory is it, if when yee be buffeted for your faults, ye ſhall take it patiently : but if when yee doe well, and ſuffer for it, ye take it patiently, this is ‖ acceptable with God.

‖ *Or, thanke.*

21 For euen hereunto were ye called : becauſe Chriſt alſo ſuffered for ‖ vs, leauing vs an example, that yee ſhould follow his ſteps.

‖ *Some reade, for you.*

22 Who did no ſinne, neither was guile found in his mouth.

23 Who when hee was reuiled, reuiled not againe ; when hee ſuffered, hee threatned not, but ‖ committed *himſelfe* to him that iudgeth righteouſly.

‖ *Or, committed his cauſe.*

24 Who his owne ſelfe bare our ſinnes in his owne body ‖ on the tree,   that

‖ *Or, to.*

that wee being dead to ſinnes, ſhould liue vnto righteouſneſſe, by whoſe ſtripes ye were healed.

25 ¶ For yee were as ſheepe going aſtray, but are now returned vnto the ſhepheard and Biſhop of your ſoules.

CHAP. III.

1 Hee teacheth the duetie of wiues and husbands to each other, 8 exhorting all men to vnitie, and loue, 14 and to ſuffer perſecution. 19 Hee declareth alſo the benefits of Chriſt toward the old world.

Ikewiſe, ye wiues, be in ſubiection to your owne husbands, that if any obey not the word, they alſo may without the word be wonne by the conuerſation of the wiues:

2 While they beholde your chaſte conuerſation *coupled* with feare:

3 Whoſe adorning, let it not bee that outward *adorning*, of plaiting the haire, and of wearing of gold, or of putting on of apparell.

4 But *let it bee* the hidden man of the heart, in that which is not corruptible, *euen the ornament* of a meeke and quiet ſpirit, which is in the ſight of God of great price.

5 For after this manner in the olde time, the holy women alſo who truſted in God adorned themſelues, beeing in ſubiection vnto their owne husbands.

6 Euen as Sara obeyed Abraham, calling him Lord, whoſe † daughters ye are as long as ye doe well, and are not afraid with any amazement.

7 Likewiſe ye husbands, dwel with them according to knowledge, giuing honour vnto the wife as vnto the weaker veſſel, and as being heires together of the grace of life, that your prayers be not hindered.

8 Finally *be ye* all of one minde, hauing compaſſion one of another, ‖loue as brethren, be pitifull, be courteous,

9 Not rendring euill for euill, or railing for railing: but contrarywiſe bleſſing, knowing that yee are thereunto called, that ye ſhould inherite a bleſſing.

10 For hee that will loue life, and ſee good dayes, let him refraine his tongue from euil, and his *lips that they ſpeake no guile:

11 Let him eſchew euil and do good, let him ſeeke peace and enſue it.

12 For the eyes of the Lord *are* ouer the righteous, and his eares are *open* vnto their prayers: but the face of the Lord *is* †againſt them that doe euill.

13 And who is hee that will harme you, if ye bee followers of that which is good?

14 But and if ye ſuffer for righteouſnes ſake, happy *are ye*, and be not *afraid of their terrour, neither be troubled:

15 But ſanctifie the Lord God in your hearts, & *be* ready alwayes to giue an anſwere to euery man that asketh you a reaſon of the hope that is in you, with meekeneſſe and ‖feare:

16 Hauing a good conſcience, that whereas they ſpeake euill of you, as of euill doers, they may bee aſhamed that falſly accuſe your good conuerſation in Chriſt.

17 For it is better, if the will of God be ſo, that yee ſuffer for well doing, then for euill doing.

18 For Chriſt alſo hath once ſuffered for ſinnes, the iuſt for the vniuſt, that he might bring vs to God, being put to death in the fleſh, but quickened by the Spirit.

19 By which alſo he went and preached vnto the ſpirits in priſon,

20 Which ſometime were diſobedient, when once the long-ſuffering of God waited in the dayes of Noah, while the Arke was a preparing: wherein few, that is, eight ſoules were ſaued by water.

21 The like figure whereunto, euen Baptiſme, doth alſo now ſaue vs, (not the putting away of the filth of the fleſh, but the anſwere of a good conſcience toward God,) by the reſurrection of Ieſus Chriſt.

22 Who is gone into heauen, and is on the right hand of God, Angels, and authorities, and powers being made ſubiect vnto him.

CHAP. IIII.

Hee exhorteth them to ceaſe from ſinne by the example of Chriſt, and the conſideration of the generall end, that now approcheth: 12 and comforteth them againſt perſecution.

Oraſmuch then as Chriſt hath ſuffered for vs in the fleſh, arme your ſelues likewiſe with the ſame minde: for hee that hath ſuffered in the fleſh, hath ceaſſed from ſinne:

2 That

† *Or, vpon.*

* Eſa. 8. 12, 13.

‖ *Or, reuerence.*

* *Or, children.*

‖ *Or, louing to the brethren.*

* Pſal. 34. 13.

2 That he no longer should liue the rest of *his* time in the flesh, to the lusts of men, but to the will of God.

3 For the time past of our life may suffice vs to haue wrought the will of the Gentiles, when we walked in lasciuiousnes, lusts, excesse of wine, reuellings, banquetings, and abhominable idolatries.

4 Wherein they thinke it strange, that you runne not with them to the same excesse of riot, speaking euil of you:

5 Who shal giue accompt to him that is ready to iudge the quicke & the dead.

6 For, for this cause was the Gospel preached also to them that are dead, that they might bee iudged according to men in the flesh, but liue according to God in the spirit.

7 But the ende of all things is at hand : be ye therefore sober and watch vnto prayer.

8 And aboue all things haue feruent charitie among your selues: for charity ‖ shall couer the multitude of sinnes.

‖ *Or, will.*

9 Vse hospitalitie one to another without grudging.

10 As euery man hath receiued the gift, *euen so* minister the same one to another, as good stewards of the manifold grace of God.

11 If any man speake, *let him speake* as the oracles of God : if any man minister, let him doe it as of the ability which God giueth, that God in all things may bee glorified through Iesus Christ, to whom be praise and dominion for euer and euer. Amen.

12 Beloued, thinke it not strange concerning the fiery triall, which is to try you, as though some strange thing happened vnto you.

13 But reioyce in as much as yee are partakers of Christes sufferings; that when his glory shalbe reueiled, ye may be glad also with exceeding ioy.

14 If ye be reproched for the Name of Christ, happie *are ye*, for the spirit of glory, and of God resteth vpon you : on their part hee is euill spoken of, but on your part he is glorified.

15 But let none of you suffer as a murtherer, or as a theefe, or as an euill doer, or as a busibody in other mens matters.

16 Yet if any *man suffer* as a Christian, let him not be ashamed, but let him glorifie God on this behalfe.

17 For the time is *come* that iudge-

ment must begin at the house of God : and if it first begin at vs, what shall the ende bee of them that obey not the Gospel of God ?

18 And if the righteous scarcely be saued, where shall the vngodly and the sinner appeare ?

19 Wherfore, let them that suffer according to the will of God, commit the keeping of their soules to him in well doing, as vnto a faithfull Creator.

CHAP. V.

1 He exhorteth the Elders to feede their flocks, 5 the yonger to obey, 8 and all to bee sober, watchfull, and constant in the faith : 9 to resist the cruell aduersarie the deuill.

 He Elders which are among you I exhort, who am also an Elder, and a witnesse of the sufferings of Christ, and also a partaker of the glory that shall be reuealed.

2 Feede the flocke of God ‖ which is among you, taking the ouersight *thereof,* not by constraint, but willingly : not for filthy lucre, but of a ready minde :

‖ *Or, as much as in you is.*

3 Neither as ‖ being lords ouer *Gods* heritage : but being ensamples to the flocke.

‖ *Or, ouerruling.*

4 And when the chiefe shepheard shall appeare, ye shall receiue a crowne of glory that fadeth not away.

5 Likewise ye yonger, submit your selues vnto the elder : yea, all *of you* bee subiect one to another, and bee clothed with humilitie : for God resisteth the proud, and giueth grace to the humble.

6 Humble your selues therefore vnder the mighty hand of God, that hee may exalt you in due time,

7 Casting all your care vpon him, for he careth for you.

8 Be sober, be vigilant : because your aduersary the deuill, as a roaring Lion walketh about, seeking whom he may deuoure.

9 Whom resist stedfast in the faith, knowing that the same afflictions are accomplished in your brethren that are in the world.

10 But the God of all grace who hath called vs into his eternall glory by Christ Iesus, after that ye haue suffered a while, make you perfect, stablish, strengthen, settle you.

11 To him bee glory and dominion for euer and euer. Amen.

12 By Syluanus a faithfull brother vnto

vnto you, (as I suppose) I haue written briefly, exhorting, & testifying, that this is the true grace of God wherein ye stand.

13 The Church that is at Babylon elected, together with you, saluteth you, and *so doth* Marcus my sonne.

14 Greete yee one another with a kisse of charity : Peace bee with you all that are in Christ Iesus. Amen.

¶ THE SECOND EPISTLE
generall of Peter.

CHAP. I.

1 Confirming them in hope of the increase of Gods graces, 5 he exhorteth them by faith, and good workes, to make their calling sure: 12 Whereof hee is carefull to remember them, knowing that his death is at hand : 16 And warneth them to be constant in the faith of Christ, who is the true Sonne of God, by the eye witnesse of the Apostles beholding his Maiestie, and by the testimonie of the Father, and the Prophets.

Imon Peter, a seruant & an Apostle of Iesus Christ, to them that haue obtained like precious Faith with vs, through the righteousnes of God, and our Sauiour Iesus Christ.

2 Grace and peace be multiplied vnto you through the knowledge of God, and of Iesus our Lord,

3 According as his diuine power hath giuen vnto vs all things that *pertaine* vnto life and godlines, through the knowledge of him that hath called vs ‖ to glory and vertue.

Or, by.

4 Whereby are giuen vnto vs exceeding great and precious promises, that by these you might bee partakers of the diuine nature, hauing escaped the corruption that is in the world through lust.

5 And besides this, giuing all diligence, adde to your faith, vertue; and to vertue, knowledge ;

6 And to knowledge, temperance ; and to temperance, patience ; and to patience, godlinesse ;

7 And to godlinesse, brotherly kindnesse ; and to brotherly kindnesse, charitie.

8 For if these things be in you, and abound, they make you that yee shall neither be barren, nor vnfruitfull in the knowledge of our Lord Iesus Christ:

9 But hee that lacketh these things, is blind, and cannot see farre off, and hath forgotten that hee was purged from his old sinnes.

10 Wherefore, the rather, brethren, giue diligence to make your calling and election sure : for if ye doe these things, ye shall neuer fall.

11 For so an entrance shall be ministred vnto you abundantly, into the euerlasting kingdome of our Lord and Sauiour Iesus Christ.

12 Wherefore I wil not be negligent to put you alwayes in remembrance of these things, though yee know them, and be stablished in the present trueth.

13 Yea, I thinke it meete, as long as I am in this tabernacle, to stirre you vp, by putting you in remembrance :

14 Knowing that shortly I must put off this my Tabernacle, euen as *our Lord Iesus Christ hath shewed mee.

* Ioh. 21. 17

15 Moreouer, I will endeuour, that you may bee able after my decease, to haue these things alwayes in remembrance.

16 For wee haue not followed cunningly deuised fables, when wee made knowen vnto you the power and comming of our Lord Iesus Christ, but were eye witnesses of his Maiestie.

17 For hee receiued from God the Father, honour and glory, when there came such a voice to him from the excellent

lent glory, This is my beloued Sonne in whom I am well pleased.

18 And this voice which came from heauen wee heard, when we were with him in the holy mount.

19 We haue also a more sure word of prophecie, whereunto yee doe well that ye take heede, as vnto a light that shineth in a darke place, vntill the day dawne, and the day starre arise in your hearts :

20 Knowing this first, that no prophecie of the Scripture is of any priuate Interpretation :

21 For the prophecie came not ‖ in olde time by the will of man : but holy men of God spake as they were moued by the holy Ghost.

‖ Or, at any time.

CHAP. II.

1 He foretelleth them of false teachers, shewing the impietie, and punishment both of them and their followers : 7 from which the godly shall bee deliuered, as Lot was out of Sodom : 10 and more fully describeth the manners of those prophane, and blasphemous seducers, whereby they may be the better knowen, and auoided.

BVt there were false prophets also among the people, euen as there shall bee false teachers among you, who priuily shall bring in damnable heresies, euen denying the Lord that bought them, and bring vpon themselues swift destruction.

2 And many shall follow their ‖ pernicious wayes, by reason of whom the way of trueth shall be euill spoken of :

‖ Or, lasciuious wayes, as some copies reade.

3 And through couetousnesse shall they with fained words, make marchandise of you, whose iudgement now of a long time lingereth not, and their damnation slumbreth not.

4 For if God spared not the Angels that sinned, but cast them downe to hell, and deliuered them into chaines of darkenesse, to be reserued vnto iudgment :

5 And spared not the old world, but saued Noah the eight person a preacher of righteousnesse, bringing in the flood vpon the world of the vngodly :

6 And turning the cities of Sodom and Gomorrha into ashes, condemned them with an ouerthrowe, making them an ensample vnto those that after should liue vngodly :

7 And deliuered iust Lot, vexed

with the filthy conuersation of the wicked :

8 (For that righteous man dwelling among them, in seeing & hearing, vexed his righteous soule from day to day, with their vnlawfull deeds.)

9 The Lord knoweth how to deliuer the godly out of temptations, and to reserue the vniust vnto the day of iudgement to be punished :

10 But chiefly them that walke after the flesh in the lust of vncleannesse, and despise ‖ gouernment. Presumptuous are they ; selfe willed : they are not afraid to speake euill of dignities :

‖ Or, dominion.
* Iude 8. 8.

11 Whereas Angels which are greater in power and might, bring not railing accusation ‖ against them before the Lord.

‖ Some read against themselues.

12 But these, as natural bruit beasts made to bee taken and destroyed speake euill of the things that they vnderstand not, and shall vtterly perish in their owne corruption,

13 And shall receiue the reward of vnrighteousnesse, as they that count it pleasure to riot in the day time : Spots they are and blemishes, sporting themselues with their owne deceiuings, while they feast with you :

14 Hauing eyes ful of † adulterie and that cannot cease from sinne, beguiling vnstable soules : an heart they haue exercised with couetous practises : cursed children :

† Gr. an adulteresse.

15 Which haue forsaken the right way, and are gone astray, following the way of Balaam the sonne of Bosor, who loued the wages of vnrighteousnesse,

16 But was rebuked for his iniquity : the dumbe asse speaking with mans voice, forbade the madnesse of the Prophet.

17 These are welles without water, cloudes that are caried with a tempest, to whom the mist of darkenesse is reserued for euer.

18 For when they speake great swelling words of vanitie, they allure through the lusts of the flesh, through much wantonnesse, those that were ‖ cleane escaped from them who liue in errour.

‖ Or, for a litle, or a while as some read.

19 While they promise them libertie, they themselues are the seruants of corruption : for of whom a man is ouercome, of the same is he brought in bondage.

20 For if after they haue escaped the pollu-

pollutions of the world through the knowledge of the Lord and Sauiour Iesus Christ, they are againe intangled therein, *and* ouercome, the latter end is worse with them then the beginning.

21 For it had bin better for them not to haue knowen the way of righteousnesse, then after they haue knowen it, to turne from the holy commandement deliuered vnto them.

22 But it is happened vnto them according to the true prouerbe : The dog is turned to his own vomit againe, and the sowe that was washed, to her wallowing in the mire.

CHAP. III.

Hee assureth them of the certaintie of Christes comming to Iudgement, against those scorners who dispute against it : 8 warning the godly for the long patience of God, to hasten their repentance. 10 He describeth also the manner how the world shall bee destroyed : 11 exhorting them from the expectation thereof, to all holinesse of life : 15 And againe, to thinke the patience of God to tend to their saluation, as Paul wrote to them in his Epistles.

His second Epistle (beloued) I now write vnto you, in both which I stir vp your pure mindes by way of remembrance :

2 That yee may be mindfull of the wordes which were spoken before by the holy Prophets, and of the Commandement of vs the Apostles of the Lord and Sauiour :

3 Knowing this first, that there shall come in the last dayes scoffers, walking after their owne lusts,

4 And saying, Where is the promise of his comming? For since the fathers fell asleepe, all things continue as they were frō the beginning of the creation.

5 For this they willingly are ignorant of, that by the word of God the heauens were of olde, and the earth †standing out of the water, and in the water,

6 Whereby the world that then was, being ouerflowed with water, perished.

7 But the heauens and the earth which are now, by the same word are

† *Gr. consisting.*

kept in store, reserued vnto fire against the day of Iudgement, and perdition of vngodly men.

8 But (beloued) bee not ignorant of this one thing, that one day is with the Lord as a thousand yeeres, and a thousand yeeres as one day.

9 The Lord is not slacke cōcerning his promise (as some men count slacknesse) but is long-suffring to vs-ward, not willing that any should perish, but that all should come to repentance.

10 But the day of the Lord wil come as a thiefe in the night, in the which the heauens shall passe away with a great noise, and the Elements shall melt with feruent heate, the earth also and the works that are therin shalbe burnt vp.

11 Seeing then that all these things shall be dissolued, What maner of persons ought ye to be in all holy conuersation, and godlinesse,

12 ‖Looking for and hasting vnto the comming of the day of God, wherein the heauens being on fire shalbe dissolued, and the Elements shall melt with feruent heat.

‖ *Or, hasting the comming.*

13 Neuerthelesse wee, according to his promise, looke for new heauens, and a new earth, wherein dwelleth righteousnesse.

14 Wherefore (beloued) seeing that ye looke for such things, be diligent that ye may be found of him in peace, without spot, and blamelesse.

15 And account that the long suffering of the Lord is saluation, euen as our beloued brother Paul also, according to the wisedome giuen vnto him, hath written vnto you.

16 As also in all his Epistles, speaking in them of these things, in which are some things hard to be vnderstood, which they that are vnlearned and vnstable wrest, as they doe also the other Scriptures, vnto their owne destruction.

17 Ye therefore, beloued, seeing yee know *these things* before, beware lest yee also being led away with the errour of the wicked, fall from your owne stedfastnesse.

18 But growe in grace, and in the knowledge of our Lord and Sauiour Iesus Christ : to him be glory both now and for euer. Amen.

✠ **THE**

¶ THE FIRST EPISTLE
generall of Iohn.

CHAP. I.

1 He describeth the person of Christ, in whome we haue eternall life, by a cõmunion with God: 5 to which we must adioine holinesse of life, to testifie the trueth of that our communion and profession of faith, as also to assure vs of the forgiuenesse of our sinnes by Christs death.

Hat which was from ỹ beginning, which wee haue heard, which wee haue seene with our eyes, which wee haue looked vpon, and our hands haue handled of the word of life.

2 (For the life was manifested, and we haue seene it, and beare witnes, and shew vnto you that eternall life which was with the Father, and was manifested vnto vs.)

3 That which wee haue seene and heard, declare we vnto you, that ye also may haue felowship with vs ; and truely our fellowship is with the Father, and with his Sonne Iesus Christ.

4 And these things write we vnto you, that your ioy may be full.

5 This then is the message which we haue heard of him, and declare vnto you, that God is light, and in him is no darkenesse at all.

6 If we say that we haue felowship with him, and walke in darkenesse, we lie, and doe not the trueth.

7 But if wee walke in the light, as he is in the light, wee haue fellowship one with another, and the blood of Iesus Christ his Sonne clenseth vs from all sinne.

8 If we say that we haue no sinne, we deceiue our selues, and the trueth is not in vs.

9 If we confesse our sinnes, hee is faithfull, & iust to forgiue vs our sinnes,

and to cleanse vs from all vnrighteousnesse.

10 If we say that we haue not sinned, wee make him a liar, and his word is not in vs.

CHAP. II.

1 He comforteth them against the sinnes of infirmitie. 3 Rightly to know God, is to keepe his commaundements, 9 to loue our brethren, 15 and not to loue the world. 18 We must beware of seducers: 20 from whose deceits the godly are safe preserued by perseuerance in faith, and holinesse of life.

Y little children , these things write I vnto you, that ye sinne not. And if any man sinne, we haue an Aduocate with the Father, Iesus Christ the righteous :

2 And he is the propitiation for our sinnes : and not for ours onely , but also for the sinnes of the whole world.

3 And hereby wee doe knowe that we know him, if we keepe his commandements.

4 He that saith, I knowe him, and keepeth not his commandements, is a lyer, and the trueth is not in him.

5 But who so keepeth his word, in him verely is the loue of God perfected: hereby know we that we are in him.

6 He that sayeth he abideth in him, ought himselfe also so to walke, euen as he walked.

7 Brethren, I write no new commandement vnto you, but an olde commandement which ye had from the beginning : the old commandement is the word which ye haue heard from the beginning.

8 Againe, a new commandement I write vnto you, which thing is true in him and in you : because the darkenesse is past, and the true light now shineth.

9 He that saith he is in the light, and hateth

hateth his brother, is in darkenesse euen vntill now.

10 Hee that loueth his brother, abideth in the light, and there is none occa-sion of † stumbling in him.

Gr. scandall

11 But he that hateth his brother, is in darknesse, and walketh in darknesse, and knoweth not whither hee goeth, because that darknesse hath blinded his eyes.

12 I write vnto you, little children, because your sinnes are forgiuen you for his Names sake.

13 I write vnto you, fathers, because yee haue knowen him that is from the beginning. I write vnto you, young men, because you haue ouercome the wicked one. I write vnto you, little children, because yee haue knowen the Father.

14 I haue written vnto you, fathers, because ye haue knowen him *that is* from the beginning. I haue written vnto you, young men, because yee are strong, and the word of God abideth in you, and yee haue ouercome the wicked one.

15 Loue not the world, neither the things that are in the world. If any man loue the world, the loue of the Father is not in him.

16 For all that is in the world, the lust of the flesh, the lust of the eyes, and the pride of life, is not of the Father, but is of the world.

17 And the world passeth away, and the lust thereof, but hee that doeth the will of God, abideth for euer.

18 Little children, it is the last time: and as yee haue heard that Antichrist shall come, euen now are there many Antichrists, whereby wee know that it is the last time.

19 They went out from vs, but they were not of vs : for if they had beene of vs, they would no doubt haue conti-nued with vs: but *they went out* that they might be made manifest, that they were not all of vs.

20 But ye haue an vnction from the holy One, and ye know all things.

21 I haue not written vnto you, be-cause yee know not the trueth : but be-cause ye know it, and that no lie is of the trueth.

22 Who is a lier, but hee that denieth that Iesus is the Christ? hee is Anti-christ, that denyeth the Father, and the Sonne.

23 Whosoeuer denieth the Sonne, the same hath not the Father: *but he that acknowledgeth the Sonne, hath the Father also.*

24 Let that therefore abide in you which yee haue heard from the begin-ning : if that which ye haue heard from the beginning shall remaine in you, yee also shall continue in the Sonne, and in the Father.

25 And this is the promise that hee hath promised vs, *euen* eternall life.

26 These things haue I written vnto you, concerning them that seduce you.

27 But the anointing which ye haue receiued of him, abideth in you : and yee need not that any man teach you : But, as the same anointing teacheth you of all things, and is trueth, and is no lye: and euen as it hath taught you, ye shall abide in ‖him.

‖ *Or, it.*

28 And now, little children, abide in him, that when hee shall appeare, wee may haue confidence, and not bee asha-med before him at his comming.

29 If ye know that he is righteous, ‖ye know that euery one which doeth righteousnesse, is borne of him.

‖ *Or, know ye*

CHAP. III.

Hee declareth the singular loue of God towards vs, in making vs his sonnes : 3 Who there-fore ought obediently to keepe his com-maundements, 11 As also brotherly to loue one another.

Eholde, what manner of loue the Father hath be-stowed vpon vs, that wee should be called the sonnes of God : therfore the world knoweth vs not, because it knewe him not.

2 Beloued, now are we the sonnes of God, and it doeth not yet appeare, what wee shall be : but wee know, that when he shall appeare, we shall bee like him : for we shall see him as he is.

3 And euery man that hath this hope in him, purifieth himselfe, euen as he is pure.

4 Whosoeuer committeth sinne, transgresseth also the lawe : for sinne is the transgression of the law.

5 And ye know that hee was mani-fested to take away our sinnes, and in him is no sinne.

6 Whosoeuer abideth in him, sinneth not : whosoeuer sinneth, hath not seene him, neither knowen him.

7 Lit-

7 Little children, let no man deceiue you : he that doth righteousnes, is righteous, euen as he is righteous.

8 He that committeth sinne, is of the deuill, for the deuill sinneth from the beginning : for this purpose the Sonne of God was manifested, that he might destroy the works of the deuill.

9 Whosoeuer is borne of God, doth not commit sinne : for his seede remaineth in him, and he cannot sinne, because he is borne of God.

10 In this the children of God are manifest, and the children of the deuill : whosoeuer doeth not righteousnesse, is not of God, neither hee that loueth not his brother.

11 For this is the ‖message that yee heard from the beginning, that wee should loue one another.

‖ Or, commandement.

12 Not as Cain, *who* was of that wicked one, and slewe his brother : and wherefore slewe hee him ? because his owne workes were euill, and his brothers righteous.

13 Marueile not, my brethren, if the world hate you.

14 Wee know that wee haue passed from death vnto life, because wee loue the brethren : he that loueth not his brother, abideth in death.

15 Whosoeuer hateth his brother, is a murtherer, and yee knowe that no murtherer hath eternall life abiding in him.

16 Hereby perceiue wee the loue of God, because he layd downe his life for vs, and wee ought to lay downe our liues for the brethren.

17 But who so hath this worlds good, and seeth his brother hath need, and shutteth vp his bowels of compassion from him ; how dwelleth the loue of God in him ?

18 My little children, let vs not loue in word, neither in tongue, but indeede and in trueth.

19 And hereby wee know that wee are of the trueth, and shall †assure our hearts before him.

† Gr, perswade.

20 For if our heart condemne vs, God is greater then our heart, and knoweth all things.

21 Beloued, if our heart condemne vs not, *then* haue wee confidence towards God.

22 And whatsoeuer we aske, wee receiue of him, because we keepe his commandement, and doe those things that are pleasing in his sight.

23 And this is his commandement, that we should beleeue on the Name of his Sonne Iesus Christ, and loue one another, as hee gaue vs commandement.

24 And hee that keepeth his commandements dwelleth in him, and hee in him : and hereby wee know that hee abideth in vs, by the spirit which hee hath giuen vs.

CHAP. IIII.

1 He warneth them not to beleeue all teachers, who boast of the spirit, but to try them by the rules of the Catholike faith : 7 and by many reasons exhorteth to brotherly loue.

Eloued, beleeue not euery spirit, but trie the spirits, whether they are of God : because many false prophets are gone out into the world.

2 Hereby know ye the spirit of God : euery spirit that confesseth that Iesus Christ is come in the flesh, is of God.

3 And euery Spirit that confesseth not that Iesus Christ is come in the flesh, is not of God : and this is that *spirit* of Antichrist, whereof you haue heard, that it should come, and euen now already is it in the world.

4 Ye are of God, little children, and haue ouercome them : because greater is he that is in you, then he that is in the world.

5 They are of the world . therefore speake they of the world, and the world heareth them.

6 We are of God : hee that knoweth God, heareth vs : he that is not of God heareth not vs, hereby know wee the spirit of trueth, and the spirit of errour.

7 Beloued, let vs loue one another ; for loue is of God : and euery one that loueth, is borne of God and knoweth God.

8 Hee that loueth not, knoweth not God : for God is loue.

9 In this was manifested the loue of God towards vs, because that God sent his only begotten Sonne into the world, that we might liue through him.

10 Herein is loue, not that wee loued God, but that he loued vs, and sent his Sonne to be y propitiation for our sins.

11 Beloued, if God so loued vs, wee ought also to loue one another.

12 No man hath seene God at any time.

time. If wee loue one another, God dwelleth in vs, and his loue is perfected in vs.

13 Hereby know wee that we dwell in him and he in vs, because hee hath giuen vs of his Spirit.

14 And we haue seene, and doe testifie, that the Father sent the Sonne *to be* the Sauiour of the world.

15 Whosoeuer shall confesse that Iesus is the Sonne of God, God dwelleth in him, and he in God.

16 And we haue knowen and beleeued the loue that God hath to vs. God is loue, and hee that dwelleth in loue, dwelleth in God, and God in him.

Gr. loue with vs.

17 Herein is †our loue made perfect, that wee may haue boldnesse in the day of Iudgement, because as hee is, so are we in this world.

18 There is no feare in loue, but perfect loue casteth out feare : because feare hath torment : hee that feareth, is not made perfect in loue.

19 We loue him : because hee first loued vs.

20 If a man say, I loue God, and hateth his brother, he is a lyar. For hee that loueth not his brother whom hee hath seene, how can he loue God whom he hath not seene?

21 And this commandement haue we from him, that he who loueth God, loue his brother also.

CHAP. V.

Hee that loueth God, loueth his children, and keepeth his Commandements: 3 which to the faithfull are light, and not grieuous. 9 Iesus is the Sonne of God, able to saue vs, 14 and to heare our prayers, which we make for our selues, and for others.

Hosoeuer beleeueth that Iesus is the Christ, is borne of God : and euery one that loueth him that begate, loueth him also that is begotten of him.

2 By this wee know that wee loue the children of God, when we loue God and keepe his commandements.

3 For this is the loue of God, that we keepe his commandements, and his commandements are not grieuous.

4 For whatsoeuer is borne of God, ouercommeth the world, and this is the victorie that ouercommeth the world, euen our faith.

5 Who is he that ouercommeth the world, but he that beleeueth that Iesus is the Sonne of God?

6 This is hee that came by water and blood, euen Iesus Christ, not by water onely, but by water and blood : and it is the Spirit that beareth witnesse, because the Spirit is trueth.

7 For there are three that beare record in heauen, the Father, the Word, and the holy Ghost : and these three are one.

8 And there are three that beare witnesse in earth, the Spirit, and the Water, and the Blood, and these three agree in one.

9 If we receiue the witnesse of men, the witnesse of God is greater : for this is the witnesse of God, which hee hath testified of his Sonne.

10 Hee that beleeueth on the Sonne of God, hath the witnesse in himselfe : he that beleeueth not God, hath made him a liar, because he beleeueth not the record that God gaue of his Sonne.

11 And this is the record, that God hath giuen to vs eternall life, and this life is in his Sonne.

12 Hee that hath the Sonne, hath life ; and hee that hath not the Sonne, hath not life.

13 These things haue I written vnto you that beleeue on the Name of the Sonne of God, that ye may know, that ye haue eternall life, and that yee may beleeue on the Name of the Sonne of God.

14 And this is the confidence that we haue ‖in him, that if wee aske any thing according to his will, hee heareth vs.

‖*Or, concerning him*

15 And if we know that he heare vs, whatsoeuer wee aske, wee know that we haue the petitions that wee desired of him.

16 If any man see his brother sinne a sinne *which is* not vnto death, hee shall aske, and he shall giue him life for them that sinne not vnto death. There is a sinne vnto death : I doe not say that he shall pray for it.

17 All vnrighteousnes is sinne, and there is a sinne not vnto death.

18 We know that whosoeuer is borne of God, sinneth not : but hee that is begotten of God, keepeth himselfe, and that wicked one toucheth him not.

19 And we know that we are of God, and the whole world lieth in wickednesse.

20 And

20 And we know that the Sonne of God is come, and hath giuen vs an vnderstanding that wee may know him that is true: and wee are in him that is true, *euen* in his Sonne Iesus Christ. This is the true God, and eternall life.

21 Little children, keepe your selues from Idoles. Amen.

¶ The second Epistle of Iohn.

Hee exhorteth a certaine honourable matrone, with her children, to perseuere in Christian loue, and beliefe, 8 lest they lose the reward of their former profession: 10 And to haue nothing to doe with those seducers that bring not the true doctrine of Christ Iesus.

He Elder vnto the elect Lady, and her children, whome I loue in the trueth: and not I onely, but also all they that haue knowen ỹ trueth:

2 For the trueths sake which dwelleth in vs, and shalbe with vs for euer:

3 Grace bee with you, mercie, and peace from God the Father, and from the Lord Iesus Christ, the Sonne of the Father in trueth and loue.

4 I reioyced greatly, that I found of thy children walking in trueth, as wee haue receiued a commaundement from the Father.

5 And now, I beseech thee Lady, not as though I wrote a new commandement vnto thee: but that which wee had from the beginning, that wee loue one another.

6 And this is loue, that wee walke after his Commandements. This is the Commandement, that as yee haue heard from the beginning, yee should walke in it.

7 For many deceiuers are entred into the world, who confesse not that Iesus Christ is come in the flesh. This is a deceiuer, and an Antichrist.

8 Looke to your selues, that wee lose not those things which wee haue ‖wrought, but that we receiue a full reward.

9 Whosoeuer transgresseth and abideth not in the doctrine of Christ, hath not God: hee that abideth in the doctrine of Christ, he hath both the Father and the Sonne.

10 If there come any vnto you, and bring not this doctrine, receiue him not into your house, neither bid him, God speed.

11 For hee that biddeth him God speed, is partaker of his euill deeds.

12 Hauing many things to write vnto you, I would not write with paper and inke, but I trust to come vnto you, and speake †face to face, that our ioy may be full.

13 The children of thy elect sister greet thee. Amen.

‖ *Or, gaine Some copies reade, which yee haue gained, but that ye receiue, &c.*

† *Gr. mouth to mouth.*

¶ The third Epistle of Iohn.

Hee commendeth Gaius for his pietie 5 and hospitalitie 7 to true preachers: 9 Complaining of the vnkind dealing of ambitious Diotrephes on the contrary side: 11 Whose euill example is not to bee followed: 12 And giueth speciall testimonie to the good report of Demetrius.

He Elder vnto the welbeloued Gaius, whom I loue ‖ in the trueth:

2 Beloued, I ‖wish aboue all things that thou mayest prosper and be in health, euen as thy soule prospereth.

3 For I reioyced greatly when the brethren came and testified of the truth that is in thee, euen as thou walkest in the trueth.

4 I haue no greater ioy, then to heare that my children walke in truth.

5 Beloued, thou doest faithfully whatsoeuer thou doest to the Brethren, and to strangers:

6 Which haue borne witnesse of thy charitie before the Church: whome if thou

‖ *Or, truely.*

‖ *Or, pray.*

thou bring forward on their iourney after a godly sort, thou shalt doe well:

7 Because that for his Names sake they went foorth, taking nothing of the Gentiles.

8 We therefore ought to receiue such, that we might be fellow helpers to the trueth.

9 I wrote vnto the Church, but Diotrephes, who loueth to haue the preeminence among them, receiueth vs not.

10 Wherefore if I come, I will remember his deeds which he doeth, prating against vs with malicious words: and not content therewith, neither doth hee himselfe receiue the brethren,

and forbiddeth them that would, and casteth them out of the Church.

11 Beloued, follow not that which is euill, but that which is good. He that doth good, is of God: but hee that doth euill, hath not seene God.

12 Demetrius hath good report of all men, and of the trueth it selfe: yea, and we *also* beare record, and ye know that our record is true.

13 I had many things to write, but I will not with inke and pen write vnto thee.

14 But I trust I shall shortly see thee, and wee shall speake †face to face. Peace bee to thee. Our friends salute thee. Greet the friends by name.

† *Gr. mouth to mouth.*

¶ THE GENERALL
Epiſtle of Iude.

Hee exhorteth them to bee conſtant in the profeſsion of the faith. 14 False teachers are crept in to seduce them: for whose damnable doctrine and manners horrible punishment is prepared: 20 Whereas the godly, by the assistance of the holy Spirit, and prayers to God, may perseuere, and grow in grace, and keepe themselues, and recouer others out of the snares of those deceiuers.

Vde the seruant of Iesus Christ, and brother of Iames, to them that are sanctified by God the Father, and preserued in Iesus Christ, & called:

2 Mercie vnto you, and peace, and loue be multiplied.

3 Beloued, when I gaue all diligence to write vnto you of the common saluation: it was needfull for mee to write vnto you, and exhort you that ye should earnestly contend for the faith which was once deliuered vnto the Saints.

4 For there are certaine men crept in

vnawares, who were before of olde ordained to this condemnation, vngodly men, turning the grace of our God into lasciuiousnesse, and denying the onely Lord God, & our Lord Iesus Christ.

5 I will therefore put you in remembrance, though ye once knew this, how that the Lord hauing saued the people out of the land of Egypt afterward destroied them that beleeued not.

6 And the Angels which kept not their ‖first estate, but left their own habitation, he hath reserued in euerlasting chaines vnder darkenesse, vnto the iudgement of the great day.

‖ *Or, principalitie.*

7 Euen as Sodom and Gomorrha, and the cities about them, in like maner giuing themselues ouer to fornication, and going after †strange flesh, are set forth for an example, suffring the vengeance of eternall fire.

† *Gr. other.*

8 Likewise also these filthy dreamers defile the flesh, despise dominion, and speake euill of dignities.

9 Yet Michael the Archangel, when contending with the deuill, he disputed about the body of Moses, durst not bring against him a railing accusation, but said, *The Lord rebuke thee.

* *Zac. 3. 2.*

10 But

10 But these speake euill of those things, which they know not: but what they knowe naturally, as brute beastes, in those things they corrupt themselues.

11 Wo vnto them, for they haue gone in the way of Kain, and ranne greedily after the errour of Balaam, for reward, and perished in the gainsaying of Core.

12 These are spottes in your feasts of charitie, when they feast with you, feeding themselues without feare: cloudes they are without water, caried about of winds, trees whose fruit withereth, without fruit, twise dead, plucked vp by the rootes.

13 Raging waues of the sea, foming out their owne shame, wandring stars, to whom is reserued the blacknesse of darkenesse for euer.

14 And Enoch also, the seuenth from Adam, prophesied of these, saying, Behold, the Lord commeth with ten thousands of his Saints,

15 To execute iudgement vpon all, and to conuince all that are vngodly among them, of all their vngodly deeds which they haue vngodly committed, and of all their heard *speaches*, which vngodly sinners haue spoken against him.

16 These are murmurers, complainers, walking after their owne lustes, and their mouth speaketh great swelling wordes, hauing mens persons in admiration because of aduantage.

17 But beloued, remember yee the words, which were spoken before of the Apostles of our Lord Iesus Christ :

18 *How* that they tolde you there should be mockers in the last time, who should walke after their own vngodly lustes.

19 These be they who separate themselues, sensual, hauing not the spirit.

20 But yee beloued, building vp your selues on your most holy faith, praying in the holy Ghost,

21 Keepe your selues in the loue of God, looking for the mercy of our Lord Iesus Christ vnto eternall life.

22 And of some haue compassion, making a difference :

23 And others saue with feare, pulling them out of the fire : hating euen the garment spotted by the flesh.

24 Now vnto him that is able to keepe you from falling, and to present you faultlesse before the presence of his glory with exceeding ioy,

25 To the onely wise God our Sauiour, be glory and maiestie, dominion and power, now and euer. Amen.

¶ THE

¶ THE REVELATION
of S.Iohn the Diuine.

CHAP. I.

4 Iohn writeth his reuelation to the seuen Churches of Asia, signified by the seuen golden Candlestickes. 7 The comming of Christ. 14 His glorious power and maiestie.

He Reuelation of Iesus Christ, which G O D gaue vnto him, to shewe vnto his seruants things which must shortly come to passe; and he sent and signified *it* by his Angel vnto his seruant Iohn,

2 Who bare record of the word of God, and of the testimonie of Iesus Christ, and of all things that he saw.

3 Blessed is hee that readeth, and they that heare the words of this prophesie, and keepe those things which are written therein : for the time is at hand.

4 Iohn to the seuen Churches in Asia, Grace *be* vnto you, & peace, from him *which is, and which was, and which is to come, and from the seuen spirits which are before his throne :

5 And from Iesus Christ, *who is the* faithful witnesse, and the *first begotten of the dead, and the Prince of the kings of the earth : vnto him that loued vs, *and washed vs from our sinnes in his owne blood,

6 And hath *made vs Kings and Priests vnto God and his Father : to him be glory and dominion for euer and euer, Amen.

7 *Behold he commeth with clouds, and euery eye shal see him, and they also which pearced him : and all kinreds of the earth shall waile because of him : euen so. Amen.

8 I am Alpha and Omega, the beginning and the ending, saith the Lord, which is, and which was, and which is to come, the Almighty.

9 I Iohn, who also am your brother, and companion in tribulation, and in the kingdome and patience of Iesus Christ, was in the Isle that is called Patmos, for the word of God, and for the testimonie of Iesus Christ.

10 I was in the spirit on the Lords day, and heard behind me a great voice, as of a trumpet,

11 Saying, I am Alpha and Omega, the first and the last : and what thou seest, write in a booke, and send it vnto the seuen Churches which are in Asia, vnto Ephesus, and vnto Smyrna, and vnto Pergamos, and vnto Thyatira, and vnto Sardis, and Philadelphia, and vnto Laodicea.

12 And I turned to see the voice that spake with mee. And being turned, I saw seuen golden Candlesticks,

13 And in the midst of the seuen candlestickes, *one* like vnto the Sonne of man, clothed with a garment downe to the foot, and girt about the paps with a golden girdle.

14 His head, and his haires were white like wooll, as white as snow, and his eyes *were* as a flame of fire,

15 And his feet like vnto fine brasse, as if they burned in a furnace : and his voice as the sound of many waters.

16 And hee had in his right hand seuen starres : and out of his mouth went a sharpe two edged sword : and his countenance was as the Sunne shineth in his strength.

17 And when I sawe him, I fell at his feete as dead : and hee laid his right hand vpon me, saying vnto mee, Feare not, * I am the first, and the last.

18 I am hee that liueth, and was dead : and behold, I am aliue for euermore,

*Exo. 3. 14.

* 1. Cor. 15. 21. coloss. 4. 18.

* Heb. 9. 14

* 1. Pet. 2. 5

* Matt. 24. 30.

* Esay. 41. 4. and 44. 6.

more, Amen, and haue the keyes of hell and of death.

19 Write the things which thou hast seene, and the things which are, and the things which shall be hereafter,

20 The mysterie of the seuen starres which thou sawest in my right hand, and the seuen golden Candlestickes. The seuen Starres are the Angels of the seuen Churches : and the seuen candlestickes which thou sawest, are the seuen Churches.

CHAP. II.

What is commaunded to bee written to the Angels, that is, the Ministers of the Churches of 1 Ephesus, 8 Smyrna, 12 Pergamus, 18 Thyatira : and what is commended, or found wanting in them.

Nto the Angel of the church of Ephesus, write, These things saith he that holdeth the seuen starres in his right hand, who walketh in the midst of the seuen golden Candlesticks :

2 I know thy workes, and thy labour, and thy patience, and how thou canst not beare them which are euil, and thou hast tried them which say they are Apostles, and are not, and hast found them lyers :

3 And hast borne, and hast patience, and for my Names sake hast laboured, and hast not fainted.

4 Neuerthelesse, I haue *somewhat* against thee, because thou hast left thy first loue.

5 Remember therfore from whence thou art fallen, and repent, and doe the first workes, or else I will come vnto thee quickly, and will remoue thy Candlesticke out of his place, except thou repent.

6 But this thou hast, that thou hatest the deeds of the Nicolaitans, which I also hate.

7 Hee that hath an eare, let him heare what the Spirit saith vnto the Churches : To him that ouercommeth will I giue to eate of the tree of life, which is in the middest of the Paradise of God.

8 And vnto the Angel of the Church in Smyrna, write, These things saith the first and the last, which was dead, and is aliue,

9 I know thy works, and tribulation, and pouertie, but thou art rich,

and I know the blasphemie of them which say they are Iewes and are not, but *are* the Synagogue of Satan.

10 Feare none of those things which thou shalt suffer : behold, the deuill shal cast some of you into prison, that ye may be tried, and yee shall haue tribulation tenne dayes : bee thou faithfull vnto death, and I will giue thee a crowne of life.

11 He that hath an eare, let him heare what the spirit saith vnto the churches. He that ouercommeth, shall not be hurt of the second death.

12 And to the Angel of the Church in Pergamos, write, These things saith hee, which hath the sharpe sword with two edges :

13 I know thy workes, and where thou dwellest, *euen* where Satans seat is, and thou holdest fast my Name, and hast not denied my faith, euen in those daies, wherein Antipas *was* my faithful Martyr, who was slaine among you, where Satan dwelleth.

14 But I haue a fewe things against thee, because thou hast there them that holde the doctrine of *Balaam, who taught Balac to cast a stumbling blocke before the children of Israel, to eate things sacrificed vnto idoles, and to commit fornication.   *Num. 25.

15 So hast thou also them that hold the doctrine of the Nicolaitans, which thing I hate.

16 Repent, or else I will come vnto thee quickly, and wil fight against them with the sword of my mouth.

17 Hee that hath an eare, let him heare what the Spirit saith vnto the Churches. To him that ouercommeth will I giue to eate of the hidden Manna, and will giue him a white stone, and in the stone a new name written, which no man knoweth, sauing hee that receiueth it.

18 And vnto the Angel of the church in Thyatira, write, These things saith the Sonne of God, who hath his eyes like vnto a flame of fire, and his feete *are* like fine brasse :

19 I know thy works, and charitie, and seruice, and faith, and thy patience, and thy workes, and the last *to bee* more then the first.

20 Notwithstanding, I haue a few things against thee, because thou sufferest that woman *Iezebel, which calleth herselfe a Prophetesse, to teach and to   *1. Kin. 16, 31.

to seduce my seruants to commit fornication, and to eat things sacrificed vnto idoles.

21 And I gaue her space to repent of her fornication, and she repented not.

22 Behold, I will cast her into a bed, and them that commit adultery with her, into great tribulation, except they repent of their deeds.

23 And I will kill her children with death, and all the Churches shall know that * I am hee which searcheth the reines and hearts : and I will giue vnto euery one of you according to your workes.

24 But vnto you I say, and vnto the rest in Thyatira, as many as haue not this doctrine, and which haue not knowen the depthes of Satan, as they speake, I will put vpon you none other burden :

25 But that which ye haue already, hold fast till I come.

26 And hee that ouercommeth, and keepeth my workes vnto the ende, to him will I giue power ouer the nations :

27 (*And he shall rule them with a rod of yron : as the vessels of a potter shall they be broken to shiuers :) euen as I receiued of my Father.

28 And I will giue him the morning starre.

29 He that hath an eare, let him heare what the Spirit saith vnto the Churches.

CHAP. III.

2 The Angel of the Church of Sardis is reproued, 3 exhorted to repent, and threatned if hee doe not repent. 8 The Angel of the Church of Philadelphia 10 is approoued for his diligence and patience. 15 The Angel of Laodicea rebuked, for being neither hote nor colde, 19 and admonished to be more zealous. 20 Christ standeth at the doore, and knocketh.

Nd vnto the Angel of the Church in Sardis write, These things saith he that hath the seuen Spirits of God, & the seuen starres; I know thy workes, that thou hast a name that thou liuest, and art dead.

2 Be watchfull, and strengthen the things which remaine, that are ready to die : for I haue not found thy works perfect before God.

3 Remember therefore, how thou hast receiued and heard, and hold fast, and repent. * If therefore thou shalt not watch, I will come on thee as a thiefe, and thou shalt not know what houre I will come vpon thee.

4 Thou hast a few names euen in Sardis, which haue not defiled their garments, and they shall walke with me in white : for they are worthy.

5 Hee that ouercommeth, the same shalbe clothed in white raiment, and I will not blot out his name out of the *booke of life, but I will confesse his name before my Father, and before his Angels.

6 Hee that hath an eare, let him heare what the Spirit saith vnto the Churches.

7 And to the Angel of the Church in Philadelphia write, These things saith he that is Holy, he that is true, he that hath the key of Dauid, he that openeth, and no man shutteth, and shutteth, and no man openeth ;

8 I know thy workes : behold, I haue set before thee an open doore, and no man can shut it : for thou hast a little strength, and hast kept my word, and hast not denied my Name.

9 Behold, I will make them of the synagogue of Satan, which say they are Iewes, and are not, but doe lie : behold, I will make them to come and worship before thy feete, and to know that I haue loued thee.

10 Because thou hast kept the word of my patience, I also will keepe thee from the houre of temptation, which shall come vpon all the world, to try them that dwell vpon the earth.

11 Beholde, I come quickly, hold that fast which thou hast, that no man take thy crowne.

12 Him that ouercommeth, will I make a pillar in the Temple of my God, and he shall goe no more out : and I wil write vpon him the Name of my God, and the name of the Citie of my God, *which is* new Hierusalem, which commeth downe out of heauen from my God : And *I will write vpon him* my New name.

13 Hee that hath an eare, let him heare what the Spirit saith vnto the Churches.

14 And vnto the Angel of the Church || of the Laodiceans, write, These things saith the Amen, the faithfull and true witnesse, the beginning of the creation of God :

15 I

Margin notes

* Iere. 11. 20. and 17. 10.

* Psal. 2. 9.

* 1. Thess. 5. 2. 2. pet. 3. 10.

* Chap. 20. 12. phil. 4. 3.

‖ *Or, in Laodicea.*

15 I know thy workes, that thou art neither cold nor hot, I would thou wert cold or hot.

16 So then because thou art lukewarme, and neither cold nor hot, I wil spew thee out of my mouth :

17 Because thou sayest, I am rich, and increased with goods, and haue need of nothing : and knowest not that thou art wretched, and miserable, and poore, and blinde, and naked.

18 I counsell thee to buy of me gold tried in the fire, that thou mayest be rich, and white raiment, that thou mayest be clothed, and that the shame of thy nakednesse doe not appeare, and anoint thine eyes with eye salue, that thou mayest see.

*Prou. 3. 11. hebr. 12. 5.

19 * As many as I loue, I rebuke and chasten, be zealous therefore, and repent.

20 Behold, I stand at the doore, and knocke: if any man heare my voyce, and open the doore, I will come in to him, and will sup with him, and he with me.

21 To him that ouercommeth, will I graunt to sit with mee in my throne, euen as I also ouercame, and am set downe with my Father in his throne.

22 Hee that hath an eare, let him heare what the Spirit saith vnto the Churches.

CHAP. IIII.

2 Iohn seeth the throne of God in heauen. 4 The foure and twentie Elders. 6 The foure beasts full of eyes before and behinde. 10 The Elders lay downe their crownes, and worship him that sate on the Throne.

Fter this I looked, and beholde, a doore was opened in heauen: and the first voice which I heard, was as it were of a trumpet, talking with me, which said, Come vp hither, and I will shew thee things which must be hereafter.

2 And immediatly I was in the spirit : and beholde, a Throne was set in heauen, and *one* sate on the Throne.

3 And he that sate was to looke vpon like a Iasper, and a Sardine stone: and there was a rainebow round about the Throne, in sight like vnto an Emeralde.

4 And round about the Throne were foure and twentie seates, and vpon the seates I saw foure and twentie Elders sitting, clothed in white rayment, and they had on their heades crownes of golde.

5 And out of the Throne proceeded lightnings, and thundrings, and voyces : and there were seuen lampes of fire burning before the Throne, which are the seuen Spirits of God.

6 And before the Throne there was a sea of glasse like vnto Chrystall : and in the middest of the throne, and round about the Throne, were foure beastes full of eyes before and behinde.

7 And the first beast was like a Lion, and the second beast like a Calfe, and the third beast had a face as a man, and the fourth beast was like a flying Egle.

8 And the foure beasts had each of them sixe wings about him, and they were full of eyes within, and they †rest not day and night, saying, * Holy, holy, holy, Lord God Almighty, which was, and is, and is to come.

†Gr. they haue no rest. *Esai. 6. 3.

9 And when those beasts giue glory, and honour, and thankes to him that sate on the Throne, who liueth for euer and euer,

10 The foure and twentie Elders fall downe before him that sate on the Throne, and worship him that liueth for euer and euer, and cast their crownes before the Throne, saying,

11 * Thou art worthy, O Lord, to receiue glorie, and honour, and power : for thou hast created all things, and for thy pleasure they are, and were created.

*Chap. 5. 12.

CHAP. V.

1 The booke sealed with seuen seales : 9 which only the lamb that was slain is worthy to opē. 12 Therfore the Elders praise him, 9 and confesse that he redeemed them with his blood.

Nd I saw in ỹ right hand of him that sate on the Throne, a booke written within, & on the backeside, sealed with seuen seales.

2 And I saw a strong Angel proclaiming with a loude voice; Who is worthy to open the booke, and to loose the seales thereof ?

3 And no man in heauen, nor in earth, neither vnder the earth, was able to open the booke, neither to looke thereon

4 And I wept much, because no man was found worthy to open, and to reade the booke, neither to looke thereon.

5 And

*Gen. 49. 9

5 And one of the Elders saith vnto me, Weepe not : beholde, *the Lion of the tribe of Iuda, the roote of Dauid, hath preuailed to open the booke, and to loose the seuen seales thereof.

6 And I beheld, and loe, in the middest of the Throne, and of the foure beastes, and in the midst of the Elders stood a Lambe as it had beene slaine, hauing seuen hornes and seuen eyes, which are the seuen Spirits of God, sent foorth into all the earth.

7 And he came, and tooke the booke out of the right hand of him that sate vpon the Throne.

8 And when he had taken the booke, the foure Beasts, and foure and twenty Elders fel downe before the Lambe, hauing euery one of them harps, and golden vials full of ‖odours, which are the prayers of Saints.

‖ Or, incense.

9 And they sung a new song, saying, Thou art worthy to take the Booke, and to open the seales thereof : for thou wast slaine, and hast redeemed vs to God by thy blood, out of euery kinred, and tongue, and people, and nation :

*1. Pet. 2. 9.

10 *And hast made vs vnto our God Kings and Priests, and we shall reigne on the earth.

11 And I beheld, and I heard the voyce of many Angels, round about the Throne, and the beasts and the Elders, and the number of them was ten thousand times tenne thousand, and thousands of thousands,

12 Saying with a lowd voice, Worthy is the Lambe that was slaine, to receiue power, and riches, and wisedome, and strength, and honour, and glory, and blessing.

13 And euery creature which is in heauen, and on the earth, and vnder the earth, and such as are in the sea, and all that are in them, heard I, saying, Blessing, honour, glory, and power bee vnto him that sitteth vpon the Throne, and vnto the Lambe for euer and euer.

14 And the foure beasts said, Amen. And the foure and twenty Elders fell downe and worshipped him that liueth for euer and euer.

CHAP. VI.

1 The opening of the seales in order, and what followed thereupon, conteining a prophesie to the end of the world.

ANd I sawe when the Lambe opened one of the seales, and I heard as it were the noise of thunder, one of the foure beastes, saying, Come and see.

2 And I saw, and behold, a white horse, and hee that sate on him had a bowe, and a crowne was giuen vnto him, and hee went foorth conquering, and to conquere.

3 And when hee had opened the second seale, I heard the second beast say, Come and see.

4 And there went out another horse that was red : and power was giuen to him that sate thereon to take peace from the earth, and that they should kill one another : and there was giuen vnto him a great sword.

5 And when hee had opened the third seale, I heard the third beast say, Come and see. And I beheld, and loe, a blacke horse : and hee that sate on him had a paire of balances in his hand.

6 And I heard a voice in the midst of the foure beastes say, ‖A measure of wheate for a penie, and three measures of barley for a penie, and see thou hurt not the oyle and the wine.

‖ The word chænix, signifieth a measure containing one wine quart, and the twelfth part of a quart.

7 And when hee had opened the fourth seale, I heard the voice of the fourth beast say, Come and see.

8 And I looked, and behold, a pale horse, & his name that sate on him was Death, and hell followed with him : and power was giuen ‖vnto them, ouer the fourth part of the earth to kill with sword, & with hunger, and with death, and with the beastes of the earth.

‖ Or, to him.

9 And when hee had opened the fift seale, I saw vnder the altar, the soules of them that were slaine for the word of God, and for the testimony which they held.

10 And they cried with a lowd voice, saying, How long, O Lord, holy and true, doest thou not iudge and auenge our blood on them that dwell on the earth ?

11 And white robes were giuen vnto euery one of them, and it was sayd vnto them, that they should rest yet for a little season, vntill their fellow seruants also, and their brethren that should be killed as they were, should be fulfilled.

12 And I beheld when he had opened the sixt seale, and loe, there was a great

great earthquake, and the Sunne became blacke as ſackecloth of haire, and the Moone became as blood.

13 And the ſtarres of heauen fell vnto the earth, euen as a figge tree caſteth her ‖vntimely figs when she is shaken of a mighty winde.

Or. greene figs.

Eſa. 34. 4

14 *And the heauen departed as a ſcrowle when it is rolled together, and euery mountaine and Iland were moued out of their places.

15 And the kings of the earth, and the great men, and the rich men, and the chiefe captaines, and the mighty men, and euery bondman, and euery free man, hid themſelues in the dennes, and in the rockes of the mountaines,

16 And said to the mountaines and rockes, *Fall on vs, and hide vs from the face of him that ſitteth on the throne, and from the wrath of the Lambe:

Luk. 23. 30.

17 For the great day of his wrath is come, and who shall be able to ſtand?

CHAP. VII.

3 An Angel ſealeth the ſeruants of God in their foreheads. 4 The number of them that were ſealed: of the tribes of Iſrael a certaine number. 9 Of all other nations an innumerable multitude, which ſtand before the Throne, clad in white robes, and palmes in their hands. 14 Their robes were waſhed in the blood of the Lambe.

 Nd after these things, I ſaw foure Angels ſtanding on the foure corners of the Earth, holding the foure windes of the earth, that the winde should not blow on the earth, nor on the ſea, nor on any tree.

2 And I saw another Angel aſcending from the East, hauing the ſeale of the liuing God: and he cried with a loud voice to the foure Angels to whom it was giuen to hurt the earth and the Sea,

3 Saying, Hurt not the earth, neither the ſea, nor the trees, till wee haue ſealed the ſeruants of our God in their foreheads.

4 And I heard the number of them which were ſealed: and there were ſealed an hundreth and fourty and foure thousand, of all the tribes of the children of Iſrael.

5 Of the tribe of Iuda were ſealed twelue thousand. Of the tribe of Ruben were ſealed twelue thousand. Of

the tribe of Gad were ſealed twelue thousand.

6 Of the tribe of Aſer were ſealed twelue thousand. Of the tribe of Nepthali were ſealed twelue thousand. Of the tribe of Manaſſes were ſealed twelue thousand.

7 Of the tribe of Simeon were ſealed twelue thousand. Of the tribe of Leui were ſealed twelue thousand. Of the tribe of Iſachar were ſealed twelue thousand.

8 Of the tribe of Zabulon were ſealed twelue thousand. Of the tribe of Ioſeph were ſealed twelue thousand. Of the tribe of Beniamin were ſealed twelue thousand.

9 After this I beheld, and lo, a great multitude, which no man could nūber, of all nations, and kindreds, and people, & tongues, ſtood before the throne, & before the Lamb, clothed with white robes, and palmes in their hands:

10 And cryed with a loude voice, ſaying, Saluation to our God, which ſitteth vpon the Throne, and vnto the Lambe.

11 And all the Angels ſtood round about the Throne, and about the Elders, and the foure beaſts, and fell before the throne on their faces, and worshipped God,

12 Saying, Amen: Bleſſing, and glorie, and wiſedome, and thankesgiuing, and honour, & power, and might be vnto our God for euer & euer, Amen.

13 And one of the Elders anſwered, ſaying vnto mee, What are these which are arayed in white robes? and whence came they?

14 And I said vnto him, Sir, thou knoweſt. And he said to me, These are they which came out of great tribulation, and haue waſhed their robes, and made them white in the blood of the Lambe.

15 Therefore are they before the throne of God, and ſerue him day and night in his Temple: and hee that ſitteth on the Throne shal *dwell among them.

*Cha. 21.

16 *They shall hunger no more, neither thirst any more, neither shall the Sunne light on them, nor any heate.

*Eſa. 49.

17 For the Lambe, which is in the middeſt of the throne, shall feede them, and shall leade them vnto liuing fountaines of waters: *and God shal wipe away all teares from their eyes.

*Eſa. 25. chap. 21.

CHAP.

CHAP. VIII.

1 At the opening of the seuenth seale, 2 seuen Angels had seuen Trumpets giuen them. 6 Foure of them sound their trumpets, and great plagues follow. 3 Another Angel putteth incense to the prayers of the Saints on the golden altar.

Nd when hee had opened the seuenth seale, there was silence in heauen about the space of halfe an houre.

2 And I sawe the seuen Angels which stood before God, and to them were giuen seuen trumpets.

3 And another Angel came & stood at the altar, hauing a golden censer, and there was giuen vnto him much incense, that hee should ||offer it with the prayers of all Saints vpon the golden altar which was before the throne.

ⁿ Or, adde it to the prayers.

4 And the smoke of the incense which came with the prayers of the Saints, ascended vp before God, out of the Angels hand.

5 And the Angel tooke the censer, and filled it with fire of the altar, and cast it into the earth : and there were voyces, and thunderings, and lightnings, and an earthquake :

6 And the seuen Angels which had the seuen trumpets, prepared themselues to sound.

7 The first Angel sounded, and there followed haile, and fire mingled with blood, and they were cast vpon the earth, and the third part of trees was burnt vp, and all greene grasse was burnt vp.

8 And the second Angel sounded, and as it were a great mountaine burning with fire was cast into the sea, and the third part of the sea became blood.

9 And the thirde part of the creatures which were in the Sea, and had life, died, and the third part of the ships were destroyed.

10 And the third Angel sounded, and there fell a great starre from heauen, burning as it were a lampe, and it fell vpon the third part of the riuers, and vpon the fountaines of waters :

11 And the name of the starre is called Wormewood, and the third part of the waters became wormewood, and many men dyed of the waters, because they were made bitter.

12 And the fourth Angel sounded, and the thirde part of the Sunne was smitten, & the third part of the Moone, and the third part of the starres, so as the third part of them was darkened : and the day shone not for a third part of it, and the night likewise.

13 And I beheld, and heard an Angel flying through the midst of heauen, saying with a loude voice, Woe, woe, woe, to the inhabiters of the earth, by reason of the other voyces of the trumpet of the three Angels which are yet to sound

CHAP. IX.

1 At the sounding of the fift Angel, a starre falleth from heauen, to whome is giuen the key of the bottomles pit. 2 Hee openeth the pit, and there come foorth Locusts like Scorpions. 12 The first woe past. 13 The sixt Trumpet soundeth. 14 Foure Angels are let loose, that were bound.

Nd the fift Angel sounded, and I saw a starre fall from heauen vnto the earth : and to him was giuen the key of the bottomlesse pit.

2 And hee opened the bottomelesse pit, and there arose a smoke out of the pit, as the smoke of a great fornace, and the sunne and the ayre were darkened, by reason of the smoke of the pit.

3 And there came out of the smoke locusts vpon the earth, and vnto them was giuen power, as the Scorpions of the earth haue power.

4 And it was commaunded them that they should not hurt the grasse of the earth, neither any greene thing, neither any tree : but only those men which haue not the seale of God in their foreheads.

5 And to them it was giuen that they should not kill them, but that they should be tormented fiue moneths, and their torment was as the torment of a Scorpion, when he striketh a man.

6 And in those daies shal men seeke death, and shall not finde it, and shall desire to die, and death shall flee from them.

7 And the shapes of the Locusts were like vnto horses prepared vnto battell, and on their heades *were* as it were crownes like golde, and their faces were as the faces of men.

8 And they had haire as the haire of women, and their teeth were as the teeth of Lions.

9 And

9 And they had brestplates, as it were brestplates of iron, and the sound of their wings was as the sound of charets of many horses running to battell.

10 And they had tayles like vnto Scorpions, and there were stings in their tayles : and their power was to hurt men fiue moneths.

11 And they had a king ouer them, which is the Angel of the bottomlesse pit, whose name in the Hebrew tongue is Abaddon, but in the Greeke tongue hath his name ||Apollyon.

‖ *That is to say, A destroyer.*

12 One woe is past, and behold there come two woes more hereafter.

13 And the sixt Angel sounded, and I heard a voyce from the foure hornes of ỹ golden altar, which is before God,

14 Saying to the sixt Angel which had the trumpet, Loose the foure Angels which are bound in the great riuer Euphrates.

15 And the foure Angels were loosed, which were prepared ||for an houre, and a day, and a moneth, and a yeere, for to slay the third part of men.

‖ *Or, at.*

16 And the number of the armie of the horsemen were two hundred thousand thousand : and I heard the number of them.

17 And thus I sawe the horses in the vision, and them that sate on them, hauing brest-plates of fire and of Iacinct, and brimstone, & the heades of the horses were as the heads of Lions, and out of their mouthes issued fire, and smoke, and brimstone.

18 By these three was the third part of men killed, by the fire, and by the smoke, and by the brimstone which issued out of their mouthes.

19 For their power is in their mouth, and in their tailes : for their tailes were like vnto serpents, and had heads, and with them they doe hurt.

20 And the rest of the men which were not killed by these plagues, yet repented not of the works of their hands, that they should not worship deuils, *and idoles of golde, and siluer, and brasse, and stone, and of wood, which neither can see, nor heare, nor walke :

* Psal. 115. 4. & 135. 15.

21 Neither repented they of their murders, nor of their sorceries, nor of their fornication, nor of their thefts.

CHAP. X.

A mightie strong Angel appeareth with a booke open in his hand. 6 Hee sweareth by him that liueth for euer, that there shall bee no more time. 9 Iohn is commanded to take and eate the booke.

Nd I saw another mighty Angel come downe from heauen, clothed with a cloud, and a rainebow *was* vpon his head, and his face *was* as it were the Sunne, and his feet as pillars of fire.

2 And hee had in his hand a little booke open : and hee set his right foote vpon the sea, and his left foote on the earth,

3 And cryed with a loude voice, as when a Lion roareth : and when hee had cried, seuen thunders vttered their voices.

4 And when the seuen thunders had vttered their voices, I was about to write : and I heard a voice from heauen, saying vnto mee, Seale vp those things which the seuen thunders vttered, and write them not.

5 And the Angel which I saw stand vpon the sea, and vpon the earth, lifted vp his hand to heauen,

6 And sware by him that liueth for euer and euer, who created heauen, and the things that therein are, and the earth, and the things that therein are, and the sea, and the things which are therein, that there should bee time no longer.

7 But in the dayes of the voice of the seuenth Angel, when he shall begin to sound, the mysterie of God should be finished, as hee hath declared to his seruants the Prophets.

8 And the voice which I heard from heauen spake vnto me againe, and said, Go, and take the litle booke which is open in the hand of the Angel which standeth vpon the sea, and vpon the earth.

9 And I went vnto the Angel, and said vnto him, Giue me the little booke. And he sayd vnto me, *Take it, and eat it vp, and it shall make thy belly bitter, but it shall bee in thy mouth sweete as hony.

* Ezek. 2. & and 3. 3.

10 And I tooke the little booke out of the Angels hand, and ate it vp, and it was in my mouth sweet as honie : and as soone as I had eaten it, my belly was bitter.

11 And he sayd vnto me, Thou must prophesie againe before many peoples, and nations, and tongues, and kings.

CHAP.

CHAP. XI.

3 The two witnesses prophesie. 6 They haue
power to shut heauen, that it raine not. 7
The beast shall fight against them, and kill
them. 8 They lie vnburied, 11 and after
three dayes and a halfe rise againe. 14
The second woe is past. 15 The seuenth
trumpet soundeth.

Nd there was giuen me a
reede like vnto a rod, and
the Angel stood, saying,
Rise, and measure the
Temple of God, and the
Altar, and them that worship therein.

2 But the Court which is without
† *Gr. cast out* the Temple †leaue out, and measure it
not : for it is giuen vnto the Gentiles,
and the holy citie shall they tread vnder
foote fourty and two moneths.

‖ *Or, I will giue vnto my two witnesses that they may prophesie.* 3 And ‖I will giue *power* vnto my
two witnesses, and they shall prophesie
a thousand two hundred and threescore
dayes clothed in sackcloth.

* *Zach. 4. 3. & 11. 14.* 4 These are the *two oliue trees,
and the two candlestickes, standing be-
fore the God of the earth.

5 And if any man will hurt them,
fire proceedeth out of their mouth, and
deuoureth their enemies : and if any
man will hurt them, hee must in this
maner be killed.

6 These haue power to shut heauen, that it raine not in the dayes of
their prophesie : and haue power ouer
waters to turne them to blood, and to
smite the earth with all plagues, as often as they will.

7 And when they shall haue finished their testimonie, the beast that ascendeth out of the bottomlesse pit, shall
make warre against them, and shall o-
uercome them, and kill them.

8 And their dead bodies shall *lie* in
the street of the great citie, which spiritually is called Sodome and Egypt,
where also our Lord was crucified.

9 And they of the people, and kinreds, and tongues, and nations, shal see
their dead bodies three dayes and an
halfe, and shall not suffer their dead bodies to be put in graues.

10 And they that dwell vpon the
earth shall reioyce ouer them, and make
merry, and shall send gifts one to another, because these two Prophets tormented them that dwelt on the earth.

11 And after three dayes and an halfe
the Spirit of life from God, entred in-

to them : and they stood vpon their
feete, and great feare fell vpon them
which saw them.

12 And they heard a great voyce
from heauen, saying vnto them, Come
vp hither. And they ascended vp to
heauen in a cloud, and their enemies beheld them.

13 And the same houre was there a
great earthquake, and the tenth part of
the city fell, and in the earthquake were
slaine † of men seuen thousand : and the
remnant were affrighted, and gaue
glory to the God of heauen. † *Gr. names of men.*

14 The second woe is past, and behold, the third woe commeth quickly.

15 And the seuenth Angel sounded,
and there were great voyces in heauen,
saying, The kingdomes of this world
are become *the kingdomes* of our Lord,
and of his Christ, and he shall reigne for
euer and euer.

16 And the foure and twentie Elders
which sate before God on their seates,
fell vpon their faces, and worshipped
God,

17 Saying, Wee giue thee thankes,
O Lord God Almightie, which art,
and wast, and art to come ; because thou
hast taken to thee thy great power, and
hast reigned.

18 And the nations were angry, and
thy wrath is come, and the time of the
dead that they should bee iudged, and
that thou shouldest giue reward vnto
thy seruants the Prophets, and to the
Saints, & them that feare thy Name,
small and great, and shouldest destroy
them which ‖destroy the earth. ‖ *Or, corrupt*

19 And the Temple of God was opened in heauen, and there was seene in
his Temple the Arke of his Testament, and there were lightnings, and
voyces, and thundrings, and an earthquake, and great haile.

CHAP. XII.

1 A woman clothed with the Sunne trauaileth.
4 The great red dragon standeth before her,
ready to deuoure her child : 6 when she was
deliuered she fleeth into the wildernes. 7 Michael and his Angels fight with the dragon,
and preuaile. 13 The dragon being cast
down into the earth, persecuteth the woman.

N D there appeared a
great ‖wonder in heauen,
a woman clothed with
the Sunne, & the Moone
vnder her feete, and vpon
her ‖ *Or, signe.*

her head a Crowne of twelue starres:

2 And shee being with childe, cried, trauailing in birth, and pained to be deliuered.

3 And there appeared another ||wonder in heauen, and behold a great red dragon, hauing seuen heads, and ten hornes, and seuen crownes vpon his heads.

Or, signe.

4 And his taile drew the third part of the starres of heauen, and did cast them to the earth : And the dragon stood before the woman which was ready to be deliuered, for to deuoure her childe as soone as it was borne.

5 And shee brought foorth a man child, who was to rule all nations with a rod of yron : and her child was caught vp vnto God, and to his Throne.

6 And the woman fled into the wildernesse, where shee hath a place prepared of God, that they should feed her there a thousand, two hundred, and threescore dayes.

7 And there was warre in heauen, Michael and his Angels fought against the dragon, & the dragon fought and his angels,

8 And preuailed not, neither was their place found any more in heauen.

9 And the great dragon was cast out, that old serpent, called the deuill and Satan, which deceiueth the whole world : hee was cast out into the earth, and his angels were cast out with him.

10 And I heard a lowd voyce saying in heauen, Now is come saluation, and strength, and the kingdome of our God, and the power of his Christ : for the accuser of our brethren is cast down, which accused them before our God day and night.

11 And they ouercame him by the blood of the Lambe, and by the word of their Testimony, and they loued not their liues vnto the death.

12 Therefore reioyce, yee heauens, and yee that dwell in them ; Woe to the inhabiters of the earth, and of the sea: for the deuill is come downe vnto you, hauing great wrath, because he knoweth that he hath but a short time.

13 And when the dragon saw that he was cast vnto the earth, hee persecuted the woman which brought foorth the man childe.

14 And to the woman were giuen two wings of a great Eagle, that shee might flee into the wildernesse into her place, where she is nourished for a time, and times, and halfe a time, from the face of the serpent.

15 And the serpent cast out of his mouth water as a flood, after the woman : that he might cause her to bee caried away of the flood.

16 And the earth helped the woman, and the earth opened her mouth, and swallowed vp the flood which the dragon cast out of his mouth.

17 And the dragon was wroth with the woman, and went to make warre with the remnant of her seed, which keepe the Commaundements of God, and haue the testimony of Iesus Christ.

CHAP. XIII.

1 A beast riseth out of the sea with seuen heads and ten hornes, to whom the dragon giueth his power. 11 An other beast commeth vp out of the earth : 14 causeth an image to be made of the former beast, 15 and that men should worship it, 16 and receiue his marke.

Nd I stood vpon the sand of the sea : and saw a beast rise vp out of the sea, hauing seuen heads, and ten hornes, and vpon his hornes ten crownes, and vpon his heads, the ||name of blasphemie.

Or, name

2 And the beast which I saw, was like vnto a Leopard, and his feet were as *the feet* of a Beare, and his mouth as the mouth of a Lion : and the dragon gaue him his power, and his seat, and great authoritie.

3 And I saw one of his heads as it were †wounded to death, and his deadly wound was healed : and al the world wondered after the beast.

†Gr. slain

4 And they worshipped the dragon which gaue power vnto the beast, and they worshipped the beast, saying, Who is like vnto the beast? Who is able to make warre with him?

5 And there was giuen vnto him a mouth, speaking great things, and blasphemies, and power was giuen vnto him to ||continue fortie and two moneths.

Or, to make warre.

6 And he opened his mouth in blasphemie against God, to blaspheme his Name, and his Tabernacle, and them that dwelt in heauen.

7 And it was giuen vnto him to make warre with the Saints, and to ouer-

ouercome them : And power was giuen him ouer all kinreds, and tongues,
and nations.

8 And all that dwel vpon the earth,
shall worship him, whose names are
not written in the booke of life of the
Lambe, slaine from the foundation of
the world.

9 If any man haue an eare, let him
heare :

10 Hee that leadeth into captiuitie,
shall goe into captiuitie : *Hee that killeth with the sword, must be killed with
the sword. Here is the patience and the
faith of the Saints.

11 And I beheld another beast comming vp out of the earth, and hee had
two hornes like a lambe, and hee spake
as a dragon.

12 And he exerciseth all the power of
the first beast before him, and causeth
the earth and them which dwell therein, to worship the first beast, whose
deadly wound was healed.

13 And hee doeth great wonders, so
that hee maketh fire come downe from
heauen on the earth in the sight of men,

14 And deceiueth them that dwel on
the earth, by the meanes of those miracles which he had power to do in the
sight of the beast, saying to them that
dwell on the earth, that they should
make an Image to the beast which had
the wound by a sword, and did liue.

15 And he had power to giue †life vnto the Image of the beast, that the I-
mage of the beast should both speake,
and cause that as many as would not
worship the Image of the beast, should
be killed.

16 And he causeth all, both smal and
great, rich and poore, free and bond, †to
receiue a marke in their right hand, or
in their foreheads :

17 And that no man might buy or
sell, saue he that had the marke, or the
name of the beast, or the number of his
name.

18 Here is wisedome. Let him that
hath vnderstanding, count the number
of the beast : for it is the number of a
man, and his number is, sixe hundred
threescore and sixe.

CHAP. XIIII.

1 The Lambe standing on mount Sion with his
company.　6 an Angel preacheth the Gospel.　8 The fall of Babylon.　15 The haruest of the worlde, and putting in of the
sickle.　20 The vintage and winepresse of
the wrath of God.

Nd I looked, and loe, a
Lambe stood on the mount
Sion, and with him an hundreth fourty and foure thousand, hauing his Fathers Name written in their foreheads.

2 And I heard a voice from heauen,
as the voice of many waters, and as the
voyce of a great thunder : and I heard
the voyce of harpers, harping with
their harpes.

3 And they sung as it were a new
song before the throne, and before the
foure beasts, and the Elders, and no
man could learne that song, but the
hundreth and fourtie and foure thousand, which were redeemed from the
earth.

4 These are they which were not
defiled with women : for they are virgines : These are they which follow
the Lambe whithersoeuer hee goeth :
These †were redeemed from among
men, being the first fruits vnto God,
and to the Lambe.

5 And in their mouth was found no
guile : for they are without fault before
the throne of God.

6 And I saw another Angel flie in
the midst of heauen, hauing the euerlasting Gospel, to preach vnto them that
dwel on the earth, and to euery nation,
and kinred, and tongue, and people,

7 Saying with a loud voice, Feare
God, and giue glory to him, for the
houre of his iudgement is come : *and
worshippe him that made heauen and
earth, and the sea, and the fountains of
waters.

8 And there followed another An-
gel, saying, *Babylon is fallen, is fallen,
that great citie, because she made all nations drinke of the wine of the wrath of
her fornication.

9 And the third Angel followed
them, saying with a lowd voice, If any
man worship the beast and his image,
and receiue his marke in his forehead,
or in his hand,

10 The same shall drinke of the wine
of the wrath of God, which is powred
out without mixture into the cup of his
indignation, and hee shall be tormented
with fire and brimstone, in the presence
of the holy Angels, and in the presence
of the Lambe :

11 And the smoke of their torment
ascendeth

*Matth. 26.
52.

†Gr. breath.

†Gr. to giue.

†Gr. were
bought.

*Psa. 146. 5
acts 14. 15.

*Esa. 21. 9.
iere. 51. 8.
chap. 18. 2.

ascendeth vp for euer and euer. And they haue no rest day nor night, who worship the beast and his image. and whosoeuer receyueth the marke of his name.

12 Here is the patience of the Saints: Here are they that keepe the Commandements of God, and the faith of Iesus.

13 And I heard a voyce from heauen, saying vnto me, Write, Blessed are the dead which die in the Lord, ||from hencefoorth, yea, saith the Spirit, that they may rest from their labours, and their workes doe follow them.

Or, from henceforth saith the Spirit, yea.

14 And I looked, and beholde, a white cloud, and vpon the cloude *one* sate like vnto the sonne of man, hauing on his head a golden crowne, and in his hand a sharpe sickle.

15 And another Angel came out of the Temple crying with a loude voice to him that sate on the cloud: *Thrust in thy sickle and reape, for the time is come for thee to reape, for the haruest of the earth is ||ripe.

* Ioel 3. 13.

|Or, dryed.

16 And hee that sate on the cloude thrust in his sickle on the earth, and the earth was reaped.

17 And another Angel came out of the Temple which is in heauen, he also hauing a sharpe sickle.

18 And another Angel came out from the Altar, which had power ouer fire, and cryed with a loud cry to him that had the sharpe sickle, saying, Thrust in thy sharpe sickle, and gather the clusters of the vine of the earth, for her grapes are fully ripe.

19 And the Angel thrust in his sickle into the earth, and gathered the vine of the earth, & cast it into the great winepresse of the wrath of God.

20 And the winepresse was troden without the citie, and blood came out of the winepresse, euen vnto the horse bridles, by the space of a thousand and sixe hundred furlongs.

CHAP. XV.

1 The seuen Angels with the seuen last plagues.
3 The song of the that ouercome the beast.
7 The seuen vials full of the wrath of God.

ND I saw another signe in heauen great and marueilous, seuen Angels hauing the seuen last plagues, for in them is filled vp the wrath of God.

2 And I saw as it were a Sea of glasse, mingled with fire, and them that had gotten the victorie ouer the beast, and ouer his image, and ouer his marke, and ouer the number of his name, stand on the sea of glasse, hauing the harpes of God.

3 *And they sing the song of Moses the seruant of God, and the song of the Lambe, saying, Great and marueilous are thy workes, Lord God Almightie, *iust and true are thy wayes, thou king of saints.

* Exo. 15. 1.

* Psal. 145. 17.

4 *Who shall not feare thee, O Lord, and glorifie thy Name? for thou onely art holy : for all nations shall come and worship before thee, for thy iudgements are made manifest.

* Iere. 10. 7.

5 And after that I looked, and behold, the Temple of the tabernacle of the testimony in heauen was opened:

6 And the seuen Angels came out of the Temple, hauing the seuen plagues, clothed in pure and white linnen, and hauing their breasts girded with golden girdles.

7 And one of the foure beasts gaue vnto the seuen Angels, seuen golden vials, full of the wrath of God, who liueth for euer and euer.

8 And the Temple was filled with smoke from the glory of God, and from his power, and no man was able to enter into the Temple, till the seuen plagues of the seuen Angels were fulfilled.

CHAP. XVI.

2 The Angels powre out their Vials full of wrath. 6 The plagues that follow thereupon. 15 Christ commeth as a thiefe. Blessed are they that watch.

Nd I heard a great voyce out of the Temple, saying to the seuen Angels, Goe your wayes, and powre out the vials of the wrath of God vpo the earth.

2 And the first went, and powred out his viall vpon the earth, and there fell a noysome and grieuous sore vpon the men which had the marke of the beast, and vpon them which worshipped his image.

3 And the second Angel powred out his viall vpon the sea, and it became as the blood of a dead man : and euery liuing soule died in the sea.

4 And

4 And the third Angel powred out his viall vpon the riuers and fountaines of waters, & they became blood.

5 And I heard the Angel of the waters say, Thou art righteous, O Lord, which art, and wast, and shalt be, because thou hast iudged thus:

6 For they haue shedde the blood of Saints and Prophets, and thou hast giuen them blood to drinke : for they are worthy.

7 And I heard another out of the altar say, Euen so, Lord God Almightie, true and righteous are thy iudgements.

8 And the fourth Angel powred out his viall vpon the Sunne, and power was giuen vnto him to scorch men with fire.

Or, burned

9 And men were ‖ scorched with great heat, and blasphemed the Name of God, which hath power ouer these plagues : and they repented not, to giue him glory.

10 And the fift Angel powred out his viall vpon the seat of the beast, and his kingdome was full of darkenesse, and they gnawed their tongues for paine,

11 And blasphemed the God of heauen, because of their paines, and their sores, and repented not of their deeds.

12 And the sixt Angel powred out his viall vpon the great riuer Euphrates, and the water thereof was dried vp, that the way of the Kings of the East might be prepared.

13 And I saw three vncleane spirits like frogs *come* out of the mouth of the dragon, & out of the mouth of the beast, & out of the mouth of the false prophet.

14 For they are the spirits of deuils working miracles, which goe forth vnto the Kings of the earth, and of the whole world, to gather them to the battell of that great day of God Almighty.

Mat. 24.
4.

15 *Behold, I come as a thiefe. Blessed is he that watcheth, and keepeth his garments, least hee walke naked, and they see his shame.

16 And hee gathered them together into a place, called in the Hebrewe tongue, Armageddon.

17 And the seuenth Angel powred out his viall into the ayre, and there came a great voyce out of the Temple of heauen, from the throne, saying, It is done.

18 And there were voices and thunders, and lightnings : and there was a

great earthquake, such as was not since men were vpon the earth, so mighty an earthquake, and so great.

19 And the great Citie was diuided into three parts, and the Cities of the nations fell : and great Babylon came in remembrance before God, *to giue vnto her the cup of the wine of the fiercenesse of his wrath.

*Ier. 25. 15.

20 And euery yland fled away, and the mountaines were not found.

21 And there fell vpon men a great haile out of heauen, euery stone about the weight of a talent, and men blasphemed God, because of the plague of the hayle : for the plague thereof was exceeding great.

CHAP. XVII.

3. 4 A woman arayed in purple and scarlet, with a golden cup in her hand, sitteth vpon the Beast, 5 which is great Babylon the mother of all abominations. 9 The interpretation of the seuen heads, 12 and the tenne hornes. 8 The punishment of the whore. 14 The victory of the Lambe.

Nd there came one of the seuen Angels, which had the seuen vials, and talked with me, saying vnto mee, Come hither, I will shew vnto thee the iudgement of the great Whore, that sitteth vpon many waters:

2 With whom the kings of the earth haue committed fornication, and the inhabiters of the earth haue beene made drunk with the wine of her fornication.

3 So he caried me away in the Spirit into the wildernesse : and I saw a woman sit vpō a scarlet coloured beast, full of names of blasphemy, hauing seuen heads, and ten hornes.

4 And the woman was arayed in purple and scarlet colour, and †decked with gold, and precious stone & pearles, hauing a golden cup in her hand, full of abominations and filthinesse of her fornication.

†Gr. gilded.

5 And vpon her forehead was a name written, MYSTERY, BABYLON THE GREAT, THE MOTHER OF ‖HARLOTS, AND ABOMINATIONS OF THE EARTH.

‖Or, fornications.

6 And I saw the woman drunken with the blood of the Saints, and with the blood of the Martyrs of Iesus : and when I saw her, I wondred with great admiration.

7 And the Angel saide vnto mee, Where-

Wherefore didſt thou marueile? I will tell thee the mystery of the woman, and of the beast that carieth her, which hath the seuen heads, and ten hornes.

8 The beast that thou sawest, was, and is not, and shall ascend out of the bottomlesse pit, and goe into perdition, and they that dwell on the earth shall wonder, (whose names were not written in the booke of life from the foundation of the world) when they behold the beast that was, and is not, and yet is.

9 And here is the mind which hath wisedome. The seuen heads are seuen mountaines, on which the woman sitteth.

10 And there are seuen Kings, fiue are fallen, and one is, and the other is not yet come: and when he commeth, he must continue a short space.

11 And the beast that was, and is not, euen he is the eighth, & is of the seuen, and goeth into perdition.

12 And the tenne hornes which thou sawest, are ten kings, which haue receiued no kingdom as yet: but receiue power as kings one houre with the beast.

13 These haue one minde, and shall giue their power and strength vnto the beast.

*1. Tim. 6. 15. chap. 19. 16.

14 These shal make warre with the Lambe, and the Lambe shal ouercome them: *For he is Lord of Lords, and King of kings, and they that are with him, are called, & chosen, and faithfull.

15 And he saith vnto me, The waters which thou sawest, where the whore sitteth, are peoples, and multitudes, and nations, and tongues.

16 And the ten hornes which thou sawest vpon the beast, these shall hate the whore, and shall make her desolate, and naked, and shall eate her flesh, and burne her with fire.

17 For God hath put in their hearts to fulfill his will, and to agree, and giue their kingdome vnto the beast, vntil the words of God shall be fulfilled.

18 And the woman which thou sawest, is that great Citie which reigneth ouer the kings of the earth.

CHAP. XVIII.

2 Babylon is fallen. 4 The people of God commanded to depart out of her. 9 The Kings of the earth, 11 with the Merchants and Mariners, lament ouer her. 20 The Saints reioyce for the iudgements of God vpon her.

Nd after these things, I saw another Angel come downe from heauen, hauing great power, and the earth was lightened with his glory.

2 And he cryed mightily with a ſtrōg voyce, saying, *Babylon the great is fallen, is fallen, and is become the habitation of deuils, and the hold of euery foule spirit, and a cage of euery vncleane and hatefull bird:

* Chap. 14. 8.

3 For all nations haue drunke of the wine of the wrath of her fornication, and the Kings of the earth haue committed fornication with her, & the Merchants of the earth are waxed rich thorow the ||abundance of her delicacies.

|| Or, power.

4 And I heard another voice from heauen, saying, Come out of her, my people, that yee be not partakers of her sinnes, and that yee receiue not of her plagues:

5 For her sinnes haue reached vnto heauen, and God hath remembred her iniquities.

6 Reward her euen as shee rewarded you, and double vnto her double according to her works: in the cup which she hath filled, fill to her double.

7 How much shee hath glorified her selfe, and liued deliciously, so much torment and sorrow giue her: for she saith in her heart, I sit a *Queene, and am no widow, and shall see no sorrow.

* Esay. 47. 8.

8 Therefore shall her plagues come in one day, death, and mourning, and famine, and she shall bee vtterly burnt with fire, for strong is the Lord God, who iudgeth her.

9 And the Kings of the earth, who haue committed fornication, and liued deliciously with her, shall bewaile her and lament for her, when they shall see the smoke of her burning:

10 Standing afarre off for the feare of her torment, saying, Alas, alas, that great citie Babylon, that mighty citie: for in one houre is thy iudgement come.

11 And the Merchants of the earth shall weepe and mourne ouer her, for no man buyeth their merchandise any more.

12 The merchandise of gold, and siluer, and pretious stones, and of pearles, and fine linnen, and purple, and silke, and scarlet, and all ||Thine wood, and all maner vessels of Yuorie, and all maner vessels of most precious wood, and of

|| Or, sweet.

of brasse, and iron, and marble,

13 And Cynamome, and odours, and ointments, and frankincense, & wine, and oile, and fine floure, and wheat, and beasts, and sheepe, and horses, and chariots, and ‖slaues, and soules of men.

Or, bodies.

14 And the fruits that thy soule lusted after, are departed from thee, and all things which were daintie, and goodly, are departed from thee, and thou shalt finde them no more at all.

15 The Merchants of these things which were made riche by her, shall stand afarre off for the feare of her torment, weeping and wailing.

16 And saying, Alas, alas, that great city, that was clothed in fine linnen, and purple and scarlet, and decked with gold, and pretious stones, and pearles:

17 For in one houre so great riches is come to nought. And euery shipmaster, and all the company in ships, and sailers, and as many as trade by sea, stood a farre off,

18 And cryed when they saw the smoke of her burning, saying, What city is like vnto this great citie?

19 And they cast dust on their heads, and cried, weeping, and wailing, saying, Alas alas, that great citie, wherein were made rich all that had ships in the sea, by reason of her costlinesse, for in one houre is she made desolate.

20 Reioyce ouer her thou heauen, and ye holy Apostles and Prophets, for God hath auenged you on her.

21 And a mightie Angel tooke vp a stone like a great milstone, and cast it into the sea, saying, Thus with violence shall that great citie Babylon bee throwen downe, and shall bee found no more at all.

22 And the voyce of harpers and musitions, and of pipers, and trumpetters, shall bee heard no more at all in thee : and no craftsman, of whatsoeuer craft hee be, shall be found any more in thee : and the sound of a milstone shalbe heard no more at all in thee :

23 And the light of a candle shall shine no more at all in thee : and the voice of the bridegrome and of the bride shalbe heard no more at all in thee : for thy Merchants were the great men of the earth : for by thy sorceries were all nations deceiued.

24 And in her was found the blood of Prophets, and of Saints, and of all that were slaine vpon the earth.

CHAP. XIX.

1 God is praised in heauen for iudging the great whore, and auenging the blood of his Saints. 7 The marriage of the Lambe. 20 The Angel will not be worshipped. 17 The foules called to the great slaughter.

AND after these things I heard a great voyce of much people in heauen, saying, Alleluia : saluation, and glorie, and honour, and power vnto the Lord our God:

2 For true and righteous are his iudgements, for hee hath iudged the great whore which did corrupt the earth with her fornication, and hath auenged the blood of his seruants at her hand.

3 And againe they sayd, Alleluia : and her smoke rose vp for euer & euer.

4 And the foure and twentie Elders, and the foure beasts fell downe, and worshipped God that sate on the throne, saying, Amen, Alleluia.

5 And a voice came out of the throne, saying, Praise our God all yee his seruants, and ye that feare him, both small and great.

6 And I heard as it were the voice of a great multitude, and as the voice of many waters, and as the voice of mightie thundrings, saying, Alleluia : for the Lord God omnipotent reigneth.

7 Let vs bee glad and reioyce, and giue honour to him : for the mariage of the Lambe is come, and his wife hath made herselfe readie.

8 And to her was granted, that she should bee arayed in fine linnen, cleane and white : for the fine linnen is the righteousnesse of Saints.

9 And hee saith vnto mee, Write, *Blessed are they which are called vnto the marriage supper of the Lambe. And he saith vnto mee, These are the true sayings of God.

* Mat. 22. 2.

10 And I fell at his feete to worship him : And he said vnto me, *See thou doe it not : I am thy fellow seruant, and of thy brethren, that haue the testimonie of Iesus, Worship God : for the testimony of Iesus, is the spirit of prophecie.

* Cha. 22. 9.

11 And I sawe heauen opened, and behold a white horse, and hee that sate vpon him was called faithful and true, and in righteousnes hee doth iudge and make warre.

12 His

12 His eyes *were* as a flame of fire, and on his head were many crownes, and hee had a name written, that no man knew but he himselfe.

* Esa. 63. 2.

13 * And hee was clothed with a vesture dipt in blood, and his name is called, The word of God.

14 And the armies which were in heauen followed him vpon white horses, clothed in fine linnen, white and cleane.

15 And out of his mouth goeth a sharpe sword, that with it hee should smite the nations : and he shal rule them with a rod of yron : and he treadeth the winepresse of the fiercenesse and wrath of Almighty God.

* Chap. 17.
14.

16 And he hath on his vesture, and on his thigh a name written, * *KING OF KINGS, AND LORD OF LORDS.*

17 And I saw an Angel standing in the Sunne, and hee cried with a lowd voyce, saying to all the foules that flie in the midst of heauen, Come and gather your selues together vnto the supper of the great God:

18 That yee may eate the flesh of Kings, and the flesh of Captaines, and the flesh of mighty men, and the flesh of horses, and of them that sit on them, and the flesh of all men both free and bond, both small and great.

19 And I saw the beast, & the Kings of the earth, and their armies gathered together to make warre against him that sate on the horse, and against his armie.

20 And the beast was taken, & with him the false prophet, that wrought miracles before him, with which he deceiued them that had receiued the marke of the beast, and them that worshipped his image. These both were cast aliue into a lake of fire burning with brimstone.

21 And the remnant were slaine with the sword of him that sate vpon the horse, which sword proceeded out of his mouth : aud all the foules were filled with their flesh.

CHAP. XX.

2 Satan bound for a thousand yeeres. 6 The first resurrection: they blessed that haue part therein. 7 Satan let loose againe. 8 Gog and Magog. 10 The deuill cast into the lake of fire and brimstone. 12 The last and generall resurrection.

ANd I saw an Angel come down from heauen, hauing the key of the bottomles pit, & a great chaine in his hand.

2 And hee laid hold on the dragon that old serpent, which is the deuill and Satan, and bound him a thousand yeres,

3 And cast him into the bottomlesse pit, and shut him vp, and set a seale vpon him, that he should deceiue the nations no more, till the thousand yeeres should bee fulfilled : and after that hee must be loosed a little season.

4 And I saw thrones, and they sate vpon them, and iudgement was giuen vnto them : & I saw the soules of them that were beheaded for the witnesse of Iesus, and for the word of God, and which had not worshipped the beast, neither his image, neither had receiued his marke vpon their foreheads, or in their hands, and they liued and reigned with Christ a thousand yeeres.

5 But the rest of the dead liued not againe vntill the thousand yeeres were finished. This is the first resurrection.

6 Blessed & holy is he that hath part in ỹ first resurrection : on such the second death hath no power, but they shall be Priests of God, and of Christ, and shall reigne with him a thousand yeeres.

7 And when the thousand yeeres are expired, Satan shall be loosed out of his prison,

8 And shall goe out to deceiue the nations which are in the foure quarters of the earth, * Gog & Magog, to gather them together to battell : the number of whom is as the sand of the sea.

* Ezech.
2. and 39.

9 And they went vp on the breadh of the earth, and compassed the campe of the Saints about, and the beloued citie : and fire came downe from God out of heauen, and deuoured them.

10 And the deuil that deceiued them, was cast into the lake of fire and brimstone, where the beast and the false prophet *are*, and shall be tormented day and night, for euer and euer.

11 And I saw a great white throne, and him that sate on it, from whose face the earth and the heauen fled away, and there was found no place for them.

12 And I sawe the dead, small and great, stand before God : and the books were opened : & an other * booke was opened, which is *the booke* of life : and the dead were iudged out of those things which

* Chap. 3

which were written in the books, according to their works.

13 And the sea gaue vp the dead which were in it : and death and ‖hell deliuered vp the dead which were in them : and they were iudged euery man according to their works.

14 And death and hell were cast into the lake of fire : this is the second death.

15 And whosoeuer was not found written in the booke of life, was cast into the lake of fire.

CHAP. XXI.

1 A newe heauen and a newe earth. 10 The heauenly Ierusalem, with a full description thereof. 23 She needeth no sunne, the glory of God is her light. 24 The kings of the earth bring their riches vnto her.

Nd *I saw a new heauen, and a new earth: for the first heauen, and the first earth were passed away, and there was no more sea.

2 And I Iohn saw the holy City, new Hierusalem comming down from God out of heauen, prepared as a bride adorned for her husband.

3 And I heard a great voice out of heauen, saying, Behold, the Tabernacle of God *is* with men, and he wil dwell with them, and they shall be his people, and God himselfe shalbe with them, *and be* their God.

4 *And God shall wipe away all teares from their eyes : and there shall bee no more death, neither sorrow, nor crying, neither shall there bee any more paine : for the former things are passed away

5 And he that sate vpon the throne, said, *Behold, I make all things new. And hee said vnto me, Write : for these words are true and faithfull.

6 And he said vnto mee, It is done : *I am Alpha and Omega, the beginning and the end. *I will giue vnto him that is athirst, of the fountaine of the water of life, freely.

7 He that ouercommeth, shall inherite all things, and I will bee his God, and he shall be my sonne.

8 But the fearefull, and vnbeleeuing, and the abominable, and murderers, and whoremongers, and sorcerers, and idolaters, and all lyars, shall haue their part in the lake which burneth with fire and brimstone . which is the second death.

9 And there came vnto me one of the seuen Angels, which had the seuen vials full of the seuen last plagues, and talked with me, saying, Come hither, I will shew thee the Bride, the Lambes wife.

10 And he caried me away in the spirit to a great and high mountaine, and shewed me that great citie, the holy Hierusalem, descending out of heauen from God,

11 Hauing the glory of God : and her light *was* like vnto a stone most precious; euen like a iasper stone, cleare as christal,

12 And had a wall great and high, and had twelue gates, and at the gates twelue Angels, & names written thereon, which are *the names* of the twelue tribes of the children of Israel.

13 On the East three gates, on the North three gates, on the South three gates, and on the West three gates.

14 And the wall of the citie had twelue foundations, and in them the names of the twelue Apostles of the Lambe.

15 And hee that talked with mee, had a golden reede to measure the citie, and the gates thereof, and the wall thereof.

16 And the city lieth foure square, and the length is as large as the breadth : and he measured the city with the reed, twelue thousand furlongs : the length, and the breadth, and the height of it are equall.

17 And he measured the wall thereof, an hundred, and fourtie, and foure cubites, according to the measure of a man, that is, of the Angel.

18 And the building of the wall of it was of Iasper, and the city was pure gold, like vnto cleare glasse.

19 And the foundations of the wall of the city were garnished with all maner of precious stones. The first foundation was Iasper, the second Saphir, the third a Chalcedony, the fourth an Emerald,

20 The fift Sardonix, the sixt Sardius, the seuenth Chrysolite, the eight Beryl, the ninth a Topas, the tenth a Chrysoprasus, the eleuenth a Iacinct, the twelfth an Amethyst.

21 And the twelue gates were twelue pearles, euery seuerall gate was of one pearle, and the streete of the city was pure golde, as it were transparent glasse.

22 And I saw no Temple therein : for

*r, hell.

Esa. 65. 17
pet. 3. 13

cha. 7. 17

, Cor. 5.

chap. 1. 8.
1 22. 13.
Esa. 55. 1.

For the Lord God Almightie, and the Lambe, are the Temple of it.

*Esai. 60. 19.

23 * And the citie had no need of the Sunne, neither of the Moone to shine in it : for the glory of God did lighten it, and the Lambe is the light thereof.

*Esai. 60. 3.

24 * And the nations of them which are saued, shall walke in the light of it : and the kings of the earth doe bring their glory and honour into it.

*Esai. 60. 11

25 * And the gates of it shall not bee shut at all by day : for there shall bee no night there.

26 And they shall bring the glorie and honour of the nations into it.

27 And there shall in no wise enter into it any thing that defileth , neither whatsoeuer worketh abomination, or *maketh* a lie : but they which are written in the Lambes booke of life.

CHAP. XXII.

1 The riuer of the water of life. 2 The tree of life. 5 The light of the Citie of God is himselfe. 9 The Angel will not be worshipped. 18 Nothing may bee added to the word of God, nor taken therefrom.

Nd he shewed mee a pure riuer of water of life, cleere as Chrystall , proceeding out of the throne of God, and of the Lambe.

2 In the middest of the street of it, and of either side of the riuer, *was there* the tree of life, which bare twelue manner of fruits, and yeelded her fruit euery moneth : and the leaues of the tree were for the healing of the nations.

3 And there shall be no more curse, but the throne of God, & of the Lambe shall bee in it, and his seruants shall serue him.

4 And they shall see his face, and his name *shall be* in their foreheads.

*Chap. 21. 23.

5 * And there shalbe no night there, and they need no candle, neither light of the sunne, for the Lorde God giueth them light, and they shall reigne for e-uer and euer.

6 And hee said vnto mee, These sayings *are* faithfull and true. And the Lord God of the holy Prophets sent his Angel to shew vnto his seruants the things which must shortly be done.

7 Beholde, I come quickly : Blessed is he that keepeth the sayings of the prophecie of this booke.

8 And I Iohn saw these things, and heard them. And when I had heard and seene, I fell downe, to worship before the feet of the Angel, which shewed me these things.

*Chap. 19. 10.

9 Then saith he vnto me, * See thou doe it not : for I am thy fellow seruant, and of thy brethren the Prophets, and of them which keepe the sayings of this booke : worship God.

10 And hee saith vnto mee, Seale not the sayings of the prophesie of this booke : for the time is at hand.

11 He that is vniust, let him be vniust still : and he which is filthy, let him be filthy still : and hee that is righteous, let him bee righteous still : and hee that is holy, let him be holy still.

*Rom. 2. 6

12 And behold, I come quickly, and my reward is with mee, * to giue euery man according as his worke shall be.

*Esa. 41. 4 and 44. 6.

13 I am Alpha and Omega, * the beginning and the end, the first & the last.

14 Blessed are they that do his commandements, that they may haue right to the tree of life, and may enter in thorow the gates into the citie.

15 For without *are* dogs, and sorcerers, and whoremongers, and murderers, and idolaters, and whosoeuer loueth and maketh a lie.

16 I Iesus haue sent mine Angel, to testifie vnto you these things in the Churches. I am the roote and the offspring of Dauid, and the bright and morning starre.

*Esa. 55.

17 And the Spirit and the Bride say, Come. And let him that heareth, say, Come. * And let him that is athirst, come. And whosoeuer will, let him take the water of life freely.

*Deut. 4. prou. 30. 6

18 For I testifie vnto euery man that heareth the wordes of the prophesie of this booke, * If any man shal adde vnto these things, God shall adde vnto him the plagues, that are written in this booke.

19 And if any man shall take away from the wordes of the booke of this prophesie, God shal take away his part out of the booke of life, and out of the holy citie, and from the things which are written in this booke.

20 Hee which testifieth these things, saith, Surely, I come quickly. Amen. Euen so, Come Lord Iesus.

21 The grace of our Lord Iesus Christ be with you all. Amen.

FINIS.